A TIBETAN-ENGLISH DICTIONARY

WITH SANSKRIT SYNONYMS

A TIBETAN-ENGLISH DICTIONARY

BY

RAI SARAT CHANDRA DAS, BAHADUR, C.I.E.

A TIBETAN-ENGLISH DICTIONARY

WITH SANSKRIT SYNONYMS

BY

SARAT CHANDRA DAS, RAI BAHADUR, C.I.E.,

AUTHOR OF "A JOURNEY TO LHASA AND CENTRAL TIBET."

REVISED AND EDITED UNDER THE ORDERS OF THE GOVERNMENT OF BENGAL

BY

GRAHAM SANDBERG, B. A.,

CHAPLAIN, H.M. INDIAN SERVICE; AUTHOR OF "A HAND-BOOK OF COLLOQUIAL TIBETAN," "MANUAL OF THE SIKKIM-BHUTIA LANGUAGE," "MILARASPA, TIBETAN POET AND MISTIC," ETC., ETC., ETC.,

AND

A WILLIAM HEYDE,

ONE OF THE REVISORS OF THE TIBETAN NEW TESTAMENT, MORAVIAN MISSIONARY ON THE TIBETAN FRONTIER.

GYAN

Published by

GYAN

Gyan Publishing House
5, Ansari Road
Daryaganj, New Delhi-110002
Phone: 011-47034999, 9811692060
E-mail: books@gyanbooks.com

Distribution Network
gyanbooks.com
India, USA, Canada, UK, Australia, France

ISBN : 978-81-212-3079-7 (PB)
First Published, 1902

2nd Impression 2020

Printed at: Gyan Press, Delhi.

A Tibetan-English Dictionary
Author: Graham Sandberg

A
TIBETAN-ENGLISH DICTIONARY

WITH SANSKRIT SYNONYMS

BY

SARAT CHANDRA DAS, Rai Bahadur, C.I.E.,

AUTHOR OF "A JOURNEY TO LHASA AND CENTRAL TIBET."

Revised and Edited under the orders of the Government of Bengal

BY

GRAHAM SANDBERG, B.A.,

CHAPLAIN, H. M. INDIAN SERVICE; AUTHOR OF "A HAND-BOOK OF COLLOQUIAL TIBETAN," "MANUAL OF THE SIKKIM-BHUTIA LANGUAGE," "MILARASPA, TIBETAN POET AND MYSTIC," ETC., ETC., ETC.,

AND

A. WILLIAM HEYDE,

ONE OF THE REVISORS OF THE TIBETAN NEW TESTAMENT, MORAVIAN MISSIONARY ON THE TIBETAN FRONTIER.

CALCUTTA:

PUBLISHED BY THE BENGAL SECRETARIAT BOOK DEPÔT.

1902.

PREFACE.

I.

Alex. Csoma de Körös, the pioneer student of Tibetan, in the preface of his Tibetan-English-Dictionary, published in 1834, wrote as follows:—

"When there shall be more interest taken for Buddhism (which has much in common with the spirit of true Christianity) and for diffusing Christian and European knowledge throughout the most eastern parts of Asia, the Tibetan Dictionary may be much improved, enlarged, and illustrated by the addition of Sanskrit terms."

The result of his investigations, to speak in Csoma's own words, was that the literature of Tibet is entirely of Indian origin. The immense volumes on different branches of science, etc., being exact or faithful translations from Sanskrit works, taken from Bengal, Magadha, Gangetic or Central India, Kashmir, and Nepal, commencing from the seventh century after Christ. And that many of these works have been translated (mostly from Tibetan) into the Mongol, Manchu, and the Chinese languages; so that by this means the Tibetan language became in Chinese Tartary the language of the learned as the Latin in Europe. In the year 1889 I brought these opinions of that original investigator to the notice of Sir Alfred Croft, K.C.I.E., the then Director of Public Instruction in Bengal, and explained to him the necessity of compiling a Tibetan-English Dictionary on the lines indicated by Csoma de Körös for the use of Tibetan students and particularly to assist European scholars in the thorough exploration of the vast literature of Tibet, which, besides indigenous works, comprises almost all the Buddhist religious works of India, including the great collections of the *Kahgyur* and the *Tangyur*. Shortly before this Sir Alfred Croft had received a communication from the late Right Hon'ble Professor F. Max Müller on the desirability of translating into English a Sanskrit-Tibetan work on Buddhist terminology, which was looked for with interest, because it was expected to throw light on many obscure points of Buddhist-Sanskrit literature. The philosophical terms of that literature, many of which were of extremely doubtful meaning, had been translated with literal accuracy into Tibetan in early times, and it was anticipated that an analysis of the meaning of these terms would elucidate that of the original Sanskrit words, of which they were the equivalent renderings. Being impressed with the importance of the proposed work, Sir Alfred Croft, in a memorandum addressed to Government, wrote as follows:—

"Babu Sarat Chandra Das has brought with him four dictionaries of the classical Tibetan; one of these being a well-known Tibetan-Sanskrit Dictionary, compiled from a large number of named Tibetan as well as standard Sanskrit works, and dating from the 13th century A.D., and another being a Sanskrit-Tibetan Dictionary, which explains the Tantrik portion of the Buddhist Scriptures. The external arrangement of the dictionary will be as follows:—The Tibetan words will be placed first in alphabetical order; next their accepted Sanskrit equivalents; next the English rendering of the Tibetan terms; then will follow what is to be a special and valuable feature of the new dictionary. The meaning of each technical term is to be illustrated by extracts, with exact references from Sanskrit-Buddhist and Tibetan works. Further, it is proposed that Babu Sarat Chandra Das should include in the dictionary words of modern Tibetan which were not known to Csoma or Jäschke. The materials which he has amassed during his two journeys to and residence in Tibet give him exceptional facilities for making the work complete."

These recommendations having received the sanction of Government in June 1889, I was placed on special duty in connection with the compilation of the proposed dictionary. In 1899, when the work of compilation was brought to a close, the Hon'ble Mr. C. W. Bolton, C.S.I., then Chief Secretary to the Government of Bengal, entrusted the revision of the work to the Revd. Graham Sandberg and Revd. William Heyde, and deputed Professor Satis Chandra Acharya, M.A., who had made Buddhist Sanskrit and Pali works his special study, to co-operate with me. My respectful thanks are, therefore, due to Sir Alfred Croft for the keen interest he took in my Tibetan studies and for his kind help at the inception of the work, and to Mr. Bolton for securing the services of the two Tibetan scholars—the Revd. Graham Sandberg and Revd. William Heyde —for its successful completion. I also record my obligations to Sir John

Edgar, K.C.I.E., formerly Chief Secretary to the Government of Bengal; to Dr. Emil Schlagintweit of Bavaria, and to the Hon'ble W. W. Rockhill, Author of *The Land of Lamas* for encouragement, assistance, and advice during the prosecution of my researches. Great is the debt of gratitude which I owe to the Revd. G. Sandberg for various acts of kindness. Without his scholarly and efficient aid this work would hardly have assumed its present shape, as he has given a scientific finish to the work which it was not in my power to do.

II.

In studying the origin and growth of Tibetan literature and the landmarks in the history of that language, Jäschke, the compiler of the second Tibetan-English Dictionary (published in 1882), noticed only two periods of literary activity. Had that critical student of Tibetan been in possession of works of modern literature, which dates from the establishment of the Dalai Lama's sovereignty over whole Tibet in the beginning of the 18th century A.D., he would certainly have modified his remarks on the subject. Neither he nor Csoma de Körös had any means or opportunities of studying either the current literature of every-day business or the refined, idiomatic literature of Tibet itself, which is quite distinct from the Indian literature that was translated or imported into the language. They do not seem to have ever during the course of their study of Tibetan come across works on drama, fiction, correspondence, etc. It is, therefore, no wonder that the compiler of the later dictionary should assign only two periods to the history of the literature of Tibet, entirely ignoring the third, which is indeed not the least important of the three.

The first period, to describe it in the language of Jäschke, is the Period of Translations, which, however, might also be entitled the Classical Period, for the sanctity of the religious message conferred a corresponding reputation and tradition of excellence upon the form in which it was conveyed. This period begins in the second half of the seventh century A.D., when Thon-mi Sambhoṭa (the good Bhoṭa or Tibetan), the minister of King Srongtsan Gampo, returned to Tibet after studying the Sanskrit language under an eminent Brahman teacher of Magadha. "His invention of the Tibetan alphabet gave two-fold impulse: for several centuries the wisdom of

India and the ingenuity of Tibet laboured in unison and with the greatest industry and enthusiasm at the work of translation. The tribute due to real genius must be accorded to these early pioneers of Tibetan grammar. They had to grapple with infinite wealth and refinement of Sanskrit; they had to save the independence of their own tongue, while they strove to subject it to the rule of scientific principles, and it is most remarkable how they managed to produce translations at once literal and faithful to the spirit of the original."

The Classical Period may be divided into three stages. The first or the earliest stage terminated with the downfall of the first historical monarchy, when King Langdarma fell by the hand of an assassin. The second stage commenced with the introduction of the system of chronology, called the Vrihaspati cycle of 60 years, in Tibet by an Indian Buddhist called Chandra Nath and Chilu Pandit of Tibet in 1025 A.D. This was the age of Milaraspa and Atisa, whose illustrious disciple, Brom-ton Gyalwai Jungné, laid the foundation of the first Buddhist Hierarchy in Tibet and established the great monastery of Rwaḍeng, with a library of Sanskrit works. Jäschke's second period evidently corresponds with this stage, when "Tibetan authors began to indulge in composition of their own" and wrote on historical and legendary subjects. The third stage began with the conquest of Tibet by the Tartar Conqueror, Chingis Khan, in 1205 A.D., when Pandit S'ākya S'ri of Kashmir had returned to Tibet after witnessing the plunder and destruction of the great Buddhist monasteries of Odantapuri and Vikrama S'ila in Magadha, and the conquest of Bengal and Behar by the Mahomedans under Baktyar Ghilji in 1203 A.D. In this last stage flourished the grand hierarchy of Sakya, which obtained supreme influence over Tibet and the country, which was then divided into 13 provinces, called Thikor Chusum, as a gift from the immediate successors of Chingis Khan. Among the most noted writers of the time were Sakya Pandit Kungah Gyal-tshan, Dogon Phag-pa, the spiritual tutor of Emperor Khubli Khan, and Shongton Lotsawa, who translated the *Kāvyādarśa* of Dandi and Kshemendra's *Avadāna Kalpalatā* in metrical Tibetan. With the opening of the 15th century Buton-Rinchen Düb introduced a new era in the literature of Tibet, and Buddhism received fresh impulse under the rule of the Phagmodu chiefs, when Tibetan scholars took largely to the study of

Chinese literature under the auspices of the Ming Emperors of China. During this period, called the age of Dā-nying (old orthography), the great indigenous literature of Tibet arose. A host of learned Lotsāwas and scholars like Tsongkhapa, Buton, Gyalwa Ngapa, Lama Tārānātha, Desri Sangye Gyatsho, Sumpa Khampo, and others flourished. This was the age of the Gelug-pa, or the Yellow Cap School of Buddhism, founded by Tsongkhapa with Gahdan as its head-quarters.

The third period begins with the first quarter of the 18th century, when Chinese suzerainty over Tibet was fully established and the last of the Tartar kings of the dynasty of Gushi Khan was killed by a General of the Jungar Tartars—an incident which transferred the sovereignty of Tibet to the Dalai Lama, who was till then a mere hierarch of the Gelug-pa Church. It is within this period that Tibet has enjoyed unprecedented peace under the benign sway of the holy Bodhisattvas, and its language has become the *lingua franca* of Higher Asia.

LHASA VILLA, DARJEELING,
July 1902.

SARAT CHANDRA DAS.

REVISORS' PREFACE.

WHEN in December 1899 the Chief Secretary to the Government of Bengal handed over to us for revision the Tibetan Dictionary upon which Sarat Chandra Das had laboured for some dozen years, we found at our disposal a work embracing a mass of new and important collections on the language, the value of which was marred by two prominent characteristics—*first*, the material had been put together in somewhat heterogeneous fashion, hardly systematic enough for a dictionary; *secondly*, the vast amount of original matter had been throughout greatly interlarded with lengthy excerpts from Jäschke's Dictionary, not always separable from the new information, and this imparted a second-hand appearance to large portions of the work, which was, in reality, by no means deserved. Moreover, in this way, no attempt had been made to improve upon Jäschke's definitions of many of the commoner Buddhist philosophical terms or to incorporate the later results of European scholarship in these instances. On the other hand, one was very often gratified to find, in the case of the more difficult philosophical terminology, that the learned Bengali had gone to original and little-explored sources of native information, such as Tsongkhapa's *Lam-rim Chhenmo*, and, by extracts from the same, furnished valuable and novel particulars under those heads.

Accordingly, the task which the Revisors set themselves was directed mainly to counteracting the errors of judgment above indicated. Such a task proved one of a more laborious character than might be at first imagined; and the fact that the work of amendment and addition has taken them upwards of two years of incessant toil sufficiently evidences its difficulty.

First, has come the business of selection and excision. The religion and philosophy of Tibetan books are properly confined to the Bon cult and to Buddhism. There had been, however, a tendency here to draw in all manner of Hindu thought and mythology, because one or two works translated into Tibetan from the Sanskrit dealt with these matters. This tendency it seemed right to curb except in those instances, not at all infrequent, where the Vedic and Puranic Hinduism, in some measure, was bound up with, or bore upon, or explained, Buddhist belief or popular practice.

Excision has had to be meted out, further, in the case of unnecessary repetition of otherwise properly-introduced information. *Secondly*, our task has been one of substitution. Many articles have had to be freshly written, or at least re-compiled. In place of the innumerable excerpts from Jäschke, already referred to, we have had to examine and to treat *de novo* the grammar and general usage of a large number of the commoner nouns, adjectives, and verbs, notably the verbs. To illustrate these new articles, we have had to substitute for Jäschke's examples a large number of original quotations from Tibetan authors as well as a certain number of made-up sentences put together to exhibit various phrases of ordinary employment. In other articles, also, where Sarat Chandra Das had not thought it necessary to do more than repeat Csoma's or Jäschke's illustrative sentences, we have looked out fresh examples to replace them. Of still greater importance was it in the case of certain doctrinal terms and phrases of Buddhism to undertake re-definition and to connote and assimilate modern discussion and research on the subject. Among those terms may be noted such as རྐྱེན, *rkyen ;* རྟེན་འབྲེལ, *rten-hbrel ;* ལྟ་བ, *lta-wa ;* རྡུལ, *rdul ;* བླ་མ, *bla-ma ;* གཡུང་དྲུང, *gyuñ-druñ ;* དེ་བཞིན་གཤེགས་པ, *de-bshin-gçegs-pa.* But while referring to these substitutions and others of a like nature, we do not wish to assume too much. We would rather repeat that, in the matter of philosophical definitions also, we have been frequently surprised and instructed by the descriptions and explanations of recondite ideas and terms which Sarat Chandra Das has himself succeeded in collecting from various native authorities. Such information would have sufficed if he had not sometimes confused it by the sudden and inconsequent linking on of Jäschke's remarks without curtailment and without any connotation of them to that which he had himself just set out. *Thirdly*, in the way of direct addition to the original work, there have been certain moderate supplementary contributions. Jäschke had dealt very fully with the Western colloquial, and we have sought to introduce a number of the colloquial words and phrases belonging to the Central and Eastern speech. Other additions have been short paragraphs on the mythological pantheon of Tibet and Mongolia, together with an attempt to give exact information on zoological and geographical points.

It may be considered by some that there is a certain lack of reference to known authorities in support of many of the statements set forth in this work. However, it should be remembered that in dealing with a language so little explored as the Tibetan (or which, indeed, in one narrow groove—that of the *Kahgyur* translations from Sanskrit—has, in some sense, been over-explored), the difficulty is to find adequate authorities for the real and more current uses of words and phrases. The stilted verbiage of the *Kahgyur* is often mere Sanskrit idiom literally rendered into Tibetan, but it gives no idea of the elastic style to be found in the innumerable indigenous productions of native Tibetan writers. Sarat Chandra Das has held familiar intercourse with modern men of learning in Tibet itself—the professors at Tashi-lhunpo, Daipung, Samye, Mindolling, and other important monastic institutions. Much, therefore, has been gleaned by him which, though absolutely reliable, cannot be given on any stated authority, but must be accepted as information obtained at first hand and now presented for the first time. This frank acceptance should also be extended to much with which the Revisors have been able to supplement the Author's original work. Both of them have been located for lengthy periods where Tibetan is the language of the people of the place, and have been in constant communication with men from Lhasa and all parts of Tibet. Under such circumstances, "authorities" cannot of course be quoted.

In dealing with philosophical terms, and in general with the forms to be met with both in the old classical works and in modern treatises, it will certainly be found, however, that our examples are constantly supported by exact references. These have been taken from writings of all kinds. Hitherto European scholars seem to have thought of the literature of Tibet as one consisting wholly of Sanskritic translation and as limited to the contents of the *Kahgyur* and *Tangyur*. The Author and the Revisors have endeavoured, by widening the sources of their quotations, to show how extensive a field is covered by mediæval and modern Tibetan writers. Geography, history, biography, political government, accounts, astrology, are all represented. It may be remarked, for example, that the official biographies of the successive Dalai Lamas alone fill some 32 volumes. Nevertheless, although these scarce memoirs are included in Sarat Chandra Das's library, we are sorry to point out that none of his examples appear to have been taken therefrom.

Knowing, however, how scanty is the range of Tibetan works available to the majority of students, we have not failed to quote largely in our examples from the *Kahgyur* and *Tangyur* collections. We may note on this point that a suggestion has been forwarded to us that, in quoting from the former, special references should be given to Mons. Feer's *Textes tirés du Kandjour*. But we are afraid that the scope for quotation would be narrowed if our references to the *Kahgyur* were confined to Mons. Feer's very limited extracts published in lithograph form over 30 years ago. As to the *Index du Kandjour*, which was issued in the publications of the Musée Guimet 20 years back, it is evident to every Tibetan student that this *Index* was only a *réchauffé* of Csoma Korösi's much clearer and fuller analysis of the *Kahgyur* printed 68 years ago in the pages of the *Asiatic Researches*. We fear, indeed, that reliance on such works as these would rather expose us to charges of non-acquaintance with more recent results of European investigation in the present field. Although working in India, we may observe, however, that we have done our best to keep pace with what European Orientalists have written on our subject; but assistance has been mainly derived from the many memoirs compiled by Russian and German scholars, and we would specially recommend to notice the collections in this field made by Prince Ukhtomski and the very recent publications of Dr. Albert Grünwedel, Dr. A. Conrady, and Professor Huth. The analyses of the *Tangyur*, issued by Professor Huth during the last three or four years, are particularly noteworthy. To return, however, to the above-mentioned suggestion, we may say that not only would the scope be too restricted, but also there is no necessity, under present conditions, to refer to any mere collection of extracts. Nearly every capital city in Europe now has obtained possession of complete copies of the *Kahgyur* volumes, and in two or three libraries the 220 volumes of the *Tangyur* may be also consulted. In St. Petersburg are three full sets of the *Kahgyur* and two sets of the *Tangyur;* in Paris is a set of the *Kahgyur;* in one or other of the great German libraries both the Tibetan encyclopœdia may be seen; in England, while curiously enough the British Museum Library owns only a small drawer-ful of loose Tibetan book-leaves, the India Office Library can boast a perfect series of both *Kahgyur* and *Tangyur;* and, lastly, in the Vatican Propaganda Library is preserved Oratio della Penna's incomplete collection of *Kahgyur* volumes.

A word as to the Sanskrit equivalents following each Tibetan term. Sanskrit scholars will perhaps consider these equivalents rather unsystematically enumerated. They have, nevertheless, with regard to the majority of them, this particular value:—they were selected by native Indian scholars of mediæval and later days in collaboration with Tibetan *lotsawas* or translators, as the appropriate Sanskrit synonyms of the respective Tibetan words. They have been taken chiefly from one celebrated Sanskrit-Tibetan Dictionary, and supplemented by a well-known Calcutta pandit and professor, Satis Chandra Acharya *Vidyabhusan*, who has also considerable acquaintance with literary Tibetan. The same learned professor has also, in numerous instances, appended a literal English rendering of the Sanskrit terms. These renderings have been placed within square brackets with the initial *S* outside the brackets, and he alone is responsible for such translations.

The system of transliteration followed is that adopted finally at the Vienna Congress of Orientalists; and this system is observed in the case of all Tibetan and Sanskrit words intended to be literally transliterated and printed in *italics*. However, when a Tibetan or Sanskrit proper name occurs in Roman characters, not as a transliteration, but in the English explanation of a word, or in any English sentence as an integral part of such explanation or sentence, the name is spelled according to the conventional English fashion and, in the case of Sanskrit terms or names, as in Sir Monier Williams's Dictionary.

A considerable number of Tibetan words at the head of paragraphs will be found in larger type. This indicates either that the word is the root of all related terms, or that it is the most common word of the series and thus ostensibly that from which the others have been derived. Two different arbitrary signs will be found prefixed to many words. The Author, it seems, has marked such words as he considers archaic or gone out of present use with a *swastika* (卐), and those words deemed by him to have been imported into Tibetan from the Sanskrit, whether directly or by derivation, he has distinguished by a double-headed dagger (‡).

In conclusion, the Revisors would point out that although they have been given, and have generally taken, the greatest freedom in correcting or rejecting the matter set forth in this work, and for that reason cannot justly shift responsibility for the accuracy or non-accuracy of that which is herein written, nevertheless they have generally not reversed the views and statements of the Author wherever these have seemed to them reasonable or fairly tenable, and to be the result of deliberately-formed opinion. They have felt, even when differing personally from the Author, that this Dictionary was Sarat Chandra Das's—not their own.

We must not omit to mention that, by the agency of the Chief Secretary to Government, certain brief comments on various portions of the Dictionary were received from Professor Bendall, and we have to thank him for his kind suggestions.

GRAHAM SANDBERG.
A. WILLIAM HEYDE.

DARJEELING, INDIA;
The 1st March 1902.

ALPHABETICAL PLAN OF THE TIBETAN LANGUAGE,

དབྱངས་ལྔ (*yāng nga*).

The five vowels:

ཨ་ཨི་ཨུ་ཨེ་ཨོ། *a, i, u, e, o.*

The four vowel signs that are attached to the basic letter ཨ are called *gi-gü*, *shabkyü*, *ḍeng-bü* and *nāro*:

ི ུ ེ ོ། *i, u, e, o.*

གསལ་བྱེད་སུམ་ཅུ་ནི (*sal-je süm-chü*).

The thirty consonants:

ཀ་ཁ་ག་ང་།	ཅ་ཆ་ཇ་ཉ།	ཏ་ཐ་ད་ན།
ka, kha, ga, ṅa.	*ca, cha, ja, ña.*	*ta, tha, dà, na.*
པ་ཕ་བ་མ།	ཙ་ཚ་ཛ་ཝ།	ཞ་ཟ་འ་ཡ།
pa, pha, ba, ma.	*tsa, tsha, dsa, wa.*	*sha, za, ḥa, ya.*
ར་ལ་ཤ་ས།	ཧ་ཨ།	
ra, la, ça, sa.	*ha, a.*	

The Dictionary order of the Tibetan letters,
with their Indo–Romanic equivalents and their pronunciation
exemplified by English words:

ཀ *k* in kill, seek.

ཁ *kh* ,, ink-horn.

ག *g* ,, gun, go, dog.

ང་ *ṅ* (=*ng*) ,, sing, king.

ཅ *c* (=*ch*) in porch.

ཆ *ch*(=*chh*),, church-hill.

ཇ *j* ,, jet, jump.

ཉ *ñ* (=*n*) ,, singe.

ཏ	*t*	in water (in Ireland).	ཞ	*sh*	in shone or *s* in leisure.
ཐ	*th*	,, nut-hook.	ཟ	*z*	,, azure or *s* in as.
ད	*d*	,, dice (more like *th* in this).	འ	*ḥ*	,, hour, honour.
ན	*n*	,, not, nut.	ཡ	*y*	,, yard, year.
པ	*p*	,, pull, page.	ར	*r*	,, ray, rope.
ཕ	*ph*	,, uphill.	ལ	*l*	,, last, large.
བ	*b*, or *w*	,, ball, boy, bard.	ཤ	*ç* (=*sh*)	,, sharp.
མ	*m*	,, man, map.	ས	*s*	,, same, soon.
ཙ	*ts*	,, parts.	ཧ	*h*	,, half, happy.
ཚ	*tsh*	,, (*ts* aspirated).	ཨ	*a*	,, far.
ཛ	*ds*	,, guards.			
ཝ	*w*	,, waft, wave.			

In all the above twenty nine letters the last letter ཨ is inherent, therefore tho Tibetan Grammarians have included it as a basis both for vowels and consonants. The letter འ (*ḥ*) called (འ་ཆུང་) the little *a* is generally joined to the basic-vowel of a letter to make its pronunciation long. When it is subjoined to the letter ཨ the compound so formed becomes equivalent to the Sanskrit आ *ā* and is pronounced as *a* in tar, far, or father. When it is subjoined to the vowel ཨི the compound so formed resembles the Sanskrit ई and is pronounced like *i* in police and so on.

The Sanskrit Alphabet and their Tibetan equivalents:

The vowels:

अ आ इ ई। उ ऊ ऋ ॠ। ऌ ॡ ए ऐ। ओ औ अं अः।

ཨ་ཨཱ་ཨི་ཨཱི། ཨུ་ཨཱུ་རྀ་རཱྀ། ལྀ་ལཱྀ་ཨེ་ཨཻ། ཨོ་ཨཽ་ཨཾ་ཨཿ

a, ā, i, ī. u, ū, r, ṛi. l, ḷi, e, ē. o, au, am, aḥ.

The consonants:

क ख ग घ ङ। च छ ज झ ञ। ट ठ ड ढ ण। त थ द ध न।

ཀ་ཁ་ག་གྷ་ང་། ཙ་ཚ་ཛ་ཛྷ་ཉ། ཊ་ཋ་ཌ་ཌྷ་ཎ། ཏ་ཐ་ད་དྷ་ན།

ka, kha, ga, gha, ṅa. tsa, tsha, dsa, dsha, ña. ṭa, ṭha, ḍa, ḍha, ṇa. ta, tha, da, dha, na.

प फ ब भ म। य र ल व। श ष स ह। क्ष।

པ་ཕ་བ་བྷ་མ། ཡ་ར་ལ་ཝ། ཤ་ཥ་ས་ཧ། ཀྵ།

pa, pha, ba, bha, ma. ya, ra, la, wa. ça, ṣa, sa, ha. kṣa.

The consonant signs representing the letters ཡ, and ར:

ྱ (ཡ་བཏགས *ya-tāg*) and ྲ (ར་བཏགས *ra-tāg*).

ལོག་ཡིག་དྲུག (*log-yig* six).

The six inverted Tibetan letters representing the Sanskrit letters:

ट ठ ड ण ष क्ष।

ཊ་ཋ་ཌ་ཎ་ཥ་ཀྵ།

ṭa, ṭha, ḍa, ṇa, ṣa, kṣa.

ཧ་བཏགས་དྲུག (*ha-tāg* six).

The six aspirates, *i.e.*, letters having ཧ subjoined to them,

घ ध भ झ ढ ल्ह।

གྷ་དྷ་བྷ་ཛྷ་ཌྷ་ལྷ།

gha, dha, bha, dsha, ḍha, lha.

གི་གུ་ཞབས་ཀྱུ་འགྲེང་བུ་ན་རོ་(or སྣ་རོ་)བཞི་བཏགས་པ་ནི།

The compounds formed with the four vowel signs of *i, u, e* and *o* called *gi-gu*—the angle ི, *shabs-kyu*—the hook ུ, *hgreṅ-bu* the 'standing' stroke ེ, and *sna-ro* 'the horns over the nose' ོ, which are joined to the consonants including the basic vowel ཨ,

ཀི་ཀུ་ཀེ་ཀོ།	*ki, ku, ke, ko.*	ཁི་ཁུ་ཁེ་ཁོ།	*khi, khu, khe, kho.*
གི་གུ་གེ་གོ།	*gi, gu, ge, go.*	ངི་ངུ་ངེ་ངོ་།	*ṅi, ṅu, ṅe, ṅo.*
ཅི་ཅུ་ཅེ་ཅོ།	*ci, cu, ce, co.*	ཆི་ཆུ་ཆེ་ཆོ།	*chi, chu, che, cho.*
ཇི་ཇུ་ཇེ་ཇོ།	*ji, ju, je, jo.*	ཉི་ཉུ་ཉེ་ཉོ།	*ñi, ñu, ñe, ño.*

ཏི་ཏུ་ཏེ་ཏོ།	*ti, tu, te, to.*	ཐི་ཐུ་ཐེ་ཐོ།	*thi, thu, the, tho.*
དི་དུ་དེ་དོ།	*di, du, de, do.*	ནི་ནུ་ནེ་ནོ།	*ni, nu, ne, no.*
པི་པུ་པེ་པོ།	*pi, pu, pe, po.*	ཕི་ཕུ་ཕེ་ཕོ།	*phi, phu, phe, pho.*
བི་བུ་བེ་བོ།	*bi, bu, be, bo.*	མི་མུ་མེ་མོ།	*mi, mu, me, mo.*
ཙི་ཙུ་ཙེ་ཙོ།	*tsi, tsu, tse, tso.*	ཚི་ཚུ་ཚེ་ཚོ།	*tshi, tshu, tshe, tsho.*
ཛི་ཛུ་ཛེ་ཛོ།	*dsi, dsu, dse, dso.*	ཝི་ཝུ་ཝེ་ཝོ།	*wi, wu, we, wo.*
ཞི་ཞུ་ཞེ་ཞོ།	*shi, shu, she, sho.*	ཟི་ཟུ་ཟེ་ཟོ།	*zi, zu, ze, zo.*
འི་འུ་འེ་འོ།	*ḥi, ḥu, ḥe, ḥo.*	ཡི་ཡུ་ཡེ་ཡོ།	*yi, yu, ye, yo.*
རི་རུ་རེ་རོ།	*ri, ru, re, ro.*	ལི་ལུ་ལེ་ལོ།	*li, lu, le, lo.*
ཤི་ཤུ་ཤེ་ཤོ།	*çi, çu, çe, ço.*	སི་སུ་སེ་སོ།	*si, su, se, so.*
ཧི་ཧུ་ཧེ་ཧོ།	*hi, hu, he, ho.*	ཨི་ཨུ་ཨེ་ཨོ།	*i, u, e, o.*

ཡ་བཏགས་བདུན་ནི (*ya-tāg* seven).

The seven basic consonants to which the letter ཡ *y* is subjoined:

ཀྱ་ཁྱ་གྱ་པྱ་ཕྱ་བྱ་མྱ། *kya, khya, gya, pya, phya, bya, mya.*

The four compounds which in their pronunciation resemble the four simple letters ཅ, ཆ, ཇ, ཉ:

པྱ	*pya*	is pronounced	as	ཅ *ca.*	ཕྱ	*phya*	is pronounced	as	ཆ *cha*
བྱ	*bya*	„	„	„ ཇ *ja.*	མྱ	*mya*	„	„	„ ཉ *ña.*

ར་བཏགས་བཅུ་གསུམ (*ra-tāg* thirteen).

The thirteen basic consonants to which the letter ར *r* may be subjoined and in which though the basic constituent is not pronounced, in Tibet proper yet the compounds so formed have a pronunciation altogether different from that of any of the constituents,

ཀྲ་ཁྲ་གྲ་ཏྲ་ཐྲ་དྲ་པྲ་ཕྲ་བྲ་མྲ་ཤྲ་སྲ་ཧྲ།

kra, khra, gra, tra, thra, dra, pra, phra, bra, mra, çra, sra, hra,
(*ṭa*), (*ṭha*), (*ḍa*), (*ṭa*), (*ṭha*), (*ḍa*), (*ṭa*), (*ṭha*), (*ḍa*), (*ma*), (*sra*), (*sa*), *hra.*

The eight compounds of which the pronunciation resembles that of the Sanskṛt cerebrals ट, ठ, ड represented in Tibetan by the inverted letters ཊ, ཋ, ཌ, :—

ཀྲ	*kra* (*ṭa*).	ཏྲ	*tra* (*ṭa*).	པྲ	*pra* (*ṭa*).	ཁྲ	*khra* (*ṭha*).
གྲ	*gra* (*ḍa*).	དྲ	*dra* (*ḍa*).	བྲ	*bra* (*ḍa*).	ཕྲ	*phra* (*ṭha*).

ལ་བཏགས་དྲུག (*la-tāg* six).

The six basic consonants to which the letter ལ *l* is subjoined :

ཀླ་གླ་བླ་རླ་སླ་ཟླ།

k̲la, gla, b̲la, r̲la, s̲la, zla (*da*).

In the compounds the མིང་གཞི *i.e.*, basic are silent except in ཟླ which is pronounced as *d*; the letters not pronounced are underlined.

དེ་ལ་ཞབས་ཀྱུ་བཏགས་པ།

The same with ུ *u* subjoined :

ཀླུ་གླུ་བླུ་རླུ་སླུ་ཟླུ།

k̲lu, glu, b̲lu, r̲lu, s̲lu, zlu (*du*).

ཝ་ཟུར་བཏགས་པ་བཅུ་དྲུག་ནི (*wa-zur tāg-pa* sixteen).

The sixteen letters with (ཝ་ཟུར) *i.e.* ྭ which is a corner of the letter ཝ *w* subjoined to them :

ཀྭ་ཁྭ་གྭ་ཅྭ་ཉྭ་ཏྭ་དྭ་ཙྭ་ཚྭ་ཞྭ་ཟྭ་རྭ་ལྭ་ཤྭ་སྭ་ཧྭ།

kwa, khwa, gwa, cwa, ñwa, twa, dwa, tswa, tshwa, shwa, zwa, rwa, lwa, çwa, swa, hwa.

ར་མགོ་བཅུ་གཉིས་ནི (*ra-go* twelve).

The twelve basic consonants with ར *r* on their head, *i.e.*, ར surmounting them :

རྐ་རྒ་རྔ་རྗ་རྙ་རྟ་རྡ་རྣ་རྦ་རྨ་རྩ་རྫ།

r̲ka, r̲ga, r̲ña, r̲ja, r̲ña, r̲ta, r̲da, r̲na, r̲ba, r̲ma, r̲tsa, r̲dsa.

(the superscribed letter being generally silent is represented by an underlined *r̲*)

ལ་མགོ་བཅུ་ནི (*la-go* ten).

The ten basic consonants with the letter ལ *l* surmounting them:

ལྐ་ལྒ་ལྔ་ལྕ་ལྗ་ལྟ་ལྡ་ལྤ་ལྦ་ལྷ།

l̲ka, l̲ga, l̲ṅa, l̲ca, l̲ja, l̲ta, l̲da, l̲pa, l̲ba, lha.

the superscribed letter where silent is represented by an underlined *l̲*.

ས་མགོ་བཅུ་གཅིག་ནི (*sa-go* eleven).

The eleven basic consonants with the letter ས *s* surmounting them:

སྐ་སྒ་སྔ་སྙ་སྟ་སྡ་སྣ་སྤ་སྦ་སྨ་སྩ།

s̲ka, s̲ga, s̲ṅa, s̲ña, s̲ta, s̲da, s̲na, s̲pa, s̲ba, s̲ma, s̲tsa.

the superscribed letter which is not pronounced is represented by an underlined *s̲*.

སྔོན་འཇུག་ལྔ (*ngon-jüg* five).

The five letters which, when prefixed to initial or basic letters to form a word, are seldom in Tibet Proper pronounced and are represented by underlined italics:

ག་ད་བ་མ་འ།

g̲, d̲, b̲, m̲, h̲.

རྗེས་འཇུག་བཅུ་ནི (*je-jüg* ten).

The ten letters which when affixed to initial letters to form a word are very softly pronounced:—

ག་ང་ད་ན་བ་མ་འ་ར་ལ་ས།

g, ṅ, d, n, b, m, h̲, r, l, s.

རྫོགས་ཚིག་བཅུ་གཅིག་ནི (*dsog-tshig* eleven).

The eleven letters which are reduplicated (to form the preterite) when joined with a terminal *o*:

གོ་ངོ་དོ་ནོ་བོ་མོ་འོ་རོ་ལོ་སོ་ཏོ།

go, ṅo, do, no, bo, mo, h̲o, ro, lo, so, to.

ལ་དོན་རྣམ་པ་བདུན་ནི (*la-don* seven).

The seven postpositions signifying to or at,

སུ་རུ་ར་དུ་ན་ལ་ཏུ།

su, ru, ra, du, na, la, tu.

འབྲེལ་སྒྲ་ལྔ་ནི (*ḏel-ḏā* five).

The postpositive particles to signify possession:—

གི་ཀྱི་གྱི་འི་ཡི།

gi, kyi, gyi, ẖi, yi.

བྱེད་སྒྲ་ནི *ché-ḏā* or *jé-ḏā*.

The instrumental particles:—

གིས་ཀྱིས་གྱིས་འིས་ཡིས།

giṣ, kyiṣ, gyiṣ, ẖiṣ, yiṣ.

སྔོན་འཇུག་ལ་བ་ཐོབ་པའི་ཀ་ཡིག་(མིང་གཞི)།

the basic (མིང་གཞི) ཀ and its compounds with the letter *b* བ prefixed,

བཀའ།	*ḇkaẖ.*	བཀང་།	*ḇkaṅ.*	བཀག།	*ḇkag.*	བཀན།	*ḇkan.*
བཀབ།	*ḇkab.*	བཀས།	*ḇkaṣ.*	བཀར།	*ḇkar.*	བཀལ།	*ḇkal.*
བཀུག།	*ḇkug.*	བཀུམས།	*ḇkumṣ.*	བསྐུར།	*ḇṣkur.*	བཀུར།	*ḇkur.*
བཀུས།	*ḇkuṣ.*	བཀོད།	*ḇkoḏ.*	བཀོལ།	*ḇkol.*	བཀྱིགས།	*ḇkyigṣ.*
བཀྱེ།	*ḇkye.*	བཀྲ།	*ḇkra.*	བཀྲག།	*ḇkrag.*	བཀྲབས།	*ḇkrabṣ.*
བཀྲམས།	*ḇkramṣ.*	བཀྲལ།	*ḇkral.*	བཀྲི།	*ḇkri.*	བཀྲུ།	*ḇkru.*
བཀྲུས།	*ḇkruṣ.*	བཀྲེན།	*ḇkren.*	བཀྲེས།	*ḇkreṣ.*	བཀྲོངས།	*ḇkroṅṣ.*
བཀྲོལ།	*ḇkrol.*	བཀྲག།	*ḇkrag.*	བསྐྱེད།	*ḇṣkyeḏ.*	བསྐྱུར།	*ḇṣkyur.*
བསྐོས།	*ḇṣkoṣ.*	བརྐོ།	*ḇṟko.*	བརྐུ།	*ḇṟku.*	བརྐྱངས།	*ḇṟkyaṅṣ.*
བརྐུམ།	*ḇṟkum.*						

བ་འཕྲུལ་སྔོན་པའི་ཅ།

the basic ཅ and its compounds with the letter བ prefixed,

བཅའ།	*b̲caḥ.*	བཅགས།	*b̲cagṣ.*	བཅངས།	*b̲caṅṣ.*	བཅད།	*b̲caḍ.*
བཅབས།	*b̲cabṣ.*	བཅར།	*b̲car.*	བཅལ།	*b̲cal.*	བཅས།	*b̲caṣ.*
བཅིལ།	*b̲cil.*	བཅིངས།	*b̲ciṅṣ.*	བཅིང་།	*b̲ciṅ.*	བཅུག།	*b̲cug.*
བཅུད།	*b̲cuḍ.*	བཅུམ།	*b̲cum.*	བཅུ།	*b̲cu.*	བཅོམས།	*b̲comṣ.*
བཅོས།	*b̲coṣ.*	བཅོལ།	*b̲col.*	བལྕིད།	*b̲l̲ciḍ.*		

བ་སྔོན་པའི་ཏ།

the basic ཏ and its compounds with the letter བ prefixed,

བཏགས།	*b̲tagṣ.*	བཏང་།	*b̲taṅ.*	བཏབ།	*b̲tab.*	བཏིངས།	*b̲tiṅṣ.*
བཏུ།	*b̲tu.*	བཏུས།	*b̲tuṣ.*	བཏུད།	*b̲tuḍ.*	བཏུབ།	*b̲tub.*
བཏུལ།	*b̲tul.*	བཏུང་།	*b̲tuṅ.*	བཏེབ།	*b̲teb.*	བརྟན།	*b̲r̲tan.*
བརྟེན།	*b̲r̲ten.*	བསྟན།	*b̲s̲tan.*	བསྟེན།	*b̲s̲ten.*	བལྟ།	*b̲l̲ta.*
བལྟས།	*b̲l̲taṣ*	བལྟར།	*b̲l̲tar.*	བལྟོས།	*b̲l̲toṣ.*	བལྟམས།	*b̲l̲tamṣ.*
བརྟུན།	*b̲r̲tun.*	བརྟུལ།	*b̲r̲tul.*	བསྟེགས།	*b̲s̲tegṣ.*	བསྟུམ།	*b̲s̲tum.*

བ་སྔོན་པའི་ཙ།

the basic ཙ and its compounds with the letter བ prefixed,

བཙག།	*b̲tsag.*	བཙན།	*b̲tsan.*	བཙའ།	*b̲tsaḥ.*	བཙས།	*b̲tsaṣ.*
བཙལ།	*b̲tsal.*	བཙིར།	*b̲tsir.*	བཙུགས།	*b̲tsugṣ.*	བཙུད།	*b̲tsuḍ.*
བཙུན།	*b̲tsun.*	བཙུམས།	*b̲tsumṣ.*	བཙེམས།	*b̲tsemṣ.*	བཙོ།	*b̲tso.*
བཙོག།	*b̲tsog.*	བཙོང་།	*b̲tsoṅ.*	བཙོད།	*b̲tsoḍ.*	བཙོན།	*b̲tson.*
བཙོངས།	*b̲tsoṅṣ.*	བཙོས།	*b̲tsoṣ.*	བརྩི།	*b̲r̲tsi.*	བརྩུབ།	*b̲r̲tsub.*
བརྩེ།	*b̲r̲tse.*	བསྩོན།	*b̲s̲tson.*	བརྩམས།	*b̲r̲tsamṣ.*		

བ་སྔོན་པའི་ག།

the basic ག and its compounds with the letter བ prefixed,

བགག།	*bgag.*	བགགས།	*bgags.*	བགད།	*bgad.*	བགམ།	*bgam.*
བགེགས།	*bgegs.*	བགོ།	*bgo.*	བགོས།	*bgos.*	བགྱངས།	*bgyańs.*
བགྱི།	*bgyi.*	བགྱིས།	*bgyis.*	བགྱིད།	*bgyid.*	བགྲང་།	*bgrań.*
བགྲངས།	*bgrańs.*	བགྲད།	*bgrad.*	བགྲེས།	*bgres.*	བགྲོ།	*bgro.*
བརྒན།	*brgan.*	བརྒོལ།	*brgol.*	བརྒྱངས།	*brgyańs.*	བརྒྱིད།	*brgyid.*
བརྒྱུད།	*brgyud.*	བརྒྱུན།	*brgyun.*	བརྒྱེ།	*brgye.*	བརྒྱན།	*brgyan.*
བརྒྱལ།	*brgyal.*	བརྒྱད།	*brgyad.*	བསྒྱིར།	*bsgyir.*	བསྒྱུར།	*bsgyur.*
བསྒྱེད།	*bsgyed.*	བསྒྲོབ།	*bsgrob.*	བསྒྲུན།	*bsgrun.*	བསྒྲུངས།	*bsgruńs.*
བསྒྲུམ།	*bsgrum.*	བསྒྲེང་།	*bsgreń.*	བསྒྲོན།	*bsgron.*	བསྒྲགས།	*bsgrags.*
བསྒྲུབས།	*bsgrubs.*						

ÇAD OR THE STOPS.

ཤད pronounced shad in Ladak and Amdo but in Tsang and Central Tibet is pronounced : Shay |

ཀྱང་ཤད or ཚེག་ཤད single perpendicular stroke | = (,) Comma.

ཉིས་ཤད double stroke || = (.) full stop.

བཞི་ཤད four-fold stroke |||| used at the end of a chapter or section.

ཚེག point, dot separating syllables.

ཚེག་ཤད stroke with dots on its top ༔ or ༄ ornamental stop.

ABBREVIATIONS OF NAMES.

A.......................*Ati-çaẖi ṟnam-thar* ཇོ་བོ་རྗེ་ཨ་ཏི་ཤའི་རྣམ་ཐར།
A. K. ....Avadāna Kalpalatā.
A. R. ....Asiatic Researches.
A. S...................Aṣṭa Sāhasrikā B. T. Society.
A. Ç. ....Anuruddha-Çataka B. T. Society.
Abhi...................Abhidhammattha-sangaho.
Ar. ....Arabic.
B. grub. ....*Bon-gyi grub-m̱thaẖ* བོན་གྱི་གྲུབ་མཐའ།
B. Nam.............Bon Nam shag.
B.T.S. ....Buddhist Text Society.
Bal. ....Baltistan.
Beẖu...................*Behu-bum s̱ñon-po* བེའུ་བུམ་སྔོན་པོ།
Beng...................Bengali language.
Bhar. ....Bharata, dialogue, ed. by Dr. A. Schiefner.
Bhot...................Bhotan, province.
Bodhi. ....Bodhicharyāvatāra, B. T. Society.
B.ch....................*Bon-chos̱* བོན་གྱི་ཆོས།
Budh. ....Buddhism.
Bum....................སྨན་འབུམ་ཆུང་ *S̱man-ẖbum chuñ.*
Burn. I. ....Burnouf, Introduction au Buddhism Indien.
Burn. II............Burnouf, Lotus de la bonne loi.
C. ....Central Tibet.
Cāṇ....................*Cāṇakya (Tsā-na-ka)* ཙ་ཎ་ཀ།
Cho-zañ. ....*Lama Chos̱-ḇzañ g̱suñ-ẖbum.*
Choi-g. ....*Chos̱-ṟgyal ḇstoḏ-pa* ཆོས་རྒྱལ་བསྟོད་པ།
Cs.......................Csoma de Körösi's Tibetan English Dictionary
Cunn. ....Cunningham General, Ladak and the surrounding country.
Çe or *Ç. doñ.* ......*Çes̱-rab s̱doñ-bu* ཤེས་རབ་སྡོང་བུ།
Ç. gya. ....*Çes̱-rab ḇrgya-pa* ཤེས་རབ་བརྒྱ་པ།
Ç. lam. ....*Çam-bha-laẖi lam-yig* ཤམ་བྷ་ལའི་ལམ་ཡིག།
Çer. ....*Çer-gyi me-loñ* ཤེར་གྱི་མེ་ལོང་།
Çil. ....*Çila* ཤཱི་ལ།
Div. A...............Divyâvadāna.
D. çel................*Dwañs̱-çel me-loñ* དྭངས་ཤེལ་མེ་ལོང་།
D. R. ....*Dul-wa Rinpo-che*, a Bon religious work.
Dran. ....*Dṟan-pa ñer g̱s̱hag* དྲན་པ་ཉེར་གཞག།
Dag....................*Dag-byeḏ g̱sal-waẖi me-loñ* དག་བྱེད་གསལ་བའི་མེ་ལོང་།

Deb. ....*Deb-ther sňon-po* དེབ་ཐེར་སྔོན་པོ།
Desg. ....Desgodins, La Mission du Tibet de 1855–1870.
Dh. ....Dharmasangraha (Max Müller).
Dham. . ...Dhammapado, B. Text Society's edition.
Do or *Dom.* ....*Mdo-maň* མདོ་མང་།
Dsam. ....*Hdsam-gliň rgyas-bçad* འཛམ་གླིང་རྒྱས་བཤད།
Dus-ye. ....*Dus-hkhor-gyi ye-çes-kyi lehu* also *Dus-hgrel ye-le.*
Dus-kho. ....དུས་འཁོར་ཊཱི་ཀཱ *Dus-hkhor ṭi-kā.*
Dug. ....*Gdugs-dkar* གདུགས་དཀར།
Dzl. ....*Mdo hdsaň-blun* an ancient collection of Legends of Buddha.
Ev. ....*E-vam* ཨེ་ཝམ།
G. Bon. ....*Rgyal-rabs bon-gyi hbyuň-gnas* རྒྱལ་རབས་བོན་གྱི་འབྱུང་གནས།
G. kah. ....*Rgyal-po bkah-thaň* རྒྱལ་པོ་བཀའ་ཐང་།
G. Sndg. ....Revd. Graham Sandberg, B.A., LL.B.
Gyal. ....*Rgyal mtshan rtsemohi gzuňs.*
Gyal. S. ....*Rgyal-rabs gsal-wahi me-loň* རྒྱལ་རབས་གསལ་བའི་མེ་ལོང་།
Glr. ....*Rgyal-rabs*, a history of the kings of Tibet quoted by Jäschke.
Gram. ....Grammar or native grammatical works.
Grub. ....*Grub-mthah çel-gyi me-loň* གྲུབ་མཐའ་ཤེལ་གྱི་མེ་ལོང་།
Gul. ....མཁས་པའི་མགུལ་རྒྱན *Mkhas-pahi mgul-rgyan.*
Gya-cher. ....*Gya-cher rol-pa*, Tib. version of the *Lalitvistara* Ed. by Foucaux.
Glu. ....*Rgyal-wa Tshaňs-dbyaňs rgya-mtshohi mgul-glu.*
Gser-phreň. ....རྒྱལ་བློན་གྱི་འཛངས་ཤིག་ལེགས་བཤད་གསེར་འཕྲེང་ by Nāgārjuna.
Gshon. ....*Gshon-nuhi mgul mgyur* གཞོན་ནུའི་མགུལ་མགྱུར།
Gyu. ....*Gyu-thog-pahi rnam-thar* གཡུ་ཐོག་པའི་རྣམ་ཐར།
Hey. ....Revd. A. W. Heyde of the Moravian Mission.
Hind. ....Hindi language.
Hook. ....Sir Joseph Hooker's Himalayan journals.
Huc. ....Abbe Huc and Gabet's Tibet.
Hbrom ....*Hbrom-ston-pahi rnam-thar* འབྲོམ་སྟོན་རྒྱལ་བའི་འབྱུང་གནས་ཀྱི་རྣམ་ཐར།
Hbum. ....*Yum-chen-mo* ཡུམ་ཆེན་མོ།
J. Zaň. ....*Dpag-bsam ljon-bzaň* དཔག་བསམ་ལྗོན་བཟང་།
Jä. ....Jächke's Tibetan-English Dictionary.
Jig. ....*Hjig-rten lugs-kyi bstan-bcos* འཇིག་རྟེན་ལུགས་ཀྱི་བསྟན་བཅོས།
K. d. ....*Bkah-hgyur mdo* བཀའ་འགྱུར་མདོ།
K. du. ....*Bkah-hgyur hdul-wa* བཀའ་འགྱུར་འདུལ་བ།
K. dun. ....*Bkah-babs bdun-ldan-gyi rnam-thar* བཀའ་བབས་བདུན་ལྡན་གྱི་རྣམ་ཐར།
K. g. ....*Bkah-hgyur rgyud* བཀའ་འགྱུར་རྒྱུད།
K. ko. ....*Bkah-hgyur dkon-brtsegs* བཀའ་འགྱུར་དཀོན་བརྩེགས།
K. my. ....*Bkah-hgyur myaň-hdas* བཀའ་འགྱུར་མྱང་འདས།
K. phal. ....*Bkah hgyur phal-po-che* བཀའ་འགྱུར་ཕལ་པོ་ཆེ།

K.P. ....Karuṇā-puṇḍarika, B. T. Society.

K. thañ. or *Kathañ.* *Padma b̲kah̲ thañ.*

Kālac. T. ....Kālachakra of Tārānātha.

Kh.....................Kham, eastern part of Tibet.

Kha. ....མཁའ་འགྲོ་མའི་བརྡའ *M̲khah h̲gro-mahi brdah̲.*

Khrid̲. ....*K̲loñ-chen H̲khrid̲-yig* ཀློང་ཆེན་སྙིང་ཞིག་གི་སྔོན་འགྲོའི་འཁྲིད་ཡིག།

Köpp. ....Köppen, die religion des Buddha.

Kun....................Kunawar, province under British protection.

Kye-rim. ....*H̲jigs̲-bye̲d b̲s̲kyed̲-rim* འཇིགས་བྱེད་བསྐྱེད་རིམ།

L. V....................Lalitavistara.

Lankā. ....Laŋkāvatāra-Sūtra, B. T. Society.

Lam-rim. ....*Byañ-chub Lam-gyi rim-pa* བྱང་ཆུབ་ལམ་གྱི་རིམ་པ།

Lam. ṭi...............*Lam-don ṭi-ka* ལམ་སྟོན་ཊི་ཀ།

Lat. ....Latin.

Ld. ....Ladak.

Ld. Glr...............*Ladak Gyal-rabs̲*, a history of Tibet, Ed. by Dr. E. Schlagintweit.

Lex or *Lexx*........Lexicon or Lexicons, native Tibetan dictionaries.

Lh. ....Lhasa.

Lh. kar...............*Lha-sah̲i d̲kar-chag* ལྷ་སའི་དཀར་ཆག།

Lha. kah̲. ....*Lha-h̲dr̲e b̲kah̲-thañ* ལྷ་འདྲེ་བཀའ་ཐང་།

Liç. ....*Li-çi gur-khañ* ལི་ཤི་གུར་ཁང་ a Tibetan glossary.

Lo. ....*Thog-mah̲i b̲lo-s̲byoñs̲* ཐོག་མའི་བློ་སྦྱོངས (*Lam-rim*).

Loñ. ....*K̲loñ-r̲dol g̲suñ-h̲bum* ཀློང་རྡོལ་གསུང་འབུམབླ་མ་ཀློང་རྡོལ་རིན་པོ་ཆེའི་གསུང་འབུམ་བ་པ 16th volume.

L. kah̲. ....*B̲lon-po b̲kah̲-thañ* བློན་པོ་བཀའ་ཐང་།

L̲jañs̲. ....*L̲jañ-gliñ-gi b̲s̲gruñs̲* ལྗང་གླིང་གི་བསྒྲུངས།

M. V. ....*Mahā Vyutpatti.*

M. vṛtti. ....*Mādhyamika Vritti* B. T. Society.

M. Wills. ....Sir. Monier William's Sanskrit-English Dictionary.

Ma. ....*Ma-h̲oñs̲ luñ-b̲s̲tan* མ་འོངས་ལུང་བསྟན Tibetan Apocalypse.

M. gu. ....*Mar̲gyud̲* མ་རྒྱུད།

Mahā. p. ....Mahāparinibbāna-sutta, Pali Text Society.

Mahā. v. ....Mahāvaṁso.

Mam....................མ་མོ་བསྐང་གསོ *Mamo b̲skañ g̲so.*

Med. ....Medical works of Tibet.

Mi. ....*Mih̲i m̲tshan-ñid̲* མིའི་མཚན་ཉིད།

Mil. ....Milaraspa's མགུར་འབུམ *m̲gur h̲bum* hundred thousand songs.

Mil. nt................*Mi-la ras̲-pah̲i r̲nam-thar* མི་ལ་རས་པའི་རྣམ་ཐར Mila's autobiography.

Miñ-r̲da....... ......*Miñ-don b̲r̲dah̲-s̲prod̲* མིང་དོན་བརྡའ་སྤྲོད (*Dag-yig*).

Mong. ....Mongolian.

Mñg. ....*Man-ñag r̲gyud̲* མན་ངག་རྒྱུད a medical work.

M̱grin. ....*M̱grin-s̱ṅon zla-wa̱hi ṟtogs-ḇrjoḏ* མགྲིན་སྔོན་ཟླ་བའི་རྟོགས་བརྗོད།

M̱gur. ....*Mi-la raṣ-pa̱hi m̱gur-ẖbum* མི་ལ་རས་པའི་མགུར་འབུམ

M̱ṅon. ....*M̱ṅon-ḇrjoḏ m̱khaṣ-pa̱hi ṟna-ṟgyan* མངོན་བརྗོད་མཁས་པའི་རྣ་རྒྱན། a Lhasa block-print work in 80 leaves compiled by Ṅag Wang Jigten Wangchûg Tagpai Dorje (ངག་དབང་འཇིག་རྟེན་དབང་ཕྱུག་གྲགས་པའི་རྡོ་རྗེ) from Sakya Paṇchhen's Tshig-gter, Tibetan translation of Amarkoṣa and other lexicons.

M̱tshan...............*M̱tshan-ñiḏ* མཚན་ཉིད།

Nāro. ....*Na-ro choṣ-dṟug* ཟབ་ལམ་ན་རོ་ཆོས་དྲུག་གི་འཁྲིད། པཎ་ཆེན་ན་རོ་པའི་རྣམ་ཐར།

Nor. ....*Nor-lha̱hi g̱zuṅṣ* ནོར་ལྷའི་གཟུངས།

Ṅag. ....*Dag-yig ṅag-s̱gron* དག་ཡིག་ངག་སྒྲོན་རྩ་འགྲེལ།

Org. ....Original texts.

Org. m. ....Original manuscripts.

Pag. ....*Ṟtogṣ-ḇjroḏ ḏpag-sam ẖkhri-çiṅ* རྟོགས་བརྗོད་དཔག་བསམ་འཁྲི་ཤིང་།

Pth. ....*Paḏ-ma thaṅ-yig* པད་མ་ཐང་ཡིག།

Pur. ....Purraṅg.

Ṟdo. ....*Ṟdo-riṅ sum-ṟtags* རྡོ་རིང་སུམ་རྟགས།

Ṟdo-phreṅ. ....*Ṟdo-ṟje phreṅ-wa.*

Ṟdsa...............*S̱gom-chen daṅ ṟdsa-ṟtsig-gi ṟnam-thar* སྒོམ་ཆེན་དང་རྫ་རྩིག་གི་རྣམ་ཐར།

Ṟgyan. ....*Ṟgyan-gyi ḇstan ḇcoṣ* རྒྱན་གྱི་བསྟན་བཅོས།

Ṟje-nam. ....*Ṟje rin-po che̱hi ṟnam-thar* རྗེ་རིན་པོ་ཆེའི་རྣམ་ཐར།

Ṟnam. ....*Ṟnam-ḇçaḏ s̱ñiṅ-ṟgyan* རྣམ་བཤད་སྙིང་རྒྱན།

Ṟtsa-g. ....*Ṟtsa-ṟgyuḏ* རྩ་རྒྱུད།

Ṟtsa. ṭi. ....*Ḏbu-ma ṟtsa ẖgrel-pa g̱ñiṣ-ka,* དབུ་མ་རྩ་བ་དང་འགྲེལ་པ་གཉིས་ཀ།

Ṟtsa-shuṅ...............*Man-ṅag ṟgyuḏ-kyi ṟtsa-wa̱hi g̱shuṅ* མན་ངག་རྒྱུད་ཀྱི་རྩ་བའི་གཞུང་།

Ṟtsi. ....*Ṟtsiṣ-kyi ḇstan-ḇcoṣ* རྩིས་ཀྱི་བསྟན་བཅོས།

Ṟtsii...............*Ṟtsiṣ-g̱shi phyogṣ-ḇsgrigṣ* རྩིས་གཞི་ཕྱོགས་བསྒྲིགས།

S. ....Sanskrit terms from Tibetan-Sanskrit Lexicons of Tibet explained by Satis Chandra Acharya, M.A.

S. del. ....*G̱sum-ẖgrel* གསུམ་འགྲེལ།

S. g. ....*Shaḏ-gyuḏ*, a medical work.

S. Lex. ....Sanskrit lexicon.

S. phreṅ. ....*Legṣ-ḇçaḏ gser-ẖphreṅ* ལེགས་བཤད་གསེར་འཕྲེང་།

S. kar. ....*Ḇsam-yaṣ ḏkar-chag* བསམ་ཡས་དཀར་ཆག།

S. lam. ....Sambhalai lam-yig.

S. leg. ....*Sa-s̱kya legs-ḇçaḏ* ས་སྐྱ་ལེགས་བཤད།

S. o. ....*G̱ser-ẖoḏ dam-pa* གསེར་འོད་དམ་པ།

S.P. ....Suvarṇa-prabhā, B. T. Society.

Samā. ....Samādhirāya-sūtra, B. T. Society.

Sām. ....*Sāmkhya-tattva Kaumudi.*

Sans. ....Sanskrit or Sanskṛt.

Sch. ....Prof. Is. J. Schmidt, Tibetisch-Deutsches Wörterbuch. and Tibetische grammatik.
Schr...................Dr. A. Schiefner.
Schl. ....Dr. E. Schlagintweit, Buddhism in Tibet.
Schtr. ....Schröter, editor of the first Tibetan Dictionary.
Ser. ....*Gser-gyi Meloñ,* གསེར་གྱི་མེ་ལོང་།
Shad...................*Sman-gyi bçad-rgyud* སྨན་གྱི་བཤད་རྒྱུད།
Shal...................ཞལ་ལྕེ *Shal-lce.*
Sikk...................Sikkim.
Situ. ....*Si-tuhi sum-rtags* སི་ཏུའི་སུམ་རྟགས (བོད་ཀྱི་སུམ་རྟགས་ཀྱི་འགྲེལ་པ་སི་ཏུ་པཎ་ཆེན་གཙུག་ལག་ཆོས་ཀྱི་སྣང་བས་མཛད་པ་མཁས་པའི་མགུལ་རྒྱན་མུ་ཏིག་ཕྲེང་མཛེས).
Sman. g................*Sman-rgyud* or སྨན་གཞུང་རྒྱུད་བཞི།
Sman....................*Bder-dge sman-bsdus chen-mo* བདེར་དགེ་སྨན་བསྡུས་ཆེན་མོ།
Sñag....................*Sñags-skad* སྔགས་སྐད a vocabulary of mystic Sanskṛt terms.
Sñan....................*Sñan ñag meloñ* སྙན་ངག་མེ་ལོང་།
Sñiñ.....................*Kloñ-chen sñiñ-thig-gi theg-mchog mdsod* ཀློང་ཆེན་སྙིང་ཐིག་གི་ཐེག་མཆོག་མཛོད།
Snd. Hbk...............Rev. G. Sandberg's Hand-book of Tibetan.
Sog. ....*Sog-gtam* སོག་པོའི་དཔེ་གཏམ།
Sorig. ....*Gso-rig chos-hbyuñ* གསོ་རིག་ཆོས་འབྱུང་།
Spyod. ....*Spyod-rnam* སྤྱོད་རྣམ།
Spyo.....................*Spyod-hjug* སྤྱོད་འཇུག།
Stg. ....*Bstan-hgyur* བསྟན་འགྱུར་ collection of commentaries.
Sukh.....................Sukhāvatī-vyūha.
Surañ. ....Surañgama Sûtra སུ་རང་ག་མ་སུ་ཏྲ།
Tan. d. ....*Bstan-hgyur-mdo* བསྟན་འགྱུར་མདོ།
Tan. sñag..............*Bstan hgyur sñags.*
Tā. ....Tārā Nātha's *Rgya-gar chos-hbyuñ*, history of the rise of Buddhism.
Theg.....................*Theg-mchog mdsod* ཐེག་མཆོག་མཛོད།
Thgr.....................*Bar-do thos-grol chen-mo* བར་དོ་ཐོས་གྲོལ་ཆེན་མོ།
Thgy.....................Thargyan, scientific treatises.
Tib. ....For Tibetan.
Trig......................Triglot a collection of Buddhist terms by Prof. Minayeff.
Ts. or *Tsañ*............*Gtsañ* གཙང་ Tsang province.
Ts. kah..................*Btsun-mo bkah-thañ* བཙུན་མོ་བཀའ་ཐང་།
Tshig. ....*Tshigs-brgya-pa* ཚིགས་བརྒྱ་པ།
Ü. ....The province of དབུས *Dbus*, Central Tibet.
V. C.......................*Vajra-chedikā.*
Vai. kar. ....*Vai-dūrya dkar-po* བཻ་ཌཱུ་རྱ་དཀར་པོ།
Vai. sñ..................བཻ་ཌཱུ་རྱ་སྔོན་པོ or (*Vai-dūry sñon-po*).
Visuddhi. ....Visuddhimaggo B. T. Society.
W. or *W. Tib.* ......Western Tibet.

Was. .... Prof. W. Wassiljew, Der Buddhismus.
Wils. .... Wilson's Grammar.
Wts. .... Wai-tsang thu-shi; a description of Tibet, Ed. by Klaproth.
Ya-sel. .... *Vai-dūra ya-sel* བཻ་ཌཱུ་རྱ་གཡའ་སེལ།
Yañ-ṭi. .... དབྱངས་ཅན་ཊཱི་ཀཱ *D̲b̲yañs̲-can ṭikā.*
Yid̲. .... *Yid̲-kyi mun-sel* ཡིད་ཀྱི་མུན་སེལ།
Yig. .... *R̲gya-bod̲ yig-tshañ* རྒྱ་བོད་ཡིག་ཚང་།
Yig. k. .... *Yig-b̲s̲kur r̲nam-gshag* ཡིག་བསྐུར་རྣམ་བཞག།
Yon. .... *Yon-g̲tan m̲dsod̲* ཡོན་གཏན་མཛོད།
Z. .... *Zañs̲-d̲kar* ཟངས་དཀར།
Zam. .... *B̲r̲dah̲-yi b̲stan-b̲cos̲ Za-ma-tog* བརྡའ་ཡི་བསྟན་བཅོས་ཟ་མ་ཏོག། (*Dag-yig*).

卐 and + prefixed to some words indicate them as (བརྡ་རྙིང་ *b̲r̲da r̲ñiñ*) belonging to the older orthography.

‡ and ‡ prefixed to some words indicate their Indian or Sanskrit origin.

* words marked with asterisks were sent by Dr. Albert Grünwedel for being incorportated in this Dictionary. They were collected by Dr. A. Schiefner.

GRAMMATICAL ABBREVIATIONS.

abbr.	abbreviated; abbreviations.
abstr.	abstraction; abstract.
acc.	according to.
accus.	accusative case.
act.	active, actively.
adj.	adjective.
adv.	adverb, adverbially.
arith.	arithmetic.
b.	books.
c.	cum, with.
c.c.	construitur cum, construed with.
c.c.a.	construed with the accusative, etc.
cf.	confer, compare.
ch.	chapter.
cog.	cognate, related in origin.
col. or colloq.	colloquial, colloquially.
collect.	collective, collectively.
com.	commonly.
comp.	compound, compounds.
conj.	conjunction.
contr.	contracted.
corr.	correct, correctly.
correl.	correlative, correlatively.
dat.	dative case.
demon.	demonstrative.
deriv.	derivative.
dub.	dubious.
E.	east.
e. g.	exempli gratia, for instance.
eleg.	elegant, elegantly.
elswh.	elsewhere.
emphat.	emphatical, emphatically.
erron.	erroneous, erroneously.
esp.	especially.
equiv.	equivalent.
euph.	euphemistical, euphemistically.
ex.	example.
expl.	explain, explainations.
extr.	extrimo, towards the end of a
fem.	feminine gender. [longer article.
fig.	figurative, figuratively.
frq.	frequently.
fut.	future tense.
gen.	general, generally.
genit.	genitive case.
gram.	grammar.
ibid.	ibidem, in the same place.
id.	idem, the same.
i. e.	id est, that is.
imp.	imperative mood.
impers.	impersonal, impersonally.
incorr.	incorrect, incorrectly.
inf.	infinitive mood.
init.	initio, at the beginning of a longer
inst.	instead. [article.
instr.	instrumentative case.
interj.	interjection.
interr.	interrogative, interrogatively.
inters.	intransitive.
i.o.	instead of.
irr.	irregularly, irregular.
lang.	language.
lit.	literally, also literature.
long.	longitude.
masc.	masculine gender.
med.	medical works. [longer article.
med.	medio, about the middle of a
metaph.	metaphorical, metaphorically.
met. or meton.	metonymical, metonymically.
myst.	mystical or mystically.
n.	name.
N.E.	north-east.
neut.	neuter gender.
ni.f.	ni fallor, if I am not mistaken.
n.p.	noun proper.
N.W.	north-west.
num.	numeral.
obs.	obsolete.
opp.	as opposed to.
orig.	for original work.
orthog.	orthography.
p.	page.
para.	paragraph.
partic.	participle.
pass.	passive, passively.
past.	past tense.
perh.	perhaps.
pers.	person, personal.

pf. perfect tense.
pl. plural number.
pleon. pleonastic, pleonastically.
p. n. proper name.
po. poetically.
pop. popular language.
poss. p. possessive pronoun.
postp. postposition.
prep. preposition.
pres. pret. present tense, preterite.
prob. probably.
pron. pronoun.
prop. properly.
prov. provincialism, provincial.
q. v. quod vide, which see.
rel. relative.
resp. respectful, respectfully.
sbst. substantive.
S.E. south-east.
sim. similar in meaning, similarly.
sing. singular number.
sh or ṣ for ष or ཥ.
symb. num. symbolical numeral.
Syn. or synon. synonymous.
termin. terminative case.
trop. tropically.
trs. transitive.
v. vide, see.
vb. verb.
vb. a. verb active.
vb. nt. verb neuter.
vulg. vulgar, low expression.
vulgo. in common life.
W. west.
w.e. without explanation.

TIBETAN-ENGLISH DICTIONARY.

ཀ

ཀ *Ka* the first letter of the Tibetan alphabet, corresponding in sound to the Sanskrit क or the English K. Of this letter we read: ཀ་ནི་རྩ་བ་ཤེས་པར་གྲགས *ka-ni ṟtsa-wa shes̱-par grags̱* ·(*K. g.* ཀ *424*) "the *ka* is called the root." As the first letter it has the sense of "the beginning": ཀ་ནས་དག་པ *ka-nas̱ dag-pa* pure from the beginning. Again, it can signify "power": སྙན་འཚེར་རུང་མ་ཞུ་ཀ་མེད *s̱ñan ẖtsher-ruñ ma-shu ka-meḏ* though unpleasant to hear, I have no power not to say it; མ་གནང་ཀ་མེད *ma g̱nañ ka-meḏ* powerless not to give; མ་འགྲོ་ཀ་མེད *ma ẖgro ka-meḏ* powerless not to go, *i.e.*, cannot avoid going. ཀ *ka* has almost the same sense in ཀ་ཅིས་ཀྱང་མི་ཕན་འཆི་བ་ལ *ka cis̱ kyañ mi-phan ẖchi-wa la* (*Lo. 35*), no resource avails at death. This letter seems to have other metaphorical meanings; thus we read: ཀ་ཤེས་བྱ་བ་འདོད་པ་ཡིན *ka shes̱ bya-wa ẖdoḏ-pa yin* (*K. g.* ཁ *179*) "*ka*, so to be called, is desire."

ཀ I: 1. when used in indicating numbers *ka* signifies one or first. 2. in modern Tibetan as an affix to many words it denotes: the, all the, the very. སྐབས་ཀ *s̱kabs̱-ka* has the same meaning as སྐབས་སུ *s̱kabs̱-su*, on a certain occasion; དེ་ཀ *de-ka* that very; གཉིས་ཀ *g̱ñis̱-ka* the two. 3. in a large number of words we find ཀ occurring as the second syllable. In some of these it has been added apparently as a differentiative particle; and in the colloq. we often find it annexed to the older monosyllabic form without explainable reason.

ཀ II: indeed; surely: སླར་ཡང་དྲན་དུ་ཀ་སོང *s̱lar yañ ḏran-du ka soñ* (*Pag. 42*) later again he indeed recollected (the separation).

ཀ *ka* for; ཀ་བ *ka-wa* a pillar.

ཀ་ཁ *ka-kha* 1. the A-B-C, or alphabet. 2. a feather: གསང་སྐད་ལ་ཀ་ཁ་ནི་སྒྲོ་འོ *ḇsañ-s̱kaḏ la ka-kha ni s̱gro-ẖo* (*K. g.* ཀ *216*) in the secret language *ka-kha* signifies a feather.

ཀ་ཁ་པ *ka-kha-pa* a beginner of the alphabet; a child.

ཀ་ཐོ *ka-tho*, also ཀ་ཁའི་ཐོ *ka-khaẖi tho*, an alphabetical register; an index.

ཀ་ཐོག *Ka-thog̱* lit. "on the top of ཀ"; n. of a celebrated Buddhist monastery in Kham belonging to the *Ṟñiñ-ma* School, the Head Lama of which is believed always to be an incarnation of his predecessor and holds the title of ཀ་ཐོག་རིག་འཛིན་ཆེན་མོ། The hill on which this monastery was built is said to have resembled the letter ཀ *ka*. འབྲི་ཆུའི་འགྲམ་སྦོམ་པོར་དང་ཉེ་བར་ཀ་ཐོག་ཅེས་པའི་གནས་དགོན། (*Deb.* ཀ *26*) On the bank of the Di-chu (*Hbri-chu*), near Pom-po, is the monastery called Kathog.

ཀ་དག *ka-dag* = ཀ་ནས་དག་པ *ka-nas dag-pa* pure from the beginning. According to the *Rñiñ-ma* School of Buddhism it means སྟོང་པ་ཉིད *stoñ-pa-ñid* (*çūnyatā*) emptiness, or the void; that which is pure from the beginning: ངོ་བོ་ཀ་དག་རང་བཞིན་ལྷུན་གྱི་གྲུབ་པའི་འདུས་མ་བྱས་ཀྱི། (*Yig. 14*) that which is not compounded, being evolved of itself, is pure from the beginning.

ཀ་སྡེ *ka-sde* कवर्ग 1. the four letters in the first group of the Tibetan alphabet, namely, ཀ་ཁ་ག་ང་། 2. in astronomy consecutive numbers: ཆུ་སྲིན་དུ་ཀ་སྡེ་ལུགས་འབྱུང་། (*Ya-sel. 45*) the order of figures in the (zodiac sign of the) crocodile is consecutive.

ཀ་པ *ka-pa* the first volume of a work or a series of works; a volume or anything else marked with the letter ཀ *ka*.

ཀ་དཔེ *ka-dpe*, also expressed ཀ་ཁའི་དཔེ *ka khahi dpe*, an A-B-C book; a primer.

ཀ་ཕྲེང་ *ka-phreñ* (*ka-theng*) = ཀཱ་ལི *kāli* the series of consonants in the Tibetan alphabet.

ཀ་མེད *ka-med* helpless, powerless.

ཀ་སྨད་སུམ་ཅུ *ka-smad sum-cu* lit. "the thirty (letters of the Tibetan alphabet) below the letter ཀ."

ཀ་རྩོམ *ka-rtsom* an acrostic; a metrical composition in which the initial letters of each line form a continuous word or sentence.

ཀ་ལི *ka-li* ordinarily written for the Tibetan Sanskṛt word ཀཱ་ལི (ཀ + ཨཱ་ལི).

‡ ཀཱ་ལི *kā-li* = ཀ་ཕྲེང་ *ka-phreñ* the series of letters gen. beginning with ཀ *ka*, *i.e.*, the consonants of the Tibetan language: ཡི་གེ་ཨཱ་ལི་ཀཱ་ལི་ཡིན *yi-ge ā-li kā-li yin* "letters are of the ཨ series, *i.e.*, vowels, and of the ཀ series, *i.e.*, consonants" (*Situ. 3*).

‡ ཀ་ཀ I: *ka-ka* काक 1. the crow. 2. the cry of the crow: ཀ་ཀ་ཅེས་ན་ནོར་རྙེད་འབྱུང་། (*Vai. kar.*) "if a crow caws, wealth will be found."

ཀ་ཀ II: excrement (nursery word); in *W.* ཀ་ཀ་ཏང་ཅེ *ka-ka tañ-ce* = French *faire caca* (*Jä.*).

‡ ཀ་ཀ་ཎི *ka-ka-ni* काकिणी 1. a small coin of Ancient India (*Cs.*): ཀ་ཀ་ཎི་འགྲོན་བུ་ཉི་ཤུའི་རིན། "*ka-ka-ni* of the value of twenty shells (*cowries*)." 2. कपर्दक the fourth part of a *paṇa*. 3. the quarter of a *māna*. 4. the seed of *Abrus precatorius*, used as a weight in medicine. 5. the shell of *Cypræa moneta*, used as money.

‡ ཀ་ཀ་རང་ *ka-ka-rañ* the cucumber is so called in Kunawar (*Jä.*).

‡ ཀ་ཀ་རི ककारि n. of a fabulous snowy mountain situated to the north of a river called *Patru*, where a medicinal plant called *Tujanaya* grows (*S. Lam. 36*).

‡ ཀ་ཀི་ཎི *Ka-ki-ni* 1. n. of a Buddhist literary work. 2. n. of a female Buddhist deity: གྲུབ་ཐོབ་མལ་བྱེ་ཚང་པ་ལ་ཀ་ཀི་ཎིའི་སྐོར། (*D. 20*) "(taught) the rites concerning the goddess *Kakini* to the saint Mal-bye Tshañ-pa."

‡ ཀ་ཀུ་སྟ *Ka-ku-sta* n. of a river (*K. d.* ད *582*).

‡ ཀ་ཀུ་བྷ་ཡ *Ka-ku bha-ya* ककुभ 1. n. of a plant used in medicine, *Terminalia arjuna.* 2.=དུག་མོ་ཉུང་གི་ཤིང་ནོར *dug-mo ñuñ-gi çiñ-nor* the "fruit of the tree of little poison" (*Ñag.*).

‡ ཀ་ཀེ་རི་ཡ *Ka-ke-ri-ya* ककेरिय n. of a tree which grew on Gṛdhrakûṭa, or the Vulture-peak Hill of Magadha (*K. ko.* ཀ *3*).

‡ ཀ་ཀོ *ka-ko* applied in Sikkim for ཀ་ཀོ་ལ *ka-ko-la.*

‡ ཀ་ཀོ་ལ *ka-ko-la* कक्कोल 1. cardamom, the fruit of *Cocculus Indicus*; a plant with a berry, the inner part of which consists of seeds with a wax-like aromatic substance. 2. नाड़ीतरङ्ग, मुञ्ज *Saccharum munja,* but is variously described as a fruit used in medicine; a poisonous tree-drug; also =एरण्ड the castor-oil plant.

Syn. ཚང་མང་ *tshañ mañ*; ཟླ་བ་གཞོན་ནུ *zla-wa gshon-nu*; ཟླ་བའི་བྱེ་མ *zla-wahi bye-ma* (*Mñon.*).

ཀ་ཙ *ka-ca* (also ཀ་ཚ *ka-cha*) धन articles, goods, effects, property, furniture: ཀ་ཙའི་རྗེས་སུ་འབྲང་བའི་རྒྱལ་པོ། the king who follows after property; ཀ་ཙས་ཚིམ་པར་བྱེད་པ property causes satisfaction.

Syn. སྤྱད་ལག *spyad-lag*; ཡོ་བྱད *yo-byad*; དངོས་ཆས *dños-chas* (*Mñon.*).

ཀ་ཙན *Ka-can* n. of a place in Tibet (*Deb.* ཀ *43*).

ཀ་ཙི *ka-ci* colloq. ཀ་རྗི *ka-rji* 1. a kind of coarse white cotton cloth largely imported into Tibet from Nepal and used for making prayer-flags. A piece of *ka-ci* is generally four to six yards long and a foot-and-a-half broad. 2. a kind of muslin; a very fine cotton cloth imported from Benares: ཀ་ཙི་ཕྲུག་རེར་འབྲུ་ཁལ་བརྒྱད། for each piece of *ka-ci* eight bushels of barley.

ཀ་ཙི་སྐྱེམ་རས *ka-ci skyem-ras* fine cotton cloth or muslin, so called from its resemblance to the superior quality of Tibetan paper called *skyems*; སྟོད་རས་སྣ་ཚོགས་ཀ་ཙི་སྐྱེམ་རས། (*S. kar. 179*) different sorts of cotton cloth, muslin, &c., brought from Upper Tibet; ཀ་ཙི་སྒྲུམ་མ an inferior kind of *ka-ci* cloth.

‡ ཀ་ཙི་ལི *ka-ci-li* कचिलि n. of a flower (*K. my.* ཀ *20*). कचिलि is identical with कचु and कच्वी, a plant with an esculent root (*Arum colocasia*) cultivated for food.

ཀ་ལྕི *ka-lci* sometimes used for ཀ་ཙི.

ཀ་ལྕོག *Ka-lcog* an abbr. of the names of two celebrated translators of the Kahgyur: ཀ་བ་དཔལ་བརྩེགས *Ka-wa Dpal-brtsegs* and ལྕོག་རོ་ཀླུའི་རྒྱལ་མཚན *Kluhi rgyal-mtshan* of *Lcog-ro.*

ཀ་ཚ *ka-cha*=ཀ་ཙ *ka-ca.*

ཀ་ཚ་ཊ *ka-cha-ṭa* a habitation, a hut (*Schtr.*).

ཀ་ཆུག *ka-chug* so, like that, accordingly; ཀ་ཆུག་མཛོད *ka-chug mdsod* means དེ་ལྟར་བྱེད *de-ltar-byed*, do like that, do accordingly: ཨ་མེས་མི་འདོད་ན་མི་བྱེད་དུ་ཀ་ཆུག་མཛོད། "if *Ame* is disinclined lot (him) not do like that" (*A. 94*).

ཀ་ཊ *ka-ta* in mystic language a term for mother (*K. g.* ཀ *216*).

‡ ཀ་ཊ་ཀ *ka-ta-ka* 1. n. of a tree. ཀ་ཊ་ཀ་དང་སྦྲང་གིས་མིག་སྨན་བྱས་ན་མིག་ནད་ཐམས་ཅད་སེལ་བར་བྱེད་དོ། if an eye-medicine be made from *kataka* and honey, all eye-diseases may be removed (*S. Lam. 38*). 2. कतक the clearing nut-plant, *Strychnos potatorum.* A seed of this plant when rubbed on the inside of a water jar produces a precipitation of the earthy particles of water.

ཀ་ཏ་མ་ཀ *ka-ta-ma-ka* n. of a kind of bird (*K. ko.* ཀ *2*).

‡ **ཀ་ཏ་ཡ** *Ka-ta-ya*, also ཀ་ཏྱ *Ka-tya* n. of a place in Ancient India, probably the country of the *Gœtae;* according to *Cs.* Scythia; n. of a district in Tibet.

‡ ཀ་ཏ་ཡ་ན་ནོག་ཅན *Ka-ta-ya-na nog-can* lit. Kātyāyana with a hump on his shoulders; one of the six heretical teachers who disputed with Buddha.

‡ ཀ་ཏཱའི་བུ *Ka-taḥi bu*=ཀཱ་ཏྱ་ཡ་ན *kā-tya ya-na* कात्यायन the son of Kātyāyanī; n. of a *Bhikṣu* (Buddhist monk) (*Ṅag. 3*).

‡ ཀ་ཏཱའི་བུ་མོ *Ka-taḥi bu-mo* कात्यायनी, उमा the goddess Umā; also the mother of the *Bhikṣu* Kātyāyana.

‡ ཀ་ཏྱའི་བུ *Ka-tyaḥi bu* कात्यायन lit. the son of Kātya. It is said that the family name of Kātyāyana was given because the patriarch of the tribe took the vows of an ascetic from the sage Nada (*K. d.* ད *127*).

‡ **ཀ་ཏ་ར** *ka-ta-ra* n. of a flower (*K. d.* ཁ *12*).

ཀ་ཏ་རུ *ka-ta-ru*=རེའུ་མིག *reḥu mig* a table of figures made of lines crossing each other and forming squares.

ཀ་ཏན *ka-tan*=རས *ras* cotton cloth (*Ṅag. 2*).

‡ **ཀ་ཏམ་བྷ** *ka-tam-bha* described as སྲོག་ཆགས་ཀྱི་མིང་ (*K. d.* ཟ *462*), n. of an insect.

‡ **ཀ་ཏོ་ར** *ka-to-ra*=གཞོང་ *gshoṅ* a basin, bowl; कतोरा (also ཀ་ཊོ་ར *ka-ṭo-ra*) the Tibetan form of the Hindi word *kaṭorā*.

‡ **ཀ་ཊ་ཀི** *Ka-ṭa-ki* कटकी a generic name for mountain; n. of a mountain (*Sch.*).

‡ **ཀ་ཊ་ཀི་ལ** *Ka-ṭa-ki-la* कटकिल n. of a city in Ancient Sind (*S. Lam. 35*); lit. a pillar of grass.

ཀ་ཊ་བོ་ཊ *Ka-ṭa Bo-ṭa* Indian n. for the town of Paro in Bhutan (*Dsam.*).

‡ **ཀ་ཊུ་ཀ** *Ka-ṭu-ka* n. of a fabulous city which is described to have been fifty *yojana* in circumference.

ཀ་ཊོ་ར *ka-ṭo-ra* v. ཀ་ཏོ་ར *ka-to-ra*.

ཀ་ཐ་ར *ka-tha-ra* in Kunawar a sort of peach (*Jä.*).

ཀ་ཐི་ཤི *Ka-thi-çi* a Chinese minister who founded the monastery of *Hi kwan-zse* (*Yig. 45*).

ཀ་ཐེ *ka-the* v. ཀ་བ *ka-wa*.

‡ **ཀ་ད་རུ་ཧ** *ka-da-ru-ha* कदरुह (prob. कदररुह a bird nestling on *khadira* trees) n. of a kind of bird (*K. ko.* ཀ *2*).

‡ **ཀ་དམ་པ** *ka-dam-pa* कदम्ब, प्रियक 1. n. of a tree; ཀ་དམ་པའི་མེ་ཏོག कदम्ब पुष्प the *kadamba* flower; the tree *Nauclea cadamba*, a tree with orange-coloured fragrant blossoms. 2. བྱ་མཐིང་རིལ་དང་ཤིང་ལྗོན་གྱི་བྱག་གི་མིང་། (*Ṅag.*) n. of a species of bird of a deep blue colour and also that of a tree. 3. a kind of grass.

ཀ་དམ་པ་ཅན *ka-dam-pa can* cloud, v. སྤྲིན་པ *sprin-pa* (*Mṅon.*).

‡ **ཀ་ཌ་ཀ** *ka-ḍa-ka* कडक also ཀ་ཌཱ་པ *ka-ḍā-pa* 1. n. of a fruit. 2. n. of a bird (*K. d.* ཡ *20*).

‡ **ཀ་ཌ་པ** *ka-ḍa-pa* कडाप n. of a fruit (*K. d.* ཡ *202*); prob. करिभ the fruit of the tree *Ficus religiosa*.

‡ **ཀ་ན་ཀ** *ka-na-kam* कनक gold; a pedantic synonym for གསེར *gser* (*Mṅon.*).

‡ ཀ་ན་ཀ་ཝརྨ། कनकवर्म n. of an Indian paṇḍit who visited Tibet (*J. Zañ.*).

‡ ཀ་ཎ་ཙ *ka-ṇa-tsa* (prob. कणीचि) lit. sprouting; generic name for a tree; the plant *Abrus precatorius*; ཤིང་ཀ་ན་ཙའི་མེ་ཏོག་རྣམས། the flowers of the *ka-na-tsa* tree (*K. g.* ཁ *227*).

‡ ཀ་ཎ་ཙ་ན *ka-ṇa-tsa-na* कणचन n. of a tree (*K. d.* ཙ *422*); कञ्चड़ the plant *Commelina Bengalensis*.

ཀ་ན་ཡ *ka-na-ya* n. of a kind of weapon; a short lance attached by a string to the arm, by which it can be drawn back after having been thrown at an object; ལག་ན་མཚོན་ཆ་གཅིག་པ་དང་ཀ་ན་ཡ་དང་མདའ་བོ་ཆེ་དང་། in the hands, a sword, a lance and a large arrow (*K. g.* ཁ *113*).

‡ ཀ་ནི་ཀ *Ka-ni-ka* also ཀ་ནིཥ་ཀ कनिष्क n. of a celebrated *Turuṣka* (Tartar) king who ruled over Palhava, Kashmir and Jalandhara (the provinces of the Panjab and Kabul) in ancient times; he embraced Buddhism and is said to have held the last great Buddhist Council for the compilation of the Mahāyāna Tripiṭaka in the first century B.C.

ཀ་གནམ *Ka-gnam* n. of a province of Tibet north-east of Kong-po; ཀ་གནམ་པ *ka gnam-pa* a native of *Ka-gnam*.

‡ ཀ་ཎ་ཡ *ka-ṇa-ya* कणय for ཀ་ན་ཡ *ka-na-ya* a kind of spear or lance. कणय and कनय, कनप are synonymous terms.

‡ ཀ་པཱ་ལ *ka-pā-la* कपाल the skull; the forehead. In Tib. Budh. *kapala* or *kapali* signifies either the skull or a drinking cup made of the human skull.

‡ ཀ་པི I: *Kapi* n. of the language that was anciently spoken in the country of Kapistan; n. of a country. The Bon *Rgyal-rabs* (a history of the kings of Tibet), according to the Bon historians, was asserted to have been written in Kapi, the language of the gods, in which the ancient Bon scriptures were mostly written. It is also stated that the Bon books were translated into the language of the Persians or *Tajik* people, from which again the Tibetans translated them into the language of Shañ Shûñ in Northern Tibet.

‡ ཀ་པི II: 1 कपित्थ gum, resin (*Jä.*); the resin extracted from a medicinal plant called *çug-pa* (*Juniper communis*). The root is gathered in autumn or spring and being thoroughly cleansed, is cut into pieces and beaten into pulp. The juice is squeezed out with a clean cotton rag, and being poured into a clean dry earthen pot is subjected to a gentle heat. As soon as it begins to thicken it is stirred with a spoon till it gains the consistency of resin. 2. the hog-plum, *Spondias magnifera*; a tree; *Pentaptira tomentosa*; the mane-fig tree; *Ficus inpectoria*. Also a wood-apple tree. 3. n. of a yellow orpiment.

‡ ཀ་པི་ཀ་ཚ *ka-pi ka-tsha* n. of a medicinal plant (*K. g.* ཙ *51*); कपिकच्छ the plant *Mucuna pruritus*.

‡ ཀ་པི་ད *ka-pi-da*=ཀ་པི *ka-pi*.

‡ ཀ་པི་ན *Ka-pi-na* कपिन n. of a king of Southern India who lived in Buddha's time and considered himself the greatest monarch of the world. His vanity was exposed by the Great Teacher, who converted him to Buddhism and ultimately raised him to the position of an *Arhat* (*K. d.* ཁ *354*).

‡ ཀ་པི་ལ་མུ་ནི་ कपिल मुनि n. of a Brāhmanical sage whose hermitage was at the mouth of the Ganges (*S. Lam.*).

‡ ཀ་པིང་ཐ *ka-piñ-tha* कपित्थ n. of a very delicious fruit (*K. d.* ཡ *20*).

‡ ཀ་པིན་ད་ཀ *ka-pin-da-ka* कपिन्दक n. of a kind of bird.

ཀ་པུ་ཏ *Ka-pu-ta* n. of a place in Ancient India where, in accordance with the curse of a holy sage, adultery and incest were punished with the burning of the house in which such crimes were committed (*Dsam.*).

ཀ་པེད *ka-ped* a gourd; a sort of medicinal fruit (*Lex.*).

ཀ་ཕ *ka-pha* a tree.

ཀ་བ I: *Ka-wa* n. of the mother of Bromton, the founder of the Buddhist hierarchy of Tibet (*Hbrom.* ཕ *37*).

ཀ་བ II: = གཟུག་པ *gzug-pa* स्थूणा, स्तम्भ a pillar, column, stake, support; also trident; ཀ་སྐེ *ka-ske* the neck of a pillar or column; ཀ་སྐེད *ka-sked* the shaft; ཀ་གཅིག་མ *ka-gcig-ma* a small house or temple having but one pillar; ཀ་ཆེན *ka-chen* the principal pillar, a very large pillar; ཀ་རྟེན *ka-rten* the base of a pillar; ཀ་སྟེགས *ka-stegs* the pedestal of a pillar; ཀ་གདན *ka-gdan* the base or pedestal on which a pillar stands; ཀ་སྤུངས *ka-spuñs* a colonnade, a number of pillars; ཀ་བ་ཤུལ་ཅན a grooved pillar; ཀ་བ་དང་ཉེ་བའི་ཀ་བའི་གྲོང་ स्थूणा ग्राम: (lit. the town of houses built with pillars and king-posts) one of the thirty-six holy places of the Buddhists; ཀ་བ་བུམ་པ་ཅན *ka-wa bum-pa-can* one of the pillars of the great Jokhang temple at Lhasa, with the upper part of its capital in the shape of a water-pot; ཀ་བ་སྦྲུལ་མགོ་ཅན *ka-wa sbrul-mgo-can* the pillar that had a serpent-shaped capital; ཀ་བ་ཤིང་ལོ་ཅན *ka-wa çiñ-lo-can* the pillar which had designs of leaves of trees round its capital; ཀ་བ་སེང་མགོ་ཅན *ka-wa señ-mgo-can* the pillar with a lion's head on its capital. These were tho names given to the four principal pillars of the Jokhang temple of Buddha at Lhasa, built by King Sroñ-btsan sgam-po about 640 A.D., after the model of the pillars in the palace of the Emperor T'ai-tsung, called Kyñ lün tin, the palace of the golden dragon. གནམ་གྱི་ཀ་བ *gnam-gyi ka-wa* आकाशस्तम्भ the pillar of heaven; ས་ཡི་ཀ་བ *sa-yi ka-wa* भूस्तम्भ the pillar of earth; མེ་ཡི་ཀ་བ *me-yi-ka-wa* वह्निस्तम्भ the pillar of fire; ཆུ་ཡི་ཀ་བ *chu-yi ka-wa* जलस्तम्भ the pillar of water,—these are the fabulous and metaphorical pillars mentioned in the astrological works of Tibet. གཡུའི་ཀ་བ *gyu-hi ka-wa* a pillar of turquoise, or one that is studded with turquoises (*Lha. kar. 13*).

ཀ་ཁོལ་མ *Ka khol-ma* n. of a historical pillar in the grand temple of Buddha at Lhasa, inside of which the earliest known MS. of Tibet, called བཀའ་ཆེམས་ཀ་ཁོལ་མ།, and said to be the will of King Sroñ-btsan Sgam-po, was alleged to have been found in the middle of the eleventh century A.D.

ཀ་མགོ *ka-mgo* the capital of a pillar.

ཀ་ཅན *ka-can* = ཀ་བ་ཅན *ka-wa-can* lit. with a pillar or pillars; a house. In the sense of being the supports or upholders of the school of Marpa, the *Tantrik* sage of Tibet, his four disciples were called ཀ་ཅན་བཞི *ka-can bshi* "the four pillars of his school." They received his *bkaḥ*, commission, regarding Buddhism, and were also called བཀའ་བབས་བཞི "the four commissioned ones." The following were the four disciples: རྔོག་ཆོས་རྡོར *Chos-rdor* of *Rṅog*; བསོད་ནམས་རྒྱལ་མཚན *Bsod-nams rgyal-mtshan*; ཏོལ་གྱི་མཚུར་དབང་རྡོ་རྗེ *Mtshur-dwaṅ rdo-rje* of *Tol*; and མི་ལ་རས་པ *Mi-la ras-pa*.

ཀ་གཅིག་སྒོ་གཅིག *ka-gcig sgo-gcig* 1. a small house with but one pillar and one door, gen. a small prison-house. 2. A mode of capital punishment is said to be called so when the culprit is fastened to a pillar in a dungeon until he dies of hunger (*Jä.*).

ཀ་འཕན *ka-ḥphan* the ornamental silk fringes and embroidered hangings made in various mythical designs for decorating the capitals of pillars.

ཀ་བ་བཟང་པོ सुस्तम्भ a strong well-finished pillar.

ཀ་བའི་སྦྱར་བཀོད *ka-wahi sbyar-bkod* a cornice; the ornamental projections, &c., which surmount a pillar; the decorative pieces which are attached to a pillar.

ཀ་མང་མ *ka-maṅ-ma* a house with many pillars.

ཀ་མིག *ka-mig* the square space (of about twelve feet) enclosed by four pillars is called a *ka-mig*; the area or enclosure of a colonnade is measured by the *ka-mig*.

ཀ་རྩེ *ka-rtse* the top of a pillar.

ཀ་རྩེ *ka-rtse* (ཀ་ཡང་རྩེ *ka-yaṅ-rtse*) the upper part or capital of a pillar.

ཀ་གཞུ *ka-gshu* स्तकाष्ठालक capital of a wooden pillar; a piece of timber in the shape of a bow fixed on a pillar to hold up the main beam (*Lex.*).

ཀ་ཡང་རྩེ the extremity of a pillar which projects over the capital (architrave).

ཀ་ཤུབས *ka-çubs*=ཀ་བའི་ཤུབས *ka-wahi çubs* the cover of a pillar, perhaps the abacus.

ཀ་བ III: a particular faculty acquired by a mystic process in which the appetites —hunger, thirst, &c.—are suppressed. This is one of the six practices of the Buddhist *Tantriks* who practise *yoga* (meditative concentration).

ཀ་བ IV: धमस्तम्भ a large vein or artery in the abdomen; a vessel in the side of the breast containing vital air (प्राणवायु), supposed to be brought into action in above mystic process.

† ཀ་པི་ཏ *kabita* कपित्थ n. of a tree, the elephant or wood-apple, *Feronia Elephantum* (*S. Lam. 38*).

† ཀ་པི་ཏ་ལ *ka-bi-ta-la* 1. n. of a tree (*K. d.* ཙ *422*). 2. probably कपितैल benzoin, storax.

ཀ་བུ་ལོ *Ka-bu-lo*, described as དྲི་ཟའི་རྒྱལ་པོ་ཞིག་གི་མིང་, n. of a *Gandharva* Rāja—Prince of the celestial musicians (*K. my.* ཀ *492*).

ཀ་བེད *ka-bed* or ཀུ་བ *ku-wa*, gourd. In the district of *Ped-ma dkod* in Tibet, just north of Assam, the gourd is called ཨ་བུམ *a-bum*: ཀ་བེད་འབྲས་བུས་ཚ་འབྲུ་གཅོད་པར་བྱེད། the gourd fruit cures fever and diarrhœa: ཀ་བེད་བསྲེག་ནས་བུ་རམ་དང་བཟའ་བར་བྱས་ན་ཁྲག་ཏུ་འབྲུ་བ་སེལ་བར་བྱེད་དོ། burnt or baked gourd eaten with molasses cures bloody diarrhœa (*K. g.* ཙ *47*).

† ཀ་བེལ *Ka-bel* n. of a city in Ancient Udyāna, *i.e.*, in ཨུ་རྒྱན་ཡུལ *U-rgyan yul* probably the modern Kabul.

† ཀ་བོ་ཀ *Ka-bo-ka* n. of a Prince of Ancient Kabul (*S. Lam. 17*).

‡ ཀ་མ་ཆ *Ka-ma-cha* or ཀ་མུ་ཚ *Ka-mu-tsha* कामखा n. of a sacred place in Assam where there is a stone-cut symbol of Kāli, the Hindu goddess.

ཀ་མ་ཏ *ka-ma-ta* the lotus (*Ńag.*).

‡ ཀ་མ་ཙི *ka-ma-tsi* कमचि a kind of medicinal plant: ཀ་མ་ཙིའི་རྩ་བ་སྤྱི་བོར་བཞག་ན་གཉིད་དུ་འགྱུར། "if the root of *ka-ma-tsi* be placed on the top of the head, sleep arises" (*K. g.* ཙ *56*).

‡ ཀ་མ་རུ *kama-ru* 1. Kāmarūpa in Assam. 2. alabaster (*Sch.*); རྡོ་ཀ་མ་རུ་པ *rdo ka-ma-ru-pa* marble.

‡ ཀ་མ་ལ *ka-ma-la* कमल 1. the water-lily, lotus *Nelumbium*. 2. a river. 3.= གྲོས་སེམས *gros sems* a consulting or reflecting mind (*Ńag.*). The word *Kamala* is variously used by the Tibetans, and the following synonyms of it (both symbolic and metaphoric) are enumerated in the work (*Ńag.*):—

Syn. སྒྲའི་སྙེ་མ *sgrahi sñe-ma* soft tones; ལྗོན་ཤིང་རྩེ་རྒྱས a branching tree; གླང་པོའི་མྱོས་བུམ *glań-pohi myos-bum* the teats of an elephant; ཐུབ་པ་རབ་མཆོག प्रवरमुनि n. of a Buddha; བདེན་སྨྲ་བ *bden-smra-wa* one who speaks the truth; ནམ་མཁའ *nam-mkhah* the sky; ནོར་བུ *nor-bu* a gem; སྣང་བྱེད་གཉིས་པ *snań-byed gñis-pa* the second luminary, the moon; བ་གླང *ba-glań* a bull; བར་གྱི་མཚམས *bar-gyi mtshams* the middle zone or boundary: བྱ་ངང་པ *bya ńań-pa* swan; སྦྲང་ཆང *sbrań-chań* beer made of honey; དབང་པོའི་གསལ *dwań-pohi gsal* a lamp, that which clears the sight; མ་ཧེ *ma-he* a buffalo; མི་མོའི་གླུ *mi-mohi glu* a woman's song; བཞོན་པའི་རྟ *bshon-pahi rta* a riding horse; ཡུལ་ཕྲན *yul-phran* a small country; རི་དྭགས *ri-dwags* a deer; ལུང་ཚགས་པ *luń tshags-pa* a collected mind; རིན་པོ་ཆེ *rin-po che* precious thing; རི་རབ་ཀྱི་རི་ཕྲན *ri-rab-kyi ri-phran* a smaller peak of the mountain Sumeru; ཤིང་རྟ *çiń-rta* a chariot; གསེར་གྱི་ཁ་དོག *gser-gyi kha-dog* the colour of gold.

‡ ཀ་མ་ལ་ཤི་ལ कमलशील a celebrated Buddhist philosopher of the ancient monastery of Vikramaçīla in Magadha, who introduced the *Yogacārya* Mahāyāna School of Buddhism into Tibet, after defeating in controversy a Chinese hoshang who wished to convert the Tibetans to the doctrine of the "do-nothing" school during the reign of King ཁྲི་སྲོང་ལྡེའུ་བཙན *Khri-sroń sde-hu btsan* about the middle of the 8th century A.D.

ཀ་མ་ལི *ka-ma-li* a very sharp sword (*Ńag. 2*): ལག་པ་དགུ་ན་སྤུ་གྲི་ཀ་མ་ལ་སྣད་དགུ་ཐོགས་པ། (*D. R.*) grasping in his nine hands nine lotus-hafted razors.

ཀ་མུ་ལ་རྡོ་རྒྱུད *ka-mu-la rdo-rgyad* n. of a sort of alabaster or steatite found in Central Tibet (*Jä.*).

ཀ་ཙ་རྐེད་ཉག *ka-tsa rked-ñag* rusty and crooked: བྱང་བུར་ཀ་ཙ་རྐེད་ཉག་ཡོད་པ་རྣམས། "the steel ribs of the coat of mail which are rusty and bent" (*Jig.*).

‡ ཀ་ཙ་ཙུ་ཙ་ཀ कचचचक n. of a kind of bird (*K. ko.* ཀ *2.*).

‡ ཀ་ཙ་ལིན་དི *ka-tsa-lin-di* (prob. काचिलिन्दिक)=ལྷ་རྫས་ཀྱི་གོས dress made of a heavenly stuff, *i.e.*, the finest kind of silk which is used for presentation at an interview, or when making an application for any favour, &c.; n. of a very fine cloth or linen made of Kācilindi (*Lex.*).

‡ ཀ་ཙང་ཀ་ལ *Ka-tsań-ka-la* n. of a *Bhikṣuṇī* (Buddhist nun) (*K. d.* ཉ *18*).

† ཀ་ཙི་ལི་བན *Ka-tsi-li-ban* the Kachili forest: ཆུ་ཀླུང་རོ་ཧི་ཏའི་བྱང་འགྲམ་ཀ་ཙི་ལི་བན་བལ་པོ་རྫོང་དང་། on the northern bank of the river Rohita there is the Kachili forest and a Nepalese stronghold (*Dsam. 21*).

ཀ་རྩ་ག་ལ *ka-ṛtsa-ga-la* the sea (*Sehtr.*).

ཀ་རྩམ *ka-ṛtsam* a species of wild oats; it differs from *yug-po* or Tibetan oats and is considered superior to buckwheat, but inferior to wheat.

ཀ་ཚལ *Ka-tshal* n. of a place situated to the east of Lhasa; དབུས་སྟོད་མལ་གྲོ་ཀ་ཚལ་ལྷ་ཁང་། the monastery known as Ka-tshal Lha-khan of Mal-gro in Upper Ü (Central Tibet).

ཀ་ཚིགས་ཆེན་པོ *Ka-tshigs chen-po* the title of a Buddhist work on the genealogy of the Kings of Tibet (*Gyal. S. 28*).

† ཀ་ཡ་གོ་ཪི गयागौरी described as རི་ཤིན་ཏུ་མཐོ་བའི་སྟེང་དུ་ཡོད་པའི་རྒྱ་གར་གྱི་མཆོད་རྟེན་ཞིག་གི་མིང་། (*Dsam.*) "n. of an Indian *Chaitya* situated on the high hill (of Gayā Gauri)."

ཀ་ར I: *ka-ra* शर्करा sugar: ཀ་ར་དང་། ཡཱ་ར་དང་ཆ་མཉམ་དུ་བཟའ་ཞིང་། ཤོ་བྷ་ཉྫ་ནའི་རྩ་བའི་ཆང་འཐུང་ན་ཆུ་མའི་རྡེའུ་འབྱིན་པར་བྱེད་དོ། having taken sugar and arsenic in equal parts, if beer made from the root of *Çobhajana* be drunk, the gravel of the bladder will be ejected; ཀ་ར་དཀར་སྨུག *ka-ra dkar-smug* brown sugar; ཀ་ར་དཀར་སྨུག་བུར་སྦྲང་ཁ་བཀར་བ། a kind of brown crystallized treacle and honey; ཀ་ར་ཏོག་ཏོག *ka-ra tog-tog* loaf sugar, sugar in lumps; རྒྱལ་མོ་ཀ་ར *Rgyal-mo ka-ra* sugar from *Rgyal-mo Roñ*, situated on the confines of Tibet and China; བྱེ་མ་ཀ་ར *bye-ma ka-ra* powdered sugar, or granulated sugar; ཤེལ་ཀ་ར *çel-ka-ra* rocky candy (*K. g.* ཙ *46*).

ཀ་ར II: tent-pole; ཀ་ར་སྡིག་པོད *ka-ra sdig-pod* a tent-pole with a grooved bulb on top used in some countries; ཀ་ར་སྡིག་མེད་པ། or ཀ་ར་སྡེ་བཞང་མེད་པ། a tent-pole without a grooved bulb on top.

† ཀ་རཉྫ *ka-rañ-dsa* करंज, मर्कटी, प्रकीर्य a medicinal fruit or berry; n. of the tree *Pongamia glabra* and *Verbesina scandens.* ཀ་རཉྫ་ནི་བའི་མེ་དྲོད་སྐྱེད། *karañdsa* produces natural warmth (in the stomach).

Syn. རུལ་བྱེད་སྐྱེས *rul-byed skyes*; མར་གྱི་གང་ *mar-gyi gañ*; རྩོད་བྱེད་མ *rtsod byed-ma*; འཇམ་འབྲས་དབྱེ་བ *hjam-hbras dbye-wa*; ཚིགས་དྲུག་པ *tshigs drug-pa*; སྙེ་མ་ལུས་ལྕིབས *sñe-ma lus-lcibs* (*Mñon.*).

† ཀ་ར་ད *ka-ra-da* n. of a bird, the cry of which is like the sound of a drum. It is described in Buddhist books as like fire in colour, and as located in the abodes of the *Asura* (*K d.* ཉ *15*).

ཀ་ར་ན་ཇུས *ka-ra-na-jus* a kind of fine Chinese satin (*Jig.*). ཀ་ར་ན་ཇུས་དམ་ཇུས་མ་སོགས་ཚོས་དང་རིས་མོའི་དབྱིབས་ཀྱིས་ཤེས་ཐུབ་སོ། the kinds of satin (called) *karanajus* and *damjus*, &c., are distinguished by their colour and the shape of the figures on them.

ཀ་ར་ན་རུས *ka-ra-na-rus* a kind of Chinese satin: པང་ཁེབས་ཕལ་ཆེར་ཀ་ར་ན་རུས་དང་ཏ་ཞིང་དག་ལས་བྱས། aprons are mostly made of *kara-narus* and *ta-shiñ* satin.

ཀ་ར་ནང་ *ka-ra-nañ* in the mystic language of the *Ḍākinī* of Tibet=the food of pigs (*K. g.* ཁ *27*).

† ཀ་ར་བི་ར *ka-ra-bi-ra* or ཀ་ར་ཝི་ར *ka-ra wi-ra* करवीर 1. a fragrant oleander, *Nerium odorum*; a species of *soma*; a

particular magical formula or spell for recovering a missile of mystic properties after its discharge. [The name *karavira* is also applied to the *daphne* plant, from the bark of which Tibetan paper is made. The creeper called the white *karavira* rubbed with the blood of the rock-lizard and the medicine *ṣmutha* rubbed with *Bhriñgirāja*, when conbined, make an ointment which cures venereal eruptions on the skin of the penis (*K. g.* ཙ *49*).] 2. a sword or scimitar.

Syn. སོ་སོར་རྒོད་ *so-sor rgod*; སོ་སོར་བཤད་ *so-sor bshad*; རྟ་གསོད་ *rta gsod*; དཔའ་བོ་ལག་པ་ *dpah-po lag-pa*; གསོད་རྟགས་མེ་ཏོག་ཅན་ *gsod rtags me-tog can*; བརྒྱད་གྱེས་ *brgyad gyes*; གཏུམ་པོ་ *gtum-po* (*Mñon.*).

† ཀ་ར་རུ་བེ་ཀ *ka-ra ru-be-ka* कररावक a kind of bird (*K. ko.* ཀ *2*).

† ཀ་ར་ཧ་རི *ka-ra ha-ri*=བུ་རམ *bu-ram* sugar (*Sman. 291*).

† ཀ་རན་ད་བ *ka-ran da-wa* कारण्डव.

† ཀ་རནྡ I: *ka-ran-ḍa* कारण्डव 1. a sort of wild duck; ཀ་རཎྜ་ནི་སྐད་སྙན་པ་ཞིག་གི་མིང་། *karaṇḍa* is the name of a sweet-voiced bird. 2. कारण्ड, also पिटक, in Sans. a basket or covered box of bamboo wicker-work used for keeping books in; a basket for flowers; མདོ་ཟ་མ་ཏོག་བཀོད་པ་ कारण्डव्यूहसूत्र n. of a Buddhist work (*K. d.* ཞ *275*).

† ཀ་རནྡ II: श्वेत, शुक्ल white.

† ཀ་རས *ka-ras*, abbr. of *Kaçikahi ras*, the Benares muslin which used to be in great demand in Tibet. In the sacred books of Tibet the gods are generally dressed in fine Benares muslin. ཀ་རས་འདྲ་བས་ཁ་རེར་འབྲུ་བྲེ་རོ། for imitation Benares muslin the price per piece is two *bre* of barley.

† ཀ་རིའི་བུ་མོ *Ka-ri-hi bu-mo* कात्यायनी the daughter of Kātyāyana; Umā.

ཀ་རུ *ka-ru* 1. a wedge (*Jä.*). 2. white (*Ñag. 3*).

ཀ་རེ *ka-re*, probably ག་རེ *ga-re*. The use of the latter is very common in Eastern Tibet. In Sikkim they say ཀ་ཏེ *ka-te*, what? which? ཨུ་པ་སི་ཀ་ཁྱོད་ཀ་རེ་དགའ Upāsaka, in what do you delight? (*A. 94*).

ཀ་ལ་ཏ *Ka-la-ta* in mysticism ཀ་ལ་ཏ་ནི་འདོད་པའི་སྐུ་བྱད། *Ka-la-ta* is described as a man of lovely appearance (*K. g.* ཀ *216*).

† ཀ་ལ་པིང་ཀ *Ka-la-piñ-ka* कलविङ्क a sparrow; a singing bird with a sweet voice. According to *Lex.* the Indian cuckoo.

Syn. རྒྱལ་གསུང་ཡན་ལག *rgyal gsuñ yan-lag*; རྗེས་འགྲོ་མཁན་ *rjes hgro mkhan*; སྙན་པའི་དཔེ་ཅན་ *sñan-pahi dpe-can*; རྣ་བའི་བཅུད་ *rna-wahi bcud*; སྒོ་ངའི་དུས་ནས་སྐད་སྨྲའི་དབང་ *sgo-ñahi dus nas skad smrahi dwañ* (*Mñon.*).

† ཀ་ལ་བུ *Ka-la-bu* कलपुत्र n. of a king: དེའི་ཚེ་ན་རྒྱལ་པོ་ཀ་ལ་བུ་ཞེས་བྱ་བ་ཁྲོ་ཞིང་གཏུམ་པ at that time (there lived) a king named Kalaputra, fierce and wrathful (*K. my.* ཀ *209*).

† ཀ་ལ་རོ་ཟན *Ka-la ro-zan*, lit. काल, the black lord of death who eats the dead; n. of a *Nāga*.

† ཀ་ལ་ཤ कलश pitcher, jar; a large waterpot.

ཀ་ལག *ka-lag* in *W.* mud; earth and water used instead of mortar; also other similar compounds (*Jä.*).

† ཀ་ལནྡ་ཀ कलन्दक=མཆིལ་པ *mchil-pa* a species of bird, probably the *Bûl-bûl*.

‡ ཀ་ལན་ད་ཀ *Ka-lan-da-ka* कलन्दक 1. a town. 2. an individual: ཀ་ལན་ད་ཀའི་གྲོང་དུ་བྱིན་ནས། having arrived at the town of Kalandaka: དེ་ནས་ཀ་ལན་ད་ཀའི་བུ་ཚེ་དང་ལྡན་པ་བཟང་བྱིན་བྱུང་བས། then appeared Zañ-jin the long-lived, son of Kalandaka (*K. d.* ཙ. *34*).

‡ ཀ་ལན་ཛ་རི་ཀ *ka-lan-dsa-ri-ka* कलञ्ज-रिक 1. a flowering plant; also the flower used in *yajña*—sacrificial fire (*K. g.* ད *33*). 2. belonging to कलञ्ज, an animal struck with a poisoned arrow; tobacco.

‡ ཀ་ལམ་ཀ *ka-lam-ka*, described as ཡུལ་ཞིག་གི་མིང་, n. of a place in Ancient India (*Dsam. 14*).

‡ ཀ་ལམ་བ *ka-lam-ba* कलम्ब the pot-herb *Convolvolus repens, Menispermum calumba*; a medicinal plant: ཀ་ལམ་བའི་ལོ་མ་ཟས་ན་ཁམས་འཕེལ་ལོ། tho leaf of *Kalamba* when eaten improves health (*K. g.* ཙ *44*).

‡ ཀ་ལཱ་པ *ka-lá-pa* कलाप 1. an aggregate of many accomplishments; an accumulation of excellent and wonderful properties in one place or thing (*Lexx.*). 2. the Buddhist Utopia; the capital of the fabulous kingdom of S'ambhala.

ཀ་ལི *ka-li* an abbreviation of the word *ka-pa-li*, a skull (*Lexx.*).

‡ ཀ་ལི་ཀ *ka-li-ka* 1. described as མེ་ཏོག་ཙམ་པ་ཀའི་འབྲས་བུའི་མིང་། the fruit of the *magnolia* flower-plant; a bud of that flower (*M̱ñon.*). 2. prob. कलिकार, a plant bearing a nut which is used as a febrifuge, grey *Bonduc.*

‡ ཀ་ལིང་ག *Ka-liñ-ga* or ཀ་ལིང་ཀ *Ka-liñ-ka* कलिङ्ग 1. one of the thirty-six Buddhist sacred places said to be situated at a distance of 60 *yojana* S. E. of Gayā—also the birth-place of Vis'wantara (*Duṣ-ye. 39*). 2. a bird, a native of an island or maritime province of India bordering on the Indian Ocean (*K. d.* ཞ *15*).

ཀ་ལེ *ka-le* or ཀ་ལེབ *kaleb* saddle-cloth (*Jä.*).

‡ ཀ་ཤ *ka-ça*=སྤང་རྩི *ṣpañ-ṟtsi* (*Ñag.*) a species of grass (*K. d.* བ *91*); कुश *Saccharum spontaneum.*

‡ ཀ་ཤི་ཀ I: *ka-çi-ka* the finest Benares muslin; cotton cloth of the finest texture formerly manufactured in Benares; ཀ་ཤི་ཀའི་རས काशिकांशुक Benares muslin which in ancient times was of great repute. It is said that even the gods longed to wear clothes made of this material. According to *Cs. ka-çi-ka* means a kind of flax as well as linen cloth; ཀ་ཤི་ཀའི་རས་དཀར་པོ། white Benares linen; ཀ་ཤི་ཀའི་འབྲུ་སྣུམ the oil of *kaçika* grain, prob. linseed oil.

‡ ཀ་ཤི་ཀ II: of Kāshi (Benares); an inhabitant of Benares.

ཀ་ཤི་ཀ་ཕྲ་མོ *ka-çi ka phra-mo* fine flax; Benares muslin.

ཀ་ཤིས *ka-çiṣ*, abbr. of ཀ་ཤི་ཀའི་རས, cotton cloth.

‡ ཀ་ཤི་རུ *Ka-çi-ru* n. of a place or island in the Indian ocean (*K. d.* ད *319*): कशेरु one of the nine divisions of Jambu-dvīpa.

ཀ་ས *ka-sa* the colloq. form of the expression བཀའ་གསལ *ḇkaẖ gsal*, a definite order or clear message. According to *Jä. kasa* and *kaso* are mutilated forms of བཀའ་བཙལ *ḇkaẖ ḇstsal*, meaning in *Ld.* "yes, sir; very well, sir; at your service."

‡ ཀ་སན་ཀ་ར *ka-san ka-ra* རྒྱ་གར་གྱི་གྲོང་ཁྱེར་ཞིག་གི་མིང་ "n. of a city of Ancient India" (*Dsam. 25*).

‡ ཀ་ཧ་ན་ཡ་ན་ཤཱི་ལ *Ka-ha-na ya-na çi-la* n. of an Indian Pandit (*Yig. 30*).

‡ ཀཀྐུ་ཊི་པ *Kak-ku ṭi-pa* n. of an Indian Buddhist sage (*K. dun. 52*).

‡ ཀཀོ་ལ *Kako-la* कक्कोल a secret abode of the Ḍākinī (*K. g.* ཀ *337*).

ཀག *kag* or ཀག་མ *kag-ma* mischief, harm, danger (*Lex.*); ཀག or གེག or སྐག implies some accident or injury; ཀག་གིས་ལངས = ཧད་ཀྱིས་ལངས *had-kyis lañs* fleeing from harm; ཀག་གིས་ལངས་ནས་འགྲོ་བ། going from a place which has not suited one owing to bad luck or any accident; also to run away from a place from fear; adv. ཀག་གིས suddenly (*Sch.*).

‡ ཀག་ཀ་བ *kag-ka-wa* कगकव n. of a species of bird living on the Vulture-peak Hill near Gayā (*K. ko.* ཀ *2*).

‡ ཀང་ཀ *kañ-ka* कङ्क, जलाटन 1. crane. 2. in Tibet a bird that feeds on dead bodies and is therefore called དུར་བྱ *dur-bya* the bird of the cemetery.

‡ ཀང་ཀ་ར *kañ-ka-ra* कङ्कर 1. n. of a flower described as growing on the Vulture-peak Hill of Gayā (*K. ko.* ཀ *4*). 2. prob. कङ्करोल the plant *Alangium hexapetalum*.

ཀང་དང་ཀིང *Kañ-dañ-kiñ* prop. n. of a terrific deity, a *Ḍākinī*. When the monastery of Sam-ye was built, the image of *Kañ-dañ-kiñ* was placed on the first floor of the principal temple (*Gyal. S. 87*).

‡ ཀང་ཚ་རངྒ *Kañ-tsha-rañga* a place in Ancient Bengal, called Gaur in the Indian language and *Gha-broñ* in the colloq. of Tibet (*S. Lam.*).

ཀད *kad* in *Ld.* sometimes used instead of the affix ཀ *ka*, *e.g.*, གཉིས་ཀད *gñis-kad*, ཙང་ཀད *tsañ-kad*; also མཉམ་ཀད *mñam-kad* (*Jä.*).

ཀན I: *kan* (see ཁ་ན *kha-na*) the side or bank: སྲི་ཆུའི་ཕར་ཀན་ན་ཇག་པའི་ཡུལ་ཡོད་པས། on the further bank of the river *Sri-chu* there being a country of brigands (*A. 27*).

ཀན II: also spelt སྐན *skan*, to cease absolutely from: ད་ནི་ཁྲོས་ཞེ་སྡང་བྱེད་དེ་ཀན། "now give up anger and passion"; ན་རེ་ཀན cease to tell anybody. Here the word ཀན *kan* is an emphatical prohibition (*Bon.*).

ཀན III: 1. तालु the palate; in *pad-kan* phlegm; lit. the plywer of the palate. 2. हारक that seizes or takes away by force. 3. कण्टक a thorn; an illness; a disease (*Lex.*). 4. n. of the pulse felt with the middle finger called *kan-ma*.

‡ ཀན་ནི་ཀ *Kan-ni-ka* कणिक district in the east of India (*K. d.* ར *267*).

‡ ཀན་ཀྱ་ཀུབ་ཛ (lit. the daughter of the hunchback) कान्यकुब्ज, also written ཀར་ཉའི་ཡུལ *Kar-nyahi yul*, a city in Ancient India, the capital of which was Kānyakubja, the modern Kanouj (*K. du.* ད *131*).

ཀན་མ *kan-ma* the middle finger.

‡ ཀན་ཙི *Kan-tsi* काञ्ची n. of a province, and also that of a city of Buddhist fame in Southern India (*Dus-ye. 39*).

‡ ཀཎ་ཊ་ཀཱ་རི *kaṇ-ta-kā-ri* कण्टकारि a wild *Rubus*; n. of a plant, *Solanum jaquini*; also the fruit of this plant; a drug useful in stopping fever; a thorny stick.

Syn. རིགས་ལྡན་མ *Rigs ldan-ma*; ཡུལ་འཁོར་སྐྱེས *yul hkhor skyes*; སྟག་ལྡན *stag ldan*; ཚེ་ལྡན *tshe ldan*; ཚེར་མ་ཅན *tsher-ma can*; རྩུབ་མོའི་རེག་བྱ *rtsub-mohi reg-bya*; ཕྱོགས་མེད་མ *phyogs med-ma*; སྐུལ་བྱེད *skul byed* (*Mñon.*).

ཀབ་ཀོབ *kab-kob*=ཀོ་བ་སྦྱར་པོ hide; untanned skin (*Ñag. 5*).

ཀབ་ཤ *kab-ça* shoe; leather shoes of Hindu fashion used by the wealthier Tibetans (*Jä.*).

† ཀཾ་ཀ *kam-ka*=ཀང་ཀ *kañ-ka*, ཛ་ལ་ཊ་ན *ja-la ṭa-na* जलाटन crane.

† ཀམ་བི་ལ *kam bi-la* a kind of tree growing on the Vulture-peak Hill near Gaya (*K. ko.* ཀ *3*); prob. the plant *Crinum Amaryllacec.*

† ཀམ་བོ་ཛ *Kam-bo-dsa* कम्बोज 1. a country in the north-west of India (*Vai. sñ.*), written *Kampo-rtse* (*Jä.*); n. of a fabulous city said to have contained an area of a hundred *yojana* (*S. Lam.*). 2. modern Cambodia, anciently called Champa.

ཀམ་བོ་ཛི་ཀ *Kam-bo-dsi-ka* n. of the country, also of the people, as well as of articles that come from it (*K. du.* ད *148*).

ཀཧུ *kahu* water-melon (*Sch.*).

ཀཧུ་ཧིས *Kahu-his* n. of a Chinese minister (*Yig. 24*).

ཀར *kar*, also *kar-kar*, great pain; suffering (*Lex.*); ཀར་ཀར་ཟུག་ལངས། aching pain (*Ñag. 4*).

ཀར་ལངས་པ *kar lañs-pa*=ནད་ཟུག་ལངས་པ *nad zug lañs-pa* (*Ñag.*), irritation or pain in sickness; exacerbation.

† ཀར་ཀ་ཊ *karka-ta* or ཀརྐ་ཊ कर्कट, the constellation of "Cancer." It is represented by the frog (སྦལ་པ) in Tibet.

† ཀར་ཀེ་ཏ *karke-ta*=ཀར་ཀེ་ཏ་ན कर्केतन, described as ནོར་བུ་གསེར་པོ, a yellow gem or precious stone (*K. d.* ཡ *295*).

ཀར་སྐྱིན *kar-skyin* loan; in polite language v. སྐྱིན *skyin* (*Jä.*).

ཀར་རྒྱལ *Kar-rgyal* a *Nāga* (*S. kar.*).

ཀར་རྒྱུད *Kar rgyud* members of the line of the *Karma-pa* hierarchy; also an abbreviation of the expression *Karma-pahi-rgyudpa.*

ཀར་ཆག *kar-chag* (also written དཀར་ཆག) a register; list; index.

† ཀར་ཎི་ཀ *kar-ni-ka* कर्णिक, कर्णिकार n. of aflower of the shape of an ear-ring (*K. g.* ཞ *2*); the flower of the tree *Pterospermum acerifolium* and of *Cassia fistula.*

† ཀར་ཎ་ཀྵ་ར *karṇa kṣa-ra*=ཚ་ལ *tsha-la* borax (*Sman. 484*).

† ཀརྣི་ཀ *karni-ka* in mystic language= དྲིལ་བུ *dril-bu*, a bell (*K. g.* ཁ *27*).

† ཀརྨ *kar-ma*=འཕྲིན་ལས *hphrin-las* or ལས कर्म commission, service; action; work; that which is produced from action; ཀར་མ་པ *Karma-pa* (in Nepal called कर्मिक) n. of a *Tāntrik* school of Buddhism. The head of that school in Tibet holds the title of *Rgyal-wa Karma-pa.* The followers of the school are generally designated by the name of *Karma-pa.*

ཀརྨ་གཉིས་པ *Karma-gñis-pa* the second head of this sect, named *Pakṣi* or *Bakṣi*, was invited to China by the Emperor Kublai Khan. The third chief, called *Karma Rañ-byuñ rdorje*, was invited to Peking by the Emperor Temur Toakwan. The fourth *Karma Rol pahi rdorje* was a friend of the last monarch of the Mongol dynasty. The fifth *Karma De bshin gçegs-pa* was invited to China in the reign of the *Ming* Emperor Yunglo (*Loñ.* ར *10*).

ཀརྨ་བསྟན་སྐྱོང་ *Karma bstan skyoñ* the last of the *Sde-ba Gtsañ-pa* or rulers of Tsang and Ü whom the Mongol Chief Gu-shi Khan overthrew (*Loñ.* ར *15*).

ཀར་མ་བདྲ *Kar-ma ba-dsra* कर्मवज्र n. of an Indian pandit who worked in Tibet for Buddhism (*J. Zañ.*).

ཀར་སྨུག *kar-smug* or ཀ་ར་སྨུག་པ *ka-ra-smug-pa* brown sugar or treacle (*Jig.*).

ཀར་ཡོལ *kar-yol* (also written དཀར་ཡོལ, meaning white ware) porcelain; china-ware; a china cup.

ཀར་ལང་བ *kar-lañ-wa* to stand up; to rise suddenly (*Jä.*).

† ཀར་ཤ་པ་ཎི *kar-ça-pa-ṇi* कार्षापण 1. a coin in Ancient India, or a weight of varying value; a *tola* or one *rupee* weight of gold; the value of two Tibet *sho*: མ་ནུ་ལྔ་སོགས་མཱ་ཥ་ཀ། *ma-nu lña sogs mā-ṣa-ka*, དེ་རྣམས་བཅུ་དྲུག་ཀར་ཥ་པ་ཎ། *de-rnams bcu-drug kar-ṣa-pa-ṇa*, དེ་བཞི་ནི་གསེར་སྲང་ངོ་། *de bshi ni gser-srañ-ño* (*Ñag.*) five *manu* make a *māṣaka*, sixteen *māṣaka* make a *kar-ṣa-paṇa*, and four of these make a gold *sran* (*i.e.*, half a *tola* of gold). 2. འགྲོན་བུ་སྟོང་དྲུག་བརྒྱའི་རིན the "value of 1,600 *cowries*." 3. कर्षापण a coin or weight of different values=*karṣa*: if of gold, weighing sixteen *māṣa*, which are variously calculated; if of silver, in value equal to 16 *paṇa* of *cowries*, *i.e.*, 1,280 *cowries*, commonly termed a *kahan*; if of copper, it weighs 80 *raktika*, or the same as of gold, about 176 grains.

ཀར་ཤུབས *kar-çubs* (abbr. of དཀར་ཡོལ་གྱི་ཤུབས *dkar-yol-gyi çubs*) the cover of a china tea-cup, generally made of iron, brass or silver: ཀར་ཤུབས་ལ་བྲེ་བཅུ *kar-çubs-la bre-bcu* (*Rtsii.*) "for the cover of a tea-cup made of silver (the price is) 10 *bre*."

ཀར་ས *kar-sa* n. of a kind of brick-tea; also called ལྗང་ཇ *ljan-ja* (green tea) or ལྗང་ཇ་པ་རི *ljañ-ja pa-ri*; also the tea that comes from the Chinese district of Jañ: ལྗང་ལམ་རྒྱུད་ལ་ཀར་ས་བོད་མཐིང་གཉིས, ད་ལྟ་ལྗང་ཇ་ཞེས་སུ་གྲགས་མོད་ཀྱིས། by the Jang route (come) both *Karṣa* and Bod-thing (teas), now well known as Jang-ja (*Jig. 23*).

ཀར་སོག *Kar-Sog*, an abbr. of *Kar-ma-pa* and *Sog-po*, followers of the *Karma-pa* sect and the Mongolians.

ཀརྟི་སྒང *Karti sgañ* n. of a place in Tibet.

† ཀལྤ *kalpa* for བསྐལ་པ *bskal-pa* कल्प, an age; a mythical period of time.

† ཀཱ་ཀ *kā-ka* काक a crow.

ཀཱ་ཁི་ལ *kā-khi-la* (mystic) door; entrance (*K. g.* ཕ *28*).

ཀཱ་འཇི *kā-hji*=ཀྭ་ཙེ *kwa-tsi* a shirt; a Chinese jacket (*Sch.*). In Chinese *Kua-tzu*.

† ཀཱ་ཏྱ་བུ་མོ *Kā-tya bu-mo* described as དབང་ཕྱུག་གི་བཙུན་མོ་ཨུ་མ། the goddess Umā, wife of Dwañ dphyug (*Mñon.*).

ཀཱ་ཏ་ཀ *kā-ta-ka* fish (*Schtr.*).

‡ ཀཱ་པ་ལི *kā-pa-li* कपाल human skull; cup made of skull: དངུལ་ཉམས་ལྗང་བར་བྱས་ཏེ་ཀཱ་པ་ལིར་བཙུག། (*A. 121*) having made the silver pieces green, (he) put them in the skull-cup.

‡ ཀཱ་བེ་རི *Kā-be-ri* कावेरी the river Cauvery in Mysore, a river said to be half a *yojana* broad and 300 *yojana* long. On the banks of this river are flower gardens (*K. d.* ར *268*).

‡ ཀཱ་ཙི་ཀཱ *kā-tsi-kā* 1. काञ्चिका, also as कुञ्चिका, a species of bamboo which when bent by the wind is said to emit fire (*K. d.* ར *287*). 2. कुञ्चिका a plant bearing a red and black seed used as a weight, *Arbus precatorius;* or another plant bearing a pungent seed, *Nigella Indica.*

‡ ཀཱ་རི་ཀཱ *kā-ri-kā* कारिका aphorism; purely Sanskṛt yet largely used in Tibetan works (ཚ་བའི་ཀཱ་རི་ཀ 7); = ཚིག་ལེའུར་བྱས་པ a *Sûtra* or *Udana* in verse.

‡ ཀཱ་ལ་ཀོ *Kā-la-ko* a country beyond the sea into which the Indus flows and where the finest coral grows (probably a marine province or island in the Persian Gulf) (*K. d.* ར *280*).

‡ ཀཱ་ལ་སྔོ་བསང *kā-la sño-bsañ* deep blue-black colour (*Sch.*).

ཀཱ་ཤ *Kā-ça* काश 1. a city in Ancient India which was twenty *yojana* in area (*S. Lam*). 2. a sort of grass, *Saccharum spontaneum.*

‡ ཀྭ *kwa* or ཀྱེ *kye* Oh! ཀྭའི་གྲོགས་པོ *kwahi grogs-po* Oh friend!

ཀྭ་ཡེ *kwa-ye* an exclamation used in calling some one, generally a subordinate.

ཀྵ *ksha* this word in its mystic signification is symbolic of the source of all *Dharma* (matter and phenomena), and demonstrates that they are subject to eternal change.

‡ ཀྵེ་ཏྲ་པཱ་ལ *kṣe-tra pā-la* क्षेत्रपाल (*Schr.*) a deity protecting the fields; in Budh. a guardian of the province of a Buddha's work.

ཀི *ki* numeral for thirty-one.

ཀི་ཀི *ki-ki* a hortative utterance in the invocation of spirits: ཀི་ཀི་སྨོ་སྨོ་དེ་རིང་ཉི་མ་དྲོ། "Hail, O, ye gods! to-day is warm!"

ཀི་ཀང *ki-kañ* 1. wild leek (*Sch.*). 2. described as མ་བདག་གི་མིང་ n. of a demi-god, a *Nāga.* It is inauspicious to do any work of merit when Kikañ comes near.

ཀི་གུ *ki-gu* a hook; the vowel sign *i*, which resembles a hook in shape.

ཀི་རྒྱུང་ *ki-rgyuñ* a mystical invocation signifying "Lord": ཀི་རྒྱུང་ང་ནི་ཕྱོགས་བར་ཞི་ཕྱུབ་དུ། "O Lord, be appeased by this prostrate (devotee)." It is a mystic charm to propitiate the *Bon-po* deity, called *Çen-gsras Mi-mgon rgyal-po* (*D.R.*).

‡ ཀི་ཏ་ཀ *Ki-ta-ka* कितक 1. a *Rākṣasa* or cannibal demon (*K. d.* ར *189*). 2. a worm or insect (*Cs.*).

ཀི་ལྡིར *ki-ldir* a shrill shout; a savage howl.

ཀི་པ *ki-pa* a volume, &c., marked with the letter ཀི.

ཀི་མ *ki-ma* according to *Schr.* a corruption of the Chinese word *khin*, a lyre with seven strings. (*Pilgrimage of Fa-Hian. Calcutta, 1848, p. 265.*)

ཀི་ཙི *ki-tsi* tickling; ཀི་ཙི་བྱེད་པ *ki-tsi byed-pa* to tickle (*Jä.*).

‡ ཀི་ར་ཎ *ki-ra-ṇa* (mystic) a flower (*K. g.* ཕ *26*).

‡ ཀི་རི་ཀན *ki-ri-kan* ह्रकच, ह्रकर a kind of pepper, *Piper chaba*; ཤིང་ཨརྐ་དཀར་པོའི་རྩ་བ་དང་། ཀི་རི་ཀན་དཀར་པོའི་རྩ་བ་དང་། (*K. g.* ཞ *210*) the roots of white *arka* tree and roots of white *kiri-kan* (are used in medicine).

‡ ཀིང་ཀ་ར *kiṅ-kara* किङ्कर a servant or an emissary.

‡ ཀིང་ཤུ་ཀ *kiṅ-çu-ka* किंशुक a kind of flower; the tree *Butea Frondosa;* a tree bearing pretty flowers.

‡ ཀིམ་པ *kim-pa* a pretty but bitter fruit, erroneously for ཀིམ་པ་ཀ *kim-pa-ka.*

‡ ཀིམ་པ་ཀ *kim-pa-ka* किम्पाक a fruit, *Cucurbitaccous* plant, *Trichosanthes palmata*; also possibly *Cucumis colocynthis.* ཀིམ་པ་ཀ་ཡི་འབྲས་བུ་མཚུངས། ཉ་མཆིལ་ཟས་ཀྱི་རིགས་ཅན་དང་། སྒྱུ་མ་བཞིན་དང་མི་རྟག་པའི། འདོད་པ་ལ་ནི་མི་རྣམས་ཞུགས། (*K. d.* ཡ *525*) men entertain desires which are transient and deceptive like the *Kimpaka* fruit and like fish that eat bait on a hook.

‡ ཀིམ་པ་ལ *kim-pa-la* or ཀིམ་བ་ལ *kim-ba-la* किम्बल a musical instrument; a cymbal (*Cs.*).

ཀི་ཧུ *ki-hu* गृञ्जनक a species of small red garlic; acc. to some carrot.

ཀིལ *kil* slowly = ག་ལེ *ga-le*: ལ་གཅིག་བརྒལ་ནས་ཀིལ་གྱིས་སླེབ། crossing a mountain pass (he) arrived slowly (*D.R.*).

‡ ཀི་ལ་ཀི་ལ *Kila-kila* किलकिल 1. an epithet of S'iva. 2. a town in Ancient India. 3. a *Rākṣasa* King (*K. g.* མ *623*). 4. an onomatopoetic for sounds or cries (*Jä.*).

‡ ཀཱི་རི་ཏ་ཀ *Kī-ri ta-ka* किरातक the country of the Sapta Kosi in Nepal inhabited by the Kirāt tribes and called Kiranta; n. of a district in མོན་ཡུལ་ Sub-Himālayā (*Duṣ-yc. 39*).

ཀཱི་ཤའི་འདབ *kī-çahi hdab* अपामार्गपत्र, ཤིང་ཨ་པ་མརྒ་ཏོ་མ the leaf of the tree *Achyranthes aspera* used in incantations, in medicine, in washing linen, and in sacrifices (*Mñon.*).

ཀཱིང་ཀང་ *Kīṅ-kaṅ* v. ཀང་དང་ཀིང *Kaṅ daṅ kiṅ.*

ཀུ I: *ku* 1. for the numeral 61. 2. (mystic) a fairy or *dākinī* (*K. g.* ཕ, *179*); ཀུ་པ *ku-pa*, the 61st (volume).

ཀུ II: a cry, moan; ཀུ་སྒྲ *ku-sgra* clamour, noise; ཀུ་སྒྲ་ཧེ་རེ་བྱེད་པ a general cry; the vociferations of many people together; ཀུ་རེང་རེ་། the noise of general conversation: དེ་ནས སོག་ཆུ་ཁར་སྦྱོན་པའི་དུས་སུ་ཁང་པ་ཞིག་ན་ཀུ་རེང་རེ་འདུག། then, when they arrived at the bank of Sog chu, there was the sound of chattering in a house (*A. 82*).

ཀུ་ཀུ *ku-ku* = སྐུ་སྐུ *sku-sku* प्रहेलिका; ལྡ་ཧུ *lda-hu* an enigma, a riddle, a puzzling question.

ཀུ་ཀུ་སྒྲོགས *ku-ku sgrogs* lit. that cries *kuku*; = བྱ་གག *bya-gag* a grey species of duck (*Mñon.*).

ཀུ་ཀུ་ར་ཙ *Ku-ku-ra-tsa* कुकुराचार्य a teacher or trainer of dogs; n. of an Indian Buddhist sage who was also called Kukuripa (ཀུ་ཀུ་རི་པ) (*K. dun. 45*).

ཀུ་ཀུར་ཏ་པཱ་དཱ *Ku-kur-ta pā-dā* कुक्कुरपादा = རི་བྱ་རྐང་པ་ཅན་ n. of a hill in Magadha (*Dsam. 17*).

ཀུ་ཀེ *Ku-ke*, erroneously for གུ་གེ *Gu-ge*, a part of the province of Nga-ri in Tibet.

ཀུ་ཅོ *ku-co* कोलाहल, कलकल, स्वन noise, clamour; ཁྱི་རྒན་ཀུ་ཅོ་འདོན་པ་ན ཀྱ་མཚན་མེད་པར་གཞན་དུ་རྒྱུག། when an old dog barks, go elsewhere without explanation (*S. leg.*). ཀུ་ཅོ་ཅན་ noisy, clamorous; ཀུ་ཅོ་ཅན་སྨྲ་བ་སྒྲུབ to speak in a loud voice (meaning nothing); to bawl out; ཀུ་ཅོ་འདོན་པ to bawl, to cry out, to make a loud noise; ཀུ་ཅོ་ཆེ་བ a great noise or tumult, an uproar.

ཀུ་ཅོར *Ku-cor*, also ཀུ་ཆོར, n. of a place in Tibet.

ཀུ་དེང་ངེ *ku-deñ-ñe*: See ante ཀུ *ku*.

ཀུ་ཐེར *ku-ther* = མཐོ་རིས་རླུང *mtho-ris rluñ* the heavenly breeze (*Mñon.*).

‡ ཀུ་ཎ་ལ *Ku-ṇa-la* कुणाल 1. the *manāl* or Himālayan pheasant; also, a bird with beautiful eyes which lives in the fabulous mount Sumeru. 2. the eldest son of As'oka.

ཀུ་བ *ku-wa* or སྐུ་བ *sku-wa* (in Chinese: *kua*) अलाबु, तुम्बक a gourd; the bottle gourd, *Lagenaria vulgaris*. In the Pemakoi district this fruit is called ཨ་བུམ *a-bum*, *i.e.*, nature's bottle. A bottle made of a dried gourd is also called ཀུ་བ *ku-wa*.

Syn. རྣམ་པར་རྒྱལ *rnam-par rgyal*; སྡོང་བུ་རིང *sdoñ-bu riñ*; དྲ་བ་ཅན *dra-wa-can*; རྔ་ཟླུམ་བྱེད *rña zlum byed*; འབིགས་བྱེད *hbigs byed*; འབྲས་མཆོག *hbras mchog*; མདའ་ལྤགས *mdah lpags* (*Mñon.*).

ཀུ་བའི་གཟིངས *ku-wahi gziñs* a float made of long-dried gourds.

‡ ཀུ་བ་ལ་མེ་ཏོག *ku-ba-la me-tog* कुवलय, also उत्पल, the water-lily; also, the jujube plant, *Zizyphus jujuba* and the fruit of that plant.

‡ ཀུ་བེ་ར *Ku-bera* कुवेर, श्रेष्ठ Kuvera, the god of riches, the chief of the Noijin known also as *Naga Kuvera* and རྣམ་ཐོས་ཀྱི་བུ *Rnam-thos kyi-bu*, the son of *Vaiçravaṇa*. According to some Tibetan writers, *Kuvera* is one of the eight keepers of the horses of *Vaiçravaṇa*. [*Kubera*, or in later Sanskrit *Kuvera*, originally the name of the chief of the evil beings of darkness bearing the epithet *Vaiçravaṇa*; afterwards the god of riches and treasures, and is regent of the northern quarter of the world, which is hence called *Kubera-gupta-dik*. Kubera is the son of *Viçrava* by *Idaviḍa*, the chief of the *Yakṣa* and a friend of Rudra.] (*M. Wills.*).

ཀུ་བྱི་མང་ཀེ *Ku-byi mañ-ke* a Bon deity who resembles the *Bodhisattva* Jampal; the god of learning and wisdom among the Northern Buddhists (*D.R.*).

ཀུ་མ་ར *ku-ma-ra* = གསེར་མཆོག *gser-mchog* लङ्कासुवर्ण leaf-gold (from China brought by way of Ceylon); it is described in (*Mñon.*): ལང་ཀ་ནས་རྫས་པའི་གསེར་མཆོག gold exported from Lankā (Ancient Ceylon).

‡ ཀུ་མུད *ku-mud* कुमुद the water-lily which opens at the appearance of the moon; said to be *Nymphæa esculenta*; ཀུ་མུད་ཚལ = ཀུ་མུ་ད་ཡི་ནགས་ཚལ a bush or cluster of water-lilies.

Syn. ཨུཏ་པ་ལ་དཀར་པོ *ut-pa-la dkar-po*; ཟླ་བའི་དྲི *zla-wahi dri*; ས་མོས *sa-mos*; ས་དགའ *sa-dgah*; སའི་གདུ་གུ *sahi gdu-gu*; སྟེང་འཐུང་དཀར་པོ *steñ hthuñ dkar-po*; ཟླ་བས་དགའ *zla-was dgah*; སི་ཏ *sita*; ས་སྒྲོག *sa-sgrog*; ས་སྟོབས *sa-stobs*; མཚན་མོ་བཤད *mtshan-mo bshad* (*Mñon.*).

‡ ཀུ་མུད་གྲོགས་ *ku-mud grogs* = བསིལ་ཟེར་ *bsil-zer* or ཟླ་འོད་ *zla-hod* moonbeams (*Mñon.*).

‡ ཀུ་མུད་དགྲ་ *ku-mud dgra*, v. ཉི་མ་ *ñi-ma*, the sun (*Mñon.*).

‡ ཀུ་མུད་ཅན་ *ku-mud can*, v. ཀུ་མུད་ཚལ་ *ku-mud-tshal* (*Mñon.*).

‡ ཀུ་མུད་གཉེན་ *ku-mud-gñen* कुमुदबन्धु lit. the friend of the water-lily; the moon.

‡ ཀུ་མུད་ལྡན་ *ku-mud-ldan*, v. ཀུ་མུད་ཚལ་ *ku-mud tshal*.

‡ ཀུ་མུད་ལོ་མ་ *ku-mud lo-ma* = ཤིང་ཡོངས་འདུ་ས་བརྟོལ། a medicinal plant of the lily species (*Mñon.*).

‡ ཀུ་མུད་ཚལ་ *ku-mud-tshal* a cluster of water-lilies.

‡ ཀུ་ཛ་ *ku-dsa* कुज 1. a tree; lit. that which grows on the earth. 2. the planet Mars.

ཀུའི་ *Kuhi* a devil or demon in Chinese demonology. In Chinese *Kuei*.

ཀུའི་ཤིན་ *kuhi-çin* a class of evil spirits (*Grub.*). In Chinese *Kuei-shen*, "devils and gods."

ཀུའི་ཙང་ *kuhi-tsañ* a Chinese work on divination (*Grub.* ཞ *5*).

ཀུ་ཡ་ *ku-ya* sediment of urine from which Tibetan physicians diagnose disease (*Med.*).

‡ ཀུ་ར་ར་ *ku-ra-ra* कुरर = ཅ་ཀུ་ར་ར་ n. of a bird; an osprey (*Mñon.*).

‡ ཀུ་ར་བ་ཀ་ *ku-ra-ba-ka* कुरबक or कुरवक the crimson amaranth; a purple or yellow *Barleria*; the blossom of the amaranth or *Barleria*.

‡ ཀུ་རང་ག་ *ku-rañ-ga* कुरङ्ग the deer; also སྲོག་ཆགས་ *srog-chags* an insect (*K. d.* ཞ *462*).

‡ ཀུ་རུ་ *Ku-ru* कुरु a city in Ancient India near Delhi one *yojana* in area; also a province (*S. Lam. 20*).

‡ ཀུ་རུ་ཀུལ་ལེ་ *Ku-ru-kul-le* कुरुकुल्ला a female Buddhist deity associated with Kuvera, the god of wealth; is goddess of might and power; she is also called རིག་བྱེད་མ་ (*Vidyā*). The first sovereign Dalai Lama is said to have acquired great power by propitiating this deity.

‡ ཀུ་རུ་པིན་ད་ *ku-ru-pin-da* = ཤ་ཉེ་ *sha-ñe* 1. कुरुविन्द lead. 2. a fragrant grass; *Cyperus rotundus*; the bud of a flower. 3. a ruby; cinnabar.

‡ ཀུ་རུ་བན་ད་ *ku-ru ban-da*, v. མོན་ལུག་ *mon-lug*, the breed of sheep in the sub-Himālayan countries (*Mñon.*).

ཀུ་རེ་ *ku-re* or ཀུ་རེས་ *ku-res* क्रीड़ा, खेला, खेला, हास्य sport, diversion, jest, horse-play; ཀུ་རེ་བྱེད་པ་ to jest; ཀུ་རེའི་ཆེད་ for the purpose of amusement or fun; ཀུ་རེའི་རིམ་པས་མི་དགའ་བ། केलिक्रमेण अरतिः not liking, disgusted with, amusements.

‡ ཀུ་ལ་ཀཱ་ *Ku-la-kā* कुलका a *Srin-mo* (goblin) that lived only on lotus flowers and lotus-honey, and resided in the fabulous island of *Ramamo* (*K. d.* ར *280*).

‡ ཀུ་ལན་ཏ་ *ku-lan-ta* कुलान्त the country inhabited by an aboriginal race of people (*Dus-ye.*).

‡ ཀུ་ལཱ་ལ་ *Ku-lā-la* for ཀུ་ཎ་ལ་ *Ku-ṇa-la*.

ཀུ་ལུ་ཏ་ *Ku-lu-ta* a place situated in the south-east of Kashmir, now called Nyûn-ti by Tibetans, by Hindus Kulu (*S. Lam. 19*).

‡ ཀུ་ཤ་ *ku-ça* 1. कुश, दर्भ the sacred grass used in certain religious ceremonies both by Brahmans and Buddhists;

Poa cynosuroides, a grass with long stalks and numerous pointed leaves: ཀུ་ཤས་ཚེ་བསྲིང་ལུས་ཤུགས་རྒྱས་པར་བྱེད། the grass *kuça* ensures longevity and increases the strength of the body. 2. n. of a city (*K. du.* ཕ *152*).

Syn. ངན་སེལ་ *ñan-sel*; ས་གནས་ *sa-gnas*, བདུད་འདུལ་གདན་ *bdud hdul gdan*; མཆོད་སྦྱིན་རྒྱན་ *mchod sbyin rgyan*; གཙང་བྱེད་ *gtsañ-byed*; ཁྲུས་ཀྱི་རྩ་ *khrus-kyi rtsa*; རྩ་མཆོག་ *rtsa-mchog*; རྩ་དབང་ *rtsa-dwañ* (*Mñon.*).

ཀུ་ཤའི་གྲོང་ཁྱེར་ *Ku-çahi groñ-khyer* कुशीनगरी (कुशिनारा) 1. Kus'ianagara, one of the thirty-six sacred places of the Buddhists, where Gautama Buddha is said to have breathed his last. 2. n. of Chakravartī Rāja (Supreme Ruler of the Universe); ཀུ་ཤ་ཆེན་པོ *Ku-ça chen-po* महाकुश n. of a Chakravartī Rāja.

ཀུ་ཤ་ན་ *ku-ça-na* n. of a flower; also n. p. མེ་ཏོག་ཀུ་ཤ་ན་བུ་བ་སྲིན་པོའི་བུ་མོ་ཁྱེད་ཀྱིས་གང་ནས་བོན། whence did you bring that Srin-po's daughter called Kusana flower (*Hbrom. 121*).

‡ ཀུ་ཤ་བན་དྷ *ku-ça-ban-dha* कुशबन्ध a gem which is said to possess the property of curing infectious diseases and plague.

‡ ཀུ་ཤ་ལ *ku-ça-la*=དགེ་བ *dge-wa* कुशल piety, holiness.

‡ ཀུ་ཤ་ལི *Ku-ça-li*, also ཀུ་སཱ་ལི *ku-sā-li* कुशली, a Buddhist sage; the title of a Buddhist monk or priest who has acquired spiritual knowledge and is more devout than learned: སྤྱིར་པཎྜི་ཏ་དང་ཀུ་ཤ་ལི་བྱ་བ་ཕྱི་ནང་གཉིས་ཀ་ལ་ཡོད, པཎྜི་ཏ་བྱ་བ་ཕྱི་ནང་གི་ཤེས་བྱའི་གནས་ལ་མཁས་པ་ལ་ཟེར། ཀུ་ཤ་ལི་བྱ་བ་སྤྲོས་པ་ཐམས་ཅད་བཅད་ནས་ནང་ལ་མཆོག་ཏུ་གཞོལ་བ་ལ་ཟེར་བ་ཡིན་གསུང་། ཡི་གེ་ལ་ཡང་ཀུ་སཱ་ལི་ཟེར་འདུག། (*Yig.*). Generally there are among both Brāhmans and Buddhists those called Paṇḍita and Kuçali. The title of *Paṇ-ḍi-ta* is applied to one who is versed in intellectual science. Those who are called *Ku-ça-li* have attained a high spiritual development by abstraction from material or intellectual enjoyments. In some works it is called *Ku-sā-li.*

ཀུ་ཤུ *ku-çu* a kind of lime; a kind of fruit; an apple (*Jä.*); ཀུ་ཤུ་ཤིང་ *ku-çu çiñ* an apple tree; ཀུ་ཤུ་འབྲས་བུས་རྒྱུ་ལོང་ཚིག་འཁྲུགས་གཟེར་བ་འཇོམས། the fruit of *Ku-çu* cures griping and acute pains in the intestines.

‡ ཀུ་སུ་ལུ *ku-su-lu* is a corrupt form of ཀུ་ཤ་ལི *Ku-ça-li.*

‡ ཀུ་ཤུའི་ཁམས *ku-çuhi khams* n. of a kind of blue flower, v. མཐིང་ *thiñ.*

Syn. དུས་ཀྱི་མེ་ཏོག *dus-kyi me-tog*; བྱ་ཁྱུང་རྡོ *bya-khyuñ rdo*; མེ་ཏོག་སྨིག་སྨན *me-tog smig-sman*; མེ་ཏོག་ཟེ *me-tog ze*; གསལ་ལྡན *gsal-ldan* གསལ་བ་ཅན *gsal-wa-can* (*Mñon.*).

‡ ཀུ་ཤེ་ཤ་ཡ *ku-çe-ça-ya* कुशेशय a kind of lotus flower (*K. d.* ར *324*); a generic name for water-lily or lotus.

‡ ཀུ་ས་ར *Ku-sa-ra* कुसर an Indian pandub who preached Buddhism in Tibet (*J. Zañ.*).

‡ ཀུ་ས་ལི་བྷ་དྲ *Ku-sa-li bhadra* कुसलीभद्र n. of an Indian Buddhist sage (*K. dun. 13*).

‡ ཀུ་སུ་མ *ku-su-ma* कुसुम 1. གུར་གུམ *gur-kum* saffron. 2. a flower (*Sman. 428*).

‡ ཀུ་སུ་ལི *Ku-su-li* a Buddhist exorcist; a Naljor or Buddhist *yogi* who carries a small hand-drum (called *damaru* which is generally made of a human skull) and a thigh-bone trumpet in his hands, and professes power of exorcising evil spirits,

ཀུ་སུ་ལུའི་སྤྱོད་པ *Ku-su-luhi spyod-pa* the practice of the *Shaman* or Buddhist exorcists; ཀུ་སུ་ལུའི་སྤྱོད་པ་མཛད་པའི་ཚེ། (*A. 26*) when practising the rites of a *Ku-su-lu* exorcist.

ཀུ་སུ་ལུ་པ *ku-su-lu-pa* is a word of *Tantrik* mysticism, its proper Tibetan equivalent being གཅོད་པ *gcod-pa*, the art of exorcism. The mystic *Tantrik* rites of the *Avadhauts*, called *Avadhūtipa* in Tibet, exist in India.

ཀུ་སེ་རྫོང་ *Ku-se-rdsoṅ* n. of a fort and also that of a district in ཁམས *Khams* (*S. kar.*).

ཀུ་བསྭོ *ku bswo* the shrill ejaculation *swo, swo*, &c., made at the time of sacrifice to the earthly gods, demi-gods and spirits by priests, &c., in Tibet: ལྷ་ཡི་དམག་ཚོགས་བསམ་གྱིས་མི་ཁྱབ་པས་བསྐོར་ནས་ཀུ་བསྭོ་ཆེ the celestial troops in inconceivable numbers surrounding them gave vent to *bswo-bswo*.

† ཀུ་ཧུ *ku-hu* कुहू the cry of the Indian cuckoo; ཀུ་ཧུའི་མགྲིན་ལྡན कुहूकण्ठ the cuckoo, *i.e.*, the bird that cries '*koohoo*'; aco. to *Cs.* a kind of ring dove.

ཀུ་ཧྲང་ *ku-hraṅ* sheep and goats: གཤེན་པ་རྣམས་ཀྱིས་རྒྱུ་འབྲས་ཀྱི་བོན་རྣམས་ཀུ་ཧྲང་དང་མ་ཧེ་དང་མཛོ་དྲེལ་རྔ་མོང་ལ་སོགས། (*G. Bon.*) among the followers of Shenrab the *Bon-po* of the *Rgyu* and *Hbras-po* sects sacrifice sheep and goats, buffaloes, dzo, mules, camels, &c.

ཀུག *kug* crooked; a hook; གྲི་ཀུག *gri-kug* (the *kukri*), a curved knife; short sabre; ལྕགས་ཀུག *lcags-kug* an iron hook; ཉ་ཀུག *ña-kug* a fish-hook.

ཀུག་ཀུག་བྱེད་པ *kug-kug byed-pa* to bend, curve, clinch (a nail) (*Jä.*).

ཀུག་ཀུག *kug-kug* altogether crooked; ཀུག་པ་ཉིད *kug-pa-ñid* crookedness (*Cs.*).

ཀུག་རྩེ *kug-rtse* cuckoo in *W* (*Jä.*).

ཀུང་ཀུ་ན *Kuṅ-ku-na* possibly the province of Konkan in Western India (*S. Lam. 33*).

† ཀུང་ཀུམ *kuṅ-kuma* कुङ्कुम saffron. Tibetan ཀུར་ཀུམ is evidently a corruption of the Sanskṛt word.

† ཀུཉྫ་ར *Kuñ-dsa-ra* कुञ्जर a fabulous silver mountain situated beyond the great sea and at a distance of 2,000 *yojana* to the south of *Ñima ldan*, where the sun never sets. It is full of precious stones, such as lapis lazuli, sapphire, &c., and on the sides of this mountain there grows a species of tree producing a race of men who live only one day; they are born at dawn, they begin to walk after daybreak, in the morning they are youths, towards evening they grow old, and at sunset they die (*K. d.* ར *276.*).

ཀུན *kun* परि, षा, निखिल, सर्व all, entire, the whole; སྤུ་ཡི་ཁུང་བུ་ཀུན་ནས། from all pores of the hair; དེ་དག་ཀུན all those; གཞན་ཀུན all the others; ཀུན་ཐམས་ཅད all, every one included; ཀུན་གྱི་ཐོས་པ་ལ in the hearing of all; མེ་ཏོག་འདི་ཀུན་དགྲམ་པར་བྱ all these flowers should be strewn about; ཀུན་གྱིས་མཐོང་བ seen by everybody; དུས་རྣམ་པ་ཀུན or རྣམ་པ་ཀུན time without interruption; at all times; colloq. ཀུན་ལ *kun-la* means "everywhere."

Syn. ཐམས་ཅད *thams-cad* all; སྣ་ཚོགས *sna-tshogs* various kinds; མ་ལུས *ma-lus* without leaving anything behind; ཟད་པར *zad-par* exhaustively; ལྷག་མེད *lhag-med* without remainder: ལུས་མེད *lus-med* nothing left (*Mṅon.*).

ཀུན་དཀྱིལ *kun-dkyil*, same as ཀུན་གྱི་དཀྱིལ *kun-gyi dkyil*, in the midst of all; in the middle of all; at the centre.

ཀུན་དཀྲིས *kun-dkris* (*kun-ti*) = ཉོན་མོངས *ñon-mons* lit. that which binds all; misery, moral corruption, general corruptness, sin.

ཀུན་བཀྲམ *kun-bkram* (*kun-tam*) or ཀུན་ཏུ་བཀྲམ *kun-tu bkram* आकीर्ण strewn about, spread over.

ཀུན་སྐྱེ *kun-skye*, same as ཀུན་ཏུ་སྐྱེ *kun-tu skye* or ཀུན་ལ་སྐྱེ *kun-la-skye* उपपत्ति, आसव, उद्भूत, अवरोह, grows everywhere: དབྱར་དུས་མེ་ཏོག་ཀུན་ཏུ་སྐྱེ flowers grow everywhere in summer time.

ཀུན་སྐྱེད་བྱེད *kun-skyed-byed* = སྙིང་ *sñiṅ* the heart, mind (*Mṅon.*).

ཀུན་སྐྱོ་བ *kun-skyo-wa* or ཀུན་ཏུ་སྐྱོ་བ *kun-tu skyo-wa* संकोप, प्रहसन, आक्षेप, to become penitent; to thoroughly regret: སེམས་ནི་ཉིན་མཚན་ཀུན་ཏུ་སྐྱོ། his mind was filled with regret day and night.

ཀུན་སྐྱོད *kum-skyod* agitated, moved; agitation.

ཀུན་སྐྱོབ་གླིང་ *Kun-skyob gliṅ* n. of a monastery in Tibet.

ཀུན་ཁེབས *kun-khebs* आच्छादन, व्योमन् any cover; the all-encompassing cover, the sky.

ཀུན་ཁྱབ I: *kun-khyab* = ནམ་མཁའ *nam mkhaḥ* आकाश, व्योमन् that which encompasses all things; the void space, the sky, the four quarters of heaven.

ཀུན་ཁྱབ II: = འཕྲོག་བྱེད *Hphrog-byed* हरि he that takes away misery; the all-pervading enemy; the snatcher; the lord of death.

ཀུན་འཁོར *kun-ḥkhor* v. ཀུན་བཟང་འཁོར་ལོ *kun-bzaṅ ḥkhor-lo*, a charm in the name of the Dhyani Buddha called Samanta Bhadra.

ཀུན་ཁྱབ་དཔལ་མོ *kun-kkyab dpal-mo* = ནམ་མཁའ *nam-mkhaḥ* the sky; n. of a goddess (*Yig. k. 16*).

ཀུན་འཁྱམས *kun-ḥkhyams* परिभ्रामक a wanderer; a beggar, a mendicant who goes to every door for alms.

ཀུན་མཁྱེན *Kun-mkhyen* = ཐམས་ཅད་མཁྱེན་པ *thams-cad mkhyen-pa* सर्वज्ञ, वैद्य the All-knowing; the Physician; an epithet of Buddha and also of the highest order of *Bodhisattva*.

ཀུན་མཁྱེན་ཀུན་གཟིགས *kun-mkhyen kun-gzigs* omniscient and all-seeing, referring to the attributes of a Buddha or *Bodhisattva*.

ཀུན་མཁྱེན་ཀློང་ཆེན *Kun-mkhyen kloṅ-chen* a religious teacher of the *Rñiṅ-ma* School who founded a sect of his own called *Kun dgaḥ lugs*.

ཀུན་མཁྱེན་ཆོས་སྐུ་འོད་ཟེར *Kun-mkhyen chos-sku ḥod-zer* the Tibetan hierarch of *Sa-skya*, who, at the request of *Khu-lugs*, the Chief of Horchen, first shaped the Mongolian alphabet.

ཀུན་མཁྱེན་ཉི་མའི་གཉེན *Kun-mkhyen ñi-maḥi gñen* सर्वज्ञ सूर्यवंश an epithet of Gautama Buddha (*Yig. k. 83*).

ཀུན་མཁྱེན་དབྱིག་གཉེན *Kun-mkhyen dbyig-gñen* n. of a lama who was given the religious title of *Kun-mkhyen*, the all-knowing.

ཀུན་འཁྲུགས *kun-khrugs* आकुल, वाप agitated; anxious: རྒྱ་མཚོའི་ཐ་གློང་ཀུན་འཁྲུགས། the waves of the sea were agitated.

ཀུན་འཁྲུལ *kun-ḥkhrul* परिभ्रम blunder; illusion; also adj. all-delusive; all-wandering.

ཀུན་གྱི་མཐའ *kun-gyi mthaḥ* the end or termination of all (merits): བསགས་པ་ཀུན་གྱི་མཐའ་ཟད་ཅིང་། བསྟུད་པའི་མཐའ་ནི་འགྱེལ་བར་འགྱུར། the end of accumulation is expenditure; the end of rising is fall (*K. d.* ཕ *330*).

ཀུན་གྱི་གནས *kun-gyi-gnas* the basis or abode of all (miseries): ན་ན་འཆི་རྒྱགས་རྒྱུ་བསྡུལ་ཀུན་གྱི་གནས། the grounds of misery are disease, old age, and death (*K. d.* མ *333*).

ཀུན་གྱི་རྩ་བ *kun-gyi, rtsa-wa*, the root of everything; wisdom, divine knowledge. མཐོང་དང་མ་མཐོང་ཡོན་ཏན་འདི། ཀུན་གྱི་རྩ་བ་ཤེས་རབ་ཡིན། This seen or unseen talent has *Prajñā* (absolute knowledge) for its basis, *i.e.*, the root of all things is wisdom (*prajña*) (*Ç. gya.*).

ཀུན་གྱིས་བཀུར་བ *kun-gyis bkur-wa* he who is respected by all; a learned man, v. མཁས་པ *mkhas-pa* (*Mnon.*).

ཀུན་གྱིས་ཕྱག་བྱས *kun-gyis phyag-byas* to whom all paid homage: འཇིག་རྟེན་ཀུན་གྱིས་ཕྱག་བྱས་ཤིང་། *hjig-rten kun-gyis phyag-byas çin*, to whom the world has bowed (*K. d.* ཁ *113*).

ཀུན་གྲུབ *kun-grub*=ཟླ་བ་དགུ་པ *zla-wa dgu-pa* or སྟོན་ཟླ་ཐ་ཆུང་ *ston-zla tha-chun* the month of October (*Rtsii.*).

ཀུན་གླིང་ *Kun-glin*, same as ཀུན་བདེ་གླིང་ *Kun-bde glin*, the place or grove of all happiness; one of the four royal monasteries of Lhasa, this one being situated in the western suburbs.

ཀུན་དགའ *kun-dgah* आनन्द, संमोद amusement; great merriment or joy.

* ཀུན་དགའ་རྒྱལ་མཚན་དཔལ་བཟང་པོ *Kun-dgah rgyal-mtshan-dpal-bzanpo* आनन्दध्वज the name of Saskya Pandita (ས་སྐྱ་པཎྜི་ཏ).

ཀུན་དགའ་སྙིང་པོ *Kun-dgah snin-po* n. of a celebrated lama of Tibet (*Lon.* ཁ *12*).

ཀུན་དགའ་ནོར *Kun-dgah Nor* a lake in Mongolia (*Lon.* ཇ *21*); probably the Gonga-nor (Egg lake). In Mongol *nor* =a lake.

ཀུན་དགའ་བ་འཛིན་པ *kun-dgah-wa hdsin-pa*=རིན་པོ་ཆེ *rin-po-che* n. of a precious article or gem (*K. d.* ར *294*).

ཀུན་དགའ་བོ *Kun-dgah-bo* आनन्द the personal attendant and cousin of Buddha.

ཀུན་དགའ་འབར *Kun-dgah-hbar* n. of the son of *Kun-dgah snin-po*, one of the chiefs of *Sa-skya* who visited India to study Buddhism (*Lon.* ཁ).

ཀུན་དགའ་འཛིན་པ *Kun-dgah hdsin-pa* a mountain in Uttara Kuru, the fabulous continent of the north (*K. d.* ར *318*).

ཀུན་དགའ་གཞོན་ནུ *kun-dgah gshon-nu*=ཧུ་སུ *hu-su* coriander (*Sman. 428*).

ཀུན་དགའ་ར་བ *kun-dgah ra-wa*=གླིང་དགའ *glin-dgah* आराम a grove; any pleasure-grove containing groups of trees, flower beds, artificial lakes, garden houses, shady walks, &c., often surrounded by a wall or fence.

ཀུན་དགའི་དབང་མོ *kun-dgahi dwan-mo* an address of courtesy for ལྷ་ལྕམ་གྱི་རིགས ladies of the class of Lhacham—her grace or ladyship: ཡིད་འཕྲོག་ཀུན་དགའི་དབང་མོ་མཆོག་གི་དྲུང་དུ། "at the (feet) of her charming ladyship" (*Yig. k. 49*).

ཀུན་མགྱོགས *kun-mgyogs* आवेग speed; also as adv. speedily, at full speed.

ཀུན་འགེབས *kun-hgebs*=ནམ་མཁའ *nam-mkhah* परिवास the sky; that which covers all; the all-covering.

ཀུན་འགོག *kun-hgog* that which hinders physical or moral growth.

ཀུན་འགྲོ I: *kun-hgro*, v. ནམ་མཁའ *nam-mkhah*, the sky (*Mnon.*).

ཀུན་འགྲོ II: snake, v. སྦྲུལ *sbrul* a serpent (*Mnon.*).

ཀུན་འགྲོ་འབད *kun-hgro hbad* आभोग to be assiduous: ལས་བྱ་བ་ཀུན་ལས་དུ་འགྲོ་བ་ལ་འབད assiduous in the manner of performance.

ཀུན་འགྲོའི་སྲོལ *kun-hgrohi srol*=ལམ *lam* a road, passage (*Mnon.*).

ཀུན་ཅིངས *Kun-cins* समापित 1. that pains, ties or entangles all at all times. 2. अनङ्ग the God of Love; also for ཀུན་ཏུ་ཅིངས *kun-tu cins*: ཉོན་མོངས་ཀྱི་ཞགས་པས་ཡིད་དུས་ཀུན་ཏུ་ཅིངས། by the fetters of misery the mind is always fastened down.

ཀུན་བཅོམ་ *Kun-bcom* आहर, यम 1. vanquished; suppressed, fully put down. 2 the vanquisher or killer of all; the lord of death. 3. n. of a son of a Brahman of Ujjayani (*S. leg.*).

ཀུན་ཆུབ་ *kun-chub* ཤེས་རབ་ *çes-rab* all-perfection; wisdom; divine knowledge (*K. d.* ཕ *26*); ཀུན་ཆུབ་པ་ अवगत he that has comprehended everything.

ཀུན་མཆོག་ལྡན་ *kun-mchog-ldan* or དུས་ཀུན་མཆོག་ལྡན་=དུས་ཀྱི་འཁོར་ལོ་ (*Mñon.*), श्रीकालचक्र, the *Tantrik* doctrine of Kālachakra.

ཀུན་འཛུག *kun-hjug* for ཀུན་དང་མཐུན་པར་འཛུག། करणं, संस्तर bringing together; putting in harmony with all.

ཀུན་འཛུག་ཕོ་ཉ་ *kun-hjug pho-ña* the messenger of harmony, that which harmonises or makes everything agreeable, hence=ཀ་ར *ka-ra*, sugar.

ཀུན་འཇོམས་ *Kun-hjoms* आखण्डल, आघातक 1. Indra, the subduer of all; that by which everything can be subdued or controlled. 2. *Yoga* or the contemplative concentration of the mind.

ཀུན་འཇོམས་མཆོག *kun-hjoms mchog* the chief all-subduing (elixir); དངུལ་ཆུས་བཙུད་ལེན་ནད་གདོན་ཀུན་འཇོམས་མཆོག། is an excellent preparation of mercury, which subdues all evil spirits and diseases.

*ཀུན་སྙིང་ *Kun-sñiṅ*=*Tāranātha*. (*Tā. 28.*)

ཀུན་ཏུ་ *kun-tu* unto all; in all; everywhere; in every direction: མེ་ཏོག་སྟེང་འོག་ཀུན་ཏུ་བཀྲམ། flowers were strewn everywhere, above and below: ཚོང་ཟོང་ཕྱི་ནང་ཀུན་ཏུ་བཀྲམ། articles of merchandise were spread in every place, inside and outside (the house). When used in reference to time, ཀུན་ཏུ *kun-tu* signifies: continually or perpetually; *dus kun-tu* same as དུས་རྒྱུན་དུ་ *dus rgyun-du* or དུས་རྟག་ཏུ, at all times, always.

ཀུན་ཏུ་བསྐྱེད་ *kun-tu bskyed* producing every where, all-producing, *i.e.*, imagination: ཡོངས་སུ་རྟོགས་པས་ཀུན་ཏུ་བསྐྱེད། imagination is all-productive (*K. d.* ཕ *36*).

ཀུན་ཏུ་འཁྱམས་ *kun-tu hkhyams* wandering everywhere: སྲིད་པ་ཉམ་ངར་ཀུན་ཏུ་འཁྱམས། in the fearful world, *i.e.*, in the unhappy states of existence, he wanders about (*K. d.* ཟ *169*).

ཀུན་ཏུ་འཁྲུགས་ *kun-tu hkhrugs* signifies གཡོ་འགུལ་ཅན་པོ་བྱུང་བ convulsed; also convulsive, subject to agitation and shaking (*Mñon.*).

ཀུན་ཏུ་གས་ *kun-tu gas*=སྤང་རྒྱན་མེ་ཏོག *spaṅ-rgyan me-tog* or སྟོན་གྱི་མེ་ཏོག (autumn flower), lit. the fully developed or blown; n. of a species of daisy which blossoms in autumn (*Mñon.*).

ཀུན་ཏུ་གོ་བ་ *kun-tu go-wa* विश्रुत well-known; well-understood; celebrated.

ཀུན་ཏུ་དགའ་བར་གྱུར་བའི་གླིང་ *Kun-tu dgah-war gyur-wahi gliṅ* a fabulous continent situated 5,000 *yojana* beyond the Western Ocean of (*Jambudvīpa*) India, where there are lions that fly in space: some of the wild animals of that continent are said to live a thousand years (*K. d.* ར *280*).

ཀུན་ཏུ་འགེངས་པ་ *kun-tu-hgeṅs-pa* विश्वम्भर he that provides for the world, the All-Provider; Providence.

ཀུན་ཏུ་འགྱེད་པ་ *kun-tu hgyed-pa* सन्विसजति to be diffused; that which goes in every direction: སྤྲུལ་པ་དང་ཕོ་ཉ spiritual emanations; envoys: འོད་ཟེར་ཚོགས་ཀུན་ཏུ་འགྱེད rays of light went in every direction.

ཀུན་ཏུ་འགྲོ=ཀུན་ཏུ་རྒྱུ་བ *kun-tu rgyu-wa* आगम, आगमुक 1. lit. going everywhere. 2. as met. wind; a bird. 3. n. of a spirit.

ཀུན་ཏུ་རྒྱས་པར་བྱེད་པ *kun-tu rgyas-par byed-pa* परिस्फारयति to fully spread; to make plentiful everywhere; to make copious.

ཀུན་ཏུ་བསྒྲིབས *kun-tu bsgribs* eclipsed; darkness: ཉི་མ་དང་ཟླ་བའི་འོད་ཟེར་ཀུན་ཏུ་བསྒྲིབས་པའོ། the rays of the sun and moon were eclipsed.

ཀུན་ཏུ་བཅུག་པ *kun-tu-bcug-pa* or ཀུན་བཅུག་པ *kun-bcug-pa* to put in; to employ, engage: སྣོད་འདི་ཀུན་ཏུ་བཅུག། put this vessel (or pot) to all uses.

ཀུན་ཏུ་ཆགས་པ *kun-tu chags-pa* व्यप, व्यग्र, विलग्न anxiety; yearning, clinging to: འདོད་ཡོན་ལ་སེམས་ཀུན་ཏུ་ཆགས། the mind remains attached to its crooked desires.

ཀུན་འཇུག་པ *kun-hjug-pa* = སྡུག་བསྔལ་བ *sdug-bsñal-wa* misery, sufferings.

ཀུན་ཏུ་འཇུག་པ་སྒྲོལ *kun-tu hjug-pa sgrol* = ལམ་བདེན་པ *lam-bden-pa* the truth about the way to *Nirvāṇa, i.e.*, out of misery.

ཀུན་ཏུ་འཇུག་བྱེད *kun-tu hjug byed* = ཀུན་འབྱུང་བ *kun hbyuñ-wa* sin.

ཀུན་ཏུ་འཇུག་བྲལ *kun-tu hjug-bral* निरोध freedom from sin, or འགོག་པ *hgog-pa*, entire stoppage of suffering.

Note.—The above four expressions are used in the higher spiritual terminology relating to *Bodhisattva* (*K. ko.* ཀ *235*).

ཀུན་ཏུ་བསྟེན *kun-tu bsten* = དད་གུས་དང་ལྡན་པ *dad-gus dañ ldan-pa* faith and reverence; also possessed of faith, respect, etc.

Syn. གུས་པ *gus-pa*; གུས་ལྡན *gus-ldan*; གུས་པར་བྱེད *gus-par byed*; མངོན་པར་ལྡན *mñon-par ldan*; གཅིག་ཏུ་སེམས *gcig-tu sems*; མོས་པ *mos-pa*; མོས་ལྡན *mos-ldan*; དད་ལྡན *dad-ldan*; དད་ཆགས་ཅན *dad-chags-can*; དད་པ་ཅན *dad-pa-can*; ཕྱག་བྱེད་པ *phyag-byed-pa*; ཤེ་ས་བྱེད *she-sa byed* (*Mñon.*).

ཀུན་ཏུ་འཐོར *kun-tu hthor* अवकीर्ण strewn over, scattered, diffused, dispersed: མེ་ཏོག་ཀུན་ཏུ་འཐོར། flowers were scattered over every place.

ཀུན་ཏུ་དོར *kun-tu dor* निरस्त perfect abandonment: ཉེས་པ་དུས་ཀུན་ཏུ་དོར། all faults should be entirely thrown out.

ཀུན་ཏུ་བདེ་བ *kun-tu bde-wa* समस्तसुख general happiness, prosperity; beatitude (*Spyod*).

ཀུན་ཏུ་འདྲེས་པ *Kun-tu hdres-pa* n. of a river in the fabulous continent of Godāniya (*K. d.* ར *331*).

ཀུན་ཏུ་གནས *kun-tu gnas* स्थिति, वसति stability; the all-abiding residence, that which remains at all times or everywhere.

ཀུན་ཏུ་བདུང་བ *kun-tu bduñ-wa* the burning rays of the sun; extremely painful; all-piercing.

ཀུན་ཏུ་གནོད་པར་གྱུར་པ *kun-tu gnod-par gyur-pa* समभिद् to do mischief everywhere.

ཀུན་ཏུ་སྣང་བ *kun-tu snañ-wa* समन्ताभास 1. the sun; n. of a Buddha. 2. all-illumined, all-enlightened.

ཀུན་ཏུ་སྤྱད *kun-tu spyad* an usual duty, habitual work; as a vb. to practise: དགེ་བ་དུས་ཀུན་ཏུ་སྤྱད། practise righteousness or religious acts at all times.

ཀུན་ཏུ་སྤྱོད་པ *kun-tu spyod-pa* free or unbridled behaviour: described as བྲམ་ཟེའི་སྤྱོད་ཚུལ the Brāhmaṇical conduct (*Mñon.*).

ཀུན་ཏུ་སྤྲས *kun-tu spras* आभूषाचित dressed in every way; adorning the body with precious ornaments.

ཀུན་ཏུ་སྦྱོར་བ *kun-tu sbyor-wa* = ཐམས་ཅད་སྤངས་པ giving up everything (*Mñon.*).

ཀུན་ཏུ་མིག་ལྡན *kun-tu mig-ldan* (lit. with eyes everywhere), described as ནོར་བུའི་ལྗོན་ཤིང་, n. of a fabulous tree on which grow glittering gems; also a plant or tree in full bloom; འདི་ཙལ་ཅེར་ལྷ་དང་ལྷ་མ་ཡིན་གྱི་ཡུལ་དང་བྱང་སྒྲ་མི་

སྙན་གྱི་ཡུལ་ན་ཡོད་པ་ཡིན་ནོ། this (kind of tree) is generally to be found in the lands of gods, demi-gods, and in the continent of Uttara Kuru (*K. d.* ཞ *16*).

ཀུན་ཏུ་རྨོངས *kun-tu rmoṅs* the all-stunning, all-obscuring; darkness of mind; ignorance: ཀུན་ཏུ་རྨོངས་པའི་དགྲ་འཇོམས་མཚོན་ཆ་ཡི, ཐབས་ཚུལ་མན་ངག་སྟོན་པའི་གྲོགས་ཀྱི་མཆོག། O, best of friends who guideth me in precepts, morals, resources, the weapons for vanquishing the all-obscuring enemy!

ཀུན་ཏུ་རྨོངས་བྱེད་ཀྱི་མདའ *kun-tu rmoṅs-byed-kyi mdaḥ* सम्मोहन the all-stupefying fascination; n. of one of the arrows of Cupid.

ཀུན་ཏུ་འཛིན་མ *Kun-tu ḥdsin-ma* अवधारणी holding to all or everything; n. of a goddess.

ཀུན་ཏུ་བཟང་པོ *Kun-tu ḥzaṅ-po* 1. समन्तभद्र lit. good to all and everywhere and at all times; n. of the first *Dhyāni Bodhisattva*, the equivalent of Samanta Bhadra; the *Khamuga-Sain* of the Mongols. 2. in the *Rñiṅ-ma* sect, n. of the first or Ādi Buddha.

ཀུན་ཏུ་བཟང་མོ *Kun-tu ḥzaṅ-mo* समन्तभद्रा 1. is a female figured in conn ection with the foregoing *Bodhisattva*. 2. a kind of flower growing on the Sumeru Mountain (*K. my.* ཀ *20*).

ཀུན་ཏུ་གཟིགས *Kun-tu gzigs* he who sees all things and everywhere by his divine eye of knowledge; n. of a Buddha, also that of the *Bodhisattva* Avalokitesvara.

ཀུན་ཏུ་ཧུར་ཧུར *kun-tu ḥur-ḥur* संरवण a great noise or uproar heard everywhere; the rattling of thunder; also the noise of wind or rain.

ཀུན་ཏུ་འོ་མ *kun-tu ḥo-ma* = སི་ཛ་ཛུ *si-dsa-dsu* (*Mñon.*) n. of a tree with milky sap.

ཀུན་ཏུ་འོད *kun-tu ḥod* समन्तप्रभा fully enlightened; ས་བཅུ་གཅིག་པ *sa ḥcu-gcig-pa* the eleventh stage of *Bodhisattva* perfection.

ཀུན་ཏུ་རབ་ཏུ་འཁྲུགས *kun-tu rab-tu ḥkhrugs* lit. very much agitated; n. of the six descriptions of earthquake (*K. d.* མ *259*).

ཀུན་ཏུ་རབ་ཏུ་འགུལ *kun-tu rab-tu ḥgul* lit. moving and shaking very greatly; n. of a form of earthquake.

ཀུན་ཏུ་རབ་ཏུ་ཆེམ་ཆེམ *kun-tu rab-tu chem-chem* प्रगर्ज्जित् lit. roaring all about; n. of a kind of earthquake.

ཀུན་ཏུ་རབ་ཏུ་ཧུར་ཧུར *kun-tu rab-tu ḥur-ḥur* loud and fearful rattling or roaring; n. of one of the six forms of earthquake in which sound comes out of the sea and the mountains.

ཀུན་ཏུ་རབ་ཏུ་གཡོས *kun-tu rab-tu gyos* lit. everywhere all shaken very much; n. of universal earthquake in which the mountains and the oceans are moved profoundly.

ཀུན་ཏུ་རིག I: *kun-tu rig* आवेद = རྣམ་པ་ཀུན་ཏུ་རིག་པ all-knowing; omniscient; n. of a deity.

ཀུན་ཏུ་རིག II: = ཤེས་རབ *ҫes-rab* wisdom (*K. d.* ཕ *26*).

ཀུན་ཏུ་གསལ *kun-tu gsal* आदीपक, आभा, आभास, the sky; clear inside and outside; very clear, lucid, illuminated.

ཀུན་ཏུ་གསུང *kun-tu gsuṅ* a flower mentioned in the Kahgyur (*K. my.* ཀ *20*).

ཀུན་ཏུ་གསོ *kun-tu gso* to heal everyone or repair everything; the healer of all.

ཀུན་གཏུམ *kun-gtum* चण्डाल lit. very fierce; དམངས་རིགས *dmaṅs-rigs* n. of lowest caste in India.

ཀུན་བཏུས *kun-ḥtus* समुच्चय n. of a religious work which is full of extracts taken from different sacred books (*Mñon.*).

ཀུན་རྟོག *kun-rtog*, same as རྣམ་རྟོག *rnam-rtog* विकल्प, संकल्प, संस्कार, fancy, illusory associations.

ཀུན་བརྟགས *kun-ḅrtags* परिकल्पन ideas and associations.

ཀུན་བརྟགས་པའི་མཚན་ཉིད *kun-ḅrtags-paḥi ṃtshan ñiḍ* परिकल्पितलक्षणम् one of the three signs, characteristics or *lakṣaṇa*, v. མཚན་ཉིད *ṃtshan ñiḍ*.

ཀུན་བརྟན *kun-ḅrtan* अवष्टम्भ 1. support. 2. negligence.

ཀུན་བསྟེན *kun-ḅsten* आराधना reliance; resignation; service or adoration.

ཀུན་མཐོང་གི་མཚོ *Kun ṃthoṅ-gyi ṃtsho* a fabulous fresh-water lake in the land of the *Lha-ma-yin* or *Asura*, situated at the centre of their chief city Shubhra Mālikā. It is said to be five *yojana* on each side. When the *Lha* fight with the *Lha-ma-yin* the signs of victory or defeat are said to be reflected on its surface.

ཀུན་དང་འཁོན་པ *kun-daṅ ḥkhon-pa* quarrelling with all: ནག་པོའི་མཆུ་ཅན་ཀུན་དང་འཁོན་པར་བྱེད། a person whose lips are black quarrels with everybody (*Tan. d. 217*).

ཀུན་དང་མཐུན་པ *kun-daṅ ṃthun-pa* = ཐམས་ཅད་དང་མཐུན་པ harmonious, concordant; agreeing or in harmony with all.

ཀུན་དོན *kun-don* सर्व्वार्थ the public weal, general interest, cause of all.

ཀུན་དྲིལ་བ *kun-dril-wa* = ཚང་མ་བསྡོམ་པ *tshaṅ-ma ḅsdom-pa* all taken together.

ཀུན་གདུང *kun-gduṅ* आविद्ध, अनङ्ग that afflicts all; the all-burning one; Cupid.

ཀུན་བདག *Kun-ḅdag* विश्वपति, विश्वात्म the Lord of All. འཇིག་རྟེན་ཀུན་བདག the Soul of the World; the Supreme Lord of the World.

ཀུན་བརྡུང *kun-ḅrduṅ* 1. an oppressor; a tyrant: སྔར་ཉི་མ་ཀྱི་སྐབས་སུ་སྦྱོར་བ་བཅུ་དྲུག་པ་ཀུན་བརྡུང 2. In astronomical calculations the sixteenth conjunction is called *Kun-ḅrduṅ*.

ཀུན་འདར *kun-ḥdar* अवधूति the pulse that always beats = རྩ་དབུ་མ *ṛtsa ḍvu-ma* n. of the central artery.

ཀུན་འདྲེན *Kun-ḥdren* the Supreme Leader; he who leads all into the way of deliverance; epithet of Buddha.

ཀུན་ནས *kun-nas*, same as ཀུན་ལས *kun-las* समन्त or समन्ततः from every place or direction; round about; wholly, thoroughly: ཕྱོགས་མཚམས་ཀུན་ནས་ར་བས་བསྐོར། in every direction it was surrounded by railings; ཀུན་ནས་འདོད་པ། to wish from the bottom of the heart.

ཀུན་ནས་དཀྲིགས་པ *kun-nas ḍkrigs-pa* entirely darkened: ཆར་སྤྲིན་ཕྱོགས་ཀུན་ནས་དཀྲིགས rain-clouds have darkened all quarters.

ཀུན་ནས་སྐྱེ *kun-nas ṣkye* समन्तज, उत्पादन produced or grown everywhere (like grass).

ཀུན་ནས་འཁུམས *kun-nas ḥkhums* कुङ्कुम; = གུར་གུམ *gur-gum* saffron (*Mṅon.*).

ཀུན་ནས་འགེགས *kun-nas ḥgegs* = བཙུན་མོའི་མོ་བྲང a residence that is closed on every side, a sanctum; residence of a queen; a convent (*Mṅon.*).

Syn. འཁོར་བའི་ཁྱིམ *ḥkhor-waḥi khyim*; ས་སྤྱོད་མ་གནས *sa-spyod-ma gnas*; སྲུང་མ་ཅན *sruṅ-ma-can*; དག་པའི་མཐའ་ཅན *dag-paḥi ṃthaḥ-can*; གཙང་གནས *gtsaṅ-gnas*.

ཀུན་ནས་འགྲོ *kun-nas ḥgro* सङ्गति communion.

ཀུན་ནས་རྒོད *kun-nas ṛgod* = བཤད་གད *ḅshad-gad* to laugh out (*Mṅon.*).

ཀུན་ནས་སྒོའི་ལེའུ་ཤེས་པའི་མདོ *Kun-nas sgoḥi leḥu shes-paḥi ṃdo* समन्तद्वारपरिच्छेदो नाम सूत्रम् the "*Sûtra* on the door or entrance from all quarters," *i.e.*, of free entrance (*K. ko.* ཁ *287*).

ཀུན་ནས་སྒྲིབ་པར་བྱེད *kun-nas ṣgrib-par byeḍ* आच्छादयति to over-shadow all round, to put into shade in all directions.

ཀུན་ནས་ཉོན་མོངས་པ་ *kun-nas ñon-moṅs-pa* संक्लिष्ट made very miserable; pained, distressed; ཀུན་ནས་ཉོན་མོངས་པ་མེད་པ། entirely free from misery (*Hbum.* ཀ *239*).

ཀུན་ནས་སྙེམས *kun-nas sñems* आक्रन्दन, अवलिप्त very haughty; arrogant.

ཀུན་ནས་བཏགས་པ *kun-nas btags-pa* उपहित, संबद्ध fastened or tied up on all sides.

ཀུན་ནས་བཏུས་པ *kun-nas btus-pa* संयुक्त, समुच्चय collected from everywhere; extracted or taken from every work.

ཀུན་ནས་འདུད་པ *kun-nas hdud-pa* आनम्र venerated by everybody or everywhere: ལུས་ངག་ཡིད་གསུམ་ཀུན་ནས་འདུད་པ། to reverence in every manner with body, speech, and heart.

ཀུན་ནས་ལྡང་བ *kuṅ-nas ldaṅ-wa* पर्युपस्थान, समुत्थान raised from every place; set up well; got-up: ཕྱོགས་ཀུན་ནས་དགྲ་ལྡང་བར་བྱེད། the enemies rose up in all directions.

ཀུན་ནས་སྡུད་པ *kun-nas sdud-pa* समाहार collected from every place; brought together from every place.

* ཀུན་ནས་སྣང་བ *kun-nas snaṅ-wa* = རྒྱལ་བ *rgyal-wa* the all-illuminator (*Schr.*).

ཀུན་ནས་འཕགས་པ *kun-nas hphags-pa* समुद्गत sprung from everywhere.

ཀུན་ནས་བྲིས *kun-nas bris* चित्र, उल्लिखित perfectly painted, described, delineated, referred to.

ཀུན་ནས་བླངས *kun-nas blaṅs* taken from every place.

ཀུན་ནས་འབར *kun-nas hbar* सन्तापक, सन्तापित inflamed; ablaze: མེ་ཕྱོགས་ཀུན་ནས་འབར་བ fire broke out in every direction.

ཀུན་ནས་སྦྱོར་བ *kun-nas sbyor-wa* संयोजन to combine; combination; སྨན་ཀུན་ནས་སྦྱོར་བ to compound or mix up medicines.

ཀུན་ནས་བརྩེགས་པ *kun-nas brtsegs-pa* अवकुटित built up everywhere; piled up; erected.

ཀུན་ནས་མཛེས *kun-nas mdses* illuminated; very beautiful: ཟླ་བའི་མཚན་ཉིད་ཀུན་ནས་མཛེས། the signs or charms of the moon are exquisitely fine; མེ་ཏོག་གི་ཚོགས་ཀྱིས་ཀུན་ནས་མཛེས་ཤིང་ཉམས་དགའ་བ། (the garden) from its collection of flowers was lovely and pleasant (*Mṅon.*).

ཀུན་ནས་བཟང་ *kun-nas bzaṅ* गम्भारि, गम्भारिका = དཔལ་གྱི་ལོ་མ *dpal-gyi lo-ma* n. of a tree the leaves of which are sweet.

Syn. ལོ་མ་མངར *lo-ma mṅar*; ལོ་མ་བཟང *lo-ma bzaṅ* (*Mṅon.*).

ཀུན་ནས་བཟོད་པ *kun-nas bzod-pa* all-forgiving; very patient (*K. d.* ར *68*).

ཀུན་ནས་ཡོངས་སུ་བསྐོར་བ *kun-nas yoṅs-su bskor-wa* entirely besieged, shut up entirely, surrounded on all sides.

ཀུན་ནས་གཡེངས *kun-nas gyeṅs* समुद्धत, समन्तपरिच्छिन्न thoroughly; very excited: སེམས་ཀུན་ནས་གཡེངས་པ། the mind agitated (not being fixed on any subject).

ཀུན་སྣང་འབར་བ *kun-snaṅ hbar-wa* = ཉི་མའི་འོད་ཟེར *ñi-mahi hod-zer* all-illuminating rays; the rays of the sun (*Mṅon.*).

ཀུན་སྤངས *kun-spaṅs* सर्वत्यागी; བྱ་བཏང་ *bya btaṅ* all-abstracted: अवधुर; འཇིག་རྟེན་གྱི་བྱ་བ་ཀུན་སྤངས་པ། one who has left off all the concerns of this world; he who has renounced all worldly matters, acts and concerns; an epithet of Buddha.

ཀུན་སྤངས་ཆེན་པོ *kun-spaṅs chen-po* = སྒོམ་ཆེན the all-renouncer; an ascetic; a hermit: ཚེ་གཅིག་སངས་རྒྱས་སྒྲུབ་པའི་ཀུན་སྤངས་ཆེན་པོའི་ཞབས་དྲུང་དུ before the feet of the Arch Renouncer who in one life has attained to Buddhahood.

ཀུན་སྤྱད *kun-spyad* 1. समुदाचार, धर्म, समय that which is to be practised at all times. 2. customary or habitual work; habit.

ཀུན་སྤྱོད་ངན་པ *kun-spyod ńan-pa* कृष्णब्राह्मन् a black or fallen Brāhman; bad habits, vicious acts or professions.

ཀུན་སྤྱོད་མཚུངས་མ *kun-spyod mtshuńs-ma*= གྲོགས་མོ *grogs-ma* a sweetheart, mistress (*Mńon.*).

ཀུན་ཕན་བདུད་རྩི་དབང་པོ *kun-phan bdud-rtsi dwań-po*= ཟླ་བ *zla-wa* the moon (*Yig. k. 16*).

ཀུན་བོར *kun-bor* all-renouncer: གཉེན་དང་ནོར་རྫས་ཡུལ་འཁོར་ཀུན་བོར། he cast off relations, wealth, properties, realm and all (*K. d.* ཅ *333*).

ཀུན་བྱེད་རྒྱལ་པོ *kun-byed rgyal-po* 1. སྔོ་སྨན་སྤང་རྩི *sńo sman spań-rtsi* a medicinal vegetable growing in the grass in Tibet. 2. in the terminology of the Nying-ma sect, the སེམས (mind) is called *kun-byed rgyalpo*, the chief agent, the prince of all doings.

ཀུན་འབྱུང་ *kun-hbyuń*= ཉོན་མོངས समुदय all-growing; misery; sin.

ཀུན་སྦྱོར *kun-sbyor* libertinism (see ཀུན་ཏུ་རུ *kun-tu-ru*).

ཀུན་མོས་དྲི་བཟང་བཞོན་པ་ཅན *kun-mos dri-bzań bshon-pa-can*= དྲི་ཞིམ་པོ *dri-shim-po* sweet perfume.

Syn. འདོད་པའི་དྲི *hdod-pahi-dri*; སྣ་ཚིམ་བྱེད *sna-tshim-byed*; ངད་བཟང *ńad-bzań*; རིང་དུ་ཁྱབ *riń-du khyab*; ལེགས་པར་ཐུལ *legs-par thul* (*Mńon.*).

ཀུན་རྨོངས *kun-rmońs* सम्भ्रम error; the all-blundering (*A. K. 72*).

ཀུན་འཛིན *kun-hdsin* सन्धर, सन्धा the all-containing; that which holds everything in itself.

ཀུན་རྫོབ་བདེན་པ *kun-rdsob bden-pa* संवृतिसत्य conditional or dependent truth; acc. to *Was.* subjective truth.

ཀུན་གཞི *kun-gshi*= སེམས་ཉིད *sems-ñid* आलय basis; the mind (*Mńon.*); ཀུན་གཞི་རྣམ་པར་ཤེས་པ आलयविज्ञान=अहमास्पद ज्ञान consciousness of self; literally the primary cause of all things, the basis of all; the soul, spirit: རྣམ་པར་ཤེས་པ། དགེ་མི་དགེ་འཁོར་འདས་ཆོས་འབྱུང་བའི་གཞི་ཡིན་པའི་ཕྱིར "*gshi* is a philosophical term for *vijñāna*, soul, which is considered to be the basis of virtue, sin, worldly or spiritual existence, &c."

ཀུན་ཟ་མེ་ཏོག *kun-za me-tog*= སྤྱི་ཤུར་ཤིང་གི་མེ་ཏོག flower of the plant called *Spyi-shur*, which gives blue tint to water (*Mńon.*).

ཀུན་གཟིགས *kun-gzigs*= ཀུན་ལ་བལྟ་མཁྱེན who sees all; the All-seeing One; that is cognizant of all (*Loń.* ཀ *15*).

ཀུན་བཟང་ *Kun-bzań* समन्तभद्र the all-good; epithet of Buddha; a *Bon* sage and teacher.

ཀུན་བཟང་འཁོར་ལོ *Kun-bzań hkhor-lo* a metrical arrangement in several squares resembling a chess-board and sometimes forming an acrostic.

ཀུན་བཟང་གླིང་ *Kun-bzań gliń* n. of a place of pilgrimage in Tibet (*Deb.* ག *43*).

ཀུན་བཟང་རྣམ་གསུམ *Kun-bzań rnam-gsum* the three good ones; the Supreme Deity of the *Bon* religion in Tibet who is explained as having three manifestations: (1) བདག་མེད་ཀུན་བཟང་ निरात्मक समन्तभद्र the impersonal God or Supreme Being, ཡེ་གྲོལ་ཡེ་སངས་རྒྱས་པ།, who from eternity has been free and all-perfect; (2) བདག་ཡོད་ཀུན་བཟང་། the personal God སེམས་ཉིད་ཀྱི་གནས་ལུགས་སོ། as manifest in the form of a sentient being (like Shenrab); (3) རྟེན་དུ་ཚོགས་པའི་ཀུན་བཟང་། the deity represented in symbol, *i.e.*, form; རིས་སུ་བྲིས་དང་འབུར་དུ་བཏོད་ལུགས་སུ་བླུག་པ། representations in painting, figures in relief or casts.

ཀུན་བཟོད་ *kun-bzod*= ས་གཞི *sa-gshi* सर्वंसहा the all-enduring; a figurative name for the earth.

ཀུན་ཆོས་གཙང་བ *Kun-chos gtsaṅ-wa* a Buddhist sect with a few monasteries bordering on Yunnan.

ཀུན་རིག *Kun-rig* सर्वविद् all-knowing; n. of a god; a learned man.

Syn. མཁས་པ *mkhas-pa*; ཀུན་ཤེས *kun-çes*; ཀུན་གྱིས་བཀུར་བ *kun-gyi bkur-wa* (*Mṅon.*).

ཀུན་ལ *kun-la* सर्वत्र to every one, to all; to everywhere.

ཀུན་ལ་བཀྲ་ཤིས་དབང་ལྡན་མ *kun-la bkra-çis dwaṅ-ldan-ma* she who gives blessings to all: དབང་ཕྱུག་གི་བཙུན་མོ་ཨུ་མའི་མིང་ a name of the goddess Umā, the wife of Mahes'wara (*Mṅon.*).

ཀུན་ལ་ཁྱབ་བྱེད་སེར་པོ *kun-la khyab-byed ser-po* गोरोचना = གི་ཝང *ghi-waṅ* (*Sman. 107*) a bright yellow pigment prepared from the urine or bile of a cow, or vomited in the shape of scidulæ by that animal; bezoar stone.

ཀུན་ལ་འཇུག *kun-la hjug* efficient; able to enter into anything: རིག་པ་སྦྱང་བས་རྩོམ་པ་ཀུན་ལ་འཇུག། the intellect being cultured becomes efficient in composing.

ཀུན་ལ་བདེ *kun-la bde* happiness to all.

ཀུན་ལ་ཕན *kun-la phan* useful or good to all.

ཀུན་ལ་འཕྲོད *kun-la hphrod* beneficial; agreeable to all: བ་མར་མར་གྱི་མཆོག་ཡིན་ཀུན་ལ་འཕྲོད། "cow butter being the best of butter is agreeable to all."

ཀུན་ལ་བཙེས་པ *kun-la btses-pa* injuring all, all-hurting, hurtful, obnoxious.

ཀུན་ལ་རེག *kun-la reg* उपसर्ग meddling, meddlesome, touching everything.

ཀུན་ལས *kun-las* = ཀུན་ནས *kun-nas* सर्वतः from every place or thing; from all; than all.

ཀུན་ལས་བཏུས་པ *kun-las btus-pa* समुद्धृत, समुच्चय selected or compiled from every book; n. of a book.

ཀུན་ཤེས་པ *kun çes-pa* सर्वज्ञ all-knowing; knowing all, omniscient.

ཀུན་ཤེས་པའི་སོ་གམ་པ *kun çes-pahi ço-gam-pa* a religious man who, being under moral discipline, has reduced his desires and requirements; lit. "an all-knowing tax-gatherer."

ཀུན་བཤད་པ *kun bçad-pa* व्याख्यात well explained; preaching all the religions, one that preaches everywhere.

ཀུན་སེམས *kun-sems* संविद् to be conscious or cognizant of all things; to think at all times.

ཀུན་སློང *kun-sloṅ* समुत्पाद, समुत्थान a general rising; rising from every direction or place; = སེམས་བསྐྱེད *sems-bskyed* चित्तोत्पाद conception; idea; the notion of a thing; a thought; དགེ་མི་དགེ་ཀུན་སློང་བའི་སེམས the mind which gives rise to thoughts of sins or merits, virtue or vice.

ཀུན་སློང་ཆེན་པོ *kun-sloṅ chen-po* comprises the three ཆགས་སྡང་རྨོངས *chags-sdaṅ-rmoṅs*, lust, anger and ignorance.

ཀུན་གསོད *kun-gsod* घातक all-killing, that which kills everybody or thing; the lord of death.

ཀུན་གསལ *kun-gsal* = ནམ་མཁའ *nam-mkhah* 1. the sky; that is fully clear, illuminated. 2. = ཉི་མ *ñi-ma*, the sun, the all-clearer.

‡ ཀུན་ཏ *kun-ta* कुत: from where? one from an unknown place; also interrogatively, come from where? It is used in mystic language (*K. g.* ཁ *26*).

ཀུན་ཏུ་རུ *kun-tu-ru* the union of the two sexes, copulation (used only in mystic language) (*K. g.* ག *216*).

‡ ཀུན་ཐི་ར *kun-thi-ra* कुन्थिर n. of a bird: ཀུན་ཐི་ར་ལས་བྱས་པའི་ཙུའི་ནང་དུ་བྱུང་བ་བཙུག་ན་ནམ་མཁའ་ལ་འགྲོ་བར་བྱེད་དོ (*K. g.* ཙ *58*).

ཀུན་ད *kun-da* भ्रम 1. mistake, blunder, illusion (*Lex.*). 2. विमरिका, कुन्द the blue jessamine, *Jasminum multiflorum* or *pubescens*.

Syn. ཆུ་སྐྱེས *chu-skyes*; དགུན་ཟླ་ཐ་ཆུང་སྐྱེས *dgun-zla tha-chuṅ skyes*; འདབ་མོའི་མཛོད *ḥdab moḥi mdsod* (*Mṅon.*).

ཀུན་ད་བྱང་སེམས *kun-da byaṅ-sems* = དངུལ་ཆུ *dṅul-chu* quicksilver (*Sman. 79*).

ཀུན་དུ་རུ *kun-du-ru* सुकुन्द, कुन्द sweet-smelling tree; a kind of incense; the resin of *Boswellia thurifera*; gum olibanum (*M. Wills.*).

Syn. སྐྱོང་བྱེད་པ *skyoṅ-byed-pa*; མུ་ཀུན་ད *mu-kun-da*; ཀུན་དུ *kun-du* (*Mṅon.*).

ཀུན་དུ་ལ *kun-du-la* = ཤིམ་བུ *shim-bu* a cat (*Mṅon.*).

ཀུན་དོང *kun-doṅ* पलाण्डु onion.

ཀུམ་པ *kum-pa* crooked; shrivelled; ཀུམ་པ་ཉིད *kum-pa-ñid* contraction; ཀུམ་ཀུམ *kum-kum* very contracted.

ཀུམ་པོ *kum-po* cringing; one in a contracted posture; ཀུམ་པོར *kum-por* cringingly; contractedly.

ཀུམ་བྷ *kum-bha* कुम्भ = བུམ་པ *bum-pa* gen. an earthen jar; a vessel for water.

ཀུམ་བི་ར *kum-bi-ra* कुम्भीर n. of a srin-po (demi-god or demon).

ཀུར་ཏི *kur-ti* to hasten; ཀུར་ཏི་ལངས་འགྲོ *kur-ti laṅs-ḥgro* to start or go off on any business; (in colloq. language) to start on an errand or mission early in the morning without having even a cup of tea.

ཀུལ་ཀར *Kul-kar*, also ཀུལ་དཀར *kul-dkar*, n. of a place in Tsang; a kind of shield manufactured in *Kul-kar*: ཀུལ་ཀར་ཕུབ་རྣམས་ཀྱ་ཡི་ཁྱད་དུ་འཕགས the shield manufactured at *Kul-kar* is of superior quality (on account of its superior metal); ཀུལ་དཀར་ཕུབ་ནི་རབ་ལ་ཞོ་ལྔ་རེ as to the *Kul-dkar* shield it costs five *sho* for the best.

ཀེ *ke* numeral for 91; *ke-pa* the 91st (volume).

ཀེ་ཀ *ke-ka* in the dialect of *Ḥphan-yul* for སྐྱ་ཀ *skya-ka*, a magpie.

‡ ཀེ་ཀཱ་པི་ནོ *Ke-kā-pi-no* केकापिन a country west of Jambudvīpa of romantic scenery, said to be filled with gardens, dales, fountains, cascades, etc., and intersected with streams, and inhabited by a race of very handsome men who eat red rice (*K. d.* ར *179*).

ཀེ་ཀིའི་སྒྲ *ke-kiḥi-sgra* the cry of the peacock (*Schtr.*).

‡ ཀེ་ཀེ་རུ *ke-ke-ru* ककतर or कर्केतन a white precious stone.

ཀེ་རྒྱུང *ke-rgyuṅ* a charm of the *Bon* deity called *Çen-sras mi mgon rgyal-po*: ཀེ་རྒྱུང་ང་ནི་རྗེ་ཡར་ནི་བྱ་པ་ད། ཀེ་རྒྱུང་མད་དོ་ཡར་བཞི་བྱ་པད (*D. R.*).

‡ ཀེ་ཏ་ཀ *ke-ta-kā* from केतक 1. a gem which has the property of purifying water; its Tibetan name is དྭངས་བྱེད or ཟུང་བྱེད, the purifier. 2. a great mountain situated north of the great forest plain beyond the north bank of the river Sita. Its peaks are described as very grand in appearance. It contains mines of gold and silver, and round its peaks are four fabulous lakes which at all seasons remain filled with lotuses and lilies. The ruler of this country in ancient times was *Vaiçravana*, whose army consisted of amazons of great beauty and valour (*S. Lam.*).

‡ ཀེ་ཏ་ར *Ke-ta-ra* a mountain, probably Kedara (केदार); part of the Himalaya (*Jä.*).

‡ ཀེ་ཏུ *Ke-tu* 1. a fabulous planet in Brāhmaincal as well as in Tibetan astrology. In Tibet the name *Ke-tu* is generally applied to comets, called also དུ་བ་མཇུག་རིང (lit. the long smoke-tailed). 2. a fiery meteor; a shooting star; the descending node. 3. n. of a demon.

ཀེ་ནེའི་བུ *Ke-neḥi-bu* n. of a sage of the time of Gautama the Buddha (*K. du.* ཀ *54*).

ཀེ་བྱེད *Ke-byed* Kārtika, the god of war (*Schtr.*).

ཀེ་རྩེ་བ *Ke-rtse-wa* n. of a *Bon* teacher: བོན་པོ་ལ་ཀེ་རྩེ་བ་གདན་དྲངས (*Deb.* ཀ *6*) the *Bonpo* priests invited *Ke-rtse.*

ཀེ་ཚེགས *Ke-tshegs* a *Nāga*; the quarter where it resides during a certain astrological period is considered inauspicious.

ཀེའུ *Keḥu* 1. a tribe in Tibet (*Vai. kar. 160*). 2. गृञ्जनक in classical Tibetan a kind of garlic. 3. a cavern, den, hollow place (*Cs.*).

ཀེའུ་རྩེ *Keḥu-rtse*, also ཀེ་རྩེ *ke-rtse*, a jacket made in the Chinese fashion; in Chinese *kwa-tzu.*

ཀེའུ་ཚང *Keḥu-tshaṅ* (in Chinese *K'u-ts'ang*, "a treasury; a store-house") n. of a sacred rock-cavern.

ཀེའུ་རི *Keḥu-ri* n. of a female deity of fearful mien.

ཀེའུ་ལི *Keḥu-li* the Tibetan and Mongolian name for Corea. In Chinese Kaoli.

ཀེའུ་ལེ *keḥu-le* ཀེའུ་ལེའི་རྒྱ customary seal (*Jä.*).

ཀེའུ་ཤ་ཡ *keḥu-ça-ya* (from *kaṣāya*) celestial robes; robes worn by the gods (*K. my.* ཀ *7*).

ཀེ་ཡ *ke-ya* wickedness: ངན་སེམས་ཀྱི་ཀེ་ཡ་ནག་པོའི་རྩ་བ་འཁྲུངས་པས the root of wickedness of a bad heart (*i.e.*, envy) having sprung forth (*J. Zaṅ.*).

‡ ཀེ་ཡུ་ར་ཀ *Ke-yu-ra-ka* केयूरक 1. a kind of grass used in ancient times in making garments for a *Bhikṣu* (*K. du.* ཕ *388*). 2. n. of a *Gandharva.*

ཀེ་རུ *Ke-ru* 1. n. of a place and monastery in the district of H̱on in Yar-lung (*J.Zaṅ. 217*). 2. སྲན་མ *sran-ma* a species of peas: ཆུ་གཏོར་བཏང་ནས་ཁྱིམ་དུ་ཁྲིད་ནས་སྲན་མ་ཀེ་རུའི་ཚོད་མ་ཕོར་གང་དྲངས། after casting water in oblation, he conducted (him) inside the house and served him with a cupful of pea-soup (*Deb.* ཀ *35*).

ཀེ་རེ *Ke-re*, v. ཀྱེ་རི *kye-ri.*

ཀེ་ལ *Ke-la* རིགས་རུས་ཞིག་གི་མིང་། n. of a tribal clan (*Yig.*).

ཀེ་ལ་ཀ *ke-la-ka* = སྒ་སྐྱ *sga-skya* ginger (*Sman. 267*).

‡ ཀེ་ལ་ཤ *ke-la-ça* = ཀཻ་ལ་ཤ *kai-la-ça* རིའི་རྒྱལ་པོ་ཏི་སེ། कैलास the king of mountains *i.e.*, Kailasa in the Himalayas.

ཀེ་ལན *Ke-lan*, prob. corruption of དགེ་ལྡན, follower of Tsongkhapa (*Huc*, vol. II).

ཀེ་ལེ *Ke-le* n. of a fabulous place or country: ཀེ་ལེ་མི་ཤ་ཟན་གྱི་ཡུལ the country of cannibals, Ke-le (*D. R.*).

ཀེ་ཤ *ke-ça* केश hair; mane; ཀི་གི་ཀེ་ཤ་ཅན letters which are surmounted with double *e* sign called *ḥgreñ-bu* or *o* sign called *naro*. Signs for long accentuation are also called *ke-ça*.

*ཀེ་ཤ་ར *ke-ça-ra* केशर mane (*Schr.*).

‡ ཀེ་ཤུ་ཀ *Ke-çu-ka* a plant, perhaps *Arum colocasia*, with edible roots; also किंशुक, v. ཀིང་ཤུ་ཀ *Kiñ-çu-ka* (*Ḥbum.* ཀ *17*).

‡ ཀེ་སར་ར *Ke-sa-ra* केशर 1. the hair; the mane of the lion. 2. the hairy filament of the lotus; a celestial flower; saffron.

ཀེག *keg*=བར་ཆད *bar-chaḍ* danger; accident, v. ཀག *kag*.

ཀེག་མ *Keg-ma*=ཀག་མ *kag-ma* (*Lex.*).

ཀེང་རུས *Keñ-rus* कङ्काल skeleton.

‡ ཀེང་ཤུ་ཀ *Ken-çu-ka* an evergreen tree, *i.e.*, of the colour of the parrot (*Ńag. 3*). This is evidently a corruption of किंशुक.

ཀེར་ཀོ *Ker-ko* a cymbal; a musical instrument: ཅང་ཏེའུ་དང་ཀེར་ཀོ་དང་གླིང་བུ་དང་ (carrying with him) a hand-drum, a cymbal, a pipe (flute) (*K. g.* ༥ *2*).

ཀེར་གྱིས *ker-gyis* suddenly (*Sch.*).

ཀེར་བ *Ker-wa* to raise; to lift up; གནམ་ལ་མཛུབ་མོ་ཀེར་བ། to point the fingers towards heaven.

ཀེར་ལངས *ker-lañs* समुत्थित suddenly stood up: ཀེར་ལངས་ནས། "suddenly standing erect and still (like a tree") (*Ńag. 3*).

ཀེར་ལེབ་སྒུར *ker leb sgur* metaph. for horse, sheep and yak: ཀེར་ལེབ་སྒུར་གསུམ་གྱི་དང་ནས་ཀེར་སྒུར་གྱི་འབབ། the tax (in kind, *i.e.*, one in a hundred) on horse and yak from among the three kinds of cattle (*Ṛtsii.*).

ཀེལ་མག *Kel-mag* possibly indicates the *Kalmuk* Tartars.

‡ ཀཻ་ཏ་ཀ *Kai-ta-ka* n. of a mythological demon.

ཀཻ་ནེ་ཡ *Kai ne-ya* कैकेय a rishi or sage; also patronymic of Rāvana (*K. d.* p. *186*).

ཀཻ་ལ་ཤ *Kai-la-ça* कैलास =རི་བོ་གངས་ཅན *Ri-wo gañs-can* the huge snowy mountain on the north shore of the Manasarowara lake called Gang Ti-se by the Tibetans and Kailāsa by the Indians.

ཀོ I: *ko* num. 121; ཀོ་པ *ko-pa* the volume marked with the letter ཀོ *ko*, or the 121st volume.

ཀོ II: ནི an expletive meaning: same, the same, very; as in འདི་ཀོ *ḥdi-ko*, the same; as འདི་ནི *ḥdi-ni*, this very: རྣམ་བཞག་འདི་ཀོ་ཙམ་པར། "these same classifications"; དེ་ཀོ *de-ko*=དེ་ནི *de-ni* that very.

ཀོ III: all, whole; quite, entirely, altogether (*Schtr.*).

ཀོ་བ *ko-wa* 1. hide, leather—that derived from yaks, buffaloes and horses as distinguished from *pags-pa* the skins of sheep, goats, foxes, &c. 2. colloq. for *ko-gru* a hide-boat.

ཀོ་ཁུག *ko-khug* a leather purse; a little leathern money-bag.

ཀོ་ཁྲོལ *ko-khrol* (*ko-ṭhol*) a sieve made of hide-strips or strings to clean peas, barley grain, &c., of gravel, &c.: ཀོ་བའི་ཁྲོལ་མ་སྲན་ནས་ཚགས་པ་ལ། (*Ṛtsii.*) for a hide-sieve for sifting peas and barley (*i.e.*, price for).

ཀོ་གྲུ *ko-gru* (*ko-ḍu*) a hide-boat a boat made of the entire hide of a *yak*; a skin coracle.

ཀོ་བཏུམ *ko-ḅtum* hide-packing. This is said to be a criminal punishment in

Central Tibet, varying in severity, *e.g.*, ལག་པ་ཀོ་བཏུམ when the culprit's hands are cut off, the stumps sewed up in leather and the poor wretch thrown as a beggar upon public charity, &c. (*Jä.*).

ཀོ་ཐག *ko-thag* strap; thong.

ཀོ་ཐུད *ko-thud* a kind of tea, probably so called on account of being sold packed in hide cases; an inferior tea: སེ་སེ་ཕུར་མེད་པའི་ཀོ་ཐུད་ལ། (*Rtsii.* 74) "to the cost of pressed brick-tea."

ཀོ་ཐུམས *ko-thums* packed up in hide; གསེར་སྲང་སུམ་ཅུ་ ཡོད་པའི་ཀོ་ཐུམས་ཤིག a leather package containing 30 ounces of gold: གསེར་གྱི་ཀོ་ཐུམས་བརྐུས་ནས་ཕྱི་ཕྲང་དུ་སྦས having stolen a bag containing gold, (we) concealed it in a marmot's (ཕྱི་བ a marmot) hole.

ཀོ་འཐགས *ko-hthags* a small instrument of leather to weave lace with (*Cs.*).

ཀོ་གདན *ko-gdan*, pronounced *kom-gdan*, skin-rug or seat; a piece of leather put under the saddle (*Sch.*): སྐྱི་འབུར་ཀོ་གདན་ཀོ་རྐྱབས་འདུ་བ་རེར for each tanned skin-rug or leather folding used for cushions (three *tanka*) (*Rtsii.*).

ཀོ་མདའ *ko-mdah* an arrow bound with hide: བྱང་གི་ཀོ་མདའ, the hide arrow used in the north (of Tibet).

ཀོ་ལྡིང *ko-ldin* a vessel or basin made of hide to keep or cleanse oil or lime-wash: ས་རྩི་གསོལ་བའི་ཀོ་ལྡིང་རེར (*Rtsii.*) for each hide vessel for holding *sa-rtsi* (such and such a price).

ཀོ་ལྤགས *ko-lpags* hide; also tanned skin; ཀོ་ལྤགས་ཀྱི་གཞི चर्मवस्तु hide or leather material or stuff included in the fourteen materials prescribed for clothing to be used by Buddhist monks.

ཀོ་ལྤགས་མཁན *ko-lpags mkhan* = ལྷམ་མཁན *lham-mkhan* चर्मकार worker in hide and leather; a shoe-maker.

ཀོ་སྤྱིན *ko-spyin* (*ko-pin*) glue: ཀོ་སྤྱིན་རྡོག་ལེབ་རེར for each stick or cake of glue (*Rtsii.*).

ཀོ་ཕོངས *ko-phons* guitar (gen. made of thin belly-skin of a cow) (*Ld.*); it is tuned in three-fourths (*Jä.*).

ཀོ་ཕོར *ko-phor* a cup made of leather and painted to look like a wooden cup; ཀོ་གཞོང *ko-gshon* a basin made of hide.

ཀོ་བ་མཁན *ko-wa mkhan* a tanner; the steersman of a hide boat.

ཀོ་བ་མཉེད་མཁན *ko-wa mñed-mkhan* a tanner.

ཀོ་བ་བྲག *Ko-wa brag* སྟོད་ཕྱོགས་ཀྱི་ཡུལ་ཞིག་གི་མིང་ n. of a district in Upper Tibet: དེ་ནས་སྟོད་ལུང་ཀོ་བ་བྲག་ཏུ་བྱོན then he visited *Ko-wa brag* in *Stod-luṅ* (*Lha. kah.* 23).

ཀོ་བུབས *ko-bubs* an entire skin: ཀོ་བུབས་རེ་ལ་སྙིང་མར་ཁལ་ཉག་གསུམ་རེ an entire skin of a sheep holds three *khar-ñag* measure of good butter (*Rtsii.* 74).

ཀོ་འབུགས *ko-hbugs* an awl; a three-sided needle for sewing leather (*Sch.*).

ཀོ་འབོ *ko-hbo* itch scab; ཀོ་འབོ་ནད་ཅན scabby. In Sikkim a measure for rice or barley made of hide.

ཀོ་སྦྲགས *ko-sbrags* a hide filled with butter; the whole package is so called.

ཀོ་ཚལ *ko-tshal* pieces of leather or hide: ཀོ་ཚལ་དང་སྦྲང་མར་སོགས་ཀྱི་ཀོ་བ་རེར for each skin of butter and honey, &c., with hide wrapping (*Rtsii.*).

ཀོ་རློན་གཏུམས *ko-rlon gtums* packed in a fresh skin: མི་ཀོ་རློན་གྱིས་གཏུམས་པ་དེ་དང་ཐོར་ལྷོད་ལྷོང་འདུ་ཡང་བསྐམས་ནས་འཁྱུག་སྐྲབས་མེད་པར་བསྐུམས་ནས་ན་ཚ་བསྐྱེད like a man packed in a fresh skin, or anything packed or fastened with raw hide which becomes shrivelled when the skin dries and illness is induced.

ཀོ་རུལ་ *ko-rul* a rotten hide.

ཀོ་ལ་ *ko-la* a grub which breeds in hides; a kind of hide-moth; ཀོ་ལ་སྦུག་མ་ཤའི་འབུ་འདྲ་ཞིག་ཞིག་གི་རིགས་ལྟ་བུ། the *Kola* moth, something like a species of vermin in flesh (*Rtsii.*).

ཀོ་ཤམ་པ་ *ko-çam-pa* (*Lex.*) one dressed in skin or having a skin for his under-clothing, v. ཀོམ་པོ་ *kom-po.*

ཀོ་ཀ *Ko-ka* a place in Bengal where in ancient times many *Tantrik* adepts lived (*S. Lam.*).

‡ ཀོ་ཀ་ལི་ཀ *Ko-ka-li-ka* कोकालिक a Bhikṣu of the Buddha's time who sided with Devadatta (*K. d.* ཤ *247*).

ཀོ་ཀི *Ko-ki* a wild mountainous country east of Bengal in the Chakma and Hamsa-vati countries which are east and south-east of Haribhadra (Manipur) (*S. Lam.*).

‡ ཀོ་ཀི་ལ *Ko-ki-la* कोकिल the Indian cuckoo, in books described as a bird that sings sweetly (*K. du.* ཁ *99*).

‡ ཀོ་ཀི་ལཀྵ *ko-ki lakṣa* n. of a tree (*Mṅon.*).

ཀོ་ཀོ *Ko-ko* (variously spelt ཀོ་སྐོ *ko-sko,* ཀོས་ཀོ *kos-ko* ཀོས་སྐོ *kos-sko*) 1. जोड़ the chin; also occasionally the throat or the neck: ཀོ་སྐོ་འདེགས་པ་=མགྲིན་པ་འདེགས་པ to raise the chin (*Ṅag.*) [see ཀོས་ཀོ]. ཀོས་ཀོ་མེད་པ chinless, or one with a small chin: ཀོ་སྐོས་བསྒྲུང་ एकजोड़ with a slightly perceptible chin; ཀོ་སྐོ་ཕག་གི་ལྟ་བུ शूकरजोड़ a chin like that of a pig; pig-faced (no chin) "beneath the chin." ཀོས་ཀོའི་འོག་མ चिबु or चिबुक the lower part of the chin. 2. a Tibetan of mixed breed, *i.e.*, born of a Chinese father and a Tibetan mother.

ཀོ་ཀོ་ཐང་མ *Ko-ko thaṅ-ma* a country in or near Ceylon (*Jä.*).

ཀོ་ཀྱ *Kokya* पवित्र pure (*Lexx.*).

ཀོ་ཁྲད་ *Ko-krad* (*ko-ṭch*) 1. ལྷམ་གྱི་ཨ་ཁྲད *lham-gyi ākrad* the worn out leather of old shoes and boots; 2. also a leather-shoe (*Jä.*).

ཀོ་སྐོ *ko-sko*ཀོ་ཀོ *ko-ko*=མགྲིན་པ neck: ཀོ་སྐོ་འདེགས *ko-sko hdegs*=མགྲིན་པ་འདེགས *mgrin-pa hdegs* raise the neck (*Ṅag. 4*).

ཀོ་ཉ *Ko-ña* ཡུལ་ཞིག་གི་མིང་ *yul-shig gi-miṅ* n. of a place in Tibet (*Yig.*).

ཀོ་ཉོན་ཙེ *ko-ñon-tse,* also ཀོ་ཉོལ་ཙེ *ko-ñol-tse* or ཀོ་ལོན་ཙེ་ *ko-lon-tse,* the kernel of the pine-apple (*Cs.*); more particularly the edible seed of the *Neosa*-pine growing in the valley of the Sutlej; it is also called སྐན་ཉན་ཙེ *skan-ñan-tse* in *Kunawar* (*Jä.*).

ཀོ་ཏན *ko-tan*=ཁྲག *khrag* blood in mystic language (*K. g.* ཀ *216*).

ཀོ་ཏམ་པ *ko-tam-pa* རི་ཞིག་གི་མིང་ n. of a mountain (*K. dun. 17*).

ཀོ་ཏམ་པའི་རས *ko-tam-pahi-ras* कोतम्बक one of the 41 materials of clothing permissible to Buddhist mendicants; a kind of grass formerly used in making clothes (*K. du.* པ *388*).

ཀོ་ཏམ་བྷག *ko-tam-bhag* same as above.

ཀོ་ཏྲ་པ *ko-tra-pa* कोद्रव, माड़व, in vulg. Nepalese *Kodu*, a kind of millet largely used in Sikkim for making *murwa* beer; it is mentioned in *K. d.* ར *333*. A species of grain eaten by the poor; *Paspatum scrobiculatum.*

ཀོ་ཏྲོག་ཅན *ko-trog-can* མི་གྲོག་གྲོག *mi krog krog* applied to a thoughtless, childish man (*K. d.* ཡ *362*).

ཀོ་ཐ *ko-tha* कोठ, कुष्ठ a kind of leprosy (*Jä.*).

ཀོ་ཐལ *ko-thal* cinders, ashes; ཀོ་ཐལ་དུ་བྱས་པ *ko-thal-du byas pa* to be reduced to ashes: ཀོ་ཐལ་འཐོར་བར་གྱུར་པ *ko-thal ẖthor-war gyur-pa* scattered about ashes.

‡ ཀོ་དཱ་ལ *ko-dā-la* कोदाल or कोदालक a tree growing in the mountain called ཁུ་བྱུག་རི Kokila Parvata (*K. d.* ར *274*).

ཀོ་པང་ཙེ *ko-pañ-tse* a sort of tea (*Schtr.*); usually called *Capinze* (*Schtr.*).

ཀོ་བི་ད་ར *Ko-bi-da-ra* कोविदार the tree of paradise on which grows the *Pārijāta* flower; also a tree the flower of which is pretty and of sweet scent, probably *Bauhinia variegata* (*K. my.* ཀ *20*); ཀོ་བི་ད་ར་ཀ कोविदारक an abode of the gods (*K. du.* ད *310*).

ཀོ་བོ *Ko-ḇo* prop. n. of a country (*Vai. kar.*).

ཀོ་བྲག་པ *Ko-brag-pa* prop. a sect of *Tantrik* Buddhists; also its founder: ཀོ་བྲག་པ་བསོད་ནམས་རྒྱལ་མཚན་གྱིས་བལ་པོ་ནས་བི་བྷུ་ཏི་ཙནྡྲ་དིང་རིར་སྤྱན་དྲངས་ནས་ཕྱིས་སྟོད་མྱང་སྟོད་དུ་ཀོ་བྲག་དགོན་པ་བཏབ། (*J. Zañ.*) *Ḇsoḏ-namṣ ṟgyal-m̱tshan* of *Ko-brag* brought Vibhūti Chandra from Bal-po (Nepal) to Ding-ri and later on founded the monastery of Ko-brag in Upper Myañ.

ཀོ་མ *ko-ma* a bird (*Vai. s̱ñ.*).

ཀོ་ཙེ *ko-tse* ཇ་བརྒྱད་པ *ja ḇrgyaḏ-pa* the Chinese name for the brick-tea used by the common people of Tibet. It is called *ja ḇrgyaḏ-pa*, the eighth or the inferior quality of tea (*S. kar. 80*).

ཀོ་ཝགས *ko-wagṣ* is meant to express the voice of a raven (*Jä.*).

‡ ཀོ་རཎྜོ *Ko-raṇḍo* कोरण्ड prop. a country, said to be in the fabulous Western Continent of Godâniya (*K. d.* ར *331*).

‡ ཀོ་ར་བ *Ko-raba* कौरव the descendants of Kuru; their party; n. of a country in the east (*K. d.* ར *267*).

ཀོ་རེ *ko-re* or ཀོ་ར *ko-ra* cup for drinking; ཤིང་ཀོར *çiñ-kor* wooden cup which every Tibetan carries with him in the pocket of his great coat next to his bosom; ཤེལ་ཀོར *çel-kor* a drinking glass.

ཀོ་ལའི་འདབ *ko-laẖi ẖdab* = གླང་པོའི་པི་པི་ལིང *glañ-poẖi pi-pi liñ* plantain leaf (*M̱ñon.*).

ཀོ་ལོང I: *ko-loñ* annoyance; dissatisfaction; the jealousy of demi-gods or of *Nāga*, &c.: ཀོ་ལོང་དུ་ང་ཕྲག་དོག་མ་བྱེད་ཤིག། "pray do not out of dissatisfaction be jealous of me." In saying grace at meal time the Gods are exhorted by the lamas not to be spiteful, jealous or angry, &c.: ཇོ་བོ་ལ་ནི་སྙིང་མི་མངའ་བས་ཀོ་ལོང་ལ་སོགས་པ་གང་ཡང་མི་མཛད་པར། the Lord (Atis'a) not being actuated by any spite did not express any dissatisfaction, &c. (*A. 58*).

ཀོ་ལོང II: is a dubious word (*Schtr.*); ཀོ་ལོང་བ *ko-loñ-wa* to hate, envy; but in a passage in *Mil.*, where the connection admits of no doubt, *ko-loñ m̱dsaḏ-pa* must be taken = disdain (*Jä.*). In Amdo ཀོ་ལོང *ko-loñ* = dispute, fight.

‡ ཀོ་ཤ་ལཱ *Ko-ça-lā* कोशला mythical river east of Jambudvīpa (*K. d.* ར *267*).

‡ ཀོ་ཤི་ལ *Ko-çi-lā* कोशिल a certain king of birds (*K. my.* ཀ *18*).

‡ ཀོཎྜི་ཉ *Koṇḍi-nya* कौण्डिन्य the son of Upāyamatī; in Tib. ཐབས་ལྡན་མ n. of a Muni or sage; n. of a grammarian; a patronymic of the poet Jayadeva.

† ཀོ་ཤམ་བི *Ko-çam-bi*, also written ཀོཽ་ཤམ་བི *Koh̲u-çam-bi* कौशाम्बी, the city of flowers; n. of an ancient city situated on the Ganges in the lower part of the Doab, in the vicinity of Kurrah; acc. to *Ńag. 3* Vatsapattana.

† ཀོ་ཤི་ཀ *Ko-çi-ka*, also written ཀོཽ་ཤི་ཀ *Ko-h̲u-çi-ka* कौशिक. 1. an epithet of Indra; n. of a drug. 2. n. of the *Vatica Robusta*; n. of a teacher; an owl; a patronymic of Vis'vāmitra, who was the grandson of Kus'ika; n. of a river, river Kosi (*K. d.* ར *267*).

Syn. ན་གུ་ལེ *na-gu-le*; སྦྲུལ་ཁས་སྡིགས་པ *sbrul khas sdigs-pa*; དྲང་སྲོང་མཛོད་ཤེས *d̲rań-s̲roń m̲dsod̲ çes* (*Ńag.*).

† ཀོ་ཥ་ཋི་ལ་ཆེན་པོ *Ko-ṣa-ṭhi-la chen-po* महाकौष्ठिल n. of a *Çrāvaka* attendant of the Buddha (*K. my.* ག *428*).

† ཀོ་ས་ལ *Ko-sa-la* कोसल, कोशल n. of a part of Ancient Oudh which in the Buddha's time was ruled by King Prasenajit.

ཀོག་པ I: *kog-pa* 1. a cover; ཀོག་ཤོག *kog-çog* the paper-cover of a letter; an envelope (*Yig. k. 2*): ཀོག་ཤོག་ལ་གཙང་སྦྲམ་རྒྱུག་དགོས the cover or envelope (of a letter) should be neat and clean. ཇ་ཀོག *ja-kog* a hide case in which tea is packed is usually called *ja-ko*; མར་ཀོག *mar-kog* a skin of butter: མར་གྱི་ཀོག་དང་ཆུ་རྡོ་ཇི་བཞིན་དུ། (*S. leg.*) "like a stone in water or package of butter." ཤུན་ཀོག *çun-kog* shell, rind; ཕྱི་ཡི་ཀོག *phyi-yi-kog* exterior shell; bark. 2. the name ཀོག་པ *kog-pa* is applied to an old man after the age of 85 (*R̲tsa shuń.*).

ཀོག་པ II: 1. vb., to splinter off, to chip; ཀོག་ལང་བ to rise suddenly and run away (*Jä.*). 2. ཀོག་པ་ཤུ་བ *kog-pa çu-wa* to peel, pare off.

ཀོག་ཙེ *kog-tse* जाल a net: acc. to (*Ńag.*) བྱ་དང་རི་དྭགས་བཟུང་བྱེད་རྒྱུས་སྐྱེས། "a net or snare to catch birds or wild animals."

ཀོང་ I: *koń*, also ཀོང་ཀོང་ *koń-koń*, concave; excavated; crooked; bent; warped. ས་ཀོང་ཀོང་ *sa koń-koń* undulating ground; ཀོང་པ་ཉིད *koń-pa-ñid̲* concavity.

ཀོང་ II: ཀོང་པོ *Koń-po*, also སྐོང་བུ *skoń-bu* गर्त्तदेश 1. cup; crucible. 2. the country of ravines, n. of a province of Tibet lying to the south-east of Lhasa and east of Tse-thang. ཀོང་གསུམ *Koń-gsum* त्रिगर्त the three divisions of *Koń-yul*; also n. of a kingdom in Ancient India which was ruled by King Susarmā. ཀོང་སྐེད *Koń-sked̲* a kind of sash or waist-band of fine wool manufactured in *Koń-po*; ཀོང་མདུང *koń-m̲duń* a kind of spear manufactured in *Koń-po* (*Jig. 32*); ཀོང་སྤང *koń-pań* planks brought from *Koń-po* (*S. kar. 179*); ཀོང་སྤྲེལ *koń-sprel* an ape from *Koń-po*; the name of an individual who made a donation to aid in repairing the monastery of Samye. ཀོང་བཟོ *kon-b̲zo* a kind of armour or weapon manufactured in *Koń-po*.

* ཀོང་ཀུན *koń-kun* कोंकण n. p. (*Schr.*).

ཀོང་ཁྲུ *koń-khru* (*koń-ṭhu*) a kind of yellow satin: གོས་ཀོང་ཁྲུ་སེར་པོ་ཕྱུག་གཅིག (*S. kar. 180*) a piece or roll of yellow satin for a gown.

ཀོང་ཇོ *Koń-jo*, in Chinese *Kung-chu*, a princess; the Tibetan name of the daughter of Emperor Tai-tsung, who was married to King *S̲roń-tsan S̲gam-po*, རྒྱ་ནག་ཡུལ་ནས་རྒྱ་བཟའ་ཀོང་ཇོ *Koń-jo*, from China; the Chinese spouse Koń-jo (*Loń.* ༡ *5*).

ཀོང་བུ *Koñ-bu* a small cup-shaped brass or copper oil-burner; མཆོད་ཀོང་ *mchod-koñ* an offering bowl, a cup for offering pure water to any divinity; སྣག་ཀོང་ *snag-koñ* ink-stand, generally for black ink; མཚལ་ཀོང *mtshal-koñ* ink-stand for red ink or vermilion; བླུགས་ཀོང *blugs-koñ* casting mould, crucible; གསེར་ཀོང *gser-koñ* a gold cup or oil-burner placed before Tibetan deities; བྱེ་ཀོང་ *bye-koñ* bowl of sand.

ཀོང་མོ *koñ-mo* གཞི a cave; a ditch.

ཀོད *Kod* boiled: ཇ་དེ་ཀོད་ནས་ཀ་ར་བྲམ་པོ་ལྔ་བྱིན་པས་ཇོ་བོ་དགྱེས *ja de kod-nas ka-ra bram-po lña byiñ-pas Jo-wo dgyes* (*A. 95*) the tea having been boiled (prepared) and given with five lumps of sugar, the *Jo-wo* was gratified.

ཀོན་པ *kon-pa*, also called ཀོན་པ་གབ་སྐྱེས *kon-pa gab-skyes*, the name of a plant that grows in solitary places, generally in the clefts of rocks. This medicine, *kon-pa gab-skyes*, is used in Tibet for stopping hemorrhage.

ཀོབ་ཀོབ *kob-kob*, same as ཀབ་ཀོབ *kab-kob*, the noise or sound produced from the stretching of hides.

ཀོམ་པ *kom-pa* to tan (skin).

ཀོམ་གདན *kom-gdan* a seat made of tanned skin.

ཀོམ་པོ *kom-po* skin which has been made soft and pliable by tanning; leather.

ཀོམ་ཤིང་ཀོང་ཇོ *Kom-çiñ koñ-jo* the princess Kom, the youngest daughter of Wen Chung, the fifth Emperor of the Tang dynasty. She was married to King Me Agtshom (*J. Zañ.*).

ཀོར *kor*, same as སྐོར *skor*. 1. is used as a ཚིག་གྲོགས or auxiliary particle used in the manner of an affix, as in སྟོད་ཀོར *stod-kor*, which signifies a cloth that surrounds or covers the upper part of one's body; hence སྟོད་ལེ *stod-le* a kind of half jacket worn by children and also by lama dancers; ཀླད་ཀོར *klad-kor* the circular dot put over the head of certain letters to signify the letter མ *ma*. 2. anything that has been cut out by the hand or a lathe, such as ཤིང་ཀོར *çiñ-kor* a wooden cup; རྫ་ཀོར *rdsa-kor* an earthen cup or vessel turned out. 3. n. of a place; ཀོར་ནི་རུ་པ *Kor-ni-ru-pa* n. of a great lama who was a native of the place called *Kor*. (*Deb.* ཀ *11*).

ཀོར *kor* also occurs in ཐན་ཀོར *than-kor*, ཉེན་ཀོར *ñen-kor*, འོད་ཀོར *hod-kor*, པད་ཀོར *pad-kor*, གདུབ་ཀོར *gdub-kor*, &c.

ཀོར་ཀོར *kor-kor* coiled: ཞག་པ་ཕུར་པ་ལ་ཀོར་ཀོར་བྱས། "a string was wound round the (exorcist's) dagger (*Vai. sñ. 82*).

ཀོར་བཟོ *kor-bzo* lit. of round make; a kind of shield of round shape (*Rtsii.*).

ཀོལ a colloq. form of ཀོར.

ཀོལ་བའི་ལམ *kol-wahi lam*=ལམ་ངན་པ *lam-ñan-pa*, a bad road (*Mñon.*).

ཀོལ་ས *kol-sa*, v. འགོལ་ས *hgol-sa* or གོལ་ས *gol-sa*.

ཀོས་ཀོ *kos-ko* ཇོཌ the chin. This word is also applied to the throat and even to the wind-pipe.

ཀྱ་ལ *Kya-la* (also called སྐྱ་ལ) petty; n. of a petty state in Tibet, the chief town of which is སྐྱ་ལ་སེང་གདོང་ (lit. the lion-face), where the Tsang-po, it is said, enters a rocky chasm in the mountains.

ཀྱ་ཨན *Kya-an* n. of a large fort in Tibet (*Dsam. 32*).

ཀྱག *kyag* or ཀྱག་ཀྱག *kyag-kyag* 1. throwing obstacles in the way of another's work out of spite. 2. thick; run into clots; ཀྱག་པ་ཉིད *kyag-pa ñid* thickness (*Cs.*).

ཀྱག་ཀྱོག *kyag-kyog* or ཀྱོག་ཀྱོག *kyog-kyog* वक्र curved; crooked; not straight.

ཀྱང་ I: *kyañ*, also ཀྱང་ཀྱང *kyañ-kyañ* or ཀྱང་པོ *kyañ-po*, 1. straight; right; very straight (*Cs.*). 2. slender as a stick (*Jä.*).

ཀྱང་ II: अपि च 1. and; and also; though; although; too; yet more; used instead of དང་ *dañ* enclitically after the letters ག་ད་བ་ས. In composition the word ཀྱང་ is placed between the subject and the predicate, for example:—མཛེས་ཀྱང་མཛེས་ལ་སེམས་ཀྱང་བཟང་ he was beautiful and his mind was also good. In the sense of "though" ཀྱང་ follows the first or contrasted verb:—གདོང་པ་མཛེས་ཀྱང་ལུས་པོ་ཀྱོག "though his face was handsome yet his body was crooked." འདི་ནི་མཛེས་ཤིང་འོད་ཀྱང་འཕྲོ། this being handsome also sheds lustre. 2. since, since that; then, therefore; likewise; whereas.

ཀྱང་ཀྱོང *kyañ-kyoñ* indolent, lazy, idle (*Jä.*).

ཀྱར་པོ *kyar-po*, also ཀྱར་ཀྱར *kyar-kyar*, flat, not globular (*Cs.*).

ཀྱར་ཀྱོར *kyar-kyor* still feeble as a convalescent after disease (*Jä.*).

ཀྱལ I: *kyal*, resp. ཞལ་ཀྱལ *shal-kyal*, a joke; also a comic or jocular look: ལན་ཅིག་ཞལ་ཀྱལ་དུ་མཛད་དེ། (*A. 113*) once having a jocular smile on his face.

ཀྱལ II: also ཀྱལ་ཀྱལ *kyal-kyal*, sometimes written as རྐྱལ་རྐྱལ *rkyal-rkyal*, long and flat, not globular. Described in (*Ñag.*) ངན་ཙ་སྡོང་པ་འཕྱག་འཕྱག་ཅེ་བའི་དོན། like straw, hollow and devoid of meaning; worthless.

ཀྱལ་ཀ *kyal-ka* केलि, प्रलाप joke, jest, tricks: ཀྱལ་ཀའི་ཚིག *kyal-kahi tshig* केलिवचन, རྩེད་མོའི་ཚིག *rtsed-mohi tshig* playful word.

ཀྱལ་པ *kyal-pa* vain, idle talk, nonsense.

ཀྱལ་ཀྱོལ *kyal-kyal* poor; ill-conditioned.

ཀྱི *kyi* 1. This syllable is primarily an inflecting affix attached to nouns, adj., participles, &c., indicating the genitive case. This affix takes the form ཀྱི only after the final letters ད, བ, or ས, and is varied to གྱི where the word to which it is attached ends in either ན, མ, ར, or ལ, and to གི where the preceding final is ག or ང་, or simply to འི if the final happens to be a vowel. Ex.: བོད་ཀྱི of Tibet, Tibetan; ལམ་གྱི of the way; བྱང་གི of the north; འགྲོ་བའི་ཚེ at the time of going. Sometimes, moreover, it is elided altogether, as in བོད་སྐད Tibetan language. 2. It is annexed to verbal roots (with the same variations of form) after the manner of a continuative particle and imparting the gerundial sense, but by some modern writers used as a finite verb. Gerundially it generally implies an antithesis which may be expressed in English by "though" followed by "yet": བུ་མོས་ཁོ་ལ་བོས་ཀྱི་མགོ་སྐྱུར་བ་མེད་ལམ་དྲང་འགྲུལ་ཡོད though the girl called to him, yet he went on the straight way without turning his head. As affix to a finite verb it is frequent in the writings of Padma Jungnas and Milaraspa, and is also used in the *C.* colloquial. Attached to the verbal root it may also carry the sense of "as much as," "as far as": ལམ་འདི་སེམས་ལ་ངེས་ཀྱི་བ་གླང་གི་རྗེས་སུ་སོང་ as far as he remembered this road, he followed the ox. 3. ཀྱི connecting the auxiliary verb with the verbal root forms a much-used present tense: ཉལ་ཀྱི་ཡོད I am lying down. But here the final vowel does not often take the simple *i* (ི), *e.g.*, ལྟ་ཀྱི་འདུག is seeing; still we have in books ཟས་ཟའི་འདུག is eating food. [*N.B.*—The use with the instrumental form ཀྱིས will come under that article.]

ཀྱི་གློང་ *kyi-gloṅ* the elbow.

ཀྱི་ལྕེ *Kyi-lce* n. of a medicinal plant, *Gentiana decumbens.* The white species of this plant called ཀྱི་ལྕེ་དཀར་པོ *kyi-lce dkar-po* is in repute for biliousness. The blue called ཀྱི་ལྕེ་སྔོན་པོ *kyi-lce sṅon-po* heals swelling in the throat or glands (*Med.*).

ཀྱི་བུན *kyi-bun* a chill; a feeling of cold (*Sch.*).

ཀྱི་ལིང་ཆུ་རྟ་སྔོན་པོ *kyi-liṅ chu-rta sṅon-po*= དངུལ་ཆུ *dṅul-chu* quicksilver (*Smān. 118*).

ཀྱི་ཧུད *kyi-hud* हा वत, हाहा, हा कष्ट, आहा 1. interj., the sound of weeping, lamentation; an expression of grief, sorrow or loss; Alas! Ah! ཀྱི་ཧུད་ཟེར་བ *kyi-hud zer-wa* हाहा वत expressing deep sorrow or lamentation. 2. one of the eight cold hells of the Buddhist purgatory.

ཀྱིག་རྩེ *kyig-rtse* unburnt brick (*Sch.*).

ཀྱིང་ *Kyiṅ* n. of a people living in the east of Asia (*Yig. 8*).

ཀྱིང་སེར་རླུང་ *kyiṅ ser-rluṅ* a violent wind with hail: acc. to *Jä.* also ཀྱ་ས *kya-sa*, onomatopoetic word; a blowing wind.

ཀྱིན *kyin* a verbal termination used alternatively with གྱིན *gyin* and གིན *gin* and after a vowel; ཡིན *yin* denoting a partic. pres. like the English '*ing*': གླུ་འདེབས་ཀྱིན་སོང་ proceed on your way singing! With ཡོད *yod* or འདུག *hdug* it forms a periphrastical present tense: སྨོན་ལམ་འདེབས་ཀྱིན་ཡོད *smon-lam hdebs-kyin yod* he is praying (just now) (*Jä.*). Most probably the common present form in *kyi*, *gi*, &c., is an excised form of this use, *e.g.*, ཡོང་གི་འདུག is coming; ལྟ་ཀྱི་རེད is looking.

ཀྱིར *kyir*, also ཀྱིར་ཀྱིར *kyir-kyir*, round; circular; a disk; a round thing; ཀྱིར་བ་ཉིད *kyir-wa-ñid* roundness.

ཀྱིས *kyis* by, with; the sign of the instrumental case, used after the letters ད, བ, or ས, and generally indicating the personal subject of the action. It is called the བྱེད་པ་པོའི་སྒྲ *byed-pa pohi sgra* (the term of the doer). Gerundially *kyis* is annexed to a verbal root to render clauses which in English would be introduced with "by," "from," &c., *e.g.*, རལ་གྲིས་མཆིན་པ་ཐིགས་ཀྱིས་བསད་དོ from the sword having pierced the liver, he was slain. Of course the prep. "from" might be omitted here. Again our "because" is often an appropriate opening to clauses terminated in ཀྱིས; གྱིས, &c.: འགོང་པོ་བྱུན་གྱིས་ཁོས་ཟུལ་སོང the demon coming, he turned aside; or, because the demon came, he, &c.

ཀྱུ *kyu* अङ्कुश a hook; ལྕགས་ཀྱུ *lcags-kyu* iron hook; an angle; a fishing hook; ཞབས་ཀྱུ *shabs-kyu* (*i.e.*, the foot-hook) a mark fixed at the foot of a letter to signify the vowel 'u' and written as ུ

ཀྱུར་ཀྱུར *kyur-kyur* twittering; the cry of a small bird: བྱིའུ་ཅོ་ག་ཀྱུར་ཀྱུར་སྒྲོག *byihu coga kyur-kyur sgrog* the swallow twitters.

ཀྱེ *kye* हे, भोः the vocative sign; O! Holla! ཀྱེ *kye* is called འབོད་པའི་སྒྲ *bbod-paḥi sgra* or interjection—the word of invocation or calling: ཀྱེ་རྒྱལ་པོ་ཆེན་པོ། O great King! ཀྱེ་ནོར་བུ་པད་མ O lotus-gem (Chenraisi).

ཀྱེ་ཀྱེ *Kye-kye*, also written ཀྱེ for abbreviation; conveys the same meaning as ཀྱེ.

ཀྱེ་རྡོ་རྗེ *Kye-rdo-rje* हे वज्र n. of a terrific *Tantrik* deity.

ཀྱེ་ག *kye-ga* n. for the magpie.

ཀྱེ་ཕང་པ *Kye-phañ-pa* n. of an idol of the Nying-ma sect, consisting, like most of the popular idols in Tibet, of an enchanted stick or log decked with rags, but much dreaded and said to be identical with *Pe-dkar Gyalpo* (*Jä.*).

ཀྱེ་མ *kye-ma* हा बत (interj.) Alas! An expression of surprise with sorrow, also of misery; ཀྱེ་མ་མ་ལ *kye-ma-ma-la* अहो बत but oh! an interjection expressive of desire for compassion or fatigue: ཀྱེ་མ་མ་ལ་གླང་པོ་འདི *kye-ma ma-la glañ-po ḥdi* alas this elephant! (*A. K. 1-36*).

ཀྱེ་རེ *kye-re* or ཀེ་རེ *ke-re*, also ཀྱེར *kyer*, upright, erect; ཀྱེ་རེ་བ *kye-re-wa* or ཀྱེ་རེ་ཉིད *kye-re-ñid* the act of standing erect.

ཀྱེ་ཧུད *kye-hud* (interj.) अहो, हा कष्टं Alas! Woe! Ah! What misery! An expression of grief or pain; ཀྱེ་ཧོ *kye-ho* What oh! Holla! ཀྱེ་ཧོ་ཀྭ་ཡེ་འབོད་པའི་ཚིག། *kye-ho* and *kwa-ye* are exclamatory words.

ཀྱོ་བ *kyo-wa* अङ्कुश a pointed iron-hook; a large pin to pierce with.

ཀྱོ་རང *kyo-rañ*, v. ཀྱོ་བ *kyo-wa*.

ཀྱོག *kyog*, also ཀྱོག་ཀྱོག वक्र, crooked, bent, winding, curved: མགོ་བོ་ཀྱོག་ཀྱོག་བྱས། having turned his head (sideways). ལམ་ཀྱོག *lam-kyog* a winding or surpentine road; a zig-zag.

ཀྱོག་པོ *Kyog-po* वक्र crooked; ཀྱོག་པོར *kyog-por* crookedly, not straight: རི་དྭགས་ཁྲིངས་རྣམས་མགྲིན་པ་ཀྱོགས་ཏེ་བྲོས་སོང (*Pag. 133*) the wild animals that conceal themselves bending their necks ran away.

ཀྱོང I: *kyoñ* or ཀྱོང་ཀྱོང *kyoñ-kyoñ* 1. बिल hollow; cavity; the hollow of a dish or tray; cognate to ཀོང་ *koñ*. 2. obstinate; unmanageable (*Jä.*). 3. hard, as in ཆུ་ཀྱོང་པོ, hard water; evidently a colloq. form of ཆུ་གྱོང་པོ.

ཀྱོང II: or ཀྱོང་བུ *kyoñ-bu* a small shovel, scraper; ཀྱོང་ཁ *kyoñ-kha* quarrel (*Sch.*).

ཀྱོམ *kyom* flexible but without elasticity; flabby, loose, lax.

ཀྱོམ་པ *kyom-pa* soft and tough; ཀྱོམ་པ་ཉིད *kyom-pa-ñid* pliancy; toughness.

ཀྱོམ་ཀྱོམ *kyom-kyom* of irregular shape, not rectilinear (*Jä.*).

ཀྱོར *kyor* or ཀྱོར་ཀྱོར *kyor-kyor* weak, feeble, unfortified (*Cs.*).

ཀྱོལ *kyol* or ཀྱོལ་ཀྱོལ *kyol-kyol*=ཀྱོར *kyor*.

ཀྲ *Kra* (*ṭa*) for ས་ཀྲ, ཀྲ་བཙུགས *kra-btsugs* established a Dharmaśālā (*A. 61*).

ཀྲ་མ་ཤར་ཥ *kra-ma çar-ṣa* n. of a kind of precious stone: "པད་མ་ར་གའི་ཁང་བརྩེགས་རབ་མཐོ་བ་ཀྲ་མ་ཤར་ཥའི་བ་གམ། (*Rtsii. 41*) a house built of ruby made lofty with a dome of *krama çarṣa*.

ཀྲག *krag* (*ṭag*)=བྲག *brag*, signifying rock.

ཀྲང་ངེ *krañ-ñe* (*ṭang-ñe*) standing; ཀྲང་ངེ་བ or ཀྲང་ངེ་བ་ཉིད an upright posture; ཀྲང་སྡོད་པ *krañ-sdod-pa* to stand.

ཀྲང་ནང་ *Krañ-nañ* (*ṭang-nang*) a gallery round a house; a covered passage; evidently an incorrect form of སྐང་ནང་.

ཀྲང་བ *krañ-wa* (*ṭang-wa*), prob. wrongly written for དྲང་པོ་བྱེད་པ, to make straight.

ཀྲད་འཁོར *krad-ḥkhor* (*ṭé-khor*) a ring used in the exercise of archery as a butt for arrows; a mark; a target.

ཀྲད་རྒྱུན *krad-rgyun* (*ṭé-gyün*) a piece of long narrow leather to mend shoes with; acc. to *Cs.* a long narrow piece of leather to fasten the sole to the upper leather of a shoe or boot.

ཀྲད་པ *krad-pa* (*ṭé-pa*) a shoe; a covering for the feet of the lower classes of people; a leathern half-boot; ཀྲད་ལྷན *krad-lhan* a patch for shoe.

ཀྲན་མ *kran-ma* (*ṭan-ma*), colloq. for སྲན་མ *sran-ma*, peas.

ཀྲབ་ཀྲབ *krab-krab* (*ṭab-ṭab*) = འཁྲབ་པ dancing or stamping of the feet: རྐང་ལག་ཀྲབ་ཀྲབ་བྲོ་འཁྲབ་པ (his) legs and arms moved as in dancing. According to *Ṅag.* ཀྲབ་ཀྲབ is equivalent to ལེབ་ལེབ, flat.

ཀྲམ *kram* (*ṭam*) cabbage; ཀྲམ་མངར sweet or fresh cabbage; ཀྲམ་སྐྱུར *kram skyur* cabbage-pickle; cabbage soaked in vinegar.

‡ ཀྲི་ཀ་རུ་ཀ *Kri-ka-ru-ka* कृकवक n. of a monastery in ancient Behar which was also known by the names of Samudra Gupta and Kusumapuri (*A. 60*).

‡ ཀྲི་ཀ་ལཱ་ཥ *kri-ka lā-ṣa* कृकलास a small lizard.[2] There is an account of this animal being once offered as a burnt sacrifice to the gods (*K. d.* ཡ *214*).

‡ ཀྲི་ཀྲི *Kri-kri* क्रिकि, कृकि n. of a Buddhist king of Benares who is said to have patronized Buddha Kās'yapa. In the Chinese version of the Vimala-kīrti-nirdes'a sûtra, he is called Kṛpin, the kind and merciful.

ཀྲི་ཁ *kri-kha* (*ṭi-kha*) the magpie; the white-breasted magpie; colloq. called *kya-ka* in Tibet.

ཀྲི་བ་ཤཱའི་གདོང *Kri-wa shaḥi-gdoñ* n. of a place in Tibet (*J. Zañ.*).

ཀྲི་མི *kri-mi* (*ṭi-mi*) = བྱ་གག *bya-gag* 1. the grey duck (*Mṅon.*). 2. कृमि a worm.

ཀྲི་ཡ *kriya* क्रिया; ཀྲི་ཡ་བྱ་བའི་རྒྱུད the ritualistic part of Sambhawa mysticism: དེ་ཀྲི་ཡའི་སྔགས་དྲུག་ཕྱག་དྲུག་གིས་བྱེད་པ་ཡིན་ནོ། (*A. 74*) the *kṛyā man-tra* having been performed by the six-armed deity.

ཀྲི་ཤོང་བ་རོ *Kri-çoñ-ba-ro* n. of an individual who did some service to Atis'a during his journey to Tibet through Nepal (*A. 142*).

ཀྲིག་ཀྲིག *krig-krig* (*ṭig-ṭig*) = ནན་ནན to beat or press with the hand or feet; to make the sound *ṭig-ṭig*.

ཀྲིག་གི *krig-gi* (*ṭig-gi*) straight: ལྕགས་ཀྱི་མདའ་ནི་ཀྲིག་གི་བཟང་ནས། the iron arrow when quite straight being good (*D.R.*).

ཀྲིག་ཆགས་མེད་པ *krig-cags med-pa* སྔར་ནས་ལུགས་སྲོལ་མེད་པ་བཅས་དོན་དག་མེད་པ། not customary or purposelessly; for nothing: རྒྱུན་དུ་སོག་པོའི་རིགས་ཀྲིག་ཆགས་མེད་པའི་ཞུ་ཞུ་ཡོད་པར། Mongol tribes without adhering to custom would always be making prayers (*D. çel.10*).

ཀྲིང་ཀང་ *kriñ-kañ* (*ṭiñ-kañ*) a weapon like the spear; a forked spear: མདུང་དང་ཀྲིང་ཀང་འདྲ་བ་མི་བཙམ་རེར། (to the cost of) a spear and lance with saw-like teeth (*Ṛtsii.*).

ཀྲིང་བག་སྒྱོ *kriñ-bag-ṣgyo* (*ṭiñ-pag-gyo*) glue or paste made of flour.

ཀྲིན་ནད་ *krin-naḍ* (*ṭin-ne'*) the colic.

ཀྲིཥྞ *Krisṇa* कृष्ण n. of sculptor; an image-maker during Atis'a's time about 1000 A.D. (*A. 121*).

ཀྲིཥྞ་སཱ་ར *Kriṣ-ṇa-sā-ra* कृष्णसार the spotted antelope (*Jä.*); a kind of black antelope which is said to possess the heart of a *Bodhisattva.* The skin of this animal is used by Hindus and Buddhists alike to sit upon; the Tibetan lamas attach much sanctity to this antelope and its skin.

ཀྲུ་ཀྲུ *kru-kru* (*ṭu-ṭu*) (*W.*) wind-pipe (*Jä.*).

+ ཀྲུ་ཀྲུ་ཏྲིས *kru-kru triṣ* (*ṭu-ṭu ṭi*) चित्रक a kind of yellow chintz resembling satin of great value, formerly highly prized in India and Tibet. It is called ཀྲུང་བང་རྒྱ་སེར་གོས་ཆེན.

ཀྲུ་ར *kru-ra* (*ṭu-ra*) = དམངས་རིགས *ḍmañṣ-rigṣ* the vulgar, or the lowest class of people in the mystical language (*K. g.* ཀ *28*).

ཀྲུང་ཀྲུང་སྒྲ་ཅན *Kruñ-kruñ ṣgra-can* (*ṭuñg-ṭuñg-ḍa-can*) n. of a country (filled with the cry of storks or cranes) said to have been visited by the Buddha (*K. du.* ཀ *302*).

ཀྲུང་ཐང་ *Kruñ-thañ* the chief Chinese minister who was resident in Tibet when Abbé Huc visited Lhasa; an official of his class (*Yig. k. 38*). Probably an error for *Chung t'ang*, a title borne by certain high officials in China.

ཀྲུམ་པ *krum-pa* (*ṭum-pa*) broken in the edge or side or nibbled, but not entirely broken to pieces.

ཀྲུམས *Krumṣ* (*ṭum*) meat: in polite language it is called གསོལ་ཀྲུམས (*sol-ṭum*), the meat that is offered to a respected person.

ཀྲེ་ཉག *Kre-ñag* (*ṭe-ñag*) n. of a place in Kham.

ཀྲེ་ནག *krag-nag* (*ṭe-nag*) the spout of a kettle (*Sch.*).

ཀྲེ་པ *kre-pa* (*ṭe-pa*) the forehead; also a colloq. spelling for དཔྲལ་པ *ḍpral-pa*, the forehead.

ཀྲེ་བོ *Kre-ḅo* (*ṭe-o*) n. of a place in Kham.

‡ ཀྲོ་དྷ་ན *kro dha-na* क्रोधना = བུད་མེད་གཏུམ་མོ a fierce woman; an amazon (*Ṃñon.*).

ཀྲོག་ཀྲོག *krog-krog* (*ṭog-ṭog*) a kind of sound produced by the grinding of hard or brittle objects together: ཀྲོག་ཀྲོག་ནི་སྒྲ་སྐད "*ṭog-ṭog* is a sound" (*Ñag.*); *ṭog-ṭog* is an onomatopoetic word meaning a grating sound.

ཀྲོང་ *kroñ* (*ṭoñ*) erect; standing: ལུས་ཐད་ཀྲོང་། the body erectly stood.

ཀྲོང་ཀྲོང *kroñ-kroñ* (*ṭong-ṭong*) standing; posing still and erect: སློབ་མ་གཉིས་ཀྱིས་མཐོང་བར་ལྷ་དངོས་སུ་ཀྲོང་ཀྲོང་བྱུང་ནུས་པ། (*A. 27*) "while the two pupils were looking on, the deity was able to appear erect as if in life." When used of persons, it means also standing on one's knees; kneeling in an upright position (*Jä.*).

ཀྲོང་རྩེ་ *kroṅ-rtse* (*toṅg-tse*) n. of a kind of round writing anciently used in China: དེ་དུས་ཀྱི་ཡི་གེ་ནི་ཀྲོང་རྩེ་ཞེས་པ་འཁོར་ཡིག་ཡིན་པ་ལ། the characters of that time were circular letters called *Toṅg-tse*. The word ཀྲོང་རྩེ *kroṅ-rtse* seems to be a corruption of the Chinese *tang-ch'ien*, copper cash. Tibetans say ཏྲང་ཙེ་བརྒྱ་ཚན་བ "a hundred cash."

ཀྲོན་ཀྲོན་ *kron-kron* (*ton-ton*) in *W.* hanging; dangling.

ཀླ་རྩི་ *kla-rtsi* musk: कस्तूरी this is an incorrect spelling of the word གླ་རྩི *gla-tsi*.

ཀླ་ཀློ་ *kl-klo* म्लेच्छ, तुरुष्क, तीवर, अनार्य्य 1. a barbarian: ཀྱི་ཧུད་གླ་གློ་དུད་འགྲོ་ཀླུ། *kyi-hud gla-glo dud hgro klu* (*Zam. 2*) "Alas, the Mleccha, the beasts, and the *Nāga*!" 2. any Musalman of India, a Hwi-hwi or Hwi-tse in China. 3. a nation without laws; a barbarous, uncivilized race.

ཀླ་ཀློ་ཁ *kla-klo-kha* = ཟངས *zaṅs* copper (*Mṅon.*).

* ཀླ་ཀློ་རྣམས *kla-klo rnams* म्लेच्छाः the barbarians (*Schr.*).

ཀླ་ཀློའི་ཁ *kla-klohi kha* म्लेच्छमुख a Musalman's mouth; = ཁ་ཆེ *kha-che* "a wide mouthman," *i.e.*, a Musalman of Kashmir.

* ཀླ་ཀློའི་ཆོས *kla-klohi chos* शब्दधर्म (*Schr.*) "religion on the lips."

ཀླ་ཀློའི་ཏིག་ཏ *kla-klohi tig-ta* several bitter roots growing in the sub-Himālayan regions; one is also called མོན་གྱི་ཏིག་ཏ *Gentiana cheretta* (*Mṅon.*).

ཀླ་ཀློའི་སྤོས *kla-klohi spos* = སྒོག་པ garlic (*Mṅon.*).

ཀླ་ཀློའི་འཕེལ *kla-klohi hphel* यवनवर्द्धन, तुरुष्कवर्द्धन n. of a Turuṣka (Tartar) King; lit. growth of the *Yavana* or the *Mleccha*; ཀླ་ཀློའི་བྱེ་བྲག *kla-klohi bye-brag* तुरुष्क विशेष a tribe of Turuṣka; a Tartar.

ཀླག་ཅོར *klag-cor* कोलाहल, ध्वनि clamour, noise: ཀླག་ཅོར་ཆུང་བ less noisy: ཀླག་ཅོར་མང་དུ་སྒྲུམ་པ་དང་། "having made a row about."

ཀླག་པ *klag-pa* 1. अध्ययन study, reading; ཀླག་པའི་སློབ་དཔོན། पाठाचार्य्य a teaching professor, a teacher: ཀླག་པའི་བརྟུལ་ཞུགས་ཡོངས་རྫོགས་པ། "has completed his vow of study" (*A. K. 30*), v. ཀློག་པ *klog-pa* to read, peruse; ཀླགས *klags* पठित, is pret. of ཀློག་པ. 2. अवतार to incarnate: ཀླགས་ལྟ་བ अवतारप्रेक्षिन् waiting for or expectant of one's advent or incarnation; in Aṣṭa. अवतारप्रेक्षिन् "one who finds fault with"; ཀླགས་མི་ཁྲུགས = ཀླགས་མི་རྙེད not incarnated or obtained an incarnated state: སྟོང་པ་ཉིད་ནས་སྟོང་པ་ཉིད་ལ་ཀླགས་མི་རྙེད་དོ། "there cannot be transmigration from one to another state of emptiness." (This is in reference to the eighteen states of *Sūnyatā.*)

ཀླགས *klags*, v. ཀློག *klog*.

ཀླད *klad* ཀླད་ཅེས་པ་གོང་ངམ་སྟེང་དུ་ཞེས་པའི་དོན། 1. "the word *klad* means above or upward" (*Ṅag.*); ཀླད་ལ་བསྐོར་ནས revolving round overhead (*A. 155*). 2. मस्तिष्क, मस्तक head; brain; it is also written as ཀླད་པ ཀླད་སྐོར, same as ང་རོ, a dot or cypher placed on the top or head of a letter to denote the abbreviation of the letter མ *ma*, which is commonly used in writing and occasionally in printing. 3. first; ཀླད་ནས from the first: གཅན་གཟན་སེང་གེའི་ཕྲུ་གུ་དེ། སྡེར་ཆགས་ཐམས་ཅད་ཀླད་ནས་འཛོམས as to lion's cubs, their claws are prominent from the first.

ཀླད་རྒྱ *klad rgya* membrane covering the brain; *pia mater*; ཀླད་རྒྱུས་ལྷ་པ the bloody marrow in the bones (*Schr.*); ཀླད་སྒོ *klad sgo* the fontanel in the infant cranium (*Schr.*).

ཀླད་ཆུང་ *klad chuñ* the cerebellum; ཀླད་གཞུང་ *klad gshuñ* the spinal marrow; ཀླད་གཟེར་ *klad gzer* painful pricking sensation in the brain; ཀླད་ཤུབས་ or ཀླད་ཤུ the thin covering of the brain.

ཀླད་ཐོ *klad-tho* the top length of a Tibetan tent, *i.e.*, the distance between its two poles.

ཀླད་དོན *klad-don* lit. signifies the meaning of the text or the original work, but is gen. used as a term for the Sanskrit names or expressions which head almost all the religious books of Tibet. The work *Mñon.* makes ཀླད synonymous with ཀླད་རྒྱས the amplification of the original text.

ཀླད་པ *klad-pa* उपरि what is uppermost; ཀླད་མ *klad-ma* आदि priority, beginning, top.

ཀླད་པ་འགེམས་པ *klad-pa hgems-pa* lit. whose brains have become confounded; to stun; to surprise; to confound; to overthrow in argument.

ཀླད་བཟོ *klad-bzo* the making of the outer side of anything: ཀླད་བཟོ་སྦུག་ཐེར་སྐབས་དང་བསྟུན་པར་བྱ། *klad bzo sbug ther skabs dañ bstun-bar bya* this outer covering and the flannel within must be made to fit in their size (*Yig. 22*).

ཀླན་ཀ *klan-ka* उपालम्भ censure, blame; ཀླན་ཀ་མི་འཚོལ་བ *klan-ka mi htshol-wa* one not seeking brawls: གཞན་ལ་སྐྱོན་འཚོལ་བ་ལ་ཀླན་ཀ་འཚོལ་བ་ཟེར casting imputations against another is called *klan-ka htshol-wa*; རྩོད་པ་བསྐོད་པ་ལ་ཡང་ཀླན་ཀ་ཟེར also fomenting a dispute is called *klan-ka*; ཀླན་ཀ་འཚོལ་བ=ཀླན་ཀ་བསམ་པ; उपालम्भप्रिय one who seeks brawls; ཀླན་བྱེད་པ or ཀླན་ཀ་བྱེད་པ or ཀླན་ཀ་འདེབས་པ or སྐུར་ཀླན to censure, blame.

ཀླན་པ *klan-pa* 1. revenge; wrong avenged; to wreak vengeance for: བྱ་རོག་གིས་འུག་པ་ལ་ཤ་ཀླན་པ་ཞེས་པས་ལེན་པའི་དོན (*Lo. 9*) the crow revenges itself upon the owl by what is called flesh-revenge.

ཀླན་བྱ *klan-bya* part to be mended or to be patched.

ཀླམ་པ *klam-pa* स्थूलकम्बल a thick blanket; also a *pagri* or turban used by Tibetans when travelling: ཀླམ་ཞེས་པ་མགོ་ལ་དཀྲི་རྒྱུའི་རས་རིང་པོའི་མིང་ (*K. du.* ཀ *121*) *klam* the term for a long piece of cloth which is tied round the head.

ཀླལ་བ *klal-wa*=བསྒྱིངས་པ *bsgyiñs-pa* or བྱ་བསྙངས་པ *bya bsñañs-pa* विजृम्भण, yawning; to yawn.

ཀླས *klas* उत्त, उग्र copious, abundant; an equivalent of ཡས *yas*, beyond, apart, as in འབུམས་ཀླས, མཐའ་ཀླས *mthah klas* or མཐའ་ཡས (अनन्त). In this case ཀླས may be taken to mean "without,' and is an equivalent of the Sanskrit ब.

ཀླིང་མ *kliñ-ma* or གླིང་མ पुलिन, the margin of a river or lake.

ཀླུ I: *klu* नाग n. of a kind of flower (*K. my.* ཀ *20*).

ཀླུ II: नाग, तक्षक, नमुचि, दिक्कमल 1. the Indian *Naga*, that is, a demi-god having the human head and the body of a serpent, which is generally supposed to live in fountains, rivers, and lakes. The *Lu* are also believed to be the guardian of great treasures under-ground; they are able to cause rain and certain maladies, and become dangerous when angry. 2. a serpent or any snake in general.

ཀླུ་ཀུན་ཏུ་དགའ་བའི་ཟློས་གར *klu kun-tu dgah-wahi zlos-gar* the drama of Nāgānanda;

ཟློས་གར་གྱི་ ཀླུ་བ་ཅོས་ དགའ་བའི་ ལུས་མཛད་པའི་མིང་། a dramatic treatise by Harṣadeva (*Ya-sel. 230*).

ཀླུ་ཁང་ *klu-khaṅ* the residence of the *Lu* or serpent gods. An imaginary palace supposed to exist at the bottom of the sea or of some lake where the *Nāga* reside: ཀླུ་ཁང་སྐྱིད་ཚལ་བཅས་བློ་ལས་གཟིགས་སོ (*Jig.*) saw the palace of the *Lu* and their grove with delight.

ཀླུ་གླང་ནག་པོ་བ་རུ་ཅན *klu-glaṅ nag-po ba-ru can*=སྡིག་སྲིན the crab which is called by the Tibetans "bull-horned black *Lu*" (*Sman. 144*).

* ཀླུ་རྒྱལ *klu-rgyal* नागराज (*Schr.*).

ཀླུ་རྒྱལ་དཀར་པོ་དུང་སྐྱོང་ *Klu-rgyal dkar-po duṅ-skyoṅ* नागराज-शुभ्र-शङ्ख-पाल n. of a certain *Nāga Rājā* or a serpent demi-god called the White Protector of Conch Shells: ཀླུ་རྒྱལ་དཀར་པོ་དུང་སྐྱོང་དང་འཛིན་པ་ལག་མང་སོགས the *Lu* ruler called white S'ankhapāla and S'ankhadhara Bahu Pāṇi, the deity with many arms, and others (*Rtsii. 44*).

ཀླུ་རྒྱལ་མཐའ་ཡས *klu-rgyal mthah-yas* अनन्त infinite; the king of the snakes described in Hindu mythology (*Mṅon.*); one of the eight ཀླུ་ཆེན *klu-chen*, great *Lu*.

ཀླུ་རྒྱལ་རིགས་ལྔ *klu-rgyal rigs-lṅa* the five classes among the *Naga Rājā* or *Lu* kings residing in the fabulous world of the snakes.

ཀླུ་སྒྲུབ *Klu-sgrub* (*Lu-ḍub*) नागार्जुन the expounder of the Madhyamika school of Buddhist philosophy.

ཀླུ་ཆེན་བརྒྱད *klu-chen brgyad* the eight chiefs of the Lu or Naga are མཐའ་ཡས अनन्त; འཇོག་པོ तक्षक; ནོར་རྒྱས वासुकी; དུང་སྐྱོང་ शङ्खपाल; པད་མ पद्म; པད་མ་ཆེན་པོ महापद्म; སྟོབས་ལྡན बलवत; རིགས་ལྡན कुलीन, कुलिक.

ཀླུ་འཇོག་པོ *klu hjog-po* तक्षक the class of *Lu* or *Nāga* called *Takṣaka*.

ཀླུ་ཐེབས *klu-thebs* the coming forth of the *Lu* in summer from their retreats. This time is fixed in Tibetan almanacs for worshipping them: དབྱར་ས་སྟེང་དུ་ཀླུ་ཧོང་བ་ལ་ཀླུ་ཐེབས་ཟེར *db yar-sa steṅ-du klu hoṅ-wa la klu-thebs zer* the coming upwards of the *Lu* from their retreats in summer is called ཀླུ་ཐེབས *klu-thebs*.

ཀླུ་ལྡོག *klu-ldog* the retiring of the *Lu* to their abodes in the nether regions is called ཀླུ་ལྡོག *klu-ldog*, which time is generally calculated by the Tibetan astrologers to fall in December.

ཀླུ་མཐར་བྱེད *klu mthar byed* शेषनाग the chief patriarch of the *Nāga*; also नागान्तक, which is a name of the Garuḍa bird.

ཀླུ་དུག *klu-dug*=ཐུལ་འབྲུམ་བླ་བའི་རྩ་བོ་ཅན། དུག་ངན་པ་ཞིག་གི་མིང 1. n. of an indolent poison. 2. n. of a very venomous snake (*Smaṅ. 350*).

ཀླུ་དུག་ཅན *klu dug-can* poisonous snakes.

ཀླུ་གདོན་འཇོམས་བྱེད *klu-gdon hjoms-byed*=རྒྱལ་པོ་སྨུག་པོ *rgyal-po smug-po* lit. that which destroys poison or kills *Lu* demons=གླ་རྩི musk (*Sman. 333*).

ཀླུ་བདུད་རྡོ་རྗེ *klu-bdud rdor-je* n. of a medicinal plant which is believed to have the property of healing all sorts of diseases caused by *Lu* or malignant spirits.

ཀླུ་མདུད *klu-mdud* prob. *Codonopsis ovata* (*Jä.*) also ཀླུའི་གནོད་པ *kluhi gnod-pa* cures all kinds of arthritis and rheumatism (*W.*).

ཀླུ་སྡིངས *klu-sdiṅs* नागसानु the peaks or flanks of a mountain where snakes reside.

ཀླུ་ནད *klu-nad* नागरोग, कुष्ठरोग the disease caused by the *Lu* or leprosy.

ཀླུ་གནས *klu-gnas* नागवृत the abode of the *Lu.*

* ཀླུ་བོད *klu-bod* नागाह्वय one of the disciples of Nāgārjuna (*Schr.*).

* ཀླུ་བྱང *klu-byañ* नागबोधि an epithet of Nāgārjuna and also that of one of his disciples.

ཀླུ་དབང་གི་རྒྱལ་པོ *klu-dwañ-gi rgyal-po* a Buddha ruling over the *Lu*, usually depicted with 4 attendant *Bodhisattva* (*Grüb. 109*).

ཀླུ་འབུམ *Klu-hbum* n. of a section of the *Sgomáñ* division of the monastery of དཔལ་ལྡན་འབྲས་སྤུངས *Dpal-ldan Hbras-spuñs* (Daipung near Lhasa): དཔལ་ལྡན་འབྲས་སྤུངས་སྒོ་མང་པའི་ཁམས་ཚན། ཧོར་གདོང་བསམ་བློ་ཀླུ་འབུམ། the Gomang sections of Daipung Monastery are the Hordong, Sam-lo and Lubum; n. of a treatise on a hundred thousand *Nāga.*

ཀླུ་འབུམ་ཁྲ་བོ *klu-hbum khra-bo* 1. n. of a religious work among the *Bon-po.* 2. ཁྲ་བོ *khra-bo* means "mottled." There are also ཀླུ་འབུམ་དཀར་པོ *klu-hbum dkar-po,* ཀླུ་འབུམ་ནག་པོ *klu-hbum nag-po. Klu-hbum,* originally a hooded snake, *cobra di capello ;* the mythological sense, however, is only understood in Tibet, where every child knows and believes in *Lu* or Nāgas, &c., cobras being unknown.

ཀླུ་མེས *klu-mes* བླ་མ་ཞིག་གི་མཚན། (*Deb. 46*) n. of a lama of Tibet.

ཀླུ་མོ *klu-mo* a female serpent; also a serpent demoness.

ཀླུ་མོ་མུ་ཏིག་ནུ་ཤོ་ཅན *klu-mo mu-tig nu-sho-can* n. of medicinal plant used for wounds or sores. Its flowers are of garnet colour; when they are plucked there oozes out a milkish sap which is said to possess healing power (*Sman. 350*).

ཀླུ་སྨན *klu-sman* n. of a medicine.

ཀླུ་གཟུགས *klu-gzugs* the body or likeness of a snake; also a *Lu* in the body of a snake; anything with the body or in the guise of a snake.

ཀླུའི་སྐད *kluhi skad* the language of the *Nāga*; according to some Tibetan authors this is the Nāgari language of India which they identify with the Prākrit. According to the earliest historians of Tibet ཀླུའི་སྐད *kluhi skad, i.e.,* the *Nāga bhāṣā,* was the language of the Chinese: རྒྱ་ནག་པ་ཀླུ་ལས་ཆད་པས *Rgya-nag-pa klu-las chad-pas,* ནཱ་ག་ཀྲི་ཏ་ཀླུའི་སྐད་དུ་སྨྲ། the Chinese having *originated* from the serpent demi-gods, speak the *Nāga kṛta,* the language of the *Lu.* ནཱ་ག་ཀྲི་ཏ *nāga kṛta* is distinguished from the Sanskrit language which is called *Deva bhāṣā,* the language of the gods. *Nāga-kṛta* means corrupt language and *Sans-kṛta* means refined language.

ཀླུའི་གྲོང་ཁྱེར *kluhi groñ-khyer* नागनगरी, भोगवती the mythological city of the *Nāga* in the nether world ruled by King S'eṣa.

ཀླུའི་འཇིག་རྟེན *kluhi hjig-rten* नागलोक the nether world or region inhabited by the *Lu* or *Nāga.*

ཀླུའི་དུག་བཅོམ *Kluhi dug-bcom* n. of a fabulous sea which lies beyond a great sandy desert. The *Lu* chieftain *Stobs-ldan* (*Balarán*) resides there and excites dissensions among living beings (*K. d.* ར *335*).

ཀླུའི་གདེངས་ཀ *kluhi gdeñs-ka* the hood or neck of a *Nāga* or of a serpent.

* ཀླུའི་སྡེ *Kluhi-sde* नागसेन (*Schr.*) n. of the celebrated Buddhist sage who answered the interrogations of King Menander (of Milinda Pannha); one of the eighty Buddhist saints of the northern school.

ཀླུའི་གནོད་པ *kluhi gnod-pa* or ཀླུའི་སྐྱོན *kluhi skyon,* plague; a disease of unknown origin;

maladies supposed to be originated from the malignity of the serpent demi-gods.

* ཀླུའི་བྱང་ཆུབ་ *kluhi byañ-chub* नागबोधि (*Schr.*).

ཀླུའི་སྦྲུལ་ *kluhi sbrul* पन्नग a class of very venomous snakes.

ཀླུའི་ཡི་གེ *kluhi yi-ge* नाग अक्षर acc. to *Cs.* the Chinese character; acc. to some authors the *Nāgari* character.

* ཀླུའི་བཤེས་གཉེན *klui bçes-gñen* नागमित्र (*Schr.*) n. of a Buddhist saint.

ཀླུ་ཡི་སྐད *klu-yi skad* नागभाषा the language of the *Nāga*: ལེགས་སྦྱར་གྱི་སྐད་དང་ཡང་ན་ཀླུ་ཡི་སྐད་དུ་གསུངས་ན་གོ་གསུངས། it is said that (he) understood (it) when related in the Sanskrit or in the language of the *Nāga*.

ཀླུ་ཡི་འཁྲི་ཤིང *klu-yi hkhri-çiñ*=སོ་མའི་འཁྲི་ཤིང n. of a leafy creeping plant (*Mñon.*).

ཀླུ་ཡི་ལྕེ *klu-yi lce*=ཤལ་རྡེས་སྨན lit. the snako's tongue; n. of a plant used in medicine.

Syn. སྔོ་སངས་འཁྲི་ཤིང *sño-sañs hkhri-çiñ*; སྔོ་སངས་མཐའ་ཡས *sño-sañs mthah-yas*; མཐའ་ཡས་རྩ *mthah-yas rtsa*; བ་གླང་བསྲུང *ba-glañ bsruñ*; མེ་ཏོག་ཕྲ་མོ *me-tog phra-mo* (*Mñon.*).

ཀླུ་ཡི་གཞི *klu-yi gshi*=ས་གཞི the earth (*Mñon.*).

ཀླུ་ཤིང *klu-çiñ* नागवृक्ष lit. the snake-tree; सुवर्णत्वक् the tree of golden bark.

Syn. བུམ་ཅན *bum-can*; སྐྱེས་བུ་མཐོ *skyes-bu mtho*; ལྷའི་འདབ *lhahi hdab*; ལྷའི་ལྕུག་མ *lhahi lcug-ma*; སེང་གེ་སྐྲོད *señ-ge skrod*; ཀླུའི་མེ་ཏོག *kluhi me-tog*; གེ་སར་མར་པོ *ge-sar mar-po*; ཀླུ་སྐྱེས *klu-skyes* (*Mñon.*).

The names of some species of trees called *nāga vṛkṣa* are the following:—ཚད་ལྡན་འདབ་མ *tshad-ldan hdab- ma*; མེ་ཏོག་རྩེ *me-tog rtse*; ས་སྲུང *sa-sruñ*; ཀླུའི་མཚན *kluhi mtshan*; སོག་ལེ་སྒྲིབ *sog-le sgrib*; ཤུན་པ་དྲི་ཞིམ *çun-pa dri-shim*; རྩ་བ་མང *rtsa-wa mañ*; སའི་ཛམ་བུ་ཀ *sahi dsam-bu-ka* भूमिजम्बूक, the plant *Flacourtia spadia* (*Mñon.*).

ཀླུ་གཅེད་གསུམ *klu gçed gsum* the names of three medicines, viz., སྡིག་སྲིན *sdig-srin*, ཞལ་ནག *shal-nag* and བྱང་ནག *byañ-nag* (*Sman.* *450*).

ཀླུང *kluñ* a valley; river; ཆུ་ཀླུང *chu-kluñ* नदी a river in general; ནགས་ཀླུང *nags-kluñ* a river passing through wooded tracts; the name ཀླུང *kluñ* is seldom applied to small streams or rivulets.

ཀླུང་རྒྱུན *kluñ-rgyun* a stream, current; ཀླུང་རྒྱུན་ལྟར like the flow of a river.

ཀླུང་སྒོག *kluñ sgog* a kind of garlic growing wild on the margins of rivers in Tibet: ཀླུང་སྒོག་མཛེ་ཡི་མ་གསོ་སྐྲངས་ཆུ་སྐེམ། wild garlic cures leprous sores and dries up the fluids in swellings (*Med.*).

ཀླུང་རྟ *kluñ-rta* (in ནག་རྩིས *nag-rtsis* the art of divination)=རླུང་རྟ *rluñ-rta*.

ཀླུང་ཕྱུགས *kluñ-phyugs* cattle living in the lower table-lands of Tibet. This term is also applied to the yaks which are kept in the lower plains of Tibet: ཀླུང་ཕྱུགས་སོ་གཉིས་ཡན་གྱི་ཀོ་བ་རེར། *kluñ-phyugs so-gñis yan-gyi ko-wa rer* "for (*i.e.*, the price of) each hide of cattle of two teeth," (*i.e.*, above two years old) (*Rtsii.*).

ཀླུང་འབབ་པ *kluñ hbab-pa* the rushing of a hill torrent; the flowing of a river.

ཀླུང་མ *kluñ-ma* a river.

ཀླུང་ཚག *kluñ-tshag* a yak of the valley; རི་ཚག *ri-tshag* a hill yak—a yak belonging to the higher elevations and hill-tops of Tibet (*Rtsii.*).

ཀླུང་ཤོད *Kluñ-çod* n. of a place in the uplands of འབྲི་གུང (*Diguñ*) situated to the north-east of Lhasa (*Loñ.* ཟ *12*).

ཀླུང་ཚོས་ *kluṅ-ços* a kind of plant growing on the margins of rivers in Tibet, and said to be efficacious when applied to sores: ཀླུང་སྒོག *kluṅ-sgog* garlic of the valley.

ཀླུངས I: *kluṅs* this term is applied to the astrological results arrived at by computing one's age in reference to that of one's parents by consulting their horoscopes. It occurs in the *Vaidurya Karpo* in expressions such as ཕ་ཀླུངས, མ་ཀླུངས། *pha-kluṅs, ma-kluṅs.*

ཀླུངས II: cultivated lands; a field: ཀླུངས་སུ་སྐྱེ *kluṅs-su skye* grow on cultivated soil: དཀར་མདངས་ཀྱི་ཀླུངས་ཚང་མ *Dkar-mdaṅs-kyi kluṅs tshaṅ-ma* all fields belonging to *Dkar-hdaṅs.*

+ **ཀླུབ་པ** *Klub-pa*, pf. ཀླུབས་པ *klubs-pa*, 1. to cover the body with ornaments (*Jä.*); to put on luxuriously (*Cs.*): གསེར་ལེབ་རྟ་ཤིང་དག་ལས་ལེགས་གྲུབ་པའི་སེང་ཁེབས་རབ་འབྲིང་ཐ་མ་གསུམ་དུ་ཀླུབས *gser leb rta çiṅ dag-las legs grub-paḥi seṅ-khebs rab ḥbriṅ tha-ma gsum-du klubs* (*Jig.*). 2. to set up (a tenant). 3. n. of a tribe in Tibet (*Vai. kar. 160*).

ཀླུས་བོད *Klus bod* नागाह्वय, *Nāgā-hvaya*, one of the 28 Buddhist sages mentioned in the *M. V.*

ཀླུས་བྱང་ཆུབ *Klus byaṅ-chub* नागबोधि, *Nāga Bodhi*, one of the chief disciples of Nāgārjuna. His essence is supposed to have been embodied in the late Kusho Seng-chen of Tashi-lhünpo.

ཀླས *klas* a rack for clothes, clothes-horse.

ཀློག་པ *klog-pa* to read, imp. ཀློགས་ཤིག *klogs-çig* also ལྷོགས་ཤིག *lhogs-çig* do read, pf. ཀླགས་པ *klags-pa* or བཀླགས *bklags*, fut. ཀླག *klag* or བཀློག *bklog*, བཀླག་པར་བྱ *bklag-par-bya* ཀློག་པར་བྱེད *klog-par-byed* is reading; ཀློག་པར་བྱེད་པ *klog-par byed-pa* the act of reading, the causing to be read; ཀློག་བྱ *klog-bya* anything to be read; ཀློག་ཏུ་འཇུག་པ *klog-tu hjug-pa* to begin or cause one to read; ཀློག་པ་པོ *klog-pa po* or ཀློག་མཁན *klog-mkhan* a reader; ཀློག་གྲྭ *klog-grva* a reading school, a school for reading; དཔེ་ཆ་སོགས་ཀློག་པ *dpe-cha sogs klog-pa* reading books, &c. ཀློག་འདོན *klog-hdon* to read aloud; ཀློག་བྱང *klog-byaṅ* गुणनिका well-read, accomplished in reading, a scholar; ཀློག་པ་ཡང་ཀློག་པ *klog-pa yaṅ klog-pa* to read again.

ཀློག་ཐོབ *Klog-thob* n. of a *Bodhisattva* (*K. ko.* ཆ *50*).

ཀློང *kloṅ* I: or ཀློང་བ *kloṅ-pa* आवर्त extent; mass, bulk, body; depth, abyss. Also a wave or any undulating thing: ཀློང་དང་བཅས་པ सावर्त with opening or reverting folds or coils as in a conch shell.

ཀློང II: this word either alone or in combination with ཡངས *yaṅs* is generally used to express the idea of vastness, infinitude or immensity. It also signifies "space" as a definite expanse, being in a measure synonymous with དབྱིངས *dbyiṅs*: ཆོས་ཀྱི་ཀློང་ཡངས the immensity or profoundness of *Dharma*; ཆོས་ཀྱི་དབྱིངས धर्मधातु the expanse of matter or infinitude of phenomena; སེམས་ཉིད་ཀྱི་ཀློང་ the depth or amplitude of the mind: རྡོ་རྗེ་འཆང་དཔང་ཆོས་སྐུ་ལྷ་ལམ་མཐའ་བྲལ་ཀློང་ཡངས་ན, རྡོ་རྗེ་རྣལ་འབྱོར་ལོངས་སྐུ་ལྷ་ལྡན་ནམ་མཁའི་ནོར་བུ་རུ་རྒྱས། this spiritual being of Dorje chang developes in the wide boundless sphere of the gods into that jewel of the heavens which comprises the five illusive bodies of Dorje Naljor (*Nāro. 1*).

ཀློང III: centre or middle; = དབུས *dbus* or དཀྱིལ *dkyil* as in དབའ་ཀློང *dbah kloṅ* or

རྦ་ཀློང་ *rba-kloṅ* the eddy or whirlpool caused by རྦ *rba* or དབའ *dbaḥ*, the waves; དབའ་ཀློང་ *dbaḥ-kloṅ* or རྦ་ཀློང་ *rba-kloṅ* is also used to signify *rba-rlabs*, a wave, billow.

ཀློང་འཁོར་ *kloṅ-khor* a whirlpool or eddy (*Mṅon.*).

卐 ཀློང་ IV: ཀློང་དུ་གྱུར་པ *kloṅ-du gyur-pa* has the meaning of དབང་དུ་གྱུར་པ, under one's subjection or power; is equivalent to अवबोध fully comprehended; overpowered. It is also used to signify perfection in mystic arts, as Jäschke renders it "a soaring into mystic perfection." The work དག་འགྲེལ explains it in the following manner: ཡོངས་སུ་རྫོགས་པར་འདུས་པ་ལའང་འཇུག། "it is also applied (to mean) whatever has arrived at complete perfection or become concentrated into one."

ཀློང་ཆེན *Kloṅ-chen* n. of a celebrated lama of Tibet who was also called ཀློང་ཆེན་རབ་འབྱམས་པ.

ཀློང་སྡེ *kloṅ-sde* a division of the Buddhist writings of the མན་ངག उपदेश class, the introduction of which is attributed to *Lo-tsava* Vaira-tsana. བོད་ཀྱི་ཡུལ་འདིར་མན་ངག་རྫོགས་པ་ཆེན་པོར་གྲགས་པ་ལ་ལ་སེམས་སྡེ་དང་ཀློང་སྡེ་དང་མན་ངག་སྡེ "in this country of Tibet (in books) known as the great *Man-ṅag rdsogs-pa*, there are the *Sems* section, the *Loṅ* section, and the *Man-ṅag* section" (*Deb.* ག *3*).

ཀློང་མ་དཀྱེལ *kloṅ-ma dkyel* 1. of great capacity. 2. कुक्षि the cavity of the abdomen.

ཀློངས་པ *kloṅs-pa* लुठित, same as དཀྲུགས་པ *dkrugs-pa*.

ཀློངས་རག *Kloṅs rag* n. of a place in Tibet; ཀློངས་རག་གྲུ་ཁ the ferry at *Kloṅs-rag* (*Yig.*).

ཀློན་པ *klon-pa* to mend, to patch shoes, &c; ཀློན་པ་པོ a cobbler, mender of shoes.

ཀྵ *kṣa* in mystic language the term signifies an evil spirit.

ཀྵ་ཡ *kṣaya*, pronounced in Tibetan as ཤ་ཡ, क्षय *phthisis pulmonalis*; but according to the Tibetan pathology ཀྵ་ཡ་ནག་པོ denotes a bilious disease, prob. black jaundice (*Jä.*). The symptoms of the disease *kṣa-ya*, as described in the medical works of Tibet, are as follows: མཁྲིས་པ་ལུས་ལ་ཁྱབ་ནས་ཟ་འཕྲུག་བྱེད། པགས་མདོག་ལྗང་ནག་སྐྲ་དང་སྨིན་མ་འབྱི་བྱེད་མེད་ཤ་སྐམ་སེན་མོ་ནག་ཐིག་ཆགས་པ་འོང་ "the bile having permeated the body, itching is set up, the skin becomes greenish-black in colour, the hair and the eyebrows fall off, loss of strength, shrivelled flesh, and black spots on the nails, will be produced" (*Med.*).

ཀྵ་སུ་ར *kṣa-su-ra* a kind of precious stone resembling crystal; it is very rare in Tibet: ཀྵ་སུ་ར་ནི་ཤེལ་དང་སྟང་ཟིལ་དངོས་རེ་རེ་ཙམ་ལས་བོད་དུ་འབྱུང་མི་འགྱུར as to Kṣasura, that crystal and the genuine staṅ-zil stone do not occur in Tibet except singly (*Yig.*).

དཀག་པ *dkag-wa* constipation; obstructed bowels.

卐 དཀན *Dkan* I: तालु, acc. to *Ṅag.* the palate, the roof of the mouth; ཡ་དཀན the upper part of the palate; མ་དཀན the lower part of the palate; དཀན་གཅེར cleft palate; དཀན་གྱི་ཡི་གེ तालव्यवर्ण the palatal letters; དཀན་གཏོར जिह्वास्फोटक an abscess in the palate; དཀན་ནད any disease of the palate.

དཀན II: is sometimes used in the place of གྱེན *gyen*, steep or up hill; དཀན་གཟར་བ

ḏkan gzar-po a steep declivity; precipice (Ñag. 5).

དཀའ *Ḏkaḫ*, དཀའ་བ *ḏkaḫ-wa* or དཀའ་བོ *ḏkaḫ-ḇo* कृच्छ्र, कठोर 1. hard, difficult; used as adj. གོ་དཀའ་བ hard to understand; རབ་ཏུ་དཀའ་བ very hard or difficult. 2. pains, exertions, sufferings; དཀའ་བ་མེད་པར་ཐོབ་པ अकृच्छ्रलाभ gain without pain or exertion; དཀའ་བ་མེད་པ without hardship or difficulty; འགྲོད་དཀའ་བ difficult of access; སྒྲུབ་དཀའ་བ *sgrub ḏkaḫ-wa* hard to accomplish or to perfect; fig. to propitiate; བརྗོད་དཀའ་བ hard to express or describe; རྙེད་དཀའ་བ difficult to find; བྱ་དཀའ་བ hard work, or hard to do; དཀའ་བ་ཉིད कृच्छ्रत्व difficulty; དཀའ་བ་བྱེད་པ दुष्करकारक one who accomplishes a difficult or hard task.

དཀའ་འགྲེལ *ḏkaḫ-ḫgrel* पञ्जिका lit. difficulties explained; a commentary; explanation of difficulties (*Jä.*): ཚིག་དོན་གོ་དཀའ་བ་འགྲེལ་པས་བཀྲོལ་བ meanings of terms which are difficult to understand are explained in a commentary (*Ñag. 5*).

དཀའ་བཅུ *ḏkaḫ-ḇcu* दशदुष्कर ten ascetical hardships; a Buddhist scholar who has acquired such great proficiency in sacred literature as to be able to interpret the meanings of a term in ten different ways.

དཀའ་ཐུབ I: *ḏkaḫ-thub* तपस्या; also श्रमण, यति, विप्र, प्रव्रजित, asceticism, also penance; an ascetic, one who is able to stand hardships or privations: དཀའ་ཐུབ་ལུས་ནི་ཆེ་བ་དང་། མཛེས་མ་གཅིག་པུར་ཉལ་བ་དང་། དཔའ་བོ་རྨ་མཚན་མེད་པ་སྟེ། འདི་གསུམ་ཡིད་མི་ཆེས་པའི་རྒྱུ། "that an ascetic's body should be fat, that a pretty woman should sleep by herself, and that a hero should be without wound-scars—these three are things the mind does not credit."

དཀའ་ཐུབ II: a name for the first month of the Tibetan calendar (*Rtsii.*).

དཀའ་ཐུབ་ཀྱི་གནས *Ḏkaḫ-thub-kyi gnas* तपोवन the residence of an ascetic; a hermitage.

དཀའ་ཐུབ་དགྲ *ḏkaḫ-thub-ḏgra*=འདོད་ལྷ་དགའ་རབ་དབང་ཕྱུག། (lit. the ascetic's enemy) a name of the god of love (*Mṅon.*).

དཀའ་ཐུབ་ཅན *ḏkaḫ-thub-can*=ཉོན་མོངས་པ *ñon-moṅs-pa* तपस्वी, तपोधन one who undergoes asceticism; a hermit; one who having renounced the worldly life has retired to solitude; an epithet of the Hindu deity Mahes'vara.

Syn. སྤང་སྤོས *spaṅ-spos*; སྤུ་ཅན *spu-can*; དྲིའི་སྲས་པོ *ḏriḫi-sras-po*; འབྱུང་པོའི་རལ་པ *ḫbyuṅ-poḫi ral-pa* (*Mṅon.*).

དཀའ་ཐུབ་སྤྱོད་པ *ḏkaḫ-thub spyoḏ-pa* the practices of an ascetic or hermit; དྲང་སྲོང *ḏraṅ-sroṅ* a rishi (*Mṅon.*); དཀའ་ཐུབ་ལ་འགོ་བ to embrace the life of an anchorite; དཀའ་ཐུབ་མེར་པོ=ཕུར་ཀུམ saffron (*Sman. 351*); དཀའ་ཐུབ་གསལ तपःप्रकाश one whose asceticism or penitence is either visible or exemplary.

དཀའ་ཟློག་བླ་མ *Ḏkaḫ-zlog ḇla-ma* n. of a snowy mountain; it is generally applied to རི་བོ་གངས་ཅན *Ri-ḇo gaṅs-can* (*Mṅon.*).

དཀའ་ཟློག་མ *Ḏkaḫ-zlog-ma* n. of the Goddess གཽ་རི *Gau-ri* (*Mṅon.*).

དཀའ་ལས་ཆེ་བ *ḏkaḫ-las che-wa* very difficult; དཀའ་ལས་མེད་པ free from difficulty; easy.

དཀར I: *ḏkar* in compounds=དཀར་པོ *ḏkar-po* white; grey.

དཀར II: sincere; དཀར་མི་ཕུམ not confessing one's guilt; not exonerated; not making a clean breast of anything.

དཀར་སྐྱ *ḏkar-skya* पाण्डुर light grey: དཀར་སྐྱོ पाण्डु pale; white.

དཀར་ཁང *ḏkar-khaṅ* a lighted house; also a store room (*S. kar. 66, 178*).

དཀར་ཁུང་ *dkar-khuṅ*=སྐར་ཁུང་ window, a sky-light; a hole in the wall of a house for the entrance of light.

དཀར་ཁྱུག *dar-khyug* anything streaked or ornamented with diverse colours.

དཀར་ཁྲིགས *dkar-khrigs* (*kar-thig*) white; shining; bright; glittering; brilliant.

དཀར་གོང *dkar-goṅ* 1. a kind of white clay; porcelain clay. 2. same as མེ་རྡོ *me-rdo* flint: དཀར་གོང་སྲིན་འདོན་གདོན་དུག་ལ་ཕན། white-clay is useful to expel worms and for the poison of evil spirits.

དཀར་རྒྱ *dkar-rgya* rose-coloured; pale pink.

དཀར་རྒྱན *dkar-rgyan* white ornament; the butter used in painting offerings made of barley flour or rice to the gods: ཞལ་ཟས་དཀར་རྒྱན་མར cakes that are painted white and red with (coloured) butter (*Rtsii.*).

དཀར་བཅུད་གསུམ *dkar-bcud-gsum* the triple white elixir, *i.e.*, the cream from the milk of the female yak, ewe, and cow: འབྲི་ལུག་བ་གསུམ་གྱི་འོ་མ་འདུས་པའི་ཁཎྜ་ "*Khaṇḍa* is the mixed milk of the female yak, ewe and cow."

དཀར་ཆག *dkar-chag* सूचिलिपि 1. an index; register. 2. whitish; grey. 3. morally good; standing on the side of virtue; sincere; candid.

དཀར་ཆབ་ཆབ *dkar-chab-chab*=དཀར་ཅེམ་ཅེམ or འོད་ཟེར་དཀར་ཅེམ་མེ glittering white rays.

དཀར་ཆུང་ལྷ་ཁང *Dkar-chuṅ lha-khaṅ* n. of a monastery in Tibet (*J. Zaṅ.*).

དཀར་ཉེ *dkar-ñe*=དཀར་བའི་ཉེ་བ a true friend; one who has come over to one's side out of sincere good will; a friendly relation.

དཀར་སྟིང་ཆ་ངམ *Dkar-stiṅ cha-ṅam* n. of a place in Kham near *Ri-wo-che*. (*Lon.* ཀ *29*).

དཀར་ཐག *dkar-thag*. the string of a bow: དཀར་ཐག་གཡོན་ཆ་འཁྲིགས་དག་མ་རེར་འབྲུ། (*Rtsii.*)

དཀར་དྲོ *dkar-dro* milk and curd: གོང་གི་རིན་ཐང་མཉམ་པའི་དཀར་དྲོ་བྱ། it will make milk and curd of equal value with the above (*Jig. 30*).

དཀར་ལྡན *Dkar-ldan* गौरी lit. the fair one; the Goddess Gauri, the wife of S'iva.

དཀར་པོ *dkar-po*, also དཀར་མོ *dkar-mo* शुचि, शुक्ल, धवल, अवदात, गौर, अर्जुन, गुण, पण्डित 1. white; pure; fair; a qualification, talent, enlightenment; (sometimes) wise. 2. दूर्वा, silver; *dub* grass; a learned man; purity: དཀར་པོ་རྣམ་པར་མཐོང་བའི་ས། शुक्ल विदर्शनाभूमि। "complete enlightenment is a stage of insight." It is one of the stages of perfection of the *Hīnayāna* School.

དཀར་པོ་ཅིག་ཐུབ *dkar-po chig-thub* a kind of medicinal plant; also, its root, which is used to kill worms; དུག་ཕྱུང་གཉན་སྲིན་འཇོམས། it draws out poisonous matter and subdues worms which infest one.

* དཀར་པོ་རྣམ་པར་འཆར་པ *dkar-po rnams-par hchar-pa* सदभ्युदय (*Schr.*).

* དཀར་པོ་འབར *dkar-po hbar* श्वेतदीप्ति (*Schr.*) white lustre.

དཀར་པོ་སྦལ་རྒྱབ *Dkar-po sbab-rgyab* རྡོ་སྨན་ཞིག་གི་མིང n. of a medicinal stone (called "white frog's back") (*Mṅon.*).

དཀར་པོའི་བསྐལ་པ *dkar-pohi bskal-pa* श्वेतकल्प the enlightened age or *Kalpa*.

དཀར་ཕིགས *dkar-phigs* used in colloq. for དཀར་ཕིབས *dkar-phibs*.

དཀར་ཕིབས *dkar-phibs* a tower or dome built on pillars or on the roof of a house for commanding a view, generally in the Chinese style: དཀར་ཕིབས་ཆེན་མོར་ཀ་རིང་སེང་གེའི་ཁ in the great domed tower is the tall pillar with a lion's mouth.

དཀར་ཕྱོགས *dkar-phyogs* शुक्लपक्ष the light half of a month; the period from the new to the full moon; the innocent side in two contending parties; དཀར་ཕྱོགས་ལྷ the gods who belong to the side of virtue; དཀར་ཕྲེང་ *dkar-phreṅ* n. of the mythical capital of the *Asura* (*Pag. 30*).

དཀར་བ *dkar-wa* शुक्ल white, v. དཀར་དཀར་བ་ཉིད शुक्लत्व whiteness: ཆོས་ལ་དཀར་བ་ཡོད་པས། "through sincerity in the doctrine"; "by piety" (*Pag. 30*).

དཀར་མི་བྱེད་པ *dkar-mi byed-pa* to plead innocence. Ṅag. explains it as རང་ལ་ནག་ཉེས་པ་ཡོད་བཞིན་དུ་མནའ་སྐྱེལ་བསམ, to show by signs or by oath that he is not guilty.

དཀར་མིན *dkar-min* असित, श्यामल not white; black; dark; chaos; bent; crooked.

དཀར་མིན་བུ *Dkar-min-bu* the son of *Dkar-min*; the offspring of chaos: दक्ष an epithet of the son of Brahmā.

དཀར་མེ *dkar-me*=ཆོས་མེ *chos me* sacred fire; especially lamps lighted before deities: དཀར་མེ་སྡོང་རས་རམ་རིགས། the kind (of cloth) fit for wicks of lamps (lighted before the images of saints and deities) (*Rtsii.*).

དཀར་མེད་མ *Dkar-med-ma* གནོད་སྦྱིན་མོའི་གཙོ་མོ (*Mṅon.*) a name of the queen of the *Yakṣa.*

དཀར་མོ *dkar-mo* 1. mutton; a sheep when slaughtered; དཀར་མོ་ལག་གཡས་དཀར་ཤ་ལག་པ་གཅིག a shoulder of mutton from the right side of a slaughtered sheep (*Rtsii.*); ལག་གི་དཀར་མོ་ལག་པའི་གསོས mutton of sheep slaughtered by the hand (as distinguished from the meat of a dead sheep) (*Jig. 9*). 2. अपराजिता, कात्यायनी an epithet of the goddess Durgā. 3. white rice.

དཀར་དམར *dkar-dmar* light red or whitish red.

དཀར་རྩི *dkar-rtsi*, also spelt དཀར་རྩེ *dkar-tse* 1. lime; white-wash; white-paint. 2. a kind of coarse cotton cloth; lint: དཀར་རྩི་ཤ་རུས་ལ་ནད་ནད་འགོགས་བྱེད lint arrests decaying disease in the flesh and bone (*S. kar. 3*). 3. दुकूल, རས་དཀར་རྩི white muslin.

དཀར་རྩིས *dkar-tsis* or སྐར་རྩིས astrology: རྒྱ་གར་ནས་བོད་དུ་དར་བའི་རྩིས་ལ་དཀར་རྩིས་ཟེར the system of reckoning introduced in Tibet from India is called *dkar-rtsis* (*D. çel. 8*).

དཀར་རྩེར་བ *dkar rtser-wa* very white or fair: རྟ་པ་གཞོན་ནུ་མ་དཀར་རྩེར་བ་ཞིག། a young maiden of very fair complexion on horseback (*A. 135*).

དཀར་འཛིན *dkar-ḥdsin* the female breast; teats.

Syn. འདོད་པའི་མྱོས་བུམ *ḥdod-paḥi myos-bum*; ལང་ཚོའི་མཚན་མ *laṅ-tshoḥi mtshan-ma*; འོ་མ་འཛིན *ḥo-ma ḥdsin*; ལོགས་སྐྱེས *logs-skyes* (*Mṅon.*).

དཀར་མཛོད *dkar-mdsod* a dispensary.

དཀར་འོད *dkar-ḥod*=སྲིན་བུ་མེ་ཁྱེར fire-fly (*Mṅon.*).

དཀར་ཡོལ *dkar-yol* procelain (*Ṅag. 5*).

དཀར་གཡེང་ *dkar-gyeṅ* is explained as ཁྲིམས་ཞིབ་ཆ་བྱེད་པ a trial or investigation under law.

དཀར་སངས *dkar-saṅs* pure white; also དཀར་སེང་ངེ་བ or དཀར་པོ་དཀར་ཀྱང་ very white.

དཀར་སེང་ངེ་བ *dkar-seṅ-ṅe-wa*=རྒྱ་སོམ་མེ་བ, v. དཀར་སངས.

དཀར་སོབ་ཡང་བའི་འོད་ཅན *dkar-sob yaṅ-waḥi ḥod-can*=ཅོང་ཞི alabaster (*Sman. 353*).

དཀར་གསལ *dkar-gsal* fair; white; light.

དཀར་གསུམ *dkar-gsum* the three white things, viz., curd, milk and butter (*A. 143*).

+ དཀུ *dku* कुक्षि; =ལུས་ཀྱི་རྩ་ཟུར (*Lex.*) the side of one's body: དཀུ་ནི་དཔྲི་མགོ་ནི་གོང་རྩམ་རྩིབ་མ་ཕྲང་ངུའི་ཐད། ལུས་ཀྱི་གཡས་གཡོན་གང་རུང་། *dku* is towards the small ribs just above the hip, whether on the right or left of the body; དཀུར་ or དཀུ་ལ་རྟེན་པ་ to carry a thing at one's side (*Zam.*); དཀུ་བརྟོལ་བ་ to open the side; དཀུ་ལྕི་ a heavy feeling in the side, as a symptom of pregnancy; དཀུ་ནད་ *ḏku-naḏ* apparently a disease of the kidneys (*Jä.*); དཀུ་ཟླུམ་ *ḏku-zlum* round and plump buttocks; the cavity of the abdomen (*Jä.*); དཔེར་ན་དྲིལ་བུ་དཀུར་བརྟེན་སོགས། for example a bell resting on its side (*Ńag.*).

དཀུ་མཉེ་ *ḏku-m̱ñe* आसन a rug to sit upon; a seat.

དཀུ་ལྟོ *ḏku-lto* contrivance, stratagem; craft; trick, especially if under some pretext one person induces another to do a thing that proves hurtful to him (*Jä.*); དཀུ་ལྟོ་བྱེད་པར་ using a stratagem.

དཀུ་སྟེ *ḏku-ṣte*=ལྷག་སྟེ शेष remaining; in excess.

卐 **དཀུ་བ** *ḏku-wa* stench; putrid smell: དཀུ་བ་ནི་དྲི་མི་ཞིམ་པའམ *Ḏku-wa* signifies anything that is not of agreeable smell; དྲི་ཆ་བ་ལ་དྲི་མ་དཀུ་ཟེར་ the smell of that which is putrid is called *ḏku-wa*. དཀུ་བ་རྣམ་པ་ལྔ the five kinds of *ḏku-wa*, *i.e.*, objects with bad strong smell, are the following:—སྒོག་པ garlic; ཙོང onion; རྒྱ་སྒོག Chinese garlic; རི་སྒོག the hill or Tibetan garlic; and შིང་ཀུན asafœtida. The use of these five are forbidden to the Buddhist *Bhikṣu* (*K. d.* ཕ *115*).

དཀོན *ḏkon* དཀོན་པ दुर्लभ 1. adj. rare, scarce; hard to acquire: ལོ་འདི་ལ་ཆར་པ་དང་འབྲུ་དཀོན། this year rain and grain are scarce; དེང་སང་བོད་ཇ་ཤིན་ཏུ་དཀོན་པ་འདུག། just now Tibetan tea is very rare; འཇིག་རྟེན་ན་དཀོན་ནོ exceedingly rare in the world; འཇིག་རྟེན་ན་དཀོན་པར་བཟང་ངོ་། it is of a quality rarely to be met with in the world; ཁྱོད་འདྲ་བ་མཐོང་ན་དཀོན་རྒྱུ་མེད། to see a person like you is nothing particularly rare; ལྕེ་བདེ་མོ་ལ་ལྷ་ཆོས་དཀོན with a prattler religion is scarce (*Jä.*). དཀོན་པ་ཉིད rarity; དཀོན་ནོར valuable property; riches; rare things. 2. sbst., a rarity. There are said to be seven *ḏkon* or rarities.

དཀོན་མཆོག *ḏkon-m̱chog* रत्न any precious object; anything very excellent or best of its kind. The oldest forms of this word are—དཀོནད་ཅོག or དཀོན་ཅོག. དཀོན་མཆོག means དཀོན་པའི་མཆོག, the chief of rarities, the rarest being or object, the Supreme Being: སྤྱིར་འཇིག་རྟེན་ན་ནོར་བུ་རིན་པོ་ཆེ་ནི་ཤིན་ཏུ་རྙེད་དཀའ་ཞིང་དཀོན་པ་ཡིན། དཀོན་པ་དེ་ལས་ཀྱང་ཤིན་ཏུ་དཀོན་པས་ན་དཀོན་པའི་མཆོག། "in general in this world a precious jewel difficult to procure is a rarity; that which is much rarer still than any rarity is *ḏkon-chog*." A precious gem of the rarest kind is useful only for worldly purposes; but Buddha, his church, and creed, are of use to all living beings, both here and hereafter, for increasing and ensuring their happiness. Apart from Buddhism, the Tibetans appear to have possessed the conception of the Supreme Deity in the term *Ḏkon-m̱chog*. This term, དཀོན་མཆོག, is used in Tibetan writings for each member of the Buddhist triad—Buddha, Dharma, and Saŋgha—separately, as also for the three collectively; in the latter case often with *gsum* annexed. Mr. W. W. Rockhill has condemned the use of this word by Christian missionaries to signify "God." But Jäschke has elaborated on the subject as follows:—"Buddhism has always sought the highest good not in anything material, but in the moral sphere, looking with indifference, and indeed with contempt, on everything merely relating to matter. It is not, however, moral perfection, or the happiness attained thereby, which is understood by the 'most precious thing,' but the mediator or mediators who procure that happiness for mankind, viz., Buddha (the originator of the doctrine), the doctrinal scriptures and the corporate body of priests, called त्रिरत्न, *dkon-mchog gsum.* Now, although this triad cannot, by any means, be placed on a level with the Christian doctrine of a triune God, yet it will be easily understood how the innate desire of man to adore and worship something supernatural, together with the hierarchical tendency of the teaching class, have afterwards contributed to convert the acknowledgment of human activity for the benefit of others (for such it was undoubtedly on the part of the founder himself and his earlier followers) into a devout, and by degrees idolatrous, adoration of these three agents, especially as Buddha's religious doctrine did not at all satisfy the deeper wants of the human mind, and its author himself did not know anything of a God standing apart and above this world. For, whatever in Buddhism is found of beings to whom divine attributes are assigned, has either been transferred from the Indian and other mythologies, and had, accordingly, been current among the people before the introduction of Buddhism, or is the result of philosophical speculation that has remained more or less foreign to the people at large. As, then, the original and etymological signification of the word is no longer current, and as to every Tibetan '*Dkon-mchog*' suggests the idea of some supernatural power, the existence of which he feels in his heart, and the nature and properties of which he attributes more or less to the three agents mentioned above, we are fully entitled to assign to the word *Dkon-mchog* also the signification of God, though the sublime conception which the Bible connects with the word, viz., that of a personal absolute Omnipotent Being, will only with the spread of the Christian religion be gradually introduced and established."

དཀོན་མཆོག་ཀུན་འདུས *dkon-mchog kun-hdus* the three gems, *i.e.*, *Buddha*, *Dharma* and *Saygha* collectively: བླ་མ་ནི་དུས་གསུམ་སངས་རྒྱས་ཐམས་ཅད་འདུས་པའི་བདག་ཉིད *lama* is tho essence of all the Buddhas of the three ages massed together; སྐུ་དགེ་འདུན་གསུང་དམ་ཆོས་ཐུགས་སངས་རྒྱས་ཀྱི་ཇོ་བོ་རྫས་དཀོན་མཆོག་ཀུན་འདུས། tho image represents the church; the scriptures represent tho heart, *i.e.*, the *Dharma*; and the holy relics (symbolical of the spirit of Buddha) complete the three gems.

དཀོན་མཆོག་གི་མཆོད་པ the service or worship of the *Dkon-mchog*.

དཀོན་མཆོག་འབྱུང་གནས *Dkon-mchog hbyuṅ-gnas* रत्नाकर a name of the first of the nine stages of *Samādhi* or ཏིང་ངེ་འཛིན the meditations of a *Bodhisattva*.

དཀོན་མཆོག་བརྩེགས་པ रत्नकूट a Sanskrit work on the names and attributes of Buddha, in one hundred chapters, out of which forty-nine chapters were translated into Tibetan; of these forty-nine only six are now extant in Tibet. The entire work was translated into Chinese by Jñāna Gupta, A.D. 589-618.

དཀོན་མཆོག་གསུམ *dkon-mchog gsum* त्रिरत्न the three *Ratna* or Precious Ones. The Buddhist triad are—(1) *Saṅs-rgyas dkon-mchog* Buddha most rare; (2) Dharma, called *Dam-chos dkon-mchog*, the holy Doctrine most rare; (3) *Dge-hdun dkon-mchog* body of priests most rare. Colloq. the phrase is frequently used as an exclamation quite in the sense of our "God knows!"

*དཀོན་མཆོག་གསུམ་གྱི་འབངས *dkon-mchog gsum-gyi hbañs* त्रिरत्नदास (*Schr.*) lit. a servant of the three gems, *i.e.*, a devout Buddhist; n. of an individual.

དཀོན་གཉེར *dkon-gñer* = སྐུ་གཉེར a priest who is in charge of a Buddhist chapel or temple and performs the daily services to the deities contained in it. The *Sku gñer* is also called *Am-chod*: ཨམ་མཆོད་དཀོན་གཉེར་བསྐངས་རྒྱུན་པ་སོགས་ཕོགས་ཐོབ་ཆར་ཅན། the priests and image-steward and others who continually officiate get the customary allowances (*Rtsii.*).

དཀོན་པོ *dkon-po* or དཀོན་མོ rare, scarce; dear, precious.

+ དཀོན་བུ *dkon-bu* a wreath; མེ་ཏོག་གི་དཀོན་བུ a flower wreath.

+ དཀོར *dkor* = རྫས द्रव्य, *dkor* is resp. for ནོར, substance, wealth, riches, property: དགེ་འདུན་གྱི་དཀོར the property of the church or that of a monastic congregation; མཐིལ་དཀོར foundation, endowment of a monastery; ཡང་དཀོར additional or occasional gifts for the support of a religious institution; ས་དཀོར landed endowments of a monastery or religious institution.

དཀོར་བདག *dkor-bdag* lit. the owner of property. It generally signifies the spirit or demi-god who is supposed to be the custodian of the images of all Buddhist deities, scriptures, symbols; in short, of all church and sacerdotal properties. In this sense the demon called *Pehar rgyal-po* of Sam-ye is a *Dkor-bdag* or custodian of religious property.

དཀོར་ནོར *dkor-nor* church property or general wealth: ལྷུན་གྲུབ་ལོངས་སྤྱོད་དཀོར་ནོར་ཕྱུག་པ་མངའ། (*D. R.*) you possess accumulated wealth and church-property.

དཀོར་པ *dkor-pa* a treasurer (*Cs.*); one in charge of the endowments and properties of a temple or monastery.

དཀོར་བླ *dkor-bla* or དཀོར་གྱི་བླ a lama who appropriates sacred property to himself (*M. V. 66*).

དཀོར་མ་འབགས *dkor-ma-hbags* not misappropriating the treasures, stores, etc., of the church: སྨོམ་དུ་ཆང་གསོལ་དགེ་འདུན་དཀོར་མ་འབགས། do not take wine for drink nor embezzle the property of the priesthood (*Kathañ. 115*).

དཀོར་མཛོད *dkor-mdsod* is a general name for wealth or property and hence is frequently used to signify བང་མཛོད་ཀ treasury; treasure-chest (*Ñag. 5*).

དཀོར་རྫོགས *Dkor-rdsogs* n. of a monastery in Southern Ladak, situated 16,000 feet above the sea level.

+ དཀོར་ཟས *dkor-zas* = ནོར་ཟས་པ spendthrift (*Ñag. 5*).

དཀོར་རིགས *dkor-rigs* वित्त, धन different properties belonging to a monastery.

དཀོལ་པ *dkol-pa* आर्त struck by calamity; afflicted; one in suffering.

+ དཀོས་ཐག *dkos-thag* = ཉམས་ཐག 1. आर्त्ति suffering, affliction. 2. उद्घाटन exciting disgust.

དཀྱར *dkyar* any appliance for crossing snow or glaciers. Stocking boots (*Sch.*). The *dkyar* used by the Tibetans and the Sharpa Bhutias of Nepal in crossing glaciers is a light circular disk of wood about a foot in diameter, with four holes through which strings are passed to fasten it to the knee. In climbing up and walking down the snowy sides of mountains, these boards are attached to the soles of the felt boots and are of great assistance to the traveller, preventing the feet from sinking in the soft snow.

དཀྱིལ *dkyil* དབུས or མཐིལ मध्य the middle, centre; तल bottom, base; དཀྱིལ་ནས *kyil-naṣ* from the middle or centre; from amidst; from the bottom; དཀྱིལ་མ the middle one; the central one; དཀྱིལ་ཆེ་བ=ཁོང་མ་ཡངས་པར་ हृद्य, खतिक with wide base; spacious interior; comprehensive understanding; also quick comprehension.

དཀྱིལ་དཀྲུངས *dkyil-dkruṅs* पर्यङ्क, परका, परिकर a cross-legged posture: དཀྱིལ་མོ་དཀྲུང་བཅས་ཏེ་ पर्यङ्कमाभुज्य sitting in a cross-legged posture for mystic meditation.

དཀྱིལ་འཁོར *dkyil-ḥkhor* मण्डल, परिवेश, नेमि 1. circle; circumference; globe; disk: ཞལ་གྱི་དཀྱིལ་འཁོར the disk of the face (मुखमण्डल); the full or whole face. 2. especially used as the equivalent of the Sanskrit *Maṇḍala*, the magic diagrams or figures formed of grain or other materials which are "offered" to deities in Tantrik Buddhist rites. In *Tantrik* rites diagrams representing supposed mansions of certain celestial *Bodhisattva* and called དཀྱིལ་འཁོར are traced on the ground or on paper. The respective places assigned to the different minor deities are painted in different colours in the design, and the central place in the diagram is occupied by the tutelary deity himself, to whom the rest are subordinate. 3. region, sphere; surroundings; suburb. According to the Buddhist cosmogony there are ས་ཡི་དཀྱིལ་འཁོར the sphere of earth, ཆུ་ཡི་དཀྱིལ་འཁོར the sphere of water, the ocean, རླུང་གི་དཀྱིལ་འཁོར *rluṅ-gi-dkyil-ḥkhor* the atmosphere, མེ་ཡི་དཀྱིལ་འཁོར the sphere of fire; each forming a stratum over the other. The upper stratum, *i.e.*, that which is beyond the atmosphere, is called the sphere of fire or light.

དཀྱིལ་འཁོར་གྲུ་བཞི་པ *dkyil-ḥkhor gru-bshi-pa* a quadrangle; square; a certain mystical figure; diagram or model. The expression རྟེན་དང་བརྟེན་པའི་དཀྱིལ་འཁོར་བརྟན་པ means the gods who constitute the རྟེན assembly in the *Vimāna* or གཞལ་ཡས་ཁང, *i.e.*, superb mansion represented.

དཀྱིལ་འཁོར་བརྒྱད་པའི་མདོ is a description of the eight mansions of eight imaginary Buddhas (*K. d.* ▪ *72*). Whoever utters the names of these Buddhas or hears the aphorisms about them is liberated from dangers caused by evil spirits, snakes, &c. By remembering and repeating them, even brigands, not to speak of kings, are said to be able to make the weapons of their enemies ineffectual against themselves.

དཀྱིལ་འཁོར་ཅན *dkyil-ḥkhor-can* मण्डलवत् anything that has a circular and mystical figure on it; also any *Tantrik* deity placed to be worshipped on the plane of his fancied celestial mansion traced on the ground.

དཀྱིལ་འཁོར་ལྡིང *Dkyil-ḥkhor-ldiṅ* n. of the grand central temple of Buddha at Lhasa, popularly known as Kinkhording.

དཀྱིལ་འཁོར་གསུམ *dkyil-ḥkhor gsum* त्रिमण्डल three cycles (of offerings): (1) རང་བཞིན་དུས་ཀྱི་དབྱིངས་ནས་ལྷུན་གྱི་གྲུབ་པ་དང the cycle of offerings for the Bon gods sprung out naturally in course of time; (2) ཏིང་ངེ་འཛིན་དཀྱིལ་འཁོར་མཁའ་ལ་ཡིད་ཀྱིས་བསྒོམ་པ་དང; the celestial mansion for contemplation formed in the sky (to imagine an aerial castle); (3) འདུས་བྱས་དཀྱིལ་འཁོར་ས་ལ་རྒྱས་ཀྱིས་བྲིས་པའོ། the mansions of gods designed on the ground for placing the offerings to them (*B. Nam.*).

དཀྱུ་རྟ *dkyu rta* or དཀྱུ་བའི་རྟ *dkyu-wahi rta* a race-horse.

དཀྱུ་པ *dkyu-pa* in Ladak: to lose colour by washing; perhaps more correctly རྐྱུག་པ.

卐 **དཀྱུ་བ** *dkyu-wa* = རྒྱུ་བ 1. to run a race; དཀྱུ་སར་དཀྱུས *dkyu-sar dkyus* = རྒྱུག་སར་རྒྱུགས running a race; བང་རྒྱུགས galloping: དཔེར་ན་རྟ་རྒྱུག་ས་ལ་རྒྱུགས་པ། (*Ñag. 5*) "for example running a race on horseback." 2. to wring out; to filter (*Sch.*). 3. to caper about (*Jä.*); དཀྱུ་བྱའི་རྟ *dkyu-byahi-rta* a race-horse.

དཀྱུ་ས *dkyu-sa* a race-course; the race ground (*Cs.*).

卐 **དཀྱུད་པ** *dkyud-pa* = བརྗེད་པ to forget; བརྩེ་བས་མི་དཀྱུད་པའི་གསུང་བྲིས། an affectionate letter to prevent one being forgotten or a letter which love will not forget (*Yig. k. 37*).

དཀྱུས *dkyus* आयत 1. length; lengthwise. 2. untruth; also adj. untrue; spurious (*Jä.*). 3. bold, insolent (*Sch.*). In lexicons it is synonymous with the term གཞུང་ *gshuñ*, meaning "lengthwise." In weaving, the threads that are stretched lengthwise are called དཀྱུས་ཐག *dkyus-thag* (the woof) and those that pass them crosswise are called སྤུན་ཐག *spun-thag*: དེ་སྟེང་བཞུགས་ཁྲི་པད་གདན་རྡོ་རྩིག་དཔངས་ལ་ཁྲུ་དོ་མཐོ་གང་། དཀྱུས་ལ་རྒྱུགས་འདོམ་གསུམ་རེ། (*S. kar. 134*) upon that stood the throne constructed of stone, having a lotus cushion, in breadth two cubits and a span, in length three running fathoms.

དཀྱུས་དཀར *dkyus-dkar* a porcelain cup of inferior quality; a common porcelain cup.

དཀྱུས་ཇ *dkyus-ja* common or inferior tea. Tea served to the public or to the congregation of monks in a monastery or in a religious service.

དཀྱུས་མ *dkyus-ma* प्राकृत common, vulgar, inferior; མི་དཀྱུས་མ *mi-dkyus ma* an ordinary man; one who is neither an official nor a religious man (*Ñag 5*): དཀྱུས་རམས་ཉག་རེ་འབྲུ (*Rtsii.*) "indigo of inferior quality is valued at so much per ཉ་ག or lb." དཀྱུས་བཏགས *dkyus-btags* a scarf of ordinary quality; ཀྱུས་བུར *dkyus-bur* treacle of inferior quality: དཀྱུས་བུར་སྒར་ཚུགས་རེར *dkyus-bur sgar tshugs rer* "coarse treacle for each thick lump" (*Rtsii.*).

དཀྱུས་མོ *dkyus-mo* = མགྱོགས་པ *mgyogs-pa* quickly, swiftly.

དཀྱུས་ཚད *dkyus-tshad* the dimensions of anything when measured lengthwise.

དཀྱུས་རིང *dkyus-riñ* = འདུན་རིང आयत, दीर्घ spacious; large; long.

卐 **དཀྱེལ** *dkyel* = ཀློང *kloñ* the compass, extent, bulk of anything: ནམ་མཁའི་དཀྱེལ the compass of the heavens: རྒྱ་མཚོའི་དཀྱེལ the stretch of sea: དཀྱེལ་ཆེ = དཀྱེལ་ཆེ་བ spacious; of wide capacity (*Ñag. 5*).

དཀྱེལ་པོ་ཆེ *dkyel-po-che* acc. to *Sch.* is the Universe; defined as ཁང་ཡངས་པ the wide house (*Lex.*).

དཀྱོར་འབྱིན *dkyor-hbyin* प्रक्ष्य capable of being thrown down; impelled or driven on; also capable of being felled down.

དཀྲམ་ཀོ་འཐུག་པ *dkram-ko hthug-pa* = སྤྱི་བརྟོལ་ཆེ་བ *spyi-brtol che-wa* 1. अत्यय transgression. 2. adj. very impudent; impertinent.

བཀྲས་ལྗོངས *Bkras-ljoṅs*, abbr. of བཀྲ་ཤིས་ལྗོངས (*Tashi jong*), n. of a district under *Lhun-grub Rdsoṅ* in Tibet.

དཀྲི *dkri* (*ṭi*) वेष्टन anything to wrap with; a tie; ཁ་དཀྲི a cloth to tie round the face or cover the mouth; muffler; ཤོག་དཀྲི vb., wrapping or winding up with paper; paper-wrapping; an envelope (*Yig. k. 2*).

+ **དཀྲི་བ** I: *dkri-wa* (*ṭi-wa*) in old Tibetan, to conduct one's pupil from one stage of learning to another stage; pf. དཀྲིས vb. a. (cf. འཁྲི་བ) in modern Tibetan, to wind; to wrap round about; དཀྲི་བ་པོ *dkri-wa-po* = དཀྲི་བར་བྱེད་མཁན one who wraps up; གོས་སོགས་དཀྲི་བར་བྱེད་པ to fold up clothes, etc.

དཀྲི་བ II: དཀྲི་བ་སྙེགས་པ་ལྟ་བུ *dkri sñegs-pa lta-bu* a snare, anything to entangle with; vb., to ensnare.

དཀྲིག *dkrig* (*ṭig*) personally: དཀྲིག་བཅར་ཞུ་ཕྱིབས་མ་དེད་ཀྱང is same as ངོ་མ་ཡོང་ནས་ཞུ་ཤག་མ་ཆོད་ཀྱང not having come personally, cannot reply or say decidedly.

དཀྲིགས I: *dkrigs* विम्बर, प्रसर a term for a thousand billions. The term དཀྲིགས་ཕྲག་ཆེན་པོ or དཀྲིགས་ཆེན་པོ महाविम्बर or महाप्रसर is used for a still larger number.

དཀྲིགས II: = འཐིབས dense; thickly-gathered: སྤྲིན་དཀྲིགས *sprin-dkrigs* (*Ṅag. 5*) := སྤྲིན་འཐིབས་པ gathering or condensing of clouds; also vb. darkened, obscured, dim, diffused: སོ་ཡི་འོད་ཟེར་མདུན་དཀྲིགས་པས (*A. K. ii. 47*) the flashing of his teeth bewildered them; དཀྲིགས་པར་འགྱུར་པར *dkrigs-par ḥgyur-par* grown dim; དཀྲིགས་པར་བྱེད་པར *dkrigs-par byed-pa* to obscure.

དཀྲིས་གྱུར *dkris-gyur* (*ṭi-gyur*) वृत surrounded, encircled, encompassed: དཔལ་གྱིས་དཀྲིས་གྱུར *dpal-gyis dkris-gyur* श्रीवृत encircled with glory.

དཀྲིས་པ *dkris-pa* परिवेष्टन 1. to surround, encircle, ensnare. 2. = བཅིངས་པ आवृति to lie round; to wind up (*Mṅon.*): སེར་སྣས་ཀུན་ནས་དཀྲིས *ser-snas kun-nas dkris* quite ensnared in avarice (*Jä.*).

དཀྲིས་ཕྲག *dkris-phrag* n. of a large number (*Ṅag. 5*).

དཀྲུ་བ *dkru-wa* (*ṭu-wa*) = དྲི་མ *dri-ma* पूति, मल abomination, pollution; also dirt, filth (*Lexx.*).

དཀྲུག་པ *dkrug-pa* (*ṭug-pa*) = སློང་བ *gloṅ-wa* मन्थ to disturb, to put in motion; the act of troubling, agitating, churning; to turn; to turn a lathe.

དཀྲུགས་པ *dkrugs-pa* = བསྲུབས་པ *bsrubs-pa* विलोड़ित, मथित, लुठित stirred up, agitated, troubled, ruffled, disturbed, confused; churned; turned (as in a lathe); confounded: དཔེ་ཆ་དཀྲུགས *dpe-cha dkrugs* the leaves of a book are confused or mixed up together; བག་ཆགས་ཀྱིས་དཀྲུགས་པའི་སེམས *bag-chags-kyis dkrugs paḥi sems* a mind troubled with passion; རླུང་གིས་དཀྲུགས་པའི་ཆུ *rluṅ-gis dkrugs-paḥi chu* water agitated by the wind.

དཀྲུགས་པ་པོ *dkrugs-pa-po* a confounder: ཕན་ཚུན་དཀྲུགས་པར་བྱེད་མཁན་གྱི་མི་དེ་ལ་དཀྲུགས་པ་པོ་ཟེར the man who causes confusion afar off and nigh is called *ṭug-pa-po*.

དཀྲུགས་ཡིག *dkrugs-yig* བོད་ཀྱི་ཡིག་རིགས་ཤིག་གི་མིང a kind of character used in Tibet which is puzzling.

དཀྲུམ་པ *dkrum-pa* (*ṭum-pa*) brittle; defined in *Lexx.* as དཀར་ཡོལ་ལྟ་བུ་སྣོད་ཆག་པ, breaking in the manner a porcelain vessel does.

✝ **དཀྲེ** *dkre* (*țe*) པོ་མཚན་གྱི་ཏོག लिङ्गकेतु the glans-penis.

དཀྲོག་པ *dkrog-pa* (*țog-pa*) = དཀྲུག་པ *dkrug-pa* 1. to churn; to agitate, mingle, trouble, &c.: ཞོ་དཀྲོག་པ *sho dkrog-pa* churning curds (for butter). 2. to rouse, scare up; to wag, *e.g.*, the tail (*Jä.*). Also = དཀྲོགས་པ *dkrogs-pa*, འོ་མ་དཀྲོགས་པ *ho-ma dkrogs-pa* to churn milk; acc. to *Ńag.* is equivalent to སྙོགས་པ *sñogs-pa*.

དཀྲོགས་སྐྱེས *dkrogs-skyes* (lit. anything produced from churning) butter (*Mñon.*).

དཀྲོགས་པ་པོ *dkrogs-pa-po* = དཀྲོགས་པར་བྱེད་མཁན *dkrogs-par byed-mkhan* one who churns.

དཀྲོགས་མ *dkrogs-ma*, v. སྲབས་མ *srabs-ma*, the churning rod; also said to = whey (*Mñon.*).

དཀྲོང་བསྐྱེད *dkroṅ-bskyed* (*țong-ke*) चयोत्पाद of instantaneous birth; instantaneous perception. Acc. to *Lex.* in meditating on a certain deity, the act of perceiving him to be a reality instantaneously is called དཀྲོང་བསྐྱེད *dkroṅ bskyed*.

དཀྲོལ *dkrol* वादन; pf. and fut. of འཁྲོལ *hkrol*: དཀྲོལ་བ་པོ *dkrol-wa-po* is defined as "one who causes music to sound or be sounded."

བཀག I: *bkag* in བཀག་ལངས *bkag laṅs* the lid or cover of a trunk; the sides of a Tibetan leather-trunk. Defined in *Rtsii.* as མདུན་གཡས་གཡོན་གྱི་ཀོ་བ་ལེབ་གཉིས་པོ་ལ both the flat pieces of leather which are at the back and front on the right and left of a trunk.

བཀག II: प्रतिहत, निषिद्ध; pf. of འགེགས་པ, obstructed, opposed; also prohibition, obstruction, hindrance.

བཀག་སྐོར་མེད་པ *bkag-skor med-pa* = འགོར་གཞི་མེད་པ without delay, as in sending anything; also without let or hinderance; བཀག་བགེགས་རུང་འགེགས not permissible and permissible, not fit and fit, unbecoming and becoming.

བཀག་ཆ་བྱེད་པ *bkag-cha byed-pa* to forbid; to put a hinderance (*Sch.*).

བཀག་སྡོམ *bkog sdom* prohibition; prohibiting one from passing by a road or from entering any garden or place.

བཀག་མོ་ཁེགས་པ *bkag-mo khegs-pa* not to be observant; to transgress, to trespass.

བཀང *bkaṅ* acc. to *Rdo. 46*, pf. of དགང་བ *dgaṅ-wa* पूरित, filled to the brim; full to the brim as in the case of a water pot; སྣོད་བཀང་བ *snod-bkaṅ-wa* a vessel filled up; གཞུ་བཀང་བ a bow with an arrow ready to shoot; འདོད་པ་བཀང་བ wish fulfilled. Acc. to *Jä.* pf. of འགེངས་པ, to fill, make full; and used in *W.* instead of འགེངས་པ.

བཀད *bkad* 1. set or placed in order; arrangement: མགོ་འཛུགས་པ same as མགོ་བཀད མགོ་སྤུའི་རིམ་པ་འམ་གྲལ་ལ་འང་། ཐགས་ཀྱི་སྣལ་མ་ཕར་འགྲོའི་དུས་ཀྱི་སྤུན་འགྲོ་བ་དེ་དང་། བཏགས་ཚར་བའི་སྣམ་བུའི་སྤུན་གྱི་རྗེས་འབུར་འབུར་ཡོད་པའི་མིང་ལ་ཡང་ཐགས་ཀྱི་བཀད་ཟེར། *mgo-spuhi rim-paham gral-lahaṅ, thags-kyi snal-ma phar hgrohi dus-kyi spun hgro-wa de daṅ, btags tshar wahi snam-buhi spun-gyi rjes hbur-hbur yod-pahi miṅ la yaṅ thags-kyi bkad zer* (*Ńag.*) the order or row (of plaits) in the hair of the head, the crosswise thread in the web of a cloth, also the ridge in the cross-wise texture of a blanket, are called the *bkad* of weaving.

བཀད་ནས *bkad-nas* having described; represented in any manner.

བཀད་ས *bkad-sa*, ནས་ཀྱི་གཡོས་ས (*Ńag.*) 1. the place where barley, corn, &c., are parched; a bake-house, kitchen, cook's shop (*Cs.*). 2. acc. to *Ńag.* ✝ བཀད་ས་ནི་རང་སྡོད་ས one's own home or residence.

3. open hall or shed erected on festive occasions (*Jä.*).

བཀན་པ *bkan-pa* 1. to up-root or turn up anything by applying a stick at its foot or root. 2. to bend: ལུས་རྒྱབ་ཏུ་བཀན (*Ńag.*) the body bent backwards: ལག་པ་བཀན to stretch the arm bending it upwards to pull anything. 3. ཡར་ལུགས་ལྡོག་ཏུ་བརྩིས་པ་ལ་ཡང་བཀན་ཟེར counting up and then backwards is called *yang-bkan* (*S. del*). It is also applied to counting from right to left (*Vai. kar.*). 4. to put; to press; to apply (*Jä.*): རྐང་པ་རྩིག་པ་ལ་བཀན་པ to press one's foot against a wall. 5. to hold fast; to extend (*Cs.*).

བཀབ་པ *bkab-pa*, pf. of འགེབས་པ = བཙང་པ च्छन्न, प्रच्छन्न, to cover; to spread over.

བཀབ *bkab* a cover; a shelter.

Syn. ཁེབས *khebs*; གཡོགས *gyogs*; བྱིབས *byibs* (*Mńon.*).

བཀམ་པ *bkam-pa* pincers or nippers: བཀམ་པ་བརྒྱབ་པ to hold or cut with pincers.

བཀའ *bkah* I: (*Vai. kar. 60*) n. of a tribe in Tibet.

བཀའ II: शासन (*A. K. XXVI*), आज्ञा, वचन: primarily means simply "word" or "speech"; but being the honorific form it usually implies an order or command. When used of a sacred personage it means his advice or precepts as well as his authoritative words, *e.g.*, བླ་མའི་བཀའ the lama's injunction; རྒྱལ་པོའི་བཀའ the king's command; དཔོན་པོའི་བཀའ the order of the chief.

བཀའ III: also signifies, especially, the enunciations and pronouncements which have issued from the Buddha. They are said to be of three kinds; so སངས་རྒྱས་ཀྱི་བཀའ has three divisions:—

(1) ཞལ་ནས་གསུངས་པ *shal-nas gsuńs-pa* precepts delivered by the Buddha personally.

(2) བྱིན་གྱིས་བརླབས་པ those conveyed through the attendant *Bodhisattva* and *S'rāvaka*, such as Subhūti, S'āriputra, &c., under inspiration from Buddha or by his sanction expressed or implied or revealed in such works as ལྷའི་ལྗོན་ཤིང *lhahi ljon-çiń* the celestial tree; རྔ་བོ་ཆེ་མདོ *rńa-bo che mdo* the great drum *sūtra*. The precepts under this head are subdivided into—(1) སྐུའི་བྱིན་བརླབས the personal blessings (of the Buddha), also the blessings received from his enchanted image; (2) གསུང་གི་བྱིན་བརླབས the blessings derived from his teachings; (3) ཐུགས་ཀྱི་བྱིན་བརླབས the blessings of the spirit. This last again is subdivided into the following:—(1) ཐུགས་ཏིང་ངེ་འཛིན་གྱིས་བྱིན་བརླབས་པ the blessings of a contemplative heart as in the work called ཤེས་རབ་སྙིང་པོ *çes-rab sńiń-po*; (2) ཐུགས་ཐུགས་རྗེས་བྱིན་གྱིས་བརླབས་པ the grace of the spirit, as in གནོད་སྦྱིན་ལ་སོགས་པས་སྨྲས་པའི་སྔགས, the *Mantras* uttered by Noijin and other goblins; (3) ཐུགས་བདེན་པའི་སྟོབས་ཀྱིས་བྱིན་བརླབས་པ the blessings inherent in a truthful spirit or mind.

(3) རྗེས་སུ་གནང་བ *rjes-su, gnań-wa* anything reproduced from memory by the successors of the Buddha under inspiration from him at the Buddhist convocation (*J. Zań.*).

Syn. ལུང *luń*; ངེས་པར་བསྟན་པ *ńes-par bstan-pa*; ཉེ་བར་བསྟན་པ *ńe-war bstan-pa*; གདམས་པ *gdams-pa*; རྗེས་སུ་བསྟན་པ *rjes-su bstan-pa*; རྗེས་སུ་གནང་བ *rjes-su gnań-wa*; ཉེ་བར་གནང་བ *ńe-war gnań-pa*; བཀའ་ལུང *bkah-luń* (*Mńon.*).

བཀའ་བཀོད་པ *bkah-bkod pa* to publish, proclaim; also publication, proclamation.

བཀའ་བཀྱོན *bkah-bkyon* according to *Ńag.* implies blaming; a verbal blow, reprimand, rebuke (given by a superior) (*Jä.*).

བཀའ་བཀྲོལ *bkah bkrol* (*ka-ṭol*) leave of absence.

བཀའ་སྐོར་མེད་པ *bkah-skor med-pa* = འགོར་གཞི་མེད་པར without delay.

བཀའ་ཁོལ *bkah-khol*, གལ་ཆེ་བའི་བཀའ very important order (*Yig. 4*): བཀའ་ཆེམས་བཀའ་ཁོལ་མ the most important will of King Sroñ-btsan sgam-po. This document having been discovered within one of the great pillars of Kinkhording temple in Lhasa is generally known by the name བཀའ་ཆེམས་ཀ་ཁོལ་མ.

བཀའ་འཁོར *bkah-hkhor*, divided into *nañ-hkor* domestic servants; *bran-gyog* servants, menials; *phyi-hkhor* attendants; བཀའ་འཁོར་བྲན་གཡོག those who wait for orders, attendants; དྲུང་འཁོར official clerks; also private secretaries and personal assistants of a high official; attendants in general.

བཀའ་ཁྱབ *bkah-khyab* a decree, manifesto, edict; a general order.

བཀའ་ཁྲིམས *bkah khrims* a law, commandment; བཀའ་ཁྲིམས་བཙན་པོ strict justice; severe punishment: རྒྱལ་པོའི་བཀའ་ཁྲིམས་གཅན་པས by the cruel order of the king (*Jä.*).

བཀའ་ཁྲིམས་པ *bkah khrims-pa* a lawyer; a magistrate.

བཀའ་གྲོས *bkah gros* (*ka-doi*) a conference, consultation; བཀའ་གྲོས་བྱེད आलोचनां करोति makes consultation; gives advice or counsel; gives instructions; བཀའ་ གྲོས་བྱེད་པ to give advice (*Jä.*).

བཀའ་གྲོས་པ *bka gros-pa* (*ka-doi-pa*) a counsellor; senator.

བཀའ་བགྲོ་བ *bkah bgro-wa* सङ्गति debating; considering; taking measures for: ནང་བློན་བཅུ་དང་བཀའ་ཞིབ་ཏུ་བགྲོས་པ་ལ deliberating carefully with the ten confidential ministers.

བཀའ་འགྲོལ་བ *bkah hgrol-wa* to dismiss; dissolve a meeting or a conference.

བཀའ་གླེགས *bkah-glegs* = ཕྱག་བྲིས *phyag-bris* or བཀའ་ཤོག *bkah-çog* a letter; an autograph: མགྲོན་གཉེར་མདུན་ཟུར་སྔོལ་བཟང་པོའི་རྒྱུན་བཞིན་བཀའ་གླེགས་གནང་རྟེན་བཅས་གནང་བ་བཀའ་དྲིན་ཆེ། "great many thanks for the gracious letter with enclosures sent by the *Donñer* according to the good customs" (*Yig. k. 12*).

བཀའ་འགྱུར *bkah-hgyur* is generally taken as a synonym for "the instructions and precepts of Buddha," and means literally "that which has become a command." This term is in fact the title of the great collection of the religious Buddhist writings (mostly, but not all, translated from Sanskrit into Tibetan) known as the Kahgyur. The Kahgyur is divided into seven series of books containing several hundred treatises, and consists properly of 108 volumes, though editions in 100, 102, and 104 volumes are also current.

བཀའ་རྒྱ་བཅུག་པ *bkah-rgya bcug-pa* issuing of an official order; also the accumulation of gold, silver, and grain in a Government treasury.

བཀའ་རྒྱ་མ *bkah rgya-ma* आज्ञापत्र, आज्ञालिपि in Hind. *Para-wana* 1. public order, permit, missive, communication, &c. 2. བཀའ་རྒྱ་མ་ནི་བཀའ་གསང་བ་ཅན (*Lex.*) in mysticism a secret precept; occult communication which is made only to the trusted few.

བཀའ་རྒྱུད ।: *bkah-rgyud* succession or descent of the dogmatic principles of Buddha. The principal school of *Tantrik* Lamaism originating from Nāro Paṇ-chen of Magadha and alleged by Milaraspa to have been introduced by Mar-pa Lo-tsava in Tibet in the beginning of the 11th century A.D. Its different sects or branches are the following:—ཀརྨ་བཀའ་རྒྱུད *Karma Bkah-rgyud*, དགེ་ལྡན་བཀའ་རྒྱུད *Dge-ldan Bkah-rgyud*, དྭགས་པོ་བཀའ་རྒྱུད *Dwags-po Bkah rgyud*, འབྲི་གུང་བཀའ་རྒྱུད *Hbri-guñ Bkah-rgyud*, འབྲུག་པ་བཀའ་རྒྱུད *Hbrug-pa Bkah-rgyud*, ཤངས་པ་བཀའ་རྒྱུད.

བཀའ་རྒྱུད་ II : བཀའ་ཡི་རྒྱུད་ *bkah-yi rgyud*, *i.e.*, the line or thread of the word, *i.e.*, the oral tradition of the word of Buddha which is supposed to have been delivered through a continuod chain of teachers and disciples apart from the written scriptures.

བཀའ་རྒྱུད་བསྟན་པའི་གསལ་བྱེད་ (lit. the illuminator of the doctrine of *Kahgyud* School) a general designation of the chief lamas of the *Bkah-rgyud-pa* sect (*Yig. k. 67*).

བཀའ་རྒྱུད་རྣམ་རྒྱལ་ *Bkah-rgyud rnam-rgyal* the *Bkah rgyud*, Chief Lama whom the Mongol Chief Gushi Khan dethroned after overthrowing the power of *Sde-pa Gtsan-pa* the ruler of Tsang and Ü in 1643 A.D. (*Lon. 13*).

བཀའ་བསྒྱུར་ *bkah-sgyur* admonition and reprehension ; བཀའ་བསྒྱུར་གཏང་བ to issue an order ; to admonish ; བཀའ་བསྒྱུར་བ to translate the words of Buddha, &c.

བཀའ་བསྒྱུར་བཏང་བ *bkah-sgyur btan-wa* to instruct a subordinate in a rough pointed manner, cautioning him against his faults ; to counsel against wrong practices.

བཀའ་སྒྲོག་པ *bkah sgrog-pa* to publish an order ; to proclaim or read an order or edict.

བཀའ་བསྒོ *bkah bsgo* आज्ञा 1. exhortation to the deity. When any one falls ill either naturally or from the supposed malignity of an evil spirit, he goes to a lama or a *Tantrik* priest and begs of him for a *bkah bsgo*—permission to invoke the deity. The lama touches the patient's head with the consecrated sceptre called *Dorje* (*vajra*), with the sacred dagger called the *phurbu*, a string of beads, an image of a Buddha or a deity or a holy book, and repeating some charms exhorts the deity to be propitious to the patient. Those who do not actually suffer from any kind of illness also ask for such protective religious measures. 2. commandment ; precept (*Jä.*).

བཀའ་བསྒོས *bkah bsgos* is pf. of བཀའ་བསྒོ *bkah bsgo*, a sentence passed.

བཀའ་མངགས་པ *bkah mnags-pa* = ངག་གཏམ་བྱེད་པ to send verbal message ; to give a reply.

བཀའ་བཅུ *bkah-bcu*, also བཀའ་བཅུ་པ *bkah bcu-pa*, one who has observed the ten commandments of Buddha. The title of *Bkah-bcu* is given to a Buddhist monk-scholar who has passed all preliminary examinations for a religious degree. There are two classes of བཀའ་བཅུ—those of *glen-bsres* and *gsan-phu* ; a བཀའ་བཅུ of Tashilhunpo monastery is called *Bkah-chen* on account of his superior prestige in religious study and practice.

བཀའ་གཅོག་པ *bkah gcog-pa* to act against an order ; to disregard an express order or command : ཡབ་ཀྱི་བཀའ་བཅག་ཏུ་མེད the order of (one's father must not be disregarded) (*Jä.*).

བཀའ་བཅོས *bkah-bcos* an abbreviation of བཀའ་འགྱུར་དང་བསྟན་བཅོས or the two great collections of Buddhist writings.

བཀའ་ཆེམས *bkah-chems* = ཞལ་ཆེམས resp. for ཁ་ཆེམས a great man's last will ; a royal testament or will : བཀའ་ཆེམས་ཀ་ཁོལ་མ་ཞེས་སོགས་ལས། in the work called *Bkah-chems ka-khol-ma*, etc. (*J. Zan.*).

+ བཀའ་མཆིད *bkah mchid* = བཀའ་ལན or གསུང་གྲོས a command in reply resp., but also word or speech of a superior person. The term likewise signifies a conference, debate, &c. : བཀའ་མཆིད་ཇི་ལྟ་བུ་མཛད what conversation did he hold? བཀའ་མཆིད་དམ་པ་བདུད་རྩི་གསུང་དུ་གསོལ། "pray, let the nectar of pious conversation be uttered !"

བཀའ་ཉན *bkah-ñan* **1.** obedient; dutiful; submissive; observant of command. 2. one's tutelary deity is also called his *bkah-ñan,* because he carries out his protégé's behest; བཀའ་ཉན་ཅི་བགྱི = ཞབས་གཡོག service; doing service (*Mṅon.*).

བཀའ་ཉན་པ *bkah ñan-pa* to obey; be obedient; བཀའ་མི་ཉན་པ to disobey; བཀའ་ཉམས་སུ་ལེན་མཁན an observer of orders or precepts.

བཀའ་གཉན *bkah gñan* the cruel commander; acc. to *Lex. btsan-pahi sa bdag,* "the mighty lord of the soil," is said to be a pre-Buddhist deity (*Jä.*).

བཀའ་གཉན་པོ *bkah gñan-pa* 1. severe retribution from guardian deities for defects in worshipping them; also the injury they do their devotees for impropriety in their conduct or language. 2. damnation into which both a teacher and his pupil fall for disclosure of secrets of their doctrine without authority.

བཀའ་གཉན་བརྗིད *bkah-gñan brjid* a weighty command or injunction.

+ བཀའ་བཏགས *bkah-btags* = ཁྲིམས་བསྒྲགས་པ 1. a proclaimed order: ཁྲིམས་བསྒྲགས་པ is also colloq. called བཀར་བཏགས *bkar-btags.* 2. नैमित्तविद् one versed in drawing omens; an astrologer (བཀའ་གཏོགས་པ) (*M. V. 61*).

བཀའ་རྟགས *bkah-rtags* mark seal; precept; maxim (*Cs.*): བཀའ་རྟགས = ཕྱག་དམ (*Yig. k. 27*).

བཀའ་སྟོད *bkah-stod* a subaltern; agent (*Sch.*)

བཀའ་ཐང *bkah-thañ* = བཀའ་ལུང *bkah-luñ* order; edict (*Jä.*); written order; command; commandment; precept (*Cs.*).

བཀའ་ཐམ *bkah-tham* = ཕྱག་དམ *phyag-dam* or དམ་ཕྲུག *dam-phrug,* seal; chief seal: བཀའ་ཐམ་རིན་པོ་ཆེ་གནང་རྟེན་གསུང་མདུད་ཕྱར་འབྱོར received the letter containing the chief seal of the Grand Lama and enclosing a scarf with charmed knots (*Yig. k. 75*).

བཀའ་དྲག་པོ་ཕབ་པ *bkah drag-pa phab-pa* to command sharply, hastily or severely (*Sch.*); to issue an ultimatum.

བཀའ་དྲིན *bkah-drin,* resp. for དྲིན *drin* प्रसाद, a favour, kindness, grace, boon: བླ་མའི་བཀའ་དྲིན་གྱིས through the kindness of the lama.

བཀའ་དྲིན་ཅན *bkah-drin-can* = བྱམས་པ་དང་ལྡན་པ *byams-pa dañ ldan-pa* kind; gracious; benevolent (*Mṅon.*).

བཀའ་དྲིན་ཆེ *bkah-drin-che* very gracious; (you are) very kind; the usual phrase for our "thank you," in acknowledgment of a kindness or favour—common in letters, &c.

བཀའ་དྲིན་ཆེ་ཞུས་པ *bkah-drin-che shus-pa* to say it is an act of great kindness; to acknowledge kindness; to thank.

བཀའ་དྲིན་རྗེས་སུ་དྲན་པ *bkah-drin rjes-su dran-pa* to remember a benefit or kindness received.

བཀའ་དྲིན་སྙིང་དཔྱངས *bkah-drin sñiñ-dpyañs* to bear in mind or remember the kindness obtained of another person.

བཀའ་དྲིན་མཛད་པ *bkah-drin mdsad-pa* to bestow a favour; to show kindness.

བཀའ་དྲིན་གསུམ་ལྡན *bkah-drin gsum-ldan* possessed of or making use of the three graces or courtesies, viz.: (1) རིག་པ་བསླབ་པ teaching of the sciences; (2) མདོ་རྒྱུད་བཤད་པ explaining the aphorisms and the *Tantra*; (3) དབང་བསྐུར་བྱིན་རླབས་བྱེད་པ blessing and ordaining.

བཀའ་དྲིན་གསོལ་བ *bkah-drin gsol-wa* to thank; to be grateful for favours.

བཀའ་དྲུང *bkah-druñ* a secretary of state.

བཀའ་གདམས *bkah-gdams* an advice; counsel; instruction from a high official.

བཀའ་གདམས་པ *Bkah-gdams-pa* 1. an adviser (*Sch.*). 2. the reformed Buddhist school of Tibet founded by འབྲོམ་སྟོན་པ་རྒྱལ་བའི་འབྱུང་གནས, the chief disciple of Atisha. It was divided into two stages: བཀའ་གདམས་རྙིང་ or བཀའ་གདམས་གོང་མ the earlier school from Bromston to Tsongkha-pa, and བཀའ་གདམས་གསར་པ or the modern school, said to be identical with that now called Gelug-pa, dating from Tsongkha-pa downwards. The earlier *Bkaḥ-gdams-pa* were distinguished for their elaborate ritual and for their power of propitiating deities. The members of the later *Bkaḥ-gdam-pa* have been remarkable for scholarship and linguistic erudition.

བཀའ་གདམས་ཕོ་བྲང་ *bkah-gdams pho-brañ* the palace whore the Grand Lama of Tashi-lhun-po resides.

བཀའ་མདའ *bkaḥ-mdah* a contraction for བཀའ་བློན་དང་མདའ་དཔོན *bkaḥ-blon-dañ mdaḥ-dpon*, minister and general (*Yig. k. 52*).

བཀའ་འདུས་ཆོས་ཀྱི་རྒྱ་མཚོ *bkaḥ-ḥdus chos-kyi rgya-mtsho* a kind of ritualistic observance of the *Rdsogs-chen* sect of the *Rñiñ-ma* Buddhist School in which a particular deity with his followers is depicted.

བཀའ་འདོགས་པ *bkaḥ ḥdogs-pa* to make into law; to proclaim; a proclamation (*Jä.*).

བཀའ་འདོམས *bkaḥ-ḥdoms* = བཀའ་སྟོན་པ or བཤད་པ instruction; order.

བཀའ་སྡོད *bka-sdod*, also written as བཀའ་བསྡོད, one waiting for orders; an attendant on a superior; an aide-de-camp; one's guardian deity is also called by this epithet: བཀའ་སྡོད་གཤིན་རྗེ་གཤེད་ཀྱི་སྒྲུབ་པ་པོ། (*A. 13*) "he who has propitiated the lord of death to serve him as his attendant spirit."

བཀའ་བསྡུ་བ *bkaḥ bsdu-wa* collection of the doctrine (*Jä.*); synopsis of the scriptures at the grand Buddhist convocations; also the convocations where the precepts of Buddha were promulged.

བཀའ་གནང་བ *bkaḥ gnañ-wa*, vb., to order, command, grant, permit; an order; permission: ངེད་བོད་ཀྱི་རྒྱལ་པོའི་བཙུན་མོ་ལ་བཀའ་གནང་བར་ཞུ I beg you will give her as a consort to our King of Tibet (*Jä.*).

བཀའ་གནམ *Bkaḥ-gnam* = ཀ་གནམ a district in the east of Kong-bu; also n. of a district of Ngari Khorsum in Western Tibet.

བཀའ་ཕེབས *bkaḥ-phebs* a great man's order.

བཀའ་ཕྲིན *bkah-phrin* (*ka-tin*) a message.

བཀའ་འཕྲིན *bkaḥ-ḥphrin* letter of command: བཀའ་འཕྲིན་བཀོད་པ to writo or issuo a lettor containing instructions.

བཀའ་བབས I: *bkaḥ-babs* an injunction; a direction.

བཀའ་བབས II: *bkaḥ-babs* the fulfilment of a commission; also the lama or saint who is commissioned with some high duty. When a lama at the command of his spiritual instructor fulfils what was entrusted to him, he is said to be a *bkaḥ-babs*.

བཀའ་བབས་བདུན *bkah-babs bdun* n. of a historical work on later Indian Buddhism by Lama Tārānātha.

བཀའ་བབས་བཞི *bkah babs-bshi* the four commissioned ones (see བཀའ་བབས).

བཀའ་བམ *bkah-bam* = བཀའ་ཤོག ordor; diploma: བཀའ་བམ་ངོ་བཟུས་ཡིག་ཆུང་སྤྲིང་དོན། the object of sending the autograph letter (*Btsii.*).

བཀའ་བྲིས *bkaḥ-bris*, resp. བཀའ་ཤོག *bkaḥ-çog*, a letter; a written authority, generally in autograph: མགྲོན་གཉེར་མདུན་བཀའ་བྲིས་གནང་རྟེན་བཅས་ཕྱག་ཕེབས་བཀའ་དྲིན་གྱི་དཔལ་དུ་ཆེ། it is very gracious of you to favour me with your autograph and enclosure presented by the hand of the Don nyer (*Yig. k. 14*).

བཀའ་དབང་ *bkah-dwañ*=བློན་པོ a minister (*Mñon.*).

བཀའ་འབབ་པ *bkah-hbab-pa* the going forth of an order or edict (*Schr.*).

བཀའ་འབུམ *bkah-hbum* the hundred thousand precepts; n. of a religious work.

བཀའ་བློ་བདེ་བ *bkah-blo bde-wa*=བཀའ་བློ་གོ་བ *bkah-blo go-wa*; ཅི་བྱས་ལ་ཉན་པ (*Ñag.*) 1. attentive; executing an instruction or order with attention; one who is cheerful at heart owing to his attention to བྱང་ཆུབ་སེམས. 2. one who easily understands what he is ordered to do; one who appreciates his superior's instruction. 3. सुवचस् speaking well; eloquent; བཀའ་བློ་མི་བདེ་བ *bkah-blo mi-bde-wa* दुर्वचस् one whose expression or delivery is not good.

བཀའ་བློན *bkah-blon* or བཀའ་ཡི་བློན་པོ *bkah-yi blon-po*, the name given to the four Cabinet Ministers who assist the Gyal-tshab or Regent in the administration of the Government of Tibet during the minority of the Grand Lama of Lhasa. The four Kālön must be laymen and are often military officers. Popularly they are styled Shāpé (ཞབས་པད): བཀའ་བློན་གཟིམས་ཤག *bkah-blon gzims-çag* the residence of a *bkah-blon*.

བཀའ་བློན་དྲུང་འཁོར *bkah-blon druñ-hkhor* the official staff of a Kālön.

བཀའ་བློན་བཞི *bka-blon-bshi* (particularly) the four ministers whom the 4th Manchu Emperor K'ien-lung (in Tibetan called *Lha-skyoñ* Protected of Heaven) appointed to conduct the state affairs of Tibet. They were ཀུན་དགའ་བཞི་ནོ་ཡོན *Kun-dgah-bshi No-yon*, ཚེ་རིང་དབང་རྒྱལ *Tshe-riñ dwañ-rgyal* of *Gyañ Roñ*, ཐོན་པ *Thon-pa*, and རྩེ་དྲུང་ *Rtse-druñ* of *Po-ta-la*. These four governed the country for twenty-seven years from the year of the *iron-sheep* (*Loñ. 16*).

བཀའ་བློན་གསུམ *bkah-blon-gsum* the three ministers who conducted the Government of Tibet from the year of the *fire-horse* to the middle of the year of the *earth-ape*. Their names were:—བཀའ་བློན་ལུམ་པ་བ *bkah-blon Lum-pa-wa*, བཀའ་བློན་ང་ཕོད་པ *bkah-blon Ña-phod-pa* of *Koñ-bu*, and བཀའ་བློན་སྦྱར་ར་བ *bkah-blon Sbyar-ra-wa*.

བཀའ་མ. *bkah-ma*=དགོངས་གཏེར spiritual or intellectual heir-loom. This is a philosophical term of the *Rñiñ-ma* School, meaning the descent of the *bkah* (Buddha's word) in an unbroken succession or without being kept concealed for a period. One who has received such a succession, or any scripture that has come down to him in such a manner.

བཀའ་མང་ཐིམ་པ *bkah-mañ thim-pa* to contain many precepts or commands; one on whom there are instructions or commissions to perform.

བཀའ་གཙང་མ *bkah gtsañ-ma* one whose morals are pure; one who has preserved his vows.

བཀའ་སྩོལ་བ *bkah-stsol-wa*, pf. *stsal*, to speak; to say (where an honoured person is the spokesman); according to circumstances, to command, ask, beg, relate, answer, &c., especially in ancient literature, in which it is almost invariably used of Buddha and of kings speaking.

བཀའ་ཚོགས *bkah-tshogs*=བཀའ་ལན *bkah-lan* or གསུང་ལན a reply in the way of instruction: ནང་མའི་བཀའ་ཚོགས་ཀྱང་གསེར་ལྡན་མའི་རྒྱུན་བཞིན་ཡོད་པ་མཛིན། "pray favour me with replies on internal affairs (uninterruptedly) like the flow of the river of gold" (*Yig. k. 15.*)

བཀའ་འཛིན *bkah-hdsin* letter of authority or commission from Government (issued to one who is on the move or who is to exercise some kind of power over the people) to afford facilities for travelling or for carrying out a mission: མི་རིམ་པའི་ཁྲིམས་རྩང་དང་ཤུགས་རྩང་ཚུར་སྤྱལ་ལ་བཀའ་འཇོན་བྲངས། (*Ṟtsii.*) a commission was issued to despatch hither a man who would frame settled laws and shew energy.

བཀའ་བཞིན་བྱེད་པ *ḇkaḥ-ḇshin byeḏ-pa* to do according to order; doing; ordered: བཀའ་བཞིན་ཉན་པ to be obedient; a faithful servant.

བཀའ་རབ་འབྱམས་པ *ḇkaḥ rab-ḥbyams-pa* a doctor of divinity among the monastic scholars of Tibet; one who has acquired the highest proficiency in the Buddhist sacred literature and is of pure morals.

བཀའ་རམས་པ *ḇkaḥ-rams-pa* one who has passed the highest examination in Buddhist metaphysics; one who has reached the highest of the 13 classes in the *Mtshan-ñiḏ grva-tshañ*, the metaphysical school in the great monastic establishments of Tibet.

བཀའ་ལ་རྩི་བ *ḇkaḥ-la ṟtsi-wa* to give heed to or attend to an instruction or precept; to listen to any advice.

བཀའ་ལུང *ḇkaḥ-luñ* an order; a precept: བཀའ་ལུང་གནང་བ to command or give orders; to issue an injunction.

བཀའ་ལོག *ḇkaḥ-log*=གྲྭ་ལོག *grba-log* (*ṭa-log*) one who has given up his religious vows; a Buddhist monk turned out of his monastery for misconduct. In *Khams* he is called *ḇkaḥ-log*; in Middle Tibet *ṭa-log*.

བཀའ་ཤག *ḇkaḥ-çag* the court or council-house of the four *kālōn* or ministers of Lhasa: བཀའ་རྒྱ་བ་འགྲོ་མི་རྣམས་ལ་བཀའ་ཤག་ནས་དེབ་སྐྱོད་སྐབས་རྩིས་ཁང་ནས་ཀྱང་བདའ་འགྲོད་བྱས། when the warrant officer registers the document at the court of *kālōn* he should also verify it at the Account Office (*Ṟtsii.*).

བཀའ་ཤོག *ḇkaḥ-çog* any writing of authority from a superior; decree; diploma; passport; official paper or letter; བཀའ་ཤོག་རྫུན་མ *ḇkaḥ-çog ṟdsun-ma* a fabricated authority; spurious writing or deed; བཀའ་ཤོག་རིམ་སྐྱེལ *ḇkaḥ-çog rim ṣkyel* to circulate a passport or an official order; serial letters sent one after another.

བཀའ་གསལ *ḇkaḥ-gsal*=བཀའ་ཤོག order; official message: བཀའ་གསལ་རིམ་བསྐྱུད་མཛད་པ to send a message or express order one after another.

བཀའི་རྔ་བོ་ཆེ *ḇkaḥi-rña-wo-che* proclamation by the beat of drum (*Yig. k. 18*).

བཀའི་ཅོད་པན *ḇkaḥi coḏ-pan* an instruction or precept to be received with perfect obedience; to value or honour an order; a command carried out with the same respect as that with which a man carries his own head-dress.

བཀའི་མདུན་བློན *ḇkaḥi ṃdun-ḇlon* resp. བློན་པོ *ḇlon-po* minister: ཁྱུས་ཆུང་བཀའི་མདུན་བློན་གྱི་མིང་འཛིན་བདག་དང་ཞབས་བྱ་སེར་སྐྱ་གཡོག་འཁོར་བཅས་ཁམས་སྟོབས my humble self bearing the title of state minister together with the circle of attendants, both lay and clerical officials, are in good health (*Yig. k. 6*).

བཀར *ḇkar* or བཀར་པ according to the law; to legalize; to make it into law (*Cs.*); to proclaim, publish (*Jä.*); བཀར་བཏགས་པ निमित्तवेदन to publish; publication: བཀར for བཀའ་རུ.

+ **བཀར་བ** 1. *ḇkar-wa* pf. of vb. དཀར་བ སོ་སོར་ཕྱེ་བའི་དོན to separate, put aside, select, banish: གནས་ནས་བཀར་པ banished from his place. 2. to ask any question captiously; to make a peevish enquiry.

བཀལ་བ *ḇkal-wa*, pf. of འགེལ་བ, but in *W.* is the primary form of the verb meaning 1. to load; to burden; put a load on (*Cs.*): བལ་བཀལ་བ to load wool: ཁལ་བཀལ་བ

to load a beast of burden, &c.: ཁྲལ་བཀལ་བ to levy a tax. 2. pf. of འཁལ་བ to spin; ཀླིམས་པ spun; twisted (*Ñag. 5*).

བཀལ་ཐགས *ḇkal-thags* a kind of stuff made of coarse goat-hair about nine inches in width: ར་སྤུ་ཉག་ལྔ་རེ་ལ་བཀལ་ཐགས་བྱས་པར། *ra spu ñag-lña re la ḇkal-thags byas-par* with every five pounds of goat's hair to weave one blanket (*Rtsii.*).

བཀས *ḇkas*, contraction བཀའ་ཡིས instr. of བཀའ.

བཀས་པ *ḇkas-pa*=སེར་ཁ 1. crack, split, cleft. 2. pf. of འགེས་པ.

བཀུ་བ *ḇku-wa* 1. elixir, quintessence (*Cs.*); སྨན་བཀུ medicinal extract. 2. with pf. བཀུམ་པ to make extract of a drug by drawing out the juice (*Lex.*); མར་བཀུ melted butter; བཀུ་བ་འབྱིན་པ to extract the spirit of; བཀུ་ཕྱུང་ *ḇku phyuñ* spirit extracted (*Cs.*); སྨན་བཀུམ་ཏེ་བོར་བ to extract medicine by infusion.

བཀུག་པ *ḇkug-pa* pf. of འགུགས་པ आकृष्ट, མདུན་དུ་བཀུག་པ, drawn or pulled forward; བཀུག་ཤོག summons (*Yig. 7*).

བཀུམ་པ *ḇkum-pa*, pf. of འགུམ་པ, but pres. in *W.* and according to *Lex.* fut. བཀུམ *ḇkum*, pf. བཀུམས་པ, to kill, to destroy; མཚམས་བཀུམ་པར་བགྱིད to cut off the edge; fix a boundary to.

བཀུར་སྟི *ḇkur-sti* भक्ति, सत्कार, सेवा, परिचर्या honour, respect, homage; mark of honour; respectful reception (by asking one to sit on a seat of honour); བཀུར་སྟི་མཆོད་པ *ḇkur-sti mchod-pa* to distinguish (a person) by marks of respect (*Zam.*); རང་ལ་བཀུར་སྟི་འབྱུང་དུས *rañ-la ḇkur-sti ḥbyuñ-dus* when honour is shewn to (one's self) yourself (*Jä.*); བཀུར་སྟིས་དྲེགས *ḇkur-stis dregs* sense of honour; self-respect: མི་ཆེན་པོ་རྣམས་ལ་བཀུར་སྟིས་དྲེགས་པ་ཡོད། *mi chen-po rnams-la ḇkur-stis dregs-pa yod* great men have the sense of dignity.

Syn. མཆོད་པ *mchod-pa*; རིམ་གྲོ *rim-gro*; བསྙེན་བཀུར *bsñen-ḇkur*; རི་མོར་བྱས *ri-mor byas*; ཞབས་ཏོག *shabs-tog*; ཞབས་འབྲིང་ *shabs-ḥbriñ*; བཀུར་བ *ḇkur-wa*; ཉེ་བར་གནས *ñe-war gnas*; ཉེ་བར་སྤྱོད *ñe-war spyod*; རྗེད་པ *rjed-pa* (*Mñon.*).

བཀུར་བ I: *ḇkur-wa*=མཆོད་པ 1. to pay homage or reverence; to esteem. མང་པོས་བཀུར་བའི་རྒྱལ་པོ महासम्मत राजा literally "the king honoured of many" was the name of the first king of the world according to the Buddhist legendary account. 2. to carry; to fetch; to convey in *W.* being also pf. of འཁུར་བ; གོང་དུ་བཀུར་བ to carry upward.

བཀུར་བ II:=ཉེས་པ, གནོང་མི་བཀུར་བ=ཁས་མི་ལེན་པ अनभ्युपगम to slander; to blaspheme; not to accept as true or correct (*Liç.* ཁ *4*).

བཀུར་བར་བྱེད་པ *ḇkur-war byed-pa* the act of respecting; to do honour; frq. to make reverence, to salute.

བཀུར་ཚིག *ḇkur-tshig*=བསྟོད་པའི་ཚིག *bstod-paḥi-tshig* words or expressions of honour, some of which are:—བསྔགས་ཧོས *bsñags-hos*; བསྔགས་པ་བརྗོད *bsñags-pa brjod*; སྟོད་སྨྲ *stod-smra*; མཆོད་ཚིག *mchod-tshig*; མཐོ་བར་བྱ *mtho-war-bya*; སྟོད་པ་སྨྲ *stod-pa smra*; ཆེ་བརྗོད *che-brjod*; མཆོག་གྱུར *mchog-gyur*; ཕུལ་བྱུང *phul-byuñ*; རྨད་བྱུང *rmad-byuñ*; ལེགས་བརྗོད *legs-brjod*; ལེགས་སྨྲ *legs-smra*; གཟེངས་བསྟོད་པ *gzeñs-bstod-pa*; ཤིན་ཏུ་བཟང *çin-tu-bzañ* (*Mñon.*).

བཀུར་ཧོས *ḇkur hos* worthy of respect; respectable.

བཀོག་པ *ḇkog-pa*, pf. of འགོག་པ.

བཀོང་བ *ḇkoñ-wa*, pf. of འཁོང་བ. When བཀོང *ḇkoñ* is joined with ཐ to form the compound word ཐ་བཀོང it means རྫིགས་པ threat, menace.

བཀོད *bkod*=བསྐོས *bskos* to appoint; to raise to the throne.

བཀོད་པ *bkod-pa*, v. འཀོད་པ ब्यूह, सञ्चय, न्यास 1. sbst. གྲལ *gral* or རིམ་པ arrangement; བཀོད་ལུགས order or arrangement; method of arranging; applied to mind, as in སེམས་ལ་བཀོད the meaning is meditation, समाधि, समाहित. 2. vb.=to build, arrange, plan, &c.

བཀོད་པ་མཐའ་ཡས अनन्तव्यूह of boundless or infinite design; the universe; n. of a great *Bodhisattva*.

བཀོད་པའི་གཙུག་གཏོར *bkod-pahi gtug-gtor*= རིག་པའི་རྒྱལ་པོ the prince of learning; science.

བཀོད་འདོམས *bkod-hdoms*=བཀོད་སྟོན་པ *bkod-ston-pa* (*Yig. k. 23*).

བཀོད་བལྟ *bkod-blta* (colloq. བཀོབ་ལྟ *bkob-lta*) the plan of an undertaking; design; plot.

བཀོད་ལྡན *bkod-ldan*=ཟླ་བ་བཅུ་གཅིག་པ *zla-wa bcu-gcig-pa* or དགུན་ཟླ་འབྲིང་པོ *dgun-zla hbriṅ-po* the eleventh month of the Tibetan year, sometimes corresponding with January (*Rtsii.*).

བཀོན་པ *bkon-pa*, pf. of འགོན་པ *hgon-pa*.

བཀོར་འདྲེ *bkor-hdre* seems to be a kind of goblin (*Jä.*).

བཀོལ་སྤྱོད *bkol-spyod* n. of a torment; torture from being boiled in water or oil: བྱོལ་སོང་བཀོལ་སྤྱོད་ཀྱི་སྡུག་བསྔལ *byol-soṅ bkol-spyod-kyi sdug-bsṅal* the sufferings of the damned through the torture of being boiled.

བཀོལ་བ *bkol-wa* occasionally pf. of འཁོལ་བ *hkhol-wa*, to boil; usually indicates འཁོལ་བ to bind to service; to employ; སྣོད་སྤྱད་བཀོལ་བ *snod-spyad bkol-wa* a boiling vessel; གཡོག་ཏུ་བཀོལ་བ *gyog-tu bko-wa* to take into service; ཟུར་དུ་བཀོལ་བ to set aside; to keep out.

བཀྱལ་བ *bkyal-wa* 1. to talk nonsense (*Jä.*). 2. ངག་འཁྱལ་བ to rave in speech; to talk nonsense: བཀྱལ་བའི་ངག प्रलाप, सम्भिन्नप्रलाप, v. ཀྱལ་ཀ.

བཀྱིག་པ *bkyig-pa* in the colloq. of Tsang=འཁྱིག་པ *hkhyig-pa* to tie (by a rope); བཀྱིགས=བཅིངས་པ bound, tied, fastened (*Mṅon.*).

བཀྱེ་བ *bkye-wa*, pf. and fut. of འགྱེད་པ, but in *W.* is used as the only form of the verb=to send, despatch; to cause to come forth: ཕོ་ཉ་བཀྱེ *pho-ña bkye* despatched an envoy: འོད་བཀྱེ *hod bkye* sent forth rays: སྤྲུལ་པ་བཀྱེ *sprul-pa bkye* caused a form to emanate: སྟོན་མོ་བཀྱེ *ston-mo bkye* made an exhibition of.

བཀྱེད་པ *bkyed-pa*, pf. to bend back; recline (vb. nt.).

བཀྱོན་པ *bkyon-pa*=རྡུང་བ *rduṅ-wa* to beat (*Jä.*); བཀའ་བཀྱོན་པ resp. to chastise with words, to scold (*Jä.*). *Schtr.* mentions བཀྱོན་བཀྱལ་བ chiding.

བཀྲ་བ *bkra-wa* (*ṭa-wa*) cog. to ཁྲ་བོ चित्र, विचित्र variegated; beautiful, blooming (of complexion); glossy, well-fed (of animals); བཀྲ་ཆེན महाचित्र a great painting; བཀྲ་བར་འདོན་པ चित्रकर a painter: བཀྲ་བའི་རི་མོ་ཅན with variegated figures; paintings: བཀྲ་བའི་འོད་དཔག་ཅན चित्रमेखला a radiant or illuminated zone or halo: བཀྲ་ཡར विभक्ति, विभक्त variegated; with shades of colour.

བཀྲ་བའི་སྐད་འབྱིན *bkra-wahi skad-hbyin* n. of the bird called *Garghoṅguta*; ཞ་གར་སྒོང་ག་ཏའི་མིང་། (*Mṅon.*).

བཀྲ་བྱེད *bkra-byed*=རི་མོ་མཁན *ri-mo-mkhan* a painter (*Mṅon.*).

བཀྲ་ཤིང་དམར *bkra çiṅ dmar* parti-coloured; on a red ground.

བཀྲ་ལམ་མེ *bkra-lam-me*=ཁྲ་ལམ་མེ glaring; in glare; ཤར་ཁ་བཀྲམ་པ་ལྷ་བུའི་མཛེས་པས་བཀྲ་ལམ་མེ་འདུག་ཅེར the beauty or effect produced by variegated colours as in a painting; the illumination of colours as set forth in a rainbow; hence splendour.

བཀྲ་ཤིས *bkar-çis* मङ्गल, स्वद्द रोचना, प्रकीर्णक, स्वस्तिक prosperity; blessing; good luck: འབངས་རྣམས་ལ་བཀྲ་ཤིས་ཤོག good fortune to my people! may they prosper! བཀྲ་ཤིས་ཀྱི་ཆུ holy-water; consecrated water or consecrating water; བཀྲ་ཤིས་ཀྱི་མལ་ auspicious bed; nuptial bed (*Cs.*); བཀྲ་ཤིས་ཀྱི་ཚིག་ words of blessing; benediction; བཀྲ་ཤིས་ཀྱི་གསོ་སྦྱོང་ *bkra-çis-kyi gso sbyoñ* मङ्गल पोषध auspicious fasting; བཀྲ་ཤིས་སྲུང་བའི་གོ་ཆ *bkra-çis sruñ-wahi go-cha* instruments used for insuring luck; sacrificial ceremony by which blessings are to be drawn down (*Jä.*); བཀྲ་ཤིས་པ propitious; lucky; བཀྲ་ཤིས་པའི་ལྟས good omens; lucky signs; བཀྲ་ཤིས་པའི་རྟགས་ *bkra-çis-pahi rtags* lucky configurations or semblances; happy omens; བཀྲ་ཤིས་མ मङ्गला n. of a goddess; the goddess of glory (*Jä.*); བཀྲ་མི་ཤིས་ misfortune; calamity; བཀྲ་མི་ཤིས་པ calamity; adj. wretched; unlucky.

བཀྲ་ཤིས་གླིང་ *Bkra-çis gliñ* n. of a place in *Khams* (*Loñ.* ༥ *25*).

བཀྲ་ཤིས་བརྒྱད་པའི་མདོ *bkra-çis brgyad-pahi mdo* n. of a short sutra in *K. d.* ༥ *76* which contains the names of eight Buddhas. Whoever recites it and meditates on the perfections acquired by the Buddhas escapes from the dangers of evil spirits and demons. Such a devotee can easily have admission into the courts of kings and address the highest authorities without let or hinderance. Remembrance of this effusion is believed to be a safeguard against bad dreams and also mishaps or accidents in war, and in repelling offensive weapons.

བཀྲ་ཤིས་སྒོ་མང *bkra-çis sgo-mañ* n. of a monastery in Amdo.

བཀྲ་ཤིས་ཅན *bkra-çis-can* अगरु n. of an incense (*Mñon.*).

བཀྲ་ཤིས་ཆོས་རྫོང་ *Bkra-çis chos-rdsoñ* the summer seat of the Government of Bhutan where the Dharma Raja resides. It is ordinarily called Tassisudon on English maps.

བཀྲ་ཤིས་བརྗོད་པ *bkra-çis brjod-pa* मङ्गलोक्ति auspicious expression; a benediction.

བཀྲ་ཤིས་རྟགས་བརྒྱད *bkra-çis rtags-brgyad* the eight auspicious signs or emblems, viz.:—(1) རིན་ཆེན་གདུགས छत्ररत्न the precious or jewelled umbrella; (2) གསེར་གྱི་ཉ सुवर्ण मत्स्य the golden fish; (3) གཏེར་ཆེན་པོའི་བུམ་པ धनकुम्भ the pot of treasures; (4) པད་མ་བཟང་པོ पद्म the excellent lotus; (5) དུང་དཀར་གཡས་འཁྱིལ दक्षिणावर्त शङ्ख the white conch-shell with whorls turning to the right; (6) དཔལ་གྱི་བེའུ श्रीवत्स the auspicious mark represented by a curled noose emblematical of love; (7) མཆོག་གི་རྒྱལ་མཚན ध्वज the chief standard of victory, *i.e.*, the emblem of royalty; (8) གསེར་གྱི་འཁོར་ལོ सुवर्णचक्र the golden wheel.

བཀྲ་ཤིས་རྟགས་ཅན *bkra-çis rtags-can* possessed of auspicious marks: ལག་པ་བཀྲ་ཤིས་རྟགས་ཅན་སྣུམ་པ་ནི། བུ་དང་ནོར་རྣམས་ཐོབ་པར་བྱེད་པ་ཡིན། a glossy hand possessing auspicious lines will cause one to obtain both a son and wealth (*K. d.* ཀོ *217*).

བཀྲ་ཤིས་དུང་ *bkra-çis duñ*=དུང་དཀར་གཡས་འཁྱིལ *duñ-dkar gyas-hkhyil* दक्षिणावर्तशङ्ख a conch-shell with its whorls turning to the right instead of to the left (*Mñon.*).

Syn. དུང་མཆོག *duñ-mchog*; སྐྱེ་བ་ལྔ་པ *skye-wa lña-pa*; རྒྱལ་པོ་འཁྱིལ་བ *rgyal-po hkhyil-wa* दक्षिणावर्त (*Mñon.*).

བཀྲ་ཤིས་ལྡན *bkra-çis ldan* स्वस्तिक, मङ्गलमय auspicious; lucky.

བཀྲ་ཤིས་པའི་རྫས *bkra-çis-pahi rdsas* मङ्गल द्रव्य, स्वस्तिक प्रकरण, स्वस्तिरूपक lucky articles.

བཀྲ་ཤིས་པའི་ཡི་གེ *Bkra-çis-pahi yi-ge* n. of a kind of (mystic) writing which is considered auspicious.

བཀྲ་ཤིས་པར་གྱུར་ཅིག *bkra-çis-par gyur-cig* मङ्गलं भवतु may you enjoy prosperity.

བཀྲ་ཤིས་བྱེད་མ *bkra-çis byed-ma* = རིག་པའི་རྒྱལ་མོ n. of a goddess (*K. g.* ད *112*).

བཀྲ་ཤིས་བླ་མ *Bkra-çis blama* 1. Tashi Lama, the name by which the Panchhen Lama of Tashilhun-po is known in India and Europe. 2. a lama priest who officiates at a marriage ceremony in Sikkim: བཀྲ་ཤིས་བླ་མས་བཀྲ་ཤིས་ཀྱི་གཏོར་མ་མནའ་མའི་མགོ་ལ་རྒྱལ་ཡོང་། the Tashi lama will touch with the auspicious offerings (for the gods) the head of the bride.

བཀྲ་ཤིས་རྩེ *Bkra-çis-rtse* (*Tashi-tse*) n. of a village in the district of *Stod-luñ* in Tibet.

བཀྲ་ཤིས་བརྩེགས *Bkra-çis-bstsegs* (*Tashi seg-pa*) n. of a brother of King *Skyid-lde Ñimahi mgon*, who settled down in *Mñah-ris* in Western Tibet (*Loñ.* ཀ *8*).

བཀྲ་ཤིས་བརྩེགས་པའི་མདོ *bkra-çis btsegs-pahi mdo* n. of a work the reading of which produced auspicious occurrences.

བཀྲ་ཤིས་རྫས་བརྒྱད the eight lucky articles are—(1) མེ་ལོང mirror; (2) གི་ཝང medicinal concretion from the brains of elephant; (3) ཞོ curd; (4) རྩ་དུར་བ *Dub*-grass; (5) ཤིང་ཏོག་བིལ་བ the wood-apple; (6) དུང་དཀར་གཡས་འཁྱིལ a right-whorled conch-shell; (7) ལི་ཁྲི *li-khri* vermillion; (8) ཡུངས་དཀར white mustard.

བཀྲ་ཤིས་རྫོགས་པ *bkra-çis rdsogs-pa* मङ्गलपूरण completion of an auspicious work or event.

བཀྲ་ཤིས་ལྷུན་པོ *Bkra-çis lhun-po* (Tashi-lhunpo) the seat of the Panchhen Rin-po-che, the second Lama in Tibet, ordinarily called Tashi Lama, ranking next to the Dalai Lama of Lhasa. The grand monastery of this name adjoining the town of Shiga-tse in Tsang harbours 4,880 monks, presided over by the Tashi Lama.

བཀྲག *bkrag* (*tag*) འོད་ལྷོང་ལྷོང་མདངས་ཡོད་པ *hod lhoñ-lhoñ mdañs yod-pa* 1. dazzling brightness; lustre; མདངས *mdañs* also བཀྲག་མདངས, *e.g.*, glitter (of jewels). 2. ཤ་བཀྲག beautiful appearance; high colour (of the face, skin); ཤ་བཀྲག་མདངས pure gloss of the skin; བཀྲག་ཆེ very bright (*Jä.*).

བཀྲག་པ *bkrag-pa* = མདོག་བཟང་བ fair or fine complexion.

Syn. མདངས་ཅན *mdañs-can*; འཚེར་བ *htsher-wa* (*Mñon.*).

བཀྲག་མེད *bkrag-med* = མདོག་ངན་པ or མདངས་མེད dull appearance; bad complexion (*Mñon.*).

བཀྲབ་པ *bkrab-pa* (*tab-pa*) pf. བཀྲབས་པ to choose or select from among many; མཆོག་ཏུ་བཀྲབ *mchog-tu bkrab* exquisite choice (*Lex.*).

བཀྲམ་པ *bkram-pa* (*tam-pa*), pf. བཀྲམས་པ, a form of འགྲེམ་པ प्रकीर्ण, प्रसार, अवकीर्ण to spread over, scatter.

Syn. དགྲམ་པ *dgram-pa*; བརྡལ་བ *brdal-pa* also གཏོར་བ *gtor-wa*; འཐོརད་པ *hthord-pa* विस्तीर्ण; གཙུགས་པ *gtsugs-pa* (*Mñon.*).

བཀྲལ་བ *bkral-wa* (*tal-wa*) 1. pf. of འགྲེལ་བ (*Cs.*) མདོ་རྒྱུད་ཀྱི་ཚིག་དོན་ལེགས་པར་བཀྲལ་བ། elucidation (of the meanings of the terms in the *Sūtra* and the *Tantra*). 2. to appoint: ལས་ལ་བཀྲལ་བ, to engage in business.

བཀྲས *bkras* in the passage ལུས་ཤེལ་ཡུང་བཙན་བཀྲས་སྐྱེལ་བ; བཀྲས here means rolled or varnished in variegated colours.

བཀྲས་པ *bkras-pa* (*te-pa*) an abbreviation of བཀྲ་ཤིས་བ, according to *Sch.* also pf. of the verb བཀྲ་བ: བཀྲས་བཏགས for བཀྲ་ཤིས་ཁ་བཏགས an auspicious scarf for presentation on the occasion of a visit or some ceremony or festivity.

བཀྲས་ལུང་ *bkras-luñ* (*Te-lung*) n. of a valley in Tibet (*Deb. 44*).

བཀྲས་ལྷུན *Bkras-lhun* (*Tei-lhun*) मङ्गलकूट a contraction of བཀྲ་ཤིས་ལྷུན་པོ (Tashi-lhun-po); also a heap or mountain of glory or auspicious objects.

卐 **བཀྲི་བ** *bkri-wa* (*ti-wa*) 1. pf. of འཁྲིད་པ to conduct according to order, *e.g.*, one after another. 2. for དཀྲི་བ वेष्टन, to wrap. 3. to draw; to try; to acquire; to search for.

བཀྲིད་དྲང *bkrid-drañ* (*ti-dang*)=མ་རུལ་བ་བརྟུལ་བའི་ནག་པོ the black discipliner of the unsubdued; the black and horrible (assumed) appearance of Mañju Ghoṣa *Bodhisattva* to lead the sinner into the path of righteousness and virtue: རུལ་བ་བཀྲིད་དྲང་གི་བྲོ་བོ the dreaded (Bon) deity who leads or drags the subdued straight onward (*D. R.*).

བཀྲིས *bkris* an abbreviation of བཀྲ་ཤིས *bkra-çis*.

བཀྲིས་པ *bkris-pa* (*ti-pa*), pf. of འཁྲིད་པ. ཐར་པ་ལ་བཀྲིས་པ *thar-pa-la bkris-pa* conducted to emancipation or *Nirvāṇa*.

བཀྲུ *bkru* (*tu*), fut. of ཁྲུས *khrus*, v. བཀྲུ་ཞིན *bkru-zin* क्षालक. བཀྲུ་བཤལ་གྱི་སྣོད *bkru bçal-gyi snod* सेचन पात्र washing bowl; to wash a vessel, plate, &c.: བཀྲུ་བྱ *bkru-bya*, རས་སོགས་གང་ཡང་ཁྲུས་རྒྱུར clothes, etc., to be washed.

བཀྲུག་པ *bkrug-pa* (*tug-pa*) probably an incorrect reading of དཀྲུག་པ.

བཀྲུས་པ *bkrus-pa*, pf. of ཁྲུས *khrus*.

བཀྲེ *Bkre* (*teh*) n. of a place in *Khams*, which is also called བཀྲེ་ནག་ཚང *Bkre-nag tshañ*.

བཀྲེ་ཧོར *Bkre-hor* (*te-hor*) n. of a section of the *Sgo-mañ* department of the monastic school of Dapung.

卐 **བཀྲེན་པ** *bkren-pa* (*ten-pa*), दीन 1. poor, indigent, hungry; ནོར་དཀོན་པ་སའི་ཕྱོགས་བཀྲེན a country where resources are scanty (*Lex.*). 2. कृपण miserly, stingy.

བཀྲེན་པོ *bkren-po*=དབུལ་པོ a beggar; destitute person.

Syn. ནོར་མེད *nor-med*; འཕོངས་པ *hphoñs-pa* (*Mñon.*).

བཀྲེས་སྐོམ *bkres-skom*, contraction of ལྟོགས་པ་དང་སྐོམ་པ, hungry and thirsty: ཐ་མ་ཁ་འདི་ནི་བཀྲེས་སྐོམ་གང་ལ་ཡང་མི་ཕན། this tobacco does not allay in any way either hunger or thirst: བཀྲེས་སྐོམ་པ་ལས་ཚིམ་པར་འདྲེན་ཏེ། leading from hunger and thirst to satiety (*Jä.*): བ་ཡི་ཝོ་མའི་དབུགས་མི་བདེ་བ་དང་བཀྲེས་སྐོམ་སེལ། the cow's milk removes hunger and thirst and hard breathing."

བཀྲེས་ནས *bkres-nas* बुभुक्षित being hungry.

卐 **བཀྲེས་པ** *bkres-pa* (*teh-pa*) to be hungry; also hunger. In *C.* resp. for "hunger"; བཀྲེས་ངར་བ to have ravenous appetite (*Sch.*); སྐུ་བཀྲེས་པ the appetite or feeling of hunger; honorific term: རི་སྟོང་གི་རྩེ་མོ་ཕྱིན་པས་སྐུ་བཀྲེས་པ་ལ་ཞལ་ཟས་འདྲེན་པ་བྱུང་བ on arriving at the top of a barren mountain, he felt hungry and was supplied with food (*Deb.* ག. 7).

卐 **བཀྲོངས་པ** *bkroñs-pa* resp. term for killed; dead.

བཀྲོལ་བ *bkrol-wa* (*tol*) pf. of *hgrol-wa* vb. trs. to untie, to loosen; also in *W.* is the only form in use: མདུད་པ་བཀྲོལ་བ *mdud-pa bkrol-wa* the knot untied. བཅིངས་པ་བཀྲོལ་བ

ḇçiṅs̲-pa ḇkrol-wa set free from bondage; ཁྲལ་བཀྲོལ་བ khral̲ ḇkrol-wa remitted revenue or rent; དགོངས་པ་བཀྲོལ་བ ḏgoṅs̲-pa ḇkrol-wa forgiven, pardoned, &c.

བཀྲོས ḇkros̲ (toi)=འདམས་པ to choose; to select; imp. བཀྲོས་ཤིག ḇkros̲-çig (Situ. 105).

བཀླགས་པ ḇklags̲-pa pf. of ཀློག་པ to have read; done reading: བཀླགས་པ་འདོད wishes to read or sing.

རྐ ṟka or ཆུའི་རྐ chuẖi-ṟka or ཆུ་རྐ=ཕ་མཆུ a gutter; a small channel on the roof of a house or at the edge of the roof for carrying off the rain ཐུར་པའི་རྐ; small furrow conveying water from a conduit to trees or plants; furrow between the beds of a garden; hence even flower-bed.

རྐ་ཆུའི་ལྷ་ཁང Ṟka chuẖi ḻha khaṅ n. of a monastery near Sam-ye.

རྐང ṟkaṅ I: 1. marrow, pith. 2. descent, extraction, origin: དཔེར་ན་ལྷ་མོའི་ཆིབས་པ་དྲེའུ་ལ་རྐང་གསུམ་ཞེས་པ་ནི། "for example, the mule on which the Goddess Paldan Lhamo rides is called ṟkaṅ gsum, on account of a so-called three-fold origin" (its father is an ass, mother a mare but in itself it is neither of them, but a mule!).

རྐང II: 1. stuff: རྐང་ཡག་པོ་འདུག it is of good stuff: རྐང་ཡག་པོ་མི་འདུག it is not of good stuff. 2. bundle; a collection: རྩྭ་རྐང་གཅིག a bundle of grass: སྐྲ་རྐང་གཅིག a tuft of hair: སྐུད་པ་རྐང་གཅིག a skein of yarn.

རྐང་པ ṟkaṅ-pa resp. ཞབས पद, पद्य 1. foot, leg, hind leg of a quadruped: རྐང་པ་མི་གཏོང नाभिक्षिप्य पादै: not throwing the foot (M̲ṅon.). 2. lower part, lower end, e.g., of a letter: རྐང་པ་ཅན having a foot, so the nine letters are called that extend below the line ཀ་ཁ་ག, etc. (Jä.). 3. a metrical line, verse. 4. base foundation: རྫུ་འཕྲུལ་གྱི་རྐང་པ་བཞི ṟdsu-ẖphrul̲-gyi ṟkaṅ-pa ḇshi ऋद्धिपाद the four feet (stages) of performing miracles.

Syn. ཞབས shabs̲; རྒྱུ་བྱེད ṟgyu-byeḏ; འགྲོ་བྱེད ẖgro-byeḏ; བགྲོད་བྱེད ḇgroḏ-byeḏ; རྒྱུག་བྱེད ṟgyug-byeḏ (M̲ṅon.).

ཀང་ཀྱོག kaṅ-kyog bandy-legged. (Jä.)

རྐང་ཀྲི ṟkaṅ-kri (kang-ti) a piece of cloth to wrap round the legs (Sch.).

རྐང་བཀོད ṟkaṅ-ḇkoḏ पादन्यास the manner of walking; རྐང་པ་བཀྲུ་བའི་ས ṟkaṅ-pa ḇkru-waẖi sa पादधावनिका the place for washing the feet.

རྐང་བཀྲ་མ Ṟkaṅ-ḇkra-ma=རི་བྱི་སྐྱེས born of the hill-rat; a name of Agastya Muni (M̲ṅon.).

རྐང་སྐྱེས ṟkaṅ-s̲kyes̲ n. for the Sudra caste (of India) which originated from the foot (of Brahmā) (M̲ṅon.).

རྐང་ཁྲ Ṟkaṅ khra (Kang-ṭha) n. of a king of Ancient India: རྒྱ་གར་གྱི་རྒྱལ་པོ་རྐང་ཁྲ་དང་རབ་སྣང་སོགས་ལྟར་ཕྲེའུ་སོགས་ལས་ཀྱང་མ་རྒྱུད་འབྱུང། "like the Indian Kings, Ṟkaṅ Khra, and Rab s̲naṅ and others, their lineage on the mother's side was also from apes, etc." (J. Zaṅ.).

རྐང་ཁྲབ ṟkaṅ khrab (kang-ṭhab) iron shoes worn along with the coat of mail; that part of armour worn like boots from the foot to the knees; greaves.

རྐང་ཁྲི ṟkaṅ-khri (kang-ṭhi=རྐང་སྙགས) foot-stool (M̲ṅon.).

རྐང་འཁུམ ṟkaṅ-ẖkhum (probably) having a foot contracted by disease (Lex.).

རྐང་འཁོར ṟkaṅ-ẖkhor bandy-legged (Sch.).

རྐང་གོས ṟkaṅ-gos̲ = གོས་ལྷམ gos̲-ḻham Tibetan boots made of felt or of coarse serge.

རྐང་མགོ *rkaṅ-mgo* पदाग्र the fore part of the foot.

Syn. རྐང་རྩེ *rkaṅ-rtse* (*Mṅon.*).

རྐང་མགྱོགས *rkaṅ-mgyogs* swift-footed: མཐུ་རྩལ་རྨད་དུ་བྱུང་བ་རྐང་མགྱོགས་རླུང་དང་མཉམ་པ་གཅིག་སྤྱན་དྲངས *mthu-rtsal rmad-du byuṅ-wa rkaṅ-mgyogs rluṅ-daṅ mñam-pa gcig spyan-draṅs* invited (brought) one who was swift-footed like the wind and possessed of miraculous powers: རྐང་མགྱོགས་ཀྱི་དངོས་གྲུབ the secret blessing of swift-footedness: རྐང་མགྱོགས་ཀྱི་དངོས་གྲུབ་ཐོབ་པས། (*K. dun. 73*) having acquired the grace of swift-footedness.

རྐང་འགྲོ *rkaṅ-hgro* (*kang-do*) पदग one who travels on foot; a vassal or subject paying his duty by serving as a messenger or porter (*Cs.*).

རྐང་འགྲོས *rkaṅ-hgros* also རྐང་བྲོས *rkaṅ-bros* 1. walking on foot. 2. domestic cattle; breeding cattle.

རྐང་གླིང *rkaṅ-gliṅ* a trumpet made of the human thigh-bone used in temples; also in travelling to keep off evil-spirits.

རྐང་རྒྱུ *rkaṅ-rgyu* རྐང་པས་རྒྱུ a foot-soldier, v. རྐང་དམག: infantry acc. to *Cs.*

རྐང་བརྒྱ *rkaṅ-brgya* or=རྐང་བརྒྱ་པ a centipede: འབུ་རྐང་བརྒྱ་ལག་བརྒྱ་ཡོད་པའི་མིང། "the name of the worm which has a hundred feet and arms" (*Mṅon.*).

རྐང་བརྒྱད་པ *rkaṅ brgyad-pa* a fabulous lion having eight feet. An imaginary lion of Buddhist design with eight legs, generally found in sculpture and in Tibetan mythological pictures.

རྐང་ངར *rkaṅ-ṅar* the leg (*Mṅon.*).

རྐང་གཅིག་པ *rkaṅ-gcig-pa* एकपदी one-footed, met. a tree; the fabulous countries of the *Huraṅ* and *Tsu-ta*, the people of which are said to walk on one foot.

རྐང་རྗེས *rkaṅ-rjes* अपदेश, कुक्कुर footstep, foot-mark; a dog; "foot-follower."

རྐང་གཉིས་པ *rkaṅ gñis-pa* mankind; རྐང་གཉིས་གཙོ་བོ the chief of bipeds; an epithet of Buddha or བཅོམ་ལྡན་འདས (*Mṅon.*): རྐང་གཉིས་རྣམས་ཀྱི་མཆོག་སངས་རྒྱས། *Saṅs-rgyas* (Buddha) is the chief of the human kind.

རྐང་གདུབ *rkaṅ gdub* नूपुर a foot ornament; a foot-bangle.

རྐང་རྟེན *rkaṅ-rten* पदाधिष्ठान a foot-stool; trestle; a raised ground or stone step on which, at the time of alighting from any conveyance, the foot is placed.

རྐང་སྟེགས *rkaṅ-stegs* or རྐང་པ་འཇོག་ས foot-stool.

Syn. རྐང་རྟེན *rkaṅ-rten*; རྐང་ཁྲི *rkaṅ-khri*; ཟླ་བ་གཅིག་པ *zla-wa gcig-pa*; ཞབས་སྟེབས *shabs-stebs* (*Mṅon.*).

རྐང་སྟེང་བུ *rkaṅ-steṅ-bu*=སྐར་མ་གསེར་ཕུར the star of the golden flight or བརྟན་པ, a name of a fixed star (*Mṅon.*).

རྐང་སྟེན་བུ *rkaṅ-sten-bu*=སྐར་མ་སྟོད་ཕུར the star of higher flight (*Mṅon.*).

རྐང་ཐང *rkaṅ-thaṅ* 1. on foot. 2.=རྐང་དམག पदातिक a foot soldier (*Mṅon.*).

རྐང་ཐང་པ *rkaṅ-thaṅ-pa* a pedestrian; རྐང་ཐང་དུ་འགྲུལ་བ one travelling on foot; to walk; to go on foot.

རྐང་མཐིལ *rkaṅ-mthil* पादतल the sole of the foot; foot-sole.

རྐང་འཐུང *rkaṅ-hthuṅ* पादप, metaph. for a tree, *i.e.*, that which drinks or draws nourishment through its feet, or roots: རྐང་འཐུང་དམར་པོ रक्तपादप, भूतवृक्ष the red tree; the devil's tree.

རྐང་དྲུག་པ *rkaṅ drug-pa* or རྐང་དྲུག་ལྡན་པ the six-footed, met. for the bee.

རྐང་དྲུག་ཚེས *rkañ-drug-tshes* = ཨ་མྲའི་ཤིང the mango tree.

རྐང་གདུབ *rkañ-gdub* नूपुर foot-ring; bangle-like ornament worn on the foot.

རྐང་འདྲེན *rkañ-hdren* also ཞབས་འདྲེན, *e.g.*, drawn by the foot; shame; disgrace.

རྐང་ལྡན *rkañ-ldan* shoes; that contains or holds the feet; also metaph. for a road, way, passage; རྐང་ལྡན་མ = ཤིང་སེང་གེའི་མཇུག་མ the lion's-tail tree (*Mñon.*).

རྐང་སྣམ *rkañ-snam* coarse woollen leggings manufactured in Tibet.

རྐང་པ་བརྐྱངས *rkñ-pa brkyañs* the legs stretched; རྐང་པ་བསྐུམས contracted legs; རྐང་འཕྱར = ཁ་ཐོར་བ to rove, wander; to disperse, separate: ཕྱུགས་བཏང་བས་ལས་དབང་གིས་རྐང་འཕྱར་ཏེ་བོད་ཡུལ་དུ་ཕེབས། banished from their country, by force of *Karma* they wandered forth and came to the country of Tibet.

རྐང་པ་འཐེང་པོ *rkañ-pa hthen-po* पादेन खञ्जः lame.

རྐང་པ་གསུམ་ལྡན *rkañ-pa gsum-ldan* = རྣམ་ཐོས་སྲས त्रिपादवान् he who is possessed of three legs or three regions; Vishṇu; an epithet of Vais'ravana.

Syn. བྱང་ཕྱོགས་བདག་པོ *Byañ-phyogs bdag-po*; རྒྱལ་པོའི་རྒྱལ *rgyal-pohi rgyal*; དཔལ་གཏེར་གསང་བདག *dpal-gter gsañ-bdag*; གཏེར་གྱི་བདག *gter-gyi bdag*; མིའི་ཆོས་ལྡན *mihi chos-ldan*; ངལ་བསོས་པོ *ñal-bsos-po*; འོད་ཡངས་ཚ་བོ *hod-yañs tsha-bo*; ཨེ་ལའི་བརྒྱུད *E-lahi brgud*; ནོར་སྦྱིན་འདྲེན་པ *nor-sbyin hdren-pa*; གནོད་སྦྱིན་རྒྱལ *gnod-sbyin-rgyal*; ནོར་གྱི་བདག *nor-gyi bdag*; དབྱིག་གི་ཆར་འབེབས *dbyig-gi char-hbebs*; བྱང་ཕྱོགས་སྐྱོང *byañ-phyogs-skyoñ* (*Mñon.*).

རྐང་པའི་སྟབས་སྒྱུར *rkañ-pahi stabs-sgyur* dancing at the cadence of a song (*Mñon.*).

རྐང་པའི་འདུ་བྱེད *rkañ-pahi hdu-byed* पदसञ्चार the movements of the feet which are described as དལ་འགྲོས *dal-hgros*; བུལ་འགྲོས *bul-hgros*; ལེ་ལོའི་འགྲོས *le-lohi hgros*; འགྱིང་འགྲོས *hgyiñ-hgros*; སྒེག་འགྲོས *sgeg-hgros*; རོལ་པའི་འགྲོས *rolpahi hgros*; བརྗིད་པའི་འགྲོས *brjid-pahi hgros*; གོམ་ཤུགས *gom-çugs*; གོམ་སྟབས *gom-stabs*; གོམ་རླབས *gom-rlabs*, གོམ་པ་ཡངས *gom-pa yañs*; གོམ་པ་འཁྱོར *gom-pa hkhyor*; ལང་མཆོང་འགྲོ *lañ mchoñ hgro*; མྱུར་འགྲོ *myur-hgro*; མགྱོགས་འགྲོ *mgyogs-hgro*; རབ་འགྲོ *rab-hgro*; རྒྱུག་པ *rgyug-pa* (*Mñon.*).

རྐང་པའི་རྩ་བ *rkañ-pahi rtsa-wa* = རྟིང་པ *rtiñ-pa* the heel (*Mñon.*).

རྐང་པའི་མཚོན་ཆ་ཅན *rkañ-pahi mtshon-cha can* = ཁྱིམ་བྱ poultry; a fowl (of which the weapon is in its feet).

རྐང་ཕྱིན *rkañ-phyin* felt for covering the legs.

རྐང་བོལ *rkañ-bol* upper part of the foot (*Jä.*).

རྐང་བྲལ *rkañ bral* विपन्न footless; helpless; involved.

རྐང་འབམ *rkan hbam* श्लीपदी a disease in the foot; swelling in the foot; also gout.

རྐང་འབྲོས *rkañ-hbros* or རྐང་བྲོས, v. རྐང་འགྲོས.

རྐང་སྦས *rkañ-sbas* (lit. hidden feet) = སྦྲུལ a snake (*Mñon.*).

རྐང་མ་རྐང་ཅིག *Rkañ-ma rkañ-chig* n. of the part of the nether world where the *Nāga* demi-gods reside.

རྐང་མར *rkañ-mar* pith; marrow: རྐང་མར་གྱི་རིགས་གང་བྱུགས་ཡན་ལག་རེངས་འཁུམས་མཉེན་པར་བྱེད། by rubbing in any kind of marrow, contracted limbs may be smoothened (*i.e.*, straightened).

Syn. མདངས *mdañs*; ཁུ་བ་བྱེད *khu-wa-byed* (*Mñon.*).

རྐང་མིག *Rkañ-mig* अक्षिपाद (अक्षपाद) n. of the founder of *Nyāya* philosophical sect in ancient India.

རྐང་དམག *rkañ-dmag* infantry; a foot-soldier.

Syn. རྐང་ཐང *rkañ-thañ* རྐང་པས་རྒྱུ *rkañ-pas rgyu*; རང་སྟོབས་ཀྱིས་བགྲོད *rañ stobs-kyis bgrod*; རྐང་ཤར་བ *rkañ çar-wa*; ལུས་ཀྱིས་འཐབ *lus-kyis hthab*; ལུས་ཀྱིས་རྒོལ *lus-kyis rgol*; མཚོན་ཆས་འཚོ་བ *mtshon-chas htsho-wa*; དཔུང་བུ་ཆུང་ *dpuñ-bu chuñ* (*Mñon.*).

རྐང་རྩ *rkañ-rtsa*, resp. ཞབས་རྩ *shabs rtsa*, general name for shoes in Tsang. In Tibet the sole of a shoe is generally made of a kind of durable grass, hence the name རྐང་རྩ *rkañ rtsa*, foot-grass, signifies a shoe.

རྐང་རྩེ *rkañ rtse* पदाग्र the fore part of the foot.

རྐང་ཚུགས *rkañ-tshugs*=འགོ་འཛུགས or རྩ་བ་ཚུགས་པ to have a firm footing; to take root.

རྐང་མཛེར *rkañ mdser* iron nails or spikes fastened to the boot-sole for climbing.

རྐང་མཛེས *rkañ-mdses*=ཤིང་མྱ་ངན་མེད་ the *As'oka* tree, *Jonesia asoka* Roxburgh (*Mñon.*).

རྐང་བཞི *rkañ-bshi*, རྐང་བཞི་པ four-footed; quadruped; a beast; also a chair or anything that stands on four legs; རྐང་བཞིའི་ནོར་ལྡན=འབྲོག་པ lit. possessed of cattle; a herdsman (*Mñon.*).

རྐང་ཡང *kañ-yañ* agile; quick in going or walking.

རྐང་རིང *kañ-riñ* I: long shanks.

རྐང་རིང II: v. ཆུའི་བྱ་གག the crane; acc. to some the grey species of duck (*Mñon.*).

རྐང་ལམ *rkañ-lam* foot-path; a passage where a man can only pass but not ride.

རྐང་ཤར་པ *rkañ-çar-pa*=རྐང་དམག a foot-soldier (*Mñon.*).

རྐང་ཤིང་ *rkañ çiñ* treadle of a loom.

རྐང་ཤུ *kran-çu* foot-sore.

རྐང་ཤུབས *rkrañ-çubs* socks; stocking.

རྐང་སོར *kañ-sor* toe.

རྐན *rkan* 1. sometimes used in the place of སྐན. 2. རྐན तालु the palate=དཀན, which is an obsolete form: རྐན་མཐའི་རྙིལ *rkan-mthahi rñil* end of the palate or "gums at the end of the palate": ཏ་ཐ་ད་ ན་ར་ལ་དྲུག, ལྕེ་རྩེ་རྐན་མཐའི་རྙིལ་ལ "the six letters t, th, d, n, r, l, arise from the tip of the tongue and the front palate."

རྐན་ཕུག *rkan-phug* the cavity of the palate: ཀ་ཁ་ག་ངའི་ཡི་གེ་བཞི, རྐན་ཕུག་ལྕེ་རྩེའི་ཆ་ལས་བྱུང་། these four letters come out from partly the cavity of the palate and partly the tip of the tongue. རྐན་དབུས the roof or centre of the palate: ཡ་ཞ་ཙ་ཚ་ཛ་ཉ་ཤ, བདུན་པོ་ལྕེ་དཀྱིལ་རྐན་དབུས་བྱུང་། these seven letters are pronounced from the centre of the tongue and the middle of the palate.

རྐན་མར *rkan-mar* the butter which is mixed with barley-flour to make a paste for the food of children and infants; barley paste made with water or milk is apt to choke infants, so the Tibetan mothers mix in butter (*Deb.* ཀ *10*).

+ **རྐམ་པ** *rkam-pa* or བརྐམ་པ of passionate desire. The latter form བརྐམ་པ is generally used; it signifies འདོད་ཡོན longing; ཆགས་ཆེན लोलुप greed; passionate: བཀུར་སྟི་དང་རྙེད་པ་ལ་བརྐམ་པ *bkur-sti dañ rñed-pa la brkam-pa* a longing for honours and gain: ཁ་ཟས་ལ་བརྐམ་པ་འགྱུར becomes eager for cakes.

རྐུ་བ *rku-wa* चोरयति, pf. བརྐུས, fut. བརྐུ or བརྐུ་བར་བྱ, imp. རྐུས, to steal, rob; pres. རྐུ་བར་བྱེད steals, robs; བརྐུ་བྱ *brku-bya* an article to be stolen; བརྐུ་བྱའི་རྫས *brku-byahi rdsas* things that may be stolen; also stolen property. The six kinds of theft acc. to Buddhism are—(1) འཇབ་བུས་ཀུ་བ *hjab-bus rku-wa* to steal or take away quietly another's property; (2) རྒྱུས་ཀུ་བ *rgyus-rku-wa* to rob a thing knowing all about it beforehand; (3) མཐུས་ཀུ་བ *mthus-rku-wa* to rob violently one's property; (4) ཕྱིས་སྦྱིན་ནོ་ཞེས་ནས་ཀུ་བ to rob a thing promising to return it; (5) བཀོགས་ཏེ་ཀུ་བ to steal by concealment; (6) གཞན་ལ་བཟློས་ནས་ཀུ་བ to rob a thing by slandering another person (*K. d.* ཁ *5*).

ཀུ་བར་བགྲང་བ *rku-war bgrañ-wa* स्तेयसंख्यातं to count as stealing.

ཀུ་སེམས *rku-sems* स्तेयचित्त a mind to steal, or thievish mind.

ཀུར་བཅུག་པ *rkur bcug-pa* हरणग्राहणयोः, ཀུ་ཐབས་སུ་གནས་པ *rku-thabs-su gnas-pa* स्तेयसंवासिक:, the ten kinds of stealing according to Tibetan authors, *viz.* :—མཐུས་ཀུ་བ *mthus rku-wa* to rob by means of incantations; སྒྱུ་ཐབས་ཀྱིས་ཀུ་བ *sgyu thabs-kyis rku-wa* to rob by producing magical illusions; འབྲིད་པས་ཀུ་བ *hbrid-pas rku-wa* to rob one by using threats; གཏམ་པས་ཀུ་བ *gtam-pas rku-wa* to rob by speech (by lying); སྙན་ཚིག་ཟེར་ནས་ཀུ་བ to rob one by soft words; ཕྱིར་བསབ་ཟེར་ནས་ཀུ་བ to rob by saying that he will return the thing afterwards; ནན་དཀྲུག་པའི་ཀུ་བ to steal by conjuring; དངན་འཐན་གྱིས་ཀུ་བ stealing by misappropriation or breach of trust; འཇམ་པོས་ཀུ་བ cheating by gentle persuasion; ཆོས་ཀུ་བ stealing by (imposing upon another in the name of) religion (*Loñ.* ཁ *15*).

ཀུ་བྱ *rku-bya*, same as སྦ་བ to keep secret, hide.

ཀུན་སྒྱིག *rkun-sgyig* thief's pouch; a sort of small wallet.

ཀུན་ཅན *rkun-can* a thief.

ཀུན་བཅོམ *rkun-bcom* plunder; highway robbery.

ཀུན་ཐབས་སུ་བླང་བ *rkun-thabs-su blañ-wa* to take away by thievish means.

ཀུན་ནོར *rkun-nor* stolen goods.

ཀུན་པོ *rkun-po*, fem. ཀུན་མོ *rkun-mo* दस्यु, चोर, a thief, a robber.

Syn. ཇག་པ *jag-pa*; གཡོས་མ *gyos-ma*; ཡན་ལག་ངན *yan-lag ñan*; ཨར་པ *ar-pa*; འཇབ་བུ་པ *hjab-bu-pa*; ཆོམ་ཀུན *chom-rkun*; གཞན་དུང *gshan-duñ*; མཚམས་ཀྱི་བྱེད་པོ *mtshams-kyi byed-po*; ཧོག་ཏུ་རྒྱུ *hog-tu-rgyu*; ཆོམ་པོ *chom-po* (*Mñon.*).

ཀུན་པོས་བསྒོ་བ *rkun-pos bsgo-wa*=ཀུན་པོས་ངན་བྱེད་པ *rkun-pos ñan byed-pa* the harm done by a thief.

ཀུན་དཔོན *rkun-dpon* the head of a gang of wandering marauders.

ཀུན་མ *rkun-ma* one who steals; a thief; also applies occasionally to theft.

ཀུན་རྫས *rkun-rdsas* stolen goods or things.

Syn. ཀུན་ནོར *rkun-nor*; ལྐོག་ནོར *lkog-nor*, stolen property (*Mñon.*).

ཀུན་སྲུང *rkun-srun* a guard; a watchman; to watch for thieves: ཀུན་མ་སྲུང་རྒྱུའི་ཆེད་དུ་ཁྱི་གསོས *rkun-ma sruñ-rgyuhi ched-du khyi-gsos* feeding dogs to guard against thieves.

ཀུབ *rkub* पायु vulgar word for the anus, backside, posterior; colloq. ཕོངས or འཕོངས.

ཀུབ་སྐྱོད་པར *rkub-skyod-par* to move or shake one's hinder parts, a mode of nautch girl's dance in India.

ཀུབ་རྒྱག *rkub-rgyag* a chair to sit upon.

ཀུབ་སྟེགས *rkub-stegs* a sitting bench; a portable rest used by coolies.

ཀུབ་ཚོས *rkub-tshos* buttocks (*Cs.*).

རྐེ་བ *rke-wa*=རིད་པ *rid-pa* (cf. སྐེམ་པ *skem-pa*) lean; meagre (*Cs.*): རྐེ་བར་འགྱུར་བར *rke-war hgyur-war* to grow lean, thin.

རྐེད་པ *rked-pa*, also སྐེད་པ कटि, जघन, the waist, more particularly that part where the girdle is worn; also the loins; also defined as གཞུའི་འཆང་བཟུང་ the ends or notches of the bow which hold the string or to which the string is attached.

Syn. སྐེ་རགས་ཡུལ *ske-rags yul*; བར་མ *bar-ma*; ལུས་ཕྲ *lus-phra* (*Mṅon.*).

རྐེད་རྒྱན *rked-rgyan* an ornament (chain) hanging from waist.

རྐེད་འཆུ *rked-hchu* नितम्ब the buttocks.

རྐེད་མདུད *rked-mdud* anything twisted at the middle; knotted-waist; n. of a biscuit (*Jig.*).

རྐེད་ནད་ཅན་མ *rked-nad can-ma*, v. བུད་མེད་ཟླ་མཚན་དང་ལྡན་པ, a woman who has her monthly courses (*Mṅon.*).

རྐེད་པ་གྱོང་པ *rked-pa gyoṅ-pa* stiff, unyielding waist: རྐེད་པ་གྱོང་བ་ཁྱོ་བོ་འཆི་བར་འགྱུར the husband of the woman with a stiff waist will die (*K. d.* ཁ *217.*).

རྐེད་པ་རྒྱུར་བ *rked-pa, rgyur-wa* (metaph.) to become a slave (female): རྐེད་པ་རྒྱུར་བ་གཞུ་འདྲ་གཡོག་མོར་འགྱུར། a woman whose waist has become bent like a bow becomes a maid servant (*K. d.* ཁ *217*).

རྐེད་པ་ཆག *rked-pa chag* (lit. broken waist) to fail in a great undertaking: སེང་གེ་མཆོང་ས་ལ་ཝ་མཆོང་ན་རྐེད་པ་ཆག if a fox (tries to) leap over a place where lions jump, he breaks his waist, *i.e.*, dies in the attempt.

རྐེད་པ་ཕྲ *rked-pa phra* a slender waist.

རྐེད་འབྲས *rked-hbras*=ཚ་བ་ལེན n. of a fruit used in fever (*Mṅon.*).

རྐེད་སྦོམ *rked-sbom* one with a large or broad waist; a corpulent person.

Syn. ལྟོ་བ་ཆེ་བ *ldo-wa che-wa*; གསུས་པོ་ཆེ *gsus-po che*; ལྟོ་ལྡིར་བ *lto-ldir-wa*; གསུས་རྡེས་ཅན *gsus-rdses can*; ལྟོ་བ་འཕྱང་བ *lto-wa hphyaṅ-wa*; གྲོད་པ་ཆེན་པོ *grod-pa chen-po*; གྲོད་པ་སྦོམ་པོ *grod-pa sbom-po* (*Mṅon.*).

རྐེད་མེད་མ *rked-med-ma* a pretty woman; =བུད་མེད་མཆོག, a woman with slender waist (*Mṅon.*).

+ རྐེད་སོ *rked-so*=རྐེད་པ *rked-pa* the waist: ལྡེ་མིག་ཆུང་ངུ་སྣ་མང་པོས་སྐུའི་རྐེད་སོ་འཁོར་བ *lde-mig chuṅ-ṅu sna-maṅ-pos skuhi rked-so hkhor-wa* (*A. 133*) many little keys of different kinds surrounded his waist.

རྐོ་བ *rko-wa*, pf. བརྐོས *brkos*, imp. རྐོས་ཤིག *rkos-çig* 1. to dig, dig out; to hoe 2. to engrave; turn up; till.

རྐོ་བྱེད *rko-byed* I: 1.=ཕག a hog; also that which digs; a mattock, shovel. 2. विशिख an arrow.

རྐོ་བྱེད II: v. བྱི་བ *byi-wa* that burrows; a rat (*Mṅon.*).

རྐོ་མ *rko-ma* a kind of small hoe for digging earth; n. of a bird called ཀོ་མ *ko-ma* (*Vai. sṅ.*).

རྐོས་མཁན *rkos-mkhan* or བརྐོས་མཁན or རྐོ་མི खनक a digger; one who hoes.

རྐོག་མ *rkog-ma* incorrectly for ལྐོག་མ *lkog-ma*.

རྐོང་པ *rkoṅ-pa*=ཟ་རྐོང *za-rkoṅ* दद्रुरोग ringworm; itch (*Cs.*).

རྐོང་པོ་འབྲས་ཆེན *rkoṅ-po hbras chen* n. of a skin disease with large eruptions; also eruptions (*Ya-sel. 28*).

རྐོད་པ *rkod-pa* engraving; =རྐོ་བ *rko-wa*, to dig or to engrave (*Cs.*).

✢ རྐོན་པ *rkon-pa* net; a fowler's net: བྱ་བཟུང་བའི་དོན་དུ་རྒྱ་སྣེ་འཛུགས་པ་ལ་རྐོན་པ་འཛུགས་ཟེར། (*Ñag.*) to set up a snare to catch birds is called *rkon-pa hdsugs-pa*.

Syn. བྱ་རྒྱ *bya-rgya*; བྱ་རྐོན *bya-rkon* (*Mñon.*).

བརྐམ་ཆགས *brkam-chags* लुब्ध passionate; also greedy.

བརྐུས *brkus* རྐུན་མ་བརྐུས་ཚར་བ *rkun-ma brkus char-wa* stolen: བརྐུས་ཏེ་བོར་བ *brkus-te bor-wa* to abandon or throw away a thing after stealing it.

བརྐོ་སྤྱོད *brko-spyod* a gouge; an instrument to scoop out (*Sch.*); an instrument to engrave; བརྐོ་བྱའི་ས *brko-byahi sa* ploughed land; བརྐོས་པ *brkos-pa* खात dug out; བརྐོས་ཕོར *brkos-phor* a mould for making clay images: ལྷ་ཐོ་ཐོ་རི་གཉན་བཙན་གྱི་རིང་ལ་སྤང་སྐོང་ཕྱག་རྒྱ་པ་དང་ས་ཚྭའི་བརྐོས་ཕོར་ཁང་སྟེང་དུ་བབས་ཏེ་དམ་པའི་ཆོས་ཀྱི་དབུ་བརྙེས། in the time of the Lhatho-thori dynasty there fell on the top of the palace a book called *Spañ skoñ phyag-rgya* and a mould for clay miniature images and brought the commencement of the holy doctrine.

བརྐོས་མ *brkos-ma* sculpture; anything that has been engraved upon.

རྐྱག་པ *rkyag-pa*, also སྐྱག་པ *skyag-pa*, dung; ordure; excrement: རྐྱག་པ་བཏོང་བ *rkyag-pa btoñ-wa* to cause purging, v. སྐྱག *skyag*.

རྐྱང I: *rkyañ* खर, गवय *Equus kyang*, or the wild ass of Tibet and Higher Asia. It is found everywhere in Tibet in large droves, and is distinct from the wild ass of Sindh and Persia. ཕོ་རྐྱང, a male *kyang*; མོ་རྐྱང a female *kyang*; རྐྱང་དར་མ an adult *kyang*; རྐྱང་རྒན an old *kyang* (*Cs.*).

རྐྱང II: or རྐྱང་པ *rkyañ-pa*, also རྐྱང་རྐྱང *rkyañ-rkyañ*. एकाकिन्, नग्न, अचेल, each; single; simple; alone: ང་རྐྱང་པས་མི་ཐུབ I alone cannot: རས་རྐྱང་པ dressed only in cotton cloth: སྐུ་ཞབས་སྐུ་རྐྱང་ཇི་ལྟར་ཐེབས will Your Honour go thus alone? ཆུ་རྐྱང་འཐུང་ནས drinking water only. ལུས་རྐྱང་ naked body; ཅིག་རྐྱང་ only one; མི་རྐྱང་, same as མི་སྐྱང་པོ, *i.e.*, a free, unemployed man, generally one that carries no burden; ཡི་གེ་རྐྱང་པ *yi-ge rkyañ-pa* a letter that forms by itself a syllable, or one that is not *brtegs-pa* (mounted) and without any other consonant or any vowel sign superscribed; རྐྱང་པའི་གྲངས said to be 1, 10, 100, and the further multiples of 10; མིང་རྐྱང་པ a word that has no affix denoting case, &c., also a name without any titles added to it.

Syn. རེ་རེ *re-re*; གཅིག་བུ *gcig-bu*; སྲབ་པ *srab-pa*; གཅེར་བུ *gcer-bu*.

རྐྱང་ཆུ *Rkyañ chu* n. of a lake in the south of Ladak, in the neighbourhood of which there are many wild asses.

རྐྱང་ཐག *rkyañ-thag* (ཐག་པ་རི་འམ་ཡང་ན་ཁང་ཐོག་ནས་མར་བཏང་བ) a rope that is lowered from the top of a mountain or from the roof of a lofty house (*Yig.*).

རྐྱང་པ 1. *rkyañ-pa* गद्य prose; writing. 2. རྐྱང་བ *rkyañ-wa* = རྐྱོང་བ *rkyoñ-wa* प्रसारित extended; spread.

རྐྱང་འཕྱེས *rkyañ-hphyes* महापद्म an immensely large number.

རྐྱང་མ *rkyañ-ma* n. of an artery often referred to in mystic meditation. It is one of the three arteries denominated *Srog-rtsa riñ-po*, and is asserted to run towards the left side.

རྐྱང་ཕྱག *rkyañ-phyag* salutation by prostrating one's self on the ground with the hands and feet stretched out (*A. 48*).

རྐྱན་ *rkyan* 1. a brass vessel like a tea-pot, with a spout; in *W.* "*o-kyan*," a milk-pot. 2. pot-belly; paunch (*Sch.*); ཆབ་རྐྱན་, a vessel for water; ཆང་རྐྱན a vessel for wine (*Jä*).

རྐྱན་བུ *rkyan-bu* = འགྲིམ་ཞལ *hgrim-shal* a kind of vessel made of brass or silver or gold of the shape of a wine glass.

རྐྱལ་ཀ *rkyal-ka* = ཀུ་རེ vain talk; *rkyal-ka byed-pa* to play a practical joke on; to make game of.

རྐྱལ་པ *rkyal-pa* चर्मखल्ली a sack or leather bag, frq. is poetical term for the body or the five aggregates, *i.e.*, ལུས་འདི་མི་གཙང་རྫས་ཀྱི་རྐྱལ་པ "the body is a bag of unclean things" (*Jä.*).

རྐྱལ་བ *rkyal-wa* सन्तरण to swim; རྐྱལ་རྩེད་པ *rkyal-rsted-pa* to amuse one's self by swimming (*Jä.*); colloq. "*khyal-gyab khan*" a swimmer.

རྐྱལ་བུ *rkyal-bu* small bag; pouch; colloq. *kyal-bu.* ར་རྐྱལ a bag of goat skin; ཕྱེ་རྐྱལ; a bag for flour ཆུ་རྐྱལ water bag or Hindi *moshuk*; མར་རྐྱལ butter bag.

རྐྱལ་བྱེད་པ *rkyal byed-pa* अवगाहन the act of swimming or bathing. In the mystic language of the *Brahmakāyika deva* རྐྱལ་བྱེད *rkyal-byed* or རྐྱལ་བ signifies སྡུག་བསྔལ་བ misery; ཉམས་པར་རྐྱལ་བྱེད or ཀུན་ཏུ་རྐྱལ་བྱེད means ཀུན་འབྱུང་བ sins; རྐྱལ་པ་མར་བྱེད denotes རྐྱལ་མར the exhaustion of misery, *i.e.*, the cessation of misery or its འགོག་པ निरोध; རྐྱལ་བ་ཐོལ་མེད signifies རྐྱལ་མར་སྒོམ་པ, *i.e.*, to meditate on the exhaustion of misery signifies ལམ or the way to *Nirvāna*. These are the terms believed to be used in the language of the celestial beings who dwell in the heaven called འཕྲུལ་དགའ निर्माणरतय (*K. ko.* ཀ *236*).

རྐྱེན *rkyen* I: In Buddhist science this important term expresses any co-operating influence which serves to shape and bring about an event as distinguished from རྒྱུ *rgyu*, its direct and obvious cause. In plain language, *rgyu* is the primary cause of anything, but *rgyu* is frequently controlled and modified by a co-ordinate influence known as *rkyen*. As a medical term, according to Jāschke, *rkyen* is differentiated from *rgyu* in that it indicates the pathological or secondary cause of disease, while the latter word denotes its primary or anthropological cause. However, while assigning to *rkyen* the primary meaning of "cause" and "occasion" in the qualified sense of being contributary only to that which comes to pass, we have to note the apparently contradictory signification—effect, occurrence, incident, event. So we meet with རྐྱེན་ངན་པ *rkyen-ńan-pa* unfortunate accident; རྐྱེན་ངན་པས་འདས he has perished by an evil incident; ཚེ་འདིར་བྱུང་བའི་རྐྱེན་ངན་རྣམས the adversities arising in this life; རང་མི་འདོད་པའི་རྐྱེན an event disagreeable to one's own self; བློ་བུར་རྐྱེན *blo-bur rkyen* a sudden accident; རྐྱེན་དེ་ལ་བརྟེན་ནས *rkyen de-la brten-nas* owing to that circumstance; མེད་པའི་རྐྱེན་ལ་བལྟས་ཏེ *med-pahi rkyen-la bltas-te* or བརྟེན་ཏེ *brten-te* considering the case of not being, not having; thus ནད་ཀྱི་རྐྱེན་དང་འཆི་བའི་རྐྱེན stands also for a cause of disease and of death; བགོལ་རྐྱེན *bgol-rkyen* any circumstance or event adverse to the success of an action, any obstacle, anything opposed or hostile to the existence of another thing: མཐུན་རྐྱེན *mthun-rkyen* a happy, favourable circumstance; furtherance; assistance; supply; མཐུན་རྐྱེན་བྱེད་པ *mthun-rkyen byed-pa* to assist in; to help to; མཐུན་རྐྱེན་འཛོམས་པ *mthun-rkyen hdsom-pa* altogether successful.

རྐྱེན II: प्रत्यय, प्रत्यय In Buddhist metaphysics there are four kinds of རྐྱེན *rkyen*, viz., (1) རྒྱུའི་རྐྱེན *rgyuhi rken* हेतुप्रत्यय relation of causality; (2) དེ་མ་ཐག་པའི་རྐྱེན *de-ma-thag pahi rkyen* समनन्तर प्रत्यय relation of posteriority; (3) བདག་རྐྱེན *bdag-rkyen* अधिपतिप्रत्यय relation of subordination or conditionality; (4) དམིགས་རྐྱེན *dmigs-rkyen* आलम्बनप्रत्यय relation of dependence (as for instance the relation of parts to the whole and *vice versâ*): རིག་པས་གཟུགས་ཅན་གྱི་རྐྱེན་བྱེད་ན་བདག་རྐྱེན་གཅིག་པོས་བྱེད, གཟུགས་ཅན་གྱིས་རིག་པ་ལ་རྐྱེན་བྱེད་ན་དམིགས་རྐྱེན་དང, བདག་རྐྱེན་གཉིས་ཀ་ཚང་དགོས, གཟུགས་ཅན་གྱི་གཟུགས་ཅན་ལ་རྐྱེན་བྱེད་ན་རྒྱུ་རྐྱེན་དང་བདག་རྐྱེན་གཉིས་ཀས་བྱེད་དོ. Besides the above four there are two other subdivisions of རྐྱེན *rkyen*, viz., ཉེར་ལེན उपादान प्रत्यय and ལྷན་གཅིག་བྱེད सहकारी प्रत्यय (*Loñ. 16*).

རྐྱེན III: misfortune; ill-luck; calamity: རྐྱེན་ཟློག་པ *rkyen glog-pa* to avert a misfortune: རྐྱེན་ཐེགས་པ *rkyen thegs-pa* to endure misfortune: རྐྱེན་ཐུབ་པ *rkyen thub-pa* to be equal to the occassion, cope with calamity.

རྐྱེན་གྱིས *rkyen-gyis*, postp. with gen. by reason of; on account of; by; དེའི་རྐྱེན་གྱིས therefore; accordingly.

རྐྱེན་གཅིག་རྟོགས *rken-gcig rtogs* = རང་སངས་རྒྱས an epithet for a *Pratyeka* Buddha (*Mñon.*).

རྐྱེན་ཆགས་འབྱུང་བ *rkyen-chags hbyuñ-wa* to die or to be abolished (*D. çel. 11*).

རྐྱེན་རྟོགས *rkyen-stogs* प्रत्येकबुद्ध also the contemplation of a *Pratyeka* Buddha and ordinary saint; a class of Buddhist devotees who meditate on *rkyen*, the co-operative cause.

རྐྱེན་ཐུབ *rkyen-thub* = བཟོད་པ patience; forbearance (*Mñon.*).

རྐྱེན་པ *rkyen-pa* यव barley.

卐 རྐྱེན་རྩི *rkyen-rtsi* = རྐྱེན་སྨན *rkyen-sman* प्रत्ययौषधि a medicine that is administered for determining the co-operative cause of a disease.

རྐྱོང་བ *rkyoñ-wa*, pf. བརྐྱངས, fut. བརྐྱང་བ or བརྐྱང་བར་བྱ, to stretch, extend, stretch forth (one's hand to a person); put out (the tongue); spread; distend (the wings, a curtain): ཞབས་གཉིས་བརྐྱོང་བསྐུམ *shabs-gñis brkyoñ bskum* one leg stretched out, the other drawn in.

Syn. བརྐྱང་བ *brkyañ-wa*; བརྐྱངས་པ *brkyañs-pa*; རྐྱངས་པ *rkyañs-pa*; རྐྱོངས་པ *rkyoñs-pa*; བསྣར་བ *bsnar-wa* (*Mñon.*).

རྐྱོང་ཙེ *rkyoñ-tse* in *W.* lamp; candle (*Jä.*).

བརྐྱང་ཤིང *brkyañ-çiñ* 1. literally "the extending-wood," an instrument of torture in Tibet; a wooden frame on which the extended arms and legs of the delinquent are fastened down, whilst burning pitch or sealing wax is dropped on his naked breast, which procedure is called བརྐྱང་ཤིང་སྦྱོད་པ or བརྐྱང་ཤིང་ལ་བཙུག་པ or བརྐྱང་བ, placing or stretching one on a cross (*Jä.*). 2. in New Testament translation adopted to signify "cross."

བརྐྱངས *brkyañs* विश्रान्त prostrated (by fatigue); stretched out; བརྐྱང་བའི་དོན་ཅན आयतनार्थं for the purpose of stretching.

ལྐུག *lkug* पण a wager: ཤོ་རྩེགས་ཀྱི་རྒྱལ "to gain a wager in dice-playing, &c."

ལྐུགས་པ *lkugs-pa* 1. dumb; mute; ཁ་ལྐུགས་པར་བྱེད་པ *kha lkugs-par byed-pa* to put to silence; ལྐུགས་པ་མ a dumb woman (*Cs.*). 2. मूर्ख, जड़ dull, stupid (*Sch.*). The following examples may belong to either 1. or 2.:—ལྐུགས་པར་སྐྱེས *lkugs-par skyes* born idiotic or mute: ལྐུགས་པར་སྐྱེས་ན་རྣམ་ཤེས་ལས་སུ་མི་...

ཏང་བས་ཆོས་བྱེད་དུ་མི་ཁོམ། if one is born a deaf-mute, one's consciousness (soul) not being suited to work, one cannot act religiously.

Syn. སྨྲ་བཅད་ *s̱mr̠a-ḇcaḏ*; ངག་གིས་དབུལ་ *ṅag-gis ḏbul*; ངག་མི་ལྡན་ *ṅag mildan*; སེམས་བེམ་པོ་ *sems bem-po*; ཚིག་ཉམས་ *tshigñams*; ཚིག་མི་གསལ་ *tshig mi-gsal*; བེམ་པོ་ལྟར་ལྐུག་ *bem-po ḻtar ḻkug*; མི་སྨྲ་ཤེས་ *mi-s̱mr̠a çes̱* (*M̱ñon.*).

ཀློག *ḻkog* I: = ཕ་གི *pha-gi* yonder. In the passage ཀློག་གི་རི་སྣ་འདི་ནས་མཐོང་ལགས་ཟེར་བས, he said "from here look to yonder hill-side": ཀློག་གི་རི་སྣ *ḻkog-gi ri s̱na* = ཕ་གི་རི་ཟུར the corner of the hill there.

ཀློག II: secrecy; ཀློག་གི་ཆུང་མ a wife kept secretly in Tibet. Where polyandry prevails any of the brothers who is not satisfied with the common spouse takes to himself a wife called *Kok-gi chung-ma*—a concubine (*Cs.*).

ཀློག་མ *ḻkog-ma*, vulg. ཨོག་འཇོལ *og-ẖjol* 1. gullet. œsophagus. 2. wind-pipe. 3. the throat; ཀློག་མའི་ལྷ་གོང *ḻkog-maẖi ḻha-goṅ* the larynx (*Sch.*); also written ཀློག་མའི་ལྷར་གོར.

ཀློག་དཀར *ḻkog-ḏkar* the ferret-badger (*Helictis monticola*).

ཀློག་གྱུར *ḻkog-gyur*, v. ཀློག་ན་མ *ḻkog-na-ma* (*M̱ñon.*); ཀློག་གྱུར་བྱས *ḻkog-gya byas̱* made secret.

ཀློག་གླུ *ḻkog-glu* a secret hummed song: གཞན་གྱི་མ་ཐོས་པར་བྱས་ནས་གླུ་ལེན་པ་ལ་ཀློག་གླུ་ཟེར a song sung so that others may not hear it is called *Kog-lu* (*Ṅag.*).

ཀློག་ཆད *ḻkog-chaḏ* secret punishment.

ཀློག་ཆོས་བྱེད་པ *ḻkog-chos̱ byeḏ-pa* to apply one's self to religious studies secretly.

ཀློག་རྙན *ḻkog-r̠ñan* a reward given secretly; a bribe.

ཀློག་ཏུ *ḇkog-tu* confidentially, secretly; ཀློག་གྱུར or ཀློག་ཏུ་གྱུར་པ परोक्ष secret; hidden; out of sight (*Jä.*); ཤིན་ཏུ་ཀློག་གྱུར *çin-tu ḻkog-gyur* very secret; most confidential.

ཀློག་ཏུ་བརྐུས *ḻkog-tu ḇrkus̱* stolen; removed secretly; ཀློག་ཏུ་གྲེན་པ to converse secretly; ཀློག་ཏུ་ཆོས a secret doctrine; to worship secretly; ཀློག་ཏུ་ལབ་པ to speak confidentially.

ཀློག་མདུད *ḻkog-m̱duḏ* = ཨོལ་མདུད the larynx.

ཀློག་འདུན *ḻkog-ẖdun* is described as meaning ཏ་མ་གོ་བར་གྲོས་བྱེད་པ, secret conversation or deliberating, so that others may not understand it.

ཀློག་ན་མ *ḻkog-na-ma* that which is not evident.

Syn. ཀློག་གྱུར *ḻkog-gyur*; མངོན་སུམ་མིན་པ *m̱ñon-sum min-pa* (*M̱ñon.*).

ཀློག་ནོར *ḻkog-nor* = རྐུན་རྫས *r̠kun-r̠das̱*, lit. secret articles; stolen property (*M̱ñon.*).

ཀློག་ཕྲ *ḻkog-phra* = ཀློག་ཏུ་ཕྲ་མ་བྱེད་པ or དཀྲུག་ཤིང་བྱེད་པ *ḏkrug-çiṅ byeḏ-pa* misunderstanding; difference (between two parties).

ཀློག་ཟན་ཟ་བ *ḻkog zan-za-wa* to take usurious interest in secret (*Sch.*); ཀློག་ཐབ་བྱེད་ནས་ལྟ་བ to watch; to witness from a lurking-place.

ཀློག་ཟས་ཟ་བ *ḻkog-zas̱ za-wa* to take food secretly.

ཀློག་ལ་བྲང་འབྱར་གྱི་རྒྱལ་ཁམས *Ḻkog-la braṅ ẖbyar-gyi r̠gyal khams̱* the name of a kingdom of the *Asura* (demons) where people have no neck, their chins being joined to the breast.

ཀློག་ཤལ *ḻkog-çal* सास्ना dew-lap (of oxen); ཀློག་ཤལ་ཅན *ḻkog-çal-can* = བ་གླང oxen in general (*M̱ñon.*).

ཀློག་སོག *ḻkog-sog* craw (of birds) (*Cs.*).

ཀློབ *ḻkob* fat, heavy, plump (*Sch.*).

ཀློལ་མདུད *ḻkol-m̱duḏ* = ཨོལ་མདུད larynx.

སྐ *s̱ka*; this word is thus explained སྐ་ཞེས་ཆོས་རྣམས་ཀྱི་ཕྱུང་པོ་ཡོངས་སུ་ཤེས་པ་རྟེན་ཏེ "*s̱ka* shows the complete knowledge of the aggregation of all *dharma* or phenomena" (*K. d.* ཉ *114*). This explanation also occurs in the aphorism on the interrogation of the Nāga-rāja Samudra (*K. d.* ག *178*), also in (*Ḥbum.* ག *283*): སྤུང་པོ་དམིགས་སུ་མེད་པའི་ཕྱིར་ཆོས་ཐམས་ཅད་ཀྱི་སྒོའོ "*ska* is the symbol of the law of Buddha (Buddhism) as it explains mystically that all things are (निरवलम्ब) not dependant; they are supportless, *i.e.*, have no real existence."

སྐ་ཅིག *ska-cig* for སྐད་ཅིག a moment.

སྐ་ཅོག *ska-cog* or ཀ་ལྕོག *ka-lcog* the names of two grammarians jointly written for abbreviation, *Ska* standing for སྐ་བ་དཔལ་བརྩེགས and *Cog* for ཅོག་རོ་ཀླུ་ཡི་རྒྱལ་མཚན *Cog-ro klu-yi rgyal-mtshan*.

སྐ་བ *ska-wa* thick (of fluids, cf. *sla-wa*); *ska-slad* consistence; density (*Jä.*).

སྐ་རགས *ska-rags* काञ्चबन्ध, कटिबन्ध, मेखला, मखिक; =ཞུགས་ཐུ also སྐེ་རགས, in resp. language; སྐུ་རགས a girdle: སྐ་རགས་འཆིང་བ to put on a girdle. སྐ་རགས་བཞུར་བ (*Sch.*) a girdle with a clasp; སྐ་རགས་པོ་ཕུ་ཅན काचहार, स्वच्छ-हार ornamental chain worn by Tibetan women on the waist.

སྐ་རགས་བཟང་པོ་མ *Ska-rags bzan-po ma*; གནོད་སྦྱིན་མོའི་གཙོ་མོའི་མིང n. of a princess of the *Noijin* demi-gods (*Mñon.*).

སྐག *skag*=ཀག *kag* or ཀེག *keg* अश्लेषा 1. n. of one of the 27 constellations, *Açleṣā*; an evil star. 2. mischief; bad luck; evil; the name of the goddess Bhogavatī; a fox ལོ་སྐག *lo-skag* an unlucky or bad year ཟླ་སྐག *zla-skag* an evil or unlucky month ཞག་སྐག *shag-skag* a bad day; དུས་སྐག *dus-skag* evil hour; inauspicious time.

Syn. གདེངས་ཅན་ལྷ་མོ *gdeṅs-can lha-mo*; ཝ *wa* (*Rtsi.* and *Mñon.*).

སྐག་རྩིས *skag-rtsis* astrology which treats of the planets and of bad omens, &c.

སྐག་ལས་སྐྱེས *skag-las skyes* केतु;=དུ་བ་མཇུག་རིང a comet; born under the constellation of *Açleṣā*.

Syn. མཇུག་ཕོད་ཅན *mjug-phod-can*; གཙུག་ཕུད་ཅན *gtsug-phud-can*; སྦྲུལ་ཅན *sbrul-can*; སྐྲ་གཉིས་པ *skra-gñis-pa* (*Mñon.*).

སྐང་བ *skaṅ-wa*=སྐོང་བ, སྐང་གསོ 1. satisfaction (*Sch.*). 2. a kind of expiatory sacrifice to make amends for a duty not performed (*Jä.*).

སྐང་ཤ *skaṅ-ça* sods cut out (*Sch.*).

སྐད *skad* I: (*keh*) भाषा, वार्त्ता 1. voice, cry, sound. Though སྐད and སྒྲ are generally used as synonymous words, yet the majority of the grammarians of Tibet apply the former to all manner of sounds and the latter to the sounds uttered by animate things only. 2. སྐད is equivalent of ཟེར in some expressions such as དེ་སྐད, འདི་སྐད, which mean "thus he said," "speaking these words," &c., and in ཇི་སྐད, ཡིན་སྐད, &c., may be traced similar significations: སྐད་ཅི་གནང་འདུག what is your pleasure? what did you say, sir? ཟེར་བ་དེ་ཅི་སྐད་ཡིན the (words) spoken what speech are they? what do they mean? (*Jä.*) འདི་སྐད་དུ "in these words" is used before a literally quoted speech and དེ་སྐད་ཅེས after it. ཟེར་སྐད also often occurs after statements meaning "it is said" or "it is rumoured." Other phrases are: དེ་སྐད་མ་བྱེད don't do that or so; སྐད་སྒྲོ་བ to give an account, to relate. 3. language: བོད་སྐད the Tibetan language; རྒྱ་གར་སྐད the Indian language; ཡུལ་སྐད་དུ

in the provincial dialect; མི་སྐད་སྨྲ speaking human language; འབྲུག་སྐད་ལྡིར་ཟེར *hbrug-skad ldir zer* the voice of thunder rattles; གླང་པོ་ཆེའི་སྐད་སྒྲ་བུའི་སྒྲ a voice like the cry of an elephant; སྡུག་བསྔལ་བའི་སྐད་འབྱིན་པ to utter painful or lamentable cries; སྙིང་རྗེའི་སྐད་འདོན་པ to send forth cries for pity; སྐད་ཀྱི་དབྱིངས धातु the root of a word.

སྐད II: ladder=སྐས་ཀ *skas-ka* (*Jä.*).

སྐད་འགག *skad-hgag* or སྐད་འཛེར་པོ *skad hdser-po* hoarseness of the voice (*Cs.*).

སྐད་རྒྱལ *skad-rgyal,* metaph. a donkey (*Sman. 2*).

སྐད་བསྒྱུར་པ *skad-bsgur-pa*=སྐད་བསྒྱུར་མཁན one who has changed his language.

སྐད་སྒྲ་ཆེ *skad-sgra che* (*ke' da-che*) the vulgar expression for "fame": ཁོ་དེང་སང་སྐད་སྒྲ་ཆེན་པོ་འདུག he is just now very famous.

སྐད་ངར *skad-ṅar* rough language: སྐད་ངར་ཟེར་བས་ཡུལ་དེའི་མིང་ཡང་ང་ར་ཐང་དུ་བཏགས། on account of their speaking rough speech the name of that place was called *Ṅa-ra thaṅ* (*Yig. 65*).

སྐད་ཅན *skad-can* having a voice; sounding.

སྐད་ཅིག *skad-cig* क्षण, चपल, प्रत्यक्ष one moment; an instant. སྐད་ཅིག་མ་ཡི་ཡུན= སྐད་ཅིག་པ is described as སེ་གོལ་གཏོགས་གཅིག་རེ་ལྔའི་ཆ, "one fifth part of the time required for the sound of the snapping of the fingers."

སྐད་ཅིག་བཅོམ *skad-cig bcom*, v. བཅོམ་པ.

སྐད་ཅིག་འདོད་ལྡན *skad-cig hdod-ldan*, v. ཕུག་རོན कपोत a pigeon (*Mṅon.*).

སྐད་ཅིག་པ *skad-cig-pa* or སྐད་ཅིག་མ वैनाशिक, क्षणिका, क्षणिक instanteneous; also ephemeral, momentary; also lightning.

སྐད་ཅིག་དབུགས *skad-cig-dbugs* lit. that takes breath only for a moment=སྲམ, an otter (*Mṅon.*).

སྐད་ཅིག་འདོད *skad-cig hdod* क्षणप्रभ sudden flash; flash of lightning.

སྐད་ཅིག་གློག་འོད *skad-cig glog-hod*=གློག lightning (*Mṅon.*).

སྐད་ཆ *skad-cha* कथा, काहिनी, आलाप, वार्त्ता news, report, discourse, conversation, topic; སྐད་ཆ་ཤག་པ to converse; to have a chat.

སྐད་གཉིས་པ *skad-gñis-pa* lit. that has two kinds of voices, *i.e.*, a parrot.

Syn. ལྕེ་གཉིས་པ *lce-gñis-pa*; འཁྱོག་པོའི་མཐུ་ཅན *hkhyog-pohi mthu-can*; ཚིག་འཇམ་ལྡན *tshig-hjam-ldan*; འཇམ་ལྗང་འདབ་ལྡན *hjam-ljaṅ hdab-ldan* (*Mṅon.*).

སྐད་གཉིས་སྨྲ་བའི་དབང་པོ *skad-gñis smra-wahi dwaṅ-po* one learned in science; one who has mastered (at least) two languages (*Yig. k. 48*).

སྐད་མཉེན་པ *skad mñen-pa* भाषाकोमल of a gentle voice; soft voiced.

སྐད་བསྙན *skad-bsñan*=བྲག་ཆ an echo (returned by a rock) (*Mṅon.*).

སྐད་སྙན་བསྒྱུར་བ *skad-sñan bsgyur-wa* to sing or whistle in a quavering, warbling manner, of birds, flute-players, &c. (*Jä.*): འགྱུར་སྐད a singing or playing of this kind.

སྐད་སྙན་པ *skad sñan-pa* कोकिल, कलस्वर one with a sweet voice; spoken of the cuckoo.

སྐད་སྙན་མ *skad-sñam-ma* the princess of the *Noijin* demi-gods; cf. གནོད་སྦྱིན་མའི་གཙོ་མོ (*Mṅon.*).

སྐད་སྟེར་བ *skad ster-wa*=སྐད་རྒྱག་པ to call to a person (*Schtr.*).

སྐད་མཐུན་པར་ *skad mthun-par* with one voice; with one accord.

སྐད་དོད་ *skad-dod* = སྐད་ཚབ་ an equivalent term in another language; the original from which another is translated: སྐད་དོད་ཡོད་མེད་ whether there are any original texts: སྐད་དོད་མེད་ it is without the original text (*Situ. 110*).

སྐད་ཀྱི་གདངས་ *skad-kyi gdaṅs* the character or tone of the voice: ངང་པ་འབྲུག་གི་སྐད་གདངས་ནོར་དང་ལྡན། བོང་རྔམ་གླང་གི་སྐད་གདངས་སྡུག་བསྔལ་ཆེ ॥ (*Mtshan.*) when the tone of one's voice is that of a goose or dragon it betokens the possession of wealth. A voice like that of an ass or ox indicates great troubles.

སྐད་གདངས་དམའ་བ་ *skad-gdaṅs dmaḥ-wa* विस्वर low sinking voice; poor voice.

སྐད་འདོན་ *skad-ḥdon* संराव bawling out; loud voice.

སྐད་པ་ *skad-pa* I: = ཞེས་བྱ་བས་ *shes bya-was* called; named (*A. 120*).

སྐད་པ་ II: 1. vb. to say, tell, relate: ཞིང་ཁམས་ཤིག་ཡོད་དོ་སྐད་པར་ཐོས that a land (of bliss) exists I heard people say. 2. interpreter; language master; teacher (*Jä.*)

སྐད་པ་ཆེ་ *skad-pa-che* or སྐད་པོ་ཆེ་ *skad-po-che* celebrated; famed.

སྐད་པོ་ཆེ་ *skad-po che* घोषणा rumour.

སྐད་འབྱིན་ *skad-ḥbyin* निकूजन singing of a bird.

སྐད་སྦྱངས་ཤིག་ *skad sbyaṅs-çig* cultivate your voice; improve the voice by exercise.

སྐད་མི་གསལ་ *skad mi-gsal* म्लेच्छ one whose language is not intelligible; a barbarian.

སྐད་རིང་ *skad-riṅ* दूरेभाष a voice heard at a distance; a high pitched voice.

སྐད་རིགས་ཆེན་པོ་བཞི་ *skad-rigs hen-po bshi* the four great divisions of language—(1) སཾསྐྲྀ་ཏ་ལྷའི་སྐད་ Sanskrit, the language of the gods; (2) པི་ཤ་ཙི་ཏྲི་ཤ་ཟའི་སྐད་ *Piçātsi*, the language of the meat-eating people; (3) རང་བཞིན་ཤེས་པ་པྲ་ཀྲྀ་ཏ *raṅ-bshin shes-pa pra-kṛ-ta* the *Prākṛta* or the natural language of the people; (4) ཨ་པ་བྷྲམ་ཤ་ཧྲང་ཚག་སྐྱ *Apa bhram-ça* corrupt language (*T. K.*).

སྐད་ལུགས་ *skad-lugs* = སྐད་རིགས་ *skad-rigs* dialect.

སྐད་ལོག་ *skad-log* clamour; screaming.

སྐད་ལེགས་མ་ *skad-legs-ma* = ལྷའི་གཟུགས་ཅན་མ་ a celestial courtezan (*Mṅon.*).

སྐན་ཏེ་ *skan-te*, *W.*, instead of སྐ་བ་ *ka-wa*.

སྐབ་ *skab* = འགོར་པོ་ *hgor-po* delay: མགྱོགས་པོས་མ་འདྲེད་སྐབ་པས་མ་ཟིན་ཅིང་། (*Rdsa. 28*) the swift not hurrying, the lingerers not finishing.

སྐབས་ *skabs* दशा, वार 1. time, opportunity, occasion, circumstance: མཐོང་བའི་སྐབས་ opportunity of seeing: སྐབས་རྙེད་པ་ *skabs rñed-pa* to find an opportunity: སྐབས་སུ or སྐབས་སྐབས་སུ now and then; sometimes. སྐབས་སུ or སྐབས་ with genit. = at the time of, on the occasion of, during, while, when: རེ་ཀ་སྐབས་སུ in a moment; instantly: སྐབས་དེར *skabs der* अथानन्तरे thereafter: སྐབས་འདིར now; here; in this case; in this place: སྐབས་རེ once for a time; each time; བར་སྐབས interval; inter-lapse of time. 2. sphere, state, situation: སྐབས་དང་སྦྱར་བ fit for; adapted; suited to the occasion. 3. སྐབས also means ལེའུ *leḥu*, chapter, and is synonymous with ཚིགས་ མཚམས་ གནས, &c., signifying section: སྐབས་བཅུ *skabs bcu*, the ten sections of the doctrine; also he that has observed them (*Jä.*). 4. mode;

method, way, manner, so the word seems to be used in *Vaiṣño*: ལྡུམ་བུའི་སྐབས་ལ་ཕུག་དང་སྐྱེས་ལུགས་འདྲ་བར། *ldum-buhi skabs la-phug dañ skyes lugs hdra-war* the manner (nature) of the plants being similar to that of a raddish as to growth (*Jä.*).

སྐབས་གཉིས་པ *skabs gñis-pa* द्विदग्ध the second chapter.

སྐབས་དོན *skabs-don* अवसरार्थं for the sake of leisure; also circumstance.

སྐབས་འདི་ལ *skabs hdi-la* अस्मिन् प्रकरणे at this opportunity; at this time; on this subject.

སྐབས་ཕྱེ་ན *skabs phye-na* अवकाशं कुर्यात् to make opportunity.

སྐབས་འབྱེད་པ *skabs hbyed-pa* अवसर leisure.

སྐབས་ལ་བབས་པ *skabs-la babs-pa* कचित् when the time came; opportunity arrived.

སྐབས་གསུམ་བཏུང་བ *skabs-gsum btuñ-wa* = ལྷའི་བདུད་རྩི the drink of the gods; ambrosia: ཡིབས་ཚོགས་ཀུན་བཟང་པོའི་སྐབས་གསུམ་བཏུང་བའི་རྒྱུན་བཞིན་སྤྱི་བོར་སྤྲོལ་ལ་མཛིན། pray send kind letters like the flow of the drink of the gods over the heads of the good (*Yig. k. 78*).

སྐབས་གསུམ་གནས *skabs-gsum-gnas* = མཐོ་རིས་ཀྱི་གནས the residence of the gods; the heaven.

སྐབས་གསུམ་པ *skabs gsum-pa* I: त्रिदिव, त्रिदश a god; a common name for gods possessed of the knowledge of their past and future births and also of those of others.

སྐབས་གསུམ་པ II: a name of the celestial musician; ལྷའི་གླུ་མཁན *lhahi glu-mkhan* (*Mñon.*).

སྐབས་གསུམ་དབང *skabs-gsum-dwañ* a name of Indra; བརྒྱ་བྱིན *Brgya-byin* or ལྷ་ཡི་དབང་པོ (*Mñon.*).

སྐབས་གསུམ་མཚོན་ཆ *skabs-gsum mtshon-cha* त्रिदशायुध thunderbolt of Indra.

སྐམ *Skam* I: སྐམ་པ n. of a tribe in Tibet (*Vai. kar. 160*).

སྐམ II: a pair of tongs; pincers; an instrument for seizing anything.

Syn. འཛིན་བྱེད *hdsin-byed*; བཟུང་བྱེད *bzuñ-byed* (*Mñon.*).

སྐམ་པ *skam-pa* शुष्क dry; སྐམ་རློན *skam rlon* lit. dry and wet; all articles (furniture, chattels, clothes, utensils, &c.) and food, drink, etc., being included in the term. སྐམ is often used as equivalent to སྐམ་ས, the dry land, hence a plain or སྐམ་ལ་སླེབས་པ *skam-la slebs-pa* to get ashore; སྐམ་ལམ journey by land, སྐམ་ཟས dry food, སྐམ་ཤ dry meat, སྐམ་སྐོམ *skam-skom* the dry or stuffed carcass of an animal; གཅན་ཟན་དང་རི་དྭགས་དང་ཐམས་ཅད་ཀྱི་སྐམ་སྐོམ། the dried carcasses of beasts and game and of all (others) (*D. R.*).

སྐམ་གློག *skam-glog* a flash of summer lightning: སྐམ་གློག་ཆེན་པོ་བྱུང་བ་ལ་བརྟེན་ཏེ་འཁོར་ཐམས་ཅད་ཀྱང་ཤིན་ཏུ་སྐྲག། "on a great flash of lightning coming forth, all his attendants became very much frightened" (*A. 17*).

སྐམ་ཆས *skam-chas* all goods except live-stock.

སྐམ་ཐལ *skam-thal* = ཙམ་ཐལ or ཙམ་རྩམ corn or barley flour to make gruel.

སྐམ་ཐུག *skam-thug* gruel made of barley-flour, dry meat and raddish.

སྐམ་དྲས *skam-dras* neat and clean (*Jig. 30*).

སྐམ་པག *skam-pag* dry, flour of barley.

སྐམ་པོ *skam-po* शुष्क, शोषित dry dried.

སྐམ་ཕོགས *skam-phogs* allowances or wages of an officer or inferior servant in barley-flour, tea or coin, etc., but not cooked food; གཞུང་གི་ངག་དོན་སྐམ་ཐོགས according to Government order; dry allowance (*J. Zań.*).

སྐམ་ལས་སྐྱེ་བ *skam-las skye-wa* स्थलज produced or born on land.

སྐམ་བཤད *skam-bçad* dry or meaningless words; hollow expressions meaning nothing: ཁ་ཕྱིར་རྐའི་སྐམ་བཤད་མཁན་པོ "one versed in talking nonsense, as if only for his mouth's sake" (or "as if on account of his mouth") (*Ev.*).

སྐམས་པ *skams-pa* = ས་སྟོང bleak and barren place (*Mńon.*).

སྐར་བ *skar-wa* I: pf. བསྐར, imp. སྐོར, to hang up; to weigh; སྐར, སྐར་ཀ, སྐར་ཁ weight; སྐར་ཚད measure; scale; སྐར་བ *skar-wa* for སྐར་ཀ, སྐར་ཚད and སྐར་མ points on a steel-yard for weight or measure: སྐར་ལྔ five points on the steel-yard weighing two *annas* of silver: སྐར་གང (one *skar*) is equal to ten ཧོན *hon*, which is a little less than an Indian *anna*.

སྐར་མ *skar-ma* ज्योतिः, ऋक्षमूल, तारा, नक्षत्र a star; a fixed star; constellation: གྲོལ་བྱེད, འཕུར་བྱེད, རྒྱུ་བའི་སྐར་མ་ཉི་ཤུ་བརྒྱད (*Vai. kar.*) the stars that are liberated and that soar on high and roam are twenty-eight in number: སྐར་མ་ཅན *skar-ma-can* with stars or figures of stars on anything, a shawl, &c.

སྐར་ཁུང *skar-khuń* वातायन, गवाक्ष, जाल a hole or small opening for the admission of light in a house; a window; same as སྒོ་ཚང, v. དཀར་ཁུང; སྐར་ཁུང་གི་སྒོ་ལེབས a plank or board for a window; shutters; སྐར་ཁུང་དྲ་བ་ཅན जालवातायन lattice window; a grated window.

སྐར་ཁོངས *skar-khońs* the sphere of a lunar mansion; a constellation together with the minor stars which are included within its sphere.

སྐར་མཁན *skar-mkhan* गणक an astrologer.

སྐར་ལྕག *skar-lcag* a rigorous enquiry; a flogging (*Jä.*).

སྐར་ཆུ *skar-chu* I: literally star-water; bathing when the star *Agastya* (*Ri-byi*) appears in October, when, according to Tibetan astrologers, water becomes pure and wholesome.

སྐར་ཆུ II: generally applied to dew which is said to come from the stars: *skar-tag tań che* (*Jä.*) to enquire rigorously; to restrict; to bind down; to flog.

སྐར་མདའ *skar-mdah* a shooting star; སྒྲོན་མ *sgron-ma* a lamp; ཏ་ལ་ལ उल्का a meteor: སྐར་མདའ་ལྷུང་བ or ལྷུང་བ उल्कापात the falling or shooting of a meteor.

སྐར་མདའི་གདོང་ངམ་སྣ *skar-mdahi gdoń-ńam sna* उल्कामुख or उल्कानास one having either his face or nose glowing as a meteor; a demon; a meteor-mouthed arrow; n. of a fire-arm anciently used in India. One of the ancestors of Gautama Buddha, directly descended from Mahasammata, the first elected king of the world.

སྐར་དཔྱད *skar-dpyad* = སྐར་རྩིས *skar-rtsis* astrology; སྐར་དཔྱད་པ = རྩིས་པ an astrologer (*Mńon.*).

སྐར་ཕྲན *skar-phran* or སྐར་ཆུང a little star.

སྐར་འཕྲེང *Skar-hpreń* 1. n. of a fabulous city situated at the foot of Rirab (Sumeru) mountain said to be the residence of the *Asura* King, Kaṇṭha-Mālī. 2. the squares in a chart of the constellations in which the figures representing the stars are written. 3. the angular distance between two stars or planets (*Cs.*).

སྐར་བ II: (*Cs.*) 1. a penning of cattle; assortment; separation; to pen; to fold; to separate, v. དཀར་བ.

སྐར་མ་སྟོད་ཕུར་ *skar-ma stod-phur* ध्रुवतारा supposed to be *Leonis*. This star is believed to be the most steady among the stars and is therefore called the sure-star or fixed-star; also called the crown-star.

Syn. བརྟན་པ་ *brtan-pa*; རྐང་སྟེང་བུ་ *rkaṅ steṅ-bu*; སྣང་ལྡན་ཤིང་རྟ་ *snaṅ-ldan çiṅ-rta*; སླུགས་བཟང་སྐྱེས་ *slugs-bzaṅ skyes*; གཟའ་ཡི་རྟེན་ *gzah-yi rten*; རྒྱུ་སྐར་ཏོག་ *rgyu-skar tog*; གན་རྒྱལ་བུ་ *gan-rgyal-bu*; གསེར་འཕུར་ *gser-hphur* (*Mṅon.*).

སྐར་མ་རྩག་རྩིག་ *skar-ma rtsag-rtsig*, also སྐར་མ་ཁྲ་ཙེམ་ཙེམ, a twinkling star; painting on a canopy or on a ceiling in starry design; རྒྱུ་སྐར་ those constellations through which the moon passes in her revolution round the heaven; བཙས་སྐར་ the constellation under which one is born; གཡང་སྐར་ a propitious constellation; the constellation under which one prospers or which brings fortune and good luck to one.

སྐར་མ་འཚེ་ *skar-ma htshe* तारापीड़न the injury caused by a malignant star.

སྐར་མའི་དཔྱོད་ *skar-mahi dpyod* ज्योतिष an examination or observation of the stars.

སྐར་མིག་བུ་ *Skar-mig-bu* "son of Star-eye or *Skar-mig*," the eagle. A certain hermit called *Skar-mig* found three eggs. These he gave to a woman in distress, saying that if she broke them after seven days they would bring her happiness. Out of impatient curiosity she broke two on the third and the sixth day. These turned into lightning and the dawn. The third she broke on the seventh day, when there sprung forth a full-fledged eagle which turning round asked what she wanted of him. In reply she wished him to kill the *Lu* demons; and this he accordingly did. Thenceforth the eagle came to be known as the son of *Skar-mig* (*Mṅon.*).

སྐར་འཛིན་ *skar-hdsin* star-catching; making sure of a propitious constellation, *e.g.*, for an intended journey (*Jä.*).

སྐར་འོད་ *skar-hod* ज्योतिःप्रभ the light emitted by a star; name of a kind of flower.

སྐར་ཡུམ་ *skar-yum* works or treatises on the stars; སྐར་ཡུམ་གཟའ་ཡུམ་ sacred works on stars and planets.

སྐལ་པ་ *skal-pa* अदृष्ट, दैव luck, chance, fortune—particularly when propitious.

སྐལ་ངན་ *skal-ṅan* दुर्भाग्य wretched; unlucky; unfortunate.

སྐལ་ཅན་མ་ *skal-can-ma*, also called སྐལ་ལྡན་མ *skal-ldan-ma* 1. भाग्यवती n. of a goddess; a blessed lady. 2. = སྤུ་ལ་འབབ་པ *spu-la hbab-pa* n. of a disease in which the hairs are affected.

སྐལ་ལྡན་ *skal-ldan* भव्य, भगवान् happy; blessed; also n. of one of the 28 ancient sages mentioned in Buddhist works.

སྐལ་ལྡན་ཤིང་རྟ་ *Skal-ldan çiṅ-rta* भगीरथ n. of a king of the solar race who is said to have brought the river Ganges to Jambu-dvīpa (India) from heaven; one of the ancestors of the Buddha S'akya-muni: ཡིག་ཚོགས་ཀྱང་སྐལ་ལྡན་ཤིང་རྟའི་འགྲོས་བཞིན་ཡོད་པ་མཛིན་ཅིག། "favour me with letters uninterruptedly like the course of the river Bhāgīrathī (Ganges)" (*Yig. k. 17*).

སྐལ་ལྡན་ཤིང་རྟའི་བུ་མོ་ *skal-ldan çiṅ-rtahi bu-mo* भागीरथी, v. གང་གཱ *Gaṅ-gā*, the daughter of Bhagīratha, the river Ganges (*Mṅon.*).

སྐལ་པ་ཅན་ *skal-pa-can* भव्य, भागिन् the fortunate: སྐལ་པ་ཅན་དུ་འགྱུར་ भागिनो भवन्ति are very fortunate.

སྐལ་པ་ཆེ་ *skal-pa-che* = དཔང་ཐང་ཆེ་བ་ महाभाग very fortunate, lucky; also powerful and rich.

སྐལ་པ་མཉམ་པ s̱kal̠-pa, m̱ñam-pa uniformly fortunate or always lucky; སྐལ་པ་དང་བཅས fortunate : མི་དང་སྐལ་པ་མཉམ་པར་སྐྱེས *mi dañ s̱kal̠-pa m̱ñam-par s̱kyes* मानुषाणां सभागतयाभ्युपपन्न born with fortune equal to that of a human being.

སྐལ་པ་བཟང་པོ *s̱kal̠-pa ḇzang-po* भद्रकल्प good fortune; སྐལ་པ་ངན་པ bad luck, unfortunate; ཚེ་འདིའི་འགྲོགས་སྐལ the matrimonial share of the present life; the connubial fate for which a person is predestined; ཆོས་ཀྱི་སྐལ་པ religious good luck; also the merit of the pious; སྐལ་ཆེ་བ very lucky; སྐལ་མེད unfortunate.

སྐལ་པ་ཡོད་པ *s̱kal̠-pa yod̠-pa* fortunate; སྐལ་པ་ལྷག་པ extra luck.

སྐལ་འཕར *s̱kal-ẖphar* enlarged fortune; lucky or of increased luck.

སྐལ་བ *s̱kal-wa*=ཆ *cha* भाग 1. portion; share; ནོར་བགོས་པའི་ཐོབ་སྐལ the apportioned share of hereditary wealth; inheritance; ཟས་སྐལ share or portion of food; ration; རང་སྐལ personal share: སྐལ་བ་མ་ཆད་པར without being deprived of any of his portion. 2. the portion of good or bad fortune that falls to a man's lot as a consequence of his former actions; lot, fate, destiny.

སྐལ་བ་ཆད་པ *s̱kal̠-wa chad̠-pa* suppressed fortune; unhappy.

སྐལ་བཟང *s̱kal̠-bzañ* सुभग 1. prosperous; of good fortune. 2. a plant—*Chrysanthemum coronarium*.

སྐལ་རིན *s̱kal̠-rin* the valuation of one's share of property; the price of one's share in any concern (*Jig.*).

སྐས *s̱kas* or སྐས་ཀ *s̱kas̱-ka*, also called སྐས་འཛེག : ཐེམ་སྐས निःश्रेणि, a stair; a flight of steps; སྐས་ཀྱི་རིམ་པ order of steps; སྐས་འགྲམ the two side-pieces of a staircase or ladder (*Cs.*); སྐས་འཛུག་པ to place a ladder; སྐས་ལ་འབབ་པ काष्टकावलम्बन to come down a ladder; སྐས་ལ་ काष्टकारोहण to climb up a ladder.

སྐས་སྐོར་ཁྲ་མ *s̱kas-s̱kor khra-ma* the lattice, rail or fencing by the sides of stairs.

སྐས་གདང་བུ *s̱kas̱-g̱dañ-bu*, abbr. of སྐས་ཛེ་གདང་རིང་པོ, a flight of long steps in a ladder: སྤྱན་འདྲེན་པ་ལ་སྐས་གདང་བུ་བདུན་དགོས་པ་ཡོད་པས། to bring him (here) a seven-step ladder was necessary (*A. 91*).

སྐས་ཚང *s̱kas̱-tshañ* signifies a flight of steps (*Jig.*).

སྐས་ལེབ *s̱kas̱-leb* the steps of a ladder or stair; the planks of a ladder.

སྐུ *s̱ku* काय, गात्र, मूर्त्ति, resp. for ལུས *lus̱*, body. 1. *s̱ku* may be prefixed to the names of parts of the body and even of anything belonging to a person, thus imparting to them the character of respectful terms. As honorific particle it can also be prefixed to nouns in general: སྐུ་ལུས the person or body of a great man; སྐུ་ཆས goods, stores or property of a man of rank; also the religious robe of a lama. སྐུ་སྐྱེས *s̱ku-s̱kyes* a present (given to or received from a respected personage); སྐུ་བསོད virtue, happiness; སྐུ་འབག image, statue; སྐུ་གཟན the wrapper used by a lama or a great man; སྐུ་ཞེར the cloak used by the lamas when attending a religious service; སྐུ་ཡོལ the inner lower garment of a man of rank. Even buildings (monasteries, &c.) are honoured by this respectful expression: སྐུ་དཀར་གསོལ་བ to white-wash a house, &c.; རྐོས་སྐུ *ṟkos̱-s̱ku* an engraved image; གོས་སྐུ tapestry; a figure worked upon satin with silk; འཇིམ་སྐུ an image of clay; ཐག་སྐུ a woven image; རྡོ་སྐུ a stone image; ལུགས་སྐུ a molten image; བྲི་སྐུ a painted image; འབུར་སྐུ a *Basso Relievo* image; བླུགས་སྐུ *ḇlugs̱-s̱ku* a cast image; གསེར་སྐུ *g̱ser-s̱ku* a golden image. 2. སྐུ or སྐུ་ཡི *s̱ku-yi* may be also used honorifically as a poss. meaning "his," "her," "yours," &c. 3. It is further employed to express the reflective verb *khyed-gañ la s̱ku ẖdeg* "why are you beating yourself?"

སྐུ་སྐལ *s̱ku-s̱kaḻ* portion or share of a respected person.

སྐུ་སྐེམ *s̱ku-s̱kem* the lean slender body of a respectable person.

སྐུ་ཁམས *s̱ku-khams̱* a great man's person; also the state of health.

སྐུ་གམ་ངོ་བཅར *s̱ku-gam ño-ḇcar* a personal interview; to approach or come before a great man personally.

སྐུ་བགེགས་ཆགས *s̱ku-ḇgegs̱ chags̱* disease caused by evil spirits.

སྐུ་ལྔ་རྒྱལ་པོ *s̱ku-ḻña ṟgyaḻ-po* the five divine Buddhas symbolical of the five highest moral virtues inculcated in Buddhism.

སྐུ་རྒྱུ *s̱ku-ṟgyu* the matter or substance whereof an image is made.

སྐུ་རྒྱུད *s̱ku-ṟgyuḏ* a scion, descendant, of a noble family.

སྐུ་བཅར *s̱ku-ḇcar* personal attendant of a greatman; gen. the attendant monks of the Dalai Lama (*S. kar. 181*); also same as སྐུ་མདུན་པ as in སྐུ་བཅར་མཁན་པོ *s̱ku-ḇcar m̱khan-po*, the domestic priest of the Dalai Lama who is also called སྐུ་མདུན་མཁན་པོ.

སྐུ་བཅར་མོ *s̱ku-ḇcar-mo* the raiment worn next to the skin (*Yig.*).

སྐུ་ཆས *s̱ku-chas̱* བླ་ཆེན་དང་དཔོན་ཆེན་རྣམས་ཀྱི་སྤྱད་ལག་ལ the chattels and other possessions of any high class person.

སྐུ་ཆོས *s̱ku-chos̱*=ཆོས་གོས robes; dress worn by great men or by lamas.

སྐུ་མཆེད *s̱ku-m̱ched* brothers and sisters: རྒྱལ་པོའི་སྲས་སུ་འཁྲུངས་པའི་སྐུ་མཆེད་དང, བླ་མ་གཅིག་གི་སློབ་མ་ཡིན་པའི་སྐུ་མཆེད་དོ། "those who are born the sons of kings are 'kum-che,' and the pupils of one lama are 'kum-che' (*Loñ.* ཟ *2*). སྐུ་མཆེད་གསུམ the three spiritual sons of Bromston—(1) པོ་ཏོ་བ་རིན་ཆེན་གསལ, (2) སྤྱན་སྔ་བ་ཚུལ་ཁྲིམས་འབར, (3) ཕུ་ཆུང་བ་གཞོན་ནུ་རྒྱལ་མཚན; འདི་གསུམ་ལ་འབྲོམ་སྟོན་གྱི་སློབ་མ་སྐུ་མཆེད་གསུམ་ཟེར (*Loñ.* ཟ *2*); these three were called the spiritual sons of Bromston.

སྐུ་མཉེད *s̱ku-m̱ñeḏ*=ལྟོ་རས *ḻto-ras̱* or ལག་རས handkerchief (*Yig. k. 55*).

སྐུ་གཉེར *s̱ku-g̱ñer* कायजीव keeper of images in a temple or monastery.

Syn. ལྷ་གཉེར *lha-g̱ñer*; ལྷའི་འཚོ་བ *ḻhaẖi ẖtsho-wa* (*M̱ñon.*).

སྐུ་བརྙན *s̱ku-ḇṟñan* I: a reflected image, v. སྐུ་འདྲ or གཟུགས་བརྙན likeness (*M̱ñon.*).

སྐུ་བརྙན II: = སྐུ་ཤ the health or flesh of a respectable person (*M̱ñon.*).

སྐུ་རྟེན *s̱ku-ṟten* an image of Buddha or of a saint. It is a contraction of the three words: *s̱ku*, *g̱suñs̱*, *thug-ṟten* the holy image, *i.e.*, of a Buddha or saint; the sacred books or volumes containing religious precepts; and the *chaitya* (*m̱choṟten*), the symbol of the resting of the *thugs̱* or heart.

སྐུ་བལྟམས *s̱ku-ḇḻtams̱*=སྐུ་འཁྲུངས birth (of a great man).

སྐུ་ཐོག *s̱ku-thog*=སྐུ་རིང lifetime; age; generation; སྐུ་ཐོག་སྔ་མ=སྐུ་ཐོག་གོང་མ or སྐུ་ཐོག་སྔོན་མ former generation; also ancestor or predecessor; སྐུ་ཐོག་རྗེས་མ=སྐུ་ཐོག་འཇུག་མ succeeding generation; སྐུ་ཐོག་མང་པོ many generations: བོད་ཀྱི་སྤྲུལ་སྐུ་རྣམ་གསུམ་ནི་སྐུ་ཐོག་མང་པོ་ཕེབས་ཤིང་བྱིན་རླབས་ཆེ་བ་ཡིན། the three incarnate beings of Tibet (*i.e.*, the Dalai Lama, Panchen Lama and Táránáth Lama) having come in many re-births are greatly blessed.

སྐུ་དྲུང་པ *sku drun-pa* a page; an attendant of a great man; a private secretary to a high official.

སྐུ་གདུང *sku-gdun* relics, remains; also lineage, descendants.

སྐུ་འདྲ *sku-hdra* (*kunda*) प्रतिमा, प्रतिबिम्ब, मूर्त्ति image; statue of Buddha or any sainted persons.

Syn. སྐུ་བརྙན *sku-brñan*; སྐུ་གཟུགས *sku-gzugs*; གཟུགས་བརྙན *gzugs-brñan*; སླར་གཟུགས *slar-gzugs*; མཆོད་བྱ *mchod-bya*; ཉེ་བར་འཇལ *ñe-war hjal*; འདྲ་བར་བཞེངས *hdra-war bshens*; འདྲ་འབག *hdra-hbag*; དེ་ལྟ *de-lta*; དེ་འདྲ *de-hdra*; དེ་མཚུངས *de-mtshuns*; དཔེ *dpe*; མཉམ *mñam*; མཚུངས *mtshuns*; དེའི་གཞི་འཛིན *dehi gshi-hdsin*; རབ་ཏུ་འདྲ *rab-tu hdra*; པྲ་ཕབ་བཞིན *pra-phab bshin*; ལེགས་པར་བཞེངས *legs-par bshens*; ལྡེར་བཟོ *lder-bzo*; སླར་གྲིབ་མ *slar-grib-ma*; སླར་བྱས་མཐུན *slar-byas mthun*; དངོས་པོ་མཚུངས *dnos-po mtshuns*; འདྲ་བ *hdra-wa*; ལྟ་བུ *lta-bu*; ཉེར་ཚད *ñer-tshad*; ངེས་སྣང *nes-snan* (*Mnon.*).

སྐུ་ལྡེམ་པ *sku ldem-pa* to be unwell, ill; ill-health.

Syn. ནད་ཀྱིས་བཏབ *nad-kyis btab*; ནད་ཕོག་པ *nad phog-pa*; ན་བ *na-wa*; ན་ཚ་འབྱུང་བ *na-tsha hbyun-wa*; ཁམས་མ་བདེ་བ *khams ma-bde-wa*; འདུ་བ་འཁྲུགས་པ *hdu-wa hkhrugs-pa*; ཉེ་བར་གདུང་བ *ñe-war gdun-wa*; ཉམས་མ་བདེ་བ *ñams ma-bde-wa*; བྲོ་འཚལ་བ *bro htshal-wa*; སྨུན་པ *snun-pa* (*Mnon.*).

སྐུ་ན *sku-na* a respectable person's age.

སྐུ་བུབ *sku-bub* a monkey of the langur class found near Bathang.

སྐུ་འབུམ *Sku-hbum* "a hundred thousand images," commonly pronounced Kum-bum. The name of the birth place of Tsongkhapa in Amdo, situated to the east of lake Kokonor; also the name of huge monastery built on the spot. Village and monastery both derive their names from a poplar tree, the leaves of which are said to bear miraculous impressions of a hundred thousand images of Buddha on them. Huc and W. W. Rockhill have given elaborate accounts of Kumbum monastery: ཨ་མདོ་སྐུ་འབུམ་བྱམས་པ་གླིང་གི་སྐུ་འབུམ་ཏོག་གི་རྒྱ་ཕིབས་བཞེངས (*Lon. 17*) he (King *Mi-dwan Phola Thaiji*) erected the gilt dome of the monastery of Chambaling above Kum-bum in Amdo.

སྐུ་སྨད *sku-smad* the part of the body below the navel; སྐུ་སྟོད་སྨད the upper and lower parts of the body.

སྐུ་ཚ *sku-tsha* a brother's son; a nephew; called ཚ་བོ *tsha-wo* in colloquial language.

སྐུ་ཚབ *sku-tshab* a representative; deputy.

སྐུ་ཚེ་སྟོད *sku tshe-stod* = སྐུ་གོང་མའི་དུས during the time of his predecessors.

སྐུ་མཚལ *sku-mtshal*, resp. for གཟུགས་ཁྲག, the blood (of a great man's) body.

སྐུ་ཞབས *sku-shabs* lit. "your honour's feet," is the correct form of the colloq. expression སྐུ་ཞོགས, meaning your honour, your lordship, your worship. It is generally pronounced as *ku-sho*.

སྐུ་གཟན *sku-gzan* = གཟན *gzan shawl* wrapper worn by lamas (*Yig. k. 55*).

སྐུ་གཟུགས་བདེ *sku-gzugs bde* = ནད་མེད་པ health; also healthy.

Syn. ཁམས་བདེ *khams bde*; ཉེར་འཚེ་མེད *ñer-htshe med*; འབྱུང་བཞི་སྙོམས *hbyun-bshi snoms*; བྲོ་མི་འཚལ *bro mi-htshal* (*Mnon.*).

སྐུ་ཡི་བབས་དང་བསྟུན *sku-yi babs dan bstun* according as his health permits; according to the state of one's health.

སྐུ་ཡི་ཟོ་མདོག *sku-yi zo-mdog*, resp. of ལུས་ཀྱི་ཁམས *lus-kyi-khams* health: དེང་སྐུའི་ཟོ་མདོག་འཛམ་བུའི་ཆུ་བོའི་གསེར་ཁམས་ལྟར་བཟང་ཞིང་། just now your health is good like the condition of the gold in the Dsam-bu river.

སྐུ་རགས *sku-rags* = སྐེ་རགས *ske-rags*, also སྐ་རགས *ska-rags*, a sash (*Yig. k. 55.*).

སྐུ་རིང་ *sku-riṅ* the period of a life—one's own or another's.

སྐུ་རིམ *sku-rim*, resp. for རིམ་གྲོ *rim-ḥgro*, reverence, respect, and thence the common word for any set service in a temple and in general for a ceremonial act of worship, and particularly in the special sense of a solemn sacrificial ceremony. སྐུ་རིམ་རྒྱ་ཁག་གསུང་སྒྲོག་གི་གཏོང་གཞི indicates the allowance granted by the Government of Lhasa for *Kurim* in the different monasteries of Tibet.

སྐུ་རུ *sku-ru* a water-wheel without a rim; such are the water-wheels of all the mills in the Himalaya (*Jä.*).

སྐུ་རུ་ཁ *sku-ru-kha* asterisks; marks generally of the figure of a cross, + also ×. The latter is common in books as an abbreviation like "ditto," to save the repeated writing at full length of the same sentence or word or expression. Some authors spell this word as ཀུ་རུ་ཁ.

སྐུ་ལུས *sku-lus* शरीर, resp. for ལུས, the body.

སྐུ་ཤ་འབྱོར་པོ *sku-ça ḥbyor-po* = ཤ་ཉམས་རྒྱས་ཤིང་རྒྱགས་པ corpulent; also corpulence; the original name of *Ḥbrom Rgyal-waḥi ḥbyuṅ gnas* (*Mṅon.*).

སྐུ་གཤེགས་པ *sku-gçegs-pa* dying; death.

སྐུ་གཤེན *Sku-gçen-gçen Rab* the great teacher of the Bon: འོད་ཟེར་དཔལ་ཞེས་བདག་གི་ཕ་ཡག་གཤེར་སྐུ་གཤེན་འབྲོམ་དུ་གདགས "*Ḥod-zer dpal* was my father, I *Sku gçen* of *Yag gsher* am called *Ḥbrom*" (*Ḥbrom.* ཁ *22*).

སྐུ་སྲས་བརྒྱད *sku-sras brgyad*, the eight spiritual sons of Bon-po S'en-rab are the following:—(1) མུ་ཆོས *Mu-chos*; (2) འོལ་དྲུག་ཐང་པོ *Ḥol-drug thaṅ-po*; (3) གཏོ་བུ་འབུམ་སངས *Gto-bu bum-saṅs*; (4) དཔྱད་བུ་ཁྲི་ཤིང *Dpyad-bu khri-çiṅ*; (5) ལུང་འདྲེན *Luṅ-ḥdren*; (6) བརྒྱུད་འདྲེན *Brgyud ḥdren*; (7) ཀོང་ཙ་དཀར་པོ *Koṅ-tsha dkar-po*; (8) ཀོང་ཙ་འཕུལ་བུ་ཆུང *Koṅ-tsha ḥphul-bu chuṅ*.

སྐུ་གསུང་ཐུགས *sku gsuṅ-thugs*, resp. for ལུས་ངག་ཡིད, body, speech, thought, which constitute the three spheres of a man's doings or sufferings; works in words and thoughts.

སྐུ་གསུམ *sku-gsum* त्रिमूर्त्ति, त्रिकाय the three personal exsistences of a Buddha, viz., ཆོས་ཀྱི་སྐུ धर्म्मकाय spiritual existence; ལོངས་སྤྱོད་རྫོགས་པའི་སྐུ सम्भोगकाय celestial existence, and སྤྲུལ་པའི་སྐུ निर्म्माणकाय bodily existence; also miraculously emanated existence.

སྐུ་གསེང *sku-gseṅ* rest and gentle exercise (of a great man) when convalescent: ཞབས་འབམ་གྱིས་སྐུ་སྐྲིམ་པའི་ཚུལ་བསྟན་སྐབས་ཅུང་ཟད་དྲངས་པ་ཉེ་བ་ན་སྐུ་གསེང་གི་དུས་ཕར་ཐེབས། when gout was indicated in the form of swelling of the body and slight improvement approached, it being the time of convalescence, he went out (*Ya-sel. 11*).

སྐུ་བསྲུངས *sku-bsruṅs* or སྐུ་བསྲུངས་པ *sku-bsruṅs-pa* तलवर्ग, अन्तिकस्थ attendant; waiter; body-guard.

སྐུགས *skugs* = རྒྱན wager; the stake in a game received by the winner. སྐུགས་སུ་འཛུགས་པ signifies སྣོད་ལག་གཏར་མ་ལ་བཞག་པ, that is, anything placed in pawn: སྐུགས་ནོར་ན་སྡུག་ངན་གྱི་མཚོ་བརྡོལ། (*D. R.*) if the wager is lost he will be plunged into an ocean of grief.

སྐུང་བ *skuṅ-wa* = སྦྲག་ཏུ་སྦས་པ to conceal in a secret place (*Ñag.*), pf. བསྐུངས *bskuṅs*, fut. བསྐུང་ *bskuṅ*. 1. to hide in the ground; to bury; to inter: བདག་གིས་གཏེར་དང་ནོར་བསྐུངས་རྙེད། I have found hidden treasures and concealed wealth (*nor.*). 2. संयोजन (*A. K. 53-55*) to fasten down; to tie, to tie on all sides (a corpse in a doubled up or twisted position before it is burnt).

སྐུངས་ས *s̱kuñs-sa* lurking place; hiding place.

སྐུད *s̱kuḏ* or སྐུད་པ जोचना; སྐུད་བུ सूत्र, कार्पास 1. thread, yarn, wire: སྐུད་པ་གཅོད་པ to cut the thread, *i.e.*, the tie of marriage; to divorce. གོས་འཚེམ་རྒྱུའི་སྐུད་པ the thread to sew a dress with; རས་སྐུད cotton thread, yarn; བལ་སྐུད woollen thread; གསེར་སྐུད gold wire; དངུལ་སྐུད silver wire; སྐུད་སེར yellow thread; དར་སྐུད silk thread; ཚོན་སྐུད coloured thread; སྐུད་རོ the frayed ends of a seam; སྐུད་བྲིས་མཁན an embroiderer; one that makes up a picture with threads of different colours; སྐུད་རིས= འཚེམས་ཕུ་བུ་བ पट्चिकर्म needle-work on cloth; སྐུད་པ་འཁལ་བར spinning thread. 2. vb. pf. བསྐུས, fut. བསྐུ, imp. སྐུས, to smear; to besmear; to daub: སྣུམ་སྐུད་པ=སྣུམ་བྱུགས་པ to be smeared with oil: སྒོ་ལ་རྩི་སྐུད་པ to paint a door: སྨན་གྱི་སྐུད་པ to anoint; to apply an ointment; སྐུད་པ་བསྒྲིམས or སྐུད་པ་བསྒྲིམས་ཟིན་པ threads twisted together.

སྐུད་པའི་འབུ *s̱kuḏ-paẖi ẖbu*=དར་གྱི་སྲིན་བུ *dar-gyi srin-bu* silk-worm (*M̱ñon.*).

སྐུད་པོ *s̱kuḏ-po*=ཆུང་མའི་སྤུན་ཟླ *chuñ-maẖi s̱pun ẕla* 1. wife's brother; brother-in-law. 2. श्वशुर father-in-law (*Jä.*). 3. in Sikkim a husband's younger brother is also called *s̱kuḏ-po*.

སྐུན་བུ *s̱kun-bu* is described as སྨྱུག་མ་ལ་བཏགས་པའི་སྣོད *s̱myug-ma-la ḇtags-paẖi s̱noḏ* a wicker-work basket; but a basket or vessel made of bamboo is called ཀོང་བུ or ཞེལ་མ (*Ñag.*).

སྐུབ *s̱kub* अधम very low (*Lex.*).

སྐུམ་པ *s̱kum-pa*, pf. བསྐུམས, fut. བསྐུམ, imp. སྐུམས, to contract; also to be drawn up; to be paralysed: ཡན་ལག་སྐུམ་པ to draw in the limbs.

སྐུར་པ *s̱kur-pa* अपवाद slander; false witness; blasphemy; abuse: སྐུར་འདེབས་པ same as སྐུར་པ་བཏབ་པ to throw abuse, cast aspersion and to bear false witness; to speak impiously of holy things: དཀོན་མཆོག་གསུམ་མི་བདེན་པར་ལྟ་ཞིང་སྐུར་པ་འདེབས་པ to blaspheme by viewing as untrue the threo most precious Ones.

སྐུར་བ I: *s̱kur-wa* or སྐུར་ཆུས་པ to slander, mock, ridicule.

སྐུར་བ II:=བཏང་བ प्रेषण a bestowing, giving, sending; also vb. a. to bestow, give, send; དབང་བསྐུར་བ अभिषेक to furnish with power; to empower or instal; འཕྲིན་སྐུར་བ to send intelligence; རྨ་སྐུར probably decorating one with the peacock's feather (as in China).

སྐུར་བ་འདེབས་པ *s̱kur-wa ẖdebs-pa* to hold as not existing what exists; to belittle.

སྐུལ་མཁན *s̱kul-m̱khan* in *W.* overseer (*Jä.*).

སྐུལ་རྒྱུ *s̱kul-ṟgyu* to render service; to exact service: མག་པ་ལོ་གསུམ་ཁྲེས་རྒྱུད་མིན་ཀྱང་སྐུལ་རྒྱུ། the son-in-law (elect), though ho is not a slave by birth, must render service for three years (to the parents of the bride).

སྐུལ་བ *s̱kul̠-wa*, pf. བསྐུལ, བསྐུལ་བར་བྱ, to excite; to exhort, admonish, enjoin: མི་ཞིག་ལས་བྱེད་པར་སྐུལ་བ to exhort a man to do a thing; to appoint: མི་ཞིག་ལས་ཀ་ལ་བསྐུལ་ཏོ imposed some work on a person: དེའི་ཚིག་གིས་བསྐུལ་ནས being induced by his words: རྣམ་ཤེས་ལས་དང་ཉོན་མོངས་ཀྱིས་བསྐུལ་ནས། the (departed) soul urged on by its former deeds and sins: ལྷ་སྲིན་མཆོད་སྐུལ་ཀྱང though I tried to bring round the gods and evil spirits by sacrifices: གླིང་སོགས་དྲག་ཏུ་སྐུལ་ཤིང arousing strongly (the actors) with flutes and other instruments. བསྐུལ་བ and more frequently བསྐུལ་མ exhortation; admonition. བསྐུལ་མ

འདེབས also སྐུལ་བྱུག་པ and སྐུལ་ཅག་བྱེད་པ to expostulate with, rebuke; incite.

སྐུལ་བྱེད skul-byed, v. ཀུཎ་ཊ་བྲུ་རི.

སྐུལ་ཚིག skul-tshig a word in the hortative or imperative mood.

སྐེ ske स्कन्ध, resp. མགུལ, neck; throat: མགྲིན་པ་གཅིག with one throat; unanimously: སྐེ་གཙོད་པ=སྐེ་གཅུབ་པ and སྐེ་འབྲེག་པ to cut one's throat; to behead: སྐེར་འཐམ་པ to seize by the throat; to worry (Sch.): སྐེར་དོགས་པ to tie round the neck (an amulet); སྐེ་འཁོར neck-lace (Schr.); སྐེ་ཆ ornament for the neck; a necklace: ཁམས་མོའི་སྐེ་ཁོར་བྱུ་རུ the coral neck-lace of a woman of Khams.

སྐེ་སྟོང་ ske-stoṅ cavity of the throat (Jä.), defined in Med. as ཡོལ་མདུད་ཀྱི་རོག་ཙམ་པ་ཀོང་ཀོང་ཡོད་པ the cavity as far down as below the larynx.

སྐེ་ཙེ ske-tse or སྐེ་ཙེ राजिका, चोद: Sinapis ramosa, black mustard; mustard seeds (Jā): བགེགས་འདུལ་སྐྲངས་དང་ལྷོག་པ་སེལ། it removes evil spirits and cures swellings and carbuncles (Med.).

སྐེ་ཚང་ Ske-tshaṅ n. of an old monastery situated in the mountains behind the monastery of Sera (Deb. ག 13).

སྐེ་རགས ske-rags=སྐ་རགས, སྐ་རགས་ཚུང་པ काञ्ची a sash; an ornament like a sash worn round the waist.

སྐེག skeg अश्लेषा n. of a constellation: སྐེག་ལ་སྐྱེས skeg-la skyes अश्लेषाभव born in the constellation of Açleṣā. [The man born in the constellation of Açleṣā is unfortunate, inasmuch as his birth is followed by the death of himself, his mother or father.]

སྐེག་ཚོས skeg-tshos paint, rouge (for the face) (Sch.).

སྐེང་ལུངས Skeṅ-luṅs n. of a place in Tibet (Deb. ག 11).

སྐེད་དཀར skyed-dkar same as སྐེ་རགས་དཀར, white sash.

སྐེད་འཇིགས sked-hjigs=དྭ་དྲུ་འཇོམས da-dru hjoms n. of a medicinal drug (Mṅon.).

སྐེད་པ sked-pa=སྐེད་པ कटि the waist: སྐུ་སྐྱེད sku skyed or སྐེད་སྐབས sked-skabs नितम्ब, the hind parts below the waist; སྐེད་པའི་ཕྱོགས मेखला waist-band. སྐེད་སོ sked-so the waists: སྐེད་པའི་ཚུར་སྐྲ་རིང་ཚུང་སྐེད་སོ་ན་མར་སླེབ་པ the length of hair reaching down even to the waist (Hbrom. ཁ 35).

སྐེད་མ sked-ma, v. སེ་འབྲུ, pomegranate (Mṅon.).

སྐེམ་ནད skem-nad consumption.

སྐེམ་པ skem-pa=སྐམ་པ शोषक, adj. रूक्ष, क्षयलक, क्षय, vb. pf. བསྐམས शोषित, fut. བསྐམ or བསྐམ་པར་བྱ, imp. སྐོམས skoms, pres. སྐེམ་པར་བྱེད་པ 1. to make dry, lean meagre; to dry up. 2. also as adj. སྐམ་པོ skam-po dry; dried up; meagre.

སྐེམ་པ skem-pa=ལུས་ཉམས་ཆུང་བ lean, thin body (Mṅon.).

སྐེམ་བྱེད Skem-byed n. of a demon that causes drought; སྐེམ་བྱེད་ཀྱི་གདོན n. of a trouble (in the body of a person) caused by an evil spirit.

སྐེམ་བྱེད་དཀར་པོ skem-byed dkar-po the resin of the sāl tree, which is burnt as an incense; same as སྤོས་དཀར white incense gum (Sman. 447.)

སྐེམ་བྱེད་མ Skem-byed-ma n. of a goddess.

སྐེམ་བྱེད་ཤ་ཟ Skem-byed ça-za=དབང་ཕྱུག་གི་བུ་ཆུང་བ་གཞོན་ནུ་གདོང་དྲུག an epithet of Kumāra, the younger son of Mahādeva (Mṅon.).

སྐེམས་པ skems-pa क्षयलक, प्रस्कन्द, v. འཛུག་པ very thin, lean.

སྐེམས་པའི་སྦྲེབས་པ skems-pahi sbrebs-pa शोषक the hunger of emaciating disease.

སྐེར་ *sker* is sometimes written as ཀེར་ *ker*.

སྐེར་ལེབ་སྒུར་ *sker leb sgur* pony, sheep, and yak; collectively cattle.

སྐོ་སྐོ་ *sko-sko* चिबुक the chin.

སྐོ་བ་ *sko-wa*, pf. བསྐོས, fut. བསྐོ or བསྐོ་བར་བྱ, to select; also to appoint, nominate, commission, charge; ལས་སུ་སྐོ་བ to appoint a person to work: གནས་ཁང་སྐོ་བའི་དགེ་སློང་བསྐོ་བར་བྱའོ། (*K. du.* ཀ *362*) should appoint a ge-long (Buddhist monk) to arrange for lodging; རྒྱལ་སར་བསྐོས་པ raised to the throne; མ་བསྐོས་ཤིང་ without mandate; unbidden; ལས་ལ་བསྐོས་པ destined; appointed to the work, *i.e.*, destined (to be a man) in consequence of his works; ངེད་ཀྱི་ལས་བསྐོས appointed by my destiny; fate (*Jä.*).

སྐོ་ཚེ་ *sko-tse* a mixture of the leaves of various kinds of leeks pounded and formed into balls and dried; when used, a small portion is broken off, fried in butter, and then added to the food. This spice forms a lucrative article of commerce and is exported from Ladak to Kashmir and from Lhasa to India (*Jä.*).

སྐོགས *skogs*=སྐོགས་པ or ཀོག་པ a hard covering; rind; bark; a shell: སྐོགས་ཅན *skogscan* adj., having a cover or shell (*Cs.*).

སྐོང་ *skoṅ*, v. ཀོང *koṅ*.

སྐོང་བ *skoṅ-wa* पूरण, pf. བསྐངས *bskaṅs*, fut. བསྐང་ imp. སྐོངས, to fulfil; also sbst. རེ་བ་སྐོང་, to fulfil a hope: ཁ་སྐོང་བ to fill up what is open; to make up a deficiency: དགེ་བའི་ཁ་སྐོང *dge-wahi kha-skoṅ* to fulfil perfectly the laws of virtue. ཁ་སྐོང or ཁ་བསྐངས also ཁས་སྐོང signify an appendix; supplement: ཕྱི་མ་དུ་ཁ་སྐོང་དུ་བཤད will be described in the appendix below: ཞུགས་དམ་བསྐང་ཇུས to do a certain ceremony fully according to your vow; སྲུང་མའི་བསྐང་གསོ the ceremony to satisfy one's guardian deity by supplementing what was wanting and making amends for the same: བསྐང་གཏོར is an offering or *torma* for a deficiency: བསྐང་མདོས offering of some representation of celestial mansions, made of coloured threads, to one's guardian deities; བསྐང་གསོ offering to the gods and guardian deities.

སྐོངས་ཤིག *skoṅs-çig*=རེ་བ་སྐོངས་ཤིག may your hope be fulfilled.

སྐོན་པ *skon-pa*=གྱོན་པ 1. sbst. v. གོན་པ. 2. vb. pf. and fut. བསྐོན to dress; to clothe another person.

སྐོབས *skobs*=སྐབས, སྐབས་སུ་ཐུད་པ, བྱ་དཀའ་བའི་སྐབས་སུ་ཐུད་ཅེས་པའི་དོན (*Ñag.*) signifies the coming occasion of doing some difficult work.

སྐོམ I: *skom* पिपासा, तृष्णा thirst; resp. ཞལ་སྐོམ *shal-skom*, བཏུང་བ་སྐོམ་གྱི་གདུང་བ tormented by thirst; ཟས་དང་སྐོམ food and drink: སྐོམ་དུ་དཀར་དང་ཇ་གསོལ་ཅིག take milk (lit. "white") and tea for thirst: སྐོམ་དུ་ཆང་གསོལ *skom-du chaṅ-gsol* take wine for thirst (*Kathaṅ. 115*).

སྐོམ II: the dry land (*Jä.*).

སྐོམ་སྐྱུར *skom-skyur* sour beer; sour fermented liquor.

སྐོམ་དད *skom-dad* or སྐོམ་དད་ཆེ thirst; མི་སྐོམས་སྐོམ་ཆེ་བ one who is very thirsty: སྐོམ་འདོད་པ་ལ་སྐོམ पानं पानार्थिभ्यः (give) drink to the thirsty; བཏུང་བ་འདོད=ཆུ་འདོད wishing for drink; ཁ་སྐོམས mouth drying; thirsty: སྐོམ་པ་དག་ནི་སྐོམ་པ་དང་བྲལ་བར་འགྱུར། the thirsty will be freed from their thirst.

སྐོམ་ནས *skom-nas* तृषित thirsty; imp. སྐོམས་ཤིག चोभय् become thirsty; སྐོམ་པ་ཉིད་འདུག पिपासित thirsty.

སྐོམ་ཤ *skom-ça* the flesh of a calf that died or was killed as soon as it was born, even before it could suck milk from its mother's teat (*Sman.*).

སྐོམས་པ *skoms-pa* पिपासी thirsty.

Syn. བཏུང་བ་འདོད *btuṅ-wa ḥdod*; ཆུ་འདོད *chuḥdod*; ཁ་སྐོམ *kha-skom* (*Mṅon.*).

སྐོར *skor* 1. class, order; appertaining to; subject; circle; body—a term often used to signify a retinue, a set of attendants, persons of one class; མདུན་སྐོར class of official staff; also court (*Yig. k. 37*); ཁྱོ་གའི་སྐོར class of husband; that which concerns a husband; བུད་མེད་ཀྱི་སྐོར class of women, about women; དེའི་སྐོར་ལ of that order; with respect to that; also of that subject; ཁྲིམས་རྩོད་ཀྱི་སྐོར་ལ on the subject of litigation; མཆོད་ཆའི་སྐོར the paraphernalia of worship; ས་སྐོར circuit, tour: བོད་བཞུགས་ཨམ་བན་ས་སྐོར་དམག་རྩིས་ལ་ལྷ་ལྡན་ནས། "the Resident Amban of Tibet (started) from Lhasa on a military tour, &c." 2. anything round, a circle; མིག་སྐོར eye-ball. In *W.* སྨྱུ་སྐོར hoop of bamboo (*Schtr.*); མིའི་ཀླག་སྐོར the (circumference) of a man's head; ཁང་ཀླག་སྐོར the top of a house. 3. section, division, *e.g.*, of a book, similar to ལེའུ chapter. 4. repetition; སྐོར་ཟླས་པ to repeat (*Schtr.*). 5. religious circumambulation, v. སྐོར་བ.

Syn. སྡེ་ཚན *sde-tshan*, རིགས *rigs*, གྲས *gras*, དོན *don* (*Mṅon.*).

སྐོར་མཁན *skor-mkhan* one who goes round; སྐོར་བ one who turns a lathe; one who circumambulates or walks round a sacred object.

སྐོར་འགོ *skor-ḥgo*, རྩིས་ཀྱི་སྐོར་འགོ་རྣམ་པ་བརྒྱད། (*Vai. kar.*) classes in astrology. There are eight heads or sections according to Indian astrology; according to Tibetan astrology there are fifteen སྐོར་འགོ heads of astrology, such as about kings, ministers, priests, sages, mystics, queens, &c.; also about birth, growth, maidens, old persons, illness, husbandry, houses, service, &c.; འཚོང་བརྒྱབ་ནས་ཁེ་ཡོང་བའི་སྐོར་ཐང། about profit in trade; སྨན་སྦྱོར་བ་སོགས་ཚད་ཀྱི་སྐོར་ཐང། profit from the compounding of medicines and drugs; དངུལ་སོགས་བསྐྱེས་འཕེལ་གྱི་སྐོར་ཐང་། interest accruing from the laying out of silver (money).

སྐོར་རྒྱུགས *skor-rgyugs* turning the enemy; getting into his rear (*Jä.*).

སྐོར་ཐག *skor-thag* the cord of a lathe.

སྐོར་ཐང *skor-thaṅ* price or rate; also interest on anything in kind; in grain given as loan.

སྐོར་ཐིག *skor-thig* a pair of compasses; སྐོར་དབྱུག a sling.

སྐོར་པ *skor-pa* or སྐོར་ར་པ or སྐོར་མཁན a turner; also one who goes on his rounds.

སྐོར་བ *skor-wa*, vb., pf., &c., fut. བསྐོར, 1. to fill with; to surround, encircle, enclose, besiege; to come again and again; to revolve: ཁང་པའི་སྐོར་བའི་གྲོང་ཁྱེར་ནི། (*A. K.*) the town that was encircled (filled) with houses: སྐོར་ཐང་ཅན སྐོར་ཐང་ཅན་གྱི་མི་གསུམ་ནི the three men of those who were surrounding them: ཡ་རྩེ་རྒྱལ་པོ་གཡའ་མས་བསྐོར། the Chief of the *Ya-rtse* mountains is surrounded by rugged rocks: ཏི་རྩེ་རྒྱལ་པོ་གངས་ཀྱིས་བསྐོར the *Ti-rtse* (*Tise*) mountain is surrounded by glaciers: ཀྱུ་ར་རྒྱལ་པོ་ཆབ་ཀྱིས་བསྐོར the *Kyura Rgyalpo* mountain is surrounded by water (*D. R*). 2. to traverse; ride round a thing. Also metaphorically in the religious sense: ཆོས་ཀྱི་འཁོར་ལོ་སྐོར་བ to preach, to propound the doctrine of Buddhism: ཚོགས་ཀྱི་འཁོར་ལོ་སྐོར་བ to make mystic offerings (*i.e.*, the symbolical offerings representing one's accumulated merits) to the *Tantrik* deities, and to observe the ceremonies thereof. 3. བསྐོར་བ or གཡས་སྐོར प्रदक्षिण the reverential ceremony of circumambulation which consists in walking round a holy object with one's right side towards it. This is also called ཆོས་སྐོར *chos-şkor* धर्मप्रदक्षिण Buddhist circumambulation. The Buddhist priests of Tibet perform this in contradistinction to བོན་སྐོར, or the ceremony of the *Bon*, who reverences a sacred object by walking round it keeping it to his left. The Bon ceremony is also called གཡོན་སྐོར, walking round a holy object keeping it to the left ཕྱག་དང་སྐོར་བ་བྱེད་པ, as a specification of religious duties, to make salutation and circumambulations. ནང་སྐོར the inner pathway for circumambulating a holy place or shrine; ཕྱི་སྐོར the outer passage for the above object; བར་སྐོར the middle pathway for the same; བསྐོར་བྱེད *ḇkor-byeḏ* one who goes round or makes a circle or traverse. Other usages of this verb are:—མགོ་སྐོར་བ or མགོ་སྐོར་བྱེད་པ to befool, delude, deceive a person; ཁ་སྐོར་བ *kha şkor-wa* to make one alter one's sentiments; to divert one from a plan, &c. བསྐོར *şkor* in མ་བསྐོར་དགུ་བསྐོར signifies if all were taken into account; the circumstances or things available (*A. 142*).

Syn. འཁོར་བ *ḫkhor-wa*; ཡང་ཡང་ཧོང་བ *yañ-yañ ḫoñ-wa* (*M̱ñon.*).

སྐོར་ཚེར *şkor-tsher* on this occasion: སྐོར་ཚེར་སྐྱིད་པ་ཞིག་བྱུང་། on this (present) occasion prosperity arose.

སྐོ་རེས *şko-reş* = རེས་མོས་བྱེད་པ in courses; in rotation, one coming after another and again going back.

སྐོར་ལམ *şkar-lam* a roundabout way; the way or passage round any sacred place, temple or town for pilgrims to circumambulate it; the pathway round about a monastery used for holy processions.

སྐོར་ལོག་པ *şkor-log-pa* a wrong turn: སྐོར་ལོག་ལ་འགྲོ་བ to walk round an object in the wrong way, keeping it to his left.

སྐོར་ཤིང་ *şkor-çiñ* a turner's lathe or tool.

སྐོལ་བ *şkol-wa* = གདུ་བ pf. and fut. བསྐོལ, to boil (vb., act., cf. འཁོལ་བ): སྐོལ་མི one who boils tea.

སྐོས་པ *şkoş-pa*, v. སྐོ་བ *şko-wa*.

སྐྱ *şkya* 1. crop; the produce of a year, *i.e.*, ལོ་ཏོག; སྐྱ་རྒྱས plenteous crop: ད་ལོ་སྐྱ་རྒྱས་པོ་བྱུང་། this year the crop has been abundant: ད་ལོ་སྐྱ་འཕམ་པོ་བྱུང་། this year the crop has been unsuccessful (lit. "a loser"). 2. a paddle; also ladle. 3. wall or partition, usually བར་སྐྱ. 4. plain, without distinguishing colour, but see སྐྱ་བ below: སྐྱ་སྒམ a plain unpainted box: སྐྱ་ཆོས a blank book: སྐྱ་ཞྭ a plain hat without riband.

སྐྱ་བག *şkya-bag* greyish colour; iron-grey colour (*Jig.*).

སྐྱ་ཀ *şkya-ka* = སྐྱ་ག magpie; in *Ld.* n. of a bird (*Cs.*).

Syn. བྱ་ཁྲ་བོ *bya khra-wo*; མགྲོན་གྱི་འཕྲིན་སྐྱེལ་བྱ *m̱gron-gyi ḫphrin-şkyel bya*; མངོན་ཤེས་ཅན *m̱ñon-çeş-can* (*M̱ñon.*).

སྐྱ་སྐྱ *şkya şkya* pale-white; grey colour.

སྐྱ་རྒྱབ་པ *şkya r̤gyab-pa* to row; to ladle.

སྐྱ་ཆེན *şkya-chen* a superior kind of plain scarf (for presentation) (*S. kar. 179*).

སྐྱ་ཉིལ *şkya-ñil* zinc.

སྐྱ་ཐ་ལེ *şkya-tha-le* of plain white colour.

སྐྱ་ཐུད *şkya-thuḏ* a kind of plain cheese made of pounded dried milk with butter but not with sugar.

སྐྱ་ཐུད་ལེབ *şkya-thuḏ-leb* a kind of cheese-cake made of dried milk and butter.

སྐྱ་ཐུམ *şkya-thum* a kind of cake or biscuit made without sugar or treacle.

སྐྱ་ཐོམ་མེ་བ *şkya thom-me-wa* glaring white: སྐྱ་ཐོམ་མེ་བ་གཅིག་རྒྱུན་དུ་ཡོད་ at all times one of

སྐྱ་ནར་ *skya-nar* पाटलि, पाटल 1. n. of a flower, *Bignonia graveolens*. 2. brown; buff.

སྐྱ་ནར་ཁྲ་བོ་ *skya-nar khra-ḇo*, also སྐྱ་སྣར་བཀྲ་བོ་ चित्र पाटल, n. of a flower; སྐྱ་སྣར་བཀྲ་ཆེན་ महाचित्र पाटल another species of *Bignonia graveolens*.

སྐྱ་ནར་གྱི་བུ་ *Skya-nar-gyi bu* पाटलिपुत्र n. of a city in ancient India, Pātalīputra, now supposed to be Patna.

སྐྱ་ནར་ལྡན་མ་ *Skya-nar ldan-ma* पाटलवती, also पाटलावती n. of a river in Ancient India; acc. to Bhavabhuti's description the river flowed by पद्मावती or modern Nārwār in Mālwa मालव (उज्जयिनी). This latter name of the river occurs in Bhavabhuti's Mālatīmādhava, written early in the 8th century.

སྐྱ་བ་ *skya-wa* I: 1. vb. pf. བསྐྱས་ *bskyas*, fut. བསྐྱ་ *bskya*, to carry; convey to a place (a quantity of stones, wood, water, &c.). 2.=འཕོ་བ་ to change place.

སྐྱ་བ་ *skya-wa* II: also སྐྱ་བོ་ *skya-wo* पाण्डर, विशद grey or whitish grey; pale-white; མི་སྐྱ་ a secular personage; one clothed in no particular colour; a layman, from the grey colour of the coarse serge which is generally worn by the lay people of Tibet: སྐྱ་བའི་དུས་ when (he was still) a layman, *i.e.*, had not entered the sacred order (*A. 126*): སྐྱ་བའི་དུས་ནས་ (*A. 126*) from the time I was a layman; སྔོ་སྐྱ་ light blue. ལྗང་སྐྱ་ light green; དམར་སྐྱ་ light red; སེར་སྐྱ་ कपिल tawny; light yellow; སྤྱོ་སྐྱ་ rice; barley without anything to eat it with; insipid miserable food; སྐྱ་བཉེད་ whiteness; faintness; སེར་སྐྱའི་གྲོང་ कपिलनगर the city of Kapila; སེར་སྐྱའི་གཞི་ कपिलवास्तु the residence of Kapila; སེར་སྐྱའི་གནས་ कपिलाश्रम the hermitage of Kapila.

སྐྱ་བ་འཛིན་ *skya-wa ḥdsin*=མཉན་པ་ *mñan-pa* or གྲུ་གཏོང་མཁན་ a rower (*Mṅon.*).

སྐྱ་བོ་ *skya-wo*=དཀར་སེར་སྨིན་པའི་ཁ་མདོག་ pale whitish yellow.

སྐྱ་བོ་སྤྱི་ *skya-wo spyi* vulgar people; the common worldly men.

སྐྱ་མ་ *skya-ma* hard and rough soil for cultivation: ས་ལ་ནག་མ་སྐྱ་མ་གཉིས་ལས་ (*Jig.*) as to soil, two kinds, the alluvial or soft and the hard or gravelly.

སྐྱ་མ་ན་ཁ་ *Skya-ma na-kha* n. of a vast grassy plain or common belonging to the Government of Lhasa in Ü (Central Tibet).

སྐྱ་རྩ་ *Skya-rtsa* dry grass.

སྐྱ་རྩེ་ *skya-rtse* a layman at the top (of a row): གདོང་གྲལ་གཡོན་དུ་སྐྱ་རྩེ་འོང་བ་ཡིན་ the front left hand row of seats should have a layman heading it (*Jig.*).

སྐྱ་རིས་ *skya-ris* outline, sketch, drawing of the outlines of a picture, which is generally done with charcoal in Tibet: དེ་ནས་སྐྱ་རིས་འདི་ལྟ་བུ་དགོས་ then outlines of this kind are necessary (*A. 108.*).

སྐྱ་རེང་ *Skya-reṅ*, also called སྐྱ་མདངས་ अरुणः, n. of the lake from which (the Yang-tse kiang) the River of the Golden Sands takes its rise.

སྐྱ་རེངས་ནུ་བོ་ *skya-reṅs nu-bo* अरुण the several stages or divisions of the dawn which are—སྐྱ་རེངས་དམར་ ताम्रकारुण the copper-red dawn; སྐྱ་རེངས་དཀར་ गोधा the white dawn (the earth); སྐྱ་རེངས་སེར་, the golden or yellow dawn; སྐྱ་རེངས་དང་པོ་ཤར་བ་ नीलारुण the first appearance of the dawn; སྐྱ་རེངས་བར་མ་ཤར་བ་ पीतारुण the appearance of the middle or the yellow dawn; སྐྱ་རེངས་ཐ་མ་ ताम्रारुण the last (stage of the) dawn.

སྐྱ་ལན་ *skya-lan* also སྐྱ་ཟ in *C.* morning; twilight; dawn.

སྐྱ་ལེབ་ *skya-leb*=སྐྱ་མདུག་ a rudder.

སྐྱ་སེང་ *Skya-seṅ* n. of a tree (*Jä.*); translation of the name Pāṇḍu.

སྐྱ་སེང་གི་བུ་ *skya-seṅ-gi bu* पाण्डव the sons of Pāṇḍu; སྐྱ་སེང་གི་བུ་ལྔའི་ཀརྣ་པ་ན་ཙན་གྱི་མིང་ the names of Karṇa, the eldest of the Pāṇḍava—ས་ཡི་ནུ་བ भूमिकर्ण, ཡང་གའི་རྒྱལ་པོ अङ्गराज, ཉི་ཉེར་སྐྱེས राधातनय, འཛོམས་བྱེད་བུ, ཉི་མ་དགའ सूर्यनन्दन, ནུ་བ་ཅན कर्ण: གཡུལ་ངོར་བརྟན་པའི་མིང་ the names of *Yudhiṣṭhira*—युधिष्ठिर, ཆོས་རྒྱལ་སྐྱེས धर्मराजपुत्र, མི་ནུ་དཀའ་ཐུབ་ཅན, ཆོས་ཀྱི་བུ धर्मपुत्र, མ་སྐྱེ་དགྲ अजातशत्रु, ཀུན་གྱི་ནུ་ཅན, རྫེས་སྐྱེས: འཇིགས་རྡེའི་མིང the names of Bhima-sena—वृकोदर; ཀླུ་ཡི་སྟོབས་ལྡན *Klu-yi stobs-ldan*, ཚོགས་ལས་སྐྱེས *Tshogs-las skyes* དཔའ་བོ་དུལ, རླུང་གི་བུ पवनपुत्र, ཐུང་རྩེ་འཛོམས: སྲིད་སྒྲུབ་ཀྱི་མིང་ *Srid sgrub-kyi miṅ*, the names of अर्जुन Arjuna—བུ་རམ་སྣ, སྟོབས་བཟང་དབང་, འདབ་བུ་ཆེ, སྙིང་པོ་མེད *Sñiṅ-po-med*, ནམ་པར་རྒྱལ་བྱེད, བརྒྱ་བྱིན་དཀར. བསྙེན་པ་དཀར་པོ, བྲེ་ཏ་གྷོ *Bre-ta gho*, དགའ་བའི་དབང་ཕྱུར: ཐ་རྒྱང་ལྷར་བཅས་ཀྱི་མིང་ the names of As'vinīkumāras Sahadeva—སྐྱེས་རྒུ་སྐྱེས *Skyes rgu skyes*, ལྷན་ཅིག་སྐྱེས *Lhan-cig-skyes*, རིགས་མེད नकुल; ལྷར་བཅས सहदेव: སྐྱ་སེང་གི་བུ་ལྔའི་ཆུང་མའི་མིང་ the names of the wife of the five Pāṇḍava—द्रौपदी; ནག་མོ་ལྔ་ལེན कृष्णा, पाञ्चाली; རི་སྐྱེས་མ *Ri-skyes-ma*, མ་ཎྜོ་བོ, སྐྱིད་མ *Skyid-ma*, བསོད་ནམས་མ, གྲགས་ལྡན་མ, མཚན་སྤྱིན་མ, རིག་བྱེད་སྐྱེས *Rigbyed skyes*, དག་ཏུ་ཡང་ཚོ་ལྡན་མ.

སྐྱ་སེར *skya-ser* white and yellow, *i.e.*, the laity and the clergy, the latter being distinguished from the former by their yellow dress.

སྐྱ་སློམས *skya-sloms* occurs in the passage ཡོངས་རྩེ་མ་རྩེ་སློམས་སྐྱ་སློམས་ཆོན་རྩེ་མེད་པའི་སྨུག་མའི་ནོ (*Rtsii.*).

སྐྱ་ལྷམ *skya-lham* leather boots put on by laymen.

སྐྱག་པ *skyag-pa* I: same as ཕང་སྐྱག 1. human excrement; also any kind of ordure. 2. bad man, the dreg or scum of society; མིག་སྐྱག secretion from the eyes; སྐྱག་པ་གཏོང་བ to ease nature.

Syn. དྲི་ཆེན *dri-chen*; བྲུན *brun* (*tun*); མི་གཙང་མ *mi-gtsaṅ-ma* (*Mṅon.*).

སྐྱག་པ II: 1.=རྒྱག་པ. 2. pf. བསྐྱགས, fut. བསྐྱག, imp. སྐྱོག to spend, lay out, expend: སྐྱག་སྒོ expenditure or items of expenditure: སྐྱག་ཐོ *skyag-tho* list or account of expenses. 3. in *W.* སྐྱོག་དང་རྩེ to slaughter, to murder (*Jä.*).

སྐྱག་པོ *Skyag-po* n. of a place in Tibet: སྐྱག་པོ་འདམ་ར the marshy plain of སྐྱག་པོ.

སྐྱང *skyaṅ* पाण्डर; དམར་སྐྱང་ལྷ་བུ reddish brown.

+སྐྱང་ནུལ *skyaṅ nul*=རྫིང་ or ལྷག་པ लेप plaster; also pavement; clay-flour; mud-flour; སྐྱང་ནུལ་བྱེད་པ=ཞལ་བ་བྱེད་ པ to pave; to plaster; according to *Sch.* to rub, polish.

སྐྱངས *skyaṅs* ashamed; in shame: སྐྱངས་ཕྱར་རྩེ being ashamed (*A. K.*).

སྐྱབས *skyabs* शरण protection, defence; help, assistance: གནས་སྐབས་ཀྱི་སྐྱབས protection for the place and for the occasion: མཐར་ཐུག་གཏན་གྱི་སྐྱབས permanent and everlasting protection which according to the Buddhists can only be obtained from taking refuge in the three holies:—(1) Buddha who is the teacher is called སྐྱབས་རྗེ་པ or the Refuge Master; (2) Dharma or the sacred doctrine called སྐྱབས་དངོས, the real protection; (3) Saṅgha, the priesthood called སྐྱབས་སྒྲུབ་པའི་གྲོགས, the friend for gaining protection. Refuge in these three completely liberates one from the miseries of the world and secures the state of omniscience for the devotee: སྐྱབས་གསུམ་དུ་འགྲོ་བའི་ཚིག་གསུམ the three formula or expressions for seeking refuge in the three holies: (1) རྐང་གཉིས་ཀྱི་མཆོག་སངས་རྒྱས་ལ་སྐྱབས་སུ་མཆིའོ། "I come for refuge to Buddha who is the chief of the two-footed"; (2) འདོད་ཆགས་དང་བྲལ་བའི་མཆོག་ཆོས་ལ་སྐྱབས་སུ་མཆི། "I come for refuge to Dharma which separates from desires"; (3) ཚོགས་ཀྱི་མཆོག་དགེ་འདུན་ལ་སྐྱབས་སུ་མཆིའོ། "I come for refuge to the priesthood, the chief of all assemblies."

སྐྱབས་མགོན་ *skyabs-mgon* helper; protector; deliverer. The *Kyap-gon* is the popular term for the Dalai Lama in Lhasa and for the Panchen Lama in Shigatse and throughout Tsang. It is also applied to other incarnate lamas by courtesy.

སྐྱབས་མགོན་སྦུག་ *skyabs-mgon sbug* original or real protector; a complementary title of the Dalai Lama: སྐྱབས་མགོན་སྦུག་གི་བཀའ་ཤུའི་དགོངས་དོན་བཞིན according to the spirit of the letter of command of the Protector.

སྐྱབས་མགོན་རྩེ་ཞོད་ *skyabs-mgon rtse-çod* lit. tho Protector (residing on the) top (of Potala and the court) below: སྐྱབས་མགོན་རྩེ་ཞོད་ལ་ལོ་ཕྱག་སྔོན་མ་དང་བཞིན་ལོ་ལྟར་ཞར་ཕྱག་མེད་པ་འབུལ། "offer, without fail annually, as before, the new year's homage to the Grand Lama and his Court."

སྐྱབས་སྒྲོན་ *skyabs-sgron* प्रदीपशरण both protector and enlightener.

· སྐྱབས་བཅོལ་ *skyabs-bcol*, རྒྱ་བོད་བླ་དཔོན་རྣམས་དང་དེའི་རྒྱལ་ཐོག་རིམ་ཅན་གྱི་འགོ་དཔོན་སྐྱབས་བཅོལ་བྱ་གནས་ཡིན་པ་དགོངས་མངགས་བཞིན.

སྐྱབས་བཅོལ་ས་ *skyabs bcol-sa* the place of refuge: སྐྱབས་བཅོལ་ས་དཀོན་མཆོག་གསུམ་ལས་མེད། except the threo precious ones there is no place of refuge.

སྐྱབས་འཇུག་ *skyabs-hjug*=མགོ་འདྲེན་ a blessing; favour; taken under protection: ཡིད་སྨོན་བཞིན་འགྲུབ་པའི་སྐྱབས་འཇུག། blessing attained in accordance with one's mental prayor (*Yig. k. 25*).

སྐྱབས་འཇུག་ཞུ་བ་ *skyabs-hjug shu-wa* to ask benediction from the higher class of incarnate lamas for protection against disease, evil spirits, and other enemies, and also for a safe journey to heaven without falling into hell, &c.

སྐྱབས་གནས་ *skyabs-gnas* the placo of refuge, shelter; also of persons, helper.

སྐྱབས་གནས་རྒྱ་ཆེན་ *skyabs-gnas rgya-chen*= མཆོད་གནས་ the great object of worship or adoration (*Mṅon.*).

སྐྱབས་པ་ *skyabs-pa*=བསྐྱབས་ *bskyabs* शरण protection; saved (*Zam.*).

སྐྱབས་བྱ་ *skyabs-bya* the person who seeks refuge.

སྐྱབས་བྱེད་ *skyabs-byed*=བསྲུང་བ, रक्षा protection, defence (*Mṅon.*).

སྐྱབས་བྱེད་པ་ *skyabs byed-pa* to protect, help, save.

སྐྱབས་འོས་ *skyabs-hos* शरण्य worthy of protection; also སྐྱབས་གསུམ་ त्रिशरण the three protectors, *i.e.*, Buddha, Dharma and Saṅgha.

སྐྱབས་སུ་འགྲོ་བ་ *skyabs-su hgro-wa* or སྐྱབས་འགྲོ་བ་ *skyabs hgro-wa* शरणगमन to seek refuge; a going unto or repairing to for protection. शरणगमन or त्रिशरणगमन has been defined in the Bodhicharyāvatāra as follows:—रत्नत्रयं मे शरणमिति त्रिशरणगमनम्। "I take refuge in the three gems." In the same work पूजना has been substituted for it and it is found in the list of seven-fold highest modes of worship.

སྐྱབས་སེམས་ *skyab-sems* སྐྱབས་སུ་འགྲོ་བའི་སེམས་བསྐྱེད། the idea of seeking refuge.

སྐྱར་ཕུ་ *Skyar-phu* a place in Tibet (*Deb. 45*).

སྐྱར་གོག། *skyar-gog* naked (in the dialect of Purang).

སྐྱར་བཅག། *skyar-bcag* to bring into recollection, to bring back into memory anything that has been forgotten.

སྐྱར་པོ་ *skyar-po* snipe; wood-cock (*Sch.*).

སྐྱར་བ་ *skyar-wa*=སྐྱོར་བ་ ཡང་ཡང་ पुनः पुनः again and again.

Syn. སྐྱར་བའི་ཚིག་ *skyar-wahi tshig*; སྐྱོར་ཚིག་ *skyor-tshig*; བཟློས་ཚིག་ *zlos-tshig*; གཉིས་གསུམ་

ཟློས་པ *gñis-gsum zlos-pa*; ཟློས་གཏམ *zlos-gtam* (*Mṅon.*).

སྐྱར་རབ *skyar-rbab* (*Cs.*) पाण्डुरोग a kind of dropsy; a greyish rheumatic swelling.

སྐྱར་མོ *skyar-mo* a kind of water fowl; according to *Sch.* a heron. The flesh of this fowl is antidote for a poison administered in Mongolia mixed with horse flesh (*Sman gshuṅ*). ཆུ་སྐྱར duck (*Cs.*, *Sch.*); bittern, but the कादम्ब of the *Lex.* is a kind of goose.

སྐྱར་ལེབ *skyar-leb* the sheldrake.

སྐྱལ *skyal* प्लवन swimming.

སྐྱལ་ཁ *skyal-kha* कूर्दन leaping; a boat.

སྐྱལ་གྱིས་སྒྲོལ *skyal-gyis sgrol* प्लविक: crossing over by swimming.

སྐྱལ་ཆེན *skyal-chen*=ཉ་པ *ña-pa* fish; a fisherman (*Mṅon.*).

སྐྱས *skyas* a changing of abode or residence; སྐྱས་ཆེན་པོ death: སྐྱས་ཆེན་པོ་ནི་འདེགས the great change of place that uplifts, *i.e.*, death; སྐྱས་འདེགས་པ to change one's dwelling place; (cf. སྐྱ་བ) སྐྱས་ཆེན་འདེགས་པ to die; vb. *skyas-pa*, pf. བསྐྱས, fut. བསྐྱ or བསྐྱ་བར་བྱ, to transfer, and hence to depart this life.

སྐྱས་མ *skyas-ma* 1. v. སྐྱེས་མ. 2. fern (in Sikkim).

སྐྱི *skyi* 1. interest on loan; སྐྱི་ནོར wealth accrued from interest, *i.e.*, money-lending; according to some borrowed wealth. 2. the outward side of a skin or hide (*Cs.*).

སྐྱི་དཀར *skyi dkar*=ཀོ་བ་རྩེ་ཁ་དཀར་པོ the white fatty side of a skin (*Ṅag.*): སྐྱི་དཀར་གྱི་པགས་པ acc. to *Cs.*, dressed leather; tanned leather, sometimes hide: སྐྱི་དཀར་གྱི་པགས་ཤོག parchment.

སྐྱི་ཁུང *Skyi-khuṅ* a place in Tibet (*Deb.* ཀ *34*).

སྐྱི་མཁར་ལྷ་ཁང *Skyi-mkhar lha-khaṅ* n. of a monastery in Tsang (*Deb.* ཀ *12*).

སྐྱི་སྒམ *skyi-sgam* a box, chest or trunk lined outside with dressed hide.

སྐྱི་བསྟུམས *skyi-bstums* anything packed or tied round with dressed hide; a skin or hide to pack with: དཀྲོང་རྩེ་སྐྱི་བསྟུམས་མ *dkroṅ-rtse skyi bstums-ma*.

སྐྱི་ནག *Skyi-nag* or སྐྱི་སྐྱི་ན་ག *skyi-skyi na-ga* n. of a pasture land in province Tsang.

སྐྱི་ལྤགས *skyi-lpags* chamois wash-leather (*Sch.*).

སྐྱི་བ *skyi-wa* I: a medicinal plant (*Med.*); acc. to *Jä.* potato.

སྐྱི་བ II: vb. pf. བསྐྱིས *bskyis*, fut. བསྐྱི *bskyi*, imp. སྐྱིས *skyis*, to borrow, especially money or goods (cf. གཡར་བ and སྐྱིན་པ *skyin-pa*).

སྐྱི་བུང *skyi-buṅ* cloud: དེ་ལ་ཀོང་རྩེ་འཕྲུལ་གྱི་རྒྱལ་པོ་ཡང་སྐྱི་བུང་གྱིས་མོང་ནས། thereupon the phantom King Kong-tse departed with the clouds (*D. R.*).

སྐྱི་བུན *skyi-bun* prob. an itching of the skin (*Jä.*).

སྐྱི་གཡའ *skyi-gyha*=འཇིགས་པ fear; dread (*Mṅon.*): སྐྱི་གཡར་བ *skyi gyaḥ-wa* to shiver, tremble with fear (*Cs.*); to be struck with panic.

སྐྱི་ཤ *skyi ça* outward and inward side of a hide (*Jä.*); according to *Sch.* the anus.

སྐྱིག་པ *skyig-pa* or སྐྱིགས་པ *skyigs-pa* also སྐྱིགས་བུ *skyigs-bu* vulgo. ཨི་ཁུག *i-khug* हिक्का, अनुबन्धि hicough; yex; also a sob: གསེར་མ་ཟ་བ་རྣམས་ཀྱིས་ཁ་ནས་གཡེགས་བྱེད་པ། "coughing by those who eat the berry (gyer-ma)" (*Ṅag.*); སྐྱིགས་བུ་བརྩེག་པར *skyigs-bu brtseg-par* to keep on sobbing.

སྐྱིང་ཁབ་ *skyiṅ-khab* in Hindi *Kiṅkab*, embroidery inlaid with gold and silk manufactured both in India and China.

སྐྱེང་སེར་ *skyeṅ ser* eagle; vulture (*Jä.*).

སྐྱིངས་ *skyiṅs* occurs in the passage བཀའ་བབས་ཡང་སྐྱིངས་བཞིན་ཐོག་གི་སྣང་ (*D. R.*).

སྐྱིད་གྲོང་ *Skyid-groṅ* n. of a well-known town in Southern Tib., near sources of the Ganduk on Nepal border, commonly called Kirong: སྐྱིད་གྲོང་གི་རི་བོད་བལ་འབར་ལ་སྒོམ་དུ་ཕྱིན་པ་ལས། having come to meditate on the mountains of Kirong between Tibet and Nepal (*Mil.*).

སྐྱིད་གླུ་ *skyid glu* song of joy; a merry song.

སྐྱིད་མགོ་ *skyid mgo* beginning of happiness.

སྐྱིད་ཆུ་ *Skyid-chu* "the river of happiness," n. of northern tributary of the great Yeru Tsangpo or Brahmaputra River, on which tributary Lhasa is situated.

སྐྱིད་ཆེས་ *skyid-ches* comfortable: ངེད་རྣམས་སྐྱིད་ཆེས་པ་ *ṅed-rnams skyid ches-pa* we have been comfortable (*A. 129*).

སྐྱིད་ཐབས་ *skyid-thabs* comforts; mode of comfortable living: བུ་དེ་བདེ་ཐབས་སྐྱིད་ཐབས་འཇམ་ཐབས་ཁོ་ན་ལ་ *bu-de bde-thabs skyid-thabs hjam-thabs kho-na-la* the son only sought for opportunities of happiness and comfort.

སྐྱིད་དར་ *skyid-dar* a silk scarf presented to the bride at the time of marriage as a token of prosperity.

སྐྱིད་ལྡེ་ཉི་མ་མགོན་ *Skyid-lde ñi-ma-mgon* n. of a King of Tibet: སྐྱིད་ལྡེ་ཉི་མ་མགོན་འདི་མངའ་རིས་སུ་ཐེབས་རྒྱལ་སྲིད་བཟུང་། this Kyi-de Ñima-gon came into Ngari and seized the kingdom (*Loṅ.*).

སྐྱིད་སྡུག་ *skyid-sdug* good and ill-luck, happiness and misery; one's general circumstances: སྐྱིད་སྡུག་ཅི་བྱུང་ཀྱང་ whatever circumstances may happen: སྐྱིད་སྡུག་བསྲེ་བ pleasure and pain intermingled.

སྐྱིད་པ་ *skyid-pa* or སྐྱིད་པོ་ *skyd-po* sbst. सुख, सौख्य, क्षेम happiness; adj. सुखिन् happy: སྐྱིད་པོ་འདོད་ན་གཅིག་པོར་སྡོད་ *skyid-po hdod-na gcig-por sdod* if you wish to be happy, live alone, *i.e.*, be a celibate (*Lo. 27*).

སྐྱིད་ཞིང་ངེ་ *skyid ziṅ-ṅe* = སྐྱི་སྟོང་ངེ་ *skyi stoṅ-ṅe* always happy; uninterrupted happiness: སྐྱིད་ཞིང་ཞིང་བྱེད་པ་ *skyid ziṅ-ziṅ bycd-pa* to be continuously happy.

སྐྱིད་ཤོད་ *Skyid-çod* the district including the tracts in the lower valley of the river *Kyi*; the central district of དབུས་ or Ü, the province of which Lhasa is the chief city.

སྐྱིད་ལྷན་ *skyi-lhan* signifies སྐྱིད་པོ་ལ་འགྲོ་བར་ *skyi-po-la hgro-war*, to be prosperous; happy (*Lo.*).

སྐྱིན་ *skyin* the Tibetan ibex, *Capra sakeen*: ཁྱེའུ་ཆུང་སྐྱིན་གྱི་རལ་ཀ་ཅན་གསེར་གྱི་རལ་གྲི་ཐོགས་པ་གཅིག་ *khyehu chuṅ-skyin-gyi ral-ka-can gser-gyi ral-gri thogs-pa gcig* (*D. R.*) a little boy who had the horns of an ibex holding a golden sword. In Ladak the female ibex is differentiated as ལྷན་མོ.

+ **སྐྱིན་གོར་** *skyin-gor* or སྐྱིན་མགོ་ *skyin-mgo* a lizard (*Lex.*); also called གངས་སྦལ་ snow-frog.

སྐྱིན་ཐང་ *skyin-thaṅ* = སེར་བ་ *ser-wa* hail and sleet (*Sch.*).

སྐྱིན་པ་ *skyin-pa* 1. sbst. a loan; money borrowed irrespective of interest; ནོར་བསྐྱེས་པའི་སྐྱིན་པ་ loan producing interest: ང་ལ་འདི་སྐྱིན་དུ་འཚལ་ *ṅa-la hdi skyin-du htshal* grant me this as a loan; སྐྱིན་པ་སྤྲོད་པ་ *skyin-pa sprod-pa* or སྐྱིན་པ་འཇལ་བ་ *skyin-pa hjal-wa* to pay back or return a loan; ནོར་སྐྱིན་ *nor-skyin* a loan of money or goods; གོས་སྐྱིན *gos-ṣkyin* a loan of clothes; སྐྱིན་པ་ལེན་པ *ṣkyin-pa len-pa* to take on credit. 2. vb. pf. བསྐྱིན *ḅṣkyin* to borrow.

སྐྱིན་པོ *ṣkyin-po* chiefly colloq. resp. ཀར་སྐྱིན *kar-ṣkyin* a loan; a thing borrowed; money advanced without interest (*Jä.*).

སྐྱིན་མི *ṣkyin-mi* acc. to *Schr.* a debtor.

སྐྱིན་ཚབ *ṣkyin-tshab* a debt; any thing paid as equivalent of thing taken on loan. In *C.* signifies same as ཚབ, the pledge for loan.

སྐྱིབས *ṣkyiḅṣ* a place giving shelter (either in a rock, under a tree, roof or cavern): བྲག་ཕུག་ཕུག་གི་ཤོག་ཁྱོག་ན་བྱ་རྣམས་བརྟེན་པས་བྲག་དེས་སྐྱིབས་ཤེས་པ་སྐྱབས་པའི་དོན། དེ་ལ་བྱ་སྐྱིབས་ཟེར because birds dwell in the hollow of an overhanging rock, such rock known as *ṣkyiḅṣ* is termed "bird-shelter" for the reason that it affords protection (*Ñag.*): བྲག་སྐྱིབས *brag-ṣkyibṣ* a sheltering place under an overhanging rock or a projecting roof: བཀའ་སྐྱིབས *ḅkaḥ-ṣkyibṣ* a covered terrace or small portico before a house: ཆར་སྐྱིབ *char-ṣkyib* shelter from rain.

སྐྱིམ *ṣkyim* dressed leather painted red or in other colours, japanned or varnished leather.

སྐྱིལ་ཀྲུང *ṣkyil-kruñ* (*kil-ṭuñ*) the posture of sitting cross-legged serenely without moving the limbs; སྐྱིལ་ཀྲུང་བྱེད་པ *ṣkyil-kruñ byeḍ-pa* पर्यङ्क to take a particular kind of posture practised by ascetics in meditation; སྐྱིལ་མོ་ཀྲུང་གི་འདུག་པ *ṣkyil-mo kruñ-gi ḥdug-pa* or བཞུགས་པ *ḅshugṣ-pa* to sit in a cross-legged posture; སེམས་དཔའི་སྐྱིལ་ཀྲུང *semṣ-ḍpaḥi ṣkyil-kruñ* the mental concentration, or the posture of sitting perfectly still, of a *Bodhisattva*: རྡོ་རྗེ་སྐྱིལ་ཀྲུང *ṛdo-ṛje ṣkyil-kruñ* वज्रपर्यङ्क the posture of sitting perfectly still without moving the body; the unchangeable posture of sitting cross-legged; རྫོགས་པའི་སྐྱིལ་ཀྲུང *ṛdsogṣ-paḥi ṣkyil-kruñ* the posture of perfection, *i.e.*, of a Buddha.

སྐྱིལ་བ *ṣkyil-wa*, pf. བསྐྱིལ་པ *ḅṣkyil-pa* or བསྐྱིལ་ཏོ *ḅṣkyil-to*, fut. བསྐྱིལ་བར་བྱ *ḅṣkyil-war bya* or *ḅṣkyil* 1. to pen up, shut up; to dam up a river; ཆུ་སྐྱིལ་བ *chu ṣkyil-wa* to bank up water; ཆུ་རྫིང་དུ་སྐྱིལ་བ *chu ṛdsiñ-du ṣkyil-wa* to collect water in a pond; ཆུ་རྫིང་བུར་སྐྱིལ་བ *chu ṛjiñ-bur ṣkyil-wa* to collect water for a pond. When the water collects itself into a pool or tank it is called ཆུ་འཁྱིལ་བ *chu ḥkhyiḷ-wa*: ཟག་མེད་བདུད་རྩིའི་བཏུང་བ་མཚོ་ལྟར་བསྐྱིལ *zag-meḍ ḅduḍ-ṛtsiḥi ḅtuñ-wa ṃtsho-ḷtar ḅṣkyil* the exhaustless drink of ambrosia stands collected like a sea. [2. to bend, esp. the legs when sitting on the ground after Oriental fashion; also to bend in another's leg by a kick from behind; to bend the bow (*Jä.*)].

སྐྱིལ་མོ་ཀྲུང་ *ṣkyil-mo kruñ* = འདུག་སྟངས posture of sitting; it is same as རྡོ་རྗེ་སྐྱིལ་ཀྲུང་ *ṛdo-ṛje ṣkyil-kruñ* (*Ṃñon.*).

སྐྱུ་གང *ṣkyu-gañ* 1. acc. to *Sch.* a gulp; draught. 2. dough made of flour with tea: སྐྱུ་གང་གི་རྣམ་པའི་སྐབས་ཟ་བའི་དུས་སྐབས་ཀྱིས་ཀོང་ཀོང་རྒྱུགས་འདུ་བ་བཙོས་ནས་མར་ཁྲ་གཟུམ་བྱེད་ཀྱི་མིང་། (*Ñag.*) at the time of eating pap of barley flour the dough becomes formed like a hollow bowl and the name of the rounded buttery lump is *kyu-gang*: ལམ་དུ་ཟ་སྤོལ་སྐབས་ཟ་དུས་མར་ཁྲ་འདབ་བསྐྱི། སྐྱུ་གང་བཙོས་ཏེ on a journey when eating barley flour mixed with butter and boiled tea the dough so made (*Lo.*).

སྐྱུ་ར་སྒང *Ṣkyu-ra-ṣgañ* one of the six districts of ཁམས *Khamṣ* designated under the name of སྒང་དྲུག. The six *Ṣgañ* are the following:—(1) སྐྱུ་ར་སྒང་ Skyu-ra Sgañ, (2) རབ་སྒང་ Rab-Sgañ, (3) སྤོ་འབོར་སྒང་ Spo-ḥbor Sgañ, (4) དམར་ཁམས་སྒང་ Dmar-Khams Sgañ, (5) ཚ་སྒང་ Tsha-Sgañ, (6) ཟལ་མོ་སྒང་ Zal-mo Sgañ.

སྐྱུ་རུ I: *skyu-ru* a kind of medicinal fruit called སྐྱེར་ཤུན *skyer-çun.*

སྐྱུ་རུ II: *skyu-ru* in Sikk. and སྐྱུར་མོ *skyur-mo* in Lhasa, signify a sour liquid or vinegar (*Jä.*).

སྐྱུ་རུ་ར *skyu-ru-ra* अम्लक, धचक 1. n. of a sour fruit said to cure the diseases of phlegm, bile and blood. 2. *Jä.* in his Dict. says: "In later times the word seems to have been used also for the olive, and *skyu-ru çiñ*, the olive tree, which in Sikkim is called *kha skyur-poḥi çiñ.*"

Syn. རྒྱལ་འབྲས *rgyal-ḥbras*; ཞི་བྱེད *shi-byed*; བཅུད་ལྔ་པ *bcud lña-pa*; ལང་ཚོ་བརྟན་བྱེད *lañ-tsho brtan-byed*; ན་ཚོད་གནས *na-tshod-gnas*; དཔལ་ལྡན *dpal-ldan*; བཅུད་གནས *bcud-gnas*; མ་མ *ma-ma* (*Mñon.*).

སྐྱུ་རུམ *skyu-rum*=ཚོད་མའི་མིང་ *tshod-maḥi miñ* (*Nag.*) 1. n. of a kind of table vegetable. 2. condiment; sauce; pickle (*Cs.*). According to others, at least in *W.*, only the resp. word for སྤགས *spags*: (*Jä.*) སྐྱུ་རུམ་སྦྱོར་བ to prepare sauce, &c.; ཤ་ཡི་སྐྱུ་རུམ sauce made of vinegar for meat; ཚོད་མའི་སྐྱུ་རུམ sauce made of vegetable or pot-herbs.

སྐྱུག་པ *skyug-pa*, pf. སྐྱུགས *skrugs* 1. उद्गीर्ण to vomit, eject, *e.g.*, blood; སྐྱུགས་ཏེ་འཇུག་པ *skyug-te hjug-pa* to cause to vomit; སྐྱུག་པ་འདྲེན་པ *skyug-pa dren-pa* to excite vomiting; ངན་སྐྱུགས *ñan-skyugs* vomit (it is the food of certain demons, and being boiled in it is one of the punishments of hell) (*Jä.*). 2. to lose colour; to stain.

སྐྱུག་ཉེས་པ *skyug ñes-pa* दुर्भुक्त that cannot be taken or eaten.

སྐྱུག་ལྡད *skyug-ldad* rumination; chewing the cud; acc. to *Sch.* eructation: སྐྱུག་ལྡད་བྱེད་པ रोमन्थायते to chew the cud as cattle.

སྐྱུག་བྲོ་བ *skyug bro-wa* (*kyug-to-wa*) or སྐྱུག་ལོག=ཞེ་མེར་བ nausea (*Mñon.*); also what is repulsive to taste or sight or smell; causing nausea; སྐྱུག་བྲོ་བའི་ནད the disease of nausea; སྐྱུག་བྲོ་བས from disgust (to eat anything); སྐྱུག་བྲོ *skyug-bro* in *C.* shameful; impure with regard to religion (*Jä.*).

སྐྱུག་སྨན *skyug-sman*=སྐྱུག་བྱེད an emetic; a medicine causing to vomit.

སྐྱུག་ལོག་པ *skyug log-pa* (*Sch.*) to feel disgust, v. སྐྱུག་བྲོ་བ *skyug bro-wa.*

སྐྱུགས་པོ *skyugs-po*=གསལ་བ *gsal-wa* 1. clear; 2. n. of a bird the bill of which is of coral colour.

Syn. བྱུ་རུའི་མཆུ་ཅན *byu-ruhi mchu-can*; ཡུལ་ངན་འབོད *yul-ñan hbod*; གྲང་རེག་ཕོ་ཉ *grañ-reg pho-ña* (*Mñon.*).

སྐྱུང་བ *skyuñ-wa*, pf. བསྐྱུངས་པ *bskyuñs-pa*, fut. བསྐྱུང་ *bskyuñ*, imp. སྐྱུངས *skauñs*, to diminish or reduce; བསྐུམ་པ *bskum-pa* or also འབྲི་བ *hbri-wa*, ཉུང་དུ་བཏང་བ *ñuñ-du btañ-wa*; སྐྱུངས *skyuñs* reduced; subdued: བསྐྱུངས *bskyuñs* ང་རྒྱལ་བསྐྱུངས་ནས་སྟན་ལ་འདུག་པ་ན (*A. 10*) "he was seated on his cushion after his pride was subdued." Acc. to *Jä.* in *C.* *skyuñ-ua*, to leave behind; to lay aside, *e.g.*, a task.

ᚐ **སྐྱུད་པ** *skyud-pa* to forget, resp. ཐུགས་བརྗེད་སོར་བ *thugs brjed çor-wa* forgetfulness; acc. to *Jä.* to leave off: བསྐྱུད་པ *bskyud-pa* (*Zam. 10*). Acc. to *Sch.* to communicate; to swallow.

སྐྱུར་བ I: *skyur-wa*, vb. pf. and fut. བསྐྱུར *bskyur* to throw, to cast; to leave off; རྒྱབ་ཏུ་སྐྱུར *rgyab-tu skyur* अपविद्ध, to cast behind; རིང་ཏུ་སྐྱུར་བ *riṅ-tu skyur-wa*, to throw at a distance: ལྷུང་བཟེད་ནམ་མཁའ་ལ་བསྐྱུར་ནས *lhuṅ-bzed nam-mkhah-la bskyur-nas* having flung his mendicant's platter towards the sky; ཆུ་ལ་སྐྱུར་བ *chu-la skyur-wa*, to throw into the water. སྐྱུར *skyur* also implies བཏང་ *btaṅ*, to mix; throw; pour out; to throw away; throw down a stone, a corpse, &c.: བདག་ཆང་འཐུང་རྒྱུ་སྐྱུར་བཞག་པ་ཡིན *bdag chaṅ hthuṅ-rgyu skyur bshag-pa yin* I have left off drinking beer. ལུད་པ་སྐྱུར་བ *lud-pa skyur-wa* to eject a phlegm; to throw off a rider; to give up, abandon a work; to forsake a friend; to abort (*A. 155.*).

སྐྱུར་པ *skyur-pa* धौत bleached; bleaching: ཟླ་བ་ལྟ་བུ like the moon bleached, or white like the moon. སྐྱུར་པོ *skyur-po* अम्ल acid; sour.

སྐྱུར་ཁུ *skyur-khu* 1. a sour soup; sour juice. 2. རང་སྐྱུར *raṅ-skyur* vinegar (in Sikkim "*skyur-ru*," in Lahoul "*skyur-mo*").

སྐྱུར་གོང་ *skyur-goṅ*, also སྐྱུར་དད *skyur-dad*, same as སྐྱུར་ངོན *skyur-ṅon*. སྐྱུར *skyur* signifies "thrown" and གོང་ *goṅ* over; hence one over-powered by wine; a drunkard: སྐྱུར་གོང་ཅེ་བ་ལ་བུད་མེད་ལ་དགའ་བ one who is over-powered by wine delights in women: མི་སྐྱུར་གོང་ཅན་ལ་ཆགས་སྨོ་ཡོད a tipsy man is contemptible: མི་ནག་ཆང་གིས་སྐྱོ་ན་སྐྱུར་འགོང་འཛར if a layman is intoxicated with beer, drunken noisiness arises (*Rdsa. 11*).

སྐྱུར་ངོམ *skyur-ṅom* or སྐྱུར་དད *skyur-dad*=ཆང་མང་པོ་འཐུང་དགོས necessity (by habit) to drink; passion for drinking.

སྐྱུར་ཅན *skyur-can* powerful; spirited.

སྐྱུར་འཇུག་པ *skyur-hjug-pa* to leaven to turn sour; to take a sour taste; ཁ་སྐྱུར་པོ *kha-skyur-po* or ཁ་ཤ་སྐྱུར་པོ *kha-ça skyur-po* olive (*Jä.*).

སྐྱུར་ཏུམ *skyur-tum* व्यञ्जन a condiment; sauce; ཚོད་བའི་མིང་ a sour vegetable curry.

སྐྱུར་བ II: अम्ल, चुक्र adj. sour, acid; more frequently སྐྱུར་པོ *skyur-po* also སྐྱུར་མོ *skyur-mo*. Also sbst. sourness.

སྐྱུར་བྱེད་གསུམ *skyur-byed gsum*=འབྲས་བུ་གསུམ *hbras-bu gsum* the three sour medicinal fruits; also called ཀུན་དང་མཐུན་པའི་སྐྱུར་བྱེད་གསུམ *kun daṅ mthun-pahi skyur-byed gsum* "the three *myrobolan* which agree with all" and are:—(1) ཨ་རུ *a-ru*, (2) བ་རུ *ba-ru*, (3) སྐྱུ་རུ *skyu-ru* (*Sman. 447*).

སྐྱུར་མ *skyur-ma* abortion; in *W.* ཆུ་སྐྱུར *chu-skyur*, གཡང་སྐྱུར *gyaṅ skyur*, capital punishment in Tibet, when the delinquent, with a weight fastened to his neck, is thrown from a rock into a river (*Jä.*).

སྐྱུར་མོ *skyur-mo* leaf of the *Elá* plant; *Elettaria cardamomum*, v. ཨེ་ལའི་འདབ (*Mṅon.*).

སྐྱུར་རྩི *skyur-rtsi*=ཤིང་ཀ་པད་ཐ *çiṅ-ka pad-tha* a kind of lemon (*Mṅon.*).

སྐྱུར་རྩི་ཆུང *rskyur-rtsi chuṅ* नागरङ्ग the smaller species of orange.

སྐྱུར་རྩི་ཆེན་པོ *skyur-rtsi chen-po* जम्बीर n. of a kind of lemon.

Syn. སོ་རྩི *so-rtsi*; ལེགས་འཛིན *legs-hdsin*; རབ་གནས་མེ་ཏོག *rab-gnas me-tog*; སྙིང་རྗེ *sñiṅ-rje*; གསོ་དགའ་བྱེད *gso-dgah-byed*; རྣམ་པར་མཛེས *rnam-par-mdses* (*Mṅon.*).

སྐྱུར་ཤིང་ *skyur-çiṅ*=རག་ཆུང་ཤིང་ *rag-chuṅ çiṅ* n. of a plant (*Mṅon.*).

སྐྱུས *skyus*, acc. to *Sch.* སྐྱུས་ཐོག་པ *skyus thog-pa* altogether: སྐྱུས་སུ་ཀློག་པ *skyus-su klog-pa* to pronounce jointly, viz., two consonants without a vowel between them (*Jä.*).

སྐྱེ *skye*, v. སྐྱེད *skyed*, and སྐྱེ་བ *skye-wa*.

སྐྱེ་དགུ *skye-dgu*=སྐྱེ་བོ་ཀུན *skye-bo kun* प्रजा all beings. This word is sometimes written as སྐྱེ་རྒུ *skye-rgu*. དགུ *dgu* "nine," in the word སྐྱེ་དགུ *skye-dgu* signifies many: སྐྱེ་དགུ་མ་རུང་བ *skye-dgu maruṅ-wa* or སྐྱེ་དགུ་མ་རུང་བའི་བསམ་པ་ཅན *skye dgu-ma ruṅ-wahi bsam-pa can* wicked and vicious animals or sensate beings (*K. du.* ག *453*).

སྐྱེ་དགུའི་བདག་པོ *skye-dguhi bdag-po*=སྐར་མ་སྣར་མ *skar-ma snar-ma* रोहिणीनक्षत्र 1. n. of the fourth constellation (*Mṅon.*). 2. ཚངས་པ the god Brahmā of the Hindus (*Mṅon.*).

སྐྱེ་དགུའི་བདག་མོ *Skye-dgu-hi bdag-mo*, महाप्रजावती the step-mother and first governess of Buddha; also a name of the goddess Paldan Lhamo.

སྐྱེ་འགྲོ *skye-hgro*=འགྲོ་བ *hgro-wa* जगत् beings or moving beings; also སྐྱེ་བོ *skye-bo* human being (*Mṅon.*).

སྐྱེ་འགྲོ་ཡོངས་ཀྱི་མདོག་གསལ *skye-hgro yoṅs-kyi mdog-gsal*=སྦྲང་རྩི honey (*Sman. 73*).

སྐྱེ་རྒས *skye-rgas*, contraction of སྐྱེ་བ་དང་རྒ་བས *skye-wa daṅ rga-was*, by birth and old age, *i.e.*, death.

སྐྱེ་སྒོ *skye-sgo* 1. entrance to rebirth, viz., to one of the six regions of birth: སྐྱེ་སྒོ་གཅོད་པ *skye-sgo gcod-pa* to prevent birth, to lock it up 2. face: སྐྱེ་སྒོ་ལེགས་པ *skye-sgo legs-pa* a handsome face; སྐྱེ་སྒོ་ཞན་པ *skye-sgo shan-pa* an ugly face; also ཁ་སྒོ་སྐྱེ་འབྲས་ལེགས་པ *kha-sgo skye-hbras legs-pa* is said for having a handsome exterior.

སྐྱེ་ངན *skye-ṅan*, माणवक lit. "a bad man," but also a dwarf.

སྐྱེ་མཆེད *skye-mched* I:=དབང་པོ आयतन the sources and places of origin of the senses. Of these there are four:—(1) ནམ་མཁའ་མཐའ་ཡས་སྐྱེ་མཆེད *nam mkhah mthah yas skye-mched* आकाशानन्त्यायतन a world as infinite as the sky; (2) རྣམ་ཤེས་མཐའ་ཡས་སྐྱེ་མཆེད *rnam-çes mthah yas skye-mched* विज्ञानान्त्यायतन a world as formless as consciousness; (3) ཅི་ཡང་མེད་པའི་སྐྱེ་མཆེད *ci-yaṅ med-pahi skye-mched* आकिञ्चन्यायतन a world as unlimited as void; (4) འདུ་ཤེས་མེད་འདུ་ཤེས་མེད་མིན་སྐྱེ་མཆེད *hdu-çes-med hdu-çes-med miṅ skye-mched* नैवसंज्ञानासंज्ञायतन a world where there is neither consciousness nor unconsciousness.

སྐྱེ་མཆེད II: the inner and outward organs of sense.

སྐྱེ་མཆེད་མུ་བཞི *skye-mched mu-bshi* is said to mean འཇིག་རྟེན་ཁམས་ཀྱི་མིང, n. of the world.

སྐྱེ་འཆི་མེད་པ *skye-hchi med-pa* without birth or death; eternal.

སྐྱེ་གནས *skye-gnas* 1. birth-place; station or locality of a plant; also=མོ་དབང་ योनि the female generative organ. 2. जाति the state or sphere of birth or rebirth; བྱོལ་སོང་གི་སྐྱེ་བ *byol-soṅ-gi skye-wa* the being born as an animal; སྐྱེ་བ་བཞི *skye-wa, bshi* or སྐྱེ་གནས་བཞི *skye-gnas bshi* the four states or ways of being born.

སྐྱེ་གནས་མཚུངས་པ *skye-gnas mtshuṅs-pa*=མིང་སྲིང *miṅ-sriṅ* brother and sister (*Mṅon.*).

སྐྱེ་བ I: *skye-wa* pf. *skyes* to be born: ང་ལ་བུ་སྐྱེས་པ་ཡིན *ṅa-la bu skyes-pa yin* I have given birth to a son, or to me a son has been born. མངལ་སྐྱེས *mṅal skyes* or མངལ་ནས་སྐྱེ་བ *mṅal-nas skye-wa* जरायुज viviparous; born of the womb. སྒོང་སྐྱེ *sgoṅ skyes* or སྒོ་ང་ལས་སྐྱེ་བ *sgo ṅa-las skye-wa* अण्डज born out of an egg or oviparous; དྲོད་གཤེར་སྐྱེས *drod-gçer skyes* संस्वेदज moisture-sprung; born out of heat and humidity; རྫུས་སྐྱེས *rdsus-skyes* उपपादुक apparitional; born in a supernatural way like the gods who, it is said, spring out from lotus flowers; also the inhabitants of the infernal regions; souls in that state of existence between death and rebirth which is called བར་དོ *bar-do*; ཕོ་སྐྱེས *pho-skyes* a male; a man; also one who has done a manly work; མོ་སྐྱེས *mo-skyes* a woman; female: སྐྱེ་ག་ན་འཆི་བའི་སྡུག་བསྔལ *skye-ga-na hchi-wahi sdug-bsnal* the evils of birth—old age, sickness and death.

སྐྱེ་བ II: *skye-wa* जाति 1. the being born; the birth; also re-birth; སྐྱེ་བ་མཐོ་བ *skye-wa mtho-wa* high birth; of high birth; nobleman; male; སྐྱེ་བ་དམའ་བ *skye-wa dmah-wa* or སྐྱེ་དམའ *skye-dmah* or སྐྱེ་དམན *skye-dman* of low birth; ignoble; also a woman: མི་ལུས་ཐོབ་ཀྱང་སྐྱེ་བ་དམན *mi-lus thob-kyan skye-wa dman* born a human being, it is true, but only a female. སྐྱེས་དམན *skyes-dman*, in colloquial *kyer-men*, a vulgar word for wife or woman: *ṅe* "*skyer-men*" my woman or wife: མིར་སྐྱེ་བ་བཞེན་པ *mir skye-wa bshen-pa* to take or assume rebirth, existence, life.

སྐྱེ་བ III: 1. to become; to begin to exist; to arise: ནད་ཀུན་མི་སྐྱེ་སྐྱེས་པའང་འཆི་བའི་ཕྱིར *ut ne morbus ullus nascatur, natus quoque sedetur* (*Jä.*), ཁྱེའུ་ཁྲོས་པའི་སེམས་སྐྱེས་ཏེ *khe-hu khros-pahi sems-skyes-te* the youth—thoughts of wrath arising (in him). 2. to grow (*nasci*): ལུང་པ་འབྲུ་སྐྱེ་བ valleys where corn grows: རུ་མགོ་ལ་སྐྱེ *ru mgo-la skye* a horn is growing on the head. 3. =འཕེལ་བ उद्गत, उदय, वृद्धिप्राप्त growing up, or grow up; thriving. 4. to grow (*crescere*); ཆེར *cher* or ཆེན་པོར་སྐྱེ་བ *chen-por skye-wa* to grow up; to grow tall: རས་ཀྱང་ལུས་ཀྱི་ཚད་དུ་སྐྱེས་སོ *ras-kyan lus-kyi tshad-du skyes-so* the garment also grew to the measure in proportion to the growth of the body, *i.e.*, རྟུལ་ཕོད་པར་སྐྱེས་སོ *rtul-phod-par skyes-so*, he grew up a valiant man; became a valiant man; to bud, germinate, sprout; in *W.* to accelerate the germinating of the seed by maceration.

སྐྱེ་བ IV: 1. v. སྐྱེ་གནས *skye-gnas* in a concrete sense the reborn individual: ཡུམ་གྱི་སྐྱེ་བ་ཡིན *yum-gyi skye-wa yin* she is the rebirth of the mother. 2. the arising, etc 3. the growing, etc.

སྐྱེ་བ་རྒྱལ *skye-wa ryal*=སྐྱེས་པ *skye-pa* a person.

སྐྱེ་བ་རྒྱུན་གཅོད *skye-wa rgyun-gcod* to stop the continuance of birth—to interrupt it.

Syn. བྲག་སྤྲས *brag-spras*; གབ་མིང་ *gab miṅ* (*Miṅ.*).

སྐྱེ་བ་ལྔ་པ *skye-wa lṅa-pa*=དུང་དཀར་གཡས་འཁྱིལ *duṅ-dkar gyas-hkhyil* दक्षिणावर्तशङ्ख a conch-shell with its coil reverting to the right instead of to the left (*Mṅon.*).

སྐྱེ་བ་སྔ *skye-wa sṅa* प्राग्जन्म former birth; anterior birth; སྐྱེ་བ་སྔ་མའི་རེ་ཁ *skye-wa sṅa-mahi re-kha* the lines or marks in the hand or head which are supposed to represent the symbols of one's acts in a former life.

སྐྱེ་བ་མཐུན་པ *skye-wa mthun-pa* is defined as རིགས་རུས་གཅིག་པར་སྐྱེ་བའམ་ཉིན་གཅིག་སྐྱེ་བ *rigs-rus gcig-par skye wahm ñin-gcig skye-wa* "the being born of one and the same lineage or the being born on one day."

སྐྱེ་བ་དང་འཇིག་པ *skye-wa daṅ hjig-pa* birth and death, or passing away; frequently of thoughts, passions, &c. (the person as well as the thing in the accusative).

སྐྱེ་བ་དྲན་པ *skye-wa dran-pa* जातिस्मरण remembrance of a former birth.

སྐྱེ་བ་བདུན་ *skye-wa bdun* seven periods of life.

སྐྱེ་བ་འདི་ལ་ *skye-wa hdi-la* in this my present period of life.

སྐྱེ་ལྡན་ *skye-ldan* = སེམས་ཅན་ *sems-can* animated beings (*Mṅon.*).

སྐྱེ་ལྡུམ་ *skye-ldum* a plantain (in Zayul) (*Snd. Hbk.*).

སྐྱེ་བ་སྤེལ་ *skye-wa spel*=འཁྲིག་པ་ *hkhrig-pa* to copulate.

Syn. དགའ་མགུར་སྤྱོད་ *dgah-mgur spyod*; ཆགས་སྤྱོད་ *ehags-spyod*; འདོད་ལོག་སྤྱོད་ *hdod-log spyod*; དབང་པོ་གཉིས་སྦྱོར་ *dwaṅ-po gñis sbyor*; ལོག་གཡེམ་ *log-gyem*; གསང་སྤྱོད་ *gsaṅ-spyod*; མི་ཚངས་སྤྱོད་ *mi-tshaṅs spyod* (*Mṅon.*).

སྐྱེ་བ་ཕྱི་མ་ *skye-wa phyi-ma*=ཚེ་ཕྱི་མ་ *tshe phyi-ma* future birth or existence.

སྐྱེ་བ་ཕྲ་མོ་ *skye-wa phra-mo*=འབུ་ཕྲ་མོ་ an animalculæ; also a small grain (*Mṅon.*).

སྐྱེ་བ་གཞན་ *skye-wa gshan* जन्मान्तर a future or previous birth.

སྐྱེ་བ་རིག་པ་ *skye-wa rig-pa* inherited intelligence: ཁམས་ཐམས་ཅད་འབྱུང་བ་ལྔར་ཤེས་པས་སྐྱེ་བ་རིག་པ་ *khams thams-cad hbyuṅ-wa lṅar çes-pas skye-wa rig-pa* that all the elements from which we spring are known to be five is hereditary knowledge.

སྐྱེ་བའི་ཆ་ཅན་ *skye-wahi eha-ean*=ཁྱི་ a dog.

Syn. རྡོ་རྗེའི་མཇུག་མ་ *rdo-rjehi mjug-ma*; སེང་གེའི་རིགས་ *seṅ-gehi rigs*; གྲོང་གི་གཅན་གཟན་ *groṅg-gi gcan-gzan* (*Mṅon.*).

སྐྱེ་བའི་ལམ་སྟེར་ *skye-wahi lam-ster*=མ་ *ma* mother (*Mṅon.*).

སྐྱེ་བས་མཐོ་ *skye-was mtho*=སྐྱེས་པ་ *skyes-pa* of high birth; man.

སྐྱེ་བས་འཐོབ་ *skye-was hthob* उपपत्तिप्रातिलम्भिक or •लम्भिक inheritance; heritage.

སྐྱེ་བོ་ *skye-bo* 1. a general name for all living creatures: མི་ལ་སོགས་པ་སྐྱེ་བོ་ *mi la-sogs-pa skye-bo* man and other living beings. 2. people; mankind; འཕྲུལ་བཅས་སྐྱེ་བོ་ *hphrul bcas skye-bo* infatuated men; སྐྱེ་བོ་མཁས་པ་གཞན་རྣམས་ *skye-bo mkhas-pa gshan rnams* other intellectual people; སྐྱེ་བོ་མང་པོའི་ཡིད་དུ་འོང་བ་ *skye-bo maṅ-pohi yid-du hoṅ-wa* beloved by many; མི་ནག་སྐྱེ་བོ་ *mi-nag skye-bo* laymen (on account of the dimness of their religious knowledge); སོ་སོ་སྐྱེ་བོ་ *so-so skye-bo* पृथग्जन 'the lower clergy, common monks, but also simple laymen if they are not quite without religious knowledge; not of saintly origin; not an incarnate Lama; སྐྱེ་བོ་ཐམས་ཅད་ལ་ཕན་ཡོན་ *skye-bo thams-chad la phan-yon* सार्व्वजनिक useful to all; of public utility.

Syn. སྐྱེ་འགྲོ་ *skye-hgro*.

སྐྱེ་བོ་བཀྲེས་པ་ *skye-bo bkres-pa* hungry person: གླིང་དེར་གནས་པའི་སྐྱེ་བོ་བཀྲེས་པ་ *skye-bo bkres-pa* the people residing in that country (or continent) are (always) hungry (*K. d.* ཀ *143*).

སྐྱེ་བོ་ངན་པ་ *skye-bo ṅan-pa* खल a charlatan; a knave: སྐྱེ་བོ་ངན་དང་འགྲོགས་པ་ཡིས། སྐྱེ་བོ་དམ་པ་རླག་པར་བྱེད་ *skye-bo ṅan daṅ hgrogs-pa-yis, skye-bo dam-pa rlag-par byed* by friendship with a bad man a holy man is spoiled (*Cāṇ.*).

སྐྱེ་བོ་དམ་པ་ *skye-bo dam-pa* सुजन a good or holy man; an incarnate being.

སྐྱེ་བོ་གནས་པ་ *skye-bo gnas-pa* ग्राम a place of habitation.

སྐྱེ་བོ་ཕལ་པོ་ཆེའི་ཕན་པ་ *skye-bo phal-po-chehi phan-pa* महते जनकायाय हितम् of good or use to the general public.

སྐྱེ་བོ་ཚན་པོ་ཆེ *skye-bo tshan-po-che* a large number of men; a crowd; ཚན་པོ *tshan-po* implying a large number.

སྐྱེ་བོ་གསོ་ཐིག *skye-bo gso-thig* n. of a treatise on ethics by Nāgārjuna (*Tan d.* གོ *176*).

སྐྱེ་བོའི་གཏམ *skyu-bohi gtam* जनवाद, जनोक्ति popular talk; rumour.

སྐྱེ་བོའི་ཚོགས *skye-bohi tshog* जनता assembly; a crowd.

སྐྱེ་བོའི་ཚོགས་ཅན *skye-bohi tshog-can* = སྨད་འཚོང་མའི་གཙོ་མོ *smad-htshoṅ mahi gtso-mo* queen of the harlots (*Mṅon.*).

སྐྱེ་བོས་བསྐུར་མ *skye-bos bskur-ma*, v. སྨད་འཚོང་མའི་གཙོ་མོ *smad-htshoṅ mahi gtso-mo* (*Mṅon.*).

སྐྱེ་བོས་དབེན་པ *skye-bos dwen-pa* a solitary man.

སྐྱེ་མེད་བཙན་ས་ཟིན་པ *skye-med btsan-sa zin-pa* attained to an exalted state of existence from which there is no rebirth.

སྐྱེ་རྨོངས *skye-rmoṅs* = སྐྱེས་བུ་རྨོངས་པ *skye-bu rmoṅs-pa* a stupid man; one who is sunk in pleasures or sordid acts.

སྐྱེ་ཚེ *skye-tshe* राजिका mustard; སྐྱེ་ཚེའི་འབྲུ *skye-tshehi hbru* राजिका तण्डुल mustard grain.

སྐྱེ་ཟླ *skye-zla* (*keh-dā*) the month or the particular phase of the moon in which one is born (*Ya-sel. 11*).

སྐྱེ་རགས *skye-rags*, v. སྐེ་རགས for *ske-rags*, girdle. The term in *Mil.* book, *skye-rags-kyi ras hdi*, seems an inversion of the intended order of the words.

སྐྱེ་ཤིང *skye-çiṅ* = སྡོང་རྐང་སྦོད *sdoṅ rkaṅ sbod* a tree with a huge trunk.

སྐྱེ་སེར་གྱི་རླུང *skye-ser-gyi rluṅ* the cold north wind called *skyeṅ-ser rluṅ* in *Mil.*: བྱང་སྐྱེ་སེར་གྱི་རླུང་པོ་མ་རྒྱབ་ན, ལྷོ་རུ་ཙན་དན་གྱི་ནགས་མི་འགུལ *byaṅ skye-ser-gyi rluṅ-po ma, rgyab-na lho-ru tsan-dan-gyi-nags mi-hgul* if the north wind does not blow, the sandal trees in the south do not move.

སྐྱེ་སྲིད་ས་བོན *skye-srid sa-bon* = प father (*Mṅon.*).

སྐྱེག *skyeg* = *keg* or *kag* misfortune.

སྐྱེགས *skyegs* 1. n. of a bird; ཆུ་སྐྱེགས *chu-skyegs* coot; water-hen (*Sch.*); རི་སྐྱེགས *ri-skyegs* a large singing bird (*Cs.*); also according to *Sch.* grouse; heath cock. 2. རྒྱ་སྐྱེགས *rgya-skyegs* shell-lac (*Jä.*).

སྐྱེང་བ *skyeṅ-wa* or སྐྱེངས་པ *skyeṅs-pa* सलज्ज to be ashamed; shame; bashfulness: ཁ་སྐྱེང་བ *kha skyeṅ-wa* or ཞལ་སྐྱེང་བ *shal skyeṅ-wa* to be unable to reply out of shame.

སྐྱེང་སེར་རླུང *skyeṅ-ser rluṅ*, v. སྐྱེ་སེར་གྱི་རླུང *skye-ser-gyi rluṅ*.

སྐྱེངས་པ་མེད *skyeṅs-pa med* विलज्ज; = ངོ་ཚ་མེད shameless (*Mṅon.*).

སྐྱེད *skyed* and སྐྱེ *skye* 1. growth; progress; increase: ཚེ་སྐྱེད *tshe-skyed* longevity or increase of life: ལུས་སྐྱེད *lus skyed* growth of the body: དབང་ཐང་སྐྱེད *dwaṅ-thaṅ skyed* growth of wealth and power: སྟོབས་སྐྱེད *stobs-skyed* increase of strength: ནུས་པ་སྐྱེད *nus-pa skyed* increase of efficacy or ability: སྐྱེད་ཆེ་བར་འགྱུར་བ *skyed che-war hgyur-wa* to grow much: གཞན་གྱི་ཟླ་སྐྱེད་པས་དེའི་ཞག་སྐྱེད་ཆེ *gshan-gyi zla skyed-pas dehi shag-skyed che* his daily growth was greater than the growth of others in a month (*Jä.*): ཡུར་བའི་ཆུ་ཡིས་ཤིང་སྐྱེད་འདུ *yur-wahi chu-yis shiṅ skyed ẖdṟa* just as the water of the irrigation canals makes growth in the fields; སྐྱེད་ཀྱིས་འཚོ་བ *s̱kyeḏ-kyis ẖtsho-wa* to nurse up; སྐྱེད་ཡོང་ *s̱kyeḏ-yoṅ* shall make progress. 2. interest; profit; gain: དངུལ་སྐྱེད *dṅul-s̱kyeḏ* profit in silver or money; འབྲུ་སྐྱེད *ẖbru-s̱kyeḏ* interest of corn loan; སྐྱེད་དུ་གཏང་བ *s̱kyeḏ-du gtaṅ-wa* to lay out or to give on interest (*Cs.*): ནད་ལ་སྐྱེད་མེད *nad-la s̱kyeḏ meḏ* (this) is of no use for that disease (*Jä.*).

སྐྱེད་སྒོ *s̱kyeḏ-s̱go*, not improbably རྒྱལ་སྒོ *ṟgyal-sgo*, principal door (*Jä.*).

སྐྱེད་ཅན *s̱kyeḏ-can* I: yielding interest or profit (*Cs.*).

སྐྱེད་ཅན II: *s̱kyeḏ-can*, v. ཙན་དན་སྦྲུལ་གྱི་སྙིང་པོ *tsan-dan s̱brul-gyi s̱ñiṅ-po*, the sandal wood called 'snake's heart' (*M̱ṅon.*).

སྐྱེད་ཅིག *s̱kyeḏ-cig* ཡར་སྐྱེད་ཅིག *yar-s̱kyeḏ cig* let it grow up, thrive.

སྐྱེད་པ I: *s̱kyeḏ-pa* vb. pf. བསྐྱེད *ḇs̱kyeḏ*, act. to སྐྱེ་བ *s̱kye-wa*, to procreate, generate, and, sometimes, to bring forth; give birth to: ཤ་ཁྲག་ལུས་འདི་བསྐྱེད་པའི་ཕ་དང་མ *ça khrag lus ẖdi, ḇs̱kyeḏ-paẖi pha daṅ ma* the parents who generated this body of blood and flesh: སངས་རྒྱས་ཐམས་ཅད་བསྐྱེད་པའི་ཡབ་དང་ཡུམ *saṅs̱-ṟgyas̱ thams̱-caḏ ḇs̱kyeḏ-paẖi yab daṅ yum* the father and mother who have begotten all the Buddhas: སྐྱེད་བྱེད *s̱kyeḏ-byeḏ* tree.

སྐྱེད་པ II: 1. to produce, form, cause; and metaph. to generate (opposite to མེད་པར་བྱེད་པ *meḏ-par byeḏ-pa* to destroy, annihilate), *e.g.*, diseases, fear, roots of virtue, merit: བསོད་ནམས་ཀྱི་ཚོགས་ས་བོན the accumulation of merits or the seed or germ of virtue. Fig. འབྲས་བུ *ẖbras̱-bu* retribution: སྤྲོ་བ་བསྐྱེད་པས, དེའི་ཕ་མ་ཡང་སྤྲོ་བ་ཅུང་ཟད་སྐྱེས་ནས *s̱pro-wa ḇs̱kyeḏ-pas̱, deẖi pha-ma-yaṅ s̱pro-wa cuṅ-zaḏ s̱kyes̱-nas̱* joy having arisen (in him), his parents also were caused a little joy: ཐམས་ཅད་ཀྱིས་བརྩོན་འགྲུས་བསྐྱེད་དོ *thams̱-caḏ-kyis̱ ḇṟtson-ẖgrus̱ ḇs̱kyeḏ-do* they all created zeal; took great pains: ཅེས་བསམ་པ་བསྐྱེད་ནས *ces̱ ḇsam-pa ḇs̱kyeḏ-nas̱* thus were thoughts generated (*Jä.*). 2. སྐྱེད་པ *s̱kyeḏ-pa* or སྐྱེད་པོ *s̱kyeḏ-po* जनयिता, जनक father.

སྐྱེད་འཕེལ *s̱kyeḏ-ẖphel* ཡོད་པས་མེད་ལ་བུ་ལོན་སྐྱེད་འཕེལ་ཐོང་ *yoḏ-pas meḏ-la bu-lon s̱kyeḏ-ẖphel thoṅ* (the rich one) who has should give loan on interest to one who has not (*Kathaṅ.* ཀ *115*).

སྐྱེད་བྱེད *s̱kyeḏ-byeḏ* applies to father or earth; also to a tree; སྐྱེད་བྱེད་པ *s̱kyeḏ byeḏ-pa* blowing: ཇི་སྲིད་རླུང་ནི་སྐྱེད་བྱེད་པ *ji s̱riḏ ṟluṅ-ni s̱kyeḏ byeḏ-pa* यद्वहति मारुतः as the wind blows (*A. K. 2-7*).

སྐྱེད་མ *s̱kyeḏ-ma* = སྐྱེད་བྱེད་མ *s̱kyeḏ-byeḏ ma* जननी mother; also छाया shadow; shade.

སྐྱེད་ཚལ *s̱kyeḏ-tshal* निकुञ्ज, उद्यान, उपवन the so-called Tibetan park; artificial grove; also སྐྱེད་མོས་ཚལ *s̱kyeḏ-mos̱ tshal.*

སྐྱེད་རིམ *s̱kyeḏ-rim* उत्पन्नक्रम the kind of *Tantrik* meditation in which one has to imagine himself to be a god with a view ultimately to be changed into a god: རྫོགས་རིམ *ṟdsogs̱-rim*, सम्पन्नक्रम, in which according to the *Tantrik* process one has to pass through five stages of development before attaining the *Bodhisatva* rank.

སྐྱེན *s̱kyen* कण्टक thorn.

སྐྱེན་པ *s̱kyen-pa* = མགྱོགས་པ *m̱gyogs̱-pa* (*Ṉag.*) 1. quick, swift: ཁྲོ་ལ་སྐྱེན་པ *khro-la s̱kyen-pa* or སྡང་སྐྱེན་པ *s̱daṅ s̱kyen-pa* swift to wrath: བྱེད་སྐྱེན་པ *byeḏ s̱kyen-pa.* 2. rash, hasty, precipitate. 3. nimble; dexterous: འཕོང་སྐྱེན་པ *ẖphoṅ s̱kyen-pa* dexterous in shooting; a skilful archer.

སྐྱེན་ལ *s̱kyen-la* colloq. *C.* "upwards" (*Snd. H̱bk. 94*).

སྐྱེམ་པ་ *skyem-pa*, resp. to be thirsty; སྐྱེམས *skyems* 1. thirst. 2. drink, beverage, especially beer; also ཞལ་སྐྱེམས *shal-skyems* or ཞལ་སྐོམས *shal-skoms*; སྐྱེམས་འདྲེན་པ *skyems hdren-pa* to offer or set before an honoured person something to drink; སྐྱེམས་བཞེས་པ *skyems bshes-pa* to accept of it; to take it; སྐྱེམས་ལ་གསོལ་རས་བྱེད་པ *skyems-la gsol-ras byed-pa* to be permitted to drink beer in company; གཅེགས་སྐྱེམས *gçegs-skyems* a carousal on the departure of an honoured person; drink-offerings to a lama on his departure (*Mil.* ཁ *12a*); གསེར་སྐྱེམས *gser-skyems* an offering of beer or wine to the gods for the good success of an enterprize, a journey, etc., also for recovery from illness: གསེར་སྐྱེམས་པ *gser skyems-pa* "the offerer of golden drink"; a *Tantrik* priest who offers the drink to the gods; among the religious dancers of Tibet the priest who offers wine to the gods for invocation is called *Gser-skyems-pa*.

སྐྱེམ་བྱེད་མ *skyem-byed-ma* ईश्वरी the Goddess Is'varī.

སྐྱེམ་ཤོག *skyem-çog* a kind of superior paper manufactured in the town of སྐྱེམས *Skyems* in the district of *Dwags-po*; this paper is of large size, generally measuring two feet by six feet in size.

སྐྱེམས *Skyems* n. of a place in དགས་སྟོད Upper *Dbags-po*.

སྐྱེམས་ཆང་ *skyems-chañ* beer; སྐྱེམས་ཆུ *skyems-chu* drinkable water; drinking water.

སྐྱེམས་སྟོང་རྫོང་ *Skyems-stoñ rdsoñ* the fort of *Skyems-stoñ*; སྐྱེམས་སྤྲགས་ལུང་ *Skyems-sprags luñ* the place where the finest *Daphne* paper called *skyems-çog* is manufactured.

སྐྱེམས་ཚུག *skyems-tshug* cup; dish (*Sch.*): སྐྱེམས་ཤིང *skyems-siñ* small beer-cup (*Jä.*).

སྐྱེམས་བཟང་ *skyems-bzañ* pleasant beverage, such as good wine or savoury tea.

སྐྱེམས་གསོལ *skyems-gsol* resp. beverage, drink: མནྡཱ་ར་བའི་གླུ་ཡ་རབས་སྐྱེམས་གསོལ *mandara-wahi glu ya-rabs skyems gsol* (the lady) Mandarava sang and offered drink to the superior (personages).

སྐྱེར་སྐྱ *skyer-skya* = ཚོས་ཁའི་མདོག་སེར་སྐྱ reddish brown (*Ñag.*).

སྐྱེར་སྐྱེར *skyer-skyer* solitary; perfectly solitary: སྐྱེར་སྐྱེར་མི་དང་འགུལ་འགུལ་ཁྱི *skyer-skyer mi dañ hgul-hgul khyi* lonely without men; where not even a dog stirs about.

སྐྱེར་ཁ *skyer-kha* a kind of dye; colour; हरित, हरिद्रा yellow dye; a light yellow colour.

སྐྱེར་ཆུ *Skyer-chu* n. of a river of སྤ་རོ (*Pa-ro*) in Bhutan.

སྐྱེར་པ *skyer-pa* the barberry; applied to the plant and its wood from which a yellow dye is extracted; the flower of this plant is said to be cure for diarrhœa, its fruit draws out bilious matters and its yellow bark is useful in dropsy, etc.; སྐྱེར་ཁཎྜ *skyer-khaṇḍa* a confection of སྐྱེར་པ *skyer-pa* useful in eye diseases.

Syn. ཁུ་བ་སེར་པོ *khu-wa ser-po*; དུས་སྐྱེས *dus-skyes*; ཞིང་སེར *çiñ-ser*; ཤི་ལ་དྲུ *çi-la-dru* (*Mñon.*).

སྐྱེར་དམན *skyer-dman* = སྐྱེས་དམན *skyes-dman* a woman. The former is a corruption of the latter and, sounded *kyermen*, is one of the most familiar terms in the colloquial for "wife" or "woman."

སྐྱེར་ཤིང་ *skyer-çiñ* तालीस, तालीसपत्र n. of a tree, *Flacourtia cataphracta*.

སྐྱེལ་འགྱུར s̱kyel-gyur सम्प्राप्ति removal of articles, furniture, etc. (to another place): སྐྱེལ་ཆེ་བ s̱kyel che-wa अतिक, अन्तिक frequent removal or changing.

སྐྱེལ་ཐུང་ s̱kyeḻ thuṅ to accompany or to escort one from the place of starting to a distance on the way: ལྷ་བཙུན་པས་ཐག་རིང་པོར་སྐྱེལ་ཐུང་མཛད་ནས *Lha ḇtsun-pas̱ thag riṅ-por s̱kyeḻ thuṅ m̱dsaḏnas̱* Lah tshun-pa having accompanied the party to a long distance (*A. 129*); སྐྱེལ་ཐུང་བྱེད་པ *s̱kyel-thuṅ byeḏ-pa* or གཅེགས་སྐྱེལ་བྱེད་པ *gçegs̱-s̱kyel byeḏ-pa* to accompany one to a short distance (generally with some wine for his refreshment). སྐྱེལ་དར *s̱kyel-dar*, acc. to *Lex.* also in colloq., presentation scarf of tho departing person to those that had accompanied him for a short distance.

སྐྱེལ་བ I: *s̱kyel-wa* pf. and fut. བསྐྱལ *ḇs̱kyal*, imp. སྐྱོལ *s̱kyol* 1. to carry, take away: ཤི་བའི་རོ་སྐྱེལ་བ *çi-waḥi ro s̱kyel-wa* to take away the body of the dead (*Cs.*): ཤིང་མ་སྐྱལ་ཅིག do not bring wood: སྐྱལ་ཤོག bring! སྐྱལ་སོང་ take away! 2. to send, *e.g.*, clothes, to somebody. 3. to risk, to stake (one's life རང་སྲོག *raṅ-srog*). 4. to use, to employ: བ་གླང་ལས་བྱེད་པ་ལ་སྐྱལ *ba g̱laṅ las̱ byeḏ-pa la s̱kyal* use an ox for work; ལས་བྱེད་པ་ལ་མི་ཚེ་སྐྱལ to devote one's whole life to work. ལེ་ལོ་ནང་ན in idleness; གཏོར་མ་གླུད་སྐྱེལ་བ *gtor-ma g̱luḏ s̱kyel-wa* to cast away as a ransom in the *torma* sacrifice; ཁ་སྐྱེལ་བ *kha s̱kyel-wa* to kiss (*Jä.*); གནོད་པ་སྐྱེལ་བ *gnoḏ-pa s̱kyel-wa* to do harm; to hurt; inflict an injury; to play one a trick; མནའ་སྐྱེལ་བ *m̱naḥ s̱kyel-wa* to swear; take an oath; བློ་སྐྱེལ་བ *lo s̱kyel-wa* to rely; depend upon; repose confidence.

སྐྱེལ་བ II: pf. and fut. བསྐྱེལ *ḇs̱kyel*, imp. སྐྱོལ *s̱kyoḻ* 1. to conduct; accompany; resp. གདན་སྐྱེལ་བ *gdan-s̱kyeḻ-wa*; སྐྱོལ་ལ་ཤོག *s̱kyoḻ-la çog* conduct him hither; བསུ་བསྐྱལ *ḇsu-ḇs̱kyal* going to meet and to accompany; གཅེགས་སྐྱལ་བྱེད་པ *gçegs̱ s̱kyaḻ-byeḏ-pa* resp. to accompany an honoured person on departing; to see him off.

སྐྱེལ་མ *s̱kyel-ma* आनुगमक an escort; convoy: སྐྱེལ་མར་ཡོད *s̱kyel-mar yoḏ* he is a guide (to me): སྐྱེལ་མ་ཞུ *s̱kyel-ma shu* grant us safe conduct. དམག་དང་བཅས་པའི་སྐྱེལ་མ *ḏmag daṅ ḇcas̱ paḥi s̱kyel-ma* a military escort; སྐྱེལ་རོགས་བྱེད་པ *s̱kyel-rogs̱ byeḏ-pa* to escort or accompany one to a place.

སྐྱེལ་མི *s̱kyel-mi* an escort: ལྷ་ས་ནས་སྐྱེལ་མི་དགོས་རིགས་སྔར་རྒྱུན་ལྟར་མི་དཔོན་ནས་གཏོང་བ་བཅས་བགྱིས *Lhasa nas̱ s̱kyel mi ḏgos̱ rig̱s̱ sṅar-ṟgyun ḻtar mi-ḏpon nas̱ g̱toṅ-wa ḇcas̱ ḇgyis̱* the *Mi-ḏpon* should arrange for the escort (*s̱kyeḻ-mi*) of those formerly entitled to that privilege from Lhasa.

སྐྱེས I: *s̱kyes̱* 1. v. སྐ *s̱ka*. 2. v. སྐྱེད *s̱kyeḏ*. 3. སྐྱེ་བ *s̱kye-wa*.

སྐྱེས II: also སྐྱས་མ *s̱kyas̱-ma* or སྐྱོས་མ *s̱kyos̱-ma*, ཁྱོས་མ *khyos̱-ma*, resp. གནང་སྐྱེས *gnaṅ-s̱kyes* सन्देश, उपहार, संवाद a present; news, tidings; འབྱོན་སྐྱེས *ḥbyon-s̱kyes̱* = ཕེབས་སྐྱེས *phebs̱-s̱kyes̱* a present given to or received from somebody on his arrival or going away; སྐྱེས་ཆང་ *s̱kes̱-chaṅ* a present of beer: སྐྱེས་ཆེན *s̱kyes chen* a present sent with a letter, etc. (*Ṅag.*); སྐྱེས་ཁུར *s̱kes̱-khur* present of cakes; སྐྱེས་ལན *s̱kes̱-lan* a present made in return (*Cs.*).

སྐྱེས III: भूत, भूत, जात birth or growth; growing or grown; རང་སྐྱེས *raṅs̱-kyes* self-grown; ཤིང་སྐྱེས *shiṅ-s̱kyes̱* born in a grove; ལྷན་སྐྱེས *ḻhan-kyes̱* सहज or सहजात born together; ཕོ་སྐྱེས *pho-s̱kyes̱* male; མོ་སྐྱེས *mo-s̱kyes̱* female; སྔགས་སྐྱེས *s̱ṅags̱-s̱kyes̱* of enchanted growth; born out of charms: ཤིང་སྐྱེས་ལྷན་ཅིག་སྐྱེས་དང་སྔགས་སྐྱེས་ཀྱི་མཁའ་འགྲོའི་ཚོགས་ཀྱིས་བུ་ལ་མ་བཞིན་དུ་བརྩེ་བར་དགོངས་ནས་དངོས་གྲུབ་ཀུན་སྩོལ་ཤིང་

བགེགས་ཀུན་ཉེ་བར་ཞི་བའི་བཀའ་དྲིན་མཛོད། *shiṅ-skyes lhan-chigskyes daṅ sṅags-skyes-kyi mkhaḥ-ḥgroḥi tshogs-kyis bu-la ma-bshin-du brtse-war dgoṅs nas dṅos-grub kun stsal-shiṅ bgegs kun ñe-war shi-waḥi bkaḥ-drin mdsod*, as the assemblage of *khadoma* fairies, who have been born in groves and born simultaneously and are of magie birth, are meditating lovingly as a mother towards a son, may the grace be granted of all manner of perfect knowledge being bestowed and of all demons being speedily soothed!

སྐྱེས་སྒྲ་ཅན *skyes-sgra can*=ར goat (*Mṅon.*).

སྐྱེས་ངེས *skyes-ṅes* अपायीन certain of being born or reborn.

སྐྱེས་ཆེན *skyes-chen* a present with or as an enclosure to a letter, explained in *Ṅag.* as ཡིག་རྟེན་ལྟ་བུ་དོན་བསྐུར་བ that which is sent as a support to a letter.

སྐྱེས་ཆེན་སྒྲུབ་གནས *skyes-chen sgrub-gnas* a hermitage of holy persons.

སྐྱེས་ཆེན་དམ་པ *skyes-chen dam-pa* a holy incarnate person: བསོད་ནམས་རྒྱ་མཚོ་སོགས་སྐྱེས་ཆེན་དམ་པ་བརྒྱ་ཕྲག་མང་པོ་ལ་གུས་འདུད་དང་དད་འབུལ་རྒྱ་ཆེར་མཛད་དོ *Bsod-nams rgya-mtsho sogs skyes-chen dam-pa brgya-phrag maṅ-po la gus-ḥdud daṅ dad-ḥbul rgya-cher mdse-do* "Sö-nam Gya-ts'o and others made salutations and offerings in full form to many hundred holy incarnate ones" (*Loṅ.* ར *14*).

སྐྱེས་མཆོག *skyes-mchog* परम or प्रधान पुरुष an incarnate personage; a *Mahātmā*: སྐྱེས་མཆོག་བཞི *skyes-mchog bshi*, རྒྱ་ནག་གི་བླ་མ་མཁས་པ་ཆེན་པོ་བཞི་ཡི་མཚན the names of four great learned lamas of China, the four incarnate ones:—(1) ཧ་ཕུ་ཅི *Ha-phu-çi*, (2) ཝེན་ཝང་ *Wenwaṅ*, (3) ཅིའི་ཀྱུང་ *Ciḥi kyuṅ*, (4) ཁུང་ཙི *Khuṅtsi* (Confucius) (*Grub.* ན *7*).

སྐྱེས་ལྡན *skyes-ldan*=མི་སྤྱི *mi-spyi* नरः mankind (*Mṅon.*).

སྐེས་སྡོང་ *skes-sdoṅ*, སྐྱེས་ལ་སྡོང་ *skyes-la sdoṅ* in Sikkim the *banana*, plantain; from Hindi *ke-la* and *sdoṅ*, a plant: *la* is dropt in conversation, hence *ke-la* and *sdoṅ* are abbreviated into "*ke-doṅ.*" In the districts of Upper Tib. and *W. ke-doṅ* signifies a layman.

སྐྱེས་ནག *skyes-nag*=མི་རྒྱུ་ནག in *C.* widower (*Jä.*). སྐྱེ་ནག *skyes-nag* stands for སྐྱེས་བུ་ནག་པོ *skyes-bu nag-po* (lit. black person) a layman=*mi-nag*: མི་ནག་གི་གྲོང་སྐད in the country dialect of the lay people.

སྐྱེས་པ I: *skyes-pa* 1. man; male person. 2.=ལོ་ཏོག उत्पन्न the year-crop; produce. 3. ཤར་བ उत्थान adult; full grown. Ex. of 1. སྐྱེས་པ་དང་བུད་མེད *skyes-pa daṅ bud-med* men and women; རྒྱལ་པོ་གཅིག་པོ་སྐྱེས་པ་ཡིན *rgyal-po* man; *gcig-po skges-pa yin* the king alone is a man (*Jä.*); སྐྱེས་པ་འདྲ་བའི་བུད་མེད *skye-pa ḥdra-waḥi bud-med*, पुरुषानुरूपिणी a woman resembling a man, *i.e.*, possessing masculine appearance and virtues.

Syn. སྐྱེས་བུ་ཕོ *skyes-bu pho*; སྐྱེས་པ་རྒྱལ *skyes-pa rgyal*; སྐྱེ་བས་མཐོ *skye-was mtho*; ཁུ་བའི་བདག་ཉིད *khu-waḥi bdag-ñid*; སྐྱོང་བྱེད *skyoṅ-byed*; འཛན་ཕོ *ḥzan-pho*; ལྷ་སྐྱེས *lha-syes*; མི་ཕོ *mi-pho*; ལིང་ག་ཅན *liṅ-ga-can* (*Mṅon.*).

སྐྱེས་པ II: pf. of སྐྱེ་བ *skye-wa*=འཕེལ་བ, also उदय, वृद्धिप्राप्त growth or grown up.

སྐྱེས་པ III:=འཁྲུངས་པ *ḥbruṅs-pa* born.

སྐྱེས་པ་དར་མ *skyes-pa dar-ma* full; manhood.

སྐྱེས་པ་འབྲུས་ཕྱུང་པ *skyes-pa ḥbrus phyuṅ-wa* according to some: an eunuch, one who is made so artificially.

Syn. ཧོག་མེད *hog-med*; དབང་པོ་ཉམས་པ *dwaṅ-po ñams-pa*; ཁྱིམ་ཁོལ *khyimkhol*; བཙུན་མོའི་ཁོལ་པོ *btsun-moḥi khol-po*; བུད་མེད་དགའ་བྲལ *bud-med dgah bral*; རལ་གུ་ཅན *ral-gu-can*; འཁྲིག་མི་ནུས *hkhrig mi-nus*; འབྲས་དབྱུང་བ *hbras dbyuñ-wa*; ཉུག་རུམ་པ *ñug-rum-pa*; བཅོས་པའི་མ་ནིང *bcos-pahi ma-niñ* (*Mñon.*).

*སྐྱེས་པའི་རྒྱུ་སྐར *skyes-pahi rgyu-skar* जन्मनक्षत्र (*Schf.*) the particular star or constellation under which one is born.

སྐྱེས་སྤོར *skyes-spor* the measure used by creditors in receiving back the loan of grain, etc.: ལྷས་སྤོར་དང་ལྷས་སྲང་གསུམ་བཞི་སྐྱེས་སྤོར་ཆེ *lha-spor dañ lhas-srañ gsum bshi skyes-spor che* "a large *kye-phor* contains 3 or 4 ounces in measure or weight."

སྐྱེས་བ་རྒྱལ *skyes-wa rgyal*=སྐྱེས་པ *skyes-pa* or མི་ཕོ a man or male person (*Mñon.*).

སྐྱེས་ཕན *skyes-phan*=ན་ཆུང युवति a damsel, maiden.

སྐྱེས་བུ *skyes-bu* पुरुष man, esp. a holy man; person; སྐྱེས་བུ་གང *skyes-bu gañ* whosoever; human (*Med.*); one: སྐྱེས་བུ་ལག་པ་བརྐྱང་བ་ཙམ་གྱིས *skyes-bu lag-pa brkyañ-wa tsam-gyis* as quick as one stretches out his hand (*Jä.*); སྐྱེས་བུ་དམ་པ *skyes-bu dam-pa* सत्पुरुष a saint; དད་ལྡན་སྐྱེས་བུ *dad-ldan skyes-bu* the believing; the faithful. According to some Tibetan grammarians སྐྱེས་བུ *skyes-bu* applies both to men and women: སྐྱེས་བུ་གང་ཟག་དད་པ་ཅན, གང་ཞིག་ལྷ་རྣམས་མཆོད་བྱེད་པ, སྟོན་པའི་བཀའ་བཞིན་བྱེད་པ་སྟེ, དེ་ནི་སངས་རྒྱས་རྣམས་ཀྱིས་བསྔགས *skyes-bu gañ-zag dad-pa-can, gañ-shig lha rnams mchod byed-pa, Ston-pahi bkah bshin byed-pa-ste, de ni Sañs-rgyas-rnams-kyis bsñags* (*K. du.* ཕ *96*) that human being who is faithful, and who worships the gods (saints) and acts according to the commands of the Teacher is praised by the Buddhas.

སྐྱེས་བུ་སྐྱེས་མཆོག *skyes-bu skye mchog* पुरुषपुङ्गव the chief among men.

སྐྱེས་བུ་ཁུ་མཆོག *skyes-bu khu-mchog* पुरुषवृषभ the leader of men.

སྐྱེས་བུ་ཅན *skyes-bu can* རྟ་དང་བཅས་པའི་སྐྱེས་བུ *rta-dañ bcas-pahi skyes-bu* a horseman; one on horseback.

Syn. རྟ་པ *rta-pa*; རྟ་ལ་གཞོན་པ *rta-la gshon-pa* (*Mñon.*).

སྐྱེས་བུ་མཆོག *skyes-bu mchog* पुरुषोत्तम a superior person; lama; also ཁྱབ་འཇུག *Viṣṇu*: སྐྱེས་བུ་ཆེན་པོ *skyes-bu chen-po* महापुरुष a great man or saint; an epithet of Buddha.

སྐྱེས་བུ་མཐོ *skyes-bu mtho*=གླུ་ཤིང *glu-çiñ* n. of a tree supposed to grow in the land of the Nāga (*Mñon.*).

སྐྱེས་བུ་ནག་པོ *skyes-bu nag-po*, same as མེང་ཅན་ནག་པོ, n. of a kind of flower (*Sman. 447*).

སྐྱེས་བུ་ཕོ *skyes-bu pho*=སྐྱེས་པ *skyes-pa* a man or male person.

སྐྱེས་བུ་འབྲིང *skyes-bu hbriñ*=སྐྱེས་བུ་བར་མ *skyes-bu bar-ma* or སྐྱེས་བུ་དབུས་མ *skyes-bu dbus-ma* मध्यमपुरुष the second person; personal pronoun in grammar.

སྐྱེས་བུའི་འཁྲུགས་པ *skyes-buhi hkhrugs-pa* अभिमान pride, self-respect.

སྐྱེས་བུའི་ངོས *skyes-buhi ños* पुम्भाव, पौरुषम् manliness; manly self-respect or confidence.

སྐྱེས་མ *skyes-ma* 1. fem. of *skyes-pa*, a female; she that has been born. 2. མནའ་མ a bride. 3. སྐྱེས་མ *skyes-ma* fern in Sikkim.

སྐྱེས་མ་ཐག *skyes-ma thag* as soon as born; newly born.

སྐྱེས་མ་ཐག་པ *skyes-ma thag-pa* a new-born infant.

Syn. བཙས་མ་ཐག་པ *btsas-ma thag-pa*; ཞོ་འཐུང་བ *sho thuñ-wa*; གཞིབ་འཐུང *gshib-hthuñ*; འཇིབ་འཐུང *hjib-hthuñ*; འཁྱུད་འཐུང *hkhyud-hthuñ*; ཧོ་མའི་མགྲིན་པ་ཅན *ho-mahi mgrin-pa-can* (*Mñon.*).

སྐྱེས་དམན་ *skyes-dman* in the vulg. language a woman; = ཆུང་མ or བུད་མེད (*Mṅon.*).

སྐྱེས་རྫོངས *skyes-rdsoṅs* cultivation; a farm.

སྐྱེས་གཟུགས *skyes-gzugs* जातरूप gold; birth; form or born-shape; stature; figure (gold).

སྐྱེས་རབས *skyes-rabs* जातक a series of alleged births of an individual, or legendary history of these, and especially accounts of the different births of Buddha.

སྐྱེས་སོ་ཅོག *skyes-so cog* ancestors: སྐྱེས་ཚད་ཐམས་ཅད *skyes tshad thams-cad*; སྔ་རབས་ཀྱི་ཕ་དང་མེས་པོ་ཡང་མེས་ལ་སོགས་པ། སྐྱེས་སོ་ཅོག་ཀྱང་རིམ་པར་ཤི་སྟེ་ད་ལྟ་ནི་མིང་གི་ལྷག་ཙམ་དུ་གྱུར *sña-rabs-kyi pha daṅ mes-po yaṅ-mes la-sogs-pa skyes-so-chog kyaṅ rim-par çi ste da-lta ni miṅ-gi lhag tsam-du gyur* father, grandfather, great-grandfather, &c., ancestors of the former generations having successively died, now nothing remains but their names.

སྐྱོ *skyo* or སྐྱོ་བ *skyo-wa*, खेद, उद्वेग, हाहा, आहा, संवेग, शोक grief; sorrow; grieving; mourning.

སྐྱོ་འགྱེད *skyo-hgyed* weariness dispersed: བདེ་བ་ཅན་དག་སྐྱོ་འགྱེད་པས, ཁྱོད་གསུང་ཀུན་དང་འཚམ་པར་འདུག། the inhabitants of the land of bliss relieved of weariness accept all your precepts (*Lam-rim.*).

སྐྱོ་ངེས *skyo-ṅes* = སེམས་སྐྱོ་བ *sems skyo-wa* to repent; repentance (*Mṅon.*).

+ སྐྱོ་ངོགས *skyo-ṅogs* quarrel; འཁྲུག་ལོང *hkhrug-loṅ* (*Lex.*), esp. སྔར་གྱི་རྩོད་པ་སླར་ཡང་སློང་བ reviving of old feuds and dissensions.

སྐྱོ་བ *skyo-wa* 1. སྔར་གྱི་རྩོད་པ *sṅar-gyi rtsod-pa* old quarrels and feuds. 2. repentance; sorrow: སེམས་སྐྱོ་བ་བསྐྱེད་ལ་རི་ཁྲོད་འགྲིམ། *sems skyo-wa bskyed-la ri-khro hgrim* he wanders on mountain ranges to induce repentance (*Lo.*).

སྐྱོ་བྲན *skyo-bran* servant; slave: མི་སེར་སྐྱོ་བ་དང་ཚེ་གང་གི་གཡོག་པོ a slave for life.

སྐྱོ་མ I: *skyo-ma* 1. quarrel; litigation. 2. thin gruel, gruel of rice and tea, thin paste of wheat or oatmeal: སྐྱོ་མ་བཤེས་པའི་རྒྱ་མཚོ་ནུབ་བ་ལང་སྤྱོད་ཀྱི་གླིང་འདས་ནས་ཡོད *skyo-ma-wa shes-pahi rgya-mthso nub Ba-laṅ-spyod-kyi gliṅ hdas nas yod* the ocean called Skyoma-wa lies beyond the continent of Godānīya (*K. d.* ར *234*).

སྐྱོ་མ II: v. ཁྲིམས་པ *khrim-pa* 1. one convicted. 2. तपन, अपपाप penitence; smaller transgression: སྐྱོ་མ་སྔ་བཙན *skyo-ma sña btsan* སྔོན་རྩོད་པ་བྱུང་བའི་དུས་སུ་ཁྲིམས་ཀྱིས་བཅད་པ one who was once convicted before on the occasion of a former dispute.

སྐྱོ་མ་ཅན *skyo-ma can* adj. slanderous (*Cs.*); སྐྱོ་མ་བྱེད་པ *skyo-ma byed-pa* a slandering (*Cs.*).

སྐྱོ་མེད *skyo-med* = མཐོ་རིས་ཀྱི་གནས *mtho-ris kyi gnas* the heaven, where there is no penitence.

Syn. དལ་འཛིན་གནས་བཟང *dal-hdsin gnas-bzaṅ*, བདེ་འགྲོ *bde-hgro*, བདེ་ལྡན *bde-ldan*, མཐོ་རིས་རྒྱལ་སྲིད *mtho-ris rgyal-srid*, སྐབས་གསུམ་གནས *skabs-gsum gnas*, སྟེང་གི་འཇིག་རྟེན *steṅ-gi hjig-rten*, གྲུབ་པའི་གནས *grub-pahi gnas*, འཆི་མེད *hchi-med*, ནམ་མཁའི་ཁྱིམ *nam-mkhahi khyim*, སུམ་རྩེན *sum-rtsen*, ལྷ་ཡི་གྲོང *lha-yi groṅ*, ལྷ་ཡི་འཇིག་རྟེན *lha-yi hjig-rten*, ལྷ་ཡི་ཡུལ *lha-yi yul*, सिद्धक a semi-divine being possessed of supernatural powers (*Mṅon.*).

སྐྱོ་མེད་ཁྱབ *skyo med-khyab* དབང་ཕྱུག་གི་གཞུའི་མིང n. of *Viṣṇu's* bow (*Mṅon.*).

སྐྱོ་ཚག *skyo-tshag* a light broth made of barley-flour with the addition of a little butter (*A. 155*): ཐོ་རངས་ཀྱི་དུས་སུ་སྐྱོ་ཚག་བསེར་མ (རླུང) མི་སྐྱེ་བ *tho-raṅs-kyi dus-su skyo-tshag bser-ma* (*rluṅ*) *mi skye-wa* early in the morning (*i.e.*, at dawn) by taking barley gruel, wind is not engendered (*A. 155*).

སྐྱོ་རས་ཚོ་ཚོགས་ *skyo-ras tsho-tshogs* n. of a kind of chintz (*S. kar. 179*).

སྐྱོ་རོགས་ *skyo-rogs* a consoler; one who consoles a person during grief: བུ་མོའི་སྐྱོ་རོགས་ཨ་མས་མི་ཐུབ the mother cannot be the consoler of her daughter's grief, *i.e.*, one cannot be of service to another in certain cases of sorrow.

སྐྱོ་ཤས་ *skyo-ças* to be sad; sorrowful: རང་ལ་ངེས་འབྱུང་དང་སྐྱོ་ཤས་སད་སུད་སྐྱེས *rañ la ñes-ḥbyuñ dañ skyo-ças sad-sud skyes* he felt (slight) repentance and sorrow.

སྐྱོ་སངས་ *skyo-sañs* to console in his grief or sorrow or repentance.

སྐྱོ་སངས་ཉིད་ *skyo-sañs ñid* freedom from fatigue.

སྐྱོ་སངས་གནས་ *skyo-sañs gnas* a pleasure garden.

སྐྱོག་ནག *skyog-nag* iron spoon or scoop.

སྐྱོགས *skyogs* 1. a spoon or ladle; also shovel. Wooden spoons for wine measure used in Tibet are called སྐྱོགས *skyogs*. There are three kinds of spoons used in Tibet for measuring liquids, salt, &c.—those which are mounted with copper are the largest; those lined with silver are of middle size; those of the smallest size are tipped with gold and called *gser-skyogs*, golden spoons. མེ་སྐྱོགས *me-skyogs* coal shovel; ཚྭ་སྣུམ་ཐོག་འཇལ་བའི་ཟངས་སྐྱོགས the copper spoon with which to measure the allowance in salt and oil for servants, etc.; ཞུ་སྐྱོགས *shu-skyogs* melting spoon or crucible. 2. drinking cup; bowl; goblet; གསེར་སྐྱོགས *gser-skyogs* དངུལ་སྐྱོགས *dñul-skyogs*, etc., gold cup, silver cup, and wooden cup are now called གཟར་བུ *gzar-bu*; ཞལ་སྐྱོགས *shal-skyogs* lip-cup; resp. eating or drinking-cup; སྲབ་སྐྱོགས the rein of a bridle; also name of tribe in Tibet (*Vai. kar.*).

སྐྱོགས་ལྟོ་འབུ *skyogs lto-ḥbu* a snail in *W.* (*Jä.*).

སྐྱོགས་པ *skyogs-pa* 1. to turn: མགྲིན་པ་སྐྱོགས་པ *mgrin-pa skyogs-pa* to turn the neck, *i.e.*, look round, back; also to turn away, aside. 2. one who uses or manufactures the coal-shovel or stone scoop, etc.

སྐྱོགས་པ *skyogs-pa* སྐྱོན་འདོགས་པ *skyon ḥdogs-pa*; दोषमुद्घाटयति to find fault with.

སྐྱོགས་མེད *skyogs-med* निर्व्यङ्क not curved; without any curvature or crookedness.

སྐྱོང་ལྡན་མ *skyoñ ldan-ma* n. of a goddess; she who protects.

སྐྱོང་བ *skyoñ-wa* पा, रच्, पालन, pf. བསྐྱངས *bskyoñs*, fut. བསྐྱང *bskyañ*, imp. བསྐྱོངས *bskyoñs* or བསྐྱོངས་ཤིག *bskyoñs-çig*, to guard; to keep; to defend; to save; preserve (the life, the body); to support; to take care of (poor people): དྲིན་བཟང་པོས་སྐྱོང་བ *drin bzañ-pos skyoñ-wa* to support by benefits, favours: ཐབས་ཀྱིས་སྐྱོང་བ *thabs-kyis skyoñ-wa* to protect by various means; to attend to: ཐུགས་དམ་གྱི་སྐྱོང་བ *thugs-dam-ghyi skyoñ-wa* to protect by the moral force of meditation: ལག་ལེན་གྱི *lag-len-gyi* by exercise: རྒྱལ་སྲིད་སྐྱོང་བ *rgyal srid skyoñ-wa* to rule; govern a kingdom: ཆོས་བཞིན་དུ་བསྐྱོང་བ *chos bshin-tu bskyoñ-wa* to protect by justice or justly: ཆོས་སྐྱོང *chos-skyoñ* धर्मपाल protector, defender of religion, is used for a certain individual deity or for a class of exorcists in some of the monasteries of Tibet. Under this head there are certain powerful deities who have taken on themselves the duty of defending Buddhism against its enemies. When co-erced they can even make their appearance in the person of the invoker. The གནས་ཆུང་ཆོས་སྐྱོང་ *Gnas-chuṅ chos-skyoṅ* living near Lhasa is a deity of this class who is generally consulted both by the State and the people of Tibet as an oracle: འཇིག་རྟེན་སྐྱོང་ *hjig-rten skyoṅ* लोकपाल guardian of the world. There are four of these, identical with the རྒྱལ་ཆེན་བཞི *Rgyal-chen bshi*, the four great spirit kings:—धृतराष्ट्र (ཡུལ་འཁོར་སྐྱོང་ *Yul-hkhor skyoṅ*) the protector of the country or kingdom; विरूढक (འཕགས་སྐྱེས་བུ *Hphags skyes-bu*); विरूपाक्ष (སྤྱན་མི་བཟང་ *Spyan mi-bzaṅ*); वैश्रवण (རྣམ་ཐོས་སྲས *Snam thos-sras*). སྐྱོང་དལ *skyoṅ-dal* assistance (in the colloquial of *W.*); སྐྱོང་དལ་བྱེད་པ *skyoṅ-dal byed-pa* to help; སྐྱོང་མ *skyoṅ-ma*, same as བརྟན་མ *brtan-ma*, the Goddess of the Earth; རྒྱལ་སྲིད་སྐྱོང་ *rgyal-srid skyoṅ* राज्यपाल a defender of the realm; same as འབངས་སྐྱོང་ प्रजापाल a defender or protector of the subject or of people: སྐྱོང་བྱེད *skyoṅ-byed* पालक one who supports or protects.

སྐྱོང་བྱེད་མ *skyoṅ byed-ma*, v. ཀུན་དུ (*Mṅon.*).

སྐྱོད་པ *skyod-pa* pf. and fut. བསྐྱོད *bskyod* सम्भ्रम, उत्क्राथ, चञ्चल; གཡོ་བ *gyo-wa* or འགུལ་བ *hgul-wa* to move (trans. vb.); also to go, pass on: རླུང་གིས་ཡལ་ག་སྐྱོད་ན if the wind moves the branches. མི་སྐྱོད་པ *Mi-skyod-pa* or མི་གཡོ་བ *mi-gyo-wa* अक्षोभ्य the unmoved; he whose mind is not agitated; n. of the second *Dhyāni* Buddha. In *W. skyod-pa* is the general respectful term for: to go; to walk. བསྐྱོད་འདོད *bskyod-hdod* is same as འགྲོ་འདོད *bgro-hdod* desirous to go or about to go: ནང་དུ་སྐྱོད "*naṅ-du skyod*" step in (if you please); "*tan-po kyot*" tread firmly! བསྐྱོད་སྐབས་ལ *bskyod skabs-la* at the time of going or coming.

སྐྱོད་བྱེད *skyod-byed*=གྲུ་སྐྱ *gru-skya* oar (*Mṅon.*).

སྐྱོན *skyon*, ཉེས་པ *ñes-pa* दोष, कलङ्क, अपचय, आपत्ति, पर्याप्ति, अवलेप, आदीनव, आविल, also རྙོག་པ *rñog-pa* 1. a fault, defect: སྐྱོན་གང་ཡང་མེད *skon gaṅ-yaṅ med* it has no fault whatever. The two words སྐྱོན *skyon* and ཉེས་པ *ñes-pa* are sometimes used together as ཉེས་སྐྱོན *ñes-skyon*, but defects in inanimate things are expressed by the word སྐྱོན *skyon* and never by the words ཉེས *ñes* or ཉེས་སྐྱོན *ñes-skyon*; slight defects in honoured persons are expressed by the words དགེ་སྐྱོན *dge-skyon*, which also signifies faults or sins in holy persons, that is, སྐྱོན *skyon* (fault) in དགེ *dge* or དགེ་འདུན *dge-hdun* (clergy): སྐྱོན་ཅི་ཡོད་འཁྲུལ་པ་ལ *skyon ci yod hkhrul-pa la*, what harm is there in erring? མི་སྐྱོན *mi-skyon* no harm; སྐྱོན་མེད *skyon-med* no harm, no matter; སྐྱོན་ཡོན་གང་ཡང་མིན *skyon yon gaṅ yaṅ min* he is without anv imperfection or perfection; སྐྱོན་དུ་མཐོང་བ *skyon-du mthoṅ-wa* to consider as a loss, also to find fault with. 2. bodily defect, fault, as lameness, derangement, disorder in the mixture of the humours. 3. spiritual defect, sin, vicious quality; རྫུན་དུ་སྨྲ་བའི་སྐྱོན *rdsun-du smra-wahi skyon* the sin of lying; སྐྱོན་གྱིས་མ་གོས *skyon-gyi ma-gos* not defiled by sin: ལར་སྐྱོན་ཆེ *lar skyon che* but that is very bad (of you). སྐྱོན་བྱེད་པ *skyon byed-pa* to commit a fault; སྐྱོན་སྤང་བ *skyon spaṅ-wa* to leave off a fault or quit it; མི་ལ་སྐྱོན་འབེབས་པ་འདོགས་པ *mi-la skyon hbebs-pa hdogs-pa* to charge one with a crime; to criminate; གཞན་གྱི་སྐྱོན་གླེང་བརྗོད་པ *gshan-gyi skyon gleṅ brjod-pa* to name the faults of others, to speak ill of them; to slander; to blame, criticise; སྐྱོན་སྤང་ཁ་ཤེ་མེད་པ *skyon-spaṅ kha she med-pa* to do any work with application and at the same time without any fault or mischief to any body ; སྐྱོན་མི་མཐོང་བ=སྐྱོན་དུ་མ་གོ་བ, not perceive a fault or defect.

སྐྱོན་སྐྱེ *skyon-skye* दोषोत्पाद अनुबन्ध conducive of sin ; sin-producing.

སྐྱོན་ངག *skyon-nag* कण्टक thorny; mischievous.

སྐྱོན་ཅན *skyon-can*=སྐྱོན་དང་བཅས་པ *skyon-dan bcas-pa* or སྐྱོན་ལྡན *skyon-ldan* कालिका, कलङ्की, दोषी faulty, defective, incorrect, sinful; guilty.

སྐྱོན་བཅོ་བརྒྱད *skyon bco-brgad* the eighteen defects are the following:—(1) མི་སྡུག་པ *mi-sdug-pa* ugliness; (2) མགོ་སྐྲ་ངན་པ *mgo skra nan-pa* bad or bristling hair ; (3) དཔྲལ་བ་ཆུང་བ *dpral-wachun-wa* small or narrow forehead; (4) མགོ་སེར་སྐྱ *mgo ser-skya* brown hair ; (5) མིག་སེར་བ *mig ser-wa* yellow eyes; (6) སྨིན་མཚམས་མ་འབྱར་བ *smin-mtshams ma-hbyar-wa* the eye-brows disjoined ; (7) སྣ་ལེབ་པ *sna leb-pa* flat nose ; (8) སོ་ལྟོ་བ *so lto-wa* bottle-teeth ; (9) དིག་པ *dig-pa* stammering ; (10) མིག་ཟླུམ་པ *mig zlum-pa* round eyes ; (11) མིག་ཆུང་བ *mig chun-wa* small eyes ; (12) སྒུར་བ *sgur-wa* crooked or bent body ; (13) ལྟོ་བོ་ཆེ་བ *lto-bo che-wa* large or pot-belly ; (14) དཔུང་པ་རྗེ་ངར་ཐུང་བ *dpun-pa rje nar thun-wa* small shoulders ; (15) སྤུ་ཅན *spu-can* hairy body ; (16) ལག་པ་དང་རྐང་པ་མི་མཉམ་པ the arms and legs with the feet not proportionate ; (17) ཚིགས་སྦོམ་པ *tshigs sbom-pa* large or swollen joints ; (18) ཁ་ལུས་པ་དྲི་མི་ཞིམ་པ་ཡོད་པ bad fœtid smell coming out of the body and the mouth.

སྐྱོན་བརྗོད་པ *skyon brjod-pa*=སྨད་པའི་ཚིག *smad-pahi tshig* to slander or speak ill of others; also slander (*Mnon.*).

སྐྱོན་དུ་འགྲང་བ *skyon-du hgran-wa* असूयता to reckon as or into sin or defect.

སྐྱོན་ནས་སྨྲ་བ *skyon-nas smra-wa* अपवाद: to ascribe a fault.

སྐྱོན་གནད་མེད་པ *skyon gnad med-pa* without the least fault or blemish.

སྐྱོན་པ *skyon-pa*, pf. བསྐྱོན *bskyon*, to put astride upon a thing (causative form of ཞོན་པ *shon-pa*) ; མི་ཤིག་རྟ་ལ་སྐྱོན་པ *mi-shig rta-la skyon-pa* to cause a man to mount ; to ride on horseback; to fix something on a stick ; མི་ཤིག་གསལ་ཤིང་ལ་སྐྱོན་པ to impale a man (*Jä.*) : བོང་བུར་སྐྱོན་ཏེ *bon-bur skyon-te* having caused him to ride a donkey (*Pag. 61*).

སྐྱོན་མེད་རྟོག *skyon-med rtog* निरामय free from disease; thinking or taking as faultless.

སྐྱོན་མེད་གནས *skyon-med gnas* अनवद्य, सावद्य remaining, living, or dwelling, in a state of innocence or faultlessness : སྐྱོན་མེད་པར་བཞུགས་པ *med-skyon par bshugs-pa* न्यास: residing without fault.

སྐྱོན་ཚིག *skyon-tshig* slander; also scandal.

སྐྱོན་འཛིན *skyon-hdsin* སྐྱོན་བློ་ཡིས་འཛིན་པ to find fault with.

སྐྱོན་ཤེས *skyon-çes*=མཁས་པ a learned man; a critic.

Syn. ཀུན་རིག *kun-rig* ; ཀུན་ཤེས *kun-çes* ; ཀུན་གྱིས་བཀུར་བ *kun-kyis-bkur-wa*. (*Mnon.*)

སྐྱོན་ཤེས་པ *skyon çes-pa*=སྨན་པ *sman-pa* वैद्य a physician (*Mnon.*).

སྐྱོན་སེལ་བ *skyon sel-wa* to remove a sin ; amend or correct a fault.

སྐྱོབ་པ *skyob-pa* त्राण, पाति, रक्षक, pf. བསྐྱབས, fut. བསྐྱབ, imp. སྐྱོབས or སྐྱོབས་ཤིག, to protect ; to defend, preserve, save ; frequently འཇིགས་པ་ལ་སྐྱོབ་པ *bjigs-pa la skyob-pa*, to protect from fear or danger or destruction : བསྐྱབས་པ the protecting power ; the preserving cause : གང་ཞིག་གང་ལ་སྐྱབས་འཚོལ་བ་དེ་ལ། སྐྱབས་སྦྱིན་པ་དེ་ནི་སྐྱོབ་པ་ཞེས་སྐྱོབ་པའོ he that gives protection to another is called སྐྱོབ་པ

s̱kyob-pa : སྐྱོབས་སྦྱིན་པ s̱kyobs̱ s̱byin-pa the giver of refuge or shelter.

· སྐྱོབ་སྟོན s̱kyob-s̱ton = སྐྱོབ་པ་པོ s̱kyob-pa-po or སྐྱོབས་པ s̱kyobs̱-pa त्रायी a protector.

སྐྱོབས s̱kyobs̱ help, assistance; seldom for སྐྱབས s̱kyabs̱; སྐྱོབས་མ s̱kyobs̱-ma and སྲོག་སྐྱོབས s̱rog-s̱kyobs̱ in colloq., preservation of life; escape; also he that saves another's life; a helper (*Jä.*); imp. of སྐྱོབ་པ s̱kyob-pa འཇིགས་པ་ཐམས་ཅད་ལས་སྐྱོབས་ཤིག protect from all the dangers.

སྐྱོབས་བྱེད s̱kyob-byed̠ त्रायमाण, त्रायी, बलभद्र one who protects; a name of Balabhadra.

སྐྱོམ་པ s̱kyom-pa, pf. བསྐྱོམས b̠s̱kyoms̱, fut. བསྐྱོམ b̠s̱kyom, imp. སྐྱོམས s̱kyoms̱ to pour; to pour out, agitate, stir up; according to *Lex.* to give; defined as ཆུ་སྣོད་ཆུ་སྐྱོགས་ཀྱིས་བླངས་ཏེ་ཟངས་ནང་དུ་བླུགས་པ་ལྟ་བུ *chu s̱nod̠ chu-s̱kyogs̱-kyis b̠lańs̱-te zańs-nań-du b̠lugs̱-pa l̠ta-bu*, taking from water-pots and water-bowls and pouring into kettles (*Ńag.*). Seldom used in colloquial language; ཆུ་སྐྱོམ་པ to stir the water; སྣོད་སྐྱོམ་པ to shake a vessel.

སྐྱོར s̱kyor, same as ཁྱོར *khyor*, the hollow of the hand filled: ཆུ་སྐྱོར *chu-s̱kyor* a handful of water (*Jä.*).

སྐྱོར. s̱kyor, འཁྱོག་པའམ་གཉེར་བ *h̠khyog-pah̠am g̠ñer-wa* bent, contracted or crooked: ཤངས་སྐྱོར *çańs̱-s̱kyor* = *s̱na h̠khyog-pa* (his) nose was bent (*A. 106*).

+ **སྐྱོར་སྐྱོར** s̱kyor-s̱kyor again and again; repeatedly.

སྐྱོར་བ s̱kyor-wa, vb. pf. and fut. བསྐྱར *b̠s̱kyar* 1. to hold up, to prop; to paste. 2. to repeat; to recite by heart: བསྐྱར་ཏེ་བཏང *b̠s̱kyar-te-b̠tań* it was repeatedly sent: ཚིག་སྐྱོར་བ *tshig s̱kyor-wa* to repeat a word; like the reciting of the *Mani, i.e.*, ཨོཾ་མ་ཎི་པདྨེ་ཧཱུྃ *om ma-ṇi pad̠-me hûm*: མི་རྒན་པ་དང་ནད་པ་དང་ཆང་གིས་བཟི་བ་གཞན་གྱིས་སྐྱོར་བས་འགྲོ་བ an old, sick, or drunken person walks being supported by another: གནད་པོ་འགྱེལ་འགྲོ་བ་ལ་སྐྱོར་བ to prop a thing that is falling or tumbling down: ཆུ་སྐྱོར་བ *chu s̱kyor-wa* the pouring of water with some force as if through a pipe or the mouth of a kettle; the sprinkling of water from a pot or vessel or a scoop; རྒྱབ་སྐྱོར to back; to help morally or religiously or otherwise one who is in difficulty, engaged in war or litigation, &c.: 3. enclosure; fence (*Jä.*).

སྐྱོར་སྦྱངས *s̱kyor-s̱byańs̱* repetition from memory: བློ་ལ་ཟིན་ཏེ་སྐྱོར་སྦྱངས་མཛད having retained in his minds, he repeated it.

སྐྱོར་ཚིག *s̱kyor-tshig*, v. སྐྱར་བ (*M̱ńon.*).

སྐྱོར་མོ་ལུང *S̱kyor-mo-luń* n. of a village with a monastery situated to the west of Lhasa containing estate of the *Shabs̱-pad̠ Sres̱ chuń-pa* (ཞབས་པད་སྲེས་ཆུང་པ).

སྐྱོལ་བ *s̱kyol-wa* sometimes for སྐྱེལ་བ *s̱kyel-wa*.

+ **སྐྱོས་པ** *s̱kyos̱-pa* = ཉམས་པ wasted; spoiled; degenerated.

སྐྱོས་མ *s̱kyos̱-ma*, v. སྐྱེས *s̱kyes̱*, སྐྱོས་མ *s̱kyos̱-ma* a present made to a friend or an acquaintance at the time of his going to a distant place, or removal to some place of residence.

སྐྲ *s̱kra* (*ṭa*), resp. དབུ་སྐྲ the hair of the head: སྐྲ་དང་ཁ་སྤུ *s̱kra dań kha-s̱pu* the hair of the head and the beard: སྐྲ་བསྒྲིལ་བ *s̱kra-b̠sgril-wa* plaited hair or curled hair: སྐྲ་ཉག་གཅིག *s̱kra ñag-gcig* a single tuft of hair: སྐྲ་ནི་འཇམ་རྩུབ་སྦོམ་ཕྲ་སྙོམས་སེར་མདངས་ཅན་སྣུམ་ལོངས་སྤྱོད་ཆེ *skra-ni ḥjam rtsub sbom phra sñoms-ser mdaṅs-can snum loṅs spyod-che* (he whose) hair is neither soft nor rough nor thick nor fine but uniform and smooth, and yellowish and glossy, becomes wealthy and prosperous (*Mtshan.*). སྐྲ་དོ་ཀེར *skra do-ker* the hair dressed and plaited together on the crown of the head; སྐྲ་དོ་ཀེར་ཅན *skra do-ker can* उत्कच-शिरः one with long flowing locks; སྐྲ་གྱེན་དུ་འགྲེང་བ་ལྟ་བུ *skra gyen-du ḥgreṅ-wa lta-bu* whose hairs stand upwards as bristles; སྐྲ་གྲོལ मुक्तकेशी with loose or carelessly worn hair; སྐྲ་སྐྲ་སྐྲི་ཅན गुल्मकेश a skein of silk or cotton attached to the flowing locks of Tibetan women; སྐྲ་བ་གླང་གི་སྤུ་འདྲ་བ *skra ba-glaṅ-gi spu ḥdra-wa* hair like that of a bull; སྐྲ་ཞགས=བུད་མེད་ཀྱི་སྐྲ locks of hair of women; སྐྲ་ཞིང thin hair (*Schtr.*); སྐྲ་བཤད་པ to comb hair; སྐྲ་བཞར་བ the shaving of one's hair; སྐྲ་གཞེར केशप्रतिग्रहण a barber; also napkin; སྐྲའི་བཀོད་པ कवरी well braided hair; also a braid or fillet of hair.

Syn. སྐྲ་ཚོགས *skra-tshogs*; སླར་སྐྱེ *slar-skye*; བྱེད་པ་ཅན *byed-wa-can*; མགོ་སྐྱེས *mgo-skyes*; མགོ་སྤུ *mgo-spu*; སྤྱི་བོ་སྐྱེས *spyi-bo skyes*; གཙུག་ཕུད *gtsug-phud*; རལ་པ *ral-pa*; ཐོར་ཚུགས *thor-tshugs*; མེ་ཏོག་ཅན *me-tog-can*; འཁྱིལ་བ *ḥkhyil-wa*; མགོ་ཉལ *mgo-ñal*; དོ་ཀེར *do-ker*; རལ་པའི་གདེངས *ral-paḥi gdeṅs*; ཟུར་ཕུད *zur-phud*; ཐོར་ཅོག *thor-cog*; དབུ་ལོ *dwu-lo*; ལྗང་ལོ *ljaṅ-lo* (*Mṅon.*).

སྐྲ་མཁན *skra-mkhan*=སྐྲ་འདྲེག་མཁན *skra ḥdreg-mkhan* a barber (*Mṅon.*).

སྐྲ་ཅན *skra-can* अरिष्टकेशिन्, केसर the mane (as of a lion); hairy.

སྐྲ་ཅན་གནས *skra-can gnas* वासर lady's bed-chamber.

སྐྲ་ཅན་མ *skra can-ma* a kind of hairy worm; also = བུད་མེད woman (*Mṅon.*).

སྐྲ་ཅན་གསོད *skra-can gsod* केशव a name of Hari, who killed the demon Keçi.

སྐྲ་གཉིས་པ *skra gñis-pa*=དུ་བ་མཇུག་རིང་ or མཇུག་ཐོད་ཅན a comet (*Mṅon.*).

སྐྲ་མདུད *skra-mdud* hair knot; acc. to *Jä.* the bow of ribands at the end of the long plaits of hair of the women in Ladak.

སྐྲ་འདྲེས་མ *skra ḥdres-ma*=ལྷའི་གཟུགས་ཚོང་མ a celestial courtezan (*Mṅon.*).

སྐྲ་གནས *skra-gnas* चपि n. of a species of sensitive plant.

སྐྲ་འབལ་བ *skra-ḥbal wa*=སྐྲ་རྐོག་པ *skra rkog-pa* or སྐྲ་ཏོག་པ *skra tog-pa* केशोल्लुञ्चन (shaving the head clean); to pull out the hair: ལ་ལ་ནི་ཉམ་ཐག་པའི་ང་རོ་འདོན་པ་ལ་ལ་ནི་སྐྲ་འབལ some sent forth cries of anguish, some pulled out the hair of their head (*Ḥbrom. 113*).

སྐྲ་མེད་མགོ *skra-med mgo* "a head without hair"; ཛཱ་ཏི *dsā-ti* जाति nutmeg; also *Jarminum grandiflorum* (*Sman. 404.*).

སྐྲ་ཚལ *skra-tsal* false hair; a peruke.

སྐྲ་རྩ *skra-rtsa* जटा clotted hair.

སྐྲ་ཚོགས *skra-tshogs*, v. སྐྲ *skra* (*Mṅon.*).

སྐྲ་མཚམས *skra-mtshams* सीमन्त the arrangement of the hair.

+ སྐྲ་ཟིངས *skra-ziṅs*=ང་རྒྱལ་ཆེ་བ vanity, pride; adj. vain, very proud.

སྐྲ་བཟང *skra-bzaṅ* a secret or mystic word (*Miṅ. 4*).

སྐྲ་བཟང་མ *skra bzaṅ-ma*=གནོད་སྦྱིན་མོའི་གཙོ་མོ n. of a *Yakṣa* goddess (*Mṅon.*).

སྐྲའི་ཁྱོན་ནམ་བྱིས་པའི་ལམ *skraḥi khyon-nam byis-paḥi lam* बालपथ hair parting.

སྐྲའི་རྒྱལ་པོ *skraḥi rgyal-po*=ལྡུམ་པ *ldun-po* केशराज a grove; a garden; n. of a vegetable.

སྐྲའི་བྱི་དོར *skraḥi byi-dor* v. སྐྲ་སད *skra-sad* (*Mṅon.*).

སྐྲའི་རྩེ་མོའི་མཐའ *skrahi rtse-mohi mthah* or ཤེ་ཙམ वालाग्रकोटि the hair-end.

སྐྲ་ལི་བ *skra li-wa* or སྐྲའི་རྣམ་འགྱུར *skrahi rnam-gyur* बर्बरी curly hair; to dress the hair.

སྐྲ་ལོ *skra-lo*=བུད་མེད་ཀྱི་སྐྲ *bud-med kyi-skra* woman's hair (*Mṅon.*).

སྐྲ་ཤད *skra-shad* प्रसाधनी hair separator; a comb.

Syn. སོ་མང *so-mań*, སྐྲའི་བྱི་དོར *skrahi byi-dor* hair cleaner (*Mṅon.*).

སྐྲག་སྐྲག *skrag-skrag*=ཁྲག་པོ *khrag-po* or སྲ་བ *sra-wa* hard.

སྐྲག་པ *skrag-pa* (*tag-pa*) to be terrified, frightened, afraid of something. This word is nearly always combined with འཇིགས་པ *hjigs-pa* as in འཇིགས་སྐྲག་པ *hjigs skrag-pa*, to be panic-struck.

སྐྲག་བྱེད་མ *skrag byed-ma*=ཉི་མའི་བཙུན་མོ *ñi mahi btsun-mo* the wife of the sun (*Mṅon.*).

སྐྲང་བ *skrań-wa* (*tań-wa*) उच्छ्राय, फुल्ल; pf. སྐྲངས *skrańs* to swell; སྐྲང་སོང *skrańs-soń* it is swollen: བྱོ་བུར་མཚོན་དང་རྡོ་དང་དབྱུག་པ་སོགས་ཐོག་ནས་སྐྲངས swollen from being suddenly struck with a stick or a stone or a sword.

སྐྲང་འབུར *skrańs-hbur* an abscess not yet open (*Sch.*); སྐྲངས་འབུར་འཇོམས *skrańs-hbur hjoms*, v. བ་སྤྲུ་ཤིང *ba-spru çiń*, n. of a medicinal tree which removes tumours or abscess (*Mṅon.*).

སྐྲངས་ཀྱི་སྤྱང་ཀི *skrań-kyi spyań-ki*, སྨན་ཐར་ནུ *sman-thar-nu* n. of a medicine (*Sman. 126*).

སྐྲངས་པོ *skrańs-po* a swelling; tumour (*Sch.*).

སྐྲན *skran* (*ten*) ལྷན་སྐྲན *lhan-skren* 1. गुल्म tumour or any fleshy excrescence in the abdomen; a concretion under the skin or in the bowels, womb, &c. (*Cs.*); a swelling of the glands (*Sch.*). སྐྲན་ནད *skran-nad* is described as a consequence of suppressed wind (*Jä.*); རྡོ་སྐྲན *rdo-skran* བད་སྐྲན two sorts of steatite.

སྐྲབ་པ *skrab-pa* (*tab-pa*) to beat the ground with one's feet; to stamp, tread; to dance; also *bro skrab-pa*: ཁ་སང་གི་བྲོ་སྐྲབ་པ་ཡག་པོ་བྱུང yesterday's dancing was excellent.

སྐྲས་ཀ *skras-ka* a ladder, v. སྐས་ཀ *skas-ka*.

སྐས་ཀ (*te-ka*) ladder, which generally consists of the notched trunk of a tree (*Jä.*); གང་སྐྲས a single ladder, *i.e.*, a ladder with one pole; རྡོ་སྐྲས *rdo skras* (*do-te*) a flight of stone steps; རྒྱ་སྐྲས *rgya-skras* a regular staircase, as in European houses; གྲུ་སྐྲས probably a flight of steps at the corner of a building.

ᚐ **སྐྲི་བ** *skri-wa* (*ti-wa*) to conduct; to send (*Cs.*): སྐྲི་ཤིག *skri-çig*=ཐོང་ཤིག *thon-shig* let him send: ངེད་བོད་ན་དེ་ལ་སྐྲི་བར་བྱེད་ཞུས་པས I asked to send him to Tibet (*A. 101*).

ᚐ **སྐྲུ་བ** *skru-wa*, pf. བསྐྲུས *bskrus*, fut. བསྐྲུ *bskru*, to wait (*Sch.*); to cut; ཟས་ལ་སྐྲུ *zas-la skru* to cut meat; སྐྲུ *skru*, ཤིང་སྐྲུས་པ *çiń krus-pa* to cut wood or a tree: བསྐྲུ་བ *bskru-wa*, རྒྱུན་དུ་དགའ་བའི་སྐྲུ་བ་ཡིས always being smitten by pleasures (*Pag. 1-35*).

ᚐ **སྐྲུད་པ** *skrud-pa* (*tud-pa*)=གཞན་ལ་ཐབས་ཀྱིས་འབྲོད་པ to make another run away by devices.

སྐྲུན་པ *skrun-pa* (*tun-pa*)=སྐྱེད་པ *skyed-pa* to produce; བསྐྲུན་པ *bskrun-pa*, བསྐྱེད་པ *bskyed-pa* जात, रोपित, जनित grown up: བསྐྲུན་བུའི་ལོ་ཏོག growing crop.

སྐྲུམ *skrum* (*tum*) meat; applied to the food of the respected; generally གསོལ་སྐྲུམ *gsol-skrum* is used in colloquial language.

སྐྲོག ṣkrog (ṭog) to beat (the drum). ཌ་མ་རུ་འཁྲོལ་བའི་དོན ḍama-ru ḥkhrol-wahi don signifies the beating of a skull-drum (*Ńag.*).

སྐྲོག་པ ṣkrog-pa to churn; stir (with a rod): ཧོ་མ་སྐྲོག་པ ḥo-ma ṣkrog-pa to churn milk (*Ńag.*).

སྐྲོད་པ ṣkrod-pa (ṭo-pa) प्रवासनीय, उत्खाटित to expel, drive out, eject: གནས་ནས་སྐྲོད gnaṣ naṣ-ṣkroḍ to expel from a place: ཕྱིར་སྐྲོད phyir-ṣkroḍ to drive out: བགེགས་སྐྲོད ḥgegṣ-ṣkroḍ to eject an evil spirit.

བསྐ་བ ḅṣka-wa = ཁར་བ, कषाय astringent; also thick.

བསྐང་མདོས ḅṣkań ṃdoṣ a slight framework made of sticks and coloured threads as an offering to the gods in cases of sickness: ལྷོ་ཡི་ཕྱོགས་སུ་བསྐང་མདོས་དང་བསྲུང་འཁོར་བཞག lho-yi-phyogṣ-su ḅṣkań-ṃdoṣ dań ḅsruń ḥkhor ḅshag place Rṣkań-ṃdoṣ and amulets on the south side (*Jig.*).

བསྐང་རྫས ḅṣkań-ṛdsaṣ a sacrificial ceremony (*Sehl. 360*).

བསྐང་གསོ ḅṣkań-gso ཡི་དམ་མཁའ་འགྲོ་ཆོས་སྐྱོང་རྣམས་ལ་བསྐང་གསོ་རྒྱས་པ to make copious religious services to the tutelar deities, angels, and the guardian spirits of the ten quarters (*Çil. 9*).

བསྐངས ḅṣkańṣ 1. ཁ་བསྐངས་པུར་ full to the brim. 2. ཐུགས་དམ་བསྐངས, ཉམས་པ་གསོས་པ ńamṣ-pa gsoṣ-pa fill to the brim (*Situ. 74*).

བསྐམ ḅṣkam " བསྐམ་བྱའི་དངོས་པོ ḅṣkam-byaḥi dṅoṣ-po " (*Situ. 77*).

བསྐམས ḅṣkamṣ past. dried, burnt: བསྐལ་མེས་མཚོ་བསྐམས by the fire (at the end of the age) the lakes dried up (*Ńag. 9*).

བསྐལ་པ ḅṣkal-pa कल्प a fabulous period of time; the various ages of the world, each of which has been presided over by its own human Buddha respectively: བསྐལ་པ་ཆེན་པོ ḅṣkal-pa chen-po the great *Kalpa*; བར་བསྐལ bar-ḅṣkal the intervening or middle *Kalpa*; བསྐལ་བཟང་པོ ḅṣkal-pa ḅzań-po भद्रकल्प the happy or glorious period in which the Buddhas appear; བསྐལ་པ་ངན་པ ḅṣkal-pa ńan-pa the evil *Kalpa*, in which no Buddhas appear (*Jä.*).

བསྐལ་པ་བཟང ḅṣkal-pa ḅzań = བསོད་ནམས पुण्य virtuous; also virtue (*Mńon.*).

བསྐལ་པ་ཤེས ḅṣkal-pa çeṣ = རྩིས་པ ṛtsiṣ-pa an accountant (*Mńon.*).

བསྐལ་མེ ḅṣkal-me = བསྐལ་པའི་མེ the fire which will destroy the world at the end of the present Kalpa (*Ńag. 9*).

བསྐལ་བཟང ḅṣkal-ḅzań ཆོས་ཤིག་གི་མཚན n. of a religious work.

བསྐུ ḅṣku = བྱུག་པ byug-pa, fut. བསྐུས ḅṣkuṣ लेप rubbed (*Ńag. 9*).

བསྐུངས ḅṣkuńṣ = མི་མཐོང་བར་སྦས་པ mi-ṃthoń-war ṣbaṣ-pa concealed; hidden (*Ńag. 10.*).

བསྐུམ ḅṣkum, pf. of སྐུམ.

བསྐུམ་མཁྱིད ḅṣkum-ṃkhyiḍ the distance or measure between the thumb and the top of the forefinger drawn in; about one-half of the measure of a span: ཞེང་སོར་གང་ཡོད་པ་རྒྱག་མཐོ་བརྒྱད་དང་བསྐུམ་མཁྱིད་གང་། (*Rtsii.*) its breadth was one finger (*i.e.*, one inch), and length eight spans and one ḅṣkum-ṃkhyiḍ.

བསྐུམ་ཁྲུ ḅṣkum-khru about a cubit measure with the fingers drawn in a fist.

བསྐུམ་འདོམ ḅṣkum-ḥdom a measure of distance by stretching apart the two arms (with "fisted hands"); a little less than a fathom's measure.

བསྐུར ḅṣkur, sbst. sending, granting; དབང་བསྐུར to bless; to grant benediction; འཕྲིན་བསྐུར (*Ńag. 9*).

བསྐུལ v. སྐུལ་བ, བསྐུལ་བརྡའ *bskul-brdah* signal to call one to his business; signal to call workmen to their respective duties..

བསྐུལ་གཞུང *bskul-gshuṅ*, གཞུང་གི་ལས་ཀ་བསྐུལ་མཁན one who gets Government works excuted: བསྐུལ་གཞུང་ནམ་གཉིས་དང་རྩུལ་མི་འདུ་བ.

བསྐུས *bskus*, pf. of བསྐུ *bsku* लिप्त anointed; stained or poisoned (*Ṅag. 9*).

བསྐོན *bskon*, pf. གོས་བསྐོན་ཏོ *gos bskon-to* to be dressed (*Situ. 64*).

བསྐོར *bskor* surrounded: འཁོར་གྱིས་བསྐོར surrounded by followers, admirers and attendants.

བསྐོས *bskos*= བཀོད *bkod*, pf. རྒྱལ་པོར་བསྐོས (*Situ. 74*).

བསྐྱང་དུ་མེད *bskyaṅ-du med* = དཔག་ཏུ་མེད numberless; immeasurable (*Zam. 10*).

བསྐྱངས *bskyaṅs* पालित protected; cherished; nursed.

བསྐྱབས *bskyabs* रक्षित protected; སྲོག་བསྐྱབས *srog-bskyabs* protected, saved life (*Situ. 74*).

+ བསྐམས *bskyams*= བསྐམས: སྣོད་མི་བསྐམས *snod mi-bskyams* the vessel has not dried. ཆུ་བསྐམས water dried up (*Situ. 74*).

བསྐྱར *bskyar*= སྐར་ཡང་ or ཡང་ཡང་ again; again and again (*Zam. 10*).

བསྐྱར་བཟོ *bskyar-bzo* repairing; mending of.

བསྐྱུར *bskyur* cast out; exhiled; driven away.

བསྐྱུར་དུ་བཅུག་པ *bskyur-du bcug-pa* to cause any one to cast or fling anything away.

བསྐྱེད་འདོད *bskyed-hdod* वर्द्धन: growth or growing; wish to grow.

བསྐྱེད་པ *bskyed-pa*, उपार्जित, जनन, प्रयुक्ति 1. a production, generation, formation. 2. उत्पादित, उत्पादय्. སེམས་བསྐྱེད་པ *sems bskyed-pa* चित्तोत्पाद to form one's mind; to have a conception of; also technically means purification of the heart as in बोधिचित्तोत्पाद.

བསྐྱེད་པ་བགྱི་འོ *bskyed-pa bgyi-ho* उत्पादयति to have a conception of.

བསྐྱེད་རིམ *bskyed-rim* उत्पत्तिक्रम the gradual development of ideas; powers of an occult nature.

བསྐྱོད་ནས *bskyod-nas*= སྤོས་ནས *spos-nas*.

བསྐྱོད་པ *bskyod-pa* प्रकम्प्य, उद्भूत, क्षोभ्य moved, agitated; མ་བསྐྱོད་པ *ma bskyod-pa* अक्षोभ्य unagitated.

བསྐྱོད་པ་ཡང་མ *bskyod-pa yaṅ-ma* अधूत्यानता moving again and again, at paroxysm.

བསྐྱོད་མེད་པ *bskyod med-pa*, གྲངས *graṅs* अपरिमित n. of an immensely great number.

བསྐྲད *bskrad* and ཕྱིར་བསྐྲད *phyir-bskrad*= ཕྱིར་བཏོན *phyir-bton* turn out, expel (*Situ. 74*): བགེགས་བསྐྲད turn out a ghost or devil.

བསྐྲུས *bskrus*, pf. of སྐྲུ་བ, ཟས་བསྐྲུས food cut up (*Situ. 9*).

བསྐྲུན *bskrun*= བསྐྱེད *bskyed* 1. མང་དུ་བཏང་བ *maṅ-du btaṅ-wa* to multiply. 2. པར་དུ་བཀོད་པ *par-du bkod-pa* to print, set up in print (*Ṅag. 9.*): དགེ་བ་བསྐྲུན་པ *dge-wa bskruna*, ལོ་ཏོག་བསྐྲུན་པ *lo-tog bskrun-pa*.

ཁ

ཁ *kha* I: the second letter of the Tibetan alphabet, being the aspirate of ཀ *ka*. In sound it resembles ख, the second consonant of the Sanskrit alphabet. 1. On registers it indicates the second, or number two. It is attached, often optionally, as an additional syllable to many words, especially in the colloquial: དགོང་ཁ *ḍgoṅ-kha* the price; ཆ་ཁ *cha-kha* a thing. 2. It implies ཁག *khag*, a part: ཁ་གཉིས་སུ *kha-gñiṣ-su*=ཁག་གཉིས་སུ *khag-gñiṣ-su* into two parts (divisions): ཁ་གང *kha-gaṅ* one part. The sixth part of a *taṅ-ka* (Tib. coin) is called *kha*. 3. Origin, source, &c.: གསེར་ཁ *gser-kha*=གསེར་གྱི་འབྱུང་ཁུངས *gser-gyi ḥbyuṅ-khuṅṣ* the source of gold, gold-mine: ཚྭ་ཁ *tshwa-kha* salt-pit: རྩྭ་ཁ *tswa-kha* pasture-land, a place where pastures abound. 4. Time: ཉི་འཆར་ཁ་རུ་དུས་གདབ་ *ñiḥchar-kha-ru ḍuṣ-gḍab* (*Situ. 21*) calculate time from the moment of sunrise; འགྲོ་ཁར *ḥgro-khar* at the time of going; at the time when he was ready to start: མོ་འཆི་ཁར་ཆོས་ལ་འདུན་པ *mo ḥchi-khar choṣ-la ḥdun-pa* she at the time of dying became religious, &c. (*Pag. 27*): བྱོན་ཁར *byon-khar* when he came; at the moment of arrival: ཡོང་ཁ *yoṅ-kha* at the time of coming; ས་དང་པོ་ཐོབ་ཁ་མ *sa daṅ-po thob-kha-ma*=ས་དང་པོ་ཐོབ་མ་ཐག *sa daṅ-po thob-ma-thag* as soon as he attained to the first stage, *i.e.*, one moment before the attainment: ཡུན་རིང་གི་ཁ་ནས *yun riṅ-gi kha naṣ*=ཡུན་རིང་གི་སྒོ་ནས *yun riṅ-gi sgo naṣ* by little and little; gradually (*Jä.*); རེ་བའི་ཁར in the hope of; ཐབས་ཀྱི་ཁ་ན just on the opportunity; "in the nick of time."

ཁ II: 1. the front side: मुख face, mouth; also the surface or upper side. ཁ is the ordinary word for "mouth," while གདོང་ is the commoner term for "face." Again, to express the surface as well as the front of any inanimate thing, ཁ is the usual form: བྲག་ཁ་ལ་གངས་རྒྱུན icicles on the face of the cliff; སྐྱིལ་ཀྲུང་མཛད་ནས་ཆུ་ཁར་བྱོན *ṣkyil-kruṅ ṃdsaḍ-naṣ chu-khar byon* (*Pag. 117*) sitting in a cross-legged posture he moved on the surface of the water; འོ་ཐུག་ཁ་ལ་འོད་ཟེར་གྱི་རི་མོ་མཐོང *ḥo-thug kha-la ḥoḍ-zer-gyi ri-mo ṃthoṅ* saw reflection of rays on the surface of milk-broth (*Pag. 113*). 2. भाषा language; conversation; वचन word: རྒྱལ་པོ་བུད་མེད་ཀྱི་ཁར་དབང་དུ་སོང་ནས the king having become powerless at (his) wife's word (*Pag. 32*).

Syn. སྨྲ་བའི་སྒོ *ṣmṛa-waḥi ṣgo*; ཟ་བྱེད *za-byeḍ*; གསུང་བར་བྱེད *gsuṅ-war-byeḍ*; ཞལ *shal*; གཏམ་གྱི་འབྱུང་གནས *gtam-gyi ḥbyuṅ-gnaṣ*; རྗོད་བྱེད *ṛjoḍ-byeḍ*; གདོང *gdoṅ*; བདུད་རྩིའི་རྟེན *bdud-ṛtsiḥi ṛten*; སྐད *ṣkaḍ*; གཏམ *gtam* (*Mṅon.*).

ཁ III: a breadth or a square of cloth, &c.

In its several inflected forms ཁ is often used as if it were a postposition governing the accusative case. These forms are ཁ་ན *kha-na*, ཁ་རུ *kha-ru*, and ཁར *khar*, and take the meaning of "on," "at," "beside," &c.: མེ་ཁར་ on the fire; ཁྲི་ཁ་ན on the chair; ཕྱོགས་བཞི་ཁ་རུ all round.

ཁ་ཀྱིལ་བ *kha kyel-wa* चुम्बन to kiss.

ཁ་ཀྲབ་པ *kha krab-pa* (*kha ṭab-pa*) to smack or cluck with the mouth.

ཁ་དཀར་པོ *kha dkar-po* = སྣང་བ་གསལ *snañ-wagsal* 1. bright: བཀྲ་ཤིས་པ *ḇkra-çis-pa.* 2. auspicious; of happy omen; agreeable; pleasant looking; ཁ་དཀར་གཏིང་ནག *kha-ḏkar gtiñnag* outside white, inside black, *i.e.*, plausible.

ཁ་དཀྲི *kha-ḏkri* (*kha-ṭi*) neck-cloth, sometimes worn as a protection against cold; a kind of raw silk stuff of narrow breadth manufactured in Assam and largely imported into Tibet, where it is used as necktie and handkerchief: ཁ་དཀྲི་བཅས་འདྲ་བ་ཁ་རེར་འབྲུ *kha-ḏkri ḇcaṣ ḫdra-wa kha-rer ḫbru* (*Ṟtsii.*) for each breadth (of cloth), which is equal to a *kha-ti*, price in barley grain.

ཁ་ལྐུག *kha-ḻkug* dumb; also of indistinct speech: ར་ཡི་མཆེར་པས་བྱིས་པའི་ཁ་ལྐུག་འབྱེད the spleen of a goat removes the dumbness of children.

ཁ་སྐད *kha-ṣkaḏ* वृत्तान्त oral account; tradition; narrative; colloquial language.

ཁ་སྐོང *kha-ṣkoñ* गण्डूष, पूरण a mouthful; completion; appendix of a book: ཁ་སྐོང་བ *kha-ṣkoñ-wa* 1. to fill up a void; to make up a deficiency. 2. to fill up the mouth with water, to rinse it.

ཁ་སྐོར་བ *kha ṣkor-wa* = སླུ་བ *ṣlu-wa* or ཁ་བསྐོར་བ *kha ḇṣkor-wa* to speak cunningly; to circumvent by speech.

ཁ་སྐྱུར་པོན *kha ṣkyur-pon* 1. sour; of an acid taste. 2. olive; olive tree (in Sikkim) (*Jä.*).

ཁ་སྐྱེངས *kha-ṣkyeñṣ* shame-facedness: མི་ཞིག་གོས་མི་གཞན་ཞིག་ལ་གསོལ་རས་སྐྱེར་གྱི་ཡོད་ན, དེ་མི་གཞན་ཞིག་གི་ལག་པ་བཟེད་ནས་དེ་ལ་མ་སྐྱེར་ན་ཁོ་ངོ་ཚ་བ་ལ་ཁ་སྐྱེངས་ཟེར, དཔེ་ལ་ཀུན་མ་ཁ་སྐྱེངས་ཀྱི་མི་བཟོད་ཟེར། If a man is about to give his garment to another man, and that other man having held out his hand, it is not given to him, he is ashamed—that is termed *kha-ṣkyeñṣ.*

ཁ་ཁ *kha-kha* I: apart, separately: ཁ་ཁ་བསྡད་ན་ཁ་མཆུ་མེད if (you) sit apart there will be no quarrel.

ཁ་ཁ II: or ཁ་ཁ་མོ *kha-kha-mo* bitter mouth; bitter taste.

ཁ་ཁེབས *kha-khebṣ* कोष a veil; a cover: གྲུ་པ་རེར་ཁ་ཁེབས་རས་ཁ་རེ *grḇa-pa rer kha-khebṣ raṣ kha-re* (at every offering) there is a square of cloth apiece as a face covering to each monk.

ཁ་ཁོར *kha-khor* = ཐ་འཁོར *tha-ḫkhor* border, edge; also the circumference.

ཁ་ཁྱག *kha-khyag* = ཁ་ཐེག་བྱེད་པ *kha-theg byed-pa* contradiction; denying one's liability.

ཁ་ཁྱག་པ *kha-khyag-pa*, same as ཁ་ཐེག་བྱེད་པ *kha-theg byeḏ-pa*, to deny having undertaken to do a thing; denying one's liability.

ཁ་ཁྱེར *kha-khyer* 1. ལན་ཀན *lan-kan*; སྟེགས་བུ *ṣtegṣ-bu* any shelf or box on which birds perch; also वेदिका an altar; a raised seat. 2. མཐའ་བསྐོར་ཁ *mthaḫ-ṣkor-kha* the surrounding line or circumference of anything; the surrounding edge of a cloth, &c.

ཁ་ཁྲ *Kha-khra* (*kha-ṭha*), v. བློ་ཁ་ཁྲ *Ḇlokha-khra* or ལོ་ཁ་བྲག *Lo kha-brag*; also n. for certain wild tribes of the border land of Tibet, namely the Aka and Mishmi tribes of eastern Tibet and Assam (*Ya-sel. 38*).

ཁ་ཁྲམ *kha-khram* (*kha-ṭham*) defined as ཁ་ཡི་གཡོ་རྒྱུ་བ་ཤད་པ cunning talk, deceitful language.

ཁ་ཁྲམ་པ *kha-khram-pa* = གཡོ་རྒྱུ་བཤད་མཁན *gyoṟgyu ḇçaḏ-ṃkhan* one who speaks cunningly so as to cheat.

ཁ་ཁྲལ I: *kha-khral* (*kha-ṭhē*) मुखदण्ड respect, regard; lit. tribute in language or in words.

ཁ་ཁྲལ II: capitation tax or poll tax.

ཁ་འཁོར *kha-ḥkhor* the circumference of the mouth (*Cs.*); ཁ་འཁོར་བ *kha ḥkhor-wa* to surround.

ཁ་འཁྱིག་བ *kha ḥkhyig-pa* to bind an animal's mouth; to gag; to strangle.

ཁ་འཁྱོམས *kha-ḥkhyoms* to be agitated outwardly: རླུང་ཆེན་པོ་དེས་རྒྱ་མཚོའི་ཁ་འཁྱོམས *rluṅ chen-po deṣ rgya-mtshoḥi kha ḥkhyoms* the surface of the sea was troubled by that great wind (*A. 16*).

ཁ་ག་པོ *kha-ga-po* difficult (*Sch.*).

ཁ་ག་མ *kha-ga-ma* or ཁ་གང་མ *kha-gaṅ-ma* the square rug that is spread over a great man's cushion or seat.

ཁ་གང *kha-gaṅ* a quadrate, square; one sixth of the Tibetan coin called *taṅka*, which is equivalent to one *anna* in India: ཁ་གང་བ *kha gaṅ-wa* adj. square.

ཁ་གང་དགར་སྨྲ་བ *kha-gaṅ-dgar-smra-wa* to talk at random; to speak at pleasure (thoughtlessly).

ཁ་གབ *kha-gab* cover, lid. (*Sch.*).

ཁ་གྱེན་ཕྱོགས *kha gyen-phyogs* उन्मुख with the face upwards (in expectation); expectantly, eagerly.

ཁ་གྲངས *kha-graṅs* (*kha-ḍaṅ*) enumeration.

ཁ་གྲུ *kha-gru* (*kha-ḍu*) or མཐའ་གྲུ *mthaḥ-gru* the corner limit or sphere of a place, also of the mouth. The width of the mouth of a vessel or pot, also the opening of the mouth. ཁ་གྲུ་ཡངས་ཤིང་དཀར་འབོལ་རྩ་མེད་མཆོག *kha-gru yaṅṣ-çiṅ dkar-ḥbol rtsa-med mchog* that being broad in space, of white and soft appearance, and without grass, is best (*Jig.*).

ཁ་གླིང *Kha-gliṅ*, མཐའ་འཁོབ་ཡུལ་གྱི་མིང *mthaḥ-ḥkhob yul-gi miṅ* n. of a border country.

ཁ་གླིང་སྒྲ *kha gliṅ-sgra* is defined as དམག་གི་སར་འབྱུང་བའི་དགྲ་སྐད་ལ the noise of the foe which arises in a battle-field (*Mṅon*).

ཁ་འགོག་པ *kha ḥgog-pa* mute; one who cannot or does not speak; gagged (*Mṅon.*).

ཁ་འགྱུར་བ *kha ḥgyur-wa* to change one's words or promises.

ཁ་འགྲིག་པ *kha ḥgrig-pa* (*kha-ḍig*) = ཁ་འཆམ་པ *kha ḥcham-pa* of the same opinion or disposition.

ཁ་འགྲིལ *kha-ḥgril* (*kha-ḍil*) the selvedge or loose tufts of thread on either edge of a cloth: གུར་གྱི་ཁ་འགྲིལ་རས་སྔོན་པོ་བཏང་བ་ལ the fringes of the tent being made with blue cotton.

ཁ་རྒོད *kha-rgod* ill or rough language; also a slanderer (*Sch.*).

ཁ་རྒན *kha-rgan* privilege of old age (*Jä.*).

ཁ་རྒྱན *kha-rgyan* ताम्बूल the betel-leaf which the Indians chew; literally the beautifier of the mouth.

ཁ་རྒྱལ་བ *kha-rgyal-wa* to win a dispute: བདུད་རིགས་ཀྱི་སེམས་ཅན་ཁ་རྒྱལ *bdud rigs-kyi sems-can kha-rgyal* the animate beings of the demon kind won the controversy.

ཁ་རྒྱུག *kha-rgyug* idle talk; unfounded assertion (*Jä.*).

ཁ་རྒྱུད *kha-rgyud*, resp. ཞལ་རྒྱུད *shal-rgyud*, same as གཏམ་རྒྱུད *gtam-rgyud*, oral tradition; also certain mystical doctrine not allowed to be written down.

ཁ་སྒོར *kha-sgor* the shoulder bone.

ཁ་སྒྱུར་བ *kha sgyur-wa* ཁ་ལོ་སྒྱུར་བ *kha-lo sgyur-wa* to govern; to rein the mouth (of a horse); to lead, guide, influence other persons.

ཁ་སྒྲོག *kha-sgrog* (*kha-ḍog*) ཁ་སྒྲོག་ནང་མ་ལོ་ཇ་ཕུང་ཉེར་བྱེད་ཡོད་པ. In this passage ཁ་སྒྲོག *kha-*

sgrog means shutting or binding up the straps of a trunk or leather box.

ཁ་བསྒོས *kha-bsgos* advice.

ཁ་ལྷ་པ *kha lha-pa*=སེང་གེ *señ-ge* the lion (*Mñon.*).

ཁ་སྔ་བ *kha sña-wa* or ཁ་སྔས་པ *kha sñas-pa* to anticipate or say something beforehand; to speak out inconsiderately.

ཁ་ཅིག *kha-cig* or ཁ་གཅིག *kha-gcig* 1. ལ་ལ *la-la*, कश्चित् a certain person; ཁ་ཤས *khaças* also འགའ་རེ *hgah-re*, འགའ་ཞིག *hgah-shig*. 2. some (*J. Zañ.*): ཁ་ཅིག་ཏུ་ཕུར་སྒྲར *kha cig-tu phur-sgrar* प्रचिसमब्द "or as somo call it a flying word"; ཁ་ཅིག་ན་རེ *kha-cig na-re* someone said.

ཁ་ཅུལ *kha-cul* or ཁ་ཅུར *kha-cur* Kashmir; a Kashmirian.

ཁ་གཅང *kha-gcañ* clever talking, cf. ཁ་སྦྱང་པོ *kha sbyañ-po* eloquent; dexterous in conversation.

ཁ་བཅུད *kha-bcud*=ཅུ་གང *cu-gañ* n. of a medicinal substance (*Sman. 149*).

ཁ་གཅོད *kha-gcod* cover; in *Ld.* cork.

ཁ་བཅོལ *kha-bcol* idle talk, prattle (*Sch.*).

ཁ་ཆག I: *kha-chag* defect in the blade (of a knife or an axe), but ཁ་ཆག་སྣ་རལ *kha-chag sna-ral*=to get the mouth damaged and nose torn; ཁ་ཐུག་པོ་སོང *kha thug-po soñ* the edge (of a knife, &c.) has become blunt; ཁ་ལོག་སོང *kha log-soñ* the blade has become turned, *i.e.*, bad; ཁ་མི་འདུག *kha mi-hdug* the sharpness is wanting; གྲིའི་ཁ *grihi-kha* or གྲིའི་སོ *grihi so* (in *Khams*) the blade of a knife.

ཁ་ཆག II: abuse; ill language (*Jä.*).

ཁ་ཆད *kha-chad*, ཞལ་ཆད *shal-chad* agreement, covenant; a truce; ཁ་ཆད *kha-chad*= ཆད་དོན *chad-don* special object or reason (*Mñon.*).

ཁ་ཆར *kha-char*=abbreviation of ཁ་བ, snow and ཆར་པ, rain.

ཁ་ཆིངས *kha-chiñs* the taming or appeasing of wild beasts, &c., by witchcraft.

ཁ་ཆུ *kha-chu* (ཞལ་ཆབ *shal-chab*) लाला, ष्ठयत् spittle; also used colloq. for ཁ་བའི་ཆུ *kha-wahi chu* snow-water.

ཁ་ཆུ་ཕུག *kha chu-phug* n. of a place on the uplands of Kha-chu (*Lon.* ཀ *32*).

ཁ་ཆེ *Kha-che* a native of Kashmir; a Mahomedan; a person that has the command over much; principal or important things (ཁ་ཆེ་བ་རྣམས *kha-che-wa rnams*); n. of a mask in the religious plays of Tibet.

ཁ་ཆེ་སྐྱེས *kha-che skyes*, ཁ་ཆེ་མཆོག *kha-che mchog*, v. གུར་གུམ *gur-gum* (*Mñon.*), काश्मीरज or कुङ्कुम saffron, the produce of Kashmir.

ཁ་ཆེ་འགྲོན་ཁང *kha-che hgron-khañ*, ཁ་ཆེ་ཟ་ཁང *kha-che za-khañ* an inn kept by a Mussalman at Lhasa or in Peking; ཁ་ཆེ་མཆོག *kha-che mchog* परम काश्मीरज the chief article, *i.e.*, saffron, which the Tibetans obtain from Kashmir; ཁ་ཆེ་ཤ་ཁ་མ *kha-che ça-kha-ma* a kind of yellow flower resembling saffron which imported from Kashmir is largely grown in Tibet; ཁ་ཆེ་ཤ་ཁ་མ་སྤོར་རེར་འབྲུ *kha-che ça-kha-ma spor rer hbru* the cost of a *spor* of Kashmir *ça-kha-ma* flower is a *bru* of barley flour (*Rtsii.*).

ཁ་ཆེམས *kha-chems*, resp. ཞལ་ཆེམས *shal-chems*, last will, testament: ཁ་ཆེམས་འཇོག་པ *kha-chems hjog-pa* to make a will; ཁ་ཆེམས་རླུང་ལ་བསྐུར *kha-chems rluñ-la bskur* sent (his) last will to the winds (*Behu.*).

ཁ་ཆོས *kha-chos* hypocrisy; religion in talk only.

ཁ་འཆལ *kha-hchal* जल्पना idle talk, prattle; talk as in a delirium: ཁ་འཆལ་བྱེད (he) prattles.

ཁ་འཆམ *kha-ḥcham*=ཁ་མཐུན *kha-mthun*. ཁ་འཆམ་པ *kha ḥcham-pa*=ཁ་མཐུན་པ *kha-mthun-pa* or ཁ་ཐུག་པ *kha thug-pa* to agree upon; ཁ་འཆམ་ཁྲུགས *kha-ḥcham khrugs*=ཕོ་མོ་ལྷན་ཅིག་ཏུ་གནས་པ residing together as husband and wife; to live harmoniously (*Mṅon.*).

ཁ་འཆེ་བ *kha ḥche-wa*, same as ཁ་ཐལ་བ *kha thal-wa*, to promise; speaking sweet words meaning nothing or evil.

ཁ་འཇམ་གཏིང་ཁག *kha-ḥjam gtiṅ-khag*=ཁ་འཇམ་གཏིང་ནག *kha-ḥjam gtiṅ-nag* ཁ་ནས་སྣ་པོ་ཟེར་གཏིང་ལ་སེམས་ངན་པ soft and polite in language but evil at heart.

ཁ་འཇལ་བ *kha-ḥjal-wa* to measure.

ཁ་འཇུག་པ *kha ḥjug-pa* to interfere; to meddle with; meddlesome.

ཁ་རྗེ *kha-rje* देव, पुष्कर the chief of the clouds; cloud-god. Acc. to *Cs.* great lord, mighty personage; good luck, good fortune; acc. to *Jä.* fortune, good, wealth.

ཁ་རྗེ་ཁྱུ་མཆོག *kha-rje khyu-mchog*=བསོད་ནམས *bsod-nams* पुण्य merit, moral virtue (*Mṅon.*).

ཁ་རྗེ་ཅན *kha-rje-can*=བསོད་ནམས་ཅན *bsod-nams can* possessed of moral merit; virtuous (*Mṅon.*).

ཁ་རྗེ་ཆེ *kha-rje che* very powerful; also high moral merit: ང་སྤུན་མིང་སྲིང་རྣམས་མེད་ན་དེ་རིང་རང་ཁ་རྗེ་ཆེ་ཡང if we brother and sister were not here, would you have been powerful to-day? (*A. 18*).

ཁ་ཉན་པ *kha ñan-pa* or ཁ་ལ་ཉན་པ *kha-la ñan-pa* to obey; ཁ་ཉན་པོ *kha ñan-po* obedient.

ཁ་ཉུང *kha-ñuṅ* sparing of words; laconic (*Sch.*): ཁ་ཉུང་ལག་གཙང *kha-ñuṅ lag-tsaṅ*, ཁ་མང་པོ་མི་ལབ་མཁན་དང་ཀུན་མ་མ་རྐུ་བ is one who does not speak many words and who does not act the thief.

ཁ་ཉོག *kha-ñog*, v. ཁ་ནོག *kha-nog*.

ཁ་མཉམ *kha-mñam*=སྐད་མཉམ *skad-mñam* of equal, *i.e.*, same words or opinion: ལྷོ་མཉམ་ཟས་ནས་ཁ་མཉམ་ལབ་པ if (you) eat together (you) should agree in speech.

ཁ་རྙིང *kha-rñiṅ* old or second-hand articles.

ཁ་བརྙོངས *kha-brñoṅs*, སེམས་ལ་མེད་པའི་ཁ་ལ་མཛེས་པོ *sems-la med-paḥi kha-la mdses-po* bad at heart, but very polite in expression (*Ṅag. 10*).

ཁ་སྙོམས *kha-sñoms* of same height; also of level surface: མཐོ་དམན་ཁ་འདྲ་འདྲ་སྙོམས་པ they were equal in height; བསིལ་རི་ཁ་སྙོམས་པའི་ཁོངས་སྐྱིབས་ན *bsil-ri kha-sñoms-paḥi khoṅs-skyibs-na* in a sheltered corner or cleft of cool mountains of level surface (*Ya-sel. 35.*).

ཁ་ཏ *kha-ta* or ཁ་ལྟ *kha-lta* good advice; lesson; ཁ་ཏ་བྱེད་པ *kha-ta byed-pa* or འཇོག་པ *ḥjog-pa* to give advice; མི་ངན་པ་ལ་ཁ་ལྟ་མི་བྱེད་པ not to give advice to a bad man (*Jig.*).

ཁ་ཏམ་ག *kha tam-ga*, ཁ་ཏྭ *kha-twa*, v. ཁ་ཊྭཾ་ག *kha-ṭbam-ga*, a club or staff with a skull at the top, the weapon of S'iva, also carried by ascetics; a trident; ཁ་ཏཾ་ག *kha tam-ga* a *Tantrik* club or staff with a skull at the top, v. ཁ་ཊྭཾ་ག *kha-ṭwam ga*, trident; the *Tantrik* staff with three skulls piled one above another at the top, the lowest one resting on a pot. This was originally introduced into Tibet by Padma Sambhava.

ཁ་ཏིག *kha-tig* bitter; bitter taste, v. ཁ་བ I: *kha-wa*.

ཁ་ཏོ་ཤིང *kha-to çiṅ* is said to be same as གསལ་ཤིང *gsal-çiṅ*, a pointed stake used for the execution of criminals (*Jä.*).

ཁ་ཏོན *kha-ton* or ཁ་འདོན *kha-ḥdon* स्वाध्याय, अनुपठ a reading or reciting from memory with a loud voice; ཀློག་གམ་ཁ་ཏོན་དུ་ནས reading or saying by heart; ཁ་ཏོན་དུ་ཤེས་པ *kha ton-du çes-pa* to know by heart; ཁ་ཏོན་བྱང་བ *kha-ton byañ-wa* वचसा परिजिता (पर्य्यञ्चिता) a clear recitation of prayer or hymns. Also explained as དཔེ་ཆ་ལྟ་མ་དགོས་པར་བློ་ལ་བཟུང་བའི་ཆོས་འདོན་པར་བྱེད་པ to recite religious tracts from memory, without having recourse to books: གཙུག་ལག་བལྟ་ཞིང་ཁ་ཏོན་བྱེད་པ "by looking at scientific works to commit to memory" (*A. 3*).

ཁ་གཏད་པ *kha gtad-pa*, same as ཁ་སྤྲད་པ *kha sprad-pa* or ར་སྤྲད་པ *ra-sprad-pa* 1. to bring together personally; to confront: འགྲོ་མ་ནུས་པར་རྟ་རང་ཁ་གཏད་འདོན་པས *hgro ma-nus-par rta rañ kha-gtad hdon pas* (*Yig.*) not being able to go, (he) let the horse go towards you. 2. to turn one's face.

ཁ་གཏམ *kha-gtam*, resp. ཞལ་གཏམ *shal-gtam*, oral tradition.

ཁ་གཏུགས་པ *kha gtugs-pa*=ཁ་ལ་ཧོ་གཏུགས *kha la ho gtugs-pa* or ཁ་ལ་ཧོ་བྱེད་པ *kha-la ho byed-pa* to kiss.

ཁ་གཏོང་བ *kha gtoñ-wa* to injure; to abuse; to call names.

ཁ་བཏགས *kha-btags* anything that is put on the face, *i.e.*, presented or placed before a person for his acceptance; hence that ubiquitous article of Tibetan social intercourse, the presentation or salutation scarf. These scarves are of various descriptions. The longest and the best ones are presented to the great lamas, high officials, and to other personages; they carry respect according to their quality, colour and length. There are different sorts of ཁ་བཏགས *kha-btags* (silk presentation scarves)—ཁ་བཏགས་ལ་ཕྱི་མཛོད་ནང་མཛོད་ཉིན་བདེ་མ *kha-btags-la phyi-mdsod, nañ-mdsod, ñin-bde-ma,* བསོད་བཏགས *bsod-btags,* ཚེ་ལྷ་མོ *tshe-lha-mo* or ཨ་ཤེ་ལྔ་སྦགས་བརྒྱད་སྦགས་བཅུ་སྦགས་སོགས་སྣ་ཚོགས་ཡོད *a çe lña-sbags brgyad-sbags, bcu-sbags, sogs sna-tshogs yod.*

ཁ་སྟན *kha-stan* a soft thin rug that is spread on a cushion; a cover for a cushion or couch.

ཁ་སྟེང་དུ *kha sten-du* above; besides; on; upon; at; towards: དེའི་ཁ་སྟེང་དུ་བཞུགས *dehi kha-steñ-du shugs* he sat upon it (*Pag. 64.*)

ཁ་སྟོང *kha-stoñ* not yet having eaten anything; lit. empty mouth.

ཁ་སྟོམས་རྒྱབ་པ *kha-stoms rgyab-pa* is defined as གཅིག་གིས་གཅིག་ལ་དོན་བདག་མེད་པར་ཁ་མ་ལེགས་པ་འཐབ་པ, to revile one another for no purpose.

ཁ་ཐྭམ་ག *kha tbam-ga*, ལྷ་ཡི་ཕྱག་མཚན *lha-yi phyag mtshan*, v. ཁ་ཊམ་ག *kha-tam-ga.*

ཁ་ཐལ *kha-thal*=ཐུག་ཐལ *thug-thal* or ཐུག་རྩམ *thug rtsam* rice or barley particles.

ཁ་ཐལ་བ *kha thal-wa*=ཁ་འཆེ་བ *kha hche-wa* to promise (*Cs.*).

ཁ་ཐི *kha-thi* a kind of satin in variegated colours.

ཁ་ཐུག *kha-thug* to the brim=གདོང་ཐུག *gdoñ-thug*: ཁ་ཐུག་སྐོང་བ *kha-thug skoñ-wa* to fill to the brim; ཁ་ནང *kha-nañ* the inside brim ཁ་ཐུག་པ *kha thug-pa* to meet in a contest, in concert with.

ཁ་ཐོག *kha-thog* top or surface; upon a thing=ཐོག་ཁ *thog-kha* on the roof, on the upper flat.

ཁ་ཐོར *kha-thor* pustules in the mouth (*Sch.*).

ཁ་མཐུན *kha-mthun*, v. ཁ་འཆམ *kha-cham.*

ཁ་མཐུན་པ *kha-mthun-pa*=ཁ་ཐུག་པ *kha-thug-pa* agreeing upon, unanimous; also together with: ཕོ་བྲང་གི་མི་རྣམས་ཁ་མཐུན་པས་ཞུས་པ, in concert with the men of the palace they petitioned (*Pag. 275*).

ཁ་འཐབ *kha-hthab* 1. regulating of stores by equalizing their quantities: ཡོ་བྱད་སོགས་མང་ཉུང་འདྲ་འདྲ་བྱེད་པ་ལ *yo-byed sogs mañ ñuñ hdra hdra byed-pa la,* རྙིང་པའི་ཆད་དང་གསར་སྤྱོད་ལ་འཐབ

རྙིང་པ་ rñiñ-paḥi chad daṅ gsar sprod-la ḥthab byed-pa (Rtsii.). 2. ཁ་འཐབ་པ་ kha ḥthab-pa= གཡུལ་སྤྲོད་པ་ gyul sprod pa or དམག་འཐབ་པ་ dmag ḥthab-pa to fight; to give battle (Mñon.).

ཁ་འཐེན་བཏང་བ་ *kha-ḥthen btañ-wa*=ལོན་བཏང་བ་ *lon btañ-wa* to send a reply, to reply; ཁ་འཐེན་པ་ *kha ḥthen-pa* (to pull the mouth) to stop a beast of draught.

ཁ་འཐོར་པ་ *kha-ḥthor-pa*=སོ་སོར་འབྲལ་བ་ *so-sor ḥbral-wa*, གྱེས་པ་ *gyes-pa* to scatter, to separate one from another; also disordered, confused, confusion: དཔེ་ཆ་ཁ་འཐོར་བ་ a book, the leaves of which have become mixed up together; གནས་ན་ཁ་འཐོར་ཙམ་ཞིག་མཆིས at the place there were a few scattered ones only (*A.* 23); དུད་འགྲོ་ལ་ཕྱིངས་གནས་དང་ཁ་འཐོར་བ་གཉིས་ཡོད among the beasts there are two classes: those that live secluded and those that are scattered (in abodes of men and gods).

ཁ་དག *kha-dag* swept clean, cleared up, entirely gone: ནོར་ཕྱུགས་ཐམས་ཅད་ཁ་དག་སོང *nor phyugs thams-cad kha-dag soñ* his wealth and cattle have all disappeared.

ཁ་དིག *kha-dig* or ཁ་ལྡིག *kha-ldig* to stammer; ཁ་ལྡིག་མཁན *kha-ldig-mkhan* a stammerer.

ཁ་དུག་ཅན *kha dug-can* विषमुख, विषास्य poisonous mouth; having poison in the mouth.

ཁ་དུམ་པ *kha dum-pa* being in concert with; having agreed.

ཁ་དུལ་པོ *kha-dul-po* (soft mouth) manageable; tractable.

ཁ་དོག *kha-dog* or ཁ་མདོག *kha-mdog*=མདངས *mdañs* colour: སྐྲ་མཐོན་མཐིང་གེ་ཁ་དོག་ཏུ་གྱུར་ཏོ the hair became blue-black; ཁ་དོག་གི་གཟུགས *kha-dog-gi gzugs* वर्णरूप; ཁ་དོག་མཐུན་པ *kha-dog mthun-pa* of one uniform colour: དགེ་སློང་ཆོས་གོས་གསུམ་ཁ་དོག་མཐུན་པར་གསོལ་པ *dge-sloñ chos-gos gsum kha-dog mthun-par gsol-pa* he wears the three garments of a monk of uniform colour. ཁ་དོག་སྒྱུར་བ *kha-dog sgyur wa* to change colour; ཁ་དོག་འགྱུར the colour changes (*Jä.*).

ཁ་དོག་དཀར་པོ *kha-dog dkar-po*=དག་བྱེད *dag-byed* or རྩྭ་ཀུ་ཤ *rtsba ku-ça* the cleanser, purifier; also a name for the *dub* grass (*Mñon.*).

ཁ་དོག་ངན་པ *kha-dog ñan-pa* दुर्वर्णा of disagreeable or bad color.

ཁ་དོག་ཆེན་པོ *kha-chen-po* metaph.=གསེར *gser* gold (*Mnoñ.*).

ཁ་དོག་ལྟ་བུ *kha-dog lta-bu* or ཁ་དོག་འདྲ་བ *kha-dog ḥdra-wa dog lta-bu* in colour; like its colour.

ཁ་དོག་སྣ་ཚོགས *kha-dog sna-tshogs* variety of colours; of different hues: ཁ་དོག་སྣ་ཚོགས་མུ་ཏིག་རབ་ཡིན་ནོ *kha-dog sna-tshog mu-tig rab yin-no* an excellent pearl is of a variety of colours (*Loñ.* ༥ *2.*).

ཁ་དོག་པ *kka-dog-pa* small hole or narrow hole.

ཁ་དོག་མཐའ་ཡས་པ *kha-dog mthaḥ yas-pa* अनन्तवर्ण variegated colours.

ཁ་དོག་གསུམ་པ *kha-dog gsum-pa* explained as ཤིང་བ་གླང་རྨིག་པའི་མིང་ *çiñ ba-glañ rmig-paḥi miñ* a name for the tree called the ox-hoof (*Mñon.*).

ཁ་དྲག *kha-drag* बल mighty, haughty; ཁ་དྲག་པ loquacious, talkative.

ཁ་དྲང་ *kha-drañ* just before; straight on.

ཁ་དྲོ *kha-dro* in *Khams* and *Amdo* signifies བཀྲ་ཤིས *bkra-çis* auspicious, of good omen or appearance.

ཁ་དྲོ་བོ *kha dro-bo*=ཁ་འཕྲོད་པོ *kha hphrod-po* agreeable, amiable, of pleasant company.

ཁ་གདངས་པ *kha gdañs-pa* विजृम्भण, जृम्भण yawning; opening the mouth; gaping; widening the mouth: ཁ་གདངས་ནས *kha-gdañs nas* having opened the mouth widely.

ཁ་མདོག *kha-mdog*, v. ཁ་དོག *kha-dog.*

ཁ་འདར *kha-ḥdar* one who speaks too fast or too loud.

ཁ་འདིག *kha-ḥdig* cork, bung, stopple.

ཁ་འདེབས *kha-ḥdebs*=ཁ་གཅིག་ཏུ་མཐུན་པ *kha gcig-tu mthun-pa* agreeing in an account.

ཁ་འདོན *kha-ḥdon*, v. ཁ་ཏོན *kha-ton.*

ཁ་འདོན་བྱེད་པ *kha-ḥdon byed-pa* to recite or mutter a charm or *mantra.*

ཁ་རྡ *kha-rda* muttering, whispering: ཁ་བརྡ་བཟང་པོ་བྱེད to mutter or speak auspiciously.

ཁ་བརྡ *kha-brda* conversation, talk, prophecy, prediction; it also signifies བཤད་པ་བཟང་པོ *bçad-pa bzañ-po* good explanation or utterance: བསྟན་པ་དར་བར་འགྱུར་རོ་ཞེས་པའི་ཁ་བརྡ་བཟང་པོ "may the doctrine (of Buddha) prosper" such was his righteous utterance (*A. 146*).

ཁ་བརྡའ *kha-brdaḥ*=སྐད་ཆ *skad-cha* verbal utterance: བུ་མོའི་མིག་མཐོང་ཡང་མ་མཐོང་བ་ལྟར་བྱས་ནས་ཁ་བརྡའ་མི་བྱེད although he had beheld the girl's eyes, he acted as if he had not seen her and gave no spoken sign.

ཁ་སྡམས *kha-sdams*=ཁ་ཏ *kha-ta* or གདམས་ཁ *gdams-kha* advice.

ཁ་སྡོམ་པ *kha sdom-pa*=ཁ་མནན་པ *kha mnan-pa* to silence; to gag or stop the speech.

✝ ཁ་ཌ་ག *kha-da-ga* खड्ग the scimitar or sabre of the Hindus.

ཁ་ན་མ་ཐོ་བ *kha-na ma-tho-wa*, lit. ཁ་ནས་མ་ཐོན་པ *kha nas ma thon-pa*, not confessed, *i.e.*, not come out of the mouth; अवद्य also वद्य, a metaphysical term defined as སྡིག་པ་དང་ཉེས་པའི་མིང, a name for sin and moral corruption. There are two kinds, viz., (1) རང་བཞིན་གྱི་ཁ་ན་མ་ཐོ་བ *rañ bshin-gyi kha-na ma-tho-wa* sins which are committed naturally and semi-consciously; (2) བཅས་པའི་ཁ་ན་མ་ཐོ་བ *bcas-pahi kha na ma tho-wa* sins of overt violation of law or religion. མི་ཁྱིམ་པ་དང་རབ་བྱུང་ཕལ་ཆེར་དང་གི་སྡིག་པ་ཉེས་པ་ཁོང་དུ་སྦས་ན་ཁ་ནས་མ་ཐོན་པས་ཁ་ན་མ་ཐོ་བ་ཞེས་པའོ Householders and monks in general, in keeping these sins and failings concealed, because they do not issue forth from the mouth, such are styled *kha-na-ma-tho-wa.* ཁ་ན་མ་ཐོ་བ་མི་མངའ་བ *kha-na ma tho-wa mi mñaḥ-wa* निरवद्य the sinless; ཁ་ན་མ་ཐོ་བ་མེད་པ *kha na ma tho-wa med-pa* अनवद्य without sin or moral corruption; ཁ་ན་མ་ཐོའི་གཏམ *kha-na-ma thoḥi gtam*=གཏམ་དང་རྩེས་སུ་འབྲེལ་བའི་མིང sinful or blasphemous speech.

ཁ་ནག་པོ *kha nag-pa*=མུན་པ་ནག་པོ *mun-pa nag-po* darkness; also of gloomy appearance; morose; wicked (*Mñon.*).

ཁ་ནང *kha-nañ* yesterday morning. But ཁ་ནང་དུ་བལྟས *kha-nañ-du bltas* अन्तर्मुखप्रवृत्त: to look inwardly: ཁ་ནང་བལྟས་ཀྱི་ཤེས་པ་ནི་རང་གི་སེམས་ལ་བཟང་ངན་དགེ་མི་དགེ་ཇི་ལྟར་འདུག་ལེགས་པར་བརྟགས་ཏེ་སྤང་བླང་བྱེད་པའོ the knowledge gained by introspection, which is carefully to examine how much of good or evil and virtue or vice exists in one's own heart, causes rejection (of evil) and acceptance (of good).

ཁ་ནད *kha nad* mouth disease.

ཁ་ནར་ཅན *kha nar-can* oblong.

ཁ་ནས *kha-nas* orally; by word of mouth; ཁ་ནས་ཁུ་བྱུག a cuckoo; also to cry or call like the cuckoo; ཁ་ནས་ཟེར་བ *kha-nas zer-wa* to speak colloquially.

ཁ་ཉིང *kha-niñ* last year.

ཁ་ཉིམ *kha-nim*=རས་ཡོལ་སོགས་ཀྱི་ཁ་མདོག་གཉིས་པ of cotton cloth, etc.; that having two colours (*Rtsii.*).

ཁ་ནོག *kha-nog* or ཁ་ཉོག *kha-ñog* clamourous; asking often and often for a thing, etc.: ཉེ་འཐོགས་དང་ཁ་ནོག་དང་ཐོག་བབས་དང་བཅས་རིམ་པ་གསུམ་པ the three may be classed together, (namely) defilement, importunity, and being stricken by lightning (*Rtsii.*).

ཁ་ནོར་སོང་ *kha-nor soṅ* he has erred in conversation.

ཁ་མནན་པ *kha mnan-pa*=ཁ་སྡོམ་པ *kha sdom-pa* to obstruct the speech; also to coerce, to silence.

ཁ་པ *kha-pa* the volume marked with the letter ཁ *kha*, *i.e.*, the 2nd volume. Anything (book or article) marked with the letter ཁ *kha*.

ཁ་པོ *kha-po* sometimes=ཁ *kha* speech, *e.g.*, ཁ་པོ་དུལ་མོ mild speech and polished language.

ཁ་པོ་ཆེ *kha-po-che*=ཁ་རྒྱག་པ *kha rgyag-pa* or ཁ་མང་པོ *kha maṅ-po* talking much: རྩི་གེ་སྲེག་ཤོར་ཟེར་བའི་ཁ་ཕོ་ཆེ *rtsi-ge sreg-çor zer-wahi kha pho-che* a shrew called *Rtsi-ge sreg-çor*, who was very talkative (*Rdsa. 31*).

ཁ་ལྤགས *kha-lpags*=ཁལ་པགས *khal-pags* lip.

ཁ་སྤུ *kha-spu* hair of the face; whiskers.

ཁ་ཕོ *kha-pho* boasting: ཁ་ཕོ་ཆེ *kha-pho-che* one who boasts much; also boasting much.

ཁ་ཕོག *kha-phog* verbal reproof.

ཁ་ཕོར *kha-phor* सरक; सारक a cup; a saucer.

ཁ་ཕྱི *kha-phyi* the outer edge.

ཁ་ཕྱིན་པ *kha phyin-pa*=གྲོས་མཐུན་པ *gros mthun-pa* unanimity in a conference; unanimous vote.

ཁ་ཕྱིར་ལྟ *kha-phyir lta*=ཕ་རོལ་ཏུ་ཁ་ཕྱོགས་པ *pha-rol-tu kha phyogs-pa* examining by appearances; also to look outside (*Mṅon.*): ཁ་ཕྱིར་བལྟས་ཀྱི་ཤེས་པ *kha-phyir bltas kyi çes-pa* knowing or judging things by their external appearance.

ཁ་ཕྱིས *kha-phyis* napkin.

ཁ་ཕྱེ་བ *kha phye-wa*=ཁ་རྒྱས་པ *kha rgyas-pa* कुसुमित, उज्जृम्भ 1. to bloom or blossom; also well developed, full blown. 2.=ཁ་འབྱེད་པ *kha hbyed-pa* जृम्भण to yawn.

ཁ་ཕྱོགས *kha-phyogs*=ཁ་ལྟ་བའི་ཕྱོགས *kha lta-wahi phyogs* the direction of one's sight.

ཁ་འཕང་བ *kha-hphaṅ-wa*=ཁ་འབུམ་དཀྲུག་པ to divulge; spread ill rumours (*Jä.*).

ཁ་འཕྱུར *kha-hphyur* खारवर्ष a solid measure for grain like བྲེ *bre* द्रोण; or འབོ *hbo*.

ཁ་འཕྲོད་པོ *kha hphrod-po*, v. ཁ་དྲོ་བོ *kha dro-bo*.

ཁ་བ I: *kha-wa* तिक्त bitter; ཁ་ཏིག *kha-tig* from ཁ་བ and ཏིག་ཏ bitter, *i.e.*, of very bitter taste: རོ་ཁ་བ *ro kha-wa* bitter taste; ཁ་མངར *kha-mṅar* bitter and sweet; ཁ་མོ *kha-mo* bitter: ཆང་ཁ་མོ *chaṅ kha-mo* beer that is very strong or of bitter taste.

ཁ་བ II: =གངས *gaṅs* हिम snow: ཁ་བ་དུང་ལྟར་གསལ *kha-wa duṅ ltar gsal* the snow (was) unsullied as shells; ཁ་བ་སྐྱེ *kha-wa skye* हिमज, शीत, वरुण snow-born or ocean-god; ཁ་གོང *kha-goṅ*=ཁ་བའི་གོང་རིལ snow ball; ཁ་ཆར *kha-char* snow and rain; ཁ་མ་ཆར *kha-ma char* sleet; ཁ་བ་ཅན *Kha-wa-can* हिमवत् Tibet, the snowy country: ཁ་བ་ཅན་གྱི་ཡུལ the country of snow, or snowy country; ང་ཡི་དུས་ནི་ལོ་བརྒྱ་ན་ཁ་བ་ཅན་གྱི་མཚོ་སྐྱི་ནས 100 years (after) my time the snowy lakes of Tibet becoming dry; ཁ་བ་ཅ་ཏ་ཀ a swallow, prob. snow-swallow. ཁ་བའི་རྡུལ *kha-wahi rtul* हिमसञ्च, हिमधूलि lumps of snow: ཁ་བའི་ཕྱེ་མ *kha-wahi phye-ma* हिमवालुका snow dust; flakes of snow; also camphor, कर्पूर; ཁ་འབབ *kha-hbab* or ཁ་བ་འབབ *kha-wa hbab* snow-fall, avalanche; ཁ་བའི་མིང་ཅན having the name of snow; ཁ་བའི་འོད हिमद्युति glare from the snow, snowy lustre.

ཁ་བ་དཀར་པོ *Kha-wa dkar-po* n. of an important religious institution in *Khams*.

ཁ་བ་རི་པ *kha-wa ri-pa*=གངས་ལྗོངས་པ *Gaṅs-ljoṅs-pa* a Tibetan; one residing in the snowy mountains (*Yig. k. 6*).

ཁ་བད་ I: *kha-baḏ* the architectural ornament of a Tibetan house formed by the projecting ends of the beams which support the roof.

ཁ་བད་ II: the humidity of the air caused by snow (*Jä.*).

ཁ་བར་བྱེད་=རེག་བཟང་ *kha-war byeḏ*=*reg-ḇzañ* of soft or pleasant touch (*M̱ñon.*).

ཁ་བུ *kha-bu* or ཁ་བུབ་པ *kha bub-pa* being turned downwards: བདག་སྡིག་པའི་གཡང་ལ་ཁ་བུབ་ཏུ་ལྷུངས I have fallen headlong into the abyss of sin (*Pag. 185*).

ཁ་བྱང *kha-byañ* अधःकृतमुख, कृतमुख with the face downwards; learned, wise.

ཁ་བྱེ་བ *kha bye-wa* विकसित in bloom.

ཁ་བྲག *kha-brag* (*kha-ṭag*) forked rocks; any forked object; also as adj. ལོ་ཁ་བྲག *Lo-kha-brag*, the mountainous wild country N. E. of Bhutan inhabited by wild tribes.

ཁ་བྲལ *kha-bral* (*kha-ṭal*) विश्लेष divorce, separation, especially of lovers or husband and wife.

ཁ་དབང་ *kha-ḏwañ* eloquent: ཁ་དབང་ཆོག *kha-ḏwañ-chog* able to speak powerfully, eloquent (*Ñag. 11*).

ཁ་དབྲག *kha-ḏbrag* literally the mouth-split: ཆུ་ཁ་དབྲག *chu kha-ḏbrag* a river which is divided or branched out; ལམ་ཁ་དབྲག a road which is branched into several paths; ཤིང་གི་ཡལ་ག་ཁ་དབྲག the branch of a tree which divides into several parts; རྨིག་པ་ཁ་དབྲག *ṟmig-pa kha-ḏbrag* a hoof which is bifurcated or split.

ཁ་འབར་མ *Kha ẖbar-ma* ज्वालामुखी n. of a goddess (*Ṟtsii.*). In the Hindu pantheon Jvālāmukhī (she with a burning or glowing mouth) is worshipped as the goddess of cholera.

ཁ་འབུ་བ *kha-ẖbu-wa*, the opening of the buds of flowers.

ཁ་འབུབ་ཏུ་ཉལ་བ *kha-ẖbub-tu ñal-wa* to lie with one's face downwards.

ཁ་འབུས་པ *kha-ẖbus-pa* कोरक, कुड्मलक-जात unblown flower, buds.

ཁ་འབྱེད་པ *kha ẖbyed-pa*=ཁ་ཕྱེ་བ *kha-phye-wa* to open a cover or pasted letter or packed article; is also used of books.

ཁ་འབྲི་བ *kha ẖbri-wa* (*kha-ḏi-wa*) to make less, to diminish; to detract from (in quality).

ཁ་སྦྱང *kha-s̱byañ* eloquence; ཁ་སྦྱང་པོ *kha s̱byañ-po* eloquent.

ཁ་སྦྱར *kha-s̱byar* or ཁ་སྦྱར་བ *kha s̱byar-wa* the mouth of a vessel or box closed or shut up: ཟངས་ཆེན་ཁ་སྦྱར་རིན་ཆེན་སིལ་མས་བཀང་ *zañs-chen kha-s̱byar rin-chen sil-mas ḇkañ* a covered copper vessel filled with precious things, etc. (*G kaẖ. 77*).

* ཁ་སྦྱོར་ཐིག་ལེ *kha-s̱byor*=*thig-le* संपुट-तिलक n. pr. (*Schr. Tā. 2, 275*).

ཁ་སྦྱོར *kha s̱byor* दशनोच्छिष्ट, सम्भुक्त anything that is left after eating or has been touched by the mouth but not eaten; ཁ་སྦྱོར་བ to kiss.

ཁ་སྦྱོར་བདུན་ལྡན=རྡོ་རྗེ་འཆང་ *kha-s̱byor ḇdun-ḻdan*=*Ṟdo-ṟje ẖchañ*, the *Tantrik* Buddha Vajradhara (*M̱ñon.*).

ཁ་མ་འཆམ *kha ma-ẖcham*=ཁ་མི་མཐུན *kha mi-m̱thun* discordant; ཁ་མི་འཆམ *kha mi-ẖcham* does not agree or live in harmony.

ཁ་མ་ཕྱེ་བ *kha ma-phye-wa* कुड्मल an opening bud; one of the twenty-one hells in which sinners are punished, being bound with ropes.

ཁ་མ་བྱེ *kha-ma bye* कोष a store or repository (*Lex.*).

ཁ་མི་ཤེས་པ *khami-çes-pa* not knowing the language.

ཁ་མུར *kha-mur* bit (of a bridle).

ཁ་མེད *kha-med* silent; cannot reply: ལབ་ན་ཁ་མེད, བཏོན་ན་རྒྱུ་མེད *lab-na kha-med, bton-na rgyu med* if asked there is no reply; if ransacked, nothing to produce (from one's pocket); ཁ་མེད་ལྐུགས་པ, ལྕེ་མེད་རེག་པ (the common saying is) "the dumb does not speak, the tongueless stammers."

ཁ་མོ *kha-mo* enchantment; irresistible influence.

ཁ་དམར *kha-dmar* lit. "red mouth"; a demon or *preta*; a ghostly apparition. This word is used in astrology and the medical works of Tibet to signify an affirmative prediction, good or bad. When such a prediction is realized it is called ཁ་དམར་ཕོག *kha-dmar phog*, when otherwise it is called ཁ་དམར་ཏོག *kha-dmar tog*.

ཁ་རྩང *kha-rtsañ*=ཁ་སང *kha sañ* yesterday forenoon: ཁ་རྩང་གི་བྱིས་པ the boy that was here yesterday forenoon (*A.*); also the day before yesterday; ཁར་སང་གཟའ་ཉི་མ *kar-sañ gzah ñi-ma* last Sunday (*Jä.*).

ཁ་རྩོད *kha-rtsod* disputation.

ཁ་ཚ *kha-tsha* bitter and acrid; hot in the mouth; pungent like pepper; acc. to *Jä.* (*a*) a very acrid sort of radish; (*b*) aphthæ thrush, a disease of the mouth incident to horses, cows, sheep, &c.; (*c*) ཁ་ཚ་རིང་ངེ་བ *kha-tsha riñ-ñe-wa* daily warm food.

ཁ་ཚར *kha-tshar* 1. fringes, such as the threads at the end of a web or cloth or rug, scarf or sash. 2. minor ingredients in a medicinal mixture: སྨན་གཅིག་གཙོ་བོ་བྱས་ནས་དེ་ལ་སྨན་གཞན་གཅིག་ཉུང་སྙད་བསྐྱབ་པ་ལ་ཁ་ཚར་བསྐྱབ་ཟེར having made one drug the principal ingredient, on adding thereto another drug in less quantity, it is called adding the *kha-tshar*.

ཁ་ཚུབ *kha-tshub* snow-storm.

ཁ་ཚོ *kha-tsho* boasting: ཁ་ཚོ་ཤིན་ཏུ་ཆེ་བ *kha tsho çin-tu che-wa* a great swaggerer (*Jä.*).

ཁ་ཚོད *kha-tshod* the weighing: ཁ་ཚོད་བལྟ་ཕྱིར་ཚིག་གི་ལན་སྨྲས་པ *kha-tshod, blta-phyir tshig-gi lan smras-pa* (*A. 6*) considering one's expression with a view to reply to it. (ཚིག་གང་འདྲ་ལབ་ཡོང་ཚོད་ལྟ་བ *tshig gañ-hdra lab-yoñ tshod lta-wa.*)

ཁ་ཚོན *kha-tshon*=ཁ་འགྲིག *kha-hgrig*, ཁ་འཆམ *kha-hcham* or ཁ་མཐུན *kha-mthun* unanimous, of one voice or opinion. Generally used with གཅོད་པ, meaning 1. as in ཐམས་ཅད་མཐུན་པར་དམ་པར་ཁ་ཚོན་བཅད (*A. 3*), all unanimously and firmly agreed upon; lit. ཁ་ཚོན *kha-tshon* colour; hence to be all of one colour in the face, *i.e.*, to be of the same opinion. 2. =ཐག་གཅོད་པ *thag gcod-pa* a final decision or resolution: ཀུན་གྱིས་རྒྱལ་སྲིད་སྤོང་བར་ཁ་ཚོན་བཅད (*A. 15*) they all resolved to forsake their kingdoms; མཐའ་གཅིག་ཏུ་ཁ་ཚོན་ཆོད་དཀའ *mthah gcig-tu kha-tshon chod dkah* it is difficult to arrive at a final decision. 3. surface or width (*Jä.*).

ཁ་མཚུལ *kha-mtshul* तुण्ड muzzle; mouth; the lower part of the human face.

ཁ་འཚངས་པ *kha htshañs-pa*=སྨོད་པ *smod-pa* to slander; to curse (*Mñon.*).

ཁ་འཚོག *kha-htshog* abuse: ཁ་འཚོག་ཆེན་པོ *kha-htshog chen-po* a great abuser, a reviler.

ཁ་འཛིན *kha-hdsin* कोकिल the cuckoo.

ཁ་འཛིན་བྱེད་པ *kha-hdsin byed-pa* to receive in a friendly spirit; to be kind; to assist (*Jä.*); also to govern; ཁ་འཛིན་པར་མཛད་པ

sent or commissioned for governing (*Ḏsam. 25*).

ཁ་འཛིན་གསུམ *kha-ḥdsin gsum* are the following three: སུག་སྨེལ *sug-smel* त्रिपुट small cardamom, *Convolvulus turpetthum*; གུར་གུམ *gur-gum* saffron; and པི་པི་ལིང *pi-pi-liṅ* long pepper (*Sman. 450*).

ཁ་འཛུམ་པ *kha ḥdsum-pa* to shut the mouth.

ཁ་ཞན *kha-shan* of inferior quality or of low position: ཁ་ཞན་པའི་སྡུག་བསྔལ the misfortune of being of low birth (*Jä.*).

ཁ་ཞུར *kha-shur* water-hen (*Sch.*).

ཁ་ཞེ *kha-she* mouth and mind: ཁ་ཞེ་མི་མཚུངས་པ *kha-she mi mchuṅs-pa* hypocrisy; hypocrite; ཁ་ཞེ་མེད་པ *kha-she med-pa* unfeigned; sincere.

ཁ་ཞེང *kha-sheṅ* breadth, expanse, *e.g.*, of the heavens.

ཁ་ཞེན *kha-shen*=*kha-lab shan-pa* modest in speech; also not able to speak well.

ཁ་ཞེས *kha-shes* food, victuals (*Cs.*).

ཁ་ཟམ *kha zam*, ཁ་ཆེ་ཟམ *kha-che zam* a kind of chintz from Kāshmir; also a kind of cloth or silk stuff in variegated colours: བལ་ཟམ *bal zam* chintz from Nepal.

ཁ་ཟས *kha-zas* food, either in general or some particular article of food: ཁ་ཟས་ལ་བརྐམ་པར་གྱུར *kha-zas la brkam-par gyur* he longed for food; ཁ་ཟས་གཙང་མ *kha-zas gtshaṅ-ma* clean food, or clean in (taking food). In Sikk. *khabze* sweet cakes, etc.

ཁ་ཟུམ་པ *kha zum-pa* to close the mouth or any opening.

‡ ཁ་ཟུར *kha-zur* or ཁ་སུར *kha-sur* खर्जूर the date fruit.

ཁ་ཟེར་བ *kha zer-wa* मुखर loquacious.

ཁ་གཟར *kha-gzar* spoon or ladle.

ཁ་གཟི *kha-gzi* or ཁ་གཟེ *kha-gze* in *W.* rake in gardening; in Spiti a carrier's load; *kha ze-pa* a coolie (*Jä.*).

ཁ་བཟང *kha-bzaṅ*=ཚིག་གི་གཏང་རག *tshig-gi gtaṅ-rag* good speech; one who speaks pleasantly (*Mṅon.*).

ཁའི་ཉིན *khaḥi-ñin* पूर्वेद्युस् the day before yesterday.

ཁ་འོག *kha-ḥog* lit. face downward; downcast; ཁ་འོག་ཏུ་བཅུག་པ *kha ḥog-tu bcug-pa* or ཆུད་པ *chud-pa* to subjugate one, or to enforce obedience upon; ཁ་འོག་ཏུ་བལྟས་ཏེ་ཤི་བ *kha ḥog-tu bltas-te çi-wa* to die falling down head-long, *i.e.*, with the face downward.

ཁ་ཡ *kha ya* lit. being one's partner or match as to speaking, but in general partner, assistant; ཁ་ཡ་བྱེད་པ *kha-ya byed-pa* to assist: ཁ་ཡི་ཡ་ང་མི་ཐུབ I am not his match, not able to compete with him; with regard to things, I am not equal to the task (*Jä.*).

ཁ་ཡིག *kha-yig* खाकार the letter ཁ, a label; a letter or writing on the cover of any parcel or letter; an inscription.

ཁ་ཡེལ *kha-yel* the spout (of a kettle or any other vessel): བུམ་པའི་ཁ་ཕྱིར་འཕྱང་བ་ཁ་ཡེལ་ལ་མཆུ་འཛིངས་པ drawing with his lips at the spout which hangs down outside the vessel (*A. 23*).

ཁ་ཡོག *kha-yog* a false charge (*Jä*): མ་ཉེ་པའི་ཁ་ཡོག་བྱུང *ma ñe-paḥi kha-yog byuṅ* (*C.*) he was unjustly accused (*Jä.*); མ་ཉེས་པར་ཀྱང་ཁ་མཆུ་དང་མི་ཁ་བྱུང་བ་སོགས་བདག་ལ་རྡུན་མེད་པའི་ཁ་ཡོག་བྱུང unfounded accusations arise such as those coming by word of mouth and by implication, though one is guiltless.

ཁ་གཡེལ *kha-gyel* wide mouth: ལྷུན་པོ་ཡོངས་རྫོགས་དབྱིབས་སྣོད་ཁ་གཡེལ་བ་འདྲ the shape of Sumeru resembled that of a vessel placed with its wide mouth upwards (*i.e.*, like a pyramid on a point) (*Ya-sel. 35*).

ཁ་གཡོགས *kha-gyogs*=ཁ་ཁེབས *kha-khebs* cover of a vessel or basket (*G. kaḥ. 77*).

ཁ་ར *kha-ra* in *W.* for ཀ་ར *ka-ra*, sugar (*Jä.*); trough; manger (*Sch.*).

ཁ་རག *Kha-rag* n. of a place in Tibet. ཁ་རག་སྒོམ་ཆུང n. of a celebrated lama of the Kādampa School of Buddhism.

ཁ་རས *kha-ras* neck-cloth; a towel.

ཁ་རི *kha-ri* or ཁ་རུ *kha-ru*, v. ཁལ་རི *khal-ri*.

ཁ་རུ་ཚྭ *kha-ru tshwa*=ཚྭ་ནག་པོ black salt used medicinally (*Mṅon.*): बचक, विड्, विड्लवण a kind of salt (procured by boiling earth impregnated with saline particles); a particular kind of salt of fetid odour (used medicinally as a tonic aperient). It is black in colour and is prepared by fusing fossil salt with a small proportion of *emblic myrobalan*, the product being muriate of soda with small quantities of muriate of lime, sulphur and oxide of iron (*M. Wills.*). *Kha-ru tshwa-yis drod skyed sbos-pa daṅ sgeg daṅ hgyiṅ khrog bad rluṅ hjoms-par byed* flatulence, accompanied with belching, rumblings, phlegm, and wind, is overcome by the medicinal salt.

Syn. རུ་ཙ་ཀ *ru-tsa ka*; སྨིན་ཚྭ *smin-tshba*; བི་ཏམ་ངོ *bi-tam ṅo* (*Mṅon.*).

ཁ་རེ་སྐྱེངས *kha-re skyeṅs*=ཁ་སྐྱེངས་པ *kha skyaṅs-pa* or ངོ་ཚ་བ *ṅo tsha-wa* to be ashamed.

ཁ་རེག་པ *kha reg-pa* to touch anything by the lips; to put one's mouth to a thing in order to eat or drink it.

ཁ་རོ *kha-ro* taste in the mouth.

ཁ་རོག *kha-rog*=ཁ་བཙུམ *kha-btsum* silent, without reply: དེ་བས་རྣ་བ་མ་ཚ་ཁ་རོག་སྡོད therefore remain silent with untingling ear! ཁ་རོག་སྡོད་ཅིག *kha-rog sdod-cig* be silent; do not speak. ཁ་རོག་པ is also freq. ཁ་རོག་ཏེ་འདུག་པ to remain silent.

ཁ་རོག་པ *kha rog-pa* तुत्थक a kind of drug, prob. sulphate of copper.

ཁ་རླངས *kha-rlaṅs* वाष्प vapour from the mouth.

ཁ་ལ་མེ་འབར *kha-la me-hbar* n. of the King of the Yi-dag or *Preta*.

ཁ་ལ་རེག་པ *kha-la reg-pa*=metaph. ཟས *zas* to eat; do eat (*K. g.* ཁ *28*).

ཁ་ལ་སླ་ཏེ་དོན་ལ་དཀའ *kha-la sla-te don-la dkah* easily spoken but difficult in meaning.

ཁ་ལན *kha-lan* mouth requital; thanksgiving; reply, especially angry reply; also requital for food received (*Jä.*): དད་ཟས་ཁ་ལན་བསམ་ངན་འདུག when disordered with evil thoughts, the food of faith is my reply (*Mil.*).

ཁ་ལས་བྱུང *kha-las byuṅ* sprung forth from the mouth.

ཁ་ལིན་པ *Kha-lin-pa* n. of a place in Tibet.

ཁ་ལེ *kha-le*, v. ཁྱ་ལེ *khya-le*.

ཁ་ལེབ *kha-leb* cover, lid.

ཁ་ལོ *kha-lo* 1. =ཁ་ཕྱོགས *kha-phyogs* towards the mouth. 2. prow of the ship (*Schr.*); according to others the helm གྲུ་གཞིང. 3. acc. to *Cs.* and *Jä.* the glans-penis.

ཁ་ལོ་སྒྱུར་པ *kha-lo sgyur-pa* or *sgyur-wa* पुरुष, सूतः; यन्ता, सारथि, चक्ता; ཁ་ལོ་སྒྱུར་མཁན *kha-lo sgyur-mkhan* one who steers; also a governor, a driver, a charioteer. See especially in narrative of early life of the Buddha in Dulwa.

ཁ་ལོ་པ *kha lo-pa*=ཁ་ཕྱོགས་པ *kha phyogs-pa* सारथि, कायाः; ཁ་ཕྱོགས་སྒྱུར་མཁན *kha phyogs sgyur-mkhan* one who leads or guides; also a shadow.

ཁ་ལོག་པ *kha-log-pa* to reply; to contradict: ཕྱི་ལ་འགྲོ་ནས་ཚུར་ཁ་ལོག་པ *phyi-la hgro-na tshur kha log-pa* walking out he returned hither.

ཁ་ཤ *kha-ça* the spotted deer (*Jä.*); elk (*Sch.*). In Sikk. the common deer of the Duars is called ཁ་ཤ. ཁ་ཤ་ཡི་ཇ་ཁུག *kha-ça-yi ja-khug* a tea bag made of deer-skin.

ཁ་ཤགས *kha-çags* jest; joke in *W.* (*Jä.*).

ཁ་ཤས *kha-ças* (sounded "*kha-she*") some; colloq. in *C.*

ཁ་ཤུགས་ཅན *kha-çugs-can* or ཁ་ཤེད་ཅན *kha shed-can* eloquent; ཁ་ཤུགས་མེད་པ *kha-çugs med-pa* one who has nothing much to say, same as སྐད་ཆ་ལབ་རྒྱུ་མེད་པ *skad-cha lab-rgyu med-pa.*

ཁ་ཤོབ *kha-çob* in colloq. lies; obscene talk; idle talk.

ཁ་ཤོར *kha-çor* breach of promise: ཁ་ཤོར་སོང *kha-çor soṅ* the mouth has run away, denoting inconsiderate talk (*Jä.*).

ཁ་ཤོལ་བ *kha-çol-wa* उपस्पर्श rinsing the mouth; sipping water and ejecting it.

‡ཁ་ཤྱ *Kha-çya* n. of a mountainous country in the north-east of India (*Tā.*); the Khasya Hills in Assam.

ཁ་གཤགས། *kha-gçags*=ཁ་རྩོད *kha-rtsod* using rough language; controversy, discussion, dispute; with *rgyag-pa* to dispute: འཛུབ་མོ་བསྒྲེངས་ཏེ་ཁ་གཤགས་རྒྱག་ཏུ་འགྲོ pointing his fingers he goes to dispute (*Rdsa. 17*).

ཁ་བཤད *kha-bçad* talk, gossip.

ཁ་སག *Kha-sag* མཐར་འཁོབ་ཀྱི་ཡུལ་ཞིག་གི་མིང་ n. of a wild country on the border of Tibet (*Ya-sel. 38*).

ཁ་སང *kha-saṅ*, v. ཁ་རྩང *kha-rtsaṅ.*

ཁ་སངས *kha-saṅs* explained as སེམས་ལ་གང་ཤར་བ་ཁ་ནས་དང་པོ་བཤད to speak one's mind; to tell honestly what has occurred in the mind.

ཁ་སུབ *kha-sub* a bribe: ཁ་སུབ་སྦྱིན་པ *kha-sub byin-pa* to offer a bribe.

ཁ་སི *Kha-si* n. of a wild hill tribe of India (of the Khasya Hills) (*Dsam.*).

ཁ་སིང *kha-siṅ* 1. the day before yesterday. 2. also=several weeks ago; sometime back.

ཁ་སུར *kha-sur*, v. ཁ་ཟུར *kha-zur.*

ཁ་སོ *kha-so* 1. abbreviation of ཁ *kha*, mouth, and སོ *so*, teeth. 2. the edge, border of a thing: ཁ་སོ་ལ་འཕང་ངོ *kha-so la hphaṅ-ṅo* =ཁ་ཁྱེར་ལ་འཕང་ངོ flung to the border (*Pag. 187*): རྫིངས་ཀྱི་ཁ་ཁྱེར་ལས་འཇའ་ལི་བྱས *rdsiṅs-kyi kha-khyer las hjah li byas*=གྲུ་རྫིངས་ཀྱི་མཐའ་ལ་ཤན་རྒྱབ *gru-rdsiṅs-kyi mthah la çan-rgyab* lined the border of the ship with iron plates (*A. 18*).

ཁ་སྲལ་ཆུང་ངུ *kha-sral chuṅ-ṅu* कल्ल deaf.

ཁ་སློབ *kha-slob*=ཁ་ཏོན *kha-ton* learning by heart; primer used by children in *W.*

ཁ་གསག *kha-gsag*, v. ཁ་བསག *kha-bsag.*

ཁ་གསར *kha-gsar* new, fresh.

ཁ་གསལ *kha-gsal* or གསལ་ཁ *gsal-kha* a message; clear language; intelligible language: ཁ་མི་གསལ་བ *kha mi-gsal-wa* obscure; not in clear terms or language.

ཁ་གསོ *kha-gso* made full by adding something more to it: བཅུད་དང་བདུད་རྩི་ཁ་གསོ་ filling with the best thing and nectar in oblation (*Rtsii.*).

ཁ་བསག *kha bsag*=ཁ་གསག *kha gsag* जल्पक talkative.

ཁ་བསྲེ་བ *kha bsre-wa* to associate with one another, viz., in drinking and smoking together.

ཁ་བསླང་དུ *kha-bslaṅ-du* turned upwards: ཁ་བསླང་བ *kha bslaṅ-pa* to lie with the face uppermost.

ཁ་བསླུས *kha-bslus* to tempt by false hopes and promises; to deceive by sweet words.

ཁ་ཧྲག *kha-hrag* forked mouth or point; the bifurcated mouth or end of anything made of iron or wood: ནུབ་ན་ཤིང་གཅིག་རྩེ་མོ་ཁ་ཧྲག་དང *nub-na çiñ-gcig rtse-mo kha-hrag dañ* in the west a tree with forked top, &c.

ཁ་ལྷག *kha-lhag* remnant of a meal.

ཁྭ *khwa* a raven: ཁྭ་སྐད་ཤེས་པའི་རིག་པ *khwa-skad çes-paḥi rig-pa* वायसविद्या the science of drawing omens from the caw of a raven.

ཁྭ་སྐྲོད་ནུས་པ *khwa skrod nus-pa* = བྱ་ཁྭ་དེད་ཐུབ་པ *bya-khwa ded thub-pa* काकवित्ताड़नासमर्थ able to scare a raven—used as attribute of Buddha; as long as a boy cannot drive away a magpie he is not considered ready (by his age) to get religious instructions.

ཁྭ་ཏ *khwa-ta* the Tibetan magpie: ཁྭ་ཏའི་ཤ་ཡིས་གདོན་ནད་སེལ་བར་བྱེད། ཁྭ་ཏའི་སྒྲོ་ཡིས་སྒྲིབ་ཤིང་བྱེད། *khwa-taḥi ça-yis gdon-nad sel-war byed, khba-taḥi sgro-yis sgrib-çiñ byed* the flesh of the magpie removes diseases caused by evil spirits; the feather of the magpie prevents the patient seeing apparitions, ghosts, &c.; spotted magpie or ཁྭ་ཏ་ཁྲ་བ *khwata khra-wa* fuller name for the magpie.

ཁྭ་བ *khwa-wa* = དཔྱ་བ *dpya-wa* rent or tax in kind: ཆོས་བཞིན་དུ་ཁྭམ་དཔྱ་འབུལ *chos bshin-du khbaham dpya-hbul* paid rent or tax according to religious law.

ཁག I: *khag* 1. means, resource; ཁག་མེད *khag-med* = ཐབས་མེད without means.

ཁག II: a task, charge, business, duty; responsibility; of importance: ཁག་ཁུར *khag-khur* = འགན་ཁུར *hgan-khur* to take charge of a thing or person, to be responsible for anything, to be surety for anyone; ཁག་འཁུར་བ *khag hkhur-wa* to assume charge of; ཁག་འགེལ་བ *khag hgel-wa* to place in charge; ཁག་ཐེག་པ *khag theg-pa* or ཁག་རྒྱག་པ *khag rgyag-pa* to guarantee; become responsible: དེར་འཚོ་བ་ཡོང་བ་ཁག་ཐེག *der htsho-wa yoñ-wa khag-theg* I warrant you will get something to eat there. ཁག་ཐེག *khag-theg* or ཁག་ཁྱག *khag-khyag* in *C.* acc. to *Jä.* = bail; ཁག་ཆེན *khag-chen* important.

ཁག III: that which is divided off; a class, part, division, section (of a book or place); བཅུ་ཁག *bcu-khag* the tenth part; tithe: ཁག་གཉིས་ལ་ཕོག་སོང *khag gñis-la phog-soñ* I have hurt myself in two places. ཡུལ་ཁག *yul-khag* a province, district; རྒྱལ་ཁག *rgyal-khag* kingdom; དཔོན་ཁག *dpon-khag* principality; དགོན་ཁག *dgon-khag* monastic estate or authority. སྡེ་དཔོན་ཁག་སོ་སོ་ནམ་མཚན་གཅིག་མཆོད་པ་ཕུལ་དགོས་པས the different divisional chiefs should make religious offerings (service) for one night (*Loñ.* ༤ *17*); སྐྱབས་འགྲོ་སེམས་སྐྱེད་ཀྱི་ཁག་ཁོ་མོ་ཅག་རྣམས *skyabs hgro sems skyed-kyi khag kho-mo cag-rnams* we who belong to the class in whom the inclination (for religion) and to seek refuge has arisen (*A. 19*).

ཁག་པོ *khag-po* difficult, hard; colloq. "*ká-le khag-po.*" ལས་ཀ་འདི་ད་ཅང་ཁག་པོ་རེད this work is very hard; ལམ་ཁག་པོ་འདུག the way is difficult; ཁག་པོ་བྱུང difficulties arose; ཁག་པོ་ཆེ་བ *khag-po che-wa* to suffer from want. 2. acc. to *Jä.* bad, spoiled, rotten: མར་ཁག་པོ་སོང the butter has become rancid (*Jä.*).

ཁང་པ *khañ-pa* = ཁང་ཁྱིམ *khañ-khyim* सदनं, मन्दिर, गृह, शाला, कुटिका, भवन, आवसथ house, residence, home; a building; སྟེང་ཁང *steñ-khañ*, འོག་ཁང *hog-khañ*, བར་ཁང *bar-khañ* upper story, lower story or ground floor, middle story; གཞུང་ཁང *gshuñ-khañ* means also the principal or central room. A *khañ-pa* is the opposite to ཕུག་པ *phug-pa*, a cavern. བཟོ་ཁང *bzo-khañ* workshop; བང་ཁང *bañ-khañ* store-house, store-room; སྒོ་ཁང *sgo-khañ* entrance, vestibule; སྐོར་ཁང *skor-khañ* or more properly སྐོར་ལམ *skor-lam*, passage running round a building or temple; ཤོག་ཁང *çog-khañ* paper house or a house where paper is kept or manufactured. In *W.* the scooping form or mould used in the manufacture of paper is so called. ཚས་ཁང་ *tshas khañ* flower bed (garden) (*Jä.*). In Buddhism ཁང་ *khañ* signifies ནང་ *nañ*, inside, *i.e.*, the heart: ཁང་ཤྲུགས་ཅིང་ཕྱིར་འཛག་པ *khañ myags-çiñ phyir ḥdsag-pa* अन्तःपूतिरवस्रुता inwardly being corrupt, the pus issues or drops from him; མྱ་ངན་གྱི་ཁང་ *mya-ñan-gyi khañ* mourning house; also the body; ཁང་གླ *khañ-gla* house rent; ཁང་ཆུང་ गोसुख a small house; a house or room reserved for decrepit parents; ཁང་ཆུང་པ *khañ chuñ-pa* an occupant of such; ཡང་ཁང་ཆུང་པ *yañ-khañ chuñ-pa* such a person of the second degree (if, during his life, his son enters into the same right) (*Jä.*); ཁང་ཆེན *khañ chen* a large house; ཁང་ཆེན་པ *khañ chen-pa* महशाल: one taking his abode in a great house or mansion (*Budh.*); old, weak persons belonging to Gautama's family.

Syn. གནས་ཁང *gnas-khañ*; གནས་གཞི *gnas-gshi*; འཇུག་པའི་གནས *ḥjug-paḥi gnas*; འདུག་ས *ḥdug-sa*; འདུག་གནས *ḥdug-gnas*; ཁྱིམ *khyim*; ཁབ *khab*; རྟེན་གཞི *rten-gshi*; རྟེན་གནས *rten-gnas*; བླ་གབ་ཅན *bla gab-can*; ཕིབས་ཧོག *phibs-hog* (*Mñon.*).

ཁང་གཉེར *khañ-gñer* गृहरक्षक, गृहपाल the steward of a house; the house-keeper; the person in whose charge a house is kept.

ཁང་སྟེང *khañ-steñ* तलकोपरि the upper roof or terrace of a house.

ཁང་ཐོག *khañ-thog* or ཁང་པའི་ཐོག *khañ-paḥi thog* छाद, पटल the roof or cover of a house; the top flat of a house.

ཁང་པ་བཀྲ་བ *khañ-pa bkra-wa* विचित्र गृह a painted house.

ཁང་པ་བཙན་པོ *khañ-pa btsan-po* a consecrated house where theives or robbers cannot have access.

ཁང་པ་བརྩེགས་པ *khañ-pa brtsegs-pa* प्रकूट a masonry building; also a storeyed house.

ཁང་པ་གཡོ *khañ-pa gyo* छदनं the roof of a house: ཁང་པ་གཡོ་བ to cover a house, to roof it; ཁང་པ་རལ་ཞིང་གྲུམ་པ *khañ-pa ral-shiñ grum-pa* or འདྲུམས་པ *ḥdrums-pa* खण्डस्फुट a delapidated house; a ruined edifice.

ཁང་པའི་ནང *khañ-paḥi nañ* अभ्यन्तर, कोष्ठ the inside of a house; a room; an apartment.

ཁང་བུ *Khañ-bu* n. of a fabulous country; a little house, cottage.

ཁང་མིག *khañ-mig* a room; a cell.

ཁང་རྩ *khañ-rtsa* the foundation of a house.

ཁང་བརྩེགས *khañ-brtsegs* कूटागार upper house or a storied room, v. ཁང་པ་བརྩེགས་པ *khañ-pa brtsegs-pa*.

ཁང་ཞབས *khañ-shabs* floor; flooring of a room.

ཁང་ཞིང *khañ-shiñ*=ཁང་པ་དང་ཞིང་ཁ *khañ-pa dañ shiñ-kha* house and the cultivated fields attached to it.

ཁང་བཟང *khañ-bzañ* प्रासाद residence; mansion. In *Budh.* धर्मेय (धर्ममठ), कीर्त्ति, कौमिनाराम monument.

ཁང་བཟོ་བ *khañ-bzo-wa* मर्माजीव mason; architect.

ཁངས་པ *khañs-pa*=རངས་པ *rañs-pa* 1. delay. 2. distance.

ཁད *khad*=1. ཐག *thag* or ཚར *tshar* near. 2. litter barrow. 3. =ལྟར *ltar* like, as ཁད་སྙམས *khad-sñams*, v. འཁོད་སྙམས *ḥkhod sñams*, equal, even; དེ་མ་ཁད *de-ma khad*=དེ་མ་ཐག *de-ma thag* not distantly; instantly; as soon as; without delay: དབུགས་ཆད་མ་ཁད་དུ *dbugs chad-ma khad-du* as soon as the breathing ceases; བུ་སྐྱེས་མ་ཁད་ཅིག *bu skyes-ma khad-cig* a child born just now; འཕུར་ལ་ཁད *hphur-la khad* about to fly; འགྲོ་ལ་ཁད *hgro-la khad* about to go; ལྷུང་ལ་ཁད *lhuṅ-la khad* near to fall; སླེབས་ལ་ཁད *slebs-la khad* as soon as (he) arrived; འཆི་ལ་ཁད *hchi-la khad* when about to die: ནུབ་ལ་ཁད་པའི་ཚེ *nub-la khad-pahi tshe* when the evening drew near; དབུགས་ཆད་ལ་ཁད་པའི་དུས *dbugs chad-la khad-pahi dus* when the ceasing of the breath approaches; ཟིན་ལ་ཁད་ཡོད་པ་ལ *zin-la khad yod-pa la* as we were just about to seize him; ཁད་དུ *khad-du* as far as: རྟིང་མ་ཁད་དུ *rtiṅ-ma khad-du* as far as the heel (*Jä.*).

ཁད་ཀྱིས *khad-kyis*=དལ་བུས *dal-bus* or རིམ་གྱིས *rim-gyis* शनैः slowly, by degrees; ཁད་ཀྱིས་ཁད་ཀྱིས *khad-kyis khad-kyis* शनैः शनैः by degrees; in slow motion.

ཁད་པ *khad-pa* the same as འཁོད་པ *hkhod-pa* to stick fast; to be seized, stopped, impeded, v. འཁད་པ *hkhad-pa*.

ཁད་པར་གྱུར་པ *khad-par gyur-pa* to be stopped or hindered; ཁད་པར་བྱེད་པ *khad-par byed-pa* to stop, hinder.

ཁན *khan* खालोप bit; small piece (*Cs.*).

† **ཁན་ད** *khan-da* खण्ड confection; a medicinal syrup; treacle or molasses partially dried; དེ་ལ་ཁཎ་ཌ་བཅོས་པ *dela khaṇḍa bcos-pa* the candy made of it (*Jä.*).

ཁན་པ *khan-pa* also ཁེན་པ *khen-pa*, wormwood (*Schtr.*); to add (arith.) (*Vai. kar.*).

ཁན་མན *khan-man* modest in *Lh* (*Jä.*).

ཁབ I: *khab*=ཕོ་བྲང *pho-braṅ* पुरी, *resp.* of ཁང་ཁྱིམ *khaṅ-khyim*, a great man's residence; a castle; court; residence of a prince; རྒྱལ་པོའི་ཁབ *Rgyal-pohi khab* राजगृह metropolis; the capital of Magadha in Buddha's time; the modern town of Rajgir in Behar: རྒྱལ་པོའི་ཁབ་ཀྱི་མི་རྣམས *Rgyal-pohi khab-kyi mi-rnams* the courtiers; the people of Rājagṛha. 2. wife, spouse; ཁབ་ཆེན་མ *khab chen-ma* the first wife (who is high in rank): དེ་ལ་ཁབ་འོས་པ་མ་རྙེད་ནས *de-la khab hos-pa ma rñed-nas* as there was not found a wife worthy of him; འདི་གཉིས་ངའི་ཁབ་ཏུ་བྱུང་བ་རྨིས་སོ *hdi-gñis ṅahi khab-tu byuṅ-wa rmis-so* I dreamt that these two would become my wives (*Jä.*); ཁབ་ཏུ་བཞེས་པ *khab-tu bshes-pa* to take for a wife (*Schtr.*); ཆུང་མར་ཁབ་པ *chuṅ-mar khab-pa* to marry; to take one for his wife.

ཁབ་བཙུན་མ *khab btsun-ma* a married lady; ཁབ་འཛིན་མ *khab hdsin-ma*=ཁྱིམ་བདག་མོ *khyim bdag-mo* गृहपत्नी housewife; the lady of the house.

ཁབ II: सूची a needle: ཁབ་སྤུ *khab-spu* a bristle; a needle like hair ཁབ་ཕྲ *khab-phra* a small, fine needle; ཁབ་སྦོམ *khab-sbom* a large needle; ཁབ་མིག *khab-mig* the eye of a needle; ཁབ་མིག་ཏུ་སྐུད་པ་འཇུག་པ *khab-mig-tu skud-pa hjug-pa* to thread a needle; ཁབ་རྩེ *kha-rtse* सूच्यग्र, पराग्र the point of a needle.

ཁབ་རལ *khab-ral* also རྩེ་མ་ཁབ་རལ *rtse-ma khab-ral* सूचीगृहकं needle-case.

ཁབ་ལེ *khab-le* in *W.* difficult (*Jä.*).

ཁབ་ལེན་རྡོ *khab-len-rdo* चुम्बक load-stone; the metal that attracts a needle: ཁབ་ལེན་རྡོ་ཡིས་མདེའུ་འབྱིན་རྒྱུད་རུས་རྩ་ནད་སེལ the load-stone draws out arrow-heads and removes diseases of the brains, bones and veins.

ཁབ་ལོང *khab-loṅ* अयस्कान्त the magnet; lit. the needle-lifter.

ཁབས *khabs* n. of a disease (*Jä.*).

ཁམ *kham* 1. colour. 2. a bit; a small piece of anything. 3. the point of a reed pen. 4. appetite (*Jä.*).

ཁམ་ཁམ་ *kham-kham*, སེར་ཁམ་ཁམ་ *ser-kham kham* or pale yellow: མདོག་སེར་ཁམ་ཁམ་སྨུག་མའི་མདོག *mdog ser kham-kham smug-mahi mdog* the colour was pale-yellow, *i.e.*, the colour of a dry bamboo.

ཁམ་ཁུམ་ *kham-khum* uneven, explained, as འབར་འབུར་རམ་གཉེར་མ་ལྟ་བུ "in ridges, like a puckered skin."

ཁམ་གང་ *kham-gañ* or ཁམ་གཅིག *kham-gcig* a bit; ཟས་ཁམ་གཅིག a mouthful of food: ཟ་དུས་དུམ་བུ་རེ་བཅད་དེ་ཁ་ལ་བཙུག་པའི་ཚད the measure of food in each piece that can be put in the mouth at once when eating; ཁམ་ཆུང་ *kham-chuñ* a morsel.

ཁམ་སྟར་ *kham-star* abbreviation of ཁམ་བུ་དང་སྟར་ཀ *kham-bu-dañ star-ga, i.e.*, peach and walnut.

ཁམ་ལྡོག *knam-ldog* faded colour, same as ཁམ་ལོག *kham-log*, want of appetite; nausea, aversion, dislike (*Jä.*).

ཁམ་པ *kham-pa* 1. fox coloured; sorrel; brownish; ཁམ་ནག *kham-nag* dark brown: རལ་པ་ཁམ་ནག *ral-pa kham-nag* dark brown locks or mane. 2. porcelain-clay; china clay. 3. *Tenacetum tomentosum*, a very aromatic plant growing on the high mountains of Tibet. 4. a native of *Khams* in Eastern Tibet.

+ ཁམ་ཕོར་ *kham-phor* सराव, शराव a cup or saucer made of (burnt) clay; a cup made of dough, used in sacrifice as lamps (*Jä.*).

ཁམ་འཕྲོ་མི་བཅད་པ *kham-hphro mi-bcad-pa* सकृ-दवच्छेदक, नक्राव्योच्छेदक refers to Buddha having enjoined that a monk must not eat a fruit or cake, etc., leaving any of it. He should not take more than what he can or should eat.

ཁམ་བུ *kham-bu* apricot; peach; in *Sikk.* ཁམ་བུའི་རྩི་གུ *kham-buhi rtsi-gu* the stone of an apricot (*Jä.*): མངའ་རིས་ཁམ་བུ *Mñah-ris kham-bu* dried apricot imported from Ngari: ཁམ་བུས་སྐྲ་སོགས་སྤྲུ་སྐྱེས་ཆུ་སེར་སྐེམ the peach dries the yellow humour of the body and promotes the growth of hair on the head (*Med.*); ཁམ་ཚིག *kham-tshig* the stone of an apricot or peach; བྱུ་རུ་ཁམ་ཚིག་ཆེ་ཙམ the cost of a coral of the size of the stone of a large apricot.

ཁམ་གཡག *kham-gyag* 1. lit. the *Bos grunniens* or *yak*-bull of ཁམས *Khams*, which is of a brown colour: སྤུ་ཁའི་མདོག་སེར་ཁམ་ཡོད་པ་ལ་ཁམ་གཡག་ཟེར *spu-khahi mdog ser-kham yod-pa la kham-gyag zer* the colour of the hair (of an animal) when pale yellow is called ཁམ་གཡག *kham-gyag*. 2. cherries, morels (*Jä.*).

ཁམ་རན་པ *kham ran-pa* परिमण्डलमालोपम a horse's bit that fits well.

ཁམ་ས *kham-sa* clay for making pottery.

ཁམ་སང་ *kham-sañ* = ཆབ་སང་ *chab-sañ*, གཅིན་པ *gcin-pa*, etc., resp. evacuation; purging; making water.

ཁམ་སེར *kham-ser* of a slightly pale-yellow; colour resembling the colour of dried bamboo, v. ཁམ་ཁམ *kham-kham*.

ཁམས I: *khams* = དངས་ག *dañs-ga* appetite.

ཁམས II: धातु the health, condition, physical constitution of the body; also root; a constituent or essential part; that which constitutes the nature of a thing. Used colloq. as in *kusho, khye'-kyi khams ta-sam?* "Sir, how are you?" (*Snd. Hlk.*): ཁམས་ཞེས་པ་སྤྱིར་རང་བཞིན་ནམ་ངོ་བོ་ལ་འཇུག་པའི་དོན་ཅན་ཡིན་ཏེ་རླུང་གི་ཁམས་ཞེས་པའི་ཁམས་དེ་ནི་རླུང་རང་གི་ངོ་བོ་ཡིན *khams shes-pa spyir rañ-bshin nam ño-bo la hjug-pahi don-can yin-te rluñ-gi khams shes-pahi khams de ni rluñ rañ-gi ño-bo yin.*

ཁམས III: the six elements, earth, air, fire, water, the heavenly ether, and *nam-shes* or the physical substance of the mind. For the last two, arterial blood and seminal fluid are sometimes substituted. Also there are the eighteen elements acc. to the Buddhists, namely, the five organs of sense, together with *manas* (mind); the six faculties or senses dependent on these and also the six ideas produced by these six faculties. Any one of the five properties or qualities of the elements observed by the organs of sense, viz., sound, tangibility, colour, flavour and smell, is also so called.

ཁམས་བཅོ་བརྒྱད་ཀྱི་མིག་སོགས་རྟེན་དབང་པོའི་ཁམས་དྲུག་དང་མིག་གི་རྣམ་པར་ཤེས་པ་སོགས་བརྟེན་པ་རྣམ་པར་ཤེས་པའི་ཁམས་དང་གཟུགས་ཁམས་སོགས་དམིགས་པ་ཡུལ་གི་ཁམས་དྲུག་དང་བཅོ་བརྒྱད་དོ *khams bco-brgyad-kyi mig sogs rten dwan-pohi khams drug dan mig-gi rnam-par çes-pa sogs brten-pa rnam-par çes-pahi khams dan gzugs-khams sogs dmigs-pa yul-gi khams-drug dan bco-brgyad-do* may be rendered.

The eighteen ཁམས *khams* or *Dhātu* acc. to the Buddhists are:—

I.—The organs themselves: མིག *mig* eye; རྣ་བ *rna-wa* ear; སྣ་བ *sna-wa* nose; ལྕེ *lce* tongue; ལུས *lus* body; and ཡིད *yid* the mind.

II.—གཟུགས *gzugs* bodily form; སྒྲ *sgra* sound; དྲི *dri* smell; རོ *ro* taste; རེག *reg* touch; ཆོས *chos*, धर्म attributes.

III.—The རྣམ་པར་ཤེས་པ *rnam-par çes-pa Vijñāna* or consciousness produced by the organs of sense, &c. The *Vijñāna* of མིག *mig*, of རྣ་བ *rna-wa*, of སྣ་བ *sna-wa*, of ལྕེ *lce*, of ལུས *lus* and of ཡིད *yid*, *i.e.*, eye, ear, nose, tongue, body, and mind.

ཁམས IV: empire; realm; territory; domain: ཡུལ་ཁམས *yul-khams* political territory; empire, in a geographical sense (*Jä.*); རྒྱལ་ཁམས *rgyal-khams* kingdom: རྒྱལ་བའི་ཁམས *rgyal-wahi khams* the province or sphere of the Buddhas, also of their spiritual influence: རྒྱལ་ཁམས་འགྲིམ་པ *rgyal-khams hgrim-pa* to roam over the kingdoms, the countries (*Jä.*): ཁམས་ཆེན empire; also the earth.

ཁམས V: लोक world: ཁམས་གསུམ *khams-gsum* त्रैलोक्य, त्रैधातु the sensual world, viz:—(1) कामधातु or कामलोक (འདོད་པའི་ཁམས *Hdod-pahi khams*) the phenomenal world; (2) रूपधातु; གཟུགས་ཀྱི་ཁམས *gzugs-kyi khams* the world of astral forms; (3) अरूपधातु; གཟུགས་མེད་ཁམས *gzugs-med khams* the spiritual world, *i.e.*, the world of formless spirits.

ཁམས VI: n. of the easternmost districts of Tibet, embracing some dozen semi-independent petty states, about half of which own allegiance to Lhasa, and the rest give joint allegiance to both China and Lhasa. ཁམས *Khams* and སྒང *Sgan* are the two lower regions of Tibet; these constitute what is called བོད་ཆེན *Bod-chen* or Greater Tibet.

ཁམས་བརྟས་པ *khams brtas-pa* or ཁམས་བརྟས་བྱེད་པ *khams-brtas byed-pa* one who draws omens: ཐེག་པ་གསུམ་གྱི་ཁམས་བརྟས་བྱེད་པ *theg-pa gsum-gyi khams-brtas byed-pa* (*J. Zan.*).

ཁམས་ཆེན་པོ *khams chen-po*=དངུལ་ཆུ *dnul-chu* mercury; quicksilver (*Mnon.*).

ཁམས་དྭངས་པ *khams dwans-pa*=ཁམས་བདེ་བ *khams bde-wa* good health. When glass is pure ཤེལ་དྲི་མ་མེད་པ *çel dri-ma med-pa* and clean it is called ཤེལ་ཁམས་དྭངས་པ *çel-khams dwans-pa*. A clear cloudless sky ནམ་མཁའ་སྤྲིན་པ་མེད་པ is said to be *Nam-khams dwans-pa*; སེམས་སྒྲིབ་པ་མེད་པ *sems sgrib-pa med-pa* the mind when it is free from defilement or sin.

ཁམས་བདེ་ *khams-bde* = ནད་མེད་པ་ *nad med-pa* free from disease; health.

Syn. སྐུ་གཟུགས་བདེ་ *sku-gzugs bde*; ཉེར་འཚེ་མེད་ *ñer-htshe med*; ཉེ་ཤོས་དྭེན་ *ñe shos-dwen*; གཉོང་མེད་ *goñ-med*; སྙུན་མེད་ *sñun-med*; ནད་བུ་མེད་ *nad-bu-med*; འབྱུང་བཞི་སྙོམས་ *hbyuñ-bshi sñoms*; བྲོ་མི་འཚལ་ *bro mi-htshal* (*Mñon.*).

ཁམས་བདེ་དྲི་སྨེད་ *khams-bde dri-smed*, སྨྲ་བ་དང་རྗེས་སུ་འབྲེལ་བ་ *smra-wa dañ rjes-su hbrel-wa* to inquire of one's health if he is well or happy (a complementary expression used on the occasion of meeting) (*Mñon.*).

ཁམས་བདེ་བ་ *khams bde-wa* or གཟུགས་བདེ་བ་ *gzugs bde-wa* good health; healthy constitution; the happy state both of the body and the mind: རྗེ་བཙུན་གྱི་ཁམས་བདེ་ལགས་སམ་ *Rje-btsun gyi khams-bde lags-sam* is your reverence well? ཁྱེད་ཁམས་བདེའམ་ *khyed khams bde-ham* are you well? (*Jä.*)

ཁམས་ལྡོག་པ་ *khams ldog-pa* = ཁམས་ལོག་པ་ *khams log-pa* want of appetite; aversion, dislike; ཁམས་རྨྱ་ *khams-rmya* nausea; falling sick (*Cs.*).

ཁམས་སྣ་ཚོགས་མཁྱེན་པའི་སྟོབས་ *khams sna-tshogs mkhyen-pahi stobs* नानाधातुज्ञानबल the power of knowing the constitution of all sorts of bodies.

ཁམས་མི་ཉག་ *Khams mi-ñag* n. of one of the petty principalities in *Khams*.

ཁམས་མི་འདྲ་བ་ *khams mi-hdra-wa*, འཇིག་རྟེན་གྱི་ཁམས་མི་འདྲ་བ་ *hjig-rten gyi khams mi hdra-wa* different or dissimilar worlds.

ཁམས་ཚན་ *khams-tshan* this term is applied to the quarters in a monastery reserved for the accommodation of the monks of a particular section of people or of some special community or those coming from one particular locality.

ཁམས་སས་ *khams-sas* rest; health; comfort (*Sch.*); recreation; recovery; restoration of health.

ཁམས་སུ་གཏོགས་པ་ *khams-su gtogs-pa* धातुपतित included in the constitution.

ཁམས་སླང་ *khams-slañ* = ཁམས་ཀྱི་སླ་ང་ *khams-kyi sla-ña* a cooking pan made in *Khams*.

ཁམས་སླེ་ *khams-sle* better kind of coarse serge of the pattern coming from Yarkand; blanket manufactured in *Khams*: སྨུག་སླེ་ཁམས་སླེ་བཅས་རྣམ་པ་རེ་ *smug sle khams sle bcas rnam-pa re* each piece of blanket costs, &c.

ཁམས་གསུམ་ *khams-gsum* त्रिलोक the three worlds—heaven, earth and the nether world.

ཁམས་གསུམ་འཁོར་ལོས་བསྒྱུར་བ་ *Khams-gsum hkhor-los bsgyur-wa* श्रीकालचक्र a name of the Kālachakra system (*Mñon.*).

ཁམས་གསུམ་ཟངས་ཁང་གླིང་ *khams-gsum zañs-khañ-gliñ* n. of the temple in the grand monastery of Sam-ye (*Bsam-yas*) built by one of the queens of King *Khri sroñ ldeñ btsan* (*Loñ.* ཇ *8*).

ཁམས་གསུམ་ལ་མ་ཆགས་པ་ *khams-gsums-la ma-chags-pa* त्रिधातुकामसक्ता is not passionately fond of or attached to the three worlds.

ཁམས་གསོས་པར་ *khams gsos-par* to repair broken health.

ཁར་ *Khar* n. of a city in *W.* (*S. Lam*).

*ཁར་བཀྲོལ་ *khar-bkrol* मम्या (*Schr.*; *Lebensh. 93*).

ཁར་རྐྱང་ *khar-rkyañ*, v. ཁ་རྐྱང་ *kha rkyañ*.

ཁར་གོང་ *khar-goñ* steatite; soap stone; probably དཀར་གོང་ *dkar-goñ* (*Sch.*).

ཁར་ཆེན་བཟའ་ *Khar chen-bzah* the Princess of Khar-chen, one of the queens of King *Khri-sroñ ldeu btsan* (*Loñ.* ཇ *8*).

ཁར་ཏ་ཏ་ *Khar Ta-ta* n. of a city or seaport on the mouth of the Indus, Tata (*S. Lam.*).

ཁར་པ *Khar-pa* कंस 1. n. of a demon of *Puranic* India who was killed by Krishna. 2. a compound of copper and zinc; bell metal.

ཁར་བ་མགར *khar-wa mgar* कंसकार a maker of bell-metal.

ཁར་རྩང *khar-ṛtsañ*=ཁར་སང *khar-sañ* col. yesterday forenoon.

‡ ཁར་ཛུ་ར *khar-dsu-ra* खर्जूर; ཤིང་གི་འབྲས་བུ *çiñ-gi ḥbras-bu* the date fruit.

‡ ཁར་ས་པ་ནི *khar-sa pa-ni* or ཁ་སར་པ་ན *kha-sar pa-na* खसर्पण he that moves in the sky; gliding through the air; a name of Avalokites'vara *Bodhisattva*; Vishṇu.

ཁར་གསེལ *khar-gsel* त्रिशूल the trident carried by mendicants of the སྔགས་ཀྱི་ཐེག་པ Tantrik School.

ཁལ *khal* 1. primarily a load or burden in general: ཁལ་འཁྱེར་བ *khal khyer-wa* to carry a burden; ཁལ་གྱི་སྟེང་ལ *khal-gyi ṣteñ-la* on the top of the baggage; ཁལ་འགེལ་བ *khal ḥgel-wa* to load; ཁལ་འབོགས་པ *khal ḥbogs-pa* to take off the burden, to unload; ལུག་ཁལ a sheep load; འཁྱེར་པའི་ཁལ a coolie load. 2. a set weight or measure, said to equal 30lb, used for dry goods, corn, salt, tea, &c. In Tibet 1 *khal*=2 *ḥbo*=20 *bre*; hence in Sikkim and *W.* ཁལ་གཅིག *"khe-chik"* has come to mean 20 or a score of anything; འདེགས་ཁལ *ḥdegs-khal* a weighing score; the weight of 20 points on the steel-yard called *ṛgya-ma*. 3. a caravan.

ཁལ་ཁ *Khal-kha* the native name of Mongolia Proper, the country of Jenghis-khan, the Tartar Conqueror ཁལ་ཁ་ཁུ་རལ་བླ་བྲང *Khal-kha khu-ral ḅla-brañ*, lit. "the sacred enclosure of Khal-kha"; the name applied to Urga in Northern Mongolia, where the incarnation of the Taranath Lama resides. The latter is sometimes styled ཁལ་ཁ་རྗེ་བཙུན་དམ་པ *Khal-kha Ṛje-ḅtsun dam-pa*, the venerable holy one of Khal-kha.

ཁལ་ཁོལ *khal-khol* stunned; insensible (*Jä.*).

ཁལ་ཅག *khal-cag* the best sort of wool for manufacturing shawls coming from the northern solitudes of Tibet.

ཁལ་རྗེས *khal-ṛjes*=དོས་རྒྱབ *dos-ṛgyab* or ཁལ་མ་རྟ *khal-ma ṛta*, གླང་སོགས་ཀྱི་རྗེས *glañ sogs-kyi ṛjes* those who conduct a caravan or follow the train of packed animals, such as pony, yaks, oxen, &c.; relay of packed animals: ཁམས་སོགས་ཐག་རིང་པའི་དོས་རྒྱ་བཁལ་རྗེས *khams sogs thag-riñ-paḥi dos-ṛgya ḅkhal-ṛjes* the relay of beasts of burden when proceeding on a long journey to *Khams, &c.*

ཁལ་པ *khal-pa* 1. wether; castrated ram. 2. sow-thistle, *Sonchus*.

ཁལ་བན *khal-ban* jug or pitcher to hold wine for 20 persons or a quantity measuring 20 བྲེ *bre*: དམངས་ཚང་ཁལ་བན་རེ་གང་རིགས jugs of ale each sufficient for 20 of the vulgar folk of whatever class.

ཁལ་མ *khal-ma* any draught animal or beast of burden: ཁལ་མ་རྣམས་འབང་ལ་སྐྱེལ་བ to drive beasts of burden to the pasture; often contracted into *khal*: མི་ཁལ་གཉིས་ཀྱི་གླ the wages of both carriers and beasts of burden.

ཁལ་རི *khal-ri*=ཁལ་རུ *khal-ru* or ཁ་རི *kha-ri* or ཁ་རུ *kha-ru* a measure of about 20 bushels.

ཁས *khas* for ཁ་ཡིས *kha-yis* instr. of ཁ *kha*.

ཁས་ཁྱགས *khas-khyags*=ཁས་ཐེགས *khas-thegs* or ཁག་ཐེགས *khag-thegs* to be witness; to give evidence.

ཁས་ཆེ་ *khas-che*=ཁས་བླངས་ *khas-blaṅs* promise.

ཁས་ཆེ་བ *khas che-wa* प्रतिज्ञा to promise; undertake: ཁས་ཆེ་བའི་དགེ་སློང་ *khas che-waḥi dge-sloṅ* प्रतिज्ञाभिक्षु a Buddhist monk who has taken the vows.

Syn. ཁས་ཆེ *khas-che*; ཕྱོགས་བཟུང་ *phyogs bzuṅ*; ངེས་པར་མཉན་བྱས *ṅes-par mñan-byas*; ཡང་དག་ཐོས *yoṅ-dag-thos*; བདག་གིར་བྱས *ḥdag-gir byas*; སོ་སོར་མཉན *so-sor mñan*; གཡར་དམ *gyar dam*; དམ་ཁས་བླངས་པར་འོས་པ *dam khas blaṅs-war ḥos-par*; དམ་བཅའ *dam-bcaḥ*; ཁས་ལེན *khas-len* (*Mṅon.*).

ཁས་བརྗོད *khas-brjod*=གླུ་དབྱངས *glu-dbyaṅs* song; singing (*Mṅon.*).

ཁས་ཉེན་དབང་ཆུང་ *kha-ñan dwaṅ-chuṅ*=མི་ཉམ་ཆུང་ *mi ñam chuṅ* a humble man.

ཁས་བླངས *khas-blaṅs*=ཁས་ལེན *khas-len* अनुज्ञा, अनुमत, संविद्, उपगम promise; consent, approval; knowledge; acceptance.

ཁས་ཞན་པ *khas shan-pa* ཉམ་ཆུང་ humble.

ཁས་ལེན་གན་ཁུར *kha-lan rgan-khur* responsibility.

ཁས་ལེན་པ *khas len-pa* or ཁ་བང་བ *kha laṅ-wa* उपगच्छति 1. to promise; to stand bail or security. 2. to presume; to arrogate; to accept, adopt with the mouth; to acknowledge, admit (*Jä.*).

ཁི *khi* numerical figure 32.

† ཁི་བི་ཛ་ལ *Khi-bi dsa-la* खिविजल n. of a city in the neighbourhood of the fabulous S'ambhala.

ཁིའུ *khiḥu* (ཁྱིན *khyiṅ* or ཁི་ཆུང་ *khi-chuṅ*) a small cutting-knife.

ཁུ *khu* numerical figure 62; also for ཁུ་བ *khu-wa* (humour or juice or sap), as in ཁུ་ཁྲག་སོགས *khu khrag sogs* रसरक्तादि, humour, blood, &c.

ཁུ་གུ *khu-gu* uncle (*Cs.*).

ཁུ་ཁྲག *khu-khrag* संक्लेद the mixture of the semen with the uterine blood by which process, according to Indian physiology, the fœtus is formed (*Med.*).

ཁུ་ཏུ *khu-tu* a hut, cottage, constructed of branches of trees (*Jä.*).

ཁུ་ཐུ་ཆི *Khu-thu-chi* the title of a Mongolian nobleman: སོག་པོའི་ཁུ་ཐུ་ཆིའི་ཆས་ཐོབ *Sog-poḥi khu-thu-chiḥi chas thob* obtained the robe of a Mongolian Chief.

ཁུ་རྡུལ *khu-rdul*=ཁུ་རྣ *khu-rna* water-spray: སྤྲིན་དང་ཁུ་རྡུལ་ཐམས་ཅད་རང་མར་དེངས the water in all its particles issued fresh from the clouds (*A. 149*): ནམ་མཁའི་ཁམས་མི་དྭངས་པར་བྱེད་པ་སྨུག་པ་དང་རྡུལ་སོགས *nam-mkhaḥi khams mi-dwaṅs-par byed-pa smug-pa daṅ rdul sogs* the firmament of the sky was obscured by mists and fogs. In medical works the seminal fluid of the male is called ཁུ *khu* and of females རྡུལ *rdul*.

ཁུ་ནུ *Khu-nu* the districts of Kunawar and Bissahar on the Upper Sutlej, bordering Tibet and inhabited in the northern part by Tibetans: ཁུ་ནུའི་རྒུན་འབྲུམ grapes from Kunawar.

ཁུ་རྣ *khu-rna*, v. ཁུ་རྡུལ *khu-rdul*.

ཁུ་པོ *Khu-po* n. of a place and also of a Lama of that place (*Deb.*).

ཁུ་བ *khu-wa*=ཞུ་བ *shu-wa*; रस, द्रवत्व, वीर्य्य, बहुल, पुष्पक, रेतः, शुक्र, कुन्द 1. fluid, liquid: ལྷུང་བཟེད་བཀྲུས་པའི་ཁུ་བ *lhuṅ-bzed bkrus-paḥi khu-wa* the liquid (water) which has washed a mendicant's bowl; ཁྲུས་ཁུ *khrus-khu* dish-wash; swill (*Jä.*); འབྲས་ཁུ *ḥbras-khu* rice-soup (*Cs.*); rice-water (*Schtr.*); ཤིང་ཁུ *çiṅ-khu* the sap of trees; རྩ་ཁུ *rtsa-khu* the sap of plants (*Cs.*); ཤ་ཁུ *ça-khu* broth; gravy; མར་ཁུ *mar-khu* melted butter. 2. semen virile.

Syn. ཟླ་བ *zla-wa*; ཐིག་ལེ *thig-le*; ས་བོན *sa-bon*; སྟོབས་ལྡན *stobs-ldan*; དབང་པོར་འགྲོ *dwaṅ-por ḥgro*; བྱང་སེམས་དཀར་པོ *byaṅ-sems dkar-po*; དྭངས་མ *dwaṅs-ma*; ཁམས་དཀར་པོ *khams dkar-po* (*Mṅon.*).

ཁུ་བ་ཀུན་ལྡན *khu-wa kun-ldan* = སྤོས་དཀར་ཤིང་ *spos-dkar çiṅ* the Sâl tree, the dried sap of which is used as incense.

Syn. ཤ་ལའི་ཤིང་ *sha-lahi çiṅ*, སྲ་རྩི་ཤིང་ *sra-rtsi çiṅ*, སྤོས་དཀར་ཤིང་ *spos-dkar çiṅ*, མཆོད་སྦྱིན་སྤོས *mchod-sbyin spos* (*Mṅon.*).

ཁུ་བ་ལྡན *khu-wa ldan*, v. ཐར་ནུ *thar-nu*.

ཁུ་བ་བྱེད *khu-wa byed* = རྐང་མར marrow; to make a soup of; also to make an infusion or decoction of: སྨན་དང་ཤ་སོགས་ཀྱི་ ཁུ་བ་བྱེད་པ། (*Mṅon.*).

ཁུ་བ་འབྱིན་པ *khu-wa ḥbyin-pa*, སྐྱེས་པའི་ཐིག་ལེ་འདོན་པ to emit semen.

ཁུ་བ་སེར་པོ *khu-wa ser-po* = སྐྱེར་བ *skyer-wa* n. of a plant from which a kind of yellow dye is made in Tibet (*Mṅon.*).

ཁུ་བའི་བདག་ཉིད *khu-wahi bdag-ñid* = སྐྱེས་པ *skyes-pa* पुरुष meton. for a male person.

ཁུ་བའི་འཕོ *khu-wahi ḥpho* शुक्रच्युति the discharge of the semen.

ཁུ་བའི་དབང་པོ *khu-wahi dwaṅ-po* शुक्रेन्द्र, पारद-रस a kind of mercurial medicine.

ཁུ་བའི་སློབ་མ *khu-wahi slob-ma* शुक्र-शिष्य = ལྷ་མ་ཡིན *lha-ma-yin* असुर the class of demi-gods on Mount Sumeru who fight with the *Lha* (*Mṅon.*).

ཁུ་བེ *Khu-be* n. of a place to the west of Lhasa.

ཁུ་བོ *khu-wo* पितृव्य uncle on the father's side, *i.e.*, ཕ་སྤུན *pha-spun*, father's brother, uncle; ཁུ་དབོན *khu-dbon* also ཁུ་ཚན *khu-tshan*, uncle and nephew: ཕའི་སྤུན་ཨ་ཁུའི་རིགས་ལ་ཁུ་བོ་ཟེར father's brother is called *A-khu* or *Khu-bo*.

ཁུ་བྱུག *khu-byug* कोकिल, हरिकण्ठ cuckoo.

Syn. དཔྱིད་ཀྱི་ཕོ་ཉ *dpyid-kyi pho-ña*; ནགས་ན་དགའ་བ *nags na dgaḥ-wa*; འདབ་མའི་ཐིག་པ *ḥdab-maḥi thig-pa*; ན་ཚོད་གནས *na-tshod gnas*; མིག་མཛེས *mig-mdses*; འདོད་པའི་ཏཱ་ལ *ḥdod-paḥi tâla*; གཞན་གྱིས་གསོས *gshan-gyis gsos*; ངག་སྙན *ṅag-sñan*; དབང་སྙན *dwaṅ-sñan*; གཞན་ལ་སེམས *gshan-la sems*; འདོད་པའི་ཕོ་ཉ *ḥdod-paḥi pho-ña*; སྐད་ལ་ལྔ་པའི་དབྱངས *skad-la lña-paḥi dbyaṅs*; སྦྲང་རྩིའི་སྒྲ *sbraṅ-rtsiḥi sgra* (*Mṅon.*).

ཁུ་བྱུག་གྲགས་ཟླ *khu-byug grags-zla* = ཟླ་བ་བཞི་པ *zla-wa bshi-pa* the fourth month of the Tibetan year corresponding with the month of May (*Rtsii.*).

ཁུ་བྱུག་མིག I: *khu-byug-mig* eyes like those of the cuckoo; red eyes.

ཁུ་བྱུག་མིག II: = ཤིང་ཀོ་ལཀྵ *çiṅ-ko lakṣa* कोकिलाक्ष n. of a tree (*Mṅon.*).

ཁུ་བྱུག་རྩ *khu-byug-rtsa* n. of a medicinal herb.

ཁུ་མག *khu-mag* purse, money-bag; colloq. for ཁུག་མ *khug-ma* (*Jä.*).

ཁུ་ཚུར *khu-tshur* मुष्टि-सन्धि the clenched hands; fist.

ཁུ་ཚུར་གྱིས་འཚོ *khu-tshur gyis ḥtsho* = གསེར་བཟོ་བ *gser bzo-wa* a goldsmith; one who makes his livelihood by the use of his fist, *i.e.*, hand-craft (*Mṅon.*).

ཁུ་ཚུར་བཅིངས་པ *khu-tshur bciṅs-pa* to clench the fist; also to hold with the fist (*Mṅon.*).

* ཁུ་ཚུར་བཅིངས *khu-tshur bciṅs* मुष्टिबन्ध fist; closed hand (*Schr.*; *Kâlac. T. 131*).

ཁུ་ཚུར་སྣུན་པ *khu-tshur snun-pa* = ཁུ་ཚུར་རྒྱབ་པ *khu-tshur rgyab-pa* to strike with the fist or the half-closed fist (*Sch.*).

ཁུ་འོད་བཟའ *Khu-ḥod bzaḥ* n. of the mother of Bromston, the founder of the Lamaic hierarchy of Tibet.

ཁུ་ཡུ *khu-yu* hornless; having no horns; also a corruption of the word *khu-ḅyug* in colloq. Tibetan.

ཁུ་ར *khu-ra,* སྣུམ་ཁུར *ṣnum-khur* cakes or pastry fried in oil or butter (*K. du. 327*).

ཁུ་ལུ *khu-lu* 1. the short soft hair of the yak, also pashm wool in general. 2. In *Lh.* venereal disease; syphilis (*Jä.*).

ཁུ་ལེ *Khu-le* 1. n. of a place in Tibet: ཁུ་ལེ་རྣམ་རྒྱལ *Khu-le ṛnam-ṛgyal* the Lama Namgyal of Khu-le; ཁུ་ལེའི་ཆ་ཧ་བོ་གངས་རི Habo Gang-ri, a part of Khule. 2. In the Dzang-lun the word is used to denote the pan in an ordinary pair of scales on which the weights are placed.

ཁུག *khug* or ཁུགས *khugṣ* 1. a corner or nook; a creek, bay, gulf, inlet; ཆུ་ཁུག *chu-khug* crook in a river: ཁུག་ཏུ *khug-tu,* in the inner recess of a cavity. 2. imp. of འགུག་པ *ḥgug-pa* संकर्षण, drawn or attracted by; གྱེན་དུ་ཁུག *gyen-du khug* called upward, *i.e.*, to good luck or fortune; ཁུག་ཐུབ *khug-thub* earned, acquired.

ཁུག་ཁྱོག *khug-khyog* solitude; solitary place; a place with few men.

ཁུག་རྟ *khug-ṛta,* ཁུག་ཏ *khug-ta* or ཨ་ལི་ཁུག་ཏ *āli-khug-ta* दिवौकस्, चातक, सारङ्ग the swallow, *Cuculus melanoleucus*, a kind of swallow (*Cs.*): ཁུག་རྟའི་གློ་བས་གློ་ནད་གཅོད the lungs of ཁུག་རྟ *khug-ṛta* suppress pulmonary diseases (*Med.*).

Syn. ཆར་སྟོད *char-ṣtoḍ*; ཆུང་ཉུང *chuñ-ñuñ*; སྤྲིན་ལ་སློང *sprin-la ṣloñ*; སྤྲིན་འདེགས *sprin-ḥdegṣ*; བཟང་མོ *ḅzañ-mo*; ཐུབ་པའི་བུ *thub-paḥi-bu*; སྒྲ་སྒྲོགས *ṣgra-ṣgrogṣ*; ཆར་དགའ *char-ḍgaḥ* (*Mñon.*).

ཁུག་སྣ *khug-ṣna* or ཁུག་རྣ *khug-ṛna,* निहार, महिका fog, mist, haze (during a calm, especially in spring time): mentioned also as ཡན་ལག་གི་ཁུག་རྣ་བརྒྱད་ཀྱི་གཅིག "one of the eight varieties of causal concatenation."

ཁུག་པ I: *khug-pa* turning like a zig-zag; also bending like a thread that is trimmed; ལམ་ཁུག་པ *lam khug-pa* the twist of a road; སྐུད་ཁུག་པ *ṣkuḍ khug-pa* entwining of a thread; དུས་ཁུག་པ *dus khug-pa* returning to mundane existence at the expiration of each term of life.

ཁུག་པ II: to find, get, earn, draw: ནོར་ཁུགས་པ་འང་སྲིད *nor khugṣ-pa ḥañ sṛiḍ* it is even possible that cash may be replenished; གཉིད་ཁུགས་པ *gñiḍ khugṣ-pa* to get asleep: སྲང་གསུམ་ཁུགས *ṣrañ gṣum khugṣ* it drew, *i.e.*, weighed three ounces (*Jä.*): ཁུག་པ་བཅོ་བརྒྱད *khug-pa ḅco-ḅṛgyaḍ* "the eighteen turns," *i.e.*, returns to life in the present *kalpa*.

* ཁུག་པ་ལྷས་རྩི *Khug-pa lhaṣ-ṛtsi* = རྟ་ནག་འགོས་ལོ་ཙཱ་བ *Ṛta-nag Ḥgoṣ Lo-tsā-wa* (*Schr.*).

ཁུག་མ *khug-ma* थोकनी also टाकनी pouch; little bag; small sack; རྒྱ་ཁུག *ṛgya-khug* Chinese bags made of leather; སྐེ་ཁུག *ṣke-khug* neck-bag; a bag with charmed objects or important letters hanging at the neck; a courier bag; གློ་ཁུག *glo-khug* bag carried at one's side; དངུལ་ཁུག *ḍñul-khug* pouch for silver, a purse; བུལ་ཁུག *bul-khug* a pouch containing soda; མེ་ལྕགས་ཁུག་མ *me-ḷcagṣ khug-ma* tinder-pouch with flint; ནུ་ཁུག *nu-khug* sucking bag for babies; རྩམ་ཁུག *ṛtsam-khug* a bag of barley flour; ཚྭ་ཁུག *tswa-khug* a salt bag; ཞིབ་ཁུག *shib-khug* little bag for flour; གཡང་ཁུག *gyañ-khug* pouch containing auspicious articles to draw good luck.

ཁུགས་པ *Khugṣ-pa* n. of a dynasty originated at a place called *Khugṣ-pa*: རྒྱལ་རབས་ཁུགས་པ་ཐུགས་རྗེ་ཆེན་པོའི་ཡང་རིག་ལས་གསང་བ་པོ་དགེ is the n. of a historical work containing accounts of the succession, dynasty, etc., of kings narrated by Khugs-pa Thugs-rje chenpo (*Yig. 9*).

ཁུང *khuñ* I: hole, pit, hollow, cavity, originally used, only of dark holes and cavities: ཁུང་ཉལ་ *khuñ-ñal* बिलेशय that sleeps in a lair or hole; a snake; སྣ་ཁུང *sna-khuñ* nostril; ཆབ་ཁུང *chab-khuñ* a sink; མཆན་ཁུང *mchan-khuñ* armpit: armhole; གཏོར་ཁུང *gtor-khuñ* a sink; a gutter; མདའ་ཁུང *mdah-khuñ* loop-hole; a hole made by an arrow; བྱི་ཁུང *by-ikhuñ* mouse-hole; བྲག་ཁུང *brag-khuñ* a cleft in a rock; བསོ་ཁུང *bso-khuñ* peep-hole; འི་ཁུང *hi-khuñ* or མིག་ཁུང *mig-khuñ*, ཏེ་ཁུང *te-khuñ* are used of any hole in walls, clothes, &c., caused by natural or artificial causes.

ཁུང་ II: = རྩ་བ *rtsa-wa* root: དེའི་ཁུང་ནའང་བོད་ཀྱི་སེམས་ཅན་དང་སངས་རྒྱས་ཀྱི་བསྟན་པ *dehi khuñ nahan Bod-kyi sems-can dan Sañs-rgyas-kyi bstan-pa* from that root the living beings of Tibet and the religion of Buddha spread out, &c. (*A. 128*).

ཁུང་དྲོགས *khuñ-drogs* soot of an oven or chimney (*Sch.*).

ཁུང་པ *khuñ-pa* or ཁུང་པོ *khuñ-po* a large hole.

ཁུང་བུ *khuñ-bu*=ཁུང *khuñ* a small hole (*Cs.*); སྤུའི་ཁུང་བུ *spu-hi khuñ-bu* the passage of perspiration; hair-hole or cavity.

ཁུང་བུ་ཅན *khuñ-bu can* full of cavities or holes.

ཁུང་ཙི *Khuñ-tsi* or ཁུང་ཕུའུ་ཙི *Khuñ phuhu tsi* Confucius, the first law-giver of China and founder of Confucianism.

ཁུངས *khuñs* origin, source: ཁུངས་སྐྱེལ *khuñs-skyel* the act of making over the charge of any office or store in a faithful manner without anything missing, making use in full of that bought over as a loan, &c.: ཆོས་ཁུངས་དག་པ *chos khuñ dag-pas* pure and uninterpolated religious work; also pure religion: རྒྱུད་པ་ཁུངས་དག་པ *rgyud-pa khuñs dag-pa* of pure origin or lineage. The word ཁུངས་དག་པ *khuñs dag-pa* is also applied to articles of the best make and quality from well-known centres of trade: འདིར་ཡོད་རྨོངས་མི་རྣམས་ནས་ཁུངས་སྐྱེལ་ཐུབ་པའི་སྙན་ཞུ་འབུལ *hdir yod rmons-mi-rnams nas khuñs-skyel thub-pahi sñun-shu hbul* the benighted people of that place petitioned stating the real state (of affairs). ཁུངས་ཐུབ *khuñs-thub* pure and real, original; ཁུངས་མེད *khuñs-med* or ཁུངས་ངན་པ *khuñs-ñan-pa* having no good origin, *i.e.*, mean, inferior: གཏམ་ཁུངས *gtam-khuñs* historical or traditional source; record; document: གཏམ་ཁུངས་ཅན་ཡིན *gtam khuñ s-canyin* the source of that speech is divine. བསྒོམས་པས་རྣམ་རྟོག་ས་བོན་དང་བཅས་པ་སྤོང་ནུས་པའི་ཁུངས་ཇི་ལྟར་ཞེ་ན If asked what is the nature of meditation, it is the secret source of being able to abandon imaginative thoughts (*rnam-rtog*) together with their seed (*Lam. ṭi., 43*).

ཁུངས་མ *khuñs-ma*=དངོས་ནས་ཡོད་པ *dños-nas yod-pa* original and really existing or སྤུས་དག་པོ *spus dag-po*, of excellent quality, same as ཁུངས་གཙང་མ་འགའ་ཞིག་ལ་གཞི་ཁུངས་མ་ནས་འབྱུང་བའི་རྒྱུ་མཚན some of pure descent had reasons arising from genuine grounds.

ཁུངས་བཙུན *khuñs-btsun* well-founded; genuine; of undefiled origin: བོན་གཞུང་གང་ཇུང་ཁུངས་བཙུན་ནས་བ་ཤད་པ as described in whatever Bon texts that have a genuine origin.

ཁུད *khud* coat-lap or any makeshift cloth; wrapper: གོས་ཀྱི་ཁུད་དུ་དྲིལ་ཏེ་ཁུར *gos-kyi khud-du dril te khur* carried wrapped in the flap of his coat; ཁུད་དུ *khud-du* aside, apart; secretly; ཁུད་དུ་འཇོག་པ *khud-du hjog-pa* to put; lay aside: ཁུད་དུ་བྱས་པ *khud-du byas-pa* to have shown one's authority over a thing which belongs to many.

ཁུད་པ *khud-pa* pocket, pouch (*Sch.*): རྫས *rdsas* or སྐྱེལ་རྫོངས *skyel-rdsons* यौतुक anything sent; a dowry; an article presented.

ཁུད་མ *khud-ma* side; edge (*Cs.*).

ཁུད་ཟེ *khud-ze* for ཁུད་ལ་གཟད *khud-la gzad* hold forth the lap of your coat!

ཁུན་ཏི *khun-ti* or ཁྱེན་ཏི *khyen-ti* is stated to be used in *Pur.* for he or she (*Jä.*).

ཁུན་པ *khun-pa* कूजन the uttering of any inarticulate sound; cooing; moaning; the rattling of wheels; rumbling of the bowels; to grunt (*Jä.*); to groan (*Sch.*).

ཁུམ་བུ *Khum-bu* n. of a place in the confines of Tibet and Nepal (*S. kar. 77*).

ཁུམ(ས) *khum(s)* crooked (*Jä.*).

ཁུམས་ལག *khums-lag*=སྐྱེ་ལག *skyes-lag*, དོན་བསྒྱུར་ཡིན *don bsgyur-yin* diminished; changed: ཁྱེད་ཀྱི་དད་པ་ཁུམས་ལག་ན if your faith be diminished (*A. 85*).

ཁུར *khur* or ཁུར་པོ *khur-po* भार burden; load for men: ཕ་དེར་པའི་ཁུར་བོག་པ the father's burden having fallen on the son (*Pag. 23*): ཁུར་རྒྱུད་པས་འཚོ་བ་ཞིག one that lives by carrying loads (*Ja.*): ཁུར་ཤིང *khur-çin* wooden pole over the neck from the ends of which loads are carried; a milkmaid's yoke-pole is called ཁུར་འཛིན *khur-hdsin*: ཁུར་ཁུར་པོ *khur-khur-po* he who carries the bodily existence is *Puñ-gala*; a corporeal being; ཁུར་གྱིས་དུབ་པ *khur-gyis dub-pa* भारच्छिन्न one worn out by carrying loads; ཁུར་གྱིས་ནོན་པ *khur-gyis non-pa* one drooping under a burden or load, also pressed down by responsibilities and sufferings: སྡུག་བསྔལ་མང་པོའི་ཁུར་གྱིས་ནོན་པར་འགྱུར were pressed down by the weight of many miseries; ཁུར་གླ *khur-gla* भारमूल्य the wage for carrying a load: ཁུར་རྔན *khur-rñan*. id.

ཁུར་ལྕི་བ *khur lci-wa* heavy load or responsibility: ནས་ཏེ་འཆི་བ་དང་ཁུར་ལྕི་བས་ངལ being old, heavy burdens and death wore them out (*Lam-rim. 74*).

ཁུར་བརྙན་པ *khur-brñan-pa*=གཡར་བ *gyar-wa* धारण (from धारि) to borrow; to take loan of.

ཁུར་ཐག *khur-thag*=ཁུར་ཡོངས་འདྲེན་ཐག *khur-yons hdren-thag* or འཕྱང་ཐག *hphyan-thag* the rope used in suspending loads from the ends of a yoke-like pole; rope to carry loads.

ཁུར་འདེགས་བྱེད *khur hdegs-byed* giving over a charge or responsibility or load.

ཁུར་འདྲེན་པ *khur hdren-pa* भारिक one who carries or draws a load; one who takes charge of.

ཁུར་པ *khur-pa* and ཁུར་མི *khur-mi* a load-carrier; a coolie.

ཁུར་འཕྲོག་པ *khur hphrog-pa* भारहार the depriving of one's charge; the robbing of one's load.

ཁུར་བ *khur-wa*, v. ཁུར་ཚོས *khur-tshos*.

ཁུར་བོར་བ *khur-bor-wa* अपगतभार he who has laid down the burden, charge or responsibility. In Buddhism ཁུར་བོར་བ *khur-bor-wa* or ཁུར་པོ་བོར་བ *khur-po bor-wa*, one who has laid down the five aggregates (*skandha*), *i.e.*, he who will not have again to take corporeal existence; one of the perfections of a *S'rāvaka*.

ཁུར་བླངས་པ *khur blan-pa* to take over charge: འབྲེལ་བཤད་ཀྱི་ཁུར་བླངས་པས *hbrel bçad kyi khur blans-pas* having undertaken the task of expounding (*Situ. 2*).

ཁུར་མང(ས) *khur-man(s)* or ཁུར་མང་པ *khur-man-pa*, ཁུར་ཚོད *khur-tshod* तिक्तिर, साकुबच्छ dandelion, or the (བ་སླང་ལྕེ *ba-glan lce*) ox-tongue (as it is called in Tibet), used as a pot-herb and medicinal plant, a kind of edible herb: ཁུར་མང་བད་སྨུག་ཚད་པ་ལ་ཕན dandelion is useful in fever and brown phlegm.

Syn. ཁུར་ཚད *khur-tshad*; བ་གླང་ལྕེ *ba-glañ lce* (*Mñon.*).

ཁུར་ཚོས *khur-tshos* or མཁུར་ཚོས *mkhur-tshos* गण्ड; कपोल the cheek, the ruddy part of the face below the eyes.

Syn. ཁུར་བ *khur-wa.*

ཁུར་བཟོད་པ *khur-bzod-pa* भारक्षम one who is able to carry a load, who has patience to carry a burden or responsibility.

ཁུར་ལ་མི་འཇིགས *khur-la mi-hjigs* = ས་གཞི *sa-gshi* the earth (*Mñon.*).

ཁུར་ལེན *khur-len* the charge of: རྫོང་སྡོད་མི་འདིས་ལོ་ཟླ་ཚེས་གྲངས་འདི་ཙམ་རྫོང་གི་ཁུར་ལེན་བྱེད་པ the resident officer in the Jong about this date of the month and year took over charge of the Jong (district).

ཁུར་བསམ་ཆེ་བ *khur-bsam che-wa* one having a sense of responsibility: སྤྱི་སྒོ་གང་བྱེད་ཁུར་བསམ་ཆེ་བ་དགོས་པའི་བཀོད general instruction for the necessity of a sense of responsibilities in an office.

ཁུལ *khul* 1. jurisdiction; province; domain; district: གཞིས་རྩེ་ཁུལ *Gshis-rtse-khul* within the jurisdiction or province of Shi-ga-tse: ལྷ་སའི་ཁུལ *Lha-sahi khul* all the places belonging to or within the town jurisdiction of Lhasa: དེའི་ཁུལ་ལ་འདུག *dehi khul la hdug* is subject to him (*Jä.*). 2. also manner, state, or circumstance: ཡང་མ་ཤེས་ན་ཤེས་ཁུལ་བྱས if you do not know, act the manner of knowing: མེད་ན་ཡོད་པའི་ཁུལ་བྱས if (you) have (it not), act as if you had: གཅིག་ཕར་ཚུར་ཚོང་སྣུན་བུ་རྒྱབ་ཁུལ་བྱེད་ཀྱི་ཡོད I have been doing a little business in buying and reselling from one party to another. 3. a ravine (in *Kunawar*). 4. the soft down of furs (*Sch.*). 5. ཁུལ་མལ *khul-mal* small basket for wool. 6. very soft wool of Tibetan goat which grows next to skin, and also called ཁུ་ལུ *khu-lu* or བལ་འཇམ *bal-hjam*: ཁུལ་སྒྱེ་མོ *khul sgye-mo* made of the softest goat-hair or yak-hair: ཁུལ་ཕྱིང *khul-phyiñ* felt made of the softest wool of goat or yak.

Syn. མངའ་ཤབས *mñah-shabs*; མངའ་ཧོག *mñah-hog* (*Mñon.*).

ཁུལ་མ *khul-ma* the bottom or the side of a thing (*Cs.*).

ཁུལ་རྩེ *khul-rtse* = ཧ་ཅང *ha-cañ* or ཤིན་ཏུ *çin-tu* to a great measure, lit. from the bottom to the top; hence entirely, greatly (*Yig. 14*).

ཁུལ་རྩིད *khul-rtsid* an abbreviation of the words ཁུ་ལུ *khu-lu* and རྩིད *rtsid*.

ཁེ *khe* numeral ninety-two (92).

ཁེ་ཁྱེ *khe-khye* or ཁེ་མ *khe-ma* 1. profit, gain; ཁེ་སྤོགས *khe-spogs* ditto; ཁེ་ཚོང་བྱེད་པ *khe tshoñ byed-pa* to trade; to traffic; to bargain; ཉམས་པའི་ཁེ་ཁྱེ gain; advantage obtained by experience. 2. tetter; herpes; ringworm (eruption on the skin) (*Sch.*).

ཁེ་གད *Khe-gad* n. of a place, the birth-place of ལོ་ཙ་བ་འཁོར་ལོ་གྲགས་པ *Lo-tsa-wa Hkhor-lo grags-pa* (*Loñ.* ཟ *30*).

ཁེ་གན་རྩེ *Khe gan-rtse* n. of a monastery in China erected by the Chinese Minister Ka-thi-shee (*Yig.*).

ཁེ་སྒྲུབ་པ *khe sgrub-pa* to mako profit, to gain: ཁེ་བརྒྱབ་པ *khe brgyab-pa* to make a good bargain (*Sch.*).

ཁེ་ཅན *khe-can* with profit; profitable.

ཁེ་ཉེན *khe-ñen* profit and loss; risk; also good and evil, *i.e.*, ཡག *yag* and ཉེས *ñes*.

ཁེ་པ *khe-pa* in Amdo = ཚོང་པ *tshoñ-pa* tradesman; dealer; one who makes profit by selling or in business; ཚོང་འདུས་ཁེ་པ *tshoṅ-hdus khe-pa* trader; middleman.

ཁེ་བྲག་མདོ *Khe brag-mdo* n. of a place in Kong-po, where the eighth incarnate *Karmapa* Lama was born.

ཁེ་མེད *khe-med* unprofitable.

ཁེ་རུ་འགྲོ་བ *khe-ru hgro-wa* to fall in price.

ཁེ་ལེ་མོན *Khe-le mon* n. of a place in Mongolia (*Yig.*).

ཁེ་སླེབས་ཆེན་པོ *khe-slebs chen-po* very profitable yielding good income.

ཁེ་གསུམ *Khe-gsum* n. of a place in Tibet (*S. kar.*).

ཁེགས *khegs*, v. ཁ *kha*.

ཁེགས་པ I: *khegs-pa* to obstruct; close: མངལ་སྒོ་ངེས་པར་ཁེགས་པར་འགྱུར་རོ (the medicine) will certainly obstruct the passage of the womb.

ཁེགས་པ II: = མུན་པ་སྤྱི *mun-pa spyi* a general name for darkness, gloom or obscurity (*Mṅon.*).

ཁེངས་གཏམ *kheṅs-gtam* boastful words or language.

Syn. དྲེགས་ཚིག *dregs-tsig*; ང་རོ *ṅa-ro* (*Mṅon.*).

ཁེངས་ལྡན་མ *kheṅs-ldan ma* = བུ་མོ་དར་མ *bu-mo dar-ma* a youthful maiden (*Mṅon.*).

ཁེངས་པ *kheṅs-pa* अहंकार, दम्भ 1. pride, haughtiness, arrogance. 2. pf. of འཁེངས་པ *hkheṅs-pa* to fill; become replete with. 3. गर्वित puffed up, haughty, arrogant: ཁེངས་པ་ཅན *kheṅs-pa-can* गर्वित् one who boasts; braggadacio.

Syn. རེངས་པ *reṅs-pa*; དྲེགས་པ *dregs-pa*; ང་རྒྱལ *ṅa-rgyal* (*Mṅon.*).

ཁེན་འདྲ *khen-hdra* a kind of cotton cloth.

ཁེན་པ *khen-pa* 1. wormwood (*Schtr.*). 2. to lean; to repose on (erroneously for བཁན་པ *bkhan-pa*) (*Sch.*).

ཁེབས *khebs* छदन, कम्बा a cover, lid, coverlet: कम्बा an enclosure round the sacrificial ground; ཁེབས་ཀྱི་དྲ་བ *khebs-kyi dra-wa* जाल a net (generally of iron) to cover anything; པང་ཁེབས *paṅ-khebs* a cover for the lap; apron; napkin; སྒ་ཁེབས *sga-khebs* a cover for the saddle; ཅོག་ཙེ་ཁེབས *cog-rtse khebs* a table cloth; ཆར་ཁེབས *char-khebs* a rain cloak: ཐོད་ཁེབས *thod-khebs* a cap; hood; གདུང་ཁེབས *gduṅ-khebs* a certain beam or board above the capital of a pillar; གདོང་ཁེབས *gdoṅ-khebs*, veil; cloth to cover the face; མདུན་ཁེབས *mdun-khebs* in *W.* apron.

ཁེབས་འགབ་པ *khebs-hgab-pa* to place a covering (over a thing); to cover.

ཁེབས་སང་བ *khebs saṅ-wa* to take the covering off.

ཁེབས་པ *khebs-pa* = གཡོགས་པ *gyogs-pa* covered, veiled; ཁེབས་མ *khebs-ma* covering (*Cs.*).

ཁེམ *khem*, v. ཁྱེམ *khyem*.

ཁེར་རྐྱང *kher-rkyaṅ* alone; solitary: མི་ཁེར་རྐྱང་གཅིག་འདུག there was only one man, a solitary man.

ཁེར་རྒྱག་པ *kher rgyag-pa* to defraud; to usurp (*Sch.*).

ཁེལ་སྒོ *Khel-sgo* n. of a district, also that of a mountain: ཁེལ་སྒོ་རི་ལ་སྡོག་རྒྱུ་ཁྱོད *Khel-sgo ri-la sdog rgyu-khyod*.

ཁེལ་བ *khel-wa* 1. to load upon; = འཁེལ་བ *hkhel-wa* (*Jä.*). 2. rely upon; depend on; བློ་ཁྱེལ་བ *blo khyel-wa*, བློ་ཆེས་བ *blo ches-wa* to have confidence in; བརྟེན་ཁེལ་བ *brten khel-wa* to be sure; to be certain; to be certain of anything; absolutely certain: དེ་རིང་ཡོང་བརྟན་ཁེལ་ཡིན *de-riṅ yoṅ brtan-khel-yin* (his) coming to-day is absolutely certain.

ཁེས་ཉིན་ *khes-ñin* the day before yesterday (*Sch.*).

ཁེས་པ་ *khes-pa* 1. to hit (the right thing): གནད་ལ་ཁེས་པ་ *gnad-la khes-pa* to strike the vital parts; to hit mortally. 2. one who makes profit or bargain by selling; a petty dealer, trader.

ཁོ་ *kho* I: numeral 122.

ཁོ་ *kho* II: the usual word for the pers. pron., 3rd pers., meaning he, she, or it. Although not an honorific term, it occurs in many authors in referring to both common personages and respected persons, especially in Milarapa and even in much earlier works where *kho* often refers to kings and lamas. However ཁོང་ *khoṅ* is the proper honorific term of the 3rd pers. pron. In certain districts and in some popular writings མོ་ *mo* is used instead of *kho* for "she," but it is considered a vulgar and illiterate usage. The plural takes ཅག་ or ཚོ་, *e. g.*, ཁོ་ཅག་ *kho-cag*, they, them; also ཁོ་ཚོ་ *kho-tsho*, commoner in *W.* In *C.* ཁོ་རང་ *kho-rang* is the popular form for "he" or "she," &c.

ཁོ་ཏི་ *kho-ti* tea-kettle, prob. Chinese (*Jä.*).

ཁོ་ཐག་གཅོད་པ་ *kho-thag gcod-pa* to acquiesce in; hope for; be resigned to: བུས་རྒྱལ་སྲིད་འཕྲོགས་པའི་ལོ་རྒྱུས་ཐོས་ནས་འཕྲེང་ཅན་གྱིས་ཁོ་ཐག་བཅད་ (*Pag. 45*) hearing the account of her son having usurped the kingdom, *Ḥphreṅ-can* acquiesced in it. The word སེམས་ *sems* often precedes this phrase.

ཁོ་མཐིང་ལྷ་ཁང་ *Kho-mthiṅ lha-khaṅ* n. of a monastery in Lhobrag, South Tibet.

ཁོ་ན་ *kho-na* 1. only, solely, exclusively. 2. just, exactly, the very: སྡིག་པ་ཁོ་ན་ *sdigpa kho-na* sin only; དགེ་བ་ཁོ་ན་ *dge-wa kho-na* piety alone: སྐད་ཅིག་ཁོ་ན་ *skad-cig kho-na* only for a moment; འདོད་ཁོ་ནས་བྲལ་བ་ *ḥdod kho-nas brel-wa* to be separated even from desire: སེམས་ཅན་ཁོ་ནས་བདེ་བར་འདོད་ཅེ་ན་ as he intended only the welfare of beings: རང་བྱེད་པའི་སྐྱོན་ཁོ་ནར་ཡོང་ (*Pag. 134*) it will be the fault only of one's own doing: རྒྱལ་པོས་འདོད་པ་ཁོ་ན་ཡིན་ that is just what has been wished for by the king (*Jä.*): སྔ་མ་ཁོ་ན་བཞིན་དུ་ just as before: འདི་ཁོ་ན་ཡིན་པར་ངེས་ the very same (man): སྲིན་བུ་ཁོ་ན་འདྲ་བ་ just like a worm: ཚུལ་དེ་ཁོ་ནས་ by the very same process: དེ་ཁོ་ན་ *de-kho-na* तत्त्व the state of being that; true state; real state; truth; reality; opposed to what is illusory or fallacious; essential nature; the real nature of the human soul as being one and the same with the supreme spirit pervading the universe; (in philosophy) truth, reality, a true principle.

Syn. ཤ་སྟག་ *ça-stag*; འབའ་ཞིག་ *ḥbaḥ-shig* (*Mṅon.*).

ཁོ་པ་ *kho-pa*=ཁོ་ཅག་ *kho-cag* or ཁོང་ཚོ་ *khoṅ tsho* they.

ཁོ་པོ་ *Kho-po* a tribal name in Tibet: ཉག་ལེ་ལ་ཁོ་པོ་དང་ཁོ་དབྲ་གཉིས་ *Ñag-le la kho-po daṅ kho dbra gñis*, the ཉག་ལེ་ *Ñag-le* tribe is divided into two—ཁོ་པོ་ *Kho-po* and ཁོ་དབྲ་ *Kho-dbra*.

ཁོ་བོ་ *kho-wo* अहं I; myself; ཁོ་བོ་ཅག་ *kho-wo cag*=ངེད་ཚོ་ we: འདི་ལ་ཁོ་བོས་ངོ་མཚར་གྱུར་ *ḥdi-la kho-wos ño-mtshar gyur* this produced admiration in me: ལུགས་འདིར་ཁོ་བོའི་སྤྲོ་བ་འཕེལ་ for this system my enthusiasm increased. In མི་ཁོ་བོའི་རྣམ་ཤེས་ the term *kho-wo* would seem to mean "himself,"—the soul of man himself.

ཁོ་བོམ་ *Kho-bom* the early Tibetan name for Khatmandu, the capital of Nepal. In East Tibet Khatmandu is still called Yam-bu.

ཁོ་མ *kho-ma*=ཁོམ *khom* knapsack; wallet (*Jä.*).

ཁོ་མོ *kho-mo* I; we (feminine).

ཁོ་གྱུ *kho-gyu* the thrashing process, which is done by driving a number of oxen fastened together round a pole that stands in the middle of the thrashing floor.

ཁོ་ར I: *kho-ra* is evidently a corruption of ཁོ་རང *kho-rañ*, མི་ཁོ་ར་རང་གི *mi kho-ra rañ-gi* of the man himself (*Ñag.*).

ཁོ་ར II: (*Cs.*) also འཁོར་ས *khor-sa* circumference; circumjacent space.

ཁོ་ར་ཁོར་ཡུག *kho-ra khor-yug* 1. space; also fence; any surrounding wall (*Jä.*); also a ditch filled with water or moat round a city or a fort. 2. ཀུན་ནས *kun-nas* समन्ततः from everywhere, from all directions; ཁོ་ར་ཁོར་ཡུག་ཏུ *kho-ra khor yug-tu* in a circle; in circumference (frequently in measuring) also roundabout, all round, *e.g.*, to encompass: ཁོར་ཡུག་ཀུན་ཏུ in the whole circuit, roundabout (*Jä.*): ཁོ་ར་ཁོར་ཡུག་ཏུ་དཔག་ཚད་ཕྱེད་པ extending over half a *yojana* or two miles all round.

ཁོ་རེ *kho-re* 1. in *Khams* an expression of displeasure or anger towards a man: ཨ་རོགས *ā-rogs* Oh friend! is the opposite of ཁོ་རེ *kho-re*. 2 one of the early kings of Tibet, son of King *Lde-cug mgon*.

ཁོ་ལ་ཆེ་བ *kho-la che-wa* 1. a large space (*Sch.*). 2. dough made of རྩམ་པ *rtsam-pa* (barley flour) and beer.

ཁོ་ལག *kho-lag*=སྐུ་ལུས *sku-lus* limbs, the entire body: ཁོ་ལག་ཡངས་པ *kho-lag yañs-pa* fully developed body or prominent limbs; ཁོ་ལག་ཡངས་ཤིང་ཆེ་བ་དང་དཔལ་དང་གཟི་བརྗིད་འབར་བ་དང his person being well-developed, was large and glowed with grace and brightness; སྤྱི་ཆེ་བ་ལ་ཁོ་ལག་ཆེ་བ་ཟེར anything that is large all over is called *kho-lag che-wa*. Also a generally well-developed shape is called *kho-lag che-wa*.

ཁོ་ལག་རྫོགས *kho-lag rdsogs*=ལང་ཚོ་དར་བ *lañ tsho dar-wa* youthfulness; full youth (*Mñon.*).

ཁོག *khog*, freq. for ཁོང་པ *khoñ-pa* 1. the interior, inside. 2. for ཁོགས *khogs* or འཁོགས *hkhogs*. 3. also for འགེགས་པ *hgegs-pa*; ཤ་ཁོག *ça-khog* the carcass of an animal for meat: ཁོག་འཛུད་ཁོག་པ་ཕྱེད་དང་ལྷུ་གཟུགས་སོགས *khog hdsud khog-pa phyed dañ lhu-gzugs sogs* (*Jig.*) the entire body and one half of the carcass and the parts of the animal (slain).

ཁོག་གཅོང *khog-gcoñ* chronic disease in the stomach or internal parts of the body.

ཁོག་ཆུད *khog-chud* for ཁོང་དུ་ཆུད *khoñ-du-chud*.

ཁོག་པ *khog-pa* 1. inside; the stomach: ཁོག་པ་ལ་ཟས་འཇུ་བ the digestion of food in the stomach. 2 the trunk of the body, containing the heart, lungs, liver, &c.: རུས་སྦལ་གྱི་ཁོག *rus sbal gyi khog* the interior of the body of a tortoise.

ཁོག་མ *khog-ma* also རྫ་ཁོག *rdsa-khog* pot; earthen vessel generally used in Tibet for cooking rice, meat, broth, &c.; རྡོ་ཁོག *rdo-khog* a stone vessel or pot used in *Khams* for cooking purposes; ཁོག་ཆེན *khog-chen* large earthen or stone vessels for cooking the food of a large number.

ཁོག་ཡངས *khog-yañs* or ཁོག་པ་ཆེ་བ *khog-pa che-wa* capacious or large interior (*Ya-sel.* 48): ཁོག་ཤིང *khog-çiñ* the core of a tree; heart-wood.

ཁོག་ཤུགས *khog-çugs* a groan; a sigh.

ཁོགས་པ *khogs-pa* 1. imp. of འགོག་པ *hgg-opa*, ར་དེ་མི་རྣག་ར་མ་བཙུག་པར་ཁོགས་ཤིག stop that goat from eating the flowers. 2. to cough (*Jä.*).

ཁོང I: *khoṅ* an honorific equivalent of ཁོ *kho*, he, she: ཁོང་གི་ཐུགས་ལ *khoṅ-gi thugs-la* in his thoughts; ཁོང་གི་སྐུ་མདུན་དུ *khoṅ-gi sku-mdun-du* in his presence; རྒྱལ་པོ་ཁོང་རང་ཡིན་དགོངས་ནས *rgyal-po khoṅ-raṅ yin dgoṅs-nas* the king supposing that he himself was meant. Plural ཁོང་ཚོ *khoṅ-tsho* they, them.

ཁོང་པ *khoṅ-pa* the interior of anything; the inside; also as adv. in the forms *khoṅ-du, khoṅ-na,* inside, within; also postp. *khoṅ-na,* into, within; *khoṅ-nas* out of. Certain phrases occur: ཁོང་དུ་ཚུད་པ to be anxious, to bear in mind, be impressed; ཁོང་ནས་བླུ་བ to repeat from memory; ཁོང་དུ་བཟུ་བ to collect in the mind; to impress on the memory; to learn (by heart); ཁོང་དུ་མ་ཚུད་པ not to appreciate (*Hbum. 239* to *249*); ཁོང་དུ་མ་ཚུད་པ་མེད་པ not that it was not understood or appreciated (*Hbum. 239* to *249*): ཁོང་ནས་སྙིང་ཕུང་བ་ལྟར *khoṅ-nas sñiṅ phuṅ-wa ltar* as if their hearts had burst out; ཁོང་ནས་སྡང་བ *khoṅ-nas sdaṅ-wa* प्रकोप to be angry or indignant; ཁོང་ནས་ཕྱུང་ *khoṅ-nas pyyuṅ*= ནང་ནས་ཕྱུང *naṅ-nas phyuṅ* was taken out; ཁོང་པའི་དྲོད་ལ་ཕན *khoṅ-pahi drod-la phan* it helps the internal heat, *i.e.*, digestion.

ཁོང་འཁྲུག *khoṅ-hkhrug* uneasiness; sorrow; anxiety.

ཁོང་ཁྲོ *khoṅ-khro* (*koṅ-tho*) or ཁོང་ཁྲོ་བ *khoṅ khro-wa* प्रतिघ the state of becoming angry; passion; also inward wrath, malice; ཁོང་ཁྲོ་ཅན *khoṅ-khro-can* कटुक bitter; angry; malicious: ལེགས་སྤྱད་གང་ཡིན་དེ་ཀུན་ཀྱང ཁོང་ཁྲོ་གཅིག་གིས་འཇོམས་པར་བྱེད even all the good that was done, by one angry outburst may be destroyed; ཁོང་ཁྲོ་སྤོང་བ *khoṅ-khro spoṅ-wa* to put away or subdue anger; ཁོང་ཁྲོ་ཟ་བ *khoṅ-khro za-wa* to conceive anger, take dislike; to be indignant; ཁོང་ཁྲོའི་རྣམ་འགྱུར་མེད་པ *khoṅ-khrohi rnam hgyur med-pa* free from the state of passion or anger (*Pag. 130.*).

ཁོང་གང *khoṅ-gaṅ* full inside; solid.

Syn. ཚོད་ཡོད *tshod-yod*; ཁོག་ཆུད *khog-chud* (*Mṅon.*).

ཁོང་སྙིང་ *khoṅ-sñiṅ* 1. the secret heart; the intention or design. 2. pith; core; ཤིང་གི་ཁོང་སྙིང the pith or inner wood of a tree (*Mṅon.*).

+ ཁོང་སྙོམ *khoṅ-sñom*= ཡིད་ཞུམ་པ *yid-shum-pa* of even temper.

ཁོང་མར *khoṅ-mar* butter used in making cake-like offerings to the gods.

ཁོང་སྨན་སེར་པོ *khoṅ-sman ser-po* the yellow medicine from the intestines, *i.e.*, bile or gall (*Sman. 66*).

ཁོང་ཚིལ *khoṅ-tsil* suet.

ཁོང་འཛིན *hkhoṅ-hdsin*= ཁོང་ཁྲོ *khoṅ-khro* anger; vindictiveness (*Mṅon.*).

ཁོང་གསེང *khoṅ-seṅ* secret holes in rocks.

ཁོང་གསེབ *khoṅ-gseb* the hollow (of a tree); the inner recess: སྔོན་དྲང་སྲོང་གོ་ཏ་མའི་ཆུང་མ་བཞོལ་མེད་མ་ཞེས་བྱ་བ་ཤིན་ཏུ་སྡུག་ཅིང་ཡིད་དུ་འོང་བ་ཞིག་ཡོད་པ་ཤིང་གི་ཁོང་གསེབ་ཏུ་སྦས in ancient times the wife of Gautama the sage, Shol-med-ma by name, being very pretty and fascinating, was concealed in the hollow of a tree (*Mṅon.*).

ཁོངས *khoṅs* the middle; the innermost; ཁོངས་སུ or ཁོངས་ན in the midst: *khoṅs-su htshud-pa* to go into the midst; to understand; *byed-sgo che phra zom-lus med-pahi khoṅs hgros yoṅ-wa* the more and less important works, not leaving out the simpler ones, should be well studied. *Hgro-wa rigs drug rtsis pahi skabs-su klu-ni dud-hgrohi khoṅs-su hdus* when reckoning the six kinds of animated beings, include the *Nāga* among the beasts; གསེར་གླིང་དང་ཟང་གླིང་སོགས་ཀྱང་འཛམ་གླིང་གི་ཁོངས་སུ་གཏོགས Ser-ling, Zang-ling, etc., are included in the continent of Dzam-ling: དེ་ཉིད་ཀྱི་ཁོངས་སུ་གཏོགས་སོ (this) is contained, *i.e.*, included in, that (*Jä.*): བཙམས་སིལ་རི་ཁ་སྙོམས་པའི་ཁོངས་སྐྱིབས་ན *bsil-ri kha snoms-vahi khons-skyibs na* in the protected cleft of the cool mountain where the snow is levelled (*Ya-sel. 35*).

ཁོངས་པ *khons-pa* कर्कश 1. highly injurious; violent; cruel; rough. 2. adv. crooked: ཁོངས་ཆ་འདུག *khons cha-hdug* it is bent, curved, warped.

ཁོངས་རིལ *khons-ril* crippled. (*Jä.*).

ཁོད *khod*=ངོས *nos* 1. the external appearance; outward look; surface: སྙོམས་པས་ཁོད་ *sa khod-snoms-pa* land of even surface; plains: སོ་ངོས་སྙོམས་པ even and regular teeth: ལས་ཀ་ལ་ཁོད་སྙོམས་པོ་གྱིས *las-ka la khod-snoms-po gyis* in doing a work (business) be of even temper: ཞལ་བ་དང་ཚོན་བཏང་རྒྱུ་ལ་ཁོད་སྙོམས་པོ་གྱིས *shal-wa dan tshon btan-rgyu-la khod-snoms-po gyis* in plastering and in painting make the surface even: མི་མང་པོའི་བཟའ་བཏུང་ལ་ཁོད་སྙོམས་པོ་གྱིས *mi man-pohi bzah btun-la khod snoms-po gyis* in giving food and drink to many people make the distribution uniform: སྲབ་འཐུག་ཁོད་སྙོམས་པོ *srab hthugkhod-snoms-po* fine and thick levelled into one. 2. v. འཁོད་པ *hkhod-pa* and འགོད་པ *hgod-pa*.

ཁོད་ཁོད་གྲངས an average number (*Ya-sel. 35*).

ཁོན I: *khon* वैरता sbst. anger; grudge; resentment; enmity: ཁོན་འཛིན་པ *khon hdsin-pa* or ཁོན་དུ་འཛིན་པ *khon-du hdsin-pa* उपनाह to feel rancour, hatred; ཁོན་བཟོད་པ *khon bzod-pa* forbear, endure, forgive; ཁོན་ཀྱུག་ཏེ་སྡད་པ *khon gug-te sdad-pa* lit. to sit waiting out of vindictiveness to take revenge upon; ཁོན་འབར *khon-hbar* in *W.* sting; the burning of anger or hatred in the soul (*Jä.*); ཁོན་པ་ལས་ཁོན་པར་གྱུར་ཤིང་ getting more and more spiteful.

ཁོན II: a technical term in Tibet and Chinese astrology applying to one of the eight mystical signs or *parkha* of divination; ཁོན་པ one whose lot is cast in this division.

ཁོབ *khob* fat; heavy; clumsy (*Sch.*).

ཁོབ་ཁྲོབ *khob-khrob* the sound caused by the tapping of one thing upon another.

ཁོམ *khom* wallet; leather trunk; felt or hide bag: གཟིགས་ཁོམས *gzigs-khoms* a great man's trunk: ཁོམ་འབོག *khom-hbog* a bag usually made of leather for carrying apparel and other articles on a journey.

ཁོམ་པ *khom-pa* 1. to have leisure, time to do a thing. 2. to be enabled to do a thing by the absence of external impediments (*Schtr.*): ཁོམ་པ་མིན *khom-pa min* I have no time; I cannot do it now; སྡོད་མི་ཁོམ *stod mi khom* no leisure to stay; ང་ཁོམ *na khom* I am versed in; མི་ཁོམ *mi khom* not practised; མི་ཁོམ་པ་བརྒྱད *mi khom-pa brgyad* अष्टावक्षणा: the eight obstacles to happiness caused by the rebirth in places or situations unfavourable to one's conversion to Buddhism. Such re-births are:—སེམས་ཅན་དམྱལ་བ *sems-can dmyal-wa* नरकजाति as hell beings; དུད་འགྲོ *dud-hgro* तिर्यक् as beasts, reptiles, flies, etc.; ཡི་དྭགས *yi-dbags* प्रेत ghosts; ལྷ་ཚེ་རིང་པོ *lha tshe-rin-po* दीर्घजीविदेव the gods who enjoy very long life; མཐའ་འཁོབ་མི *mthah hkhob-mi* प्रत्यन्तजनपद the border (wild) people; དབང་པོ་མ་ཚང་བ *dwan-po ma-tshan-wa* इन्द्रियवैकल्य those who are defective in the faculties of the mind or of the body; ལོག་པར་ལྟ་བ *log-par lta-wa* मिथ्यादर्शन following false or heretical doctrines or theories; དེ་བཞིན་གཤེགས་པ་རྣམས་མ་བྱུང་བ *de-bshin gçeg-pa rnams ma byun-wa* तथागतानामनुत्पाद the place where the Tathāgata has not (yet) made his appearance.

ཁོར་མོ་ཡུག *khor-mo yug* incessantly; continually (*Sch.*), v. ཁོར་ཡུག *khor-yug*.

ཁོར་མོར་སྤྱོད་པ *khor-mor spyod-pa* continual and uninterrupted suffering (in the hell): དམྱལ་བར་སྐྱེས་ན་ཆོ་ཀྱང་གི་ སྡུག་བསྔལ་ལ་ཁོར་མོར་སྤྱོད་པས་ཆོས་བྱེད་དུ་མི་ཁོམ when born in hell, being subjected to torments in the miseries of heat and cold, the performance of religion is impracticable.

ཁོར་ཟུག *khor-zug* an obsolete form of ཁོར་ཡུག *khor-yug*, also ཉེ་འཁོར *ñe-ḥkhor* परिसमन्त.

ཁོར་ཡུག *khor-yug* 1. ཉེ་འཁོར *ñe-ḥkor*; ཀུན་ནས *kun-nas* समन्ततः चक्रवाल the horizon; the outmost limit; the outer line or circumference; ཉིན་མཚན་ཀུན་ཏུ at all times, day and night. 2. ཉིན་མཚན་ཁོར་ཡུག་གཉིད་མེད་དུ་བཞག kept them without sleep at all times, day and night (*Yig*): ཁོར་ཡུག་ཆེན་པོ *khor-yug chen-po* महाचक्रवाल acc. to the Buddhists, the outer wall of the world; the greater horizon from the top of Sumeru.

ཁོར་ས *khor-sa*=ཁོ་ར *kho-ra*.

ཁོལ *khol* or ཁོལ་བུ *khol-bu* abridgment; epitome; ཁོལ་དུ་ཕྱུང་བ *khol-du phyuñ-wa* abridged (*Cs.*).

ཁོལ་མཆུ *khol-mchu* the mouth of a bellows.

ཁོལ་དུ *khol-du*=ཟུར་དུ *zur-du* in a corner; marginally.

ཁོལ་པ *khol-pa* boiled (*Cs.*); boiling; bubbling (*Sch.*).

ཁོལ་པོ *khol-po*=གཡོག་པོ *gyog-po* दास a servant; ཁོལ་བྲན *khol-bran* a slave; ཁོལ་པོར་རྗེས་སུ་བཟུང་བ *khol-por rjes-su bzuñ-wa* to take; to hire for a servant: འཇིག་རྟེན་སྲིད་པའི་ཁོལ *hjig-rten srid-pahi khol* the world is a servant of the evolving principle. ཁོལ་མོ *khol-mo* a maid-servant; a female slave; ཁོལ་པོ་སྒོག་སྐྱའི་ཁུར་པོ་ཅན *khol-po sgog-skyahi khur-po-can* name of kind of vegetable medicine applied to wounds and sores, &c. (*Sman. 350*).

ཁོལ་བུ *khol-bu* a bit; a small piece.

ཁོལ་མ *khol-ma*=སྐར་ཁུང *skar-khuñ* गवाच 1. a window; a hole in the wall or roof of a house to serve the purpose of a window or sky-light; acc. to *Sch.* an outlet for the smoke in a roof. 2. anything boiled: ཇ་དང་ཆུ་སོགས་བསྐོལ་པའི་ཁོལ་མ *ja dañ chu sogs bskol-pahi khol-ma* tea or water that has been boiled: དམྱལ་བའི་ཁྲོ་ཆུ་ཁོལ་མ *dmyal-wahi khro-chu khol-ma* the boiling or molten matter of hell: ཧོ་ཐུག་ཁོལ་མ *ho-thug khol-ma* boiling gruel.

ཁོལ་མོ: *khol-mo* 1. གཡོག་མོ *gyog-mo* दासी maid servant. 2. a coarse sort of blanket usually given to slaves in *C.* (*Schtr.*). 3. mowed corn; a swath (*Jä.*). 4. among the herdsmen called *Dog-pa*, a bellows made of an entire goat skin.

ཁོས་རྒྱུད *khos-rgyud*, mis-spelt for ཁོལ་རྒྱུད, a slave family or mean extraction: མག་པ་ལོ་གསུམ་ཁོས་རྒྱུད་མིན་ཀྱང་སྐུལ་རྒྱུད་ཡིན *mag-pa lo-gsum khos rgyud min-kyañ skul-rgyud yin* though the son-in-law (elect) is not a slave (by birth) yet he should be made to serve (the bride's parents) for three years.

ཁོས *khos* imp. of གས་པ *gas-pa* to split: དགྲ་བོའི་མགོ་ཁོས་ཤིག *dgra-bohi mgo khos çig* split the head of the enemy.

ཁྱ་ཧི་ཙེ *khya-hi-tse* the running handwriting of the Chinese.

ཁྱ་ལེ *khya-le* or ཁ་ལེ *kha-le* as much as fills the hollow of the hand; handful, *e.g.*, of water (*Cs.*).

ཁྱག་པ I: *khyag-pa*, seldom ཁྱགས་པ *khyags-pa* 1. frozen. 2. the frost; ice; ཁྱག་ཐོག་ཁར *khyag thog-khar* on the ice; འཁྱག་པའི་བོད་ཡུལ *hkhyag-pahi Bod-yul*, Tibet, the country of frost; ཁྱག་ལ་སྦྱར་སོང *khyag-la sbyar soṅ*, it has stuck fast by freezing: ཁྱག་ཞུ་ཀོ་ཀོ *khyag-shu ko-ko* acc. to *Jä.* in Tsang, mud caused by a thaw; snow-water; ཁྱག་སྲན་ཅན *khyag sran-can* hardened by frost; ཁྱག་རུམ *khyag-rum* or ཁྱག་རོམ *khyag-rom* ice; pieces of ice; floating blocks of ice.

ཁྱག་པ II: to undertake; to be surety for: འདི་ཁྱོད་ཁུར་ཁྱག་གམ་མི་ཁྱག *hdi kkyod-khur khyag-gam mi kkyag* can you undertake to do this or not: བུ་ལོན་སོགས་ལ་ཁ་ཁྱག་བྱེད་པ to stand as security for a loan, etc.

ཁྱད *khyad* 1. difference, distinction: གང་བཏང་ན་ཁྱད་མེད *gaṅ btaṅ-na khyed-med* it is no matter which you give me; ང་དང་ཕྲད་པ་དང་ཁྱད་མེད *ṅa daṅ phrad-pa daṅ khyad-med* it is quite the same as if they came to myself; སེམས་ལ་ཁྱད་བྱུང *sems-la khyed-byuṅ* a difference of opinion arose (*Jä.*). 2. something excellent; superior; ཁྱད་ཆེས་འཕགས་པ greatly exalted; བཟོ་ཁྱད *bzo-khyad* an excellent work of art; བསྒྲུབས་པའི་ཁྱད་ཡོན *bsgrubs-pahi khyad-yoṅ* there will be some advantage in accomplishing it; ཁྱད་ནོར *khyad-nor* the principal or chief wealth; ཁྱད་དོན *khyad-don* the principal sense or reason; advantage. 3. is added to an adj. to express the notion derivable from any quality: སྟོམ་པོ thick; སྟོམ་ཁྱད thickness; ཡངས་པ wide; ཡངས་ཁྱད width; གོམས་པ accustomed; གོམས་ཁྱད a habit or custom.

ཁྱད་ཁྱུད *khyad-khyud*, said to be གྲངས་ཀྱི་མིང, n. of a number (*Ya-sel. 57*).

ཁྱད་ཆོས *khyad-chos* superior or excellent doctrine; a good religious discourse, hence those who possess special qualification for miracles are called གཞན་ལས་ཁྱད་པར་དུ་འཕགས་པ "in sublimity superior to others."

ཁྱད་དུ *khyad-du*=ཁྱད་པར་དུ *khyad-par-du* or བྱེ་བྲག་ཏུ *bye-brag-tu* especially, particularly; also superior and excellent; ཁྱད་དུ་གསད་པ *khyad-du gsad-pa* to contradict; also to do the contrary (out of pride or vanity); to despise: ང་རྒྱལ་དབང་གིས་དམའ་ལ་ཁྱད་དུ་གསད *ṅa-rgyal dwaṅ-gis dmah-la khyad-du gsad* from pride he speaks ironically to the lowly.

ཁྱད་པར *khyad-par*=*khyad-du* 1. difference, distinction: ང་དང་ཁྱོད་གཉིས་ཁྱད་པར་ཆེ *ṅa daṅ khyod dṅis khyad-par che* between you and I there is a great difference; དེ་དང་ཁྱད་པར་མ་མཆིས་པའི་རྟེན *de daṅ khyad-par ma mchis-pahi rten* an image not differing from this; མིང་གི་ཁྱད་པར་ཡིན *miṅ-gi khyad-par yin* it is (only) a difference of name. 2. sort, kind: འབྲས་བུའི་ཁྱད་པར་ཀུན *hbras-buhi khyad-par kun* all sorts of fruit; རི་དྭགས་ཀྱི་ཁྱད་པར་ཞིག *ri-dwags-kyi khyad-par shig* a particular kind of game; ཡུལ་གྱི་ཁྱད་པར *yul-gyi khyed-par* a particular place or province.

ཁྱད་པར་བཀོད་པ *khyad-par bkod-pa*, རྒྱལ་པོའི་ཕོ་བྲང *rgyal-pohi pho-braṅ* an edifice of special design; palace of superb make.

ཁྱད་པར་གྱི་འཆིང་བ *khyad-par-gyi hchiṅ-wa* विषय that which binds particularly, *i.e.*, worldliness.

ཁྱད་པར་ཅན *khyad-par-can* special; specially good; superior, excellent, capital: ཁྱད་པར་ཅན་གྱི་མཛད་པ་གཉིས *khyad-par can-gyi mdsad-pa dṅis* the two special achievements or exploits (*Yig.*): བླ་མ་ཁྱད་པར་ཅན་ཅིག *bla-ma khyad-par-can cig* an excellent spiritual teacher.

ཁྱད་པར་དུ *khyad-par-du*, adv. particularly, chiefly, especially: ཁྱད་པར་དུ་འཕགས་པ *khyad-par-du hphags-pa* particularly eminent, noble; ཁྱད་པར་དུ་སྨོད་པར་བྱེད *khyad-par-du sod-par byed* he scorns, despises, ridicules, vilifies.

ཁྱད་པར་གནས *khyad-par gnas*=བྱང་ཆུབ་ལྗོན་ཤིང་ the *Bodhi* or *Pipal* tree (*Mṅon.*).

ཁྱད་པར་ལོ་མ *Khyad-par lo-ma* excellent leaf; विशाख n. of an individual (*A. K.*).

ཁྱད་ཚར་ཅན *khyad tshar-can*=ངོ་མཚར་ཅན *ṅo mtshar-can* wonderful; curious; strange.

ཁྱད་གཞི *khyad-gshi* the superior basis. A superior basis is alone possessed of *khyad-chos*, *i.e.*, virtues which cannot be found elsewhere. The god Brahmā is called ཁྱད་གཞི་ཚངས་པ *Khyad-gshi tshaṅs-pa*, the god of excellent basis, for Brahmā is possessed of superior moral merits, resplendence, and longevity.

ཁྱབ་པ *khyab-pa*=རྒྱས་པ *rgyas-pa* व्यापिन्, व्याप्त, स्फुरण 1. to fill, penetrate; also to embrace, estimate, comprise: འབྲུམ་པ་མང་པོས་ཁྱབ་པ *hbrum-pa maṅ-pos khyab-pa* full of, or quite covered with, pustules; མཁྲིས་པས་ཁྱབ་པ *mkhris-pas khyab-pa* filled, impregnated with bile; གྲངས་འདས་པའི་བསྐལ་པ་གྲངས་མེད་དཔག་ཏུ་མེད་པ་བསམ་གྱིས་མི་ཁྱབ་པའི་ཕ་རོལ་ཏུ unnumbered immeasurable *kalpas* ago; beyond what the mind is able to estimate. In grammar: capable of being joined to any word, inclusive of all; ཁྱབ་ཆེ་བ *khyab-che-wa* comprehensive; everywhere and nowhere; to be met everywhere; used also in the way of censure (*Jä.*). ནམ་མཁའི་མཐའ་ཁྱབ་པ་ནི་སངས་རྒྱས་ཀྱི་མཁྱེན་པའི་ཡེ་ཤེས the wisdom of Buddha encompasses the bounds of heaven; ཤེས་བྱའི་ཡུལ་རྣམས་ནི་ནམ་མཁའ་མཐའ་དང་མཉམ་པའི་ཁྱབ་པ the domain of knowledge is commensurate with the very extremity of the heavens. 2. ཁྱབ་སོང་བ *khyab soṅ-wa* all-sufficing; all-covering.

ཁྱབ་ཆ *khab-cha*=བྱ་བ *bya-wa* duty, general business (of a man); work: *lugs zuṅ-gi khyab-cha lhos med-du mcis* am executing without relaxation the general duties of both parts of life (*i.e.*, the spiritual and temporal) (*Yig. 44.*).

ཁྱབ་འཇུག *Khyab-hjug* विष्णु the All-pervading One, *i.e.*, Vishṇu. His several names are:—དགའ་བའི་དབང་པོ་གོ་བིནྡ *Dgah-wahi dwaṅ-po* गोविन्द the Lord of Pleasures, Govinda; ཐིག་ལེ་དྲུག་པ་འགྲོ་བའི་ཏོག *Thig-le drug-pa hgro-wahi tog*; ཐ་གུའི་ལྟོ་ཅན་སྲེད་མེད་བུ *Tha-guhi lto-can sred med-bu*; གཡོ་མེད་གླང་རྫི་སྐྲ་ཅན་གསོད *Gyo-med glaṅ-rdsi skra-can gsod* the immovable *Gopāla*—the killer of Kes'i; མི་ཡི་ཐེག་པ་དཔའ་བོ་བརྒྱུད *Mi-yi theg-pa dpah-bo brgyud*, ཉེ་དབང་དཔལ་གྱི་བེའུས་མཚན *Ñe-dwaṅ dpal-gyi behus mtshan* उपेन्द्रश्रीवत्स लाञ्छन the sign S'rīvatsa on the breast of Vishṇu; པདྨའི་ལྟེ་བ་འོག་དབང་སྐྱེས *Padmahi lte-wa hog dwaṅ skyes*; དཔལ་གྱི་ལག་པ་གཡུང་དྲུང་ཅན *Dpal-gyi lag-pa gyuṅ druṅ can*; དབྱིག་གི་ལྟོ་བ་ནབས་སོ་སྐྱེས *Dbyig-gi lto-wa nabs-so skyes*; སྦྱོར་བ་བརྒྱ་པ་དཔལ་གྱི་བདག *Sbyor-wa brgya-pa dpal-gyi bdag*; འཇུག་པ་བཅུ་པ་མིའུ་ཐུང *Hjug-pa bcu-pa mihu thuṅ* वामन the dwarf; he of the ten incarnations; གོམ་གསུམ་གནན་དང་སྟོབས་ལྡན་བསླུ *Gom gsum gnan daṅ stobs-ldan bslu*; མཁའ་ལྡིང་རྒྱལ་མཚན་འཁོར་ལོ་ཕྱག *Mkhah ldiṅ rgyal-mtshan hkhor-lo phyag*; ཟླ་བའི་སྙིང་པོ་པད་དཀར་མིག *Zla-wahi sñiṅ-po pad-dkar mig* पुण्डरीकाक्ष the lotus-eyed; Vishṇu; མ་འཛག་དང་ནི་རྭ་གཞུ་ཅན *Ma hdsag daṅ ni rwa gshu-can*; སྣ་ཚོགས་གཟུགས་ཅན་ཁྱུ་མཚོག་ལྟོ *Sna-tshogs gzugs can khyu-mtshog lto*. དགའ་བ་བརྒྱ་པ་མཐོན་པོའི་ལྷ *Dgah-wa brgya-pa mthon-pohi lha*; སྦྱིན་སྐྱེས་དགྲ་བོ་གོས་སེར་ཅན *Sbyin-skyes dgra-bo gos-ser-can*; མེ་ཏོག་ལྟོ་བ་མཁར་བའི་དགྲ *Me-tog lto-wa mkhar-wahi dgra*; མི་ཡི་སེང་གེ་ཁྱབ་འཇུག་གོ *Mi-yi seṅ-ge Khyab hjug-go* नरसिंह, विष्णु Vishṇu or Nrisimha.

ཁྱབ་འཇུག་རྐང་པ *Khyab-hjug rkaṅ-pa*=river Ganges.

ཁྱབ་འཇུག་སྐྱེས་ *khyab-ḥjug skyes*=ཙན་དན་སྦྲུལ་གྱི་སྙིང་པོ *tsan-dan sbrul-gyi sñiṅ-po* उरगसारचन्दन the fragrant sandal wood tree. Snakes generally coil round its branches; images made of it fetch very high prices.

ཁྱབ་འཇུག་དགའ་མ *Khyab-ḥjug dgaḥ-ma*=ཁྱབ་འཇུག་ཆུང་མ *khyab-ḥjug chuṅ-ma* विष्णुरमा Vishṇu's lover or wife.

ཁྱབ་འཇུག་ཆུང་མ *khyab-ḥjug chuṅ-ma* विष्णुप्रिया *Viṣṇu's* wife. Her different names are:—པདྨ་ཅན *Padma-can*, पद्मावती; འཕྲོག་བྱེད་ཡུམ *Ḥphrog-byed yum*, དཔལ་མོ *Dpal-mo*, ཁྱབ་འཇུག་དགའ་མ *Khyab-ḥjug dgaḥ-ma*.

ཁྱབ་འཇུག་དྲེགས་པའི་གདོང *khyab-ḥjug dregs-paḥi gdoṅ*=སྨན་ཆེན *sman-chen* aconite (*Sman. 97*).

ཁྱབ་འཇུག་གནས *Khyab-ḥjug gnas* विष्णुपद a place of pilgrimage in Gaya, the temple where there is a footprint of Vishṇu.

ཁྱབ་འཇུག་གནོན་པ *khyab-ḥjug gnon-pa*=སྤང་རྒྱན *spaṅ-gyan* lit. the ornament of grass or སྟོན་གྱི་མེ་ཏོག *ston-gyi me-tog*, an autumnal flower (*Mṅon.*).

ཁྱབ་འཇུག་བཞོན་པ *Khyab-ḥjug bshon-pa* the golden eagle on which Vishṇu rides: ཁྱབ་འཇུག་གི་བཞོན་པ་བྱ་ཁྱུང་གི་མིང་ the different names of Garuḍa, the conveyor of Vishṇu—སྐྱ་རེངས་ནུ་བོ *Skya-reṅs nu-bo* the younger brother of the dawn; འོད་སྲུངས་སྐྱེས *Hod sruṅs skyes* काश्यप; མཁའ་འགྲོང་དབང་ཕྱུག *Mkhaḥ ḥgroṅ dwaṅ phyug*, ཀླུ་མཐར་བྱེད *Klu-mthar byed* नागान्तक; གསེར་གྱི་འདབ་ཅན *Gser-gyi ḥdab can* རྡོ་རྗེའི་མཆུ *Rdo-rjeḥi mchu*, འདབ་ཆགས་སེང་གེ *Ḥdab-chags seṅ-ge* ལྟོ་འགྲོ་ཟ *hlto ḥgro-za*, ཉེ་དབང་ཤིང་རྟ *Ñe-dbaṅ çiṅ-rta*, རྣམ་དུལ་སྐྱེས *Rnam dul-skyes*, སྐར་མིག་བུ *Skar mig-bu*, དུག་འཇོམས་ལྡན *Dug-ḥjoms ldan*, འདུལ་སྐྱེས *ḥdul-skyes*, འདབ་ཆགས་རྒྱལ་པོ *Ḥdab-chags rgyal-po*, མཁའ་ལྡིང *Mkhaḥ-ldiṅ* (*Mṅon.*).

ཁྱབ་འཇུག་གཟེར *Khyab-ḥjug gzer* or ཁྱབ་འཇུག་ནད *khyab-ḥjug nad*, also ར་ཧུ་ལེ་ནེ *Ra-hu le ne*, epilepsy, which is supposed to be sent or caused by the planets or the Hindu deity Vishṇu.

ཁྱབ་གདལ *khyab-gdal* spread out slowly and uniformly in all directions; to absorb all, as does *Çūnyatā*; voidity: ཁྱབ་ནི་ནམ་མཁའ་ཉི། འོད་ཀྱིས་ཁྱབ་པ་ལྟ་བུ་ཆོག་གྲོས་གདལ་ཞེས་པ་ས་ཐམས་ཅད་ཁོད་སྙོམས་པར་གདལ་བ་ལྟ་བུ་ཆོས་ཐམས་ཅད་ལ་ཁྱབ་པའི་སྟོང་ཉིད་དང་ཆོས་ཉིད་ལ་ཡང་ཁྱབ་གདལ་གྱི་སྒྲ་འཇུག་པ་ཡོད་ཅེས (*Ṅag.*).

ཁྱབ་བདག *khyab-bdag* विभु the all-pervading lord.

ཁྱབ་འདོད *khyab-ḥdod* wishing everything.

ཁྱབ་བརྡལ *kkyab-brdal*=ཁྱབ་གདལ *khyab-gdal* all absorbing; all-encompassing: སྣང་བ་དཀར་པོའི་ཁྱབ་བརྡལ་དུ་སྤེལ *snaṅ-wa dkar-poḥi khyab-brdal du-spel* widely diffused like the sunlight.

ཁྱབ་པར་འགྲོ་བ *khyab-par ḥgro-wa* to move, covering everything in the way.

ཁྱབ་པར་འཛིན་པ *khyab-par ḥdsin-pa* निघ्नति: to envelope.

ཁྱབ་བྱེད *khyab-byed*=རུ་རྟ *ru-rta* 1. n. of a vegetable drug. 2. met. the eye. 3. met. the sun.

ཁྱམས *khyams* 1. yard, courtyard; gallery (*Cs.*);=སྲང་ག *sraṅ-ga* the hall of a house; impluvium; (*khyams* is termed *sgo-ra* in a poor house). 2. open; uncovered place in the upper stories of a house where people sit for airing or to enjoy light, air and sun. ཡུལ་འཁོར་འདི་ན་སྐྱེས་བུ་ཇི་སྙེད་ཡོད་པ་ཐམས་ཅད་འཁོར་གྱི་ཁྱམས་སུ་འདུས་ཤིག *yul-ḥhor ḥdi-na skyes-bu ji-sñed yod-pa thams-cad ḥkhor-gi khyams su ḥdus-çig* bring to the courtyard all the people as many as there are in this country to be my followers (*K. d. 210 to 214*).

ཁྱམས་སྟོད *khyams-stod* upper courtyard; ཁྱམས་སྨད *khyams-smad* the lower courtyard.

ཁྱམས་པ *khyams-pa*, ཁྱར་བ *khyar-wa* or ཁྱལ་པ *khyal-pa*, v. འཁྱམས་པ *hkhyams-pa*, &c.

ཁྱམས་ར *khyams-ra* open space before a house or on the roof of a house used for airing, walking, or sitting; also play-ground.

ཁྱི *khyi*, in Tsang pronounced as *kyi* or *kih*, कुक्कुरः, श्वन्, श्वलर्कं, जिह्वाप hound, dog; ཁྱི་མོ *khyi-mo* a bitch; ཁྱི་སྨུག་ཡོང *the dog will bite*; ཁྱི་བོས་ནས་མ་བརྡུང *khyi bos-nas ma-brduṅ* "after calling a dog, do not beat him" is a Tibetan common saying to explain that it is not proper to beat or insult an invited person even if he be a bad person. Acc. to *Sch.* ཁྱི་རྐང་གཉིས *khyi-rkaṅ gñis* a bastard dog, a cur; prob. an inferior breed is meant. ཁྱི་ཡི་ལྕེ་ཡིས་རྨ་རྣམས་འདྲུབས་པར་བྱེད *khyi-yi lce-yis rma rnams hdrubs-par byed* the tongue of the dog causes wounds to heal; ཁྱི་ཡི་རླིག་པས་བུ་རོ་འབྱིན *khyi-yi rlig-pas bu ro hbyin* the testes of a dog draw out the dead child (from the womb); ཁྱི་ཡི་ཀླད་པས་འགྲིབ་མིག་ལ་ཕན *khyi-yi klad-pas hgrib mig-la phan* the brains of a dog are useful for the cataract of the eye; ཁྱི་ཡི་ཁྲག་གི་མཛེ་ནད་སེལ dog's blood removes leprosy: ཁྱི་ཡི་ཤ་ཡིས་ཆུ་ནད་སྐེམ་པར་བྱེད a dog's flesh dries up water, *i.e.*, heals dropsy; ཁྱི་ཡི་སྤུ་གསོབ་ལྷོག་སྐྲངས་གནོན *khyi-yi spu gsob lhog skraṅs gnon* the burnt hair of a dog absorbs swollen ulcers; ཁྱི་ཡི་དྲུན་གྱིས་གདོན་འཇོམ་སྐྲངས་པ་ཞི *khyi-yi drun-gyis gdon hjom skraṅs-pa shi* the excrement of the dog subdues evil spirits in one's body and soothes swellings; ཁྱི་ཐུག་ཆུ་ཡིས་ཁ་ཡི་རུལ་རྡོལ་གཅོད *khyi-thug chu-yis kha-yi rul-rdol gcod* the urine of a dog is a cure for ulcers in the gums (*Sman.*); ཁྱི་ཡི་སྤྱོད་པ *khyi-yi spyod-pa* the habits of the dog described by *Masurakṣa* are as follows: མང་དུ་ཟད་པ *maṅ-du zad-pa* voraciousness, ཉུང་ཟད་ཚོག *cuṅ-zad chog* contentment with a small quantity, ལེགས་པར་གཉིད་ལོག *legs-par gñid-log* always sleeping, མྱུར་བར་སད *myur-war sad* easily wakeful, དཔལ་ལ *dpal-la* intrepidity, སྙིང་ཉེ *sñiṅ-ñe* faithfulness, བརྟན་པ *brtan-pa* firmness. ཁྱི་ཉལ་རྒྱུག་ལྷོང *khyi-ñal rgyug-lhoṅ* is a common saying, to cause a sleeping dog to get up by poking him with a stick, *i.e.*, to rouse to action one who is silent.

Syn. རྡོ་རྗེའི་མཇུག་མ *rdo-rjehi mjug-ma*; གསོ་བྱེད *gso-byed*; འདོད་དབང *hdod-dwaṅ*; སེང་གེའི་རིགས *seṅ-gehi rigs*; སྐྱེ་བའི་ཆ་ཅན *skye-wahi cha-can*; རྫི་གསང་བ *rdsi gsaṅ-wa*; གྲོང་གི་གཅན་གཟན *groṅ-gi gcan-gzan*; ཤ་ཁྱི *ça-khyi* (*Mṅon.*).

ཁྱི་ཀླུང *Khyi-kluṅ* n. of a place and valley in Tibet.

ཁྱི་དཀར་དུང་གི་ཐག་པ་ཅན *khyi dkar duṅ-gi thag-pa-can* n. of a vegetable possessing medicinal properties for healing wounds and sores (*Sman. 350*).

ཁྱི་སྐད *khyi-skad* the barking of a dog.

ཁྱི་ཁང *khyi-khaṅ* dog kennel.

ཁྱི་གུ I: *khyi-gu* in *W.*, bud (of leaves and branches, not of blossoms); the eye (of a plant).

ཁྱི་གུ II: a puppy; a dog.

ཁྱི་ཁྱོ *Kyi-kyo* n. of a place, also of a fabulous country to the east of Asia, prob. Kamschatka (*J. Zaṅ.*).

ཁྱི་སྟོན་ཇོ་ཡེ *Khyi-ston jo-ye* n. of a Buddhist teacher of Tibet.

ཁྱི་དམ *khyi-dam* lit. dog's seal; a mark burnt in; stigma.

ཁྱི་དུག *khyi-dug* the poison of hydrophobia (*Sch.*).

ཁྱི་མདུད་པ *khyi mdud-pa* pairing of dogs.

ཁྱི་པལ་ཇོར *kyi-pal jor* in *W.*, *Blitum virgatam.*

ཁྱི་ཕུལ་ *khyi-pul* a dog kennel; dog-house (*Jä.*)

ཁྱི་སྤྱང་ *khyi-spyañ* (*khib-jung*) a jackal.

ཁྱི་བྲུ་ *khyi-bru* a vicious, biting dog (*Sch.*).

ཁྱི་ར་པ་ *khyi-ra-pa* = རྔོན་པ་ *rṅon-pa*, व्याध, श्वपद, शबर 1. a huntsman; one who kills wild animals by chasing them with dogs, &c. 2. ཀི་ར་ཏ *Kirāta* किरात a tribe in Nepal who live by hunting.

ཁྱི་སྦྲང་ *khyi-sbrañ* a flea; lit. dog's fly.

*ཁྱི་མོ་ *khyi-mo* bitch or female dog: བུད་མེད་དེ་ཁྱི་མོ་དམར་མོ་ཞིག་ཏུ་སོང་ནས "the woman having transmigrated into a red bitch" (*Mil.*).

ཁྱི་སྨྱོང་ *khyi-myoñ* a rabid dog; also canine madness; hydrophobia.

ཁྱི་ཚང་ *khyi-tshañ* a dog-house.

ཁྱི་འཚེད་ *khyi-ḥtshed* भर्जक the baker or seller of parched rice, millet, &c.

+ཁྱིའུ་ཀ *khyiḥu-ka* the remainder of anything cut or chopped off.

ཁྱིའུའི་ཁྱིའུ *khyiḥuḥi-khyiḥu*, ཁྱི་ཕྲུག *khyi-phrug* or ཁྱི་གུ *y-khigu*, puppy; pup: ཁྱིའུའི་ཁྱིའུ་དབྱུང་བའི་ཚུལ་དུ *khyi-ḥu-ḥi-khyiḥu ḏbyuñ-ᴜaḥi tshul-du* श्वनिप्रत्याभिनिर्हारयोगेन in the manner of a puppy being brought forth.

ཁྱི་ར་ *khyi-ra* chasing, hunting, especially of a single huntsman, not of a party; in *W. khyi-ra la ca-çe*, to go hunting: ཁྱི་ར་ལ་ཆགས་ཅན *khyi-ra la chags-can* one who is fond of hunting; sportsman.

ཁྱི་ལ་ཝ་རི *khyi-la ᴜa-ri* = སེང་ལྡན *señ ldan* खदिर the tree *Acacia catechu*; also *Terra japonica*.

ཁྱི་ཤིག *khyi-çig* चत्पात् कीट a flea.

ཁྱི་ཤིང་ *khyi-çiñ* a tree-drug which cures diseases of the lungs and the eye. It also expectorative (*Med.*).

ཁྱི་སོ་རྒྱབ་པ *khyiso-rgyab-pa* the bite of a dog: ཁྱི་སོ་ཏབ་ཤེ *khyiso tab-çe* the dog will bite—Ladak dialect.

ཁྱིག *khyig*, v. འཁྱིག་པ *ḫkhyig-pa*.

ཁྱིད *khyid* breadth of the hand with the thumb extended to form a span.

ཁྱིམ *khyim* 1. resp. ཁབ *khab* गृह, आगार a home, residence, dwelling-place: ཁྱིམ་ན *khyim-na* at home; ཁྱིམ་དུ *khyim-du* at home, in the house; ཁྱིམ་བདག་རིན་པོ་ཆེ *khyim-ḫdag rin-po-che* गृहपतिरत्न the ideal householder (of the Buddhists). 2. राशि the signs of zodiac; ཁྱིམ་བཅུ་གཉིས *khyim-ḫcu-gñis* द्वादशराशि the twelve signs of the zodiac; राशिचक्र or ཁྱིམ་གྱི་འཁོར་ལོ *khyim-gyi ḫkhor-lo* the zodiac; मेष, ལུག *lug* the ram; वृष, གླང *glañ* the bull; मिथुन, འཁྲིག་པ *ḫkhrig-pa* (husband and wife in union) the twins; कर्कट, ཀར་ཀ་ཊ *kar-ka-ṭa* the crab; सिंह, སེང་གེ *señ-ge* the lion; कन्या, བུ་མོ *bu-mo* the virgin; तुला, སྲང *srañ* the balance; वृश्चिक, སྡིག་པ *sdig-pa* the scorpion; धनुः གཞུ *gshu* (or bow) the archer; मकर, ཆུ་སྲིན *chu-srin* the sea-monster (capricorn); कुम्भ, བུམ་པ *bum-pa* water-pot; water-bearer; and मीन, ཉ *ña* fish. Besides these there are mentioned twenty-four minor signs of the zodiac such as वामन, མིའུ་ཐུང *miḫu thuñ* the dwarf; उपकुम्भ, ཉེ་བའི་བུམ་པ *ñe-ᴜaḫi bum-pa*, འབྲིན་གར *ḫbrin-gar*, &c., which raise the list of the signs to thirty-six (*K. g.* ད *129*). Acc. to *Jä.* there is moreover a division into twenty-seven lower mansions much in use, v. རྒྱུ་སྐར *rgyu-skar*. 3. double hours; the time of two hours; the time of the passing of a sign of the zodiac through the meridian (*Jä.*).

4. halo or circle round the sun or moon (*Cs.*). 5. symbolic numeral 21 (*Jä.*).

ཁྱིམ་སྐྱེས *khyim-skyes* गृहज domesticated; indigenous.

ཁྱིམ་སྐྱོང་བ *khyim skyoṅ-wa* to have a household; to gain a livelihood (*Jä.*); to stick to home and look after it.

ཁྱིམ་ཁོལ *khyim-khol* = སྐྱེས་པ་འབྲུས་ཕྱུང་བ *skyes-pa hbrus-phyuṅ-wa* an eunuch; also कुटुम्बिक a domestic slave; one belonging or related to a family.

ཁྱིམ་གྱི་ཀུན་དགའ་ར་བ *khyim-gyi kun-dgah ra-wa* = སྐྱེད་ཚལ *skyed-tshal* a grove or garden attached to a house (*Mṅon.*).

ཁྱིམ་གྱི་གཏོར་ཟ *khyim-gyi gtor-za* ཆུའི་བྱ་གག *chuhi bya-gag* a grey species of duck (*Mṅon.*).

ཁྱིམ་གྱི་དག་ར *khyim-gyi dag-ra*, དངས་ར *daṅs-ra* गृहाङ्गन yard, courtyard. The དག་ར *dag-ra* of a temple or tomb is called འཁོར་ས *hkhor-sa* or ཉེ་འཁོར *ñe-hkhor*.

ཁྱིམ་གྱི་ནོར་བུ *khyim-gyi nor-bu* (lit. the gem of the house) = སྒྲོན་མེ *sgron-med* or མཚན་མོའི་སྣང་བྱེད *mtshan-mohi snaṅ byed* and འབར་བའི་རལ་པ *hbar-wahi ral-pa* a lamp, light (*Mṅon.*).

ཁྱིམ་གྱི་གཡབས *khyim-gyi gyabs* सरणि verandah or portico.

ཁྱིམ་གྱི་ས་ཚིས *khyim-gyi sa tsis* household; house-keeping; farming.

ཁྱིམ་ཉ *khyim-ña* a whale; a fish of the size of a house; a mythological fish (*Sch.*).

ཁྱིམ་ཉེ་བའི་རིན་པོ་ཆེ *khyim-ñe-wahi rin-po-che* गृहोपरत्न the perfect ideal of a lay subject of a king and second only to the ཁྱིམ་བདག་རིན་པོ་ཆེ *khyim-bdag rin-po che*.

ཁྱིམ་ཐབ *khyim-thab* or ཁྱིམ་ཐབས *khyim-thabs* husband; frequently also wife; ཁྱིམ་ཐབ་ལ་སློང་བ *khyim thab-la sloṅ-wa* to give in marriage; to give away a woman for a wife; ཁྱིམ་ཐབ་མོ *khyim thab-mo* wife; house-wife (*Cs.*); ཁྱིམ་ཐབ་ལས་མ་འགྱུར་བ पतिव्रता a devoted wife: བདག་ཁྱོད་དང་ཁྱིམ་ཐབས་བྱར let you and me be married.

Syn. ཁྱོ་ཤུག *khyo-çug*; བཟང་ཚོ *bzaṅ-tsho*; བཟའ་ཚང *bzah-tshaṅ* (*Mṅon.*).

ཁྱིམ་དང་ཁྱིམ་ན *khyim daṅ khyim-na* house to house; each in his house.

ཁྱིམ་དུ་ཉལ *khyim-du ñal* = བྱ་མཆིལ་པ *bya-mchil-pa* the swallow (*Mṅon.*).

ཁྱིམ་བདག *khyim-bdag* गृहपति a house-holder; a master of the house; husband; owner of a house; a citizen. Very freq. in the older writings ཁྱིམ་བདག་གི་རིགས་ཤིང་སཱ་ལ་ཆེན་པོ་ལྟ་བུ། गृहपतिमहाशाल कुल the house-holder class is like a great *Sāla* tree.

ཁྱིམ་བདག་དྲག་ཤུལ་ཅན *khyim-bdag drag-çul can* a rough uncultured householder.

ཁྱིམ་བདག་དཔལ་སྦྱིན *khyim-bdag dpal-sbyin*, ཞེས་པ་ནི་བཅོམ་ལྡན་འདས་ཀྱི་དུས་སུ་བྱུང་བའི་ཁྱིམ་བདག་ཞིག་གི་མིང་ श्रीदत्त n. of a householder who was devoted to Buddha (*K. ko.* ཙ *335*).

ཁྱིམ་བདག་མོ *khyim-bdag-mo* गृहपत्नी a house-wife; also a female householder.

Syn. བརྟུལ་ཤུགས་མ *brtul shugs-ma*; ཁྱིམ་འཛིན་མ *khyim hdsin-ma*; ཁབ་འཛིན་མ *khab-hdsin-ma*; རིགས་སྐྱོང་མ *rigs skyoṅ-ma*; རིགས་ཀྱི་མ *rigs-kyi-ma*; ཁྱིམ་བདག་མ *khyim-bdag-ma* (*Mṅon.*).

ཁྱིམ་ལྡན *khyim-ldan*, v. རྩངས་པ *rtsaṅs-pa* a lizard (*Mṅon.*).

ཁྱིམ་ནས་འབྱུང་བ *khyim-nas byuṅ-wa* = ཐེག་ཆེན་བྱང་ཆུབ་ལྗོན་ཤིང་གི་ལོ་མ *theg-chen byaṅ-chub ljon-çiṅ-gi lo-ma* a leaf of the Bodhi-tree (*K. d.* ན *327*).

ཁྱིམ་གནས *khyim-gnas*, བྲམ་ཟེའི་རིགས་བཞི་ཡི་གཅིག་ལ་ཁྱིམ་གནས *bram-zehi rigs-bshi-yi gcig la-khyim gnas* गृहस्थाश्रम acc. to Brāhmaṇical religion, the worldly life, a house-holder's life (*Ya-sel.*, *55*).

ཁྱིམ་པ *khyim-pa* layman; married man: ཁྱིམ་པའི་ཕྱོགས་སུ་སྦྱིན་པ *khyim-pahi phyogs-su sbyin-pa* to give away to a layman: ཕྱིས་ཁྱིམ་པའི་ཚུལ་ཅན་གྱི་རྣལ་འབྱོར་པ *phyis khyim-pahi tshul can-gyi rnal-hbyor-pa* a devout man or *yogi* who lives outwardly in the manner of a layman.

ཁྱིམ་པའི་སྤོད་པ་ཅན *khyim-pahi spod-pa can* he who betakes to the life of *yogi*; གཞོན་ནུ་གདུང་དྲུག *gshon-nu gduṅ-drug* an epithet of Kumāra Shaḍānana (*Mṅon.*): ཁྱིམ་པའི་ལུས་སུ་མ་ལྡུར་ཅིག do not revert to tho life of a layman (*Mṅon.*).

ཁྱིམ་པ་རྟག་པའི་དཔྱད *khyim-pa rtag-pahi dpyad* वास्तुविद्या the science of discerning the fit place for the residence (of a householder).

ཁྱིམ་པར་གནས་པ *khyim-par gnas-pa* वास्तु, गृहस्थ one that abides in his house; one living in his house; a worldly man; ho who lives as a layman.

ཁྱིམ་ཕུབ *khyim-phub* living in divided families (*K. d.* ས 75).

ཁྱིམ་བྱ *khyim-bya* (*khyim-cha*) कुक्कुट, कुक्कुभ domestic fowl; cock; hen; poultry.

Syn. ཟངས་ཀྱི་གཙུག་ཕུད *zaṅs-kyi gtsug-phud*; མྱ་ངན་མེད *mya-ṅan-med*; ཟུང་གི་སྒྲ་སྒྲོགས *zuṅ-gi rags sgrogs*; ཐོ་རངས་སྐད *tho-raṅs skad*; མཚན་མོ་སྐད *mtshan-mo skad*; བདེ་ལེགས་ཅན *bde-legs chn*; ཡོངས་ཟླུམ་མིག *yoṅs-zlum mig*; དགའ་བྱེད *dgah-byed*; འཕེལ་བྱེད *hphel-byed*; ནོར་བུའི་མགྲིན་ཅན *nor-buhi mgrin-can*; འོད་ཀྱི་སྡེ *hod-kyi sde*; སྔ་བར་སྒྲ་སྒྲོགས *sṅa-war sgra-sgrogs*; ཟངས་ཟི་ཅན *zaṅs-zi-can*; པགས་པའི་གཙུག་ཕུད *pags-pahi gtsug phud*; མཚན་མོ་རིག *mtshan-mo rig*; རྐང་པའི་མཚན་ཆ་ཅན *rkaṅ-pahi mtshan-cha can* (*Mṅon.*).

ཁྱིམ་བྱ་མཚལ་ལུ *khyim-bya mtshal-lu* a very large species of fowl which is also called སྤྲེ་བོ་མཚལ་ལུ. The bile of this bird is believed to be a cure for poison.

ཁྱིམ་བྱའི་སྤྱོད་པ *khyim-byahi spyod-pa* the four habits of the cock acc. to *Masurakṣi* are tho following:—ཐོ་རངས་ལྡང་དང *tho-raṅs ldaṅ daṅ* crowing before dawn; འཐབ་པ་དང་ལྡན *hthab-pa daṅ-ldan* always fighting; གཉེན་ལ་ཁ་ཟས་སྙོམས་པར་བྱེད *gñen-la kha-zas sñoms-par byed* dividing food equally with his friend; མོ་ལ་རབ་གནོན་ཉེ་བར་སྤྱོད *mola rab-gnon ñe-war spyod* always keeping the hen under control and chucking her.

ཁྱིམ་ཚང *khyim-tshaṅ* a family; a household.

ཁྱིམ་མཐེས *khyim-mthes* a neighbour; ཁྱིམ་མཚེས་དུས་པ་བཏང་འབྲེལ *khyim-mtshes dus-pa btaṅ-hbrel* nearness of residence; neighbourhood so near that the smoke from the fire-place of one house mixes up with that of another; ཁྱིམ་མཚེས་པ *khyim-mtshes-pa* a male neighbour; ཁྱིམ་མཚེས་མ *khyim-mtshes-ma* a female neighbour.

ཁྱིམ་ཞག *khyim-shag* a zodiacal day.

ཁྱིམ་ཟླ *khyim-zla* a zodiacal month.

ཁྱིམ་ལ་འོང་བ *khyim-la hoṅ-wa*, གཏོང་བ *gtoṅ-wa* to get married, to be given in marriage on tho female part (*Jä.*).

ཁྱིམ་ལ་ཞེན་པ *khyim-la shen-pa* a lover of home; one attached to his home; homesick.

ཁྱིམ་སུན་འབྱིན་པ *khyim-sun hbyin-pa* कुलदूषक vituperating or blaming the secular state or a domestic abode.

ཁྱིམ་སོ *khyim-so* गृहव्याकुलिक homesick.

ཁྱིམ་སོ་སོར་བསྒོ་བ *khyim so-sor bsgo-wa* कुलप्रतिसम्भेदक one who creates dissensions in a family.

ཁྱིམ་གསར་མ *khyim-gsar-ma*=བག་མ *bag-ma* or ལག་འཛིན་མ *lag-hdsin-ma*, also ལྷན་ཅིག་སྤྱོད་མ *lhan-cig spyod-ma* a bride; wife (*Mṅon.*).

ཁྱུ *kyu* flock; herd: ལུག་གི་ཁྱུ *lug-gi khyu* a flock of sheep; རྟའི་ཁྱུ *rtahi khyu* a herd of horses; གནག་གི་ཁྱུ *gnag-gi khyu* a herd of cattle; བྱའི་ཁྱུ *byahi khyu* or ཚོགས *tshogs* a flock of birds. ཁྱུ་གསགས་པ་ *khyu gsags-pa* to collect or gather in flocks (*Sch.*); ཁྱུ་སྐྱོང་བ་ *khyu skyoñs-wa* to keep; tend a flock or herd; company; band; gang; troop: མི་ཁྱུ་ *mi-khyu* a company of men (*Cs.*); བུ་མོ་ཁྱུ་ *bu-mo-khyu* a bevy of girls; དམག་ཁྱུ་ *dmag-khyu* a troop of soldiers. ཁྱུ་ནས་འབུད་པ་ *khyu-nas hbud-pa* to exclude from the flock or company; ཁྱུ་སྣ་འདྲེན་པ་ *khyu sna hdren-pa* to go before; to take the lead of a troop or of a flock; *Bya ser-po khyu-re hgrogs mañ-po* yellow birds; many companions in each flock (*A. 34*).

ཁྱུ་མཆོག *khyu-mchog* पुङ्गव, ऋषभ, भूवर, वृषभ, विष्णु 1. chief; king; the bull; Vishnu. 2. ཟླ་བ་གསུམ་པ་ *zla-wa gsum-pa* the third month of the Tibetan year generally corresponding with April.

Syn. དཔྱིད་ཐ་ཆུང་ *dpyid-tha chuñ* वृषभ, चैत्र; ནག་པ་ *nag-pa*; སྦྲང་ཟླ་ *sbrañ-zla*; སྨྱོས་བྱེད་ *myos-byed*; དྲི་ཞིམ་ལྡན་ *dri-shim ldan*; ཡིད་སྲབས་ *yid-srabs*; འདོད་འདུས་ *hdod-hdus*; མིང་བཟུགས་ *miñ-bzugs*; འབྲུག་ཟླ་ *hbrug-zla*; ཟླ་བ་གསུམ་པ་ *zla-wa gsum-pa*, the third month of the Tib. year (*Rtsii.*).

ཁྱུ་མཆོག་བགྲོད་པ་ *khyu-mchog bgrod-pa* = བྱ་མཆིལ་པ་ *bya-mchil pa* कलन्दक a kind of swallow (*Mñon.*).

ཁྱུ་མཆོག་རྒྱལ་མཚན་ *khyu-mchog rgyal-mtshan* = དབང་ཕྱུག་ཆེན་པོ་ *dwaañ-phyag chen-po* वृषध्वज n. of Mahādeva (*Mñon.*).

ཁྱུ་མཆོག་ཅན་ *khyu-mchog can* = ཟླ་བ་བརྒྱད་པ་ *zla-wa brgyad-pa* or སྟོན་ཟླ་འབྲིང་པོ་ *ston-zla hbriñ-po* tho eighth month of the Tibetan year corresponding with November (*Rtsii.*).

ཁྱུ་མཆོག་མཚན་པ་ *khyu-mcog mtshan-pa* 1. वृषाङ्क one with the marks or signs of a bull or one who carries the bull ensign. 2. n. of a drug called वासक (the plant *Jastica genderussa*), which is used for purifying the blood.

ཁྱུ་ལྟོ་བ་ *khyu lto-wa* वृषोदर with a belly resembling that of a bull.

ཁྱུ་འདུས་པ་ *khyu hdus-pa* वृन्द collected in a herd or flock; also heap, multitude; an aggregate.

ཁྱུ་ལྡན་ *khyu-ldan*, v. ཚ་བ་ལེན་ *tsha-wa len* पिचुल, the tamarisk (*Mñon.*).

ཁྱུ་བྱུག *khyu-byug* erroneously used for ཁུ་བྱུག་ *khu-byug*, n. of a large bird of sweet note, which, according to the Tibetans, migrates in summer to cooler regions and in cold weather returns to the warmer zones. In *Jä.* ཁུ་བྱུག་གུ་རུ་ probably signifies the note of the black Indian cuckoo.

ཁྱུག *khyug*, v. འཁྱུག་པ་ *hkhyug-pa.*

ཁྱུག་ཁྱུག་ *khyug-khyug* གློག་གི་འོད་ཁྱུག་ཁྱུག་བྱེད་ *glog-gi hod khyug-khyug byed* a zig-zag flash of lightning.

ཁྱུག་ཙམ་ *khyug tsam* = ཏིག་ཙམ་ *tig-tsam* or ཏིབ་ཙམ་ or སྲིབ་ཙམ་ *srib-tsam* a little; a little while.

ཁྱུང་ I: *khyuñ* herd, multitude.

ཁྱུང་ II: (*Sch.* also *khyuñ-mo*) the *garuḍa* bird, mythical chief of the feathered race; the golden eagle: ཁྱུང་སྐྱུག་ *khyuñ-skyug* a kind of gem said to have been brought from the Sumeru mountain by Garuḍa and vomited by him: ཁྱུང་སྐྱུག་སོགས་ནད་ཀུན་འཇོམས་པའི་མཆོག *khyuñ-skyug dug sogs nad kun hjoms-pahi mchog*, the *khyuñ-skyug* (the eagle's vomit) is the chief remedy against the effects of poisonous drugs: ཁྱུང་གི་སེན་མོས་ཀླུ་ནད་འཇོམས་ *khyud-gi sen-mos klu nad hjoms* the toe of an caglo is used as an antidote for leprosy. ཁྱུང་ཕྲུག་སྐྱུག་པའི་བདུད་རྩི་ཆག་པའི་ཁ་ཆུ་ *khyuñ phrug skyug-pahi bdud rtsi-chag pahi kha-chu* the watery substance vomited by locusts; a mystical expression (*Miñ. 4*).

ཁྱུང་སྔོན་སྐྱེས I: *khyuṅ ṣṅon-ṣkyeṣ* 1. गरुडाग्रज the first-born of heaven; the one that was born before *garuḍa*; an epithet of Aruna, the charioteer of the sun. 2. = སྐྱ་རེང་ *ṣkya-reṅ* dawn. 3. ཁྱུང་གཤོག་ཅན *khyuṅ çog-can* the early morning which advances with the wings of an eagle; a name of Vajrapāṇi *Bodhisattva*.

ཁྱུང་སྔོན་སྐྱེས II: ཉི་མའི་ཁ་ལོ་པ *ñi-maḥi kha lo-pa* the charioteer of the sun (*Mṅon.*).

ཁྱུང་ཐུར་ཅན *khyuṅ-thur can*=གོ་ཆ *go-cha* or གོ་ཁྲབ *go-khrab* coat of mail (*Mṅon.*).

ཁྱུང་སྡེར *khyuṅ-ṣder* claws of an eagle (*Med.*; *Cs.*); (Garuḍa-claw) the n. of a medicinal root: ཁྱུང་སྡེར་དཀར་མོ *khyuṅ-ṣder ḍkar-mo* the white species of this vegetable drug, so called on account of its resemblance to the claw of an eagle: ཁྱུང་སྡེར་སྨུག་པོ *khyuṅ-ṣder ṣmug-po* the dark brown species of the root, in appearance like the claws of an eagle. Both these roots are used to neutralize snake poison, &c.

ཁྱུང་པོ *khyuṅ-po* many collected or assembled together.

ཁྱུང་དཔྱད *khyuṅ-ḍpyaḍ* a small round basket of reed (*Cs.*).

ཁྱུང་རྩེ་དགོན *Khyuṅ-ṛtse ḍgonpa* monastery in the valley of Panam in Tsang.

ཁྱུང་རིལ *khyuṅ-riḷ* is said to be a large cylindrical basket, the same as *kun-dum* in *Ld.*, v. རྐོན་པ *ṛkon-pa*.

ཁྱུད་པ *khyuḍ-pa* परिपूजन to worship, adore.

ཁྱུད་མོ *khyuḍ-mo* 1. རྟ་ཆས *ṛta-chaṣ* the equipments of a horse. 2. rim of vessel (*Sch.*).

ཁྱུར་པོ *khyur-po*=རིལ་པོ *riḷ-po* or སྒང་པོ *ṣgaṅ-po* entire; full.

ཁྱུར་མིད་པ *khyur miḍ-pa* to swallow; to eat the food without chewing, in the manner of birds, snakes and fish: ཁྱུར་མིད་དུ་སོང་སྟེ *khyur miḍ-du soṅ-ṣte* suffering himself to be swallowed.

ཁྱུས *khyuṣ* wall side (in Tsang) ? (*Jä.*).

ཁྱེ་པ *khye-pa* प्रसर wide.

ཁྱེ་བོ *khye-bo*, བུ་ཚ *bu-tsha* children.

ཁྱེ་མ *khye-ma* n. of a disease (*Med.*; *Jä.*).

ཁྱེད I: *khyeḍ* n. of a tribe in Tibet (*Vai. kar. 150*).

ཁྱེད II: pers. pron. thou, you; is the ordinary resp. form of ཁྱོད: ཁྱེད་ཅག *khyeḍ-cag*, plur. of ཁྱེད *khyeḍ*, is generally used in addressing lamas, but seldom in addressing superiors, such as parents, uncles, and brothers; is used to those senior in age, and sometimes contemptuously. ཁྱེད་རང *khyeḍ-raṅ* is common colloquially for *khyeḍ*; ཁྱེད་ཅག ཁྱེད་རྣམས, ཁྱེད་ཚོ you or you all: དགེ་ཚུལ་ཁྱེད་གཉིས *ḍge-tshuḷ khyeḍ ḡñiṣ* you two novice monks; ཁྱེད་ཚོའི་བློ་མངའ་ ལྟར་ཡོང it will be as you (all) think.

ཁྱེན་ཏེ *khyen-te* in Purang he; she (*Jä.*).

+ ཁྱེབས *khyebṣ*=ཁེབས *khebṣ* cover.

ཁྱེམ *khyem*=ཁེམ *khem* a shovel: ཁྱེམ་དང་འཐེན་པ to shovel away; to cast out with a shovel; ཁྱེམ་གྱི་འདབ་མ *khyem-gyi ḥdab-ma* the blade of a shovel (*Jä.*): ཁྱེམ་གྱི་ཡུ་བ *khyem-gyi-yu-wa* the handle of a shovel (*Cs.*); གྲུ་ཁྱེམ *gru-khyem*, ཆུ་ཁྱེམ *chu-khyem* oar; in *W.* ལྕགས་ཁྱེམ *ḷcagṣ khyem* iron spade; མེ་ཁྱེམ

me-khyem fire-shovel; ཝ་ཁྱེམ *wa-khyem* a scoop; ཁྱེམ་བུ *khyem-bu* a spoon (*Cs.*).

ཁྱེའུ *khyeh̲u* दारक, also मानवक, शिशु 1. a boy; an infant child. 2. a youth, esp. in *Dzang-lun*.

ཁྱེའུ་ཁ *khyeh̲u kha* = ཤིང་ལོ་གསར་དུ་ཁ་འབུས་པ *çiñ-lo g̲sar-du kha h̲bus̲-pa* the tender shoots of leaves (*M̲ñon.*).

ཁྱེའུ་མཐོན་པ *khyeh̲u m̲thon-pa*, ཁྱེའུ་བྱེ་བ *khyeh̲u bye-wa* the delivery of a child; child-birth. In *Kahgyur* and *Tangyur* ཁྱེའུ་མཙས་པ *khyeh̲u m̲tsas̲-pa* = བུ་སྐྱེས་པ *bu s̲kyes̲-pa* the birth of a male child.

ཁྱེར་རྐྱང *khyer-r̲kyañ* one who is specially authorized or responsible to make payment or receive deposits in money or in kind in a Jong or district: ཡོང་སྒོས་ཆེ་ཕྲའི་རིགས་རྫོང་སྡོད་ཁྱེར་རྐྱང་ནས་བསྡུ་བ *yoñ-s̲gos̲ che phrah̲i rigs̲ R̲dsoñ-s̲dod̲ khyer-r̲kyañ nas̲ b̲sdu-wa* all proceeds (collections) large or small should be collected by the officer resident in the Jong (*R̲tsii.*).

ཁྱེལ་བཞུགས་པ *khyel b̲shugs̲-pa* n. of a posture in *yoga*; a mode of sitting: འདུག་སྟངས་ཀྱི་མིང *h̲dug-s̲tañs̲ kyi miñ* or རྩོག་རྩོག་པུར་འདུག་པ *r̲tsog-tsog pur h̲dug-pa* (*M̲ñon.*).

ཁྱོ *khyo* or ཁྱོ་བོ *khyo-b̲o* a husband; ཁྱོ་བྱེད་པ *khyo b̲yed̲-pa* to act as a husband; also to take a wife: *khyod̲-ñah̲i khyo mi byed-na* if you do not marry me (*Jä.*).

ཁྱོ་ག *khyo-ga* husband; also emphatically man, as སྐྱེས་བུ་ང་ཧོར་པ་ཁྱོ་ག་ཡིན *s̲kyes̲-bu ña Hor-pa khyo-ga yin*, I, a Tartar, am a man (as distinguished from effeminate people).

ཁྱོ་ག་པོ *khyo-ga-po* a hero.

ཁྱོ་འདམ་མ *khyo h̲dam-ma* = བག་མ *bag-ma* a bride.

ཁྱོ་ཕོ *khyo-pho* husband: ཁྱོད་ཀྱི་ཁྱོ་ཕོ་དེ་ཆེ་ཞིག་ལྟ་བུ *khyod̲-kyi khyo-pho de che-shig l̲ta-bu* what like is your husband (*Sñiñ.*).

ཁྱོ་མེད་པ *khyo-med̲-pa*, अधवा, विधवा a widow.

ཁྱོ་རེ *khyo-re* to stand erect, upright (*Yig. 51*).

ཁྱོ་ཤུག *khyo-çug* दम्पती husband and wife; a married couple; same as བཟའ་ཚོ *b̲zah̲-tsho* or བཟའ་མི *b̲zah̲-mi* (*Liç.* ཁ *4*).

ཁྱོ་ཤུག་གནས *khyo-sug g̲nas̲* वासर the place where a married couple pass their honey-moon.

ཁྱོག་ཐོང *khyog-thoñ* (abbr. of ཁྱོ་ག *khyo-ga* and ཐོང *thoñ*) in *W.* a young man; a youth (*Jä.*).

ཁྱོག་པོ *khyog-po* crooked; curved; bent (*Cs.*); also cunning (*Jä.*).

ཁྱོགས *khyogs̲*, ཕེབས་བྱམས *phebs̲-byams̲* दुलि, दोला 1. a *sedan* chair, palankeen; also a scaffold (*Cs.*). 2. litter, bier (*Jä.*).

* ཁྱོགས *khyogs̲* दोलक a swing (*Schr.*; *Kālac. T. 146*).

ཁྱོགས་པ *khyogs̲-pa* = ཐེག་པ *theg-pa* a vehicle or conveyance.

ཁྱོང *khyoñ* = སྐྱོང *s̲kyoñ*, or ཁོང་བ *khoñ-wa*, in colloq. ཉིན་ཁྱོང *ñin-khyoñ*, one day's entertainment.

ཁྱོད *khyod̲* pers. pron., 2nd pers., thou, you—is the ordinary form of address to inferiors or to equals: ཁྱོད་ཀྱི *khyod̲-kyi* your, thine; ཁྱོད་ཅག་གི *khyod̲ cag-gi* your, of you all: ཁྱོད་ཚོ *khyod̲-tsho* or ཁྱོད་རྣམས *khyod̲-r̲nams̲* you, ye: ཁྱོད་རང *khyod̲-rañ* thou, you, yourself—very common in the colloq. of *C.* in place of the simple *khyod̲*.

ཁྱོད་ཤུགས *khyod̲-çugs̲* मिथुन a pair; pairing, v. ཁྱོ་ཤུག *khyo-çug*.

ཁྱོན *khyon*, **आयत, इयु, योग** the measure or dimensions, area, extent, size; width; circumference; height: this term can be applied to things material or immaterial; ཤེས་བྱའི་ཁྱོན་ཀུན *çes-byahi khyon-kun* the whole extent of learning or knowledge; ནམ་མཁའི་ཁྱོན་ཀུན the extent of the void space or sky.

ཁྱོན་སྒྲིལ *khyon-sgril* altogether; all taken together: སྡོང་རས་ཁྱོན་སྒྲིལ་གོས་སྣམས *sdoñ-ras khyoñ-sgril gos snams* cotton cloth for wicks all together (*Rtsii.*).

ཁྱོན་ཆེ་བ *khyoñ-che-wa* **विस्तीर्ण, आयत** broad; very widely spread.

ཁྱོན་སྡོམ *khyon-sdom* all together; sum total; contents; acc. to *Cs.* narrow extent.

ཁྱོན་ནས *khyon-nas* thoroughly; ཁྱོན་ནས་མི་སྡིག་ཅན an out-and-out sinner; ཁྱོན་ནས་མེད་པ not at all (*Jä.*).

ཁྱོམ་ཁྱོམ *kyom-khyom* oblique; awry; irregularly shaped.

ཁྱོར་བ I: to move totteringly; to stumble; be dizzy: defined in a native author as ཉིད་མེད་པ་གྲོད་པ་ལྟོགས་ནས་འགྲོ་ཡོད་པ་ལྟ་བུ་འགྲོ་བ "moving as if one went with a hungry belly and without strength"; རང་བཞི་བཀམ་རྒས་ནས་འགྲོ་དུས་གོམ་པ་ཁྱོར to walk as an old or drunken person; ཚད་པས་ན་ནས་ཁ་ཁྱོར *tshad-pas na-nas kha khyor* speaking irregularly as in a feverish delirium; ཤིང་གི་སྣོད་ཁྱོར་བ *çin-gi snod khyor-wa* bobbing as a wooden vessel.

ཁྱོར་བ II: as much as fills the hollow of the hand; ཁྱོར་བ་གང *khyor-wo gañ* a handful (of anything); ཁྱོར་བ་དོ *khyor-wa do* two handsful.

ཁྱོལ་བ *khyol-wa*, v. འཁྱོལ་བ *hkhyol-wa*, to be brought or carried or ཁྱོས་མ *khyos-ma*.

ཁྲ I: *khra* (*thā*) **वञ्चक** 1. a cheat. 2. a kind of hawk or falcon; sparrow-hawk used for hunting: ཁྲ་ཡི་སྒོ་ངས་ས་བོན་འཛག་པ་བསྲུང *khra-yi sgo-ñas sa-bon hdsag-pa bsruñ* the egg of the hawk is curative of the disease of involuntary discharge of the semen; ཁྲ་ཡི་མཇུག་སྒྲོམ་མོ་ནད་སེལ the feathers from a hawk's tail remove female diseases; ཁྲ་ཡི་བྲུན་གྱིས་སྐྲངས་པ་རྣག་ཏུ་འགུགས *khra-yi brun-gyis skrañs-pa rnag-tu hgugs* the excrement of the hawk prevents accumulation of pus in a boil; ཁྲ་མིག་གཟའ་ནད་འབྱུང་པོའི་གདོན་ཀུན་ཐུབ a hawk's eye overcomes all demons that produce apoplexy.

Syn. འདབ་ཆགས་དང་མ *hdab-chags dañ-ma*; རི་བོང་ཟ *ri-boñ-za*; བྱ་ཁྲ *bya-khra*; གཡོ་བ *gyo-wa* (*Mnoñ.*).

ཁྲ II: n. of a tribe in Tibet (*Vai. kar. 100*).

ཁྲ III: **अलीक** 1. a lie, falsehood; also a liar. 2. n. of a *Nāga* Rāja (snake king).

ཁྲ IV: or ཁྲ་མ *khra-ma* (*tha-ma*) a letter; སྐྱེས་ཁྲ *skyes-khra* a letter with a present.

ཁྲ་ཁྲ *khra-khra* (*tha-tha*) = ཁྲ་བོ *khra-wo* party-colour (*Ñag. 10*).

ཁྲ་ཁྲོ་ཅན *khra khro-can* (*tha-tho-can*) defined as ཁོང་ཁྲོ་ཆེ་བཀམ་ཞེ་སྡང་ཆེ་བ a passionate or wrathful individual.

ཁྲ་རྒྱུ *khra-rgyu* variegated colour: སྣུམ་ལག་རྐེད་ལྷས་ལ་དཀར་པོ་ཁྲ་རྒྱུ་དགོས་ཤིང *snum lag rked lhas la dkar-po khra rgyu dgos çin*.

ཁྲ་བརྒྱན *khra-brgyan* variegating an ornament (amulet or bracelet, &c.) with precious stones.

ཁྲ་སྒྲིགས *khra-sgrigs* (*tha-dig*) ཁྲ་རིམ་བཞིན་སྒྲིགས་པ *khra-rim bshin sgrigs-pa* arranging in variegated colours with rows of turquoise, corals, pearls, &c.

ཁྲ་སྣ་ཀེ་རུ *Khra-sna-ke-ru* n. of a place near ཧོན *Hon* in Tibet.

ཁྲ་པ *khra-pa* a falconer.

ཁྲ་བོ *khra-bo* (*ṭhā-o*) चित्र, शबल, ख्युल, तिलक, कर्बुर 1. many coloured, with one predominating colour as in chintz; party-coloured, as in the case of cattle and wild animals, such as a tiger or leopard, and in birds. In དཀར་ཁྲ *dkar-khra*, the white (*dkar*) is supposed to prédominate. In དམར་ཁྲ *dmar-khra*, red predominates. In the common saying སྟག་གི་ཁྲ་བོ་ཕྱི་ལ་ཡོད, མི་ཡི་ཁྲ་བོ་ནང་ལ་ཡོད *stag-gi khra-bo phyi-la yod, mi-yi khra-bo nań-la yod*, the tiger is party-coloured externally, but man is so internally—the meaning, of course, is that it is difficult to know a man even by the traits of his mind. 2. Acc. to *Jä.* a distinction is to be drawn between *khra-wo* and *khra-wa*, the first signifying only two-coloured or piebald, and the second party or many-coloured. We have not found this distinction ourselves. The significations of the various compounds of ཁྲ *khra* have all a reference to the peculiar effect produced on the eye by the blending of two or more colours together, especially when seen from a distance; so ཁྲ་ཙེམ་མེ *khra cem-me* is said of a rainbow, tinted meteor, etc.; ཁྲ་ལམ་མེ *khra lam-me* or ཁྲ་ལྷམ་མེ *khra lham-me* of a similar phenomenon; ཁྲ་ཆེམ་ཆེམ *khra chem-chem* of a flight of birds: ཁྲ་ཆམ་སེ་ཁྲ་ཆེམ་མེ *khra cham-se khra chem-me* or ཁྲ་ཆེམ་སེ *khra chem-se* in *C.* = ཆེམ་ཁྲ་སྤྲིང་ངེ *chem khra sprin-ńe* in *Ld.* Such compounds have also assumed the character of an adverb, as in ཁྲ་མེ་རེ *khra-me-re*, together; altogether.

ཁྲ་མ *khra-ma* 1. a register, index. 2. a judicial decree. 3. a kind of grain, འབྲུ *hbru* काङ्ग. 4. acc. to *Vai. sṅ.* = མགྱོགས་ནས *mgyogs-nas* a kind of barley grain, growing and ripening rapidly within 60 days, v. གྱོ་ཁྲམ *gyo-khram.*

ཁྲ་མ་གཉིས་སྒྲོམ *khra-magñis sgrom* in jewellery or lacquer work when there is a variegating with two colours.

ཁྲ་མར *khra-mar* a kind of biscuit made in twisted cross ribs and painted red. These are given only to Government officials at state dinners in Tibet.

ཁྲ་རྩེ *khra-rtse* a kind of biscuit or pastry made in the shape of a grating.

ཁྲ་ཟུར *khra-zur* a species of eagle (*Sch.*).

ཁྲ་ཟླ *khra-zla* (*ṭha-da*) = ཟླ་བ་གཉིས་པ *zla-wa gñis-pa* or དཔྱིད་ཟླ་འབྲིང་པོ *dpyid-zla hbrin-po* the second Tibetan month corresponding with March (*Rtsü.*).

ཁྲ་རིང *khra-riń* a striped long scarf. This is also called བཀྲ་ཤིས་ཁྲ་རིང *bkra-çis khra-riń*, the auspicious long striped scarf which is generally attached to flag poles:—*lhag-par pho-brań rtse-nas khra-riń dań dar-phan duń dań rol-mo sogs sbro*, moreover they exhibited from the top of the palace long scarves and pendant silk and played on trumpets and cymbals, &c.

ཁྲ་ཤིག་ཤིག *khra çig-çig* in dazzling array (*J. Zań.*).

ཁྲ་སེམས་ཤེས *khra-sems çes* n. of a bird (*K. ko.* ཀ *3*).

ཁྲག *khrag* (*ṭhag*) སྐུ་མཚལ *sku-mtshal*, resp. रुधिर, असृज, लोहित, रक्त, शोणित blood: པང་ཁྲག *pań-khrag* blood of child-bed. ཤང་ཁྲག *shań-khrag* or vulgarly ཛང་ཁྲག *dsań-khrag* signifies blood of the menses; གཤུང་ཁྲག *gshuń-khrag* healthy and nourishing blood (*Cs.*); ནད་ཁྲག *nad-khrag* bad or diseased blood. In Sikkim *khrag* is pronounced *khyak.* ཁྲག་གཅོད *khrag-gcod* n. of a medicinal herb which stops bleeding (*Med.*):

ཁྲག་གཅོད་པ to stop bleeding; ཁྲག་ཆད་པ cessation of bleeding: སྙིང་ཁྲག་འཁོལ་ལ་རག in *W.* I feel my blood throbbing, *e.g.*, from ascending a steep hill. ཁྲག་འཛག་པ flowing of the blood, generally applied to menstruation; ཁྲག་ཆག་པ clotted blood; gore (*Cs.*).

Syn. རྨ་སྐྱེས *rma-skyes*; ཤར་འགྱུར་བྱེད *çar hgyur-byed*; ཤ་ཡི་ས་བོན *ça-yi sa-bon*; མཚན་བསྣུན་སྐྱེས *mtshan-bsnun skyes*; ཁྱབ་གནས *khyab-gnas*; མི་ལྷུང *mi-lhuñ*; ལུས་སྐྱེས *lus-skyes*; རྨ་ལས་འབབ་པ *rma-las hbab-pa* (*Mñon.*).

ཁྲག་སྐེམ *kkrag-skem*, སྤང་རྩི *spañ-rtsi* n. of a vegetable medicine very useful in stopping bleeding (*Sman. 86*).

ཁྲག་ཁྲིག *khrag-khrig* (*thag-thig*) नियुत also प्रयुत 1. one hundred thousand million, or an indefinitely large number (*Cs.*); this number has twelve figures; ཁྲག་ཁྲིག་ཆེན་པོ *khrag-khrig chen-po* महानियुत this has thirteen figures, cf. དཀྲིགས་པ *dkrigs-pa.* 2. in vulgar language ཁྲག་ཁྲིག *khrag-khrig* is expressed as ཁྲ་གི་ཁྲི་གི *khra-gi khri-gi* and means moving and oscillating about: དེ་ནས་རྫིངས་ཆེན་པོ་ཁྲག་ཁྲིག་ཙམ་ཡང་མེད་པར *de-nas rdsiñs chen-po khrag-khrig tsam yañ med-par* then (in) a large ship which did not even roll.

ཁྲག་ཁྲིག་སྣང་བ *khrag-khrig snañ-wa*=སྨིག་རྒྱུ *smig-rgyu* a mirage; an optical illusion (*Mñon.*).

ཁྲག་ཁྲུག *khrag khrug* (*thag-thug*) all in disorder; promiscuous state; like a troop of fighting men, or like the loose leaves of a book when out of order (*Zam.*).

ཁྲག་འཁྲུགས *khrag-hkhrugs* agitation; flutter; orgasm of the blood (*Sch.*).

ཁྲག་ཁྲོག *khrag-khrog* (*thag-thog*), v. ཁྲག་ཁྲུག *khrag-khrug.*

ཁྲག་གེ་ཁྲུག་གེ *khrag-ge khrug-ge* (*thag-ge thug-ge*) when two men do not agree with each oher, there is said to be *thag-ge thug-ge* among them—a falling-out, disagreement.

ཁྲག་རྒྱུན *khrag-rgyun* शोणिताटन the running of the blood in the veins; circulation.

ཁྲག་ཆགས་རྟ *khrag ehags-rta* a blood bred horse, *i.e.*, a real horse, opposed to a metaphysical one (*Mil.*).

ཁྲག་འཐུང *khrag-hthuñ* 1. a class of terrifying deities of the Bon and *Tantrik* Schools. 2. སྐྱུ་རུ་ར *skyu-ru-ra* आमलकी; *Myrobalaum emblica* (*Sman. 304*).

ཁྲག་འཐུང་འབུ *khrag hthuñ-hbu* the worm that drinks blood.

ཁྲག་འཐུང་སྲིན་བུ *khrag-hthuñ srin-bu* a leech (*Mñon.*).

ཁྲག་ལྡན *khrag-ldañ* व्याघ्र tiger; ཤིང་དམར་རམ་གཤེར་ཤིང་ *çiñ-dmar ram gçer çiñ* n. of a red tree; the red pine called कुन्द; a species of mahogony (*Mñon.*).

ཁྲག་ལྡན་མ *khrag-ldan ma* described as བུད་མེད་ཟླ་མཚན་དང་ལྡན་པ a woman at her monthly period (*Mñon.*).

ཁྲག་པོར་སྐྱེ་བ *khrag-por skye-wa* a botanical term applied to the leaves of plants (*Vai. sñ.*).

ཁྲག་འབབ *khrag-hbab*=ཆུ་བོ་སི་ཏ *chu-bo si-ta* a name of the river Sita (*Mñon.*).

ཁྲག་རོ *khrag-ro* clotted blood.

ཁྲག་ལིང *khrag-liñ* a clot of blood.

ཁྲག་ཤས་ཆེ་བ *khrag-ças che-wa* plethoric (*Med.*; *Jä.*).

ཁྲག་ཤོར *khrag-çor* hemorrhage; bloody-flux (*Med.*; *Jä.*).

ཁྲག་བཤལ *khrag-bçal* flooding after child-birth; profuse mensturation: བུ་མོ་ནད་མེད་པའི་ཕང་རག་གེས་རྒྱུ་གཟེར, ཁྲག་བཤལ་གཅོད it stops the flooding and internal spasms in the blood discharge of a healthy woman: རག *rag*=ཁྲག *khrag.*

ཁྲང་ *khrañ* (*thang*), v. མཁྲང་ *mkhrañ*.

ཁྲད་པ *krad-pa* (*the-pa*) stretched out: ཁྲད་པོར་སྡོད་པ *khrad-por sdod-pa* to sit with the legs stretched out (*Jä.*).

ཁྲབ *khrab* (*thab*) पत्त्रिकासन्नाहः shield; buckler; coat of mail. The coat of mail used in Tibet and Bhutan is generally made of iron rings or thin disks resembling the scales of a fish netted together. Two kinds of *khrab* are known in Tibet; one is called ཆ་ལུང་གི་ཁྲབ, which is made of iron rings or scales; བྱང་བུའི་ཁྲབ, that made of thin plates or iron foils. There are accounts of coats of mail made of silver and gold for the use of kings. The common quilted cloth armour used in Mongolia and China is called སྙིང་བལ་ཁྲབ. In Mongolia it is called *dasa*.

ཁྲབ་ཁྲབ *khrab-khrab* (*thab-thab*) a weeper; one that sheds tears on every occasion (*Sch.*).

ཁྲབ་མཁན *khrab-mkhan* one who makes or wears armour.

ཁྲབ་ཅན *khrab-can* scaled; scaly; wearing a coat of mail.

ཁྲབ་བྱང་གུ *khrab-byañ gu* scales or iron foils used in a coat of mail (*Rtsii.*).

ཁྲབ་བྱིན་ལུས་ཁེབ *khab-byin lus kheb* a coat of mail for covering the whole body (*Rtsii.*).

ཁྲམ *khram* (*tham*), ཕྲ་མ *phra-ma* a false word; कपटि a cunning man.

ཁྲམ་ཁ *khram-kha* (*tham-kha*) 1. ལྷ་འདྲེ་བྱེ་བྲག་གི་ཁྲོ་བའི་ཁ་དོག་ཁྲ་ཁྲ *lha-hdre bye-brag-gi khro-wahi kha-dog khra-khra* (*tha-tha*) spotted and party-coloured appearance of the wrathful demi-gods the Lhan-de (*Ñag.*). 2. chart used in witchcraft or necromancy: ལྷ་འདྲེའི་རྩིས་ཀྱི་མིང *lha hdrehi rtsis-kyi miñ*, ཁྲམ་ཁ་ལ་བབས *khram-kha la babs* is explained: མི་ལ་གནོད་པ་འབྱུང་རྒྱུའི་རྩིས་ཐུམ་ཏེ་གང་ལ་བབས་པ་དེ་ལ་གནོད་པ་བྱེད་པའི་རྟགས the sign or mark of one's ruin having been incident on the chart (of fate). 3. cross marks or lines cut into a piece of wood so as to cross one another as an ornament: ཁྲམ་ཁའི་ཤིང *khram-khahi-çiñ* a club-like implement, carved with lines, representing the attributes of a god and containing squares with mystic figures in them which serve as a means to make attempts of witchcraft to injure a person ineffectual; ཉག་ཁྲམ *ñag-khram* a notch (*Jä.*).

ཁྲམ་ཁྲུམ *khram-khrum* fragments; baked fragments: ས་ཕག་ལ་པར་བརྐོས་ནས་མེ་ལ་བསྲེགས་པ་དེ་ཁྲམ་ཁྲུམ་བརྡུངས་ཏེ་བསྒོལ (raw) brick containing prints or engravings thereon when burnt are said to be baked fragments.

ཁྲམ་ལྡན *khram-ldan* व्याघ्र a tiger.

ཁྲམ་པ *khram-pa* (*tham-pa*) = ཕྲམ་མ धूर्त, कपट, भ्रामक, चतुर 1. a liar; a swindler; artful person: སླུ་བར་བྱེད་པའི་ཁྲམ་པ *byed-pahi* for seducing or deceiving: ཁྲམ་སེམས་ཅན *khram sems-can* lying; mendacious (*Cs.*). 2. lively, brisk, quick, like boys, kids, &c. (the contrary of གླེན་པ *glen-pa*, slow, indolent, apathetic): *khram-pa che* in *W.* a wish of god-speed addressed to one going on a journey, such as Good success! May all go well! 3. modest; attentive to the wishes of others (*Jä.*). ཁྲམ་པ་གཅོད *gcod* lit. means to get out of mishaps caused by the evil machinations of enemies; to make the evil-charms of enemies ineffectual.

ཁྲམ་བྱེད *khram-byed*, v. གཡོ་ཅན *gyo-can* or ཕྲ་མ་བྱེད *phra-ma byed*; ལྕེ་གཉིས་པ *lce gñis-pa* double-tongued or double-dealer (*Mñon.*).

ཁྲམ་ཤིང་ *khram-çiñ* or ཁྲིམས་ཀྱི་ཁྲམ་ཤིང་ *khrims-kyi khram-çiñ* a board on which the body of a culprit is stretched to flog him on tho back (*Ñag.*).

ཁྲལ་ *khral* (*thal*) बाछिक, दण्ड 1. tax; tribute; duty; forced service. 2. punishment; chastisement for sins; visitations: ཁྲལ་བཀལ་བ་ *khral bkal-wa* to levy taxes: དངུལ་ཁྲལ་ *dṅul-khral* tax to be paid in money: འབྲུ་ཁྲལ་ *hbru-khral* tribute paid in corn: ཏིལ་དམར་ཁྲལ་ *til-dmar khral* tax to be paid in red sesamum.

Syn. དཔྱ་ *dpya*; སྡུད་པ་ *sdud-pa*; གཡར་ཁྲལ་ *gyar-khral*; ཧོ་གམ་ *ço-gam*; ཁྲལ་རིགས་ *khral-rigs* (*Mṅon.*).

ཁྲལ་རྒྱུག་པ་ *khral rgyug-pa* to perform forced service (*Rtsii.*).

ཁྲལ་འཇལ་བ་ *khral-hjal-wa* or ཁྲལ་སྐོར་བ་ *khral skor-wa* to pay taxes or customs duty.

Syn. ཁྲལ་འབུལ་བ་ *khral hbul-wa*; དཔྱ་འཇལ་བ་ *dpya hjal-wa*; ཁྲལ་སྤྲོད་པ་ *hhral sprod-pa* (*Mṅon.*).

ཁྲལ་སྡུ་བ་ *khral sdu-wa* to collect taxes; pf. ཁྲལ་བསྡུས་ *khral-bsdus*, pf. ཁྲལ་བསྡུས་ཚར་ *khral-bsdus tshar*, fut. ཁྲལ་བསྡུ་ བར་བྱ་ *khral-bsdu war-bya*.

ཁྲལ་གསར་ *khral-gsar* levying of a new tax: ཞིང་མེད་པའི་ཁྲལ་གསར་བཀལ་ནས་ཞི་མི་སེར་ལ་སྡུག་པོ་གཏང་ by levying fresh taxes to oppress the tenants.

ཁྲལ་ཁྲུག་ *khral-khrug* (གྲངས་) n. of a very large number (*Ya-sel.*).

ཁྲལ་ཁྲུལ་ *khral-khrul* is defined as སྣོད་ལག་ལྷ་བུ་ཆགས་སོང་བ་ལ་ཡང་ཟེར་ applied to any broken things, such as furniture or utensils.

ཁྲི་ I: *khri* (*thi*), ཁྲི་ཁྲག་ *khri-khrag*, ཁྲི་གྲངས་ *khri-grañs* for number: अयुत ten thousand; a myriad: ཁྲི་བྱེ་བ་ *khri bye-wa* कोटि, प्रवेद ten millions.

ཁྲི་ II: खट्, पीठ seat, chair, throne, couch; also frame, sawing jack, trestle; ཀུ་ཁྲི an European chair; ཁྲིའུ་ *khrihu* पीठिका 1. a bedstead or stool; a small chair or table; ཁྲི་ལ་བསྐོ་བ་ *khri-la bsko-wa* to raiso to the throne; to place on the chair; ཁྲི་ལ་འཁོད་པ་ *khri-la hkhod-pa* to presido; to occupy the chair; སེང་གེ་ཁྲི་ *señ-ge khri* throne; a chair borne (in relief) by a carved lion for rulers and incarnate lamas; གསེར་ཁྲི་ *gser-khri* golden seat or chair; seat for royalty; སྔས་ཁྲི་ *sñas-khri* a contrivance to serve the purpose of a pillow; ཆོས་ཁྲི་ *chos-khri* a professoral chair; pulpit; reading desk; table for books; school tablo; ཉལ་ཁྲི་ *ñal-khri* resp. གཟིམས་ཁྲི་ *gzims-khri* bedstead. 2. མཆོད་རྟེན་གྱི་བང་རིམ་ the upper pedestal of a chaitya or Buddhist votive tomb.

Syn. ཉལ་ཁྲི་ *ñal-khri*; རྒྱུན་ཁྲི་ *rgyun-khri*; འདུག་ཁྲི་ *hdug-khri*.

ཁྲི་རྐང་ཅན་ *khri rkañ can* खट्वाङ्ग a seat furnished with legs; a bedstead.

ཁྲི་ཁ་ *khri-kha* = ཁྲིའི་ཁ་ *khrihi kha* or ཁྲིའི་སྟེང་ *khrihi steñ* on the chair: ཁྲི་ཁ་ན་ *khri kha-na*, on the chair or seat (*A. 57*).

ཁྲི་ཆེན་ *khri-chen* a great chair; a title of the abbot of Galdan monastery.

* ཁྲི་ཆེན་ངག་དབང་མཆོག་ལྡན་ *Khri-chen Ñag-dwañ mchog-ldan* དྲིན་ཅན་ངག་དབང་མཆོག་ལྡན་ *Drin-can ñag-dwañ mchog-ldan* (*Schr. 17 A*).

* ཁྲི་ཆེན་ངག་དབང་སྙན་གྲགས་ *Khri-chen ñag-dwañ sñan-grags* n. pr. (*Schr.*).

* ཁྲི་ཆེན་བློ་བཟང་བསྟན་པའི་ཉི་མ་ *Khri-chen Blo-bzañ bstan-pahi ñi-ma* = བློ་བཟང་ཉི་མའི་ཞབས་ *blo-bzañ ñi-mahi shabs* (*Schr.*).

ཁྲི་སྙན་ *khri-sñan* n. of a Buddhist physician of Lhasa; སྨན་པ་ཆེན་པོ་དུང་གི་ཐོར་ཅོག་ཅན་གྱི་སྲས་ the son of the celebrated physician named *Duñ-gi thor-can*. (*Yu thog-pa*) (*Gyu. 33*).

ཁྲི་སྙན་ས་ལེ་ *khri sñan sa-le* skin of the black antelope; कृष्णसार a devotee sitting on it remembers the vows as well the duties of a *Bodhisattva* ; ཁྲི་སྟན་ས་ལེ་ཞིག་ན་གདན་དུ་བཏིང spreading a skin of black antelope for a seat (*A. 11.*).

ཁྲི་སྟན་ཆེན་པོ *khri stan chen-po* महासन a large couch or bed ; ཁྲི་སྟན་མཐོན་པོ *khri-stan mthon-po* उच्चासन a high couch or bed (forbidden to the devout).

ཁྲི་གདུགས *khri-gdugs* the sun.

* ཁྲི་ལྡན་སེང་གེའི་མཛོད *khri-ldan señ-gehi mdsod* आसनसिंहकोश (*Schr.*; *Tā. 2, 44*).

ཁྲི་ཕྱེད་དང་གཉིས *khri-phyed dañ gñis* two thousand and half ; ཉི་ཁྲི *ñi-khri* twenty thousand.

ཁྲི་འཕང *khri-hphañ* the height of a chair ; a high chair (*Cs.*) ; also the official rank.

ཁྲི་མིན=བཙོན་ཁང་ *btson-khañ* a prison ; jail (*Mñon.*) ; also ཁྲི་མུན *khri-mun* a prison ; dungeon.

ཁྲི་ཧུར *khri-hur* བྱ་ཞིག་གི་མིང་ n. of a bird (*Ya-sel. 7*).

ཁྲི་ལེ་བ *khri le-wa* fear, in *C.* (*Jä.*).

ཁྲི་ཤིང་ I : *khri-çiñ* or ཁྲིའུ *khrihu* a chair.

ཁྲི་ཤིང་ II : (*thi-s'ing*) वल्लि a creeping plant ; a creeper.

ཁྲི་སྲོང་ལྡེ་བཙན *Khri-sroñ lde-btsan* the celeberated King of Tibet who formally introduced Buddhist monarchism into Tibet, erected the great monastery of Sam-ye, and caused numerous Buddhist sacred books to be translated into Tibetan.

ཁྲིའི་རྐང་པ་ཆོས་པ *khrihi rkañ-pa chos-pa* पादकसम्पादन a bed furnished with legs or supports ; fig. to discipline the mind so that religion may take hold of it.

ཁྲིའི་རྐང་རྟེན *khrihi rkañ-rten* प्रतिपादक the legs of a chair.

ཁྲིག་ཁྲིག *khrig-khrig* (*thig-thig*) 1. proper, suitable ; not less nor more : ཁྲིག་བསྒྲིགས་སོང *khrig-khrig bsgrigs-soñ* it has suited well ; it fits exactly. 2. quivering, as of the body with cold, or chattering of the teeth. 3. v. ཁྲིབ་ཁྲིབ *khrib-khrib*.

ཁྲིགས *khrigs* (*thig*) གྲལ་ཁྲིགས་པ *gral khrigs-pa* 1. arranged in proper order or row without deviation from the right course or line : ཁྲིགས་ཆགས་སུ་བཀོད་པ *khrigs chags-su bkod-pa* seated or arranged in proper order where men, women, the old and the young, the great and the low, all are put in their respective order ; 2. also in reference to a priest conducting a religious service, his demeanour when he does not look this side or that side but is intent on his duties and ceremonial observances ; he is then said to be ཁྲིགས་ཆགས་སུ་བཀོད་པ *khrigs chags-su bkod-pa*.

ཁྲིགས་སེ *kharigs-se* plentiful, abundant ; thorough ; ཁྲིགས་སེ་གང *khrigs-se gañ* quite well ; ཁྲིགས་སེ་བྱེད་པ *khrigs-se byed-pa* to treat ; to entertain plentifully (*Sch.*).

ཁྲིད I : *khrid* (*thi*) instruction, tutelage ; ཡོན་ཏན་ཁྲིད་པ *yon-tan khrid-pa* instruction, teaching ; ཁྲིད་འདེབས་པ *khrid hdebs-pa* to give instruction ; to instruct : ཁྲིད་པས་ཆོག *khrid-pas chog* I am willing to give instruction ; you may have lessons with me (*Jä.*). ཁྲིད་ཟབ་པོ *khrid zab-po* thorough instruction ; སླུ་ཁྲིད *slu-khrid* instruction to an evil purpose ; seduction ; ཁྲིད་བཤད་པ *khrid bçad-pa* to give instruction ; to make admonitory speeches.

ཁྲིད II : or གྲལ श्रेणी row ; order ; serial order or arrangement : དེ་སྙེད་ན་བྱང་ཆུབ་ལམ་གྱི་རིམ་པའི་ཁྲིད་ལ་བཞི in the same manner there are four stages in the way to saintly perfection (*Lam-rim. 4*).

ཁྲིད III: pf. of འཁྲིད་པ.

ཁྲིད་ཕྲུག *khrid-phrug* (*thi-thŭg*) scholar; pupil (*Jä.*).

ཁྲིབ་ཁྲིབ *khrib-khrib* (*thib-thib*) གྲངས་ཀྱི་མིང་ n. of a large number (*Ya-sel.*).

ཁྲིམས *khrims* (*thim*), शासन, न्याय, नियम law or right in general; the laws of a state; any particular law. There are two kinds of laws—ཁྲིམས་ལ་ཆོས་ཁྲིམས་དང་རྒྱལ་ཁྲིམས་གཉིས་ཡོད *khrim-la chos-khrims dan rgyal-khrims gñis yod* state law and spiritual or religious law. The proverb says: རྒྱལ་ཁྲིམས་གསེར་གྱི་གཉའ་ཤིང་, ཆོས་ཁྲིམས་དར་གྱི་མདུད་པ་ལྟ་བུ་ཡིན *Rgyal-khrims gser-gyi gñah çiñ, chos-khrims dar-gyi mdud-pa lta-bu yin* the state law is a golden yoke, but the religious law is like a silken knot: ཁྲིམས་ཀྱི་སྐབས་སུ་བཀའ་ཁྲིམས་བཅའ for laws they pass decrees, statutes: ཁྲིམས་ལ་གནས་པ *khrims-la gnas-pa* to be subject to law: འཕགས་རིགས་དང་སྐྱེ་མ་བུ་དམ་པ་རྣམས་ཁྲིམས་ལ་གནས་པ་ཡིན holy personages and the incarnate race are also subject to law.

Syn. for laws of state:—ལུགས *lugs*; འཇིག་རྟེན་ཁྲིམས *hjig-rten khrims*; ཡུལ་ཆོས *yul-chos*; ཁྲིམས *khrims*; ཁྲིམས་ལུགས *khrims-lugs* (*Mñon.*).

ཁྲིམས་ཁང་ *khrims-khañ* court or place of justice.

Syn. ཁྲིམས་རྔའི་ཁང་པ *khrims-rñahi khañ-pa*; སྒྲ་ལྡན་ཅན *sgra-ldan can*; ཁྲིམས་ཀྱི་ར་བ *khrims-kyi ra-wa*; དྲིལ་སྒྲོག་ས *dril-sgrog-sa* (*Mnon.*).

ཁྲིམས་ཀྱི་ཁ་ལོ་པ *khrims-kyi kha lo-pa*, བློན་པོ *Blon-po* a minister; a legal officer (*Mñon.*).

ཁྲིམས་བསྒྲགས་པ *khrims bsgrags-pa*, v. བཀའ་བཏགས *bkah-btags*, a proclamation or proclaimed order.

ཁྲིམས་གཅོད *khrims-gcod*=ཉེས་པ་གཅོད *ñes-pa gcod* to inflict punishment (*Mñon.*).

ཁྲིམས་འཇགས *khrims-hjags* = ཁྲིམས་ཀྱི་དོན་བཞིན *khrims kyi don bshin* acc. to the meaning or spirit of the law (*Ñag.*).

ཁྲིམས་སྦྱོར=ཁྲིམས་ལ་སྐྱལ་བ *khrims la skyal-wa* to deliver up to justice.

ཁྲིལ *khril* (*thi*), v. འཁྲིལ *khril.*

ཁྲིས *khris* (*thi*), ཁྲིས་འཇོགས་པ *khris hjogs-pa* peace, v. འཇུགས་པ *hjugs-pa.*

ཁྲུ *khru* (*thû*) ཁྲུ་མ *khru-ma* हस्त one-fourth of a འདོམ *hdom* or fathom; a cubit; རྩེ་ཁྲུ *rtse-khru* or the measure of eighteen inches, from the elbow to the extremity of the middle finger: ཁྲུ་གང་ཚམ *khru-gañ rtsam* हस्तमात्र about the measure of 15 inches from the elbow to the fisted middle finger is called བསྐུམ་ཁྲུ *bskum-khru*, or cubit measure; ཁྲུ་འཇལ་བ *khru hjal-wa* to measure with a cubit measure (*Cs.*).

ཁྲུ་བ *khru-wa* (*thu-wa*), sometimes for འཁྲུ་བ *hkhru-wa*, to wash.

ཁྲུ་གཟར *khru-gzar* a kind of stew-pan (*Sch.*).

ཁྲུ་སློག *khru-slog* or ཁྲུ་རློག *khru-rlog* tilling the ground; acc. to *Sch.* a pit filled with corn: ཁྲུ་སློག་པ *khru-slog-pa* digging; breaking up the soil; gardening.

ཁྲུང་ཁྲུང་ *khruñ-khruñ* (*thung-thung*) क्रौञ्च crane, *grus cinerea*; also the stork: ཁྲུང་ཁྲུང་རུས་པས་ཆུ་འགགས་སེལ *khruñ-khruñ rus-pas chu-hgags sel* the bones of the crane remove the stoppage of urine. When milk mixed with water is given to a crane it will drink the milk, leaving the water in the basin. The reason of this, according to *K. d.*ད *110*, is that as soon as the bill of the crane touches the milk it turns into curds, which are eaten up, leaving the water in the basin.

Syn. མགྲིན་པ་རབ་རིང་ *mgrin-pa rab-riṅ*; མིག་སྨན་མཇུག་མ་ *mig sman mjug-ma*; ཀྲུཉྩ *kruñ-ca* (*Mṅon.*).

ཁྲུང་ཁྲུང་འཇོམས་ *khruṅ-khruṅ hjoms*=དབང་ཕྱུག་གི་བུ་ཆུང་བ་གཞོན་ནུ་གདོང་དྲུག *dbaṅ-phyug-gi bu chuṅ-ba gshon-nu gdoṅ-drug* a name of Kumāra the second son of Is'vara (*Mṅon.*).

ཁྲུད་པ *khrud pa*, ལུས་ཁྲུད་པ *lus khrud-pa* to wash; cleanse out dirt or filth from the body (*Ṅag.*).

ཁྲུན *khrun* (*thun*) आरोह, परिमाण height; length; extension (*Cs.*): ཁྲུན་ཕང་སྲིད *khrun phaṅ srid* height and breadth (equal).

ཁྲུམ་ཁྲུམ *khrum-khrum* (*thum-thum*) (*Sch.*): ཁྲུམ་ཁྲུམ་བྱེད་པ *khrum-khrum byed-pa* or ཁྲུམ་ཁྲུམ་ བརྡུང་བ *khrum-khrum brduṅ-wa* to pound in a mortar.

ཁྲུམས *khrums* (*thum*) भाद्र-पद n. of a constellation: ཁྲུམས་སྟོད *khrums-stod* the name of the 24th constellation, पूर्व्व-भाद्र-पद.

Syn. བྱ་མཆུ *bya-mchu*; རིའི་ལྷ་མོ *rihi lha-mo*; གནས་མ *gnas-ma*; བ་གླང་རྐང་ *ba-glaṅ rkaṅ* (*Mṅon.*).

ཁྲུམས་སྟོད་ཀྱི་ཉ་བ *khrums-stod-kyi ña-wa* भाद्र-पद-पौर्णमासी the full moon of the month of भाद्र पद, July.

ཁྲུམས་སྨད *khrums-smad* the name of the 25th constellation, उत्तर-भाद्र-पद; acc. to Hindu astronomy the 26th lunar mansion, figured by a conch, and comprehending two stars, of which one is Andromeda.

Syn. ཟེའུ *zehu*; སྦྲུལ་འཆིང *sbrul-hchiṅ* (*Mṅon.*).

ཁྲུམས་ཟླ *khrum-zla* (*thum da*), v. ཟླ་བ་བརྒྱད་པ *zla-ba brgyad-pa* पितृपच, पूर्व्वभाद्र, the eighth month of the Tibetan year.

Syn. འབུགས་པ *hbugs-pa*; བྱ་མཆུ *bya-mchu*; ནོར་ལྡན *nor-ldan*; ཁྱུ་མཆོག་ཅན *khyu-mchog can*; བ་ལང་རྐང་བཟང་ *ba-laṅ rkaṅ-bzaṅ*; སྤྲིན་བཟང་ *sprin-bzaṅ*; ལེན་པ *len-pa*; བྱའི་ཟླ་བ *byahi zla-wa*; སྟོན་ཟླ་འབྲིང་པོ *ston-zla hbriṅ-po* (*Mṅon.*).

ཁྲུལ *khrul* (*thul*), ཁྲུལ་གཏོང་བ *khrul gtoṅ-wa* to let fall; to drop (several things at intervals); མཆི་མ་ཁྲུལ་བཤེད *mchi-ma khrul bshed* to shed tears: ཟླ་ཁྲུལ *zla-khrul* in *W.* intercalary month (*Jä.*).

ཁྲུལ་པོ *khrul-po* in *C.* 1. cheerful; merry. 2. fornicator (*Jä.*).

ཁྲུལ་མ *khrul-ma* 1. in *W.* crooked crank, handle (*Jä*). 2. a whore. 3. ཁུ་བ་ཁྲུལ་མ *khu-wa khrul-ma* rice-water or water in which millet is washed.

ཁྲུས *khrus* (*thus*) मज्जनम्, स्नान, आप्लव, मर्ज bath; washing; ablution.

ཁྲུས་ཀྱི་བརྟུལ་ཞུགས་ཅན *khrus-kyi btul-shugs can*=དྲང་སྲོང་ *draṅ-sroṅ* a *Ṛṣi* or sage who observes the vow of ablution: ཁྲུས་བྱེད་པའི་ལྟུང་བྱེད *khrus byed-pahi ltuṅ-byed* स्नान-प्रायश्चित्तिक faults committed while bathing: ཁྲུས་བྱས་གོས་གཙང་གྱོན་ཏེ་དཀར་གསུམ་ཟོས having bathed put on clean clothes and take milk, curds and butter (*Loṅ.* ཀ *32*).

Syn. ཀུན་ཏུ་རྒྱུ *kun-tu rgyu*; དཀའ་ཐུབ་ཅན *dkah-thub-can*; ངག་བསྡམས་པ *ṅag bsdams-pa*; དགེ་བར་སློང་བ *dge-war sloṅ-wa*; ཉོན་མོངས་ཐུལ *ñon-moṅs thul*; དབང་པོ་ཐུལ *dbaṅ-po thul*; སྨྲ་བ་ཅད་པ *smra-ba cad-pa*; གཏང་བར་གནས་པ *gtaṅ-bar gnas-pa*; ཚངས་པར་སྤྱོད་པ *tshaṅ-par spyod-pa*; རིག་བྱེད་ཀློག་པ *rig-byed klog-pa* (*Mṅon.*).

ཁྲུས་ཀྱི་རྩ *khrus-kyi rtsa*, ཀུ་ཤ *ku-ça* the grass *Ku-ça* (*Mṅon.*).

ཁྲུས་ཀྱི་རྫིང་ *khrus-kyi rdsiṅ* ཁྲུས་རྒྱབ་སའི་རྫིང་ *khrus rgyab-sahi rdsiṅ* a bathing tank.

ཁྲུས་ཁུ *khrus-khu* water for bathing (*Jä.*).

ཁྲུས་ཁང་བརྩེགས་པ *khrus-khaṅ brtsegs-pa* the making of a bath or bathing place.

ཁྲུས་མཁན་ *khrus-mkhan* स्नातक one who bathes; he that has bathed.

ཁྲུས་ཆལ་ *khru-chal* स्नानीय washing materials, soda, soap, etc.

ཁྲུས་ཆུ་ *khrus-chu* bathing water; water consecrated by a deity being washed in it.

ཁྲུས་དར་ *khrus-dar* scraf or good linen towel for the toilet; scarf of silk used in washing the images of deities (*Rtsii.*).

Syn. བུམ་དར་ *bum-dar*; སོ་སོར་ཁྲུས་བཏགས་རི *so-sor khrus btags-ri* (*Mñon.*).

ཁྲུས་སྡེར་ *khrus-sder* basin; washing bowl.

ཁྲུས་པ *khrus-pa* (*thus-pa*) उत्सेक, परिप्लुतम्, धाव washed; also washing.

Syn. ཁྲུས་བྱ *khrus-bya*; འཁྲུད *hkhrud*; ཁྲུ་བ *khru-wa* (*Mñon.*).

ཁྲུས་བུམ *khrus-bum* कमण्डलु washing pot or jug.

ཁྲུས་མ་ཁྲུད་མ *khrus-ma khrud-ma* washings of rice or any other millet; also the remnant of water in which rice, &c., is boiled.

ཁྲུས་རྫས *khrus-rdsas* articles of washing or to wash with such as soap, etc.

Syn. ལྡག་ཆལ *ldag-chal*; ཁྲུས་རྩི *khrus-rtsi*; དག་བྱེད *dag-byed* (*Mñon.*).

ཁྲུས་གཞོང *khrus-gshoñ* सेचन-पात्र bathing tub; basin used for a bath.

ཁྲུས་རས *khrus-ras* स्नानशाटक a towel; a bathing towel.

ཁྲུས་གཤེར *khrus-gçer* bathing water. Acc. to *Jä.* this word (in Ladak) relates to a certain medical procedure or method of curing.

ཁྲུས་གསོལ་བ *khrus-gsol-wa* resp. for ཁྲུས་བྱེད་པ *khrus-byed-pa*, *i.e.*, when applied to bathing places used by divine beings and great men: ལྷ་མི་ཁང་པ་སོགས་ལ་ཁྲུས་བྱེད་པ *lha-mi khañ-pa sogs la khrus byed-pa* "gods or men taking a bath in their abodes and so forth," to administer a bath to another, especially as a religious ceremony, consisting in sprinkling with water.

ཁྲེ *khre* (*the*) millet: ཁྲེ་ནི་ལྕི་བསིལ་ལྡན་པས་རྨ་འདས་བྱེད, རུས་པ་ཆག་ཞུམ་གསེས་རྣམས་སྦྱོར་བར་བྱེད millet, being both heavy and chilling, causes wounds to swell, but bones which have been dislocated or fractured it causes to unite. ཁྲེ་རྒོད *khre-rgod* wild millet; ཁྲེ་རྒོད་འཁྲུ་བ་གཅོད་ཅིང་དུག་སེལ་བྱེད wild ཁྲེ stops diarrhœa and removes the poison.

ཁྲེ་ཙེ *khre-tse* Chinese vermicelli (*Jä.*).

ཁྲེགས་པ *khregs-pa* (*theg-pa*), v. མཁྲེགས་པ *mkhregs-pa*.

ཁྲེམ་གཉེར *khrem-gñer*, v. ཆུ་གཉེར *chu-gñer* (*Mñon.*).

ཁྲེལ་པོ *khrel-po* shameful.

ཁྲེམས་པ *khrems-pa* (*them-pa*) 1. irrigation; also to water gardens and cultivations; to sprinkle water. 2. n. of a book: བྱང་ཁོག་ཁྲེམས་ཀྱི་ལུང་རིན་ཆེན་འོད་འཕྲོ་བ *byañ-khog khrems-kyi luñ rin-chen hod hphro-wa* (*Sorig. 81*).

ཁྲེལ *khrel* (*thel*) resp. ཐུགས་ཁྲེལ *thugs-khrel* 1. प्रियंगु a kind of millet. 2. अपत्रपा shame; diffidence; bashfulness; modesty. 3. piety acc. to *Jä.*, especially in *W.* 4. in *C.* disgust; aversion.

ཁྲེལ་གད *khrel-gad* a scornful laughter.

ཁྲེལ་ཅན *khrel-can* possessed of shame; ཁྲེལ་ཅན *khrel-can* bashful (*Cs.*); also earnest, conscientious.

ཁྲེལ་ལྟོས *khrel-ltos* pusilanimous; shamefaced.

ཁྲེལ་གདོང *khrel-gdoñ* (lit. a face capable of shame) a bashful face.

ཁྲེལ་འདོད་ཅན *khrel-hdod-can* in *W.* ready to shame others.

ཁྲེལ་ལྡན *khrel-ldan*, v. ངོ་ཚ་ཤེས་པ *ño-tsha çes-pa* अपत्रपिन् modest.

ཁྲེལ་བ to be ashamed; to provoke shame: ཁྲེལ་བ་དང་ངོ་ཚ་བ་མེད *khrel-wa daṅ ṅo-tsha-wa med* he has no shame or modesty.

ཁྲེལ་མེད་པ *khrel-med-pa*, ཁྲེལ་མེད་མ *khrel-med-ma* अनपत्रप immodest, shameless.

ཁྲེལ་ཡོད *khrel-yod* अपत्रपा modesty; chastity; decency; ཁྲེལ་ཡོད་པ *khrel-yod-pa* to be chaste: ཁྲེལ་ཡོད་པར་བྱེད་པ *khrel yod-par byed-pa* to behave chastely, with modesty.

ཁྲེས *khres* or (*the*) ཁྲེས་པོ *khres-po*, (*the-po*) a load, burden: མི་ཁྲེས་ཆུང་ཅན *mi khres chuṅ-can* a man with a small load (*A. 10*). ཁྲེས་པོ་དེའི་ནང་ནས *kres-po dehi naṅ-nas* from within that package: གཞུང་དོན་གྱི་བསངས་ཤིང་ཁྲེས་ཕྱེད *gshuṅ-don-gyi bsaṅs çiṅ khres phed* half a bundle (or load) of fire-wood for the use of government (*Rtsii.*).

Syn. ཁུར་པ *khur-pa*; ཁུར་འདྲེན་པ *khur hdren-pa*; རྒྱབ་ཀྱིས་ཐེག་པ *rgyab-kyis theg-pa*; ཁུར་རྩ་པ *khur stsa-pa* (*Mṅon.*).

ཁྲེས་ཁྲེས *khres-khres* (*the-the*) unable to sit erect; falling down: མི་གཅིག་ཁྲེས་ཁྲེས་ན་བ་གཟིགས་ནས་སྨན་པ་ལ་ཅིས་ཕན་དྲིས་པས *mi-gcig khres-khres na-wa gzigs nas sman-pa la cis phan dris-pas* (*A. 44*) seeing a man very ill so as to be unable to sit erect, he asked the physician what would be of use.

ཁྲོ *khro* (*tho*) सरकं a kind of bronze, of about same quality and worth as bell-metal (འཁར་བ *hkhar-wa*), but inferior to *li*. The kind of bronze called *khro-nag* or dark bronze is also called *lchags khro* on account of the predominance of iron in the compound. The kind called ཁྲོ་དཀར *khro-dkar*, white bronze, has more zinc and ཟངས་ཁྲོ *zaṅs-khro* has more of copper in it than iron. The dark-bronze is largely manufactured in China; the white-bronze is much prized by the Tibetans. Huge bronze caldrons used in the great monasteries of Tibet for boiling tea are made of the white bronze; ཚོགས་ཁྲོ *tshogs-khro* large bronze caldrons used in cooking tea, &c., for the use of the congregation in the monasteries of Tibet: ཁྲོ་ནག་གདོན་གཟེར་སྲིན་དང་དུག་ནད་འཇོམས *khro-nag gzer-srin daṅ dug-nad hjoms* dark bronze dissipates worm-spasms and poisonous complaints.

ཁྲོ་རྒྱན *khro-rgyan* ornaments made of bronze. ཁྲོའི་ཁུག་ཏིལ *khrohi khug-til* bronze pot to boil tea.

ཁྲོ་ཆུ *khro-chu* 1. liquid or melted bronze; acc. to some author melted iron before it is cast. 2. n. for དངུལ་ཆུ *dṅul-chu* quicksilver; (a mystic) term (*Miṅ.*).

ཁྲོ་ཆུ་སྡོམ་པ *khro-chu sdom-pa* to fill up joints, grooves, &c., with melted bronze; to solder.

ཁྲོ་འཇོམས་པ *khro hjoms-pa* to suppress anger or wrath: གང་ཞིག་བསྒྲིམས་ཏེ་ཁྲོ་འཇོམས་པ། དེ་ནི་འདི་དང་གཞན་དུ་བདེ *gaṅ-shig bsgrims-te khro hjoms-pa, de-ni hdi-daṅ gshan-du bde* (*Spyod.*) he who can subdue his anger will be happy here and hereafter.

ཁྲོ་ཉམས *khro-ñams* = རྔམ་བརྗིད *rṅam-brjid* or རྔམ་འཇིགས *rṅam-hjigs* or རྔོམ་བརྗིད *rṅom-brjid* to sit in an angry mood (*Mṅon.*).

ཁྲོ་གཉེར *khro-gñer* भ्रुकुटि, भ्रूकुटि wrinkles on the face and forehead expressive of wrath, indignation, anger; also indignant.

ཁྲོ་གཉེར་ཅན *khro-gñer-can* भ्रुकुटि she whose face is wrinkled with anger; also frowning.

* ཁྲོ་གཉེར་ཅན་མ *khro-gñer can-ma* (*Sehr. 36 C.*).

ཁྲོ་གཉེར་མེད་པ *khro-gñer med-pa* अपगतभ्रुकुटि free from frowning or anger.

ཁྲོ་གཉེར་གཟི་བརྗིད་ལྡན་པ *khro-gñer gzi-brjid ldan-pa*, ཤུ་དག *çu-dag* n. of a medicinal root (*Sman. 102*).

ཁྲོ་པ *khro-pa* in *W.* for ཁྲོ *khro*.

ཁྲོ་གཏུམ་པོ *khro-gtum-po* furious with rage.

ཁྲོ་བ *khro-wa*, (*tho-wa*) བརྩེ་བ *brtse-wa* मन्यु, अरिका sbst. anger, wrath; also adj. angry, wrathful: ཁོང་ཁྲོ་བ *khoṅ-khro-wa* smouldering wrath: ཁྲོ་བ་བཟོད་པ *khro-wa bzod-pa* subduing or abstaining from anger: ཁྲོ་བ་བཟོད་པ་ངེས་བཅོམ་པ་སླར་ཡང་སྐྱེ་བར་མི་འགྱུར་རོ *khro-wa bzod-pa ṅes bcom-pa slar-yaṅ skye-war mi-hgyur-ro* anger having been subdued and inwardly suppressed, it will not grow again (*K. d.* ར *68*): ཁྲོ་བའི་དུག་གི་སྨན་མཆོག་ཏུ་བཟོད་པ the chief remedy for the poison of anger is forbearance (*K. d.* ར *68*): ཁྲོ་བའི་སེམས་འདི་གཅིག་བཅོམ་ན, དགྲ་དེ་ཐམས་ཅད་བཅོམ་དང་འདྲ if the wrathful mind be once subdued it is tantamount to subduing all the enemies one has. ཁྲོ་བར་བྱེད་པ or ཁྲོ་བར་འགྱུར་བ to be or to grow angry (*Cs.*); ཁྲོས་ཀྱང་སྣང་མི་ཁྲོ་བར་བྱ though angry, to be as if not angry; ཁྲོ་བས་ལྟ=མིག་ཁྲོ་བས་ལྟ་བ angry looks; to look back with anger (*Mṅon.*).

ཁྲོ་བ་མ *Khro-wa-ma* क्रोधना n. of a goddess.

ཁྲོ་བོ *khro-wo* (*tho-wo*) क्रोधी, भैरव an angry spirit; a god or *Bodhisattva* in his assumed wrathful mood or manifestation.

*ཁྲོ་བོ་ཁམས་གསུམ་རྣམ་རྒྱལ་སྤྲུལ་བཅད *khro-wo khams-gsum rnam-rgyal sprul-bcad* क्रोधत्रैलोक्यविजयनिर्म्मितभाषा (*Schr.*; *Tā. 2, 276*).

ཁྲོ་བོ་ཆེན་པོ *khro-wo chen-po* महाक्रोधी an appellation of Mahākāla, the Lord of Death—the terrific god or guardian of Buddhism.

*ཁྲོ་བོ་རྟ་མགྲིན *khra-wo rta-mgrin* क्रोधहयग्रीव (*Schr. 71 C.*).

*ཁྲོ་བོ་སྟོབས་པོ་ཆེ *khro-wo stobs-po-che* महाबलक (*Schr. 73 B.*).

*ཁྲོ་བོ་བདུད་རྩི་འཁྱིལ་པ *khro-wo bdud-rtsi hkhyil-pa* क्रोधामृतावर्त (*Schr.*; *Tā. 2, 103*).

*ཁྲོ་བོ་འདོད་རྒྱལ *khro-wo hdod-rgyal* टक्किराज (*Schr. 72 A.*).

*ཁྲོ་བོ་རྡོ་རྗེ་ས་འོག *khro-wo rdo-rje sa-hog* वज्रपाताल (*Schr. 74 B.*).

*ཁྲོ་བོ་དབྱུག་པ་སྔོན་པོ *khro-wo dbyug-pa sṅon-po* नीलदण्ड (*Schr.*; *Tā. 2, 161*).

*ཁྲོ་བོ་མི་གཡོ་བ *khro-wo mi-gyo-pa* क्रोधाचल (*Schr. 58 C.*).

*ཁྲོ་བོ་སྨེ་བ་བརྩེགས་པ *khro-wo sme-wa brtsegs-pa* (*Schr. 58 A.*).

*ཁྲོ་བོ་གཙུག་ཏོར་འཁོར་བསྒྱུར *khro-wo gtsug-tor hkhor-bsgyur* उष्णीषचक्रवर्त्ती (*Schr.*).

*ཁྲོ་བོ་གཞན་གྱིས་མི་ཐུབ་པ *khro-wo gshan-gyis mi-thub-pa* (*Schr. 71 A.*).

*ཁྲོ་བོ་གཤིན་རྗེ་གཤེད *khro-wa gçin-rje-gçed* यमान्तक्रोध (*Schr. 71 B.*).

ཁྲོ་བྱེད *khro-byed* रोषण, चट frightful.

ཁྲོ་བྱེད་མ *khro byed-ma* चण्डी 1. a name of the goddess Paldan Lhamo. 2. བུད་མེད་གཏུམ་མོ *bud-med gtum-mo* क्रोधना a fearful woman (*Mṅon.*).

ཁྲོ་མིག *khro-mig*=མིག་གི་རྣམ་འགྱུར *mig-gi rnam-hgyur* or སྡང་མིག *sdaṅ-mig* an expression of the eye; angry eyes (*Mṅon.*).

ཁྲོ་མོ *khro-mo* a female terrific deity or spirit.

ཁྲོ་མོན *khro-mon* prison (*Sch.*).

ཁྲོག *khrog* (*thog*) in ཁྲོག་བརྒྱབ་པ *khrog brgyab-pa* to drink hastily; to gulp down: ཁྲོག་ཆུང་པ་ཡིས་ཁྲག་སྐོར་གཅོད་པའི་མཆོག *khrog chuṅ-pa yis khrag-çor-gcod-pahi-mchog.* Thog-chung is best for stopping bleeding.

ཁྲོག་ཁྲོག *khrog-khrog* (*ṭhog-ṭhog*) 1. one who speaks irrelevantly and is not steady in his acts or words. Described as མི་བརྟན་པོ་མེད་པ་ཁ་ཚད་ཅིག་དོན་ལ་མི་གནས་ཤིང་སྐད་ཆ་མི་འདུ་བ་མང་པོ་ལབ་པས་ཆ་བཞག་ས་མེད་པ་སྨྲ་ཚིག་ཚུབ་བྱེད་པའི་མི། 2. acc. to *Jä.* in *W.* the sound caused by something falling heavily on the ground.

ཁྲོག་ཆུང་ *khrog-chuñ* an herb with leaves resembling a saw in shape.

ཁྲོག་པོ *khrog-po* botanical term, used of leaves standing round the stem scattered or alternately.

ཁྲོག་སྨན *khrog-sman* the raw unprepared substance of a medicine (*Sch.*): སྨན་ཁྲོག *sman-khrog* is defined as སྨན་མ་བརྡུངས་པ་སྣ་ཚོགས་ལ *sman-ma brduñs-pa sna-tshogs-la*, the unpulverized ingredients of a medicine.

ཁྲོང་ངེ *khroñ-ñe* (*ṭhoñg-ñe*) upright, straight, erect (*Jä.*).

ཁྲོང་པོ *khroñ-po* close-fisted, stingy (*Jä.*).

ཁྲོད་ *khrod* (*ṭhod*) crowd, assemblage, mass, multitude; མི་ཁྲོད *mi-khrod* a troop; crowd of men; རི་ཁྲོད *ri-khrod* a range of mountain peaks; རྩ་ཁྲོད *rtsa-khrod* a heap, stack, rick (of hay); ནགས་ཁྲོད *nags-khrod* a dense forest; མུན་ཁྲོད *mun-khrod* thick darkness; དུར་ཁྲོད *dur-khrod* a cemetery; ཁྲོད་དུ in the crowd; རི་ཁྲོད=also a hermit.

ཁྲོན *khron* (*ṭhon*) claw: ཁྲོན་གྱིས་རྐོ་བའི་སྡེ *khron kyis rko-wahi sde* the class of gallinaceous birds (*S.g.*; *Jä.*).

ཁྲོན་པ *khron-pa* (*ṭhon-pa*), कूप, वापि, वसुक, उदपान well; spring: ཁྲོན་པའི་ཆུ *khron-pahi chu* well-water; also called དོང་ཆུ *doñ-chu*; ཁྲོན་བུ *khron-bu*, a little well: ཁྲོན་པའི་སྙིང་པོ *khron-pahi sñiñ-po* जलकूपी; ཁྲོན་པས་རུང་བ *hron-pas ruñ-wa* उदपानकल्प water in a well that has been made fit (by the priesthood) for drink.

ཁྲོན་བུ *khron-bu* 1. a medicinal root; a vegetable purgative. 2 ཁྲོན་བུས་འཇམ་པོར་སྦྱོང་བྱེད་གྲོགས་ཀྱི་མཆོག *khron-bus hjam-por sbyoñ-byed grogs-kyi mchog* thron-bu acts as a gentle purgative.

ཁྲོམ *khrom* (*ṭhom*) a market place; a bazar; crowd of people; multitude of persons; ཁྲོམ་ཆེན *khrom-chen* a great crowd; ཚོགས་པའི་ཁྲོམ་རྣམས *tshogs-pahi khrom-rnams* the assembled crowd; ཕོ་ཁྲོམ *pho-khrom* multitude of men; རྒྱལ་ཁྲོམ *rgyal-khrom* a royal gathering: acc. to *Cs.* ཁྲོམ་ཆེན་པོ *khrom-chen-po*, chief market-place, also principal street: ཁྲོམ་སྐོར་བ *khrom-skor-wa* to wander about the market; to ramble through as if in a market; གསང་སྔགས་ཁྲོམ་དུ་ཀློག *gsañ-sñags khrom-du klog* secret spells (magic formulas) are read in the market.

ཁྲོམ་སྐོར་མ *khrom-skor-ma* harlot; strumpet; street woman (*Cs.*).

ཁྲོམ་ཐོག་ཆོད *khrom-thog chod* a person well dressed, well equipped, and possessed of personal accomplishments; one above the crowd; above his fellows.

ཁྲོམ་པ *Khrom-pa* 1. n. of a province in Tibet; ཁྲོམ་པོ་པ *khrom-po-pa*, an inhabitant of *Khrom* (Thom). 2. a market vendor.

ཁྲོམ་དཔོན *khrom-dpon* officer who is charged with the supervision of a market.

ཁྲོམ་མེ *khrom-me* sparkling; glittering: ཟིལ་པ་ཁྲོམ་མེ *zil p-akhrom-me* sparkling dew.

drop. ཁྲོམ་དམར་ནག་འཁྱིལ་བ *khrom dmar nag ḥkhyil-wa* a motley crowd; a throng, black and red intermingled.

ཁྲོམ་ཚོགས *khrom-tshogs* (*thom-tsho*) the gathering of buyers and sellers, &c., in a market: ཤ་ཁྲོམ *ça-khrom* the section of the market where meat is sold; meat market; དཔེ་ཁྲོམ *dpe-khrom* book market; རྟ་ཁྲོམ *rta-khrom* the section where ponies and horses are sold.

ཁྲོམས *khroms*, v. འགྲེམ་པ *ḥgrem-pa*.

ཁྲོལ *khrol* (*thol*), v. འཁྲོལ་བ *ḥkhrol-wa* and འགྲོལ་བ *ḥgrol-wa* 1. a sound (*Jä.*). 2. ग्रन्थिमोचन loosening; unfastening; that which is unfastened. མགོ་ཁྲོལ་ནི་ཤ་པ་ལུག་མགོ་སོགས་ལེགས་པར་བཙོས་ནས་ཤ་རུས་སོ་སོར་འགྲོ་བ by *mgo-khrol* is meant the separating of meat from the bones by the sheep's head having been boiled well. ནང་ཁྲོལ *nañ khrol* the contents of a slaughtered animal, including the stomach, entrails, lungs, liver, spleen, &c. The expression རང་གི་ནང་ཁྲོལ་ཕྱི་ལ་སྟོན་པ *rañ-gi nañ-khrol phyi-la-ston-pa* means "one's own blunders exposed to outward show": ཁྲོལ་གྱིས་སོང་ *khrol-gyis soñ* (the ring) slid sounding (across the azure floor).

ཁྲོལ་ཁྲོལ *khrol-khrol* (*thol-thol*)=ཁྲོལ་པོ *khrol-po* bright, shining; ཁྲོལ་ཁྲོལ་བྱེད་པ *khrol-khrol byed-pa*=མིག་ཁྲོལ་ལེ་ཁྲོལ་ལེ་ལྟ་བ *mig khrol-le khrol-le lta-wa* to stare at.

ཁྲོལ་དོང *khrol-doñ* is said to denote a large hand-bell.

ཁྲོལ་ཆ *khrol-cha* release (as of monks from a religious service or of school-boys from class work; acc. to *Sch.* the act of forgiving; pardon.

ཁྲོལ་པོ I: *khrol-po* (*thol-po*) 1. cheerful, merry; sparkling, glittering, dazzling. 2. fornicator.

ཁྲོལ་པོ II: 1. sparkling: འོད་ཁྲོལ་པོ *ḥod khrol-po* brightness (on water when the sun shines upon it). 2. acc. to *Jä.* in *W.* distinct; intelligible.

ཁྲོལ་མ *khrol-ma*, ནས་ཚགས *nas-tshags* a seive for cleansing and sifting barley, grain, etc.

ཁྲོལ་མོ *khrol-mo* in *W.* brittle, fragile; opposite to མཉེན་པོ *mñon-po*, tough.

ཁྲོལ་ཚགས *khrol tshogs* a sieve (*Cs.*); ལྕགས་ཚགས *lcags tshags* iron sieve.

ཁྲོལ་ལོག *khrol-log*=ཁྲོག་ཁྲོག *khrog-khrog* in *W.* cf. འཁྲོལ་བ *ḥkhrol-wa.*; also 1. kettle. 2. a sound.

ཁྲོས་པ *khros-pa* ཐུགས་ཁྲོས་པ *thugs khros-pa* वह, कुपित enraged; wrath-seeming; appearance of wrath: ཕྱག་ན་རྡོ་རྗེ་ཤིན་ཏུ་ཁྲོས་པའི་ཚུལ་བསྟན་པ *phyag-na rdo-rje çin-tu khros-paḥi tshul bstan-pa* Chagna Dorje in a very wrathful form manifested himself: ཁྲོས་པའི་གར *khros-paḥi gar* dance in wrathful mood.

ཁྲོས་མ *khros-ma* (*thoi-ma*) or ཁྲོ་མ *khro-ma* the wrathful female deity or *Rudrānī*; such female divinities as outwardly show themselves to be of terrific and frightful aspect.

ཁྲོས་ཚིག *khros-tshig* angry words.

Syn. རྙན་འཕྱར *rñan-ḥphyar* or སུན་འབྱིན *sun-ḥbyin* (*Mñon.*).

མཁན *mkhan* an affix which, annexed to substantives and verbal roots, answers in colloq. very much the same purposes as the Hindustani appendix *wala*; ས་མཁན *sa-mkhan* one who has to do with the soil; ལམ་མཁན *lam-mkhan* one who knows the way, a guide; ཤིང་མཁན *çiñ-mkhan* a worker in wood, carpenter, joiner, &c. Affixed to a verbal root, signifies he who performs an action, whether only just now or habitually; ཡོང་མཁན་ *yoñ-mkhan* comer; འགྲོ་མཁན་ *ḥgro-mkhan* the goer; one who moves; བྲི་མཁན་ *bri-mkhan* the writer, one who has written it; ཨང་མཁན་ *añ-mkhan* (in Sikkim) one who speaks falsehoods, a liar; ཤེས་མཁན་ *çes-mkhan* he who knows; བསྟན་མཁན་ *bstan-mkhan* the shower, explainer; འདོགས་མཁན་ *ḥdogs-mkhan* one who is binding, fastening; also with an objective case, ངའི་བུ་མོ་འདོད་མཁན་ *ñaḥi bu-mo ḥdod-mkhan*, such as are desiring my daughter; བསད་མཁན་ *bsad-mkhan* the man who is killed or who kills; a murderer. In colloq. language *mkhan* seems to have entirely displaced the termination པ་ *pa*, signifying in general the agent: གདུང་མ་ཁྱེར་མཁན་གྱི་མི་ *gduñ-ma khyer-mkhan gyi mi* the men carrying the beam. Contrary to its original signification, it is even used to form the relative: བསད་མཁན་གྱི་ལུག the sheep which was killed.

མཁན་རྒྱུད་ *mkhan-rgyud*= བླ་ཆེན་དང་མཁན་པོའི་རྒྱུད་ *Bla-chen dañ mkhan-poḥi rgyud* the lineal spiritual descendants of *Bla-chen* and *Mkhan-po*, those through whom the vows formulated by them are handed down (*Yig.*).

མཁན་པ I: *mkhan-pa* ferns of two species. The one growing in Tibet is called མཁན་དཀར་ *mkhan-dkar*, or the white fern; the other species belonging to the Cis-Himalaya is called མཁན་ནག་ *mkhan-nag*, black fern: *mkhan-pa* is deemed useful in healing fresh cut wounds; it is also applied to swellings.

མཁན་པ II: incense; frankincense: མཁན་པ་བ་ལུ་རྣམས་གཙོ་བའི་དྲི་ལྡན་གྱི་སྤོས་སྣ་ཚོགས the various kinds of incense in which the scent of such as *khan-pa*, *Bālu*, etc., predominates (*Rtsii.*).

མཁན་པོ *mkhan-po*, প্রশাস্তা, উপাধ্যায a professor employed to teach; the head of a monastery. In Tibet the head of a particular college attached to a monastery, high priests who give vows to the junior or inferior lamas, and professors of sacred literature, are called *mkhan-po*; also learned men, who as such are endowed with the མཁན་རྒྱུད་ *mkhan-rgyud* or spiritual gifts or descended heritage from their spiritual ancestors, are called *mkhan-po*. Again, learned men such as are sent to China as representatives of the Grand Hierarch are also styled *mkhan-po*. Besides these, those who serve the Grand Lama as his domestic chaplains, teachers or advisers, such as སྐུ་བཅར་མཁན་པོ་ *Sku-bcar Mkhan-po* Khan-po, who sits in company of the Grand Lama; གཟིམས་དཔོན་མཁན་པོ་ *gzim-dpon mkhan-po* the chamberlain khan-po; མཆོད་དཔོན་མཁན་པོ་ *mchod-dpon mkhan-po* the domestic chaplain; གསོལ་དཔོན་མཁན་པོ་ *gsol-dpon-mkhan-po* the steward in charge of the Grand Lama's tea and food; མཁན་སྡེ་ཕྱི་ཀ་ *mkhan-sde phyi-ka* outside khan-po—those that enjoy this distinction but partially. Other designations of this kind are མཁན་པོ་ལ་རྣམ་པ་བཞི་སྟེ་ *Mkhan-po la rnam-pa bshi ste*:—(1) མཁན་པོ་ཆོས་ཀྱིས་སྡུད་ལ་ཟང་ཟིང་གིས་མ་ཡིན་པའང་ཡོད་ *mkhan-po chos-kyis sdud-la zañ-ziñ-gis ma-yin pahañ-yod* the professor who conveys to his pupil instruction, not wealth; (2) ཟང་ཟིང་གིས་སྡུད་ལ་ཆོས་ཀྱིས་མ་ཡིན་པའང་ཡོད་ *zañ-ziñ-gis sdud-la chos-kyis ma-yin pahañ yod* the professor who gives riches but not religious instructions; (3) མཁན་པོ་ཆོས་ཀྱིས་སྡུད་ཅིང་ཟང་ཟིང་གིས་སྡུད་པ་ཡང་ཡོད་ *mkhan-po chos-kyis sdud-ciñ zañ-ziñ-gis sdud-pa yañ yod* the professor who gives both wealth and religious instruction to his pupil; (4) མཁན་པོ་ཆོས་ཀྱིས་ཀྱང་མི་སྡུད་

ཅིང་ཟང་ཟིང་གིས་ཀྱང་མི་སྡུད་པ་ཡོད་ *m̱khan-po chos-kyis kyaṅ mi-s̱duḏ-chiṅ zaṅ-ziṅ-gis kyaṅ mi s̱dud-pa yoḏ* the professor who neither imparts instruction nor wealth.

མཁན་བུ *m̱khan-bu* pupil, scholar (*Jä.*).

མཁན་མོ *m̱khan-mo* mistress, intructress (*Cs.*).

མཁན་རབས *m̱khan-rabs* the succession of khan-po or abbots in a great monastery.

མཁན་རིམས *m̱khan-rims* the respective prospects of being elected abbot as depending on the different ranks of the expectant candidates; the order of the succession of abbots.

མཁན་སློབ *m̱khan-s̱lob* for མཁན་པོ་དང་སློབ་མ *m̱khan-po daṅ s̱lob-ma* the professor and his pupil; also (according to some) མཁན་པོ་དང་སློབ་དཔོན *m̱khan-po daṅ s̱lob-ḏpon* the professor and the teacher: བླ་མ་མཁན་སློབ་ཀྱི་བཀའ *ḇla-ma m̱khan-s̱lob-kyi ḇkaẖ* the words or commands of the lama, abbot and teachers.

མཁའ *m̱khaẖ* ख the heaven; the sky; generally ནམ་མཁའ *nam-m̱khaẖ*.

མཁའ་ཀློང་ *m̱khaẖ-ḵloṅ*, མཁའ་ཁྱབ *m̱khaẖ-khyab*, མཁའ་དབྱིངས *m̱khaẖ-ḏbyiṅs* the whole compass or extent of the heavens (*Cs.*).

མཁའ་སྐྱེས *m̱khaẖ-s̱kyes* heaven-born; a name for the year Fire-tiger མེ་སྟག of the Tibetan calendar (*M̱ṅon.*).

མཁའ་ཁྱབ *m̱khaẖ-khyab* आस्फारणकः that which encompasses space or the sky: མཁའ་ཁྱབ་ཏིང་ངེ་འཛིན *m̱khaẖ-khyab tiṅ-ṅe ẖdsin* आस्फारणक समाधि the all-comprehending (all absorbing) meditation; n. of a *Samādhi*.

མཁའ་ཁྱིམ་ཅན *m̱khaẖ khyim-can* दिवौकस् he whose abode is in the sky; the sun.

* མཁའ་མཁའ་རོ *m̱khaẖ-m̱khaẖ ro* खखरस (*Schr; Kālac. T. 46*).

མཁའ་གོས་ཅན *m̱khaẖ-gos can* clouds (*M̱ṅon.*).

མཁའ་འགྲོ *m̱khaẖ-ẖgro* (*kha-ḏo*) lit. "the sky-goer"; a god; a bird; arrow.

Syn. ལྷ་རྣམས *lha-ṟnams*; འདབ་ཆགས *ẖdab chags*; བྱ *bya*; མདའ *m̱daẖ*; བྱ་ཁྱུང་ *bya-khyuṅ*; ཌཱ་ཀི་ནི *ḍā-ki-ni*; གཙོ་མོ *gtso-mo* (*M̱ṅon.*).

མཁའ་འགྲོ་མ *m̱khaẖ-ẖgro--ma* a class, mainly of female sprites, akin to our witches, but not necessarily ugly or deformed. There are two kinds of *khadoma*:—those still in the world and those that have passed out of the world or are about to pass away from it. Of the latter or those called ཡེ་ཤེས་ཀྱི་མཁའ་འགྲོ་མ *ye-çes kyi m̱khaẖ ẖgro-ma*, goddessess of wisdom, they are five kinds, viz., Buddha *Ḍākinī*, Vajra *Ḍākinī*, Ratna *Ḍākinī*, Padma *Ḍākinī*, and Karma *Ḍākinī*. Of these *Ṟdor-je Phag-mo*, *Seṅ gdoṅ-ma*, &c., have each a hundred thousand *ḍākinī* followers. They are said to be possessed of supernatural powers and resemble fairies in their attributes. Among the worldly *Ḍākinī* there are two classes, those belonging to the pantheon of the Brāhmaṇs and those devoted to the cause of Buddhism. In Tibet we read of ཚེ་རིང་མཆེད་ལྔ *Tshe-riṅ m̱cheḏ-lṅa*, the five long-lived sisters: བསྟན་མ་བཅུ་གཉིས *Ḇstan-ma ḇcu-gñis* the twelve nymph sisters who undertook to guard Buddhism, &c.

Syn. འགྲོ་བའི་སྒྲོན་མེ *ẖgro-waẖi s̱gron-me*; སྲིད་པའི་སྒྲོན་མེ *s̱riḏ-paẖi s̱gron-me*, the lamp of the world, the light of the universe (*M̱ṅon.*).

མཁའ་འགྲོ་སྐྱེས *m̱khaẖ-ẖgro s̱kyes* खसरज born of those that move in the sky.

མཁའ་འགྲོ་བརྡ་ཡིག *m̱khaẖ-ẖbro ḇrda-yig* ཞེས་པ་རྙིང་མའི་གཏེར་ཡིག་ལ་མཁའ་འགྲོ་བརྡ་ཡིག a form of Deva nāgari character used by the *Ṟñiṅ-ma* sect in their mystical writings.

མཁའ་འགྲོ་གསང་བ་ཡེ་ཤེས *M̱khaẖ-ẖgro gsaṅ-wa ye-çes* n. of a deified lady, who was, in her former existence, the wife of a king called (Ratna Dāsa) དཀོན་མཆོག་འབངས. She is adored in Tibet as the goddess of mystical learning.

མཁའ་འགྲོའི་རྒྱལ་པོ *mkhaḥ-ḥgrohi rgyal-po*= གསེར་གྱི་བྱ་གཙུག་ཕུད་ཅན *gser-gyi bya-gtsug phud-can* the golden bird (eagle) with a crest: བྱ་འདིའི་སྤྱི་མདོག་བེ་ཌཱུར་ལྟར་དངས་ཤིང་གཤོག་པ་རྣམ་པར་བཀྲ་བ་ཡོད་ཟེར the crest of this bird is in colour resplendent as *lapis lazuli*, and its wings are said to be chequered all over.

མཁའ་འགྲོའི་དབང་ཕྱུག I: *mkhaḥ-ḥgrohi dwaṅ-phyug* खगेश्वर, खग, व्योमचारिन् the lord of the sky.

མཁའ་འགྲོའི་དབང་ཕྱུག II: = विष्णु; ཁྱབ་འཇུག *khyab-ḥjug* Vishṇu (*Mṅon.*).

མཁའ་མཉམ *mkhaḥ-mñam* like the heavens; infinite: མཁའ་མཉམ་པ *mkhaḥ mñam-pa* a name of Buddha (*Mṅon.*).

མཁའ་རྟེན *mkhaḥ-rten* व्योमक the firmament; sky supporting; a sort of ornament.

མཁའ་ལྡིང་ *mkhaḥ-ldiṅ* गरुड़, पचीम met. the eagle, the bird that soars on high.

མཁའ་ལྡིང་དཀར་པོ *mkhaḥ-ldiṅ dkar-po* ངང་པ་སྤྱིའི་མིང་ चक्राङ्ग, हंस a general name for the swan species (*Mṅon.*).

མཁའ་ལྡིང་རྒྱལ་མཚན *mkhaḥ-ldiṅ rgyal-mtshan*, ཁྱབ་འཇུག *khyab-ḥjug* गरुड़ध्वज, *Viṣṇu* (*Mṅon.*).

མཁའ་ལྡིང་དབང་པོ *mkhaḥ-ldiṅ dwaṅ-po*=ཁྱུང་ *khyuṅ* the king of birds (*Yig. k. 29*).

མཁའ་ལྡིང་གཤོག་པ *mkhaḥ-ldiṅ gçog-pa*, v. མར་གད *mar-gad* मरकत, n. of a green gem (*Mṅon.*).

མཁའ་སྤྱོད *mkhaḥ-spyod* व्योमचारिन्, खेचर, गन्धर्व, नभश्चारिन् 1. that which has attained to the sky, a *gandharva* (celestial musician). 2. celestial enjoyment; residing in heaven: མཁའ་སྤྱོད་དུ་ལུས་མ་སྤངས་པར་བགྲོད་པ་མཁའ་སྤྱོད་ཀྱི་དངོས་གྲུབ *mkhaḥ-spyod du lus ma-spaṅs par bgrod-pa mkhaḥ-spyod kyi dṅos-grub* the blessing of entering into a heavenly existence without losing one's present form: མཁའ་སྤྱོད་དུ་གཤེགས་པ gone to the state of beatitude, *i.e.*, to heaven.

མཁའ་སྤྱོད་པ *mkhaḥ spyod-pa* खसर्पण: n. of Avalokites'vara *Bodhisattva*.

མཁའ་སྤྱོད་དབང་མོ *mkhaḥ-spyod dwaṅ-mo* an epithet of the goddess Dorje Phag-mo and of the abbess of the Yamdok Samding monastery: རྗེ་བཙུན་མཁའ་སྤྱོད་དབང་མོའི་ཞབས་པད་རིན་པོ་ཆེའི་དྲུང་དུ before the precious lotus feet of the venerable one who has attained the heavens (*Yig. k. 20*).

མཁའ་དབྱུག *mkhaḥ-dbyug* खट्वाङ्ग lit. sky-sticks; a bedstead.

* མཁའ་མིག *mkhaḥ-mig* खाच. (*Schr.; Kālc. T. 48*).

མཁའ་ཡི་སྙེ་མ *mkhaḥ-yi sñe-ma*=རྒྱལ་མཚན *rgyal-mtshan* ध्वज the sacred ensign (*Mṅon.*).

མཁའ་རོལ་པ *mkhaḥ rol-pa* divine musician; that plays or moves merrily in the sky.

མཁའ་ལ་རྒྱུ 1. *mkhaḥ-la rgyu* नभश्चर that moves in the sky. 2. བྱ *bya* a bird (*Mṅon.*): མཁའ་ལ་རྒྱུ་བ *mkha-la rgyu-wa* to wander or move in the sky: མཁའ་ལ་རྒྱུ་བའི་ཡི་དྭགས the *Preta* that moves in the sky: མཁའ་ལ་ལྡིང་བ *mkhaḥ-la ldiṅ-wa* to soar in the air. 3. ether, as the fifth element 4. symbolical numbers; cypher, naught.

མཁའ་གསང་ *mkhaḥ-gsaṅ*=མོ་མཚན *mo-mtshan* स्त्रीलिङ्ग the female sex (*Mṅon.*).

མཁའི་གོས་ཅན *mkhaḥi gos-can* खावरक cover or dress of the sky; the night; མཁའི་རྒྱལ་མཚན *mkhaḥi rgyal-mtshan* नभोध्वज the sky-ensign; མཁའི་པགས་པ *mkhaḥi pags-pa*=the space; the void sphere; the skin or cover of the sky, *i.e.*, darkness, gloom; མཁའི་ནོར་བུ *mkhaḥi* gem of heaven; the sun, moon, star.

མཁའི་ཟིལ་བ *mkhaḥi zil-ba*=fog (*Mṅon.*).

མཁར *mkhar* कोट्ट, कुटी a castle, a nobleman's seat or mansion; manor house; freq. a citadel; fort: མཁར་དཔོན *mkhar-dpon* governor of a castle; commander of a fortress.

མཁར་ཁ *Mkhar-kha* n. of a place situated, to the north of Gyan-tse in Tsang; the birthplace of *Grub-chen Gtsaṅ smyon He-ru-ka*, one of the celebrated Buddhist *Tantrik* saints of Tsang.

མཁར་རྒྱའི་ཁལ *mkhar rgyaḥi-khal* contains 768 *Dbus sho*=640 *mgyur-sho*.

མཁར་རྔ *mkhar-rña* पणव, पणविक a drum; (according to somo) a minstrel.

མཁར་ཆེན་བྲག་དཀར *Mkhar-chen brag-dkar* བོན་གནས་སོ་བདུན་གྱི་ནང་གཅིག་གི་མིང་ n. of one of the 37 sacred places of the Bon (*G. Bon. 38*).

མཁར་ཆེན་རྫོང་ *Mkhar-chen rdsoṅ* n. of a fort near Tengri Nor.

མཁར་ཆེན་བཟའ *Mkhar-chen bzaḥ* ཉེས་པ་ཉི་སྒྲོན་དཔོན་པདྨ་འབྱུང་གནས་ཀྱི་ཇོ་མོ་ཞིག་གི་མཚན one of the wives of Padma Sambhava (*Loṅ.* ༢ *8*).

མཁར་ཉག་གི་ཁལ *mkhar-ñag-gi khal* on the Tibetan steel-yard མཁར་ཉག་གང *mkhar-ñag gaṅ* of gold weight=38 *sho* of *Dbus* plus 8 *skar* of gold.

མཁར་ཉལ *mkhar-ñal* that sleeps on space; a general name for gods and birds.

མཁར་རྟ *Mkhar-rta* n. of a place on the confines of Tibet and Nepal (*S. kar. 77*).

མཁར་ལྟག *Mkhar-ltag* an abbreviation of མཁར་རྩེ་དང་ལྟག་རྩེ་རྫོང་ *Mkar-rtse daṅ Ltag-rtse rdsoṅ*, the forts of *Mkhar-rtse* and *Ltag-rtse*.

མཁར་ཐོག *Mkhar-thog* n. of Tibet.

མཁར་རྡོ *mkhar-rdo* (ཟླ་ཉ) कंसमाक्षी n. of a medicine; a metalic substance in large grains; a sort of pyrites.

མཁར་སྡེར *mkhar-sder*, कंस, कंस्य a plate or dish made of bell-metal.

མཁར་བ *mkhar-wa* I: कंस, कंसक bell-metal.

མཁར་བ II: (also འཁར་བ *ḥkhar-wa*) in *B.* and *C.* staff, stick: མཁར་གསིལ *mkhar-gsil* a staff of the Buddhist mendicant priests, the upper part of which is hung with jingling rings (*Jä.*): ཕྱག་མཁར *phyag-mkhar* resp. for མཁར་བ *mkhar-wa*.

མཁར་བའི་དགྲ *mkhar-baḥi dgra*, कंसारि enemy of Kañça an epithet of *Viṣṇu* (*Mñon.*).

མཁར་རྩེ *Mkhar-rtse* n. of a རྫོང *Rdsoṅ*, or fort in *Phan-yul* in Tibet.

མཁར་ཟམ་ལྷ་ཁང་རྫོང་ *Mkhar-zam Lha-khaṅ rdsoṅ* n. of a fort and town in Tibet.

མཁར་བཟོ་བ *mkhar-bzo-wa* कंसकार, कंसकर्म्मा a maker of articlos of bell-metal.

མཁར་རུའི་སྤོར་གང *mkhar-ruḥi spor gaṅ* one *spor* of *Mkhar-ru* measure is equal to one silver *sraṅ*.

མཁར་སྲུང་ *mkhar-sruṅ* कोट्टपाल the guard or garrison of a fortross (*Cs.*).

མཁར་གསིལ *mkhar-gsil* metal cymbal.

མཁལ་མདོག *mkhal-mdog* kidnoy-coloured; dark rod (*Cs.*).

མཁལ་ནད *khal-nad*=མཁལ་མའི་ནད *mkhal-maḥi nad* disease of the kidnoys.

མཁལ་མ *mkhal-ma* I: the kidneys: *mkhal-ma gaṅ yin tsha-graṅ nus pa mthun daṅ mkhal-nad lgaṅ-wa rked-paḥi nad-la phan* the kidnoy (of cattle, etc. taken as food) equalizes the temperature, and is beneficial in kidney disease and also for ailments of the bladder and groin.

མཁལ་མ II: said to be kind of fruit of two species used in kidney disease.

མཁས་གྲུབ *mkhas-grub* (མཁས་པ་དང་གྲུབ་པ *mkhas-pa dan grub-pa*) a Buddhist scholar who being learned has attained perfection.

* མཁས་གྲུབ་རྗེ *Mkhas-grub rje* = མཁས་གྲུབ་དགེ་ལེགས་དཔལ་བཟང *Mkhas-grub Dge-legs dpal-bzan* one of the chief disciples of Tsoṅ-khapa.

མཁས་མཆོག *mkhas-mchog* पटुतम a profound scholar; eminent among the learned.

མཁས་བརྟན *mkhas-brtan* धीर steady and wise; of reliable knowledge མཁས་པ་བརྟེན་པ *mkhas-po brten-pa*.

མཁས་པ *mkhas-pa* पण्डित, सुकर्म्मार, कुशल, चतुर, विचक्षणः, निपुण, विद्वान्, प्रवीणः, प्राज्ञः, निष्ठितः, दक्ष, प्रतीतः, पटु, बुद्ध, कृतिन् wise, learned, sagacious: སྨན་པ་མཁས་པ *sman-pa mkhas-pa* skilful physician: ཆོས་ལ་མཁས *chos-la mkhas-pa* versed in religion: སློབ་མ་སྐྱོང་བ་ལ་མཁས་པ efficient in managing pupils.

Syn. བྱ་བ *bya-wa*; རིག་ལྡན *rig-ldan*; རྣམ་གསལ *rnam-gsal*; རིག་པ་ཅན *rig-pa-can*; བློ་ལྡན *blo-ldan*; སྐྱོན་ཤེས *skyon-çes*; ཡོན་ཏན་ཤེས *yon-tan-çes*; གྲངས་ཅན *grans-can*; མཛངས་པ *mdsans-pa*; སྙན་ངག་མཁན *snan-nag-mkhan*; ཤེས་རབ་ཅན *ças-rab-can*; དམ་པ *dam-pa*; རིག་པའི་དཔའ་བོ *rig-pahi dpah-po*; གོ་བ་ཅན *go-wa-can*; ཀུན་རིག *kun-rig*; བརྟན་པོ *brtan-po*; སེམས་ཤེས་པ *sems çes-pa*; ཐོས་ལྡན *thos-ldan*; སྤྱོད་ལྡན *spyod-ldan*; རྣམ་པར་དབང *rnam-par-dbans*; རིང་དུ་མཐོང་བ *rin-du mthon-wa*; གྲགས་པ་ཐོབ་པ *grags-pa thob-pa*; གསལ་བའི་སྒོ *gsal-wahi sgo*; དུས་ཡིག་ཅན *dus-yig-can*; ཀུན་ཤེས *kun-ças*; དྲན་པའི་དབང་པོ *dran-pahi dwan-po*; བློ་བཟང *blo-bzan*; བློ་གྲོས *blo-gros*; མིག་ལྡན *mig-ldan*; ཀུན་གྱིས་བཀུར་བ *kun-gyis bkur-wa*. (*Mṅon.*)

མཁས་པ་ཅན *mkhas-pa-can* विद्वान् wise; learned; skilful; experienced; prudent; shrewd.

མཁས་པ་ལྟ་བུ *mkhas-pa lta-bu* पटुकल्प, पटुदेश्य like a dexterous man; appearing skilful.

མཁས་པ་སྨད་པ *mkhas-pa smad-pa* पटुदेश्य of inferior attainments.

མཁས་པ་བཞིན་བྱེད *mkhas-pa bshin byed* showing as one skilful, but not really so.

མཁས་པའི་མགུལ་རྒྱན *mkhas-pahi mgul rgyan* སི་ཏུ་ཆོས་ཀྱི་འབྱུང་གནས་ཀྱི་སུམ་རྟགས་ཀྱི་འགྲེལ་པ n. of a commentary on Tibetan grammar called མཁས་པའི་མགུལ་རྒྱན *mkhas-pahi mgul-rgyan* by *Si-tu Chos-kyi hbyun-gnas*.

མཁས་པའི་དགའ་སྟོན *mkhas-pahi dgah-ston* ཟུར་མཁར་བློ་གྲོས་རྒྱལ་པོའི་སུམ་རྟགས་འགྲེལ་པ་མཁས་པའི་དགའ་སྟོན n. of a commentary on Tibetan orthography (*Sum-rtag*) by *Blo-gros rgyal-po* of *Zur-mkhar*.

མཁས་པའི་རྒྱན *mkhas-pahi rgyan* ཧོ་ཕུག་པ་ཀརྨ་རབ་རྒྱས་ཀྱི་སུམ་རྟགས n. of a grammatical work by *Karma Rab-rgyas* of *Ho-phug*.

མཁས་པའི་རང་བཞིན་ཅན *mkhas-pahi ran-bshin can* पण्डितजातीय possessed of the nature of the learned; naturally wise or skilful.

མཁས་པའི་རིགས *mkhas-pahi rigs* पटुजातीय of the learned class: མཁས་པའི་རིགས་ལས་སྐྱེས *mkhas-pahi rigs las skyes* born of the race of *Dakṣa*.

མཁས་པར་རློམ་པ *mkhas-par rlom-pa* (མཁས་རློམས *mkhas-rloms*) पण्डितम्मन्य, समुन्नद्ध conceited person; a pedant.

མཁས་པས་དྲེགས *mkhas-pas dregs* pedantic: ཡོན་ཏན་ཅན་པོ་རྣམས་ལ་མཁས་པས་དྲེགས་པ་ཡོད among the cultured there is much pedantry in learning.

མཁས་པོ *mkhas-po* or མཁས་པ *mkhas-pa* a learned man; སྔོན་གྱི་མཁས་པོ་རྣམས *snon-gyi mkhas-po rnams* learned men of former times.

མཁས་བླུན *mkhas-blun* wise and foolish; wisdom and folly.

མཁས་མ *mkhas-ma* = བུད་མེད་བློ་ལྡན་མ *bud-med blo-ldan ma* a noble, learned woman (*Mṅon.*).

མཁས་བཙུན་ *mkhas-btsun* learned and righteous; མཁས་བཙུན་བཟང་ *mkhas-btsun bzañ* learned; conscientious and good.

མཁས་ཅོད་ *mkhas-çod* पटुतरः, पटीयान् most skilful or dexterous.

མཁུན་པ *mkhun-pa* (*Sch.*), v. ཁུན་པ *khun-pa.*

མཁུར་བ *mkhur-wa* the cheeks: མཁུར་བར་ཤ་འཇོར་ཚུང་ཡོད་ལོངས་སྤྱོད་ལྡན a little fleshiness in the cheeks forebodes wealth (*Mi.*): མཁུར་ཚོས *mkhur-tshos*, v. ཁུར་ཚོས *khur-tshos*, cheeks: རབ་དམར་མཁུར་ཚོས་ཉི་གཞོན་འཆར་ཁའི་འོད her very ruddy cheeks glow like the rising sun.

མཁོ་བ *mkho-wa* necessary; desirable; also vb. to want: ང་ལ་མཁོ་བ་མེད I don't want it. མཁོ་བའི་ཡོ་བྱད *mkho-wahi yo-byad* indispensable things; necessary articles; ཉེ་བར་མཁོ་བ *ñe-war mkho-wa* or ཉེར་མཁོ *ñer-mkho* requisites, wants, desiderata; most necessary things: སྔ་མཁོ་བཞིན according as was wanted before; as heretofore.

མཁོ་བྱེད *mkho-byed*, colloq. *kho-che*, necessary things; what may be needed: *khyö-la kho-che yö-pe rik di dir nyo ma chok* the kind which you wanted cannot be bought here.

མཁོས་ཕབ *mkhos-phab* acc. to *Kag.* signifies a fancy for a thing; a liking for; also to wish, want something.

མཁྱིད་གང *mkhyid-gañ* the measure with the fist made with thumb extended, about six inches: འབེབས་བཀུམ་མཁྱིད་གང་ (its) length when folded is one *mkhyid* (*Yig. k.*).

མཁྱུད་པ *mkhyud-pa*, v. འཁྱུད་པ 1: *hkhyud-pa* to keep, to hold, to retain; དཔེ་མཁྱུད་པ *dpe mkhyud-pa*, དཔེ་མཁྱུད་ཅན *dpe mkhyud-can* unwillingness to lend books (*Cs.*); དཔེ་མཁྱུད་བྱེད་པ *dpe-mkhyud byed-pa* to be unwilling to lend books.

མཁྱུད་སྤྱད *mkhyud-spyad* 1. a sort of bag or vessel for carrying medicine. 2. sorcery, witchcraft (*Sch.*): ཕ་དམ་པའི་མཁྱུད་སྤྱད་སྣ་ཚོགས a little instruction or various subjects like the alms-bag of the saint Phadam-pa (which contained different medicines).

མཁྱུད་སྤྱད་པ *mkhyud spyad-pa* = སྨན་པ *sman-pa* a medicine man; a physician (*Mñon.*).

མཁྱེན *mkyen*, v. མཁྱེན་པ *mkhyen-pa.* རྗེ་བཙུན་གྱིས་ཐུགས་མཁྱེན་གྱི་གཟིགས་པ་ལགས་སམ *rje btsun-gyis thugs mkhyen-gyi gzigs-pa lags-sam* Has your reverence seen by your prophetic sight? སྐུ་མཁྱེན *sku-mkhyen* form of abject entreaty: I appeal to your honour's wisdom; གསུང་མཁྱེན to your honour's sacred words; ཐུགས་མཁྱེན to your honour's heart; མཁྱེན་མཁྱེན you know full well; you will understand: བླ་མ་ཁྱེད་མཁྱེན་མཁྱེན O Lama, thou knowest all! མཛད་པར་མཁྱེན་མཁྱེན of your wisdom permit to be done!

མཁྱེན་མཁན *mkhyen-mkhan* very learned: ཆོས་གང་ལ་ཡང་རྒྱ་མཚོ་ལྟ་བུ་མཁྱེན་མཁན profound like the ocean in every (department of) religion.

མཁྱེན་རྒྱ་ཅན *mkhyen-rgya-can* possessed of much understanding; very learned: ཡེ་མཁྱེན *ye-mkhyen* = མངོན་མཁྱེན *mñon mkhyen* possessed of prophetic knowledge; fore-knowledge; ཐུགས་མཁྱེན *thugs-mkhyen* knowledge of a higher kind; prophetic sight.

མཁྱེན་པ *mkhyen-pa* resp. for ཤེས་པ *çes-pa*, རིག་པ *rig-pa*, གོ་བ *go-wa* 1. to know; also knowledge; ཐམས་ཅད་མཁྱེན་པ *thams-cad mkhyen-pa* सर्वज्ञ all-knowing. 2 རྣམ་ཤེས *rnam-çes* = རྣམ་མཁྱེན *rnam-mkhyen* विज्ञ, such terms though applicable to Buddha are now applied to the Grand Lamas of Tibet out of courtesy or for the purpose of flattering them: མཁྱེན་པ་ཐོགས་པ་མི་མངའ་བ whose knowledge has no bound (*Lam-rim.*); མཁྱེན་པའི་ཡེ་ཤེས superior wisdom; མཁྱེན་པའི་ཡོན་ཏན attainments; accomplishments of a high order; མཁྱེན་པར་གྱུར་ཏོ perceived, found out, discovered; བསམ་པ་དག་པར་མཁྱེན་པས perceived the sentiments to be pure.

མཁྱེན་དཔྱོད་ཡངས་པ *mkhyen-dpyod yańs-pa* wide and critical knowledge; wide discriminating wisdom.

མཁྱེན་སྤྱན་ཡངས་པ *mkhyen-spyan yańs-pa* (with) broad views and wisdom; wide prophetic vision or sight.

མཁྱེན་བརྩེ *mkhyen-brtse* omniscient mercy.

མཁྱེན་གཟིགས *mkhyen-gzigs* supernatural perception; attributes of a high incarnate lama or a *Bodhisattva*.

མཁྱེན་རབ *mkhyen-rab* the wise; also ཤེས་རབ *çes-rab* प्रज्ञा wisdom.

མཁྱེན་ཤིང་ངམ *mkhyen-çiń-ńam* = མཁྱེན་ནམ *mkhyen-nam* did you understand it?

མཁྱེན་གསུམ *mkhyen gsum*:—གཞི་ཤེས *gshi-çes*, आलय, or विषय ज्ञान the knowledge of the subject; basic knowledge: ལམ་ཤེས *lam-çes* knowledge of the way (to Nirvāṇa); knowing the way. རྣམ་མཁྱེན *rnam-mkhyen* = རྣམ་པར་ཤེས *rnam-par çes* विज्ञान चैतन्य cognition of all things.

མཁྲང་པ *mkhrań-pa* (*thang-pa*) acc. to *Jä.* is the fourth stage of the development of the fœtus.

མཁྲང་པོ *mkhrań-po* = ཧྲང་པ *hrań-pa* or སྲ་བར་འགྱུར་བ *sra-war hgyur-wa* a robust, hard and sound constitution: ལུས་ཀྱི་ཤེད་ཆེ་བ་ལ་མཁྲང་པོ in the great strength of his body there is sound health (*Ńag*). The soundness of one's constitution is ascertained by examining the urine deposited in a bottle; when it is natural the physician declares མཁྲང་འདུག *mkhrań-hdug*, or colloquially ཧྲང་གིན་འདུག *hrań-gin hdug*, it (the constitution) is sound, &c.

མཁྲང་བ *mkhrań-wa* (*thań-wa*), or མཁྲངས *mkhrańs* also ཁྲང *khrań* hard; solid; compact; སྲ་མཁྲང་ཅན་འགྱུར་མེད *sra-mkhrań-can hgyur med* firm; hearty; sound; of a robust constitution (*Jä.*).

མཁྲིག་མ *mkhrig-ma* (*thig-ma*) the wrist of the hand (*Jä.*); the part of the hand which (in women) is adorned with bangles. It is also called ནོར་བུ་འཆིང་བ *nor-bu chiń-wa*, the part where jewels are bound.

མཁྲིགས་པ *mkhrigs-pa* (*thig-pa*) sometimes for མཁྲིག་མ *mkhrig-ma*.

མཁྲིས་ནད *mkhris-nad* bilious disease.

མཁྲིས་པ *mkhris-pa* (*thi-pa*) पित्त 1. the vesicle of the gall; the gall-bladder, as part of the intestines. 2. generally the bile itself; the bilious fluid: མཁྲིས་པ་སྣ་ཚོགས་བསྡུས་པ་རྨ་དང་དུག་མཁྲིས་མིག་ལ་ཕན *mkhris-pa sna-tshogs bsdus-pa rma dań dug mkhris mig-la phan* a mixture of the biles of different animals is useful for sores; and the bile of poisonous animals is useful for eye-disease: མཁྲིས་པའི་གསལ་བྱེད་བཞི the four animal biles that are used in medicine:—(1) དོམ་མཁྲིས *dom-mkhris* bear's bile; (2) རི་བོང་མཁྲིས་པ *ri-boń mkhris-pa* hare's bile; (3) འཕྱི་བའི་མཁྲིས་པ *hphyi-wahi mkhris-pa* marmot's bile; (4) ཉ་མཁྲིས *ña-mkhris* fish bile (*Sman. 175*).

མཁྲིས་པ་ཅན *mkhris-pa-can* splenetic; a short-tempered person.

མཁྲིས་མ *mkhris-ma* acc. to *Jä.* = འཁྲིས *hkhris*.

མཁྲིས་ཚད *mkhris-tshad* bilious fever; གྲང་མཁྲིས *grań-mkhris* a feverish chill.

མཁྲིས་རིམས *mkhris-rims* applied to a fever in which the liver is conjested.

མཁྲིས་ཤས་ཆེ་ mkhris-ças che, མི་ལ་མཁྲིས་པའི་ནད་མང་བའི་དོན one in whose constitution the bilious diseases predominate.

མཁྲེགས་པ mkhregs-pa (theg-pa) कठोर, कठिन hard; that cannot be broken; cannot be divided; also fearless; and acc. to *Jä.* མགོ་མཁྲེགས་ཅན *mgo mkhregs-can* obstinate, stiffnecked, stubborn.

Syn. སྲ་བ *sra-wa*; མི་ཤིགས *mi-çigs*; མི་འཇིག *mi-hjig*; མི་ཕྱེད *mi-phyed* (*Mṅon.*).

འཁང་བ *ḥkhaṅ-wa*, སེམས་མི་དགའ་བ་ལྟ་བུ *sems mi-dgaḥ-wa lta-bu* 1. to hurt at heart or offend, also to irritate. 2. vindictiveness: ཁྱོད་ལ་འཁང་ཚིག་གཅིག་ཀྱང་འདུག་པས *khyod la ḥkhaṅ-tshig cig-kyaṅ ḥdug-pas* (*Ḥbrom. 51*) you use all manner of vindictive words. 3. bickering, quarrelling; འཁང་མང many quarrels: དཔོན་སློབ་རེ་འཁང་འབྱུང *dpon slob re ḥkhaṅ-ḥbyuṅ* there arose mutual differences between masters and scholars. རེ་འཁང་བྱེད་པ *re ḥkhaṅ byed-pa* to make mischief (*Mil.*).

འཁད་པ *ḥkhad-pa*, especially in *W.* 1. to sit; to sit firm: རྔ་མོང་ལ་འཁད་པ to sit on the back of a camel. 2. to remain sitting; to stick fast; to be stopped; kept back (*Jä*); རྐང་པ་འཁད་དེ་འགྱེལ་བ to get entangled with the foot so as to fall: སྒོ་འཁད་འདུག the door sticks.

འཁམ་པ *ḥkham-pa*=བརྒྱལ་བ *brgyal-wa* to sink or fall down senseless; to faint away; to swoon. 2. to take into one's mouth (*Sch.*).

འཁར *ḥkhar*=ཞེན་པ *shen-pa* or ཆགས་པ *chags-pa* desire; passion; attachment (*Ńag.*).

འཁར་སྒོང *ḥkhar-sgoṅ* white pebbles called དཀར་གོང *dkar goṅ* in medical works: གཡས་གཡོན་གཉིས་སུ་འཁར་སྒོང་དང་སྲན་མ *gyas-gyon gñis-su ḥkhar-sgoṅ daṅ sran-ma* on both his right and left there were white pebbles and peas.

འཁར་བ I: 1. *ḥkhar-wa* a walking stick, staff, clutcheon: ཆུ་ཤིང་གི་འཁར་བ་ཐོགས་པ་ཞིག་དང་འཕྲད he met (a man) who carried a stick of *chu-çiṅ* (water-tree) (*A. 131*). 2. कंस, कंसास्थि bell-metal: འཁར་བའི་གཡའ་ཡིས་མིག་ནད་སེལ the rust (sulphate) of bronze, or of gong-metal, removes eye disease. འཁར་བ is a compound of bell-metal with copper, &c.; འཁར་བའི་ཆུ *ḥkhar-waḥi chu* molten, liquid bronze; འཁར་བའི་མེ་ལོང *ḥkhar-waḥi me-loṅ* a metallic mirror.

འཁར་བ II. vb. to adhere to; to stick to. འཁར་རྔ *ḥkhar-rña* or རྒྱ་རྔ *rgya-rña* 1. gong used in Tibet and China to call people to their work or lamas to religious service. 2. a drum of bell-metal, large bell-metal disk, producing when struck loud sound like that of a bell.

འཁར་གཞོང *ḥkhar-gshoṅ* dish of bell-metal. འཁར་ཟངས *ḥkhar-zaṅs* a metallic kettle. འཁར་གསིལ *ḥkhar-gsil* the staff carried by mendicant priests having a *chaitya* fixed on its top end, from which hang down sixteen rings: ཐམས་ཅད་ཀྱང་འཁར་གསིལ་མཛེས་པར་བཟུངས་པ (*A. 22*) they all grasped beautiful mendicant's staves.

འཁར་གསིལ་གྱི་མདོ *ḥkhar-gsil-gyi-mdo* (*K. d.* ཨ. *425*) a tractate on the merit accruing from the use of the mendicant's staff.

འཁལ *ḥkhal* when spinning the thread stretched across is called *ḥkhal*, and that lengthwise is called *sgrim*; sometimes this word is spelt as འཁེལ *ḥkhel* (*Dag-yig.*).

འཁལ་བ *ḥkhal-wa* 1. to spin: བལ་འཁེལ་བ *bal ḥkhel-wa* to spin wool. 2 in *W.* to send; to forward things.

འཁུ་འཁྲིག *hkhu-hkhrig* or འཁང་བ *hkhañ-wa* denotes certain passions that disturb the tranquility of the mind, such as malignity and covetousness; acc. to *Cs.* to emulate, contemn, hate; also to long for; acc. to *Sch.* pride (*Jä.*).

✝ **འཁུ་བ** *hkhu-wa* འགྲན་པ *hgran-pa*= स्पर्द्धा, द्रोह to vie with, contend; also wrathfully rebelling: ཞེ་སྡང་དུ་ཧང་བཅད *she sdañ-du-hañ hçad*, དོན་ལ་རྒྱུན་དུ་གནོད་པའི་སེམས་འཆང་བ *don-la rgyun-du gnod-pahi sems hchañ-pa* the real signification is always to harbour thoughts of doing mischief. Acc. to *Jä.* to offend, insult, injure; also injury.

འཁུ་བའི་བསམ་པ *hkhu-wahi bsam-pa*= ལོག་ལྟ *log-lta* मिथ्यादर्शन a false creed; heresy (*Mñon.*).

འཁུན་པ *hkhun-pa* 1. groan; a deep sigh, from suffering or disease. 2. on account of fullness of the stomach, beasts such as cows and buffaloes make this hollow sound at the time of chewing the cud: འཁུན་སྒྲ་ཁང་པ་ཁེངས *hkhun-sgra khañ-pa kheñs* he filled the house with groanings: སྡང་བའི་དགྲ་ལ་གཡག་ལྟར་འཁུན *sdañ wahi dgra-la gyag ltar hkhun* he groans (or grunts) like a yak against a fierce enemy (*Jä.*).

འཁུམ་པ *hkhum-pa*, pf. ཁུམས *khums* (cf. སྐུམ་པ *skum-pà*), ཐོས་པ *thos-pa* to comprehend; to shrink; ཡན་ལག་འཁུམས་པ *yan-lag hkhûms-pa* to be contracted of the limbs; རྐང་ལག་འཁུམས་པ *rkañ-lag hkhums-pa* contracted hands and feet: ཡུར་ར་རང་བཞིན་ འཁུམ་བྱེད་ཡིན *yur-ra rañ-bshin hkhum byed yin* the ditch will get narrower of itself (*Jä.*).

འཁུམས་པ *hkums-pa* 1. shrunk, shriveled, contracted; fig. reduced; restricted; deprived of power: བློ་འཁུམས་པ *blo hkhums-pa* a contracted mind; an easily frightened heart; one who is much afraid of (*Ñag.*): acc. to *Sch.* to practise; to impress on the mind.

འཁུར་དུ་ཐོགས་ཏེ *hkhur-du thogs-te* taking up in order to carry; taking on one's back; ལག་པར་ཁུར་བྱེས *lag-par khur-byes* in *W.* to hold in one's hand (*Jä.*); སེམས་ལ་འཁུར་བ *sems-la hkhur-wa* to bear in mind; འཁུར་ཐག *hkhur-thag* girth or rope; strap for carrying.

འཁུར་བ *hkhur-wa* sbst. pastry; vb. to carry, as in ཁུར་འཁུར་བ་པོ *khur hkhur-wa-po*, one who carries a burden; འཁུར་བྱེད *hkhur-byed*, འཁུར་བཞིན་པ *hkhur bshin-pa* carrying: མི་ཐེག་པར་འཁུར་བ *mi-theg-par hkhur-wa* to carry very heavy loads; to carry what one is not able to carry. *Khur-çog*, bring it! *Khur-song*, take it away!

འཁུར་ཚོས *hkhur-tshos*, v. ཁུར་ཚོས *khur-tshos*.

འཁུར་ར *hkhur-ra*=སྣུམ་འཁུར *snum-hkhur* bread or pastry baked with or in oil (*Ñag.*).

འཁུལ་བ *hkhul-wa* acc. to *Ñag.* to subdue; to subject one by argument and language to service; acc. to *Cs.* to be uneasy about; ཁྲལ་འཁུལ་བ *khral hkhul-wa* acc. to *Jä.* perh. to force a tax, a rate, on a person.

འཁེགས་པ *hkhegs-pa*, pf. of འགེགས *hgegs*, to hinder, stop, shut off, debar: ཇི་ལྟར་བཀག་རུང་མ་འཁེགས་པས *ji-ltar bkag ruñ-ma hkhegs-pas* although they prohibited, in whatever way, he was not stopped: ཉེས་སྐྱོན་འཁེགས་པ་པོ *ñes-skyon hkhegs-pa-po* one who has stopped evils and dangers: འཁེགས་བྱེད *hkhegs-byed* one who stops.

འཁེངས་པ་ *hkheńs-pa*, pf. ཁེངས *kheńs*, to be replete; to be full: ཁྲག་གིས་ཁེངས་ཡོད་པ was filled with blood; བློ་གྲོས་མ་ཁེངས་ཏེ *blo-gros ma kheńs-te* his mind not being satiated (*Jä.*).

འཁེབ་པ་ *hkheb-pa*, pf. ཁེབས *khebs*, to cover; to spread over; ཡོངས་སུ་ཁེབས་ཏེ *yońs-su khebs-te* being covered all over; ཁ་ཐམས་ཅད་ཁེབས་ཏེ *kha thams-cad khebs-te* being covered over the whole face; to overshadow (*Jä.*).

འཁེལ་བ་ *hkhel-wa*, འགེལ་བ *hgel-wa*, pf. ཁེལ *khel*, གདེང་འཁེལ་བ *gdeń hkhel-wa*, to put on; to pack on; to load: བཅུ་ཐོག་ཁེལ་བ *bcu thog khel-wa* when the ten storeys shall have been put on (erected).

འཁོ་བ་ *hkho-wa* (cog. to མཁོ་བ *mkho-wa*) to wish; to want; to think useful, serviceable, necessary; to have occasion for: འཁོ་རྒྱུ་འོང it will be of use; he will be able to make use of it: འཁོ་འམ་མི་མཁོ will it be useful or not, or in *W. hkho-ce med*, I do not want it; I do not like it. འཁོ་བཟེད fit for use; useful (*Jä.*).

འཁོགས་པ་ I: *hkhogs-pa* very infirm from old age; decrepit; decayed. Gen. signifies རྒན *rgan* or རྒྱས་འཁོགས *rgyas-hkhogs* worn out by age: ཞོ་ཁོག *sho-khog*, སྐྱ་ཁོག *skya-khog* complexion blue or pale from old age.

འཁོགས་པ་ II: चरण, शव, विहार, भव, भ्रमण migration; wandering; fig. worldly existence.

འཁོགས་པ་ III:=གློ་འགོག་པ *glo hgog-pa* to cough (*Mńon.*).

འཁོང་བ་ *hkhoń-wa* (cf. སྒོང་བ *sgoń-wa*) to draw in one's limbs; to sit in a cowering position; to squat; to hide one's self; དཔའ་འཁོང་བ *dpah hkhoń-wa* to be discouraged, disheartened (*Jä.*).

འཁོད *hkhod*, fut. of བཀོད *bkod*=ཁོད *khod* 1. surface; superficies; ས་ཡི་འཁོད་སྙོམ་པ *sahi hkhod sñom-pa* to remove inequalities of the surface; to level; to plane; འཁོད་སྙོམས་པ *hkhod sñoms-pa* levelled; made even; plain; frequently བར་གྱི་ཁོད་སྙོམས *bar-gyi khod-sñoms* gaps were filled up, *i.e.*, distinctions of rank, wealth, &c., were done away with. 2. a mill stone; ཡ་འཁོད *ya-hkhod* the upper stone; མ་འཁོད *ma-hkhod* the nether stone (*Jä.*).

འཁོད་པ་ *hkhod-pa*=སྡོད་པ *sdod-pa* to sit down; to sit; also to live, to dwell; to be set down; to be put: *rgyal srid-la hkhod-pa* raised to the throne; གནས་སུ་འཁོད་པ settled at a place; གྲལ་དུ་འཁོད་པ seated in rank or order; སྟེང་དུ་འཁོད་པ *steń-tu hkhod-pa* placed above; འོག་ཏུ་འཁོད་པ placed under.

འཁོན I: *Hkhon* n. of an ancient family in Tibet: ས་སྐྱ་འཁོན་གྱི་རིགས *Sa-skya hkhon-gyi rigs*, *Sa-skya* (hierarchs) belonged to the race of *Hkhon* (*Ńag.*).

འཁོན II:=ཞེ་འཁོན *she-hkhon* malice; dispute; war; spite (*Ńag.*); འཁོན་ནས *hkhon-nas* from the state of dispute or war; འཁོན་མེད་པར *hkhon-med-par* honestly, without evil intentions; also without quarrel or dispute; འཁོན་ཟུགས་པ *hkhon sugs-pa* to be spiteful or quarrelsome.

འཁོན་པ *hkhon-pa*, also འཁོན་ཡོད་པ *hkhon-yod-pa* to bear a grudge or ill-will against a person; to be dissatisfied with a thing; also to be malicious, spiteful.

འཁོན་པོ *hkhon-po* discord; dissension (*Jä.*).

འཁོབས ẖkhobs, བྱ་བའི་འཁོབས bya-waẖi ẖkhobs the sphere of one's doing or work (*Zam.*); also=ཁྱབ་པ *khyab-pa*. Acc. to *Jä.* to be startled, agitated, alarmed.

འཁོབས་ཤག *ẖkhobs-çag* not fitting to a place; become larger or smaller: འཁྱགས་ནས་འཁོབས་ཤག་ཆེར་ཆེར་སོང *ẖkhyags-nas ẖkhobs-çag cher-cher soñ* being frozen it does not fit, it having grown larger (*Ñag.*).

+ **འཁོབ་པ** *ẖkhob-wa*=ངན་པ *ñan-pa* bad; wicked; low; barbarous; rough; rude; མཐའ་འཁོབ *mthaẖ ẖkhob* border; also border country; ཡང་འཁོབ *yan-ẖkhob* distant border land.

འཁོར I: *ẖkhor* an attendant who is inferior to a friend in rank and superior to a servant: འཁོར་གྱི་ནང་ན་འདུག་ཀྱང་རུང་ even if he be allowed to be among the attendants.

འཁོར II: 1. for འཁོར་ལོ *ẖkhor-lo* a wheel; མེ་འཁོར *me-ẖkhor* the fire-wheel; ཆུ་འཁོར *chu-ẖkhor* a mill or wheel turned by water; རླུང་འཁོར *Rluñ-ẖkhor* wheel turned by wind; ལག་འཁོར *lag-ẖkhor* a wheel turned by the hand; a millstone. 2. circle; circumference; the persons or objects encircling; that which surrounds (a certain point or place): ལྟེ་བ་དང་དེའི་འཁོར་རྣམས *lte-wa dañ deẖi ẖkhor-ṟnams* the navel and the circumjacent parts; དེ་ཁོར་ལ *de khor-la* thereabouts. ཉེ་འཁོར *ñe-ẖkhor* retinue, attendants; also waiters: འཁོར་དང་བཅས་པས *ẖkhor dañ ḇcas-pa* (सपरिवार) with the attendants or suite; འཁོར་དགྲ་བཅོམ་པས *ẖkhor dgra-ḇcom-pas* surrounded by the retinue of *Arhats*: འཁོར་དུ་བསྡུས་པོ *ẖkhor-du ḇsdus-po* gathered round as his retinue; also frequently the train of thoughts, reminiscences, &c., which the soul, when passing into a new body, cannot take along with it (*Jä.*).

*འཁོར *ẖkhor* भ्रमति (*Schr.*; *Kālac. T. 22*).

འཁོར་ཀུན་ཏུ་གྲགས *ẖkhor kun-tu grags*, सर्वपर्षदानुरञ्जिता resounding in every company.

འཁོར་ཁ *ẖkhor-kha*, ཟླ་བ་དང་ཞག་འཁོར་བ་ལ *zla-wa dañ shag ẖkhor-wa la* return or each rotation (of a month, day, or year): མང་བའི་རིགས་ལ་འཁོར་ཁའི་ལྷག་འཁྱིལ་ཡོང་གི་འདུག་པ *mañ-waẖi rigs la ẖkhor-khaẖi ḻhag ẖkhyil yoñ-gi ẖdug-pa* those articles which are found in excess at the termination of the period should be sent round (*Ṟtsii.*).

འཁོར་མཁན *ẖkhor-ṃkhan* one who turns a wheel; a wheel that is turned; those who come and go with somebody.

འཁོར་གྱི་དཀྱིལ་འཁོར *ẖkhor-gyi ḏkyil-ẖkhir* पर्षद्मण्डल the circle of attendants.

འཁོར་གྱི་སྐྱེ་བ *ẖkhor-gyi s̱ke-wa*, परिजन dependants.

*འཁོར་གྱི་སྐྱེ་བོ *ẖkhor-gyi s̱ke-bo* परिजन (*Schr.*; *Kālac. T. 21*).

འཁོར་གྱི་འཁྱམས *ẖkhor-gyi ẖkhyams* courtyard; an open space near a temple or a residential house where people assemble to witness a spectacle; also the passage round a temple or monastery for devotees to walk round for religious merit.

འཁོར་གྱི་གཙོ་བོ *ẖkhor-gyi gtso-ḇo* the chief of the attendants or followers.

འཁོར་གཅིག *ẖkhor-gcig* one attendant; འཁོར་རྣམས *ẖkhor-ṟnams* domestics; household servants; ལོ་འཁོར *lo-ẖkhor* a cycle of years: ལོ་འཁོར་བཅུ་གཉིས *lo-ẖkhor ḇcu-gñis* or དྲུག་བཅུ *dṟug-ḇcu* a cycle of twelve or sixty years.

འཁོར་ཉན *ẖkhor-ñan* निषाद the first of the seven musical notes.

འཁོར་ཏོ *ẖkhor-to* n. of a tribe in Tibet (*Vai. kar. 190*).

འཁོར་གཏན *hkhor-gtan*=སྒོའི་ཐེམ་པ *sgohi them-pa* इन्द्रकील: steps at the threshold or at the entrance of a house.

འཁོར་དུ་བསྡུས *hkhor-du bsdus* to enlist; to recruit; to take as one's followers. བྱང་ཆུབ་སེམས་དཔས་སེམས་ཅན་འཁོར་དུ་བསྡུས་ནས་དོན་བྱེད A *Bodhisattva* taking animated beings as his followers works for their good; or a *Bodhisattva* having brought animated beings into his followers, does work for the cause of men: འཁོར་འདུས་པ་འདུག *hkhor-hdus-pa hdug* all the attendants had collected together.

འཁོར་པ *hkhor-pa* or འཁོར་པོ *hkhor-po* male attendant.

* འཁོར་ཕག་མོ *hkhor phag-mo* (*Schr.*, 53 *A.*)

འཁོར་བ *hkhor-wa* I: to turn round; to circumambulate, to walk all round; also to elapse, to be completed. 2. to be formed, perfected: ཁྱག་པར་འཁོར་བ་མེད the frost has formed; ཟིལ་པ་འཁོར dew has arisen.

འཁོར་བ II: the world; rotatory existence; the round of transmigration within the six classes of beings: འཁོར་བ་ལ་སྐྱོ་ཤས་སྐྱེས *hkhor-wa la skyo-ças skyes* to repent at having come into transmigratory existence.

Syn. མ་རིག *ma-rig*; མངོན་ཆགས *mṅon-chags*; སྲིད་པ *srid-pa*; འཇིག་རྟེན *hjig-rten*; ཡང་སྲིད *yaṅ-srid*; གཞི་འཛིན་པ *gshi hdsin-pa*; གཙུག་ལག་དང་པོ *gtsug-lag daṅ-po*; ཐུན་མོང་ཆོས *thun-moṅ chos*; སྡུག་བསྔལ་འབྱུང་གནས *sdug-bsṅal hbyuṅ-nas*; འཁོར་བ *hkhor-wa* (*Mṅon.*).

འཁོར་བ་འཁོར་མོར *hkhor-wa hkhor-mor* to transmigrate in the world (*Pag. 291*).

འཁོར་བ་འཇིག *hkhor-wa hjig* क्रकुच्छन्द तथागत the breaker or destroyer of transmigratory existence; the name of a former Tathāgata.

* འཁོར་བ་དང་ལྡན་ཆེན་པོ *hkhor-wa daṅ-ldan chen-po* महाधामी (*Schr.*; *Kālac T. 145*).

འཁོར་བ་དོང་སྤྲུག *hkhor-wa doṅ-sprug*=སེམས་ཅན་ཐམས་ཅད་སངས་རྒྱས་འཁོར་སྟོང་དུ་འགྲོ་བ་ལ་ཟེར the passing of all animals to be followers of the thousand past Buddhas.

འཁོར་བ་ལས་སྒྲོལ་མཁན *hkhor-wa las sgrol-mkhan* one who has been liberated from transmigratory existence; also one who liberates another from that state.

འཁོར་བའི་ཁྱིམ *hkhor-wahi khyim*=བཙུན་མོའི་ཕོ་བྲང *btsun-mohi pho-braṅ* the residence of a queen (*Mṅon.*).

འཁོར་བའི་དགྲ *hkhor-wahi dgra* संसारशत्रु the enemy of the world, *Māra*.

འཁོར་བའི་རྒྱ་མཚོ *hkhor-wahi rgya-mtsho* the ocean of worldly existence: རྣམ་རྟོག་མ་རིག་ཆེན་པོ་སྟེ, འཁོར་བའི་རྒྱ་མཚོར་ལྟུང་བར་བྱེད the *Vikalpanā* (the wrong impression); thrown into the ocean of worldly business (*Grub.* ང 76).

འཁོར་བའི་འཆིང་བ *hkhor-wahi hchiṅ-wa* the entanglements or ties of the world: འཁོར་བའི་འཆིང་བ་དྲག་པོ་སྟེ, སེམས་ཅན་དམྱལ་བ་ཀུན་གྱི་རྒྱུ the strong fastenings to this world are the cause of the suffering in hell of all animated nature (*K.* ཕ *114*).

འཁོར་བའི་སྡུག་བསྔལ *hkhor-wahi sdug-bsṅal* the miseries of the worldly existence.

འཁོར་བའི་བླ་མ *hkhor-wahi bla-ma*=འདོད་ལྷ་དགའ་རབ་དབང་ཕྱུག *hdod-lha dgah-rab dbaṅ-phyug* Cupid, the god of Love (*Mṅon.*).

འཁོར་བའི་བཙོན་ར *hkhor-wahi btson-ra* the prison-house of worldly existence.

འཁོར་བའི་ལམ *hkhor-wahi lam* संसारवर्त्म the path of transmigratory existence.

འཁོར་བར་འཁོར *hkhor-war hkhor* to come in and go out of this world very often.

འཁོར་བར་འཁོར་བ་པོ *hkhor-war hkhor-wa-po* one who transmigrates.

འཁོར་བར་འཁྱམས *hkhor-war hkhyams* འགྲོ་མཆོག wandering purposelessly in this world.

འཁོར་མ་ཚགས *h̲khor-ma tshags* without interruption.

འཁོར་མང་ཅན *h̲khor mañ-can*=ཤིང་ཀ་དམ་པ *çiñ ka-dam-pa* कदम्ब the tree *Cadamba* (*M̲ñon.*).

འཁོར་མེད *h̲khor-med*, ཆད་མེད *chad̲-med̲* uninterrupted: བཀའ་དྲིན་འཁོར་མེད *b̲kah̲ drin h̲khor-med̲* uninterrupted mercy (*Yig. 42*).

འཁོར་ཞག *h̲khor-shag* the date of return; the term or period for which leave is granted to monks or soldiers at the expiration of which they are bound to return to duty.

འཁོར་ཟུག *h̲khor-zug*, v. འཁོར་ཡུག *h̲khor-yug*.

འཁོར་ཡུག *h̲khor-yug*, चक्रवाल the horizon; the wall surrounding a city or fort; rampart: འཁོར་ཡུག་ཏུ *h̲khor-yug-tu* or འཁོར་མོ་ཡུག་ཏུ *h̲khor-mo yug-tu* within the limits of the horizon; everywhere; at all times.

* འཁོར་ཡུག *h̲khor-yug* वृत्तं (*Schr.; Kālac. T. 12*).

འཁོར་གཡའ *h̲khor-g̲yah̲* latch.

འཁོར་གཡོག *h̲khor-g̲yog* परिवार, परिषद् attendants and servants, companions and domestics: མདུན་འཁོར *m̲dun-h̲khor* waiting servant; *valet de chambre*; ནང་འཁོར *nañ-h̲khor* household servants; domestics: གཙོ་འཁོར *gtso-h̲khor* master and servant: དཔོན་འཁོར *dpon-h̲khor* the chief and his servant; སྟོན་འཁོར *ston-h̲khor* the teacher and his pupils; དྲུང་འཁོར *d̲ruñ-h̲khor* a secretary or clerk; ཕྱི་འཁོར *phyi-h̲khor* servants outside the domestics.

* འཁོར་རལ་གཅིག་མ *h̲khor ral-g̲cig-ma* (*Schr. 53 B.*).

འཁོར་ལེགས་པ *h̲khor-legs-pa* good attendants.

འཁོར་ལོ I: *h̲khor-lo* and other weapons of war included in the following list of weapons or མཚོན་ཆ *m̲tshon cha*:—གཡུལ་དུ་འཛིན་པ *g̲yul-du h̲dsin-pa*; ཐོ་བ *tho-wa*; རྡུང་བྱེད *r̲duñ-byed̲*; འཛོམ་བྱེད *h̲dsom-byed̲*; དབྱུག་པ *d̲byug-pa*; ལྕགས་བཅིངས *l̲cags-b̲ciñs*; དབྱིག་པ *d̲byig-pa*; འཕང་མདུང *h̲phañ-m̲duñ*; ཤང་ལང *çañ-lañ*; གསོར་མདུང *g̲sor-m̲duñ*; ཙ་ཀྲ *tsa-kra* འཁོར་ལོ *h̲khor-lo* (*M̲ñon.*).

འཁོར་ལོ II: 1. चक्र, रथांग, सुदर्शन, जिह्मा an orb, circle, disk; a wheel: འཁོར་ལོ་ཆེན་པོར་འཇུག་པའི་ཡེ་ཤེས་ཀྱི་ཕྱག་རྒྱ महाचक्रप्रयोग-ज्ञान-मुद्रा the symbol of entering into the great circle. 2. the round of life; orb or state of existence; སྲིད་པའི་འཁོར་ལོ *s̲rid̲-pah̲i h̲khor-lo* भवचक्र the chart or cycle of existence: ལྷ་དང་མི་རྣམས་ཀྱི་འཁོར་ལོ་བཞི *lha dañ mi r̲nams-kyi h̲khor-lo b̲shi* the four states of existence of gods and men:—(1) མཐུན་པའི་ཡུལ་དུ་གནས་པ *m̲thun-pah̲i yul-du g̲nas-pa* प्रतिरूपदेशवास residence in a place where there is agreement or which is agreeable; (2) སྐྱེས་བུ་དམ་པ་ལ་བརྟེན་པ *s̲kyes-bu dam-pa la b̲rten-pa* सत्पुरुषाश्रय to take refuge with or shelter under good men; (3) བདག་ཉིད་ཀྱི་ཡང་དག་པའི་སྨོན་ལམ *b̲dag ñed̲-kyi yañ-dag-pah̲i s̲mon-lam* आत्मनः सम्यक् प्रणिधान perfect determination of one's self; (4) སྔོན་ཡང་བསོད་ནམས་བྱས་པ *s̲ñon yañ-b̲sod̲-nams byas-pa* पूर्व्वकृत पुण्य moral merit acquired in a former existence: འཁོར་ལོ་ཅན (1) *h̲khor-lo can* चक्री one who is possessed of a disk; (2) སྦྲུལ *s̲brul* a snake (*M̲ñon.*); (3) v. བྱ་ངུར་བ *bya ñur-wa* चक्रवाक (*M̲ñon.*).

འཁོར་ལོ་བསྒྱུར *h̲khor-lo b̲s̲gyur*, འཁོར་ལོས་སྒྱུར *h̲khor-los-s̲gyur* चक्रवर्त्ति राज an Universal Emperor.

Syn. མ་ལུས་རྒྱལ་པོ *ma-lus r̲gyal-po*; རྒྱལ་ཀུན་འདུད *r̲gyal-kun h̲dud̲*; ལྷག་པའི་དབང་ཕྱུག *lhag-pah̲i d̲wañ-phyug*; ས་ཀུན་དབང *sa-kun d̲wañ*; ཡང་དག་རྒྱལ་པོ *yañ-dag r̲gyal-po*; མི་ཡི་ལྷ *mi-yi lha*; གནམ་བསྐོས *gnam-b̲skos* (*M̲ñon.*).

འཁོར་ལོས་སྒྱུར་རྒྱལ་གྱི་བཙུན་མོ *ḥkhor-los sgyur rgyal-gyi btsun-mo* the wife of the Universal Emperor.

Syn. མི་ཡི་ལྷ་མོ *mi-yi lha-mo*; བུད་མེད་རིན་ཆེན *bud-med rin-chen*; གནམ་བསྐོས་མ *gnam bskos-ma*; ལྷག་པའི་དབང་ཕྱུག་མ *Lhag-paḥi dwaṅ-phyug ma*; འཇིག་རྟེན་བཙུན་མོ *ḥjig-rten btsun-mo.* (*Mṅon.*)

འཁོར་ལོ་འཇོམས *ḥkhor-lo ḥjoms*, v. ད་དྲུ་འཇོམས *da-dru ḥjoms* སྨན་བཟང་པོ, vegetable medicine for ringworm.

འཁོར་ལོ་དང་ལྡན་པའི་རི *Ḥkhor-lo daṅ ldaṅ paḥi-ri* चक्रपर्वत n. of a fabulous mountain situated beyond the great ocean where the horizon touches the earth. At its centre it has an impenetrable golden hill called *Vajra nābhi parvata.* It is filled with fruit trees in consequence of which there are innumerable species of monkey living there (*K. d.* ར *282*).

འཁོར་ལོ་དང་འཁོར་ལོ་ཆེན་པོ་ལྷའི་མེ་ཏོག *ḥkhor-lo daṅ ḥkhor-lo chen-po lhaḥi me-tog* (*K. d.* ཆ *368*) n. of a celestial flower; idem ཙ་ཀྲ་དང་ཙ་ཀྲ་ཆེན་པོ *tsa-kra daṅ tsa-kra chen-po.* (*K. d.* ཞ *156.*)

འཁོར་ལོ་དྲི་མེད *ḥkhor-lo dri-med* चक्रविमल n. of flower.

འཁོར་ལོ་གདོང *ḥkhor-lo gdoṅ*=ཕག་པ *phag-pa*, चक्र, चक्रा a pig; one with a circular muzzle.

འཁོར་ལོ་འདབ་བརྒྱ *ḥkhor-lo ḥdab-brgya* चक्रशतपत्र n. of a flower.

འཁོར་ལོ་འདྲ *ḥkhor-lo ḥdra*=དོང་ག *doṅ-ga.* Syn. རྒྱལ་པོའི་ཤིང *rgyal-poḥi çiṅ*; སོར་མོ་བཞི་པ *sor-ma gshi-pa*; ལོ་མ་བཟང *lo-ma bzaṅ* (*Mṅon.*).

འཁོར་ལོ་འདྲ་བ *ḥkhor-lo ḥdra-wa* चक्रवत्, चाक्रिक: like a circle; resembling a wheel.

འཁོར་ལོ་སྡོམ་པ *ḥkhor-lo sdoma-pa* चक्रसम्बर n. of Buddhist *Tantrik* deity.

འཁོར་ལོ་དབང་སྒྱུར *ḥkhor-lo dwaṅ-sgyur* བོན་གྱི་སྟོན་པ་ཞིག n. of a Bon teacher (*G. Bon. 1*).

འཁོར་ལོ་འབྱེད་པ *ḥkhor-lo ḥbyed-pa* चक्रभेदिनी one who can penetrate into the designs or machinations of others.

འཁོར་ལོ་རྩིབས་སྟོང *ḥkhor-lo rtsibs-stoṅ* the fabulous wishing wheel which is possessed of one thousand radiating spokes: རྒྱལ་པོའི་མདུན་ན་གསེར་གྱི་འཁོར་ལོ་རྩིབས་སྟོང་ཡོད་པ in the presence of the king was the golden wheel with one thousand radiating ribs; རྩིབས་རེ་རེ་ལ་ཟས་ཕྲ་རེ་རེ་བཞག་ནས་འདྲེན་པ་ལ on each spoke, where it touched the felloe, there was placed a dainty dish; གང་འདོད་པ་དེ་མདུན་དུ་བསྐོར་ནས་འདྲེན from the wheel was brought before him whatever he wished; མི་འདོད་པ་དེ་རྒྱབ་ཏུ་བསྐོར་ནས་འཇོག་པ that which he did not like turned away from him (*A. 2*).

འཁོར་ལོ་གཡོ *ḥkhor-lo gyo* कुन्द n. of a flower.

འཁོར་ལོའི་རྐང *ḥkhor-loḥi rkaṅ* round foot; elephant; གླང་པོ *glaṅ-po* (*Mṅon.*).

འཁོར་ལོའི་མགོན་པོ *ḥkhor-loḥi mgon-po* the lord or chief of all: མཁས་བཙུན་བཟང་པོའི་དཔལ་མངའ་འཁོར་ལོའི་མགོན་པོ་བཀའ་དྲིན་མཚུངས་མེད་དགེ་བའི་བཤེས་གཉེན་ཆེན་པོའི་ཞབས་དྲུང་དུ before the feet of *Kalyāṇamitra* who is the paramount lord possessing the grace of the noble, wise, and good, whose kindness is unequalled.

འཁོར་ལོའི་མགྲིན *ḥkhor-loḥi mgrin* as met.=རྔ་མོང *rṅa-moṅ* the camel. (*Mṅon.*)

འཁོར་ལོའི་མཐའ *ḥkhor-loḥi mthaḥ* नेमि, नाभि the circumference of a circle.

འཁོར་ལོའི་རྣམ་པ་ཅན *ḥkhor-loḥi rnam-pa can*, described as སྟག་གི་སེན་མོ་ཞེས་བྱ་བའི་དྲི་རྫས, a scent called "tiger's-claws."

འཁོར་ལོའི་ཡན་ལག *ḥkhor-loḥi yan-lag*=ངང་པ་སྤྱིའི་མིང *ṅaṅ-pa spyiḥi miṅ* चक्राङ्ग, हंस a general term for the goose species (*Mṅon.*).

འཁོར་ལོའི་ལུས I: *ḫkhor-loḫi lus* = སྤུ་ཤེལ་ཙེ *pu-çel tse* amber.

Syn. བྱ་ཟས *bya-zas*; ཉ་ཡི་འཁོར་པ *ña-yi ḫkhor-pa*; ལུས་ངན་མིག *lus-ñan mig* (*Mñon.*).

འཁོར་ལོའི་ལུས ii: = གདུགས *gdugs* an umbrella.

Syn. ཆར་སྐྱོབ *char-skyob*; ཚ་བ་སྒྲིབ *tsha-wa sgrib*; ཚད་སྐྱོབ *tshad-skyob* (*Mñon.*).

འཁོར་ལོས་འགྲོ་བ *ḫkhor-los ḫgro-wa*, ཤིང་རྟ་སྤྱི་དང་བྱེ་བྲག *çiñ-rta spyi-dañ bye-brag* wheeled; carriage or vehicle (*Mñon.*).

འཁོར་ལོས་སྒྱུར *ḫkhor-los sgyur*, v. རེག་བཟང *reg-bzañ* (*Mñon.*).

འཁོར་ལོས་འཚོ *ḫkhor-los ḫtsho*, v. རྫ་མཁན *rdsa-mkhan*, a potter; one who lives by turning the (potter's) wheel (*Mñon.*).

འཁོར་ས *ḫkhor-sa* प्रदक्षिण-पथिका the path for circumambulation round a sacred building or other object; the positions of attendant demi-gods of a principal deity round his mansion.

འཁོར་གསུམ *khor-ḫgsum* man, horse and cow: ཞིབས་ལས་གནོལ་ཏེ་འཁོར་གསུམ་ཕྱུང་དུ་ཕུལ, alighting from his horse, he presented the three objects, viz., a servant, a horse, and a cow to him (*A. 7*).

འཁོར་གསུམ་རྣམ་པར་དག་པ *ḫkhor-gsum rnam-par dag-pa* the alms-giver, alms-giving, and the receiver of alms, when those three are of pure motives.

འཁོལ་བ *ḫkhol-wa*, pf. བཀོལ *bkhol*, imp. ཁོལ *khol* 1. to make a person a slave; to bind as a servant; to cause to serve one. བྲན་ཁོལ *bran-khol* or ཁོལ་པོ *khol-po* a slave; *bkol-spyod-kyi sdug-bsñal* the miseries of servitude; *gshan-dag-gis dwañ-med-par bkol-wa* to be enslaved by others, without ability to help oneself. 2. acc. to *Cs.* to save; to spare; to enjoy with moderation. 3. acc. to *Sch.* to become insensible; to be asleep; to get benumbed in reference to the limbs. In *Med.* 4. to boil (with pf. ཁོལ *khol*): འཁོལ་འདུག་པ to make one boil; place for boiling (*Jä.*).

འཁོལ་ཐུབ་པ *ḫkhol thub-pa* explained in *rañ-gis bsgo-waḫi ñag la ñan-ciñ las gañ bskul-wa thams-cad sgrub-par byed, sems kyañ ḫgyur-wa-med na bran gyog-tu ḫkhol-thub-pa yin, de-ltar ma-byuñ-na bran gyog-tu gyur-kyañ ḫkhol mi thub-pa red* (*Ñag.*) extracting voluntary service, *i.e.*, if a servant obediently gives effect to the wishes of his master, otherwise, although the servant may be in his service, he has not rendered service.

འཁོལ་མ *ḫkhor-ma* a female attendant (*Cs.*).

འཁོལ་མོ *ḫkhol-mo* दासी maid-servant.

འཁོས *ḫkhos* or འཁོས་ཀ *ḫkhos-ka* worth, value, importance; also necessity: འཁོས་ཅན *ḫkhos-can* important; mighty; of great influence; འཁོས་མེད *ḫkhos-med* uninfluential; འཁོས་སུ་ཕབ་པ *ḫkhos-su phab-pa* to draw as a blister or poultice; དངོས་པོ་དགའ་ཚང་ཅིག་ཡོད་ཀྱང་སྣོད་ཀྱི་འཁོས་ཀཧམ *dños-po dgaḫ tshañ cig yod kyañ snod-kyi ḫkhos-kaham* (*A. 142*) although there have existed some articles pretty complete, there was necessity for a vessel to receive (deserve) them; འཁོས་ཀ་ཆུང་བ *ḫkhos-ka chuñ-wa* of less necessity; འཁོས་ཆུང་བ *ḫkhos chuñ-wa* = ལས་བྱ་བར་ཆུང་བ *las-bya-war chuñ-ba* less active or less energetic (*Mñon.*).

འཁོས་བསྟུན *ḫkhos bstun* = ཧོས་བབས *hos babs*, དོན་དང་བསྟུན *don dañ bstun* suited to one's intention or object; fitness; suitability.

འཁོས་དཔག *ḫkhos-dpag* according to the measure of one's ability.

འཁོས་སུ་ཕེབས་པ *ẖkhos̱-su phebs̱-pa*=ལོགས་སུ་བཞག་པ *logs̱-su ḇshag-pa* to put in opposition.

འཁྱགས་པ *ẖkhyags̱-pa* शीत, हिम, शिशिर vb. intrans. 1. to freeze either into ice or hard; to coagulate, crystalise: ཆུ་འཁྱགས་ཀྱི་ཡིན the water will be freezing; བུལ་ཚྭ་ཁ་རུ་ཁྱབ་སྡང the soda has congealed on the salt-lake. In Sikkim *khyek* or *khek*=ice. 2. to feel cold, become numbed: འཁྱགས་འབྱུང *ẖkhyags̱-ẖbyuñ* they felt cold (*M̱ñon.*).

འཁྱགས་རུམ *ẖkyags̱-rum* or འཁྱགས་རམ *ẖkhyags̱ ram* an ice-slip; also ice in blocks.

འཁྱམ་ཁྱི *ẖkhyam-kyi* a stray dog.

འཁྱམས་པ I: *ẖkhyams̱-pa* fig. to rove, wander: འདོད་པས་ཡོངས་སུ་བསླུས་པ་ཡིས, འཇིག་རྟེན་འཁོར་ལོ་བཞིན་དུ་འཁྱམས being completely deluded by desire, they rove the world as a wheel (*K. d.* ༡ *380*): འཁོར་བར་འཁྱམས་པ་དང *ẖkhor-war ẖkhyams̱-pa dañ* or བར་དོར་འཁྱམས་པ *bar-dor ẖkhyams̱-pa* to rove (in the world or in the interval between death and regeneration) for no purpose.

འཁྱམས་པ II: =དོན་མེད་དུ་འགྲོ་བ *don-meḏ-du ẖgro-wa* सम्भिन्न-प्रलाप, भ्रमयन्त, घूर्ण, विगाढ, विगाढ; pf. འཁྱམས་པར་གྱུར *ẖkhyams̱-par gyur* 1. to ramble about; to wander purposelessly; to wander in a strange country. At certain seasons many monks wander about Tibet, Mongolia and China, *vide* Huc. विभ्रमण, विघूर्ण; རྣམ་པར་འཁྱམས་པ *ṟnam-par ẖkhyams̱-pa*, to wander about continually; to move about unceasingly: འཁྱམ་དུ་འཇུག་པ *ẖkhyam-du ẖjûg-pa* to cause to ramble or rove about; to become strayed, lost; wandering; vagrant; erroneous; erring; ཆུ་འཁྱམ་པ *chu ẖkhyam-pa* inundation; flood.

འཁྱམས་པོ *ẖkhyams̱-po* 1. erroneous; a vagabond. 2. n. of a disease.

འཁྱར་བ *ẖkhyar-wa* to err, to go astray, to deviate from the right path: མི་འཁྱར *mi-ẖkhyar* erring or blundering man; ཁྱི་འཁྱར *khyi ẖkhyar* a stray dog; ཡི་གེ་འཁྱར་བ་པོ *yi-ge ẖkhyar-wa-po* one who makes mistakes in writing (a letter, &c.); སྐད་ཆ་ལ་འཁྱར་མ་བཅུག do not err in conversation. འཁྱར་དོགས་ཡོད one should be afraid of making mistakes, of going astray; དཔེ་འཁྱར་པོ *ḏpe ẖkhyar-po* a defective simile (*Jä.*).

འཁྱལ་བ *ẖkhyal-wa*=འཆལ་བ *ẖchal-wa* irrelevant: ངག་འཁྱལ་བ speaking unconnectedly.

འཁྱལ་ཚིག། *ẖkhyal-tshig* irrelevant speech; speaking nonsense: གཞོན་ནུ་འདྲེན་པར་མི་བྱེད་པའི, འཁྱལ་ཚིག་སྨྲ་ན་ཁྲིམས་དང་འགལ if one speak misleading words which cause the youthful not to go straight, it infringes the law (or justice).

འཁྱི་བ *ẖkhyi-wa*, acc. to *Sch.* འཁྱིལ་བ *ẖkhyil-wa*.

འཁྱིག་པ *ẖkhyig-pa*, बन्धन to bind; to take prisoner. बध्वानीतम्, also in *C.*, to strangle; suffocate; ཐག་པས་འཁྱིག་པ་པོ *thag-pas̱ ẖkhyig-pa-po* one who binds with a rope.

Syn. འཆིང་བ *ẖchiñ-wa*; སྡོམ *s̱dom*; འདོགས *ẖdogs*; གདགས *gdags̱*; བཅིང་པ *ḇciñ-wa*; བཀྱིག་པ *ḇkyig-pa*.

འཁྱིགས་པ *ẖkhyigs̱-pa*, pf. བཀྱིགས *ḇkyigs*, bound.

卐 **འཁྱིད་པ** *ẖkyiḏ-pa*༢=འབྱིན་པ *ẖbyin-pa* to draw out; strain; also to roll, revolve: མིག་འཁྱིད་པ *mig-ẖkhyiḏ-pa* to turn or roll one's eyes: འཁོར་བར་འཁྱིད་པའི་རྒྱུའི་གཙོ་བོ་ནི་ཇི་ལྟར་སྣང་བའི་དངོས་པོ་འདི་དག་ལ *ẖkhor-war ẖkhyiḏ-paẖi ṟgyuẖi gtso-ḇo ni ji-ḻtar s̱nañ-waẖi ḏños̱-po ẖdi dag la* the chief of the causes of revolving in the world lies in how one appears outwardly (*Lam. ti, 36*).

འཁྱིམ་པ *hkhyim-pa*=ཆུ་འཁོར་བ *chu hkhor-wa* to whirl (as of water) (*Mñon.*).

འཁྱིམས་པ *hkhyims-pa* परिवेश, आहृत्ति, described as *ñi-ma dañ zla-wa sogs la hod sgor-sgor-du hkhyims-pa*, to be encircled with a halo, like the sun and moon; འོད་འཁྱིམས་ *hog-hkhyims* परिधि nimbus; halo: འཇའ་འོད་འཁྱིམས *hjah-hod hkhyims* a rainbow encircling (him): ན་བུན་ *na-bûn* or སྨུག་པ་འཁྱིམས *smug-pa khyims* དུད་པ་འཁྱིམས *dud-pa hkhyims* fog, mist, or smoke enveloped him (*Jä.*).

འཁྱིར་བ *hkhyir-wa* to turn round: དབུ་ལ་གདུགས་བསྐོར་བའི་འཁྱིར་པ *dbu-la gdugs bskor-wahi hkhyir-pa* (*Ñag.*) to turn a parasol round in a circle over the head.

འཁྱིལ་བ *hkhyil-wa* आवर्त, आवृत्त, vb. intrans. to wind; to twist; to whirl round; *skra* hair (*Mñon.*): ཆུ་རང་ཤུགས་ཀྱིས་འཁྱིལ་བ *chu-rañ çugs-kyis hkhyil-wa* water of itself whirls round, *i.e.*, turns into a whirlpool; དུང་དཀར་གཡས་འཁྱིལ་གཡོན་འཁྱིལ *dûñ-dkar gyas-hkhyil gyon-hkhyil* a white shell wound to the right or wound to the left; སྦྲུལ་འཁྱིལ་བ *sbrul hkhyil-wa* to coil up like a snake; to being wound in the manner of a snake: ཆུ་ཆེན་པོ་འཁྱིལ་འདུག *chu chen-po hkhyil hdug* much water has accumulated surrounding a place or inside a place forming itself in a whirlpool; འོད་དུ་འཁྱིལ་ཞིང་ *hod-du hkhyil-shiñ* as if wreathed with light; ཉ་གསེར་མིག་འཁྱིལ་བ་ཡོད *ña gser mig hkhyil-wa yod* the fish was revolving its golden eyes: མི་མང་པོ་དེ་རུ་འཁྱིལ་བར་གྱུར་ཏེ *mi mañ-po de-ru hkhyil-war gyur-te* there many people having crowded together or assembled together: ཆུ་ལ་འཁྱིལ་ལྡོག་མེད་ཀྱང་ས་གཞི་ཟབ་ཏུ་བྲུ although there was no swirl in the waters they dug deeply into the ground.

Syn. འཁོར་བ *hkhor-wa*; འཇུག་པ *hjug-pa* (*Mñon.*).

འཁྱིལ་བ་བརྒྱ *hkhyil-wa brgya* शतावर्त्तः one hundred coils: འཁྱིལ་ལྡན *hkhyil-ldan* कुण्डली anything that is possessed of coils; wound together.

འཁྱིལ་བ་ཅན *hkhyil-ba can*=རྣ་རྒྱན *rna-rgyan* an earring.

Syn. རྣ་བ་མཛེས་བྱེད *rna-ba mdses-byed*; རྣ་བར་འཁྱིལ *rna-war hkhyil*; སྙན་རྒྱན *sñan-rgyan* कर्णिका (*Mñon.*).

འཁྱིས་པ *hkhyis-pa*, v. འཁྱིད་པ *hkhyid-pa*, to evolve.

འཁྱུ་བ *hkhyu-wa* or འཁྱུས་པ *hkhyus-pa*=ཀྱོག་པོ *kyog-po* 1. bent; not straight (*Ñag.*). 2. pf. འཁྱུས *hkhyus* run away.

Syn. ཡོ་བ *yo-wa*; བྲོས་པ *bros-pa* (*Mñon.*).

འཁྱུག་པ *hkhyug-pa* चलन; pf. ཁྱུག *khyug* to run, move swiftly; said to imply མྱུར་བའི་དོན *myur-wahi-don*, the meaning of rapidity; འཁྱུག་པོ *hkhyug-po* runner. གློག་འཁྱུག་པ *glog-hkhyug-pa* rapid motion of lightning: གློག་ལྟར་འཁྱུག་པ *glog ltar hkhyug-pa* to run or move rapidly like the flash of lightning: འཁྱུག་པོ་འཁྱུ་པ *hkhyug-po hkhyu-pa* to run away swiftly: འཁྱུག་ཙམ *hkhyug-tsam* in or about a moment or in a flash: སྐུ་འཁྱུག་ཙམ་ཕེབས་པ *sku hkhyug-tsam phebs-pa* your honour has come for a rapid visit: ཁྱེད་རང་དེ་རིང་འཁྱུག་ཙམ་ཕེབས་རོགས *khyed-rañ de-riñ hkhyug-tsam phebs rogs* will you come here to-day just for a trice: འཁྱུག་ཙམ་གཟིགས *hkhyug-tsam gzigs* see for about an instant: སེམས་འཁྱུག *sems hkhyug* the mind travels quickly. ཁྲ་ཁྱུག་པ *khra khyug-pa* to gleam; to twinkle with light; to shine in various colours: ཡིད་ནི་རྣམ་མཛངས་འཁྱུགས་པར་འགྱུར (*Lam. ti. 35.*) the mind moves (restless) with suffering; ཟེར་འཁྱུག་གེ་བ glittering in yellow lustre; to glitter; to shine (of the rainbow).

འཁྱུག་ཡིག *hkhyug-yig* running hand; current handwriting.

འཁྱུག་ཤར་ཅན *hkhyug-çar-can* in *W.* hasty; hurrying; careless.

འཁྱུད་འཐུང་ *hkhyud-hthuñ*=སྐྱེས་མ་ཐག་པ *skyes-ma thag-pa* as soon as born (*Mñon.*).

འཁྱུད་ནས་ལྡོང་བའི་མ་ནིང་ *hkhyud nas ldoñ-wahi ma niñ* आसक्त षण्ढ पण्डक one that becomes an hermaphrodite after being embraced.

འཁྱུད་པ I: *hkhyud-pa* आलिङ्गित, आलिङ्गन 1. to embrace; embraced: མགུལ་ནས་འཁྱུད་པ *mgul-nas hkhyud-pa* to clasp round the neck; to hug; to encompass by spanning. 2. to glide in or into (as serpents): མངལ་དུ་འཁྱུག་པ *mñal-du hkhyug-pa* entering of the soul into new conception. 3. to be able: ལང་བར་མི་འཁྱུད *lañ-war mi hkhyud* unable to rise (from bed). The word is also illustrated as རྩིག་པ་ལ་རྟེན་ནས་འགྲོ་བ་ལྟ་བུ *rtsig-pa la rten nas hgro-wa lta-bu*, to move supporting himself on a wall, &c.

འཁྱུད་པ II: =འཁྲིག་པ *hkhrig-pa* मैथुन, आलिङ्गन sexual embrace (*Mñon.*).

འཁྱུར་བ *hkhyur-wa* or འཁྱུར *hkhyur*, fut. of བསྐྱུར *bskyur*, to be separated; divorced (*Cs.*): to stop; to put an end to. Acc. to *Jä.*, to be deserted: བསྐྱུར་བས་འཁྱུར་ཉེས་པས being separated, he was, so to speak, bereft.

འཁྱུས *hkhyus*, v. འཁྱུ་བ *hkhyu-wa*.

འཁྱེང་བ *hkhyeñ-wa* to be filled up, v. འགེངས་པ *hgeñs-pa*.

འཁྱེད་པ *hkhyed-pa* 1. to be sufficient, to suffice, to be enough; to hold out; colloq. འདི་ཁྱེད this is enough: མི་ཁྱེད there is not enough. 2. in *C.* to gain (a law suit); to be acquitted (*Jä.*). 3. ཕྱིར་ཁྱེད་པ *phyir khyed-pa* to bow without uncovering one's head, as a less humble way of saluting (*Jä.*).

འཁྱེར་བ *hkhyer-wa* नय to carry away, to take away; sometimes, to bring: ཆུ་ཡིས་འཁྱེར *chu-yis hkhyer* carried away by water; ལེ་ལོས་འཁྱེར *le-los hkhyer* to be overcome, carried away by idleness. ལྡེ་མིག་ཁྱེར *lde-mig khyer* take the key; ཁྱེར་ཤོག *khyer-çog* bring; ཁྱེར་སོང *khyer soñ* carry off, take away; akin to the *le-au* and *le-jao* of Hindustani.

འཁྱེར་སོ *hkhyer-so* 1. bearing; appearance; demeanour; neatness. 2. colloq. advantage; superiority; pleasantness.

འཁྱེལ་བ *hkhyel-wa Ld.* to hit, to strike.

འཁྱོག་འཁྱོག *hkhyog-hkhyog* bent, crooked (*Ñag.*).

འཁྱོག་འགྲོ 1 *hkhyog-hgro*=གཟའ་སྤེན་པ *gzah spen-pa* the planet Saturn or གོས་སྔོན *gos-sñon*; he in blue robe (*Mñon.*). 2. =འབབ་ཆུ *hbab-chu* a stream; waterfall (*Mñon.*); སྦྲུལ་འཁྱོག་འགྲོ *sbrul hkhyog-hgro* the snake because it creeps in a bent course (*Mñon.*).

འཁྱོག་ཅན *hkhyog-can* or འཁྱོག་འཁྱོག *hkhyog-hkhyog* tortuous.

འཁྱོག་སྟོན་པ *hkhyog ston-pa* to fly into a passion (*Seh.*).

འཁྱོག་པ *hkhyog-pa*, pf. ཁྱག *khyag*, imp. ཁྱོག *khyog* 1. to lift; lift up. 2. to carry; tob ring: གསོལ་ཇ་ཁྱོག *gsol-ja khyog* bring in the tea (*C.*).

འཁྱོག་པོ *hkhyog-po* or ཁྱོག་པོ *khyog-po* crooked; bent: ཁྱོག་པོའི་རི་མོ *khyog-pohi ri-mo* a crooked figure; a curve, flourish, crescent, &c.: ཉས་ཕར་འཁྱོག་ཚུར་འཁྱོག *ñas phar hkhog-tshun-hkhyog* the fish writhing hither and thither.

འཁྱོག་པའི་ས་བོན *hkhyog-pahi sa-bon* वक्रबीज crooked seeds.

འཁྱོག་པོ *hkhyog-po* = དྲང་པོ་མིན་པ *drañ-po min-pa* वक्र, वृजिन,वक्रा, नत, विच्छिन्न, कुटिलम् not upright; not straight, *i.e.*, crooked.

འཁྱོག་པོའི་མཐུ་ཅན *hkhyog-pohi mthu-can* the bent-bill; a toucan.

འཁྱོག་པོའི་སྡེ *hkhyog-pohi sde* = པོ་སོན་ཆ *po-son cha*, ཆང་རྩི *chañ-rtsi* a kind of churn or mixer to make wine with.

Syn. གོང་བུ་ཅན *goñ-bu can*; གསེར་གྱི་ལག *gser-gyi lag*; དབུགས་འབྱིན་ཤིང *dbugs-hbyin çiñ*; ཆང་ཤིང *chañ-çiñ*; ལག་པའི་ཚོང་དུས *lag-pahi tshoñ-dus*; མྱོས་བྱེད *myos-byed.*

འཁྱོག་པོའི་ཚིག *hkhyog-pohi tshig* = ཚིག་གི་གཏང་རག *tshig-gi gtañ-rag* rough language; not straightforward (*Mñon.*).

འཁྱོག་དཔྱང *hkhyog-dpyañ* a lath or pole for carrying burdens (*Sch.*).

འཁྱོག་གྲལ *hkhyog-gral* = དྲང་ལམ *drañ-lam* straight road (*Mñon.*).

འཁྱོག་འབར *hkhyog-hbar* མེ་ལྗེའི་མིང blaze or flame (*Mñon.*).

འཁྱོག་མེད *hkhyog-med* = དྲང་པོ *drañ-po* or སྲོང་པ *sroñ-pa* straight (*Mñon.*).

འཁྱོག་བཤད *hkhyog-bçad* a crooked, out-of-the-way construction or explanation.

འཁྱོགས *hkhyogs* or ཁྱོགས *hkhyogs*, रथ a palanquin; sedan chair; litter.

འཁྱོང་བ *hkhyoñ-wa* or འཁྱོངས *hkhyoñs* སྐྱོང་བ་དང་སྐྱོངས་པའི་དོན་དང་མཚུངས *skyoñ-wa dañ skyoñs-pahi don-dañ mtshuñs* to observe: ཉིན་འཁྱོངས *ñin-hkhyoñs*, དགོན་པ་ལ་སྦྱིན་བདག་གིས་ཉི་མ་གཅིག་གི་བསྙེན་བཀུར་བཞུ་བ *dgon-pa la sbyin-bdag-gis ñi-ma gcig-gi bsñen-bkur shu-wa* 1. to observe a day's religious service in a monastery. 2. acc. to *Jä.* and Ramsay *khyong* in Ladak signifies to bring.

འཁྱོམ་པ *hkhyom-pa* तरल, fluid hence fig. giddy or giddiness; also to reel; to be giddy: བཟི་འཁྱོམ་འཁྱོམ་རྒྱུག *bzi hkhyom hkhyom rgyug* dizzy with intoxication: ཡང་ཤིང་སོགས་འཁྱོས་དང་འཁྱོར་ཞིང་འཁྱོག *yañ çiñ sogs hkhyos dañ hkhyor-shiñ hkhyog* the trees being moved (by the wind) were bent (*Ñag.*); so the words འཁྱོམ *hkhyom* and འཁྱོག *hkhyog* are somewhat similar to each other. ཁྱོམ་ཁྱོམ་དོ་བ *khyom-khyom do-wa* in *C.* to reel, stagger: ཆང་གི་འཁྱོམ་པ་འདུག *chañ-gi hkhyom-pa hdûg* he is staggering under the influence of beer; མཚོ་འཁྱོམ *mtsho-hkhyom* dizziness; vertigo: ལུག་ཀླད་མགོ་འཁོར་འཁྱོམ་པ་གསོ *lug-glad mgo-hkhor hkhyom-pa gso* the brain of a sheep (taken as food) cures reeling or dizziness of the head (*Med.*).

འཁྱོར་བ *hkhyor-wa* विकल to be unsteady; to miss, fail; not to hit (*Cs.*); to reel, stagger, from intoxication; to warp (of wood or wooden vessels): འགྲོ་ན་གོམ་པ་འཁྱོར in walking his steps reeled (*Rdsa.*).

འཁྱོལ་པ *hkhyol-pa*, pf. འཁྱོལ *hkhyol*, cf. སྐྱེལ་བ *skyel-wa*, to be carried; to be brought; to arrive at, come to, reach: མཐར་མ་འཁྱོལ་བར་ལུས་སོང on reaching the end, it was left (unfinished).

འཁྱོས་པ *hkhyos-pa* = འཕྱོས་པ *hphyos-pa* (*Sch.*).

འཁྱོས་མ *hkhyos-ma*, same as སྐྱས་མ *skyas-ma*, a present, gift.

འཁྲ་བ *ḥkhra-wa* (*ṭha-wa*), vb., pf. probably འཁྲས *ḥkhras*, to lean to; to incline towards (*Cs.*).

འཁྲ་ས *ḥkhra-sa* a support to lean against; a prop; the back (of a chair): འཁྲ་སར་འཁྲས *ḥkhra-sar ḥkhras*=རྟེན་ལ་བརྟེན་པ *rten-la brten-pa* firm in support (*Ñag.*).

འཁྲངས *ḥkhrañs* (*ṭhañ*) खरः hard; འཁྲང་བ *ḥkhrañs-wa*, བཀྲང་བ *bkrañ-wa* adj. hard.

འཁྲད་པ *ḥkhrad-pa* (*ṭhad-pa*), in colloq. Tib. to expel; turn out: བགེགས་འཁྲད་བྱེད *bgegs ḥkhrad byed* to expel the devil (from one's body).

འཁྲབ་པ *ḥkhrab-pa* (*ṭhab-pa*) उच्चार, पव; pf. བཀྲབ *bkrab* or སྐྲབ་པ *skrab-pa*, 1. to strike; to beat (in regular strokes, as in swimming and rowing); to thrust, stamp, tread heavily; བྲོ་འཁྲབ་པ *bro ḥkhrab-pa* to dance in that manner. 2. to winnow; to fan. 3. to blink, twinkle, wink with the eyes. 4. to jest; to joke; to crack jokes. 5. to leap, jump (*Sch*); jump for joy (*Schr.*). 6. to scoop out; to bail out (*Sch.*). 7. to fight; to combat in *C.* and *W.* (*Jä.*).

འཁྲལ་འཁྲུལ *ḥkhral-ḥkhrul* (*ṭhal-ṭhul*)= ཁྲལ་ལེ་ཁྲུལ་ལེ *khral-le khrul-le* (*ṭha-le ṭhu-le*) confused; dazed; confounded; also as adv. མི་ཆ་བཟུང་མེད་པ་སྐད་ཆ་རྣམ་པ་སྣ་ཚོགས་ལབ་ཞིང, སྡོད་མི་ཐུབ, པ་ཡར་ཕྱིན་ཚུར་ཡོང་སྤྱོད་ལག་ཀྱང་ཚགས་མི་ཐུབ་པ་ལ་ཟེར་ཡོང also applied to one who is confused in his ideas and speaks unconnectedly and ravingly, and being unable to sit moves up and down and cannot even preserve his own goods.

འཁྲས *ḥkhras* (*ṭhe*)=སེམས་ཆགས་སྡོད་པ *sems-chags sdod-pa* hopeful; also attached.

འཁྲི *ḥkhri* (*ṭhi*) reduction; discount.

འཁྲི་རྐང *ḥkhri-rkañ* ध्वज, said to be=རྒྱལ་མཚན *rgyal-mtshan*, the Buddhist flag of victory.

འཁྲི་སྒྲུབ *ḥkhri-sgrub* payment of stipulated revenue or dues: ཁྲལ་འམ་བུ་ལོན་སོགས *khral-ḥam bu-lon sogs*, རང་གི་མགོ་ལ་བབས་པ་ནི་འཁྲི་བ *rañ-gi mgo-la babs-pa-ni ḥkhri-wa* liabilities on account of rent or debt, &c.

འཁྲི་བ *ḥkhri-wa*, pf. འཁྲིས *ḥkhris*, cf. དཀྲི་བ *dkri-wa* cognate. 1. to wind; compress; entangle; hold fast: ཁྱིམ་ཐབ་ཀྱི་འཁྲི་བ *khyim tkab-kyi ḥkhri-wa* conjugal embrace; འཁྲི་ཤིང *ḥkhri-çiñ* or འཁྲིལ་ཤིང *ḥkhril-çiñ* a creeper; a creeping plant: ཁྲལ་འཁྲི་བ་དང་བུ་ལོན་འཁྲི་བ to be tied by taxes and entangled in debt. 2.= ཆགས་པ *chags-pa* mostly as a sbst. thrall; attachment, but as vb. also: རང་དོན་གྱི་འཁྲིས་པ *rañ don-gyi ḥkhris-pa* to be attached to one's interest or advantage; བུ་མེད་ཀྱི *bu-med-kyi* to wife and children: འཁྲི་བ་ཆོད *ḥkhri-wa-chod*=ཞེན་པ་དང་འབྲེལ་ཐག་ཆོད *shen-pa-dañ ḥbrel-thag chod* fondness; attachment. ཞེན་འཁྲིས *shen-ḥkhris* passionate attachment.

འཁྲི་འབབ *ḥkhri-ḥbab* assessment of revenue or རྩ་ཆུ་ཤིང་གསུམ་གྱི་འཁྲི་འབབ *rtsa-chu çiñ gsum-gyi ḥkhri-ḥbab*, levy for the three—grass, water, wood (to be supplied to privileged travellers or officials) (*Rtsii.*).

འཁྲི་ཤིང *ḥkhri-çiñ*=འཁྲིལ་ཤིང *ḥkhril-çiñ* लता, वल्ली, लतिका, कल्लीषि, व्रतति a creeping plant.

Syn. ཡལ་གའི་རལ་པ *yal-gaḥi ral-pa.*

འཁྲི་ཤིང་མཆོག་ལྡན *ḥkhri-çiñ mchog-ldan*, ཤིང་བཟང་པོ་ཞིག་གི་མིང n. of a kind of tree.

Syn. པྲི་ཡང་ཀུ *pri-yañ ku*; བུད་མེད་མིང་ཅན *bud-med miñ-can*; སྣ་ཚོགས་སྡེ *sna-tshogs sde*; འབྱུང་པོའི་མེ་ཏོག *ḥbyuñ-poḥi me-tog*; ས་ལ་ཕྱག་འཚལ *sa-la hyag-ḥtshadl* (*Mñon.*).

འཁྲི་ཤིང་ཐོགས་མེད་ *hkhri-çiñ thogs-med* སྤོས་དཀར་ཤིང་གི་མིང་ a name for the Sâl tree.

Syn. སཱ་ལའི་ལྗོན་པ *sā-lahi ljon-pa*; སཱ་ལའི་ཤིང *sā-lahi çiñ*; སྲ་རྩི་ཤིང *sra-rtsi çiñ* कर्षैकार, हन्तक (*Mñon.*).

* **འཁྲིག་པ** *hkhrig-pa* 1. मिथुन (*Schr.*). 2. གཉིས, *gñis* mystic number signifying "two" (*Rtsii.*). 3. vb. to cohere; to stick together, become thick, intermingled: གནམ་འཁྲིག *gnam-hkhrig* the sky is thick: འོད་ཟེར་དང་འཇའ་འོད་འཁྲིག་པ *hod-zer dañ hjah-hod hkhrig-pa* beams of light and rainbow hues intermingled: འཁྲིགས་གྱུར་པ *hkhrig gyur-pa*, སྙིང་རྗེའི་གེ་སར་འཁྲིགས་པ to become adherent being intimately mixed up with the saffron of mercy. 4. coitus; sexual intercourse: འཁྲིག་པ་སྤྱོད་པ to perform such. འཁྲིག་སྐད *hkhrig-skad*=འཁྲིག་ཚིག *hkhrig-tshig* amorous speech; obscene language; འཁྲིག་ཐབས *hkhrig-thabs* वैमिक amorous dalliance; འཁྲིག་འདོད་མ *hkhrig hdod-ma* कामुकी a voluptuous woman. 5. मिथुनराशि the twins in the Zodiac.

Syn. of No. 4. དབང་པོ་གཉིས་སྦྱོར *dwañ-po gñis-sbyor*; གྲོང་པའི་ཆོས *groñ-pahi chos*; ཉེ་ཟུངས *ñe-zuñs*; ལག་བསྡམས *lag-bsdams*; འདོད་པ་སྤྱོད *hdod-pa spyod*; བཅོས་པ *bços-pa*; ཤེ་སྦྱོར *çe-sbyor*; མི་ཚངས་སྤྱོད *mi tshañs spyod*; གསང་སྤྱོད *gsañ-spyod*; ཉེ་རེག *ñe-reg*; དགའ *dgah*; རྨོངས *rmoñs*; སྦྱོར་བ *sbyor-wa*; ཀུན་སྦྱོར *kun-sbyor*; སྐྱེ་བ་སྤྱོད *skye-wa spyod*; དགའ་མགུར་སྤྱོད *dgah mgur-spyod*; དགའ་བ་རོལ *dgah-wa rol*; འཁྱུད་པ *hkhyud-pa*; ཆགས་སྤྱོད *chags-spyod*; འདོད་ལོག་སྤྱོད *hdod-log spyod*; ལོག་གཡེམ *log-gyem* (*Mñon.*).

འཁྲིག་པ་དང་ལྡན་པར་སྨྲ་བ *hkhrig-pa dañ ldan-par smra-wa* मैथुनाभाषण speaking of copulation or of sexual union.

འཁྲིག་པ་འབྱིན་པ *hkhrig-pa hbyin-pa* to talk smut.

འཁྲིག་པ་སྦེད *hkhrig-pa sbed* བྱ་རོག་གི་མིང n. for the crow (*Mñon.*).

འཁྲིག་པའི་ཆོས་རྟེན་པ *hkhrig-pahi chos rten-pa* to be given up to voluptuousness.

འཁྲིག་པའི་བསམ་གཏན་མ *hkhrig-pahi bsam-gtan ma*, or བུད་མེད་འདོད་ལྡན་མ *bud-med hdod-ldan ma* a voluptuous or licentious woman (*Mñon.*).

འཁྲིག་སྦེད *hkhrig-sbad* गुह्य मैथुन, v. འཁྲིག་པ་སྦེད *hkhrig-pa sbed*.

འཁྲིག་མ *hkhrig-ma* or འཁྲིགས་མ *hkhrigs-ma*, ལག་པའི *lag-pahi* मणिबन्ध करभ the wrist (of the hand).

འཁྲིགས་པ *hkhrigs-pa* collected or assembled together, of སྤྲིན *sprin* (clouds).

འཁྲིད་པ *hkhrid-pa* (*thid-pa*) विनीत, pf. ཁྲིད *khrid*, pf. བཀྲི *bkri* नयति, to lead; to conduct; bring to a place; especially used in connection with animals and children, also of leading an army: བུ་ཚ་འཁྲིད་བྱུང་ *bu-tsha hkhrid byuñ* led out their children.

འཁྲིམས *hkhrims* (*thim*), འཇིགས་སྐྲག *hjigs skrag* (*Ñag.*) terror, panic, fear: འབྲེད་ནས་འཁྲིམས *hbred-nas hkhrims* (*Lex.*; *Jä.*).

འཁྲིལ་བ *hkhril-wa* (*thil-wa*) འཁྲི་བ *hkhri-wa* to wind, coil round (of serpents); draw close; embrace closely; to clasp round; འཁྲིལ་མཁན *hkhril-mkhan* an embracer; འཁྲིལ་ལྡན *hkhril-ldan* a plant furnished with tendrils or claspers; ཁ་འཁྲིལ་བ *kha hkhril-wa* in *W.* to speak imperfectly like children; to lisp, to stammer.

འཁྲིལ་ལྡེམ *hkhril-ldem* fig. very handsome and young; འཁྲིལ *hkhril* union. ལྡེམ *ldem* waving; moving.

འཁྲིལ་ཤིང *hkhril-çiñ*=ཁྲི་ཤིང *hkhri-çiñ* a climbing plant, a creeper.

འཁྲིས *ḥkhris* (*ṭhi*) निकट, समीप near, neighbouring bank, shore, coast; also postp. འཁྲིས་སུ and འཁྲིས་ན close to; very near; against: *sbrel zla-wa med-pa rnams-kyaṅ srid-skyoṅdeḥi ḥkhris-su min-pa zla yod ma gtogs raṅ-ñid gcig-por gshuṅ-las mi byed* one should not singly (venture) to do Government work unless assisted by a colleague under the king (*D. çel. 12*).

Syn. འགྲམ *ḥgram*; རྩར *rtsar*; དྲུང་ *druṅ* (*Mṅon.*).

འཁྲིས་འཛིན *khhris ḥdsin*, ར་གན *ra-gan*, पित्तल brass.

འཁྲུ་བ *ḥkhru-wa* (*ṭhu-wa*) = འཁྲུད་པ *ḥkhruḍ-pa* प्रक्षालन to wash; to bathe: འཁྲུར་འཇུག་པ *ḥkhrur ḥjug-pa* धवन, धावति causing to be washed.

འཁྲུ་བ་གཅོད་པ *ḥkhru-wa gcoḍ-pa* संग्रहण stoppage of looseness or diarrhœa.

འཁྲུ་གཞི *ḥkhru-gshi* 1. diarrhœa. 2. འཁྲུ་སྦྱོངས *ḥkhru-sbyoṅ*, འཁྲུ་ནད *khru-naḍ*, འཁྲུ་སྐྱུག *ḥkhru-skyug* अतिसार diarrhoea with vomiting.

* **འཁྲུག** *ḥkhrug* संग्राम (*Schr.; Kālac. T. 121*).

འཁྲུག་གོས *ḥkhrug-gos* = གོ་ཆ *go-cha* or གོ་ཁྲབ *go-ḥhrab* war-dress; coat of mail (*Mṅon.*).

འཁྲུག་ལྷ་པ *ḥhhrug-lha-pa* the drumming to battle; stated (*Mṅon.*) to mean also གཡུལ་གྱི་སར་འབྱུང་བའི་སྒྲ་སྐད the clamour which arises on the battle-field.

འཁྲུག་པ I: *ḥkhrug-pa* (*ṭhug-pa*) संग्राम, विनाश, रणाच, सङ्कुलम्, कलह, युद्ध, आयोधन, समर, आनर्त, 1. vb. pf. འཁྲུགས་པ *ḥkhrugs-pa*, cf. དཀྲུག་པ *dkrug-pa*, དཀྲུག་པ *ḍkrug-pa* to be in commotion; commotion; to be disturbed; to be panic-stricken: འཁྲུག་པར་མི་འགྱུར་བ *ḥkhrug-par mi-ḥgyur-wa* न क्षुभ्यति will not become angry; get disordered: རྩ་ཐམས་ཅད་འཁྲུག་ཏུ་བཅུག *rtsa thams-caḍ ḥkhrug-tu ḅcug* it made all his veins disordered (blood to boil). 2. to be angry; also to quarrel, fight, contend: དེ་གཉིས་འཁྲུག་ནས *de-gñis ḥkhrug-nas* the two quarrelling. Also as sbst. fight, disruption, row: འཁྲུག་པ་ཤོར *ḥkhrug-pa çor* disorder arose; quarrel took place. འཁྲུག་པ་བྱེད་པ to show fight; to take up arms; to rebel: འཁྲུག་པ་བྱེད་པའི་དུས་སུ in times of war: དམག་འཁྲུག *dmag-ḥkhrug* = འཐབ་འཁྲུག *ḥthab-ḥkhrug* war. མི་འཁྲུགས་པ *Mi ḥkhrug-pa* a name of Buddha, who does not become agitated or ruffled at heart. འཁྲུག་པའི་ས་གཞི *ḥkhrug-paḥi sa-gshi* = གཡུལ་གྱི་ས་གཞི *gyul-gyi sa-gshi* or དམག་གི་ས་གཞི *dmag-gi, sa-gshi* battle-field (*Mṅon.*).

འཁྲུག་དཔོན *ḥkhrug-dpon* = དམག་དཔོན . *dmag dpon* general; commanding in war.

འཁྲུག་ལོང *ḥkhrug-loṅ* = སྐྱོ་ངོགས *skyo-ṅogs* 1. contest, strife. 2. གཡུལ་སྤྲོད་པ *gyul-sprod pa* or དམག་འཐབ་པ *dmag-ḥthab-pa* (*Mṅon.*).

འཁྲུགས *ḥkhrugs* (*ṭhug*) defined as མ་རྣལ་བ་གཡོ་འགུལ་ཆེན་པོ་ལྡང་བ, quaking, trembling, shaking (*Mṅon.*): འཁྲུགས་མཁན *ḥkhrugs-mkhan* in *W.* having small cracks, flaws, of potter's ware (*Jä.*): འཁྲུགས་པ *ḥkhrugs-pa* = སྡང་བ *sdaṅ-wa* also ཁོང་ནས་ལྡང་བ *khoṅ-nas ldaṅ-wa* कुपित, प्रकोप, क्षुब्ध, क्षुभित was stirred up, agitated, confused, also rage, anger; greatly angry; passionate. འཁྲུགས་ཚད *ḥkhrugs-tshaḍ* fever caused by overwork and fatigue.

འཁྲུགས་ལོང *ḥkhrug-loṅ* खेटन war, fight: འཁྲུག་ལས *ḥkhrug-las* work of dispute; quarrel.

འཁྲུང་བ *ḥkhruṅ-wa* (*ṭhuṅ-wa*) or འཁྲུངས་པ *ḥkhruṅs-pa* resp. for སྐྱེ་བ *skye-wa* जात,

सम्भूत 1. to be born: སྐུ་འཁྲུངས་བ *sku-hkhruṅ-wa* = སྐུ་བལྟམས་པ *sku bltams-pa* to be born; also the birth of a great man, prince or lama: འཁྲུངས་རབས *hkhruṅs-rabs* = སྐྱེས་རབས *skyes-rabs* जातक birth stories or legends connected with one's birth. 2. to arise; come from: ཁྱེད་རང་གི་ཐུགས་ལ་འཁྲུངས་པའི་ཚིག words as they may just arise in the mind of yourself; ཏིང་ངེ་འཛིན་འཁྲུངས་པས *tiṅ-ṅe-hdsin hkhruṅs-pas* meditation arising: སྙིང་རྗེ་ཐུགས་ལ་འཁྲུངས་པ *sñiṅ-rje thugs-la hkhruṅs-pa* compassion arose in his mind. 3. to come up, shoot, sprout, grow (of seeds and plants) (*Jä.*).

འཁྲུངས་རབས་གསོལ་འདེབས *hkhruṅs-rabs gsol hdebs* reverence shown to a great lama or saint by enumerating the names of his supposed successive embodiments.

འཁྲུད་པ *hkhrud-pa* (*thud-pa*) क्षालन, pf. འཁྲུས *hkhrus*, fut. བཀྲུ *bkru*, to wash; to cleanse; to bathe; to wash off: གོས་དྲི་མ་འཁྲུད་པར་བྱེད *gos dri-ma hkhrud-par byed* the dirt of clothes should be washed out: ནད་ལ་བ-ཤལ་སྨན་བཏང་ནས་འཁྲུད་པར་བྱེད *nad-la* in illness, by giving purgatives, one may be cleansed: འཁྲུད་པར་བྱེད cause to be washed.

འཁྲུད་མ *hkhrud-ma* the washings of plates and dishes after dinner, which are given to pigs, dogs, &c.

འཁྲུན་ཆོད *hkhrun-chod* (*thun-chod*) = དོན་དག་ཐག་ཆོད *don dag thag-chod* finally deciding or determining any matter (*J. Zañ.*: དམག་དང་ཁ་མཆུ་ལྟ་བུ་ཐག་ཆོད *dmag-dañ kha-mchu lta-bu thag-chod* to decide upon a war or a law suit.

འཁྲུན་མཐོ་བ *hkhrun mtho-wa* = འཕང་མཐོ་བ *phañ mtho-wa* of high rank.

+ འཁྲུན་རིང *khrun-riñ* = དཀྱུས་སུ་རིང་བ *dkyus-su riñ-wa* lengthwise; in length.

འཁྲུལ I: *hkhrul* (*thul*) or འཁྲུལ་པ *hkrul-pa* भ्रम, विभ्रम, 1. भ्रान्ति sbst. mistake; frenzy; madness; error; illusion; also adj. mistaken; deranged; deluded: འཁྲུལ་གྱིས་ཕོགས་པ་མ་ཡིན mistakes are not profitable; འགྲོ་བ་འཁྲུལ་པ *hgro-wa hkhrul-pa* the deluded beings (of this world).; འཁྲུལ་བ *hkhrul-wa* to be mistaken; to be deceived: རང་སྣང་འཁྲུལ་པར་འདུག *rañ-snañ hkhrul-par hdug* I have mistaken; it was a deception of the senses; སྣང་འཁྲུལ་ཧམ་འཁྲུལ་སྣང *snañ hkhrul-ham hkhrul-snañ* illusion; delusion: འཁྲུལ་སྣང་ཅན *hkhrul-snañ can* delusive; erring: as a syn. of ནོར་བ *nor-wa*: ཁྱོད་ཅག་འཁྲུལ་པའི་འཇིག་རྟེན་པ *hhyod-cag hkhrul-pahi hjig-sten pa* ye deluded children of the world! 2. to be insane, deranged. Syn. of སྨོས་པ་འཁྲུལ་སོ *smos-pa hkhrul-so* occasion for making mistake; wrong way; peril.

འཁྲུལ II: (*thul*) in the words མིག་འཁྲུལ *mig-hkhrul* is a little different from འཕྲུལ *hphrul*; it applies to moral or intellectual mistakes as distinct from external blunders. In the same manner it differs from the word ནོར་བ *nor-wa* or ནོར་འཁྲུལ *nor hkhrul*. ནོར་བ *nor-wa* applies to external or phenomenal blunders: ནང་གི་སེམས་མ་འཁྲུལ་ན་ཕྱི་ཡི་བྱ་བ་མི་ནོར if the inner heart does not err, one's doings in the outside world will also not be wrong; अविद्या ignorance: མ་རིག་འཁྲུལ་པའི་དབང་གིས་འཁོར་བར་འཁྱམས *ma-rig hkhrul-wahi dwañ-gis hkhor-war hkhyams* by the influence of unrighteous errors (we) wander in the cycles of existence.

འཁྲུལ་འཁོར *hkhrul-hkhor* यन्त्र machine; contrivance; artifice. Acc. to *Cs.* this is same as འཕྲུལ་འཁོར *hphrul-hkhor*.

*འཁྲུལ་འཁོར *hkhrul-hkhor* यन्त्र (*Schr.*; *Kālac. T. 12ā.*).

འཁྲུལ་འཁོར་ཁྱིམ *hkhrl-hkor-mkhyim*, v. བཙོན་ཁང *btson-khañ*, a prison-house (*Mñon.*).

འཁྲུལ་འཁོར་མཁན་ *ḥkhrul-ḥkhor ṃkhan* a juggler.

འཁྲུལ་དགའ་ *Ḥkhrul-ḍgāḥ* (wrongly for འཕྲུལ་དགའ་ *ḥphrul-ḍgaḥ*) ལྷ་གནས་ निर्माण रतय: n. of a celestial mansion.

འཁྲུལ་སྣང་ *ḥkhrul-ṣnañ*, v. འཁྲུལ་བའི་སྣང་བ་ *ḥkhrul waḥi ṣnañ-wa*, illusive vision or exhibition.

Syn. འཁྲུལ་པའི་སེམས་ *ḥkhrul-waḥi semṣ*; འཁྲུལ་པའི་ཡིད་ *ḥkhrul-paḥi yiḍ* (*Ṃñon.*).

འཁྲུལ་བྱེད་མ་ *ḥkhrul byeḍ-ma* བུད་མེད་འདོད་མའི་མིང་ a woman that decoys others.

འཁྲུལ་མེད་ *ḥkhrul-med*, v. ནོར་མེད་ *nor-meḍ* or འཆུག་མེད་ *ḥchug-med*, unmistakeably; without mistake.

འཁྲུལ་ཞིག་ *ḥkhrul-shig*, སྟོང་ཉིད་རྟོགས་པའི་བླ་མ་འམ་གང་ཟག་ *ṣtoñ-ñiḍ ṛtogṣ-paḥi ḅla-ma ḥam gañ-zag* a lama or any person who meditates on the theory of emptiness (*i.e.*, the voidity of all nature).

འཁྲུལ་གཞི་ *ḥkhrul-gshi* cause or basis of error; fundamental mistake. It is usually illustrated thus: If one mistakes a fine rope for a snake, the rope is the basis or cause of mistake, and འཁྲུལ་ཤེས་ *ḥkhrul-çeṣ* is the idea or notion of a snake conveyed to the mind by the sight of the rope: ཐག་པ་མཐོང་ནས་སྦྲུལ་འཛིན་གྱི་ཤེས་པ་སྐྱེས་པ་ནི་འཁྲུལ་ཤེས་ཡིན་ཏེ། དེ་བཞིན་དུ་བདག་ཅག་མ་རིག་འཁོར་བའི་སེམས་ཅན་རྣམས་མི་བདེན་པ་བདེན་པར་བཟུང་། མི་རྟག་པ་ལ་རྟག་པ་བཟུང་། སྡུག་བསྔལ་བ་ལ་བདེ་བར་བཟུང་སྟེ་འཁྲུལ་འཁོར་བ་འདི་ཡིན *thag-pa ṃthoñ-naṣ ṣbrul-ḥjin-gyi çeṣ-pa ṣkyeṣ-pa ni ḥkhrul-çes yin-te, de-ḅshin-du ḅdag-cag ma-rig ḥkhor-waḥi sems-can ṛnamṣ mi-ḅden-pa ḅden-par ḅzuñ, mi-ṛtag-pa la ṛtag-pa ḅzuñ, ṣdug-ḅṣñal-wa la ḅde-war ḅzuñ-ṣte ḥkhrul-waṣ ḥkhor-wa ḥdi yin* in the same manner we animated beings, deluded by *Avidyā*, mistake falsehood for truth, the transient for the permanent, misery for happiness; hence this transmigratory existence.

འཁྲུལ་ཡས་ *ḥkhrul-yaṣ* (གྲངས) a very large number.

འཁྲེགས་ *ḥkhregṣ*=སྲ་བ་ *sṛa-wa* प्रकृढ very stiff or hard.

འཁྲིན་པ *ḥkhren-pa* (*ṭhen-pa*)=ཞེན་པ་ *shen-pa* desire; passion; to wish; to long for: 1. ཟས་སྐོམ་འཁྲན་པ་ *zaṣ-ṣkom ḥkhran-pa* to wish for food and drink. 2. to look upon with envy; jealousy (*Jä.*).

འཁྲོ་བ་ *ḥkhro-wa* pf. ཁྲོས་ *khroṣ* to be angry.

འཁྲོལ་བ་ *ḥkhrol-wa* (*ṭhol-wa*), pf and fut. དཀྲོལ་ *ḍkrol*, imp. ཁྲོལ་ *khrol* 1. to cause to sound; to make a noise; play: *rol-mo ḥkhrol-wa* to play on a musical instrument; *dril-bu ḥkhrol-wa* to ring a bell. 2. vb. intrans. to sound; resound: ཁ་ཐུད་དཀྲོལ་ the avalanche resounded; རྒྱ་ལོང་འཁྲོག་ཤིང་ *ṛgya-loñ khrog-çiñ* a rumbling in the bowels (*Med.*); སྦོ་འཁྲོག་ *ṣbo-ḥkhrog* in the belly: འཁྲོག་ཁྲོག་ *ḥkhrog-khrog* roaring; rushing; buzzing (*Jä.*).

འཁྲོགས་ *ḥkhrogṣ* dislocated: རྒན་མོ་པུས་ཅིག་འཁྲོགས་ཀྱང་འགྲོ་སྙིང་འདོད་ the old woman yet wishes to walk, though her knee has been dislocated (*Ṛdsa. 17.*).

ག

ག I : *ga* is the third letter of the Tibetan alphabet corresponding with Sanskrit ग. It is pronounced as soft *k* when alone or when placed without a prefix at the beginning of a word or syllable. When used as a final letter it sounds as *k* or is often barely pronounced. If a prefix precede ག or if it carry a surmounting letter, it sounds as a hard *g*. When used to represent a numerical figure it signifies the third, *i.e.*, the ordinal III, and as such is generally used in marking volumes of books, &c. ག *ga* is sometimes used as an affixed particle of a word to complete it, as in ཡལ་ག *yal-ga*, the branch of a tree.

ག II: in mystical language signifies born of a goat; also a he-goat : བསང་སྐད་ལ་ར་སྐྱེས་ཡིན *bsañ skad-la ra-skyes yin* (*K. g.* ཁ, *28*).

ག III: 1. in mystio Buddhism ག *ga* means the hidden entity or the essence of Buddha : ག་ཞེས་པ་ནི་དེ་བཞིན་གཤེགས་པའི་གསང་བའི་སྙིང་པོ་སྟེ། སེམས་ཅན་ཐམས་ཅད་ལ་སངས་རྒྱས་ཀྱི་རང་བཞིན་ཡོད་ཅེས་པའོ༎ that which is styled *ga* being the hidden essence of the Tathāgata, it may be said (ཅེས་པ) that all sensate beings have the nature of Buddha (*K. my.* ཀ *207*). 2. ག་ནི་བགྲོད་དང་བགྲོད་མེན་ཡིན as to *ga* it moves and it is also motionless : རྒྱུ་ཡང་ག་ཡིན་སྒྲ་ཡི་ངོ་བོ་ཉིད "the cause is *ga*, the real nature or origin of sound" (*Hbrom. 88*). Again we read definitions of this sort: ག་ནི་གང་ལ་གང་གང་ཆགས་མེད་པ "that which belongs to no place anywhere is *ga*" (*Hbrom. 88*).

ག་ཁྲལ *ga-khral* (*ga-thal*) tax, duty (on cattle, butter, &c.) (*Jä.*).

ག་ག *ga-ga* a title of honour in *W.* (*Jä.*).

ག་ག་ཚིལ *ga-ga tshil* tickling : ག་ག་ཚིལ་བྱེད་པ, to tickle: སྔོན་གྲྭ་པ་བཅུ་དྲུག་གིས་གྲྭ་པ་གཅིག་ལ་ག་ག་ཚིལ་བྱས་པས། རང་དབང་མེད་པར་ གད་མོ་མང་བོ་ཤོར་ནས་རླུང་གྱེན་དུ་འཐུགས་ཏེ་དུས་ལ་བབ་པོ ༎ in ancient time sixteen monks tickled one monk and from the excessivo laugther he involuntarily sent forth, the mystio wind passing upwards inside him, his end came" (*K. du.* ཅ, *228*).

ᚐ ག་གེ་མོ *Ga-ge-mo* 1. n. of a certain place in Tibet. 2. ཆེ་གེ་མོ *chege-mo*, such a one; such a thing; such and such (*Cs.*).

ག་གོན *Ga-gon* त्रपुष 1. one of the two merchants whom Buddha met immediately after his six years' asceticism under the *Bodhi* treo. 2. ག་གོན་གྱི་རྒྱལ་པོ *Ga-gon-gyi rgyal-po* घोयाख the king of a country in Southern India. 3. a melon (acc. *Cs.*, *Lex.*, cucumber; others; barley) (*Jä.*).

ག་འགྲིག *ga-hgrig* (*ga-dig*) a saddle; སྒ་སྒྲིག *sga-sgrig* equipment of a riding horse.

ག་ཅེན *ga-cen* or ག་ཆེན *ga-chen* some or a good many; good deal (*Jä.*).

ག་ཆད *ga-chad* involuntarily; without causo, *e.g.*, to weep (*Med.*, *Ja.*).

ག་ཆད་པ *ga chad-pa* fatigued; very tired; ཡི་མུག་ག་ཆད་པ, ཞུ་ཟུག་ག་ཆད་པ giving up in despair; being quite exhausted (*D. R.*).

ག་སྙོད *ga-snod* अजाजि cummin seed, *Nigella Indica.*

‡ **ག་ཏ** *ga-ta* गाता or गाथा ག་ཏའི་སྡེ་ཚན *ga-tahi sde tshan* a kind of Indian handwriting, evidently referring to the *Gatha* or *Kaithi* character, in which the original *Māgadhi* used to be written. The Tibetan ག *ga* is ordinarily pronounced as *K*, hence ཀ་ཏ *ka-ta*, or *kaithi.*

‡ **ག་ད** *ga-da* गदा a club; a mace.

ག་དུར *ga-dur* an astringent medicinal root: རིམས་དང་གློ་ཚད་རྒྱུ་ནད་སེལ it removes remittent fever, diseases of the lungs and of the bowels.

ག་དོར *ga-dor*=གྭ་དོར *gwa-dor* also གོ་དོར *go-dor* the tender growthof fresh horn in the three animals, rhinoceros, stag, and antelope: *gwa-dor gsum-gyis rnag dañ chu-ser skem* the three *ga dor* dry up pus and yellowish discharges: ཤ་བའི་ག་དོར the growth of a new branch on a stag's horn (*Sch.*).

ག་འདྲས *ga-hdras*=གང་འདྲས *gañ-hdras* (colloq. "*gánde*") how? of what kind? what sort?

ག་ན *ga-na* (*ka-na*) གང་ན *gañ-na* कावन where? ག་ན་བ *ga-na-wa* and གང་ན་བ *gañ-na-wa*, the same as a sbst., the whereabouts of a person, his place of residence: རྒྱལ་པོ་ག་ན་བར་དེར་སོང་ he went here where the king was.

ག་ན་མེད *ga-na med* (in *W.*) absolutely; at all events: ག་ན་མེད་བཀལ་དགོས it must be sent by all means: ག་ན་མེད་ལོག་སླ་བཏང་ཡིན། I shall give it back at all events (*Jä.*).

‡ **ག་ཎ་པ་ཏི** *Ga-ṇa pa-ti* गणपति ལྷ་ཆེན་ཚོགས་བདག་གི་མིང་ *Lha-chen Tshogs-bdag-gi miñ* the name of the great God, called the Lord of the Multitude (*Sñag.*).

‡ **ག་བ་ཏ་བ་རི་ཎི** *Ga-wa ta-wa ri-ṇi* गवतवरिणि [कपोतवर्णी small cardamom]. Also the n. of a flower (*K. kon.* ཀ, *4*).

‡ **ག་བུར** *ga-bur* I: 1. n. of several plants, probably *Gentiana cherayta, Curcuma, Zerumbet,* &c. 2. ཧྲིང་ཤེལ་ག་བུར is a kind of stone like ཙོ་ཙང་ཧྲིང་ཤེལ (*Miñ. 4*).

ག་བུར II: कर्पूर, विधु camphor; ཤེལ་ག་བུར *çel ga-bur* crystal-like camphor; མང་ག་བུར *mañ ga-bur* camphor resembling yak's lard in appearance; *ga-bur tsha-wa rgyas-pa thog-hbab gcod* camphor, where the fever has increased, cures by lowering its height; *rñiñ-shiñ shan-pahi tsha-wa rtsa-nad gcod* it also cures long-standing fever and disease of the fundament; *ga-bur ti-los glo-rims tshad-pa sel* the kind of camphor called Tilo cures inflamation of the lungs and fever.

Syn. ཁ་བའི་ཕྱེ་མ *kha-wahi phye-ma*; འོད་དཀར་ཅན *hod-dkar-can*; ནུས་ལྡན *nus-ldan*; སྤྲིན་གྱི་སྙིང་པོ *sprin-gyi sñiñ-po* ཟླ་བའི་ཐལ་བ *zla-wahi thal-*; *wa*; རོའི་གེ་སར *rohi-ge-sar*; ཤིང་གི་སྙིང་པོ *çiñ-gi sñiñ-po* (*Mñon.*).

ག་བུར་ནག་པོ *ga-bur nag-po* defined as ཕག་བྲུན་མེ་ལ་བསྲེགས་པའི་ཐལ་བ *phag-brun me-la bsregs-pahi thal-wa.* 1. the ashes of the burnt dung of pigs. 2. a secret name (*Miñ. 4*).

ག་བུར་འཛིན་པ *ga-bur hdsin-pa* कर्पूरधर meton. ཟླ་བ *zla-wa* the moon.

ག་བྲ *ga-bra* (*ga-ṭah*) n. of a medicine; a twig; also the fresh shoot on a tree:

ga-bra rluṅ-tshad rims-nad sel-war byed (this medicine) removes the epidemic fevers and the heat induced by *rluṅ* (wind).

‡ ག་མུ *ga-mu* from the Sans. गम go; in mystical language go or go away! (*K. g.* ཁ *27*).

ག་མོ་བྱི་ལ *ga-mo byi-la* n. of a species of wild cat: ག་མོ་བྱི་ལས་ཉལ་ནས་བྱིའུ་འཛིན the *ga-mo byi-la* catches little birds by lying in wait (*Rdsa.*).

ག་ཙམ *ga-tsam*=ཇི་ཙམ *ji-tsam* how much; how many; how long; interr. and correl., as much as, *e.g.*, as much as you like.

ག་བཙོན *ga-btson* (in *W.*) an irruption of the skin (*Jä.*).

ག་ཚོད *ga-tshod* how much; colloq. "*rin di ka tsŏ*" what is the price; how much? In Sikkim *gong-di ka-dzŏ-mo?* (*Snd. Hbk.*).

ག་ཛན་ཏ *ga-dsan-ta* गजन्त a precious stone used in curing infectious fevers and other diseases, also to relieve one from the influence of malignant spirits.

ག་ཤ *ga-sha*=ག་གཤའ *ga-gshah* or ག་ཤ *ga-ça*, more properly the last word, *i.e.*, ག་ཤ *ga-ça* signifies བཤད་གད *bshad-gad* a laughter, jest, joke: ག་ཤ་དང་རྩེད་མོ་རྩེ they jest and play: དེ་རིང་ག་ཤ་མི་འདུག he is not in good humour, or in good spirits, to-day (*Jä.*); also "to-day there is no fun."

ག་ཟུག *ga-zug* (in *W.*) how, interr. and correl (*Jä.*).

ག་གཟི *ga-gzi* squinting (in *W.*).

གའུ *gahu* सम्पुट an amulet; a brooch containing charms (v. གམ *gam*).

Syn. ཁ་སྦྱར *kha-sbyar* (*Mṅon.*).

གའུ་ཁ་སྦྱར *gahu kha-sbyar* charm box the lids of a which are joined edge to edge: མི་དབང་ཁྱོད་བཞུགས་གནས་ཤིན་ཏུ་དབེན་པ་ཉི, གནམ་ས་གའུ་ཁ་སྦྱར་ལྟ་བུས་མཛེས O Mi-wang (O king), thy residence is very solitary and so beautiful, as if the heaven and the earth kiss each other there, like the lids of an amulet (*Hbrom. 89*).

གའུ་ལེ *gahu-le* account book; list (of cases, also of cash and balance); also a short note kept on the margin: ལོགས་སུ *logs-su* in a separate place that is not in the body of a book, but on the foot or margin or corner, *i.e.*, ཟུར་དུ *zur-du*, of a book or note-book: ཟླ་ཚེས་གྲངས་འདི་ཙམ་རྫོང་གི་ཁུར་ལེན་བྱེད་པའི་བར་ལ་ཁྲིམས་ཤགས་འདི་ཙམ་བྱུང་ཟེར་བའི་འཕོར་ཆེ་ཆུང་ཁྲིན་བསྡོམས་ནས་བྱས་བྱུང་སྐར་གྱི་གའུ་ལེར་འཇོག་པ since the date of the month, etc., of taking over charge of the *Rdsoṅ* (District office) as many criminal cases as may be, and the receipts large and small all bound together should be kept in the registration book (*Rtsii.; G. Sndg.*).

‡ ག་ཡ་ག་རིའི་མདོ *Ga-ya gau-rihi mdo* a *Sûtra* delivered by the Buddha on the mountain of Gayā Gauri.

ག་ཡིག *ga-yig* गवर्ण the letter ग *g*.

‡ ག་ར་ཁ་ཏཎ་ཌུ་ལའི་རྩ་བ *ga-ra kha-tan ḍu lahi rtsa-wa* कर्कतण्डुलमूल excellent rice; the root of a kind of plant: ག་ར་ཁ་ཏཎ་ཌུ་ལའི་རྩ་བ་དང་རྟ་དྲི་དང་ཏིལ་དང་ནས་དང་བུ་རམ་རྣམས་མཉམ་པོར་བྱས་ནས་ཟོས་ན་གཞོན་ནུ་བར་འགྱུར་རོ by taking a confection made of equal quantities of the root of *Garka Tandula rta-dri*; sesame, barley and treacle, one becomes youthful (*K. g.* ཙ *45*).

ག་རི *ga-ri*, for དགའ་རིས *dgah-ris*, ག་ཤ *ga-sha* (in *W.*) dejected: ག་རི་མི་རག I am in low spirits (*Ja.*).

ག་རུ *ga-ru* in colloquial གང་དུ *gañ-du* whither; which way; to which place; where?

† **ག་རུ་ཌ** *ga-ru-da* गरुड; =ཁྱུང *khyuñ* the fabulous chief of the feathered race.

ག་རེ *ga-re* 1. in Lhasa very com. colloq. form for "what," sounded *káre*. 2. where, whence: ག་རེ་འདི་འདྲ་ཨ་ཀྱང་རང་དྲག་བྱུང *ga-re ḥdi-ḥdṛa a-kyañ rañ-dṛag byuñ* whence comes this oppression, over-powering (*Ṟdsa. 10*).

ག་རོ *Ga-ro* རྒྱ་གར་ན་ཡོད་པའི་ཡུལ་ཞིག་གི་མིང n. of a place in India; the Garo hills (*Ḇsam. 28*).

ག་ལ *ga-la* 1. येन whither: བཅོམ་ལྡན་འདས་ག་ལ་བ་དེར་ཐལ་མོ་སྦྱར་བ་ཕྱོགས་སུ་ཕྱག་འཚལ་ནས་ येन भगवान् तेन प्रणम्य with the palms of the hands joined he bowed in the direction where the Victorious One was. 2.=ཇི་ལ *ji-la* for what; owing to what: ག་ལ་ཕན to what does this serve? of what use is this? ག་ལ་འགྲོ་གིན་ཡིན་པ where are (you or they) going?

† **ག་ལ་གོ་ལི་ཀ** *ga-la go-li-ka* गलगोलिक n. of an insect which subsists, it is said, by inhaling the air only (*K. d.* ཀ *464*).

ག་ལེ *ga-le* शनैः शनैः slowly, softly, gently. To a departing guest one says: ག་ལེ་ཕེབ "*ka-le pe'p*" go gently. To the host you answer: ག་ལེ་བཞུགས "*ka-le shu*" stay quietly, remain in peace! ག་ལེ་ཤོག *ga-le çog* come slowly or gently: གཏམ་དཔེ་ལ་ག་ལེ་ག་ལེ་འགྲོ་ན་བོང་བུས་རྒྱ་ནག་བསྐོར་ནས་ཡོང it is a common saying (in Tibet) that by walking slowly and slowly the ass can travel all round China.

ག་ལོག *ga-log* (in *W.*) squinting.

ག་ཤ I: *ga-ça* laughter: གད་མོ་བགད *gad-mo ḇgad*, ག་ཤར་བཅུག *ga-çar ḇcug* to cause laughter.

ག་ཤ་སྒྲོག *ga-ça-sgrog* loud laughter; *ga-ça sgrog-ciñ glu-gar rol-mo ḇbul* loudly laughing they danced, sang, and made music (*A. 11*).

ག་ཤ II: n. of a place in Upper Tibet (*A. 20*).

ག་ཤ III: v. ག་ཤ *ga-sha* उत्तरीयवस्त्र a raiment used by *Tantrik* priests.

ག་ཤ IV: a string of beads; a necklace; a string of human skulls or bone-bits worn by *Tantrik* Lamas: ཁ་ནས་ཁྲག་འཛག་མི་མགོ་འི་ཕྲེང་བ་ཡི་ག་ཤ་རབ་འབྱུང་མི་བཟོད་བདུད་དཔུང་གི་ང་རྒྱལ་དྲེགས་པ་འཇོམས་པ་ཁྱོད་ལ་བསྟོད blood drops from her mouth, a string of human heads hangs down from her neck, to thee be my praise who hast subdued the intolerable pride and arrogance of the host of demons (*Choi-g.*).

ག་ཤར *ga-çar* 1. defined in these passages; ཕྱོགས་གཅིག་དཔུང་པ་ལ *phyogs-gcig ḏpuñ-pa la*; ཕྱོགས་གཅིག་མཚན་ཧོག་ལ *phyogs-gcig ṃtshan-ḫog la*; གཞུ་དཀར་གཅིག་ག་ཤར་གྱོན་པ *gshu-ḏ gcig ga- kar çar gyon-pa* (*A. 135*). Girth or rope hung across the breast and the shoulder in order to draw or carry anything; also a dog harness; a shoulder-belt worn as a badge of dignity by constables and the like officers. 2. སྒོམ་ཐག *sgom-thag*, the cord worn round the shoulder and the waist at the time of meditation. ག་ཤར་དང་གཤམ་ཐབས་ཀྱི་མཛེས་པ *ga-çar dañ gçam-thabs-kyi ṃdses-pa* (*D. R.*) Looking nice (on account) of (his) *ga-çar* and petticoat.

ག་ཤས *ga-ças*=ཁ་ཤས *kha-ças* some; part; a few, com. in colloq.

ག་ཤེད *ga-çeḏ* 1. prob. གང་ཤེད *gañ-çeḏ* uncertain; not definitely known. 2. an approximate but uncertain direction, region or quarter: ག་ཤེད་གཅིག་ལ་ཡོད it is at a certain place; it is somewhere: ཞིབ་མོ་མི་འཆད་པར་ག་ཤེད་དུ་ཕྱིན་གྱི་སོང without explaining minutely (*i.e.*, the particulars), he proceeded instantly somewhere (*A. 135*).

ག་ཤེལ *ga-çel* glass beads; glass pearls (*Sch.*).

གཱ *Gā* n. of a *Dākinī*, a goddess (*K. g.* ཁ, *179*).

གྭ་པ *gwa-pa* the white mark or patch on the forehead of the *kyañ* (the wild ass of Tibet).

+ **གག** *gag* 1. silver in bars, ingots, small pieces, &c., uncoined (in *W.*). 2. wad; wadding (for loading muskets) (*Jä.*).

གག་པ *gag-pa*=ལྷོག་པ *lhog-pa* or གག་ལྷོག *gag-lhog* is a swelling in the throat; a quinsy: *nad mi dañ dud-hgrohi ske-dañ mgrin-pa-la skrañ-nas rnag thon-te drag-yod* is a malady of men and animals in which the neck and throat become swollen, but matter issuing forth, it is eased; གག་ནས་ཤི་ཡོད death occurs from obstruction. སྤྱིར་གག་ལྷོག་ཅེས་མིང་སོ་སོར་བཤད་ཀྱང་ངོ་བོ་གཉན་ནད་དུ་གཅིག་རིམས་ནད་ཀྱི་གྲས *spyir gag-lhog-ces miñ so-sor bçad-kyañ ño-wo gñan-nad du-gcig rims-nad-kyi gras* though the disease in general is differently expressed by the names *gag* and *lhog*, its real nature is but one among pestilential diseases and it belongs to the class of (विषम-ज्वर) fatal fevers.

གག་ཚེ *gag-tshe*=བྱ་གག *bya-gag* a water fowl (*Cs.*).

གགས *gags* प्रतिबद्ध obstructed.

གང་ག་ཆུང I: *gañ-ga-chuñ* a kind of flower which resembles a chorten (chaitya) in shape, growing in the sandy crevices of rocks in Tibet. It is used as an antidote against poison and also diarrhœa, གཡའ་གསེབ་བྱེ་མའི་ལོགས་ལ་སྐྱེ *gyah-gseb bye-mahi logs-la skye* གང་ག་ཆུང་གིས་དུག་དང་ཚ་འཁྲུ་གཅོད *gañ ga chuñ-gañ-ga chuñ-gis dug dañ tsha-hkhru gcod*.

གང་གཱ *gañga* གངྒཱ *gañgā* गङ्गा the river Ganges; གང་གཱའི་ལྷ་མོ *Gañ-gāhi Lha-mo* गङ्गा-देवी the goddess of the river Gaŋgā. Its different names are:—ཡན་ལག་བརྒྱད་ལྡན *Yan-lag brgyan-ldan*, འཆི་མེད་ཆབ *Hchi-med chab*, ནམ་མཁའི་ཆུ་བོ *Nam-mkhahi chu-bo*, དྲག་པོའི་ཐོད *Drag-pohi thod*, ཛ་ཧྣུའི་བུ་མོ *Dsa-uuhi bu-mo* (जाह्नवी), རྒྱུན་གསུམ་པ *Rgyun-gsum-pa*, ལམ་གསུམ་འགྲོ *Lam-gsum hgro*, གླང་ཆེན་ཁ་འབབ *Glan-chen kha-hbab* (गोमुखी), འཇིགས་སྡེ་མ *Hjigs-sde ma*, ཁྱབ་འཇུག་རྐང་པ *Khyab-hjug rkañ-pa*, ཆུ་བྱིན་མ *Chu-byin-ma*, སྐལ་ལྡན་ཤིང་རྟའི་བུ་མོ *Skal-ldan çiñ-rtahi bu-mo* (भागीरथी), ལྷ་ཡི་ཆུ་བོ *Lha-yi chu-bo* (*Mñon.*).

གང་གཱ་འཛིན I: *gañ-gā hdsin* गङ्गाधर an epithet of S'iva. He who holds Gaŋ-gā on his head, *i.e.*, from whose head the Ganges flows: མཐོ་རིས་ཀྱི་གནས་ཐམས་ཅད་བསྐལ་པའི་མེས་བསྲེགས་པའི་སྐབས་སུ་ལྷ་མོ་གང་གཱ་ལྷུང་ནས་བྱུང་བ་ན་ནམ་མཁའ་ལ་རལ་པ་བརྐྱངས་ནས་རལ་པའི་སྟེང་དུ་བཟུང་བས་སོ *mtho-ris-kyi gnas thams-cad bskal-pahi mcs bsrcgs-pahi skabs-su Lha-mo Gañ-gā lhuñ-nas byuñ-wa-na nam-mkhah la ral-pa bkyañs-nas ral-pahi steñ-du bzuñ-was-so* when all the celestial regions were burnt by the fire of the *Kalpa*, Gaŋgā as goddess appeared on this earth having fallen from heaven. Her locks were spread out in the sky and held up aloft by S'iva (for which he is called Gañgādhara, the holder of Gañgā) (*Mñon.*).

གང་གཱ་འཛིན II: རྒྱ་མཚོ་ཆེན་པོ *rgya-mtsho chen-po* the great ocean which holds the entire discharge of Gaŋgā (*Mñon.*).

གང *gañ* what, which.

གང་གི་དུས *gañ-gi-dus* when; at which time.

. གང་གི་ཕྱིར *gañ-gi-phyir* यस्मात्, यत्कृते for which; for the sake or reason of which.

གང་ཉིད *gañ-ñid* यदेव whichever; whatever.

གང་འཐད *gañ-hthad* = གང་འགྲིགས *gañ-hgrigs* what (you) like; also what suits you? དེར་ཚེ་སྲོག་ལ་བར་དུ་གཅོད་པ་བྱུང་ནའང་ཅུ་ཅག་ལ་ཁག་མི་འབྱུང་སྟེ་གང་འཐད་གང་རིགས་ཞེས་གཙོ་བོ་གཅིག་གིས་སྨྲས་པ། even if any accident happened to life there, to us no hardship occurring, wo can do whatever suits us, so ono *Tso-wo* expressed himself (*Hbrom. 136*).

གང་དག *gañ-dag* केचन some; གང་དག་གི་ཕྱིར *gañ-dag-gi phyir* येषां कृते for whom or what; for the sake of whom or what.

གང་དག་ཉིད *gañ-dag-ñid* यदेव whichover.

གང་དག་འདིར *gañ-dag-hdir* यावित, यदद those two who are here; all those here; whoever present.

གང་དུ *gañ-du* कुत्र, यत्र where? whero.

གང་དུའང་ *gañ-duhañ* कचित् at whatever time; whorevor; seldom; where.

གན་དྲན་དྲན་དུ་བཤད་པ *gan dran-dran-du bçad-pa* = བརྫུན་བཤད་པ *brdsun bçad-pa* to speak at random; to say what occurs in the mind; to speak falsehood.

. གང་འདྲ *gañ-hdra* यादृशो how, like what: གང་འདྲ་མཐོང་ *gañ-hdra mthoñ* what have you soen?

གང་ན *gañ-na* क्वचन where?

གང་རྣམས་ཀྱི *gañ-rnams-kyi* येषा of what; pertaining to what?

གང་མགོ *gañ-mgo* (in *C.*) bowl of a tobacco-pipe; གང་མཇུག *gañ-mjug* mouthpiece or tip of it.

གང་པོར *gañ-por* in a lump, mass.

གང་བ I: *gañ-wa* = ཁེངས་པ *kheñs-pa* पूर्ण to fill; to make full; filled up; also piled up: གང་བའམ་བརྩེགས་པ *gañ-waham brtsegs-pa* piled up or mado full.

Syn. ཚན་ཅན *tshan-can*; ཁེངས *kheñs*; བྱུར་བུ *byur-bu*; ཕྱུར་བུ *phyur-bu* (*Mñon.*).

གང་བ II: अलम्, पूर्ण finished; completed; ལུང་ཆུས་གང་བ *luñ-chus gañ-wa* a valley filled with water: ཟླ་བ་ཉ་གང་བ "tho moon as full fish"; in the fullness of the crescent.

གང་བ་མེད་པ *gañ-wa med-pa* असम्पूर्ण incomplete.

* གང་བ་བཟང་པོ *gañ-wa bzañ-po* पूर्णभद्र (*Schr.; Tā. 2, 181*) completely happy or gentle; also n. of a serpent demon.

* གང་བའི་ཟླ་བ *gañ-wahi zla-wa* पूर्णचन्द्र (*Schr.; Bull. 1848, 298*); lit. the full moon; n. of a *Bodhisattara*.

གང་བུ *gañ-bu* वल्लरि, मञ्जरि fresh shoots of leaves; a pod or sheath; also cluster of buds. Acc. to *Sch.* flower bud: འབྲུ་གང་བུ་ཅན *hbru gañ-bu-can* grains which have husks such as whoat, sesamum, &c.: འོད་ཟེར་གྱི་གང་བུར་འཁྲིལ་ནས enveloping himself in a veil of rays; wrapping himself in a sheath of light.

གང་བྱེད *gañ-byed* यत् करोति whatever he does, has been doing, is doing.

གང་མོས *gañ-mos* नाना 1. various; difforent sorts. 2. གང་འདོད *gañ-hdod* whatever is wished for.

གང་ཙམ *gañ-tsam* a small quantity; not a considerable quantity.

གང་ཙུག་ཡིན *gañ-tsug-yin* = གང་ནས་ཡིན *gañ-nas-yin* or གང་ན་སྡོད་མཁན་ཡིན *gañ-na sdod mkhan-yin*; ཁྱེད་གང་ཙུག་ཡིན་གར་འགྲོ་དྲིས་པས *khyed gañ-tsug-yin gar-hgro dri-pas* he asked whence are you; whither are you going (*A. 131*).

གང་ཞིག *gañ-shig* यः, यत् which.

གང་ཞེ་བསྟན་པ *gaṅ-she bstan-pa* य उपदिष्टः which has been explained, shewn.

གང་ཟག I: (ཞལ་ཟག *shal-zag*) tobacco-pipe, not the *hukka*, but a long straight sort, similar to the European smoking pipe, generally made of metal.

གང་ཟག *gaṅ-zag* II: 1. पुद्गल, पुद्गल, भूतात्मन्। पूर्यति गलति च इति पुद्गलः that which becomes full and then undergoes decay (Sāṁ.); an animated being; a corporeal being that is subject to decay and destruction. 2. man, as an intellectual being; a person: གང་ཟག་གཞན་གྱིས་བརྡ་སྤྲད་པས *gaṅ-zag gshan-gyis brda sprad-pas* another person describing it to you (opposite to what we know by our own perception and observation), hence a philosophical term for "self": བསྟན་བཅོས་ལ་མཁས་པའི་གང་ཟག་རྣམས learned or lettered men; men of science, especially in relation to religion: ཆོས་ཕྱི་བཤོལ་བྱེད་པའི་གང་ཟག་རྣམས men who postpone religion, not troubling themselves about it: འཕགས་པའི་གང་ཟག་རྣམས་ཀྱི་རྒྱལ་པོ the prince of the reverend (band of) persons, *i.e.*, Buddha: ལོག་ལྟ་ཅན་གྱི་གང་ཟག inferior heretical people: གང་ཟག་ཕལ་པ *gaṅ-zag phal-pa* or ཐ་མལ་པ *tha-mal-pa*, common or vulgar people (*Jä.*).

གང་ཟག་བཞི *gaṅ-zag bshi* the four kinds of human beings or higher beings are—(1) तमस्तमः परायणः; མུན་ཁྲོད་ནས་མུན་ཁྲོད་དུ་འགྲོ་བ *mun-khrod nas mun-khrod du hgro-wa* that go on from darkness to darkness; (2) ज्योतिः परायणः; མུན་ཁྲོད་ནས་སྣང་བར་འགྲོ་བ *mun-khrod nas snaṅ-war hgro-wa* that go from darkness unto light; (3) ज्योतिस्तमःपरायणः; སྣང་བ་ནས་མུན་ཁྲོད་དུ་འགྲོ་བ *snaṅ-wa nas mun-khrod du hgro-wa* that go again from light into darkness; (4) ज्योतिर्ज्योतिःपरायणः; སྣང་བ་ནས་སྣང་བར་འགྲོ་བ *snaṅ-wa nas snaṅ-war hgro-wa*, that advance from light to a greater enlightenment. The term གང་ཟག *gaṅ-zag* has sixteen different synonyms:—བདག *bdag*; སྲོག *srog*; སེམས་ཅན *sems-can*; སྐྱེ་བ *skye-wa*; གསོ་བ *gso-wa*; སྐྱེས་བུ *skyes-bu*; ཤེད་བདག *çed-bdag*; ཤེས་ལས་སྐྱེས *çes-las skyes*; मानव, मनुज man; བྱེད་པ་པོ *byed-pa-po*; བྱེད་དུ་འཇུག་པ་པོ *byed-du hjug-pa-po*; ཚོར་བ་པོ *tshor-wa-po*; ཤེས་པ་པོ *çes-pa-po*; མཐོང་བ་པོ *mthoṅ-wa-po*; ཟ་བ་པོ *za-wa-po*; སློང་བ་པོ *sloṅ-wa-po* (*Mṅon.*). These are all applied to signify an animate being. There are two kinds of གང་ཟག, ordinary and extraordinary; the ordinary གང་ཟག literally means that which is subject to decay, from གང *gaṅ*, what, and ཟག *zag*, decay. The Buddhist meaning is as follows:—(1) རང་རྒྱུད་སྡིག་པ་ཉོན་མོངས་ཀྱིས་གང་ཞིང་ཡོན་ཏན་དང་དགེ་བའི་རིགས་གསོག་མི་ཐུབ་པར་ཟག་འགྲོ་བས་སེམས་ཅན་ཕལ་བའི་གང་ཟག *raṅ-rgyud sdig-pa ñon-moṅs kyis gaṅ shiṅ yon-tan daṅ dge-wahi rigs gsog mi-thub-par zag hgro-was sems-can phal-wahi gaṅ-zag* one's own nature being filled (གང *gaṅ*) with sin he cannot acquire and retain virtue, which ཟག *zag* leaks out or decays, therefore an ordinary living being is called གང་ཟག *gaṅ-zag*; (2) རང་རྒྱུད་དགེ་བ་དང་བཟང་པོའི་ཡོན་ཏན་ཐམས་ཅད་ཀྱིས་གང་ཞིང་ཉོན་མོངས་ཀྱི་སྐྱོན་ཐམས་ཅད་ཟག་འགྲོ་བས་སངས་རྒྱས་གང་ཟག *raṅ-rgyud dge-wa daṅ bzaṅ-pohi yon-tan thams-cad-kyis gaṅ-shiṅ ñon-moṅs-kyi skyon thams-cad zag hgro-was saṅs-rgyas gaṅ-zag* Buddha is གང་ཟག because his nature is full of all virtues or merits and sin has been thrown out of it or has altogether been destroyed; (3) རང་རྒྱུད་ལ་ཡོན་ཏན་གྱི་རིགས་གང་བྱུང་བ་མི་ཉམས་པར་བྱེད་པ་དང་སྐྱོན་གྱི་རིགས་བྱུང་བ་རྣམས་ཐབས་ཀྱི་ཟག་ས་སུ་བཙུག་པ་ནི་ཐེག་ཆེན་ཐེག་དམན་ལམ་ཞུགས་པ་གང་ཟག་རྣམས་ས་དེ་ཡང་གྲུབ་མཐའ་སྨྲ་བ་དང་ལྟ་བ་འདོད་ཚུལ་འཆད་པ་ཙམ་ལ་ཐེག་ཆེན་གང་ཟག when one's own nature retains whatever virtue it possessed undeteriorated and whatever faults there was in it have been thrown out from exertion, one has entered either the *Mahā yānā* or *Hīnayāna* path. Persons in such a stage, whatever docrtine or theory they may hold for salvation, belong indeed of the *Mahāyāna.* In གང་ཟག *gañ-zag* of the ordinary kind his very nature is གང་ *gañ, i.e.,* filled with deeds (*las*), sin, suffering, and misery; moreover, all virtue and talents having become exhausted, *i.e.,* ཟག *zag*, his animated being becomes what is called *Pudgal.* In the strict sense of the word, a Buddha is also a *Pudgala,* though of the extraordinary kind, he on the contrary being full of virtues and talents and all defects, sins, &c., being exhausted in him. The following are the twenty གང་ཟག *gañ-zag* (*Pudgala*) of the *Çrāvaka* School:—(1) स्रोतआपन्न; རྒྱུན་དུ་ཞུགས་པ *rgyun-du shugs-pa* one having entered the regular course performs *Samādhi* (deep meditation); (2) सप्तकृत्भवपरम; དེ་ལྟར་ཐོགས་ན་སྲིད་པ་ལན་བདུན་པ *de-ltar thogs-na srid-pa lan bdun-pa* after having thus spiritually cultured the mind he has to pass into seven births in the world; (3) कुलंकुल; རིགས་ནས་རིགས་སུ་སྐྱེ་བ *rigs-nas rigs-su skye-wa* after the second stage, his birth is ensured in his own state, *i.e.,* if he is a god he is reborn as a god, if man he is reborn as a man, but he never goes to any lower stage of birth; (4) सकृदागामी; ལན་གཅིག་ཕྱིར་འོང་བ *lan-gcig phyir hoñ-wa* (as such) he has only once to come to this world for doing good; (5) एकवीचिक; བར་ཆད་གཅིག་པ *bar-chad gcig-pa* he has only one interruption before full fruition; (6) अनागामि; ཕྱིར་མི་འོང་བ *phyir mi-hoñ-wa* he will not come again to this existence; (7) अन्तरा परिनिर्व्वायिन्; བར་མ་དོར་ཡོངས་སུ་མྱ་ངན་ལས་འདའ་བ *bar-ma-dor yoñs-su mya-ñan las hdah-wa* he will attain to *Nirvāṇa* not from this life but from the intermediate state or *Bardo*; (8) साभिसंस्कारपरिनिर्व्वायिन्; མངོན་པར་འདུ་བྱེད་པ་དང་བཅས་པས་ཡོངས་སུ་མྱ་ངན་ལས་འདའ་བ *mñon-par hdu-byed-pa dañ bcas-pas yoñs-su mya-ñan las hdah-wa* he escapes from misery save that a vestige of the *Skandha* still remains; (9) अनभिसंस्कारपरिनिर्व्वायिन्; མངོན་དུ་འདུ་བྱེད་པར་མེད་པར་ཡོངས་སུ་མྱ་ངན་ལས་འདའ་བ *mñon-du hdu-byed par med-par yoñs-su mya-ñan las hdah-wa* he attains to *Nirvāṇa*, the *Skandha* being utterly destroyed, *i.e.,* without the least vestige remaining; (10) ऊर्ध्वस्रोतस् གོང་དུ་འཕོ་བ *goñ-du hpho-wa* he will in his spiritual progress reach up to the *Akaniṣṭha* heavens; (11) कायसाक्षी; ལུས་ཀྱི་མངོན་སུམ་དུ་བྱེད་པ *lus-kyi mñon sum-du byed-pa* he will obtain the body of supreme intelligence or knowledge; (12) श्रद्धानुसारी; དད་པའི་རྗེས་སུ་འབྲང་བ *dad-pahi rjes-su hbrañ-wa* he will here have completely subdued the senses or passions; (13) धर्मानुसारी; ཆོས་ཀྱི་རྗེས་སུ་འབྲང་བ *chos-kyi rjes-su hbrañ-wa* all his intellectual and moral faculties become so as to be directed effectually to all good works; (14) दृष्टिप्राप्त; མཐོང་བས་ཐོབ་པ *thoñ-was thob-pa* having heretical views or having insight into religion; (15) समयविमुक्त; དུས་ཀྱིས་རྣམ་པར་གྲོལ་བ *dus-kyi rnam-par grol-wa* getting salvation in time; (16) असमयविमुक्त; དུས་དང་མི་སྦྱོར་བར་རྣམ་པར་གྲོལ་བ getting salvation not in proper time; (17) उभयतोभागविमुक्त; གཉིས་ཀའི་ཆ་ལས་རྣམ་པར་གྲོལ་བ *gñis-kahi cha-las rnam-par grol-wa* getting salvation in time as well as without reference to time; (18) उपपद्यपरिनिर्व्वायी; སྐྱེས་ནས་ཡོངས་སུ་མྱ་ངན་ལས་འདའ་བ *skyes-nas yoñs-su mya-ñan las hdah-wa* entering into the state of *Nirvāṇa* immediately after one's birth; (19) प्रज्ञाविमुक्त; ཤེས་རབ་ཀྱིས་རྣམ་པར་གྲོལ་བ *çes-rab kyis rnam-par grol-wa* fully delivered by means of absolute or transcendental knowledge; (20) श्रद्धाविमुक्त। delivered by means of faith.

གང་ཡ *gañ-ya* a very large figure or number (*Ya-sel.* 56).

གང་ཡང་ *gañ-yañ* कश्चित्, यश्च whosoever; whatever; any one.

གང་ལ *gañ-la* कुत्र where; in whom.

གང་ལོ *gañ-lo* an empty pod, freed from the kernels (in *W.*) (*Jä.*).

གང་ཤར *gañ-çar* གང་སེམས་ལ་བསམས་པ anything that occurs (in the mind); what is thought; a thought.

གང་སུ་དག *gañ-su dag* ये केचित् whichever of those.

གངས *gañs* हिम 1. glacier; glacier-ice. 2. snow (usually *kha*). 3. the sclerotic of the eye (*Sch.*).

གངས་རྒྱུད *gañs-rgyud* a chain of snowy mountains.

གངས་ཅན *gañs-can* हिमवत् 1. one of the native names of Tibet. 2. abounding in snow; snowy; full of glaciers: *Gañs-can-las hbyuñ-wahi chu* the water issuing from a glacier: *Gañs-can-gyi skad* the language of Tibet.

གངས་ཅན་མཁས་པའི་གཙུག་རྒྱན *Gañs-can mkhas-pahi gtsug-rgyan* a complementary name of Tsongkha-pa, the great Buddhist reformer of Tibet whose religious name was རྒྱལ་བ་བློ་བཟང་གྲགས་པ *Rgyal-wa Blo-bzañ grags-pa*; his other names were :—རྗེ་རིན་པོ་ཆེ *Rje rin-po che*; རྗེ་ཙོང་ཁ་པ *Rje Tsoñ-kha-pa*; གངས་ཅན་ཤིང་རྟ *Gañs-can çiñ-rta*; ཤར་ཙོང་ཁ་པ *Çar Tsoñ-kha-pa*; འཇམ་མགོན་བླ་མ *Hjam mgon blama.*

གངས་ཅན་མགོན་པོ *Gañ-can mgon-po* or སྤྱན་རས་གཟིགས *Spyan-ras gzigs* the patron saint of Tibet, Avalokites'vara, also styled :—འཇིག་རྟེན་མགོན་པོ *Hjig-rten mgon-po*; ཐུགས་རྗེ་ཆེན་པོ *Thugs-rje chen-po*; འགྲོ་བའི་མགོན་པོ *Hgro-wahi mgon-po.*

གངས་ཅན་རྒྱལ་པོ *Gañs-can rgyal-po* King of Tibet; and in books occasionally applied to the Dalai Lamas of Lhasa.

གངས་ཅན་རྒྱལ་པོའི་བཞི་གནས *Gañs-can rgyal-pohi bzhi-gnas* as also ཆོས་འཁོར་དཔལ་གྱི་ལྷ་ས *chos-hkhor dpal-gyi Lha-sa* used to designate Lhasa, the capital of Tibet (*Yig. k. 31*).

གངས་ཅན་ཆེན་པོ *gañs-cañ chen-po* sometimes applied to mountainous region covered with eternal snow extending from Ladak to the Kailas range. Also the name of a fabulous mountainous region the chief peak of which is said to be about 1,500 miles round and filled with *Yakṣa*, *Rakṣa* and other demi-gods.

གངས་ཆེན *Gañs-chen* any great range of snowy mountains or a great glacier; n. of a village at the south-western foot of the Kañchenjunga mountain. གངས་ཆེན་མཛོད་ལྔ (Kanchenjunga in Sikkim) lit. the five great repositories of snow.

གངས་ཆེན་ཆོས་རྒྱལ *Gañs-chen Chos-rgyal* the Grand Lama of Tibet; also the name of a guardian deity of Buddhism in Tibet; a name of Yama, the Lord of Death, who is worshipped in Tibet under the name of *Dam-chen Chos-rgyal.*

གངས་ལྗོངས་ཡུལ *Gañs-ljoñs yul*=བོད *Bod* Tibet.

Syn. གངས་ཅན་ཞིང *gañs-can shiñ*; གངས་རི་ར་བའི་སྐོར་བའི་ཞིང་ཁམས *gañs ri ra-wahi skor-wahi shiñ-khams*; གངས་ཅན་ས་ལྷའི་སྨན་ལྗོངས *gañs-can sa-lhahi sman-ljoñs* (*Mñon. and Yig. k.*).

གངས་འབབ *gañs-hbab* avalanche; it snows.

གངས་སྦལ *gañs-sbal*, also called དཀྱིལ་འཁོར *dkyil-hkhor* गोधा, the snow lizard with circular marks on its skin resembling the common Indian lizard (*Lex.*); a frog of fabulous origin: the male frog is said to live on the top of the snowy mountains and the female frog in the abyss of the deep gorge below the mountain; when the sun passes over the tropic of cancer (*karkaṭa* or crab), the male frog descends to the foot of the mountain and the female frog ascends there to meet him midway. Before meeting each other the male frog remains more powerful; but after they have united, the female becomes the stronger of the two (*Sman.*).

གངས་རི I: *gańs-ri* हिमाद्रि, हिमगिरि snowy mountain or snow-mountains—a common designation for many of the great ranges in Tibet; གངས་ཉི་ཤུ *gańs-ñi-çu* the twenty principal mountains of Tibet:—(1) ཐང་ལྷ *Thańlha*, (2) ཏི་སེ *Ti-se* (*Kailāça*), (3) མང་མཁར *Mań-mkhar*, (4) བུ་ལེ *Bu-le*, (5) སྟར་སྒོ *Star-sgo*, (6) ཕོ་ལ *Pho-la*, (7) མཁའ་རི *Mkhaḥ-ri*, (8) ཇོ་མོ་ཁ་རག *Jo-mo kha-rag*, (9) རྡོ་རྗེ *Rdo-rje*, (10) གང་བཟང་ *Gań-bzań*, (11) རྩེ་རྡུམ *Rtse-rdum*, (12) ལ་ཕྱི *La-phyi*, (13) ཚེ་རིང་ *Tshe-riń*, (14) སྣ་ནམ *Sna-nam*, (15) ཏེ་སྒྲོ *Te-sgro*, (16) འོད་དེ་གུང་རྒྱལ *Hod-de guń-rgyal*, (17) ཡར་ལྷ་ཤམ་པོ *Yar-lha çam-po*, (18) གསལ་རྗེ *Gsal-rje*, (19) ཧ་བོ་གངས་བཟང་ *Ha-bo gańs-bzań*, (20) ཙ་རི་ང་ལའི་གངས *Tsa-ri ńa lahi-gańs* (*Kathań.* ཀ, *168*).

གངས་རི II: ཤུ་དག་དཀར་པོ *çu-dag dkar-po* n. of a vegetable drug (*Mńon.*).

གངས་སྲག *gańs-srag* = གངས་འཕྲེད *gańs-hphred* along or across the glacier.

གངས་སྲུལ *gańs-srul* an avalanché; a slip in the snowy side of a mountain; a snow-slip.

གངས་ཐིག *gańs-thig* n. of a stone or mineral substance resembling stone; it is said to be a cure for fever that is produced from the liver.

གངས་པ་ཤེའུ *Gańs-pa çe-hu* the name of a celebrated lama and philosopher of the *Kadampa* School of Tibet.

གཉྫི་ར *gañ-ji-ra* lit. posessed of treasure or མཛོད་ལྡན *mdsod-ldan*; an ornamental pinnacle on a temple, house or chorten constructed after the prescribed model given in Buddhist books. This is a Sanskrt word though sometimes Tibetanized, being written as འགན་འཇི་ར *hgan-hji-ra*.

གད *gad* as in གསེར་གད *gser-gad* 1. pure, genuine, unalloyed. 2. a rock.

གད་སྐྱིབས *gad-skyibs* a rock cavern; a place of shelter under the cleft or nook of a rock: དངུལ་གྱི་ལྷང་པ་དེ་རྣམས་གད་སྐྱིབས་ཤིག་ཏུ་བཞག kept the bars of silver in the nook of a rocky hill.

གད་ཁ *gad-kha* प्रस्थः wide, broad; breadth; with breadth.

གད་མོ *gad-mo,* हास्य a laughing; laughter: གད་མོ་དགོད *gad-mo dgod* हसति utters a laugh; གད་མོ་བགད་བྱུང་ *gad-mo-bgad byuń* I have laughed; གད་མོ་བགད་སོང་ *gad-mo bgad-soń* he has laughed. གད་མོ་རྒོད *gad-mo rgod* to laugh; གད་མོ་ཤོར་བྱུང་ *gad-mo çor-byuń* laughter sprang forth; གད་མོ་ཤོར་སོང་ *gad-mo çor-soń* idem; གད་མོས་འདེབས་པ *gad-mos hdebs-pa* to laugh at a person; འཇིག་རྟེན་པའི་གད་མོ *hjig rten-pahi gad-mo* laughter of worldly-minded people: ངའི་གད་མོའི་གནས this is to me an object of laughter; it is ridiculous to me (*Jä.*). གད་རྒྱངས་ཅན *gad-rgyańs-can* अट्टहास. བསྡིགས་པའི་གད་མོ *bsdigs-pahi gad-mo* (हाहा *Ha Ha*) loud laughter; སྡིག་པའི་གད་མོ *sdig-pahi gad-mo* (हिहि *hihi*) coquettish laugh; དགྱེས་པའི་གད་མོ *dgyes-pahi-gad-mo* (हेहे *he-he*) laugh of merriment or rejoicing; ཟིལ་གྱིས་གནོན་པའི་གད་མོ *zil-gyis gnon-pahi gyad-mo* हो हो a laughter of triumph; ཁྲོ་བོའི་བཞད་པ་བརྒྱད *khro-wohi bshad-pa brgyad* the eight laughs of indignation and wrath, &c.

གད་རྒྱལ *gad-rgyal* the walls of conglomerate rock through which mountain-torrents have cut their way.

གད་སྙིགས *gad-s̤ñigs̤* dust; refuses; swept-out: *phyags-mas̤ gad-s̤ñigs̤ phyags̤* sweep with a broom the dust, refuse, etc. (*Ñag.*).

གད་དར *gad-dar* sweeping, cleansing; གད་དར་བྱེད་པ *gad-dar-byed-pa* cleansing; sweeping well a place; keeping it clean.

Syn. ཕྱག་དར *phyag-dar*; བྱི་དོར *byi-dor*; གད་དར *gad-dar*; གཙང་བར་བྱེད *gtsañ-war-byed*; རྡུལ་འཕངས *rdul-hphañs* (*Mñon.*).

གད་མདའ་ལ *Gad-mdah-la* n. of a mountain; the lowlands at the foot of a *Gad*.

གད་མདལ་ལ་ཚུན *gad mdal-la tshun* this side of the mountain called *Gad-dala*.

གད་པ I: *gad-pa* or གད་མཁན *gad-mkhan* a sweeper; a cleanser; ཕྱག་དར་བྱེད་མཁན, གད་མ་ཆུ་མ་སོགས་སོགས་དགོས་རིགས the class (of menial servants) requiring wages (such as) sweepers, dusters and water carriers. གད་གཙང་མ any place or object well dusted or cleansed.

གད་པ II: 1. a precipitous cliff of conglomerate such as often walls in the mountain rivers: 2. wide crack in a conglomerate rock.

གད་ཕུག *gad-phug* a cavern or cleft in a conglomerate rock: གཞུང་གིས་སྟག་དཀར་གྱི་གད་ཕུག་ཏུ་ཞག་ལྔ་བཞུགས *gshuñ-gis̤ stag-dkar-gyi gad phug-tu shag-lña bshugs̤* meanwhile they halted for five days in the rocky cavern of *S̤tag-dkar*.

གན *gan=rtsar* near: དེད་དཔོན་དེའི་གན་དུ་སོང་སྟེ་དྲིས་པ *ded-dpon dehi gan-du soñ-s̤te dris̤-pa* going near to the chief of the merchants (caravan), he asked. གན *gan* (=གམ *gam* in *C.*) signifying nearness, proximity; is used in such connection as གན་དུ to, towards, up to: ངའི་གན་དུ་ཤོག come up to me; རྒྱལ་པོའི་གན་དུ he went unto the king; ཁང་པའི་གན་དུ་སོང་ he went towards the house; རྒྱལ་པོའི་གན་ནས་བྱུང he came from the king; དོག་པོ་གན་དུ in *W.* close by the brook; ཆུར་གན་དུ *chur gan-du* in *W.* hard by the water; རིར་གན་པ *rir gan-pa* one living close to a mountain or hill.

གན་ཀྱལ *gan-kyal* or གན་རྐྱལ *gan-rkyal*, पतन supine; lying on the back with the face upward: གན་ཀྱལ་དུ་ཉལ་བ to lie in that position: གན་ཀྱལ་དུ་འགྱེལ་བ to fall on the back.

གན་རྒྱ *gan-rgya*=འགན་རྒྱ *hgan-rgya*, vulg. གམ་རྒྱ *gam-rgya*, a written contract; an agreement (*Cs.*).

གན་དར *gan-dar*, a silk handkerchief offered as a present in exchanging compliments on meeting (*Sch.*).

† གན་དྷ་བྷ་དྲ *gan-dha bha-dra* गन्धभद्र, a kind of drug used in liver derangement.

† གན་དྷ་རིའི་སྔགས *gan-dha rihi s̤ñags̤* गन्धारी-मन्त्र a Buddhist *mantra* or charm which has the power of enabling one to move in space.

† གན་དྷོ་ལ *gan-dho-la*, गन्धालय, गन्धकूट the temple of fragrance; hall of worship built after the model of a *chaitya* with many doors. It is generally attached to a great monastery. In Tibetan it is called དྲི་གཙང་ཁང *Dri gtsañ-khañ*, the name being applied to the particular chapel where the image of Buddha is placed. The great temple of Buddha at Gaya was called *Mahā gandhola Caitya*. *Phyi gan-dho-la nañ-du lha-khañ byas̤-pa* its inside was a god's house or chapel and the outside a *gandhola*.

† གན་དྷི *gan-dhi* गन्धिन् a mineral substance used as a cure for leprosy.

‡ གཎྚའི་ཏོག *gaṇ-ṭaḥi-tog* or གན་ཐི་པར་ན *gan-thi par-na* a medicinal plant.

‡ **གཎྚི** *gaṇ-ṭi* घण्टि a piece of thick plank measuring about 6 feet by 12 inches either of white sandal wood or of deodar, which when struck with a hammer or another piece of thick hard wood, produces a kind of ringing sound which is heard from a great distance. It is used on special occasions to summon the monks of a monastery to attend any special religious service, &c.

གན་གཡོག *gan-gyog* or གཎྚི་ཐེ་ཨུ *gaṇ-ṭi the-ḥu* घण्टि कोटक the rod or hammer with which the *ghaṇṭi* (wooden gong) is struck or beaten.

‡ གཎྜ་པ་སི *gaṇḍa-pa si* (mystic) avarice; greed for gain (*K. g.* ཀ *26*).

‡ **གཎྜི** *gaṇ-ḍi* रागपुष्प in books the gong or bell to call monks to monastic services.

གན་མཛོད *gan-mdsod* = བང་མཛོད *bañ-mdsod* store-room, store-house.

卐 **གབ་ཁུང** *gab-khuñ*, defined as པུས་མོའི་རྒྱབ་ཀྱི་སྒྱིད་ཁུང *pus-mohi rgyab-kyi sgyid-khuñ*, the cavities behind the knee bones.

གབ་སྒྲ *gab-sgra* a belch (in *W.*) (*Jä.*).

གབ་པ *gab-pa* to hide; to conceal one's self: རྒྱལ་བའི་འབྱུང་གནས་འདི་ཡོན་ཏན་ཐམས་ཅད་གབ་ནས་མི་སྟོན་པར་གདའ་བས *Rgyal-wahi hbyuñ-gnas hdi yon-tan thams-cad gab-nas mi ston-par gdah-was*. This *Rgyal-wahi hbyuñ-gnas* having concealed all his talents does not exhibit them (*Hbrom.* ཀ 2).

Syn. ཡིབ་པ *yib-pa*; སྦས་པ *sbas-pa*; གཡོགས་པ *gyogs-pa*; མི་མངོན་པར་བྱ་བ *mi mñon-par bya-wa* (*Mnoñ.*).

གབ་ཕྱུང *gab-phyuñ* n. of a religious treatise on the occult doctrine of Buddhism.

གབ་ཙེ *gab-tse* = གབ་རྩེ *gab-rtse* चक्र or གབ་ཚེ *gab-tshe* a plan or table of points for computing the figures of divination in magical computations. In this connection, ས་ལ་གནས་པའི་ས་བདག་གི་རྩིས *sa-la, gnas pahi sa-bdag-gi rtsis* refers to calculating the identity and deeds of mischief done by a local "god of the soil." Again བར་སྣང་ལ་གནས་པའི་བཟའ་སྐར་གྱི་རྩིས refers to astrological calculations worked with the *gab-tse*. གཞན་ཡང་སྐུ་ཡི་གབ་ཙེ is a mystic chart used for bodily prognostics; གསུང་གི་གབ་ཙེ one for the speech; ཐུགས་ཀྱི་གབ་ཙེ་དང་ one for the heart. སྤྱིར་གབ་ཙེ་ལ་ས་ཡི་གབ་ཙེ་གནམ་གྱི་གབ་ཙེ་ བར་གྱི་གབ་ཙེ་སོགས་ཀྱི་ཐ་སྙད་མང་པོ་ཡོད In the general term *gab-tse* are included many particular significations, that for the soil, that for the sky, that for the intermediate space, etc.

གབ་ཚད *gab-tshad* slow, insiduous fever; according to *Sch.* a hectic, consumptive fever.

གབ་ཚིག *gab-tshig* मन्त्र, प्रहेलिका riddle; also mystical words or expressions used in magic to stupify one's enemies without killing them. Also the 16 ornamental mystical allusions employed to excite laughter in a play, etc., and to convey hidden meanings in an assembly, etc. The names of these are as follows:—ཀུན་ཏུ་ཚོགས་པའི་གབ་ཚིག *kun-tu tshogs pahi gab-tshig*; དེ་བཞིན་དུ་སླུ་བྱེད་ཀྱི་རིམ་པ་དང་བྲལ་བའི་གབ་ཚིག *de-bshin-du slu byed-kyi rim-pa dañ bral-wahi gab-tshig*; རབ་བཅོམ་གྱི་གབ་ཚིག *rab-bcom-gyi gab-tshig*; མཐུན་གཟུགས་ཀྱི་གབ་ཚིག *mthun gzugs-kyi gab-tshig*;

རྩུབ་མོའི་གབ་ཚིག *rtsub-moḥi gab-tshig*; གྲངས་ཀྱི་གབ་ཚིག *grañs-kyi gab-tshig*; རབ་བཏགས་ཀྱི་གབ་ཚིག *rab btags-kyi gab-tshig*; མིང་དུ་འདུས་པའི་གབ་ཚིག *miñ-du ḥdus-paḥi gab-tshig*; སྒྲིབ་པའི་གབ་ཚིག *sgrib-paḥi gab-tshig*; མཐུན་པའི་སྒྲའི་གབ་ཚིག *mthun-paḥi sgraḥi gab-tshig*; རྨོངས་པའི་གབ་ཚིག *rmoñs-paḥi gab-tshig*; ཡོངས་ཕྲོགས་ཀྱི་གབ་ཚིག *yoñs phrogs-kyi gab-tshig*; གཅིག་བསྒྲིབས་ཀྱི་གབ་ཚིག *gcig bsgribs-kyi gab-tshig*; གཉིས་ཀ་བསྒྲིབས་པའི་གབ་ཚིག *gñis-ka bsgribs-paḥi gab-tshig*; ཡོངས་འདྲེས་ཀྱི་གབ་ཚིག *yoñs ḥdres-kyi gab-tshig*.

གབ་ཡིག *gab-yig* 1. in the medicinal works of Tibet the names of certain drugs and medicines are written in words which are not ordinarily understood, having secret meanings assigned to them. 2. in figurative language, meanings of names and words which are not ordinarily understood. Such are called གབ་མིང *gab-miñ*, *i.e.*, secret names.

གབ་ས *gab-sa* སྦས་ས *sbas-sa* or ཡིབ་ས *yib-sa* hiding-place; place of concealment: གསེར་མང་པོ་ཁྱེར་འོངས་བ་ལ་གབ་ས་དང་འགྲོ་ས་ནི་མེད we came bringing much gold with us, but we were without a hiding-place or a place to go to (*A. 120*).

གམ *gam* **निकट** near, v. གན *gan*.

Syn. གམ་ཡོ *gam-yo*; དྲུང *druñ*; ཉེ་འཁོར *ñe-ḥkhor* (*Mṅon.*).

གམ་གུམ *gam-gum* a number, གྲངས་གནས *grañs-gnas* (*Ya-sel. 57*).

གམ་སྤངས *gam-spañs* panels or little boards beneath the cornice of a roof, often filled up with paintings (*Jä.*).

‡ **གམ་བུ་ར** *gam-bu-ra*, **जम्बिर** in *W.* a citron; lemon (*Jä.*).

གམ་འབྲོག *gam-ḥbrog* a dairy in the neighbourhood of one's residence. *Gam-ḥbrog rgyañ ḥgrog bzañ-wa rtsa-yi dge* Near and distant dairy farms become thriving through the abundance of pastures (*Jig.*).

གམ་འཛིན *gam-ḥdsin* abbr. of གན་རྒྱ་དང་འཛིན *ganrgya dañ ḥdsin*, a receipt, acknowledgment; the letter of transfer, exchange, &c., for buying and selling or transaction of money business, &c.: གམ་འཛིན་བྱེད་པ་འདོད་སྦྱར་གྱི་བཀོད་པ་གོ་བརྡའ་འཕྲོད་ངེས *gam-ḥdsin byed-pa ḥdod sbyargyi bkod-pa go-brdaḥ ḥphrod ñes* certainly, the receipt and the deed of agreement should be satisfactorily explained (*Rtsii*).

+ གམ་ཡོ *gam-yo* (གམ་གཡོག *gam-gyog*) = ཉེ་འཁོར *ñe-ḥkhor* attendant.

གའུ *gaḥu* **सम्पुट** 1. a little box or case; when containing a talisman or amulet, it is worn suspended round the neck.

གར I: *gar* or གར་བྲོ *gar-bro* **नृत्य, नाट, भाव** dance; acting in a dramatic play; gesticulation; གར་བས་བསྐོར *gar-was bskor* surrounded by dancing girls or actors; གར་བྱེད་པ *gar-byed-pa* to dance; གླུ་གར་རྩེད་མོ་བྱེད་པ *glu-gar rtsed-mo byed-pa* to sing; to dance and play; གར་ཟས *gar-zas* the food given to performers; *gar ḥkhrab-mkhan gyi zas-la* for the food of those who perform dancing; གར་ལ་དགའ་བ *gar-la dgaḥ-wa* **ताण्डवप्रिय** very fond of dancing; གར་ལ་བལྟ *gar-la blta* **नृत्येक्षण** attending a dance; witnessing a performance.

གར་གྱི་ལྟད་མོ *gar-gyi ltad-mo* **नटरङ्ग** dancing entertainment or amusement.

གར་གྱི་དབང་པོ *gar-gyi dwañ-po* = གྲུབ་ཆེན *grub-chen* or རྣལ་འབྱོར་པ་ཆེན་པོ *rnal-ḥbyor-pa chen-po* fig. a *yogi* or ascetic engaged in meditation: སྐུ་མཆོག་གར་གྱི་དབང་པོ་མཛེས་བརྗིད་རྫོམས་ཤིང་ *sku-mchog gar-gyi dwań-po mdses brjid ńoms-çiń* your holiness the lord of the dancers (peacock), equal in beauty and splendour (*Yig. k. 28*).

གར་གྱི་གཙོ་བོ *gar-gyi gtso-bo*=གླུ་གར་གྱི་མཁན་པོ *glu-gar-gyi mkhan-po* or གཙོ་བོ *gtso-bo* teacher or director of a dance or dancing performance (*Mńon.*).

གར III: or ག་རུ *ga-ru*, or གང་དུ *gań-du*, whither; where; གར་ཡང *gar-yań* anywhere: གར་ཡང་སྐྱེ་བ *gar-yań skye-wa* growing anywhere: གར་ཡང་མི་འགྲོ་བ *gar-yań mi hgro-wa* to go nowhere. གར་མེད *gar-med* in *W.* at all events; by all means; ག་ན་མེད *ga-na-med* or གར་བབ *gar-bab* at random; haphazard (*Sch.*).

གར་མཁན *gar-mkhan* or བྲོ་མཁན *bro-mkhan* नर्त्तक dancer 1. a dancer, performer, *e.g.*, even a Buddha or any saint dances when displaying miracles. 2. name of a god, acc. to *Sch.* S'iva (*Jä.*).

གར་མཁན་མ *gar-mkhan-ma*=གར་མ *gar-ma* नटी, चुट्टा dancing girl. The thirteen modulations of voice or musical notes: (1) གར་མ *gar-ma* कैषिक; (2) རོལ་རྩེད་མ *rol-rtsed-ma* गान्धार; (3) དལ་མ *dal-ma* निषाद; (4) མྱུར་མ *myur-ma* धैवत; (5) བར་མ *bar-ma* मध्यम; (6) ཚིག་རྡེག *tshig-rdeg* षड्ज; (7) བྱ་བའི་དུས *bya-wahi-dus* पञ्चम; (8) བྱ་བའི་ཚད *bya-wahi tshad* ऋषभ; (9) ཏ་ཏྭ *ta-tva* (तत्त्व) reality; (10) ཨོ་གྷ *o-gha* (ओघ) flow; (11) གྷ་ནི *gha-ni* घन compact; (12) ལ་ཡ *la-ya* (लय) absorption; adherence; (13) སཱ་མྱ *sā-mya* (साम्य) equality.

གར་འཆམ *gar-cham* the frantic dance of the lamas of Tibet which is chiefly observed by the *Rńiń-ma* schools of Tibet. It is of two kinds ཕུར་པའི་རྩ་འཆམ *phur-pahi rtsa hcham* the dance of the enchanted club, and འཁྲུབ་འཆམ *hkhrub-hcham* the dance of the lamas at the time of offering sacrifice.

གར་སྟབས *gar-stabs* dancing gesture or motion.

གར་པ *gar-pa* नाटक a dancer; also a dance.

གར II: the encampment of an army; a camp.

གར་རྒྱབ *gar-rgyab* encampment; གར་རྒྱབ་པ *gar-rgyab-pa* to encamp; also for གང་རྒྱབ *gań-rgyab*, རྡོ་མདའ་སོགས་གར་རྒྱབ *rdo-mdah sogs gar-rgyab* fling at him stone or arrow, etc., whatever (you can) (*Hbrom.* ཕ *6*).

+ གར་ཅིག *gar-cig*=གང་ཞིག *gań-shig*, which one; whichever one.

གར་གདོང་བཙན *Gar gdoń-btsan* the famous general of King *Sroń-btsan sgam-po*, who visited the capital of China and induced Emperor Taitsung to give one of the princesses imperial in marraige to his sovereign, about 630 A.D.

གར་རྡེབ *gar-rdeb* ཆུས་ཁྱེར་གར་རྡེབ་སོགས་ལ *chus-khyer gar-rdeb-sogs-la* lands, fields, houses, &c., that have been devastated by a river by the over-flowing of its banks, &c. (*Rtsii.*).

གར་ནག *gar-nag* name of a medicine.

གར་པོ I: *gar-po* in colloq. language the word དཀར་པོ *dkar-po* is pronouned as གར་པོ *gar-po* and also written as such. It is usual to pronounce དཀར་པོ *dkar-po* as གར་པོ *gar-po* in the vulgar language (*Grub.* ཞ *2*).

གར་པོ II: घन, also གར་མོ *gar-mo*, thick; dense; condensed; not fluid.

གར་བ 1. *gar-wa* བསྐ་བ *bska-wa* कषाय astringent. 2. strong; གར་ཆང་ *gar-chaṅ* strong beer (*Jä.*).

གར་བཙན་འཕགས་པ *Gar btsan hphags-pa* name of a monastery and also of a deity in Tibet (*Jig. 3.*).

† **གརྫ** *gar-dsa* or བི་གརྫ *bi gar-dsa*, गर्जा, विगर्जा n. of a tree or kind of wood ཤིང་ *çiṅ* (*K. ko.* ཀ, *3*).

གར་ཞ *gar-sha* the native name of the district called La-hul or La-hol by the Hindus (*Jä.*).

གར་ལོག *gar-log* acc. to the Tibetans rapacious mountain tribes belonging to the far north-east of Tibet. ཏུ་རུཥྐ་ཀ་ཞེས་པ་བོད་སྐད་དུ་གར་ལོག་ཡིན་ཞེས་ལི་ཤི་གུར་ཁང་དུ་བཤད་ཡོད those styled in the Tibetan tongue *Gar-log* are described in the Li-s'i Gur-khang as Turushka. The གར་ལོག *Garlog* were a different people from the མགོ་ལོག *Mgo-log.* གར་ལོག་གི་རྒྱལ་པོ་ལ་སྐུ་ལུས་བཏང་བས་ཆོས་ཕྱིར་སྲོག་ཀྱང་བཏོང་བའི་རྒྱལ་པོ་ཡིན *Gar-log gi rgyal-po la sku-lus btaṅ-was chos-phyir srog-kyaṅ btoṅ-wahi rgyal-po yin.* In Atīs'a's biography it is mentioned that the King of the Gar-log in the first part of the 11th century, A.D., came from the Indian side and made the King of Tibet a captive when he was there on a visit to Purang. Probably they were the earliest Mohamedan invaders of Kashmir.

གར་ཤ *gar-ça* the muscles of the thumb (*Med.*) (*Jä.*).

+ **གལ** I: *gal*=ནན *nan* pressing; གལ་གྱིས *gal-gyis* pressingly, urgently.

གལ II: importance གལ་དུ་འཛིན་པ *gal-du hdsiṅ-pa* to consider of importance; to esteem.

Syn. གནད *gnad*; མདོ *mdo* (*Mṅon.*).

གལ III: 1. constraint; compulsion: *ṅa-la gal-juṅ* in *C.* "I have been compelled" (*Jä.*). 2. trap; snare: in colloq. གལ་འཛུག་པ *gal hdsug-pa* to set a snare (*Jä.*).

གལ IV: v. གང་ལ་ལ *gaṅ la-la.*

གལ་འགག *gal-hgag*=གནད་འགག important; གལ་འགག་ཆེ་བ very important.

གལ་ཆུང *gal-chuṅ* unimportant; insignificant; undervalued; slighted.

གལ་ཆེ་བ *gal-che-wa* very important: ཚེ་འདི་དང་ཕྱི་མ་གཉིས་ལས་ཕྱི་མ་གལ་ཆེ་བ of the two, this life and the future, the latter is of greater importance: དོན་མེད་འབྱམས་འགྲོ་བ་ལས་ཡོན་ཏན་བསླབ་ན་གལ་ཆེ it is of greater importance to acquire accomplishments than to go roving about without purpose: བསླབ་བྱ་གལ་ཆེ་བ important moral precepts.

Syn. གནད་ཆེ་བ *gnad-che-wa*; རྩ་ཆེ་བ *rtsa-che-wa*; ཁག་ཆེ་བ *khag-che-wa*; གཙོ་ཆེ་བ *gtso-che-wa* (*Mṅon.*).

གལ་ཏེ *gal-te* conj. if; in case of; implies a conditional possibility. It is placed as the first word in a conditional sentence while ན *na*, its complement, stands after the verb at the end; together they signify "if." གལ་ཏེ, however, is sometimes omitted, ན still meaning "if." In colloq. expression གལ་ཏེ *gal-te* is seldom used; but "*gal-shi*" is a common substitute: གལ་ཏེ་བདེ་བ་ཀུན་འདོད་ན, འདོད་པ་ཐམས་ཅད་ཡོངས་སུ་སྤངས if you wish to enjoy all happiness, you must entirely leave off all desire: གལ་ཏེ་རྟག་ཏུ་མཛེའ་འདོད་ན, ཚོ་ཉ་ཙོར་གྱི་ཁ་སྒོགས་དང་ ཡིད་ཆེས་ཆུང་མ་ལ་

བསྐྱུ་བ, ཉེས་པ་གསུམ་པོ་སྤང་བར་བྱ if you wish at all times to live in friendship (with the three Holies), you should avoid the three dangers, viz. of looking at your loving wife, thinking of profit, and of confiding in an envoy.

གལ་མདོ *gal-mdo*=གལ་འགག *gal-hgag* or གནད་འགག *gnad-hgag* 1. really, essentially of importance. 2. n. of a disease (*Med.*).

གལ་པོ *gal-po* probably same as གལ *gal.* གལ་པོ་ཆེའི་ཁྱིམ་དཔོན the important, indispensable master of the house (family).

གལ་བ *gal-wa* to force, to press some thing on a person: མི་ལ་བཙོན་གལ indoor confinement is forced on men (*Jä.*).

གལ་བར་བྱེད་པ *gal-war byed-pa* བརྩོན་བཏང་བ *brtson btañ-wa* उद्वर, उद्गुर to be assiduous.

གལ་བཟུང *gal-bzuñ* (lit. got hold of the important thing), =སྤུན་འབྱིན renunciation.

གལ་རོ *gal-ro* in *W.* refuse; rubbish.

གས *gas*, v. འགས་པ *hgas-pa.*

གི *gi* I. numeral for 33, v. affix instead of ཀྱི *kyi* after ག and ང; for signification v. ཀྱི *kyi.*

གི་གུ *gi-gu* the vowel sign ི for *i.*

གི་གུ་ཞེལ *gi-gu çel*=གི་གུ་ཤ *gi-gu-ça*, having a white speck in the eye; wall-eyed (of horses) (*Sch.*).

གི་ལྡི་བིག *gi-lji-big* or ཀོ་ཙི་བིག *ko-tsi-big* tanned skin of a kind of deer obtained from Mongolia and China (*Jig.*).

‡གུ་ནེ་རུ *Gu-ne-ru* n. of an Indian *yoginī* or female ascetic (*K. dun. 38*).

གི་ཝང *gi-wañ* and also གི་ཧང *gi-hañ* गोरोचना, रोचना, वचक, सिङ्गण a yellow pigment, an anthelminthic medicine; विङ्क n. of a concretion in the entrails of some animals, used for medicine. Acc. to the medical works of Tibet this concretion is formed in the liver of certain animals and seldom in men, and it resembles in appearance and size the boiled yolk of a hen's egg. There are also smaller ones. Acc. to some lexicographers this concretion is formed in two or three *strata* or folds. The best quality of *gi-wañ* is that which is obtained from an elephant, and those obtained from the ox called *gorocanā* are of second quality. A kind of གི་ཝང *gi-wañ* is also obtained from minerals and clay, and is of reddish-yellow colour. All these are supposed to be possessed of wonderful healing power. གི་ཝང་དང་སྦྲང་རྩི་མིག་སྨན་བྱས་ནས་མིག་གཉིས་ལ་བསྐུས་ནས་གཞི་ལ་ཡོད་པའི་གཏེར་ཐམས་ཅད་མཐོང་བར་འགྱུར་རོ (*K. g.* ང *308*). *Gi-wañ* mixed with honey, if applied to both the eyes as a medicine, will give one such a clear vision, enabling one to see all the treasures which are in the earth.

‡གི་རི་བྷན་དྷ *Giri bhan-dha* n. of a mountainous country: *Gi-ri bhan-dhahi yul-gyi mthahi ri khoñs-su kla-klohi rigs mi-hdra-wa beu yod-par rgya-gar-pa dag-la grags-çiñ* it being known to the Indians that in the mountains skirting the country of Giribandha there are ten different La-lo tribes (*Dsam.*).

གི་ལིང *gi-liñ* a strong-bodied horse (*Sch.*).

གི་ལིན *gi-lin* a fabulous animal.

གི་ཤང་རྒྱ་ *Gi-çaṅ rgya* n. of a tribe in Tibet.

‡ གིང་ *giṅ* किङ्कार probably a little drum, or the beating of it as an accompaniment in dancing (*Jä.*).

གིམ *gim* སྒྲ་སྙན་གྱི་གྲས་ཤིག *sgra-sñan-gyi gras-shig* n. of a soft musical tone. (*K. my.* ཀ *803*).

གིར་མོ *gir-mo, Ld.*, the Indian rupee; in *C.* it is called གོར་མོ *gor-mo* or སྒོར་མོ *sgor-mo*.

གིས *gis* instead of ཀྱིས *kyis* after a final ག or ན.

གུ *gu* 1. numerical for 63 = ཧུ *hu*. 2. sign of diminutives, *e.g.*, ཁྱི་གུ *khyi-gu* a puppy; little dog. 3. extension; extent; room; space; གནས་ས་གུ་དོག *gnas sa gu-dog*, ལུང་པ་གུ་དོག *luṅ-pa gu-dog*, ལམ་གུ་དོག *lam gu-dog*, སེམས་གུ་དོག་པོ *sems gu-dog-po* narrow-minded; a narrow place, valley or road; གུ་ཡངས་པ *gu-yaṅs-pa* spacious; roomy; wide; གུ་ཡངས་པ་འདུག *gu yaṅs-pa hdug* there is much room here.

གུ་ཡངས་པོ *gu yaṅs-po* = དོགས་པོ་མེད་པ *dogs-po med-pa* spacious; capacious: ས་ཆ་གུ་ཡངས་པ *sa-cha gu yaṅs-pa* a spacious, wide place: སྡོད་ས་གུ་ཡངས་པ *sdod-sa gu yaṅs-pa* a commodious residence: སེམས་གུ་ཡངས་པ *sems gu-yaṅs-pa* a broad, generous heart.

གུ་གུ་ཤ *gu-gu-ça* enamelled plates, cups, &c.; generally enamels on copper.

‡ གུ་གུལ *gu-gul* or གུག་གུལ *gug-gul*, धूपन, देवधूप, गुग्गुल a costly incense, one kind of which is white, another black. It is used in medicine and its smell drives away evil spirits.

Syn. བུམ་མཁན *bum-mkhan*; འདྲེ་འཇིགས *hdre-hjigs*; ནལ་མོ་འདྲ *nal-mo hdra* (*Mṅon.*).

‡ གུ་གུལ་ཤིང *gu-gul-çiṅ* उलूखल, पटीर, पद्मपर्णी *Amyris galloca* the plant from which the incense is obtained.

གུ་གེ *Gu-ge* n. of a province in the West of Tibet. Also n. of a section and school in the Sera monastery. The people of the province of གུ་གེ *Gu-ge* are called གོ་གེ་པ *Go-ge-pa*.

གུ་ཏན *Gu-tan* also called *Go-tan*, the elder grandson of ཇེན་གིས་ཁན *Jen-ghis Khan*, who invited Sakya Paṇḍita to Mongolia in order to introduce Buddhism there.

གུ་ཏི *gu-ti* in *W.* deaf (*Jä.*).

‡ གུ་ཎ་མི་ཏྲ *Gu-ṇa mi-tra* गुणमित्र a Buddhist monk about whom mention is made in the *Phar-phyin* section of the sacred books of Tibet.

གུ་ཟུལ *gu-zul* (for རལ་གུ་ཟུལ་མ *ral-gu zul-ma*) hair-pendants of precious stones of women in Tibet: མོ་རང་གི་རལ་གུ་ཟུལ་ཕུད་ནས་ཕུལ taking off her hair-ornaments, she offered them (*A.* ཀ *102.*).

གུ་ཡར *gu-yar* in *W.* slowly; gently; without noise (*Sch.*).

གུ་ཡུ *gu-yu* पारद quick-silver.

གུ་ཡོག *Gu-yog* 1. བྱའི་རྒྱལ་པོ་ཞིག *byahi rgyal-po shig* n. of a king of birds (*K. my. 18*). 2. n. of the second son of Jengis Khan, who ruled over Eastern Mongolia.

‡ གུ་རུ *gu-ru* गुरु spiritual teacher; a teacher; father-confessor; བླ་མ *bla-ma*, སློབ་དཔོན *slob-dpon*. Often in Milarapa.

གུ་རུ་མཚན་བརྒྱད *Gu-ru mtshan-brgyad* the eight manifestations of the Great Teacher; also the eight names of Padma Sambhava.

གུ་རུག *gu-rug* 1. in *Ld.* a colt or foal of an ass (*Jä.*). 2. n. of a celebrated lama who was tutor to *Rog Çes-rab.*

གུ་ལང་ *gu-laṅ* n. of a deity propitiated by mothers (in Tibet) for the well-being of their children. According to some this deity blesses mothers with children.

གུ་ལིང་ *gu-liṅ* 1. pure gold picked out from a mine. 2. also spelt གུ་གླིང་ *gu-gliṅ*, gold embroidered cloth or silk: གུ་གླིང་གི་ཆོས་གོས་གཅིག་ཕུལ་ནས having presented a religious garment of embroidered silk (to him).

གུ་ལེ *gu-le* in *W.* for ག་ལེ *ga-le* slowly; softly; gently.

‡ **གུ་ཤྲཱི** *Gu-çrī* said to be a corrupt form of the Chinese title of *Kauçiri*, which is conferred on Buddhist monks and religious men, but it is evidently the corruption of the Sanskrit title of *gau-çrī*, the lord of religion or *guṇa-çrī*: in Tibetan ཡོན་ཏན་དཔལ *yon-tan-dpal*, the blessed, learned or talented one. In Mongolian *Kau-çri* signifies a *Paṇḍit* or a learned man.

གུ་ཤྲཱི་སོག་པོ *Gu-çrī sog-po* Gus'ri the Mongolian, in Tib. called གུ་ཤྲཱི་བསྟན་འཛིན་ཆོས་རྒྱལ *Gu-sri bstan-ḥdsin chos-rgyal*, the *Dsuṅgarian* Chief, who conquered Tibet and established the supremacy of the Dalai Lama in 1643 A.D. over all Tibet; also an *Œleuth* Mongolian who belonged to Gus'ri's banners.

གུ་སུ *gu-su* occurs in (*Vai. kar.*) a garment, dress (*Jä.*).

གུག་གུ་བཅན *gug-gu, bçan* an oblation cup: གུག་གུ་བཅན་ནི་ཧོར་གྱི་ཏིང་ལས་ལོད *gug-gu bçan-ni Hor-gyi tiṅ las lod* this name is now applied to enamelled cups made in China (*Jig.*).

‡ གུག་གུལ *gug-gul*, v. གུ་གུལ *gu-gul.*

གུག་པ *gug-pa* 1. དུད་པ *dud-pa*, དད་པས་གུག་པ *dad-pas gug-pa* अवनत bent as in reverence, to bend in salutation: གུག་བཅས *gug-bcas* with humility, humbleness, modesty. 2. In *W.* to rub or scratch gently; to tickle.

གུག་གུག *gug-gug* bend low: མགོ་ལུས་གུག་གུག་གསུམ་གྱིས་ཕྱག་བྱས *mgo-lus gug-gug gsum-gyis phyag-byas* he saluted thrice, bending low his head and body.

གུག་གེ་བ *gug-ge-wa* bent; bent downwards (of leaves) (*Vai. sñ.*), v. གུག་པ *gug-pa.*

གུག་སྲང་ *gug-sraṅ* weight of gold according to the standard formerly used in the province of གུ་གེ *Gu-ge*, a *Sraṅ* or ounce of གུ་གེ *Gu-ge*: གསེར་གུག་སྲང་གསུམ་བརྒྱ་ཕུལ་ནས having presented gold of the weight of 300 ounces (of *Gu-ge*) (*A. 79*).

གུང་ I: *Guṅ* an imperial title, belonging to the second class of nobility in China; it is second only to the distinction of *Wang* or Prince, and is very much prized in Tibet. The recipient wears a ruby button and three plumes of the peacock.

གུང་ II: द्विपिन् variously applied (1) to a species of leopard-cat found in Tibet.

which is smaller than the Himalayan leopard, and (2) to the broad-headed tiger of Central Asia, kharakula of the Mongols, which lives in the forests of the Amur and of North-Western China. The flesh of latter is used in paralysis, and also as an antidote against evil spirits.

གུང་ III: the middle; central; also generally the meridian; noon; midday; as well as, less frequently, midnight; ཉིན་གུང་ *ñin-guñ* midday; noon; མཚན་གུང་ midnight.

གུང་ལ་ *guñ-la* in the middle: སྟོད་ཀྱི་གུང་ནས་ཐོན་ *ṣtoḏ-kyi guñ-naṣ thon* taken or come out of the middle of Upper Tibet.

གུང་དུ་བྱེད་པ་ *guñ-du byeḏ-pa* to divide through middle; to dissect anatomically; དབྱར་གྱི་གུང་ལ་ *dwyar-gyi guñ-la* in the middle of summer; ནམ་གྱི་གུང་ལ་ *nam-gyi guñ-la* at the midnight hour; the middle watch of night.

གུང་རྒྱལ *Guñ-ṟgyal* n. of one of the early kings of Tibet (*Yig.*).

གུང་ཇ་ *guñ-ja* midday tea; also the religious service conducted in a Buddhist monastery at midday when tea is served to the congregated monks.

གུང་གཉིས་ *guñ-gñiṣ* the two middle times, midday and midnight.

གུང་ཐང་ *Guñ-thañ* lit. central plain, n. of a part of Ngāri Khorsum; n. of a monastery in Ngāri.

ཕུལ་གུང་ཐང་ district of Gungthang in western Tsang, the birth-place of *Nag-tsho Lo-tsa-wa Tshul-khrimṣ ṟgyal-wa*, who brought Atis'a to Tibet.

གུང་ཐང་འཇམ་དབྱངས་ *Guñ-thañ Ḫjam-ḏbyañs* n. of an incarnate Lama of Amdo, who became the high priest of *Tashi Gomañ* monastery of Amdo and erected a lofty chorten-temple 360 feet high; and founded a monastery with a library containing 20,000 block-print volumes.

གུང་ཐང་རྩའི་ཀོ་རོན་ *Guñ-thañ Ṟtsaḫi ko ron* the birth-place of *Milaraṣpa* the poet and saint.

གུང་པ་ *guñ-pa* = འབྲིང་པོ་ *ḫbriñ-po* मध्यम the second of three brothers; the middle one.

གུང་འབབ་པ་ *guñ ḫbab-pa* to take rest at noon on a journey; གུང་ཚིགས་ *guñ-tshigṣ* dinner (*Sch.*).

གུང་འཛུག་ *guñ-ḫdsug* मध्याङ्गुलि also *gung-mo*, the middle finger.

གུང་རི་གུང་བཙན་ *Guñ-ri guñ-ḇtsan* the son and successor of King ཁྲི་སྲོང་ལྡེའུ་བཙན་ *Khri-ṣroñ ḻdeḫu-ḇtsan* who reigned in Tibet about 733 A.D.

གུང་ལ་ཕུག *guñ-la phug* or གུང་དམར་ལ་ཕུག་ *guñ ḏmar-la phug* carrot.

གུང་སངས་ལ་འགྲོ་བ་ *guñ-sañṣ la ḫgro-wa* to take a walk about midday, also generally to take a walk གུང་ལོན་ *guñ-lon* at noon.

གུད *guḏ* 1. slope; declivity (*Cs.*). 2. separation; solitude; seclusion (*Sch.*).

གུད་དུ་ *guḏ-du* = ལོགས་སུའམ་སྒེར་དུ་ *logs suham ṣger-du* aside; apart: ཡང་ཇོ་བོས་ཕྱག་དར་སྟོན་པ་ལ་གུད་དུ་གསུངས་པ་ again *Joḇo* spoke to *Phyag-dar ṣton-pa* while alone in a solitary place (*A. 5*).

གུད་དུ་འབོར་བ་ *guḏ-du ḫbor-wa* 1. to place aslant or to one side; གུད་དུ་གཀེགས་པ་ *guḏ-du gegṣ-pa* to separate (*Jä.*), disperse. 2. to buy dear, at a loss; synonymous with གུན་གོད་ *gun-goḏ*; in *Lad.* heavy or thick of hearing; གུད་ནག་ *guḏ-nag* quite deaf; deaf as a post. 3. གུད་དུ་འཇུག་པ་ *guḏ-du ḫjug-pa* = ལོགས་སུ་བཞག་པ་ *logṣ-su ḇshag-pa* or ཞན་དུ་བཙུག་པ

shan-du bcug-pa to humiliate; deprecate; to place in a false or inferior position.

གུད་པ *gud-pa*=འགུད་པ *hgud-pa*.

གུད་པོ *gud-po* dear; expensive, v. རྒུད་པོ *rgud-po*.

གུན *gun* loss; damage: ང་ལ་གུན་ཕོག *ṅa-la gun-phog* in *W*., I have suffered loss (prop. damago has como to me) (*Jä.*). གུན་ཁ་གསབ་པ to make up a loss: གཞན་གུན་ན་ཕར་ལ་ང་རྒྱལ་གྱི་དྲེགས་པ་བཙོངས་པས་ཉིན་རེ་ཙམ་གྱི་གུན་ཁ་གསབས in all other placos, on the other hand, they out of pride almost daily tried to replenish their loss (*Hbrom.* ཁ *33*).

གུན་དུམ *gun-dum* a bottlo-shaped or cylindrical basket for fruit in *Ld.* (perhaps akin to *rkon-pa*) (*Jä.*).

གུན་པོ *gun-po* in *Ld.* expensive; doar.

གུམ་སྟེ *gum-ste*=ཤི་ནས *çi-nas* or ཤི་སྟེ *çi-ste* having died or been dead: དེ་ནས་ཡུན་མི་རིང་བར་བྲམ་ཟེ་གུམ་སྟེ *de-nas yun mi-riṅ war Bram-ze gum-ste* thon, not long aftor, the Brāhmaṇ having died (*Hbrom. 162*).

གུམ་པ *gum-pa*, v. འགུམ་པ *hgum-pa*.

གུར *gur* खरपटह, पञ्जर, प्रासाद a tent; also a house made of hay or straw or grass; དབུ་གུར *dwu-gur* a sleeping tent; བཞུགས་གུར *bshugs-gur* a tent used by a great man for his residence; གུར་ཡོལ *gur-yol* the ceiling of a tent; གུར་ཁེབས *gur-khebs* the cover or canopy; རས་གུར *ras-gur* tent of cotton cloth; རྒྱལ་གུར *rgyal-gur* royal pavilion; དམག་གུར *dmag-gur* a military tent; གུར་མཆོག *gur-mchog* a magnificent tent; གུར་ཐག *gur-thag* tent robes; གུར་བེར *gur-ber* in *W*., or གུར་ཤིང *gur-çiṅ*, the tent poles; གུར་ཐོག *gur-thog* the upper covering or outer-fly of a tent; ཐབ་གུར *thab-gur* hearth-tent; that which is used as a kitchen; གུར་གྱི་ཤམ་བུ *gur-gyi çam-bu* the outer canopy-liko cover of a tent; the upper part of a doublo tent; གུར་ཕུར *gur-phur* the pegs or pins used for pitching a tent: གུར་གཞོལ *gur-gshol* the walls of a tent; གུར་གླད *gur-glad* the top or crown of a tont; the passage for the smoke out of a tent; གུར་འགྲམ *gur-hgram* lattice in tho side of a tent; གུར་ལྕམ *gur-lcam* stakes supporting the roof of a tent (*Sch.*).

གུར་ཁང་ *gur-khaṅ* the imaginary pavilion or mansion of tho gods, which is formed in the sky, canopied by rain-bows, walled by rays of light, supported by diamond posts and carpetted with variegatod clouds, for the use of the gods when they come to witness religious entertainmonts or performancos of the pious on this earth.

གུར་གྱི་མགོན་པོ *Gur-gyi mgon-po* a divinity of the Sakya-pa School.

གུར་དྲག *Gur-drag* n. of a Buddhist deity of tho Sakya-pa School.

གུར་ནག *gur-nag* these of tho black tent, or the Black-tent Mongols; གུར་དཀར *gur-dkar* tho Whito-tent tribes of Mongolia; གཅོད་གུར *gcod-gur* the tent used by itinerant mendicants or *Shamans*.

གུར་པ་གྲྭ་ཚང *gur-pa grba-tshaṅ* a Buddhist congregation at རྒྱང་རྩེ *Gyaṅ-tse*.

གུར་ལྤགས *gur-lpags* a perforated skin; a hide full of holes (*Sch.*).

གུར་སེར *gur-ser* the tribe of the Mongols who used to live in yellow tents. The Tāranātha Lama of Urga (Tah Khureh) in Mongolia still uses the yellow tent.

× **གུར་གུམ** *gur-gum* or གུར་ཀུམ *gur-kum* कुङ्कुम, काश्मीरज saffron, crocus, marigold, calendula, and similar yellow flowers (*Jä.*) : གུར་གུམ་མཆིན་ནད་ཀུན་སེལ་རྩ་ཁ་སྡོམ *gur-gum m̱chin-naḏ kun sel ṟtsa kha s̱dom* saffron cures liver-disorders and contracts the surface of the bowels (*Ṟtsii.*). There are three kinds of saffron known to the Tibetans ; བལ་པོ་གུར་གུམ *Bal-po gur-gum* the saffron of Nepal ; ཁ་ཆེ་གུར་གུམ *kha-che gur-gum* the Kashmir saffron, which is the best, and ཀྲི་ཡང་ཀུ or ཀྲི་ཡ་ཀ, that is brought from distant regions (Spice-islands).

Syn. ཚིམ་བྱེད་དམར *tshim byeḏ ḏmar* ; འདབ་བརྒྱ་བ *ẖdab ḇṟgya-wa* ; རྫིང་དྲུང་སྐྱེས *ṟdsiń ḏṟuń s̱kyes* ; མེ་ཏོག་དོན་ཅན *me-tog don-can* ; ཀུན་ནས་འཁུམས *kun-nas ẖkhums* ; མེ་ཏོག་ཉི་མ *me-tog ñi-ma* ; ཕྲ་མ་ཅན *phra-ma-can* ; ཁ་ཆེ་སྐྱེས *kha-che-s̱kyes* ; དྲི་ཞིམ *ḏṟi-shim* ; ལུས་དམར *lus-ḏmar* ; མེའི་རྩེ་མོ *meẖi ṟtse-mo* ; བདེ་བྱེད *ḇde-byeḏ* ; འཐུང་བྱེད *ẖthuń-byeḏ* ; མཆོག་ལྡན *m̱chog-ḻdan* ; དཔའ་པོ་བརྟན་པ *ḏpaẖ-po ḇṟtan-pa* (*M̱ńon:*).

གུར་གུར *gur-gur* in *Ld.* a small churn used for preparing tea. (*Jä.*)

གུར་ཏིག *gur-tig* a kind of drug used for healing or drawing sores, &c. ; རྨ་གས་རྩ་ཚད་མཁྲིས་ནད་སེལ *ṟma gas ṟtsa tshaḏ m̱khris naḏ-sel* it inflames sores, cures bilious fever.

གུལ་གུལ *gul-gul* a quaking ; shaken as if by a strong wind : ཁྲོ་བོའི་སྟང་སྟབས་མཛད་པས་ཡུལ་ཆེན་པོ་གཅིག་གུལ་གུལ་བྱུང་སྐད *khro-ḇoẖi s̱tań-s̱tabs m̱dsaḏ-pas yul chen-po gcig gul-gul byuń s̱kaḏ* It is said that because they assumed the attitude of a wrathful deity, a great country trembled (as if by an earth-quake).

གུལ་ནག *gul-nag*, lit. the black གུ་གུལ *gu-gul* or གུག་གུལ་ནག་པོ *gug-gul nag-po*, n. of a medicine.

གུས་པ *gus-pa* श्रद्धा, सम्भ्रम, आदर, भक्ति गौरव, अभिवादन, सौरभ्यं, समाप्ति, नम्र, मान, sbst. humility, respect, reverence, devotion ; also adj. respectful, devout ; very common in the phrase *gus-pas phyag ẖtshal-lo*, saluted with reverence ; མ་གུས་པ *ma-gus-pa* unsubmissive, undevout ; གུས་པ་དང་བཅས་པ *gus-pa dań ḇcas-pa* सगौरव respectfully ; with dignity and honour ; གུས་པར་འགྱུར་བ *gus-par ẖgyur-wa* to be respectful ; to humble one-self (*Cs.*) ལུས་ངག་ཡིད་གསུམ་གུས་པས་ཕྱག་འཚལ་ལོ I offer salutation reverentially with the three—my heart, speech and body : གུས་པ་ཆེན་པོས་བསྟེན་པར་བྱིན་གྱིས་རློབས *gus-pa chen-pos ḇs̱ten-par byin-gyis-ṟlobs* may the blessing be granted to maintain the greatest devotion. གུས་པར་བསྒྲིམ་པ *gus-par ḇs̱gṟim-pa* to behave with respect ; གུས་པར་ཉན *gus-par ñan* शुश्रूषा to serve or attend respectfully ; to listen with respect ; གུས་པར་བྱེད་པ to regard.

གུས་པོ *gus-po* in *C.* and *W.* expensive, costly, dear, v. གུད་པོ *guḏ-po* or རྒུད་པོ *ṟguḏ-po*.

གུས་སོ *gus-so* वनति becomes very dear ; respects ; worships.

གེ *ge* num. for 93.

གེ་བ *ge-wa* is an auxiliary particle signifying did (emphatically) : ཡ་སོའི་མཆེ་བས་བྲང་ཁ་ནོན་མ་སོའི་མཆེ་བས་དཔྲལ་བ་ན་ཡར་ལ་ལྷག་གེ་བ *ya-soẖi m̱che-was brań kha non, ma-soẖi m̱che-was ḏpral-wa na yar-la lhag ge-wa* by the upper tusk he pressed on his breast, by his lower tusk he opened asunder up to the forehead (*H̱brom. 139*).

གེ་ར *Ge-ra* n. of a country : གེ་རའི་རྒྱལ་པོ་ཤེས་པའང་བྱུང་འདུག *Ge-raẖi ṟgyal-po shes-pahań byuń-ẖdug* also there was one, called the King of གེ་ར *Ge-ra* (*K. du.* ཞ *281*).

གེ་ར་ལྷ་པ *Ge-ra lha-pa* name of a Tibetan chief, said to have descended from the royal line of kings, *i.e.*, from *Sroṅ-btsan sgam-po*, and belonging to a place called གེ་ར་ལྷ *Ge-ra lha* situated to the east of Lhasa on the Yaru Tsang-po beyond Chethang.

གེ་ཤ *ge-ça* a kerchief for the head hanging down behind from the shoulders.

‡ **གེ་སར** I: *ge-sar* सुरभिगन्धि, केशरं, किञ्जल्क, काश्मीरज, प्रियक saffron, the corolla of a flower. There are three kinds of གེ་སར *ge-sar* viz:—ན་ག་གེ་སར *na-ga ge-sar* नागकेशर, པུཥ་པ་གེ་སར *pus-pa ge-sar* पुष्पकेशर, and པད་མ་གེ་སར *pad-ma ge-sar* पद्मकेशर (*Miṅ.*). Acc. to *Cs.* གེ་སར is a flower; it is said to grow in Nepal and is called པད་མ་གེ་སར *pad-ma ge-sar*; acc. to *Sch.* pistil, but like ཟེ་འབྲུ *ze-hbru* it signifies undoubtedly the organs of fructification in general.

‡ **གེ་སར** II: *Ge-sar* n. of a powerful king ruling in Shensi in China, who on account of his martial valour was deified and raised to the position of the God of War. There are various accounts of him. The people of Kham in Tibet own him for their national war-god, while the Mongolians say that གེ་སར *Ge-sar* was a king of Mongolia. According to some authors, he lived in the 7th century A.D. According to the collection of heroic songs called the རྒྱལ་དྲུང *Rgyal-druṅ*, King *Ge-sar* lived in the 8th century A.D. His origin is, however, lost in myth.

གེ་སར་གྱི་སྒྲུང *ge-sar-gyi sgruṅ* stories from the works called གླིང་དང་འཇང *Liṅg* and *Jaṅg*; also extracts from the fabulous history of Ge-sar.

གེ་སར་ཅན *ge-sar-can* केसर the lotus flower; the filament of a lotus.

གེ་སར་དམར་པོ *ge-sar dmar-po*, ཀླུ་ཤིང *glu-çiṅ*, Nāga Vṛkṣa (*Mṅon.*).

གེ་ཧྱ *ge-hya*, གནས *gnas* a secret abode—used as གསང་སྐད *gsaṅ-skad* (a mystic word) in the *Tantra* (*K.* ག *g. 215*).

གེགས *gegs*=གགས *gags* विबन्ध, प्रतिबन्ध hindrance; stoppage; obstacle: གེགས་ཆགས་ *gegs-chags*=བར་ཆད *bar-chad* interruption by an accident; danger; ཐེ་ཚོམ་དང་གེགས་སེལ་བ to remove doubts and hindrances (*Mil.*); གེགས་བྱེད་བགེགས a malignant spirit causing mischief or impediments; ཆོས་མཛད་ཡོངས་ལ་གེགས་བྱེད་པ to hinder effectually religious doings; སངས་རྒྱས་མི་ཐོབ་པའི་གེགས་བཞི four obstacles to the attainment of Buddhahood: ཐོབ་པའི་གྲོགས་འགྲོའམ་གེགས་སུ་འགྲོ *thob-paḥi grogs ḥgroḥam gegs-su ḥgro* will you help me or hinder me in obtaining; འགྲུབ་པའི་གེགས *ḥgrub-paḥi gegs* impediment to the attainment of perfection.

+ **གེལ་པ** *gel-pa* the trunk of a tree with a spiral top: གེལ་བ་ནི་ཤིང་ཕུང་ངམ་རྩ་བ་སྦོམ་ཤིང་རྩེ་མོ་རྒྱས་པ *gel-wa ni çiṅ phuṅ ṅam rtsa-wa sbom çiṅ rtse-mo rgyas-pa* the term *gelwa* is when the stem or thick roots of a tree grow into a branching top.

གེལ་ཤིང *gel-çiṅ* स्तम्भ a log; a post.

གཻན་དར་པ *Gain-dar-pa* བྱའི་རྒྱལ་པོ་ཞིག་གི་མིང n. of a king of birds. (*K. my.* ཀ, *18*).

གོ I: *go* 1. numerical sign for 123. 2. abbr. for དགུ་བཅུ *dgu-bcu* in the nineties; གོ་གཅིག *go-gcig* 91; also གོ་གཉིས *go-gñis* 92, etc.

གོ II:=in mystic language ཁྱུ་མཆོག *khyu-mchog* पुङ्गव, ऋषभ, वृष the chief of a herd or company (*K. g.* ཁ, *28*).

གོ III: 1. place; room; space (prob.= གུ *gu*); in this sense it is used in མཚམས་མེད་པར *m̱tshams̱ meḏ-par*, without intermediate space, *i.e.*, close together, continuous: འབྲུ་སྣ་ཚོགས་གོ་མཚམས་མེད་པར་སྐྱེས *ẖbru s̱na-tshogs̱ go m̱tshams̱ meḏ-par s̱kyes̱* grain of every kind grew densely, luxuriantly: གོ་མཚམས་མེད་པར་གང་བ *go-m̱sthams meḏ-par gaṅ-wa* closely filled. An important compound of *go* is found in གོ་ཆོད *go-choḏ*, the space is cut off, or filled, *i.e.*, the matter is done with, settled; satisfaction has been made; colloq. also I have got enough; I am full: དེས་རྒྱལ་བའི་གོ་མི་ཆོད་པ *des̱ ṟgyal-wahi go-mi choḏ-pa* by this the victory has not yet been fully decided: ཐོས་བསམ་སྒོམ་གསུམ་གྱི་གོ་ཆོད *thos̱-ḇsam s̱gom g̱sum-gyi go-choḏ* there is intermission of hearing; thinking; meditation: ཁྱེད་ལ་གོ་མི་ཆོད་པའི་ཆོས *khyed-la go-mi-choḏ paẖi chos̱* doctrine not satisfactory to you: བུ་ཚབ་ང་སྤྱུགས་ཅི་ཕྱིར་གོ་མི་ཆོད *bu-tshab ṅa s̱pyugs̱ ci-phyir go-mi-choḏ* why should it not be sufficient that I be banished instead of my son? 2. place, position, rank, condition of life: ཕ་ཡི་གོར *pha-yi gor* in the place of his father; གོ་ནས *go-nas̱* according to; in proportion to (*Jä.*): གོ་རྒས་ན *go ṟgas̱-na* when rank and dignity are grown old and gone; when the position in life has been lost: ངང་གི་གོ་འདུག that is my place; my business. 3. a way, a space, in the more general sense: སྤྲིན་གྱི་གོ་བར་ཕྱེ་ནས་འོངས *s̱prin-gyi go-war phye-nas̱ ẖoṅs̱* have come parting the clouds: ཨ་མའི་གོ་ན *a-maẖi go na* at the place of my mother; with my mother (*Jä.*). གོ་ལྡོག་པ *go ḻdog-pa* to change place, especially to turn to the contrary (*Sch.*); ནད་གོ *naḏ-go* the seat of disease (*Sch.*).

གོ་སྐབས *go-s̱kabs̱* अवकाश, स्थान, अन्तर, अवसर, मध्य interval; leisure; space; opportunity; in the meanwhile: བར་མཚམས་ཚིག་གྲོགས་ཀྱིས་དལ་བ་དང་ཁོམ་པ་དང་དབང་དང་ལོང་ཡོད་མེད occasionally with companion words *go-s̱kabs̱* signifies slowly, at leisure, or in power; just at the time: བདེ་བར་བསྡད་པའི་གོ་སྐབས་མེད *ḇde-war ḇs̱daḏ-paẖi go s̱kabs̱-meḏ* there is no chance of my sitting at ease: དེ་ཕྱིར་བདག་ལ་གོ་སྐབས་སྩལ་དུ་གསོལ *de-phyir ḇdag-la go-s̱kabs̱ s̱tsal-du g̱sol* (*A. 16*) therefore I pray for leave to avail myself of this opportunity.

གོ་སྐལ *go-s̱kal* the share or portion due to a person in accordance to his rank (*Jä.*).

གོ་ཁང་ *go-khaṅ*, གོ་ཆའི་ཁང་པ *go-chaẖi khaṅ-pa* arsenal (*Schtr.*).

གོ་ཁྲབ *go-khrab*= གོ་ཆ་དང་ཁྲབ *go-cha daṅ krab* coat of mail with helmet; armour, v. གོ་ཆ *go-cha*.

གོ་གྱོན་པ *go-gyon-pa*, གོ་ཆ་གྱོན་པ *go-cha gyon-pa* to wear a coat of mail, etc.; to put on war dress.

Syn. གོ་བགོས *go-bgos*; གཡུལ་གྱི་ཆས་ཞུགས་པ *g̱yul gyi chas̱ shugs̱-pa*; ཡ་ལད་བགོས *ya-laḏ ḇgos̱* (*M̱ṅon.*).

གོ་གྲལ *go-gral* or གོ་གྲས *go-gras̱* rank; dignity (*Cs.*).

གོ་བགོས་པ *go-ḇgos pa* सज्जीकरण the act of equipping or arraying:= གོ་ཆ་གྱོན་པ *go-cha gyon-pa* to equip with armour; put on harness, v. གོ་ཆ *go-cha*.

གོ་ཙ *go-ca*, v. གོ་ཆ *go-cha*.

གོ་ཆ *go-cha* सज्ज, वर्म, सन्न, सन्नाह, कञ्चुक निर्मोक, दंशन; कवच armour; harness; gear; implements; tools; བཀྲ་ཤིས་ཀྱི་གོ་ཆ *ḇkra-çis-kyi go-cha* the implement of good luck; an amulet.

Syn. ཡ་ལད *ya-laḏ*; མཚོན་སྐྱོབ; *m̱tshon-s̱kyob*; ལུས་སྐྱོབ *lus̱-s̱kyob*; ལུས་བསྲུང *lus̱-s̱ruṅ*; ལྕགས་གོས *ḻchags-gos*; ཞུབ་ཅན *shub-can*; དཔ་ཅན

dra-wa can; འཁྲུག་གོས *hkhrug-gos*; ལྕགས་ཀྱི་བགོ་བ *lcags-kyi bgo-wa*; ཁྲབ *khrab*; རྨོག *rmog*; མགོ་སྐྱོབ *mgo skyob*; རྨོག་ཞུ *rmog-shu*; ལྕགས་ཞུ *lcogs-shu*; རྨོག་ཐུར *rmog-thur*; ཁྱུང་ཐུར་ཅན *khyuṅ-thur can*; གོ་ཁྲབ *go-khrab* (*Mṅon.*).

གོ་ཆ་གྱོན་པ *go-cha gyon-pa*, v. གོ་གྱོན་པ *go gyon-pa* or གོ་བགོས་པ *go bgos-pa*.

* གོ་ཆ་དང་བཅས *go-cha daṅ bcas* सगुल (*Schr.*; *Kālāc. T. 139*) with a ball.

* གོ་ཆའི་སྐྲག་བྱེད་མ *go-chahi Skrag byed-ma*. (*22 B.*) (*Schr.*)

* གོ་ཆའི་བསྐྱོད་བྱེད་མ *go-chahi Bskyod-byed-ma*. (*Schr.*) (*22 C.*)

* གོ་ཆའི་རྟ་མཆོག *go-chahi Rta-mchog*. (*Schr.*) (*21 A.*)

* གོ་ཆའི་རྡོ་རྗེ་ཉི་མ *go-chahi Rdo-rje ñi-ma*. (*Schr.*) (*20 C.*)

* གོ་ཆའི་རྡོ་རྗེ་སེམས་དཔའ *go-chahi Rdo-rje sems-dpah*. (*19 B.*)

* གོ་ཆའི་རྣམ་སྣང *go-chahi Rnam-snaṅ*. (*19 C.*)

* གོ་ཆའི་པད་མ་གར་དབང *go-chahi Pad-ma gar-dwaṅ*. (*Schr.*) (*20 A.*)

* གོ་ཆའི་རྨོངས་བྱེད་མ, *go-chahi Rmoṅs-byed-ma*. (*Schr.*) (*22 A.*)

* གོ་ཆའི་ཙཎྜི་ཀ *go-chahi Tsaṇ-ḍi ka*. (*Schr.*) (*23 A.*)

* གོ་ཆའི་གཤིན་རྗེ་མ *go-chahi Gçin-rje-ma*. (*Schr.*) (*21 C.*)

* གོ་ཆའི་ཧེ་རུ་ཀ་ནག་པོ *ge-chhi He-ru-ka nag-po*. (*Schr.*) (*20 B.*)

གོ་ཆོད་པོ *go-chod-po*=ཕན་ཐོག་པོ *phan-thog-po* useful; serviceable. ལས་དོན་གང་བྱེད་ཀྱང་བསྒྲུབ་ནུས་པའམ་མཐར་ཕྱིན་པའི་མི་ལ་གོ་ཆོད་པོ་ཟེར *las don gaṅ-byed kyaṅ bsgrub-nus paham mthar phyin-pahi mi-la go-chod-po zer* the term *go-chod-po* is applied to a man who is successful or who accomplishes any business or duty successfully: མི་འདི་གོ་ཆོད་དམ *mi-hdi go chod-dam* will this man be of service? (*A. 127*).

གོ་སྙོད *go-sñod* षजाजी cummin seed (*Zam. 24*).

‡ གོ་དཱ་བ་རི *go-dā wa-ri* the Godavari river. ཐུགས་ཀྱི་གནས་བརྒྱད་ཀྱི་གཅིག་བེ་ཏའི་ཡུལ་གྱི་ལྷོ་ཐག་ཉེ་སར་ཡོད, ཧོ་མའི་ཆུ་མིག་སོགས་གནས་ཡ་མཚན་ཅན་མང *thugs-kyi gnas brkyad kyi-gcig, be-tahi yul-gyi lho-thag ñe sar-yod, ho-mahi chu-mig sogs gnas-ya mtshan-can maṅ* Godāvari, one of the holy rivers of Southern India, a place on its bank near Vidharva where there is spirit-symbol of Buddha. It contains a milky spring (*Dsam. 36*).

‡ གོ་དམ་བཱ *go-dam bā* n. of a drug

Syn. ཡངས་པ་ཅན *yaṅs-pa can*; རི་མོ་ཅན *ri-mo can*; བ་གླང་མིག *ba-glaṅ mig*; མཆོག་སྦྱིན་མ *mchog sbyin-ma*; དབང་པོ་བཀྲ་བ *dbaṅ-po bkra-wa*; ཀཾ་ཀ་ཆེན་པོ *kam-ka chen-po* (*Mṅon.*).

གོ་བདེ་བ *go-bde-wa* simple; easy; that which is easily understood: གོ་བདེ་བ་ལ་བསམས་ནས་དཔེར་བརྗོད་ན *go-bde-wa la bsam-nas dper-bjod na* he uttered an example with a view to make it easily understood (*Situ. 101*).

\+ གོ་འདུན *go-hdun*, defined as སྣ་ཚོགས་སམ་གང་མོས་པ *sna-tshogs-sam gaṅ mos-pa* what you like of different kinds.

གོ་འདྲིས་ཁྱེར་བ *go-hdris khyer-wa*=དགའ་པོ་ཉེས་པོ་བྱེད་པ to be friendly; intimate (*A. 145*).

* གོ་ཌ *go-ḍa* गौड़वर्द्धन; གོ་ཌ་འཕེལ་བྱེད *Go-ḍa hphel-byed* n. pr. (*Schr.*) (*Tā. 2, 82*).

གོ་འཕང *go-hphaṅ*=གོ་གནས rank; place; position: རྣམ་མཁྱེན་སངས་རྒྱས་ཀྱི་གོ་འཕང་ཐོབ་པར་བྱིན་གྱིས་བརླབས may the blessing be accorded me to gain the rank of an omniscient Buddha (*Mil.*).

གོ་བ *go-wa* to understand; to perceive mentally: དང་པོ་པཎྜི་ཏ་ཀུན་གྱི་གོ་བ་བྱུང *daṅ-po paṇ-ḍi-ta kun-gyi go wa byuṅ* first of all it was understood by all the Paṇḍits.

གོ་བ་ཅན *go-wa can* = མཁས་པ a learned, clear-headed person; གོ་བ་ཅན་གྱི་མི་རྣམས wise men.

གོ་བོ *go-ḅo* or བྱ་གོ་བོ *ḅya-go-ḅo* a kind of vulture: གོ་བོའི་གྲེ་བས་ཤ་མ་ཞུ་བ་དང་, མ་ཞུ་བའི་རིགས་རྣམས་འཇུ་བར་བྱེད *go-woḥi gre-waṣ ça-ma shu-wa dañ, ma-shu-waḥi rigṣ-ṛnamṣ ḥju-war byeḍ* the larynx of the vulture causes indigestible meat and different kinds of food which are not digested, to become digested (*Ṣman.*).

གོ་བྱེད *go-byeḍ* acc. to *Jä.* is a quality of the air.

གོ་བཟློག *yo-ḅzlog* (*go-ḍog*) = གོ་ལོག *go-log* misunderstand; misapprehend; to attach a wrong meaning (*Situ. 110*).

‡ གོ་ཡུ *go-yu* (Beng. গুবা) areca nut: གོ་ཡུས་མཁལ་མའི་ནད་སེལ་སོ་རྩི་མཆོག areca nut is the best essence for the tee'h and cures kidney disease (*Ṣman.*).

+ གོ་ར *go-ra* = བཙོན་ར *ḅtson-ra* jail; prison.

གོ་རིམ *go-rim* order, arrangement: གོ་རིམ་དང་མཐུན་པར་ཇུང་ཟད་བཀོད་པས have arranged it so as to agree with the order of things, etc. (*Situ. 101*).

+ གོ་རེ *go-re* = རྫོགས་པ *ṛdsogṣ-pa* perfected; finished; completed.

+ གོ་རེ་ལོང་ *go-re loñ* = མངག་གཞུག་པ *ṃṅag gshug-pa* or རང་དབང་མེད་པ *rañ-ḍwañ meḍ-pa* spontaneously; as a matter of course; without power to exert one's self in any matter; necessarily (*K. du.* ཕ *175*).

གོ་ལ *go-la*, རྒྱ་ནག་གི་སྲ་རྩིའི་རྒྱུ་སེ་ཤིང་གི་ཁུ་བ *ṛgya-nag gi sra-ṛtsiḥi ṛgyu-se çiñ-gi khu-wa* 1. a kind of gum, prob. acacia imported to Tibet from China; ashes which have burnt without ignition. 2. མགྲོན་བུ་མེར་བསྲེག་པའི་ཐལ་བ lime of burnt shell or cowries. 3. the areca nut brought from the sub-Himalayan district or from India is called སྨན་གོ་ལ *ṣman go-la, i.e.*, the globular medicine; རྒྱ་གར་གོ་ཡུ *ṛgya-gar go-yu* the Indian areca nut, or མོན་གོ་ཡུ, areca nut from the sub-Himalaya; these two are called སྨན་གོ་ལ *ṣman-go-la* (*Ṣman.*).

གོ་ལའི་རླུང *go-laḥi-ṛluñ* ཉི་ཟླ་གཟའ་སྐར་རྒྱུ་བ་འི་རླུང་གི་མིང the wind which, acc. to Tibetan astronomers, keeps the sun and the stars moving in space: ཕེབས་ཚོགས་ཀྱང་གོ་ལའི་རླུང་འགྲོས་ལྟར་འགོག་མེད་དུ་ཞུ *phebṣ-tshogṣ kyañ Go-laḥi ṛluñ-ḥgroṣ ḷtar ḥgog-meḍ-du shu* your letters should also be without let or hindrance, like the wind which keeps the heavenly bodies always in motion (*Yig. k. 87*).

གོ་ལེ *go-le* = ག་ལེ *ga-le* or དལ་པོ *dal-po* slowly.

གོ་ཥ *go-ṣa*, ཨོ་རྒྱན་ལམ་བར་གྱི་གྲོང་ཁྱེར་ཞིག་གི་མིང་ n. of a town in the way to Udyāna, prob. in Ancient Kabul (*S. Lam. 17.*).

གོ་ལོག *go-log* the reverse; opposite to what was; back again; also for གོ་ས་ལོག་པ *go-sa log-pa* degraded; position changed as in the case of a superior officer subordinated, or an inferior officer promoted to a higher position:—དཔོན་པོ་གཡོག *ḍpon-po gyog* master made a subordinate or servant, or གཡོག་པོ་དཔོན *gyog-po ḍpon*, a servant raised to the position of a master; ཕན་པར་སྨྲས་པ་ལ་གནོད་པར་གོ་བ་ལྟ་བུ *phan-par smraṣ-pa la gnoḍ-par go-wa ḷta-bu* to take a useful advice as intended for mischief; also སྦྱིན་པ་གོ་ལོག opposed to charity or misunderstand charity; ཚུལ་ཁྲིམས་གོ་ལོག reversing, misinterpreting character or morality; བཟོད་པ་གོ་ལོག *ḅzoḍ-pa go-log*, བརྩོན་འགྲུས་གོ་ལོག *ḅṛtson-ḥgrus go-log* to misunderstand one's forbearance or industry; བསམ་གཏན་གོ་ལོག performance of the wrong *Dhyāna*; ཤེས་རབ་གོ་ལོག perverse or distorted knowledge or wisdom; སྙིང་རྗེ་གོ་ལོག *ṣñiñ-ṛje go-log* tired of showing sympathy or compassion; བྱམས་པ་གོ་ལོག *byamṣ-pa go-log* tired of loving.

གོ་ས *go-sa*, = གོ་གནས or གོ་འཕང་ rank; office; dignity: བླ་མ་མཁན་པོ་རྒྱལ་བློན་སོགས་ཀྱི་གོ་ས་ལྟ་བུ་ལ *bla-ma mkhan-po rgyal-blon sogs-kyi go-sa lta-bu-la* like unto the position of the lamas, professors, officers, etc.

‡ ག་ཏ་མ *gau-ta-ma* = གཱོ་ཏ་མ *Gohu-ta-ma* རིགས་རུས་ཀྱི་མིང་། गौतम n. of a family in Ancient India (*K. du.* ₅ *133*); n. of Buddha S'ākyamuni.

གོག *gog* in *W.* for གོང་པོ *goṅ-po* a lump.

གོག་ཐལ *gog-thal* ashes; burnt fragments.

གོག་པ *gog-pa* 1. to crawl. 2. to crumble off; to scale off (of the plaster of a wall) (*Jä.*).

གོག་པོ = ཤིག་རལ་བྱུང་བ *shig-ral byuṅ-wa* or ཉམས་ཆག་བྱུང་བ *ñams-chag byuṅ-wa* dilapidated; damaged; in ruins; worn out: ལྷ་ཁང་གོག་པོ a temple in ruins: མཆོད་རྟེན་གོག་པོ a chorten in ruins: ཁ་ཅིག་གོག་པོ་འགོག་ཙམ་ན་འཆི་བའང་ཡོད there are some who even die worn out when they crawl about (as little children) (*Khrid. 13*).

*གོ་བཟློག་ལྷན་སྐྱེས *go-bzlog lhan-skyes* (*Schr.*) (*30 A.*).

*གོ་ལའི་རི་མོ *go-lahi ri-mo* गोलरेखा (*Kālac. I. 52 58*) a circle; circular.

གོང་ *goṅ* 1. price; value; also གོང་ཐང *goṅ-thaṅ* གོང་ཚད *goṅ-tshad*; ནོར་རྫས་ཀྱི་རིན་གོང་གི་ཚད *nor-rdsas kyi rin goṅ-gi tshad* the price or valuation of things or property: གོང་དཔྱད་པ *goṅ dpyad-pa* to apprize; to fix a price: གོང་བརྒྱབ་པ *goṅ brgyab-pa* or གོང་སྒྲིག་པ *goṅ sgrig-pa* id. In Sikkim: "*di goṅ ka dzô mo*" what is the price of it? (*Snd. Hbk.*) 2. = སྟེང *steṅ* or སྔོན *sṅon* or ཐོག་མ *thag-ma* also ཀླད *klad* उपरि, उत the above; in space as well as in time (in *Khams*, *e.g.*, it is used as a sbst. signifying elevated, alpine pasture grounds). གོང་དང་མཐུན *goṅ daṅ mthun*, གོང་དང་འདྲ་བར *goṅ-daṅ hdra-war*, གོང་བཞིན *goṅ-bshin*, གོང་མཚུངས *goṅ-mtshuṅs* as above (mentioned); like the above or aforesaid similar to the above.

གོང་འཁོད *goṅ-hkhod* stated above; གོང་དུ་ཡོད་པ *goṅ-du yod-pa* existing above; གོང་དུ་གསལ་བར *goṅ-du gsal war*, set forth or elucidated above; གོང་གི *goṅ-gi* the former; the above; གོང་གི་དེ་རྣམས *goṅ-gi de rnams* those preceding; གོང་གི་ཤེས་སྨོས་པ *goṅ-gi shes smos-pa* the above statement that; སྔ་གོང་བོད་ཀྱི་རྒྱལ་པོ *sṅa goṅ Bod-kyi rgyal-po* the ancient or former Tibetan kings; གོང་གི་བཤད་པ་ལྟར *goṅ-gi bçad-pa ltar* as has been stated above; གོང་དུ *goṅ-du* over it; above; གོང་དུ་འཕགས་པ *goṅ-du hphags-pa* उन्नय taken upwards; gone upwards; improved; progressed; གོང་དུ་ཕུད *goṅ-du phud* placed in a position of dignity; kept on the top; གོང་དུ་འཕོ་བ *goṅ-du hpho-wa*, जर्ध्व यातः spiritually developed, lit. gone upwards; གོང་དུ་སྦྱོར་བ *goṅ-du sbyor-wa* उद्युक्त ready; གོང་དུ་མོས་པ *goṅ-du mos-pa* the above mentioned; གོང་ན *goṅ-na* on it; above; གོང་ནས *goṅ-nas* from above; གོང་ནས་གོང་དུ *goṅ-nas goṅ-du* उत्तरोत्तर more and more; higher and higher. གོང་པ *goṅ-pa* अति very much (*Lex.*); one above; the senior (one) = སྒོ་གོང་དུ *sgo goṅ-du* over the door; ཡབ་ཀྱི་གོང་དུ་འདས *yab-kyi goṅ-du hdas* died before his father; དེའི་གོང་དུ *dehi goṅ-du* before that or that time; མ་ཚོགས་གོང་དུ *ma-tshogs goṅ-du* before they assembled or congregated together.

གོང་དཀར་རྫོང་ *Goṅ-dkar-rdsoṅ* n. of a fort and town on the Tsang-po, where convicts are generally sent for punishment. It is situated S.-E. of Lhasa, in the district of Mal-gro.

གོང་ཁྲི་བདལ་འོད་འབར *Goṅ khri-bdal, hod-hbar* n. of a Bon saint believed to exist in astral form in the north-west quarter. (*G. Bon. l*).

གོང་པོ *goṅ-po*=གོང་བུ *goṅ-bu* समज्या a meeting; assembly; fame; renown; globular.

གོང་ཕུད་པ *goṅ-phuḏ-pa*=གོང་དུ་ཕུད་པ *goṅ-du phuḏ-pa* to lift up; to ride up.

གོང་ཕེབས *goṅ-phebs̱*, or གོང་གི་བཀའ་ཕེབས *goṅ-gi ḇkaẖ-phebs̱*, the instructions from higher authorities; also those arrived or received earlier.

གོང་བ *goṅ-wa* in *W.* collar: གོང་བ་ནས་འཛིན་པ *goṅ-wa nas̱ ẖdsin-pa* to seize by the collar.

གོང་བུ *goṅ-bu* 1. पिण्ड, सपिण्ड, मूर्त्ति, मान a globular mass, lump, heap; གོང་བུ་ཅན *goṅ-bu-can* पिण्डवत् clot; clotty; in lump; in heaps; གོང་བུ་སོ་སོ *goṅ-bu so-so* प्रतिश्या, प्रतिश्याय catarrh or cold; གོང་བུར་བྱས *goṅ-bur-byas̱* made into globular mass or lump. 2. agglomeration of atoms; དྲི་རོ་རེག་གཟུགས་བཞི་སྟེ་རྡུལ་རྫས་བརྒྱད་འདུས་གོང་བ་ཡིན *dṟi ro reg gẕugs̱ ḇshi-s̱te ṟdul-ṟdsas̱ ḇrgyaḏ ẖdus̱ goṅ-wa yin* acc. to the Buddhist metaphysical conception that which produces the sensation of smell, taste, touch and sight is formed of the following eight atoms:—(1) རྡུལ་ཕྲ་རབ *ṟdul phra-rab*, (2) རྡུལ་ཕྲན *ṟdul-phran*, (3) ལྕགས་རྡུལ *lcags̱-ṟdul*, (4) ཆུ་རྡུལ *chu-ṟdul*, (5) རི་བོང་རྡུལ *ri-boṅ-ṟdul*, (6) ལུག་རྡུལ *lug-ṟdul*, (7) གླང་རྡུལ *glaṅ-ṟdul*, (8) ཉི་མའི་འོད་ཟེར་གྱི་རྡུལ *ñi-maẖi ẖoḏ-zer-gyi ṟdul* (*Sorig. 7.*)

གོང་མ *goṅ-ma* अधि, उपरि, उत्तम, उत्तर superior; the former; the first-named; གོང་མ་ཆེ *goṅ-ma-che* or གོང་མ་ཆེན་པོ *goṅ-ma chen-po* the most high; རྒྱ་ནག་གོང་མ *Ṟgya-nag goṅ-ma* the Emperor of China; གོང་མ་རྣམས *goṅ-ma-ṟnams̱* the gods and superior beings. གོང་མ་ཆེ་དྲུག *goṅ-ma che dṟug*, the six superior things of the བོན་པོ *Bon-po* are the following:—གསང་བ་འདུས་པ *gsaṅ-wa ẖdus̱-pa* mysticism; སྟི་ཁར *s̱ti-ghar*; མི་ལུས་བསམ་ལེགས *mi-lus̱ ḇsam legs*; ཡེ་ཤེས་སྙིང་པོ *yi-çes̱ s̱ñiṅ-po*; སྣང་བ་མདོག་ཅན *s̱naṅ-wa m̱dog-can*.

གོང་མ་ཆེན་ལུང་རྒྱལ་པོ *Goṅ-ma Chen-luṅ ṟgyal-po* the Tibetan name of the fourth Manchu Emperor Kyun-luṅ is ལྷ་སྐྱོང་རྒྱལ་པོ *Lha-s̱kyoṅ ṟgyal-po*, the king protected by the gods. འདི་མན་ཇུའི་རྒྱལ་པོ་བཞི་བ་ཏ་ཙང་མངའ་ཐང་ཆེན་པོ་བྱུང་ཆོས་ལ་ཤིན་ཏུ་དགའ་བ་པཎ་ཆེན་དཔལ་ལྡན་ཡེ་ཤེས་གདན་འདྲེན་ཏེ་ཆོས་ཞུས་གཙུག་ལག་ཁང་སྐུ་གསུང་ཐུགས་རྟེན་མང་པོ་བཞེངས་པ་སོགས་རྣམ་ཐར་ཡ་མཚན་ཆེ་ལོ་དྲུག་ཅུ་རྒྱལ་སྲིད་བསྐྱངས He became very powerful, was devoted to Buddhism, invited the Pan-chen Rin-po-che called Tashi Lama Pal-dan Ye-s'e (friend of the first Governor General of India, Mr. Warren Hastings). He erected many temples and chaityas, and his life was a record of miracles. He reigned upwards of sixty years.

གོང་མ་མཆོད་ཡོན *goṅ-ma m̱choḏ-yon* the Dalai Lama being the spiritual lord and the Emperor of China being the temporal lord: གོང་མ་མཆོད་ཡོན་གྱི་ཐུགས་རྗེར་འདིར་ཡང་འཚོ་ཁམས་བདེ་ཞིང་འཕྲིན་ལས་ཞབས་འདེགས་ལ་ལྷོད་མེད་དུ་མཆིས *goṅ-ma m̱chon-yon-gyi thugs̱-ṟjer ẖdir-yaṅ ẖtsho-khams̱ ḇde-shiṅ ẖphrin-las̱ shabs̱-ẖdegs̱ la lhoḏ-med-du m̱chis̱* by the grace of the Grand Lama and the Emperor (of China) here too I being in good health have been in the discharge of public service without relaxation (*Yig. k. 18*).

གོང་མ་བཞིན *goṅ-ma ḇshin*=སྔོན་མ་བཞིན *s̱ṅon-ma ḇshin* पूर्ववत् as before; as the above mentioned; like the aforesaid; as the previous one.

གོང་མའི་གོང་མ *goṅ-moẖi goṅ-ma* उत्तरोत्तर a superior's superior; also more and more; more in future.

གོང་མོ 1. *goṅ-mo* the upper one; ལག་པའི་གོང་མོ *lag-paḥi goṅ-mo* मध्याङ्गुलि the middle finger. 2. the white grouse, but applied to various birds in Tibet of the *Tetraonidæ* family: *lha-bya goṅ-mo* is the *Crossoptilon Tibetanum*, and *gong-gyag* the *Ithaginis geoffryoi*, etc. (*Snd. Hbk. pp. 170-1*). བྱིའུ་ཙོ་ཀ་གཉིས་ཀྱིས་གོང་མོ་ལ་སྨྲས་པ *byiḥu co-ka gñis kyis goṅ-mo la smras-pa* the two little *Coka* birds said to the grouse (*Rdsa.*). གོང་མོའི་ཤ་ཡིས་རོ་ཙ (འདོད་ཆགས) ཆུ་སེར་མོ་ནད་སེལ *goṅ-moḥi ça-yis ro-tsa chu-ser mo-nad sel* the flesh of the grouse stimulates the sexual desire and also cures discharge of whites: གོང་མོའི་མཇུག་སྒྲོའི་མོ་ནད་སེལ *goṅ-moḥi mjug sgroḥi mo-nad sel* the feathers of the grouse cure female diseases: གོང་མོའི་སྒོ་ངས་མེ་ལྷའི་གདོན་ནད་གསོ *goṅ-mohi sgo-ṅas me-lhaḥi gdon-nad gso* the eggs of the grouse cure illness caused by the demons of the fire-god.

གོང་མོ་སྲེག *goṅ-mo sreg* a pheasant, *Phasianus decollatus*.

གོང་ཞུ *goṅ-shu* = གོང་དུ་ཞུ *goṅ-du shu* 1. as stated or prayed above. 2. a paper lantern (*Jä.*); in colloq. Tibetan "*gam-shu*," a lantern.

གོང་འོག *goṅ-ḥog* = ལྟག་འོག *ltag-ḥog* पूर्व्वपश्चात् upper and lower; གཞི་གོང *gshi-goṅ* folio; གོང་སྐུ་གཞོགས *goṅ-sku gshogs* a title of honour, signifying his highness, excellence, etc.

གོང་རོལ་དུ *goṅ-rol-du* = སྔ་རོལ་དུ *sña-rol-du* or སྔོན་ལ *sṅon-la*, before, prior to: དམག་མ་བྱུང་གི་གོང་རོལ་དུ before the war took place.

གོང་ལ *goṅ-la* above.

གོང་ས *goṅ-sa* उद्युक्त one in supreme authority or position; the sovereign.

གོང་ས་ཡས་ཕྱིན་པ *goṅ-sa yas phyin-pa* = ཡ་རབས་གོང་མ *ya-rabs goṅ-ma* those superior persons gone before; persons in superior or more exalted stations.

གོད *god* loss; damage; གོད་འགྱུར་བ *god ḥgyur-wa* to suffer loss; ནོར་ལ་གོད loss of money and property; གོད་ཁ *god-kha*, ནོར་ཕྱུགས་ལ་ནད་སྣ་ཚོགས་བྱུང་ནས་ཤི་བ *nor phyugs la nad sna-tshogs byuṅ-nas çi-wa* loss in property or in cattle by disease and other accidents: སྒོམ་སྒྲུབ་ཅི་བྱས་ཀྱང་གོད་མེད *sgom sgrub ci-byas kyaṅ god-med* there was no loss whatever whether he performed meditation or propitiation.

གོད་མ *god-ma* = འཇིག་པ *ḥjig-pa* भय, व्यय; fear, loss.

གོན *gon* the common gourd; pumpkin in *W.* (*Jä.*).

གོན་པ *gon-pa* (གྱོན་པ) to put on clothes, shoes, etc.; གོན་པ་འདྲ་བ་རེ་རེ *gon-pa ḥdra-wa re-re* the cost of a set of anything to wear (*Rtsii.*); མགོ་ལ་ཞྭ་གོན་པ to put a cap on the head. 2. coat, clothing (*Sch.*).

གོན་སྣམ *gon-snam* (གྱོ་སྣམ) serge or broadcloth for making robes, etc. (*Rtsii.*).

གོན་ཕྱིང *gon-phyiṅ* felt used for wearing.

གོན་ལྷམ *gon-lham* = གྱོན་ལྷམ *gyon-lham* shoes to put on.

གོབ་ནོན *gob-non* (spelling uncertain) in *W.* to tease; vex; irritate (*Jä.*).

གོམ་པ *gom-pa* पाद, पद, लङ्घनम्, क्राम a pace; step: རྐང་འགྲོས *rkaṅ-ḥgros* to make a step; གོམ་པ་འབོར་བ *gom-pa bor-wa* to pace: གོམ་པ་བདུན་འབོར་བ *gom-pa bdun bor-wa* to make seven steps (as a ceremony, which may also be counted equivalent to a religious pilgrimage, the actual performance of which is not possible).

གོམ་པའི་སྟབས *gom-paḥi stabs* any peculiar manner of stepping whether in procession or in dancing.

གོམ་འགྲོས *gom-hgros* walking in step like soldiers or a procession: འགྲོ་ན་གོམ་འགྲོས་འཁྱོར *hgro-na gom-hgros hkhyor* in walking he missed the measure of the paces.

གོམ་སྟངས *gom-stańs* पदबन्ध the manner of pacing; walking in measured step.

གོམ་གསུམ *gom-gsum* त्रिपाद three paces; fig. the heavens, earth and the nether region.

གོམ་གསུམ་པ *gom-gsum-pa* one with three steps.

གོམ་གསུམ་གནོན *gom-gsum gnon*, ཁྱབ་འཇུག *kyab-hjug* त्रिविक्रम; त्रिपादविक्रम a name of Vishṇu when he deceived Bali in his *Bāmana* or Dwarf incarnation (*Mṅon.*).

གོམས་པ *goms-pa* 1. अभ्यास one practised in any work; skilled; wont; ཀློག་པ་ལ་གོམས་པ practising or practised in the art of reading; གོམས་པ་ཅན *goms-pa-can* कृती one who is skilled or practised in any art, གོམས་པར་བྱེད་པ *goms-par byed-pa* अभ्यस्त one who is skilled or accustomed; གོམས་པར་བྱས་པ *goms-par byas-pa* अनुशीलयति one who has practised or studied.

གོར *gor* or ཕྱུགས་གོར *phyugs-gor* = ནོར་ནད *nor-nad* murrain (*A.* ཀ *103*).

གོར་བུ *gor-bu* 1. चतुरस्रकं quadrangle. 2. कलन्दिका wisdom.

གོར་མ *gor-ma* རྡོ་ལ་ཞེ་ས་བྱས་པ *rdo-la she-sa byas-pa* a term of respect for stone, or a general name for stone (*Cs.*); large and small pebbles; stones; rubble; boulder stones (*Sch.*).

+ **གོར་མ་ཆག** *gor-ma chag* = གོར་མ་བཀུམ་པ *gor-ma bkum-pa*, ཐེ་ཚོམ་མེད *the-tshom med* or ངེས་པ *ńes-pa* नून, निःसंशय certain; sure; indubitable: དེ་འབྱུང་བ་གོར་མ་ཆག་གོ *de-hbyuń-wa gor-ma chag-go* his coming is quite certain.

+ གོར་མོ *gor-mo* = རྡོ *rdo*, སྡང་བའི་སེམས་ལ་ཡང་འཇུག *sdań-wahi sems-la yań hjug* གོར་མོ *gor-mo* is also applied to signify an irritable or angry temper.

‡ གོར་ཤི་ཤ *gor-çi-ça*, गोशीर्ष a kind of sandal wood.

གོལ་བ *gol-wa*, v. འགོལ་བ *hgol-wa*.

གོས *gos* वस्त्र, वसन, चीवर, निवसन, वास, कंबल, आच्छादन, अम्बर, क्षौम, चेल, चीन, परिच्छद, परिवार, अंशुक cover; dress; garment. The common word for coat or clothing; there are seven kinds of stuffs for priests, &c.: བལ་གོས *bal-gos* woollen cloth; ཤ་ནའི་གོས *ça-nahi gos* cloth of flax; ཟར་མའི་གོས *zar-mahi gos* linen; དུ་ཀུ་ལའི་གོས *du-khu lahi gos* silk cloth; རས་བལ་གྱི་གོས *ras-bal-gyi gos* cotton cloth; ཀོ་ཏམ་པའི་གོས *ko tam-pahi gos* jute cloth; ཉི་ཧོག་གི་གོས *ñi-hog-gi gos* European cloth, &c. གོས་ཀྱི་རྒྱུའི་འབྱུང་ཁུངས་བསྟན་པ *gos-kyi rgyuhi hbyuń-khuńs bstan-pa* enumeration of the materials for cloth:— སྲིན་བུ *srin-bu* silk-worm; ར་ལུག་དང་རི་དྭགས་ཀྱི་སྤུ་དང་པགས་པ་སྣ་ཚོགས *ra lug dań ri-dwags-kyi spu-dań pags-pa sna-tshogs* various hairs and skins of sheep, goats and wild animals; ཤིང་གི་ཤུན་པ bark or fibres; ཤིང་གི་འབྲས་བུ fruits; ཟར་མ་སོགས *zar-ma sogs* fibres, etc.; རས་བལ་སོགས *ras-bal sogs* wool, cotton, etc.; དུ་ཀུ་ལའི་མིང *du-khu-lahi miń* silk cloth, satin, etc.; གོས་གསར *gos-gsar* new cloth; དྲི་མེད *dri-med* clean cloth; གོས་སོ་མོ *gos-so-mo* new or fresh cloth; དྲི་མ་ཅན *dri-ma can* dirty cloth; གོས་རྙིང་པ *gos rñiń-pa* old, worn out clothes; ཟད་པ *zad-pa* or ཧྲུལ་པོ *hrul-po* rags or ragged dress; སྟོད་གོས *stod-gos* उत्तरासङ्ग upper garment of Buddhist monks; བླ་གོས *bla-gos* = སྣམ་སྦྱར *snam-sbyar* the sacred raiment containing thirty-two patches; སྟོད་གཡོགས *stod-gyogs* upper cover; སྨད་གཡོགས *smad-gyogs* or སྨད་གོས *smad-gos* lower garment; བཾ་ཙ་ལི་ཀ *bań-tsa-li-ka* an apron of five colours; འདོམས་དཀྲིས *hdoms-dkris* folds round loins like the *dhuti* of the Hindus;

སྨད་དཀྲིས *smaḏ-ḏkriş* the back folds of *dhuti*; སྨད་ཤམ *şmaḏ-çam* under cloth or garment; མཐང་གོས or ཤམ་ཐབས the petticoat-like clothes worn by the Tibetan monks; *ṟgyan-goş* fine dressing clothes; *ṟgyun-goş* an every-day coat (*Jä.*); *choş-goş* clerical garb or garment; *pho-goş* male dress; *ḇla-goş* an upper garment, a kind of toga; *mo-goş* a woman's gown; *gzab-goş* holiday or gala clothes; གོས་གྱོན་པ *goş gyon-pa* to put on dress; གོས་འབུད་པ *goş ẖbuḏ-pa* to take off dress; གོས་བརྗེ་བ *goş ḇṟje-wa* to change dress or clothes; གོས་བརྩེགས་པ *goş ḇṟtsegş-pa* to put one garment over the other; གོས་བཏེག་པ *goş ḇteg-pa* to tuck up, by drawing the front skirts under the girdle; གོས་ལྡབ་པ *goş ḻdab-pa* to lay or fold a coat together.

གོས་ཀྱི་ཁྱིམ *goş-kyi khyim* (तांबु) गुल्मी a tent; a diseased man's wardrobe; གོས་ཀྱི་གར *goş-kyi gar* चीवरवंश a bamboo or bar to hang or keep the dress; གོས་ཀྱི་ཆོག་ཤེས་པ *goş-kyii chog çeş-pa* चीवरसन्तुष्ट one who has enough of clothes; གོས་ཀྱི་གདང་ཤིང *goş-kyi g̱daṅ-çiṅ* नागदन्तक a rope or string to hang clothes.

གོས་དཀར *goş-ḏkar* white dress; གོས་དཀར་ཅན *goş-ḏkar can* पाण्डरवासिन् one dressed in white; the Goddess Sarasvatī.

གོས་སྐུད *goş-şkuḏ* yarn or silk thread.

གོས་ཁ་བརྒྱ་ཐམ་པ *goş-kha ḇṟgya-tham-pa* one hundred breadth-measure of blankets.

གོས་ཁུམས་པ *goş khumş-pa* གོས་ལ་གཉེར་མ་བྱུང་བ ऊर्म्मि a cloth folded as to look like waves or wrinkles.

གོས་གུར *goş-gur* a tent of cloth or satin; ཕྱིང་གུར *phyin-gur* a tent of felt; སྦྲ *şbra* or རེ་གུར *re-gur* tent of yak-hair blanket or felt.

གོས་འགྱེད་པ *goş ẖgyeḏ-pa* चीवरभाजक the folds in the garment of a monk; one who folds clothes.

གོས་གྲུམ *goş-grum* a square rug made of Chinese satin.

གོས་སྒབ *goş-şgab* skirt or flap of a coat or robe.

གོས་སྒམ *goş-şgam* box; chest or press for clothes; wardrobe.

གོས་སྔོན་ཅན *goş-şṅon-can* नीलाम्बर 1. one dressed in a blue dress; the sky. 2. ཕྱག་རྡོར वज्रपाणिबोधिसत्त्व Chag-na Dorje *Bodisattva*, སྟོབས་བཟང *ştobş-ḇzaṅ*, बलभद्र the brother of Krishṇa said to be an *avatāra* of Vishṇu. 3. གཟའ་སྤེན་པ *gzaẖ şpen-pa* the planet Saturn.

གོས་ཅན *goş-can* चन्दन a kind of sandal.

* གོས་ཅན *goş-can* 1. पट्टिका (*Schr.*; *Lebensb.* 86) a tablet; a piece of cloth. 2. གོས་ཅན་ཙན་དཀར *goş-can tsan-ḏkar* पट्टिका satin.

གོས་ཆེན *goş-chen* silk fabrics; Chinese satin, of which the different kinds known in Tibet are:—ཧོར་གོས *hor-goş*, ཐོན་ཐི *thon-thi*, ནོར་བུ་ཆབ་བདུན་མ *nor-bu chab ḇdun-ma*, མཛོད་གོས *m̱dsoḏ-goş*, སྐྱིན་ཁབ *şkyin-khab* (*Kincob*) embroidered satin; ཇུས *juş*, རྒྱན་བཞི་མ *ṟgyan ḇshi-ma*, རྒྱན་དྲུག་མ *ṟgyan dṟug-ma*, འབྲུག་རིས་མ *ẖbrug riş-ma*, འབྲུག་བརྒྱ་མ *ẖbrug ḇṟgya-ma*.

གོས་ཆེན་པོ *goş-chen-po* = དུ་ཀུ་ལའི་རས *du-ku laẖi raş* silk-cloth (*M̱ṅon.*).

གོས་མཆོག *goş-m̱chog* the finest satin or silk-cloth.

Syn. གོས་བཟང *goş-ḇzaṅ*; ཀུན་དགའི་གོས *kun-ḏgaẖi goş*; སྲུབས་མེད་གོས *şṟubş-meḏ goş* (*M̱ṅon.*).

གོས་ཉོ *goş-ño* क्रय्यवस्त्र a purchased dress; a cloth fit to be purchased.

གོས་རྙིང *goş-ṟñiṅ* = གོས་རྙིང་པ *goş ṟñiṅ-pa* or བེམ་པོ *bem-po* in *Ld.* dialect, an old coat or dress.

Syn. ཟད་པོ *zaḏ-po*; ཧྲུལ་པོ *hrul-po*; དྲུག་པ *dug-pa* (*M̱ṅon.*).

གོས་བརྙན *goş-ḇṟñan* चीवरभाजक a mendicant who puts on a ragged garment; a ragged dress.

གོས་ཐུང *gos-thuṅ* trousers.

གོས་མཐའ *gos-mthaḥ* skirt of dress or robe.

གོས་དུག་པ *gos dug-pa* old cloth; ragged cloth; torn cloth; གོས་དྲི་མ་ཅན *gos dri-ma-can* dirty clothes; གོས་དྲི་མེད *gos dri-med* clean cloth.

གོས་འདུག *gos-ḥdug* or ཆུ་གོས *chu-gos* bathing cloth.

གོས་པ 1. *gos-pa* लिप्त, pf. of བགོ་བ *bgo-wa*, to apply on; to paste or rub. 2. उपलेप a liniment.

གོས་ཕྱེད་ཕུ་ལུང་ *gos-phyed phu-luṅ* sleeveless robe or garment (in Sikk.).

གོས་ཕྲ *gos-phra* अंशुक fine-silk; muslin.

གོས་བྱེད *gos-byed* प्रतिपत्ति gain; acceptance; performance; honour.

གོས་བྲལ *gos-bral* नग्न, विवस्त्र naked; without dress or cover for the body.

གོས་སྦེད་པ *gos sbyed-pa* चीवर-गोपक one concealing his mendicant's clothes.

གོས་མིན *gos-min* पटल a roof; veil; film over the eyes; multitude.

གོས་མེད *gos-med* दमथ, नग्नक, निर्ग्रन्थिक a devotee who has cut off worldly ties.

གོས་དམར་སྡེ *gos-dmar sde* ताम्रशाटीय classes of Buddhists who are dressed in red.

གོས་ཙམ *gos-tsam* अंशुक satin.

གོས་བཙེམས་ཉེས་པ *gos-btsems ñes-pa*,=གོས་སྐྱོགས་ཚེམ་ངན་པ badly-sewn clothes.

གོས་ཤིག་པ *gos-shig-pa* ऊर्मिका a wave, a plait or fold in a garment.

གོས་ཟད་པོ *gos zad-po* worn-out clothes.

གོས་ཟས་ཀྱི་འཚོས་མ *gos-zas-kyi ḥtshos-ma* पटवासिनी a female mendicant clothed in suitable dress; one who lives doing nothing more than eating and dressing.

གོས་ཟེགས *gos-zegs* worn out clothes; old clothes (*Rtsii. 5*).

གོས་ཡུག *gos-yug* piece or cloth or satin, enough for making a robe.

གོས་ལག *gos-lag* colloq. (in Sikk.) "*ko-lak*," a coat; dress; clothes.

གོས་སེར་ཅན *gos-ser can*, पीताम्बर a name of Vishṇu, one covered with a yellow cloth.

གོས་ལྷོད་པ་ *gos-lhod-pa* to let go a robe which has been grasped: གོས་ནས་འཇུས་པར་ཐོང་ཟེར་སླུ་རིན་སྤྲོད་ཟེར་སྲང་གསུམ་སྤྲད་དེ་གོས་ལྷོད་སྒོ་བཅད *gos-nas ḥjus-par thoṅ zer slu-rin sprod-zer sraṅ-gsum sprad-de gos lhod sgo-bcad* one said: "see you are held fast by your clothes;" and he said: fix a price for the ensnarement;" and three *srang* being allotted, the cloth was let go and the door shut. (*G. Sndg.*).

གོས་པོ *gos-po* or གྱོས་པོ *gyos-po* श्वशुर father-in-law; གོས་པོས་བསྲུངས་པ *gos-pos bsruṅs-pa* श्वशुररक्षित protected by one's father-in-law.

གྱ *gya* num. used in the abbreviated form, in the place of བརྒྱད་ཅུ *brgyad-cu* 80; གྱ་གཅིག *gya-gcig* 81; གྱ་གཉིས *gya-gñis* 82; གྱ་གསུམ *gya-gsum* 83; གྱ་བཞི *gya-bshi* 84; གྱ་ལྔ *gya-lṅa* 85; གྱ་དྲུག *gya-drug* 86; གྱ་བདུན *gya-bdun* 87; གྱ་བརྒྱད *gya-brgyad* 88; གྱ་དགུ *gya-dgu* 89.

གྱ་གྱུ *gya-gyu*=གཡོན་ཅན *gyon-can* कद्म, जिह्म dissimulation; crookedness; intrigue; secret machinations: དེ་ཉིད་གྱ་གྱུ་མེད་པའི་རྣམ་པ་ཡིན་པས་ *de-ñid gya-gyu med-paḥi rnam-pa yin-pas* he was a person absolutely free from deceitful intentions. གནོད་སེམས་དང་སླུ་བའི་གྱ་གྱུ་སོགས *gnod-sems daṅ slu-waḥi gya-gyu sogs* malice and beguiling intrigues, etc.

གྱ་གྱུ་ཅན *gya-gyu-can* कुटिल, कुटिलक crafty, deceitful, fraudulent.

གྱ་གྱུ་བྱེད་པ *gya-gyu byed-pa* to intrigue; to plot.

གྱ་གྱུར་འགྲོ *gya-gyur ḥgro* that which goes not in the direct way; a frog; smoke; a snake; a river: གྱ་གྱུར་འགྲོ་བ *gya-gyur ḥgro-wa* serpentine-motion; to move circuitously.

གྱ་མ་གྱུ *gya-ma gyu* (meandering of rivers, &c.) quiet; calm; gently flowing along (*Jä.*). Of a man: cautious; scheming so that one does not know what to think of him.

གྱ་ཉེས *gya-ñes* marvellous; inexplicable, of men, occurrences, &c.

+ གྱ་ཐོ *gya-tho*=རྣ་རྒྱན *rna-rgyan* an ornament for the ear; an ear-ring.

གྱ་དོ *gya-do* उरश्छद a breast plate.

+ གྱ་ནོག་སྣང *gya-nog snaṅ* सुदृश beautiful; of nice appearance.

གྱ་ནོམ་སྣང་བ *gya-nom snaṅ-wa* n. of a celestial mansion, the residence of the gods.

+ གྱ་ནོམ་པ *gya nom-pa*, ཕུན་སུམ་ཚོགས་པ *phun-sum tshogs-pa* वैशारद्य, सम्पन्न, प्रणीत; དབང་ཐང་ཆེ་བ *dwaṅ-thaṅ che-wa* one in abundance; in plenty; possessed of wealth and power.

གྱ་པ *gya-pa* or གྱ་བ *gya-wa*=ཉམས་པ *ñams-pa* नष्ट spoiled; degenerated. Acc. to *Cs.* deformed; disfigured; having lost his or her former beauty.

+ གྱ་ཙོམ *gya-tsom* or གྱ་རྩོམ *gya-rtsom* [illegible] (to become dry?) acc. to *Cs.* haste; hurry; rashness.

+ གྱ་ཚོམ *gya-tshom*, सहसा; མ་བརྟགས་པ *ma brtags-pa* momentary; unstable; without deliberation; consideration: གྱ་ཚོམ་དུ་འགྲོ་བར་མི་བྱའོ *gya tshom-du ḥgro-war mi-byaḥo* should not go all on a sudden, without deliberation.

གྱ་ཚོམ་ཅན *gya-tshom-can* 1. कीटक a bard of the Māgadha tribe. 2. one in doubt.

+ གྱག་པ *gyag-pa*=བརླག་པ *brlag-pa* मथुर destroyed; ruined; acc. to *Cs.* diminished, v. འགྱག་པ *ḥgyag-pa*.

གྱང *gyaṅ* or གྱིང *gyiṅ* clay stamped into moulds, and frequently used as building material in Spiti, Ladak and other parts of Tibet; གྱང་སྐོར *gyaṅ-skor* earthen wall round an estate or village; གྱང་སྒྲོམ *gyaṅ-sgrom* pisé mould.

གྱང་ཙེ *gyaṅ-tse* pisé terrace; wall of dry earth in Ladak.

གྱང་ར *gyaṅ-ra* cattle-yards constructed of clay or mud.

གྱང་རིམ *gyaṅ-rim* pisé layer or one layer of pisé, *i.e.*, as much as is stamped in at a time, about one ell in height; this frequently serves for a measure of the depth of the snow (*Jä.*).

གྱང་རིས *gyaṅ-ris* fresco or wall painting: ཕུག་པའི་གྱང་རིས་སོགས་ལ *phug-paḥi gyaṅ-ris sogs-la* in the frescoes, &c., of the caves (*Ya-sel. 45*).

གྱད *gyad* मल्ल, वीर a champion; a man of great physical strength; an athlete: ད་དུང་གྱད་ཀྱི་རྩལ་འགྲན *da duṅ gyad-kyi rtsal ḥgran* let us compete once more in athletic dexterity. གྱད་ཀྱི་འཛིན་སྟངས *gyad-kyi ḥdsin staṅs* संघाटो मल्लस्य, मंडलम् the mode of seizing in wrestling; གྱད་ཀྱི་ཤུགས *gyad-kyi çugs* the prowess or strength of a champion.

གྱད་རྡོ *gyad-rdo* 1. giant stone; a quoit. 2. n. of a tribe in Tibet.

*གྱད་གཡུང་པོ *gyad gyuṅ-po* पुलिन्द, पुक्कस, डोम्ब (*Schr.; Lebensh. 98*) n. of a barbarous tribe.

གྱམ *gyam* a shelter; a recess in a rock, large and wide but not deep; བྲག་གྱམ *brag-gyam* a shelter under a rock: གད་གྱམ *gad-gyam* a grotto beneath a conglomerate rock; a shelter in the steep side of a rock; ཕོང་གྱམ *phoṅ-gyam* or ཕ་བོང་གྱམ *pha-boṅ gyam* a shelter under a beetling rock (*Jä.*); གྱམ་བུ *gyam-bu* a little cover or shelter (*Cs.*).

གྱར་གྱོད *gyar-gyod*, probably གྱོད་ཁ *gyod-kha* གོད་པ *god-pa*, loss, damage (*Jä.*).

གྱི *gyi* for གི *gi*, after ན, མ, ར, ལ, v. ཀྱི *kyi*.

གྱི་གླིང *Gyi-gliṅ* Kulti, n. of a place.

གྱི་ལྗང་ *Gyi-ljaṅ* n. of a place in Tibet.

གྱི་ཐན *Gyi-than* n. of a place and also of a tribe in E. Tibet: བར་ན་ཀོ་འཇེ་རག་ཤི་གཉིས in the middle (country) are the two, viz., *Ko-hje* and *Rag-çi*; སྨད་ན་མི་ཉག་གྱི་ཐང་གཉིས *smad-na Mi-ñag Gi-thaṅ gñis* in the lower country are *Mi-ñag* and *Gyi-than* (*Yig.*).

གྱི་ན་བ *gyi-na-wa* 1. coarse; poor; miserable, of food, clothes, &c.: གྱི་ན་འཚོ་བ a miserable, starving life. 2. unsteady; fickle (*Sch.*).

གྱི་འཕྱོ *gyi hphyo*, in གཙམ་ཡས་བགྲང་ཡས་གྱི་འཕོ་དང་ *gcam-yas bgraṅ-yas gyi-hpho daṅ*, n. of a number inconceivably large (*Ya-sel. 57*).

གྱི་ནའི་གཡང་ *gyi-naḥi gyaṅ*=སྙོམ་ལས་པ *ṣñom las-pa*, or ལས་ཀ་ཆེར་མ་ཐུབ་པ *las-ka cher-ma thub-pa*, state of inactivity, idleness: ལོག་ཆོས་ཐམས་ཅད་གྱི་ནའི་གཡང་ལ་བསྐྱུར *log chos thams-cad gyi-naḥi gyaṅ la bskyur* threw all heretical doctrines into the abyss of inaction. (*A. 158.*)

གྱི་ལིང *gyi-liṅ* name of a good breed of horses from Amdo where there are twelve different breeds, གྱི་ལིང *gyi-liṅ* and གནམ་ས་ *gnam-sa* being the best among them (*Jig.*)

གྱི་ལིང་ཆུ་རྟ་སྔོན་པོ *gyi-liṅ chu-rta ṣṅon-po*=དངུལ་ཆུ quick-silver (*Sman. 118*). གྱི་ལིང་ཆུ་རྟ་དཀར་པོ *gyi-liṅ chu-rta dkar-po*=འཛིན་པ་དཀར་པོ *ḥdsin-pa dkar-po* n. of a mineral medicine, probably mercury. (*Sman. 447.*)

གྱིག *gyig* caoutchouc; India rubber.

གྱིག་ཤིང *gyig-çiṅ* or གྱིག་སྡོང་ *gyig-sdoṅ* caoutchouc tree (Sikk.).

གྱིང་ *Gyiṅ* n. of a deity, prob. ཀིང་ཀང *Kiṅ-kaṅ*.

གྱིང་མོ *gyiṅ-mo* in *W.* gently sloping; gradually descending or subsiding.

གྱིན *gyiṅ*, v. ཀྱིང་ *kyiṅ*.

གྱིམ་བག *gyim-bag* amalgam; གྱིམ་བག་གིས་བསྐུག་པ to gild in the fire. (*Schtr.*)

གྱིམ་ཤང་རིན་ཆེན་སྤུངས་པ *Gyim-çuṅ Rin-chen ṣpuṅṣ-pa* n. of an astrological work.

\+ གྱིམ་ཤིང *gyim-çiṅ*, རོལ་མོ *rol-mo* music, cymbal.

གྱིས *gyis* 1. instead of ཀྱིས *kyis*, after the letters ན *na*, མ *ma*, ར *ra*, ལ *la*. 2. imp. of བགྱིད་པ *bgyid-pa*, work honestly;

behave well; do (so); དྲང་པུར་གྱིས *drañ-pur-gyis* do it straight: གྱིས་ཤིག *gyis-çig*, कुरु do or let him do.

+ **གྱུ་བ** *gyu-wa* = བཀུར་བ *bkur-wa* to honour; to esteem.

གྱུང་རོ *gyuñ-ro*, v. གྱོང་ར *gyoñ-ra*.

གྱུར *gyur* imp. and pf. of འགྱུར་བ.

གྱུར་དུ་ཟིན *gyur-du zin* = གྱུར་དུ་ཆུག *gyur-du chug*.

གྱུར་ན *gyur-na* स्यात्, अभविष्यत् if it so happened; if it became so.

གྱུར་པའི་རྣམ་པ *gyur-pahi rnam-pa* परिणाम anything changeable; subject to change.

གྱེ་གུ *gye-gu* कुब्ज crookedness; curve; hunch; hump; crooked back; གྱེ་གུར་གྱུར་པ *gye-gur gyur-pa* द्विकुब्ज double hump-back; met. a Bactrian camel.

གྱེ་གོར *Gye-gor* n. of a Bon-po deity.

གྱེ་རེ *Gye-re* n. of place on the Tsang-po, to the south-east of Lhasa: གྱེ་རེ་ལྷ་པ *Gye-re Lha-pa* n. of a very old noble family of Tibet.

གྱེང *gyeñ*, v. གྱང *gyañ*.

གྱེད་པ *gyed-pa*, v. འགྱེད་པ *hgyed-pa*.

གྱེན་དུ *gyen-du* up; upward; uphill: གྱེན་དུ་འགྲོ *gyen-du-hgro* उद्यान, उत्पतनं going or flowing upwards; གྱེན་དུ་འཛེག climb up; གྱེན་གྱི་དྲི *gyen-gyi-dri* सुगन्धि fragrance; sweet scent; fragrant; གྱེན་དུ་བལྟ་བ *gyen-du blta-wa* = ཡར་ལྟ་བ *yar lta-wa* उल्लोकन to look upwards.

གྱེན་རྒྱུ *gyen-rgyu* གྱེན་རྒྱུའི་བུ་ག *gyen-rgyuhi bu-ga* (ཁ་དང་སྣ *kha-dañ-sna*) the mouth and the nose through which the wind passes upwards or downwards; གྱེན་རྒྱུའི་མཐུ *gyen-rgyuhi mthu* n. of a disease (*Med.*).

གྱེན་རྒྱུ *gyen-rgyu* उदान that runs upwards; fire; names of the five vital (प्राणवायु) winds in the human body.

གྱེན་རྒྱུག་པ *gyen-rgyug-pa* to gallop uphill; to pass upwards; to climb up.

གྱེན་ཆད *gyen-chad* in *W.* (opp. to མན་ཆད *man-chad*) 1. the upper part of a country; པུ་རིག་གྱེན་ཆད *Pu-rig Gyen-chad*, the Upper Purig (*Jä.*) 2 an ascent.

གྱེན་དུ་འདེགས་པ *gyen-du hdegs-pa* to lift high; to praise.

གྱེན་དུ་འདྲེན *gyen-du hdren* उद्वाहन drawing upwards; also marriage.

གྱེན་དུ་བརྫིས་པ *gyen-du brdsis-pa* उत्तरण to turn up; to cock (a hat or cap).

གྱེན་དུ་ལུས་པ *gyen-du lus-pa* to keep above (water).

གྱེན་མིག *Gyen-mig* विताल, वितल the second of the seven lower regions under the earth.

གྱེན་གཟར་པོ *gyen gzar-po* a steep ascent.

གྱེན་བཟློག་པ *gyen-bzlog-pa* उद्गार, to vomit.

གྱེན་ལ་དྲང་པོ *gyen-la drañ-po* in *W.* perpendicular; vertical.

གྱེར *gyer*, v. དགྱེར་བ *dgyer-wa*.

གྱེར་བསྒོམ *gyer-bsgom* the kind of meditation practised by the Bon-po.

གྱེར་ལིང *gyer-liñ* རྟ *rta* कुलीन a high breed horse, or pony.

གྱེས *gyes* = སོ་སོར *so-sor*, v. འགྱེ་བ *hgye-wa*.

` གྱེས་བརྗེས *gyes-brjes* उन्नत raised up; magnanimous; noble.

གྱེས་པ *gyes-pa* विश्लेषः to analyse, resolve, separate; to split asunder.

གྱོ་དུམ *gyo-dum* = ཀ་ར *ka-ra* शर्करा, उपल 1. sugar. 2. potsherd. 3. brick tile (*Sch.*).

གྱོ་མོ *gyo-mo* कङ्कर 1. gravel; grit. 2. potsherd. 3.=གྱེ་མགོ *gye-mgo* clay vessel.

གྱོག་པ *gyog-pa* crooked; curved: རྐང་གྱོག *rkañ-gyog* bent or crooked leg.

གྱོག་པོ *gyog-po* left-handed; awkward (*Sch.*).

གྱོགས *gyogs* for སྒྱོགས *sgyogs* cannon; a large gun.

གྱོང *gyoñ* want; need; indigence: གྱོང་འཁུར་བ *gyoñ hkhur-wa* to be reduced to want.

གྱོང་པོ *gyoñ-po* खर, बक्र;=རིག་དཀའ་བ *rig dkah-wa* crooked; rough; hard to understand; ཁ་གྱོང་པོ *kha gyoñ-po* hard-mouthed (*i.e.*, pulling at the reins); སེམས་གྱོང་པོ *sems gyoñ-po* harsh; resembling a horn or hide that can hardly be made soft; མི་གྱོང་པོ *mi gyoñ-po* a crooked man; an obstinate man (*A. 134*); སྐད་གྱོང་པོ *skad gyoñ-po* imperfect language; ཚིག་གྱོང་པོ *tshig gyoñ-po* impolite words; དགྲ་གྱོང *dgra gyoñ* a hard, cruel, dangerous enemy.

གྱོང་བ *gyoñ-wa* ब्रातङ्क; ཁ་གྱོང་ཆེ *kha gyoñ-che* very rude; impudent (*Jä.*).

གྱོང་རུ་བ *gyoñ-ru-wa* कर्कश rough.

+ **གྱོང་རལ** *gyoñ-ral*=ས་ཤག *sa-shag* a film of dirt, formed of dust and other substances, on the surface of water; scum.

གྱོང་རོ *gyoñ-ro* dried body; a mummy (*Sch.*).

གྱོད *gyod*, v. འགྱོད་པ *hgyod-pa*.

གྱོད་ཁ *gyod-kha* remorse; quarrel; law-suit.

གྱོད་གཞི *gyod-gshi*=འཁྲུག་པའི་རྩ་བ *hkhrug-pahi rtsa-wa* the basis or grounds of a quarrel or fight: ཆ་མ་ཆགས་སྡང་གི་གྱོད་གཞི the last is the ground of contention between lust and passion.

གྱོན་པ *gyon-pa* परिधित, परिहित, वस्त्रित to put on; to dress; to wear: གྱོན་པ་ལུས་ལ་གྱོན་པའི་གོས *gyon-pa lus-la gyon-pahi gos* putting on the garment that one wears: གྱོན་རྒྱུ *gyon-rgyu* materials for clothing.

གྱོན་པོ *gyon-po*=གནབས་པ *gnabs-pa* or ན་བཟའ *na-bzah* वस्त्र the garment or dress to be worn.

གྱོལ *gyol* पल्लव green shoots of leaves or twigs; གྱོལ་པོ *gyol-po* नीलकण्ठ a blue-necked jay.

+ **གྱོས་པོ** I: *gyos-po* श्वशुर wife's father; father-in-law: གྱོས་པོས་བསྲུང་བ श्वशुर-रक्षित protected by the father-in-law.

གྱོས་མོ *gyos-mo* mother-in-law; the matron of a family; also any old lady of a family: གྱོས་སྒྱུག *gyos-sgyug* parents-in-law.

གྲ *gra* (*da*) one of the six early tribes of Tibet: བོད་མི་མཆེད་པ་སེ་རྨུ་ལྡོང་སྟོང་དང་གྲ་འབྲུ་སྟེ་རུས་དྲུག་ཟེར *bod-mi mched-pa se-rmu ldoñ stoñ dañ gra hbru-ste rus-drug zer*, the six tribes:—*Hbru*, *Gra*, *Stoñ*, *Ldoñ*, *Rmu* and *Se* (originated from) the five Tibetan brothers (bearing the same names) (*J. Zañ.*).

གྲ་རྒྱས *gra-rgyas* thick and abundant (as of the mane on the neck of the lion, horse etc.): ཞོ་གྲོད་བཀལ་དང་གཅན་གཟན་གྲ་རྒྱས་འདྲ *sho-grod bkal-dañ gcan-gzan gra-rgyas hdra* (the land is well-preserved) as curds carried in a sheep's paunch or like the thickly-grown mane of wild animals (youth in good circumstance is also so described): ཁོ་གྲ་རྒྱས་པོ་འདུག *kho gra-rgyas-po hdug* he is very bright and cheerful (*Jig.*).

གྲ་སྒྲིག *gra-sgrig* to make proper preparation or arrangement or equipment for any business, &c.

གྲ་སྒྲིག་པོ *gra sgrig-po* everything put in order; also looking neat and clean.

གྲ་ཆགས་པོ་ *gra-chags-po* 1. nice and smooth or glossy; very fine; fit and outwardly appearing nice. 2. appropriate; elegant; looking well (*A. 126*).

གྲ་དོལ *gra-dol* abbr. of the two names of places called Lho-gra (Lho-ḍa) and Nang-dol (*Rtsii. 25*).

གྲ་སྡེབས *gra-sdebs* proper order, arrangement; also མི་མང་ཁ་སྡེབས *mi-maṅ kha-sdebs* uniform deposition: མདུན་དང་བོག་གཡས་གཡོན་གྱི་གྲ་སྡེབས the arrangement in the front and of the right and left sides (*Rtsii.*).

གྲ་པད *gra-pad* 1. n. of a great Lama who is said to have unearthed many Buddhist religious and medical works. 2. a net before the window to prevent passers-by from looking into the room. 3. carvings in wood; གྲོ་སོགས་གྲ་པད་ཀྱི་ཤིང་ཕུག་རིགས *gro sogs gra pad kyi çiṅ phug rigs* films and hollowed pieces of wood with carvings, etc. (*Rtsii.*).

གྲ་ཕུབ *gra-phub*, གྲ་དང་ཕུབ *gra-daṅ phub* the bristles of barley grain and its chaff: གྲོ་ནས་སོགས་བདང་ནས་འབྲུ་སོག་གཉིས་སོ་སོར་ཕྱེ་བའི་ཚེ་གྲ་དང་ཀོག་པ་གཉིས་འདྲེས་པ་ལ་གྲ་ཕུབ་ཟེར།

གྲ་ཕྱི *Gra-phyi* (*ḍa-chyi*) and གྲ་ནང་ *Gra-naṅ* (*ḍa-naṅ*) are names of two villages in Lho-kha (*Rtsii.*).

གྲ་ཕྱི་ཚོང་འདུས *Gra phyi tshoṅ-ḥdus* n. of a great mart of trade in Lho-kha during the 11th century A.D. (*A. 90*).

གྲ་སྦུག *gra-sbug*, also called རྒྱ་ནག་གི་སྦུག་ཆ *rgya-nag gi sbug-cha*, a musical instrument of Chinese make, perhaps the cymbal: གྲ་སྦུག་ཆ་རེ་རེ *gra-sbug cha-re-re* the cymbal each pair (*Rtsii.*).

གྲ་མ *gra-ma* (*ṭa-ma*) किंशारु, शूक 1. awn, beard, bristle, the ears of cereals and wild grasses have: གྲོ་ནས་དང་འབྲས་རྣམས་སྨིན་དུས་རྩེ་རྩ་ཀུ་ཤ་ལྟ་བུ་ཡོད་པ་དེ་དག་ལ་འབྲུ་གྲ་མ་ཅན་ཟེར། "when the fruits of wheat and barley spring forth, to those which come in points like the Poa grass, the name of bearded grain is given." The term འབྲུ་གྲ་མ་ཅན *ḥbru gra-ma-can*, bearded, awned plants, is opp. to འབྲུ་གང་བུ་ཅན *ḥbru gaṅ bu-can*, leguminous plants. 2. trellis-work, lattice. 3. a tree or shrub, probably the Tibetan furze, Caragana versicolor.

གྲ་མ་ཉམས་གྲ་ཟུར་མི་མང་གྲུང་པོ་རྣམ་དག་ནི *gra-ma ñams gra-zur mi maṅ gruṅ-po rnam-dag ni* in the (irregular cornered) cell many learned and holy men lived (*Jig. 36*).

གྲ་མ་ཆེ *Gra-ma che* n. of a king of ancient time; མི་ལས་སྐལ་ལྡན་གྲ་མ་ཆེ *mi-las skal-ldan gra-ma che* among men the blessed Gra-ma-che (*Yig.*).

གྲ་ཟུར *gra-zur* (*ḍa-zur*) सन्धि the corner or junction of sides also called གྲྭ *grwa*.

གྲ་ལེགས་པ *gra legs-pa* (*ṭa leg-pa*) or གྲ་མ་ལེགས་པ *gra ma-legs-pa* the hairs of wild animals such as tiger or leopard, &c., when thick and glossy are called *gra-legs-pa*.

གྲྭ I: *grwa* (*ṭa*) 1. कोण angle; corner; side གྲྭ་ནི་ཕྱོགས་ནི་ཀུན་ཏུ་ཡང་ *Grwa* is quarter or direction 2. lap; lappet; extremity; གོས་ཀྱི་གྲྭ *gos-kyi-grwa* coat-tail: ལོ་ཙཱ་བས་ཆོས་གོས་ཀྱི་གྲྭ་ནས་བཟུང་སྟེ་བཅུམས་པས་ཀྱང་མ་གནང *Lo-tsa-was chos-gos kyi grwa-nas bzuṅ-ste bçums-pas kyaṅ ma-gnaṅ* though the Lo-tsa-wa wept seizing the lappet of his garment, yet he (Atis'a) would not bestow it.

གྲྭ II: a school; ཀློག་གྲྭ *klog-grwa* a reading school (*Cs.*); སྒོམ་གྲྭ *sgom-grwa* a school for meditation; སྔགས་གྲྭ *sṅags-grwa* a school for mystical Buddhism (*Cs.*); འདུལ་གྲྭ *hdul-grwa* a training school; seminary; སྨན་གྲྭ *sman-grwa* a medical school; རྩིས་གྲྭ *rtsis-grwa* a school where mathematics is taught; ཡིག་གྲྭ *yig-grwa* a writing school (*Cs.*).

གྲྭ་ཁང་ *grwa-khaṅ* अट्टाल, हर्म्य 1. top-house; a dome. 2. school-house, sometimes also monk's residence.

གྲྭ་གྲངས *grwa-graṅs* (*ṭa-ḍaṅ*) the number of candidtae monks in a monastery.

གྲྭ་ཐང་ *grwa-thaṅ* (*ḍa-thaṅ*) कोणस्थल corner or nook in a plain.

གྲྭ་པ *grwa-pa* (*ṭa-pa*) छात्र 1. a school boy; a scholar; disciple. 2. generally a monk-pupil or novice belonging to a monastery.

གྲྭ་དཔོན *grwa-dpon* school master; chief *ṭa-pa* or monk.

གྲྭ་ཕྲུག *grwa-phrug* a little boy who reads.

གྲྭ་ཚང་ *grwa-tshaṅ* (*ṭa-tshaṅ*) चतुष्पाठी school where monks are instructed in sacred literature; a section in a great monastery, where the monks belonging to one particular school of studies live together.

གྲྭ་ཚོགས *grwa-tshogs* (*ṭa-tshog*) a congregation or convention of monks.

གྲྭ་བཞིར *grwa-bshir* (*ṭa-shor*) चतुष्कोणेषु in the four corners: the real meaning according to Tibetan authors is चतुष्पार्श्वेषु, on the four sides of a house.

གྲྭ་ཟུར *grwa-zur* a corner room or monk's cell.

གྲྭ་ས *grwa-sa* (*ṭa-sa*) a monastery; གྲྭ་ས་ཆེན་པོ *grwa-sa chen-po* (*ṭa-sa chen-po*) great departmental school attached to large monastery; མཚན་ཉིད་གྲྭ་ས་ཞིག *mtshan-ñid grwa-sa shig* a school where the Buddhist metaphysics is taught.

གྭ་ཏི *grwa-ti* plate; dish in *Ld.* (*Jä.*).

གྲག་སྟོང་ *grag-stoṅ* echo; described as བྲག་ཆ་ལྟ་བུ་སྟོང་ཉིད་ཀྱི་སྒྲ *brag-cha lta-bu stoṅ-ñid kyi sgra*, a name for anything of empty sound as an echo from a rock: *skye-med grag-stoṅ tshig-gi ṅa-ro sgrogs* an echo without any real existence proclaims a loud cry of words (*A. 14*); *lo shes bya-wa grag-stoṅ sñan-pahi glu-dbyaṅs* a low noiseless refrain is called *lo* (*A. 146*): ཁྱེད་ཀྱི་གྲག་སྟོང་བསྒྲགས་པ་ཡིས, ཁོ་བོའི་བློ་གྲོས་གས་པར་བྱས *khyed-kyi grag-stoṅ bsgrags-pa yis; kho-bohi blo-gros gas-war byas* the echoes (or reverberations) of the sounds you sent forth have split my senses (*Hbrom.* ཕ *10*).

གྲག་པ *grag-pa* or གྲགས་པ *grags-pa* 1.= སྒྲ་འབྱིན་པ *sgra hbyind-pa* नाद the tone; pitch of a sound or voice. 2. fame; noise; rumour; talk. 3. the principal or most distinguished amongst several persons (*Jä.*). 4. occasionally=འགྲག་པ.

གྲགས *grags* किल hope; contempt.

གྲགས་པ I: *grags-pa* 1. acc. to *Jä.* to bind or fasten up a load; so also in the colloq. 2. pf. of འགྲག་པ *hgrag-pa*.

གྲགས་པ II: यशः, अभिख्या, कीर्त्ति, आख्या, ख्याति, श्लोक, भग, ललाम glory; also fame, reputation, character by report; གྲགས་པ་ངན་པ notoriety; ill name; bad repute; rumour; report: དེའི་གྲགས་པ་ཆེན་པོ་བྱུང་ the report of it spread, was circulated (in most cases it signifies good name, renown): སྙན་པ་དང་གྲགས་པས་སའི་སྟེང་ཐམས་ཅད་ཁྱབ་པ *sñan-pa daṅ grags-pas sahi steṅ thams-cad khyab-pa* the whole earth was filled with his fame and renown; སྙན་གྲགས *sñan-grags* reputation.

གྲགས་ཅན *grags-can* 1. famous; renowned; beautiful; splendid; glorious; proud; haughty; གྲགས་ཆེན *grags chen* महायशाः; of great fame; celebrated; renowned; well known. 2. सार्थवाह a merchant; གྲགས་སྙན་དཀར་བ *grags-sñan dkar-wa* शुचियशः good name; pure fame; reputation; གྲགས་འདོད་ཅན *grags-hdod-can* ambitious; desirous of gaining glory, of being famous; གྲགས་ལྡན *grags-ldan* यशस्वी, यशस्वान् one who is celebrated or possessed of fame: སྙན་པའི་གྲགས་པས་ཕྱོགས་རྣམས་ཀུན་ཏུ་སྒྲོགས *sñan-pahi grags-pas phyogs-rnams kun-tu sgrogs* (his) fame spread in all quarters (everywhere).

* གྲགས་པ་རྒྱལ་མཚན *Grags-pa rgyal-mtshan* यशोध्वज (*Schr.; Tā. 31*), lit. banner of glory; n. of a governor of Tibet.

གྲགས་པ་ཅན *grags-pa-can* = སྙན་གྲགས་ཅན *sñan-grags-can* प्रसिद्ध, विश्रुत, अवघुष्ट, प्रतीत, नादित illustrious; renowned; ཤིང་ནས་གྲགས་པ་ཆེ་བ of great renown; of celebrity, fame, glory; རྙེད་པ་དང་གྲགས་པ་ལ་ཆགས་པ greedy of gain and fame.

གྲགས་པ་ཐོབ་པ *grags-pa thob-pa* = མཁས་པ *mkhas-pa*, a learned man.

* གྲགས་པ་འོད་ཟེར *Grags-pa hod-zer* n. pr. (*Schr.*).

* གྲགས་པའི་བཤེས་གཉེན *Grags-pahi bçes-gñen* यशोमित्र n. pr. (*Schr.; Tā. 2, 205*).

གྲགས་བྱིན *Grags-byin* यशोदत्त one of the devoted attendants of the Buddha: བཅོམ་ལྡན་འདས་འཁོར་ལྔ་སྡེ་དང་གྲགས་བྱིན་དང་འཆར་ཀ་ལ་སོགས.

གྲགས་མ *grags-ma* Paldan Lhamo, also called དཔལ་ལྷ་མོ *Dpal lha-mo, i.e., Çrī-Devī*.

གྲགས་མུ་ཁྱུད *Grags mu-khyud* यशोनेमि n. of a legendary king, the sphere or circle of whose fame was very wide.

གྲགས་འཛིན་མ *Grags hdsin-ma* (*dag-dsin-ma*) यशोधरा the wife of the Buddha S'ākya-muni.

གྲགས་ཡས *Grags-yas* 1. विख्यात of world-wide fame; of boundless celebrity. 2. n. of a number. 3. n. of a district in *Khams*.

གྲང་བ *grañ-wa* (*tang-wa*), also གྲང་མོ शीत, adj. cold, cool; colloq. partakes of the nature of a verb in such phrases as གྲང་གི་འདུག *grañ-gi hdug*, he feels cold; གྲང་ངོ *grañ-ño* it is cold. In such phrases, however, it is common to insert the word གནམ *nam*, the sky, *e.g.* (colloq.) *nam tang-mo re*, the sky is cold, *i.e.*, "it is cold"; གྲང་སྐྱོབ *grañ-skyob* तनुत्राण protection from cold; warm woollen clothes: གྲང་བ་དང་དྲོ་བ་ཤེས་བྱའི་བྱ *grañ-wa dañ dro-wa shes-byahi bya* the bird called the शीतोष्ण cold and warmth; this fabulous bird is a native of the forest called in Tibetan སྒྲིབ་པ་སྔོན་པའི་ནགས *Sgrib-pa sñon-pahi nags*, the primeval shady forest; its sight relieves one from the effects of cold or heat: གྲང་བ་ནི་དྲོ་བར་འགྱུར the cold will be changed into warmth; གྲང་བས་གཟིར frozen or congealed by cold; གྲང་འགྲོ་བར་འདུག it will grow cold.

Syn. ལྷགས་གྲང *lhags-grañ*; འཁྱགས *hkhyags*; ལྷགས་པ *lhags-pa*; བསིལ་བ *bsil-wa*; བསེར་བ *bser-wa*; གྲང་རེག *grañ-reg*; གྲང་ངད *grañ-ñad* (*Mñon.*).

གྲང་བ་སེལ *grañ-wa sel* अशिशिर warm; where there is no cold to remove.

གྲང་བའི་དུས *grañ-wahi dus* शिशिर, शीत-काल the cold season.

གྲང་བའི་ནད *grañ-wahi-nad* प्रतिशीत the cold fit of the ague; གྲུམ་པུ *grum-pu* gout; rheumatism; arthritic pain; གྲང་དྲོ *grañ-dro* cold and warmth, temperature; གྲང་ཤུམ་བྱེད་པ *grañ-çum byed-pa* to shiver with cold.

གྲང་བའི་གནས *grañ-wahi gnas* a cool place.

གྲང་ཀླུང *grañ-kluñ* lit. cold valley; n. of a large village under Kamba Jong on the other side of the Kangchen Juñga mountain.

གྲང་དམྱལ་བརྒྱད་ *grañ-dmyal brgyad* the eight cold hells, v. དམྱལ་བ *dmyal-wa*.

གྲང་གཞི *grañ-gshi* disease induced by cold, gen. dispepsia.

གྲང་རེག་ཕོ་ཉ *brañ-reg pho-ña*=བྱ་སྐྱུང་ཀ *bya-skyuñ-ka* the jack-daw (*Mñon.*).

གྲང་རླུང་ *grañ-rluñ* वात a disease allied to rheumatism, also cold in the stomach.

གྲངས *grañs* (*dañg*) संख्या number; ཕན་གྲངས་དུ་མར a multiplied number, many times; གྲངས་མེད་པར innumerable; གྲངས་མ་མཆིས་པར *grañs ma-mchis-par* having no number or without number; numberless; གྲངས་འདེབས་པ *grañs hdebs-pa* or རྩིས་པ *rtsis-pa* to count; also an accountant; གྲངས་བརྡ *grañs-brda* symbolical numerals of certain nouns, which in some books are used instead of the usual numerals, for instance མིག *mig*, the eye for "two" (*Cs.*). 1. लिङ्ग sign. 2. गणक astrologer.

གྲངས་ཀྱི་རྣམ་གྲངས *grañs-kyi rnam-grañs* arithmetical enumeration; enumeration of the numbers used in the sacred books of Tibet as compiled from the work called (མཛོད་འགྲེལ) *mdsod-hgrel* are:—(1) གཅིག *gcig* one; (2) བཅུ *bchu* 10; (3) བརྒྱ *brgya* 100; (4) སྟོང་ *stoñ* 1000; (5) ཁྲི *khri* 10,000; (6) འབུམ *hbum* 100,000; (7) ས་ཡ *sa-ya* 1,000,000; (8) བྱེ་བ *bye-wa* 10,000,000; (9) དུང་ཕྱུར *duñ-phyur* 100,000,000; (10) ཐེར་འབུམ *ther-hbum* 1,000,000,000; (11) ཐེར་འབུམ་ཆེན་པོ *ther-hbum chen-po* 10,000,000,000; (12) ཁྲག་ཁྲིག *khragkhrig* 100,000,000,000; (13) ཁྲག་ཁྲིག་ཆེན་པོ *khrag-khrig chen-po*, 1,000,000,000,000; (14) རབ་བཀྲམ *rab-bkram* 10,000,000,000,000; (15) རབ་བཀྲམ་ཆེན་པོ *rab-bkram chen-po* 100,000,000,000,000; (16) གཏམས *gtams* 1,000,000,000,000,000; (17) གཏམས་ཆེན་པོ *gtams chen-po* 10,000,000,000,000,000; (18) དཀྲིགས *dkrigs* 100,000,000,000,000,000; (19) དཀྲིགས་ཆེན་པོ *dkrigs chen-po* 1,000,000,000,000,000,000. Next, the following are progressive numbers increasing by multiples of ten up to 60 figures: 20, མི་འཁྲུག *mi-hkhrug*; 21, མི་འཁྲུག་ཆེན་པོ *mi-hkhrug-chen-po*; 22, ཁྱད་འབྱིན *khyad hbyin*; 23, ཁྱད་འབྱིན་ཆེན་པོ *khyad-hbyin chen-po*; 24, སྤང་རྟེན *spañ-rten*; 25, སྤང་རྟེན་ཆེན་པོ *spañ-rten chen-po*; 26, དེད་འདྲེན *ded-hdren*; 27, དེད་འདྲེན་ཆེན་པོ *ded-hdren-chen-po*; 28, མཐའ་སྣང *mthah-snañ*; 29, མཐའ་སྣང་ཆེན་པོ *mthah-snañ chen-po*; 30, རྒྱུ་རིགས *rgyu-rigs*; 31, རྒྱུ་རིགས་ཆེན་པོ *rgyu-rigs chen-po*; 32, འོད་མཛེས *hod-mdses*; 33, འོད་མཛེས་ཆེན་པོ *hod-mdses chen-po*; 34, དབང་པོ *dwañ-po*; 35, དབང་པོ་ཆེན་པོ *dwañ-po chen-po*; 36, ལེགས་འབྱིན *legs-hbyin*; 37, ལེགས་འབྱིན་ཆེན་པོ *legs-hbyin chen-po*; 38, རྟོགས་འགྲོ *rtogs-hgro*; 39, རྟོགས་འགྲོ་ཆེན་པོ *rtogs-hgro chen-po*; 40, འབྱིང་རྡུལ *hbyiñ-rdul*; 41, འབྱིང་རྡུལ་ཆེན་པོ *hbyiñ-rdul chen-po*; 42, རྒྱ་རྟགས *rgya-rtags*; 43, རྒྱ་རྟགས་ཆེན་པོ *rgya-rtags chen-po*; 44, སྟོབས་འཁོར *stobs-hkhor*; 45, སྟོབས་འཁོར་ཆེན་པོ *stobs-hkhor chen-po*; 46, བརྡའ་ཤེས *brdah-çes*; 47, བརྡའ་ཤེས་ཆེན་པོ *brdah-çes chen-po*; 48, རྣམ་འབྱུང་ *rnam-hbyuñ*; 49, རྣམ་འབྱུང་ཆེན་པོ *rnam-hbyuñ chen-po*; 50, སྟོབས་མིག *stobs-mig*; 51, སྟོབས་མིག་ཆེན་པོ *stobs-mig chen-po*. Up to this number there are Sanskrit equivalents; from 53 to 60 there are no Sanskrt equivalents, the Tibetans having introduced new names to replace lost originals. 53, བྱམས་པ *byams-pa*; 54, བྱམས་པ་ཆེན་པོ *byams-pa chen-po*; 56, སྙིང་རྗེ *sñiñ-rje*; 56, སྙིང་རྗེ་ཆེན་པོ *sñiñ-rje chen-po*; 57, དགའ་བ *dgah-wa*; 58, དགའ་བ་ཆེན་པོ *dgah-wa chen-po*; 59, བཏང་སྙོམས *btañ-sñoms*; 60, བཏང་སྙོམས་ཆེན་པོ *btañ-sñoms chen-po*. These sixty numbers are used in astronomical and astrological calculations.

གྲངས་ཅན *grañs-can* महापद्म 1. a countless number. 2. མཁས་པ *mkhas-pa* or རིག་པ་ཅན *rig-*

pa-can पण्डित an intelligent man; a learned man (*Mñon.*).

གྲངས་ཅན་པ *grañs̱-can-pa* सांख्य the oldest of the atheistic philosophical sects of the Brahmans, called *Sāñkhya.*

གྲངས་བཅས *grañs̱-ḇcas̱* 1. उषा the dawn, or the goddess of the dawn. 2. lit. "together with the number."

གྲངས་འབྱམས *grañs̱-ẖbyams̱* असंख्या numberless; countless.

གྲངས་མང་ཆ *grañs̱ mañ-cha* [चतुरभ्यस्त, repeated four times]*S.*

གྲངས་མེད *grañs̱-meḏ* 1. असंख्य countless; numberless. 2. श्वित्र a crawling; श्वितरोग white leprosy: གྲངས་མེད་ཀྱི་ཁྱད་པར *grañs̱-meḏ kyi khyaḏ-par* the distinction of being countless, numberless; གྲངས་མེད་ཅན *grañs̱-meḏ-can* परम supreme.

གྲངས་མེད་གཅིག *grañs̱-meḏ gcig* (the numberless one). In the work called *Mañju çrī-mūla Tantra* (འཇམ་དཔལ་རྩ་རྒྱུད) the following numbers are said to have been in use in Ancient India among the laity for worldly purposes:—From 1 to 10, *i.e.*, གཅིག *gcig* to ཐེར་འབུམ *ther-ẖbum*, and 11, ཤུ་རྡོག *çu-ṟdog*; 12, མཆོག་ཉལ *mchog-ñal*; 13, སྐྱ་འཕྱིས *s̱kya-ẖphyis̱*; 14, བྱེ་མ *bye-ma*; 15, ནུབ་ནུབ *nub-nub*; 16, མཚོ་ཡས *mtsho-yas̱*; 17, ལྡབས་ཕྱོར *ḻdabs̱-phyor*; 18, རྫི *ṟdsi*,—all these being each a multiple of another by ten. In the work called ཕལ་པོ་ཆེ *phal-po-che* the numbers vary after the eighth, *i.e.*, བྱེ་བ *bye-wa*; such as ཁོད་ཁོད *khoḏ-khoḏ*, ཐད་དགུ *thaḏ-dgu*, ཁྲིག་ཁྲིག *khrig-khrig*, ཐམས་ཐམས *thams̱-thams̱* and so on up to 128 places, increasing by multiples of one hundred. In the *Lalita Vistara* there are thirty-two numbers, also increasing in multiples of a hundred.

གྲངས་སུ་གཅེར *grañs̱-gçer* to enumerate; count the number one by one.

གྲངས་སུ་འགྲོ *grañs̱-su ẖgro* संख्यां गच्छति goes into numbers; is counted: གྲངས་སུ་བཙུག་པ *grañs̱-su ḇcug-pa*, put into numbers; counted: གྲངས་སུ་ཡང *grañs̱-su yañ* संख्यामपि even in number.

གྲབ་རྒྱབ *grab-ṟgyab* pride; boasting (*Sch.*).

གྲབས I: *grabs̱* ཀུ་སོམ་བྱེད *gçom-byeḏ*; གྲ་སྒྲིག *gra-s̱grig* 1. preparation; arrangement; measures; contrivance; གྲབས་བྱེད་པ to make preparation for; འགྲོ་བའི་གྲབས་བྱེད་པ to prepare to go: གསོད་གྲབས་ཡོད་པའི་ཚེ་ན just as preparations were being made for slaughtering them (*Mil*). 2. defined as ངེས་མ་ཐག་ངེས་པར་འབྱུང་བའི་དོན "signifies the certainty about the time of immediate action": ཡོང་གྲབས་འདུག *yoñ-grabs̱ ẖdug* was on the point of coming, or am just coming; བརྡུང་གྲབས་བྱས་བྱུང *ḇṟduñ-grabs̱ byas̱-byuñ* was about to beat or strike; ཤི་གྲབས་བྱས་བྱུང *çi-grabs̱ byas̱-byuñ* was almost dying or dead; གསད་གྲབས་བྱས་བྱུང *gsaḏ-grabs̱ ḇyas̱-ḇyuñ*, was about to kill: ཐོབ་གྲབས་ཡིན was about to get or gain; སྔོར་གྲབས་ཡིན is about to slip or run away; ཚར་གྲབས་ཡོད is about to finish; ནང་ནང་གཉིས་གྲབས་མཐུན་ནི on mutual agreement. 3. deliberation: ངེད་ཕྱིར་གྲབས་བྱེད་བྱིན་འདུག they were deliberating about me (in *W.*).

གྲབས II. चिन्तास्थल place or object of reflection, thought, etc.: གྲབས་ཡུལ་ལྟ་བུ *grabs̱-yul ḻta bu*, གྲབས་ཀྱིས *grabs̱-gyis̱*, སྟོན་མོ་ལྟ་བུ *s̱ton-mo ḻta-bu*.

གྲམ *gram* (*ḏam*) 1. ཆུ་ནང་གི་རྡོ *chu nañ-gi ṟdo* a kind of stone found in water (*Ñag*). 2. གྲམ་པ *gram-pa* swamp; marsh; fen (*Lex.*). 3. འགྲེམ་པ *ẖgrem-pa* (*Miñ.*).

གྲམ་པ་ཁམ་བུ *Gram-pa kham-bu* one of the places of pilgrimage of the Bon (*G. Bon. 38*).

གྲམ་ས *gram-sa* উচ্ছকৰ stony.

གྲལ *gral* (*ḍal*) འཕྲེང་བ *ḥphreṅ-wa* পংক্তি row, range series; also a rope, cord; আহার, আলি, class, stratum.

གྲལ་མགོ *gral-mgo* or གྲལ་གྱི་ཐོག་མ *gral-gyi thog-ma* the upper end of a row; the uppermost place; the seat at the head of a table; གཡས་གྲལ *gyas-gral* the right hand row; གཡོན་གྲལ *gyon-gral* the left hand row; ཚོགས་གྲལ *tshogs gral* 1. the order or file of monks in a religious congregation; གྲྭ་པ་མང་པོ་ཡ་ཡོ་མེད་པར་སྒྲིག་ནས་བཞུགས་པ many novices sitting in rows without being awry; བཞུགས་གྲལ *bshugs-gral* the order of seats, also the order or row in which lamas and chiefs, high and low, sit according to their position or rank in any public or social gathering; རྟེན་གྲལ row of religious symbols; མཆོད་གྲལ row of offerings for the gods or offerings placed in one or more rows; སྐུ་གྲལ the order or row in which the images are placed in a temple; མི་གྲལ row or order in which men are seated; གྲལ་གཏམ house-talk (*Jä.*); དབང་གྲལ the row of supplicants waiting for benediction: མཆེད་གྲོགས་དང་དབང་གྲལ་མཉམ་དུ་ས་སུ, when you are sitting with your brethren (fellow-believers) in one row.

གྲལ་སྒྲིག *gral-sgrig* or གྲལ་དུ་སྒྲིག་པ *gral-du sgrig-pa* to arrange in order, dispose in rows.

གྲལ་ཚེས *gral-tshes*=ཚེས་གྲངས *tshes-graṅs* date; a consecutive date.

གྲལ་རིམ I: *gral-rim* পংক্তি line; row; file in which monks sit in any religious service or congregation: རྒན་གཞོན་གྲལ་རིམ *rgan-gshon gral-rim* the order in which the young and old sit; the right of seniority; གྲུབ་ཐོབ་རིམ་གྲོ་གྲལ་རིམ་བཞིན the religious services of the perfected saints according to the order of seniority (*Zam.*).

Syn. གྲལ་དུ་སྒྲིགས་པ *gral-du sgrigs-pa*; ཚར་དུ་དངར *tshar-du dṅar*; ཕྲེང་བཀོད *phreṅ-bkod*; ལུ་གུ་རྒྱུད *lu-gu rgyud*; ཁྲིག་ཆགས་བཀོད *khrig chags bkod* (*Mṅon.*).

གྲལ་རིམ II: (*ḍal-rim*) acc. to *Jä.* claim; title.

གྲལ་སྐྱོང་བ *gral skyoṅ-wa* কায়া a shadow.

གྲལ་པ *gral-pa* a beer-house customer (*Jä*).

གྲལ་མ *gral-ma* a small beam; rafter (*Cs*); གྲལ་བུ་གྲལ་ཕྱམ *gral-bu gral-phyam* roof-laths; sticks which are laid close together and covered with earth (*Jä.*).

གྲས *gras* class, order, series; rank, dignity; tribe (*Cs.*).

གྲས་པ *gras-pa* 1. to bind, for དྲས་པ *dras-pa*. 2. (Bengali) কাঠকরি wooden beams or rails.

གྲི *gri* (*ḍi*) অসি, মল্ল, কর্ত্তি a knife, weapon; খড়্গ sabre. Different kinds of weapons:—ཆུ་གྲི *chu-gri*, གྲི་ཐུང *gri-thuṅ*, རལ་གྲིའི་བུ *ral-grihi bu*, གྲི་གུག *gri-gug*, གྲི་འཁྱོག་པོ *gri ḥkhyog-po*, དགྲ་སྟ *dgra-sta*, སྟ་རི *sta-ri*, སྟ་གྲི *sta-gri*, རལ་གྲིའི་འཁྲུལ་འཁོར *ral-grihi ḥkhrul-ḥkhor*, གྲི་སྒུར *gri-sgur*, ས་རང *sa-raṅ*.

Syn. ཤང་ལང *çaṅ-laṅ*; བརྡེག་ཆ *brdeg-cha*; རྗེས་སུ་གཅོད *rjes-su gcod*; ལག་སྐྱོང *lag-skyoṅ*; ཟླ་བ་འཛུམ་བྱེད *zla-wa ḥdsum-byed*; གཡུལ་དུ་འཛིན *gyul-du ḥdsin*; མཚོན་ཆའི་གཞི *mtshon-chahi gshi*; སྒྲོལ་བྱེད *sgrol-byed*; དཔལ་གྱི་སྙིང་པོ *dpal-gyi sñiṅ-po*; གཅོད་བྱེད *gcod-byed*; ཤ་མ་ཀ *ça-ma-ka* (*Mṅon.*).

གྲི་ཁ *gri-kha* the edge of a knife.

གྲི་གུ *gri-gu*=ཁུག་ཅིག *khug-cig* niche; corner (*A. 57*): ཡང་རྡོ་རྗེ་གདན་གྱི་གྲི་གུ་ན་བུད་མེད་ཅིག *yaṅ Rdo-rje gdan-gyi gri-gu na bud-med cig* again a woman in a niche of the temple, &c., at Vajrāsana.

གྲི་གུ་ཆུང་ *gri-gu chuṅ* कर्त्तरि small knife.

གྲི་གུག *gri-gug* कर्त्तरि a short crooked sword.

གྲི་གུམ་བཙན་པོ *Gri gum-btsan-po* one of the ancient kings of Tibet, son of *Srib-khri-btsan*, who was assassinated with a knife.

གྲི་ནོན *gri-non* चय n. of a disease.

གྲི་བྱ་གག་གི་གཙོག་པ་ལྟ་བུ *gri bya gag-gi gçog-pa lta-bu* खड्गः कुक्कुट-पक्षकप्रव a knife of the shape of the wings of a cock.

གྲི་བྱ་རོག་གི་མཆུ *gri bya rog-gi mchu* खड्ग-काक-चञ्चुक a knife of the shape of the crow's bill.

གྲི་མག *gri-mag*, v. གྲིབ་མ *grib-ma*.

གྲི་དམར *gri-dmar* (lit. the red knife) knife of superior quality manufactured in Tibet.

གྲིའི་སོ *grihi-so* sharp edge of a knife.

གྲིའི་རྩེ་མོ *grihi tse-mo* कर्त्तर्यग्र the point of a scimitar or sword.

གྲིའུ *grihu* a small knife.

གྲི་ཤ *gri-ça* explained as སྐྱེས་པ་དར་མ་གྲི་ལ་ཤི་བའི་ཤ *skyes-pa dar-ma gri-la çi-wahi ça*, flesh of an adult man who has been killed with a sword (this flesh being used in sorcery).

གྲིར་ཧྲམ་པ *grir ṛham-pa* or གྲིར་གསོད་པ *grir gsod-pa* or གྲིར་འགུམ་པ *grir hgum-pa* to kill (or being killed) with a knife.

གྲིན་པ *grin-pa* (*din-pa*) prob. སྒྲིན་པོ *sgrin-po* skilful; clever (*Jä.*).

གྲིབ *grib* (*dib*) shade; defilement; stain or spot; filth; contamination, mostly in a religious sense: གྲིབ་ཡོང *grib-yoṅ* contamination, pollution will arise: རོ་གྲིབ *ro-grib* defilement by or from a corpse; གྲིབ་སེལ *grib-sel* the removal of defilement; also one in whom there is no defilement; n. of a Buddha. ཟས་གྲིབ *zas-grib* unclean food or pollution of food; གོས་གྲིབ dirty clothes, or defilement in clothes; ཡུགས་གྲིབ *yugs-grib* or pollution of widowhood; བག་གྲིབ or the defilement that is brought by different people assembled in a marriage; དམར་གྲིབ *dmar-grib* or pollution of blood or anything slain red-handed; དམ་གྲིབ pollution by the breach of a vow; unchastity; འཁོན་གྲིབ defilement by quarrel or fight; བ་ཤན་གྲིབ defilement in slaughter pertaining to butchers, or defilement from murder; མནའ་གྲིབ defilement caused by oath or by the barbarous custom of killing animals and swearing over their blood (prevailing among the Kham-pa tribes); ནལ་གྲིབ defilement from incest.

གྲིབ་ཀྱི་ཕུ *grib-kyi phu* shady valley, generally on the north side of a mountain range (cf. སྲིབས *sribs*); གྲིབ་ཕྱོགས *grib-phyogs* the shady side of a hill or mountain, the side not exposed to the sun.

གྲིབ་ཁྲུས *grib-khrus* the washing of defilement.

གྲིབ་ཅན *grib-can* stubborn; refractory (*Jä.*).

གྲིབ་མདོས *grib-mdos* offerings made to Bon deities for removing some defilement.

གྲིབ་གནོན *grib-gnon* 1. आच्छादक, छाया shadow, or 2. བཙོག་པའི་གྲིབ *btsog-pahi grib* defilement from unclean things, filth, night-soil, &c.: ཆོས་གྲྭར་གྲུལ་བུམ་གྲིབ་གནོན་བསྲུངས *chos-grwar grul-bum grib-gnon bsruṅs* in a religious school there should be protection against defilement from harpies (*Zam. 2.*).

གྲིབ་གནོན་གྱི་གདོན་ *grib-gnon gyi gdon* a demon that defiles and poisons food; a harpy.

གྲིབ་མ་ *grib-ma* shade; shadow; གྲིབ་དང་གྲིབ་མའི་གྲོལ་ *grib-daṅ grib-mahi grol* (*Zam. 2*) छाया; ཤིང་གི་གྲིབ་མ་ *çiṅ-gi grib-ma* the shadow of a tree.

གྲིབ་མ་སྔོན་པོའི་ནགས་ *Grib-ma sṅon-pohi nags* forest of the dark-blue shado in the fabulous northern continent of Uttara Kuru.

གྲིབ་མའི་ལམ་ *grib-mahi lam* छायापथ the milky-way; also a path by the shady side of a mountain or in the valley.

གྲིབ་མའི་ལུས་ *grib-mahi lus* छायाङ्ग, the shadowy body, *i.e.*, body of defilements.

གྲིབ་སེལ་ *grib-sel* the removing of pollution or defilement of any symbol, image, sacred books, or offerings by religious rites.

གྲིབ་སོ་ *grib-so* the quickly vanishing, at sunset, of the shadows of trees, &c.; གྲིབ་སོ་མངོན་པར་རབ་ཏུ་བབས་པ་ अभिप्रलम्बते hanging down, also lengthening of shadows before they vanish in the shade of night; གྲིབ་སོ་ཆེར་བབས་པ་ अभ्यवलम्बन long projection of shadows.

གྲིབ་སྲུང་ *grib-sruṅ* guarding against defilement.

གྲིབ་བསངས་ *grib-bsaṅs* cleansed or purified of defilement; purification of defilement.

གྲིབ་ལྷགས་ *grib-lhags* cool shade (*Sch.*).

གྲིམ་པ་ *grim-pa* to hasten; to hurry (*Sch.*).

གྲིམ་ཙེ་ *grim-tse*, acc. to *Jä.* a pair of scissors (in Sikkim sounded "*kyimtse*").

གྲིམས་པ་ *grims-pa*, चतुर, पटु clever; skilful; dexterous; also careful; on the alert; རིག་པ་གྲིམས་པ་ *rig-pa grims-pa* to be careful; on the alert: གྲྭ་ས་གྲིམས་ཤིག་ *grwa-sa grims-çig* be attentive in the monastic school: རི་བྲོད་གྲིམས་ཤིག་ on a hill range take care!

གྲིལ་ *gril* (*dil*) (cf. འགྲིལ་བ *hgril-wa*) a roll; ཤོག་གྲིལ་ *çog-gril* rolled paper; a paper roll: ཤོག་དུམ་གྲིལ་ནས་བཞག་བྱུང་ kept rolled up in paper: གོས་གྲིལ་ *gos-gril* a roll of satin or cloth; a garment folded up (*Cs.*).

གྲིལ་ཁ་བྱེད་པ་ *gril-kha byed-pa* to make up a parcel. (*Sch.*)

གྲུ་ I: *gru* 1. a figure, corner, tip, anything with length and breadth; གྲུ་བཞི་ *gru-bshi* a figure with four corners, gen. a square; ཡུལ་གྲུ་ *yul-gru* a country with certain dimensions, *i.e.*, the division of a country in provinces or districts. 2. lustre; གྲུ་དམར་ *gru-dmar* a reddish lustre from precious stones. 3. a district of Tibet lying to the east and north of *Dbus* (*Jig.*).

གྲུ་ II: नौः, नाव्य, तरणी, पोत, यान general term for boat, raft, vessel; also གྲུ་ཤན་ *gru-çan* a boat, ferry.

Syn. རྟགས་གསུམ་པ་ *rtags gsum-pa*; གྲུ་ཡི་རབ་ *gru-yi rab*; སྒྲོལ་བར་བྱེད་ *sgrol-war byed*; ཕ་མཐར་སྒྲོལ་ *pha-mthar sgrol*; སེང་གེ་ཅན་ *seṅ-ge-can*; རྟ་མགོ་ཅན་ *rta-mgo-can*; ཆུའི་ཤིང་རྟ་ *chuhi-çiṅ-rta* (*Mṅon.*).

གྲུ་དཀར་ *gru-dkar* (*du-kar*) a kind of turquoise.

གྲུ་སྐྱ་ *gru-skya* स्फारिच that which falling on water strikes it; an oar (*Mṅon.*).

Syn. སྐྱོད་བྱེད་ *skyod-byed*; བསྒྲལ་བའི་ཤིང་རྟ་ *bsgral-wahi çiṅ-rta.*

གྲུ་ཁ་ *gru-kha* or གྲུ་ཤན་ཁ་ *gru çan-kha* or གྲུ་བཏང་ས་ *gru btaṅ-sa* landing place on the side of a river, etc.; a ferry. See maps in Survey Report of A. K.'s journey.

གྲུ་ཁུག་ *gru-khug* the keel of a slip.

གྲུ་མཁན་ *gru-mkhan* नाविन् navigator; a ferry man.

གྲུ་ག *Gru-ga* 1. clew; hank. 2. n. of a country. 3. stone or paint of whitish-blue colour.

གྲུ་གུ *gru-gu* 1. a thread-ball; yarn in round ball. 2. མཚོན་གྱི་གྲུ་གུ *Mtshon-gyi gru-gu* n. of a village in Tibet (*Jig.*).

གྲུ་གུ་རྒྱ་ར *Gru-gu Rgya-ra* n. of a village in Khaṁ (*Loṅ. 27*).

གྲུ་གླ *gru-gla* passage money at a ferry; a boatman's fee.

གྲུ་ཆར *gru-char* 1. rains; rainy season: ཡུལ་གྲུ་ཀུན་ལ་ཁྱབ་པར་འབེབས་པའི་ཆར *yul-gru kun-la khyab-par hbebs-pahi char* rains that fall over the whole country and produce a good harvest. 2. a fine, fertile rain (*Sch.*).

གྲུ་མ *gru-ma* (*du-ma*) angle; corner; convex or concave; also edge, border, brim. (*Cs.*).

གྲུ་ཆོད *gru-chod* or གྲུབ་ཟིན *grub-zin* कोण corner; angle.

གྲུ་གསུམ *gru-gsum* त्रिकोण a triangle; གྲུ་བཞི *gru-bshi* a square; གྲུ་དྲང *gru-draṅ* a right angle; གྲུ་ཡོན *gru-yon* or གྲུ་གཡེལ *gru-gyel* oblique angled.

གྲུ་བཞི *gru-bshi* n. of a stone: གྲུ་བཞིས་ཀླད་པ་གསོ་ཞིང་ཆུ་སེར་འདྲེན *gru-bshis klad-pa gso shiṅ-chu-ser hden* the stone called *Grub-bshi* heals the brain and draws out pus.

གྲུ་འདྲེན *gru-hdren* नियामकं, defined as གྲུ་ནང་དུ་འཇུག་པའི་སྐྱེ་བོའི་མིང *gru naṅ-du hjug-pahi skye-bohi miṅ*, person conveyed in a boat. People who journey by boat are:—མགྲོན་པོ guest; ཚོང་མཁན merchant, trader; གྲུ་ལ་ཞོན boat passengers.

གྲུ་པ *gru-pa* ferryman.

གྲུ་བོ *gru-bo*=གྲུ་གཟིངས *gru-gziṅs* ship (*Jä.*).

+ གྲུ་བཙས *gru-btsas* boatman's fee; གྲུ་བཙས་པ *gru btsas-pa*, ཆུ་ལ་ཁྲལ་སྡུད་པ་པོ *chu-la khral sdud-pa-po tol* collector of a ferry.

གྲུ་ཚུགས *gru-tshugs*, གྲུ་བཏོང་ས *gru-gtoṅ-sa* a ferry or *ghat*: *de nas Se-dmar gyi-gru-tshugs-la byon-nas*, then he arrived at the ferry of *Se-dmar* (*A. 91*).

གྲུ་ཚུམས་པ *gru-tshums-pa*=ཁ་ཚུམས་པ or ཁ་རོག་སྡོད་པ to sit silent, without speaking.

གྲུ་འཛིན *gru-hdsin* पोतलक, पोतल 1. n. of a mountain in the south of India; also the residence of Avalokites'vara on the small island of Puto off Shanghai; n. of the residence of the Grand Lama at Lhasa. 2. an harbour.

གྲུ་ཡི་ཡན་ལག *gru-yi yan-lag*=གྲུ་སྐྱ *gru-skya* an oar (*Mṅon.*).

གྲུ་ཡི་རབ *gru-yi rab*=གྲུ་ཤན *gru-çan* a ship (*Mṅon.*).

གྲུ་ཡི་གཤོག་པ *gru-yi gçog-pa*=གྲུ་སྐྱ *gru-skya* oar; the wings of a boat (*Mṅon.*).

Syn. གྲུའི་ཡན་ལག *gruhi yan-lag*; གཡོབ་བྱེད *gyob-bye*; སྐྱ་བ *skya-wa* (*Mṅon.*).

གྲུ་ཡིས་སྒྲོལ *gru-yis sgrol* नाविक a navigator.

གྲུ་ལས་འདས་པ *gru-las hdas-pa* अतिनौः one who has made a voyage.

གྲུ་ཤན *gru-çan*=གྲུ་ཡི་རབ *gru-yi rab* a ship; གྲུ་ཤན་ཁ *gru-çan kha*=གྲུང་གཏང་ས *gruṅ-gtaṅ sa* starting or landing place of a ferry; གྲུ་ཤན་པ *gru çan-pa* ferryman; གྲུ་ལ་ཞོན་པ *gru-la shon-pa* to go on a ferry-boat.

གྲུ་མོ *gru-mo* (*du-mo*) the elbow; གྲེ་མོ *gre-mo*, ཀུ་ནི *ku-ni*, कुर्पर the elbow, or ཀ་ཨུ་ནི *ka-au-ni* काउनि, ལག་པའི་ཚིགས་པ་བར་པའི་རྩེ་ཏོག *lag-pahi-tshigs-pa bar-pahi rtse-tog* the top-most piece of the middle joint of the arm: གྲུ་མོར་ཁ་ཊྭཾ་ག་བཟུང་བ *gru-mor kha tvam-ka* holding a trident in the hollow of his elbow. ལག་པའི་གྲུ་མོ *lag-pahi gru-mo* is defined as *ñe-wahi dpuṅ-pa*; གྲུ་མོའི་ཁྲག the hollow of the elbow joint: ལག་པའི་གྲུ་མོ་རེ་ཇོ་བོའི་པུས་མོའི་སྟེང་ན་བཞག *lag-paẖi gru-mo re-jo-woẖi puş-moẖi şteñ-na ḇshag* resting each elbow on the knees of the lord (*A. 135*).

གྲུག་པ *grug-pa* to break into small pieces; to crumble; to bruise; གྲུག་པའི་འབྲས *grug-paẖi ẖbraş* bruised rice (*Sch.*); གྲུགས་བུ *grugş-bu* something broken.

གྲུང་པོ I: *gruñ-po* (*ḍuñ-po*) = གྲུང་བ *gruñ-wa*, སྦྱང་པོ *şbyañ-po*, རིག་པ་གྲིམས་པ *rig-pa grimş-pa* 1. very intelligent; चतुर clever; wise; prudent. 2. meek; mild; gentle (*Cs.*).

གྲུང་པོ II: the corn seed that is not rotten (*Jig.*).

གྲུབ *grub* I: (*ḍub*) pronounced *rub*, in the upper Himalaya's and Shar-Khombu, signifying in *Ld.* all: གྲུབ་ཤི་སོང *grub-çi-soñ* all are dead (*Jä.*). *Rûb-te*: altogether, jointly.

གྲུབ II: सिद्ध; བྱེད་པ་པོ་དངོས་སུ་མེད་པར་རང་རང་གིས་གྲུབ་པ *byeḏ-pa-po ḏños-su meḏ-par rañ-rañ giş grub-pa* anything accomplished or done by itself without any agent.

གྲུབ་མཆོག *grub-m̱chog* = གྲུབ་ཆེན a great saint; གྲུབ་མཆོག་མ *grub-m̱chog-ma* सिद्धेश्वरा a female saint.

གྲུབ་ཐོབ *grub-thob*, सिद्धा a saint, occurs in the following passage of (*Zam. 2*):—གྲུབ་ཐོབ་རིམ་གྲོ་གྲལ་རིམ་བཞིན *grub-thob rim-gro gral-rim ḇshin* གྲུབ་བརྙེས *grub-ḇṟñeş* one who has gained perfection.

གྲུབ་མཐའ I: *grub-m̱thaẖ* 1. सिद्धान्त, समयतन्त्र established conclusion; opinion; theory (*Zam.*): ཕྱི་ནང་གི་གྲུབ་མཐའ་མ་འཚམས་པར there being no conformity of doctrinal principles between the Brāhmans and the Buddhists.

གྲུབ་མཐའ II: = ཐར་པའི་བློ་གྲོས *thar-paẖi ḇlo-groş* resolution for liberation from miseries; determination for obtaining *Nirvāṇa* (*M̱ñon.*).

གྲུབ་པ *grub-pa* I: 1. सिद्ध, सिद्धा, सम्पन्न, प्रसाधनी, क्षेम, शुभ, साधक; pf. of འགྲུབ་པ to accomplish 2. གྲུབ་པར་བྱེད་འཛུག *grub-par byeḏ ẖzug* सहाय, सिद्धक a saint: གྲུབ་པས་བཏགས་པ *grub-paş ḇtagş-pa* सिद्धोपनीत accomplished by a saint; གྲུབ་པས་བསྟན་པ taught or preached by a saint; གྲུབ་པར་གྱུར་ཅིག *grub-par gyur-cig* सिद्धिरस्तु be it ready, complete, perfect.

གྲུབ་པ II: ཟིན་པ *zin-pa* निष्पत्, सिद्धि existing; success; མ་གྲུབ་པ *ma grub-pa* not existing (*Jä.*): གྲུབ་པ་དང་བདེ་བ *grub-pa dañ ḇde-wa* योग सुख the happiness arising from *yoga* or union with the supreme spirit (in Brahmaṇism) and with the eternal *Çûnyatā* or void in Buddhism: གྲུབ་པ་ལུས *grub-pa luş*, the formed body, either the frame, the structure, the body, or more prob. an abbreviation of ཕུང་པོ་ལྔ་ལས་གྲུབ་པའི་ལུས, the body that is made of the five *skandha* (aggregates); གྲུབ་པའི་དོན་ཅན *grub-paẖi don-can* what is necessary in the charms of necromancy for propitiation; सर्षप mustard.

གྲུབ་པའི་དབང་ཕྱུག *grub-paẖi ḏwañ-phyug* = གྲུབ་ཆེན *grub-chen* great saint (*Yig. k. 11*).

གྲུབ་པའི་རང་བྱོན་སྤྱན་རས་གཟིགས *Grub-paẖi rañ-byon şpyan-raş gzigş* the saint originated or existing by himself; the self-formed Avalokites'vara; ལྷུན་གྲུབ *lhun-grub* or ལྷུན་གྱི་གྲུབ་པ *lhun-gyi grub-pa* सहजसिद्ध self-originated or self-formed: དོན་གྲུབ *Don-grub* or དོན་ཐམས་ཅད་གྲུབ་པ *Don thamş-caḏ grub-pa* सर्वार्थसिद्ध a name of the Buddha, in whom there is the fulfilment of every purpose; also the name of a magie spell or formula.

གྲུམ་པ *grum-pa* the Tibetan badger: རླུང་སེམས་འཛིན་པ་ཕྱི་བ་དང་གྲུམ་པས་ཀྱང་ཤེས་གསུང *ṟluñ semş ẖdsin-pa phyi-ḇa-dañ grum-paş kyañ-çeş gsuñ* he said both the badger and the marmot know how to suspend animation and rlung—a reflection upon the the practices of Tibetan ascetics or *nal-jor* (*A. 70*): གྲུམ་པའི་རྒྱུ་མས་སྒྱུ་གཟེར་འཇོམས *grum-pahi rgyu ma sgyu-gzer hjoms* the intestines of the badger overcome colic.

གྲུམ་པོ *grum-po* a maimed person; a cripple.

གྲུམ་བུ *grum-bu* (*dum-bu*) or གྲུམ་ནད *grum-nad* also called ཏྲེམ *trem*, gout or rheumatism. ཤ་གྲུམ *ça-grum*, acc. to *Jä.* དྲེག་གྲུམ *dreg-grum* podagra; a feeling of lameness in the limbs; རུས་གྲུམ *rus-grum* gout affecting the bones; རྩ་གྲུམ *tsa-grum* rheumatic pain in the muscles. ཆུ་གྲུམ *chu-grum*, གྲུམ་དཀར *grum-dkar*, གྲུམ་ནག *grum-nag* seem to be varieties of small-pox.

གྲུལ་བུམ *grul-bum* (*dul-bum*) कुम्भाण्डक, कुम्भाण्ड a class of vampire-ghouls feeding in cemeteries; གྲུལ་བུམ་མ *grul-bum-ma* कुम्भाण्डी females of the above.

གྲུལ་བུམ་ཅན *Grul-bun-can* n. of a medicinal drug; an esculent root, *Arum campanulatum* (a cure for piles).

Syn. རྩུབ་མོ *rtsub-mo*; ག་གོན *ga-gon*; ཨར་ཤ་འཇོམས *arça-hjoms* अर्शोघ्न that which cures piles: བྲ་བོ་རྒོད *bra-bo rgod*; འདེད་བྱེད་སྤོང་པོ *hded-byed spon-po* (*Mñon.*).

གྲུལ་བུམ་ཟླ་བའི་ནུ་ཞོ་ཅན *grul-bum zla-wahi nu sho-can* are the following three:— ཀླུ་དུག *klu-dug* (ནག *nag*), གཟའ་དུག *gzah-dug* (དཀར *dkar*), གཉན་དུག *gñan-dug* (ཁ) *kha* (*Sman. 350*).

གྲུས་པོ *grus-po* (*du-po*) a yak only two or three years old (*Jä.*).

གྲེ *Gre* (*deh*) पूर्व्वफाल्गुनी the eleventh of the twenty-seven constellations mentioned in works on astronomy.

Syn. མཚོ་སྐྱེས *mtsho-skyes*; རྟ་ཆུ *rta-chu*; འཚོ་སྐྱེས *htsho-skyes* (*Mñon.*).

གྲེ་སྐྱེས *gre-skyes* प्राक्फाल्गुनीभव born in the constellation of पूर्व्वफाल्गुनी.

གྲེ་ག *gre-ga* a sheet of paper (*Jä.*).

གྲེ་སྣ *Gre-sna* n. of a place in the province of *Koñ-po* in Central Tibet.

གྲེ་བ *gre-wa* (*de-wa*)=མགྲིན་པ *mgrin-pa* or གློ་ཡུ *glo-yu* ग्रीवा, कण्ठ the fore part of the neck, the throat, both wind-pipe and the gullet; voice: གྲེ་བ་བདེ་མོ *gre-wa bde-mo* a good voice; གྲེ་བ་འགགས་པ *gre-wa gags-pa* obstruction in the throat; hoarseness; གྲེ་བ་དར་བ *gre-wa, dar-wa* a stertorous voice; གྲེ་བསལ་བཏང་བྱེད *gre-bsal btañ-byed* in *W.* to hawk; to hem; to clear the throat (*Jä.*).

གྲེ་བོ *gre-bo* a species of demons; གྲེ་མོ *gre-mo* female demons of this kind.

གྲེ་མག *gre-mag* vulg. for གྲ་མ *gra-ma* awn of barley or of Poa grass.

གྲེ་མོག་འབུ *gre-mog hbu* in *W.* ant; emmet (*Jä.*).

གྲེན *gren* occurs in གྲེན་གྱི་དོང་དུ་བཅིངས་པའི་རི་མོ་ཅན *gren-gyi don-du bciñs-pahi ri-mo can.* (*Jig. 32*).

གྲེན་ཚག *gren-tshag* plaited wicker-work in straight rows.

+ གྲེའུ I: *grehu*, or དྲེའུ *drehu*, a young bear: ཅོ་རོས་གྲེའུ་གཅིག་ཕུལ་བས *co-ros grehu-gcig phul-was* Cho-ro having presented a young bear (*A. 63*).

གྲེའུ II: माष pea, peas; མོན་སྲན་གྲེའུ *mon-sran grehu* a kind of pea growing in the Sub-Himalayas.

གྲེས་མ *gres- ma* 1. the flashing lightning (*Schtr.*). 2. དྲེས་མ *dres-ma* a kind of plant: གྲེས་མའི་གེ་སར་སྲིན་གསོད་གླང་ཐབས་འཇོམས *gres-mahi ge-sar srin-gsod glañ-thabs hjoms* the pistil of *dresma* kills worms and overcomes the diseases called *glañ-thabs*.

གྲོ *gro* गोधूम wheat; གྲོ་སྐམ *gro-skam* dry wheat.

གྲོ་ག *gro-ga* (*do-ga*) or གྲོ་ཁ *gro-kha* लेखन, or ཤིང་སྟག་པའི་པགས་པ *çiñ-stag pahi pags-pa*, white birch bark used for writing charms on; also acc. to *Jä.* used for ornamenting bows: རང་ཡུལ་དུ་སྐྱེས་པའི་གྲོ་གའམ་ཤིང་ཤུན་རམ་ཏ་ལའི་ལོ་མའམ་གོས་དཀར་པོ་ལ་སྔགས་འདི་བྲིས wrote these mantras on white cloth or paper or leaves of the palmyra or the bark of the birch which grew in their country (*Surañ.*).

གྲོ་དོང *gro-doñ* the winter granary of wheat in Tibet; an under-ground cell where wheat is kept during the winter.

གྲོ་ཚག *gro-tshag* sieve for sifting wheat.

གྲོ་བ *gro-wa* or གྲོ་མོ *gro-mo* reddish grey.

གྲོ་བཞིན *Gro-bshin* श्रवणा नक्षत्र the twenty-second or twenty-third constellation in the astronomical works of Tibet and India.

Syn. འཕྲོག་བྱེད *hphrog-byed*; བོན་པོ *bon-po*; བྱ་སྦོ *bya-sbo* (*Mñon.*).

གྲོ་བཞིན་གྱི་ཉ་བ *Gro-bshin gyi ña-wa* श्रावणी पूर्णिमा the full moon in the month of July-August.

གྲོ་བཞིན་གྱི་ཟླ་བ *Gro-bshin-gyi zla-wa* or ཟླ་བ་བདུན་པ *zla-wa bdun-pa* the month of *Çrāvaṇa*.

གྲོ་བཞིན་བྱེད *gro-bshin-byed* (*do-shin-ché*) hole under the ground where wheat is kept in winter (*A. K.*).

གྲོ་ཡོས *gro-yos* (*do-yo*) parched wheat or corn.

གྲོ་རིལ *gro-ril* ball of dough, or lump made of moistened wheat flour.

གྲོ་སོག *gro-sog* (*do-sog*) stalks of wheat, wheat-straw.

གྲོ་མ *gro-ma* (*do-ma*) मद्दारस, कसेरु 1. the sweet potato of Tibet. 2. name of a herb (*Vai-sñ.*) [the grass *Scirpus Kysoor*]*S.* རྒྱ་གྲོ *rgya-gro* or རྒྱའི་གྲོ་མ *rgyahi gro-ma* the potato introduced from India: གྲོམ་མངར་ཡང་ནུས་བསིལ་ཚ་འཁྲུ་གཅོད the potato being sweet is cooling and stops diarrhœa.

གྲོ་མ་ལུང *Gro-ma luñ* n. of a place in the north of Tibet (*Ka-thañ. 168*).

གྲོ་ལུང *Gro-luñ* n. of a village in the province of Lho-kha.

གྲོ་ལོ་མ *gro-lo-ma* (*do-lo-ma*) གོས་ཆེན *gos-chen* a kind of satin; silk stuff.

གྲོ་ས *Gro-sa* village in the district of Phenyul.

གྲོ་ཧོ *Gro-ho* (*do-ho*) ཕྱག་རྒྱ་རྣམས་སོ *phyag-rgya rnams-so* a mystical word used in the *Mahāmudrā Tāntrik* rites (*K. g.* ག *215*).

གྲོག *grog*=གྲོག་མ *grog-ma* or གྲོག་མོ *grog-mo* (*dog-mo*) पिपीलक, भूता ant; emmet.

Syn. སྲིན་ཕྲན་མ *srin phran-ma*; རྒྱུ་རྒྱུ་ར *rgyu-rgyu-ra*; གཤིན་རྗེའི་བུ *gçin-rjehi-bu* (*Mñon.*).

གྲོག་སྐེད *grog-sked* waist of the ant; also narrow as that is.

གྲོག་མཁར *grog-mkhar* वल्मीक ant-hill.

Syn. བརྒྱ་བྱིན་སྤྱི་བོ *brgya-byin spyi-wo*; ནོར་ལྡན་བརྩེགས *nor-ldan brtsegs*; གྲོག་མའི་ཚང *grog-mahi-tshhñ*; གྲོག་མའི་མཁར *grog-mahi mkhor* (*Mñon.*).

གྲོག་པོ *grog-po* 1. श्वभ्र a deep ravine in which a torrent flows; the sides of such ravines are termed *gad-pa*, ཆུ་ཆེན་པོས་བྲུས་ནས་བྱུང་བའི་གྲོག་པོའམ, གད་པ་ཡང་ཟེར *chu chen-pos brus-nas byun-wahi grog-poham, gad-pa yan-zer*, that which is caused by the erosion of great waters is also styled *grogs-po* or *gad-pa*.

གྲོག་སྦུ to *grog-sbu*, v. གྲོག་མ *grog-ma*, ant (*Ñag.* 52).

གྲོག་ཚང *grog-tshan*=གྲོག་མའི་ཚང *grog-mahi tshan* ant-hill.

གྲོག་ཞིང་ I: *grog-shin* or འབྲོག་ཞིང་ cultivation in uneven narrow ground away from villages or gen. in wild places where cattle are pastured.

གྲོག་ཞིང་ II: རྨ་དང་གཟེར་སྐྲངས་ཆུ་སྲི་སེལ *rma-dan gzer skrans chu sri-sel* n. of a medicine which cures obstruction of the urine; a kind of moss growing on the sides of chorten, and old walls, etc.

གྲོག་གཡང་ *grog-gyan* lateral gully on hill-side: གྲོག་ཆུ *grog-chu*, brook; rivulet, v. གྲོག་པོ *grog-po*.

གྲོག་གཟར *grog-gzar* a torrent pouring down a ravine.

གྲོགས *grogs* सङ्ग, समिति, मैथुन, सगत, सखा, धव a friend, companion, fellow-labourer, assistant; paramour, also husband; ཁ་གྲོགས *kha-grogs* a seeming friend; a friend in words; a false friend; རྟིང་གྲོགས *rtin-grogs* or སྙིང་གྲོགས *snin-grogs* true friend, bosom friend, associate, companion, comrade, fellow; གྲོགས་ཁྱེ *grogs-khye* playmate or play-fellow; དཔུང་གྲོགས *dpun-grogs*, fellow combatants comrades; འདུག་གྲོགས *hdug-grogs* or བཞུགས་གྲོགས *bshugs-grogs* fellow-lodger; དགའ་གྲོགས *dgah-grogs*, གཏན་གྲོགས *gtan-grogs* spouse; husband; wife; འདོད་གྲོགས *hdod-grogs* or འདོད་རོགས *hdod-rogs* sweetheart; མཛའ་གྲོགས *mdsah-grogs* a lover; གཟིམ་གྲོགས *gzim-grogs* bed-fellow (not only concubine); དམག་གྲོགས *dmag-grogs* ally, confederate (in war); ལས་གྲོགས *las-grogs* colleague; journeyman; under-workman; ཚིག་གྲོགས, *tshig-grogs* an auxiliary word. [*N.-B.*—In pop. works and colloq. language the word གྲོགས sounded *ro* or *rog* is combined with verbs in the imp. To give a polite turn to any request; "*nang-ro-nang*" please give; "*tön-rog-nang*" "will you kindly shew," etc.

གྲོགས་ངན *grogs-nan* a bad friend.

གྲོགས་དན *grogs-dan* सहायता help or assistance.

གྲོགས་འདྲིས *grogs-hdris* mutual friendship.

གྲོགས་པོ *grogs-po* (*tog-po*) सखा, मित्र, पक्ष friend; ally.

གྲོགས་བྱེད་པ I: *grogs-byed-pa* to be friend; to make friendship; to assist; to be friends. ཕན་ཚུན་གྲོགས་བྱེད་པ to cultivate friendship, to be mutual friends.

གྲོགས་བྱེད II: सहाय, पक्ष assistance; aiding.

གྲོགས་བྱེད་པ *grogs-byed-pa* is synonymous with རོགས་རམ *rogs-ram*; in writing sometimes སྡོངས་གྲོགས *sdons-grogs* is also used.

གྲོགས་མོ *grogs-mo* a female friend; also a mistress.

Syn. ཟླ་མོ *zla-mo*; ན་མཉམ་མ *na mñam-ma*; ཕོ་ཉ་མོ *pho ña-mo*; ཀུན་སྤྱོད་མཚུངས་མ *kun-spyod mtshuns-ma*; འཕྲིན་སྐྱེལ་མ *hphrin skyel-ma* (*Mnon.*).

གྲོགས་བཟང་ *grogs-bzan* or གྲོགས་བཟང་པོ *grogs-bzan-po* सौहृदम्, सुसखा friendship, also sweetheart.

གྲོང་ I: *gron* or *grons* pf. of འགྲོང་བ to die; གྲོང་འཇུག *grun-hjug* resurrection bringing life to a dead body, translating the soul from one body to another: བསྟན་འགྲོའི་དོན་མཛད་ཅིང་སྐལ་ལྡན་གྱི་གྲོང་འཇུག་ལན་བཞིར་མཛད་པར་གྲགས་ཤིང་ having done service to religion, and living beings he is said to have four times performed the noble work of translating a soul from one body to another (*J. Zañ.*).

གྲོང་ II: 1. ग्राम, पुरी an inhabited place; a village; hamlet; also house; བརྒྱ་གྲོང་ *brgya-groñ* a place of a hundred; སྟོང་གྲོང་ *stoñ-groñ* thousand houses or households (*Jä.*); གྲོང་ལ་འགྲོ *groñ-la-hgro* ग्रामं गच्छन् going or gone to the village: གྲོང་གསུམ་མཐར་བྱེད *groñ-gsum mthar-byed* त्रिपुरान्तक he who has destroyed the three habitable spheres, the god S'iva.

གྲོང་ཁྱེར *groñ-khyer* (*doñ-khyer*) पुर्, मन्दिर, नगर, पत्तन, पुर a town or city; a place which is surrounded by a wall, originally a palace. That is called a country or ཡུལ *yul* where there are 100 *lakhs* of households, a place where there are 100,000 households is called ཡུལ་འཁོར *yul-hkhor* or province. In a city (གྲོང་ཁྱེར *groñ-khyer*) which is gen. fortified there should be at least 10,000 households; a town with population less than 800 is called a གྲོང་ *groñ* in Sans. ग्राम.

Syn. ཕོ་བྲང་འཁོར *pho-brañ hkhor*; མི་གྲོང་ *mi-groñ*; གྲོང་ཁྱིམ *groñ-khyim*; ལུས་ཅན་གནས *lus-can-gnas*; དམངས་འདུལ་གནས *dmañs-hdul-gnas*; མུར་ག་ཏི *mur-ga-ti*; ས་བསྐོས *sa-bskos*; སྤྱོད་པའི་ཕུར་བུ *spyod-pahi phur-bu*; འཇིགས་མེད་གནས *hjigs-med-gnas*; མི་བསྐྱོད་གནས *mi-bskyod-gnas*; སྲུང་བྱེད *sruñ-byed*; སྐྱོང་བྱེད *skyoñ-byed* (*Mñon.*).

གྲོང་ཁྱེར་དགྲ *Groñ-khyer dgra* पुरारि the enemy of the city, S'iva.

གྲོང་ཁྱེར་འཇིག *Groñ-khyer hjig* पुरन्दर Indra.

གྲོང་ཁྱེར་རྗེ *groñ-khyer rje*=ཡུལ་གྱི་བདག་པོ *yul-gyi bdag-po* or ཡུལ་འཁོར་དབང་ *yul-hkhor dwañ* sheriff, also the chief of a city; also རྒྱལ་ཕྲན *rgyal-phran* a petty *Rājā* (*Mñon.*).

གྲོང་ཁྱེར་སྤྱོད *Groñ-khyer spyod* met. for a crow.

* གྲོང་ཁྱེར་དཔལ་ཡོན་ཅན *groñ-khyer dpal-yon-can* औदाधिनगर (*Schr.*; *Tā. 2, 166*).

* གྲོང་ཁྱེར་མེ་ཏོག *groñ-khyer me-tog* कुसुमपुर (*Schr.*) lit. the city of flowers; it is the same as Pāṭaliputra or Patna.

གྲོང་གི་གཅན་གཟན *groñ-gi gcan-gzan* कुक्कुर met. for dog (*Mñon.*).

གྲོང་གི་བརྗོད་པ *groñ-gi brjod-pa* पौरं provincialism; country or rural language; གྲོང་གི་ཉེ་འཁོར *groñ-gi ñe-hkhor* ग्रामोपकण्ठ the suburbs: གྲོང་གི་འཐབ་མོ *groñ-gi hthab-mo* feuds and quarrels (among villagers).

གྲོང་གི་བདག *Groñ-gi bdag* ग्रामाधिप, ग्रामणी the headman of a village.

གྲོང་དྲ་བ་ཅན *groñ dra-wa-can* चक्रचारिन् (གྲོང་མཐའ་ལ་དྲ་བ་བསྐོར་བ *groñ-mthah la-dra-wa bskor-wa*) a town surrounded with fortifications; གྲོང་གི་དྲ་བ *groñ-gi dra-wa* चक्र a circle or circuit of a village; fortification round a city: གྲོང་གི་འཕྲེང་ལྡན་མ *groñ-gi hphreñ ldan-ma*, पुरमालिनी the village flower-woman: གྲོང་གི་གཙོ་བོ *Groñ-gi gtso-wo* the chief man in a town or village; a headman.

གྲོང་གྲངས *groñ-grañs* the number of houses in a village or town.

གྲོང་མཆོག *groñ-mchog* chief city; also scene; sphere.

གྲོང་བསྙེན *groñ-bsñen* a གྲོང་དུ་མཚམས་བསྙེན་སྒྲུབ་བྱེད་པ་ a lama who performs meditations or asceticism remaining inside a village or town; དབེན་ན་མི་བསྟེན་པའི་གྲོང་བསྙེན་དར་བ་དང *dben-na mi bsten-pahi groñ bsñen dar-wa dañ* one not performing the practice of asceticism by going to any solitude (*Ya-sel. 21*).

གྲོང་གཏམ *groṅ-gtam* country speech or language.

གྲོང་བདག *groṅ-bdag*=གྲོང་པའི་གཙོ་བོ *groṅ-paḥi gtso-bo* the headman of a village or city.

གྲོང་རྡལ *groṅ-rdal*=གྲོང་བརྡལ *groṅ-brdal* जनपद, निगम a large town (which is not enclosed by a wall) together with its suburbs.

གྲོང་སྡེའི་ཕྲ་མ་མཁན *groṅ-sdeḥi phra-ma mkhan* =དཀྲུགས་ཤིང་བྱེད་མཁན *dkrugs-çiṅ byed-mkhan* one who causes or excites brawls, feuds, etc., among village people or communities.

གྲོང་པ *groṅ-pa* a villager; one holding a house; a tenant.

གྲོང་པའི་ཆོས *groṅ-paḥi chos*=ཕོ་མོ་འཁྲིག་པ *pho-ḥkhrig-pa* sexual union (*Mṅon.*).

གྲོང་པའི་ཆོས་ཀྱིས་མ་གོས་པ *groṅ-paḥi chos kyis-ma gas-pa*=བུ་མོ་ཕོ་དང་མ་ཕྲད་པ *bu-mo pho-daṅ ma phrad-pa* virgin purity; a maiden not touched by a male (*Sman 289*).

གྲོང་དཔོན *groṅ-dpon* ग्रामणी, वन्द्य, पुरोभास the chief of a town or village.

གྲོང་བ *groṅ-wa* (*doṅg-wa*) in *C.* acc. to *Jä.* used for གྲང་བ *graṅ-wa*: cold.

གྲོང་བར *groṅ-war* the middle of a village or hamlet.

གྲོང་སྤངས *groṅ-spaṅs* निर्मुक्त one who is liberated or has abandoned the life of a layman or householder.

གྲོང་ཚིག *groṅ-tshig* ग्राम्य provincialism: གྲོང་ཚིག་གིས་མ་སླད་པར *groṅ-tshig gis-ma sla-dpar* =གྲོང་སྐད་ཀྱིས་མ་འདྲེས་པར *groṅ-skad kyis-ma-ḥdres par* not mixed up with provincialisms.

གྲོང་ཚོ *groṅ-tsho* large village; town; several hamlets taken together.

གྲོང་མཚོ་མེར་མོ *Groṅ-mtsho mer-mo* n. of a village in the district of ཨེ *E* in Lhokha: ཨེ་ལབ་ཀྱི་འདབ་གྲོང་མཚོ་མེར་མོ *E lab-kyi ḥdab Groṅ mtsho mer-mo* (*Loṅ.* ཀ *30*).

གྲོང་གཞི *groṅ-gshi* an estate; farm (*Sch.*).

གྲོང་ཡུལ *groṅ-yul* country place (*Jä.*).

གྲོངས *groṅs* (*doṅg*), v. འགྲོང་བ resp. to die; རང་གིས་ཤི་བ་ལ་ནི་ས་ཟུམ་པ is resp. for natural death.

གྲོད་པ *grod-pa* or གསུས་པ *gsus-pa* belly; generally the paunch of ruminating animals; in collcq. language it is sometimes applied to the stomach or ཕོ་བ *pho-wa*: མར་གྲོད *mar-grod* butter kept in the dried paunch of a sheep.

གྲོད་སྦོམ *grod-sbom* (*doi-bom*) a large belly; also the dried paunch of a bullock to keep oil.

གྲོན་ཅན *gron-can* (*don-can*) disadvantageous; injurious.

གྲོན་ཆེ *gron-che* very noxious (*Jä.*); གྲོན་མེད *gron-med* harmless; innoxious (*Lex.*).

གྲོན་པ I: *gron-pa* (*don-pa*) explained as འགྲོ་སྒོ་ཆེན་པོ *ḥgro-sgo chen-po*, much expenditure; expensive; also to expend, squander: བོད་ཀྱི་མི་ནོར་མང་པོ་གྲོན་པ་དང་ *bod-kyi mi nor maṅ-po gron-pa daṅ* having squandered much wealth and men of Tibet: སྣག་ཤོག་གྲོན་པ *snag-çog gron-pa* (*Ṅag.*) waste or expenditure of much paper and ink.

གྲོན་པ II: explained by མི་ཚན་ཆེའམ་བཟོད་ཆེའམ་བསྲན་ཆེ་བ *mi-tshan cheḥam bzod-cheḥam bsran che-wa*, applied to a great or illustrious family, to one who is very patient or forbearing, a thing that is very durable and hard.

གྲོན་ཤས *gron-ças* འགྲོ་སྒོ *ḥgro-sgo* item of expenditure; also the account of the distribution and lending of grain.

གྲོམ་པ་རྒྱང་ *Grom-pa rgyaṅ* (*ṭom-pa-gyang*) n. of a place in Tsang which contained one of the twelve temples said to have been erected by King *Sroṅ-btsan sgam-po* (*Ya-sel. 41*).

གྲོལ *grol* (*ḍol*) मुक्ति (*Schr.; Kālāc. T. 5*) release; deliverance.

གྲོལ་ཉིན *Grol-ñin* (*ḍol-ñin*) the day when the annual assembly of the lamas dissolve.

གྲོལ་སྟོན *Grol-ston* (*ḍol-ton*) a festival on the day when lamas relax after the term of the special devotions is over.

གྲོལ་འདོད *grol-hdod* मुमुक्षु wishing to be emancipated or set free from transmigratory existence and misery, etc.; abbreviation of འཁོར་བ་དང་སྡུག་བསྔལ་སོགས་ལས་གྲོལ་བར་འདོད་པ *hkhor-wa daṅ-sdug-bsṅal sogs-las grol-war hdod-pa*.

གྲོལ་བ *grol-wa* (*ḍol-wa*) pf. of འགྲོལ་བ *hgrol-wa*; also sbst. निःसरण, मोच, तार, मोचन मुक्ति deliverance; deliverance from worldly existence.

གྲོལ་བ་ཅན *grol-wa can* मौक्तिक 1. relating to emancipation; deliverance. 2. sbst. pearl: मुक्ता that has been delivered from the oyster.

Syn. མུ་ཏིག *mu-tig*; ན་ལེ་ཤམ *na-le çam* (*Mṅon.*).

གྲོལ་བུའི་ལྷ་ལྔ *Grol-buhi lha-lṅa* the five demigods or, perhaps, Nāga demi-gods.

གྲོལ་མེད་འཇོམས *Grol-med hjoms* नमुचिसूदन the killer of Namuci; an epithet of Indra.

གྲོས I: *gros* (*ḍoi*) = མོལ་བ *mol-wa* 1. advice; counsel. 2. = གཏམ *gtam* speech; talk; བཀའ་གྲོས *bkah-gros* conference; committee.

གྲོས II: acc. to *Cs.* care, heed, caution.

གྲོས་གྲོགས *gros-grogs* (*ḍoi-ḍog*) a consulting friend; anyone consulted with.

གྲོས་ཅན *gros-can* careful; cautious.

+ གྲོས་གཅམ *gros-gcam* 1. consultation. 2. = གྲོས་བྱེད་པ *gros byed-pa* to consult.

གྲོས་མཐུན་པར *gros mthun-par* unanimously; by unanimous decree.

གྲོས་འདྲི་ས *gros hdri-sa* (*ḍoi-ḍi-sa*) the place where advice may be asked; an oracle.

གྲོས་འདེབས་པ *gros hdebs-pa* giving advice.

གྲོས་འདྲི་བ *gros hdri-wa* to ask (a person's) advice; to consult (with one).

གྲོས་པ *gros-pa* (*ḍoi-pa*) adviser; counsellor; senator; also advice; གྲོས་བྱས་པ *gros byas-pa* (*ḍoi-je-pa*) to have consulted; लोचना consultation; conference; གྲོས་བྱེད་པ *gros byed-pa* (*ḍoi-je-pa*) सम्प्रधारण to consider; to deliberate; to resolve; decide after consderation, deliberation, etc.

གྲོས་མི *Gros-mi* (*ḍoi-mi*) consulting man; an adviser; sometimes in Sikkim the headman of a village.

གྲོས་མེད *gros-med* without asking or consulting anybody; self-sufficient; careless; heedless.

གྲོས་ཚོད *gros-tshod* (*ḍoi-tshoi*) the real points or object of a conference: གྲོས་ཚོད་འཛིན་དང་ཡ་རབས་སྤྱོད་པ *gros-tshod hdsin-daṅ ya-rabs spyod-pa* to catch the leading and salient points in a conference (*Jig.*).

གྲོས་ཡ *gros-ya* (*ḍoi-ya*) a secretary; a councillor.

གླ *gla* wages; pay; fee or remuneration for any work done: དགེ་སློང་བརྒྱ་རྩ་བརྒྱད་ཀྱི་འཚོ་བ་གླ་ནས་སྦྱར *dge-sloṅ brgya-rtsa brgyad-kyi htsho-wa gla-nas sbyar* the maintenance of one hundred and eight monks was met from the fees (he received) (*A. 61*).

གླ་བ *gla-wa* कस्तुरिमृग the musk deer, *Moschus moschiferus*, of which there are three varieties or perhaps even species in Tibet. Another species occurs in Amdo: *Moschus Sifanicus*; གླ་རྣའི་པགས *gla-rnahi pags*, གླ་བ་དང་རྣ་བའི་པགས་པ *gla-wa dan rna-wahi pags-pa* the skin of the *Nao* antelope and the musk-deer.

Syn. དྲི་བཟང་དབང་པོ *dri-bzan dwan-po*; གླ་རྩི་ཅན *gla-rtsi can*; ས་ལུས *sa-lus*; རླུང་བསྲེག *rlun-bsreg* (*Mnon.*).

གླ་གོར་ཞོ་ཤ *gla-gor sho-ça* n. of a fruit.

གླ་བླངས་པ *gla blans-pa* has taken or received his wages for work.

གླ་སྒང *gla-sgan* मुस्त, नागर n. of a medcinal herb; मुस्त *Cyperus rotundus*: नागर the root of *Cyperus pertennis*.

གླ་རྔན *gla-rnan*, abbr. of གླ་དང་རྔན་པ *gla-dan rnan-pa*, wages and remuneration.

གླ་པ *gla-pa* or གླ་པོ *gla-po* or གླ་བུ *gla-bu* one who works on wages; a servant employed on a fixed salary; also a day-labourer or hired workman; གཡོག་གླ *gyog-gla* पण service money; salary.

གླ་ཕོར *gla-phor* a kind of tree the wood of which is good in turning and for making plates and cups.

གླ་ཕྲུག *gla-phrug* the young one of a musk-deer.

གླ་མི *gla-mi* भृत्य, दास a servant; a hired workman.

གླ་མོ *gla-mo* 1. a hired female servant. 2. musk-doe: གླ་བའི་ནོར་བུས་སྦྲུལ་སོགས་དུག་སྲུང་བྱེད *gla-wahi nor-bus sbrul-sogs dug-srun byed* the jewel of the musk deer (the musk-pod) is a protection against snake poison, etc.

གླ་རྩི *gla-rtsi* मद, मृगनाभि, कस्तुरी musk: གླ་རྩི་གྲོ་ཡི་ཚིག་མ་འདྲ *glo-rtsi gro-yi tshig-ma hdra* musk is like burnt-wheat grains: གླ་རྩི་འཇམ་མཁྲེགས་དྲི་ཆེ་བཟང་ the musk that is slightly soft, tough besides being of strong scent, is good: གླ་རྩིས་དུག སྦྲིན་མཁལ་ནད་གཉན་ཚད་སེལ musk eradicates snake-poison, kidney disease, plague.

Syn. རི་དྭགས་ལྟེ་བ *ri-dwags lte-wa*; སྦྲུལ་སྐྲག་བྱེད *sbrul-skrag byed*; མྱོས་པའི་མཚན་མ *myos-pahi mtshan-ma*; དྲི་ཡི་ཐོད *dri-yi thod*; དྲི་ཡི་གོས་ཅན *dri-yi gos-can*; རི་དྭགས་ཆང་ *ri-dvags chan*; རི་དྭགས་རྩི *ri-dwags rtsi*; གླ་བའི་ནོར་བུ *gla-wahi nor-bu* (*Mnon.*).

གླ་རྩིའི་མེ་ཏོག *Gla-rtsihi me-tog* n. of a flower, the *Pedicularis megalantha*.

གླ་ལྟོ *gla-lto* food and wages.

གླག *glag* or བྱ་གླག *bya-glag* a bird described as resembling an eagle, but smaller than the vulture and larger than the hawk, of blackish chocolate colour; carries away kids and lambs. This bird is numerous in Mongolia, Central Tibet and Kham. Probably the lammergayer.

གླག་ཁྲ་མོ *glag-khra-mo* a spotted species of eagle.

✢ **གླག་པ** *glag-pa*=ལྟག་པ *ltag-pa* upper or back part or side: མགོའི་ལྟག་པ *mgohi ltag-pa* the crown or upper part of the head. Defined as གྲི་དང་སྟ་རེའི་ལྟག་པ, the upper back part or blunt side of a knife or axe.

གླག་པ་ལམ *Glag-pa lam* n. of a place in Tibet (*Deb.*).

གླགས *glags* अवसर opportunity, occasion, possibility: གླགས་འཚོལ་བ *glags htshol-wa* to seek for an opportunity: ད་གླགས་རྙེད་པར་འདུག *da glags rned-par hdug* now the favourable time seems to have come; esp. opportunity of doing harm to another, of getting a hold on him (*Jä*): གླགས་རྙེད་པར་མི་འགྱུར *glagş ẖñed-par mi ẖgyur* he will not get an opportunity to do you harm. གཟོད་གླགས་མེད intolerable; insupportable: གསོ་གླགས་མེད there is no possibility of helping him; he is incurable (*Jä*): གླགས་མི་ཁེལ not able to do injury or some interruption to one's actions.

卐 གླགས་པ *glagş-pa* to go; be going; to proceed; to be on the point of.

གླང་ I: *Ġlañ* n. of a place in Tibet.

གླང་ II: वृष, ऋषभ 1. ox; bullock. 2. one of the signs of the Zodiac, the Bull: གླང་གི་མཁྲིས་པས་སྦྱར་དུག་མིག་ལ་ཕོག་པར་ཕན *glañ-gi m̲khriş-paş şbyar-dug mig-la phog-par phan* the bile of the ox is useful when contagious poison strikes upon the eye: གླང་གི་མཆེར་བས་རྨ་དང་དུག་ལ་ཕན the spleen of the ox is useful in sores and poisons: གླང་གི་མཁལ་མས་མཁལ་ཚདས་སེལ the kidney of the ox removes kidney diseases: གླང་གི་ཁྲག་གིས་དུག་ཕྱིར་འདྲུད the blood of the ox (with food) draws out blood poison.

Syn. འགྲོ་བྱེད *ẖgro-byeḏ*; འདྲེན་བྱེད *ẖdren-byeḏ*; སྟོབས་ལྡན *ştobş-ḻdan*; བཟང་པོ *ḇzañ-po*; ཁྱུ་མཆོག *khyu-m̲chog* (*M̲ñon.*).

གླང་ III: or གླང་ཐབས *glañ-thabş*, also called གཟེར་གླང་ *gzer-glañ*, colic, gripes, spasms in the stomach and similar affections (*Jä.*).

གླང་ཐབས *glañ-thabş*=གློ་བུར, *glo-bur* 1. sudden; suddenly: གླང་ཐབས་ཀྱི་དགྲས་ངེས་པ was suddenly defeated by the enemy. 2. n. of a disease, prob. hysterical fit.

གླང་ཁྱིམ *glañ-khyim* गोपुरी, गोपुर a shed or fold where cows are kept; an ornamented gateway.

གླང་ཁྱུ་མཆོག *glañ-khyu m̲chhog* वृषभ a bull; ox.

གླང་ཁྱུ་བ *glañ-khyu-wa* ऋषभवान् a bull kept for breeding purpose.

གླང་གླད *glañ-glaḏ* 1. the brains of the bullock or ox. 2. in Tsang=soap.

གླང་རྒོད *glañ-ṟgoḏ* a wild ox. This term is applied in Tibet to the buffalo (in Tib. མ་ཧེ *maẖ-he*).

གླང་ཆེན *glañ-chen*=གླང་པོ་ཆེ *glañ-po-che* मातङ्ग, गज, हस्तिन्, नाग, स्तम्बेरम, पीलु, करिन्, पुष्कर, इभ, दन्तिन्, वारण the elephant; elephant in rut: གླང་ཆེན་པགས་པས་འབྲུམ་ནག་ནད་ལ་ཕན the skin of the elephant is useful in black small-pox: གླང་པོ་རྗེས་སུ་མཐུན་པའི་རྫས་སོ་སོའི་མིང་ *glañ-po ṟjeş-su m̲thun-paẖi ṟdsaş so-soẖi miñ*, *i.e.*, the names of various apparatus necessary for an elephant are the following:—ཤྲམ *çram* श्रम; ཤྲིམ་ག་མ *çrim-ga-ma* शृङ्ग; གླང་པོའི་རྒྱན *glañ-poẖi ṟgyan*; འདོགས་པའི་ཀ་བ *ẖdogş-paẖi ka-wa*; ཨ་ལ་ན *a-la-na*; आलान the post to which an elephant is tied; ལྕགས་ཀྱུ *ḻcagş-kyu* the conductor's hook; ཤྲི་ཏི, ཤྲེ་ཁི; མཆིལ་བ *m̲chil-wa*; བྲི་ཀྵ་ཀ་ཀྵ་བ་ར་ཊ *bri-kşa ka-kşa ba-ra-ṭa* वृचक-चवरट or གླང་པོའི་ཐག་པ *glañ-poẖi thag-pa*. ཧཀ་ཀོ་གཛ་ཛ *hak-ko gdsa-dsa* हेक्कोगज्ज=འབོད་པ་ཞིས་འདུག *ẖboḏ-pa shiş-ẖdug* (*M̲ñon.*).

Syn. སོ་ལྡན *so-ḻdan*; སོ་གཉིས *so-gñiş*; ལག་ལྡན *lag-ḻdan*; གཉིས་འཐུང *gñiş-ẖthuñ*; མང་པོ་འཐུང *mañ-po ẖthuñ*; མྱོས་བུམ་ཅན *myoş bum-can*; ནགས་ཚལ་དགའ *nagş-tshal ḏgaẖ*; མཆེ་བ་སྟོབས་ལྡན *m̲che-wa ştobş-ḻdan*; ས་ལུད་ཉལ *sa-luḏ ñal*; ཐིག་ལེ་ཅན *thig-le can*; འཁོར་ལོའི་རྐང *ẖkhor-loẖi ṟkañ*; ཛ་ལ་ཀ *dsa-la ka*; མྱོས་རྔུལ་ཅན *myoş-ṟñul can*; དབྱུག་པའི་རྣ་ཅན *ḏbyug-paẖi ṟna-can*; མཆོད་རྟེན་བྱེད *m̲chod-ṟten byeḏ*; སྟོབས་ལྡན *ştobş-ḻdan*.

གླང་ཆེན་ཐལ་དཀར *glañ-chen thal-ḏkar* the white elephant, or one having a white fore-head; the chief of the elephants (*Ñag.*): གླང་ཆེན་མཁྲིས་པས་དུག་གིས་ཉ་ཉམས་གསོ the bile of the elephant cures emaciation caused by poison, etc.: གླང་ཆེན་ཤ་ཡིས་གདོན་ནད་སེལ་བར་བྱེད the flesh of elephant (taken as food) cures the diseases attributed to devils (in *W.*).

གླང་ཆེན་རྩི་ *glañ-chen rtsi* गोरोचना the secretion of the elephant; also elephant-musk.

Syn. གི་ཝང་ *gi-wañ* (in magic) or གབ་ཚིག mystic term (*Miñ 3*).

གླང་མཛིང་ཡོན་ *Glañ mjiñ-yon* a name of Prince *Sad-na legs-mjiñ yon*, son of King *Khri-sroñ ldehu-btsan*. He was so called on account of his prowess: མཛིང་པ་ཡོན་ལ་སྐུ་དབང་ཆེ་བས་གླང་མཛིང་ཡོན་དུ་གྲགས *mjiñ-pa yon-la sku-dwañ che-was glañ-mjiñ yon-du grags*.

གླང་རྟོ་ *glañ-to* the Indian bull (*Bos taurus Indicus*).

གླང་ཐང་ *Glañ-thañ* n. of a plain to the east of Lhasa.

གླང་ཐུག *glañ-thug* or གླང་འོག་ཅན *glañ-hog can* a bull (not castrated): གླང་ཐུག་རྭ་ཅོས་མགོ་ཆག་ལ་ཕན *glañ-thug rwa-cos mgo-chag-la phan* the horn of uncastrated bull is useful in the fracture of the head: *glañ-thug nag rwa-cos mdse-la phan-par-byed* the horn of a black uncastrated bull is used in leprosy: གླང་གི་རྭ་གཞོབ་མཆིན་པའི་ཚ་བ་སེལ *glañ-gi rwa-gshob mchin-pahi tsha-wa-sel* the ashes of a burnt bull's horn taken internally cures inflamation of the liver.

གླང་དར་མ *Glan-dar-ma* 1. a youthful ox. 2. n. of the King of Tibet who persecuted the Buddhists in the ninth century A.D.

གླང་འདེད *glañ-hded*=ཐོང་མཁན *thoñ-mkhan* the husbandman, a rustic.

གླང་པོ་སྐྱོང་ *glañ-po-skyoñ*=གླང་རྫི *glañ-rdsi* गोपाल a cow-herd; one who tends or looks after cows (*Mñon.*).

གླང་པོ་མཆོག *glañ-po-mchog* गन्धहस्तिन् the chief of the elephants, lit. a scent-elephant.

Syn. གླང་པོའི་རྒྱལ་པོ *glañ-pohi rgyal-po*; སྤོས་ཀྱི་གླང་པོ *spos-kyi glan-po*; ཁྱུ་ཡི་མགོན་པོ; *khyu-yi mgon-po*; ཁྱུ་ཡི་བདག་པོ *khyu-yi bdag-po*; ཐལ་ཀར *thal-kar*; མཆེ་བ་དྲུག་ལྡན *mche-aw drug-ldan*; གཉིས་འཐུང་དབང་པོ *gñis-hthuñ dwañ-po* (*Mñon.*).

གླང་པོ་གཏུམ་པོ *glañ-po gtum-po*=གླང་པོ་སྨྱོན་པ *glañ-po myon-pa* a wild, mad elephant (*Mñon.*).

གླང་པོ་འདོད་པས་དྲེགས་པ *glañ-po hdod-pas dregs-pa*=གླང་པོ་རྒོད *glañ-po rgod* wild elephant; an elephant turned wild and mad for union with a she-elephant.

Syn. ཆགས་པས་མྱོས་པ *chags-pas myos-pa*; ལྕགས་ཀྱུས་གདུལ་དཀའ་བ *lcags-kyus gdul-dkah-wa*; གཡོ་བ་ཅན *gyo-wa-can*; གླང་པོ་རྒོད *glañ-po rgod*; གླང་པོ་ཆང་གིས་མྱོས་པ *glañ-po chañ-gis myos-pa*; གླང་པོ་གཏུམ་པོ *glañ-po gtum-po*; ཆང་གིས་དྲེགས་པ *chañ-gis dregs-pa*; གླང་བཟི *glañ-bzi*; གླང་པོ་སྨྱོན་པ *glañ-po smyon-pa*.

གླང་པོ་སྣའི་གླིང་སྨད *Glañ-po snahi gliñ-smad* n. of a place within the district of Shiga-tse in Tsang.

གླང་པོ་ཤོངས *Glañ-po çoñs* n. of a place (in Tib.); also one which was situated near the ancient city of Kapilavāstu.

གླང་པོའི་ཁ་ལོ་པ *glañ-pohi kha-lo-pa*=གླང་རྫི *glañ-rdsi* conductor of an elephant (*Mñon.*).

གླང་པོའི་རྒྱལ་པོ *glañ-pohi rgyal-po*=གླང་པོ་མཆོག *glañ-po-mchog* (*Mñon.*).

གླང་པོའི་སྟོབས *Glañ-pohi stobs*, हस्तिबल n. of a very powerful giant-like king; སྤང་རྟེན་མང་འཛིན་གླང་པོའི་སྟོབས *spañ-rten mañ-hdsin glañ-pohi stobs* (*Ya-sel. 57*).

གླང་པོའི་གནས *glañ-pohi-gnas*=གླང་པོ་ཆེའི་གནས *glañ-po-chehi gnas* the stable where elephants are kept (*Mñon.*).

གླང་ཕྲན *glañ-phran*=གླང་ཕྲུག *glañ-phrug* a young elephant (*Mñon.*).

གླང་བྲེས *glañ-bres* गोशाल ox-manger; གླང་པོའི་བྲེས *glañ-pohi bres* elephant-stall.

གླང་མ *glañ-ma* 1. a medicinal plant: གླང་མས་མོ་ནད་དང་ནི་ཚད་པ་སེལ *glañ-ma* cures fever and female diseases. 2. a large kind of alpine willow.

གླང་མོ *glaṅ-mo* or ལག་ལྡན་མ *lag-ḷdan-ma* she-elephant: གླང་མོའི་འོ་མས་རབ་ཏུ་བརྟན་པར་བྱེད the milk of a she-elephant is very sustaining: གླང་མོའི་པགས་པས་མོ་ནད་དང་ཚད་པ་སེལ the skin of a she-elephant cures female disease and fever.

གླང་དམར *glaṅ-ḍmar* a stallion ox: གླང་དམར་ཟུག་པའི་གསོན་ཁྲག་དྲོན་མོ་ཡིས, དུག་ནད་ཙ་ཡི་འགྲོས་འཕྲང་སྡོམ་པར་བྱེད with the warm blood of a living stallion ox the circulation of poison in the blood can be neutralized.

གླང་རྫི I: *glaṅ-ṛdsi* गोविन्द a cow-keeper; a chief herdsman.

གླང་རྫི II: गोपाल the keeper of an elephant; keeper of cows; Kṛishṇa.

Syn. གླང་པོའི་ཁ་ལོ་པ *glaṅ-poḥi kha-lo-pa*; གླང་པོ་སྐྱོང *glaṅ-po ṣkyoṅ* (*Ṃṅon.*).

གླང་གཡག་དྲི་ལྡན *glaṅ-gyag dṛi-ḷdan* 1. གི་ཝང *gi-waṅ* गोरोचना the musk-like, scented secretion in the brains or in the stomach of an elephant. 2.=དོམ་མཁྲིས *dom-ṃkhriṣ* bear's bile (*Ṣman. 353*).

གླང་རི་ལུང་བསྟན *Ḡlaṅ-ri luṅ-ḅstan* n. of a Sûtra in the *Kaḥgyur*, said to have been delivered by Buddha when on a visit to Li-yul.

གླང་རུ *glaṅ-ru* a bullock's horn; also a large forked stick used by the Tibetan soldiers to rest the musket on when firing.

གླང་ལུང་གནས་ཁྲ་མོ *Ḡlaṅ-luṅ gnaṣ-khra-mo* n. of a place in Kham.

གླང་ཤིང *glaṅ-çiṅ*=གླང་མ་ཤིང *glaṅ-ma-çiṅ* or མཛོ་མོ་ཤིང *ṃdso-mo-çiṅ* a kind of tree growing largely in Tibet, the leaves of which are burnt as incense (གབ་མིང mystical term) (*Miṅ.*).

གླང་ཤུ *glaṅ-çu* a kind of sore-hoof.

གླངས་ཁམས་པ *Ḡlaṅṣ-khamṣ-pa* n. of a learned lama come from a place called *Ḡlaṅ-khamṣ*, who was invited by King *Khri-ṣroṅ ḷdeḥu-ḅtsan* to his capital on account of the fame of his learning.

གླད *glaḍ* or གླད་པ *glaḍ-pa* मस्तक the head; brains; cf. ཀླད *ḵlaḍ*: གླད་ལ *glaḍ-la* on the top, on the head; also used as postposition in the sense of over, close over: ཆུའི་གླད་ལ *chuḥi glaḍ-la* close above the river or water.

གླད་རྒྱ *glaḍ-ṛgya*=གླད་པའི་རྩ *glaḍ-paḥi ṛtsa* the veins of the brain.

གླད་པ *glaḍ-pa* generally written as ཀླད་པ *ḵlaḍ-pa* (*Sch.*), cf. ལྷད *lhaḍ* or སླད་པ *ṣlaḍ-pa*.

གླན་པ *glan-pa* also གློན་པ *glon-pa* 1. to patch up; to mend: གོས་སོགས་ལ་རྡོལ་ཞུག་ཡོད་པ= ལྷན་གླན་པ *lhan glan-pa* to sew up or patch up torn clothes, etc. (*Ṅag.*); གླན་བརྒྱབ་པ to sew on a patch. 2. to return; ལན *lan* an answer to reply; rejoin (*Lex.*). 3. colloquial for གླེན་པ *glen-pa*.

གླན་གླེན *glan-glen*, v. གླེན་པ *glen-pa* dumb.

卐 གླམ་པ *glam-pa* or སྣམ་བུ་འཐུག་པོ *ṣnam-bu ḥthug-po* a kind of thick blanket.

གླལ་བ *glal-wa* जृम्भ 1. to yawn or gape: འགའ་དོར་འགྱིང་བའི་བརྡའ *ḥgaḥ dor-ḥgyiṅ waḥi ḅrdaḥ* a relaxation of the body by stretching the limbs and yawning. 2. a terrific attitude or posture of sitting: སེང་གེ་རྣམ་བསྒྱིངས *seṅ-ge ṛnam-ḅṣgyiṅṣ*=སེང་གེ་གླལ་བ *seṅ-ge glal-wa* a lion's attitude on his vanquished foe is called *glal-wa*.

གླས་འཚོ་བ *glaṣ ḥtsho-wa* one who subsists on salary or wages.

གླིང I: *gliṅ* दर्भ, कुश a kind of sacred grass.

གླིང II: 1. द्वीप, क्षेत्र island; isolated place; limb or part of the globe; division of lands, large or small; continent, in fabulous Indian sense: གླིང་གཞན་ནས་སྐྱེས་པ་ཚུལ་བྱེད་མི་འདྲ་བ *gliṅ gshan-nas skyes-pa tshul-byed-mi hdra-wa* भिन्नकल्पद्वीपान्तरा: being of other continents they are of a different manner of birth.

གླིང་ III: a large monastery; a monastery isolated in its greatness and separate from other jurisdiction.

གླིང་ཆེན་བཅུ་གཉིས *gliṅ-chen bcu-gñis* the twelve continents according to Bon cosmography are the following:—(1) གཡུང་དྲུང་བཀོད་པའི་གླིང་ (ཤར) *Gyuṅ-druṅ bkod-pahi-gliṅ*; (2) དགའ་ལྡན་ལྷ་ཡི་གླིང (གཡས) *Dgah-ldan lha-yi gliṅ*; (3) འདུལ་བ་ཁྲིམས་ཀྱི་གླིང (གཡོན) *Hdul-ba khrims-kyi gliṅ*; (4) བདུད་འདུལ་སྔགས་ཀྱི་གླིང (གཡས) *Bdud-hdul sṅags-kyi gliṅ*; (5) ཚད་མེད་བྱ་བ་གླིང་ (ལྷོ) *Tsad-med bya-wa gliṅ*; (6) སྦྱིན་པ་མཐའ་ཡས་གླིང (གཡོན) *Sbyin-pa mthah-yas gliṅ*; (7) མི་གཡོ་བསམ་གཏན་གླིང (ནུབ) *Mi-gyo bsam-gtan gliṅ*; (8) དགེ་རྒྱས་ཡོན་ཏན་གླིང (གཡས) *Dge-rgyas yon-tan gliṅ*; (9) ཚད་མེད་བྱམས་པའི་གླིང (གཡོན) *Tshad-med byams-pahi gliṅ*; (10) གནོད་སྦྱིན་ནོར་གྱི་གླིང་ (བྱང་) *Gnod-sbyin nor-gyi gliṅ*; (11) ཡོན་ཏན་རྒྱས་པའི་གླིང (གཡས) *Yon-tan rgyas-pahi gliṅ*; (12) རིན་ཆེན་སྤུངས་པའི་གླིང(གཡོན) *Rin-chen spuṅs-pahi gliṅ*; or འོལ་མོ་གླིང (དབུས) *Hol-mo gliṅ* (*G. Bon. 5*). The seventeen sub-continents attached to the twelve continents are the following:—(1) རྒྱལ་རིགས་རྒྱལ་ས་འཛིན་པའི་གླིང་ *Rgyal-rigs rgyal-sa hdsin-pahi gliṅ*; (2) རྗེའུ་བཀོད་པའི་གླིང་ *Rjehu bkod-pahi gliṅ*; (3) དྲང་སྲོང་འགྲོ་འདུལ་གླིང་ *Draṅ-sroṅ hgro-hdul-gliṅ*; (4) མྱ་ངན་མེད་པའི་གླིང་ *Mya-ṅan med-pahi gliṅ*: (5) བྲམ་ཟེ་གཙང་བའི་གླིང་ *Bram-ze gtsaṅ-wahi gliṅ*; (6) བྲམ་ཟེ་ཧས་མོ་གླིང *Bram-ze has-mo gliṅ*; (7) འབྲི་མིག་མཚོ་ཡི་གླིང་ *Hbri-mig mtsho-yi gliṅ*; (8) དམངས་རིགས་གདོལ་བའི་གླིང་ *Dmags-rigs gdol-wahi gliṅ*; (9) སྟོབས་ཆེན་གྱད་ཀྱི་གླིང་ *Stob-chen gyad-kyi gliṅ*; (10) ཨ་བ་ད་རའི་གླིང་ *A-ba-da-rahi gliṅ*; (11) འགྲོ་བ་འདུལ་བའི་གླིང་ *Hgro-wa hdul-wahi gliṅ*; (12) ཁྲི་དང་འཐབ་པའི་གླིང་ *Khri daṅ hthab-pahi gliṅ*; (13) རྒྱ་ལག་འོད་མའི་གླིང་ *Rgya-lag hod-mahi gliṅ*; (14) རྒྱལ་མོ་མོ་ཁྲོས་གླིང་ *Rgyal-mo mo-khros gliṅ*; (15) མཁའ་འགྲོ་མི་རྐུན་གླིང་ *Mkhah-hgro mi-rkun gliṅ*; (16) མིཧམ་ཅི་ཡི་གླིང་ *Miham ci-yi gliṅ*; (17) ལྷ་ཀླུ་མན་དྷ་སྤྲེའུ་གླིང་ *Lha-klu man-dha sprehu gliṅ* (*G. Bon. 6*).

གླིང་ཀ *Gliṅ-ka* a garden or pleasure grove.

གླིང་ངན *gliṅ-ṅan* dispute; quarrel.

གླིང་དཀར་རྫོང་ *Gliṅ-dkar rdsoṅ* n. of a district in Tibet.

གླིང་དར *gliṅ-dar* पुष्कर n. of a kind of cloud.

གླིང་ལྡན་མ *gliṅ-ldan-ma*, མཚོ *mtsho* द्वीपवती, द्वीपी a lake which contains islands.

གླིང་བུ *gliṅ-bu* वंश, घनिनल a reed-pipe; a musical reed; flageolet; the common musical instrument of herdsmen, and consists of two pipes joined together; ཕྲེད་གླིང་ *phred-gliṅ* flute; piccolo-flute, mostly of metal; དགེ་གླིང་ *dge-gliṅ*, generally written རྒྱ་གླིང་ *rgya-gliṅ*, a larger musical instrument like a hautboy, used in sacred ceremonies; རྐང་གླིང་ *rkaṅ-gliṅ* trumpet made of the human femoral bone.

གླིང་མ *gliṅ-ma* पुलिन the margin of a lake or river.

གླིང་ཡགས་པ *Gliṅ-yags-pa* n. of the chief preist of *Galdan* who was born at *Gliṅ-yags*.

གླིང་ལོག *gliṅ-log* revolution; internal dissension: དེར་འབྲི་ཁུང་པ་ལ་གླིང་ལོག་ཆེན་པོ་བྱུང་ there arose much civil disturbance there in Dikhuṅ, *i.e.*, among the members of the *Hbri-khuṅ* monastery.

གླུ *glu* गीतं, गेय, ऋषभ, पञ्चम song; ditty; also a tune; གླུ་གར་དང་རྗེས་སུ་འབྲེལ་བ་དག accompaniments of musical performance, etc.; བྷ་ར་ཏ *bha-ra-ta*, भरत; གར་དག *gar-dag* an actor; a stage-player; རྐང་པའི་རྒྱབས་སྒྲ *rkaṅ-*

pahi stabs-sgyur falling of the feet at the music or cadence of the song; གར་གྱི་གཙོ་བོ *gar-gyi gtso-bo* stage-master; རྔ་པ *rña-pa* the drummer; རྔ་བརྡུང་བ *rña brduṅ-wa* drum-beater; ཕེབ་རྡོབ་པ *pheb rdob-pa*, झर्झर; ཐལ་མོ་རྡོབ *thal-mo rdob* the clapper; གླིང་བུ་བ *gliṅ-bu wa* trombone blower; གླིང་བུ་མཁན *gliṅ-bu mkhan* the flute-player; པི་ཝང *pi-waṅ* guitar, violin; པི་ཝང་མཁན *pi-waṅ-mkhan* the violin player; གླུ་བ *glu-wa* the singer; གར་མཁན *gar-mkhan* dancer; འགྱུར་བག་མཁན *hgyur-bag-mkhan* one who shows various appearances in different dresses, such as the clown, etc. (*Mṅon.*).

གླུ་སྒྲ *glu-sgra* time in singing.

གླུ་ཆུང *glu-chuṅ* a little song; ditty.

གླུ་སྙན་ལེན་པ *glu-sñan len-pa* to sing a sweet song.

གླུ་དབྱངས *glu-dbyaṅs* संगीति singing; གླུ་དབྱངས་ཀྱི་ངེས་པ་བདུན *glu-dbyaṅs-kyi ṅes-pa-bdun* the seven kinds of harmonical pitch or measures of the compass of the musical tones. These are:—བར་མ *bar-ma* मध्यम, དྲང་སྲོང *draṅ-sroṅ* ऋषभ, ས་འཛིན *sa-hdsin* गान्धार, དྲུག་ལྡན *drug-ldan* षड्ज; ལྔ་པ *lṅa-pa* पञ्चम; བློ་གསལ *blo-gsal* धैवत, འཁོར་ཉན *hkhor-ñan* निषाद. Then, too, there are various definitions of songs and modes of singing. Such are: རྒྱུད་དང་མགྲིན་ལས་སྐྱེས་པའི་དབྱངས *rgyud-daṅ mgrin-las skyes-pahi dbyaṅs*, འཁོར་ཉན་གླང་པོའི་སྒྲ་ལྟ་བུ *hkhor-ñan glaṅ-pohi sgra lta-bu*, ཁྱུ་མཆོག་བ་གླང་སྐད་ཀྱི་སྦོས *khyu-mchog ba-glaṅ skad-kyi sbos*, དྲི་འཛིན་(རྨ་སྐད)སྐྱེས་ནི་ར་ཡི་སྐད *dri-hdsin skyes-ni ra-yi skyad*, དྲུག་སྐྱེས་རྨ་བྱའི་སྐད་ལྟར་སྒྲོགས *drug-skyes rma-byahi skad-ltar sgrogs*, བར་མ་ཁྲུང་ཁྲུང་སྒྲ་སྒྲོགས་བཞིན *bar-ma khruṅ-khruṅ sgra-sgrogs bshin*, བློ་གསལ་རྟ་སྐད་ལྟ་བུར་འཚེར *blo-gsal rta-skad lta-bur htsher*, ལྔ་པ་མེ་ཏོག་ལྡན་དུས་སུ, ཁུ་བྱུག་སྒྲོགས་པ་ལྟ་བུ *lṅa-pa me-tog-ldan dus-su, khu-byug sgrogs-pa lta-buho* རྩེད་མོ་རློམ་པར་བླང་བ་ནི, ལྔ་པ་དང་ནི་བར་མའི་དབྱངས *rtsed-mo rlom-par blaṅ-wa-ni, lṅa-pa daṅ-ni bar-mahi dbyaṅs* དཔའ་བོ་དྲག་པོ་ངོ་མཚར་དུ, དྲུག་སྐྱེས་ཁྱུ་མཆོག་དེ་བཞིན་ནོ *dpah-po drag-po ṅo-mtshar-du, drug-skyes khyu-mchog de-bshin-no* ས་འཛིན་པ་དང་འཁོར་ཉན་དབྱངས, སྙིང་རྗེའི་རོ་ལ་བླངས་པར་བྱ *sa hdsin-pa daṅ hkhor-ñan dbyaṅs, sñiṅ-rjehi ro-la blaṅs-par bya* འཐབ་མོ་འཇིགས་དང་བཅས་པ་ལ, བློ་གསལ་དབྱངས་ནི་བླངས་བའོ *hthab-mo hjigs-daṅ bcas-pa-la, blo-gsal dbyaṅs-ni blaṅs-waho*.

གླུ་དབྱངས་ཀྱི་ཁང་པ *glu-dbyaṅs kyi khaṅ-pa* संगीति-प्रासाद a stage; a place where singing is done.

གླུ་དབྱངས་མཁན *glu dbyaṅs-mkhan* a singer; one who sings or instructs in singing.

Syn. གླུ་ལེན་པ *glu len-pa*, གླུ་མཁན *glu-mkhan* (*Mṅon.*).

གླུ་རེས *glu-res* alternate songs.

གླུ་ལེན་མ *glu-len-ma* = གླུ་མཁན་མ *glu mkhan-ma* a songstress.

གླུད *glud* a thing given as a ransom; སྲོག་གི་གླུད a ransom for life: ཁོའི་གླུད་དུ་ལུག་བརྒྱ་གསོད *khohi glud-du lug brgya-gsod* slaughter a hundred sheep as a ransom for him, གླུད་ལ་བཏང *glud-la btaṅ* to ransom a scape-goat.

གླུད་ཚབ *glud-tshab* the ransom offered to some malignant spirit, consisting of one's effigy made of barley or wheat-straw, and its interior filled with grain, edibles, cloth, medicines, and precious articles such as gold, silver or coins, and then thrown in the direction from which the evil spirit is supposed to have come. There are several varieties of this kind of ceremony.

གླུམ *glum* or སྦང་གླུམ *sbaṅ-glum* fresh fermented rice, barley, or wheat, used instead of malt in brewing beer. ཆང་བཙོས་ཁབ་བཏབ་བསྐྱལ་ནས་ཡངས་པ་ཆང་གི་གླུམ་མམ་སྦང་གླུམ་ཡང་ཟེར

chaṅ ḅtsos phab ḅtab ḅsñal-nas laṅs-pa chaṅ-gi glum-mam sbaṅ glum yaṅ-zer.

གླེ *Gle* a small uncultivated island; also a grove; same as ཚལ *tshal* or གླིང་ཀ *gliṅ-ka.*

གླེ་འདམས་མ *gle ḥdams-ma* 1. one having the disease in which urine and fœcal matter pass together, *i.e.*, by the rectum (*K. du.* ད *413*). 2.=सम्भिन्न-व्यञ्जन; མཚན་མེད་མ་ནིང་ *mtshan-med ma-niṅ* a hermaphrodite; having neither the sign of male nor of female.

གླེགས *glegs* table; plate; board; any flat piece: སྒོ་གླེགས་གཞུག་གོ *sgo-glegs gshug-go* there was a door panel placed.

གླེགས་ཆབ *glegs-chab* a buckle, clasp or ring attached to the thong.

གླེགས་ཐག *glegs-thag* a thong, &c., fastened round a book.

གླེགས་བམ *glegs-bam* पुस्तक, पुथि a volume; a book; leaves placed between flat boards.

གླེགས་བུ *glegs-bu* 1. a label; explained as ཆོས་གོས་ལ་གླིང་གླིང་གྲུ་བཞི་བཅད་པའི་གྲ་བཀག་པ *chos-gos la gliṅ-gliṅ gru-ḅshi bcad-paḥi gra ḅkag-pa*, a square or rectangular piece of cloth or paper put as label containing the name of books, chapters, pages, etc. (*Ṅag.*). 2. a tablet. 3. བཀའི་གླེགས་བུ *ḅkaḥi-glegs-bu* or བཀའ་ཤོག *ḅkaḥ-çog* a diploma; ཟངས་ཀྱི་གླེགས་བུ copper plate or tablet.

གླེགས་མ *glegs-ma*, v. གླེགས *glegs.*

གླེགས་ཤིང་ *glegs-çiṅ* the wooden boards which in a Tibetan book supply the binding.

གླེང་བ *gleṅ-wa* or གླེངས་པ *gleṅs-pa* संवर्ण to say, converse, relate, describe: གཏམ་དུ་གླེང་བ *gtam-du gleṅ-wa* or གསུང་གླེང་བ *gsuṅ gleṅ-wa* to relate a story: ལམ་ལ་མ་ཐར་ཤེས་གླེངས་ནས *lam-la ma-thar shes gleṅs-nas* as the word was sent, the road is not passable! གཏམ་གླེང་བ་ཉི་འདུག་ཞེས་བྱས I have made this speech: གཅིག་གླེང་གཉིས་གླེང་རིམ་པས་མཚེད་དེ་བཙུན་མོའི་བར་དུ་གླེང་ཞིང the rumour spreading from one to another, until it came before the lady. ཆོས་ཀྱི་སྒྲོག་གླེང་བྱེད་པ *chos-kyi sgrog-gleṅ byed-pa* to preach religious discourses; གྲོས་གླེང་ *gros-gleṅ* council; consultation.

གླེང་བ་པོ *gleṅ-wa-po* or གླེང་མོ་མཁན *gleṅ-mo mkhan* a story-teller.

གླེང་འབུམ *Gleṅ-ḥbum* a hundred thousand stories; the title of a book in the *Ḥdul-wa* division of the Kahgyur or Tibetan Buddhist scriptures, which contains different stories on the behaviour of devotees, monks, nuns, &c , who adopted the Buddhist faith, and who violated the rules of monastic discipline laid down by Buddha.

གླེང་མོ *gleṅ-mo* or ལབ་གླེང་ *lab-gleṅ* གླེང་བརྗོད *gleṅ-brjod* कथा, काहिनी, वार्त्ता, आलाप talk; conversation; story; account.

གླེང་གཞི *gleṅ-gshi* or གླེང་བསླངས་པ *gleṅ bslaṅs-pa* तोथं, निदान any subject; primary cause: གླེང་གཞི་འདི་ལ *gleṅ-gshi ḥdi-la* अस्मिन् निदाने in this narration. 1. narration. 2. the subject of a discourse (*Cs.*). 3. table of contents; index. 4. place, scene of a conversation or discourse.

གླེན་ལྐུགས *glen-lkugs*, abbr. of གླེན་པ་དང་ལྐུགས་པ *glen-pa daṅ-lkugs-pa*, very stupid and idiotic: གླེན་ལྐུགས་བཀོལ་སྤྱོད་ཀྱི་སྡུག་བསྔལ *glen-lkugs bkol spyod-kyi sdug-bsṅal* the misery of being stupid, of dumbness and servitude.

གླེན་པ *glen-pa* मूर्ख, जड़, अज्ञ, धिक्, मूढ़ stupid, foolish, ignorant; a thick-headed fool; an idiot: བྱོལ་སོང་ལས་ཀྱང་གླེན་པ more stupid than a brute: ཁྱོད་རྣམས་རེ་གླེན fools that you are each of you: གླེན་པ་གཏི་མུག་ཅན muddled ones.

Syn. ལྡར་བ *ldar-wa*; གླན་གླེན *glan-glen*; མི་གསལ་བ *mi gsal-wa*; ལྟོ་འགེངས *lto-hgeñs*; ལེ་ལོ་བ *le-lo-wa*; ཐ་ཤལ *tha-çal* (*Mñon.*).

གླེབ་པ *gleb-pa*, pf. གླེབས *glebs*, to make flat, plain (*Cs.*); ལེབ་མོར་གླེབ *leb-mor-gleb* make flat.

+ གླེབས་པ *glebs-pa*, निक्रम् to trample; to tread down; to press down by the feet (*Ñag.*).

གླེམ་པ *glem-pa* to press, squeeze; to crush, squash (*Jä.*).

གློ *glo* or ལྡོ *ldo*, in *Ld.* resp. གཞོགས *gshogs*, 1. the side, esp. of the body: གློས་ཕབ་པ *glos-phab-pa* to lie down on one's side. 2. a cough.

གློ་དཀར *glo-dkar* or འཐོང་ཀ *hthoñ-ka* गवाक्ष a small window in (the side of) a house to let in light.

གློ་བཀྲ *Glo-bkra* n. of a country in Tibet (*Jig.*).

གློ་ཀློགས་པ *glo-lkogs-pa* उत्कासन to cough; to clear the throat.

གློ་སྐར *glo-skar*=གློ་དཀར *glo-dkar* or སྐར་ཁུང *skar-khuñ* a small door or window.

གློ་ཁ *glo-kha* n. of a colour like the blood of the lungs; pale-red.

གློ་ཁུག *glo-khug* a small money-bag attached to the sash or girdle of a Tibetan.

གློ་འགོགས་པ *glo hgogs-pa*=གློ་འགོགས་པ or གློ་རྒྱག་པ *glo rgyag-pa* to cough; to feel stifled (*Mñon.*).

གློ་འགྲམས *glo-hgrams* चत, n. of a disease.

གློ་རྒྱས *glo-rgyas* a disease of the lungs; asthma.

གློ་གཅོང *glo-gcoñ* a disease of the lungs which increases during the night.

གློ་དོང *glo-doñ* wind-pipe (*Cs.*).

གློ་རྡོག *glo-rdog*=གློ་བུར *glo-bur* sudden (*Ñag.*).

གློ་རྡོལ *glo-rdol*=རྣག་རྡོལ *rnag-rdol* excessive expectoration.

གློ་སྤིར *glo-spir* n. of a kind of shield: ཀུལ་དཀར་ཕུབ་ནི་རབ་ལ་ཞོ་ལྔ་སྟེ, གློ་སྤིར་ཞོ་རེ་ཕུབ་སྐོར་ཞོ་ཕྱེད་ཡིན *kul-dkar phub-ni rab-la sho-lña-ste, glo-spir sho-re phub-skor sho-phyed yin* the best *Kul-dkar* shield costs five *sho* and that of *Glo-spir* costs a *sho* for each disk on it (*Jig.*).

གློ་ཕུག *glo-phug* place where things are kept—either in a wall or a corner of a house, &c.: ཕྲུས་པ་དེས་གསེར་རྣམས་གློ་ཕུག་ཅིག་ན་པར་བཞག that boy kept the gold in a niché.

གློ་བ *glo-wa* फुफ्फुस् क्लोम the lungs; གློ་བ་བུ་ལྔ *glo-wa bu-lña* the five anterior lobes of the lungs; གློ་བ་མ་ལྔ *glo-wa malña* the five posterior lobes of the lungs.

གློ་བུར *glo-bur* अकस्मात् sudden; adv. གློ་བུར་དུ *glo-bur-du* suddenly; all on a sudden; instantaneously: གློ་བུར་དུ་མི་མང་པོ་ཤི་བའི་སྡུག་བསྔལ *glo-bur-du mi-mañ-po çi-wahi sdug-bsñal* the misery or calamity of many men dying suddenly. གློ་བུར་དུ་ཧོངས་པ *glo-bur-du hoñs-pa* आगन्तुक one who has come all on a sudden; གློ་བུར་བའི་དོན *glo-bur-wahi don* the signification of suddenness.

གློ་བུར་རྒྱལ་པོ *Glo-bur rgyal-po* a name of the King of Tibet about 900 years ago.

གློ་བུར་ནད *glo-bur-nad* a disease that arises suddenly.

གློ་བུར་བ *glo bur-wa* suddenness.

གློ་འབུར *glo-hbur* प्रधान a projection; uprising: འབུར་དུ་སྡོད་པ *hbur-du sdod-pa* to rise up into sitting posture.

གློ་སྦུབ *glo-sbub* wind-pipe.

གློ་ལ་བ *glo-la-wa* convulsions of the lungs; cough.

གློག *glog* विद्युत, तड़ित, ह्रादिनी, चाका-लिका, अमनि, चपला, चञ्चला, स्फूर्जथु, चला lightning; flash of lightning; སྤྲིན་ཕན་ཚུན་འཐབ་པ་ལས་བྱུང་བ *sprin-phan-tshun ḥthab pa las byuṅ-wa* that produced from the concussion or collision of clouds. The names of different kinds of lightning are mentioned in the *Kah-gyur*:—གློག་གཞི་འབྱིད་ཅན *glog gzi-ḥbyid-can* the lightning with flash; གློག་སྟུག་འོད *glog-stug hod* the lightning of dense lustre, sheet-lightning; གློག་མཛེས་ཕྲེང་ཅན *glog-mdses phreṅ-can* the lightning of beautiful strings or zig-zags, &c. (*K. g.* ཀ, *115*). The lightning that comes from the south is called སྐད་བརྒྱ་པ *skad-brgya-pa*, that of a hundred rattles; that coming from the west is called འོད་ཉམས་པ *hod-ñams-pa*, that of fading lustre; that which comes from the north is called རྒྱུན་གྱི་བདག་པོ *rgyun-gyi bdag-po*, lord of streaming flashes (*K. g.* ཀ, *324*).

Syn. འཇུག་པ་བརྒྱ་པ *hjug-pa brgya-pa*; གཞི་སྔོན་སྐྱེས *gshi-sṅon skyes*; སྤྲིན་གྱི་ལྕུག་མ *sprin-gyi lcug-ma*; གསེར་འོད་ཅན *gser-hod can*; ལུས་ཕྲ *lus-phra*; བདེ་འཐུན *bde-ḥthuṅ*; སྐད་ཅིག་འོད *skad-cig hod*; སྐད་ཅིག་གསལ་བ *skad-cig gsal-wa* (*Mṅon.*)

གློག་ལྡན *glog-ldan* तड़िल्वत full of lightning; flashed cloud.

གློང་ཐང་ *Gloṅ-thaṅ* n. of a place in Tibet proper and also in Kham.

གློང་ཐང་སྒྲོན་མའི་ལྷ་ཁང་ *Gloṅ-thaṅ sgron-maḥi lha-khaṅ* n. of a monastery and temple in Kham.

གློག་པ *glog-pa* रजत silver.

གློག་པའི་ནད *glog-paḥi-nad* n. of a disease mentioned in grammar, but not found in the medical works. Acc. to *Jä.* གློག་ནད is another name of the disease called གློག་པ *lhog-pa*=cancer.

གློད་པ *glod-pa*=ལྷོད་པ *lhod-pa* to relax; to loosen བཅིངས་པ་གློད *bciṅs-pa-glod*=བསྡམས་པ་གློད *bsdams-pa-glod* slacken binding; སེམས་གློད་པ to relax the mind, be at ease; གློད་ལ་རྒྱུན་དུ་བཞུགས *glod-la rgyun-du bshugs* you may stay here always with easy mind; མ་བཟུང་མ་གློད་པར *ma-bzuṅ ma-glod-par* without any regard to taking or giving.

གློན་པ *glon-pa* or གླན་པ *glan-pa* 1. to return an answer; to reply. 2. to patch, mend.

卐 **གློས་པ** *glos-pa* or རྨོངས་པ *rmoṅs-pa* stupidity; ignorance.

གློས་ཕབ་པ *glos-phab-pa* to lie on one side or on the side: ལུས་ཀྱི་གཞོགས་ཕབ་ནས་གླང་ཉལ་བ་ལྟ་བུ to lie on the side like an ox lying down.

དགག་པ *dgag-pa*, fut. of འགེགས་པ to hinder.

དགག་པ་དང་བྲལ་བ *dgag-pa daṅ bral-wa*=དགག་པ་མེད་པ *dgag-pa med-pa* विप्रतिषेध open; without let or hinderance; unobstructed.

དགག་ཕྱེ *dgag-phye*, v. དགག་དབྱེ་བྱེད *dgag-dbye byed*.

དགག་དབྱེ *dgag-dbye*=དགག་ཕྱེ *dgag-phye* प्रवारित stopped; obstructed.

དགག་དབྱེ་བྱེད *dgag-dbye byed* प्रवारक one who stops or obstructs.

དགག་ཚིག *dgag-tshig* or དགག་པའི་ཚིག *dgag paḥi tshig* न चेत word of prohibition; objection.

དགང་དཀའ་བ *dgaṅ-dkaḥ-wa*, ཁེངས་དཀའ་བ *kheṅs-dkaḥ-wa* दुर्भरता hard to fill up.

དགང་བ *dgaṅ-wa*, fut. of འགེངས་བ *hgeṅs-wa*, to fill; fill up.

དགང་བླུག *dgaṅ-blug* पूर्णाहुतिपात्र a ladle to pour butter in sacrificial fire.

དགང་གཟར *dgaṅ-gzar* स्रावी sacrificial spoon or ladle: སྦྱིན་སྲེག་བླུགས་བྱེད་ཀྱི་གཟར་བུ་དང་སྐྱོག་ལྟ་བུ *sbyin-sreg blugs byed-kyi gzar-bu daṅ skyog lta-bu* there are two kinds of spoons in *homa* sacrificial fire, one is large called *Dgañ-gsar*, and the other smaller *blug-gsar*, which is used to pour butter on fire.

དགང་གཟར་ཤིང་ *Dgañ-gzar çiñ* n. of a tree, the tree resembling tiger's feet.

Syn. སྟག་གི་རྐང་པ *stag-gi rkañ-pa*; ཚེར་མ་ཞིམ *tsher-ma shim*; ས་འཚོ *sa-ḥtsho*; ཚིག་མང་ *tshig mañ* (*Mñon.*).

དགང་སླ་བ *dgañ-sla-wa* full to the brim; replete: སྣོད་དུ་ཁེངས་མ་ཁེངས *snod-du kheñs-ma kheñs*.

དགབ་པ *dgab-pa*, fut. of འགེབས་པ *hgebs-pa*.

དགབ་བྱ *dgab-bya* garment; dress (*Mñon.*).

དགའ་བ *dgaḥ-wa* मदन, सम्भोग, नन्दन, प्रश्रय, स्पृहा, आनन्द, मोद, रमण, प्रेमा, रति, प्रमद, प्रीति, सन्तोष, आमोद, रभस, रङ्ग, कौतुक 1. delight; happiness; joy. 2. vb. neut. to rejoice; དགའ་བ་ཡིན་པ to be pleased; དགའ་བ་མ་ཡིན་པ to be displeased; also དགའ་བར་བྱེད་པ to make glad: མི་དགའོ was displeased: རབ་ཏུ་དགའ་ནས rejoicing greatly.

Syn. མགུ་བ *mgu-wa*; རངས་པ *rañs-pa*; སྤྲོ་བ *spro-wa*; ཤིན་ཏུ་དགའ *çin-tu dgaḥ*; ཡང་དག་དགའ *yañ-dag dgaḥ*, ཡིད་རང་ *yid-rañ*; དགྱེས་པ *dgyes-pa*; མཉེས་པ *mñes-pa*; ཚིམ་པ *tshim-pa*; བདེ་སྐྱིད *bde-skyid*; ཡིད་བདེ *yid-bde*; སེམས་སྣུམ་པ *sems snum-pa*; རབ་དགའ *rab-rdgaḥ*; འཛོ་སྟེར་བ *ḥdso-ster-wa* (*Mñon.*).

དགའ་རྐྱང *dgaḥ-rkyañ* (གྲངས་གནས) n. of a large numerical figure (*Ya-sel. 75*).

དགའ་སྐྱེས *dgaḥ-skyes* हृष्ट very pleased; glad.

དགའ་སྐྱོ་ཟུལ་གསུམ *dgaḥ-skyo zul-gsum* the abbreviation of the names of the three places situated to the west of Lhasa, viz., དགའ་བ་གདོང *Dgaḥ-wa-gdoñ*, སྐྱོ་མོ་ལུང *Skyo-mo-luñ* and ཟུལ་པོ *Zul-po*, in each of which there is a monastery.

དགའ་གྲོགས *dgaḥ-grogs* lover; spouse; wife; an intimate friend (*Mñon.*).

དགའ་དགུ *dgaḥ-dgu* संसर्ग intercourse; association; merriment; དགའ་དགུར་སྤྱོད་པ *dgaḥ-dgur spyod-pa* संसर्गं चर्या to perform conjugal rites; also to indulge in sexual enjoyment.

དགའ་ཅན་གྱི་མདོ *Dgaḥ-can gyi-mdo*, the *Sûtra* of དགའ་བ་ཅན *Dgaḥ-wa-can* in (*K. d.* ཝ *421*), which contains:—སྲོག་གཅོད་པའི་ཉེས་དམིགས་བཅུ *srog gcod-paḥi ñes-dmigs bcu* (10); རྫུན་དུ་སྨྲ་བའི་ཉེས་དམིགས་བཅུ *rdsun-du smra-waḥi ñes-dmigs bcu* (10); ཆང་འཐུང་བའི་ཉེས་དམིགས་སུམ་བཅུ་སོ་ལྔ *chañ hthuñ-waḥi ñes-dmigs sum-bcu so-lña* (35); མ་བྱིན་པར་ལེན་པའི་ཉེས་དམིགས་བཅུ *ma-byin-par len-paḥi ñis-dmigs bcu* (10); ལོག་པར་གཡེམ་པའི་ཉེས་དམིགས་བཅུ *log-par gyem-paḥi ñes-dmigs bcu* (10).

དགའ་སྟོན *dgaḥ-ston* उत्सव, क्षण, कौतुक festival.

Syn. མཆོད་པ *mchod-pa*; དུས་སྟོན *dus-ston*; རྒོད *rgod*; ཉེར་དགའ *ñer-dgaḥ* (*Mñon.*).

དགའ་སྟོན་སྐྱེས *dgaḥ-ston-skyes* producing mirth.

དགའ་སྟོན་སྦྱིན *dgaḥ-ston sbyin* क्षणद an astrologer; water.

དགའ་བདེ *dgaḥ-bde*, colloq. "gan-de," joy and happiness.

དགའ་དར *dgaḥ-dar* or དགའ་བའི་ཁ་བཏགས *dgaḥ-waḥi kha-gtags* a scarf presented for pleasing or consoling; a scarf of congratulation.

དགའ་གདོང་ *Dgaḥ-gdoñ* n. of a monastery near Dapung which has an oracle and a divinity called Ga-dong Chokyong, whose duty it is to cause rain during a drought.

དགའ་ལྡན I: *Dgaḥ-ldan Gă-dan*) तुषित a paradise of the Buddhists; the residence of those sainted beings who enjoy beatitude, which is the peculiar privilege of the *Mahâyana* Buddhists. It is presided over by the coming Buddha, now the *Bodhisattva* Maitreya. The gods residing in it are said to live 4,000 years, the duration of a day of which is equal to 400 human years; and the length of one's body is a furlong (*Sorig.*). མགོན་པོ་བྱམས་པས་ལུགས་གཉིས་ཀྱི་རྒྱལ་སྲིད་མཛད་ནས་ཐེག་པ་ཆེན་པོའི་ཆོས་ཀྱི་དགའ་བ་དང་ལྡན་པས་ན་དགའ་ལྡན་ཏེ། དེ་ན་གནས་པ་རྣམས་ཀྱི་ལུས་ཀྱི་ཚད་ནི་རྒྱང་གྲགས་ཡིན་ལ ཚེ་ཚད་ནི་མི་ལོ་བཞི་ བརྒྱ་ལ་ ཞག་ཏུ་ བྱས་པའི་རང་ལོ་བཞི་སྟོང་ཐུབ་པོ owing to Lord Maitreyas' spiritual and temporal rule the celestial people are possessed of the joy of a righteous life.

དགའ་ལྡན II: (pronounced Gāndan) the great monastery of Gāndan situated 35 miles N.E. of Lhasa, which was founded by the Buddhist reformer Tsong-kha-pa. It contains twenty-six divisions or wards for the residence of monks. གྲྭ་ས་དགའ་ལྡན *Grva-sa Dgaḥ-ldan* the quarters for the residence of the monks of Gāndan are divided into two sections 1. called གྲྭ་ཚང་གོང་བྱང་རྩེ་ *grva-tshañ goñ Byañ-rtse* which has the following divisions or ཁམས་ཚན *khams-tshan*:—(1) ཧར་གདོང་ *Har-gdoñ*; (2) བསམ་བློ *Bsam-glo*; (3) ཀྲེ་བོ *Kre-ḅo*; (4) ཚ་པ *Tsha-pa*; (5) གསེར་ཁང་ *Gser-khañ*; (6) རྡོ་ར *Rdo-ra*; (7) ཀླུ་འབུམ *Klu-ḥbum*; (8) བྲག་ཉི *Brag-ñi*; (9) སྤ་ཏི *Spa-ti*; (10) རྒྱལ་རོང་ *Rgyal-roñ*; (11) གོ་བ *Go-wa*; (12) ཀོང་པོ *Koñ-po*; (13) མངའ་རིས *Mñaḥ-ris* (*Loñ.* ༤ *14*). 2. called གྲྭ་ཚང་འོག་ཤར་རྩེ *grva-tshañ ḥog Çar-rtse*, which has the following divisions or ཁམས་ཚན *khams-tshan*:—(1) རྡོ་ཁང *Rdo-khañ*; (2) ཕོ་ཁང་ *Pho-khañ*; (3) ལྷོ་པ *Lho-pa*; (4) ཉག་རེ *Ñag-re*; (5) ཅོ་ནེ *Co-ne*; (6) ཐེ་བོ *The-ḅo*; (7) ཟུང་ཆུ *Zuñ-chu*; (8) སོག་པོ *Sog-po*; (9) རྟ་འོན *Rta-ḥon*; (10) མངའ་རིས *Mñaḥ-ris*; (11) ཆ་པ *Cha-pa*; (12) ཉང་པོ *Ñañ-po*; (13) གུང་རུ *Guñ-ru* (*Loñ.* ༦, *14*). The name Gāndan is generally fixed before the names of monasteries and institutions which belong to the *Dgaḥ-ldan-pa* or Gelug-pa sect.

དགའ་ལྡན་ཁང་གསར *Dgaḥ-ldan Khañ-gsar* 1. formerly the residence of King *Dpon-po Mi-Dwañ*: དཔོན་པོ་དབང་གི་ཕོ་བྲང་ *Dpon-po dwañ-gi pho-brañ* near Lhasa (*Loñ.* ༢, *18*). 2. the residence of King *Dgaḥ-ldan Tshe-wañ* is situated to the back of the royal monastery of *Tsho-mo-gliñ* in Lhasa: རྒྱལ་པོ་དགའ་ལྡན་ཚེ་དབང་གི་ཕོ་བྲང་དེ་ལྷ་ས་མཚོ་མོ་གླིང་གི་རྒྱབ་ལ་ཡོད (*Rtsii.*).

དགའ་ལྡན་ཁྲི་པ *Dgaḥ-ldan khri-pa* the lineal successor of Tsong-kha-pa in the ecclesiastical throne of the great monastery of Gāndan. He is the chief of the ordinary non-incarnate lamas and occupies the third place in the hierarchical precedence of Tibet.

དགའ་ལྡན་ཆོས་འཁོར་གླིང་ *Dgaḥ-ldan chos-ḥkhor gliñ* n. of a monastery in Higher Tibet. It is a very common name by which several monasteries are designated.

དགའ་ལྡན་ཕུན་ཚོགས་གླིང་ *Dgaḥ-ldan Phun-tshogs gliñ* the monastery of Phunts'o Ling situated to the west of Tashi-lhunpo in Tsang. It contains a large number of block-prints and religious works. It was (formerly) Lama Taranatha's monastery. གཙང་བཀྲ་ཤིས་ལྷུན་པོའི་ནུབ་ལ་ཡོད,ཇོ་ནང་ཏཱ་རཱ་ནཱ་ཐའི་དགོན་པ་ཡིན *Gtsañ Bkra-çis-lhun-poḥi nub-la yod, Jo-nañ tḫa-rḫa-nḫa thaḥi dgon-pa yin*, སྐུ་གསུང་ཐུགས་རྟེན་དང་, ཆོས་ཀྱི་པར་མང་པོ་ཡོད *sku-gsug thugs-rten dañ, chos-kyi phar mañ-pa yod*.

དགའ་ལྡན་ཕོ་བྲང་ *Dgaḥ-ldan pho-brañ* also called སྡེ་པ་གཞུང་ *Sde-pa gshuñ* the Government-house in Lhasa, also the Government of Lhasa (*Rtsii. 14*).

དགའ་སྤྱོད *dgaḥ-spyod* मज्ञचर्य्या entertainment; merriment; also good behaviour.

དགའ་སྤྲོ་ཅན་ *ḏgaẖ-spro-can* ऊर्जितः possessed of cheerfulness and enthusiasm.

དགའ་བ་འཁྱིལ་བ་ *ḏgaẖ-wa ẖkhyil-wa* 1. स्वस्तिक the all-good; that exists by itself; the emblem of purity; purity typified. 2. n. of a gem. 3. the king's palace.

Syn. གཡུང་དྲུང་ *gyuṅ-druṅ*; རྒྱལ་པོའི་ཕོ་བྲང་ *rgyal-poẖi pho-braṅ* (*Mṅon.*).

དགའ་བ་བརྒྱ་པ་ *Dgaẖ-wa ḇrga-pa* (ཁྱབ་འཇུག་གི་མིང་) one of the names of Vishnu; one of a hundred joys (*Mṅon.*).

དགའ་བ་ཅན་ *ḏgaẖ-wa-can* सुखालु cheerful; merry.

Syn. དགའ་བ་མྱོང་ *ḏgaẖ-wa myoṅ*=འཁྲིག་པ *ẖkhrigpa* or ཁྱིམ་པའི་ཆོས *khyim-paẖi chos*, sexual enjoyment (*Mṅon.*).

དགའ་བ་དམན་པ *ḏgaẖ-wa ḏman-pa* sordid pleasure; one delighting in sexual pleasures; met. a cock.

དགའ་བ་བཞི *ḏgaẖ-wa ḇshi* the four pleasures or delights are the following:—(1) ལྐོག་མ་མི་བདེ་གླུ་ལ་དགའ *ḻkog-ma mi-bde glu-la ḏgaẖ*; (2) དམངས་རིགས་སྟན་མཐོ་ལ་དགའ *ḏmaṅs-rigs stan-mtho la ḏgaẖ*; (3) དབུལ་པོ་གཏོང་ལ་དགའ *ḏbul-po gtoṅ-la ḏgaẖ*; (4) ཤིང་རྒན་པོ་གཞོན་ནུ་མ་ལ་དགའ *shiṅ-rgan-po gshin-nu-ma-la ḏgaẖ* (*Cāṇ.*).

དགའ་བ་འོད་འཕྲོ *Dgaẖ-wa hoḏ-ẖphro* n. of Atis'a's residence at Nye-thang near Lhasa: ཇོ་བོའི་གཟིམས་ཆུང་དགའ་བ་འོད་འཕྲོ་ཞེས་པའི་གླིང་། *Jo-ḇoẖi gzims chuṅ Dgaẖ-wa hoḏ-ẖphro shes-paẖi gliṅ* (*A. 98*).

དགའ་བའི་གྲགས་པ་ II: *Dgaẖ-waẖi grags-pa* रामयशा the Brāhmaṇa at whose request the Kashmirian poet Kshemendra wrote Avadāna Kalpalatā and several other Sanskrit poems.

* དགའ་བའི་གྲགས་པ་ II: नन्दकीर्त्ति (*Schr.; Bull. 184, 294*).

དགའ་བའི་བུ་ག *ḏgaẖ-waẖi bu-ga* रतिकुहर the female organ.

དགའ་བའི་དབང་པོ་ I: *ḏgaẖ-waẖi ḏwaṅ-po* हृषीकेश; ཁྱབ་འཇུག *khyab-ẖjug* a name of Vishnu (*Mṅon.*).

དགའ་བའི་ཚལ *Dgaẖ-waẖi tshal*=རྒྱལ་པོའི་སྐྱེད་ཚལ *rgyal-poẖi skyeḏ-tshal* royal gardens; also नन्दनवन the celestial gardens.

དགའ་བའི་བཞིན *Dgaẖ-waẖi ḇshin* (ཡུལ་ལྗོངས *yul-ljoṅs*) n. of a place; ཤར་ཕྱོགས *çar-phyogs* the Orient, the East (*K. d.* ར, *267*).

དགའ་བའི་རོ *ḏgaẖ-waẖi ro* रतिरस sexual enjoyment.

* དགའ་བའི་བཤེས་གཉེན *ḏgaẖ-waẖi ḇçes-gñen* नन्दमित्र (*Schr.*).

དགའ་བའི་ས་གཞི *ḏgaẖ-waẖi sa-gshi* the female organ.

Syn མོ་རྟགས *mo-rtags*; མོ་མཚན *mo-mtshan* (*Mṅon.*).

དགའ་བའི་སླད *ḏgaẖ-waẖi slaḏ* प्रियाय for the sake of pleasure.

དགའ་བར་བྱེད *ḏgaẖ-war byeḏ*=དགའ་གྲོགས *ḏgaẖ-grogs* or མཛའ་གྲོགས *mdsaẖ-grogs* or ཁྱོ་བོ *kyoẖ-ḇo* a friend; sweetheart; a hubsand (*Mṅon.*).

དགའ་བས་བཅིངས *ḏgaẖ-was ḇciṅs* प्रेमबन्ध love-bound; bond of love.

* དགའ་བོ I: *ḏgaẖ-wo* नन्द (*Schr.; Tā. 2, 69*).

དགའ་བྱེད *Dgah-byeḏ* राम, नन्दक, नन्दन, मोदक, रामिल, प्रियकार, मुदिर Rāma, the hero of the epic Rāmāyana; n. of a cloud.

* དགའ་བྱེད་སྙན་པ *ḏgaẖ-byeḏ sñan-pa* नन्दप्रिय n. pr. (*Schr.; Tā. 2 102*), dear to or fond of Nanda (the delightful).

དགའ་བྱེད་དགྲ་སྟ་ཅན *Dgaẖ byeḏ Dgra-sta-can* परशुराम the third accepted incarnation of Vishnu; his other names are—དཔའ་བོ་ཛ་མ

Dpaḥ-po dsa-ma; ཨག་ནིའི་སྲས Ag-niḥi sras; དབང་ཆེན Dwañ-chen; རྟུལ་བཟང་སྐྱེས Ṛtul-bzañ skyes; མཚོན་ཆ་མཁན Mtshon-cha mkhan; སྲིད་སྒྲུབ Srid-sgrub; ལུས་སྐྱེས Lus-skyes; གཅོད་བྱེད Gcod-byed; རྡུལ་ཅན་མའི་བུ Ṛdul-can-maḥi bu; ངན་སྤོང་སྐྱེས Ñan-spoñ skyes; ཕ་ལད Pha-lad; ཨ་ག་ནི་དགའ་བྱེད Aga-ni dgaḥ-byed (Mṅon.).

དགའ་བྱེད་ཤིང་ dgaḥ-byed çiñ कुथि the tree called སྤྱི་ཤུར་ཤིང spyi-shur çiñ.

Syn. གདུང་བྱེད gduñ byed; ལུས་ངན lus ñan; ཀུ་ནི ku-ni; འོད་ལྡན ḥod-ldan; འཁྱོག་པོ ḥkhyog-po (Mṅon.).

དགའ་འབྱམས dgaḥ-ḥbyams प्रमदा she who is full of enjoyment; a number.

དགའ་མ Dgaḥ-ma रति, रम्या, हृद्या, वनिता the beautiful; a name of Rati, the wife of Cupid; དགའ་མའི་བདག Dgaḥ-maḥi bdag रतिपति the husband of Rati.

དགའ་མོ dgaḥ-mo प्रीति good; lovely.

དགའ་ཚང dgaḥ-tshañ=ཡག་པོ yag-po, བཟང་པོ bzañ-po and ལེགས་པ legs-pa good; fine; handsome: དེའི་ནང་ན་དངོས་པོ་དགའ་ཚང་ཅིག་ཡོད་ཀྱང among them there was one article which was very pretty (A. 14).

དགའ་ཚད་པ dgaḥ-tshad-pa=སེམས་དགའ་ཚོར་བྱམས་པ to be sufficiently pleased (Khrid. 32).

དགའ་བཞི་པ dgaḥ bshi-pa प्रिय-चतुर: possessed of the four joys—piety, wealth, men and lands: ཆོས་ནོར་མི་ས་བཞིའཛོམ་པའི་དགའ་བཞི་པ chos nor mi sa-bshi ḥdsom-paḥi dgaḥ bshi-pa.

དགའ་ཡས dgaḥ-yas विमद boundless joy or pleasure.

དགའ་ཡི་སྐྱེ་བར dgaḥ-yi skye-war प्रियजन्मा born or grown out of joy or enjoyment.

དགའ་རབ་རྡོ་རྗེ Dgaḥ-rab Ṛdo-rje n. of a celebrated Lama of the Ṛdsog-chen sect of the Ṛñiñ-ma School (Grub. ཕ 13).

དགའ་རབ་དབང་ཕྱུག Dgaḥ-rab dwañ-phyug the Lord of Love, Cupid.

དགའ་རིངས dgaḥ-riñs दीर्घरति met. for the hog ["long in copulation"; a dog] S.

དགར dgar 1. n. of a place; n. of a district in Tibet. 2.=དགའ་བར dgaḥ-war རང་དགར rañ-dgar at pleasure, ad libitum; frq. ཅི་དགར chi-dgar what is your pleasure; according to Jä. why?

དགར་བ dgar-wa उच्चाटन to separate; confine; place apart (men, cattle, goods): དགར་བྱའི་ཕྱུགས dgar-byaḥi phugs cattle to be penned in a fold (Cs). གནས་ནས་དགར་བ gnas-nas dgar-wa to banish from a place; to exile; དགར་བའི་དོན་དུ dgar-waḥi don-du in special sense; in particular (Sch.). In W. "gar-te bor-ce" to set apart, exclude, shut out; to lock up, shut up; to lay up or by; to preserve (Jä.); Dgar-rgya eo-ee to store up.

དགལ་བ dgal-wa, fut. of འགེལ་བ ḥgel-wa.

དགས་པ dgas-pa, v. འགས་པ ḥgas-pa; སེར་ག་དགས་པ ser-ga dgas-pa to have cracks or be cracked.

དགུ dgu 1. nine; དགུ་བཅུ dgu-bcu or དགུ་བཅུ་ཐམ་པ dgu-bcu tham-pa ninety. 2. as met. =many: དགུས་ཐབས་གསགས dgus-thabs gsags gathered by many efforts, with great difficulty. 3. also sign of plural: ཁམས་གསུམ་སྐྱེ་དགུ khams-gsum skye-dgu the people of the three worlds: མི་འདི་མི་ཤེས་དགུ་ཤེས་པ་འདུག this man says many things he knows not. མི་ཤེས་དགུ་ཤེས་པོ one who knows everything; ཟེར་དགུ or སྨྲས་དགུ many talks; many things to say; སྐྱེ་དགུའི་བདག་པོ Skye-dguḥi bdag-po प्रजापति the lord of all living beings; སྐྱེ་དགུའི་བདག་མོ Skye-dguḥi bdag-mo प्रजापति, प्रजावती the name of the step-mother who nursed Gautama Buddha; ཡོད་དགུ those that are; the existing many or beings; ནོར་ཡོད་དགུ་ཅིག the goods that one has; property; བཟང་དགུ the many good and brave; also ལུས་འདོད་དགུར་སྒྱུར་བ *lus-hdod dgur sgyur-wa* to be changed, transformed *ad libitum*; ངན་དགུ་ཐུབ་པ *ṅan-dgu thub-pa* one who can suppress the wicked; also to overcome every evil: མི་བྱེད་དགུ་བྱེད་མི་ཡོང་དགུ་ཡོང་ *mi-byed dgu-byed mi-yoṅ dgu-yoṅ*, according to *Cs.*, *Jä.*, if you do many things which ought not to be done, many things will take place which ought not to take place; ཤི་བ་ཡིད་ཀྱི་དགུ་ལ་མི་བྱེད་དེ not counting upon death among things to be thought of; དགུ་ཁྲི *dgu-khri* the chair or conveyance for the many, *i.e.*, for the dead; litter; bier (*Jä*). དགུ་གླིང་བཅུ་གཉིས *dgu-gliṅ bcu-gñis* the twelve continents inhabited by living beings. Here *dgu* would seem to act as mere plural sign.

དགུ་གཏོར *dgu-gtor* offerings made to evil spirits on the 29th day of the last month of the Tibetan calender in the monasteries of Tibet. དགོན་པ་རྣམས་སུ་ལོ་རེ་བཞིན་ཟླ་བ་བཅུ་གཉིས་པའི་ཉི་ཤུ་དགུ་ལ་གཏོར་མ་འཐང་བ་ལ་དགུ་གཏོར་ཟེར, དེ་དུས་འཆམ་བརྒྱབ་པ་སོགས་ལྟད་མོ་ཆེན་པོ་ཡོད་

དགུ་ཐུབ *dgu-thub* able to subdue the many; one full of resources; the all-conquering one.

དགུ་པ *dgu-pa* the ninth; having, comprising, measuring nine, *e.g.*, ཁྲུ་དགུ་པ *khru dgu-pa*, measuring nine cubits (in length, height, etc.); དགུ་པོ *dgu-po* नवम the ninth, the nine, those nine; ལན་དགུ *lan-dgu* nine times.

དགུ་ཕྲུགས *dgu-phrugs* or དགུ་སྡེབས *dgu-sdebs* a stage of meditation which is dependent upon the regulation of the breath; རླུང་སྒོམ་པའི་དུས་སུ་དང་པོ *rluṅ sgom-paḥi dus-su daṅ-po*. The first stage in the regulation of the breath in the art of meditative concentration.

དགུ་བ *dgu-wa* 1. vb. to bend; to make crooked. 2. sbst. the act of bending, stooping, bowing; inflection. 3. adj. bent; stooping.

དགུ་རྩེགས *dgu-rtsegs* n. of a yellow flower (*Cs.*).

དགུ་ཚིགས *dgu-tshigs* or དགུ་ཚིགས་སྐྱ་མོ *dgu-tshigs skya-mo* the milky-way constellation.

Syn. ནམ་མཁའི་སྐྱེ་རགས *nam-mkhaḥi skye-rags*; གནོད་སྦྱིན་ཁ་རླངས *gnod-sbyin kha-rlaṅs* (*Mṅon.*).

དགུ་ཟི་གླང་པོ་སྣ *dgu-zi glaṅ-po sna* n. of the enchanted sword of *Gri-gum btsan-po*; one of the early kings of Tibet who was assasinated (*Yig. 58*).

དགུ་གཤུང་ *Dgu-gshuṅ* n. of a place in Tibet (*Rtsii. 70*).

དགུག་པ *dgug-pa*, v. འགུག་པ *hgug-pa*.

དགུག་བྱང་ *dgug-byaṅ* urgent call; དགུག་གཤུག *dgug-gshug*=དགུག་ཤུགས *dgug-çugs* id.

དགུང་ *dguṅ* रात्रि generally applied to midnight, but at times to noon as well. Sometimes is made equivalent to གུང་ *guṅ*, but properly speaking དགུང་ *dguṅ* signifies sublimity, loftiness and also profundity; and གུང་ *guṅ* signifies the middle part, centre. ཉིན་དགུང་མཚན་དགུང་ is sometimes written as ཉིན་གུང་མཚན་གུང་། The direct sense occurs in རི་མཐོན་པོ་དགུང་ལ་སྙེགས་པ *ri mthon-po dguṅ-la sñegs-pa*, a high mountain rising aloft; དགུང་སྔོན་ནམ་མཁའི་དབྱིངས་སུ=ཉིན་མོའི་དགུང་ at noon, the middle of the day (*Ṅag.*).

དགུང་ཁག *dguṅ-khag* division of time.

དགུང་མཁའ *dguṅ-mkhaḥ* midnight sky.

དགུང་ཆར *dguṅ-char*=ཆར་པ *char-pa* rain (*Mṅon.*).

དགུང་སྙིང་ *dguṅ-sñiṅ* a year; a year of one's life.

དགུང་ཐིག *dguṅ-thig* the meridian line; དགུང་ཐིག་གི་དཀྱིལ་འཁོར *dguṅ thig-gi dkyil-ḥkhor* the meridian circle.

དགུང་དུ་ dguṅ-du or དགུང་ལ་གཤེགས་པ་ ḏguṅ-la gçegs-pa gone to heaven, *i.e.*, dead.

དགུང་བདུན་ dguṅ-ḇdun seven nights; a week.

དགུང་དོ་ནུབ་ dguṅ-do-nub this evening; to-night.

དགུང་འདེགས་ ḏguṅ ḥdegs = གཡོ་མེད་པར་བཞུགས་པར seated steadily without moving or leaning on any side; raised to the sky.

དགུང་མོ་ dguṅ-mo रात्रि the early night; evening; the time from 4 P.M. to 7 P.M.

དགུང་ཞག་ ḏguṅ-shag a day's halt; halt.

དགུང་ལ་རེག་པ་ ḏguṅ-la reg-pa touching, the sky; the meridian.

དགུང་ལོ་ ḏguṅ-lo the age of a respectable or high personage: སྐུ་ཞབས་ཀྱི་དགུང་ལོ་ sku shabs-kyi ḏguṅ-lo what is your honour's age?

དགུང་ལོ་མཐོན་པ་ dguṅ-lo m̱thon-pa = རྒན་པ་ ṟgan-pa an elderly person, 61 to 72 years old (*Mṅon.*).

དགུང་གསེབ་ ḏguṅ-gseb or དགུང་དཀྱིལ་ ḏguṅ-ḏkyil the middle of the sky.

དགུན་ dgun शिशिर; དགུན་ཀ་ dgun-ka the winter.

*དགུན་གྱི་རྒྱལ་མོ་ dgun-gyi ṟgyal-mo (*Schr.; 84 C.*).

དགུན་ཉི་ལྡོག་ dgun-ñi ldog the winter solstice: དགུན་ཉི་ལྡོག་གི་ཐིག་ dgun-ñi ldog-gi thig or ཁོར་ཐིག་ khor-thig the line of the winter solstice; the tropic of Capricorn.

དགུན་སྟོད་ dgun-stod the first part of winter.

དགུན་འབྲུམ་ dgun-ḥbrum winter grapes.

དགུན་སྨད་ dgun-smad शिशिर the after part of the winter season; དགུན་སྟོད་ཁ་དུས་ཧེམནྟ་ dgun-stod kha dus hemanta time of snow in the beginning winter; དགུན་སྨད་གྲང་དུས་ time of cold, about the end of the winter (*Rtsii.*).

དགུན་ཚིགས་ dgun-tshigs = དགུན་དུས་ (ḏgun-dus) winter time.

དགུན་ཟླ་ dgun-zla the mid-winter months, ཟླ་བ་བཅུ་པ་ zla-wa ḇcu-pa, ཟླ་བ་བཅུ་གཅིག་པ་ zla-wa ḇcu-gcig-pa, ཟླ་བ་བཅུ་གཉིས་པ་ zla-wa ḇcu-gñis-pa.

དགུན་ཟླ་ཐ་ཆུང་ dgun-zla tha-chuṅ माघ the month of January-February.

དགུན་ཟླ་འབྲིང་པོ་ ḏgun-zla ḥbriṅ-po पौष December-January.

དགུན་ཟླ་ར་བ་ dgun-zla ra-wa मार्गशीर्ष January; lit. the beginning of the year, *i.e.*, November-December.

དགུན་ས་ dgun-sa हैमन्तिक वास winter residence.

དགུམ་པ་ dgum-pa, fut. of འགུམ་པ་ ḥgum-pa.

དགུར་ I: dgur crooked: དབྱིབས་དགུར་བ་ ḏbyibs-ḏgur wa of crooked stature: སེམས་ཀྱིས་ཚུགས་ཀྱང་ལུས་ཀྱིས་དགུར་མ་ཚུགས་ sems-kyis tshugs-kyaṅ lus-kyis ḏgur-ma tshugs although the mind may bend, yet do not let your body bend (*Rdsa.*): རྒུར་ཤིག་ ṟgur-shig stoop down! སྒུར་ཏེ་ sgur-te writhing (with pain); མགོ་དགུར་བ་ to bend; to submit; to humble one's self; ཚིགས་དགུར་ a crooked-back; ལག་དགུར་ drawn bent hands.

Syn. རྒུར་ ṟgur; སྒུར་ sgur (*Mṅon.*).

དགུར་ II: many; all; འཁོར་གྱི་དཀྱིལ་འཁོར་ཡོད་དགུར་ཡང་ཡོད་དགུར་ ḥkhor-kyi ḏkyil-ḥkhor yoḏ-dgur yaṅ yoḏ ḏgur signifies ཡོད་པ་ཀུན་ yoḏ-pa kun all or all of those existing.

དགུར་འགྲོ་ dgur-ḥgro a snake; one of a stooping gait.

དགུར་པོ་ dgur-po anything crooked; a crooked man; སྒུར་པོ་ sgur-po hump-backed; དགུར་མོ་ dgur-mo a crooked woman.

དགེ་བ་ I: dge-wa स्वस्ति, कल्याण, शुभ, कुशल श्रेयः, क्षेम, सुकृत, शिव, भद्र, साधु, शं, भव्य, चरित्र happiness, welfare, virtue; also adj. happy, propitious, virtuous: དགེ་བའི་སེམས

dge-wahi sems a virtuous mind; ལས་དགེ་བ་མི་དགེ་བ *las dge-wa mi-dge-wa* virtuous and evil actions; དགེ་བའི་རྩ་བ *dge-wahi rtsa-wa* fundamental virtues: དགེ་བའི་རྩ་བ་རྒྱ་ཆེན་པོ་གཅིག་བྱུང་བ་དགོས some mighty act of virtue should be performed (*A.* 65); དགེ་རྩ་སྐྱེད་པ *dge-rtsa skyed-pa* to conceive the idea of a meritorious act. There are two kinds of དགེ་བ *dge-wa*, ཟག་བཅས་ཀྱི་དགེ་བ *zag-bcas kyi dge-wa* and ཟག་མེད་ཀྱི་དགེ་བ *zag-med-kyi dge-wa*; the former, called पुण्य or བསོད་ནམས *bsod-nams*, belongs to the world of desires and is subject to decay; the latter is undestructible, consisting of the enduring works of piety performed by saints belonging to the ཁམས་གོང་མ *khams goñ-ma* superior states of existence. There are two other kinds of *dge-wa*, viz.:—འདུས་བྱས་ཀྱི་དགེ་བ *hdus-byas-kyi dge-wa* and འདུས་མ་བྱས་ཀྱི་དགེ་བ *hdus-ma byas-kyi dge-wa*, the former consists of works done for gain or happiness in this world; འདུན་དུ་བྱས་པའི་དགེ་བ *hdun-du byas-pahi dge-wa* consists in paying reverence to and worshipping the Tathāgata and the incarnate saints. དགེ་བ may mean fasting, abstinence, as in the phrase དགེ་བ་སྲུང་བ *dge-wa sruñ-wa*, to fast, to abstain from food. Also alms, charity; that which is done as a religious work. ཤི་དགེ་གསོན་དགེ *çi dge gson dge* benevolences bestowed or given in one's life time when dying; དགེ་བ་འདོད་པར་བྱེད *dge-wa hdod-par byed* शुभकाम्यति wishes for prosperity; ཡང་དགེ་བ་ལ་འཇིག་རྟེན་པའི་དགེ་བ་དང་, འཇིག་རྟེན་ལས་འདས་པའི་དགེ་བ་ཡོད *yañ dge-wa la hjig-rten-pahi dge-wa dañ, hjig-rten-las hdas-pahi dge-wa yod. Dge-wa* are of two kinds—the worldly religious works, and the same for spiritual cultures; the former consists in ཕར་ཤེས་པ *phar-çes-pa*, appreciating or regarding one's father or knowing him as such; མར་ཤེས་པ *marçes-pa* knowing the mother, *i.e.*, to be grateful to her; to regard as one's mother; དགེ་སྦྱོང་དུ་ཤེས་པ *dge-sbyoñ-du çes-pa* to venerate or revere one as a member of the Buddhist church; བྲམ་ཟེར་ཤེས་པ *bram-zer çes-pa* to respect or pay homage to a Brāhmaṇ; རིགས་ཀྱི་ནང་ན་རྒན་པ་ལ་རིམ་གྲོ་བྱེད་པ *rigs-kyi nañ-na rgan-pa la rim-gro byed-pa* to pay respect to the elders of a family; སྦྱིན་པ་གཏོང་བ *sbyin-pa gtoñ-wa* to give alms in charity; དགེ་བཅུ *dge-bcu* the observance of the ten virtuous acts; འདུ་ཤེས་དགུ་དང་ *hdu-çes dgu-dañ* the nine *Samskāra*; དྲན་པ་བཅུ *dran-pa bcu* the ten remembrances.

དགེ་སྐྱེས *dge-skyes* शोभा charm; good appearance; n. of a goddess.

དགེ་སྐྱོན *dge-skyon*=སྐྱོན་ཕྲན་བུ *skyon phran-bu* སྐྱོན་ཅུང་ཟད *skyon cuñ-zad* slightly defective; a little fault.

དགེ་སྐྱོས *dge-skyos* or དགེ་བསྐྱོས *dge-bskyos*, उपधिवारिक a supervisor or director of monks in a monastery. A sort of provost-sergeant in the larger monasteries who keeps strict order and punishes transgressors. He is also called ཆོས་འཁྲིམས་པ *Chos-hkhrims-pa* in some monasteries. Rockhill calls this officer at Kumbum the Ge-kor.

Syn. ཙེ་རྒོད *tse-rgod* (*Mñon.*).

དགེ་རྒན *Dge-rgan* I: surety; moral bail; a monk that is made answerable for the moral conduct of another who is placed under his care (*Jä.*).

དགེ་རྒན II: lit. an old man of the religious order. དགེ་འདུན་རྒན་པ *dge-hdun rgan-pa* ordinarily signifies a schoolmaster, tutor: འཇིག་རྟེན་དགེ་རྒན་དང་ཆོས་དགེ་རྒན་གཉིས both the spiritual teacher and worldly teacher.

དགེ་རྒྱས *Dge-rgyas* n. of a celestial region (*B. ch.* 6); one of the *Rupa-dhātu* or worlds of form.

དགེ་རྒྱས་བྱེ་མ་གླིང་ *Dge-rgyas bye-ma gliñ* n. of a monastery near Sam-ye founded by *Hbroñ-za*, wife of King *Khri-soñ d:hu-btsan*.

དགེ་ངལ་བ *dge ñal-wa*=དགེ་སློང་ novice monk.

དགེ་བཅུ *dge-bcu*=དགེ་བ་བཅུ *dge-wa-bcu* the ten virtues, which are as follows:—(1) སྲོག་མི་གཅོད་པ *srog mi-gcod-pa*, (2) མ་བྱིན་པར་མི་ལེན་བ *ma-byin-par mi-len-pa*, (3) ཚངས་པར་སྤྱོད་པ *tshañs-par spyod-pa*, (4) བདེན་པར་སྨྲ་བ *bden-par smra-wa*, (5) ཚིག་འཇམ་པོར་སྨྲ་བ *tshig hjam-por smra-wa*, (6) ངག་མི་འཆལ་བ *ñag mi-hchal-wa*, (7) ཕྲ་མ་མི་བྱེད་པ *phra-ma mi-byed-pa*, (8) གཞན་གྱི་ནོར་ལ་ཧམ་པ་མི་བྱེད་པ *gshan-gyi nor-la ham-pa mi-byed-pa*, (9) གཞན་ལ་གནོད་པའི་སེམས་མི་བསྐྱེད་པ *gshan-la gnod-pahi sems mi-bskyed-pa*, (10) ཡང་དག་པའི་ལྟ་བ *yañ-dag-pahi lta-wa*. Those are: not taking life; not to take what is not given; to observe purity of morals; to speak the truth; to speak gently, politely; not to break a promise; not to speak slander; not to covet another's property; not to do mischief or think of doing injury to others; to regard the purest doctrine.

དགེ་ཆུ *dge-chu* sacred water.

དགེ་ཆུང་ *Dge-chuñ* one of the celestial regions.

དགེ་ཆེ་མེད་པ *dge-che med-pa* དོན་དག་ཆེན་པོ་མེད་པ *don-dag chen-po med-pa* without some important object or business: མགྱོགས་པར་དགེ་ཆེ་མེད་པས་སྐབས་དང་སྦྱོད if there be nothing very important to be done quickly, work according to circumstance (*D. çel. 7*).

དགེ་བསྙེན *Dge-bsñen* उपासक Buddhist devotee with only eight vows to observe.

དགེ་བསྙེན་ཆོས་འཕེལ *Dge-bsñen Chos-hphel* the original name of འབྲོམ་སྟོན་རྒྱལ་བའི་འབྱུང་གནས *Hbrom-tson Rgyai-wahi hbyañ-gnas* the founder of the Buddhist hierarchy of Tibet (*Grub.* ཀ 5).

དགེ་བསྙེན་མ *Dge-bsñen-ma* उपासिका a female Buddhist devotee.

* དགེ་བསྙེན་དྷརྨ *Dge-bsñen dharma*=ཆོས་སྐྱོབ *chos-skyob* (*Schr.*).

དགེ་བཏོན་རྐྱེན་གསང་ *dge-bton rkyen-gsañ*, དགེ་བཏོན་རྐྱེན་གསང་གི་མཐུན་འགྱུར་ལེགས་སྤེལ་བྱ་རྒྱུ་རྣམས་ཁྱེད་རང་ལ་བཀོད་མངགས་སྔོན་ཡོང་ལྟར *dge-bton rkyen gsañ-gi mthun-hgyur legs-spel bya-rgyu rnams-khyed-rañ la bkod-mñags sñon yoñ-ltar*.

དགེ་ལྟས *dge-ltas* propitious prognostic.

དགེ་འཐུད *dge-hthud*=དགེ་བ་འཐུད་པ *dge-wa hthud-pa* an uninterrupted payment of allowances or endowments attached to religious offices or institutions; a connected series of pious actions or works; also the performance of some religious observances by several persons one following another: དྲུང་འཁོར་དུ་ཡུན་རིང་བསྡད་པ་འཚོ་བར་དགེ་འཐུད་བབས་དང་། *druñ-hkhor-du yun-riñ bsdad-pa htsho-war dge-hthud babs dañ* the estimated permanent allowances to the *Druñ-hkhor* (civil employes) for food and lodging (*D. çel. 4*).

དགེ་དྲུང་ལྷ་ཁང་ *Dge-druñ lha-khañ* n. of a monastery in Tsang.

དགེ་འདུན *dge-hdun*, सङ्घ the third component of the Buddhist triad or དཀོན་མཆོག་གསུམ may be rendered as "the priesthood," "the assemblage," or "the church." The term *dge-hdun* is composed of two words, དགེ *dge* and འདུན *hdun*; འདུན *hdun* means འདོད་པ *hdod-pa* desire: དགེ་བ་དང་ཐར་པ་སྒྲུབ་པར་འདོད་པས་ན་དགེ་འདུན *dge-wa-dañ thar-pa sgrub-par hdod-pas na dge-hdun* he is དགེ་འདུན *dge-hdun* who longs for piety and emancipation: དགེ་འདུན་བཙུན་པ་རྣམས་བསན་དུ་གསོལ *dge-hdun btsun-pa rnams bsan-du gsol* I beg the venerable body of monks would hear me. In this sentence *dge-hdun* has the general meaning of an assembly of religious folk. There are in particular two kinds of དགེ་འདུན *dge-hdun*: སོ་སོར་སྐྱེ་བོའི་དགེ་འདུན *so-sor skyebohi dge-hdun* the ordinary clergy, and འཕགས་པའི་དགེ་འདུན *hphags-pahi dge-hdun* the sainted clergy. Four individuals of the former class collectively, *i.e.*, when they assemble together, form what is called *Saŋgha-ratna* དགེ་འདུན་དཀོན་མཆོག *dge-hdun dkon-mchog*. An individual of the latter class, *i.e.*, the sainted clergy, may singly form the *Saŋgha-ratna*. The *Saŋgha* of the Mahāyāna School differed from that of the Hīnayāna School. In the *Abhisamaya* of Maitreya, twenty classes of Saŋgha are enumerated as belonging to the Hīnayāna School. The S'rāvaka, Pratyeka Buddha, Bodhisattva and the Dharmapāla, who protect Buddhism, are also included in the *Saŋgha-ratna*. དགེ་འདུན་ལ་རག་ལུས་པ *dge-hdun-la rag-lus-pa* सङ्घाधीन belonging or subject to the church; དགེ་འདུན་ལ་རུང་བ *dge-hdun-la ruṅ-wa* सङ्घकल्प suitable for the use of the clergy.

དགེ་འདུན་སྐྱེས *dge-hdun skyes* = རི་ཤོ *ri-ço* 1. n. of a medicinal plant; གབ་མིང་ *gab-miṅ* (*Miṅ*) mystic. 2. n. of a lama.

དགེ་འདུན་གྱི་དུས *dge-hdun-gyi dus* हैमन्तिक belonging to the months following autumn when the lamas perform religious meditations, &c.

དགེ་འདུན་གྱི་སྡེ *dge-hdun-gyi sde* the clerical order or class of the clergy.

དགེ་འདུན་གྱི་དབེན་བྱེད་པ *dge-hdun-gyi dben byed-pa* सङ्घ-भेदक one who produces differences or disunion among the clergy; to produce such disunion.

དགེ་འདུན་རྒྱ་མཚོ *Dge-hdun Rgya-mtsho* n. of the Dalai Lama who died in 1851.

དགེ་འདུན་གྲུབ་པ *Dge-hdun grub-pa* the founder of the hierarchy of the Dalai Lama.

དགེ་འདུན་བསྡུ་བའི་ཕྱིར་ *dge-hdun bsdu-wah-phyir* for the purpose of assembling the clergy.

དགེ་འདུན་ཕལ་ཆེན་པ *dge-hdun phal-chen-pa* the clergy of the Mahāsaṅghika School.

* དགེ་འདུན་འཕེལ *dge-hdun hphel* संघवर्द्धन n. of a Buddhist saint; pr. (*Schr.; Tā. 278*).

* དགེ་འདུན་འབངས *Dge-hdun hbaṅs* संघदास n. pr. (*Sch.; Tā. 2, 127*).

* དགེ་འདུན་བསྲུང་བ *dge-hdun bsruṅ-wa* संघरक्षित n. of a Buddhist sage pr. (*Schr.; Tā. 2, 104*).

དགེ་ལྡན *dge-ldan* = དགེ་བ་ཅན *dge-wa can* possessed of virtue or of piety; pious.

དགེ་ལྡན་པ *Dge-ldan-pa* a name of the དགེ་ལུགས་པ *Dge-lugs-pa* sect of Lamas founded by Tsong-kha-pa.

དགེ་སྤྱོད *dge-spyod* religious acts; acc. to the *Bon-po* དགེ་སྤྱོད *dge-spyod* consists in erecting tombs, images, *caitya*, painting of holy personages and printing of the sacred texts, making moulds of images of gods and saints, uttering *mantras* and, generally, acquiring moral merits.

དགེ་ཕྲུག *dge-phrug* pupil-monk; young boy trained as a novice monk.

དགེ་བ་སྦྱོང་ *dge-wa sbyoṅ* or དགེ་སྦྱོང་ *dge-sbyoṅ* श्रमण a religious ascetic. In this term are included all those who have taken the vows of renouncement, *i.e.*, प्रव्रज्या; so both དགེ་ཚུལ *dge-tshul* and དགེ་སློང་ *dge-sloṅ* are within its signification; in the Southern School only the དགེ་སློང་ *dge-sloṅ*, *i.e.*, the Bhikshu, can have claim to this title provided they live in conformity with the rules of the *Vinaya*. The qualifications of a *dge-sbyoṅ* are the following:—དུལ་པ་དང་ *dul-pa dań* moral discipline; ཅང་ཤེས་པ་དང་ *cań çes-pa dań* wisdom; ཚུལ་ཁྲིམས་ཀྱི་ཕུང་པོ་ཡོངས་སུ་དག་པ་དང་ *tshul-khrims kyi phuń-po yońs-su dag-pa dań* purity of morals; ཉིང་ངེ་འཛིན་ལ་འཇུག་པ་ཤེས་པ *ńe hdsin-la hjug-pa çes-pa* knowing to perform *Samādhi* or meditation.

དགེ་བ་སྦྱོམ་པ *dge-wa sbyom-pa*, explained as དགེ་བ་བྱས་པ་དོན་མེད་པར་གཞན་ལ་སྒྲོགས *dge-wa byas-pa don-med-par gshan-la sgrog-pa*, to trumpet or advertize one's acts of charity; དགེ་བ་མི་སྦྱོམས་པ *dge-wa mi-sbyoms-pa* प्रतिच्छन्नकल्याण to do virtue secretly, *i.e.*, without any fuss or trumpeting or advertizement.

དགེ་བའི་བདག་ཉིད *dge-wahi dag-ñid* भाग्य fortune; good luck.

དགེ་བའི་གནས *dge-wahi-gnas* a place of piety; a pious man.

དགེ་བའི་དབང་པོ *dge-wahi dbań-po*, སྙན་ངག་མངོན་བརྗོད་སྡེབ་སྦྱོར་གསུམ་ལ་མཁས་པ *sñan-ńag mńon-brjod sdeb-sbyor gsum-la mkhas-pa* one versed in poetry, *Abhidhāna*, and in rhetoric like the great poet Kshemendra of Kashmir.

དགེ་བའི་རྩ་བ་བསྐྲུན་པའི་བསྐྱེད་པ *dge-wahi rtsa-wa bskrun-pahi bskyed-pa* अवरोपितकुशलमूल one who has done some religious acts.

དགེ་བའི་ལས *dge-wahi las* कुशल-कर्म्म good actions.

དགེ་བའི་བཤེས་གཉེན་མགུ་བར་བྱ་བ *dge-wahi bçes-gñen mgu-war bya-wa* कल्याणमित्राराधना paying reverence, &c., to please a *Kalyāṇamitra* (a Buddhist monk-scholar).

དགེ་བར་གྱུར་ཅིག *dge-war gyur-cig* शुभमस्तु good luck to you.

དགེ་བྲལ *dge-bral* अपसम्पत् devoid of virtue or piety.

དགེ་སྦྱོང་ཆེན་པོ *Dge-sbyoń chen-po* महाश्रमण an epithet of Buddha; དགེ་སྦྱོང་ལྟར་བཅོས་པ *dge-sbyoń ltar bcos-pa* श्रमणप्रतिरूपक in the manner of a religious ascetic.

དགེ་སྦྱོང་དུ་ཁས་འཆེ་བ *dge-sbyoń-du khas-hche-wa* श्रमण-प्रतिज्ञ one who has avowed to betake to the life of a *dge-sbyoń* or *Çramaṇa*.

དགེ་སྦྱོང་བྱེད་པ *dge-sbyoń byed-pa* श्रमण-कारका the performance of asceticism in the manner of a Buddhist *Çramaṇa*: དགེ་སྦྱོང་བྱེད་པའི་ཆོས་བཞི *dge-sbyoń byed-pahi chos-bshi* चत्वारः श्रमणकारका धर्म्माः, the four duties of a true *Çramaṇa*, which are as follows:—(1) གཤེའང་སླར་མི་གཤེ་བར་བྱ *gçehań-slar mi-gçe war bya* आक्रुष्टस्य प्रत्याक्रोष्टव्यम् do not curse others though you have been abused by them; (2) ཁྲོས་ཀྱང་སླར་མ་ཁྲོ་བར་བྱ *khros-kyań slar-ma khro-war-bya* रोषितस्यप्रतिरोषितव्यम् do not be angry with others though you have been enraged by them; (3) མཚང་བྲུས་ཀྱང་སླར་མི་བྲུ་བར་བྱ *mtshań-brus kyań slar-mi bru-war-bya* भण्डितस्यप्रतिभण्डितव्यम्। do not commit injury to others though you have been injured by them; (4) བརྡེག་ཀྱང་སླར་མི་བརྡེག་པར་བྱ *brdeg-kyań slar mi-brdeg-par bya* ताडितस्य प्रतिताडितव्यम् do not beat others though you have been beaten by them.

དགེ་སྦྱོང་མ་ཡིན་པར *dge-sbyoń ma-yin-par* अश्रमण not being a *Çramaṇa*.

དགེ་སྦྱོར *dge-sbyor* ཆོས་དགེ་ལས་བྱེད་པ *chos dge-las byed-pa* one who has attained to a stage of holiness by religious devotion and works: མཚན་དུས་དགེ་སྦྱོར་གྱི་རྒྱུན་ལ་ཅུང་ཟད་གནས་པའི་ཚེ *mtshan-dus dge-sbyor-gyi rgyun-la cuń-zad gnas-pahi tshe* at night when he was absorbed in the state of pious devotion (*Ya-sel. 11*).

དགེ་མ *dge-ma*=བཙུན་མ *btsun-ma* 1. a Buddhist nun. 2. शान्ति peace.

དགེ་ཚུལ *Dge-tshul* श्रामणेर generally a novice-monk; the first stage of a monk after he has taken the vow of *Pravrajyā* or renunciation, when he has to observe.

thirty-six vows before he is qualified to be ordained as a དགེ་སློང་ *Dge-sloṅ*; as long as he is not admitted into the latter order he will continue as a *Çamaṇera* though even to eighty years old.

དགེ་ཚུལ་མ *Dge-tshul-ma* श्रमणेरिका a nun young or old that has not yet taken the vows of ordination belonging to the order of *Bhikṣuṇī*.

དགེ་མཚན *dge-mtshan* कुमललचण, कौतूहल lucky omen; also entertainment, amusement or amusing; དགེ་མཚན་ཅན *dge-mtshan-can* सकुन्य bearing lucky marks.

དགེ་གཞོན *Dge-gshon* a young student who is studying under a tutor called དགེ་རྒན *dge-rgyan*, who is responsible for his education, behaviour and moral training. He is required to attend, when necessary, his monk-tutor as a servant. When he is very young he is called དགེ་ཕྲུག *dge-phrug*.

དགེ་གཡོག *Dge-gyog* boy or youth attending upon a monk and who works with a view himself to enter the holy order. When he has passed the prescribed examinations for admission, he gets the position of a དགེ་གཞོན *Dge-gshon*.

དགེ་ལུགས་པ I: *Dge-lugs-pa.* Tsong-kha-pa founded the monastery of དགའ་ལྡན་རྣམ་པར་རྒྱལ་བའི་གླིང་ *Dgah-ldan rnam-par rgyal-wahi gliṅ*, situated on the hill called འབྲོག་རི་བོ་ཆེ *Hbrog-ri-bo che*, and resided there during the last part of his life. His school was called ཆོས་རྗེ་དགའ་ལྡན་པའི་ལུགས *chos-rje Dgah-ldan-pahi lugs* and vulgarly དགའ་ལྡན་པའི་ལུགས *Dgah-ldan-pahi-lugs* or དགའ་ལྡན་ལུགས་པ *Dgah-ldan lugs-pa*, which term has assumed the form དགེ་ལུགས་པ *Dge-lugs-pa* (*Grub. 3 1*).

དགེ་ལུགས་པ II: *Dge-lugs-pa* one belonging to the sect of *Dgah-ldan-pa* founded by Tsong-kha-pa.

དགེ་ལེགས *dge-legs* or དགེ་བ *dge-wa* श्रेयस्, शुभ, कल्याण piety; good and auspicious action.

Syn. བདེ་ལེགས *bde-legs*; ཞི་བ *shi-wa*; མྱང་འདས *myaṅ-hdas*; རེ་སྐོང་ *re-skoṅ*; གནམ་བསྐྲོས *gnam-bskros*; སྔོན་བསགས་མཐུ *sṅon-bsags-mthu*; ཁ་རྗེ *kha-rje*; རབ་བསྔགས *rab-bsṅags*; སྐལ་བའི་ཕུལ *skal-wahi phul*; བསྔགས་ཧོས *bsṅags-hos*; ཡིད་བཞིན་འགྲུབ *yid bshin-hgrub*; བདེ་བའི་འབྱུང་གནས *bde-wahi hbyuṅ-gnas*; རབ་ཞི *rab-shi*; ལེགས་ལྡན *legs-ldan*; ཧུན་ཚོགས *hun-tshogs* (*Mṅon.*).

དགེ་ལེགས་ཅན *dge-legs-can* श्रेयसी blessed; glorious.

* དགེ་ལེགས་དཔལ་བཟང་ *Dge-legs dpal-bzaṅ* = མཁས་གྲུབ་རྗེ *Mkhas-grub rje* (*Schr.; Org. 105, 5*).

* དགེ་ལེགས་བཤེས་གཉེན *Dge-legs bçes-gñen* कल्याणमित्र (*Schr.; Tā. 2, 211*) a good counsellor; a pious Buddhist monk.

དགེ་ཤིས *dge-çis* प्रशस्त; དགེ་བ་དང་ཤིས་པ *dge-wa daṅ çis-pa* piety and blessedness.

དགེ་བཤེས *Dge-bçes* कल्याणमित्र a contraction of དགེ་བའི་བཤེས་གཉེན *dge-wahi bçes-gñen*, a Buddhist gelong who has mastered metaphysics and the important branches of sacred literature. Monks, also, who have got the titles of རབ་འབྱམས་པ *Rab-hbyams-pa*, རྡོ་རམས་པ *Rdo-rams-pa*, &c., are by courtesy addressed with the title of དགེ་བཤེས *Dge-bçes* कल्याणमित्र; others who lead a pure life and are possessed of learning and good character are also generally addressed as དགེ་བཤེས *Dge-bçes*, *i.e.*, དགེ་བའི་བཤེས་གཉེན *Dge-wahi bçes-gñen*.

* དགེ་སྲུང་ I: *dge-sruṅ* कल्याणगुप्त n. pr. (*Schr.; Tā. 2, 219*).

* དགེ་སྲུང་ II: कुमलरचित (*Schr.; Bull. 1848, 292*).

དགེ་སློང་ *Dge-sloṅ* श्रीघन, भिक्षु, a Buddhist monk who after finishing his probationary period in a monastery has been ordained into the highest order. He has to observe 253 vows. དགེ་སློང་ལ་དོན་དམ་པའི་དགེ་སློང་དང་ཀུན་རྫོབ་པའི་དགེ་སློང་གཉིས་ཡོད་ among *gelong* there are two classes: *para mârtha Bhikṣu* and *Samvṛti Bhikṣu*. The following seven, *i.e.*, Buddha and *Bodhisattva*, *Pratyeka Buddha*, *Arhats*, such saints as on account of their pious acts will not be born again or will be born only once, those who have attained to the stage of *Srotāpanna*, *i.e.*, gone on the path of *Nirvāṇa*, belong to the higher class or *Paramārtha Bhikṣu*. These or some of these while even they reside in human habitation, being possessed of divine knowledge and wisdom, continue in the class of *Paramārtha Bhikṣu*. Ordinary gelong or *Bhikṣu*, such as wear the yellow garments, have shaven their heads and betaken to the life of *Pravrajya* or renunciation of all worldly concerns, and observe the vow belonging to the order, are called *Samvṛti Bhikṣu*.

དགེ་སློང་དུ་མི་རུང་བ *dge-sloṅ-du mi-ruṅ-wa*, དགེ་སློང་མ་ཡིན་པ *dge-sloṅ ma-yin-pa* अभिक्षु one unworthy the position of a gelong.

དགེ་སློང་མ *Dge-sloṅ-ma* भिक्षुणी an ordained nun; she has 364 vows or restrictions to observe; དགེ་སློང་མ་སུན་ཕྱུང་བ *dge-sloṅ-ma sun-phyuṅ-wa* भिक्षुणीदूषक one who finds fault with or slanders a Buddhist nun.

དགེ་སློང་ཤིང་ *dge-sloṅ-çiṅ* acc. to *Jä.* is a provincial name for the (*Cedrus deodara*) *Deodar* tree.

དགེ་སློབ་མ *Dge-slob-ma* शिक्षमाणा a pupil monk; one who is preparing himself for being admitted into the higher order.

དགེང་ལ *dgeṅ-la*, more properly དགང་ལ *dgaṅ-la* on; upon; in; at (in *Ts.*, *Jä.*).

དགེར་བ *dger-wa*=གཡོ་བ *gyo-wa* to parch or fry (food); འབྲང་བ་དགེར་བ to fry pastry.

དགེར་འབད *dger-ḥbad*=དགེ་བ་ལ་འབད *dge-wa la-ḥbad* to exert one's self in acts of piety; a pious man.

དགེས་པ *dges-pa*=དགྱེས་པ *dgyes-pa* or མཉེས་པ *mñes-pa* or དགའ་བ *dgaḥ-wa* delighted, pleased or cheered.

དགེས་པ་རྡོ་རྗེ *Dges-pa Rdo-rje*, also written as དགྱེས་པ་རྡོ་རྗེ *Dgyes-pa Rdo-rje*, name of the *Tantrik* deity ཧེ་བཛྲ *He-vajra*: རྣལ་འབྱོར་གྱི་དབང་ཕྱུག་དགེས་པ་རྡོ་རྗེ་ཞལ་གཟིགས་པ *rnal-ḥbyor-gyi dwaṅ-phyug dges-pa Rdo-rje shal-gzigs-pa* he saw (miraculously) the face of the deity *Dges-pa Rdo-rje*, the Chief of the Nal-jor (*A. 28*).

དགོ་བ *dgo-wa* a species of antelope living on high mountains, *Procapra picticaudata* (Hodgson); colloq. "*go-â*" Mongol; *gura*. དགོ་བ་མ *dgo-wa-ma*, female of the above (*Cs.*): དགོ་བའི་རྭའི་འབྲུ་བ་གཅོད *dgo-wohi rba-hi hkhru-wa gcod* the horn of the *go-â* taken as medicine cures diarrhœa.

+ དགོག་དུ་ཕྱིན་པ *dgog-du phyin-pa* 1. पर्य-तुषाय to become aged. 2. acc. *Lex.* སྐོག་ཏུ་ཕྱིན་པ *lkog-tu phyin-pa*.

Syn. རྒས་པ *rgas-pa* (*Mṅon.*).

དགོག་པ *dgog-pa* abstraction: དགོག་པའི་སྙོམས་འཇུག་ཅེས་པ *dgog-pahi sñoms-ḥjug ces-pa* sat perfectly abstracted, being absorbed in meditation on the emptiness of all worldly things.

དགོང་རྒྱུ *dgoṅ-rgyu* मत्यं, मतं opinion.

དགོང་མོ *dgoṅ-mo* or དགོངས་མོ *dgoṅs-mo* सन्ध्या, सन्धि the evening; the junction of the day and the night; ཕྱི་དྲོ་ཉིན་མོའི་མཐའ *phyi-dro ñin-moḥi mthaḥ* the evening which is the end of the day (*Rtsii.*); དགོང་ཇ *dgoṅ-ja* evening tea; དགོང་ཤོག *dgoṅ-shog* evening and morning.

དགོངས་སྐོར *dgoṅs-skor* leave in general; also leave (from a superior official); suing somebody in a court to do him harm.

དགོངས་འགལ་མེད་པ *dgoṅs-ḥgal med-pa* = ཐུགས་ཁྲོ་བ་མེད་པ *thugs khro-wa med-pa* without incurring displeasure, or displeasing.

དགོངས་བཅད *dgoṅs-bcad* judgment; decision on any case or law-suit.

དགོངས་པ *dgoṅs-pa* I: 1. vb. to think, reflect, meditate, consider: 2. sbst. the act of thinking, reflection, cogitation. ཐུགས་དགོངས *thugs-dgoṅs* = ཐུགས་འདོད wish, consideration; མཉམ་པ་ཉིད་ལ་དགོངས་པ *mñam-pa ñid la dgoṅs-pa* to take one as his equal or as a match for him; དུས་གཞན་ལ་དགོངས་པ to think of or at other times; གང་ཟག་གཞན་ལ་དགོངས་པ to think of another person; དོན་གཞན་ལ་དགོངས་པ to reflect on some other object or business; དགོངས་པ་ཁྲེལ་བ *dgoṅs-pa khrel-wa* resp. ཁོང་ཁྲོ་ཟ་བ *khoṅ-khro za-wa* to become angry; to take offence; བཀའ་ལས་ནམ་ཡང་མི་འདའ་ཞིང་དགོངས་པ་ཁྲེལ་བ *bkaḥ-las nam-yaṅ mi ḥdaḥ-shiṅ dgoṅs-pa khrel-wa* never to be disobedient and to be angry (*Ya-sel. 16*): དགོངས་ཕྱོགས་མ་ལོག་ན *dgoṅs-phyogs ma-log-na* if his opinion does not change.

དགོངས་པ II: अभिप्राय् vb. to purpose, intend; usually with termin. of the inf. འཐབ་པར་དགོངས་སོ intended to fight.

དགོངས་ཕྱོགས་རི *dgoṅs phyogs-ri* to be partial; to act with partiality.

དགོངས་མོ *dgoṅs-mo* = དགོང་མོ *dgoṅ-mo* रात्रि night.

དགོངས་འབྲེལ *dgoṅs-ḥbrel* वृत्ति, टीका commentary.

དགོངས་ཞུ *dgoṅs-shu* to ask for leave or permission to do any thing.

དགོངས་ཟབ *dgoṅs-zab* serious consideration; as very important.

དགོད་པ I: *dgod-pa*, pr. tense, हसन, हास to laugh; laughter.

དགོད་པ II: a jest; joke (*Sch.*); cf. བགད་པ *bgad-pa*; བདེ་བ་ལ་དགོད་ཀྱིན་འདུག *bde-wa la dgod-kyin ḥdug* laughing, being in happiness; གད་མོ་དགོད་ཀྱིན་འདུག *gad-mo dgod-kyin ḥdug* laughing a loud laughter.

དགོད་ཡས *dgod-yas* (གྲངས *grañs*) खवर n. of a very large number.

དགོད་ར *dgod-ra* "དགོད་ར་ལ་འཁོར་རྣམས་མ་འཚམས་པར་རྩོད་ཅིང་ *dgod-ra-la ḥkhor rnams ma ḥtsham-par rtsod-ciṅ* (*Yig. 28*).

+ **དགོན་དུང** *dgon-duṅ* ཆུ་མེད་པའི་ས་ཕྱོགས *chu-med-paḥi sa-phyogs* a desert; a desolate wilderness where there is no water.

དགོན་པ *dgon-pa* (pr. "*gom-pa*") or དགོན *dgon* अरण्य, कान्तार, जटी 1. wilderness; solitary place, waved-leaf fig-tree. Hence 2. a *vihāra*; a monastery, a hermitage, so called on account of its original situation in earlier times in lonely places abounding in *Bodhi* trees. A *gŏm-pa* should be situated at least a thousand yards distant from a village or town (*K. du.* ཅ, *304*). Later on these hermitages became converted into monasteries. Monasteries in later times assumed the size of large castles and collections of dwelling houses.

Syn. ཆོས་ཀྱི་འདུན་ས *chos-kyi ḥdun-sa*; ཆོས་ཀྱི་ཚོང་བརྡལ *chos-kyi tshoṅ-brdal*; ཀློག་གྲྭའི་གནས *klog-grbaḥi-gnas*; མཁས་པའི་འབྱུང་གནས *mkhas-paḥi hbyuṅ-gnas*; ཆོས་ཀྱི་ཕུར་བུ *chos-kyi phur-bu*; འདུལ་བའི་གནས *hdul-wahi-gnas* (*Mṅon.*).

དགོན་པ་པ *dgon-pa-pa* आरण्यक one residing in the wilderness, or in a hermitage or *gömpa*; དགོན་པ་མ *dgon-pa-ma* a female of the above.

དགོན་གཞི *dgon-gshi* landed endowments of a monastery; an estate belonging to a monastery for the support of its monks.

དགོལ *dgol* (prob. for དགྲོལ *dgrol*) སྣ་རེ་བསྡུས་ཀྱང་སྣ་རེ་དགོལ *sna-re bsdus kyaṅ sna-re dgol* when some are collected, others disperse.

དགོས་ངེས *dgos-ṅes* urgent necessity; urgently needed.

དགོས་ཆ *dgos-cha* necessary objects; indispensables.

དགོས་འདོད 1. *dgos-hdod* necessary expenses; what is wished for as very necessary (*Cs.*). 2. དགོས་འདོད wishes and wants: དགོས་འདོད་འབྱུང་བའི་དཔལ *dgos-hdod hbyuṅ-wahi dpal* a treasure out of which all wishes and wants are met.

དགོས་པ I: *dgos-pa* (*goi-pa*) प्रयोजन, अर्थ, समायोगि implies necessity and what is due or desired; to be necessary; to be obliged or compelled; to want; to stand in need of; also where we use 'ought' *dgos* is generally used added to the verbal root, *e.g.*, ཟ་དགོས, must eat: ང་ལ་དགོས *ṅa-la dgos* I want; I stand in need of: ཅི་ཞིག་ཏུ་དགོས *ci-shig-tu dgos* for what purpose did he want them? བཞེངས་མ་དགོས *bsheṅs-ma-dgos* he was not obliged to erect. In commanding, the word is used to paraphrase the imperative of a verb: ཧོང་བར་དགོས *hoṅ-war gdos* come! *i.e.*, you must come. In entreating, the respectful term is chosen: འབྱོང་དགོས *hbyoṅ-dgos* should practise good works: ང་ལ་གཡུ་དགོས་པ་མེད *ṅa-la gyu dgos-pa med* I have no use for the turquoise, I do not want it.

དགོས་པ II: necessary; due; needful; useful; མེད་ཀྱང་དགོས་པའི་ཁྲལ་བསྡུད *med-kyaṅ dgos-pahi khral bsdud* a tax necessary to be paid; unrelentingly exacted: རང་ལ་དགོས་པའི་སྐལ་བ the portion due to you: དགོས་པ་ཅིའི་ཕྱིར for what purpose? དགོས་པ་ཆུང་བའི being of little use; དགོས་པ་མེད *dgos-pa-med* not necessary: དགོས་པ་ཡིན *dgos-pa-yin* it is requisite; མི་དགོས་པ *mi-dgos-pa* useless; unnecessary; མི་དགོས་པའི་ཕྲ་མེན *mi-dgos-pahi phra-men* pernicious witch-craft; དགོས་པའི་བསླབ་བྱ *dgos-pahi bslab-bya* useful doctrines; དགོས་བྱེད *dgos-byed* useful: དོན་དགོས་བྱེད་ཅི་འདུག *don-dgos-byed ci-hdug* what is there in it of useful contents.

དགྱེ་དགྱེ *dgye-dgye*=མགོ་རྒྱབ་ཕྱོགས་སུ་དགྱེ་བ *mgo-rgyab-phyogs-su dgye-wa* to bend the head backwards.

དགྱེ་བ *dgye-wa* to bend; to be curving or crooked; དབྱིབས་དགྱེ་བ *dbyibs dgye-wa* stooping; cringing; writhing: མ་སྡོད་རྒྱབ་ཕྱོགས་སུ་དགྱེ་བ *ma-sdod rgyab phyogs-su dgye-wa* don't wait, turn and go away: དགྱེ་དགྱེ་བའི་བྲང་མ་སྟོན *dgye-dgye-wahi braṅ-ma-ston* do not stretch or heave up the breast by bending or stooping backwards. དགུར་དགུར་གྱི་ཕྱག་འཚལ *dgur dgur-gyi phyag htshal* salutation by bending the head low.

དགྱེ་བོ *dgye-wo* वङ्किःकुब्ज a bent man.

དགྱེར་བ *dgyer-wa* or གླུ་དགྱེར་བ *glu dgyer-wa* for གླུ་ལེན་པ *glu len-pa* to sing, chant; an expression of the Bon-po.

དགྱེལ་བ *dgyel-wa* or སྒྱེལ་བ *sgyel-wa* to fall down, tumble down.

དགྱེས་པ *dgyes-pa* (*ge-pa*) (elegant term) དགའ་བ *dgah-wa* सन्तुष्ट 1. to rejoice; to be glad; also cheerfulness: ཐུགས་དགྱེས་པ *thugs-ḏgyeş-pa* the heart cheered: རྗེ་བཙུན་བླ་མ་དགྱེས་པའི་འཛུམ་དཀར་ཅན *rje-ḇtsun Ḇla-ma dgyeş-paẖi ẖdsum-ḏkar-can* the reverend lama smiled with cheerfulness. 2. to be pleased to; to choose: ཇོ་བོ་འགྲོན་པ་ལ་ཐུགས་དགྱེས་པར་འདུག the Lord in walking is pleased, *i.e.*, likes to walk. མི་དགྱེས་ཏེ *mi-ḏgyeş-te* sorrowful, sad, discomfited, dejected; angry, indignant.

དགྱེས་པ་རྡོ་རྗེ *Ḏgyeş-pa Ṟdo-ṟje* the *Tantrik* god called Hē Vajra; his other names are:—དཔལ་ལྡན་ཁྲག་འཐུང་ཧེ་རུ་ཀ *Ḏpal-ḻdan khṟag ẖthuñ he-ra-ka*; དཔྱིད་རྡོ་རྗེ *Ḏpyiḏ Ṟdo-rje*; རྡོ་རྗེ་གྲི་གུག *Ṟdo-ṟje gri-gug*; རོལ་པའི་རྡོ་རྗེ *Rol-paẖi Ṟdo-ṟje*; ཀྱེ་རྡོ་རྗེ *Kye Ṟdo-ṟje* (*Mñon.*).

* དགྱེས་པའི་རྡོ་རྗེ་རྒྱན་གྱི་སྙིང་པོ *dgyeş-paẖi ṟdo-ṟje ṟgyan-kyi şñiñ-po* **हेवज्रतन्त्र** (*Schr.; Tā. 2, 192, 275*) n. of a *Tantra* work.

དགྱེས་ཞལ *dgyeş-shal* cheerful countenance: མྱུར་བར་དགྱེས་ཞལ་དངོས་མཇལ་ཞུ་ཆོག་པ *myur-war dgyeş shal ḏños-ṃjal shu chog-pa* may soon be permitted to have an interview; may meet or see your cheerful countenance soon.

དགྱེས་སུ་འཇུག་པ *dgyeş-su ẖjug-pa* to bend; to double down (*Sch.*), v. དགྱེ་བ *ḏge-wa*.

དགྲ *dgra* (*ḏa*) also དགྲ་བོ *ḏgra-wo* **शत्रु, दस्यु, द्विट्, कैतव, अरि, दुष्ट, रिपु, प्रत्यमित्र** enemy; foe; འཆི་དགྲ *ẖchi-ḏgra* mortal enemy; སྡང་བའི་དགྲ *şdañ-waẖi-ḏgra* the hating enemy, opp. བྱམས་པའི་གཉེན *byams-paẖi-gñen*, the loving friend; ད་དགྲ *da-ḏgra* or ད་ལྟའི་དགྲ *da-ḻtaẖi ḏgra* present enemy; སྔ་དགྲ *şña-ḏgra* former enemy; ཕྱི་དགྲ *phyi-ḏgra* a future foe; more properly the outer enemy, *i.e.*, an ordinary enemy, not the inner foe; also a foreign enemy.

Syn. སྡང་བྱེད *şdañ-byeḏ*; འཁོན་འཛིན *ẖkhon-ẖdsin*; བཤེས་མི་བྱེད *ḇçeş mi-byeḏ*; མཛའ་བྲལ *ṃdsaẖ bral*; མཛའ་མེད *ṃdsaẖ-meḏ*; ཕ་རོལ་པོ *pha-rol-po*; ཕྱིར་རྒོལ *phyir-ṟgol*; ཕས་ཀྱི་རྒོལ་བ *phaş-kyi ṟgol wa*; དགྲ་ཟླ *ḏgṟa-zla*; འགྲན་ཟླ *ẖgran-zla*; འཁུ་བྱེད *ẖkhu-byeḏ* (*Mñon.*).

དགྲ་ཁང *dgra-khañ* an enemy's house or camp.

དགྲ་གང *ḏgra-gañ*=བ་གམ *wa-gam* **अट्टाल; हर्म्य** a dome, a turret built on the top of a castle.

དགྲ་ངན *Ḏgra-ñan* **दुर्योधन** bad or ungenerous enemy; a name of the king of the Kaurava, son of Dhṛtarāṣṭra.

དགྲ་བཅོམ་པ *Ḏgṟa-ḇcom-pa* **अर्हत, अर्हन्, वड्वम**; དགྲ་བཅོམ་ཚར་བ *dgra-ḇcom tshar-wa* one who has subdued his enemy; one who has subdued his inner enemy (that brings on sufferings) and by practising religion becomes an *Arhat* of the Mahāyāna School. The *Arhat* of the Mahāyāna School is he who has attained to the first stage of *Bodhisattva* perfections. An *Arhat* of the *Tantrik* School is one who has attained to the fourth order in the five orders of the *Tantrik* School, *i.e.*, རྫོགས་རིམ་གྱི་རིམ་པ་བཞི་པ *ṟdsogş rim-gyi rim-pa ḇshi-pa*.

དགྲ་བཅོམ་པ་གསོད་པ *Ḏgra-ḇcom-pa gsoḏ-pa* **अर्हद्-घात** killing of an *Arhat* or Buddhist saint.

དགྲ་ཆས *dgra-chaş* the equipments of war; weapons; arms.

དགྲ་འཇོམས *dgra-ẖjomş* **रिपुवराघात** one who has subdued his enemy; subduing the enemy.

དགྲ་འཇོམས་པ *dgra ẖjomş-pa* **अरिहनक, अरिघातक** killer or subduer of one's enemy.

* དགྲ་ཉམས *dgra-ñamş* **शत्रोर्नाश** (*Schr.; Kā-lac. T. 110*) destruction of the enemy.

དགྲ་ཉམས་པར་གྱུར་ཅིག *dgra ñamş-par gyur-cig* **मत्रुहन** (let the enemy be destroyed or injuriously dealt with).

དགྲ་བོ་ *dgra-bo* (*da-o*) enemy: "གང་ཞིག་དགྲ་བོ་དག་ལ་ཡང་, གཡོ་མེད་སེམས་ཀྱིས་ཕན་བྱེད་པ, དེ་ལ་དགྲ་བོ་ཐམས་ཅད་ཀྱང་, ཕྱལ་མོ་བྱེད་པ་ཉིད་དུ་བྱེད to whatever enemy one does good with an unruffled mind, even to him all the enemies also will show reverence.

དགྲ་ལྷ *dgra-lha* the war-god.

དགྲ་ལྷ་དཔང་བསྟོད *dgra-lha dpań-bstod* hymns to the war-god; religious service for the war-god.

དགྲ་སྟ *dgra-sta* परशु an axe the blade of which is semi-circular; a sector-like disk; a weapon of war.

Syn. སྟ་རེ *sta-re*; དགྲ་སྟ *dgra-sta*; ཐོ་བ *tho-wa* (*Mńon.*).

དགྲ་སྟ་ཅན *dgra-sta-can* कराल, खड्ग, परशुधर frightful.

དགྲ་སྟ་བ *dgra-sta-wa* पारश्वधिक one who holds the axe (such as Paras'urāma).

དགྲ་དག་པ *dgra-dag-pa* निर्यातन giving pains; taking vengeance on an enemy.

དགྲ་རྡེལ *dgra-rdel* (*Rtsii. 51.*).

དགྲ་འདུལ་བ *dgra hdul-wa* अरिन्दम to subdue an enemy.

དགྲ་བོ་གདུང་བ *dgra-wo gduń-wa* शत्रुन्तप, द्विषन्तप one who has destroyed his enemy; lit. foe-paining.

དགྲ་བྱེད་པ *dgra-byed-pa*, དགྲ་རུ་ལྡང་བ *dgra ldań-wa*, ལང་བ *lań-wa* to act in a hostile manner.

དགྲ་ཟོན *dgra-zon* always on guard; careful.

དགྲ་ཟླ *dgra-zla* (དགྲ་བོའི་ཟླ་བོ *dgra-bohi zla bo*) प्रतिद्वन्द्विन् rival; opponent; adversary.

* དགྲ་ཡི་ཁྱིམ *dgra-yi khyim* शत्रुवेश्म, रिपुभवन (*Schr.; Kālāc. T. 137*) the enemy's house.

དགྲ་ལས་རྒྱལ་བ *dgra-las rgyal-wa* जितारि, शत्रुञ्जय triumphant over an enemy.

དགྲ་ཤགས *dgoa-çags* a substitute in cattle supplied for killing another's horse, yak or sheep, etc.: དགྲ་ཤགས་ཕན་མ་ཐུབ་ན་མིང་ངང་མ་འདོད་ཅེས if you cannot give a substitute do not call me by my name.

དགྲ་སློང་བ *dgra sloń-wa* to search for one's enemy.

དགྲ་གསོད་དཔའ་བོ་དཀར་པོ *dgra-gsod dpah-wo dkar-po* = ག་བུར *ga-bur* कर्पूर camphor (*Sman. 107*).

དགྲད་པ *dgrad-pa* (*da-pa*) विस्तृत spread.

དགྲན་ཟླ *dgran-zla* (*dan-da*) = དགྲ་བོ *dgra-bo* or དགྲ་ཟླ *dgra-zla* enemy; adversary; rival; foe (*Mńon.*).

དགྲམ་པ *dgram-pa* (*dam-pa*) fut. of འགྲེམ་པ *hgrem-pa* མེ་ཏོག་དགྲམ་པ *me-tog dgram-pa* अवकीर्ण, flowers to be strewn; དགྲམས *dgrams* that which is to be arranged or set out.

དགྲར་སེམས་པ་འཛིན་པ *dgrar sems-pa hdsin-pa* to look upon one as an enemy.

དགྲོང་པ *dgroń-pa* resp. of ཤི་བ *çi-wa* to die; *da dgroń-gin hdug* now he is dying.

དགྲོལ་བ *dgrol-wa*, fut. of འགྲོལ་བ *hgrol-wa* मोचन, छन्दः, to set free; also free-will; བཅིངས་པ་དགྲོལ *bcińs-dgrol* a knot or tie loosened.

བགག་པ *bgag-pa* pf. tense of འགེགས་པ *hgegs-pa*, བཀག་པ་སུ་གྱུར་པའི་(ཆ་བཤག་པ)རག་ལུས་པ *bgags-su gyur-pahi* (*cha bshaj-pa*) *rag lus-pa* settled or decided upon obstructing or hindering, opposing, etc.; ལམ་སོགས་བཀགས་པ *lam-sogs bgags-pa* प्रतिबन्ध obstructed the road.

བགད་པ *bgad-pa* to laugh; a laugh; བགད་མོ་བགད་པ *bgad-mo bgad-pa* id. cf. དགོད *dgod*; བཞད་གད *bshad-gad* आवहासि a smile; laughter.

卐 བགམ་པ *bgam-pa* to eat; to gobble; to throw into the mouth.

བགེགས I: *bgegs* གེགས *gegs* a demon. བགེགས་ལ་གང་ཟག་དང་གང་ཟག་མ་ཡིན་པ་གཉིས་ཡོད *bgegs-la gaṅ-zag daṅ-gaṅ zag-ma yin-pa gñis-yod* the *bgegs* are of two classes, those mortal and those spirit-like; these cause hinderance, obstruction. བགེགས་ཀྱི་རྒྱལ་པོ *bgegs-kyi rgyal-po* བི་ནཱ་ཡ་ཀ *vi-nā-ya-ka*, Ganes'a, the remover of obstacles, the leader of the *Gaṇa*—class of demons.

བགེགས II: विबन्ध, विघ्न hinderance; obstacle; བགེགས་ཀྱི་རྒྱལ་པོ *bgegs-kyi rgyal-po* विघ्नराज is the chief of the evil spirits who are of 80,000 different kinds. Some cause heavy rains, hail storms, etc., to injure the crops; some bring on famine and so on.

བགེགས་ཀྱི་བདག་མོ *bgegs-kyi bdag-mo* शङ्करी a goddess.

བགེགས་བག་པ *bgegs bag-pa* གནོད་པའི་འདྲེས་སྒྲིབ་པ་ལ *gnod-pahi hdres sgrib-pa-la* འདི་ལོ་བགེགས་བག་པ་མིན་ན་ཆུང་བའི་འཇམ་པ་ཙམ་འདུག་རུང་ *bdi-lo bgegs bag-pa min-na chuṅ-wahi hjam-pa tsam-hdug-ruṅ* (*Rtsii.*).

བགེགས་བྱེད་པ *bgegs byed-pa* प्रतिबन्ध, विघ्नकर that which causes obstruction; to cause obstruction.

བགེགས་སེལ་བ *bgegs sel-wa*; སྐྱོན་སེལ་བ *skyonsel-wa* to remove obstruction, calamity, disease, epidemic, &c.: ངན་ལམ་ཞུགས་མི་ཡོང་བའི་ཆེད་དུ་བགེགས་སེལ *ṅan-lam shugs-mi yoṅ-wahi ched-du bgegs-sel* performed some religious ceremonies that no mishap may occur on the way, etc. (*Rtsii. 65*).

བགོ་སྐལ *bgo-skal* སོ་སོའི་ཆ *so-sohi-cha* भाग, सपिण्ड, दायाद प्रत्यंश portion; a kinsman or claimant. 1. སྔོན་གྱི་ལས་ཀྱི་བགོ་སྐལ the portion or lot on account of one's former acts; also share, lot. 2. the doctrine of strict retribution.

བགོ་སྐལ་ལ་སྤྱོད་པ *bgo-skal-la spyod-pa* (རང་གིས་གང་ཐོབ་པའི་སྐལ་བ་དེ་ལ་སྤྱོད་པ *naṅ-gis gaṅ-thob pahi-skal-wa de-la spyod-pa*) दायाद-चर्य्यां to enjoy one's own share.

བགོ་བ I: *bgo-wa* वस्त्र clothes; clothing; བགོ་བ་དང་བཟའ་བ *bgo-wa daṅ bzah-wa* food and clothes (*Jä.*).

བགོ་བ II: 1. to put on clothes, pf. imp. བགོས *bgos*; ལྷམ་རྟག་ཏུ་བགོས *lham-rtag-tu bgos* always wear shoes. 2. subst. apparel, etc.: བགོ་བ་ངན་པ *bgo-wa ṅan-pa* कुप्रावरण.

བགོ་བ III: fut. of བགོད་པ *bgod-pa*.

བགོ་བྱ *bgo-bya* dividend; the number or quantity to be divided.

卐 **བགོ་རེ** *bgo-re*=བ་གམ *ba-gam* also the parapet on the roof of a house; a square turret or castellated room on the top of a castle: ཟོག་སྐྱན་བད་དང་ཁང་པ་གྲུ་བཞིའི་དབྱིབས་ཐའང་ཟེར "it is applied to a building four-cornered in shape with an edge of crockets on the top."

བགོ་བ་ཤ *bgo-bça*=བགོ་བ་ཤའ *bgo-bçah* or བགོ་སྐལ *bgo-skal*, संविभाग, ཕ་མ.

བགོ་བ་ཤའ་བྱེད་པ *bgo-bçah byed-pa* to distribute, allot, apportion. Often also བགོ་བ་ཤའ་རྒྱབ་པ.

བགོད་པ *bgod-pa*, fut. བགོ *bgo*, pf. བགོས *bgos* सन्नाह, अवस्थान to divide; ནོར་བགོ་བ *nor-bgo-wa* to divide property; to divide in ciphering a གྲངས *graṅs* number; to distribute ཤས་ཤས་སུ into shares; མི་རྣམས་ལ among people.

བགོད་པ་པོ *bgod-pa-po* the divider; བགོད་བྱེད *bgod-byed* divisor.

བགོད་ཡས *bgod-yas* अवन 1. protection. 2. n. of a number (*S. Lex.*).

བགོད་ར *bgod-ra* apportionment; share: ནང་ཟན་གཏན་སྡོད་རྣམས་ལ་སྙོམས་བརྡད་ཡེང་ཡོང་བའི་བགོད་ར་བྱེད *naṅ-zan gtan sdod rnams-la sñoms-brdad yeṅ-yoṅ-wahi bgod-ra byed* divide everything (that is left over) equally among the permanent residents of the family, &c. (*Ṟtsii. 61*).

བགོམ་བྱ *ḇgom-bya* पथ way; road.

བགོམས་པ *ḇgoms-pa* लङ्घन, गति, also བགོམ་པ *ḇgom-pa*, to walk, to step, to stride, to pace: འཐེམ་པ་ལ་བགོམས་པ stepped over the threshold. བགོམ་འགྲོ་བ to pace; to walk slowly.

བགོར *ḇgor*, supine of བགོ་བ *ḇgo-wa*.

བགོར་བ *ḇgor-wa* or འགོར་བ *ẖgor-wa* (*Cs.*); ལམ་དུ་འགོར *lam-du ẖgor* to linger or loiter in the way; delay.

བགྱངས་པ *ḇgyańs-pa*, v. རྒྱོང་བ *ṟgyoń-wa*.

བགྱིད་པ *ḇgyiḏ-pa*, pf. བགྱིས *ḇgyis*, fut. བགྱི *ḇgyi*, imp. གྱིས *gyis*. Is elegant form of བྱེད་པ करण: 1. to do; to act; to perform. 2. to make; to manufacture: གྱིས་ཞེར་བའི་གཟུགས the images regarding which there had been said, 'make them,' *i.e.*, the bespoken, ordered images (*Jä.*). ལས་བགྱིད་པ to do a work; བཀའ་བཞིན་དུ་བགྱིའོ according to order, it will be done; ཉེ་གནས་བགྱིད་པ to act the disciple; to be a disciple. མི་ལ་གནོད་པ་བགྱིས I have hurt the man; I have done him harm; བུ་ཡོད་པར་གྱིས་ཤིག make, bring it about, that a child be (born): རྒྱལ་པོ་མ་ནོར་གྱིས་ཤིག *ṟgyal-po ma-nor gyis çig* see that you do not let the prince escape; ཞེས་བགྱི་བ the so-called (*Jä.*).

བགྱིས *ḇgyis* कृत्य, कार a deed, act.

བགྱེར་བ *ḇgyer-wa*, past. of འགྱེར་བ *ẖgyer-wa*, ཀློར་ཊྲགས་པས་ཚིག་བཏང་དུས་སྐད་གདངས་སྙན་པོས་འདོན་པ ejaculating; chanting: གསང་སྔགས་སྦྱ་ཧེ་བཞིན་པར་བགྱེར་ནས, ཚིས་ཚོག་ལ་འགོད་པ་ཞིག་བྱུང་ accordingly in the chanting of the *Mantra*, there was some mistake (*A. 66*).

བགྲང་ *ḇgrań* संख्या number; figure.

བགྲང་རྟོགས *ḇgrań-ṟtogs* n. of a very great number (*Ya-sel. 57*).

བགྲང་འཕྱེས *ḇgrań-ẖphyes* n. of a great number; བགྲང་འཕྱོས *ḇgrań ẖphyos* n. of a great number occurring in the passage བགྲང་འཕྱོས་བགྲང་འཕྱེས་ལ་བསྒྲེས་པ *ḇgrań-gphyos ḇgrań-ẖphyes-la ḇsgres-pa* (*Ya-sel. 57*).

བགྲང་འཕྲེང་ *ḇgrań-ẖphreń* अक्षमाला, जपमाला rosary-beads.

བགྲང་བ *ḇgrań-wa* गणित to number, count, calculate: འཕྲེང་བ་བགྲང་བ་བྱ *ẖphrań-wa ḇgrań-wa bya* should count the beads of his rosary.

བགྲང་བ་ཡང་ *ḇgrań-wa yań* गणनामपि even counting.

བགྲང་བྱ *ḇgrań-bya* what may be numbered; numberable—years, time.

བགྲང་ཡལ *ḇgrań-yal* अवर low; n. of a great number (*S. Lex.*).

བགྲང་ཡོལ་ *ḇgrań-yol* अमेय that cannot be measured: བགྲང་ཡོལ་གཉིས་དང་མི་འཇལ་གཉིས *ḇgrań-yol gñis dań mi-ṉjal gñis* (*Ya-sel. 57*).

བགྲངས་པ *ḇgrańs-pa* संख्येय capable of being counted.

བགྲངས་པ་ལ་འདས་པ *ḇgrańs-pa la ẖdas-pa* गण-नामतिक्रान्त that is past counting.

བགྲད་པ *ḇgraḏ-pa*=1. གདངས་པ *gdańs-pa* to open wide; མིག་བགྲད་པ *mig-ḇgrad-pa* to stare; to goggle; ཁ་བགྲད་པ *kha-ḇgraḏ-pa* to gape; རྐང་པ་བགྲད་པ *ṟkań-pa ḇgraḏ-pa* to part the legs wide; to straddle. 2. to scratch (*Sch.*), spelt more correctly འབྲད་པ *ẖbraḏ-pa* (*Jä.*).

བགྲམ་པ *ḇgram-pa* व्यग्र separated; anxious.

བགྲིལ་བ *ḇgril-wa* to fall down; to drop down: གཡང་ལ་བགྲིལ fell into the abyss (*Situ. 74*).

བགྲུང་བ *bgruṅ-wa* or བགྲུངས *bgruṅs*, = དྭངས་སུ་བཅུག་པ *dwaṅs-su bcug-pa* to strain; to depurate; ཆུ་ཡི་རྙོག་མ་དྭངས་སུ་བཅུག་པ *chu-yi rñog-ma dwaṅs-su bcug-pa* to strain the impurities out of water.

བགྲུད་པ *bgrud-pa*, pf. བགྲུས *bgrus*, fut. བགྲུ *bgru* to clear of husks; to shell; བགྲུས་པའི་འབྲས *bgrus-pahi hbras* husked rice.

བགྲེ་བ *bgre-wa* resp. རྒས་པ *rgas-pa* or བགྲེས *bgres*, वृद्ध old; grown in age.

Syn. ན་སོ་རྒས་པ *na-so rgas-pa* old; བགྲེས་པོ *bgres-po*; རྒད་པོ *rgad-po* or རྒན་པོ *rgan-po* (*Mṅon.*).

བགྲེང *bgreṅ* occasionally for 1. སྒྲེང་བ *sgreṅ-wa*; 2. བགྲང་བ *bgraṅ-wa*.

བགྲེང་ཕྲེང *bgreṅ-phreṅ* जपमाला a rosary to count the names of saints, Buddhas, &c.

བགྲེན་པ *bgren-pa* (*den-pa*), v. བཀྲེན་པ *bkren-pa* (*Sch.*).

བགྲོ *bgro* (*do*) संगीत a song.

བགྲོ་གླེང་པ *bgro-gleṅ-pa* = གྲོས་བྱེད་པ *gros-byed-pa* to argue, discuss: ཁོང་གི་གྲྭ་པ་མཁས་ཤིག་ལྷ་རྗེ་ལ་བགྲོ་གླེང་བྱེད་དུ་བྱུང་སྟེ *khoṅ-gi grwa-pa mkhas-shig lha-rje-la bgro-gleg byed-du byuṅ-ste* one of his learned scholars having come to confer with *Lharje* (*Deb.* ཀ *8*).

བགྲོ་བ *bgro-wa* (*do-wa*) (pf. བགྲོས *bgros*), resp. བཀའ་གྲོས *bkah-gros* with གླེང་བ *gleṅ-wa* 1. to argue, discuss, confer with, consider: ཤེས་ཕན་ཚུན་དུ་བགྲོས་ནས *shes phan-tshun-du bgros-nas* thus mutually discussing; ཇི་ལྟར་བྱ་ཤེས་བགྲོས་ནས *ji-ltar-bya shes bgros-nas* deliberating what they should do. 2. to resolve, decide.

བགྲོ་བའི་ཁང་པ *bgro-wahi khaṅ-pa* = གླུ་དབྱངས་ཀྱི་ཁང་པ *glu-dbyaṅs-kyi khaṅ-pa* संगीत-प्रासाद the stage; a music booth.

བགྲོང་བ *bgroṅ-wa* (*doṅ-wa*) = བགྲང་བ *bgraṅ-wa* to count (*Jä.*).

བགྲོད *bgrod* (*doi*) व्रजन्ति 1. progress; gait (*Schr.; Kālāc. T 25*); going. 2. it also signifies the number 2 (*Rtsii.*). བགྲོད་དཀའ་བ *bgrod-dkah-wa* दुर्गम difficult progress; difficult to pass; བགྲོད་དཀའ་བའི་གནས *bgrod-dkah-wahi gnas* कान्तार a wilderness; a place or desert which is difficult to traverse; བགྲོད་དཀའ་བའི་ལམ *bgrod-dkah-wahi lam* दुर्गमपथ a difficult passage; an inaccessible path.

བགྲོད་པ गति, अयन, यान 1. to walk; to get over; wander: བགྲོད་ལ་ཕན *bgrod-la-phan* is useful in getting along. ལམ་བགྲོད་པ *lam-bgrod-pa* to travel over; to get through: ཆུ་བགྲོད་པར་དཀའ་བ *chu-bgrod-par dkah-wa* a river difficult to cross. 2. declination; अयन; ཉི་མ་ལྷོ་བགྲོད *ñi-ma lho-bgrod* the sun's going to the south; the sun's south declination; བྱང་བགྲོད *byaṅ-bgrod* the sun's north declination; བགྲོད་དུས་གཉིས *bgrod-dus gñis* both declinations; བུད་མེད་ལ་བགྲོད་པ *bud-med-la bgrod-pa* to lie with a woman (*Cs.*).

བགྲོད་བྱ *bgrod-bya* (*doi-ja*) कलत्र a road in general; met. a woman (*Mṅon.*).

བགྲོད་ཡས *bgrod-yas* विचार walking; a mover (*Lex.*).

བགྲོད་ལམ *bgrod-lam* 1. a road; passage. 2. met. the female organ (*Mṅon.*).

བགྲོས *bgros* (*doi*) = བཀའ་གྲོས *bkah-gros* conference, consultation (*Situ. 75*); བགྲོས་ངན་བྱས *bgros-ṅan byas* made conspiracy; holding unlawful conference: ཡང་སང་ཉིན་ཁོང་གཉིས་ཀྱིས་བགྲོས་ངན་བྱས་པས *yaṅ saṅ-ñin khoṅ-gñis kyis bgros-ṅan byas-pas* (*Rdsa. 14*) again yesterday both of them held evil conference.

མགར *mgar* the work or craft of a smith; གསེར་མགར *gser-mgar* goldsmith.

མགར་ཁང་ *mgar-khaṅ* or མགར་ས *mgar-sa* smithy.

མགར་ཁྲི་སྒྲ་འཛི་ཐུན . *Mgar-khri sgra-dsi thun*; n. of a celebrated minister of Tibet.

མགར་སྤྱོད *mgar-spyod* (*gar-choi*) कर्म्मारचर्य्या the practice or craft of a smith.

མགར་བ *mgar-wa* लोहकार, सुकर्म्मार, कर्म्मकार, अयस्कार blacksmith; one of low caste.

Syn. ལྕགས་བཟོ་པ *lcags-bzo-pa*; ལྕགས་མགར་བ *lcags-mgar wa*; མཚོན་ཆ་མཁན *mtshon-cha-mkhan*; རྡེག་ཆ་མཁན *rdeg-cha-mkhan* (*Mṅon.*).

མགར་རྩན་གཉའ་ལྡོམ་བ *Mgar-rtsan gñaḥ ldom-ba* n. of the celebrated minister Gar of Tibet, who was sent to China to negotiate for the marriage of the daughter of emperor Thaṅ Tai-tsung with his master king *Sroṅ-btsan sgam-po*.

མགལ་བ *mgal-wa* jaw; jaw-bone; ཡ་མགལ *ya-mgal* the upper jaw-bone; མགལ་བ *mgal-wa* or མ་མགལ *ma-mgal* the lower jaw-bone. In colloq. both jaws together are called ཡ་ལེ་མ་ལེ *ya-le ma-le*. མགལ་ཆག *mgal-chag* a broken jaw-bone; མགལ་བུད *mgal-bud* a dislocated jaw-bone.

མགལ་དུམ *mgal-dum* वन्यालात a large piece of wood split or cut, or half burnt.

མགལ་པ *mgal-pa* or འགལ་པ *hgal-pa* a billet of wood.

མགལ་མེ *mgal-me* आलात, fire-brand; torch consisting of long chips of wood.

མགལ་མེ་བསྐོར་བ *mgal-me bskor-wa* अलातचक्र to whirl round a fire-brand.

མགལ་མེའི་འཁོར་ལོ *mgal-meḥi ḥkhor-lo* a circle of light produced by whirling round a fire-brand.

* **མགུ** *mgu* तुष्ट (*Schr.*; *Kālāc. T. 3*). [satisfied]*S*.

མགུ་བ *mgu-wa* सन्तोष, उदग्र, हृष्ट, तुष्टि, आह्लाद 1. to rejoice; to be glad, joyful, content; མགུ་ནས *mgu-nas* delighted: མགུ་བའི་ལན་མ་བྱུང *mgu-waḥi lan ma-byuṅ* did not receive a gratifying or satisfactory answer. 2. to exhilarate; to gladden; to make content. དགའ་དགུ་བ *dgaḥ-dgu-wa*, དགའ་དགུ་རང་བ *dgaḥ-dgu raṅ-wa*, མགུ་བ་བྱ་བ *mgu-wa bya-wa* आराधना are frq. intensive forms to express joy or exultation in the older classics.

Syn. དགའ་བ *dgaḥ-wa* (*Mṅon.*).

མགུར *mgur* 1.= མགུ་བར *mgu-war*. 2. कण्ठ throat; neck; that which comes out of the མགུར *mgur* is called a མགུར་མ *mgur-ma*, a song: རྗེ་བཙུན་མི་ལའི་མགུར *rje-btsun mi-laḥi mgur* the venerable Mila's songs. 3. voice; མགུར་སྙན་པ *mgur-sñan-pa* sweet voice; harmonious voice. 4. song, air, melody; hence a religious song. Used as honorific form for གླུ, especially in Milarapa, each of the doctrinal ditties in that work being preceded by the words མགུར་འདི་གསུངས་སོ, he uttered this song.

མགུར་ཆུ *mgur-chu*, མཆོད་རྟེན་གྱི་བུམ་གདན *mchod rten-gyi bum-gdan* the pedestal on which the cupola of a chaitya rests.

མགུར་དུ་གསུངས་པ *mgur-du gsuṅs-pa* anything sung or put into verse.

མགུར་ན་པ *mgur na-pa* = མགུལ་རྒྱན *mgul-rgyan* ornament worn round the neck (*Mṅon.*).

མགུར་འབུམ *mgur-ḥbum* the hundred thousand sacred songs; name of one of *Milaraspa's* two great works, which are both interwoven with numerous religious songs.

མགུར་ཞོ *mgur-sho* or སེ་བ *se-wa* 24; of the weight of 24 *rattee*; a weight equal to $7\frac{1}{3}$ (*Skar-ma* སྐར་མ).

མགུར་བསལ་བ *mgur-bsal-wa* 1. to deliver a song with emphasis. 2. to clear the throat; to hawk; to hem (*Jä.*).

མགུར་ལྷ *mgur-lha* a god of hunting with the Mongol Shamans (*Sch.*).

མགུར་ལྷ་མཆེད་བཞི *mgur-lha mched-bshi* the four brothers (sylvan gods) from whom the four great tribes of Tibet are said to have originated.

མགུལ་པ *mgul-pa* कण्ठ, ग्रीवा, गल, कन्धर neck; throat; resp. for མགྲིན་པ *mgrin-pa*; མགུལ་དུ་འདོགས་པ *mgul-du hdogs-pa* to tie, fasten on the neck, *e.g.*, magic objects; རང་གི་མགུལ་པ་གཅོད་པ *rañ-gi mgul-pa gcod-pa* to cut one's own throat; to commit suicide, suicidal; མགུལ་པ་ནས་འཁྱུད་པ *mgul-pa nas hkhyud-pa* to fall on a person's neck; to embrace; མགུལ་པ་ནས་འཛིན་པ or འཛུ་བ to seize by the throat.

Syn. སྐེ *ske*; མགྲིན་པ *mgrin-pa*; མགུར *mgur*; མགོ་རྟེན *mgo-rten*; མགོ་འཛིན *mgo-hdsin*; resp. རི་མོ་གསུམ་པ *ri-mo gsum-pa*; དུང་འདྲའི་མགྲིན *duñ-hdrahi mgrin*; བུམ་པའི་མགུལ་ཅན *bum-pahi mgul-can* (*Mñon.*).

མགུལ་གླུ *mgul-glu*, resp. གླུ *glu*, ཚངས་དབྱངས་རྒྱ་མཚོའི་མགུལ་གླུ *Tshañs-dbyañs rgya mtshohi mgul-glu*, n. of a work of the second Dalai Lama *Tshañ-dbyañs rgya-mtsho*.

མགུལ་རྒྱན *mgul-rgyan* कण्ठाभरण, वचक necklace; a neck ornament.

Syn. མགྲིན་པའི་རྒྱན *mgrin-pahi rgyan*, མགུར་ན་སྤ *mgur-na spa*; སྐེའི་རྒྱན *skehi-rgyan*; མགུལ་པའི་རྒྱན *mgul-pahi-rgyan* (*Mñon.*).

མགུལ་སྔོན *mgul-sñon* = མགྲིན་སྔོན *mgrin-sñon* नीलकण्ठ, नीलकन्धर 1. he with a blue neck. 2. a peacock.

མགུལ་ཆིང་དཀར་པ *mgul-chiñ dkar-pa* a white neck-cloth.

མགུལ་ཆུང *mgul-chuñ* a small amulet worn on the neck.

མགུལ་དར *mgul-dar* or དཔའ་དར *dpah-dar* 1. a silk scarf tied round the neck as a badge of honour. 2. the shoulder of a mountain; གཡོན་མགུལ་ན *gyon-mgul na* on the left slope (*Jä.*).

མགུལ་གདུབ *mgul-gdub* हर्ष the neck-bangle or necklace worn by the Indians.

མགུལ་ནད *mgul-nad* disease of the throat.

མགུལ་པའི་རྒྱན *mgul-pahi-rgyan* = མགུལ་རྒྱན *mgul-rgyan* or མགྲིན་པའི་རྒྱན *mgrin-pahi rgyan* (*Mñon.*).

མགུལ་རིང *mgul-riñ* अतिग्रीव a long neck.

མགེའུ *mgehu* same as མགོའུ *mgohu*, v. མགོ *mgo*.

མགོ I: *mgo* शिरः, मूर्द्धा, उत्तमाङ्ग, मस्तक the head: མགོ་འཇོག་པས་ལུས་ཤེས *mgo-hjog-pas lus-çes* by the movement of the head the body is known; མགོ་ལ་མེ་འབར་བ་ལྟ་བུ *mgo-la me-hbar-wa lta-bu* आदीप्त-शिरोज्वलोपम as if glowing with fire on his head. མགོ་རུས *mgo-rus* कपाल the head-bone; frontal bone; མགོ་བོང་བུ་ལྟ་བུ *mgo boñ-bu lta-bu* खरशीर्ष a head like that of an ass: མགོ་སྒྱུར་སློག་སློག་བསྡད་འདུག *mgo-sgyur slog-slog bsdad-hdug* he sat (at times) bending his head (*Rdsa.*).

མགོ II: 1. summit, height, top: རི་མགོ་ཁ་བས་གཡོགས the hill tops were covered with snow. 2. first place; principal part; མགོ་བྱེད་པ *mgo-byed-pa* to lead; to command; to be at the head of; དབུ་མཛད་པ *dwu-mdsad-pa* to inspect, look after, superintend, control: བུ་མོ་ཞིག་གིས་མགོ་བྱེད་པའི་མི་མང་པོ *bu-mo shig-gis mgo-byed-pahi mi-mañ-po* a number of (labouring) people were superintended by a girl (the farmer's daughter) (*Jä.*). 3. beginning: གྲོས་མགོ *gros-mgo* the beginning of a consultation. མགོ་འཛུགས་པ *mgo-hdsug-pa* to begin: བོད་སྡུག་པའི་མགོ་འཛུགས *bod sdug-pahi mgo-hdsug* that was the beginning of the misfortunes of Tibet;

བརྟན་གྱི་སྐྱིད་མགོ་དེ་ནས་ཚུགས *brtan-gyi skyid-mgo de-nas tshugs* with this my constant good fortune commenced; ལོ་མགོ་ལ *lo-mgo la* at the beginning of the year; མགོ་ནས *mgo-nas* from the beginning. 4. in grammar a superscribed *r, l, s, e, i;* ར་མགོའི་ཀ *ra-mgohi ka;* ཀ *k* with *r* superscribed; དེ་རྣམས་བས་ཕུལ་ས་མགོའི་ཀཱའོ *de-rnams bas-phul sa-mgohi kaho* theso are the words boginning with བ་ས་ཀ *b, s, k* (*Jä.*).

མགོ III: मृगशिरा: n. of a constellation (the 5th) consisting of stars resembling tho head of an antelope.

Syn. རི་དྭགས་མགོ *ri-dbags-mgo*; མགོ་སྐྱེས *mgo-skyes*; སྨལ་པོ *smal-po*; ཟླ་སྐྱེས *zla-skyes* (*Mñon.*).

མགོ་ཀླད *mgo-klad* the brain.

མགོ་དཀྱིལ *mgo-dkyil* colloq. crown of the head; vertex.

མགོ་སྐོར *mgo-skor* imposture, deceit: བདུད་ཀྱི་མགོ་སྐོར་དེ་ང་མི་འདོད *bdud-kyi mgo-skor de ña-mi-hdod* I detest these diabolical tricks (*Jä.*).

མགོ་སྐོར་བ *mgo-skor-wa* to cheat, swindlo, confuse; མི་མགོ་མ་སྐོར *mi-mgo ma-skor* do not cheat people.

མགོ་དགུ་བ *mgo dgu-wa*=དགུར་བ *dgur-wa*= དགུ་བ *dgu-wa*.

མགོ་སྐྱ *mgo-skya* a gray head; མགོ་སྐྱ་ཅན *mgo-skya-can* a gray-hoaded person.

མགོ་སྐྱེས *mgo-skyes*, v. མགོ *mgo* III.

མགོ་སྐྱེས་དཀར་བ *mgo-skyes dkar-wa*=རྒན་པ *rgyan-pa* or རྒས་པ *rgyas-pa* an old man; gray hairs (*Mñon.*).

མགོ་སྐྱོང *mgo-skyoñ* or མགོ་འདྲེན *mgo-hdren* a protector; patron.

མགོ་སྐྱོབ *mgo-skyob*=རྨོག *rmog* a helmet.

མགོ་ཁྲ *mgo-khra* (*go-tha*) scald-head.

མགོ་མཁྲེགས་ཅན *mgo-mkhregs-can* (*go-theg-chen*) obstinate, portinacious, stubborn, esp. in buying and bartoring; selfish; bargaining; haggling.

མགོ་རྒྱན *mgo-rgyan* मुण्डाभरण, दीक्षता 1. head ornament. 2. n. of a placo in Tibet.

མགོ་ལྗི་ཡོག་པ *mgo-lji yog-pa* मुण्डभारि a heavy head.

མགོ་ཉལ *mgo-ñal* hair of tho head.

མགོ་ཉོག *mgo-ñog* bewildered, confused; troublesome: དུ་རེས་ཀྱི་བྱ་བ་འདི་མགོ་ཉོག *du-res-kyi bya-wa hdi-mgo ñog* work at theso times is very troublesome (*Rdsa. 26*).

མགོ་མཉམ་གསུམ *mgo-mñam-gsum* the three things of simultaneous occurrence; they are:—(1) འཆི་བ་དྲན་པ་རྒྱུད་ལ་སྐྱེས་པ *hehi-wa dran-pa rgyud-la skyes-pa* the thought of death arising in the mind; (2) ཚེ་འདི་བློས་ཐོངས་པ *tshe-hdi blos-thoñs-wa* renouncing of worldly affairs; (3) ཆོས་བྱེད་པ *ehos-byed-pa* to practise religion. The contrary of the three are the following:—(1) མི་འཆི་སྙམ་པ *mi-hehi-sñam-pa* the thought that one will not die; (2) ཚེ་འདི་ལ་འཐམས་པ *tshe-hdi-la hthams-pa* to remain attached to worldly affairs; (3) སྡིག་པ་བྱེད་པ *sdig-pa byed-pa* commission of sin (*Lo. 45*).

མགོ་བསྙུང *mgo-bsñuñ* लिङ्गग्रीवशिरा: stiff-neck.

མགོ་བཏགས་ཞུ་བ *mgo-btags shu-wa* to seek protection under one who is superior to himself; to seek refuge under such.

མགོ་རྟག་ཆོད་པ *mgo-rtag-ehod-pa* one who can give decided advice.

མགོ་རྟེན *mgo-rten* that on which the head rests, *i.e.*, the throat or མགོ་འཛིན *mgo-hdsin* that holds the head; ग्रीवा the neck (*Mñon.*).

མགོ་སྟོང *mgo-stoñ* a giddy-headed man; an idiot; one who cannot think for himself.

མགོ་ཐུག *mgo-thug*=འདྲ་འདྲ *hdra-hdra* an equal, a match, a rival.

མགོ་ཐོད *mgo-thod* शेखर top or crown of the head; on the summit.

མགོ་ཐོན་པ *mgo-thon-pa* one who by his own ability can direct others.

མགོ་འཐོམ་པ *mgo-hthom-pa* confounded.

མགོ་འདོན་པ *mgo-hdon-pa*=མགོ་འདྲེན་བྱེད་པ *mgo-hdren byed-pa* to favour, preserve, make safe: དགེ་བསྙེན་བཞིའི་ཡོ་བྱད་ཐམས་ཅད་མགོ་འདོན་དུ་བཅུག་པོ all the properties of four Upāsakas he caused to be kept secure (*A. 22*).

མགོ་ན *mgo-na* मुण्ड-व्यथा headache.

མགོ་ནན *mgo-nan*, ཐོག་མ *thog-ma* प्रथम first, foremost.

མགོ་སྦུག *mgo-sbug* the head together with the meat of a slain goat, sheep or yak, &c.

མགོ་བ *mgo-wa* शिर: the head.

[མགོ་བོ *mgo-bo*=ཡན་ལག་མཆོག *yan-lag mchog* मस्तक the chief of the limbs of the body (*Mñon.*): མགོ་བོ་གདུགས་འདྲ་ཟླུམ་པའི་མི་ཡི་དབང་པོར་འགྱུར he who has a round head resembling an umbrella becomes a lord of men.

མགོ་བོ་སྤྱི་ཐེར་བ *mgo-wo spyi-ther-wa* a bald-head.

མགོ་མི་བསྒྱུར *mgo mi-bsgyur* न शीर्ष प्रचोदक does not change his residence or head-quarters.

མགོ་མོ་གཡོག *mgo-mo-gyog* head-cover.

མགོ་སྨོས་པས་གོ་བ *mgo-smos-pas go-wa*=ཅུང་ཟད་ལབ་པ་ཙམ་གྱིས་གོ་བ *cun-zad lab-pa tsam-kyis go-wa* to easily perceive the meaning from a slight movement of the head.

མགོ་ཚོག *mgo-tsog* round protuberant head: ཡོ་བྱད་གང་ཅུང་གི་མགོ་ཚོག་ཚོག་ཡོད་པ་ལ on the heads of whatsoever things that may be round.

མགོ་འཛིན *mgo-hdsin* शिरोरोधि the head of an office, or work-leader.

མགོ་འཛུག་པ *mgo-hdsug-pa* उपक्रम to begin (a work or subject, etc.).

མགོ་ཟླ་བ *mgo-zla-wa* मार्गशिरः, मार्गशीर्ष November-December of Indian calendar. The eleventh month of the Tibetan calendar.

མགོ་ཟླུམ *mgo-zlum* (*go-dum*) or མགོ་རེག *mgo-reg* मुण्डन, प्रव्रजित, पलितकेश shaven head, also round bald-head; a Buddhist monk; མགོ་ཟླུམ་གནས *mgo-zlum-gnas* a place where the shaven heads reside; a monastery; མགོ་ཟླུམ་པ *mgo-zlum-pa* a shaven head; a monk.

མགོ་ཟླུམ་ལམ་ནག *mgo-zlum lam-nag*=སྒྲ་གཅན *sgra-gcan* राहु the sounding planet; a comet (*Mñon.*).

མགོའུ་ཆུང *mgohu-chuñ* अशीर्षक with a small or no head; the running-hand character of Tibet.

མགོ་གཡོག་པ *mgo-gyog-pa*=བསླུས་པ *bslus-pa* or མགོ་སྐོར *mgo-skor* to cheat, deceive; མགོ་གཡོག་མགོ་སྐོར་གྱི་བསླུ་ཁྲིད *mgo-gyog mgo-skor-gyi bslu-khrid* to rob one by deception or cheating.

མགོ་རུག *mgo-rug*=མགོ་གུག་གུག་བྱེད་པ *mgo-gug gug byed-pa* to bend the head; to bow down the head: ཇ་བུར་འདྲེན་པའི་མགོ་རུག་བྱེད་པ *ja-wur hdren-pahi mgo-rug byed-pa* he made obeisance presenting tea and treacle.

མགོ་ལིང་ཅན *mgo-liñ-can* विटपी; ཤིང *çiñ* a tree;=མགོ་འདན་པ *mgo hdan-pa* shaking the head as a signal or from illness.

མགོ་རེག *mgo-reg* or མགོ་བྲེགས *mgo-bregs* Buddhist monk.

མགོ་ལྷག་ཕྱེད་པ *mgo-lhag phyed-pa* or མགོ་སྙོམས་བྱེད་པ *mgo-sñoms byed-pa* to make all equal; not to make any invidious distinction between parties; to deal evenly: ཐམས་ཅད་མགོ་ལྷག་ཕྱེད་པར་གྱིས་ཤེས *thams-cad mgo lhag-phyed-par-gyis shes* thus commanded, all behave fairly among yourselves (*A. 115*).

* མགོན་དཀར་ཡིད་བཞིན་ནོར་བུ *mgon-dkar yid-bshin nor-bu* (*Schr.; 77 A.*).

མགོན་པོ་ *mgon-po* according to some grammarians the word མགོན *myon* is an abbreviation of the words མགོ་འདྲེན *mgo-hdren* (འདྲེ *hdre* being eliminated), signifying नाथ protector, patron, principal, master, lord, tutelary god; so the word is applicable to Buddha, saints, and also ordinarily to any protectors and benefactors in general. When མགོན་པོ occurs as a proper name it denotes either Buddha or Avalokites'vara or Mahádeva. Among the མགོན་པོ *mgon-po* are also classed Gaṇes'a, the Dikpāla or guardians of the world and of Buddhism, besides many other spirits who are represented as possessing four, six, and sometimes eight arms. This class of gods is also numerous in both the Tantrik and Bon pantheon. མགོན་པོ་ཞལ་བཞི་ཕྱག་བཅོ་བརྒྱད *mgon-po shal-bshi phyag bco-brgyad* the Lord with four faces and eighteen arms. Sambhara (བདེ་མཆོག) of the Bon-po has three faces and six arms. In Buddhist India there were worshipped three Nātha नाथ, or མགོན་པོ *mgon-po*, viz.:—(1) འབབ་སྟེགས་མགོན་པོ *Hbab-stegs mgon-po* the spirit invoked to inspire one by entering one's body; (2) ནག་པོ་མགོན་པོ *Nag-po mgon-po* the black-spirit; (3) བྲམ་ཟེ་མགོན་པོ *Bram-ze mgon-po* the *Brāhma nātha, i.e.*, Brāhmaṇa's spirit (*K. dun. 50*).

* མགོན་པོ་གྲི་གུག *Mgon-po gri-gug* n. pr. (*Schr.*).

མགོན་པོ་རྟ་ནག་ཅན་ཕྱག་བཞི་པ *mgon-pa rta-nag can phyag bshi-pa* (*Schr.*).

* མགོན་པོ་སྟག་ཞོན *Mgon-po stag-shon* (*Schr.; 87 A.*).

མགོན་པོ་སྤྱན་རས་གཟིགས *Mgon-po Spyan-ras gzigs* = འཕགས་པ་སྤྱན་རས་གཟིགས *Hphags-pa Spyan-ras gzigs* अवलोकितेश्वर the patron Lord Avalokites'vara (*Mṅon.*).

* མགོན་པོ་ཕྱག་དྲུག་པ *Mgon-po phyag-drug-pa* (*Schr.*).

* མགོན་པོ་ཕྱག་བཞི་པ *Mgon-po phyag-bshi-pa* (*Schr.; 81 C.*).

* མགོན་པོ་བེང *Mgon-po Beṅ* (*Schr.; 85 C.*).

* མགོན་པོ་བྲམ་གཟུགས *Mgon-po bram-gzugs* n. pr. (*Schr.*).

* མགོན་པོ་མི་ཕམ་པ *Mgon po mi-pham-pa* अजितनाथ (*Schr.; Tā. 2, 111*) [invincible Lord] *S.*

མགོན་པོ་འོད་དཔག་མེད *Mgon-po hod-dpag med* अमिताभ lit. immeasurable light; a n. of the 4th Dhyāni-Buddha.

* མགོན་པོ་ཞལ་གཅིག *Mgon-po shal-gcig* (*Schr.*).

* མགོན་པོ་ཞལ་བཞི *Mgon-po shal-bshi* (*Schr.*).

* མགོན་པོ་ལེགས་ལྡན *Mgon-po legs-ldan* (*Schr.*; (*Org. m. 110, 20*).

མགོན་མངས *mgon-maṅs* many patrons or defenders of religions; many small pyramidal sacred erections (*Cs.*).

མགོན་མེད *mgon-med* अनाथ unprotected, helpless; མགོན་མེད་ཟས་སྦྱིན *Mgon-med zas-sbyin* अनाथ-पिण्डद n. of a certain house-holder who accommodated Buddha in the Jetavana grove of S'rāvasti. He was the chief house-holder devotee of Buddha.

མགོན་བཙུན་ཕྱའི་གྲོང་ཁྱེར *Mgon-btsun phyahi groṅ-khyer* n. of a city in the paradise of the Bon-po.

མགྱོགས་འགྲོ *mgyogs-hgro* horse, wind.
Syn. རླུང *rluṅ*; རྟ *rta* (*Mṅon.*).

མགྱོགས་འགྲོའི་བྲུན *mgyogs-hgrohi brun*, met. for རྟ་ཡི་སྦངས *rta-yi sbaṅs*, horse-dung (*Sman. 186*).

མགྱོགས་པ *mgyogs-pa* जव, सपदि, आशु, क्षिप्र, जावनं, तूर्णं adj. and adv. rapid, swift, quick; speedily: མགྱོགས་པོ་འགྲོ་ན་རྟ་དང་གླང་ཆེན་འཆད, ག་ལེ་འགྲོ་ན་བོང་བུས་རྒྱལ་ཁམས་བསྐོར by quickly going the horse and the elephant become prostrate; by slowly walking the donkey travels round a kingdom. In modern works and colloq. མགྱོགས་པོ as adj. and མགྱོགས་པོར as the adv. are the commoner forms.

མགྱོགས་པ་དྲི་ལྡན་ *mgyogs-pa dri-ldan*, ཤིང་ཀུན་ *çiñ-kun* assafœtida (*Sman 109*).

མགྱོགས་པོར་ *mgyogs-por* quickly, speedily, soon.

མགྱོགས་ལམ་ *mgyogs-lam* a straight, short way; རྐྱང་མགྱོགས་ *rkyañ-mgyogs*, v. རྐང་ *rkañ*, a short-cut; སུ་མགྱོགས་ *su-mgyogs* a race; a running-match (*Jä.*).

མགྲིན་སྐྱེས་ *mgrin-skyes* = ཀླུ་དབྱངས་ *klu-dbyañs* song; music (*Mñon.*).

མགྲིན་སྔོན་ *mgrin-sñon* नीलकण्ठ Mahâdeva; he with a blue neck; the peacock. When the ocean was churned by the gods and the Asuras, there came out the sun and moon and then Lakṣmī the goddess of wealth and fortune, and afterwards nectar was the result. Lastly came forth a pot of poison which would have destroyed the world. The God Mahādeva out of compassion for all living beings of the world, himself drank the potion, in consequence of which his neck turned blue.

Syn. ལྷ་དབང་ཕྱུག་ *Lha-dwañ-phyug*; རྨ་བྱ་ *rma-bya* (*Mñon.*).

མགྲིན་གཅིག་ཏུ་ *mgrin gcig-tu* with one voice; unanimously.

མགྲིན་བཅུ་ *Mgrin-bcu* दशकण्ठ a name of Rāvana, King of Ceylon and the son of Pulasta.

མགྲིན་བཅུའི་དགྲ་བོ་ *mgrin-bcuhi dgra-bo*, རྒྱལ་པོ་ར་མ་ཎ་ *Rgyal-po Ramaṇa*, King Rāma (*Mñon.*).

མགྲིན་ཐུང་བ་ *mgrin thuñ-wa* a short neck, throat, or voice.

མགྲིན་ལྡན་ *mgrin-ldan*, कलकण्ठ the cuckoo or Indian *koel.*

Syn. ཁུ་བྱུག་ *khu-byug.*

མགྲིན་པ་ *mgrin-pa* (*din-pa*) ग्रीवा, कन्धर, कण्ठ, शिरोधि, कम्बु the neck; མགྲིན་རིང་བ་ *mgrin riñ-wa* a long neck.

Syn. གྲེ་བ་ *gre-wa*; མགུར་ *mgur*; མགུལ་པ་ *mgul-pa*; མགོ་རྟེན་ *mgo-rten*; མགོ་འཛིན་ *mgo-hdsin*; སྐེ་ *ske*; རི་མོ་གསུམ་པ་ *ri-mo gsum-pa*; དུང་འདྲའི་མགྲིན་ *duñ-hdrahi mgrin*; བུམ་པའི་མགུལ་ཅན་ *bum-pahi mgul-can* the last three are used in polite language (*Mñon.*). གྲེ་བ་ *gre-wa* is a corrupt form of the Sanskrt word ग्रीवा *grīvā* (*Liç.*).

མགྲིན་པ་ཅན་ *mgrin-pa-can* peaked mountain.

མགྲིན་པ་བཏེགས་ *mgrin-pa btegs* raised head (as if out of panic or alarm).

མགྲིན་པ་རབ་རིང་ *mgrin-pa rab-riñ* = ཁྲུང་ཁྲུང་ *khruñ-khruñ* the stork (*Mñon.*).

མགྲིན་པའི་རྒྱན་ *mgrin-pahi rgyan* = མགུལ་རྒྱན་ *mgul rgyan* or སྐྱེ་ཡི་རྒྱན་ *skye-yi rgyan* necklace (*Mñon.*).

མགྲིན་པའི་སྒྲ་ *mgrin-pahi sgra* voice.

མགྲིན་པའི་ཕྱོགས་ *mgrin-pahi phyogs*, जत्रु the mouth [the collar-bone]*S.*

མགྲིན་པའི་རྩ་ *mgrin-pahi rtsa* कण्ठमूल the root or base of the neck.

མགྲིན་པའི་རླུང་ *mgrin-pahi rluñ* उदानं breath.

མགྲིན་དམར་ *mgrin-dmar* रक्तग्रीव red-throat; n. of a bird.

མགྲིན་མཛེས་ *mgrin-mdses* सुग्रीव a handsome neck; མགྲིན་བཟང་ *Mgrin-bzañ* n. of the friend and general of Rāma in his exile.

མགྲིན་བཟང་ *mgrin-bzañ* one with a loud, clear voice.

* མགྲིན་བཟང་མ་ *mgrin-bzañ-ma* (*Schr.; 92 R.*).

མགྲིན་བཟང་བཙུན་མོ་ *mgrin-bzañ btsun-mo* 1. n. of a goddess. 2. = གི་ཝང་ *gi-wañ* गोरोचना n. of concretion found in the brains of elephants or stomach of cows (*Sman. 94*); a bright yellow pigment.

མགྲིན་སྔོན་ཟླ་བའི་རྟོགས་བརྗོད་ *Mgrin-sñon zla-wahi rtogs-brjod* n. of a Tibetan romance containing 133 block-print leaves, composed by Lama *Blo-bzan Bstan-pahi rgyal-mtshan* of Tshor-phu in Tibet.

མགྲོན I: *mgron (don)* is also sometimes wrongly spelt as འདྲོན *hdron* अतिथि, निमन्त्रण feast, treat, banquet, entertainment, resp. སྐུ་མགྲོན *sku-mgron*; སྐུ་མགྲོན་འབུལ་བ *sku-gron hbul-wa* to entertain; མགྲོན་ལ་འབོད་པ *mgron-la hbod-pa*, resp. མགྲོན་དུ་སྤྱན་འདྲེན་པ *mgron-du spyan-hdren-pa* उपनिमन्त्रण to invite to an entertainment; མགྲོན་དུ་གཉེར་བ to regale, treat (*K. du.* ན, *87*).

མགྲོན II: in Buddhism signifies object of invocation; and any person invoked is called མགྲོན་པ *mgron-pa*. The latter are of four classes:—(1) དཀོན་མཆོག་སྲིད་ཞུའི་མགྲོན *dkon-mchog srid shuhi mgron* the holy ones form the object of invocation in the world. The holy ones are:—Buddha, Dharma, Sañgha, one's lama (Guru) and one's tutelary deity: (2) མགོན་པོ་ཡོན་ཏན་གྱི་མགྲོན *mgon-po yon-tan-gyi mgron*, the *Nātha* who are a class of fearful deities, the celestial *Dākinī*, the *Dharmapāla* and the guardian gods of Buddhism; (3). རིགས་དྲུག་སྙིང་རྗེའི་མགྲོན *rigs-drug sñiṅ-rjehi mgron* the six classes of animate beings such as human beings, gods, demons, the animal kingdom, the *Preta* or ghosts, and the hell-beings; (4) གདོན་བགེགས་ལན་ཆགས་ཀྱི་མགྲོན *gdon-bgegs lan-chags-kyi mgron*; here the invoked are 360 demons called གདོན *Gdon* and 80,000, evil spirits called བགེགས *Bgegs*. These do mischief to all living beings on account of their own misdeeds of a former existence. It is necessary to invoke such and to appease them by offerings. According to the Bon-po there are chiefly two kinds of མགྲོན *mgron*, *i.e.*, objects of invocation:—(1) a person or deity invoked for worship; (2) a person invoked out of compassion (*D.R.*).

མགྲོན་ཁང་ *mgron-khaṅ* अतिथिशाला a house for the accommodation and temporary board of guests, strangers, &c.

མགྲོན་གྱི་འཕྲིན་སྐྱེལ་བྱ *mgron-gyi hphrin-skyel bya*; བྱ་སྐྱ་ཀ *bya skya-ka* the mag-pie (*Mṅon.*).

མགྲོན་གཉེར *mgron-gñer* or མགྲོན་བུ་འབོད་པ *mgron-bu hbod-pa* to invite or call a guest; མགྲོན་བུ་གཉེར་བ *mgron-bu gñer-wa* lit. the receiver of guests; an officer whose duty it is to introduce others to the king or to the great lamas of Tibet. He is also called ཡར་གསལ་ཞུ་མཁན *yar-gsal shu-mkhan*, he who communicates the wishes or mandates of a superior person to an applicant.

མགྲོན་དུ་འགྲོ་བ *mgron-du hgro-wa* to go to an entertainment; ཟས་མགྲོན a feast; ཇ་མགྲོན a tea party; ཆང་མགྲོན a treat with beer or wine.

མགྲོན་པོ *mgron-po* अतिथि, आगन्तुक one newly come; a guest.

Syn. གསར་དུ་འོང་བ *gsar-du hoṅ-wa*; གློ་བུར་འོང་བ *glo-bur hoṅ-wa*; མགྲོན་དུ་འོང་བ *mgron-du hoṅ-wa* (*Mṅon.*).

མགྲོན་པོ་བོས་པ *mgron-po bos-pa* to call or invite a person.

མགྲོན་བུ་ཐལ་བ *mgron-bu thal-wa* name of a medicinal drug which is alleged to stop bleeding; it is useful in fracture and sores.

འགག *hgag* 1. obstruction; stoppage; ཡིད་འགག *yid-hgag* want of appetite; གཅིན་འགག *gcin-hgag* also འགག *hgag* strangury. 2. a place or spot that has to be passed by all that proceed to a certain point: ཟམ་པའི་འགག་ཏུ་འགུག་ན་རྐུ་མ་འཛིན་ཐུབ *zam-pahi hgag-tu hgug-na rku-ma hdsin-thub* a thief may be arrested if you be on the look-out for him in the passage of a bridge; རི་བོ་དཔལ་འབར་གྱི་འགག the place on *Pal-hbar* mountain where there is a narrow passage; སྒོ་འགག *sgo-hgag* the door of the house because through it all that enter or leave have to pass; ཁ་འགག *kha-hgag* the mouth, through which everything must pass that is eaten; fig. ཐར་ལམ་གྱི་གནད་འགག *thar-lam-gyi gnad-hgag* the main point for salvation. འགག་གཅིག་ཏུ་དྲིལ་བ *hgag-gcig-tu dril-wa* to unite; to be concentrated in one point (*Jä.*).

འགག་སྐྱོར *hgag-skyor* anything like a fencing that is put round a field or garden or a house to stop ingress from outside.

འགག་པ *hgag-pa*, or འགགས *hgags* निबद्ध 1. pf. form of འགེགས་པ *hgegs-pa* to stop, to cease; to be at a stand-still; mostly in the perfect form: ཁ་འགགས the appetite is gone; the passions having been suppressed. 2. door-keeper, v. སྒོ་འགག *sgo-hgag*.

འགག་པ་མེད *hgag-pa med* अनिबद्ध free, unobstructed; the sky; also voidity or that which is in a simple or uncompounded state.

འགང *hgañ*, v. རྒང *rgañ*.

འགང་(པོ) *hgañ (po)* the burden of an office, business, commission.

འགངས་ཆེན *hgañs-chen* also འགང་ཆེན *hgañ-chen* important; very valuable; གདན་འགངས་ཆེན་རྣམས་བཀོལ་བདེ་དང་ངོ་ནོར་མེད *gdan hgañs-chen rnams bkol bde dañ ño-nor med*, གནས་འགངས་ཆེན་རྣམས *gnas hgañs-chen rnams* important or chief places of pilgrimage, &c.; རྟེན་འགངས་ཆེན very sacred symbols; རྫས་ལག་འགངས་ཆེན valuable things; དོན་འགངས་ཆེན important meaning or object.

Syn. རྩ་ཆེ་བ *rtsa che-wa*; དྲག་པ *drag-pa*; ཡག་པོ *yag-po* (*Mñon.*).

འགངས་མཐུན *hgañs-mthun* equal; ཕལ་ཆེར་མཐུན *phal-cher mthun* in thorough agreement; in harmony: ལྷོ་གླིང་གསུམ་གཅིག་ཏུ་བྱས་པའི་ཚད་དང་ཡང་འགངས་མཐུན *lho-gliñ-gsum gcig-tubyas-pahi tshad-dañ yañ hgañs-mthun* (it was about) equal to the area which the three southern places together occupy (*Ya-sel. 19*).

འགངས་པ *hgañs-pa* difficult, troublesome (*Sch.*).

འགན་འཁུར་བ *hgan-hkhur-wa* to stand security for; to guarantee; to take responsibility on one's self; འགན་བསྐྱུར་བ *hgan-bskyur-wa* to impose responsibility.

འགན་དཀྲིས *hgan-dkris* (*gan-ti*) making over charge; making responsible.

འགན་རྒྱ *hgan-rgya*=གན་རྒྱ *gan-rgya* agreement, covenant.

འགན་ཅན *hgan-can* responsible.

འགན་ཐེག་པ *hgan-theg-pa* to undertake anything; to take charge of: རང་དོན་ལ་ཐུག་ན་ལུས་པོང་བུས་ཀྱང་འགན་ཐེག when self-interest is concerned even the donkey understands his duty.

འགམ་པ *hgam-pa* to cram into the mouth, especially of dry edibles; ཕྱེ་འགམ་པ་པོ *phye hgam-pa-po* an eater of flour (*Situ. 84*).

འགལ་བ *hgal-wa*=མི་མཐུན་པ *mi-mthun-pa* to contradict; to disagree; to mistake; འགལ་སྤོང་བ *hgal-spoñ-wa*=འགལ་བ་སྤོང་བ *hgal-wa spoñ-wa* not to make mistake; to avoid errors; འགལ་མེད *hgal-med* without mistake.

འགལ་ཟླ *hgal-zla*=འགལ་བའི་གྲོགས *hgal-wahi grogs* or མི་མཐུན་པའི་གྲོགས *mi-mthun-pahi grogs* an enemy: རང་དང་མི་མཐུན་པའི་འགལ་ཟླ་རྣམས་དང་བསྡོངས་ནས having joined with such of the enemy as were not in agreement with one another (*Khrid. 116*).

འགས་པ *hgas-pa* to split, to crack, to burst apart.

འགུད་པ *hgud-pa*, v. གུད་པ *gud-pa*.

འགུགས་པ *hgugs-pa* to summon; bring back; འགུགས་པ་པོ *hgugs-pa-po* one who is called to; a waiter (*Situ. 84*).

+ **འགུམ་པ** *dgum-pa* to die (of natural death, of disease): དེའི་རིང་ལ་ལོ་ཙཱ་བའི་འཁོར་ཡང་ཕལ་ཆེར་ཚད་པས་འགུམ at that time most of those of the attendants of the *Lo-tsa-wa* who were smitten with fever died (*A.* 65).

འགུལ་བ *hgul-wa* to move, quake, shake; ས་གཡོ *sa-gyo* = ས་འགུལ *sa-hgul* earthquake; འགུལ་བ་པོ *hgul-wa po* or འགུལ་བྱེད *hgul-byed* shaker; fut. འགུལ་བཞིན *hgul-bshin* = འགུལ་གྱིན, *hgul-gyin*.

འགུར་ཞོ *hgur-sho*, same as མགུར་ཞོ *mgur-sho* ཏཾ་ཀ་བརྒྱད་ལ་མགུར་ཞོ་གཅིག *tam-ka brgyad-la mgur-sho-gcig*, one *Mgur-sho* is equal to eight tan̂-ka.

འགེགས་བྱེ *hgeg-bye* = ཁྱོ་བོ *khyo-wo* or མཛའ་གྲོགས *mdsah-grogs* husband (*Mṅon.*).

+ **འགེམས་པ** *hgems-pa* = འཇོམས་པ *hjoms-pa* to confound; to subdue प्रत्यस्थित; མགོ་འགེམས་པ་པོ *mgo hgems-pa-po* one who confounds or bewilders.

འགེམས་པར་བྱེད་པ *hgems-par byed-pa* दिदंशति repeatedly bites; acc. to *Cs.* another form for འགུམ་པ *hgum-pa*, to kill, to destroy (*Sch.*); ཀླད་པ་འགེམས་པ *klad-pa hgems-pa* to surprise; to over-throw an argument by reason; མགོ་གེམས *mgo-gems* stupid (*Sch.*).

འགེགས་པ *hgegs-pa* प्रसिध्, निषिध्, प्रतिषिध् to hinder, obstruct, keep back or in; fut. དགགས *dgags*, pf. བཀག *bkag*: དགག་པ་ལ་མེད་དགག་དང་མ་ཡིན་དགག་གཉིས་ཡོད *dgag pa-la med-dgag dan̄ ma-yin dgag gñis-yod* ཡིན་མིན་ལྟ་བུ *yin-min lta-bu* preventing what is and what is not, etc., in Buddhist metaphysics.

འགེངས་པ *hgeṅs-pa*, pf. བཀང་ *bkan̄*, fut. དགང་ *dgan̄*, imp. ཁོང་ *khon̄*, to fill up; also to satiate.

འགེབས་པ *hgebs-pa*, pf. བཀབ *bkab*, fut. བགབ *bgab*, imp. ཁོབ *khob*, to cover up; to put on; to conceal.

འགེལ་བ *hgel-wa* = འགྱེལ་བ *hgyel-wa*, pf. བཀལ *bkal*, fut. དགལ *dgal*, imp. ཁོལ *khol*: 1. to load; to lay on a burden; ཁྲལ་འགེལ་བ *khral hgel-wa* to impose tax or rent; to commission; to charge with; to make, appoint, constitute; to put; to place on or over: གདུང་མ་བཀལ་བ་ *gdun̄-ma bkal-wa* a beam placed over it; to set or put on, *e.g.*, a pot; to hang up; གོས་འགེལ་གདང་ *gos hgel-gdan̄* a stand to hang clothes on; fig. འཆི་བར་ནུས་པའི་ཐོག་འགེལ་དགོས *hchi-war nus-pahi thog-hgel dgos* one must set on it the roof of being able to die, *i.e.*, one must crown the whole edifice of life by being free from fear of death (*Jä.*); to impose a fine; to give punishment.

འགེལ་བྲེལ *hgel-brel* old; འགེལ་བྲེལ་ན་ལྡན *hgel-brel na-ldan* the old, aged.

འགེལ་གཡག *hgel-gyag* = ཁལ་གཡག *khal-gyag* laden yaks.

འགེལ་ལུགས *hgel-lugs* the method of imposing fine or punishment.

འགེས་པ *hges-pa*, pf. བཀས *bkas*, fut. དགས *dgas*, imp. ཁོས *khos*, to split, cleave, divide; བཀས་ཤིང་ *bkas-çin̄* (*Lex.*) cleft or chopped wood; དུམ་བུར་དགེས་པ *dum-bur dges-pa* to divide into pieces; to cut up or open.

འགོ *hgo*, same as མགོ *mgo*, origin, source; प्रमुख 1. foremost; in front; དམག་འགོ *dmag-hgo* commander of an army; མཁར་འགོ *mkhar-hgo* or རྫོང་འགོ *rdson̄-hgo* commander of a fort, of a district: ཆོས་ཀྱི་འགོ་སངས་རྒྱས་ལ་ཐུག *chos-kyi hgo san̄s-rgyas-la thug* the origin of *Dharma* (Buddhism) is traced to Buddha; ཆུ་ཡི་འགོ་གངས་ལ་ཐུག the source of a river is traced to the snows. 2. beginning; the first: འགོར *hgor* in the beginning; སེར་བའི་འགོར *ser-wahi hgor* the beginning of the hail.

Syn. ཐོག་མ *thog-ma*; དང་པོ *dan̄-po*; རྩ་བ *rtsa-wa* (*Mṅon.*).

འགོ་ལྟབ་པ *hgo ltab-pa* apricots?

འགོ་ནན་ *hgo-nan*=ཐོག་མ *thog-ma* beginning; first.

འགོ་སྣམ *hgo-snam* broad-cloth; also the superior kind of blanket.

འགོ་པ *hgo-pa* the headman of a village.

འགྲོ་དཔོན *hgro-dpon* rector, director, head-master, principal.

འགོ་ཕིབ *hgo-phib* ག་སུབ *ga-sub* a cover; also a canopy or dome over a temple or tomb.

འགོ་བའི་ལྷ་ལྔ *Hgo-wahi lha-lna* the five superior demi-gods, which are the following: (1) མོ་ལྷ་ཧམ་ཞང་ལྷ *mo-lha ham shan-lha*, (2) སྲོག་ལྷ *srog-lha*, (3) དགྲ་ལྷ *dgra-lha*, (4) ཕོ་ལྷ *pho-lha*, (5) ཡུལ་ལྷ *yul-lha*. These are the inseparable companions of humanity, and rejoice when we do good actions and become sorry when we sin. There are several treatises on the rites to propitiate them.

འགོ་ཕེར *hgo-pher*=གོ་ཆོད་པ *go chod-pa* useful: ལོ་ཆུང་ནས་འགོ་ཕེར from early years, *i.e.*, from boyhood, he has been useful.

འགོ་བ *hgo-wa* लेप, pf. གོས *gos*, or འགོས *hgos*, cf. བསྒོ་བ *bsgo-wa* 1. to stain; to lose colour; to dirty, sully one's self. 2. संचर to infect with a disease; འགོ་བའི་ནད *hgo-wahi nad*, འགོ་བའི་རིམས *hgo-wahi rims* a contagious or epidemic disease, a plague; འགོ་ནད or འགོ་བའི་ནད, རིག་དུག་དང་རིམས, उपसर्गः an infectious disease; also a contagious disease.

འགོ་མ *hgo-ma* beginning, origin, source.

འགོ་མི *hgo-mi* headman.

འགོག་ཀུ *hgog-ku* prob. derived from the Chinese, signifying the goddess of the elements. Acc. to the Chinese the fundamental elements are tree, fire, earth, iron, and water. Each of these is presided over by a goddess.

འགོག་པ I: *hgog-pa* निरोध, संरोध, अवरोध, प्रवारण, प्रत्यादेश, प्रतिबन्ध, v. བར་དུ་བཅོད་པ *bar-du bcod-pa*, འགེགས་པ *hgegs-pa*.

འགོག་པ II:=འཇོག་པ *hjog-pa* निक्षेप, न्यास, उपनिधि to keep; to place; to arrange; a deposit; pledge.

འགོག་པ III: pf. བཀོག *bkog*, fut. དགོག *dgog*, imp. ཁོག *khog* 1. to take away forcibly; to snatch, tear away, pull out; རྩ་བ་འགོག་པ *rtsa-wa hgog-pa* to pull up the root; འགོག་པ་པོ *hgog-pa-po* one who takes or draws out. 2. to take off a cover, a lid, a pot from the fire, in *W.* (*Jä.*).

འགོག་པ་རི *Hgog-pa-ri* the hill on which the monastery of Gahdan is situated: འགོག་པ་རི་ནས་རྗེ་བླ་མས་དགའ་ལྡན་གྱི་དུང་གཏེར་ནས་བཏོན *Hgog-pa ri-nas Rje bla-mas dgah-ldan-gyi dun gter-nas bton* (*J. Zan.*).

འགོག་སྤྱོད་པ *hgog-spyod-pa* अर्हन् =སེམས་ཀྱི་རྣམ་རྟོག་འགོག་པ *sems-kyi rnam-rtog hgog-pa* to stop the arising of imaginations or fancies in the mind.

འགོག་བྱེད *hgog-byed* संयत discipline, and from འགོག་པ *hgag-pa*, there arise 1. ཞི་བ *shi-wa* शान्ति peace; 2. རྒྱ་ནོམ་པ *gya-nom-pa*=ཕུན་སུམ་ཚོགས་པ *phun-sum tshogs-pa* प्रतिष्ठित perfected state; 3. ངེས་པར་འབྱུང་བ *nes-par hbyun-wa* निःसरण firm conviction.

འགོགས I: *hgogs*=བཀག་པ *bkag-pa* (*Mnon.*).

འགོགས II: पर्यय, लङ्घन passing over; transit; crossing; getting over.

འགོགས་པ *hgogs-pa*=འགེགས་པ *hgegs-pa* to prevent; to avert unfortunate events, as danger, fatal consequences; to suppress the symptoms of a disease by medicine; to drive back or away; to expel, *e.g.*, spirits, ghosts; to repel people that are trying to land: བདུད་རྣམ་པ་ལྔ་ཡིས་འགོག་སྟེ bdud rnam-pa lña-yis hgog-ste it having been averted by the five kinds of demons (*D.R.*).

འགོང་པོ་རྡོ hgoñ-po rdo, or ཕ་ཝང་ལོང་བུ pha-wañ loñ-bu, a kind of stone of liver colour, believed to be sacred to the God Dam-chen who rides on a goat—the peculiarity of this stone being that it breaks in cube-like pieces (*Sman. 404*).

འགོང་བ *hgoñ-wa*=འདའ་བ *hdah-wa* or སྨད་པ *smad-pa* विघ्न to bewitch, enchant; also to pass over, get the better of: འདི་ལ་སུ་ཡིས་འགོང་བར་ནུས *hdi-la su-yis hgoñ-war nus* who can overpower this, *i.e.*, who can enchant him; འགོངས་ནས *hgoñs-nas* समुत्क्रान्त having crossed, passed over.

འགོང་བ་པོ *hgoñ-wa po* or འགོང་པོ *hgoñ-po* an enchanter; འགོང་བ་མོ *hgoñ-wa mo* an enchantress, a sorceress.

འགོང་བོ *hgoñ-bo* विघ्न a class of demons which bring disease on men and cattle.

འགོད་པ *hgod-pa*, pf. བཀོད *bkod*, fut. དགོད *dgod*, imp. ཁོད *khod*, cf. ཁོད་པ *khod-pa* न्यास, व्यूह 1. to design; to project; to plan (*Sch.*). 2. to found; to establish; to lay out (a town); to build (a house); to manufacture; to form; to frame. 3. to put; to fix; to transfer into a certain state or condition; བདེ་བ་ལ་འགོད places in a state of happiness; ཐར་པའི་ལམ་ལ་འགོད puts into the way of salvation; སངས་རྒྱས་ཀྱི་ས་ལ་འགོད་པ *sañs-rgyas-kyi sa-la hgod-pa* establishes in the realm of Buddhahood. 4. to set or place in order: གྲལ་ཕྱམ་བཀོད་པ་འདྲ *gral-phyam bkod-pa hdra*, as the rafters of a roof are placed side by side (*S.g.*) མཐར་དགོད་པ *mthar dgod-po* to add, place at the end (*Vai-kar.*); བཀོད་པར་མཛེས་པ *bkod-par mdses-pa* beautiful as to arrangement; nicely ordered; བརྒྱན་དགོད་པ *brgyan dgod-pa* to arrange ornaments (tastefully); to decorate, adorn; to construct or adjust grammatical forms, sentences (*Zam.*). 5. to set down in writing; ཡི་གེ་ལ་འགོད་པ *yi-ge-la hgod-pa* to record: མིང་ཀ་བ་ལ་འགོད་པ *miñ ka-wa-la hgod-pa* to write name on a column; to compose, draw up, write a narrative, etc. Frequently to mention; to insert in a writing; to publish; to make known. 6. to rule; to govern (*Sch.*): བྱོལ་སོང་བཀོད་པའི་རྒྱལ་པོ་ཡིན *byol-soñ bkod-pahi rgyal-pa yin* he is king over all subjugated animals (*Jä.*). The participle pf. བཀོད་པ *bkod-pa* is also sbst.: (1) ground-plan; outline of a building; delineation; sketch; ཞིང་བཀོད *shiñbkod* map; design; (2) form, shape, figure (*Sch.*); sample; copy; even of one's own body, *e.g.*, where a person multiplies himself by magic virtue སྤྲུལ་བ *sprul-wa*; (3) building; edifice; structure: བཀོད་པ་མཛེས *bkod-pa mdses* the structure is beautiful; (4) frame; form; བཀོད་པ་ལུས *bkod-pa lus* the structure of the body: ངའི་བཀོད་པ་ནམ་མཁའི་རང་བཞིན *ñahi bkod-pa nam-mkhahi rañ-bshin* my form of an etherial nature.

འགོམ་པ *hgom-pa* 1. to tread: བླ་མ་སློབ་དཔོན་སོགས་ཀྱི་གྲིབ་མ་དང་, བཞུགས་གདན་ན་བཟའ་སོགས་དང་ཟ་བཏུང་སོགས་འགོམ་ན་ཉེས་པ་ཆེ *bla-ma slob-dpon sogs-kyi grib-ma dañ, bshugs-gdan na-bzah sogs dañ za-btuñ-sogs hgom-na ñes-pa-che* treading on the shadows of lamas, teachers, &c., also on their chairs, seats or clothes, or objects of food and drink, is sinful. 2. acc. to *Sch.*=འགེམ་པ *hgem-pa*, འགུམ་པ *hgum-pa* to pass over; འགོམ་པ *hgom-pa*=འགྲོ་བ *hgro-wa* to go; going (by passing); སྟེང་ནས་འགོམ་ཤེས་པས *steñ-nas hgom shes-pas*=གོམ་པ་བརྒྱབ་ནས་འགྲོ་བ to pass over a thing; leap over it.

འགོམ་ཡུག་པ *hgom-yug-pa*=ཕར་འགོམ་ཚུར་འགོམ་བྱེད་པ *hphar-hgom tshur-hgom byed-pa* to cross or pass over from one side to another (*Khrid.*): རྐང་པས་འགོམས་ཤིང་འགྲོ walks pacing with the feet.

འགོར *hgor* 1. in the beginning; འགོ་གྲལ་འགོར at the top or head of a row or order: ཆུ་འགོར at the source of a river. 2. supine of འགོ་བ *hgo-wa*.

འགོར་བ *hgor-wa*=ཐོགས་པ *thogs-pa* विलम्ब, मन्दः to tarry, linger, loiter: ལམ་དུ་འགོར་བ *lam du hgor-wa* to linger on the way.

Syn. གུལ་བ *gul-wa*.

འགོར་གཞི *hgor-gshi* delay; འགོར་གཞི་མེད་པ *hgor-gshi med-pa* without delay.

འགོལ་བ *hgol-wa* अपांग्र; pf. གོལ *gol* 1. to part, to separate; vb. n. འགོལ་བའི་གནས *hgol-wahi gnas* a hermitage; འགོལ་པོ *hgol-po* hermit, recluse. 2. to deviate; err; go astray.

འགོལ་ས *hgol-sa* 1. the place where two roads separate so as to create doubt in the mind regarding the right path. 2. error; mistake.

འགོས *Hgos* n. of a monastery, *Tā.*, also n. of a tribe and of a minister of Tibet: བློན་ཆེན་འགོས་ཀྱིས་ཞལ་ཆེ་དགའ་གསུམ་དུ་བཅད *Blon-chen hgos-kyis shal-che dgah gsum-du bcad* (*Ya-sel. 4*).

འགོས་པ *hgos-pa* 1. v. འགོ་བ *hgo-wa*: འགོ་བའི་ནད་འགོས་ཡོང *hgo-wahi nad hgos-yon* it will catch contagion. 2. लिपित a liniment; a medicine to be rubbed on; लिप्त anointed, besmeared.

* འགོས་གཞོན་ནུ་དཔལ *Hgos Gshon-nu dpal* n. pr. (*Schr.*; *Tā. 2, 60*).

འགྱག་པ *hgyag-pa*, cf. སྐྱག་པ *skyag-pa*, to be sold, spent, expended (*Cs.*).

འགྱང་བ *hgyan-wa*, pf. འགྱངས *hgyans*; विलम्बित, विप्रकृष्ट, दविष्ठ to be delayed, deferred, postponed; farthest: ཕྱིར་འགྱང་ན *phyir hgyan-na* if one defers it; ལོ་མང་པོ་མི་འགྱང་བར not many years shall have passed; དུས་འགྱངས a long time after.

འགྱངས་མེད *hgyans-med* without delay (*Yig. k. 26*).

འགྱིངས་པ *hgyins-pa* विभ्रम, लीला an appearance of greatness or of pride.

འགྱིང་བ *hgyin-wa* 1. to assume air or appearance of greatness; to sit lifting up the body in the manner of a lion. 2. to look haughtily; to look down upon; to slight a person; མི་ལ་འགྱིང་བ *mi-la hgyin-wa* also of things, to despise, contemn, neglect them. སྟེངས་སུ་འགྱིང་བ seems to be an intensified form, meaning to scorn loftily; to look down on as from a summit.

འགྱིང་བག *hgyin-bag* attitude; posture; gesture; also manner in reference to. གཟུགས *gzugs* form, or དབྱིབས *dbyibs*, appearance.

འགྱིངས་འཁར *hgyin-hkhar* a staff consecrated to a fearful deity, or having on its top a head with wide yawning mouth or in some fearful attitude.

འགྱིངས་པ *hgyins-pa*, v. འགྱིང་བ *hgyin-wa*.

འགྱིམ་པ *hgyim-pa* परिधि the circumference.

འགྱུ་བ *hgyu-wa*, pf. འགྱུས *hgyus*, to move quickly to and fro, *e.g.*, as lightning, the quivering air in a mirage, the motion and versatility of the mind, &c.

འགྱུར་བ *hgyur-wa* वर्तते, सञ्जायते, pf. གྱུར་ཏོ *gyur-to* or གྱུར་པ *gyur-pa*, imp. གྱུར་ཅིག *gyur-cig*, cf. སྒྱུར་བ *sgyur-wa* 1. to become; to grow, increase, change: དགེ་སློང་དུ་འགྱུར་བ *dge-slon-du hgyur-wa* to become a monk; རྒྱལ་པོར་

འགྱུར་བ *rgyal-por ḥgyur-wa* to become a king; སྦྲུམ་མར་འགྱུར་བ *ṣbrum-mar ḥgyur-wa* to get with child; བདུན་དུ་འགྱུར *ḇdun-du ḥgyur* to reach the number of seven: ཁྱོད་པས་བརྒྱ་འགྱུར་པས་ལྷག་པར་བཟང་བ་ཡོད *khyoḍ-paṣ ḇrga ḥgyur-paṣ lhag-par ḇzañ-wa yoḍ* there are those which grow a hundred times better than you; གསུམ་འགྱུར་ལྟ་བུར *gsum ḥgyur ḻta-bur* three times as much; ད་གཉིས་འགྱུར་ཙམ་ཞིག *da gñiṣ-ḥgyur tsam-shig* one twice as large as that; འགྱུར་སྐད a changing voice. 2. sbst. change, alteration, revolution, vicissitude: དུས་བཞིའི་འགྱུར་བས *da ḇshiḥi ḥgyur-waṣ* through the change of the fourth season; འགྱུར་རྟེན་བཞག་པ *ḥgyur-ḇrten ḇṣhag-pa* to pay money in hand as an earnest that the bargain is not to be retracted. འགྱུར་དུ་མེད་པ *ḥgyur-du meḍ-pa* अविवर्त unchangeable, invariable: མཐུ་སྟོབས་ནད་མེད་པ, གཟི་རྗིད་ཡོངས་སུ་འགྱུར་བ *ṃthu-ṣtobṣ naḍ meḍ-pa, gzi-ṛjiḍ yoñṣ-su ḥgyur-wa* the total decay of strength, health and esteem (in old age); བདག་གི་སེམས་མ་གྱུར་མ་ཉམས་པ *ḇdag-gi semṣ ma-gyur ma-ñamṣ-pa* my mind has not been altered nor weakened; དད་པ་འདི་ལས་མ་འགྱུར་ཅིག *daḍ-pa ḥdi-laṣ ma-ḥgyur-cig* do not depart from this belief. འགྱུར་དུ་ཡོད་པ *ḥgyur-du yoḍ-pa* changeable, variable: ཕོ་མོ་འགྱུར་པ *pho-mo ḥgyur-pa* male changing into female and *vice versâ*; སེམས་འགྱུར་བ to change the mind; ཡོད་པར་འགྱུར་བ to become; begin to exist; to gain possession: སྲོག་ལ་མི་ལྟ་བར་འགྱུར་པའི་དངོས་པོ་འདི་དག these acts of having become indifferent to life; ཅང་མི་སྨྲ་བར་གྱུར་ཏོ *cañ mi ṣmra-war gyur-to* he became speechless. 3. འགྱུར་བ *ḥgyur-wa* annexed to an infinitive may denote either the perfect or the future tense, the context deciding in every instance how it is to be understood: སུ་ཞིག་རྒྱལ་སྲིད་བྱེད་པར་འགྱུར *su-shig ṛgyal-sṛiḍ byeḍ-par ḥgyur* who shall have the Government? who shall rule? དེ་རྒྱལ་པོར་འགྱུར་བར་ཤེས་སོ *de ṛgyal-por ḥgyur-war çeṣ-so* they knew that this man would become king. ཡ་མཚན་དུ་འགྱུར་བ *ya-ṃtshan-du ḥgyur-wa* to be surprised, astonished; གནས་སུ་འགྱུར་བ *gnaṣ-su ḥgyur-wa* to come to a place; to arrive at: འདོད་པའི་དངོས་གྲུབ་ཏུ་འགྱུར་བ *ḥdoḍ-paḥi ḏños-grub-tu, ḥgyur-wa* to be endowed with the perfect gift of wishing, viz., of having every wish fulfilled; གཡོས་པར་འགྱུར་བ to become moving; to begin to move. 4. to be translated; བོད་དུ་འགྱུར་བ to be translated into Tibetan; བཀའ་འགྱུར *ḇkaḥ-ḥgyur* the translated word; འགྱུར་བྱུང *ḥgyur-byuñ* was translated.

འགྱུར་བའི་ཆོས *ḥgyur-waḥi-choṣ* changeable (and therefore perishable) things (*Cs.*).

*འགྱུར་བར་འགྱུར *ḥgyur-war ḥgyur* भविष्यत (*Schr.*; *Kālāc. T, 89*) it will become.

འགྱུར་བྱེད *ḥgyur-byeḍ* a changer; one who brings about changes.

འགྱུར་མེད *ḥgyur-meḍ* अचर unchangeable; infallible.

འགྱུར་ཚིག *ḥgyur-tshig* the translated words; according to some authors words that have been translated into another language: རྒྱུད་རང་གི་འགྱུར་ཚིག་དངོས་གནས་སུ་འཇོག *ṛgyuḍ rañ-gi ḥgyur-tshig ḏños-gnaṣ-su ḥjog* keep the original terms of the *Tantra* intact with their translation (*Ya-sel. 38*).

འགྱེ *ḥye*=འོད *ḥoḍ* चोद light; a whip.

འགྱེ་བ *ḥgye-wa*, pf. and imp. གྱེས *gyeṣ*, 1. to be dispersed; to be divided, *e.g.*, a river that is divided into several branches; རྣམ་པ་གཉིས་སུ *ṛnam-pa gñiṣ-su* (a ray of light) divided into two parts; to separate; to part: བེམ་རིག་འགྱེས་དུས *bem-rig ḥgyeṣ-duṣ* when body and soul part from each other. 2. to issue, proceed, spread, branch from: དེ་དག་ལས་གྱེས་སོ they have proceeded from those (their ancestors).

འགྱེག *hgyeg* = གནད་ *gnad* the sense; the real meaning; essence: བོན་ཐམས་ཅད་ཀྱི་འགྱེག་མན་ངག་ལ་ཐུག་པས *Bon thams-cad-kyi hgyeg-man-ṅag-la thug-pas* the essence of all the Bon meets in the Man-ṅag.

འགྱེད *Hgyed* 1. n. of a district in north Tsang: གཙང་གི་རུ་གཉིས་ནི་རུ་ལག་ཤང་འགྱེད *Gtsaṅ-gi Ru gñis-ni Ru lag Çaṅ hgyed* (*Loṅ.* ཨ *6*). 2. alms in money or eatable things; འགྱེད་གཏོང་པ *hgyed gtoṅ-pa* to distribute alms. This expression is defined by Tibetan writer as ཚོགས་ལ་དངུལ་ལྟ་བུ་མི་རེ་རེ་ལ་བགྲིམས་ཏེ་སྐྱེར་བ to bestow silver and the like in an assembly, distributing to each man.

འགྱེད་སྟོབས *hgyed-stobs* बाहुव्यायाम athletic feat; exercise of arms.

འགྱེད་པ *hgyed-pa*, pf. བགྱེས, *bgyes* fut. བགྱེ *bkye* विग्रह; विवाद, संचोदन 1. to divide (trs.), to scatter, disperse; འོད་ཟེར་འགྱེད་པ *hod-zer hgyed-pa* to diffuse rays of light: སྤྲུལ་པ་འགྱེད *sprul-pa-hgyed* sends forth an emanation; ཕོ་ཉ་འགྱེད་པ *pho-ña hgyed-pa* to send a messenger; to dismiss; ཚོགས an assembly. 2. to institute, set going; འཐབ་མོ་འགྱེད་པ to start a combat; གཡུལ་འགྱེད་པ to fight a battle; གཡུལ་འགྱེད་པ་པོ one who gives battle; *hgyed-pahi tshe* in the dispute. 3. to give an entertainment, banquet; to hold a feast.

འགྱེད་མ *hgyed-ma* = ཕྲ་མེན་པ *phra, men-pa* n. of a goddess—one that brings on division, dissension, or disunion.

འགྱེར་བ *hgyer-wa* or སྤོང་བ *spoṅ-wa* वर्जन to drop or let fall; to throw down; to quit, abandon, throw away (*Sch.*).

འགྱེལ་བ *hgyel-wa* to fall; to tumble down: གན་རྐྱལ་འགྱེལ *gan-rkyal hgyel* fell on his back, face upwards; ས་ལ་འགྱེལ *sa-la-hgyel* tumbled on the ground; རླུང་སོགས་ཀྱིས་འགྱེལ་བ *rluṅ-sogs-kyi hgyel-wa* to be thrown by the wind, &c.; ནད་ཀྱིས་འགྲོ་མི་ཐུབ་པར་འགྱེལ་བ stricken down by illness so as to be unable to walk: རྡོ་ལ་ཐོགས་ནས་འགྱེལ་བ he fell by stumbling on a stone; དེའི་ཚེ་ན་ཧོ་མོ་བརྒྱམས་ཏེ་ས་ལ་འགྱེལ་བ་དང་ then I, fainting away, fell to the ground.

འགྱེས་པ *hgyes-pa*, another form of འགྱེ་བ *hgye-wa* ཕན་ཚུན་སོ་སོར་འགྱེས་པ *phan-tshun so-sor hgyes-pa*, to separate asunder or between two parties.

འགྱོག་ཐེལ *hgyog-thel* = ལས་དམ *las-dam* seal; འགྱོག་ཐེལ་ཆབས་བཅས propeities under seal (*Rtsii.*).

འགྱོག་པ *hgyog-pa* to ascend; གྱེན་དུ་འགྱོག་པ་པོ *gyen-du hgyog-pa-po* one who climbs up (*Situ. 84*).

འགྱོད་པ *hgyod-pa* कौकृत्यं, अनुताप, अनुशय, कोप, विप्रतिसार to repent; to grieve for. 1. lament, relent, not only for bad, but also for good actions, when the latter are attended with disadvantage. 2. sbst. regret: འགྱོད་པ་བསྐྱེད་པ *hgyod-pa bskyed-pa* regret arises at last; ང་འགྱོད་པ་བསྐྱེད་པ *ṅa hgyod-pa bskyed-pa* I felt regret; ང་འགྱོད་པའི་སེམས་མེད་པར་ཁྱོད་ལ་སྦྱིན་ནོ *ṅa hgyod-pahi sems med-par khyod-la sbyin-no* I gave it to you readily without regret.

འགྱོད་པ་རྣམ་གསུམ *hgyod-pa rnam-gsum* the three kinds of regret are illustrated as follows:—(1) དགྲ་ཕྱིས་ཕ་མ་འདུལ་རང་ཡུལ་འགྱོད not being able to defeat an enemy out of one's country, or དཔའ་རེས་ཕྱས་གཅིག་ཐུང་ན་སེམས་ངོ་འགྱོད to be sorry for an occasional defeat after one has behaved himself as a hero; (2) འགྲོན་གཉིས་ཕུ་མ་ཕྱས་ཕྱིས་ཕུ་འགྱོད to be sorry, when out on a journey, at not being properly equipped with provisions, etc; མགྲོན་ཆེས་ཁ་གཅིག་ཐུང་དུས་ང་རེ་འགྱོད to be sorry on inviting an important person when there is no proper arrangement for his entertainment or reception; (3) རྟ་པོ་གཞིས་སུ་མ་གསོ་ཕྱིས་སུ་འགྱོད to be sorry for not having fed one's horse when on a journey; also རྟ་ཤི་སྒ་ཁུར་ཕྱུང་དུས་ང་རེ་འགྱོད to be sorry when the horse dies, one has to carry the saddle on one's own back; (4) ལྷ་ཆོས་གཞོན་དུས་མ་བྱས་རྒས་དུས་འགྱོད to be sorry in old age for not having done religious works as a youth; (5) འཆི་བདག་བདུད་པོ་དེ་ཕྱུང་དུས་འགྱོད "when that Devil the lord of death has come, he repents."

འགྱོད་པའི་དྲི་མ *ḥgyoḍ-paḥi dṛi-ma* regret after a gift has been made; འགྱོད་མེད *ḥgyoḍ-meḍ* अनताप without regret or repentance.

འགྱོད་རྨོ་བ *ḥgyoḍ-ṛmo-wa* to cause repentance; to make one suffer, feel, or pay for a thing: གནོང་འགྱོད *ḥnoṅ-ḥgyod* repentance proceeds from consciousness of guilt (*Jä*). འགྱོད་ཚངས་བྱེད་པ *ḥgyod-tshaṅs byed-pa* to apologise: འགྱོད་ཚངས་བྱེད་པར་གནང་བ to accept an apology.

འགྱོད་ཟིན་པ *ḥgyoḍ zin-pa* having repented.

འགྱོད་བཤགས *ḥgyod-ḅçags* confession and repentance.

འགྲགས་གྲགས *ḥgrags-gras*, or གྲགས་འགྲགས *grags-ḥgrags* अतिप्रभ, very bright.

འགྲགས་པ I: *ḥgrags-pa* (*ḍag-pa*), pf. གྲགས *grags* 1. to sound forth; to utter a cry or sound, of men, animals, thunder, &c.; to shout: དེའི་རྣ་བར་དུ་འགྲགས་པར་འགྱུར་ན if it should be shouted into his ear. 2. to be famous; to be called; ཤེས་གྲགས *shes-grags* so it is called; so he was called; by this name he goes; under that name he is known.

འགྲགས་པ II: *ḥgrags-pa* to bind, v. གྲགས་པ *grags-pa*.

འགྲང་བ *ḥgraṅ-wa* (*ḍang-wa*) 1. to number; to count, v. བགྲང་བ *ḅgraṅ-wa*. 2. to satisfy with food; to satiate; འགྲངས་རྗེས *ḥgraṅs-rjes* after having eaten one's fill; ཤ་བ་བསད་པས་མི་འགྲངས་ཏེ not yet having enough of deer killing.

འགྲངས *ḥgraṅs* (*ḍang*) भुक्त fully fed; eaten to the full extent; filled up.

འགྲངས་པ *ḥgraṅs-pa* = གྲོད་པ་འགེངས *groḍ-pa ḥgeṅs* or གསུས་པ་འགེངས *gsus-pa ḥgeṅs* bellyful, stomachful; ལྟོ་བ་འགེངས *ḷto-wa ḥgeṅs* eaten to one's fill; also ངོམས་པ *ṅoms-pa* eaten to satiety; with ཚིམ་པ *tshim-pa* satiated; ཆོག་པ *chog-pa* contented (*Mṅon.*).

འགྲད་པ *ḥgraḍ-pa* or བགྲད་པ *ḅgraḍ-pa* (*ḍepa*) to spread; to enter.

འགྲན *ḥgran* (*ḍen*), v. འགྲན་པ *ḥgran-pa* आहूत, ह्वय, ऐ, ओ, औ, ह्वै challenged; invoked.

འགྲན་གྱི་དོ་མེད *ḥgran-gyi do-meḍ* = འགྲན་ཡ་མེད *ḥgran-ya meḍ* without a rival; matchless; unequalled (applied to things).

Syn. འགྲན་གྱི་དོ་ཟླ་མེད་པ *ḥgran-gyi do-zla med-pa*; འགྲན་ཟླ་མེད་པ *ḥgran-zla med-pa* (*Mṅon.*).

འགྲན་ཐུབ་པ *ḥgran thub-pa* = འགྲན་ནུས་པ *ḥgran nus-pa* or འགྲན་བཟོད་པ *ḥgran ḅzoḍ-pa* to suffer rivalry; to stand rivalry.

འགྲན་དུ་འཇུག་པ *ḥgran-du ḥjug-pa* 1. to place in opposition; to enter into competition. 2. in a general sense, to defend one's self; to make resistance (*Ṛdsa.*).

+ འགྲན་དོ *ḥgran-do* = འགྲན་ཟླ *ḥgran-zla*.

འགྲན་པ *ḥgran-pa* (*ḍen-pa*) प्रतिस्पर्द्धा, प्रतिगज, संहर्ष (1) to vie with, contend with; to strive (for victory); ཕྱུག་ཁྱད་རྣམ་ཐོས་སྲས་དང་འགྲན་ཏེ *phyug-khyaḍ ṛnam-thos sras-daṅ ḥgran-te* to cope even with Vais'ravaṇa as to riches: བསྟོད་པར་འགྲན *ḅstoḍ-par ḥgran* let us vie with one another in uttering praise; འགྲན་པས་ཆོག let us now draw a parallel between (these two).

འགྲན་ཚིག *hgran-tshig* words of contention, bickering.

འགྲན་ཟླ *hgran zla* (*den-da*) 1. rival, competitor. 2. equal match; འགྲན་ཟླ་དང་བྲལ་བ *wa* unrivalled; matchless.

Syn. འགྲན་ཡ *hgran-ya*; འགྲན་གྱི་དོ་ཟླ *hgran-gyi do-zla*; འགྲན་དོ *hgran-do* rival; match.

འགྲན་སེམས *hgran-sems* 1. contention; emulation. 2. jealousy. 3. quarrelsome temper; spirit of controversy; འགྲན་སེམས་གཅོག་པ to stop; put an end to contention, rivalry.

འགྲམ *hgram* (*dam*) bank; shore; side; neighbourhood, as རྩིག་པའི་འགྲམ the foot of the wall; ཆུ་ཡི་འགྲམ *chu-yi hgram* river-side or bank; མེ་ཡི་འགྲམ *me-yi hgram* fire-side; དགོན་པའི་འགྲམ *dgon-pahi hgram* neighbourhood of a monastery; གྲོང་པའི་འགྲམ *aroṅ-pahi hgram* vicinity of a village; ལམ་གྱི་འགྲམ *lam-gyi hgram* roadside: ལུང་པ་ཆུ་ཡིས་གང་ན་འགྲམ་རྡོ་སྐམ་པོ་མི་ལུས if the river fills the valley, a stone on its bank does not remain dry (a proverb). Often used as a postp. with or without *du* or *la* annexed: གཡང་པོའི་འགྲམ་དུ at the brink of the precipice; མཚོའི་འགྲམ་ལ at the lake; close to the lake; འགྲམ་དུ is also used as adv. meaning near; close by.

འགྲམ་དཀྱུས *hgran-dkyus*=འགྲམ་པ *hgram-pa*.

འགྲམ་ངོགས *hgsam-ṅogs* तीर्थ, तट a bathing-place; a shore.

འགྲམ་ལྕག *hgram-lchag* a slap on the face; a box on the ear.

འགྲམ་པ *hgram-pa* हनु, गण्ड cheek (cf. ཁུར་ཚོས *khur-tshos*) ལག་པ་འགྲམ་པ་ལ་རྟེན་པ *lag-pa hgram-pa la rten-pa* to lay one's hand on the cheek; as vb. to proclaim, publish.

འགྲམ་པོ *hgram-po* जम्भदन्त one living or residing in the neighbourhood; one possessing crushing teeth; a demon.

འགྲམ་གཞི *hgram-gshi* foundation; basis; འགྲམ་གཞི་འདིང་བ *hgram-gshi hdiṅ-wa* to lay a foundation.

འགྲམ་ཡིག *hgram-yig* edict, proclamation, publication; ལོ་རྒྱུས་གནས་ཚུལ་གྱི་ཡི་གེ་འགྲམ་པ *lo-rgyus gnas-tshul-gyi yi-ge hgram-pa* to publish accounts of biography or history, &c.

འགྲམ་རུས *hgram-rus* cheek-bone; jaw-bone.

འགྲམ་གཅོག *hgram-gcog* the hinder part of the jaw-bone (*Sch.*).

འགྲམ་སོ *hgram-so* aco. to *Jä.* cheek-tooth; molar-tooth; grinder.

འགྲམས་པ *hgrams-pa* to spread over; མེ་ཏོག་སོགས་འགྲམས་པ་པོ *me-tog sogs hgrams-pa-po* one who spreads or scatters flowers, etc.: འདི་ནི་མི་ལ་འགྲམས་པ this will be spread over the man; ས་ལ་འགྲམས་པ to spread on the ground; ཕྱོགས་ཕྱོགས་སུ་འགྲམས་པ *phyogs-phyogs-su hgrams-pa* to scatter to the different quarters; ལུས་ལ་ནད་འགྲམས་པ *lus-la nad hgrams-pa* to infect the body with disease.

འགྲམས་ཚད *hgram-tshad* over-mastering fever.

འགྲས་འགྲུས *hgras-hgrus*=གྱ་གྱུ *gya-gyu*; जिह्म serpentine, crooked, bent.

འགྲས་པ *hgras-pa* (*de-pa*) ཕན་ཚུན་མི་མཐུན་པ *phan-tshun mi-mthun-pa* 1. disagreement; difference between two parties. 2. द्विष्, विद्विष् to hate; to bear ill-will; to have spite against.

འགྲིག་འགྲིག *hgrig-hgrig* (*dig-dig*) 1. arranged properly; ཚིག་འགྲིག་འགྲིག་པ *tshig hgrig-hgrig-pa* to arrange words properly. 2. gelatine; jelly of meat (*Jä.*).

འགྲིག་པ *hgrig-pa* (cf. སྒྲིག་པ *sgrig-pa*) to suit, agree, correspond; to be right; སྟབས་འགྲིག་པ *stabs hgrig-pa* suitable occasion; རྟེན་འབྲེལ་འགྲིག་པ *rten-hbrel hgrig-pa* good or auspicious coincidence; དུས་ཚོད་འགྲིག་པ *dus-tshod hgrig-pa* the time suits; གྲལ་འགྲིག་པ *gral hgrig-pa* to make everything ready; ཁ་འགྲིག་པ *kha hgrig-pa* unanimity in deposition; all of one expression or speech; བློ་སེམས་འགྲིག་པ *blo-sems hgrig-pa* to agree in opinion; ཁ་མཆུ་འགྲིག་པ *kha-mchu hgrig-pa* compromise in a law-suit or case (civil or in criminal).

འགྲིབ་པ *hgrib-pa* 1. हानि to grow dim; to get dark (*Cs.*) (cf. སྒྲིབ་པ *sgrib-pa*). 2. अपाय loss; diminution; also to grow less; to decrease, to be diminished, to decay; མི་འགྲིབ་མི་ལུད་པ *mi-hgrib mi-lud-pa* neither to grow less nor to flow over; འཕེལ་བ *hphel-wa* is opposed to འགྲིབ་པ *hgrib-pa*; བསྐལ་པ་མར་འགྲིབ་པ *bskal-pa mar-hgrib-pa* the *kalpa* (period) diminishes.

འགྲིམ *hgrim*, v. འགྲིམ་པ *hgrim-pa* in ལག་འགྲིམ *lag-hgrim* ལག་འགྲིམ་གྱིས་བརྒྱུས་པས *lag-hgrim gyis brgyus-pas*, passing from hand to hand.

འགྲིམ་འགྲུལ *hgrim-hgrul* communication; also travellers, either merchants or pilgrims: རྡོ་རྗེ་གདན་དུ་སོག་པོའི་འགྲིམ་འགྲུལ་ཆད *Rdo-rje gdan-du sog-pohi hgrim-hgrul chad* the communication of the Tartars with Dorjedan (Gaya) was interrupted (*A. 19*).

འགྲིམ་པ *hgrim-pa* 1. sometimes for འབྲིམ་པ *hbrim-pa*. 2. pf. འགྲིམས *hgrims* to march about, perambulate; to rove or stroll about; walk round; རྒྱལ་ཁམས་འགྲིམ་པ *rgyal-khams hgrim-pa* to rove over the countries; རི་ཁྲོད་འགྲིམ་པ *ri-khrod hgrim pa* to wander on a mountain range; ཆུ་དང་ལུང་ལ་ཡང་འགྲིམ་ནས་འགྲོ་བ *chu-dan lun-la yan hgrim nas hgro-wa* to go about crossing rivers and valleys, &c.

འགྲིམ་མོད *hgrim-mod* doing or accomplishing any work: ལ་ལ་ནི་ལས་ཀྱི་དབང་གིས་མངལ་སྒོ་གཞན་ཡང་འགྲིམ་མོད་ཀྱིས་མཐར་བདེ *la-la ni las-kyi dwan-gis mnal-sgo gshan-yan hgrim-mod-kis mthar bde* some in consequence of *las* (*i.e. karma*) entered the womb, others having accomplished good deeds, were happy enough to escape (here མཐར་=ཐར) (*Hbrom.* ཁ, *24*).

འགྲིམས *hgrims* (*dim*) or འགྲིམས་པ *hgrims-pa* अपकर्ष, अनल्प inferiority; inequality or also less in quantity or quality; རིག་པ་འགྲིམས་པ *rig-pa hgrims-pa* failing in intellect; growing foolish.

འགྲིལ་བ *hgril-wa* (*dil-wa*), pf. གྲིལ *gril* (cf. སྒྲིལ་བ *sgril-wa*) 1. to be twisted or wrapped round, for འཁྲིལ *hkhril* (*Sch.*), to be collected, concentrated; to flock or crowd together; ཀུན་འགྲིལ་ནས *kun hgril-nas* all in a heap; all together. 2. to be turned, rounded, made circular or cylindrical, *e.g.*, a stick (*Jä.*). 3. to fall, drop down.

འགྲིས *hgris* (*di*), v. འདྲིས *hdris*; འགྲིས་མ་ཐག་ཏུ་སྙིང་གཏམ་མི་བཅད་ཅིང་ *hgris-ma thag-tu snin-gtam mi-bcad-cin* immediatly after acquaintance not expressing one's heart's words, (*i.e.*, revealing one's secret) (*Jig.*).

འགྲུ་བ *hgru-wa*, (*du-wa*) pf. གྲུས *grus* 1. to bestow pains upon a thing; སློབ་པ་ལ་འགྲུ་བ to take pains in studying. 2. n. of a tribe in Tibet: དབྲའ་འགྲུ་ལྡོམ་གསུམ་ལྒ་དང་བཞི *dbrah-hgru ldom-gsum lga-dan bshi* (*Jig.*).

འགྲུབ་པ *hgrub-pa* (*dub-pa*) pf. གྲུབ *grub* (*Situ. 69*) to be accomplished without any perceptible agent; to be made ready; to be finished; འགྲུབ་པར་འགྱུར་རོ *hgrub-par hgyur-ro* will be finished: འགྲུབ་པར་གྱུར་ཅིག *hgrub-par gyur-cig* let it be finished or performed; འགྲུབ་པར་འགྱུར or འགྲུབ་ཡོང་ will be finished, performed; འགྲུབ་པ་མི་སྲིད *hgrub-pa mi-srid* it cannot be accomplished or done; མ་གྲུབ་པར *ma-*

grub-par before accomplished or performed: མ་འགྲུབ་པ་རྣམས་འགྲུབ་པར་འགྱུར་ར likt those deeds not yet effected be accomplished. ལྷུན་གྱིས་གྲུབ་པ *lhun-gyis grub-pa* spontaneously grown or produced, *i.e.*, in a supernatural way: འགྲུབ་པར་ཤོག *hgrub-par çog* सम्पद्यतु may it be accomplished!

འགྲུབ་སྦྱོར I: *hgrub-sbyor* or འགྲུབ་པ་དང་སྦྱོར་བ *hgrub-pa dañ sbyor-wa* anything accomplished and perfected (as a reward).

འགྲུབ་སྦྱོར II: is an expression occurring in almanacks relative to the proving true of certain astrological prognostics of good luck; similar to, but not identical with, རྟེན་འབྲེལ *rten-hbrel.*

འགྲུམ་པ *hgrum-pa* (*dum-pa*), pf. གྲུམ *grum* (cf. གྲུམ་པ *grum-pa*), to pinch or nip off (the point of a thing); to cut off; to prime, lop, clip the wings (*Jä.*).

འགྲུལ་པ *hgrul-pa* (*dul-pa*)=ལམ་གྱི་མགྲོན་པོ *lam-gyi mgron-po* a traveller, passenger; also a pilgrim: བོད་ལ་ད་ལོ་སོག་པོ་འགྲུལ་པ་མང་པོ་སླེབས་བྱུང, འགྱེད་མང་ཇ་ཡག་པོ་བྱུང *Bod-la da-lo sog-po hgrul-pa mañ-po slebs-byuñ, hgyed mañ-ja yag-po byuñ* this year many Mongol pilgrims have come to Tibet; there were liberal alms-doles, and tea for many.

འགྲུལ་བ *hgrul-wa* 1. to walk; to pass; to travel; འགྲུལ་བར་བྱེད་པ *hgrul-war byed-pa* to cause to go; to send off, despatch, a messenger; འགྲུལ་བ་པོ *hgrul-wa po* a walker, post, traveller, pedestrian; sbst. འགྲུལ *hgrul* passage; the possibility of passing: གཉའ་ནང་གི་འགྲུལ་ཆད་པས *Gñah-nañ-gi hgrul chad-pas* the passage from Nyanang being stopped (by snow). 2. fig. to walk; to live, act, or behave. 3. to pass as good; to be current (of coins).

འགྲུལ་ཞུད *hgrul-shud* passage, communication.

+ འགྲུས་འགོག *hgrus-hgog*=བརྩོན་འགྲུས *brtson-hgrus* assiduity, industry.

འགྲུས་པ *hgrus-pa* (*dui-pa*) 1. pf. འགྲུ་བ *hgru-wa.* 2. sbst. zeal, enthusiasm, diligence, endeavour; more frequently བརྩོན་འགྲུས *brtson-hgrus* (*Jä.*)

འགྲེ་བ *hgre-wa* (*de-wa*) (རིགས་ལྟ་བུ *rigs lta-bu*) पेयाल to roll one's self; ས་ལ་འགྲེ་བ *sa-la hgre-wa* to roll on the ground; འགྲེ་ལྡོག *hgre-ldog* or འགྲེ་ལོག་བྱེད་པ *hgre-log byed-pa* to roll on the ground from pain or despair, &c.; also of horses, &c.

འགྲེ་ལྡོག་ལྡོག་པ *hgre ldog-ldog-pa* to roll on the ground from pain, etc.; to wallow: རྟ་སོགས་ཕར་ཚུར་འགྲེ་ལོག་རྒྱབ་པ *rta-sogs phar-tshur hgre-log rgyab-pa* the horses, etc., roll hither and thither; སྡུག་བསྔལ་མི་བཟོད་པས་འགྲེ་ལྡོག་ལྡོག་བྱེད་ཀྱིན་འདུག *sdug-bsñal mi-bzod-pas hgre ldog-ldog byed-kyin hdug* unable to bear pain they were rolling (on the ground) (*Khrid. 39*).

འགྲེང་བ *hgreñ-wa* (*deñ-wa*) (cf. སྒྲེང་བ *sgreñ-wa*) प्रोन्नत, उत्थित to stand: དོང་གི་ཁར་འགྲེང་ནས standing at the mouth of the pit; དངངས་པ་ལྟར་འགྲེང་བར་འགྱུར *dñañs-pa ltar hgreñ-war hgyur* they started up as if afrighted. མི་འགྲེང་གསུམ *mi-hgreñ gsum* three lengths of a man (*Jä.*).

འགྲེང་བུ *hgreñ-bu* (*deñ-bu*), also འགྲེང་པོ *hgreñ-po*, sign of the vowel ◌ེ "*e.*"

འགྲེམ་པ *hgrem-pa*, pf. བཀྲམ *bkram*, fut. དགྲམ *dgram*, imp. ཁྲོམས *khroms* 1. to spread (as of grain, for drying), or འགྲེམས་པ *hgrems-pa* (*dem-pa*) (ཆུ་ལྟ་བུ *chu lta-bu*) अवकिरण to sprinkle (water). 2. to put or lay down in order, *e.g.*, beams, &c.; to spread out; to display; to scatter; to draw (a curtain).

* འགྲེལ་ཆུང་དོན་གསལ *hgrel-chuñ don-gsal.* गुणप्रभ n. pr. (*Schr.; Tä. 2, 200*).

འགྲེལ་པ *hgrel-pa* 1.=འཚོལ་པ *htshol-pa* ज्ञप्ति, कारिका to beg, supplicate. 2. to put in, arrange; ཚིག་དོན་འགྲེལ་པ *tshig-don hgrel-pa* the arranging or paraphrasing the meanings of words. 3. to explain, comment upon.

* འགྲེལ་བཤད *hgrel-bçad* कारिका (*Schr.*)

འགྲེས་པ *hgres-pa ex*-officer; late officer.

* འགྲོ་གླིང་ *Hgro-gliñ* द्रमिल n. pr. (*Schr.*; *Tā. 2, 222*), n. of a country (prob. Tamil); of a lexicographer [prob. द्राविड़].

འགྲོ་སྒོ *hgro-sgo* = འགྲོ་སོང་བ *hgro-soñ-wa* expenditure, cost; anything expended.

འགྲོ་ལྡིང་ I: *Hgro-ldiñ* n. of a country in the south of India, *i.e.*, Dravira.

འགྲོ་ལྡིང་ II: द्रमिल (*Schr.*; *Tā. 2, 27*).

འགྲོ་བ *hgro-wa*, pf. སོང་ *soñ*, imp. སོང་ *soñ*, but negative form of imp. མ་འགྲོ *ma-hgro* 1. to go, in all its significations, *i.e.*, to go away, proceed to, walk, &c. 2. sbst. a living creature; that which moves; འགྲོ་བ རིགས་དྲུག the six classes of living things. 3. to live; be living; move; exist; to be.

Syn. རྒྱུ་བ *rgyu-wa*; འདོང་བ *hdoñ-wa* (*Mñon.*).

འགྲོ་བ་པོ *hgro-wa po*=འགྲོ་བྱེད *hgro-byed* one who goes; goer; walker; traveller; passenger; pres. འགྲོ་བཞིན་འདུག *hgro-bshin hdug*= འགྲོ་གིན་འདུག *hgro-gin hdug* proceeding; going; fut. འགྲོ་བར་འགྱུར *hgro-war hgyur*.

འགྲོ་བ་རིགས་དྲུག *hgro-wa rigs-drug* the six kinds of moving beings:—(1) ལྷ *lha* देव the gods; (2) ལྷ་མ་ཡིན *lha-ma yin* असुर the demons; (3) མི *mi* मनुष्य humanity; (4) དུད་འགྲོ *dud-hgro* तिर्य्यक् beasts, etc.; (5) ཡི་དྭགས *yi-dhags* प्रेत the ghosts; (6) དམྱལ་བ *dmyal-wa* नरक hell-beings.

. འགྲོ་བའི་མགོན་པོ *hgro-wahi mgon-po* जगन्नाथ an epithet of Avalokiteçvara; སྤྱན་རས་གཟིགས *Syan-ras gzigs* a name of Buddha, of Vishnu (*Mñon.*).

འགྲོ་མྱོང་ས *hgro-myoñs* = འགྲོ་ཉོང་ *hgro-ñoñ* previously visited.

འགྲོ་ལས་ཆེ *hgro-las che*=འགྲོ་ཤས་ཆེ *hgro-ças che* or འགྲོ་ཉེན་ཆེ *hgro-ñen che*, adv. very probably; in all probability; also ལས་ཆེ alone is used: གསོ་བ་རིག་པ་འདི་བོད་ན་སྨན་མེད་པས་ནུབ་ནས་འགྲོ་ལས་ཆེ *gso-wa rig-pa hdi bod-na sman med-pas nub-nas hgro-las che* the science of healing, there being no medicine in Tibet, may in all probability disappear (*A. 35*).

འགྲོགས་པ *hgrogs-pa* to associate with; to keep company; to be in the company of; to accompany: དམ་པ་དག་དང་འགྲོགས་པར་བཙུན *dma-pa dga-dañ hgrogs-par, bcun* try to associate with the holy ones.

འགྲོགས་པ་པོ *hgrogs-pa-po* or འགྲོགས་པར་བྱེད *hgrogs-par byed* associate; one who accompanies, goes together.

Syn. རྗེས་ཆགས *rjes-chags*; ཡོངས་སྦྱོར *yoñs-sbyor*; ཡང་དག་འགྲོགས *yañ-dag hgrogs* (*Mñon.*).

འགྲོ་ལུགས *hgro-lugs* (custom) manner.

འགྲོན་བུ *hgron-bu* ཆོ་ལོའི་ས་བོན *cho-lohi sa-bon* cowries; dice (*Mñon.*).

* འགྲོ་མ *hgro-ma* गामना (*Schr.*; *Kālāc. T. 119*).

* འགྲོ་བཟང་མ *hgro bzañ-ma* (*Schr.*; *92 A.*).

འགྲོ་བྱེད *hgro-byed*=གླང་པོ *glañ-po* an elephant (*Mñon.*).

འགྲོལ་བ I: *hgrol-wa*, pf. བཀྲོལ *bkrol*, fut. དགྲོལ *dgrol*, to unravel; to make loose; to set free; to unfasten; དོན་དུ་མདུད་པ་འགྲོལ་བ *don-du mdud-pa hgrol-wa* to cut the knot; འགྲོལ་བ་པོ *hgrol-wa po* or འགྲོལ་བྱེད *hgrol-byed* one who unravels, loosens; འགྲོལ་གྱིན་འདུག *hgrol-gyin hdug* is being set free; འགྲོལ་བར་འགྱུར *hgrol-war hgyur* will be set free.

འགྲོལ་བ II: to escape, be liberated, be released from. The pf. here is གྲོལ *grol.* Generally used in the distinctive Buddhist sense of escape from the necessity of living, re-birth, etc.

འགྲོས *ẖgros* མི་རྟ་སོགས་ཀྱི་འགྲོ་ལུགས *mi-ṟta sogs-kyi ẖgro-lugs* gait; manner of walking of men, horses, etc.: ཉི་ཟླ་གཟའ་སྐར་ལ *ñi-gzlaẖ s̱kar la*:—རང་འགྲོས་རླུང་འགྲོས་གཉིས་རེ་ཡོད *rañ-ẖgros ṟluñ-ẖgros gñis re-yod* those that are self-moving, such as sun, moon and planets, etc., and those that are moved; ངང་པ་ནེ་ཙོའི་འགྲོས་ཅན་ཀུན་གྱིས་བཀུར those whose manner of walking is like the goose or the parrot are respected by all; གླང་ཆེན་སེང་གེ་ཁྱུ་མཆོག་འགྲོས་ལྡན་མིས, ལོངས་སྤྱོད་མང་པོའི་བདག་པོ་བྱེད་པར་འདོད *glañ-chen señ-ge khyu-m̱chog ẖgros-ḻdan mis, loñs-s̱pyoḏ mañ-poẖi ḇdag-po byeḏ-par ẖdoḏ* those that walk in the manner of elephant, lion or bull become rich and wish to be master of many people; ཁྱི་ཕག་བོང་འགྲོས་ཅན་གང་སྡུག་བསྔལ་འཐོབ whosoever walks in the manner of dog, pig and donkey gains unhappiness (*Mi.*).

རྒ་བ *ṟga-wa*, pf. རྒས་ *ṟgas* जरा 1. to be old, aged; also sbst. old age. 2. to go down; to set (of the sun, etc.) (*Jä.*).

རྒ་ཝང་ཀྲད་ཀྱི *ṟga-wañ kraḏ-kyi* bat, flitter-mouse (*Jä.*).

* རྒ་ལོ *ṟga-lo* (*Schr.; Tā 2, 252*).

རྒ་ཤི *ṟga-çi* जरामरण old age and death; རྒ་ཤིས་གཟིར་བ *ṟga-çis gzir-wa* to suffer under the infirmities of old age.

རྒང་ *ṟgañ* also འགང་གཟེར་མ *ẖgañ-gzer-ma* hedge-hog, the second term designating two species: *Erinaceus auritus* and *Erinaceus amurensis*, the latter found in Kökönur district.

རྒད་པ *ṟgaḏ-pa*=resp. རྒན་པ *ṟgan-pa* old; aged.

རྒད་པོ *ṟgaḏ-po*=རྒས་པ *ṟgas-pa* also=བགྲེས་པོ *ḇgres-po* an old man; a man gray with age.

Syn. ལང་ཚོ་ཡོལ *lañ-tsho yol*; ན་ཚོད་ཡོལ *na-tshoḏ yol*; ལོ་མང་ཁུར་ལྡན *lo-mañ khur-ḻdan*; དྭང་པོ་ཉམས *ḏwoñ-po ñams*; འཁོགས་པ *ẖkhogs-pa*; མགོ་སྐྱེས་དཀར་བ *m̱go-s̱kyes ḏkar-wa*; བཞི་པའི་གནས་སྐབས *ḇshi-paẖi gnas-s̱kabs*; སྐུ་ན་སྨིན་པ *s̱ku-na s̱min-pa*; དགུང་ལོ་མཐོན་པོ *ḏguñ-lo m̱thon-po*; རྒན་པ *ṟgan-pa* (*M̱ñon.*).

རྒད་མོ *ṟgaḏ-mo* an old woman.

རྒན་རྒོན *ṟgan-ṟgon* (རྒད་པོ་རྒད་མོ *ṟgaḏ-po ṟgaḏ-po*) old man and old woman.

རྒན་པ *ṟgan-pa* ज्येष्ठ, महत्तर an elder; senior. In Tibetan astrology a person aged between 60 and 72 is called རྒན་པ.

རྒན་པོ *ṟgan-po* वृद्ध, मूल, जीर्ण 1. an old man; elder. 2. the headman of a village.

རྒན་པོའི་ཐིག *ṟgan-poẖi thig*, གོ་བ *go-wa* vulture; also met. for rainbow (*M̱ñon.*).

རྒན་པོའི་ཐིག་ལེ *ṟgan-poẖi thig-le* वृद्ध-पुत्रक met. an old man's son.

རྒན་པོའི་ལས *ṟgan-poẖi las* the work of an elderly man.

རྒན་མོ *ṟgan-mo* जर्जरिका, जीर्णा, वृद्धा an old woman; one infirm and worn out.

རྒན་ཤུགས *ṟgan-shugs* महल्लक those that are grown old; elderly people.

རྒན་རབས *ṟgan-rabs* ज्येष्ठ the venerable, aged.

རྒན་རིམས *ṟgan-rims* वृद्धान्त of the older class.

རྒན་ལ་ཉན་པ *ṟgan-la ñam-pa* वृद्धश्रव: to listen to the advice of the old.

རྒན་སོང *ṟgan-soñ* वाजय्य has become old.

རྒལ rgal तरण, अनुयुक्त;=རབ rab a ford; ཆུ་རྒལ chu-rgal the ford in a river: རྒལ་དཀའ་བ rgal dkaḥ-wa difficult to ford or to cross.

རྒལ་པ rgal-pa or རྒལ་བ rgal-wa pf. and fut. བརྒལ brgal, imp. རྒོལ rgol, to ford (a river); to travel through; to pass over; to surmount a pass: རྒྱ་མཚོ་ལ་གྲུ་གཟིངས་ཀྱི་རྒལ་ཏེ rgya-mtsho la gru-gziṅs-kyi rgal-te after having crossed the sea in a ship; ལ་བརྒལ་བའི་བྱང་ངོས la brgal-waḥi byaṅ ṅos the north side (face) of the mountain-pass that has been crossed.

རྒལ་ཚིགས rgal-tshigs पृष्ठमांस, सन्धि the joints of the back; hip-joint; according to *Sch.* རྒལ་ཚིགས rgal-tshigs=སྒལ་ཚིགས sgal-tshigs the spine.

རྒལ་ཅིག rgal-cig a lizard; བླ་མ་རྒལ་ཅིག bla-ma rgal-cig the chameleon.

རྒས rgas=རྒ་བ rga-wa old, ripe.

རྒས་ཀ rgas-ka old age.

རྒས་པ rgas-pa=རྒད་པོ rgad-po जराक्रान्त, जीर्ण aged, old; exhausted; infirm; sbst. an old man.

རྒས་པ་བསོ་བ rgas-pa, bso-wa an elixir (which has the property of giving the appearance of youth in old age); བཅུད་ལེན་གྱི་སྐོར bcud-lengyi skor (*Mṅg. 90*).

རྒས་བྱེད rgas-byed जराहित that makes one look old and haggard.

རྒས་བྱེད་མ rgas byed-ma जराहिणी a woman whose company makes a youth look old.

རྒས་མེད rgas-med निर्जर that never grows old, a name of the celestial beings.

རྒུ rgu=དགུ-dgu many; དགུ་ཐུབ dgu-thub one able to overcome many.

རྒུ་དྲུས rgu-drus a mixture of many ingredients healing sores, joining veins and removing pains in the intestines, as in རྒུ་དྲུས་རྨ་འདྲུབ་རྩ་མཐུད་རྒྱུ་གཟེར་འཇོམས rgu-drus rma-ḥdrub rtsa-mthud rgyu-gzer ḥjoms (*Med.*).

རྒུད་པ rgud-pa व्यसन, विपत्ति, विद्रव, आपदा: 1. disadvantage; trouble. 2. to decline, to sink, grow frail: རྒས་པ་དང་ན་བ་དང་མྱ་ངན་དང་སྡུག་བསྔལ་གྱིས་ལུས་སེམས་རྒུད་པ rgas-pa daṅ na-wa daṅ mya-ṅan daṅ sdug-bsṅal gyis lus-sems rgud-pa (his) body and mind become deteriorated from misery, sorrow, disease and age; དར་རྒུད dar-rgud rise and decline.

རྒུད་པོ rgud-po, v. གུད་པོ gud-po.

རྒུད་ཕྲན rgud-mun=དབུལ་ཕོངས་ཀྱི་མུན་པ dbul-phoṅs-kyi mun-pa a destitute person; destitute.

རྒུན rgun=རྒུན་འབྲུམ rgun-ḥbrum द्राक्षा grapes; རྒུན་དཀར rgun-dkar the white species of grape: རྒུན་འབྲུམ་གློ་ནད་སེལ་ཞིང་ཚད་པ་སྦྱོང rgun-ḥbrum glo-nad sel-shiṅ tshad-pa sbyoṅ the grape removes diseases of the lungs and cures fever.

རྒུན་སྐྱེམས rgun-skems wine or drink made from grapes.

རྒུན་རྒོད rgun-rgod wild grapes; according to *Jä.* raisins in *W.*

རྒུར་པོ rgur-po or སྒུར་པོ sgur-po कुब्ज hunchback; one bent by age, v. དགུར dgur.

རྒུར་རེ rgur-re རྒུར་རྒུར་བྱས་ནས་སྡད་པ rgur-rgur byas-nas sdad-pa sit downcast, bending the head downwards.

རྒོ rgo, sometimes for སྒོ sgo.

རྒོ་བ rgo-wa=དགོ་བ dgo-wa a species of antelope Procapra picticaudata v. *Jä.*

རྒོངས་མོ rgoṅs-mo=དགོང་མོ dgoṅ-mo in older writings the evening.

རྒོད rgod 1. adj. wild; བྱ་རྒོད a vulture; a bird of prey; ར་རྒོད wild goat; ཕག་རྒོད wild boar; གཡག་རྒོད=འབྲོང་ a wild yak. 2. མི་རྒོད་ལྷ་ཆ,

mi-rgod lta-bu like a wild man; a savage; a robber; a ruffian; མི་རྒོད་བྱེད་པ *mi-rgod byed-pa* to rob (usually named together with murdering and lying).

རྒོད་སྐམ་མ *rgod skam-ma* a barren mare.

རྒོད་པ *rgod-pa* 1. to laugh. 2.=གཡེང་བ *gyeṅ-wa* to grow weak, languid, or indolent.

+ རྒོད་བག་ཅན *rgod bag-can*, described as ཡོན་ཏན་མེད་ཅིང་སེམས་དཔང་མཐོ་བ *yon-tan med-ciṅ sems dwaṅ mtho-wa* 1. a vain person pretending to be great and powerful, but devoid of wisdom. 2.=སེམས་རྣམ་པར་མི་ཞི་བ *sems rnam-par mi-shi-wa* the disturbed state of the mind (*K. d.* ན *355*). 3. weak; languid (*Jä.*).

རྒོད་བྱེད *rgod-byed* अर्धनयन laughing; laughter.

རྒོད་མ *rgod-ma* वामी, वाड़वा a mare.

རྒོད་མ་སྐྱེས *rgod-ma skyes* 1. a name of the physician of the gods. 2. born of the mare. One of the wives of the God of the Sun who, unable to bear the glare of his rays, ran away in the guise of a mare to the northern continent, Uttara Kuru. The sun followed there, and caused her to give birth to the celestial twins called As'vinī kumāra.

རྒོད་མའི་ཚོགས *rgod-maḥi tshogs* वाड़व a herd of mares.

རྒོད་ཡས *rgod-yas* a numerical figure.

རྒོལ *rgol*, v. རྒོལ་བ *rgol-wa*.

རྒོལ་ཕྱི་རྒོལ *rgol-phyi rgol* a posture of witchcraft against evil spirits: རྒོལ་ཕྱི་རྒོལ་གྱི་གདན་བཅམས *rgol phyi-rgol gyi-gdan bçams* (*A. 33*) prepared the seat for a defiant attitude to suppress evil spirits.

རྒོལ་བ *rgol-wa*=རྩོད་པ *tsod-pa* वाद, pf. and fut. བརྒོལ *brgol*, to dispute, combat, fight, make controversy; ཚིག་གིས་རྒོལ་བ to hold discussion, verbal disputation; དཔུང་དང་སྟོབས་ཀྱིས་རྒོལ་བ to fight by means of troops and powers; རྒོལ་བའི་ཞུ་དོན *rgol-wahi, shu-don* a challenge; a speech provoking a quarrel; ཕས་རྒོལ a quarrel or contest begun by the counter party (*Sch.*); ཕས་རྒོལ་མི an adversary, opponent; སྔ་རྒོལ *sña-rgol* पूर्ववादी the plaintiff in a law suit, but generally signifies an aggressor, assailant; ཕྱི་རྒོལ *phyi-rgol* परवादी defendant; ཕྱིར་རྒོལ་བའི་གནོད་པ *phyir-rgol-wahi gnod-pa* is an external danger against which every one tries to protect himself and chiefly by charms and witchcraft; སྔ་རྒོལ *sña-rgol* and ཕྱི་རྒོལ *phyi-rgol* are also said to signify such students as hold religious controversies with one another. སྔ་རྒོལ *sña-rgol* is the party putting the questions; ཕྱི་རྒོལ *phyi-rgol* is the party answering the questions.

རྒོལ་ཚིག *rgol-tshig* threatening words.

Syn. སྤྱོ་ཚིག *spyo-tshig*; བསྡིགས་ཚིག *bsdigs-tshig* (*Mṅon*).

རྒྱ I: *rgya* मुद्रा seal, stamp, token, mark, sign; རྒྱ་འདེབས་པ *rgya-ḥdebs-pa* to seal; to stamp: རྒྱ་གཅོག་པ *rgya gcog-pa* to break or open a seal; རི་རྒྱ་ལུང་རྒྱ་བཞུག་པ *ri-rgya luṅ-rgya bshug-pa* to seal up hills and valleys, *i.e.*, to protect the living beings inhabiting them from being harmed by huntsmen or fishermen; an annual religious performance of the Dalai Lama, consisting in a variety of spells and incantations for the safety of animals.

Syn. ཐེའུ་ཙེ *thehu-tse*; ཕྱག་དམ *phyag-dam*; དམ་ཕྲུག *dam-phrug* (*Mṅon.*).

རྒྱ II: animal of the deer class, in appearance like the *Nilgai*, possibly the saiga-antelope.

རྒྱ III: जाल, कल a net, a trap; ཉ་རྒྱ *ña-rgya* a fishing net; བྱ་རྒྱ *bya-rgya* a fowling net; རི་དྭགས་ཀྱི་རྒྱ *ri-dwags kyi rgya* a net or trap to catch birds or wild animals.

རྒྱ IV: 1. extent; size: རྒྱའི་ཚད་ནི་ཅི་ཙམ *rgyahi tshad-nichi-tsam* how much was its extent? རྒྱ་དཔག་ཏུ་མེད་པ *rgya dpag-tu med-pa* immeasurable in extent. 2. भारत a name for India but sometimes for China, which are both vast countries; also fullness, complete state, or perfection. རྒྱ་རིམ་པ་བདུན་རྒྱས་བཏབ་པ *rgya rim-pa bdun-rgyas btab-pa* there are seven kinds of mark used in dividing a volume; they are the following:—(1) ཚིག་འབྲུ་མི་འཁྲུགས་ཚིག་གི་རྒྱ *tshig-hbru mi-hkhrugs tshig-gi rgya* the sign or mark for distinguishing one verse from another, so that the verses may not be confused; (2) ཚིག་རྐང་མི་འཁྲུགས་པ་ཤད་ཀྱི་རྒྱ *tshig-rkañ mi-hkhrugs-pa çad-kyi rgya* the marks or stops used at the end of a sentence or the line of a verse; (3) ཚིག་དོན་མི་འཁྲུགས་པ་ལེའུའི་རྒྱ *tshig-don mi-hkhrugs-pa lehuhi rgya* to mark the chapters: (4) ཤོ་ལོ་ཀ་མི་འཁྲུགས་པ་བམ་པོའི་རྒྱ *ço-lo-ka mi-hkhrugs-pa bam-pohi rgya* the marks so that the lines may not be carried from one chapter to another; (5) བམ་པོ་མི་འཁྲུགས་པ་བམ་པོའི་གྲངས་ཀྱི་རྒྱ *bam-po mi-hkhrugs-pa bam-pohi grañs-kyi rgya* marks to shew the number of parts in each volume; (6) མཐའ་མི་འཆལ་བ་སྣེ་ཐིག་གི་རྒྱ *mthah mi-hchal-wa sne thig-gi rgya* the marks to shew the end of book, part or chapter; (7) གླེགས་བམ་མི་འཁྲུགས་པ་གདོང་ཡིག་གམ་སྤྱན་ཁྱེར་གྱི་རྒྱ *glegs-bam mi-hkhrugs pa gdoñ-yig gam spyan-khyer-gyi rgya* the serial number used in marking the volumes of a collection.

རྒྱ་གྲམ *rgya-gram* (*gya-tam*) a cross; the *Svastika* sign; རྡོ་རྗེ་རྒྱ་གྲམ *rdo-rje rgya-gram* a cross made of two *Vajra*, one placed upon another crosswise.

རྒྱ་སྐད *rgya-skad* Indian or Chinese language.

རྒྱ་སྐས *rgya-skas* a staircase, cf. སྐས་ཀ *skas-ka.*

རྒྱ་སྐྱེགས *rgya-skyegs* लाक्षा, जतु lac; a kind of resin; རྒྱ་སྐྱེགས་ཀྱི་རྣམ་འགྱུར *rgya-skyegs kyi rnam-hgyur* जतुः a sort of lac of the colour of *Mañjiṣṭhā.*

རྒྱ་སྐྱེགས་ཤིང *rgya-skyeg çiñ* मज्जन, लोध्र, सावर a kind of tree the twigs of which are used to clean the teeth.

རྒྱ་བསྐུམ་པ *rgya bskum-pa* to contract; to diminish in extent.

རྒྱ་དཀར *rgya-dkar* large orb; disk: ཉི་ཟླའི་རྒྱ་དཀར་ཤར *ñi-zlahi rgya-dkar çar* the bright orbs of the sun and the moon appear (*Jä.*).

རྒྱ་བསྐྱེད་པ *rgya bskyed-pa* to widen, enlarge, extend, augment.

རྒྱ་ཁམས་པ *rgya khams-pa* the Khampa tribes residing on the confines of China and Tibet.

རྒྱ་ཁྱི *rgya-khyi* a Chinese lap-dog.

རྒྱ་ཁྱོན *rgya-khyon* or རྒྱ་འམ་ཁྱོན *rgya ham khyon*, v. རྒྱ *rgya.*

རྒྱ་གར **Rgya-gar** said to stand for *Rgya-dkar*, because *dkar* becomes གར *gar* when joined to the word རྒྱ *rgya* भारत; Tibetan n. for India, the extensive country where the people dress in white. The different names for India are—(1) འཕགས་ཡུལ *Hphags-yul* आर्यदेश Ārya des'a; (2) འཕགས་འཁྲུངས *Hphags-hkhruñs* birth (place) of the Holy ones; (3) བསོད་ནམས་ས་གཞི *Bsod-nams sa-gshi* पुण्यभूमि *Puṇya-bhū-mi* for Magadha; (4) སའི་སྙིང་པོ *Sahi sñiñ-po* भूमण्डल.

*རྒྱ་གར་ཕྱག་ན་ *Rgya-gar phyag-na* (*Schr.; Tā. 2, 249*).

རྒྱ་གྲམ་ *rgya-gram*, v. རྒྱ་ཀྲམ་ *rgya-kram.*

རྒྱ་གྲོལ་ *rgya-grol* उन्मुक्त set free, liberated.

རྒྱ་བརྒྱབ་པ་ *rgya bgyab-pa* or རྒྱ་བཏབ་པ་ *rgya-btab-pa* to lay a net or trap.

རྒྱ་རྒྱུ་ར་ *rgya-rgyu-ra*, met. for གྲོག་མ་ *grog-ma* the ant (*Mṅon.*).

རྒྱ་སྒོ་ *rgya-sgo* द्वार a gate; a principal door or entrance.

རྒྱ་སྒྱུར་ *rgya-sgyur* met. an ant (*Mṅon.*).

+ རྒྱ་ཅང་ *rgya-caṅ* སྐེ་རགས་སྦུབ་ཅན་ཨབ་བཏབ་པ་ *ske-rags sbub-can ab btab-pa* narrow, long money-bag made of net and securely joined to the sash.

རྒྱ་ལྕོག་ *rgya-lcog* Chinese table.

རྒྱ་ཆད་ *rgya-chad* partiality; invidious distinction.

རྒྱ་ཆེ་བ་ *rgya che-wa* or ཐུལ་ཆེ་བ་ *gthul che-wa* great, large, copious, diffused; སྟོན་པ་རྒྱ་ཆེ་བ་ *ston-pa rga che-wa* a great master or teacher.

རྒྱ་ཆེར་རོལ་པ་ *Rgya-cher rol-pa* Tibetan edition of the Lalitavistara.

རྒྱ་ཆེ་ལམ་ *rgya-che lam* राजपथ = རྒྱ་ལམ་ *rgya-lam* main road.

རྒྱ་ཆེན་པོ་ *rgya-chen-po* = རྒྱ་ཆེ་བ་ *rgya che-wa* प्रथित large, copious, wide; ས་ཆ་རྒྱ་ཆེན་པོ་ *sa-cha rgya-chen-po* an extensive country or large place; སེམས་རྒྱ་ཆེན་པོ་ *sems rgya-chen-po* a generous broad heart; ཆོས་རྒྱ་ཆེན་པོ་ *chos rgya-chen-po* a voluminous religious work; religious observances on a large scale.

རྒྱ་ཆེར་བཤགས་པ་ *rgya-cher bśags-pa* विस्तीर्णवर्णना copious or abundant description.

རྒྱ་ཇོག་ *rgya-jog* or རྒྱ་འཇོག་ *rgya-hjoga* a long table; a bench.

རྒྱ་རྟགས་ *rgya-rtags* 1. मुद्रा mark, sign, signature, stamp. 2. (གྲངས་ *grañs*) n. of a numeral.

རྒྱ་ཏམ་ *rgya-tam* the Indian rupee.

རྒྱ་ཐེལ་ *rgya-thel* a kind of seal or stamp.

རྒྱ་མཐོང་ *rgya-mthoṅ* lit. wide view; a platform or open pavilion on the top of a house.

རྒྱ་མདའ་ *Rgya-mdah* n. of a district in upper Kong-po (*Yig. k. 25*).

རྒྱ་འདྲེ་ *rgya-hdre* or རྒྱམ་འདྲེ་ *rgyam-hdre* a quarrel.

རྒྱ་ནག་ *Rgya-nag* महाचीन China, *i.e.*, the great and extensive country where people dress in black.

རྒྱ་རྣམས་ *Rgya-rnams* or རྒྱ་མི་རྣམས་ *Rgya-mi-rnams* the Chinese people.

རྒྱ་སྣ་རུ་ *rgya-sna ru* in mystic language copulation (གབ་ཚིག་དོན་ལ་འཁྲིག་པ་ *gab-tshig don-la hkhrig-pa*).

རྒྱ་སྤོས་ *rgya-spos* तगरः the Chinese incense stick or *Joss*-stick.

རྒྱ་ཕུགས་ *rgya-phugs* छादन a full covering.

རྒྱ་བ་ *rgya-wa* = ཕན་པ་ *phan-pa*, བསམ་པ་འབད་པ་ *bsam-pa, hbad-pa* to be useful and of service; to exert one's self: སངས་རྒྱས་ཀྱི་བསྟན་པ་ལ་རྒྱ་བ་ཡིན་པས་ *sans-rgyas-kyi bstan-pa la rgya-wa yin-pas* (*A. 133*) he was of great service to the religion of Buddha.

རྒྱ་བོ་ *rgya-wo* the beard; colloq. "gyan."

རྒྱ་བོད་ *rgya-bod* or རྒྱ་ནག་དང་བོད་ *Rgya-nag-daṅ Bod* China and Tibet. बहिर्भोट; also Ulterior or Chinese Tibet.

རྒྱ་བྱིན་གཞུ་ *rgya-byin gshu* इन्द्रधनु: rainbow.

རྒྱ་མ་ *rgya-ma* a steel-yard. In Amdo the term རྒྱ་རྨ་ *rgya-rma* signifies secondary syphilis.

རྒྱ་མེན་མེ་ཏོག་ *rgya-men me-tog* a flower used as medicine: རྒྱ་མེན་མེ་ཏོག་ཁྲག་འཁྲུག་རེ་རྨོད་གཉེར་ལ་ཕན, the flower *Gyamen metog* is useful in diseased blood and in pains in the shoulders.

རྒྱ་མོ་ *rgya-mo* a net; also a Chinese woman.

རྒྱ་སྨུག *rgya-smug* of the colour of the liver; purple. Acc. to *Jä.* violet colour.

རྒྱ་རྩངས *rgya-rtsaṅs* a kind of lizard (*Sman 322*).

རྒྱ་རྩི *rgya-rtsi* (ས་རྩི *sa-rtsi*) a Chinese varnish: རྒྱ་རྩིས་རྨ་ཤུ་འབྲས་སྐྲན་རྔོ་ལ་ཕན *rgya-rtsis rma-çu hbras-skron rṅo-la phan* Chinese varnish cures sores, wounds, skin-iruption, itch, etc.

རྒྱ་བརྩོན་འགྲུས་སེང་གེ *Rgya-brtson hgrus Seṅ-ge* n. of the learned Tibetan *Lo-tsā-wa* who twice visited Vikramas'ila in Magadha with a view to take Atis'a to Tibet.

རྒྱ་ཚྭ *rgya-tshwa*=སིན་ཏུ་ལན་ཚྭ་བ *çin-tu lan-tshwa-wa* sal-amoniac.

Syn. ཀ་པོ་ཏ *ka-po-ta*; ལྕེ་འབིགས *lche-hbigs* (*Mṅon.*).

རྒྱ་ཚོས *rgya-tshos* vermilion.

རྒྱ་མཚོ *rgya-mtsho* समुद्र, सागर, जलेन्द्र 1. the ocean; the sea. 2. dropsy. 3. it also signifies the number four: མཁས་པ་ལེགས་བཤད་ཀྱིས་མི་ངོམས, རྒྱ་མཚོ་ཆུ་ཡིས་ངོམས་པ་མེད *mkhas-pa legs-bçad kyis mi-ṅoms, rgya-mtsho chu-yis ṅoms-pa med* no amount of elegant sayings or writings is adequate for the learned; no quantity of water is sufficient for the ocean. རྒྱ་མཚོ is a common personal name in Tibet.

Syn. ཆུ་གཏེར *chu-gter*; ཆུ་དག *chu-dag*; ཆུའི་ཕུང་པོ *chuhi phuṅ-po*; རིན་ཆེན་འབྱུང་གནས *rin-chen hbyuṅ-gnas*; ཟླ་བས་འཕེལ *zla-was hphel*; ཟླ་བའི་གྲོགས *zla-wahi grogs*; ཕ་རོལ་མི་མངོན *pha-rol mi-mṅon*; རྒལ་དཀའ་བ *rgal-dkah-wa*; ཆུ་སྲིན་འབྱུང་གནས *chu-srin hbyuṅ-gnas*; ཆུ་སྲིན་བདག *chu-srin bdag*; ཆུའི་སྲིན་པོའི་གྲོང་ཆེ *chuhi srin-pohi groṅ-che*; སིན་དྷུའི་བདག་པོ *sin-dhuhi bdag-po*; གང་གཱ་འཛིན *gaṅ gha-hdsin*; རི་ཡི་འོད་ཅན *ri-yi hod-can*; རོ་ལྡན་མ *ro ldan-ma*; ས་མཆོད་མ *sa-mchod ma*; དུག་ཅན་གནས *dug-can gnas*; ཉལ་འགྲོའི་གཏེར *ñal-hgrohi gter*; དལ་འབབ་མཛོད *dal-hbab mdsod*; ཆུ་སྲེལ *chu-srel*; ཆུ་སྲིན་རྒྱལ་མཚན་ཅན *chu-srin rgyal-mtshan can*; ཟླ་བའི་མ་མ *zla-wahi ma-ma*.

རྒྱ་མཚོ་དགའ *rgya-mtsho dgah* समुद्रानन्दन the moon; རྒྱ་མཚོའི་ཟླ *rgya-mtshohi zla* सोमसिन्धु reflection of the moon in the ocean; རྒྱ་མཚོ་པ་འམ་མཆོད་ཀྱི་དཔྱད *rgya-mtsho pa-ham mchod-gyi dpyad* समद्रलचण a seaman or anything belonging to the sea.

* རྒྱ་མཚོ་སྦས་པ *Rgya-mtsho sbas-pa* Samudra Gupta; क्रकचक n. of ancient monastery found buried under sand by King Dharmapāla, near site of which was founded the monastery of Vikramas'ila.

+ རྒྱ་མཚོའི་མཆིང *rgya-mtshohi mchiṅ*=རྒྱ་མཚོའི་མཛིངས *rgya-mtshohi mjiṅs* or ཀློང་དཀྱིལ *kloṅ-dkyil* the vast expanse of the sea.

རྒྱ་མཚོའི་དུང་ཕྲེང *rgya-mtshohi duṅ-phreṅ*=ཚ་ལ *tsha-la* billows; waves of the sea; also borax (*Sman. 166*).

རྒྱ་མཚོའི་རྡོ་བ *Rgya-mtshohi rdo-wa* n. of a medicine.

རྒྱ་མཚོའི་ལྦུ་བ *rgya-mtshohi wu-wa*, v. རྒྱ་མཚོའི་དབུ་བ *rgya-mchohi dbu-wa* समुद्रफेन, a kind of medicine [(1) sea-foam, (2) cuttle-fish bone]*S.*

རྒྱ་བཞི *rgya-bshi* in *W.* is stated to be a kind of *gtor-ma* offering to demons and demi-gods as a substitute for animal sacrifice (*Jä.*).

རྒྱ་གཟེབ *rgya-gzeb* acc. *Sch.* a large net; a large rake used in reaping.

རྒྱ་ཡན *rgya-yan*=གཡེང་བ *gyeṅ-wa* laziness; remissness: རྣམ་ཀུན་རྒྱ་ཡན་དུས *rnam-kun rgya-yan dus* during the time I am found negligent (of religious duties) (*Yig. k. 22*).

+ རྒྱ་ཡི་འབུར *rgya-yi-hbur* engravings on a seal; རྒྱ་ཡི་འབུར *rgya-yi hbur*=དམ་ཕྲུག་གི་རི་མོ *dam-phrug gi ri-mo* the raised figures or inscriptions on a seal; ཕྱག་རྒྱ *phyag-rgya* in mystic rites the symbolical gestures of the hand or the fingers, to express certain charms and language.

རྒྱ་ཡུལ *rgya-yul* the country of India or China.

རྒྱ་རི་ *rgya-ri* व्यञ्जन painted figures, etc.; a portion of meat (*Jä.*). It also denotes a measure = half *dum* or one fourth of *lhu*.

རྒྱ་རོག *rgya-rog* = ཨག་ཚོམ *aga-tsom* beard.

རྒྱ་ལབ *rgya-lab* talk, gossip.

རྒྱ་ལམ *rgya-lam* high road, main way.

རྒྱ་ཤུག *rgya-çug* the juniper tree; a species of fir from China and the Himalayas; a species of jujube; རྒྱ་གར་དང་རོང་གི་ཤུག་པ་འབྲས་བུ་ཆུང་ཆུང་ཡོད་པ་ཞིག *rgya-gar-dan roṅ-gi çug-pa hbras-bu chuṅ-chuṅ yod-pa shig* (*Khrid. 33*); རྒྱ་ཤུག་གི་འབྲུ *rgya-çug-gi hbru* कुवल, बदर फल jujube, fruit.

Syn. བྱ་རྒོད་སེན་མོ *bya-rgod sen-mo*; འབྲས་ཟླུམ་ཅན *hbras-zlum-can*; དདལ་སྐྱེས *ddal-skyes*; ས་སྟོབས *sa-stobs* (*Mṅon.*).

རྒྱ་ཤུག་འཁྱིལ *rgya-çug hkhyil* (རྒྱ་ཤུག་གི་སྡོང་པོ་བཟང་པོ *rgya-çug-gi sdoṅ-po bzaṅ-po*) a species of juniper.

རྒྱ་ཤུབས *rgya-çubs* or པུས་ཤུབས *pus-çubs* light trousers worn by the Chinese.

རྒྱ་ཤོག *rgya-çog* Chinese paper.

རྒྱ་ཤོས *rgya-ços* = རྒྱ་ཚོས *rgya-tshos* vermilion.

རྒྱ་སེར *rgya-ser* 1. gap, cleft, fissure chasm in rocks, glaciers, &c. 2. a dog with yellow spots about the nose. 3. རྒྱ་སེར་པ a Russian.

རྒྱ་སོག *rgya-sog* or རྒྱ་སོག་ལེ *rgya-sog-le* 1. a saw imported from India or China. 2. a Tartar of Turkistan.

རྒྱ་སྲང *rgya-sraṅ* a wide opening or passage; a street; a balance.

རྒྱ་སྲན *rgya-sran* कुलत्थ (འབྲུ *hbru*) a kind of pulse; gram.

རྒྱག་པ *rgyag-pa* another form for རྒྱབ་པ *rgyab-pa*, used esp. in *C.*, to throw, cast, fling; མདའ་རྒྱག་པ *mdah rgyag-pa* to shoot arrows; དགོན་པ་ཞིག་རྒྱག་པ *dgon-pa shig rgyag-pa* to found a monastery. Has, in general, all the significations of འདེབས་པ.

རྒྱགས་པ I: *rgyags-pa* चमस provisions, victuals, food; འཚོ་བའི་རྒྱགས *htsho-wahi rgyags* provisions for living; ལམ་རྒྱགས *lam-rgyags* provisions for a journey; དགུན་རྒྱགས *dgun-rgyags* provisions for the winter; རྒྱགས་ཟོང་ *rgyags-zoṅ* merchandise to buy or barter victuals with.

རྒྱགས་པ II: मद, दर्प, मान; དྲེགས་པ *dregs-pa* arrogance, pride. Adj. arrogant and inebriated. There are eight kinds of རྒྱགས་པ *rgyags-pa*:—(1) རིགས་བཟང་བས་རྒྱགས་པ *rigs bzaṅ-was rgyags-pa* pride of high birth; (2) གཟུགས་ཀྱིས་རྒྱགས་པ *gzugs-kyis rgyags-pa* pride of appearance; (3) ལང་ཚོས་རྒྱགས་པ *laṅ-tshos rgyags-pa* pride of youth; (4) ནད་མེད་པས་རྒྱགས་པ *nad med-pas rgyags-pa* pride of freedom from sickness; (5) ནོར་གྱིས་རྒྱགས་པ *nor-gyis rgyags-pa* pride of wealth; (6) དབང་ཡོད་པས་རྒྱགས་པ *dwaṅ yod-pas rgyags-pa* pride of power; (7) བཟོ་རིག་ཤེས་པས་རྒྱགས་པ *bzo-rig çes-pas rgygas-pa* pride of technical knowledge; (8) མང་དུ་ཐོས་པས་རྒྱགས་པ *maṅ-du thos-pas rgyags-pa* pride of versatile perception.

རྒྱགས་པའི་དགའ་སྟོན *rgyags-pahi dgah-ston* fat, stout (*Sch.*); also mighty, powerful, proud.

རྒྱང་ *rgyaṅ* = རྒྱང་ *rgyaṅ* 1. wall. 2. दूर distance.

རྒྱང་གྲགས *rgyaṅ-grags* क्रोश the distance of about two miles; the reach of hearing.

རྒྱང་མཆོང་བཏང་གིན *rgyaṅ-mchoṅ btaṅ-gin* moving forward by long leaps.

རྒྱང་ཐུང་བ *rgyaṅ thuṅ-wa* near; མིག་རྒྱང་ *mig-rgyaṅ* distance of sight, *i.e.*, the distance from which a man may be well distinguished.

རྒྱང་དུ་ལུས་པ *rgyaṅ-du lus-pa* lingering behind (*Sch.*).

རྒྱང་ནས་ཕོག་པ *rgyaṅ-nas phog-pa* दूरविध् ear shot; hit from a distance.

རྒྱང་པ *rgyaṅ-pa*, used for བརྐྱང་བ *brkyaṅ-wa*, stretched: རྒྱང་ནས་བཞག་པ *rgyaṅ-nas bshag-pa* they laid him down stretched out (*Jä.*).

རྒྱང་ཕན་པ *Rgyaṅ phan-pa* or རྒྱང་འཕེན་པ *rgyaṅ phen-pa* a sect of Hindu philosophers who were scorned by the Buddhists and called atheists; འཇིག་རྟེན་རྒྱང་ཕན་པ lit. the cast out by the world, *i.e.*, the despised of the people, the *Lokāyata* sect of Ancient India.

རྒྱང་མ *rgyaṅ-ma* distance; great way off; རྒྱང་མ་ནས *rgyaṅ-ma-nas* at a distance; from afar. རྒྱང་མ་ནས་གྲགས་པ་ཆེ་བ *rgyaṅ-ma-nas grags-pa che-wa* famous, celebrated; heard from afar. Very common in older as well as in modern works.

རྒྱང་མིག་མི་མཐོང་མཁན *rgyaṅ-mig mi-mthoṅ-mkhan* short-sighted.

རྒྱང་ཙེ *Rgyaṅ-tse* ordinary pronunciation of རྒྱལ་རྩེ *Rgyal-rtse*, the chief town in the district of Nyang in Southern Tsang.

རྒྱང་ཚམ *rgyaṅ-tshas* not far from.

རྒྱང་རིང་པོ *rgyaṅ-riṅ-po* far, remote; རྒྱང་རིང་པོ་ནས་ལེན་པ *rgyaṅ riṅ-po-nas len-pa* taken or brought from a great distance.

རྒྱང་རིང་བ *rgyaṅ-riṅ-wa* विप्रकृष्ट, उपवर्तं, आरात् delaying; procrastinating.

རྒྱང་བསྲིངས་པ *rgyaṅ bsriṅs-pa* lengthened to a great distance.

རྒྱངས *rgyaṅs* adv. far; རྒྱངས་བསྐྱེད་དེ *rgyaṅs bkyed-de* moving far away, *e.g.*, in order to increase one's distance from an unpleasant neighbour at table (*Jä.*).

རྒྱངས་ཏེ *rgyaṅs-te* arriving as in haste: ཤེལ་གྱི་འཁར་བ་ཞིག་ཐོགས་ནས་ཁོང་གི་རྩར་རྒྱངས་ཏེ་བྱུང *çel-gyi hkhar-wa-shig thogs-nas khoṅ-gi rtsar rgyaṅ-te byuṅ* carrying a crystal staff he arrived near him (*A. 138.*).

རྒྱངས་ཤིང *rgyaṅ-çiṅ*, also wrongly written as རྐྱངས་ཤིང *rkyaṅ-çiṅ*= སྐུ་ཐང་རི་མོ་བྲི་རྒྱུའི་རས་གཞི་རྒྱོང་བའི་ཤིང་སོགས་དང་མི་སོག་རྒྱང་བ *sku-thaṅ ri-mo bri-rgyuhi ras-gshi rgyoṅ-wahi çiṅ sogs daṅ mi-sog rgyaṅs-wa* 1. castle. 2. the board on which the body of a culprit is stretched for flogging; the board or canvas on which cloth or pasteboard is placed for making a picture.

རྒྱན I: *rgyan*, colloq. *rgyan-cha* आभरण, अलंकार, विभूषण, संस्कृत ornament, decoration; རྒྱན་གྱིས་བརྒྱན་པ *rgyan-gyis brgyan-pa* decked with ornaments; དབུ་རྒྱན *dwu-rgyan* the ornament of the head; a diadem; སེམས་ཀྱི་རྒྱན *sems-kyi rgyan* a blessing; an ornament of the heart: ཡོན་ཏན་དང་འདྲ་ལུས་ཀྱི་རྒྱན་གཞན་མེད, སེམས་དམ་དང་འདྲ་ལུས་ཀྱི་སྡུག་བསྔལ་མེད, no ornament of the body equals mental talents; the miseries of the body are not equal to anxiety of the mind (*Çe. 13*).

Syn. ཆས *chas*; ལེགས་བྱེད *legs-byed*; མཛེས་བྱས *mdses-byas*; རྒྱན་བྱས *rgyan-byed*; བཀོད་པ *dkod-pa*; སྤྲས *spras* (*Mṅon.*).

རྒྱན II: སྐུགས *skugs* 1. a stake or pledge at play. 2. lot; རྒྱན་རྒྱབ་པ *rgyan-rgyab-pa*, to cast lots—without religious ceremonies.

* རྒྱན་མཁན་པོ *rgyan mkhan-po* अलंकारपण्डित (*Sehr.; Tā 2, 187*) one versed in rhetoric.

རྒྱན་འགྱེད་པ *rgyan hgyed-pa* दुरोदर to lay a wager.

རྒྱན་མཆོག *rgyan-mchog* कर्णपूर earring.

རྒྱན་དུ་འཆར *rgyan-du hchar* it proves a blessing for the heart; a moral advantage.

རྒྱན་དྲུག *rgyan-drug* षडाभरण the six kinds of ornaments used by the Aryan people of India.

རྒྱན་འདོགས་པ *rgyan-hdogs-pa* to adorn one's self.

རྒྱན་ནེའུ་ལེ་ཅན *rgyan nehu le-can* नकुलक ornament made in the shape of a weasel's head.

རྒྱན་པ *rgyan-pa*= བཞག་པ *bshag-pa* मण्डित adorned, bejewelled.

རྒྱན་པོ *rgyan-po* द्यूतक्रीड़ा throwing dice; also རྒྱན་བཞག་མཁན *rgyan bshag-mkhan* one who joins in a wager; gambler.

རྒྱན་པ་བྱེད་པ *rgyan-pa byed-pa* to lay a wager.

རྒྱན་དོར་བ *rgyan dor-wa* or བཞག་པ *bshag-pa* अक्षधूर्त a dice-rogue; a gamester; one who throws dice.

རྒྱན་ཕྲན *rgyan-phran* सामन्नक commonly or slightly ornamented.

རྒྱན་བྱས *rgyan-byas*, v. རྒྱན *rgyan.*

རྒྱན་ཟླ་གམ *rgyan zla-gam* चन्द्रक a semi-circular necklace.

རྒྱབ *rgyab* पृष्ठ, पश्चात् 1. the back of the body; the back part of anything; རྒྱབ་ཀྱི་ཕྱོགས *rgyab-kyi phyogs* behind; རྒྱབ་ཀྱིས་ཕྱོགས་པར་བྱེད་པ *rgyab-kyis phyogs-par byed-pa* to put to flight; རྒྱབ་ཁལ *rgyab-khal* a burden carried on the back; རྒྱབ་སྒུར་པོ *rgyab gur-po* haunch-back; རྒྱབ་སྙས *rgyabsñas* a cushion or pad for the back. 2. a load; བལ་རྒྱབ a load or pack of wool; དྲེལ་རྒྱབ་གསུམ three mule-loads.

རྒྱབ་ཏུ *rgaab-tu* རྒྱབ་ན *rgyab-na*, and རྒྱབ་ལ *rgyab-la* are in common use both as adverbs and as postp., in the latter form governing the geuit. case, signifying afterwards or after, behind, at the back, etc. : རྒྱབ་ལ་རྒྱུག *rgyab-la rgyug* run behind; ཁོའི་རྒྱབ་ཏུ་ཉལ་སོང they lay down behind him; དགོན་པའི་ཐོག་ཕྱིག་པའི་རྒྱབ་ནས after building the roof of the monastery.

རྒྱབ་ཏུ་ཞོན *rgyab-tu shon* mounts on the back.

རྒྱབ་རྟེན *rgyab-rten* अपाश्रय a back-support; something to lean against; a safe retreat; prop, support.

རྒྱབ་རྟེན་པ *rgyab rten-pa* to lean one's back against; to lean or rest on; to rely upon, confide in.

རྒྱལ་རྟེན་བྱེད་པ *rgyal-rten byed-pa* to make a support; to back.

རྒྱབ་སྟོན་པ *rgyab ston-pa* to turn one's back; to turn round.

རྒྱབ་གནོན *rgyab-gnon* confirmation.

རྒྱབ་པ *rgyab-pa*, pf. and fut. བརྒྱབ *brgyab*, imp. རྒྱོབ *rgyob*, to throw, to fling; to hit, to beat, to strike; རྡོ་རྒྱབ་པ *rdo-rgyab-pa* to throw or pelt stones at; ཤིང་རྒྱབ་པ *çiñ-rgyab-pa* to put wood (on fire, &c.); འོ་རྒྱབ་པ *ho-rgyab-pa* to kiss; ཕྱུགས་ནགས་སེབ་ཏུ་རྒྱབ་པ *phyugs-nags seb-tu rgyab-pa* to let the cattle run into the thickets. བཟློག་པ་རྒྱབ་པ *bzlog-pa rgyab-pa*, also བཏབ་པ *btab-pa* to clap; འོ་མ་རྒྱབ་པ *ho-ma-rgyab-pa* to pour or mix milk; ཚྭ་རྒྱབ་པ *tshba-rgyab* to salt (a curry or meat).

རྒྱབ་ཕྱོགས་པ *rgyab phyogs-pa* to turn one's back to a person or thing; to leave it behind; to be indifferent.

རྒྱབ་བྱེད་པ *rgyab byed-pa* to protect; to back.

རྒྱབ་འབོལ *rgyab-hwol*, རྒྱབ་རྟེན *rgyab-rten* cushion for the back.

རྒྱབ་དམག *rgyab-dmag* = རྗེས་དམག *rjes-dmag* re-inforcement; reserve.

རྒྱབ་རྩིས *rgyab-rtsis* intend to make; hint.

རྒྱབ་རྫི *rgyab-rdsi* one standing behind working people in order to watch and superintend them.

རྒྱབ་གཞུང *rgyab-gshuñ* the spine, the backbone.

རྒྱབ་ཡས *rgyab-yas*, གྲངས *grañs* हेरव (or हेवर) a number.

རྒྱབ་རིང *rgyab-riñ* दीर्घपृष्ठ the long-back; met. a fish or a snake.

རྒྱབ་ལོག་བྱེད་པ *rgyab-log byed-pa* to turn one's back; to rebel; revolt.

རྒྱབ་ལོགས *rgyab-logs* the back; back part; the reverse of a thing.

རྒྱམ་ཚྭ *rgyam-tshba* = རྒྱ་ཚྭ *rgya-tshba* सिन्धुक, सिन्धुलवण a kind of rock-salt (brought from Sind) used in medicine.

རྒྱལ I: *rgyal* (སྐར་མ *skar-ma*) तिष्या, पुष्या नक्षत्र the eighth constellation in the Hindu and Buddhist astronomy.

Syn. བླ་མའི་ལྷ་ལྡན་མ *bla-mahi lha-ldan-ma*; སྦྱོར་ལྡན་མ *sbyor ldan-ma*; ཚིམ་བྱེད་མ *tshim-byed-ma*; གྲུབ་པ་མ *grub-pa-ma*; རྒྱལ་སྨད *rgyal-smad* (*Mnon.*).

རྒྱལ II: 1. फल. 2. the five penalties for theft.

རྒྱལ III: (used only in compounds) royal, victorious; also great, chief.

རྒྱལ་ཀུན་འདུད *Rgyal-kun hdud*=འཁོར་ལོས་སྒྱུར་བའི་རྒྱལ་པོ *Hkhor-los sgyur-wahi rgyal-po* a Chakravartī Rājā (*Mnon.*).

རྒྱལ་དཀའ *Rgyal-dkah* अजित, दुर्जय, अजय invincible; the unconquerable.

རྒྱལ་གྱི་མཚན་མོ *rgyal-gyi mtshan-mo* पौषरात्रि a December night; རྒྱལ་གྱི་ཟླ་བ *rgyal-gyi zla-wa* पौषमास the month of December; རྒྱལ་གྱི་ཉ་བ *rgyal-gyi ña-wa* पौष पूर्णिमा the full-moon day of December-January.

རྒྱལ་ཁང *rgyal-khan*=རྒྱལ་པོའི་ཕོ་བྲང *rgyal-pohi pho-bran* the king's residence; palace.

Syn. རྒྱལ་པོའི་ཁབ *rgyal-pohi khab*; བསོད་ནམས་ཁང་པ *bsod-nams khan-pa* (*Mnon.*).

རྒྱལ་ཁབ་ཆེན་པོ *rgyal-khab chen-po* the main government; imperial government (*Yig. k. 18*).

རྒྱལ་ཁྲིམས *rgyal-khrims*=རྒྱལ་པོའི་ཁྲིམས *rgyal-pohi khrims* court law; the king's law: རྒྱལ་ཁྲིམས་གསེར་གྱི་གཉའ་ཤིང་ the law is a golden yoke.

རྒྱལ་མཁན་པོ *rgyal-mkhan-po* पण्डित (*Schr.; Tā. 2, 230*) learned.

རྒྱལ་རྒྱུད *rgyal-rgyud* royal family or lineage.

རྒྱལ་རྔ *rgyal-rña* जयढाक drum of victory: རྒྱལ་རྔ་རབ་འབྱམས་ཞིང་ཀུན་ཁྱབ་པར་བསྒྲགས *rgyal-rña rab-hbyams shin kun-khyab par-bsgrags* the drum of victory diffusing far and wide proclaims your fame all over the world (*Yig. k.*).

རྒྱལ་ཆེན་སྡེ་བཞི *Rgyal-chen sde-bshi*=རྒྱལ་ཆེན་བཞི *Rgyal-chen bshi* चतुर्महाराज, चतुर्महाराज-कायिक; they are: (1) ཡུལ་འཁོར་སྲུང་ *Yul-hkhor srun* धृतराष्ट्र, (2) འཕགས་སྐྱེས་པོ *Hphags skyes-po* विरूढक, (3) སྤྱན་མི་བཟང་ *Spyan mi-bzan* विरूपाक्ष, (4) རྣམ་ཐོས་སྲས *Rnam-thos sras* वैश्रवण

* རྒྱལ་མཆོག *rgyal-mchog* जिनवर, उज्जयन n. p. (*Schr.; Tā. 2, 3*) victorious; subduer.

* རྒྱལ་མཆོག་རིན་ཆེན *Rgyal-mchog rin-chen* (*Schr.; 27 A.*).

རྒྱལ་འདབ *rgyal-hdab* शतपत्र n. of a tree [a lotus]*S.*

* རྒྱལ་སྡེ་དཀར་ཆུང་ *Rgyal-sde dkar-chun* जयसेन (*Schr.; Tā. 2, 212*).

རྒྱལ་པོ I: *rgyal-po* राजा, अध्यक्ष, क्षत्रिय, नृप king, chieftain, ruler; རྒྱལ་པོར་བསྐོ་བ *rgyal-por bsko-wa* to inaugurate a king; to raise (him) to the throne: རྒྱལ་པོ་རང་གི་ཡུལ་ན་བཀུར, ཡོན་ཏན་ལྡན་པ་ཀུན་ཏུ་བཀུར the king is honoured in his own country, the learned is everywhere respected; འགྲོ་ཐང་གི་རྒྱལ་པོ the ruling deity of Do-thang: ང་རྒྱལ་པོ་མི་འདོད I do not wish to be king: རྒྱལ་པོ་མི་ཐོབ་ན if I do not attain royalty.

Syn. ས་སྐྱོང་ *sa-skyon*; ས་གཞི་སྐྱོང་ *sa-gshi skyon*; ས་བསྲུང་ *sa-bsrun*; ས་བདག *sa-bdag*; སྤྱོད་ *sa-spyod*; ས་དབང *sa-dwan*; དཔུང་པ་སྐྱེས *dpun-pa skyes*; ལག་ལས་སྐྱེས *lag-las skyes*; རྣམ་པར་སྐྱེས *rnam-par skyes*; འགྲོ་བའི་དབང *hgro-wahi dwan*; སྐྱེད་གུའི་བདག་པོ *skyed-guhi bdag-po*; མི་རྗེ *mi-rje*; མི་བདག *mi-bdag*; མིའི་དབང་ཕྱུག *mihi dwan-phyug*; མིའི་དབང་པོ *mihi dwan-po*; མིའི་འདྲེན་པ *mihi hdren-pa*; གནམ་གྱི་རྒྱལ་པོ *gnam-gyi rgyal-po*; འཇིགས་སེལ་བྱེད *hjigs-sel byed*; དམའ་སྐྱོབ *dmah-skyob*; སྤྱི་བོར་དབང་བསྐུར *spyi-wor dwan-bskur*; མི་ཡི་མགོན་པོ *mi-yi mgon-po*; ས་འཛིན *sa-hdsin*; ས་འཚོ *sa-htsho*; སའི་དབང་ཕྱུག *sahi dwan-phyug* (*Mnon.*).

རྒྱལ་པོ II: that which is excellent; something superior in its kind; ཏིང་ངེ་འཛིན་རྒྱལ་པོ *tiṅ-ṅe-ḥdsin rgyal-po* Samādhi-rāja, the excellent work on meditation.

རྒྱལ་པོ་འཁུན་པ་གྲོས་འདེབས *rgyal-po ḥkhun-pa gros ḥdebs*=དཀར་པོ་ཅིག་ཐུབ *dkar-po chig-thub* n. of a medicinal root (*Sman. 104*).

རྒྱལ་པོ་འཁྱིལ་བ *rgyal-po ḥkhyil-wa* 1. a medicine. 2. राजावर्त्त, राजपट्ट a kind of precious stone said to be brought from Virātdes'a; a royal fillet.

Syn. མུ་མེན *mu-men* (*Mṅon.*).

རྒྱལ་པོ་ངེས་པར་འཚོ་བ *rgyal-po ṅes-par ḥtsho-wa* राजजीव supported by the king.

རྒྱལ་པོ་ཅན *rgyal-po-can* royal; kingly.

རྒྱལ་པོ་འཇོམས *rgyal-po ḥjoms* राजघ्न one who has killed the king; regicide.

རྒྱལ་པོ་སྨུག་པོ *rgyal-po smug-po*=གླ་རྩི *gla-rtsi* musk (*Sman. 333*).

རྒྱལ་པོ་མཚོན་བྱེད *rgyal-po mtshon-byed* कुक्कुट the cock.

རྒྱལ་པོ་བཞིན *rgyal-po bshin*=རྒྱལ་པོ་ནང་ལྟར *rgyal-pa naṅ-ltar* राजवत् in the manner of a king; right royally.

རྒྱལ་པོ་བཞུགས་པ *rgyal-po bshugs-pa* राजकुलं the race of kings.

རྒྱལ་པོ་ཟས་གཙང *Rgyal-po zas-gtsaṅ* King S'uddhodana; བཅོམ་ལྡན་འདས་ཀྱི་ཡབ *bcom-ldan ḥdas-kyi yab* the father of S'akya-muni.

རྒྱལ་པོ་གཡུ་སྡོང་གསེར་འགོ *Rgyal-po gyu-sdoṅ gser ḥgo* वासिका n. of a medicinal plant (*Sman. 77*) [the plant *Justicia Janderussa*]*S.*

རྒྱལ་པོ་ར་མ་ཎ *Rgyal-po Ra-ma-ṇa* King Rāma-chandra of the Rāmāyaṇa.

Syn. ར་གྷུའི་བུ *Ra-ghuhi-bu*; དཀའ་ཐུབ་ཅན *Dkah-thub-can*; ཚུལ་བཟང *Tshul-bzaṅ*; དགའ་བྱེད *Dgah-byed*; འཕོངས་སྐྱེན *Hphoṅs-skyen*; ཤིང་རྟ་བཅུ་པའི་སྲས *Çiṅ-rta bcu-pahi sras*; མགྲིན་བཅུའི་དགྲ་བོ *Mgrin bcuhi-dgra-wo*; སི་ཏའི་བདག་པོ *Si-tahi bdag-po*; འཛམ་གླིང་རྒྱལ་པོ *Hzam-gliṅ rgyal-po*; དགའ་བྱེད་བཟང་པོ *dgah byed-bzaṅ-po*; ཕོ་བྲང་མི་ཏོག་ཅན *Pho-braṅ mi-tog can* (*Mṅon.*).

རྒྱལ་པོ་རབ་སྣང *Rgyal-po rab-snaṅ* described as བཅོམ་ལྡན་འདས་འཁྲུངས་པའི་དུས་སུ་བྱུང་བའི་རྒྱལ་པོ་ཆེན་པོ་ཞིག་གི་མཚན n. of a king who was born on the day Buddha was born.

རྒྱལ་པོ་ཤ་ར་བ *Rgyal-po ça-ra-wa* शरव= ; བཅོམ་ལྡན་འདས་འཁྲུངས་དུས་བྱུང་བའི་རྒྱལ་ཆེན་ཞིག་གི་མཚན.

རྒྱལ་པོ་གསང་བ་སྤྱན་གཅིག *Rgyal-po gsaṅ-wa spyan-gcig*=ཤང་དྲིལ་དམར་པོ *çaṅ-dril dmar-po* n. of a medicine (*Sman. 224*).

རྒྱལ་པོའི་སྐུ་བསྲུངས་པ *rgyal-pohi sku-bsruṅs-pa* a king's body-guard.

Syn. བསྲུང་མའི་ཚོགས་པ *bsruṅ-mihi tshogs-pa*; སྐུ་བསྲུངས་པ *sku bsruṅs-pa*; བ་ཏྲའི་སྡེ *ba-trahi sde*; བསྲུང་བ *bsruṅs-wa* (*Mṅon.*).

རྒྱལ་པོའི་སྐྱེད་ཚལ *rgyal-pohi skyed-tshal*=རྒྱལ་པོའི་ཚལ *rgyal-pohi tshal* or དགའ་བའི་ཚལ *dgah-wahi tshal* royal gardens; park (*Mṅon.*).

རྒྱལ་པོའི་སྐྱེས་བུ *rgyal-pohi skyes-bu*=རྒྱལ་པོའི་མི *rgyal-pohi mi* राजपुरुष personage of the king's family; an official.

རྒྱལ་པོའི་ཁབ *rgyal-pohi khab* राजगृह the king's residence; palace; capital Rājagir in Magadha.

Syn. ཁྱད་པར་བཀོད་པ *khyad-par bkod-pa*; འཕེལ་བ་ཅན *hphel-wa-can*; བཀྲ་ཤིས་ཅན *bkra-çis can*; བསོད་ནམས་ཁང་པ *bsod-nams khaṅ-pa*; ཀུན་ནས་བཟང *kun-nas bzaṅ*; བ་གམ་ཅན *ba-gam-can*; ས་བདག་ཁྱིམ *sa-bdag khyim*; གཡུང་དྲུང་འཁྱིལ་བ *gyuṅ-druṅ ḥkhyil-wa*; རྒྱལ་ཁང *rgyal-khaṅ*; རྒྱལ་པོའི་ཕོ་བྲང *rgyal-pohi pho-braṅ*; རྒྱལ་པོའི་བསྟི་གནས *rgyal-pohi bsti-gnas* (*Mṅon.*).

རྒྱལ་པོའི་ཁམས *rgyal-pohi khams*=རྒྱལ་སྲིད *rgyal-srid* राज्य kingdom.

རྒྱལ་པོའི་རྟགས *rgyal-pohi rtags* the signs of royalty, such as the umbrella, the *chowry*, etc.; royal paraphernalia.

རྒྱལ་པོའི་གདུང *rgyal-pohi gduṅ*=རྒྱལ་སྲས *rgyal-sras* the son of a king; a prince; a scion of the royal family; a royal descendant.

རྒྱལ་པོའི་དཔྱད *rgyal-pohi dpyad* বলি, উপহার present; tribute (to a king).

རྒྱལ་པོའི་མྱུ་གུ *rgyal-pohi myu-gu* the son of a king; a prince.

+ རྒྱལ་པོའི་སླས *rgyal-pohi slas*=བཙུན་མོའི་སྡོད་ས *btsun-mohi sdod-sa* the queen's apartments in a palace, also her attendants.

Syn. བཙུན་མོའི་འཁོར *btsun-mohi hkhor*; ཕོ་བྲང་འཁོར *pho-brañ hkhor* (*Mṅon.*).

རྒྱལ་པོས་བཀྲབས་པ *rgyal-pos bkrabs-pa*=རྒྱལ་པོས་འདམས་པ *rgyal-pos hdams-pa* chosen, selected gain and loss; win by the king.

རྒྱལ་ཕམ *rgyal-pham* victory and defeat; wining and losing.

རྒྱལ་ཕྲན *rgyal-phran* (*gyal-than*), a petty king; a feudatory prince.

Syn. རྒྱལ་རིགས་ཆ་ཤས *rgyal-rigs cha-ças*; ཡུལ་འཁོར་དབང *yul-hkhor-dwañ*; ཡུལ་གྱི་བདག་པོ *yul-gyi bdag-po*; གྲོང་ཁྱེར་རྗེ *groñ-khyer-rje*; སྡེ་དཔོན *sde-dpon*; ས་ཡི་ཐིག་ལེ་འཛིན *sa-yi tihg-le hdsin*; ཁམས་ཀྱི་རྒྱལ་པོ *khams-kyi rgyal-po* (*Mṅon.*).

རྒྱལ་བ I: *rgyal-wa* जय, v. neut. 1. to be victorious; to win; to conquer; to subdue; to overpower; ནག་པོའི་ཕྱོགས་ལས་རྒྱལ་བ *nag-pohi phyogs-las rgyal-wa* to be victorious over the powers of sin, *i.e.*, the side of darkness; གཡུལ་ལས་རྒྱལ་བ *gyul-las rgyal-wa* to be victorious in battle; ཚོད་ལྟ་བ་ལས་རྒྱལ་བ *tshod lta-wa las rgyal-wa* to pass an examination successfully; རྩོད་པ་ལས་རྒྱལ་བ *rtsod-pa-la rgyal-wa* to win a contest. 2. the number twenty-four.

རྒྱལ་བ II: जय 1. the act of conquering; victory. 2. the conquering party or person; he that prevails; the conqueror (opp. to ཕམ་པ *pham-pa*, the vanquished).

རྒྱལ་བ III: जिन, भगवत् 1. the conqueror, most high, *i.e.*, the Buddha. 2. the earliest known Buddha, Adi-Buddha; the conqueror of passions.

རྒྱལ་བ IV: adj. victorious; superior; eminent; excellent: རྣམ་པར་རྒྱལ་བའི་ཁང་བཟང *rnam-par rgyal-wahi khañ-bzañ* the mansion completely excellent.

* རྒྱལ་བ་ཅན *rgyal-wa can*, n. p. (*Schr.*; *Bull. 1848, 288*).

* རྒྱལ་བ་མཆོག་གི་སྐྱེད་མཛད *rgyal-wa mchog-gi skyed-mdsas* जिनवरजन (*Schr.*; *Kālāc. T. 21*).

རྒྱལ་བ་གཉིས་པ *Rgyal-wa gñis-pa* the second Buddha of this age; an epithet which once belonged to Nāgārjuna, now given to Tsong khapa, *i.e.*, རྗེ་རིན་པོ་ཆེ *Rje-rin-po-che*, རྒྱལ་བ་གཉིས་པའི་བསྟན་པའི་རྒྱལ་མཚན་སྲིད་རྩེར་བསྒྲེངས *rgyal-wa gñis-pahi bstan-pahi rgyal-mtshan srid-rtser bsgreñs*, he uplifted in the kingdom the banner of the creed of the second Buddha (Tsong-khapa) (*Yig. k. 22*).

* རྒྱལ་བ་ཚུལ་ཁྲིམས *rgyal-wa tshul-khrims* one of the four great Teachers of the Bon religion (*G. Bon. 35*).

རྒྱལ་བ་ཚེ་དཔག་མེད *Rgyal-wa tshe-dpag-med* जिन-अमितायुः (*Schr.*; *29 A.*) n. of a Dhyāni-Buddha.

* རྒྱལ་བ་ཤཱཀྱ་ཐུབ་པ *Rgyal-wa çhakya thub-pa*, ཏ་ཐཱ་ག་ཏ་མུ་ནི *ta-tya-thha mu-ni* (*Schr.*; *33 A*).

རྒྱལ་བ་རིན་པོ་ཆེ *Rgyal-wa Rin-po-che* the "most precious Jina" is the ordinary title in Tibet of the Grand Lama of Lhasa—the Dalai Lama.

རྒྱལ་བའི་ཅོད་པན *Rgyal-wahi cod-pan* जयापीड़ n. of a famous king of Kashmir who reigned about the seventh century A.D.

རྒྱལ་བའི་བསྟན་པ *Rgyal-wahi bstan-pa*=སངས་རྒྱས་ཀྱི་བསྟན་པ *sañs rgyas-kyi bstan-pa* the religion of Buddha; Buddhism (*Yig. k. 10*).

རྒྱལ་བའི་ཐུགས་སྲས *rgyal-wahi thugs-sras* जिनौरसः the spiritual son of Buddha.

རྒྱལ་བའི་སྤྱན *rgyal-wahi spyan* = ལུག་མིག་མེ་ཏོག *lug-mig me-tog* a flower resembling in appearance the eye of a Buddha and used in medicine (*Sman. 421*).

རྒྱལ་བའི་དབང་པོ *Rgyal-wahi dwaṅ-po* जिनेन्द्र the chief Buddha; also an occasional appellation of the Grand Lama of Lhasa: རྒྱལ་བའི་དབང་པོ་ཐམས་ཅད་མཁྱེན་ཅིང་གཟིགས་པ་ཆེན་པོ the Gyal-wai Wang-po is the great seer and one who knows all things (*Yig. k. 1*).

* རྒྱལ་བའི་དབང་པོའི་བློ་གྲོས *rgyal-wahi dwaṅ-pohi blo-gros* जिनेन्द्रमति (*Schr.; Bull. 1848, 94*) one whose mind is devoted to the Lord Buddha.

རྒྱལ་བའི་མྱུ་གུ *rgyal-wahi myu-gu*, v. རྒྱལ་སྲས *rgyal-sras* जिनाङ्कुर [a nascent Buddha.] *S.*

རྒྱལ་བའི་རྒྱལ་ཚབ *rgyal-wahi rgyal-tshab* = རྒྱལ་བ་རིན་པོ་ཆེའི་སྐུ་ཚབ *Rgyal-wa rin-po chehi sku-tshab* the Regent of Tibet who administers the country during the minority of the Dalai Lama; now called *Rgyal-tshab Rin-po che* or *Bod-Rgyal-po* (*Pö-gye po.*).

རྒྱལ་བའི་ཚབ *rgyal-wahi tshab* the vice-regent of Buddha; a name of Maitreya Bodhisattva.

རྒྱལ་བའི་གཞི *rgyal-wahi gshi* जिनाधार *byaṅ-chub sems-dpah* or *Bodhisattva*.

རྒྱལ་བའི་འོད *Rgyal-wahi hod* जयप्रभा, जिनरुचि the glory of Buddha; name of a *Bodhisattva*.

རྒྱལ་བའི་སྲས *rgyal-wahi sras* = རྒྱལ་སྲས *rgyal-wa* जिनपुत्र; *Bodhisattva*, a Buddhist monk; an ordained *Bhikṣu*.

* རྒྱལ་བའི་ལྷ *rgyal-wahi lha* जयदेव (*Schr.; Tā. 2, 146*).

* རྒྱལ་བར་དཀའ *rgyal-war dkah* दुर्जय (*Schr.; Kālāc. T. 22*) one of the ten stages of perfection or भूमि.

རྒྱལ་བུ *rgyal-bu* राजपुत्र, कुमार the son of a king; a prince; རྒྱལ་བུ་རྒྱལ་བྱེད *rgyal-bu rgyal-byed* n. of a prince in Kos'ala in Buddha's time.

Syn. བསོད་ནམས་སྟོབས *bsod-nams stobs*; ཟིལ་གནོན་བུ *zil-gnon-bu*; རྒྱལ་རིགས་ཐིག་ལེ *rgyal-rigs thig-le*; རྒྱལ་པོའི་གདུང *rgyal-pohi gduṅ*; རྒྱལ་སྲས *rgyal-sras*; ནོར་འཛིན་བདག་པོའི་སྲས *nor-hdsin bdag-pohi sras*; རྒྱལ་པོའི་མྱུ་གུ *rgyal-pohi myu-gu* (*Mṅon.*).

རྒྱལ་བྱེད་མ *Rgyal byed-ma* जया, अपराजिता n. of a goddess.

རྒྱལ་བྱེད་ཚལ *Rgyal-byed-tshal* जेतवन n. of the grove which was purchased by Anāthpiṇḍada a merchant of S'rāvasti and where the Buddha resided for a long time.

* རྒྱལ་དབང་ལྔ་པ་ཆེན་པོ *Rgyal-dwaṅ lṅa-pa chen-po* = ཀུན་གཟིགས་བློ་བཟང་རྒྱ་མཚོའི་ཞབས *kun-gzigs blo-bzaṅ rgya-mtshohi shabs* (*Schr.; 16 A*).

རྒྱལ་དབང་པདྨ *Rgyal-dwaṅ padma* = སངས་རྒྱས་གཉིས་པ *saṅs-rgyas gñis-pa* or སློབ་དཔོན་རིན་པོ་ཆེ *Slob-dpon Rin-po-che* an epithet of the saint Padma Sambhava given him by the *Rñiṅ-ma* sects (*Yig. k. 27*).

རྒྱལ་བློན *rgyal-blon* the king and his minister, also the state minister.

རྒྱལ་མོ *rgyal-mo* राज्ञी the queen; wife of the king.

རྒྱལ་མོ་ཀ་ར *Rgyal-mo ka-ra* (སྨན *sman*) a शर्कर, a coarse sugar used in medicine.

རྒྱལ་མོ་རོང *Rgyal-mo-roṅ* = རྒྱལ་རོང *Rgyal-roṅ* n. of a country on the confines of S. E. Tibet (*Situ. 56*).

རྒྱལ་མོའི་ག་གོན *rgyal-mohi ga-gon* कर्कटिका n. of a place.

རྒྱལ་ཚབ *rgyal-tshab* युवराज 1. the Desi (*Bde-srid*) or regent of Tibet. 2. the would-be successor of a king; crown prince.

རྒྱལ་མཚན 1: *rgyal-mtshan* ध्वज, केतु, शकुन, ललाम 1. the armorial flag or banner of victory of Buddhism; is the orthodox standard of the Buddhist. 2. used as a personal name of *Bodhisattvas* and individuals such as:—བྱང་ཆུབ་སེམས་པ་མི་བརྗེད་པའི་རྒྱལ་མཚན *Byañ-chub sems-pa mi brjed-pahi rgyal-mtshan*, རྟོགས་པའི་རྒྱལ་མཚན *Rtogs-pahi rgyal-mtshan*, ཡོངས་སུ་རྟོག་པ་དང་བྲལ་བའི་རྒྱལ་མཚན *Yoñs-su rtogs-pa dañ bral-wahi rgyal-mtshan*. 3. ཕོ་དབང་*phod-wañ*. The Gyal-tshan or Buddhist banner is seen as a kind of decoration of cloth in various colours and of cylindrical shape erected upon a flagstaff or carried on a pole. It is also made in brass and wood. In Tibetan Buddhism the following are the རྒྱལ་མཚན *rgyal-mtshan*, to combat with the powers of evil:—(1) ཚུལ་ཁྲིམས་ཀྱི་རྒྱལ་མཚན *tshul-khrims-kyi rgyal-mtshan*, (2) ཏིང་ངེ་འཛིན་གྱི་རྒྱལ་མཚན *tiñ-ñe-hdsin-gyi rgyal-mtshan*, (3) ཤེས་རབ་ཀྱི་རྒྱལ་མཚན་ *çes-rab-kyi rgyal-mtshan*, (4) ཡེ་ཤེས་ཀྱི་རྒྱལ་མཚན་ *ye-çes-kyi rgyal-mtshan*, (5) རྣམ་པར་གྲོལ་བའི་རྒྱལ་མཚན *rnam-par grol-wahi rgyal-mtshan*, (6) སྙིང་རྗེ་ཆེན་པོའི་རྒྱལ་མཚན་ *sñiñ-rje chen-pohi rgyal-mtshan*, (7) སྟོང་པ་ཉིད་དང་མཚན་མ་མེད་པའི་སྨོན་པ་མེད་པའི་རྒྱལ་མཚན་ *stoñ-pa-ñid-dañ mtshan-ma med-pahi smon-pa med-pahi rgyal-mtshan*, (8) ཐབས་ཀྱི་རྒྱལ་མཚན་ *thabs-kyi rgyal-mtshan*, (9) སེམས་ཅན་མེད་པ་དང་སྲོག་མེད་པ་དང་གང་ཟག་མེད་པའི་རྒྱལ་མཚན *sams-can med-pa-dañ srog med-pa-dañ gañ-zag med-pahi rgyal-mtshan*, (10) རྟེན་ཅིང་འབྲེལ་པར་འབྱུང་བ་ཁོང་དུ་ཆུད་པས་མཐར་ལྟ་བུ་དང་བྲལ་བའི་རྒྱལ་མཚན *rten-ciñ hdrel-par hbyuñ-wa khoñ-du chud-pas mthar lta-bu dañ bral-wahi rgyal-mtshan*, (11) རང་གི་སེམས་ཡོངས་སུ་དག་པས་སངས་རྒྱས་ཀྱི་བྱིན་གྱིས་བརླབས *rañ-gi sems-gi sems yoñs-su dag-pas sañs-rgyas-kyi byin-gyis brlabs*.

རྒྱལ་མཚན་གྲགས་ *rgyal-mtshan grags* ललाम fame; ornament.

* རྒྱལ་མཚན་མ *rgyal-mtshan-ma* मंगलध्वज (*Schr.; 99 B*) ensign of good fortune.

* རྒྱལ་མཚན་སེང་གེ *rgyal-mtshan señ-ge* ध्वज-सिंह (*Schr.; Org. m. 111, 25*).

རྒྱལ་ཟླ *rgyal-zla* पौष मास the month of December.

རྒྱལ་རབས *rgyal-rabs* genealogy of kings.

རྒྱལ་རབས་བོན་གྱི་འབྱུང་གནས *Rgyal-rabs Bon-gyi hbyuñ-gnas* n. of a work on the origin of the Bon religion.

རྒྱལ་རིགས *rgyal-rigs* राजकुल; क्षत्र, क्षत्रिय the military caste of India; royal race; the race of a king.

རྒྱལ་རིགས་སྐྱེས *rgyal-rigs skyes* मागध क्षत्रिय born of the military caste, also of the royal family; resident of Magadha.

རྒྱལ་རིགས་ཆ་ཤས *rgyal-rigs cha-ças*=རྒྱལ་ཕྲན *rgyal-phran* a petty king; a vassal or feudatory prince (*Mñon.*).

རྒྱལ་རིགས་ཐིག་ལེ *rgyal-rigs thig-le*=རྒྱལ་བུ *rgyal-bu* the son of a king; a prince.

རྒྱལ་རིགས་མོ *rgyal rigs-mo* क्षत्रियाणी a lady of the military caste of India.

རྒྱལ་རོང *rgyal-roñ*, v. རྒྱལ་མོ་རོང *rgyal-mo-roñ*.

རྒྱལ་ས *rgyal-sa* capital seat of Government, royal place; the place or position of a king.

རྒྱལ་སྲས *rgyal-sras*=རྒྱལ་པོའི་སྲས *rgyal-pohi sras* the son of a king or prince.

* རྒྱལ་བཤེས *rgyal-bçes* पुष्यमित्र n. pr. (*Schr.; Was. 55*).

རྒྱལ་སྲིད *rgyal-srid* राज्य, मण्डल a kingdom; empire; state.

རྒྱལ་སྲིད་རྒྱས་པ *rgyal-srid rgyas-pa* सम्राज्य empire.

རྒྱལ་སྲིད་རིན་ཆེན་སྣ་བདུན *rgyal-srid Rin-chen sna-bdun* the seven different precious articles of royalty, viz:—འཁོར་ལོ *hkhor-lo* चक्र the wheel; ནོར་བུ *nor-bu* मणि gem; བཙུན་མོ *btsun-mo*, स्त्री queen; བློན་པོ *blon-po* मन्त्री minister; གླང་པོ *glañ-po* हस्ती elephant; རྟ་མཆོག *rta-mchog* अश्व spirited horse; ཁྱིམ་བདག *khyim-bdag* गृहपति house-holder; དམག་དཔོན་རིན་པོ་ཆེ *dmagpon rin-po che* सेनापति commander-in-chief.

རྒྱལ་སྲིད་སྲུང་བ ṟgyal-sṟiḏ sṟuṅ-wa राज्य-रक्षा to defend a state against enemies.

རྒྱས་འགྲེལ ṟgyaṣ-ẖgrel = རྒྱས་པར་བཤད་པའི་འགྲེལ་པ ṟgyaṣ-par ḇçaḏ-paẖi ẖgrel-pa comprehensive commentary: སུམ་ཅུ་པ་དང་རྟགས་ཀྱི་འཇུག་པའི་གཞུང་གི་རྒྱས་འགྲེལ an elaborate commentary on the texts of *Sum-cu-pa* and *Ṟtagṣ ẖjug-pa* (*Situ. 137*).

Syn. འཕེལ་བ *ẖphel-wa*; རྫོགས་པ *ṟdsogṣ-pa*; གང་བ *gaṅ-wa*; ཁ་བྱེ་བ *kha-ḇye-wa*; ཁྱབ་པ *khyab-pa*; ཆེ་བ *che-wa*; ཚིམ་པ *tshim-pa* (*M̱ṅon.*).

རྒྱས་པ I: व्यास n. of a great sage of Ancient India, the reputed author of the Māhābhārata; དྲང་སྲོང་རྒྱས་པ *Draṅ-sṟoṅ ṟgyaṣ-pa* व्यासऋषि the sage Vyāsa.

རྒྱས་པ II: (prop. pf. to རྒྱ་བ *ṟgya-wa*) 1. vb. to increase in bulk or quantity; to augment; to spread: བ་ཡི་ནུ་ལྟར་རྒྱས *ba-yi nu-ḻtar ṟgyaṣ* swells like a cow's dug; བསྟན་པ་རྒྱས་ཤིང་ *ḇstan-pa ṟgyaṣ-çiṅ* the doctrine (of Buddha) spreading; to grow, develope. 2. adj. extensive, large, ample, wide, manifold, numerous, copious, complete, full; ཟླ་བ་རྒྱས་པ *zla-wa ṟgyaṣ-pa* full moon; the adverbial form is frequent: རྒྱས་པར་འདོད་ན *ṟgyaṣ-par ẖdoḏ-na* if you wish to know it fully.

རྒྱས་པར་བྱེད་པ *ṟgyaṣ-par byeḏ-pa* 1. to make bigger; to augment; to increase. 2. to describe, narrate, state at large.

རྒྱས་པར་བཤད་པ *ṟgyaṣ-par ḇçaḏ-pa* निर्देशन elucidation; full explanation; དོན་རྒྱས་པར་བྱེད་པ *don ṟgyaṣ-par byeḏ-pa* to be very useful; to exert a beneficial influence.

རྒྱས་བྱེད *ṟgyaṣ-byeḏ* भारत the land of plenty; a name of India.

རྒྱས་བྱེད་འབྱུང་པོའི་ལག་པ *ṟgyaṣ-byeḏ ẖbyuṅ-poẖi lag-pa* = དབང་ལག *ḏwaṅ-lag* n. of a medicinal plant growing below the limit of snow in the Himalayas and resembling the human hand in appearance (*S̱man. 416*).

རྒྱས་བྱེད་མ *Ṟgyaṣ-byeḏ-ma* भारती n. of a goddess—Cornocopia, the goddess of plenty.

* རྒྱས་ཤིང་ *ṟgyaṣ-çiṅ* पुष्टि (*Schr.*; *Kālāc. T. 110*) thriving.

རྒྱུ I: *ṟgyu* घातानं a kind of blanket.

རྒྱུ II: 1. matter; substance; material; རྒྱུ་བ *ṟgyu-wa* superior quality: རྒྱུ་གཙང *ṟgyu-g̱tsaṅ* any stuff, wool or cotton, &c., when cleansed and washed for making cloth; also pure origin. རྒྱུ་སྒོག *ṟgyu-ṣgog* n. of a medical drug; wild garlic. ཆང་རྒྱུ *chaṅ-ṟgyu* ingredients for making beer: རྒྱུ་དགེ་བ་བསགས་པས་ཐོབ་པ་ཡིན *ṟgyu ḏge-wa ḇsagṣ-paṣ thob-pa yin* the substance has been obtained by means of accumulated merits: ང་ལ་དགོས་རྒྱུ་ཆུང་ *ṅa-la ḏgoṣ-ṟgyu chuṅ* I have few wants. བཟོ་རྒྱུ *ḇzo-ṟgyu* material to make or manufacture anything with; ཟ་རྒྱུ་མེད *za-ṟgyu-meḏ* nothing to eat: ད་ལྟར་རྒྱུ་ཞིག་སྣང་ངོ *da-ḻtar ṟgyu-shig ṣnaṅ-ṅo* an opportunity will presently offer itself (*Jä.*). 2. In *W.* arrangement; preparation. In a special sense material; stuff for weaving; warp; chain (*Jä.*).

རྒྱུ III: हेतु 1. cause, namely, the primary cause as distinguished from རྐྱེན the secondary or co-operating cause; the direct cause for any event; also reason, motive, main condition: མྱ་ངན་ལས་འདས་པའི་རྒྱུར་འགྱུར་ *mya-ṅan laṣ ẖdaṣ-paẖi ṟgyur-ẖgyur* it becomes the cause of passing out of misery, *i.e.*, *Nirvāṇa*; ངན་སོང་རྒྱུ་རུ་འགྲོ *ṅan-soṅ ṟgyu-ru ẖgro*, རྒྱུས *ṟgyuṣ* with genit. by reason of; on account of; in virtue of; in consequence of; ཅིའི་རྒྱུས *ciẖi ṟgyuṣ*, why: རྒྱུ་མེད་དུ *ṟgyu meḏ-du* = རྒྱུ་མེད་པར *ṟgyu meḏ-par* without any actual cause; spontaneously; without sufficient reason; without good cause; རྒྱུ་དང་རྐྱེན *ṟgyu-daṅ ṟkyen* primary and secondary cause, which sometimes coincides with 'cause and effect'; རྒྱུ་དང་རྐྱེན་དེའི་ཕྱིར་ *rgyu-daṅ rkyen-dehi phyir*, དེའི་རྒྱུ་ *dehi rgyu*, དེའི་རྐྱེན་གྱིས་ *dehi rkyen-gyis*, དེའི་རྒྱུ་རྐྱེན་ *dehi rgyu-rkyen* therefore; on that account. ཉེ་བའི་རྒྱུ་ *ñe-wahi rgyu* in medicine the three anthropological causes or conditions of diseases; the three 'humours,' wind, bile, and phlegm; རིང་བའི་རྒྱུ་ *riṅ-wahi rgyu* the ultimate cause of diseases and of every evil, viz., ignorance; མ་རིག་པ་ *ma rig-pa*, སྐྱེད་བྱེད་རྒྱུ་ *skyed byed-rgyu* the creative cause; འཕེལ་བའི་རྒྱུ་ནི་ལྟེ་བ་ *hphel-wahi rgyu-ni lte-wa* the efficient cause of growth is the navel-string; རྒྱུ་བྱེད་པ་ *rgyu byed-pa* to be the principal cause of; to lie at the bottom of a matter; རྒྱུ་སྐྱེད་པ་ *rgyu skyed-pa* to lay the foundation of. There are six kinds of རྒྱུ་ *rgyu, i.e.*, རྒྱུ་དྲུག *rgyu-drug*:—བྱེད་པའི་རྒྱུ་ *byed-ahi rgyu*, ལྷན་ཅིག་འབྱུང་བའི་རྒྱུ་ *lhan-cig hbyuṅ-wahi rgyu* ? རྣམ་སྨིན་གྱི་རྒྱུ་ *rnam-smin-gyi rgyu*, མཚུངས་པར་ལྡན་པའི་རྒྱུ་ *mtshuṅs-par ldan-pahi rgyu*, ཀུན་ཏུ་འགྲོ་བའི་རྒྱུ་ *kun-tu hgro-wahi rgyu*, སྐལ་མཉམ་གྱི་རྒྱུ་ *skal-mñam kyi rgyu*. 2. attached to a verbal root *rgyu* often indicates the supine and, colloquially, the infinitive; འགྲོ་རྒྱུ་འདོད་ wishes to go. Also forms a future tense when connecting the root with the auxil. verb. ཟ་རྒྱུ་ཡིན་ will eat: ངའི་དྲུང་དུ་འོང་རྒྱུ་ཡིན་པ་ those that will come to me; དེ་ལ་རྒྱལ་སྲིད་གཏང་རྒྱུ་ལ་ when the government was to be entrusted to him; རྟ་འདོར་རྒྱུ་མེད་ horses were not to be had (*Jä.*); དཀོན་རྒྱུ་མེད་ *dkon-rgyu med* that is not a very precious thing; there is nothing particular in that; གཞན་པས་ལེགས་རྒྱུ་མེད་ *gshan-pas legs-rgyu med* he is not more beautiful than others; ཡ་མཚན་རྒྱུ་མེད་ *ya-mtshan rgyu-med* that is not to be wondered at.

རྒྱུ་རྐྱེན་ *rgyu-rkyen* हेतुप्रत्यय reason; cause; acc. to *Jä.* connection: རྒྱུ་རྐྱེན་བཤད་དུ་གསོལ་ *rgyu-rkyen bshad-du gsol* please explain to me the connection. རྒྱུ་ཆ་ *rgyu-cha* colloq. that which belongs to a thing; appurtenance; necessary implement, &c.; also property. རྒྱུ་འབྲས་ *rgyu-hbras* cause and effect or consequence; gen. in a moral sense; actions and their fruits (ལས་ཀྱི་རྒྱུ་འབྲས་ *las-kyi rgyu-hbras*); ལས་རྒྱུ་འབྲས་ཀྱི་ཆོས་ *las rgyu hbras-kyi-chos* the doctrine treating on this subject; the doctrine of retribution; the principal dogma of Buddhism; ལས་རྒྱུ་འབྲས་ལ་ཡིད་ཆེས་པ་ *las-rgyu hbras la-yid ches-pa* to believe in the doctrine of retribution.

རྒྱུ་སྐར་ *rgyu-skar* नक्षत्र, चरत "the moving stars." The constellations through which the moon passes in her revolution round the heavens are called རྒྱུ་སྐར་ལྷ་མོ་ཉི་ཤུ་རྩ་བརྒྱད་ *rgyu-skar lha-mo ñi-çu rtsa-brgyad*, the twenty-eight goddesses, moving-stars, believed to be the daughters of the four guardian-kings of the world. The constellations are thus named:—(1) ཐ་སྐར་ *Açvinī* (དབྱུག་གུ་ *dbyug-gu*); (2) བྲ་ཉེ་ *Bharaṇī*; (3) སྨིན་དྲུག *Kṛttikā* the Pleiades; (4) *Rohiṇī* (བེ་རྩེ་ *be-rdse*); (5) མགོ་ *Mṛgaśiras* (སྨལ་པོ་ *smal-po*); (6) *Ārdrā*, ལག་; (7) ནབས་སོ་ *Punarvasū*; (8) རྒྱལ་ *Puṣyā* (རྒྱལ་སྟོད་ *rgyal-stod*=ནམ་སོ་ *nam-so*); (9) སྐག་ *Açleṣā* (བ་ *wa*); (10) མཆུ་ *Maghā* (རྟ་པ་ *rta-pa*) or རྟ་ཆེན་ *rta-chen* with Regulus bright star; (11) གྲེ་ *Pūrvaphalguṇī* or རྟ་ཧུ་ *rtahu* or རྟ་ཆུང་ *rta-chuṅ*; (12) དབོ་ *Uttaraphalguṇī* or ཁྲ་ *khra*; (13) མེ་བཞི་ *Hasta* or བྱ་མ་ *bya-ma*; (14) ནག་པ་ *Citrā* (or བྱཱ་ཧུ་ *byahu* with Spica); (15) ས་རི་ *Svāti*; (16) ས་ག་ *Viçākhā* (17) ལྷ་མཚམས་ *Anurādhā* or ལག་སོར་ *lag-sor*; (18) སྣྲོན་ *Jyeṣṭhā*, or ལྡེ་ཧུ་ *lde-hu* (with Antares); (19) སྣྲུབས་ *Mūla*, or སྲོག་པ་ *srog-pa*; (20) ཆུ་སྟོད་ *Pūrvā āṣādhā*; (21) ཆུ་སྨད་ *uttarā āṣādhā* or ཕུལ་ *phul*; (22) གྲོ་བཞིན་ *Abhijit*; (23) བྱི་བཞིན་ *Çravaṇā* གཉིས་ *gñis*; (24) མོན་གྲེ་ *Dhanasta* or མོན་དྲེ་ *mon-dre*; (25) མོན་གྲུ་

Çatavisā or སྒྲོག *sgrog*; (26) ཁྲུམས་སྟོད *Pūrva-bhādrapada* or (27) ཁྲུམས་སྨད *uttarabhadra-pada*; (28) ནམ་གྲུ *Revati* or ཤེ་ས *çe-sa*.

*རྒྱུ་སྐར་དུས *rgyu-skar dus* (*Sch.*; *Kālāc. T. 48*).

རྒྱུ་སྐར་མུ་ཁྱུད *rgyu-skar mu-khyud* नक्षत्रनेमि the moon which is surrounded by the constellations.

རྒྱུ་སྐར་མང་པོ་རི *Rgyu-skar maṅ-po ri* n. of a mountain; the fabulous north polar mountain (*K. d.* ར *342*).

རྒྱུ་སྐར་ལམ *rgyu-skar lam* the milky-way; नक्षत्र-पथ the starry path.

རྒྱུ་གང་ *rgyu-gaṅ* for what reason.

རྒྱུ་ངེས *rgyu-ṅes* the certain or real cause.

རྒྱུ་མངའ *rgyu-mṅah* = རྒྱུ་མཚན *rgyu-mtshan* cause; reason.

རྒྱུ་ཅན *rgyu-can* = རྒྱུ་ལྡན one who knows about a thing; well-informed.

རྒྱུ་མཐུན *rgyu-mthun* cause sufficient to produce observed effect.

རྒྱུ་ལྡན *rgyu-ldan* 1. निर्झर [a cave]*S.* a hill, also a fountain; a rich man. 2. = རྒྱུ་ཅན.

རྒྱུ་ནད *rgyu-nad* disease of the bowels. Symptoms are :—རྒྱུ་ཁྲོལ *rgyu-khrol* causing much sound in the stomach; རྒྱུ་འཁྲིལ *rgyu-hkhril* causing much griping in the stomach; རྒྱུ་འགྱིངས *rgyu-hgyiṅs* where the stomach or the intestines remain swollen and stiff with wind, etc.; རྒྱུ་འགགས *rgyu-hgags* obstruction of the bowels; རྒྱུ་གཟེར *rgyu-gzer* aching or pains in the stomach.

རྒྱུ་སྤུན *rgyu-spun* the threads stretched lengthwise and crosswise to make cloth.

རྒྱུ་བ *rgyu-wa* चरण, चर to go, walk, move, wander, range; ཆུ་ལ་རྒྱུ་བའི་འདབ་ཆགས *chu-la rgyu-wahi hdab-cags* birds frequenting the water; ཀུན་ཏུ་རྒྱུ་བ *kun-tu rgyu-wa* to wander from place to place. This verb is generally used instead of འགྲོ་བ in Sikkim.

རྒྱུ་བ་མེད་པ *rgyu-wa med-pa* अपचर that does not move; motionless, still.

རྒྱུ་བའི་བརྟུལ་ཞུགས *rgyu-wahi btul-shugs* चरव्रत the vow of walking.

རྒྱུ་བྱེད *rgyu-byed* चरण, पाद feet; that which moves.

རྒྱུ་སྦྱིན *rgyin* वारिद met. the cloud.

རྒྱུ་སྦྱོར་བ *rgyu-sbyor-wa* སྦྱིན་བདག *sbyin-bdag* an alms-giver; the maker of a gift.

རྒྱུ་མ *rgyu-ma* अन्त्र entrails; intestines; bowels, more especially the small intestines; རྒྱུ་འཁྲོག་པ *rgyu hkhrogpa* the croaking of the bowels; རྒྱུ་སྒྲོག *rgyusgrog* the envelope of the lower intestines; རྒྱུ་སྟོད *rgyu-stod* the upper bowels. Colloq. *rgyu-ma* is also a term for "sausages." (*G. Sndg.*).

རྒྱུ་མེད་པ *rgyu med-pa* without cause; evidence devoid of (*lakṣmaṇa*) or characteristic.

Syn. རྒྱུ་ཡིས་སྟོང་ *rgyu-yis stoṅ*; མཚན་ཉིད་བྲལ *mtshan-ñid bral* (*Mṅon.*).

རྒྱུ་མཚན *rgyu-mtshan* निमित्त 1. cause; concatenation of events; circumstances; རྒྱུ་མཚན་འདྲི་བ *rgyu-mtshan hdri-wa* to ask after the cause: ངའི་ནང་ནས་ཕྱེ་ཁྱེར་བའི་རྒྱུ་མཚན་ཤོད *ṅahi naṅ-nas phye khyer-wahi rgyu-mtshan çod* tell me the circumstances of your fetching the flour from my house 2. प्रमाण token, sign, characteristic, proof, evidence; འདུག་པའི་རྒྱུ་མཚན *hdug-pahi rgyu-mtshan* as an evidence of being (*Jä.*).

རྒྱུ་མཚན་རིག *rgyu-mtshan rig* कारणिक: relating to proof or cause or reason.

རྒྱུ་གཟེར *rgyu-gzer* अतिसारक colic; [dysentery]*S.* ཤེས་བྱ་བའི་ནད་ནི་རིམས་ཚད་སྤྱི་དང་འདྲ་བ་ལ, གཉན་ནད་ལ་བབས་ན་རྒྱུ་གཟེར་ཤེ་པའོ, ངོ་བོ་མཚིན་ཚད་ཕྱང་དུ་བབས་པ་ལ་གཉན་ནད་ཆུ་སེར་མཁྲིས་ཚད་བསྐྱང་བ་ཡིས་རྒྱུ་མ་གཟེར་ཞིང་འབྲུ་བས་རྒྱུ་གཟེར་ཡིན *she bya-wahi nad-ni rims-tshad spyi daṅ hdra-wa la, gñan-nad la babs-na rgyu gzer she-paho, ṅo-wo mchin-tshad thuñña babs-pa la yñan-nad chu-ser mkhris-tshad bstañ-wa yis rgyu-ma gzer-shiñ hkhru-was rgyu-gzer yin,* དེ་ལ་དོན་འཁྲུ་སྣོད་འཁྲུ་སྟོབས་ཆེན་དང་ *de-la don-hkhru-snod hkhru stobs-chen dañ,* རྒྱུ་གཟེར *rgyu-gzer* རྒྱུ་འཁོར *rgyu-hkhor* རྒྱུ་འཁྲོལ *rgyu-hkhrol* རྒྱུ་ལྐུགས *rgyu-lkugs.* We read of, also, རྒྱུ་གཟེར་གཅོག་པའི་ཐོ་བ་གསུམ *rgyu-gzer gcog-pahi tho-wa gsum* the three hammers to break the nails of colic.

རྒྱུའི་རྒྱུན *rgyuhi rgyun* कारणस्रोतः the stream of cause.

རྒྱུའི་བྱེད *rgyuhi byed* हेतु-भूत that has become a cause; excuse.

རྒྱུའི་གཙོ་བོ *rgyuhi gtso-bo* प्रधान-हेतु the chief or primary cause.

རྒྱུའི་རིག *rgyuhi rig* हेतु-विद्या the science of reasoning.

རྒྱུ་ཡང་དག་པར་བཅད་པ *rgyu yañ-dag-par bcad-pa* that has fully stopped or terminated the cause; the consequence.

རྒྱུ་ཡིས་ཁྱད་པར *rgyu-yis khyad-par* जनक the chief cause; the agent.

རྒྱུ་རིག་ཅེན་པོ *rgyu-rig cen-po* (གྲངས *grañs*) महाहेतु a number.

རྒྱུ་ལ་འབྲས་བུ་བཙགས *rgyu-la hbras-bu btsags* कारणे कार्योपचार to attach a fruit to cause.

རྒྱུ་ལས་བྱུང་ *rgyu-las byuñ* हेतुक produced or originated from cause.

རྒྱུ་ལུས་ཀྱི་འབྱུང་བ *rgyu-lus-kyi hbyuñ-wa*= གཟུགས་ཁམས *gzugs-khams* the body; form.

རྒྱུ་ས *rgyu-sa*=(ལམ *lam*) road, passage.

རྒྱུ་སྲང་ *rgyu-srañ* track, passage, road: བཙན་གྱི་རྒྱུ་སྲང་ *btsan-gyi rgyu-srañ* the road that is frequented by a *Btsan* (demon).

རྒྱུད *rgyud* I: तन्तु a string; chain; that which joins things together; a connection, whether physical or mental; རི་རྒྱུད chain of hills.

རྒྱུད II: तन्त्र Tantrik treatise; ritual book for coercing deities and for other magical ceremonies. One of the large divisions of the Kah-gyur is styled རྒྱུད because it contains innumerable magical treatises. There are said to be four classes of Tantras, རྒྱུད་སྡེ་བཞི, namely, (1) བྱ་བའི་རྒྱུད, (2) སྤྱོད་པའི་རྒྱུད, (3) རྣལ་འབྱོར་རྒྱུད, (4) རྣལ་འབྱོར་བླ་ན་མེད་པའི་རྒྱུད. In the Tan-gyur the collection of Tantras is named བརྒྱུད *brgyud.*

རྒྱུད་པ *rgyud-pa* I: vb. to tie, fasten, connect together.

རྒྱུད་པ II: religious teacher; especially a teacher of mysticism.

རྒྱུད་པ III: extraction; lineage; belonging to a family or race; family.

Syn. བརྒྱུད་པ *brgyud-pa*; རྩ་འཁྲིད *rtsa-hkhrid*; རིགས་འབྱུང་ *rigs-hbyuñ*; རིགས་རྒྱུད *rigs-rgyud*; ས་བོན་ལས་བྱུང་ *sa-bon las-byuñ*; གདུང་རྒྱུད *gduñ-rgyud*; རུས་རྒྱུད *rus-rgyud*; ཚོ་འབྲང་ *cho-hbrañ*; ཅ་ཉེ *ça-ñe*; སྣག་ལས་སྐྱེས *snag-las-skyes*; རིགས *rigs* (*Mñon.*).

རྒྱུད་པ་གསུམ *rgyud-pa gsum* the three kinds of lineage are:—(1) གདུང་རྒྱུད *gduñ-rgyud* family; descent; personal; (2) སྐུ་རྒྱུད *sku-rgyud* descent (of the spirit in emanations, etc., as in the case of incarnate lamas); (3) སློབ་རྒྱུད *slob-rgyud* spiritual descent (ministerial succession by disciples).

རྒྱུན *rgyun* continuity; *rgyun-du* always; at all times; continually.

རྒྱུན་ཁྲི *rgyun khri* settled seat or throne; དུས་རྒྱུན་ས་གནས་གཅིག་ཏུ་འཇོག་པའི་ཁྲི *dus-rgyun sa-gnas gcig-tu hjog-pahi khri* the chair which always remains in one place.

རྒྱུན་སྐྱོངས *rgyun-khyoñs* always to protect.

རྒྱུན་གྱི་མྱུ་གུ *rgyun-gyi myu-gu*=ཆར་ཟིལ *char-zil* rain-drops or dews (*Mñon.*).

རྒྱུན་བབ་ཚ *rgyun-bab tsha*=ཆར་དྲག *char-drag* heavy rain (*Mñon.*).

རྒྱུན་གཏན *rgyun-gtan*=དུས་རྒྱུན *dus-rgyun* at all times; the stream of time: རྒྱུན་གཏན་གདུང་

དོན་ཡིན་ངེས་ནམས real business; transactions of a public character must always be reliable (*D. çel. 7*).

རྒྱུས་པ *rgyus-pa* sinews; tendons.

རྒྱོ *rgyo* मिथुन, शृङ्गार (a colloq. and obscene term) sexual union; copulation.

རྒྱོ་བ *rgyo-wa*, pf. བརྒྱོས *brgyos*, fut. བརྒྱོ *rgyo*, imp. རྒྱོས *rgyos*, to have sexual intercourse; acc. to *Cs.* to deflower, ravish.

རྒྱོགས *rgyogs* कठयन्त्र; མེ་རྒྱོགས་རྡོ་རྒྱོགས *mergyogs rdo-rgyogs* gun; missile.

རྒྱོང་བ *rgyoń-wa*, pf. བརྒྱངས *brgyańs*, fut. བརྒྱང་ *brgyań*, seems to be a secondary form of རྐྱོང་བ *rkyoń-wa*, to extend, stretch, spread forth, distend.

རྒྱོར་བ *rgyor-wa* मारय to kill.

ལྒ *lga* this word is seldom used, its modern form being སྒ *sga*. 1. ginger fresh or dried; ལྒ་རློན *lga-rlon* fresh ginger. In medical works both ལྒ *lga* and སྒ *sga* are used to imply སྒ་སྨུག *sga-smug*, the brown ginger. 2. རུས་ཀྱི་མིང་ *rus-kyi miń* n. of a tribe; དབྲའ་འགྲུ་ལྡོང་གསུམ་ལྒ་དང་བཞི *dbrah-hgru ldoń-gsum lga-dań bshi* the four tribes were *Dbrah*, *Hgru*, *Ldoń* and *Lga*.

ལྒ་ཕོ་ཆེ *lga pho-che*=རྒྱམ་ཚྭ *rgyam-tshba* a mystical word; oxide of mercury; also signifies སྨན་སྒ *sman-sga*, medicinal ginger.

ལྒང་ངེ *lgań-ńe* marble white. སྐྱ་ལྒང་ངེ *skya lgań-ńe* is stated to mean perfectly white (*Jä.*).

ལྒང་པ *lgań-pa* or ལྒང་ཕུག *lgań-phug* acc. to *Jä.* the urinary bladder (*Med.*).

Syn. ཆུ་སོ *chu-so*; ལྒང་བུ *lgań-bu* (*Mńon.*).

ལྒང་པ *lgań-pa* relating to the bladder (*Lex.*).

ལྒང་བུ *lgań-bu* urinary bladder; same as ལྒང་པ *lgań-pa*; acc. to *Jä.* husk, pod, shell.

ལྒང་བུག *lgań-bug*=དྲི་ཆུའི་སྣོད *dri-chuhi snod* the bladder (*Sman.*).

ལྒའུ་གཅེར *lgahu-gçer*=སྒ་རློན *sga-rlon* fresh ginger.

ལྒར་མ་མེས་པོ *Lgar-ma mes-po* patriarch of the tribe of *Lgar-ma*; a tribal name: ལྒ་ཡི་ལྒར་མ་མེས་པོ་ཐོབ *lga-yi lgar-ma mes-po thob* the tribe of *Lga* obtained the name of *Lgar-ma mespo*.

ལྒོ *lgo* a common kind of fungus like the lycoperdon or puff-ball.

ལྒྱམ་ཚྭ *lgyam-tshva*, སྨན་སྒ *sman-ga* 1. ginger, v. ལྒ་ཕོ་ཆེ *lga pho-che*. 2. acc. to *Jä.* a kind of rock salt.

སྒ *sga*=ལྒ *lga* आर्द्रक, रेचनि, पल्यङ्क 1. ginger. 2. saddle, resp. ཆིབ་སྒ *chib-sga*, a saddle for a horse; ཆིབ་སྒ་བསྟད་པ *chib-sga bstad-pa* to lay the saddle on; to saddle; གཡག་གི་སྒ *gyag-gi sga* a saddle for a yak.

སྒ་སྐྱ *sga-skya* ginger: སྒ་སྐྱས་བད་རླུང་སེལ་ཞིང་ཁྲག་འཁྱག་འཇུ *sga-skyas bad-rluń sel-shiń khrag-hkhyag hju* ginger removes phlegm and wind and liquifies the blood.

སྒ་ཁེབས *sga-khebs* saddle cloth; the leather cover or coating of a saddle.

སྒ་གློ *sga-glo* saddle girth.

སྒ་སྒྲོན་པ *sga-sgron-pa* described in *Hbrom.* as meaning: to saddle a horse.

སྒ་ཏིག་ནག་པོ *Sga-tig nag-po* the flower of a bitter species of ginger: སྒ་ཏིག་ནག་པོས་དམུ་རྫིང་ཆུ་སེར་འདྲེན *sga-tig nag-pos dmu rdsiń chu-ser hdren* the flower of *Sgatic* used as a medicine draws out the yellow water of dropsy.

སྒ་ཐག *sga-thag* ropes or straps used in adjusting a saddle.

སྒ་པ *sga-pa* 1. a young horse just fit for the saddle. 2. གཡག་ཐོད་པ་དཀར་པོ་ལ་སྒ་པ་ (also ག་པ་)ཟེར *gyag thod-pa dkar-po la sga-pa zer* a yak with a white forehead is called *sga-pa* (*Rtsii.*).

སྒ་ཕོང་ *sga-phoṅ* bat; flitter-mouse (*Sch.*).

སྒ་སྨུག *sga-smug*, also written སྨུག་སྒ *smug-sga*, brown ginger.

སྒ་ཚ *sga-tsha* the flower of gingor plant: སྒ་ཚས་དྲོད་སྐྱེད་རུལ་གཅོད་ཆུ་སེར་འདྲེན *sga-tshas drod-skyed rul-gcod chu-ser hdren* ginger flower (used) as a stimulant, cures sores and draws out pus.

སྒ་ཚྭ *sga-tsha* ग्रन्थिकद्रक pungent ginger.

སྒ་ལག *sga-lag* frame of the saddlo; saddle-bow; saddle-treo (*Cs.*).

སྒ་སེར *sga-ser* हरिद्रा turmeric; yellow ginger; a spice used in cooking meat for the table.

སྒ་ཤ *sga-ça* straps for fastening the travelling-baggage to the saddle, cf. ཤ་སྟག *ça-stag*.

སྒག་ཐུང་ *Sgag-thuṅ* n. of a small silk scarf used in religious servicos in Tibet: དབང་ལྡན་མ་དང, སྒག་ཐུང་, སྲིད་བདེ་མ *dwaṅ-ldan ma-daṅ, sgag-thuṅ, srid bde-ma* (*S. kar. 179*).

སྒག་པ *sgag-pa* धर्षण to ravish; to copulate; to embrace in sexual union.

སྒང་ *sgaṅ* 1. a hill-spur; the ridgo or top of a hill: ཅོག་ཙེའི་སྒང་ལ་བཞག *cog-tsehi sgaṅ-la shag* keep on the top of the table. 2. time; occasion: སང་ལས་ཀ་བྱེད་པའི་སྒང་ *saṅ las-ka byed-pahi sgaṅ* to-morrow at the time of doing work; ད་ལྟ་ལྟོ་ཟ་བའི་སྒང་ *da-lta lto-za-wahi sgaṅ* just now while taking food. 3. ཆུ་སྒང་ *chu-sgaṅ* a blister caused by manual work, by long marches, &c., cf. བསྒང་ *bsgaṅ*.

Syn. སྟེང་ *steṅ*, མཐོ་བ *mtho-wa* (*Mṅon.*).

སྒང་ཁ *sgaṅ-kha*=སྒང་ཁུལ *sgaṅ-khul* 1. a hill-spur: སྒང་ཁ་ལ་ཡོད tho (village) is situated on a mountain spur. 2. full, entire: སྲོག་ཆགས་གཅིག་བསད་ཀྱང་སྡིག་པ་སྒང་ཁ་རེ་སོ་སོར་ཡོང་ *srog-chags gcig bsad-kyaṅ sdig-pa sgaṅ-kha re so-sor yoṅ* even if (you) kill one living being there will bo the full (amount of) sin in oach separate case.

སྒང་ཁུལ *sgaṅ-khul* aco. to *Jä.* samo as སྒང་ཁ *sgaṅ-kha*.

སྒང་གི་ལིང་ *sgaṅ-gi-liṅ* a species of partridge.

སྒང་མཐོན་པོ *sgaṅ mthon-po* a high hill.

སྒང་བ *sgaṅ-wa*, pf. བསྒངས *bsgaṅs*, fut. བསྒང་ *bsgaṅ*, to grow or become full (*Cs.*): བུད་མེད་ན་སོ་སྒང་ *bud-med na so-sgaṅ* a full grown woman; marriageable girl.

སྒང་བུ *sgaṅ-bu* full quantity; entire piece: ང་རྒྱལ་སྒང་བུ་རལ་བར་མ་གྱུར་ཏམ has not his pride been entirely broken-down within (*A. 11*).

སྒང་གཞོང་ *sgaṅ-gçoṅ* उन्नत-निम्नस्थल elevations and depressions on a hillside.

སྒངས *sgaṅs* पुलिन 1. bank or elevated place on the margin of a river. 2. n. of districts in S.E. Tibet.

སྒབ་འདྲེ *sgab-hdre* a class of demon; a ghost that remains concealed: སྔགས་འཆང་ལུགས་དང་མཐུན་པས་སྒབ་འདྲེ་བསྐྲད *sṅags-hchaṅ lugs-daṅ mthun-pas sgab-hdre bskrad* if tho *Tantrik* priest properly performs exorcism, the ghosts are scared away.

སྒབ་པ *sgab-pa* 1. secondary form of འགེབས་པ *hgebs-pa*, to cover; covering: བྱ་མས་བུ་ལ་སྒབ་པ *bya-mas bu-la sgab-pa* the covering of a young bird by its mother. 2. གོས་སྒབ *gos-sgab* skirt or lap of a coat; སྒབ་ཐུང་ *sgab-thuṅ* a short skirt.

སྒམ *sgam* मञ्जूषा, कोष, पिट box, trunk, chest; also the testes: སྒམ་སྒོ་མང་ *sgam-sgo maṅ* a chest of drawers; ལྕགས་སྒམ *lcags-sgam* an iron-chest; ཀོ་སྒམ *ko-sgam* a leather trunk; རོ་སྒམ་ *ro-gams* or སྤུར་སྒམ *spur-sgam* a coffin.

Syn. སྒྲོམ *sgrom*; སྣོད *snod*; མཛོད *mdsod*; སྒྲོམ་བུ *sgrom-bu*; བང་པ *baṅ-pa*; ཐབ་སྒྲོམ *thab-sgrom*.

སྒམ་ཆུང་ *sgam-chuṅ* a small box.

སྒམ་པ *sgam-pa*=ཟབ་པ *zab-pa* गभीर deep; profound; མི་སྒམ་པ *mi sgam-pa* = མི་ཟབ་པ *mi zab-pa* shallow; not deep.

སྒམ་པོ *sgam-po*, adj. full or fully accomplished; one who is deep: རྒྱལ་པོ་སྲོང་བཙན་སྒམ་པོ *Rgyal-po Sroṅ-btsan sgam-po*, King *Sroṅ-btsan* who was *Sgam-po*, *i.e.*, fully accomplished. Acc. to *Sch.* prudent, quiet: བློ་སྒམ་པ *blo sgam-pa*=ཐུགས་ཤིན་ཏུ་སྒམ་པོ *thugs çin-tu sgam-po* he (the prince) was very profound.

སྒར *sgar*, defined as གུར་མང་པོ་ཕུབ་ནས་བསྡད་པ *gur maṅ-po phub-nas bsdad-pa*, pitching many tents (at a place); camp; encampment; དམག་སྒར a military encampment; སྒར་འདེབས་པ to encamp; to pitch a camp.

སྒར་སྣང *Sgar-snaṅ* respectable men.

སྒར་མིང་ *sgar-miṅ* (བསོ་སྒྲ *bso-sgra*) watch-word; parole (*Jä.*).

སྒལ *sgal* a load that is carried on the back; load of a beast of burden; རྟ་སྒལ *rta-sgal* a horse-load; ཤིང་རྟའི་སྒལ *çiṅ-rtahi sgal* cart-load; waggon-load.

སྒལ་རྟ *sgal-rta* pack-horse.

སྒལ་ཕྱུགས *sgal-phyugs* beast of burden.

སྒལ་འཕང་བ *sgal hphaṅ-wa* to throw a load off; སྒལ་འབོགས་པ *sgal hbogs-pa* to take out a load; སྒལ་བསྲང་བ *sgal bsraṅ-wa* to adjust or balance a load.

སྒལ་པ *sgal-pa* 1. the back of man or beast of burden; རྒྱབ་ལ་འཁུར་ནས་འགྲོ་བ *rgyab-la hkhur-nas hgro-wa*=སྒལ་པ་ལ་འཁུར་ཏེ་འགྲོ *sgal-pa la hkhur-te hgro* the carrying a thing on one's back. 2. the small of the back; སྒལ་འདབས *sgal-hdabs* the lumber region. 3. croup; crupper.

སྒལ་བ *sgal-wa* to carry a load (on one's back) or to cause a load to be carried on the back of a beast of burden; སྒལ་འགེལ་བ *sgal hgel-wa* to put on a load.

སྒལ་རྨ *sgal-rma* a sore on an animal's back caused by the load.

སྒལ་ཚིགས *sgal-tshigs* the spine in general; the backbone of a beast of burden.

སྒལ་ཚིགས་ཉི་ཤུ་རྩ་བརྒྱད *sgal-tshigs ñi-çu rtsa brgyad* the twenty-eight joints in the backbone; མི་ཡི་སྒལ་ཚིགས *mi-yi sgal-tshigs* the joints in the human spinal column.

སྒལ་ཚིགས་ཉི་ཤུ་རྩ་བཞི *sgal-tshigs ñi-çu rtsa-bshi* there are twenty-four joints in the backbone of a beast of burden.

སྒལ་ཚིགས་སྲང་བ *sgal-tshigs sraṅ-wa* a beast of burden of which the backbone is straight, *i.e.*, not bent by work.

སྒིར་མོ *sgir-mo* སྒོར་སྒོར *sgor-sgor* वृत्त round; orb-like; globular.

སྒུ *sgu*, adj. bent; སྒུ་སྟེགས *sgu-stegs* 1. a foot-stool. 2. acc. to *Sch.* elbow; angle.

སྒུ་རྡོ *sgu-rdo* sling-string, explained as ཧུར་རྡོ་འཕན་བྱེད་ཀྱི་ཐག་པ *hur-rdo hphan byed-kyi thag-pa* the string that is coiled round a stone for flinging it; a sling.

སྒུ་ཕྱོགས *sgu-phyogs* (སྒྱེ་ཕྱོགས *sgye-phyogs*)= མདུན་ལ་འཁྱོག་པ *mdun-la khyog-pa* bent-forward: སྒྱེ་ཕྱོགས་སྒུ་ཕྱོགས་ཤེས་པ་ཤིན་ཏུ་གཅེས *sgye-phyog sgu-phyogs çes-pa çin-tu gces* those that are bent forward and bent round were valuable? (*Jig.*).

སྒུ་མོ *sgu-mo* = ཧུར་རྡོ *hur-rdo* a sling.

སྒུག་པ *sgug-pa* प्रतीक्ष (in Pali पटिखा) to wait, pf. བསྒུགས *bsgugs*, fut. བསྒུག *bgug*, imp. སྒུགས *sgugs* (or སྒུགས་ཤིག *sgugs çig*); མི་ཡོང་རྒྱུ་སྒུག་བསྡད་པ *mi yoṅ-rgyu sgug bsdad-pa*, to wait for a man's arrival; སྒུག་པར་བྱེད *sgug-par byed* one who waits for; or སྒུག་པ་པོ *sgug-pa po* a waiter; ལམ་ན་སྒུག་པ *lam-na sgug-pa* to wait on the road; སྒུག་ཏུ་འཇུག་པ *sgug-tu hjug-pa* to cause to lie in wait (for a person); to cause to way-lay.

སྒུང་ *sguṅ* in *Ld.* clap; crack; crash; report (of a gun) (*Jä.*).

སྒུད་པོ *sgud-po*, acc. to *Sch.* father-in-law; སྒུད་མོ *sgud-mo* mother-in-law.

སྒུམ་མདའ *sgum-mdah*, acc. to *Schr.* the butt-end of a gun; gun-stock.

སྒུར *sgur*, v. དགུར *dgur*.

སྒུར་རྒྱབ *gur-rgyab* a bent-back.

སྒུར་པོ *sgur-po* कुब्ज, भग्नकुब्ज bent; crooked back.

Syn. སྒུར་འཁྱོག *sgur-hkhyog*; སྒུ *sgu* (*Mṅon.*).

སྒུར་བ *sgur-wa*, भीत, विभ्रम to become afraid.

སྒུལ་སྐྱོད *sgul-skyod* क्षोभ agitation.

སྒུལ་བ *sgul-wa*, pf. བསྒུལ *bsgul*, fut. བསྒུལ *bsgul* (cf. འགུལ་བ *hgul-wa*) to move, agitate, put in motion: རྒྱུད་ཀྱང་མ་སྒུལ་ཏོ *rgyud-kyaṅ ma-sgul-to* he could not even move the bow-string: ལག་པས་རྡོ་བསྒུལ་ཏོ *lag-pas rdo bsgul-to* with his hand he shook the rock.

སྒེ་ཁུང་ *sge-khuṅ*, སྒོ་ཆུང་ *sgo-chuṅ* a small door; a window.

སྒེག *sgeg* लावण्य grace, charm in the person.

སྒེག་པ *sgeg-pa* शृङ्गार, विलास, लासिन्, रस, लावण्य 1. the grace or charm of youth: སྒེག་པ་ནི་ཆགས་པས་གཟུགས་མཛེས་པའི་རྣམ་འགྱུར་རྟེན་པ *sgeg-pa* is the fascination arising at the appearance of a body of beautiful shape. 2. sensual enjoyment; flirtation. 3. acc. to *Cs.* to brag, boast; airs of coquetish girls (*Jä.*).

Syn. རོལ་པ *rol-pa*; འཇོ་བ *hjo-wa* (*Mṅon.*).

སྒེག་པའི་རྡོ་རྗེ *Sgeg-pahi Rdo-rje* लावण्यवज्र, लीलावज्र n. of a Buddhist sage of Ancient India who visited Udyāna (Ancient Cabul) and spread Buddhism there.

སྒེག་མ *Sgeg-ma* n. of the goddess of beauty.

སྒེག་མོ *sgeg-mo* लास्या नर्त्तकी a dancing-girl; a charming damsel.

སྒེག་རྫས *sgeg-rdsas* perfumery, pomades, &c., articles which (according to Buddhism) are incentives to sensual pleasures.

སྒེང་ལ *sgeṅ-la* or དགེང་ལ *dgeṅ-la*, acc. to *Jä.* on; upon; perhaps a wrong spelling of the word སྒང་ *sgaṅ*.

སྒེའུ *sgehu* 1. diminutive of སྒ *sga*, ginger. 2. v. སྒོག་པ ı: *sgog-pa* (*K. g.* ཞ *46*).

སྒེའུ་ཆུང་ *sgehu-chuṅ* लशुन garlic.

སྒེའུ་གསེར *sgehu-gser* आर्द्रक ginger.

སྒེར *sger* private; semi-independent; སྒེར་དུ *sger-du* specially; privately.

སྒེར་རྟ *sger-rta* a horse for the use of a private party, not for a public officer.

སྒེར་དོན *sger-don* one's own interest, private or special reason or object: སྒེར་གཞུང་མེད་དུ་བ་གནམ་བཏང *sger gshuṅ med du-wa gnam-btaṅ* neither private nor public (but an independent family) sending forth smoke from house-fire.

སྒེར་པ *sger-pa* a private land-holder; གཞུང་ཁྲལ་ཆེན་པོ་མེད་པར་རང་ལ་མི་སེར་ཡང་ཡོད་པ་ལས་ཁྲལ་བསྡུས་ནས་ཞ་བཟོད་མཁན *gshuṅ-khral chen-po med-par raṅ-la mi-ser yaṅ yod-pa las khral-bsdus nas sa bsdad-khan* a land-holder who without paying a large tax to Government enjoys an estate is called སྒེར་པ *sger-pa*, also one who holds land fee-simple; སྒེར་ལྷ *sger-lha* or སྒེར་གྱིས་མཆོད་པའི་ལྷ *sger-gyi mchod-paḥi lha*, a special deity, *i.e.*, a deity specially adored by a class of people or by an individual or by a particular family; སྒེར་ཁག *sger-khag* semi-independent estate.

སྒེར་གཡོག *sger-gyog* private servant, also one who does his own work; servant or employé of an independent party or estate which has no connection with the Government.

སྒེར་ལོ *sger-lo*, རང་སྒེར་གྱི་ཞིང་ལོ་ཏོག *raṅ-sger gyi shiṅ lo-tog* the produce of a private estate.

སྒོ *sgo* द्वार, मुख, प्रतीहार, पच a door; an entrance or doorway; the aperture itself as well as the wood-work of the door; སྒོ་བཅད་པ *sgo bcad-pa* or སྒོ་དགག་པ *sgo dgag-pa* to shut or close a door; སྒོ་ཕྱེ་བ *sgo phye-wa* or སྒོ་འབྱེད་པ *sgo byed-pa* to open a door; སྒོ་འཇུག་པ *sgo hjug-pa* to put in a door; to hang a door; སྒོ་རྒྱབ་པ *sgo rgyab-pa* to shut a door; སྒོ་གཏན་པ *sgo gtan-pa* acc. to *Sch.* to lock up, to bolt, to bar; སྒོ་བཀུམ་པ *sgo bkum-pa* or བསྐུམ *bskum*, acc. to *Cs.* resp. to shut (a door); སྒོ་བདུང་བ *sgo bduṅ-wa* to knock or rap at the door; རྒྱ་སྒོ *rgya-sgo* large, or the principal, door or entrance; སྒོ་ the gate or gate-way; ཕྱི་སྒོ *phyi-sgo* the outer door; བར་སྒོ *bar-sgo* the middle door; ནང་སྒོ *naṅ-sgo* the inner door; གསང་སྒོ *gsaṅ-sgo* the secret or private door; མཛོད་སྒོ *mdsod-sgo* the door to the store-room; གནམ་སྒོ *gnam-sgo* an aperture in the roof for light; sky-light; སྟེང་སྒོ *steṅ-sgo* the upper door; འོག་སྒོ *hog-sgo* the lower or under door; མཆོད་ཁང་སྒོ *mchod-khaṅ sgo* the chapel-door; ཐབ་ཚང་སྒོ *thab-tshaṅ sgo* kitchen door; གཉེར་ཚང་སྒོ *gñer-tshaṅ sgo* the store-house door; ཆབ་ཁང་སྒོ *chab-khaṅ sgo* the bathroom door. In Sikkim *gom*=door.

སྒོ II: often *Sgo-mo*, the admission to, the medium or means of, the passage of, knowledge or learning and, as such, the science itself, &c.; ཆོས་ཀྱི་སྒོ་མོ *chos-kyi sgo-mo* the service of *Dharma* (religion); རྩིས་ཀྱི་སྒོ་མོ *rtsis-kyi sgo-mo* the science of arithmetic or numbers; སྨན་ཀྱི་སྒོ་མོ *sman-kyi sgo-mo* science of medicine: སྒྲོལ་མའི་སྒོ་ནས་གཡུལ་མདོས་གཏོང་ *Sgrol-maḥi sgo-nas gyul-mdos gtoṅ* in the religious service of Dolma—the *mdos* for victory (in war) should be offered: སངས་རྒྱས་ཀྱི་བསྟན་པ་ལ་འཇུག་པའི་སྒོ་དམ་པ་སྐྱབས་སུ་འགྲོ་བ *Saṅs-rgyas kyi bstan-pa la hjug-paḥi sgo dam-pa skyabs-su hgro-wa* as a door for entering the religion of Buddha, it is necessary to take refuge in the holy ones: ཐེག་ཆེན་ལ་འཇུག་པའི་སྒོ་བྱང་ཆུབ་ཀྱི་སེམས *theg-chen-la hjug-paḥi sgo byaṅ-chub-kyi sems* for entering the Greater Vehicle doctrine the means is a saintly heart (the purified heart of a *Bodhi-sattva*); ཡོན་ཏན་འབྱུང་བའི་སྒོ་བརྩོན་འགྲུས *yon-tan hbyuṅ waḥi sgo brtson-hgrus* the means of acquiring learning is diligence and industry; ཉེས་པ་འབྱུང་བའི་སྒོ་ལེ་ལོ་བག་མེད་པ *ñes-pa hbyuṅ waḥi-sgo le-lo bag-med-pa* being idle and immodest forms a way to the springing up of vice.

སྒོ་ཀུན་འགྲོ *sgo kun-gro* सर्व्वतोमुख in every way.

སྒོ་སྐྱོང་ *sgo-skyoṅ* द्वारपाल porter; door-guard.

སྒོ་སྐྱོར *sgo-skyor*, v. སྒོ་སྤེ *sgo-spe*.

སྒོ་ཁང་ *sgo-khaṅ* or སྒོ་སྟེང་ *sgo-steṅ* निर्य्यूह the entrance into a house; vestibule; porch; portal; also a small house on the gate.

སྒོ་ཁུང་ *sgo-khuṅ* opening of the door; an apperture in a door; སྒོ་ཁང་སྟེང་གི་གསིལ་ཁང་ *sgo-khaṅ steṅ-gi gsil-khaṅ* the verandah room on the porch of a house.

སྒོ་ཁྱི *sgo-khyi* watch-dog.

སྒོ་འཁོར་ *sgo-ḥkhor* hinge of a door or gate; the pivot on which the door turns.

སྒོ་གླེགས་ *sgo-glegs* a small beam used to bar or bolt a door.

སྒོ་འགྲམ་ *sgo-ḥgram* the space near the door.

སྒོ་རྒྱབ་ *sgo-rgyab* the space behind the door or within the door.

སྒོ་གླེགས་ *sgo-glegs* द्वारकपाट, निष्कुट, वाथठ tho board or plank of a door; the lintel; frame work on the four sides of a door [a bier, the bed on which a dead body is carried] *S.*

སྒོ་ང *sgo-ṅa* अण्ड eggs, spawn; སྒོ་ང་ཅན་ *sgo-ṅa-can* egg; producing or possessing or having spawn.

སྒོ་ངའི་མཛོད་ *sgo-ṅaḥi mdsod* मुष्क the testicles.

སྒོ་ལྕགས་ *sgo-lcags* तालकं the lock of a door.

སྒོ་ཆོར་ *sgo-chor*, v. སྒོ་སྤེ *sgo-spe.*

སྒོ་སྙོད་ *sgo-sñod*=གོ་སྙོད་ *sgo-sñod* cummin seed.

སྒོ་བསྙན་ *sgo bsñan* n. of a Bon deity who has eighteen hands and holds eighteen different weapons of war, which are as follows:—(1) བཏེག་པའི་མདའ་ *bteg paḥi mdaḥ* an arrow for shooting; (2) འབུགས་པའི་མདུང་ *ḥbugs paḥi mduṅ* a spear to pierce with; (3) གཅོག་པའི་སྟ་རེ *gcog paḥi sta-re* an axe to split with; (4) གཅོད་པའི་གྲ་སྟ *gcod-paḥi gra-sta* a chopper to cut off; (5) འཐུབ་པའི་རལ་གྲི *ḥthub-paḥi ral-gri* a sword to cut into pieces; (6) བསྟིམ་པའི་ཆུ་གྲི *bstim-paḥi chu-gri* a dagger to pierce through; (7) འཆོག་པའི་ཐོ་ལུམ *ḥchog-paḥi tho-lum* a cannon ball for battering in; (8) འབུགས་པའི་གསོར་ཆེན *ḥbugs-paḥi gsor-chen* a pin to bore through; (9) འབྲལ་བའི་སོག་ལེ *ḥbral-waḥi sog-le* the saw to separate or cut asunder; (10) དགྲ་བོའི་སྤུ་གྲི *dgra-woḥi spu-gri* a razor-knife to cut the enemy; (11) བསྐོར་བའི་འཁོར་ལོ *bskor-waḥi ḥkhor-lo* a disk to whirl round; (12) སྒྱུར་བའི་ཡ་ལད *sgyur-waḥi ya-lad* an armour to ward off; (13) ཉམ་ཐག་གཅོད་པའི་ཀ་མ་ལི *ñam-thag gcod-paḥi ka-ma-li* a sword to cut off; (14) སྲེག་པའི་གཏར་ཏོ *sreg-paḥi gtar-to*; (15) འཆིང་བའི་ལྕགས་སྒྲོག *ḥchiṅ-waḥi lcags-sgrog* iron chain to bind with; (16) དཔལ་ཟེར་གྱི་ཆུ་ཁོལ *dpal-zer-gyi chu-khol* boiling water; (17) འོད་ཟེར་གྱི་མེ་དཔུང་ *hod-zer-gyi me dpuṅ* a heap of glowing fire; (18) དྲག་རྩལ་གྱི་ཐོག་མདའ *drag-rtsal gyi thog-mdaḥ* a thunder-bolt for chivalrous exercises.

སྒོ་གཏན *sgo-gtan* a bar or bolt of a door; སྒོ་ཐེམ *sgo-them* threshhold; also the head-piece of a door.

སྒོ་དར *sgo-dar* the scarf that is attached to the door at the time of a marriage in Sikkim.

སྒོ་དེབ *sgo-deb* enumeration of persons; the counting of persons of a village or town, &c.

སྒོ་གདན་ཟུང་ཅན *sgo-gdan zuṅ-can* कृका a circular disk with string attached to it that is put on each side of the door to open it by tho hand.

སྒོ་འགྲིག *sgo-ḥgrig* door-frame; window frame.

སྒོ་ལྡང་ *sgo-ldaṅ* each side of the door.

སྒོ་ནག *sgo-nag* the dark door, *i.e.*, the door of the dark room where a dead body is kept before disposal (*D. çel. 8*).

སྒོ་རྣམ *sgo-rnam* a single board, *i.e.*, of the floor.

སྒོ་པ *sgo-pa* दौवारिक, or སྒོ་དཔོན *sgo-dpon* or སྒོ་བདག *sgo-bdag* 1. the door-keeper, porter; 2. also the headman of the village.

Syn. སྒོ་སྲུང་ *sgo-sruṅ*; སྒོ་སྐྱོང་ *sgo-skyoṅ*; ཆབ་སྒོ་བ *chab-sgo-wa*; སྒོ་ཡི་མེལ་ཚེ་མཁན *sgo-yi mel-tshe-mkhan* (*Mṅon.*).

སྒོ་ཕུར *sgo-pur* fore-skin; prepuce.

སྒོ་པོ *sgo-po* also སྒོ་བོ *sgo-bo* outward looks; stature; bodily appearance (*Jä.*); སྐྱེ་སྒོ *skye-sgo* the face; countenance; སྐྱེ་སྒོ་ལེགས *skye sgo-legs* a beautiful face; ཞན་སྒོ *shan-sgo* an ugly face.

སྒོ་སྤང་ *sgo-spaṅ* 1. lintel. 2. སྒོ་ཡི་ཐེམ་སྤང་པའི་རྣལ་འབྱོར་པ་ཡང་ཡོད *sgo-yi them-pa spaṅ-pahi rnal-hbyor-pa yaṅ-yod* there are even *yogi* who have only left the lintel and threshold of their home (and no more).

སྒོ་སྤེ *sgo-spe* a projection of the roof of a house above the principal door of a house, under which one can sit or sleep, or where servants wait: དོ་ནུབ་བི་ཀྲ་མའི་སྒོ་སྤེའི་འོག་ཏུ་ཉོལ *do-nub bi-kra-mahi sgo-spehi hog-tu ñol* (*A. 130*) to-night sleep under the portico of Vikramas'ila.

Syn. སྒོ་སྐྱར *sgo-skyar*; སྒོ་མཚོར *sgo-mchor*; སྒོ་འབྱར *sgo-hbyar* (*Mṅon.*).

སྒོ་ཕར *sgo-phar*, སྒོ་རིམ་མང་པོ *sgo-rim maṅ-po* the name for a series of doors.

སྒོ་འཕར *sgo-hphar* कपाट-पुट, v. སྒོ་གླེགས *sgo-glegs* [the junction of the leaves of a door]*S.*

སྒོ་བ *sgo-wa* pf. བསྒོ *bsgo* also བསྒོས *bsgos*, to say; to speak, mostly to bid; to order (used in old works, now become obsolete).

སྒོ་འབྱར *sgo-hbyar*, v. སྒོ་སྤེ *sgo-spe*.

སྒོ་འབྱེད *sgo-hbyed* a kind of grass used as a medicine in eye-disease (*Sman. 353*).

སྒོ་མ *sgo-ma* 1. panel or square of a door; the fold of a folding door. 2.=གཏོར་རྒྱབ་སྐབས་ཀྱི་སྒོ་སྲུང་གི་ལྷ *gtor-rgyab skabs-kyi sgo-sruṅ-gi lha*, the deity who guards the door on the occasion of offering *torma*; སྤྲུལ་པ་ཡེ་ཤེས་ཀྱི་སྒོ་མ་བཞིའི་མིང་ *sprul-pa ye-çes kyi sgo-ma bshihi miṅ* the names of the four miraculous divinities (of the *Bon-po*):—(1) སྟག་གདོང་དཀར་མོ་ལྕགས་ཀྱུ་བནྡྷ་འཛིན *Stag-gdoṅ dkar-mo lcags-kyu banda-hdsin*; (2) ཕག་གདོང་སེར་མོ་ཞགས་པ *Phag-gdoṅ ser-mo shag-pa*, (3) སེང་གདོང་དམར་པོ་ལྕགས་སྒྲོག, *Seṅ-gdoṅ dmar-po lcags-sgro*; (4) སྦྲུལ་གདོང་ལྗང་ཁུ་དྲིལ་བུ *sbrul-gdoṅ ljaṅ khu dril-bu.*

སྒོ་མོ *sgo-mo* (1) a large door; a gate; castle-gate; town-gate; (2) the beginning: རྩིས་ཀྱི་སྒོ་མོ *rtsis-kyi sgo-mo* the beginning of a new epoch.

སྒོ་ཙམ *sgo-tsam* a little (*Sch.*).

སྒོ་རྩ *sgo-rtsa*=སྒོའི་རྩ་བ *sgohi rtsa-wa* at the door; སྒོ་རྩར near or at the door.

སྒོ་མཚམས *sgo-mtshams* door-junction; also the chink left between a door-post and the door, when the latter does not perfectly fit.

སྒོའི་ལྕོག *sgo-hi lcog* चतुष्क raised place or stools placed on either side of a door [a place where four roads meet]*S.*

སྒོའི་ཐེམ་པ *sgohi them-pa* the threshold.

སྒོ་ཡི་མེལ་ཚེ་མཁན *sgo-yi mel-tshe mkhan*, v. སྒོ་པ *sgo-pa.*

སྒོ་ཡིག *sgo-yig* 1. inscription. 2. lampoon; label on the door; sign-board. 3. a magisterial advertisement fastened at the door.

སྒོ་ར་བ *sgo-ra-wa*=སྒོ་སྲུང་བ *sgo sruṅ-wa* a door-keeper; a door-guard.

སྒོ་ལོ *sgo-lo* 1. body. 2. face (*Jä.*).

སྒོ་བཅད *sgo bçad*=སྒོ་ལ་བཅད་པ *sgo-la bçad-pa* an inscription on the door; a sign-board.

སྒོ་གསུམ *sgo-gsum* the three media, *i.e.*, of body (ལུས *lus*), speech (ངག *ṅag*), and the mind (ཡིད *yid*).

སྒོ་བསྲུངས་བ sgo bsruṅ-wa = སྒོ་ར་བ sgo ra-wa द्वार a door-keeper.

སྒོག་སྐྱ, sgog skya or སྐྱ་སྒོག skya-sgog white garlic used in medicine; *Allium nival Jacqm*; སྒོག་སྔོན sgog-sṅon a blue species of garlic, very common in the Himalayas, perh. *Allium rubellum* (*Jä.*); སྒོག་གཅིག་མ sgog-gcig-ma a garlic grown on a single root; སྒོག་བཅུད་གསུམ sgog-bcud gsum three species of garlic which have three different properties:—(1) ཙོང་དམར tsoṅ-dmar red onion; (2) སྒོག་སྐྱ sgog-skya the common white garlic; (3) སྒོག་སྔོན sgog-sṅon the blue species of garlic.

སྒོག་ཏིང་ sgog-tiṅ mortar; སྒོག་གཏུན sgog-gtun pestle for bruising leek (*Jä.*).

སྒོག་ཏུམ sgog-tum or སྒོག་རྡོག sgog-rdog a number of garlic roots bunched in one.

སྒོག་པ I: sgog-pa लशुन, रसुन garlic; leek; *allium*; རི་སྒོག ri-sgog *Allium sphaerocephal* a species of garlic growing wild in the hills of Tibet.

Syn. ཀུན་དོང kun-doṅ; རོ་ལྡན ro-ldan; གུང་དཙུན guṅ dsun; སྙེཧུ sṅehu; སྒེཧུ sgehu; ལྷ་མིན་ཁྲག lha-min khrag; ཀླ་ཀློའི་སྤོས kla-klohi spos (*Mnon.*).

སྒོག་པ II: acc. to *Cs.* pf. བསྒགས bsgags, fut. བསྒག bsgag, to make one swear; སྒོག་པོ sgog-po one that makes a person swear (*Jä.*).

སྒོག་གསིལ sgog-gsil a single garlic root or seed.

སྒོང་ I: sgoṅ also སྒོང་ང་ sgoṅ-ṅa an egg. In Sikkim "sgoṅ-do" (*Snd. Hbk.*).

སྒོང་ II: n. of a country, prob. ཀོང་པོ Koṅ-po.

སྒོང་སྐྱེས sgoṅ-skyes = སྒོ་ང་ལས་སྐྱེས་པ sgo-ṅa-las skyes-pa अण्डज born of or produced from an egg.

སྒོང་སྤྲི sgoṅ-spri the white of an egg or more properly the thin film which wraps the contents of an egg.

སྒོང་ཐོག་པ sgoṅ thog-pa n. of a plant.

སྒོང་བ sgoṅ-wa, pf. བསྒོངས bsgoṅs, fut. བསྒོང་ bsgoṅ, imp. སྒོང་ (ས) sgoṅ (s) or སྒོངས་ཤིག sgoṅs-çig पिण्डय 1. to make in tea balls to eat; to make round balls of dough (*Cs.*). 2. to hide; to conceal (a thing) (*Sch.*). 3. སྒོངས་པའམ་སྒོར་མོ sgoṅs-paham sgor-mo a laughing speech or exclamation.

སྒོད་ཡས sgod-yas n. of a numeral སམ་བྱེད་བྲང་བྲིང་སྒོད་ཡས (*Ya-sel*).

སྒོབ་སྒོབ sgob-sgob unable; deficient; wanting in strength (*Sch.*).

སྒོམ sgom, see སྒོམ་པ sgom-pa.

སྒོམ་ཆེན sgom-chen 1. a Buddhist ascetic who remains absorbed in deep meditation. 2. species of fieldmouse, *Lagomys badius*, so called from its hybernating disposition. See Hooker's Himalayan Journals.

སྒོམ་ཉེས་པ sgom ñes-pa = སེམས་ལ་བསམ་ལུགས་ཉེས་པ sems-la bsam-lugs ñes-pa or ནོར་བ nor-wa, to blunder in meditation.

སྒོམ་ཐག sgom-thag योगपट्ट meditating-cord; a long piece of cloth about four inches wide which is worn by the *Yogi* when he sits in meditation; it is stretched round the neck and under the knees while sitting. About the 10th and 11th centuries A.D. Buddhist ascetics used to wear it in the manner the sacred thread is worn by the Brāhmans, passing round the right shoulder to the side below the arm-pit: སྒོམ་ཐག་ཆེན་པོ་ཞིག་ཉིད་དཔུང་པ་ནས་མཆན་དུ་ཀ་ཤར་བཅུག let a large sgom-thag pass from the shoulders over the bosom (*A. 11*). Acc. to *Jä.* a cord or rope is slung round the body in order to facilitate the effort of maintaining an erect and immoveable posture during meditation, which expedient of course is scorned by the more rigid devotees.

སྒོམ་སྡེ *Sgom-sde* n. of a section of the school of monks called སེར་བྱས་སྒྲ་ཚང་ *Ser-byas grba-tshañ* of Tibet (*Loñ.* 3 *16*).

སྒོམ་པ *sgom-pa* भावना, vb. pres. སྒོམ་གྱིན *sgoms-gyin*, or སྒོམ་བཞིན *sgom-bshin*, pf. བསྒོམས *bsgoms*, fut. བསྒོམ *bsgom*, imp. སྒོམ *sgom* or སྒོམས *sgoms*, resp. ཐུགས་སྒོམ *thugs-sgom* 1. originally to fancy, imagine; now to meditate, contemplate systematically (c. accus. and dat.); to have; to entertain; to re-produce (in one's mind), with the accus. termin. or with double accus. 2. sbst. སྒོམ་པ *sgom-pa*, has come to signify systematic meditation of the Buddhist saint. Four degrees of this meditation are to be distinguished, viz., ལྟ་བ *lta-wa* contemplation; སྒོམ་པ *sgom-pa* meditation, properly so called (which requires གསལ་དང་མི་རྟོགས་མ་གཡེངས་གསུམ *gsal-dañ mi-rtogs ma-gyeñs gsum*, *i.e.*, that it be so performed in a clear and decided manner without suffering one's self to be disturbed or distracted by anything); the third degree སྤྱོད་པ *spyod-pa* consummation; and འབྲས་བུ *hbras-bu* fruition.

སྒོམ་པ་པོ *sgom-pa po* = སྒོམ་བྱེད *sgom-byed*, *i.e.*, སྒོམ་མཁན *sgom-mkhan* an ascetic who meditates.

སྒོམ་པ་ཚང་ *Sgom-pa tshañ* the term used in Amdo to signify སྒོམ་ཆེན *sgom-chen*, a Buddhist ascetic who meditates, &c.

སྒོམ་བྱ *sgom-bya* and སྒོམ་རྟེན *sgom-rten* the object of meditation.

སྒོམ་འབྲོག *sgom-hbrog* 1. the wilderness or solitude where hermits dwell for meditation. 2. holly in Sikkim (*Jä.*)?

སྒོམ་ཡན་ལག *sgom yan-lag* अङ्गतपः a branch or form of ascetical meditation [lit. burning the limbs; it is a kind of penance in which the whole body is exposed to four heaps of fire in four quarters and to the sun on the head] *S.*

སྒོམ་ལམ *sgom-lam* the practice of ascetical meditation, also སྒོམ་གྱི་ལམ *sgom-gyi lam*, the way to *Nirvāna* by means of meditation: ས་གཉིས་པ་དྲི་མ་མེད་པ་ནས་སྒོམ་ལམ་ལ་ཞུགས from the second stage of perfection free from defilement he entered on the practice of meditation.

སྒོམ་ཤིང *sgom-çiñ*, योगदण्ड the stick on which the ascetic fixes his gaze while engaging himself in meditation.

སྒོམ་གསུམ *sgom-gsum* three kinds of སྒོམ་པ *sgom-pa* or mystical meditation, viz.:—(1) meditation performed in the three, four or six periods into which a day may be divided for that purpose ཐུན་སྒོམ་ནི, ལས་དང་པོ་དུས་གཉེན་པོ་ཕར་འདེབས་ཀྱི་དྲན་པ་ཡིན་པས, ཐུན་མཚམས་ཕྱེ་ལ་བསྒོམ་པའོ *thun-sgom-ni, las dañ-po dus gñen-po phar hdebs-kyi dran-pa yin-pas, thun-tshams phye-la bsgom-paho*; (2) ངང་སྒོམ་ནི, མྱོང་ཚུར་འདེབས་ཀྱི་དྲན་པ་ཡིན་པས, འགྲོ་འདུག་ཟ་ཉལ་ལས་སྤྱོད་ཅི་བྱས་ཀྱང་འབྲལ་མེད་དུ་ངང་གིས་གནས་སོ *ñañ-sgom-ni, myoñ-tshur hdebs-kyi dran-pa yin-pas, hgro-hdug za-ñal las spyod ci-byas-kyañ hbral med-du ñañ-gis gnas-so*, སྒོམ་ནི་ཅི་ཡང་མེད་པ་ལ་ངང་དང་ངང་གིས་ངང་ཐག་བསྲིང་བསྲེང *sgom-ni ci-yañ med-pa la ñañ-dañ ñañ-gis ñañ-thag bsriñ-bsreñ*; (3) ཀློང་སྒོམ་ནི, ནང་སེམས་མུ་ཐག་ཆོད་པས, བསྒོམ་བྱ་སྒོམ་བྱེད་ཀྱི་བློ་དང་བྲལ་བའོ *kloñ-sgom ni, nañ-sems mu-thag chod-pas, bsgom bya-sgom-byed-kyi blo-dañ bral-waho*.

སྒོམས *sgoms* (ལྷ་ལྟ་བུ *lha lta-bu*) भाव्य a deity thought of for propitiation.

སྒོར *sgor* a spindle in a turning-lathe (*Jä.*).

སྒོར་སྒོར *sgor-sgor* round.

སྒོར་སྒོར་འཁྱིལ *sgor-sgor hkhyil* forming into an eddy or whirlpool (*Ñag. 12*).

སྒོར་བ *sgor-wa* 1. pf. and fut. བསྒར *bsgar* to boil down; to condense by boiling, *e.g.*, བུ་རམ *bu-ram* sugar. 2. to turn on a lathe (*Jä.*).

སྒོར་མེད *sgor-med* without interruption or break: (རིས་མེད་ལམ་འགྲོ *ris-med lam-hgro*) to go on a journey without break, *i.e.*, without having to turn back.

སྒོར་མོ *sgor-mo*, v. 1. སྒོངས *sgoṅs*. 2. ཟླུམ a ball, globe; also a disk; hence an Indian *rupee* is called ཕྱི་གླིང་སྒོར་མོ *phyi-gliṅ sgor-mo*; བུ་རམ་སྒོར་མོ *bu-ram sgor-mo* a ball of treacle; སྒོར་ཐིག *sgor-thig* a pair of compasses; སྒོར་ཐིག་ཕྱེ་བ *sgor-thig phye-wa* or ཕྱེད་ཀ *phyed-ka* semi-circular (*Cs.*; *Schtr.*).

སྒོས *sgos*=སྒེར་དུ *sger-du* or ལྷག་པར *lhag-par*, specially, particularly, chiefly, &c.; in compounds and as adverb: private, separate, distinct; also as opposed to སྤྱི *spyi*, *e.g.*, སྤྱི་གདུགས *spyi-gdugs* a parasol for several persons; awning; shelter; སྒོས་གདུགས *sgos-gdugs* a parasol for one person; སྒོས་སྐལ *sgos-skal* share of a single person; individual lot.

སྒོས་ཁུར *Sgos-khur* ཡི་དྭགས་ཤིག་གི་མིང་ n. of a yi-dwag or *preta*.

སྒོས་པ *sgos-pa* to choose; to find the right thing (*Sch.*).

སྒོས་སུ *sgos-su* or སྒོས *sgos* adv.=ཁྱད་པར་དུ *khyad-par du* or སྒེར་དུ *sger-du* (opposite to སྤྱིར *spyir*), particularly, especially. སྒོས་ཀྱི་དཔོན *sgos-kyi dpon* a subaltern officer (*Cs*): སྒོས་སུ་ བཀའ་གདམས་ཀྱི་བསྟན་པ་རིན་པོ་ཆེ *sgos-su bkah-gdams-kyi bstan-pa rin-po che* particularly the precious doctrine of the *Bkah-gdam-pa* School (*A. 124*).

སྒྱིག་གུ *sgyig-gu* or སྒྱིའུ *sgyihu* a bag, purse: སྒྱིག་གུ་ཆད་པོའི་དྭང་དུ་སོང་ནས *sgyig-gu chad pohi dwaṅ-du soṅ-nas* our purse being in the way of breaking, *i.e.*, at low ebb; དངུལ་སྒྱིག *dṅul-sgyig* purse to keep silver pieces.

སྒྱིང་བ *sgyiṅ-wa*, pf. བསྒྱིངས *bsgyiṅs*, fut. བསྒྱིང *bgyiṅ*. 1. ཟྭམ to yawn, gape.

Syn. གྱིང་བ *hgyiṅ-wa*; གླལ་བ *glal-wa* (*Mṅon.*).

སྒྱིད *sgyid* 1. the hollow of the knee; bend of the knee; or སྒྱིད་པ *sgyid-pa* knee-joint; སྒྱིད་པ་གཅོད་པ *sggid-pa gcod-pa*, to lame the knee-joint; hamstring (a horse). 2. the calf (of the leg).

སྒྱིད་སྒྱུར *sgyid-sgyur* आलस्य idleness; langour: སྒྱིད་སྒྱུར་ནི་བྱ་བ་གཅིག་བྱེད་འགོ་ལ་གཅིག་བྱེད་པ་ནི་ལེ་ལོ་ངན་པ (*Ńag.*) སྒྱིད་སྒྱུར *sgyid-sgyur* is the vicious indolence of beginning a new work before he has finished the one he has in hand.

སྒྱིད་སྐྱུར་པ *sgyid skyur-pa* acute pain in the knee and leg, *e.g.*, of a woman with child.

སྒྱིད་ཁུང *sgyid-khuṅ* the hollow of the knee.

སྒྱིད་ཁྱོལ *sgyid-khyol* one lame in his legs (*Cs.*).

སྒྱིད་འཁྲིལ *sgyid-hkhril* ऊर्ध्वजानु (lit. raised knee, that is, squatting and doing nothing) langour; laziness.

Syn. སྒྱིད་སྙོམས *sgyid-sñoms*; སྒྱིད་ལུག *sgyid-lug*; རྨུགས་པ *rmugs-pa*; འཇས་པ *hjas-pa* (*Mṅon.*).

སྒྱིད་བུ *sgyid-bu*, also སྒྱེད་བུ *sgyed-bu* चुल्लि a hearth, fire-place, consisting of three stones on which the kettle is placed; ལྕགས་སྒྱིད *lcags-sgyid* iron trevet, tripod, cf. སྒྱེད་པོ *sgyed-po*.

སྒྱིད་ལུག་པ *sgyid-lug-pa* अलस slothful; idle *Cs.* and *Lex.* ཡིད་ཞུམ་པ *yid shum-pa* prostrate with fatigue or mental lassitude.

སྒྱིར་རྐང་ *sgyir-rkaṅ*, གོས་དང་གུར་སོགས་ཀྱི་མཐའ་ལ་འདྲིལ་བཏང་བའི་མཐའ་བཅག the fringe that is attached to the border of robes or of tents, &c.

སྒྱུ *sgyu*=གཡོ་སྒྱུ *gyo-sgyu* craft; deception; pretext. སྒྱུ་ཅན *sgyu-can* artful; crafty; cunning (*Cs.*).

སྒྱུ་འཕྲུལ *sgyu-hphrul* माया magical deception; སྒྱུ་འཕྲུལ་མ *sgyu-hphrul-ma* माया the name of Gautama, Buddha's mother.

སྒྱུ་མ *sgyu-ma* माया illusion; fancy; imposition whether natural or intentional; སྒྱུ་མ་མཁན *sgyu-ma mkhan* मायाकार a juggler; སྒྱུ་མ་ཅན *sgyu-ma-can* वञ्चक an imposter; one who plays deception; སྒྱུ་མ་ལྟ་བུ *sgyu-ma lta-bu* मायोपम like illusion; illusive; སྒྱུ་མ་སྤྲུལ་བ *sgyu-ma sprul-wa* to exhibit a false show (*Cs.*): ངས་སྣང་བ་ཐམས་ཅད་སྒྱུ་མར་ཤེས *ṅas naṅ-wa thams-cad sgyu-mar çes* I know that all phenomena are only illusions. སྒྱུ་མ་བྱེད་པ *sgyu-ma byed-pa* मायावी, मायादच one dexterous in magical show; a magician; སྒྱུ་མ་མེད་པ *sgyu-ma med-pa* अमायावी free from guile; guileless; སྒྱུ་མའི་ནོར *sgyu-mahi nor* illusive riches, hence general wealth: སྒྱུ་མའི་ནོར་ལ་ཆོག་ཤེས་མེད, ཉེན་པས་བསགས་ཀྱང་ཤུལ་དུ་ལུས, རང་གིས་བསགས་ཀྱང་གཞན་གྱིས་སྤྱོད the mind is not satisfied with the illusive wealth, though accumulated by desire it remains behind, and though acquired by yourself it is enjoyed by others.

སྒྱུ་མའི་དཔེ་བཅུ་གཉིས *sgyu-mahi dpe-bcu-gñis* the twelve expressions illustrative of illusion:—(1) སྒྱུ་མ་ལྟ་བུ *sgyu-ma lta-bu*; (2) ཆུ་ཟླ *chu-zla* the image of the moon in water; (3) མིག་ཡོར *mig-yor* scenes that appear in a vision; (4) སྨིག་རྒྱུ *smig-rgyu* mirage; (5) རྨི་ལམ *rmi-lam* dream; (6) སྒྲ་བརྙན *sgra-brñan*, echo; (7) དྲི་ཟའི་གྲོང་ཁྱེར *dri-zahi groṅ-khyer* castle in the air; (8) མིག་འཕྲུལ *mig-hphrul*; (9) དབང་པོའི་གཞུ *dbaṅ-pohi gshu* rain-bow; (10) གློག *glog* lightning; (11) ཆུ་བུར *chu-bur* bubble; (12) མེ་ལོང་གི་གཟུགས་བརྙན་ལྟ་བུ *me-loṅ-gi gzugs-brñan lta-bu* reflection or reflected image in a mirror.

སྒྱུ་རྩལ *sgyu-rtsal* कला art, skill, dexterity: སྒྱུ་རྩལ་གནས་ཀྱང་དྲང་པོར་རྒྱུར *sgyu-rtsal gnas-kyaṅ draṅ-por rgyur* कलालयोऽपि सरल though dexterous (artful) he was sincere. There are 64 arts, of which 30 are distributed in handicrafts, 18 in music, 7 in singing, 9 in dancing.

སྒྱུ་རྩལ་ས *sgyu-rtsal sa*=རྒྱལ་པོའི་སྐྱེད་ཚལ *rgyal-pohi skyed-tshal* the royal gardens where in ancient time kings used to try feats of arms, etc. (*Mṅon.*).

སྒྱུ་ལུས *sgyu-lus* 1. the immaterial body of the soul while in the *Bardo*. 2. the animal and human body in general, inasmuch as it is only an apparent body; a phantom, when considered from a higher philosophical point of view.

སྒྱུག་མོ *sgyug-mo* श्वश्रू, श्वसा, श्वश्रु mother-in-law; མནའ་སྒྱུག *mnah-sgyu* both daughter-in-law and mother-in-law: སྒྱུག་མོས་བསྲུངས་པ *sgyug-mos bsruṅs-pa* श्वश्रूरक्षिता watched by one's mother-in-law.

སྒྱུར་བཀོད *sgyur-bkod* strong advice.

སྒྱུར་བ *sgyur-wa* वर्तन, pf. and fut. བསྒྱུར *bsgyur*, trans. form of འགྱུར་བ *hgyur-wa*. 1. to transform, alter, change (colour, one's mind); to correct; to translate; to revise. 2. to cast aside; to dissuade, divert; to turn; to cause to turn; འཁོར་ལོ་སྒྱུར་བ *hkhor-lo sgyur-wa* or སྐོར་བ *skor-wa* to turn a wheel; སྐད་སྒྱུར་བ *skad sgyur-wa* to vary or modulate the voice, also to hum a tune; to sing or whistle. 3. to govern, steer, control: རྟའི་ཁ་སྲབ་ཀྱིས་སྒྱུར, *rtahi-kha srab-kyis sgyur* a horse's mouth by a bridle: འདོད་ཆགས་ངན་པས་ཁ་སྒྱུར *hdod-*

chags ñan-pas kha-sgyur he is governed by evil passions; ཁ་ལོ་སྒྱུར་བ *kha-lo sgyur-wa* to govern; also a driver; ཁ་ལོ་ཤིང་རྟ་སྒྱུར་བ *kha-lo çiñ-rta sgyur-wa* to drive a carriage; དབང་སྒྱུར་བ *dwañ sgyur-wa* to have command, control of; to dominate; to command.

སྒྱེ *sgye* (སྣོད *snod*), धोकनि, प्रसेव a vessel [a sack; a Cathern bottle]*S.*

སྒྱེ་སྒུར *sgye-sgur* crooked (*Sch.*).

སྒྱེད་སྒྱུ་སྒྱུར་བ *sgyed-sgyu sgyur-wa* द्विकुब्ज bent forward and hump-backed.

སྒྱེ་བོ *sgye-bo* बहिःकुब्ज 1. hump-back; acc. to *Jä.* 2. one of the lower classes of officials or noblemen.

སྒྱེ་མོ *sgye-mo* ཁུག་པ *khug-pa*, स्योन, स्यूत 1. sbst. a small pouch; རས་སྒྱེ *ras-sgye* a bag of cotton stuff. 2. adj. quiet, gentle (in Spiti) (*Jä.*).

སྒྱེའུ *sgyehu* a small bag.

སྒྱེད་པོ *sgyed-po* पच a small fire-place; hearth-stone.

སྒྱེད་བུ *sgyed-bu* चुल्लि a make-shift fire-place.

སྒྱེན་པ *sgyen-pa* to be on the move.

སྒྱེལ་བ *sgyel-wa*, pf. and fut. བསྒྱེལ *bsgyel*, transit. form of འགྱེལ་བ *hgyel-wa*, to throw down; to over-turn; to lay or put down (a bottle, a book); to thwart (the charm of an enemy); to kill (horses) (*Jä.*).

སྒྱོགས *sgyogs* कट, लाघयन्त्र a warlike engine to shoot darts or to fling stones with; mortar; cannon: སྒྱོགས་ཀྱི་འཕྲུལ་འཁོར *sgyogs-kyi hphrul-hkhor* id; སྒྱོགས་རྡོ *sgyogs-rdo* stone flung from such a machine. མེ་སྒྱོགས *me-sgyogs* and རྡོ་སྒྱོགས *rdo-sgyogs*= cannon: མེ་སྒྱོགས *me-sgyogs* now called དབ *dob* in Tibet; རྡོ་སྒྱོགས *rdo-sgyogs* a stone-thrower is used in Bhutan.

* སྒྱོགས་མདའ *sgyogs-mdah* यष्टि (*Schr.*; *Kālac. T. 128*) catapult.

སྒྱོང་བ *sgyoñ-wa*, pf. བསྒྱོངས *bsgyoñs*, fut. བསྒྱོང *bsgyoñ*, perh. originally=སྒོང་བ *sgoñ-wa* to hide. 1. to fill; to stuff (a sausage). 2. colloq. in *W.* to put into (the pocket): གླ་ཕྱིར་སྒྱོང་བ *gla-phyir sgoñ-wa* to return the wages due to another person (*Sch.*).

སྒྲ *sgra* (*da*) शब्द,वर्ण, ध्वनि, स्वर, गीत, घोषः, नाद, प्रतिध्वनि, टङ्कार 1. sound, noise, voice: སྒྲ་ལ་ཟིན་པའི་སྒྲ་དང་མ་ཟིན་པའི་སྒྲ་གཉིས་ཡོད *sgra-la zin-pahi sgra-dañ ma-zin-pahi sgra-gñis yod* there are two kinds of sound, viz:—ཟིན་པའི་སྒྲ *zin-pahi sgra, i.e.*, sound that can be caught or heard and understood; མ་ཟིན་པའི་སྒྲ *ma-zin-pahi sgra* which cannot be heard or understood; indistinct sound; མིང་སྒྲ *miñ-sgra* a mere word. 2. word, syllable. 3. a language.

སྒྲ་སྐད *sgra-skad* sound; voice; fame; སྒྲ་སྐད་སྙན་པ *sgra-skad sñan-pa* sounding; sonorous.

སྒྲ་བསྐྱུང་བ *sgra bskyuñ-wa* अल्पमन्दा one who speaks few words.

སྒྲ་བརྒྱ་པ *sgra brgya-pa*=འབྲུག *hbrug* मतङ्ग्दा thunder.

* སྒྲ་བསྒྱུར་མར་པ་ལོ་ཙྪ *Sgra-bsgyur mar-pa lots tsha*=མར་པ *Mar-pa* the translator and lo-tsā-wa.

སྒྲ་སྒྲགས་པ *sgra sgrags-pa* (*da-dag-pa*) लक्ष्यकाण्ड the sound returned by the target when the arrow hits it.

སྒྲ་སྒྲོག་པར་བྱེད *sgra sgrog-par byed* (*da-dog-par ceh*) रावण one who proclaims much; a great self-advertiser.

སྒྲ་སྒྲོགས *sgra-sgrogs* ख्यात, रावण, प्रतिश्रुत 1. the famous. 2. n. of the king of *Lañkā* (Ceylon) with whom *Rāma* waged war, described in the epic of Rāmāyan by Vālmiki.

སྒྲ་སྒྲོགས་པ *sgra-sgrog-pa* (*ḍa-ḍog-pa*) to produce sounds, noises, etc.

སྒྲ་ངེས་པར་སྦྱོར་བ *sgra ńes-par sbyor-wa* = ཚིག་གི་སྒྲ་དག་པར་སྦྱོར་བ *tshig-gi sgra dag-par sbyor-wa* निर्वचन the correct formation of words.

སྒྲ་གཅན *Sgra-gcan* राहु, तमस्, कवन्ध 1. n. of an *Asura* demon, who fought with the gods and drank nectar obtained by churning the ocean. 2. fabulous planet of Chinese and Brahminical astrology which exercises malignant influences on the destinies of mankind; specially known by being at enmity with the sun and the moon, on whom it is continually wreaking vengeance. Eclipses are caused by *Sgra-gcan* swallowing the sun or moon. His different names are the following:— བསོད་ནམས་ལྡན *Bsod-nams ldan*; མུན་པ་ཅན *Mun-pa can*; མཐོ་རིས་སྣང་བྱེད *Mtho-ris snań-byed*; བཟའི་རྣ་བ *Bzahi rna-wa*; མགོ་ཟླུམ *Mgo-zlum*; ལམ་ནག *Lam-nag*; ཟླ་བའི་དགྲ *Zla-wahi dgra*; སེང་གེ་མོའི་བུ *Señ-ge mohi bu*; ཟླ་བ་འཇོམས *Zla-wa hjoms*; ཉེ་བར་འཕར་འགྲོ *Ñe-war hphar-hgro*; ཤ་ཟ *Ça-za*; སྤྲིན་ལས་རྣམ་རྒྱལ *Sprin-las rnam-rgyal*; བྲ་ཉེ་སྐྱེས *Bra-ñe skyes*; ཁམས་གསུམ་རྣམ་རྒྱལ *Khams-gsum rnam-rgyal* (*Mńon.*).

སྒྲ་གཅན་འཛིན *Sgra-gcan-hdsin* राहुल the only son of Gautama Buddha who, according to the southern Buddhists, was born on the day Siddhārtha left the world. According to the northern Buddhists he was conceived in the womb of his mother Yasodharā long before the renunciation took place, and saw light six years after, on the day when Buddha finished his six years asceticism, on the bank of the river Nairañjanā; he was so named being born on the day when there was an eclipse.

* སྒྲ་གཅན་འཛིན་བཤེས་གཉེན *Sgra-gcan hdsin bçes-gñen* राहुलमित्र (*Schr.; Tā. 2-249*) [friend of Rāhula]*S.*

སྒྲ་གཅན་ལུས་འཇོམས *sgra-gcan lus hjoms* राहुमूर्त्तिभिद् the god who subdued Rāhu, the demon, by cutting him into two.

སྒྲ་ཆེ *sgra-che* far-famed, renowned; སྒྲ་ཆེན *sgra-chen* महारव great; sound; སྒྲ་ཆེན་པོ *sgra chen-po* महाराव high loud sound; སྒྲ་ཆེར་གྲགས་པ *sgra-cher grags-pa* well-known, famous; སྒྲ་ཉན་པ *sgra ñan-pa* to hear; to hear sound; སྒྲ་ཉམས་པ *sgra ñams-pa* अपमन्द sinking voice; low sound; སྒྲ་སྙན *sgra-sñan* कलकण्ठ, श्री a well-sounding, agreeable voice; a guitar; སྒྲ་བརྙན *sgra-brñan* (བྲག་ཆ *brag-cha*) प्रतिश्रुत, प्रतिशब्द an echo.

སྒྲ་ཏོག *sgra-tog* sound made by the tongue striking on the roof of the mouth: ཁོ་བོ་མི་མཐོང་བའི་ཚེ་ཤ་བྲག་གི་རོ་ལ་རྐན་སྒྲ་ཏོག་པ་ལ when I happened not to see him he by striking the roof of the mouth with his tongue signified the relish of meat, &c. (*Hbrom. 118*).

སྒྲ་དག་པ *sgra dag-pa* pure; clear-voiced.

སྒྲ་དོན *sgra-don* शब्दार्थ meaning of a word.

སྒྲ་དྲག་པོ *sgra drag-po* निर्घात sound made by a sudden blow.

སྒྲ་ལྡན *sgra-ldan* 1. noisy. 2. (བྱ་རོག *bya-rog*) घोषा, ध्वांक्ष met. a crow.

སྒྲ་ལྡར *sgra-ldar* sounding; sonorous.

* སྒྲ་བ *sgra-wa* भाषा (*Schr.*) [speech]*S.*

སྒྲ་འབྱིན་པ *sgra-hbyin-pa* पर्यायेण नदति; སྐད་འདོན་པ *skad hdon-pa* to resound, groan, cry loudly.

སྒྲ་བྱུང་ལོ *sgra-byuń lo* सस्वर [resounded]*S.*

སྒྲ་བྱེད *sgra-byed* sound-maker; སྒྲ་བྱེད་དོ *sgra byed-do* शब्दायते makes sound.

སྒྲ་དབྱངས *sgra-dbyańs* निर्घोष pleasing tone; harmony; euphony (*A. k. 111-8*).

* སྒྲ་དབྱངས་རྒྱལ་པོ *Sgra-dbyańs rgyal-po* (*Schr.*; (*46 B.*).

སྒྲ་དབྱངས་ལྷ་མོ *Sgra dbyańs lha-mo* the Goddess Svarasvatī.

Syn. ལྷ་མོ་དབྱངས་ཅན་མ *Lha-mo dbyaṅs-can-ma*; དབྱངས་ཅན་མ *Dbyaṅs-can-ma*; ཚངས་སྲས་མོ *Tshaṅs-sras-mo*; མཚོ་བྱུང་ལྷ་མོ *Mtsho-byuṅ lha-mo*; ཚངས་བའི་སྲས་མོ *Tshaṅ-wahi sras-mo*; ངག་དབང་ལྷ་མོ *Ṅag-dwaṅ lha-mo* (*Mṅon.*).

སྒྲ་སྦྱོར་མ *sgra sbyor-ma* a coalition or connection of letters.

སྒྲ་མི་སྙན *Sgra-mi-sñan* कुरु of disagreeable voice. According to the fabulous geography of the Buddhists the northern continent which is said to be square in shape, and where a language is spoken not intelligible to the people of India.

སྒྲ་མེད *sgra-med* अघोष soundless; voiceless.

སྒྲ་མེད་སྤྲིན *sgra-med sprin* a cloud without thunder.

སྒྲ་ཙམ *sgra-tsam* स्वननं only a voice.

སྒྲ་ཚད *sgra-tshad* (སྒྲ་དང་ཚད་མ *sgra-daṅ tshad-ma*) grammar and logic.

སྒྲ་འཛིན=རྣ་བ *sgra-hdsin*=*rnawa* शब्दग्रह that catches the sound; the ear.

སྒྲའི་སྐྱེ་གནས *sgrahi skye-gnas* शब्दयोनि, धातु the origin or root of a word.

སྒྲའི་རྒྱན *sgrahi-rgyan* रूपक, यमक metaphor in rhetoric.

སྒྲའི་སྙེ་མ *sgrahi sñe-ma* tender tones and half tones, &c.; also the name of a book (*Ṅag.*).

སྒྲ་འོད་ཟེར་གསུམ *sgra hod-zer gsum* the three rays of sound which are incident on the soul in the *Bardo*: སྒྲ་ཡིས་དངངས་སོ *sgra-yis dṅaṅs-so*; འོད་ཀྱིས་འཇིགས་སོ *hod-kyis hjigs-so*; ཟེར་གྱིས་སྒྲག་གོ *zer-gyis sgrag-go*.

སྒྲ་ཡི་སྡེ *sgra-yi sde* मन्नुसैन्य (*Schr.*; *Kālāc. T. 124*) [soldiers of the adversary]*S.*

* སྒྲ་ཡི་གནས *sgra-yi-gnas*=རྣ་བ *rna-wa* शब्दाधिष्ठान the ear.

སྒྲ་རིག་པ *sgra-rig-pa* शब्दविद्या, शब्दचुञ्चु, शब्दवन the science of words; grammar [one versed in lexicography]*S.*

སྒྲ་ལ་མཁས་པ *sgra-la mkhas-pa* शाब्दिक one versed in the science of words; a grammarian.

སྒྲ་སེང་རིག་པའི་བློ་གྲོས *Sgra-seṅ rig-pahi blo-gros*=འཇམ་དཔལ་དབྱངས *Hjam-dpal dbyaṅs* मञ्जुश्री a *Boddhisattva* and God of Learning of the northern Buddhists.

སྒྲ་གསལ *sgra-gsal* स्फोट articulate; intelligible.

སྒྲགས *sgrags* 1. together with; jointly. 2. n. of a place in Tibet.

སྒྲགས་ཀྱི་དར་ཕུག *Sgrags-kyi dar-phug* n. of a sanctuary situated in a rock-cavern of Tibet (*Deb.* ག *44*).

སྒྲགས་ཀྱི་ཡང་རྫོང་ *Sgrags-kyi Yaṅ-rdsoṅ* district in *Lho-brag* in S. Tibet.

སྒྲང་བ *sgraṅ-wa* (*dang-wa*) pf. བསྒྲངས *bsgraṅs*, fut. བསྒྲང་ *bsgraṅ*, imp. སྒྲོང་ *sgroṅ* 1. to enumerate; to reckon up separately. 2. to upbraid; to reproach.

སྒྲལ་བ *sgral-wa* (*dal-wa*) 1. to cut into small pieces, viz., the picture of an enemy whom one wishes to destroy (*Jä.*). 2. ཆུ་སོགས་ལས་སྒྲལ་བ *chu-sogs las sgral-wa* to pass over or travel upon a river or sea.

སྒྲས་མངོན་པར་གོ་བར་བྱེད *sgras mṅon-par go-war byed* स्वरेणाभिविज्ञापयति by voice or sound he causes to be understood.

སྒྲིག *sgrig* (*dig*) or གྲལ་སྒྲིག་པ *gral sgrig-pa* well arranged; good arrangement; v. སྒྲོལ *sgrol.*

སྒྲིག་པ *sgrig-pa*, pf. བསྒྲིགས *bsgrigs*, fut. བསྒྲིག *bsgrig*, imp. སྒྲིག *sgrig* or སྒྲིགས *sgrigs* གྲལ་དུ་སྒྲིག་པ *gral-du sgrig-pa*, to arrange in order or row; to lay or put in order; to arrange, adjust; to put or fit together; to join (the separate parts); སྒྲིགས་པར་བྱེད་པ *sgrigs-par byed-pa* ग्रथ्नाति to compile (books); to stitch close (books, &c.); आच्छादयति covers.

སྒྲིག་ལད་ *sgrig-lad* defect in fixing gems on ornaments : ནུ་མེད་ཀྱི་སྒྲིག་ལད་དཀའ་ཞིག་བྱུང་འདུག་དུང་ even though there was some defect in fixing a sapphire (*Rtsii.* and *Yig. 17*).

སྒྲིག་ལམ *sgrig-lam* arrangement according to usage; custom: སྒྲིག་ལམ་ཞིག་སོང་བ *sgrig-lam shig soñ-wa* there was a custom.

སྒྲིགས *sgrigs*, imp. of སྒྲིག་པ *sgrig-pa.*

སྒྲིན་པོ *sgrin-po* (*ḍin-po*) पटु skilful, clever, prudent, expert.

Syn. མཁས་པ *mkhas-pa*; སྤྱང་པོ *spyañ-po* (*Mñon.*).

སྒྲིབ *sgrib* (*ḍib*), ཉི་ཟླ་སྒྲ་གཅན་གྱི་སྒྲིབ་པ *ñi-zla sgra-can-gyi sgrib-pa*, to eclipse; to cover over, v. སྒྲིབ་པ I : *sgrib-pa.*

སྒྲིབ་ཆག *sgrib-chag*, དུས་རྒྱུན་གྱི་རྩིས་ལས་མར་འགྲིབ་ཅིང་ཆག་པ *dus-rgyun-gyi rtsi-las mar-hgrib ciñ chag-pa* reduction; anything below the average calculation; also discount.

སྒྲིབ་གཉིས་ཀྱི་དབྱེ་བ *sgrib-gñis-kyi dbye-wa* distinction between the two defilements.

སྒྲིབ་པ I : *sgrib-pa* 1. sbst. आवरण, छद, अपिधान, अपवारण, संविधान sin; mental and moral defilement; the state of being obscured, darkened; obscuration. 2. पटल, [a roof, cover] *S.* མ་རིག་པའི་སྒོ་ངའི་སྦུགས་ཀྱི་སྒྲིབ་པ *ma-rig pahi sgo-ñahi sbugs-kyi sgrib-pa* hidden inside the egg of ignorance.

སྒྲིབ་པ II : 1. vb. pf. བསྒྲིབས *bsgribs*, fut. བསྒྲིབ *bsgrib*, imp. སྒྲིབ *sgrib* (ས *s*) to obscure; to cover; to darken, defile: ཉི་མའི་འོད་ཟེར་བསྒྲིབ་ནས *ñi-mahi hod-zer bsgrib-nas* the light of the sun being obscured : སྤྲིན་པས་ཉི་མ་སྒྲིབ་པ *sprin-pas ñi-ma sgrib-pa* the sun is covered by the clouds. 2. ཡོངས་སུ་བསྒྲིབས *yoñs-su bsgribs* परिवारण utterly obscured or covered.

སྒྲིབ་པ III : adj. dark; sbst. darkness; sinner.

སྒྲིབ་པ་ལྔ *sgrib-pa lña* the five kinds of moral obscurations are the following :—(1) ལས་ཀྱི་སྒྲིབ་པ *las-kyi sgrib-pa*, or འདོད་སྲིད་ཀྱི་སྒྲིབ་པ *hdod-srid-kyi sgrib-pa* defilements or sins of passionate desires; (2) གནོད་སེམས་ཀྱི་སྒྲིབ་པ *gnod-sems-kyi sgrib-pa* sins of an evil heart, *i.e.*, of the wish to do evil to others; (3) རྨུགས་རྒོད་ཀྱི་སྒྲིབ *rmugs-rgod-kyi sgrib* sins of laziness and indolence; (4) གཉིད་ཀྱི་སྒྲིབ་པ *gñid-kyi sgrib-pa* sins of sleep; (5) ཐེ་ཚོམ་གྱི་སྒྲིབ་པ *the-tshom gyi sgrib-pa* sins of doubt.

སྒྲིབ་པ་གཉིས *sgrib-pa gñis* or སྒྲིབ་གཉིས *sgrib-gñis* the two kinds of moral and mental obscuations are :—(1) ཉོན་མོངས་པའི་སྒྲིབ་པ क्लेशावृति defilement of misery that caused by habits, etc.; ཤེས་བྱའི་སྒྲིབ་པ ज्ञेयावृति the sin produced from the objects of cognition; acc. to the *Mahāyāna* doctrine these two sins vanish as soon as one has attained to the eight stage of *Bodhisattva* perfection; acc. to the *Hinayāna* these remain even when one has become an *Arhat.* Acc. to the Bon religion, sins which bring sufferings encompass the living beings of the three worlds, sins that appertain to knowledge only affect such saints, གཡུང་དྲུང་སེམས་པ *Gyuñ-druñ sems-pa* and རིག་འཛིན་སེམས་པ *Rig-hdsin sems-pa*, as belong to the tenth stage only.

སྒྲིབ་པ་རྣམ་སེལ *Sgrib-pa sgrib-pa rnam-sel* n. of a *Bodhisattva.*

སྒྲིབ་ཤིང་ *Sgrib-çiñ* (*ḍib-çing*) invisible by the power of charms or by certain articles of influence on men and devils: ཁྭ་ཏའི་སྒྲོ་ཡིས་སྒྲིབ་ཤིང་བྱེད *khwa-tahi sgro-yis sgrib-çiñ byed* made invisible by the feathers of a magpie.

སྒྲིམ་པ *sgrim-pa* (*ḍim-pa*), pf. བསྒྲིམས *bsgrims* (*ḍim*), fut. བསྒྲིམ *bsgrim*, imp. སྒྲིམ (ས) *sgrim* (*s*).

1. to hold fast; to force or twist together; to endeavour; (*Cs.*) to squeeze in, crowd in; (*Sch.*) to be confused: བློ་དང་རིག་པ་སྒྲིམ་པ *ḅlo-dań rig-pa ṣgrim-pa* to be careful both in mind and intelligence, that is, not to forget any important point or say a foolish word in conducting a case; to bring all the intelligence into play; སྐུད་པ་སྒྲིམ་པ *ṣkuḍ-pa ṣgrim-pa* to twist the threads together that they may become a compact plait.

སྒྲིལ་ཁ *ṣgril-kha* a piece rolled together: ཁ་ཉི་ཤུ་རྩ་གཅིག་ཡོད་པའི་སྒྲིལ *kha ñi-çu ṛtsa-gcig yoḍ-paḥi ṣgril* a roll containing twenty-one pieces.

སྒྲིལ་བ *ṣgril-wa*, pf. and fut. བསྒྲིལ *ḅṣgril* (cf. འགྲིལ་བ *ḥsgril-wa* and འཁྲིལ་བ *ḥkhril-wa*). to make a roll of; to roll, wrap up; to wind into a spool; ཐག་པ་དང་ཤོག་བུ་སྒྲིལ་མཁན *thag-pa dań çog-bu ṣgril-mkhan* he who rolls up ropes or paper; རིལ་བུར་སྒྲིལ་བ *ril-bur ṣgril-wa* to roll or form into a pill; གང་ལྷོད་པ་སྒྲིལ་བ *gań lhoḍ-pa ṣgril-wa* to roll up tightly what has got slack.

སྒྲིས་ཁྲིམས *ṣgris-ṣkhrims* rules or regulations of admission; སྒྲིས་བཙུག་པ *ṣgriṣ ḅcug-pa* to admit; to introduce.

སྒྲུག་པ *ṣrug-pa* (*ḍug-pa*) = འཐུ་བ *ḥthu-wa*, pf. བསྒྲུགས་པ *ḅṣgrugs-pa*, fut. བསྒྲུག *ḅṣgrug*, imp. སྒྲུག *ṣgrug* or སྒྲུགས *ṣgrugs* to collect, gather, pluck, pick up, *e.g.*, wood, nuts, vermin, &c.: ཤིང་སྒྲུག *çiń-ṣgrug* = ཤིང་འཐུ་བ་ *çiń ḥthu-wa*; ཤིང་ཅིག་སྒྲུགས་དང་གསུང་ནས *çiń cig ṣgrugs-dań gṣuń-nas* having requested that some wood should be collected.

སྒྲུང་ I: *Ṣgruń* (*dung*) n. of a Tibetan king of the Bon period.

སྒྲུང་ II: or སྒྲུངས *ṣgruńs*, described as སྔོན་གྱི་ལོ་རྒྱུས་བདེན་རྫུན་སྣ་ཚོགས *ṣńon-gyi lo-ṛgyus ḅden-ṛdsun ṣna-tshogs*, various anecdotes, true and false, of former times; སྒྲུང་མཁན *ṣgruń-ṃkhan* one who narrates fables or stories (*Cs.*): སྒྲུང་རྒྱུད *ṣgruń-ṛgyuḍ* the stories or fables that have come down to us; སྒྲུང་འཆད་པ *ṣgruń ḥchaḍ-pa* to relate fables, stories, &c.; སྒྲུང་གཏམ *ṣgruń-g̣tam* legends; tales of ancient time.

སྒྲུང་ལྡེའི་གནམ་བོན *ṣgruń-ḷdeḥi gnam-bon* the heavenly or celestial Bon-po teachers who flourished before the time of King *Di-gum ḅtsan-po* and his successors in the mythological period.

སྒྲུང་པ *ṣgruń-pa* a relater of legends.

སྒྲུང་བ *ṣgruń-wa* = སྒྲུང་བཤད་མཁན *ṣgruń ḅçaḍ-ṃkhan* 1. one who relates fables or stories. 2. vb. pf. བསྒྲུངས *ḅṣgruńs*, fut. བསྒྲུང་ *ḅṣgruń*, to mix; to invent; to feign (*Cs.*); སྒྲུང་བབས *ṣgruń-babṣ* the inspired story-tellers of Tibet, whose profession it is to narrate fables for a living; he puts a square cap on his head and goes on telling stories without pause.

+ **སྒྲུན་པ** *ṣgrun-pa* (*ḍun-pa*), pf. and fut. བསྒྲུན *ḅṣgrun* प्रतिगर्जे 1. to resound; to reply in the same tone; to rival. 2. to compare; to emulate, vie, contend with (*Cs.*).

Syn. འགྲན་པ *ḥgran-pa* (*Ṃńon.*).

སྒྲུབ་པ *ṣgrub-pa*, vb. pf. བསྒྲུབས *ḅṣgrubṣ*, fut. བསྒྲུབ *ḅṣgrub*, imp. སྒྲུབ *ṣgrub* (cf. འགྲུབ་པ *ḥgrub-pa*) नियम्, यम, साधन to complete, finish, perform, carry out, accomplish; to achieve, manufacture, attain to; དོན་སྒྲུབ་པ *don ṣgrub-pa* to attain to one's aim; to obtain a blessing, a boon; ཚེ་འདིའི་དོན་སྒྲུབ་པ *tshe-ḥdiḥi don ṣgrub-pa* to care for the wants of this life; to accomplish the ends of this life; རྒྱགས་ཕྱེ་སྒྲུབ་པ *ṛgyags-phye ṣgrub-pa* to procure flour as provision for a journey; ནོར་སྒྲུབ་པ *nor ṣgrub-pa* to gain riches;

also to furnish with, to supply; ལྷ་སྒྲུབ་པ *lha sgrub-pa* to propitiate a god. Acc. to *Jä.* ལྷ་སྒྲུབ་པ *lha sgrub-pa* implies, in accordance with Brāmanic-Buddhist theology, not so much the making of a deity propitious to man, as rendering a god subject to human power, forcing him to perform the will of man. Whilst the *conatus*, the labouring in this arduous undertaking is often called སྒྲུབ་པ *sgrub-pa*, the arriving at the wished-for end is designated འགྲུབ་པ *hgrub-pa*.

སྒྲུབ་དཀའ་བ *sgrub dkah-wa* दुःसाध्य very difficult to propitiate, to perform, to execute.

སྒྲུབ་ཁང་ *sgrub-khan* the house or place where one sits to meditate or propitate a deity, or where the rites and ceremonies are observed for the same.

སྒྲུབ་མཁན *sgrub-mkhan* साधक one who propitiates; a propitiator.

སྒྲུབ་བླ *sgrub-gla*=སྒྲུབ་ཡོན *sgrub-yon* remuneration for propitiating (*Mñon.*).

སྒྲུབ་འཆག *sgrub-hchag* building or making and dismantling or destroying; the term is defined in གསར་བ་སྒྲུབ་རྒྱུ་དང་རྙིང་པ་ནས་མར་འཆག་རྒྱུ *gsar-wa sgrub-rgyu dan rñin-pa nas mar-hchag rgyu* constructing a new one and breaking down the old one.

སྒྲུབ་རྟགས *sgrub-rtags* token; proofs of the attainment of perfection in accomplished saints.

སྒྲུབ་ཐབས *sgrub-thabs* साधन, संग्रह the method of effecting the propitiation of a deity, of obliging a god to make his appearance. There are two kinds of སྒྲུབ་ཐབས *sgrub-thabs*: ཞི་བའི་སྒྲུབ་ཐབས་དང་ཁྲོ་བོའི་སྒྲུབ་ཐབས་གཉིས *shi-wahi sgrub-thabs dan khro-wahi sgrub-thabs gñis* the propitiation or co-ercion of gods in their mild aspect, and of those of wrathful aspect.

* སྒྲུབ་ཐབས་རྒྱ་མཚོ *sgrub-thabs rgya-mtsho* साधन संग्रह (*Schr.*; *Tā. 2, 330*) the ocean of coercion.

སྒྲུབ་དང་སུན་འབྱིན *sgrub-dan sun-hbyin* propitiating and discomfitting.

སྒྲུབ་ནུས *sgrub-nus* साधकत्व the power to perform or propitiate.

སྒྲུབ་པ་དཀའ་བརྒྱད *Sgrub-pa dkah-brgyad* the eight gods who according to the རྙིང་མ *Rñin-ma* sect of Tibet are difficult to propitiate. They are the following:—འཇམ་དཔལ་སྐུ *Hjam-dpal sku*, པད་མ་གསུང *Pad-ma gsun*, ཡང་དག་ཐུགས *Yan-dag thugs*, བདུད་རྩི་ཡོན་ཏན *Bdud-rtsi yon-tan*, ཕུར་པ་འཕྲིན་ལས་འཇིག་རྟེན་འདས་པའི་སྡེ་ལྔ *Phur-pa hphrin-las hjig-rten hdas-pahi sde-lña*, མ་མོ་རྦོད་གཏོང *Ma-mo rbod-gton*, དམོད་པ་དྲག་སྔགས *Dmod-pa drag-sñags*, འཇིག་རྟེན་མཆོད་བསྟོད *Hjig-rten mchod-bstod* (*Grub.* ཁ *11*).

སྒྲུབ་པར་བྱེད་པ *sgrub-par byed-pa* to cause ecstasy in meditation.

སྒྲུབ་པོ་མཆོག *sgrub-po mchog* करणं highest stage of consummation.

སྒྲུབ་བྱ *sgrub-bya* सिद्धिकर, साध्य anything to be propitiated; a god. There are two kinds of deities, male and female, who having in view the good of all living beings do many kind services when invoked; they are manifested in aspects, calm and peaceful, or terrific and wrathful. For instance, the Goddess Dolma when she is propitiated is a mild deity and is called ལྷ་མོ་སྒྲུབ་བྱ *lha-mo sgrub-bya*, *i.e.*, the goddess to be propitiated; the man who propitiates being called སྒྲུབ་པ་པོ *sgrub-pa-po*, and the manner of exhorting her is called སྒོམ་ཚུལ *sgom-tshul*; the propitiatory rites are called སྒྲུབ་ཐབས *sgrub-thabs*. སྒྲུབ་པར་བྱེད་པ *sgrub-par byed-pa* includes the persons who observe the rites, who meditates on her and officiates at the service. When the goddess has been propitiated, *i.e.*, བསྒྲུབས *bsgrubs*, she appears before the devotee and grants him his prayers or wishes.

སྒྲུབ་བྱེད་ *sgrub-byed* साधक, सम्प्रधारण, क्रियाकर 1. he that accomplishes the propitiation or coercion. 2. a kind of bile.

སྒྲུབ་རན་ *sgrub-ran* or སྒྲུབ་ངན་ *sgrub-ńan* दुर्विध cannot easily be propitiated or accomplished.

སྒྲུབ་ལེ་ *sgrub-le* དབང་ལེ་དང་སྒྲུབ་ལེ་ *dwań-le dań sgrub-le.*

སྒྲུབ་གཤེན་ *Sgrub-gçen* a deity of the Bon to be propitiated; the Bon doctrine (*Jä.*).

སྒྲུབ་སླ་བ་ *sgrub sla-wa* सुसाध्य easy to perform, or easy of accomplishment.

སྒྲེ་བ་ *sgre-wa* (*de-wa*) 1. uncovered: ཆོས་ཀྱི་གླེགས་བམ་སྒྲེ་བ་ལ་བཞག་མི་རུང་ *chos-kyi glegs-bam sgre-wa la bshag mi-ruń* a sacred volume should not be kept uncovered. 2. adj. gen. + སྒྲེ་བོ་ *sgre-bo* bare; naked; སྒྲེ་མོ་ *sgre-mo*, ས་སྒྲེ་བོ་ *sa sgre-bo*=ས་ཁོད་མི་སྙོམས་པ་ *sa-khod mi-sńoms-pa* or ས་གཅེར་བུ་ *sa gcer-bu* bare uneven ground. 3. vb. pf. and fut. བསྒྲེ་ *bsgre* to repeat; to put or place in order; to put together; to collate.

སྒྲེག་པ་ *sgreg-pa* (*deg-pa*) vb. pf. སྒྲེགས་ *sgregs*, sbst. उद्गार, निगार to belch; also sbst. eructation.

Syn. གསུད་པ་ *gsud-pa* or གསུས་པ་གྱེན་བཟློག་ *gsus-pa gyen-bzlog* eructation that rises upwards.

སྒྲེང་སྒྲེང་ *sgreń-sgreń* firm and well-fixed: ལྟག་རྩ་སྒྲེང་སྒྲེང་རང་མེད་པ་འདིས་ལེན་ *ltag-rtsa sgreń-sgreń rań med-pa hdis-len.*

སྒྲེང་བ་ *sgreń-wa* (*deńg-wa*)=གྱེན་དུ་སླང་བ་ *gyen-du slań-wa* उच्छ्रित, समुच्छ्रय, vb. pf. བསྒྲེངས་ *bsgreńs*, fut. བསྒྲེང་ *bsgreń*, imp. སྒྲེང་ *sgreń* or སྒྲེངས་ *sgreńs*, cf. འགྲེང་པ་ *hgreń-pa* 1. to lift, hoist or rise up: དར་ལྕོག་དང་རྒྱལ་མཚན་སོགས་གྱེན་དུ་སྒྲེང་བ་ fix or erect the house-flags and the sacred standard. 2. to stretch out.

སྒྲེན་མོ་ *sgren-mo* (*den-mo*) नग्न; གོས་མེད་གཅེར་བུ་ *gos-med gcer-bu* naked; without cover; destitute; bleak.

སྒྲེན་མོ་གསུམ་ *sgren-mo gsum* (*den-mo sum*) the three *denmo* according to a Tibetan saying are the following:—(1) ཀླུང་ནི་ཆུ་མེད་སྒྲེན་མོ་སྟེ་ *kluń-ni chu-med sgren-mo ste* a valley is bleak when it is without water; (2) ཡུལ་འཁོར་མགྲོན་མེད་སྒྲེན་མོ་ *yul-hkhor mgron-med sgren-mo* a country without a protecting deity is destitute; (3) གལ་ཏེ་མིང་པོ་བཅུ་ཡོད་ཀྱང་, ཁྱོ་མེད་བུད་མེད་སྒྲེན་མོའོ་ *gal-te miń-po-bcu yod-kyań, khyo-med bud-med sgren-moho* that woman who is without husband though she may have got ten brothers is *denmo, i.e.*, destitute.

སྒྲེས་པ་ *sgres-pa* (*deh-pa*) n. of a numeral figure used in Buddhist astrology: སྒྲིག་པ་ཤིན་ཏུ་བརྟན་པའི་ཉེས་བ་ཟད་དེ་འདི་ལ་གྲངས་གནས་བཅུ་དང་ཉེར་བརྒྱད་འབྱུང་ཞིང་ (*Ya-sel. 57*).

སྒྲོ་ *sgro* 1. a large feather, esp. quill-feather, used for an ornament of arrows, as a charm, etc.: སྒྲོ་ལྡན་ *sgro-ldan* feathered race; a general name for birds as being possessed of feathers; also an arrow. 2. སྒྲོ་བ་ *sgro-wa* to elevate, exalt, increase (*Cs.*); to exaggerate (*Jä.*). 3. sack; bag; ཐལ་སྒྲོ་ *thal-sgro* a sack full of ashes (*Jä.*), v. སྒྲོ་བ་ *sgro-wa.*

སྒྲོ་རྐང་ *sgro-rkań* (*do-kang*) a species of tall fir; the feather-fir.

སྒྲོ་སྐུར་ *sgro-skur* (*do-kūr*) is an abbreviation of the expression; སྒྲོ་འདོགས་པ་དང་སྐུར་པ་འདེབས་པ་ *sgro hdogs-pa dań skur-pa hdebs-pa* decorating with feathers and casting abuse, *i.e.*, exaggeration and depreciation: ང་ནི་སྒྲོ་སྐུར་མེད་པའི་དགེ་སློང་ཡིན་ *ńa-ni sgro-skur med-*

paḥi ḏge-ṣloṅ yin I am a monk (Bhikṣu) who neither flatters nor speaks ill of others.

སྒྲོ་ཁྱིམ *ṣgro-khyim* (*ḏo-khim*) སྒྲོ་ཁྱིམ་ཡངས་པ་མགོ་བོ་བྲ་བོ་ཅན (*Jig. 32*).

སྒྲོ་ག *ṣgro-ga* (*ḏo-ga*) 1. the little bubbles in sparkling beverages. 2. the ropes used to pack cloth; cord, fetter; ལྕགས་སྒྲོ *lcags-ṣgro* iron fetters; ལྕགས་སྒྲོ་ལག་པ་སྦྲེལ་ནས *lcags-ṣgro lag-pa ṣbrel-naṣ* the hands chained together; ལྷམ་སྒྲོ *lham-ṣgro* shoe-strap; lace; latchet.

སྒྲོ་གུ *ṣgro-gu* (*ḏo-gu*) string; strap for binding, fastening, strapping: སྒྲོ་གུ་རྟེན་པ *ṣgro-gu ṟten-pa* the steel point or blade of an arrow to which a feather is attached.

སྒྲོ་བཏགས་པ *ṣgro ḇtagṣ-pa* आरोप vb. to make a false show; to pretend much; sbst. vanity; presumption: རྣམ་པར་རྟོག་པས་སྒྲོ་བཏགས་པའི་བདག་ཉིད་ཅན་ཡིན (*Lam-ṭi. 42*) imaginary thoughts are possessed of the nature of vain and unreal assertion.

སྒྲོ་འདོགས *ṣgro-ẖdogṣ* (*ḏo-dōg*) doubts; སྒྲོ་འདོགས་གཅོད *ṣgro-ẖdogṣ gcoḏ* free from doubts: བླ་མ་དམ་པའི་གདམས་ངག་གིས་ནང་གི་སྒྲོ་འདོགས་གཅོད་པ་ཡིན by the (*upadeça*) precepts of the holy Lama his doubts were dissolved (*A. 77*).

སྒྲོ་འདོགས་མ་ཆོད *ṣgro-ẖdogṣ ma-choḏ* his doubts were not cleared (*A. 27*).

སྒྲོ་ཕུག *ṣgro-phug* n. of a place in Tibet.

སྒྲོ་ཕུག་པ n. of a celebrated Nying-ma Lama who lived in Dophug: སྒྲོ་སྟོན་གྱི་ལྷ་ཁང་སྒྲོ་ཕུག་ཏུ་བརྩིགས་པ་ལགས་སོ the temple of Do-ton was built at Do-phug (*Deb.* ཀ *6*).

སྒྲོ་བ I: *ṣgro-wa* (*ḏo-wa*) a leather or hide bag for keeping barley-flour, peas, etc. Those that are carried on horseback are called རྟ་སྒྲོ *ṟta-ṣgro*; small leather bags are called ལག་སྒྲོ *lag-ṣgro* hand-bag; གསང་སྒྲོ *gsaṅ-ṣgro* or the mystic bag is a term for the scrotum.

Syn. སྒྱེ་མོ *ṣgye-mo*; སྒྱེའུ *ṣgyeḥu*; ཚུགས་སྣོད *tshugṣ-ṣnoḏ*; ཕད་ཚེ *phaḏ-tshe* (*Mṅon.*).

སྒྲོ་བ II: sbst. 1. acc. to *Vai-sṅ.* and *Sch.* the bark of a species of willow. 2. in C. Tib. the penis.

སྒྲོ་བ III: vb. pf. བསྒྲོས *ḇṣgros*, fut. བསྒྲོ *ḇṣgro*, imp. སྒྲོ *ṣgro*, to debate, discuss, chatter freely.

སྒྲོ་མདོངས *ṣgro-mdoṅṣ* (*ḏom-doṅ*) a peacock's plumes or feathers (*Ḫbrom.* ཕ *11*); a Chinese decoration used to adorn the hat worn by the chiefs and noblemen of Tibet, China, &c.

སྒྲོག *ṣgrog* (*ḏog*) strap, as in ལྷམ་སྒྲོག *lham-ṣgrog* (*lham-ḏog*); shoe-strap; ལྕགས་སྒྲོག *lcagṣ-ṣgrog* iron fetters or chain; བརྒྱངས་ཞིང་ལ་སྒྲོག *ḇṟgyaṅṣ-çiṅ-la ṣgrog*.

སྒྲོག་གདན *ṣgrog-gdan* (*ḏog-daṅ*) the triangular patch generally made up of satin on the པང་གདན *paṅ-gdan*, *i.e.*, the bibu which covers the front of a woman's petticoat.

སྒྲོག་གདུབ *ṣgrog-gdub* (*ḏog-dûb*) a bangle made of cord or straps also of jade.

སྒྲོག་པ *ṣgrog-pa* (*ḏōg-pa*) कथ, रणित, ध्वन्, नि-नद्, pf. བསྒྲགས *ḇṣgragṣ*, fut. བསྒྲག *ḇṣgrag*, imp. སྒྲག *ṣgrag* or སྒྲགས *ṣgragṣ* to call, shout forth; to publish, proclaim, declare; སྒྲོག་པ་པོ *ṣgrog-pa po* a declaimer, preacher; གསུང་སྒྲོག་པ *gsuṅ ṣgrog-pa* to read the sacred words. Used in *Mil.*, also, of birds sending forth their cries. སྒྲོགས་པའམ་གསལ་བ *ṣgrogṣ-paḥm gsal-wa* उद्गत; ཆོས་སྒྲོགས་པ *choṣ ṣgrogṣ-pa* or ཆོས་ཀྱི་སྒྲོགས་གླེང་མཛད་པ *choṣ-kyi ṣgrogṣ-gleṅ ṃdsaḏ-pa* to preach; དྲིལ་སྒྲོགས་པ *dṟil ṣgregṣ-pa* to publish by ringing a bell.

སྒྲོག་རིལ *ṣgrog-ril* (*ḏog-ril*) button, round button; སྒྲོག་རིལ་སྒྲོག་པ *ṣgrog-ril ṣgrog-pa* to button up (*Sch.*).

· སྒྲོག་རུས་པ *sgrog rus-pa* (*dog-rui-pa*) हंसहट [a shelter for swans]*S.*

སྒྲོགས་ལྡན *sgrogs-ldan* कक्कोलिनी a river.

སྒྲོགས་ཞུམ *sgrogs-shum* (*dōg-shum*) scream.

སྒྲོད་པ *sgrod-pa* (*doi-pa*) another form of འགྲོད་པ *hgrod-pa as in* ཕྱི་ལ་སྒྲོད་པ *phyi-la sgrod-pa* to go outside; not much used.

སྒྲོན་བསྐལ *sgron-bskal* (*don-kal*) the enlightened age, opp. to མུན་བསྐལ *mun-bskal* or the dark age.

སྒྲོན་ཆས *sgron-chas* the articles such as butter, oil, &c., for lighting lamps in a chapel during the eight holy days in a month.

སྒྲོན་ཏེ *sgron-te*=ཕུལ་ཏེ *phul-te* having offered: དཀོན་མཆོག་གསུམ་ལ་རས་མདའ་ཞིག་སྒྲོན་ཏེ having offered to the *Triratna* (the three precious ones) a wick (*Rtsii. 32*).

སྒྲོན་དེབ *sgron-deb* the list of people able to give lamps in a town or on a large estate.

སྒྲོན་དྲེགས *sgron-dregs* lamp-black.

སྒྲོན་པ *sgron-pa*, vb., pf. and fut. བསྒྲོན *bsgron* 1. to cover; to lay over, adorn, decorate; to light; to kindle. 2. n. of a kind of arrow which shoots like a meteor.

སྒྲོན་མ I: *sgron-ma* (*don-ma*) light, lamp, lantern, torch. The word སྒྲོན *sgron* is used to various persons as a title of honour; གསེར་སྙན་སྒྲོན *gser-sñan sgron* is intended for royalty; ཞལ་གསེར་སྒྲོན *shal-gser sgron* the golden enlightener, term of address to great lamas; ན་བཟའ་སྒྲོན *na-bzah sgron* is applied to the dress of royalty; གསོལ་བ་སྒྲོན *gsol-wa sgron* to the food served to a prince; གསོལ་ཇ་སྒྲོན *gsol-ja sgron* to his tea.

卐 སྒྲོན་མ II: आलोक (*Schr.; Bull. 1848 291*). [light]*S.*

སྒྲོན་མ་དྲུག *Sgron-ma drug* the six lamps used to signify the six religious discourses of *Panchen* Naropa generally called ནཱ་རོ་ཆོས་དྲུག *Na-ro chos-drug*.

སྒྲོན་མེ *sgron-me* दीप, प्रदीप, उल्का a burning lamp; prop. a lamp as religious offering: ལག་ན་སྒྲོན་མེ་ཡོད་ཀྱང་ནི, ལོང་བས་ལམ་ནི་མཐོང་མི་འགྱུར though a lamp be in his hand, the blind will not see the way (*Çe. doṅ. 16*). རིན་ཆེན་སྒྲོན་མེ *rin-chen sgron-me* रत्नप्रदीप the precious light; name of a book.

Syn. མཚན་མོའི་སྣང་བྱེད *mtshan-mohi snaṅ-byed*; སྣུམ་ལ་དགའ *snum-la hgah*; ཁྱིམ་གྱི་ནོར་བུ *khyim-gyi nor-bu*; སྣུམ་ཟ *snum-za*; འབར་བའི་རལ་པ་ཅན *hbar-wahi ral-pa can*; སྣང་གསལ *snaṅ-gsal*; མར་མེ *mar-me* (*Mṅon.*).

སྒྲོན་མེ་ཤིང་ *sgron-me-çiṅ*, v. སྒྲོན་ཤིང་ *sgron-çiṅ*.

སྒྲོན་གཞི་ཁ *Sgron gshi-kha* n. of a large estate in the district of Lhun-tse in Tibet.

སྒྲོན་ཤིང་ *sgron-çiṅ* or སྒྲོན་མེ་ཤིང་ *sgron me-çiṅ* the yew-leaf fir, *Pinus picca*; in Sikkim *Pinus longifolia* is so called. སྒྲོན་ཤིང་བད་རླུང་ཆུ་སེར་གྲང་བ་སེལ *sgron-çiṅ* removes mucous, wind, and cold in the stomach.

སྒྲོབ *sgrob* (*dob*) haughtiness, arrogance, pride.

སྒྲོབ་ཆེ་བ *sgrob che-wa*=ཉམས་ཆེ་བ *ñams che-wa*, one with great airs; bumptious, pretentious person: རྫོང་དཔོན་འགའ་རེ་སྒྲོབ་ཆེ་བས་ཡུལ་འཁོར་ཡོང་གི་ཡོད་འདུག་པ་བཅས (*D. çel. 7*) Some Jong-pöns are as over-bearing, as if the whole country belonged to their circuit.

སྒྲོབ་ཆེན *sgrob-chen* and sometimes སྒྲོམ་ཆེན *sgrom-chen* are provincial words used to signify pretentiousness or self-assumption; སྒྲོ་ཆེ་བ *sgro che-wa*=བརྫུ་བྱས་པ *brdsu byas-pa* pompous: མི་སྒྲོབ་ཆེན་དང་སྒྲོམ་ཆེན་སོགས་བརྫུ་བྱས་པའི་དོན་གྲོང་སྐད་ཡིན (*Ñag. 18*) mi dob-chen and dom-chen etc. signify pretentiousness in provincial language.

སྒྲོམ *sgrom* (*ḍom*) पिटकम्, पेटक a trunk or portmanteau; a box the inside of which is made of wood or wicker work and the outside lined with leather; a large leather box. [पिटक may be regarded as the Pali form of Sanskrit पीठक, a seat, an altar] *S.* མཆོད་སྒྲོམ *mcho-sgrom* a chest to keep articles of religious service; ཐབ་སྒྲོམ *thab-sgrom* a box to keep utensils, plates, &c., for cooking, generally covered with tanned tiger skin.

Syn. སྒམ *sgam*.

སྒྲོམ་བུ *sgrom-bu* a small box; སྨྱུག་སྒྲོམ *smyug-sgrom* = གཤེབ་མ *gsheb-ma* a chest made of wicker work.

སྒྲོལ་དཀར *Sgrol-dkar* and སྒྲོལ་ལྗང་ *sgrol-ljañ* 1. are known as the White and Green manifestations of the Goddess Dolma or Tārā, the two wives of King *Sroñ-Btsan Sgam-po*, being deified and worshipped as their incarnations. 2. names of females of frequent occurrence in Tibet.

སྒྲོལ་དཀར་ཀུན་བློ་མ *Sgrol-dkar kun blo-ma*, སྒྲོལ་མ་ཀུན་རྒྱལ་མ *Sgrol-ma kun-rgyal-ma*, སྒྲོལ་མ་རྒྱལ་བཟང་མ *Sgrol-ma rgyal-bzañ-ma* are other different manifestations of the Goddess Dolma.

སྒྲོལ་བ *sgrol-wa*, pf. and fut. བསྒྲལ *bsgral* 1. to save, rescue, deliver; to set free; to liberate; ཆུ་དང་སྡུག་བསྔལ་དང་འཇིགས་པ་དང་འཁོར་བ་ལས་སྒྲོལ་བ to save from the water, from misery, fear, and from transmigratory existence: སྒྲོལ་བའི་དེད་དཔོན་དུ་འགྱུར *sgrol-wahi ded-dpon du hgyur* he becomes a guide to salvation. 2. to transport, carry; to cross (a river) by boat or ferry: འཁོར་བ་བསྒྲལ་བའི་གྲུ་གཟིངས་ཡིན *hkhor-wa bsgral-wahi gru-gziñs yin* it is a boat that will carry you over the river of transmigration. 3. to remove, expel, drive away: འདྲེ་རྣམས་ཕྱིའི་རྒྱ་མཚོ་ཆེན་པོ་ལ་བསྒྲལ *hdre-rnams phyihi rgya-mtsho chen-po la bsgral*, the demons were banished to the uttermost parts of the sea; བདུད་སྒྲོལ་བ *bdud sgrol-wa* to expel the devil.

སྒྲོལ་བ་པོ *sgrol-wa-po* तारकः the deliverer, met. for saviour.

* སྒྲོལ་བའི་དབང་ཕྱུག *sgrol-wahi dwañ-phyug* मुक्तेश्वर, मुक्ताखामी (*Schr.*; *Bull. 1898, 295*) the Lord of final deliverance.

སྒྲོལ་བྱེད *sgrol-byed* तारकः, तरी a deliverer; met. for a boat, ship.

སྒྲོལ་མ *sgrol-ma* (*Ḍol-ma*) तारा, तारिणी the Goddess Dolma, she that saves from transmigratory existence; one of the most popular deities in Tibet, and of whom there are supposed to be many *sprul-ku* or branch emanations. Some *Sgrol-ma kyil-hkhor* exhibit twenty-one different manifestations of the goddess. The several appellations of སྒྲོལ་མ *Sgrol-ma* are:—ཨོཾ་མཛད *Om-mdsad*; རྒྱལ་ཡུམ *Rgyal-yum*; མཆོག་གི་མ *Mchog-gi ma*; མྱུར་སྐྱོབ *Myur-skyob*; འཇིག་རྟེན་དབང་སྲས་མོ *Hjig-rten*; *Dwañ sras-mo*; ཞི་མ་ཕོངས་སྐྱོབ *Shi-ma phoñs-skob*; ལེགས་བྱིན་མ *Legs-byin ma*; ཆོས་ཀྱི་དཔལ་མོ *Chos-kyi dpal-mo* (*Mñon.*).

སྒྲོལ་མ་ཀུ་རུ་ཀུལླེ *Sgrol-ma ku-ru kulle* one of the twenty-one manifestations of the Goddess Dolma (*K. g.* ང *266*).

སྒྲོལ་མ་ཆེ *Sgrol-ma che* महातारा Mahā Tārā or the great Goddess Dolma.

* སྒྲོལ་མ་ཉིན་ཞི་མཚན་ཁྲོ *Sgrol-ma ñin-shi mtshan-khro* (*Schr.*; *45 A*) "Dolma, mild by day and wrathful by night."

* སྒྲོལ་མ་ནོར་སྦྱིན་མ *Sgrol-ma nor-sbyin-ma* (*Schr.*; *46 B*) Dolma, the wealth-giver.

སྒྲོལ་མ་དཔལ་ཆེན *Sgrol-ma dpal-chen* तारामहाश्री Dolma, the most glorious.

* སྒྲོལ་མ་དམར་མོ *Sgrol-ma dmar-mo* (ས་ལུགས *sa-lugs*) (*Schr.*; *46 A*) the Red Dolma.

སྒྲོལ་མ་ཞི་མ་ *Sgrol-ma shi-ma* तारिकाशिनी Dolma in her mild aspect.

* སྒྲོལ་མ་ཡིད་བཞིན་ནོར་བུ *Sgrol-ma yid-bshin nor-bu* (*Schr.*; *46 C*) Dolma the wish giving gem.

* སྒྲོལ་མ་སེར་མོ *Sgrol-ma ser-mo* (*46 C.*; *Schr.*).

* སྒྲོལ་མའི་སྒྲུབ་ཐབས་བརྒྱ་རྩ *Sgrol-mahi sgrub-thabs brgya-rtsa* तारासाधनशतक (*Tā 2, 156*) n. of a book consisting of one hundred stanzas composed for propitiating the Goddess Dolma.

སྒྲོལ་ཤེར *Sgrol-çer* abbreviation of the expressions སྒྲོལ་མ་འདོན་རྒྱུ *sgrol-ma hdon-rgyu* and ཤེས་རབ་སྙིང་པོ *çes-rab sñiñ-po*.

སྒྲོས *sgros* (*doi*) manner; method; way; བཤད་སྒྲོས *bçad-sgros* manner of explaining; གཏམ་སྒྲོས *gtam-sgros* way of speaking (*Cs.*); བླ་མ་རྣམས་ཀྱི་གསུང་སྒྲོས *bla-ma rnams-kyi gsuñ-sgros* conference of the lamas; སྒྲོགས་བཤད་སྒྲོས *sgrogs bçad-sgros* the method of instruction which is to be proclaimed (*Sch.*). མཆུ་སྒྲོས *mchu-sgros* is same as མཆུ་བསྒྲིགས་པ *mchu-bsgrigs-pa*, མཆུ་སྒྲོས་བིམ་བ་ལྟར *mchu-sgros bim-ba ltar*, his graceful lip was like the fruit called *Bimba*. 1. edge, brim, lip (*Cs.*). 2. scar, also a mark from a wound (*Sch.*).

བགྲད་པ *brgad-pa* = བགད་པ *bgad-pa* to smile; smile on.

བརྒལ *brgal*, pf. of རྒལ་བ *rgal-wa* བརྒལ་ལེན *brgal-len*, controversy, disputation.

བརྒལ་དཀའ་བ *brgal dkah-wa* the ocean (that which is difficult to cross) (*Mñon.*).

བརྒལ་པ *brgal-pa* अनुयुक्त [enjoined; asked; censured]*S*.

བརྒོལ་བ *brgol-wa* to disagree; to act in opposition; to be disposed to contrariety.

བརྒྱ *brgya* शत one hundred; བརྒྱ་མཆོད *brgya-mchod* a hecatomb of 100 lamps; one hundred offerings; བརྒྱ་སྟོང *brgya-stoñ* शतं सहस्र one hundred thousand; བརྒྱ་ཐམ་པ *brgya tham-pa* full one hundred; བརྒྱ་འོད *brgya-aod* = གྲྭ་པ་བརྒྱ་ཐམས་པས་སྐུ་རིམ་བྱེད་པའི་གླ་ཡོན་ལ remuneration to one hundred monks for conducting a religious service; ཡང་བརྒྱ་མཆོད་ཀྱི་དངུལ་འབྲུ་སོགས, &c., remuneration in silver, grain, etc., for conducting the religious service of one hundred offerings; བརྒྱ་འདངས *brgya-hdañs* about a hundred; nearly one hundred.

བརྒྱ་པ *brgya-pa* शतिक, शतमायुः centenarian; one of a hundred years of age.

བརྒྱ་པོ *brgya-po* consisting of one hundred.

བརྒྱ་ཕྲག *brgya-phrag* शत the hundred; a century; ཕྲན་ཚེགས་བརྒྱ་ཕྲག་མི་ཕམ་མགོན *phran-tshegs brgya-phrag mi-pham mgon* (*A. 21*).

བརྒྱ་བམ *brgya-bam* anything kept in groups of one hundred; བརྒྱ་རེ་རེ་ཐུམ་པ་རྒྱབ་ནས་བཞག་པ (*Zam. 4*).

བརྒྱ་བྱིན *Brgya-byin* 1. n. of a medicinal root; དུག་མོ་ཉུང་ *dug-mo ñuñ* a mystic word or གབ་ཤིག (*Miñ. 3*). 2. शतक्रतु one who has performed one hundred *yajña* (sacrifices); an epithet of Indra. Acc. to Buddhist mythology there are two Indras, the senior Indra rules over the gods, the junior, riding on the great elephant called Airāvata, keeps guard over the celestial regions, having in his immediate charge the quarters of the East.

བརྒྱ་བྱིན་སྐྱེས *brgya-byin skyes* शक्रज Indra's son; born of Indra.

བརྒྱ་བྱིན་གྲོང་ *brgya-byin groñ* शक्रनगरी the residence of Indra; the celestial metropolis.

Syn. འཆི་བ་མེད་ལྡན *hchi-wa med-ldan*; ལྟ་ན་སྡུག *lta-na sdug*; སུམ་ཅུ་རྩ་གསུམ *sum-cu rtsa-gsum*; ཁང་བཟང་རྣམ་པར་རྒྱལ་བ *khañ-bzañ rnam-par rgyal-wa*; རྣམ་པར་རྒྱལ་བྱེད་ཕོ་བྲང་ *rnam-par rgyal-byed pho-brañ* (*Mñon.*).

བརྒྱ་བྱིན་སྤྱི་བོ *brgya-byin spyi-wo* = གྲོག་མཁར *grog-mkhar* ant-hill; also ant's foot.

བརྒྱ་བྱིན་སྤྲོས *brgya-byin spros*; ཨ་རུ་ར *Myrabalan arjuna* the delight of Indra.

བརྒྱ་བྱིན་མ *Brgya-byin ma* = བརྒྱ་བྱིན་བཙུན་མོ *Brgya-byin btsun-mo* मघोनी the celestial queen; the wife of Indra. Her different names are:—འཆི་མེད་དབང་མོ *Hchi-med dwań-mo*; ལྷའི་བཙུན་མོ *Lhahi btsun-mo*; ལེགས་བརྗོད་མ *Legs-brjod ma*; དབང་ཆེན་མ *Dwań-chen ma*; པུ་ལོམའི་སྲས་མོ *Pu-lohi sras-mo*:; བདེ་སོགས་མ *Bde-sogs ma* (*Mńon.*).

བརྒྱ་བྱིན་གཞུ *brgya-byin gshu* इन्द्रधनुः 1. the bow of Indra, *i.e.*, rainbow. 2. a kind of medicinal fruit.

བརྒྱ་བྱིན་ལྷ་ཡི་དབང་པོའི་མིང་ *Brgya-byin Lha-yi dwań-pohi miń* the different names of Indra:—མཐོ་རིས་འདྲེན་པ *Mtho-ris hdren-pa*; མཐོ་རིས་རྒྱལ *Mtho-ris rgyal*; ལྷ་ཡི་རྒྱལ་པོ *Lha-yi rgyal-po*; འཇེར་འཇིགས *Hjer-hjigs*; ལྷའི་རྔ་ཅན *Lhahi-rńa-can*; གཙང་བྱེད་མགོན་པོ *Gtsań-byed mgon-po*; རྡོ་རྗེ་ཅན *Rdo-rje-can*; སྟོབས་ལྡན་དགྲ་བོ *Stobs-ldan dgra-wo*; ལྷ་ཡི་བདག *Lha-yi bdag*; འཆི་མེད་རྒྱལ་པོ *Hchi-med rgyal-po*; ལེགས་བྲིས་གཙོ *Legs-bris gtso*; གྲགས་པའི་མུ་ཁྱུད *Grags-pahi mu-khyud*; མཆོད་སྦྱིན་བརྒྱ་པ *Mchod-sbyin brgya-pa*; བདེ་སོགས་བདག *Bde-sogs bdag*; ལྷ་དབང་ *Lha-dwań*; ལེགས་སྐྱོབ *Legs-skyob*; སྐབས་གསུམ་དབང་ *Skabs-gsum dwań*; རྒན་ལ་ཉན *Rgan-la ńan*; ཤིས་བརྗོད་ཉན *Çis-brjod ńan*; གནས་ཀྱི་བདག་པོ *Gnas-kyi bdag-po*; སྤྲིན་ལ་ཞོན *Sprin-la shon*; བཟོད་དཀས་རངས *Bzod-dkas rańs*; བཤེན་བསྙེམས་བཟོད *Bshen-bsńems bzod*; ཆར་འབེབས་གྲོང་འཇོམས *Char-hbebs groń-hjoms*; གྲོལ་བྱེད་འཇོམས *Grol-byed hjoms*; པུ་ལོ་མ་དགྲ *Pu-lo ma-dgra*; གང་པོ་འབོད *Gań-po hbod*; ཧ་རིའི་རྟ་ཅན *Ha-rihi rta-chan*; སྨིན་པ་གསོད *Smin-pa gsod*; ཚིག་མདའི་མགོན་པོ *Tshig-mdahi mgon-po*; མིག་སྟོང་ཅན *Mig-stoń-can*; ཀོཧུ་ཤི་ཀ *Kohu çi-ka* (*Mńon.*).

བརྒྱ་འཛིན *brgya-hdsin* शतधृति that contains or holds one hundred objects, etc.

བརྒྱ་ལས་འདམ་པ *brgya-las hdam-pa* བརྒྱ་ཐམ་པ་ལས་གཅིག་འདམ་པ *brgya-tham-pa las gcig-hdam-pa*.

བརྒྱག་བརྙན *Brgyag-brńan* n. of a Bon god who is also called ལྷ་བསངས *Lha-bsańs*.

བརྒྱགས *brgyags* सम्बल victuals; provision, as in མཚམས་བརྒྱགས *mtshas-brgyags*, ལམ་བརྒྱགས *lam-brgyags* provision for the journey.

བརྒྱང་བ *brgyań-wa* सन्तनय्, pf. བརྒྱངས *brgyańs*, fut. བརྒྱང་ *brgyań*, imp. རྒྱོངས *rgyońs* or རྒྱོངས་ཤིག *rgyońs-çig* 1. to extend, stretch out, set out or arrange; ཀོ་བ་དང་ཐག་པ་བརྒྱང་བ *ko-wa dań thag-pa brgyań-wa* to stretch hide and rope; སྣོད་བརྒྱང་བ *snod rgyań-wa* to set out a vessel; མཆོད་མེ་བརྒྱང་བ *mchod-me brgyań-wa* to put in array lamps as offerings. 2. to call a person from a distance.

བརྒྱད *brgyad* अष्ट eight.

Symbolic Syn. བཀྲ་ཤིས *bkra-çis*; ལྷ *lha*; ཀླུ *klu*; ནོར *nor*; གདེངས་ཅན *gdeńs-can*; སྲིད་པ *srid-pa*; ལྟོ *lto*; འགྲོ *hgro* (*Rtsii.*).

+ བརྒྱད་བཀག *brgyad-bkag* = བཀའ་བཀྱོན་པ *bkah bkyon-pa* निग्रह rebuke; reproof; reflection on one's conduct or act.

བརྒྱད་བཀུག *brgyad-bkug* or སྐུད་པ་བརྒྱད་སྒྲིལ *skud-pa brgyad-sgril* thread in eight-fold twists.

བརྒྱད་བཅུ *brgyad-bcu* अशीति eighty.

བརྒྱད་ཆུང་ *Brgyad-chuń* n. of a kind of tea which is of inferior quality, largely consumed by Tibetans in general.

བརྒྱད་སྟོང་པ *Brgyad-stoń-pa* अष्टसाहस्रिका one of the abridged sacred scriptures of the northern Buddhists containing 8,000 s'lokas.

བརྒྱད་སྟོན *Brgyad-ston* अष्टमीक the festival on the eighth lunar day of the month.

བརྒྱད་པ *brgyad-pa* अष्टम 1. the eighth. 2. ཚར་བཅད་པ *tshar bcad-pa* he who finishes or puts an end to; the destroyer.

བརྒྱད་པོ *ḇṟgyaḏ-po* consisting of eight; the eight.

བརྒྱད་ལྷག *ḇṟgyaḏ-lhag* lit. eight in excess (of one hundred); निष्क a rosary which consists of one hundred and eight heads.

བརྒྱན་པ *ḇṟgyan-pa* (*gyen*) अलङ्कृ, अलङ्कार, मण्डन, vb. to adorn, decorate; to provido with: རིན་ཆེན་རྒྱན་གྱིས་བརྒྱན་པ *rin-chen ṟgyan-gyis̱ ḇṟgyan-pa* adorned with precious ornaments, cf. རྒྱན *ṟgyan*; sbst.

བརྒྱལ་བ *ḇṟgyal-wa*=མྱོག་ཆེས་བྱེད་པ *myog-ches̱ byeḏ-pa* मूर्छां गम् 1. to fall down senseless; to lie senseless; to sink down unconscious; to faint. 2. to howl, of a fox (*Sch.*); ངོ་བརྒྱལ་ཏེ *ẖo ḇṟgyal-te* fainting with fatigue; བརྒྱལ་བོག་པ *ḇṟgyal bog-pa* laid prostrate and unoonscious: ཐམས་ཅད་བརྒྱལ་བོག་པ་བཞིན *thams̱-caḏ ḇṟgyal bog-pa ḇshin* all as if prostrate and sensoloss (*A. 76*).

བརྒྱས *ḇṟgyas̱*=ལྷན་རྒྱས *lhan-ṟgyas̱* together with.

བརྒྱུགས *ḇṟgyugs̱*, pf. of རྒྱུག་པ धावति, धावन used as sbst. a race; also running a raco.

བརྒྱུངས་པ *ḇṟgyuñs̱-pa* the marrow in the back-bone (*Cs.*).

བརྒྱུད *ḇṟgyuḏ*, cf. རྒྱུད *ṟgyuḏ* परम्पर, वंश, सन्तान, གཅིག་ནས་གཅིག་ཏུ་བརྒྱུད་པ *cig-nas̱ gcig-tuṟgḇyuḏ-pa* descent from one to another. 1. family, lineage, ancestors, offspring. 2. race, people, nation: བོད་ཀྱི་མི་བརྒྱུད *boḏ-kyi mi-ḇṟgyuḏ* the Tibetan nation, people. རིགས་བརྒྱུད *rigs̱-ḇṟgyuḏ* relations; གདུང་བརྒྱུད *gduñ-ḇṟgyuḏ* descendants; བླ་བརྒྱུད *ḇla-ḇṟgyuḏ* the succession or line of Lamas. 3. Tantras and mystic manuals, v. རྒྱུད; ཆོས་ཀྱི་བརྒྱུད་པ *chos̱-kyi* religious arguments and deductions.

བརྒྱུད་བརྒྱུགས *ḇṟgyuḏ-ḇṟgyugs̱* a continuous succession (*Sch.*).

བརྒྱུད་ཅན *ḇṟgyuḏ-can* possessed of descendants; fruitful.

བརྒྱུད་པ *ḇṟgyuḏ-pa* 1. belonging to a raco or family. 2. v. རྒྱུད *ṟgyuḏ* and རྒྱུད་པ *ṟgyuḏ pa*.

བརྒྱུད་པ་རྣམ་པ་ལྔ *ḇṟgyuḏ-pa ṟnam-pa ḻña* there were five different schismatic successions among the Buddhists in Auciont India; they wore the following:—(1) འདུལ་བའི་རྒྱུད *ẖdul-waẖi ṟgyuḏ* or विनयतन्त्र the generation observing moral discipline; (2) གསང་སྔགས་ཀྱི་རྒྱུད *gsañ-s̱ñags̱-kyi ṟgyuḏ* or गुह्यतन्त्र the mystical succession; (3) རྒྱ་ཆེན་སྤྱོད་རྒྱུད *ṟgya-chen s̱pyoḏ-ṟgyuḏ* or वैपुल्यतन्त्र the succession of abundant performances; (4) ཟབ་མོ་ལྟ་རྒྱུད *zab-mo ḻta-ṟgyuḏ* गम्भीरतन्त्र [tho profound succossion]*S.*; (5) སྙིང་པོ་དོན་རྒྱུད *s̱ñiñ-op don-ṟgyuḏ* or tho *Occult* race सारतन्त्र (*Grub.* ད *6*).

བརྒྱུད་འཕེལ་བ *ḇṟgyuḏ ẖphel-wa* to increaso the race or progeny; to multiply; to increase the family.

བརྒྱུད་མ *ḇṟgyuḏ-ma* 1. one belonging to a family; a scion; one well acquainted with the secrets, well informed; acc. to *Cs.*= བརྒྱུད་ཅན *ḇṟgyuḏ-can*. 2. in *W.* fruitful; fertile. 3. བརྒྱུད་མ་རྒྱབ་པ *ḇṟgyuḏ-ma ṟgyab-pa* to perpotuato family lineage; བརྒྱུད་འཛིན *ḇṟgyuḏ-ẖdsin* वंशधर heir; successor.

བརྒྱུད་ཡས *ḇṟgyuḏ-yas̱* विमद n. of a numorical figuro (*Ya-sel. 56*).

བརྒྱུས་པ *ḇṟgyus̱-pa* ग्रथित to make a string of; to stitch together.

བསྒག་པ *ḇs̱gag-pa*, v. འགེགས་པ *ẖgegs̱-pa* and སྒོག་པ *s̱gog-pa*.

བསྒང *ḇs̱gañ* or སྒང *s̱gañ*=དངོས་གཞི *ḏños̱-gshi* point of time; moment; instant; conjuncture: ལོ་གསར་བསྒང་གི་ལྷགས་པ *lo-gsar ḇs̱gañ-gi lhags̱-pa* a chilling gale on the opening of the new year; བྱ་བའི་བསྐང་ the proper time for doing a thing; འབྲི་བའི་ བསྐང་ the time for writing; ཟ་བའི་བསྐང་ the time of eating.

བསྒངས་པ *bsgaṅs-pa* to form into; གོང་བུ་བསྒངས *goṅ-bu bsgaṅs* made a ball of; གཅིག་ཏུ་བསྒོངས *gcig-tu bsgoṅs* collects into one.

བསྒར *bsgar*, pf. of སྒོར་བ.

བསྒུགས་པ *bsgugs-pa* pf. of སྒུག་པ *sgug-pa* to wait (for one's arrival or return).

བསྒུལ་བསྐྱོད *bsgul-bskyod* tremulous; to shake and tremble: སེམས་ཅན་འགྲོ་འདུག་དང་བསྒུལ་བསྐྱོད་བྱེད the living beings move, stand and tremble (*Khrid. 47*).

བསྒུལ་པ *bsgul-pa* प्रकम्प to shake, tremble, quake, quiver Gen. སྒུལ་བ.

བསྒོ་བ *bsgo-wa* उद्योजन 1. to direct, instruct, v. སྒོ་བ *sgo-wa*. 2. to rub with; to apply on སྣུམ་བསྒོས་པ *snum bsgos-pa*; to stain, anoint; to infect with disease; བསྒོས་པ *bsgos-pa* pf. of བསྒོ་པ to command, order; also བཀའ་བསྒོས་པ *bkah bsgos-pa* to give directions; issue commands; also the coercive bidding of the mystic exorcist towards an evil spirit. བག་ཆགས་བསྒོས་པ *bag-chags bsgos-pa* defiled with moral impurity (*Ṅag. 19*).

Syn. ཁས་བླངས་བྱེད *khas-blaṅs byed*; དུལ་བ་འཛིན *dul-wa hdsin*; ཚིག་བརྟན་པ *tshig brtan-pa*; བསྒོ་བ་ཉན་པ *bsgo-wa ñan-pa*; དབང་དུ་གྱུར *dwaṅ-du gyur*; བསྙེན་པ *bsñen-pa*; ཞི་བ *shi-wa*; དུལ་བ *dul-wa*; ཉེར་ཞི་བ *ñer shi-wa* (*Mṅon.*).

བསྒོ་བ་བཅག་པ *bsgo-wa bcag-pa* आज्ञाविच्छेटन to disobey; to disregard directions.

བསྒོ་བ་རྣ་ལ་གཟོན་པ *bsgo-wa rna-la gzon-pa*= བསྒོ་བ་མི་ཉན་པ *bsgo-wa mi-ñan-pa* not listening to instructions or directions.

བསྒོ་བ་རྣམ་པ་གསུམ I: *bsgo-wa rnam-pa gsum* the three religious instructions or directions:— 1. དགེ་འདུན་གྱིས་བསྒོ་བ instructions issued by the church. 2. ཚེས་བསྒོ་བ those issued by a section of the church. 3. དགེ་འདུན་གནས་བརྟན་གྱིས་བསྒོ་བ directions emanating from the senior member of the holy order.

བསྒོ་བ་རྣམ་པ་གསུམ (II): 1. སློབ་དཔོན་གྱིས་བསྒོ་བ the order of the principal of a college or the superior of a monastery. 2. མཁན་པོས་བསྒོ་བ the command of the Khanpo (abbot). 3. དགེ་འདུན་གྱིས་བསྒོ་བ *dge-hdungyis bsgo-wa*.

བསྒོ་བ་རྣམ་པ་གསུམ III: 1. དགེ་འདུན་གྱིས་བསྒོ་བ the vows of the holy order. 2. གང་ཟག་གིས་བསྒོ་བ vows of ordinary men. 3. སོ་སོར་ཐར་པས་བསྒོ་བ vows for individual emancipation in the ordinary way (*K. du. 42*).

བསྒོ་བ་བཞིན་ཉན་པ *bsgo-wa bshin ñan-pa* or རྗེས་སུ་འཇུག་པ *rje-su hjug-pa* अनुविधीयमान to follow, do as directed. [One who acts as directed]*S.*

བསྒོ་བ་ལ་མི་ཉན་པ *bsgo-wa la mi-ñan-pa* བསླབ་བྱ་ལ་མི་ཉན breach of religious discipline; आज्ञाविच्छेटन not to act according to instruction.

བསྒོམ་པ *bsgom-pa* भाव contemplation; = གོམས་པ *goms-pa*; བསྒོམ་པ་དང་གོམས་པ་གཉིས་ལམ་ལ་སྦྱར་ན་དོན་གཅིག་ཡིན *bsgom-pa* and *goms-pa* in their application to road have one and same meaning.

བསྒོམ་སྐྱེས *bsgom-skyes* भावज, भावात्म produced from contemplation, also reflection; བསྒོམ་པ་བྱུང་བ *bsgom-pa byuṅ-wa* भावनामयी sprung from contemplation; བསྒོམ་པ་ལ་དགའ་བ *bsgom-pa la dgah-wa* delighting in contemplation.

བསྒོམས་པ *bsgoms-pa*, pf. of སྒོམ་པ *sgom-pa*.

བསྒྱིངས་པ *bsgyiṅs-pa* = འགྱིང་བ *hgyiṅ-wa* 1. विजृम्भ्, जृम्भ् to yawn. 2. = སྦོ་བ *sbo-wa*.

བསྒྱུར་བ I: *bsgyur-wa*, another form of སྒྱུར་བ *sgyur-wa* परिणामन, आवर्तन, to change; ཁ་དོག་བསྒྱུར་བ *kha-dog bsgur-ba* changing colour; གོས་བསྒྱུར་བ to change clothes; to change the cover (like a snake);

to translate; རྒྱ་གར་ནས་ཆོས་བསྒྱུར་བ *rgya-gar nas chos bsgyur-wa* to translate books brought from India; ཚིག་བསྒྱུར *tshig-bsgyur* to translate words; དོན་བསྒྱུར *don-bsgyur* to alter the meaning; ཐད་བསྒྱུར *thad-bsgyur* to change the direction; འཆོལ་བསྒྱུར *hchol-bsgyur*, ལུས་བསྒྱུར *lus-bsgyur* to change one's body (miraculously); མིང་བསྒྱུར *min-bsgyur* to change one's name; མདོག་བསྒྱུར *mdog-bsgyur* to change the complexion or colour; སྤུས་བསྒྱུར *spus-bgyur* to change the quality; བསྔོས་བསྒྱུར *bsnos-bsgyur, i.e.*, to change one's intention; ཕྱི་ནང་བསྒྱུར *phyi-nan bsgyur* to invert the object; ཆོས་ལུགས་བསྒྱུར *chos-lugs bsgyur* conversion; སྐད་བསྒྱུར *skad-bsgyur* to change the language.

བསྒྱུར་བ II: गुणित to multiply, increase.

Syn. བསྣུན *bsnun*; བསྒྲེས་པ *bsgres-pa*; སྤེལ་བ *spel-wa*; གསིལ་བ *gsil-wa* (*Mnon.*).

བསྒྱུས་པ *bsgyus-pa* स्नायु muscle.

བསྒྲག་ཕྲེང་ *Bsgrag-phren* (*dag-theng*) n. of a Jong in Tibet.

བསྒྲགས *bsgrags* (*dag*) (ཆོས་ཀློག་ཚར་བ *chos klog-tshar-wa*) कीर्त्तित, निखन proclaimed; read or recited loudly.

བསྒྲགས་པ *bsgrags-pa* sung; diffused.

བསྒྲང་བ *bsgran-pa* 1. to enumorate, count up (*Cs.*). 2. to cause to grow cold.

བསྒྲད་པ *bsgrad-pa*=བགྲད་པ *bgrad-pa* to open wide; མིག་བགྲད་པ *mig bgrad-pa* to stare; རྐང་པ་བགྲད་པ *rkan-pa bgrad-pa* to part the legs wide; to straddle.

བསྒྲལ *bsgral* सर्य्यं, तीर्ण [crossed; passable]*S.*

བསྒྲལ་བ *bsgral-wa* उत्‌-तर् to pass; cross over.

བསྒྲལ་བའི་ཤིང་རྟ *bsgral-wahi cin-rta* a boat, also=གྲུ་སྐྱ *gru-skya* an oar of a boat (*Mnon.*).

བསྒྲལ་བྱ *bsgral-bya* तरणी, तरी met. a boat.

བསྒྲལ་ཡས *bsgral-yas* खरर: a numerical figure used in Buddhist astrology.

བསྒྲིགས *bsgrigs* (*dig*) मेलर, ग्रन्थ, ग्रन्थित put in order, arranged, arrayed; བསྒྲིགས་པ *bsgrigs-pa* ग्रथित formed into string.

བསྒྲིབས་པ *bsgribs-pa* (*dib-pa*), pf. of སྒྲིབ *sgrib* निहृता, गोपायित, चाहृत, च्छादित covered.

བསྒྲིབས་པའི་ལུང་དུ་མི་སྟོན་པ *bsgribs-pahi lun-du mi-ston-pa* निहृतव्याकरण to abstain from obscure predictions: དགེ་མི་དགེ་གང་ཡང་མིན་པ་ལ་ལུང་མ་བསྟན: do not prophesy or predict what is not known either to be good or bad.

བསྒྲིམས་པ *bsgrims-pa* (*dim-pa*) (སྤྲས་པ *spras-pa*) བརྟན་བརྟན་བྱས་པ *brtan-brtan byas-pa*, v. སྒྲིམ་པ *sgrim-pa*, *rig-pa bsgrims-pa* perverted skill; also chaotic acquirements; confused information.

བསྒྲུན་པ *bsgrun-pa*, akin to འགྲན *hgran* प्रतिगर्जे, to rival, vie with; to reply to: བསྒྲིན་མི་ཕོད *brgrin mi-phod*=འགྲན་ཟླ་བྱེད་མི་ནུས་པ *hgran-zla byed mi-nus-pa* cannot compete or be a match for.

བསྒྲེང་ *bsgren*=བཙུགས་པ *btsugs-pa*, རྒྱལ་མཚན་ལྟ་བུ *rgyal-mtshan lta-bu* समुच्छ्रित, उच्छ्राय, प्रसार up-lifted; hoisted.

བསྒྲེངས *bsgrens* (*deng*), pf. of སྒྲེང་ *sgren*, imp. སྒྲེངས་ཤིག *sgrens-cig*, བསྒྲེངས་བྱའི་རྒྱལ་མཚན *bsgrens-byahi rgyal-mtshan*, a flag that is to be hoisted (*Situ. 77*).

བསྒྲེས *bsgres* (*de*) (བསྒྲེ *bsgre*) old, aged; སྐུ་བསྒྲེས *sku-bsgres*, དེ་བགྲས་མུ་ཡལ་བསྒྲེས *de-bgras mu-yal bsgres* (*Ya-sel.*). དབུ་ཆོས་བསྒྲེས་རིམ *dbu-chos bsgres rim* aged respectable lamas.

བསྒྲེས་པ *bsgres-pa* परिवर्त्त changed.

བསྒྲེས་ཡས *bsgres-yas* a numerical figure used in Buddhist astrology.

ང

ང་ *ṅa* I: is the fourth consonant of the Tibetan alphabet. It corresponds to the Sanskrit letter ङ and sounds like *ng* in the English word "song." As a final the pronunciation is therefore easy enough; but in its frequent occurrence as an initial letter the difficulty of sounding it properly comes in. As an initial ང་ must be pronounced as a nasal g. To acquire the sound, first say *un-ga*; and then, dropping the u, try to say the *nga*.

ང་ II: 1. it represents the numerical figure 4. 2. stands for ལྔ་བཅུ in the consecutive numbers ང་གཅིག 51; ང་གཉིས 52; ང་གསུམ 53; ང་བཞི 54; ང་ལྔ 55; ང་དྲུག 56; ང་བདུན 57; ང་བརྒྱད 58; ང་དགུ 59.

ང་ III: in mystical Buddhism is symbolical of the dissolution of all *Samskāra* (combinations either phenomenal or material). ང་ཞེས་པ་ནི་འདུ་བྱེད་ཐམས་ཅད་ཞིག་པའི་མཚན་ཉིད་དོ། "the term ང་ is the sign of the synthesis of all matters which phenomenally exist in a compounded state" (*K. my.* ཀ *207*). ང་ནི་འཛིན་པ་མེད་པའི་སྒོ, འཛིན་བྲལ་ཐམས་ཅད་གྲོལ་བར་སྟོན (*K. g.* ཕ *42*) "ང་ is symbolical of the state where there is no cohesion; it explains that all that are without adherence (attachment) will be liberated."

ང་ IV: अहं pers. pron., first person, singular I: ང་མི་རྒན old man that I am; ང་རྒྱལ་པོ་སྲོང་བཙན་སྒམ་པོ་དང་། "I with *Sroṅ-btsan sgam-po*"; བླ་མ་ང་ I the Lama. ངའི or ང་ཡི my, mine: ངའི་ཡིད་འོང་ my charming (wife), *i.e.*, dearest; ང་ཡི་ཡིན=བདག་གི་ཡིན it is mine; མི་ངའི་རྣམ་ཤེས soul of me a man; ངའི་འདི this my; ངའི་རྗེ་བཙུན my venerable master. Colloq. the common form for ང་ *nga* is ང་རང་ *ṅa-raṅ* "I."

ང་ཁོ་ན *ṅa kho-na* I myself; I alone.

ང་ཉེད *ṅa-ñed*, ང་ཉིད, ང་རང་ अस्मद्, अहं, स्व I myself.

Syn. ཁོ་བོ *kho-wo.*

ང་ཅག *ṅa-cag*, ང་ཚོ *ṅa-tsho*, ང་རྣམས *ṅa-rnams*, are the several plurals of ང་ signifying we.

ངས *ṅas* for ང་ཡིས *ṅa-yis* by me, v. ང་ *ṅa*.

ང་རྒྱལ *ṅa-rgyal* अग्र, दर्प, मान, अहंकार (lit. "I, the chief"), *i.e.*, pride, arrogance: ང་རྒྱལ་གྱི་སྟེང་ལ་ཡོན་ཏན་གྱི་ཆུ་མི་ཆགས། "on the height of pride the water of merit does not accumulate"; ང་རྒྱལ་སྐྱེད་པ to be proud. ང་རྒྱལ་གཅོག་པ to break (another's) pride; to humble; ངར་སྙམ་པའི་ང་རྒྱལ=the pride of assertion of self; lit. the pride of reflecting "I am."

Syn. རྒྱགས *rgyags*; དྲེགས *dregs*; འཕྱར་གཡེང་སྙེམས *hphyar-gyeṅ-sñems*; མངོན་པའི་ང་རྒྱལ *mṅon-pahi ṅa-rgyal*; ང་ལྡན *ṅa-ldan* (*Mṅon.*).

ང་རྒྱལ་ཅན *ṅa-rgyal-can* अहंकारी, अतिमानिक, महाभद्रौ; proud, boastful; rivalling.

Syn. ང་རྒྱལ་ལྡན་ *ṅa-rgyal-ldan*, དྲེགས་ལྡན *dregs-ldan* (*Mṅon.*).

ང་རྒྱལ་ལས་ཀྱང་ང་རྒྱལ मानातिमान supreme pride.

ང་ཕོད *Ṅa-phod* n. of a district in the province of Kong-po (*Loṅ.* ཉ, *16*).

ང་བ *ṅa-wa*=ཡང་བ *ya ṅa-wa* भीषण 1. bad; dangerous; fearful. 2. rarely for ངན་པ bad; དྲི་ང་བ a bad smell.

ང་མེད *ṅa-med* अमम lit. without self; without vanity; not thinking of one's self or self-interest.

ང་མེན་ཆོས་པོ *ṅa-men chos-po* (he who is personified by worldliness), the name by which *Māra*, the lord of worldliness of the Buddhists, is known to the Bon (*B. Nam.*).

ང་ཉུར *ṅa-ṅur* a species of duck, v. ངུར་པ *ṅur-pa*, perh. *Anas casarca*.

ང་ཤི *ṅa-çi*, lit. I die; cry of fear with wonder; evidently a Bengali expression of wonder—"मरि or हा मरि I die, alas! I die," which Atis'a introduced in Tibetan—ཨ་ཙ་ང་ཤི་རྒྱ་གར་ན་དུང་ངོ་མཚར་ཅན་གྱི་གཏམ་ཡོད། (*A. 107*) "Oh, I die from wonder! yet there are wonderful stories in India (to be told)."

ང་མོ *ṅa-mo* for རྔ་མོ the camel: ཁུར་བ་ངུར་སྐྱེར་འདྲངས་ཤིང་ང་མོ་མགྱོགས། *khur-wa ṅur skyer draṅs çin ṅa-mo mgyag* the camel, grunting with loads, travels quickly (*Jig. 22*).

ང་འཚེང་ *ṅa-ḥtsheṅ* self-sufficient or self-sufficiency; pride; egotism (*A. 90*).

ང་ཡིར་མེད *ṅa-yir med* अमाय want of selfishness: ང་ཡིར་འཛིན་པ=བདག་གིར་འཛིན་པ or གང་ཟག་བདག་ཏུ་འཛིན་པ the cognition of personality which may be styled the self or བདག.

ང་ར *ṅa-ra* 1. noise; sound. 2. cold air: ང་གངས་ཀྱི་ང་རས་མི་འཇིགས། I am not afraid of the air of the glaciers (*Mil.*).

ང་ར་ཅན I: *ṅa-ra-can* 1. loud, noisy, roaring. 2. a crier, brawler, noisy fellow.

ང་ར་ཅན II: rarified; cold.

ང་ར་ཐང་ *Ṅa-ra thaṅ* n. of a place in Tibet: ཟངས་སྒམ་དེ་ཁ་ཕྱེ་བས་སྐད་ངར་ར་ར་ཟེར་བས་ཡུལ་དེའི་མིང་ཡང་ང་ར་ཐང་དུ་བཏགས། (*Jig. 65*) when the lid of the copper-coffin was opened, there came out from it the cry *ṅa-ra-ra*; hence the name of that place became known as *Ṅa-ra-thaṅ*.

ངར་ར་ར *ṅar ra-ra* expression of extreme pain and suffering.

ང་རུ *Ṅa-ru* n. of a place in Ancient Tibet, which *Hod*, one of the four sons of King *Se-sbreg-pa*, had chosen for his residence (*Deb.* ཀ, *19*).

ང་རོ *ṅa-ro*, स्वर 1. a loud, deep voice; a cry; སྐད་ཀྱི་ང་རོ་དྲག་ཞན the pitch of the voice loud and low. 2.=*visarga*, *i.e.*, ཿ. དབྱངས་ཐུང་བ་ལྔའི་མཐར་ཐིག་ལེ་ང་རོ་ཡོད་པ་དབྱངས། at the end of the five short vowels, there being the *visarga* dots (they should be regarded as a) vowel (*Ya-sel. 47*). 3. སེང་གེ་དང་སྟག་གི་ངར་སྐད། the roaring sound of the lion or the tiger: སྟག་གི་ངར་སྐད་འདོན་པ་ན, སྤྲེའུ་ཤིང་གི་རྩེ་ནས་ལྷུང་། the tiger's growl issuing forth, the monkey drops down from the top of the a tree; སྐད་ཀྱི་ང་རོ་ཆེན་པོས་བསྒྲགས་སོ they proclaimed, shouting at the top of their voice; གདུག་པའི་ང་རོ voices foreboding mischief; ཀྱེ་ཧུད་ཀྱི་ང་རོ་འདོན་པ to raise woeful cries.

ང་རོ་སྒྲོག་པ *ṅa-ro sgrog-pa* 1. to roar; to rage. 2. the circlet used on the top of a letter to signify མ turns into ང, ཉ, ན and མ before words beginning with any of these.

ང་རོ་བྱིན་པ *ṅa-ro byin-pa* आर्त्तनाद, आर्त्तस्वर, आक्रन्दन crying; bewailing; to cry or bewail loudly on account of pain or grief.

ང་ལ་ནུ *Ṅa-la nu* also ང་ལས་ནུ *Ṅa-las nu* मान्धाता n. of a mythological king who ruled as a Chakravarti-rājā over heaven and earth and shared the celestial throne with six successive Indras. N. of an ancestor of Gautama Buddha: བྱིས་པས་ནུ་མ་ང་ལ་ནུ་གསུངས་པ་ལ་བརྟེན་མིང་ཡང་ང་ལ་ནུ་ཞེས་གྲགས་སོ། the child having cried "give me suck," was called Ña-la-nu (*Pag. 14*).

ངག *ňag* वाच्, वाणी, इरा, भारती, गौः speech; talk; word; ངག་གི་ཉེས་པ sins committed with the tongue (in words); ངག་འཇམ་པོ polite speech; gentle words; ངག་སྡོམ་པ वाक्संयम or ངག་བཅད་པ मौनव्रत silence, observed as a monastic duty or religious exercise; the vow of not speaking, *i.e.*, of keeping silence for a definite time.

Syn. ཚིག *tshig*; སྒྲ་བརྗོད་པ *sgra-bjod-pa*; དབྱངས་ཅན *dbyaňs-can*; གཏམ *gtam*; ལོ་རྒྱུས *lo-rgyus*; སྐད་སྨྲ་བ *skad-smra-wa* (*Mňon.*).

ངག་སྐྱེས *ňag-skyes* वाणीज born or produced from speech.

ངག་འཁྱལ *ňag-hkhyal* प्रलाप, भिन्नलाप, विभिन्नलाप delirium; unconnected speech; foolish talk; ravings (*Ňag.*).

ངག་གི་རྒྱལ་པོ *Ňag-gi rgyal-po* मञ्जुघोष; འཇམ་དབྱངས the *Bodhisattva* Mañju-s'ri ghosha, who is believed by Buddhists to be the god of speech; ངག་གི་རྒྱན *ňag-gi-rgyan* दीपक a figure of rhetoric or speech; gen. amplication of an idea by the use of apt expressions; ངག་གི་ཕྱག་རྒྱ वाङ्मुद्रा the symbolic speech or mode of expression by the configuration of the fingers; this is described as གསང་བའི་བརྡ་སྐད་བ་སྟོད་པ་གཙོ་བོ, mystical language in which expression by signs, *i.e.*, with the configuration of the fingers, forms the principal feature; ངག་གི་དབང་ཕྱུག, वागीश्वर the lord of speech—Jam-yang or Mañ-ju-s'rī ghosha: ངག་གི་དབང་ཕྱུག་འཇམ་པའི་དབྱངས་ལ་ཕྱག་འཚལ་ལོ། salutation to Jampai-yang, the prince of speech (*Situ. 3*); ངག་གི་དབུལ *ňag-gi dbul* one poor in speech; a dumb person, v. ལྐུག་པ *lkug-pa* (*Mňon.*).

ངག་འགྲོས *ňag-hgros* manner of speaking or uttering words (*Cs.*).

ངག་རྒྱས་པ *ňag rgyas-pa* वाग्विस्तर too much talking; full and detailed discussion.

ངག་རྒྱུན *ňag-rgyun* प्रबन्ध a discourse; also oral tradition, not recorded history.

ངག་འཆལ *ňag-hchal*=ངག་འཁྱལ irregular or senseless speech.

Syn. འཆལ་ཚིག *hchal-tshig*; ཆ་མེད་གཏམ *cha-med gtam*; ཀླག་ཅོར *klag-cor*; བབ་ཅོལ *bab-col*; མུ་ཅོར *mu-cor* (*Mňon.*).

ངག་སྙན *ňag-sňan* 1.=as met. the cuckoo. 2. pleasant voice or sweet language; one who speaks in sweet language.

ངག་གཏམ *ňag-gtam* verbal message; also oral tradition.

ངག་བསྡམས་པ *ňag-bsdams-pa* वाचि संयम, वाक्संयत one who has controlled his speech or tongue.

ངག་འདབ *ňag-hdab* or ངག་གི་འདབ་མ *ňag-gi hdab-ma* (lit. the leaf of speech) रसना the organ of tasting; རོ་འཛིན the tongue, v. ལྕེ *lce*: (*Mňon.*).

ངག་འདོན་པ *ňag-hdon-pa* लपन to express in words; to cry; to speak.

ངག་ལྡན *ňag-ldan* वाङ्मान्, वाग्मिन् eloquent; possessed of (the power of) speaking.

ངག་བྱེད *ňag-byed* लपमान; the speaker.

ངག་དབང་ *ňag-dwaň* a title of learning given to some of the Grand Lamas of Tibet. Is also the first name of the present or 14th Dalai Lama of Lhasa.

ངག་དབང་ཡེ་ཤེས་རྒྱ་མཚོ *Ňag-dwaň Ye-çes rgya-mtsho* the Lama who with the help of Lhabzañ, King of the country round lake Kökönor, conducted the Government of Tibet for thirteen years (*Loň.* ༢, *16*).

ངག་དབང་ལྷ་མོ *Ňag-dwaň lha-mo* वागीश्वरी देवी the goddess of speech; དབྱངས་ཅན་མ an epithet of Sarasvatī (*Mňon.*).

ངག་སྦྱོར་ *ṅag-sbyor* वाग्योजना arrangement of speech (*Cs.*).

ངག་མ *ṅag-ma* वाचा the speech itself.

ངག་མ་ཚང་བ *ṅag-ma tshaṅ-wa* = ལྐུག་པ काह्ल 1. one of imperfect or defective speech; a stupid person. 2. indistinct speech.

ངག་མི་ལྡན *ṅag-mi-ḻdan* a dumb person; also one who cannot express himself in clear language.

Syn. ལྐུག་པ *ḻkug-pa*; ཚིག་མི་གསལ *tshig-mi-gsal*; སེམས་བེམ་པོ *sems-bem-po* (*Mṅon.*).

ངག་མེད *ṅag-meḏ* समाधि meditation; a state in which there is no use of speech.

ངག་ཚབ *ṅag-tshab* representation in writing: ངག་ཚབ་ཀྱི་དོ་ཚིག the principal points in a representation or petition.

ངག་མཚུངས *ṅag-mtshuṅs* समो of uniform and consistent speech, *i.e.*, where there is no contradiction, redundancy, or irrelevancy.

ངག་ཡིད *ṅag-yiḏ* वाङ्मन: the speech and the heart.

ངག་ལམ་ཞུ་བ *ṅag-lam shu-wa* to apply, or pray to, verbally.

ངག་གཅེར *ṅag-gçer* in vulg. ཁ་གཅེར or གདོང་གཅེར, in Sikk. cross-examination; also deposition of the plaintiff and defendant in the presence of each other.

ངག་ཤོར *ṅag-çor* committing to words; a promise.

ངག་གསལ *ṅag-gsal* वाक्लिपा, वाक्लेप clear speech or lucid language.

ངག་ལྷ་མོ *Ṅag lha-mo* वाग्देवी the Goddess of Speech.

ངང་ I: *ṅaṅ* = ཀློང་ or དབྱིངས निसर्ग 1. the nature, being, idiosyncracy; the very essence of any person or thing. 2. sphere; province; domain: སྟོང་པའི་ངང = སྟོང་པའི་དབྱིངས the essentiality of vacuity (*Çūnyatā*): ནམ་མཁའི་ངང་ the sphere of the void space: སེམས་ཀྱི་ངང་ = སེམས་ཀྱི་དབྱིངས the natural constitution of the mind: ཐུགས་མཉེས་བཞིན་པའི་ངང་ལ in a cheerful state of the mind (*Thgr.*); སྟོང་པའི་ངང་ཉིད the very essence of vacuity itself (*Glr.*): ཏིང་ངེ་འཛིན་གྱི་ངང་ལ་ཞུགས་པ to enter into the state of deep meditation: ཆགས་མེད་ཀྱི་ངང་ལ་གནས་པར་གྱིས། continue in that state of mind which is free from attachment, etc.: འཇིགས་སྐྲག་གི་ངང་ནས་འཆི་བ། to die of fear or panic.

ངང་ II: character; disposition: ངང་ངན or ངང་རྒྱུད་ངན་པ a naturally bad disposition; ངང་རྒྱུད་བཟང་པོ a naturally good disposition (*Sch.*; *Jä.*).

ངང་གིས *ṅaṅ-gis* adv. spontaneously; naturally; also, acc. to *Jä.* and *Schr.*, slowly, gradually, gently.

ངང་ཅན *ṅaṅ-can* natural capacity: གཏོང་བའི་ངང་ཅན त्यागमाली one who is naturally capable of renouncing or giving up; able to abandon. ངང་ནས is generally used like སྒོ་ནས.

ངང་བག་ཡོད *ṅaṅ-bag-yoḏ* naturally modest: ངང་བག་ཡོད་ཀྱི་སྒོ་ནས་ཚུལ་ཁྲིམས། his moral character in regard to his natural modesty (*A. 53*).

ངང་མ་ཐུང་ *ṅaṅ ma-thuṅ* do not be short-tempered: ཁོ་བོས་མཁའ་འགྲོ་མ་ལ་ཞུ་ཡིས་ངང་མ་ཐུང་ཞེར་ནས། when I had said to the *kha-do-ma* "pray be not short-tempered" (*Ḇbrom. 93*).

ངང་ཚུལ *ṅaṅ-tshul* natural disposition or temperament; ངང་ཚུལ་བཟང་པོ 1. good conduct; a naturally good disposition. 2. n. of a Buddhist sage and author of Ancient India, included in the list of twenty-three sages (*M.V.*).

ངང་རིང་ *ṅaṅ-riṅ* or ངང་རྒྱུད་རིང་བ forbearing; long-suffering; of cool nature: དོན་ཆེན་སྒྲུབ་པ་ངང་རིང་། བྱེད་དགོས། in accomplishing important business one should work with great patience.

ངང་པ *ṅaṅ-pa* हंस the male goose.

ངང་རྐང་ *ṅaṅ-ṛkaṅ* लुबद्दा that which waddles.

ངང་སྐྱ *ṅaṅ-ṣkya* बलाका grey teal of Tibet.

Syn. པད་ཟླུམ་མགྲིན *pad-zlum mgrin*.

ངང་སྒྲོ *ṅaṅ-ṣgro* the quill of the goose.

ངང་ངུར *ṅaṅ-ṅur* चक्रवाक the ruddy goose, realy *Tadorna rutila*, the sheldrake.

ངང་པ་གསེར་ལྡན *ṅaṅ-pa gser-ḷdan* 1. the yellow or golden goose. 2. རྟ་ངང་པ་གསེར་ལྡན་ཁྲིར་ཤོག་གསུངས། he said "fetch the horse called *Ṅaṅ-pa gser-ḷdan*" (*Yig.*).

ངང་པའི་རྒྱལ་པོ *ṅaṅ-paḥi ṛgyal-po* the "king-goose" and flamingo; also the plant *Jasminum zambac*.

ངང་པའི་ནགས *Ṅaṅ-paḥi-nags* a mythological grove called the swan's grove (as) situated beyond the Cuckoo's hill on this side of the ocean. It is filled with numberless flocks of ducks, geese and swans, with bills of coral, ruby, sapphire, and other precious stones. The lakes in that grove are filled with lotuses of the colour of glittering gold; and the grove extends over ten thousand miles (*K. d.* ར *272*).

ངང་པའི་ཚོགས *ṅaṅ-paḥi tshogs* कदम्ब a flock of wild geese.

ངང་མོ *ṅaṅ-mo* हंसी a goose.

ངད I: *ṅad* nice smell; aroma fragrance: ངད་ཡལ the fragrancy, the aroma evaporates; སྤོ་ངད aromatic herbs.

Syn. བསུང་ *ḅsuṅ*; བསུང་ངད *ḅsuṅ-ṅad* (*Mṅon.*).

ངད II: acc. to *Jä.* cog. to ངར air; ཐྲིམ་གྱི་ངད་ལྡན་པ the rising of an aromatic breeze; also vapour; ཁ་ངད vapour from the mouth; also snowy vapour; ཆུ་ངད aqueous vapour.

ངད་ཅན *ṅad-can* fragrant; also acc. to *Jä.* 1. fresh, cool. 2. rough, impetuous.

ངད་བཟང་ *ṅad-ḅzaṅ* good smell: ཡིགས་ཚོགས་ག་བུར་གྱི་ངད་བཟང་ཡང་ནས་ཡང་དུ་ཡོང་བ་མཛོད། let the breeze of your letters laden with the aroma of camphor come again and again to me, *i.e.*, pray write me often.

ངན *ṅan* evil; mischief; misfortune; defilement: ངན་ཆེན་པོ་བྱས། it has done great mischief; esp. harm done by sorcery and witchcraft; ངན་དུ་བརྗོད་པ to revile (a person).

ངན་འགྲོ *ṅan-ḥgro* I: दुर्गति going or about to go to the undesirable state, *i.e.*, the state of the damned, comprising those in hell and those wandering about in distorted forms.

II: जायानुजीवन 1. one who follows the dictates of his wife and is led by the nose by her in all his works. 2. कपरूव dissimulation.

III: तड़ित lightning.

ངན་དགུ *ṅan-ḍgu*. all kinds of evil or mischief.

ངན་སྐྱེས *ṅan-ṣkyes* अन्त्यज of low birth; also भूमिज lit. anything produced from the soil and manure; the planet Mars.

ངན་རྒྱུ་ཅན *ṅan-ṛgyu-can* one who does mischief, speaks ill of others; ངན་རྒྱུ་ཅན་མེད one that does not speak evil of anybody (*A. 139*).

ངན་ངོན *ṅan-ṅon* अवर, अवरक sordid, vile, mean, pitiful: ངན་ངོན་ཙམ་གྱི་དད་པ or ངན་ངོན་ཙམ་གྱི་ཚིག་ཤེས་པ अवरमात्रकप्रसाद to be satisfied with anything be it ever so little or poor; =འདོད་པ་ཆུང་བ unambitious.

ངན་རྙེད *ṅan-ṛñed* कच्छुर 1. scabby; itchy. 2. unchaste; libidinous.

ངན་ཐབས *ñan-thabs* = ཕྲ་མ *phra-ma* or ཁྲམ་པ *khram-pa* पुक्कस, पुकस vile language; mean, vulgar conversation; abuse.

ངན་འདེབས་པ *ñan-ḥdebs-pa* to curse, execrate; མཐུ་ངན་འདེབས་པ to curse by means of witchcraft; cf. མངན.

ངན་ན་བ *ñan-na-wa* the bad.

ངན་པ I: *ñan-pa* क्रु, धूर्त, पापिष्ठ, मन्द, शठ, खल, कुटिल bad; miserable; poor; wicked; ugly; also a scoundrel, slanderer, rogue; the vile, vulgar, low, mean.

ངན་པ II: 1. excrement; ordure; manure: ངན་པ་རྒྱབ་པས་ཞིང་དུ་གསོབ་པར་འོང་། by the use of manure the soil becomes very fertile.

Syn. མི་གཙང་མ *mi-gtsañ-ma*; སྐྱག་པ *skyag-pa* (*Mñon.*).

ངན་པ་བརྗོད་པ *ñan-pa brjod-pa* अभ्याख्यान to blaspheme.

ངན་པ་གཉའ་རེངས *ñan-pa gñaḥ-reñs* a stiff-necked villain (*Rtsii. 13*).

ངན་པ་དཔུང་བསྡེབས *ñan-pa dpuñ-bsdebs* conspirators; evil-minded men who intrigue, form a league to do mischief to others.

ངན་སྤོང་སྐྱེས *Ñan-spoñ skyes* = དགའ་བྱེད་དགུ་རྒྱ་ཅན or ངན་སྤོང་བུ Paras'u Rāma; རྡུལ་ཅན་མའི་བུ the son of *Rdul-can-ma* (*Mñon.*); an epithet of S'ukra and also of the planet Venus (གཟའ་པ་སངས).

+ ངན་བུ *ñan-bu* in earlier Tibetan the word ངན་བུ was used in the place of the modern expression ཉན or ཉན་བདག, my humble or little self.

ངན་བྱ་བ *ñan bya-wa* धिक्कृत reproached; deceived; cheated.

ངན་སྨྲ *ñam-smra* अपवाद, निह्नव notoriety; bad reputation; disgrace.

ངན་བཅོས་མ་བྱས་པ *ñan-bzos ma-byas-pa* अकर्मारकृत not reclaimed; made useless.

ངན་གཡོ *ñan-gyo* = ཁྲམ་པ or ཁྲམ कपटता hypocrisy (*Mñon.*); ངན་གཡོ་ཅན (or གཡོ་སྒྱུ་ངན་པ་ཅན कुक्कुटिक 1. a hypocrite; a fox. 2. of a low caste.

ངན་རིངས་མ also ངང་རིངས་མ दुर्दुरा procrastinating, delaying; always throwing a duty or anything to a distance.

ངན་རོག *ñan-rog* = ངན་རྙེད *ñan-rñed*.

ངན་ལམ *ñan-lam* = ལང་ལ་སོང་བ 1. bad habit, indulgence in any kind of work, behaviour, or eating, of a degrading nature. 2. n. of a place in Tibet (*Deb.* ག, *2*).

ངན་ཤི *ñan-çi* अपमृत्यु death from starvation or from an accident or epidemic or plague, etc.; any person or animal that has died from starvation.

ངན་སེལ *ñan-sel* that which removes the defilement and purifies: ངན་སེལ་ཞེས་པ་ཀུ་ཤ་, དུར་བ་དང་ནི་ཆུ་ཡི་མིང་། *ñan-sel* is a term for water and also for tufts of *kuça* and *dub* grass (*Mñon.*).

ངན་སོང *ñan-soñ* अपाय those actually gone to damnation.

ངན་གསོ *ñan-gso* to feed and foster persons or animals that have suffered from starvation.

ངན་ཧྲུལ *ñan-hrul* low and destitute; delapidated; decomposed: མི་སེར་ངན་ཧྲུལ་རྣམས་སོར་སྐྱོན། "(agricultural) tenants who have become scattered and destitute" (*Rtsii.*).

ངམ་དཀར *ñam-dkar* grey colour; not very white.

ངམ་གྲོག *ñam-grog* = གཡངས་ཆས deep ravines with precipitous eroded banks, which are impassable and inhospitable in aspect. Acc. to *Cs.* a torrent; acc. to *Sch.* the bank of a river grown ridgy and steep by having been gradually washed out by currents.

ངམ་གྲོག་ཆེན་པོ *ñam-grog chen-po* महाश्वभ्र a poetic name of Tibet which is called ངམ་གྲོག་ཅེ, the country of deep ravines.

ངམ་པ *ṅam-pa* दम्भ 1. arrogance. 2. गह्वर a ravine.

ངམ་མཐོང་ཅན *ṅam-mthoṅ-can* दाम्भिक a proud, bumptious person; one who assumes the appearance of greatness.

ངམ་དུར་ཅན *ṅam-dur-can* given to gluttony and drinking (*Jä.*).

ངམ་རིང་ *Ṅam-riṅ* n. of a district in Upper Tsang with a fort and monastery subject to Tashi-lhunpo.

ངམ་རུ *ṅam-ru* n. of a disease (*Med.*).

ངམ་ཤིང་ *Ṅam-çin* n. of a snake-demi-god of the nether regions.

ངམ་ཤུགས *ṅam-çugs*=རང་ཤུགས as a matter of course; by one's own force (of nature) or accord.

ངམ་ཤོད *Ṅam-çod* 1.=སྟེང་འོག *steṅ-hog* upper and lower: དེ་ནས་མཆེད་དེ་ངམ་ཤོད་ཐམས་ཅད་ཆུར་སོང་། thence spreading over inundated the upper and lower parts (of the country) (*A. 92*). 2. n. of a place in Lhokha—the south-eastern district of the province of Ū (*Loṅ.* ཥ *5*): མ་ཤོད་སྨད the lower part of ངམ་ཤོད (*Deb.* ག, *19*).

ངར *ṅar* 1. fore side; front side; ངར་གདོང་ front surface; forepart, esp. of the leg, the shin-bone, also knuckle; ལག་ངར forearm; རྐང་ངར lower part of the leg; རྡོ་ངར acc. to *Jä.* an appellation for both. 2. termin. of ང་ 'to one's self'; ངར་འཛིན अहङ्कार; ང་ ཡིར་འཛིན་པ=བདག་འཛིན pride; selfishness; self-interest. 3. ངར་འདོན་པ to set on or against; to instigate.

ངར་སྐད *ṅar-skad* the sound of the roaring of lions, etc.

ངར་ངར་པོ *ṅar-ṅar-po* hoarse, husky, wheezing, *e.g.*, in old age (*Thgy.*); ངར་གླུད *ṅar-glud* hoarseness and phlegm (*Med.*); གྲེ་བ་ངར་བ *gre-wa ṅar-wa* a hoarse throat (*Med.*; *Jä.*); ངར་ངར་འཕྲུན་སྒྲ a hoarse groaning.

ངར་སྣབས *ṅar-snabs* mucus of the nose.

ངར་པ *ṅar-pa* stalk of plants (*Med.*).

ངར་བ *ṅar-wa* 1. strength; vigour; hardness (of steel); གྲི་སོགས་ཀྱི་ངར་འཇམ་པོ *gri-sogs-kyi ṅar-hjam-po* the hard or soft temper of (the metal of) knife; etc. 2. cold; frost; cold wind (*Mil.*); (cf. ར་ར) ངར་གླུད་པ to steel; to temper.

ངར་ཅན *ṅar-can* 1. strong; vigorous. 2. ductile; ངར་ལྡན id., སེམས་ངར་ལྡན, strong-minded; ངར་མེད weak; soft.

ངར་པོ *ṅar-po* grim; strong; ferocious, (of beasts) (*Jä.*).

ངར་གླུད *ṅar-glud* sbst. 1. valour and strength: དཔའ་བོའི་ངར་གླུད་ཁ་ལྟས་ཁྱབ་པར་རྒྱུ the valour of a hero is indicated in his face (physiognomy). 2. vb. ངར་གླུད་པ or ངར་བཏང་བ to temper and sharpen a steel-weapon or instrument.

ངར་འབོལ *ṅar-hbol* strong in quality; ཇའི་མདོག་དམར་པོ་ངར་འབོལ་པོ་ཡོད་པ the red colour of tea is its strength.

ངར་མ *ṅar-ma* 1. irritable, passionate, impetuous (*Sch.*). 2. strong, powerful, *e.g.*, a powerful protection (*Mil.*, *Jä.*).

ངར་འཛིན, v. ངར།

ངལ་བ *ṅal-wa* श्रम, आयास fatigue; weariness; resp. སྐུ་ངལ་བ also ཡོངས་ངལ परिश्रम; ཐུགས་ངལ་བ or མཉེལ་བ tired mentally; विश्रान्त, क्लम, श्रान्त to be fatigued, wearied; prostrate with exercise of the body.

Syn. ཐང་ཆད་པ *thaṅ-chad-pa*; དུབ་པ *dub-pa*; ངལ་དུབ་པ *ṅal-dub-pa* (*Mṅon.*).

ངལ་རྐེན་པ *ṅal-rkcn-pa* (ནད *nad*) किलास a kind of disease. [1. a kind of white leprosy. 2. weariness, languor]*S.*

ངལ་ཆད་པ *ṅal chad-pa* to be prostrate by fatigue.

ངལ་འཇུག་པ *ṅal-ḥjug-pa* vb. a. to tire; to cause to be weary.

ངལ་སྟེགས *ṅal-stegs* I: a rost; a sort of wooden crutch to support a load on the back while resting in a standing posturo.

ངལ་སྟེགས II: or ངལ་ཚུགས a bench or seat inviting repose.

Syn. བསྟི་བ *bsti-wa*; སྡོད་པ *sdod-pa* (*Mṅon.*).

ངལ་དུབ་པ *ṅal-dub-pa* intensivo form of ངལ་བ, to be very tired.

ངལ་ཕོང་ *ṅal-phoṅ* fatigued; bocomo tirod.

ངལ་མེད *ṅal-med* अश्रान्त not wearied; untired; untiring.

ངལ་འཚོ *ṅal-ḥtsho* rofreshment.

ངལ་གསོ་བ *ṅal-gso-wa* lit. to curo woarinoss; to take rest: विश्राम, विराम, विरति rest, resting.

ངལ་གསོས *ṅal-gsos* श्रमण met. for an ascetic.

ངི་ *ṅi* num. fig. 34.

ངུ་ *ṅu* 1. num. fig. 64. 2. v. ངུ་བ *ṅuwa*.

ངུ་བ *ṅu-wa* रोदन, क्रन्दन to cry; to weep; pf. ངུས, resp. ཤུམ་པ། ངུས་པའི་མཆི་མ, tears that have been shed (*Dzl.*); ག་ཅད་ངུས་པ weeping without cause; hysterical weeping (*Med.*); ངུ་བ་པོ *ṅu-wa-po* a weeper; ངུ་མཁན *ṅu-mkhan* id.

ངུ་འདོད *ṅu-ḥdod* रुरुदिषति wishing to cry; going to weep.

ངུ་བྲོ *ṅu-bro* was about to cry or weep.

ངུ་འབོད *ṅuḥ-bod* 1. bewailing; crying or weeping loudly. 2. रौरव n. of a hell: ངུ་འབོད་ཆེན་པོ महारौरव the hell greater in suffering than *Raurava*.

ངུ་རྫི *ṅu-rdsi W.* sbst. a loud crying; bawling out; lamenting (*Jä.*).

ངུ་རུ *ṅu-ru* teal.

ངུ་རུ་འཇུག་པ *ṅu-ru ḥjug-pa* to cause to weep.

ངུ་ཤུར་ཅན *ṅu-çur-can* acc. to *Sch.* a child that is continually crying.

ངུད་མོ *ṅud-mo* a sob (*Cs.; Schr.*).

ངུག་པ *ṅug-pa*=ངུར་བ to grunt; to snore; to pur.

ངུར་སྒྲ་ཅན *ṅur-sgra-can* that which grunts; a pig; a yak.

ངུར་པ *ṅur-pa* चक्रवाक duck, esp. the red wild duck, *Anas nyroca*.

Syn. ཤིང་རྟའི་ལུས *çiṅ-rtaḥi-lus*; འཁོར་ལོ་ཅན *ḥkhor-lo-can*; གཉིས་གཉིས་སྤྱོད *gñis-gñis-spyod*; མཚན་མོ་འབྲལ *mtshan-mo-ḥbral*; འདོད་པ་ལྡན *ḥdod-pa-ldan*; ཅོ་ཀ *co-ka*; འདབ་ཆགས་གསེར་ལྡན *ḥdab-chags gser-ldan* (*Mṅon.*).

ངུར་པ་ཆེན་པོ *ṅur-pa chen-po* 1. sheldrake. 2. n. of a celebrated Lama of Tibet mentioned in the *Mṅon* (*Deb.*).

ངུར་བ *ṅur-wa* to grunt (of pigs and yaks).

ངུར་ཀ *ṅur-ka* as red as fire; fiery-red (*Jä.*).

ངུར་སྨྲིག *ṅur-smrig* कषाय is described as ཀུར་ཀུམ་གྱི་མདོག་དམར་སེར reddish yellow; saffron-colour.

ངུར་སྨྲིག་གོས *ṅur-smrig gos* the robe of an ordained monk which ought to be, but is not often so in Tibet, of orange-colour; he who wears the reddish-yellow; a Buddhist mendicant dressed in reddish-yellow clothes.

ངུར་སྨྲིག་ཆེན་པོ *ṅur-smrig chen-po*=ངུར་སྨྲིག་འཛིན་པ कषायहस्तिक a great Buddhist monk; a monk who is great on account of his orange robe.

ངེ *ñe* num. fig. *94*.

ངེད *ñed* अहं pers. pron. first person, sing. in *C.* for ང་, I; ངེད་ཀྱི my or mine; ངེད་རྣམས་ཀྱི our.

ངེད་ཉིད *ñed-ñid*=ངེད་ཁོ་ན, ངེད་རང་ I myself; we ourselves.

ངེད་གཉིས *ñed-gñis* we two; ངེད་སྤུན་གསུམ we three brothers.

ངེད་རྣམས *ñed-rnams*, ངེད་ཅག, ངེད་ཚོ, ངེད་དག are variously used for the plural of ངེད to signify we.

ངེད་རང་ *ñed-rañ* I, or I myself.

ངེས་ཁ་རག *Ñes-kha-rag* n. of place in Tibet (*Deb.* ག *25*).

ངེས་པ *ñes-pa* **निश्चय, ध्रुव, निश्चित्ति, नियत** certain, true, sure, firm; also truth, reality, certainty: བདག་ལ་ངེས་པ་ཞིག་སྨྲ་ལ་དུ་གསོལ I ask you to communicate to me something certain, *i.e.*, authentic news: འཆི་བ་ངེས death is certain (*Jä.*); རྩིས་འཕྲོ་ལ་ངེས་པ *rtsis hphro la ñes-pa* to be sure of a mathematical calculation, *i.e.*, to hold it as a certain result.

Syn. བདེན་པ *bden-pa*; མི་བསླུ་བ *mi-bslu-wa*; རྫུན་པོ་མ་ཡིན་པ *rdsun-po ma-yin-pa* (*Mñon.*).

ངེས་ཁྱབ *ñes-khyab* निर्धार;=ཁྱབ་བྱའི་ཡུལ་ཕྱི་ནང་གང་ཆེ་ཆུང་ལ the proportion of space inside a country to that which is outside, whether large or small; ཁྱབ་བྱེད་གང་གིས་ངེས་པར་ཁྱབ་པ that which is fully encompassed or covered over by another object is called *khyab-byed*.

ངེས་གྲོལ *ñes-grol* (*ñe-dol*) निर्मोच, स्वर्ग=ངེས་པར་གྲོལ, *i.e.*, འཁོར་བ་དང་ནད་དང་སྡུག་བསྔལ་ལས་གྲོལ། liberation from the transmigratory existence, disease, and suffering.

ངེས་འགྲོ *ñes-hgro* transmigration; ངེས་པར་འགྲོ་ངན་སོང་མཐོ་རིས་དག་ཞིང་སོགས་སུ། return to another state of existence after death, either to hell or heaven, or to any non-earthly place.

ངེས་རྒྱལ *ñes-rgyal*=ངེས་པར་རྒྱལ निस्तरण certain victory; triumph. དགྲ་བདུད་ཉོན་མོངས་ལས triumph over enemies, the devil and misery, is described as *ñes rgyal*.

ངེས་སྒྲ *ñes-sgra* निह्राद a real sound; སེམས་ལ་ངེས་པའི་སྒྲ་ཐོས་པ any sound that has made an impression in the mind.

ངེས་སྒྲོགས *ñes-sgrogs* निर्घोष emphasis; any proclamation; reading letters or sacred writings loudly that there may not be any mistake about them.

ངེས་ཆེར་མེད *ñes-cher-med* it is not quite sure; I do not know for certain.

ངེས་འཇུག་པ *ñes-hjugs-pa* आश्वास assurance; to assure; དགེ་བ་དང་སྡིག་པའི་ལས་སོགས་ལ་ངེས་འཇུག་པ to enter on good and bad actions.

ངེས་འཇོམས *ñes-hjoms* fully subduing an enemy, the devil, etc.

ངེས་བརྗོད *ñes-brjod* a true and authoritative expression; ངེས་བརྗོད་ཀྱི་རིག་བྱེད ऋग्वेद, ऋच: the Rig Veda; true sayings or revelations.

ངེས་ཉམ *ñes-ñam* the certain fall or degeneration.

ངེས་ཐོབ *ñes-thob* निष्ठा the real or certain gain; it is explained thus: འཇིག་རྟེན་གྱི་ནོར་རྫས་སམ, གོ་ས་སོགས་སངས་རྒྱས་ཀྱི་ས་ལམ་ གོ་འཕང་སོགས་ངེས་པར་ཐོབ། *ñes-par-thob is* the gaining of wealth, honour, or sainthood, Buddhahood, the stages to it, &c.

ངེས་དག *ñes-dag* निष्पात:;=ངེས་པར་དག purification; cleansing; སྐྱོན་དང་དྲི་མ་སྡིག་སྒྲིབ་སོགས་དག་པ sure cleansing of faults, defilements, stains, sins, etc.

ངེས་དོན *ñes-don* नीतार्थ;=ངེས་པའི་དོན or དོན་དམ་པ certain and true meaning or import; also immediate or absolute knowledge of the truth.

ངེས་གདུང་ *ńes-gduń* उपाक=ངེས་པར་གདུང་བ anything that gives sure pain: སྡུག་བསྔལ་དང་ཉོན་མོངས་ཀྱི་མེ་དང་ཉི་མས་ངེས་པར་གདུང་བ misery and sufferings which like fire and rays of the sun burn with certainty.

ངེས་སྣང་ *ńes-snań*=དངོས་པོ་མཚུངས or འདྲ་བ *hdra-ba* similar things; also similarity in things (*Mńon.*).

ངེས་པ་ཅན *ńes-pa-can* real; actual.

ངེས་པ་ཉིད་དུ *ńes-pa ñid-du* in reality; truly; in truth; really.

ངེས་པའི་ཕུང་པོ *ńes-pahi phuń-po* नियतस्कन्ध =ངེས་པ་ཐམས་ཅད all things perceivable and realisable: དཔེར་ན་གཟུགས་ཀྱི་ཕུང་པོ་ཞེར་ན་གཟུགས་སུ་གྱུར་པ་ཐམས་ཅད་བསྡུས་པ་ལྟ་བུ། for example, *rūpa-skandha* signifies all that has been transmuted into bodily form collected together.

ངེས་པར *ńes-par* अवश्य, नून adv. certainly; surely; really; to be sure.

Syn. གོར་མ་ཆག་པ *gor-ma chag-pa* (*Mńon.*).

ངེས་པར་ཀུན་སྦྱིན *ńes-par kun-sbyin* अपादान removal; ངེས་པར་འགྲོ་བ་ཀུན་ལ་སྦྱིན་པས giving in charity to all living beings; ཡང་རང་གི་དངོས་པོ་ཀུན་ངེས་པར་སྦྱིན་ན། or consists in giving over one's properties to others.

ངེས་པར་སྐྱེ་བ *ńes-par skye-wa* sure produce or infallible results; for instance ཐོས་པ་ལས་ཡོན་ཏན་ངེས་པར་སྐྱེ་བ from study knowledge is the sure result; བསྒོམས་པ་ལས་རྟོགས་པ from meditation true thought (enlightenment) is produced; སྨོན་ལམ་གྱི་དབང་གིས་དག་ཞིང་དུ from the power of resolute will, birth in a happier state is ensured; ལས་ཀྱི་དབང་གིས་ངེས་པར་སྐྱེ by force of *las* (*i.e.* of *Karma*) one is born in the transmigratory state; རྒྱུ་ལས་འབྲས་བུ་འབྱོར་ from cause fruit is evolved.

ངེས་པར་དགའ་བ *ńes-par dgah-wa* perfect satisfaction; to be really pleased.

ངེས་པར་འགུགས *ńes-par hgugs* निङ्कुपित the act of bringing under one's own sure possession or power any wished-for property or person by the exercise of occult powers.

ངེས་པར་འགྱུར་བ *ńes-par hgyur-wa*=མ་འོངས་པ नियाम the future; that will be; that is destined to come.

ངེས་པར་འགྲོ་བ *ńes-par hgro-wa* निस्सरणं to go to certainty, *i.e.*, to *Nirvāṇa* or emancipation from the sufferings of the world.

ངེས་པར་རྒྱལ་བ *ńes-par rgyal-wa* to be completely victorious; to bring a certain thing or person under one's command or control.

ངེས་པར་བརྒལ་བ *ńes-par brgal-wa*,=མཐར་ཕྱིན་པ निस्तार one who has arrived at a sure conclusion; one who has attained to an absolute state; one who has been saved or emancipated.

ངེས་པར་གཅོད་པ *ńes-par-gcod-pa* lit. to cut sure; to make certain; अवश्यभव्य something that will certainly happen; ངེས་པར་ཆོད *ńes-par-chod* to prevent the occurrence of ominous events by means of mystical charms.

ངེས་པར་འཇུག་པ *ńes-par-hjug-pa* to establish firmly.

ངེས་པར་མཉན་བྱས *ńes-par mñan-byas*=ཁས་བླངས་པ anything promised; an undertaking (*Mńon.*).

ངེས་པར་རྟོགས་པ *ńes-par rtogs-pa* or ཞུ་རྗེ་རྟག་བ निरूपण true investigation; same as ལེགས་པར་རྟོགས་པ अवकल्पना, to arrive at the truth of a thing or in a wider sense to reflect on the true signification or import of a word or expression, as to whether the right conclusion has been arrived at, etc.

ངེས་པར་བརྟན་པ *ńes-par brtan-pa* ध्रुव, निष्पाप certainty; the state free from sin; the state of reality.

ངེས་པར་བསྟན་པ *ńes-par bstan-pa* ग्राह्मं established religion or doctrine.

ངེས་པར་གནོད་མཛད *ńes-par gnod-mdsad* lit. one who really does mischief; निग्रह an epithet of a deity of wrathful mien.

ངེས་པར་བརྣགས་པ *ńeş-par brnagş-pa* = ངེས་པར་བསམས་པ to be convinced of a thing or occurrence; conviction.

ངེས་པར་སྤངས་པ *ńeş-par şpańş-pa* प्रतिनिसर्ग perfect renunciation.

ངེས་པར་བྱེད་པ *ńeş-par byeḍ-pa* to fix, settle, establish; to make certain.

ངེས་པར་འབྱིན་པ *ńeş-par ḥbyin-pa* नैर्य्याणिक to be evolved; to draw or pull out.

ངེས་པར་འབྱུང་བས་བརྟེན नैष्क्रम्यस्त ;= འཁོར་བ་ལས་ངེས་པར་འབྱུང་བས་བརྟེན། based upon the certain liberation from transmigratory existence; acc. to *Schtr.* deliverance from the round of transmigration.

ངེས་པར་འབྱེད་པའི་ཆ་དང་མཐུན་པའི་རིམ་བཞི, निर्भेदभागियाः the four distinct orders agreeing with tho analytical stages of saintly perfection are:—(1) དྲོ་བར་གྱུར་བ ऊष्मागतम् process of moral development; (2) རྩེ་མོ मूर्द्धा the climax, *i.e.*, reaching the crowning stago; (3) བཟོད་པ क्षान्ति perfect patience; (4) འཇིག་རྟེན་པའི་ཆོས་ཀྱི་མཆོག लौकिकाग्रधर्म्म tho highest worldly good.

ངེས་པར་སྦྱོར *ńeş-par-şbyor* संविनियोजन permanently-engaged or fully-employed.

ངེས་པར་འཛིན་པ *ńeş-par-ḥdsin-pa* प्रतिनिर्द्धारण holding firmly; to be convinced.

ངེས་པར་བཟུང་ *ńeş-par-bzuń* विनीत lit. held fast; brought under discipline.

ངེས་པར་ལེགས་པ *ńeş-par legş-pa* निःश्रेयस really blessed and good; deliverance from transmigratory existence; *summum bonum.*

ངེས་པར་སེམས་པ *ńeş-par semş-pa* to make up the mind; to form a resolution; ངེས་པར་སེམས་པ་བྱེད to ascertain.

ངེས་པོ *ńeş-po* निष्ठ the certain, fixed; the inevitable.

ངེས་སྤེལ *ńeş-şpel* or ངེས་པར་སྤེལ प्रणीत real progress; རིགས་རྒྱུད་དང་བསྟན་པ་ངེས་སྤེལ advancement or spread of family and religion.

ངེས་འབབ *ńeş-ḥbab* सङ्घटन a veritable event.

ངེས་འབྱུང་ *ńeş-ḥbyuń,* निःसरण one of the three principal ways to *Nirvāṇa* that are called ལམ་གྱི་གཙོ་བོ་རྣམ་གསུམ. It is described as འཁོར་བ་ལ་ཞེ་ལོག་ནས་ཡིད་སྐྱོ། repentance caused by disgust at worldly matters. སེམས་ཅན་ཀུན་ལ་ཡོངས་པའི་རྒྱུ་མཚན་ཞུས་པས་ངེས་འབྱུང་དྲག་པོ་སྐྱེས Having inquired the whole of what would happen to all living beings, a strong aversion to matters worldly arose.

ངེས་མེད *ńeş-meḍ* 1. n. of a number. 2. uncertain; undefined; homeless.

ངེས་སྨོད *ńeş-şmoḍ* निर्वाद curse.

ངེས་ཚིག *ńeş-tshig* निरुक्त, निपात lit. real term; real signification; real meaning.

ངེས་ཚོགས *ńeş-tshogş* निचय many; a multitude.

ངེས་ཤེས་སྐྱེས *ńeş-çeş şkyeş* birth of faith, also the growth of the knowledge of reality in the mind; full faith in the doctrine of retribution (*Karma* and *Phala*).

ངེས་གསལ *ńeş-gsal* निकाश elucidation.

ངེས་ཡམ་ཤུང་ *Ńeş-yam-çuń* n. of a place in Tibet (*Deb.* ག *25*).

ངོ *ńo* I: num. fig. 124.

ངོ II: मुख, resp. ཞལ་ངོ, face; countenance; air; look; the original. བདག་གི་ངོ་ལ་གཟིགས་ནས when (she, my mother) shall have seen my face; རང་གི་ཕུ་བོ་རྣམས་ཀྱི་ངོ་བལྟ་དགོས you must watch the looks of your elder brothers.

ངོ་ཀྲོ *ńo-kro* (*ńo-ṭo*) n. of a capitation tax (*Yig.*); lit. tax on the face, *i.e.*, head-tax.

ངོ་དཀར་པོ *ńo-ḍkar-po* a cheerful face.

ངོ་བསྐྱོད་པ *ńo-bşkyoḍ-pa* to go or move personally.

ངོ་ལྐོག *ńo-lkog* adj. public and private; open and secret.

ངོ་ཁྲལ *ño-khral* मुखदण्ड poll-tax.

ངོ་གྲངས *ño-grañs* = དངོས་གྲངས individual number; enumeration of individual things.

ངོ་ཆེ *ño-che* personal appreciation; recognition of one's service or kindness: ལོ་ཙཱ་བས་དཀའ་བ་དཔག་ཏུ་མེད་པ་མཛད་ནས་ངོ་ཆེ་ལགས་རེ་ཞུས་པས་ཀྱང་མ་གནང་། (*A. 103*) the *Lo-tsa-wa* (on the ground of) having undergone immeasureable hardships, prayed for the acceptance of his request, but it was not acceded to.

ངོ་ཆེན *ño-chen* (lit. the great self) a man of influence; ངོ་ཆེན་བྱེད་པ to intercede (only men of higher position being able to intercede); མི་ལ་ངོ་ཆེན་འཚོལ་བ to seek a great man to intercede; to seek intervention.

ངོ་ལྟོས *ño-ltos* = དཔོན་གཡོག master and his servant.

ངོ་བསྟོད *ño-stod* praise to the face of a person; open flattery.

ངོ་ཐོག *ño-thog* true; genuine; really.

ངོ་ཐོན་པ *ño-thon-pa* = ངོ་ཐོ་ཡོད་པ one in rank or position; to rise to dignity.

+ ངོ་མཐོན་པ *ño-mthon-pa* = ནན་གྱིས earnestly; pressingly; with persistence.

ངོ་ནག कालमुख 1. "black-face"; ངོ་ནག་པར་འདུག་པ to sit with a gloomy face: ངོ་ནག་པར་འགྱུར་པ to grow sorrowful; to turn dark with fright, pain, etc. 2. n. of an *Asura*; ངོ་གནགས་ཏེ frowning or becoming gloomy with sorrow. 3. n. of one of the 28 "curious religious sects" of Ancient India, followers of which used to paint their faces black (*M.V.*).

ངོ་གནོང་བ *ño-gnoñ-wa* to be ashamed; unable to show one's face for shame.

ངོ་སྤྲོད་པ *ño-sprod-pa* to indentify; to point out; acc. to *Jä.* to lay open the features; to show the nature of a thing; to explain.

ངོ་བོ *ño-bo* भाव, स्वभाव essence; substance; intrinsic nature; རང་གི་ངོ་བོས in itself; acc. to its own nature; by nature; naturally.

Syn. དངོས་པོ *dños-po*; རང་བཞིན *rañ-bshin*; རང་གཞུགས *rañ-gjugs*; ངོ་བོ་ཉིད *ño-bo-ñid* (*Mñon.*).

ངོ་བོ་ཉིད *ño-bo-ñid*, v. ངོ་བོ སེམས་ཀྱི་ངོ་བོ་ཉིད temperament; acc. to *Was.* character.

ངོ་འབབ་པ *ño hbab-pa* to be dejected; adj. discouraged; downcast; in *W.* bashful.

ངོ་མ *ño-ma* the original, v. ངོ.

ངོ་མི་རྟག་པ *ño mi-rtag-pa* unsteady; changeable; one who is vacillating; one who has no personality (*Yig.*).

ངོ་མི་ཆོད་པ *ño mi-chod-pa* = ངོ་མི་ཐོད་པ or ངོ་མི་བཟློག་པ उपरोधशील one who listens to or does a thing to please another which he would not otherwise have done; to be unable to refuse or oppose.

ངོ་མི་ཤེས་པ *ño-mi-çes-pa* not knowing or recognizing; unknown; *incognito*.

ངོ་མིག *ño-mig* in *W.* boldness; ངོ་མིག་ཅན or ངོ་མིག་ཆེན་པོ bold; courageous; daring (*Jä.*).

ངོ་མེད་ལྐོག་མེད *ño-med lkog-med* acc. to *Cs.* acting in the same manner in public as in private life; ingenuous.

ངོ་ཚ *ño-tsha* लज्जा, ह्री, त्रपा shame; blushing of the face: ངོ་ཚ་ཞུམ pf. blushed; felt shame; ངོ་ཚ་རུ་འཇུག་པ ह्रेपयति to put to shame.

Syn. ཞུམ་བྱེད *shum-byed*; མིག་དམའ *mig-dmah*; ངོ་དམའ *ño-dmah*; འཛེམ་མདོག *hdsem-mdog*; བག་ཡོད *bag-yod*; བག་ལྡན *bag-ldan*; ངོ་ཚ་ཤེས *ño-tsha-çes*; ཁྲེལ་ཡོད *khrel-yod*; ཁྲེལ་ལྡན *khrel-ldan*; ངོ་ཚའི་ཚུལ་ཅན *ño-tshahi tshul-can* (*Mñon.*).

ངོ་ཚ་ཅན *ño-tsha-can* one who has shame; is bashful.

ངོ་ཚ་བ *ño tsha-wa* or ངོ་ཚ་ཤེས་པར་བྱེད་པ to feel shame; blush.

ངོ་ཚ་མེད་ *ṅo-tsha-med* or ངོ་ཚ་ཁྲེལ་མེད་ shameless; immodest; impudent.

Syn. ལོག་པར་སྤོབས་ *log-par-spobs*; སྤྱི་བརྟོལ་ཅན་ *spyi-brtol-can*; དཔྲལ་མགོ་སྟུག་པོ་ *dpral-mgo-stug-po*; གདོང་ཆེན་ཅན་ *gdoṅ-chen-can*; འཚེར་བ་མེད་ *htsher-wa-med*; སྐྱེངས་པ་མེད་ *skyeṅs-wa-med*; མུ་ཅོར་ཚུགས་མེད་ *mu-cor tshugs-med*; ངོ་མི་བསྲུང་ *ṅo-mi-bsruṅ*; གནོང་མེད་ *gnoṅ-med* (*Mṅon.*).

ངོ་ཚབ་ *ṅo-tshab*=སྐུ་ཚབ་ *sku-tshab* a representative; a proxy (*Yig. k. 53*).

ངོ་མཚར་ *ṅo-mtshar* wonder ངོ་མཚར་ཅན་ अद्भुत wondering; wonderful; ངོ་མཚར་ཆེ་ amazement; ངོ་མཚར་བ་ exciting curiosity; to be curious; to wonder.

ངོ་རྫུན་རྒྱབ་པ་ *ṅo-rdsun rgyab-pa* to disguise; to put under a false garb; also to garble.

ངོ་གཡོག་ *ṅo-gyog* or ངོ་མ་དང་གཡོག་པོ་=དཔོན་གཡོག་ master (himself) and servant.

ངོ་རུ་ *ṅo-ru* or ངོར་ in the face; =ངོ་ངར་དུ་ in the face of; before the eyes.

ངོ་ལོག་མཁན་ *ṅo-log-mkhan* a rebel, mutineer; ངོ་ལོག་ཅན་ seditious; faithless; rebellious.

ངོ་ལོག་པ་ *ṅo-log-pa*=ངོ་ལྡོག་པ་ to turn the face against; to revolt; to rebel against; to oppose.

ངོ་ཤུས་ *ṅo-çus* a copy from the original.

ངོ་ཤེས་པ་ *ṅo-çes-pa* प्रत्यभिज्ञान to know a person or thing; to recognize an acquaintance.

ངོ་སོ་ *ṅo-so* joy; sometimes for ངོ་བསོ་ a high title or dignity: ངོ་སོ་ཆེ་བར་འོང་ you will have great joy; he will obtain high dignity; སྦྱིན་པ་ངོ་སོ་བྱེད་པ་ to make presents or give alms to another to his full satisfaction.

ངོ་སྲུངས་ *ṅo-sruṅs* 1. regard to the opinion of others; an aiming at applause. 2. body-guard: ང་ལ་དཔོན་མེད་གཡོག་མེད་ངོ་བསྲུང་མེད་ *ṅa-la dpon-med gyog-med ṅo-bsruṅ-med* I have no master, no servant, none to guard me (*A. 7*).

ངོ་བསོ་མཐོན་པོ་ *ṅo-bso mthon-po* a high title or position; one in exalted position.

ངོ་བསོད་བྱ་བ་ *ṅo-bsod bya-wa* to praise one to the face; to flatter; to eulogise.

ངོག *Ṅog* n. of a place in Tibet where the monastery of Shong was founded by Lama *Çes-rab-mchog* of Myur (*Deb.* ཀ *4*).

ངོགས *ṅogs* तीर the bank of a river or lake; འཇུག་ངོགས་=ཆུ་ངོགས་ a place on the bank of a river where people crossing it; land. Acc. to *Jä.* mountain side; slope; ghaut.

Syn. འགྲམ་ *hgram.*

ངོགས་ཐོབ *ṅogs-thob* n. of a number (*Ya-sel. 57*).

ངོམ *Ṅom* 1. n. of a place in Tibet (*Deb.* ཀ *30*). 2. satisfaction: ངོམ་དུ་ཉུང་བ་ཞིག་ཕོ་བོས་བྱེད་པ་ཡིན་མོད་ I indeed accomplished something very satisfactory (*A. 152*).

ངོམ་པ་ *ṅom-pa*, pf. ངོམས་པ་ तृप्त, सन्तुष्ट; ནོར་ངོམས་ལྟ་བུ་ to satisfy one's self with gain; to be contented: མ་ངོམས་ I am not satisfied; ངོམས་ཚད་འཐུང་བ་ to drink one's fill.

ངོམས་པ་ *ṅoms-pa* sbst. 1. तृप्ति contentment; satisfaction. 2. oblation for quenching the thirst of the Yidag. 3. a hermit; a recluse in the wilderness who enjoys contentment; ངོམས་པ་མེད་པ་ insatiable: ངོམས་པར་འགྱུར་ विगतपिपासः भवति his thirst will be quenched; his desire will be fulfilled.

Syn. ཚིམ་པ་ *tshim-pa*; ཆོག་པ་ *chog-pa*; ཡོངས་བསྲུང་ *yoṅs-bsruṅ*; ལག་པ་འགེབས་ *lag-pa-hgebs* (*Mṅon.*).

ངོར *Ṅor* 1. v. under ངོ་ *ṅo*. 2. n. of a monastery of the *Sa-skya-pa* School; n. of a district in Tibet.

ངོས *ṅos* पच्च 1. side; margin; edge; surface; མདུན་ངོས front side; ལྷོ་ངོས *lho-ṅos* southern side or slope; ངོས་གཅིག one side. 2.=ངང་ in the state of: བདེ་བ་བཞུགས་པའི་ངོས་ནས། while in the state of being happy; while prosperous; མེ་ལོང་གི་ངོས=མེ་ལོང་གི་ལོགས the surface of a mirror; སའི་ངོས the surface of the earth. 3. basis or foundation.

ངོས་རྒྱུད *ṅos-rgyud*=དངོས་བརྒྱུད personally.

ངོས་འབྱོར་རྟགས *ṅos-ḥbyor rtags* 1. a receipt or sign of having received a thing. 2. original sign or signification.

ངོས་ཟིན་པ *ṅos-zin-pa*=དངོས་ཟིན་པ vb. 1. to be selfish. 2.=ངོས་ལོང་ self interested: དེ་བས་རང་རྐྱེན་ངོས་ལོང་གསལ་བར་ཤོད། therefore, clear of self-interest, confess your faults (*Rdsa.* *15*).

ངོས་ཡངས *ṅos-yaṅs* विपुलपार्श्व breadth.

ངོས་ཤུས *ṅos-çus* a copy from the original.

ངོས་སུ *ṅos-su* openly; publicly; plainly.

དངགས་སྙན *dṅags-sñan*=ངག་སྙན, v. སྙན་ངགས काव्य poetry; a poem.

དངང་བ *dṅaṅ-wa*, pf. དངངས त्रासित, to be out of breath; to pant; to feel oppressed, *e.g.*, when plunged into cold water, but especially when frightened and terrified. 2. to be frightened; to fear; to be afraid of: ཅེས་དངངས་ནས thus being affrighted.

དངངས་སྐྲག *dṅaṅs-skrag* त्रास, त्रातङ्क in colloq. great fear; panic.

Syn. འཇིགས་སྐྲག *jigs-skrags.*

དངངས་པ *dṅaṅs-pa* त्रास 1. fear དངངས་པར་གྱུར་ཏེ he became frightened. Often pleonastically joined with སྐྲག or འཇིགས or with both. 2.=དྲི་བྲལ निर्मल pure; clean.

དངན་འཐེན་པ *dṅan-ḥthen-pa* misappropriation; not returning things taken away from another.

དངར *dṅar* or དངར་བ 1. nectar; sometimes used for མངར sweet; དངར་རོ sweet taste. 2. ཚར་དུ་དངར་བ=གྲལ་བསྒྲིགས to put in order; to arrange properly.

དངུད་མོ *dṅud-mo*=ངུད་མོ *ṅud-mo* (*Sch.*).

དངུལ *dṅul* कलधौत, रजत, रूप्य silver; money. The kind of silver called མཚོག་ཙན is imported into Tibet from Khorasan. The silver current in Tibet consists of ingots, Indian rupees, and a thin native coin, the *chō-tang* or *tang-ka.*

དངུལ་སྐམ *dṅul-skam* पारारस oxide of mercury.

དངུལ་སྐུད *dṅul-skud* silver-wire.

དངུལ་སྐེད *dṅul-skyed* silver-belt.

དངུལ་ཁ *dṅul-kha* रूप्य-खनि silver mine; silver vein; དངུལ་ཁ་འདོན་པ to work a silver mine.

དངུལ་ཁུག *dṅul-khug* or དངུལ་སྒྱིག money-bag; purse for silver coins.

དངུལ་འགག *dṅul-ḥgag* a silver cup or silver slate.

དངུལ་རྐྱན *dṅul-rkyan* goblet made of silver: དངུལ་རྐྱན་ཆང་ལ་དངུལ་དམ་ཨ་རག་ཏོད། silver goblet for beer and silver cup for *arrack* (*Jig.*).

དངུལ་ཆུ *dṅul-chu* पारद, घनसार quicksilver.

Syn. འདེད་བྱེད *ḥded-byed*; འཕྲོག་བྱེད *ḥphrog-byed*; ས་བོན *sa-bon*; མེས་འཛིན་ *mes-ḥehiṅ*; དངུལ་བྱེད *dṅul-byed*; དག་པའི་ཁམས *dag-paḥi-khams*; ཁམས་ཆེན་པོ *khams-chen-po*; མཚལ་སྐྱེས *mtshal-skyes*; རྒྱུག་བྱེད *rgyug-byed* (*Mṅon.*).

དངུལ་ཏིག *dṅul-tig* one of the six kinds of bitters which are, viz:—གཟེར་ཏིག, ཟངས་ཏིག, དངུལ་ཏིག, ལྕགས་ཏིག, སུམ་བཅུ་ཏིག, གུར་ཏིག, stated to possess wonderful healing virtues.

དངུལ་རྟ་མིག་མ *dṅul-rta-mig-ma* silver ingots in the shape of a horse-hoof, weighing about 165 *tolas* or rupees imported into Tibet from China.

དངུལ་དམ *dṅul-dam* wine-cup made of silver.

དངུལ་དུལ་མ *dṅul dul-ma* silver-ink (*Sch.*).

དངུལ་རྡོ *dṅul-rdo* रूप्यमाचिक hœmatite ore of iron; this term is also applied to a kind of stone on which silver is tested.

དངུལ་ཕོར *dṅul-phor* रूप्यखोलक wooden cup mounted with silver used by the higher classes in Tibot for drinking tea.

དངུལ་རྨིག *dṅul-rmig* bar or ingot of silver.

དངུལ་ཚགས *dṅul-tshags* silver-work on copper, brass, or iron; plating of silver on articles made of those metals.

དངུལ་བཟོ *dṅul-bzo* रूप्यकर्मी silversmith.

དངུལ་ཧོ་ཁ་མ *dṅul-ho-kha-ma* the purest silver imported into Tibet from China.

དངུལ་ལི *dṅul-li* one tenth of the measure called ཧོན *hon*.

དངུལ་སྲང *dṅul-sraṅ* an ounce of silver; used as an equivalent of current money in Tibet, = to one Chinese *tael.*

དངོ *dṅo* 1. edge; also = ཆུ་ཡི་ངོགས shore; bank. 2. = གྲི་ཡི་སོ the edge of a knifo; རྟ་ལྕགས་ཀྱི་དངོ། "edge of whip-cord"; lash of a whip (*Jä.*). 3. = གྲི་ཡུ handle of a knife (*Cs.*).

དངོམ་པ *dṅom-pa* = དངོམ་བརྗིད brightness splendour.

དངོམ་བ = དངོམ་ཅན shining; bright (*Cs.*); དངོམ་ཆེ *dṅom-che* very bright, cf. ངོམ་པ.

དངོས *dṅos* (in Gram.) मूल 1. original; reality; real; very self; དངོས་དང་སྒྱུམ reality and illusion; སངས་རྒྱས་དངོས tho real Buddha; ལྷ་དངོས the real god (not the image); དངོས is equivalent to ངོ་བོག real; reality. 2. proper; genuine; true; positive (opp. to negative); personal; དངོས་ཡོད་པ personally present. 3. གཙོ मुख्य chief, principal; དངོས་སུ in bodily form, *e.g.*, to appear bodily: འ་ཡིག་དངོས་སུ་མེད་ཀྱང་། even though the letter འ is not actually written there.

དངོས་སྐྱེས *dṅos-skyes* personal present: ལེ་རྒྱམ་ཕྱུག་གི་མཚན་ཡིག་གསལ་གྱི་དངོས་སྐྱེས་ཉམས་མེད་འབྱོར། one roll of fine serge, as specified in the letter, sent as a personal present has without damage arrived (*Yig. k.*).

དངོས་གྲུབ *dṅos-grub* (*ṅoi-dub*) सिद्धि 1. the accomplishment or acquisition of the real thing sought for; gen. perfection or excellence; anything superior; acc. to *Jä.* honour, riches, talents, and esp. wisdom, higher knowledge, and spiritual power, as far as they are not acquired by ordinary study and exercise, but have sprung from within spontaneously or in consequence of long and continued contemplation. In Buddhism དངོས་གྲུབ seems to denote consummation of worldly as well as spiritual objects. Temporal acquirements are called ཐུན་མོང་གི་དངོས་གྲུབ, general or ordinary consummation (in reference to material objects); the other is called མཆོག་གི་དངོས་གྲུབ, the supreme consummation, which is the attainment of Buddhahood, *i.e.*, *Nirvāṇa*. The following are the eight ordinary *dṅos-grub* or ཐུན་མོང་གི་དངོས་གྲུབ as enumerated in the sacred books of the Northern Buddhists:—(1) རལ་གྲིའི་དངོས་གྲུབ the enchanted sword made so by some mystical religious process; for instance, if any one touching it wishes to acquire any object, merit, power, etc., he gets it; (2) རིལ་བུའི་དངོས་གྲུབ efficacy of magical pills; by some religious charms medicated pills are made to possess wonderful healing properties; by their use one may become healthy and fine looking; (3) མིག་སྨན་གྱི་དངོས་གྲུབ a medicine for the eye by the use of which one is able to see things in an occult manner; (4) རྐང་མགྱོགས་ཀྱི་དངོས་གྲུབ the power of walking miraculously and swiftly, generally by the efficacy of some enchanted leaf or leaves; (5) བཅུད་ལེན་གྱི་དངོས་གྲུབ the magical elixir by using which an old man of eighty may look like a young man of twenty; (6) མཁའ་སྤྱོད་ཀྱི་དངོས་གྲུབ the occult process of miraculously vanishing bodily into the state of the gods; (7) མི་སྣང་བའི་དངོས་གྲུབ the power of miraculously disappearing from an assembly, etc., without being seen by anybody; (8) ས་འོག་གི་དངོས་གྲུབ the power of passing through a wall, mountain, or earthly barrier, without any difficulty.

དངོས་ངན *dṅos-ṅan* = རིད་པ or སྦེད་པ *sbed-pa* कृश lean (in body); thin; emaciated.

དངོས་འཇུག *dṅos-hjug* the matter or the subject of a work (*Tsa-ṭika.*).

དངོས་རྙེད *dṅos-rñed* real or substantial gain; also obtaining one's object; anxious; thoughtful.

དངོས་དོད *dṅos-dod* the original text; the principal part of a work.

དངོས་པོ *dṅos-po* वस्तु, मूल, अर्थ, द्रव्य, पद, भवत्व 1. property in gold or silver; substance; belongings; goods; furniture; utensils; article; position: ངས་དངོས་པོ་དམར་དམར་སྤྲད་པ་ཡིན། I have given cash, lit. red cash or gold: ཇོ་བོ་བུད་མེད་དང་འབྲེལ་བའི་དངོས་པོ་གང་ཡང་ཕྱག་ཏུ་མི་བཞེས། (*A.* 50) the Lord (Atis'a) does not touch (receive) with his hand any article connected with (*i.e.*, belonging to) woman. དངོས་པོ་མེད་པ immaterial, unreal; also worthless, poor, hollow; དངོས་པོ་མཚན अनुभव experience; དངོས་པོར་བྱས་པ = རྫས་སུ་བྱས་པ वस्तुकृत made material, substantial; དགའ་བའི་དངོས་པོ object or matter of rejoicing. 2. occurrence, events, action 3. in Buddhism subject matters; properties; virtue: དངོས་པོ་ལ་བཞི་འམ་དགུ་འམ་ཉི་ཤུ་རྩ་དགུའི་དབང་དུ་བྱས་ནས་ཆོས་རྣམས་བསྡུས་ཚེ་ངས་གང་དུ་བསྟན་པ་དེ་ནི་མདོ་སྡེ་ཡིན་ནོ། I have compiled subject-matters classifying them under four, nine or twenty-nine heads, that is *Sūtrānta*, wherein I have explained religious matters (*K. d.* ཆ *73*).

དངོས་པོ་སྒྲུབ་པ *dṅos-po sgrub-pa* to bring a thing about; to set it on foot or a-going; as a philosophical term, substance, matter; དངོས་པོར་འཛིན་པ the belief in the reality of the existence of matter, holding it as simple and absolute. In Buddhist ontology there are eight kinds of དངོས་པོ भावत्व or states:—(1) རྣམ་མཁྱེན wisdom; (2) ལམ་ཤེས་ཉིད knowledge of the ways and means; (3) ཐམས་ཅད་ཤེས་པ་ཉིད सर्वज्ञता omniscience; (4) རྣམ་ཀུན་མངོན་རྫོགས་རྟོགས་པ the contemplation of (the possibility of) bringing all things into perfection; (5) རྩེ་མོར་ཕྱིན་པ reaching the climax; the state of attaining to the highest point of moral excellence; (6) མཐར་གྱིས་པ attainment to finality, *i.e.*, emancipation; (7) སྐད་ཅིག་མ་གཅིག་གིས་མངོན་པར་རྫོགས་པར་བྱང་ཆུབ་པའི་སྦྱོར་བ། to attain to the perfected state of enlightenment in an instant; (8) ཆོས་ཀྱི་སྐུ धर्मकाय the supreme, spiritual existence.

དངོས་པོ་མཚུངས *dṅis-po mtshuṅs*, v. ངེས་སྣང

དངོས་པོ་བཞི *dṅos-po gshi*, abbr. of བསོད་ནམས་ཀྱི་དངོས་པོ་བཞི the four articles of merit.

དངོས་མ *dṅos-ma* orginal; natural; natural productions (*Cs.*).

དངོས་མིང *dṅos-miṅ* 1. the proper or real name of a thing. 2. the noun substantive.

དངོས་མེད *dṅos-med* དངོས་པོ་མེད་པ अभव unreal; that was never born nor existed: ཆོས་ཐམས་ཅད་དངོས་པོ་མེད་པ अवस्तुक सर्वधर्मा *(M. V.)* all objects are unsubstantial, immaterial, not existing (*Cs.* and *Was.*).

དངོས་གཙང *dños-gtsañ* lit. pure in substance; originally pure; of the first or superior quality.

དངོས་འཛིན *dños-hdsin* identification; also holding as one's own; possession of worldly objects: འཇིག་རྟེན་གྱི་ ཡོ་བྱད་དང་ སྡུད་ལག་ རྣམས་ལ་ བདག་ཏུ་ འཛིན་པ། to hold as real and belonging to one's self things worldly which are unreal and therefore nobody's.

དངོས་གཞི *dños-gshi* मूल, वस्तु, मूल the basis of a thing; the thing itself.

དངོས་ཤུགས *dños-çugs* abbr. of དངོས་བསྟན and ཤུགས་བསྟན, honest belief in a doctrine and also apparent belief in it.

དངོས་སུ *dños-su* in actual substance.

དངོས་སློབ *dños-slob* direct or personal disciple—Ananda was the personal disciple of Buddha.

མངག་པ *mñag-pa*, pf. མངགས, to commission, charge, send, delegate, *i.e.*, a messenger, commissary, etc.

མངག་གཞུག *mñag-gshug* also མངག་གཞུག་པ प्रेष्य, किङ्कर a messenger, emissary, servant, slave.

Syn. གཡོག་པོ *gyog-po*; བྲན *bran* (*Mñon.*).

མངགས་པ་ཅན *mñags-pa-can* दूत a messenger; envoy.

མངགས་བྱ་བྱེད *mñags-bya-byed* one executing a mission; a commissioner.

+ **མངན** *mñan* शाप མཐུ་ཧྲུ་བུ a curse; a necromantic injury; མངན་བགྲང་བ enumeration of curses (*Cs.*).

མངན་པ *mñan-pa* to curse; to execrate.

མངའ *mñah* resp. for དབང་ might, dominion, sway, power; མངའ་མཛད་པ to govern, to rule; མངའ་རྙེས་པ to obtain power; མངའ་སྒྱུར་བ *mñah-sgyur-wa* to have mastered a thing; to understand thoroughly.

མངའ་བརྙེས་པ *mñah brñes-pa*=དབང་ཐོབ་པ to get authority, power, etc.; to be authorized, v. མངའ་མཛད་པ (*Mñon.*).

མངའ་ཐང་ *mñah-thañ* power, might.

Syn. བསགས་རྒྱབ *bsags-rgyab*; སྔོན་བསགས *sñon-bsags*; ལྷས་བསྟན་པ *lhas-btan-pa*; བགོ་སྐལ *bgo-skal*; སྔོན་བྱས *sñon-byas*; སྔོན་གྱི་ལས *sñon-gyi-las*; ལྷས་བསྐྱབ *lhas-bskyob*; གནམ་བསྐྱོས *gnam-bskyos*; ཆས་བསྐྱོས *chas-bskyos*; སྐལ་ལྡན *skal-ldan*; དབང་ཐང་ *dwañ-thañ* (*Mñon.*).

མངའ་ཐང་ཅན *mñah-thañ-can* powerful; one in power.

མངའ་བདག *mñah-bdag* विभु, अधिपति, प्रभु lord; owner; master; sovereign; an epithet of Buddha (*M.V.*).

མངའ་བདག་ཁོ་རེ *Mñah-bdag kho-re* n. of a certain early king of Tibet (*Loñ.* ཞ 7).

མངའ་བདག་ཁྲི་རལ་པ *Mñah-bdag Khr Ra* or Ralpachan, the famous king of Tibet who greatly patronized Buddhism and also extended the limits of his dominions to the borders of China proper. Under his orders Buddhist works were translated from Sanskrit into Tibetan. He reigned about the end of the 9th century A.D. (*Deb.* ག *41*).

མངའ་བདག་ཉང *Mñah-bdag-ñañ* n. a ruler of the province of Nyang; also གྲུབ་ཐོབ་ཞིག་གི་མཚན that of a Buddhist saint (*J. Zañ.*).

མངའ་བདག་འོད་ལྡེ *Mñah-bdag Hod-lde* n. of a king of Tibet (*Loñ.* ཞ, 7).

མངའ་བདག་ལྷ་ལྡེ *Mñah-bdag Lha-lde*, བོད་རྒྱལ་ཁོ་རེའི་སྲས "the son of King Kho-re of Tibet" (*Loñ.* ཞ *9*).

མངའ་ལྡན་མ *mñah ldan-ma* अन्तरपत्नी a mistress, sweetheart, a secret wife.

མངའ་བ *mñah-wa* 1. vb. to own; to possess; also sometimes resp. for ཡོད་པ to be; to have: རྒྱལ་པོ་ལ་སྲས་གསུམ་མངའ་སྟེ། the king having three sons: བཙུན་པའི་སྐུ་ལ་བསྟུང་མི་མངའ་ལགས། your majesty is not unwell. 2. adj. (partic.) being owned by; belonging to. 3. མངའ་ལྡན་པ having, owning, or being in possession of (*Jä.*).

མངའ་འབངས *mṅaḥ-ḥbaṅs* = མངའ་ཞབས प्रजा a subordinate; a tenant; a subject.

མངའ་མཛད *mṅaḥ-mdsad* विभु lord, master; མངའ་མཛད་པ = དབང་སྤྱོད་པ vb. to lord, rule ovor; also to own.

མངའ་འཛིན་མ *mṅaḥ-ḥdsin-ma* she who has assumed power; she who controls her husband.

མངའ་ཞབས *mṅaḥ-shabs* = མངའ་འབངས.

མངའ་འོག *mṅaḥ-ḥog* མངའ་ཞབས་པ subject; subjection; also under the power of; within tho jurisdiction or dominion of (*Situ. 1*).

མངའ་རིས *Mṅaḥ-ris* 1. = མངའ་ཞབས or མངའ་འབངས. 2. n. of the westernmost provinco of Tibet now known as Ngari Khorsum. It formerly consisted of throe districts, Purang, Shangshung, Maṅ-yul, which were apportioned to the threo princes of the royal family of Tibot, viz., བཀྲ་ཤིས་མགོན། དཔལ་གྱི་མགོན and ལྡེ་གཙུག་མགོན. From this circumstance the province came to be known by the name of *Mṅaḥ-ris* (*A. 63*). Out of these throe districts, Purang, Gugé (Shangshuṅ), aud Maṅ-yul, were afterwards formed, whon the province of མངའ་རིས་བསྐོར་གསུམ became an important part of Tibet. They are poetically described:— སྤུ་རངས་གངས་ཀྱིས་བསྐོར Puraṅg surrounded by snowy mountains; གུ་གེ་གཡའ་ཡིས་བསྐོར Gugé surrounded by rocky cliffs; མང་ཡུལ་མཚོ་ཡིས་བསྐོར Maṅ-yul filled with lakes. The whole country round the sources, and the upper courses of the Indus and the Sutlej, together with some of the more western parts is now called (མངའ་རིས་འཁོར་གསུམ) Ngari Khorsum. It also includes Rudok.

མངའ་རིས་ཁམ་བུ *mṅaḥ-ris kham-bu* apricots from Baltistan and Nga-ri.

མངའ་རིས་སྟག་མོ *Mṅaḥ-ris Stag-mo* n. of a celebrated lama of མངའ་རིས *Mṅaḥ-ris*.

མངའ་རིས་ཤ *mṅaḥ-ris-ça* a kind of apricot grown in མངའ་རིས.

མངའ་གསོལ་བ *mṅaḥ-gsol-wa* 1. to be installed in power; to bc nominated or appoiutod to a dignity or position. 2. to praise; བཀྲ་ཤིས་མངའ་གསོལ་བ to wish auspicious success; to congratulato.

མངའ་གསོལ་བ, v. རྣམ་ལེགས་པ།

མངར་བ *mṅar-wa* = མངར་མོ मधुर, स्वादु, रसन swcet; delicious; མངར་གསུམ་དཀར་གསུམ *mṅar-gsum dkar-gsum* the three swcots and the threo whites:—བུ་རམ *bu-ram* molassos; སྦྲང་རྩི *sbraṅ-rtsi* honey; and བྱེ་མ་ཀ་ར *bye-maka-ra* sugar (the three whites being milk, curds and butter).

མངལ *mṅal* गर्भ, resp. ལྷུམས जरायु, कुक्षि tho uterus; tho womb; also the side of the breast, whence Buddhas are generally born lost they be contaminated by the impurities of the womb.

མངལ་སྐྱེས *mṅal-skyes* जरायुज all animals that are born of the womb.

མངལ་གྲོལ་བ *mṅal-grol-wa* प्रसव, गर्भमोचन child-delivery; child-birth; to be born.

མངལ་སྒྲིབ *mṅal-sgrib* contamination of the womb or pollution caused from child-birth.

མངལ་ཆགས *mṅal-chags* or མངལ་དུ་ཆགས་པ गर्भः-सत्वा, आपन्नसत्वा 1. conception; the formation in the womb. 2. the fœtus or embryo.

མངལ་འཇུག་པ *mṅal-ḥjug-pa* or མངལ་དུ་འཇུག་པ गर्भावक्रान्ति entering the womb (relative to a Buddha); his incarnating himself; his assuming corporeal frame.

མངལ་ཐུར *mñal-thur* a spoon used in midwifery for extracting a dead child.

མངལ་འཛིན་པ *mñal-hdsin-pa* or མངལ་དུ་འཛིན་པ to conceive; to be big with child.

མངལ་ནད *mñal-nad* प्रदर mœnorrhagia; disease of the womb.

མངལ་བ *mñal-wa* = ཁ་མངལ་བ bad offensive smell from the mouth.

མངལ་རླུགས་པ *mñal-rlugs-pa* गर्भपातन abortion; མངལ་རླུགས་པར་བྱེད་པ to force delivery or cause abortion.

མངོན་པ *mñon-pa* I: अभिव्यक्ति manifestation (this occurs in the works of the *Tirthikas*); conspicuous; visible; evident; manifest; clear; མངོན་པར་འགྱུར་བ to become manifest; to be verified, proved; as a vb. to be evident; to appear clearly: བདེན་པར་མཆིས་མངོན that which is true is evident.

མངོན་པ II: = ཆོས་མངོན་པ་མངོན་པའི་སྡེ་སྣོད the *Abhidharmma Piṭaka*; the metaphysical—part of the Buddhist scriptures. At the beginning of the *Abhidharma* of the *Mahāyāna* School a salutation is made to *Bodhisattva* Jam-pal.

མངོན་ཁྱབ *mñon-khyab* समुच्छ्रायण encompassing fully; covering all.

མངོན་དགའ *Mñon-dgah* 1. n. of a mythological garden and also world: ཤར་ཕྱོགས་མངོན་པར་དགའ་བའི་ཞིང་ཁམས "in the east there exists the World of Joy" (*J. Zañ.*). 2. n. of a section of *Çar-rtse* theological school in the monastery of Gahdan (*Loñ.* a *12*). 3. ཚོང་དཔོན་གྱི་བུ་མངོན་དགའ n. of a merchant's son who was devoted to Buddha.

མངོན་དགོངས *mñon-dgoñs* अभिसन्धि deliberation; design; premeditated plan.

མངོན་འགྲོ་བ *mñon-hgro-wa* a pioneer; vb. to proceed; to go away.

མངོན་བཅོམ *mñon-bcos* अभिहत killed, slain, destroyed.

མངོན་བརྗོད *mñon-brjod* अभिधान clear explanation of terms; one of the four parts of the science of words (शब्दविद्या); a dictionary which is in two parts: (1) in which one meaning is conveyed by several terms. (2) in which by one word several meanings are expressed.

མངོན་ཉིད *mñon-ñid* अभिसर the state of being manifest; manifestation.

མངོན་རྟགས *mñon-rtags* proof; argument; sign or token of the truth of a thing.

མངོན་རྟོགས *mñod-rtogs* or མངོན་པར་རྟོགས་པ अभिसमय practice, culture. 1. ཉན་ཐོས་ཀྱི་ཐེག་པ་མངོན་པར་རྟོགས་པའི་རིགས། श्रावकयानाभिसमयगोत्र those that by their power of discrimination have fully and clearly comprehended the doctrine of the *Çrāvaka* School. 2. རང་སངས་རྒྱས་ཀྱི་ཐེག་པ་མངོན་པར་རྟོགས་པའི་རིགས། प्रत्येकबुद्धयानाभिसमय-गोत्र those that have fully and clearly comprehended the doctrine of the *Pratyekya-Buddha* School. 3. དེ་བཞིན་གཤེགས་པའི་ཐེག་པ་མངོན་པར་རྟོགས་པའི་རིགས། तथागत-यानाभिसमय-गोत्र those that have fully and clearly comprehended the vehicle or *yana* of the *Tathā-gata*. 4. མ་ངེས་པའི་རིགས། अनियतगोत्र those that have not been able to rightly comprehend any particular doctrine. 5. རིགས་མེད་པ། अगोत्रक those who have not entered any of the schools.

མངོན་མཐོ *mñon-mtho* अभ्युदय; མཐོ་རིས་དང་ལྷ་དང་མི comprises a god or a human being, (स्वर्ग) heaven; those of exalted birth or state.

མངོན་དུ་གྱུར་པ *mñon-du gyur-pa* अभिमुक्ति one of the ten stages of *Bodhisattva* perfection, to be made manifest. It is explained := དེ་ཁོ་ན་ཉིད་མངོན་དུ་གྱུར་པས་མངོན་པ་སྟེ the state in which the *tattva* (reality) is manifest.

མངོན་དུ་ལྡང་བ *m̱ñon-du ḻdañ-wa* or ལྡངས་པ प्रत्युत्थान, अभ्युत्थान getting up (from one's seat out of respect to another person); removal from a place; going away.

མངོན་དུ་ཕྱོགས་པ *m̱ñon-du phyogs-pa* अभिमुख lit. going to the front; moving forward; proceeding.

མངོན་དུ་བྱས *m̱ñon-du-byas* साक्षात्कृत, made manifest.

མངོན་དུ་འབྱིན་པ *m̱ñon-du ḥbyin-pa* to disclose, reveal; to make known (one's wishes).

མངོན་དུ་འོང *m̱ñon-du-ḥoñ* अभिक्रमण advent, arrival, coming in.

མངོན་འདོད *m̱ñon-ḥdod*, अभीप्सा, अनुकर्म्म, अभिमत to wish for; earnest desire.

མངོན་ནོ *m̱ñon-no* प्रज्ञायते स्म is made known or evident.

མངོན་པ་པ *m̱ñon-pa-pa* a student of *Abhidharma*; one versed in that part of the Buddhist scriptures.

མངོན་པའི་ང་རྒྱལ *m̱ñon-paḥi ña-ṟgyal* अभिमान self-respect; pride.

མངོན་པར *m̱ñon-par* adv. manifestly, openly; evidently; entirely; highly; greatly; very; མངོན་པར་སྐབས་ཡོད་པ, अभ्यवकाशिक one who has leisure or opportunity to do an act of piety or a self-sacrifice; an ascetic; one who remains in an uncovered spot to practise religious austerity.

མངོན་པར་བསྐྱེད *m̱ñon-par ḇskyed*, v. རྗེས་སུ་དྲན་པ, remembrance; any thought dawning in the mind (*M̱ñon.*).

མངོན་པར་ཁྱབ་པ *m̱ñon-par khyab-pa* अभिसिद्धा to cover or encompass well; well-accomplished.

མངོན་པར་ཁྲོ *m̱ñon-par-khro* अतीन्द्रिय sbst. wrath; terrible mien.

མངོན་པར་མགུ་བར་བྱ་བ = མཉེས་པར་བྱ་བ अभिराधना to be rendered propitious; མངོན་པར་གྱུར་པ become manifest, clear; མི་མངོན་པར་གྱུར་པ, तिरोभावना to disappear, vanish from the sight.

མངོན་པར་རྒྱལ *m̱ñon-par-ṟgyal* आभिजात्य pride.

མངོན་པར་རྒྱུག་པ *m̱ñon-par ṟgyug-pa* अभिधावन to follow with speed; to run after.

མངོན་པར་སྒྲུབ *m̱ñon-par sgrub* अभिसम्पन्न well-finished; well-accomplished.

མངོན་པར་ངེས་མྱང *m̱ñon-par ñes-myañ* अभिनिर्भोग enjoyment.

མངོན་པར་ཆགས *m̱ñon-par chags*, v. འཁོར་བ 1. the transmigratory existence (*M̱ñon.*). 2. रुचि fondness; attachment; the state of being very much attached.

མངོན་པར་ཆལ་དུ་བཀྲམ་པ *m̱ñon-par chal-du ḇkram-pa* विकीर्ण to spread over; diffused.

མངོན་པར་མཆོད་པ *m̱ñon-par chod-pa* पू, पुरस्कृ honour; to make reverence to a kind friend or to a noble or venerable person.

མངོན་པར་བརྗོད *m̱ñon-par ḇrjod*, अवदान, अभिलापनता, अभिलाप्य full expression; elucidation.

མངོན་པར་བཏུད་པ *m̱ñon-par ḇtud-pa*, अभिनमित to pay homage; to bow down out of respect.

* མངོན་པར་རྟོགས་པ *m̱ñon-par ṟtogs-pa* अभिनिरूपणा, अभिसमय 1. right discernment; right knowledge; a clear comprehension; མངོན་པར་རྟོགས་པ་དང་ལྡན་པ one possessed of right judgment and discernment; མངོན་པར་རྟོགས་པའི་མཐའ་ལས་བྱུང་བ, अभिसमयान्तिक one who has been purified and perfected by the thorough exercise of right judgment. 2. a hymn-like discription (of a deity).

མངོན་པར་བསྟོད་པའི་གྲགས་པ अभिनन्दितयश enlightening fame.

མངོན་པར་མཐོ་བ *m̱ñon-par m̱tho-wa*, अभ्युदय exalted; become sublime.

མངོན་པར་དྲངས *m̱ñon-par drañs*, अभिनीति one who has been conducted to the path of deliverence—from the sufferings of transmigratory existence.

མངོན་པར་འདུ་བྱེད་ *m̱ṅon-par ẖdu-byeḏ*, अभिसंस्कार 1. sublime associations, ideas, views. 2. possessing origination, continuance and extinction: ཆོས་ཐམས་ཅད་ནི་མངོན་པར་འདུ་བྱེད་པ་མེད་པ, अनभिसंस्काराः सर्वधर्माः objects are not produced, they are without origination or extinction (*M.V.*).

མངོན་པར་འདུད་པ *m̱ṅon-par ẖduḏ-pa* अभिनमन bowing; bending reverentially.

མངོན་པར་འདུལ་ཧོས་པ *m̱ṅon-par ẖdul ẖos-pa* fit to be brought under religious discipline.

མངོན་པར་འདོན་པ *m̱ṅon-par ẖdon-pa* अभ्युद्धार drawing out; bring out; exposing; dragging out.

མངོན་པར་སྡེ་སྣོད, अभिधर्म्म पिटक, *Abhidharma-piṭaka*, one of the three classes of Buddhist sacred writings, v. སྡེ་སྣོད་གསུམ.

མངོན་པར་སྤྱོད་ *m̱ṅon-par s̱pyoḏ*=དྲག་པོའི་ལས, अभिचार witchcraft; mystical measures for the suppression of an enemy.

མངོན་པར་སྤྲོ་བ *m̱ṅon-par s̱pro-wa*, अभ्युत्साह enthusiasm; zeal for any work.

མངོན་པར་ཕྱོགས *m̱ṅon-par-phyogs̱*=མངོན་ཕྱོགས.

མངོན་པར་འཕགས་པ *m̱ṅon-par ẖphags̱-pa* (འཁོར་བ་ལས) अभ्युद्गत gone or come out of transmigratory existence.

མངོན་པར་བྱང་ཆུབ *m̱ṅon-par ḇyaṅ-chub*, अभिसम्बोधि highest state of a *Bodhisattva;* on the brink of the position of a Buddha.

མངོན་པར་དབང་བསྐུར་བ *m̱ṅon-par ḏwaṅ-s̱kur-wa* अभिषेक the initiation of a monk into the order of gelong or *Bhikṣu*.

མངོན་པར་སྦྱོར *m̱ṅon-par-s̱byor*, अभियोग, अभियुक्त full application of meanings, words and expressions in reference to religion.

མངོན་པར་བྱུང་བ अभिभाव occurs (in *Tirthika* works) in the sense of manifestation.

མངོན་པར་འབྱུང་བ *m̱ṅon-par ẖbyuṅ-wa* (འཁོར་བ་ལས) अभिनिष्क्रमण perfect renunciation; escape from worldly existence with the resolution to go to *Nirvāṇa*.

མངོན་པར་བརྩོན་པ *m̱ṅon-par ḇrtson-pa* assiduity, industry.

མངོན་མཚན *m̱ṅon-m̱tshan* अभिलक्षण an evident sign.

མངོན་པ་མཚན་ཉིད་པ *m̱ṅon-pa m̱tshan-ñiḏ-pa* (तत्त्व) he who has clearly realized the true state of things has become M̱ṅon-pa.

མངོན་པར་འཛིན *m̱ṅon-par-ẖdsin*, अभिग्रह attachment; passionate love.

མངོན་པར་རྫོགས་པ *m̱ṅon-par ṟdsogs̱-pa* complete fulfilment; perfection in all accomplishments, virtues, etc.; མངོན་པར་རྫོགས་པར་སངས་རྒྱས་པ अभिसम्बुद्ध fully enlightened; མངོན་པར་རྫོགས་པར་འཚང་རྒྱ་བ the attainment of perfect enlightenment, *i.e.*, the state of Buddha.

མངོན་པར་རབ་ཏུ་འཕྱང་ *m̱ṅon-par rab-tu ẖphyaṅ* अभिप्रलम्बते hangs down straightly or suspends (some ornamental fringes or silk cloth).

མངོན་པར་རིག་པའི་སྣང་བ *m̱ṅon-par rig-pahaṃ s̱naṅ-wa* cognition; knowing of.

མངོན་པར་ཤེས་པ *m̱ṅon-par çes̱-pa* अभिज्ञान prescience; resp. མངོན་པར་མཁྱེན་པ *m̱ṅon-par m̱khan-pa* अभिज्ञ certain gifts of supernatural perception, of which six kinds are enumerated: (1) ལྷའི་མིག་གི་མངོན་ཤེས दिव्यचक्षुर्विज्ञान seeing anything clearly as if with divine sight. By the exercise of this power one can see (realize) the sufferings of all kinds of living beings; (2) ལྷའི་རྣ་བའི་མངོན་ཤེས दिव्यश्रोत्रम् divine hearing in a perfect manner. By the exercise of this knowledge one can hear the sound of བུ་མོ་ད (the smallest insect) and understand the different languages articulate and inarticulate of all living beings; (3) ཕ་རོལ་གྱི་སེམས་ཤེས་པ་དང་ परचित्त-ज्ञानम् knowledge of another's heart; སེམས་ཀྱི་རྣམ་གྲངས་ཤེས་པའི་མངོན་ཤེས་གཞན་སེམས་ཤེས་པའི་མངོན་ཤེས knowing of another's thoughts; चेतः पर्य्यायज्ञानम् serial knowledge of the heart; (4) རྫུ་འཕྲུལ་གྱི་བྱ་བ་ཤེས་པའི་མངོན་ཤེས ऋद्धि विधि ज्ञानम् knowledgo of the four forms of miracle. By the oxercise of this knowledge one knows the events of his former and future states of existence, and also the circumstances of his death and birth. By the exercise of one's miraculous knowledge it is possible to move one's body without being seen; (5) སྔོན་གྱི་གནས་རྗེས་དྲན་པའི་མངོན་ཤེས། पूर्व्वनिवासानुस्मृतिज्ञानम् the power of remembering the acts of one's former existence or life; (6) ཟག་པ་ཟད་པ་ཤེས་པའི་མངོན་ཤེས་པ आश्रवक्षयज्ञानम् knowledge of the destruction of the passions. By the exercise of the knowledge of (ཟག *zag* and ཟད *zad*) decay and destruction, one can quickly attain to the state of the omniscient (सर्व्वज्ञ) by purifying himself of all impurities of the heart. By the exercise of the power of knowing all living beings one can perceive as well the stages of their moral perfection or culture.

མངོན་པར་ཤེས་པ་དྲུག་དང་ལྡན་པ षड्भिज्ञ the possessor of the six kinds of fore-knowledge; an epithet of Buddha (*M. V.*).

མངོན་པར་ཤེས་པའི་ཤེས་པ *mṅon-par çes-paḥi çes-pa* अभितोज्ञान fore-knowledge.

མངོན་པར་སེམས *mṅon-par-sems* अभिमानस *Samādhi*; contemplation; reflection.

མངོན་པར་སེལ *mṅon-par-sel* अभिस्थान coagulated; congealed.

མངོན་པར་སོང་ *mṅon-par-soṅ* अभिपन्न involved; fully occupied; engrossed.

མངོན་པར་ལྷག་པ *mṅon-par lhag-pa* आगन्तु, अतिथि a new-comer; new arrival; one just come.

མངོན་ཕྱོགས *mṅon-phyogs*=ཁ་ལྟས་པ अभिप्रति, उन्मुख, सम्मुख in colloq. 1. towards; forward; straight ahead. 2. moving towards; སྐྱེ་བ་ལ་མངོན་དུ་ཕྱོགས་པ *skye-wa la mṅon-du phyogs-pa* proceeding to birth; འཆི་བ་ལ་མངོན་དུ་ཕྱོགས་པ rushing on to death; སངས་རྒྱས་པ་ལ་མངོན་དུ་ཕྱོགས་པ moving towards the attainment of Buddhahood.

མངོན་ཕྱོགས་ཏེ *mṅon-phyogs-te* अभ्येत्य having gone on; proceeded.

མངོན་ཕྲ *mṅon-phra* dissimulation.

མངོན་དུ་བྱེད་པ *mṅon-du byed-pa* to be manifest; to make public; to make clear or manifest to one's self.

མངོན་ཞེན *mṅon-shen* अभिनिवेश application; devotion.

མངོན་རློམས *mṅon-rloms* अभिमनस् having the mind directed towards; longing-for.

མངོན་ཤེས *mṅon-çes* fore-knowledge.

མངོན་ཤེས་ཅན *mṅon-çes-can* 1. v. བྱ་སྐྱ་ཀ (*Mṅon.*) the mag-pie. 2. one possessed of fore-knowledge; one who can read the mind of others.

མངོན་སུམ *mṅon-sum* प्रत्यक्ष open, public, manifest; cognizable by the senses.

Syn. མངོན་དུ *mṅon-du*; དབང་པོའི་ཡུལ *dwaṅ-poḥi-yul* (*Mṅon.*).

མངོན་སུམ་དུ *mṅon sum-du* 1. manifestly; adv. openly, publicly. 2. དངོས་སུ=*dṅos-su*, *e.g.*, bodily, personally; by one's own personal experience; མངོན་སུམ་དུ་སྐྱེས *mṅon-sum-du skyes* अभिजात, अभिजन really born, not of imaginary birth; མངོན་སུམ་དུ་འདུལ་བར་འོས་པ सम्मुख-विनय proper to place under moral discipline; one fit to be brought under religious control.

མངོན་སུམ་ཕྱོགས་མིན་པ *mṅon-sum phyogs-min-pa* पराङ्मुख not forward; unable to succeed; turned back; failed; unsuccessful in an enterprise.

མངོན་སུམ་མིན་པ *mṅon-sum min-pa* परोक्ष beyond the range of sight; imperceptible; unknown; unintelligible.

མངོན་གསལ *mṅon-gsal* lucid, clear, evident; making known; manifesting, v. མངོན་པར་གསལ.

རྔ *rña* डिण्डिम tambour; कवच a drum used in battle; आनक a large military drum beaten at one end; ढक्क drum; kettle-drum འཁར་རྔ *hkhar-rña*, v. འཁར *hkhar*; རྫ་རྔ *rdsa-rña* a drum made of earthenware; རྒྱལ་རྔ *rgyal-rña* जयढक्क the drum of victory; བག་རྔ *bag-rña* drum at a wedding: ཁྲིམས་ཀྱི་རྔ་བོ་ཆེ་བརྡུངས་ཏེ *khrims-kyi rña-bo-che brduṅs-te* having beaten the large drum for the Government edicts.

རྔ་དཀར *rña-dkar* or རྔ་མ་དཀར་པོ a white hairy tail; རྔ་དཀར་པོའི་རྔ་གཡབ a fan of the white yak-tail or the *chowry*.

རྔ་མཁན *rña-mkhan* mower; reaper.

རྔ་ཁྲི *rña-khri* (*ña-ṭhi*) a stool on which the larger drums are set for being beaten.

རྔ་སྒྲ *rña-sgra* (*ña-ḍa*) 1. तूर्य sound of the drum. 2 an epithet of Buddha Amogha Siddha; རྔ་སྒྲ་འབྱིན་པའི་སྒྲ་ཞེས་བྱ་བའི་ནགས n. of a forest situated on the mountains *Sprin-dkar rgyu-wa* in the fabulous continent of Uttara Kuru.

རྔ་རྔོག *rña-rṅog* abbr. of རྔ་མ་དང་རྔོག, the tail and the crest-hair (mane) of a yak, horse or mule: རྔ་རྔོག་ཐམས་ཅད་ལ་དར་ཁ་དོག་སྣ་ལྔ་བཏགས་པ to all their tails and manes scarves of five different colours were attached (*A. 141*).

རྔ་ལྕགས *rña-lcags* a drum-rod; gen. a bent rod used as a drum-stick.

རྔ་ཆུང་ *rña-chuṅ* 1. a small drum. 2. a small camel; a young camel.

རྔ་དར *rña-dar* a scarf tied to a drum.

རྔ་པ *rña-pa* a drummer.

རྔ་དཔོན *rña-dpon* chief drummer.

རྔ་ལྤགས *rña-lpags* drum-skin.

རྔ་བ *rña-wa*, vb. pf. བརྔས *brñas*, fut. བརྔ *brña*, imp. རྔོས *rños*, to mow, to reap, to cut with the sickle; sbst. the seeding of corn, barley, wheat or paddy; བཙས་མ་བརྔས་པ *btsas-ma brñas-pa* the reaped corn.

རྔ་བོ་ཆེ *rña-wo che* यशोभेरि fame; also large drum; a drum announcing fame.

རྔ་བ་ཆེ་བའི་མདོ a Sūtra in the *Kahgyur* of a metaphysical nature (*K. d.* ཙ *142*).

རྔ་བོང་ *Rña-boṅ* 1. n. of an Indian sage who is said to have flourished a thousand years before Buddha. 2. n. for camel in *W*.

རྔ་བྲན *rña-bran* n. of an animal: ཟས་ནི་རྔ་བྲན་ཤ་གསར་དང his food was the fresh meat of *ña-bran* (*Sman. 212*).

རྔ་དབྱུག *rña-dbyug* drum-stick.

རྔ་སྦུག *rña-sbug* drum and cymbal.

རྔ་མ *rña-ma* पुच्छ the tail; the hairy tail of a beast; རྔ་མ་རྒྱས་པ་བྱེད *rña-ma rgyas-pa byed* उत्पुच्छयति puffing out the tail.

རྔ་མུ་ཀུན་ད मुकुन्द a kind of drum.

རྔ་མོང *rña-moṅ* or རྔ་མོ *rña-mo* उष्ट्र, करभ the camel; རྔེ་ཧུ *rñe-hu* a young camel; the smaller species of camel: ཡུལ་ས་ཐག་རིང་པོར་གཤེགས་པའི་སྐད་ཐོས་པས, རྔ་མོ་དྲེའུ་སྟོར་བ་ལྟར་ཐུགས་བཏུལ་ཆེན་པོར་གྱུར་ཏེ hearing the news of his having gone to a distant country, he became greatly grieved, as if he had lost his camel or mule (*Hbrom. 113*).

རྔ་མོ་ཉུད་ཀ *rña-mo ñud-ka*, a *srinbu*, *i.e.*, worm with a black head. In whatever place the worm was found on its back, that place suffered from visitations of various kinds of calamities, such as war, famine, disease, devastations and destructions (*K. ko.* ཀ *237*).

རྔ་ཐེར *rña-ther* serge cloth made of camel's hair.

རྔ་བཟོ་བ *rña-bzo-wa* ढक्किक a drum-maker.

རྔ་ཟླུམ *ṟña-zlum* (*ña-dum*) मृदङ्ग, आनक kind of drum played at Indian concerts.

རྔ་ཟོར *ṟña-zor* n. of a demi-god.

རྔ་ཟླུམ་ཅན *ṟña-zlum-can* मुकुन्द species of flower [a kind of drum; the resin of *Boswellia thurifera*]*S.*

རྔ་ཡུ *ṟña-yu* handle of a kettle-drum which is supported by a stick sometimes fixed on the ground but generally held by the hand.

རྔ་ཡབ *Ṟña-yab* चामर, प्रकीर्णक 1. lit. "the father of tails," *i.e.*, a yak's tail, used for fanning and sometimes for dusting. 2. n. of a fabulous continent said to exist to the north of Jambudvīpa.

རྔ་ཡབ་མཇུག་མ་ཅན a term for horses in general; lit. that has the yak's tail (*Mṉon.*).

Syn. གཡོག་བྱེད *gyog-byeḏ*; བུང་པ་སྐྲོད་བྱེད *buñ-pa s̱krod-byeḏ* (*Mṉon.*).

རྔ་གཡོག *ṟña-gyog* आनक a military drum.

རྔ་རིང *ṟña-riñ* long tail.

རྔ་ཤིང་ *ṟña-çiñ* the wooden body of a drum; also the wooden support.

རྔ་སྒོང་ *ṟña-çoñ* kettle-drum; music (*Sch.*).

རྔ་གསངས *ṟña-gsañs* or རྔ་བསངས a loud beat or roll of the kettle-drum (*Sch.*).

རྔད *ṟñaḏ* རྔད་ཡང་ཡི་དམ་ལྷ་རུ་རྔད, བཞེས་ཡང་མ་དང་མཁའ་འགྲོ་བཞེས.

རྔན་བགྲང *ṟñan-bgrañ* enumerating another's faults: ཕ་ཕས་བུ་ལ་རྔན་བགྲང་ཉིད་དང་མཚུངས like enumerating the sins or misdoings of a family, *i.e.*, from father to son (*Yig. k.*).

རྔན་ཅན *ṟñan-can* or རྔན་ཆེན *ṟñan-chen* अवगणित, अवमत jeering; disdain: (ངན་པས་རྔན་ཅན་བྱེད་དུའང་འོང *ñan-pas ṟñan-can byeḏ-duhañ ẖoñ*) the evil hearted also came to scoff at him (*H̱brom. 37*).

Syn. བརྙས་པ *bṟñas-pa*; ཚོ་ཁྱད *tsho-khyaḏ* or ཁྱོད་ཚོ *khyoḏ-tsho* (*Mṉon.*).

རྔན་པ I: sbst. *ṟñan-pa*=སྐུག་པ remuneration for a service done; reward; fee; hire; wages; vb. pf. བརྔན to pay hire to: རྔན་པ་སྦྱིན་པ or རྔན་པ་གཏོང་བ to pay wages or remuneration; sometimes to bribe; to corrupt.

རྔན་པ II: acc. to *Jä.* a kind of sacrifice in C. Tibet.

རྔན་འཕྱར་བ *ṟñan-hphyar-wa* to insult, defame.

རྔབ་པ *ṟñab-pa* 1. to be hungry: བཀྲེས་རྔབ་པ *ḇkres ṟñab-pa* to be greedy; to have a craving appetite; acc. *Jä.* 2. cf. རྔམ་པ to crave; to desire earnestly. 3. in *W.* colloq. for རྔ་བ, to mow.

རྔབ་ཚ་བ *ṟñab tsha-wa* oppressive: རྒྱལ་ཁྲིམས་ཇི་ལྟར་རྔབ་ཚ་ཀྱང་ even if the laws (of government) be oppressive.

རྔབས་ར *ṟñabs-rba*=འཛིབ་རུ a surgical instrument, made of horn, for drawing out blood by suction.

རྔམ་རྔམ *ṟñam-ṟñam* 1. threateningly. 2. with dazzling splendour; རྔམ་རྔམ་ཇིག་ཇིག་བྱེད་པ anything tidy and very fine.

རྔམ་ཅན *ṟñam-can* 1. adj. rageful; avaricious; covetous; ཟ་རྔམ་པ raging; gluttonous; ravenous.

རྔམ་བརྗིད *ṟñam-bṟjiḏ* 1. expression or appearance of wrath. 2.=རྔོམ་བརྗིད *ṟñom-bṟjiḏ* splendour; magnificence (*Jä.*).

Syn. རྔམ་འཇིགས *ṟñam-ẖjigs*; ཁྲོ་ཉམས *khro-ñams* (*Mṉon.*).

རྔམ་པ *ṟñam-pa* 1. to rage at; to be furious; to devastate; རྔམ་པའི་ང་རོ a voice of terror. 2. to breathe violently; to pant for; to desire ardently; སྲོག་གཅོད་པ་ལ་རྔམ་པ *s̱roggcoḏ-pa-la ṟñam-pa* to be blood-thirsty; རྔམ་པའི་ཚུལ་གྱིས ravenously (devouring).

རྔམ་པ་ཕག་མགོ *Rňam-pa phag-mgo* n. of a deity with the head of a wild boar.

རྔམ་པོ་ཆེ *rňam-po-che* very frightful.

རྔམ་གསས *rňam-gsas* the occupying of one's body by a god or spirit according to Bon-po notions; a woman when inspired riding on any demon is called གསས་མོ.

རྔམས *rňams*=དཔངས height or depth; རྔམས་སུ in height or depth; ཆུ་དཀྱིལ་རྔམས་སུ་དཔག་ཚད་འབུམ་ཕྲག་བརྒྱད། (*Yig.*) the depth at the middle of the waters was 800,000 *yojana.*

རྔམས་པ अद्भुत wonder, surprize; pathos in music.

རྔམས་ཆེ *rňams-che*, དཀའ་ལས་ཆེ་བ very difficult; causing much hardship.

རྔས *rňas* (མལ་གྱི) उपबर्ह, v. སྔས *sňas*, pillow; a bolster.

རྔས་འབོལ *rňas-hbol* गेण्डक a stuffed cushion; a football.

རྔུ *rňu*=ཟུག་རྔུ *zug-rňu* pain.

རྔུ་ཆུ *Rňu-chu*, colloq. for རྔུལ་ཆུ (*Loň.* ༥ 5).

རྔུ་མ *rňu-ma* or མིག་སྐྱག *mig-skyag* चक्षुर्मल rheum in the eye.

✢ **རྔུབ་པ** *rňub-pa*=ནང་དུ་འདུས་པ *naň-du hdus-pa* or འཇུག་པ *hjug-pa*, pf. བརྔུབས *brňubs* or རྔུབས་ *rňubs*, fut. བརྔུབ *brňub*, imp. རྔུབས *rňubs* to draw in; དབུགས་རྔུབ་པ *dbugs rňub-pa* to inhale; to breathe in.

རྔུལ *rňul* or རྔུལ་ཆུ *rňul-chu* स्वेद, विपाक perspiration; sweat; རྔུལ་འདོན་པ *rňul-hdon-pa* to cause to sweat or prespire.

Syn. ཆད་སྐྱེས *chad-skyes*; ལུས་ཆུ *lus-chu*; ལུས་འབབ *lus-hbab*; ལུས་རྔུལ *lus-rňul* (*Mňon.*).

རྔུལ་ཆུ *Rňul-chu* n. of a river in Kham. It is formed by the joining of the rivers རྒྱལ་མོ་རྔུལ་ཆུ *Rgyal-mo rňul-chu* of Kham and *Rdsa-khog Ňag-chu* of Sze-chuan.

རྔུལ་བ *rňul-wa*, vb. pf. བརྔུལ *brňul*, to sweat, perspire.

རྔུལ་གཟན संकचिका [belonging to the armpit]*S.*

རྔུལ་གཟན་གྱི་གཟན *rňal-gzan-gyi gzan* प्रतिसंकचिका.

རྔེ་ཆུ *rňchu* or རྔེ་ཆུ་ཆུང་ རྔ་ཆུང་ 1. a little drum. 2. རྔ་མོང་གི་ཕྲུ་གུ *rňa-moň-gi phru-gu* a small camel; a young camel.

རྔོ *rňo* skin disease causing painful itching which is contagious and affects dogs, sheep, and goats.

རྔོ་ཐོག་པ *rňo-thog-pa* to be capable: རྔོ་ཐོགས་ལགས Sir, I can do (it); རྔོ་ཐོག་མི་ཐོག incapable or not able.

རྔོ་བ *rňo-wa* to be able (*Cs.*); རྔོ་མི་ཐོགས not able; not competent; incapable.

རྔོ་བག་ཅན *rňo-bag-can* 1. a disease of the skin with painful itching. 2. acc. *Cs.*= རྔམ་བག་ཅན.

རྔོ་ཡས *rňo-yas* n. of a number (*S. Lex.*).

རྔོ་ལེན་པ *rňo-len-pa* to roast; to fry (*Sch.*), v. རྔོད་པ *rňod-pa.*

རྔོག I: *rňog* or རྔོག་མ *rňog-ma*=ཟེ་རྔོག *ze-rňog* 1. the mane; རྟ་རྔོག *rta-rňog* mane of the horse, &c. 2. acc. *Lex.* the hunch or hump of an animal. 3. acc. *Cs.* འདྲེ་རྔོག *drchu-rňog* a kind of stuffed seat; mattress; a thick-haired carpet (*Sch.*).

རྔོག II: n. of a tribe in Tibet to which belonged the celebrated *Lo-tsā-wa* Lama *Rňog Blo-ldan Çes-rab* (*Loň.* ༩ 9).

རྔོག་ཅན *rňog-can* or རྔོག་ལྡན *rňog-ldan* having a mane.

རྔོགས་ཆགས *rňogs-chags* a beast that has a mane.

རྔོད་པ་ *rṅod-pa*, pf. བརྔོས་ *brṅos*, fut. བརྔོད་ *brṅod*, acc. to *Cs.* and *Jä.* བརྔོ་ *brṅo*, imp. རྔོད་ *rṅod* or རྔོས་ *rṅos*. 1. to parch (barley, wheat, or rice); to bruise; to roast; to fry, *e.g.*, meat in a pan. 2. acc. to *Cs.* to deceive.

རྔོབ་པ་ *rṅob-pa* in *Ld.* to be able, v. རྔོ་བ་ *rṅo-wa*.

རྔོམ་བརྗིད་ *rṅom-brjid* (cf. རྔམ་པ་) splendour; stateliness; majesty; རྔོམ་བག་ཅན་ *rṅom-bag-can* grand; majestic; terrible.

རྔོམ་པོ་ *rṅom-po* bright; brilliant; majestic; shining.

རྔོལ་བོན་ *Rṅol-Bon* the earliest stage of the Bon religion of Tibet known by the name of ཡུང་དྲུང་ or *Svastika*, which flourished before the second century B.C.; said to have been introduced in Tibet during the reign of the seventh descendant of King གཉའ་ཁྲི་བཙན་པོ་ (*J. Zañ.*).

རྔོས་ཁྱེར་ *rṅos-khyer* one who has caught the skin disease called རྔོ་ *rṅo*.

ལྔ་ *lṅa* पञ्च five: ལྔ་ག་ *lṅa-ga* or ལྔ་ཀ་ all the five; each of the five; ལྔ་བརྒྱ་ *lṅa-rgya* पञ्चशत five hundred; ལྔ་བཅུ་ *lṅa-bcu* पञ्चाशत् fifty; ལྔ་བཅུ་ང་གཅིག་པ་ पञ्चाशेात्तर the fifty-first: ལྔ་ཆ་ *lṅa-cha* पञ्चभाग, पञ्चमांश the fifth part or share.

ལྔ་མཆོད་ *lṅa-mchod* lit. the five offerings; but the term signifies the religious service with illumination on the anniversary of the birth of Tsong-khapa, the great Buddhist reformer of Tibet, which generally falls in the month of November, *i.e.*, about the 25th of the 9th Tibetan month. It is observed in every house in Tibet.

ལྔ་སྟོང་ *lṅa-stoṅ* पञ्चसहस्र five thousand.

ལྔ་སྟོན་ *lṅa-ston* पञ्चमक the fifth festive ceremony generally observed.

ལྔ་ཐམ་ *lṅa-tham* a Buddhist monk who does not possess any knowledge of the ritual and the contemplative practice of Buddhism.

ལྔ་བདོ་ *lṅa-bdo*, ལྔ་བདོ་སྙིགས་མ་མ་རུངས་ཚེ་ *lṅa-bdo sñigs-ma ma-ruṅs tshe* (*Hbrom. 25*).

ལྔ་དྲུག་འགྲོ་ *lṅa-drug-hgro* in Tibet when one borrows grain he has, as a rule, to give back one measure more for every five measures he had taken. This is called the payment—six for five measures of agricultural loan.

ལྔ་ལྡན་ *Lṅa-ldan* पञ्चाल n. of a city in ancient Kho-ten known in Tibet under the name of Li-yul.

ལྔ་སྡེ་བཟང་པོ་ *Lṅa-sde bzañ-po* the five early disciples of Buddha:—Kauṇḍinya, Açvajit, Vāṣpa, Mahānāmān, and Bhadrika, who first received his teachings (*Yig.*).

+ ལྔ་པ་ *lṅa-pa* पञ्चम 1. the fifth; पञ्चमी the fifth day after the full or new moon, पञ्चक. 2. n. of a tribe in Tibet. 3. ལྔ་པ་ནི་མཐང་གོས a name for a Buddhist monk's raiment. 4. the fifth path: ལམ་ལྔ་པ་བཅུ་སྔོན་དུ་སོང་ the ten have gone before on the fifth path (*Yig.*).

ལྔ་པ་ཉིད་ *lṅa-pa ñid* पञ्चता the fifth state, *i.e.*, death.

ལྔ་པོ་ *lṅa-po* पञ्च the five.

ལྔ་པའི་དོན་ *lṅa-pahi-don* = རིག་པའི་གནས་ལྔ་པ the five sciences.

ལྔ་པའི་དབྱངས་སྙན་ n. of a singing bird, v. འཇོལ་མོ.

ལྔ་པའི་ལམ་ *lṅa pahi-lam* = འཆི་བ the way to the fifth state, *i.e.*, death.

ལྔ་བ་ *lṅa-wa* a flash (of lightning).

ལྔ་རྩེན་ *Lṅa-rtsen* पञ्चिका or རྩེན, a game played with five dice; कुबेर n. of the Yaksha who is custodian of wealth; one of the eight generals of Vais'ravaṇa (*Yig.*).

ལྔ་ཚིགས *ḻña-tshigs* = ཐུན་གསུམ་པ तृतीय प्रहर 1. the third watch (of night or day). 2. ཀོ་ས་ལའི་རྒྱལ་པོ་གསལ་རྒྱལ་གྱི་སྲས་ལྔ་ཚིགས་ཅེར n. of a son of Prasenajit, King of Kos'ala (*J. Zañ.*). 3. ཡན་ལག་ལྔའི་ཚིགས་ལྔ the five joints of the five limbs.

ལྔ་རིག *ḻña-rig* = རིག་པའི་གནས་ལྔ་ཤེས་པ पण्डित one who is versed in the five sciences; a learned man; a scholar.

ལྔ་ལེན *ḻña-len* पञ्चाल, पञ्चालक also 1. ancient name of a province in the north-west part of India, one of the 36 sacred places of the Buddhists (*M. V.*). 2. पञ्चत्वं five times. 3. ཕུང་པོ་ལྔ་ལེན་པ to be born, *i.e.*, assumption of the five (*skandha*) aggregates; body.

སྔ *şña* पूर्व before; soon; early—referring mostly to time not place: འདའ་བ་ནི་ཉ་ཚང་ཡང་སྔ་ཆེས་སོ deliverance takes place much too soon: ང་ནི་ཐེམ་པ་སྔ་བཅལ་ཡིན I was the foremost, the first, (earliest) to cross the threshold (*Glr.*); བསྟན་པ་སྔ་དར་བར་དར་ཕྱི་དར་གསུམ the first, intermediate, and the last propagation of the (Buddhist) doctrine (*Glr.*). སྔོན or སྔོན་ལ is the ordinary adverbial form; gen. སྔ is used with postpositions or in compounds: སྔ་མཁོ *şña-m̱kho* the olden time; སྔ་སྔ *şña-şña* very early; སྔ་དུས in bygone times.

སྔ་གུང *şña-guñ*, abb. of སྔ་དྲོ་དང་གུང, morning and noon.

སྔ་གོང *şña-goñ* 1. adv. before; previously; at first; a little while ago; just now (*Mil.*); སྔ་གོང་ནས formerly; སྔ་གོང་ཡབ your late father (*Glr.*); སྔ་གོང་བོད་ཀྱི་རྒྱལ་པོ the earlier Tibetan kings (*Glr.; Jä.*).

སྔ་དགོངས *şña-ḏgoñs* morning and evening (*Sch.*).

སྔ་རྒོལ *şña-ṟgol* पूर्ववादिन् in a religious disputation, he who first begins the discussion; a plaintiff in a case.

སྔ་སྔོ *şña-şño* v. སྔོ *şño*, vegetables; greens (*Jä.*).

སྔ་ཆད *şña-chaḏ* = སྔོན་ཆད *şñon-chaḏ* formerly; hitherto; till now; up to this time.

སྔ་ཆོས *şña-choş* = ཆོས་གྲངས་སྔ་མ 1. earlier date. 2. the indistinctness: ཤོག་བུ་སྔོན་པོ་ལ་སྣུམ་པ་སྔོ་ཆོས་སྐྱ་ཆོས inelligibility of the writing on blue paper with blue ink is here alluded to (*Ṟtsii.*).

སྔ་རྟོག *şña-ṟtog* early crop; the first-fruit of the harvest.

སྔ་རྟིང་དུ *şña-ṟtiñ-du* earlier or later; not at the same time.

སྔ་ལྟས *şña-ḻtaş* foreboding; prognostic; presage.

སྔ་ཐོག *şña-thog* early; in the forenoon.

སྔ་དྲོ *şña-ḏro* पूर्वाह्ण, प्रातः, प्रत्यूष early morning: སྔ་དྲོ་འདུལ་བ *şña-ḏro ẖdul-wa* to tame the mind in the morning lest evil may enter it later.

སྔ་ན *şña-na* before, previously, betimes.

སྔ་ནུར་ཕྱི་འགྱངས་མེད་པ *şña-nur phyi-ẖgyañş meḏ-pa* early in the morning, not late in the day; without delay.

སྔ་པ *şña-pa* 1. vb. pf. སྔས to be the first; to come first; to be beforehand. 2. adj. ancient; belonging or referring to former ages; རྒྱ་ནག་གི་རྒྱལ་པོ་སྔ་བ an ancient king of China.

སྔ་ཕྱི *şña-phyi*, abbr. of དུས་ཚོད་སྔ་བ་དང་ཕྱི་བ पौर्वापर्यम्, early and late; སྔ་ཕྱི་མེད अपूर्वाचरम not early not late; that has no beginning or end.

སྔ་ཕྱི་རྒོལ *şña-phyi ṟgol*, abbr. of སྔ་རྒོལ་དང་ཕྱི་རྒོལ *ṟña-ṟgol dañphyi-ṟgol* पूर्ववादिन् परवादिन्, the plaintiff and defendant in a law-suit.

སྔ་ཕྲོས *şña-phroş* early or first work; the earlier position of a work.

སྔ་བ *sña-wa* = སྔ་པ or སྔ་བར = ཐོ་རངས प्रातः dawn; very early in the morning: སང་སྔ་བར་ to-morrow early morning.

སྔ་མ *sña-ma* पूर्व, प्राची, प्राक् the former; the first-named; the earlier one; anterior in time and place; the first; the foremost in a series; སྔ་མ་བཞིན་ पूर्ववत् as before; as the one gone before; as the earlier one; སྔ་མའི་དུས in early times.

སྔ་མོ *sña-mo* earlier; bygone; སྔ་མོ་ནས long before; from former time.

སྔ་ཟ *sña-za* breakfast; the morning food; food taken early in the morning.

སྔ་རོལ *sña-rol* of old time; past ages; སྔ་རོལ་དུ before; in time past; gone before.

སྔ་ལགས *sña-lags* = ལེན་པོ in Tsang a return visit or entertainment.

སྔ་ཤ *sña-ça* = རྟ་སྒའི་སྔ་ཟ straps for binding things to a saddle; རྗེ་ཤ the straps which go round the hind part, and called ཤ་བཏགས་སྒའི་སྔ་ཤ་ལ་ནད་རྒྱལ་དང (*Lhamo bstod-pa*).

སྔ་ཤས *sña-ças* very early.

སྔ་ཤུགས་འདྲེན་པ *sña-çugs hdren-pa* the accenting of the first syllable.

སྔ་སོར *sña-sor* पूर्व 1. before; in the first place; first of all; at first. 2. anciently; in olden times.

Syn. སྔར *sñar*; སྔོན་དུ *sñon-du*; སྔ་མ *sña-ma* (*Mñon.*).

སྔ་ཧར *sña-har* a kind of tea.

སྔག་པ *sñag-pa*, also སྔགས་པ, pf. བསྔགས, fut. བསྔག, imp. སྔོག *sñog*, to praise, commend, extol; to recommend: འགྲོ་བར་སྔགས it is recommended to go; བསྟོད་བསྔགས་པ praising; singing praise; བསྔགས་པ་པོ a praiser, commender (*Cs.*); བསྔགས་པར་འོས་པ worthy of praise; བསྔགས་ལྡན praised; also n. of Buddha's horse; བསྔགས་གསོལ thanksgiving.

སྔགས *sñags* 1. praise; encomium (*Cs.*). 2. मन्त्र magical formula consisting mostly of strings of Sanskṛt syllables in the recital of which perfect accuracy is required. These are used in invoking and coercing deities and demons, and are the equivalents of the famous mantras and dhārani of Sanskṛt Buddhism; སྔགས་སྒྲུབ་པ *sñags-sgrub-pa*, སྔགས་སྤེལ་བ *sñags-spel-wa*, to recite mantras; to pronounce charms or incantations; སྔགས་ཀྱི་ཐེག་པ मन्त्रयान the mystical or *Tantrik* doctrine of the Buddhists, v. ཐེག་པ *theg-pa*; སྔགས་ཀྱི་དག་བྱེད हविः clarified butter (used in the sacrificial fire); སྔགས་ཀྱི་སྤྱོད་པ *sñags-kyi spyod-pa* मन्त्रचर्या mysticism; the practice of the mystic cult.

སྔགས་འཆང་ *sñags-hchañ* मन्त्रधर one who ministers charms, a professor of mysticism; སྔགས་འཆང་བ or སྔགས་འཛིན་པ to carry dhārani charms about one's self.

སྔགས་བཏུ་བ *sñags-btu-wa* समुच्चय extracts of *mantra* or charms.

སྔགས་སྡེ་གསུམ *sñags-sde-gsum* acc. to the Buddhist as well as the Bon-po = ཕྱི་རིགས་སྔགས the external or ritualistic science. 1. the external spells by which a god or goddess is propitiated or brought under one's power so as to obey the wishes; ནང་གསང་སྔགས गुह्यमन्त्र the secret charms by the efficacy of which a *Tantrik Bodhisattva* either in his wrathful manifestation or in his milder form is propitiated. By dint of charms, he mysteriously unites with a female who having acquired similar perfections and merits like himself, is thus prepared spiritually for such a union. Both having attained to the same degree of spiritual culture and sitting in each others embrace vanish, it is believed, into the state of *Nirvāṇa*. This practice is called མཉམ་སྦྱོར

mkhah-spyod. 2. གསང་སྔགས secret written charms; གཟུངས་སྔགས धारणीमन्त्र charms which contain efficacious significations and are capable of over-powering or coorcing spirits. These charms are generally inscribed on cloth, paper, or wooden boards. 3. རིག་སྔགས, v. རིག spells.

སྔགས་པ *sňags-pa* तान्त्रिक् one versed in the *Tantra* cult of the Buddhists; one who practises mysticism.

Syn. ནུས་པ་ཅན *nus-pa-can*; མཐུ་བོ་ཆེ *mthu-bo-che*; སྔགས་འཆང *sňags-hchaň*; བསྲུང་འཁོར་པ *bsruň-hkhor-pa*; བསྟན་བདག *bstan-bdag*; འཇོམས་བྱེད *hjoms-byed*; རྡོ་རྗེ་འཛིན *rdo-rje-hdsin*; སྔགས་ཆེན *sňags-chen* (*Mňon.*).

སྔགས་བོན *sňags-bon* for སྔགས་པ and བོན་པོ *Bon-po.*

སྔགས་བཙུན་མར་གྱི་རྐྱལ་པ་ཅན *sňags-btsun mar-gyi rkyal-pa-can* n. of an ointment for wounds and sores (*Sman. 350.*).

སྔགས་རིགས *sňags-rigs* ब्राह्मण Brâhman.

སྔངས *sňaňs*=དངངས, v. དངང་བ.

སྔངས་སྐྲག *sňaňs-skrag*=དངངས་སྐྲག panic; sudden fear.

སྔངས་བྱེད *sňaňs-byed* भीषण very fearful, terrific; panic stricken.

སྔན *sňan* for སྔ or སྔོན *sňon*, སྔན་ཆད formerly; before; previously, opp. to now: འཆར་ཀ་སྔན་ལ་སྔངས Charka was sent proviously or at first.

སྔན་བུ *sňan-bu* a medicinal herb.

སྔར *sňar* पुरस्तात्, पूर्व्वं adv. of time, used for སྔ་རུ *sňa-ru*, before; beforehand; previously; formerly; at first; སྔར་ནས from before; སྔར་མེད་པ what has not existed before; an innovation; སྔར་མ་བྱས་པ what was not done before; སྔར་ལངས to get up first; one who has risen first or early; སྔར་གྱི་སྒྲིག་གསོལ to have or avail of a former arrangement or system; སྔར་གྱི་ཡི་གེ་རྙིང་པ་རྣམས old or early records; the writings of antiquity; སྔར་བ the former; first mentioned; སྔར་གྱི་བས=སྔར་ལས་ཀྱང or སྔར་བས་ཀྱང than, before: རྒྱལ་བུ་སྔར་གྱི་བས་ཀྱང་ཁྱད་པར་དུ་འཕགས་པ་ཙམ་དུ་གྲགས་པ་ལ། "the prince was superior even to those who preceded him, *i.e.*, even he excelled his predecessors." Although སྔར occurs almost exclusively as a temporal adv., it is used in the sense of a local postp. in the honorific expression སྤྱན་སྔར, before his eyes, in his presence.

སྔར་སྐྱེས *sňar-skyes*=ཨ་ཇོ; अग्रज an elder brother.

སྔར་ཁྱུན་ལྟར *sňar-khyun ltar* or སྔར་རྒྱུན་ལྟར as usual; in the ordinary course; as formerly.

སྔར་ཁྲིམས *sňar-khrims* (*ňar-thim*) early laws; previous punishment or conviction.

སྔར་འཁྱུར *sňar-hkhyur*=སྔ་མའི་སྲོལ former custom or usage.

སྔར་རྒྱས *sňar-rgyas* early diffusion or earlier propagation.

སྔར་འཇགས *sňar-hjags* given as before; as before.

སྔར་རྗེས་ཅན *sňar-rjes-can* one who follows or acts according to precedents; སྔ་མའི་ལམ་ལུགས་སྲོལ *sňa-mahi lam-lugs-srol* the old or former customs.

སྔར་རྟོགས *sňar-rtogs*=སྔ་མ་ནས་རྟོགས *sňa-ma-nas rtogs* premeditated; thought of before; anything done after much consideration.

སྔར་ལྟར *sňar-ltar* as before.

སྔར་འཐུང *sňar-hthuň* anything that is to be drunk first; an early drink.

སྔར་དྲངས *sňar-draňs* (སྔོན་འདྲེན་པ *sňon-hdren-pa*) पूर्व्वका formerly invited.

སྔར་གནོད *sňar-gnod* aggression; doing mischief without provocation.

སྔར་མ *sňar-ma* sharp, intelligent, quick of apprehension.

སྔར་མེད་རྙེད་ *sṅar-med-rñed* योग gaining or acquiring what one was without before; སྔར་མེད་གསར་སྒྲོགས innovation; new introduction; སྔར་མེད་གསར་བྱུང་ what did not exist before (in the usage, custom or institutions), but has been introduced.

སྔར་ཚིམ *sṅar-tshim* पूर्व्व पुर early satisfaction; previous contentment.

སྔར་བཞིན *sṅar-bshin* as before, as usual.

སྔས *sṅas* resp. དབུ་སྔས *dbu-sṅas* pillow; cushion; bolster: ཡོ་བྱད་སྔས་སུ་འཇུག་པ using their things as a pillow; སྔས་རྒྱ or སྔས་འགོལ pillow; རྒྱབ་སྔས a cushion for the back; སྔས་མལ a couch of pillows.

སྔས་པ *sṅas-pa*, v. སྔ་བ.

སྔུན *sṅun*, adv. of time; in colloq. signifying previously; first; ago.

སྔུར་བ *sṅur-wa* to snore (cf. ངར་བ also སྔུར་བ་འཛེར).

སྔེཧུ *sṅehu* the kind of pulse or peas growing in the Sub-Himalayan regions called སོན་སྣར་, v. གྲེཧུ *grehu*.

སྔོ I: *sṅo* or སྔོ་དབགས *sṅo-dbags* (སན་སྲེས *sansres*).

སྔོ II: a root signifying green; as sbst. plant, herb, green vegetable; སྔོ་སྐྱེན *sṅo-skyen* early growth; when it is verdant.

སྔོ་སྐྱ *sṅo-skya* pale-green.

སྔོ་ཁྲ *sṅo-khra* painting on a blue body in variegated colours.

སྔོ་སྒ *sṅo-sga* officinal herb; green ginger: སྔོ་སྒའི་ཚ་བས་མཁྲིས་ཚད་མགོ་ནད་སེལ the pungency of green ginger removes headache and congested liver (*Sman.*).

སྔོ་ལྗང་ *sṅo-ljaṅ* bluish-green.

སྔོ་ཏོག *sṅo-tog* unripe fruits; green fruits.

སྔོ་དྲེགས *sṅo-dregs* mire or bluish-green mud.

སྔོ་ནག *sṅo-nag* blue-black; deep-blue.

སྔོ་སྣེ *sṅo-sne* ornaments made of coloured glass-beads.

སྔོ་སྤྲིན *sṅo-sprin* = ཁྱག་རོང་ (mystic expression) (*Miṅ.*).

སྔོ་བ I: *sṅo-wa Cs.* also སྔོད་པ *sṅod-pa*, pf. བསྔོས *bsṅos*, fut. བསྔོ *bsṅo*, imp. སྔོས *sṅos* to become green; སྔོ་བོ *sṅo-bo* green; verdant.

སྔོ་བ II: དགེ་བ परिणाम, कल्याण 1. to bless; to pronounce benediction. 2. to design; to intend: ང་ལ་བསྔོས་པའི་གཡུ *ṅa-la bsṅos pahi gyu* the turquoise intended for me.

སྔོ་སྨན *sṅo-sman* a medicinal herb.

སྔོ་རྩྭ *sṅo-rtsba* green grass, as distinguished from སྐྱ་རྩྭ, whitish-green shoots of grass.

སྔོ་ཚོད *sṅo-tshod* vegetables; herbs.

སྔོ་རྫབ *sṅo-rdsab* n. of a colour or paint.

སྔོ་ཡས *sṅo-yas* n. of a number.

སྔོ་ལོ *sṅo-lo* green leaf; the leaf of a plant (*Cs.*): སྔོ་ལོ་འཆར་བ *sṅo-lo hchar-wa* 1. to sprout. 2. "to become notorious."

སྔོ་བསངས *sṅo-bsaṅs* श्यामल pale or rather Greenish blue; སྔོ་བསངས་མ *sṅo bsaṅs-ma* श्यामा the goddess Paldan Lhamo; the sky.

སྔོ་བསངས་ལུས *sṅo-bsaṅs-lus* श्यामतनु pale-blue body.

སྔོག་པ *sṅog-pa*, prob. pf. བསྔོགས *bsṅogs*, fut. བསྔོག *bsṅog*, imp. སྔོགས *sṅogs*, to vex; to annoy; to cause petty irritation; to disturb from rest.

སྔོན *sṅon* पुरा, पूर्व्व, आदि former; formerly; before; previously; སྔོན་སངས་རྒྱས *sṅon-saṅs-rgyas* आदिबुद्ध the earliest Buddha:

སྔོན་གྱི་རྒྱལ་བ་བཞུགས་བཞུགས་པ *ṣñon-gyi rgyal-wa shugs-bshugs-pa* पूर्व्वजिनाध्यासित when the first Buddha was still living; སྔོན་གྱི་འཆར་གཞི *ṣñon-gyi-hchar-gshi* former matter or subject; སྔོན་གྱི་ཆོ་ག *ṣñon-gyi cho-ga* पुराकल्प the preliminary ceremonies or rites; སྔོན་གྱི་མཐའ *ṣñon-gyi-mthah* पूर्व्वान्त, the end of a preceding one; སྔོན་གྱི་མུ *ṣñon-gyi mu* पूर्व्वकोटि former boundary or limit; the starting point; སྔོན་གྱི་དུས་སམ་ཚེ *ṣñon-gyi dus-sam-tshe* पूर्व्वकाल or पुरा former or olden times. This word has more commonly the temporal signification, whilst སྔོན་ལ refers most frequently to place and position.

སྔོན་སྐྱེས *ṣñon-ṣkyes* ब्राह्मण, पूर्व्वज, अग्रज, the first-born; born before; the first-born of Brahmā; a Brāhmaṇ; an elder brother.

སྔོན་གྱི་རབས *ṣñon-kyi rabs* 1. पुराणम् ancient history; legends. 2. former generation.

སྔོན་འགྲོ *ṣñon-hgro* पुरस्सर, अयेग one going before; precursor: སྔོན་དུ་འགྲོ *ṣñon-du hgro*, སྔོན་དུ་སྩོགས་པ *ṣñon-du ṣtsogs-pa* पूर्व्वयोग the preamble or the introduction of a work.

Syn. གནའ་བོ *gnah-bo* (*Mñon.*).

སྔོན་ཆད *ṣñon-chad* in former times; anciently: སྔོན་མེད་མ་ཡིན་སྔོན་ཆད་མ་གྲགས་པ *ṣñon-med ma-yin ṣñon-chad ma-grags-pa* not that it did not exist before, but it was not known formerly.

སྔོན་འཇུག *ṣñon-hjug* anything fixed to the fore; a prefix; a prefixed letter.

སྔོན་དུ *ṣñon-du* or སྔོན་ལ *ṣñon-la*, adv. and postp. before; formerly; at the head; in advance; in front of. Of the various forms of cognate meaning, this is the most usual and regular; སྔོན་དུ་འགྲོ་བ *ṣñon-du* to go before; precede; སྔོན་དུ་འཇུག་པ *ṣñon-du hjug-pa* to put or place before; སྔོན་དུ་འདྲེན་པ *ṣñon-du hdren-pa* पुरःसर: one drawing before, leading; a guide; སྔོན་དུ་གནས་པ *ṣñon-du gnas-pa* placed or located in front; existing from before; སྔོན་དུ་བྱས *ṣñon-du-byas* पुरस्कृत, साचात्कृत promoted; remunerated; honoured; visited; སྔོན་དུ་བྱས་ནས *ṣñon-du byas-nas* साचात् कृत्वा being respected; སྔོན་དུ་བཞག་པ *ṣñon-du bshag-pa*=མདུན་དུ་བཞག་པ placed before.

སྔོན་དུས *ṣñon-du* पुरा ancient time; olden times; of yore.

སྔོན་དྲན *ṣñon-dran* recollecting the events of former times; རྗེས་ཡོང་སྔོན་དྲན་གྱི་གཏམ *rjes-yoñ ṣñon-dran-gyi gtam* stories of olden times (which have) come down.

སྔོན་ནས *ṣñon-nas* from a former time.

སྔོན་པོ *ṣñon-po* or སྔོན་མོ *ṣñon-mo* 1. v. སྔོ *ṣño* नील blue. 2. stale; old.

སྔོན་པོ་བཞིན *ṣñon-po bshin*=ནམ་མཁའ the blue sky, the nature of which is blue as of old; སྔོན་པོར་འགྱུར *ṣñon-por-hgyur* (མི་དྭང་ མི་བཏུབ) to go out of use; become old and useless.

སྔོན་ཕྱུག *ṣñon-phyug* rich from the beginning; rich at first; formerly rich.

སྔོན་ཕྱུག་པར་གྱུར *ṣñon phyug-par gyur* was formerly rich.

སྔོན་བུ *Ṣñon-bu* a vegetable; n. of a medicinal plant, *Delphinium Cashmirianum*: སྔོན་བུས་ཆུ་སེར་ནད་རྣམས་འཇམ་པོར་སྦྱོང *ṣñon-bus chu-ser nad-rnams hjam-por ṣbyoñ*.

སྔོན་བྱུང *ṣñon-byuñ* इतिहासकम्, पुरावृत्त, अधिसर्ग history; ancient account: སྔོན་བྱུང་བ *ṣñon-byuñwa* भूतपूर्व्व anything happened before; early events; gone before.

སྔོན་བྱུས *ṣñon-byus* विधि, भाग्य destiny; fate.

སྔོན་འབུམ *Ṣñon-hbum* n. of a botanical work; 'the hundred thousand vegetables' (*Cs.*).

སྔོན་སྦྱངས *ṣñon-ṣbyañs* culture of a former birth; early development; སྔོན་སྦྱངས་ཀྱི་ཕྱུགས

sñon-sbyañs-kyi çugs by dint of culture in a previous existence (*Yig. 7*).

སྔོན་མ *sñon-ma* 1. प्राचीन, the former (when two persons or things are spoken of); སྔོན་མ་རྣམས *sñon-ma rnams* the former (persons or things). 2. beginning; ལྷ་ཁང་བརྩིག་པའི་སྔོན་མ་ལྷ་ས་ལ་བྱས་སོ a beginning to build temples was made at Lhasa.

Syn. སྔ་མ *sña-ma*; ཐོག་མ *thog-ma*; དང་པོ *dañ-po*; འགོ་མ *hgo-ma*; གནའ་བ *gnah-wa* (*Mñon.*).

སྔོན་མོ *sñon-mo* शाक the first; a vegetable.

སྔོན་མོ་ཆབ་འདྲན *sñon-mo chab-hdran* (lit. the vegetable which draws out water). 1. n. of a medicinal plant which is largely used in dropsy. It grows on the plains as well as in the clefts of rocks in Tibet. 2. དང་ཡ་ཀུན་སྐྱུག་པོ (སྔོ་སྨན), སོ་དཀར་སྐྱུག་པོ་གཅིག་ཡིག (*Miñ. 4*).

སྔོན་དམར་ཅན *sñon-dmar-can* नीललोहित 1. blue and red; purple. 2. an epithet of S'iva.

སྔོན་ཚེ *sñon-tshe* olden times.

སྔོན་བཞིན *sñon-bshin* as formerly.

སྔོན་ཡང་བསོད་ནམས་བྱས་པ पुण्यंकृत पुण्याम् merits of former existence (*M.V.*).

སྔོན་རབས *sñon-rabs* पुराण ancient history; former generation; སྔོན་རབས་ཀྱི་གཏམ *sñon-rabs-kyi gtam* traditions of antiquity.

སྔོན་རོལ *sñon-rol*=སྔ་རོལ *sña-rol* by-gone time or period.

སྔོན་ལ་བཅད *sñon-la bçad* पुरायक्त previously stated; explained before or said before.

སྔོན་ལས *sñon-las* नियति, विधि, दैव, समय former actions; an accident; an event over which one has no control; from before.

སྔོན་བསགས་མཐུ *sñon-bsags-mthu* power due to merits formerly acquired, v. མཐོ་རིས་གནས or དགེ་ལེགས. 1. virtue; piety. 2. paradise. (*Mñon.*).

བརྙ་བ *brña-wa* to reap.

བརྙ་ཡས *brño-yas* n. of a number.

བརྙད *brñad* 1.=བྲང་ 2. ནས་བསྙོད་པ *nas bsñod-pa* to crop barley. 3. འབྲིད་པ लोभयत to tempt (*Situ. 77*).

བརྙད་པ *brñad-pa* to seduce deceitfully (a woman or man) (*Sch.*); also to draw out; to distill; to extract the juices of.

བརྙད་བ *brñad-wa*, v. རྙ་བ.

✢ བརྙན་པ *brñan-pa*=མཆོད་པ *mchod-pa* पूजन to honour; to worship.

བརྙབ་པ *brñab-pa* 1. acc. to *Sch.*=བརྙད་པ. (2) acc. to *Lex.* རྙབ་པ or རྙམས་པ.

བརྙམས *brñams*=འདོད་པ་ཆེ་བ passionate (*Situ. 99.*).

བརྙའ *brñah* crops; བརྙའ་བྱའི་པོ་ཏོག harvest fit for the sickle (*Situ. 77*).

བརྙས *brñas* reaped; འཆམ་མ་བརྙས reaped the harvest (*Situ. 75*).

བརྙས་པ *brñas-pa* लुभ् tempted, entrapped.

བརྙུབ *brñub*, pres. དབུགས་བརྙུབ *dbugs-hrñub*, བརྙུབས *brñubs*, past "དུ་བ་བརྙུབས *du-wa brñubs* (*Situ. 75*); བརྙུབ་བྱའི་སྨན *brñub-byahi sman* medicine to be inhaled.

བརྙུབས *brñubs* पावित drawn in (breath or water); འཐུངས་ཚར་བ drunk.

བརྙུལ *brñul* pf. of རྙུལ་བ *rñul-wa*.

བརྙོག་པ *brñog-pa* to point out anothers' fault; seek out faults; also to search out a lost article.

བརྙོད *brñod* 1. pf. བརྙོད་བྱའི་ནས *brñod-byahi nas* barley to be cropped (*Situ. 77*). 2. སླུ་བ to seduce, deceive: བུད་མེད་བརྙོད་པ *budmed-brñod-pa* to seduce a woman (*Situ. 75*).

བརྙོན *brñon* प्रतिभेद dividing (discovery) pf. རི་དྭགས་བརྙོན་ཏོ *ri-dbags brñon-to* hunted a wild animal (*Situ. 77*).

བརྔོན་པ་ brñon-pa, vb. pf. and fut. བརྔོན brñon 1. to pursue wild beasts; to hunt; to seduce བུད་མེད་ bud-med, esp. to sensual indulgence (*Jä.*): རྔོན་པས་རི་དྭགས་ལ་བརྔོན་ *rñon-pa sri-dbags-la brñon* a huntsman chases a wild animal. 2. sbst. व्याध, शबर, लुब्धक fowler; huntsman; मृगया, आखेट hunting; རྔོན་པ་མོ་ *rñon-pa-mo* a hunting woman; a huntress (*Cs.*): རི་དྭགས་བརྔོན་ཏོ་ *ri-dbags brñon-to* have been hunting game.

བསྔགས་ལྡན་ *bşñags-ldan* कण्टक, कण्ठक n. of Gautama's horse on which he left his home.

བསྔགས་པ་ *bşñags-pa* = བསྟོད་པ་ སྔན་པར་བརྗོད་པ་ 1. praise, eulogy; परिश्लिष्ट, प्रशस्त praised; བསྔགས་འོས་ *bşñags-ḥos* प्रशस्य, श्लाघ्य praise-worthy. 2. description.

བསྔལ་བ་ *bşñal-wa* to be faint or exhausted (*Cs.*), v. སྡུག་བསྔལ་ *sdug-bşñal.*

བསྔས་པ་ *bşñas-pa* to place the head or body upon a cushion; to recline.

བསྔོ་བ་ *bşño-wa* 1. परिणाम the end v. སྔོ་བ་ *şño-wa.* 2. a blessing, བདག་གཞན་གྱི་དོན་དུ་ *bdag-gshan gyi don-du* cf. སྔོ་བ་ *şño-wa.* 3. mouldy; rotten (*Cs.*).

བསྔོགས་པ་ *bşñogs-pa* — མཚང་དུམ་པ་, pf. བསྔག *bşñag*, imp. སྔོགས་ཤིག *şñogs-çig* (*Situ.* 75).

བསྔོས་པ་ *bşños-pa* संकल्प resolution: བསྔོས་པས་བསྒྱུར་བ་ *bşños-pas bsgyur-wa* परिणामना 1. to make a firm resolve to go the way of *Nirvāṇa* or to do any act of piety. 2. final consequences of Budhhistic enlightenment, viz., showering of blessings on the afflicted. Compare—

यत् किञ्चिद् जगतो दुःखं तत् सर्व्वं मयि पच्यताम्।
बोधिसत्त्वशुभैः सर्व्वैः जगत् सुखितम् अस्तु च॥ (*Bodhi*)

"Let whatever sufferings the world has, come to me! may the merits of the *Bodhisattvas* make the world happy!"

ཅ

ཅ *ca*, the fifth letter of the Tibetan alphabet, corresponding in pronunciation to the Sanskrit च or to English *ch* in the word "child." Acc. to Tibetan grammarians, the Sanskrit च is equivalent to ཙ, the seventeenth letter of the Tibetan alphabet. Thus Tibetans write the Sanskrit word चन्द्र (moon) as ཙནྡྲ *tsan-dra* and not as ཅནྡྲ *can-dra*.

ཅ 1. as num. fig. 5. 2. ཅ *ca*=ལྕ *lca* excrement; alvine discharges: ཅ་འདོར་བ to discharge excrements (*Jä.*).

ཅ་ཅིར *ca-cir* bark (in *Ld.*) (*Jä.*).

ཅ་ཅུས *ca-cus* warped; distorted; awry (*Sch.*).

ཅ་ཅོ *ca-co* 1.=ཀི་ལི་ཀི་ལ कोलाहल, कलकलध्वनि clamour, noise, cry; the noise produced by many people talking with one another. 2.=བཤད་གད; སྙིང་ཚིམ་གྱི་ཅ་ཅོ exclamation of joy: ད་ཅ་ཅོ་མ་ཟེར now do not make such a noise! (*Mil.*) *Ki-li ki-la*, noise of laughter. 3. डिम्ब-कूजन chirping, twitter (of birds).

ཅ་ཅོ་སྒྲོགས *ca-co-sgrogs* कलधौत, कामध्वनि 1. expression of love in birds; a low or pleasing tone. 2.=ཕུག་རོན कपोत pigeon.

ཅ་ཅོ་ཅན *ca-co-can* shouting, bawling; talkative, loquacious (*Jä.*).

ཅ་ཅོ་ཆེ *ca-co-che* ཀླག་ཅོར་ཆེ a babel; confused noise (as in a market) (*Ñag.*).

ཅ་ཅོ་མེད་པ *ca-co med-pa* नास्तिरवितम् free from noise or chatter; without fuss; an attribute of Buddha (*M. V.*); one of the eighteen independent conditions of Buddhahood (*Dh.* sect. LXXIX).

ཅ་ཕྱི *ca-phyi*=མི་མཐུན་པ disagreement; not in accordance with.

ཅ་ར་མ་ར *ca-ra ma-ra* raving; adj. irrelevant: སྐད་ཆ་ཅ་ར་མ་ར་བཤད་ཀྱི་འདུག། he is speaking irrelevant things, talking unconnectedly.

ཅ་ར་ར *ca-ra-ra* the noise produced by the falling of rain in high wind.

ཅ་རི *ca-ri* in *W.* a bug (*Jä.*).

ཅ་རེ *ca-re*=ཅར *car* continually; always (*Jä.*).

ཅ་རེ་ཉ་རེ *ca-re ña-re* drippingly; little and little (*A. 52.*).

ཅ་ལེ་ཅོ་ལེ *ca-le co-le*=ཆ་ལེ་ཆོ་ལེ irregular: ཁྱེད་རང་ཚུལ་ཁྲིམས་ཅ་ལེ་ཅོ་ལེར་སོང་བ་མིན་ནམ (*A. 107*) has not your conduct become irregular and slack?

ཅག *cag* termination of plur. of pers. pron. as in ང་ཅག we, ཁྱེད་ཅག you, ཁོ་ཅག they.

ཅག་ཀྲུམ *cag-krum*=ཆག་ཀྲུམ *chag-krum* 1. sbst. broken pieces (of glass or any brittle thing). 2. cartilage; gristle; སྣའི་ཅག་ཀྲུམ *snaḫi cag-krum* bridge of the nose (*Jä.*).

ཅག་དཀར *cag-dkar*=ཅག་རྡོ in *W.* quartz (*Jä.*).

ཅག་ག *cag-ga* care; vb. ཅག་ག་བྱེད་པ to take care of; ཅག་ག་དག་པོ acc. to *Jä.* in colloq. careful, orderly, regular, tidy.

ཅག་ཅག *cag-cag* crunching sound in eating: ཅག་ཅག་མི་བྱ do not crunch so!

ཅག་ཅེར་རེ *cag-cer-re* closely pressed or crowded in standing or sitting (in *Ld.*) (*Jä.*).

ཅག་ཅོབ *cag-cob* = ཅག་ཅག (*Ñag.*).

ཅག་རྡོ *cag-rdo*, v. ཅག་དཀར in *W.*

ཅང་ *cañ* contraction of ཅི་ཡང་ anything, whatever, everything: ཅང་མི་གསུངས་པར་བྱུར he did not say anything whatever; ཅང་མི་སྨྲ་བ to say nothing.

ཅང་ཏེའུ *cañ-tehu* also ཅང་ཅང་ཏེའུ डमरु a kind of small drum; a hand drum. Those used by the *Tantriks* are made of a human skull; ཅང་ཏེའུ་བརྡུང་རྡེང་ beating a hand-drum (*A. 32*).

ཅང་རིག *cañ-rig* = སྤྱང་པོ wise, prudent; knowing everything.

ཅང་ཤེས *cañ-çes* आजानेय one who knows all about (a subject); ཅང་ཤེས་པ wise, well-informed, good; ཅང་མི་ཤེས་མཁན = ཅི་ཡང་མི་ཤེས་མཁན one not knowing anything; blockhead, simpleton [अजानमान not well informed]*S.*; ཅང་མ་མཐོང་ did not see anything: ཁྱོད་ལ་བཙར་བའི་མཛའ་བཤེས་ཅང་མ་མཐོང་། I have never seen a friend who was intimate with you (*Rdsa. 13*).

ཅང་སྲིད *cañ-srid* what; what is it?

ཅངས་པོ *cañs-po* clever, skilful.

ཅན *can* an affix signifying having, possessing, being provided with, corresponding to the English adj. terminations—ous,—y,—ly,—ful: ཚེར་མ་ཅན thorny. Sometimes also = like, or ish: བོན་ཅན Bon-like; ཁྱོད་ཅན you or one like you; ཧིན་དུ་ཅན a Hindu, Hinduish. ཡོན་ཏན་ཅན = ཡོན་ཏན་དང་ལྡན་པ having or being possessed of merit, qualifications; སྐྱོན་ཅན = སྐྱོན་ཡོད་པ faulty, with faults; ཚེར་མ་རྣོན་པོ་ཅན having sharp thorns; སེང་གེའི་མགོ་ཅན having a lion's head. It is sometimes affixed to verbs: བྱེད་པ་ཅན doer; ལས་ཀ་ཅན worker; sometimes signifies belonging to: བོད་ཅན Tibetan, ཕྱི་གླིང་ཅན European. In *C.* is also used for the possessive pron. ང་ཅན, ཁོ་ཅན my, his or her.

ཅན་ཅིལ *can-cil W.* the green shell of a walnut (*Jä.*).

ཅན་ཅེ *can-ce*, ཅན་ཅེར, ཅན་ཇེ in colloq. ཇ་ཕོར 1. tea-cup (made either of wood or of china (*Ñag.*). 2. a small bowl or dish (*Sch.*). 3. continually (*Cs.*).

\+ ཅན་དུ *can-du* postp. c. accus. to; with: ཁོ་ཅན་དུ་མི་འགྲོ། I do not go to him; ང་ཅན་དུ *ña-can du* with me, in my possession.

ཅན་བཞི་རྒྱལ་པོ *Can-bshi rgyal-po* believed to be an incarnation of Padma Sambhava or *Guru rin-po-che*. ཅན་བཞི་རྒྱལ་པོས་དགྲ་བགེགས་ཙ་རུ་སྐྱོལ། saves one from enemies, evil spirits and *Rudra* (*Lh. kar. 35*).

卐 **ཅབ་ཅབ** *cab-cab* patting or clapping with the hands to express approbation. འབྲོམ་ཡང་རྔོག་ལ་ཕྱག་ཅབ་ཅབ་མཛད་ནས། also bowing to and patting *Rñog* (*Hbrom. 116*).

ཅབ་ཅོབ *cab-cob* (ཁ་ཅག་ཅག་ལྟ་བུ) 1. the sound of tasting. 2. nonsense: ཅབ་ཅོབ་སྨྲ་བ། to talk nonsense.

ཅམ *cam* 1. slow (*Cs.*). 2. quietly, without any noise or fuss; ཅམ་མེ་བཞག་པ or ཅམ་གྱིས་འཇོག་པ to place quietly; in *Sikk.* ཅམ་སྡོད keep silent or sit still. 3. in *W.* acc. to *Jä.* whole, unimpaired: ས(རྩྭ)ཅམ་མེ་ཡོད the whole store of hay is still left. 4. glistening, glittering cf. ལྕམ་མེ (*Jä.*).

ཅམ་པ་ཏ་ལོ *cam-pa ta-lo* in Tsang, the mallow (*Jä.*).

ཅམ་པོད *cam-pod* in *Ld.* a bunch of flowers, sprigs, etc., a handful of ears of corn (*Jä.*).

ཅར *car* 1. (*Lex.*) ཅར་རེ; acc. to *Cs.* ཅ་རེ continually, always; with numerals; གཅིག་ཅར at the same time, opp. to one after the other, successively (viz., doing or suffering a thing, sleeping, dying, etc.). 2. at once, on a sudden, opp. to gradually; ལྔ་ཅར all the five together.

ཅར་མར *car-mar* always, continually (*Sch.*).

ཅར་རས *car-raṣ* = འདོམས་རས a small apron to cover the privy parts.

ཅར་རེ *car-re*, v. ཅར *car*.

ཅལ *cal* or ཅལ་ཅལ noise (*Cs.*); ཅལ་སྒྲོག rumour, (false) report. ཆལ་ཅོལ or ཅལ་ཅོལ་གཏམ idle talk, nonsense (*Jä.*).

ཅས་ཅུས *caṣ-cuṣ* 1. ཕན་ཚུན་ལ་འཆུམས་པ distorted; to be obstinately perverse; twisted; awry. 2. acc. to *Sch.* = ཅ་ཅུམ.

ཅི I: num. fig. 35.

ཅི II: किम्, कथं 1. gen. used in books though not commonly in colloq.: what? ཅིའི of what? ཅིའི་ཕྱིར or ཅི་ཕྱིར why, for what, for what object? ཅིའི་དོན་དུ in whose interest, for what purpose? ཅིའི་ཆེད་དུ or ཅིའི་སླད་དུ why? དེ་ཅིའི་ཕྱིར་ཞེ་ན this wherefore? why this? "if so it is asked." ཅིའི་འབྲས་བུ what sort of fruit; the fruit of what? ཅིའི་རི what kind of mountain, hill; ཅི also like an adj., is placed after the word to which it belongs: རྒྱུ་ཅི་ལས for what reason; on what account? 2. why? wherefore? བདག་ལ་དེས་ཅི་མ་ཆོག། "why should not that suffice me"? ཅི་མི་སྒྲུབ why do you not procure; བསམས་ན་ཅི་མ་ལེགས། I (you) considered, why would not that be a good thing? དེ་འབྱུང་ན་ཅི་མ་རུང་། if that happened, why should it not be desirable? 3. in conjunction with other words ཅི signifies how? 4. inst. of a note of interogation, *e.g.*, in: ཅི་གནང་ for གནང་ངམ, གཤེགས་པར་ཅི་གནང་། "do you allow (me) to come"? (*Jä.*) In the colloq. of *C.* ཅི *ci* is almost invariably re-placed by གང་ *gaṅ* both in the sense of "what" and "which"; whereas, properly གང་ means "which" only, and ཅི means "what."

ཅི III: correlatively which, what; whatsoever; everything. ཅི as a correlative ought properly always to be written ཇི; yet not even in decidedly correlative sentences is this strictly observed: ཅི་བྱེད་ན་འང་། whatever I may do; ཅི་བགྱི་བཀའ་ཙམ་ཏེ་ངེད་ཀྱིས་བསྒྲུབ། whatever we may be bidden to do, we shall obediently perform. ཅི་མྱུར also ཅི་མྱུར་ཞིག་ལ as quickly as possible; also ཅི may = at any rate: སྤྱན་ཅི་དྲངས he must be invited here at all events (*Jä.*).

ཅི་ག *ci-ga* what? colloq. ཅི་དགར, ཅི་དགར་བར whatever one may wish; at pleasure; *ad libitum.* ཅི་ག་ཅི་ཡིན་ནམ what is it? ཅི་གར = ཅི་ལྟར in what manner, how?

ཅི་བགྱི *ci-bgyi* किङ्कर a servant, valet; one who does what he is ordered to do.

ཅི་འགྲོ *ci-hgro* = གང་དག whatever is good: ཕྱོགས་ཐམས་ཅད་ནས་ཁྱོད་ཀྱི་ཅི་མ་སུ་ཅི་འགྲོ་བྱེད། from all sides, whatever is good is accredited (accounted) to you (*A 133*).

ཅི་ཅོག *ci-cog* = ཅི་ཡོད what or whatever is.

ཅི་བརྗོད *ci-brjod* किमुक्तम् what has been stated or told.

ཅི་ཞིག *ci-shig* whatever; something; anything: ཅི་ཞིག་ཏུ་དགོས་པ for what purpose it is wanted.

ཅི་སྙེད་ *ci-sñed*, v. སྙེད་ *sñed*.

ཅི་ལྟར་ *ci-ltar* कीदृश like what? ཅི་ལྟར་བྱུང་བའི་གཏམ་བྱས་སོ "he related how it happened."

ཅི་སྟེ *ci-ste* but if; if however.

ཅི་སྟོ *ci-sto* what does it matter?

ཅི་དྲག *ci-drag* what to do; what is to be done; what is the matter?

ཅི་བདེ་བ *ci-bde ba* किं ह्लादयति 1. what is well, good; what pleases; as it pleases them; as they like. 2. name of a section of *Tantrik* Buddhists in the monastery of Vikramas'ila during Atis'a's time.

ཅི་འདོད་པ *ci-hdod-pa* पर्याप्त whatever one wishes; as much as desired; whatever (they) wish; ཅི་འདོད་པ་བཞིན་ཐོབ་པ to get according to what one wishes [an attribute of a *Bodhisattva* (*M. V.*)].

ཅི་འདྲ་བ *ci-hdra-wa* कीदृश like what? similar to what? ཅི་འདྲ་མཐོང་ what have you seen?

ཅི་སྨྲ་བར་བྱེད *ci-smra bar-byed* किं वक्तव्यम् किमुक्तम् what is there to say?

ཅི་ཙམ *ci-tsam* how much.

ཅི་ཙུག *ci-tsug* how? in what manner?

ཅི་མཚན *ci-mtshan* किंलिङ्ग of what sex?

ཅི་ཤེས་བསྟན་པ *ci-shes bstan-pa* whatever has been demonstrated.

ཅི་ཟེར *ci-zer* what does he say?

ཅི་ཟེར་བརྟག་པའི་ཚིག *ci-zar brtag-pahi tshig* the interrogative expression *ci-zar* (किं वचन) is used to signify:—ཅོ་འདྲི *co-hdri*; འགོག་ཚིག *hgog-tshig*; འགལ་བ་བརྗོད *hgal-wa-brjod*; ཧོག་ལེན་པ *hog-len-pa*; སད་མདའ *sad- mdah* (*Mñon.*).

ཅིའང *cihañ* = ཅི་ཡང (*Situ. 125*).

ཅི་ཡང་ *ci-yañ* = ཅང་ किञ्चन whatever; anything; ཅི་ཡང་མི་ནུས not able to do anything.

ཅི་ཡང་མེད་པ *ci-yañ med-pa* अकिञ्चन nothing whatever; not any; one who has got nothing.

ཅི་ཡང་མེད་པའི་སྐྱེ་མཆེད *ci-yañ med-pahi skye-mched* आकिञ्चन्यायतन [lit. realm of nothingness; one of the eight kinds of *Vimokṣa*—salvation. The sixth stage in which one perceives nothing. Comp. Mahā-p. 30]*S.*

ཅི་ཡང་རུང་བ *ci-yañ ruñ-wa* whatever is permissible, suitable.

ཅི་ཡིན *bi-yin* = ཅི་ག *ci-ga* what?

ཅི་ཡོད *ci yod* किमस्ति what has happened?

ཅི་རིགས་པ *ci-rigs-pa*, adj. यथायोगं, adv. ཅི་རིགས་པར 1. in some measure; to a certain degree; in part; partly. 2. of every sort.

ཅི་རུ *ci-ru* whither: ཅི་རུ་འགྲོ་བ, གང་ལ་ཡང་མ་ལྟ་བར་འགྲོ་བ། to go without looking at anything.

ཅི་ལ *ci-la* कुत्र why? wherefore? ཅི་ལ་ཅི་ལ why? for what? ཅི་ལ་མ་རག་པར་ཆས་པ། gone without being obstructed; ཅི་ལ་ཡང་ कोऽपि for whatever; ཅི་ལ་ཡོད कुतः why is this? whence? ཅི་ལས कस्मात् from what?

ཅི་ཞུལ *ci-çul* ལས་ཅི་བྱས་པའི་རྗེས། after whatever has been done.

ཅིར *cir*, ཅི་རུ *ci-ru*, termin. of ཅི 1. where to, etc. 2. with ཡང་; everywhere; in every direction; for any purpose; by all means; with a negative=nowhere.

ཅིར་མི་རྟོག *cir-mi-rtog* = ཅི་ལ་མི་རྟོག་པ why not consider the matter or subject.

ཅིས *cis* instr. of ཅི by what? whereby; ཅིས་ཡིད་ཆེས་པར་འགྱུར by what am I to believe it? what shall make me believe it? whereby can I know it to be true? ཅིས་ཀྱང་མི་སྐྲག་པ he is not to be frightened by anything. ཅིས་ཀྱང་ and ཅི་ནས་ཀྱང་ used as adv.: by all means, at any rate: ཅིས་ཀྱང་འགྲོ་ན if you wish to go by all means, at all hazards; ད་ཅིས་ཀྱང་མི་ཕན now nothing will help or be of any use; ཅིས་ཀྱང་བཞེས་པ་ཞུ I beg of you at least to accept it; ཅིས་ཀྱང་སློབས teach it to me at any rate! (*Jä.*).

ཅི་རྒོད *ci-rgod* wild millet.

† ཅི་ཅེར *ci-cer* = མགོ་ལ་སྐྲ་མེད་པ without hair on the head; bald head.

† ཅི་ཆིབ *ci-chib* = མཐར་ཕྱིན exhaustive; brought to perfection; to the farthest limit.

ཅི་ཙེ *ci-rtse* कोद्रव a kind of millet; a species of grain eaten by the poor.

ཅི་ཚེ *ci-tshe* = ཅི་ཙེ *ci-tse*.

ཅིག *cig* modified form of གཅིག one, and changing to ཞིག after vowels or after ང, ན, མ, ར, or ལ. 1. a; a few; a little; some: ལུག་ཅིག་ཉོ་ནས་ནང་དུ་ཁྲིད་སོང་ having bought a sheep, they led it inside; མི་ལྔ་ཙམ་ཞིག some five people. 2. when affixed to verbs it is a sign of the imperative mood. ཅུང་ཟད་ཅིག་སྡོད་ཅིག wait a little while! ལམ་སྟོན་ཞིག show the path!

ཅིག་ཅར *cig-car* or གཅིག་ཅུ 1. together; with one accord: ཅོད་པན་བེ་ཅོན་ཅིག་ཅར་སྤང་། he left off his crown and sceptre together (*Zam.*). 2. सत्वर quickly.

ཅིག་ཅར་ཤེས *cig-car shes* = ལན་གཅིག་ཙམ once; equally; ཅིག་ཆར = ལན་གཅིག युगपत् once; all at once.

ཅིག་ཤོས *cig-s̤os* or གཅིག་ཤོས इतर the other; the latter; some other.

ཅིང I: *ciṅ* = ཤིང, or ཞིང, a gerundial particle, the initial letter of which is changed acc. to the rules obtaining for ཅིག; corresponds to the English participle '*ing*' and is used in sentences beginning with "when," "after," "as," and is affixed to verbal roots and adjectives; in the latter case including the auxilliary verb to be: mostly concludes minor clauses and interposed participial sentences, never ending main clauses: བུ་མོ་གཞན་དེ་ཤིང་ཁར་འཛེག་ཅིང་མེ་ཏོག་བཏོགས་ནི the other girl climbing up the tree picked the flower: བྲོས་ཤིང་གབ་པས having hid themselves after running away; frq. also when co-ordinate ideas are in English connected by 'and' or 'but': ཤ་ལ་ཟ་ཞིང་ཁྲག་ལ་འཐུང་བ། eating flesh and drinking blood; ཆེ་ཞིང་ལེགས་པ། tall and well shaped; དྲོད་གནོད་ཅིང་བསིལ་བ་ཕན། heat is hurtful, (but) cold is beneficial. It is also used like the ablative of the gerund in Latin: ཉ་གསོད་ཞིང་འཚོ we live by fishing (*Jä.*).

ཅིན་ཅི་ལི *Cin-ci-li* a creeping plant (in Tsang).

ཅིཧུ་རི *Ciḥu-ri* n. of a female demon (*Jä.*).

ཅུ *cu* 1. num. fig. 65. 2. inst. of བཅུ used in compound numerals for the tens, when the preceding numeral ends with a consonant: སུམ་ཅུ, དྲུག་ཅུ, བདུན་ཅུ, བརྒྱད་ཅུ.

✗ ཅུ་གང *Cu-gaṅ* (སྨན) 1. वंशलोचना bamboo-manna; substance secreted in the joints of bamboos and used in medicine both in India and Tibet. 2. kind of lime used in medicine (*Cs.*): ཅུ་གང་རྨ་ཚད་ཀུན་སེལ་མ་ཚད་གཅོག། *cu-gang* breaks sores and cures inflammation of the lungs.

ཅུ་ལི *cu-li*, ཅོ་ལི *co-li* 1. in *W.* a fresh apricot (*Jä.*). 2. dried apricots. 3. a sort of wild-growing vegetable in Sikk. In *W.* ཅུ་ལི་ཁ་གིར the pulp of apricots boiled down to a conserve and formed into cakes (*Jä.*).

ཅུག་ཅུག *cug-cug*, v. ཙག་ཙག (*Sch.*).

ཅུང *Cuṅ* 1. in *C.* gourd; pumpkin. 2. n. of a place. 3. = ཅུང་ཞིག a little: ད་ཕྱིན་ཅུང་འགྱངས་པ་ཡིན you are a little too late now; ཅུང་ཡོ་བ a little slanting (*Jä.*).

ཅུང་ཞིག *cuṅ-shig*, v. ཅུང་ཟད *cuṅ-sad* a little.

ཅུང་ཤོག *cuṅ-shog* a little (piece), a trifle.

ཅུང་ཟད་ *cuṅ-zad* a littlo; slight, trifling; a little while: ཅུང་ཟད་ཀྱང་མི་ནུས=ཅི་ཡང་མི་ནུས not at all able; ཅུང་ཟད་ཁྲོ་བ a little angry: ཅུང་ཟད་གོད་ a little smiling; ཅུང་ཟད་ཀྱི་ཕྱིར even for the sake of a trifle: ཅུང་ཞིག་ཕན་ནམ་བལྟ I shall see whethor it will help a little; ཅུང་ཟད་ཅིག་སྡོད wait a little, a while; ཅུང་ཟད་མ་བདེ་བ a little unwell; ཅུང་ཟད་ཉམས་པའི་ང་རྒྱལ my self-respect is (made) small.

ཅུང་ཟད་པ an epithet of a Nāgarāja (*M.V.*)

ཅུང་ཟད་ཙམ *cuṅ-zad-tsam* some little.

ཅུང་འགག *cuṅ-hgag* a brass plate or dish (*Ṛtsii.*).

ཅུང་ཞོ *cuṅ-sho* or ཟན་ཆ་གཙོང་ཞི a medicinal white stone alleged to cure diarrhœa (*Jä.*).

ཅུར *cur* colloq. without leaving any remnant; ཅུར་མིད་པ to devour it all up.

† ཅུར་ཎི *cur-ni* (ཞིབ་མོ or ཕྱེ་མ चूर or चूर्ण) 1. powder; in the work called *Li-gur* it is stated to have been derived from the dialect of *Shaṅ-shuṅ*, but it is evidently Sanskṛt. 2. meal, flour (occurring only in medical writings) (*Jä.*).

ཅེ *ce*, num. fig. 95.

ཅེ་ཅང་ *ce-caṅ*, v. ཅེ་སྤྱང་.

ཅེ་ན *ce-na* its other grammatical forms: ཤེ་ན, ཞེ་ན inst. of ཅེས་སྨྲ་བ 'if one says so, asks, so,' etc.

ཅེ་སྤྱང་ *ce-spyaṅ* = ཅེ་ཅང་ used for སྤྱི་སྤྱང་ सिवा, श्रगाल जम्बूक jackal; fox.

ཅེ་སྤྱང་ར *ce-spyaṅ ra*, ཅེ་སྤྱང་ར་ཡིས་ནོར་ཕྱུགས་ནད་རྣམས་སྲུང་། the horn of the (fabulous) jackal; is a protection against cattle disease; n. of a precious stone.

ཅེ་ཙེ *ce-tse* (अनुपाल, also काद्रव *M. V.*) कोद्रव a kind of millet, *Paspalum scrobiculatum.*

ཅེ་ཙེ་རྒོད *ce-tse-rgod*=ཁྲེ་རྒོད wild millet (*M. V.*).

ཅེ་ཧུ *cehu* a reed for sucking up beer. It is called ཙུག་ལི *tsug-li* in Sikk.

ཅེ་ཧོ *ceho*, किल certain.

ཅེ་རེ *ce-re* or ཅེར་རེ staring (fixed-eyes): མིག་ཅེ་རེ་ལྟ་གྱིན་འདུག (he was) looking at it with fixed eyes (*Ñag.*); ཅེ་རེ་ལ་ལྟ་བ *ce-re-la lta-wa* looking with fixed stare: འགོམས་ཤིང་ཕྱིན་མིག་ཅེ་རེ་ལ་མ་མཐོང་བར he paced forward with his eyes staring and open without seeing (it) (*A. 73*).

ཅེང་ཀེ *ceṅ-ke* (གྲི་དཔར་ཏམ) a kind of long knife with thin but broad blade: ལག་མ་ཐོངས་པའི་ཅེང་ཀེ་ཚམ་ལ་འབྲུ་ཁལ for a *Ceṅ-ke* about a little less than an arm's length the price is one khal of grain (*Ṛtsii.*).

ཅེམ་ཙེ *cem-tse* scissors (*Jä.*).

ཅེར་བུ *Cer-bu* n. of a place in Tibet (*B. ch. 4*).

ཅེར་རེ *cer-re* = ཅེ་རེ *ce-re.*

ཅེས *ces* (its other grammatical forms: ཤེས, ཞེས) इति so, thus; *ces* is generally used after ག, ད, བ, as in བདག་ཅེས་བྱ་བ I, the so-named; ཡོད་ཅེས་པ thus existing; ཐོབ་ཅེས so gaining; in ancient literature ཅེས is regularly placed after words or thoughts that are literally quoted, and so continuing the sentence; the quotation itself is generally preceded by འདི་སྐད་དུ or འདི་སྙམ་དུ. In later literature ཅེས and the introductory words are often omitted; in colloq. language always. Inst. of ཅེས་སྨྲས་སོ or ཅེས་གསུངས་སོ so he said, thus he spoke, so has been said or spoken, so it is said; often only ཅེས་སོ is used and in like manner ཅེས་པ for ཅེས་སྨྲས་པ this word, this speech: ཅེས་པ་ལ་སོགས་པ "these and similar words."

ཅེས་བྱ་བ *ces-bya-wa* or ཅེས་པ the so-called, frq. after names; ཅེས་སུ rarely for ཅེས.

ཅོ *co* num. fig. 125.

ཅོ་ག *Co-ga* also written ཛོ་ག=བཙ་ཀ in colloq. བྱིའུ་ཅོག་མོ a small singing bird; the lark: ཅོ་གའི་གྲེ་བས་སྐད་འགགས་སེལ the larynx of *Co-ga* removes hoarse voice.

ཅོ་ག་ཀླད་སྨན *co-ga, klad-sman*=འབྲུ་སུ་དྲང་ (mystic expression) (*Miñ. 4*).

ཅོ་གྲས *co-gras* (*co-tch*) a colt one year old, when Tibetans clip its mane and tail for the first time.

ཅོ་ཏོ *co-to* a tuft of hair on the head; ཅོ་ཏོའི་ཏོར་ག hair plaited and dressed on the crown of the head: སྔགས་པའི་མགོའི་སྐྲ་རྫོག་རྫོག་བསྡམས་ནས་ཐོར་ཅོག་བྱེད་པ to make the hair of a sorcerer's head into ཐོར་ཅོག it (the hair) is gathered into a tuft.

ཅོ་དིར *co-dir*=ཅར་དིར.

卐 ཅོ་འདྲི་བ *co-hdri-wa*, विहेठन, विडम्बना 1. to blame, reproach, scoff at; to vie with: In *K. du.* this term is described as signifying to be jealous of, and as equivalent of ཁྲེལ་བགད་བྱས་པ, acc. to *Ñag.* ཅོ་འདྲེ v. ཅི་ཟེར་བ what does he say. 2. མགོ་བསྐོར་བ to deceive, to cheat (*Ñag.*).

ཅོ་ནི *Co-ni* n. of a district in Amdo.

ཅོ་རེ *co-re* same as ཅོར་ཅོར, the *cor-cor* sound produced by straining fermented beer (*Ñag.*).

ཅོ་ལེ་བ *co-le-wa*=ཐོ་རེ་བ or ཐ་རེ་ཐོ་རེ a little; ཅོ་ལེ་ཙམ=ཐོ་རེ་ཙམ somewhat; rather: བྱང་ཆུབ་སེམས་པའི་བསླབ་པ་ལ་ཉེས་པ་ཅོ་ལེ་ཙམ་གྱིས་གོས། in his instruction of the *Bodhisattva* he was somewhat culpable (*A. 52*).

卐 ཅོག *cog* 1. all; also a plural sign; acc. to *Schr.* all (people): ཡོད་དོ་ཅོག all that exists: ཐོས་སོ་ཅོག all that has been heard; མཐོང་ངོ་ཅོག all that has been seen; ཡིན་ནོ་ཅོག those that exist; གཅེས་སོ་ཅོག those that are valuable. 2. ཤིང་ཐགས.

ཅོག་ཅིག་ཅར *cog-cig car*=ཐམས་ཅད་མཉམ་དུ altogether: དུས་གསུམ་རྒྱལ་བ་ཡིན་ནོ་ཅོག་ཅིག་ཅར་འདུས the Buddhas of the three ages all assembled together (*Ya-sel. 28*).

ཅོག་ཅོག་པ *cog-cog-pa* in *W.* grasshopper; cricket (*Jä.*).

ཅོག་པ *cog-pa* to have leisure: ཅོག་ན་ཡོང་དགོས if you have leisure you should come; དེ་རིང་ཅོག་ཀ་མེད to-day I have no leisure.

ཅོག་བུ *Cog-bu* a small square tent to accommodate only one person used by anchorites of Tibet when they retire to solitary places for practising religious austerities.

ཅོག་བུ་པ *cog-bu-pa* 1. one who lives in a lonely mountain cavern or in a small tent that accommodates but one man. 2. [नैषद्यिक sitting and not lying down; one of the twelve ascetic practices]*S.*

ཅོག་བུར adv. *cog-bur* the manner of sitting up at night awake (*Ñag.*).

ཅོག་ཙེ *cog-tse* is a corruption of the Chinese word ཅོ་ཞ་ཙེ meaning a small dining table. It has been Tibetanized in ཅོག་བཙེགས or ཅོག་ཙེ, ཅོག་ཙེ་ཞབ་ཕྱག་མ་ཡང་འདེར་བཤད་དོ།

(*Jig.*) (a small) table the legs of which resemble those of a pig is here indicated; ཅོག་བརྩེགས་མི་གང་མ a table just suitable for one man to sit at.

ཅོག་རོ *Cog-ro* n. of a place in the district of *Tsañ-dkar* in E. Tibet.

ཅོག་ལ་མ *cog-la-ma* a mineral substance used for medicinal purposes.

ཅོང་ *coñ*, in colloq. ཤོང་ 1. a musical instrument (*Lex.*); a bell (*Schtr*). 2. acc. to *Jä.* a precipice: ཅོང་ལ་སྒྱུར་བ to push down a precipice in order to kill (a man). 3. v. གཅོང་ *gcoñ*.

ཅོང་ཅི *coñ-ci* small bowl or dish (*Sch.*); v. ཅན་ཅེ.

ཅོང་ཅོང་ *coñ-coñ* jagged, indented, serrated (*Jä.*).

ཅོང་བ *coñ-wa* (ངུ་འབོད་ཅོང་བ *ñu-hbod coñ-wa*) to raise wailings, loud lamentations (at funerals); cf. གཅོང་སྐད *gcoñ-skad*.

ཅོང་མོ *coñ-mo* in colloq. for ལྕུང་མོ.

ཅོང་ཞི *coñ-shi*=ཅུང་ཤོ *čuñ-sho* सोम the *Soma* plant said to be useful in diarrhœa, in phlegm and fever; ཅོང་ཞིའི་ཆུ juice or water of the *soma* plant.

ཅོང་རོང་ *coñ-roñ*, perh.=ཅོང་ཅོང་, ཅོང་རོང་ཙེར་མ a kind of thistle.

ཅོར་ཅོར *cor-cor* an onomatopoetic word expressive of effervescing; beer is described in fermenting as making the sound '*cor-cor*': ཆང་སྒྲ་ཅོར་ཅོར་ཟེར་ནས་འཚག་པ། (*Ñag.*) after the sound ཅོར་ཅོར of fermenting beer has ceased, it must be strained.

ཅོལ་ལེ *col-le*=ཞེང་ངེ or ཟེང་ངེ adj. hanging or dangling: ཡུལ་དེ་ན་རི་བྲག་ནག་པོ་མང་པོ་ཅོལ་ལེ་ཡོད་པ། in that country many black rocky hills overhang (*Hbrom. 117*).

ཅོལ་ལེ་བ *col-le-wa*, v. ཟོར་རེ་བ or ཟ་རེ་ཟོ་རེ adj. lying irregularly or promiscuously (*Mñon.*).

ཅོད་པན *cod-pan*, मुकुट, उष्णीष, मौलि 1. tiara, diadem, crown worn by kings. 2. the crest of gallinaceous birds.

Syn. དབུ་རྒྱན *dbu-rgyan*, དཔུང་རྒྱན *dpuñ-rgyan*; ཟླ་བ་ཅན *zla-wa-can*; རྩེ་གསུམ་བགོ་རྒྱན *rtse-gsum bgo-rgyan*; རྩེ་བྲན *rtse-bran* (*Mñon.*).

ཅོད་པན་སྣ་ཚོགས་དཔལ་གྱི་གཙུག विचित्र-मौलि श्रीचूड़, literally, handsomely-crested bird; n. of a king of birds (ནམ་མཁའ་ལྡིང་ *nam-mkhah-ldiñ*) (*M. V.*).

ཅོར་གང་ *cor-gañ* or ཅོར་ཅིག a mouthful; a gulp.

ཅོལ་ཆུང་ *col-chuñ* childish prattle or babbling.

གཅགས་པ *gcags-pa* (*A.K. 1, 24*) 1. to apprehend; to grasp (with the understanding); to impress, gen. with ཡིད་ལ on the mind; ནན་གཅགས་པ well-impressed; impressive; བཀའ་ནན་གཅགས་ཆེན་པོ་གནང་བ། to give a very thorough instruction; གཅགས་པོ་བྱེད་པ། to lay emphasis on. 2. relative to persons it may be synon. with ཆགས་པ, to love.

གཅང་པོ *gcañ-po* clever; lively, sprightly; in *W.* also attentive to; regardful of; གཟང་པོ་དྲང་པོ=གཅང་དྲང་ལྡན་པ clever and sagacious; གཅང་ sbst. sagacity, cleverness; ཁ་གཅང clever words; clever speech (*Cs.*).

གཅད་པ *gcad-pa*, v. གཅོད་པ *gcod-po*=གཏུབ་པ cut into pieces (*Mñon.*).

གཅན་གཟན *gcan-gzan* श्वापद carnivorous animal; beast of prey; the cat and the dog not being included in the term; གཅན་གཟན་ཐ་མ the lowest of the beasts of prey; གཅན་གཟན་གྲི་བ चमूरुग ferocious, wild animals (*Mñon.*); चमूरुग literally signifies a warrior-beast.

གཅམ་པ I: *gcam-pa* = བྱས་པ made: གྲོས་གཅམ = གྲོས་བྱས་པ made a conference; talked over (*Ńag.*).

གཅམ་པ II: = བྱམས་པ *byams-pa* loyal and loving: ཀོང་ཙེ་འཕྲུལ་གྱི་རྒྱལ་པོ་ལ་གཅམ་པའི་ཚིག་གནང་བའི་མདོ། the *Sūtra* for expressing loving words to the miraculous king Kong-tse (*D. R.*).

✝ **གཅམ་བུ** *gcam-bu* adj. artificial, not natural; artificial expression of feeling; insincere demonstration: གཅམ་བུའི་ཚིག་སྨྲ་བ, speaking words of outward regard. Also humbleness, servility, flattery: གཅམ་བུའི་ཚིག, a servile speech (*Sch.*).

གཅམ་བུ་པ *gcam-bu-pa* = ངང་པོ་མི་བྱེད་མཁན། an obsequious, insincere person.

གཅམ་ཡས *gcam-yas* n. of a number.

གཅར་བ *gcar-wa* acc. to *Sch.* cut out; put out; knocked out; cf. བཙར་བ (*Jä.*).

གཅལ་བ *gcal-wa* to spread, display; lay out, *e.g.*, precious stones, jewels, on a table, on the ground (*Jä.*); གཅལ་དུ་བཀྲམ་པ *gcaldu bkram-pa* having laid out.

གཅི་བ *gci-wa* प्रस्राव 1. vb. v. གཅིད་པ to discharge urine; to make water. 2. གཅིན་གཅི་བ་པོ one who is making water. 3. གཅི་བྱའི་ཆུ urine to be discharged.

གཅིག *gcig* एक 1. the number one; གཅིག་པུང་ one only; one and the same; དུས་གཅིག་ཏུ at the same time; at one time; དུས་ཅིག་ན་ or དུས་གཅིག་ན once; one day. 2. one only: ཡབ་གཅིག my only father or མ་གཅིག, the only mother, the mother of several brothers or sisters but idiomatically the common wife of several brothers; ཤིན་ཏུ་གདུང་བའི་མ་གཅིག my only beloved mother: མ་གཅིག་ཡབ་གྱི་སྒྲོན་མ the venerable mother *Labdron*; གཅིག་གིས་གཅིག or གཅིག་ལ་གཅིག, etc., one another, each other; མི་གཅིག་པ different (*Jä.*).

གཅིག་ཀ *gcig-ka* single, only, opp. to several.

གཅིག་ཙར *gcig-car* or གཅིག་ཆར alone, v. ཙར.

གཅིག་ཅིག *gcig-cig* certain; some one (*Jä.*).

གཅིག་གཅིག *gcig-gcig* 1. one at a time; separately; alone. 2. of the same kind; not different. 3. adv. by one's self; only; solely.

གཅིག་གཙོག *gcig-gcog* एकमुख्य, वृन्दारक one principal; the leader; ring-leader.

གཅིག་ཆོག *gcig-chog* all-sufficient (*Jä.*).

གཅིག་རྗེས *gcig-rjes* (ལམ) एकपदी a passage (for one man to pass); lit. fit for one foot only.

གཅིག་ཉིད *gcig-ñid* सख्य, एकत्व friendship; state of unity; the state of being one; oneness; unity.

གཅིག་ཏུ *gcig-tu* एकत्र 1. together with; into one; into one body; གཅིག་ཏུ་སྡུ་བ to unite; to collect into one. 2. at once; wholly; altogether. 3. only, solely; གཅིག་ཏུ་གྱུར་པ एकीभाव be turned into one uniform state; གཅིག་ཏུ་ངེས་པ ऐकान्तिक to be intent on one object; one object for certain; གཅིག་ཏུ་བསྡུས་ནས एकत्र पिण्डीकृत्य, अभिसंक्षिप्य having agglomerated, abbreviated; གཅིག་ཏུ་འདུས་ནས एकीभूय having come together; being united; གཅིག་ཏུ་འདུས་ཤས་སྤྲད་ནས सम्भूय having joined or being united together; གཅིག་ཏུ་འཛིན་པ the holding together or to hold together; ཕྱོགས་གཅིག་ཏུ in one direction; in a certain direction; ཡུལ་གཅིག་ཏུ in a certain place; སྣོད་གཅིག་ཏུ in one vessel; ནང་གཅིག་ཏུ in, one house.

གཅིག་ཏུ་མཛེས་པ *gcig-tu mdses-pa* एकान्त रञ्जक 1. lit. one who can perfectly please. 2. n. of a *Bodhisattva* (*M. V.*).

གཅིག་ཏུ་ཡོད *gcig-tu-yod* व्यतिमृति all existing together; in one place.

གཅིག་ཏུ་སེམས་པ *gcig-tu sems-pa* 1. to be all attention (to any subject or person); to pay homage; to be respectful. 2. དད་གུས་དང་ལྡན་པ། or ཕྱག་བྱེད་པ, གུས་པ to be possessed of faith and respect (*Mňon.*).

གཅིག་འཐོབ *gcig-hthob* 1. expectant (that he will get something). 2. कुशीलव an actor; a bard.

གཅིག་དུ *gcig-du*, acc. to *Jä.* unity and plurality; གཅིག་དུ་བྲལ not having these qualities (*Was.*).

གཅིག་ནས་གཅིག་ཏུ *gcig-nas gcig-tu* परम्परा परम्पर्या from ono to another; in succession; གཅིག་ནས་གཅིག་ཏུ་རྒྱུད་པ सन्तान lineal descent or lineal descendant; one unbroken line of succession; གཅིག་ནས་གཅིག་ཏུ་འདུས་ནས परम्परया, एकं भूत्वा become one or united by succession; གཅིག་ནས་གཅིག་ཏུ་བསྡུ་བ *gcig-nas gcig-tu bsdu-wa* to accumulate for each other; གཅིག་ནས་རྟོགས་པ *gcig-nas rtogs-pa* एकविचारक one who deliberates with undivided attention; གཅིག་ནས་གཅིག་ཏུ་ཞེན་པ *gcig-nas gcig-tu shen-pa* successive thoughts combining together.

གཅིག་པ *gcig-pa* 1. the first. 2. of one kind, not different or manifold; མི་གཅིག་པ different.

གཅིག་པུ *gcig-pu* 1. एकक alone, single, only; གཅིག་པུས་མི་སྟོང་ཐུབ་པ། to be able to cope alone with a thousand men; གཅིག་པུར་ལུས་པ forsaken, abandoned; to be left alone; བུ་གཅིག་པུ the only son. 2. གཅེར་བུ, རྐྱང་པ bare, naked, single; in vulg. ཁེར་མ, ཁེ་རྐྱང་.

Syn. རེ་རེ *re-re*; རྐྱང་རྐྱང་ *rkyań-rkyań*; ཟླ་མེད *zla-med*; ཡ་གྱལ *ya-gyal* (*Mňon*).

གཅིག་པུ་དབེན་པ *gcig-pu dben-pa* = སྙོག་ཏུ་སོང་བ། एकाकिनोऽरण्यगतता residing alone in retirement; one of the conditions of *yoga* (*M. V.*).

གཅིག་པུ་མ *gcig-pu ma* एका a woman without any husband, or living alone.

གཅིག་པོ *cig-po* 1. alone: རྒྱལ་པོ་གཅིག་པོ་སྐྱེས་པ་ཡིན། "the king alone is a man (one possessed of manliness)." 2. being one, or the one: མ་གཉིས་ལ་སྐྱེས་པའི་བུ་གཅིག་པོ། one son of two mothers, viz., claimed by two. 3. the one (*Jä.*).

གཅིག་པོ་པ *Gcig-po-pa* n. of a solitary mountain said to be one hundred *yojana* long and 500 *yojana* high; from which a great river (the Tsang-po) issuing flows eastward towards tho ocean (*K. d.* ར *268*).

གཅིག་བྱས *gcig-byas* केवल only.

གཅིག་མིན *gcig-min* अनेक except one.

གཅིག་ཚིག *gcig-tshig* the singular number (*Situ. 119*).

གཅིག་ལ་གཅིག་མེད་པ *gcig-la gcig med-pa* इतरेतराभाव mutual non-existence; absence of one thing in relation to another thing—a technical term of the *Nyāya* philosophy.

གཅིག་ལས་འཕྲོས་པའི་ལུང་ *gcig-las hphros-pahi-luń* एकोत्तरिकागम n. of a religious work.

གཅིག་ཤོས *gcig-ços* the only one; the othor, when speaking of two.

གཅིད་པ *gcid-pa*, also གཅི་བ pf. གཅིས, fut. གཅི, imp. གཅིས, to make water; to piss.

གཅིན་ནད *gcin-nad* प्रमेह disease of the urine, prob. spermatorrhœa.

གཅིན་པ *gcin-wa* मूत्र, प्रस्राव 1. urine; གཅིན་གཅིད་པ or གཅིན་གཅི་བ to make water. 2. tight, firm, unshaken.

Syn. དྲི་ཆུ *dri-chu*; རྒྱུན་འབབ *rgyun-hbab*; རབ་འཛག *rab-hdsag* (*Mṅon.*).

གཅིན་ཤོར *gcin-çor* involuntary discharge of urine.

གཅིན་འགག *gcin-hgag* retention of urine (*Med.*).

གཅིན་སྙེ *gcin-sñe* प्रमेह prob. gonorrhœa; also a disease of the kidneys in which urine is frequently and involuntarily discharged.

གཅིན་མང་ *gcin-mañ* बहुमूत्र diabetes.

གཅིན་ཡང་ *gcin-yañ* = གཅིན་མང་ *gcin-mañ*, making water again and again.

གཅིན་སྲི་བ *gcin sri-wa* मूत्रकृच्छ्र pain or smarting in discharging urine.

གཅིའུ *gcihu* 1. = ཅིའུ clyster-pipe; གཅི་ཨུའི་སྨན clyster (*Ṅag.*).

གཅིལ་བ *gcil-wa* to spoil; to destroy (*Sch.*).

གཅུ་གལ *gcu-gal* = དོ་གལ་ཆེ་བ (adj. and sbst.) importance; important.

གཅུ་ཏི *gcu-ti* = ཙུ་ཏི *cu-ti*.

གཅུ་དོང་ *gcu-doñ* screw-box.

གཅུ་བ *gcu-wa* = སྒྲིམ་པ 1. to squeeze; to strain; to whirl; turn round like the twisting of a screw: ཡི་མིག་གཅུ་བ་ཞིག་བྱས། (*A. 131*). he made a twist with his eyes. 2. to punish by striking; to correct. 3. = སྒྲུ་བ, v. གཅུད་པ; གཅུ་སྐོར in *W.* གཅུས་བུ screw. གཅུ or སྒྲུ་འཁོར (*Cs.*).

གཅུག *gcug* difference, discord.

གཅུག་མེད *gcug-med* = མཐུན་པ without difference; harmony (*Ṅag.*).

གཅུགས་པ *gcugs-pa* भाव planted, cultivated, acquired or gained; མཛའ་གཅུགས་པ cultivated friendship; འཁོན་གཅུགས་པ to sow or create discord, dissension: ཁོན་པ་ལས་ཁོན་པར་གྱུར་པ། "from hatred to hatred, or hatred increased more and more"; མཛའ་བ་ལས་མཛའ་བོར་གྱུར་པ། to improve friendship; to become more and more friendly; to increase intimacy: མི་མཐུན་པ་ལས་མི་མཐུན་པར་གྱུར་པ། "from disagreement to disagreement, or the misunderstanding became more and more intense still." 5. = བརྟན་པ firm: ཡིད་ལ་གཅུགས་པ། to be firm in the mind, *i.e.*, ཡིད་གཅུགས་པ.

+ **གཅུང་པོ** *gcuñ-po* = སྤུན་ཆུང་བ a younger brother (*Ṅag.*).

གཅུད་པ *gcud-pa*, pf. གཅུས, སྒྲུས fut. གཅུ or སྒྲུ, to turn; to turn round; to twist; to twine; to plait; to braid.

གཅུད་བོར *gcud-bor* 1. adj. is explained in (*Ṅag.*) ལས་ཀ་ཧུར་ཐག་བྱེད་པ་དང་ཅི་བྱེད་ཉན་པ། "doing work with zeal and earnestness and also obediently." 2. གཅུད་ལ་འདོར་བ acc. to *Sch.* to forsake; to cast out; to reject.

གཅུན་པ *gcun-pa* = འཇུན་པ to reprove (one's servants, &c.); to subdue, tame (an animal) (*Ṅag.*); གཅུར་ཉེད་གཅུན་པ to beat or press a thing until it is soft.

གཅུར་པ *gcur-pa* 1. pf. of འཇུར་བ *hjur-wa* (*Ṅag.*) བར་དོའི་འཕྲང་རིང་གི་མཐའ་ལ་གཅུར། shuns the long narrow passage in the confines of the *Bar-do*. 2. a coarse sort of vermicelli.

གཅུས་པ *gcus-pa* to interfere; to meddle with (*Ṅag.*): ལག་པ་གཅུས་པ id.

གཅུས་བུ *gcus-bu* anything that is screwed in; what has got jammed in.

གཅེ་བ *gce-wa*, to esteem; to hold dear; to love (*Sch.*).

+ **གཅེན** *gcen* or གཅེན་པོ or སྔོན་སྐྱེས་པ *sñon-skyes-pa* अग्रज, resp. for སྤུན་ཆེ་བ *spun-che-wa*, 1. an elder brother (*Ṅag.*): དེ་ནས་གཅེན་གསུམ་

གདན་འདྲེན་ལ་ཕྱིན་པས། then he came to invite the three elder brothers. 2. acc. to *Zam.* first-born.

གཅེའུ *gceḫu*, acc. to *Jä.* 1. clyster-pipe = ཅེའུ, གཅེའུ་ཁ་མང་ a flageolet; a kind of musical pipe with many holes in it.

གཅེར *gcer* anything naked, *i.e.*, bare and uncovered; གཅེར་སྐྱོབ a covering for the body; raiment.

གཅེར་སྒྲིབ *gcer-sgrib* lit. that which covers the nakedness of the body; met. clothes or dress.

གཅེར་བ *gcer-wa*, v. བཅེར.

གཅེར་བུ *gcer-bu* नग्न, अचेल, क्षपणक 1. naked; གཅེར་བུར་འབྱིན་པ to make naked; to strip off. 2. = རྐྱང་པ or གཅིག་པུ alone, solitary, without a companion, single.

གཅེར་བུ་པ *gcer-bu-pa* निर्ग्रन्थ a naked person; n. of a sect of homeless mendicants; གཅེར་ཉལ་མཁན of the *Jaina* sect of India; also a Hindu *sanyāsi*.

གཅེར་བུ་གཉེན་གྱི་བུ *gcer-bu gñen-gyi bu* निर्ग्रन्थज्ञातिपुत्र n. of the founder of the *Jaina* heretical school, one of the six *Tirthika* teachers of Buddha's time (*M. V.*).

གཅེར་བུ་མ *gcer-bu-ma* a naked woman; the Goddess Kāli.

གཅེར་བུ་ལག་རྡུམ *Gcer-bu lag-rdum* (མ་བདག) n. of a mischievous armless demi-god.

གཅེར་མོ *gcer-mo* or གཅེར་བུ་མ नग्नका a woman who walks naked.

གཅེས་གཅེས་པ *gces-gces-pa* = བྱམས་པོ་བྱམས་པོ་བྱེད་པ། to show more and more affection for one; to love very much.

གཅེས་བཏུས *gces-btus* choice extracts, &c. (*Cs.*).

གཅེས་པ I: *gces-pa* 1. བྱམས་པ dear; beloved: ངེད་ཀྱི་མི་གཅེས་པ a man dear to us; our beloved; གཅེས་ཕྲུག our darling child: འཇིག་རྟེན་འདི་ན་གཅེས་པ་རང་སྲོག་ཡིན། the dearest thing in this world is one's own life. 2. Also precious; very important; useful: ཤིན་ཏུ་གཅེས་པའི་ཡི་གེ་ལྔ the five very important letters; འཁོར་བར་གཅེས་པ་རང་སྲོག one's life is most precious in this world; ཤེས་པ་གཅེས it is of importance to know.

གཅེས་པ II: (བརྩོན་པ) eager; diligent.

གཅེས་པར་བྱ་བ *gces-par bya-wa* to esteem; to regard with affection.

གཅེས་སྤྲས *gces-spres* (*ce-ṭeḫ*) esteem; གཅེས་སྤྲས་བྱེད་པ to hold dear; to love; to esteem; also to exert one's self; གཅེས་སྤྲས་སུ་བྱས་པ exerted one's self; made exertion: མངོན་པར་ཤེས་མེད་པས་སྔོན་སྐྱབ་པ་ལ་ནན་ཏན་གཅེས་སྤྲས་སུ་བྱས་པར་དཀའ། (*Ḫbrom.* ཁ *2*) without fore-knowledge it is difficult for one to exert himself with assiduity to counteract a former life.

གཅོག་པ *gcog-pa*, pf. བཅག *bcag*, imp. ཆོག or ཆོགས, to break; དུམ་བུར་གཅོག་པ to break into pieces; to burst asunder; to cleave; to split, blast; to violate (a promise, a vow, a law, etc.); to break out from: ཐ་གུ་བཅག་པ་ཡིན་ཏེ the rope having been broken.

གཅོག་རྩིས *gcog-rtsis* reduced account; reduction, discount.

གཅོང *gcoṅ* 1. a chronic disease; གློ་གཅོང chronic bronchitis; ཁོག་གཅོང chronic cough. 2. a defile; རོང་གཅོང a rocky defile.

གཅོང་སྐད *gcoṅ-skad* 1. a low fine musical note or voice. 2. cry of sorrow, lamentations, wailing (*Ṅag.*).

Syn. ཆོ་ངེ *cho-ṅe*; ཡེ་གེ་བྲལ *ye-ge bral*; མ་ལ *ma-la*; ཉེར་སྐད *ñer-skad*; ཟེར་ཟེར་སྐད *zer-zer skad*; ངུད་མོ *ṅud-mo* (*Mṅon.*).

གཅོང་ཆེན་ནད་དྲུག *gcoṅ-chen nad-ḏrug* the six chief chronic diseases: (1) མ་ཞུ་བའི་ནད dyspepsia; (2) སྐྲན; (3) སྐྱ་རབ; (4) ཐོར་ནད; (5) དམུ་ཆུ dropsy in the chest or in the pericardium; (6) གཅོང་ཆེན་རྨ་བྱེད phthisis (*M. gu.*).

གཅོང་བ *gcoṅ-wa* 1. pf. བཅོངས to excavate, wash out, undermine through the action of water: ཟུར་དུ་གཅོང་བར་མ་གྱུར་ཏོ། have not been undermined (by water). 2. to get faint, languid, wearied in mind (*Jä.*).

གཅོང་མེད *gcoṅ-meḏ* without illness.

གཅོང་ཞི *gcoṅ-shi*, v. ཙོང་ཞི.

གཅོང་རོང་ *gcoṅ-roṅ* is described in (*Ṅag.*): རོང་དམའ་བ་བགྲོད་མི་ནུབ་པ། an impassable narrow defile.

གཅོད་རྟོགས *gcoḏ-ṟtogs* (གྲངས) कुट्टचिन्न n. of a number; one versed in that chapter of arithmetic which treats of dividend.

གཅོད་པ *gcoḏ-pa*, pf. བཅད *ḇcaḏ*, fut. གཅད *gcaḏ*, imp. གཅོད or ཆོད *choḏ* छेदन, कुट्ट (*M̱ñon.*) to cut, to cut asunder (ཁམས་ཚད་དུ into small bits); to cut off, chop off (the hands); to cut down, to fell (trees); to cut out (the tongue); to rend asunder; to break (a thread, a rope, chain, fetter). This verb has a very varied metaphorical use, and is especially employed to denote that the course of anything has been stopped or "cut off." Thus it can signify to cure (a disease); to suppress (a passion); to stop a road; to wake up from sleep; སྲོག་གཅོད་པ to kill, to murder, to stop life, to obviate, prevent, avert; to avoid; to lock (the door); བར་དུ་གཅོད་པ to throw obstacles in a person's way; to hinder, impede; frq. སྲོག་ལ་བར་དུ་གཅོད་པ་དེ་དག these life-endangering beings; to stop, to make a pause (in reading); to judge, condemn. Again we have རྗེས་གཅོད་པ to follow after; ཚར་གཅོད་པ to search into; to investigate.

གཅོད་བྱེད *gcoḏ-byeḏ* दमन teeth; छिलर knife; hand; the king; executioner.

Syn. མཆེ་བ *m̱che-wa*; གྲི *gri*; ལག་པ *lag-pa* (*M̱ñon.*).

གཅོད་འབྲེག་པ *gcoḏ-ḇbreg-pa* to make a brief abstract of the grounds of any complaint or application made to a court of justice: སྔ་བོན་ལ་ཡང་གཅོད་འབྲེག་གི་རིགས་སྔོན་དུ་བྱེད་པ་གལ་ཆེ། (*D. çel 7*) it is of much importance previously to make some sort of abridgment; གཅོད་འབྲེག་གི་ཁྲིམས capital punishment in which the culprit is either maimed by cutting off his limbs or is beheaded.

གཅོད་མཚམས *gcoḏ-m̱tshams* the limit or point to be cut for a defined boundary of disputed land; an agreement or definite treaty.

གཅོད་ལུགས *gcoḏ-lugs* Tantrik or mystical system of Buddhism.

གཅོད་ལུགས་བདུད་བཞི *gcoḏ-lugs ḇduḏ-ḇshi* the four chief evil spirits according to the *Tantras* are:—(1) ཐོགས་བཅས་ཀྱི་བདུད། devil that can be stopped or averted; (2) ཐོགས་མེད་ཀྱི་བདུད། devil that comes unhindered or cannot be stopped; (3) དགའ་བྲོད་ཀྱི་བདུད། devil of enjoyment and mirth; (4) སྙེམས་བྱེད་ཀྱི་བདུད། devil of arrogance and pride.

གཅོམ *gcom* for བཅོམ *ḇcom* that which is over-powering; haughtiness, arrogance.

+ གཅོམ་སྐྱུངས *gcom-ṣkyuṅṣ* terror-stricken.

གཅོར་བ *gcor-wa* to spread, scatter, disperse (*Cs.*).

གཅོར་ཟླ *gcor-zla*, ཟླ་བའི་སྐོར་འགོ་འཛིན་ལུགས, གཅོར་འགོ་འཛིན་ལུགས་པ་རང་ལུགས (*Ya-sel.*).

བཅག *ḇcag* or བཅག་པ, v. གཅོག་པ and འཆག་པ 1. व्याकोट्टन cut, ground or divided; ཤིང་བཅག;

རྡོ་བཅག to split wood; to break stone. 2. ས་བཅག་པ to cultivate; till ground (*Situ.* 77).

བཅག་ཐག *bcag-thag* taking care of (one's body, property, chattels, &c.): ངག་བཀོད་ལྟར་གྱི་བཅག་ཐག་སེང་ནོར་མེད་པ་བྱེད། according to (my) verbal direction take care (of the articles, &c.) without mistake.

བཅགས *bcags*, pf. of འཆག་པ, subdued, disciplined, down-trodden: ཞབས་ཀྱིས་བཅགས trodden on by his feet, *i.e.*, brought under discipline (*Situ.* 75).

བཅང་བ *bcaṅ-pa*, pf. བཅངས *bcaṅs*, fut. of འཆང་བ *hchaṅ* 1. to hold: ལག་ཏུ་བཅངས held or carried in the hand (*Situ.* 77). 2. acc. to *Sch.* adj. comprising, comprehensive extensive; བཅང་རྒྱ་ཆེན་པོ comprising much; བཅང་རྒྱུར་མཛད་པ resp. to apply one's self; to bestow pains upon.

བཅད *bcad* in ཚིགས་སུ་བཅད་པ cut or put to metre; poetry. བཅད་ཀ in *W.* a whole that has been cut into, or a piece cut off (*Jä.*).

བཅད་བརྡར *bcad-brdar* critical examination; cutting and rubbing (a thing) for testing.

བཅད་ལྡན *bcad-ldan* a kind of Chinese satin.

བཅད་པ *bcad-pa*, pf. of གཅོད་པ *gcod-pa*, to cut; to separate; to decide; to distinguish, discriminate; to close (a road): རྣམ་པར་བཅད (*A. K.* 1-48) having rent or pierced, cut, separated, decided, distinguished, etc. ཞིབ་བཅད investigate. བཅད་ནས having cut. བཅད་པའི་ཁ་ན་མ་ཐོ་བ་དང་བཅས་པ प्रतिक्षेपणसावद्य one of the disciplinary duties of a Buddhist monk; lit. rejecting or getting rid of what is blamable.

བཅད་པོ *bcad-po* in *W.* something old, torn, worn out (*Jä.*).

བཅད་འཕྲོ *bcad-hphro* = བཅད་ལྷག too few or too many (བཅད and ལྷག) faults in writing or printing.

བཅད་བྱ *bcad-bya* what is to be cut (off); anything to be killed or slain.

བཅད་མཚམས *bcad-mtshams* = གཅོད་མཚམས also དཔྱད་མཚམས rules or laws, especially for monks in monasteries; decision, settlement, agreement.

བཅད་ལྷུག *bcad-lhug*, abbr. of ཚིགས་བཅད་དང་ལྷུག་པ, poetry and prose.

བཅབས *bcabs* गुप्तकृत made secret, concealed; ཕྱག་བཅབས salutation in secret; ཉེས་པ་བཅབས concealed or hidden fault (*Situ.* 75); རང་བཅབས = རང་གིས་སྦས་པ or གསངས་པ self concealed (*Ṅag.*).

Syn. གསང་བ *gsaṅ-wa*; སྦས་པ *sbas-pa* (*Mṅon.*).

བཅམ་བཅོམ *bcam-bcom* trivial things; medley; hodge-podge (*Sch.*).

བཅའ་འགྲིག *bcah-hgrig* full equipment: བཅའ་འགྲིག་རྟ་སྒ་འཁོར་ཆ་འགྲིག full equipment of horse, saddle, and retinue in full array.

བཅའ་སྒ *bcah-sga* शुण्ठि dried ginger.

བཅའ་འཕྲང *bcah-hphraṅ* declivity; precipice (*Sch.*).

བཅའ་བ *bcah-wa*, v. ཆ་བ., sbst. a drinking or drink.

བཅའ་བ་བྱེད་པ *bcah-wa byed-pa* to give notice: བཅའ་བ་བྱེད་ཀྱི་དོན་དུ་ཕར་ཕྱིན་པ་དང་། he arrived for the purpose of giving notice or information (*Yig.* 23).

བཅའ་ཡིག *bcah-yig* letter of notice, official notice; regulation for public guidance.

བཅར་བ I: *b̲car-wa* 1. sbst.=ཉེ་བ near; adj. intimate: ཁྱོད་ལས་བཅར་བའི་མཛའ་བཤེས་ཅང་མ་མཐོང་། (*Rdsa. 13*) I have not seen a more intimate friend than you. 2. vb. to interview; སྐུ་བཅར་ཆོག་པ to be permitted to interview (a great man).

བཅར་བ II: 1. acc. to *Jä.* བཅར་བ=བཙིར་བ, to squeeze, to press (in a press); to crowd, to throng. 2. to pull or force from; to wrest (*Cs.*). 3. acc. to *Sch.* ཟོགས་སུ་བཅར་བ, to prop sideways.

བཅར་བཞུགས་པ *b̲car b̲shugs-pa* to have a permanent residence.

བཅལ་བ *b̲cal-wa*, pres. pf. of འཇལ་བ to weigh; to pay; pay back; ནོར་བཅལ estimated wealth; བྲེ་ལ་བཅལ measured in a *bré* (*Situ 75*).

བཅལ་ལུང་ *b̲cal-luṅ*=གཡོག་པོ *gyog-po* a waiter for orders; a servant (*Mṅon.*).

བཅས *b̲cas* and བཅས་པ also བཅས་ཏེ *b̲cas-te* सह, सहित, सार्द्ध a word used as a conjunction and as adj. It is annexed to nouns by means of the conjunction དང་ signifying together with, connected with, having, possessing, containing a thing: འཁོར་དང་བཅས་པ together with the attendants, with retinue or suite; frq. བུ་མོ་བོད་བློན་དང་བཅས་པས་བསྐོར་ཏེ། surrounded by (ten) virgins together with the Tibetan ambassadors: བཙུན་མོ་དང་སྲས་སུ་བཅས་ཏེ། with his wife and son; གོས་དང་བཅས་སུ with; having his clothes on; ཞལ་འཛུམ་པ་དང་བཅས་ཏེ། with a smiling face; སེར་སྣ་དང་བཅས་པ། subject to avarice; འཁྲུལ་བཅས infatuated, fascinated. When the form is བཅས་སུ *b̲cas-su*, the construction is adverbial, and the words introduced with it are to be taken adverbially as qualifying the proximate verb., *e.g.*, བུ་མོས་ཐུར་མ་དང་བཅས་སུ་མེ་ལ་མར་བླུགས་སོ, the girl poured butter on the fire with her spoon. It is also used as a kind of plural; also like ལ་སོགས་པ, meaning "etc.," or "and such like." So, too, we read བརྒྱགས་དང་བཅས་བསྐྱལ་ལོ། provisions and other necessaries are sent.

བཅས་པའི་ཁྲིམས *b̲cas-pahi khrims* Buddhist canon; religious regulations.

བཅས་རང་ *b̲cas-raṅ* प्रज्ञप्ति 1. notification, information. 2. transgression: བཅས་ནི་སངས་རྒྱས་ཀྱིས་ཁྲིམས་སུ་བཅས་པ, རང་ནི་རང་བཞིན་གྱི་ཉེས་པ། In *b̲cas-raṅ*, *b̲cas* is law or rule laid down by Buddha and *raṅ* is *raṅ-b̲zin-gyi ñes-pa*, *i.e.*, natural corruption, hence it signifies transgression caused by violating the law of Buddha.

བཅིང་བ 1. *b̲ciṅ-wa* and བཅིངས་པ are parts of འཆིང་བ *h̲chiṅ-b̲a* बन्ध, to bind. 2. sbst. bond, fetters (whether of a material, moral, or magical nature); ཞགས་པས་བཅིངས tied with rope (*Situ. 75*).

བཅིངས་ཐག *b̲ciṅs-thag*=ཞགས་པ *shags-pa* पाश string or rope to bind with; fetter.

བཅིངས་པ་གྲོལ་བ *b̲ciṅs-pa grol-b̲a* बन्धमोचन lit. to untie what is bound; liberation; emancipation.

བཅིན *b̲cin*, v. ཅིན.

࿕ **བཅིབས** *b̲cibs*, pf. of འཆིབ་པ, signifying ཞོན་པ, to mount or ride on a horse; ཆིབས་ལ་བཅིབས rode on a horse (*Situ. 75*).

བཅིར་བ *b̲cir-wa*, v. འཚིར་བ.

࿕ **བཅིལ་བ** *b̲cil-b̲a*, pf. of འཇིལ་བ (*R̲do. 46*) to abandon, give up; to bring under subjection: དབང་པོའི་སྒོ་ལྔའི་ཆགས་སྡང་གི་སྤྱོད་པ་ཅུང་ཟད་ཙམ་ཡང་ཕྱིར་བཅིལ་ཏེ་བསྡམས་སོ (*H̲brom.* ཀ *36*) he brought himself under control by abandoning, at least to a certain extent, the passions of the five senses.

བཅུ *bcu* or བཅུ་ཐམ་པ ten; བཅུ་ཕྲག a decade; བཅུ་པ the tenth; བཅུ་པ་དང་པོ the first ten (of a series); བཅུ་པོ the tenth; བཅུ་ཁ tithe levied as duty, hence customs-duty; བཅུ་སྒྱུར ten-fold; བཅུ་ཁག་འདོན་པ to tithe; to take a tenth.

Syn. སྟོབས *stobs*; སོར་མོ *sor-mo*; ཕྱོགས *phyogs*; འཇུག་པ *hjug-pa*; ཁྲོ་བོ *khro-wo*; འབྱོར་པ *hbyor-pa* (*Rtsi.*).

བཅུ་བརྒྱད་བཀར་ཁོངས *Bcu-brgyad bkar-khoṅs* n. of one of the state treasuries of Tibet.

བཅུ་གཅིག *bcu-gcig* एकादश eleven.

Met. Syn. བདེ་བྱེད *bde-byed*; བདེ་འབྱུང *bde-hbyuṅ*; དབང་ཕྱུག *dwaṅ-phyug*; དྲག *drag*; བྱེད་པ *byed-pa* (*Rtsi.*).

བཅུ་གཅིག་ཞལ *Bcu-gcig-shal* the eleven-faced deity—a name for the *Bodhisattva* Avalo-kites'vara.

བཅུ་གཉིས *bcu-gñis* द्वादश twelve.

Met. Syn. ཉི་མ *ñi-ma*; རྟེན་འབྲེལ *rten-hbrel*; ཁྱིམ *khyim* (*Rtsi.*).

བཅུ་ཐེབས *bcu-thebs* tenfold; also a group or a batch of ten.

བཅུ་དྲུག *bcu-drug* sixteen.

Met. Syn. མི་བདག *mi-bdag*; རྒྱལ་པོ *rgyal-po* (*Rtsi.*).

བཅུ་དྲུག་ཆ *bcu-drug-cha* 1. one sixteenth portion. 2.=कला the lunar crescent—each of which is one sixteenth of the full moon.

བཅུ་དྲུག་བདག་པོ *bcu-drug bdag-po* 1. the full moon; བཅུ་དྲུག་བདག་པོའི་དཀྱིལ་འཁོར། the disk of the full moon: སྐུ་འཚོ་བཅུ་དྲུག་བདག་པོའི་དཀྱིལ་འཁོར་དྲི་མེད་ལྟ་གསལ། his healthy person shone like the spotless disk of the full moon (*Yig.*). 2. སྐྱུ་རུ་ར आमलकी, पञ्चरसा *Emblic myrobalan*.

Syn. སྒྲ་མཁན *sgra-mkhan*; སྒྲ་མཁས *sgra-mkhas*; མེ་བཞི་སྐྱེས *me-bshi-skyes*; འབར་བ་ལྡན *hbar-wa-ldan*; སྣ་ཚོགས་གཙུག་ཅན *sna-tshogs gtsug-can*; ཉི་མའི་རིགས་སྐྱེས *ñi-mahi-rigs skyes*; མཐོ་རིས་ཐོབ *mtho-ris-thob*; རིག་བྱེད་བདག *rig-byed-bdag*, also ལྷ་ཡི་བླ་མ *lha-yi bla-ma*; ལྷ་ཡི་སློབ་དཔོན *lha-yi slob-dpon* (*Mñon.*).

བཅུ་གཉིས་མིག་ལྡན *bcu-gñis mig-ldan* an epithet of Kumāra or Saḍānana, the youngest son of Mahādeva.

བཅུ་དྲུག་བདེ་བའི་ཆ་ཤས maiden of sixteen.

བཅུ་དྲུག་འོད་ལྡན *bcu-drug hod-ldan* शुक्र a name of the planet Venus.

བཅུ་དཔོན *bcu-dpon* a corporal over ten soldiers.

བཅུ་ཕོག *bcu-phog* an allowance every ten days (given to every monk) in the state monasteries of Tibet.

བཅུ་བ *bcu-wa*=འཆུ་བ.

བཅུ་བན *bcu-ban* a mug for keeping wine or beer enough for ten persons.

བཅུ་བཞི *bcu-bshi* fourteen.

Met. Syn. སྲིད *srid*; ཡིད *yid*; མ་ནུ *ma-nu*; ཤེད་བུ *çed-bu* (*Rtsi.*).

བཅུ་བཞི་སྟོན *bcu-bshi ston* चतुर्दशीका a festival kept on the 14th day, *i.e.*, before the full or new moon.

བཅུ་གལ *bcu-gal*=དོ་གལ་ཆེ་བ important; ཕྱིང་པ་འཆག་པ་ཁྲི་ལག་བཅུ་གལ་མེད། (*Rdsa. 21*).

བཅུ་གསུམ *bcu-gsum* thirteen.

Met. Syn. འདོད་པ *hdod-pa*; ལུས་མེད *lus-med*; མྱོས་བྱེད *myos-byed*; གདུགས *gdugs*; རིམ *rim*; སྣ་ཚོགས *sna-tshogs* (*Rtsi.*).

བཅུག་ནས *bcug-nas*=ལྷུགས་ནས निक्षिप्त thrown or having poured into.

བཅུག་པ *bcug-pa*, pf. of འཇུག་པ with, also, the special meanings of; to meddle; to interfere: ངེད་ཀྱི་དོན་ལ་ཁྱོད་ལག་བཅུག་དོན་མེད། you have no business to interfere in my affairs (*Rdsa.*).

བཅུད *bcud* रस, चार 1. sap, juice, moisture. 2.=སྙིང་པོ or essence: ས་ཡི་བཅུད the essence of the earth or soil, by which the produce of the field, medicinal plants and precious metals and stones, &c., are said by Tibetans to be produced; therefore this essence is the natural fecundity of the soil and is not the same as moisture or manure; ཟས་ཀྱི་བཅུད the food nutriment which sustains life and also by which living beings thrive and grow; ཟླ་བའི་བཅུད the fructifying effect of the moon on the vegetable world which is compared to the nectar of the gods. 3. invigorating cordial; quintessence.

བཅུད་ཀྱི་མ *bcud-kyi-ma*, v. ह्वे रसना organ of taste; रसमातृका the tongue, lit. the mother of all taste.

བཅུད་སྐྱེས *bcud-skyes* रस agreeable taste.

བཅུད་ལྔ་པ *bcud lña-pa*=སྐྱུ་རུ་ར आमलकी *Emblic myrobalan.*

བཅུད་ལྔ་ལྡན་པ *bcud-lña lñan-pa*=བུང་བ the bee; भ्रमिकर a kind of poisonous insects.

བཅུད་ཅན *bcud-can* nutritious; བཅུད་མེད not nutritious; also insipid.

བཅུད་བརྟུལ་ཞུགས *bcud brtul-shugs*=བཅུད་འཛིན that takes or holds the elixir or essence (*Mñon.*).

བཅུད་ལྡན་ཆེ *bcud ldan-che* रसातल the nether world.

བཅུད་ཕྲ་མོ *bcud phra-mo* मधुर lit. of mild taste; sweet.

བཅུད་སྦྱིན *bcud-sbyin*=བཅུད་འཛིན.

བཅུད་མོ་ལྡན *bcud-mo-ldan* रसवत् possessed of the essence; sweet, juicy, succulent.

བཅུད་སྨིན་པ *bcud smin-pa* ripe; ripeness.

བཅུད་འཛིན་མ *bcud hdsin-ma*=འབབ་ཆུ a cataract; cascade (*Mñon.*).

བཅུད་ལེན *bcud-len* or བཅུད་ཀྱི་ལེན रसायन the art of extracting essences for prolonging health and longevity, such essences as being of different kinds, viz.:—ཏིང་ངེ་འཛིན་གྱི་བཅུད་ལེན the elixir of meditation; མེ་ཏོག་བཅུད་ལེན the elixir drawn from flowers, *i.e.*, honey; རྡོ་བཅུད་ལེན the elixir drawn from pebbles, &c. Animate beings are metaphorically called བཅུད and this world འཇིག་རྟེན is called བཅུད་ཀྱི་སྣོད the receptacle of life; animated nature.

བཅུད་ལེན་གྲུབ *bcud-len grub* गन्धर्वं [a class of demi-gods] *S.*

བཅུད་ལེན་གྲུབ་པའི་དངུལ་ཆུ पारारस, रसायन mercurial preparation for making an elixir of life.

བཅུམ་པ *bcum-pa*=བསྐུམ་པ also བཟུང་བ 1. to become contracted; contraction ཛིངས་ཀྱི་ཤར་ནུབ་གཉིས་ནས་བཅུམ་སྟེ། the east and west (sides) of the ship having contracted (*A. 18*). 2. pf. tense of འཛུམ་པ. 3. acc. to *Sch.* to use artifices; to chicane.

བཅུར་པ *bcur-pa* 1. to be flattened down (*Sch.*). 2. colloq. to bar, obstruct block up by snow; obstructing a road; cf. འཇུར་བ (*Jä.*) སྣང་དུ་བཅུར་ཏེ (*Situ. 77*).

བཅུས་པ *bcus-pa*, pf. of བཅུ་བ (ཆུ་བཅུས) उत्क्षत 1. to draw out water; to irrigate. 2. to distil (*Situ. 75*).

བཅེར་བ *bcer-wa* 1. to heap or pile up; to collect in one place: མཁའ་འགྲོ་མ་མང་པོས་སྔགས་ཀྱི་གླེགས་བམ་མང་པོ་བཅེར་ནས། (*A. 37*) many volumes of *Mantras* having been collected by many *Khado-ma*. 2. to glare at: བཅེར་ཏེ་གཟིགས་ནས་ཞལ་ནས་འདི་སྐད་གསུངས། having looked closely at them, he spake thus. 3. colloq.=བཙེར་བ to squeeze; to press.

བཅོ *bco* for བཅུ in, བཅོ་ལྔ 15, and བཅོ་བརྒྱད 18.

བཅོ་བརྒྱད *bco-brgyad* eighteen.

Syn. ཉེས *ñes*; སྐྱོན *skyon*; ཁམས *khams* (*Rtsi.*).

བཅོ་ལྔ *bco-lña* fifteen.

Met. Syn. ཚེས *tshes*; ཉིན *ñin*; ཞག *shag* (*Rtsi.*).

བཅོ་ལྔ་མཆོད་པ *Bco-lña mchod-pa* the religious service that is observed on the fifteenth of the first Tibetan month (February-March) at Lhasa wheu the Kinkhording, the grand temple of Buddha, is illuminated.

བཅོ་པ *bco-pa* a colt one year old.

བཅོ་བ *bco-wa* pf. and imp. བཅོས, prop. root of the fut. tense of འཆོས་པ, but in *W.* the usual word for བྱེད་པ, to make, perform; to prepare, mauufacture, construct. It is employed in all kinds of phrases (*Jä.*).

བཅོག་པ *bcog-pa* to reduce, cut down: ཟླ་བ་རེར་བཅུ་ཟུར་བཅོག "every month makes it less by ten" (*Rtsii.*); བཅོག་རྩིས the account or calculation of reduction (of pay, allowances, &c.).

བཅོམ *bcom* भग success; victory; triumph.

བཅོམ་བསྐྱུངས་པ *bcom-bskyuṅs-pa* to speak in low voice or to keep silent (out of fright); འཕྲོག་བཅོམ robbery and acts of violence.

བཅོམ་ལྡན *bcom-ldan* victorious, blessed, triumphant (over enemies).

བཅོམ་ལྡན་འདས *Bcom-ldan hdas* भगवान् the victorious one who, having subdued the host of Māra, has passed away from misery; epithet attached specially to the Buddha S'akyamuni, acc. to *Sch.* 'the victoriously-consummated.'

བཅོམ་ལྡན་འདས་རྒྱལ་བ भगवान् जिन the blessed Jina, the conquerer of his (moral enemies).

བཅོམ་ལྡན་རལ་གྲི *Bcom-ldan ral-gri* n. of a fancied Buddha.

བཅོམ་པ *bcom-pa*, pf. of འཇོམས་པ *hjoms-pa* निहत, घात, निर्घात, conquered, subdued, killed. Also broken down, dispersed; མངོན་བཅོམ अभिहत fully subdued (*A. K. 1-2*).

བཅོམ་རླག *Bcom-rlag* मथुरा n. of an ancient city of India near Agra iu the early times of Buddhism.

བཅོམས *bcoms*, pf. གཞོམས, fut. འཇོམས. (*Rtsii. 46*).

བཅོལ་དམ *bcol-dam* taking care of things entrusted to one's charge; བཅོལ་དམ་བྱ, བཅོལ་དམ་ཟིན, ཡག་པོ་བཅོལ་བ or དམ་པོ་བྱས་ཏེ.

བཅོལ་བ *bcol-wa* pf. and fut. of འཆོལ་བ.

བཅོལ་མ *bcol-ma* a thing committed to a person's charge; a trust.

བཅོལ་བཞོག་པ *bcol bshog-pa* to entrust a thing to another's charge; བཅོལ་གཏམ་བྱེད་བཞག་པ། to settle about the trust; to entrust a thing to a person's charge (with an understanding): བཅོལ་ཧྲོགས=ཟླུས་ཐོག.

བཅོས *bcos* or བཅོས་བུ कृत्रिम artificial.

བཅོས་ཐབས *bcos-thabs* 1. the method of curing. 2. doing a thing for the sake of appearances, or for form's sake; བཅོས་སུ་བྱེད་པ performing a show work: གཞི་ནས་བསྒྱུར་ཅིང་བཅོས་ནས་གཏན་ལ་ཕབ་བོ། changing or modifying it radically, he published the artificial one (*A. K. 74*). 3. made or contrived by art; མ་བཅོས artless; unaffected; genuine.

བཅོས་ཐབས་མེད *bcos-thabs-med* निष्प्रतिकार no means of cure (disease) or mending matters.

བཅོས་པ *bcos-pa* संस्कार to refine; प्रतिकृति, भृति to cure, remedy; healing or mending; कृत्रिम artificial, affected, feigned; mixed up: མཁས་ཀྱང་བཅོས་སུ་མེད་ he cannot be cured even by the wisest.

བཅོས་པའི་ནགས *bcos-pahi-nags* an artificial grove attached to one's residence.

Syn. སྐྱེད་མོས་ཚལ *skyed-mos tshal* or ཁྱིམ་གྱི་ཚལ *khyim-gyi-tshal* (*Mṅon.*).

བཅོས་པའི་མ་ནིང *bcos-pahi ma-niṅ* one who is artificially made a eunuch.

Syn. ཧོག་མེད་པ *hog-med-pa*; སྐྱེས་པ་འབྲུས་ཕུང་བ *skyes-pa hbrus phuṅ-wa* (*Mṅon.*).

བཅོས་བུའི་རས *bcos-buhi-ras* a coloured cloth (*Ṅag.*).

བཅོས་མ *bcos-ma* sbst. and adj. anything artificial; anything ficticious, alloyed (metal or thing), counterfeit, mock, sham, not genuine.

བཅོས་མ་བྱེད་པ *bcos ma-byed-pa* क्रियावादी a section of the *Tantrik* school which practises mysticism.

ལྕེ *lce*, in *Ld.* for ལྕི་བ, excrement, dung, (of cattle) (*Jä.*).

ལྕ་སྒ *lca-sga*=བཙའ་སྒ white ginger, v. སྒ.

ལྕ་བ *lca-wa* 1. a sort of carrot (*Cs.*). 2. कम्बल a garment made of wool or felt: ལྕ་བས་ཆུ་སེར་མཁལ་ནད་གྲང་བ་སེལ། felt cures watery discharges, kidney disease, and cold in the loins (*Med.*).

ལྕག *lcag* 1. whip, rod, switch, stick: རྟ་བཟང་ཀྱང་ལྕག་ཅིག་དགོས། even a good horse requires a whip; ལས་ལ་བསྐུལ་ལྕག་མཛད་ to get work done, urging on is necessary; རྟ་ལྕག horse-whip; གླང་ལྕག ox-whip; རྔ་ལྕག stick to beat a kettle-drum; ལྕག་ངག willow-twig; osierswitch; སྨྱུ་ལྕག a cane or bamboo whip; ཚིག་ལྕག sharp words for reproof, rebuke. 2. stroke, blow, cut; མགོ་ལྕག a blow on the head; འགྲམ་ལྕག a smack on the cheek (*Cs.*); ཞལ་ལྕག slap on the face. 3. forepart of a coat of mail (*Sch.*). 4. a kind of daphne paper, v. རེ་ལྕག་པ

ལྕག་རྡོ *lcag-rdo* in *W.* flint; flint-stone; ལྕག་འབྲུམ whip-cord (*Jä.*).

ལྕག་ལྕིག *lcag-lcig* n. of a number: ལྕག་ལྕིག་ཕྱུང་ཆེམ་ཆེམ་དང་། (*Ya-sel. 56*).

ལྕག་ཐོགས *lcag-thogs*=འབྲོག་པ lit. one who carries a whip (in hand) (*Mṅon.*); yak-herd; also shepherd.

ལྕག་སིལ *lcag-sil*, occurs in རྫང་ཚས་ཕུལ་རྒྱ་ལྕག་སིལ.

+ ལྕག་པོད *lcag-pod*=ཚམ་མགོ་ཅན་གྱི་སྐེ་རགས *chab-mgo can-gyi ske-rags* is described as a girdle made of plaited wire and interlaced scales resembling a chain.

ལྕག་འབྲིང་ *lcag-hbriṅ*=ལྕག་དང་ lash of whip.

ལྕག་ཚན *lcag-tshan* or རྟ་ལྕག a whip in general; a horse-whip.

ལྕག་ཡུ *lcag-yu* the handle of a whip.

ལྕགས I: *Lcags* n. of a place eight miles to the south-east of Tashi-lhunpo in Tsang.

ལྕགས II: लोहक, मल, कृष्ण 1. iron; ལྕགས་བརྐོན་མཁན one who digs out iron; རྒྱ་ལྕགས Chinese iron; ཐོ་ལྕགས steel; an inferior sort of iron; མོ་ལྕགས a finer and ductile sort of iron; acc. to *Cs.* steel. 2. any iron instrument or tool, esp. lock (of doors), fetter, shackle: སྒོ་ཐམས་ཅད་ལྕགས་བརྒྱབ་ཅིང་། having locked every door; གནམ་ལྕགས a thunderbolt; also a flash of lighting just striking an object; མེ་ལྕགས a steel to strike fire with; a tinder-pouch.

ལྕགས་ཀྱི་འཁྲུལ་འཁོར *lcags-kyi hkhrul-hkhor* 1. an enchanted iron-horse; the magic iron-horse, *i.e.*, a name said to be given to the railways of India by the Tibetans.

ལྕགས་ཀྱི་གར་བུ *lcags-kyi gar-bu* अयःपिण्ड iron-ball.

ལྕགས་ཀྱི་ཐོ་ལུམ *lcags-kyi tho-lum* अयोगुड a lump of iron; a hammer.

ལྕགས་ཀྱི་ཕུང་པོ་ཞེས་བྱ་བའི་རི a fabulous mountain which extends eastward over a distance of 12,000 miles from the ocean and is filled with iron ore and iron-dust (*K. d.* ར *341*).

ལྕགས་ཀྱི་བཙའ *lcags-kyi-btsah* rust; ལྕགས་ཀྱི་བཙའ་ཡིས་མཆིན་པའི་ནད་ལ་ཕན། rust or oxide of iron is useful in liver disease.

ལྕགས་ཀྱི་ཚ་ཚ *tsha-tsha* अयस्पपातिका red-hot particles of iron flying under the smith's hammer.

ལྕགས་ཀྱི་ཚོགས *lcags-kyi tshogs* rust of iron, scoria.

ལྕགས་ཀྱི་གཞོངས་རིང *lcags-kyi gshoṅs-riṅ* अयोद्रोणिका iron vessel; iron-tray or bowl.

ལྕགས་ཤལ་མ་ལི་བན *lcags-çal ma-li-ban* अयःशाल्मलीवन the wood of iron bristles; n. of one of the subdivisions of hell (*M. V.*).

ལྕགས་ཀྱི་སིལ་ཁྲོལ *sil-khrol* झाझरी iron bells or rings tied to the necks of donkeys and mules, etc.

ལྕགས་ཀྱུ *lcags-kyu* अङ्कुश 1. iron pin to guide and punish elephants; fish-hook: ལྕགས་ཀྱུས་གདུལ་དཀའ་བ *lcags-kyus gdul dkah-wa* an elephant that is difficult to tame or manage with the iron-pin. 2. n. of an officinal plant used to allay the effect of poison.

ལྕགས་ཀྱུས་སྒྱུར་ཐབས *lcags-kyus sgyur-thabs* अङ्कुशग्रह an elephant-driver, also the art of disciplining elephants.

ལྕགས་དཀར *lcags-dkar* tin; tinned iron-plate.

ལྕགས་སྐམ *lcags-skam* iron pincers.

ལྕགས་སྐུད *lcags-skud* iron-wire; a thin wire made of steel.

ལྕགས་ཁ *lcags-kha* iron colour or iron-grey.

ལྕགས་ཁུ *lcags-khu* iron wash: ལྕགས་ཁུས་མཆིན་ཚད་མིག་ནད་བྲུ་བ་སེལ། iron-wash (water containing oxidized iron) removes inflammation of the liver, and eye-abscess (*Med.*).

ལྕགས་ཁྱེམ *lcags-khyem* लोहकुशी a spade.

ལྕགས་ཁྲོལ *lcags-khrol* an iron caldron.

ལྕགས་མགར *lcags-mgar*=མགར་བ *mgar-wa* लोहकारक ironsmith; smith.

ལྕགས་མགུ *lcags-mgu* or ལྕགས་ཀྱི་མགུ་ཙེ an iron pot.

ལྕགས་མགོ *lcags-mgo*=ལྕགས་སྐྱོག *lcags-skyog* iron laddle.

ལྕགས་སྒོར *lcags-sgor* iron pan.

ལྕགས་སྒྱིད *lcags-sgyid* trevet; tripod.

ལྕགས་སྒྲོག་མ *lcags-sgrog-ma* iron-chain, shackle; n. of a Tibetan work printed at Narthang.

ལྕགས་སྒྲོལ *lcags-sgrol* an iron pan; steel pan.

ལྕགས་མཆོག *lcags-mchog* or ལྕགས་མཆོག་ཡིད་ཝང་། (*Mṅon.*) 1.=gold. 2. iron of superior quality that came from Orissa. It is said that swords made of this metal were so sharp and hard that an elephant could be cut into pieces with them. The finest and hardest iron called *mi-tshe-ri* (མི་ཚེ་རི) used to be obtained from the country of Lagmana.

ལྕགས་སྙིགས *lcags-sñigs*=ལྕགས་དྲེག iron slag or dross of iron (*Mṅon.*).

ལྕགས་ཏིག *lcags-tig* n. of a species of gentian, v. ཏིག་ཏ: ལྕགས་ཏིག་མ་ཚད་རིམས་ཚད་སེལ། Gentian removes intermittent fever and also sores (*Med.*).

ལྕགས་ཐུམ *lcags-thum*=ལྕགས་ཏྲོག लोहकन्दु an iron ladle; any cooking utensil of iron such as a boiler or a saucepan.

ལྕགས་དྲེག *lcags-dreg* medicinal preparation of iron for weak and painful eyes: མིག་ནད་སྒྲོངས་དང་གཉེར་ནད་ འཇོམས.

ལྕགས་མདའ *lcags-mdah* एषण an iron arrow; an iron or steel probe; खराशिक steel-pointed arrow; steel arrow.

ལྕགས་མདའ་སྒྲ་ཅན *lcags-mdah sgra-can*=ལྕགས་སྦུབས་ཅན *lcags sbubs-can* a kind of steel-tipped arrow from which when flung a whizzing sound came forth (*Mňon.*).

ལྕགས་རྡོ *lcags-rdo*=ཉག་རྡོ 1. flint-stones: 2, iron-stone or iron-ore.

ལྕགས་ཐག *lcags-thag* dross and slime of the intestines.

ལྕགས་ཐབ *lcags-thab*=ལྕགས་སྒྲིད.

ལྕགས་ཐལ *lcags-thal* लोहभस्म oxide of iron obtained, red-hot iron being repeatedly dipped in the urine of cows, &c.: མཆིན་དུག་དམུ་རྫིང་སྐེམ་པའི་མཆོག། iron-ash is the best remedy for liver disease, poison and dropsy.

ལྕགས་ལྡེལ *lcags-ldel*, abbr. of སྒོ་ལྕགས་དང་ལྡེ་མིག *sgo-lcags dan lde-mig* door-lock and key.

ལྕགས་སྤུ *Lcags-spu* n. of a place in Tibet.

ལྕགས་འཕེལ *Lcags-hphel* n. of a district of Tibet to the north-east of Kashmir (*Lam. 19*).

ལྕགས་སྦུགས *lcags-sbugs* a match-lock made (formerly) in India.

ལྕགས་དམར *lcags-dmar* लोहिताय: copper.

ལྕགས་མག *lcags-mag* tinder-case.

ལྕགས་ཤོལ *lcags-shol* n. of a weapon.

ལྕགས་གཟར *lcags-gzar* आयसदर्विका an iron spoon.

ལྕགས་བཟོ་པ *lcags-bzo-pa*=མགར་བ iron-smith, black-smith (*Mňon.*).

ལྕགས་གཡའ *lcags-gya* rust.

ལྕགས་ར *lcags-ra* n. of a place on the confines of Tibet and China; a wall round a house, an estate, or a town.

ལྕགས་རི *lcags-ri* (ཐུམ) प्राचीर, प्राकार a strong wall.

ལྕགས་ཤན *lcags-çan* iron-hoop; hasp; cramp-iron.

ལྕགས་སོལ *lcags-sol* powdered coal: ལྕགས་སོལ་མིག་སེར་ཏུམ་ཞེན་འདོན་པར་བྱེད། powder of mineral coal (called in Hindi *Surma*) is used as a cure for the eyes.

ལྕགས་བསྲོ *lcags-bsro* smoothing iron (*Sch.*).

ལྕགས་སླང *lcags-slan* a large iron pan for roasting or kiln-drying corn (*Jä.*).

ལྕང་སྐྱ *Lcan-skya* 1. n. of a place in the province of Kham. 2. grey or pale white.

ལྕང་སྐྱ་སྟག་སྒམ *lcan-skya stag-sgam* a sort of trunk first made under the direction of *Cãn-skya* Lama, with tanned tiger skin.

ལྕང་སྐྱ་རོལ་པའི་རྡོ་རྗེ *Lcan-skya Rol-pahi rdo-rje* n. of a celebrated lama born at *Cãn-skya* in Kham and who became the chief-priest of the lamaic section of the Chinese Buddhists of Peking during the reign of Emperor Kyenlung, about 1770 A.D.

ལྕང་ལྕོང *lcan-lcon* = སང་སོང (*Cs.*) a craggy place; broken eroded country.

ལྕང་ཕྱིའི་ཉང *Lcan-phyihi ñan* n. of a place in Tibet visited by Atis'a in the beginning of the eleventh century A.D.

ལྕང་མ *lcan-ma* 1. willow, *Salix viminalis*. 2. a general name for trees that are planted in the vicinity of villages; वेतस the ratan, *Calamus rotang*.

ལྕང་མ་བྲག *Lcañ-ma brag* n. of a place in upper Tibet.

ལྕང་རྩགས *Lcañ-rtsags* n. of a place near *Ñam-çod* in Tibet.

ལྕང་ར *lcañ-ra*=ལྕང་སྲེབ *lcañ-sreb* a grove of willows, poplar and other trees.

ལྕང་ར་རྫོང *Lcañ-ra rdsoñ* n. of a district in Tibet.

ལྕང་རློམ *lcañ-rlom* a flat basket made of willow twigs.

ལྕང་ཤིང *lcag-çiñ* willow tree; willow wood.

ལྕང་ཤོས *lcañ-ços* the red willow (*Sch.*).

ལྕང་སིལ *lcañ-sil* coolness, shade under willow-trees.

ལྕང་ལུང་པཎྜི་ཏ *Lcañ-luñ pan-di-ta* a celebrated lama-author of Mongolia.

ལྕང་ལོ *lcañ-lo* 1. willow leaves. 2. वेणी braided hair; अलक a curl; lock of hair; जटा coiled hair, long plait of hair.

Syn. སྐྲ་རིང་པོ *skra riñ-po*; དབུ་ལོ *dbu-lo* (*Mñon.*).

ལྕང་ལོ་ཅན *Lcañ-lo-can* अलकावती 1. the abode of Kuvera or Vais'ravana. 2. n. of a village near Gyañ-tso in Tsang. 3. अटकावती n. of a place in Ancient India, also of another on the fabulous Sumeru.

ལྕང་ཤེས *lcañ-çes*=ཅང་ཤེས the finest breed of horse in Tibet.

ལྕམ *lcam* 1. a lady, a nobleman's wife; ལྷ་ལྕམ a princess or lady of rank; ལྕམ་ཆུང young unmarried lady of noble rank. 2.=ཅམ acc. to *Jä.* lath, pole, rafter, spar of a roof.

ལྕམ་དཀྲིས *lcam-dkris* वलितक wrinkled; n. of an ornament.

ལྕམ་དཀྲིས་ཅན *lcam-dkris-can* possessed of wrinkles.

ལྕམ་དྲལ *lcam-dral*=མཆེད་ལྕམ་དྲལ brother and sister.

ꕗ **ལྕམ་པ** *lcam-pa*=སྲག་ལྕམ 1. n. of an officinal herb used for healing wounds: ལྕམ་པས་ཆུ་འགགས་སྐོམ་དང་འཁྲུ་བ་སེལ། *Lcam-pa* removes obstruction of urine, thirst, and diarrhoea. 2. gentle; polished; ལྕམ་པ་ཐུགས་རྒྱལ་ཆུང་བ mild and humble (*A. 134*).

ལྕམ་པོ *lcam-po* upright; in erect position ལྕམ་པོར adv. སྐུ་འགྱིང་མི་བྱེད་པར་ལྕམ་པོར་གཤེགས་པ། (*A. 33*) he walked in an upright posture without bending the body.

ལྕམ་མེ *Lcam-me* 1. n. of a celebrated lady of Tibet who received Atis'a with much hospitality (*A. 5*). 2. bright, glittering.

ལྕམ་མེ་བ *lcam me-wa* shining, dazzling, variegated (*Jä.*).

ལྕམ་མོ *lcam-mo*, an abbr. of ལྕམ and སྲིང་མོ *sriñ-mo*; acc. to some a sister.

ལྕམ་ལེགས་སྨིན *Lcam-legs smin* n. of a མཁའ་འགྲོ་མ or *Dākinī*; རྒྱལ་པོ་ཨིནྡྲ་བོ་དྷི། ལྕམ་ལེགས་སྨིན། *Rgyal-po Indra bodhi, lcam-legs-smin* King Indra Bodhi and the Lady Legmin (*A. 40*).

ལྕི་བ *lci-wa* गुरु adj. heavy, substantial, weighty: ཁྱེད་ཀྱི་སྐྱེས་དང་བཀའ་རྩལ་ལྕི་བ་དེས *khyed-kyi skyes-dañ bkah-stsal lci wa-des* in consequence of your weighty presents and requests; ཁ་ན་མ་ཐོ་བ་ལྕི་བ a heavy deadly sin: ཡང་ལྕི 1. light and heavy, *i.e.*, gravity or weight. 2. dung, esp. of cattle; བ་ལྕི cowdung; ལྕི་བ་སྐམ་པོ *lci-wa skam-po* करीष: dried dung of cattle, &c.; ལྕི་རློན *lci-rlon* fresh dung or droppings of cattle; ལྕི་བའི་ཕུང་པོ

गोमय-निकाय heap of cow-dung (dung in general).

ལྕི་མདའ *Lci-mdah* n. of a place in Tibet; ལྕི་མདའ་ཟམ་པ bridge at that place.

ལྕིག་ལྕིག *lcig-lcig* slightly moving: འབུ་སྲིན་ལ་སོགས་པ་ཆང་འབག་གི་སྦྲང་མ་བཞིན་ལྕག་ལྕིག་ཡོད་པ་ལ། moving as little worms and insects do, like grain, &c., in fermentation.

ལྕིད *lcid*, sometimes written for ལྕི་བ, heavy.

ལྕིབས *lcibs* 1. gloves (*Sch.*); ཚ་ལྕིབས pot-cloth (to take or lift up pots from fire); མིག་ལྕིབས or སྤྱན་ལྕིབས eye-lids that protect the eyes; མིག་གི་ལྕིབས་ཐོར stye in the eye; ཉ་ལྕིབས fish-gills. 2. acc. to *Jä.* contrivances to facilitate the handling of different objects, as the handles of pots and vessels; the handles, loops, etc., of knives, scissors, pincers, and other tools. 3. a shield: རྟོག་པའི་མདའ་འཕངས་དར་དཀར་ལྕིབས་ཀྱི་སྐྱུང་། the arrow of illusive thoughts having been flung, a white scarf came forth as a shield of protection.

ལྕུ་བ *lcu-wa*, v. གཅུ་བ.

ལྕུག་མདལ *lcug-mdal* creeping plant (*Mñon.*).

ལྕུག་པ *lcug-pa* शाखा a supple branch; ལྕུག་གུ the tender twig or the bend of a twig; ལྕུག་ཕྲན *lcug-phran* twigs of a plant or creeper.

ལྕུག་མ *lcug-ma* a root-shoot of a willow or of a poplar-tree; a rod, switch; ལྕུག་ལྕུག་བྱེད་པ, to bud repeatedly (*Cs.*).

ལྕུགས *lcugs* soft, pliable, not hard or tough: རྒྱལ་པོ་འདི་ཡང་ལྕུགས་ལ་ཚད་དམར་འཛིན། (*Hbrom.* ཀ *30*) the king being susceptible, was seized with red fever.

ལྕུང་ཀ *lcuñ-ka* = སྐྱུང་ཀ *skyuñ-ka* colloq. jackdaw.

ལྕུང་མོ *lcuñ-mo* thimble (*Jä.*).

ལྕུད་པ *lcud-pa*, v. གཅུད.

ལྕུམ *lcum* or ལྕུམ་རྩ a plant, the stalks of which are used as a purgative (*Cs.*); ལྕུམ་རྩས་དུག་ཚད་རྡོལ་ཚད་བད་ཀན་སྤྱོང་ the root of ལྕུམ་རྩ cures poison, fever, uterus fever, and phlegm, &c.

ལྕུམ་དཀར *lcum-dkar* a white species of the above plant.

ལྕེ *lce* जिह्वा, रसना, ललन the tongue; ལྕེ་རྐྱང་བ *lce rkyañ-wa* to put forth, to stretch out the tongue. Also met. a tongue: གྲི་ལྕེ the tongue or blade of a knife; ལྕེ་འབེབས་པའི་གློག། a tongue or flash of lightning; མེ་ལྕེ tongue of fire; ལྕེ་གྱིགས *lce-kyigs* the *frenum* of the tongue (*Cs.*).

Syn. རོ་འཛིན *ro-hdsin*; རོ་ཤེས *ro-çes*; རོ་མྱང་བ *ro-myañ-wa*; བདུད་རྩི་འཛག *bdud-rtshi-hdsag*; བཅུད་ཀྱི་མ *bcud-kyi-ma*; ངག་གི་འདབ་མ *ñag-gi hdab-ma*; སྨྲ་བའི་བབས་སྟེགས *smra-bahi babs-stegs*; ལྗགས *ljags*; སྨྲ་བྱེད *smra-byed* (*Mñon.*).

ལྕེ་བརྒྱ་པ *Lce brgya-pa* lit. he with a hundred tongues—epithet of Varuṇa, the god of the sea; the sea, the waves being so many tongues, &c. (*Mñon.*).

ལྕེ་བསྒྲིལ་བ *lce bsgril-wa* ललाजिह्वा to stretch out or wag the tongue, to grasp or twist it round a thing as the cow does.

ལྕེ་ཆུང *lce-chuñ* उपजिह्वा uvula: ལྕེ་ཆུང་འབབས inflammation of the uvula.

ལྕེ་གཉིས་པ *lce gñis-pa* 1. lit. the two-tongued, *i.e.*, snake or parrot. 2. double-tongued, deceitful; ལྕེ་གཉིས་བྱེད་པ *lce-gñis byed-pa* to be double-tongued; to have double dealings.

ལྕེ་སྙིང་མེད་ *lce sñiṅ-med* met. a thunder-bolt (*Mṅon.*).

ལྕེ་ཐེབ *lce-theb* or ལྕེ་འདུ a fleshy excrescence below the tongue (*Cs.*).

ལྕེ་བདེ *lce-bde* a nimble tongue; a babbler.

ལྕེ་ཕུང་སྟེ་ཟས་མི་ཟ *lce phuṅ-ste zas-mi-za* not eating food by licking (a prohibition to monks).

ལྕེ་འབར་བ *lce hbar-wa*=འབར་འབར burning flame=ཚོག (*Mṅon.*).

ལྕེ་འབིགས *lce-hbigs*=རྒྱ་ཚྭ *rgya-tshva* sal-ammoniac (*Mṅon.*).

ལྕེ་འབུར *lce-hbur* eruption on the tongue.

ལྕེ་མེད *lce-med* (སྦལ་བ) अजिह्व lit. without tongue; a frog (which is supposed to have no tongue).

ལྕེ་མྱང་ཚྭ *lce myaṅ-tshba* alum.

ལྕེ་རྩ *lce-rtsa* or ལྕེའི་རྩ་བ *lcehi rtsa-wa* जिह्वामूल the root of the tongue: ལྕེ་རྩ་ཅན *lce-rtsa can* जिह्वामूलीय a letter pronounced from the root of the tongue; the gutturals, viz., ཀ, ཁ, ག, ང, ཨ, ཧ, ཨཿ; the *visarga* before ཀ and ཁ, and also རྀ *r*, and ལྀ, *lr*, are called जिह्वामूलीय; ལྕེའི་རྩེ་མོ the tip of the tongue: ལྕེའི་རྩེ་མོ་ཅན a letter sounded from the tip of the tongue.

ལྕེ་རྩེ་གཡོ་བ *lce-rtse gyo-wa* लोला 1. to loll out the tongue and move it too and fro. 2. fig. the fickle or changeable one. 3. an epithet of the goddess of fortune.

ལྕེ་གཞུང་ *lce-gshuṅ* जिह्वामध्य the middle of the tongue; ལྕེ་བཞར *lce-bshar* जिह्वानिर्लेखनिका a tongue-scraper.

ལྕེའི་སྐྱེ་མཆེད *lcehi skye-mched* जिह्वायतन the organ of taste (*M. V.*).

ལྕེག *lceg* a coat of mail for horse (*Sch.*).

ལྕེབ་པ *lceb-pa* आत्महत्या 1. to kill one's self; to commit suicide: ཁྱོད་དེ་ཙམ་དུ་ལྕེབ་པ་ལ་ཐུག་ན། "if, for even that, you kill yourself" (*Hbrom. 124*); ལྕེབ་བྱས་པ committed suicide. 2. used of insects that fly into the flame.

ལྕོག *lcog* (ཁང་པའི) 1. खोड़क a pot; खोड़कशीर्ष the arched roof of a house, a turret on a house-top, a pinnacle. 2. n. of an aquatic plant, *Trapa bispinosa*.

ལྕོག་ག *lcog-ga* the swallow, but, according to some authors, the lark.

ལྕོག་རྩེ *lcog-rtse*, resp. གསོལ་ལྕོག, a small very low table on which food and drink are served in Tibet; ལྕོག་ཁེབས a cover for such a table, table-cloth; རྒྱ་ལྕོག Chinese or European table; མདུན་ལྕོག 'fore-table,' one before an image of Buddha or of some deity for placing offerings on.

ལྕོག་རྩེ་ལ *Lcog-rtse-la* n. of a mountain in Tibet the top of which is flat like a table.

ལྕོག་རས *lcog-ras* piece of cloth put over iron helmet worn in war-dance in Tibet.

ལྕོག་ལ་བྲག་ཁུང་ *Lcog-la brag-khuṅ* n. of a rock-cavern on Chogla pass in Tibet.

ལྕོགས་པ *lcogs-pa* or ལྕོག་པ I: 1. to be agitated, shaken; to tremble. 2. མེ་ཏོག་མགོ་ལྕོགས a flower shaking, waving its head (*Jä.*).

ལྕོགས་པ II: 1. vb. to be able: དེ་མ་ལྕོགས་ན if (he) is not able (to do that); ཅི་ལྕོགས་ཀྱི as much as possible; to the utmost (*Jä.*). 2. adj. able; ཤེད་ཀྱིས་མི་ལྕོགས་པ། feeble (in strength) failing in strength, weak; རིག་པས་མི་ལྕོགས་པ། ignorant, poor in intelligence.

ལྕོང་ *lcoṅ*=སྦལ་ལྕོང་ a frog in its first stage of development; a tadpole (*Jä.*).

ལྕོངས *lcoṅs*=ཀོང་ཀོང་ undulating; an un-even place.

ཆ

ཆ *cha* I: the letter ཆ *cha*, which is the aspirated ཅ, resembling the Sanskrit छ in pronunciation, though acc. to Tib. Gram. छ=ཚ *tsha*. As num. fig.=6; ཆ་པ *cha-pa* the volume marked with ཆ signifying the sixth volume.

ཆ II: 1. a part or fraction; भाग share, portion, anything divided; opp. to the whole; thus, ཕྱེད་ཆ one-half, གསུམ་ཆ one-third, བཞི་ཆ one-fourth, and so on; བརྒྱ་ཆ one hundredth part; སྟོང་གི་ཆ one thousandth part; བང་མཛོད་གསུམ་ཆ་གཅིག one-third of the treasury (or its contents); དབུའི་ཆ་ཙམ་ཅིག་གསེར་གྱིས་མ་ཁོང་བར there being still wanting a portion of as much gold as would about equal his head (*Glr.*); ནམ་གྱི་ཆ་སྟོད the first portion of the night; ནམ་གྱི་ཆ་སྨད the second, the last half of the night. ཆ་གཉིས་བསྲེ་བ *cha-gñis bsre-wa* to put together two parts; རང་ཆ one's own share. ནང་པར་ཐ་བའི་ཆ the following day's first part, *i.e.*, the following morning (*Mil.*); ས་ཆ (lit. part of the earth) a piece of land; territory; country in general. 2.=ཟུང་ युग a pair; ལྷམ་ཆ་གཅིག a pair of boots; ཉད་ཆ་གཅིག a pair of shoes. ཆ་སྒྲིག་པ to pair, to match, to couple, to arrange in pairs or proportionately; ཆ་མཐུན་པ proportionate, similar. ཆ་མ་ཡིན་པ not forming a pair or match; unfit, improper, discordant. དགག་གཅོག་པ་ནི་ཆ་མ་ཡིན not obeying; will not do; is out of place (*Ta. 110, 11*; *Jā.*).

ཆ III: 1. news, intelligence, word, sound; སྐད་ཆ topic; གཏམ་ཆ་འདྲི་བ to ask any news; བྲག་ཆ echo returned from a rock. 2. prospect, auspices: ཁྱིམ་ཆ prospects regarding the household; དགྲ་ཆ prospects or expectations as to one's enemies. 3.=ཆ་ག things; གོས་ལུས་ཆ a complete suit of clothes for a person; རྒྱན་ཆ ornaments or articles of adornment; དགོས་ཆ necessary things, requisites; མཚོན་ཆ weapons; ཡིག་ཆ articles of writing, deeds, documents; རས་ཆ cloth; ལག་ཆ implements, utensils, &c.

ཆ IV: कला 1. a sixteenth part of the month (*Bull. 1848, 295*). 2. कण a particle (*Kālac. T. 7*).

ཆ་དཀར *Cha-dkar* n. of a district in Lhokha, in Tibet. ཆ་དཀར་སྲང *Cha-dkar-sraṅ* n. of the junction of several public roads in *Chakar*, ཆ་དཀར་དུ་ཆ་དཀར་སྲང་གི་བལ *Cha-dkar-du Cha-dkar sraṅ-gi bal* in Chakar the wool (sold at) Chakar cross-roads.

ཆ་རྐྱེན *cha-rkyen* share of destiny, of fate (*Sch.*).

ཆ་ག *cha-ga* (འདབ or མཐའ) hem, edge, border; གོས་ཀྱི་ཆ་ག=གོས་ཀྱི་མཐའ the border or edge of a robe. ཆ་ག་འདེབས་པ=ཆ་ག་བརབ་པ, (གོས་ལྷ་ཐ) to put a fringe to a robe, to hem, to turn in (the edge of cloth). ཆ་ག་མ *cha-ga-ma* a dress with linings on the edge of the sleeve, etc. ཕོ་གོས་སྔོན་པོ་ཆ་ག་མ་རེ་ལ (the price) for each blue male robe with turned-back borders. ཆ་ག་མེད་པ robe with plain edge.

ཆ་ག་པ *cha-ga-pa* locust; also a grasshopper: ཆ་གའི་མགོ་ཡིས་བུང་དུག་འཇོམས the head of a grasshopper applied on the sting of a hornet (འབུ་བུང་ཁྲ) removes its poison.

ཆ་གྲུམ *cha-grum* a square rug.

ཆ་འགྲིག *cha-ḥgrig* a complete set or suit of any furniture or clothes.

ཆ་མཁན *cha-mkhan* fortune-teller, soothsayer (*Sch.*).

ཆ་ཅན *cha-can* भांशक consisting of a pair, forming a pair.

ཆ་ཚོ *cha-cho* a thing homogeneous; matched (*Sch.*).

ཆ་འཇོག་པ *cha-ḥjog-pa* to stick to, adhere to any work; to come to a conclusion on any matter; to arrive at a definite settlement.

ཆ་ཉམས *cha-ñams* कलाहीन, परिणत impaired, degenerated, fallen down, grown worse.

ཆ་གཉིས *cha-gñis* द्विभाग two parts; उभय both or a pair; colloq. two pairs.

ཆ་གཉིས་བསྲེ་བ *cha-gnis sre-wa* to mix or mingle two equal parts.

ཆ་སྙོམས *cha-sñoms* or ཆ་མཉམ equal parts (without difference in size, number or quantity); ཆ་ཙམ or ཆ་འདྲ་ཙམ in part, in some measure; ཆ་མ་འདྲ་བ or ཆ་མ་མཐུན་པ partly, not equal, differing a little; ཆ་ཙམ་ཤེས་ཀྱང even if one knows but a little (*Jä.*); ཆ་ཚང་བས being complete in every part, entire, integral (*Sch.*); ཆ་མཉམ་པ adj. even.

ཆ་གཏེར *cha-gter* कलानिधि the moon, that which shines in crescent parts.

ཆ་དེ *cha-de* for ཆ་ཡོད་པ་དེ *cha yod-pa-de*.

ཆ་བདག་སྐྱེས *cha-ḥdag skyes*, v. ཆང་ *chañ* wine.

ཆ་འདྲ་ཙམ *cha-ḥdra tsam*, v. ཆ་སྙོམས *cha-sñoms*.

ཆ་ལྡན *cha-ldan* भाग possessed of some share; fortunate.

ཆ་ཕྲ *cha-phra* कृपण a miser.

ཆ་བ I: *cha-wa*=བརྒྱན་པ or བཞག་པ मण्डन vb. to adorn, bedeck, wear (*S. Lex.*).

卐 **ཆ་བ** II:=प्रस्थान to go away, to start, to leave (a place): སླེབས་ཏུ་ཆ་བའི་ཚེ *slebs-tu cha-wahi tshe* when they were on the point of arriving; ཆ་བར=འགྲོ་བར to go, going (*A. 138*).

ཆ་བུ *cha-bu* ornament worn in the ears.

ཆ་བྱེད *cha-byed* वेश 1. dress, clothing; མི་སྡུག་པའི་ཆ་བྱེད་ཅན shabbily dressed; poorly clad; ragged: ཆ་བྱེད་འདི་བཞིན་བྱས he was (in this manner) dressed. 2. implement, instrument (*e.g.*, a musical instrument, a surgical instrument) also external appearance of animals (*Jä.*).

ཆ་མ་མཆིས *cha-ma-mchis* (it has no equal, not another like it to form a pair) matchless (*D.R.*).

ཆ་མ་མཐུན་པ *cha-ma mthun-pa*, v. ཆ་སྙོམས.

ཆ་མ་འདྲ་བ *cha-ma ḥdra-wa*, v. ཆ་སྙོམས.

ཆ་མེད་པ *cha-med-pa* to be companionless; to be left alone; to be without an equal.

ཆ་མེད་གཏམ *cha-med-gtam*=དག་འཆལ nonsense; irrelevant speech (*Mñon.*).

ཆ་ཙེ *cha-tse* is said to be a Chinese word;=ཁ་སྟེན *kha-sten* or ཚིག་སྟེན *tshig-sten*.

ཆ་ཙམ *cha-tsam*, v. ཆ་སྙོམས *cha-sñoms*.

ཆ་ཚང་ *cha-tshañ* complete in all its parts; complete suit of ornament, dress, &c.

ཆ་ཚད *cha-tshad*, v. ཆག་ཚད *chag-tshad*.

ཆ་ཚན *cha-tshan* species, division, class (*Sch.*).

ཆ་ཚོགས *cha-tshogs* (གྲངས) n. of a large number.

ཆ་མཛེས *cha-mdses* अप्रतीक symmetrical.

ཆ་འཛིན་པ *cha-ḥdsin-pa* 1. to select from among many; to pick one out of a number (for identification). 2.=རོལ་མོ a pair of cymbals.

ཆ་རྫོགས *cha-ṛdsogs*, v. ཆ་སྙོམས *cha-ṣñoms*.

ཆ་བཞག་པ *cha-ḅshag-pa* to rely or depend upon, to confide in; sbst. trust, confidence: གཏམ་དེ་ལ་ཆ་བཞག་ཡོད་ན if that information is reliable. To adhere, cling to; to follow, obey (laws): སངས་རྒྱས་ཀྱི་བཀའ་ལ་ཆ་བཞག they adhere to the words of Buddha; རྒྱལ་པོའི་བཀའ་ལ་ཆ་བཞག་པ to obey the king's commands.

ཆ་ཡི་རྩེ *cha-yi ṛtse* = ཡང་རྩེ sublime.

ཆ་ར *cha-ra* also མོན་ཆ་ར *mon cha-ra* Himalayan oak with pointed, ever-green leaves, a tree inferior to the English oak; ཆ་ར་ཕྲིའུ the stunted or dwarf species of oak.

ཆ་རི *cha-ri* = ཆ་ལི or ཆ་ལུ a coarse blanket made of yak's hair (*Jä.*).

ཆ་རི་སི *cha-ri-si* ཉ་ག a steel-yard.

ཆ་རུ *cha-ru* a peg to which to fix the ropes of a tent.

ཆ་ལག *cha-lag* = ལག་ཆ implements required for carrying on business.

ཆ་ལང་ *cha-lañ* or སྦུབ་ཆལ *ṣbub-chal* pair of cymbals.

ཆ་ལམ *cha-lam* = ཉ་ལམ some; for the most part; rather.

ཆ་ལི *cha-li*, v. ཆ་རི *cha-ri*.

ཆ་ལུ *cha-lu*, v. ཆ་རི *cha-ri*.

ཆ་ལུགས *cha-lugs* वेष (*A. K. 1, 38*) appearance, clothing, costume; colloq. artificial badge or mark of distinction.

ཆ་ལུགས་ངན་པ *cha-lugs ñan-pa* विकृत disfigured; of bad dress.

ཆ་ལུགས་མཛེས་པ *cha-lugs ṃdses-pa* finely dressed; elegant manner of dressing.

ཆ་ཤས *cha-ças* अवयव, अंश, कला shape; part, portion, share; ལུས་ཀྱི་ཆ་ཤས a part of the body, a limb; also shape of the body.

ཆ་ཤས་ངན་པ *cha-ças ñan-pa* = ཉུང་ཟད་ངན་པ slightly bad; also of bad shape or parts.

ཆ་ཤས་མཆེ་གཙིག *cha-ças ṃche-gtsig* (?) उत्कर-मकूट hill; heaved-up portion of the earth.

ཆ་ཤས་འཕྲོག་པ *cha-ças ḥphrog-pa* अंशहर a sharer.

ཆ་ཤས་བྱེད *cha-ças-byeḏ* बिन्दु particles.

ཆ་ཤས་སྦྱང་པ *cha-ças ṣbyañ-pa* = གསེར, (ས་རིམས་རྩེ་མ་ཀྱི་ཆ་ཤས་སྦྱང་བ) कलधौत gold.

ཆ་སྲོལ *cha-ṣrol* = ལུགས་སྲོལ *lugs-ṣrol* custom, usage.

ཆ་བསགས་པ *cha-ḅsags-pa* lit. many parts or particles accumulated together (ས་གཞི་དང་རིའི་མིང་རྡུལ་གྱི་ཆ་བསགས་པ). 1. a term signifying the earth; a mountain. 2. कलाप the capital of the fabulous S'ambhala.

ཆ་ཧར *Cha-har* Chahar, n. of a Mongol tribe.

ཆག *chag* 1. gram or other grain for horses, &c. ཆག་ཕད the bag containing grain which is tied to the mouth of a horse or donkey from which it eats. ཆག་གཞོང་ trough, manger, crib (*Jä.*). 2. the fourth finger (*Med.*). 3. resp. for shoe, also for ཕྱག་ལྷམ. 4. = ཆག་ཕེབས་པ incorrectly for ཕྱག་ཕེབས་པ signifying welcome (*Jä.*). 5. ཆག་གང་ prob. for ཕྱག་གང་ the breadth of a fist.

ཆག་ཀྲུམ *chag-krum* piece, fragment; ཆག་ཀྲུམ་ལ་སོང་ *chag-krum la soñ* it has gone to pieces (*Jä.*).

ཆག་སྐྱ་བ *chag-ṣkya-wa* (*Sch.*) having only one purpose, pursuing but one aim; unremitting, indefatigable.

ཆག་ཁོངས *chag-khoñs* = འཁོར་ཆག a basket for measuring grain.

ཆག་ག་ཆོག་གེ *chag-ga chog-ge* for ཕྱག་ག་ཕྱོག་གེ things mixed up or thrown together.

ཆག་རྒྱག་པ *chag-rgyag-pa* to doubt (*Sch.*).

ཆག་ཆག I: *chag-chag* 1. with བྱེད་པ or འདེབས་པ to sprinkle: ཁང་པའི་ནང་ཕྱག་དང་ཆག་ཆག་བྱས་ཏེ having swept and sprinkled the inside of the house. ཆག་ཆག་ལེགས་པར་བཏབ་པ सुस्नात well bathed or washed, also to cleanse a house or road with water. 2. ཆག་ཆག་གདབ་པ to starch, to stiffen (*Sch.*). 3. in *W.* to tread, to trample, *e.g.*, the narrow path or furrows between garden beds. 4. to clap the hands (*Jä.*).

ཆག་ཆག *chag-chag* colloq. anything broken. སྡེར་མ་ཆག་ཆག broken dish or plate.

ཆག་ཆད *chag-chad* rent, break, rupture (*Sch.*).

ཆག་དུམ *chag-dum* fragment, scrap, bit.

ཆག་འདིང་ *chag-hdiṅ* doubtful, incredible (*Sch.*).

ཆག་པ *chag-pa* 1. a large bunch of flowers, ears of corn, etc. 2. pf. of འཆག་པ broken; མ་ཆགས་པ and esp. adv. མ་ཆགས་པར also ཆག་མེད་པ uninterrupted, unremitting, (*Jä.*); རྒྱུན་མ་ཆག་པར *rgyun ma-chag-par* without interruption; without breaking the continuity or course; གས་ཆག་མེད without a crack, flaw, or chink. 3. ལམ་ཆག་པ, v. འཆག་པ II: ཆག་ཤིང་ wooden splint for a broken limb (*W.*) (*Jä.*).

Syn. ཤིག་པ *shig-pa*; འཐོར་བ *hthor-wa* (*Mṅon.*).

ཆག་པོ *chag-po* a broken vessel, pot, etc.; ཙེལ་ཆག་པོ a broken dosser or pannier (*Jä.*).

ཆག་ཕད *chag-phad* the bag containing grain tied to the mouth of a horse from which it eats.

ཆག་ཕེབས *chag-phebs* for ཕྱག་ཕེབས welcome.

ཆག་བུ *chag-bu* diminutive of ཆག་པ a little bunch.

ཆག་བྲོམ *chag-brom* in *W.* colloq. "*chakrum*" ice.

ཆག་མོ *chag-mo* bunch; འབྲས་བུ་ཆག་མོ a fruit growing in clusters, like the grapes of the vine, the berries of the elder (*W.*) (*Jä.*).

ཆག་ཙེ *chag-tse* a small grain, *e.g.*, of ground grits; ཆག་ཙེ་ཅན grauulous (*W.*) (*Jä.*).

ཆག་ཚང་པ *chag-tshaṅ-pa*=ཐབ་ཁ་པ or མ་ཆེན a cook (*Mṅon.*).

ཆག་ཚད *chag-tshad* or ཆ་ཚད (*Sch.*) the right measure; དུག་སྟེར་ཆག་ཚད *dug-ster chag-tshad* a sufficient quantity of poison administered to a person (*Med.; Jä.*).

ཆག་གཞོང *Chag-gshoṅ*, v. ཆག *chag*.

ཆག་ལོ *Chag-lo* n. of a celebrated lama of Tibet. ཆག་ལོ་མཚོ་དཀྱིལ་ཡོད་པར་འདོད་པ it was asserted that Chag Lo-tsā-wa had been into the middle of the lake (*Ya-sel. 33*).

ཆག་ཤིང་ *chag-çiṅ*, v. ཆག་པ *chag-pa*.

ཆགས་པ I: *chags-pa* 1. to be fond of, to be attached to, to love; བུ་མོ་ལ་ཆགས་པ to love a girl; སྐྱེས་པ་དང་ན་ཆུང་གཅིག་ཆགས་པ *skyes-pa daṅ na-chuṅ gcig chags-pa* the mutual affection between a man and a maiden; ཡིད་ལ་ཆགས་པའི་བུ་མོ་རྣམས my dearly beloved daughters (*Pth.*). 2. to cling to, *e.g.*, ལུས་དང་སྲོག་ལ་ཆགས་པ *lus-daṅ srog-la chags-pa* to body and to life; ཡུལ་ལ to one's home, to one's native country; often to suffer one's self to be enticed by a thing, to indulge in; ཆགས་པར་མི་བྱ་འཇིགས་པར་མི་བྱ་སྟེ allowing neither desire nor fear to have any influence upon himself (*S. Lam.*, also *Jä.*).

ཆགས་པ II: vb. 1. to be begotten, produced; མ་ཆགས་པ not produced in the usual way of propagation, but རྫུས་ཏེ་སྐྱེས་པ *rdsus-te skyes-pa*, or ལྷུན་གྱིས་གྲུབ་པ *lhun-gyis* *grub-pa* (*Pth.*); frq. མངལ་དུ་ཆགས་པ to be produced in the womb, as the foetus is; hence ཆགས in compounds = animal; འདབ་ཆགས bird; གཤོག་ཆགས *gṣog-chags* winged animal; སྲོག་ཆགས *srog-chags* living being. 2. to arise, spring up, originate, come forth; to come to light, to appear: ས་གཞི་ལ་ཆགས་པ the growth or founding of (towns, monasteries, institutions, etc.) on the earth; ཟས་ལ་བཅུད་ཆགས་པ the causing of nutrition in food; མི་ལ་ནོར་ཆགས་པ the accumulation or growth of fortune to a person; ཤིང་ལ་ཁམ་བུ་ཆགས་བྱུང་ apricots had sprung forth on the tree; རབ་ཏུ་ཆགས་པ = རབ་ཏུ་འབྱུང་བ to become a cleric; ཆགས་རབས genesis, history of the beginning esp. of the world; ཆགས་ཚུལ manner of being produced, peopled: ཐོག་ཆེན་པོ་དྲུག་ནམ་མཁའ་ལ་ཆགས་འདུག་པ་མཐོང་། I saw six large pinnacles appearing in the sky.

ཆགས་པ III: 1. प्रणय, स्नेह, अनुराग, राग, कामगुण, आसक्ति sbst. love, lust, passion for, affection, attachment: ཆགས་པ་སྐྱེས་སོ *chags-pa skyes-so* he fell in love (*Dzl.*); ཆགས་པ་སྤྱོད་པ *chags-pa spyod-pa* = འཁྲིག་པ་སྤྱོད་པ *ḥkhrig-pa spyod-pa* to copulate: ཆགས་པ་མེད་ན་འཁོར་བ་མེད if there is no attachment, there cannot be any transmigratory existence (*D.R.*). 2. लोभ greed for gain, acquisitiveness. འདོད་ཡོན་ལ་སེམས་ཆགས the mind runs after the objects of desire. 3. formation, congelation, agglutination; ཁྱགས་པ་ཆགས ice formed on water; ཆགས་པ་མེད་པ निरुपलेप without any covering, formation of film. ཆགས་པའི་བསྐལ་པ *chags-paḥi bskal-pa* निवर्तकल्प the age when worlds are formed.

ཆགས་སྐྱོད་བྱེད་པ *chags-skyod byed-pa* रञ्जन the act of affecting or agitating the heart or producing sensation of pleasure in it.

ཆགས་འཁྲི *chags-ḥkhri* रागलता fig. the creeping plant of love which entwines.

ཆགས་སྒོ *chags-sgo* extenuation of fault; ཉེས་པ་ཅན་ལ་ཆགས་སྒོ་དང་བུག་པ་ཅན་ལ་གླན་པ to shield the faulty and to put a patch or lid over the place (hollow).

ཆགས་ཅན *chags-can*, prov. राग, 1. time in music. 2. passionate, lustful.

ཆགས་ཆེན་མ *chags-chen-ma* रागिणी, कामिनी a musical air; a wife; a young woman.

ཆགས་འཇོམས *chags-ḥjoms* one who has subdued his passions, a general epithet of Buddha (*Mṅon.*).

ཆགས་གཏམ *chags-gtam* amorous conversation.

Syn. འཁྲིག་ཚིག *ḥkhrig-tshig*; ཆགས་ཚིག *chags-tshig*; འདོད་གཏམ *ḥdod-gtam* (*Mṅon.*).

ཆགས་རྟགས་པ *chags-rtags-pa* to remain for a long time at one place.

ཆགས་ལྡན་མ *chags-ldan-ma* कामुकी a lustful woman.

ཆགས་སྡང་ *chags-sdaṅ* passion for; passionate attachment.

ཆགས་པའི་རྒྱལ་མཚན *chags-paḥi rgyal-mtshan* the male organ or penis.

ཆགས་པའི་གདོན་ཅན་མ *chags-paḥi gdon-can-ma* = བུད་མེད་འདོད་ལྡན་མ a lustful woman (*Mṅon.*).

ཆགས་པར་འགྱུར་པ *chags-par ḥgyur-pa* रञ्जनीय lovely, fascinating, charming.

ཆགས་པས་མྱོས་པ *chags-pas myos-pa* = འདོད་པས་དྲེགས་པ *ḥdod-pas dregs-pa* intoxicated with love or desire for any object (*Mṅon.*).

ཆགས་སྤྱོད *chags-spyod* = འཁྲིག་པ copulation; fornication.

ཆགས་བྱ *chags-bya* मोच्य an object of attachment; that which has been affected with love.

ཆགས་བྱེད *chags-byed* or ཆགས་བྱེད་འོད་དཀར सोम an epithet of the moon (*Mṅon.*).

* ཆགས་བྲལ *chags-bral* वीतराग without attachment (*Kālac. T. 3*).

ཆགས་བྲལ་ཅན་ *chags-bral-can* निर्मुक्त one who is free from passion or attachment.

ཆགས་ཚིག་ *chags-tshig* = ཆགས་གཏམ་ *chags-gtam* or འདོད་གཏམ་ *ḥdod-gtam* amorous conversation; talk of love.

ཆགས་ཞེན་ *chags-shen* hankering after wealth or worldly objects.

ཆགས་ཟད་ *chags-zad* रागक्षीण passionless, attachment exhausted.

ཆང་ *chaṅ* मद, सुरा, मधु, माधवी, आसव, गन्धमादनी, मोद, आमोद, दैत्या fermented liquor, whether beer or wine. ཆང་གི་དབྱེ་བ different sorts of beer or wine:—འབྲུ་ཆང་ beer from corn; ནས་ཆང་ barley-brewed ale; འབྲས་ཆང་ white rice beer; བུ་རམ་ཆང་ treacle-beer; སྦྲང་རྩི་ཆང་ wine of honey, pulse, mead; མེ་ཏོག་ཆང་ wine of certain flowers such as the मधूक of Magadha; ཤིང་ཤུན་ཆང་ wine from certain barks of trees such as cinnamon; ལྗོང་བཙུད་ཆང་ fermented juice of certain trees; རུས་ཆང་ beer of bones; སློང་ཆང་ proposal-wine, *i.e.*, wine sent as a present to negotiate for the marriage of a girl; སྨན་ཆང་ medicinal wine; རྒུན་ཆང་ *rgun-chaṅ* wine from grapes; དར་བའི་ཆང་ wine of whey or curds; བསུ་ཆང་ present of wine sent for the reception of a guest or friend or an official; ཨ་རག arrack or spirit.

Syn. ཡོངས་འབབ *yoṅs-ḥbab*; ཆ་བདག་སྐྱེས *cha-bdag-skyes*; དཔའ་མོ *dpaḥ-mo*; ལྷ་མིན་ཉིང་ཁུ *lha-min ñiṅ-khu*; སྟོབས་བཟང་ *stobs-bzaṅ*; དགའ་མ *dgaḥ-ma*; བཅོལ་ལྡན་མཉེས *bçol-ldan mñes*; མྱོས་བྱེད *myos-byed*; དགའ་བྱེད *dgaḥ-byed*; མྱོས་འགྱུར *myos-ḥgyur*; དྲི་མཆོག *dri-mchog*; དྲི་རབ *dri-rab*; སྤོས་ངད་ལྡན *spos-ṅad-ldan*; ཆུ་མ *chu-ma*; བཅོལ་མ *bçol-ma*; མཆོག་ལྡན་མ *mchog-ldan-ma*; ཅ་ཅོ་བྱེད *ca-co byed*; ཡོངས་སུ་ཐོབས *yoṅs-su thobs*; གནོད་སྦྱིན་ཆང་ *gnod-sbyin chaṅ*; ཧ་ལཱ *hā-lā* (*Mṅon.*).

ཆང་སྐྱོགས *chaṅ-skyogs* चषक goblet for wine; also ladle to help wine.

ཆང་ཁང་ *chaṅ-khaṅ* pot-house, tavern, place where wine and beer are sold.

+ ཆང་ཁྲུ་འཚོག *chaṅ khyu-ḥtshog*, ཁུ་ཚུར་གྱིས་བརྡུང་བ to beat with the clenched hand or fist.

ཆང་གི་ཉིང་ཁུ *chaṅ-gi ñiṅ-khu* = ཆུར་རྩི or ཉིང་ཁུ spirit; བདུད་རྩི་སྙིང་པོ essence of nectar.

ཆང་གི་ཕྱ་དར *chaṅ-gi phya-dar* the place where boiled barley, rice, etc., after being mixed with yeast, is spread for fermentation.

ཆང་གིས་གཡེངས་པ *chaṅ-gis gyeṅs-pa* to be drunk.

ཆང་གྲལ *chaṅ-gral* the order or row of seats at a carnival.

ཆང་འགག *chaṅ-ḥgag* = ཆང་སྣོད *chaṅ-snod* vessel for keeping wine.

ཆང་རྒྱུ *chaṅ-rgyu* the substance of which beer or wine is made.

ཆང་ཆུང་ *chaṅ-chuṅ* in colloq. = ཆང་ངེ་ཆུང་ངེ་ some few, also miscellaneous; acc. to *Sch.* a little.

ཆང་ཆེམ་ཅན *chaṅ-chem-can* an intoxicated person.

ཆང་ཉམས *chaṅ-ñams* = met. ཐོག *thog* (*Mṅon.*).

ཆང་རྙིང་ *chaṅ-rñiṅ* = ཆང་རྒན *chaṅ-rgan* in Sikk. old beer or wine.

ཆང་བསྙལ *bchaṅ-bsñal* intoxicated.

ཆང་ཏིག *chaṅ-tig* vessel for measuring wine.

+ ཆང་ཐུབ *chan-thub* a drinking being, *i.e.*, one subject to decay and destruction.

ཆང་དད་ཅན *chaṅ-dad-can* a drunkard, tippler: ཆང་དད་ཆེ་བའི་ཁྱོ་ག་འཆལ་བ་དང་། ཁྲོ་དད་ཆེ་བའི་བུད་མེད་འཆལ་མོ་གཉིས། ཁྱིམ་གཅིག་ནང་དུ་འཛོམས་ན་འགྲིག་པ་མེད॥ a husband of intemperate habits and an immoral wife can have no harmony if they dwell together in one home.

ཆང་རྡོད *chañ-dod* silver or other articles with which wine or beer is exchanged.

ཆང་དྲེགས *chañ-dregs* or ཆང་གིས་དྲེགས་པ *chañ-gis dregs-pa*=ཆང་གིས་མྱོས་པ *chañ-gis myos-pa* intoxication (*Mñon.*).

ཆང་འདོན *chañ-hdon*=ཆང་སྣོད *chañ-snod* wine-glass or cup (in Sikk.).

ཆང་གནས *chañ-gnas* or ཆང་འཐུང་གནས a place of drinking; greg-shop.

ཆང་པ་སྟོང་བ *chañ-pa stoñ-wa* erroneously written for འཆང་པ་སྟོང་པ *hchañ-pa stoñ-pa* रिक्तमुष्टि; lit. open fist, or an empty hand; fig. nothing to give in charity to the poor.

ཆང་སྤགས *chañ-spags* dough of barley soaked in beer.

ཆང་ཕུད *chañ-phud* the first distillation of wine—the best beer or wine.

ཆང་ཕོག *chañ-phog* allowance in beer.

ཆང་བུ *chañ-bu*, described in རྩམ་པ་བཙིར་བ་སྐྱུར་སོར་བཅངས་ནས་སོར་མོའི་བར་འདོན་པ་དེ་ནི་འབྱུང་པོ་རྣམས་སྐྱེར་བྱ་ཡིན། the dough of barley-flour squeezed or pressed within the hand and coming out between the fingers is given to the ghosts.

Syn. རྡོག་པ *rdog-pa*; ཆངས་པ *chañs-pa* (*Mñon.*).

ཆང་མ *chañ-ma*, v. ཆང་འཚོང་མ (*Mñon.*) a woman selling wine.

ཆང་མལ *chañ-mal* grog-shop, tavern.

ཆང་རྩི *chañ-rtsi* dry barm, lees, yeast (of beer).

ཆང་ཚང་ *chañ-tshañ* grog-shop; ཆང་ཚང་ལས་འོངས་པ come or coming from a grog-shop.

Syn. ཆང་མལ *chañ-mal*; ཆང་ཁང་ *chañ-khañ* (*Mñon.*).

ཆང་ཚང་ལས་འོང་བ *chañ-tshañ las hoñ-wa* a drunkard; one who is just coming out of a grog-shop.

ཆང་འཚོང་མ *chañ-htshoñ-ma* barmaid.

Syn. མྱོས་བྱེད་འཚོང་ *myos-byed-htshoñ*; ཆང་མ *chañ-ma*; ཆང་བྱེད་མ *chañ-byed-ma* (*Mñon.*).

ཆང་འཚོང་མའི་ཁང་པ *chañ-htshoñ-mahi khañ-pa* गञ्ज lit. wine-selling woman's house.

ཆང་ཟས *chañ-zas* roast meat taken at the time of drinking.

ཆང་བཟུང་ *chañ-bzuñ* for འཆང་བཟུང་ मुष्टि closed hand, fist.

ཆང་གཡོས *chañ-gyos* or ཆང་གིས་གཡོས पानसात्र parched rice, barley, &c., taken with wine.

ཆང་ར *chañ-ra* आपान, abbr. of ཆང་ and ཨ་རག, beer and arrack; a drinking party.

ཆང་ས *chañ-sa* 1. a beer-house. 2. beer carousal: ཆང་ས་ཆེན་པོ་བྱེད་པ to give or arrange for a great beer-drinking party.

ཆངས་པ *chañs-pa*, v. ཆང་བུ *chañ-bu*.

ཆད I: *chad* time; ཕྱིན་ཆད in after time, henceforth; སྔོན་ཆད formerly, heretofore.

ཆད II: 1. special promise, agreement or engagement; ཆད་འབུལ special presentation, special request, compliments at the commencement of a letter. ཁ་ཆད oral, verbal engagement; ལག་ཆད pledge of faith by the hand (*Jä.*). 2. in compounds for ཆད་པ punishment; ལུས་ཆད corporeal punishment.

ཆད་དོན *chad-don* or ཁ་ཆད a promise, contract; ཆད་དོན་བྱེད་པ to give a promise, make a contract; གཏོང་བའི་ཆད་དོན་བྱེད་པ to agree about giving; ཆད་དོན་སྐྱར་བྱེད་པ to keep, fulfil, a promise.

ཆད་མདོ *chad-mdo* or ཁ་ཆད the purport or the main object; a promise or contract.

ཆད་པ I: *chad-pa* उन्मुक्त, उद्गारण, अत्यय, छेद 1. to open, to separate, liberate; to give out. 2. to promise, bind one's self.

Syn. ཕྱེད་མ *phyeḏ-ma*; དབྱེ་བ *ḏbye-wa* (*Mñon.*).

ཆད་པ II: sbst. resp. བཀའ་ཆད निग्रह, दण्ड punishment; ལུས་ཆད corporeal punishment; fig. punishment with the rod. རྒྱལ་པོའི་ཆད་པ king's punishment, *i.e.*, punishment that the law inflicts on any person. ངལ་ཆད punished with fatigue, worn out. ཆད་པ་ཅན *chaḏ-pa-can*=བཙའ་ལྡན दण्डिक, दण्डवान् a convict; one who has been convicted of an offence. ཆད་པའི་ཚར་གཅད་པ *chaḏ-paḫi tshar-gcaḏ-pa* or ཆད་པས་གཅོད་པ निग्रह to convict, to sentence, to punish.

Syn. དབྱུག་པ *ḏbyug-pa*.

ཆད་པ III: vb. to be descended from; to be born of or with; gen. with ལས or ནས.

ཆད་པ་ཕོག་པ *chaḏ-pa phog-pa* to award punishment, to punish in any way.

ཆད་པས་བཅད་པ *chaḏ-paṣ ḇcaḏ-pa* to be visited with punishment.

ཆད་པོ *chaḏ-po* 1. rent, torn, worn-out, ragged, tattered (*Jä.*). 2. a limited time, a term (*Sch.*).

ཆད་ཡིག *chaḏ-yig* a written contract: ཆད་མལ་གྱི་ཡི་གེ id. (*Glr.; Jä.*).

ཆད་ལུས་པ *chaḏ-luṣ-pa* not to obtain the things hoped for, to be disappointed (*Sch.*).

ཆད་སོ *chaḏ-so* or ཆད་སོར=ཆད་གསབ 1. a limited time, a term. 2. a time-purchase (*Sch.*). 3. an agreement (*Tā.; Jä.*).

ཆན *chan* I: (དཔེ་ལ་ཆན་ལྷ་བུ) टिप्पनी a marginal note or foot-note to explain the meaning of a term or expression in the text.

ཆན II: sop, mash, pulp, etc.; འབྲས་ཆན rice-pap; ནས་ཆན barley-pap (*Jä.*).

ཆན་གྲི *chan-gri*=ཚེམ་གྲི *ḫtshem-gri* (lit. a tailor's knife); कृपाणी a pair of scissors.

ཆན་པ *chan-pa*=འཚེམ་གྲི scissors, shears: དགེ་སློང་གི་སྐྲ་ཆན་པས་འབྲེག་པར་མི་བྱར (*K. d.* ཀ *106*) the hair of a gelong should not be cropped with scissors.

ཆབ I: *chab* [resp. and eleg. for ཆུ *chu*] water, in any form; but never used like *chu* to signify a river. དྲི་ཆབ scented water. ཁྲུ་ཆབ or ཁྲི་ཆབ water which at the beginning and close of religious meetings in the larger monasteries is passed round, and of which every one present takes a few drops on his tongue, as a symbol of purification in the place of full ablutions. སྤྱན་ཆབ tears; ཞལ་ཆབ spittle; ཆབ་གསང་ urine.

ཆབ II: power, dominion, sway; ཆབ་འོག under one's sway: ཆབ་འོག་ཏུ་བསྡུ་བ to bring or collect under one's power or sway.

ཆབ་རྐྱན *chab-ṛkyan* brass can, brass tea-pot with a long spout for pouring out tea (*Jä.*).

ཆབ་སྐྱ *chab-ṣkya*=དར་བ *dar-wa* whey.

ཆབ་ཁུང་ *chab-khuñ* urinal, a privy.

ཆབ་སྒོ *chab-ṣgo* door; ཆབ་སྒོ་བ *chab-ṣgo-wa*=སྒོ་རག་པ a door keeper.

ཆབ་གཏོར *chab-gtor*=ཆུ་གཏོར *chu-gtor* तर्पण oblations to the dead; water religiously offered to quench the thirst of Yidag or *Preta* in the प्रेतलोक।

ཆབ་ནག *Chab-nag* n. of a monastery in Kong-po in Eastern Tib.

ཆབ་བྲོམ *chab-brom* ice (*Jä.*).

ཆབ་འབངས *chab-ḫbañṣ*=འབངས་གཡོག प्रजा a servant; a subject; one owing allegiance.

ཆབ་བླུག *chab-ḇlug* 1. a spittle pot. 2. acc. to *Jä.* a vessel for rinsing one's mouth with water.

ཆབ་མ *chab-ma* lid, valve; ཆབ་རྩེ *chab-rtse* or ཆབ་ཙེ *chab-tse* buckle, clasp.

ཆབ་མིག *chab-mig* = ཆུ་མིག a fountain, spring.

ཆབ་རྩེ *chab-rtshe*, v. ཆབ་མ *chab-ma*.

ཆབ་ཚོད *chab-tshod* (lit. water-measure for time) a watch, a clock.

ཆབ་གཤུག *chab-gshug* a bath; also the bathing festival of the Tibetans in August and September.

ཆབ་འོག་པ *chab-hog-pa* a vassal, a subject; ཆབ་འོག་གི་རྒྱལ་པོ a vassal king, feudal chief.

ཆབ་རིལ *chab-ril* the vessel of consecrated water passed to monks of a congregation before dispersing.

ཆབ་རིལ་པ *chab-ril-pa* one who passes through water, v. ཆག་ཁྲུས.

ཆབ་རོམ *chab-rom* = ཆུ་འཁྱགས་པ ice, frozen water.

ཆབ་ཤོག *chab-çog* = བཀའ་ཤོག eleg. for an official letter, a diploma, etc.

ཆབ་སེར *chab-ser* eleg. for ཆུ་སེར matter, pus.

+ ཆབ་སྲིད *chab-srid* = རྒྱལ་སྲིད *rgyal-srid*- dominion, kingdom, territory.

ཆབ་གསང་ *chab-gsañ* urine; ཆབ་གསང་འདང་བ to make water.

ཆབ་གསིལ་བ *chab gsil-wa* to discharge urine, make water (*Ñag.*).

卐 **ཆབས་ཅིག** *chabs cig* = ལྷན་ཅིག or མཉམ་དུ सह, सार्द्धम् together with, all together.

ཆམ *cham* headlong, full length; also completely, utterly.

卐 **ཆམ་དུ** *cham-du* = གཏན་དུ always, continually; ཆམ་དུ་འབེབས་པ pouring continually.

ཆམ་པ *cham-pa* प्रतिश्याय a cold or catarrh; གྲེ་ཆམ *gre-cham* bronchial catarrh; གློ་ཆམ catarrh in the lungs; སྣ་ཆམ *sna-cham* nose cold (cold in the head); རིམས་ཆམ influenza.

ཆམས་བཞག *chams-bshag* = ཅམ་བཞག, བཏང་སྙོམས་སུ་བཞག་པ། to be in a tranquil state; colloq. to keep quiet མི་མཐུན་པ་རྣམས་ཆམས་བཞག་ནས་ཇོ་བོའི་གསུང་བཞིན་མཛད་པས (*A. 119*) those who did not assent keeping quiet: it was effected according to the precepts of the lord (Atis'a).

ཆར *char* or ཆར་པ *char-pa* वर्षा काल rain.

Syn. སྤྲིན་བཅུད *sprin-bcud*; སྦྲང་ཆར *sbrañ-char*; ཆུའི་ས་བོན *chuhi-sa-bon*; སྤྲིན་གྱི་མེ་ཏོག *sprin-gyi me-tog*; མཁའ་ལས་བབ *mkhah-las-bab*; རླུང་གི་འབྲས་བུ *rluñ-gi hbras-bu*; རྒྱུན་བབ *rgyun-bab*; དགུང་ཆར *dguñ-char*; གྲུ་ཆར *gru-char*; ལོ་ཏོག་གཉེན *lo-tog-gñen* (*Mñon.*).

ཆར་སྐྱིབས *char-skyib* a shelter, pent roof, protection from rain.

ཆར་སྐྱེས *char-shyes* वर्षभू lit. rain-born; met. a frog.

ཆར་སྐྱོབ *char-skyob* 1. protection against rain, also opp. to ཚད་སྐྱོབ *tshad-skyob* protection against heat (of the sun). 2. = གདུགས an umbrella (*Mñon.*).

ཆར་སྐྱོར *char-skyor* undecided (cases or disputes).

ཆར་ཁེབས *char-khebs* cover or dress for protection against rain, rain-cloak.

ཆར་གྱང་ *char-gyañ*, འབྲས་སོ་བའི་ཆར་གྱང་རིམ་པ་གསུམ་ཙམ་རེ་བབས (*Ya-sel. 33*).

ཆར་གྱི་ཟེགས་མ *char-gyi zegs-ma* = ཆར་ཐེལ.

ཆར་དགའ *char-dgah* lit. that delights in rains, ཁྲུག་རྟ (*Mñon.*).

ཆར་རྒྱུན *char-rgyun* प्रवर्ष incessant rain.

ཆར་ཅན *char-can* 1. = ཆར་ལྡན. 2. ལུགས་སྲོལ custom, usage (*W.*). 3. n. of a hero बलदेव (Baladeva) (*Lex.*).

ཆར་བཅུག་པ *char-bcug-pa* उद्योजित; བྱེད་དུ་བཅུག་པ made to be done or worked out.

ཆར་ཆེས *char-ches* for ཆར་པ་ཆེན་པོ.

ཆར་གཏོགས་པ *char gtogs-pa*, v. ཆ, included in the division of; = ཁོངས་སུ་གཏོགས་པ or ཕྱོགས་སུ་གཏོགས་པ.

ཆར་སྟོན *char-ston* met. the swallow.

ཆར་དུས *char-dus* the rainy season.

ཆར་དྲག་པ *char-drag-pa* आषाढ़ lit. heavy rain; the month of heavy rains, corresponding with July.

Syn. དྲག་བབ *drag-bab*; ཡོངས་ལྷུང་ *yoń-lhuń*; རྒྱུན་བབ་ཚ *rgyun bab-tsha* (*Mṅon.*).

ཆར་རྡུལ *char-rdul* = ཆར་ཟིལ.

ཆར་ལྡན *char-ldan* rainy; ཆར་ལྡན་སྤྲིན་དང་དབྱར་དུས་ལའོ in the summer season are rain-clouds (*Mṅon.*).

ཆར་སྣ་རླུང་ཁྲིད *char-sna rluń-khrid* an idiomatic expression signifying guided; lit. as wind leads the rain.

ཆར་པ *char-pa*, v. ཆར.

ཆར་སྤྲིན *char-sprin* जीमूत rain-cloud; ཆར་སྤྲིན་ཅན cloud containing rain.

ཆར་ཕོབས *char-phobs* वार्षेय to cause rain.

ཆར་འབབ་མཁས་པ *char-hbab mkhas-pa* gen. a *Tantrik* lama; lit. one who is skilled in bringing down rain (by the efficacy of his charms).

ཆར་འབེབས *char-hbebs* or ཆར་པ་འབེབས बलाहक, मिहिर that causes rain; rain-cloud.

ཆར་འབེབས་གྲོང་འཇོམས *char-hbebs groń-hjoms* an epithet of Indra (*Mṅon.*).

ཆར་མེད་ཐོན་པ *char-med thon-pa* = སྐྱིང་འབར drought, rainlessness.

ཆར་ཤོད *char-shod* good and beneficial rain: འདི་ལོ་ཆར་ཤོད་ལེགས་པར་བབས this year rain has copiously fallen.

ཆར་ཤོད་ཆེ་སྟབས *char-shod che-stabs* (idiomatic phrase) a matter of great importance.

ཆར་ཟིལ *char-zil* rain drop, rain particles or drops.

Syn. ཆར་རྡུལ *char-rdul*; ཆུ་ཡི་ཟེགས་མ *chu-yi zegs-ma*; རྒྱུན་གྱི་སྨྱུ་གུ *rgyun-gyi myu-gu*; ཆུ་ཡི་ཟེར *chu-yi-zer*; ཆུ་རྡུལ *chu-rdul*; ཆར་གྱི་ཟེགས་མ *char-gyi zegs-ma* (*Mṅon.*).

* ཆར་བཟང་འབེབས་པ *char-bzań hbebs-pa* सुवर्षक n. pr. (*Tā. 2, 271*).

ཆར་གཡོགས *char-gyogs* = ཆར་ཁེབས house; cover or dress for protection against rain.

ཆར་ལེན *char-len* the coping or water-tile of a wall (*Cs.*).

ཆལ *chal* resp. སྐུ་ཆལ belly, abdomen (*Cs.*).

ཆལ་ཆལ *chal-chal* the sound of falling oars.

ཆལ་ཆིལ *chal-chil* wavering, fluctuating (*Sch.*).

ཆལ་ཆོལ *chal-chol*, v. འཆལ་འཚོལ or འཆལ་ལེ་འཚོལ་ལེ.

ཆལ་དུ་བཀྲམས་པ *chal-du bkrams-pa* विकीर्ण scattered, strewn over, fully spread, widespread.

ཆལ་མར་བརྡལ་བ *chal-mar brdal-wa* (vb. a.) to spread equally, uniformly.

ཆས *chas* 1. thing; tool; requisite, etc.: བག་མར་སྟོང་བའི་ཆས things to be given to a bride as dowry; ལྕགས་ཆས iron tools or utensils; ལྟོ་ཆས food; དམག་ཆས military stores, requisites for war; འཚོ་ཆས provisions; ལག་ཆས tools, instrument. 2. dress, garment; ཕོ་ཆས man's dress. 3. in a more general sense: appearance, form, shape: བུད་མེད་ཀྱི་ཆས་སུ་བྱ་སྟེ appearing in the guise of a woman; ཧོར་ཆས་

བྱེད he puts on a Tartar dress; བུ་མོའི་ཆས་སུ་ཞུགས he has assumed a girl's dress; disguised himself as a girl.

ཆས་ཀ *chas-ka* or ཆས་ཁ सम्बल one's property, resources, requisites; all that one possesses or requires for his use.

ཆས་སྒྱུར་བ *chas-sgyur-wa* to put on, to assume another's dress.

ཆས་ཆོད *chas-chod* पराभव, अभिभव, v. བརྙས་པ *brñas-pa.*

ཆས་པ *chas-pa* [originally the pf. of ཆ་བ but always used as a separate vb.] 1. to set forth, depart: ཆས་དགོས་པར as it is necessary to depart (*Thgy.*); བོད་དུ་ཆས་སོ they set out for Tibet (*Glr.*); དུས་གཅིག་ཏུ་ཆས་སོ they departed together (*Dzl.*); ཆས་སུ་འཇུག་པ to send away, dispatch. 2. to prepare for, set about, to start; གསོད་པར་ཆས they started killing; འགྲོ་བར་ཆས་པ་ལས having made arrangements to depart (*Dzl.*): ད་ཕྱིར་འདོང་ངོ་ཞེས་ཆས་པས 'now we will return' they said, and they made preparations (*Dzl.; Jä.*)

ཆས་བཟོ *chas-bzo*=ལུས་ཆས a full suit of clothes (for the body).

ཆི *chi* num. fig. 36.

ཆི་ག *chi-ga* in *W.* wallet, knap-sack (*Jä.*).

ཆི་ལི་ལི *chi-li-li* onomatopoetic word for snuffing up scent by the nose; ཞིམ་ཞིམ་དྲི་མ་ཆི་ལི་ལི་ཕྱིར (*Cs.*) snuffing sweet odours that are borne; མེ་ཏོག་དྲི་མ་ཆི་ལི་ལི the perfumes of flowers are perceptible (*Mil.*; *Jä.*).

ཆིག *chig* used for གཅིག as the first part of compound numbers:—ཆིག་བཅུ 10; ཆིག་བརྒྱ 100; ཆིག་སྟོང 1,000; ཆིག་ཁྲི a myriad, etc.

ཆིག་རྐྱང *chig-rkyań* acc. to *Schtr.* separate, single, one alone.

ཆིག་རྒྱུ་ཉིས་སྤུན *chig-rgyu ñis-spun* a kind of blanket in the weaving of which one longitudinal thread is crossed by two.

ཆིག་ཐུབ་པ *chig-thub-pa* 1. to be able to do a thing alone. 2. n. of a plant used in medicine (*Jä.*).

ཆིག་དྲིལ *chig-dril* rolled, wrapped, packed up in one parcel or bundle (*Sch.*).

ཆིག་ལབ་བྱེད་པ *chig-lab byed-pa* to talk to one's self, to hold a soliloquy (*Schtr.*).

ཆིག་ཤད *chig-çad* one stroke, or stop: དོན་ཚིགས་ཚིགས་བཅད་ཀྱི་མཐར་ཆིག་ཤད་བྱ། at the close of each line of a verse (forming a sentence), put one stroke, *i.e.*, full stop (*Situ.*).

ཆིངས *chińs*, v. འཆིང་བ बन्धन, that which binds. ཆིངས་ལྔ the five binding things:—(1) ཁོག་དབུག་སྟོང་ཧུན་གྱི་ཆིངས *khog-dbug stoń-'hun-gyi chińs*; (2) ས་དཔྱད་རྣམ་འབྱེད་ཀྱི་ཆིངས *sa-dpyad rnam-hbyed-kyi chińs*; (3) འབྲེལ་པ་འབྲུ་འགྲེལ་གྱི་ཆིངས *hbrel-pa hbru-hgrel-gyi chińs*; (4) བསྡུས་དོན་གྱི་ཆིངས *bstus don-gyi chińs*; (5) ལག་ལེན་མན་ངག་གི་ཆིངས *lag-len man-ńag-gi chińs* (*Sman.*).

ཆིད་པ *chid-pa*, v. ཕྱིད་པ

✝ **ཆིབ་པ** *chib-pa* 1. ཁྱབ་པ व्याप्त encompassing, covering all. 2. acc. to *Sch.* equal, uniform, suitable.

ཆིབས *chibs* or ཆིབས་པ resp. term for རྟ *rta* a horse; generally a riding horse; a saddle horse; ཆིབས་ལ་འཆིབ་པ riding on a horse, to get on horse-back; ཆིབས་ལས་གཤོལ་བ to dismount: ཆིབས་གཤོལ་བ་ལ་གནང (*C.*) I beg you to dismount; ཁྱེད་ཀྱི་ཆིབས་སུ་འབུལ I give it you for a riding horse (*Jä.*).

ཆིབས་བསྐྱོད་གནང་བ *chibs-bskyod gnań-wa* (lit. to ride on a horse)=ཆིབས་བསྒྱུར་གནང་བ to start for a journey, to go to a place.

ཆིབས་ཁ་འཁྲིད་པ *chibs-kha hkhrid-pa*=ཆིབས་ཁ་བསྒྱུར་བ to lead a horse by the bridle (*Sch.*).

ཆིབས་ཁ་ཐུབ་པ *chibs-kha thub-pa* to have the command of the bridle; fig. to be expert in ruling.

ཆིབས་སྒ *chibs-sga* resp. for སྒ saddle.

ཆིབས་ལྷ་ལྡན *Chibs-lha-ldan* also called བསྔགས་ལྡན, the horse on which Gautama Buddha used to ride.

ཆིབས་ལྕག *chibs-lcag* resp. a whip.

ཆིབས་ཆས *chib-chas* a horse's furniture, harness; (*Cs.*) the equipments of a horse.

ཆིབས་ཆེན *chibs-chen* a charger; the best horse in the stable.

ཆིབས་རྟ *chibs-rta* a riding horse of a great man.

ཆིབས་ཐུར *chibs-thur* horse's head-piece.

ཆིབས་དཔོན *chibs-dpon* chief groom.

† ཚིར *chir* from the Hindi छिट, chintz.

ཚིལ་སྒྲོག *chil-sgrog*, v. ཆུ་གཉེར *chu-gñer*.

ཆུ I: *chu* num. fig. 66.

ཆུ II: जल, उदक, अपः, पयः, &c. 1. water, the universal and common term in all senses. 2. a river; the general term.

Syn. གཏུང་བྱ *gtuñ-bya*; གཏུང་བྱེད *gtuñ-byed*; སྒོ་ཀུན་འགྲོ *sgo-kun-hgro*; སྤྲིན་གྱི་མེ་ཏོག *sprin-gyi me-tog*; སྤྲིན་གྱི་བཅུད *sprin-gyi-bcud*; དག་བྱེད *dag-byed*; ངན་སེལ *ñan-sel*; འབྲུ་ཕན *hbru-phan*; སྤྲིན་གྱི་མྱུ་གུ *sprin-gyi myu-gu*; ཐུར་བགྲོད *thur-bgrod*; ཀུན་འགྲོ *kun-hgro* (*Mñon.*).

ཆུ་ཀླུང *chu-kluñ* नदी a river is a term often occuring in books, but rarely in conversation. ཆུ་ཀླུང་སྣ་ཚོགས་ཀྱི་མིང the names of various rivers both real and mythical which occur in the sacred books of Tibet and according to Buddhistic geography:—(1) ཟབ་མོའི་ཆུ *zab-mohi chu*, (2) རབ་ཏུ་དང་བའི་ཆུ *rab-tu dañ-wahi chu*, (3) གཙང་བའི་ཆུ *gtsañ-wahi chu*, (4) འོ་མའི་ཆུ *ho-mahi chu*, (5) རྒྱུན་འབྲུའི་ཆུ *rgyun-hbruhi chu*, (6) ཟླ་བ་རྒྱུ་བ *zla-wa rgyu-wa*, (7) འོ་ཐུག་གི་འདམ *ho-thug-gi hdam*, (8) གྲམ་སག་གི་ཆུ *gram-sag-gi chu*, (9) ངང་ངུར་གྱིས་གང་བ *ñañ-ñur-gyis gañ-wa*, (10) ངང་པ་ཀུན་ཏུ་སྒྲ་འབྱིན་པ *ñañ-pa kun-tu sgra hbyin-pa*, (11) དབྱངས་སྙན་པ *dbyañs sñan-pa*, (12) སེམས་འགྲོ་བ *sems hgro-wa*, (13) ཧུ་རུ་རུའི་སྒྲས་འབབ་པ *hu-ru-ruhi-sgras hbab-pa*, (14) རླབས་འབྱུང་བ *rlabs hbyuñ-wa*, (15) བདེ་བའི་ཆུ *bde-wahi chu*, (16) ཀ་དམ་པ་འཁོད་པ་ཉིད *ka-dam-pa hkhod-pa-ñid*, (17) ནོར་བུའི་མཆུ་ཅན་རྣམས་ཀྱིས་འཛིན་པ *nor-buhi mchu-can rnams-kyis hdsin-pa*, (18) ཆུ་སྲིན་ཀུརྨ་མང་བ་ཉིད *chu-srin kurma mañ-wa-ñid*, (19) ཉ་རོ་ཧི་འཁོར་བ *ña ro-hi hkhor-wa*, (20) རུས་སྦལ་གྱིས་གང་བ *rus-sbal-gyis gañ-wa*, (21) ཆུ་སྲིན་ན་ཀྲས་བསྐོར་བ *chu-srin na-kras bskor-wa*, (22) ཡིད་བདེ་བར་འབབ་པ *yid bde-war hbab-pa*, (23) དབུ་བའི་ཕྲེང་བ *dbu-wahi phreñ-wa*, (24) རབ་ཏུ་དགའ་བར་གྱུར་པའི་ཆུ *rab-tu dgah-war gyur-pahi chu*, (25) རླུང་མཚུངས་པ *rluñ mtshuñs-pa*, (26) ཆར་དང་ཆར་གྱི་རྗེས་སུ་འབྱུང་བའི་ཆུ་ཀླུང *char dañ char-gyi rjes-su hbyuñ-wahi chu-kluñ*, (27) དབྱངས་ཅན་གྱི་མདོག་ཏུ་འབབ་པ *Dbyañs-can-gyi mdog-tu hbab-pa*, (28) དུས་སུ་འབབ་པ *dus-su hbab-pa*, (29) རིང་པ *riñ-pa*, (30) རྩེ་མོའི་ངང *rtse-mohi ñañ*, (31) གསེར་གྱི་ཆུ *gser-gyi chu*, (32) དངུལ་གྱི་མདོག *dñul-gyi mdog*, (33) མུ་ཏིག་གི་བྱེ་མ་ལྡན་པ *mu-tig-gi bye-ma ldan-pa*, (34) རི་བོ་ལ་རྒྱུ་བ *ri-bo-la rgyu-wa*, (35) སྤྲིན་འཁོར་བ *sprin hkhor-wa*, (36) མུ་སཱ་ར་གལ་པ་རྒྱན་དུ་བྱས་པ *mu-sā-ra gal-pa rgyan-du byas-pa*, (37) བི་དྲུ་མའི་ཤིང་དང་ལྡན་པ *vi-dru-mahi çiñ dañ ldan-pa*, (38) དཔྱིད་དགའ་བ *dpyid dgah-wa*, (39) དབྱར་སྤྲིན་རབ་ཏུ་དང་བའི་ཆུ་འབབ་པ *dbyar-sprin rab-tu dañ-wahi chu hbab-pa*, (40) རྩེ་མོ་ལ་འཇུག་པར་དགའ་བ *rtse-mo la hjug-par dgah-wa*, (41) གངས་ཡོད་པ *gañs yod-pa*, (42) ཉི་མ་ཤར་བར་གྱུར་པས་མི་རེག་པ *ñi-ma çar-war gyur-pas mi reg-pa*, (43) མྱུར་བའི་ཆུ *myur-wahi chu*, (44) རླབས་རབ་ཏུ་འཇུག་པ *rlabs-rab-tu hjug-pa*, (45) ཨ་ཏུ་པཱ *a-tu pā*, (46) ཙུ་ལུན་ད་འབབ་པ *tsu-lun-da hbab-pa*, (47) དྲིའི་ཆུ *drihi-chu*, (48) ཀེ་ཏ་ཀའི་དྲིས་བསྒོས་པ *ke-ta-kahi-dris bsgos-pa*, (49) དབྱར་དགའ་བ *dbyar dgah-wa*, (50) དྷུན་དྷུ་མཱ་རཱ *dhun-dhu mā-rā*, (51) ཉེ་འཁོར་ན་ཁྱབ་པ *ñe-hkhor-na khyab-pa*, (52) དཔག་མེད་པ་འབབ་པ *dpag med-pa hbab-pa*, (53) རྒྱབ་ནས་ཀླུང་ཀུན་ཏུ་གང་རབ་ཏུ་འབབ་པ *rgyab-nas klun kun-tu-gan rab-tu hbab-pa*, (54) དམའ་བའི་ཆུ *dmah-wahi chu*, (55) དགའ་བས་འཇུག་པ *dgah-was hjug-pa*, (56) སྔོན་གྱི་དུ་བའི་སྟོབས *snon-gyi du-wahi stobs*, (57) སྤྲིན་གྱི་འགྲོས *sprin-gyi hgros*, (58) དྲི་ཟའི་དབྱངས་ཅན *dri-zahi dbyans-can*, (59) རྔའི་སྒྲའི་དབྱངས་ཅན *rnahi sgrahi dbyans-can*, (60) སྐད་ཀྱི་དབྱངས་ཅན *skad-kyi dbyans-can*, (61) ཀླུ་ཡི་བུ་མོ་མངོན་པར་དགའ་བ *klu-yi bu-mo mnon-par dgah-wa*, (62) རིག་པ་འཛིན་པ་རྩེ་དགའ་བས་གནས་པ *rig-pa hdsin-pa rtse-dgah was gnas-pa* (*K. d.* ར *298*).

ཆུ་ཀླུང་སྐྱེས *chu-klun skyes*, རྒྱལ་བྱེད་ཤིང་གི་མིང་ n. of a tree called जयन्ती [*Sesbania Ægyptiaca*]*S.*

ཆུ་ཀླུང་མགོན *chu-klun mgon* the lord of rivers.

ཆུ་ཀླུང་ཅན *chu-klun-can* a place which is intersected by streams, or where there are many rivulets.

ཆུ་ཀླུང་དག་པ *chu-klun dag-pa* नदीस्नात lit. purified by bathing in a river; a Tīrthika.

ཆུ་ཀླུང་བདག *chu-klun-bdag* सरित्पति the lord of rivers; the ocean. ཆུ་ཀླུང་དམར *chu-klun-dmar* शोण नदी the red river, *i.e.*, the river Sone.

ཆུ་ཀླུང་མཚོ *chu-klun-mtsho* (མཐོ་རིས་ཀྱི་མཚོ) the wide expanse of the heaven; an imaginary lake in heaven; the sea.

ཆུ་ཀློང་ *chu-klon* the main, deeper channel of a river, v. ཀློང་ *klon*.

ཆུ་དཀྱིལ *chu-dkyil* ཆུ་གཞུང་ the middle of a river.

ཆུ་རྒྱལ *chu-rgyal* a leather bag for water, a *moshug* (*Cs.*).

ཆུ་སྐད *chu-skad* the voice of water, the sound of rushing water.

ཆུ་བསྐོལ་པ *chu bskol-pa* boiled water, boiling water.

ཆུ་སྐོར *chu-skor* or རང་ཐག་ཆུ་སྐོར *ran-thag chu-skor* water-mill, *i.e.*, self-grinding mill.

ཆུ་སྐྱ *chu-skya* = དར་བ whey.

ཆུ་སྐྱར *chu-skyar* कलहंस a species of water fowl—the spoon bill.

Syn. ཉ་འབིགས་བྱེད *na-hbigs-byed*; རྒྱལ་བྱེད *rgyal-byed*; རྐང་གཅིག་པ *rkan-gcig-pa*; གངས་སྦལ *gans-sbal*; མཛའ་མོ *mdsah-mo*; ཆུ་ཅན *chu-can* (*Mnon.*).

ཆུ་སྐྱུར *chu-skyur* 1. the bittern. 2. also n. of a plant. 3. acidulous mineral waters. 4. vinegar (*Jä.*).

ཆུ་སྐྱེས *chu-skyes* जलज, अम्बुज, अब्ज 1. lit. the water-born, the lotus. 2. the moon, the planets Neptune and Venus.

ཆུ་སྐྱེས་དཀར *chu-skyes dkar* पुण्डरीक the white lotus. ཆུ་སྐྱེས་སྔོན་པོ *chu-skyes snon-po* उत्पल the blue lotus.

ཆུ་སྐྱེས་མངལ *chu-skyes mnal* पद्मयोनि, ब्रह्मा; = ཚངས་པ་ཆེན the great Brahmā.

ཆུ་སྐྱེས་ཅན *chu-skyes-can* सरोजिनी pond where lotuses grow.

ཆུ་སྐྱེས་བདག *chu-skyes-bdag* सरोजपति the lord of the lotus, the sun.

ཆུ་སྐྱེས་རྩ་བ *chu-skyes rtsa-wa* मृणाल the white tuberous root of the lotus.

ཆུ་སྐྱོད *chu-skyod* ग्रीवा met. the neck.

ཆུ་ཁུག *chu-khug* a creek; bay, gulf.

ཆུ་ཁུར་ཏུ་འཛིན *chu-khur-tu hdsin* वारिवाहधर [1. "that which holds clouds," *i.e.*, the sky. 2. "having clouds for a vehicle," an epithet of Indra]*S.*

ཆུ་འཁུར *chu-hkhur*, met. སྤྲིན་པ *sprin-pa* cloud.

ཆུ་ཁེབས *chu-khebs* = ཆར་ཁེབས cloak worn for protection against rain.

ཆུ་ཁོལ *chu-khol* ཆུ་ཚུག. [1. boiled water. 2. जलतापिन् the Hilsa or sable fish]*S.*

ཆུ་འཁོར *chu-hkhor* जलाटन, काजल, सधम a whirlpool, an eddy. ["a water-goer," *i.e.*, a heron or a leech]*S.*

Syn. ཀློང་འཁོར *kloṅ-ḥkhor* ; འཁྱིམ་པ *ḥkhyim-pa* ; ཟེག་མའི་ལྟེ *zeg-maḥi lte* ; ཆུ་ཡི་འཁོར་ལོ *chu-yi ḥkhor-lo* འཁོར་ཆུ *ḥkhor-chu* (*Mṅon.*).

ཆུ་འཁོར་བ *chu-ḥkhor-wa* the turning of a water-mill.

ཆུ་འཁྱགས *chu-ḥkhyags* ice, frozen water. Syn. ཐབ་རོམ *bhab-rom* ; འཁྱག་པ *gkhyag-pa*.

ཆུ་འཁྱིལ *chu-ḥkhyil* puddle, pool.

ཆུ་འཁྱོགས་པ *chu ḥkhyogs-pa* वङ्क नदी any tortuous or meandering river.

ཆུ་འཁྲི་ཤིང་ *chu-ḥkhri-çiṅ*=ཆུའི་ཐ་རླབས a wave.

ཆུ་མཁྲིས *chu-mkhris* जलपित्त water and bile [" the bile of water," *i.e.* fire]*S.*

ཆུ་འཁྲུག *chu-ḥkhrug*=ཆུའི་ཐ་རླབས a wave; ruffle on the surface of water.

ཆུ་གང་ *chu-gaṅ* full of water.

ཆུ་གྲི *chu-gri* छुरिका a small knife; acc. to *Schr.* razor.

ཆུ་གྲོག *chu-grog* acc. to *Sch.* 1. rivulet, brook. 2. dish-water, rinsings (*Jä.*).

ཆུ་གླང་ནག་པོ *chu-glaṅ nag-po* or ཆུ་གླང་ནག་པོ =རྭ་ཅོ་ཅན *rwa-co-can* སྡིག་པ་རྭ་ཅོ *sdig-pa rwa-co* (*Sman. 108*).

ཆུ་གླིང་ *chu-gliṅ* पुलिन any islet in a river.

ཆུ་མགྲིན་ཅན *chu mgrin-can*=ཆུ་སྲིན कुम्भीर; जलकण्ठ said to be the crocodile.

ཆུ་མགོ *chu-mgo* source or head of a river, a feeding spring.

ཆུ་འགགས་པ *chu ḥgags-pa* मूत्ररोध stoppage or retention of urine.

ཆུ་འགོ་རྟ་རིང་ *Chu-ḥgo rta-riṅ* one of the thirty-seven holy places of the Bon (*G. Bon. 38*).

ཆུ་རྒྱན *chu-rgyan* कमल the ornament of the water, *i.e.*, the lotus flower.

ཆུ་རྒྱུན *chu-rgyun* प्रवाह the current or flow of a river.

ཆུ་རྒྱུས *chu-rgyus* स्नायु sinews, ligaments and nerves; ཆུ་རྩ gland.

ཆུ་སྒང་ *chu-sgaṅ* a blister.

ཆུ་སྒོང་ *chu-sgoṅ* the water-egg, po. for the moon which (mythologically) sprung out of the great ocean.

ཆུ་སྒྲ *chu-sgra* the murmur of a stream.

ཆུ་བསྒྱུར་བ *chu bsgyur-wa*=ཆུ་ཁ་བསྒྱུར་བ the change of the course of a river.

ཆུ་ངན་ལམ་བཤུགས *chu-ṅan lam-bshugs*=སྲོལ་ངན་པ་བྱུང་བ *srol ṅan-pa byuṅ-wa* (idiomatic expression) the introduction of a bad custom; following a bad usage.

ཆུ་ངོགས *chu-ṅogs* bank of a river or lake; ཕ་རོལ་ངོགས the opposite side or bank, called also ཕར་ང and ཆུ་རོལ་ངོགས this side of the river; བྱེ་མ་ངོགས sandy bank; བྱེ་ཐང་ sandy plain on the side or margin of a river.

ཆུ་རྔམས *chu-rṅams*=ཆུའི་ཐ་རླབས a wave (*Mṅon.*).

ཆུ་བཅུད *chu-bcud*=ལན་ཚྭ *lan-tshba* table-salt.

ཆུ་ལྕག *chu-lcag* निचुल water streaming down from rock [the tree *Barringtonia acutangula*]*S.*

ཆུ་ཆག *chu-chag* grain or grass, &c., given to cattle mixed with water.

ཆུ་ཆུ *chu-chu*=ལ་ཆུ rhubarb; ཆུ་རྩ its root is used as dye and laxative in Tibet.

ཆུ་ཆུང་དུ *chu chuṅ-du* (ཆུ་སྟོད་ཀྱི་ཟླ་བ) the sixth month of the Tibetan calendar, *i.e.*, July.

ཆུ་ཆུང་ཉི་ལ *chu chuṅ-nḥi la* (ནོར་བུ) precious stone, a gem of fabulous properties like ཆུ་སྙིང་ containing the essence of water, the finest pebble or crystal.

ཆུ་ཉལ *chu-ñal* also ཆུ་རྫིང jalāśaya a tank.

ཆུ་ཉུང་ *chu-ñuṅ*, v. ཁྱིམ་བྱ चातक the swallow.

* ཆུ་ཉུལ་བ *chu-ñul-wa* = ཉུལ་བ or འཁོར་བ.

ཆུ་གཉེར *chu-gñer* wavelets or ripples in water.

Syn. མཚར་གཡོ *mtshar-gyo*; ཆིལ་སྒྲོག *chil-sgrog*; ཁྲེམ་གཉེར *khrem-gñer*; རླབས་ཀྱི་རི་མོ *rlabs-kyi ri-mo* (*Mṅon.*).

ཆུ་མཉམ་པ *Chu-mñam-pa* n. of a fabulous sea situated beyond the ocean called སྦྲུའི་དུག་བཅོམ; lit. (cure against snake-poison) (*K. d.* ར, *335*).

ཆུ་རྙོག་མ་ཅན *chu rñog-ma-can* turbid or muddy water.

Syn. ལྡམ་བུ *ldam-bu*; མི་དངས *mi-daṅs*; རྙོག་མ་ཅན *rñog-ma-can*; འདམ་རྫབ *hdam-rdsab*; འབྱིན་བྱེད *hbyin-byed*; འཇིམ་པ *hjim-pa* (*Mṅon.*).

ཆུ་སྙིང *chu-sñiṅ* 1. a precious stone; believed to possess fabulous properties such as the power of keeping off fire, and the effects of thunder and lightning. 2. salt.

ཆུ་གཏིང་ཐུང་བ *chu-gtiṅ thuṅ-wa* shallow water.

Syn. གཏིང་གཤལ་ནུས *gtiṅ gshal-nus*; ས་ལེ་བ *sa le-wa*; མི་ཟབ་པ *mi zab-pa* (*Mṅon.*).

ཆུ་གཏིང་ཟབ་པ *chu-gtiṅ zab-pa* deep water.

Syn. གཏིང་མེད *gtiṅ-med*; ཟབ *zab*; གཏིང་དཔག་དཀའ *gtiṅ-dpag-dkah*; འོག་གཞི་མི་རིག *hog-gshi-mi rig*; རབ་མེད *rab-med* (*Mṅon.*).

* ཆུ་གཏེར *chu-gter* རྒྱ་མཚོ་ཆེན་པོ जलधि the ocean; also symb. the number four (*Rtsi.*).

ཆུ་གཏེར་མུ་ཁྱུད *chu-gter mu-khyud* अब्धिनेमि an island.

* ཆུ་གཏེར་ཟུར *chu-gter-zur* अब्धिकोण a creek of the sea (*Kālac. T. 135*).

ཆུ་རྟ་མོ *Chu rta-mo* n. of a medicinal plant called སྟག་ཤ *stag-ça* (*Sman. 258*).

ཆུ་སྟེང་སྦྱིན *chu steṅ-sbyin* कुमुद the water-lily.

ཆུ་སྟོད *chu-stod* पूर्वाषाढ the month of July.

ཆུ་སྟོད་ཀྱིས་ཉ་བ *chu-stod-kyis ña-wa* आषाढी पूर्णिमा the full moon of July.

ཆུ་སྟོད་སྐར་མ *chu-stod skar-ma* the constellation བྲེ་ཆུ་ལྷ་ལྡན་མ *bre-chu lha ldan-ma* ཀླུ་མོ; पूर्वाषाढ (*Rtsi.*).

ཆུ་སྟོད་སྐྱེས *chu-stod-skyes* (སྤར་མིག་དམར) मङ्गल-ग्रह the planet Mars.

ཆུ་ཐགས *chu-thags* वारियन्त्र water-mill.

ཆུ་ཐིག *chu-thig* जलबिन्दु drop of water, water-drop.

ཆུ་ཐོགས་པ *chu thogs-pa* विगाहन to bathe in water.

ཆུ་མཐའ *chu-mthah* or ཆུ་མཐའ་རྒྱ་ཆེ་བ the broad side or bank of a river.

ཆུ་མཐོངས *chu-mthoṅs* = ནམ་མཁའ *nam-mkhah*.

ཆུ་འཐོར *chu-hthor* = ཆུའི་ཐིགས་མ particles of water. ཆུ་འཐོར་གཏམ *chu-hthor-gtam* speaking and spitting together.

ཆུ་འཐོར་བ *chu-hthor-wa* प्रतिसिञ्च् to sprinkle.

Syn. ཆུར་སྒྲོགས *chur-sgrogs*; ཆུར་འཇུག *chur-hjug*; ཆུའི་འདབ་ཆགས *chuhi hdab-chags*.

ཆུ་དང་ཞེང་དུ་ལྡན་པ *chu-daṅ sheṅ-du ldan-pa* आरोहपरिणाहसम्पन्न a long wide river.

ཆུ་དར *chu-dar* a small prayer-flag stuck on the bank of a river, in order to avert inundations (*Jä.*).

ཆུ་དུག *chu-dug* acc. to *Sch.* hemlock.

ཆུ་བདག *chu-bdag* or ཆུ་ཡི་བདག = ཆུ་ལྷ the god of water (*Mṅon.*); also a fox.

ཆུ་བདག་སྐྱེས *chu-bdag-skyes* = ཆང་དཀོར alcohol (*Mṅon.*).

ཆུ་དྲོ་འཇམ *chu-dro hjam* कोष्णोदक tepid water, slightly warm water.

ཆུ་དྲོན་ *chu-dron* or ཆུ་དྲོན་མ་ *chu dron-ma* उष्णोदक hot or warm water.

ཆུ་མདའ་ *chu-mdah* a jet of water.

ཆུ་མདོ་ *chu-mdo* confluence of rivers.

ཆུ་འདོད་ *chu-hdod*=སྐོམས་པ་ *skoms-pa* or ཁ་སྐོམས *kha-skoms* (*Mñon.*) thirst; also thirsty.

ཆུ་འདྲེན་ *chu-hdren* बलाहक lit. that draws water; a cloud.

ཆུ་རྡུགས་ཁྱེར་ *chu-rdugs khyer* water-fright; cattle being confounded by fright while crossing a river.

ཆུ་རྡུལ་ *chu-rdul*, v. ཆར་ཐིལ་ particles of water or rain drops (*Mñon.*).

ཆུ་རྡོ་ *chu-rdo* rounded pebbles found in brooks; a kind of crystal. ཆུ་རྡོ་གྲང་མོ་ cool crystal (used for spectacles) (ཆུ་རྡོ་གྲང་མོའི་དྭགས་ཀྱིས་ཁྲག་གཟེར་འཇོམས).

ཆུ་ལྡུར་ *chu-ldur* (རྟའི་ཆུ་རྫམ) flour and water mixed up together as the food of horses.

ཆུ་ཉིང་ *chu-niñ* years ago.

ཆུ་རྣག *chu-rnag* matter, pus (*Sch.*).

ཆུ་ཕུག *chu-phug* a cavern in a rock at the head of a river or brook.

ཆུ་ཕྱག་པ *chu-phyag-pa* (lit. one who sweeps over water), *i.e.*, a ferry-man (*Jä.*).

ཆུ་ཕྲན *chu-phran* a little river, a brook.

ཆུ་འཕྲད་པ *chu hphrad-pa* कपोटपाल a rudder, or a large oar used as such.

ཆུ་བ *chu-wa* a large gland of which there are sixteen acc. to Tibetan anatomy (*Jä.*). ཆུ་བ་སྒྲོག་པ a contraction of the sinews (*Cs.*).

ཆུ་བན *chu-ban* jug; water-pot.

Syn. ཆུ་སྣོད *chu-snod*; ཆུ་རྫ *chu-rdsa*; ནོར་བུ་ཅན *nor-bu-can*; སྣོད་པོ་ཆེ *snod-po che*; ཆུ་བུམ *chu-bum* (*Mñon.*).

ཆུ་བལ *chu-wal* शैवाल, जलवल, मत्सुल water-moss.

ཆུ་བུན *chu-bun* white paint for the face (*Sch.*).

ཆུ་བུམ *chu-bum*=ཆུ་བན *chu-ban*.

ཆུ་བུར *chu-bur*=ཆུའི་ལྦུ་བ *chuhi lbu-wa* स्फार (*Mñon.*) 1. bubbles of water, also froth. 2. watery eruptions on the skin, vescicles, blister, occasioned by a burn. 3. acc. to *Jä.* boil, ulcer, abscess.

ཆུ་བུར་ཅན *Chu-bur-can* अर्बुद n. of one of the cold hells. 2. acc. to *Schtr.* the eye.

ཆུ་བོ *chu-wo* वाहिनी, नदी 1. river: ཆུ་བོ་ནམ་པ་བཞིའི་རྒྱུན་བཞིན་རྩོལ་ལ་པ་མཆིན liko the strcams of the four great rivers (let your letters) flow towards me (*Yig. k. 13*). 2. also signifies the number four (*Rtsi.*).

ཆུ་བོ་ཆེན་པོ་ལྔ *chu-bo chen-po lña* the five great rivers of the continent of Godaniya (བ་ལང་སྤྱོད *Ba-lañ-spyod*), which acc. to Buddhist cosmogony are the following:—(1) ཡངས་པ་ཅན, (2) ཙན་ཙུམ་པ་ཐི, (3) ཟླ་བའི་ཤུག་པ, (4) ཆུ་བཟང་པོ, (5) ཀུན་ཏུ་འདྲེས་པ.

The seventeen great rivers of the continent of Pûrva Videha (ཤར་ལུས་འཕགས་པ) are:—(1) ཕྱི་མ་འདྲེས་པ, (2) ཤ་མྲེ་ཌཱ *Sña mre-ḍā*, (3) ཆུ་གཡོ་བ, (4) ཀླུའི་ཆུ *Kluhi-chu*, (5) ནགས་ནས་འབྱུང་བ, (6) ཙ་ར་ཙ, (7) འབྲི་ཞིང་གོས་གཡོགས་པ, (8) རྩེ་མོ་ལ་འཁོར་བ, (9) ཆུ་ནག་པོ, (10) ཟོ་མ་ཐུར་དུ་འབྱུང་བ, (11) དུ་བ་དཀར་བ, (12) ཉི་ཚོ་ལུཧ་འབབ་པ, (13) དྲང་སྲོང་དགའ་བ་སྔོན་འབབ་པ *Drañ sroñ dgah-wa sñon hbab-pa*, (14) བཟང་པོ (these flow down from the mountain called རྨ་བྱའི་ཚོགས་ཀྱི་རི *Rma-byahi tshogs-kyi ri* in Pûrva Videha), (15) རྭ་གསུམ་པ *Rwa gsum-pa*, (16) ཙ་ཙོ་པ *Ca-co-pa*, (17) རྡོ་བ་འགྲིམ་པ *Rdo-wa hgrim-pa* (*K. d.* ར *337*).

ཆུ་བོ་འདྲ་བ *chu-bo hdra-wa*; ཆུ་བོའི་སྟ་ཟུར *chu-bohi sta-zur* ओघ; ཆུ་བོའི་འདོམས *chu-bohi hdoms?*

ཆུ་བོ་གངྒཱ *Chu-wo Gañgā* the river Ganges.

ཆུ་བོ་ཡ་མུ་ན *Chu-bo Ya-mu-na* the different names of the river Yamunā: ཉི་མའི་བུ་མོ *Ñi-maḥi bu-mo*, གདུང་བྱེད་མ *Gduṅ byed-ma*, ཞི་བའི་སྲིང་མོ *Shi-waḥi sriṅ-mo*, རྩོད་ཅན *Rtsod-can*, ཀཱ་ལིནྡའི་བུ་མོ *Kā-lindaḥi bu-mo*, གཤིན་རྗེའི་སྲིང་མོ *Gçin-rjeḥi sriṅ-mo* यमु.

ཆུ་བོ་རབ་མེད *Chu-bo rab-med* नदीवैतरणी the great unfordable river of hell.

ཆུ་བོ་རི *Chu-bo ri* n. of a monastery situated 32 m. S. W. of Lhasa on the top of a hill opposite the iron bridge over the Yeru Tsang-po. It is also called ལྕགས་ཟམ་ཆུ་བོ་རི *Lcags-zam Chu-bo-ri.*

ཆུ་བོ་སི་ཏཱ *Chu-bo Si-tā* the river Sitā= the great Tsang-po of Tibet: བརྒྱར་གྱེས *Brgyar-gyes*, ཞགས་གྲོལ *Shags-grol*, དཔུང་པས་བྱིན *Dpuṅ-pas byin*, སྲིད་སྒྲུབ་མ *Srid-sgrub-ma*, རྟགས་ཏུ་འབབ *Rtags-tu ḥbab*, ཁྲག་འབབ *Khrag-ḥbab*, དབྱིག་གི་ཁུ་བ *Dbyig-gi khu-wa*, ལག་པའི་ཆུ་བོ *Lag-paḥi chu-bo.*

ཆུ་བོ་སིན་དྷུ *Chu-bo Sin-dhu* different names of the river Sindhu (Indus): རྩེད་འཇོའི་ཆུ་བོ *Rtsed-ḥjoḥi chu-bo*, སྔོན་གྱི་གང་གཱ *Sṅon-gyi gaṅ-gā* (पूर्वगङ्गा), ཟླ་བ་སྐྱེས *Zla-wa skyes*, རི་བོའི་བུ་མོ *Ri-boḥi bu-mo*, མང་པོ་བྱིན *Maṅ-po byin*, རེ་བཱ་ཆུ་བོ *Re-bā chu-bo.*

ཆུ་དབུས *chu-dbus*=ཆུ་གཞུང *chu-gshuṅ* the central course or main stream of a river.

* ཆུ་དབུས་པ *chu-dbus-pa* मध्यान्तिक Pāli: Majjhāntiko (*Tā. 2, 9*).

ཆུ་འབབ *chu-ḥbab* निम्नस्रोता: a hill-torrent; ཆུ་འབབ་སྒྲ *chu-ḥbab sgra* the sound of a torrent.

ཆུ་བྱ *chu-bya* water-fowl, water-bird; ཆུའི་བྱ་གག *chuḥi bya-gag* the grey duck.

ཆུ་འབྱུང *chu-ḥbyuṅ* (གྲངས *grañs*) a number (*Ya-sel. 57*).

ཆུ་འབྱེད *chu-ḥbyed* said to be the swan (*D. R.*).

ཆུ་བྲུག་པ *chu brug-pa* (ཆར་པ་ཆེན་པོ་བབས་ཏེ་ཆུ་ལོག་ཁྲུག་པ) नदीपूर over-flowing of a river; any inundation (*Zam. 5*).

ཆུ་ལྦག *chu-lbag*, v. ལྦག bubbles.

ཆུ་སྦུར *chu-sbur* acc. to *Sch.* 1. drifted wood and the like; thin pieces of wood, chips, chaff, etc., floating on the water. 2. water-beetle (*Jā.*).

ཆུ་སྦྲུལ *chu-sbrul* a harmless water-snake said to abound in the hotsprings of Tibet.

ཆུ་སྦྱིན *chu-sbyin*=तर्पण offerings of water to the yi-dag.

ཆུ་མ *chu-ma* 1. a water-carrier. གད་པ་ཆུ་མ་སོགས་བོགས་དགོས་རིགས། classes of men such as sweepers and water-carriers, &c., to whom allowances should be paid (*Rtsii.*). 2. cultivation which requires irrigation.

ཆུ་མ་རྩི *chu-ma-rtsi* a water-plant: ཆུ་མ་རྩི་ལྷིམ་ཆུ་སེར་དམ་ཆུ་སྐྱོང་། *chu-ma rtsi* cures or dries pus and serum.

ཆུ་མིག *chu-mig* जलाच 1. spring, fountain. 2. n. of a vein. [3. जलाची an aquatic plant, *Commelina salicifolia*]*S.*

ཆུ་དམར་པོ *chu-dmar-po* a sea of red water where the Nāga people and the Asura fight together every day after taking their food (*K. d.* ར *334*).

ཆུ་སྨད་སྐར་མ *chu-smad skar-ma* the constellations of उत्तराषाढ़ are the following:— ཕུལ *phul*, སྣ་ཚོགས *sna-tshog*, ལྷ་ལྡན་མ *lha-ldan-ma* (*Rtsi.*).

ཆུ་རྩམ *chu-rtsam* water with flour; gen. the grain mixed with water that is given to horses.

ཆུ་ཚགས *chu-tshags* परिस्रावण 1. a strainer, sieve. 2. n. of a demi-god of the nether world. ཆུ་ཚགས་ཀྱིས་རུང་བ *chu-tshags kyis ruṅ-wa* परिस्रावकल्प; a monk permitted to use filtered water, *i.e.*, fit to use filtered water,

3. ཆུ་ཚགས་གྲུ་གསུམ *chu-tshags gru-gsum* खञ्जक triangular filtering sieve [a leather water-bag]*S.*

ཆུ་ཚན *chu-tshan* any hot-spring, large numbers of which occur everywhere in Tibet.

ཆུ་ཚུབ་སྐྱ་རེང་ *chu-tshub skya-reṅ*, ཚུགས་པ་ཞིང་ ཆུ་ཚུབ་སྐྱ་རེང་གིས་བྲོས་ཏེ་གང་ཆུར་སོང་ཡང་ཆ་མེད་པར་སོང་ངོ (*D.R.*).

ཆུ་ཚྭ *chu-tshwa* salt from water.

ཆུ་ཚོད *chu-tshod* दण्ड lit. the measure of time by a water-clock; the Indian hour, one-fifth of a ཁྱིམ or 24 minutes.

ཆུ་ཚོད་འཁོར་ལོ *chu-tshod hkhor-lo* घड़ी; घटिका 1. the clepsydra or water-clock of Ancient India. 2. now=clock in general or watch.

ཆུ་འཛིན *chu-hdsin* 1. भग the female organ. 2. जलधर, जलधि cloud. In *Mṅon.* we read རྒྱ་མཚོ་ལས་བྱུང་བའི་ཆུ་རྡུལ་འཛིན་པའི་ཕྱིར་རོ། it is so called because of its holding the particles of water that rise from the ocean.

Syn. of 2. སྤྲིན་པ *sprin-pa*; ནམ་མཁའི་གླང་པོ *nam-mkhahi glaṅ-po*; ཚ་ཟེར་འཇོམས *tsha-zer-hjoms*; མཁའ་གོས་ཅན *mkhah-gos-can* (*Mṅon.*).

ཆུ་རྫ *chu-sdsa* earthen water-jar.

+ཆུ་ཞེང་ *chu-sheṅ* आरोह area; ཆུ=དཀྱུས་རིང་ཐུང་ *dkyus-riṅ-thuṅ*; ཞེང་=ཁ་ཞེང *kha-sheṅ* superficial area of a globe or circle.

ཆུ་ཞེང་འགབ་པ *chu-sheṅ hgab-pa* परिमण्डल; परिणाह acc. to *Schtr.* proportionate, symmetrical; acc. to others, beautiful, stately.

ཆུ་ཞེང་མཐའ *chu-sheṅ mthah* चक्रवाट् circumference.

ཆུ་བཟོམ *chu-bzom* a covered bucket for carrying water.

ཆུ་ཟེམ *chu-zem* प्रतितोय water-tub (*Jä.*).

ཆུ་ཟླ *chu-zla* or ཆུའི་ཟླ *chuhi-zla* उदकचन्द्र 1. the image of the moon in water, reputed to be a deception of the senses by witchcraft. 2. the water-month, the first month (*Jä.*).

ཆུ་གཟར *chu-gzar* a large ladle (*Cs.*).

ཆུའི་སྐྱེ་གནས *chuhi-skye-gnas* कपोट्योनि (ཆུ་ནང་གི་སྲོག་ཆགས་ཚང་མ) water insects, worms, etc. (may also mean "fire").

ཆུའི་འཁྲིལ་ཤིང་ *chuhi-hkhril-çiṅ* creeping plants growing in water.

ཆུའི་འཁྲུལ་འཁོར. *chuhi-hkhrul-hkhor*=ཆུ་འཛིན mirage (*Mṅon.*).

ཆུའི་གད་མོ *chuhi gad-mo*=ཆུའི་ལྦུ་བ *chuhi lbu-wa* [जलहास 1. cuttle-fish bone, considered as the petrified foam of the sea. 2. water-bubbles]*S.*

ཆུའི་སྒུར་འཁྱོག *chuhi-sgur hkhyog* सूकर a pig.

ཆུའི་ཉ་ཕྱིས *chuhi ña-phyis* शम्बुक shell; also a snail.

ཆུའི་དྲ་བ *chuhi dra-wa* कर्कन्धु (ཆུ་འཐོར་བ) [the jujube-tree]*S.*

ཆུའི་དོང་ *chuhi-doṅ*=ཆུ་དོགས [जलकूपी a well, spring or pool]*S.*

ཆུའི་འདབ་ཆགས *chuhi hdab-chags* water-fowl v. ཆུ་འཐོར་བ.

ཆུའི་རྡོ་བ *chuhi-rdo-wa* (ཆུ་ནང་གི་རྡོ) कुकुन्दर [n. of a plant]*S.*

ཆུའི་འདྲེ་ལོག *chuhi hdre-log*=ཆུའི་རྦ་རླབས waves (*Mṅon.*).

ཆུའི་དཔལ་ཡོན *chuhi dpal-yon* (ཆུ་སྲ) वर्द्धनी (རྒྱ་མཚོ་ཟླ་བར་རྟེན་ནས་འཕེལ) flow and ebb-tide.

ཆུའི་རྩྭ *chuhi-rtswa* शैवाल watermoss; (ཤུ་དག) the rush.

ཆུའི་ཞལ་ཏ་པ *chuhi-shal-ta-pa* पानीयदारिका a woman who supplies water to a lady.

ཆུའི་གཞི *chuhi-gshi* जलाशय a lake; a place filled with fresh water.

ཆུའི་ཟེགས་མ *chuhi zegs-ma* particles of water; spray.

Syn. ཆུ་འཐོར *chu-hthor*; ཉར་མ *ñar-ma*; ཆུའི་ཟེར་མ *chuhi zer-ma*; ཆུ་ཟིལ *chu-zil*; ཆུ་ཐིག *chu-thig*; དབའ་རླབས་སྐྱེས *dbah rlabs-skyes* (*Mṅon.*).

ཆུའི་གཟུགས་བརྙན *chuhi gzugs-brñan*=སྨིག་རྒྱུ (*smig-rgyu*) mirage.

ཆུའི་ལོ་མ *chuhi lo-ma* (གཉེར་མ) ripples in water.

ཆུའི་ཤིང་རྟ *chuhi çiṅ-rta* (གྲུ་ཤན) वारिरथ met. a boat, ship.

ཆུའི་ས་བོན *chuhi sa-bon*, v. ཆར་པ.

ཆུ་འོབས *chu-hobs* water-ditch (*Sch.*).

ཆུ་ཡི་འཁོར་ལོ *chu-yi hkhor-lo* whirlpool, v. ཀློང་འཁོར *kloṅ-hkhor* or ཆུ་འཁོར.

ཆུ་ཡི་ཧྲགས་པ *chu-yi sñags-pa*, a shell; met. a monkey.

ཆུ་ཡི་སྙིང་པོ *chu-yi sñiṅ-po* 1.=ཆུ་ཡི་རོ salt (*Mṅon.*). 2. n. of tank filled with lotus flowers.

ཆུ་ཡི་ཐུབ་པ *chu-yi thub-pa* or ཆུ་ཡི་དབང་པོ अम्भल the god of water; also animals living in water. However, in Tibetan mythology there is no general god of water. Irrigation streams and channels are under the protection of a special deity and the various large rivers have each a protecting river-god respectively; but if an universal ཆུའི་ལྷ is ever mentioned in books, it must be a mere phrase of the author's fancy.

ཆུ་ཡི་ཕུང་པོ *chu-yi phuṅ-po*, वारिराशि;=རྒྱ་མཚོ་ཆེན་པོ the ocean.

ཆུ་ཡི་ཚེར་མ *chu-yi tsher-ma* the lotus plant, flower, etc.

ཆུ་ཡི་འཛུམ་དཀར *chu-yi hdsum-dkar*=ཆུའི་ལྦུ་བ froth of water, also bubble.

ཆུ་ཡི་ཟེགས་ལྡན *chu-yi zegs-ldan* कङ्कणावती that which contains particles of water; rain or cloud.

ཆུ་ཡི་ཟེགས་མ *chu-yi zegs-ma*, v. ཆར་ཟིལ.

ཆུ་ཡི་འོད་ཕྲུག་སྔོན་པོ *chu-yi hod-phrug sñon-po* =དངུལ་ཆུ quick-silver.

ཆུ་ཡི་རོ *chu-yi-ro* salt.

ཆུ་ཡི་ལང་ཚོ *chu-yi laṅ-tsho* पद्म the lotus.

ཆུ་ཡི་སྲིན་པོའི་གྲོང་ཆེ *chu-yi srin-pohi groṅ-che* =རྒྱ་མཚོ་ཆེན་པོ the great city of sea monsters, *i.e.*, the ocean (*Mṅon.*).

ཆུ་རགས *chu-rags* dam, dyke (*Jä.*); same as ཆུ་ལོང་ *chu-loṅ* (*Mṅon.*).

ཆུ་རི *chu-ri* (lit. water-hill) a billow.

ཆུ་རུག *chu-rug* n. of a medicinal root: ཆུ་རུག་རུས་པའི་ཚད་པ་སེལ་བར་བྱ *chu-rug* will remove inflammation in the bones.

ཆུ་རླབས *chu-rlabs*, v. ཆུའི་ཐ་རླབས ऊर्मि, wave, billow.

ཆུ་ལས་འབྱུང་བ *chu-las hbyuṅ-wa* जलौका: a leech.

ཆུ་ལོ *chu-lo* n. of an aquatic edible plant.

ཆུ་ལོག *chu-log* floods (*Jä.*).

ཆུ་ལོན་ *chu-lon* dam, dyke. * ཆུ་ལོན་གྱི་ཐུབ་པ་བདུན *chu-lon-gyi thub-pa bdun* (*Tā. 2, 71*) the seven rulers over irrigation channels and the watering of crops.

ཆུ་ཤིང་ *chu-çiṅ* कदली, रम्भा, निचुल 1. the plantain. 2. acc. to *Jä.* drift-wood. [3. also the ratan plant]*S.*

Syn. རྩ་ཡི་སྙིང་པོ *rtsa-yi sñiṅ-po*; རྒྱུན་རྣམས་འཛིན *rgyun-rnams-hdsin*; ནད་ཀྱི་འབྲས་ཅན *nad-kyi hbras-can*; འཆི་འབྲས་ཅན *hchi-hbras-can*; གླང་པོའི་ལྕུག་མ *glaṅ-pohi lcug-ma*; མཛོད་ལུས *mdsod-lus*; གྲོལ་བ *grol-wa*; ཤིང་འཛིན *çiṅ-hdsin* (*Mṅon.*).

ཆུ་ཤིང་དཀར་པོ *chu-çiṅ dkar-po* [काण्डपाटला, श्वेतद्रुहती white aconite, *Aconitum ferox*].*S.*

Syn. གཞོན་ནུ་ཅན *gshon-nu can*; ལོ་མ་ཁ *lo-ma kha* (*Mṅon.*).

ཆུ་ཤིང་གི་མཁར་བ་ *chu-çiñ gi mkhar-wa* a stick made of *chuçiñ* plant (*Hbrom. 160*).

ཆུ་ཤིང་བརླ་ཅན་མ་ *chu-çiñ brla-can-ma* lit. a woman whose loins resemble the plantain plant, *i.e.*, a harlot, prostitute (*Ya-sel. 54*)

ཆུ་ཤུར་ *Chu-çur* n. of a district in Tibet. (*Btsii.*). ཆུ་ཤུར་རྫོང་ *Chu-çur-rdsoñ* the *Jong* or fort of *Chu-çur* near Lhasa.

ཆུ་ཤུལ་ *chu-çul* जलखण्ड channel or drain for water [little drops of water adhering to a vessel after it has been emptied]*S.*

ཆུ་ཤེལ་ *chu-çel* उदकहर्षण, स्फटिक crystal. [चन्द्रकान्तमणि the "moon-stone" described by Sanskrit poets as having the power of emitting water at the sight of the moon]*S.*

ཆུ་ཤེལ་དབང་གི་དཀྱིལ་འཁོར་ *chu-çel dwañ-gi dkyil hkhor* = the crystal disk, *i.e.*, the moon (*Yig. k. 30*). ཆུ་ཤེལ་དབང་པོ་ *chu-çel dwañ-po* = ཟླ་བ the moon: སྐུ་འཚོ་ཆུ་ཤེལ་དབང་པོར་རབ་ཏུ་གསལ་ཞིང་ལེགས་མཛད་ཀྱི་འོད་དཀར་ཡར་རྒྱས་རིང་ནས། while the light of your good works has been increasing in brightness, your health has become resplendent as the lord of the crystal disk (*Yig. k. 85*).

ཆུ་ཤེལ་ཞུན་མ་ *chu-çel shun-ma* lit. melted crystal; met. the moon (*Yig. k. 18*).

ཆུ་གསོང་ *chu-gçoñ* a ravine containing water (*Jä.*).

ཆུ་སེར་ *chu-ser* matter, pus.

ཆུ་སོ་ *chu-so* वास्तेय 1. the bladder. 2. the external and internal urinary organs (*Jä.*).

* ཆུ་སྲང་ *chu-srañ* शिरा; ཆུ་སྲང་གསུམ་ *chu-srañ gsum* त्रिशिर (*Kālac. T, 62*).

‡ ཆུ་སྲིན་ཀེ་ཀེ་རུ་ *Chu-srin Ke-ke-ru* n. of a crocodile; also that of a place in Ancient India (*A. 20*).

ཆུ་སྲིན་རྒྱལ་མཚན་ *Chu-srin rgyal-mtshan* मकरध्वज n. of a king whose royal standard was a crocodile; an epithet of Cupid.

Syn. ཆུ་གཏེར་ *chu-gter* (*Mñon.*).

ཆུ་སྲིན་ཆེན་པོ་ *chu-srin chen-po* or ཆུ་སྲིན་ཤ་ཀྲ་ *chu-srin ça-kra* ग्राह, कुम्भीर mythological monster-fish with body like a hill, and furnished with eighteen heads (*K. d.* ༥ *82*).

ཆུ་སྲིན་བདག་ *chu-srin-bdag* said to be = རྒྱ་མཚོ་ཆེན་པོ the sea.

ཆུ་སྲིན་རྡོ་རྗེ་རི་མོའི་བྲན་མོ་ *Chu-srin rdo-rje ri-mohi bran-mo* a goddess who rules over the forest of Kong-po and is believed to possess the power of stopping at will the course of the great river Yeru Tsang-po.

ཆུ་སྲིན་སྡེར་མོ་ *chu-srin sder-mo* medicinal herb useful in leprosy.

ཆུ་སྲིན་བྱིས་པ་གསོད་ *chu-srin byis-pa-gsod* a river-crocodile which carries away and eats children (*K. d.* ཞ *24*).

ཆུ་སྲིན་འཛིན་ཁྲི་ *chu-srin hdsin-khri* a throne supported on carved crocodiles.

ཆུ་སྲིབ་ *chu srib* प्रमेह gonorrhœa.

ཆུ་སྲུབ་ *chu-srub* = ཆུ་དཀྲུག་པ་ *chu-dkrug-pa* convulsed state of a lake by wind; ruffling or churning of the waters.

ཆུ་སྲེལ་ *chu-srel* = རྒྱ་མཚོ་ཆེན་པོ་ the ocean.

ཆུ་སྲོལ་ *chu-srol* dried-up bed of river.

ཆུ་ལྷག་ *chu-lhag* a kind of tree.

Syn. རི་འཇོམས; *ri-hjoms* ར་བ་ཤིང་ *ra-wa çiñ* (*Mñon.*).

ཆུ་ལྷའི་ཞགས་པ་ *chu-lhahi shags-pa* पाश, नागपाश the snake-noose—the weapon of the god of water.

ཆུ་ལྷའི་ཤིང་ *chu lhahi-çiñ* वरण वृक्ष an Indian tree, the tree *Cratæva roxburghii.*

ཆུག *chug*, imp. of འཇུག་པ *hjug-pa*; གཅེན་རིན་པོ་རབ་ཏུ་འབྱུང་དུ་ཆུག་ཅེས་གསུངས he said: admit the elder brother into the priesthood! (*Hbrom. 36*).

ཆུང་ 1. *chuṅ* or ཆུང་བ *chuṅ-wa* अल्प, मृदु, ईषत्, मनाक् little, small, young, junior, inferior; ཆུང་ཆེས་པས when he was very young; ཟླ་ཆུང་བ or ཆུང་ངུ་; ཆུང་བ་དཔལ་གྱི་སྙིང་པོ་ཡང་རབ་ཏུ་བྱུང་སྟེ (his) younger brother S'rīgarbha also having entered the Buddhist order; སྲས་ཆུང་ངུ་ the younger or youngest son; ལོ་ཆུང་ young in years; ཨ་ཕ་ཆུང་བ the junior father, *i.e.*, the second joint-husband of one's mother; ཆུང་ནས from infancy; ཆུང་གྲོགས an early friend, a friend of younger days. Sometimes includes vb. to be, as in སྙིང་མ་ཆུང་ཅིག be not small in courage!

Syn. ཉུང་བ *ñuṅ-wa*; ཉུང་ཤས་ཙམ *ñuṅ-ças-tsam*; ཚོད་ཙམ *tshod-tsam*; ཉུང་ངུ *ñuṅ-ṅu*; ཆུང་ངུ *chuṅ-ṅu*; ཕྲ *phra*; ཕྲ་མོ *phra-mo*; བག་ཙམ *bag-tsam*; ཟེགས་མ *zegs-ma*; ཟེར་མ *zer-ma*; འཐོར་མ *hthor-ma* (*Mṅon.*).

ཆུང་གྲི *chuṅ-gri* = གྲི་ཆུང་ a small knife.

* ཆུང་ངུ *chuṅ-ṅu* लघु small, little (*Kālac. T. 141*).

ཆུང་ངུན *chuṅ-ṅun* a very little part; ཆ་སྟོང་ལ་སྟོང་ཆུང་ངུན་ཡང་ཟེར་(*Yig.*) one thousandth part is called *stoṅ chuṅ-ṅun*.

ཆུང་ཆུང་ *chuṅ-chuṅ* = ཞ་ཆུང་ very small, little.

ཆུང་ཆེས་པ *chuṅ-ches-pa* अल्पतर a little more, yet still small in quantity.

ཆུང་འཇུག *chuṅ-hjug* a kind of tea (*Rtsii.*).

ཆུང་ཉུང་ *chuṅ-ñuṅ*, v. ཁུག་རྟ *khug-rta*.

ཆུང་བྱེད *chuṅ-byed* कृशाङ्ग slender [also fire] *S.*

ཆུང་མ *chuṅ-ma* जाया, कलत्र wife, consort, partner; ཆུང་མ་ལེན་པ to take a wife, to marry; མི་ཞིག་གི་ཆུང་མར་བྱེད་པ to be made a man's wife, to be married; ཆུང་མ་ལོག་གཡེམ་དང་ཅེ་སྤྲོངས to abandon an adulterous wife (*Çe. 1*).

ཆུང་མའི་སྤུན་ཟླ *chuṅ-mahi spun-zla* brothers of one's wife (*Mṅon.*).

ཆུང་ཟད *chuṅ-zad* = ཉུང་ཟད a little.

ཆུང་ངུས་གྲོལ *chuṅ-ṅus-grol* (དཀའ་བ་ཆུང་ངུས་འཁོར་བ་ལས་གྲོལ) स्तोकेन मुक्त to gain salvation with little asceticism; a state which precedes sainthood.

ཆུང་ལུག *chuṅ-lug* a lamb.

ཆུང་ལུང་ *Chuṅ-luṅ* n. of a place in Tibet.

ཆུང་ཤ *chuṅ-ça* = ལུག་ཤ mutton.

ཆུང་ཤོས *chuṅ-ços* the smallest or the youngest.

ཆུང་སུག *chuṅ-sug* the limbs of a kid.

ཆུད་པ *chud-pa* प्रविश्; = འཇུག་པ to get into, to enter, to put into, insert, etc.; ཐུགས་སུ་ཆུད་པ resp. to impress on one's mind; ཁོང་དུ་ཆུད to comprehend or get into the mind fully; དབང་དུ་ཆུད་པ to subject, to put under.

ཆུད་མ་གསོན *chud-na-gson* = ཆུད་མ་གཟོན not exhausted, exhaustless (*Ṅag.*).

ཆུད་མི་ཟ་བ *chu mi-za-wa* or ཆུད་མི་འཛད་པ inexhaustible, unwasteable; to be successful.

ཆུད་འཛའ་བ *chud hdsah-wa* = ཆུད་ཟ་བ to be fruitless or unsuccessful (in any work or action).

ཆུད་གཟོན་པ *chud-gzon-pa* to waste, make away with, to squander; ཆུད་ཟོད་པ *chud-zod-pa* to be wasted, become barren: ཆུད་ཟོས་ལ་སོང་ཚར་བ when it had been consumed, they went quite away.

ཆུན *chun* occurs in ཞིང་ཆུན one that is watering or taking care of fields, ཚལ་ཆུན gardens, ཐང་ཆུན meadows (*Jä.*).

ཆུན་གྱི་བྲག་དམར *Chun-gyi brag-dmar* one of the thirty-seven holy places of the Bon (*G. Bon. 37*).

ཆུན་པ *chun-pa* 1. to bunch or bundle together. 2. in *W.* the common designation of one that takes care of fields.

ཆུན་པོ *chun-po* दामन्, माला 1. bunch, bundle; དར་གྱི་ཆུན་པོ a bundle of silk scarves; a skien of silk. 2. a collection, pile, heap. 3. tuft, tassel, as ornament, etc.

ཆུན་པོ་ཅན *chun-po-can* wreathed.

ཆུན་འཕྱང་བ *chun-hphyan-wa* to wear a wreath or garland of flowers.

ཆུབ་པ *chub-pa* accomplished, perfected as in བྱང་ཆུབ་སེམས་དཔའ་ཀུན་ཆུབ་པར་བྱེར a *Bodhisattva* is to be perfected in all matters.

ཆུམ *chum* rice (in Sikk.).

卐 ཆུམ་པ *chum-pa* भीत;=ཁྲེམ་པ *khrem-pa* to be frightened, also to shrink; འཇིགས་ཆུམ་པ to crouch with fear. 2.=ཆགས་པ animals living on the surface of water; also ཆུའི་བྱིད་པ a kind of cuttle-fish called Pilha (པི་ལྷ) supposed to move on the surface of water and to pull down men and cattle when they swim.

ཆུར *chur* termin. of ཆུ; ཆུར་འཆི་བ to be drowned.

ཆུར་སྒྲོགས *chur-sgrogs* or ཆུར་འཇུག n. of a kind of water-fowl.

ཆུར་འདྲེས *chur-hdres*=མ་ཧེ महिष buffalo (*Mñon.*).

ཆུར་བ *chur-wa* or ཆུར་ར किलाट a kind of cheese or curd extracted from milk after boiling and evaporation: ཆུར་ར་སྟོབས་བསྐྱེད་ཁུ་བ་འཕེལ *chur-ra* gives strength and increases the seminal energy.

ཆུར་མི་ལྷུང་ *chur-mi lhuñ*=སྔོན་ཤིང་ द्रुम a magic tree (*Mñon.*).

ཆུར་ལྷུང་ *Chur-lhuñ* पातञ्जल n. of a sage, the expounder of the *Yoga* philosophy.

ཆུས *chus* instr. of ཆུ; ཆུས་གཏོང་བ to gild, to overspread with liquid gold or silver.

ཆུས་འཇིག་པ *chus-hjig-pa* अपः-संवर्त्तना destruction or devastation from water.

ཆུས་བྲན་པ *chus-bran-pa*, ཆུས་ཅུང་ཟད་སྦྲང་མ་པ to slightly wet or moisten with water.

ཆུས་མི་ཉམས་པ *chus mi-ñams-pa* thunder-bolt, v. ཐོག (*Mñon.*).

ཆུས་མི་འཚུབ *chus-mi-htshub* met. fish (*Mñon.*).

ཆེ *che* 1. num. fig 96. 2. v. ཆེ་བ great.

ཆེ་ཀ *che-ka* acc. to *Sch.* chiefly; the plurality.

ཆེ་ཁྱད *che-khyad* size, greatness.

ཆེ་གེ *che-ge* दाम a garland, wreath.

ཆེ་གེ་མོ *che-ge-mo* (in Beng.) अमुक 1. such a one, such a person: ལོ་ཆེ་གེ་མོ་ཞིག་ལ in such and such a year; ཆེ་གེ་མོ་ཁྱོད such as you are; ཆེ་གེ་མོ་སྐྱབས་མཛོད་ཅིག let such a one protect (me or him). 2.=གང་ཟག་ཀྱི a term for animated beings in general.

ཆེ་དགུ *che-dgu* the upper classes or races; དགུ in ཆེ་དགུ *che-dgu* signifies many and ཆེ *che* the upper races: བལ་པོའི་ཆེ་དགུ་ཐམས་ཅད་ཀྱིས་རྟ་དང་ཤིང་རྟ་དང་གླང་པོ་ཆེ་དང all the upper classes of Nepal possess horses, chariots and elephants (*A. 148*).

ཆེ་རྒྱུ *che-rgyu*=ཆེ་བ *che-wa.*

ཆེ་བརྒྱུད *che-brgyud* the descendants of the eldest son.

ཆེ་ཆུང་ *che-chuñ* सपत्नी 1. joint wife. 2. great and small; the dimensions or size.

ཆེ་ཆེ *che-che* for ཆེན་པོ་ཆེན་པོ *chen-po chen-po*; སྔོན་དུ་ཉེས་དམིགས་ཆེ་ཆེ་རྣམས་སྤངས first leave off the most serious moral faults (*Behu 40*).

ཆེ་ཆེར་རྒན་པ *che-cher rgan-pa* पोषित, पालित growing older, becoming more and more an old man; ཆེ་ཆེར་རྒན་མོ *che-cher rgan-mo* पालिता growing older, becoming more and more an old woman.

ཆེ་མཆོག *che-mchog* महा; विशिष्ट chief and great.

ཆེ་བརྗོད *che-brjod*=བསྟོད་ཚིག *bstod-tshig* or བཀུར་ཚིག *bkur-tshig* words of praise, eulogy (*Mṅon.*).

ཆེ་ཐབས *che-thabs* arrogance, haughtiness; སྡེ་པའི་ཆེ་ཐབས *sde-pahi che-thabs* the arrogance of the Depa (chief of a tribe or place).

ཆེ་ཐབས་ཅན *che-thabs-can* proud, arrogant, haughty.

ཆེ་དོན *che-don* for ཆད་དོན *chad-don* a missive to an inferior, an edict (*Jä.*). In a letter the word ཆེད་དོན *ched-don* expresses some special wish or object.

ཆེ་འདོན *che-hdon* the coming to full age, attaining the age of majority.

ཆེ་དཔང་པོ *che-dpaṅ-po* साक्षिश्रेष्ठ witness in chief.

ཆེ་བ *che-wa* महत्, अतिमात्र, स्फीत, स्थूल 1. often in compounds ཆེ *che*: great, large, powerful. ཆེ alone often=very. In conversation ཆེན་པོ *chen-po* is the usual form and in Ladak ཆེན་མོ *chen-mo* both in books and in talk. 2. sometimes used as a vb. with perf. ཆེས: དེ་ནི་བསོད་ནམས་ནི་སྔ་མ་བས་མཆོག་ཏུ་ཆེའོ his piety is much greater than before (*Dzl.*).

ཆེ་བཙན *che-btsan* majesty, greatness in rank and power: ཆེ་བཙན་དང་སྙན་གྲགས་མི་རྟག་པས (*Khrid.*) greatness and fame being transient.

ཆེ་ཤེ *che-she* a female adorned with jewellery (*K. d.* ན *326*).

+ ཆེ་གཞི *che-gshi*=དཔང་པོ *dpaṅ-po* a witness.

ཆེ་བཞག་ཆུང་སྐྱུར་བ *che-bshag chuṅ-skyur-wa* to keep everything in proper order, *e.g.*, placing larger or smaller things in their respective order.

ཆེ་རེ *che-re* with ལྟ་བ to stare at, to look with fixed eyes (*Hbrom. 105*).

ཆེ་ལོང *che-loṅ*=དགོས་པ or དགོས་རིམ उदारिक [sufficient, excessive, noble] *S.*: ཆེ་ལོང་དོན་ཙམ་མཐོང་བས་ཚོག་ཤེས་སྐྱེད། having perceived a sufficient meaning he obtained contentment.

ཆེ་ལོངས *che-loṅs* 1. grown up, adult (*Jä.*). 2. many, much: སྟོན་པའི་མཛད་པ་ལས་ཆེ་ལོང་ཙམ་བསྡུས་ན། if collected largely from the actions of the teacher (*J. Zaṅ.*).

ཆེ་ཆོས *che-ços*,=ཆེས་ཆེ་བ साधिष्ठ the greatest, greater than all others, chief (*Mṅon.*).

ཆེད *ched* or ཆེད་དུ *ched-du* निमित्त, कृते 1. postp. for, for the purpose of, with a view to, for the sake of, because of, on account of; ཆེད་དུ་བྱིན་པ given for, made a gift on account of; ཆེད་དུ་བྱ་བ to be done on account of; ལྟ་བའི་ཆེད་དུ་ཡིན it is in order to see. 2. adv. on purpose, expressly.

Syn. དོན་དུ *don-du*; དོན་ལ *don-la*; ཕྱིར་དུ *phyir-du*; ཆེད་གཉེར *ched-gñer* (*Mṅon.*).

+ ཆེད་འགའ *ched-hgah*=རེས་འགའ some, a good number of.

ཆེད་ཆེན་པོ *ched chen-po* a special thing, an important business.

ཆེད་ཆེར *ched-cher* more and more; ཆེད་ཆེར་བྱེད to increase: གཉིད་དང་རྨུགས་པ་ལ་ཆེད་ཆེར་མ་བྱས་པར་བུའི་རྗེས་སུ་ཞུགས་སོ། *gñid-daṅ rmugs-pa la ched-cher ma-byas par buhi rjes-su shugs-so* (*Hbrom.* ཁ *20*) without indulging more and more in sleep and laziness, he followed the example of my son.

ཆེད་བརྗོད་པའི་སྡེ *Ched brjod-pahi sde* a class of Buddhist scriptures which includes four divisions:—(1) དབྱངས་སྙན, (2) ལུང་དུ་བསྟན, (3) ཚིགས་བཅད, (4) ཆེད་བརྗོད.

ཆེད་གཉེར *ched-gñer*, v. ཆེད.

ཆེད་དུ་བརྗོད་པའི་ཚོམས *ched-du brjod-pahi tshoms* this expression is described as:—ཆོས་ཀྱི་དོན་གྱི་སྙིང་པོ་བསྡུས་ཏེ་ཚིགས་བཅད་དུ་བསྒྲིགས་པ (*K. d.* ཞ *327, 400*) the compilation of the substance of the Doctrine, and arranging it in verses.

ཆེད་དོན *ched-don*=ཆེ་དོན special signification, etc.

ཆེད་པ *ched-pa*=ཁྱབ་པ प्रसर to spread over.

ཆེད་སྤེལ་བ *ched-spel-wa* (ཆེད་མངགས་གཏང་བ) to send any special message (*Yig.*).

ཆེད་སོ *ched-so*=ཆེད་དོན great object, special reason: ལོ་ཙཱ་བ་ཡང་དང་པོའི་ཆེད་སོ་ཡོད་པས (*A. 84*) again the *Lo-tsā-wa* having a special reason for the first (course).

ཆེན་པོ *chen-po* महा, महत्, उदार, गुरु, वृहत् great, large, chief; མི་ཆེན་པོ a great man; བླ་མ་ཆེན་པོ a great lama. Sometimes ཆེན་མོ: གསུང་གི་གཟུངས་འབུམ་ཆེན་མོ a huge jar containing magic spells.

ཆེན་ཆུང་ *chen-chuṅ* first wife and second wife (*Jä.*).

ཆེན་སྣང་ *chen-snaṅ* स्थूलावलोकन magnifier; seeing a thing larger than its real size.

ཆེན་པོ་འགྱུར་བ *chen-po hgyur-wa* to become great, to increase, to grow up.

ཆེན་པོ་ལྔ *chen-po lṅa* lit. the five greats, *i.e.*, void space. In Buddhism, the sky is so called as having the five attributes of greatness, viz.:—གཟུགས་མེད it is immaterial, ཐོགས་པ་མེད limitless, རྟག་པ eternal, མི་འགྱུར་བ unchangeable, མི་འཇིག་པ undestructible.

ཆེམ *chem* or ཆེམ་ཆེམ *chem-chem* rattling sound like thunder; also any loud noise expressive of anger. Also ཆེམ་པ to thunder forth: རབ་ཏུ་ཆེམ་མོ he made a thundering noise (*D.R.*).

ཆེམས *chems* compounds: ཁ་ཆེམ or ཁ་ཆེམས resp. ཞལ་ཆེམས, བཀའ་ཆེམས farewell exhortation; last will, testament; སྲས་ལ་ཁ་ཆེམས་འཇོག་པ to deposit a testamentary disposal for a son (*Jä.*).

ཆེམ་ཆེམ *chem-chem* n. of a number (*Ya-sel. 56*).

ཆེམ་མེ་བ *chem me-wa* stillness, silence (*Cs.*); ཆེམ་མེར་འདུག་པ (*Sch.*) ཆེམ་མེར་འཁོད་པ to sit still without speaking (*Jä.*).

卐 **ཆེམས་པ** *chems-pa* (འཕྲིན་པ) to inform, to deliver a message.

ཆེལ་པ *chel-pa* defined as རང་སྟོབས་ཀྱིས་འཚུན་པ or ཐུབ་པ able by one's own power or might (*Ṅag. 26*).

ཆེས *ches* 1. instr of ཆེ. 2. pf. of ཆེ་བ as adv. ཁ་ཟས་ངན་ཆེས་ཀྱི as the food is very bad (*Jä.*); ཆེས་སྒྲིན་པ་ very prudent or clever (*Sch.*); ཆེས་དར་བར་གྱུར་ཏོ it spread very much (*Jä.*); ཆེས་དཀོན་པར་སྣང་ it becomes exceedingly valuable or scarce (*Situ. 55*).

ཆེས་མགྱོགས *ches-mgyogs*, v. ཆེས་མྱུར *ches-myur* very quick, speedy.

ཆེས་རྒས་པ *ches-rgas-pa*, རྙིང་པ or རྒས་པ old, worn out.

ཆེས་ལྗི་བ *ches-lci-wa* गुरुतर very heavy.

ཆེས་ཆུང་བ *ches chuṅ-wa* अल्पतर much less.

ཆེས་ཆེ་བ *ches che-wa* (ཆེ་ཤོས) very much; supreme, the greatest or highest.

ཆེས་མཆོག *ches-mchog* वरिष्ठ the supreme.

ཆེས་ཉེ་བ *ches-ñe-wa* आसक्त very attached; very intimate.

ཆེས་འཐུང་བ *ches-hthuṅ-wa* to drink much.

ཆེས་སྡོམ་པ *ches sdom-pa* to preserve one's vows very carefully.

ཆེས་པ *ches-pa* 1. pf. of ཆེ་བ to be great, to increase: དམག་དཔུང་ཆེས་པ the army having become great; དཔང་ཆེས་པས being very powerful. 2. to believe, but only when preceded by ཡིད (resp. ཐུགས): ཡིད་མི་ཆེས does not believe.

ཆེས་མང་ *chcs-mañ* or ཆེས་མང་བ बहुतर, भूयः rather large or too many.

ཆེས་མྱུར *chcs-myur* क्षिप्रतर very quick, rapid.

ཆེས་གཞོན་པ *chcs-b̲shon-pa* अतियुव very youthful; also कनिष्ठ very young or youngest.

ཆེས་ལྷག་པ *chcs-lhag-pa* अधिकतर in much excess; a great deal in excess.

ཆོ *cho* 1. num. fig. 126. 2. substantial, of meaning; ཆོ་མེད (དོན་མེད) meaningless, for nothing, no object, in vain; མི་ཆོ་མེད an empty-headed man.

ཆོ་ག *cho-ga* विधि, विधान, नीति 1. the way or method of doiug a thing, *e.g.*, of solving an arithmetical problem, of curing maladies, esp. used in magical performances. 2. prescribed rites and observances (in religious services, etc., ཆོ་ག་ལ་གནས་པ observant of rites). 3. specially, any magical rite. 4. आचार behaviour; ཆོ་ག་ཕུན་སུམ་ཚོགས་པ चरित्रसम्पन्न of good character, possessed of good morals; ཆོ་ག་ཉམས་པ आचारविपन्न of bad morals, fallen. ཆོ་ག་བཅུ or the ten kinds of religious rites observed by the Buddhists of Tibet are:—(1) བཞེང་དཀྱིལ་འཁོར་ཆོ་ག rites of magical circles and figures painted on the ground and also on paper; (2) རིམ་པ་དབང་གི་ཆོ་ག rites of mystical initiation and religious service; (3) བྱིན་རླབས་རབ་གནས་ཀྱི་ཆོ་ག rites of consecration; (4) ཆེ་འདས་རོ་སྲེག་གི་ཆོ་ག *che-h̲das ro-sreg-gi cho-ga* funeral rites and ceremonies; (5) ལྷོ་སྒོ་སྦྱོངས་ཀྱི་ཆོ་ག *lho-sgo sbyoñs-kyi cho-ga* the art of sleight of hand, etc.; (6) མཉེས་བྱེད་མཆོད་པའི་ཆོ་ག rites for propitiation (of a deity or spirit); (7) མགྲོན་མཆོད་གཏོར་མའི་ཆོ་ག rites for torma offerings to a deity; (8) སྐུ་གཟུགས་སྐུ་ཚའི་ཆོ་ག the art of making casts of miniature images; (9) མཆོད་སྦྱིན་ཆུ་གཏོར་གྱི་ཆོ་ག offering of sacrificial fire and also of water to the manes of the dead; (10) བཀྲ་ཤིས་ཚེའི་ཆོ་ག rites to secure a happy and long life.

ཆོ་གའི་ངང་ཚུལ་ཅན *cho-gah̲i ñañ-tshul can* आचारशील one naturally of good behavior.

ཆོ་ངེ *cho-ñe* or ཆོ་ངེས is explained as (མིག་ཆུ་གཏོང་བ) shedding of tears (*M̲ñon.*), lamentation, wailing, esp. lamentations for the dead, dirge; ཆོ་ངེས་འདེབས་པ आर्त्तस्वरं क्रन्दति throwing up lamentations.

ཆོ་ངེ་དིར *cho-ñe-dir* loud lamentations (*D.R.*).

ཆོ་འཕྲུལ *cho-h̲phrul* प्रातिहार्य्य, ऋद्धि miracles. ཆོ་འཕྲུལ་གསུམ *cho-h̲phrul-gsum* three kinds of miracles performed by the Buddha:—(1) རྫུ་འཕྲུལ་གྱི་ཆོ་འཕྲུལ *rdsu-h̲phrul-gyi cho-h̲phrul* ऋद्धिप्रातिहार्य्य magical and miraculous exhibitions; (2) ཀུན་ཏུ་བརྗོད་པའི་ཆོ་འཕྲུལ *kun-tu b̲rjod̲-pah̲i cho-h̲phrul* आदेशनप्रातिहार्य्य miraculous exhibition by speech; (3) རྗེས་སུ་བསྟན་པའི་ཆོ་འཕྲུལ *r̲jes-su b̲stan-pah̲i cho-h̲phrul* अनुशासनप्रातिहार्य्य miraculous effects of teaching the doctrine. We read also of ཆོ་འཕྲུལ་གྱི་བསམ་རྣམས miraculous thoughts.

ཆོ་འཕྲུལ་མཆོད་པ *cho-h̲phrul m̲chod̲-pa* religious service to commemorate the miraculous exhibitions of Buddha.

ཆོ་བ *cho-wa* to set on or incite; ཁྱི་རེ་ཆོ་ཆོ་བ to set the dog at any one repeatedly (*Cs.*).

ཆོ་བབས་སྐོར *chos-babs skor* = རྩིས་ཡོང་བབས revenue, income; འབྲས་ཁུལ་ཆོ་བབས་སྐོར the earnings or income from the state of Sikkim.

+ ཆོ་འབྲང་ *cho-h̲brañ* (རྒྱུད or གདུང་རྒྱུད) (*M̲ñon.*) family; extraction; especially the maternal relations, the mother's family or lineage.

ཚོ་མ *cho-ma* n. of a number (*Ya-sel.* 56).

ཚོ་རིགས *cho-rigs* father's lineage, descent by the father's side.

ཚོ་རིས *cho-ris* वार्त descent, extraction; ཚོ་རིས་པ་ནས་བཙུན་པ from the beginning or always of honourable descent.

ཚོ་ལོ *cho-lo* 1. a shrub from the dried leaves of which a yellow dye is prepared for the clothes of the lower classes. 2. दुरोदर, पण, द्यूत gambling dice; ཚོ་ལོ་མཁན *cho-lo mkhan* a dice-player (*Cs.*); ཚོ་ལོ་རྒྱལ་ལོ *cho-lo rgyal-lo* आचिक he excels in dice-throwing.

ཚོ་ལོ་རྩེ་བ *cho-lo rtse-wa* द्यूतक्रीड़ा, अचक्रीड़ा: to play at dice.

ཚོ་ལོ་རིས *cho-lo-ris* diagram; a stamped mark or figure on a dice.

ཚོ་ལོའི་སྐུགས་པ *cho-lohi-skugs-pa* पणद्यूत, दुरोदर to lay a wager in gambling and to exhort your side to win.

ཚོ་ལོས་ཐུལ་ལོ *cho-los thul-lo* आचिक one who has been defeated, *i.e.*, has lost in dice-play.

ཚོ་ལོའི་ས་བོན *cho-lohi sa-bon* = འགྲོན་བུ *hgron-bu* (*Mñon.*) a kind of shell; the *cowrie* used as a coin in India and also as a substitute for dice.

ཚོག *chog*, see ཚོག་པ III below: it is generally used as a permissive particle after a verb: འགྲོ་ཚོག you can go; ཡོང་ ཚོག you may come; བྱས་ཚོག may be permitted to be done.

ཚོག་པ *chog-pa* I: अलङ्कृत; རྒྱན་པ adorned, ornamented (*Lex.*).

ཚོག་པ II: पर्याप्ति to suffice, to be sufficient: ངེད་ལ་དེ་ཀས་ཚོག that is sufficient for us; རྟ་དེ་རྣམས་ཚོམ་གྱིས་ཚོག་པ་ཡོད they had about enough of those horses; འདི་ཚོག་པ་མ་ཡིན this is not sufficient. Adv. ཚོག་པར sufficiently; ཚོག་པར་སྦྱིན་པ to give sufficiently; ཕྱིན་པས་ཚོག་གི it being sufficient (for the present) that I have come; ཐམས་ཅད་ལ་ཚོག་པར་གྱུར་ཏོ there was enough for all; ཚོག་པར་འཛིན་པ to deem a thing sufficient; to be contented or satisfied with it.

ཚོག་པ III: to be permitted, to be allowable. In books gen. with the instrumental participle: ཆང་འཐུང་བས་མི་ཚོག drinking beer is not allowed; ཕྱིར་འོང་བས་ཚོག་ཡོང་ it will be permitted to come back (*Mil.*). In colloq. ཚོག is annexed direct to the verbal root: མཐོན་པོ་ཐབ་མི་ཚོག talking loudly is not allowable; ནང་ལ་འགྲོ་ཚོག you may go inside, or into the house.

ཚོག་པ་མེད་པ *chog-pa med-pa* appetite (ངང་ག or ངང་ག་བདེ་བ) good appetite (*Mñon.*).

ཚོག་ཤེས་པ *chog-çes-pa* सन्तोष contentment; to be contented or satisfied with.

ཚོང *choñ* or མཚོང transparent variegated half-precious stone brought from India to *Ld.* and considered less valuable than ག་ཟི (cat's eye), perh. cornelian or sardonyx (*Jä.*).

ཚོད *chod* 1. a decision. 2. a partition wall; ཚོད་རྒྱག་པ to construct a partition wall (*Sch.*). 3. v. གཅོད་པ.

ཚོད་པ *chod-pa* I: 1. छेद to be cut off; བར་ལ་ཐག་རིང་པོ་ཆད་པ to be separated by a long interval; ལམ་སྒོ་གཉིས་ཁ་བས་ཚོད་དེ both approaches being cut off or obstructed by snow; མི་ཚོད་རྡོ་རྗེ a diamond that cannot be cut to pieces; an epithet of a firm unbending king. 2. to be decided, settled, fixed; ཡོང་ཐང་དཔྱད་ཀྱི་མི་ཚོད the value (of the stone) cannot be fixed, though one should attempt to appraize it, *i.e.*, it is priceless, invaluable (*Jä.*).

ཆོད་པ II: (སྒྲིབ་པ) आवरण, निवरण to cover over, put into shade; also a shade, cover.

ཆོད་སོ་བདོག་པ *chod-so bdog-pa*=ཁ་ཆད་ཡོད་པ also ཁས་བླངས་པ to promise, to undertake to do a thing: སློབ་དཔོན་གནས་བརྟན་དང་ཆོད་སོ་བདོག་པ་ཐུགས་ལ་མངའ་མོད (*A. 84*) he indeed bore in mind that he had made a promise to the Sthavira the chief teacher.

ཆོན *chon* in *W.* 1. useless, to no purpose; རིན་ཆོན་སོང་ the payment has been useless, thrown away; gen. adv. ཆོན་ལ gratuitously, in vain, for nothing. 2. tent; ཆོན་ཐག tent-rope; ཆོན་ཕུར tent-peg (*Jä.*).

ཆོམ *chom* or ཆོམས robbery; ཆོམས་ཀྱིས་ཟས་འཚོལ་བ to live by robbery; ཆོམ་སྒྲ=ཅུར་སྒྲ a fearful rattling sound (resembling that of a thunder or a cannon), gen. made by robbers when invading a village or house to frighten the inmates out.

ཆོམ་པ *chom-pa* to be finished, accomplished, in *W.* (*Jä.*).

ཆོམ་པོ *chom-po* or ཆོམས་པོ *choms-po* तस्कर, दस्यु, चौर a robber; ཆོམ་པོ་ཀུན་མ robber and thief, gen. ཆོམ་ཀུན; ཆོམ་ཀུན་གྱི་འཇིགས་པ fear of robbers and thieves.

ཆོལ *chol* 1. inconstant (*Cs.*); དཔྱིད་ཆོལ fickle spring-weather (*Jä.*). 2. for ཆོ་ལོ in compounds, རུས་ཆོལ a dice made of bone; ཤིང་ཆོལ a wooden dice; དུང་ཆོལ a shell used in the place of a dice.

ཆོལ་ཁ *chol-kha* 1. a country, province: དབུས་གཙང་གཉིས་དམ་པ་ཆོས་ཀྱི་ཆོལ་ཁ། Ü and Tsang were the countries of holy religion; མདོ་སྟོད་མིའི་ཆོལ་ཁ *Mdo-stod*, the province abounding with population; མདོ་སྨད་རྟའི་ཆོལ་ཁ་སྟེ, *i.e.*, *Mdo-smad*, the province of horses; ཆོལ་ཁ་གསུམ་ཕུལ་ནོ presented the three provinces (*Loñ.* ན *13*). 2. acc. to *Sch.* a hole made by a blow; a nest.

ཆོལ་འགྲོ་བ *chol-hgro-wa* or ཆོལ་གྱི་འགྲོ *chol-gyi hgro*=ཉམས་འགྲོ་བ or འཆལ་འགྲོ་བ to be decayed, become degenerate (*A. 70*).

卐 **ཆོལ་ཟངས** *chol-zañs* (ཆལ་ཏིག) 1. bed-pan; also a vessel to contain washings, &c.; impure-water. 2. acc. to *Sch.* a shallow shore.

ཆོས *chos* धर्म 1. religious doctrine; religion; more especially the doctrine of Buddha. Generally speaking, *chos*, *i.e.*, *dharma*, consists of all phenomena, all matter, and all knowledge of things worldly as well as spiritual. It includes ཤེས་བྱ all that can be known, གཞལ་བྱ all that is cognizable by the senses, ཡོད་པ all that exists, གཞི་ཁྱབ basis and material. 2. a particular doctrine, tenet, or precept; གསང་བའི་ཆོས་ཤིག an esoteric doctrine, a mystical doctrine; ཁྱད་ཆོས for ཁྱད་པར་ཅན་གྱི་ཆོས sublime or excellent religion; འཇིག་རྟེན་གྱི་ཆོས་བརྒྱད the eight worldly doctrines or principles, viz.:—རྙེད་པ लाभ gain, profit; མ་རྙེད་པ अलाभ loss; སྙན་པ यशः fame, reputation; མི་སྙན་པ अयशः bad name, notoriety; སྨད་པ निन्दा scandal, slander; བསྟོད་པ प्रशंसा praise; བདེ་བ सुख happiness; སྡུག་བསྔལ་བ दुःख misery or unhappiness. 3. system of morality, ethics (faith, exercise of religion). 4. any way, manner, method; a custom, usage. 5. is sometimes used to signify a thing, substance, property.

The word ཆོས is also explained as རང་སེམས་བཅོས་ཤིང་འདུལ་བར་བྱེད་ན་ཆོས *Chos* consists in placing under discipline a mind already formed. *Chos* or the religion of Buddha is again divided into two classes which are of scriptural and contemplative nature. The scriptural *chos* is collected in the three *sde-snod* or *piṭaka*, viz.:—the *Vinaya*, the *Sûtra* and the *Abhidharma*. The meditative *chos* consists of the three trainings viz.:—moral discipline, meditation and *Prajñā* or the absolute knowledge of all things. The first three are studied and the last three are practised. The *chos* for the purification of sins have been also subdivided as follows:—(1) ཕར་ཕྱིན་དྲུག the six transcendental moral virtues; (2) སྟོང་ཉིད་བཅོ་བརྒྱད་ the eighteen metaphysical voidities; (3) དྲན་པ་ཉེ་བར་བཞག་པ་བཞི the four remembrances; (4) ཡང་དག་པར་སྤོང་བ་བཞི the four renunciations; (5) རྫུ་འཕྲུལ་གྱི་རྐང་པ་བཞི *ṟdsu-ẖphrul-gyi ṟkañ-pa ḇshi* the four bases for magical transformations; (6) དབང་པོ་ལྔ the five powers; (7) སྟོབས་ལྔ five fortitudes; (8) བྱང་ཆུབ་ཀྱི་ཡན་ལག་བདུན the seven *Bodhyañga* or attributes of *Bodhisattva*; (9) འཕགས་པའི་ལམ་ཡན་ལག་བརྒྱད the eight subdivisions of the noble paths; (10) རྣལ་འབྱོར་གྱི་ལམ་བྱང་ཕྱོགས་གསུམ་བཅུ་སོ་བདུན the thirty-seven northern paths of ascetism.

ཆོས་ཀྱི་སྐུ *chos-kyi-sku* धर्मकाय the spiritual form or the existence (of a Buddha).

ཆོས་ཀྱི་སྐྱེ་མཆེད *chos-kyi skye-mched* धर्मायतन 1. religious capacity, spiritual development. [2. the mind]*S*.

ཆོས་ཀྱི་ཁྱུ་མཆོག་འབྲོང *chos-kyi khyu-mchog ẖbroñ* (རིགས ཀུལ) धर्मानुचारी (ཁྱུ་མཆོག་ནི་གཙོ་བོ། དེའི་རྗེས་སུ་འབྲང་) following a leader.

ཆོས་ཀྱི་འཁོར་ལོ *chos-kyi ẖkyor-lo* धर्मचक्र comprises three:—(1) བདེན་པ་བཞིའི་ཆོས་འཁོར (འདུལ་བ), (2) ལེགས་པར་རྣམ་པར་འབྱེད་པའི་ཆོས་འཁོར (ཐེག་ཆེན་གྱི་མདོ་དང་རྒྱུད), (3) མཚན་ཉིད་མེད་པའི་ཆོས་འཁོར. The three are explained as the original, the amplified and the abridged *yum* (ཡུམ་རྒྱས་འབྲིང་བསྡུས་གསུམ).

* ཆོས་ཀྱི་གྲགས་པ *Chos-kyi grags-pa* धर्मकीर्त्ति n. of a Buddhist philosopher (*Bull. 1848, 287*).

ཆོས་ཀྱི་རྒྱལ་མཚན *Chos-kyi ṟgyal-m̱tshan* धर्म-ध्वज n. of a Buddhist philosopher and author.

ཆོས་ཀྱི་སྒྲ *chos-kyi-sgra* धर्मशब्द the loud recitation of religious formulæ, or singing of hymns; preaching of a sermon.

ཆོས་ཀྱི་ངང *chos-kyi ñañ*, v. ཆོས་ཀྱི་དབྱིངས *chos-kyi ḏbyiñs*.

ཆོས་ཀྱི་ཆོས་ཉིད *chos-kyi chos-ñiḏ* the natural properties of matter, such as མེ་གྱེན་དུ་འབར་བ *me-gyen-du ẖbar-wa* the property of fire to run up; ཆུ་ཐུར་དུ་འབབ་པ that of water to run down.

ཆོས་ཀྱི་གཏིང་སླེབས་པ *chos-kyi g̱tiñ slebs-pa*= ཆོས་ཉིད་མངོན་སུམ་དུ་རྟོགས་པ reflecting on the virtues of matter and phenomena.

ཆོས་ཀྱི་བསྟོན་པ *chos-kyi ḇston-pa* स्मृति recitation of the scripture; remembrance thereof.

ཆོས་ཀྱི་འདུན་ས *chos-kyi ẖdun-sa* དགོན་པ a monastery or convent.

ཆོས་ཀྱི་རྣམ་གྲངས *chos-kyi ṟnam-grañs* धर्म-पर्य्याय enumeration of scriptures.

ཆོས་ཀྱི་འཕོངས་པར་འགྱུར་བ *chos-kyi ẖphoñs-par ẖgyur-wa* धर्मव्यसन to become irreligious, sacrilegious.

ཆོས་ཀྱི་བར་དུ་གཅོད་པ *chos-kyi bar-du g̱cod-pa* धर्मान्तराय to obstruct the course of nature.

ཆོས་ཀྱི་བུ *Chos-kyi-bu* धर्मपुत्र a name of Yudhisthira the eldest of the five Pāṇḍava brothers.

ཆོས་ཀྱི་དབང་ཕྱུག *chos-kyi ḏwañ-phyug* धर्मेश्वर, described as སངས་རྒྱས་སྤྱིའི་མཚན *sañs-ṟgyas spyiẖi-m̱tshan* (*M̱ñon.*) an epithet applicable to the Buddhas in general.

ཆོས་ཀྱི་དབྱིངས *chos-kyi ḏbyiṅş* धर्मधातु the sphere or purview of religion; ཆོས་ཀྱི་དབྱིངས་ཀྱིས་གྲུབ་པ(?) धर्म-धातुपरम [versed in the element of law or religion]*S.*

ཆོས་ཀྱི་རྩ་འཁོར *chos-kyi ṟtsa-ẖkhor* चित्त met. the heart (*Mṅon.*).

ཆོས་ཀྱི་རྩ་བ *chos-kyi ṟtsa-wa* धर्ममूल the root or the fundamental principles of religion.

ཆོས་ཀྱི་མཚོང་བརྡལ *chos-kyi tshoṅ-ḇrdal* met. a monastery (*Mṅon.*).

* ཆོས་ཀྱི་ཚོང་དཔོན *chos-kyi tshoṅ-ḏpon* धर्म-श्रेष्ठ a divine; a priest; one whose profession is religion (*Tā. 2, 53*).

ཆོས་ཀྱི་བཞོན་པ་ཅན *chos-kyi ḇshon-pa-can* धर्म-वाहन the conveyance of *chos* or *dharma.* ["one whose vehicle is *dharma* personified as the bull," *i.e.*, S'iva]*S.*

ཆོས་སྐད *chos-ṣkaḏ* book language.

ཆོས་སྐྱོང་ *chos-ṣkyoṅ* धर्मपाल 1. the protector or defender of Buddhism; ཆོས་སྐྱོང་ཆེན་མོ the great guardian of Buddhism; the equivalent of པེ་དཀར or Po-har. 2. name sometimes given to the four Dik-rajas or guardian kings of Buddhism: ཆོས་སྐྱོང་གྱི་འཛུགས་གཏོར offerings for the guardian spirits of the doctrine. 3. popular astrologers, votaries of Pe-har at Lhasa.

* ཆོས་སྐྱོང་དྲེགས་པ་ལྕམ་སྲིང་ *Chos-ṣkyoṅ dṟegs-pa ḻcam-sṟiṅ* (*Org. m. 113, 32*) a terrific female guardian deity.

* ཆོས་སྐྱོབས *chos-ṣkyobş* धर्मत्राता n. pr. (*Tā. 2, 297*); n. of an Indian Buddhist who taught Buddhism in China.

ཆོས་ཁྲི *chos-khri* book-shelves or table to keep sacred books upon; also the chair on which the priest sits while delivering a religious sermon; acc. to *Jä.* reading-desk, pulpit.

ཆོས་ཁྲིམས *chos-krims* धर्मयाज्ञ religious or monastic discipline; ཆོས་ཁྲིམས་པ *chos-khrims-pa* དགེ་བསྐོས one who enforces discipline in a monastery.

ཆོས་འཁོར *chos-ẖkhor* prayer-wheel.

ཆོས་འཁོར་རྒྱལ *Chos-ẖkhor ṟgyal* n. of the place where the first Dalai Lama was born, and where there is a large monastery which is generally visited once by the successive Grand Lamas of Lhasa.

ཆོས་འཁོར་སྒང *Chos-ẖkhor-ṣgaṅ* n. of a place in Tibet.

ཆོས་འཁོར་གནས *Chos-ẖkhor-gnaş* n. of a place in Tibet.

ཆོས་གོས *chos-gos* चीवर the religious robe worn by a Buddhist monk. ཆོས་གོས་ཀྱི་སྒྲོག་མ *chos-gos-kyi ṣgrog-ma* चीवर करण्डक strings or bands for fastening a religious robe. [a basket for containing religious robes]*S.*

ཆོས་གོས་ཀྱི་སྣོད *chos-gos-kyi ṣnoḏ* चीवरभाण्डिका a pocket in the upper garment of a monk; ཆོས་གོས་ཀྱི་གཏུར་བུ *chos-gos-kyi gtur-bu* चीवर-तूषिका the bag in which a monk puts robes.

ཆོས་གོས་ཟླུམ་པོར་བགོ་བ *chos-goş zlum-por ḇgo-wa* परिमण्डलचीवर one dressed in a petticoat like robe; also to put on a such robe.

ཆོས་གྲྭ *chos-grwa* धर्मसंघ a school for religious instruction, *i.e.*, generally a class in a monastic institution where religious discussions are held. The school at Tashi-lhunpo is called གྲུབ་པའི་ཆོས་གྲྭ *grub-paẖi chos-grwa*, the school of religious attainments.

* ཆོས་གྲགས *chos-gragş* धर्मकीर्त्ति (*3 C*).

ཆོས་རྒྱལ *chos-ṟgyal* or ཆོས་ཀྱི་རྒྱལ་པོ धर्मराज 1. a king who rules acc. to Buddhist laws. 2. n. of the lord of death གཤིན་རྗེ་རྒྱལ་པོ. 3. also applied to a great personage by courtesy, and is a general epithet of Buddhas (*Mṅon.*).

ཆོས་རྒྱལ་སྐྱེས *Chos-ṟgyal-ṣkyeş* धर्मराजपुत्र a name of Yudhisthira, the eldest Pāṇḍava; also that of Ajāta-s'atru, the son of king Bimbisāra.

* ཆོས་རྒྱལ་གྱི་སྒྲུབ་ཡུམ་བཅས *Chos-rgyal-gyi sgrub yum-bcas* (*Org. m. 113, 33*; *Pallasiix, vii*, 4. II, 9).

* ཆོས་རྒྱལ་ནང་སྒྲུབ *Chos-rgyal nan-sgrub* (*80 B*).

* ཆོས་རྒྱལ་ཕྱི་སྒྲུབ *Chos-rgyal phyi-sgrub* (*80 A*).

* ཆོས་རྒྱལ་ཡབ་རྐྱང་ *Chos-rgyal yab-rkyan* (*Org. m. 113, 34*).

* ཆོས་རྒྱལ་གསང་སྒྲུབ *Chos-rgyal gsan-sgrub* (*80 C*).

ཆོས་རྒྱུགས *chos-rgyugs* lessons, or tasks imposed by a teacher on his pupil.

ཆོས་རྒྱུད *chos-rgyud* religious instructions descending to pupils and their sub-pupils, &c.; religious tradition, also creed; རྗེ་བཙུན་གྱི་ཆོས་རྒྱུད་འཛིན་པ་རྣམས those embracing the religious traditions of his reverence; ཆོས་རྒྱུད་གཅིག་པ one confessing ancestral religion. ཆོས་རྒྱུད་འཛིན་པ *chos-rgyud hdsin-pa* (*Tā. 2, 233*).

* ཆོས་རྒྱུན་གྱི་ཏིང་ངེ་འཛིན *Chos-rgyun-gyi tin-ne hdsin* स्रोतोऽनुगतनामसमाधि (*Tā. 2, iii*).

ཆོས་ཅན *chos-can* धार्म्मिक pious, devout.

ཆོས་ཅན་རིང་ *chos-can-rin* met. a donkey (*Mnon.*).

ཆོས་བཅས་མ *chos-bcas-ma* met. a bride.

Syn. ཁྱིམ་གསར་མ *khyim-gsar-ma*; ཀྱོ་འདམ་མ *kyo-hdam-ma* (*Mnon.*).

ཆོས་ཆས *chos-chas* the requirements of a religious service; also religious dress.

* ཆོས་མཆོག *Chos-mchog* धर्म्मोत्तम n. pr. (*Tā. 2, 223*); धर्मोत्तर a logician, author of Nyāyabindu ṭikā.

ཆོས་འཆད་པ *chos hchad-pa* to explain or set forth religion; ཆོས་སྟོན་པ to teach religion; ཆོས་ཀྱི་སྒྲོག་གླེང་མཛད་པ *chos-kyi sgrog-glen mdsad-pa* to demonstrate or expound the doctrine; ཆོས་འཆད་པའི་འདུན་ཁང་ place where sermons are delivered; ཆོས་ཉན་པ to hear religious discourses; ཆོས་ཞུ་བ to ask religious instruction; ཆོས་བྱེད་པ to act or live religiously or practice religion.

ཆོས་འཆོང་པ *chos-hchon-pa* धर्म्मधारण Lord of the faith, viz., 1. Buddha. 2. a title of honour given to distinguished scholars. 3. Tibetan exorcists who are believed to be coerced by a god or demi-god who has been invoked for the purpose of inspiring them.

ཆོས་རྗེ་ནག་དཀར *chos-rje nag-dkar* the black and the white (Buddhist) exorcists.

ཆོས་ཉིད *chos-ñid* = དེ་བཞིན་ཉིད धर्म्मत्व, धर्म्मता 1. quality, nature. 2. existence, entity.

ཆོས་ཉིད་ཀྱིས་རྙེད་པ *chos-ñid kyis rñed-pa* धर्म्मताप्राप्तिलभिक one who has acquired a religious disposition; also religiousness.

ཆོས་ཉིད་ཀྱིས་འཐོབ་པ *chos-ñid kyis hthob-pa* धर्म्मताप्राप्तिलब्धिक id.

ཆོས་སྙམ་སྒྲུབ་པ་པོ *chos-sñam sgrub-pa po* = ཆོས་དང་སྙམ་དུ་སྒྲུབ་མཁན one who, having acquired great proficiency in sacred literature, has become protected by mystic arts.

* ཆོས་རྟོལ *chos-rtol* (*Tā. 1, 216*).

ཆོས་སྟེགས *chos-stegs* = ཆོས་ཁྲི *chos-khri*.

ཆོས་སྟོན *chos-ston* an entertainment given in honour of a saint.

ཆོས་ཐམས་ཅད *chos-thams-cad* सर्व्वधर्म्म matter; all things; phenomena.

ཆོས་ཐོབ *chos-thob* धर्म्मागमिन् one who has become religious; a convert to Buddhism.

ཆོས་མཐུན *chos-mthun* or ཆོས་མཐུན་པ in conformity with religion, in harmony with Buddhism.

ཆོས་དར་བ *chos-dar-wa* to propagate Buddhism; also the place where Buddhism was introduced.

ཆོས་དྲངས་པ *chos-draṅs-pa* 1. righteous in reference to the laws of Buddhism 2. justice, righteousness.

ཆོས་དྲུག *chos-drug* षड्धर्म the six tenets of Buddhism.

ཆོས་དྲེད་ *chos-dred* ཆོས་ལ་ཞེ་ལོག་པ one who is disgusted with Buddhism, *i.e.*, has no faith in that religion.

ཆོས་དོན་དུ་གཉེར་བ *chos-don-du gñer-wa*=ཆོས་འདོད་པ धर्माधिक to be devout.

ཆོས་འདོད *Chos-hdod* the son of Cupid.

ཆོས་འདོད་པ *chos-hdod-pa* धर्मेच्छक to be fond of religion; to delight in Buddhism.

ཆོས་ལྡན *chos-ldan* or ཆོས་དང་ལྡན་པ धार्म्मिक one who is devout.

ཆོས་ལྡན་ཞིང་ཁམས *Chos-ldan shiṅ-khams* gen. used to signify བོད་ཡུལ Tibet ཆོས་ལྡན་ཞིང་ཁམས་ཀྱི་རྒྱལ་པོ་རིན་པོ་ཆེ the precious majesty of the religious kingdom (Buddhist realm) (*Yig. k. 59*).

* ཆོས་ལྡན་རབ་འབྱོར *Chos-ldan rab-hbyor*, धार्म्मिकसुभूति (*Tā. 2, 90*).

ཆོས་སྡེ *chos-sde* a certain term for Buddhist monasteries in Tibet, where studies are not altogether neglected. ཆོས་སྡེ་ཆེན་པོ *chos-sde chen-po* the grand religious institution or monastery (*Yig. k. 66*).

ཆོས་རྣམས་གང་དག *chos-rnams gaṅ-dag* ये धर्माः n. of a kind of contemplation; and a literal translation of the first part of the Sanskrit formula *ye dharmā hetu*, &c.

ཆོས་སྣང་བའི་སྒོ *chos-snaṅ-bahi sgo* धर्मालोकमुख the door or entrance to Buddhism. [the initiatory light of religion]*S.*

ཆོས་པ *chos-pa* a monk.

ཆོས་སྤུན *chos-spun* a brotherhood formed by two devotees who before starting on a pilgrimage are blessed by a priest who casts lots on the occasion.

* ཆོས་འཕེལ *Chos-hphel* धर्मवर्द्धन n. pr. (*Tā. 2, 103*).

ཆོས་བློན *chos-blon* a Buddhist minister, a minister well disposed towards Buddhism.

* ཆོས་འབངས *Chos-hbaṅs* धर्मदास n. pr. (*Tā. 127*).

ཆོས་འབྱུང་ *chos-hbyuṅ* works on the origin, growth, and development, of Buddhism.

* ཆོས་འབྱུང་བྱིན *Chos-hbyuṅ-byin* धर्माकरदत्त n. pr. (*Tā. 2, 219*).

* ཆོས་འབྱུང་ཞི་བ *Chos-hbyuṅ shi-wa* धर्माकरशान्ति n. pr. (*Tā. 2, 252*).

ཆོས་སྦྱིན *chos-sbyin*, ཆོས་ཀྱི་སྦྱིན་པ *chos-kyi sbyin-pa* religious gift, religious charity.

ཆོས་མ *chos-ma* a Buddhist nun.

ཆོས་མི་འགྱུར་བ་ཉིད *chos-mi-hgyur-wa ñid* (སྟོང་ཉིད) धर्मनियमता that the nature of things is unalterable.

ཆོས་མིན *cho-min* अधर्मः, अधार्म्मिक un-Buddhistic, irreligious.

ཆོས་མིན་སྤྱོད་པ *chos-min spyod-pa*=ཆོས་དང་མི་མཐུན་པའི་ཚུལ་ངན any practice opposed to Buddhism.

ཆོས་མེད *chos-med* चण्डाल; གདོལ་པ the uncivilised; a name for a *Caṇḍāla*, the lowest class of men in India.

ཆོས་སྨྱོན *chos-myon* religious frenzy, mad with religion; a religious bigot.

ཆོས་སྨྲ་བ *chos-smra-wa* धर्मभाष to preach Buddhism; to deliver a sermon.

ཆོས་ཚོང་བ *chos-tshoṅ-wa* धर्मपचन to trade in religion.

ཆོས་རྫོང་ *Chos-rdsoṅ* n. of a monastery and of a fort in Nye-thang, near Lhasa.

* ཆོས་བཞི་བའི་དབྱངས *Chos-bshi-wahi dbyaṅs* धर्मशान्तिघोष n. pr. (*Tā. 2, 213*).

ཆོས་གཞི *chos-gshi* endowment for the support of a religious institution.

ཆོས་ཤོག *chos-shog* priest-craft (*Jä.*).

ཆོས་བཟང་ *chos-bzañ* 1.=ཚུལ་བཟང་ प्रतियश good custom. 2. सुधर्म्म Buddhism; piety; pious. (3) n. of an individual; a complimentary address for monks.

* ཆོས་བཟང་བསྐལ་པ *Chos-bzañ bskal-pa* सुधर्म्म-कल्प (*Kālac. T. 14*) age of good fortune; the lucky age in which Buddhas appear.

* ཆོས་བཟང་སྤྲིན *Chos-bzañ sprin*, or *Saddharma megha* (*Tā. 2, 277*). [one of the ten *bhūmis* or stages of perfection]*S.*

ཆོས་ལུགས *chos-lugs* 1. नीति, व्यवहार usage. 2. a denomination, sect.

ཆོས་ཤེས་པར་འདོད *chos çes-par hdod* जिज्ञास्यति धर्म्मः inquiring after religious matter, wishing to know of religion.

ཆོས་སེམས *chos-scms* religious temper, piety.

ཆོས་སེམས་ཁང་བུ *chos-scms khañ-bu*=རི་ཁྲོད a mountain hermitage; a cave used by Buddhist recluses for meditation.

ཆོས་སེམས་ཅན *chos-sems-can* inclined to religion, pious.

ཆོས་སྲིད *chos-srid* (ཆོས་ཀྱི་སྲིད *chos-kyi-srid* धर्म्मराज्य) religious government: འབངས་རྣམས་ཆོས་སྲིད་ཀྱིས་སྐྱོང་ས *hbañs-rnams chos-srid kyis-skyoñ* the subjects weie protected (governed) by religious government (*Yig. k. 27*).

མཆང་གནས *mchañ-gnas* occurs in ཧོ་ན་མཆང་གནས་ཤིག་ཞུ་ཟེར་རོ *ho-na mchañ-gnas çig shu zer-ro* (*A. 95*).

མཆད་པ *mchad-pa* मृतगृह 1. tomb, sepulchre. 2. མཆད་པར་བྱ་བ महिमन् greatness; also the magical power of increasing one's size at will. 3. acc. to *Jä.* प्रमारित killed, slain; but མཆད་པ་མེད་པ=entire, perfect.

མཆན *mchan* 1. a footnote, v. མཆན་བུ. 2. कक्ष the side of the breast; མཆན་གྱི་བུ bosom-child, darling; མཆན་གྱི་མཆིས་བྲང་ bosom-wife; མཆན་དུ་འཇུག་པ *mchan-du hjug-pa* to put into one's bosom.

མཆན་ཁུག *chan-khug*=མཆན་ཁུང་ कक्षपुट arm-pit.

Syn. མཆན་ཧོག *mchan-hog*; མཆན་ཤབས *mchan-shabs* (*Mñon.*).

མཆན་བུ *mchan-bu* 1. note, annotation, foot-note in a book; ཡི་གེའི་མཆན་བུ words or lines written or printed in smaller character than the original and inserted in the མ་ཡིག (main-work). 2. a helper, an apprentice (*Jä.*). 3. v. མཆིས།

མཆན་ཤབས *mchan-shabs*, v. མཆན་ཁུག.

མཆན་ཧོག *mchan-hog*, v. མཆན་ཁུག.

མཆི་བ *mchi-wa* 1. eleg. for to come, to go, to appear: ཕྱིད་བཞིན་པར་མཆིའོ I shall come later; སྐྱབས་སུ་མཆིའོ शरणं गच्छामि go under the protection of, take refuge: འབངས་སུ་མཆིའོ I will obey (as a subject, servant) (*Mil.*); མཆི་ལགས= ཡོང་ས་ལགས yes sir, it will be or it will do. 2. to say, in the phrase ཞེས་མཆིའོ thus he said. (*Jä.*). 3. v. མཆིས.

མཆི་མ *mchi-ma* resp. སྤྱན་ཆབ, མིག་ཆུ अश्रु tears; མཆི་མ་བཏུ to shed tears; མཆི་མ་སྐྱེམ་པ *mchi-ma skyem-pa* to dry tears; མཆི་མ་འཕྱི་བ to wipe away tears; མཆི་མས་བཏང་བ to be choked with tears, acc. to *Sch.* to sob violently. མཆི་མ་བསྒྲིལ v. མཆི་མ་བཏུ; མཆི་མ་འཁྲིན་པ to shed tears; མཆི་མའི་ཐིགས་པ अश्रुकणा tear drops; མཆི་མ་འདོག or མཆི་མ་ལྷུང་བ अश्रुपात to cry, to shed tears.

མཆིག *mchig* (གཏུན) शिला stone for grinding spice, etc.

མཆིག་གུ *mchig-gu* 1. a small mortar, a mortar. 2. a pestle. 3. the nether mill-stone.

མཆིག་སྐོར་བ *mchig skor-wa* to grind (*Sch.*).

མཆིག་མ *chig-ma* the runner or upper mill-stone (*Sch.*).

མཆིང་བུ *mchiṅ-bu* 1. काच glass ornaments, trinkets, v. འཆིང་བུ. 2. n. of a place in Tibet. 3. a precious stone.

Syn. of 3. ནོར་བུ་མཛེས་བཟང་རོལ་པོ *nor-bu mdses-bzaṅ rol-po*; རིན་ཆེན་འགྱུར་བྱེད *rin-chen hgyur-byed* (*Mṅon.*).

མཆིད *mchid* or བཀའ་མཆིད 1. resp. talk, discourse, speech (of an honoured person). 2. letter: བཀའ་མཆིད་ཕེབས་རྒྱགས་ཀུང་ལྷའི་ཆུ་བོའི་རྒྱུན་བཞིན་རྒྱལ་བ་མཛེད། "pray let your letters come to me uninterruptedly like the flow of the divine river (Ganges)" (*Yig. k.*).

མཆིན་པ *mchin-pa* (resp. སྐུ་མཆིན acc. to *Lex.*). 1. acc. to *Jä.* the liver. 2. n. of a fruit called མཆིན་པ་ནོ་ཤ.

མཆིན་དྲི *mchin-dri* or མཆིན་རི the midriff or diaphragm.

མཆིན་ནད *mchin-nad* liver disease.

མཆིན་ནན *mchin-nan* lit. liver-pressing, *i.e.*, keeping the liver in order. མཆིན་ནན་བྱེད་པ to breakfast. It is believed that taking food early in the morning keeps the liver in good order.

མཆིན་ཚད *mchin-tshad* liver-fever; ལྕགས་ཁྲུས་མིག་ནད་མཆིན་ཚད་སེལ iron-mixture cures eye-disease and congested liver (*Med.*).

མཆིམས *Mchims* n. of a village near the great monastery of Sam-ye; n. of a tribal family.

མཆིམས་བཟའ *Mchims-bzah* princess of *Mchims* who was married to king *Khri-sroṅ ldehu btsan*.

མཆིལ་ཁྲ *mchil-khra* the sparrow-hawk.

མཆིལ་མགོ *mchil-mgo* a fabulous stone, resembling a sparrow's head, supposed to possess marvellous qualities (*Jä.*).

མཆིལ་པ I: *mchil-pa* अङ्कुश 1.= *lcags-kyu* an iron hook; described as གླང་པོའི་རྗེས་སུ་མཐུན་པའི་རྫས (*Mṅon.*) the thing which makes the elephant obey his conductor. 2. fishing hook; མཆིལ་པས་ཉ་འཛིན་པ to fish with a hook.

མཆིལ་པ II: ཅིཉ कलविङ्क the common sparrow.

Syn. ཉེར་ཆགས *ñer-chags*; ཁྱིམ་དུ་ཉལ *khyim-du-ñal*; ཁྱུ་མཆོག་འགྲོད་པ *khyu-mchog hgrod-pa*; རྒྱབ་བཀྲ *rgyab-bkra*; མགྲིན་སྔོན *mgrin-sṅon* (*Mṅon.*).

མཆིལ་མ *mchil-ma* (resp. ཞལ་མཆིལ) spittle.

Syn. ཁ་ཆུ *kha-chu*; ཞལ་ཆབ (*Mṅon.*).

མཆིལ་མའི་ཐལ་བ *mchil-mahi thal-wa* particles of saliva: རྒྱལ་སྲིད་མཆིལ་མའི་ཐལ་བ་བཞིན་དུ་སྤངས *rgyal-srid mchil-mahi thal-wa bshin-du spaṅs* he threw off his kingdom in the manner one throws out spittle (*A. 11*).

མཆིལ་མའི་སྣོད *mchil-mahi-snod* resp. (ཞལ་བཞེད) कटाहक, श्लेष्मकटाहक spittoon, spitting-box.

མཆིལ་ལུད *mchil-lud* or མཆིལ་སྣབས mucous.

མཆིལ་ལྷམ *mchil-lham* उपानत् shoe, boot: མཆིལ་ལྷམ་གཉིས་འདོར་བ to lose both the shoes; མཆིལ་ལྷམ་མཁན shoe-maker, cobbler, seller of boots; མཆིལ་ལྷམ་གྱི་ལུ་བ the leg of a boot (*Cs.*): ཀར་ཥ་པ་ཎི་དོག་མ་ལྔ་མཆིལ་ལྷམ་ཟུང་ཅིག་རྣམས་ཕུལ། he presented him with five pieces of *Karṣapaṇa* and a pair of shoes (*Yig.*).

མཆིས་པ I: *mchis-pa* pf. of མཆི་བ (ཡོད་པ) सन्ति, eleg. མཆིས་ལགས་པ to be, to be there, to exist: ཏུ་མཆིས how much was there, how many were there? (*Cs.*). སུ་ལ་དམ་པའི་ཆོས་མཆིས་པ whoever has the holy doctrine.

མཆིས་པ II: pf. of མཆི་བ to come: ཐག་རིང་པོ་ནས་མཆིས་ཏེ having come from afar.

+ མཆིས་བྲང་ *mchis-brañ* (lit. a house where one exists, resides) 1. a housewife, partner. 2. eleg. dwelling, abode, domicile; also when speaking of one's own dwelling: བདག་གི་མཆིས་བྲང་ my humble residence, cf. ཕོ་བྲང་ palace, བླ་བྲང་ lama's residence.

Syn. ཆུང་མ *chuñ-ma*; བག་མ *bag-ma*; ཁྱིམ་བདག་མོ *kyim bdag-mo* (*Mñon.*).

མཆིས་མལ *mchis-mal* bed, bedstead (*Cs.*).

མཆུ *mchu* I: तुण्ड, ओष्ठ 1. the lips; ཡ་མཆུ the upper lip; མ་མཆུ the lower lip. 2. beak or bill of a bird, also called མཆོ་ཇོ in Sikk.: ཁྱིའུ་མཆུ་རིངས་དང་ཏིང་ཏིང་མ་ཟེར་བ་གཉིས་ཡོད, "there were two, the bird called the long-beaked and the Ting-ting-ma" (*Rdsa.*). མཆུ་ལ་ཐོགས་ཏེ་འགྲོ་བ going off, carrying something in the bill. མཆུ་བིམ་པ་ལྟར་དམར་བ the lips were red like the *Bimba* fruit. མཆུ་རྐང་དམར *mchu-rkañ-dmar* lit. red bill and feet=ངང་པའི་རྒྱལ་པོ a gander (*Mñon.*). མཆུ་ཅན *mchu-can* possessed of fine lips; མཆུ་རྡོ *mchu-rdo* beak, the bill of a bird; མཆུ་ནོན་པ *mchu-non-pa* pointed beak; མཆུ་མེད *mchu-med* अनोष्ठक one whose lips are very small, one who has no lips. མཆུ་ཞེང་ *mchu-sheñ* आयाम;=དཀྱུད *dkyud* and ཁ་ཞེང་ length and breadth.

Syn. མཆུ་སྒྲོས *mchu-sgros*; སྒྲོས་དམར *sgros-dmar*; སོ་ཡི་གཡོགས *so-yi-gyogs*; སོ་སྐྱོབས *so-skyobs*; སོ་སྒྲིབ *so-sgrib*; སོ་གོས *so-gos* (*Mñon.*).

མཆུ II: constellation called *Maghā* in Sanskṛt; one of the lunar mansions, v. རྒྱུ་སྐར.

Syn. ཕ་མོ་ལྷ་སྐྱེས *pha-mo lha-skyes*; སྙན་ངག་མཁན *sñan-ñag-mkhan*; རྟ་ཆེན *rta-chen*; མ་གྷ *maghā* (*Mñon.*); also ཚིགས་བརྒྱའི་དབང་པོ *tshigs brgyahi dwañ-po*; བཅུ་དྲུག་འོད་ལྡན *bcu-drug hod-ldan* (*Mñon.*).

མཆུ་སྡེ་ལྔ *Mchu-sde-lña* n. of a chapter in the *Mdo* series of Buddhist sacred books.

+ མཆུ་རིང་ *mchu-riñ*=དཀྱུས་སུ་རིང་པོ *dkyus-su riñ-po* long, lengthwise.

མཆུ་རིངས *mchu-riñs* (འཁྲུན་རིང་ *hkhrun-riñ*) 1. བྱ་ཕུ་ཤུད (*Mñon.*) the long-beaked-bird, the hoopoe, the crane. 2. ཕག་རྒོད the wild boar; long-snout. 3. acc. to *Jä.* mosquito.

མཆུ་ལས་སྐྱེས *mchu-las skyes* मघाभव born under the constellation of *Maghā*.

མཆུམ་པོ *mchum-po* (མུ་ཏིག) pearl; also string of pearls.

མཆེ་བ *mche-wa* दन्त, दंष्ट्र, विषाण tooth, generally canine tooth, the eye-tooth, fang; མཆེ་ཀུག elephant's tusk.

མཆེ་གཙིགས་པ *mche-gtsigs-pa* कराल in *W.* to show one's teeth, to grin; མཆེ་བ་ཅན་གྱི་སྡེ the class of tusked animals, viz., the carnivora and the tusked pachydermata.

མཆེ་སྡེར *mche-sder* མཆེ་བ་དང་སྡེར་མོ *mche-wa dañ sder-mo* teeth and claws of wild animals.

མཆེ་བ་གཅིག་པ *Mche-wa gcig-pa* एकदन्त a name of Gaṇapati, the son of the goddess Umā.

མཆེ་བ་ལྡད་བྱེད་པ *mche-wa ldad-byed-pa* विजृम्भ to chew the cud, ruminate.

མཆེ་བ་སྟོང་ལྡན *mche-wa stoñ-ldan* (ཉ་ཡི་རྒྱལ་པོ) fish, said to possess one thousand teeth (*Mñon.*).

མཆེ་བ་སྟོབས་ལྡན *mche-wa stobs-ldan*=གླང་པོ an elephant.

མཆེ་བ་དྲུག་ལྡན *mche-wa drug-ldan* षड्दन्त n. of the king of elephants on whom Indra rides.

* མཆེ་བའི་སྡེ *Mche-wahi-sde* दंष्ट्रसेन n. pr. (*Tā. 2, 212*).

མཆེད *mched* (སྐུ་མཆེད *sku-mched*, མཆེད་ལྕམ *mched-lcam*) resp. for brother, also for sister; མཆེད་གཉིས two brothers; སྲས་མོ་ལྷ་ལྕམ་མཆེད་བཞི four princesses, sisters; དེའི་མཆེད his brother, in reference to a king, prince, etc., esp. of gods; མཆེད་བཞི four divine brothers; མཆེད་གྲོགས or གྲོགས་མཆེད clerical brothers, politely addressed as brother. མཆེད་གྲོགས་མང་པོ་ཚོགས་པར where many clerical brothers assemble; མཆེད་གྲོགས་དམ་ཚིག་གཅིག་པ betrothed brothers, religious brothers (ཆོས་སྤུན *chos-spun*); an intimate friend. མཆེད་པོ་ལྔ the race that originated from the five early patriarchs of Tibet. སྨུར་ལྷ་མཆེད་བཞི four brothers called:—སྨུར་ལྷ་ *Mgur-lha*: (1) གཉེན *Gñen*, (2) དམུ *Dmu*, (3) གླུ *Glu*, (4) ཚ *Tsha*.

མཆེད་ཟླ *mchid-zla*=སྤུན་ཟླ *spun-za*) brothers; also brother and sister.

མཆེད་པ *mched-pa* प्रसवित, वृद्धिप्राप्त, आयतन: to spread, gain ground; to increase, multiply; the word མཆེད་པ is seldom used except of fire, plague, etc.: བདག་གི་འདོད་ཆགས་ཀྱི་མེ་མཆེད་པས as the fire of voluptuousness spread or increased within me; མར་མེ་གཅིག་ལ་གཅིག་མཆེད་ལྟར as one kindles one light by another; གཅིག་གླེང་གཉིས་གླེང་རིམ་པས་མཆེད་དེ *gcig-gleṅ gñis-gleṅ rim-pas mched-de* as (the news) spread more and more passing from one to another. སྐྱེ་མཆེད *skye-mched*, v. སྐྱེ *skye* སྐྱེས་པའི་མཆེད *skyes-paḥi mched*. མཆེད་ཆེ་མིན་པ *mched che min-pa* very widely spread, very largely. འབྲུམ་པ་ཡང་མཆེད་ཆེ་མིན་པའི་ཡང་ལྕི་སྣ་ཚོགས *ḥbrum-pa yaṅ mched-che min-paḥi yaṅ lci sna-tshogs* (*Ya-sel.* 17) also several cases of small-pox of virulent and light (types) were very widely spread.

Syn. ཁྱབ་པ *khyab-pa*; རྒྱས་པ *rgyas-pa*; ཆེ་རུ་སོང་བ *che-ru soṅ-wa*; མང་དུ་འགྲོ་བ *maṅ-du ḥgro-wa*; སྐྱེ་བ *skye-wa*; འཕེལ་བ *ḥphel-wa*; འགྲིམ་པ *ḥgrim-pa* (*Mṅon.*).

མཆེར་པ *mcher-pa* (also spelt འཆེར་པ) acc. to *Jä.* the mult, spleen.

མཆེལ *mchel* অবলম্বন a support, help: ལག་པའི་མཆེལ the hand stretched to rescue (*A. K. 111, 21*).

མཆོག *mchog* অগ্র, পরম, বর, প্রধান, উত্তম, শ্রেষ্ঠ, শ্রেয়:, প্রবর, মহান্ the best, the most, the most excellent of its kind; དཀོན་མཆོག the greatest rarity, the Deity; v. also under དཀོན—ཤིན་ཏུ་མཆོག *çin-tu mchog* the very excellent or superior, sublime, exalted; ཆོས་མཆོག *Chos-mchog* ধর্মোত্তর n. of a Buddhist philosopher who wrote the ন্যায়-বিন্দুটীকা. མཆོག་གི་མཆོག *mchog-gi mchog*=རབ་ཀྱི་རབ, བླ་མའི་བླ་མ the most excellent, the best of the best, superior of the superior; སྐྱེས་བུ་མཆོག *skyes-bu mchog* the chief of great beings, also Buddha; མིའི་མཆོག the greatest of men, a king, also Buddha: རྐང་གཉིས་རྣམས་ཀྱི་མཆོག দ্বিপদানাং শ্রেষ্ঠ the chief of the bi-peds, *i.e.*, of men, any Buddha. ང་ནི་འཇིག་རྟེན་འདི་ན་མཆོག I am the highest in this world (says Buddha immediately after his birth). གཞུང་མཆོག chief of the fundamental doctrine. གནས་མཆོག་པོ་ཏ་ལ Potala is the chief of (holy) places. རོ་མཆོག excellent taste or flavour, delicious. མཁས་མཆོག་རྣམས most learned men: མི་མཆོག་ཁྱོད thou best of men. མཆོག་དམར the great and the low; མཆོག་དང་ཐ་མང་ the nobles and the commons; མཆོག་དང་ཕལ་པ the great and the vulgar. As adv. མཆོག་ཏུ অত্যন্ত very, most (used with verbs).

Syn. གཙོ་བོ *gtso-wo*; ཆེ་གོས *che-ços*; ཆེས་ཆེ་བ *ches che-wa*; ཕུལ་བྱུང་ *phul-byuṅ*; ཆེན་པོ *chen-po*; རྩེ་མོ *rtse-mo*; རབ *rab*; བླ་ན་མེད *bla-na med*; རྒྱ་ནོམ་པ *gya-nom-pa*; དཔོན *dpon*; གོང་མ *goṅ-ma*; དང་པོ *daṅ-po*; ཕུད་དུ་བསྐུར *phud-du-bskur*; རྩེ་མོར་སོན *rtse-mor-son*; ལེགས་པ *legs-pa*; ལེགས་གནས *legs gnas*; ཡང་རབ *yaṅ-rab*; གོང་མའི་གོང་མ *goṅ-maḥi* goṅ-ma; དཔའ་བོ *dpaḥ-bo*; ཅང་ཤེས་པ *caṅ çes-pa* (*Mṅon.*).

མཆོག་སྐྱོང་ *mchog-skyoṅ* the chief protector.

མཆོག་གི་རྒྱན *mchog-gi rgyan* = བཙུན་མ the chief ornament; pure-born; a holy lady (*D.R.*).

མཆོག་གི་ལྕུག་མ *mchog-gi lcug-ma* the principal of the women in a family (*Mṅon.*).

མཆོག་གི་བདག *mchog-gi-bdag* the lord of the best; the principal among the nobles or lamas.

མཆོག་གི་རྒྱལ་མཚན *mchog-gi rgyal-mtshan* n. of a gem, v. བཀྲ་ཤིས་རྟགས་བརྒྱད the eight auspicious objects.

མཆོག་གི་དང་པོའི་སངས་རྒྱས *Mchog-gi daṅ-poḥi Saṅs-rgyas* the Supreme Adi-Buddha, v. དུས་ཀྱི་འཁོར་ལོའི་མཚན *Dus-kyi ḥkhor-loḥi mtshan*.

མཆོག་གི་བདུད་རྩི *mchog-gi bdud-rtsi* अमृतसार the best elixir; n. of a medicine.

མཆོག་གི་མ *mchog-gi-ma* the chief mother; epithet of the goddess Dolma (*Mṅon.*).

མཆོག་དགའ *mchog-dgaḥ* or མཆོག་ཏུ་དགའ་བ वरामोद, प्रमोद्य great joy, ecstasy.

མཆོག་ཉལ *mchog-ñal* (གྲངས) निखर्व n. of a number (*Ya-sel. 56*).

མཆོག་ཏུ་བཀྲབས *mchog-tu-bkrabs* श्रेयस् the chosen.

མཆོག་ཏུ་འགྲོ་བ *mchog-tu ḥgro-wa* to become great or attain to the position of the great, to be elevated to an exalted position. མཆོག་ཏུ་གྱུར་པ *mchog-tu gyur-pa*, id.

མཆོག་ཏུ་རྒྱན་པ *mchog-tu rgyan-pa* to be very well-dressed.

མཆོག་ཏུ་ཕུན་སུམ་ཚོགས་པ *mchog-tu phun-sum tshogs-pa* to become very prosperous.

* མཆོག་ཏུ་ཚ་བའི་དཔའ་བོ *mchog-tu tsha-waḥi dpaḥ-bo* वरकरकभर (*Kālac. Tā. 2, 162*).

མཆོག་ཏུ་མཛེས་པ *mchog-tu mdses-pa* दिव्यद्युति very handsome, lustrous.

མཆོག་ཏུ་ཡིད་འཐད *mchog-tu yid-ḥthad* परममनोज्ञ exquisite, very pleasant.

མཆོག་ཏུ་རིང་བ *mchog-tu riṅ-wa* very remote.

མཆོག་ཏུ་བསམ་པ *mchog-tu bsam-pa* well-thought of.

མཆོག་བདག *bchog-bdag* met. the earth.

མཆོག་བདེ *mchog-bde* met. a fish.

མཆོག་འདོད *mchog-ḥdod* सूर्य met. the sun.

མཆོག་ལྡན *mchog-ldan* (གྲངས) 1. n. of a great number. 2. གུར་གུམ कुङ्कुम saffron (*Mṅon.*).

མཆོག་སྦྱིན *mchog-sbyin* 1. वरुण, धर्म्म the god of water. 2. पारद quick-silver.

མཆོག་སྦྱིན་ཕྱག་རྒྱ *mchog-sbyin phyag-rgya* a gesture made in practicing magic, in conjuring up or exorcising ghosts.

མཆོག་སྦྱིན་མ *mchog-sbyin-ma* = པོ་དུམ་པུ (སྨན་བཟང་) n. of a medicine (*Mṅon.*).

མཆོག་སྦྱོར་བ *mchog-sbyor-wa* वरयोजन to unite the principal ones, also to mix up the chief ingredients of medicines.

མཆོག་ཟུང་ *mchog-zuṅ* the model pair; the two most excellent amongst Buddha's disciples, S'āri-putra and Maudgalyāyana.

མཆོག་འོད *mchog-ḥod* or མཆོག་སྲིད *mchog-srid* वररुचि n. of the celebrated Sanskṛt grammarian who wrote during the reign of king Vikramāditya.

མཆོག་ཡས *mchog-yas* (གྲངས) प्रवर n. of a great number.

མཆོག་ཤེས *mchog-çes* = ཤེས་རབ་ཏུ་ཕྱིན wisdom.

མཆོག་སེམས *mchog-sems* 1. = བྱང་སེམས a saint, purified soul, प्रचेतस्. 2. वरुण; ཆུ་ལྷ the god of water, also called མཆོག་སྦྱིན.

མཆོག་སྲིད *Mchog-srid*, कात्यायन, वररुचि: 1. n. of a great Buddhist sage who first composed the Pali grammar. 2. one of the nine sages who adorned the court of king Vikramāditya.

མཆོག་གསུམ *mchog-gsum* = དཀོན་མཆོག་གསུམ the most precious ones: མཆོག་གསུམ་བྱིན་མཐུས་འདིར་ཡང་ལུས་ཁམས་བདེ here I am in good health by the grace of the three chief ones (*Triratna*) (*Yig. k. 15*).

མཆོང་ *mchoṅ* = ཆོང་ *choṅ* n. of a gem which is believed to have the property of curing paralysis.

མཆོང་བ *mchoṅ-wa* लङ्घन; pf. མཆོངས to leap up, to jump (into the water, etc.), also to bathe in water: སེང་གེ་མཆོང་ས་ལ་ཝ་མཆོང་ན་རྐེད་པ་ཆག when the fox jumps in the place where lions leap, he breaks his waist; ཆུར་མཆོངས་ཏེ having leapt into the water.

Syn. འགེངས་པ *ḥgeṅs-pa*; བརྒལ་བ *brgal-wa* (*Mṅon.*).

མཆོད་པ *mchod-pa* (vb.) आराधना, पूजन, अर्चना, मानना 1. to honour, to worship, to revere, respect; to receive with honour. ཕྱིའི་མཆོད་པ formal worshipping, *i.e.*, to honour saints or deities by offering articles of food, flowers, perfumes, etc.; ནང་གི་མཆོད་པ to honour Buddha, *Bodhisattvas*, etc., in faith by meditating on their virtues. མཆོད་པར་འོས་པས་མཆོད་པ *mchod-par ḥos-pas mchod-pa* पूज्यपूजित because worthy of being honoured; (he) is honoured. 2. sbst. offering, oblation, libation; མཆོད་པ་འབུལ་བ to make offerings; རོལ་མོ་མཆོད་པར་འབུལ་བ to bring an offering of music; མཆོད་པ་སྣ་ཚོགས་ཐོག་སྟེ carrying along with them all sorts of offerings; མཆོད་པའི་ཁྱད་པར་བཅུ the ten kinds of offerings; ལྷ་མཆོད offerings or libations to the gods; བླ་མ་མཆོད་པ offerings made to the lamas in order to honour them; འབྲུ་མཆོད an offering consisting of grain; དུས་མཆོད offering presented on prescribed occasions; རྒྱུན་མཆོད daily or usual offering or religious service. 3. = དགའ་སྟོན festivity, festive entertainment (*Mṅon.*).

མཆོད་ཀོང *mchod-koṅ* small oil-burners generally made of bell-metal, brass, copper, silver or gold.

མཆོད་ཁྲི *mchod-khri* the chair or seat of the priest performing any religious service. Also མཆོད trestle, table, altar or frame for placing offerings on = མཆོད་སྒྲོགས, v. *Jä.*

མཆོད་ཁང་ *mchod-khaṅ* पूजागृह a chapel.

མཆོད་ལྕོག *mchod-lcog* a table or altar on which the offerings are put.

མཆོད་ཆས *mchod-chas* utensils necessary in making offerings.

མཆོད་མཆོག *mchod-mchog* वरक्रतु a grand religious service; chief or principal service [n. of Indra] *S.*

མཆོད་བརྗོད *mchod-brjod* the invocations, praises, &c., of the deities and saints worshipped.

མཆོད་རྟེན *mchod-rten*, चैत्य, स्तूप lit. means "receptacle of offerings," but is the common term for a chaitya; in Tibet this takes the shape of small and tall masonry monuments of settled form crowned with the ཉི་ཟླ (emblem of the sun and moon) and generally having in some cavity inside the ashes of a saint or other relics.

མཆོད་རྟེན་གྱི་འཁོར་ས *mchod-rten-gyi ḥkhor-sa* चैत्याङ्गन the walk or passage round a chörten for devotional circumambulation.

མཆོད་རྟེན་ཤིང་ *Mchod-rten-çiṅ* चैत्यद्रुम lit. the tree which grows on the (brick) *chaitya*; or which is venerated on account of Buddha having attained to the state of Buddha under its shadow; *C.* བྱང་ཆུབ་ཤིང་ the *Bodhi* or *pipal* tree.

མཆོད་རྟེན་བྱེད *mchod-rten-byed* met. an elephant (*Mṅon.*).

མཆོད་སྟེགས *mchod-stegs* offering-table, altar.

མཆོད་སྟོད *mchod-stod* an offering with a hymn of praise (*Sch.*).

མཆོད་སྟོན *mchod-ston* an entertainment, as a sort of libation, given to the priests.

མཆོད་ལྡན *mchod-ldan* सूर्य the sun (*Mñon.*).

མཆོད་ལྡན་མ *mchod-ldan-ma* माहेश्वरी an epithet of Umā. (*Mñon.*).

མཆོད་སྡོང་ *mchod-sdoń* = མཆོད་རྟེན *mchod-rten* 1. यष्टि, यूपधातु a stick [a sacrificial post] *S.* 2. offering-lamp (*Sch.*). 3. the wick of such a lamp (*Jä.*).

མཆོད་སྡོང་ཅན *mchod-sdoń-can* a kind of water-fowl (*Mñon.*).

མཆོད་སྡོང་ཆེན་པོ *mchod-sdoń chen-po* རྒྱལ་བ་ལྷ་བལ the great offering trunk or Bodhi tree. བསྐལ་འགྲོའི་བསོད་ནམས་ཀྱི་མཆོད་སྡོང་ཆེན་ པོར་བསྐལ་ བརྒྱར་གཡོ་མེད་དུ་བཞུགས། seated unmoved for a hundred *Kalpa*, as the worshipful Bodhi tree: by the good merits of all religious beings. (*Yig. k. 20*).

མཆོད་གནས *mchos-gnas* 1. objects to which offerings are made. མཆོད་པའི་གནས་ལ་གང་ཟག་དང་རྟེན་གཉིས, གང་ཟག་ནི་བླ་མ་སངས་རྒྱས་དགེ་འདུན་སོགས, རྟེན་ནི་སྐུ་གསུང་ཐུགས་རྟེན་སོགས་ཡིན the objects to which veneration is shown comprise two: persons and symbols; the persons are the assembly, Buddha, and the lamas; the symbols are images, the receptacles of what has been said, relics, and such like. 2. the officiating priest, the sacrificator.

མཆོད་པ་པོ *mchod-pa-po* a sacrificer, one who gives an offering.

མཆོད་པའི་སྤྲིན *mchod-pahi-sprin* पूजामेघ (མཆོད་པའི་ཚོགས་སྤྲིན) ["a cloud of worship" described in the Bodhi. II, to be a magnificent mode of worship in which incenses, lamps, garlands of flowers, etc., are profusely used] *S.*

མཆོད་པའི་ཚིགས *mchod-pahi-tshigs* མཆོད་པ་འབུལ་བ་ལ་འདོན་རྒྱུའི་ཚིགས་བཅད the *Gatha* or verses recited at a religious service.

མཆོད་པར་བྱེད *mchod-par-byed* पुष्पाञ्जलि worshipping, paying reverence.

མཆོད་པར་འོས་པ *mchod-par hos-pa* (སྦྱིན་གནས or མཆོད་གནས) पूज्य worthy of veneration, worshipful; they are three such, viz.:—(1) སློབ་དཔོན आचार्य the teacher or spiritual guide; (2) མཁན་པོ उपाध्याय the high priest; (3) those who are elders or superiors.

མཆོད་ཕྱིར་ཐོགས *mchod-phyir-thogs* यज्ञोपवीत, མཆོད་པ་འབུལ་དུས་གོས་ཆེན་ནམ་ཁ་བཏགས་ལྷ་བུ་གྲུ་བཞི་ལག་ཏུ་བཟུང་ནས་མཆོད་པ་བཞག་ནས་ཐོགས་པ the sacred raiment made of silk or a square satin scarf which is held in the hand while making any offerings to a deity; also an image or figure of a deity.

མཆོད་བྱ *mchod-bya* object of worship.

མཆོད་བྱེད *mchod-byed* = འབུལ་བ offerings, libations.

མཆོད་འབུལ *mchod-hbul* the offerings in a sacrifice (*Cs.*).

མཆོད་སྦྱིན *mchod-sbyin* मन्यु, यज्ञ, क्रतु, यजन a religious service where sacrifices of small figures are made. མཆོད་སྦྱིན་ལྔ the five *Yajña* (sacrifices) are:—(1) ཚངས་པའི་མཆོད་སྦྱིན་ཀློག་འདོན་པ *tshańs-pahi mchod-byin klog hdon-pa* the Brahma *Yajña*, which consists of recitation of the Vedas; (2) ལྷའི་མཆོད་སྦྱིན—སྦྱིན་སྲེག་བྱེད *lhahi mchod-sbyin—sbyin-sreg-byed* the *Deva Yajña*, consisting of burnt offerings to the gods; (3) མིའི་མཆོད་སྦྱིན་མགྲོན་འོང་མཆོད *mihi mchod-sbyin mgron-hoń mchod* the human *Yajña* consisting of hospitality to those present; (4) ཕ་མེས་མཆོད་སྦྱིན་མཚུན་ཚིམ་བྱེད *pha-mes mchod-sbyin mtshun-tshim-byed* the *Yajña* for ancestors consists in giving them (their souls) satisfaction; (5) འབྱུང་པོའི་མཆོད་སྦྱིན་གཏོར་མའོ *hbyuń-pohi mchod-sbyin gtor-mahо*, *Bhuta Yajña*, consists in making torma offerings of cakes to the ghosts.

Syn. སྦྱིན་སྲེག *sbyin-sreg*; རྒྱུད་བདུན་པ *rgyud bdun-pa*; མཐོ་རིས་དོན *mtho-ris don*; ཨ་དྷ་ར *a-dhara* (*Mñon.*).

མཆོད་སྦྱིན་གྱི་རིག་བྱེད *mchod-sbyin-gyi rig-byed* यजुर्वेद the *Yajur* Veda of the Brāhmaṇs.

མཆོད་སྦྱིན་ཅན *mchod-sbyin-can* मघवन् an epithet of Indra.

མཆོད་སྦྱིན་འཇོམས *mchod-sbyin-hjoms* क्रतुध्वंसी one who destroys a sacrifice; a *Yavana*, Mahomedan [an epithet of S'iva as destroyer of Dakṣa's sacrifice]*S.*

མཆོད་སྦྱིན་འཛིན *mchod-sbgin hdsin* = མཆོད་སྦྱིན་གྱི་ལས་བྱེད་མཁན *mchod-sbyin-gyi las byed-mkhan* priests who recite the ritual at a sacrificial offering.

མཆོད་སྦྱིན་དགྲ་བོ *mchod-sbyin dgra-wo* = ལྷ་མ་ཡིན an *Asura*, a demon.

མཆོད་སྦྱིན་འདོན་མ *mchod-sbyin hdon-ma* सवित्री met. mother.

མཆོད་སྦྱིན་གནས *mchod-sbyin gnas* = མཆོད་སྦྱིན་བྱེད་པའི་ཁང་པ the house or place where *Yajña* sacrifices are performed.

མཆོད་སྦྱིན་སྤོ *mchod-sbyin spo* = སྤོས་དཀར *spos-dkar* lit. white incense, the resin of the *Sāl* tree (*Mñon.*).

མཆོད་སྦྱིན་སྤྱོད *mchod-sbyin-spyod* the performance of *Yajña*.

མཆོད་སྦྱིན་ཕྱུགས *mchod-sbyin-phyugs* gen. the object that is sacrificed in a *Yajña*.

མཆོད་སྦྱིན་བྱས *mchod-sbyin-byas* याज्ञिक one who performs a *Yajña* sacrifice.

མཆོད་སྦྱིན་བྱེད་དུ་འཇུག་པ *mchod-sbyin byed-du hjug-pa* याजन to make one perform a *Yajña* sacrifice.

མཆོད་སྦྱིན་སྦྱར *mchod-sbyin-sbyar* = བདག་ཉིད आत्म the self.

མཆོད་སྦྱིན་ལྷག *mchod-sbyin-lhag* अमृत nectar.

མཆོད་མེ *mchod-me* offering of lighted lamps in honour of a deity.

མཆོད་རྫས *mchod-rdsas* गव्य, द्रव्य the articles of *Yajña*, particularly clarified butter, *i.e.*, articles of religious service (མཆོད་ཆས or མཆོད་པའི་ཡོ་བྱད sacrificial utensils), requisites for festive processions in honour of a deity.

མཆོད་སྙོམས *mchod-çoms* or མཆོད་བཤམས the arrangements for a religious service and the placing of the offerings on the table before the deity to be worshipped.

མཆོད་ཚིག *mchod-tshig* (བསྟོད་ཚིག or བཀུར་ཚིག) स्तोत्र words of praise to a deity or saint.

མཆོད་འོས *mchod-hos* 1. सूर्य met. the sun (*Mñon.*). 2. worthy of worship, worshipful.

མཆོད་འོས་གནས *mchod-hos-gnas* = གཙུག་ལག་ཁང་ a sanctuary or Gandhagṛha (དྲི་གཙང་ཁང་ *dri gtsaṅ-khaṅ*) or *Vihāra* (*Mñon.*).

མཆོད་ཡོན *mchod-yon* remuneration to a priest or lama performing any religious service.

Syn. ཉེ་རེག *ñe-reg*; ཞལ་བསིལ *bshal-gsil*; ཁ་བཤལ་བ *kha bçal-wa*; ཡོན་ཆབ *yon-chab*; འཐོར་འཐུང *hthor-thuṅ* (*Mñon.*).

མཆོད་གཡོག *mchod-gyog* one who serves in a religious or sacrificial service.

མཆོད་རོ *mchod-ro* remnants of offerings consisting of cakes, etc., that have already been presented to a deity.

མཆོར་པོ *mchor-po* sometimes also འཕྱོར་པོ *hphyor-po* 1. pretty, handsome, neat, elegant; ཕོ་མཆོར་པོ a handsome man; བུད་མེད་མཆོར་མོ a pretty woman, esp. a smart gaily-dressed female. 2. in *W.* also vain, conceited(*Jä.*).

འཆག *hchag* constitutional walk; in colloq. is called ལྟོ་འཇུ་བ *lto hju-wa* constitutional walk for the digestion of food; in eleg. language of the lamas it is called རླུང་སངས་འགྲོ་ཆེད་ *rluṅ-saṅs hgro-ched* "a walk for clearing the wind." མ་ཉལ་འགྲོ་དང་འཆག་དང་རྩེ་བ་དང་། to play, to walk, and to move about, not lying down (*A. 14*).

འཆག་ཅན་ *hchag-can* in colloq. trodden, stamped; solid, firm, compact.

འཆག་པ་ *hchag-pa* I: pf. ཆག or ཆགས 1. to break, be broken; སྣོད་ཆག་པ *snod-chag-pa* a broken vessel; fig. ང་རྒྱལ་ཆག་པ humiliation, breaking one's pride; དེར་འགྲོན་སྐབས་ཆག the opportunity of going there has been cut off; ལམ་ཆག་པ *lam-chag-pa* a beaten, practicable road. 2. to abate, beat down from the price: ཁ་ཆག་མེད་པར there being no room for either asking or abating (*Jä.*).

འཆག་པ་ II: also ཆགས་པ, pf. བཅགས, fut. བཅག 1. to tread, to walk, to move, esp. when speaking respectfully or formally: ཡབ་མེས་ཀྱི་ཞབས་ཀྱིས་བཅགས་པའི་ས་ཆ the place where my ancestors did walk; ཞབས་ཆགས་པའི་ཕྱག་ཕྱིར་འགྲོ follow me on my walk (*Jä.*); འཆག་ཏུ or འཆག་ཏུ་འགྲོ་བ to take a walk.

འཆག་ས *hchag-sa* चंक्रमण (ཞབས་འཆག་ས་ལྟ་བུ) a place for walking in; འཆག་སར་འཆག་པ to take a constitutional walk within a limited distance.

འཆག་པར་བྱེད *hchag-par-byed* चाचंक्रमेत takes constitutional walk after dinner; also the place for this purpose.

འཆག་སའི་བུག་པ *hchag-sahi bug-pa* an artificial cavern where a recluse takes rest or retires.

འཆགས་པ་=བཤགས་པ 1. confession: སྡིག་པ་འཆགས་སོ *sdig-pa hchags-so* I have confessed my sins. 2. v. འཆག་པ. 3. sometimes for འཆེག་པ *hcheg-pa* (*Jä.*).

འཆང་བ *hchaṅ-wa*=འཛིན་པ *hdsin-pa*, pf. བཅངས, imp. ཆོང་ or ཆོངས 1. to hold, to take hold of, to keep, to bear; also possession; धारण, धृति; ལག་ཏུ་འཆང་བ to hold in the hand; སེམས་ལ་འཆང་བ to bear in the mind, also to retain in the memory: ཟན་གྱིས་གསོས་པའི་ཁྱི་རྒན་གྱིས, ནམ་ཞིག་རང་ལ་འཆང་བ་མཐོང་། *zan-gyis gsos-pahi khyi-rgan gyis, nam-shig raṅ-la hchaṅ-wa mthoṅ* one night I beheld the old dog which I had fostered with food laying hold on my own self. དབང་པོ་རྡོ་རྗེ་འཆང་བའི་ལྷ *dwaṅ-po rdo-rje hchaṅ-bahi lha* the god Vajradhara—n. of the ideal Buddha of the *Gelugpa* school acc. to the *Tantrik* section of it. ཚུལ་ཁྲིམས་ཆེན་པོ་འཆང་བའི་མཆོག *tshul-khrims chen-po hchaṅ-bahi mchog* a very good character is the chief of possessions. 2. to carry, to wear, to carry about with one, *e.g.*, amulets, etc. 3. to have, to assume, *e.g.*, the body of a goddess, of a *Rakṣasī* (*Jä.*). 4. to bite or bark at.

འཆང་ཟུངས *hchaṅ-zuṅs* handle, crook of a stick.

འཆངས་པ *hchaṅs-pa* in *W.* a (closed) handful, *i.e.*, of dough; འཆངས་ཟ a clod (of clay), a snow-ball, etc., formed in the hand (*Jä.*).

འཆད་པ I: *hchad-pa* 1. pf. ཆད vb. n. to གཅོད་པ; like ཆད་པ छेदन, चंक्रमण to be cut into pieces, to be cut off, to decay, to separate or break asunder: ཐག་པ་ལྟ་བུ་ཆད་པ cut like a rope. 2. to cease, end, stop: དབུགས་འཆད་གྱིན་འདུག he is stopping for breath; to die away, to become extinct (of a family, a generation); to be consumed (of provisions, of bodily strength) (*Jä.*).

འཆད་པ II: pf. and fut. བཤད, imp. ཤོད भाषण, निर्देशन to explain; explanation, explaining: ད་ལྟ་འཆད it is now explained; ཆོས་འཆད་གྱིན་འདུག he is explaining the doctrine; ཡིད་ལ་ཟུམ་ཤིག་དང་བཤད give heed, and I will explain it to you; འཆད་པར་འགྱུར आख्यायति;

འཆད་ཉན་པ to listen to an explanation (*Sch*).; འཇིག་ཆོས་གཏམ་འཆད་པ to teach the transitoriness of existence (*Sch.*).

འཆད་མཁས་པ *ḥchad-mkhas-pa* = བརྗོད་བཟང་ or ཕན་བཟང་ one skilful in explaining a thing; also a clever description. In Bon terminolgy འཆད་པ = a convincing explanation, where there is no room for doubt.

འཆད་འདོད *ḥchad-ḥdod* विवचा (ངག་ནས) desire for explanation of any discourse.

འཆད་པ III: = ཤི་ཁང་ मृतगृह dead-house, a shed where the corpse is kept.

卐 **འཆབ་པ** *ḥchab-pa* pf. བཅབས, fut. བཅབ, imp. ཆོབ, སྦེད་པ *sbed-pa* प्रतिच्छदयति to conceal, to keep secret. འཆབ་པ་མེད་པའི་སེམས a candid mind, open-heartedness (cog. to འཇབ་པ). The word is also explained as རང་གི་སྐྱོན་མི་མངོན་པར་བྱ་བ *rañ-gi skyon mi-mñon-par bya-wa* not to make evident one's fault, to hide it.

འཆམ་པ I: *ḥcham-pa* = མཐུན་པ (pf. བཅམ *Lex.*), also adj. and sbst., to accord, to agree, agreeing, agreement: སྲིད་ལ་མི་འཆམ་པས *sri-la mi-ḥcham-paṣ* as they did not agree about the government. འཆམ་བྱེད་པ *ḥcham-byed-pa* to make agree, to reconcile; ཁ་འཆམས་པ to agree upon, to concert: བློན་པོ་རྣམས་ཁ་མ་འཆམ་ནས the officers having disagreed (*Pth.*).

འཆམ་པ II: གར་འཆམ, གར་འཆམས नर्तन to dance; also a dancer: ཁྲོ་འཆམ་པ *khro-ḥcham-pa* who dances in frantic leaps wearing a frightful mask; གར་འཆམ a dramatic or stage dance (*Jä.*).

འཆམ་པོ *ḥcham-po* or འཆམ་པ་པོ 1. a dancer. 2. མཐུན་པོ harmony, concord: རྒྱལ་པོ་ཕན་ཚུན་གཉིས་འཆམ་པོ་བྱེད་ཀྱི་བར་དུ་བཞུགས the king sat between the two parties to reconcile them to each other (*Yig. k. 52*).

འཆམ་དཔོན *ḥcham-dpon* director of a dance, a stage-master.

འཆམ་ཡིག *ḥcham-yig* a book on dancing.

འཆམས *ḥchamṣ* नृत्य a dance, dancing.

འཆའ *ḥchaḥ* in *Ld.*, a cup-board (*Jä.*).

འཆའ་བ I: *ḥchaḥ-wa* 1. pf. བཅས rarely; འཆས fut. བཅའ *bcaḥ* imp. ཆོས *choṣ* to draw up, prepare, construct, adjust. གནས་འཆའ་བ *gnaṣ ḥchaḥ-wa* to prepare a place, or abode; to settle. མལ་འཆའ་བ *mal ḥchaḥ-wa* to prepare a bed; དམག་གར་འཆའ་བ *dmag-gar ḥchaḥ-wa* to pitch a camp; སྐྱིལ་ཀྲུང་འཆའ་བ *skyil-kruñ ḥchaḥ-wa* to adjust in cross-legged posture; ཁྲིམས་ར་འཆའ་བ *khrimṣ-ra ḥchaḥ-wa* encamp, to establish a court of justice; རྒྱལ་ཁྲིམས་འཆའ་བ *rgyal-khrimṣ ḥchaḥ-wa* to draw up a law, to give laws. 2. with དམ *dam* to make a vow, to promise, assert; frq. ཡི་དམ་འཆའ་བ *yi-dam ḥchaḥ-wa* to promise by oath; བློ་གཏད་འཆའ་བ *blo-gtad ḥchaḥ-wa* to place confidence in. 3. with ཞེན་པ *shen-pa* or ཆགས་པ *chagṣ-pa* to be attached to.

འཆའ་བ II: to snap at, mangle; གཅིག་ལ་གཅིག་འཆའ་ཞིང་ཟ་བ *gcig-la gcig ḥchaḥ-shiñ za-wa* to maul and devour one another; ཤིང་འཆའ་བ *çiñ-ḥchaḥ-wa* to gnaw at a piece of wood (*Jä.*).

འཆའ་རློམ་པ *ḥchaḥ-rlom-pa* = ཁ་ལ་ཟ་རྒྱུ་ལ་རློམ་པ *kha-la za-rgyu la rlom-pa* one very fond of munching; a greedy person.

འཆར *ḥchar* उदय rising, appearance (as of the sun).

འཆར་ཀ *Ḥchar-ka* उदयी n. of an attendant of Buddha, who became a *Bhikṣu*.

འཆར་སྐྱེམས *ḥchar-skyems* (བློ་གྲོས་ལྟ་བུ *blo-gros lta-bu*) habit.

འཆར་ག *ḥchar-ga* the rising, the appearance.

འཆར་སྒོ *hchar-sgo* thought, idea, conception: སེམས་ཅན་སོ་སོའི་སྣང་བའི་འཆར་སྒོ་ལས *sems-can so-sohi snan-wahi hchar-sgo las* from the thoughts that dawn (in the mind) of different animated beings (*Ya-sel. 43*).

འཆར་སྟེངས་པ *Hchar-stens-pa* n. of a celebrated Lama of Charteng (*Deb.* ཀ *44*).

འཆར་བ *hchar-wa* (pf. ཤར་བ) उदय, उदयन, उद्गत to arise, to start up, become visible, to shine: ཚོགས་དྲུག་ཞེན་མེད་རྒྱུན་དུ་འཆར the six objects of perception free from fascination continually arise. གཟུགས་འཆར་བ་བྱེད་པ to cause an image to be reflected (in water); ཡིད་ལ་འཆར་བ (thoughts) dawning or rising in the mind; གྲོགས་སུ་འཆར (they) appear as friends; རྒྱན་དུ་འཆར it turned into an ornament, *i.e.*, a blessing.

འཆལ *hchal* प्रलाप random talk or speech: འདི་འཆལ་འདུག་པས་ད་རང་རེ་རྣམས་འགྲོ། as this is meaningless talk, let us, every one of us, now go.

འཆལ་འཆོལ *hchal-hchol* or འཆལ་ལ་འཆོལ་ལེ confused, pell-mell.

འཆལ་གཏམ *hchal-gtam* meaningless talk; ཐབས་པ་མེད་པ་ལ་བཟུང་བའི་འཆལ་གཏམ meaningless talk where nothing practical comes out; འཆལ་གཏམ་སྨྲ་བ to rave, talk nonsense.

འཆལ་པ I: *hchal-pa* (ཤེས་རབ་ལྟ་བུ) a kind of supernatural wisdom; འཆལ་པའི་ཤེས་རབ दौष्प्रज्ञा mischievous wisdom or knowledge; འཆལ་པའི་ཁྲིམས दुःशील bad morals; immoral.

འཆལ་པ II: or འཆལ་པོ *hchal-po* lecher, fornicator; འཆལ་པ་རྣམས་ཀྱི་ཚིག *hchal-pa rnams-kyi tshig* obscene language (*Jä.*).

འཆལ་བ *hchal-wa* 1. to lose one's wits, to be confused, to be in disorder. བསླབ་པ་འཆལ་བ to break moral discipline; to make confusion of the doctrine. 2. to hesitate, fluctuate in mind, be irresolute. 3. to fornicate, to commit adultery; བུད་མེད་ཚུལ་འཆལ་བྱེད་པ a woman that has lost her purity; a whore, harlot (*Jä.*).

འཆལ་མོ *hchal-mo* a whore (*Jä.*).

འཆལ་ཚིག *hchal-tshig* = ངག་འཆལ delirium, vain talk.

* འཆི *hchi* मृत्यु death (*Kālac. T. 109*).

འཆི་གུ *hchi-gu* = གཡུན་ཐུ sling, string-weapon.

འཆི་ཁ *hchi-kha* ཤི་བའི་སྐབས the point of death, just when dying; འཆི་ཁ་མ at the time of dying; འཆི་ཁ་བར་དོ་རང་གྲོལ n. of a religious work, which if read to a dying person his soul will not wander in the *Bardo* (the state between death and re-birth).

འཆི་རྟགས *hchi-rtags* sign of death.

འཆི་རྟགས་མཚན་མ་རང་གྲོལ *Hchi-rtags, mtshan-ma ran-grol* another work which is read when the sign of approaching death is perceived. It is read in order to hasten death so that after death the deceased may go to some ascertained place in the next world.

འཆི་ལྟས *hchi-ltas*, अरिष्ट, अप्रास forebodings of death; ཉི་མའི་འཆི་ལྟས་འཕེལ་བ increasing the signs of the sun's death (by the approach of the eclipse) (*Ya-sel. 51*).

འཆི་བདག *Hchi-bdag* = གཤིན་རྗེ यम, मृत्युपति Yama, the lord of death.

འཆི་ནད *hchi-nad* a fatal disease.

འཆི་འཕོ *hchi-hpho* or འཆི = འཆི་དང་འཕོ་བ च्युति-संक्रम, भवसङ्क्रान्ति termination of worldly concerns, death.

འཆི་འཕོ་བ *hchi-hpho-wa* = ཚེ་འཕོ་བ to change one's place of existence, to transmigrate.

འཆི་འཕོ་མེད *hchi hpho-med* = སྐྱེ་འཆི་མེད अच्युता not subject to change, without birth and death.

འཆི་བ *ḥhci-wa*, मरण, मृत्यु, अन्तमय्या, देहयात्रा; साधन, सन्न, परिसर, मृङ vb. to die: རང་འཆིའོ *raṅ-ḥchiḥo* I will seek death; འཆི་བ་ཡིན he is about to die; འཆི་བར་བྱེད་པའི་ཆུ water causing death; འཆི་བའི་ཆར་གཏོགས मरणाधिक appertaining to death, relating to death.

Syn. ལྔ་བའི་གནས་སྐབས *ḽṅa-wahi gnas-skabs*; ལུས་ཞིག་པ *lus shig-pa*; དུས་ཀྱི་ཆོས་ཉིད *dus-kyi chos-ñid*; སྐལ་འཇིག *skal-ḥjig*; ཚེ་འགྲོ *tshe-ḥgro*; བལྟ་བའི་མཐའ *bḽta-wahi mthah*; ཏིལ་བཅས་ཁྱོར་ཆུ་སྦྱིན་པའི་ཡུལ *til-bcas khyor-chu sbyin-pahi yul*; ཚེ་འདའ *tshe-ḥdah*; ཚེ་འཕོ *tshe-ḥpho*; འཆི་འཕོ *ḥchi-ḥpho* (*Mṅon.*).

འཆི་བ་མེད *ḥchi-wa-med*, अमर immortal, v. འཆི་མེད.

འཆི་བ་ལས་རྒྱལ་བ *ḥchi-wa las-rgyal-wa*, मृत्युञ्जय he who has conquered death; an epithet of Buddha.

འཆི་བ་བསླུ་བ *ḥchi-wa-bslu-wa*, मृत्युवञ्चन to deceive death, to ransom the life of a dying man.

འཆི་མེད *ḥchi-med*, अमर, अमृत, अरिष्ट 1. मुक्ति emancipation, immortality. 2. met. the raven which is famous for longevity.

འཆི་མེད་དགའ་བ *ḥchi-med dgah-wa*, n. of a religious work (*Ya-sel. 60*).

འཆི་མེད་རྔ *ḥchi-med-rṅa*, or འཆི་མེད་རྔ་བོ་ཆེ, ལྷའི་རྔ་བོ་ཆེ lit. celestial drum; n. of a Buddhist work (*Yig. k. 20*).

འཆི་མེད་ཆབ *Ḥchi-med-chab*—ཆུ་བོ་གང་གཱ a name of the river Ganges (*Mṅon.*).

འཆི་མེད་མཆོད་ཡོན *ḥchi-med mchod-yon*, an epithet of the river Ganges (*Ya-sel. 76*).

འཆི་མེད་ལྗོན་ཤིང *ḥchi-med, ljon-çiṅ*, = ལྷའི་དཔག་བསམ་གྱི་ཤིང the celestial wishing-tree: སྐུ་འཚོ་འཆི་མེད་ཀྱི་ལྗོན་ཤིང་ལྟ་བ་བརྟན་པར་རྟག་ཤིང may your health remain as steady as the celestial wishing-tree (*Yig. k. 35*).

འཆི་མེད་བདུད་རྩི *ḥchi-med bdud-rtsi* the immortal elixir of life, Ganges water: བཀའ་མཆིད་ཕྲིན་ཚིགས་འཆི་མེད་བདུད་རྩིའི་རྒྱུན་བཞིན་རྫོགས་པ་མཐེན pray let your letters, communication, &c., flow like the deathless elixir—the stream of the Ganges (*Yig. k. 12*).

འཆི་མེད་བུ་མོ *ḥchi-med bu-mo* a goddess.

འཆི་མེད་མཛོད *ḥchi-med-mdsod*, अमरकोष n. of a Sanskṛt Dictionary composed by Amara Siṁha.

འཆི་མེད་རིལ་བུ *ḥchi-med ril-bu* (ཚེ་རིལ) lit. life-pill; the life-giving pills. The abbess of Samding monastery and other sacred personages have such pills at their disposal.

འཆི་མེད་དབང་མོ *ḥchi-med dwaṅ-mo*, अमरेश्वरी the queen of the immortals; a name of the wife of Indra.

* འཆི་མེད་སེང་གེ *ḥchi-med seṅ-ge*, अमरसिंह (*Bull. 1898, 296*).

འཆིག་པ *ḥchig-pa* 1. = འཆིག་བུ शिला a pestle. 2. said to = ཆོས་མ་ཡིན་པ་ལ་དམ་དུ་འཛིན་པ to hold as holy that which is not *Dharma* (Buddhism) (*K. d.* ང *355*).

འཆིང་བསྒྲིགས *ḥchiṅ-bsgrigs* an agreement.

འཆིང་ཉེན་པ *ḥchiṅ-ñen-pa* to become connected or related by marriage: བནྒ་ལ་རུ་ཁོ་བོ་འཆིང་ཉེན་གཏང in Bengal I entered into marriage relations (*A. 14*).

འཆིང་པ *ḥchiṅ-pa* बन्धन bond, binding.

འཆིང་བ I: *ḥchiṅ-wa* बन्धि, नाह, यमन, (pf. བཅིངས fut. བཅིང imp. འཆིང or འཆིངས) to bind, tie up, make fast to exorcise.

འཆིང་བ II: sbst. any binding-material. 1. ribbon; མགུལ་ཆིངས necklace, neck-cloth, neckerchief. 2. cord, fastenings, fetter, shackle: ལས་ཀྱི་འཆིང་བ་རྣམས कर्मसंयोजन the fetters of *Karma*, also fig. for magic curse, anathema. 3. used in colloq. for cramp or convulsions.

Syn. བཀྱིག་པ *bkyig-pa*; འཁྱིག་པ *ḥkhyig-pa*; བཅིང་བ *bciṅ-wa*; pf. འཆིངས་པ *ḥchiṅs-pa* = བཀྱིགས་པ

ḇkyigs-pa; འཁྱིགས་པ ḫkhyigs-pa; བཅིངས་པ ḇciṅs-pa, signifying བསྡམས་པ ḇdams-pa (Mṅon.).

འཆིང་བྱེད ḫchiṅ-byed = རྙེ ṟñe or རྙེ་ཐག ṟñe-thag (Mṅon.).

འཆིང་བྱེད་མ ḫchiṅ-byed-ma a general term for women.

འཆིང་བ་སྦྱིན་མ ḫchiṅ-wa sbyin-ma a handsome woman; maiden.

འཆིང་བར Ḫchiṅ-war n. of a village in འཕྱོང་རྒྱས, in Tibet (Rtsii.).

འཆིང་ཟབ ḫchiṅ-zab = གཏིང་ཟབ or ཀློང་ཟབ ḵloṅ-zab depth, profundity (Yig.).

འཆིང་བུ ḫchiṅ-bu trinket; glass-bangle for feet.

འཆིང་བུའི་སྣོད ḫchiṅ-buhi snod a glass vessel.

འཆིབ་པ ḫchib-pa or འཆིབས་པ, pf. བཅིབས, fut. བཅིབ, imp. ཆིབས, resp. to mount a horse or carriage; ཆིབ་པ་འཆིབས་པ to ride, to mount a horse.

འཆིམས་ཕུག Ḫchims-phug n. of a holy place with a small temple near Sam-ye.

འཆིམས་པ ḫchims-pa to be full, to get full (Sch.).

འཆིར་བ ḫchir-wa evidently a form of ཅིར་བ cir-wa to press, to squeeze. འཆིར་བ has pf. བཅིར, fut. གཅིར, to press, to wring, &c.; འཆིར་བ and ཅིར་བ being mere corruptions of the foregoing, though Jä. has them.

འཆིལ་པ ḫchil-pa sometimes stands by mistake for མཆིལ་པ mchil-pa, a sparrow.

འཆུ་བ I: ḫchu-wa acc. to Jä. 1. vb. n. to be twisted, distorted, pf. འཆུས. 2. sbst. curvature, crookedness, distortion. 3. adj. as འཆུས་པ crooked; ཁ་འཆུས the mouth distorted.

འཆུ་བ II: pf. བཅུས, fut. བཅུ, imp. ཆུས 1. to scoop up or ladle water; ཆུ་མིག་ལ་ཆུ་འཆུ་བ to draw water from a spring; ཆུ་ཟོམ water-bucket. 2. to irrigate, to water.

འཆུག ḫchug said to = ཕྱིན་ནས་སླེབས་པ་ལ phyin-nas slebs-pa la having reached; arrived at (Yig.).

འཆུག་མེད ḫchug-med = ནོར་འཁྲུལ་མེད་པ nor-ḫkhrul med-pa without mistake (Rtsii.); འཆུག་མེད་དགོས་རྒྱུ sure necessaries; unmistakeable wants.

འཆུན ḫchun or འཆུན་པ under one's control, hence. 1. to be tamed, subdued, made to yield; སྟོབས་ཀྱིས་འཆུན retained by force; ལས་ཀྱིས་འཆུན་པ subdued or overpowered by hard work; འཆལ་སར་འཆུན entangled in vicious indulgences (Sch.).

འཆུམ་པ ḫchum-pa 1. to wish, to long for. 2. sbst. = སེར་སྣ ser-sna covetousness (Mṅon.).

འཆུས་པ ḫchus-pa = གྱོག་པོ gyog-po कदर्य awkward, acc. to Sch. also left-handed; acc. to Cs. curved, crooked.

འཆེ་བ ḫche-wa (pf. བཅེས, fut. བཅེ, imp. ཆེས) to attest, to promise ཁས་འཆེ་བ resp. ཞལ་གྱིས་འཆེ་བ id.

འཆེག་པ I: ḫcheg-pa related to འཆགས་པ (pf. བཤགས, fut. བཤག, imp. ཤོག çog) 1. to cut in twain, cleave, split; ཤིང་འཆེག་པ to split wood; སོག་ལེས་འཆེག་པ to cut with a saw (Cs.). 2. to confess, to acknowledge (Jä.). 3. to be afraid of.

+ **འཆེམས་པ** ḫchems-pa pf. བཅེམས, fut. བཅེམ to chew (Med.; Jä.).

འཆེར་པ ḫcher-pa (ནང་གྲོལ) यकृत the spleen.

+ **འཆེལ་བ** ḫchel-wa or འཆེལ་བ = ཉེན་པ or འདོད་པ सक्त desire, wish; acc. to Jä. and Cs. to believe, to give credence to.

འཆེས་པ *hches-pa* sometimes spelt as མཆེས་པ happy advent.

འཆོག་པ *hchog-pa* हन्यते to smite; acc. to *Sch.* a wall.

འཆོག་ཐོག *hchog-thog* the sound of a falling article or thing.

འཆོང་བ *hchoṅ-wa* or འཆོངས་པ=འཛང་བ पालन, धारण to be holding, keep fast.

+ འཆོབས་ཤིག *hchobs-çig*=གསོངས་ཤིག made secret.

འཆོམས་པ *hchoms-pa*=འཛམས་པ vb. n. to འཛོམས་པ.

+ འཆོར་ཉན *hchor-ñan*=ཤོར་ཉན, རང་རེས་ཛ་ཅིགས་ལས་ནོན་འཆོར་ཉན་འདུག (*Rdsa.*).

འཆོར་པོ *hchor-po* occasionally for མཆོར་པོ.

འཆོར་བ *hchor-wa* I: vb. n. pf. ཤོར 1. to escape, flee or steal away; also to flow out, ooze; ཚ་ཁྲག་འཆོར་བ the blood exuding; བཀྲག་འཆོར without splendour, lustreless; ནོར་འཆོར the money has fled; སྡོམ་འཆོར the vow is dissipated; མེ་ལ་འཆོར་བ to be consumed by fire; ཆུ་ལ་འཆོར་བ to be carried away by water. 2. to come out, to break forth, frq. of fire; འཁྲུག་པ་ཤོར *hkhrug-pa-çor* a quarrel, a war broke out, also of water breaking through an embankment. 3. to go over, to pass, be transferred.

འཆོར་བ II: vb. a., pf. བཤོར, fut. གཤོར, to pursue, chase, go after; རི་བོང་རྒྱས hares by means of nets; ཉ་འཆོར་བ to fish; འཆོར་སྣིག a seducer; a swaggerer (*Sch.*).

འཆོལ་བ *hchol-wa* I: 1. adj. topsy-turvy, upside-down. 2. to mistake or deviate from an order; འཆོལ་བར་བྱེད་པ to put into disorder, to confuse, to confound. 3. pf. བཅོལ to entrust, lay upon, to commit a thing to another's charge; to make, appoint; དེ་ལ་རྒྱལ་པོ་འཆོལ་ལོ they appointed him king; བཙུན་མོ་ལ་རྟ་རྫི་བཅོལ་ལོ they made the queen tend the horses; ཐབ་གཡོག་འཆོལ་ཤིག he may be employed as a scullion; དབང་མེད་དུ་འཆོལ་བ to make one powerless, to compel authority; བཅོལ་བའི་གཉེར manager. ལས་འཆོལ་བ or (resp. ཕྲིན་ལས འཆོལ་བ) to commission one with an affair or transaction; བང་སོ་ཡུལ་དེའི་ལྷ་སྲུང་རྣམས་ལ་ཕྲིན་བཅོལ་མཛད་དོ། *ban-so yul dehi lha-sruñ rnams-la phrin-bcol mdsad-do* he entrusted the sepulchre to the tutolary gods of the country. 4. to be thrown together confusedly, e.g., of the loose leaves of a book: དགེ་སྡིག་འཆོལ་བར་འགྱུ virtue and vice are intermixed. 5. to rave, to be delirious, to talk confusedly whilst heavy with sleep (*Jä.*).

འཆོལ་མ *hchol-ma*, acc. to *Cs.* 1. a thing committed to another's care. 2. a sly, crafty woman. 3. acc. to *Sch.* a dissolute woman (*Jä.*).

+ **འཆོས་པ** I: *hchos-pa*=བཅོས་པ: 1. pf. བཅོས or འཆོས, fut. བཅོ, imp. ཆོས, supine བཅོས་སུ, to make, make ready, prepare; to construct, build, etc.: འཆོས་སམ am I to build? དྲེས་མ་ཐག་པར་འཆོས་པ to make ropes out of *dres-ma* grass, prop. to make ropes out of it. གཟབ་འཆོས་པ to dress, to train one's self up (*Sch.*); གསར་དུ་འཆོས་པ to renew, renovate, repair (*Sch.*); ཟུང་བ་ཕྱིར་འཆོས་པ to retouch, amend, correct, improve. ཚུལ་འཆོས hypocrisy, a mere outward performance of religious rites and observances: ཚུལ་འཆོས་མ་བྱས་སྤྱོད་པ *tshul-hchos ma-byas spyod-pa* to live without hypocrisy. ཚུལ་འཆོས་མཁན hypocrite. ཚུལ་འཆོས་པ or བཅོས་པ acc. to *Cs.* an established rule or canon (*Jä.*).

འཚོས་པ II: *htshos-pa* 1. adj. disorderly, dissolute, immoral. 2. sbst. disorderly conduct, dissoluteness: འཆོལ་པ་སྣ་ཚོགས་སྤྱད་པ committing various acts of immorality.

ཇ

ཇ *ja* I: this the seventh letter of the Tibetan alphabet, according to the grammarians of Tibet, was not borrowed from India, its equivalent being unknown in any of the Indian languages of the seventh century, A. D., when the Tibetan written language was shaped by Thon-mi Sambhoṭa. In sound it corresponds with the English J, but as an initial it is pronounced in *C.* as Jh. However when it is surmounted by any letter or has a prefix preceeding it, as in the words རྗེ *rje* and མཇལ *mjal,* it then resumes the sound of a pure J.

ཇ II: 1. tea; word derived from the Chinese *ca*, signifying tea. The resp. form for *ja* is གསོལ་ཇ *gsol-ja.*

ཇ་ཀོ *ja-ko* a hide bag for packing tea (*Rtsii.*).

ཇ་དཀྲུག *ja-dkrug* a twirling stick, the tea churning-piston.

ཇ་ཁ *ja-kha* of the colour of tea; n. of a Chinese scarf of brick-red colour.

ཇ་ཁུག *ja-khug* a vessel or bag in which tea is kept.

ཇ་ཁྲ *ja-khra* a large tea-pot made of copper, silver, &c., for serving tea to the congregation of monks at a religious service.

ཇ་རྒྱབ *ja-rgyab* lit. "after tea." In Tibet and Sikkim table-talk commences after tea has been served.

ཇ་མཆོད *ja-mchod* libation of tea.

ཇ་འཐག *ja-hthag* or ཇ་བཏག *ja-btag* tea-grinder (in Tibet powdered tea is put in boiled water); grinding stone, used for kitchen purposes.

ཇ་དཔོན *ja-dpon* one who is in charge of tea-drinking meetings; head tea-cook.

ཇ་ཕུད *ja-phud* the first preparation of tea which is sometimes offered to the gods; first quality of tea.

ཇ་འབིང་ *ja-hbiñ* tea-pot, tea-kettle. This word, sounded *cham-bing*, is the common term used in *C.*

ཇ་སྦྱོར *ja-sbyor* a mixture of tea with butter and salt (*Rtsii.*).

ཇ་མ *ja-ma* tea-maker, tea-cook, a cook who prepares tea and gruel, &c. (*Rtsii.*).

ཇ་ཚགས *ja-tshags* a sieve to strain tea (*Rtsii.*).

ཇ་ཡཱ་ཇུ *Ja-yā-ju* n. of a kind of tea (*Rtsii.*). ཇ་ཡུ *Ja-yu* another kind of tea (*Rtsii.*).

ཇ་རིལ *ja-ril* in *W.* acc. to *Jä.* grinding-stone; also a skull.

ཇ་ལག་གཉིས *ja-lag-gñis* an abbr. of ཇ་མ and ལག་བདེ, *i.e.*, one who prepares tea and another who serves it (*Rtsii.*).

ཇ་ལུང་ *ja-luñ* the handle straps of a leathern-trunk.

ཇ་ཤིང་ *ja-çiñ* tea plant. In Tibet the tea-plant is styled རྒྱ་ནད་སེལ་ཤིང་, *i.e.*, the plant which cures Indian or Chinese diseases, as being an antidote against malarial fever.

ཇ་སང་ *ja-sañ* plain decoction of tea: ཇ་སང་བཅས་པའི་ཆས་སྐྱོབ get plain tea with its accessories! (*Rtsii.*).

ཇ་སིགས་ *ja-sigs* used in ཇོ་བོ་ཇ་སིགས་ཇི་སྙེད་དང་ *Jo-ḅo ja-sigs ji-s̤ñed-dań* (*J. Zań.*).

ཇ་སུན་ *ja-sun* time when tea is served.

ཇ་སུན་ཅན་ *ja-sun-can* acc. to *Sch.* a cup of tea; as much as a cup of tea.

ཇ་སེར་ *ja-ser* yellow tea exported from Amdo into Eastern Tibet.

卐 ཇ་ཧོང་ *ja-hoń*=བཙོད་མདོག *ḅcod-mdog* or དམར་སེར་ *dmar-ser* मञ्जिष्ठा yellowish-red, acc. to *Jä.* ཇ་ཧོད་ *ja-ḥod* is yellow-red.

ཇག *jag* चौर robbing, robbery; ཇག་རྒྱག་པ *jag rgyag-pa* to commit robbery.

ཇག་པ *jag-pa* डमर one who terrifies by shouts and gestures; a robber. མི་སེར་ཇག་པའི་གྲིམ་ས་ཡིན it is a lurking place of husbandmen who rob, or who are robbers (*Mil.*). In this passage ཇག་པ might be almost a verb "to rob."

ཇག་དཔོན *jag-dpon* captain of a gang of robbers; a brigand chief.

ཇལ *Jal* n. of a place in Tibet; ཇལ་གྱི་ཕུ *Jal-gyi-phu* the uplands of *Jal* (*Deb.* ག *41*).

ཇི *ji* I: 1. num. fig 37. 2. the correlative form of the pron. ཅི *ci* what.

ཇི II: is used in expressions illustrating examples, comparison, measurement, dimensions, also extent of time. ཇི and ཅི are of same signification; but Tibetan grammarians discriminate their use as follows:—དཔེ་དང་ཚད་གཞལ་བ་ལ་ཇི་སྦྱོར། དངོས་ལ་ཅི་སྦྱོར། in making comparisons and measurement use *ji*, in the case of direct significations use *ci*.

ཇི་སྐད་ *ji-skad* यथोक्त, यथाज्ञ what, whatever, relative to words spoken: ངས་ཇི་སྐད་སྨྲས་ཀྱང་ whatever I may have said; ཇི་སྐད་སྨྲས་པ་བཞིན་དུ་བྱེད་པ यथा वादी तथा कारी doing in accordance with what one has said.

卐 ཇི་ག *ji-ga*=བརྟག་པ when examined or searched into: ཇི་ག་སྐྱེས་བུ་དེ་ངོ་མཚར་བྱེད་པ་ཡིན་ནམ *ji-ga s̤kyes-bu de ño-mtshar byed-pa yin-nam* (*K. d.* ཅ *4*) if looked into, is not that person really wonderful?

ཇི་སྙམ་པ *ji-s̤ñam-pa* equal to what?

ཇི་སྙེད *ji-s̤ñed*,=ཇི་ཙམ तावत्, यावत्, कियत्: 1. as much as; as great as. 2. whatever is or may be possible. 3. just about (so much).

ཇི་ཡོད or གང་ཡོད what is, or as much as is (*Dag. 8*).

ཇི་ལྟ *ji-lta* or ཇི་ལྟ་བ 1. यथा, यादृक्, कथं how, of what kind, of what nature. 2. sbst. quality, nature, condition (*Cs.*); ཇི་ལྟ=དེ་ནས अथ then.

ཇི་ལྟར *ji-ltar*, यथा adv. as, in what manner; ཁོས་ཇི་ལྟར་ཟེར་བ་བཞིན་དུ acc. to what he has said; ཇི་ལྟ་ཇི་ལྟར in as much as, in the measure of. ཇི་ལྟ་ཇི་ལྟར་ཆོག་ཤེས་པ in the proportion as one shall be contented. ཇི་ལྟ་བུ *ji-lta-bu* such as, like as. ཇི་ལྟར་དེ *ji-ltar de* यथैव=ཇི་ལྟར་ཡིན་པ་དེ་ལྟར; ཇི་ལྟར་དྲངས कथं नीयते how to be taken? བླ་མ་ལ་གསོལ་བ་ཇི་ལྟར་དྲངས་དགོས in what manner should I convey requests to the lama? ཇི་ལྟར་འབྱོར་པ *ji-ltar ḥbyor-pa* यथायोग acc. to the measure of one's means or attainments. ཇི་ལྟར་ཡང, *ji-ltar yań*=དཔེར་ན तद्यथा for example, thus.

ཇི་སྟེ *ji-s̤te* is said to=ཅི་སྟ་དེ་ནས *ci-s̤ta de-nas* अथ so and so. It also is a conjunction meaning but if, nevertheless.

ཇི་ནས *ji-nas*=ཅི་ནས་ཇི་ལྟ་བ or ཇི་ལྟར *ji-ltar* also འདི་ནས as for instance; henceforth.

ཇི་ནུས་ཀྱིས *ji-nus-kyis*=ཅི་ནུས་ཀྱིས as much as possible; to the utmost, to the best of one's ability, as far as it lies in one's power.

ཇི་མ་རུང་ *ji-ma-ruń*=ཅི་མ་རུང་ཨེ་མ exclamatory phrase akin to ཨ་ལ, ཀྱི་མ or ཀྱི་ཧུད बत, alas!

ཇི་ཙུག *ji-tsug*=གང་འདྲ how, like what? in what manner? སྐྱབས་གནས་ཐུགས་རྗེ་ཅན་རྣམས་ཅི་ཙུག་ལ་སོང་ (*A. 128*) "how the merciful ones, the refuge (of the helpless), have passed away!

ཇི་ཙམ *ji-tsam* कियत् how much? ཇི་ཙམ་ནས as soon as, when; ཇི་ཙམ་ཐུང་ how many have been got?

ཇི་ཤིག *ji-shig* कदाचित्; ཅི་ཤིག, ཇི་ཤིག་ཙམ་ཕྱིར कदाचिदेव seldom.

ཇི་བཞིན *ji-bshin* how, like what?

ཇི་བཞིན་དུ *ji-bshin-du* accordingly.

+ ཇི་འོས *ji-hos*=འཚམས་པ 1. in accordance with, conformity with. 2. གང་འོས་པ whatever is fit, is becoming (*Dag. 8*).

ཇི་སྲིད *ji-srid* यावत् as long as; ཇི་སྲིད་འཚོ་བའི་བར་དུ यावज्जीवन all the life long; as long as one lives.

ཛིང་ *jiñ* the Chinese term for Buddhism which in Tibetan is ཆོས, in Sanskrt धर्म्म.

ཛུ *ju* num. fig. 67.

ཛུ་ཐིག *ju-thig* denotes a drawing of lots by threads of different colours, whence a class of Bon-po is called ཇུ་བོན་ཇུ་ཐིག་ཅན (*Jä.*).

ཛུ་པོ *ju-po* a globular stone used for grinding spices=ཛ་རིལ (*Jä.*); acc. to *Mñon.* ཛུ་པོ=གཏུན, a pestle.

ཛུ་རུ་ཛ *ju-ru-ja* a kind of tea (*Rtsii.*).

ཛུ་ཤེས *ju-ços* a kind of satin.

ཛུན་ཝང་ *Jun-wañ* n. of a celebrated Tibetan chief under whose orders the sacred series of works called Kahgyur and Tangyur were engraved on wooden blocks at Lhasa (*Loñ.* ༢, *17*).

ཛུབ་ཕབ *jub-phab* a kind of tea (*Rtsii.*).

ཇུས *jus* strategy (*Jä.*).

ཇུས་མཁས་པོ *jus mkhas-po*=ཐབས་མཁས་པ one skilful in means, one full of resources.

ཇུས་ལེགས I: *jus-legs*=ཇུས་ལེགས ཆ་ཧེ་ཏུ one who has conquered his enemies; a Buddhist saint of the *Hīnayāna* School.

Syn. འཐབ་རྩོད་རྒྱལ *hthab-rtsod-rgyal*; གཡུལ་ལེགས་པ *gyul-legs-pa*; དགྲ་བཅོམ་པ *dgra-bcom-pa*; དགྲ་ལས་རྒྱལ *dgra-las-rgyal* (*Mñon.*).

ཇུས་ལེགས II: 1. acc. to *Sch.* possessed of good manners, of propriety of conduct; decent, agreeable; ཇུས་བདེ sincere. 2. acc. to *Cs.* clever, skilled, able, experienced; ཞིང་གི་ལས་ལ་ཇུས་བདེ skilful in agriculture; དམག་ལ ཇུས་ལེགས་པ dextrous in military matters.

ཇུས་མ *jus-ma* a sort of silk stuff (*Cs.*).

ཇེ *je* 1. num. fig. 97. 2. a particle, used for expressing the comparative degree of an adj. or adv., and esp. a gradual growing or increase, often with termin. case or ལ; ཇེ་ཆེ་ཇེ་ཆེ=ཆེ་རུ་ཆེ་རུ grew larger and larger: ཆུ་ཕྲན་མང་པོ་ཇེ་ཆེ་ཇེ་ཆེ་ལ་རྒྱས་ནས་སོང་། many streamlets increased in size becoming larger and larger (*Behu. 50*). ཇེ་མང་འགྲོ (they) go on increasing in number; ཇེ་གསལ་དུ་སོང་ it has become more evident; ཇེ་ཉེ་ཇེ་ཉེ་སོང་སྟེ going nearer and nearer; ཇེ་མཐོ་ཇེ་མཐོ higher and higher; ཇེ་བཟང་ཇེ་བཟང་དུ་འགྲོ་བ to grow better and better. 3. progress: ཆོས་ཀྱི་འདུན་ས་འདིར་ཇེ་ཅི་ཞིག་མཐོང་ (*Surañ. 5*) whatever progress you observe in the advance of the doctrine in this place (association). 4. acc. to *Lex.* དབྱངས sound, voice (*Jä.*). 5. acc. to *Schtr.* a hortative particle, often connected with a vocative.

ཇེ་ཁ *je-kha* a deed.

ཇེ་ཁྱོད *je-khyod* acc. to *Sch.* now you, you first.

ཇེ་དང་པོ *je-dañ-po* the very first. ཇེ་སྲ=སྲ་རུ་སྲ་རུ thinner and thinner or finer and finer.

ཇེ་དབུལ་བ *jc-dbul-wa* = ཉམ་ཐུང་དུ་འགྲོ་བ to grow poorer, become more and more destitute.

ཇེ་ཞིག *je-shig* = རེ་ཞིག a little while, sometime.

ཇེ་རིང་ *je-riñ* = རིང་དུ་འགྲོ་བ growing longer and longer.

ཇེང་ *jeñ* = 1. དང་པོ *dañ-po* or རེ་ཞིག प्रथम, आदि the first or earliest. 2. སྒྲ, घोष sound, voice.

ཇོ *jo* 1. num. fig. 127 = ཇོ་བོ or ཇོ་མོ.

ཇོ་ཇོ *jo-jo* अग्रजभ्राता elder brother (*Dag. 8*); = ཨ་ཇོ in *C.* and ཨ་ཙུ in Sikk.

Syn. ཕུ་བོ *phu-bo*, སྔོན་སྐྱེས *sñon-skyes*, ཐོབ་མ་སྐྱེས *thob-ma skyes*, ངེས་འཛིན *ñes-hdsin*, ཐུ་བོ *thu-bo*, གཅེན་པོ *gcen-po* (*Mñon.*).

ཇོ་གདན *jo-gdan* = ཇོ་ནང་གི་གདན་ས the seat or head-quarters of the Jo-nang-pa sect of Buddhism in Tibet.

ཇོ་ནང་ *Jo-nañ* or ཇོ་མོ་ནང་ n. of a place with a lofty *Chorten* and a convent situated about 100 miles to the N.W. of Tashilhunpo; the place where *Phyogs-las Rnam-rgyal* the founder of the Jonang-pa sect was born, and whence the name Jonang-pa was derived.

ཇོ་བོ *jo-wo* प्रभु, स्वामी, आर्य; ཇེ་ཙུ also ཇེ་རིགས lord, master, noble, venerable; also one of the nobility.

Syn. གཙོ་བོ *gtso-wo*; མགོན་པོ *mgon-po*; མགོན་འདྲེན *mgon-hdren* (*Mñon.*).

ཇོ་བོ་ཇ་མ་ལི *Jo-wo Ja-ma-li* n. of an image of Buddha in Yambu the ancient capital of Nepal.

ཇོ་བོ་རྗེ *Jo-wo rje* (lit. the noble lord) the Tibetan title of Atis'a.

ཇོ་བོ་ཕྱིང་དཀར་བ *Jo-wo phyiñ dkar-wa* n. of a demi-god (*Rtsii*).

* ཇོ་བོའི་ལུགས་ཀྱི་རྟ་མགྲིན *Jo-wohi lugs-kyi rta-mgrin* (*56c*) the deity Hayagriwa acc. to the system of *Jo-wo*.

ཇོ་མོ *jo-mo* 1. आर्या the female head of a household, a woman that governs as mistress of her own servants. 2. a cloistress, nun.

ཇོ་མོ་ཁ་ནག *Jo-mo kha-nag* snowy mountain in S. Tibet towards Bhotan.

ཇོ་མོ་གངས་དཀར *Jo-mo gañs-dkar* lit. the lady of the white snows, a Tibetan name for Mount Everest.

ཇོ་མོ་ལྷ་རི *Jo-mo lha-ri* the snowy mountain between Tibet and Bhotan ordinarily called Chumalari.

ཇོ་རྩི *jo-rtsi* varnish for wooden furniture.

ཇོ་རྩི་གསེར་ཤོག *jo-rtsi gser-çog* lustrous gold-leaf for painting purposes.

ཇོ་རྫོང་ *Jo-rdsoñ* or ཇོ་མོ་རྫོང་ *Jo-mo rdsoñ* n. of a fort and district in Tibet (*Rtsii.*).

* ཇོ་ལུགས་སྒྲོལ་དཀར *Jo-lugs sgrol-dkar* (*2A.*)

མཇལ་བ *mjal-wa* resp. for འཕྲད་པ समागम; imp. མཇོལ *mjol* 1. to meet; to interview, obtain access to an honoured person, to wait on, to pay one's respects to a person: ཡབ་དང་མཇལ་འཚལ་བོ I will pay a visit to my father; ཕྱིས་མྱུར་དུ་མཇལ་དུ་ཡོང་ *phyis myur-du mjal-du yoñ* I shall take the liberty of soon coming back; མཇལ་བར་ཞུ་བ to ask for an audience; མཇལ་དུ་མི་བཏུབ cannot get in, cannot obtain admittance; མཇལ་ཕྲད་དང་དགའ་བའི་གཏམ་མང་པོ་མཛད they exchanged many compliments and expressions of joy; གནས་མཇལ་བ to visit a sanctuary or a holy place; to go on a pilgrimage; གནས་མཇལ་པ a pilgrim. 2. གོ་བའི་མཇལ་བ *go-wahi mjal-wa* ज्ञा to understand, comprehend; དོན་མཇལ་བ to understand the meaning.

མཇལ་ཁ *mjal-kha* audience, access to a great man's presence, admittance; མཇལ་ཁ་གཏོང་བ or གནང་བ to give audience, grant interview; མཇལ་ཐུད་བྱེད་པ to have an interview with; to meet.

མཇལ་རྟེན *mjal-rten* a present made at an interview with a great man.

མཇལ་དར *mjal-dar* the scarf that is presented on the occasion of an interview.

མཇལ་སྣ་པ *mjal-sna-pa* an introducer, master of ceremonies (*Cs.*).

མཇལ་ཕྱག *mjal-phyag* salutation.

མཇལ་མང་ *mjal-mañ* a visit paid by many together, a grand reception (*Cs.*).

མཇལ་ཞུ *mjal-shu* a prayer made on the occasion of an interview or meeting.

མཇིང་པ *mjiñ-pa* = འཇིང་པ 1. कृकाटक the neck (*Dag. 8*). 2. = རྩ་མཇིང་ meadow (*Schtr.*).

མཇིང་བསྣོལ *mjiñ-bsnol* explained as སྐྱེའམ་མགྲིན་པ་ཕན་ཚུན་བསྣོལ་བ་ གཅིག་གིས་གཅིག་ལ་སོས་བྲུགས་ པ་ལྟ་བུ among birds or animals, for instance one hugging or embracing the neck of another to pick or tickle each other with the teeth; ཟུར་བཞིར་རྨ་བྱ་མཇིང་བསྣོལ་མཛེས་པར་བྱིས let the four corners be made beauteous with peacocks crossing each other's necks (*A. 4*).

མཇིངས་ཟབ *mjiñs-zab*, v. ཀློང་ཟབ *klon-zab*.

མཇུག *mjug* the back, the tail; what is behind, the hinder part, of anything, resp. སྐུ་མཇུག posteriors, backside, tail (*Dag. 8*). མཇུག་སྒོར་བ colloq. to turn one's back (on another). With regard to time = the end: ཟླ་བ་བརྒྱད་པའི་མཇུག་ལ at the end of the eighth month; མཇུག་ལ or མཇུག་ཏུ as adv. and postp. are colloquially in common use to signify: at the end of, at last, behind, after, with genit. of the verbal root; also ཡང་གི་མཇུག་མ = the last, the last one.

མཇུག་སྒྲོ *mjug-sgro* lower or inferior part, underpart, buttocks; tail-feather (*Sñiñ.*).

མཇུག་སྒྲོ་ཅན *mjug sgro-can* = རྨ་བྱ कलापी peacock.

མཇུག་བསྔོ་བ *mjug bsño-wa* to make a prayer after having done some act of merit.

མཇུག་བསྔོས *mjug-bsños* (མཐར་ཕྱིན་པ་བསྙད *mthar phyin-pa hsñad*) निगम्य gone to the extremity; attaining thoroughness in any subject.

མཇུག་དོ *mjug-do* the bone of the tail: ལུག་གི་མཇུག་དོས་མཁལ་རྐེད་རླུང་ནད་སེལ (*Sman.*) the sheep's tail-end cures kidney, pains in the waist and disease caused by རླུང་ *rluñ*.

མཇུག་རྡུམ *mjug-rdum* = མཇུག་མ་ཆད་པ with short tail, tail cut off; an ill-conditioned improvident person who at the end disappoints or behaves ungratefully.

མཇུག་ཕོད་ཅན *mjug-phod-can* = དུ་བ་མཇུག་རིང་ केतु a comet (*Mñon.*).

མཇུག་མ *mjug-ma* or འཇུག་མ *hjug-ma* लाङ्गूल, पुच्छ, ललामन् the tail, the posterior that hangs down; མཇུག་མ་སྒྲིལ་བ *mjug-ma sgril-wa* to wag the tail; fig. the further progress and final issue of an affair; the consequences; ཡང་གི་མཇུག་མ the last.

Syn. རྔ་མ *rña-ma*; ཤུ་གུ *shu-gu* (*Mñon.*).

* མཇུག་རིངས *mjug-riñs* or དུ་བ་མཇུག་རིངས *Du-wa mjug-riñs* केतु comet (*Kālac. T, 49*).

མཇུག་རིང་ केतु one of the nine planets of Hindu Astronomy.

མཇེ *mje* लिङ्ग, पुंलिङ्ग the penis (*Dag. 8*); in the Tantras it is called གསང་བའི་རྡོ་རྗེ; མཇེ་ལངས་པ or དབང་པོ་ལས་སུ་རུང་བ erection of the penis; མཇེ་མགོ the glans penis; མཇེ་རླིག *mje-rlig* the penis and the testicles. མཇེ་ཤུབས the membraneous covering or the sheath of the penis (*Jä.*).

Syn. ཕོ་རྟགས *pho-rtags*; ཕོ་དབང་ *pho-dwaṅ* (*Mṅon.*).

མཛེད་པ *mjed-pa* सह suffering, enduring, bearing patiently; acc. to *Cs.* obnoxious; མི་མཛེད prop. free; gen. acc. to Buddhist ideas the world, the universe.

འཇག་པ *hjag-pa* pf. ཇགས *jags* (*Cs.*); acc. to *Sch.* to establish, settle, fix, found; hence prob. བདེ་འཇགས and ཁྲིམས་འཇགས *khris-hjags*, འཇགས་ཁྲིམས prob. འཇགས་རིང་ time of prosperity, of peace, of rest; a time without disturbances, war, epidemic, etc. (*Jä.*).

འཇག་སྐྱ *hjag-skya*, v. འཇག་མ.

འཇག་གདན *hjag-gdan* a seat made of the grass called འཇག་མ; a cotton-rug with its edges turned up with red cloth.

འཇག་མ *hjag-ma* वीरण 1. a fragrant grass, *Andropogon muricatus.* 2. acc. to *Sch.* a coarse and thick grass of inferior quality used in roofing huts. 3. a blade (of grass); stalk (of corn); འཇག་མ་རེའི་སྟེང་ན on every blade of grass; ཀུ་ཤའི་འཇག་མ་ཐོན་ཅིག a bundle of blades of *Kuça* grass. འཇག་ཚོད acc. to *Sch.* horse-tail, pewter grass, *Equisetum* (*Jä.*). འཇག་མའི་རྩ also called འཇག་རྩ वीरण मूल the roots of this grass. In Tsang འཇག་མ is called ཁྱིམ, འཇག་མ being colloq. a word of *C.*; in Tsang we hear ས་ཞིང་ཕྲུ་རློག་བྱེད་རྒྱུའི་ཁྱིམ *sa-shiṅ phru-rlog byed-rgyuhi khyem* a shovel with which soil is overturned (*Rtsii.*).

འཇགས *hjags* v. under འཇག་པ 1.=བཞག as ཐུགས་འཇགས=སེམས་འཇགས remember, keep in mind: རིང་མིན་ངོས་མཇལ་ཐུབ་ཅིག་པ་ཐུགས་མཚོར་འཇགས་པར་མཛོད pray bear in the ocean of your mind that we may meet before long (*Yig. k.* 26). 2. clay or mud (*Dag.* 8).

འཇགས་པ *hjags-pa* in *C.* to give, to make a present, to formally present (*Georgi's Alphabetum Tibetanum*).

འཇགས་རིང་ *hjags-riṅ*=བདེ་བའི་ཡུན་རིང་ the time of happiness or prosperity.

འཇང *Hjaṅ* place in N. W. Tibet which once formed the kingdom of *Hjaṅ* (*J. Zaṅ.*).

འཇང་གི་རྒྱང་མཁར *Hjaṅ-gyi rgyaṅ-mkhar* one of the thirty-seven holy places of the Bon (*G. Bon.* 38).

འཇང་བ *hjaṅ-wa* to devour, swallow (*Sch.*).

འཇང་ཚ་ལྷ་དབང་ *Hjaṅ-tsha Lha-dwaṅ* the son of king ཁྲི་ལྡེ་གཙུག་བརྟན *Khri lde-gtsug-brtan* betrothed to the sister of the Emperor *Jūṅ*, *Jūṅ* the fifth of the *Tang* dynasty. He died before his would-be spouse could reach Tibet. His father, however, married her as she would not go back to China without becoming a queen.

འཇང་སོ *hjaṅ-so*=ས་མཚམས *sa-mtshams.*

འཇངས་ཤབས *Hjaṅs-shabs* n. of a place in Kham (*Loṅ.* ཇ, 12).

འཇངས་ས་ཐམ *Hjaṅs-sa-tham* n. of a place in Kham (*Loṅ.* ཇ, 12).

卐 འཇན་པོ *hjan-po* a consort; properly འཇན་པོ=husband, and འཇན་མོ=wife.

འཇབ་གདན *hjab-gdan* a soft rug made of wool (*Rtsii.*).

འཇབ་པ *hjab-pa* pf. prob. བཇབས fut., བཇབ, to sneak, slink, creep privily; to lie in wait, in ambush; ཚེ་ལ་འཇབ་པ to make an attempt on a person's life.

འཇབ་བུ་བ *hjab-bu-wa*=རྐུན་པོ *rkun-po* or རྐུན་མ *rkun-ma* (*Mṅon.*) a thief; འཇབ་བུས་མ་བྱིན་པར་ལེན་པ to steal clandestinely.

འཇབ་ཙེ *hjab-tse* a pair of scissors, nippers, teezers.

འཇབ་ཙེ་ཁ *hjab-tse-kha* a kind of rug made of སྡེར་མ *sder-ma* (*Jig.*).

འཇམ་པ *hjam-pa* कोमल, मृदु, मन्द tender, soft, lovely, charming.

Syn. མཉེན་པ *mñen-pa*; འབོལ་བ *hbol-wa* (*Mñon.*).

འཇམ་གླས *hjam-klas* प्रसर, ऋजु straight.

འཇམ་མགོན *Hjam-mgon* मञ्जुनाथ; v. འཇམ་དཔལ.

འཇམ་མགོན་ཆོས་ཀྱི་རྒྱལ་པོ *Hjam-mgon chos-kyi rgyal-po* the complimentary title by which Tsong-khapa is addressed in Tibet: འཇམ་མགོན་ཆོས་ཀྱི་རྒྱལ་པོའི་ཞབས་རྡེན་པད་མོའི་དྲུང་དུ། to the lotus feet of the king of the Doctrine, Jam-pal.

འཇམ་མགོན་བསྟན་པའི་སྲོག་ཤིང *Hjam-mgon bstan-pahi srog-çiñ* Jam-gon the life-tree of the Doctrine.

འཇམ་མགོན་བླ་མ *hjam-mgoa bla-ma* an address of politeness to the hierarchs of the S'akya school.

འཇམ་ཇུས *hjam-jus*=རྐྱང་ཇུས a *rkyañ-jus* a kind of silk scarf or satin.

འཇམ་འཇམ *hjam-hjam* polite words: ངན་པ་ཐ་འང་ཚིག་འཇམ་འཇམ་གྱི་སྣན་འདེབས "polite language should be used even towards the meanest person." Also. in *C.* softly, gently.

འཇམ་ལྗང་འདབ་ལྡན *hjam-ljañ hdab-ldan* a parrot or the bird with light green plumage (*Mñon.*).

འཇམ་གཉེན་མ *hjam gñen-ma* a woman of fascinating speech.

འཇམ་ཐབས *hjam-thabs* gentle means, milder measures.

འཇམ་པའི་རྡོ་རྗེ *Hjam-pahi rdo-rje* मञ्जुवज्र n. of a deity; a *Bodhisattva.*

* འཇམ་པའི་དབྱངས *Hjam-pahi-dbyañs* मञ्जुघोष, མཻ་ཏྲི *Maitri* རྡོ་བརྩོན (*Org. m. 113, 35*).

འཇམ་པའི་རིགས *hjam-pahi rigs* मन्दजातीय humbler classes (opp. to རྩུབ་པ *rtsub-pa*), soft, tender, smooth, mild, *e.g.*, of cloth, hair; a meadow, a plain without stones or rocks, of fruit, the air, the character of a person, a person's way of speaking.

འཇམ་པོ *hjam-po* 1. soft, gentle, not rough or cross; གྱོང་པོ་མ་ཡིན་པ *gyoñ-po-ma yin-pa* not stiff. 2. मृदुत्व, फत्करीकं mild; alum.

འཇམ་པོས་ལེན *hjam-pos-len* to draw out information or any secret from another by using fascinating or smooth language.

འཇམ་པོར་སྨྲ *hjam-por-smra* speak softly, gently.

འཇམ་དཔལ *Hjam-dpal* मञ्जुश्री n. of the third *Dhyani Bodhisattva,* who is regarded as the deputy of the third Dhyani Buddha, Dzin-sten Jung-do. Is popular throughout Nepal and Tibet. His several names are:—འཇམ་དབྱངས मञ्जुघोष the soft-voiced; ཤེས་རབ་ཀྱི་ལྷ *Çes-rab-kyi-lha* the god of wisdom; བརྟན་པའི་འཁོར་ལོ *Brtan-pahi hkhor-lo*; རལ་གྲི་ཅན *Ral-gri-can*; ཟུར་ཕུད་ལྔ་པ *Zur-phud lña-pa*; བློ་ཡི་གཏེར *Blo-yi-gter*; ངག་གི་དབང་ཕྱུག *Ñag-gi dwañ-phy-ug*; སེང་གེ་རྩེན *Señ-ge-rtsen*; སྨྲ་བའི་རྒྱལ་པོ *Smra-wahi rgyal-po*; སྨྲ་བའི་ལྷ *Smra-wahi-lha*; ཡེ་ཤེས་མེ་ལོང *Ye-çes meloñ*; ཡེ་ཤེས་སྐུ *Ye-çes-sku*; ཤེས་རབ་འཁོར་ལོ *Çes-rab hkhor-lo*; ཤེས་རབ་སྐུ *Çes-rab-sku*; རྡོ་རྗེ་རྣོན་པོ *Rdo-rje rnon-po*; ངག་གི་རྒྱལ་པོ *Ñag-gi rgyal-po* (*Mñon.*).

འཇམ་དཔལ་གནས་པ मञ्जुश्रीविहार the residence or sphere in the heavens of Jam-pal.

* འཇམ་དཔལ་གྲགས *Hjam-dpal-grags* मञ्जुश्रीकीर्त्ति (*Bull. 1848, 295*).

འཇམ་དཔལ་རྒྱ་མཚོ *Hjam-dpal rgya-mtsho* n. of the eighth Dalai Lama of Lhasa who died in the year 1805, aged 46. From the birth of Tsong-khapa to the 20th year of the Dalai Lama *Hjam-dpal rgya-mtsho* 420 years elapsed (*Loñ.* ༢ *16*).

* འཇམ་དཔལ་ང་སྒྲ *Hjam-dpal rña-sgra* मञ्जुश्रीदुंदुभीश्वर n. of a Buddha (*Tā. 2, 279*).

འཇམ་དཔལ་སྙིང་པོ *Hjam-dpal sñiṅ-po* the name under which Tsong-khapa is now believed to be known in the *Tuṣita* regions.

འཇམ་དཔལ་གྱི་སངས་རྒྱས་ཀྱི་ཞིང་གི་ཡོན་ཏན་བཀོད་པ मञ्जुश्री-बुद्ध-क्षेत्र व्यूह n. of a Buddhist religious book giving description of the region where dwells Mañ-jus'ri or Jam-pal.

* འཇམ་དཔལ་གཞོན་ནུར་གྱུར་པ *Hjam-dpal gshon-nur gyur-pa* मञ्जुश्रीकुमारभूत a manifestation of Jam-pal.

* འཇམ་དཔལ་བཤེས་གཉེན *Hjam-dpal bçes-gñen,* मञ्जु श्री मित्र.

འཇམ་དབྱངས *Hjam-dbyaṅs* मञ्जुघोष v. འཇམ་དཔལ called also the principal *Bodhisattva* among ཉེ་བའི་སྲས་ཆེན་བརྒྱད the eight spiritual sons of the Buddha.

* འཇམ་དབྱངས་དཀར་པོ *Hjam-dbyaṅs dkar-po* a white image or manifestation of Jam-pal. A yellow ditto:—འཇམ་དབྱངས་དམར་སེར *Hjam-dbyaṅs dmar-ser.*

* འཇམ་དབྱངས་སྨྲ་སེང *Hjam-dbyaṅs smra-seṅ* ཝ་གྷི་ཤྭ་ར *Wa-ghi çva-ra* वागीश्वर Lord of speech.

འཇམ་འབྲས *Hjam-hbras* n. of medicinal fruit reputed useful in diseases of the kidney (*Med.*); འཇམ་འབྲས་མཁལ་མའི་ནད་ནི་སེལ་བར་བྱེད.

འཇམ་འབྲས་དབྱེ་པ *hjam-hbras dbye-pa,* v. करञ्ज (*Mñon.*), a medicinal fruit. [the tree *Pongamia glabra*]S.

འཇམ་མ *hjam-ma* 1.= ཇེ་འཇམ resp. for ཐུག་པ gruel, broth. 2. goddess of fortune.

འཇམ་མོ *hjam-mo* post-stage (*Sch.*).

འཇམ་རྩི *hjam-rtsi* निरूह a purging clyster; a mild purgative medicine.

འཇམ་ཡས *hjam-yas* n. of a number (*Ya-sel. 57*).

འཇམ་བསླུས་མགོ་སྐོར་བ *hjam-bslus mgo-skor-wa* to deceive by sweet and fascinating language.

འཇའ *hjah* or འཇའ་ཚོན इन्द्रधनुः, इन्द्रचाप, इन्द्रायुध rainbow; also the colours of the rainbow; འཇའ་ཚོན་ཡལ་བ *hjah-tshon yal-wa* the vanishing of the rainbow; འཇའ་འོད *hjah-hod* light or splendour of the rainbow; འཇའ་ལུས the body of a saint vanishing in the rainbow or in the manner of the colours of the rainbow.

Syn. དབང་པོའི་མཚོན *dwaṅ-pohi mtshon*; བརྒྱ་བྱིན་གཞུ *brgya-byin gshu*; རླུང་གི་རྒྱལ་མཚན *rluṅ-gi rgyal-tshan*; རླུང་གི་བལ *rluṅ-gi bal*; རླུང་གི་འབྲས་བུ *rluṅ-gi hbras-bu*; འོད་ལྔ་པ *hod lṅa-pa*; གཞའ་ཚོན *gshah-tshon*; འཇའ་རིས *hjah-ris*; རྒན་པོའི་ཐིག *rgan-pohi thig*; ལྷ་རྒྱལ་མཚོན་ཆ *lha-rgyal mtshon-cha*; སོས་ཀ་བཤད *sos-ka bshad*; དབང་གཞུ *dwaṅ-gshu*; ལྷ་ཡི་ཚན་རིས *lha-yi tshan-ris*; དབང་པོའི་ཤིང་བལ *dwaṅ-pohi çiṅ-bal* (*Mñon.*).

འཇའ་བ *hjah-wa* 1. also འཇའ་མོ acc. to *Sch.* lame, gen. ཞ་བོ; འཇའ་བར་བྱེད་པ *hjah-war byed-pa* to make lame, to lame. 2. to bespeak, to concert, to confederate (*Sch.*)

འཇའ་མ *hjah-ma* laces or needle-work representing the colours of the rainbow; generally Chinese shoes are made with such laces.

འཇའ་ས *hjah-sa* or འཇའ་མོ edict, diploma, a permit (*Cs.*); said to be a Chinese word Tibetanized.

འཇའ་རིས *hjah-ris,* v. འཇའ.*hjah.*

འཇའ་ས *hjah-sa,* མངའ་ཞབས་བཟང་པོ faithful servant of the king.

འཇར་བ *hjar-wa* acc. to *Cs.*=འབྱར་བ to stick together, to cohere.

འཇལ་བ *hjal-wa,* pf. བཅལ, fut. གཞལ, imp. འཇོལ (*Rdo. 46*) 1. to weigh. འཇལ་བྱེད་སྲང (a pair of) scales for weighing. 2. to measure: རིང་ཐུང་ཚད་འཇལ་བ to measure the length. 3. to appraise, to tax; to weigh in one's mind, to ponder; more fully expressed by བློས་གཞལ་བ *blos-gshal-wa* (मानन, मिमीते) to understand. 4. to pay; pay back, repay; བུ་ལོན་འཇལ་བ to pay a debt; སྐྱིན་པ་འཇལ་བ *skyin-pa hjal-wa* to repay a loan; ཁྲལ་འཇལ to pay rent or tax, esp. with ལན; ལན་ལན་གནོད་པས་འཇལ or ལེགས་ པའི་ལན་ཉེས་པས་འཇལ to retaliate, return, repay, return evil for good; also in the way of a fine or punishment. In the Tibetan penal code ཁྲི་འཇལ *khri-hjal, i.e.*, payment in ten thousand fold is necessary for making good the loss of sacred life or objects; བརྒྱད་བཅུ་འཇལ in eighty-fold for the property of the clergy; དགུ་འཇལ nine-fold is compensation for the property of ordinary men. འཇལ་བྱའི་དངོས་པོ the articles or essentials of payment in purchase or of exchange in barter.

འཇལ་ཁ *hjal-kha* the act or business of measuring; འཇལ་བགྱི मित measured.

འཇལ་བར་བྱེད *hjal-war-byed* = ཚད་དུ་བྱེད or མཉམ་བྱེད मिमीते paying in price; འཇལ་བས *hjal-was* माय dry or liquid measurement or weighment.

འཇལ་བྱེད *hjal-byed* द्रोण = 4 ādhakas; a measure; a measure of capacity.

འཇས་པ *hjas-pa*, v. སྤྱིད་སྐྱུར་བ (*Mnon.*).

'**འཇི་བ** *hji-wa* 1. or འཇི་ཤིག = ཁྱི་ཤིག a flea, also ལྗི་བ *lji-wa*. 2. acc. to *Cs.* = འཇེམ་པ. 3. soft, smooth. 4. acc. to *Sch.* disgusting, nasty, *e.g.*, of a filthy smell.

འཇིག་རྟེན I: *hjig-rten* = འཁོར་བ संसार 1. the transmigratory existence (*Mnon.*); འཇིག་རྟེན་ལས་འདས་པ or འཁོར་བ་ལས་འདས་པ passed out of the world. 2. symbolically the number three (*Rtsi.*).

འཇིག་རྟེན II: मर्त्यलोक receptacle of all that is perishable. 1. the external world, the universe; འཇིག་རྟེན་གྱི་ལྷ the god of the world (who is also subject to death); འཇིག་རྟེན་ལས་འདས་པ *hjig-rten las hdas-pa* one that has escaped from this world, emancipated, blessed; འཇིག་རྟེན་གསུམ *hjig-rten-gsum* the three divisions of the world: earth, the heavens and hades; འཇིག་རྟེན་གྱི་བྱ་བ *hjig-rten-gyi bya-wa* worldly things or affairs; འཇིག་རྟེན་ལ་དགོས་པའི་བསླབ་བྱ *hjig-rten-la dgos-pahi bslab-bya* useful maxims of life, moral rules; འཇིག་རྟེན་གྱི་ཆོས་བརྒྱད अष्टलोकधर्म्म the eight worldly objects:—(*a*) རྙེད་པ *rñed-pa* लाभ gain; (*b*) མ་རྙེད་པ *ma rñed-pa* अलाभ loss; (*c*) སྙན་པ यशः fame; (*d*) མི་སྙན་པ अयश notoriety or ill-fame; (*e*) སྨད་པ निन्दा slander or scandal; (*f*) བསྟོད་པ प्रशंसा praise; (*g*) བདེ་བ सुख happiness; (*h*) སྡུག་བསྔལ *sdug-bsñal* दुःख misery. འཇིག་རྟེན་གྱི་མཛད་པ་ལྔ the five temporal acts of a Buddha:—Conception in the mother's womb, birth, youthful achievements, marriage, and reigning over the kingdom. འཇིག་རྟེན་ལས་འདས་པའི་མཛད་པ་ལྔ the five works leading to the passing out of the world of a Buddha: (*a*) རབ་ཏུ་བྱུང་བ (प्रव्रज्या) renunciation; (*b*) དཀའ་བ་སྤྱད་པ (तपस्या) asceticism; (*c*) ཆོས་འཁོར་བསྐོར་བ *chos-hkhor bskor-wa* (धर्म्मचक्रप्रवर्त्तन) turning the wheel of Law, *i.e.*, preaching religion; (*d*) ཆོ་འཕྲུལ་སྟོན་ཅིང་བདུད་བཏུལ་བ *cho-hphrul ston-cin bdud btul-wa* subduing the devil (Māra) by exhibiting religious miracles; (*e*) སངས་རྒྱས་པ the attainment of *Nirvāṇa*. 2. world, as a more general term: བདེ་བ་ཅན་གྱི་འཇིག་རྟེན *bde-wa-can gyi hjig-rten* the Sukhāvati or the world of bliss. There are two kinds of worlds:—(*a*) མ་དག་པའི་འཇིག་རྟེན the impure or defiled world, *i.e.*, the world of sin; (*b*) དག་པའི་འཇིག་རྟེན the sanctified world, *i.e.*, the world of purity. Most Buddhists include our world, in the *Madag-pahi Hjig-rten*. The following five include the pure worlds or *Dag-pahi hjig-rten*: (*a*) བདེ་བར་གཤེགས་པ་བདུན་

ཀྱི་ཞིང་ཁམས the worlds which have been sanctified by the presence of the sevon Sugata Buddhas or tho happily-passed-away Buddhas; (*b*) the worlds presided over by tho Buddhas of the ton quarters and the five Dhyāni Buddhas; (*c*) the world of beatitude called མངོན་དགའ་བ or མངོན་པར་དགའ་བའི་ཞིང་ཁམས; (*d*) the world called པདྨ་ཅན *pad ma-can*; (*e*) De-wa-chan or the World of Bliss of tho Northern Buddhists (*Sorig.*). Our present world is divided into two:—(*a*) ཕྱི་སྣོད་ཀྱི་འཇིག་རྟེན *Phyi-snod-kyi hjig-rten* the physical or inorganic world, (*b*) ནང་བཅུད་ཀྱི་འཇིག་རྟེན the living or animated world.

འཇིག་རྟེན་ཁམས *hjig-rten-khams* लोकधातु the world.

Syn. ས་རྟེན *sa-rten*; བཅུད་ཀྱི་སྣོད *bcud-kyi snod*; གནས་རྟེན *gnas-rten*; རང་སྐྱེད *rañ-skyed*; ས་བོན *sa-bon* (*Mñon.*).

འཇིག་རྟེན་ཁམས་ཀྱི་ཆ་ཤས *hjig-rten-khams kyi cha-ças* लोकधात्वंश part of the world.

* འཇིག་རྟེན་མཁའ་འགྲོ *Hjig-rten mkhah-hgro* n. of a nymph.

འཇིག་རྟེན་མཁྱེན་པ *hjig-rten mkhyen-pa* लोकविद् tho knower of the world, *i.e.*, of all that happens in the world.

འཇིག་རྟེན་ཁྲིམས *hjig-rten-khrims*=རྒྱལ་ཁྲིམས *rgyal-khrims* the laws or institutes for governing (*Mñon.*).

འཇིག་རྟེན་གྱི་གཏམ *hjig-rten-gyi gtam* worldly saying, common saying, proverb.

འཇིག་རྟེན་གྱི་ཐད *hjig-rten-gyi thad* व्यावहारिका worldliness; in the direction of worldliness, or usage, custom, etc.

འཇིག་རྟེན་གྱི་བར *hjig-rten-gyi bar* लोकान्तरिका in the world a dark space, n. of a hell.

འཇིག་རྟེན་གྱི་གཙོ་བོ *Hjig-rten-gyi gtso-bo* the lord of the universe (*M. V.*).

འཇིག་རྟེན་གྱི་ཚུལ *hjig-rten-gyi tshul* लोकयात्रा worldly manner, according to custom, or usage.

འཇིག་རྟེན་མགོན་པོ *Hjig-rten mgon-po* लोकनाथ the patron or protector of the world; an epithet of the *Bodhisattva* Avalokites'vara; also n. of tho Buddha.

འཇིག་རྟེན་འཇིག་པ *hjig-rten hjig-pa* लोकाभिभवन the destruction of tho world.

འཇིག་རྟེན་ཐམས་ཅད་ལ་མངོན་པར་མི་དགའ་བའི་འདུ་ཤེས सर्व-लोकेऽनभिरतिसंज्ञा an aversion to the concerns of this world, being the outcome of adherence to the Doctrine.

འཇིག་རྟེན་འདུལ *hjig-rten-hdul* (སངས་རྒྱས་སྤྱིའི་མཚན *sañs-rgyas spyihi-mtshan*) लोकजित् one who has conquered tho world—a general epithet of Buddha (*Mñon.*).

འཇིག་རྟེན་པ *hjig-rten-pa* लौकिक, लोकत: a worldly man, a layman.

འཇིག་རྟེན་དཔང་པོ *hjig-rten dpañ-po*=ཉི་མ also लोकेश, संसारसाची the sun, the witness of tho world.

འཇིག་རྟེན་ཕ་རོལ *hjig-rten pha-rol* परलोक the next world.

འཇིག་རྟེན་བྱེད་པོ *Hjig-rten byed-po* the maker of the universe, an epithet of ལྷ་དབང་ཕྱུག་ཆེན་པོ Mahes'vara (*Situ. 8*).

འཇིག་རྟེན་བྱེད་པོ *Hjig-rten byed-po*=ལྷ་ཚངས་པ *lha-tshañs-pa* a name of Brahmā (*Mñon.*).

འཇིག་རྟེན་དབང་ཕྱུག *Hjig-rten dwañ-phyug* लोकेश्वर a name of Avalokites'vara (*Mñon.*).

* འཇིག་རྟེན་དབང་ཕྱུག་ཡི་གེ་བདུན *Hjig-rten dwañ-phyug yi-ge bdun* the seven letters symbolical of Avalokites'vara (*A. 24*).

འཇིག་རྟེན་མིག *hjig-rten-mig*=ཉི་མ लोकचक्षु: the sun as the eye of the world (*Mñon.*); n. of a Rishi, the founder of *Lokāyata* sect of Indian atheists (*Grub.* ཀ *5*).

འཇིག་རྟེན་མེས་པོ *Hjig-rten mes-po* (ལྷ་ཚངས་པ) the ancestor of the world; an epithet of Brahmā (*Mñon.*).

* འཇིག་རྟེན་ཟླ་བ *hjig-rten zla-wa* लोकेन्द्र (*Kālac. T, 74*).

འཇིག་རྟེན་ལས་འདས་མ *Hjig-rten las hdas-ma* a n. of the queen of the Noi-Jin demons (*K. g.* ད *130*).

འཇིག་རྟེན་ཤིང་རྟ་མ *hjig-rten çiñ rta-ma*=འབབ་ཆུ *hbab-chu* a hill torrent (*Mñon.*).

འཇིག་པ I: *hjig-pa*=འཇིག་པ भङ्ग breaking down, destruction, ruin.

འཇིག་པ II: 1. vb. act. pf. བཤིག, fut. གཤིག, imp. ཤིག (*Rdo. 46.*) to destroy, to devastate, to devour, to abolish, to do away with, dissolve (an enchantment). 2. vb. n. pf. བཤིག or ཞིག *shig* to be lost; undermined; to decay, perish: འཇིག་པར་ཤིན་ཏུ་སླ (earthly good) may be easily lost again; འཇིག་པ་ཞིག་གསོས་བྱེད་པ to restore repair. 3. to suck, draw out moisture (*Sch.*), v. འཇིབ་པ.

འཇིག་པ་ཅན *hjig-pa-can* frail, perishable (*Cs.*); མི་འཇིག་པ imperishable.

འཇིག་པའི་བསྐལ་པ *hjig-pahi bskal-pa* संवर्त्तकल्प the period of dissolution of the universe.

འཇིག་པའི་ངང་ཅན *hjig-pahi ñañ-can* विनश्वर subject to destruction.

འཇིག་པར་ལྟ་བ *hjig-par lta-wa* भयदर्शी apprehensive of danger, fearful.

འཇིག་ཚོགས *hjig-tshogs* lit. collection of the destructibles, *i.e.*, the worldly things; भीषण terrible.

འཇིག་ཚོགས་ལ་ལྟ་བ *hjig-tshogs-la lta-wa* the doctrine of regarding everything as destructible; described as ལྟ་བ་ཉོན་མོངས་པ་ལྔ་ཡོད་པའི་གཅིག one of the five schools of philosophy that aimed at freedom from misery, holding that worldly existence is comprised of five miseries; the doctrines opposed to it were:—(1) མི་འཇིག་ལྟ; (2) མཐར་ལྟ; (3) ལྟ་བ་མཆོག་འཛིན; (4) བརྟུལ་ཞུགས་མཆོག་འཛིན; (5) ལོག་ལྟ. [The Sanskrt equivalents may be thus rendered:—(1) सत्कायदृष्टि regarding the body as permanent; (2) अन्तग्राहदृष्टि pondering on death; (3) मिथ्यादृष्टि false conception, *i.e.*, denial of future existence; (4) दृष्टिपरामर्श hesitation or doubt about truths; (5) शीलव्रतपरामर्श doubt about rules of conduct] *S.*

འཇིགས=*hjigs*, བ་རུ་ར *ba-ru-ra* a medicinal fruit.

འཇིགས་པ *hjigs-pa* I: भी vb. to fear, be afraid, be terrified. Frq. both in old and recent lit., also common in colloq. In books occurs with the instrumental case of the object: གྲོང་ཁྱེར་འཇིག་པར་ནུས་པ་དེ་དག་གིས་འཇིགས་ཏེ fearing those who were able to destroy the city; but in later writings and in colloq. takes ལ: ཁྲོ་བ་འབྱུང་བས་ལྷ་མོ་ལ་འཇིགས་པར་གྱུར་ཏོ because her anger was arising, he became afraid of the goddess (*Mil.*): ང་ཁྱོད་ལ་འཇིགས་སོ་ཞེས་ཟེར I am afraid of you, thus he said. The form of the supine seems to be འཇིགས་སུ not འཇིགས་པར and is in common use: རོབས་ཀྱི་ནང་ན་སྦྲུལ་གདུག་པས་འཇིགས་སུ་རུང་བས་གང་ངོ་ as it was proper to fear the poisonous snakes in the trench, they filled it (with water) (*G. Sndg.*). Intensive forms of this verb are very frq. in early lit., འཇིགས being combined with either སྐྲག or དངང་ or with both; esp. common in the Kah-gyur treatises: འཇིགས་སྐྲག་པར་གྱུར grew afraid; འཇིགས་དངང་སྐྲག་སོང་ was sore affrighted.

འཇིགས་པ II: sbst. fear, apprehension, dread. Often with genit. case: རྒྱལ་པོའི་འཇིགས་པ *rgyal-pohi hjigs-pa* standing in fear of the king; ཇུ་འཕྲོག་འཇིགས་པ་བྲལ་བས་བདེ because free from fear of robbery, I am happy; ཟད་པའི་འཇིགས་པ་མེད་པས་བདེ when having no apprehension of expenditure, he felt happy.

Syn. སྐྲག་པ *skrag-pa*; དོགས་པ *dogs-pa*; དངངས་པ *dñañs-pa*; སྐྱི་གཡའ *skyi-gyah*; སྐྱི་བུན *skyi-bun*; བག་ཚ་བ *bag-tsha-wa* (*Mñon.*).

* འཇིགས་སྐྱོབས *hjigs-skyobs* མེའི *mehi*... ཆུའི *chuhi*...སེང་གེའི *señ-gehi*...གླང་པོའི *glañ-pohi*..,

ཆད་པའི་ *chad-pahi*... ཀླུའི་ *kluhi*... མཁའ་འགྲོའི་ *mkhah-grohi*... མི་རྒོད་ཀྱི་ *mi-rgod-kyi*... (*Schr.*).

འཇིགས་སྐྲག *hjigs-skrag* fear, panic; also a terrible object: འཇིགས་སྐྲག་ཏུ་སོང་ he has become frightened.

འཇིགས་མཁན *hjigs-mkhan* one who is frightened.

འཇིགས་བཅས *hjigs-bcas* सभय, भीत with fear, possessed of fear.

འཇིགས་བཅས་ལམ *hjigs-bcas-lam* a bad, unsafe road (*Mñon.*).

འཇིགས་ཆུམ་པ *hjigs-chum-pa*, v. ཆུམ་པ.

* འཇིགས་སྟེར *hjigs-ster* भयदा (*Kālac T. 152*) [inspiring fear, causing danger]*S.*

འཇིགས་སྡང་ *hjigs-sdaṅ* भयङ्कर fierce, terrible; also a term for wine.

འཇིགས་སྡེ *Hjigs-sde* भीष्म, भीमसेन, भयानक terrible, a name of the second Pāṇḍava, also Bhishma.

འཇིགས་གནས *hjigs-gnas* 1. lit. a fearful place; a cemetery, where dead bodies are left or disposed of. 2.=འབྱོར་པ विभव wealth, prosperity.

Syn. དུར་ཁྲོད *dur-khrod*; རོ་ཡི་གནས *ro-yi-gas* (*Mñon.*).

འཇིགས་པ་ཅན *hjigs-pa-can* 1. fearful, timorous. 2. dreadful, frightful (*Cs.*).

འཇིགས་པ་བཅུ་པ *hjigs-pa bcu-pa*=མ་ཧེ *ma-he* प्रतिभय a buffalo.

འཇིགས་པ་མེད *hjigs-pa-med* अभय fearless.

འཇིགས་པ་སེལ་བྱེད *hjigs-pa sel-byed* the remover of all fears; a kind or ruler; also=རྒྱལ་བ a Jina, who removes all fears.

Syn. མིའི་མགོན་པོ *mihi mgon-po*; ས་གཞི་སྐྱོང་ *sa-bshi skyoṅ* (*Mñon.*).

འཇིགས་པར་འགྱུར *hjigs-par-hgyur* बिभेति becomes frightened; འཇིགས་པར་བྱེད *hjigs-par byed* भाययति frightened.

འཇིགས་བྱེད་སྐྱེས *hjigs-byed-skyes* भीष्मज born of Bhīshma.

* འཇིགས་བྱེད་བསྡུས་པ *Hjig-byed bsdus-pa* (*Schr.*).

འཇིགས་བྱེད་མ *Hjigs-byed-ma* 1. n. of a princess of the *Yakṣa* or Noijin demi-gods. (*K. g.* ང, *130*). 2.=ཉེས་པའི་ལམ the way to sin (*Mñon.*).

* འཇིགས་བྱེད་རོ་ལངས་བརྒྱད་སྐོར་གྱི་སྒྲུབ་ཐབས भयकरवेतालाष्टकसाधन propitiating eight fearful goblins (*Schr.*).

འཇིགས་རུང་ (བ) *hjigs-ruṅ-(wa)* भयानक, प्रतिभय, बीभत्स, रौद्र, भीषक, भैरव, भीम fearful, loathsome; one of the names of the second son Pāṇḍu Rāja.

འཇིགས་ས *hjigs-sa* dangerous quarters or place.

འཇིགས་ས་ཆེ *hjigs-sa-che* a place where there is much occasion for being afraid.

འཇིགས་སུ་རུང་བ་མ *hjigs-su ruṅ-wa-ma* रोषणी, रोषण, भीलुक: n. of a goddess of fearful mien.

འཇིང་ I: *hjiṅ* a mineral substance applied on old sores.

འཇིང་ II: seems to mean the midst, as well as the expanse, the whole bulk; རྒྱ་མཚོ་ཡི་འཇིང་ *rgya-mtsho-ye hjiṅ* the whole surface of the sea; ལུས་འཇམ་འཇག་པོ་མཚོ་འཇིང་འཇུག *lus-hjam hjag-po mtsho hjiṅ-hjug* the smooth-bodied Takshaka (snake) enters into the midst of the lake.

འཇིང་པ *hjiṅ-pa* also མཇིང་པ neck, resp. སྐུ་འཇིང་. འཇིང་ཀྱོག *hjiṅ-kyog* a wry neck (*Cs.*); འཇིང་ཕྲང་ the nape of the neck (*Jä.*); འཇིང་རྒྱབ the back part of the neck (*Cs.*); འཇིང་ནུབ अग्रीव (lit. sunk-neck) a short-neck (in a man).

འཇིངས *hjiṅs* मध्य, मध्य the center, the pith or དབུས, རྒྱ་མཚོའི་འཇིངས=རྒྱ་མཚོའི་དབུས the depths of the sea; the centre of ocean (*Dag. 8*).

འཇིབ་འཐུང་ *hjib-hthuṅ* lit. that drinks as soon as it is born=སྐྱེས་མ་ཐག་པ *skyes-ma thag-pa* an infant just born.

འཇིབ་པ I: *hjib-pa* or འཇིབས་པ pf. བཞིབས also གཞིབས *gshibs*, fut. བཞིབ or གཞིབ to suck, *e.g.*, of a baby; མཆུས་འཇིབས་པ to suck with the lips (*Dag. 8*). ཁྲག་འཇིབས to suck blood; also to blister.

འཇིབ་པ II: or འཇིབས་པ, cf. ཞིམ་པ to relish, also to taste.

འཇིབ་རྩི *hjib-rtsi* acc. to *Cs.* a syrup, a medicinal plant.

འཇིབ་རྩི་ཆེན་པོ *hjib-rtsi chen-po* n. of a medicinal plant; it is said of it: ཁ་ཡི་ནད་དང་སོ་དང་མཆིན་པའི་ཚད་པ་སེལ་བར་བྱེད it cures inflammation of the liver and the teeth and diseases of the mouth.

འཇིམ་པ *hjim-pa* कर्दम mud, clay, also muddy water (*Mṅon.*). འཇིམ་སྐུ mud image or statue. འཇིམ་སྐོང་ *hjim-skoṅ* a small cup of clay; a crucible (*Cs.*). འཇིམ་གཟུགས a figure formed of clay.

འཇིམ་ལས་པ *hjim-las-pa* one of the four classes of the rural people who make mud houses; those who work in mud, cultivators of the soil (*Ya-sel. 55*).

འཇིལ་བ *hjil-wa* 1. to shed blood. 2. pf. བཅིལ *bcil*, fut. གཞིལ to expel, eject, remove, turn off. ཕྱིར་འཇིལ་བ *phyir hjil-wa* to banish out (noxious animals, vices, etc.).

‡ འཇིལ་ན་ཤན *Hjil-na-çan* river mentioned in early history of India (*K. my.* ཁ *198*).

འཇིལ་ལི *hjil-li*=ཁྲིའུ་ཤིང *khrihu-çiṅ* a chair, wooden stool; also=འཇའ་རིས *hjah-ris* colours of the rainbow: རྫིངས་ཀྱི་ཁ་ཁྱེར་ལས་འཇིལ་ལི་བྱས་ནས *rdsiṅs-kyi kha khyer-las hjil-li byas-nas* (*A. 18*) a seat was furnished him by his being carried on the deck of a vessel.

འཇུ་བ I: *hju-wa* vb. 1. pf. འཇུས to seize, grasp, lay hold of, with ལ (*Dag. 8*): དཔྲལ་བའི་མདའ་ལ་འཇུ་བ *dpral-wahi mdah-la hju-wa* grasping the arrow (that was) sticking in his forehead; གཅིག་ལ་གཅིག་འཇུ་བ taking firmly hold of each other; ལག་པ་ནས་འཇུ་བ to grasp by the hand (*Jä.*). 2. pf. བཞུས, fut. བཞུ to melt, to digest; ཟས་འཇུ་བ to digest the food; འཇུ་སླ་བ easily digestible; འཇུ་དཀའ་བ difficult for digestion; ཟོས་པ་དང་འཐུངས་པ་དང་འཆམས་པ་དང་མྱངས་པ་རྣམས་ལེགས་པར་བདེ་བར་འཇུ whatever has been eaten, drunk, or tasted with perfect ease (pleasure) becomes well digested.

འཇུ་བ II: 1. digestion; འཇུ་བ་ལ་སྒོ *hju-wa-la-sgo* the digestion is in order, is easy (*Med.*); འཇུ་རྫིབས་ཆུང་ the digestive power is weak (*Med.*; *Jä.*). 2.=འཇི་བ a flea (*Sch.*).

འཇུག I: *hjug*, སྟབས *stabs* to plant, fix, pitch; འཇུག་བདེ་བ *hjug-bde-wa*=སྟབས་བདེ་བ *stabs-bde-wa* easy to plant or to fix.

འཇུག་འཁྲུན་ཆོད་པ *hjug-hkhrun chod-pa* to make the last settlement, settle a thing once for all.

འཇུག་བརྒྱ་པ *hjug-brgya-pa*=གློག *glog* सतावर्त lightning; banks, margin.

འཇུག་ངོགས *hjug-ṅogs*, तीर n. of Vishṇu; ཆུ་རབ a ford, where one may cross a river, also the margin of a river.

འཇུག་ལྡོག *hjug-ldog* obstacles.

འཇུག་སྡུད *hjug-sdud* for མཇུག་སྡུད निगमन insertion, also conclusion in a syllogism.

འཇུག་པ I: *hjug-pa* गमन, प्रवेश, निर्वेश, वर्त्तन pf. and imp. ཞུགས *shugs* 1. to go into, to enter; ཆུའི་ནང་དུ་འཇུག་པ to enter into the water; རྒྱ་མཚོར་འཇུག་པ to start on the sea; ལམ་དུ་འཇུག་པ to set out, start, to proceed on a journey. Gen. འཇུག་པ is used with the termin. case, but sometimes it occurs with ལ: རྗེ་བླ་མའི་བྱིན་རླབས་རི་ལ་ཞུགས by the blessing of the reverend lamas I have entered the mountains (*Mil.* ཁ *278*); བསམ་གཏན་དང་པོ་ལས་བྱུང་ནས། བསམ་གཏན་གཉིས་པ་ལ་ཞུགས and when they had emerged from the first stage of Samtan abstraction (*i.e.*, *dhyāna*), they entered into the second stage (*Dzl.*). In this passage, we find the termin. case employed: འཁྱགས་ན་སྟོང་ཉིད་ཀྱི་ར་བར་འཇུག when I feel cold, I enter into the fold of the very Void (*Mil.* ཀ *92*). དགེ་བ་ལ་འཇུག་པ to betake to pious works; འཇུག་པའི་ལས works that are a consequence of having really entered upon the practice of virtue, positive good works; ཆོས་ལ་འཇུག་པ = ཆོས་ལ་བབས to turn to religion, to be converted; བསྟན་པ་ཞིག་ལ་འཇུག་པ *bstan-pa shig-la hjug-pa* to adopt a certain religion, a certain doctrine. 2. almost analogous to 1. is another common signification: to begin, to set about. Here the vb. is always coupled to the participle by ལ: དགོངས་པ་ལ་འཇུག་པ to begin to think upon; སྟོན་པ་ལ་འཇུག་པ to begin showing; གཅིག་ལ་གཅིག་རྣམ་པར་བརླག་པ་ལ་ཞུགས་པས having started entirely exterminating one another (*Jä.*).

འཇུག་པ II: = ཕོན་པ sbst. the going into, the entering; the beginning; the first stage of a disease (*Mṅy.*); also can signify: अवतार the incarnation of a deity. འཇུག་པ་བཅུ *Hjug-pa-bcu* दशावतार the ten incarnations of the Supreme Being (Vishnu), viz., ཉ मत्स्य the Fish; རུས་སྦལ कूर्म Tortoise; ཕག वराह the Pig; མིའི་སེང་གེ नृसिंह the Man-lion; མི་འུ་ཐུང་ वामन the Dwarf; སྟུག་པ་ནག་པོ कृष्ण Krishna or rather his elder brother Balarâma; དགའ་བྱེད་ར་མ་ཎ परशुराम Paras'u Rāma; རྒྱས་པ་ར་མ་ཎ रामचन्द्र Rāmacandra; སངས་རྒྱས बुद्ध Buddha; ཀིང་གྷི་རྩེ *Kiṅ-ghi rtse* कल्कि Kalki.

འཇུག་པ III: pf. བཅུག (perh. also འཇུགས *Lex.*), fut. གཞུག (*Rdo. 46*), imp. ཆུག vb. 1. to put into, insert; to infuse, inject; to fix. མི་ཞིག་ཆོས་ལ་འཇུག་པ to convert a man, to induce him to adopt a certain religion. 2. to appoint, constitute; also to manifest, place out, settle. 3. to command, induce. 4. to permit, allow, suffer. In last two senses with termin. case of root of verb.

འཇུག་པ་གཅིག *hjug-pa-gcig* = མགྲིན་གཅིག of one opinion, of the same party; ཕྱོགས་མཐུན; ཕྱོགས་མཚུངས; བསམ་བྱ་མཚུངས (*Mṅon.*).

འཇུག་པའི་གནས *hjug-pahi-gnas* met. house, residence (*Mṅon.*).

འཇུག་པར་འདོད་པ *hjug-par hdod-pa* to wish to take up any work.

འཇུག་པར་བྱེད་པ *hjug-par-byed-pa* to undertake.

འཇུག་བྱ *hjug-bya* 1. road. 2. dwelling.

འཇུག་རིངས *hjug-riṅs* (for མཇུག་རིངས) *mjug-riṅs* केतु comet.

+ **འཇུངས་པ** *hjuṅs-pa* = སེར་སྣ་ཆེ་བ 1. avarice; avaricious (*Dag. 8*). 2. कृपण a miser; འཇུངས་པ་ཅན *hjuṅs-pa-can* avaricious.

+ **འཇུད་པ** *hjud-pa* and more frq. འཛུད་པ a secondary form of འཇུག་པ cf. ཆུད་པ, འཆུད་པ.

+ འཇུད་མཐུན་མ *hjud-mthun-ma* or འཇུད་འཐུན་མ = སྨད་འཚོང་མ गणिका a prostitute, harlot. (*Dag. 8*); འཇུད་མཐུན་བྱེད་པ *hjud-mthun byed-pa* to play the harlot.

འཇུན་འགར *Hjun-hgar* a tribe of Eleuth Mongols who invaded Tibet and destroyed monasteries *circa* 1645 (*Loṅ.* ཞ *12*).

འཇུན་པ *hjun-pa* pf. བཅུན *bcun*, fut. གཞུན *gshun* (cf. བཞུན *bshun*, ཞུན *shun*) acc. to *Cs.*, to subdue, make tame; to make confess; to make soft, to soften, to punish (by words or blows); to convert. ཐབས་ཀྱིས་འཇུན་པ་པོ one who can tame by certain means or strategy.

འཇུམ་ཁྱད *hjum-khyad* = ཉུང་དུ་འགྲོ་བ་མར་ཆག་པ to diminish, to become less (*Rtsii.*).

འཇུམ་པ *hjum-pa* or འཇུམས་པ pf. འཇུམ *bjum*, fut. བཀུམ, imp. ཁུམ, prop. to cause to shudder, but is frq. as neut. vb. to contract; ཤ་འཇུམ་པ contraction of the muscles, shrinking (*Sch.*).

འཇུར་གེགས *Hjur-gegs* n. of a kind of Yidag whose throat is so contracted that a drop of water can hardly pass through it to quench his ever-burning thirst.

འཇུར་གྱིས *hjur-gyis* suddenly, all at once: ན་བཟའི་ཕག་ན་ཚུར་དངུལ་གྱི་མནྜལ་ཁྲུ་གང་པ་ཞིག་འཇུར་གྱིས་བཏོན *na-bzahi phag-na tshur dnul-gyi man-dal khru gañ-pa shig hjur-gyis bton.* from the pocket of his robe he suddenly drew forth a silver *mandal* tray one cubit square (*Hbrom. 14*).

འཇུར་བ *hjur-wa* (pf. བཅུར q.v.) 1. to draw tight; འཇུར་བར་འགྱུར་བ to be entangled; འཇུར་མདུག wrinkled, as the skin is in old age; འཇུར་མིག *hjur-mig* a wire-drawing hole or vice. 2.=འཛུར་བ to evade, to shun, to go out of the way; འཇུར་མེད unavoidable (*Jä.*).

འཇུར་བུ *hjur-bu* the act of busying one's self in worldly concerns and thereby remaining tied to them, འཇུར་བུས་བཅིངས་པའི་སེམས་ཉིད་ནི, གྲོད་ན་གྲོལ་བར་ཐེ་ཚོམ་མེད (*Lo. 40*).

འཇུས *hjus* seized, held by the hand, v. འཇུ་བ.

འཇེ *hje* sometimes written for མཛེ.

+ **འཇེབས་པ** *hjebs-pa* or འཇེབས་པོ well sounding, beautiful, handsome; also of sweet sounds; སྙན་འཇེབས harmony, euphony (*Jä.*).

འཇེམ་པ *hjem-pa* also འཇེམས་པ or འཇེམས་པོ 1. dexterity, cleverness. 2. skilled, clever.

འཇེར་འཇིགས *Hjer-hjigs* an epithet of Indra (*Mñon.*).

འཇོ་བ *hjo-wa* I:=སྒེག་པ *sgeg-pa* लास्या fascinating, charming, seductive. འཇོ་བགམས་ཕྱོས་པ *hjo-bgam phyos-pa*=འཇོ་བག་ཅན or འཚོས་པ सलील playful, coquettish. འཇོ་སྒེག *hjo-sgeg*: 1. beauty, charm (*Yig. 50*). 2. a coquettish, alluring posture; འཇུད་མཐུན་འཇོ་སྒེག་འཇོག the harlot places herself alluringly (*Jä.*). འཇོ་སྟེར་བ *hjo ster-wa*=དགའ་བ giving delight, charming (*Mñon.*).

འཇོ་བ II: pf. བཞོས, fut. བཞོ, imp. འཇོས दोहन to milk; མཛོ་མོ་འཇོ་བ to milk a yak-cow. འདོད་འཇོའི་བ *hdod-hjohi-ba* कामधेनु a cow yielding all desires; a cow that gives milk at pleasure.

འཇོ་མཁན *hjo-mkhan* one who milks a cow; also འཇོ་བ་པོ *hjo-wa-po.*

འཇོ་བ་མོ *hjo-wa-mo* a milkmaid.

འཇོ་མ *hjo-ma* a milch-cow.

Syn. བ་མོ *ba-mo*; འབབ་བྱེད *hbab-byed*; ཡོངས་འཇོམ *yoñs-hjom* (*Mñon.*).

འཇོ་ཤ *hjo-ça* and འཇོ་ཤ་ཀ་ཆེན་པོ *hjo-ça-ka chen-po* are celestial flowers.=ལྷའི་མེ་ཏོག *lhahi me-tog* flowers of the gods (*K. d.* ཞ *156*).

འཇོག་པ *hjog-pa* I: स्थापन, निक्षेप, प्रक्षेप, स्थापित, अवक्षेपण; pf. བཞག, fut. གཞག, imp. ཞོག: 1. to put, place, make a place for, settle; to assign: ཁྱོད་ཀྱིས་འཇོག་ཐོད་ན་ཉེ་གནས་ཀྱི་ལས་ཀ་བྱེད་དགོས (*A. 95*) if you can employ me I must do the work of an attendant. ལས་སུ་འཇོག་པ to set one a task, to employ one in a certain service; རྫུན་གྱི་དཔང་པོ་ཁ་ཅིག་ལ་འཇོག་པ to set up some person as false witnesses; སེམས་ལ་འཇོག་པ to bear in mind; ཕྱིར་འཇོག་པ to leave behind, to leave out, to put by, to lay aside. ནོར་གསོག་འཇོག་མེད treasure and articles were not put by. གསོག་འཇོག་མཁན one who hoards up wealth. 2. to leave, to leave behind; ལག་རྗེས an impression; རང་གི་ཡུལ་འཇོག་པ to leave one's own country; ཐོངས་པར་མ་བཞག་པར so that it is not left to poverty; གདུང་བརྒྱུད་འཇོག་པ to leave offspring behind, to propagate the species (*Jä.*).

འཇོག་པ་ II: pf. ཞོགས, བཞོགས, fut. གཞོག, imp. ཞོག to cut, to hew, to square (a pen, timber, etc.), to carve, to chip (a thin piece of wood, etc.) (*Jä.*).

འཇོག་པོ *Hjog-po* = འཇག་པོ तक्षक n. of a species of Nāga or Lu. རྡོ་འཇོག तक्षशिला Taxila, n. of an ancient city in the Panjab which was visited by Alexander the Great. ཀླུ་རྒྱལ་དགའ་བོ་འཇོག་པོ *Klu-rgyal dgaḥ-bo Hjog-po* Nāga-rāja Nanda Takshaka.

འཇོག་བྱེད *hjog-byed* n. of a bitter medicinal plant.

འཇོང་ *hjoṅ* 1. = ལྕོང་ *lcoṅ* tadpole. 2. a hoe, pick-axe: འཇོང་ཆེན *hjoṅ-chen*, ཏོག་ཙེ a large hoe, also pick-axe: བདུད་ཀྱི་ཐོ་ཆེན་འཇོང་ཆེན་གཉིས the hammer and hoe are both of the devil (*D.R.*). 3. of egg-form (དབྱིབས་སྒོང་ང་ལྟ་བུ) (*Dag. 8*).

འཇོང་པོ *hjoṅ-po* also *hjoṅ-hjoṅ* oblong, longish, oval, elliptical, cylindric, bottle-shaped, etc.; also applied to stature: tall; འཇོང་ཉམས་ཅན oblong shaped, in relation to leaves, cones of firs, etc.; ལོ་མ་འཇོང་རྣམས་ཉག་ཉག་ཅན slips; leaves split into narrow slips. (*Vai. sn.*); དབྱིབས་འཇོང་ an oval form (*Jä.*).

འཇོང་ཙེ *hjoṅ-tse* = ལྕོག་ཙེ a small low table (used as dining table for a single person in Tibet).

འཇོན་དམར *hjon-dmar* = ཟངས copper (*K. du. 19*).

* འཇོམས *hjoms* भग्न broken (*Kālac. T. 144*).

འཇོམས་པ *hjoms-pa*, pf. བཅོམ, or བཅོམས also of ཆོམ, fut. གཞོམ (*Rdo. 46*), imp. ཆོམས 1. उन्मूलन, प्रहसन, ध्वंस, घात, विनाशन, विहेठन, परिघ to conquer, subdue, put down, suppress; ནད་འཇོམས to root out a disease; དམག་ལ་འཇོམས་པ to defeat in a war; བློ་མུན་འཇོམས་པ *blo-mun hjoms-pa* to keep down or suppress a wicked person; འདོད་ཆགས་ཀྱིས་ཀུན་ནས་འཇོམས་པ to be quite overpowered by lust; རབ་ཏུ་འཇོམས་པ་འདི the following overpowering (charm); འཇོམས་པར་འགྱུར हनिष्यति will be killed, destroyed; བཅོམ་མོ an exclamation: I am done for! (*Jä.*). 2. to oppress, tyrannize over, plunder: འཇོམས་པའི་སྐབས་བྱས་པ་ལ as they were on the point of plundering him. རྒྱལ་པོས་བཅོམས་པ་ཐམས་ཅད་ཀུན་གྲོལ་བར་མཛད་དོ all who were oppressed by the king were delivered. From this verb is derived the well-known appellation of Buddha, བཅོམ་ལྡན་འདས, meaning "he who, possessed of victory, has passed beyond."

འཇོམས་བྱེད I: *hjoms-byed* 1. a charm, a magical formula. 2. an exorcist who suppresses the vanquisher.

Syn. མཐུ་བོ་ཆེ *mthu-bo-che*; རྡོ་རྗེ་འཛིན་པ *rdo-rje hdsin-pa* (*Mṅon.*).

* འཇོམས་བྱེད II: ममनीय the conqueror; conquerable (*Kālac. T. 153*).

འཇོམས་བྱེད་བུ *Hjoms-byed-bu* the eldest of the five Pāṇḍava brothers (*Mṅon.*).

འཇོར *hjor* = གཞོར 1. hoe, grubbing hoe, mattock, pick-axe; འཇོར་ལྕགས the iron of a mattock (*Cs.*). 2. the supine of འཇོ་བ as in འཇོར་གྱིས་རྐོ་བ *hjor-gyis rko-wa* to turn up with the hoe; འཇོར་བུ a small hoe.

འཇོར་པོ *hjor-po* a large mattock, spade; འཇོར་ཡུ *hjor-yu* the handle of the hoe.

འཇོལ་བ I: *hjol-wa* 1. to hang down, གོས་ལྟ་བུ *gos lta-bu* as of a robe, grament. 2. occurs for འབྱོལ་བ *hbyol-wa* to turn aside, to make way.

འཇོལ་བ II: a sbst. acc. to *Cs.*=འཇོལ་འཇོལ *hjol-hjol* or གཤོལ་བ *gshol-wa* train, trail, retinue; འཇོལ་གོས *hjol-gos* or འཇོལ་བེར *hjol-ber* क्षौम a linen cloth, a robe or garment with a train; འཇོལ་ཅན *hjol-can* having a train; ཐོས་བསམ་སྒོམ་པའི་འཇོལ་ཁྲབ་གྱོན put on the protecting robes of listening, reflection, meditation (*Mil.* ཀ. *92*).

འཇོལ་འཇོལ *hjol-hjol* hanging belly or paunch *Jä.*; (གོས་ལྷ་བུ་མར་ནར་ནར་ རིང་པོ་ས་ལ་རེག་པ like a flowing robe touching the ground while walking) (*Dag. 8*).

འཇོལ་ལེ *hjol-le* hanging; cf. ལྡུང་ངེ or གྲོད་པ་འཇོལ་ལེ hanging-belly, paunch.

འཇོལ་མོ *Hjol-mo* 1. a singing bird of very sweet note, said to be abundant in the juniper groves near Lhasa and in Lhokha: འཇོལ་མོའི་གྲེ་བས་ཚངས་པའི་དབྱངས་ལྟ་བུ་སྐྱེད *hjol-mohi gre-was tshaṅs-pahi dbyaṅs lta-bu skyed* from the throat of the Jol-mo comes out a voice-liko that of Brahmā. In *Snd. Hbk.* mention is made of two species of Jol-mo: འཇོལ་ནག said to be a species of blackbird identical with *Merula ruficollis*, and འཇོལ་ཁྲ a middle-sized piebald bird described as white in colour with yellow markings and with a daub of red behind each ear.

Met. Syn. ལྔ་བའི་དབྱངས་སྙན *lṅa-wahi dbyaṅs-sñan*; གྲེ་འགྱུར་མཁན *gre-hgyur-mkhan*; དུས་ཚིགས་ཀུན་འགྲོ *dus-tshigs kun-hgro* (*Mṅon.*).

རྗང་མ *rjaṅ-ma*=རྫང་མ store-room (*Jä.*).

རྗིད་པ *rjid-pa* acc. to *Cs.* lean; gen. རིད་པ.

རྗིབ་ལས *rjib-las* in *W.*=service done in socage; compulsory service in the fields, on roads etc. (*Ja.*).

རྗུད་པ *rjud-pa*=རྒུད་པ *rgud-pa* आपद्, आपत trouble, danger, disadvantage (*Dag. 8*).

རྗེ *rje* स्वामी, आर्य्य, प्रभु lord, master, superior, chief; མི་རྗེ་ཆེན་པོ his lordship, his majesty; a title of rulers and chiefs. In Tibet this title is also applied to ministers and to officials up to the rank of མདའ་དཔོན *Mdah-dpon* (general) if appointed from among the hereditary nobles of the land. ཡུལ་གྱི་རྗེ་མཛད་ནས *yul-gyi rje mdsad-nas* having acted the part of a sovereign of the country.

རྗེ་ཁྲི་སྒྲ་སྤུངས་ཅན *Rje Khri sgra spuṅs-can* one of the kings of Tibet (*Yig.*); རྗེ་ཁྲི་ཐོག *Rje khri-thog* the reigning king (of Tibet).

རྗེ་དགེ་འདུན་གྲུབ *Rje Dge-hdun-grub* Gedun-dub, the famous Lama of Lhasa who founded the monastery of Tashi-lhunpo in Tsang, and who was one of the most distinguished disciples of Tsongkhapa. *Note*: the title of Dalai Lama was not assumed until 200 years later.

རྗེ་ངར *rje-ṅar* जङ्घा the loin; but acc. to *Jä.* the lower part of the leg.

* རྗེ་ལྕང་སྐྱ་རོལ་པའི་རྡོ་རྗེ *Rje lcaṅ-skya rol-pahi rdo-rje* or ལྕང་སྐྱ་རོལ་པའི་རྡོ་རྗེའི་ཞབས *Lcaṅ-skya rol-pahi rdo-rjihi-shabs* (*18B*), v. *Rolpahi Rdorje*.

རྗེ་ཉིད *rje-ñid* प्रभुत्व your lordship, reverence.

རྗེ་ཐོག་རྩན *Rje-thog-rtsan* n. of a king of Tibet (*Yig.*).

རྗེ་བ *rje-wa*, pf. བརྗེས, fut. བརྗེ, imp. བརྗེས परिवर्त्तन to change, barter, to give or take in exchange: འདི་དག་གིས་བརྗེར it may be changed for these; to shift, pass on; རྗེ་བུའི་ནོར articles of barter.

རྗེ་བོ *rje-ho* ईश्वर, आर्य्य, स्वामी, प्रभु 1. lord, master, ruler, king: བོད་ཁམས་ཀྱི་རྗེ་བོར་གྱུར he became sovereign of Tibet; ས་ཡི་བདག་པོ་མི་ཡི་རྗེ *sa-yi bdag-po mi-yi rje* the lord of the soil, ruler of the people; རྗེ་བོ་དང་བྲན master and servant; རྗེ་གཡོག master and slave; རྗེ་བློན king and minister; རྗེ་ཅི་ལགས *rje-ci lags* sir, what for, why? 2. a title of honour for dreaded persons or deities.

Syn. གཙོ་བོ *gtso-bo*; དམག་འདྲེན *dmag-hdren*; མགོ་དཔོན *mgo-dpon*; དཔོན་མགོ *dpon-mgo* (*Mñon.*).

རྗེ་འབངས *rje-hbañs* the king and his subjects.

རྗེ་མ *rje-ma*=གཙམ་མ acc. to *Cs.* a lady of rank; རྗེ་མ་ཆུང་ young lady.

རྗེ་མོ *rje-mo* ईश्वरी mistress, lady.

རྗེ་བཙུན *rje-btsun* भट्टारक reverend, worshipful. This title is applied to saints, hermits, learned lamas, *e.g.*, to Milaraspa, the author and peripatetic teacher.

* རྗེ་བཙུན་དམ་པ་བློ་བཟང་བསྟན་པའི་རྒྱལ་མཚན *Rje-btsun dam-pa blo-bzañ bstan-pahi rgyal-mtshan* *Sehr.*

* རྗེ་བཙུན་དཔལ *rje-btsun-dpal* श्रीमट्टारक honourable sir! (*Bull. 1848, 301*) *Sehr.*

* རྗེ་བཙུན་བྱམས་པ *Rje-btsun byams-pa* or བྱམས་པ་མགོན་པོ your beneficient reverence! (*1 A.*) *Schr.*

རྗེ་བཙུན་མ *rje-btsun-ma* देवी lady who has entered the order of ge-long-ma. Applied also to any very charitable or devout woman. བསྟན་འགྲོའི་དཔལ་མགོན་མཚུངས་མེད་རྗེ་བཙུན་མ་སྐུ་ཞབས་མཆོག་གི་ཞབས་དྲུང་དུ to the feet of the venerable lady who in her devotion to the cause of religion and in beneficence is unrivalled (*Yig. k. 14*).

* རྗེ་བཙུན་མ་ཀཱ་པ་ལི་ཏཱ་ར *Rje-btsun-ma kā-pa-li tā-ra* (*54 A.*) * རྗེ་བཙུན་མ་འཕགས་མ་སྒྲོལ་མ *Rje-btsun-ma hphags-ma sgrol-ma* महामाद्दारिका आर्या तारा titles of the goddess Dolma (*Tā. 2, 151*).

རྗེ་རིགས *rje-rigs* the caste of the nobility; རྗེའུ་རིགས the caste of the smaller lords, *i.e.*, gentlemen.

Syn. བརླ་བྱུང་ *brla-byuñ* (sprung from the loins); བརླ་སྐྱེས *brla-skyes* (loin-born); ས་རེག *sa-reg*, རྗེའུ་རིགས *rjehu-rigs* (*Mñon.*).

རྗེ་རིན་པོ་ཆེ *Rje Rin-po-che* the epithet by which Tsong-khapa is commonly known in Tibet. His real name was ཀུན་དགའ་བློ་བཟང་གྲགས་པ in Sans. सुमतिकीर्त्ति.

རྗེའུ་རིགས *rjehu-rigs*, v. རྗེ་རིགས *rje-rigs*.

རྗེ་ས *rje-sa*=ཞེ་ས deference, respect; ཞེ་ས་བྱེད་པ to show respect, to pay one's respect.

卐 རྗེད་པ *rjed-pa* अर्चना, pf. and fut. བརྗེད *brjed* 1. to honour, reverence; མཆོད་ཅིང་བརྗེད to honour and worship; བརྗེད་པའི་འོས venerable, worthy of honour. 2. विस्मृति to forget; བརྗེད་དུ་འཇུག་པ *brjed-du hjug-pa* to make forget, to cause to forget: རང་ཡུལ་རང་གིས་བརྗེད་དེ having gradually forgotten my native land (*Mil.*).

རྗེད་ངས་ཅན *rjed-ñas-can* acc. to *Lex.* consulted; by *Jä.* मुषितस्मृति; forgetful, oblivious; *Cs.* gives instead of it རྗེད་ངེས་ཅན.

རྗེད་ཆུ *rjed-chu* draught of oblivion, water of forgetfulness.

རྗེད་ཐོ *rjed-tho* list of notes, memorandum, journal, note-book, etc.

རྗེད་རྡོ *rjed-rdo* prob. memorial stone (*Jä.*).

རྗེད་བྱང་ *rjed-byañ* specification or list of goods, luggage, etc., which the Tibetans mark with letters of the alphabet.

རྗེད་བྱེད *rjed-byed* or རྗེད་བྱེད་ཀྱི་གདོན 1. a demon that takes away the power of memory. 2. अपस्मार epilepsy.

རྗེད་ཟས *rjed-zas* the meal of forgetfulness (*Cs.*); any food that produces oblivion.

རྗེན་པ *rjen-pa* नग्न, अचेल 1. stark, bare, naked; རྐང་རྗེན་ bare-footed, unshod; ཞབས་རྗེན་པར་གཤེགས་པ to go bare-footed; གདོང་རྗེན་དུ་སྡོད་པ *gdoṅ-rjen-du sdod-pa* to sit with unveiled face; མགོ་རྗེན་ with uncovered head; རྒྱབ་རྗེན་པ *rgyab-rjen-pa* naked backside; རྗེན་པར་འདོན་པ to strip perfectly; དམར་རྗེན quite naked (*Sch.*); རལ་གྲི་རྗེན་པ *ral-gri rjen-pa* a naked sword; ས་རྗེན་པ the bare ground, an unoovered ground; རྗེན་ནེ་བ undisguised, obvious to the understanding, manifest. 2. raw, not roasted or cooked; དམར་རྗེན red raw meat; མར་རྗེན butter not melted; ནས་རྗེན raw barley, not parched; also the meal of it; བྲ་རྗེན buck-wheat meal (*Sch.*). 3. unripe (chiefly from *Jä.*).

རྗེན *rjen* raw; ཤ་རྗེན 1. raw meat. 2.= ཡང་ན་ལུས་ལ་གོས་མེད་པ a naked person (*Dag. 8*).

Syn. གཅེར་བུ *gcer-bu*; རྐྱང་པ *rkyaṅ-pa*; སྒྲིབ་མེད *sgrib-med*; གཡོགས་མེད *gyogs-med* (*Mṅon.*).

རྗེན་བཏགས *rjen-btags* raw barley or peas ground, without being first parched.

རྗེན་ཕྱེ *rjen-phye* unparched barley, pea, or wheat flour (*Rtsii.*).

རྗེན་རིགས *rjen-rigs* victuals that may be eaten raw (*Cs.*).

རྗེན་ཟས *rjen-zas* uncooked meal or victuals.

རྗེས *rjes* has primarily the signification of a mark left, an imprint made on the ground; and this meaning is more exactly expressed in such terms as རྐང་རྗེས *rkaṅ-rjes*, a foot-mark, the trace of one's foot and ལག་རྗེས the impression or mark left of one's hand, hence fig. an action or deed. 2. However, from this the primary sense of རྗེས there is derived the second and more ordinary signification of the word, *i.e.*, that which comes after, that which follows, the consequence. Hence we obtain the most common usage of all, namely its use as an adv., signifying after, afterwards; and the postp. རྗེས་སུ, རྗེས་ལ, or simply རྗེས, meaning after, behind, &c. རྗེས་སུ་འགྲོ་བ to follow; ཤ་བའི་རྗེས་ལ་འབྲངས་སོང་ pursued after the stag. Also, conjunction དེ་རྗེས therefore, consequently. 3. the hinder-parts, v. *Pth. 270*, line *6*.

རྗེས་ཁུགས་པ *rjes-khugs-pa* अनुवर्त्ते to recall or find out afterwards.

རྗེས་ཁྲིད *rjes-khrid* नत्तु, किल certainty, sureness.

རྗེས་སུ་སྐྱབ་པ to recover, to re-acquire, v. རྗེས་མ (*Situ. 110*).

རྗེས་དངོས *rjes-dṅos* real.

རྗེས་གཅོད *rjes-gcod*=གྲི knife (*Mṅon.*).

རྗེས་གཅོད་པ *rjes-cod-pa* अनुच्छेद 1. acc. to *Sch.* to destroy, blot out, efface a track or trace; in *Med.* to eradicate the trace of a disease, to cure thoroughly. 2. to separate, disjoin. 3. In *W.* acc. to *Jä.* to follow a trace or track, to find or to come upon the track.

རྗེས་ཆགས *rjes-chags* अनुरक्त attachment, attached; compassion.

Syn. རྗེས་སུ་བརྩེ *rjes-su-brtse*; སྙིང་རྗེ *sñiṅ-rje*. འགྲོགས་པ *hgrogs-pa* (*Mṅon.*).

རྗེས་ཆགས་སྐྱེ *rjes-chags-skye*=བསྔོད་ཚིག or བཀུར་ཚིག eulogy, praise (*Mṅon.*).

རྗེས་འཇུག *rjes-hjug* 1. a final consonant. རྗེས་འཇུག་བཅུ the ten finals, *i.e.*, ག, ང་, ད, ན, བ, མ, འ, ར, ལ, ས, which are affixed to others to form a syllable or word. 2. adj. following, subsequent; ཕྱི་རབས་རྗེས་འཇུག་ཐམས་ཅད all the following generations.

རྗེས་བརྗོད *rjes-brjod* अनुवाक् imitative words; a copy; also postscript, anything said or written afterwards; an after-expression.

རྗེས་སྙེགས་པ *rjes-sñegs-pa* to follow after (in *Sikk.*).

རྗེས་ཐོག *rjes-thog*=རྗེས་ལ afterwards.

རྗེས་ཐོབ་པ 1. cessation of meditation to take food, but no more of it than is absolutely necessary for preservation of life. 2. पृष्ठलब्ध, अनुलाभ profit, gain. 3. to find the track.

རྗེས་མཐུན་པ *rjes-mthun-pa* अनुकाय (*A. K. III. 38*) to make similar, to adjust afterwards.

རྗེས་དྲན *rjes-dran* अनुस्मृति remembrance, recollection.

རྗེས་གནང་ *rjes-gnaṅ* अनुज्ञा, अनुमति, समक्षि, आज्ञप्ति permission, leave, consent.

རྗེས་པ *rjes-pa*, v. རྗེ་བ *rje-wa*.

རྗེས་དཔག *rjes-dpag* 1. अनुमान conjecture, guessing or guess. 2. consideration, deliberation. 3. acc. to *Was.* a syllogism consisting of three propositions.

རྗེས་འབྲང་ *rjes-ḥbraṅ* अनुगत a follower, an adherent.

རྗེས་མ *rjes-ma* 1. चरम last, final; the final one. 2. sometimes for རྗེས *rjes*. 3. the hinder part (*Cs.*).

Syn. ཕྱི་མ *phyi-ma*; རྟིང་མ *rtiṅ-ma*; ཕྱི་ཆོས *phyi-ços*; གཤམ་མ *gçam-ma*; མཇུག་མ *mjug-ma*; རྗེས་སུ་བགྱིད *rjes-su-bgyid*; རྗེས་སུ་སྒྲུབ *rjes-su sgrub* (*Mṅon.*).

རྗེས་མེད *rjes-med* without leaving any traces, trackless; རྗེས་མེད་འཇིག་པ to destroy without trace being left.

རྗེས་འཛིན *rjes-ḥdsin* acquirements; accomplishments: རྗེས་འཛིན་རིག་པའི་ཡང་རྩེ་འདི་ནམ་ཡང་མི་ཉམས *rjes-ḥdsin rig-paḥi yaṅ-rtse-ḥdi nam-yaṅ mi-ñams* these acquirements—the *summum bonum* of knowledge—can never fade.

རྗེས་བཟུང་ *rjes-bzuṅ* अनुग्रह the taking or receiving at last; a favour or kindness done (*A. K. XXX. 3*).

རྗེས་ཤེས *rjes-çes* अनुज्ञान, अनुज्ञप्ति knowledge; knowing after.

རྗེས་སུ *rjes-su* adv. afterwards.

རྗེས་སུ་སྐྱེས *rjes-su-skyes* = མཐུན་པར་སྐྱེས *mthun-par-skyes*, v. རྗེས་སྐྱེས *rjes-skyes*, अनुज a younger brother; also करण a deed, act.

རྗེས་སུ་ཁྱོད *rjes-su khyod* प्रतिमा a statue, representation; a figure representing some person or deity.

རྗེས་སུ་འགུགས་པ *rjes-su-ḥgugs-pa* to recall; to summon; to order to do according to one's instructions.

རྗེས་སུ་བགྲོད *rjes-su-bgrod* gone behind, followed.

རྗེས་སུ་འགྲོ་བ *rjes-su ḥgro-wa* अन्वय to follow, go behind; to imitate.

རྗེས་སུ་བསྒྲུབ་པ *rjes-su bsgrub-pa* अनुविधान lit. doing after an order; following, obeying.

རྗེས་སུ་གཅོད *rjes-su gcod* = met. a knife (*Mṅon.*).

རྗེས་སུ་ཆགས *rjes-su chags* = རྗེས་ཆགས अनुराग atttachment; अनुरक्त attached, fond of; རྗེས་སུ་ཆགས་བཅས with love or fondness; also सवेग with motion, or force.

རྗེས་སུ་འཇིགས *rjes-su-ḥjigs* = འགྱོད་པ *ḥgyod-pa* a repentance (*Mṅon.*).

རྗེས་སུ་འཇུག་པ *rjes-su ḥjug-pa* अनुसारि or अनुसारिणी, अनुवर्त्ति imitation; imitator; follower.

རྗེས་སུ་རྟོགས་པར་བྱ *rjes-su rtogs-par bya* अनुमन्तव्य should ponder on, consider, reflect upon.

རྗེས་སུ་བསྟན་པ *rjes-su bstan-pa* अनुशासना orders, ruling instruction; བཀའ་ལུང་ or རྗེས་སུ་གནང་བ precepts, instructions left (*Mṅon.*); in colloq. མགོ་འདྲེན་བྱེད་པ *mgo-ḥdren byed-pa* to instruct a disciple in spiritual learning; also to protect, patronise.

རྗེས་སུ་ཐོས *rjes-su-thos* अनुश्रुत्य hearing afterwards, anything heard after.

རྗེས་སུ་མཐུན་པ *rjes-su mthun-pa* अनुलोम, अच्छा regular, harmonious; faith. རྗེས་སུ་མཐུན་པའི་ཆོས་དྲུག षडनुलोमिकधर्म्म six regular virtues:—(1) རྗེས་སུ་མཐུན་པའི་བཟོད་པ अनुलोमिकक्षान्ति resignation to natural consequences; (2) རྗེས་སུ་མཐོ་རིས अनुस्वर्ग character; (3) རྗེས་སུ་མཐོང་བ समनुपश्यत् disposition to view a thing properly; (4) རྗེས་སུ་གདུང་བ अनुताप remorse; (5) འགྱོད་པ *hgyod-pa* अनुशय, कौकृत्य sorrow for good as well as bad acts; (6) རྗེས་སུ་འདོད་པ *rjes-su hdod-pa* अन्वेषण right ambition.

རྗེས་སུ་དྲན་པ *rjes-su dran-pa*,=རྗེས་དྲན अनुस्मृति subjects of recollection, which are six:—(1) སངས་རྒྱས་རྗེས་སུ་དྲན་པ बुद्धानुस्मृति the remembrance of the Buddha; (2) ཆོས་རྗེས་སུ་དྲན་པ धर्मानुस्मृति the remembrance of the *Dharma*; (3) དགེ་འདུན་རྗེས་སུ་དྲན་པ सङ्घानुस्मृति the remembrance of the *Sañgha*; (4) ཚུལ་ཁྲིམས་རྗེས་སུ་དྲན་པ शीलानुस्मृति the rememberance of religious duty; (5) གཏོང་བ་རྗེས་སུ་དྲན་པ त्यागानुस्मृति the recollection of renunciation; (6) ལྷ་རྗེས་སུ་དྲན་པ देवानुस्मृति the remembrance of the gods.

རྗེས་སུ་ལྡན *rjes-su-ldan* अभ्यस्त practised, habituated.

རྗེས་སུ་གནང་བ *rjes-su gnañ-wa*, v. རྗེས་སུ་བསྟན་པ *rjes-su bstan-pa* to propound; to grant religious instruction.

རྗེས་སུ་དཔག *rjes-su-dpag* or དཔོག अनुमान to weigh, to deliberate upon.

རྗེས་སུ་སྤྱོད་པ *rjes-su spyod-pa*=རྗེས་སུ་འགྲོ་བ or ཕྱིར་འབྲང་ (*Mñon.*) to perform or practise.

རྗེས་སུ་འཕྲོག་པ *rjes-su-hphrog-pa* अनुच्छेद to deprive, to plunder, to rob, to snatch.

རྗེས་སུ་བྱེད་པ *rjes-su byed-pa*=རྗེས་སུ་འགྱུར་བ *rjes-su hgyur-wa* अनुकरण to do like another, to imitate; imitation.

རྗེས་སུ་འབྱུང་བ *rjes-su hbyuñ-wa* अनुभव feeling, thinking.

* རྗེས་སུ་འབྲང་བ *rjes-su hbrañ-wa* अनुसार going after; usage, custom (*Bull. 1848, 291*).

རྗེས་སུ་འབྲང་བ *rjes-su hbrañ-wa* अनुसरण to follow.

རྗེས་སུ་འབྲེལ་བ *rjes-su hbrel-wa* अर्चना to adore, to worship.

རྗེས་སུ་མི་མཐུན་པ *rjes-su mi-mthun-pa* प्रतिलोम discordant, in contradistinction to another.

རྗེས་སུ་བརྩེ་བ *rjes-su brtse-wa* अनुकम्पा to pity; to favour out of compassion (*Mñon.*).

རྗེས་སུ་ཚོལ་བ *rjes-su tshol-wa* अन्वेषणा searching after; अनुप्रार्थि imploring help, favour, etc.

རྗེས་སུ་འཚོ *rjes-su-htsho* सेवक, एषणा being supported or backed by another, maintained or favoured with sustenance.

རྗེས་སུ་ཞུགས *rjes-su-shugs* प्रविष्ट involved with.

རྗེས་སུ་མི་འཛིན་པ *rjes-su mi-hdsin-pa* not retaining; not retentive.

Syn. མི་འཛིན *mi-hdsin*; དེ་ངང་འགལ *de-ñañ-hgal* (*Mñon.*).

རྗེས་སུ་འཛིན་པ *rjes-su hdsin-pa* 1. अनुधारण to follow (one in reading or in making a speech, etc.); to welcome or receive kindly. 2. to believe; to have the impression of, to retain.

Syn. མངོན་པར་བསྐྱེད *mñon-par-bskyed* (*Mñon.*).

རྗེས་སུ་ཡི་རང་བ *rjes-su yi-rañ-wa* to rejoice in ecstasy.

རྗེས་སུ་བཤད་པ *rjes-su bçad-pa* अनुव्याख्यान to explain; explanation, description.

རྗེས་སུ་སློབ་པ *rjes-su slob-pa* अनुशिक्षा teaching according to another's system.

རྗོད་པ pf. and fut. བརྗོད, to say, to recite (དཔེ་ལྟ་བུ from a book); pronounce, utter, *e.g.*, a charm or magic formula; to annouce, promulgate (ཆོས a religious doctrine); to enumerate, set forth, ལེགས་པ or ཉེས་པ the good or bad qualities, actions etc.; to treat of a subject in writing.

བརྗིད *brjid*=གཟི་བརྗིད *gzi-brjid*, དཔལ་བརྗིད *dpal-brjid* glory, halo, splendour, lustre; བརྗིད་ཀྱིས་བརྗིད *brjid-kyis brjid* shines with still greater brightness.

བརྗིད་ཅན་ *brjid-can* = གཟི་བརྗིད་ཅན་ कान्त lustrous, refulgent; very able and accomplished.

བརྗིད་ཆགས་པ་ *brjid-chags-pa* = བག་ཆགས་པ or འདུ་ཆགས་པ (*Dag. 8*).

བརྗིད་ནོན་ *brjid-non* bringing another under one's power by the spell of speech, learning, or force of character; subduing one by will-power or by the fascination of one's charms, &c. ཡོང་སྡུད་བརྗིད་ནོན་ཆེ་ཤིང་ *yoṅ-sdud brjid-non che-çiṅ* (*Rtsii.*).

བརྗིད་པ *brjid-pa* to shine, glitter.

བརྗིད་པའི་འགྲོས *brjid-pahi-hgros* = ཀང་པའི་འདུ་བྱེད walking with a dancing gait (*Mṅon.*).

བརྗེ *brje* परिवर्त sbst. change, barter.

བརྗེ་བ *brje-wa* to be absorbed in thought; བརྗེ་བ་བྱང་ཆུབ་ཀྱི་སེམས behaviour after the manner of a *Bodhisattva* whose self is lost in the thought of the well-being of others. As a vb. དངོས་པོ་ཡན་ཆད་བརྗེ་བ to change, transfer, barter property.

བརྗེ་བོ *brje-bo* a making up, a compensation by barter; བརྗེ་བོ་བྱེད་པ to exchange, to give an equal measure in bartering, *e.g.*, of salt for barley, &c.

བརྗེ་མཚམས *brje-mtshams* taking over office, when a new officer takes charge of a post from an old officer (*Rtsii.*).

བརྗེད *brjed* = བསྐུད་པ *bskud-pa* oblivion.

བརྗེད་ང་བའི་འཚེ་བ *brjed-ṅa-wahi htshe-wa* the danger of forgetting.

བརྗེད་ངས་པ *brjed-ṅas-pa* मुषितस्मृति one whose recollection (memory) has been robbed. ཞེས་བྱ་བ་ནི་ཆོས་རྣམས་ལ་མི་དྲན་པ་གང་ཡིན་པའོ "it signifies that which has been forgotten in reference to a religious discourse" (*K. d.* ང *355*).

བརྗེད་ཐོ *brjed-tho* memorandum. Syn. དྲན་ཐོ *dran-tho*; བརྗེད་བྱང་ *brjed-byaṅ* (*Mṅon.*).

བརྗེད་ཐོ་བཏགས་པ *brjed-tho-btags-pa* to keep a memorandum; མ་བརྗེད་པའི་ཕྱིར་ཐོ་འགོད་པ to keep note with a view not to forget a thing: ཇོ་བོ་ངོ་མཚར་ཅན་གྱི་གཏམ་ལ་དགེས་པས་བརྗེད་ཐོ་བཏགས the lord (Atis'a), being pleased with the wonderful account, took a note of it (*A. 50*).

བརྗེད་པ *brjed-pa* विस्मृति, सम्प्रमोष to forget. Stated by lamas to be the correct spelling of རྗེད་པ *rjed-pa*.

བརྗེད་པ་མེད་པ *brjed-pa med-pa* असम्प्रमोष without forgetfulness, oblivion.

བརྗེད་སྤྲོད *brjed-sprod* prob. mis-spelt for བརྗིད་སྤྲོད *brjid-sprod* to give or make over charge of an office or duty.

བརྗེད་བྱེད *brjed-byed* अपस्मार forgetfulness (*Zam. 11*).

བརྗེད་བྱེད་ཀྱི་གདོན *brjed-byed-kyi gdon* demon who brings in forgetfulness (*Mṅg. 77, 79*).

བརྗེད་སྦྱང་བ *brjed sbyaṅ-wa* to recall to the mind what has been forgotten and to retain it by exercise.

བརྗེས་པ *brjes-pa* pf. of བརྗེ་བ q.v.

བརྗོད *brjod* संगीति, उदीरित (निगदित *Kālac. T, 101*) speech, clear expression; a phrase, utterance. བརྗོད་ཀྱིས་མི་ལང་བ vb. to be inexpressible. རེ་རེའི་མིང་ནས་བརྗོད་མི་ལང་ one cannot mention or enumerate each by its name: བརྗོད་ཀྱིས་མི་ལང་བའི་ཕྱིར་མི་བཀོད *brjod-kyis mi-laṅ-wahi phyir mi-bkod* I do not write it down, because it is impossible to relate everything (*Jä.*).

བརྗོད་ཉམས་ཚིག *brjod-ñams-tshig* = ཚིག་བཟང་པོ་མེད་པ *tshig bzaṅ-po med-pa* bad language, vulgar speech.

བརྗོད་དུ་མེད་པ *brjod-du med-pa* अनभिलाप्य 1. indescribable, inexpressible, ineffable;

བརྗོད་དུ་མེད་པ་ལས་བརྩམས་པ अनभिलाप्य परिवर्त recording what is unspeakable. 2. (གྲངས) n. of a number.

བརྗོད་དོ *brjod-do* उक्त said, described.

བརྗོད་བདེ་བ *brjed-bde-wa* agreeable speech; also one able to speak with facility.

བརྗོད་འདོད *brjod-hdod* acc. to *Schtr.* a mere supposition.

བརྗོད་པ་ཡིན *brjod-pa-yin* कथित it is said, related, v. རྗོད་པ *rjod-pa*.

བརྗོད་པར་འདོད་པ *brjod-par hdod-pa* wishing to speak; also विवक्षा to desire to talk of one's own self, conceit.

བརྗོད་པར་བྱ་བ *brjod-par bya-wa* वाच्यम् fit to be spoken; བརྗོད་པར་བྱེད་པ *brjod-par byed-pa* वद to speak; sbst. वाचक a speaker.

བརྗོད་བྱ *brjod-bya*=དོན *don* meaning; वाच्य, वाक्य, अर्थ, अभिधेय, परिघोष an expression, anything said; an attribute (*Zam. 11*).

བརྗོད་བྱ་ཅན *brjod-bya-can*=དོན་ཅན *don-can* possessed of meaning; explainable.

བརྗོད་བྱ་ལྡན *brjod-bya-ldan* वराक, सुतक met. a child.

བརྗོད་བྱ་བྲལ *brjod-bya-bral* = བརྗོད་བྱ་མེད་པ अवाच्य that cannot be said, or described.

བརྗོད་བྱའི་རྟགས *brjod-byahi-rtags* sign of expression; प्रत्यर्थन begging back.

བརྗོད་བྱའི་རབ *brjod-byahi-rab*, བརྗོད་བྱེད་རབ प्रवचनीय fit to be proclaimed, praiseworthy.

བརྗོད་མི་བདེ་བ *brjod-mi bde-wa* one who is not able to speak well.

བརྗོད་མེད *brjod-med* 1. the unspeakable, the transcendental. 2. a speech not earnestly meant; empty words, mere talk. 3. གྲངས་གནས n. of a very large number. དཔག་ཐག་གཉིས་དང་བརྗོད་མེད་གཉིས *dpag-thag-gñis dañ brjod-med-gñis* (*Ya-sel. 57*).

བརྗོད་བཟང་ *brjod-bzañ*=སྨྲ་བ་བཟང་ or ལབ་བཟང་ good speech, also a good speaker; good delivery (*Mñon.*). མངོན་བརྗོད synonymy, explanation of words; imagery. མཆོད་བརྗོད praise, eulogy; acc. to *Sch.* invocation of a deity. ཆེ་བརྗོད complimentary expression, adulation. ཆེད་དུ་བརྗོད་པ acc. to *Schtr.* preface, introduction; acc. to *Jä.* in *C.* to approve, commend, sanction; acc. to *Was.* the title of a book called उदानवर्ग, class of *gāthā* delivered by Buddha out of joy.

བརྗོད་ཡས *brjod-yas* (གྲངས) n. of a large number.

ལྗག་མ *ljag-ma* fine satin generally spread on cushions used by the great of Tibet.

ལྗག་མོ་གླིང་ག *Ljag-mo gliñ-ga* n. of a state grove in Tibet (*Rtsii.*).

ལྗགས *ljags* resp. for ལྕེ *lce* जिह्वा, रसना the tongue; ལྗགས་ཀྱིས་ཆབ་འདོར་བ *ljags-kyis chab-hdor-wa* to spit, to spit out; ལྗགས་ཆབ *ljags-chab* spittle, saliva; ལྗགས་དབུགས *ljags-dbugs* breath. ལྗགས་ཀྱི་དབང་པོ *ljags-kyi dwañ-po* जिह्वेन्द्रिय the organ of taste, the tongue.

Syn. རོ་འཛིན *ro-hdsin*; ལྕེ *lce* (*Mñon*).

ལྗགས་བསྙེན་པ *ljags-bñen-pa*=སྔགས་བཟླས་པ *sñags-bzlas-pa* to ejaculate charms or *mantras*.

ལྗང་ *Ljañ* also spelt, ལྗངས a place one day's journey to the west of Lhasa.

ལྗང་བཀྲ་ཤིས་དགོན་པ *Ljañ-bkra-çis dgon-pa* n. of an ancient monastery in Jang (*Deb. 40*).

ལྗང་གུ *ljañ-gu* green (light).

ལྗང་ཇ *ljañ-ja* also called ལྗང་ཇ་པ་རི *ljañ-ja-pa-ri* green tea, exported from the Chinese district of Kang-tse Rapak situated on the confines of Tibet (*Rtsii.*).

ལྗང་དུང་ *ljañ-duñ* in *W.* acc. to *Jä.* solid, not hollow; it also prob. signifies, bar-silver, *i.e.*, silver beaten.

ལྗང་སྐྱ *ljaṅ-skya* greenish-white.

ལྗང་ཁུ *ljaṅ-khu* also spelt ལྗང་གུ *ljaṅ-ga* हरित, श्याम green (*Dag. 8*).

ལྗང་ཁྲ *ljaṅ-khra* party-coloured on a green base; different colours on green back ground.

ལྗང་ནག *ljaṅ-nag* कालश्यामल blackish-green.

ལྗང་དམར *ljaṅ-dmar* greenish-red.

ལྗང་སེར *ljaṅ-ser* greenish-yellow.

ལྗང་པ *ljaṅ-pa* adj. 1. green, not ripe. 2. green corn in the first stage of its growth, green leaves of barley and oats. 3. silver-plate, pure silver: དངུལ་གྱི་ལྗང་པ་དེ་རྣམས་གད་སྐྱིབས་ཤིག་ཏུ་སྦས *dṅul-gyi ljaṅ-pa de-rnams gad-skyibs çig-tu sbas* they concealed the plates of silver in certain crevices of the cliff (*A. 121*).

Syn. མ་སྨིན་པ *ma-smin-pa*; སྔོ་སངས *sṅo-saṅs*; ངེས་སྒྲིབ *ṅes-sgrib* (*Mṅon.*).

ལྗང་བུ *ljaṅ-bu* the seedlings of rice, when they grow a foot high and are fit to be transplanted; greenness, verdure (grass, foliage, shrubs); ལོ་ལྗང་བ a green leaf, also having a green leaf.

ལྗང་མ *ljaṅ-ma*=ལྗང་བུ *ljaṅ-bu*.

ལྗང་མོ *Ljaṅ-mo* a district in Lithang beyond Kham.

ལྗན་ལྗིན *ljan-ljin* परिक्लेद defilement, filth, dirt, dust, sweepings: བག་ཆགས་དྲི་མ་ལྗན་ལྗིན་ཁྲུས་ཀྱིས་བཀྲུ་བའི་ཕྱིར for washing off by consecrated water the defilement and the mucus of lust (*D.R.*).

ལྗབ *ljab* in *W.* flat, plain, even (*Jä.*).

ལྗབ་ལྗབ *ljab-ljab* a large number.

ལྗི *lji*=ལྗི sbst. भार heaviness.

ལྗི་ཏིང *lji-tiṅ* heavy, depressed, as if pressed with a stone: སྟོན་པའི་ཐུགས་ལྗི་ཏིང་གིས་སྨྲས་ནས་ཇོ་བོ་ལ Stonpa's mind having become depressed, he said to the lord (*A. 115*).

ལྗི་བ *lji-wa* or ལྗི་མོ *lji-mo* adj. 1. भारि, गुरु heavy, weighty. 2. a flea.

ལྗི་མེད *lji-med* light, not heavy.

ལྗིད་གནོན *ljid-gnon* also ལྗིད་ནོན *ljid-non* साद्यं oppressive.

ལྗིད་ཅན *ljid-can* heavy; ལྗིད་ཆེ་བ *ljid-che-wa* very heavy.

ལྗིད་པ *ljid-pa* गुरुत्व heaviness, weight: གསེར་དང་ལྗིད་པ་ཉམས་པ་དགོས *gser-daṅ ljid-pa ñams-pa-dgos* it must be weighed up with gold (*Jä.*). དེ་དང་ལྗིད་ཉམས་པ *de-daṅ ljid ñams-pa* of equal weight, equal in weight: ལུས་ཐམས་ཅད་ཀྱི་ལྗིད་ཕབ *lus-thams-cad-kyi ljid-phab* he sat down with the whole weight of his body (*Cs.*); ལྗིད་ཙི་ཙམ *ljid-ci-tsam* what is the weight of.

ལྗུར *ljur* prob. for ལྡུར *ldur*.

ལྗེན་པ *ljen-pa* to enter, to penetrate; བློ་ལ་ལྗེན་པ *blo-la ljen-pa* to be perceived, understood; ཚོན་ལྗེན *tshon-ljen* a dye or colour penetrating and remaining fixed in cloth, etc. (*Jä.*).

ལྗོང་དར *ljoṅ-dar*=མདའ་དོང་གི་དར *mdaḥ-doṅ-gi dar* a scarf that is used to cover a quiver; ལྗོང་དར་རེར་འབྲུ *ljoṅ-dar rer ḥbru* bre (བྲེ) of corn for each scarf (*Rtsii.*).

ལྗོངས *ljoṅs* 1.=གཞོང་ a cultivated valley; སྨན་གཞོང *sman-gshoṅ* or སྨན་ལྗོངས *sman-ljoṅs* a valley of medicinal herbs. 2. a province or district; ལྗོངས་ཆེན་པོ *ljoṅs-chen-po* a large country; ཁ་བ་ཅན་གྱི་ལྗོངས *Kha-wa-can-gyi ljoṅs* हिमवत् प्रदेश the snowy provinces. མུ་གེའི་ལྗོངས *mu-geḥi ljoṅs* starving country, a poor country where food is scarce. ཀམས་ལྗོངས

nags-ljoṅs woody district. ལྗོངས་མི་རྣམས *ljoṅs-mi rnams* provincial people. ལྗོངས་སུ་རྒྱུ་བ *ljoṅs-su rgyu-wa* to rove about: སློབ་དཔོན་ཛེ་ཏཱ་རི་ལྗོངས་རྒྱུར་བྱོན་པས *slob-dpon dse-tā-ri ljoṅs-rgyur byon-pas* when the teacher Jetāri was roaming in the district (जनपद), *i.e.*, at a place round about his monastery after the summer recess (*Sñiñ*). ལྗོངས་རྒྱུར་བ *ljoṅs-rgyur-wa* the time at the end of the summer confinement in the monastery when monks are allowed holiday to roam about in the country.

ལྗོངས་གསུམ *ljoṅs-gsum* 1. ལྷོ་ནུབ་མཚམས་ན་སྦས་ཡུལ་འབྲས་མོ་ལྗོངས *lho-nub mtshams-na sbas-yul Hbras-mo ljoṅs* on the south-western confines (of C. Tib.) is the hidden country of *Hbras-mo-ljoṅs* (Demojong or Sikkim). 2. ནུབ་བྱང་མཚམས་ན་སྦས་ཡུལ་མཁན་པོ་ལྗོངས *nub-byañ mtshams-na sbas-yul Mkhan-po-ljoṅs* on the north-west boundary (of C. Tib.) is the hidden country of firs. 3. བྱང་ཤར་མཚམས་ནས་སྦས་ཡུལ་ལུང་གསུམ་ལྗོངས *byañ-çar mtshams-nas sbas-yul Luñ-gsum-ljoṅs* on the north-east boundary (of C. Tib.) is the hidden country of the three valleys. (*Kathañ. 168*). *Note*:—Huc's *San-chuan*.

ལྗོན་པ *ljon-pa* an immortal paradise, or country of the gods. ལྗོན་པའི་ནགས a sublime forest.

ལྗོན་ཤིང་ *ljoñ-çin* द्रुम, वृक्ष, तरु a tree; a magic tree in Dewachan.

Syn. ལྗོན་པ་ཤིང་ *ljon-pa-çiñ*; ཡལ་ག་ཅན *yal-gal-can*; འདབ་ལྡན *hdab-ldan*; རྐང་འཐུང་ *rkañ-hthuñ*; རྐང་པས་འཐུང་ *rkañ-pas-hthuñ*; རླན་ལས་སྐྱེས *rlan-las-skyes*; ཆུར་མི་ལྷུང་ *chur-mi-lhun*; རྩེ་མོ་ཅན *rtse-mo-can*; མགོ་ལྡིང་ཅན *mgo-ldiñ-can*; ཡལ་ག་འཛིན *yal-ga-hdsin*; འདབ་མ་ཅན *hdab-ma-can*; ཕུང་པོ་ཅན *phuñ-po-can*; འགྲོ་འགོག *hgro-hgog*; འགྲོ་མེད *hgro-med*; སྟེང་སྐྱེས *steñ-skyes*; ས་སྐྱེས *sa-skyes*; ཡལ་ག་འབྲེལ *yal-ga-hbrel* (*Mñon.*).

ལྗོན་པ་ལུང་ *Ljon-pa-luñ* n. of a district in Kong-po in South-Eastern Tibet.

ལྗོན་པ་སེར་པོ *ljon-pa ser-po*=ཐང་ཤིང་ देवदारुवृक्ष the *deodara* tree.

ལྗོན་ཤིང་རྩ་ཆས *ljon-çiñ rtsa-chas* a branching magic tree (*Mñon.*).

ཉ

ཉ *Ña* I: the eighth letter of the Tibetan alphabet corresponds in sound to the Sanskrit ञ. The sound of this letter, when followed by *u*, may be heard in English in such words as neuter, new, &c.

ཉ II: in general Buddhism this letter signifies ཤེས་རབ wisdom, knowledge (*K. my.* ཀ *207*); in Tantrikism: ཉ་ནི་སྤྱོད་དང་བྲལ་བའི་སྒོ, བྱ་བ་མེད་པས་ཐམས་ཅད་གྲོལ། *ña* is the symbol of passive existence; being free from action it leads to *Nirvâṇa* (*K. gu.* ཐ *42*).

ཉ III: symb. num. for eight.

ཉ་ཉེར *ña-ñer* n. of a number གཉལ་གཞི་འཁྱོང་འགྱུར་ཉ་ཉེར་དང་ ། (*Ya-sel 57*).

ཉ IV: मीन, अनिमिष, अर्भक, अण्डज the general term for a fish; means also the egg-born, the fixed; རྒྱལ་པོའི་གསོལ་ཉ the king's table fish; འདམ་ཉ an eel (*Cs.*).

Syn. སྒོང་སྐྱེས *sgoñ-skyes*, མིག་མི་འཛུམ་པ *mig mi-hdsum-pa*, འགྲོ་ལྡན *hgro-ldan*, རྣམ་འཕྱོ *rnam-hphyo*, སྣ་ཚོགས་རྒྱུ *sna-tshogs rgyu*, གསེར་གྱི་མིག་ཅན *gser-gyi mig-can*, ཆུས་མི་འཚུབ *chus mi-htshub*, ཆུར་ཉལ *chur-ñal*, རྒྱབ་རིང *rgyab-riñ* (*Mñon.*).

ཉ་ཀྱུ *ña-kyu*, described as ཉ་འཛིན་པའི་ལྕགས་ཀྱུ *ña hdsin-pahi lcags-kyu*, iron hook for catching fish.

Syn. ཉ་འབིགས *ña-hbigs*, ཉ་འཛིན *ñy-hdsin*, ལྕགས་ཀྱུ *lcags-kyu* (*Mñon.*).

ཉ་རྐྱལ *ña-rkyal* the bladder of a fish (*Cs.*).

ཉ་སྐྱོགས *ña-skyogs*=ཉའི་ན་བ gills (*Miñ.*).

ཉ་ཁྲ *ña-khra* probably *Pandion haliaëtus*, the osprey; but in *W.* is the n. given to *Polioaëtus humilis*, Hodgson, also of *Polioaëtus ichthyaëtus*; two species of grey fishing eagle.

ཉ་ཁྲབ་ཅན *ña-khrab-can* carp; ཉ་ཁྲབ་ཆེན *ña-khrab chen* sturgeon (*Sch.*).

ཉ་དགྲ་དཀར་མོ *ña-dgra dkar-mo*=དཀར་ཀ་མ *dkar-ka ma* a species of white crane, a fish-eating bird (*Rtsii.*).

ཉ་རྒྱ *ña-rgya* आनाय a fishing net.

ཉ་ཉི་མ་དགའ *ña ñi-ma dgah* संचाल lit. sun-loving fish, *i.e.*, that basks in the sun.

Syn. ཚོགས་ཀྱི་སྲད་བུ *tshogs-kyi srad-bu*, རྡོལ *dol* (*Mñon.*).

ཉ་རྒྱབ *ña-rgyab* coping, covering of the top of a wall; acc. to *Jä.* earth heaped up (like the back of a fish) on the top of the outer walls of a house.

ཉ་སྒོང *ña-sgoñ* fish-spawn, roe of fish.

ཉ་ལྩིབས *ña-lcibs* शुक्तिका 1. mother-o'pearl, a kind of oyster. 2. fish-gills (*Cs.*). 3. n. of a medicinal root: ཉ་ལྩིབས་མེས་ཚིག་ཆུ་སྐྱེམ་འཚོ *ña-lcibs mes-tshig chu-skyem htsho* the root of *ña-cib* heals scalds and blisters.

ཉ་ལྩིབས་ཀྱི་སྨིན་འགྱུ *ña-lcibs kyi smin-hgyu* head ornaments made of mother-o'pearl used by women of rank in Kham.

ཉ་ལྩིབས་ཁོག་པར་སྨིན་པ *ña-lcibs khog-par sminpa* may be taken to indicate མུ་ཏིག the pearl.

ཉ་ལྩིབས་པ་ཕོག་གནམ་སྐྱེས *ña-lcibs pa-phog nam-skyes* शुक्तिबीज lit. the sky-born pearl-seed. Acc. to the common belief, drops of rain falling in the mouth of river-mussels become converted into pearls.

ཉ་དོལ *ña-dol* धारक, पानिली fishing-net.

ཉ་དོལ་པ *ña dol-pa* a fisherman; such as those living on the southern shores of Yamdok Tsho.

Syn. སྐྱལ་ཆེན *skyal-chen*, ཉ་འཆིང་ *ña-hchiñ*, དྲ་བ་འཛིན *dra-wa hdsin*, ཉ་ཡིས་འཚོ་བ *ña-yis htsho-wa* (*Mñon.*).

ཉ་དོས *ña-dos* a load of fish.

ཉ་ཕྱིས *ña-phyis* शुक्ति mother-of-pearl; an oyster shell; it is believed that any food or drink kept in a vessel of mother-of-pearl never becomes poisonous.

ཉ་འབིགས *ña-hbigs* fishing hook; ཉ་འབིགས་བྱེད कलहंस, v. ཆུ་སྐྱར a kind of wild duck (*Mñon*).

ཉ་མིད་ཆེན་པོ *ña-mid chen-po* n. of a sea-monster; ཆུ་སྲིན་ཉ་མིད་ཆེན་པོར་བྱས་ཏེ་མདུན་བཀག། taking the form of the sea-monster called *Ña-mid*, he obstructed our passage. ཉ་རློན་མིད་ཆེན་པོ་ཡང་མཐོང་གསུང་ he said:—"we also saw the *Ña-rlon mid chen-po*" (*A. 16*).

ཉ་མོ *ña-mo* a female fish.

ཉ་མོའི་ཡུལ *ña-mohi çul*=ཉའི་སླབ་པ.

ཉ་ཚེར *ña-tsher* fish-bones (*Sch.*).

ཉ་ཟན मत्स्याशन *ña-zan* 1. n. of an aquatic monster, perhaps the crocodile. 2. an aquatic bird, a fish-eater.

ཉ་གཤོག *ña-gçog* the fin of a fish (*Cs.*).

ཉ་སག *ña-sag* fish-scale.

ཉ་སོག *ña-sog* the saw-like fringe on the back of a fish.

ཉ V: acc. to *Jä.* 1. tendon, sinew. 2. in colloq. mark left by a blow, a weal; in *W.* ཉ་ཐངས the blow has left a weal. 3. acc. to *Sch.* a lock. ཉ་བཞི the four muscles, viz., those of the arms and the calves of the leg. ཉ་ཆུ *ña-chu* tendon, sinew; perh. also a large nerve in the nape of the neck. ཉ་ལོག *ña-log* a contraction or wasting of the sinews (*Mñon*).

ཉ VI: पौर्णमासी, पूर्णिमा, पञ्चिणी the day of the full moon; ཉ་ཚེས a day in the increasing phase of the moon; ཟླ་བའི་ཉ་དྲུག་ལ on the sixth day of the moon; ཉ་གང་ *ña-gañ* the full moon; ཉ་གང་བ पूर्णिमा full moon; filled with fish; ཉ་རྒྱས *ña-rgyas* (ཟླ་བ *zla-wa*) the full phase of the moon; ཉ་སྟོན *ña-ston* पाञ्चदशीकं a festival observed on a full-moon day.

ཉ་ཁྲར *ña-khrar* a kind of brick tea.

ཉ་ཁྲི *Ña-khri* p. n. the youngest son of king གྲི་གུམ་བཙན་པོ Digum-tsanpo.

ཉ་ག *ña-ga* or ཉག *ñag* a steel-yard.

ཉ་བོ *ña-bo* body, figure (*Sch.*).

ཉ་མ *ña-ma* I: acc. to *Sch.* mistress of the house, house-wife; hearer of a lama, without being a regular disciple (*Jä.*).

ཉ་མ་ཕོ་མོ་རྣམས *ña-ma pho-mo rnams* hearers, male and female.

ཉ་མ II: 1. in the colloq. of *C.* a woman; the word occurs in the Gurbum of *Mila-ras-pa* where it applies to a lady who helped the saint. 2. in Amdo colloq. the vagina.

ཉ་མོ་གངས *Ña-mo gañs* n. of a snowy mountain in Tibet to the north of Palpa in Nepal.

ཉ་བཟུང་མ *ña bzuñ-ma*=བག་མ a bride.

Syn. དང་པོའི་རྡུལ་ཅན་མ *dañ-pohi rdul can-ma*; ཁྱོ་འདམ་པ *khyo hdam-pa* (*Mñon*).

ཉ་ར *ña-ra* care; ཉ་ར་བྱེད་པ to take care of, to provide for a person, to keep a thing safe; cf. གཉེར་ཁ.

ཉ་ར་ཉོ་རེ *ña-ra ño-re* weak, fragile, frail.

ཉ་རི *Ña-ri* n. of a place situated to the north-east of Tashi-lhunpo.

ཉ་ལྷོག *ña-lhog* n. of a disease.

ཉྭ་སུལ *ñwa-sul*, defined in སེམས་ཅན་གང་རུང་གི་རྐང་པའི་ཉྭ་ཡི་སུལ *sems-can gañ-ruñ-gi rkañ-pahi ñwa-yi sul* the muscular ridges of the legs of any living creature.

ཉག *ñag* 1. v. ཉ་ག, ཉག་གང་ one measure on the steel-yard=4 *srañ* and 1 *skar*=four and one-fourth ounces. 2.=ཉག་མ. 3. also ཉག་ག or ཉག་ཁྲམ notch, indenture; ལོ་མ་ཐྲ་བ་ཉག་ག་ཅན having multifold leaves, like those of caraway (*Jä.*; *Vai-sñ*); ཉག་ག་མེད་པ not cleft, not indented. 4. of wool, ཉག་ཏུ་འདྲེན་པ *hdren-pa* to draw out into threads, to spin (*Mil.*; *Jä.*).

ཉག་རྐྱང་ *ñag-rkyañ* obstinately; ཉག་རྐྱང་བཏང་བ=མ་ཉན་པར་བཏང་བ to send anything obstinately, not listening to any one.

ཉག་སྐྱག *ñag-skyag*=ཕོ་ན in Sikk. dialect: གཉེན་ཆང་སྐྱལ་ཆོག་པ་ཞིག་ཉག་སྐྱག་བཏང་དགོས should only press the application to be permitted to send the *Nañ-chañ* (proposal-wine for marriage).

ཉག་གཅིག *ñag-gcig*=ཕོ་ན alone, the only: སྐྱབས་ཀྱི་ཉག་གཅིག་དཀོན་མཆོག་གཙོ the only refuge is (in) *Dkon-mchog gtso* (*Hbrom.* ཕ *28*): སངས་རྒྱས་ཉག་གཅིག only Buddha (*Jä.*).

ཉག་མ *ñag-ma* single; སྤུ་ཉག་མ *spu ñag-ma* or སྤུ་ཡི་ཉག་མ a single hair.

ཉག་ཉིག *ñag-ñig* filth, dirt (*Sch.*).

ཉག་ཉུག *ñag-ñug*=སྣ་ཚོགས various, of different kinds.

ཉག་ཉོག *ñag-ñog* 1. not clear, turbid; mixed with foul matter (as water mixed with mud). 2. confusedly, speaking irrelevantly; also contradicting one statement by another.

ཉག་ཐག *ñag-thag* thread, chain (of gold or iron), cord for stringing turquoises (*Jä.*).

ཉག་མཐིལ *ñag-mthil* scale of a steel-yard.

ཉག་རྡོ *ñag-rdo* the weight of a steel-yard.

ཉག་ཤིང་ *ñag-çiñ* the beam of a steel-yard.

ཉག་པ *ñag-pa* notch, indenture=སྣ་ཉག notch or hole in the nose, or a notched nose (*Sñiñ*).

+ ཉག་ཕྲན *ñag-phran*=མདའ མར an arrow; acc. to *Cs.* a beam, a pole.

ཉག་མོ *ñag-mo* acc. to *Sch.* a woman.

ཉག་རེ *Ñag-re* 1. n. of a place in Kham (*Loñ.* • *9*). 2. single.

ཉག་རོང་ *Ñag-roñ* n. of a small principality ruled by a petty king in Kham.

ཉག་ལེ *Ñag-le* n. of a place in Tibet.

ཉང་ *Ñañ* the district of Tsang of which Gyang-tse is the chief city. It is sometimes spelt མྱང་ *Myañ* signifying tasteful, sweet (on account of its water). So in *Mil.* ཀ *26*: ཉང་སྟོད་རི་ནང་དུ་བླ་མ་དང་མཇལ met with the lama in the mountains of upper Nyang.

ཉང་གྲུམ *ñañ-grum* the square carpet-rug manufactured in the district of *Ñañ*.

ཉང་ཆུ *Ñañ-chu* the tributary of the Yeru Tsang-po which, rising from the mountains in the district of Phagri, flows N.N.W. and falls into the Tsang-po near Shiga-tse.

ཉང་ཆུ་སྐྱ་མོ *ñañ-chu skya-mo* a feeder of the *Ñañ-chu*.

ཉང་སྟོད *ñañ-stod* upper Ñang containing the town of Gyang-tse.

ཉང་པོ I: *Ñaṅ-po* n. of a place in Tibet visited by Atis'a: ཉང་པོར་ཡང་བྱོན he also visited *Ñaṅ-po* (*A. 27*).

ཉང་པོ II: n. of a district in the province of Kong-po.

ཉང་རྩི་བྲག *ñaṅ-rtsi brag* a kind of yellow fibrous root largely exported from Tibet to China: ཉང་རྩི་བྲག་ཉག་རེ་རེ་འབྲུ a *ñag* "weight of *ñaṅ-tsi-brag* is so much a piece, &c." (*Rtsii.*).

ཉང་རོ་བཤམ་པོ་མཁར *Ñaṅ-ro bçam-po mkhar* a small town in Tsang: ཉང་རོ་བཤམ་པོ་མཁར་གྱི་རི་རྩེ་ལ on the top of the hill of *Ñaṅ-ro bçam-po mkhar* (*Yig*).

ཉང་རོང་ *Ñaṅ-roṅ* n. of a battle-field where the people of Tibet fought with one of their kings (*Yig*).

ཉང་ཀ *ñaṅ-ka* or ཉང་གེ *ñaṅ-ge* in Sp. a currant (*Jä.*).

ཉང་ནོན *ñaṅ-non* = ཉམས་ལེན espionage.

ཉན་པ *ñan-pa* श्रवण, 1. imp. ཉོན to hear, to give ear to, to listen; sbst. hearing or a hearer श्रोता. ཉན་པར་བྱེད शृणोति hears or does hear. ཉན་བྱེད = རྣ་བ श्रव the ear. ཉན་ཟིན अश्रुषोत् have heard. སློབ་དཔོན་གྱི་ཞལ་དུ་ཆོས་ཉན་པ to attend to the religious instructions of the teacher; ངག or ཚིག་ཉན་པ to listen to the word (of the teacher); ཁ་ལ་ཉན་པ to obey; བཀའ་ལ་ཉན་པ to obey the commands or orders, to yield; ངས་ཇི་སྐད་ཟེར་བའི་ཁ་ལ་ཉན listen to my words as I speak. ཁ་ལ་ཉན་པོ or ཁ་ལ་ཉན་མཁན one who is obedient; ཁ་ལ་མི་ཉན་མཁན one who is disobedient. 2. to be able: འགྲོ་མ་ཉན་པས not being able to walk (on account of illness); in *W.* ཉན་ཡིན yes, I shall be able. In this sense ཉན is used also as a formative, added to the root of a verb, signifying capability, possibility, &c. གཙང་པོ་འདི་རྐྱལ་ཉན་འདུག the river is fordable.

ཉན་ཐོས་པ *ñan-thos-pa* श्रावक; ཆོས་ཉན་ཞིང་ཐོས lit. one who hearing the *Dharma* understands it; a follower of the *Hīnayāna* school.

Syn. ཐུབ་དབང་གསུང་སྐྱེས *thub-dwaṅ gsuṅ-skyes*; ཐོས་སྒྲོག་པ *thos grog-pa*; ཐེག་ཆུང་སྐྱེས་བུ *theg-chuṅ skyes-bu*; བརྟུལ་ཞུགས་དབང་ *brtul-shugs dwaṅ*; སྦྱངས་པའི་ཡོན་ཏན་ལ་གནས་པ *sbyaṅs-pahi yon-tan la gnas-pa* (*Mṅon.*).

ཉན་ཐོས་ཀྱི་ས་བདུན *ñan-thos kyi sa-bdun* सप्तश्रावकभूमि the seven stages of perfection acc. to the S'rāvaka school: (1) शुक्लविदर्शनाभूमि; དཀར་པོ་རྣམ་པར་མཐོང་བའི་ས the white illuminated stage; (2) गोत्रभूमि; རིགས་ཀྱི་ས the exalted stage of noble birth; (3) दर्शनभूमि; མཐོང་བའི་ས the stage through sight; (4) तनुभूमि; བསྲབས་པའི་ས the fine or subtle stage; (5) विगतरागभूमि; འདོད་ཆགས་དང་བྲལ་བའི་ས the stage which is free from passions (desires, etc.); (6) कृतभूमि; བྱས་པ་སྲུང་བའི་ས the finished or perfected stage; (7) अष्टमभूमि; བརྒྱད་པའི་ས the eighth stage.

ཉན་ཐོས་བཅུ་དྲུག *ñan-thos bcu-drug* the sixteen chief disciples of S'ākya-muni, *i.e.*, the གནས་བརྟན or *Sthavira* of the S'rāvaka school.

ཉན་ཐོས་མ *ñan-thos-ma* श्राविका a female hearer of the *Hīnayāna* school.

ཉན་འདོད་པ *ñan-hdod-pa* = གུས་པ शुश्रूषमाना, शुश्रूषा respectful, respectful service.

ཉན་རྣ *ñan-rna* messenger, envoy, ambassador.

Syn. ཕོ་ཉ *pho-ña*; གཏམ་སྐྱེལ *gtam skyci* (*Mṅon.*).

ཉན་རྣ་པ *ñan-rna-pa* उपश्रव to overhear; an overhearer.

ཉན་པ་མོ *ñan-pa-mo* a female listener.

ཉན་པོ *Ñan-po* the birth place of a celebrated Lama called ཤཱཀྱ་རྒྱལ་མཚན *Çākya rgyal-mtshan* (*Loñ.* ꣸ *10*).

ཉམ *ñam* locust; also ཉམ་ཉིག acc. to *Jä.* a cricket.

ཉམ་ང *ñam-ña* or ཉམས་ང་ उपायास despair anxiety, dread, fear (of a thing); ཉམས་ང་ལས་ཐར་བ to be delivered from anxiety.

ཉམ་ང་བ *ñam-ña-wa* = དོགས་པ सङ्कट, विपद्, आतंक sbst. danger, fear, anxiety; also adj. anxious, fearful; vb. n. to be alarmed, to be in great anxiety: དེས་ན་ཉམ་ང་བའི་འཁོར་བའི་དུག་ཅན་གནས་སུ། so it is, in that pernicious sphere where the cycle of anxious cares prevails (*J. Zañ.*). ཉམ་ང་བ་ཉུང་བ अव्यातङ्का less risky, beset with danger.

ཉམ་ང་མེད *ñam-ña med* intrepid, fearless. Syn. སྙིང་སྟོབས་ཅན *sñiñ-stobs-can*, འཇིགས་མེད *hjigs-med*, སྟོབས་ཅན *stobs-can* (*Mñon.*)

ཉམ་ཆུང་ *ñam-chuñ* दुर्बल weak, feeble.

ཉམ་ཆུང་དབང་པོ *ñam-chuñ dwañ-po* भृङ्ग met. a fly, a bee.

ཉམ་ཐག་པ *ñam thag-pa* आर्त to be stricken, exhausted.

ཉམ་སྣང་ *ñam-snañ* आभास a sudden flash; also a hint.

ཉམ་པའི་ལམ *ñam-pahi lam* = ལམ་ངན་པ a bad dangerous road (*Mñon.*).

ཉམ་ཡོས *ñam-yos* in Sikk. locust. = the Tib. ཆ་ག་འབུ or ཆ་ག་པ.

ཉམས *ñams* or སེམས་ཉམས resp. ཐུགས་ཉམས 1. thought, apprehension of ideas: སེམས་ལ་ཉམས་སུ་བླང་བ आशितिक्रिया to comprehend, to acquire the meaning or import of a thing; ཆོས་ཉམས་སུ་བླང་བ to commit religious instructions to memory and to comprehend their meaning. 2. the soul, mind, spirit, as an entity: ཉམས་ཀྱི་གྲོགས companions of the soul when in retirement (*Mil.*); ཉམས་ཀྱི་ཆང་ wine of the soul, *i.e.*, religious knowledge (*Mil.*); ཉམས་སྐྱེ *ñams-skye* or ཉམས་ཤར a thought springing up in the mind. 3. manner, extent, degree, condition, state; ཉམས་ཀྱི་ཚོད་བྱེད་པ to try, to put to test, *e.g.*, one's strength; ཐུགས་དམ་གྱི་ཉམས་སད་པ to try the degree of a person's devotion or spiritual progress (*Mil.*); སྨྲ་ཉམས pleasing, agreeable manner of speaking; སྤྱོད་ཉམས pleasing manner of doing or dealing; ཉམས་དགའ་བ *ñams dgah-wa* ललामन् pleasant, delightful, agreeable, charming: སྐྱེད་མོས་ཚལ་རབ་ཤིན་ཏུ་ཉམས་དགའ་བར in the most delightful grove (*A. 16*).

ཉམས་དགུ *ñams-dgu*, v. ཉམས་ཐབས *ñams-thabs*.

ཉམས་འགྱུར *ñams-hgyur* काम्यता handsome, elegant, to be elegant, comfortable.

ཉམས་རྒྱུད *ñams rgyud* = ཉམས, ཉམས་རྒྱུད་ལ་སྦྱང་བ intellectually skilled, well-versed.

ཉམས་ཆུང་ *ñams-chuñ* 1. humble; faint, weak. 2. = བུང་བ *buñ-wa* a bee.

ཉམས་ཆེན་པོ *ñams chen-po* pride.

ཉམས་བརྟས་བྱེད་པ *ñams-brtas byed-pa* to strengthen, restore: ཉམས་བརྟས he recovered, grew well, got up again (*Jä.*).

ཉམས་རྟོགས་བྱེད་པ *ñams-rtogs byed-pa* to inquire fully into any subject.

ཉམས་སྟོང་གསལ *ñams stoñ-gsal*, v. གསལ་པོ.

ཉམས་སྟོབས *ñams-stobs* strength.

ཉམས་ཐག་པ *ñams thag-pa*, v. ཉམ་ཐག་པ suffering, tormented, exhausted: ཉམས་ཐག་པའི་ང་རོ the cry of suffering, doleful cries; ཉམས་ཐག་པའི་ང་རོ་འབྱིན་པ आर्तस्वरेण क्रन्दति bewailing under agony, to utter cries of suffering.

ཉམས་ཐབས *ñams-thabs*, ཉམས་དགུ appearance, colour, figure (*Jä.*).

ཉམས་དང་བ *ñams-dañ-wa* bright appearance.

ཉམས་བདེ་བ *ñams bde-wa* काम्य happy, comfortable.

ཉམས་འདུས *ñams-hdus* met. मेढ्र the male organ.

ཉམས་པ *ñams-pa* 1. विनाश, विपन्न, विनष्ट, हीन injured, hurt, spoiled, damaged, impaired, imperfect. མ་ཉམས་པ uncorrupted, untouched, not weakened. 2. defiled, polluted. ཉམས་པར་འགྱུར་བ to grow weak, become deteriorated, to degenerate. 3. sbst. degeneration: ཉམས་པ་གསུམ the three deteriorations or impairments:—(1) ཚུལ་ཁྲིམས་ཉམས་པ depravity of morals; (2) ལྟ་བ་ཉམས་པ vicious principles; (3) ཆོ་ག་ཉམས་པ mistaken religious observances, rites, &c. (*K. d.* ང *52*). ཉམས་པ་དྲུག *ñamṣ-pa-drug* the six kinds of degeneration:—(1) བདག་ཉམས་པ degeneration in one's self; (2) གཞན་ཉམས་པ the fall of others; (3) ལྟ་བ་ཉམས་པ degeneration in religion; (4) ཚུལ་ཁྲིམས་ཉམས་པ bad or deteriorated-morals; (5) སྤྱོད་པ་ཉམས་པ *spyod-pa ñamṣ-pa* bad behaviour; (6) འཚོ་བ་ཉམས་པ bad habits, living. Besides these qualities are others with which the word ཉམས་པ is joined:— འདུལ་བ་ཉམས་པ, ལོངས་སྤྱོད་ཉམས་པ, བསོད་ནམས་ཉམས་པ, རིགས་ཉམས་པ, རིག་པ་ཉམས་པ, ཚེ་ཉམས་པ shortened life; ལུས་ཉམས་པ of impaired health; ཡོན་ཏན་ཉམས་པ of impaired talents, loss of ability; དབང་པོ་ཉམས་པ impaired faculties; བཅུད་ཉམས་པ degenerated vitality; ནུས་པ་ཉམས་པ loss of energy, depreciation of ability, of efficacy, &c.

ཉམས་པ་མེད་པ *ñamṣ-pa med-pa* अच्युत not damaged, unimpaired, uninjured, indistructible.

ཉམས་པའི་མ་ནིང་ *ñamṣ-puhi ma-niñ* पण्डक impotent, useless.

ཉམས་པར་བྱ *ñamṣ-par bya* ग्लायत, ग्लायते to be languid or weary; to despond.

ཉམས་པར་བྱེད་པ *ñamṣ-par byed-pa* सीदति;= ཉམས་སུ་འཇུག་པ *ñamṣ-su hjug-pa.*

ཉམས་པོ *ñamṣ-po* हानि injury, damage.

ཉམས་དཔྱོད་པ *ñamṣ dpyod-pa* to investigate; examine minutely.

ཉམས་བྱེད *ñamṣ-byed* नष्ट that which damages.

ཉམས་འབྲུ་བ *ñamṣ hbru-wa* to irritate, vex, provoke.

ཉམས་མི་བདེ་བ *ñamṣ mi-bde-wa*= ཁམས་མ་བདེ་བ bad health, unwell, ill.

Syn. འདུ་བ་འཁྲུགས་པ *hdu-wa hkhrugṣ-pa*; ནད་པ *nad-pa*; ན་ཚ་བྱུང་བ *na-tsha byuñ-wa*; ན་བ *na-wa* (*Mñon.*).

ཉམས་ཞིབ་ཀྱིས་སྦུག་དོན་ངེས་བྱུང་བ *ñamṣ-shib-kyiṣ sbug-don ñeṣ-byuñ-wa* by minute inquiry to ascertain the real state of things or secret of any matter.

ཉམས་མེད *ñamṣ-med* अपहानि undamaged, that cannot be spoiled; also strengthless.

ཉམས་དམས *ñamṣ-dmaṣ*= དམའ་རུ་སོང་བ *dmah-ru soñ-wa* degenerated.

ཉམས་མྱོང་ *ñamṣ-myoñ* experience; but acc. to *Jä.* enjoyment, delight. ཚོར་བའི་ཉམས་མྱོང་ *tshor-bahi ñamṣ-myoñ* experience acquired through the medium of the senses.

ཉམས་སྨད་པ *ñamṣ smad-pa* अपहृत, id.

ཉམས་རྩལ *ñamṣ-rtsal* skill; dexterity.

ཉམས་མཚར་བ *ñamṣ mtshar-wa* wonderful, most beautiful.

ཉམས་བཞག་པ *ñamṣ bshag-pa* is said to be= དྲན་པ་ཉེ་བར་བཞག་པ *drañ-pa ñe-war bshag-pa.*

ཉམས་ཡོད་པ *ñamṣ yod-pa* बल to be in possession of.

ཉམས་ལེན *ñamṣ-len* a memorial verse, a rhyme or verse for retaining things in memory (*Mil.; Jä.*).

ཉམས་ལེན་པ *ñamṣ len-pa* 1. v. ཉང་ནོན *ñañ-non* 2. to take the measure of, the dimensions of, to survey (in respect of land); inquiring into the state of any object, &c., to explore; to take an inventory, to ascertain or compute the state of any property.

ཉམས་སུ་མྱོང་བ *ñamṣ-su myoñ-wa* अनुभव to suffer, undergo, experience. ཉམས་སུ་འཇུག་པ to injure, spoil, render useless.

ཉའི་ཚེར *ñahi tshir* झष a large fish.

ཉར *ñar* 1. v. ཉ་ར *ña-ra.* 2. acc. to *Cs.* oblong; ཉར་ཉར *ñar-ñar* oblong.

ཉར་ཉེར *ñar-ñer* मेलु n. of an immensely large number.

ཉར་དུ་ལི་ཁ་ར *Ñar-du li-kha-ra* n. of a place lying between India and Tibet (*Yig*).

ཉར་གདོང་ *ñar-gdoṅ*=ངར་གདོང་ in *W.* shin, shin-bone (*Jä.*).

ཉར་མ *ñar-ma* ཆུའི་ཐིགས་མ particles of water, spray (*Mṅon.*).

ཉལ་བ *ñal-wa* शयन, शय्या, स्वपिति imp. ཉོལ *ñol.* to lie down, to sleep: ཉལ་དུ་སོང་ *ñal-du soṅ* he has gone to sleep; མལ་ཏིང་ལ *mal-tiṅ la* on the bed; ཉལ་འདུག་གོ *ñal hdug-go* he slept. Sometimes: གཉིད་དུ་ཉལ་བ to go to sleep; ཉལ་བར་འདོད *ñal-war hdod* wishing to sleep.

ཉལ་ཁྲི *ñal-khri*=མལ་ཁྲི *mal-khri* a bedstead, couch, sofa.

ཉལ་གོས *ñal-gos* counterpane, quilt, blanket (*Sch.*).

ཉལ་འགྲོ *ñal-hgro*=འབབ་ཆུ a river, stream.

ཉལ་འགྲོའི་གཏེར *ñal-hgrohi gter* receptacle of rivers, the sea wherein all the rivers flow (*Mṅon.*).

ཉལ་ཐག *ñal-thag* bands or ropes stretched to sleep upon.

ཉལ་པོ *ñal-po* ग्राम 1. a village. 2. coition; ཉལ་པོ་བྱེད་པ *ñal-po byed-pa* to practise cohabitation.

ཉལ་བུ *ñal-bu* bastard, whore-son.

ཉལ་སློང་ *ñal-sloṅ* 1. शेमुषी [understanding, intellect]*S.* 2. ཤེས་རབ प्रज्ञा wisdom, spiritual knowledge (*Mṅon.*).

ཉལ་ས *ñal-sa*=མལ་ས or གཟིམས་མལ also, གཟིམས་ས board to sleep on, a bed to sleep upon, a sleeping place.

ཉི *ñi* 1. num. fig. 38. 2. num. used inst. of གཉིས *gñis* in compounds: ཉི་བརྒྱ two hundred; ཉི་ཁྲི *ñi-khri* twenty thousand, etc. 3. for ཉི་མ the sun.

ཉི་སྐྱེས *ñi-skyes* ब्राह्मण, शनैश्चर, सूर्यपुत्र a Brahmaṇa, son of the sun.

ཉི་ཁུད *Ñi-khud* a lake in Nepal (*Jä.*).

ཉི་ཁྱིམ *ñi-khyim* भ्रामक, जामाता a traveller, a son-in-law; also halo or circle round the sun.

ཉི་ཁྲི *ñi-khri* (*ñi-ṭhi*) the title of a book; the Prajñā-Pāramita containing 20,000 ślokas.

ཉི་དགའ *ñi-dgah*=ལྕམ་པ *lcam-pa* a mystical term (*Miṅ. 4*); a flower.

ཉི་དཀྱིལ *ñi-dkyil* disk of the sun (*Sch.*).

ཉི་གུང་ *ñi-guṅ* noon, midday.

ཉི་ཆ *ñi-cha* the sunny parts or flanks of a hill or mountain.

ཉི་སྟོན *ñi-ston* ककुभ the lotus flower; the tree *Terminalia arjuna.*

ཉི་དྲོས *ñi-dros* morning time, from 8 A.M. to 10 A.M., when the sun is warm and pleasant.

ཉི་ལྡོག *ñi-ldog* the solstice; དགུན་ཉི་ལྡོག *dgun ñi-ldog* the winter solstice; དབྱར་ཉི་ལྡོག *dbyar ñi-ldog* the summer solstice.

ཉི་ནུབ *ñi-nub* sunset.

ཉི་མ *ñi-ma* 1. सूर्य, अरुण, आदित्य the sun: ཉི་མ་འཆར the sun is rising; ཉི་མ་ཤར the sun has risen, shines; ཉི་མ་རྒས or ཉི་མ་ནུབ the sun is setting or sets; ཉི་མ་ནུབ་ཚེ་བར until sunset (*Sch.*). 2.=ཉིན་མོ *ñin-mo* the day: ཉི་མ་གཉིས two days; ཉི་མ་རེ་རེ every day.

Syn. ཚ་ཟེར *tsha-zer*; སྣ་ཚོགས་ཤིང་རྟ *sna-tshogs çiṅ-rta*; མི་སྦྱིན་སྐྱེས་པ *mi-sbyin skyes-pa*; པད་མའི་གཉེན *pad-mahi gñen*; དུས་ཀྱི་བདག་པོ *dus-kyi bdag-po*; མུན་པའི་དགྲ *mun-pahi dgra*; འཇིག་རྟེན་མིག *hjig-rten mig*; དུས་ལ་དགའ *dus-la dgah*; འགྲོ་བའི་སྒྲོན་མེ *hgro-bahi sgron-me*; བཅུ་གཉིས་བདག *bcu-gñis bdag*; ལོ་ཡི་ཤིང་རྟ *lo-yi çiṅ-rta*; ཀུ་མུད་དགྲ *ku-mud dgra*; སྲིད་པའི་སྒྲོན་མེ *srid-pahi sgron-me*;

ཉིན་མོར་བྱེད་ *ñin-mor byed*; སྣང་བྱེད་ *snań-byed*; འོད་བྱེད་ *hod-byed*; ནམ་མཁའི་ནོར་ *nam-mkhahi nor*; རྟ་ལྗང་ *rta-ljań*; གཟའ་བདག *gzah-bdag*; འོད་སྟོང་འབར་ *hod stoń-hbar*; འོད་ལྡན་ *hod-ldan*; མུན་སེལ་ *mun-sel*; ཉིན་མོའི་ནོར་ *ñin-mohi nor*; འོད་གཟུགས་ *hod-gzugs*; འོད་འདྲེན་ *hod-hdren*; ཉིན་མོའི་འབྱིན་ *ñin-mohi hbyin*; བསྲུབ་བྱེད་ *bsrub-byed*; འོད་གཙང་ *hod gtsań*; འོད་འགྲོ་རྒྱས་བྱེད་ *hod-hgro rgyas-byed*; མཁའ་འགྲོ་ *mkhah-hgro*; རྣམ་སྒྱུར་འགྲོ་ལུས་ *rnam-sgyur hgro-lus*; གསལ་བའི་ནོར་ *gsal-bahi nor*; ཚ་ལྡན་ *tsha-ldan*; ངེས་སྲེག་ *ńes-sreg*; འོད་ཟེར་ལྡན་ *hod-zer ldan*; འོད་ཀྱི་རྒྱུན་ *hod-kyi rgyun*; ཕྱོགས་སྣང་བྱེད་ *phyogs-snań byed*; གདུང་བྱེད་ *gduń-byed*; ཚ་བྱེད་ *tsha-byed*; རྣམ་སྣང་བྱེད་ *rnam-snań byed*; མུན་འཇོམས་ *mun-hjoms*; ལུས་སྐྱོབ་ *lus-skyob*; འདམ་སྐྱེས་མཚན་ *hdam-skyes mtshan*; མཆོད་ལྡན་ *mchod-ldan*; བདུན་གྱི་བདུན་པ་ *bdun-gyi bdun-pa*; ཕྱོགས་བདག་ *phyogs-bdag*; མཆོག་འདོད་ *mchog-hdod*; ཆར་འབེབས་ *char-hbebs*; འཛིན་བྱེད་ *hdsin-byed*; སྣང་བའི་མུ་ཁྱུད་ *snań-bahi mu-khyud*; སྣང་ལྡན་ *snań-ldan*; མིག་གཟུགས་ *mig-gzugs*; རྣམ་གསལ་བྱེད་ *rnam-gsal byed*; འོད་འགྱེད་ *hod-hgyed*; བསྟེན་བྱ་ *bsten-bya*; བདུད་ལས་རྒྱལ་ *bdud-las rgyal*; མ་ཟླུམས་ *ma-zlums*; འཕྲོག་བྱེད་ *hphrog-byed*; རྩེན་པ་ *rtsen-pa*; ཕྱོགས་དགོད་བྱེད་ *phyogs-dgod byed*; གཏུམ་པའི་འོད་ *gtum-pahi hod*; འོད་ཀྱི་སྐྲ་ཅན་ *hod-kyi skra-can*; སྣ་ཚོགས་འོད་ *sna-tshogs hod*; སྣང་བའི་མཛོད་ *snań-bahi mdsod*; ནོར་གྱི་མཛོད་ *nor-gyi mdsod*; རྒྱུ་བའི་བརྟུལ་ཞུགས་ *rgyu-wahi brtul-shugs*; གཟའ་བཤེས་ *gzah-bçes*; མཆོད་འོས་ *mchod-hos*; འོད་ཀྱི་ནོར་ཅན་ *hod-kyi nor-can*; པད་མའི་ལག་པ་ *pad-mahi lag-pa*; རྟག་ཏུ་འཆར་ *rtag-tu hchar*; རིག་བྱེད་འབྱུང་ *rig-byed hbyuń*; ལས་སྣ་ཚོགས་ *las sna-tshogs*; ཁྱབ་བྱེད་ *khyab-byed*; ནད་མེད་ *nad-med*; འཐུང་བྱེད་ *hthuń-byed*; འོད་ཀྱི་འཕྲེང་ཅན་ *hod-kyi hphreń-can*; མིག་གཟུགས་ *mig-gzugs*; འོད་སྣང་ *hod-snań*; འོད་སྟོང་འཛིན་པ་ *hod stoń hdsin-pa*; ཁྲི་ཅན་ *khri-can*; ལོང་བའི་ཁ་ལོ་པ་ *loń-bahi kha lo-pa*; ལམ་སྟོན་ *lam-ston*; སྲིད་བྱེད་ *srid-byed*; ཤིང་རྟ་མཐོ་ *çiń-rta mtho*; དབྱིག་གི་ཁུ་བ་ *dbyig-gi khu-wa*; ཟླུམ་པོ་འཛིན་ *zlum-po hdsin*; དུས་ཀྱི་བྱེད་པོ་ *dus-kyi byed-po*; ནམ་མཁའི་མིག་ *nam-mkhahi mig*; འཇིག་རྟེན་དབང་པོ་ *hjig-rten dwań-po*; འོད་ཕུང་པོ་ *hod phuń-po*; འོད་ཟེར་གཟུགས་མང་ *hoh-zer gzugs-mań*; ནམ་མཁའི་ཏོག་ *nam-mkhahi tog*; ཕྱོགས་ཀྱི་མ་ཁྱུད་ *phyogs-kyi ma-khyud*; ཚངས་པའི་རྟ་ *tshań-pahi rta*; ནམ་མཁའི་ཐིག་ལེ་ *nam-mkhahi thig-le*; སྣ་ཚོགས་འོད་ *sna-tshogs hod*; རྟ་བདུན་པ་ *rta bdun-pa* (*Mńon.*).

ཉི་མ་གང་ཤར་ *ñi-ma gań-çar* sun-flower, *Helianthus.*

ཉི་མ་དགའ་ *Ñi-ma dgah* 1. a name of Karṇa, the king of Anga. 2. n. of a medicinal plant.

ཉི་མ་སྔ་དྲོ་ *ñi-ma sńa-dro* early morning.

ཉི་མ་བཅུ་གཉིས་ *ñi-ma bcu-gñis* twelve demi-gods who acc. to Chinese astronomy represent 12 divisions of the day (as of other periods) and are therefore called ཉི་མ; they are བྱི་བ་ *byi-wa* (mouse), གླང་ *glań* (ox), སྟག *stag* (tiger), ཡོས་ *yos* (hare), འབྲུག *hbrug* (dragon), སྦྲུལ་ *sbrul* (serpent), རྟ་ *rta* (horse), ལུག *lug* (sheep) སྤྲེལ་ *sprel* (monkey), བྱ་ *bya* (bird), ཁྱི་ *khyi* (dog), ཕག *phag* (pig).

ཉི་མ་ཐང་ *Ñi-ma thań* n. of a place situated to the west of Lhasa (*Loń.* ཞ *4*).

ཉི་མ་ལྡན་པའི་རི་ *Ñi-ma ldan-pahi ri* n. of a mythological mountain believed to be situated 5,000 *yojana* beyond the Southern Ocean (*K. d.* ར *275*).

ཉི་མ་ནག་ཆེན་ *ñi-ma nag-chen* and ཉི་མ་ནག་ཆུང་ are the names of two (*Sa-bdag*) demi-gods.

ཉི་མ་ཕྱི་དྲོ་ *ñi-ma phyi-dro* पराह्ण, पराह्न afternoon.

ཉི་མ་ཕྱི་མ་ *ñi-ma phyi-ma* a future day.

ཉི་མ་ཕྱེད་ལྷག *ñi-ma phyed-lhag* मध्यन्दिसूर्य्यं lit. more than one half of the sun, *i.e.*, from early morning to the afternoon.

ཉི་མ་སྦས་ *Ñi-ma sbas* सूर्य्यगुप्त one of the successors of Buddha in the Buddhist hierarchy of India.

ཉི་མ་བཟང་པོ་ *ñi-ma bzań-po* सुदिन a good or auspicious day.

ཉི་མ་ཤར་བ *ñi-ma çar-wa* सूर्योदय sunrise.

ཉི་མ་ལྷོ་བྱང་འགྲོད *ñi-ma lho-byañ ḫgrod* the course of the sun to the south and to the north (of the equator).

ཉི་མའི་ཁ་ལོ་པ *ñi-maḫi kha lo-pa* the charioteers of the sun are:—སྐྱ་རེངས *skya-reñs*, བླ་མེད *ḇla-med*, འོད་སྲུང *hod-sruñ*, ཁྱུང་སྔོན་སྐྱེས *khyuñ-sñon skyes* (*Mñon.*).

ཉི་མའི་ཁོར་ཡུག *ñi-maḫi khor-yug* the surroundings of the sun.

ཉི་མའི་འཁོར *ñi-maḫi ḫkhor* the attendants of the sun; they are:—གནས་བྱེད *gnas-byed*, དབྱུག་པ་ཅན *dbyug-pa can*, དམར་སེར *dmar-ser*.

ཉི་མ་འཁྱིམས་པ *ñi-ma ḫkhyims-pa* सूर्यपरिवेश the circumference of the sun.

ཉི་མའི་གུང *ñi-maḫi guñ* मध्याह्न when the sun is at the meridian, midday, noon.

ཉི་མའི་གུར་ཁང *ñi-maḫi gur-khañ* the sun's pavilion, the halo of five different colours which surrounds the sun; ཉི་མའི་ལྡིང་ཁང *ñi-maḫi ldiñ-khañ* the floating castle of the sun; ཉི་མའི་ཁྱིམ the sun-sphere.

ཉི་མའི་རྒྱུད *ñi-maḫi rgyud* आङ्गिरस the descendants of the sun.

ཉི་མའི་གཉེན *ñi-maḫi gñen* आदित्यबन्धु relative of the sun, epithet of S'ākya-muni.

ཉི་མའི་རྟ་བདུན *ñi-maḫi rta-ḇdun* the seven horses of the sun are the following:—རླུང *rluñ*, ཡིད་མགྱོགས *yid mgyogs*, མདོག་ལྔ་པ *mdog lña-pa*, ཐིག་ལེ་ཅན *thig-le can*, ངེས་བརྗོད *ñes-ḇrjod*, ཤིན་ཏུ་རྒྱལ་མཚན *çin-tu rgyal-mtshan*, རི་བོ་འཇོམས *ri-wo hjoms*. To these are occasionally added four others:—རྩེན་པའི་འོད *rtsen-paḫi hod*, ནམ་མཁའི་གྲུ *nam-mkhaḫi gru* གསེར་གྱི་དབྱངས *gser-gyi dbyañs*, ཉི་མའི་ཤིང་རྟ་རལ་གྲིའི་ཕྲེང *ñi-maḫi çiñ-rta ral-griḫi phreñ* (*Mñon.*).

ཉི་མའི་གདུགས *ñi-maḫi gdugs* lit. the umbrella of the sun, *i.e.*, the day (*Zam. 13*).

ཉི་མའི་མདའ *Ñi-maḫi mdaḫ* an epithet of the god of love.

ཉི་མའི་དཔལ *ñi-maḫi dpal* सूर्यश्रीः n. of a Buddhist author of ancient India.

ཉི་མའི་བུ *ñi-maḫi bu* सूर्यपुत्र; སྤེན་པ *spen-pa* the son of the sun, the planet Saturn.

ཉི་མའི་བུ་མོ *ñi-maḫi bu-mo* the daughter of the sun, a name of the river Yamunā or Pākshu (*Mñon.*).

ཉི་མའི་བཙུན་མོ *ñi-maḫi ḇtsun-mo* the wives of the sun-god are:—རྒྱལ་མོ *Rgyal-mo*, ལེགས་འདོད *Legs-ḫdod*, རྡུལ་བཟང *Rdul-ḇzañ*, འོད་སྐྱེས་མ *Hod skyes-ma*, གཤིན་རྗེ་ཀཱ་ལིན་དི *Gçin-rje kā-lin-di*, ནམ་གྲུ *Nam-gru*, མ་ནུ་སྦྱིན་སྐྱེད *Ma-nu sbyin skyed*, སྐྲག་བྱེད་མ *Skrag byed-ma* (*Mñon.*).

ཉི་མའི་གཟུགས་བརྙན *ñi-maḫi gzugs-ḇrñan* the reflected image of the sun.

ཉི་མའི་འོད *ñi-maḫi hod* the following are the names of the sun's rays:—འོད་ཆགས་སྣང་བ *hod-chags snañ-wa*; ནམ་མཁའ་འཇལ *nam-mkhaḫ hjal*; གདུང་བྱེད *gduñ-byed*; ཚ་ཟེར *tsha-zer*; ཆུ་འཐུང་འོད *chu-ḫthuñ hod*; མཚན་མོ་འཇོམས *mtshan-mo hjoms*; འོད་ཀྱི་ཆར *hod-kyi char*; ཀུན་སྣང་འབར་བ *kun snañ ḫbar-pa* (*Mñon.*).

ཉི་མའི་འོད་སྐོར *ñi-maḫi hod-skor* the circle of light round the sun.

ཉི་མའི་འོད་མཉམ *ñi-maḫi hod mñam* n. of a flower (*K. gu.* ཀ *446*).

ཉི་མའི་འོད་ཟེར *ñi-maḫi hod-zer* the rays of the sun, sunbeam.

ཉི་མའི་རིགས་སྐྱེས *ñi-maḫi rigs-skyes*=ཉི་མའི་རིགས་འཁྲུངས *ñi-maḫi rigs-ḫkhruñs* born of the race of the sun; occurs as a name of Buddha Sākya Simha.

ཉི་མའི་རུས *ñi-maḫi rus* सूर्यवंश the race of the sun, a section of the warrior caste of India claiming descent from the sun.

ཉི་མའི་ལུས *ñi-maḫi lus* सूर्याङ्ग 1. the body of the sun; 2. ཟངས copper.

ཉི་མའི་ལྷ་མོ *ñi-maḫi lha-mo* सूर्याणी the wife of the sun-god.

ཉི་མས་བཤད *ñi-mas ḇshad* met. a lotus (*Mñon.*).

ཉི་སྨྱུར *ñi-myur* evening, a little before dusk; the hour of sunset.

ཉི་ཚེ *ñi-tshe* acc. to *Sch.* 1. the time or duration of one day, a very short time. 2. acc. to *Lex.* प्रदेश direction; sphere, country.

ཉི་ཚེ་བ *ñi tshe-wa* 1. ephemeral, single, simple. 2. n. of a class of infernal beings. 3. very small, minute (*Grub.* ན *2*); ཉི་ཚེ་བ culæ (*Lam-ṭi.*). 4. animals that do not live more than a day, very short-lived animate beings.

ཉི་ཚོད *ñi-tshod* ཉི་ཚོད་ཀྱི་འཁོར་ལོ वेलाचक्र a sun-dial; also a wheel to ascertain time, a watch.

ཉི་ཟེར་གྱི་རྡུལ *ñi zer-gyi rdul* वातायनच्छिद्ररजः the dust seen flying in the rays of the sun coming through apertures of a window; a mote floating in a sunbeam.

ཉི་ཟླ *ñi-zla*, lit. sun and moon; but is the term designating the topmost ornament of a chorten, which takes the form of a ball superimposed on a crescent. This *nyi-da* ornament is also placed above the *gyal-tshan* or Buddhist trophy of victory.

ཉི་ཟླ་དབང་པོ *ñi-zla dwañ-po* n. of a Dākinī (*Loñ.* ང *9*).

ཉི་འོག *ñi-hog* lit. below the sun; अपरान्त the western limit; ཉི་འོག་གི་རྒྱལ་ཁམས *Ñi-hog-gi rgyal-khams* Aparāntaka the western continent or kingdom.

ཉི་འོག་གི་གོས *ñi-hog-gi gos* अपरान्तकम् or dress of the ancient people from Bactria.

ཉི་འོད *ñi-hod* सूर्यांशु, सूर्यप्रभा the rays of the sun, sunbeam, light of the sun.

ཉི་ཡོལ *ñi-yol* a screen, awning.

ཉི་ཤ *ñi-ça* fresh meat.

ཉི་ཤར *ñi-çar* = སྔ་དྲོ *sña-dro* sunrise, early morning.

ཉི་ཤུ *ñi-çu* (inst. of ཉིས་བཅུ) विंशति twenty; ཉི་ཤུ་ཐམ་པ the twenty; ཉི་ཤུ་ཙམ about twenty; ཉི་ཤུ་རྩ་གཅིག twenty-one; རྩ་གཅིག alone sometimes signifies twenty-one. In *Sikk.* and *B.* and *C. Tib.* ཉི་ཤུ་ཉེར་གཅིག or ཉེར་གཅིག is used to denote twenty-one. In the same manner the use of the abbreviated form ཉེར་གཉིས or རྩ་གཉིས for ཉི་ཤུ་ཉེར་གཉིས or ཉི་ཤུ་རྩ་གཉིས is common, and so on.

ཉིག་ཉིག *ñig-ñig* in *W.* loose, slack, lax, not tight or tense (*Jä.*).

ཉིང་ཁུ *ñiñ-khu* मण्ड 1. the juice, essence of any substance, the pith or སྙིང་ *sñiñ* (heart, soul) q. v. 2. spirit (of wine) कारोत्तर; ཆང་ལྷ་བུའི་ཉིང་ཁུ. [yeast, the froth of the liquor]*S.*

ཉིང་སྒོ་ཕུགས *ñiñ-sgo-phugs* the private or inner (hidden) door of a castle or palace: རྒྱལ་པོ་དང་ལྷན་ཅིག་ཏུ་གནས་པར་པོ་བྲང་གི་ཉིང་སྒོ་ཕུགས་མ་ཕྱེ་བར་སྒོ་ནང་ནས་བཙུམས་ཏེ། while residing with the king, he fastened the secret door of the palace from within so that it was not to be opened (*Hbrom. 162*).

ཉིང་ཏོ *ñiñ-to* acc. to *Sch.* sure, trustworthy.

+ ཉིང་གཏོར *ñiñ-gtor* = ངེས་པར certain, sure.

ཉིང་སྤྲུལ *ñiñ-sprul* acc. to *Jä.* an emanation or incarnation. ཡང་སྤྲུལ *yañ-sprul* an emanation of an incarnate being.

ཉིང་མཚམས་སྦྱོར་བ *ñiñ-mtshams sbyor-wa* प्रतिसन्धाति to be reborn, to be transmigrated in regular routine; the re-appearing of the soul after death in one of the four forms of birth, *i.e.*, the linking of the limits of existence.

ཉིང་ལག *ñiñ-lag* प्रत्यङ्ग 1. minor or secondary members of the body, such as the forehead, nose, chin, fingers, ear, eyes, etc. The अङ्ग or limbs of the body called ཡན་ལག are the head, arms, legs, &c. 2. a division, section, part, subdivision. *N.B.*—Sumpa includes the following in the ཉིང་ལག; ལག་པ, མིག, བྲང་, ཕུས་མོ, སྣ, མཁྲིན་པ, རྐང་པ, ཇྀ་ངར, རྒྱབ, སོང་ཚིགས, སྣ་སེར་བགྲ་བ་པོ &c. Acc. to *Jä.* members of a second order, parts of the ཡང་ལག, *i.e.*, of the limbs.

ཉིང་སློབ *ñiṅ-slob*=སློབ་མའི་སློབ་མ a pupil's pupil: ཉིང་སློབ་གཉིས་ཏེ་བཅུ་ལ་བརྟེན་ནས (*A. 124.*) the two *Ñiṅ-slob* depending on the ten (*i.e.*, being supported by them).

卐 ཉིང་ཤ *ñiṅ-ça* one's own flesh; the expression ཉིང་ཤ་ཉིང་གིས་ཟ་བ in the older form of Tibetan signifies རང་ཤ་རང་གིས་ཟ་བ one eating his own flesh, *i.e.*, ruining himself.

ཉིད *ñid* तत्व, एव, तद् 1. self, same, opp. to other persons; སྐུ་ཉིད your (honour's) self: ང་ཉིད=ང་རང་ I myself; མ་ཉིད the mother herself; མི་དེ་ནི་རྒྱལ་པོ་ཉིད་ཡིན་ནོ this man is you (yourself), O king! (*Jä.*). 2. the very, just, etc.: ལས་བྱེད་པའི་གནས་ཉིད་ལ just where I am working; དེའི་དྲུང་ཉིད་ན *dehidruṅ ñid-na* close by, at the very spot; དུས་དེ་ཉིད་དུ at the very moment; མཆོད་བྱ་ཉིད that which is honourable in itself. 3. when added to adjectives it denotes abstract nouns, as in English the terminations:—ness,—ship,—ty,—cy,—y, etc., but it is chiefly limited to the language of philosophical writings (*Jä.*). 4. in the more recent literature it is used resp. for ཁྱོད *khyod* thou, you; ཉིད་ཀྱི thy, your; ཉིད་རང་ you, in *W.* 5.=ཁོ་ན only གྲངས་ཀྱི་ལྔ་ཉིད only the numeral ལྔ; ཟ་ཉིད་དོ the letter *za* (ཟ) alone.

卐 ཉིད་འགྲུལ *ñid-hgrul* a very low caste.

ཉིན་མོ *ñin-mo* दिन, वार, महारोहा, अहः the day; the time lighted or illuminated by the sun. འདི་ན་མདངས་འབར་དང་, གསལ་བར་སྣང་དང་སྣང་ལྡན་དང་ *hdi-na mdaṅs-hbar daṅ, gsal-war snaṅ-daṅ snaṅ-ldan-daṅ,* མུན་སེལ་པདྨ་བཤད་པའི་དུས *mun-sel pad-ma bshad-pahi-dus* (*Rtsii.*).

ཉིན་དཀར *ñin-dkar* a white, a lucky day (*Sch.*).

ཉིན་སྐར *ñin-skar* the star that is visible during the day time: མཐུན་པའི་གྲོགས་ནི་ཉིན་སྐར་འདྲ an agreeable friend is like the day-star (*Hbrom. 55*).

ཉིན་སྐྱོང་ *ñin-skyoṅ* the observance of a fast, rite, etc., for one day.

ཉིན་འཁྱོངས *ñin-hkhyoṅs* for one day, one whole day: མཆོད་པ་སྣ་ལྔ་བརྒྱ་མཚར་ཉིན་འཁྱོངས་ཀྱི་ཐོབ་གཞི། 500 various and wonderful offerings as the allowance for one full day (*Rtsii.*).

ཉིན་གང་ *ñin-gaṅ* all the day long, during the whole day; ཉིན་གུང་ *ñin-guṅ* noon; ཉིན་གླ a day's hire.

ཉིན་གྱི་རིང་ལ *ñin-gyi riṅ-la* during the day time.

ཉིན་ཅིག *ñin-cig* one day, once; ཉིན་ཅིག་བཞིན་དུ daily; ཉིན་པར during the day time, by the day light; དེའི་ཉིན་པར on that day; དེའི་ཕྱི་ཉིན the following day, on the following day; ཚེས་བཅོ་ལྔའི་ཉིན the 15th day, on the 15th day; བསྟན་པ་ཉིན་པར་མཛད་པའི་སྐྱེས་བུ a person who brings to light the faith.

ཉིན་ཆས *ñin-chas*=ཉིན་རེའི་དགོས་སྤྱད *ñin-rehi dgos-spyad* the requirements of every day; daily necessities (*Rtsii.*).

ཉིན་ལྟར་ཆོས་ཆས *ñin-ltar chos-chas* the daily needs for religious services.

ཉིན་མཐར་བྱེད *ñin-mthar-byed* दिनान्तक;=མུན་པ *mun-pa* darkness (*Mṅon.*), v. ཉིན་མོའི་སྒོ་ང *ñin-mohi sgo-ṅa*.

ཉིན་ཐུང་སྐབས *ñin-thuṅ-skabs*, ཉི་མ་ཐུང་དུས *ñi-ma thuṅ-dus* the period of short days; when the day becomes short.

ཉིན་པར *ñin-par* during the day-time, v. *Pth. 268 b*, line *4*.

ཉིན་ཕྱེད་ *ñin-phyed* 1. midday, noon. 2. half a day, *i.e.*, six hours.

ཉིན་བྱེད་ *ñin-byed* दिवाकर 1. the sun—the maker of the day. 2. མཚལ་ *mtshal* vermilion (*Sman. 355*). 3. कुङ्कुम saffron.

ཉིན་བྲལ་ *ñin-bral* अह्नन् without day, dayless.

ཉིན་སྦྲེལ་ *ñin-sbrel* the accumulated works of several days (*Rtsii.*).

ཉིན་མེད་མཚན་མེད་ *ñin-med mtshan-med* without interruption during day and night, continually.

ཉིན་མོའི་སྒོ་ *ñin-mohi-sgo* प्रत्युष the opening of the day, day-break; ཉིན་མོའི་སྒོང་ दिनाण्ड; the egg of the day, dawn [the egg or embryo whence day proceeds; hence darkness]*S*. ཉིན་མོའི་མཐའ་ मध्याह्न the noon, the highest limit or climax of the day; ཉིན་མོའི་བདག་ सूर्य्य, दिनपति, अहःपति the lord of the day, the sun; ཉིན་མོའི་འདྲེན་པ་ the sun, that brings on the day; ཉིན་མོའི་ནོར་བུ་ दिनमणि the gem of the day, the sun; ཉིན་མོའི་བུ་ the planet Saturn, the son of the sun.

ཉིན་མཚན་ *ñin-mtshan* अहोरात्र day and night.

ཉིན་མཚན་མཉམ་པ་ *ñin-mtshan mñam-pa* विषुव the time of the equinox; ཉི་མ་དཀྱིལ་འགྲོ་འཕེལ་འགྲིབ་མཚམས་ when the sun passes over the meridian not causing increase or decrease (in the hours of the day). Described as འཕེལ་འགྲིབ་མེད་ན་ཐད་ཀར་འགྲོ་ when there is neither increase or decrease but the sun passes direct (over the head) (*Rtsii.*).

ཉིན་ཞག་ *ñin-shag* 1. day; ཉིན་ཞག་གསུམ་ three days. 2. अहोरात्र, प्रतिदिवा every day. 3. as a symbol num. 15.

ཉིན་ཞག་ཕྲུགས་གཅིག་ *ñin-shag phrugs-gcig* a day of twenty-four hours; རྫོགས་མ་ཡིན་པའི་ཕ་རོལ་ཏུ་ཕྱིན་པའི་ལུགས་ཉིན་ཞག་ཕྲུགས་གཅིག་གི་བྱ་བ (*A. 74*).

ཉིན་རང་ *ñin-rañ*=ཐོ་རངས day-break, morning twilight (*Schtr.*).

ཉིན་རིང་སྐབས་ *ñin-riñ-skabs*, ཉི་མ་རིང་བའི་དུས the time when the days become long.

ཉིན་རེ་བཞིན་ *ñin-re-bshin* every day, daily.

ཉིན་ལམ་ *ñin-lam* a day's journey, daily march.

ཉིན་ཤད་མཚན་ཤད་ *ñin-çad mtshan-çad*,=ཉིན་མཚན་མེད་པ་ without interruption, day and night (*A. 150*).

ཉིལ་བྱེད་པ་ *ñil-byed-pa* or ཉིལ་ཉིལ་བྱེད་པ, also ཉིལ་ལེ་བྱེད་པ་ *ñil-le byed-pa*, to trickle down, fall in drops (of tears, etc.): ལེགས་པའི་ཤེས་རབ་བཞེངས་ཏེ་ སྤྱན་ཆབ་སྲན་རྡོག་ཙམ་ཉིལ་ལེ་བྱུས་ནས། (*Brom. 25.*) *Legs-pahi çes-rab* rose up and tear-drops like peas trickled down.

ཉིས 1. instr. of ཉི. 2. in compounds for གཉིས as in ཉིས་བརྒྱ two hundred, ཉིས་སྟོང་ two thousand, ཉིས་འགྱུར double.

ཉིས་རྒྱུ་ཆིག་པ་ *ñis-rgyu chig-pa* serge cloth in which two threads cross, one stretched lengthwise (*Rtsii.*).

ཉིས་བལྟའི་མི་ *ñis-bltahi mi* one who looks to the interests both of the State and of the Church; also one who serves two masters (*D. çel. 5*).

ཉུ་ *ñu* num. fig. 68.

ཉུ་གུ་སྤང་ལེབ་ *ñu-gu spañ-leb* n. of a kind of worm (*Rtsii.*).

ཉུ་ཏི་ *ñu-ti* a pear (*Ld.*).

ཉུག་ ཉུག་པ་ *ñug ñug-pa* to stand out, to project.

ཉུག་རུམ་ *ñug-rum* lit. the testes cut out; ཉུག་རུམ་ or ཉུག་རུམ་པ=སྐྱེས་པ་འབྲུམ་ཕྱུང་བ་ eunuch, one whose testes have been extracted (*Mñon.*).

ཉུག་པ་ *Ñug-pa* I: n. of a place in the province of Tsang.

ཉུག་པ II: 1. to besmear, to rub gently; སྤོས་ཉུག་པ *spos-ñug-pa* to rub perfume; acc. to *Sch.* to stroke, to caress. 2. to touch; feel for. 3. to protrude, stretch out: ཆུ་ནས་མགོ་ཉུག་པ to stretch one's head out of water; ཏུ་ཉུག་མཛོད་པ to look or peep out, to take a peep at.

ཉུག་རྩ་མེ་ཏོག *ñug-rtsa me-tog* Carthusian pink (*Jä.*).

ཉུང་བ *ñuṅ-wa* अल्प, कनिष्ठ not many, little, a few; minor; ཉུང་ཤས་ཙམ a very little quantity, a little.

ཉུང་སྐྱོན *ñuṅ-skyon* slight defect.

ཉུང་ངུ *ñuṅ-ṅu* स्वल्प, अल्प less, little, small: ཉུང་ངུ་སྨྲ་བ་ཡིན speaks little.

Syn. ཆུང་བ *chuṅ-wa*, ཉུང་དུ *ñuṅ-du* (*Mṅon.*).

ཉུང་མ *ñuṅ-ma* turnip, turnip soup; ཉུང་མའི་ལོ་མ गुग्गुलु turnip leaf, a fragrant gum resin; ཉུང་རློན *ñuṅ-rlon* fresh turnip.

ཉུང་རུམ *ñuṅ-rum*, v. ཉུག་རུམ *ñug-rum*.

ཉུལ་བ *ñul-wa* to wander or rove about, to step gently or steal through, to creep. ཉུལ་མི a detective; ས་ཉུལ a spy.

ཉེ *ñe* 1. num. fig. 98. 2. for ཉེ་བ near.

ཉེ་སྐོར *ñe-skor* = ཐོག་སྐོར *thog-skor* समन्तक those about (us), retinue, v. ཉེ་འཁོར.

ཉེ་སྐྱོན *ñe-skyon* fault of partiality (*e.g.*, in a *Jongpon* district chief or judge). ཉེ་སྐྱོན་ཕྱོགས་ལྷུང lit. the inclining to one side.

ཉེ་མཁོན *ñe-mkhon* = ཉེ་རིང (*Cs.*).

ཉེ་འཁོར *ñe-ḥkhor* समन्त, उपविचार, निकट, उपवर्त्तन, उपवर्णिक 1. an attendant, one near or in waiting; relations, kindred, neighbour. 2. n. of one of the hells. 3. neighbourhood: ཁོ་རང་གི་ཉེ་འཁོར་གྱི་སློང་མོ་བ a beggar belonging to his neighbourhood. 4. उपालि (Upāli) the disciple of Buddha who narrated the *Vinaya piṭaka*.

ཉེ་འཁོར་གྱི་མིག *Ñe-ḥkhor-gyi mig* n. of a great ocean lying between the continents of Godāniya and Uttara Kuru (*K. d.* ར *330*).

ཉེ་དགའ *ñe-dgaḥ* उपनन्द a king of the *Nāga*.

ཉེ་བསྒྱུར *ñe-bsgyur* उपसर्ग trouble, misfortune.

ཉེ་གྲོགས *ñe-grogs* fellow creature, neighbour (*Cs.*).

ཉེ་གྷེ *ñe-ghe* a tribal name in Tibet, one of the three:—ཤུག་པ *shug-pa*, སྟོང་ཉེ *stoṅ-ñe*, ཉེ་གྷེ *ñe-ghe* (*Yig*).

ཉེ་ཆར *ñe-char* 1. at present or very shortly: (*Yig. k. 29*). ས་དབང་རམ་པ་ལས་ཚ་དཔོན་འཁོར་བཅས་ཉེ་ཆར་ཕེབས་རྒྱུ་ཡིན the governor Rampa with his officers and chiefs will come very shortly. 2. at the close of.

ཉེ་ཆོས *ñe-chos* समय, आह्निक time; usage; neighbour; near.

ཉེ་ཏི *ñe-ṭi* a pear (*Schtr.*), v. ཉུ་ཏི *ñu-ṭi*.

ཉེ་དག *ñe-dag* relations (*Cs.*).

ཉེ་དུ *ñe-du* ज्ञाति, कुटुम्ब kindred, relations: ཉེ་དུའི་ནང་ན་འདུག་རུང་དུང ज्ञातिमध्यगतकल्प (he) is certainly fit to be among the kinsmen.

ཉེ་དུས *ñe-dus* now-a-days.

ཉེ་འདབ *ñe-ḥdab* स्वजन one's own people, friends or admirers.

ཉེ་གནས *ñe-gnas* उपस्थ = (ཕོ་དབང) 1. the male organ. 2. उपस्थानीय disciple: ཁྱེད་ཀྱི་ཉེ་གནས་བགྱིད I shall be your attendant, or I wish to become your disciple; ཉེ་གནས་སུ་མཆི་འོ I am becoming a follower.

ཉེ་ཚན *ñe-tshan* relative, kinsman.

ཉེ་ཚལ *ñe-tshal* or ཉེ་བའི་ཚལ उपवन an artificial grove, garden.

+ ཉེ་རིག་པ *ñe-rig-pa* 1.=འཁྲིག་པ *ḥkhrig-pa* (*Mñon.*) copulation. 2.=ཁྲུས་བྱེད་པ *khruṣ-byed-pa* to wash.

ཉེ་རིགས *ñe-rigṣ* near relation.

ཉེ་བ *ñe-wa* 1. समीप-स्था, सन्निकट-भू, अन्तिक-भू vb. to be near, to approach: དུས་བྱེད་དུ་ཉེ་བས when he was near dying; ཟླ་བ་ཚང་དུ་ཉེ་བས (when she was) near the completion of the months, *i.e.*, the time of giving birth to a child (*Jā.*); སློབ་དཔོན་པར་ཕྱིན་དུ་ཉེ་བས when the time of the teacher's return drew near; ཟིན་དུ་མི་ཉེ་སྟེ being not near having done; གནས་དེར་སླེབ་ཏུ་ཉེ་བའི་ཚེ when he was near arriving at the place. 2. also as an adj.=near: ཐམ་རིང་གི་གཉེན་པས་ཁྱིམ་མཚེས་ཉེ the neighbour is nearer than a kind man living far off; ཀ་བ་དང་ཉེ་བའི་སར at a place near the pillar; ཤག་ཉེ་བ near. རི་ཤག་ཉེ་བ་ཞིག frq. in colloq. neighbouring hill, standing near, being closely connected with by consanguinity; ཉེ་བ་རྣམས those who are near, near relations; མཚམས་མེད་པ་ལྔ་དང་དེ་དང་ཉེ་བའི་སྡིག་པ the five worst sins and those coming nearest to them. 3. as an adv. the form is generally ཉེ་བར *ñe-war* almost, near, nearly: དེ་དག་ཉེ་བར་ཕྱིན་ནས when they had come near. Sometimes the form is ཉེ་བ་ན, as in ཞག་བདུན་དེ་རྣམས་ཉེ་བ་ན་རྫོགས་ཏེ these seven days being almost ended. 4. as a postp. it requires དང to connect it with the word it governs: ཁང་པ་དང་ཉེ་བར་ཕྱིན་པས་རོལ་མོ་དང་གར་བྱེད་པ་ཐོས་ནས when he came near to the house he heard music and dancing; འགྲོ་རན་པ་དང་ཉེ་བར་བབས it came near to the time of going.

ཉེ་བའི་དགའ་བྱེད་མ *ñe-wahi dgaḥ-byed-ma*=གནོད་སྦྱིན་མོའི་གཙོ་མོ n. of the queen of the Noijin or *Yakṣa* demi-gods.

ཉེ་བའི་རྣ་རྒྱན *ñe-wahi rna-rgyan* उपकर्णिक ear-ornaments beside the ear-ring.

ཉེ་བའི་དབྱངས *ñe-wahi dbyañs* उपगीत musical airs, musical notes to help in singing.

ཉེ་བའི་མ་མ *ñe-wahi ma-ma* धात्री 1. a foster-mother, a wet-nurse. 2. उपमाता step-mother.

‡ ཉེ་བའི་ཙན་དྷོ་ཧ *ñe-wahi tsa-tshan dho-ha* उपच्छन्दन hortative expression used in exorcism.

ཉེ་བའི་ཚལ *ñe-wahi tshal*=སྐྱེད་ཚལ *skyed-tshal* उपवन a grove.

ཉེ་བའི་རི་མོ་ཅན *ñe-wahi ri-mo can*=ཞར་ནུ उपचित्रक (*Mñon.*) n. of a medicinal plant. [the plants *Salvinia cucullata*, and *Croton polyandra*]*S.*

ཉེ་བའི་རིན་ཆེན་བདུན *ñe-wahi rin-chen bdun* the seven secondary adjuncts of royalty:—(1) ལྷམ shoes, (2) པགས་པ skin-rug, (3) གོས dress, (4) མལ couch, (5) ཚལ grove, (6) ཁྱིམ house, (7) རལ་གྲི sword.

ཉེ་བའི་ས *ñe-wahi sa* उपत्यका table-land, plateau, plains on or by the side of a hill.

ཉེ་བའི་སར་གྱུ *ñe-wahi sar-gyu*=བསྙེན *bsñen* आसन्नीभूत become intimate, near.

ཉེ་བའི་སྲས་ཆེན་བརྒྱད *ñe-wahi sraṣ-chen brgyad* अष्टमहाउपपुत्र the eight chief spiritual sons of the Buddha described under that title are said to be:—(1) मञ्जुश्रीकुमारभूत; འཇམ་དཔལ་དབྱངས་གཞོན་ནུར་གྱུར་པ; (2) वज्रपाणि; ཕྱག་ན་རྡོ་རྗེ; (3) अवलोकितेश्वर; སྤྱན་རས་གཟིགས་དབང་ཕྱུག; (4) क्षितिगर्भ; ས་ཡི་སྙིང་པོ; (5) सर्वनिवारणविष्कम्भि; སྒྲིབ་པ་རྣམ་སེལ; (6) आकाशगर्भ; ནམ་མཁའི་སྙིང་པོ; (7) मैत्रेय; བྱམས་པ; (8) समन्तभद्र; ཀུན་ཏུ་བཟང་པོ.

ཉེ་བར་བཀོད *ñe-war bkod* उपन्यास appropriate arrangement, good design.

ཉེ་བར་མཁོ་བ *ñe-war mkho-wa* 1. of urgent necessity. 2.=ཉེར་འཕེལ rapid increase or growth; it increases rapidly.

ཉེ་བར་འཁྱུད *ñe-war ḥkhyud* उपासिक devotee.

ཉེ་བར་གུས *ñe-war guṣ* उपनिषत् lit. humbly near; the Upanishad or Vedic literature treating of Brahma.

ཉེ་བར་དགོངས *ñe-war dgoṅs* उपन्यास tale, story, romance.

ཉེ་བར་བརྒལ་བ *ñe-war brgal-wa* अतिक्रम, (उपक्रम) to pass over.

ཉེ་བར་ཆགས་པ *ñe-war chags-pa* उपराग, ग्रहण 1. eclipse. 2. कन्दल quarrel.

ཉེ་བར་ཚིམ་ཚོགས *ñe-war tshim-tshogs* सन्तोष contentment.

ཉེ་བར་མཆོད་པ *ñe-war mchod-pa* समुपहृत, सत्कृत to honour, respect.

ཉེ་བར་མཇལ *ñe-war mjal* or incorrectly ཉེ་བར་འཇལ, v. སྐུ་ཤ *sku-ça* 1. health (*Mñon.*); =སྐུ་འདྲ *sku-hdra*, གཟུགས་བརྙན उपमान, मूर्त, प्रभ. 2. image, likeness (*Mñon*).

ཉེ་བར་འཇོག་པ *ñe-war hjog-pa* उपस्थान lit. to stand near; to worship, to wait upon.

ཉེ་བར་བསྙེན་པ *ñe-war bsñen-pa* उपसेवा service; to attend or take care of.

ཉེ་བར་རྟོགས་པ *ñe-war rtogs-pa* उपपरीक्षण to inquire into; investigation.

ཉེ་བར་བརྟེན་པ *ñe-war brten-pa* उपसेवन enjoying, serving, honouring.

ཉེ་བར་བསྟན *ñe-war bstan* उपदेश advice, counsel.

ཉེ་བར་བསྟན་པ *ñe-war bstan-pa* to command, instruct (*Mñon.*).

ཉེ་བར་གདུང *ñe-war gduṅ*=one attacked with disease.

ཉེ་བར་འདུག་པ *ñe-war hdug-pa* उपोषध to fast on the prescribed days.

ཉེ་བར་གཞང་བ *ñe-war naṅ-wa* =བཀར་ལུང.

ཉེ་བར་གནས *ñe-war gnas*=བཀུར་སྟི adulation, also flattery; ཉེ་བར་སྤྱོད *ñe-war spyod* उपासना supplication. ཉེ་བར་གནས་པ नैकटिक to be near, in attendance (*Mñon.*).

ཉེ་བར་སྤྱོད་པ *ñe-war spyod-pa* उपभोग to enjoy.

ཉེ་བར་ཕན *ñe-war phan* समुपहित put together, constructed, produced.

ཉེ་བར་ཕན་འདོགས *ñe-war phan-hdogs* उपयुज्यते is fit for, suits.

ཉེ་བར་འཕར་འགྲོ *ñe-war hphar-hgro*=སྒྲ་གཅན राहु the demon who causes the eclipse of the sun (*Mñon.*).

ཉེ་བར་བྱེད *ñe-war-byed*=ཞུས་པ उपास्ति service, veneration.

ཉེ་བར་སྦྱོར *ñe-war sbyor* उपनय friendship, harmony; ཉེ་བར་རྫོགས་མ=སྡུད་པ उपसंहार fulfilment, completion, conclusion.

ཉེ་བར་མི་རིག *ñe-war mi-rig*=ཉེ་བར་མི་འགྲོ or ཁམས་མི་ལེན.

ཉེ་བར་དམིགས *ñe-war dmigs* उपलम्बन prop. support.

ཉེ་བར་བཞག་པ *ñe-war bshag-pa* to make use of, to employ; དྲན་པ་ཉེ་བར་བཞག་པ स्मृत्युपस्थान earnest meditation, v. དྲན་པ་ཉེ་བར་བཞག; སངས་རྒྱས་ལ་དཀོན་པའི་འདུ་ཤེས་ཉེ་བར་བཞག་པ to apply to Buddha the notion of rareness.

ཉེ་བར་ཞི *ñe-war shi* उपशम relief; it is also applied in reference to ཉོན་མོངས, མེ and བཟོད་པ, to signify putting out, and forbearance (*Mñon.*).

ཉེ་བར་ལེན་པ *ñe-war len-pa* I: ཉེ་བར་ལེན་པའི་ཕུང་པོ་ལྔ the five *upādāna* or *vija* or fundamental skandha are:—(1) रूपस्कन्ध; གཟུགས་ཀྱི་ཕུང་པོ; (2) वेदनास्कन्ध; ཚོར་བའི་ཕུང་པོ; (3) संज्ञास्कन्ध; འདུ་ཤེས་ཀྱི་ཕུང་པོ; (4) संस्कारस्कन्ध; འདུ་བྱེད་ཀྱི་ཕུང་པོ; (5) विज्ञानस्कन्ध; རྣམ་པར་ཤེས་པའི་ཕུང་པོ.

The Sanskrit equivalents may be rendered as follows:—

[(1) Form-group; (2) sensation-group; (3) names or idea-group, *i.e.*, verbal association. (4) predisposition-group; (5) knowledge-group]*S*.

ཉེ་བར་ལེན་པ II: to seize eagerly, to strive for earnestly, to aspire to; also ཉེར་ལེན་པ.

ཉེ་བར་སྲེག་པར་བྱེད་པ *ñe-war sreg-par-byed-pa* उपदाह [to set fire to, to burn]*S*.

ཉེ་དབང་ *ñe-dbañ* उपेन्द्र a name of Vishnu.

ཉེ་འབྲེལ *ñe-hbrel* connection, kindred, relations.

ཉེ་ཚིག *ñe-tshig* उपपद a secondary word which limits the idea contained in the principal word.

ཉེ་ཚེ་བ *ñe-tshe-wa* प्रादेशिक provincial.

ཉེ་ཚེའི་སངས་རྒྱས *ñe-tshehi sañs-rgyas* प्रत्येकबुद्ध Pratyeka Buddha.

ཉེའུ *ñehu* small fish: བདག་འདྲའི་སྐྱེ་བོ་མ་དག་པ, ཉེའུ་སྐམ་ལ་འཐོན་པར་གྱུར an impure man like myself will be a small fish cast out on dry land.

ཉེ་ཤོ *ñe-sho* 1.=ཕྱོགས་རི partiality. 2. mishap.

+ཉེ་ཤོ་མེད་པ I: *ñe-sho med-pa*=ཉེས་སྐྱོན་མེད་པ *ñes-skyon med-pa* without defect, without mishap: ཉེ་ཤོ་མེད་པར་སླེབས་པ་ལེགས *ñe-sho med-par slebs-pa legs* it is well that you have arrived without any accident (*A. 12*).

ཉེ་ཤོ་མེད་པ II: पूरित filled, complete; without damage.

ཉེ་ཤོས་དབེན *ñe-shos dwen*=ནད་མེད་པ or ནད་མེད without disease; healthy (*Mñon.*).

ཉེ་ཟུངས *ñe-zuñs*=འཁྲིག་པ *hkhrig-pa* copulation (*Mñon.*).

+ཉེའུ་གྱི *ñehu-gyi*=བཅུད་ཆོར *bcud-chor*.

ཉེ་གཡོག་བྱ་བར་འོད་པ་ལྔ *ñe-gyog bya-war hod-pa-lña* the five persons that are worthy of being served are: (1) ཕ father, (2) མ mother, (3) མཁན་པོ teacher, (4) སློབ་དཔོན spiritual guide, (5) ནད་པ a sick man.

ཉེ་རིང *ñe-riñ* 1. near and far. ཉེ་བ་ཉེ་རིང near and distant relations. 2. distance: སྒོར་ཉེ་རིང་ཅི་ཙམ་ཡོད how far is it from here to the gate? 3. partial: རྒྱལ་པོ་ཉེ་རིང་ཆེས the king is very partial. ཉེ་རིང་མེད་པ impartial.

ཉེ་ལམ *ñe-lam*=ཐག་ཉེ་བའི་ལམ close or shorter road.

ཉེ་ལོགས *ñe-logs*=ཐག་ཉེ་བ समीप, सन्निकर्ष near, in the neighbourhood (*Mñon.*).

ཉེ་ཤིང *ñe-çiñ* उपवृक्ष n. of a tree. the root of which is used in medicine.

Syn. དྲང་སྲོང་བཅད *drañ-sroñ bcad*; འཇིགས་མེད་འདབ *hjigs-med hdab*; དབང་མཆོག *dwañ-mchog*; མཆོག་ལྡན *mchog-ldan*; མཆོག་རྒྱལ་མ *mchog-rgyal-ma*; རྩ་བ་བརྒྱ་བ *rtsa-wa brgya-wa*; བུ་མང *bu-mañ*; སྲིད་སྒྲུབ་བུ *srid-sgrub-bu* (*Mñon*).

ཉེང་བྱེད་པ *ñeñ-byed-pa* to glance at an object by lifting up the head a little: ཕོ་བྲང་གི་སྒོར་ཉེང་བྱས་ནས་སྤྲུལ་པའི་ལྷ་ཕྲུག་ཅིག་ཐོན་ལགས་སམ is it a child of the gods who has come and who has been obtained by just glancing at the door of the palace? (*Hbrom. 123*).

ཉེད་པ *ñed-pa*=མཉེད་པ *mñed-pa*.

ཉེན *ñen* व्याप्ति, परिणाम 1. perhaps=sickness, thinness (*A. K. III, 20*). གདུང་བའི་ཉེན तापार्त्ति. 2. sbst. a relative, kinsman. 3. danger, liability, risk. This meaning is probably derived from ཉན *ñan* which in *C.* is invariably pronounced *ñen* and which signifies: capability, chance, etc. Like ཉན also, it is annexed to verbal roots: དམྱལ་བར་འགྲོ་ཉེན་གདའ *dmyal-war hgro-ñen gdah* there is a danger of going to hell; སྲོག་གི་བར་ཆད་དུ་འགྲོ་བའི་ཉེན་ཡོད *srog-gi bar-chad-du hgro-wahi ñen-yod* there is the danger of risking one's life.

ཉེན་ཀོར *ñen-kor* seems to=ཐག་ཉེ་བ *thag ñe-wa* near (*Ñag.*).

ཉེན་སྐོར *ñen-skor*=གཉེན *gñen* a relative; ཉེན་སྐོར་ཞིག *ñen-skor shig* he is a relative, kinsman.

ཉེན་ཁ་ཆེ་ཙམ *ñen-kha che-tsam* may become dangerous, full of danger; ཉེན་ཅན *ñen-can* dangerous; ཉེན་སྣར་བསྐྱོད་པ *ñen-snar bskyod-pa* continually moving towards danger; ཉེན་པའི་ལམ *ñen-pahi lam*=ལམ་ཉན་པ *lam ñan-pa* a dangerous road, a road which leads to anger (*Mñon.*).

ཉེན་པ ñen-pa 1.=ཉེག་ཐག ñeg-thag, v. ཉག་མ ñag-ma. 2. an enemy. 3. to be pained, pinched, pressed hard, *e.g.*, by hunger; to labour, to drudge, v. བང་ bañ.

ཉེར ñer 1. ཉེ་བར ñe-war. 2. used in lieu of ཉི་ཤུ ñi-çu in counting numerals from 20 to 30. 3.=མྱ་ངན *mya-ñan* affliction, pain.

ཉེར་སྐད *ñer-skad*=གཅོང་སྐད *gcoñ-skad* suffering, cry of suffering.

ཉེར་བསྐྱོད *ñer-bskyod* उपपत्ति suitability.

ཉེར་བསྐྲུན *ñer-bskrun* उत्पत्ति, आत्म said to =བདག་ཉིད self.

ཉེར་འཁོད *ñer-hkhod* आसन्न near.

ཉེར་དགའ *ñer-dgah* उपानन्द delight.

ཉེར་དགུ *ñer-dgu* 29; also the 29th day of each month when offerings are made to the demons.

ཉེར་བསྒྱུར *ñer-bsgyur* उपप्लव unlucky accident.

ཉེར་སྔོགས *ñer-sños* theme, task (*Sch.*).

ཉེར་ཉེར *ñer-ñer*=ཉེར་ཞེ in *W.* dregs, sediment (*Jä.*).

ཉེར་སྤྱོད *ñer-spyod* उपचार offerings; पञ्चोपचार or the five kinds of offerings to be made to the gods in worshipping them:—(1) མེ་ཏོག पुष्प flowers; (2) བདུག་སྤོས धूप incense; (3) མར་མེ आलोक lamps; (4) དྲི गन्ध odours; (5) ཞལ་ཟས नैवेद्य eatables, cakes (*Ya-sel. 53*).

ཉེར་བྱུང *ñer-byuñ* उद्भव origination.

ཉེར་བྱེད *ñer-byed* met. a tree.

ཉེར་སྦས *Ñer-sbas*=ཉེ་བར་སྦས उपगुप्त the Buddhist priest who was spiritual guide to As'oka.

ཉེར་ཚད *ñer-tshad* उपद्रव, उपराग, विप्लव personal danger (*Mñon.*). ཉེར་ཚད་མེད *ñer-tshad-med*=ནད་མེད་པ *nad-med-pa* or འབྱུང་བཞི་སྙོམས *hbyuñ-bshi sñoms* without danger to health (*Mñon.*).

ཉེར་ཚད *ñer-tshad*=སྐུ་འདྲ *sku-hdra*, v. ཉེ་བར་མཇལ *ñe-war mjal.*

ཉེར་ཞི་བ *ñer-shi-wa* 1. བསྒོ་བ་བཞིན་ཉན་པ *bsgo-wa bshin ñan-pa* to listen to an instruction or direction. 2. ཉེ་བར་ཞི་བ उपशम alleviation, pacification.

ཉེར་ལེན་པ *ñer len-pa*=ཉེ་བར་ལེན་པ or རྒྱུའི་རྒྱུ the cause of a cause, the original cause (*Jä.*).

ཉེར་པ *ñer-pa* 1. acc. to *Sch.* to tan, dress, make soft. 2. acc. to *Jä.* in *W.* to snarl, growl. 3. to tarry, stay, linger.

ཉེར་མ *ñer-ma* in *W.* for གཡེར་མ red pepper (*Jä.*).

ཉེལ་བ *ñel-wa* to fall ill; become sick (*Sch.*).

ཉེས་པ *ñes-pa* I: दोष, अपराध, अत्यय 1. sbst. any evil or misfortune or injurious occurrence: ཉེས་པ་ཐམས་ཅད་དེའི་ལུས་ལ་འདུས all things noxious are massing together upon his body; ལོ་ཉེས a year of calamities, bad harvest; ལོ་ཉེས་བྱུང་བའི་ཚེ when the harvest had been bad; ཉེས་པ་གསུམ also གནོད་བྱེད་ཉེས་པ་གསུམ the three humours of the body, viz: वात རླུང་ wind; पित्त མཁྲིས་པ bile; श्लेष्म བད་ཀན phlegm. 2. moral fault, offence, crime; ཉེས་པའི་སྤྱོད the failings of immoral acts; ལུས་དང་ངག་གི་ཉེས་པ guilt of speech and bad action; ཉེས་པ་བྱེད་པ in reference to the body,=to commit a fault, a crime, to sin; but the word used for "sin" in the *N. Testament* and in the Christian sense is not ཉེས་པ but སྡིག་པ. ཉེས་པ་ཐོབས lit. wages of faults, *i.e.*, retribution, punishment.

ཉེས་ཆད་ *ñeş-chad̲* = ཉེས་པ་འགལ་རྒྱུ་ crime, also fine.

ཉེས་ལྟུང་ *ñeş-ltuṅ* a moral slip, trespass: ཉེས་ལྟུང་གིས་ཐོག he has met with a moral fall (*Mil.*).

ཉེས་པ་ཁས་མི་ལེན་ *ñeş-pa khaş mi-len* not to confess fault or guilt.

ཉེས་པ II: vb. to commit an offence: འདིས་ཅི་ཉེས་ཏེ་བཟུང་ *h̲diş-ci ñeş-te b̲zuṅ* for committing what offence has he been seized; སྔར་མ་སྦྲན་པ་ཉེས་སོ *şñar ma-şbran-pa ñeş-so* not reporting earlier, you did wrong; གཡོགས་པ་ཉེས་སོ you have committed a fault by covering it; བདག་ཉེས་ན if harm is done to me; ཁྱེད་ཅི་ཉེས་པ་སྨྲོས་ཤིག *khyed̲-ci ñeş-pa şmroş-çig* tell me what has befallen you; མི་དྲན་ནམ་ཅི་ཉེས is she out of her senses; ཅི་ཉེས་ན what is the matter (with her)? མ་ཉེས་པའི་འགྲོ་བ innocent beings; མ་ཉེས་པ་ཕྱིར་བྱུང་ he came out again unhurt. The commoner verbal usage is with བྱེད་པ annexed. Thus, in their *N. Testament* translation, the Moravian missionaries invariably use ཉེས་པ་བྱེད་པ in the sense of to trespass, commit a fault.

Syn. ནོངས་པ *noṅş-pa*; སྐྱོན་ཅན *şkyon-can*; ངེས་བཟུང་ *ñeş-b̲zuṅ*; སྡོམ་འཆིང་ *şdom-h̲chiṅ*; ཁྲིམས་གཅོད་ཡུལ *khrimş-gcod̲-yul*; མཐོང་བ་མེད *m̲thoṅ-wa med̲* (*M̲ṅon.*).

ཉེས་པ་སྦོམ་པོ *ñeş-pa şbom-po* स्थूलात्यय a great sin, serious fault.

ཉེས་པར་གནན་བྱས *ñeş-par gñan-byaş*, v. ཁས་བླངས has been promised (*M̲ṅon.*).

ཉེས་དཔྱད་སྣར་སྤྱོད *ñeş-d̲pyad̲ şnar-şpyod̲* continually committing mischief or trespasses.

ཉེས་སྤྱད *ñeş-şpyad̲* दुश्चर्या bad habit, immoral conduct.

ཉེས་བྱས *ñeş-byaş* a wicked action.

ཉེས་པ་བྱེད་པའི་ཤོ་གམ་པ *ñeş-pa byed̲-pah̲i ço-gam-pa* a tyrant; oppressive tax-gatherer or ruler.

ཉེས་དམིགས *ñeş-d̲migş* आदीनव, उपालम्भ reproach; punishment for faults: ཁྱིམ་གྱི་ཉེས་དམིགས་ཆེས་ཆེར་བསམས་པ་ལ considering the punishments of lay life to be great, *i.e.*, ever increasing (*A. 11*). In *C.* "*nye-mig*" is a term for punishment, penalty.

ཉོ *ño* 1. num. fig. 128. 2. carrot (*Cs.*).

ཉོ་ཏི *ño-ti* pear in *Ld.* (*Jä.*).

ཉོ་བ *ño-wa*, क्रय, pf. and imp. ཉོས to buy, to obtain by payment; ཉོ་པ a "buyer," of the bride at a Ladak wedding; ཉོ་མཁན a buyer: གང་བྱུང་མང་བྱུང་ལ་ཉོ་ལེ whether any or many wants arise he buys, *i.e.*, a constant customer; ཉོ་ཐོ account, bill; ཉོས་པོ anything bought, commodity to be bought; ཉོ་འཚོང་ buying and selling, commerce, traffic; ཉོ་འཚོང་བྱེད་པ क्रयविक्रय to trade; ཉོ་བའི་ཆེད *ño-wah̲i ched̲* for buying.

ཉོ་ལོ *ño-lo* inferior animals which cannot carry burdens: ཐ་མའི་དྲེའུ་འགེམས་པ་དང་ཐོ་ཐོག་གཉིས་ལ་ཤས་ཆུང་བས་ཉོ་ལོ་ཆུང་བར་བཤད stupid mule-colts and mules of the worst sort whether adult or small are said to be "little *ño-lo*" (*Jig.*).

ཉོག་པ *ñog-pa* or ཉོག་མ कलुषित soiled, dirtied, made unclean, *e.g.*, of victuals; ཆུ་ཉོག་མ muddy or foul water.

ཉོག་ཉོག་པ *ñog-ñog-pa* confused, mixed up.

ཉོགས་བྱིང་ *ñogş-byiṅ* (*Sch.*). too soft; ཉོག་ཉོང་ *ñog-ñoṅ* soft, maudlin, weak. ཤས་ཉོག་ཅན *çaş ñog-can* in *W.* for གཅེས་ཉོག་ཅན fondling anything (*Jä.*).

+ **ཉོད་པ** *ñod̲-pa* = ཟས अन्न food.

ཉོན་མོངས་པ क्लेश 1. misery, trouble, distress, any misfortune. 2. vb. to be troubled, in misery: ཚ་བས་ཉོན་མོངས་ཏེ molested by the heat; ཉོན་མོངས་པར་འགྱུར་བ to get into trouble, to be distressed; ཉོན་མ་མོངས་སམ had you not any trouble? prob. you had no troubles. 3. often has the technical meaning of misery as the result of ignorant clinging to existence and the world, and therefore, in the Buddhist sense, the misery of sin: ཉོན་མོངས་པ་ལས་ཐར་བའི་དོན་མེད this does not avail for being delivered from such a misery; ཉོན་མོངས་པ་མེད་པ free from troubles, perhaps also sinless: ཉོན་མོངས་ཅན་གྱིས་ཉ་ཤ་ཉོས the sinner buys the flesh of fish (*Jä.*).

ཉོན་མོངས་པའི་ས *ñon-moṅs-pahi sa* acc. to Buddhism (*K. d.* ཞ *355.*) the ten smaller causes of moral misery are:—ཁྲོ་བ wrath, འཁོན་འཛིན spite, རྫུན་པ ostentation, show, འཚིག་པ adherence to what is contrary to Buddhism, སྒྱུ illusion, གཡོ deception, ཕྲག་དོག jealousy, envy, སེར་སྣ covetousness, ང་རྒྱལ pride, ལྷག་པའི་ང་རྒྱལ arrogance.

ཉོན་མོངས་པའི་ས་ཆེན་བཅུ *ñon-moṅ-pahi sa-chen ḇcu* the ten greater causes of moral or mental misery:—མ་དད་པ want of faith; འགྱོད་པ *hgyoḏ-pa* repentance or regret; བརྗེད་ངས་པ bartering, also vacillating; སེམས་གཡེངས་པ inattention or changing the mind; ཤེས་རབ་འཆལ་བ confusion or mental derangement; ཚུལ་བཞིན་མ་ཡིན་པ་ཡིད་ལ་བྱེད་པ practising actions inaccordant with custom; ཐོག་པར་མོས་པ irreverence; རྒོད་པ laughing aloud; མ་རིག་པ ignorance; བག་མེད་པ immodesty.

ཉོན་མོངས་མེད་པ *ñon-moṅs meḏ-pa* निष्-क्लेश, अनंगन free from pain or misery.

ཉོན་མོངས་ཚིག *ñon-moṅs tshig*=ལེ་ལོའི་ཚིག words of idleness (*Mṅon.*).

ཉོབ་ཉོབ *ñob-ñob* weak, feeble-minded (*Sch.*).

ཉོར *ñor* 1.=ཉོ་བར. 2. a rectangle (*Cs.*).

ཉོལ *ñol*, imp. of ཉལ་བ.

ཉོས *ños* pf. of ཉོ་བ: ཉོས་མི a man who has been bought, a slave (*Cs.*).

གཉགས *gñags* n. of a place in Tibet (*Deb.* ཀ *2*).

གཉན *gñan* I: 1. n. of a place in Tibet (*Deb.* ཀ *2*). 2. very powerful and at the same time fearful.

གཉན II: 1. a pestilential disease, epidemic, infectious sickness, plague; མཛེ་དང་འབྲུམ་བུ་གཉན leprosy and small pox are pestilential diseases. The following diseases are mentioned under the term of གཉན pestilence (*S̱man. 108*): གཟེར་ཐུག *gzer-thug*, ནག་པོ་རྒྱུག་འགྱེལ *nag-po ṟgyug-ḥgyel*, ཀླད་གཟེར *ḵlaḏ-gzer*, འཛུམ་ཁ་རྩེག *ḥdsum kha-ṟtseg*, འཛུམ་ལྟག་དགྱེ *ḥdsum ḻtag-ḏgye*, ཉྭ་ལོག *ñḇa-log* or བྱིན་ལོག *byin-log*, ཕོ་གླང *pho-glaṅ*, རྣ་རྩ་ཕུས་འདེབས *ṟna-ṟtsa phuṣ-ḥdebṣ*, ངམ་རུ *ṅam-ru*, གཉན་སྲིན *gñan-sṟin*, གཉན་ནད་རྐུན་པོ *gñan-naḏ ṟkun-po*, གཉན་འབྲས *gñan-ḥbraṣ*, གཉན་འབུར *gñan-ḥbur*, ལྷོག་པ *lhog-pa*, གག་པ *gag-pa*. The four remedies prescribed in Tib. medical works for *gñan* called གཉན་གསོད plague killers:—ཨ་རུ or *lagerstrœmia*, བཙན་དུག arsenic, ཤུ་དག and གླ་རྩི musk (*S̱man. 450*). 2. a class of mischievous demi-gods (ས་བདག), also called གཉན་ཁྲ the parti-coloured *gñan*, གཉན་ལྗང the green *gñan*, and གཉན་ཁྲ་ཐུག་པོ.

གཉན III: a species of wild sheep, not the *Ovis ammon* but the *Ovis Hodgsoni*. Its range is throughout Tibet, but never in the Sikkim-Himalaya. In the Kuen-lün and Altan Tag ranges, both this species and the true *Ovis ammon* occur.

གཉན་ཐབ་པ *gñan-thab-pa* certain medicinal roots so called on account of their curative virtues in plague, namely:—རྟག་ཀ, ཞིག་ཅན, ལྕགས་ཀྱུ *ḻcags-kyu* (*Miṅ. 2*).

གཉན་འདུལ་པ *gñan hdul-pa* root of a plant used in the disease called *Gñan-gzer tsha-wa* of which high fever and severe aching in the body are chief characteristics.

གཉན་པ *gñan-pa* or གཉན་པོ चण्ड 1. cruel, fierce, severe: གཉན་པ་བོན་དང་བཙུན་པ་ཆོས the Bon religion is cruel and Buddhism is noble (*Gyal. S.*). ལྷ་གཉན་ནམས deities of terror; ཁྲིམས་གཉན་པ severe justice, cruel laws; དམ་ཚིག་གཉན་པ rigid vow, a solemn oath. 2. wild, rugged, precipitous: གཉན་ས a rugged country.

གཉའ་བ *gñah-wa* (in composition, often གཉའ only) 1. neck, nape: གཉའ་བ་བསྐུངས the neck is contracted or shortened. 2.=སྙིང་རྗེ प्रतिभूचम partizan, one backing a side.

གཉའ་ཀོ *gñah-ko* hide or leather of a beast's neck.

གཉའ་ཁོབས *gñah-khobs* screen to protect the neck attached to a helmet.

གཉའ་ཁྲི་བཙན་པོ *Gñah-khri Btsan-po* the first king of Tibet who was carried in a sedan-chair and was therefore called the "neck-chaired."

གཉའ་གོང་དུ་མི་སྣོལ *gñah-goṅ du mi-snol*, སྣད་= གཉའ.

གཉའ་རྒྱབ *gñah-rgyab* in *C.* castellations, parapet.

གཉའ་ནང *Gñah-naṅ* a village on the confines of Tibet and Nepal, but belonging to the former.

+གཉའ་པོ *gñah-po* a witness, one that gives evidence; གཉའ་པོ་བྱེད་པ to vouch for, to be surety for: བསྐྱི་གཉའ་ཁས he became surety for the loan.

གཉའ་རྩེ *gñah-rtse* the cervical vertebra with its projecting process (*Jä.*).

གཉའ་ཚིགས *gñah-tshigs* spinal joints.

གཉའ་རེངས *gñah-reṅs* stiff-necked, obstinate: ངན་པ་གཉའ་རེངས་སེར་སྨུག་གཏམ་འདི་ཉོན (*Rdsa. 28*) *Ser-smug*, thou obstinate wretch, listen to this my word. གཉའ་རེངས་ཅན *gñah-reṅs-can* stiff-necked, obstinate.

གཉའ་ཤིང *gñah-çiṅ* युग yoke (for oxen); གཉའ་ཤིང་འཛིན *Gñah-çiṅ hdsin* one of the seven fabulous mountains of Buddhist cosmogony so called on account of its standing out like the yoke of oxen.

གཉལ *Gñal* n. of a place in Tibet; གཉལ་པ a native of *Gñal*; གཉལ་པ་གྲྭ་ཚང *Gñal-pa grba-tshaṅ* the section of Daipung monastery where monks from *Gñal* are admitted (*Loṅ.* ཟ *3*).

གཉི་ག *gñi-ga*=གཉིས་ཀ उभय both.

གཉི་ཟེར *gñi-zer* sometimes for ཉི་ཟེར sunbeam (*Lex.*).

གཉིག་ཏུ *gñig-tu* एकान्त;=གཅིག་ཏུ into one, aimed at one, having only one object in view; but གཉིག་པོ་མཛའ་འདུག seems to= the two loved as one.

གཉིད निद्रा, तन्द्रा, मिद्ध, स्वप्न, शयन sleep; གཉིད་དུ་འགྲོ་བ to fall asleep: གཉིད་མ་ཐོབ I am sleepless; གཉིད་མ་ཡོང sleep has not come, I cannot find sleep; གཉིད་ཐུམ་པ one uninterrupted portion of sleep; གཉིད་མཐུག་པོར་སོང he fell into a sound sleep; གཉིད་སྲབ light sleep, a slumber. གཉིད་ཀྱི་ལོག་པ *gñid-kyi log-pa* अपस्वापन to fall asleep, to sleep: གང་ཞིག་ངན་མང་པོ་དང་བྲལ་བའི་མི་དེ་བདེ་བར་གཉིད་ལོག་པར་འགྱུར he who is free from misery will sleep happily; སྦྱོར་ལམ་དྲོད་ཐོབ་པ་ནས་ཉོན་མོངས་པའི་གཉིད་མི་ཡོང (*S. phreṅ. 288*) he who has attained to the stage of *Sbyor-lam* will not fall asleep. གཉིད་ཅན निद्रालु sleepy, drowsy; གཉིད་ཆག जागरित sleep interrupted, roused from slumber. གཉིད་དུ་སོང has gone to sleep.

Syn. གཉིད་བྲོ *gñid-bro*; གཉིད་འདོད *gñid-ḥdod*; གཉིད་གཡུར་བ *gñid gyur-wa*; རབ་ཏུ་འཐིབས་པ *rab-tu ḥthibs-pa*; མནལ *mnal*; གཟིམ *gzim*; གཉིད་ཁུག་པ *gñid khug-pa*; རྨོངས་པའི་གྲོགས་པོ *rmoṅs-paḥi grogs-po*; མིག་འཛུམ་པ *mig ḥdsumpa* (*Mñon.*).

གཉིད་འདོད *gñid-ḥdod* wishing to sleep.

གཉིད་རྡོལ *gñid-rdol* somnambulism.

གཉིད་མ་བྱུང་བ *gñid ma-byuṅ-wa* जागरूक wakefulness, sleeplessness.

Syn. གཉིད་མེད *gñid-med*; གཉིད་མ་ཁུག *gñid-ma-khug*; གཉིད་ཆག་པ *gñid chag-pa*; གཉིད་ཡར་བ *gñid-yar-wa* (*Mñon.*).

གཉིད་མོ *gñid-mo* स्वप्नालु, सुप्त asleep, in sleep.

གཉིད་རྨུགས *gñid-rmugs* dazed, stupid with sleep: གཉིད་རྨུགས་ལེ་ལོ་རབ་སྤངས་ཤིང་, རྟག་ཏུ་བརྩོན་འགྲུས་འབད་པར་བྱ (*Ḥbrom.* ཁ *13*) leaving off sleepiness and indolence, (you) should be always industrious.

གཉིད་གཡུར་པ *gñid gyur-pa* to be overcome by sleepiness.

གཉིད་ལམ *gñid-lam*=རྨི་ལམ *rmi-lam* dream.

གཉིད་ལོག་འདོད་པ *gñid-log ḥdod-pa* to desire sleep, to be sleepy.

གཉིད་ས *gñid-sa* bed, place of sleep.

Syn. ཉལ་ས *ñal-sa*; མལ་སྟན *mal-stan*; མལ་ས *mal-sa* (*Mñon.*).

གཉིད་སད་པ जागरित, जागरूक awakened, to awake; གཉིད་སད་པར་འགྱུར जागृ to become awake.

གཉིལ་བ *gñil-wa* to be dessicated, to crumble away; to thaw.

གཉིས *gñis* द्वि, द्वय 1. two: ཁྱོད་དང་ང་གཉིས་བཟའ་མི་བྱེད we two shall marry each other; ང་དང་དེ་གཉིས either of us: ཕྱི་ནང་གཉིས་ཆོས་ལུགས་གང་བཟང་། which is the better of the two religions, Brahmanism or Buddhism? བྲམ་ཟེ་གཉིས a Brâhman couple (man and wife). 2. both: ཇོ་བོ་དང་བྱམས་མགོན་གཉིས both Maitreya and the lord (Atis'a); ཁྱོད་དང་ང་གཉིས both you and I.

གཉིས་ཀ *gñis-ka* उभय the two, both: གཉིས་ཀའི་དོན उभयार्थ the meaning of both; the interests of both parties; གཉིས་གཉིས *gñis-gñis* two each.

གཉིས་ཀྱི་གཉིས་སྤྲད་པ *gñis-kyi gñis sprad-pa* द्वयद्वयसमापत्ति placed in two and two (in pairs).

གཉིས་སྐྱེས *gñis-skyes* द्विज, द्विजाति, ब्राह्मण the "twice-born," *i.e.*, a Brahman; used, also, of birds in general, and of human teeth.

གཉིས་ག *gñis-ga*=གཉིས་ཀ *gñis-ka* both.

གཉིས་དགའི་ཁྱིམ *gñis-dgaḥi khyim* रतिगृह met. for the female organ.

གཉིས་བརྒྱུད *gñis-brgyud*=ཟངས copper.

གཉིས་ཆ *gñis-cha* युगपत् half.

གཉིས་གཉིས་སྤྱོད *gñis-gñis spyod* क्रौञ्च, कङ्क said to be either the curlew or lapwing.

གཉིས་གཉིས་ཟུང་ *gñis-gñis zuṅ* pairing, also male and female living together.

གཉིས་འཐུང་ *gñis-ḥthuṅ* द्विप met. for elephant; གཉིས་འཐུང་དབང་པོ the king of elephants.

གཉིས་ལྡབ *gñis-ldab* two-fold, double, twice.

གཉིས་ལྡན *gñis-ldan* द्विवार, द्वापर twice; also the second age, the age according to Brâhmanical astrology in which two measures of virtue were left to humanity.

གཉིས་ལྡན་དུས *gñis-ldan-dus* द्वापरयुग the second age of the present *Kalpa*.

གཉིས་པ *gñis-pa* द्वय, द्वितीय 1. the second. 2. having two, possessed of two, *e.g.*, མགོ་གཉིས་པ *mgo gñis-pa* having two heads, the two-headed; ལྕེ་གཉིས་པ *lce gñis-pa* double-tongued; གཉིས་པ་རྣམས all the second ones; གཉིས་པ་ཙམ द्विका the second only.

གཉིས་པོ *gñis-po* द्वय both, the two.

གཉིས་མེད་གསུང་པ *gñis-med gsuṅ-pa* an epithet of Buddha. གཉིས་སུ་མེད་པ་གསུངས་པ

अद्वयवादी a propounder of the non-dualist doctrine; epithet of Buddha.

གཉིས་འཛིན་ *gñis-hdsin* द्वयस्थ holding to two; doubt, unsteadiness, wavering.

གཉིས་འཛིན་ལྟ་བ་ *gñis-hdsin lta-wa* to look upon two things as differing, to think them different.

གཉིས་ཤད་ *gñis-çad* the strokes put after a complete sentence (*Situ.*).

གཉིས་སུ་མེད་པ་ *gñis-su med-pa* अद्वय, अद्वितीय 1. matchless; identical: ང་དང་རྒྱལ་པོ་གཉིས་སུ་མེད། the king and I are not two indubitably, are the same. 2. n. of the Tantrik work of S'rī Kāla-chakra དཔལ་ལྡན་དུས་འཁོར (*Mñon.*).

གཉིས་གསུམ་ཟློས་པ་ *gñis-gsum zlos-pa* = སྐྱོར་ཚིག *skyor-tshig* or སྐྱར་བའི་ཚིག *skyar-wahi tshig* repetition (*Mñon.*).

གཉུག་མ *gñug-ma* acc. to *Cs.* 1. natural, opp. to བཅོས་མ *bcos-ma* artificial, hence (*Sch.*) དངོས་མ *dños-ma*. 2. innate, peculiar; སེམས་གཉུག་མ peculiar mind; གཉུག་མའི་སེམས *gñug-mahi sems*; གཉུག་མའི་ཡེ་ཤེས innate wisdom; གཉུག་མའི་དོན innate signification or worth; མ་བཅོས་གཉུག་མའི་ངང་དུ་འདྲེས *ma-bcos gñug-mahi ñañ-du hdres* dissolved into the uncreated primordial existence (*Jä.*).

གཉུང་དཀར *gñuñ-dkar* rape seed.

གཉུལ་བ *gñul-wa* = ཉུལ་བ *ñul-wa*.

གཉེ་བ *gñe-wa* to woo, court.

གཉེའོ *gñeho* = སྨྱེ་བོ *smye-bo* a wooer, courtier (*Jä.*).

གཉེ་མ *gñe-ma* (ནང་ཁྲོལ *nañ-khrol*), अन्त्रगुण the coiled intestine (*Zam.*), the twisted part of the colon or great gut (*Jä.*).

གཉེན *gñen* बन्धु, बान्धव, सुहृद्, resp. སྐུ་གཉེན *sku-gñen* kinsman, relation: བྱམས་པའི་གཉེན beloved relation; གཉེན་ལ་བྱམས་པ་བྱེད་པ to love one's relations; གཉེན་གྱི་སྒྱུག་མོ mother-in-law by relation; as a degree of relationship; གཉེན་བྱེད་པ *gñen byed-pa* to marry, to become related by marriage; གཉེན་གྱི་ཕྱོགས friends and relations; གཉེན་གྱི་ཕྱོགས་ལ་འདོད་ཆགས་ཆུ་ལྟར་གཡོ attachment towards friends quivers like water, &c. (*Lo. 24*); ཕ་གཉེན *pha-gñen* relations on father's side; མ་གཉེན *ma-gñen* relations on mother's side; བཤེས་གཉེན *bçes-gñen* कल्याणमित्र spiritual friend, generally a lama scholar who is versed in the Buddhist metaphysics.

གཉེན་པོ *gñiñ-po* helper, friend, assistant, esp. spiritually; རྒྱུ་གཉེན་པོ་བཟང་བར་བྱིན་གྱིས་རློབས། bless, that it may become a good spiritual help; གཉེན་པོ་ལ་མ་ལྟོས་པར without looking upon a spiritual adviser; བོད་འདུལ་བའི་གཉེན་པོ the spiritual discipliner of Tibet (Avalokites'vara); (applied to things) remedy, means, expedient, antidote; ནད་ལ་གསོ་བར་བྱེད་པའི་གཉེན་པོ assistants in curing maladies (*e.g.*, medicine, diet, etc.); དེའི་གཉེན་པོར *dehi gñen-por* as a remedy for; སྒྲུབ་པའི་ཐབས་མི་ཤེས་པའི་གཉེན་པོར *sgrub-pahi thabs mi-çes-pahi gñen-por* as a remedy for helplessness in acquiring a certain object, *i.e.*, direction or instruction how to obtain it (*Jä.*).

Syn. མཐུན་ཕྱོགས *mthun-phyogs*; ཡིད་བཙུགས *yid-bcugs*; མཛའ་བཙུགས *mdsah-bcugs*; ཟུན *zun*; འཁོར་མེད *hkhor-med*; ཡིད་མཐུན་པ *yid mthun-pa*; མཛའ་བཤེས *mdsah-bçes*; གྲོགས་པོ *grogs-po*; མཛའ་བས་བཅིངས *mdsah-was bciñs*; བློ་ཉེ་བ *blo-ñe-wa*; རང་ཕྱོགས *rañ-phyogs* (*Mñon.*).

གཉེན་ཅན *gñen-can* बन्धु used in polite language for གཉེན *gñen*.

གཉེན་ཉེ་བ *gñen ñe-wa* or གཉེན་ཉེ་མོ *gñen ñe-mo* कुटुम्ब, निकटकुटुम्ब near relations, cousins.

གཉེན་ཉེ་འབྲེལ *gñen ñe-hbrel*, v. relatives by blood or marriage connection.

གཉེན་སྡེ་ *gñen-sde*, གཉེན་ཚན་ *gñen-tshan*, གཉེན་སྲིད་ *gñen-srid* are words signifying relatives.

གཉེན་འདབ་ *gñen-ẖdab*, v. གཉེན་ *gñen*.

གཉེན་འདུན་ *gñen-ẖdun* 1. relatives; ཕ་ཡང་མ་ཡིན་གཉེན་འདུན་མིན་ *pha-yañ ma-yin gñen-ẖdun min* neither father nor relations. 2. acc. to *Sch.* concord, harmony, amongst kinsmen: གཉེན་འདུན་ཟད་པ་ཡིན་ *gñen-ẖdun zad-pa yin* the harmony ceased.

གཉེན་པ་ *gñen-pa* ज्ञाति kinsman: གཉེན་པས་བསྲུང་བ་ *gñen-pas bsruñ-wa* ज्ञातिरक्षित preserved or protected by (his) kinsman.

Syn. གཉེན་གཤིན་ *gñen-gçin*; གཉན་འདབ་ *gñan-ẖdab*; སྣག་གི་གཉེན་ *snag-gi gñen*; ཉེ་འབྲེལ་ *ñe-ẖbrel*; མཛའ་བཤེས་ *mdsah-bçes*; རྩ་ལག་ *rtsa-lag*; རིགས་རུས་གཅིག་པ་ *rigs-rus gcig-pa*; ཚོ་འབྲང་མཚུངས་པ་ *cho-ẖbrañ mtshuñs-pa*; ཉེ་དུ་ *ñe-du* (*Mṅon.*).

གཉེན་པོ་ *gñen-po* प्रत्यनीक, प्रतिहर, प्रतिपक्ष adversary, antagonist; adverse, in opposition. གཉེན་པོ་ཆོས་དབྱིངས་གཉེན་པོར་ཤར་ *gñen-po chos-dbyiñs gñen-por çar* (*Hbrom.* ཁ *33*).

གཉེན་བྱེད་པ་ *gñen byed-pa* विवाह marriage.

གཉེན་འབྲེལ་བ་ *gñen ẖbrel-wa* to be related, connected by marriage or friendship.

གཉེན་ཟླ་ *gñen-zla* consort; companion by marriage: ཁྱོད་རྣམས་ཀྱང་ངེད་རྒྱ་ནག་པའི་གཉེན་ཟླ་ as ye (Tibetans) may enter into connubial connexion with us (Chinese). གཉེན་ཟླ་མ་རྙེད་ཀྱིས་ *gñen-zla ma-rñed-kyis* a match not being available; ཁྱོད་དང་གཉེན་ཟླ་མིན་ *khyod-dañ gñen-zla min* you are not a consort fit for me; also not related to you.

གཉེན་ཡིག་ *gñen-yig* friendly letter.

གཉེན་རིང་པོ་ *gñen riñ-po* दूरकुटुम्ब distant relation.

གཉེན་གཤིན་ *gñen-gçin*, v. གཉེན་ *gñen*.

གཉེན་བཤེས་ *gñen-bçes* relatives and friends: ཁྱོད་ལ་གཉེན་མེད་བཤེས་ཀྱང་མེད་ *khyod-la gñen-med bçes-kyañ-med* you have neither relations nor friends.

གཉེར་ *gñer* 1. meaning, occasion: དེའི་གཉེར་ཅི་ཡོད་ *dehi-gñer ci-yod* what was the meaning of that (*A. 33*).

གཉེར་ཀ་ *gñer-ka* or གཉེར་ཁ་ *gñer-kha* attention, care; གཉེར་ཀ་བྱེད་ *gñer-ka byed* = དོ་དམ་བྱེད་ *do-dam byed* take care (of a thing, property or person), to supervise, to pay attention to: ཁྱོད་རང་གཉེར་ཀ་བྱེད་ལོ་གྱིས་ *khyod-rañ gñer-ka byed lo-gyis* would you take care (or take charge of) (*A. 115*); ཡུལ་རྗེའི་གཉེར་ཁ་མེད་པས་བདེ་ when I am free from the attentions of village officials I am happy (*Mil.*).

གཉེར་ཀ་གཏད་པ་ *gñer-ka gtad-pa* to commit a thing to a person's charge, to put a person in trust of.

གཉེར་དུ་གཏད་པ་ *gñer-du gtad-pa* = བློ་བཏད་པ་ *blo gtad-pa* to entrust, confide in.

གཉེར་པ་ *gñer-pa* भाण्डारी a store-keeper; ཞིང་གཉེར་ farm-steward: ས་ནམ་སྐྱོང་ཞིང་འཁོར་མཁས, གསོག་འཇོག་ཤེས་པ་གཉེར་པ་ཡིན་ (*Gul.*) he was the steward, wise in protecting agriculture and its surroundings and knowing how to collect and to keep accounts. དཀོན་གཉེར་ *dkon-gñer* keeper of precious (religious) objects; སྐུ་གཉེར་ *sku-gñer* temple-minder; དགོན་གཉེར་ *dgon-gñer* the steward of a monastery; གཞི་གཉེར་ *gshi-gñer* manager of an estate or farm; ཁང་གཉེར་ *khañ-gñer* one in whose charge a house or house properties are left, house-keeper: དིང་རིར་བསླེབས་ནས་ཁང་གཉེར་ལ་དྲིས་ having arrived at Dingri, they asked the house-keeper; སློབ་གཉེར་ *slob gñer* a student: སློབ་གཉེར་གང་དུ་བགྱིས་ *slob-gñer gañ-du bgyis* where did you study. གཏད་གཉེར་ *gtad-gñer* to entrust a thing. མགྲོན་གཉེར་ *mgron-gñer* (lit. receiver of guests but) practically a general manager or secretary under a king, minister, or landlord.

Syn. མིག་གི་ཆོས་ཅན་ *mig-gi chos-can*; ལྡེ་མིག་པ་ *lde mig-pa*; ནང་གི་གྲུ་འཛིན་ *naṅ-gi gru-ḥdsin*; སྐུ་གཉེར་ *sku-gñer* or སྐུ་གཉེར་པ་ a keeper of images of gods, &c. (*Mṅon.*).

གཉེར་བ་ *gñer-wa* or གཉེར་བྱེད་པ་ *gñer byed-pa* to tend, to take care of, to provide for; to seek for; to procure, to acquire. དོན་གཉེར་བ་ *don gñer-wa* to earn money, to take interest on money; དོན་དུ་གཉེར་བ་ *don-du gñer-wa* to provide for, to strive to procure; ཡོ་བྱད་དོན་དུ་གཉེར་བ་རྣམས people who desire to have property; དོན་གཉེར་ *don-gñer* exertion, effort, zeal; དོན་གཉེར་ཆེན་པོ་དགོས *don-gñer chen-po dgos* great exertions are necessary; རྒྱུ་དང་རྐྱེན་གཉིས་ལ་དོན་གཉེར་བྱེད་པ investigating both the primary and secondary causes; དོན་གཉེར་ཅན *don-gñer can* zealous, pains-taking.

གཉེར་མ *gñer-ma* वली wrinkles (of the face), a fold of the skin; གཉེར་མ་དངས *gñer-ma daṅs* विततवलीक defined wrinkles; གཉེར་མ་མང་ वलीप्रचुरता with many wrinkles; གཉེར་མ་རེངས་པ་འགྱུར the wrinkles have become settled or rigid, vb. གཉེར་པ *gñer-pa* to wrinkle; སྣ་གོང་གཉེར་བ *sna-goṅ gñer-wa* to knit the brows, to frown. ཁྲོ་གཉེར भ्रुकुटि a frown, a severe, angry look; ཁྲོ་གཉེར་ཅན *khro-gñer can* with frowning looks; the goddess Dolma in her terrific, frowning manifestation is called སྒྲོལ་མ་ཁྲོ་གཉེར་ཅན *Sgrol-ma Khro-gñer-can* भ्रुकुटितारा.

གཉེར་མ་ཁུམས་པ *gñer-ma khums-pa*, དོན་མ་གྲུབ་ the object not fulfilled (*A. 65*).

གཉེར་མ་ཅན *gñer-ma can* wrinkled.

གཉེར་མའི་གདོང་ *gñer-maḥi gdoṅ* lit. the wrinkled-faced; met. a monkey.

གཉེར་ཚང་ *gñer-tshaṅ* store or store-room; house where provisions are stored up: གཉེར་ཚང་གཏོང་བྱེད *gñer-tshaṅ gtoṅ-byed* issuing of articles from the stores; one who issues such.

གཉེལ་བ *gñel-wa* = ངལ་བ *ṅal-wa* श्रम fatigue, also श्रान्त tired, to get tired; acc. to some authors, the proper spelling is མཉེལ་བ *mñel-wa*.

གཉོག་པ *gñog-pa* to desire, wish earnestly (*Cs.*), v. སྙོག་པ *sñog-pa* (*Jä.*).

གཉོད *gñod* strength, durability, stoutness; གཉོད་ཅན *gñod-can* strong; གཉོད་ཆུང་ *gñod-chuṅ* or གཉོད་མེད *gñod-med* weak; ལུས་གཉོད་ཆུང་ *lus gñod-chuṅ* a weakly body or feeble constitution (*Jä.*).

+ **གཉོད་ཀ** *gñod-ka* = འཁོས་ཀ *ḥkhos-ka* importance, worth. གཉོད་ཀ་ཆུང་ = 1. unimportant, worthless. 2. generous or charitable.

གཉོས *gños* n. of a tribe in Tibet (*Loṅ. 23*).

མཉན *mñan* boat, skiff, wherry.

མཉན་པ *mñan-pa* boatman, ferry-man. མཉན་པ་ཉ་ཡི་ཀོ་བཤར a fish-skin (*Sman. 350*). མཉན་ཡོད *mñan-yod* श्रावस्ती n. of a city in Kos'ala where Buddha resided for many years. Occasionally མཉན་པ occurs erroneously for ཉན་པ to hear.

མཉེད་པ *mñed-pa* pf. and imp. མཉེས, fut. མཉེ 1. to rub, between the hands or feet, *e.g.*, ears of corn. 2. to tan, curry, dress; ཀོ་བ་མཉེད་པ to tan skin. 3. to coax (*Cs.*).

མཉམ *mñam* सम, समापन्न similar, equal, like (*Mṅon.*).

Syn. འདྲ་བ *hdra-wa* or ལྟ་བུ *lta-bu* also དེ་ལྟ *de-lta*, དེ་མཚུངས *de mtshuṅs*.

མཉམ་དཀར *mñam-dkar*; མཉམ་སྐྱེས *mñam-skyes* समकर्म्मी colleague, brethren in the same work or profession.

མཉམ་འགྱུར་བསྐལ་པ *mñam-hgyur bkal-pa* the age or *Kal-pa* next to terminate (*D.R.*).

མཉམ་འཇོག *mñam-hjog* = མཉམ་པར་འཇོག་པ ध्यान, समाधि contemplation, preserving the equanimity of the mind.

མཉམ་ཉིད *mñam-ñid* = ཕྱམ་ཆད *phyam-chad* समता, समानता impartiality, evenness, equality; justice. མཉམ་ཉིད་ཡེ་ཤེས *mñam-ñid yeçes* the knowledge to be acquired by contemplation, *i.e.*, by *Samādhi*.

མཉམ་མཉམ *mñam-mñam* समसम level, very even; smooth.

མཉམ་དུ *mñam-du* 1. together, in company with. མཉམ་དུ་འགྲོ་བ *mñam-du hgro-wa* going together. 2. in *Mṅon*. समीन yearly, annually.

མཉམ་ལྡན་བསྐལ་པ *mñam-ldan bskal-pa* the *Kalpa* that is continuing (*D.R.*).

མཉམ་གནས *mñam-gnas* समस्थ residing together; also of equal position.

མཉམ་པ *mñam-pa*, सम, युगपत्, सम्यक्, समाहित 1. like, alike, equal, same: མཉམ་པོ་ཡོད *mñam-po yod* they are alike, equal, not differing; ལྷ་དང་མཉམ་པ་ཡོད *lha-daṅ mñam-pa yod* they are like unto the gods. ཟླུམ་པོ་མཉམ་པ *zlum-po mñam-pa* roundish; རིགས་མཉམ་པ *rigs mñam-pa* of equal birth, rank; དུས་མཉམ་པ *dus mñam-pa* contemporary, simultaneous; མཉམ་པར་འགྱུར་བ to become equal, to be equal. 2. even, level, flat; ལག་མཐིལ་ལྟར་མཉམ་པ *mñam-pa* flat like the palm of the hand.

མཉམ་པ་བརྗོད་པ *mñam-pa brjod-pa* समाहूत to invite impartially.

མཉམ་པ་མེད་པ *mñam-pa med-pa* असम वर्त्तमान uneven; unequally.

མཉམ་པར་འཇོག་པ *mñam-par hjog-pa* समाधि to adjust for contemplation.

མཉམ་པར་བཞག་པ *mñam-par bshag-po* समाहित, समादधाति, प्रणिहित, प्रणिधान to compose the mind to perfect rest for meditation.

མཉམ་པར་བྱེད་པ *mñam-par byed-pa* to make even or level, to equalize; to divide equally; སེམས་མཉམ་པོ *sems mñam-po* imperturbability, evenness of mind; not to be affected by kindness or by the reverse. མི་མཉམ་པ *mi-mñam-pa* unequal, uneven.

མཉམ་བྲལ *mñam-bral* तुल्यं नास्ति unequalled, matchless.

མཉམ་མེད *mñam-med*, v. མཉམ་བྲལ *mñam-bral*.

མཉམ་གཟུང *mñam-gzuṅ* समापन lit. receiving equally; finishing.

མཉེ་བ *mñe-wa* or མཉེ་བཞིན་པ *mñe bshin-pa* संवाह, परिमर्द्दन to tan, to rub; མཉེ་བར་བྱས tanned, rubbed; མཉེ་བར་བྱ will tan or rub, v. མཉེད་པ *mñed pa*.

མཉེ་འབོལ *mñe-hbol* cushion, a pillow.

མཉེན་པ 1. *mñen-pa* resp. ཕྱག་མཉེན་པ *phyag mñen-pa* मृदु, स्निग्ध flexible, pliable, supple, soft. 2. = མཉེན་པོ *mñen-po* कोमल tender, soft.

མཉེན་ལྕུག *mñen-lcug* soft and pliant or flexible.

མཉེན་མཉེལ་བ *mñen mñel-wa* to make soft by tanning (*Sch.*).

མཉེན་མཉེས་གཅིན་པ *mñen-mñes gçin-pa* to caress, to fondle (*Sch.*).

མཉེན་པར་འགྱུར་བ *mñen-par hgyur-wa* to become soft.

མཉེན་པར་བྱེད་པ *mñen-par byed-pa* अभिष्यन्दय to make soft, smooth, flexible.

+ **མཉེལ་བ** *mñel-wa* = ངལ་བ *ṅal-wa* or ཐང་ཆད་པ *thaṅ chad-pa* to be tired, fatigued.

མཉེས *m̱ñeş* स्निग्ध smoothened; made soft (like leather).

མཉེས་པ *m̱ñeş-pa* तोषित resp. for དགའ་བ, same as དགྱེས་པ *dgyeş-pa* to be glad, to take delight in; also pleased, delighted: བླ་མའི་ཐུགས་མཉེས་པ *ḇla maẖi thugş m̱ñeş-pa* the lama's heart was delighted.

མཉེས་པར་བྱེད་པ *m̱ñeş-par byeḏ-pa* to make glad, to give pleasure.

མཉེས་བྱེད *m̱ñeş-byeḏ* मानना, आराधना adoration, paying respect.

མཉེས་གཅིན *m̱ñeş-gçin* वत्सल, स्निग्ध, प्रणयिन् loving, affectionate (*A. K. 1-10*). མཉེས་གཅིན་པ *m̱ñeş gçin-pa*=སྙིང་སྡུག *şñiṅ-şdug* beloved. Acc. to *Sch.* to love much; to be rejoiced at.

མཉོ *m̱ño* fond; མཉོ་མཉོ་ཅན *m̱ño m̱ño-can* in *W.* fondling, petting (སྤུ་སྤུ་ལ) a child (*Jä.*).

རྙ་བ *Ṟña-wa* n. of a place in Tibet. (*Deb.* ཀ *11*).

རྙ་ལོ *ṟña-lo* or སྣ་ལོ *şña-lo* several wild-growing species of *Polygonum* (*Jä.*).

རྙང་རྙིང *ṟñaṅ-ṟñiṅ* worn-out clothes, rags (*Cs.*).

རྙང་བ *ṟñaṅ-wa*=བཤལ་བ *ḇçal-wa* to rinse; in *W.* to suffer from diarrhœa. རྙང་ནད *ṟñaṅ-naḏ* diarrhœa; རྙང་པ *ṟñaṅ-pa* or རྙང་མ *ṟñaṅ-ma* diarrhœtic stool (*Jä.*).

རྙན *ṟñan*=གཉན *g̱ñan* the Tibetan argali (Ovis ammon).

རྙབ་རྙབ་པ *ṟñab-ṟñab-pa* to seize or snatch together (*Sch.*).

རྣབས་པ *şñabş-pa* stretching out the hand to catch; བྱིའུ་ཡི་ལག་པ་མེ་ལ་རྙབས་པ་ཡིས *khyeẖu yi lag-pa me-la ṟñabş-pa yis* holding out the hands of a child to the fire.

རྙས *ṟñaş* sometimes used for བརྙས་པ *ḇṟñaş-pa.* རྙས་བྱེད་པ *ṟñaş-byeḏ-pa* अवज्ञा to scorn, to look down on with contempt.

རྙི *ṟñi* जाल net, snare or trap for capturing wild animals or birds. རྙི་འཛུགས་པ *ṟñi ẖdsug-pa* to lay snares; ཕུར་རྙི *phur-ṟñi* mouse-trap consisting of a flat stone supported by a little stick or pin (ཕུར་པ *phur-pa*).

Syn. རྙི་ཐག *ṟñi-thag*; རི་དྭགས་རྒྱ *ri-dḇagş ṟgya*; རི་དྭགས་འཛིན *ri-dḇagş ẖdsin*; རི་དྭགས་དྲ་བ *ri-dḇagş dṟa-wa*; དྲ་བ་ཅན *dṟa-wa-can*; ངན་པའི་འཁྲུལ་འཁོར་བྱ་དང་རི་དྭགས་འཆིང་བྱེད *ṅan-paẖi ẖkhrul-ẖkhor bya-daṅ ri-dḇagş ẖchiṅ-byeḏ* (*M̱ṅon.*).

རྙི་ཐག *ṟñi-thag*, v. རྙི *ṟñi.*

རྙིང *ṟñiṅ*, v. རྙིང་པ *ṟñiṅ-pa.*

རྙིང་པ *ṟñiṅ-pa* जीर्ण, प्रत्न, आविल, पुराण 1. old, ancient (of things, *i.e.*, clothes). 2. muddy. གསར་རྙིང *gsar-ṟñiṅ* new and old; སྔར་གྱི་ཡི་གེ་རྙིང་པ་རྣམས *şṅar-gyi yi-ge ṟñiṅ-pa ṟnamş* the ancient records; བརྡ་རྙིང *ḇrda-ñiṅ* the ancient orthography; ལོ་རྙིང *lo-ṟñiṅ*=ན་ནིང *na-niṅ* last year (*Wts.*); དྲང་སྲོང་རྙིང་པ *dṟaṅ-sṟoṅ ṟñiṅ-pa* the old rishi or sage.

Syn. རྒན་པོ *ṟgan-po*; ཐར་པོ *thar-po*; སྔོན་སྐྱེས *şṅon-şkyes*; སྔོན་དུས་མ *şṅon-duş-ma*; ཡུན་རིང་མ *yun riṅ-ma*; རྙིང་མ *ṟñiṅ-ma*; ཐོག་མ *thog-ma*; རྒས་པ *ṟgaş-pa*; ཆོས་རྒས་པ *chos ṟgaş-pa* (*M̱ṅon.*).

རྙིང་བ *ṟñiṅ-wa* vb., pf. བརྙིངས *ḇṟñiṅş* to age, wax old; གོས་བརྙིངས *goş-ḇṟñiṅş* worn clothes; ལྷམ་བརྙིངས *lham-ḇṟñiṅş* old shoes; རྙིང་བར་འགྱུར་བ *ṟñiṅ-war ẖgyur-wa*, རྙིང་བར་བྱེད་པ *ṟñiṅ-war byeḏ-pa* to wear out in a short time (*Jä.*).

རྙིང་མ *Ṟñiṅ-ma* 1. general term for the various unreformed red-cap sects of Buddhism in Tibet. 2. particular name for one of the oldest of these same sects.

3.＝རྙིང་པ *rñiṅ-pa*, རྙིང་མ་དེ་ལ་རབ་གནས་ཀྱང་མཛད *rñiṅ-ma de-la rab-gnas kyaṅ mdsad* he also consecrated that old one (*A. 93*); རྙིང་མའི་གཏེར་གཞུང *rñiṅ-mahi gter-gshuṅ* the religious works which, it is said, were unearthed by *Gter-ston-pa* belonging to the Nying-ma school of Tibet.

རྙིང་ཚད *rñiṅ-tshad* old fever; chronic disease.

རྙིང་ཧྲུལ *rñiṅ-hrul* worn-out, old and rotten (things).

རྙིངས་པ *rñiṅs-pa*＝རེངས་པ *reṅs-pa* जीर्ण worn out; delapidated; cast off.

རྙིད་པ *rñid-pa* pf. བརྙིད *brñid*, བརྙིས *brñis* fut. གཉིད *gñid*. 1. to fade. 2. to grieve (vb. n.) (*Sch.*).

རྙིལ *rñil* or སྙིལ *sñil* gen. as སོ་རྙིལ *so-rñil* the gums.

རྙིལ་བ *rñil-wa*, v. སྙིལ་བ *sñil-wa*.

རྙིས་པ *rñis-pa*＝སྙིངས་པ *sñiṅs-pa* pf. ग्लान, जीर्ण to be worn out, become old, faded.

རྙེད་པ I: *rñed-pa* 1. vb., pf. བརྙེད *brñed* or བརྙེས *brñes* fut. བརྙེད *brñed*. लाभ, पूरण, परिगत, उदय to find, discover, acquire, meet with, get: དེ་ནི་གང་ནས་རྙེད *de-ni gaṅ-nas rñed* where did you get that? མི་རྙེད་དུ་མི་རུང་ངོ *mi rñed-du mi ruṅ-ṅo* it must be procured by all means; མ་རྙེད་པ *ma rñed-pa* not finding; ཟས་དང་སྐོམ་མ་རྙེད་དེ *zas-dan skom-ma rñed-de* having not found anything to eat or to drink; ད་ནི་རེ་བ་བརྙེད་དོ *da-ni re-wa brñed-do* now that my hopes are fulfilled; གྲི་རྙེད་པས *gri rñed-pas* as he found a knife (from *Jä.*).

རྙེད་པ II: sbst. profit, gain, property, goods; རྙེད་པ་མང་པོ་རྙེད་པ *rñed-pa maṅ-po rñed-pa* to gain much profit: རྙེད་པ་དང་བཀུར་སྟི་ལྷུར་བྱེད་པས་དགེ་སློང་ཉམས་པར་འགྱུར་ལ, རྙེད་པ་དང་བཀུར་སྟི་འདི་ནི་དགེ་བའི་ཆོས་ཐམས་ཅད་ཀྱི་བར་ཆད་པའི་རྒྱུ་ཡིན་ནོ (*K. d.* ཁ *36*) by exerting himself for gain and honour a gelong will be ruined; these riches and honours are the causes of interruption to all works of piety: བདག་རྙེད་པ་དང་ལྡན་ན་མི་དགའ *bdag rñed-pa daṅ ldan-na mi-dgah* if I am possessed of earnings, he is aggrieved. རྙེད་སྡུ་བ *rñed sdu-wa* collecting of riches; རྙེད་ཕྲོག་པ *rñed phrog-pa* to take booty, to plunder (*Sch.*). རྙེད་རློམ *rñed-rlom* pride of wealth or gain: ཟ་རློམ་འཆར་རློམ་རྙེད་རློམ་ཁ་ནས་རྒྱུ (*Khrid. 125*).

རྙེད་དཀའ་བ *rñed dkah-wa* दुर्लभ; རྙེད་པར་དཀའ་བ difficult to find, rare. The five hardly obtainable things are (see *K. d.* བ *475*):—(1) དལ་འབྱོར་གྱི་མི་ལུས the human body which is slowly prepared; (2) གླ *gla* (*Mṅon.*) wages, remuneration for work done, rent; (3) སངས་རྒྱས་ལ་དད་པ faith in Buddha; (4) the conception of saintly ideas, *i.e.*, the enlightened heart of a *Bodhisattva*; (5) སངས་རྒྱས་འབྱུང་བ the appearance of a Buddha.

རྙེད་བཀུར *rñed-bkur*＝ཐོབ་ནོར *thob-nor* riches and honour.

རྙེད་འདོད *rñed-hdod*＝འདོད་ཆགས *hdod-chags* inclination for gain (*Mṅon.*).

རྙོག་པ *rñog-pa* (cf. ཉོག་པ *ñog-pa*) vb., pf. བརྙོགས *brñogs*, fut. བརྙོག *brñog* to trouble, to stir up (*Cs.*); also adj. thick, turbid; ཆུ་རྙོག་པ *chu rñog-pa* muddy or dirty water. རྙོག་པ་ཅན *rñog-pa can*: 1.＝སྐྱོན་ཅན *skyon-can* faulty. 2. dirty, turbid, troubled རྙོག་མ་ཅན *rñog-ma can*, miry, muddy.

རྙོགས་པ *rñogs-pa*, आविल, कलंक dirt, scum, stain; རྙོགས་པ་མེད *rñogs-pa med* निष्कलङ्क stainless, clear, purified, washed; ཆུ་རྙོག་མེད

chu-rñog med=ཆུ་གཙང་བ *chu tsaṅ-wa* pure water (*Mṅon.*).

རྙོགས་ཚད *rñogs-tshad* n. of a disease (*Jä.*).

+ རྙོང *rñoṅ*=གལ *gal* जाल trap, snare.

རྙོང་བ *rñoṅ-wa* pf. བརྙངས *brñoṅs* fut. བརྙོང *brñoṅ*, imp. རྙོངས 1. to ensnare, trap (*Cs.*). 2.=རྐྱང་པ *rkyaṅ-pa* प्रतिपात to stretch out.

སྣ་ནང *sña-naṅ*=གཉའ་ནང *gñaḥ-naṅ*.

སྣ་ལོ *sña-lo*=རྙ་ལོ *rña-lo*.

སྣག་པ *sñag-pa* col. for སྙེག་པ *sñeg-pa*.

སྙགས *sñags*=དབྱངས *dbyaṅs* music, harmony (*Jä.*).

སྙད *sñad* 1.=རྒྱུ་རྐྱེན *rgyu-rkyen* reason; སྙད་མེད་པར *sñad-med-par* without reason, pretence or provocation: ཇོ་བོ་སེམས་ཅན་གྱི་དོན་ལ་བོད་དུ་བྱོན་དུ་འཇུག་པའི་སྙད་ཡིན (*A. 62*) the reason of Atis'a's undertaking to proceed to Tibet was the welfare of animate beings. 2. སྙད་འདོགས་པ *sñad hdogs-pa*=སྐྱོན་བརྗོད་བྱེད་པ *skyon brjod byed-pa* अवद्य; སྐྱོན་མེད་པར་སྐྱོན་བཏགས་པ *skyon-med-par skyon btags-pa* to impute fault where there is none, malicious accusation or imputation; སྙད་འཛུག་པ *sñad hdsug-pa* to bring an action against, to prosecute; སྙད་བྱེད་པ *sñad byed-pa* (with a dat.) to use a pretence or pretext.

སྙད་པ *sñad-pa* pf. and fut., བསྙད *bsñad*, imp. སྙོད *sñod* to relate, to report; ལོ་རྒྱུས་སྙད་པ *lo-rgyus sñad-pa* to relate a story; རྨི་ལམ་སྙད་པ *rmi-lam sñad-pa* to relate a dream; གཏམ་སྙད་པ *gtam sñad-pa* to state, inform, give notice; to rehearse.

སྙད་མེད་སྙད་དཀྲིས *sñad-med sñad-dkris* imputation without cause; false charge.

སྙན *sñan* कर्ण, श्रोत्र, resp. for རྣ་བ *rna-wa* the ear: རྒྱལ་པོའི་སྙན་དུ་ཐོས *rgyal-poḥi sñan-du thos* it came to the king's hearing. སྙན་ཁུང *sñan-khuṅ* the ear-hole, hearing.

སྙན་གྱི་གོང་རྒྱན *sñan-gyi goṅ-rgyan* अवतंसक, कर्णपूर ornament worn on the tip or up-por lap of tho oar; སྙན་རྒྱན *sñan-rgyan* कुण्डल an ear-ring; རྣ་རྒྱན *rna-rgyan* कर्णिका ear-ornament.

སྙན་སྒྲོགས་མ *sñan sgrogs-ma*=བུད་མེད་བློ་ལྡན་མ *bud-med blo-ldan-ma* (*Mṅon.*) a noble and generous lady.

སྙན་ངག *sñan-ṅag* lit. speech which is agreeable to the ear. 1. काव्य, कविता poetry as one of the four divisions of the science of words. 2.=པ་སངས *pa-asṅs* शुक्र the planet Venus.

སྙན་ངག་མཁན *sñan-ṅag mkhan*, 1. कवि a describer, poet. 2. a learned man (*Mṅon.*).

སྙན་ངག་མཁན་པོ *sñan-ṅag mkhan-po* शुक्र the planet Venus; the spiritual guide of the *Asura* demi-gods.

Syn. གཟའ་པ་སངས *gzaḥ-pa saṅs*; ངན་སྤོང་བུ *ṅan spoṅ-bu*; ལྷ་མིན་བླ་མ *lha-min bla-ma* (*Mṅon.*).

སྙན་ངག་མཁས་དབང *sñan-ṅag mkhas-dwaṅ* कवीन्द्र chief poet; a complimentary address to the learned.

སྙན་ངག་རོ་ལྡན *sñan-ṅag ro-ldan*=ཚིག་གི་གཏང་རག lit. a humorous expression; but includes དགེ་བའི་གཏམ a religious discourse, འཇམ་པོར་སྨྲ soft language ཁ་བཟང sweet words ཞི་བའི་ཚིག conciliatory mild expressions; ཚིག་བཟང pleasant words ལེགས་བཤད moral sayings (*Mṅon.*).

སྙན་གྲགས *sñan-grags* fame, reputation.

སྙན་འཇེགས *sñan-hjegs* polite and gentle (*Yig. k*).

སྙན་བརྗོད *sñan-brjod* वर्ण graphic description.

སྙན་གཏོད་པ *ṣñan-gtod-pa* to give ear to: ཀྱེ་རྒྱལ་པོ་ཆེན་པོ་བདག་གི་ཚིག་འདི་ལ་སྙན་གཏོད་ཅིག *kye rgyal-po chen-po bdag-gi tshig ḥdi-la ṣñan gtod-cig* O great king, do lend your ears to my speech (*Ḥbrom. 136*).

སྙན་ནང་ *Ṣñan-nañ* also called མནའ་ནང་ *Mnaḥ-nañ* n. of a district in N. Western Tibet.

སྙན་པ *ṣñan-pa* 1. like གྲགས་པ *grags-pa* यशः, अभिख्या fame, renown, glory, praise: ཁྱོད་ཀྱི་སྙན་པ་ཕྱོགས་བཅུར་གྲགས your fame has spread in the ten quarters, *i.e.*, all over the world; དེའི་སྙན་པ་རྒྱང་ནས་ཐོས *deḥi ṣñan-pa rgyañ-nas thos* his praises are heard far and wide; ཅེས་དེའི་སྙན་པ་བརྗོད་ཅིང་ *ces deḥi ṣñan-pa brjod-ciñ* thus speaking praisingly of him; ཅེས་པའི་སྙན་པ་ལ་རྟེན་ནས *ces-paḥi ṣñan-pa-la rten-nas* relying on a rumour of this purport; ཅེས་སྙན་པ་དང་གྲགས་པ་ཆེན་པོ་བྱུང་ *ces ṣñan-pa dañ grags-pa chen-po byuñ* so his praise and great fame arose; དེའི་སྙན་དུ *deḥi ṣñan-du* to his praise, or to his hearing. 2. adj. well-sounding, sweet to hear; སྙན་པར་སྨྲ་བ *ṣñan-par smra-wa* प्रियंवद sweet expresion, sweet and polite language; སྙན་པར་བྱེད *ṣñan-par byed* प्रियकार that does pleasant things; སྙན་པའི་དཔེ་ཅན *ṣñan-paḥi dpe-can* n. of a warbling bird, v. ཀ་ལ་པིང་ཀ *ka-la piñ-ka* (*Mñon.*). དགེ་སློང་དབྱངས་རབ་ཏུ་སྙན་པ a monk having a well-sounding voice; ཚིག་སྙན་པར *tshig ṣñan-par* with pleasant words; སྙན་སྐད *ṣñan-skad* melodious language. 3. vb. to praise, extol, glorify. 4.=གོར་མ་ཆག *gor ma-chag* नून without interruption (*Lex.*).

མི་སྙན་པ *mi-ṣñan-pa* 1. discordant, grating; སྐད་ནི་མི་སྙན་པ་ཟེར་བ *skad-ni mi-ṣñan-pa zer-wa* to utter discordant cries; (*Jä.*). 2. offensive, insulting: གང་ཞིག་བདག་ལ་རྩོད་ཅིང་མི་སྙན་བརྗོད *gañ-shig bdag-la rtsod-ciñ mi-ṣñan brjod* he who in a dispute says to me insulting words. མི་སྙན་པར་ཟེར་བ་དང་དུ་ལེན་པ *mi-ṣñan-par zer-wa dañ-du len-pa* to put up with offensive remarks.

གཏམ་སྙན་པ *gtam ṣñan-pa* 1. good joyful news, glad tidings; གཏམ་སྙན་བྱེད་པ *gtam-ṣñan byed-pa* to bring glad tidings. 2. pleasing conversation (*Cs.*);=སྙན་གྲགས *ṣñan-grags*, v. གྲགས *grags*; སྙན་རྒྱུད *ṣñan-rgyud*=བཀའ་རྒྱུད *bkaḥ-rgyud* oral instructions of lamas.

སྙན་ཕྲ་ཞུ་བ *ṣñan-phra shu-wa* to slander, to backbite.

སྙན་འཕྲིན *ṣñan-ḥphrin* 1. good tiding, gospel. 2. n. of a bird which lives very long (*Mñon.*).

སྙན་ཚིག *ṣñan-tshig* साम, སྙན་ཚིག་གི་རིག་བྱེད *ṣñan tshig-gi rig-byed* सामवेद the third *Veda* of the Hindus. སྙན་ཚིག་བྱུང་ *ṣñan-tshig byuñ* सामज grown out of the *Sāma-Veda*.

སྙན་ཤུ *ṣñan-shu* petition, memorial; སྙན་ཤུ་འབུལ་བ *ṣñan-shu ḥbul-wa* to present a petition.

སྙན་ཤལ *ṣñan-çal* the flap of the ear.

སྙན་གསན་འབེབས་པ *ṣñan-gsan ḥbebs-pa*, आमन्त्रण invitation; to invite, to call attention to.

སྙན་སྲབ *ṣñan-srab*=ཉན་དད་ཆེ་བ *ñan-dad che-wa* credulous: རྗེའི་སྙན་སྲབ *rjeḥi ṣñan-srab* the king's credulity (*Gyal. 2*).

སྙན་ལྷོང་བ *ṣñan-lhoñ-wa* to make dear.

སྙབ་པ *ṣñab-pa* to smack with the lips (*Sch.*).

སྙམ་པ *ṣñam-pa* 1. vb. to think, consider, imagine: བདག་ཅག་རིན་པོ་ཆེ་བཏང་སྙམ་མོ we thought we should give up the jewels; ང་ལྕེབ་དགོས་སྙམ་ནས *ña-lceb dgos-ṣñam-nas* thinking I should commit suicide; ཡོན་ཏན་དང་ལྡན་པར་སྙམ་སྟེ *yon-tan dañ ldan-par ṣñam-ste* considering him to be possessed of talents. 2. sbst. thought, sense, mind, sensation: ཆོས་བྱས་ན་སྙམ་པ་ཡོང་གིན་གདའ *chos byas-na ṣñam-pa yoñ-gin gdaḥ* we have thoughts of practising religion; འཇིགས་སོ་སྙམ་པ་ཡོད་རེ་སྐན *ḥjigs-so ṣñam-pa yod* re-şkan I am far from any thought of fear; སྙམ་བྱེད, ཕན་སྙམ་བྱེད་ཀྱང་ though one may imagine that it will help; སྐྱུག་པ şkyug-pa, བརྡུངས་དཀྲིས་སྙམ་བྱེད b̲rduṅs-d̲kriş şñam-byed̲ there arises a feeling like that of nausea, like that of being beaten, of being (tightly) wrapt up (*Jä.*).

སྙལ་ཡས *şñal-yaş* (གྲངས་གནས) n. of a number; ཡ་མེད་སྙལ་ཡས་འདྲུབ་འདེབ་དང་། (*Ya-sel.* 57).

སྙི *şñi*, v. རྙི *r̲ñi*.

སྙི་སྟེང་ *şñi-şteñ* = གཉའ *gñah̲* neck; nape of neck.

སྙི་པོ *şñi-po* = སྙིང་པོ *şñiñ-po* the heart.

སྙི་ཕུལ *şñi-phul* corn of luxuriant growth; abundant harvest.

སྙི་བ *şñi-wa* 1. a dwarf. 2. softness. 3. n. of a plant.

སྙི་བོ *şñi-wo* मृदु adj. gentle, soft, delicate, tender.

སྙི་མ *şñi-ma* for སྙེ་མ *şñe-ma* (*Jä.*).

སྙི་ཤང་ཀ་ཏྱ *Şñi-çañ ka tya* or སྙི་ཤང་གུར་རྟ *Şñi-çañ gur-r̲ta* name of mountains in Nepal (*Jä.*).

སྙིགས་དུས *şñigş-duş* or སྙིགས་མའི་དུས *şñigş-mah̲i duş* कलि or कलि the degenerate age, or the age of sin.

སྙིགས་བྱེད་མ *şñigş byed̲-ma* acc. to the Bon n. of the god of air (*D.R.*).

སྙིགས་པ *şñigş-pa* degenerated, grown worse, v. སྙིགས་མ *şñigş-ma*.

སྙིགས་མ *şñigş-ma* कषाय, निकषाय, माष 1. a whet-stone. 2. ཟས་ལྷག impurity in food, poison or defilement in food; impure sediment; མར་གྱི་སྙིགས་མ *mar gyi şñigş-ma* impurities in butter; དངས་སྙིགས་འབྱེད་པ to separate the clear (fluid) from the sediment; སྙིགས་མ་ཐམས་ཅད་སེལ་བ *şñigş-ma thamş-cad̲ sel-wa* to clear out all the impurities. ཞིང་སྙིགས་མ *shiñ şñigş-ma* भूमिकषाय a yellowish sprout growing up on land. 3. ཚིགས་མ *tshigş-ma* a member between two joints.

སྙིགས་མ་ལྔ་ནི *şñigş-mal̲ña-ni* the five impurities are:—(1) ཚེའི་སྙིགས, आयुःकषाय; མར་འགྲིབ་པ *mar h̲grib-pa* the decrease of the duration of life; (2) ལྟ་བའི་སྙིགས་མ, दृष्टिकषाय; = ཕྱིན་ཅི་ལོག་ཏུ་ཁ་ཕྱུར་བ perversity in thoughts, religious disbeliefs, &c. 3. ཉོན་མོངས་པའི་སྙིགས་མ क्लेशकषाय; = དུག་ལྔ་ཁ་རག་པ the five poisons; (4) སེམས་ཅན་གྱི་སྙིགས་མ, सत्व-कषाय; འདུལ་དཀའ་བ difficulty to convert; (5) དུས་ཀྱི་སྙིགས་མ, कल्पकषाय རྩོད་ལྡན *r̲tsod̲-l̲dan* degenerate ages or times.

སྙིང་ *şñiñ* वक्षः, हृदय, मनस् 1. the heart, both met. and physically: སྙིང་འདར་ཞིང་འགུལ *şñiñ-h̲dar shiñ-h̲gul* the heart throbs with fear; བདག་གི་ལུས་ཀྱི་སྙིང་ལྟར་གཅེས *b̲dag-gi luş-kyi şñiñ-l̲tar gceş* as dear to me as my own heart. 2. चित्त the disposition. སྙིང་དགའ་བ *şñiñ-d̲gah̲-wa* or སྙིང་བདེ་བ *şñiñ b̲de-wa* gladness, cheerfulness; སྙིང་དང་མིག་འཕྲོག་པ *şñiñ-dañ mig h̲phrog-pa* to transport, to ravish (*Sch.*). 3. courage; སྙིང་མ་ཆུང་ཤིག be not afraid! སྙིང་གདོན་གྱིས་བསླུས *şñiñ gdon gyiş b̲sluş* the heart is infatuated by a demon. སྙིང་ནས *şñiñ-naş* (i) heartily, zealously, earnestly, *e.g.*, looking for or to a thing; with all one's heart, most earnestly, devoutly, *e.g.*, to say one's prayer; (ii) actually, really: ཁོང་སྙིང་ནས་མི་འབྱིང་པ་ཡིན *khoñ şñiñ-na mi-h̲byiñ-pa yin* really he does not sink. 3. for སྙིང་པོ, སྙིང་འགེམས་པ *şñiñ h̲gems-pa* stupified, confounded, depressed (*D.R.*).

Syn. of No. 1. ཐུགས *thugş*; ཤ་ཡི་མཆོག *ça-yi mchog*; ཆོས་ཀྱི་རྩ་འཁོར *choş-kyi r̲tsa-h̲khor*; ཀུན་སྐྱེད་བྱེད *kun-şkyed̲ byed̲*; སྲོག་གི་གནས *şrog-gi gnaş*; སེམས་ཀྱི་ཁང་པ *semş-kyi khañ-pa*; རྣམ་ཤེས་རྟེན *r̲nam-çeş r̲ten* (*M̲ñon.*).

སྙིང་ཁ *ṣñiṅ-kha* हृदय the heart; སྙིང་ཁར *ṣñiṅ-khar* on the heart, at heart.

སྙིང་ཁམས *ṣñiṅ-khamṣ* the heart; acc. to *Sch.* courage.

སྙིང་ཁུ *ṣñiṅ-khu* = ཉིང་ཁུ *ñiṅ-khu.*

སྙིང་ག *ṣñiṅ-ga* the breast: སྙིང་གར་སྤུ་མང་སྐྱེས་པ་བདེ་བར་འཚོ *ṣñiṅ-gar ṣpu-maṅ ṣkyeṣ-pa ḇde-war ḥtsho* he will live to be happy on whose breast grows much hair (*Mi.*).

སྙིང་དགའ་བ *ṣñiṅ dgaḥ-wa* हृदयोल्लास heart's content, joy, cheerfulness.

སྙིང་གྲོགས *ṣñiṅ-grogṣ* सुहृद्, वल्लभ, a sympathizing friend, a bosom friend.

སྙིང་ཅན *ṣñiṅ-can* courageous, spirited, bold.

སྙིང་རྩེས་པ *ṣñiṅ ṛtseṣ-pa,* v. སྙི་རྗེ་བ *ṣñi ṛje-wa* कृपा mercy, compassion.

སྙིང་ཆུ་བཞུག *ṣñiṅ-chu ḇshug* in *W.* afflicted with dropsy in the pericardium (*Jä.*).

སྙིང་རྗེ *ṣñiṅ-ṛje* करुणा, दया, अनुकम्पा kindness, mercy, compassion: མི་ལ་སྙིང་རྗེ་སྒོམ་པ to meditate with pity for all men. སྙིང་རེ་རྗེ *ṣñiṅ-re ṛje,* occurs in ཁྱོད་བོད་རྣམས་སྙིང་རེ་རྗེ *khyod Bod-ṛnamṣ ṣñiṅ-re-ṛje* I pity you ye Tibetans (*A. 65*).

Syn. ཐུགས་རྗེ *thugs ṛje*; བརྩེ་བ *ḇtse wa*; རྗེས་ཆགས *ṛjeṣ chagṣ*; རྗེས་སུ་བརྩེ *ṛjeṣ-su ḇtse* (*Mṅon.*).

སྙིང་རྗེ་སྐད *ṣñiṅ ṛje ṣkad* lamentation; cry of compassion.

སྙིང་རྗེ་ཅན *ṣñiṅ-ṛje-can* कृपालु merciful, kind hearted; a merciful person.

སྙིང་རྗེ་ཆེན་པོ *Ṣñiṅ ṛje chen po,* སྙིང་རྗེའི་ལྷ *Ṣñiṅ ṛjeḥi lha,* are names of Avalokites'vara.

སྙིང་རྗེ་ཆེན་པོ་པད་དཀར *ṣñiṅ ṛje chen po pad dkar* करुणा-पुण्डरीक n. of a sūtra in the *Kaḥ gyur,* vol. ཆ, *Mdo* section.

སྙིང་རྗེ་བྲལ *ṣñiṅ-ṛje bral* = སྙིང་རྗེ་མེད་པ *ṣñiṅ-ṛje med-pa* निष्करुण devoid of mercy or compassion, merciless, cruel. The following ten acc. to Buddhism are included in the category of those who are called *ṛñiṅ-ṛje-bral*:—བཤན་པ butchers; བྱ་གག་འཚོང་པ sellers of ducks; ཕག་འཚོང་པ sellers of pigs or pork; ཉ་པ fishermen; རི་དྭགས་ཀྱི་རྔོན་པ hunters; བྱ་པ bird-catchers; བོང་བུ་སོགས་ལ་ཁལ་ལྕི་བཀལ་ཏེ་བརྡུང་མཁན drivers of donkeys and other beasts of burden who lading them heavily beat them; ཆོམ་རྐུན་པ robbers and way-layers; གཤེད་མ་པ murderers; བ་གླང་གསོད་པ་པོ slayers of oxen, etc. (*K. du.* ད *204*).

སྙིང་རྗེ་མོ *ṣñiṅ-ṛje mo* 1. compassionate: you are compassion personified. Acc. to *Jä.* in ཁྱོད་སྙིང་རྗེ་མོ་དང་ཞིག་འདུག you are much to be pitied. 2. colloq. dearest, most beloved, amiable, charming.

སྙིང་ཉེ་བ *ṣñiṅ ñe-wa* 1. = མཛའ་བོ *mdsa-ḇo,* or ཉེ་བོ *ñe-wo,* friendly, amicable, loving, affectionate. Figurative expression for it is ཡིད་ཀྱི་ཟེའུ་འབྲུ *yiḏ-kyi zeḥu ḥbru* (*Yig. k. 1*). 2. dear and near relatives. 3. कार्षापण money.

སྙིང་སྟོབས *ṣñiṅ-ṣtobs* सत्व, त्रिवर्ग; गुण, प्रकृति fortitude; character; courage, spirit, virtue: མཁས་ཤིང་མཛངས་ལ་གསལ་བ་སྤྲོ་བ་སྙིང་སྟོབས་ཆེ་བ། ལེ་ལོ་དང་སྤྱོད་པ་ངན་པའི་རྗེས་སུ་མི་འགྲོ་བ fortitude and enlightenment increasing in the wise and learned; they go not after evil deeds and indolence (*Ld.; Glr.*).

སྙིང་སྟོབས་ཅན *ṣñiṅ-ṣtobṣ can* सात्विक, fearless; possessed of fortitude, moral courage.

Syn. དཔའ་པོ *dpaḥ-po*; ཉམ་ང་མེད *ñam-ṅa meḏ*; ཞུམ་པ་མི་མངའ *shum-pa mi-mṅaḥ*; སྟོབས་ཆེན *ṣtobṣ-chen*; ཕ་རོལ་གནོན *pya-rol gnon* (*Mṅon.*).

སྙིང་སྟོབས་ཆེ *ṣñiṅ-ṣtobṣ-che* परिवाह, महासत्व great soul, one of great fortitude.

སྙིང་གཏམ *ṣñiṅ-gtam* confidential speaking a secret: སྙིང་གཏམ་ཡིན་གྱི་སེམས་ལ་ཞོག *ṣñiṅ-gtam yin gyi semṣ-la shog,* (*Lo. 30.*) put away in your mind talk which is confidential; བརྩེ་བའི་སྙིང་གཏམ *ḇtse-baḥi, ṣñiṅ-gtam* the secret speech of kindness or of love; ཕན་པའི་སྙིང་གཏམ *phan-paḥi sñiṅ-gtam* useful admonition.

སྙིང་སྟོབས་གཏེར *sñiṅ-stobs gter* सत्वनिधि;=སྙིང་སྟོབས་ལྡན་པ सत्ववान्, सत्वशालिन् intrepid, one whose heart is stored with courage (*A. K. 1, 18*).

སྙིང་དུ་སྡུག་པ *sñiṅ-du sdug-pa* or སྙིང་སྡུག་པ charming, handsome; སྙིང་དུ་འབབ་པ=གཟུགས་མཛེས་པ *gzugs mdses-pa* very handsome person, charming (*Mñon.*); in *W.* liked, beloved, darling, favourite; སྙིང་སྡུག་ཞིག་འདུག *sñiṅ-sdug shig-ḥdug* he is a general favourite; སྙིང་མ་སྡུག *sñiṅ ma-sdug* not handsome, not charming; acc. to *Jä.* bad people.

སྙིང་བརྡོམ *sñiṅ-bdom* ornamental equipments of a riding horse, generally what is put on its breast (*Rtsii.*).

སྙིང་འདོད་པ *sñiṅ ḥdod-pa* to wish, to desire, to long for; ཟ་སྙིང་འདོད་པ *za-sñiṅ ḥdod-pa* to long to eat, to be craving for food; འགྲོ་སྙིང་འདོད་པ ardently wishing to go.

སྙིང་སྡུག *sñiṅ-sdug* a beloved one; a sweetheart (*Ṅag. 29*).

སྙིང་ནད *sñiṅ-nad* 1.=སྙིང་ན་བ *sñiṅ na-wa* disease of the heart, but not often any physical disorder; heart-sickness; grief on account of injury suffered from others. 2. defined as སེམས་ལ་ནག་པོ་ཤག་པ *sems-la nag po shag-pa* vindictiveness, to keep a grudge at heart: 'མྱ་ངན་སེམས་འཁྲུགས་ཡི་མི་བདེ་ཤིང་ལྟོ་ཆག་གཉིད་ཆག་ཤེ་སྡང་དྲག་པོས་སྙིང་ནད་སྐྱེད *mya-ṅan sems-ḥkhrugs yi mi-bde shiṅ lto-chag gñid-chag she-sdaṅ drag-pos sñiṅ-nad skyed. Sñiṅ-nad* is caused by fits of anger, sleeplessness, starvation, despair and mental derangement from troubles, etc. The disease is of seven kinds:—(1) སྙིང་ཆུ dropsy of the heart, (2) སྙིང་འཁྱུམས, (3) སྙིང་ནད་ཁ་ལེ་ནག་པོ, (4) སྙིང་འཛེབས, (5) སྙིང་ཚད, (6) སྙིང་གཟེར, (7) སྙིང་སྲིན (*Mṅg. 34*).

སྙིང་པོ I: *sñiṅ-po*, सार; हृदय, गर्भ the pith, essence, heart; སྙིང་པོ་མ་ཡིན་པ་མེད་པར་གྱུར *sñiṅ-po ma-yin pa med-par gyur* अपगतफल्गु far from being useless; useful. སྐད་ཀྱི་སྙིང་པོ *skad-kyi sñiṅ-po* the substance of a speech; ཆོས་ཀྱི་སྙིང་པོ *chos-kyi sñiṅ-po* the essential part or purport of a work or the main substance of a doctrine; དོན་སྙིང་འབྱིན་པ *don-sñiṅ ḥbyin-pa* to draw out a summary, the sum and substance (of a writing): 'སེམས་ཅན་ཐམས་ཅད་སངས་རྒྱས་ཀྱི་སྙིང་པོ་ཅན་ཡིན་ན *sems-can thams-cad saṅs-rgyas kyi 'sñiṅ po can yin-na* if all living beings have the pith and essence of, *i.e.*, partake of the nature of, Buddha; དེ་བཞིན་བཤེགས་པའི་སྙིང་པོ *de-bshin bçegs-paḥi sñiṅ-po* the spirit of Tathāgata; བྱང་ཆུབ་སྙིང་པོ *byaṅ-chub sñiṅ-po*; the spirit of the *Bodhisattva*, *i.e.*, Buddhahood. སྲོག་གི་སྙིང་པོ་འབུལ་བ *srog-gi sñiṅ-po ḥbul-wa* to offer one's heart's blood, to pledge one's own life. The five chief essences or *sñiṅ-po* of food are:—ཚྭ salt, ཤིང་ཏོག fruits, བུ་རམ treacle, སྦྲང་རྩི honey, ཏིལ་དམར red sesame (*Rtsii.*).

སྙིང་པོ II: 1. མེ་ཏོག flower. 2. वज्र the thunder-bolt. 3. मण्डल, गोकिल a heap, a plough. 4. इन्द्रनील a kind of precious stone, sapphire.

སྙིང་པོ་མཁྲེགས་པ *sñiṅ po mkhregs pa*=སྙིང་པོའི་གཞི *sñiṅ poḥi gshi* धरणी the earth, that holds everything, all substances.

སྙིང་རེ་རྗེ *sñiṅ re rje* pity; to be pitied: འདི་རྣམས་སྙིང་རེ་རྗེ *ḥdi rnams sñiṅ re rje* these people are indeed much to be pitied. As an adj. སེམས་ཅན་སྙིང་རེ་རྗེ *sems-can sñiṅ re rje* the poor creatures (*Jä.*); སྙིང་རེ་རྗེ་བའི་སྡིག་ཅན the pitiable sinners.

སྙིང་པོ་ཅན *sñiṅ po can* हृदयालु, सारवत् substantial; also courageous.

སྙིང་པོ་ཆེ་ *sñiñ-po che* (སྙིང་ཆེན་པོ་བྱས་ཤིང་ཐུགས་སེམས་མི་སྡུག་པར་བསམ་བློ་རྒྱ་ཆེན་པོ *sñiñ chen-po byas-çiñ thugs-sems mi-sdug-par b̲sam-b̲lo r̲gya chen-po*) noble-hearted, intrepid, adventurous, enterprizing: སྙིང་པོ་ཆེ་བྲང་ལོག་ཏུ་བཏུག་པའི་སོ་ནམ་མཛད་དགོས་པ་ཡིན O, noble-hearted (sire) you have been required to do husbandry bending on your chest (*A. 127*).

སྙིང་པོ་མཆོག *sñiñ po m̲chog* अपमत n. of a number.

སྙིང་པོ་ཐེག་པའི་ཡང་རྩེ *sñiñ-po theg-pahi yañ-r̲tse* n. of the chief works of the *Anuttara* mystics of Tibet and of Ancient India.

སྙིང་པོ་ལྡན་མ *sñiñ-po l̲dan ma* सारवती an article that is possessed of some real properties, or of intrinsic value.

སྙིང་པོ་བསྡུ་བ *sñiñ-po b̲sdu-wa* सारसंग्रह n. of a work composed by Atis'a (*A. 66*).

སྙིང་པོ་མེད་པ *sñiñ po med̲ pa* 1. असार, फल्गु, लघु;=དོན་མེད་པ worthless, null, void, false, hollow. 2. n. of अर्जुन the third Pāṇḍava, the hero of the Mahābhārata (*M̲ñon.*).

སྙིང་པོ་སོ་སོར *sñiñ-po so sor* (ཙན་དན་དཀར *tsan-dan d̲kar*) पीतसार, white species of sandal wood; a yellow gem, a topaz.

སྙིང་པོའི་ཁང་པ *sñiñ-pohi khañ pa*=རི་ཁྲོད a recluse's cell or hermitage in the midst of a group of hills (*M̲ñon.*).

སྙིང་པོའི་དབེན་པ *sñiñ-pohi d̲ben-pa* void, worthless; sbst. solitude.

སྙིང་འབབ་དྲི *sñiñ h̲bab d̲ri* agreeable scent (*M̲ñon.*).

སྙིང་རྩ *sñiñ r̲tsa* heart-vein; the veins connected with the heart.

སྙིང་རྩེ *sñiñ r̲tse* the tip or apex of the heart; the focus of attention, *i.e.*, when all attention is concentrated.

སྙིང་བརྩེ་ལྡན *sñiñ b̲r̲tse l̲dan*, སྙིང་རྗེ་ཅན *sñiñ r̲je can* loving, affectionate (*M̲ñon.*).

སྙིང་ཚིམ *sñiñ tshim* gratification, satisfaction, consolation; also pleasure felt at the discomfiture or death of an enemy or adversary; སྙིང་ཚིམ་འདེབས་པ *sñiñ tshim h̲debs pa* to show such pleasure; also vb. སྙིང་རེ་ཚིམ་པ *sñiñ re tshim-pa* to gratify or console; to become gratified.

སྙིང་ཚིལ *sñiñ tshil* the fat about the heart (*Cs.*).

སྙིང་ཤོས་ཤ *sñiñ shos ça* n. of a fruit which in appearance is like the heart (*R̲tsii.*).

+ སྙིང་བཤོས་ཏེ་སྨྲ་བ *sñiñ b̲shos te s̲mra-wa*= སྙིང་གཏམ་དང་གསང་གཏམ་སྨྲ་བ *sñiñ g̲tam dañ g̲sañ g̲tam s̲mra wa* to speak out a secret or reveal a confidential thing.

སྙིང་རི *S̲ñiñ-ri* n. of monastery in Tibet.

སྙིང་རུས *sñiñ rus*=བརྩོན་རུས 1. assiduity, firmness of mind, perseverance. 2. courage.

སྙིང་རླུང *sñiñ r̲luñ* 1.=ཁོང་ཁྲོ་ལོངས་པ anger, indignation. 2. low spirits, melancholy (*Sch.*). སྙིང་རླུང་དུག་པོ་ལྡན become indignant.

སྙིང་ལ་ཁུགས *sñiñ-la khugs* प्रत्युरस upon the breast.

སྙིང་ལ་ཉལ *sñiñ-la ñal*=ཡིད་ལ་ཉལ lit. that lies down on the mind; a name of Kāma, the Indian Cupid (*M̲ñon.*).

སྙིང་ལ་འབབ་པ *sñiñ-la h̲bab-pa* 1. हृदयङ्गम fully comprehending, appreciating. 2. अमृत nectar.

སྙིད་པ *sñid̲-pa* prob. རྙིད་པ *r̲ñid̲-pa* (*Jä.*).

སྙིད་མོ *sñid̲-mo* ननन्दा younger sister of a woman's husband.

Syn. ཁྱོ་གའི་ནུ་མོ *khyo-gahi nu mo*; བདག་པོའི་སྲིང་མོ *b̲dag-pohi s̲riñ mo* (*M̲ñon.*).

སྙིན་པ *sñin-pa*, སྙིན་པོ *sñin-po*, སྙིན་ཏེ *sñin-te* =སྙི་བོ *sñi-wo*.

+ **སྙིམ་པ** *sñim-pa* or སྙིམ་པོ *sñim-po*=ཐལ་མོ *thal-mo* अञ्जलि two handsful; a measure for liquids, as well as for flour, grain and the like, as much as may be taken up by both hands placed together: ཇོ་བོས་འགྲོན་བུ་སྙིམ་པ་གང་བསྣམས་ཏེ་བྱོན *jo-wos hgron-bu snim-pa gan bsnams-te byon* (*A. 69*) the lord carrying both hands full of cowries arrived.

སྙིམས *snims*=མཛེས་པ *mdses pa* beautiful, handsome (*Ńag. 29*).

སྙིལ *snil*=རྙིལ *rnil*, སྙེ་མའི་ཕུང་པོ *sne mahi phun po* a bunch of ears of corn (*Ńag. 29*).

སྙིལ་བ *snil-wa* or རྙིལ་བ *rnil-wa* pf. and fut. བསྙིལ *bsnil* (cf. གཉིལ་བ *gnil-wa*) 1. to push or throw down, to break down, to destroy (houses, rocks, etc.); ཕྱེ་མར་སྙིལ་བ *phye-mar snil-wa* to reduce to powder (*Sch.*). 2. ཕྱིར་སྙིལ་བ *phyir snil wa* to expel, banish, exile (*Sch.*) (from *Jä.*).

སྙུག་པ *snug-pa* also སྨྱུག་པ *smyug-pa*, pf. བསྙུགས *bnugs*, fut. བསྙུག *bsnug* to dip in, to immerse (*Jä.*).

སྙུག་མ *snug-ma* more frq. སྨྱུག་མ *smyug-ma* reed, rush, bulrush.

སྙུག་གུ *snug-gu* reed-pen; སྙུག་བཟོ *snug bzo* wicker-work.

སྙུག་འཛིན *snug hdsin* lit. one holding the reed-pen, a writer. སྙུག་འཛིན་དབང་པོ *snug hdsin dwan po* a chief clerk in Tibet; ཐུང་ཡིག་ཡི་ཞེ་ལ་མཁས་པ one versed in writing: དཔལ་ལྡན་ཐུ་མིའི་རིང་ལུགས་ཡང་དག་པར་འཛིན་པ་སྙུག་འཛིན་དབང་པོ་གང་དེའི་ཐུང་དུ། to the chief writer who is well versed in the art of writing which was introduced by the noble Thu-mi (*Yig. k. 49*).

སྙུག་རུམ *Snug-rum* n. of a place in Tibet (*Loń.* ༣ *3*).

སྙུག་ཤིང *snug çin* bamboo:

སྙུག་སི *snug-si* dark yellow-colour; སྣོ་སྣམ་སྙུག་སི broad-cloth of dark yellow colour (*Rtsii.*).

སྙུགས *snugs* duration, continuity, time (*Cs.*).

སྙུགས་ཆེན *snugs-chen* continual (*Ńag. 29*); སྙུགས་སྲིངས་ཡུན་ཚད *snugs-srins yun-tshad* protracted, lengthened out (*Jä.*).

སྙུགས་སྦྲུལ *snugs-sbrul* a species of lizard (*Sch.*).

+ སྙུགས་སུ *snugs su*=ཡུན་དུ in a long time.

སྙུགས་སྲིང་ *snugs-srin* आयाम lengthened or continual.

སྙུང་ *snun*=སྙུན resp. for ནད disease, illness, sickness: བཙུན་པའི་སྐུ་ལ་སྙུང་མི་མངའ་འམ *btsun pahi sku la snun mi mnah ham* your honour I suppose is not unwell ?

སྙུང་བ *snun-wa* I: vb., pf. བསྙུངས *bsnuns*, fut. བསྙུང་ *bsnun* 1. to make less, to reduce, to diminish; acc. to *Sch.* to disparage. 2. to be ill, sick, indisposed; ཐུགས་སྙུང་བའི་མི people that are disagreeable, annoying to others (*Jä.*).

སྙུང་བ II: sbst. the state of being ill; illness, indisposition.

སྙུང་བུ *snun bu* awl, pricker, punch.

Syn. རྩེ་རྣོ་ *rtse rno*; ཀོ་བ་འབིགས་བྱེད *ko wa hbigs byed* (*Mṅon.*).

སྙུང་གཞི *snun gshi*=ནད་གཞི 1. illness, disease. 2. བསྐྲད་པ་རྒྱག་བྱེད་པ banishment; to expel, eject.

སྙུན *snun* रोग illness, disease, sickness: སྐུ་ལ་སྙུན་གྱིས་བཟུང་ *sku la snun gyis bzun* he was taken ill. Acc. to *Jä.* སྙུན་འདྲི་བ *snun dri-wa* or སྙུན་གསོལ་བ *snun gsol-wa* are expressions of inquiry after a person's health. ན་དྲི་ཞུ་བ *na-dri shu-wa* or སྙུན་དྲི་ཞུ་བ *snun-dri shu-wa* to wait on, to pay one's respects (*Jä.*).

སྙུན་དངས་པ *s̱ñun dbaṅs-pa* आराम cured from a disease, recovered from an illness, convalescent.

Syn. ནད་སངས་པ *nad̲ saṅs-pa*; ནད་གསོས་པ *nad̲ gsos pa*; ནད་ཀྱིས་བཏང་བ *nad̲ kyis b̲tañ wa*; ནད་ལས་གྲོལ་བ *nad̲ las̱ grol wa*; ནད་ལས་ཐར་བ *nas̱ las̱ thar wa* (*M̲ñon.*).

སྙུན་པ *s̱ñun-pa* 1. pf. and fut. བསྙུན *b̲s̱ñun* to be ill, to labour under a disease. 2.= ནད་པ *nad̲ pa*, ནད་ཕོག་པ *nad̲ phog pa*, ཉམས་མ་བདེ་བ *ñams̱ ma b̲de wa*, འདུ་བ་འཁྲུགས་པ *b̲du wa khrugs̱ pa*, ཁམས་མ་བདེ་བ *kyams̱ ma b̲de wa*.

སྙུན་མེད *s̱ñun med̲* free from illness.

+ སྙུན་རྨེད *s̱ñun ṟmed̲* (སྙུན illness, རྨེད *ṟmed̲*=དྲི་བ *dṟi-wa*) to inquire, to inquire after one's health: ཇོ་བོ་ལ་སྙུན་རྨེད *jo b̲o la s̱ñun ṟmed̲*, འདི་སྐད་མཛད་དེ (*A. 75*) thus inquiring if the lord was well.

སྙེ་མ *s̱ñe-ma*=སྙེ་མ or དོག་པ वल्लरी, मञ्जरी 1. ears of corn. 2. འབྲུའི་དོག་པ *h̲bruh̲i dog-pa* corn forming ears (v. ལྗང་པ *ljañ pa*).

སྙེ་དཀར *s̱ñe d̲kar* diseased ears of corn; སྙེ་མགོ *s̱ñe m̲go* སྙེ་མ *s̱ñe ma* ears of corn.

སྙེ་ཐང *S̱ñe-thañ*, also written མཉེས་ཐང *m̲ñes̱ thañ*, n. of a village situated about ten miles S.W. of Lhasa city. It was at Ñethang that the celebrated Atis'a spent his last days and died.

སྙེ་ཐང་གླིང་ག *S̱ñe-thañ gliñ-ga* the large grove in neighbourhood of the monastery where Atis'a resided. It contains the chorten or chait where his remains were interred.

སྙེ་མདོ *S̱ñe-m̲do* n. of a village in Tibet (*Deb. 43*).

སྙེ་ཕུ *S̱ñe-phu* n. of a small town in Tibet.

སྙེ་འཕྲེང *S̱ñe-h̲phreñ* n. of a large grove in Tibet (*R̲tsii.*).

སྙེ་འབོལ *s̱ñe h̲bol*=སྔས་འབོལ pillow or cushion to rest the head upon (*Ñag. 29*).

སྙེ་མ་མིག་ཅན *s̱ñe-ma mig-can* ears of corn which have just got or formed grains. ད་གྲོའི་སྙེ་མ་མིག་ཐོན now the ears of wheat have got grains.

སྙེ་མ་ལུས་ལྕེབས *s̱ñe-ma lus̱-l̲cebs̱* करञ्ज the tree *Pongamia glabra*, used medicinally (*M̲ñon.*).

སྙེ་མོ *S̱ñe-mo* n. of a district situated between Ü and Tsang (*R̲tsii.*).

སྙེ་མོ་འཕྲང་རྫོང *S̱ñe-mo H̲phrañ-ṟdsoñ* n. of a fort situated on a precipice in *S̱ñe-mo* (*R̲tsii*).

སྙེ་མའི་ཕུང་པོ *s̱ñe-mah̲i phuñ-po* मञ्जरी a bunch formed of ears of corn.

སྙེགས *s̱ñegs̱* straight or stretched out (*Jä.*): ལག་པས་སྙེགས *lag pas̱ s̱ñegs̱* with the hand stretched out.

སྙེགས་པ *s̱ñegs̱-pa* pf. བསྙེགས་པ *b̲s̱ñegs̱ pa* fut. བསྙེག *b̲s̱ñeg* imp. སྙོགས *s̱ñogs̱* 1. c. accus. to hasten or run after, to pursue; frq. also with རྗེས་ནས *ṟjes̱ nas̱*, རྗེས་སུ *ṟjes̱ su*, རྗེས་བཞིན་དུ *ṟjes̱ b̲shin-du*, ཕྱི་བཞིན་དུ *phyi b̲shin-du*. རང་འགྲོ་ས་སྙོགས *rañ h̲gro sa s̱ñogs̱* hasten towards your destination; བསྙེག་ཏུ་འདོང་པ *b̲s̱ñeg tu h̲doñ pa* or སྙེགས་སུ་འདོང་བ *s̱ñegs̱ su h̲doñ wa* to walk hastily, to make haste or speed (*Jä.*). 2. to overtake; སྙེག་མ་ནུས་པས *s̱ñeg ma nus̱-pas̱* not being able to reach. 3. c. dat. to hasten (to some place) ལྟད་མོ་ལ་སྙེག *l̲tad̲-mo la s̱ñeg* hasten to the play; གནམ་ལ་སྙེག *nam la s̱ñeg* hastening up to heaven (as a flame). 4. to strive or struggle for, to aspire to; ནོར་ལ་སྙེག *nr la s̱ñeg* to aspire to riches; སྡེ་ཆེན་ལ་སྙེག *s̱de chen la s̱ñeg* to aspire to the increase of territory; ཞིང་ཁམས་བཟང་ལ་སྙེག *shiñ khams̱ b̲zañ la s̱ñeg* to aspire to the region of eternal bliss. སྙེག་མ *s̱ñeg-ma* a pursuer (from *Jä.*).

སྙེང་བ *sñeṅ-wa* 1. to stretch. 2. also སྙེངས་པ *sñeṅs-pa* to fear (pf. བསྙེངས *bsñeṅs*, fut. སྙེང་, resp. རྒྱལ་པོས་མ་སྙེངས་ཤིག *rgyal pos ma sñeṅs çig* do not be afraid of the king (*Jä.*).

སྙེད *sñed* 1. the crupper attached to a saddle. 2. in ཇི་སྙེད་ལྟ་བུ *ji-sñed lta-bu* འདི་སྙེད་ཅིག *hdi-sñed-cig* or དེ་སྙེད་ཅིག *de sñed-cig* so much, so many, frq. used for how many: ཡོན་ཏན་འདི་སྙེད་མངའ་བ so many excellent qualities has he. ཅི་སྙེད or ཇི་སྙེད how much, how many? 3. after numbers: about, near: སྟོང་སྙེད *stoṅ-sñed* about or near a thousand; སྟོང་ཇི་སྙེད *stoṅ-ji sñed* about a thousand also: how many thousands? (*Jä.*).

སྙེད་པ *sñed-pa* is mistake for རྙེད་པ *rñed-pa* लाभ, प्रतिलब्ध to gain, profit, acquire: སྙེད་པ་བླ་ན་མེད་པ *sñed-pa bla na med-pa* लाभोऽनुत्तरस्य the very highest gain or supremest state.

སྙེན་པ *sñen-pa* or སྙེན་མ *sñen-ma*, acc. to *Cs.* 1. to come, go near, approach. 2. to gain, to procure.

སྙེམས་ཆུང་ *sñems-chuṅ* 1. unpretentious, humble, affable. 2. sbst. poor, indigent.

སྙེམས་པ *sñems-pa* 1. vb. pf. བསྙེམས *bsñems* to be proud or arrogant, to boast; ང་རྒྱལ་སྙེམས་པས *ṅargyal sñems-pas* being swollen or puffed up with pride; མཐུ་རྩལ་སྙེམས་པས *mthu rtsal sñems pas* proud of one's strength. 2. sbst. गर्व; དྲེགས་པ *dregs-pa* pride, haughtiness; སྙེམས་པ་ཅན *sñems-pa-can* full of pride, proud.

སྙེས *sñes*, v. སྙེ་བ *sñe-wa*. དབུ་ལ་སྙེས *dbu-la sñes* (*Ṅag. 29*) reclined your head on the pillow; སྙེས་འབོལ *sñes-hbol* pillow.

སྙོ་བ *sño-wa* sometimes for སྨྱོ་བ *smyo-wa*.

སྙོགས་པ *sñogs-pa* or བསྙོག་པ *bsñog-pa* (*Ṅag. 29*) 1. secondary form of སྙེག་པ *sñeg-pa* esp. when signifying to wish earnestly, to crave for or implore; also ཁ་སྙོགས་པ *kha sñogs pa* id. ལག་པས་ཆུ་སྙོགས་པ *lag-pas chu sñogs-pa* to ask for water stretching out the hand. 2.=རྗེས་སུ་སྙོག *rjes-su sñog* अनुयाति following; ཡར་སྙོག་མར་སྙོག *yar-sñog mar-sñog* went up and down; now gone towards the uplands, then towards the lowlands.

སྙོངས་པ *sñoṅs-pa*=ཆུག་པ लेपन, लेप to apply (an ointment).

སྙོད *sñod*=གོ་སྙོད *go-sñod* caraway.

སྙོད་པ I: *sñod pa* pf. བསྙོད *bsñod* བསྙོས *bsños*, fut. བསྙོད *bsñod* 1. to draw out and twist, as in spinning (*Jä.*). 2. acc. to *Cs.* to tell, relate. 3. སྙད་པ *sñad pa*.

སྙོད་པ II: to feed, to give to eat and to drink: འོ་མས་སྙོད་ཅིང་སྟོབས་པ *ho-mas sñod ciṅ stobs pa* fed and strengthened with milk.

སྙོན་པ I: *sñon-pa* अपलाप 1. pf. and fut. བསྙོན *bsñon* to deny, disavow (dishonestly); བསྙོན་བྱེད་པ *bsñon byed pa* to assert falsely.

སྙོན་པ II:=སྨྱོན་པ *smyon-pa*.

སྙོན་མོངས *sñon moṅs*=ཆགས་པ; དངོས་པོ་དང་བྱེད་པའི་ཁྱད་པར (*Ṅag. 29*).

སྙོབ་པ *sñob-pa* pf. བསྙོབས *bsñobs*, fut. བསྙོབ *bsñob*, imp. སྙོབས *sñobs* 1. to stretch forth; ལག་པ་སྙོབས *lag pa sñobs* stretched out the hand (*Ṅag. 29*). What is given as food is always placed in the instr. case, while the animal or person fed takes the dative: བཙུན་མོ་ལ་ཉུང་ལ་ཕུག་གིས་སྙོབས་སོ the queen was fed with turnips and radishes (*Ld.*; *Glr.*). 2. to reach by stretching one's self out; to arrive at.

སྙོམ I: *sñom* or སྙོམས་ལས *sñoms-las* तन्द्रा, किलास, आलस्य indolence, unconcern, esp. religious indifference.

སྙོམ 11: or སྙོམས་པ *snoms-pa*=འདྲ་འདྲ་ཁོད་སྙོམས་པ *hdra hdra khod snoms pa* very similar.

སྙོམ་པ *snom-pa* or སྙོམས་པ *snoms-pa* तन्द्रा; གཡེང་བ or གཡེལ་བ 1. weariness, lassitude, laziness, idleness; ལུས་སྙོམས་ལྕི་བ་ཡིན *lus-snoms lci-wa-yin* one is exhausted and dull; སྙོམ་ལ་ཉལ་བ *snom-la ñal-wa* to be tired and exhausted. 2. ཉེ་རིང་མེད་པར་འདྲ་འདྲ་བྱེད་པ impartial, to treat impartially, *i.e.*, in equal terms རྒྱ་དང་མི་རྒྱ་སྙོམ་ཉིད་ཉེ་རིང་མེད, དེ་རིང་ཁྱོད་ཀྱི་བཟུ་དང་དཔང་ཚུལ་ཞིག (*Yig.*); མགོ་སྙོམས *mgo snoms* impartial.

སྙོམ་པར་འཇུག་པ་དྲུག་པ *snom-par hjug-pa drug-pa* the six *Samāpanna* sages are:—(1) རང་སྤྱོད་ཀྱི་བུ་ལྷག་སྤྱོད *Rañs spyod kyi bu Lhag spyod*; (2) སྒྱུ་རྩལ་ཤེས་ཀྱི་བུ་རིན་ཕུར *Sgyu rtsal çes kyi bu Riñ phur*; (3) ཀུན་ཏུ་རྒྱུ་ལེགས་བཟང *kun tu rgyu Legs bzañs*; (4) བྲམ་ཟེའི་ཁྱིའུ་རྒྱལ *bram zehi khyihu Rgyal*; (5) དྲང་སྲོང་མ་བཅིངས་པ *drañ sroñ ma bciñs pa*; (6) ལྟེང་རྒྱས་འོད་སྲུང་རལ་པ་ཅན *lteñ rgyas hod sruñ ral pa can.*

སྙོམ་པོ *snom-po*=སྙོམ་པོའི་ལས *snom-pohi las* (*Ñag.* 29).

སྙོམས *snoms* for སྙོམས་པ सम; སྙོམས་དུ་མེད *snoms-du med* without an equal.

སྙོམས་པ *snoms-pa* vb., pf. བསྙོམས *bsnoms*, fut. བསྙོམ *bsnom* 1. to make even, to level; ས་ལ་སྙོམས་པ *sa-la snoms-pa* to level (with the ground), to demolish. 2. to equalize (different things), to arrange uniformly: ཟས་སྙོམས་པ *zas snoms-pa* to arrange (uniformly) one's meals, *i.e.*, not cold and warm promiscuously; ཐམས་ཅད་ན་སྙོམས་ན་བདག་ཀྱང་སྙོམས་པར་མཛད་དུ་ཚལ I wish to be treated fairly on a par with all others; ཁ་ལ་སྙོམས་པ *kha-la snoms-pa* to regulate (a matter), to manage or direct (a business) justly, uniformly.

སྙོམས་པ *snoms-pa* क्लमथ; དུབ་པ *dub-pa* fatigue, exhaustion.

སྙོམས་པོ *snoms-po* equal, even, uniform (*i.e.*, in every part equally thick) (*Jä.*).

སྙོམས་པར་འཇུག་པ *snoms par hjug pa* समापत्ति evenness or calmness of mind, equanimity. The nine *Samāpatti* are as follows:—(1) स सर्व्वशो रूपसंज्ञानां समतिक्रम्य प्रतिघसंज्ञानाम् अस्तंगमात् नानात्वसंज्ञानाम् अमनसिकारात् अनन्तम् आकाशम् इत्याकाशानन्त्यायतनम् उपसम्पद्य विहरति। Having completely passed the form-group and crossed the aggregate of passions and not thinking of the varieties, he remains realising in his mind the infinite expanse of the sky, viz., that the sky is limitless. (2) सर्व्वश आकाशानन्त्यायतनं समतिक्रम्य अनन्तं विज्ञानानन्त्यायतनम् उपसम्पद्य विहरति। Having completely passed the infinite expanse of sky, he remains realising in his mind the infinite extent of knowledge, viz, that knowledge is unbounded. (3) स सर्व्वशो विज्ञानानाम् अनन्त्यायतनं समतिक्रम्य नास्ति किञ्चन्यायतनम् उपसम्पद्य विहरति। Having thoroughly passed the boundless extent of knowledge, he remains realising in his mind the realm of nothingness, viz., that there is nothing. (4) स सर्व्वश आकिञ्चन्यायतनं समतिक्रम्य नैवसंज्ञानासंज्ञायतनम् उपसम्पद्य विहरति। Having thoroughly passed the realm of nothingness, he remains realising in his mind the region of conscious-nonconsciousness [*M.V.*]. In Tibetan we find these four thus expressed:—(1) དེ་རྣམ་པ་ཐམས་ཅད་དུ་གཟུགས་ཀྱི་འདུ་ཤེས་རྣམས་ལས་ཡང་དག་པར་འདས་ཏེ་ཐོགས་པའི་འདུ་ཤེས་རྣམས་ནུབ་པར་གྱུར་ཅིང་སྣ་ཚོགས་ཀྱི་འདུ་ཤེས་རྣམས་ཡིད་ལ་མི་བྱེད་པས་ནམ་མཁའ་མཐའ་ཡས་སོ་སྙམ་ནས་ནམ་མཁའ་མཐའ་ཡས་སྐྱེ་མཆེད་རྫོགས་པར་བྱས་ཏེ་གནས་སོ། (2) དེ་རྣམ་པ་ཐམས་ཅད་དུ་ནམ་མཁའ་མཐའ་ཡས་སྐྱེ་མཆེད་ལས་ཡང་དག་པར་འདས་ཏེ་རྣམ་པར་ཤེས་པ་མཐའ་ཡས་སོ་སྙམ་ནས་རྣམ་ཤེས་མཐའ་ཡས་སྐྱེ་མཆེད་རྫོགས་པར་བྱས་ཏེ་གནས་སོ། (3) དེ་རྣམ་པ་ཐམས་ཅད་དུ་རྣམ་ཤེས་མཐའ་ཡས་སྐྱེ་མཆེད་ལས་ཡང་དག་པར་འདས་ཏེ་ཅི་ཡང་མེད་དོ་སྙམ་ནས་ཅི་ཡང་མེད་པའི་སྐྱེ་མཆེད་རྫོགས་པར་བྱས་ཏེ་གནས་སོ། (4) དེ་རྣམ་པ་ཐམས་ཅད་དུ་ཅི་ཡང་མེད་པའི་སྐྱེ་མཆེད་ལས་ཡང་དག་པར་འདས་ནས་འདུ་ཤེས་མེད་འདུ་

ཤེས་མེད་མིན་སྐྱེ་མཆེད་རྫོགས་པར་བྱས་ཏེ་གནས་སོ། The other five are:—(5) ཐོད་རྒལ་དུ་སྙོམས་པར་འཇུག་པ། व्यतिक्रान्तसमापत्ति। (6) མཐར་གྱིས་གནས་པའི་སྙོམས་པར་འཇུག་པ་དགུ། नवानुपूर्व्वीहारसमापत्ति। (7) འབྱུང་བ་ཆེན་པོ་མཉམ་པ། महाभूतासमतासाधनम्। (8) འདུ་ཤེས་མེད་པའི་སྙོམས་པར་འཇུག་པ། असंज्ञासमापत्ति। (9) ཚོར་བ་མེད་པའི་སྙོམས་པར་འཇུག་པ། व्यास्कन्दक समापत्ति।

སྙོམས་ལས་བྱེད་པ *s̲ñoms las byed̲ pa* to be lazy, indolent, indifferent. སྙོམས་ལས་ཅན *s̲ñoms las can* उन्मनाः, तन्द्रालु adj. a lazy and idle person; an absent-minded person. སྙོམས་ལས་མེད *s̲ñoms-las-med̲* अतन्द्रालु one who is not lazy or indolent.

Syn. ལེ་ལོ་ཅན *le-lo-can*; གྱི་ན་བ *gyi-na wa*; གཏོང་སྙོམས་ཅན *gtoṅ-s̲ñoms-can*; བློ་ཆུད་ཟོས *b̲lo chud̲ zos̲* (*M̲ñon.*).

སྙོལ་བ *s̲ñol-wa* pf. and fut. བསྙལ *b̲ñal* (cf. ཉལ་བ *ñal wa*) to lay anything down; to bed a person, to assign him couch or bed; ཕྲུ་གུ་མལ་དུ་སྙོལ་བ *phru gu mal du s̲ñol wa* to lay a child on its bed; ཉལ་དུ་བཞག་པ *ñal du b̲shag pa* to lay or put down; མེ་ཉལ་བ *me ñal wa* to put the fire to bed, *i.e.*, to scrape it together and cover it with ashes; སྤུ་སྙོལ་བ *s̲pu s̲ñol-wa* lit. to smooth down the hair, fig. to abate one's anger by the touch, *i.e.*, as if to pat a cat or dog; ལུས་ངག་ཡིད་ཀྱི་ཞེ་སྡང་ཞི་བར་བྱེད *lus̲ ṅag yid̲ kyi she s̲daṅ shi war byed̲* (*Ṅag. 29*) to pacify anger physically, by words and by the heart.

བརྙ་བ *b̲r̲ña-wa* pf. བརྙས *b̲r̲ñas̲* 1.=གཡར་བ *gyar-wa* to borrow (*Ṅag. 30*). 2.=ཉོ་བ *ño-wa* to buy, to take on lease (*Ṅag. 30*). 3. to seize (by force), to usurp (*Sch.*). བརྙས་པ *b̲r̲ñas̲-pa* purchased, bought, borrowed. བརྙས་ཐབས *b̲r̲ñas̲ thabs̲* arrangement to borrow, to take loan of; བཞན་ལས་བརྙས *b̲shan-las̲ b̲r̲ñas̲* borrowed from others; བརྙན་པོའི་བརྙས *b̲r̲ñan-poh̲i b̲r̲ñas̲* interest for a loan, rent for a thing borrowed (*Sch.*).

བརྙང་བ *b̲r̲ñaṅ-wa*=འཁྲུ་བ *h̲khru-wa.*

བརྙད་པ *b̲r̲ñad̲-pa* for བསྙད་པ *b̲s̲ñad̲-pa.*

བརྙན་པ *b̲ñan-pa*=གཡར་བ to borrow: བརྙན་པོའི་གོས *b̲r̲ñan poh̲i gos̲* borrowed dress. Acc. to *Cs.* a garment marked with the figures of the rainbow, also fig. borrowed, reflected. གཟུགས་བརྙན *gzugs̲ b̲r̲ñan* or སྣང་བརྙན *s̲naṅ b̲r̲ñan* प्रतिबिम्ब a reflected image, frq. also image, picture in general; even a little statue. རྨི་ལམ་གྱི་གཟུགས་བརྙན *r̲mi lam-gyi gzugs̲ b̲r̲ñan* vision, visionary image. སྒྲ་བརྙན *s̲gra b̲r̲ñan* प्रतिशब्द returned sound, *i.e.*, echo. མགོ་བརྙན *m̲go b̲r̲ñan* a mask, a fearful apparition. ཕྱག་བརྙན *phyag b̲r̲ñan* servant (*Cs.*).

བརྙན་ཏོལ *b̲r̲ñan-tol*=ཁ་མཆུ་འཛུགས *kha-m̲chu h̲dsugs̲* to begin a case or lawsuit.

བརྙབས་པ *b̲r̲ñabs̲-pa* diligence, painstaking; to take pains (*Sch.*).

བརྙས་པ I: *b̲r̲ñas̲-pa*, v. བརྙ་བ *b̲r̲ña-wa.*

བརྙས་པ II: पराभव, अभिभव, अवज्ञा contempt; also to despise, contemn, c. dat., frq. མ་བརྙས་ཤིག *ma b̲r̲ñas̲ çig* do not despise; བརྙས་པ་བྱེད་པ *b̲r̲ñas̲ pa byed̲ pa* to treat contemptuously; བརྙས་བཅོས *b̲r̲ñas̲-b̲cos̲* contempt, scorn. བརྙས་པའི་ཁྱད་དུ་བསོད་པ *b̲r̲ñas̲ pah̲i khyad̲ du b̲sod̲ pa* अवमान, अवगणन disrespectfulness, contempt.

བརྙས་པར་བྱེད *b̲r̲ñas̲-par byed̲* one who is not respectful; one devoid of love and regard.

Syn. དད་མེད *dad̲ med̲*; མ་མོས་པ *ma mos̲ pa*; གུས་པ་ཞན *gus̲ pa shan*; དད་འདུན་བྲལ *dad̲ h̲dun bral* (*M̲ñon.*).

བརྙས་སྨད *b̲r̲ñas̲ s̲mad̲* scorn and slander.

བརྙས་སེ *b̲r̲ñas̲-se* (བརྙས *b̲r̲ñas̲* contempt སེ= slightly) adv. disrespectfully, slightingly

ཨ་མེས་བྱང་ཆུབ་ལ་ཡང་བརྙས་སེ་བྱས་པས *A-mes byañ-chub la yañ brñas-se byas-pas*, *Ames* even had behaved disrespectfully to the *Bodhisattva* (*A. 94*).

བརྙིངས *brñiñs* 1. pf. of རྙིང་བ *rñiñ-wa*. 2. adj. old, worn-out.

བརྙེས་པ *brñes pa*=བདུད་རྩི *bdud rtsi* or མངའ་བརྙེས *mñah brñes* 1. nectar, ambrosia, the food of the gods. 2. प्राप्त vb. pf. of རྙེད་པ *rñed pa* got, received.

卐 བརྙོངས *brñoñs* explained as སེམས་ལ་མེད་པའི་ཁ་ལ་མཛེས་པ *sems la med pahi kha la mdses-pa* one promising but not meaning to keep his word; polite in speech but different at heart (*Ñag. 30*), *i.e.*, one suiting himself to or framing his speech according to the circumstances of the moment; and hence, doubtless, comes the definition by *Sch.*, convenient, suitable.

卐 བསྙད *bsñad* pf. of སྙད་པ *sñad-pa*=བཤད་པ *bçad pa* आख्यात 1. stated, or related to others; རྒྱུ་མཚན་ལ་བསྙད *rgyu mtshan la bsñad* having stated the reasons (*Situ. 7*). 2. གཞན་བརྙད་པ *gshan brñad pa*=to have oppressed the weak.

བསྙད་པ *bsñad-pa* (གྲངས) मलर n. of a high number.

བསྙམས་པ *bsñams-pa* pf. of སྙམས་པ, ཕན་ཚུན་བསྙམས་པ reconciled, ཁོད་བསྙམས་པ made even, level (*Situ. 75*).

བསྙལ *bsñal* pf. of སྙོལ *sñol*; འཕྲེད་ལ་བསྙོལ *hphred la bsñol*, ཐང་བསྙལ *thañ bsñal*, མར་སར་བསྙལ *mar sar bsñal* (*Situ. 73*).

བསྙལ་ཡས *bsñal-yas* विवर n. of a numerical figure.

བསྙིགས་པ *bsñigs-pa* 1. to return, restore, deliver up (*Cs.*). 2. sediment (*Jä.*).

བསྙིགས་པ *bsñigs pa*=རྙིང་པ *rñiñ-pa* or ཉམས་པ *ñams-pa* stale, old, less efficacious; ལྷུང་བཟེད་བསྙིགས *lyuñ bzed bsñigs* an old alms-bowl, བྱིན་རླབས་བསྙིགས *byin rlabs bsñigs* a benediction less efficacious (*Ñag. 30*).

卐 བསྙིལ་བ *bsñil-wa* pf. of སྙིལ་བ to throw down, destroy; squander: རི་བསྙིལ *ri bsñil* (*Situ. 75*) the hills were thrown down. འདོད་རྒུ་འབད་མེད་ཆར་དུ་བསྙིལ་བ *hdod rgu hbad med char du bsñil wa* to squander wealth earned without exertion (*Yig. k. 2*). བསྙིལ་སྦུད་པ *bsñil sbud pa* नाशित संग्रह to waste amassed wealth.

བསྙུག་པ *bsñug-pa* pf. བསྙུགས *bsñugs* to become full (*Sch.*); སྐྱུ་གང་བསྙུག *skyu gañ bsñug* a full draught; དམར་ཁུ་བསྙུགས *dmar khu bsñugs* (*Situ 75*), filled up with red fluid (*i.e.*, blood).

བསྙུངས *bsñuñs*=ཉུང་བ་བསྙུན slightly laid up (*Ñag. 30*); संलोप; ཉུང་ངར་བྱས་པ made less, belittled, ཡོ་བྱད་བསྙུངས *yo byad bsñuñs* (*Situ. 75*).

卐 བསྙུན *bsñun* form of བསྙུང་ *bsñuñ*=ན་བ *na wa* to be ill, laid up; ནད་ཀྱིས་བསྙུན་ཏོ *nad kyis bsñun to* or བསྙུག་གཞིས་བསྙུན *bsñug gshis bsñun* ill of or laid up with an illness (*Situ. 75*).

卐 བསྙུལ་བ *bsñul-wa* to be rubbed (*Ñag. 30*), also to wash.

བསྙེགས་པ *bsñegs-pa* pf. of སྙེག་པ *sñeg-pa* གོ་ས་གོ་འཕང་བསྙེགས་པ (his) position and dignity raised.

卐 བསྙེངས་པ *bsñeñs-pa*=འཇིགས་པ *hjigs-pa* भय fear, also to be afraid of མི་བསྙེངས *mi bsñeñs*=མི་འཇིགས་པ *mi-hjigs-pa* not to be afraid གནས་སུ་བསྙེངས *gnas su bsñeñs* (*Situ. 75*).

བསྙེངས་བྲལ *bsñeñs bral* fearless, intrepid, =དཔའ་བོ *dpah-po* hero.

Syn. ཉམ་ང་མེད *ñam ña med*; ཤུམ་པ་མི་མང *shum pa mi mañ*; སྙིང་སྟོབས་ཅན *sñiñ stobs can* (*Mñon.*).

བསྙེན་པ *bsñen-pa*=བསྟེན་པ *bsten-pa* or བསྒྲུབ *bsgrub* आसेवित; བསྒོ་བ་བཞིན་ཉན་པ *bsgo-wa bshin* ñan-pa to serve as directed, as prescribed (*Mñon.*). 1. to approach, to come near, c. dat. also དྲུང་དུ *druñ du*, ཁོ་བོའི་དྲུང་དུ་བསྙེན་ཅིག *kho-wohi druñ-du bsñen-cig* come to me; གོམ་པ་རེ་རེ་བོར་ཞིང་འཆི་བ་ལ་བསྙེན་པ་ལྟར as with every step we come nearer to our death; to join, to stick to a person. 2. भजन, सेवा, निषेवन to propitiate a deity, to soothe or satisfy him. 3. to accept, to receive, admit; ཡི་དམ་ལྷ་ཡི་བསྙེན་པ་བཏང *yi-dam lha-yi bsñen-pa btañ* ejaculated many *mantras* of his tutelary deity.

བསྙེན་བཀུར I: *bsñen-bkur*, བསྔགས་པ *bsñags-pa* संवर्त्तन, उपस्थान, उपचरित, शुश्रूषा, श्लाघा reverence, veneration, respect; བསྙེན་བཀུར་བྱེད་པ *bsñan bkur byed-pa* to pay one's respect, esp. to the priesthood by various services.

བསྙེན་བཀུར II: पर्युपासना; ཞབས་ཏོག་ཞུས་པ *shabs-tog shus-pa* to worship, to do religious service. དགེ་འདུན་ལ་བསྙེན་བཀུར་ཞུས *dge-hdun la bsñen-bkur shus* (*Ñag. 30*) venerated the clergy; also asked permission of the clergy to do some religious service.

བསྙེན་བཀུར་གནས *bsñen bkur gnas* पर्युपास्य worthy of worship, veneration, adoration.

བསྙེན་བསྒྲུབ *bsñen bsgrub* सेवासाधना; = གསུང་བསྙེན *gsuñ-bsñen* service and worship.

བསྙེན་གནས *bsñen gnas* उपवास, उपवासी fasting, also one who fasts (as a religious duty).

བསྙེན་གནས་སྲུང་བ *bsñen-gnas sruñ-pa* to observe fasting as a religious duty, abstinence; to fast, to abstain from food.

བསྙེན་པར་དཀའ་བ *bñen-par dkah-wa* hard to propitiate.

བསྙེན་པར་རྫོགས་པ *bsñen par rdsogs pa* उपसम्पन्न to be ordained, consecrated.

བསྙེན་བསྲིང *bsñeh bsriñ* = ཉེ་རིང *ñe riñ*.

卐 **བསྙེམས** *bsñems* = ང་རྒྱལ་ཆེ་བ *ña-rgyal che-wa* गर्व, दर्प very proud, great pride, haughtiness; ཚངས་པར་བསྙེམས *tshañs-par bsñems* (*Situ. 75*).

བསྙེར་བ *bsñer-wa* to make grimaces or gesticulations (*Cs.*).

བསྙེར་མ *bsñer-ma* wrinkles; གདོང་གི་དཔྲལ་བ་སོགས་ཀྱི་བསྙེར *gdoñ-gi dpral-wa sogs-kyi bsñer* wrinkles of the forehead, or of the cheeks, etc. (*Ñag. 30*).

卐 **བསྙེལ་བ** *bsñel-wa* resp. of བརྗེད *brjed* to forget; ཐུགས་མི་བསྙེལ་བར *thugs mi-bsñel-war* not forgetting, not forgetful; བསྙེལ་མེད *bsñel med* not forgetting, not minding; ཐུགས་མི་སྐྱོ་མི་བསྙེལ་དང་རང་ཡུལ་ལགས་པས་འགྲོན་པ་ཞུ (*Ñag. 30*) སྙེལ་གསོ་བ *sñel-gso-wa* to remind, to put one in mind of a thing.

བསྙེལ་བ་མེད་པ *bsñel-wa med-pa* नास्ति सुषिता there is no oblivion; or नास्ति सुदिता there is no gladness. བསྙེལ་བའི་བརྗེད་པ forgetfulness.

བསྙོགས *bsñogs* = དྭངས་པོ་མེད་པ *dbañs po med pa* not clear, not sparkling; ཆུ་བསྙོགས *chu-bsñogs* turbid, dirty water (*Situ. 75*).

བསྙོད་པ *bsñod-pa* to give to one another: སྤགས་ཀྱི་སྐྱུ་གང་ཟས་བསྙོད *spags-gi skyu-gañ zas-bsñod* (*Ñag. 3*).

བསྙོན་ཅན *bsñon can* = མི་སྲིད་པ *mi srid pa*, གཞན་ལ་བསྙོན་ཏོ *gshan-la bsñon-to* (*Situ. 75*).

བསྙོན་ཏོལ *bsñon-tol* = བསྙོན་ཅན *bsñon-can* (*Zam. 10*).

བསྙོན་དོར *bsñon-dor* = བསྙོན་ཅན *bsñon-can* (*Ñag. 30*).

བསྙོན་མེད *bsñon-med* untrue or false: སྦུགས་འབྱར་བསྙོན་མེད་ཅི་ཡིན་ལ *sbugs-hbyar bsñon-med ci yin la* (*D. çel. 7*).

བསྙོར་བ *bsñor-wa* to sort, sift, divide: ནས་སོགས་ལག་པས་མར་བསྙོར *nas-sogs lag-pas mar bsñor* separates the butter from the barley, etc., with his hands (*Ñag. 30*).

ཏ

ཏ *ta* I: is the ninth letter of the Tibetan alphabet corresponding to the Sanskrit letter त; it has practically the pronunciation of an English *t*.

ཏ II: 1. as a num. fig. it represents 9. 2. in Budh.: (*a*) ཏ་ཤེས་པ་ནི་ཆོས་ཐམས་ཅད་ཀྱི་སྒོ་སྟེ *ta shes-pa ni chos thams-cad-kyi sgo-ste* the letter called ཏ is a door of admission to all things (*Bum.* ཀ *283*); (*b*) ཏ་ནི་ཐ་སྙད་མེད་པའི་སྒོ, བརྗོད་པ་མེད་པས་ཐམས་ཅད་གྲོལ *ta-ni tha-sñad med-pahi sgo, brjod-pa med-pas thams-cad grol,* ཏ is a symbol of that which is free from grammatical rules or pedantry; without being uttered it liberates all (*K. g.* ཕ *42*).

ཏ་སྡེ *ta-sde* तवर्ग the four letters classed under ཏ, viz., ཏ, ཐ, ད, ན.

ཏ་ཡིག *ta-yig* तकार the letter ཏ.

ཏ་ཀ་རི *ta ka-ri* (Hindi) scales for weighing (in *Ld.*) (*Jä.*).

ཏ་ཀུ *Ta-ku* in *W.* 1. n. of a place and fort in N. China. 2. stick with a hook; a hooked-cane; a crutch. 3. crooked, contracted, crippled (*Jä.*).

‡ ཏ་གར *ta-gar* तगर n. of a flower; also of a city in ancient India.

ཏ་གིར *ta-gir* in *W.* bread; esp. the flat bread-cakes of India (*Jä.*).

ཏ་ཇ *ta-ja* a kind of Chinese tea imported into Tibet (*Rtsii.*).

ཏ་བག *ta-bag,* in *W.* ཐ་བག *tha-bag,* in Tsang a plate; ཏ་བག་སྐོར་སྐོར *ta-bag skor-skor* a soup plate, a round deep plate (*Jä.*).

ཏ་བེར *ta-ber* in *W.* a fence of boards or laths (*Jä.*).

‡ ཏ་མཱ་ལ *ta-mā la* तमाल, सिन्धुवार n. of tree with a very dark bark and white blossoms, *Xanthochymus pictorius*; also the small tree *Vitex negundo.*

Syn. དབང་པོའི་ཆང་ *dwañ-pohi chañ*; ནག་པོ་ཕུང་པོ *nag-po phuñ-po*; མུན་པ་འཛིན *mun-pa hdsin*; མཚོ་ཅན *mtsho-can*; དབང་པོ་ཅན *dwañ-po can*; མཚོ་མཆོག *mtsho-mchog* (*Mñon.*).

ཏ་མ་ལའི་ལོ་མ *ta-ma-lahi lo-ma* तमालपत्र lit. the leaf of *Tamāla* tree, acc. to *Lex.* with flowers supposed to be very acceptable to gods as offerings from their devotees (*Bum.* ཀ *17*). ཏ་མའི་བཅུད *ta-mahi bcud* or ཏ་མ་ལའི་བཅུད *ta-ma-lahi bcud* तमालरस the juice or elixir extracted from the fruit of *Tamāla.*

‡ ཏ་ཟིག *Ta-zig* for སྟག་གཟིག *stag-gzig* Persia, *i.e.*, the country of the Tajik people.

ཏ་ཟུང *to-zuñ* सुचिविन्द a flower.

ཏ་ཡས *ta-yas* नेत्र a number in Buddhist astrology.

* ཏ་ར་ནཱ་ཐ *Ta-ra nā-tha* तारानाथ n. of one of the historiographers of Tibet whose རྒྱ་གར་ཆོས་འབྱུང "Rise of Indian Buddhism" has been translated into German. He

was known by the name of ཇོ་ནང་ཏཱ་ར་ནཱ་ཐ or རྗེ་བཙུན་ཏཱ་ར་ནཱ་ཐ Tāranātha of the Jonang sect; his religious name was ཀུན་དགའ་སྙིང་པོ *Kun-dgaḥ ṣñiñ-po.* He is supposed to be still undergoing re-births in the person of each successive chief of the lamas of the Mongols who resides in great state at Urga on the Siberian border.

‡ ཏ་ར་ནི *ta-ra ni* तरणी a kind of flower (*K. ko.* ཀ *4*); a species of rose, *Rosa glandulifera* (*K. d.* བ *126*).

‡ ཏ་རུ་ཀ *ta-ru-ka* तरुक or more properly ཏུ་རུ་ཀ *tu-ru-ka* तुरुष्क Turkistan: ཟེར་གཅིག་གིས་མཐའ་ཏ་རུ་ཀའི་ཕོ་བྲང་ལ་ཕོག་པས *zer gcig-giṣ mthaḥ Ta-ru kaḥi pho-brañ-la phog-paṣ* (*A. 19*) one of the rays at length having fallen on the palace of Turkistan.

ཏ་རེ *ta-re*, v. རེ *re*.

‡ ཏ་ལ *ta-la* ताल the palmyra tree, *Borassus flabelliformis*: ཏ་ལ་ཤིང་བཅད་ན་སླར་སྐྱེ་བ་མ་ཡིན *Ta-la-çiñ ḅcaḍ-na ṣlar ṣkye-wa ma-yin* if the palmyra tree be cut it does not grow again (*K. my.* ཀ *228*).

‡ ཏ་ལ་ལ *ta la-la* उल्का, = སྒྲོན་མེ *ṣgron-me* lamp, lantern; a meteor. ཏ་ལ་ལའི་མདོ *ta la-laḥi ṃdo* n. of a *Sūtra* in the Kah-gyur.

ཏ་ལའི་རྐང་པ་ཅན *ta-laḥi ṛkañ-pa can* lit. one with palm legs, *i.e.*, legs erect, *i.e.*, a human being (*Mñon.*).

ཏ་ལའི་རྒྱལ་པོ *ta-laḥi ṛgyal-po* v. བེ་ཏ་ཤིང *be ta-çiñ* the cane, *Calamus rotung*; also acc. to some authors: ན་རི་ཀེལ (नारिकेल) the cocoanut tree, "so called because of its being tall and majestic like the palm and more graceful than it" (*Mñon.*).

ཏ་ལའི་འདབ *ta-laḥi ḥdab* palm leaf.

ཏ་ལའི་སྨྱུ་གུའམ་ཡལ་ག *ta-laḥi myu-guḥam yal-ga* branch or stalk of the palm.

ཏཱ་ལེ་བླ་མ *Ta-le ḅla-ma* the name by which the Grand Lama of Lhasa is known in Mongolia and China. His Tibetan designation is རྒྱལ་བ་རིན་པོ་ཆེ *Ṛgyal-wa Rin-po-che* which seems to be sounded throughout Tibet as "*Gye-wa Rimpoche.*" The Mongol term, really spelt Dalai Lama, signifies "ocean lama."

ཏ་སི་གི་ས *ta-si gi-sa* a kind of satin (*Jig.*).

ཏ་ཧུན *ta-hun* red Chinese satin (*Jig.*).

ཏཱ་བོ་ཐཱ *Tā-bo-thā* n. of a large and lofty chorten at *Riḅo ṛtse-ḷña* in W. China. During the days of Buddha Kās'yapa a certain king named As'vaka is said with the help of the demons to have erected in one night 84,000 *caitya* which all contained relics of past Buddhas. One of these is said to have been located at Tābothā near *Riḅo ṛtse-ḷña*.

ཏཱ་མིང *Tā-miñ* (in Chinese ཏཱ *tā* great, མིང *miñ* n. of a family) the great Ming dynasty overthrown in 1643 A.D. by Shunte, the founder of the reigning Manchu dynasty of China. ཏཱ་མིང་གྱུང་ལོ་རྒྱལ་པོ *Tā-miñ gyuñ-lo ṛgyal-po* Emperor Yunglo of the Ming dynasty who greatly encouraged lamaism and sent an invitation to Tsong-khapa to visit China.

ཏཱ་ཚྭ *tā-tshwa* also ཏཱ་ཚྭང *tā-tshwañ* are two kinds of Chinese tea greatly used in Tibet.

‡ ཏཱ་ལི་ཀ *tā-li ka* n. of a goddess; a mystic word for a *ḍākinī*. ཏཱ་ལི་ཀ་ནི་མཁའ་འགྲོ་མའོ Tālika is a kha-do-ma fairy (*K. g.* ཕ *28*).

ཏཱ་ལའི་ཕྲེང་བ *Tā-laḥi phreṅ-wa* n. of a fabulous mountain situated five thousand *yojana* beyond the southern ocean. ཏཱ་ལའི་ཕྲེང་བ་ཞེས་བྱ་བའི་རི་རིང་དུ་དཔག་ཚད་སྟོང་ཕྲག་ལྔ། (*K. d.* ར *275*).

† ཏཀ་ཤ་ཤི་ལ *Tak-ṣa çi-la* तक्षशिला; རྡོ་འཇོག the capital of the Panjab in ancient India, visited by Alexander the Great; the Taxila of the Greeks. The name Takshaçi-la frequently occurs in *K. d.* ཤ.

ཏག་ཏག *tag-tag* in *W.* the imitative sound of knocking. ཏག་ཏག་ཟེར there is a knock (*Jä.*).

ཏང་ *taṅ* through, v. ཏོང་ and ལྟེང་ *lteṅ* (*Jä.*).

ཏང་ཀུན *taṅ-kun* root used to allay inflammation of the heart and fever: ཏང་ཀུན་སྙིང་གི་ཚད་པ་དུག་ནད་སེལ།

† ཏཏ་ཀཱ་ལ *tat kā-la* तत्काल;=དེའི་དུས *deḥi-dus* or དུས་སྦྱོར *dus-sbyor* at that time; the occasion; a sequence of happy moments; acc. to *Jä.* the present moment.

ཏན་དུར *tan-dur Ld.*, a hard cake or bread, resembling biscuit or rusk (*Jä.*).

ཏབ་ཏབ་པོར *tab-tab-por* 1. समधम suddenly: ཏབ་ཏབ་པོར་མི་གསུང་བའི་ཕྱིར་མ་ཏབས་པའོ he tapped so as not to speak suddenly. 2. v. ཏོབ་ཏོབ *tob-tob*.

ཏར་ཏར *tar-tar* in *Ld.*, smooth or even under pressure (as wrinkles or folds in cloth, paper, etc., are removed).

ཏར་བུ *tar-bu* (སྨིན་པ *smin-pa*) ཙུ་ཀ *tsu-ka?*

ཏལ་པ *tal-pa* or ཏལ་མ *tal-ma* acc. to *Cs.* a moment. ཏལ་པར *tal-par* or ཏལ་མར *tal-mar* 1. instantly, immediately, quickly: ཏལ་པར་སོང་ *tal-par soṅ* go quickly, without delay; སྤྱན་སྔར་ཏལ་གྱི་བྱོན *spyan-sṅar tal-gyi byon* went before him quickly. 2. acc. to *Sch.* completely, quite, thorough; ཏལ་པར་གཅོད་པ *tal-par gcod-pa* to cut quite through; ཏལ་མར་འབིགས་པ *tal-mar ḥbigs-pa* also ཏལ་འབིགས་པ *tal ḥbigs-pa* to bore through, to perforate.

ཏལ་བ *tal-wa* a tool with holes in it used by nailers (*Sch.*).

ཏི *ti* 1. represents num. fig. 39. 2. not originally Tibetan, designating water; has found its way into *Ld.* in ཁ་ཏི *kha-ti* saliva (water of the mouth) and སྣ་ཏི *sna-ti* water from the nose. 3. v. སྤྱི *spyi Jä.*

† ཏི་ཀ *ti-ka* used for ཊཱི་ཀཱ *ṭi-kā* (टीका) explanation, commentary.

† ཏི་སྐག *ti-skag* सारिका a bird, said to be the Indian mynah.

+ ཏི་སྒ *ti-sga* chopped meat (in Sikk.).

† ཏི་ཏི་བྷ *ti-ti bha* तित्तिभ n. of an insect, cochineal (*K. d.* ཟ *462*).

† ཏི་ཏྲིག *ti-trig* (བྱིའུ *byiḥu*), तित्तिरि the francoline partridge, a small bird (*Rtsii.*).

ཏི་ཐུག *ti-thug* (acc. to *Sch.* གཏི་ཐུག *gti-thug*) bad, mean, silly (*Cs.*); obstinate, stubborn (*Schtr.*).

ཏི་ནག *ti-nag* heath-cock (*Sch.*).

† ཏི་པུ་རི *ti-pu-ri* त्रिपुरी the modern Tippera in East Bengal; ཤར་ཕྱོགས་ཏི་པུ་རིའི་ཡུལ་གྱི་རྒྱལ་པོ་ཞིག་ཡིན (he) was a king of the country of Tipuri in the eastern quarter (*K. dun. 13*).

ཏི་ཕུ *ti-phu* pigeon; acc. to *Sch.* ཏི་ཕུ་མཇུག་རིང་ *ti-phu mjug-riṅ* the long-tailed pheasant.

ཏི་བྱི *ti-byi* n. of a giant sea-fish: རྒྱ་མཚོ་ན་ཏི་བྱི་ཞེས་བྱ་བས་རྐང་བཅས་དང་ མཐོང་བར་དཀའ་བས་མི་འབྱིང

མི་ནུབ་པ་ལྟར just as the fish called the *Tibyi* liking to see light or rays does not sink below (*K. my.* ཁ *357*).

‡ ཏི་མུ་ས *ti-mu-sa* n. of a plant (prob. तिमिष *Benincasa cerifera*): ཏི་མུ་ས་ཡིས་འཁྲུ་བ་གཅོད་པར་བྱེད *ti-mu-sa-yiṣ ḫkhru-wa gcoḏ-par byeḏ* the plant *Timusa* (used medicinally) stops diarrhœa.

卐 ཏི་ཙ *ti-tsa* 1. a mineral drug; ཏི་ཙ་དཀར་པོའི་དུད་པས་མིག་ལ་ཕན *ti-tsa ḏkar-poḫi duḏ-paṣ mig-la phan* the smoke of white *Ti-tsa* is useful for the eyes. 2. (acc. to *Sch.* = ཏུ་ཚ *tu-tsha*) an anvil.

ཏི་རྩེ *Ti-ṟtse* or ཏི་སེ *Ti-se* n. of a three-peaked mountain (fabulously described in Buddhist works) lying north of the Himalayas near Manasarowar lake. Beyond its northern flanks is the residence of Viruḍhaka the guardian king of the West. ཏི་རྩེ་ཞེས་བྱ་བའི་རི་དཔག་ཚད་ལྔ་བརྒྱ་པ་གངས་ཅན་རིའི་བྱང་ངོས་ནས་རིང་དུ་འདས་པ་ན་ཡོད། the mountain called Ti-ṟtse five hundred *yojana* long is situated at a distance from and on the north of the Himavat mountains (*K. d.* ར *287*). Under the name གངས་ཏི་སེ there is a long account in Milaraspa's Gurbum of a contest between a Bon priest and the author for jurisdiction over the mountain. In modern days Tise or Kailas is still an object of pilgrimage; and four monasteries stand on its flanks. During the past 100 years only two Europeans have reached the neighbourhood of this famous mountain; Moorcroft in 1812, and Lieut. Strachey in 1846. Its height in the main peak is about 22,300 ft. above sea-level.

ཏི་ཚ *ti-tsha* 1. same as ཏི་ཙ, of which there seem to be two kinds, the white and the yellow: ཏི་ཚ་སེར་པོས་རྨ་འཇུབ་མིག་ལ་ཕན (*Mṅg.*) the yellow *titsha* absorbs sores and cures eye disease. 2. a musical instrument, constructed of metal (*Sch.*).

ཏི་རུག *ti-rug* the Indian rupee (in Sikk.).

‡ ཏི་ལ *ti-la* तिल sesamum.

‡ ཏི་ལ་ཀ་ནཱ་ཐ *Ti-la-ka nā-tha* त्रिलोकनाथ n. of a Brahmanical sanctuary of Mahādeva near Nāhri.

‡ ཏི་ལོ་པ *Ti lo-pa* or ཏི་ལླི་པ *Til-li-pa* त्रिलोप n. of an Indian Buddhist sage born in Chittagong, East Bengal, in the beginning of the 10th century A.D. His religious name was Prajñā bhadra (in Tib. *Çeṣ-rab bzań-po*). He was called Tillipa or Tilopa by the Tibetans, on account of his having done the work of thrashing sesamum for oil. རྒྱ་གར་གྱི་གྲུབ་ཐོབ་ཆེན་པོ, བོད་པས་ཏི་ལོ་པ་ཟེར, ཏིལ་བརྡུང་གི་བྱ་བ་མཛད་པས་ཏི་ལླི་པར་གྲགས, མཚན་དངོས་པྲ་ཛྙཱ་བྷ་དྲ་ཤེས་རབ་བཟང་པོ, ཤར་ཕྱོགས་བང་ག་ལའི་ཙ་ཏི་ག་རོ་ཞེས་བྱ་བའི་གྲོང་ཁྱེར་དུ་བྲམ་ཟེའི་རིགས་སུ་འཁྲུངས་ཤིང་། (*K. dun. 31*).

ཏིག *tig* 1. a fluid measure, five སྐྱོགས་ལྔ *ṣkyogṣ* or five *ḏkar-tshaḏ* make one *tig* (*Ṟtsii.*). ཏིག་གང *tig-gań* one *tig* measure. 2. in Sikk. the great hornet (*Jä.*). 3. to be sure; ཡང་ཏིག really, in fact, surely.

‡ ཏིག་ཏ *tig-ta* तिक्तक, किरात-तिक्त, चिर-तिक्त 1. the stalks of a bitter plant *Gentiana chiretta* growing in the Himalayas, largely used as an antidote against fever and liver complaints: རྒྱ་ཏིག་བོད་ཏིག་བལ་ཏིག་གསུམ, ཏིག་ཏ་རྣམ་པ་གསུམ་ཞེས་བྱ, ཏིག་ཏས་མཁྲིས་པའི་ཚ་བ་མ་ལུས་སེལ (*Miñ.*) there are three species of chiretta, Indian *tigta*, Tibetan *tigta*, and Nepal *tigta*; it cures all kinds of bilious fever. 2. n. of several trees and plants, viz., *Trichosanthes disica*, *Agathotes chirayta*, *Terminalia catappa*, the last growing in Tibet.

ཏིག་པོ་ *tig-po*=བརྟན་པ་ or གོ་ཆོད་པ steady, useful: ཁོ་བོ་ལ་མིའི་ཏིག་པོ་མི་བརྙེད་པས having not got an intelligent steady man (*A. 123*).

ཏིག་མེན *tig-men* (in *Ld.* ཏིག་རྩེ) ribands wound round the felt gaiters that cover the lower part of the legs (*Jä.*).

ཏིག་ཚ *tig-tsha*=ཏི་ཙ *ti-tsa*.

ཏིང་ *tiṅ* or ཡོན་ཆབ་ཀྱི་ཏིང་ *yon chab-kyi tiṅ* 1. cups made of silver, bell-metal, brass, or copper to hold oblation water which are placed before the images of deities in Buddhist chapels. 2. the sound of metal. 3. तान a note of cadence introductory to a song, etc. ཇོ་བོའི་ཞལ་འཛུམ་ནག་ཏིང་གིས་མཛད་ནས a repellent smile of the Jo-bo having been signified by the sound of a *ting*.

ཏིང་ངེ་འཛིན *tiṅ-ṅe-ḥdsin* समाधि, समथ acc. to *Was.* समापत्ति, intense contemplation, profound meditation, perfect absorption of thought into the object of meditation. (cf. བསམ་གཏན ध्यान, and སྒོམ་པ भावना) ཏིང་ངེ་འཛིན་བྱེད་པ=ཏིང་ངེ་འཛིན་དུ་འཇུག་པ to be absorbed in deep and devout meditation; ཏིང་ངེ་འཛིན་འཁྲུངས *tiṅ-ṅe-ḥdsin ḥkhruṅs* devout meditation took place; also meton. the faculty, the power of meditating (*Jä.*).

ཏིང་ངེ་འཛིན་གྱི་དཀྱིལ་འཁོར *tiṅ ṅe-ḥdsin-gyi dkyil-ḥkhor* समाधिमण्डल the mystic circle which is described on the place one occupies when meditating; a circle of meditation.

ཏིང་ངེ་འཛིན་གྱི་རྒྱལ་པོ *tiṅ ṅe-ḥdsin-gyi rgyal-po* समाधिराज n. of a Mahāyāna Sūtra contained in the Kahgyur, *Mdo* section, marked *ta-pa*.

ཏིང་ངེ་འཛིན་གྱི་ཟས་ཀྱིས་འཚོ་བ *tiṅ ṅe-ḥdsin-gyi zas-kyis ḥtsho-wa* living on the food of contemplation: བསྐལ་པ་མང་པོའི་བར་དུ་ཏིང་ངེ་འཛིན་གྱི་རོའི་ཟས་ཀྱིས་འཚོ་ཞིང་སེམས་རབ་ཏུ་ཞི་བས་ཅི་ལ་མི་ཆགས་པར་བདེ་བར་གནས་སོ། he being happily not attached to anything, the mind being at peace by tasting the food of contemplation during great periods of time (*K. d.* ཇ *362*).

ཏིང་ངེ་འཛིན་དགུ *tiṅ ṅe-ḥdsin dgu* the nine meditations of a *Bodhisattva*, are:—(1) रत्नसमुद्गत, རིན་ཆེན་ཀུན་ཏུ་འཕགས complete coming forth of jewels; (2) सुप्रतिष्ठ, ཤིན་ཏུ་གནས་པ well-established; (3) अकम्प; མི་གཡོ་བ unagitated; (4) अविनिवर्तनीय; ཕྱིར་མི་ལྡོག་པ not liable to return; (5) रत्नाकर; དཀོན་མཆོག་འབྱུང་གནས abode or mine of jewels; (6) सूर्य-प्रभातेजः, ཉི་མའི་འོད་ཀྱི་གཟི་བརྗིད brilliance like sunshine; (7) सर्वार्थसिद्ध, དོན་ཐམས་ཅད་གྲུབ་པ successful in effecting all objects; (8) ज्ञानालोक, ཡེ་ཤེས་སྣང་བ light of knowledge; (9) प्रत्युत्पन्न बुद्ध सम्मुखावस्थितसमाधि, ད་ལྟར་གྱི་སངས་རྒྱས་མངོན་སུམ་བཞུགས་པའི་ཏིང་ངེ་འཛིན་ནི meditation attained in presence of the future Buddha.

ཏིང་ངེ་འཛིན་རྣམ་གསུམ *tiṅ-ṅe-ḥdsin rnam-gsum* the three kinds of ཏིང་ངེ་འཛིན acc. to Bon rules are:—(1) དེ་བཞིན་ཉིད་ཀྱི་ཏིང་ངེ་འཛིན་གཞི་ཡི་གནས་ལུགས་ཁྱབ་གདལ; (2) རབ་ཏུ་སྣང་བའི་ཏིང་ངེ་འཛིན་འགྲོ་ལ་ཚད་མེད་བཞི་སྐྱེད་པར; (3) རྒྱུའི་ཏིང་ངེ་འཛིན་ཡིག་འབྲུ་གནས་སུ་དག་པ་ལ་ལྷ་བསྐྱེད་པར (*D.R.*).

ཏིང་རྗིང *tiṅ-rjiṅ* a n. given to several species of shrew in Sikkim.

ཏིང་ཏི་ལིང *tiṅ-ti liṅ* acc. to *Jä.* a snipe (*Ld.*).

ཏིང་ཏིང་ *tiṅ-tiṅ* 1. is an auxiliary (ཚིག་གྲོགས) to another word to intensify its meaning (རྒྱས་སྐྱེད་བྱེད་པ to emphasize it); ནག་ཏིང་ཏིང་ *nag tiṅ-tiṅ* intensely black, jet black. 2. acc. to *Jä.* clean, well-swept (*Ld.*; *Ts.*).

ཏིང་ཏིང་མ *tiṅ-tiṅ-ma* n. of a small bird: ཕྱིའུ་མཆུ་རིང་མ་དང་ཏིང་ཏིང་མ་ཞེས་བ་གཉིས་འདུག་པས། there were two small birds, one called *mchu-riṅ-ma* (the long-beak) and another *tiṅ-tiṅ-ma*.

ཏིང་ཏིང་ཤག། *tiṅ tiṅ-çag* or ཏིང་ཤགས 1. a kind of cymbal. 2. little bell moved by the wind (*Sch.*).

+ ཏིང་ཏུ་ཀ *tiṅ-tu ka*=ཤིང་ཏིག་གི་ཤིང་ a tree, prob. the tamarind (*K. ko.* ཀ *3*).

‡ ཏིང་དུ་ཀ *tiṅ-du ka* तिन्दुकः n. of one of two trees *Diospyros embryopteris* or *Diospyros glutinosa*; a *Karsa* is said to= the weight of the Tinduka fruit.

ཏིབ་རིལ *tib-ril* resp. གསོལ་ཏིབ in *W.*= tea-pot; ཟངས་ཏིབ copper tea-pot; རྫ་ཏིབ an earthen tea-pot (*Jä.*).

ཏིམ་པི *tim-pi* goat's leather, kid-leather from India, dyed green or blue (*Jä.*).

ཏིམ་པི་ཅ *tim-bi ca* horse imported into Tibet from India.

ཏིམ་བི *tim-bi* (*Ts.*) funnel.

‡ ཏིར་ཧུ་ཏ *Tir-hu-ta* modern Tirhut: ཡུལ་ཡངས་པ་ཅན་ནས་ཤར་ཕྱོགས་སུ་མི་རིང་བ་ན་ཏིར་ཧུ་ཏ་ཞེར་བའི་ཡུལ་ཡོད at not long di tance from Yang-pa-chan towards the east is the country called Tirhuta (*Dsam.*).

‡ ཏིལ *til* तिल sesamum; ཏིལ་དཀར *til-dkar* white sesamum; ཏིལ་ནག *til-nag* black sesamum; ཏིལ་གྱི་ཕྱེ *til-gyi phye* powdered sesamum; ཏིལ་སྙིགས་མ *til sñigs-ma* mixed sesamum; a so an inferior quality of sesamum; ཏིལ་བརྡུངས *til-brduṅs* तिलम्भुट thrashed or beaten sesamum [also a sesamum-grinder]*S*.

ཏིལ་མར *til-mar* तैल sesame oil, seed-oil.

ཏིལ་སེར་ཅན *til ser-can* उरण, पिण्या, ग्रहि n. of a medicine; the plant *Cassia alata* or *Cardiospermum halicacabum* (*Mṅon.*).

ཏུ *tu* 1. num. fig. 68. 2. an affix denoting the terminative case, generally used to express direction to, as represented by the English "into" or "unto;" it is joined to the final consonants ག, ད, and བ, as in ཐོག་ཏུ *thog-tu*; མཇུག་ཏུ *mjug-tu*; རྒྱབ་ཏུ *rgyab-tu*; གསེབ་ཏུ *gseb-tu*; also after what is called དདྲག *da-drag* as in the words:— ཀུནད་ཏུ *kund-tu*; ཕ་རོལད་ཏུ *pha rold-tu*; ཐརད་ཏུ *thard-tu*, cf. དུ *du*, རུ *ru*, སུ *su*.

‡ ཏུ་རུ་ཀ *tu-ru-ka* तुरुष्क the Turks, sometimes used historically as a general term for Mahomedans.

ཏུ་ཙ *tu-tsa*, v. ཏི་ཙ *ti-tsa*.

ཏུག་གིས *tug-gis* suddenly; as if by surprise: ནགས་ཚལ་གླིང་ལ་ལམ་དུ་ཏུག་གིས་འཕྲད I suddenly met him on the way to the forest land (*D.R.*).

ཏུག་རིང *tug-riṅ* or ཏུག་ཆུམ *dug-chum* prob. =ཏུག་ཆེམ *tug-chem* (*Cs.*) noise of a wooden rattle; also of the trotting of horses heard in the distance (*Sch.*).

ཏུབ་ཏུག *tub-tug* either, or: whether I be able (to do it) or not (*Lex.* and *Sch*).

ཏུར་ཆུང *tur-chuṅ* hardly any, nothing definite, little clearly: སེམས་ལ་རེ་དོགས་ཏུར་ཆུང་ཡོད *sems-la re-dogs tur-chuṅ yod* in his mind he entertained hardly any hope or fear (*D.R.*).

‡ ཏུར་ཏུར *tur-tur* त्वरा 1. quickly, with haste, swiftly: ཏུར་ཏུར་བྱེད་པ *tur-tur byed-pa*= ལས་མྱུར་དུ་བྱེད་པ *las myur-du byed-pa* to do work quickly (*Mṅon.*). 2. also defined as སྣང་བ་ལ་དཀར་ཁྲ་དམར་ཁྲ་ཤར་བ appearing white spotted or red-spotten (to the mind or in vision).

ཏུར་ཕོག་པ *tur phog-pa*=ལྷོང་ཕོག་པ *lhoṅ-phog-pa* or ཙང་ཙད་ཞེབས་པ slightly affected.

ཏུར་བ *tur-wa* in W. Tib. to darn (stockings) (*Jä.*).

ཏུར་མེན *tur-men* (Chinese) one at a time in order or in a row.

ཏུར་རེ *tur-re* clear, distinct; cog. to ཝལ་ལེ *wal-le:* ཡིད་ཏུར་རེ་འདུག it is clear to my mind; ཏུར་རེ་བཟུང་ *tur-re bzuṅ* prob. watch it! have a sharp eye upon it! (*Jä.*). ཞེ་སྡང་འབངས་རྟགས་ཏུར་རེ་གྱིས take care lest an emotion of anger arises in your mind! ཏུར་གྱིས་སད prob. he awakes, stirs, is evidently roused; ཏུར་རེ་བ *tur-re-wa* adj. (or abstract noun): རྗེད་ཡེང་མེད་པར་ཏུར་རེ་བ *rjed-yeṅ med-par tur-re-wa* clear, firm with regard to perceptions, opinions, etc., without omissions or digression (*Jä.*).

✢ ཏུ་ཪྻཱ་བྷ་བ་ནི *Tur-yā Bha-wa-ni* n. of image of Ārya Tārā in a temple situated on the bank of Godāvarī, and famed for its sanctity througout India (*Dsam.*).

ཏུལ་དྲི་ཅན *tul dri-can* (prob. རུལ་དྲི་ཅན *rul dri-can*) पुतिगन्ध putrid, of offensive smell.

ཏུལ་བ *tul-wa*=དགོད་པ *dgod-pa* to laugh (mystic) (*K. gu.* ཁ *26*).

ཏེ *te* ཀྷ 1. num. fig. 99. 2. an affix denoting the gerund, and used after the final letters ན, ར, ལ, ས ; in subordinate sentences may be conveniently rendered by: when, after, as, etc.; and also used as a finite tense and in that case followed by འདུག or ཡོད or sometimes without any auxiliary. May be also denominated a continuative particle.

ཏེ་གྲེར n. of a place in Upper Tibet.

✢ ཏེ་པོར *te-por*=ལེགས་པར *legs-par* अस, अतिमात्रा 1. excellent, noble, intense, strong. 2. acc. to *Sch.* very, really, actually: ཏེ་བོར་དྲག་པ *te-wor drag-pa* (གྲོས་མི་ལྷ་བུ really good (adviser).

Syn. ཤིན་ཏུ *çin-tu*, དམ་པ *dam-pa*, སྲ་བ *sra-wa*, དྲག་པ *drag-pa*, ཚབ་ཆེ་བ *tshab che-wa* (*Mṅon.*).

ཏེ་བོར *te-wor* acc. to *Sch.* constantly, continually.

ཏེ་ལོ *te-lo* n. of a bird: ཏེ་ལོའི་ཀླད་པས་དུག་དང་སྙིང་བཅས་སེལ། the brains of the *Telo* cures (the effect) of poison applied and heart disease.

ཏེ་སེ *Te-se* 1. n. of a demi-god of the nether regions: ས་བདག་ཐེ་སེ་རྒྱལ་པོའི་སྲས the son of Thésé king of the Sadag demons. 2. v. ཏི་སེ.

ཏེའུ *tehu* (*Ld. Glr.*) (*Schtl f. 25. b.*); ཏེའུ་སེར་པོ *tehu ser-po* (*Mil. 59, 4* of *Jä.* edition); ཏེའུ་ཤིང་ཁྲི *tehu çiṅ-khri* acc. to *Sch.* a square table.

ཏེག་པ *teg-pa*=འཇེགས་པ to pack up, put up; to put in or into: ཨམ་ཕྲག་ལ་ཏེག put into your breast-pocket.

ཏེལ་པ *tel-pa* acc. to *Cs.* an instrument for burning; ལྕགས་ཏེལ a burning instrument made of iron.

✢ ཏཻ་ལིཾ་ག *Tai liṅ-ga* the modern Telingana, the birth place of the Buddhist sage and author Dignāga: དཔལ་ཕྱོགས་ཀྱི་གླང་པོའི་འཁྲུངས་ས་ཏཻ་ལིཾ་ག་ཞེར་ཡོད་པ there is Tailiṅga the birthplace of S'ri Dignāga (*Dsam.*).

ཏོ *to* 1. num. for 129. 2. (styled རྫོགས་ཚིག) an affix added to certain verbs when they terminate a sentence.

ཏོ་ཏོ་ལིང་ལིང་ *to-to liṅ-liṅ W.* an adverb denoting a swinging motion (*Jä.*).

ཏོག *tog* केतु, केतन, पद्म, ललाम the top of anything, a top ornament; esp. the button on the cap of the Tibetan and Chinese dignitaries, as a mark of distinction; ཏོག་དཀར *tog-dkar* श्वेत-केतु the name by which Gautama Buddha was known in the Tuṣita heaven before his last incarnation. རྒྱལ་མཚན་གྱི་ཏོག *rgyal-mtshan-gyi tog* the top-point of a banner; ཞྭ་མོའི་ཏོག *shba-mohi tog* the point of a helmet or Chinese cap. In medical works ཏོག *tog* signifies སྙིང་ཁུ or སྙིང་པོ essence, pith. མདུང་ཏོག the point of a spear. སྐབས་ཏོག=now, at present (in *Ld.*) (*Jä.*).

ཏོག་གེ *tog-ge* (འབྲུ་སྣོར་སྣོད) wicker work vessel for grain, ཊོ་ཀ་ནི *ṭo-ka ni* टोकनी (*Mṅon.*).

ཏོག་སྒྲ *tog-sgra* or ཏོག་ཏོག་སྒྲ any cracking or snapping sound.

ཏོག་ཅན *tog-can* स्तम्भ a pillar with a capital.

ཏོག་ཏིལ *tog-til* a bump or swelling from a knock on the head (*Jä.*)

ཏོག་ཙེ *tog-tsc* (also called འཇོར or ས་རྐོ་བྱེད་ཀྱི་འཇོར) खनित्र hoe, mattock; ཏོག་ལྕགས *tog-lcags* the iron of the hoe. ཏོག་ཙེ་བརྐོས་པོ *tog-tse brkos-po* कौद्दालिक, कौद्दालिक one who digs soil with a hoe.

ཏོག་ཙེ་འཚོ་བ *tog-tse htsho-wa* one who lives by hoeing.

ཏོག་ཡུ *tog-yu* the handle of a hoe.

ཏོང་ཏོང་བྱེད་པ *toṅ-toṅ byed-pa* to perforate; also to produce a whirling noise with a whip.

ཏོབ་ཅི *tob-chi*, more properly ཐོབ་ཅི *thob-ci*, a button.

ཏོབ་ཏོབ་སྨྲ་བ *tob-tob smra-wa* to talk confusedly (*Sch.*).

ཏོའུ་ལོ *tohu-lo* the polecat.

ཏོལ་བ *tol-wa* 1. to arrive at, to reach: ཏོལ་མེད་སླེབས་ཀྱུ་མེད he did not arrive and is not coming. ཏོལ་ལོ v. ཏོལ་ལོ=ཕེབས་སོ arrived: ནམ་ཐུན་ཅིག་ལ་དཀའ་ཐུབ་ཀྱི་ནགས་སུ་མཆོད་རྟེན་རྣམ་དག་གི་དྲུང་དུ་ཏོལ་ལོ (*Yig*) in one watch of the night he arrived at *Chorten rnam-dag* (the *Chaitya* of purity) in the forest of *Dkaḥ-thub* (*i.e.*, Nirvana). *Sch.* quotes ཏོལ་གཅོད་པ)=ཏལ་གཅོད་པ.

ཏྲ *tra* (སྲག *srag*) मर्कट an ape.

ཏྲམ་པ *tram-pa* 1. hard, tough, stiff: ཤ་ཏྲམ tough meat; རུས་ཏྲམ hard bone; རྩ་ཏྲམ *rtsa-tram* tough muscle. 2. acc. to *Jä.* ཏྲམ་དཀར *tram-dkar*, ཏྲམ་ནག *tram-nag* are different species of gout.

ཏྲི *tri*=གཟུགས་ཅན *gzugs-can* शरीरी possessing form or body, anything that has form, a living being (mystic) (*K. gu.* ཁ *179*).

ཏྲི་ཀེད *tri-ked* ཊི་ཀེད *ṭi-ked*.

ཏྲི་པ་ཏི *tri-pa ti*=ཞུ་བ *shu-wa* a prayer, a petition (mystic) (*K. gu.* ཁ *26*).

† ཏྲི་པུ་རི *tri pu-ri*, གྲོང་གསུམ་པ त्रिपुरी the three cities, name of a part of Lan-kā (modern Ceylon); three strong cities of gold, silver, and iron, in the sky, air, and earth, built by Maya for a celebrated Asura, and burnt by S'iva (*Dus-ye. 40*).

ཏྲི་བ *tri-wa* उद्ग्रह taking up; any object that may be accomplished by religious acts.

ཏྲི་མ *tri-ma* a kind of bee the sting of which is very painful. It is said in Sikkim that an ox dies if he has received the sting of this bee seven times. The honey of this bee is claimed by the Raja of Sikkim as a duo from his subjects. ལྷ་ལྕམ་འདི་སྦྲང་བུ་ཏྲེ་མ་ཞེག་གི་ལུས་བླངས་ནས་ཡོད the princess is now living, having taken the body of the bee called *Tre-ma* (*Khrid*).

‡ ཏྲི་མེར *tri-mer* n. of a sweet-scented flower (*K. du.* ད *319*).

‡ ཏྲི་ཤ་ཀུ་ནཻ *tri-ça ku-nai* 1.=རྒྱུ་མཚན་གསུམ three reasons or signs. 2. n. of a holy place in Persia (*Duş-ye. 39*).

‡ ཏྲི་ཤུ་ལ *tri-çu-la* त्रिशूल trident.

ཏྲེ་ཏྲེ་ཧ *tre-tre-ha* (by the context) a dangerous disease of the stomach or a serious symptom of it (*Jä.*).

ཏྲེ་བ་ཅན *tre-wa-can* coloured (*Sch.*).

ཏྲེ་སམ *tre-sam* in ཏྲེས་སམ་སྨན་ཕྱེ་མ་གཞན་ཕྱེ་མའི་མིང་ *treş-sam şman phye-ma gshan phye-maḫi miñ* (*Liç.*); *tre-sam* is a medicine in the shape of a powder.

ཏྲེ་མེད་དུང་མཛེས *tre-med duñ-mdseş* n. of a king of Tibet of the Bon period (*Yig.*).

ཏྲེ་ཤོད་གངས་ཀྱི་ར་བ *Tre-çod gañş-kyi ra-wa* n. of a place in Kham, the birthplace of the seventh head of the Karma-pa sect (*Loñ.* ཀ *20*).

‡ ཏྲོན *tron* जोष 1. གཙུག་ལག་ཁང་དུ་དགེ་བསྐོས་ལ་བརྟེན་ནས་ལས་ཀྱི་གྲོགས་བྱེད་པའི་མིང་ (*K. du.* ཇ *399*) a monastic official; in old days an assistant superintendent of a Buddhist monastery whose position resembled that of the modern *dge-şkoş* (*q.v.*). 2. diligence, industry (*Cs.*); ཏྲོན་བྱེད་པ to be diligent, to exert one's self.

གཏག་གཏོང་ *gtag-gtoñ* (*Lex. w. e.*) གཏག་གཏོང་བ *gtag-gtoñ-wa* to disperse (*Sch.*).

གཏག་པ *gtag-pa* any species of white-flowering rhododendron, all of which kind are held by Tibetans to be of the male sex. གཏག་མ *gtag-ma* red-flowering rhododendrons, which are considered to be female shrubs.

གཏང་རག *gtañ-rag* thank, thanksgiving, and prob. also thank-offering, esp. rendering thanks to a deity; གཏང་རག་བྱེད་པ or གཏང་རག་འབུལ་བ to render thanks (*Jä.*).

གཏད *gtad* (v. གཏོད་པ *gtod-pa*) 1. in the direction of, towards: གཡོན་གྲལ་དུ་གཏད་ཕྱིན་ནས *gyon-gral du gtad phyin-naş* going towards the left end of the row. 2.=མནན་པ अभिचर to press, urge, v. གཏོད་པ also གཏད་པ. 3. sbst. steadiness, firmness; གཏད་པ་མེད it has no hold, no firmness; གཏད་མེད་འཆལ་བ to vacillate, to waver, to be unsteady.

གཏད་པ *gtad-pa* समर्पित; ཕུལ་བ *phul-wa* to be made over, entrusted to. In Buddhism there are four kinds of གཏད་པ *gtad-pa* :—(1) བློ་ཕུགས་ཆོས་ལ་གཏད; (2) ཆོས་ཕུགས་སྤྲང་ལ་གཏད; (3) སྤྲང་ཕུགས་ཤི་ལ་གཏད; (4) ཤི་ཕུགས་གྲོག་པོ་སྟོང་པར་གཏད (*Lo. 14*).

གཏད་རབས་བདུན *gtad-rabş bdun* the first seven (Buddhist) hierarchs in succession to Gautama Buddha. Mahā-kā-s'yapa is said to have succeeded Gautama. Kās'yapa entrusted the headship of the order to Ānanda; Sanavastri succeeded Ānanda; Ārya Upagupta followed Sanavastri, who in his turn gave the charge to Ārya Krishna. Dhitika succeeded Krishna and before his death appointed Ārya Sudars'ana to the Buddhist headship.

Note.—This order of succession is partly founded on Brahmanic tradition; and Buddhaghosha gives a different series.

གཏད་སོ *gtad-so* a refuge, resource; also store of provisions; གཏད་སོ་ཞག་པ prob. གཏེད་གསོགས་འཞག་པ to keep a store of food.

གཏན *gtan* I: a husband, a consort: གཏན་གྱི་རང་འགྲོས་མ་ཤེས་ན། དོན་ལ་བླ་མེད་ཀྱི་ཁྱོ་བོ་ཡིན། (*Lo. 28*).

གཏན II: 1. order, system. 2. put in order, arranged, reduced to a system. གཏན་ལ་ལྟ་ཁང་ན་གཏན་ལ་ཕབས་པའི་བོ་དོ་ཅན (*A. 126*).

གཏན་ཁྲ *gtan-khra*, གཏན་ཚིག་གི་ཡི་གེ་ཁྲམ་དཔྱད་མཚམས agreement, stipulation, convention; also order or decision passed; a decree; གཏན་ཁྲ་ཆེད་རིས important decrees (*D. çel. 7*).

གཏན་ཁྲིམས *gtan-khrims* established law.

གཏན་འཁེལ *gtan-ḥkhel* perfectly certain, quite sure.

གཏན་གྱི *gtan-gyi* constant, continual.

གཏན་གྱི་གྲོགས *gtan-gyi grogs* husband, a friend or partner for life (*Mñon.*).

གཏན་གླེང་འཁེལ་བ *gtan-gleñ ḥkhel-wa*=ལས་ཀ་བ་གང་ཅེད་དགོས་པ་དེ་ལ་ཆ་གནས་འདོག་པ to adhere resolutely or come to a decision on work or business; to work steadily. རང་སེམས་གཏན་པ *rañ-sems gtan-pa* in a mystic sense: to regulate, to fashion, to train, to set right.

གཏན་འཇག *gtan-ḥjag*=དུས་རྒྱུན་གནས་པ permanent, enduring, perpetually abiding (*Rtsii.*).

གཏན་དུ་བ *gtan du-wa*=རྟག་པ, བརྟན་པ to be or to make continual (*Mñon.*). As an adj. आत्यन्तिक complete; གཏན་དུ *gtan-du* always, continually, for ever.; གཏན་དུ་བཞུགས་པ living or residing continually.

གཏན་ལ་ཕབ་པ *gtan-la phab-pa* प्रश्ननिर्णय to decide a question.

གཏན་པ *gtan-pa* कपाट door-bar.

གཏན་ཕན *gtan-phan* केवलं only, alone; absolute; absolutely.

གཏན་ཕེབས *gtan-phebs* निश्चय explained by ཞིབ་ཞིབ་ཅུས་ཚད་པ་ གཏན་ལ་ཕེབས published after being thoroughly revised or completely got ready.

གཏན་ལ་འབེབས་པ *gtan-la-ḥbebs-pa* to put any matter into writing; to publish after the composition has been corrected; also to fix, to arrange.

གཏན་མེད *gtan-med* असत्वित: perishable; अत्यन्ताभाव without duration or continuation.

གཏན་ཚིགས *gtan-tshigs* (ཚིག་དང་དོན་ལ་འགྱུར་རྒྱུ་མེད་པ) 1. an expression of fixed meaning. 2. हेतु=རྟགས *rtags*; རྒྱུ་མཚན *rgyu-mtshan* not deviating from what has been first settled. 3. उपपत्ति, प्रत्यय, प्रमाण proof, demonstated conclusion.

གཏན་ཚིགས་མེད་པར་སྨྲ་བ *gtan-tshigs med-par smra-wa* to argue illogically; also irrational exposition.

གཏམ *gtam*=ཚིག་ལྷུ་ཐ or ཟློལ वृत्तान्त, कथा, वार्त्ता, आलाप, किलकथा 1. speech, conversation, talk. 2. news, tidings, intelligence, account of anything; also report, rumour: དེ་ཡུལ་འཁོར་བའི་གཏམ་རྒྱལ་པོས་ཐོས་ནས when the king heard the report that it had been given; ཐག་རིང་གི་གཏམ *thag-riñ-gi gtam* accounts of bygone events; བདག་གིས་གཏམ་དུ་ཐོས་ནས as I have learned, have been told (*Jä.*); གཏམ་གླེང་བ *gtam gleñ-wa* or གཏམ་དུ་གླེང་བ *gtam-du gleñ-wa* to converse, to discourse; ཇི་ལྟར་གྱུར་པའི་གཏམ་བྱས he gave an account of how it happened. གཏམ་སྐྱེལ་བ *gtam skyel-wa*=འཕྲིན་སྐྱེལ་བ *ḥphrin skyel-wa* to send a message; also a messenger.

གཏམ་འགལ *gtam-ḥgal*=སྐད་ཆ་མི་བརྟན་པ *skad-cha mi rtan-pa* discrepancy in speech, contradictory language or talk.

གཏམ་རྒྱུད *gtam-rgyud* आख्यान oral tradition, legend: དེའི་གཏམ་རྒྱུད the legend of him; བྱིས་པ་ན་རེ་གཏམ་རྒྱུད་དུ་བཤད་དམ the boy said, has it been described in history? (*Ḥbrom. 54*).

གཏམ་ངན *gtam-ñan* evil report.

གཏམ་ཅན *gtam-can* काक, वायस met. the crow.

གཏམ་སྙན་ *gtam-s̃nan* मधुरकथा, मधुरालाप elegant saying; pleasant conversation.

གཏམ་འདྲེས་པ་ *gtam hdres-pa* चालमका mixed-up stories, garbled accounts.

གཏམ་པ་ I: *gtam-pa* वदन the face.

གཏམ་པ་ II: pf. གཏམས་པ་ 1.=ཁེངས་པ་ to fill up, to make full: སྤུ་གྲི་གཏམས་པ་ *spu gri gtams-pa* quite full of razors; acc. to *Jä.* is frq. spelt བརྟམས་པ. 2. धान to appoint, to commission (*Jä.*): གཏམས་པ་ཞེན་དང་གཉའ་བོ་དང་ it is not proper (not safe) to take charge of property. 3. निचेप to be surety for or security (*K. du.* ད *200*).

གཏམ་དཔེ *gtam-dpe* proverb, common saying, maxim.

གཏམ་བསྒྲགས་པ to declare, to proclaim.

གཏམ་དྲིས་པ to make inquiry.

གཏམ་གཞོན *gtam-gshon* तरस् strong or emphatic (speech).

གཏམ་ག-ཤགས་པ *gtam-gçags-pa* to make confession: འདི་གཉིས་གནོད་དྲིས་མི་ཞེན་པའི་ཁར་དུ་གཏམ་ག-ཤགས་འདི་འདུ་བསམ these two by avoiding the question of mischief appeared to make confesssion by the fact (*Rdsa. 16*).

གཏའ་མ *gtah-ma* a pawn, pledge; གཏའ་མར་འཇུག་པ to pawn, to give as a pledge (*Cs.*); མི་གཏའ་མ *mi gtah ma* a hostage (*Cs.*).

གཏར་བ *gtar-wa* or གཏར་ཁ་བྱེད་པ has been described as སེམས་ཅན་མི་སོགས་ལ་ཁྲག་དང་མེ་རྒྱབ་པ (*Ya-sel. 9*) to bleed or to blister human beings, animals, &c., in the way of medical treatment. རྩ་བ་ལ་གཏར་བར་བྱེད་པ or གཏར་ག་འདེབས་པ =to let out blood from a vein. Colloq. གཏར་ཀ་རྒྱབ་པ to bleed.

གཏི་ཁེ *gti-khe* a kind of louse (*Sch.*).

གཏི་ཐུག *gti-thug* =ཏི་ཐུག *ti-thug* acc. to *Sch.* insane, mad.

✢ **གཏི་བ** *gti-wa* to question, to speak.

གཏི་མུག I: *gti-mug* मोह gloom, mental darkness, ignorance, stupidity. Seems to be also used in the physical sense of stupour or comatoseness: མཚན་མོ་གཏི་མུག་གཉིད་དུ་སོང་། 'at night I fell into profound coma. In a special sense it is a subdivision of the lowest of the three qualities of humanity, viz:—सत्व, रजः, तमस् virtue, passion and ignorance. གཏི་མུག is symbolized by a pig in the *Bhavacakra* or སྲིད་པའི་འཁོར་ལོ (cycle of existence) and is placed at its centre along with the serpent and cock which are typical of anger and lust. གཏི་མུག་བྲལ विगत-मोह he who is entirely free from *gti-mug;* གཏི་མུག་མེད་པའི་དགེ་བའི་རྩ་བ अमोहकुशलमूल, གཏི་མུག་ཤས་ཆེ་བ तीव्रमोह stolid indifference, also stupidity.

གཏི་མུག II: (as stated above) met. a pig (in mysticism) also as ཕག་གི་སྣ the snout of a hog (*Mñg. 11*).

གཏིགས་པ *gtigs-pa* to trickle down, to fall in drops, to drip.

གཏིང་ *gtiñ* bottom; depth;=ཞབས or མཐིལ: ཆུ་ལ་གཏིང་ཟབ deep bottom of a river; མི་ལ་གཏིང་ཆེ་བ in a man, great depth; དེང་དང་གཡང་གཟར་པོ་ལ་གཏིང་རིང་ with regard to the declivity, great depth. རྒྱ་མཚོའི་གཏིང་དཀྲུགས *rgya-mtshohi gtiñ-dkrugs* he turned up the bottom of the sea; གཏིང་དུ་རྒྱབ་པ to sink to the bottom; གཏིང་ཟབ་པོ it is very deep; གཏིང་རིང་བ deep; གཏིང་ཉེ་བ not deep, shallow; རྒྱ་མཚོ་བས་གཏིང་ཟབ་པོ it is deeper than the sea; གཡང་ས་གཏིང་རིང་བ a deep abyss; ཆུ་བོ་གཏིང་ཟབ་པོ་ཞིག a deep river. གཏིང་ནས *gtiñ-nas* from the bottom (of the heart); ཁ་དཀར་གཏིང་

ནག white above, and black beneath; གཏིང་ཅན profound (fig. with regard to the mind), considerate; reserved, difficult to fathom; གཏིང་མེད shallow, superficial.

གཏིང་དོན་ལེན་པ *gtiṅ-don len-pa* to sound the heart or to know a secret design.

གཏིང་དྲོངས་པ *gtiṅ droṅs-pa* fathomed, penetrated, ascertained.

གཏིང་རྡོ *gtiṅ-rdo* a stone or piece of lead fastened to a rope, and used as a plummet, or an anchor; also a heavy weight as a means for drowning delinquents.

གཏིང་སྡིབ *gtiṅ-sdib* socket; མིག་ཀྱང་གཏིང་ལ་སྡིབ *mig-kyaṅ gtiṅ-la sdib* his eyes also sunk in the sockets (*Rtsii.*).

གཏིང་སྐྱེས *Gtiṅ-skyes* n. of a district of Tibet immediately to the north of the Kanglachen pass. It is known under the name of Tiṅ-kye-Jong or གཟར་གཏིང་སྐྱེས་རྫོང་; also we hear གཏིང་སྐྱེས་པ *Gtiṅ skyes-pa* a native of Ting-kye.

གཏིང་དཔག་དཀའ་བ *gtiṅ-dpag dkaḥ-wa* दुरवगाह unfathomable, difficult to dive to the bottom of; hard to get at the bottom of one's heart (*Mṅon.*).

གཏིང་ཕྱིན་པ *gtiṅ phyin-pa*=དཔྱིས་ཕྱིན་པ to examine or fathom thoroughly; མཐར་ཕྱིན་པ *mthar phyin-pa* अन्तग going to the bottom; probing the mind; also a perfect saint.

གཏིང་གཞལ་ནུས *gtiṅ gshal-nus* fathomable; ཆུ་གཏིང་ཐུང་བ shallow water (*Mṅon.*).

གཏིང་ཟབ *gtiṅ-zab* or གཏིང་རིང་བ निगूढ़, गभीर the deep recesses (of the mind).

གཏིབ་པ *gtib-pa* or གཏིབས་པ *gtibs-pa* to be gathering (of clouds); སྤྲིན་ཕུང་གཏིབ་པ thick clouds gathering; བདུག་སྤོས་སྤྲིན་བཞིན་གཏིབ *bdug-spos sprin-bshin gtib* incense passes along like clouds; མུན་པ་གཏིབ darkness envelopes.

གཏིབས་ཧོག *gtibs-hog*, occurs in ཁྲིམས་པའི་གཏིབས་ཧོག་ནང་ནས་ཕྱིར་ལ་ལྕུར་གྱིས་ཕྱུང་ *khrims-paḥi gtibs-hog naṅ-nas phyir-la lcur-gyis phyuṅ* (*D.R.*) outside the subterranean obscurities of lawyers, entanglements are removed.

གཏིམ་པ *gtim-pa*, v. ཐིམ་པ *thim-pa*.

✝ **གཏུ་ལུམ** *gtu-lum*=བཟི་བ drunkenness; also intoxicated, drunk.

གཏུག་པ *gtug-pa* pf. གཏུགས, also བཏུག་པ स्पृश्, निपत् cognate to ཐུག་པ 1. to reach, to meet with, to fall down to; to touch, to join. ཡི་དམ་གྱི་ཐུགས་ཀར་གཏུགས་ནས putting or pressing (his forehead) against the breast of the image (of his tutelary god); མི་ཞིག་གི་ཞབས་ལ་མགོ་བོས་གཏུག་པ or only ཞབས་གཏུག་པ *shabs gtug-pa* to touch as suppliant a person's feet (or the skirt of his robe), to cast one's self at another's feet. 2. acc. to *Sch.* to sue, to bring an action against a person.

གཏུག་སྦྱངས་པ *gtug-sbyaṅs-pa* to supplicate or pray (touching the feet of the king) འཕྲུལ་དུ་ཞུ་བ་མེད་པའི་འདི་གར་གཏུག་སྦྱངས་སུ་ཡོང་དགོས་དང་ (*D. çel. 7*).

གཏུན *gtun*=मुसल, शिला, शिलापत्र a pestle; also a stone ball or club; the nether mill-stone; acc. to *Sch.* ཏུན pestle.

གཏུན་ཁུང excavation in a piece of rock or stone to serve for a mortar where grain is pounded with a pestle; གཏུན་གྱིས་རྡུང་བ to pound with a pestle. གཏུན་པོ *gtun-po* a mortar (*Cs.*); གཏུན་བུ *gtun-bu* pestle; གཏུན་ཧོས *gtun-hos* मुसल्य a mallet, a knocker.

གཏུན་ཤིང་ *gtun-çiṅ* a pestle made of wood to pound Indian corn or paddy (used in Sikkim).

གཏུབ་པ *gtub-pa* pf. གཏུབས་པ (*M̱ñon.*) 1. to cut to pieces, to cut up; to chop; to mince; གཏུབ་སྦྱད a chopper (*Sch.*). 2.=བཏུབ་པ to be able: ཕྱིར་ལོག་དུ་བཏུབ་པས shall you really be able to come back. མི་བཏུབ་པ to be unable, to be unwilling, to have no mind (to do a thing) (*Jä.*).

གཏུམ་དྲག *gtum-ḏrag* one who is fierce, powerful. གཏུམ་དྲག་གི་སྡིང་ཅན met. for a bear.

གཏུམ་པ *gtum-pa*=གདོལ་པ चण्डाल 1. the Hinduized savage people or wild tribes of the lands S. of Tibet. 2. चण्ड, कराल fierce, furious. 3. sbst. ferocity, rage; ཁྲོ་ཞིང་གཏུམ་ལ་སྙིང་རྗེ་མེད in furious wrath, merciless; གདུག་ཅིང་གཏུམ་པའི་ཀླུ *gdug-ciñ gtum-paḫi ḵlu* a *Nāga* in a deadly rage; གཏུམ་པའི་ང་རོ་སྒྲོག་པ to roar furiously; ཁྲོ་གཏུམ་པ furious with rage; གཏུམ་ཞིང་རྒོད་པ obstinate and wild; གཏུམ་ཅན or གཏུམ་ལྡན cruel, fierce (*Jä.*).

གཏུམ་པའི་འོད *gtum-paḫi ḥoḏ* प्रचण्डरश्मि, सूर्य्य the sun, v. ཉི་མ *ñi-ma.*

གཏུམ་པ *gtum-pa* for བཏུམ་པ or འཐུམ་པ to veil, to cover; to wrap up, *e.g.*, the head (*Jä.*).

གཏུམ་པོ *gtum-po* I: 1. चण्ड fierce; sbst. दैत्य, अन्तेवासिन्, नाग, रोषण an Asura; an uncivilized Hindu tribe generally residing in the suburbs of a town. 2. v. ཀ་ར་སྦྱིར (*M̱ñon.*). 3. a fierce-looking short-nosed man.

གཏུམ་པོ II: चण्ड often གཏུམ་མོ *gtum-mo,* in the more developed mysticism, the special internal heat which arises after protracted meditation when such meditation has been accompanied by the peculiar technical inner absorption of the breath. Milaraspa speaks of "the blessed warmth of the *gtum-mo.*"

གཏུམ་པོ་རྗེ *G̱tum-po ṟje* n. of a fierce Bon deity (*D.R.*).

གཏུམ་པོ་ནག་པོ *gtum-po nag-po*=བོང་ང་ནག་པོ (*S̱man. 125*) the black species of aconite or wolf's-bane.

གཏུམ་པོ་འབར *gtum-po ḥbar* the arising of warmth in meditation. The veins, viz., རོ་མ, རྐྱང་མ and དབུ་མ are symbolically represented by (ཨ་ཤད), *i.e.*, the second half of an ཨ *a*, hence (ཨ་ཤད་གཏུམ་པོ) the three-veins meditation-warmth (*Mil.; Jä.*).

གཏུམ་པོ་རབ་སྣང *G̱tum-po rab-ṣnañ* प्रचण्डप्रभ n. of a king of ancient India (*Yig.*).

གཏུམ་མ *gtum-ma* चण्डी, रौद्री an epithet of the goddess Durgā.

གཏུམ་མོ *gtum-mo* चण्डाली, कौलिकी, दुर्गा, क्रोधना 1. a fierce or violent woman, a female of the *Caṇḍāla* tribe, etc. 2. as an adj. violent, fearful; རླུང་གཏུམ་མོ *ṟluñ gtum-mo* a violent wind, a hurricane. 3. mystic heat.

གཏུམ་མོ་མ་མ *gtum-mo ma-ma* चण्डिका, अम्बिका Paldan Lha-mo, a fierce goddess.

གཏུམ་མོའི་ཆ་ཤས *gtum-moḫi cha çaṣ* दण्ड stick, club.

གཏུམ་སྲས *gtum-ṣras* also གཏུམ་གསུམ n. of a female deity of the Bon (*D.R.*).

✝ **གཏུར་བུ** *gtur-bu* 1. ཆོས་གོས་ཀྱི་ཕུབས, དུ་ཕད a Buddhist monk's religious wrapper. 2. bag, sack, wallet (*Cs.*).

གཏུལ་བ *gtul-wa* to grind, to pulverize (colours, medicinal substances, etc.); cf. འཐག་པ.

གཏེ་པ *gte-pa,* གཏེ་བ, གཏེ་མ in *C.* acc. to *Lex.* གཏེང་པ pawn, pledge, bail (acc. to *Sch.* a present).

གཏེར *gter* निधि, निधान, कोश 1. treasure, store-place; ཆུ་གཏེར the repository of water, the ocean. In the *Ṟñiñ-ma-pa* School of Tibet there are Buddhist scriptures (generally spurious) called གཏེར་མ, the authorship of which is attributed to gods and holy lamas, also called ཞལ་གཏེར; others said to have been mysteriously discovered or composed by learned lamas of that school are called དགོངས་གཏེར.

There are different classes of treasures such as ཡོན་ཏན་གྱི་གཏེར the treasures of learning of which again are eight:—(1) བརྗེད་པ་མེད་པས་དྲན་པའི་གཏེར treasure of learning always present in the memory and which cannot be forgotten; (2) བློ་རབ་ཏུ་འབྱེད་པས་བློ་གྲོས་ཀྱི་གཏེར the treasure of learning which develops the mind; (3) རྟོགས་པའི་གཏེར (མདོ་སྡེ་ཐམས་ཅད་ཀྱི་དོན་གྱི་རྣམ་པ་ཁོང་དུ་ཆུད་པས etc.) the treasure for meditation and reflection: (4) གཟུངས་ཀྱི་གཏེར, (ཐོས་པ་ཐམས་ཅད་ཀུན་ཏུ་འཛིན་པས etc.) the treasure of learning to be retained in the mind as having been heard or understood, sometimes in the form of a formula धारणी; (5) སྤོབས་པའི་གཏེར (ལེགས་པར་བཤད་པས་སེམས་ཅན་ཐམས་ཅད་ཚིམས་པར་བྱེད་པ) the treasure of fortitude; (6) ཆོས་ཀྱི་གཏེར (དམ་པའི་ཆོས་ཡོངས་སུ་སྲུང་བས *dam-pahi chos yońs-su sruń-was*, etc.) the treasure of secret learning or scriptural knowledge; (7) བྱང་ཆུབ་ཀྱི་སེམས་ཀྱི་གཏེར, (དཀོན་མཆོག་གསུམ་གྱི་རིགས་རྒྱུན་མི་གཅོད་པས etc.) the treasure of a *Bodhisattva's* saintly heart, *i.e.*, of unflagging faith in the three Holies; (8) སྒྲུབ་པའི་གཏེར (མི་སྐྱེ་བའི་ཆོས་ལ་བཟོད་པ་ཐོབ་པས *mi-skye-wahi chos-la bzod-pa thob-pas*, etc.) the treasure of perfection, etc. (*K. d.* ཁ *325*).

གཏེར་ཁ *gter-kha* a mineral vein, mine: ནོར་གྱི་གཏེར་ཁ་རྙེད་པ to find a mine (of precious metals or stones).

གཏེར་དགུ *gter dgu* the nine oceans which are repositories of treasures according to the Bon are:—(1) པད་མ་ཅན the ocean of lotus or the repository of countless precious things, gems, pearls, etc.; (2) དུང་ཅན the ocean of shells or mines of fossil, etc.; (3) པད་མ་ཆེན་པོ ocean or mine of precious things larger than པད་མ་ཅན; (4) ཆུ་སྲིན་ཅན ocean filled with crocodiles and other sea-monsters; (5) རུས་སྦལ་ཅན ocean filled with turtles, etc., and other sea-monsters; (6) ཛ་ཅན; (7) དགའ་བ་ཅན; (8) སྔོན་པོ; (9) འཇོག་བྱེད (*B.N.*).

གཏེར་ཆེན *gter-chen* 1. a great store of hidden wealth, hidden books, etc. 2. महापद्म n. of an immensely large number.

གཏེར་ཆེན་པོའི་བུམ་པ *gter chen-pohi bum-pa* n. of one of the eight auspicious symbols of the Northern Buddhists,—the pot of treasure, *i.e.*, the wishing-pot which yields whatever precious object is sought.

གཏེར་སྟོན *gter-ston* a discoverer of hidden treasures, generally of sacred books which are supposed often to be kept concealed under rocks and ground for fear of being destroyed by heretics and unbelievers. Learned lamas are deemed to be expert *gter-ston*.

གཏེར་བལྟ་ཤེས་པ *gter-blta. çes-pa* खनिवादी one who knows or can tell where treasures are hidden or where they can be found.

གཏེར་བདག *gter-bdag* धनाधिप a wealthy man; n. of the god of wealth, Kuvera, in Tibetan called དཔལ་གཏེར (*Mnon.*).

གཏེར་གནས *gter-gnas* the place where a concealed treasure is unearthed. Acc. to the *Rñiṅ-ma* school, Buddhist sacred books have been unearthed in the following places in Tibet:—(1) གློ་བོ་དགེ་ཀ *Glo-bo dge-ka*; (2) སྤུ་ན་རྫ་རི *Spu-rna rdsa-ri*; (3) ཀློང་ཐང་སྒྲོལ་མ *Kloń-thań-sgrol-ma*; (4) གཡུ་ཕུ་རྫ་ལྷུང་ *Gyu-phu rdsa-lhuń*; (5) བྱམས་པ་སྤྲིན *Byams-pa sprin*; (6) བྱང་གཏེར་གཏེར་ཕྲན *Byań-gter gter-phran*; (7) འབུམ་ཐང་རྩི་ལུང་ *Hbum-thań rtsi-luń*; (8) སྙིང་དྲུང་ཤངས་བྲག *Sñiń-druń çańs-brag*; (9) གཙང་གི་རི་བོ་ཆེ *Gtsań-gi ri-bo che*; (10) བལ་ཡུལ་ཨེ་ཡིག་གཙུག་ལག་ཁང་ *Bal-yul e-yig gtsug-lag khaṅ*; (11) ལྷོ་ཁ *Lho-kha*; (12) གཙང་གི་རུ་མཚམས *Gtsaṅ-gi ru-mtshamş*; (13) མོན་ཁ་བུམ་ཐང་ *Mon-kha bum-thaṅ*; (14) དགེ་རྒྱས་ཧས་པོ་རི *Dge-rgyaş haş-po ri*; (15) ཞ་ཡི་ལྷ་ཁང་བི་མ *Sha-yi lha-khaṅ bi-ma*; (16) ཇོ་མོ་གླིང་གསུམ *Jo-mo gliṅ-gsum*, (17) མཆིམས་ཕུ་ཁོ་མཐིང་ *Mchims-phu kho-mthiṅ*; (18) སྲིན་མོ་སྤར་རྗེས་ཁོ་མཐིང་ *Srin-mo şpar-rjeş kho-mthiṅ*; (19) གྲོམ་པ་རྒྱང་ *Grom-wa rgyaṅ*; (20) པད་མ་ཤེལ་ཕུག *Pad-ma çel-phug*; (21) གནམ་སྐས་མཁར་ཆུ *Gnam-şkaş mkhar-chu*; (22) ཟངས་ཡག་བྲག *Zaṅş-yag brag*; (23) གངས་པར་ཕུག་མོ *Gaṅş-par phug-mo*; (24) གཡའ་མ་སྤ་གོང་ *Gyaḥ-ma şpa-yoṅ*; (25) རྡོ་བོད་མཚམས *Rdo-bod mtshamş*; (26) ལྷོ་མོན་ཕྱོགས *Lho-mon phyogş*; (27) དབུ་ཞལ་གསེར་ཁང་ *Dbu-shal gser-khaṅ*; (28) ཧུ་ཡུག་གཡག་སྡེ *Hu-yug gyag-şde*; (29) མོན་ཁ་སྤ་གྲོ *Mon-kha şpa-gro*; (30) ཧུ་ཤང་རྡོ *Hu-çaṅ rdo*; (31) ཁམས་ཀྱི་སྲིན་མོ་རྫོང་ *Khamş-kyi srin-mo rdsoṅ*; (32) དྭགས་པོ་ལྡང་ལ་བྲག *Dwagş-po ldaṅ-la brag*; (33) མོན་ཁ་ཆུ་ཕུག *Mon-kha chu-phug*; (34) འབྲིན་ཐང་ཀོ་རོ་བྲག *Hbrin-thaṅ ko-ro brag*; (35) ཤེལ་གྱི་བྲག་ཕུག *Çel-gyi brag-phug*; (36) སྟག་ཚང་ཟབ་ལུང་ *Stag-tshaṅ zab-luṅ*; (37) བསམ་ཡས་མཚམས་ཕུ *Bsam-yaş mtshamş-phu*; (38) ཡུམ་བུ་ལ་སྒང་ *Yum-bu la sgaṅ*; (39) ཤ་ཧུག་སྟག་སྒོ *Ça-hug ştag-şgo*; (40) མཆོད་རྟེན་དཀར་པོ *Mchod-rten dkar-po*; (41) གཡས་རུ་གཙང་འགྲམ *Gyaş-ru gtsaṅ-hgram*; (42) རྩིས་ཀྱི་ལྷ་ཁང་ *Rtsiş-kyi lha-khaṅ*; (43) ཀོང་པོ་བུ་ཆུ *Koṅ-po bu-chu*; (44) ཀོང་པོ་ཕྱིང་ལུང་ *Koṅ-po phyiṅ-luṅ*; (45) མེ་འབར་མཚོ *Me-hbar mtsho*; (46) ལྷོ་ཀོང་བྱང་ཀོང་ *Lho-koṅ byaṅ-koṅ*; (47) དཔྱལ་གྱི་བྲག *dpyal-gyi brag*; (48) ཁྱུང་ཚང་བྲག *Khyuṅ-tshaṅ brag*; (49) ཁ་རག་ཕུག *Kha-rag phug* (*Bkaḥ-thaṅ.*, *159*).

གཏེར་བསྲུང་སྦ་བ *gter-bsruṅ şba-wa* to keep concealed a disease, one's learning, coveted treasures, etc: སྨས་པའི་གཏེར་བསྲུང་སྦ་བ་ལྟར་སྐྱེ་བ་རྣན་པ in the manner of one who keeps his goitre concealed (*A. 15*).

གཏེར་བསྲུང་ *gter-bsruṅ* lit. one who guards treasures; local deities, such as Shibdag and Lu, who are supposed to be the custodians of hidden treasures, mines, etc.

གཏོ *gto* or གཏོ་བཅོས a magic ceremony for the purpose of averting misfortunes.

གཏོ་རྒྱལ་ཡེ་མཁྱེན *gto-rgyal ye-mkhyen* the supreme Bon deity resembling in his attributes མར་མེ་མཛད or Dīpaṁkara Buddha in the Buddhist series (*D.R.*).

གཏོ་བུ་དོད་དེ *gto-bu dod-de*=ཐུགས་རྗེ་བཟུང་ནས *Thugş-rje bzuṅ-naş* taking compassion or having mercy upon (*D.R.*).

གཏོ་བུ་བུམ་སངས *Gto-bu bum-saṅş* a disciple of Bon S'en-rab and the analogue of Ananda.

གཏོའི་བཀའ་སྒྲོམ *gtohi bkaḥ-sgrom* n. of a Bon work.

གཏོག་པ *gtog-pa* 1. like འཐོག་པ to grab, pluck, gather, tear out. 2. v. སེ་གོལ.

གཏོགས་པ *gtogş-pa* पर्यापन्न (पर्यासन्न) 1. to assign, classify. 2. to belong to, appertain to; belonging to: རྒྱལ་པོའི་གདུང་ལ་གཏོགས་པ་ཡིན you belong to the royal blood or family; དེའི་ནང་དུ་མི་གཏོགས་སམ am I not included in them? འཛམ་བུའི་གླིང་ལ་གཏོགས་པ belonging to *Dsam-buhi-gliṅ* (Jambudvīpa). མ་གཏོགས་པ as adv. མ་གཏོགས་པར not included, except, besides.

གཏོགས་འདོད་པ *gtogş-hdod-pa* acc. to *Sch.* to love, to like, to wish.

གཏོང་དགོས་མཆོད་ཆས *gtoṅ-dgoş mchod-chaş* articles necessary for religious observances (*Rtsii.*).

གཏོང་སྒོ *gtoṅ-şgo* allowances in money or in kind for religious observances (*Rtsii.*); གཏོང་དེབ *gtoṅ-deb* a register for such, etc.

གཏོང་ཕོད *gtoṅ-phod* generosity; གཏོང་ཕོད་ཅན वदान्य one who is able to give; liberal; bounteous.

གཏོང་བ *gtoṅ-wa* pf. བཏང་, fut. གཏང་, imp. ཐོང་ 1. to send, to let go, to permit to go, to dismiss: ཅིའི་ཕྱིར་བདག་ཅག་རྣམས་ཀྱིས་གཏོང་ why should we let you go? མ་གཏོང་ do not let him go. 2. to let in, to admit; སྒོ་ནས་གཏོང་བ admit through the door; ནང་དུ་གཏོང་བ let in, to permit to enter. 3. to let have, to give: གུར་གྱི་ཁ་འཁྱིལ་རས་སྔོ་བ་བཏང་བ having given blue cotton for the fringes of the tent; སྨན་གཏོང་བ to administer medicine; གཏོང་ཚུལ the manner of dispensing, or giving away of medicine. གཏོང་བས་མཛའ་བཤེས་འཕེལ་བར་འགྱུར by generosity or friendship the number of friends increases. གཏོང་བའི་དང་ཙན् त्यागशील one who is able or has the heart to give away (many things, &c.) in charity; གཏོང་སེམས liberality, bounty; ཆོས་ལ་གཏོང་བ to give a person to religion, *i.e.*, to destine him for the priesthood (*Jä.*). In *W.* གཏོང་བ is the common term for the verb to give; the pf. form བཏང་ *btaṅ* being used as pres. tense. 4. to give up, abandon, forsake, leave.

གཏོང་ལུགས *gtoṅ-lugs* the manner of distributing, of giving away; also of forgiving.

གཏོད་པ I: *gtod-pa*=གཏད་པ pf. བཏད or གཏད, fut. གཏད, imp. གཏོད or བཏོད 1. to deliver up, hand over, to commit to another, to bestow, confer: དགེ་འདུན་ལ་དབང་གཏད་པ to confer important offices on the priesthood; གཅིག་སྙིང་གཅིག་ལ་གཏད་པ to communicate one's feelings to one another. 2. to lean against or upon, to press on, to put against. 3. to direct, to turn: མི་ལ་མགོ་བོ་གཏོད་པ to turn one's face towards a person, to take refuge or seek protection under some one; མི་ལ་མཛུབ་མོ་གཏོད་པ to point at a person with the finger, also in the way of threat; སྒོ་ལྷོ་ཕྱོགས་བལ་པོའི་ཡུལ་དུ་གཏོད the door points south, towards Nepal; འབེམ་ལ་གཏོད་པ to take aim, to aim at; ན་བའི་དབང་པོ་གཏད་པ to listen to, to give a person a hearing; ཐུགས་གཏོད་པ to confide in a person. འོད་ཟེར་ལ་གཏད་ནས་གཟིགས་པས turning after a ray of light, following it with the eye (chiefly from *Jä.*). རྒྱལ་པོ་ལ་མགོ་གཏད་པ to submit to the king's authority. རྟ་ཆ་ཁར་གཏོད་པ to place a horse in pasture.

གཏོམ་པ *gtom-pa* to talk, to speak (*Sch.*).

གཏོམས་པ *gtoms-pa* filled up, full, for བརྟམས་པ, གཏམས་པ (*Sch.*).

གཏོར་བ *gtor-wa*=བཀྲམ་པ *bkram-pa* cf. འཐོར་བ *hthor-wa* अवकीर्ण, अवकीर्ण 1. to scatter, strew, spread over (*Mṅon.*): མེ་ཏོག་གིས་གཏོར་རོ strewed flowers; ང་ལ་ས་གཏོར་མཁན he that threw earth upon me; ས་ལ་གཏོར་བ to scatter on the ground. 2. to cast, throw (books into the water, a ring into the air); to throw out, *e.g.*, spittle into a person's ear for healing purposes (འདོར་བ); to cause to circulate the chyle through every part of the body; to waste, to dissipate (occasionally with the the accus. of the vessel containing the substance thrown out): ཟ་མ་གཏོར a cow emptying its udder by discharging the milk. 3. acc. to *Sch. srub gtor-wa* to rend, to tear to pieces (*Jä.*).

གཏོར་མ *gtor-ma* बलि sacrificial objects, *i.e.*, that which is strewn or scattered or given away. The *gtor-ma* offering may consist of ཞལ་ཟས, གསོལ་ཟ cakes (not cooked or baked) made of rice, barley flour, wheat, &c., and offered as an appeasing gift to gods, saints, evil-spirits, *Nāga* demi-gods, &c., to avert dangers to the living and to guard against visitations of epidemics, plague, drought, famine, &c. Generally the torma is shaped into a conical form, the stuff of which it is made being cemented together with butter into a firm consistency. It is an essential that, after dedication, the thing offered shall be burnt or cast away. W. W. Rockhill in his "Land of the Lamas" gives an excellent account of one kind of torma offering (pp. 113, 114). གཏོར་མ་སྦྱིན་པ to offer a torma; གཏོར་མ་བསྔོ་བ *gtor-ma bsño-wa* to devote something for it. སྒྲུབ་གཏོར offerings made to a deity that it may give anything asked for; རྒྱུན་གཏོར usual or customary offerings; *glud-gtor* offerings made to ransom a life; བགེགས་གཏོར offerings made to avert the dangers caused by an evil spirit; ཆུ་གཏོར oblation of water offerings made to the manes of the dead, *i.e.*, to *Preta*. Other terms are རྟག་གཏོར, ཟུན་གཏོར, དུས་གཏོར, མདོས་གཏོར, ཐེབས་གཏོར, འཐེན་གཏོར, བྲུལ་གཏོར, དབང་གཏོར, འབྱུང་བ་བཞི་གཏོར, ལྷ་མའི་གཏོར་མ, དམར་ གཏོར, ཚེ་གཏོར, ཚོགས་གཏོར, མཚུན་གཏོར, ཡི་དམ་གཏོར, *bzlog-gtor*, ལན་ཆགས་གཏོར, *bsruñ-mahi gtor*, all being offerings made to the guardian deities; these offerings are made of various designs and colours to suit the supposed fancy of the deities to be conciliated.

གཏོར་རྒྱབ *gtor-rgyab* offerings of pyramidal shape and painted in red and white colours as if flames of fire were inscribed on them, and which are often burnt inside a human skull.

གཏོར་རྒྱུ *gtor-rgyu* the ingredients of which a torma offering is made.

གཏོར་སྟེགས *gtor-stegs* trays and tables on which the torma offerings are placed.

གཏོར་དར *gtor-dar* scarves placed over offerings at the time of presenting them to the gods, &c.

གཏོར་གདན *gtor-gdan* (in certain *Tantrik* rites) the grain placed on the ground, on which the offerings are put.

གཏོར་མ་རྒྱས *gtor-ma rgyas* बलितुष्ट, वायस one that delights in torma or, rather, in the offering when cast away, *i.e.*, the the crow.

གཏོར་མ་བཞེས་ནས *gtor-ma bshes-nas* बलिं भुक्त्वा having accepted the offerings.

གཏོར་མ་ཟ *gtor-ma za* बलिभुक् met. the crow.

གཏོར་མ་ཟན *gtor-ma zan* acc. to *Jä.* oblation of the remnants of a meal to creatures of every description.

གཏོར་རྩམ *gtor-rtsam* barley-flour for making torma offerings.

གཏོར་བཟློག *gtor-bzlog* offerings to gods and spirits for averting epidemics, etc.

གཏོར་གསོས *gtor gsos* cakes of the size of the thumb offered to gods and demons morning and noon.

+ གཏོལ *gtol* प्रहर a division of time.

གཏོལ་བ *gtol-wa* acc. to *Sch.* to perforate, pierce; to discover, disclose, v. རྟོལ་བ.

གཏོལ་བྲལ *gtol-bral*, བཟའ་རྒྱུ་མ་རྙེད་ཅི་བྱ་གཏོལ་བྲལ་ཚེ *bzah-rgyu ma-rñed ci-bya gtol bral-tshe* at the time when we were without resource having nothing to eat (*Jig.*).

གཏོལ་མེད *gtol-med*=ཆ་མེད, རྒྱུས་མེད or ཐབས་མེད unknown, a stranger; also strange; one without any knowledge of a place or thing; acc. to (*Jä.*) not known, dubious; ཕོའམ་མོའམ་གཏོལ་མེད་དོ one who does not know yet whether will come a boy or a girl; ཅི་བྱ་བའི་གཏོལ་མེད not knowing what to do; གར་ཐལ་བའི་གཏོལ་མེད not knowing where she had gone: བདག་ལ་གཏོལ་མེད I am without knowledge of it.

གཏོས *gtos*=བོངས་ཚོད size, dimension: ཡི་དགས་ལ་ལྟོ་བ་རི་བོའི་གཏོས་དང་མཉམ the belly of the yidag (*Preta*) equals the size of a mountain; རིམ་གྲོ་གཏོས་ཆེ་བ homage or religious observances of great magnitude.

བཏག་པ *btag-pa*, v. འཐག་པ (བཏག་པར་བྱ ought to be tied) བཏག་བྱའི་རྒྱན an ornament to be worn.

བཏགས་པ *ḇtags̱-pa* 1. v. འདོགས་པ bound, tied, as in ཁྱི་བཏགས་པ bound or chained the dog; རྒྱན་བཏགས་པ ornament worn; ཁ་བཏགས་པ anything bound to the face or placed in front of any one for acceptance. 2. ground, crushed; ཞིབ་བཏགས reduced to fine powder, to flour; སྨན་བཏགས medicine pulverized.

བཏང་ *ḇtang.* pf. of གཏོང་བ and used in *W.* instead of the latter.

བཏང་སྙོམས *ḇtañ-s̱ñoms̱* उपेक्षा equanimity; even treatment of all things. 1. བཏང་སྙོམས་ཞེས་བྱ་བ་ནི, དགྲ་ལ་ནི་ཞེ་སྡང་བཏང་, གཉེན་ལ་དགའ་གདུང་བཏང་, སེམས་ཅན་ཐམས་ཅད་ལ་ཉེ་རིང་དང་ཆགས་སྡང་མེད་པར་སྙོམས་ལ་བཏང་སྙོམས་ཟེར *Ḇtañ-s̱ñoms̱* is a word signifying impartial and equal treatment of friend or foe, *i.e.*, to abstain from anger or affection for friends and relations, equal treatment to all living beings without either attachment or hatred. 2. acc. to *Jä.* perfect apathy 3. acc. to *Sch.* perfect impartiality.

བཏང་སྙོམས་ཅན *ḇtañ-s̱ñoms̱ can* उन्मनाः indifferent, indolent, apathetic person.

Syn. ལེ་ལོ་ཅན *le-lo can*, སྙོམས་ ལས་ཅན *s̱ñoms̱-las̱ can* (*M̱ñon.*).

བཏང་བཟུང་ *ḇtañ-ḇzuñ* मुचिलिन्द a species of flower; also n. of a mythical mountain. བཏང་བཟུང་ཆེན་པོ *ḇtañ-ḇzuñ chen-po* महामुचिलिन्द a larger species of Muchilinda flower.

བཏང་ཡས *ḇtañ-yas̱* (གྲངས) n. of a number (*Ya-sel. 56*).

བཏད་པ *ḇtaḏ-pa*=ཕུལ་བ समर्पित made over, entrusted, presented to.

བཏབ *ḇtab* उप्त, रोपित sewn (*Zam. 8*).

བཏབ་པ *ḇtab-pa* pf. of འདེབས་པ.

བཏིག་པ *ḇtig-pa* pf. བཏིགས་པ acc. to *Cs.* to drop, to let fall in drops. རྣ་བར་སྨན་བཏིག་པ to drop medicine in the ears, v. འཛིག་པ.

བཏིང་བ *ḇtiñ-wa* 1. v. འདིང་བ *ẖdiñ-wa.* 2. अवस्तर spread, anything spread (*Zam. 8*); संस्तृत, स्तृत; གདན་བཏིང་བ to spread a rug.

བཏུ་བ *ḇtu-wa*, v. འཐུ་བ *ẖthu-wa.*

བཏུག་པ *ḇtug-pa*, v. གཏུག་པ *g̱tug-pa.*

བཏུང་བ *ḇtuñ-wa* 1. pf. of འཐུང་བ *ẖthuñ-wa* to drink. 2. पान; (*Zam. 8*) पीत, पेय drink, anything for drinking.

བཏུང་འདོད *ḇtuñ-ẖdoḏ*=སྐོམས་པ *s̱koms̱-pa* thirsty (*M̱ñon.*).

卐 **བཏུངས་པ** *ḇtuñs̱-pa* कुट्टित; =བསད་པ killed.

བཏུང་སྣོད *ẖtuñ-s̱noḏ* drinking glass.

བཏུད་པ *ḇtuḏ-pa* अवजित, प्रहृत subdued, v. འདུད་པ.

བཏུད་ནས *ḇtus̱-nas̱* प्रणम्य, प्रणत्य, प्रणिपत्य having bowed, paid reverence; adv. reverentially.

བཏུད་མར *ḇtuḏ-mar* in rapid or close succession (*Jä.*).

བཏུབ *ḇtub* 1. རུང་ fit, becoming; convenient, practicable: ཕྱི་རོལ་པ་དང་རྩོད་པ་མི་འོང་བས་བཏུབ (*A. 33*) it is proper not to have controversy with outsiders (unbelievers). མ་བཏུབ་པོ *ḇtub-po* it is not convenient.

བཏུབས་པ *ḇtubs̱-pa* छिन्न, संभिद्य cut into pieces, v. གཏུབ་པ *g̱tub-pa.*

བཏུམ་པ *ḇtum-pa* pf. of གཏུམ་པ to wrap round, to envelope; hence in *W.* to shut (a book).

བཏུམ་ཕོག *ḇtum-phog* acc. to *Jä.* bunch or knot produced by money and the like being tied up in the girdle.

བཏུལ་བ *g̱tul-wa* विनीय, pf. of འདུལ་བ *ẖdul-wa*, also བཏུལ་ཏོ; བདུད་དང་དགྲ་བཏུལ་བ to subdue an enemy, to vanquish the devil.

བཏུས་པ *ḇtus̱-pa* 1.=བཙུས་པ उद्धृत, उत्क्षिप्त extracted, quoted. 2. བདམས་པ or བཏགས་པ

विवित ; རྣམ་པ་སྤྲེ་བ, 3. བསྡུས་པ་or མདོར་བསྡུས་པ abbreviated, concise, taken in short, in few words (*Mṅon.*).

བཏེག་བཏེག་བྱེད་པ *bteg-bteg byed-pa* to haul upwards: ཡར་མགོ་ཇེང་ཇེང་བྱས, དར་དཀར་གྱི་ཐྲིབས་ཅོགས་ཏེ་ རྒྱལ་པའི་དབུ་བཏེག་བཏེག་བྱས་ཏེ (*Hbrom. 125*).

བཏེགས་པ *bteg-pa*, v. འདེགས་པ; also used in the common saying:—བུ་ལ་ཕས་བཏེགས་པའི་སྟག་ཤར, བུ་མོ་ལ་མས་བཏེགས་པའི་དམན་ཤར "when the father maintains the son, a tiger is produced, when the mother the daugther a drudge appears."

བཏོན་པ *bton-pa* v. འདོན་པ *hdon-pa*.

རྟ *rta* or, occasionally, རྟ་པོ *rta-po* अश्व, हय, हरि, तुरङ्ग a horse; the feminine form for which is usually རྒོད་མ a mare. རྟ་འདུལ་བ to break in or train a horse; རྟ་རྒྱུག་པ to gallop, to race; རྟ་ལ་ཞོན་པ to ride on horseback. Horses are largely bred in Tibet, several of the Dog-pa tribes north of Lhasa devoting themselves exclusively to roaring horses. Both Shigatse and Gyangtse are famous horse-markets, and from the latter place numbers are imported into Nepal and Sikkim. རྟ་ཡི་རྐན་ཁྲག་རྨ་ལ་ཕན the blood from the horse's palate cures sores; རྟ་ཡི་མཁལ་མས་མཁལ་ནད་སེལ tho kidney of the horse removes kidney disease; རྟ་ཡི་མཁྲིས་པས་རྨ་ལ་ཕན the bile of the horse is useful for sores; རྟ་ཡི་གྲེ་བས་སྐད་སྐྱར་ཐོབ tho larynx of the horse improves the voice; རྟ་ཡི་ལྒང་པས་མེས་ཚིག་རྨ་ལ་ཕན urinary bladder of the horse is useful for scalds and burns; རྟ་ཡི་ཚིལ་གྱིས་ཟ་ཕྲུག་ཕྲང་བུ་སེལ horse-fat dissipates itching and eruptions on the skin.

Syn. མཆོད་སྦྱིན་ཕྱུགས *mchod-sbyin phyugs*; དཔལ་གྱི་བུ *dpal-gyi bu*; རྒྱབ་འཛིན *rgyab-hdsin*; རྔ་ཡབ་མཇུག་མ་ཅན *rṅa-yab mjug-ma-can*; རླུང་གི་ཤིང་རྟ *rluṅ-gi çiṅ-rta*; རླུང་ལས་སྐྱེས *rluṅ-las skyes*; སིན་དྷུ་སྐྱེས *sin-dhu skyes*; མགྱོགས་འགྲོ *mgyogs-hgro*; འདྲེན་བྱེད *hdren-byen*; རྨིག་པ་ཅན *rmig-pa-can*; བློ་གསལ *blo-gsal*; སྐལ་ལྡན *skal-ldan*; མྱུར་འགྲོ *myur-hgro*; རྣམ་པར་གནོན *rnam-par gnon*; རྒྱ་མཚོ་སྐྱེས *rgya-mtsho skyes*; རྟག་ཏུ་ཟ *rtag-tu za*; རྔོག་མ་ཅན *rṅog-ma-can* (*Mṅon.*).

རྟ་ཀ *rta-ka* or རྟ་རྐ = རྨིག་ལྕགས *rmig-lcags* lit. hoof-iron, horse-shoe.

རྟ་རྐྱ་པ *rta rkya-pa* or རྟ་རྐྱ་པ one skilled in horsemanship.

རྟ་སྐྱིན *rta-skyin* lit. "the horse ibox"; is a curious large heavy animal peculiar to Tibet, but straying also into North Assam, the *Budorcas taxicolor*, known to sportmen as the *takin*. Two species are recorded, one found by Pére David in the ranges of Moupin on the Chinese border, the other occurring in the mountains of the Mishmi and Abor territory.

རྟ་བསྐྲགས *rta-bskrags* a clattering train of horsemen.

རྟ་གོ *rta-go*, རྟའི་ཁྲབ་ཆ་ཚང་ coat of mail for a horse; དེ་དམག་དཔོན་རྣམས་ཀྱི་རྟ་ཆས་ཡིན tho horse-equipment for generals (*Rtsii.*).

རྟ་གལ *rta-gal* saddle-bag.

རྟ་གྲལ *rta-gral*, རྟ་མང་པོ་གྲལ་སྒྲིགས་ནས་བཞག་པ a number of horses kept in a row, prop. cavalry in martial array.

རྟ་གྲས *rta-gras* = རྟ་ར *rta-ra* stable.

རྟ་བགད *rta-bgad* a horse-laugh; རྟ་བགད་ཀྱིས་འདེབས་པ to set up a horse-laugh (*Sch.*).

རྟ་མགོ *rta-mgo* a horse's head. རྟ་མགོ་ཅན = གྲུ་ཤན *gru-çan* boat (*Mṅon.*).

རྟ་མགྲིན *Rta-mgrin*, (*Tamdin*) हयग्रीव n. of deity with a man's body but having the head of a horse and which neighs fearfully to frighten beings who are mischievous to Buddhism. The Hindu analogue of Tamdin is Hayagriwa, and shrines to this doity are not uncommon at the present day in Assam.

རྟ་སྒ *rta-sga* or རྟའི་སྒ saddle; རྟ་སྒ་འཁོར or རྟ་སྒ་འཁོར་ཆ་འགྲིག the equipments of a riding horse (*Rtsii.*).

རྟ་སྒམ *rta-sgam* a large trunk or chest generally carried on horseback.

རྟ་སྒོ *rta-sgo* the entrance for a horse or pony, a gate-way.

རྟ་སྒྱེལ *rta-sgyel* gen. connected with མི་བསད the slaughtering of men and killing of horses.

རྟ་བསྔགས་ལྡན་བཟང་པོ *rta bsňags ldan bzaň-po* n. of the horse on which Buddha used to ride when he was still a prince.

རྟ་ཅན *rta-can*, བྲམ་ཟེའི་རིགས n. of a class of Brāhmaṇs (*Mňon.*).

རྟ་ལྕག *rta-lcag* horse-whip; whip in general.

རྟ་ཆག *rta-chag* dry fodder or provender given to horses, such as peas, corn, oats.

རྟ་ཆས *rta-chas*=རྟ་ལ་དགོས་པའི་སྤྱད་ལག equipments of a riding horse, including the cloth that is wrapped round its breast.

རྟ་ཆུང *rta-chuň*, v. གྲེ *gre* पूर्व्वफाल्गुनी a constellation (*Rtsii.*).

རྟ་མཆོག *rta-mchog* अश्वरत्न "the best horse," the ideal horse which makes its possessor a wealthy man; the mythological horse of Indra, a sort of Pegasus which partakes of divine properties. He is called Balāhaka the prince of horses or in Tibetan རྟ་ཡི་རྒྱལ་པོ་ཅང་ཤེས་བ་ལ་ཧ་ཀ.

Syn. ཅང་ཤེས་པ *caň çes-pa*; ལེགས་འགྲོ *legs-hgro*; རླུང་གི་གཤོག་པ་ཅན *rluň-gi gçog-pa-can*; རླུང་ལས་རྒྱལ *rluň-las-rgyal*; རྣམ་པར་དུལ *rnam-par-dul*; རིགས་ལྡན *rigs-ldan*; གྱི་ལིང *gyi-liň*; རླུང་རྟ *rluň-rta* the horse of fortune or good luck (*Mňon.*).

རྟ་མཆོག་ཁ་འབབ *Rta-mchog kha-hbab* lit. "the down-flowing mouth of the best horse." This is the appellation of the Yeru Tsang-po or Brahmaputra during the earlier portion of its course in Western Tibet. Throughout Ngari it is known as *Tamjo Kha-bab*. The river is supposed to issue from a rock shaped like a horse's mouth, but in reality rises in a swamp in a mountain-locked valley 12 miles east of Gur-lha in West Purang.

རྟ་ལྗང *rta-ljaň* हर्य्यश्व, हरिताश्व a grey-green horse or a horse the colour of which is grey-green like a leaf.

རྟ་གདོང་མེ *rta gdoň-me* वड़वानल a great submarine fire which is believed to exist in the southern limits of the great ocean: རྟ་གདོང་མེ་དང་དུས་མཐའི་རླུང་ལྟ་བུ *rta-gdoň med-duň dus-mthahi rluň lta-bu* (devastating) like the submarine fire and the wind at the end of time (*Rtsii.*).

རྟ་བདག་བརྒྱད *Rta-bdag brgad* an epithet of the god of wealth (*Rtsii.*).

རྟ་བདུན་པ *rta bdun-pa* सप्ताश्व an epithet of the sun, whose chariot is said to be drawn by seven horses; also n. of Varuṇa the god of the oceans (*Mňon.*).

རྟ་ནག *Rta-nag* (*Tanag*) n. of a district in Tibet situated a few miles to the north of Tashi-lhunpo in Tsang.

རྟ་ནག་གནས་ག *Rta-nag gnas-ga* n. of a village in Tanag; རྟ་ནག་རིན་ཆེན་རྩེ n. of a town in Tanag with a monastery called *Rin-chen-tse*.

རྟ་གནས *rta-gnas* a stable.

Syn. རྟ་ཁང *rta-khaň*; མགྱོགས་འགྲོའི་གནས *mgyogs-hgrohi gnas* (*Mňon.*).

རྟ་རྣ *rta-rna* the horse's-ear, one having the ears of a horse.

རྟ་སྣ་རི *Rta-sna ri* अश्वकर्ण one of the seven golden mountains of Buddhist mythology, so called from its shape being like the nose of a horse.

རྟ་པ *rta-pa* अश्वक a horseman, a rider; རྐང་ཐང་རྟ་པ अश्व-पदातिक infantry and cavalry (*Ya-sel. 55*). The terms signifying a horseman are: རྟ་པ, རྟ་ལ་ཞོན་པ, སྐྱེས་བུ་ཅན *skyes-bu-can*, རྣམ་པར་གནོན (*Mňon.*).

རྟ་པ་རྟ་ཞོན *rta-pa rta-shon* in *Ld.* a balancing board, see-saw (*Jä.*).

རྟ་པའི་དཔུང་ *rta-pahi dpuṅ* cavalry (*Cs.*).

རྟ་ལྤགས *rta-lpags* a horse's skin; n. of a medicinal herb. རྟ་ལྤགས་ལྤ་བ་འཛིན་ཞིང་ཚ་སེར་སེལ.

རྟ་ཕོ་ཐལ་དཀར *rta-pho thal-dkar* a stallion of ash-colour (*K. du.* ད *18*).

རྟ་ཕྲུག *rta-phrug* foal, the young of the horse.

Syn. ཐུ་རུ *thu-ru*; རྟེ་ཧུ *rte-hu*; རྟ་ཡི་བུ *rta-yi bu*; རྟེ་ཐུར *rte-thur*; རྟ་ཕྲན *rta-phran* (*Mṅon.*).

རྟ་བབས *rta-babs* तोरण 1. a raised place or large stone generally kept at the entrance of a house or monastery or temple for alighting from a horse. 2. ཁང་པའི་རྟ་བབས the pediment of a large door-way; acc. to *Jä.* the arch of a gate-way.

རྟ་བེལ *rta-bel* a horse's forelock.

རྟ་བྲེས *rta-bres* अश्वशाला a stable; manger.

རྟ་བོན *rta-bon* is described as *lag-pahi naṅ-phyog rba hdra-wa dri ṅan-pa* nasty filth, such as that which occurs in fissures inside the hand.

རྟ་བོན་པ *rta bon-pa* तुरङ्गी a mare.

རྟ་དབྱངས *Rta-dbyaṅs* अश्वघोष a celebrated Buddhist sage who was converted to Buddhism, better known by the name of Virācharya for his heroie devotion to the cause of that faith. He wrote an epistle to king Kaniṣka, also a commentary on the *Sûtrānta.* དང་པོ་ཕྱི་པའི་པཎྜི་ཏ་ཤིན་ཏུ་མཁས་པ་ཞིག, རྗེས་སུ་ཨཱ་ཙ་ར་དེ་བས་བཀུལ་ནས་ནང་པ་ལ་བཙུད་པས, སློབ་དཔོན་དཔའ་བོ་ཞེས་མཚན་གྲགས་ཀྱི་བསྟན་པ་རྒྱ་ཆེན་པོ་མཛད, མདོ་སྡེ་དྲན་པ་ཉེར་གཞག་གི་དོན་བསྡུས་སློབ་དཔོན་རྟ་དབྱངས་ཀྱིས་མཛད་པ. At first (in the first part of his life) he was a learned *Tirthika* Pandit, afterwards he was converted to Buddhism, when being called Achārya Vira he greatly furthered the cause of Buddhism. Achārya As'va Ghosha wrote a commentary on the (Buddhist scriptural) workc alled *Dran-pa ñergshag* (*D. çel. 12*).

རྟ་སྦངས *rta-sbaṅs* horse-dung; རྟ་སྦངས་སྲིན་སེལ་མཁྲིས་སྐྱུང་སྐྱུག་པ་གཅོད horse-dung (strained) removes worms and bilious vomiting.

རྟ་དམག *rta-dmag* cavalry.

རྟ་རྨིག *rta-rmig* 1. a horse's hoof; རྟ་རྨིག་མ or རྟ་རྨིག་གཟུགས silver ingots prepared in the shape of a horse-hoof, weighing variously from 125 to 156 rupees-weight. 2. वार्ताकु a plant the leaves of which resemble the horse's hoof; རྟ་རྨིག་མ་གསོ་རྣམས་སྦྱོར་ཙ་སྔོ་འགགས.. [the egg-plant *Solanum melongena*]*S.*

རྟ་རྫི *rta-rdsi*, or རྟ་འཚོ་མཁན, one that tends horses; a groom. ནལ་འབྱོར་པ་གོང་འོག་འདི་ཀུན་ཡང་རྟ་རྫི་དང་ also all the ascetics mentioned above and below with the horse-minder (*A-119*).

རྟ་གཙང་ *rsa-gtsaṅ* the pure horse necessary for the sacrificial purposes of the Vedic Brāhmaṇas: རྟ་གཙང་མཆོད་སྦྱིན अश्वमेधयज्ञ the Brāhmaṇical sacrifice of the horse according to the Vedic rites.

རྟ་ཞུན *rta-shun* a good horse.

རྟ་བཟང་ལྕག་བཞིན *rta-bzaṅ lcag-bshin* (lit. as a whip is necessary to keep even a good horse in order) is said to be a common saying in Tibet for one person sending his remembrances to another.

རྟ་ཟམ *rta-zam* lit. horse bridge, has a double meaning: first, a government post-station on the main roadway from provincial centres to Lhasa, the place where horses, &c., are changed; secondly, it is applied to the post-rider or government messenger himself. The best known *tazam*, or *tajam* as the word is often heard, are those situated on the great postal track which stretches from Leh, viâ Gartok and the north bank of the Tsang-po, to Shiga-tse and Lhasa. The proper term for the post-rider himself is རྟ་ཟམ་པ; however usage has contracted it into རྟ་ཟམ.

རྟའི་བུ *rtahi-bu* अश्वायन ; རྟའི་ཉིན་ལམ *rtahi ñin-lam* आश्वीन a day's journey on horse back. རྟའི་ཧུ་ལག *rtahi hu-lag* a compulsory service for the supply of oxen, mules, and horses. རྟའི་ར་བ *rtahi ra-wa* मन्दुरा an enclosure for horses, a stable.

རྟ་ཧོན *Rta-hon* n. of a monastic club for discussing metaphysical topics in the monasteries of Daipung, Sera and Gahdan (*Lon.* ཞ *14*).

རྟ་ཡི་མཇུག་མ *rta-yi mjug-ma* (lit. the horse's tail) n. of a medicinal plant.

Syn. གཡོ་ལྡན་མ *gyo ldan-ma* ; ཟླ་བའི་ལོ་མ *zla-wahi lo-ma* ; འདུར་བྱེད་སྐྱེས *hdur-qyed skyes* ; ཡལ་གའི་མེ་ཏོག *yal-gahi me-tog* ; མཐོན་པོ་མ *mthon-po ma* ; འགྲོ་ལྡན *hgro-ldan* ; བོང་བོའི་མེ་ཏོག *boñ-bohi me-tog* (*Mñon.*).

རྟ་ལའི་ཀོང་ *Rta-lahi koñ* n. of a mythological race in ancient India (*Yig.*).

རྟ་ཤ *rta-ça* 1. horse-flesh. 2. the oblique abdominal muscles of the hips.

རྟ་ཤད *rta-çad* curry-comb (*Sch.*).

རྟ་སྲེ *rta-sre* पृषदश्व a pie-bald horse. ['Having pie-bald horses'; an epithet of Marut or the wind-god]*S.*

རྟ་གསར *rta-gsar* a new horse, a horse not yet broken in or dressed (*Schtr.*); རྟ་གསར་སྐྱ་པ a colt three years old newly broken and saddled.

རྟ་གསེབ *rta-gseb* a stallion: རྟ་གསེབ་སྔོན་པོའི་ཕྱང་གྲིས་ཁྱི་སྨྱོན་ནད་ལ་ཕན the dung of a stallion of blue colour is a preventive of hydrophobia.

རྟ་གསོད *rta-gsod*=ཀ་ར་བྷི་ར *ka-ra bhi-ra* the oleander, *Nerium odorum* (*Mñon.*).

རྟག་པ *rtag-pa* ध्रुव, शाश्वत, नित्य, also नित्यता, अनुबन्ध, सिद्धि 1. continuous, enduring, lasting, eternal. 2. perpetuity, duration to all futurity (a quality which, according to Buddhist views, can be ascribed only to absolute emptiness—སྟོང་པ་ཉིད, *Çūnyatā*): རྟག་པ་ཐམས་ཅད་ཀྱི་མཆོག་ནི་ནམ་མཁའ the chief of all permanent things is voidity. མི་རྟག་པ impermanent, not durable, perishable: དེ་ཡང་མི་རྟག་ཚུལ་དུ་གདའ that, too, is subject to the law of perishableness; རྟག་པ་རེ་ཞིག ("*tāk-pa re-shi*") is the common colloq. expression in *C.* for always, constantly (*Snd. Hbk.*).

Syn. བརྟན་པ *brtan-pa* ; ཐེར་ཟུག་པ *ther-zug-pa* ; གཏན་དུ་བ *gtan du-wa* ; རང་བཞིན་གནས *rañ-bshin gnas* ; མི་འགྱུར་བ *mi hgyur-wa* ; གཡུང་དྲུང་ *gyuñ-druñ* ; མི་གཤིག *mi-gshig* ; མི་གཡོ *mi-gyo* ; གཡོ་མེད *gyo-med* ; གཞོན་མེ *gshon-me* (*Mñon.*).

རྟག་འཁྲུས་ཆེ *rtag-hkhrus che* always washed =assiduity.

རྟག་ཆད *rtag-chad* lasting and transitory; an abbr. of རྟག་པར་ལྟ་བ་དང་ཆད་པར་ལྟ་བ་གཉིས the theory of eternal existence or annihilation: རྟག་ཆད་ལོག་པའི་ལམ་ཕྱོགས་ཁྱོད་ཀྱིས་འདོམས you have avoided the false doctrine of perpetual existence (*Hbrom.* ཁ *29*).

རྟག་སྙོམས་ལ *rtag-sñoms-la* adv. uniformly, equally.

རྟག་ཏུ *rtag-tu* सदा, सर्व्वदा, अनिमिष, शाश्वत always, continually, perpetually: རྟག་ཏུ་བླ་མ་ལ་སྐྱབས་སུ་འཆི always do I seek refuge in my lama (Buddha).

རྟག་ཏུ་ཁོལ *rtag-tu khol* चिरदास a slave, perpetual servant: ཐབས་མཁས་བློན་པོའི་ཁོལ a servant of a resourceful minister (*Hbrom. 152*).

རྟག་ཏུ་དགའ *rtag-tu dgah* सदानन्द always cheerful ever happy; an epithet of Mahādeva.

རྟག་ཏུ་ངུ *Rtag-tu ñu* 1. n. of a Buddhist saint who used to weep when observing the miseries of mundane existence. He devoted all that he possessed to others and by his religious ascetism and study of the *Prajñā-pāramitā* he attained to the position of a *Boddhisattva* (*Hbum.* ཕ *501*). 2. n. of a medicinal flower on which dew is formed at all times on account of which it is said to be always in tears. It grows on high altitudes in Tsari the most easterly district of Central Tibet.

རྟག་ཏུ་སྤྱོད་ *rtag-tu spyod* पावक met. the fire, which is always at work.

རྟག་ཏུ་བ *rtag-tu-wa* eternal, perpetual; also acc. to *Cs.* perpetuity, eternity.

རྟག་ཏུ་འབབ *rtag-tu hbab* a name of the river Sitā, the river of continual flow (*Mṅon.*).

རྟག་ཏུ་འབྱུང་ *rtag-tu hbyuṅ* of eternal or perpetual growth.

རྟག་ཏུ་སྦྱིན *rtag-tu sbyin* (རྟག་ཏུ་བསྒྲོད་དེ) नैत्य perpetually giving or yielding.

རྟག་ཏུ་བརྩོན नित्योद्युक्त always assiduous, ever-applying.

རྟག་ཏུ་ཟ *rtag-tu za* lit. that eats at all times, met. a horse.

རྟག་ཏུ་ལང་ཚོ་ལྡན་མ *rtag-tu laṅ-tsho ldan-ma* she who is at all times youthful, an epithet of Draupadi द्रौपदी the common wife of the Pāṇḍava brothers.

རྟག་ལྟ *rtag-lta*=རྟག་པར་ལྟ་བ the doctrine of the immortality of the soul and of all things.

རྟག་བདེ་བྱེད *rtag-bde byed* (lit. happy at all times) an epithet of རྣམ་ཐོས་སྲས Vais'ravana the god of wealth (*Mṅon.*).

རྟག་སྡོད *Rtag-sdod* land-steward or overseer. རྟག་སྡོད་ལྷ་གསེལ the resident manager of the estate of *Lha-gsel* in Tibet (*Rtsii.*).

རྟག་པ་ཐེར་ཟུག་སྨྲ་བའི་ལྟ་བ *rtag-pa ther-zug smra-bahi lta-wa* the doctrine of a Brāhmaṇical sect in Ancient India: དོན་རྟག་པ་འགྱུར་མེད་ཆེན་པོ་ལ་རང་བཞིན་མ་ངེས་པར་འདོད་པར (they) did not believe in the great unchangeable and eternal principle (*Theg. 33 to 39*).

རྟག་པ་དོན་མཚོན་པའི་ལྟ་བ *rtag-pa don mtshon-pahi lta-wa* the doctrine or view as to the eternity of matter and its attributes (*Theg. 33 to 39*).

རྟག་པར *rtag-par* सदा adv. always.

རྟག་པར་འཛིན་པ *rtag-par hdsin-pa* to look upon what is transitory as lasting, and hence to be worldly-minded, a worldling; ཉལ་བ་ལ་རྟག་པ steady in lying down, *i.e.*, to be continually at rest.

རྟག་པོ *rtag-po* adj. lasting, durable, reliable.

རྟག་མ *rtag-ma* सती eternity personified, the eternal goddess; an epithet of Durgā.

རྟག་སྨྱོས *Rtag-myos* सदामोद an epithet of the god of love.

རྟག་འཛིན་ཅན *rtag hdsin-can*=རྟག་པ་འཛིན་མཁན he who holds that things are permanent.

རྟག་ཞི་པ *rtag shi-pa* सदाशिव is an epithet of Avalokitesvara *Bodhisattra* and S'iva.

རྟག་རེས་འཁོར *rtag-res hkhor* 1. नैत्यक constantly recurring. 2. རྟག་རེ་འཁོར་བ acc. to (*Sch.*) constant change.

རྟགས *rtags* 1. प्रकृति, निमित्त, चिह्न, लिङ्ग resp. ཕྱག་རྟགས sign, manual, badge, token, mark, characteristic, prognostic, &c. བཟང་རྟགས good sign or token; ངན་རྟགས evil mark or bad sign; བཀྲ་ཤིས་པའི་རྟགས auspicious sign or mark; རྟགས་བརྒྱད or བཀྲ་ཤིས་པའི་རྟགས་བརྒྱད the eight auspicious symbols or objects, v. བཀྲ་ཤིས་བརྒྱད. We have in ཡོང་མི་ཡོང་གི་རྟགས the sign of being or not being, sufficiency or insufficiency, &c. སྐྱེ་འཆིའི་རྟགས *skye-hchihi rtags* the signs of birth and death; རྟགས་བྱེད་པ to make a mark; རབ་ཏུ་བྱུང་བའི་རྟགས་ཡོད་པ the badge or distinction of monkhood; one having the marks of an ecclesiastic; མངོན་རྟགས proof, clear evidence; རྟགས་བཙ=दृष्टनिमित्त: ཅི་རྟགས་པ་ནས་བཟུང on what evidence have they seized him? རྟགས་པ་ཞིག་དགོས a proof is necessary: རྟགས་པའང་མི་འདུག there is even no evidence or mark. རྟགས་ཅན कलङ्कित, चिह्नित having a mark upon it or marked, stained; also ominous. རྟགས་ཅན་མ=སྨད་འཚོང་མ a harlot (*Mṅon.*). 2.=མཚན་མ लिङ्ग

gender; the organ of generation; རྟགས་མེད *rtags-med* अलिङ्गक hermaphrodite. ཕོ་རྟགས male organ; མོ་རྟགས female organ. རྟགས་འཇུག *rtags-hjug* the description of the distinction of the sexes; ལུང་སྟོན་པ་རྟགས་ཀྱི་འཇུག་པ, ཞེས་བྱ་བ ब्याकरण लिङ्गावतारनाम, id., a grammatical treatise on the same (by Thon-mi Sambhota). རྟགས denotes also marks of grammatical distinction, such as terminations etc.: རྟགས་འཇུག་པ using such marks, making grammatical distinctions.

རྟགས་ཐུགས *rtags-thugs* intimate connection.

རྟགས་དམ་ཕྲུག *rtags dam-phrug* sign and seal (*Yig. k. 2*).

རྟགས་གསུམ *rtags-gsum* met. an oar (*Mṅon.*).

རྟབ་པ *rtab-pa* acc. to *Jä.* = སྟབ་པ or བརྟབས་པ to be in a hurry, to be confused, frightened, in a state of alarm (acc. to *Zam.* = བྲེད་པ).

རྟབ་རྟབ་པོ *rtab rtab-po* = འཚབས་འཚབས confused, confounded with fear, perplexed: འཁོར་རྣམས་རྟབ་རྟབ་པོར་གྱུར་ཏེ་ཐམས་ཅད་ཀྱིས་བཟློག *hkhor-rnams rtab-rtab-por gyur-te thams-cad-kyis bzlog* all the attendants becoming panic-struck turned back (*Khrid. 140*); རྟབ་རྟབ་པོར་སོང་ནས having become quite startled and confounded.

རྟབ་རྟབ་ལ *rtab-rtab-la* also རྟབ་རྟོབ་ལ adv. helter-skelter, pell-mell; also in haste. རྟབ་རྟབ་པོར id. ཞིབ་མ་བཅད་པར་རྟབ་རྟབ་པོར་ཁྲིམས་གཅོད་བྱེད་ལ་དང་མི་རུང་ it is not proper while perplexed or confused to come to a legal decision without minute investigation (*Rdsa. 16*).

རྟས་པ *rtas-pa*, v. བརྟ་བ *brta-wa*.

རྟས་གཙང་གི་མཆོད་སྦྱིན *rtas gtsaṅ-gi mchod-sbyin* अश्वमेध-यज्ञ the *Vedic* sacrificial ceremony in which horse's flesh is used for entertaining the invoked deities.

རྟིག་གི *rtig-gi* in *Tsang* for རྟེའུ *rtehu* foal, colt.

རྟིང *rtiṅ* what is behind or after (with regard to space, but more particularly to time). རྟིང་དུ *rtiṅ-du*, རྟིང་ན *rtiṅ-na*, རྟིང་ལ *rtiṅ-la*, adv. and postp. afterwards, after: རྟིང་དུ བཅོས་སོ *rtiṅ-du bcos-so* they were made afterwards; བྱོན་རྟིང་ལ *byon-rtiṅ la* after their appearance; བྱུང་རྟིང *byuṅ-rtiṅ* after he has come; དེ་རྟིང་ལ *de rtiṅ-la* after that.

རྟིང་བསྐུལ *rtiṅ-bskul* earnest entreaty or exhortation (*Sorig. 134*).

རྟིང་ལྕགས *rtiṅ-lcags* a spur; རྟིང་ལྕགས་རྒྱབ་པ *rtiṅ-lcags rgyab-pa* to spur, to prick with the spur.

རྟིང་འཇུག *rtiṅ-hjug* remaining part, remainder.

རྟིང་པ *rtiṅ-pa* 1. the end, extremity, lowest part, *e.g.*, of a stick; gen. the heel of the foot རྐང་པའི་རྫ་བ (*Mṅon.*). 2. ཕྱི *phyi* latter.

རྟིང་བལ *rtiṅ-bal* hair of the foot of goat, sheep, etc.

རྟིང་མ *stiṅ-ma* adj. and sbst. latter, the last; གཏམ་གྱི་རྟིང་མ་ཡིན *gtam-gyi rtiṅ-ma yin* it is the end of a speech, conversation or discourse, this is my last and farewell-speech; རྟིང་མ་ཉི་མ *rtiṅ-ma ñi-ma* the following day.

Syn. ཕྱི་མ *phyi-ma*; རྗེས་མ *rjes-ma*; རྗེས་སུ་བགྱིད *rjes-su bgyid*; རྗེས་སུ་སྒྲུབ *rjes-su sgrub*; གཤམ་མ *gçam-ma*; མཇུག་མ་ཕྱི་ཆོས *mjug-ma phyi-ços* (*Mṅon.*).

རྟིབ་པ *rtib-pa* pf. བརྟིབས *brtibs*, fut. བརྟིབ *brtib*, imp. རྟིབ *rtib* or རྟིབས *rtibs* to break or pull down (cf. རྡིབ་པ *rdib-pa*); in Sikk. to beat or thrash thoroughly.

རྟུག་པ *rtug-pa*, མི་གཙང་མ विष्ठा 1. human excrement; རྟུག་སྐམ or རྟུག་སྐེམ *rtug-skem* dry excrement. 2. in *C.* wind, flatulency. 3. བརྟུག or རྟུག *rtug*, v. under ཤོགས་པ.

རྟུང་བ *rtuṅ-wa* pf. བརྟུངས, fut. བརྟུང་ also སྟུང་བ to make less, to shorten, to contract, *e.g.*, a rope, a dress: གཉའ་བ་བརྟུངས his neck is contracted (*Jä.*).

རྟུན *rtun* v. གཏུན *gtun*; རྟུན་རིལ *rtun-ril* a trituration-bowl (*Sch.*).

རྟུན་པ *rtun-pa* diligence; རྟུན་པའི་སྐྱེད་པ *rtun-paḥi skyed-pa* to be diligent (*Zam.*); cf. དྲུན་པ.

རྟུལ་པོ *rtul-po* or རྟུལ་བ कुण्ठ blunt, dull, stupid; མཚོན་རྟུལ a blunt weapon (*Cs.*); དབང་པོ་རྟུལ་པོ blundering; བློ་རྟུལ *blo-rtul* weak intellect.

རྟུལ་ཕོད་པ *rtul phod-pa* पराक्रम, परिणाह, वीर bold, intrepid; also sbst. courage.

རྟུལ་བཟང་སྐྱེས *Rtul-bzaṅ skyes*=རྟུལ་ཅན་མའི་བུ the son of *Rtul-can-ma*, one of the ten incarnations of Vishnu; a name of परशुराम; དཀའ་བྱེད་དགྲ་རྒྱ་ཅན.

རྟེ་ཐུར *rte-thur*=རྟེའུ किशोर foal, colt; རྟེའུ་འབྱུང་བ to bring forth a colt, to foal (*Cs.*).

རྟེན *rten* 1. सम्भव, अनुभव, वस्तु, परायण, गुण, आश्रय a hold, support, esp. in compounds: ཀ་རྟེན the plinth or base of a pillar (*Cs.*); རྐང་རྟེན or ཞབས་རྟེན a footstool (*Cs.*) 2. आश्रय, अधिकरण in Gram. the case which denotes the place of a thing or person, the locative. 3. शरीर that which holds, contains, or supports a thing: སྐུ་རྟེན lit. the holder or receptacle of a person himself, *i.e.*, an image of a deity, of a Buddha or *Bodhisattva*; གསུང་རྟེན=ཡིག་འབྲུ letters, writings, holders of the doctrine, gen. consisting in a volume of the holy writings. ཐུགས་རྟེན *thugs-rten* "the holder of the heart or mind" as manifest in a holy person. The term རྟེན་གསུམ is often applied to the foregoing three. གདུང་རྟེན *gduṅ-rten* receptacle for the bones or relics of a saint; མཆོད་རྟེན *mchod-rten* a holder or depository for oblations, a chaitya; རིག་པའི་རྟེན *rig-paḥi rten* receptacle of the soul, *i.e.*, the body (*Schtr.*); རིག་པ་རྟེན་མེད་པ, རྟེན་དང་བྲལ་བ the houseless, bodiless soul: སྙིང་ནི་ཚེ་སྲོག་སེམས་ཀྱི་རྟེན *sñiṅ-ni tshe-srog sems-kyi rten* the heart is the seat of life and of the soul. Similarly རྟེན is often a term for a temple or shrine: རྟེན་གྱི་གཙོ་བོ the deity in a shrine; again we have ཞུ་རྟེན *shu-rten* resp. ཕྱག་རྟེན *phyag-rten* a present, gift, offering, *i.e.*, "the holder or support of a request."

རྟེན་ཁེབས *rten-khebs* पूजावस्त्र the cover for religious offerings.

རྟེན་ཁྲི *rten-khri*=མཆོད་པ་ཉམས a chapel or cabinet to hold images with accommodation for keeping offerings before them and for religious books (*Rtsii.*).

རྟེན་ཅིང་འབྲེལ་བར་འབྱུང་སྙིང་པོའི་ཆོ་གའི་གཟུངས *rten-ciṅ ḥbrel-war ḥbyuṅ sñiṅ-poḥi-cho gaḥi-gzuṅs* प्रतीत्यसमुत्पाद-परिहृदय-धारणी n. of a *dhāraṇi* expressing the essence of the doctrine of relative existence or origination (*K. gu.* པ *288*).

རྟེན་ཆས *rten-chas* things, articles.

རྟེན་པ *rten-pa* 1. vb., pf. and fut. བརྟེན imp. རྟོན to keep, to hold, to adhere to, to lean on; འཁར་བ་ལ་རྟེན་པ to lean on a staff; ཀ་བ་ལ་རྟེན་པ to keep or hold against a pillar; ལག་པ་འགྲམ་པ་ལ་རྟེན to keep the hand on one's cheeks, to lean one's head on one's hand in meditating; fig. to depend or rely on; བརྟེན་པའི་བླ་མ the priest to whom one holds; ཚིལ་ལ་རྟེན་པ to keep to the fat, *i.e.*, to eat much fat; འཁྲིག་པའི་ཆོས་ལ་རྟེན་པ to be given to sensuality. A frequent form of the vb. is རྟེན་ནས *rten-nas*: ཁྱེད་ཀྱིས་གསུང་བ་ལ་བརྟེན་ནས following, depending on your orders; ངའི་ནུས་པ་ལ་རྟེན་ནས relying on my strength; hence བརྟེན་ནས is frq. used for in consequence of, with respect to, concerning, etc.:

རྐྱེན་དེ་ལ་རྟེན་ནས in consequence of that event; ཡུལ་ཁྱད་པར་ཅན་ལ་རྟེན་ནས in connection with a noble object; ལྷོ་ཕྱོགས་ལ་རྟེན་ནས *lho-phyogs la rten-nas* to be situated towards the south; འོད་ཟེར་ལ་རྟེན་ནས་གཟིགས་པ to look after or pursue with one's eye a ray of light. 2. sbst. that which holds, keeps up; རྒྱལ་པོའི་རྟེན་པའོ these are the supports of king; བརྟེན་པ་རུས་པའི་གནས་ལུགས་བསྟན་པ 'the doctrine of the hold-giving bones' *i.e.*, osteology. 3. adj. attached to, faithful (*Jä.*).

རྟེན་པའི་རྐྱེན *rten-paḥi rkyen* dependent cause; ཆུ་ཚ་ལ་རྟེན་པའི་རྐྱེན་འཁྱགས་པ the dependent cause of (the formation of) ice is water.

རྟེན་འབྲེལ *rten-ḥbrel* is said to be a contraction of རྟེན་པར་འབྲེལ་བར་འགྱུར་བ *rten-par ḥbrel-war ḥgyur-wa* प्रतीत्यसमुत्पाद 1. it is best defined not as causal concatenation but as the inter-dependent causes which have originted matter and all phenomena. These mutually contributory causes, however, according to Buddhist theory, properly centre in or spring forth from *avidyā* (Tib. མ་རིག་པ) or the ignorant belief that all which seems to us to exist does so exist when it is really non-existent. 2. संयोग omen; circumstances combining to found a judgment or prognostic; diagnosis. Milaraspa says of *rten-ḥbrel*: སྲིད་འཁོར་འདས་ཀྱི་ཆོས་ཐམས་ཅད་རྟེན་འབྲེལ་དུ་གོ་ཉིད་ understanding *rten-ḥbrel* to be the whole doctrine of transmigration in general. However, he deviates from the purer philosophy by averring that the co-operating cause at work in *rten-ḥbrel* is produced by the deep mysteries of ཟབ་མ and མན་ངག (*Mil.* ཀ, *89*). The doctrine involved in *rten-ḥbrel* is fully dealt with in Tsong-khapa's great work, the *Lam-rim chen-mo*. He sums up the argument thus: འདི་ཀུན་ངོ་བོས་སྟོང་པ་དང་། འདི་ལས་འདི་འབྲས་འབྱུང་བ་ཡི། ངེས་པ་གཉིས་པོ་ཕན་ཚུན་དུ། གེགས་མེད་པར་ནི་གྲོགས་བྱེད་པ། འདི་ལས་ངོ་མཚར་སྒྱུར་བ་དང་། འདི་ལས་རྨད་དུ་བྱུང་བ་གང་།། The certitude that all these things are in their very essence void and yet that from the one its fruit the other springs forth, the two uninteruptedly hither or thither mutually assisting each other—what can be more wonderful than this, and what has arisen more stupendous than it!

རྟེན་འབྲེལ་གྱི་འཁོར་ལོ *rten-ḥbrel-gyi ḥkhor-lo* प्रतीत्यसमुत्पाद-चक्र the wheel illustrating the process of the working of successive existences and helpful in meditating on them and in methods for getting rid of their influences, etc. In the tractate རྟེན་འབྲེལ་གྱི་འཁོར་ལོ་མི་འདྲ་བ་བཅོ་བརྒྱད *rten-ḥbrel gyi-ḥhor-lo mi ḥdra-wa bco-brgyad* (*A. 35*) there are eighteen different descriptions of the wheel illustrating the cycle of *Pratītya samutpāda*, the earliest one having been designed by Nāgārjuna as contained in *Tan. d.* གོ *32*. In it are contained indications of human destiny, luck, happiness and misery, which are drawn up in set formulas. རྟེན་ཅིང་འབྲེལ་བར་འབྱུང་བ་དང་པོ་དང་རྣམ་དབྱེ་བསྟན་པའི་མདོ the Sûtra describing the relative existences and the distinctive features contained in them (*K. d.* ས *203*). In it are described the science of divination, the art of drawing omens from different occurrences and signs.

རྟེན་འབྲེལ་བསྒོམ *rten-ḥbrel bsgom* = རང་སངས་རྒྱས an epithet for a *Pratyeka* Buddha (*Mṅon.*).

རྟེན་འབྲེལ་རྟོགས་པ *rten-ḥbrel rtogs-pa* to investigate significant or ominous incidents and draw inferences therefrom; རྟེན་འབྲེལ་ཤེས་པ to know such, or one who knows them (*e.g.*, a physician when treating a patient must try to find out the auspices). རྟེན་འབྲེལ་བཟང་ good auspices; རྟེན་འབྲེལ་ངན་ bad omens.

རྟེན་འབྲེལ་ཡན་ལག་བཅུ་གཉིས *rten-hbrel yan-lag bcu gñis* the twelve inter-dependent contributories to the orignation of all phenomena. Or, more fully:—The twelve inter-dependent elements which together contribute to the production of all phenomena; the twelve, however, being theoretically not simultaneous in origination but occurring in a certain sequence; each indeed being dependent on its predecessor, though not exactly evolved from it, because by a process of re-action the predecessor is also dependent for manifestation on its successor. Thus, while the succeeding contributories may be said to be evolved in a measure from the preceding ones, there is a mutual dependence which makes all the twelve co-ordinate also. The twelve inter-dependent originations in the Pratītya Samutpāda are:—(1) མ་རིག་པ अविद्या ignorance; (2) འདུ་བྱེད संस्कार association or impressions; (3) རྣམ་ཤེས विज्ञान consciousness; (4) མིང་གཟུགས नामरूप name and form; (5) སྐྱེ་མཆེད *skye-mched* षडायतन the six sense-organs; (6) རེག་པ स्पर्श contact; (7) ཚོར་བ वेदना feeling; (8) *sred-pa* སྲེད་པ तृष्णा desire or hankering after; (9) ལེན་པ उपादान sensual enthralment; (10) སྲིད་པ *srid-pa* भव procreation; (11) སྐྱེ་བ *skye-wa* जाति birth; (12) རྒ་ཤི जरामरण old age and death.

རྟེན་མ *rten-ma* prop, support, pillar.

རྟེན་དམན་པ *rten dman-pa* subordinate; of lower position or order, junior; a ge-tshul is subordinate to a ge-long, a ge-nyen is inferior to a ge-tshul or Çramaṇera: ཁོང་རྟེན་དམན་པས་ལུས་ཀྱི་ཕྱག་མ་མཛད་པར he being inferior in rank, *i.e.*, in the religious order, he did not make salutation with his body (*A.* 56).

རྟེན་གཞི *rten-gshi* 1. basis, foundation आधार. 2.=ཁང་ཁྱིམ་འདུག་ས residence, home (*Mṅon.*). རྟེན་གནས *rten-gnas*, id.

རྟོག *rtog* 1. in རྟོག་ཁང *rtog-khaṅ* कुतूहलशाला a room or place of amusement on the top of a house or building. 2. केतु for ཏོག *tog*.

རྟོག་པ I: *rtog-pa* तर्क, कल्पना sbst. 1. consideration, deliberation, reflection; རྟོག་པ་སྐྱེ་བ *rtog-pa skye-wa* or རྟོག་པ་ལ་འཇུག་པ to reflect on a thing, to indulge in musings. 2. scruple, hesitation: རྟོག་པ་སྐྱེས་ཏེ *rtog-pa skyes-te* to grow doubtful, hesitating.

རྟོག་པ II: vb., pf. བརྟགས or བརྟག imp. རྟོག or རྟོགས प्रेक्षते to consider, examiue, search into, muse upon=བསམ་མནོ་བ or མནོ་བསམ་པ (*Mṅon.*): བརྟགས་ན་མི་ཤེས though one meditates (upon the soul), one cannot understand. To trouble one's head about a thing is considered a fault much to be guarded against, and the more so, as religious faith as well as meditation require the mind to be strictly free from distraction, and especially in meditation to be concentrated on a single object only: མ་རྟོག་ཏིང་ངེ་འཛིན contemplation without any disturbing reflections.

རྟོག་གེ *rtog-ge* तर्क the act of arguing, reasoning; dialectics (*Cs.*); རྟོག་གེ་པ *rtog ge-pa* तार्किक an arguer, disputer, reasoner (*Cs.*): རྟོག་གེའི་སྤྱོད་ཡུལ་མ་ཡིན་པ *rtog-gehi spyod-yul ma-yin-pa* अतर्कावचर not being the object of controversy or arguing.

རྟོག་པ་དང་བྲལ་བ *rtog-pa daṅ bral-wa* कल्पनारोध without imagination, free from sophistication.

རྟོག་པའི་དགྲ *rtog-pahi dgra* जयन्तवृक्ष n. of a tree.

Syn. རྒྱལ་བྱེད་ཤིང *rgyal-byed çiṅ*, ཆུ་ཀླུང་སྐྱེས *chu-kluṅ skyes* (*Mṅon.*).

རྟོག་པར་བྱེད་པ *rtog-par byed-pa* भावक to fancy, to imagine.

རྟོག་དཔྱོད་ *rtog-dpyod*=བསམ་མནོ, or མནོ་བསམ (*Mñon.*) विचार consideration; examination, trial: རྟོག་དཔྱོད་མེད་པ निर्विचार without examination or reflection (*A. K. 1-36*). རྟོག་དཔྱོད་གཏོང་བ to identify, to discern to recognize as, *e.g.*, མཁྲིས་པར་བརྟག it is ascertained to be bile, to be caused by bile. སོ་སོར་རྟོག་པ to identify as being different (*Jä.*).

རྟོག་མེད་ *rtog-med* निर्विकल्प simple, unsophisticated; also simplicity; singleness of heart. དེ་ལ་རྟོག་འཛུག་མི་བྱེད it should not be interfered with; he does not meddle with that (*Jä.*).

རྟོག་མེད་ལོག་ཤེས *rtog-med log-çes*=རྟོག་པ་ལོག་ཤེས mistakes caused by wrong or false conclusions, such as while passing in a boat to maintain that the trees and houses on the bank of a river are moving; in the same manner holding that all phenomena are permenant, &c. (*Loñ.* པ *15*).

རྟོགས་དཀའ་བའི་གནས *rtogs dkah-wahi gnas*=ཤིན་ཏུ་བཙན་པའི་ས a very inaccessible and fearful place.

རྟོགས་འགྲོ *rtogs-hgro* गति a number; རྟོགས་འགྲོ་ཆེན་པོ महागति a great number.

རྟོགས་བརྗོད *rtogs-brjod* or རྟོགས་པ་བརྗོད་པ अवदान lit. discriminative speech, the utterance of what is fully grasped; a common designation for the recital of the events of an ideal life, full of instructive lessons.

རྟོགས་བརྗོད་བརྒྱ་པ *rtogs-brjod brgya-pa* अवदानशतक n. of a work contained in the Kah-gyur (*K. d.* ༥).

རྟོགས་བརྗོད་རིན་པོ་ཆེ་དཔག་བསམ་ཁྲི་ཤིང་ *rtogs-brjod rin-po-che dpag-bsam khri-çiñ* अवदान कल्पलता the great work of the Kashmirian poet Kshemendra on the deeds of the Buddha, in 108 chapters, translated into metrical Tibetan by Shon-ton *Lo-tsa-wa*, and forming the 93rd volume of the Tangyur collection.

རྟོགས་དེབ *rtogs-deb*=བརྗེད་ཐོའི་དེབ་ཡིག *brjed-thohi deb-yig* a memorandum book (*Rtsii.*).

རྟོགས་འདོད་ཅན *rtogs-hdod can* desirous of knowing or learning; inquisitive (*Jä.*).

རྟོགས་ལྡན *rtogs-sdan* बुद्ध, महामति;=མཁས་པ a sage, a general term to signify such.

རྟོགས་པ *rtogs-pa* I: बोधि, ज्ञान, अवबोध, उपलक्षण, समय, गति sbst. thorough perception, infallible knowledge. It is stated that ordinary mortals are incapable of cogitating on the merits and qualities of Buddhas and *Bodhisattvas*. The true *Rtogs-pa* cannot be acquired in the first instance, the དོན (meaning of a thing) first must be understood (གོ་བ་ཉིད་པ) and that may lead to the acquirement of knowledge by བསླབ་པ शिक्षा study; then comes reflection or meditation, and last of all is *Rtogs-pa* the full comprehension. Thus we can define རྟོགས་པ as: 1. the true perception of all things in general, which leads to the attainment of the སོ་སོ་སྐྱེའི་ས *so-so skyehi-sa* stage of ordinary perfection. 2. a true metaphysical development leading the way to what is called འཕགས་ལམ, that is, to *Nirvāṇa*. This last is called མངོན་པར་རྟོགས་པ or अभिसमय, the clear understanding or perception, the same as སྟོང་པ་ཉིད or metaphysical voidity or nothingness.

Syn. ཁོང་དུ་ཆུད་པ *khoñ-du chud-pa* गतिज्ञत; མཁས་པ *mkhas-pa*; विचक्षण, གོ་བ *go-wa*; अवबोध, རྟགས་པ *rtags-pa*; निरूपण, བྱང་བ *byañ-wa* निपुण.

རྟོགས་པ II: vb. to perceive, to know, to understand: དཔྱད་ན་མ་རྟོགས་ས they did not understand; though they inquired into it; རྟོགས་པར་འགྱུར་བ to obtain information; to convince one's-self of a thing; རྟོགས་པར་བྱེད་པ to teach, demonstrate, to convince a person. མ་རྟོགས་པ stupid, ignorant; ignorance. སེམས་རྟོགས self-knowledge.

རྟོགས་པ་འཁྲུངས་པ *rtogs-pa hkhruṅs-pa* भावबोधजन्म the growth of ideas, thought.

རྟོགས་པ་ཆེན་པོ་ཡོངས་སུ་རྒྱུས་པའི་མདོ *rtogs-pa chen-po yoṅs-su rgyus-pahi mdo* a metaphysical work in the Kah-gyur (*Mdo.* ཞ *413*); རྟོགས་པའི་གཏེར *rtogs-pahi gter* or མདོ་སྡེ་ཐམས་ཅད་ཀྱི་དོན་གྱི་རྣམ་པ་ཁོང་དུ་ཆུད་པས་རྟོགས་པའི་གཏེར another work in the Kah-gyur (*Mdo. 325*).

རྟོགས་སྤྱོད *rtogs-spyod* theory and practice. རྟོགས་སྤྱོད་བྱེད་པ *rtogs-spod byed-pa* to know and to practise; རྟོགས་སྤྱོད་ལ་མཁས་པ *rtogs-spyod la mkhas-pa* theoretically and practically religious.

རྟོགས་ཞིབ *rtogs-shib* thorough inquiry; investigation of minute details.

རྟོགས་ཡས *rtogs-yas* (གྲངས) समता n. of a numerical figure.

རྟོགས་སླ *rtogs-sla* easily comprehended, or easy to understand.

རྟོད་པ *rtod-pa* = བཀྱིག or འཁྱིག (*Mṅon.*) 1. vb. to fasten, to secure, tether (v. བརྟོད་པ); རྟོད་བརྒྱབ་པ to drive in a stake or peg (*Jä.*). 2. sbst. = རྟོད་ཕུར a stake in the ground for fastening a horse, a boat, etc.; a peg in a wall for hanging up things; རྟོད་ཐག id.

རྟོན་པ *rton-pa* (བརྟེན་པ or བརྟན་པ) अनुसरण, प्रतिसरण to place confidence in a person, to rely on, to adhere to, to act in accordance with. In connection with the meaning of *rton-pa* common sayings prevail among the learned of Tibet:—(1) བོད་ཀྱི་བསྟན་བཅོས་རྣམས་སུ་ཚིག་ལ་མི་རྟོན་དོན་ལ་རྟོན rely on the import of words, do not depend on their literal signification; (2) གང་ཟག་ལ་མི་རྟོན་ཆོས་ལ་རྟོན do not depend on the personality of a teacher but rely on his doctrine; (3) ངང་དོན་ལ་མི་རྟོན་ངེས་དོན་ལ་རྟོན rely on ascertained statements not on those quoted from memory; (4) རྣམ་ཤེས་ལ་མི་རྟོན་ཡེ་ཤེས་ལ་རྟོན rely on absolute knowledge, not on mere perception.

Syn. ཡིད་རྟོན་པ *yid rton-pa*; བློ་བསྟད་པ *blo bstad-pa*; ཡིད་ཆེས་པ *yid ches-pa*; རྗེས་སུ་འབྲང *rjes-su hbraṅ* (*Mṅon.*).

རྟོལ *rtol* in ཆོས་རྟོལ acc. to *Schr.* the pith or marrow of a doctrine; རྟོལ་ཤེས་པ to know thoroughly (*Schr.*).

རྟོལ་མོ *rtol-mo* a cross back to the yak by breeding an animal three-parts of Indian parentage with a pure-bred yak.

རྟོལ་བ *rtol-wa* pf. བརྟོལ 1. to bore, to pierce, to perforate. 2. to be present in or at; to reach: དྲིས་པ་ཞིག་ཡོད་པ་མང་ཡུལ་དུ་ལུས་ནས་བོད་དུ་མ་རྟོལ་ཏོ (*A. 74*) there was a manuscript which being left in Maṅ-yul could not reach Tibet (*i.e.*, be extant there). རྟོལ་མ་རྟོལ *rtol ma-rtol* arrived or not arrived; ཡོངས་འདུས་བརྟོལ acc. to *Schr.* पारिजातक the coral-tree *Erythrina Indica*; also a tree of paradise.

རྟོལ་ཤེས *rtol-çes* = རང་བཞིན་གྱི་ཤེས་པ prescience, intuitive knowledge, knowing without being taught: ཆོས་མང་པོ་རྟོལ་ཤེས་བྱུང་ཟེར་རོ it is said he knew intuitively many religious doctrines (*J. Zaṅ.*).

ལྟ *lta* 1. v. under ལྟར *ltar*. 2. v. *Jä.* in loco.

ལྟ་བ *lta-wa* I: vb. pf. བལྟས, fut. བལྟ, imp. ལྟོས or བལྟ resp. གཟིགས་པ 1. to look, take a look at, espy. ལྟ་བ implies a special visual act, whereas མཐོང་བ is the general power or habit of seeing, beholding, etc.: ཅི་འདྲ་འདུག་བལྟས་པས when you have seen what it is like; ཆུང་མས་ཁྱེའུ་བླངས་ཏེ་བལྟས་ན། ཁྱེའུ་མཚན་དང་ལྡན་བཟང་པོ་ཞིག་ནས། རབ་ཏུ་དགའ་སྟེ the wife, having taken the boy and looked at him, because he was a fine comely child, greatly rejoiced (*Dzl.*); བལྟས་ན་མི་མཐོང though you look (for it), you do not see it (*Mil.*); the imp. ལྟོས་ཤིག look! in *C.* is often both written and spoken ལྟོས་ཤོག and we even hear ལྟོས་དང "*tö-tang*" with the same meaning.

བལྟ་ན་སྡུག་པ pleasing when looked upon; also name of the chief city of Indra on the top of Mount Sumeru; ལྟ་རུ་སོང་ go there and look (at it)! ཕྱོགས་བཞིར་ཕར་ལྟ་བ to gaze all round; ཕར་ཚུར་དུ་ལྟ་བ to look up and down; ཕྱི་མིག or ཕྱིར་ལྟ་བ to look back. Colloq. in the sense of to look at *lta-wa* is usually preceded by མིག the eye: དེ་ལ་མིག་ལྟ་ནས looking at it. 2. to look for, to search for; in this sense common in *W.*, *e.g.*, རྟ་མ་ལེབ་པས་ལྟ་བ་ལ་སོང་ the horse has not come, go and look for it. 3. to view mentally, to consider, look into; also to examine, investigate: ངས་མ་བརྟས་ན if I did not examine it; རྩ་ལྟ་བ to feel a person's pulse; ཕན་ནམ་བལྟ་བ to consider if it will be useful. སུ་ཆེ་བལྟ let us see who is greater or taller; རྗེང་སོར་བལྟ we shall see that afterwards; ཡང་དག་པར་ལྟ་བ to examine or search into minutely; ཚོད་ལྟ་བ is the expression most in use for to examine, to test, to try; དུ་འདུག་བལྟ let us see how many there are; ལྟ་རྟོག་བྱེད་པ to investigate closely. 4. a fourth and not unimportant usage of ལྟ་བ is to express a stage in mystic meditation wherein it means to be in the first or contemplative stage, during which one must be especially oblivious to all sounds and to all that is occurring around one, the sight and that limited to a single object being the only sense in action: ཁྱིའི་སྐད་མཆིལ་པའི་སྐད་ཙམ་དུ་ཐོས་དགོས་མ་རྒྱུ། ཐོས་པ་ཡོད་ན་ལྟ་བ་མེད there must not be attention to even so much as the bark of a dog or the chirp of a sparrow; if there is hearing, there is no contemplation (*Mil.* ཀ).

ལྟ་བ II: sbst. 1. a look, the act of looking. 2. contemplation (mystical). 3. दर्शन opinion, doctrine, theory, philosophical system, school. རྟག་པར་ལྟ་བ the theory of perpetual existence or duration (of worldly things). ངན་པར་ལྟ་བ = ལོག་ལྟ a false opinion or heretical view (*Jä.*).

ལྟ་བ་ངན་པ *lta-wa ṅan-pa* कुदृष्टि jealous sight, spiteful or mischievous sight.

ལྟ་བ་ཉམས་པ *lta-wa ñams-pa* दृष्टिविपन्न of heretical views. ལྟ་བའི་རྟུལ་ཤུགས་མ *lta-waḥi rtul shugs-ma* दृष्टिमती having obscured vision or heretical views.

ལྟ་བས་མི་ངོམས *lta-was mi-ṅoms* not satisfied with a glance, *i.e.*, wishing to look at it more; hence = གཟུགས་མཛེས་པ a very handsome shape or person (*Mṅon.*).

ལྟ་བས་ཆོག་མི་ཤེས *lta-was chog-mi-çes* the sight of which is never enough, met. a very handsome person (*Mṅon.*).

ལྟ་བྱེད *lta-byed* met. the eye (*Mṅon.*).

ལྟ་ལོག *lta-log* or ལོག་ལྟ false statement; false doctrine, heresy; acc. to *Jä.* any irreligious impulses of the mind, perverse and sinful thoughts.

ལྟ་བུ *lta-bu* I: इव, सदृश, सन्निभ, उपम may be described as an adj., though often used in the manner of a postp. instead of ལྟར and ལྟ. It is generally conjoined with the substantive vb. with the signification of to be like, to be as (another), to be equal to: བདག་རང་ལག་པ་མང་བའི་སྤྱན་རས་གཟིགས་ལྟ་བུ་མ་ཡིན I myself am not like Chenrezig with many hands, or I have not myself many hands like Chenrezig; ཀན་གསུམ་ལྟ་བུ་མཁས་པ་ཞིག one as wise as three village-elders (*i.e.*, the village council); ཁྱོད་ལ་ལབ་གྲོགས་གདམས་ཀ་སྟོན་པ་ལྟ་བུའི་སྐད་ལགས་སོ you have a voice like that of a companion giving advice; ཕ་ཞིག་ལྟ་བུར་གྱུར་ཏོ he became (to him) like a father; བའི་རྫི་མ་ལྟ་བུ་དང་ལྡན་ཏེ having eye-lashes like those of a cow (*Stg.*).

ལྟ་བུ *lta-bu* II: = གཟུགས་བརྙན *gzugs-brñan* or སྐུ་འདྲ *sku-ḥdra* a likeness, reflected image, image (*Mṅon.*).

ལྟ་བུ III: v. སྐུ་ཤ *sku-ça* (*Mṅon.*).

ལྟ་ཉུལ་པ *lta ñul-pa* a spy, scout; ལྟ་ཉུལ་བྱེད་པ to spy, to explore, v. ཉུལ་བ *ñul-wa*.

ལྟ་སྟངས *lta-staṅs* 1. a glance or aspect, look; ཞི་བའི་ལྟ་སྟངས a mild look or countenance (*Cs.*); ཁྲོ་བའི་ལྟ་སྟངས་ an angry or fierce look (*Cs.*). 2. the magical and powerful look employed by Tantrik experts in order to control or subdue demons; ལྟ་སྟངས་ཤིག་མཛད་པ to cast such a magical magnetizing look. In the narratives ascribed to Milaraspa, frequent mention is made of his exercising this power.

ལྟག་པ *ltag-pa* 1. described as མགོ་བོ་ད་པའི་རྒྱབ་འབུར་འབུར the projecting parts at the back of the crown of the head. 2. the back part of the neck, the nape. 3. the upper or back part of any thing; གྲི་ལྟག་པ the back of a knife; ཁྱིམ་ལྟག the back of a house; སྟ་རེའི་ལྟག་པ the back of an axe; ལྟག་སྤུ *ltag-spu* neck-hair; mane of the horse, or that of the lion.

ལྟག་ཀོར *ltag-kor* the bones of the neck.

ལྟག་ཁུང་ *ltag-khuṅ* = ལྟག་རོག་གི་ཀོང་ཀོང་ "the curved bones below the nape of the neck."

ལྟག་སྒོ *ltag-sgo* the back-door of a house. As the cottages in a Tibetan village mostly stand on hill-side, the back-door is also the upper door.

+ ལྟག་སྒྲེ *ltag-sgre* or ལྟག་འོག = སྔ་ཕྱིའམ anterior or posterior; གོང་འོག་ upper and lower.

ལྟག་གཅོད *ltag-gcod* or ལྟག་ཆོད 1. decapitation. 2. acc. to *Sch.* changeable, fickle, inconstant.

ལྟག་མདུད *ltag-mdud* the hole in the occiput, the connexion of the brain with the spinal marrow (*Jä.*).

ལྟག་སྤྲོད་བྱེད་པ *ltag-sprod byed-pa*, to transpose; to put in alternation: སྨན་རེ་མོས་བྱས་ནས་གཏོང་བ to administer medicines alternately or one after another. ཐོད་པ་ལྟག་སྤྲོད་བྱས་པའི་ཌཱ་མ་རུ the hand-drum made of pieces of skull put in alternation; འགལ་བ་ལ་ལྟག་སྤྲོད་ཟེར it is described as bringing the necks together opposite each other.

ལྟག་འབིག *ltag-ḥbig* (མདུན་ནས་རྒྱབ་ཏུ་ཐོན་པ) (*Jig.*) the piercing right through from the breast to the back of the neck.

ལྟག་མ *ltag-ma* what is uppermost, *e.g.*, words written over other words.

ལྟག་རྩ *ltag-rtsa* = རྒྱབ the back; ལྟག་རྩ་སྒྲེང་སྒྲེང་ *ltag-rtsa sgreṅ-sgreṅ* the back stiff and unbending (*Rdsa. 29*).

ལྟང་ *ltaṅ* 1. a bale of goods carried on one side of a beast of burden, half a load; ལྟང་གཉིས two bales, or a whole load. 2. also = རྟིང་ in *W.* adv. through, quite through: ཕྱི་ལྟ་ནས་ནང་ལ་ལྟང་མཐོང་འདུག one sees from the outside into the interior; ལྟང་ཐུག་སོང་ bore through; ལྟང་སོང་ཏེ་ཆ་འདུག he is passing through, he does not make a stay here (*Jä.*).

ལྟང་ཕུལ *ltaṅ-phul* occurs in བོན་བློ་བའི་མཛོད་དང་ལྷ་ཡི་ཕྱོགས་བུ་མང་པོ་ཡིས་ལྟང་ཕུལ་ནས་ཞལ་ཆེམས་ཆོས་པའི་མདོ་སྡེར་པ་ལགས (*D. R. 300*).

ལྟངས་སྤྱད་པ *ltaṅs-spyad-pa* explained as ཡག་ཉེས་ཞིབ་སྤྱད་པ to minutely examine; whether a thing is good or bad, etc. (*Yig. 16*).

ལྟད་མོ *ltad-mo* यात्रा, यापन, कौतुक, रङ्ग, कुतूहल a sight, scene, spectacle; exhibition, musical entertainment; ལྟད་མོར་འགྲོ to go to an entertainment, to some amusement; གྲོང་ཡུལ་གྱི་ལྟད་མོ་མ་དྲན་ཤིག do not remember or recall the scenes of a country life. ལྟད་མོ་ཆེ *ltad-mo che* कुतूहल great display, entertainment: ཡབ་ན་རེ་ཡ་མཚན་དང་ལྟད་མོ་ཆེ་རྒྱུ་ཅི་ཡོད the father said, what is the cause of this grand display and prodigy? (*Mil.*).

ལྟད་མོ་ཁང་ *ltad-mo khaṅ* a play-house, exhibition, stage, etc.; ལྟད་མོ་མཁན *ltad-mo mkhan* or ལྟད་མོ་སྟོན་པ a show-man, actor, mimic, etc.

ལྟད་མོ་ལྟ་བ *ltad-mo lta-wa* to look at a scene, to witness a play or scene: ལྟད་མོ་ལྟ་བའི་ས *ltad-mo lta-waḥi sa* a place where there is something to be seen for amusement; a theatre; ལྟད་མོ་པ *ltad-mo-pa* a spectator, a visitor: ལྟད་མོ་ལ་བཙོགས *ltad-mo la ḥtshogs* they came together to (a sight); an entertainment; ལྟད་མོའི་དགེ་མཚན་ *ltad-moḥi dge-mtshan* innocent amusement, entertainment.

ལྟད་མོ་སྣ་ཚོགས་ *ltad-mo sna-tshogs* different kinds of amusements and entertainments, as:—གླང་པོ་ཆེས་འགྲེད་པ elephant fighting; དཔུང་བུ་ཆུང་གིས་འགྲེད་པ a tournament; ཞར་པ་འཐབ་པ to scuffle; ཤིང་འཛེག climbing up; མཆིལ་བ་འཐབ་པ bulbul fight; ཁྱི་གག་དང་ཞར་བ་འཐབ་པ. མ་ཧེས་འགྲེད་པ buffalo fight; ཕྲག་པ་ནས་མཆོང་བ to jump from upon the shoulder of one person to that of another person; རྒྱལ་མཚན་གྱི་རྩེ་མོ་དང་སྟོབས་ཀྱི་མཆོག་དང་ exhibiting the summits of the royal standards and the supreme power; དམག་གི་ཚོགས་མང་པོ་དང་ a review of troops (*K, du.* ད *501*).

卐 ལྟན་པ *ltan-pa*=འབྱོར་པ ভর, যুক্ত joined together.

ལྟབ་པ *ltab-pa* pf. བལྟབས, fut. བལྟབ, imp. ལྟོབ to fold or gather up; to lay or put together; རྐྱང་ལྟབ་པ to fold single; གཉིས་ལྟབ་པ to fold double.

ལྟབ་བྱེད་པ *ltab-byed-pa* to fold np; གསུམ་ལྟབ་བྱེད་པ to fold or bend together three-fold (*e.g.*, a corpse previous to cremation or anything else).

ལྟབ་མ *ltab-ma* a fold, crease, plait (*Cs.*); ལྟབ་གྲི clasp-knife. ལྟབ་མ་དགུ་རྩིགས་ཅན *ltab-ma dgu-rtsigs can* one with nine folds piled one upon another, *i.e.*, nine-thick (*Sorig. 119*).

ལྟམ་ལྟེམ *ltam-ltem* immaterial, ephemeral, unsubstantial, toy-like; the meaning may be conveyed by the words ཆང་ཆུང་ or སྙིང་པོ་མེད་པ col. ཆང་ཏེ་ཆུང་ཏེ and ཐམས་ཅད་ཀྱི *Dge sbyor ltam-ltem thams-cad ma-rig-pahi rkyen-gyis ḥdu-byed yin-te* (*A. 51*) Oh, *Çramaṇa*, all those immaterial toy-like things are brought together (made phenomenal) by means of ignorance.

ལྟམས་པ *ltams-pa* pf. བལྟམས, fut. བལྟམ 1. to be full, also གཏམས་པ. 2. जाति resp. to be born; སྐྱེད་པའི་ཡབ་དང་བལྟམས་པའི་ཡུམ *skyed-pahi yab-dan bltams pahi yum* the father by whom one is begotten, and the mother by whom one is born (*Jä.*).

ལྟར *ltar* or ལྟ་ལ *lta-la* and sometimes simply ལྟ *lta*, words akin to ལྟ་བུ but more directly used as postp. governing accus.; and the first two, also, as adv.—like, as, after the manner of; ཤེས་རབ་ཀྱི་ཕ་རོལ་ཏུ་ཕྱིན་པ་ལྟར་བཅོས་པ प्रज्ञापारमिता-प्रतिवर्णिक made like as the work Prajñāpāramitā; ལྟར་ཉན་ནས having heard so, being told so; ཕྱག་བྱེད་པ་ལྟར་བྱེད་པ making a gesture like making salutation; ས་བདག་གིས་ནི་ཀོ་ཕུབ་ལྟ་ལ་ཤ་མོ་ཁུར་ནས the demi-god of the place was carrying a fungus as a shield; བསེ་རུ་ལྟ་གཅིག་པུར lonely as a rhinocerus; ཐང་ཤིག་ལྟར་རྦ་བས་རྦོབས undulating like a steppe. འདི་ལྟར=thus, as follows; དེ་ལྟར or དེ་ལྟ་ན like that, in that way. Colloq. འདྲ or འདྲ་བ are generally substituted for ལྟར, etc.: དེ་འདྲ་བྱེད་ཀྱི་འདུག he is doing so.

ལྟར་ལྟར *ltar-ltar* or ལྟར་ལྟར་པ पेसी the early stage of the embryo while it is being formed in the womb.

ལྟས *ltas* I: for ལྟོས see; also ལྟས་ཚར or ལྟས་ཟིན has seen. Should be བལྟས.

ལྟས II: or ཇི་ལྟས (similar to རྟགས), निमित्त omen, prognostic, but generally used for a bad omen; ལྟས་ངན་འབྱུང་བ उत्पात accident, a danger befallen; ངོ་མཚར་བའི་ལྟས miraculous sign, prodigy, a miracle; བཀྲ་ཤིས་པའི་ལྟས a propitious omen; རྨི་ལྟས་བཟང་པོ *rmi-ltas bzan-po* a good sign in a dream; དགེ་ལྟས a favourable omen ངན་ལྟས or ལྟས་ངན a bad sign; ལྟས་ཀྱི་རིག་པ ग्रहनविद्या the science of drawing omens.

ལྟས་པ *ltas-pa* नैमित्तिक a diviner, astrologer.

ལྟས་སུ་འབྱུང་བ *ltas-su hbyuñ-wa* उत्पात meeting with an accident.

ལྟི་རི *lti-ri* pitcher (*Sch.*).

ལྟིག་ཐུང་ *ltig-thuñ* in *C.* a person of small stature, perh. a corruption of ལྟེ་ཐུང་ *lte-thuñ* (*Jä.*).

ལྟིབ་པ *ltib-pa* to fall through (*Sch.*).

ལྟིར *ltir* अतिपूर्ण full; ལྟིར་གྱིས་གང་བ *ltir-gyis gañ-wa* full to the brim.

ལྟིར་བ *ltir-wa*, v. ལྡིར་བ *ldir-wa*.

ལྟུང་ *ltuñ* पतति, fut. and pf. of ལྷུང་བ *lhuñ-wa* to fall, to fall down: ཤིང་ཁ་ནས་ལྟུང་སྟེ having fallen from the tree; མཐོ་བ་དེ་ཡང་མཐར་ལྟུང་ངོ་ even what is high will eventually fall down: ཉེས་ལྟུང་ a moral fall, a sinful deed.

ལྟུང་བྱེད *ltuñ-byed* पापात्मिका a transgression, crime; ངན་སོང་དུ་ལྟུང་ fallen into damnation; ལྟུང་འདོད wishing to fall, to sin; also apt to fall.

ལྟུང་བ *ltuñ-wa* आपत्ति, पातक, निपत्ति sbst. fall (ངན་སོང་དུ), esp. moral fall; ལྟུང་བས་གོས་པ stained with sin; ལྟུང་བ་བཤགས་པ confession of sin; ལྟུང་བ་མ་འདྲེས་པ *ltuñ-wa ma-hdres-pa* शबलपापात्मिका not mixed with sin; ལྟུང་བ་ལས་བསླང་བ *ltuñ-wa las bslañ-wa* आपत्तिव्युत्थान to raise up from a slip into sin. ལྟུང་བར་འགྱུར་བའི་ཆོས *ltuñ-war hgyur-bahi chos* acts or doctrines which cause falling into sin; unrighteous actions or unscrupulous principles; ལྟུང་མེད *ltuñ-med* अनापत्ति sinless.

ལྟེ་བ *lte-wa* or ལྟེ་པ *lte-pa* नाभि, कोशेय 1. navel གླ་བའི་ལྟེ་བ मृगनाभि; musk-pod of musk-deer: ལྟེ་བ་ལ་ནི་ཉེད་བྱེད་ན, ཁ་ཟས་བཟར་བར་འདོད་པའོ *lte-wa la ni ñed byed-na, kha-zas bzah-war hdod-paho* (*K. gu.* ང *50*) if the navel be rubbed, there will be desire to eat food. ལྟེ་བ་ཟབ་ཟླུམ་གཡས་འཁྱིལ་དོན་གྲུབ་བཟང་ *rte-pa zab-zlum gyas hkyyil don-grub bzañ* a navel, deep, round, or coiled to the right, is a good sign of success (*M.*). 2. navel-string, umbilical cord: ལྟེ་བ་གཅོད་པ *lte-wa gcod-pa* to cut the umbilical cord; ཁོང་རང་གི་ལྟེ་བ་གུང་ཐང་དུ་བཅད་པ *khoñ-rañ gi lte-wa guñ-thañ du bcad-pa* his navel string was cut at *Guñ-thañ*, *i.e.*, he was born there. 3. fig.=the middle of a thing or centre; དཀྱིལ་འཁོར་གྱི་ལྟེ་བ the centre of a circle or disk. མུ་ཁྱུད་གསུམ་གྱི་ལྟེ་བར *mu-khyud gsum-gyi lte-war* in the middle of three concentric circles or disks; རང་བཞག་གི་ལྟེ་བ the navel or axle-tree of a water-wheel; ས་ཡི་ལྟེ་བ the navel of the earth, *i.e.*, Gayā in Magadha.

ལྟེ་བ་སྐྱེས *lte-wa skyes* नाभिजन्मा, नाभिज born from the navel is met. for ཅ་རོག a raven; also an epithet of Brahmā (*Mñon.*).

ལྟེ་བ་འཁྱིལ *lte-wa hkhyil* नाभिका n. of a medicine.

ལྟེ་བ་བལ་ཅན *lte-wa bal-can* मर्कट (lit. in whose navel there is a store of wool) met. the spider (*Mñon.*).

ལྟེ་བ་གཞུང་རང་ *lte-wa gshuñ-rañ* the central place of government in Tibet, *i.e.*, Lhasa.

ལྟེ་བ་བཟང་ *Lte-wa bzañ* one of the names of Mount Tisé in Ngari (*Mñon.*).

ལྟེ་ལེ *lte-le* prob. the polecat.

ལྟེང་ཀ *lteñ-ka* 1. acc. to *Jä.* v. ལྟང་ *ltañ*. 2.=ལྟེང་རྒྱས n. of a Buddha. 3. विल pool, pond. 4. उरुविल्व n. of a disciple of Buddha.

ལྟེབ *lteb* pocket in the fold of garment: ན་བཟའི་ལྟེབ་ཏུ་བཅུག་ནས་བྱོན *na-bzahi lteb-tu bcug-* (*A. 72*) putting (the gold) in the pocket of his robes he went on.

ལྟེབ་པ *lteb-pa* (cog. to ལྟབ་པ) to double down, to turn in; མཐའ་ལྟེབ་པ to turn in the edge, cf. སྣེ་མོ *sne-mo*.

ལྟེམ་རྒྱང་ *ltem-rgyañ* whim, caprice.

ལྟེམ་པ *ltem-pa* the state of being full, *e.g.*, a vessel full of water; full, over flowing; ལྟེམ་པོ *ltem-po* full; ལྟེམ་ལྟེམ *ltem-ltem* so full that it runs over (*Jä.*).

ལྟོ *lto* 1. अन्न food, victuals; ལྟོ་བཟའ་བ *lto bzah-wa* to eat; also to gain one's living; ལྟོ་ཡང་མ་ཟོས *lto-yañ ma-zos* he did not eat his meal, *i.e.*, anything. ལུག་ལ་ལྟོ་སྟེར *lug-la lto-ster* feed the sheep; ལྟོ་གཡོ་བ *lto gyo-wa* to prepare food; ལྟོ་ཉོ་སྲོག་ཚོང་ *lto-ño srog-tshoñ* he risks his life in order to procure food; གླ་ལྟོ *gla-lto* wages and food; ལྟོ་གོས *lto-gos* or ལྟོ་རྒྱབ *lto-rgyab* food and clothes; ལྟོ་རྒྱབ་སྐྱིད *lto rgyab-skyid* food, clothes and comfort; ལྟོ་ཆུང་ *lto-chuñ*, ལྟོ་རན *lto-ran* acc. to *Sch.* a person temperate in eating. ལྟོ་འདུན་ཅན *lto hdun-can* an epicure, parasite (*Jä.*). 2. goat's-beard (*Tragopogon*) used as a kitchen vegetable.

ལྟོ་ཀླུང་བདབ་པ *lto-kluñ bdab-pa* v. ལྟོ་ལོང་བདབ་པ *lto-loñ bdab-pa*.

ལྟོ་དཀར *lto-dkar* श्वेतोदर white-belly; an epithet of *Rnam-sras* or Kuvera.

ལྟོ་སྐུར་ཆོད་པོ་བཏབ་པ *lto-skur chod-po btab-pa* to greatly slander, spread scandal (*D.R.*) ལྟོ་སྐུར་ཆོད་པུ་བཏབ་པས *lto-skur chod-pu btab-pas* id.

ལྟོ་འགེངས *lto-hgeñs*=གླེན་པ *glen-pa* a fool, an imbecile (*Mñon.*); ལྟོ་བ་འགེངས་པ *lto-wa hgeñs-pa* उदरम्भर full-stomach; ཟོད་པ་འགེངས་ཚིམ་པ satiated with food (*Mñon.*).

ལྟོ་འགྲོ *lto-hgro* उरग 1. met. a snake. 2. symb. num. 8.

ལྟོ་འགྲོ་དགྲ *lto hgro-dgra* गरुड़ an eagle; an epithet of the conveyer of Vishnu (*Mñon.*).

ལྟོ་བ *lto-wa*=གྲོད་པ (*Yasel. 36*) जठर, उदर belly, stomach; ལྟོ་བ་མཚུངས་པ *lto-wa mtshuñs-pa* समानोदर्य्य of equal stomach or having a belly of similar size; met. brother.

ལྟོ་ཅན *lto-can*=མདའ or ཐུ་ལྡན an arrow (*Mñon.*).

ལྟོ་ཆས *lto-chas* provisions.

ལྟོ་ཆེ་བ *lto che-wa*=ཟ་ཕོད་པ *za phod-pa* घस्मर a large belly, voracious.

Syn. གསུས་པོ་ཆེ *gsus-po che*; ལྟོ་བ་འཕྱང་བ *lto-wa hphyañ-wa*; ལྟོ་ལྡིར་བ *lto ldir-wa*; རྐེད་སྦོམ *rked-sbom*; གསུས་རྫིང་ཅན *gsus-rdsiñ-can* (*Mñon.*).

ལྟོ་བ་ལྡིར *lto-wa ldir* globular, bulbous; གསེར་གྱི་བུམ་པ་ལྟོ་བ་ལྡིར *gser-gyi bum-pa lto-wa ldir* a golden pot with a huge bulb (*Hbrom. 9*).

ལྟོ་སྣུམ་པ *lto snum-pa* rice-cakes with butter or any oily substance.

ལྟོ་འཕྱེ *lto-hphye* महोरग, उरोगति a snake, a reptile that creeps.

ལྟོ་འཕྱེ་ཆེན་པོ *lto-hphye chen-po* महोरग a python; also described as ས་བདག་དཔང་ཆེ་བ་ཞིག demi-god, or huge god of the soil of the serpent-kind.

ལྟོ་སྦོས *lto-sbos* आह्मार a swollen belly.

ལྟོ་ཡུས་ཅན *lto-yus can* आत्मम्भरी conceited, selfish person.

ལྟོ་རས *lto-ras* handkerchief, napkin.

ལྟོ་ལན་ཙ *lto-lan tsa* or ཏོ་ལན་ཙ thick cotton cloth used in India for spreading on the floor; evidently a corruption of the Hindi word सतरञ्जि.

ལྟོ་ལོང་ *lto-loñ*=ལྟོ་ཀླུང་ *lto-kluñ*, ཧུ་བུ་འཕོགས་སུ་བཙུན་མོས་ལྟོ་ཀླུང་བཏབ་གསུང་བས *hu-bu hphogs-su btsun-mo lto-kluñ btab gsuñ-was* (*D.R.*).

ལྟོགས་འདྲེ *ltogs-hdre* a demon (*Sch.*); prob. the same as འདྲེ་ལྟགས *hdre-ltags*.

ལྟོགས་པ་ *ltogs-pa* 1. क्षुधित, बस hunger: ལྟོགས་པའི་གཟིར་ *ltogs-pahi gzir* क्षुधाक्रान्त suffering from hunger; ལྟོགས་ཕྱུག *ltogs-phyug* hunger, *i.e.*, poverty and wealth. 2. vb. to be hungry: ལྟོགས་སོ་ I am hungry (*Cs.*). ལྟོགས་པ་འཚོར་བ to suffer a person to be hungry, to starve. 3. acc. to *Sch.* to regret: ལྟོགས་ཉལ་མ་བྱེད do not always lie down in regret! ལྟོགས་པར་བཞུགས་པ resp. to be full of regret (?). 4. adj. hungry: སེམས་ཅན་ལྟོགས་པ་རྣམས *sems-can ltogs-pa rnams* the hungry animals; ལྟོགས་པར་འགྱུར་བ *ltogs-par hgyur-wa* to grow hungry.

ལྟོགས་གྲི *ltogs-gri* starvation. In colloq. hunger: འདི་དག་ལྟོགས་གྲི་འམ་འཁྱག་གྲིར་འཆི་བ་འམ *hdi-dag ltogs-gri ham hkhyag-grir hchi-wa ham* are these going to die from hunger or cold?

ལྟོང་ཀ *lton-ka* the groove at the lower end of an arrow to fit it on the bow-string.

ལྟོང་ག *ltoñ-ga* 1. notch, incision, indentation; མདའ་ལྟོང་ *mdah-ltoñ* the notch in an arrow. 2. a depression; རི་ལྟོང་ *ri-ltoñ* depression in a ridge of mountains; ལ་ལྟོང་ *la-ltoñ* the indentation of a mountain-pass (*Jä.*).

ལྟོངས *ltoñs* summit (*Jä.*) (?)

ལྟོངས་པ *ltoñs-pa* मूर्ख a dunce, an unlettered person.

ལྟོབ་ཆས *ltob-chas* (ལྟོ་ཆས) food, provisions, etc. (in Sikk.).

ལྟོབས *ltobs* v. སྡོབས *sdobs*; in གོས་སོགས་ལྟོབས (*A. 104*).

ལྟོམས་པ *ltoms-pa*=དགོས་པ or འདོད་པ: ཇོ་བོའི་ཞུགས་དགོངས་ལ་ལྟོམས་པའི་གཉེར་གཅིག (*A. 104*) the twenty-one objects desired by the Lord (Atis'a).

ལྟོར *ltor* a bastard; སྲས་ལྟོར *sras-ltor* a bastard prince (*Jä.*). ལྟོར་ཞུགས་པ *ltor shugs-pa* to be in the womb being illegitimately conceived; bastard conception: ཁྱེའུ་འདི་ལྟོར་ཞུགས་པ་ནས་ནད་ཞི་བར་གྱུར (*K. du.* ད *261*) from the time the child was conceived in the womb her illness was alleviated.

རྟོལ *rtol*=རྟོལ *rtol* a calf bred by a yak-bull on a མཛོ་མོ or female cross of a yak and cow (*Rtsii.*).

ལྟོས *ltos*=འཁོར 1. attendants. ལྟོས་བཅས=འཁོར་བཅས together with attendants (*Yig.*). 2. v. ལྟ་བ. 3.=གཏོས (*Sch.*).

ལྟོས་པ *ltos-pa* vb. to attend to; to look at, on, or to. Is akin to ལྟ་བ and always governs the dative ཁྱོད་དེ་ལ་ལྟོས་མི་དགོས་པ་ཞིག་ཡིན *khyod-de la ltos mi-dgos-pa shig-yin* you need not attend to that; དེ་ལ་ལྟོས་ན *de-la ltos-na* if I look at or consider this taking it for example; རེ་རེ་ལ་ལྟོས་པ་མེད་པར་གཅིག་ཟུང without looking at each, take one.

ལྟོས་སྤགས *ltos-spags* meat and rice cooked together (Sikk.).

ལྟོས་མེད *ltos-med* अजस्र, अनवरत, अनवस्था continual, without interruption, in a continual stream or flow.

སྟ *sta* is defined thus: སྟ་ཞེས་བྱ་བ་ནི་རྟོད་པ་མི་དམིགས་པའི་ཕྱིར་ཆོས་ཐམས་ཅད་ཀྱི་སྒོ་འོ (*Hbum,* ཀ *283*).

སྟ་གོན *sta-gon*=ཉེར་བསྔོགས *ñer-bsños*, or སྔོན་དུ་འགྲིག་པ *sñon-du hgrig-pa* अधिष्ठान, सम-भक preparation, early arrangement. སྟ་གོན་བྱེད་པ *sta-gon byed-pa* to make preparation, to make arrangement for a person's reception: ཟུགས་ཐག་བཅད་ནས་གཉིམས་པའི་སྟ་གོན་བྱས་པའི་ཚེ having decided what course to follow, when he was preparing to sleep (*A-67*); འཚོ་བའི་སྟ་གོན་ལ་བཞེངས he rose up to make preparations for food (*Mil.*).

སྟ་གྲི *sta-gri* pick-axe, v. སྟ་རེ *sta-re* (*Mñon.*).

སྟ་རྣོན་སྡེ་རྣོན ṣta-ṛnon ṣde-ṛnon occurs in the passage:—བདུད་ཀྱི་སྟ་རྣོན་སྡེ་རྣོན་གྱིས ḇduḏ-kyi ṣta-ṛnon ṣde-ṛnon gyiṣ (D.R.).

སྟ་བོན ṣta-bon occurs in the passage: དེ་ནས་སྙིང་པོ་སྟ་བོན་ལ་གནས་པ་ནི་རྫས་ཀྱི་སྟ་བོན་ཚིག་བཅད་ཀྱི་བོན de-naṣ ṣñiṅ-po ṣta-bon la gnaṣ-pa ni ṛdsaṣ-kyi ṣta-bon tshig-ḇçaḏ kyi-bon (D.R.).

སྟ་ཟུར ṣta-zur=དཔྱི་མགོ dpyi-m̱go श्रोणि, कुचि hip, hip-bone, *e.g.*, as the seat of strength: སྟ་ཟུར་ཡན་ཆད ṣta-zur yan-chaḏ from the hip upwards (*Jä.*).

སྟ་རེ ṣta-re=སྟ་གྲི frequently སྟ་རི कुठारिका; मंकुला axe, hatchet.

སྟག *ṣtag* शार्दूल, व्याघ्र the Bengal tiger, which is not, however, found in Tibet. In the far S. E. districts the thick-furred Chinese variety of tiger is said to be occasionally met with; but in general, to Tibetans, the tiger is only an animal of legend and literature, though actual tiger-skins are imported into the country. སྟག་ཕྲུག a tiger cub; སྟག་མོ a tigress; སྟག་ཚང་ a tiger's den; སྟག་རིས the stripes on a tiger's skin; སྟག་གི་མཆེ་བས་སོ་ཡི་གཟེར་འཇོམས་བརྟན a tiger's tooth overcomes toothache; སྟག་གི་སྤུ་ཡིས་སྣ་ཁྲག་གཅོད *ṣtag-gi ṣpu-yiṣ sna-khrag gcoḏ* tiger's hair inhaled as smoke stops bleeding from the nose; མགོ་ལུས་གཟེར་ཀུན་འཇོམས་པར་བྱེད and cures all pains in the body and the head; སྟག་གི་རུས་པས་ལྷུ་བ་འཇུ tiger's-bone softens disease of the bones (perhaps caries).

Syn. དྲི་སྙོམ *ḏri-ṣnom*; རྣགས་ཀྱི་ཤན *ṛnags-kyi çcan*; འཚེ་བྱེད *ḫtshe-byeḏ*; བརྟུལ་ཕོད *ḇrtul-phoḏ*; ངར་སྐད་ཅན *ṅar-ṣkaḏ-can*; གཅན་གཟན་ཁྲ་བོ *gcan-gzan-khra-ḇo*; ལུས་བཀྲ *luṣ-ḇkra* (*M̱ñon.*).

སྟག་དཀར *ṣtag-ḏkar* lit. white tiger; n. of a demi-god belonging to the *ḵlu* or *Nāga* class and which is believed to be striped.

སྟག་ཁྲ་པོ *ṣtag-khra-po*=ཕྱེ་མ་ལེབ་ཁྲ་བོ *phye-ma leb khra-po* a marbled or striped butterfly (*Miñ. 4*).

སྟག་གི་རྐང་པ *ṣtag-gi ṛkaṅ-pa*=དཀར་གཟར་ཤིང་ n. of a tree or plant.

Syn. ཚིགས་མང་ *tṣhigṣ-maṅ* (*M̱ñon.*).

སྟག་གི་སེན་མོ *ṣtag-gi sen-mo* कारस्क lit. the tiger's nail; n. of a sweet-scented plant.

Syn. ལག་སྐྱེས *lag-ṣkyeṣ*; སྦྲུལ་གྱི་མཚོན་ཆ *ṣbrul-gyi m̱tshon-cha*; འཁོར་ལོའི་རྣམ་པ་ཅན *ḫkhor-loḫi ṛnam-pa can* (*M̱ñon.*).

སྟག་གྲས *ṣtag-graṣ* occurs in the passage སྟག་གྲས་སྟེང་གང་ཞོ་བཞི་སྐར་གསུམ. (*Ṟtsii.*).

སྟག་ཆས *ṣtag-chaṣ* articles carried by travellers such as tinder-case, smoking implements, weapons, etc. (in striped skin bags).

སྟག་ལྡན *ṣtag-ḻdan* कण्टकारी, चुड़ the plant *Solanum jacquini* (*K. d.* ཡ *214*).

སྟག་དོང་ *ṣtag-doṅ*=མདའ་དོང་ quiver. སྟག་དོང་གཟིག་ཤུབས a quiver for arrows lined with leopard's skin (*Ṟtsii.*).

སྟག་སྡེ *Ṣtag-ṣde* n. of a place in Tibet: ནུབ་ན་སྟག་སྡེ་གཟིག་འཕན་གཉིས to the west are two places called Tag-de and Zig-phan.

སྟག་རྣ *Ṣtag-ṛna* शार्दूलकर्ण n. of the son of Tri-S'anku king of the Sudra class who by the force of his logic had induced a rich Brāhman to give his daughter in marriage to his son Sārdulakarṇa.

སྟག་པ *ṣtag-pa* the birch-tree; a large species occurs in Tibet. སྟག་ཤུན *ṣtag-çun* birch bark.

Syn. གྲོ་ག *gro-ga*; གདུགས་ཁེབས *gdugṣ-khyebṣ*; པགས་པ་ཅན *pagṣ-pa can*; ཡི་གེའི་གཞི *yi-geḫi gṣhi*; རེ་ཁའི་འདབ *re-khaḫi ḇdab*; ཤུན་པ་འཇམ *çun-pa ḫjam*; ཤྤགས་པ་མཉེན *ṣpagṣ-pa m̱ñen* (*M̱ñon.*).

སྟག་འབྲོས་པའི་སྔགས *stag hbros-pahi-sṅags* the charm to make a tiger run away, माम्भेमाम्भे (*K. gu.* ཅ *52*).

སྟག་མ *stag-ma* n. of a medicinal plant: སྟག་མའི་མེ་ཏོག་ཁྲ་དོག་ནག་ཞིམ་མཆོག.

སྟག་རྩེ་རྫོང་ *Stag-tse rdsoṅ* n. of an ancient fort situated to the east of Lhasa: སྟག་རྩེ་གཙིགས་པ་བོད་ཀྱི་མཁར་གྱི་དང་པོ་ཡིན the walled fortress of *Stag-rtse* was the earliest fortress of Tibet (*J. Zaṅ.*).

སྟག་ཚང *Stag-tshaṅ* (lit. the tiger's den); a place in Tibet well known for being the birth place of སྟག་ཚང་ལོ་ཙཱ་བ *Stag-tshaṅ Lo tsā-wa.*

སྟག་ཚང་ར་བ་སྟོད *Stag-tshaṅ Ra-wa stod* n. of a well-known hermitage situated in the mountains to the west of Lhasa (*Loṅ.* ཞ *3*).

སྟག་ཚལ་བ *Stag tshal-wa* (lit. tiger's-grove) n. of a place in Tsang: ཇོ་བོ་དེ་ཅི་ནས་ཀྱང་སྤྱན་དྲངས་དགོས་སྙམ་ནས་གཙང་སྟག་ཚལ་བའི་ལོ་ཙཱ་བ (*A-65*) thinking that the *Jo-wo* (Atis'a) should under any circumstance be brought to Tibet, the Lo-tsā-wa of *Stag-tshal* in Tsang, etc.

སྟག་གཟིག *stag-gzig* (ས་བདག *sa-bdag*) lit. "tiger-leopard." 1. n. of a demi-god residing in the nether world. 2. a corruption of the name Tajik by which Persia and the Persians are known to the Tibetans.

སྟག་རས *stag-ras* a kind of chintz with stripes resembling those of a tiger.

སྟག་རི་གཉན་གཟིགས *Stag-ri gñan-gzigs* n. of an early king of Tibet (*J. Zaṅ.*).

སྟག་རུས *Stag-rus* n. of a clan or tribe in Tibet.

སྟག་ལུང་ *Stag-luṅ* n. of a district situated to the north of Tsang (*Loṅ.* ཁ *5*).

སྟག་ཤ *stag-ça* a herb growing in pasture land with leaves resembling those of the pea.

སྟག་ཤར *stag-çar* a full grown youth.

སྟག་ལྷ་མེ་འབར *stag-lha me-hbar* lit. the tiger-god of burning fire, the chief Bon god who resembles the Buddhist deity अमृत-कुण्डल (བདུད་རྩི་འཁྱིལ) in his attributes.

སྟང་ཟིལ *staṅ-zil* there are three kinds of this stone, viz., the black, golden, and silver *zil*: གསེར་ཟིལ་དངུལ་ཟིལ་རྣམ་མདོག་འཛིན. Also =ག་བུར camphor.

སྟངས *staṅs* also སྟངས་ཀ manner, style, posture: འགྲོས་པའི་སྟངས manner of walking, gait: ཆུ་ཁ་ནས་ཁྲོ་བོའི་སྟངས་སྟབས་མཛད་པས (*A. 27*) from the bank of the river he (with eyes fixed on a certain person as if to kill him) assumed the manner and posture of a wrathful deity.

སྟད་པ *stad-pa* pf. and fut. བསྟད imp. སྟོད to load, to put on, to lay on; རྟ་ལ་སྒ་སྟད་པ to saddle a horse.

སྟན *stan* resp. གདན आसन a seat, mat, anything to sit upon; སྟན་ལས་ལངས་ to get up from a seat; སྟན་འདིང་བ to spread a rug or mat on the ground; སྟན་བཀོས་བ to lay a mat on; ཁྲི་སྟན a chair, also a rug or carpet spread on a bedstead; མལ་སྟན resp. བཞུགས་གདན a cushion or carpet to sit or lie upon; ས་སྟན seat on the ground: སྟན་རྣམ་པ་ལྔའི་སྟེང་དུ་འདུག་པར་མི་བྱ་སྟེ *stan rnam-pa lṅahi steṅ-du ḥdug-par mi bya ste* (a monk) should not sit upon the five seats intended for honourable persons. སྟན་ཕྲོལ *stan-phrol* occurs in དར་ཟབ་སྟན་ཕྲོལ་ཁྲི་སྟན་ས་ལེ་ཞིན (*A. 114*). In the following passage the sense is fairly clear: འཇིག་རྟེན་པའི་དར་གྱི་སྟན་དང་བྱལ་བཙུག་ལ་ཕྱག་ཆེན་ལ་བོས་པའི་རི་དྭགས་ཁྲི་སྟན་མ་ཞེའི་པགས་པའི་སྟན་ཞིན and སྟན་ཞིན=a seat of state.

སྟབ *stab* 1. v. རྟབ *rtab.* 2. acc. to *Sch.* སྟབ་སྟངས་པ to suffer; to tolerate; to yield.

སྟབ་ཀ *Stab-ka* n. of a place in Tibet. སྟབ་ཀ་པ *Stab-ka-pa* a native of that place or district (*Loṅ.* ཞ *3*).

སྟབ་སེང་ *stab-seṅ* the sap of a tree; སྟབ་སེང་རུས་ཆག་སྦྱོར་ཞིང་རུམ་ཚད་སེལ *Stab-seṅ* causes broken bones to join, and removes rheumatism.

སྟབས I: *stabs* compliments: སྟབས་འབུལ་བ *stabs-hbul-wa* to present compliments (*Yig. k. 47*).

སྟབས II: (cog. to ཐབས also synonymous with སྟངས) 1. mode, manner, way, measure: སེང་གེའི་སྟབས་ཀྱིས་འགྲོ་བ to walk in the manner of a lion; གར་སྟབས་ manner of dancing, v. གར. 2. opportunity, ཕྱིན་སྟབས manner of walking; an opportunity for going; རིངས་སྟབས་སུ hastily, speedily; དཀོན་སྟབས scarcity, dearth. *Stabs* may be used as a formative, converting the adj. into its related substantive.

སྟབས་ཁྲི་བཟུང་མོན་ཁེང་ *Stabs-khri bzuṅ-mon kheṅ* n. of a king of Tibet (*Yig.*).

སྟབས་བདེར *stabs-bder* = སླུམ་བདེར *slum-bder* best compliments, felicitations.

སྟར *star* for སྟ་རེ *sta-re* q. v.

སྟར་ཀ *star-ka* or སྟར་ག, སྟར་ཁ तिन्दुक 1. the tree *Diospyros embryopteris* or *glutinosa*, the fruit of this tree. 2. a *Karṣa*, a weight = the weight of the dry *Tinduka* fruit: སྟར་ཀ་བྱེད་པ to be in weight a *Tinduka* fruit. 2. acc. to authors the black species of walnut. སྟར་གའི་ཤིང་ *star-gahi-çiṅ* the walnut tree; སྟར་སྐོགས *star-skogs* nut-shell; སྟར་སྡོང་ *star-sdoṅ* walnut tree.

སྟར་བ *star-wa* pf. and fut. བསྟར imp. སྟོར 1. to file on a string, *e.g.*, pearls; to tie, fasten to; སྟར་ལ་བརྒྱུད་པ id. 2. to clean, to polish. 3. (*Sch.*) to ornament.

སྟར་བུ *star-bu* or སྟར་བུན अम्लवेतस the berries of *Hippophae rhamnoides*, a shrub very frequent in Tibet, esp. near river-beds in the Indus and Sutlej districts of W. Tib.

Syn. སྤྲིན་གྱི་རྦ་ཅན *sprin-gyi rba-can*; མེ་ལྡན་མ *me ldan-ma*; ཡུལ་ག་སྐྱུར *yul-ga skyur* (*Mṅon.*).

སྟི་བ *sti-wa* pf. བསྟིས *bstis*, fut. བསྟི *bsti*, imp. སྟིས *stis* 1. to rest, to repose, to refresh one's self; སྟི་བའི་གནས a resting place. 2. to honour; སྟི་སྟང་ sbst. respect, reverence, honour; སྟི་སྟང་བྱེད་པ to honour a person, to show a person honour.

སྟིང་བསྐུལ *stiṅ-bskul* = ཞབས་བསྐུལ अनुप्रेषण service.

སྟིང་བ *stiṅ-wa* pf. བསྟིངས *bstiṅs*, fut. བསྟིང་ imp. སྟིངས उत्क्षपन to rebuke, scold, abuse.

སྟིབ་པ *stib-pa* or སྟིབས་པ to offer (sacrifice) (*Jä.*).

སྟིམ་པ *stim-pa*, pf. བསྟིམས *bstims*, fut. བསྟིམ *bstim*, imp. སྟིམས *stims*, prop. vb. causative to འཐིམ་པ, to enter, to penetrate, pervade, to be absorbed in: ཐུགས་ཆོས་ཉིད་ཀྱི་ཀློང་དུ་སྟིམ *thugs chos-ñid-kyi kloṅ-du stim* the soul is absorbed in the expanse of the spirit (ཆོས་ཉིད).

སྟུ *stu* योनि the vulgar term for a woman's private parts.

སྟུག་པ *stug-pa* or སྟུགས་པ (མི་གཙང་བ पुरीष 1. ordure, excrement. 2. thickness, density. 3. a wind, flatulence.

སྟུགས་པོ *stugs-po* = སྟུག་པོ घन, नीरन्ध्र thick, opaque, solid, dense. དཔལ་སྟུགས श्रीघन really or solidly noble, an epithet of Buddha. སྟུག་པོ་བཀོད་པའི་ཞིང་ཁམས अकनिष्ठ = འོག་མིན

Hog-min the highest of the Buddhist heavens.

སྟུད་པ *stud-pa* pf. and fut. བསྟུད to repeat, to reiterate, to give, offer repeatedly (medicine, food, etc.): བསྟུད་ན if it is repeated; སྦྲིད་པ་མང་པོ་སྟུད་ཅིང་འོང་ repeated sneezing ensues; བསྟུད་ནས་ན་བ to be always ill (*Sch.*); cf. བཙུད་མར (from *Jä.*).

སྟུན་པ *stun-pa* pf. and fut. བསྟུན to agree; to be accordant with.

སྟུན་ཤིང་ *stun-çiñ* मुसल an iron-club.

སྟུབ་པ *stub-pa* 1. in *Ld.* for བཏུབ་པ *btub-pa* (*Jä.*). 2. same as སྟུབས་པ *stubs-pa* काट, to cut into pieces (ཤ་ལྟ་བུ *ça-lta-bu* like meat).

སྟེ *ste* (क्त्वा) an affix for the gerund, inst. of ཏེ after ག, ང, and vowels, v. ཏེ. As སྟེ contains the copula it may be added also to other words than verbs, *e.g.*, ཁྱོད་རིགས་ཆེ་ཞིང་མཐོ་བ་སྟེ *khyod-rigs che-shiñ mtho-wa ste* as you are of high and noble extraction; like འདི་ལྟ་སྟེ it is also used for namely, to wit, videlicet (viz.), that is to say, esp. before translations of foreign words and names. After an enumeration of several things it serves to point back, or to comprise: ཞ, ཟ, འ, ཡ, ཤ, ས, སྟེ་དྲུག་ནི the six letters ཞ, ཟ, etc. གསུམ་ན་ཪོ་གི་གུ་འགྲེང་བུ་སྟེ the three signs as *o*, *i*, and *e*. ད་སྟེ་ཞག་བདུན་ན as to the being now, in seven days, *i.e.*, in seven days from to-day (*Dzl.*) (from *Jä*). As a gerundial affix སྟེ or ཏེ is most correctly annexed to the present tense only, while ནས forms the perf. or pluperf. gerund.

སྟེ་པོ *ste-po*=སྟེའུ *stehu* an axe with its blade athwart the handle used by Indian and Tibetan carpenters; སྟེ་ལྟག *ste-ltag* the back of the axe; སྟེ་ཡུ *ste-yu* its handle; སྟེ་ཁ *ste-kha* its edge. སྟེ་བཞོག་གཏོང་བ *ste-bshog gtoñ-wa* to smooth, to hew with the axe (*Jä.*).

སྟེགས *stegs* I: a bridge over narrow gaps or along precipitous paths, torrents, &c.; fig. the saints or sages by whose agency men are led out of this world to *Nirvāṇa*: བླ་མ་དེ་རྣམས་གྲུབ་པ་ཐོབ་པའི་སྟེགས་རིམ་ལ་བརྒྱུད་པ those lamas have spiritually descended by the connecting bridge of those who have gained sainthood (*A. 42*).

སྟེགས II: also སྟེགས་བུ sbst. a rest, support, upholder, shelf, etc.; ཆོས་སྟེགས book-stand, bookshelf; འདུག་སྟེགས a board, stool, bench, to sit on (*Cs.*); གཞག་སྟེགས a board to place things on (*Cs.*); ཇ་སྟེགས or གསོལ་སྟེགས *gsol-stegs* dining table (*Schtr.*); ཀུབ་སྟེགས stool, portable resting stick for sitting on. ལ་སྟེགས a candle-stick.

སྟེགས་བུ *stegs-bu* 1. a turret where sparrows make their nests. 2. སྟེགས་བུ་ཡ་ཐ *stegs-bu ya-tha* occurs in སྟེགས་བུ་ཡ་ཐ་དེར་གཤེགས་མཆོད་གནས་ཀྱི་མགྲོན་ལ་དེ་རྣམས་དགོས་སོ; in the same work སྟེགས་བུ་མ་ཐ *stegs-bu ma-tha* occurs in སྟེགས་བུ་མ་ཐ་ཡི་སྟེང་དུ་ཁམས་གསུམ་སེམས་ཅན་སྡིང་ངེ (*D.R.*).

སྟེང་ *steñ* उपर, उत्त, अग्र, ऊर्द्ध that which is above, the upper part, top, surface: སྟེང་གི་ནམ་མཁའ *steñ-gi nam-mkhaḥ* the heavens above; སྟེང་གི་ཕྱོགས the zenith; སྟེང་འོག above and below; སྟེང་འོག་གི་གདོན the demons of the upper and nether regions; སྟེང་གི་འཇིག་རྟེན ऊर्द्ध-लोक the upper world; མཐོ་རིས the heavens; སྟེང་གི་དབང་པོ उपेन्द्र an epithet of Vishnu; སྟེང་སྐྱེས *steñ-skyes*, ལྡོན་ཤིང་ lit. that grows upwards; met. a tree. (*Mñon.*); སྟེང་སྐྱོབ *steñ-skyob* a canopy; སྟེང་ཁང་ upper story of a house, garret; སྟེང་ཁེབས upper cover, cover. In Gram. སྟེང་འཇུག and འོག་འཇུག a surmounting and subjoined letter respectively (*Yig. k. 1*).

སྟེང་འཐུང་ *steñ-hthuñ* lit. that drinks or draws nourishment from above; fig. the water-lily. སྟེང་འཕྱང་དཀར་པོ कुमुद the white species of water-lily.

སྟེང་དུ *steṅ-du* and སྟེང་ན *steṅ-na* adv. = upwards, etc.; and as postp.: above, on the surface, upon; also besides, in addition to. སྟེང་དུ་འདྲེན *steṅ-du ḥdren* उत्क्षेपण drawn upwards, promoted; also thrown upwards. སྟེང་དུ་འཛེག་པ *steṅ-du ḥdseg-pa* ऊर्ध्वम् आरोहति to ascend, ascending, climbing; སྟེང་ནས *steṅ-nas* down from.

སྟེང་འཕྱུར་དབང་པོ *steṅ-ḥphur dwaṅ-po* an epithet of the god Mahādeva (*Mṅon.*). སྟེང་འཕྱུར་གཤེར་ལྡན, ཟླ་བ चन्द्र the moon (*Mṅon.*).

སྟེང་འབར *steṅ-ḥbar* = ཐན་པ *than-pa* drought, want of rain (*Mṅon.*).

སྟེང་གཡོགས *steṅ-gyogs* = ཟླ་གམ उत्तरवासन the upper garment of a religious mendicant; also = ཤོགས་མ *shogs-ma* ऊर्ध्वच्छादन the upper covering.

སྟེན་པ *sten-pa*, pf. and fut. བསྟེན, imp. སྟེན 1. to keep close to, to adhere to, to retain to depend upon; akin to རྟེན་པ but c. accus.: བླ་མ་མཁས་པ་སྟེན་པ to adhere to a learned lama; ཆོས་དམ་པའི་ཁོང་སྨན་སྟེན་ཤིག *chos dam-paḥi khoṅ sman sten shig* keep to the internal medicine of the holy doctrine. 2. to side with; partake of; serve; སྟེན་བྱེད་པ *sten-byed-pa* or རབ་ཏུ་བསྟེན་པ to serve reverentially or respectfully (*Mṅon.*).

སྟེམ་པ *stem-pa*, pf. and fut. སྟེམས seems to occur in popular literature and in colloq. with the sense of—to shut or fasten (a door), to block it with a beam or bar.

སྟེམས *stems* curse, cf. བྱད *byad*. (?)

སྟེའུ་ཀ་མ *steḥu ka-ma* भल्ल a kind of missile. སྟེའུ་སྟག *steḥu-stag* क्षुरप्र a searp arrow, v. སྟེ་པོ *ste-po*.

སྟེར་བ *ster-wa*, pf. and fut. བསྟེར द 1. to grant, to give, to bestow: གསོལ་རས་ཆེན་པོ་སྟེར་སོང gave remuneration or much *bakshish*; ནང་དུ་འགྲོ་སྟེར to grant to come indoors. 2. in *W.* in a special sense: to give (ཟས་ལྟ་བུ) to eat or to drink, to feed (animals, infants) (*Jä.*). *Ster-wa* is the common colloq. for to give in *C. Tib.* just as in *W.* གཏོང་བ is always used. སྟེར་དུ་འཇུག་པ *ster-dug hjug-pa* to make or cause one to give; སྟེར་འདོད willing or wishing to give; སྟེར་བའི་ཆེད for the purpose of giving, bestowing.

སྟེར་སྒོ *ster-sgo* 1. aid, contribution; allowance, expenditure. 2. dowry, presents made by parent to daughter on giving her away in marriage.

+ **སྟེས་དབང** *stes-dbaṅ* ways, or means. རྣམས་ལེགས་པ good manners. སྟེས་དབང་གིས by the power of fate (*Schtr.*).

སྟེས *stes* वेग force, motion (*A. K. 1-48*).

སྟོ *Sto* n. of a tribe in Tibet (*Jig.*).

སྟོ་ཐག *sto-thag* a rope (*Sch.*). སྟོ་ར *sto-ra W.* a circle of dancers (*Jä.*).

སྟོ་བ *sto-wa* most frq. in colloq. phrase; ཙང་མི་སྟོ (= ཙང་མི་རྩོག) it does not matter, it makes no difference, it is all the same. ཤི་ཙང་མི་སྟོ་བ་འདུག it does not matter if they die; ཤི་ཡང་ཅི་སྟོ་སྟེ what does it matter if they die? (*Jä.*).

སྟོང *Stoṅ* I: n. of a tribe in Tibet (*J. Zaṅ.*).

སྟོང II: 1. or སྟོང་ཕྲག सहस्र a thousand; སྟོང་ཕྲག་བརྒྱ་པ शतसाहस्रिक the Mahāyāna scriptures comprising a hundred thousand *s'loka*. སྟོང་གསུམ 'the three thousands,' viz., (*a*) སྟོང་སྤྱི་ཕུད་ཀྱི་འཇིག་རྟེན་གྱི་ཁམས; (*b*) སྟོང་གཉིས་པ་བར་མའི་འཇིག་རྟེན་གྱི་ཁམས; (*c*) སྟོང་གསུམ་གྱི་སྟོང་ཆེན་པོའི་འཇིག་རྟེན་གྱི་ཁམས. 2. a fine for manslaughter to be paid in money or in goods to the relatives of the person killed; ཆེ་ཆུང་གི་སྟོང་བྱེད་པ to proportion this fine to the rank of the man killed (*Jä.*).

སྟོང་དཔོན *stoṅ-dpon* a commander over a thousand soldiers: དེང་སང་མདའ་དཔོན་ཟེར "now-a-days he is called *Mdaḥ-dpon.*" སེང་གེའི་རྩལ་ནི་དགུ་དང་རབ་ལྡན་ཞིང་ བློ་ལྡན་འཕྲུལ་ཆེ་ཁེ་ཉེན་རིག་པ་དང་། གོ་བསྲ་མཚོན་རྣོ་དཔའ་རྟ་མགྱོགས་པའི་མི་དེ་འཇིག་རྟེན་འདི་ན་སྟོང་དཔོན་ཡིན། *seṅ-geḥi rtsal-ni dgu-daṅ rab-ldan shiṅ blo-ldan ḥphrul-che khe-ñen rig-pa daṅ, go-bsra mtshon-rno dpaḥ rta-mgyogs-paḥi, mi-de ḥjig-rten ḥdi-na stoṅ dpon yin* that man is a commander over a thousand men in this world who, riding on a swift charger, has a sharp weapon and a coat of mail; he possesses the nine adroitnesses of the lion, is very intellectual and miraculously skilful as well as noble.

སྟོང་ཁུན *Stoṅ-khun* n. of an ancient king of China the fame of whose wealth was known in India even in Atis'a's time. རྒྱ་ནག་སྟོང་ཁུན་རྒྱལ་པོའི་ལོངས་སྤྱོད་དང་འདྲ་བ་ཡོད་གསུང་ *rgya-nag stoṅ-khuṅ rgyal-poḥi loṅs-spyod daṅ ḥdra-wa yod gsuṅ* they say his wealth was like that of Tong-khung Emperor of China (*A. 26*).

སྟོང་འཁོར་ལོ *stoṅ ḥkhor-lo* 1. a wheel with a thousand spokes (of fabulous properties). 2. སྟོང་འཁོར་ཞབས་དྲུང་ n. of an incarnate Lama of the monastery of *Stoṅ-ḥkhor* near Koko Nor in Amdo.

སྟོང་ཁྱབ་ནག་མོ *stoṅ-khyab nag-mo*=ཁྲོ་བོ་རྒྱས་འདེབས n. of a wrathful Bon deity.

སྟོང་ཆ *stoṅ-cha* शून्य empty, vacant.

སྟོང་ཐུན *Stoṅ-thun* 1. n. of a mythological king. 2. a number (*Ya-sel. 60*).

སྟོང་པ *stoṅ-pa* शून्य, विमानक, ख, empty, void, hollow; clear, blank; barren, without substance: ནང་མིག་དེ་སྟོང་པ་རེད the room is empty; སྒྲུབ་ཐོབ་ཀྱིས་སྔགས་གསང་རྣམས་བྲེལ་བས། འབྲུམ་ནད་བཅོམ་ཀྱིས་འབྲུམ་བུ་སེལ་ཏེ་བུ་མོའི་ལུས་སྟོང་བ་བྱུང་ secret incantations having been recited by the saint, as the small-pox was subdued, the pustules were removed and the body of the girl became clear. ཐང་སྟོང་ a desert plain; ཤོག་སྟོང་ blank paper; བྲག་སྟོང་ a rocky desert; ལུང་སྟོང་ a desolate valley; མི་སྟོང་པ a man without anything to carry; ཁང་སྟོང་ an empty house; ས་སྟོང་རི་སྟོང་ a desert place with mountains only; སྣོད་སྟོང་པ an empty vessel; ནམ་མཁའ་སྟོང་པ the void space (sky).

Syn. གསོག་གསོབ *gsog-gsob*; ཡ་མ་བརླ *ya-ma brla*; སྙིང་པོ་མེད *sñiṅ-po med*; འབྲས་བུས་སྟོང *ḥbras bus-stoṅ* (*Mṅon.*).

སྟོང་པ་ལ་རེག་པ *stoṅ-pa la reg-pa*=མེད་དོ nothing (mystic) (*K. gu.* ཁ *28*).

སྟོང་པ་ཉིད *stoṅ-pa ñid*=ཡེ་འབྱམས शून्यता, शून्यत्व emptiness, the void, vacuity; non-existence, unreality, the false or illusory nature of all things or existence. Of this we read: ཆོས་ཀྱི་རང་བཞིན་མ་གྲུབ་པའི་དོན it signifies that no object in this world is absolute, *i.e.*, simple in its nature. In Budh. metaphysics there are described eighteen kinds of *Çunyatā* or voidness :—(1) ནང་སྟོང་པ་ཉིད अध्यात्मशून्यता; (2) ཕྱི་སྟོང་པ་ཉིད अध्यात्मवहिः-शून्यता; (3) ཕྱི་ནང་སྟོང་པ་ཉིད वहिरध्यात्मशून्यता; (4) སྟོང་པ་ཉིད་སྟོང་པ་ཉིད शून्यता शून्यता; (5) ཆེན་པོ་སྟོང་པ་ཉིད महाशून्यता; (6) དོན་དམ་པ་སྟོང་པ་ཉིད परमार्थ-शून्यता; (7) འདུས་བྱས་སྟོང་པ་ཉིད संस्कृतशून्यता; (8) འདུས་མ་བྱས་སྟོང་པ་ཉིད असंस्कृतशून्यता; (9) མཐའ་ལས་འདས་པ་སྟོང་པ་ཉིད अत्यन्तशून्यता; (10) ཐོག་མ་དང་ཐ་མ་མེད་པའི་སྟོང་ཉིད अनवराग्रशून्यता; (11) དོར་བ་མེད་པའི་སྟོང་པ་ཉིད अनवकारशून्यता; (12) རང་བཞིན་སྟོང་པ་ཉིད प्रकृतिशून्यता; (13) ཆོས་ཐམས་ཅད་སྟོང་པ་ཉིད सर्वधर्म-शून्यता; (14) རང་གི་མཚན་ཉིད་སྟོང་པ་ཉིད स्वलक्षणशून्यता; (15). མི་དམིགས་པ་སྟོང་པ་ཉིད अनुपलम्भशून्यता; 16) དངོས་པོ་མེད་པ་སྟོང་པ་ཉིད अभावशून्यता; (17) ངོ་བོ་ཉིད་སྟོང་པ་ཉིད स्वभावशून्यता; (18) དངོས་པོ་མེད་པའི་ངོ་བོ་ཉིད་སྟོང་པ་ཉིད अभावस्वभाव शून्यता.

སྟོང་བྱེད་ *stoṅ-byed* expenses, expenditure.

སྟོང་མ་ *stoṅ-ma*=སྟོང་དཔོན་ or སྟོང་སྡེ་, called ཨབ་ཕྲུག *ab-phrug* in *Khams* and in *Ñag-roṅ*, a general commanding one thousand soldiers.

སྟོང་ཟད་ལ་ཚེ་སྐྱེལ་བ *stoṅ-zad la tshe-skyel-wa* to sqander, waste one's life.

སྟོང་ཞིལ *stoṅ-zil* or སྟོང་རི་ཞིལ also called གཟན་དུག་པ *Corydalis meifolia* (*Jä.*) རིམས་དང་ཚད་རིགས་འཇོམས it subdues infectious fevers, etc.

སྟོང་གསོངས *Stoṅ-gsoṅs* n. of a place in lower Takpo or *Dwags-sman* (དྭགས་སྨན) (*Rtsii.*).

སྟོང་སོབ *stoṅ-sob* फल्गु hollow like chaff. སྟོང་སོབ་ཆེན་པོ महाफल्गु very worthless; bloated; sponge-like.

སྟོངས་གྲོགས *stoṅs-grogs* 1. adj. help, co-operation, assistance (*Mṅon.*): མི་མེད་ལུང་དུ་ཕྱིན་ཡང་ལྷ་ཀླུ་ས་སྟོངས་གྲོགས་བྱེད though he visited a place where there were no men, yet he was be-friended by gods and *Nāgas* (*D.R.*). 2. sbst. a companion, a helper: ཆོས་མཛད་རྣམས་ཀྱི་སྟོངས་གྲོགས་ཡིན is a companion of those who act religiously (*Mil.* ཀ. 262).

སྟོངས་པ *stoṅs-pa* 1. pf. བསྟངས fut. བསྟང་ to accompany: ཅིས་ཀྱང་མི་སྟོངས་པ་འཆི I die without anything accompanying me. 2. to make empty; to be empty, to become waste or desolate: རང་གི་གནས་སྟོངས་ཤིང་, རང་ཡུལ་སྟོངས་ནས your own place becoming desolate; སྟོངས་ཉེ་བར་གྱུར to have become nearly empty; was almost spent or exhausted; མིས་སྟོངས་པའི་ཁང་རོ ruins forsaken by men; ས་གཞིར་སྟོངས་པ to level with the ground, to raze, to demolish entirely [from (*Jä.*).]

སྟོངས་བསྐལ *stoṅs-bskal* or སངས་རྒྱས་ཀྱི་སྟོངས་པ the period during which no Buddha appears; a state of unhappiness or མི་ཁོམ་པ, v. ཁོམ་པ *khom-pa*.

སྟོད *stod* उपर पूर्व संस्थान the upper, higher, fore, former part (of a thing): ལུས་ཀྱི་སྟོད resp. སྐུ་སྟོད the upper part of the body; ནམ་སྟོད the first portion of the night.

སྟོད་སྐོར *stod-skor* or སྟོད་ཁོར खर्व चेल a waist-coat.

སྟོད་ཁུང་སྡེ་ལྔ *stod-khuṅ sde-lṅa* the five sub-districts in the district of Toi-lung (*Deb.* ག *21*).

སྟོད་ཁོག *stod-khog* or སྟོད་པོ the upper part of the carcase (*Sch.*).

སྟོད་ཁེབས *stod-khebs* a sort of frill or ruffle of the lamas.

སྟོད་གོས *stod-gos* over-coat, upper gar-ment. སྟོད་འགག *stod-hgag* doublet worn by lamas without sleeves.

སྟོད་མངའ་རིས་སྐོར་གསུམ *Stod Mṅah-ris skor-gsum* three districts in *W.* or upper Tibet.

སྟོད་ཛ *stod-za* खदिर catechu, the resin of *Acacia catechu* (Tib. སེང་ལྡེང་ *seṅ-ldeṅ*).

སྟོད་ཐུང་ *stod-thuṅ* a short coat.

སྟོད་ཕྱོགས *Stod-phyogs* the region about the Kailas mountains, in *W.* or upper Tibet.

སྟོད་འབྲེལ *stod-hbrel* n. of a commentary written in upper West Tibet.

སྟོད་ཕུར *stot-phur*=བརྟན་པ ध्रुव the polar star.

སྟོད་སྨད *stod-smad* अद्धृषि: the upper and the lower part (of anything); also the dimensions; སྟོད་གཡོགས *stod-gyogs* lit. cover-ing the upper parts, but is explained as meaning ངག་འཇུག་དང་ཁ་སྦྱར་ལྟ་བུ (to lie) as if the face were joined to one's lower parts; also as the lid fits to the lower part of a box.

སྟོད་ར *stod-ra* (for སྟོད་སྒྲ) flattering language or speech (Sikk.); སྟོད་རས cotton cloth imported into Tibet from the direction of Ladak (*Rtsii.*).

སྟོད་ལུང་ཕུ་ཙ་ཀྱི་མོ *Stod-luṅ phu-rtsa gye-mo* district N. W. of Lhasa where is the monastery of Tshor-phug, chief seat of the Karmapa sect (*Loṅ.* ཞ *2*).

སྟོད་ལུང་མ་ཎི་ལྡན་སྐྱོག *Stod-luṅ Ma-ṇi ldan-skyog* n. of a place in Tö-lung (*Rtsii.*).

སྟོད་ལུང་ཚལ་བདེ *Stod-luṅ Tshal-bde* a sub-district of Tö-lung of which the chief town is བདེ་ཆེན་རྫོང་ *Bde-chen* Jong.

སྟོད་ལུང་མཚོ་སྨད *Stod-luṅ Mtsho-smad* part of Tö-lung: སྟོད་ལུང་མཚོ་སྨད་དུ་ཕྱིན་པའི་དུས་སུ at the time of visiting *Stod-luṅ Mtsho-smad* (*A. 27*).

སྟོད་ལེ *stod-le* 1. a jacket. 2. the upper or higher part of a country.

སྟོད་གསེར *stod-gser* gold from upper Tibet.

སྟོད་ཧོར *Stod-hor*=སྟོད་སོག *Stod-sog* the Tartars of Bokhara and Khoten (*Loṅ.* ཉ *12*).

སྟོད་པ *stod-pa* 1. vb., pf. and fut. བསྟོད to praise, commend, laud; བདག་སྟོད་པ आत्मप्रशंसा praising of one's self; རང་སྟོད་ཅན a self-admirer, self-flatterer; to extol, to glorify (men, gods, etc.), frq. སྟོད་ཅིང་བསྔགས་པ to glorify and praise; སྟོད་ཚིག praise; སྟོད་བསྔགས mystic words of praise. 2. sbst. श्लाघा praise, eulogy, compliments; complimentary phrases, *e.g.*, in letters.

N.B.—By native writers and teachers the verb in its simplest form is held to be བསྟོད་པ not སྟོད་པ.

སྟོད་གླུ *stod-glu* hymn of praise.

སྟོད་པར་བྱེད་པ *stod-par byed-pa* to praise, to extol; སྟོད་འོས laudable, commendable, worthy of praise.

སྟོད་དབྱངས *stod-dbyaṅs* the voice of praise.

སྟོན *ston* or སྟོན་ཀ 1. शरद् the autumn: སྟོན་བརྒྱ་མཐོང་བར་ཤོག་ཅིག may he live to see a hundred autumns! དགའ་བསྐྱེད་འབྲས་ལྡན་དུས་ཟླ་བ ཤ་ར་ཏ་མདའ་སྦྱིན་སྟོན་ཀའི་མིང་ s'arata the arrow-gift was formerly the name of autumn the fruitful season when joy sprang forth (*Rtsii.*). སྟོན་གྱི་མེ་ཏོག *ston-gyi me-tog* the flowers of autumn.

སྟོན་ཀ་སྤྱོད *ston-ka spyod* खञ्जन met. the swallow (lit. that pairs in autumn).

Syn. བ་མོ་བྱེའུ *ba-mo byeḥu* (*Mṅon.*).

སྟོན་ཁ *ston-kha*=སྟོན་ཀ *ston-ka*.

སྟོན་ཐོག *ston-thog*=ལོ་ཐོག harvest, autumnal crop: སྟོན་ཐོག་སྡུ་བ to gather in the harvest.

སྟོན་དོད *ston-dod*=སྟོན་མའི་སྐྱལ་བ་གསེར་དངུལ་འབྲུ་སོགས་སྐྱུད་པ the instalment of taxes in gold, silver or grain, payable in autumn just after the harvest time in Tibet (*Rtsii.*).

སྟོན་ཟླ་ཐ་ཆུང *ston-zla tha-chuṅ* कार्त्तिक the month from the middle of October to the middle of November.

སྟོན་ཟླ་འབྲིང་པོ *ston-zla ḥbriṅ-po* आश्विन from the middle of September to the middle of October.

སྟོན་ཟླ་ར་བ *ston-zla ra-wa* भाद्रपद from the middle of August to the middle of September.

སྟོན་ལྗང་ *Ston-ljaṅ* n. of a district in Tibet containing the monastery of སྟོན་ལྗང་བཀྲ་ཤིས་དགོན (*Ston-Ljaṅ Bkra-çis dgon*).

སྟོན་པ I: *ston-pa* pf. and fut. བསྟན. 1. to show, indicate. A vb. much used in ordinary talk as well as in books; the person shown anything taking the dat. c. and the object he is shown standing in the accus., *e.g.*, ང་རང་ལ་བཀྲ་ཤིས་ལྷུན་པོའི་ལམ་འདི་སྟོན་གནང་ (or སྟོན་དང་) please shew me the way to Tashi-lhunpo; དེ་དག་གིས་ཇག་དཔོན་ལ་སྒྲོག་ཆས་གང་ཡོད་རྣམས་བསྟན་ནོ they shewed the robber captain the provisions which they had. Occurs often with only the proximate object: དེ་སྟོན་རྒྱུ་ཡོད་ན་འཇིག་བྱར་བ་ཡིན་པས if it can be pointed out it shall be destroyed; སངས་རྒྱས་ཀྱིས་ཐར་པའི་ལམ་བསྟན་པར་འགྱུར Buddha will shew the path of emancipation. 2. to show, exhibit, display: དེ་འདྲ་བའི་རྫུ་འཕྲུལ་སྟོན་རྒྱུ་ཡོད miracles such as that should be shewn; ལྟད་མོ་རྩེ་བ

there was no limit to human life; (2) སྟོན་པ་ཉམས་བསྟན pantomime and frolics were displayed; ཁྱོད་ཀྱིས་དཔའ་བ་གང་བསྟན་པ་ལ་ཕོ་བོ་མཉེ the bravery which you have shewn is exhilarating to me (*Tā. 21. 13*). 3. to teach, instruct, explain: བུ་མོ་ལ་ཆོས་བསྟན་ཏེ་དད་པ་བསྐྱེས་སོ having taught the girl the doctrine, faith was born in her; དགོས་པའི་བསླབ་བྱ་བསྟན་ནས necessary precepts having been imparted. From this signification of the verb is derived the important sbst. བསྟན་པ meaning that which has been taught, and, hence, religious tenets and doctrine, and so the Buddhist religion itself in its doctrinal aspect. 4. to exemplify by overt action, to shew faith; to cause to undergo; to inflict: མི་ལ་སྡུག་བསྔལ་བསྟན་པས having visited misfortunes on the man.

སྟོན་པ II: sbst. प्रणेता, a teacher, esp. a religious teacher, commonly the founder or promulgator of a particular doctrine. Buddha is called སྟོན་པ, the teacher of Buddhism, and གཤེན་རབ་མི་བོ is the སྟོན་པ or teacher of the Bon tenets. སྟོན་པ་གང་ཟག་ཟླ་མེད་པ། གཅིག་པུ་ཚིག་ནི་གཅིག་གསུང་སྟེ། གསུང་བ་དེ་ནི་ངེས་ལེགས་པས the Teacher is without an equal, he alone has said the word and what he has said is certain (*K. du.* ད *197*). སྟོན་པའི་བསྟན་པ *ston-pahi-bstan-pa* शास्तुःशासन the religion of the teachor (Buddhism).

The ten teachers of the Bon located in the ten quarters are said to be the following:—(1) སྟོན་པ་ཞི་བ་འོད; (2) སྟོན་པ་འཁོར་ལོ་དབང་སྒྱུར; (3) སྟོན་པ་པད་མ་ཡེ་མཛེས; (4) སྟོན་པ་ཟླ་ལ་འོད་ཀྱན; (5) སྟོན་པ་ཁྱབ་བརྡལ་ཆེན་པོ (6) སྟོན་པ་ཁྱབ་པ་བདེ་མཆོག་འཁོར་ལོ; (7) སྟོན་པ་གོང་ཁྲི་བདལ་འོད་འབར; (8) སྟོན་པ་བདེ་བ་རྒྱས་འོད; (9) སྟོན་པ་བདེ་ཁྱབ་བདེ་ལྡང; (10) སྟོན་པ་འོར་བུ་རིན་ཆེན (*G. Bon. 1*). The succession of teachers སྟོན་རབས of the Bon are the following:—(1) སྟོན་པ་མི་འགྱུར་གཙུག་ཕུད appeared in this world when འབུམ་ཁྲི་གློག་གི་ལྡེ་ཙན appeared in this world when men lived a hundred thousand years; (3) སྟོན་པ་ཁྲི་པའི་རབ་བརྟན came into this world when men lived ten thousand years; (4) སྟོན་པ་གཏོ་རྒྱལ་ཡེ་མཁྱེན appeared in this world when tho duration of human life was five hundred years; (5) སྟོན་པ་གཤེན་རབ་མི་བོ came to this world in the present *Kalpa* when the duration of life is one hundred years. The first attendants of སྟོན་པ་གཤེན་རབ, the great Bon teacher, were the following:—(1) ནམ་མཁའི་བ་དན་ཅན; (2) ཁྱུང་གི་རྭ་མཚན་ཅན; (3) མ་བུའི་ཟླིམ་རྒྱང་ཅན; (4) རྒྱོད་ཀྱི་འཕོར་འདབ་ཅན; (5) ཆེ་རྒྱལ་ཀོད་ཞུ་ཅན; (6) གཅོད་པ་ཁྲ་སྔོག་ཅན; (7) དྭག་པོ་དཔལ་སྔོག་བདུད་རྩི་ཚར་སྔོག་ཅན་འཁོར་དང་བཅས (*D.R.*).

སྟོན་མུན *ston-mun* one belonging to the school of Hoshang Mahāyāna, the doctrine of absoluto inaction.

སྟོན་མོ *ston-mo* यात्रा, उत्सव festivity, feast, banquet, entertainment: སྟོན་མོ་འགྱེད་པ *ston-mo hgyed-pa* to distribute the dishes in a feast; དམངས་ཀྱི་སྟོན་མོ་འགྱེད་པ to distribute the viands of the table to the common people (*Mil.*); སྟོན་མོ་འདྲེན་པ *ston-mo hdren-pa* to serve a feast; དགའ་སྟོན festive entertainment, jubilee; རྣ་བའི་དགའ་སྟོན a feast or treat to one's ears; ཆོས་སྟོན a religious feast, or feast of charity to the poor (including monks); དུས་སྟོན a periodical feast; མིང་སྟོན feast given at the name-giving ceremony of a child; རབ་སྟོན a feast after settling some important business (*Cs.*).

སྟོབ་པ *stob-pa* दान pf. བསྟབ (acc. to *Cs.* pf. and fut. བསྟབ) imp. སྟོབ acc. to *Jä* to put into another's mouth, osp. food, to feed; also applied to a mare that shows tho grass to her foal; ནན་ཏན་གྱིས་སྟོབ་པ to press a person to accept a dish, etc. In a more general sense: ཡང་ཞི་སྟན་སྟོབ་པར་བྱེད་པ rising to offer one's own seat, to make a donation;

also ཕ་བྱད་ཐམས་ཅད་ཀྱིས་སྟོབ་པ to provide a person with every thing within one's power.

སྟོབས *stobs* or སྟོབས་པོ बल, सत्त्व, तेजः, शक्ति 1. the semen. 2. strength, vigour, force, prowess, fortitude. སྟོབས་ཅན powerful; ལུས་སྟོབས bodily vigour, physical strength; སྙིང་སྟོབས mental strength, more properly moral strength; འཇུ་སྟོབས digestive power. སྟོབས་ཀྱིས is a post. p. by means of, through.

སྟོབས་ལྔ *stobs-lṅa* पञ्चबल the five forces: (1) དད་པའི་སྟོབས श्रद्धा बल the force of faith; (2) བརྩོན་འགྲུས་ཀྱི་སྟོབས वीर्य्यबल force of energy; (3) དྲན་པའི་སྟོབས स्मृतिबल force of recollection; (4) ཏིང་ངེ་འཛིན་གྱི་སྟོབས समाधिबल force of contemplation; (5) ཤེས་རབ་ཀྱི་སྟོབས प्रज्ञाबल force of wisdom. The five སྟོབས acc. to the Bon are:—(1) བྱམས་པ་ཆེན་པོའི་སྟོབས strength of love; (2) ཡེ་ཤེས་ཆེན་པོའི་སྟོབས strength of knowledge; (3) ཞི་བ་ཆེན་པོའི་སྟོབས strength of peace; (4) སྦྱིན་པ་ཆེན་པོའི་སྟོབས strength of charity; (5) ཡངས་པ་ཆེན་པོའི་སྟོབས strength of generosity.

སྟོབས་བཅུ *stobs-bcu* दशबल a Buddha is he who is possessed of the ten kinds of strength enumerated in the sacred books, viz:—(1) བསམ་པའི་སྟོབས आशयबल the power of reflection; (2) ལྷག་པའི་བསམ་པའི་སྟོབས अध्याशयबल power of concentration; (3) སྦྱོར་བའི་སྟོབས प्रतिपत्तिबल power of acquisition; (4) ཤེས་རབ་ཀྱི་སྟོབས प्रज्ञाबल or ज्ञानबल power of wisdom; (5) སྨོན་ལམ་གྱི་སྟོབས प्रणिधानबल power of resolute prayer; (6) ཐེག་པའི་སྟོབས यानबल power of creed; (7) སྤྱོད་པའི་སྟོབས चर्य्याबल power of accomplishment or bringing to pass; (8) རྣམ་པར་འཕྲུལ་པའི་སྟོབས विकुर्व्वनबल power of changing shape; (9) བྱང་ཆུབ་ཀྱི་སེམས་དཔའི་སྟོབས बोधिसत्त्वबल power of enlightenment; (10) ཆོས་ཀྱི་འཁོར་ལོ་རབ་ཏུ་བསྐོར་བའི་སྟོབས धर्म्मचक्रप्रवर्त्तनबल power of setting the wheel of religion in motion. Again we meet with དེ་བཞིན་གཤེགས་པའི་སྟོབས་བཅུ or the ten moral virtues of a Tathāgata; these are the following:—(1) གནས་དང་གནས་མ་ཡིན་པ་མཁྱེན་པའི་སྟོབས स्थानास्थानज्ञानबल force of the knowledge of what is possible and impossible; (2) ལས་ཀྱི་རྣམ་པར་སྨིན་པ་མཁྱེན་པའི་སྟོབས कर्म्मविपाकज्ञानबल force of the knowledge of the consequences of actions; (3) མོས་པ་སྣ་ཚོགས་མཁྱེན་པའི་སྟོབས नानाधिमुक्तिज्ञानबल force of the knowledge of the different dispositions of men; (4) ཁམས་སྣ་ཚོགས་མཁྱེན་པའི་སྟོབས नानाधातुज्ञानबल force of the knowledge of different elements; (5) དབང་པོ་མཆོག་དང་མཆོག་མ་ཡིན་པའི་སྟོབས इन्द्रियपरापरज्ञानबल force of the knowledge of the higher or lower mental powers of men; (6) ཐམས་ཅད་དུ་འགྲོ་བའི་ལམ་མཁྱེན་པའི་སྟོབས सर्वत्रगामिप्रतिपथज्ञानबल force of the knowledge of the progress that leads everywhere; (7) བསམ་གཏན་རྣམ་པར་ཐར་པ་དང་ཏིང་ངེ་འཛིན་དང་སྙོམས་པར་འཇུག་པའི་ཀུན་ནས་ཉོན་མོངས་པ་རྣམ་པར་བྱང་བ་དང་ལྡན་པ་ཐམས་ཅད་མཁྱེན་པའི་སྟོབས सर्वध्यानविमोक्षसमाधिसमापत्तिसंक्लेशव्यवदान व्यवस्थान ज्ञानबल force of the knowledge of all which concerns the origin of miseries of every kind and which will lead to equanimity, mystic meditation, complete emancipation and *dhyāna*; (8) སྔོན་གྱི་གནས་རྗེས་སུ་དྲན་པ་མཁྱེན་པའི་སྟོབས पूर्वनिवासानुस्मृतिज्ञानबल force of the knowledge of remembering afterwards former abodes; (9) འཆི་འཕོ་བ་དང་སྐྱེ་བ་མཁྱེན་པའི་སྟོབས च्युत्युपपत्तिज्ञानबल force of the knowledge of birth and death; (10) ཟག་པ་ཟད་པ་མཁྱེན་པའི་སྟོབས आस्रवक्षयज्ञानबल force of the knowledge of the destruction of afflictions.

སྟོབས་ཀུན་སྟོབས *stobs-kun stobs* n. of number (*Ya-sel.* 57).

སྟོབས་བསྐྱེད་པ *stobs-bskyed-pa* बलाधान the special qualities which *Bodhisattvas* only can acquire:—(1) དྲན་པའི་སྟོབས་བསྐྱེད་པ *dran-paḥi stobs bskyed-pa* स्मृतिबलाधान memory; (2) བློ་གྲོས་ཀྱི *blo-gros kyi* मतिबलाधान intelligence; (3) རྟོགས་པའི विचारबलाधान discrimination; (4) ངོ་ཚ་ཤེས་པའི लज्जाबलाधान shame; (5)

སེམས་པའི་ भक्तिबलाधान faith; (6) བསོད་ནམས་ཀྱི་ पुण्यबल virtue; (7) གཟུགས་ཀྱི་ रूपबल physical grace; (8) སྤོབས་ཀྱི་ प्रतिभानबल self-confidence; (9) གཟུངས་ཀྱི་ धारणीबल the recitation of religious charms; (10) ལོངས་སྤྱོད་ཀྱི་ *loṅs-spyod kyi* सम्भोगबल delightfulness; (11) ལུས་ཀྱི་ कायबल bodily grace; (12) སེམས་ཀྱི་ मनोबल mental powers; (13) རྫུ་འཕྲུལ་གྱི་ ऋद्धिबल magical knowledge; (14) ཆོས་སྟོན་པའི་ धर्मबल religion; (15) བདུད་ཚར་གཅོད་པའི་ मारविजयबल vanquishing evil spirits; (16) ནན་ཏན་གྱི་སྟོབས་བསྐྱེད་པ *nan-tan-gyi stobs bskyed-pa* उद्यमबल assiduity (*K. d.* ན *353*).

སྟོབས་བསྐྱེད་གསུམ *stobs-bskyed gsum* three producers of bodily vigour: ཁྲུས་བྱས་འོ་མ་ ཆུ་སྐྱོད་ཤ, འཕྲལ་དུ་སྟོབས་བསྐྱེད་གསུམ་ཡིན་ནོ (*can.*) bathing, milk, the meat of the duck—these three quickly produce strength.

སྟོབས་ཆུང་ *Stobs-chuṅ* a n. of the son of king Bimbisāra (*J. Zaṅ.*).

སྟོབས་ཆེན *stobs-chen* महाबल a rammer, pile-driver.

སྟོབས་འཇིག *Stobs-hjig* बलभित; གཤིན་རྗེའི་གཤེད་པོ (*D. R.*) an epithet of Shin-je the lord of death, acc. to the Bon cult. [Indra, the slayer of *Bala*]*S.*

སྟོབས་ལྡན *stobs-ldan*=ལྷ་མིན असुर, बलवत्, प्रबल, दृढ very powerful; also नारायण an an epithet of Vishnu, Asura or demon.

སྟོབས་ལྡན་བསྙེམས *stobs-ldan bsñems* an epithet of Kāma (*Mṅon.*).

སྟོབས་ལྡན་བུ *Stobs ldan-bu* बलिपुत्र, वैरोचन the son of Bali.

སྟོབས་ལྡན་མ *stobs-ldan-ma* बलिनी a powerful woman, an amazon.

སྟོབས་པོ་ཆེ *stobs-po che* महाबल title of a *dhāraṇī* for causing rain during a drought (*K. gu.* མ *474*).

སྟོབས་མང་པོ *stobs maṅ-po*=met. iron;= མོང་བྱ, with syn. གསེར་གྱི་དགྲ (*Mṅon.*).

སྟོབས་མིག *stobs-mig* बलाक्ष n. of a number (*Ya-sel. 56*); སྟོབས་མིག་ཆེན་པོ=སྟོབས་མཆོག महाबलाक्ष another number.

སྟོབས་བཟང་ *Stobs-bzaṅ* 1. बलभद्र n. of the elder brother of Krishna. 2.=ཆང་དངོས spirit, alcohol (*Mṅon.*).

སྟོབས་བཟང་མ *stobs bzaṅ-ma* उरण, पिच्छा n. of a medicinal plant (*Mṅon.*).

སྟོབས་ལས *stobs-las* साहस courage, intrepidity.

སྟོར་བ *stor-wa*=ཤོར་བ also ཤོར་སྟོར་བ to go astray, to be lost; བུ་སྟོར་རོ a child has been lost; *lus-daṅ srogs stor-wa* to lose one's life; སེམས་སྟོར་བ to lose one's senses; སྟོར་མ་མེད it cannot be lost; རྫས་ལག་སྟོར་བ to lose an article; བྱ་བ་སྤྱོད་ལམ་སྟོར་པ to be misguided, lose one's character: ཐར་པའི་གཡོས་སྐལ་ངེས་པར་སྟོར་བའི་ཚེ (*A. 9*) when he was losing most certainly the good luck of emancipation; སྟོར་བ་རྙེད་པས་ཤིན་ཏུ་རྒྱས་པར་འགྱུར *stor-wa rñed-pas çin-tu rgyas-par hgyur* (*Hbrom. 57*) having regained the (thing) lost he will be very pleased.

+ སྟོར་ཁུང་ *stor-khuṅ* 1. उदकभ्रम a mirage. 2. defined as བཙོག་ཆུ་ཐམས་ཅད་རོར་མ, ལ་ཁ or དོ་མཆུ a ditch where all impurities are deposited; also a gutter or drain.

+ **བརྟ་བ** *brta-wa* fut. རྒྱས་པར་བྱ་བ pf. བརྟས་པ to grow wide, expand; be copious, abundant. བརྟས་བྱེད་པ id.; འགྱོད་པ་བས big with repentance; བག་ཆགས་བརྟས་པ inflated with passion.

བརྟག་པ *brtag-pa* ཤིང་ཆ (བརྟག་པ) परीक्ष, परीक्षित examined, v. རྟོག་པ सुपरीक्षा careful or minute inquiry or investigation, examination; རྨི་ལམ་བརྟག་པ examination of dreams; རིན་པོ་ཆེ་བརྟགས་པ་ལ་མཁས skilful in testing precious stones (*Ja.*).

བརྟག་པ་ཞུས་པ *brtag-pa shus-pa* to make inquiry, invesigatition

བརྟག་ཡས *btag-yas* (གྲངས) n. of a number.

བརྟག་དཔྱད *brtag-dpyad*=ཞིབ་དཔྱད examination, careful weighing of all the details of a ease, deliberation: རྟག་དཔྱད་མེད་པར་བྱས་ན་ཕུགས་ནས་འགྱོད (*Rdsa. 12*) if anything be done without deliberation, one repents at the end.

བརྟགས *brtajs*=བརྟོགས་པ *brtogs-pa* निपुण 1. dextrous, skilful. 2. चपला fickle, lightning.

བརྟད *brtad* अभिचार a kind of formal curse, which consists in hiding the effigy and name of an enemy in the ground and imploring some deity to kill him: བརྟད་འཛུགས་པ to perform that ceremony (*Jä.*).

+ བརྟད་པ *brtad-pa*=གློ་བུར་བ *glo bur-wa* 1. new, recent; sudden. 2. haste, speed, (*Sch.*).

བརྟན་ཁེལ་བ *brtan khel-wa* to be sure or certain of.

བརྟན་ལྡན *brtan-ldan* धीर steadfast, quiet, steady.

བརྟན་པ I. *brtan-pa* or བརྟན་པོ स्थिर, धीर, दृढ, स्थाणु, मन्द, ध्रुव, दृप्त, सक्त, स्थास्नु, नित्य 1. adj. and abstract noun: firm, steadfast, safe. 2. firmness; བརྟན་པར་གནས་པ to last, hold out, abide, centinue; བརྟན་པ་ཐོབ་པ acquire firmness and durability; བརྟན་པར་འགྱུར་བ to become firm. བརྟན་གྱི་སྐྱིད *brtan gyi skyid* a continued or abiding happiness; དཔང་བརྟན firm strength, their strength is holding out; བརྟན་དུ་འཛུགས་པ to watch, keep, preserve carefully; དམ་བཅས་པ་བརྟན་པར་ཤེས he knew his word to be inviolable; ཡི་དམ་ལ་བརྟན་པས because he firmly kept his word; དུས་བརྟན་གྱི་བདེ་བ eternal welfare, everlasting happiness; དད་པ་བརྟན་པ firmfaith (*Jä.*).

Syn. འབད་པ *bbad-pa*; གནས་པ *gnas-pa* བཅུགས་པ *bcugs-pa*; མི་གཡོ་བ *mi gyo-wa* (*Mṅon.*).

བརྟན་པ II:=རྟེན་བྱེད་མ or ས་གཞི the earth; ཕྱི་སྣོད་འཇིག་རྟེན་གྱི་ཁམས the physical or material world.

བརྟན་པ III: ध्रुव the fixed star, polar star.

Syn. of III: གསེར་ཕུར *gser-phur*; སྟོད་ཕུར *stod-phur*; རྐང་རྟེང་བུ *rkaṅ rteṅ-bu*; སྣང་ལྡན་ཤིང་རྟ *snaṅ-ldan śiṅ-rta*; ལུགས་བཟང་སྐྱེས *lugs-bzaṅ skyes*; གཟའ་ཡི་རྟེན *gzah-yi rtan*; རྒྱུ་སྐར་ཏོག *rgyu-skar tog*; གན་རྒྱལ་བུ *gan rgyal-bu* (*Mṅon.*).

བརྟན་པ་བཟུང་ *brtan-pa bzuṅ* an epithet of the *Asura* (ལྷ་མིན *lha-min*).

བརྟན་པའི་ཆོས *brtan-pahi chos* स्थिरधर्म the enduring religion, *i.e.*, Buddhism.

བརྟན་པར་བྱས་པ *brtan-par byas-pa* दृढीकृत; firmly rooted or established.

བརྟན་པོ *brtan-po*=མཁས་པ, སེམས་ཤེས་པ (*Mṅon.*); བརྟན་པོའི་དྲེགས་པ *brtan-pohi dreg-pa* (mystic); for རྡོ་དྲེགས *rdo-dregs*. (*Mṅg. 11*).

བརྟན་པར་བྱེད *brtan-par byed* स्थापयति causes to be established; the establisher.

བརྟན་བྱེད་མ *brtan byed-ma* the goddess of earth; ས་ཡི་ལྷ་མོ་ཡོངས་སུ་བརྟན་བྱེད་མ the goddess of the earth who is thoroughly steadfast (*D.R.*).

བརྟན་འཚོལ་བ *brtan htshol-wa* in བརྟན་འཚོལ་ན་ཕ་བཟང་གི་བུ་མོ་འཚོལ if you seek reliability, search for the daughter of a good father.

བརྟན་ཞལ *brtan-shal* a complimentary address or title of respect to good and honourable man.

བརྟན་གཡོ *brtan-gyo* स्थावरजङ्गम the animate and inanimate world; གཡོ་ནི་དང་བཅས་ཀྱི་སེམས་ཅན *gyo* signifies animated nature.

བརྟན་མ *brtan-ma*=1. བརྟན་པའི་ཕུང་པོ धैर्यराशि the aggregate of stability (*A. K. 1-28*). 2. v. བརྟན་མ.

བརྟབས་པ *brtabs-pa* 1.=ཁྲུམས་པ་ཐྲིམས་པ. 2.=འཚབས་པ to be afraid of, to apprehend: སྡིག་པ་ལ་བརྟབས feared sin (*Situ. 75*).

བརྟས་པ *brtas-pa* 1.=ཡར་བསྐྱེད་པ *yar bskyed-pa* grown up, anything full blown. 2. to be delighted: གསུང་བྲིས་ཞིབ་ཆ་རྟེན་ལྷ་རེག་བཅས་གནང་འབྱོར་ཡིད་མཆོག་ཏུ་བརྟས (*Yig. k. 27*) I received the note containing the particulars you have sent together with enclosure of silk scraf, and have been greatly pleased.

བརྟུན་པ *brtun-pa*=བརྩོན་པ आतापिन् assiduity, assiduous.

བརྟུན་ངེས་པ *brtun nes-pa*=གཟུ་ལུམ་དང་རང་བཙོ rash and self-sufficient; བརྟུན་ངེས་འཇུག་པ *brtun-nes hjug-pa* to be self-confident.

བརྟུམ་པ *brtum-pa* पराक्रम power, prowess.

བརྟུལ *brtul* pf. and fut. of འདུལ་བ (*Rdo-riñ. 45*).

\+ བརྟུལ་པ *brtul-pa* or བརྟུལ་པོ་བ=ཞུམ་པ or འཇམ་བ मृदु mild, gentle.

བརྟུལ་ཕོད *brtul-phod* or བརྟུལ་ཕོད་པ=དཔའ་པོ་སྙིང་སྟོབས་ཅན वीर 1. a hero, champion; བརྟུལ་ཕོད་ཁང་ abode of a hero, a tiger's den. 2. (གཡུལ་ངོར) to subdue an enemy in battle.

བརྟུལ་བ *brtul-wa*=ཉེ་བར་སྦྱོར་བ *ñe-war sbyor-wa* or ཉེ་བར་སྒྲུབ་པ 1. to conquer. 2. deportment, behaviour (*Cs.*). 3. diligence, painstaking (*Sch.*).

བརྟུལ་མ *brtul-ma* or བརྟུལ་མོ=विकुण्ठ [not blunted]*S.* བརྟུལ་མའི་བུ वैकुण्ठ heaven.

བརྟུལ་ཞུགས *brtul-shugs* व्रत, परिकर, संयमनो, व्रति, पराक्रम 1. vow; acc. to *Cs.* manner, way of acting. 2. acc. to *Sch.* exercise of penance; བརྟུལ་ཞུགས་བྱེད་པ or བརྟུལ་ཞུགས་སྤྱོད स्वर्गारिह to perform such exercises, to do penance. 3. penitent.

བརྟུལ་ཞུགས་ཅན *brtul-shugs can*=དྲང་སྲོང་ व्रति, ऋषि an ascetic; one who is penitent; a maker of penance; a sage.

Syn. དྲང་སྲོང་ *drañ-sroñ*; ཀུན་ཏུ་རྒྱུ *kun-tu rgyu*; དཀའ་ཐུབ་སྤྱོད་པ *dkah-thub spyod-pa*; ངག་བསྡམས་པ *ñag bsdams-pa*; གཙང་བར་གནས་པ *gtsañ-war gnas-pa* (*Mñon.*).

བརྟུལ་ཞུགས་དབང་ *brtul-shugs dwañ*=ཉན་ཐོས श्रावक any novice monk or disciple of the *Hinayāna* school.

བརྟུལ་ཞུགས་མ *brtul-shugs-ma*=ཁྱིམ་བདག་མོ or ཁྱིམ་བདག་མ a house-wife (*Mñon.*).

བརྟེན་པ *brten-pa* सेवित, निश्रय, v. རྟེན.

བརྟོལ *brtol*=ཕུག་པ *phug-pa* a cavern (*Mñon.*).

བལྟ *blta* fut. of ལྟ་བ we will see, let us see; also sbst. a view, prospect.

བལྟ་ན་སྡུག་པ *blta-na sdug-pa* दर्शनीय, सुदर्शन pleasant to look upon, n. of the city of Indra.

བལྟ་བའི་ཆེད *blta-wahi ched* for seeing.

བལྟ་བའི་མཐའ *blta-wahi mthah* limit of sight; met. death.

Syn. འཆི་བ *hchi-wa*; ཚེ་འདའ *tshe-hdah*; ཚེ་འཕོ *tshe-hpho*; འཆི་འཕོ *hchi-hpho* (*Mñon.*).

བལྟ་བྱ *blta-bya* चाक्षुष visible.

བལྟབས *bltabs* pf. of ལྟབ་པ, གོས་བལྟབས་པ (*Situ. 75*).

བལྟམས་པ *bltams-pa* pf. of ལྟམ་པ=འཁྲུངས་པ *hkhruñs-pa*.

Syn. སྐྱེས་པ *skyes-pa*; བཙའ་བ *btsah-wa*; བཙས་པ *btsas-pa* (*Mñon.*).

བལྟས *bltas* pf. of ལྟ་བ *lta-wa*.

བལྟས་ནས *bltas-nas* concerning, regarding, as to; used as a postp. with ལ.

བསྟང་བ *ḇstañ-wa*, v. སྟོངས་པ *stoñs-pa*.

བསྟད *ḇstaḏ*=ངོས *ños* or ཕྱོགས surface; direction: བསིལ་རི་ཕྱོགས་ལ་བསྟད on the side of a cool hill (*Ya-sel. 38*).

བསྟན *ḇstan*, दर्शन demonstration, explication (*Zam. 10*).

+ བསྟན་དཀའ་བ *ḇstan dkaẖ-wa* hard to explicate (དཔེ ग्रन्थ) a religious work or doctrine.

བསྟན་འགྱུར *ḇstan-ẖgyur* a miscellaneous collection of literary works, both sacred and general, consisting of 225 volumes. Very few of the Tangyur treatises belong to Tibetan authorship; they are mostly translations into Tibetan from Chinese and Sanskrit texts. A fine copy of this collection is stored at the India office.

བསྟན་རྒྱས་གླིང *ḇstan-ṟgyas gliñ* a monastery presided over by one of the four incarnate lamas of Lhasa from among whom by turn the *Ṟgyal-tshab*, *i.e.*, the Regent of the Dalai Lama, is selected. The monastery stands in the northern quarter of Lhasa within the walls of the city; and the title by which the lama of Tan-gye-ling is known in Tibet is བདེ་མོ་རིན་པོ་ཆེ *Ḇde-mo Rin-po-che*.

བསྟན་བཅོས *ḇstan-ḇcos* शास्त्र, आगम, श्रुति, शासन a religious commentary.

བསྟན་བཅོས་ལས་འབྱུང་བ་རྣམས *ḇstan-ḇcos las ẖbyuñ-wa ṟnams* शास्त्रीय works relating to the S'āstras: (1) དོན་མེད་ཀྱི་བསྟན་བཅོས *don-meḏ-kyi ḇstan-ḇcos*; (2) དོན་ལོག་གི་བསྟན་བཅོས *don-log-gi ḇstan-ḇcos*; (3) དོན་དང་ལྡན་པའི་བསྟན་བཅོས *don-dañ ḻdan-paẖi ḇstan-ḇcos*; (4) ཐོས་པ་ལྷུར་ལེན་པའི་བསྟན་བཅོས *thos-pa lhur-len-paẖi ḇstan-ḇcos*; (5) རྩོད་པ་ལྷུར་ལེན་པའི་བསྟན་བཅོས *ṟtsoḏ-pa lhur-len paẖi ḇstan-ḇcos*; (6) སྒྲུབ་པ་ལྷུར་ལེན་པའི་བསྟན་བཅོས *sgrub-pa lhur-len-paẖi ḇstan-ḇcos*; (7) ངན་གཡོ་དང་འབྲེལ་བའི་བསྟན་བཅོས *ñan-gyo dañ ẖbrel-waẖi ḇstan-ḇcos*; (8) བརྩེ་བྲལ་གྱི་བསྟན་བཅོས *ḇrtse bral-gyi ḇstan-ḇcos*; (9) སྡུག་བསྔལ་སྤོང་བྱེད་ཀྱི་བསྟན་བཅོས *sdug-ḇsñal spoñ-byeḏ-kyi ḇstan-ḇcos*.

བསྟན་པ *ḇstan-pa* शासन 1. doctrinal teaching in general. 2. a single doctrine or a system of doctrines. སངས་རྒྱས་ཀྱི་བསྟན་པ *sañs-ṟgyas-kyi ḇstan-pa* the doctrine or religion of Buddha; ཐུབ་བསྟན *thub-ḇstan* for ཐུབ་པའི་བསྟན་པ *thub-paẖi ḇstan-pa* id.; བཤད་པ व्याख्यान; སྒྲུབ་པ साधन; ཡོངས་སུ་བསྟན་པ परिनिर्वृति (*Intr. A. K.*). v. སྟོན་པ. གནས་ལུགས་བསྟན་པ explanation of the real state (of the body of illusion).

བསྟན་པའི་སྒྲོན་མེ *ḇstan-paẖi sgron-me* the lamp of religion, a spiritual guide, a complimentary title for a learned lama (*Yig. k. 30*).

བསྟན་པའི་མངའ་བདག *ḇstan-paẖi m̱ñaẖ-ḇdag* the lord of religion. དཔལ་ལྡན་ན་རོ་ཏའི་ཟབ་གསང་བསྟན་པའི་མངའ་བདག་མཚུངས་མེད་དམ་པའི་ཞབས་དྲུང་དུ to the feet of his holiness *Çri Narota*—the matchless lord of the profound mystic doctrines (*Yig. k. 10*).

བསྟན་པར་བྱ་བ *ḇstan-par bya-wa*=གོ་བར་བྱ་བ प्रतिपाद्य: to make intelligible, to elucidate.

བསྟན་མ *ḇstan-ma* seems to be a name given to certain female subterranean spirits living in mountainous districts. One such, in the expanded history of Gautama, under the title of འཛམ་བུ་གླིང་སོགས་དབང་ཆེན་གསེར་གྱི་ཚང་མའི་ལྷ་མོ *ẖdsam-bu-gliñ-sogs ḏwañ-chen g̱ser-gyi tshañ-maẖi lha-mo*, was, after his victory over Māra the devil, cited as a witness to his exploits. In both Milaraspa and Padma Tang-yig, we read of "the twelve *ḇstan-ma*" said to haunt the upper peaks of Mount Everest. Padma Sambhava constituted them protectors of the Doctrine in that region. Milaraspa speaks also of a གཙོ་མོ or mistress of the twelve *ḇstan-ma* whom he describes as a *khadoma* able to raise mirages before worldly eyes. (v.

Mil. ཁ, *262*). In *Rtsii.* mention is made of: བསྟད་མའི་གསོལ་མཆོད *bstad-mahi gsol-mchod* the food offerings for the guardian deity of the monastery of འབྲས་སྤུངས *hbras-spuns* (Dai-pung) called བསྟད་མ.

བསྟན་རྩིས *bstan-rtsis* a chronology; dates relative to the year of Buddha's death; བསྟན་འཛིན a follower of Buddhism, a Buddhist; an adherent of a doctrine; བསྟན་བཤིག colloq. a destroyer of the doctrine, an obnoxious person.

བསྟན་ཡས *bstan-yas* विभिह n. of a number.

བསྟན་སྲུང *bstan-srun* 1. guardian of the doctrine. 2. a guardian in general.

བསྟབས་པ *bstabs-pa* = བྱིན་པ दत्त ; བྱིན་ལེན་བྱས་པར་བཏང་བ། ཁ་ཟས་བསྟབས gifts having been freely dispensed, food was set forth (*Situ. 75*).

བསྟར་བ *bstar-wa* = ཕྱི་དོར་ལེགས་པ 1. to sweep, clean, cleanse; also adj. nice and elegant. 2. to appreciate; to be aware of (*Lig.*); བསྟར་ཆོག་པ *bstar chog-pa* = ཉམས་སུ་ལེན་ཆོག་པ to be able to comprehend, appreciate (*Yig. k. 45*).

བསྟི་བ *bsti-wa* = ངལ་བསོ་བ to take rest.

བསྟི་ཁང *bsti-khan* private house, sanctum.

+ བསྟི་གནས *bsti-gnas* འབྱུང་ཁུངས་ཀྱི་མཐིལ 1. the place of origin, source. Under this term are said to fall: སྡོད་གནས residence; ཁྱིམ home; བླ་བྲང lama's residence; ཕོ་བྲང palace; གཙུག་ལག་ཁང *Vihāra* or monastery; ཀུན་དགའ་ར་བ *Ārāma* grove or park where religious sermons are given; དགོན་པ, རི་ཁྲོད hermitage, sanctuary, retreat of वानप्रस्थ. 2. སྙིང་པོ essence.

+ བསྟི་བསྟང *bsti-bstan* = ཞེ་ས respect; ལུས་ཀྱི་ཕྱག་འདུད bowing, physically shewing respect. ང་ལ་ཟང་ཞིང་གི་བསྟི་བསྟང་གི་རི་མོར་བྱས་ཤིག (*Ya-sel. 34*).

བསྟི་མཚུངས *bsti-mtshuns* सतीर्थ a fellow religious student.

བསྟིང *bstin* = བསྒྲམས་པ आक्षीर्ण ।

བསྟིང་ཚིག *bstin-tshig* or བསྟིངས་ཚིག *bstins-tshig* उज्ञापन satire, irony; also reflecting upon conduct in polite language; censure concealed under sweet language.

Syn. འཕྱ་ཚིག *hphya-tshig*; ཚིག་གིས་བསྟིངས *tshig-gis bstins* (*Situ. 75*).

བསྟིར *bstir* supine of སྟི་བ *sti-wa.*

卐 **བསྟིར་མེད** *bstir-med* = 1. བར་མེད अवीचि one of the infernal regions. མནར་མེད་དམྱལ་བ the hell of endless torments. 2. acc. to *Jä.* restlessness.

བསྟུ་བ *bstu-wa* संग्रह to bring together discordant elements; to collect in one heap things unlike one another. The four entities which may be so drawn together བསྡུ་བའི་དངོས་པོ་བཞི are:—(1) སྦྱིན་པ दान; (2) སྙན་པར་སྨྲ་བ प्रियवादिता; (3) དོན་ལ་སྤྱོད་པ *don-la spyod-pa* अर्थचर्या; (4) དོན་མཐུན་པ समानार्थ.

བསྟུགས་པ *bstugs-pa* to make lower, to lower (*Sch.*).

བསྟུངས *bstuns* pf. ཐུང་བ, ཞག་བསྟུངས (*Situ. 75*).

བསྟུད་པ *bstud-pa*, v. སྟུད་པ.

བསྟུན་པ *bstun-pa* to be compared; ཐབས་མཁས་པ་བསྟུན་གྱིས་བསྟུ་ས་པ་དང he by skilful comparison imposed on them (*A. 127*); ཆེ་ཆུང་མཐོ་དམན་དང་བསྟུན were compared as to size and height and depth (*Yig. k. 1*).

བསྟེན *bsten* ཡོངས་སུ་ཉེ་བར་བསྟེན to attend, wait upon, respectfully, to serve; पर्युपासति lit. being ranged quite closely together, quite huddled together; also sticking most closely (*A. K. 111-3*).

བསྟེན་འདོད་གནས *bsten-ḥdod gnas* the object or person on which one wishes to rely.

བསྟེན་པ *bsten-pa* 1. pf. of *sten-pa*. 2. sbst. संभजन, vb. v. སྟེན་པ confidence;= བརྟོན་པ *brton-pa* (*Jä.*).

སྟེན་བྱ *bsten-bya* जुष one to be served, waited upon.

བསྟེན་འོས *bsten-ḥos* सेव्य fit to be respected or served.

བསྟོད་པ *bstod-pa* 1. (ཕྱུར་པ་ལ་ཐག་པས་ར་ལུག་རྟ་སོགས་བཏགས་པ) to tether cattle such as horses, sheep, goats, etc.; ཐག་པས་བསྟོད to tether with a string (*Situ. 75*). 2. eulogium, expression of praise, v. སྟོད་པ *stod-pa*.

བསྟོད་རས་བྱེད་པ *bstod-ras byed-pa* prob. བསྟོད་སྒྲ་བྱེད་པ, བསྟོད་པ to praise, to compliment; in colloq.= བསྟོད་ར or བསྟོད་སྒྲ: མཁས་བཙུན་བཟང་གསུམ་གྱི་བསྟོད་རས་ཆེ་བསྟོད་ནས being greatly praised by the learned, noble, and good (*A. 126*).

ཐ

ཐ I: *tha* the tenth letter of the Tibetan alphabet and the second consonant of the dental class. It is the aspirated form of ཏ *ta*; and in English its sound might be found in the word "Thames."

1. num. fig. 10. 2. every thing, all, total (*Sch.*).

ཐ II: defined as གླེན་པ་གཏི་མུག་པའི་དོན signifying foolishness and mental darkness.

ཐ III: In Budh. ཐ *tha* is the entrance to the cognition of all things, of matter and phenomena: (*a*) ཆོས་རྣམས་ཀྱི་གནས་དང་གནས་མ་ཡིན་པ་མཐས་པ་རྟེན་ཏོ། it demonstrates that all things are phenomenal (*K. d.* ན *114*); (*b*) གནས་མི་དམིགས་པའི་ཕྱིར་ཆོས་ཐམས་ཅད་ཀྱི་སྒོའོ it is symbolic of the instability of all things (*Ḫbum.* ཀ, *283*).

ཐ་ཀོ *tha-ko* n. of a fruit, a species of walnut. ཁམ་རྡུང, ཐ་ཀོ་འབྲས་བུ (*Sam. k. 179*).

ཐ་སྐར *tha-skar* अश्विनी 1. n. of a constellation represented in Buddhist astronomy by a woman on horseback. 2. n. of the goddess presiding over that constellation.

Syn. རྟ་ལྡན་མ *rta ldan-ma*; དབྱུ་གུ་གཅིག་པ *dbyu-gu gcig-pa*; གསལ་བའི་བུ་མོ *gsaı-wahi bu-mo* (*Rtsi.*).

ཐ་སྐར་གྱི་བུ་གཉིས *tha-skar-gyi bu-gñis* अश्विनीकुमारद्वय the two sons of *Açvinī* who are divine physicians. ཐ་སྐར་གྱི་ཟླ་བ *tha-skar-gyi zla-wa* the month of *Āçvina* (October). ཐ་སྐར་གྱི་ཉ *tha-skar-gyi ña* आश्विन पौर्णमासी the full moon in the month of *Āçvina*.

ཐ་ཁབ *tha-khab* a large needle (in *Lh.*) (*Jä.*).

ཐ་ག་ན *tha-ga-na* occurs in the work ཐ་ག་ནའི་མཚན་བརྗོད་ཀྱི་འགྲེལ་པ་ལ་སོགས་པ་གསང་སྔགས a commentary on the description of the names of *Tha-ga-na* and other terms of mysticism (*Deb.* ཀ, *27*).

+ ཐ་ག་པ *tha-ga-pa* तन्तुवाय, धावनी = ཐགས་པ་འཐག་མཁན 1. a weaver, one of the weaving caste in India. 2. in Tib. a term for the lowest class (རིགས་ངན) of people.

+ ཐ་གི *tha-gi* = ཞི་བ *shi-wa* शान्ति, मङ्गल peaceful; mild aspect.

ཐ་གུ *tha-gu* दाम, vulg. ཐི་གུ *thi-gu* a wreath, a short cord or rope; twine for making garlands; a chain or fetter.

ཐ་གུའི་ལྟོ་ཅན *tha-guhi lto-can* दामोदर an epithet of Vishnu on whose belly hang garlands (*Mṅon.*).

ཐ་གུས་ལྕི *tha-gus lci* under the weight of chains; bound by fetters or ropes: མི་གཞི་ངན་པའི་ཐོལ་སྒྱུར་ཐ་གུས་ལྕིས a man of wicked nature lies under the weight of the chain of fraud (*Khrid. 9*).

ཐ་གྲུ *tha-gru* वैपुल्य acc. to *Jä.* originally ཐག་གྲུ = རྒྱ་ཁྱོན *rgya-khyon* 1. largeness, spaciousness; abundance, plenty. 2. acc. to *Jä.* extent, width, breadth: འཛམ་བུ་གླིང་གི་ཐ་གྲུ་ཀུན་ལ *Ḫdsam-bu gliṅ-gi tha-gru kun-la* in the wholo extent of Jambudvīpa (*Glr.*).

ཐ་གྲུ་ཆེ་བ *tha-gru che-wa*=ཡངས་པ or གྲུ་ཆེ་བ very wide, spacious; extensive.

ཐ་གྲུ་ཡངས་པ *tha-gru yaṅs-pa* very spacious, abundant (*M̱ṅon.*).

ཐ་རྒྱོད *tha-r̲gyod̲* obtuse, rounded off (*Sch.*).

+ ཐ་ཅད *tha-cad̲* or ཐ་ཆད *tha-chad̲* खल, प्रतिकुष्ट, अधम, क्षुद्र base, sordid, vile (*Çer. 5*).

Syn. ཐ་རམ *tha-ram*; ཐ་ཤལ *tha-çal*; ངན་པ *ṅan-pa*; ཐ་མ *tha-ma* (*M̱ṅon.*).

ཐ་ཆུང *tha-chuṅ* 1. the last month of a season, *e.g.*, དཔྱིད་ཟླ་ཐ་ཆུང *d̲pyid̲-zla tha-chuṅ* the last month of spring, opp. to ར་བ *ra-wa* the first month. 2. the youngest of three or more sons: སྤུན་དགུའི་ཐ་ཆུང་གཉིས the youngest or last two of the nine brothers.

ཐ་སྙད *tha-s̲ñad̲* 1.=ལག་པ *lag-pa* पाणि the hand. 2. संज्ञा seems to be used of a word when employed in some peculiar sense rather than in its strictly etymological meaning; for example, as a proper name. A derived or compounded word can only be called a *tha-s̲ñad̲* when the idea it expresses does not clearly appear on analysis; ཐ་སྙད་དུ་གོ་བ understanding the sense. 3. designation; metaphor; phrase; ཞེས་ཐ་སྙད་དུ་གྲགས་སོ *shes tha-s̲ñad̲-du grags-so* so it is said to be styled. ཐ་སྙད་པའི་བདེན་པ conditional truth (*Jä.*). 4. व्यवहार behaviour, practice, dealing, business; pecuniary transaction.

ཐ་སྙད་པ *tha-s̲ñad̲-pa* दुरोदर, धव one who plays at dice; gaining at dice; one who lays stakes at play.

ཐ་སྙད་གཅིག་པ *tha-s̲ñad̲ g̲cig-pa* 1. of the same nomenclature. 2. n. of a school of doctrine.

ཐ་སྙད་དབྱེ *tha-s̲ñad̲ d̲bye* लेखक a writer.

ཐ་ཐོར *tha-thor*=ཐར་ཐོར *thar-thor* a few here and there: འཚེ་ཞིང་སྤེན་པ་ཐ་ཐོར་ཡོད་པ་ཞིག *h̲tshe-çiṅ s̲pen-pa tha-thor yod̲-pa shig* there were a few scattered bristles of *h̲tshe-çiṅ* (*R̲dsa. 18*).

ཐ་དད་པ *tha-dad̲-pa*=མ་འདྲེས་པ *ma-h̲dres-pa* पृथक्, नाना, भिन्न, असम्भिन्न distinction, separated, not mixed up together. ཐ་དད་ལྔ *tha-dad l̲ña* the five kinds of distinctions are:— (1) སྟོན་པ་ཐ་དད difference in the teachers (founders) of religions; (2) ཆོས་ཐ་དད difference in the doctrines taught by them; (3) དགེ་འདུན་ཐ་དད *d̲ge-h̲dun tha-dad̲* difference in the classes of monks; (4) ལས་ཐ་དད *las tha-dad̲* difference or varieties in works; (5) ལམ་ཐ་དད *lam tha-dad̲* difference in the ways, different methods or ways of reaching the goal (*K. du.* པ *88*). ཐ་དད་ཀྱི་མཁན་རབས the different sages or schools of sages (*Yig. 3*). ཐ་དད་བྱ་བ་ཅི་ཡིན *tha-dad̲ bya-wa ci-yin* किं नानाकारणम् what are the various doings or causes?

ཐ་དད་དུ *tha-dad̲-du* separately, variously, apart: ཐ་དད་དུ་འདུ་ཤེས་མེད་པ नास्ति नानासंज्ञा one of the eighteen ཆོས་མ་འདྲེས་པ unmixed theories of Buddha (*M.V.*). ཐ་དད་དུ་དབྱེ་ན *tha-dad̲-du d̲bye-na* if differentiated? also: synthetically, differentially. ཐ་དད་དུ་མི་འཇུག་པ *tha-dad̲-du mi h̲jug-pa*=ཐ་དད་དུ་མི་གནས་པ not differing, not being different, not admitting of differentiation.

ཐ་དད་གླིང་ལྡན v. ཐར་ནུ *thar-nu.*

ཐ་ན *tha-na* 1. polite inquiry at any time regarding a Buddhist monk's comforts while he is taking any meal, etc. This forms a part of the training in manners given to monks. 2. even, so far as, up to: ཐ་ན་གཞད་གད་བྱ་བར་བསམས་ཏེ even having thought that (one) was laughing at. ཐ་ན་

སྲོག་ཆགས་གྲོག་སྦུར་ཡན་ཆད even above the smallest insect, *i.e.*, above the ants.

ཐ་པག *tha-pag*, v. ཐར་དཔག *thar-dpag*.

ཐ་པི་ཐུ་པི *tha-pi thu-pi* confusion, disorder (*Sch.*).

ཐ་བ *tha-wa* = རེངས་པ स्तब्ध 1. (མ་སོགས) rigid, hard, compact, firm (*J. Zañ.*). 2.= ཐུ་བ *thu-wa* bad (*Mil.*). 3.= ཞེ་སྡང anger.

ཐ་བ་ངན་པ་ལྟར *tha-ba ñan-pa ltar* ऊःखलील or वीला one of the stages of *yoga* (v. ཉལ་འབྱོར་ཡན་ལག).

ཐ་བེ *tha-be* जीवक a medicinal plant *Terminalia tomentosa.*

ཐ་འབན *tha-hban* cast-off clothes; rags thrown out; སྒོ་ངོར་ཐ་འབན་རྡུལ་ཕྲོད་ནས from the heap of cast-off rags at the entrance of a house (*Pag. 180*).

ཐ་མ *tha-ma* 1. अन्तक, अन्त, प्रान्त, इतर, अधम vile, inferior, poor, humble. 2.= རྗེས་མ or མཐའ་མ the last, lowest, uttermost; ཕོ་ཐ་མ་ནོར་གྱིས་ཕྱུག་ཙ་པ་ཡིན the lowest class of male is he who is rich in wealth (*Hbrom. 51*); the last of several things, with respect to number, time, or rank: གཅན་ཟན་གྱི་ཐ་མ the meanest of the carnivorous animals; འདུས་པའི་ཐ་མ་ནི་འབྲལ the end of every meeting is parting; གཉེན་གྱི་ཐ་མས་བསྐོར *gñen-gyi tha-mas bskor* he sees his relations for the last time around him; ཟས་ཀྱི་ཐ་མ་ཟ *zas-kyi tha-ma za* he eats for the last time (*Jä.*).

ཐ་མ་ལ *tha-ma-la* 1. adv. finally, at last. 2. postp.: at the end of, after = རྗེས་ལ.

ཐ་མར *tha-mar* to the utmost, at the end, lastly; ཐ་མར་དགེ་བ *tha-mar dge-wa* पर्यवसाने कल्याण piety, auspiciousness: ཡོན་ཏན་ཐ་མར་འདུག *yon-tan tha-mar hdug* lastly, there was talent (*Hbrom. 51*).

ཐ་མ་ལས *tha-ma las* अन्ततः at the least, at all events, in any case.

‡ ཐ་མ་ཁ *tha-ma-kha* tobacco: རྫས་ངན་ཐ་མ་ཁ་ཞེས་གྲགས་པ་འདི་ནི, སྔོན་སངས་རྒྱས་མྱ་ངན་ལས་འདས་ནས་ལོ་བརྒྱ་ཙམ་སོང་བ་ན་བྱུང་། in ancient time about one hundred years after the *Nirvāṇa* of Buddha, this evil drug called *Thamakha* appeared (*Chu-bzañ.* ག, *43*). Mention is also made of tobacco in the writings of *Mucig Lab-don* dated the 12th century A.D.

ཐ་མ་ག *tha-ma-ga* also ཐ་མག *tha-mag* 1. is a Mongolian word = Tib. ཕྱག་དམ *phyag-dam* the official seal, or a warrant containing it; also tablet with the seal of authority: དཔོན་གྲགས་དར་གྱིས་སེ་ཆེན་ལས་ཐ་མ་ག་ལུང་ལས་བླངས་ཞིང་། the governor *Grags-dar* having received the warrant of official command from the Emperor *Se-chen* (Khublai-khan) (*J. Zañ.*). 2. in *W.* tobacco.

ཐ་མལ་པ *tha-mal-pa* सचराचर ordinary, mean, coarse, vulgar, common, general, usual: ཐ་མལ་པར་འདུག་པ to live like the vulgar; ཐ་མལ་པ་མ་ཡིན that is no usual thing, no common or ordinary thing (*Jä.*).

ཐ་ཚིག *tha-tshig* = ཁས་བླངས་དམ་བཅས་པ or ཁ་ཆད་ཚིག་དན vow, promise, solemn word: མ་གཡེལ་མ་གཡེལ་སྔོན་གྱི་ཐ་ཚིག་དགོངས forget not, forget not, reflect on your former vows! སྔོན་གྱི་ཐ་ཚིག་གཅན་པོ་ཉེར་དགོངས་ལ in thinking closely on thy former rigid vows. In the common saying ཁ་དཔེ་ལ་ཐ་དམ་ཚིག *kha-dpe la tha dam-tshig* the words *tha dam-tshig* signify solemn vow.

ཐ་ར་ཐོ་རེ *tha-ra tho-re* in *W.* wide asunder, wide; ཐ་ར་ཐོ་རེ་བཞག་པ *tha-ra tho-re bshag-pa* to scatter, to throw loosely about (*Jä.*).

✦ ཐ་རམ *tha-ram* 1. खल vile, mean: གཤེན་རབ་ལ་གསོལ་བ། ཐ་རམ་ལྕགས་ཀྱིས་བསྡམ་ན he prayed to *Gçen-rab* that the vile ones should be laid under chains (*Bon*). 2. a medicinal herb in *Lh.*, *Plantago major* (*Jä.*) ཐ་རམ་འཁྲུ་བ་གཅོད་པར་བྱེད *tha-ram hkhru-wa gcod-par byed* the herb *tharam* stops diarrhœa. 3. the breadth of a plain (*Sch.*).

ཐ་རམས *tha-rams* = གཏམས་པ *gtams-pa* adj. full.

ཐ་རུ *tha-ru* the utmost limit (*Schf.*).

ཐ་ལོང *tha-loṅ* in *W.* a sort of red cloth (*Jä.*).

ཐ་ཤལ *tha-çal* पिशुन, खल, कुत्सित 1. modest, lowly; base, ugly. 2. a mischievous person, one who is inferior, cruel, and mischief-making: གང་ཟག་མཆོག་གི་སྐྱེ་བ་དེང་སང་ཁམས་ཆེ་བའི་ཚུལ་མི་སྟོན་པར་ཐ་ཤལ་བའི་ཚུལ་དུ་བཞུགས (*Ya-sel. 11*) now-a-days the incarnations of great and sanctified souls do not make show of greatness but live in modest and humble manner. སྐྱེས་བུ་ཐ་ཤལ་ཉིད *skyes-bu tha-çal ñid* a n'er-do-weel.

ཐག I: *Thag* 1. n. of a place in Tibet: ཐག་གི་རྒྱ་བོར་ཡང་དག་གི་སྒྲུབ་པ་མཛད་པའི་ཚེ at the time he was engaged in the acquirement of perfection at *Rgya-bo* in Thag (*Deb. 5*). 2. for ཐག་འགྲམ the palate. ཐག་འགྲམ *thag-hgram* = འགྲམ་སོ *hgram-so* जिह्म the human palate; swelling of the tongue.

ཐག II: distance: ཐག་ཅི་ཙམ *thag ci-tsam* how far; མ་ཐག *ma-thag* only now, just now, gen. with a verbal root: སླེབས་མ་ཐག་ཡིན་པ he that has arrived just now (*Glr.*); རྫར་བ་བཤད་མ་ཐག་པ (the passages) that have been explained just now; as an adv. gen. མ་ཐག་ཏུ *ma thag-tu* or only མ་ཐག *ma-thag* frq., *e.g.*, ཐོས་མ་ཐག་ཏུ as soon as he had heard; དེ་མ་ཐག་ཏུ *de-ma thag-tu* immediately (from *Jä.*).

ཐག་ཉེ་བ *thag ñe-wa* or ཐག་ཉེ་མོ *thag-ñe-mo* निकट near; proximity; ཐག་ཉེ་བོ་མ་བྱེད do not be familiar, keep at a distance. ཐག་ཉེ་སར་སྡད *thag ñe-sar sdad* sit near, in the vicinity.

Syn. ཉེ་ལོག *ñe-log*; ཉེ་འཁོར *ñe-hkhor*; དྲུང་ན་མོ *druṅ-na-mo*; གློ *glo*; ཐོ་འཁོར *tho-hkhor* (*Mṅon.*).

ཐག་རན *thag-ran* fibre from the bark of plants or trees, &c., v. རན་མ *ran-ma*.

ཐག་རིང *thag-riṅ* दूर; distance; distant: ཐག་རིང་པོ་མ་བྱེད *thag-riṅ-po ma-byed* do not make it distant; ཐག་རིང་གཉེན་ལས་ཁྱིམ་མཚེས་བརྒྱ་དག a neighbour is a hundred times better than a relation residing at a distance. ཐག་རིང་སྦྱང་, v. སྦྱང་པ.

Syn. འགྱངས *hgyaṅs*; རྒྱང་རིང *rgyaṅ-riṅ*; བསྐལ *bskal*; ཆེས་རིང་བ *ches-riṅ-wa* (*Mṅon.*).

ཐག་རིང་པོ *thag-riṅ-po* or ཐག་རིང་མོ *thag riṅ-mo* far distant, a great distance; ས་ཐག་རིང *sa-thag riṅ* a far or remote country. ཐག་རིང་པོ་ནས *thag riṅ-po nas* from afar, from a distance.

ཐག་གཅོད་པ *thag gcod-pa* vb. a. (ཐག་ཆོད་པ *thag chod-pa* or ཐག་ཆད་པ *thag-chad-pa* vb. n. or passive) 1. to cut the cord, sever, disconnect; to abandon: བདག་ཉེ་དུ་དང་འབྲེལ་ཐག་བཅད་པས་བདེ *bdag ñe-du daṅ hbrel-thag bcad-pas bde* I am glad at having severed the connection with my family; འགྲོ་བའི་རེ་ཐག་ཆད the hope of going has been given up. Acc. to *Schtr.* ཧོ་ཐག་གཅོད་པ *ho-thag gcod-pa* = to wean (a child); བློ་ཐག་ཆོད *blo-thag chod* deliberation is cut off, the matter is decided or resolved upon. 2. to decide, resolve, determine: རྒྱལ་པོ་བསྒྲོང་བར་ཐག་བཅད་པ it was determined to murder the king; ཁྱོད་གཉིས་ང་ལ་ཆུང་མ་མི་ལེན་ཐག་ཆོད་པ་ན if you both positively refuse to give me a wife. ཐག་ཆོད་པ་བྱེད་པ to be sure, to decide, be certain: གྲོངས་པར་ཐག་བཅད་པ as it is quite certain that he has died; ཡོད་ཐག་ཆོད *yod thag-chod* there are certainly: ཆོས་དར་ཧོན་ཐག་ཆོད་ *chos dar hon thag-chod* it is quite certain that religion will spread; ཀླས་པས་ཐག་བཅད་ནས being immovable in contemplation.

ཐག་བཅད་པ *thag bcad-pa* is same as ཐག་བཅད་མེད་པ नियत decided, finished. ང་ནི་ཕྱོགས་དེ་ལ་མི་ཐིག་ཐག་ཆོད་ཟེར *ṅa-ni phyogs de-la mi-thig thag-chod zer* (*Rdsa. 31*).

Syn. བཟླས་པ *bzlas-pa*; ཕྱང་ཆད *phyaṅ-chad* (*Mṅon.*).

ཐག་ཆོད *thag-chod* certainty; surety, evidence: འོན་ཀྱང་ཐག་ཆོད་བྱེད་དགོས but one should know for certain, one must be sure of it (*Mil.*); ཁྱེད་པ་ཐག་ཆོད་ཀྱི་རྣལ་འབྱོར་པ you, the ascetic (*yogi*), firm in meditation (*Jä.*).

ཐག་ཐག *thag-thag* the noise made by the fingers on a door, etc., an onomotopetic word; སྒོ་ལ་ཐག་ཐག་བྱེད་པ to knock on or at the door.

ཐག་པ *thag-pa* or པ་ཐག 1. लता a creeping plant, root. 2. रज्जु गुण a rope, cord; བལ་ཐག *bal-thag* rope made of wool; རྩིད་ཐག *rtsid-thag* rope of the long hair of the Yak; རྩ་ཐག *rtsa-thag* or ཕོན་ཐག *phon-thag* rope of grass; ལྕགས་ཐག *lcags-thag* iron-chain, wire-rope; རས་ཐག *ras-thag* cotton-rope, bandage (*Jä.*). ཐག་མིག *thag-mig* mesh of a net (*Sch.*); ཐག་ཟོ *thag-zo* rope-work; rope maker's work; ཐག་ཁྲ་སྦྲུལ་མཐོང་བ *thag-khra sbrul-mthoṅ-wa* lit. mistaking a spotted string for a snake; fig. to be helpless, to be very afraid of. ཐག་པས་བཏགས་སྦྱར་པ पाशावकीलिता to be attached or tied by a rope (*A. K. 1-16*). བདག་ཅག་གིས་སྙིང་ཐག་པ་ནས་སྐྱོང་ཞིང་བསྲུང་། we shall watch, defending you in all sincerity (*Surañ. 124*).

ཐག་པ་གསུམ *thag-pa gsum* fig. the three fetters: (1) མི་གཡེངས་པའི་དྲན་ཐག་བསྲིང་ to preserve an undisturbed or undeviated memory; (2) མ་བཅོས་པའི་ངང་ཐག་བསྲིང་ for a long time to remain unagitated and without expressing pain; (3) མི་སྐྱོད་པའི་གཟུགས་ཐག་བསྲིང་ to sit still for a long time unmoved (*Bon*).

ཐག་གྲུ *thag-gru* = ཐ་གྲུ *tha-gru*.

ཐག་འགྱངས *thag-ḥgyaṅs* = ཐག་རིང་ *thag-riṅ* distant, remote; also late. ས་གནི་ཐག་འགྱངས་ཀྱི་ནད་པ་ཡུན་སོང་གཡལ་ཆེའི་རིགས important cases of long-suffering patients coming from a distance (*D. çel. 11*).

ཐག་མ *thag-ma* = འཇམ་པ *hjam-pa* or གཉེན་པ *gñen-pa* soft or fine (of cloth, woollens, etc.); ཐག་མ་སྣུ་མ་རྣམ་གཉིས་ལས of the two kinds of grey (woollens) of fine texture (*Jig.*).

ཐག་བཟང་རིས *Thag-bzaṅ ris* an epithet of the lord of the *Asura* or ལྷ་མིན demi-gods.

ཐགས *thags* texture, web. ཐགས་ཀྱི་རྒྱུ *thags-kyi rgyu* तन्तुवाय any stuff with which to weave, warp.

ཐགས་ཁྲི *thags-khri* वेम weaver's loom.

ཐགས་མཁན *thags-mkhan* ऊर्णनाभ, तन्तुवाय 1. the spider, a weaver. 2. ཚེར་ཐགས *tsher hthag* a fence of thorny plants (*Mṅon.*). ཐགས་མཁན་འབུ *thags-mkhan ḥbu* lit. the weaving insect; a spider.

ཐགས་སྒྲུ་བུ *thag-sgru bu* or གྲུ་གུ *gru-gu* balls of thread or yarn to weave with.

ཐགས་ཐོགས *thags-thogs* impediments (*Cs.*).

ཐགས་འཐག་པ *thags ḥthag-pa* 1. वयन to weave. 2. = ཐགས་འཐག་མཁན *thags ḥthag-mkhan* a weaver.

ཐགས་སྣལ་མ *thags snal-ma* thread or yarn.

ཐགས་སྤུན *thags-spun* प्रसर thread stretched cross-wise in weaving.

ཐགས་བྲན་བྱེད་པ *thags-bran byed-pa* to begin the warp (*Jä.*).

ཐགས་ར *thags-ra* weaver's yard.

+ ཐགས་རན *thags-ran* = བཏགས་པ *btags-pa* attached, tied, bound, fastened.

ཐང་ *thañ* I: = སྐད་ཅིག *skad-cig* क्षण, पल a moment, an instant; ཐང་གཅིག *thañ-gcig* one moment, a very short time; ཐང་འགའ་འབྱུང་བ तत्क्षणिका momentary; ཚིག་ཐང་ *tshig-thañ* one moment; བཞི་ཐང་ *bshi-thañ* four moments; ཐང་ཙམ *thañ-tsam* = ཡུད་ཙམ or ཡུན་ཙམ a little while.

ཐང་ II: 1. a plain, steppe; but the Tibetan plain is never level and always of a basin-like or hollowed configuration. གྲམ་ཐང་ *gram-thañ* a fenny or swampy plain (*Cs.*). སྤང་ཐང་ *spañ-thañ* a green grassy plain, meadow; རྩ་ཐང་ *rtsa-thañ* steppe; བྱང་ཐང་ *Byañ-thañ* the northern steppes of Tibet, commonly called the Jang-thang. བྱེ་ཐང་ *bye-thañ* sandy plain or desert. ཧོལ་ཐང་ *hol-thañ* ground covered with clover, pasture ground, grassy plain, (*Jä.*); ཤག་ཐང་ *çag-thañ* a gravelly plain. 2. when used with the word རིན, *thañ* signifies price, value. It is also used pleon. རིན་ཐང་ id. རིན་ཐང་ཅན *rin-thañ-can* dear, precious; ཡོང་ཐང་ *yon-thañ* in *W.* income, profit; in *C.* = the measure of anything. ལོ་ཐང་ *lo-thañ* the measure of produce, *i.e.*, grain; also yearly tribute; ལོ་ཐང་གཅོད་པ *lo-thañ gcod-pa* to fix yearly tribute; ཟ་ཐང་ *za-thañ* (a person's) measure of food taken at each meal; capability of eating. 3. clear, serene: ནམ་ཐང་ *nam-thañ* a cloudless sky, fine weather; བཀའ་ཐང་ *bkah-thañ* clear order or command; ཐང་ཡིག *thañ-yig* plain or clear decree or order. པད་མ་ཐང་ཡིག *pad-ma thañ-yig* is the abridged collection of legends about Padma Sambhava. 4. ཐང་ *thañ* in སྨན་ཐང་ signifies potion, plain decoction, or mixture to be drunk after a medicinal pill has been taken; ཇ་ཐང་ *ja-thañ* plain tea. རྐང་ཐང་ *rkañ-thañ* on foot (*Jä.*).

ཐང་ཀ *thañ-ka* or ཐང་ག *thañ-ga* 1. a plain, a flat field, alluvial plain. 2. resp. ཞལ་ཐང་ *shal-thañ* a portrait, a painting; ཐང་སྐུ *thañ-sku* or སྐུ་ཐང་ *sku-thañ* a picture or representation of a deity on cloth or paper.

ཐང་དཀར *thañ-dkar* 1. white-tailed eagle (*Sch.*). 2. a greyhound.

ཐང་སྐྱ *Thañ-skya* (lit. white plain), a locality near Lhasa; ལྷ་ས་ནུབ་ཕྱོགས་ཐང་སྐྱ་དགོན་པ་ཞེས་པའི་དགོན་པ་ཞིག་ལྷ་སའི་ནུབ་ཕྱོགས་ལ་ཡོད to the west of Lhasa in that place there was a monastery called *Thañ-skya dgon-pa* (*Deb.* ག, *18*).

ཐང་ཁྲག *thañ-khrag* cedar used medicinally (*Med.*). ཐང་རག *thañ-rag* colloq. of ཐང་ཁྲག *thañ-khrag*. ཐང་འབྲུ *thañ-hbru* ceder nuts (*Sch.*).

ཐང་ཁྲུང་ *thañ-khruñ* 1. bastard (*Sch.*). 2. = ཐང་ཆུ *thañ-chu*.

ཐང་ཁྲོམ *thañ khrom* धुस्तूर = ཐང་ཕྲོམ *thañ-phrom* a medicinal herb of white and black species; bears the thorn-apple used for intestinal worms.

ཐང་ཆུ *thañ-chu* gum.

Syn. དཔལ་གོས *dpal-gos* (*Mñon.*); ཚི་བ *tshi-wa* (*Med.*).

ཐང་ཆུང་གཙང་པོ *Thañ-chuñ gtsañ-po* n. of a river passing by Thang Chung in Tibet (*Deb.* ག, *34*).

ཐང་བྲང་ *thañ-brañ* lit. a place in a plain, an encampment on a plain: ནུབ་མོ་ཆུ་སྐམ་ཅིག་ཏུ་ཐང་བྲང་བཅའ་ནས་བཞུགས at night he stayed encamping in a (dried) water-course (*A.* *74*).

ཐང་མ་མེ་སྒྲོན *Thañ-ma me-sgron* an epithet of a deity of the Bon pantheon resembling Maitreya in his attributes: སྟོན་པ་གཙོ་མཆོག་ཀུན་བཟང་ནས་ཐང་མ་མེ་སྒྲོན་གྱི་བར་བཅོ་བརྒྱད་བྱུང་ between the chief great teacher Kunzang and *Thañ-ma me-sgron* there arose eighteen (*B. grub. 1*).

ཐང་མར *thañ-mar* (lit. tree-butter or oil) a balsam; acc. to *Cs.* tar.

ཐང་ཚྭ *thañ-tshwa* salt obtained from a dry place, quarried salt: ཐང་ཚྭམ་འདི་འདུལ་ཉེམ་པ་གསུམ་སྐྱེད rock-salt (collected from dry places) soothes evil-spirits and produces the three evils—phlegm, bile and wind (*Med.*).

ཐང་གཤལ་ *thañ-gshal*=ཐང་འཇལ་ *thañ-hjal* survey; map or plan of a place (*Rtsii.*).

ཐང་གཞི་ *thañ-gshi*=རིན་ཐང་ price, market-price; ཐང་གཞི་ཆག reduction of the cost price: the market price abates (*Jä.*).

ཐང་པོ་ *thañ-po* enduring, able to stand fatigue; able and hardy, strong, tense; fig. tight, firm, also tenseness: གཟུགས་པོ་ཐང་ངམ *gzugs-po thañ-ñam* are you strong? ང་གཅོད་པ *thañ gcod-pa* to tire, fatigue.

ང་ཆད་པ *thañ chad-pa* or ཐང་ཆོད་པ *thañ chod-pa* fatigue; to be fatigued, tired, wearied. Syn. ངལ་བ *ñal-wa*; དུབ་པ *dub-pa*; ཉོན་མོངས་པ *ñon-moñs-pa* (*Mñon.*).

ཐང་ཤ་གཅོད་པ *thañ-ça gcod-pa* to strain, to stretch: དགེ་བའི་ཕྱོགས་སུ་ཐང་ཤ་ཆོད exert yourself on the side of virtue (*D.R.*).

ཐང་ལྷོད *thañ-lhod* tight and loose; the fit of clothing. ཐང་ལྷོད་མེད་པ *thañ-lhod med-pa* neither strict nor mild or relaxed. ཞིབ་ཆ་ཐོན་རིགས་ཀྱི་ཐང་ལྷོད་མེད་པའི་ཆ་འདོག་ཅིང་ (*D. çel. 11*) as to arriving at detail, making the investigations without relaxation or strictness.

ཐང་ཇུ *Thañ-ju* n. of one the emperors of China of the great T'añ dynasty. ཐང་ཐེ་ཇུང་ *Thañ-the juñ* emperor T'aijung whose daughter was married to king *Sroñbtsan sgam-po* about the year 633 A. D.

ཐང་ཐུང་ *thañ-thuñ*=ཐང་ཆུང་ inferior, unimportant; བཟོ་རིགས་ཐང་ཐུང་གི་གྲངས་ཆ included in the inferior class of artizans (*Rtsii.*).

ཐང་དུ *thañ-du* 1. in the opinion of; ཉུང་ཟད་དགའ་བའི་རེ་བ་ཡོད་ཀྱང་ལ་ལའི་ཐང་དུ although little reliable hope remained, yet in the opinion of some (*J. Zañ.*). 2. for ཐང་ཡིག་ཏུ *thañ-yig-tu*.

+ ཐང་ལ *thañ-la*=བཀྲམ་པ *bkram-pa* spread over.

ཐང་ཤིང་ *thañ-çiñ* क्रमिक, देवदारु, पूतिकाष्ठ, fir, pine; deodar tree.

Syn. བཅུད་འཛིན *bcud-hdsin*; ཐང་ཆུ་ཤིང་ *thañ-chu-çiñ*; ལྗོན་པ་སེར་པོ *ljon-pa ser-po*; གསོམ་ཤིང *gsom-çiñ* (*Mñon.*).

ཐང་སག *Thañ-sag* n. of a district in Phanyul, W. N. W. of Lhasa (*Loñ. 11*).

ཐང་ཐང་ *thañ-thañ* strained to utmost: ཤ་ཐང་ཐང *ça-thañ-thañ* to the utmost of one's muscles.

ཐད *thad* 1. aside, in one direction. ལུས་སྲོག་ཐད་ལ་བཏང་ནས leaving aside body and soul, *e.g.*, sacrificing his body and soul (for the sake of his religion). དེའི་ནུབ་ཐད་ཀྱི situated on the direct west of it (*A. 65*); ཤའི་ཐད་ན་ཆོད cut off from the flesh only. 2. in *C.* entire, whole, untouched (*Jä.*).

ཐད་ཀ *thad-ka* 1. the direction, straight forward. སྟེང་དང་འོག་དང་ཐད་ཀ་ཐམས་ཅད་དུ upward and downward, and in every direction; སྟེང་འོག་ཐད་ཀར straight upward and downward: ཇོ་བོ་བཞུགས་པའི་ཐད་ཀ་ནས་ཅོག་ཀྲངས་དང་ཅུར་སྒྲ from the direction where Atis'a resided were noises and voices in the distance (*A. 27*); ཐད་ཀར་འགྲོ go straight on, in the direction of that which moves or walks horizontally, *i.e.*, तिर्यक्।

ཐད་ཀའི་འཇིག་རྟེན་གྱི་ཁམས *thad-kahi hjig-rten-gyi khams* तिर्यग्लोकधातु the animal kingdom; one of the twenty-four regions of the world (*M.V.*).

ཐད་ཀར *thad-kar* each for himself (*Glr.*) (*Jä.*).

ཐད་ཀྱ *thad-kya* or ཐད་ཀར་ལ *thad-kar la* 1. straight on; just so, in colloq. 2.=དེ་འདྲ *de-hdra* like that, so.

ཐད་དགུ *thad-dgu* n. of a number (*Ya-sel. 56*).

ཐད་དུ་ *thad-du* towards, in straight direction; over against, in presence of; exactly in the direction of a thing.

ཐད་དྲང་ *thad-drañ* straight, not bent or crooked: སྒོ་གཉིས་ཐད་དྲང་ཕུག་མ་གསལ two doors directly opposite to one another illumined the inside space (*Jig.*).

ཐད་དྲང་ན *thad drañ-na* directly ahead.

ཐད་དོ *thad-do* the remnant of the carcase of a sheep killed.

ཐིམད *thamd* abbr. of ཐམས་ཅད *thams-cad* whole, all.

ཐན *than* = ལན a reply (esp. in the dialect of Upper Tibet); ཐན་བསྐུར *than bskur* = ལན་བསྐུར་བ *lan-bskur-wa* to send a reply: ཡང་ཕྱིན་ཉིང་མར་ལོག་ནས་ཐན་བྱ་བ་མ་ཐུབ་ again having gone (there) and come down back, he could not send a reply (*A. 15*).

ཐན་ཀོར *than-kor* or ཐན་སྐོར *than-skor* = རྒྱལ་ཕྲན सामन्तक a vassal or feudatory chief; acc. to *Sch.* surrounding country.

ཐན་ཐུན *than-thun* a little (*Sch.*).

ཐན་པ *than-pa* = ཆར་མི་འབབས་ अवग्राह rainlessness, drought, want of rain; also ominous: རྒྱལ་པོ་དེ་སྐོམ་པ་རྣམ་བྱེད་ན་འཇིག་རྟེན་དུ་ཐན་པ་འོང if the king (*Cakravartti-rāja*) feels thirsty drought comes into this world (*A. 26*).

Syn. གནམ་གྱི་འཇིགས་པ *gnam-gyi hjigs-pa*; གནམ་གྱི་སྐྱོན *gnam-gyi skyon*; ཆར་མེད་སྟེང་འབར *char-med steñ-hbar*; ཚ་བས་ཉེན *tsha-was-ñen*; མུ་གེ་བསྐྱེད *mu-ge bskyed*; ཤོད་ཀྱི་བགེགས *shod-kyi bgegs*; གནམ་གྱི་ཉེར་འཚེ *gnam-gyi ñer-htshe*; གནམ་དམག *gnam-dmag* (*Mñon.*).

ཐན་བྱ *than-bya* lit. the bird of drought, *i.e.*, of ominous appearance and cry, defined as འུག་པ་དང་སྲིན་བྱ་སོགས་ལྟས་ངན་གྱི་སྐད་འདོན་པའི་བྱ the owl and other monster birds the cry of of which prognosticates evil.

ཐབ *thab* or མེ་ཐབ *me-thab* 1: रन्धनकुण्ड। resp. གསོལ་ཐབ *gsol-thab* fire-place, hearth; ལྕགས་ཐབ *lcags-thab* iron-stove; ཐབ་ཆོར *thab-çor* the hearth is running over, *i.e.*, the food placed on it runs over in boiling; ལྟོ་ཐབ *lto-thab* a hearth to cook food; སྦྱིན་སྲེག་གི་ཐབ *sbyin sreg gi thab* an oven to burn sacrificial offerings; ཐབ་ཀྱི་ས་ཚིག་རྒྱ་མའི་སྲིན་འབུ་སེལ the burnt clay of a hearth purges intestinal worms (*Med.*).

ཐབ་ཀ *thab-ka* or ཐབ་ཁ *thab-kha* अग्निक, चुल्ल hearth, fire-place; ཐབ་ཀ་ཚམ་ཡོད *thab-ka tsam-yod* how many fire-places, *i.e.*, households, are there? (*Jä.*). དེ་ནས་བན་དེ་མོས་ཇོ་བོའི་ཐབ་ཁ་བཅོས་པས then the female Bandé prepared a hearth for cooking food for the lord (Atis'a) (*A. 103*).

Syn. ཐབ་སྒྱིད *thab-sgyid*; སྒྱིད་བུ *sgyid-bu*; གཡོས་ཐབ *gyos-thab*; མེ་ཐབ *me-thab*; གཡོས་ས *gyos sa* (*Mñon.*).

ཐབ་ཀ་བ *thab ka-wa* or ཐབ་ཁ་པ *thab kha-pa* = མ་ཆེན *ma-chen* a cook.

Syn. ལག་བདེ *lag-bde*; འདྲེན་ཐང *hdren-thañ*; ཆག་ཚང་བ *chag-tshañ-wa*; ཟས་གཉེར *zas-gñer*; ཟས་བྱེད *zas-byed*; འཚེད་བྱེད་མ *htshed-byed-ma*; ཟན་མ *zan-ma*; གཡོས་མ *gyos-ma*; ཐབ་ཀ་པ *thab ka-pa*; གཡོས་དཔོན *gyos-dpon*; ལག་བདེའི་དཔོན་པོ *lag-bdehi dpon-po* (*Mñon.*).

ཐབ་ཁག *thab-khag* different kinds of hearth: ཐབ་ཁག་མང་པོ་ཡོད་པ་ལ there were many kinds of hearths (*Rtsii.*).

ཐབ་ཁང *thab-khañ* रन्धन गृह kitchen, cook-house = ཐབ་ཚང *thab-tshañ*.

Syn. ཚང་བང *tshañ-bañ*; བསྲོ་ཁང *bsro-khañ*; གཡོས་ཁང *gyos-khañ*; འཚོད་པའི་གནས *htshod-pahi gnos*; གསོལ་ཁང *gsol-khañ* (*Mñon.*).

ཐབ་ཁྲོ *thab-khro* a cauldron or large bell-metal vessel to cook food, tea etc.

ཐབ་སྒྱིད *thab-sgyid* = ཐབ་ཀ *thab-ka* hearth, a cooking tripod.

ཐབ་སྒྲོམ *thab-sgrom* a chest or basket wherein cook's utensils, etc., are kept.

ཐབ་གདན་ཆ *thab gdan-cha* cooking furniture, utensils, etc.

ཐབ་བསུ *thab-bsu* receiving a great man by waiting on the way he comes with cooking appliances, etc., to serve him with warm tea and cooked food.

ཐབ་ལྷ *thab-lha* the deity presiding over the hearth. If milk or broth boil over, he must be appeased by casting butter in the fire; and, often, by more elaborate ceremonial, sometimes even by digging up the hearth.

ཐབ་ལྷ་སེ་ཤར *Thab-lha se-çar* (མ་བདག) n. of a hearth-god.

ཐབ་ཐབ *thab-thab* flapping noise: ཤོག་པ་ཐབ་ཐབ་ལན་གསུམ་བྱས *çog-pa thab-thab lan-gsum byas* its wings thrice flapped (*Rdsa. 17*).

ཐབ་ཐིབ *thab-thib* (གྲངས) वीजग n. of a large number.

ཐབས *thabs* उपाय, योग, निःसरण, उपक्रम 1. opportunity, chance, possibility: མཐོང་ or འགྲུལ་ཐབས་མ་བྱུང་ I had no opportunity of seeing or going; ཐབ་ཤིག་ཉིད་རང་ནས་མི་འབྱུང་ན in *W.* if you offer no chance, if on your part it is not made possible; ཐབས་མི་ཐུབ I am not able, I cannot; གདན་དྲངས་པའི་ཐབས་མེད there will be no chance of bringing (the princess); འབྲོས་པའི་ཐབས་མེད there is no chance of escaping; ལམ་ལ་གཡོལ་ཐབས་མེད there is no occasion for tarrying on the road. ཐབས་བཞི *thabs-gshi* the four resources are the following:—(1) དཔུང་དང་མཐུ་བརྗོད་ལྡན་པའི་ཐབས, (2) བང་མཛོད་ནོར་གྱིས་གང་བའི་ཐབས, (3) དབྱེན་ན་བསྡུམས་པར་བྱེད་པའི་ཐབས, (4) བསྡུམས་ན་ངོ་སྲུང་བྱེད་པའི་ཐབས. 2. way, manner, mode: ཀློག་ཐབས way of reading; ཀུན་ཐབས in a thievish manner, by theft; རྒྱལ་པོའི་ཐབས་གཏོང་བ to give up the way (of life) of a king, *i.e.*, to renounce royalty. ཐབས་གཅིག་ཏུ *thabs gcig-tu* together, in company with; ཐབས་གཅིག་ཏུ་བཞུགས་སོ jointly sat down, stayed, resided in company; ཐབས་གཅིག་ཏུ་འགྲོ going together to a place. 3. means, measures: ཐབས་བྱེད་པ to use means, to take measures; ཐབས་ཀྱིས by (various) means; བློ་ཐབས་འཚོལ་བ to contrive means. འཚོ་ཐབས livelihood, subsistence; ཞི་བའི་ཐབས་ཀྱིས by pacific means, amicably, in a fair way; ཐབས་ལ་མཁས་པ or ཐབས་ཤེས་པ चक्रिका skilful, dexterous, clever, full of devices; ཐབས་མིན *thabs-min* a stupid man who has no resources, resourceless: ད་བོད་དུ་འགྲོ་ཐབས་གྱིས་ཤིག now take steps, make preparations, for a journey to Tibet; དེ་གསོན་པའི་ཐབས་ཡོད་དམ is there a means of recalling these men to life? 4. ཆོ་ག *cho-ga* ritualistic observances, mystical operations; ཐབས་ཀྱིས་གཞན་ནོར་འགུགས་པ *thabs-kyis gshan-nor hgugs-pa* drawn (gathered) another's wealth by (occult) means; ཐབས་ཀྱི་རྣམ་གྲངས *thabs-kyi rnam-grañs* enumeration of skilful means (*K. d.* པ *265*); ཐབས་ཀྱི་ཕ་རོལ་ཏུ་ཕྱིན་པ *thab-kyi pha-rol-tu phyin-pa* उपायपारमिता the supreme skilfulness in resources.

ཐབས་ཆག=ཨ་ལ་མ་ལ a shift, makeshift, surrogate.

ཐབས་དང་ཤེས་རབ *thabs-dañ çes-rab*=ཐབས་ཤེས 1. ritual and divine knowledge. 2. acc. to *Jä.* the mystical union of art and science; acc. to *Sch.* of matter and spirit (cf. *Was. 144*).

ཐབས་རྡུགས *thabs-rdugs*=ལས་ཐང་མེད་པ *las-thañ med-pa* having no spirit for work or no ability to do any work; stupid, always blundering.

ཐབས་ལ་མཁས་པ *thabs-la mkhas-pa* उपायकौशल्य ready in contrivance; possessed of resources.

ཐབས་ལ་མཁས་པའི་མདོ *thabs-la mkhas-pahi mdo* उपायकौशल्यसूत्र n. of a sūtra on skilful means in *K. d.* པ *405*.

ཐབས་ལམ་ *thabs-lam* उपायमार्ग a resource.

ཐབས་ཤེས་ལྡན་པ་ *thabs-çes ldan-pa* उपायज्ञ possessed of resources (*A. K. 1-4*).

ཐབས་ཤེས་བདག་ཉིད་ *Thabs-çes bdag-ñid* श्रीकालचक्र = དཔལ་དུས་ཀྱི་འཁོར་ལོ་ Kálachakra doctrine.

ཐམ་ག། *tham-ga* or ཐམ་ཀ *tham-ka* a seal, sign (*Cs.*); incorrect forms ཐ་མ་ག *tha-ma-ga* and ཐ་མག *tha-mag*, v. དམ་ཁ *dam-kha*.

ཐམ་ཐམ *tham-tham* or ཐམ་མེ་བ *tham me-wa* uncorrected, scattered, dispersed. ཐམ་ཐམ་བྱེད་པ *tham-tham byed-pa* = འཐམ་པ *htham-pa* (*Jä.*).

ཐམ་པ *tham-pa* (sometimes ཐེམ་པ *them-pa*) complete, full—almost exclusively used as a pleonastic addition to the tens up to a hundred.

+ **ཐམ་ལག** *tham-lag* = མན་ངག *man-ṅag* उपदेश precept, moral instruction.

ཐམས་ཅད *thams-cad* सकल, सर्व्व sbst. and adj. the whole, all; added to the singular number it gives a plural sense: རྒྱལ་ཁམས་ཐམས་ཅད the whole empire; ལུས་ཐམས་ཅད་ན the whole body ails; བོད་ཀྱི་ཟངས་ཐམས་ཅད all the copper of Tibet; དེ་ཐམས་ཅད all those; ཐམས་ཅད་ཀྱིས་སོ་སོ་ནས all of them one by one; ཐམས་ཅད་ཀྱི་ཐམས་ཅད *thams-cad-kyi thams-cad* सर्व्वेष सर्व्वः or सर्व्वसर्व्वः: all in all; everything out of the whole.

ཐམས་ཅད་སྐྱོབས *Thams-cad skyobs* (Vis'vabhu) the third of the six earthly Buddhas, who succeeded each other prior to the appearance of Shakyamuni.

ཐམས་ཅད་མཁྱེན་པ *thams-cad mkhyen-pa* = ཀུན་མཁྱེན सर्व्वज्ञ the omniscient, the all-knower, an epithet of Buddhas and *Bodhisattvas*. The incarnate lamas of Tibet are also by courtesy addressed by this title.

ཐམས་ཅད་སྒྲོལ *thams-cad sgrol* विश्वान्तर 1. a general epithet of Buddha, lit. the deliverer of the universe. 2. Vis'vantara, name of a prince believed to have been Buddha Gautama in his last-but-one birth.

ཐམས་ཅད་རྟོགས *thams-cad rtogs* = ཐམས་ཅད་མཁྱེན་པ विश्वबोधि a general epithet of Buddhas and *Bodhisattvas*.

ཐམས་ཅད་མཐོང་ *thams-cad mthoṅ* सर्व्वदृक् lit. the all-seeing; an epithet of Buddha.

ཐམས་ཅད་རྣམ་པར་འབྱེད *tham-cad rnam-par hbyed* सर्व्वविक्षेपिता renouncing or giving up every thing.

ཐམས་ཅད་པ *thams cad-pa* सर्व्वका, सर्व्वक all.

ཐམས་ཅད་ཚེ *thams-cad tshe* सर्व्वदा at all times; also, frequently (*A. K. 1-2*).

ཐམས་ཅད་གཟིགས *thams-cad gzigs* = ཀུན་ལ་བལྟ་མཁན सर्व्वदर्शी epithet of *Bodhisattvas* of higher order like Avalokites'vara.

ཐམས་ཅད་ཡོད་པར་སྨྲ་བའི་སྡེ་བདུན *Thams-cad yod-par smra-wahi sde-bdun* the seven sections of the Sarvāstivādin school of early Buddhism:—(1) ས་སྟོན་པ Mahīs'āsaka, (2) འོད་སྲུངས་པ Kās'yapīya, (3) ཆོས་སྲུང་བ Dharma gupta, (4) གོས་དམར་ཅན Tāmra s'ātiya, (5) རྣམ་པར་ཕྱེ་སྟེ་སྨྲ་བ Vibhajya vādin, (6) མང་དུ་ཐོས་པ་ལ་ཕྱུང་བ་པ Bahus'rutīya, (7) Mūlasarvāstivāda.

ཐམས་ཅད་ལས་འདས *thams-cad las hdas* अतीतसर्व्व passed beyond all, out of the reach of all.

ཐམས་ཅད་གསང་བ་ཞེས་བྱ་བའི་རྒྱུད་ཀྱི་རྒྱལ་པོ་ सर्व्वगुह्यनामतन्त्रराज n. of a mystical treatise containing metaphysical discussions on the nature of the soul, etc. (*K. g.* ३ *207*).

ཐམས་པ *thams-pa* 1. to lock together, to hold fast with the arms, either in love, or with anger. སོ་ཐམས་པ *so thams-pa* lock-jaw. 2. to stick fast; བྱེ་མ་ཐམས་སུ་འཛུག་པ to stick fast in sand: ཛ་བོའི་སྐྱུ་རྒྱབ་ཀྱི་ཙི་ག་ངོས་ལ་ཐམས་ཀྱིས་སོང་ནས་ཙྲི་བི་བི་འདུག་སྐད there was heard the cry of a lagomys mouse clinging fast to the wall behind Atis'a's back (*A. 106*).

ཐའི་ཤང་ལོའུ་ཀྱུན *Thahi-çań Lohu-kyun* in Chinese = རབ་མཆོག the most excellent; or གཙོ་བོ་བདག་པོ the chief lord; epithets of the founder of Taoism (*Grub.* ན *14*).

ཐའུ *thahu* 1. capsule (*Vai-sń.*). 2. peach (*Wts.*).

ཐར *tkar* for ཐར་ཐོར *thar-thor*.

ཐར་ཆུང་པ *thar chuń-pa* = ཁྲོན་བུ *khron-bu* a small well (mystic) (*Miń-rda.*).

ཐར་ཐོར *thar-thor* scatteredly, not together.

Syn. ཐ་རེ་ཐོ་རེ *tha-re tho-re*; ཐོར་རེ་བ *thor re-wa*; ཙོ་ལེ་བ *co le-wa* (*Mńon.*).

ཐར་ནུ *thar-nu* a kind of medicinal root used as a purgative: ཐར་ནུས་ཚ་གྲང་ནད་ཀུན་སྦྱོང་བར་བྱེད *Thar-nu* cures all disease caused by heat and cold (*Med.*).

Syn. རེ་མོ *re-mo*; ཉེ་བའི་རེ་མོ་ཅན *ñe-wahi re-mo can*; བདེ་བྱེད་མ *bde byed-ma*; ཁུ་བ་ལྡན *khu-wa ldan*: ཐ་དད་ཕྲེང་ལྡན *tha-dud phreń-ldan*; བུའི་ཕྲེང་ལྡན *buhi phreń-ldan*; ཆར་འབབ *char-hbab*; བྱི་བའི་ལོ་མ *byi-wahi lo-ma* (*Mńon.*).

ཐར་པ I: *Thar-pa* n. of a place near Dong-tse in Tibet. ཐར་པ་ལོ་ཙཱ་བ, ཉི་མ་རྒྱལ་མཚན n. of a Sanskrit scholar of Tibet who belonged to Tharpa.

ཐར་པ II: मोक्ष, मुक्ति, अपवर्ग, निर्मोक, क्षिर, क्षिव 1. freedom, salvation, liberty, emancipation, *Nirvāṇa*, supreme happiness, escape: ཐར་པའི་རྒྱུར་འགྱུར it will be serviceable for (my) liberty (*Jä.*). ཐར་མེད་ཀྱི་དམྱལ་བ hell from which there is no escape. 2. adj. free; ཐར་བར་འགྱུར་བ to become free; ཐར་བར་བྱེད་པ *thar-war byed-pa* to make free, liberate, to save.

Syn. བྱང་གྲོལ *byań-grol*; ཞི་བ *shi-wa*; མྱ་ངན་འདས *mya-ńan hdas*; འཆི་མེད *hchi-med*; རྣམ་གྲོལ *rnam-grol*; བྱང་ཆུབ་པ *byań chub-pa*; རྡུལ་མེད *rdul-med*; རྡུལ་བྲལ *rdul-bral*; ཡང་སྲིད་མེད *yań srid-med*; དོན་དམ *don-dam*; ངེས་ལེགས *ńes-legs* (*Mńon.*).

ཐར་ཐབས *thar-thabs* the means of release, liberation; བཙོན་ནས་ཐར་ཐབས means to escape from prison.

ཐར་པ་ཆེན་པོའི་མདོ *Thar-pa chen-pohi mdo* the sūtra on complete deliverance of the soul (*K. d.* ཅ *328*).

ཐར་པའི་བློ་གྲོས *thar-pahi blo-gros* = གྲུབ་མཐའ the inclination for liberation; the metaphysical conclusions of religion; n. of a metaphysical work (*Mńon.*).

ཐར་པོ *thar-po* old, worn out; རྙིང་པ *rñiń-pa*, རྒས་པ *rgas pa* (*Mńon.*).

ཐར་པ་གཞོན་ནུ *thar-pa bshon-nu* n. of a Bon. arch-devil (*G. Bon. 22*).

ཐར་དཔག *thar-dpag* or ཐར་འབག *thar-hbag* a large plate, dish, platter.

ཐར་བ *thar-wa* 1. to be freed, to be liberated, absolved. 2. escape, to get through, to be able to pass; ཆུ་ལ་ཐར་བ *chu-la thar-wa* to get through water: ཟས་མི་ཐར *zas mi-thar* the food cannot pass through. ཐར་དུ་འཇུག་པ *thar-du hjug-pa* to set at liberty, to acquit; སྲོག་ཐར་ལ་བཏང་བ to pardon (a malefactor), to grant him his life, frq. to let live (animals) (*Jä.*); རྣམ་པར་ཐར་བ to be saved, fully released, gen. from any further transmigration.

ཐར་རྩེ *Thar-rtse* n. of monastery; also that of the residence of the lama of *Ńor* in Tsang (*Loń.* ཁ *31*).

ཐར་ལམ *thar-lam* or ཐར་པའི་ལམ मुक्तिमार्ग the way to *Nirvāṇa* or emancipation.

ཐར་ལེགས་པ *thar-legs-pa* मुक्तात्मा purified; one who has acquired the means to escape sufferings.

ཐར་ས *thar-sa* place of refuge, means of escape; ཐར་ས་མི་འདུག there is no escape.

ཐར་སོང་ *thar-soṅ*=ཐར་པོ་སོང་ 1. has become old, worn out (*Ṛtsii.*). 2. has been saved, has escaped.

ཐལ *thal* पाटली the trumpet flower.

ཐལ་བ I: *thal-wa* भस्म, धूलि, रजः dust, powder, ashes; གོག་ཐལ *gog-thal* fire ashes; ཐུག་ཐལ *thug-thal* roasted barley dried and portable; བྱ་ཐལ *bya-thal* dung of birds; ཐལ་གོང་ burning embers. ཐལ་ཆུ *thal-chu* lyo, ash-water used instead of soda for making tea. ཐལ་ཆེན *thal-chen* ashes of the dead; also a sort of gray earth used for bedaubing the face in masquerades (*Mil.*; *Jä.*). ཐལ་ཐག *thal-thag* (*Ld.*) bread baked in ashes; ཐལ་མདོག *thal-mdog* ash-coloured; ཐལ་ཕྱགས *thal-phyags* broom, dusting rag (*Sch.*).

ཐལ་བ II:=འཐལ་བ *ḥthal-wa* (*Cs.*) 1. to pass, to pass by, to step beyond; to miss a mark: ཆུ་ཐལ་ཐལ་འོང་ the waves come flowing past (*Mil.*). 2. to elapse, be passed; to change or pass from: ལོ་ལྔ་བཅུ་ཐལ་ནས fifty years has been passed (*Vai-sṅ.*); སྔོ་བ་ལས་ཐལ་ནས་དམར་ཉིད་ changing or turning from blue to red; སྒྲུབ་པ་ལ་རྩེ་གཅིག་ཏུ་ཐུགས་ནས་ལོ་དགུ་ཙམ་ཐལ about nine years passed by, while he sat in meditation single-minded (*Ḥbrom.* ཁ *10-12*). ཁ་ཐལ་བ to be forward in speaking, bold. 3. to go or pass through: བྲག་ལ་ཡར་ཐལ་མར་ཐལ to soar up and down before a rock; ཕར་ཐལ་ཚུར་ཐལ་དུ་འགྲོ་བ to pass actually through it (the saints not being subject to the physical laws of matter); to shine, to light through: ཐལ་འབྱུང་དུ་འགྲོ་བ to go straight forward, to act without ceremony or disguise (*Jä*). 4. to come, to get to, to arrive at: ཐལ་ནས་ལོ་གསུམ་སོང three years elapsed since they arrived; ཕ་མ་གར་ཐལ་བའི་གཏོལ་མེད where the parents have gone it is not known; བཟང་ཐལ safe arrival; ཡར་ཀྱི་བཟང་ཐལ་ཆེན་པོར་འགྲོ་བ to arrive at: to attain (a blessed state) in a pleasant and speedy manner. 5. to be over, past, finished, done; ཐལ་སོ it is over, finished; དྲུག་ཅུ་ཐལ་སོ the number sixty is completed; ཡལ་ཐལ་བ having disappeared, vanished; ཇོར་ནས་ཐལ he is undone it is all over with him; རིམ་གྱིས་ཧྲི་ཤུད་ཐལ by degrees it vanishes or dies away; སྔར་ཆད་ཚིག་ཐལ the former agreement is no longer valid (*Jä.*).

ཐལ་ཐུང་ different lengths, one object projecting beyond another; ཐལ་ཆེས་པ to exceed the due measure (*Sch.*).

ཐལ་ཀ་རྡོ་རྗེ *thal-ka rdo-rje* एरण्ड a medicinal fruit; is described as དབྱིབས་ཁྱིའི་པོ་མཚན་འདྲ "in shape like a dog's penis." ཐལ་ཀ་རྡོ་རྗེས་རྣ་སེར་ནད་རྣམས་སེལ Thal-ka rdorje relieves suppurations (*Med.*).

ཐལ་ཀར I: *thal-kar* or ཐལ་དཀར a white elephant; གླང་ཆེན་ཐལ་དཀར་མཆེ་བ་དྲུག n. of the fabulous white elephant with six tusks; also the leader-elephant in a herd (*Yig.*).

Syn. གླང་པོའི་རྒྱལ་པོ *glaṅ-poḥi rgyal-po*; ཁྱུ་ཡི་མགོན་པོ *khyu-yi mgon-po*; གླང་པོའི་མཆོག *glaṅ-poḥi mchog*; སྤོས་ཀྱི་གླང་པོ *spos-kyi glaṅ-po* (गन्धहस्ति) (*Mṅon.*).

ཐལ་འགྱུར *thal-ḥgyur* प्रसङ्ग adherence; association; connected language. ཐལ་འགྱུར་པ *thal-ḥgyur-pa* one belonging to the *Prasaṅgika* school of the Buddhists.

ཐལ་ཆེས་པར་འགྱུར *thal ches-par ḥgyur* अतिप्रसङ्ग absence of connection; absence of adherence.

ཐལ་ལྕག *thal-lcag* a slap (on the cheek); ཐལ་ལྕག་རྒྱབ་པ *thal-lcag rgyab-pa* to slap on the cheek, to give a box on the ear.

ཐལ་བརྡབ་པ *thal brdab-pa* a clap with the hands (out of joy or scorn).

ཐལ་ཐལ *thal-thal* पल a particular number.

ཐལ་དྲེས *thal-dres* उत्पल n. of a medicinal flower of the lily species; also अनन्तमूल; *Anantamūla.*

Syn. ས་འཚོའི་བུ་མོ *so-ḥtshoḥi bu-mo*; མཐའ་ཡས་རྩ *mthaḥ-yas rtsa*; སྔོ་སངས་འཁྲི་ཤིང *sño-sañs ḥkhri-çiñ*; ཀླུ་ཡི་ལྕེ *klu-yi lce*; མེ་ཏོག་ཕྲ་མོ *me-tog phra-mo*; བ་གླང་བསྲུང *ba-glañ bsruñ*; སྔོ་སངས་མཐའ་ཡས *sño-sañs mthaḥ-yas* (*Mñon.*).

ཐལ་ཕྱོགས *thal-phyogs* the party victorious in a metaphysical disputation.

ཐལ་བྱི *thal-byi* the grey or cat-squirrel.

ཐལ་བའི་སྙིང་པོ *thal-baḥi sñiñ-po* अगरु, भस्मगर्भो a kind of sandal wood.

ཐལ་བར་འགྱུར *thal-war ḥgyur* प्रसङ्ग connection.

ཐལ་བྱུང་འགྲོ་བ *thal byuñ-ḥgro-wa* 1. to move or walk or rush fearlessly. 2. sbst. a hero. Syn. དཔའ་བོ *dpaḥ-wo*; འཇིགས་མེད *ḥjigs-med*; སྙིང་སྟོབས་ཅན *sñiñ-stobs-can* (*Mñon.*).

ཐལ་མ *thal-ma* through and through (*Sch.*).

ཐལ་མོ *thal-mo* the palm of the hand: ཐལ་མོ་སྦྱར་བ *thal-mo sbyar-wa* प्रगृहीताञ्जलि to fold the palms of the hands in devotion; ཐལ་མོ་སྣན་པ *thal-mo snan-pa* to give a slap on the cheek, or box on the ear; ཐལ་མོ་ཐལ་བར་བྱེད *thal-mo thal-war byed* अञ्जलिं मुञ्चति separated the hands that were joined to show reverence.

ཐལ་ལ་ཚལ *Thal-la tshal* n. of a place in ནག་རོང *Nag-roñ* in *Khams*: ནག་རོང་གི་ཐལ་ལ་ཚལ་དུ་དེ་འབངས་འཐབ at Thal-la tshal in *Ñag-roñ* rtsibs the chieftain and his subjects fought (*Yig.*).

ཐལ་ཚང *thal-tshañ* (གསང་སྤྱོད) closet, privy.

ཐལ་ཚྭ *thal-tshwa* a kind of salt, gen. burnt salt: ཐལ་ཚྭས་གྲང་སེལ་ཕོ་བ་སྐྲངས་པ་འཇོམས burnt salt subdues cold and swelling of the stomach.

ཐལ་ཡས *thal-yas* (གྲངས) n. of a number.

ཐལ་ལེ *thal-le* straight on; forthwith; (*Ḥbrom.* ཁ *10*).

ཐའི་ཛི *Thaḥi-dsi* (Mongolian) the title by which the descendants of Jenghis Khan the great Tartar conqueror are known. According to Mongol law the fact of one's bearing the title of *Thaḥi-dsi* exempts one from taxation.

ཐི *thi* num. fig. 40.

ཐི་གུ *thi-gu* rope, string: གནམ་ནས་གསེར་གྱི་ཐི་གུ་ཅིག་བྱུང a golden cord descended from heaven (*Yig.*).

ཐི་བ *thi-wa* कपोत 1. sandpiper, but acc. to *Sch.* stock-dove; also = ཏི་བོ plover, lapwing. 2. = ཐེ་བ in *C.* (*Jä.*).

ཐིག *thig* 1. = ཐུང་ཀོར "0" or numeral for zero. 2. a line: ཐིག་འདེབས་པ सूत्रपातन to draw a line; ནག་ཐི or སྣག་ཐིག a black line; ཚལ་ཐིག a red line; ཚངས་ཐིག diameter. 3. also ཐིག་སྐོར carpenter's cord or string to mark lines with any instrument used in drawing lines; སྐོར་ཐིག *skor-thig* a pair of compasses; གཡའ་ཐིག slate-pencil, lead pencil; also a line drawn with a lead-pencil (*Jä.*).

ཐིག་སྐུད *thig-skud* सूत्र thread, yarn; also straight line.

ཐིག་མཁན *thig-mkhan* सूत्रधार sawyer.

ཐིག་ནག *thig-nag* कालसूत्र 1. one of the eight hot hells where the damned are sawn to pieces, lines being drawn upon them, v. ཚ་དམྱལ. 2. black spot.

ཐིག་ཙམ *thig-tsam* a little, about the size of a line, a drop.

ཐིག་ཚད *thig-tshad* proportion, symmetry (*Cs.*). ཐིག་ཚད་བྱེད་པ *thig-tshad byed-pa* to proportion.

ཐིག་ཤིང་ *thig-çiñ* ruler for ruling lines; also a level.

ཐིག་པ *thig-pa*, v. ཐིགས་པ *thigs-pa*.

ཐིག་མ *thig-ma* cotton or woollen chintz, on which there are different designs.

ཐིག་འབུམ *thig-ḥbum* समुद्र the sea, ocean.

ཐིག་ལེ *thig-le* (ཁུ་བ शुक्र) 1. semen virile. 2. बिन्दु, चित्र; ཐིག་ལེ་ལྷ་བུའི་རྒྱན or མདངས तिलक star or mark tatooed on the forehead as an ornament; an eye on a peacock's feather. 3. the concentration of what is diffused; par-excellence; ས་ཡི་ཐིག་ལེ *sa-yi thig-le* भूतिलक the chief or supreme person, king (*A. K. 1-4*); painting, mark, spot; ཐིག་ལེ་ཅན spotted, concentred in spots; ཆོས་ཐིག་ལེ་ཉག་ཅིག the best or concentration of all religions. 4. निःशेषक, विशेष [complete, special]*S.* 5. zero, naught (*Vai-sñ.*). 6. a phase of mystic contemplation in which the seminal fluid is supposed to be inwardly absorbed into the arteries; also, the mystic fluid, itself: རོ་རྐྱང་གཉིས་ཀྱི་ཐིག་ལེ་འཕེལ་བ་ཡིན the semen of the *roma* and *kyañma* becomes increased (*Mil.*). སྙིང་ཁ་ཆོས་ཀྱི་འཁོར་ལོ་འདི་ཐིག་ལེས་གང་བ་ཡིན *sñiñ-kha chos-kyi ḥkhor-lo ḥdi thegs-le gañ-wa-yin* that globe of the doctrine, his heart, has been filled with the mystical fluids. 7. said to=ཟླ་མཚན the female monthly discharge. 8. as met. may=གླང་པོ *glañ-po*.

ཐིག་ལེ་མཆོག་མ *thig-le mchog-ma* तिलोत्तमा n. of a celestial courtezan; a centre of all religions in which finally all the sects must unite.

ཐིག་ལེའི་ལུས *thig-leḥi lus* a leopard, snake (*Mñon.*).

ཐིགས་པ *thigs-pa* also spelt ཐིག་པ=ཟིལ་བ *zil-wa* 1. a drop (*A. K. 111-26*): ཐིགས་པ་རེ་རེ་ནས from every drop; in drops, by drops; ཆར་ཐིགས rain drops; གསེར་ཐིག་པོ a drop or globule of gold. 2. vb. to sprinkle or throw in drops.

ཐིང་ *thiñ*, v. འདིང་བ *ḥdiñ-wa*.

ཐིང་ཤིང་ *thiñ-çiñ* राजपट्ट n. of a dye.

ཐིང་གི *thiñ-gi* མི་རབས་ཐིག་གི་མིང་ n. of a line or succession of noblemen in Tibet (*Yig.*).

ཐིད་ཡུག *thid-yug* a number (*Ya-sel. 57*).

ཐིབ་པ *thib-pa*, v. འཐིབ་པ *ḥthib-pa* and གཏིབ་པ *gtib-pa*; ཐིབ་ཐིབ *thib-thib* very dark, dense; སྨུག་པ་ཐིབ་ཐིབ *smugs-pa thib-thib* fogs thickening.

ཐིབས་པོ *thibs-po* अन्तर्धान 1. vanishing, disappearing. 2. गहन, तिमिर dark, dense, obscure, v. འཐིབ་པ *ḥthib-pa* and གཏིབ་པ *gtib-pa*; བྱིན་རླབས་ཐིབས་ཐིབས a blessing devolving upon a person.

ཐིབས་མོ *thibs-mo* dense, dark.

ཐིམ་པ *thim-pa* (ཕག་མ་ཁུགས་ལ *phags-ma khugs la*) विलीन, लीन, नाश to be lost (in some thing else), to melt down; to be dissolved being mixed up with another object; =འཐིམ་པ གཏིམ་པ and ཐིམ་པ; gen. with ལ or ནང་དུ to disappear by being imbibed, to be absorbed; to pass into, to evaporate (of fluids); of a snake; to creep away, to disappear in a hole; frq. of the vanishing of rays of light, of a god, etc.; དྲན་མེད་དུ་ཐིམ་པ to pass or sink into unconsciousness.

Syn. སིམ་པ *sim-pa*; ཤུ་བ *shu-wa* (*Mṅon.*).

ཐིམ་ཐིམ *thim-thim* n. of a number (*Ya-sel. 57*).

ཐིཨུ་ཀྭན་ཐིང་མུར *Thihu kwan-thiṅ-mur* n. of one of the Tartar Emperors of China belonging to the great Yuan dynasty. He invited the celebrated Karma Lama *Raṅ-byuṅ Rdorje* to Peking (*Loṅ.* ཞ *10*).

ཐིལ་ཆུང *Thil-chuṅ* n. of a place in Tibet (*Loṅ. 8*).

ཐིལ་སྟོན *thil-ston* prob. for མཐིལ་སྟོན་པ *mthil ston-pa* to enter into the depth of a conversation or expression; to fathom a secret.

ཐུ *thu* 1. num. fig. 70. 2. spittle: ཐུ་ཐུ་བ to spit out of scorn or contempt at anybody (*K. du.* ད *416*).

ཐུ་པ *thu-pa* skirt of a robe, coat-flap (*Khriḍ*).

ཐུ་བ *thu-wa* 1. vb. प्रचय to pluck or collect flowers. 2.=ཐུ་ལུ་བཏབ་པ. 3. ཐུབ་པ *thub-pa* able, powerful, capable of: ངན་སོང་གི་གཏིང་ཇི་ཙམ་འཇལ་བ་ལ་མི་ལས་ཐུ་བ་མེད (*Sñiṅ.*) in measuring the bottom of perdition (with a fathoming stone) there is none more capable than man. 4. malicious, wicked, vicious: སྡུག་བསྔལ་ཐུ་བ *sdug-bsṅal thu-wa* a malignant suffering or severe accident. 5. vb., v. འཐུ་བ *hthu-wa*.

ཐུ་བོ *thu-wo* 1. ज्येष्ठ chief, senior, an elder brother. 2. हलाहल, कलह quarrel, poison. 3.=ཐུག་པ *thug-pa* यवागू gruel made of barley flour.

Syn. ཇོ་ཇོ *jo-jo*; ཨ་ཇོ *ā-jo*; ཕུ་བོ *phu-ḇo*; ཐོག་མ་སྐྱེས *thog-ma-skyes*; སྔོན་སྐྱེས *sṅon-skyes*.

ཐུ་མོ *thu-mo* lady, mistress (*Cs.*).

ཐུ་མེད་ཨལ་ཐན་རྒྱལ་པོ *Thu-meḍ āl-than rgyal-po* a king of Mongolia who was famed for his patronage of Buddhism, *althān* in Mongolian signifying "golden." (*Loṅ.* ཞ *11*).

ཐུ་རེ *thu-re* uninterrupted (*Sch.*).

ཐུ་ལུ *thu-lu* spittle; ཐུ་ལུ་བཏབ་པ or འདེབས་པ to spit, to throw spittle; *thu-lu nag-po* occurs in *Glu. 3* as=withered flower.

ཐུ་ལུམ *thu-lum* a lump of metal; in *W.* acc. to *Jä.* a cannon-ball.

ཐུག *thug* postp. c. accus. until, up to; in reference to time and space ད་ཐུག until now; ཞག་བཞི་བཅུ་ཐུག for forty days; དགོན་པའི་ཁ་ཐུག over against the gompa, at the gompa. Adv.=only.

ཐུག་སྒྲ *thug-sgra* or ཐུག་འཚམས great noise: ད་རེ་ཐུག་འཚམས་དང་བ་ཐུར་གྱི་སྒྲ་ཆེན་པོ་བྱས now each made great noise and rattling sounds (*Rdsa. 9*).

ཐུག་རྔ *thug-rṅa* (ཐུག་གཡག་གི་རྔ་མ) the hairy tail of a yak fixed with a flag on the top of a Tibetan house. ཐུག་ཚོམ *thug-tshom* the flag staff with a silken flag, or a yak's tail and hay attached to the top of a post and fixed on the roof of a monastery or house in Tibet (*Rtsii.*).

ཐུག་པ I: *thug-pa* sbst. soup, broth; འབྲས་ཐུག *hbras-thug* rice-soup; བག་ཐུག *bag-thug* यवागू meal-soup; barley-soup. ཐུག་པ་འགྲིམ་པ *thug-pa hgrim-pa* यवागूचारक to make barley gruel; the cook who prepares such; རྒྱ་ཐུག *rgya-thug* Chinese porridge, a sort of vermicelli-soup; ཐུག་ཐལ *thug-thal*=ཐུག་རྩམ *thug-rtsam* flour of barley for making gruel or broth.

ཐུག་པ II: 1. to reach, arrive at, come to; c. dat. or termin: ཚེའི་མཐར་ཐུག་པ to reach the close of life; རྩམ་པ་ལ་ཐུག to reach to the very bone; ཤི་ལ་ཐུག་ཆེ or འཆི་བར་ཐུག་པ་ལ at the point of death; བཟུང་ལ་ཐུག he was just on the point of seizing her. 2. to interview, to encounter; to meet, to light upon: ཐུག་ཕྲད་བྱེད་པ to have an interview with (*Hbrom.* ཁ *7*); ཇག་པ་དང་ཐུག་པ to fall in with robbers; གདོང་ཐུག་པ resp. ཞལ་མཇལ *shal-mjal* personal interview. 3. colloq. to touch, to hit or strike against: ལག་པ་མི་ཐུག་ཡིན I shall not touch it, I shall not come near with my hand (*Jä.*).

ཐུག་ཆད *thug-chad* agreement (*Sch.*).

ཐུག་ཡས *thug-yas* 1. not to be reached, endless (*Cs.*). 2. n. of a very great number (*Ya-sel. 37*).

ཐུག་པ་མེད་པར་འགྱུར *thug-pa med-par-hgyur* अनवस्था प्रसङ्ग possibility of the fallacy of *ad infinitum* (*Gram.*). ཐུག་མེད་ལས་བསྒྲེས་པ *thug-med las bsgres-pa* अनवस्था-परिवर्त chapter on the fallacy of *ad infinitum.*

ཐུགས *thugs* 1. चित्त, मनस् the heart, gen. ཐུགས་ཀ *thugs-ka* breast, the heart: ཐུགས་ཀྱི་སྤྲུལ་པ the incarnation of a deity, originating in a ray of light which proceeds from the breast of that deity. 2. heart (in a spiritual sense), mind, soul, spirit, used resp. for སེམས; ཐུགས་སུ་ཆུད་པ=ཐུགས་སུ་འཚུད་པ to be kept in the mind, in memory. 3. purpose, intention. In this sense it occurs in the well-known compound word ཐུགས་རྗེ mercy, a favour. དེ་ལྟར་སྐྱེ་ན་སྐྱེ་བ་དོན་མེད་ཐུགས་མེད་དུ་འགྱུར if so born the birth will be useless and for no purpose (*Lam.-ṭi.*). ཐུགས་རབ *thugs-rab*=ཤེས་རབ wisdom, good heart; ཐུགས་རུས *thugs-rus*=སྙིང་རུས assiduity, exertion; ཐུགས་ཤེས་པ *thugs çes-pa* resp. for ཡིད་ཤེས་པ *yid-çes-pa* to believe; to know one's mind. *Thugs* is used also like *sems* in the colloq. pleonastically when mental feelings are expressed: ཉིད་རང་མཐོང་རྒྱུ་ལ་ངའི་ཐུགས་ལ་དགའ་བ་ཡོད I am glad to see you; *lit.* "there is joy in my mind to see you."

Syn. སྙིང་ *sñiṅ*; ཀུན་སྐྱེད་བྱེད *kun-skyed-byed*; རྣམ་ཤེས་རྟེན *rnam-çes rten*; སྲོག་གི་རྟེན *srog-gi rten*; སེམས་ཀྱི་ཁང་པ *sems-kyi khaṅ-pa*; ཤ་ཡི་མཆོག *ça-yi-mchog* (*Mṅon.*).

ཐུགས་གཏོང་བ *thugs gtoṅ-wa* resp. བསམ་བློ་གཏོང་བ to muse, meditate, reflect.

ཐུགས་སྤྲོ་བ *thugs-spro-wa* to be cheerful; to be merry.

ཐུགས་དཀར་བ *thugs dkar-wa* 1. white (clean) heart, sincerity. 2. there are 360 Bon gods called *Thugs-dkar*; and those who conduct religious rites to propitiate them are called *Thugs-dkar-wa* (*Rtsii.*). ཐུགས་དཀར་ཡེ་ཤེས one of the seven Bon sages (*G. Bon. 35*).

ཐུགས་བསྐྱེད *thugs-bskyed*=སེམས་བསྐྱེད मनउत्पाद 1. imbibing faith, an idea dawning in the mind. 2. kind remembrance: ཐུགས་བསྐྱེད་གཡོ་བ་མེད་པ་སྔར་བཞིན་ནས་གསུང་མཛད་ཀྱང་ཡང་ཡང་ཡོད་པ་མཛད། also may it please you to write me often as heretofore without becoming unsteady in your kind remembrance of me (*Yig. k. 25*).

ཐུགས་མཁྱེན *thugs-mkhyen* resp. for མངོན་ཤེས fore-knowledge.

ཐུགས་འཁུར་ཆེ་བཞེས *thugs-hkhur che-bshes* to accept responsibility: ཐུགས་འཁུར་ཆེ་བསྐྱེད་ཡོད་པ་གཞིར་བཅས at the bottom there having been engendered a sense of responsibility.

ཐུགས་འཁྲུགས *thugs-hkhrugs* resp. for ཁོང་འཁྲུགས *khoṅ-hkrugs* agitation of the mind.

ཐུགས་དགོངས *thugs-dgoṅs* resp. for དགོངས་པ consideration, thought, opinion, view.

ཐུགས་རྒྱལ *thugs-rgyal* resp. for anger, wrath, indignation: ཐུགས་རྒྱལ་བཞེངས anger arises, is roused (*Jä.*).

ཐུགས་ངན *thugs-ṅan* grief, sorrow, affliction.

ཐུགས་ངལ་བ *thugs-ṅal-wa*=སེམས་ངལ *sems-ṅal* to be sorrowful; sorrow: སེམས་གསོ་ཐུགས་ངལ་མ་མཛད་ཅིག be consoled, do not be grieved (*Bdsa. 19*).

ཐུགས་རྗེ་ *thugs-rje* lit. noble purpose or heart; generosity, pity, commiseration, compassion; a grace, favour, mercy, blessing: ང་ལ་ཐུགས་རྗེས་གཟིགས pray, look graciously upon me; ས་བོན་རིག་ཐུགས་རྗེ་གཟིགས་དགོས pray, be so kind as to send me some seeds (*Jä.*). ཐུགས་རྗེ་ཅན *thugs-rje-can*=སྙིང་བརྩེ་ལྡན gracious, merciful, generous (*Mṅon.*). ཐུགས་རྗེ་ཆེ་བ *thugs-rje che-wa*, བྱམས་པ་དང་ལྡན་པ merciful and loving (*Mṅon.*). ཐུགས་རྗེ་ཆེ *thugs-rje che* is one of the common expressions of thanks and courtesy=our "many thanks," "you are most kind," etc.

ཐུགས་རྗེ་ཆེན་པོ *Thugs-rje chen-po* an epithet of Avalokites'vara; the all-merciful one, a Buddha.

ཐུགས་རྗེ་བྱམས་མ *Thugs-rje byams-ma* an epithet of སྐྱེ་དགུའི་བདག་མོ *Skye-dguhi bdag-mo* aunt and foster-mother of Gautama Buddha.

ཐུགས་རྗེ་འཛིན་པ *thugs-rje hdsin-pa* to be compassionate, merciful; ཐུགས་རྗེ་མཛད་པ *thugs-rje mdsad-pa* to shew mercy, to behave kindly.

ཐུགས་རྗེའི་ལྷ *Thugs-rjehi lha* an appellation of Avalokites'vara. There are four gods bearing the name of ཐུགས་རྗེ་ཆེན་པོ in the Bon pantheon of the later period; they are called by their attributes:—(1) འཁོར་བ་ལ་རྒྱུན་ཆད་མེད་པའི་ཐུགས་རྗེ་ཆུ་བོ་འདྲ་བ mercy flows to all the world uninterruptedly like a river; (2) འཁོར་བ་ལ་མ་ཟད་པའི་ཐུགས་རྗེ་གཞི་འདྲ་བ mercy inexhaustible as the basis of all things for the world of migratory existence; (3) ཀུན་ལ་སྙོམས་པའི་ཐུགས་རྗེ་ཉི་མ་ལྟ་བུ blessings to all living beings evenly like as with the sun; (4) དཔག་ཏུ་མེད་པའི་ཐུགས་རྗེ་ནམ་མཁའ་ལྟ་བུ mercy boundless like the sky.

ཐུགས་ཉིད *thugs-ñid*=སེམས་ཉིད *sems-ñid*.

ཐུགས་ཐུབ *thugs-thub* resp. for ཐུབ་ཚོད 1. self-sufficient, not caring; thinking no danger or injury will accrue from such and such action or steps, etc. 2. misappropriation of anything to one's self thinking that no notice will be taken: འབྲས་བྲེ་ཕྱེད་ཐུགས་ཐུབ་ཏུ་སྤྱད་པས་ཡི་དྭགས་ཤིན་ཏུ་དབང་ཆུང་བར་སྐྱེས་པ (*A. 75*) because he had misappropriated to himself half a pound of rice, he was born as a *Preta* of most insignificant power; ཐུགས་ཐུབ་ཏུ་སྤྱད་པ *thugs thub-tu spyad-pa* to work with self-reliance, being confident of one's own abilities (*A. 75*).

ཐུགས་དམ *thugs-dam*=ཡི་དམ *yi-dam* 1. lit. holy opinion; advice. 2. oath, vow, solemn promise: ཐུགས་དམ་བཅའ་བ to take an oath, to make a vow. 3. a prayer, a wish in the form of a prayer;=སྨོན་ལམ. 5. contemplation, the act of contemplating a deity (cf. སྒོམ་པ and སྒྲུབ་པ *sgrub-pa*), meditation in general: ཐུགས་དམ་འཕེལ meditation increases, proceeds successfully; devotion. 4. a deity, a tutelar god or saint: ཐུགས་དམ་རྡོ་རྗེའི་སྐྱབས་ཁོལ་ནས་འཕྲལ་ཕྱིན་ཀུན་ཏུ་མི་འདོར་ཞིང་ not expelling me at any time outside the protection of the dorje of my tutelary god.

ཐུགས་བདེ *thugs-bde* happy, cheerful.

ཐུགས་འདུན *thugs-hdun*=ཐུགས་ཀྱི་འདུན་པ *thugs-kyi hdun-pa* or ཐུགས་འདོད *thugs-hdod*. དངོས་མཇལ་ཞུས་ཆོག་པའི་ཐུགས་འདུན་བཅས་བརྩེ་འདོར་མེད་པ་མཛད་ཅིག let your affection to me not be cast aside that I may be permitted to have a gracious interview (*Yig. k. 25*).

ཐུགས་ནང་གཤིན་པ *thugs-naṅ gçin-pa* very affectionate, loving letters: ཐུགས་ནང་གཤིན་པའི་ཡིག་འབྲས་ཚོགས་ཀྱང་གོ་ལའི་རླུང་འགྲོས་ལྟར་འགོག་མེད་དུ་ཞུ། I pray that your affectionate letters may also come to me unhindered as the motion of the wind (*Yig. k. 87*).

ཐུགས་མུག *thugs-mug*=ཡི་མུག *yi-mug* despair.

ཐུགས་བརྩེ་བ *thugs brtse-wa* love, affection of the heart, compassion; resp. for སྙིང་བརྩེ་བ; frq. ཐུགས་བརྩེ་བར་དགོངས་པ, གཟིགས་པ to look upon compassionately, to remember in mercy.

ཐུགས་སུ་འགྲོ་བ *thugs-su hgro-wa* = ཡིད་དུ་འོང་བ to think well of, approve of; to be agreeable; also adj. agreeable, pleasant, delightful; also sbst. pleasure, delight.

ཐུགས་སྲས *thus-sras* spiritual son; an appellation given to distinguished disciples of saints. Mañju-s'rī, Avalokites'vara, Vajrapāṇi, etc., are spiritual sons of Gautama acc. to the Mahāyāna School. Among the Bon, *Ha-sho*, *Mdo-sdud* and other saints are the spiritual sons of Shenrab.

ཐུང་ང་ *thuṅ-ṅa* three years old, of animals (*Sch.*).

ཐུང་བ *thuṅ-wa* 1. short, low in size, of small dimensions: སྡོང་ཐུང་བ a short stem. ཐག་རིང་ཐུང་ distance in general; གཟུགས་ཀྱི་ཐུང་ short in size, a dwarf. ཐུང་བ་བཞི *thuṅ-wa bshi* the four shortnesses of the members of the human body which are regarded as defects, viz:—མགྲིན་པ་ཐུང་བ short neck; རྐང་པ་ཐུང་བ short legs; རྒྱབ་ཐུང་བ short back; ཧྲེང་ར the lower parts of the arm or legs (*Mi.*). ཐུང་ངུ་ *thuṅ-ṅu* ह्रस्व diminutive, short; ཐུང་ངུ་འགྲོ་བ to become shorter. 2. अचिरात्; དུས་ཀྱི་ཐུང་བ brief in respect of duration, of time.

Syn. དམའ་བ *dmah-wa*; སྲིད་ཐུང་ *srid-thuṅ*; ཐུང་ངུ་ *thuṅ-ṅu*; མི་མཐོ་ *mi-mtho*; རྩེ་དམན *rtse-dman* (*Mṅon.*).

ཐུད *thud* (ཀ་བའི) कोटर 1. the hollow of a pillar. 2. coagulated milk, thickened milk with butter a dainty with yak herdsmen of Tibet. མར་དང་བུར་བདང་ཐུ་རམ་བསྲེས་ནས་ཟོས་པ ate pastry made of treacle and dried curds with butter; ཧོ་ཐུད *ho-thud* milk-cheese; also a mess of rice, milk and sugar; ཐུད་ལེབ་ལྔ five cakes of milk cheese (*Rtsii.*). ཐུད་སྒྲོམ *thud-sgrom* a box in which milk-cheese is packed for sale.

ཐུད་སོར་བ *thud ċor-wa* lit. careless; erring, blundering; defined as ལས་ཀ་སོགས་ཁྲབ་པ neglect of work, etc.; ཐུད་སོར་དུ་མ་སོང་བ not to be negligent.

ཐུད་ཐུད *thud-thud* n. of a number (*Ya-sel. 56*).

ཐུན I: *thun* = ཆུ་ཚོད याम, प्रहर a period of three hours, the eighth part of a day according to Buddhist astrology. Acc. to *Jä.* a fixed length of time; as long as a man is able to work without resting; a shift of six, four or three hours. ཆུ་ཚོད་ཐུན་འཁོར the night-watch is over; ཐུན་གཉིས་པ द्वितीययाम, द्वितीय प्रहर the second watch (of day or night); ཐུན་ཐ་མ་ལ पश्चिमे यामे in the last watch of night; ཐུན་དང་པོ་ལ प्रथमे यामे in the first watch (of night); ཐུན་བར་པ་ལ मध्यमयामे in the middle watch (of night). ནམ་གྱི་གུང་ཐུན་ལ *nam-gyi guṅ thun-la* at or about midnight.

ཐུན་མ *thun-ma* याम्य relating to the watch of the night.

ཐུན་བཞི་པ *thun bshi-pa* चतुर्थी the fourth lunar crescent, *i.e.*, the fourth day after the full or the new-moon.

ཐུན་བཞིའི་རྣལ་འབྱོར *thun-bshihi rnal-hbyor* an ascetic who meditates or keeps the mind abstracted from worldly objects, &c., continuously during the four watches of the day; the meditation of a whole day.

ཐུན་བསྲུང་བ *thun bsuṅ-wa* to keep the watch, *i.e.*, not let slip the time without fully using it either in meditation or in the performance of any other work.

ཐུན་གསུམ་པ *thun gsum-pa* त्रियामा 1. one who remains engaged in devotion three times during the day (twenty-four hours).

2. तृतीया the lunar crescent on the third day after a new or full moon. [3. night] *S.*

ཐུན་པ *thun-pa* = བསྣུན་པ *bsnun-pa* to cling to, to adhere.

ཐུན II: = མཚམས 1. सन्ध्या, सन्धि, योग the junction of the day and night, twilight and day-break: མཚམས་པ་སྒོམ་ཆེན་རྣམས་ཉིད་ངེ་འཛིན་གློད་དུ་བཏང་བའི་ཐུན་བཞི་ཡོད་ there are four periods or junctions in which those called Tsham-pa Gom-chen can relax their meditation (*Çil. 8*). ཐུན་མཚམས *thun mtshams* the day and the night; at sunset or at day-break. བདུད་རྩི་ཐུན་མཚམས अमृतयोग an auspicious conjunction of time. 2. state of abstraction and isolation, real or suppositional, of a lama sitting to meditate. Often even applied to the room where he is sitting.

ཐུན་མཚམས་རྟོགས *thun-mtshams-rtogs* is a སྲིན་པོ or cannibal demon that longs for the gloom betwixt day and night to be able to search for prey.

ཐུན་མཚམས་སྟོབས *thun-mtshams stobs* सन्ध्याबल strong in twilight, a demon or Rākshasa.

ཐུན III: (prob. for མཐུན) in sorcery: bodies or substances which are supposed to be possessed of magic virtues, such as sand, barley, sesame, mustard, etc. ཐུན་གཏོར *thun-gtor* offerings made to evil spirits. ཐུན་དོང *thun-doṅ* a hole in which magical articles are buried or concealed in Shaman rites. ཐུན་མདའ *thun-mdaḥ* a magical arrow to shoot people or devils. ཐུན་བྲབ་པ *thun brab-pa* to cast or throw enchanted articles, also to perform magical rites with them, also to slay people or evil-spirits.

ཐུན་རྭ *thun-rwa* an enchanted horn on which figures of scorpions, alligators, etc., are engraved for witch-craft.

ཐུན IV: one who collects; a gatherer (from འཐུ་བ); ཤིང་ཐུན one who picks up or gathers sticks; རྩྭ་ཐུན a gatherer of grass (*Jä.*); སྙེ་ཐུན a gatherer of ears of corn (*Cs.*). ཐུན་ཟོར reaping-hook, sickle (*Sch.*).

ཐུན་མཚོན *thun-mtshon* a weapon that is fixed or stuck on.

ཐུན་ངང་མ་མོ *thun-ṅaṅ ma-mo* the mother of the arch-devil, said to = བདུད་ཁྱབ་པ་ལག་རིང the long-armed devil. However ལག་རིང is the demon who measured lances with Shenrab the Teacher of the Bon (*D.R.*).

ཐུན་མོང *thun-moṅ* or ཐུན་མོང་བ उत्सर्ग, सामान्य, साधारण ordinary, general, common, usual; that which is done or happens every day. ཐུན་མོང་ཆོས *thun-moṅ chos* = འཁོར་བ transmigratory existence, worldly life, the works that one does in ordinary life (*Mṅon.*). The ཐུན་མོང་གི་ཆོས as specified in Buddhist works are:—(1) བསམ་གཏན་བཞི the four (*Dhyāna*) kinds of meditation; (2) ཚད་མེད་བཞི the immeasurable virtues; (3) གཟུགས་མེད་པའི་སྙོམས་པར་འཇུག་པ་བཞི the four kinds of sitting in abstraction in the formless state; (4) མངོན་པར་ཤེས་པ་ལྔ the five kinds of fore-knowledge. Again ཐུན་མོང་གི་རྣལ་འབྱོར་ལྔ = the five sorts of ordinary ascetics which are:—(1) ནང་ཐུབ་ཆོས་སྒོད་ཀྱི་རྣལ་འབྱོར a *yogi* who meditates in the mornings and evenings; (2) སྔོན་འགྲོ་གཏོར་མའི་རྣལ་འབྱོར a *yogi* who propitiates a divinity by first offering him cakes; (3) བཟའ་བ་ཟས་ཀྱི་རྣལ་འབྱོར an ascetic who practises asceticism for getting food; (4) གཏུང་བ་སྐོམ་གྱི་རྣལ་འབྱོར a thirsty ascetic who practises penance for the sake of liquor; (5) སྤྱོད་ལམ་རྒྱུན་གྱི་རྣལ་འབྱོར an ascetic whose behaviour is uniform at all times (*Ḥbum.* ག *78*).

Syn. སྤྱི *spyi*; སྤྱི་མ *spyi-ma*; སྤྱི་ཐོག *spyi-thog* (*Mṅon.*).

ཐུན་མོང་བ *thun-moṅ-wa* = ཐུན་མོང་.

ཐུན་མོང་མ་ཡིན་པའི་ཆོས *thun-moṅ ma-yin-paḥi chos* in Budh. extraordinary doctrines said to comprise :—དྲན་པ་ཉེ་བར་བཞག་པ་བཞི, སངས་རྒྱས་ཀྱི་ཆོས་མ་འདྲེས་པ་བཅོ་བརྒྱད་ཀྱི་བར་རྣམས, ཕར་ཕྱིན་དྲུག་མ་བཅུའི་ཡོན་ཏན་ཐམས་ཅད. It is stated that they are called extraordinary because they can only be practised and comprehended by the *Bodhisattvas* of the ten stages and are incomprehensible to the followers of the Hīnayāna school.

ཐུན་མོང་བུད་མེད *thun-moṅ bud-med* = སྨད་འཚོང་མ a public woman (*Mṅon.*).

ཐུན་མོང་ས *thun-moṅ-sa* unclaimed grounds, public gardens, a place for public sports and athletic exercises (*Mṅon.*).

ཐུན་ཚེགས *thun-tshegs* = ཕྲན་ཚེགས *phran-tshegs*.

ཐུབ *thub* समर्थ; བློ་ཐུབ་པ *blo thub-pa* 1. capable; also sbst. a mighty one. ཀུན་ཐུབ one who is able to do everything, able to fight out all enemies (*Yid. 124*). 2. मुनि a wise man, a sage, a saint in general.

ཐུབ་པ *thub-pa* I: potential vb. with accus. or root of another verb: 1. to be able, to be capable of, to withstand, be equal to: དུག་གིས་མ་ཐུབ་ཅིང་ as the poison could not do him any harm; སེར་ཁྲལ་གྱིས་ནི་སེར་བ་འཇོམས་ཐུབ་ཅན་པ one able to keep off hail; གཞན་གྱིས་མི་ཐུབ་པ invincible; ངན་དགུ་ཐུབ་པ to be able to subdue all evil. མི་ཡིས་ཐུབ་པར་དཀར is not easily borne by man, *e.g.*, does not agree with him; རས་རྐྱང་ཐུབ་པ to be able to bear a simple cotton dress; མལ་ཁྲིང་ལ་ཉལ་མ་ཐུབ was not able to lie on his bed; ཐོ་རངས་ནལ་རྩེ་ཐུག་འབྱོར་མི་ཐུབ་ཡོང་ I shall not be able to reach the pass-top to-morrow. 2. the common Tibetan epithet of Sākya-muni—ཤཱ་ཀྱ་ཐུབ་པ. 3. the mighty or capable one.

ཐུབ་ཚོད *thub-tshod* साहस courage (*A. K. 1-24*).

ཐུབ་ཚོད་ཅན *Thub-chod-can* = གདོལ་པ चण्डाल one of the fierce wild tribes of India that did not submit to the *Aryas*; the lowest of the Hindu tribes (*Mṅon.*).

ཐུབ་པ་ཉིད *thub-pa ñid* मुनि a sage.

ཐུབ་པ་ཆེ *thub-pa che* महामुनि a great sage; an epithet of Buddha.

ཐུབ་བསྟན *thub-bstan* मुनिशासन the doctrine of Buddha: ཐུབ་བསྟན་དྲི་མ་མེད་པ་ཡུན་མཐར་གནས་ཤིང་ the stainless doctrine of Buddha enduring to the end of time (*Yig. k. 27*).

ཐུབ་པ་དྲུག *thub-pa drug* the manifestations of Buddha in the six states of existence acc. to the Nying-ma sect:—(1) in the abodes of gods, (2) in the world of demons, (3) in the land of men, (4) as *Seṅge Rab-brtan* in the world of beasts, etc., (5) as Guru Vairotsana in the abode of the Yidag or *Preta*, (6) as Vikrama in hell.

ཐུབ་པ་རབ་མཆོག *thub-pa rab-mchog* Pravara muni; n. of a *Tathāgata*.

ཐུབ་པ་སངས་རྒྱས *Thub-pa saṅs-rgyas* शाक्यमुनि Sākya-muni.

ཐུབ་པའི་གནས *thub-pahi gnas* आश्रम a hermitage.

ཐུབ་པའི་བུ *thug-pahi-bu* = ཁྱུག་རྟ.

ཐུབ་པའི་དབང་པོ *thub-pahi dwaṅ-po* मुनीन्द्र an epithet of Buddha.

ཐུབ་དབང་གསུང་སྐྱེས *Thub-dwaṅ gsuṅ-skyes* an epithet of a *Çravaka*, a monk of the Hīnayāna school (*Mṅon.*). Also ཐེག་ཆུང་སྐྱེས་བུ *theg-chuṅ skyes-bu*.

ཐུམ། *thum* or ཐུམ་ཐུམ = འདོག་ཐུམ anything packed in a bag, a parcel, anything packed or wrapped up: འབྲུ་ཐང་ཐུམ་བཅས *hbru-thaṅ thum-bcas* together with a package of grained tea.

ཐུམ་ཏི *thum-ti* = བསྒྲུམས་པ anything cut into pieces.

ཐུམ་པ *thum-pa* a while, a moment: མཉལ་ཐུམ་པ་ཞིག་བྱུང་ took a nap for a moment.

ཐུམ་བུ *thum-bu* 1. a piece, bit: ནོར་རྫས་གཞན་མ་དགེས་པར་ཐུམ་བུ་འདི་འདོད་ཀྱིས་ཤིག་ཅེས་བསྒོས not accepting anything else, (but) this piece he would have; thus he expressed himself (*Hbrom. 144*). 2.=ཐོམ་བུ a large spoon, a ladle; རག་ཐུམ a brass ladle; ཟངས་ཐུམ a copper ladle.

ཐུམས *thums*=1. ཐུར་བ spoon, ladle. 2. piece of cloth, linen (རས་ཐུམ་ལྟ་བུ *ras-thum lta-bu*); acc. to *Cs.*=ཐུམ་པ 3. cover, covering, wrapper of a book or a parcel, also the parcel itself. ཐུམས་རྒྱབ་པ to put (a cover round a thing), to wrap up; ཐུམས་ཅན having a cover, packed.

ཐུར *thur* a slope; ཐུར་ཐུར adv. down; ཐུར་ལམ *thur-lam* down-hill road, a steep descent; ཐུར་དུ *thur-du* or ཐུར་ལ *thur-la* downwards; ཐུར་ལ་རྒྱབ་པ to cast down into; ཐུར་ལ sink down; མགོ་ཐུར་དུ་བསྟན་ཏེ head down or head over heels; ཐུར་འགྲོད *thur-hgrod* that which runs downward, as met. water (*Mñon.*).

ཐུར་མགོ *thur-mgo* 1. the tip of a spoon ཐུར་མགོ་ཙམ *thur mgo-tsam* about the tip of a spoon, a spoon measure. 2.=ཐུར་མགོ *thur-mgo* a halter; ཐུར་ཐག *thur-thag* the rope attached to ཐུར་མགོ; ཐུར་མཐའ *thur-mthah* the end of that rope.

ཐུར་པོ *thur-po* the lowest part, the lower side (of a hill): ཐུར་ཐུར་གྱི་ཐུར་པོ་ལ at the very lowest possible point, in the bottom-most part (*e.g.*, of a deep ravine between two hill-sides).

ཐུར་སེལ *thur-sel* that which clears the downward passage, a purgation; ཐུར་སེལ་གྱི་རླུང *thur-sel-gyi rluṅ* अपान the wind that passes downward, *i.e.*, through the rectum.

ཐུར་བུ *thur-bu* or ཐུར་རུ *thur-ru* foal, colt, filly (*Jä.*).

ཐུར་མ *thur-ma* 1. शलाका a stick, chopstick; ཐུར་མ་བརྒྱ་པ *tur-ma brga-pa* an umbrella which is made on a frame work of (lit. a hundred) many sticks (*Mñon.*). 2. spoon. 3. a whole class of surgical instruments (*Jä.*).

ཐུར་ཞོ *thur-sho* a pair of scales.

ཐུར་ཤིང *thur-çiṅ* शलाका pole, the stick with which loads are supported (being attached to its two ends).

ཐུར་སྲང *thur-sraṅ* an ounce of silver (*Yig.*). ཐུར་སྲང་གི་ཞོ་ལ (*Rtsii.*).

ཐུལ *thul* from འདུལ་བ *hdul-wa* used substantively: ཐུལ་དེ་མིན besides that way of converting (people) (*Jä.*). ཐུལ་འོག་ཏུ་འཇུག་པ *thul hog-tu hjug-pa* to keep under one's power or control; to keep a tight hand over a person, to discipline one; དབང་ཐུལ विजितेन्द्रिय (*A. K. 1-8*) one who has controlled his passion; ཞིང་གི་ཐུལ་འདེབས་པ to clear land for tillage (*Schl.*).

ཐུལ་གྱིས *thul-gyis* suddenly, immediately: ཐུལ་གྱིས་བྱོན *thul-gyis byon* he arrived suddenly (*A. 43*).

ཐུལ་པ *thul-pa* acc. to *Cs.*=ཐུལ་པོ *thul-po* dress made of the skins of animals, a fur coat or cloak; ལུག་ཐུལ *lug-thul* dress of sheep skin; ར་ཐུལ *ra-thul* dress of goat-skin.

ཐུལ་བ *thul-wa* 1. imp. ཐུལ་ཅིག *thul-cig* दम्यताम् to restrain, tame, curb, check: ངས་འདྲེ་རྣམས་ཐུལ་ནས the goblins having been subdued by me; ལས་ཉོན་མོངས་ཐུལ་བ་དཀའ it is difficult to check a sinful deed. As a participle: tamed, civilized; converted. 2. rolled or wound up.

ཐུལ་ལུ *thul-lu* the common sheep-skin dress.

ཐུལ་ལེ *thul-le* (*Ld.*) impressive.

ཐུས་པ *thus-pa* or འཐུས་པ 1.=འགྲིགས་པ fit, appropriate: ཁ་ལས་ཐོན་ཚད་ལབ་ན་ཐུས་ཡོང་ངམ whether it will be appropriate if coming forth from the lips, *i.e.*, expressed in words (*Rdsa. 15*). v. འཐུ་བ *hthu-wa*.

ཐེ *the* 1. for ཐེ་མོ and ཐེ་ཚོམ. 2. num. 100.

ཐེ་ཁྱིམ *the-khyim*, v. ཐེ་སེ *the-se*.

ཐེ་ཆུང *the-chuñ* the smallest toe.

ཐེ་བ *the-wa* pf. ཐེས *thes* (*Sch.*) 1. to belong, appertain to; ཐེ་མཁན belonging to a thing; མ་ཐེ་བར=མ་གཏོགས་པར; ཐེ་རེག relation of owner-ship: ང་ལ་ཡབ་ཀྱི་ཐེ་རེག་མེད to this my father has no claims. 2. to occupy one's self with a thing, to meddle with, to interfere.

ཐེ་པ *the-pa* or ཐེབ་པ *theb-pa*=གཏོགས་པ pertaining to; to be applied to; to be of use: ཞབས་བསྐྱལ་ཞུ་བར་ཐེ་པ་ཙམ those who are fit to enter service (*Ya-sel. 31*).

ཐེ་བོ *The-ḇo* n. of a place in *Khams-Amdo* (*Loñ.* ཇ *14*).

ཐེ་མོ *the-mo* resp. ཕྱག་ཐེ (originally the thumb or thumb impression) a seal, signet, stamp. ཐེ་ཙེ *the-tse* id.

ཐེ་ཚོམ *the-tshom* संशय, वितर्क, विचिकित्सा, सन्दिग्ध, संदेहन, विमति, द्वापर, त्रुटि hesitation; doubt, uncertainty, perplexity: ཐེ་ཚོམ་སྐྱེས doubt arises, or ཐེ་ཚོམ་དུ་གྱུར I am doubtful. ཐེ་ཚོམ་ཞིག་འདྲི་བ to utter a doubt. In Budh:—1. དོན་འགྱུར་གྱི་ཐེ་ཚོམ doubt regarding alteration of signification. 2. དོན་མི་འགྱུར་གྱི་ཐེ་ཚོམ doubt as to the meaning remaining unchanged. 3. ཆ་མཉམ་པའི་ཐེ་ཚོམ equal doubt in reference to both (*Loñ.* པ *15*): ཐེ་མི་ཚོམ *the mi-tshom* not doubting, also=རྟོག་པ་རྫིད་པ without being afraid of, boldly: ལས་འབྲས་བདེན་རྫུན་ལ་ཐེ་མི་ཚོམ་པར་སྒྲུབ་པ་ཉམས་སུ་བླངས he practised (the rites) for the attainment of occult powers without being exercised by the thought of *karma*, retribution, truth and untruth (*Hbrom.* ཁ *3*).

Syn. སོམ་ཉི *som-ñi*; ཉེམ་ནུར *nem-nur*; འཕྱང་མོ་ཉུག *hphyañ-mo ñug*; མ་ངེས *ma-ñes*; ཡིད་གཉིས *yid-gñis* (*Mñon.*).

ཐེ་རྟོག *the-rtog* scruple doubt, uncertainty, hesitation.

ཐེ་ཚོམ་མེད *the-tshom med* unquestionable, certain=རྟོག་པ་མེད་པ doubtless: ཕ་ནོར་བུ་ཡིས་འཛིན་པ་ཐེ་ཚོམ་མེད that the son should inherit the father's property is undoubted.

ཐེ་ཚོམ་ཟ་བ *the-tshom za-wa* to doubt, to suspect, to be suspicious, doubtful. ཐེ་ཚོམ་ཟ་བ་རྣམས *the-tshom za-wa rnams* scrupulous irresolute persons.

ཐེ་ཚོམ་ལོག་གེ *the-tshom log-ye* groundless doubt, false scruple, or suspicions: ད་དུང་ཟད་གཅོད་ཅིག་བྱེད་རང་བྱེད་དགོས་སྙམ་ཐེ་ཚོམ་ལོག་གེའི་འདུག་ཡོད as groundless suspicions remain, make a further investigation should you think it necessary to be done (*Rdsa 12*).

ཐེ་ཧན *The-han* (Chinese)=གནམ heaven. ཐེ་ཧན་ནུ *The han-nu* or ཐེ་ཡན་ནུ (Chinese)=གནམ་མཁའི་བདག་པོ the lord of heaven (*Grub.* ཤ *16*).

ཐེ་རེ *the-re* col. straight, upright, firm, smooth, without folds or wrinkles: ཐེ་རེ་ཐིང *the-re thiñ* or ཐེ་རེ་ཐེན *the-re then* draw the (carpet) smooth (*Jä.*).

ཐེ་རང *The-rañ*, v. ཐེའུ་རང *thehu-rañ*.

ཐེ་རང་མིག་གཅིག་པའི་རྒྱལ་ཁམས *the-rañ mig gcig-pahi rgyal-khams* the fabulous kingdom of one-eyed giants, of cyclops; ཐེར or ཐེ་རང a class of demons (*Yig.*).

ཐེ་རེལ *the-rel* in *W.* incomplete, defective, unfinished.

ཐེ་ལེ *the-le* तिलक black spots tatooed on the forehead of Hindu women of Bengal. ཐེ་ལེ་ལྟ་བུའི་རྒྱན *the-le lta-buhi rgyan* is rendered: ornament resembling the eye of a peacock's feather.

ཐེ་སེ *The-se* a king of the ས་བདག demi-gods residing in the nether regions. ཐེ་ཁྱིམ *The-khyim* n. of his principal wife. ཐེ་སེ་གྲུམ་བུ *The-se grum-bu* one of the minor chiefs of *Sa-bdag* demi-gods (*Rtsii.*).

ཐེ་ལེ་ལེ *the-le-le* evil-hearted, vicious: ལ་ལ་ན་རེ་ཀོང་ཙེ་འཕྲུལ་གྱི་རྒྱལ་པོ་མནར་ཟན་པོ་ཐེ་ལེ་ལེ་ཟེར some said that the miraculous king Kong-tse was blasphemous and vicious (*D.R.*).

ཐེག་པ *theg-pa* I 1. to support: དགེ་འདུན་རྟག་ཏུ་ཐེག always supports the clergy. 2. to lift, raise, hold up. 3. to endure, to be able to carry: ཇི་ཐེག་པ as much as you are able to carry; མིས་ཐེག་ཚད་གཅིག as much as one man is able to carry; མ་ཐེག he was not able to hold him up; མི་ཐེག་ཁུར་ཅན unportable, not to be carried; ཡ་ཐོག་འདི་ཁ་བ་མང་ཙམ་ཐེག་མ་ཡོང་ཐེན་ཅིག་གི་ཚེའི་བཞིན་དུ་ཐེག་མི་ཐུབ the roof will not bear so much snow; it cannot be supported for the space of a moment; ཁོང་རྣམས་ཀྱི་ནན་མ་ཐེག་པར not being able to stand their urgent demands; སྐྱིད་ཐེག་སྡུག་ཐེག to be able to bear good fortune and ill fortune, cf. འཐེགས་པ, འདེགས་པ. 4. यान, वाहन any vehicle for transit, carriage, conveyance, even riding-beast: རྟའི་ཐེག་པ་ལ་ཞོན་པ he mounted on a carriage drawn by horses; ཐེག་པ་ལྔ་བརྒྱ་བཙམས he procured or gathered five hundred conveyances (horses, elephants, chariots); ཐེག་པའི་བཞོན་པ one who mounts chariots. Not used in this sense in modern writings.

ཐེག་པ II : यान 1. a method of doctrinal religion and conduct, a vehicle whereby one may be conveyed to higher and higher stages of progress to Buddhistic perfection and so ultimately to Nirvāna. Buddhism is supposed to be divided, primarily and also as a matter of history, into two great methods of observance and spiritual advance, these methods being designated ཐེག་པ (Sans. *yāna*) or vehicles to carry you onwards. The first or earliest was the ཐེག་པ་དམན་པ otherwise ཐེག་ཆུང་ the *Hīnayāna* school or following, now generally estimated as the meanest because the easiest vehicle to go by. This school may be taken to have been now long since extinct. The second and later development, said to have been first authoritatively promulgated by Kanishka at the council of Kusāna in Kashmir (about A.D. 78), is designated the ཐེག་པ་ཆེན་པོ *theg-pa chen-po* or Great Vehicle, otherwise the Mahāyāna school. A leading feature in this system was the introduction of the series of Bodhisattwas (བྱང་ཆུབ་སེམས་དཔའ), and eventually of Dhyāni Buddhas (ཡེ་ཤེས་སངས་རྒྱས) and Dhyāni Bodhisattwas (ཡེ་ཤེས་སེམས་དཔའ), into the curriculum of progress. As the Bodhisattwas are beings who have voluntarily and indefinitely delayed their own absorption into Nirvāna for the sake of helping forward others on the ཐར་པའི་ལམ or path of deliverance, so much the greater and more noble and beneficent is a system deemed which has included such principles as part of itself than that of the Hīnayāna or Lesser Vehicle which is destitute of the idea. The Mahāyāna in all other respects, likewise, is a more elaborate and intricate method of advance and therefore is, Buddhistically, considered the higher and better; while the Hīnayāna is held to be as crude and unsophisticated as it is frankly selfish. Historically, the Lesser or Lower Vehicle may be taken as the primitive curriculum of Doctrine and Practice as taught in the early period in Magadha and transported thence into Ceylon and even to Kambodia. Nevertheless, Trans-Himalayan Buddhism, as propagated from North India into Tibet China, and Japan, has never known any other form than the Mahāyāna. Indeed all records of the prevalence of ཐེག་དམན or Hīnayāna are so vague that theories invalidating its existence altogether as a practised sphere of Buddhism have been propounded. One theory allows to it only a paper existence set forth to contrast the greater glory of the Mahāyāna system, in the works of which system alone all first references to it occur. Another theory lately expounded by Professor Satis Chandra Acharya of Calcutta (See Journal Royal Asiatic Soc., Jan. 1900) endeavours to classify Brahmanism and Jainism with the doctrine of heretical Buddhists as together comprising the Hīnayāna system as referred to in Mahāyāna writings; and it is urged that Buddhist authers would naturally speak scornfully of the Brahmanism, etc., which had gone before as being a Hīnayāna, a less or lower means of conveyance to salvation. However, Professor C. Bendall, in a note on the last proposition, points to the matter-of-fact reference of the Chinese pilgrim Hiuen Tsang to the two systems as being both of them schools of solely Buddhist practice prevalent in his own day in the countries he visited, describing in particular some of the Ceylon Buddhists as of "the Little Vehicle." We may add, moreover, that ཉན་ཐོས the well-known term for a Buddhist hearer or Sr'āvaka is always defined in the *Mṅon-brjod* and other similar Tibetan treatises as a ཐེག་ཆུང་སྨྲ་བ or ཐེག་ཆུང་རྣམ་སྨྲད, that is, a follower of the Hīnayana school. 2. the word seems to have a second or more general technical meaning, signifying: doctrine in overt action, the practice of any doctrine, whether particular or part of a system or the whole system itself; also conduct.

ཐེག་པ་གསུམ *theg-pa gsum* the Three Vehicles. Although the great primary division of Buddhism is ordinarily set forth as only two-fold, the trinitarian tendency arises here, as elsewhere, and we read, therefore, of a set of three doctrinal vehicles also. These are:—(1) ཐེག་དམན or ཉན་ཐོས་ཀྱི་ཐེག་པ *Hinayāna* or *Çrāvaka yāna*; (2) རང་སངས་རྒྱས or རང་རྒྱལ་གྱི་ཐེག་པ *Pratyeka Buddha yána* or *Pradeçika yāna*; (3) བྱང་ཆུབ་སེམས་དཔའི་ཐེག་པ or ཐེག་པ་ཆེན་པོ the *Bodhisattva yāna* or *Mahāyāna* or *Ekayāna*, "སེམས་ཅན་ཐམས་ཅད་ཀྱི་དོན་གྱི་ཕྱིར་རྫོགས་པའི་བྱང་ཆུབ་ཏུ་སེམས་བསྐྱེད་པའི་ཕྱིར for the good of all sentient beings so that they may imbibe faith in the doctrine of the all-perfect Buddhahood." Again, the Mahāyāna school has been further divided into departments which under Tantrik influence, have assumed the position of independent and even superseding systems, deemed preferable to the generating source from which they took origin. The principal derivative of *Mahāyāna* origin is the *Mantra yāna* (སྔགས་ཀྱི་ཐེག་པ) or *Vajrayāna* (རྡོ་རྗེ་ཐེག་པ) which follows mysticism and deals in a measure with esoteric Buddhism. The *Mantra-yāna* is divided into two classes called རྒྱུའི་ཐེག་པ (*Hetu-yāna*) vehicle of Cause and འབྲས་བུའི་ཐེག་པ (*Phala-yāna*) the vehicle of Effect. Acc. to the Bon and also the *Rdsogs-chen-pa* sect of the *Ñiṅ-ma* school there are nine vehicles (ཐེག་པ་དགུ). Of these བཞི་རྒྱུའི་ཐེག་པ are the four subdivisions of the doctrine of Cause:—

ཕྱུག་ཐེག་པ, ང་ཐེག་པ, ནསྲིད་ཐེག་པ, འཕྲུལ་ཐེག་པ; while བཞི་འབྲས་བུའི་ཐེག་པ=four subdivisions of the doctrine of Effect:—དགེ་ཐེག་པ, དྲང་ཐེག་པ, ཨ་ཐེག་པ, ཡེ་ཐེག་པ; and lastly is བླ་མེད or བླ་ན་མེད་པའི་ཐེག་པ अनुत्तरयान which is common to both the series just mentioned.

ཐེག་པའི་སྟོབས *theg-pa͟hi-s̤tobs̤* यानबल one of the ten spiritual strengths of a *Bodhisattva* so called on account of the superiority of doctrine, v. སྟོབས་བཅུ *s̤tobs̤-b̤cu.*

ཐེག་ཆེན་ཐུགས་རྗེ་སེམས་དཔའ *theg-chen thugs̤-r̤je sems̤-d̤pa͟h*=སེམས་ཙམ་པ a follower of the *Yogācārya* school of Buddhism an offshoot of the Mahāyāna School.

ཐེག་མཆོག་གླིང་ *Theg-m̤chog-gliñ* n. of a monastery within the suburbs of Lhasa presided over by an incarnate Lama. Seems to be identical with the *Tshe-m̤chog* Ling.

ཐེང་ཀྭན *Theñ-kwan*=དྲི་མེད་གཟིགས (*Vimala dṛṣṭi*) n. of a celebrated Chinese Buddhist scholar well-versed in Sanskṛt and who is said to have compiled 300 works. He lived during the reign of Emperor Ming hûang of the T'ang dynasty and was greatly revered both by the people and the Emperor (*Grub.* ད, *11*).

ཐེང་པོ *theñ-po* or ཐེང་བུ *theñ-bu* खञ्ज lame, maimed in the leg; in *W.* limping, hobbling.

ཐེངས *theñs̤* वार time, times: ཐེངས་གཅིག एकवार one time, once; ཐེངས་ལྔ five times; དབུགས་ཐེངས་ཅིག་ལ in one drawing of breath; at a stretch, without intermission (*Jä.*).

ཐེན *then* 1. explained as ཚུར་འདོན་རྒྱུ *tshur h̤don-r̤gyu* drawing out or pulling towards one: བཅད་ཁྲ་བཀོད་ལུགས་བཅས་ཐེན་འཁྱེར་མི་ཡོང་ *b̤cad-khra b̤kod̤-lugs̤ b̤cas̤ then-h̤khyer mi-yoñ* (*R̤tsii.*). 2.=སྲིབ *sr̤ib* or ཧྲིབ་ཙམ *hrib-tsam* चण a little while, a moment: ཐུང་ཤིག་ཐེན་ཙམ་མཛོད་དང་ཚིག་གསུམ་ཞུ pray do wait for a little while and I shall speak but three words (*R̤dsa. 22*).

ཐེན་པ *then-pa* tax, duty, impost (*Sch.*).

ཐེན་མེད *then-med̤*=ཤ་ཚ་མེད་པ (*D. çel. 8*).

ཐེབ *theb* 1. for ཐེམ *them* full. 2. for ཐབས *thabs̤* (*Glr.*).

ཐེབ་མོ *theb-mo* or ཐེབ་ཆེན the thumb; ཐེབ་ཆུང་ *theb-chuñ* the little finger, v. མཐེ་བོང་.

ཐེབས I: *thebs̤* series, order, succession (*Sch.*). ཐེབས་རེ་བྱེད་པ to do successively; ཐེབས་པ *thebs̤-pá*, v. འཐེབས་པ *h̤thebs̤-pa.*

ཐེབས II: 1. signifies ཡོང་བ *yoñ-wa* coming out, issuing; thus ཀླུ་ཐེབས=ཀླུ་ས་སྙིང་དུ་ཡོང་བ the coming out of snakes or *nagas* from underneath the ground. 2.=ཁ་ལྟ་ཕྱོགས, སྒྲ་གཅན་ཐེབས: so *s̤gra-can thebs̤*=སྒྲ་གཅན་ཁ་ལྟ་ཕྱོགས *s̤gra-g̤can kha-l̤ta phyogs̤.*

ཐེབས་པ *thebs̤-pa* I: 1. to reach, arrive at: ད་རེས་ངའི་ལག་པ་ལ་ཐེབས་བྱུང་ it has come to my hand. རྣ་བ་ལ་ཐེབས་པ to reach the ear, to come to one's hearing: འགྲོན་དུ་མ་བཞེད་ན་ཡང་སྙན་དུ་ཐེབས་པར་མཛོད if you do not like to go, at least let it come to your hearing (give audience) (*A. 128*). 2.=འཛོམ་པ *h̤dsom-pa* to collect, assemble: སྡེ་བརྒྱད་ཐེབས=སྡེ་བརྒྱད་ཚོགས་པ assembling together of the eight classes of demons. 3. to be taken, be captured, to fall into; རྙི་ལ་ཐེབས་མ་ཐེབས whether an animal has fallen in the snare or not; རྙི་བཙུགས་ནས་ཐེབས་མ་ཐེབས having laid the trap, see if any fall in it or not.

ཐེབས་པ *thebs̤-pa* II: to adjust, to fit or cause to fit, to make appropriate, to make suitable: ལན་ཐེབས་པ to give a suitable or appropriate reply; ལྕགས་གཟེར་ཐེབས་སོང་ *lcags-gzer thebs-soṅ* a rivet or nail has been fitted into it; ཟས་འཐུང་ཐེབས་སོང་ food and drink have been applied, fitted, distributed; སྒོ་ལྕགས་ཐེབས་མ་ཐེབས does the lock fit or not?

ཐེབས་རང་ *thebs-raṅ* = ཐེའུ་རང་ *theḥu-raṅ* or ཐེ་བྲང་ *the-braṅ* a class of demon.

ཐེམ་པ I: *them-pa* 1. सोपान, निःश्रेणि, आरोहण threshold; ཐེམ་པ་འགལ་བ to cross the threshold; སྒོ་ཐེམ *sgo-them* door-sill; ཡ་ཐེམ *ya-them* head piece of a door-frame, lintel; མ་ཐེམ *ma-them* sill, threshold. 2. rank, dignity. 3. series, set; ཐེམ་སྐས *them-skas* staircase, flight of steps, a ladder; ཐེམ་རིམ *them-rim* the several steps of a staircase; རྡོ་ཐེམ *rdo-them* stone-stair; འཁོར་ཐེམ *ḥkhor-them* winding stair (*Cs.*).

ཐེམ་དེབ *them-deb* registration or record of the thresholds of houses with a view to levy house-tax: མི་སེར་སྡེ་གྲོང་ཐེམ་དེབ་ནང་གསལ a statement or list of tenants, villages and towns is set forth herein (*Rtsii.*).

ཐེམ་པ II: 1. to be full, complete: ཟླ་དུས་ཐེམ་པ་དང་ when the (specified) space of months was fulfilled; ཞག་གཅིག་མ་ཐེམ་པ་ལ one day being still wanting; བརྒྱ་ཐེམ་པ one hundred being full or the limit of a hundred having been reached. 2. in *W.* to be sufficient, enough (from *Jä.*).

ཐེམ་བུ *them-bu* closing, shutting up (*Sch.*).

ཐེམ་རྩ *them-rtsa* = སྒོ་ཐེམ་གྱི་རྩ་བ (*Lo. 8*).

ཐེམ་མཚམས *them-tshams* stopping, a stoppage.

ཐེམས་ཡིག *thems-yig* memorial (*Sch.*).

ཐེའུ་རང་ *theḥu-raṅ*, ཐེ་རང་ a set of demons.

ཐེར *ther* bare, denuded; also ཐེར་ཐེར *ther-ther* unruffled, flat.

ཐེར་འབུམ *ther-ḥbum* (གྲངས) पद्म; ཐེར་འབུམ་ལ་གནས་པ་བརྒྱ, *i.e.*, 1,000,000,000. ཐེར་འབུམ་ཆེན་པོ *ther-ḥbum chen-po* महापद्म; = 10,000,000,000.

ཐེར་མ *ther-ma* a kind of serge-cloth resembling flannel; རས་ཐེར *ras-ther* drill; བལ་ཐེར *bal-ther* shawl made of sheep's wool; སྣམ་ཐེར *snam-ther* very thick serge resembling blanket; ལེ་ཐེར *le-ther* serge made of very soft goat's wool; ཐེར་སྦག *ther-sbag* (ཐེར་མཐུག་པ) a coarse kind of serge (*Rtsii.*); ཐེར་གཟན *ther-gzan* a wrapper made of sergo which the lamas wrap round their body; ཐེར་གཟན་དམར་པོ *ther-gzan dmar-po* red plaid-shawl (*Rtsii.*).

ཐེར་ཟུག *ther-zug* = ཐེར་ཟུག་པ or འགྱུར་བ་མེད་པ *ḥgyur-wa med-pa* शाश्वत constant, enduring, unchangeable.

Syn. རྟག་པ *rtag-pa*; བརྟན་པ *brtan-pa*, (*Mṅon.*).

ཐེལ་བ *thel-wa* in *W.* = སླེབ་པ *sleb-pa* to arrive, cf. ཐལ་བ *thal-wa*.

ཐེལ་མ *thel-ma* leather strap (*Rtsii.*).

ཐེལ་ཚེ *thel-tshe* (ཐམ་ཀ) seal, stamp; ཐེལ་སེ *thel-se* = ཐེ་ཚེ *the-tshe* seal, stamp (*Sch.*).

ཐེས་པ *thes-pa* pf. to ཐེ་བ *the-wa* (*Sch.*).

ཐོ *tho* 1. num. for 130. 2. register, list, catalogue, index, memorandum: བརྗེད་ཐོ་བཏགས keeping memoranda. ཐོ་འབྲི་བ *tho ḥbri-wa* to registor, to make out a list or catalogue (*Schtr.*); སླེབ་ཐོ *sleb-tho* or འབྱུང་ཐོ *ḥbyuṅ-tho* account of receipts; སོང་ཐོ *soṅ-tho*, བུད་ཐོ *bud-tho*, སྐྱག་ཐོ *skyag-tho* account of expenditures; བཏང་ཐོ *btaṅ-tho* account of money or goods lent or sent out; ངོ་ཐོ *ṅo-tho* bill, account of goods purchased; ལོ་ཐོ *lo-tho* or ཟླ་ཐོ *zla-tho* calendar, almanac; དེའི་ལག་ཏུ་ཕྲིན་བོར་ཐོ list of orders or directions given to one (lit. laid down on his hand); དེའི་རྒྱུད་ལ་ཐོབ་ཐོ a list of things which his relations shall receive, *i.e.*, inherit (*Jä.*); ཐོ་ཡིག་ལོགས་སུ་བཀོད་པ *tho-yig logs-su bkod-pa* to make a separate list of things (*Yig.*). ཐོ་ཟུར *tho-zur* corner or marginal note; ཐུག་པར་གཟིགས་རྒྱུའི་ཐོ་ཡིག list, catalogue, for reference.

ཐོ་འཁོར *tho-ḥkhor* adj. and adv. near; sbst. neighbourhood.

Syn. ཐག་ཉེ་བ *thag ñe-wa*; ཉེ་འཁོར *ñe-ḥkhor* (*Mṅon.*).

ཐོ་གར *Tho-gar* or ཐོ་དཀར *tho-dkar* n. of a kingdom situated N. and N.W. of Kashmir, including Kho-ten. Tukhara, n. of a place and people in the north-west of India; *Jä.* suggests it is the Togarmah of the Bible. ཐོ་དཀར་གྱི་དམག་མང་པོ་རམ་ཧྲར་དྲངས they brought Ramdar a large number of troops from *Tho-dkar* (*Grub* ཆ *15*).

ཐོ་ཅོ *tho-co* jocular talk, nonsense-chatter; ཐོ་ཅོ་བྱེད་པ *tho-co byed-pa* to speak nonsense, meaningless words. This word and ཐོ་ཆོ *tho-cho* are evidently identic.

ཐོ་ཆོ་སྙེན་ཚིག་ཡ་སྒྲ་དང *tho-cho sñen-tshig ya-sgra dañ* to speak with dissimulation; to speak gently by concealing one's anger (*D.R.*).

ཐོ་ཕྱི *tho-phyi* 1. in *Pth.* seems to signify the sky (*Jä.*); acc. to *Schr.* love. 2. dissimulation.

ཐོ་ཐོ *tho-tho* prob. a Chinese word, signifying boundary demarcation; thus རྒྱ་མི་ཐོ་ཐོ *rgya-mi tho-tho* is the designation of the boundary marks put by the Chinese between Nepal and Tibet.

ཐོ་ཐོ་རི་གཉན་བཙན *Tho-tho-ri gñan-btsan* the first historical king of Tibet; during his reign Buddhism was first introduced in Tibet: ཐོ་ཐོ་རི་གཉན་བཙན་གྱི་རིང་ལ་དམ་པ་ཆོས་ཀྱི་དབུ་བརྙེས་ཤིང་། the commencement of the holy doctrine occurred in the times of Tho-tho-ri nyan-tsan (*Deb.* ཀ *2*).

ཐོ་རྡོ *tho-rdo* stone boundary: རྡོའི་ཐོ་ཐོ་བཙུགས་པ putting boundary marks of piled stones.

ཐོ་བ *tho-wa* = མཐོ་བ a hammer; ཐོ་བ་མགར་བའི blacksmith's hammer; परिघ, मुद्गर; ཐོ་བས་རྡུང་བ to hammer, to forge; རྡོ་ཐོ *rdo-tho* a stone hammer; ཤིང་ཐོ *çiñ-tho* a wooden hammer, mallet; ཐོ་ཆུང *tho-chuñ* a small hammer, the cock of a gun; a soldering stick.

ཐོ་བཙམས་པ *tho btsams-pa* pf. of ཐོ་འཚམས་པ *tho ḥtshams-pa* (*Ñag.*).

ཐོ་འཚམ་པ *tho-ḥtsham-pa* विहेठना sbst. 1. contempt, scorn, a scoffer, also ཐོ་འཚམས་པ (བརྙས་བཅོས་བྱས་མཁན) (*Ñag.*). 2. to scorn, scoff, jeer, sneer at, mock: སྔོན་ཆད་ཐོ་འཚམས་པ་བཟོད་པར་གསོལ pardon our having sneered at you before.

ཐོ་ཡོར *tho-yor* pyramid of stones heaped up as votive pile, a cairn.

ཐོ་རི་སྙན་ཤལ *Tho-ri sñan-çal* another name of king *Tho tho-ri gñan-bisan* (*Loñ.* ཆ *8*).

ཐོ་རངས *tho-rañs* or ཐོ་རེངས *tho-reñs* प्रातः, उषा, प्रत्युष dawn, break of day, early morning; ཐོ་རངས་ཀྱི་དུས་སུ early in the morning; chiefly used in *W.* 2. the following morning, also adverbially: དེ་དང་མཇལ་བའི་ཐོ་རངས on the morning after having met him (*Jä.*). ཐོ་རངས་སྣང་བ *tho-rañs snañ-wa* to-morrow. ཐོ་རེ *tho-re* acc. to *Jä.* in *W.* to-morrow; = སང *sañ.*

ཐོ་རེ་བ *tho-re-wa* 1. acc. to *Cs.*=ཐོ་ཙལ *tho-tsal.* 2. ཉུང a few: པཎྜི་ཏའི་བཀོད་ལུགས་ཐོ་རེ་བ་ཞིག་གསུངས་པས according to the manner of speech of *paṇḍits*, he said a few words (*A. 104*). ཐོ་རེ་ཙམ *tho-re tsam* a little while, time (*J. Zañ.*).

ཐོ་ལུམ *tho-lum*=ཐུ་ལུམ *thu-lum* a kind of hammer with a knob at its head; ལྕགས་ཀྱི་ཐོ་ལུམ་མེ་འབར་བ a red-hot iron hammer (*Sorig*).

ཐོ་ལེ *tho-le* 1.=ནར་ནར་རིང་པོ a projection; defined also as ལག་མཐིལ་བརྡུང་བ clapping the palms of the hand (*D.R.*). ཐོ་ལེ་འདེབས་པ *tho-le hdebs-pa* to spit, c. ལ *la* at or on (cf. ཐུ *thu*). 2. a button. 3. ཐོ་ལེ་དཀར་པོ chalk (*Jä.*).

ཐོ་ལེ་རིང་ *tho-le riñ* ནམ་མཁའ་ལ་འོད་དཀར་པོར་འཁྲོལ་ནས་ཐོ་ལེ་རིང་གེས་སོང་ངོ་ being diffused as white light in the sky it was projected in a long column (*D.R.*).

ཐོ་ལོག *tho-log* hinny, offspring of a horse and she-ass; a flummel. ཐོ་འདྲེའི་དྲེའུ་འགྲེམས་དང་ཐོ་ལོག་གཉིས two hinnies with the stupidest mule-colt of the lot (*Jig.*).

ཐོ་ཤོ་ལེགས *Tho-ço legs* n. of a tribe in Tibet (*Yig.*).

ཐོ་ཧུན *tho-hun* a Chinese word, meaning pale-white or grey colour.

ཐོག I: *thog* (ནམ་མཁའི) অশনি, বজ্র thunder-bolt, lightning; ཐོག་དང་སེར་བ lightning and hail: ཐོག་སེར་གྱི་གནོད་པ damage done by lightning and hail. ཐོག་འབབ་པ lightning descending, falling of a thunderbolt; ཐོག་རྒྱབ་པ striking with lightning; ཐོག་བབས་ལྟ་འཕྱོན་པ to arrive, to approach quick or suddenly like lightning; ཐོག་གསད་ཅན་པས་རྒྱུ་གཉེར་དམར་བ་བཀལ་འཇོམས་པར་བྱེད by the touch of a bone of an individual killed by lightning, colic and diarrhœa are cured. ཐོག་གིས་གསོད་པ or ཐོག་བབ་སྟེ་འཆི་བ dying from a thunderbolt; to be killed by lightning: ཐོག་ཆེན་པོ་དྲུག་ནམ་མཁའ་ལ་ཆགས་འདུག་པ་མཐོང་ I saw six great lightnings burst asunder in the sky (*A. 16*).

Syn. རྡོ་རྗེའི་ཆར་པ *rdo-rjeḥi char-pa*; ཆུ་འཛིན་སྐྱེས *chu-ḥdsin skyes*; མེ་ཆར་འཕྲོ་འཇོམས *me-char ḥphro ḥjoms*; ལྕེ་འབར་བ *lce ḥbar-wa*; སྤྲིན་གྱི་འོད་ཟེར *sprin-gyi ḥod-zer*; ཆུ་ལས་འབར *chu-las ḥbar*; ནམ་མཁའི་ཐོ་བ *nam-mkhaḥi tho-wa*; ལྕེ་སྙིང་མེད *lce sñiñ-med*; ཆང་ཉམས *chañ-ñams*; སྤྲིན་གྱི་མེ་པོ་ཆེ *sprin-gyi me-po che*; རྡོ་རྗེའི་ཟེགས *rdo-rjeḥi zegs*; ཆུས་མི་ཉམས *chus mi-ñams*; གནམ་ལྕགས *gnam-lcags*; སྤྲིན་གྱི་ཟེར་འཕྲོ་བ *sprin-gyi zer ḥphro-wa*; རི་འཇོམས *ri-ḥjoms*; འབིགས་བྱེད *ḥbigs-byed* (*Mñon.*).

ཐོག་རྒྱག *thog-rgyag*=གློ་བུར or ཅར་རྒྱག suddenly; also any sudden rattling noise; fig. sudden accident or mishap at a time when nothing was expected.

ཐོག་ལྕགས *thog-lcags* meteoric iron, a thunderbolt (*Mñon.*). ཐོག་རྡོ *thog-rdo* id. (*Mñon.*).

ཐོག་རི་འཇོམས *thog-ri ḥjoms* thunder, the chief weapon of Indra with which he strikes the mountains (*Mñon.*).

ཐོག II; (ཁང་པའི་ཐོག) a roof, a cover, top; ཐོག་འདུབས་པ or ཐོག་འགེལ་བ to put a roof on a house; also fig. to finish an enterprise or task; ཐོག་རྡིས་གཏོང་བ to roof, to finish a roof by beating and stamping down the earth or sods of which the covering consists; also fig. to impress (*Jä.*). ཐོག་དཀར *thog-dkar* opening for smoke in a roof; ཡ་ཐོག *ya-thog* ceiling; མ་ཐོག *ma-thog* floor of a room; དགུ་ཐོག *dgu-thog* having nine storeys or floors. The *ñi-zla* or crowning finial of a chait or chörten is also styled the *thog*; so, too, architecturally, the apex or culminating point of any structure. The following forty-three terms are enumerated in connection with a storeyed house:—ཡང་ཐོག *yañ-thog*, ཆུ་སྐྱོབ་ཐོག *chu skyob-thog*, དཀར་གསལ *dkar-gsal*, སྐས་ཀ *skas-ka*, སྐྱང་ནུལ *skyañ-nul*, ཁོལ་མ *khol-ma*, གྲོང་ཁྱེར་སྒོ *groñ-khyer sgo*, རྒྱ་ཕིབས *rgya-phibs*, སྒོ་ཁང་ *sgo-khañ*, སྒོ་གླེགས *sgo-glegs*, སྒོ་གཏན *sgo-gtan*, སྒོ་དྲུང་ *sgo-druñ*, སྒོ་མདུན *sgo-mdun*, སྒོ་འཕར *sgo-hphar*, སྒོ་ཕིབས *sgo-phibs*, སྒོ་མོ་ཆེ *sgo-mo che*, སྒོ་ཡི་ཁྱིམས *sgo-yi khyims*, སྒོ་ཡི་ཁྱམས *sgo-yi khyams*, གླང་རྒྱབ *glañ-rgyab*, གླང་པོའི་སེན *glañ-pohi sen*, ཆབ་སྒོ *chab-sgo*, འཇུག་བྱེད *hjug-byed*, རྟ་འབབ *rta-hbab*, གཏན་པ *gtan-pa*, ཐེམ་སྐས *them-skas*, དྲ་མིག *dra-mig*, མདའ་ཡབ *mdah-yab*, སྣང་བའི་ཁུང་ *snañ-wahi khuñ*, པུ་ཤུ *pu-çu*, ཕྱི་རོལ་སྒོ *phyi-rol sgo*, ཕྲེད་གཏན *phred-gtan*, བ་གླང་མིག *ba-glañ mig* गवाच, བྱ་སྐྱིབས་ཅན *bya-skyibs can*, འཛེག་སྐས *hdseg skas*, འཛེག་པའི་རྟེན *hdseg-pahi rten*, ཤལ་ཤལ *shal-shal*, ཡ་གད *ya-gad*, ཡ་ཕུབ *ya-phub*, ཡན་ལག་གཞི་མདོ *yan-lag gshi-mdo*, ལན་ཀན *lan-kan*, རླུང་སྒོ *rluñ-sgo*, ས་བཅིངས *sa-bciñs*, སྲང་མདའ *srañ-mdah* (*Mñon.*).

ཐོག III: head, top, in a general sense: ཐོག་འདྲེན་པ *thog-hdren-pa* to be at the head, to lead; ཐོག་ཁ or ཐོག་ཁར on, upon, ཁྱག་ཐོག་ཁར on the ice; དམག་ཐོག་ཏུ at head of the army.

ཐོག་ཏུ and ཐོག་ཐོག adv. up, up to, above; ཡང་ཐོག་ཏུ quite at the top. སེམས་ཐོག་ཏུ་ཕྱི་བར་ བྱུང་ནས lying heavy, weighing heavily, upon one's mind. Also postp. c. gen. 1. on, upon, *e.g.*, to lay on, to place upon: ངའི་ ཐོག་ཏུ་བྱུང་ *ñahi thog-tu byuñ* it smote right upon me (*i.e.*, on my heart). 2. towards, in the direction of: མའི་ཐོག་ཏུ *mahi thog-tu* towards (its) mother; བོན་ཆེན་དེ་གནམ་མཁའི་ཐོག་ཏུ་ ཕྱིང་སྟེ the Bon priest soaring towards the skies. 3. postp. c. accus. during, as long as, throughout; whilst (ཐོག gen. without ཏུ) དགུན་ཐོག *dgun-thog* throughout the whole winter; བགྲོས་ཐོག *bgros-thog* during the walk; སྔ་ཐོག *sña-thog*, ཕྱི་ཐོག *phi-thog* lit. during forenoon, during afternoon, as sbst. in *W.* morning, evening, or forenoon and afternoon. 4. just upon, directly after: བཞོས་ ཐོག་འོ་མ *bshos-thog ho-ma* milk just after being milked (*Jä.*). ཐོག་ནས *thog-nas* above, more than; ལོ་ལྔ་བཅུ་ཐོག་ནས་མ་ལུས they remained, *e.g.*, lived, not more than fifty years (*Ld.*).

ཐོག IV: 1. fruit, produce; དཀར་ཐོག v. དཀར་པ; ཞིང་ཐོག *shiñ-thog* produce of the fields; ལོ་ཐོག *lo-thog* year's produce; ཤིང་ ཐོག *çiñ-thog* fruit, produce of a tree or other plant; གསར་ཐོག *gsar-thog* new produce, the year's crop; ཐོག་ཕུད *thog-phud* first fruit, as an offering. 2. in *W.* fortune, wealth, property; སྤྱི་ཐོག common property, property belonging to the community or congregation (*Jä.*). 3. रक्तफल lit. red fruit, n. of a plant and its fruit. Has these synonyms: གཟུགས་ཅན་མ *gzugs-can-ma*; པི་ལུའི་འདབ *pi-luhi hdab* पिलुपत्र; འབྲས་བུ་དམར *hbras-bu dmar*; འཛིན་བྱེད *hdsin-byed*; བསིལ་བ་འཛིན *bsil-wa hdsin*; གཞན་རྒྱལ *gshan-rgyal*; ཐོག་གི་ལོ་མ *thog-gi lo-ma* (*Mñon.*).

ཐོག་གྲངས་པ *thog-grañs-pa* 1. to be the leader of, to lead against, to lead forward, to conduct: ཤཱཀྱ་མིང་ཆེན་དང་བཅས་པས་ཐོག་གྲངས་ཀྱིས and headed by Sākya together with Mahānāma (*Yig.*).

ཐོག་ཐག *thog-thag* 1. in the dialect of the *Dok-pa* herdsmen of Tibet = ཆོས religion. 2. or ཐག་ཐོག during, as long as, whilst, quite: ཉི་མ་གཅིག་གི་བར་དུ་ཐོག་ཐག during a whole day; ལམ་ཐོག་ཐག་གང་ངོ་ the road was quite full (of snow); བཟུངས་པའི་ ཐོག་ཐག་ལ whilst they began to fill up འདིའི་ཕན་ཡོན་རྟག་ཏུ་ཉིན་ཐོག་ཐག་སྐད་རྒྱུན་མི་འཆད་པར the; benefit of this will be permanent as long as the sun endures (*Surañ. 123*).

ཐོག་མཐའ་བར *thog mthah-war* first and last, from beginning to end; at all times continuously (*S. kar. 5*). ཐོག་མཐའི་རྒྱུ་རྐྱེན *thog-mthahi rgyu-rkyen* the first and the last cause, the entire cause or origin.

ཐོག་མ *thog-ma* आदि, अग्र, प्रथम 1. what is uppermost, the upper end, the foremost place, the top; གྲལ་གྱི་ཐོག་མ་ལ་འདུག་པོ they sat down at the top of the row. 2. the first, earliest, ancient; also origin, beginning; ཐོག་མ་སྐྱེས་ནས already at his birth, from his very birth; ཐོག་མ་ཚེ་རིགས་ མཐོ་བ of noble birth, as regards his birth very high; ཐོག་མ་ནས from the very beginning; of itself (*Jä.*); ཐོག་མ་མེད་པའི་དུས་ནས or དུས་ཐོག་མེད་ནས from eternity, from time immemorial. ཐོག་མར་དགེ་བ आदौ कल्याण blessing, good or prosperity at the beginning (of anything).

ཐོག་མའི་ལོ་མ *thog-mahi lo-ma* fresh shoots of leaves.

ཐོག་མ་སྐྱེས I: *thog-ma-skyes* अग्रज the first born (of brothers and sisters); the eldest brother.

Syn. སྔོན་སྐྱེས *sṅon-skyes*; ཇོ་ཇོ *jo-jo*; ཕུ་བོ *phu-wo*; ཨ་ཇོ *a-jo* (*Mṅon.*).

ཐོག་མ་སྐྱེས II: the first born (of Brahmā), *i.e.*, Brāhmaṇa caste of India.

ཐོག་མ་དང་མཐའ་མ་མེད་པའི་སྟོང་པ་ཉིད *thog-ma daṅ mthah-ma med-pahi stoṅ-pa-ñid* अनवराग्रशून्यता one of the 18 kinds of emptiness (*M. V.*).

ཐོག་མའི་མགོན་པོ *thog-mahi mgon-po* = ཀུན་ཏུ་བཟང་པོ or རྡོ་རྗེ་འཆང་། (*Yig. k. 26*) आदिनाथ epithet applied to the Adi-Buddha.

ཐོག་མའི་བྱེད་པ *thog-mahi byed-pa* आदिकरण first rites, duties, or business, to be done at the outset.

ཐོག་མར *thog-mar* 1. adv. at first, first. 2. postp. c. genit. before, at the beginning of.

ཐོག་ཚད *thog-tshad* or ཐོག་སོ (ཁང་པའི) storey of a house.

ཐོག་ཚ་དཔའ་བོ *Thog-tsha dpah-bo* n. of a section of the *Sa-skya* ruling family (*Loṅ.* ཞ *30*).

ཐོགས *thogs* v. འདོགས་པ *hdogs-pa* and འཐོགས་པ *hthogs-pa*.

ཐོགས་པ *thogs-pa* 1. धार, सङ्ग to bear aloft; ལག་ཏུ་བསྣམས་པ to hold up in the hand; ཉི་གདུགས་ཐོགས་པ छत्रधर a king; one over whose head an umbrella is held as a mark of honour. 2. प्रतिहत, प्रतिघ, क्षेप to strike, stumble, run against, to throw against or on, to be impeded, delayed: ཐོགས་པ་དང་བཅས་པ with obstruction or impediments. ཐོགས་པ་མེད་པ अप्रतिहत, अप्रतिघ unhindered, unobstructed; also two classes of devils, v. བདུད་བཞི. མི་ཁྱི་གང་ལ་འང་ཐོགས་པ་མེད་དུ without being hindered by men, dogs, or any thing else.

Syn. འཆང་བ *hchaṅ-wa*; འཛིན་པ *hdsin-pa* (*Mṅon.*).

ཐོགས་པ་མེད *thogs-pa med* = ཐོགས་མེད, ཐོགས་བརྡུགས་མེད or ཐོགས་བརྡུག་མེད 1. असङ्ग; v. preceding para., also = all-searching, all-penetrating, all-pervading. 2. असङ्ग Āryāsaṅga the founder of the Yogācharya school of Buddhism. He was called the sage of Achinta-puri Vihār, now called Ajunta, the cave and temples of which still bear testimony to the glory of his time; and is said to have lived 150 years. Acc. to some Tibetan authors he was the brother of the celebrated Vasu Bandhu (*K. g.* ད, *450*).

ཐོང *thoṅ* 1. a plough. ཐོང་ལྕགས *thoṅ-lcags* फाल, फलक the iron of the plough share. 2. a trunk, box (*A. K. 1-14*); ཐོང་གོས *thoṅ-gos* clothes in a leather trunk, also the lining of the inside of a leather trunk (*Rtsii.*).

ཐོང་ཀ *thoṅ-ka* or ཐོང་ག *thoṅ-ga* = བྲང་ or བྲང་ཁ the breast: ཐོང་ག་ནས་བཟུང་བྲང་ they (fought) holding each other breast to breast.

ཐོང་ཁོར *tkoṅ-khor* = གར་བུ dense, thick; also sbst. density.

ཐོང་པ *thoṅ-pa* 1. ལུག་ཟ་ལོ་གཉིས་འཁོར་གསུམ་པ་ཁ་ལྷམས་པ a ram two years old just entering its third year. 2. acc. to *Cs.* a ram that is castrated, wether; ར་ཐོང་ *ra-thoṅ* a castrated he-goat; ཐོང་པའི་ལོ *thoṅ-paḥi-lo* the years between childhood and manhood; juvenile years (*Sch.*). 3. हाल, हल also ཐོང་པོ *thoṅ-po* cf. ཐྲག་ཐོང་ a plough. ཐོང་པའི་འཆང་བཟུང་ *thoṅ-paḥi ḥchaṅ-ḇzuṅ* = ཞོལ་པར་བྱེད་ हलीषा to plough, to hold the plough.

ཐོང་སྤུ *thoṅ-ṣpu* mane of the camel (*Sch.*).

ཐོང་གཙོལ *thoṅ-gçol* लाङ्गल, हल the ploughshare: ཐོང་གཙོལ་ཅན *thoṅ-gçol can* one who ploughs, a tiller of the soil.

ཐོངས་འཛིན *thoṅṣ-ḥdsin* a receipt: འབུད་ཤིང་བཙམ་པ་ཐོངས་འཛིན་ལྷུབ the fuel having been supplied take a receipt for it (*Rtsii.*).

ཐོད I: *thod* 1. postp. over or above; ཁ་ཐོད་ལ = ཁ་ཐོག་ལ up, upon; also as adj. higher, upper: བལ་ཡུལ་ཤྲིབ་ཅན་ཐོད་ཁྲིལ་ཤིན་ཏུ་ཆེ the windings of the higher ravines and gorges of Nepal are very considerable (*Jig.*). ཐོག་ཁེབས *thog-khebs* = སྟེང་ཁེབས *ṣteṅ-khebṣ* cover, outside cover, anything to cover over. 2. = ཞ *shḇa* शेखर, शिरोवज्र, शिरोवेष्टन also བླ་ཐོད *ḇla-thod* or དབུ་ཐོད *ḏbu-thod* crown of the head, ornament or covering for the head. ཡ་ཐོད *ya-thod*, མ་ཐོད *ma-thod* a loft in the rafters of the upper and lower storey of a house.

ཐོད་རྒལ *thod-rgal* उत्कर्षक, व्याक्रन्दक; ཐོད་རྒལ་ཆེ་བ *thod-rgal che-wa* angry, wrathful.

ཐོད་ཐོད *thod-thod*, v. སུ *su*.

ཐོད་པ *thod-pa* 1. कपाल skull; skull of dead person, death's head; ཐོད་སྐམ *thod-ṣkam* a dry skull; ཐོད་རློན *thod-ṛlon* a fresh skull; ཐོད་ཁྲག *thod-khrag* a skull filled with blood; ཐོད་ཕོར *thod-phor* drinking cup made of a skull used by *Tantrik* lamas in propitiating spirits, ghosts, etc. 2. or ཐོད་དཀྲིས *thod-ḏkriṣ* a turban, not however worn in Tibet. 3. मस्तक the forehead, brow: ཐོད་རྩ *thod-ṛtsa* vena frontalis. ཐོད་རྒྱན *thod-ṛgyan* शिरोभूषण the ornament for the head.

ཐོད་མོ་ཁོར *thod-mo-khor* = ཐོད་ལེ་དཀར a species of conch-shell which when burnt makes fine lime. ཐོད་མོ་ཁོར་གྱི་ཕྱེ་མ *thod-mo khor-gyi phye-ma* खटिका-प्रलेपक lime-wash for walls of buildings.

ཐོད་ལེ་ཀོར *thod-le kor* or ཐོད་ལེ་སྐོད *thod-le ṣkod* said to mean alabaster (*Ṅag*).

ཐོད་ལེ་དཀར *thod-le ḏkar* खटिका chalk; ཐོད་ལེ་དཀར་གྱི་ཕྱེ་མ *thod-le ḏkar-gyi phye-ma* lime-wash or powder.

ཐོན *thon* 1. v. འཐོན་པ, འདོན་པ so; ཐོན་མཚམས་སུ at the time of, also time of coming out, at the time of his departure; ཁྱད་ཐོན *khyāḏ-thon* = ཁྱད་པར་དུ་བྱུང་བ turning out excellent, particularly good. 2. n. of a village at the foot of the Khambala ridge on the south side of the Yeru Tsangpo, famous for being the birth-place of Thon-mi Sambhoṭa the father of Tibetan literature. ཐོན་པ *Thon-pa* a native of Thon, also a member of the family of Thon-mi Sambhoṭa; བཀའ་བློན་ཐོན་པ n. of a Tibetan minister born of the family of Thon-mi Sambhota (*Loṅ.* ཐ *8*). ཐོན་མི *Thon-mi* or ཐོན་མི་སམ་བྷོ་ཊ *Thon-mi Sam-bho-ṭa*, called also ཐུ་མི་སམ་བྷོ་ཊ, the minister of king *Sroṅ-ḇtsan Sgam-po* who resided for many years in

India in order to study Sanskṛt and on his return to Tibet framed the Tibetan characters and laid the basis of Tibetan literature about the middle of the seventh century A.D.

ཐོན་ཀ *thon-ka* greenish-blue: ལྗང་ཐོན་དངས་པ་ཐོན་ཀའི་མིང་དུ་འདོད (*Jig.*) bright green-blue bears the name of *thon-ka*. ཐོན་ཐི *thon-thi* n. of a kind of Chinese satin shot with green and blue (*S. kar. 179*).

ཐོབ *thob*, v. ཐོབ་པ *thob-pa*, an exhortation as in གསོལ་བ་ཐོབ། མ་ཐོར་ཐོབ, v. འདེབས་པ *ḥdebs-pa*.

ཐོབ་ཆུ *thob-chu* acc. to *Schr*. button (ཐོབ་ཅི).

ཐོབ་པ I: *thob-pa* आलब्ध, लब्ध, यात, प्राप्त 1. vb. to find, to get, obtain; is practically synonymous with རྙེད་པ *rñed-pa*, which verb in the colloq. it has to a large extent superseded, though in certain parts of Central Tibet *rñed-pa* is often heard. In *W*. and Sikkim ཐོབ་པ only is in use both conversationally and in letters. In literature ཐོབ་པ occurs in the sense of "to get, obtain, procure, receive"; but not in the proper sense of "to find, discover" which is the special meaning belonging to རྙེད་པ. Thus in books a common phrase is དད་པ་ཐོབ་སོང they obtained or acquired faith; དེ་དག་ཐོབ་མཐར at the end have got the དེ་དག (in grammatical construction). ཐོབ་པ་དང་འབྲེལ प्राप्तानुषङ्ग gaining [having a close adherence; closely connected; consequent on]*S*. 2. to become; རྒྱལ་པོ་ཐོབ་པ to become king; སངས་རྒྱས་ཐོབ་པ to become a Buddha, to attain to Buddhahood; ཆོས་ཐོབ་པ to be religious; སྡུག་བསྔལ་ཐོབ་པ to be miserable, to be unhappy; ཐར་པ་ཐོབ་པ to be saved, emancipated; བདེ་བ་ཐོབ་པ to become happy, *i.e.*, to attain to *Nirvāṇa*.

ཐོབ་པ II: sbst. लाभ gain, profit, that which has been got or obtained; the sum, result, of gain. ཐོབ་ནོར in *W*. adj. that which is to be got or received (*Jä.*); ཐོབ་ཀྱིས་འཇལ་བ=ཐབས་ཀྱིས་འཇལ་བ निष्पेष्टकत्व to draw or acquire somehow or other another's property.

ཐོབ་ག *thob-ga*, v. ཐོབ་ལོ.

ཐོབ་ཁ་མ *thob-kha-ma*=དེ་མ་ཐག also ཐོབ་ཐ་མག immediately, *e.g.*, ཕྱིན་གྱི་ཐོབ་ཁ་མ་ལ directly he had arrived (*Mñon.*).

ཐོབ་རྒྱུ *thob-rgyu* colloq. lit. anything to be got, as income, profit, gain.

ཐོབ་རྒྱལ *thob-rgyal* 1. ཐོབ་པ་དང་རྒྱལ་བ *thob-pa dañ rgyal-wa* to gain and win; this expression occurs in the passage ཐ་བ་རྡུང་རྒྱལ, རྩ་མི་ཐོབ་རྒྱལ, འབྲས་བུ་ཡོག་རྒྱལ where it signifies ལམ་ཐོབ་རྒྱུ, *i.e.*, acquiring, finding, the way (to *Nirvāṇa*), getting at the root or gaining the fruit in the phraseology of the *Ñiñ-ma* sect (*Khrid*). 2. n. of a district with a monastery in Tsang: གཙང་ཐོབ་རྒྱལ་གྱི་ཤར་ཀྱི་ཕ་རི་གཙང་ཆུའི་འགྲམ་དུ་གཙང་འགྲམ་བྱེ་མའི་ལྷ་ཁང the temple of the River-bank Sands is situated on a hill on the further bank of the Tsangpo in the direction of Thob-gyal in Tsang (*Loñ*. ཉ *6*). In Thob-gyal was born པཎ་ཆེན་བསྟན་པའི་དབང་ཕྱུག the Panchen Lama Tanpai Wangchug, who was the successor of the Tashi Lama Tan-pai Nyi-ma whom Capt. Samuel Turner had interviewed in 1786 A.D. 3. occurs in ཐོབ་རྒྱལ་བྱེད་པ *thob-rgyal byed-pa* acc. to *Sch*. to despoil, pillage, plunder.

ཐོབ་ཆ *tho-cha* a share, due; the share which one gets. Also ཐོབ་ནོར.

ཐོབ་འདོད *thob-ḥdod*=ཆགས *chags* स्पृहा expectation, longing for.

ཐོབ་ཚིར *thob-tshir* lit. the turn of getting; may be taken as=claim, right, due: ཐོབ་ཚིར་ང་ལ་ཡོད *thob-tshir ña-la yod* I have a claim, a right to it (*Jä.*). ཐོབ་རིམ *thob-rim* the order or turn of getting.

ཐོབ་ཡིག *thob-yig* repertory, index.

ཐོབ་ལོ *thob-lo*=ཐོབ་ག *thob-ga* vanity, false show: ཁོ་ཡོན་ཏན་ཐོབ་ལོ he is conceited, he is not talented but he makes a show. བཤད་པའི་སྒོར་ཞུགས་པ་དེ་ཡང་ཆོས་ཞུགས་ལོ་ཐོབ་ལོ་ཙམ་གྱིས he who makes show of religion, of having acquired it, while just entered at the door of its exposition (*Khrid.*).

ཐོབ་སྲོལ *thob-srol* prob.=ཐོབ་ཚིར *thob-tshir* right of succession.

ཐོབ་ཤ *thob-ça* contest, scramble, *e.g.*, for money thrown among people.

ཐོམ་བུ *thom-bu*, v. ཐུམ་བུ (in the dialect of Amdo) a large wooden spoon or ladle ordinarily called གཟར་བུ: ཇོ་བོ་ལ་གཞན་དང་མ་མཚུངས་པར་མ་ཧེའི་ཞོ་ཐོམ་བུ་རེ་དང་ཀ་ར་འི་ཐང་མཛོ་རེ་བ་ལྷག་པར་འབྲིན regarding the Jowo as not like others he presented him with an additional spoonful of buffalo-cow's curds and a handful of crystaline sugar (*A. 35*); བཏུང་ཐོམ་བུ་གང་ཁྱེར brought one spoonful of drink (*A. 116*).

ཐོམས་པ *thoms-pa*, v. འཐོམས་པ *hthoms-pa*.

ཐོའུ་ཀྭན *Thohu-kwan* the last emperor of China of the Ta-yuan or Tartar dynasty: ཀརྨ་རང་བྱུང་རྡོ་རྗེ་རྒྱ་ནག་ཐོའུ་ཀྭན་གྱིས་གདན་དྲངས *Karma Rañ-byuñ rdo-rje* was invited to China by (emperor) *Thohu kwan* (*Loñ.* ཆ *10*).

ཐོར *thor* anything gathered into a single point; what is in a tangle drawn out fine. ཐོར་ཅོག *thor-cog* or ཐོར་ཅོགས or ཐོར་ཚུགས (also ཏ་ཀེར) कबरी, शिखाबन्ध a plaited tuft of hair, toupet: ཐོར་ཅོག་དར་སྣ་ལྔ་བཅིངས he bound the tuft of hair with silk-string of five colours.

ཐོར་ཁོད *Thor-khod* or ཐོར་གོད *Thor-god* n. of a Mongol tribe. ཐོར་གོད་སྤྱི་ཁང *Thor-god spyi-khañ* n. of quarters in the monastery of Tashi-lhunpo where monks coming from ཐོར་གོད *Thor-god* generally reside. མཁས་པའི་དབང་པོ་ཐོར་གོད་ཤེས་རབ་སྦྱིན་པ (*Loñ. 15*) the most learned *Çes-rab sbyin-pa* of *Thor-god* &c.

ཐོར་མགོ *thor-mgo* 1. v. ཐུར་མགོ *thur-mgo*. 2. the commencement of the dawn, of the morning.

ཐོར་ཆགས *thor-chags*=ཐོ་ཡི་ནང་ལ་འཁོད་པ entered into the list; registered: རྫོང་སྡོད་བསམ་པ་ཆེ་བས་ཐོར་ཆགས the resident official of a *Jong* generously put into the list (*Rtsii.*).

ཐོར་ཏོ *thor-to*=རྩེ་མོ the top point of hair, etc.

ཐོར་པ *thor-pa*, also འཐོར་པ, small-pox (*Sch.*), pimples, pustule; སྲིན་ཐོར *srin-thor* cutaneous disorders, pustules, pimples on the skin (*Jä.*).

ཐོར་བ *thor-wa* 1. v. འཐོར་བ *hthor-wa*. 2. ཐོར་པ *thor-pa*.

ཐོར་བུ I: *thor-bu* 1. acc. to *Jä.* denotes a whole class of diseases comprising dyspepsia as well as cutaneous disorders. དམར་ཐོར *dmar-thor* measles (*Sch.*); ཐོར་ནག *thor-nag* some kind of pimples or eruption on the skin (*Ya-sel. 28*). 2. single, separate (*Jä.*); སྣ་མ་ཐོར་བུ་པ separate little things, works, books, etc. (*Schr.*).

ཐོར་མོ *thor-mo* the growing fat of cows, goats, etc., in consequence of sterility (*Sch.*).

ཐོར་གཙུག *thor-gtsug* उष्णीष;=གཙུག་ཐོར *gtsug-thor* or གཙུག་ཏོར *gtsug-tor* a turban.

ཐོར་ཚུགས *thor-tshugs* शिखाबन्ध, कबरी= plaited hair bound up on the head in a spiral.

ཐོར་རེ *thor-re* or ཐར་རེ་ཐོར་རེ, འགྲོག་པ་བསྐྱེད་བཞིན་དུ་ཐོར་རེ (*A. 119*).

ཐོར་རེ་བ *thor-re-wa*, v. ཐར་ཐོར.

ཐོལ་བ *thol-wa* 1. v. འཐོལ་བ *hthol-wa* pf. to རྟོལ་བ *rtol-wa* what has come forth, what has been raised, elevated (*Sch.*); ཐོལ་བྱུང་ *thol-byuṅ* arisen, begun suddenly.

ཐོས *Thos* I: or ཐོས་རུས *Thos-rus* n. of a clan among the ancient Tibetans (*Yig.*).

ཐོས II: (in Sikk.) = གོ་བ understanding; ཐོས་ཆུང་ *thos-chuṅ* of less understanding; ཐོས་པར་བརྗོད to express intelligibly; ཐོས་པ་བླ་ན་མེད་པ श्रवणानुत्तर्य absolute comprehension; fully understanding or hearing, one of the six བླ་ན་མེད་པ, v. བླ.

ཐོས་པ *thos-pa* 1. vb. to hear; now used in the ordinary sense of hearing anything with one's own ears just as is the verb ཉན་པ *ñan-pa*; but ཐོས་པ seems to have had originally the meaning of hearing something at second hand, *i.e.*, from others. This signification it still bears also. Hence we derive the further meaning: 2. to hear of, to have word of, to understand: ཀལ་ཀ་ཏའི་ཕྱི་གླིང་གི་གཏམ་ཐོས་སམ have you heard of the English or Europeans of Calcutta? ཐོས་པ་བཞིན། यथाश्रवण, यथाश्रुत as reported. 3. श्रुति one of the 18 sciences or विद्या; *Veda*, v. རིག་པའི་གནས.

ཐོས་གྲོལ *thos-grol* or ཐོས་པ་དང་གྲོལ श्रुतिमुक्ति set free (from the world as soon as he) heard (it); an abbreviated n. of a book called ཐོས་པ་ཙམ་གྱིས་གྲོལ་བ་ཐོས་པའི་ཆོས the work by the hearing of which one is instantly saved. It is read over deceased persons or to the soul of the deceased.

ཐོས་པ་ལེགས *thos-pa legs* श्रावक a follower of the Hīnayāna school (*Mṅon.*).

ཐོས་ཆུང་ *thos-chuṅ* of little experience; ignorant.

ཐོས་སྒྲོགས *thos-sgrogs* or ཐོས་སྒྲོག་པ 1. met. བྱ་རོག *bya-rog* the crow. 2. ཉན་ཐོས श्रावक a hearer; a follower of the Hīnayāna school (*Mṅon.*).

ཐོས་རྟུལ *thos-rtul* less read or imperfectly informed.

ཐོས་ལྡན *thos-ldan* पण्डित learned man.

Syn. མཁས་པ *mkhas-pa*; ཤེས་རབ་ཅན *çes-rab-can*; རིག་པ་ཅན *rig-pa can* (*Mṅon.*).

ཐོས་ལྡན་དབང་ *thos-ldan dbaṅ* the chief among the learned; complimentary address for a learned man.

ཐོས་པ་དགའ *thos-pa-dgaḥ* n. given to the Buddhist saint *Mi-la ras-pa*.

ཐོས་འཛིན *thos-ḥdsin* = རྣ་བ *rna-wa* श्रुतिधर hearing; also ཐོས་པའི་སྒོ the organ of hearing. ཐོས་འཛིན་རྒྱན *thos-ḥdsin rgyan* = རྣ་རྒྱན *rna rgyan* कर्णिक ear-ornament.

ཐོས་ལོ *thos-lo* hear-say; hearing (a thing) but not understanding: དེ་ལྟར་མ་ཡིན་པར་གོ་ལོ་དང་ ཐོས་ལོར་བཞག་ནས་ཉམས་སུ་མ་བླངས་ན not being so, as if one pretended to have heard and to understand without really having taken into the mind (*Khriḍ. 40*).

མཐང་ *mthaṅ* अधःशरीर the lower part of the body; མཐང་གོས *mthaṅ-gos* अन्तर्वास a vestment for it, a sort of petticoat (*Cs.*); acc. to others: a toga worn by the lamas. མཐང་སྤྲད་པ *mthaṅ sprad-pa* काय-संसर्ग mutual touching of the body, lying or sleeping together (as husband and wife): མཐང་སྤྲད་པ་ཙམ परिष्वजमात्र just on the point of embracing; མཐང་སྦྱར་བ आलिङ्गन embracing (for company).

མཐངས *mthaṅs* = ཀུན all: མཐངས་ཀྱིས་ཚོར་བ perceived by all, heard by all.

མཐའ *mthaḥ* (cf. ཐ་མ) 1. the end, whether relative to space or time; so = edge, margin, brink; termination, conclusion, limits: མཐའ་སྐོར་བ to go round the confines (of a place); མཐའ་འགྲིལ *mthaḥ-ḥgril* skirts or edge of a gown or vestment tied up; མཐའ་ལས་འདས་པ exceeding all bounds, very great; རྒྱལ་པོ་བཞུགས་པའི་མཐའ་ལ་བསྐོར to walk round him that sits on a throne (*Glr.*); ལས་མཐའ་ལ་མ་ལོག་པ not returning to former works; to the last *karma*; དེ་མཐའ *de-mthaḥ* round that (mountain); མཐའ་དབུས་ཀུན་ཏུ at the frontiers and in the interior, everywhere (*Jä.*); མཐའི་རྒྱལ་ཁམས border region; མཐའ་བཞི the four borders, *i.e.*, all the surrounding territory, frq. མཐའི་ནོར, the treasures of the border-country; མཐའ་འདུལ་བ *mthaḥ ḥdul-wa* to conquer or convert the people on the frontier; མཐའ་འདུལ་ཡང་འདུལ་གྱི་གཙུག་ལག་ཁང་ the monasteries (founded) to convert the wild people of the borderland and also those beyond (*Ṛtsii.*); མཐའི་དམག *mthaḥi-dmag* border-war, *i.e.*, the invading armies (from China, India, Nepal or Khoten): དམའ་ས་བཟུང་ན་སྐྱོམས་ཆུང་མཐའ་ལ་འདུད if the lower lands are seized, tranquility will be reduced to a *minimum* (*Ṛdsa. 22*). 2. In grammar: terminal letters; ན *na*, མ *ma*, ར *ra*, ལ *la* ཞེས་རྣམས; མཐའ་ཅན *mthaḥ-can* words ending in n, m, r, l; ག་མཐའ *ga-mthaḥ* a final (ག *ga*). 3.=ཆ་ཤས *cha-ças*. 4. apparently is sometimes used as adj.=the utmost, the last, *e.g.*, རབ་མཐའ་ལས་སྡུ་ངན་ལས་འདས having been delivered from misery and from the utmost prosperity (*Khor-de*).

མཐའ་གཅིག་ཏུ *mthaḥ gcig-tu* 1. on the one hand; in part; in a certain degree and in some respects (*Jä.*). 2. keeping all on one side, or taking from one end or from one side (of a subject or question); བདག་ལྟ་བུས་མཐའ་གཅིག་ཏུ་བཤད་པར་སླ་བ་མ་ཡིན it is not easy for one like me to explain only one side (*Situ. 2*); མཐའ་གཅིག་པ *mthah gcig-pa*=བསམ་བློ་མཚུངས་པ of one opinion, view or thought; unanimous.

མཐའ་གཅོད་པ *mthaḥ gcoḍ-pa* 1. final sentence or judgment, a decision. 2. to adjudge, decide, come to a conclusion: མཐའ་གཅོད་པའི་ཕྱིར *mthaḥ gcoḍ-paḥi phyir* in order to settle it definitely, to come to a conclusion, or decision. ཡང་དག་མཐའ *yañ-dag mthaḥ* पर्यन्त the true end, the farthest limit. 3. the rest, remainder: རེ་དོགས་ཀྱི་མཐའ་ཐུངས having given up the last remnant of hope and fear.

མཐའ་བཞིར་རྒྱས་པ *mthaḥ-bshir ṛgyaṣ-pa* चतुरन्तविजेता one who expands even unto the four limits of the universe; an epithet of a *Cakravarti Rāja* (*M.V.*).

མཐའ་ཀླས *mthaḥ-ḳlaṣ*=མཐའ་མེད་པ limitless, boundless.

མཐའ་སྐོར *mthaḥ-ṣkor* आनन्तपट्टिका all round; also as sbst. the whole circumference, the perimeter.

མཐའ་ཁོབ *mthaḥ-khob* or མཐའ་འཁོབ प्रान्त border, outskirts, etc. མཐའ་ཁོབ་མི་འམ་སྐྱེ་བ *mthaḥ-khob miḥam ṣkye-wa* प्रत्यन्तजनपद any border-land occupied by uncivilized people; also one of the eight unhappy states, v. མི་ཁོམ་པ. མཐའ་འཁོབ་ཡུལ *mthaḥ-ḥkhob yul* प्रान्तभूमि barbarian's country; also any country where Buddhism has not penetrated.

མཐའ་གེབས་པ *mthaḥ gebṣ-pa* 1.=ལ་ཕུག་གི་ལོ་མ a raddish leaf. 2. नियम rule, regulation.

མཐའ་གྲུ *mthaḥ-gru*=རྒྱ་ཆེན་པ། वैपुल्य copiousness; spacious, extensive.

མཐའ་གྲོགས *mthaḥ-grogṣ*=ཕུགས་གྲོགས or གཉེན་གྲོགས lit. friend to the limit of life, *i.e.*, spouse.

མཐའ་ངོས *mthaḥ-ños* लज्जा bashfulness, modesty.

མཐའ་ལྕགས *mthaḥ-lcagṣ* the form of a mirror, etc. (*Schr.*).

མཐའ་ཅན *mthaḥ-can* शाखा met. a branch.

མཐའ་ཆགས *mthaḥ-chagṣ* living at the border or edge; the border of a robe.

མཐའ་གཉིས *mthaḥ-gñiṣ* lit. the two extremes, namely, རྟག་པ་དང་ཆད་པ *ṛtag-pa dañ chaḍ-pa*. In ancient India the sages held that there was either immortality or total annihilation, Buddha discovering the golden mean or middle path. མཐའ་གཉིས་སྤངས་ *mthaḥ-gñis spañs* = མ་ནིང་ *ma-niñ* a hermaphrodite, who is neither man nor woman (*Mñon.*). མཐའ་གཉིས་སུ་དོགས་པ་ = ཐེ་ཚོམ doubt.

མཐའ་ཉི *mthaḥ-ñi* the sun at the end of summer and winter.

མཐའ་དག *mthaḥ-dag* समस्त, निखिल, अभितः, सकल several, sundry, all; = སོ་སོ.

མཐའ་དག་མིན *mthaḥ-dag min* frq. མང་ཚིག་མཐའ་དག *mañ-tshig mthaḥ-dag* the plural sign མཐའ་དག *mthaḥ-dag* (gram.).

མཐའ་དམ *mthaḥ-dam* or མཐའ་དམ་ཚིག *mthaḥ-dam-tshig* = the difference separating ruler and subject (*Yig. k.*)

མཐའ་བརྡུལ *mthaḥ-brdul* n. of a number (*Ya-sel. 57*). མཐའ་སྣང་ *mthaḥ-snañ* तितिम n. of number of twenty-eight figures; མཐའ་སྣང་ཆེན་པོ *mthaḥ-snañ chen-po* (གྲངས) महातितिम n. of number of twenty-nine figures.

མཐའ་བེར *mthaḥ-ber* कवचिका a kind of lasso with which the body of an enemy is entangled.

མཐའ་བྲལ *mthaḥ-bral* 1. the sky, space. 2. boundless; as with the ocean (*Mñon.*).

མཐའ་འབྱམས *mthaḥ-ḥbyams* चरम n. of a very large number (*Ya-sel. 57*).

མཐའ་མ *mthaḥ-ma* अन्त, निर्दम 1. the end; the outermost or extreme side or thing. 2. border, hem, seam, of dresses. དེང་མཐོང་བ་མཐའ་མ to-day we see (him) for the last time.

མཐའ་མི *mthaḥ-mi* प्रान्तवासी border people; barbarians.

མཐའ་བརྟན་པ *mthaḥ brtan-pa* = ཕུགས་བརྟན་པ *phugs brtan-pa* secure future, eventually for good.

མཐའ་བཞི *mthaḥ-bshi* चतुरन्तं the four limits of the globe; མཐའ་བཞིར་རྣམ་པར་རྒྱལ་བ चतुरन्तं विजितवान् one who has conquered everywhere.

མཐའ་ཡས *mthaḥ-yas* 1. प्रतिज्ञार्य्यं, अनन्त, शेष infinite, endless. 2. n. of the king of Kashmir during whose reign Kshemendra wrote the Avadāna Kalpalata. N. of a king of *Nāga* demi-gods (*Mñon.*). 3. = ས་གཞི *sa-gshi* the world.

མཐའ་ཡས་མ *Mthaḥ-yas-ma* अनन्त the ocean, a name of the goddess Paldan Lhamo (*Mñon.*).

མཐའ་ཡས་རྩ *mthaḥ-yas rtsa* अनन्तमूल n. of a vegetable medicine.

Syn. ཐལ་དྲེས་སྨན *thal dres-sman*; ཨ་ཏ་པལ *a-ta-pal* (*Mñon.*).

མཐའ་རས *mthaḥ-ras* piece-goods imported from border countries such as India, China, Kashmir or Nepal (*Rtsii.*).

མཐའ་ལས་འདས་པ་སྟོང་པ་ཉིད *mthaḥ-las ḥdas-pa stoñ-pa ñid* अत्यन्तशून्यता one of the eighteen kinds of emptiness (*M. V.*).

མཐའ་ལས་ཡས = རྒྱ་མཐའ་རྒྱ་ཆེ་བ (*Mñon.*).

མཐའ་གསལ *mthaḥ-gsal* wholly clear, illuminated.

མཐའ་གསེབ *mthaḥ-gseb* = མཐའ་ཡི་བར.

མཐར *mthar* 1. adv. at last, lastly, finally, in conclusion; acc. to *Jä.* perh. also: to the very last, wholly, altogether. Also postp. after, behind; རྒྱལ་རབས་སུམ་བརྒྱའི་མཐར *rgyal-rabs sum-brgyaḥi mthar* after three hundred royal generations; ས་མཐར་ཤིང་ the progressive particle ཤིང་ *çiñ* is (to be written) after a final ས. 2. or མཐའ་རུ *mthaḥ-ru* towards the end, at the end; frq. ཚེའི་མཐར་ཐུག་པའི་གྲངས the number of those that reach the natural end of life; མཐར་ཐུག་པ་མེད་པ *mthar thug-pa med-pa* not to be got through, inexhaustible; མཐར་ཕྱིན་པ reached the extreme limit or མཐར་ཐོན་པ *mthar* *thon-pa* fully crossed or passed over the limit; as a sbst. a perfect holy person, a saint who has acquired all virtues and has gone to the farthest limit of learning or has acquired all that is knowable. མཐར་བྱེད་པ *mthar byed-pa* to end a work, to destroy, to put an end to, to demolish. མཐར་ཕྱིན *mthar-phyin* or མཐར་བྱིན་པ अन्तग, निष्ठागत the sky. མཐར་བྱེད *mthar-byed* कृतान्त, अन्तक the lord of death who puts an end to every thing. མཐར་འབྱིན *mthar-hbyin* अन्तग going to the limit.

མཐར་གྱིས་གནས་པའི་སྙོམས་པར་འཇུག་པ་དགུ *mthar-gyis gnas-pahi snoms-par hjug-pa dgu* the gradually-acquired nine stages of tranquil posture. They comprise the states of བསམ་གཏན་བཞི the four *Dhyana*; གཟུགས་མེད་པ་བཞི the four *Arûpa* and འགོག་པའི་སྙོམས་འཇུག.

མཐར་སྐྱེལ་བ *mthar-skyel-wa* to carry out fully; to depose without reserve, to dwell upon a subject exhaustively.

མཐར་གྱིས *mthar-gyis*=རིམ་གྱིས *rim-gyis* adv. by degrees, gradually, at length.

མཐར་ཐུག་པ *mthar thug-pa* and ཤིན་ཏུ་མཐར་ཐུག་པ, མི་རྟོག་པ་དང་ཉིང་མཚམས་སྤྱོད་པ་མེད་པ *mi rtog-pa dañ ñiñ-mtshams spyod-pa med-pa* are attributes of the gods of the highest heaven (*K. ko.* ཀ *237*).

མཐར་ཐུག་པ *mthar thug-pa*= མུར་ཐུག་པ *mur-thug-pa* touching or carried to the limit as regards quality, good or bad.

མཐས་ཀླས *mthas-klas*, v. མཐའ་ཀླས *mthah-klas*.

མཐས་གཏུགས་པ *Mthas gtugs-pa* n. of a place.

མཐིང་ *mthiñ* 1. नील sky-blue, azure. 2. n. of a flower, used as a medicine for eye-disease. 3. acc. to *Cs.*=indigo; མཐིང་ཤིང *mthiñ-çiñ* indigo-plant. 4. indigo colour (*Jä.*).

མཐིང་སྐྱ *mthiñ-skya* light blue. མཐིང་ཁ *mthiñ-kha* blue colour. མཐིང་ག *mthiñ-ga* n. of a bird of deep-blue colour (*G. Bon. 12*). མཐིང་ཁྲ *mtkiñ-khra* a kind of silk-scarf with white spots on a blue ground (*Rtsii.*). མཐིང་གི *mthiñ-gi* (སྔོན་གྱི་མི་རབས) n. of an ancient dynasty (*J. Zañ.*). མཐིང་རྒྱུས *mthiñ-rgyus* a kind of stone used medicinally. མཐིང་སྔོན *mthiñ-sñon* n. of a blue-stone used in medicine, lapis lazuli (*Med.*). མཐིང་རིལ *mthiñ-ril* acc. to *Sch.* wild duck. མཐིང་ཧྲིལ *mthiñ-hril* किरिटि a smaller bird (*Jä.*) [the fruit of the marshy date tree]*S.*; མཐིང་རྡོ *mthiñ-rdo*=ལྕགས་རྡོ *lcags-rdo* superior steel, of bluish-red colour, highly prized in Tibet (*Jig.*).

Syn. མིག་སྨན་སྔོན་པོ *mig-sman sñon-po*; བྱ་ཁྱུང་རྡོ *bya-khyuñ rdo*; གསལ་ལྡན *gsal-ldan*; གསལ་པ་ཅན *gsal-pa can*; མེ་ཏོག་མིག་སྨན *me-tog mig-sman*; ཀུ་ཤུའི་ཁམས *ku-çuhi khams*; དུས་ཀྱི་མེ་ཏོག *dus-kyi me-tog*; མེ་ཏོག་ཟེ *me-tog ze* (*Mñon.*).

མཐིང་ཤུན *Mthiñ-shun* n. of a place on the Tibeto-Chinese frontier; མཐིང་ཤུན་གཡུའི་རྡོ་རི on a hill of turquoise-stone (shone as it were) melted lapis lazuli (*Yig.*).

མཐིང་ཤིང་ *mthiñ-çiñ* राजमठ monolyth of turquoise.

མཐིའུ *mthihu*, v. མཐེའུ *mthehu*.

མཐིལ *mthil* 1. तल, sbst. the bottom, the lowermost part, the depths: བྱི་ཁྲུང་གི་མཐིལ་ཟབ་མོ་ལ at the deep bottom of a marmot's burrow; གོས་རིམ་གྱི་མཐིལ the bottom or undermost of the pile of clothes. 2. the hollow part of anything, chiefly used of the hand or foot: ལག་མཐིལ the palm of the hand; རྐང་མཐིལ the sole of the foot; དཔེར་བབ་གྱིས་ན། ཐང་ལག་མཐིལ་ཙམ་ལ་སྲོག་ཆགས་གྲོག་བུར་རི་སྙེད་ཡོད་ལ for a hasty illustration, there might be so many ants clinging to life on the flat palm of the hand (or, on the palm of the hand as on a plain) (*Khor-de*). 3. the centre, the principal or chief part, of a town; the principal place: གདན་ས་མཐིལ *Gdan-sa mthil* the capital or the central place of a country where the government is located; also n. of the chief monastery of Tibet in Yar-lung, three day's journey to the east of Sam-ye.

མཐུ *mthu* = प्रभाव, अनुभव, शक्ति, तेजस्, बल, वीर्य force or power of an inherent nature; innate energy; capacity, resource. Is a word chiefly used as denoting magic powers; but not invariably so. མཐུ་དང་ལྡན་པ strong, powerful, efficacious; ནག་ཕྱོགས་འཇོམས་པའི་མཐུ the capacity of suppressing the powers of darkness; སྲོག་གཅོད་པ་སྤངས་པས་དངོས་པོ་རྣམས་བཟང་ཞིང་མཐུ་ཆེ་བའི་སར་སྐྱེ་བར་འགྱུར་རོ because he has abandoned the taking of life, he shall be born in a land of great resources and fine natural productions. མཐུ་མེད *mthu-med* also འཐུད་མེད powerless, feeble, unable; མཐུས *mthus* by virtue of, frq. མཐུ་རྩལ or མཐུ་དང་རྩལ प्रभाव, magic, witchcraft; མཐུ་གཏོང་བ, མཐུ་འདེབས་པ to cast magic spells, to bewitch.

མཐུ་བསྒྱིངས *mthu-bsgyins* विष्फूर्जति roaring expressive of one's might and prowess མཐུ་ཆེན་རྣམས *mthu-chen rnams* महानुभव; མཐུ་སེར་གཏད་གསུམ་པོ་ཐོགས་པར་བསླབས conjuring, raising tempests, exorcising ghosts, these three I have learned thoroughly.

མཐུ་བ *mthu-wa* ओझ (མཐུ་སྤྱད་མཁན) an exorcist, one who practises witchcraft. མཐུ་བོ་ཆེ *mthu-wo che* རྟོགས་པ, རྟོགས་ཆེན one versed in mysticism, in the *Tantrik* cult, an exorcist lama (*Mnon.*).

མཐུ་མོ་ཆེ *mthu-mo che* n. of a *preta* (ཡི་དྭགས): *yi-dwags mthu-mo cher skyes* was born as a powerful female *preta* (*Khrid.*).

མཐུ་རྩལ *mthu-rtsal*=མཐུ་རྩལ, *mthu-rtsa rmad-du. byun-wa rkan-mgyogs rlun-dan mnam-pa gcig spyan-dsans* brought in one who in walking was swift as wind and wonderfully skilful in feats of arms, &c.

མཐུ་ཡོད་པ *mthu yod-pa*=ནུད་པའོད प्रतिबलोभवति efficacious.

མཐུག་པ *mthug-pa*, v. འཐུག་པ घन thick, dense.

མཐུང་བྱེད *mthun-byed*, v. གུར་གུམ *gur-gum* (*Mnon.*).

མཐུད་པ *mthud*, v. འཐུད་པ *hthud-pa*.

མཐུད་མེད *mthud-med*, འཐུད་མེད *hthud-med*.

མཐུན་པ *mthun-pa* (ཆ་སྙོམས་ འདོན་པ་ལྟ་བུ) प्रदक्षिण, समादान, समान, अनुलोमी, अनुकूल, अनुरूप (*blo lta-bu*) साढ़ to agree with, to be accordant, to be on a par with: མཐུན་པར་བྱེད་པ to make agree, to bring to agreement, reconcile; to be in sympathy with. ཁ་མཐུན་པ unanimous; གྲོས་མཐུན་པ, ཁྲིམས་མཐུན་པ to live in harmony, unanimous in judgment; ཆོས་ལུགས་མཐུན་པ accordant in form of religion. ཚོང་མཐུན་པ सार्थवाह merchants, men of one and the same avocation; ཕན་ཚུན་མཐུན་པ mutual agreement. བྱ་བ་སྤྱོད་ལམ་མཐུན་པ similarity or agreement in acts and behaviour. མི་གཞན་དང་མཐུན་པར in harmony with other men; ཚིག་མཐུན་པ or ཚིག་དང་མཐུན་པར in conformity with one's words, expressions; ཡུལ་དུས་མཐུན་པ agreement in reference to time and place; ལུས་མཐུན་པ personal union as of husband and wife; ཟས་སྤྱོད་མཐུན་པ agreeing in the habits of life, in the manner of food and drink, etc.; རིགས་རུས་མཐུན་པ of equal birth and extraction; ལས་མཐུན་པ of the same or similar profession, also persons whose *karma* is similar; སེམས་མཐུན་པ mental unity, of the same thought or mind, agreement; མཐུན་པའི་སྡེ *mthun-pahi sde* समकुल same or equal rank or class. མཐུན་པར་སྐྱེས་པ समनुजात similar extraction or birth. མཐུན་པར་སྣང་བ equal or similar culture or enlightenment. ཁྲིམས་དང་མཐུན་པར་ཁྲལ་འཇལ་བ paying taxes according to law; སྐད་ཆ་མ་མཐུན་པར་ཅི་བྱེད་པ་མི་ཤེས or ཅི་བྱེད་དམ་མི་ཤེས the news being contradictory I do not know what to do; མི་གཉིས་གཅིག་དང་གཅིག་མ་འཆམ་པས། ཁྲིམས་མ་ཞུས་ཏེ་གྲོགས་པོ་ཞིག་གིས་མཐུན་པར་བྱས་སོ the two men having disagreed, they did not go to law but a friend made them agree; ཡུལ་པ་རྣམས་ཀྱི་ཏོག་གི་ནོར་གྱི་སྐོར་ལ་མཐུན་པར་མ་ཐུབ་པས་དཔོན་པོ་ཞབས་ནས་མཐུན་བཅུག་གོ because the villagers could not agree on question concerning their common property, the headman of the village came causing them to agree. It will be noted from certain of the foregoing examples that མཐུན་པར may be used as a postp. coupled to the word it governs by the affix དང་.

མཐུན་པར་རྩེ་བ *m̱thun-par ṟtse-wa* अनुक्रीड़ति playing without disagreement. .

མཐུན་པའི་རྐྱེན *m̱thun-paẖi ṟkyen* or མཐུན་རྐྱེན *m̱thun-ṟkyen* necessary articles; also, as predicate, requisite, indispensable: ཟས་སྐོམ་སོགས་འཚོ་བའི་མཐུན་རྐྱེན food and drink, &c., are the requisites of living; གོས་ལ་སོགས་མཁོ་བའི་མཐུན་རྐྱེན clothes, etc., are the articles of necessity which one must have; ནད་མེད་པ་ནང་མཐུན་རྐྱེན, སེམས་བདེ་བ་གསང་བའི་མཐུན་རྐྱེན health is a requisite of domestic happiness and a peaceful mind is necessary for inner enjoyment. གླང་པོ་ཆེ་གཉིས་ལ་མཐུན་པའི་རྐྱེན་རྣམས་བཀལ་ཏེ lading on the two elephants all the necessary articles (*A. 22*). བསྟན་འཛིན་སྐྱེས་བུའི་མཐུན་རྐྱེན་བསྒྲུབ་པ *ḇs̱tan ẖdsin s̱kyes-buẖi m̱thun-ṟkyen ḇs̱grub-pa* to have secured all things requisite for a religious man (*Yig.*). མཐུན་རྐྱེན་བྱེད *m̱thun-ṟkyen byeḏ*=རོགས་རམ་བྱེད་པ to co-operate, to help, to be-friend (*M̱ñon.*).

མཐུན་ཅན *m̱thun-can*. in *W.* gentle, peace (*Jä.*).

མཐུན་འཇུག་པ *m̱thun ẖjug-pa* or མཐུན་པར་འཇུག་པ to cause to agree, to fit in, to bring in accordant elements (*Yig.*).

མཐུན་པའི་གྲོགས *m̱thun-paẖi grogs̱* friends of great mental affinity; མཐུན་འགྱུར་གྱི་ཡི་གེ letter of recommendation.

མཐུན་པའི་དངོས་གྲུབ *m̱thun-paẖi ḏños̱-grub* wished-for blessings.

མཐུན་པའི་ཡུལ་དུ་གནས་པ *m̱thun-paẖi yul-du gnas̱-pa* प्रतिरूप-देशवास residence in a country of congenial characteristics (*M.V.*).

མཐུན་པའི་རླུང་ *m̱thun-paẖi ṟluñ* favourable wind (for a vessel sailing).

མཐུན་སྦྱོར *m̱thun-s̱byor* friendship, relationship, favourable coincidence of time, circumstances, etc., particularly when matrimonial relationship is formed.

Syn. མཐུན་ཕྱོགས *m̱thun-phyogs̱*; མཛའ་བྱེད *m̱dsaẖ-byeḏ*; ཉེ་བར་སྦྱོར *ñe-war s̱byor*; མཚམས་སྦྱོར *m̱tshams̱-s̱byor* (*M̱ñon.*).

མཐུན་ཕྱོགས *m̱thun-phyogs̱* अनुपक्ष;=གཉེན་ཕྱོགས relations, friends (*M̱ñon.*).

མཐུན་མོང་པ *m̱thun moñ-pa* or མཐུན་མོངས सामान्य ordinary, usual; also=སྤྱི་པ *s̱pyi-pa* general, common; also common property.

མཐུན་རྩིས *m̱thun-ṟtsis̱* the astrological calculation to ascertain if a bride and bridegroom will live in harmony or not after marriage.

མཐུར *m̱thur* also མཐུར་མགོ=རྟའི་མཐུར straps or rope for a horse's head to which another rope is tied to fasten him. མཐུར་མདའ *m̱thur-m̱daẖ* or མཐུར་ཞགས a halter, rope tied to the muzzle of a horse, &c.; མཐུར་མགོ reins: མཐུར་མདའ་མགོ་རྒྱན་ལ་ཡང་རིན་པོ་ཆེའི་རྒྱན་དུ་མ even on the halter and the head gear there were many precious gems (*A. 141*).

མཐུས་ *mthus* instr. of མཐུ, by magical power, by dint of (*A. K. 111-16*). མཐུས་བཙིར་བ *mthus brtsir-wa* बलात् उपक्रान्त to be subdued; gen. overpowered by witchcraft.

མཐེ་བོ་ *mthe-bo* अङ्गुष्ठ; also col. མཐེ་ཆེན, མཐེབ་མོ or ཐེ་བོ *the-bo* the thumb. རྐང་པའི་མཐེ་བོ *rkañ-pahi mthe-bo* the big toe.

Syn. སོར་མོ་ཐེ་བོ *sor-mo the-bo*; མཐེ་བོང་ *mthe-boñ* (*Mñon.*).

མཐེ་ཆུང་ *mthe-chuñ*=མཐེའུ or སོར་མོ་ཆུང་བ अनामिका the little finger; the little toe.

མཐེ་བོང་ *mthe-boñ*=མཐེ་བོ *mthe-bo*.

མཐེབ་ཀྱུ *mtheb-kyu* 1. button. 2. a symbol resembling a finger which is placed with the torma (offerings made to gods and demi-gods, &c.) (*Rtsii.*).

མཐེའུ *mthehu* or མཐེའུ a little hammer. Also, the little toe.

མཐོ *mtho* (ལག་པའི *lag-pahi*) वितस्ति 1. a span, from the tip of the thumb to the tip of the middle finger when extended. མཐོ་རེ་ཁྲུ་རེ་ཙམ་དུ་འཕར་བ they increased each about a cubit and span measure (*Hbrom. 163*). མཐོ་ཡོངས=མཐོ་གང་ཡོངས་པ (*Jig.*). མཐོ་འཇལ་བ or མཐོ་གཞལ་བ to span, to measure by the hand with the fingers extended; མཐོ་གང་, མཐོ་རེ་ཙམ a span in length; མཐོ་གཉིས or མཐོ་དོ द्विवितस्ति two spans. 2. v. མཐོ་བ.

མཐོ་གོང་ *mtho-goñ* a little triangular receptacle into which the effigy of an enemy is placed, to whom one wishes to do harm by witchcraft (*Jä.*).

མཐོ་རྒྱབ་པ *mtho rgyab-pa* to give earnest money in *W.* (*Jä.*).

མཐོ་ངག *mth-ñag*=མཐོ་བཅད *mtho-bcad* grandiloquence, high speech with little meaning. ཆོས་རྒྱལ་དེའི་དུས་ཀྱི་ལྟ་བ་མཐོ་ངག་ཡིན་ཏེ the doctrines of the time of that Buddhist king were only high-flown theories (*A. 77*).

མཐོ་བ *mtho-wa*=སྣང་ उच्छ्र, तुङ्ग, उच्च, उत 1. sbst. elevation, prominence; height; also adj. high, lofty, elevated, raised. *Jä.* makes it primarily a verb: to be high. རིགས་ཆེ་ཞིང་མཐོ་བ་ལ་སྐྱེ being of high and noble birth; དེ་ལས་མཐོ་བ higher than that; རྒྱལ་མཚན་དེ་དག་ཡ་ཐོག་གི་སྟེང་དུ་མཐོ་བ་ཡིན the sacred insignia are high up above the roof; པོ་ཏ་ལའི་མཐོ་བ་ནི་ཐོག་རིམ་བཅུ་གཅིག་ལ་འབེབས the height of Potala reaches to eleven stories; ང་མཐོ་ན *ña-mtho-na* when I am high, when I rise in position. མཐོ་བ་གནོན་པ to lower what is high, to bring down, to humble, frq. ངས་མགོ་མཐོ་ཁྱམ་པས་དམའ་དམའ་བྱུང་ the more I was aspiring, the more I was brought low (*Jä.*). 2. for ཐོ་བ hammer; མཐོ་བ་རྡོག stone used as a hammer (*Cs.*). མཐོ་ཁྱད *mtho-khyad* height, highness.

མཐོ་སྤྱོད *mtho-spyod* in *W.* haughty manner (*Jä.*). མཐོ་དཔང་ *mtho-dpañ* occurs in ཁང་པ་སོགས་དཔང་མཐོ་བ.

མཐོ་བར་བརྩེགས་པ *Mtho-war brtsegs-pa* n. of a lofty mountain in the fabulous continent of Uttara Kuru where there are trees with leaves of gold, lapiz lazuli, coral, diamond, ruby, etc., and trunks of silver. At night light is emitted from the leaves of trees, etc., to enable the gods and nymphs to make themselves merry and to revel, &c. (*K. d.* ར *309*).

མཐོ་བར་སེམས་པ *mtho-war sems-pa* उन्नमस् to think highly of, to extol (one's own religion, doctrine, &c.). མཐོ་བར་བྱ་བ *mtho-war bya-wa* to eulogise, to flatter, to praise, to exalt;=ཆེས་བརྗོད་པ, བསྔགས་པ་བརྗོད་པ, also as sbst.=བསྟོད་ཚིག, བཀུར་ཚིག.

མཐོ་དམན *mtho-dman* height: མཐོ་དམན་མཉམ་པ of equal height; མཐོ་དམན་ཅན undulating; having high and low lands.

མཐོ་མཚམས *mtho-mtshams* evil design, mischievous mind or intention, brewing mischief. སྟོན་པ་ལ་མཐོ་མཚམས་ཞིང་། བར་དུ་གཅོད་པར་འདོད *ston-pa la mtho-mtshoms shiñ, bar-du gcod-par hdod* designing mischief to the teacher in the meantime he wished to injure it (*Yig*). ས་སྐྱོགས་བྱེད་དེ་དག་ནང་དུ་ཞུགས་ཏེ་ནང་པ་ལ་མཐོ་འཚམས (*Hbrom.* ཀ *31*).

Syn. མཐོ་འཚམས *mtho-htshams*; གནོད་སེམས *gnod-sems*; འཚེ་བྱེད *htshe-byed* (*Mñon.*).

མཐོ་རིས *mtho-ris* I: स्वर्ग, सिद्धक, नाक, देव, ख, गौः heaven, paradise, the abode of the gods: ངན་སོང་གསུམ་དུ་སྐྱེས་པ་ཆེ་མང་ཞིང་མཐོ་རིས་སུ་སྐྱེས་པ་ཉི་ཟུང་ persons gone to tho three spheres of damnation being very many and persons gone into bliss being few (*Khor-de.*).

Syn. མཐོ་རིས་རྒྱལ་སྲིད *mtho-ris rgyal-srid*; ལྷ་ཡི་ཡུལ *lha-yi yul*; ས་བླ *sa-bla*; སྟེང་གི་འཇིག་རྟེན *steñ-gi hjig-rten*; དལ་འཛིན་གནས་བཟང་ *dal-hdsin gnas-bzañ*; རོལ་པའི་ས *rol-pahi sa*; བདེ་འགྲོ *bde-hgro*; སྐྱོ་མེད *skyo-med*; སྐབས་གསུམ་གནས *skabs-gsum gnas*; ལྷ་ཡི་འཇིག་རྟེན *lha-yi hjig-rten*; ལྷ་ཡི་གྲོང་ *lka-yi groñ*; སུམ་རྩེན *sum-rtsen*; འཆི་མེད *hchi-med*; གྲུབ་པའི་གནས *grub-pahi gnas*; ནམ་མཁའི་ཁྱིམ *nam-mkkahi khyim*; བདེ་ལྡན *bde-ldan* (*Mñon.*).

མཐོ་རིས་ཀྱི་ཡོན་ཏན་བདུན *mtho-ris-kyi yon-tan bdun* the seven attributes or advantages of paradise are:—རིགས་ལྡན noble birth, གཟུགས་བཟང་ fine form, ལོངས་སྤྱོད་ཆེ great enjoyment, ཤེས་རབ་ཕུན་ཚོགས mental accomplishment and merit, དབང་ཕྱུག་ལྡན power and prosperity, ནད་མེད freedom from disease, ཤིན་ཏུ་ཚེ་རིང་བ extreme longevity (*Mñon.*).

མཐོ་རིས་ཀྱི་མཚོ *mtho-ris-kyi mtsho* the lake of heaven.

Syn. ཆུ་ཀླུང་མཚོ *chu-kluñ mtsho*; རྩེ་བའི་མཚོ *rtse-wahi mtsho* (*Mñon.*).

མཐོ་རིས་ཀླུང་ *mtho-ris kluñ*=ལྷའི་ཆུ་བོ the celestial river, the river of the Mandākini (or glacial streams).

མཐོ་རིས་དགེ་བ *mtho-ris dge-wa* worldly virtues, good, etc., (heaven being inside such world).

མཐོ་རིས་ཐོབ *mtho-ris thob* बृहस्पति the spiritual guide or teacher of the gods.

Syn. ཕུར་བུ *phur-bu*; སྒྲ་མཁན *sgra-mkhan*; སྒྲ་མཁས *sgra-mkhas*; ལྷ་ཡི་བླ་མ *lha-yi bla-ma* (*Mñon.*).

མཐོ་རིས་རྣམས *mtho-ris rnams*=ལྷ་རྣམས the gods including the planet Rāhu.

མཐོ་རིས་སྨན་པ *mtho-ris sman-pa* अश्विनीकुमार the physician of the gods.

Syn. ཐ་སྐར་སྐྱེས *tha-skar skyes*; ལྷའི་སྨན་པ *lhahi sman-pa* (*Mñon.*).

མཐོ་རིས་སྨད་འཚོང་ *mtho-ris smad-htshoñ*=ལྷའི་སྨད་འཚོང་མ celestial courtezan (*Mñon.*).

མཐོང་ཁ *mthoñ-kha* or མཐོང་ག chest, breast; མཐོང་ག་ནས་འཛིན་པ to seize by the breast (*Jä.*).

མཐོང་བ I: *mthoñ-wa* 1. to see, to view, in the broad sense of the term as an ordinary faculty; to look, to see, in a general way: མཐོང་ནས दृष्ट्वा having seen; མཐོང་བར་གྱུར अपश्यत् was seen; མཐོང་བར་བྱེད་པ to cause to see: མིག་གི་ཉེ་མཐོང་རིང་མི་མཐོང་། he sees only when the object is near, not when it is far (*Sch.*); མཚན་མོ་ནི་ཁྱོད་ཀྱིས་ཐག་རིང་པོ་ཐུག་ལ་མཐོང་ངམ can you see to a far distance at night time? 2. to perceive or behold any particular object; བོད་ཀྱི་རི་མཐོང་བའི་རི an eminence from whence one can see the mountains of Tibet; མི་གཞན་གྱིས་མཐོང་སར a place where one can be seen by others; དེ་བུ་མོས་མཐོང་བར་མཛད་དོ he made it visible to the girl, he made her see it; མཐོང་བ་ཞིག་ཡོད་ན if there is one that has seen it, if there exists a witness; དེ་མཐོང་ནི་ཤེས seeing this, I came to know, *i.e.*, from this I saw, I percieved; མཐོང་ཐོས་དྲན་རེག frq. seeing, hearing, touching, remembering; acc. to

Jä. thinking of (*e.g.*, a form of prayer, or magic formula); colloq. མཐོང་བ is usually coupled with མིག, the eye, quite pleonastically: ཡ་གི་ལ་ལྟོས་ཤིག་དགོ་བ་གསུམ་མིག་མཐོང་ནུས look up there, you can see three goa deer. 3. to witness, observe (mentally): ཀྱཻ་མ་ ཁ་ལ་ལ་འཛམ་བུ་གླིང་དུ་ཆོས་ཀྱི་འཁོར་ལོ་གཉིས་པ་ བསྐོར་བ་མཐོང་ངོ་ཉིས་ཆེད་དུ་བརྗོད་པས་སོ O capital, capital, for the second timo have I witnessed the Doctrine preached in the metropolis! thus designedly he cried. 4. colloq. to experience, to endure: སྡུག་བསྔལ་མང་མཐོང་བ་ཡིན has experienced many troubles.

མཐོང་བ II: slight; in Budh. མཐོང་བ་ལ་རྣམ་པ་གཉིས་ཏེ *mthoṅ-wa la rnam-pa gñis-te* of two kinds: 1. མཚན་མོས་མཐོང་བ perception by inference: རྒྱང་ནས་དུད་པ་མཐོང་བ་ཞེས་བྱ་སྟེ, ཡང་དག་པར་མེ་མ་མཐོང་སྟེ etc., by seeing smoke from a distance to hold that I have seen fire although really I have not seen fire, etc. 2. མངོན་སུམ་དུ་གསལ་བར་མཐོང་བ actual sight by personal observation (*K. my. 437*).

མཐོང་ཕྱོགས *mthoṅ-phyogs*=ལྟ་ཕྱོགས explained as དབྱིབས་འདྲ་ བར་མཐོང་ཕྱོགས object of sight; a view, scene, aspect (*Ya-sel. 41*).

མཐོང་དུག *mthoṅ-dug* दृष्टिविष ('sight-poison') evil eye (*Sch.*); envy, grudge, jealousy [a snake]*S*.

མཐོང་བྱེད *mthoṅ-byed*=མིག *mig* 1. that which sees, the eye (*Mṅon.*). 2. a species of kite.

མཐོང་ལམ *mthoṅ-lam* the true way 1. བདེན་པ་མཐོང་བའི་ལམ the state or stage of perfection in which one perceives the truth, *i.e.*, the reality of *Nirvāṇa*: དེ་ལྟར་ས་དང་པོ་རབ་ཏུ་དགའ་བ་ནས, མཐོང་ལམ་ཆེ་བ་ཉིད་བདེན་པ་རྟོགས་ཏེ accordingly from the first stage of perfection or ecstasy he passes to the meditative stage called མཐོང་ལམ where he perceives the true state of *Dharma*. 2. acc. to *Was.* (*139*): the path of obtaining the power of sight, a mystical state.

མཐོང་ལུགས *mthoṅ-lugs* the way of viewing a thing; notion, theory, opinion.

མཐོང་བ་དོན་ལྡན *Mthoṅ-wa don-ldan* n. of an image of Buddha, the sight of which brought merit to any one (*Yig. k. 21*).

མཐོང་ན་དགའ *mthoṅ-na dgaḥ*=གཟུགས་མཛེས་པ very handsome, of beautiful form.

མཐོང་ཕུལ་ཆུང་བ *mthoṅ-phul chuṅ-wa*=མཐོང་རྒྱ་ཆུང་བ, as in མཐོང་ཕུལ་ཆུང་ངམ་སྙན་ཁྲུང་ཞན tiniest thing visible or faintest thing audible (*D.R.*).

མཐོང་བ་བླ་ན་མེད་པ *mthoṅ-wa bla-na med-pa*=བདེན་པ་མཐོང་བ दर्शनानुत्तार्य perceiving the supreme truth v. བླ་ན་མེད་པ.

མཐོང་བ་མེད་པ *mthoṅ-wa med-pa* खलाटिक fatalist.

མཐོང་བའི་ཆོས *mthoṅ-waḥi chos* दृष्टधर्म actions of present life. མཐོང་བའི་ཆོས་ལ་མྱོང་བར་འགྱུར་བ *mthoṅ-waḥi chos-la myoṅ-war ḥgyur-wa* दृष्टधर्मवेदनीयम् (Karma) manifesting itself in the actions of this life. མཐོང་བའི་ཆོས་ལ་བདེ་བར་གནས་པ दृष्टधर्मविहार one of the stages in technical meditation.

མཐོང་བས་སྤང་བྱ *mthoṅs-was spaṅ-bya* that which is renounced when seen; མཐོང་བས་གྲོལ *mthoṅ-was sgrol* deliverance at sight.

མཐོང་ཚོར *mthoṅ-tshor* वत्सल explained by མཐེ་བོང་གིས་ནི་སྲིན་ལག་ལ་རེག་པ་འཚེ་བར་མི་འགྱུར་ར (*K. gu.* ང་ *90*).

མཐོངས *mthoṅs*=མིག་གིས་མཐོང་ས 1. आदर्श view, prospect, sphere; illuminated space: ནམ་མཁའི་མཐོངས་རྣམས་འཇའ་ཚོན་གུར་གྱིས་གཏམས the expanses of sky were filled with rain-bow canopies. 2. opening in the wall or roof of a house for the entrance of light or for egress of smoke: ངའི་རྫས་ཁར་མི་རེང་དཀར་པོ་ཞིག་ སྦུག་ཁང་གི་མཐོངས་ཕྱི་ནས་བྱུང་སྟེ on the side of my pillow there came a solitary white man opening wide the cleft-holes of the bamboo house (*A. 129*). ཁྱམས་མཐོངས an opening to the sky in the middle of a building. རྒྱ་མཐོངས=མཐོངས 3. མཐོངས་ཁ *mthoṅs-kha* platform on a flat-roof. མཐོངས་ཀ *mthoṅs-ka* silk ornaments, fringes on the borders of paintings (*Cs.*) མཐོངས་ཆེ་བ *mthoṅs che-wa*= རྒྱ་མཐོངས dome.

མཐོངས་པ *mthoṅs-pa* 1. to lose one's senses; one who has lost his senses. 2. acc. to *Jä.* perh.=འཐོམས་པ *hthoms-pa*.

མཐོན་ཀ *mthon-ka* or མཐོན་ཀ also མཐོན་ཀ་ཆེན་པོ *mthon-ka chen-po* 1. महानील blue gem of great value; acc. to *Jä.* one of the five celestial gems. 2. नील azure, sky-blue.

མཐོན་ཏེ *mthon-te* उत्तीर्य coming out successfully, surmounted, climbed up.

མཐོན་པོ *mthon-po* high, elevated, exalted; deep, loud. Practically the same as མཐོ་བ and in colloq. much more frq.; occurs also as མཐོན་མོ *mthon-mo*.

Syn. མཐོ་བ *mtho-wa*; གཟེངས་མཐོ *gzeṅs-mtho*; རྔམས་ཆེ *rṅams-che*; དཔངས་མཐོ *dpaṅs-mtho*; རྩེ་མོ་རིང་ *rtse-mo riṅ* (*Mṅon.*).

མཐོན་མཐིང་ *mthon-mthiṅ* 1. इन्द्रनील; sapphire. 2. the high blue colour (of things).

མཐོན་པོའི་ལྷ *mthon-pohi lha* an epithet of Vishnu (*Mṅon.*).

མཐོར་འཐུང་ *mthor-hthuṅ* आचमन washing the mouth with a potion of water.

མཐོལ་བ *mthol-wa* or འཐོལ་བ=བཤགས་པ to confess, confession; from the word ཐལ་མོ *thal-mo*; and is defined as ལག་པ་གཉིས་ཐལ་མོ་སྦྱོར་བའི་དོན it signifies joining the palms of the hands in contrition: ཉེས་ན་མཐོལ་བར་མཛོད if you are guilty make confession (*Hbrom.* ཕ 19); མཐོལ་བར་རོས་པ་ནི་འཐོལ་ནས་ཉེས་པ་དང་ཞག་ཏུ་མི་འགྲོགས་པ one fit to confess not keeping company for a day with a sinner after he has confessed (*A. 52*). མཐོལ་བཤགས *mthol-çags* confession.

མཐོལ་ཚངས *mthol-tshaṅs* (cf. འགྱོད་ཚངས) confession, acknowledgment of guilt. མཐོལ་ཚངས་བྱེད་པ *mthol-tshaṅs byed-pa*=མཐོལ་བ་བཤགས་པ to make confession, to confess, which acc. to Buddhism implies atonement and remission of sins (*Jä.*).

མཐོས *mthos* abbreviated form of མཐོ་རིས.

འཐག *hthag* a mill; mill-stone; colloq. འཐག་གི *hthag-gi* anything pulverized in a mill; འཐག་གི་འདུག grinding or ground in a mill.

འཐག་པ *hthag-pa* pf. བཏགས *btags*, fut. གཏག, imp. ཐོག 1. to grind, crush; རང་ཐག་གིས to grind in a mill; རྩམ་པ་འཐག་པ to make flour of roasted corn, barley, wheat, &c.; ཕྱེ་མར་འཐག་པ *phye-mar hthag-pa* to grind into flour, to pulverize. 2. to weave: སྣམ་བུ་འཐག་པ to weave woolen cloth; འཐག་པ་པོ a weaver; དར་འཐག་བུ་མོ the daughter of a silk-weaver (*Glr.*); འཐག་སྣན loom (*Sch.*); འཐག་ཏུ་འཇུག་པ to cause cloth to be woven.

འཐང་གོས *hthaṅ-gos*=མཐང་གོས अन्तर्वास the under-garment or petticoat worn by the lamas called also ཤམ་ཐབས.

འཐང་སྤྲད་པ *hthaṅ sprad-pa* कायसंसर्ग bodily union as in conjugal relations.

འཐང་པོ *hthaṅ-po* lower parts of body: གཟུགས་པོ་འཐང་པོ a bodily defect or personal deformity.

འཐད *hthad* liking, pleasure; good will; joy (*Jä.*).

འཐད་པ I: *hthad-pa* (ཡིད་ལ་འདོད་པ) रम्य 1. to be delightful; pleasant, agreeable, well-pleasing. མི་འཐད་པ=མི་འདོད་པ not agreeable, repulsive: གསུང་དེ་ཀུན་ཤིན་ཏུ་སེམས་ལ་འཐད་པ་ཞིག་བྱུང་ all these sayings have pleased me very much. 2. (not governing a case) to please, to be acceptable, to be considered as good, to be (generally) admitted. མི་འཐད་པར་མཐོང་། I see that (this reading) is not generally accepted (*Zam.*); ཞེས་པ་འང་འཐད་དོ it occurs also in this form; མི་འཐད་དེ wrong (*Was. 294*); to be fit, proper, suitable (from *Jä.*). སེམས་ཞེས་པ་མི་འཐད་ལ as it is not proper to call it soul, as it cannot fitly be called soul. 3. འཐད is a familiar word very frq. in *W.* almost the only word for *dgaḥ-wa*: སེམས་འཐད་དེ cheerfully, joyfully; འཐད་རྒྱུ་མེད་པ་ཙམ་ཞིག་ལ as it was not agreeable (to him); འཐད་འཐད་འདྲ་ཡང་། though apparently rejoicing. 4. at pleasure, at will: ལོག་པ་འཐད let us turn back; རང་ཉིད་འཐད་ལ voluntarily, spontaneously (*Jä.*).

འཐད་ལེགས *ḥthad-legs* n. of a large numeral (*Ya-sel. 58*).

འཐད་པ II: acc. to *Sch.*=འཐན་པ *ḥthan-pa* འཐད་ལྡན *ḥthad-ldan*=འཐན་པོ *ḥthan-po*.

འཐན *ḥthan*=ནན་ཏན *nan-tan* pressure; urging. འཐན་འདྲེ *ḥthan-ḥdre* a demon (*Sch.*).

འཐན་པོ *ḥthan-po* steady, persistent: མི་འཐན་པོ *mi ḥthan-po* a steady man, a resolute man (*Cs.*).

འཐབ་པ *ḥthab-pa* आजि, दण्डिका, विवाद to fight; to quarrel, to dispute, to brawl. ཁ་རླུང་དང་འཐབ་པ to struggle with snow-storm (*Mil.*); འཐབ་པ་མེད་ཅིང་ཤི་བ to die peaceably without a struggle; also used when quarrelling persons are reconciled (*Jä.*); ཁ་འཐབ verbal altercation. As sbst. also འཐབ་མོ *ḥthab-mo* a fight, a battle; འཐབ་ཀྲོལ *ḥthab-krol* dispute, contest (*Lex.*) + འཐབ་ཀྲོལ་ཅན་ནི་གནོད་པའི་རྒྱུ་སྒྲུབ་པ one who quarrels is one who produces cause for mischief. འཐབ་འཁྲུག *ḥthab-ḥkhrug* समर fighting, war.

འཐབ་ཡ *ḥthab-ya* antagonist: ཁྱོད་ཀྱིས་ངའི་འཐབ་ཡ་བྱེད་དགོས you must be my rival in fight; འདུད་མོའི་འཐབ་ཡ a fighting cantankerous female; གནས་སྐབས་ཀྱི་འཐབ་ཡ occasional rival; a rival for the time being; acc. to *Jä.* the antagonists of life, *i.e.*, the family and relations a secular man has to struggle with.

འཐབ་རགས *ḥthab-rags* intrenchments, breast-work, ramparts.

འཐབ་བྲལ *ḥthab-bral* 1. thus explained: ལྷ་མིན་གྱི་འཐབ་རྩོད་དང་བྲལ་བས་ན་འཐབ་བྲལ་ཏེ if one is free from troubles with the *Asura*, it is *Thabḍal*—signifying that one of the heavens of the Buddhist theogony is free from strife. This region lies above the *Trayas trimsa* heaven. 2. acc. to Bon= མཚེ་མ *mtshe-ma*.

འཐབ་འབུ *ḥthab-ḥbu* silk-worm.

འཐམ་པ I: *ḥtham-pa* pf. འཐམས *ḥthams* आसक्त 1. to seize, to lay hold of, to clutch, to attach oneself to, to realise mentally. 2. to join together, to enlock: གྲོགས་སུ་འཐམ་པ or གྲོགས་བུར་འཐམ་པ to unite in friendship; བྱ་བར་འཐམ་པ to join in any undertaking (*Jä.*).

འཐམ་པ II:=སྤྱོ་བ *spyo-wa* परिभाषा blaming, scolding; to scold, to blame.

+ **འཐམས་པ** *ḥthams-pa* to clasp out of affection. གྲོགས་སུ་འཐམས་པ to seal friendship under a solemn oath.

འཐལ་བ *ḥthal-wa*, v. ཐལ་བ *thal-wa*.

འཐས་པ *ḥthas-pa* क्रूर 1. not straightforward, double-dealing. 2. hard, solid: སྲ་འཐས *sra-ḥthas* sinewy, strong, robust (*Sch.*).

འཐིག་པ *ḥthig-pa* 1. vb. n., pf. འཐིགས to drop, to fall in drops, to drip from:

ཁྲག་མ་འཐིགས་པར without any blood dropping out. 2. vb. a., pf. བཐིགས, fut. བཐིག to cause to fall in drops, to distil, etc. (*Jä.*).

+ **འཐིང་སླད** *hthiṅ-slad*=སྨོད་པ *smod-pa* slander, a term of blame or abuse (*Cs.*).

འཐིབས་པ *hthibs-pa*, pf. ཐིབས or གཏིབས *gtibs* to be covered, darkened: ནད་ཀྱིས་ལུས་སེམས་འཐིབས་པ the body and mind being covered with disease; ན་བུན་བཞིན་དུ་འཐིབས་པར་གྱུར་ཏོ became darkened as with a fog; vb. n. ལྗོན་ཤིང་ཐམས་ཅད་དགའ་བའི་ཚལ་དུ་འཐིབས all the trees afford a delightful shade; གཉིད་འཐིབས drowsiness overcomes me; ཤེས་པ་འཐིབས *çes-pa hthibs* consciousness grows dim (*Jä.*).

འཐིབས་པོ *hthibs-po* dark, close, dense. འཐིབས sbst., a covering.

འཐིམ་པ *hthim-pa* fut. of ཐིམ་པ *thim-pa*: ས་ལ་འཐིམ་ཡོང་། it would vanish into the earth; also would be absorbed in the soil.

འཐུ་བ *hthu-wa* 1. adj. v. ཐུ་བ *thu-wa*. 2. vb., also འཐུན་པ, pf. འཐུས, བཏུས, fut. བཏུ, imp. ཐུས་བཏུ or to gather, collect, pick up: ཤིང་དང་རྩ་རྩེ་འཐུ་བ to collect wood and roots for fuel; ཐོར་ཆ་འཐུ་བ to pick up things strewn about; ཐུས་མི an assemblage of men, council (*Cs.*).

འཐུག་པ *hthug-pa*=མཐུག་པ also འཐུག་པོ adj. and abstr. sbst. thick: པགས་པ་འཐུག་པོ a thick skin; ཀོ་བ་མཐུག་པོ a thick hide; སྣམ་འཐུག་པོ a thick rug. མཐའ་འཐུག thicker towards the margin or edge, gen. of woven stuffs, opp. to སྲབ་པ *srab-pa* (*Jä.*); སྲབ་འཐུག thickness in consistency, as of liquids; also adj. dense, strong: ནགས་འཐུག dense forest; གཉིད་འཐུག་པོ a sound sleep; བག་ཆགས་འཐུག་པོ a strong inclination (*Jä.*).

འཐུང་བ *hthuṅ-wa* pf. བཏུངས *btuṅs* or འཐུངས *hthuṅs* to drink, to imbibe fluid: ངོམས་པ་འཐུང་བ to drink one's fill; འཐུངས་པ་ཙམ་གྱིས immediately after drinking; ཆུ་འཐུང་བ་པོ one who will drink water; a water-drinker (*Situ. 84*); འཐུང་དུ་རུང་བ drinkable; allowable to drink; འཐུངས་སོ they were engaged in drinking; have drunk; བཏུང་བ sbst. drink; བཏུང་བ་འཐུང་ to drink (any) liquid: བཟའ་བ་དང་བཏུང་བ eating and drink; བཟའ་བཏུང་ food and drink; བཏུང་ཆུ *btuṅ chu* water for drinking; འཐུང་ཆུ་ཞིང་ཆུ་ལེགས་ན་ཆུ་ཡི་དགེ if drinking water and irrigation water be good, there is water prosperity (*Jig.*).

འཐུང་བྱེད *hthuṅ-byed* सूर्य met. the sun (he that drinks, *i.e.*, draws out moisture by his heat) (*Mṅon.*).

འཐུད་པ *hthud-pa*=མཐུད་པ to add on, make longer; to piece on, to prolong; ཐག་པ་ཆད་པ་མཐུད་པ to add a piece to a string when a part of it has broken off; སྐྱེ་བ་འཐུད་མི་དགོས he has no need of an additional re-birth.

འཐུད་མ *hthud-ma* 1. assistance, help in general. 2. an added piece; prolongation: ཁུར་ཙ་པ་འཐུད་མའི་ཆད་ཀ་གཟུང་དང་ make an agreement for, engage, more coolies! འཐུད་མེད *hthud-med* or འཐུད་ཉོར་མེད=ཆད་ལྷག་མེད་པ without any omission or addition, *i.e.*, to make or do a thing perfectly well.

འཐུན་པ 1. *hthun-pa*, v. མཐུན་པ. 2. a gatherer: ཤིང་འཐུན a gatherer of wood; རྩ་འཐུན a gatherer of grass.

འཐུབ་པ *hthub-pa* pf. འཐུབས *hthubs* or བཏུབ, fut. གཏུབ་པ, imp. ཐུབ to cut into pieces, to split: དུམ་བུར་འཐུབ་པ་པོ one who cuts into pieces, a splitter (*Situ. 84*); ཤ་གཏུབ་པ to cut meat into pieces, to mince; ཤིང་གཏུབ་པ to split wood in chips.

འཐུམ་པ *hthum-pa* a form of གཏུམ་པ, pf. འཐུམས or བཏུམས, fut. འཐུམ or བཏུམ, imp. ཐུམ or འཐུམ to cover or lay over, to put over, to coat; to wrap up, to envelop. v. གཏུམ་པ; གོས་ཀྱིས་མགོ་འཐུམ་པ to cover or wrap up the head with clothes.

འཐུམས *hthums* barren, sterile; addled (eggs). བློ་འཐུམས stupid.

འཐུར *hthur* supine of འཐུ for འཐུ་བར in colloq. ཤིང་འཐུར་འགྲོ=ཤིང་འཐུ་བ་ལ་འགྲོ goes collecting wood.

འཐུལ་བ *hthul-wa* 1. adj. volatile. 2. sbst. the subtle particles that are carried by the wind to produce the sensation of smell. 3. to raise, to spread; to smell of: དུ་བ་འཐུལ་བ to raise smoke; དྲི་མ་བཟང་ངན་འཐུལ་བ to diffuse good or bad smell; ག་བུར་འཐུལ it smells of camphor; རྡུལ་མི་འཐུལ་བར་བྱས་པའི་འོག་ཏུ after having laid the dust; ལ་ལས་བདུག་སྤོས་འཐུལ some persons were spreading perfumes (*Jä.*).

འཐེགས་པ *hthegs-pa* 1. to prepare for a journey, to pack up. 2. to depart; it prob. signifies the same as ཐེག་པ, to lift, raise, take up; cf. གཞི་བདག་ཅེས or འདེགས་པ to shift, to change (lodging), to remove; ཐེག་ཁུག carpet bag, knap-sack.

འཐེང *hthen* or འཐེང་བ ཁྱཱ adj. lame (person or animal); to be lame, to go lame, cf. ཐེང་པོ; རྐང་པ་ཞ་ནས་འཐེང་བར་གྱུར་པ became lame the leg being maimed.

འཐེན་པ *hthen-pa* 1. to draw, to pull: ཐག་པ་འཐེན་པ to pull a rope; གྱེན་ལ་འཐེན་པ to pull up, hoist; མདུན་དུ་འཐེན་པ to pull towards; ཕར་ཚུར་འཐེན་པ to pull this way and that way; ཕར་འཐེན་ཚུར་འཐེན they pulled to and fro; ཐུར་ཀྱིས་འཐེན་པ pulling by jerks, by little and little; ཡོལ་བ་འཐེན་པ to draw a curtain. 2. acc. to *Jä.* to stop, to stop short, to halt: འཐེན་པ་བཟང་ it will be advisable to stop. 3. in *W.* also=རྟེན་པ to lean, recline upon (*Jä.*).

འཐེན་པ II: acc. to Bon terminology is the line of a རྒྱལ་རྒྱུད or dynasty, the term being thus applied because each member was metaphorically drawn up towards heaven by his ancestors. The eleven dynasties of Bon kings or གནམ་གྱི་འཐེན་པ (lit. heavenly lines) were called (1) གནམ་འཐེན་རྗེ, (2) ཡེ་ཤུ་ལ་འཐེན, (3) མ་མངས་ལ་འཐེན, (4) སྤུ་ལ་མངས་གཡེན་ལ་འཐེན, (5) གཡེན་མངས་ཕྱུ་ལ་འཐེན, (6) ཕྱུ་མངས་འོལ་ལ་འཐེན, (7) འོལ་མངས་ཡུམ་ལ་འཐེན, (8) ཡུམ་མངས་རྐོང་ལ་འཐེན, (9) ཡུམ་མངས་འོད་ལ་འཐེན, (10) རྒྱང་མངས་འོད་ལ་འཐེན, (11) འོད་གསལ་ལྷ་ལ་འཐེན which is also called དམུ་འཐེན (*G. Bon.* 23).

འཐེབ *htheb*=ལྷག་པ overplus, extra, supernumerary: གོས་འཐེབ a supernumerary dress; ཁྱོད་ལ་གོས་འཐེབ་ཡོད་ན་བདག་ལ་གཡར་རོགས་ཀྱིས if you have an extra dress please lend it to me; མལ་གོས་འཐེབ་ཀྱིས་འཐུམ་པ to wrap up in an extra blanket; ཞག་གཅིག་འཐེབ one day over, or too much. (*Jä.*). འཐེབ་པ *htheb-pa* acc. to *Sch.* to have too much (?).

འཐེབས་པ *hthebs-pa* pf. ཐེབས a pass. form of འདེབས་པ 1. to be thrown, overthrown; seized by or with: ནད་ཀྱིས་འཐེབས་པ seized with disease; འཐེབས་ཤིང instrument for holding fast cloth etc. in sewing. 2. to be opened out, be spread about: གསལ་འཐེབས་པ to be opened out clearly, made plain; ས་བོན་འཐེབས་པ seed having been strewn; ལྕགས་ཐེར་གྱིས་ཐེབས་པའི་ས་སྲན hard soil which had been broken up with iron bars. 3. sometimes occurs as act. vb. instead of འདེབས་པ.

འཐེམས་པ *hthems-pa* 1. གྲངས་ཚང་བ the completion of a specified number; སྔགས་བགྲངས་ནས་འཐེམས completed counting the number of charms (*mantra*). 2. to shut in, comprise, cover, include, v. འཐམས་པ. 3. to suffice = འགྲིད་པ or ལྡང་བ (*Jä.*).

འཐེར་པོ *hther-po* or འཐེར་བ smooth and glossy: དྲིལ་བུའི་དབྱིབས་འཐེར་འཐེར *dril-buhi dbyibs hther-hther* surface of the bell well polished (*Jig.*).

འཐོ *htho* sometimes written instead of མཐོ *mtho* a span.

འཐོག་པ I: *hthog-pa* acc. to *Cs.* = གཏོག་པ *gtog-pa* acc. to *Sch.* འཐག་པ *hthag-pa.*

འཐོག་པ II: pf. འཐོགས imp. लुम्पति 1. to take, bear away, carry: བྱ་སྐྱ་ཏ་མཆུ་ཡིས་འབུ་སྲིན་སོགས་འཐོགས་པ the magpie carries away worms, insects, etc., with its bill; ཤ་འཐོགས་པ་པོ one who places or carries the meat; རོལ་མོ་འཐོགས་པ one carrying cymbals (musical instruments, etc.) having cymbals in his hand (*Situ. 84*). 2. for ཐོབ་པ *thob-pa* to receive. 3. for འདོགས་པ as ཕན་འཐོགས་པ useful. 4. to name, to call (*Jä.*).

འཐོན་པ *hthon-pa* (pf. and imp. ཐོན་པ) 1. to go out, to come forth, depart; ནང་ནས་ཕྱིར་འཐོན་བ to come from within; ས་ནས་ཡར་འཐོན་པ to isuse forth from the ground: ཀུན་ཕྱིར་འཐོན་ཏེ all having come out; ཆུ་ཕ་རྐར་ཐོན་ནས when I emerged on the other side of the river. In *W.* colloq. is a common usage for འོང་བ to come, and འབྱུང་བ to arise. 2. acc. to *Jä.* = to occur, as in ཚོང་བསྐྱུར་ནས་འཐོན་འདུག (these goods) occur as imported, are imported: རིག་པ་ཅན་མིང་འཐོན་ཡིན་ཏེ his name occurs (*i.e.*, goes forth) as one who is knowing, *i.e.*, he is reputed sagacious.

འཐོན་མི་འཁྲིང་པོ་རྒྱལ *Hthon-mi hkriṅ-po rgyal* n. of a descendant of king *Lde-phrin btsan* (*Yig.*).

འཐོབ་པ *hthob-pa* sometimes as a fut. of ཐོབ་པ *thob-pa*: འཐོབ་པ་དང་འབྲེལ་བ *hthob-pa daṅ hbrel-wa* प्राप्त्यनुबन्ध the accompaniment of what will be gained; result of gain or profit. འཐོབ་པ་མེད *hthob-pa med* अप्राप्ति not getting, not to be got.

འཐོམ་པ *hthom-pa*, pf. འཐོམས་པ also ཐོམས་པ to be confused, puzzled, to grope, to be stunned. མགོ་འཐོམས་པ = མགོ་འཁོར་བ: མགོ་འཐོམས་ནས his head being turned, puzzled; ཡེ་ཤེས་མིག་མེད་མུན་པར་འཐོམས being devoid of the eye of fore-knowledge he groped in darkness; མགོ་བོ་འཐོམ his head becomes dizzy, confounded (*Hbrom. 15*). Acc. to *Jä.* is now used in *W.* for to doze, slumber.

འཐོམ་ཡོར *hthom-yor* idiot, or dumb-confounded: གྲིབ་ལྐུགས་འོན་ལོང་འཐོམ་ཡོར་དང་གསུམ the three miseries of idiots, dumbness, deafness and blindness (*Khrid. 47*). In *C.* colloq. མི་འདི་འཐོམ་འཐོམ་རེད this man is very stupid or quite dazed.

འཐོར་བ *hthor-wa* pf. བཏོར *btor*, fut. གཏོར *gtor*, imp. འཐོར 1. prop. v. n. to be strewn or scattered, विकीरण, उपकर, प्रकीर्ण; ཆུ་འཐོར to sprinkle water; འབྲུ་འཐོར་བ to scatter grain: ཆར་པ་འཐོར་འཐོར་འབབ་པ་འདུག the rain comes drizzling down. 2. to be dispersed, dessicated, to burst (of a gun): ཆུ་འཐོར་བ་པོ one who throws or sprinkles water (*Situ. 84*).

འཐོར་བྱེད *hthor-byed* a parrot (*Mṅon.*).

འཐོར་འཐུང *hthor-hthuṅ* आचमन libation = ཆུ་གཏོར (*Cs.*; *Sch.*).

འཐོར་མཐོ *hthor-mtho* तुङ्गशृङ्ग lofty peak.

འཐོལ *hthol* མི་སྒྲིད་པ or མཉགས་པ revealing, giving out, confessing; same as མཐོལ་བ *mthol-wa* प्रतिदेश confession.

ད

ད *da* is the eleventh letter of the Tibetan alphabet and the third letter of the third group of consonants. It is equivalent to the Sanskrit द, being more dental in its pronunciation than the English *d*.

ད I: num. figure for 11.

ད II: द, दा. 1. metaphorically it symbolises a gift: སྦྱིན་པ་ཆེན་པོ་སྦྱིན་པ་སྟེ། ཐེག་པ་ཆེན་པོ་ཡིན་པར bestowing great charity is the Mahâyâna (personified) (*K. my.* ཀ *208*). 2. the signification and virtues of this letter according to the fancies of mystic authors may perhaps be gathered from such statements as these: ད་ནི་སྟོང་དང་བྲལ་བའི་སྒོ, ཞེན་པ་མེད་པས་ཐམས་ཅད་གྲོལ the letter ད is a symbol of being deprived of nothing; it takes away nothing, hence it sets free everything, *i.e.*, gives salvation (*K. g.* ཕ *42*); also ཆོས་ཐམས་ཅད་ཀྱི་སྒོ་སྟེ། ཆོས་རྣམས་དུལ་བ་དང་ཞི་བ་ཉིད་དུ་སྟོན་ནོ being the state of entrance to all *Dharma* (*i.e.*, source of knowledge), it explains all matter and phenomena both in their passive and regulated or active states (*K. d.* ན *114*); དུལ་བ་དང་དུལ་བའི་གནས་སུ་ཡོངས་སུ་ངེས་པའི་ཕྱིར་ཆོས་ཐམས་ཅད་ཀྱི་སྒོར as it fully makes sure the *Vinaya* (moral discipline) and the objects of *Vinaya*, it is called the entrance to all *Dharma* (*Hbum.* ག *282*).

ད III: 1. now, at present, just, esp. before the imp. mood: ད་ནང་ལ་སོང་ in *C.* just go home! in *W.* now go inside! In later works and especially in modern colloq. the ད *da*, now, is ད་ལྟ *da-lta*, usually heard in colloq. as "*tanda.*" Other combinations are ད་ལྟ་ལམ་སང་ "*tanda lamsang*" at once; ད་ལྟ་འཕྲལ་དུ "*tanda t'eltu*" directly, immediately. 2. this time, the present: ད་ལོ this, the present year. ད *da* in ད་ཆོག་ལྟ་བུ *da-chog lta-bu* then, now, चद्य.

ད་ཀོ་ཤ *Da-ko-ça* n. of an island called the Sandal-wood island (*Kathañ. 121*).

ད་ཁ *da-kha* 1. now, just now, presently. 2. acc. to *Jä.* a horse-shoe: ད་ཁ་རྒྱབ་པ *da-kha rgyab-pa* to shoe a horse.

ད་སྒོས. *da-sgos*=ད་ལྟ *da-lta* or འདི་སྐབས *hdi-skabs* now, this time, this occasion.

ད་ཅི *da-ci* 1. then what: ད་ཅི་བསམ then what do you think; བློ་ཉེས་པ་ཁོས *blo ñes-pa khos.* ད་ཅི་ནས་འབྱུང་ཞེན་གྱིས་གསུངས་ནས་གསོལ་དུ་མ་འདོད (*Khrid. 78*). 2. what was, lately: ད་ཅི་ནས་ད་ལྟ་ཕན་ལ from lately until now. 3. sickle-hook for cutting briars (*Jä.*).

ད་ཆ *da-cha* in future, henceforward.

ད་ཉིད *da-ñid* or ད་ལྟ་ཉིད the present time; but just now; ད་ལྟ་ཉིད་དུ *da-lta ñid-du* instantly.

ད་ལྟ *da-lta*, v. ད III.

ད་ལྟ་བ *da-lta-wa* or ད་ལྟ་ཡང་ *da-lta-yañ* even now: ད་ལྟ་ཡང་བཀའ་དྲིན་ཆེ even now he is very kind. ད་ལྟར *da-ltar* for the present, at the present time; ད་ལྟར་གྱི་བྱ་བ *da-ltar-gyi bya-wa* or དངོས་པོ *dños-po* a person's experience or actions during the present period of his life; ད་ལྟར་བ *da-ltar-wa* the present time, present; the present tense; ད་ལྟར་བྱུང་བ་ *da-ltar byuñ-wa* प्रत्युत्पन्न presence of mind; also, born or grown for the current age or current times.

ད་སྟེ *da-ste* henceforth, from this time forward. Also ད་ཕྱིས *da-phyis.*

ད་དུང་ *da-duṅ* or ད་རུང་ *da-ruṅ* still, still more; but in *C.* this latter form is in common use for དང་ and ད་དུང་སྟོང་ give still more: ད་རུང་ལེགས་པར་གསུང་བར་ཞུ please explain it once more; ད་རུང་ཡང་ again and again.

In colloq. ད་དེ often stands for *da-ruṅ.*

ད་དྲག *da-drag* 1.=ད་དགའ་མོ་རེད *da dgaḥ-mo red* that is good. 2. a term used in grammar for the now obsolete ད *da* when second final after the letters ན, ར, ལ, *e.g.*, in ཀུནད or འབྱོརད, changing the terminative ཏུ into དུ, also ནོ, རོ or ལོ, into ཏོ. Thus in the place of ཀུན་ནོ was formerly in use ཀུནད་ཏོ *kund-to,* and for འབྱོར་རོ was written འབྱོརད་ཏོ *ḥbyord-to* ; now, although the final *d* is no longer used, a relic of its former use survives in the concluding particle ཏོ *to.*

ད་གདོད *da-gdod*=ད་དུང་ still, still more (*Ṅag. 25*).

ད་ནང་ *da-naṅ* or ད་ནངས *da-naṅs* 1. presently. 2. this morning; lately this day; ད་ནང་ཀློགས *da-naṅ klags* read just now.

ད་ཚུག *da-tsug*=ད་གང་ *da-gaṅ* : ད་ཚུག་བྱེད *da-tsug byed* now what to do, or what is to be done; ཨ་པ་ང་ཤི་བ་འདུག་ད་ཚུག་བྱེད་སྙམ་པའི་ཤེས་པ་སྐྱོ་ཞིང་སྙིང་གྲང་ལྷུང་གི་འགྲོ.

ད་གཟོད *da-gzod*=ད་གཟོད་གོ་འབྱུང་ now (at last) I understand: ཁྱོད་ཀྱིས་ད་གཟོད་དོན་ལྡན་དུ་ཁས་བླངས now (at last) you have understood and accepted the real doctrine (*Ḥbrom. 17*).

ད་ཧུར *da-ḥur*=གློ་བུར *glo-bur* suddenly, instantly: མི་ཡི་ཁྲོ་ནས་ད་ཧུར་བབ fell suddenly from humanity (*D.R.*).

ད་རན *da-ran*=ད་ལན *da-lan* this time (in Sikk.).

ད་རངས *da-raṅs* this morning.

ད་རེ *da-re*=དེ་རིང་ this day, to-day: ད་རེ་ཐུག་འཚམས་དང་འ་ཧུར་གྱི་སྒྲ་ཆེན་པོ་ཐུས་ཡོང་བ་ཅི་ཡིན། what is this terrible noise and confusion to-day (*Rdsa. 17*). ད་རེ or ད་རེས in *W.* means also: heretofore, sometime ago.

ད་ལམ *da-lam*=དེང་སང་ now-a-days: ད་ལམ་ནུབ་ཕྱོགས་ཨུ་རྒྱན་གྱི་ཡུལ་དུ now-a-days in the country of Urgyen in the west (*Ya-sel. 11*).

‡ ད་དྲུ་འཇོམས *da-dru-ḥjoms* दद्रुघ्न, ভবম the plant *Cassia alata*, the root of which cures ringworm; several synonyms for this bulbous root, called *ol* in Bengal, are mentioned: རབ་མཐོ *rab-mtho*; གླང་པོ་དཀར་པོ *glaṅ-po dkar-po*; འཁོར་ལོ་འཇོམས *ḥkhor-lo-ḥjoms*; སྦྱེད་འཇིགས *sbyed-ḥjigs*; འདོར་ཁ་བ *ḥdor kha-wa*; ཤིན་ཤུན་ཅན *çin-çun-can*; ཕུག་རོན་རྐང་ *phug-ron rkaṅ*; པི་ཉྭ *pi-ṇya*; འོད་ལྡན་འཁྲི་ཤིང་ *hod-ldan ḥkhri-çiṅ*; དཀའ་ཐུབ་ཅན *dkaḥ-thub can*; ཏེ་ལ་སེར་ཅན *te-la ser-can*; ཕག་མོ་གདོང་ *phag-mo gdoṅ*; སྐྱོབ་བྱེད་མ *skyob-byed-ma.* Another species of *Cassia* is called སྟོབས་བཟང་མ *stobs-bzaṅ-ma.*

‡ ད་ནུ་ཀ་རི *da-nu ka-ri* or ད་ནུ་སྐ་རི *da-nu ska-ri* दनुकरि, or दनुस्करि n. of a flower (*K. d.* ཛ *368*).

ད་ཁྲི་བཙན་པོ *Da-khri btsan-po* the name of one of the sons of king *Mu-khri btsan-po.*

ད་ཆུ *da-chu*=དངུལ་ཆུ *dṅul-chu* mercury (*Sman.*): ད་ཆུ་རུས་པ་ཆག་པ་སྦྱོར་བར་བྱེད *Da-chu* causes fractured bones to unite.

ད་ཏྲིག *da-trig* 1. n. of a vegetable medicine (prob. tamarind): ད་ཏྲིག་ཚ་གྲང་འཁྲུ་བ་གཅོད་པ་བྱེད *da-trig tsha-graṅ ḥkhru-wa gcod-pa byed da-trig* stops diarrhœa caused by heat or cold (*Rtsii.*). Syn. སོ་བརྩི་མ *so brtsi-ma*; སྐྱུར་མོ *skyur-mo*; འདབ་མ་ཕྲ་མོ *ḥdab-*

ma phra-mo (*Mṅon.*). 2. in Bon terminology=devil: ད་ཏྲིག་མ་སངས་གསལ་ཟེར་འབར *da-trig ma-saṅs gsal zer hbar* the devil Masang exhibited radiant light (*D.R.*).

ད་ཕྲུག *da-phrug* or དྭ་ཕྲུག *dwa-phrug* or ད་ཙེ *da-tse* an orphan.

ད་བྱིད *da-byid* गोघा a lizard of Ladak: ད་བྱིད་ཤ་ཡིས་ར་ཚ་དང་ སྐམ་ནད་གྱུང་བ་ཅན་ལ་ཕན.

Syn.ས་འཛིན *sa-hdsin*; ས་འཛིན་སྐྱེས *sa-hdsin skyes*; ཏེའུ་ལེ་བ *tehu le-wa*; བདག་སྐྱེས *bdag-skyes* (*Mṅon.*).

ད་བེར *da-ber*, v. ཏ་བེར *ta-ber*, མདའ་བེར *mdah-ber*.

ད་ཨུ *dahu*=རྒྱ་ཚད *rgya-tshad* Indian fever, typhus fever: དེ་དུས་ན་རྒྱ་བརྩོན་སེང་ན་ལེནྡྲ་ན་ཚད་པ་དུས་ཐེབས་ནས་ཡོད་པ། at that time Gyatson-seng was laid up with typhus fever at Nalendra (*A. 71*).

ད་ར *da-ra* 1. कबन्ध a class of headless ghosts. 2.=དར་བ तक्र buttermilk which is half or three-fourths water.

‡ ད་ར་ད *Da-ra-da* n. of a country to the N.W. of India, prob. the modern Dardistan (*K. d. 23*).

‡ ད་ལིས *da-lis* (prob. from तलिस) same as བ་ལུའི་མེ་ཏོག a species of dwarf rhododendron with fragrant leaves: ད་ལིས་བད་ཀན་གྲང་བ་སེལ་ཤིང་ཚེ་བརྟུད་བྱེད *Dali* cures phlegm, gonorrhoea, and gives longevity.

དྭ་བ *dwa-wa* a plant yielding an acrid drug: དྭ་བའི་རྩ་བས་སྲིན་གསོད་རུས་འཛེར་འགོག *dwa-wahi rtsa-was sringsod rus-hdser hgog* the root of *da-wa* kills worms and checks bony excrescences (*Med.*). དྭ་ཚུར *dwa-tshur* vinegar of *dwa-wa* plant, which made into a gargle removes fetid smell from the mouth and heals diseases of the bone (*Med.*).

དྭའི་འཆིང་བཱ་དུར *Dwahi-hchiṅ bā-dur* a Mongolian king who reigned over Tibet for seven years (*Loṅ.* ན *12*).

དྭ་ལས་བཱ་དུར *Dwa-las bā-dur* the Mongol name of the son of king *Mi-waṅ Phola* ' *Bsodnams Stob-rgyas*. His real Tibetan name was *Hgyur-med Rnam-Rgyal*, and the Emperor of China conferred on him the title of Wang (*Loṅ.* ན *18*).

དག *dag* 1. sign of the plural, oleg. for རྣམས *rnams;* often added to the pronouns དེ and འདི and sometimes to numerals; also in the combination དག་རྣམས *dag-rnams*. 2. in translation of Sanskṛt denotes the dual number: ང་དག we two; ཁྱེད་དག you two; acc. to *Jä.* often used for ང་ལྟ་བུ་དག my equals. 3. in colloq.: certainly, it is true: ལགས་དག sir, it is so.

དག་ཁ *dag-kha* is said to be used in Tsang for དེ་ཁ (*Jä.*).

དག་ག་དོག་གེ *dag-ga dog-ge* 1. uneven, also adv. unevenly; anything placed not quite on a level. 2. acc. to *Jä.*=དོག་དོག *dog-dog*.

དག་གུ *dag-gu*=ཕྱེ་མ *phye-ma* powder.

དག་པ *dag-pa* I: (prop. pf. of འདག་པ *hdag-pa*) शुद्धि, शुद्ध, पूत, पवित्र, शोधित, अवदात 1. clean, pure; cleansed; དྲི་མ་དག་པ purified (of dirt, defilement, stain, etc.); སྡིག་པ་དག་པ purified of sin. 2. sublime, exalted, passionless. Also may occur as abstr. noun: purity: དག་པ་ཅན *dag-pa can* possessing purity. དག་ཐེར་བ *dag ther-wa* or དག་ཐེར་བྱེད་པ; acc. to *Sch.*: to make clean, cleanse; དག་སྐྱིར་(ཅེར)་མཛད་པ id. དག་པར་བསྒྱུར་བ to become clean, purified; དག་པར་བྱེད་པ to make clean, to cleanse, to purify; དག་པར་འཁྲུ་བ to wash clean; དག་པར་བྱས पूत, उन्मृष्ट, पावनीय, शोधित made clean, cleansed; རིགས་མ་དག impure or defiled blood or caste; ལུས་དང་ངག་དང་ཡིད་ཀྱི་ལས་ཡོངས་སུ་དག་པ། quite pure in the works of the mind, in word, and in body; དག་པར་འཚོ་བ to lead a pure virtuous life; སྨོན་ལམ་དག་པ a right and proper prayer; རྣམ་པར་དག་པ विशुद्धि, विशुद्ध quite pure, most holy, also the state of purity; མི་དག་པ impure; impurity, defilement; བཀྲུས་ན་མི་དག་པ་མེད་དོ *bkruṣ-na mi-dag-pa med-do* when they have bathed they are freed from impurity. 3. स्नात, मृष्ट, मार्जित bleached, bathed, washed clean, rubbed, dusted, swept out: གདོང་མཆི་མས་དག་པ his face washed with tears; དག་པ་ཡོངས་སུ་དག *dag-pa yoṅṣ-su dag* washed completely clean.

དག་འགྲེལ *dag-ḥgrel*=དག་ཆའི་འགྲེལ་པ a commentary on orthography.

དག་ཅི *dag-ci* mint, aromatic plant, *Mentha royliana* (*Jä.*).

དག་བརྗོད *dag-brjod* or དག་པ་བརྗོད་པ correct expression, right spelling.

ཡང་དག་པ *yaṅ-dag-pa* सम्यक्, v. ཡང་ *yaṅ*.

དག་པ་ཉིད *dag-pa ñid* शुद्धता, पावनी the state of being pure; purification.

དག་པ་རིག་པ *dag-pa rig-pa* संवित्; = དག་པ་ཤེས་པ pure consciousness.

དག་པ་གསུམ *dag-pa gsum* the three requirements of purity in religion as explained in Tsong-khapa's *Lam-rim Chenmo,* viz.:—(1) སློབ་དཔོན་གྱི་ངག་དག་པ purity in the speech of a spiritual teacher; (2) སློབ་མའི་རྒྱུད་དག་པ purity in the innate nature of a pupil; (3) བཤད་བྱའི་ཆོས་དག་པ purity in the doctrine to be explained.

དག་པའི་དཀྱིལ་འཁོར *dag-paḥi dkyil-ḥkhor* the disk of purity, the immaculate orb, *i.e.*, the moon: མཛེས་སྐུ་ཆུ་གཏེར་དག་པའི་དཀྱིལ་འཁོར་ཆུ་འཛིན་གྱིས་དབེན་ཞིང་ the disk of purity, though like waters stored in a beauteous body, is yet deprived of all clouds (*Yig. k. 15*).

དག་པའི་ཁམས *dag-paḥi khamṣ*=शुद्धधातु met. for mercury, quick-silver (*Mñon.*).

དག་པའི་མཐའ *dag-paḥi mthaḥ* or དག་པའི་རབ= ཡང་དག་པའི་མཐའ.

དག་པའི་ཞིང་ *dag-paḥi shiṅ* the region of purity, the pure mansion; hence Dewachan the heaven of Amitābha Buddha where there is no impurity.

དག་བྱེད I: *dag-byed* पावक, पवन 1. water, air, the wind-god, fire, and the sacrificial grass *kuçā*. 2. fair complexion (*Mñon.*).

དག་བྱེད II: also पावनी, पवित्र 1. holy. 2. a holy river (as a purifier of dirt and sin). དག་བྱེད་བཞི the four holy rivers, namely, Sindhu, Pukṣu, Sitā and Gaṅgā: ཐུགས་རྗེའི་ར་གུར་ནས་མི་འགྱུར་བའི་བཀའི་བདུད་རྩི་དག་བྱེད་བཞིའི་ཀླུང་རྒྱུན་བཞིན་སྤྱི་བོར་སྐྱོལ་བ་མཛོད pray bestow the nectar of your commands upon my head from the canopied enclosure of your compassion like the streams of the four holy rivers which are never diverted (*Yig. k. 6*). 3. विशद, धवल white, bleached. 4. ཨ་རུ *a-ru Myrobolana arjuna.*

དག་བྱེད III: correct spelling (in a composition); also any revision, correction.

དག་སྦྱོར *dag-ṣbyor* or དག་པའི་སྦྱོར་བ *dag-paḥi ṣbyor-wa* holy combination; also exact coincidence (*Çil. 6*).

དག་ར *dag-ra* गृञ्जन a species of garlic.

དག་ཡིག *dag-yig* orthography; རྙིང་གི་དག་ཡིག or བརྡ་དག the earlier (now obsolete) orthography.

དག་ལས་གཡོ *dag-laṣ-gyo*=དག་པ་མ་ཡིན་པ not holy, profane.

དག་ཤིང་ *dag-çiṅ* སྭཀྵ 1. small splinter of wood or bamboo for cleansing the teeth. 2. bark of a tree. 3. scale of a fish.

དྭགས *dwags* bright, *i.e.*, in reference to openness, cheerful appearance of a place: ས་དཔྱད་ཐོག་མར་མདུན་རྒྱབ་དྭགས་སྒྲིབ་བཞི in the selection of a site for building are four chief points, the frontage, back, openness and the shade (*Jig.*).

དྭགས་སྟོད *Dwags-stod* the upper or higher portion of the district of Dwag-po in Tibet. དྭགས་སྟོད་ལྕང་ར *Dwags-stod lcaṅ-ra* n. of a grove in the upper portion of the district of Dwag-po (*Rtsii.*).

དྭགས་པོ *Dwags-po* the district of Dwag-po, situated between the S. E. of the province of Ü and Kong-po, the birth place of the present Dalai Lama Lobzang Thubdan Gya-tsho. དྭགས་པོ་བཀའ་རྒྱུད *Dwags-po bkaḥ-rgyud* a section of the School of the Kah-gyu-pa which was powerful in Tibet before the supremacy of the Dalai Lama was established in 1644 A.D. དྭགས་པོ་ཟླ་འོད་གཞོན་ནུ *Dwags-po zla-hod gshon-nu* n. of celebrated lama of this school (*Loṅ.* ༤ *9*). དྭགས་ཕོར *dwags-phor* wooden cups turned in Dwag-po. དྭགས་ཤོག *dwags-çog* *Daphne* paper manufactured in Dwag-po. དྭགས་སླེ *dwags-sle* the striped woollen wrapper cloth manufactured in Dwag-po.

དང་ I: *daṅ* is a peculiarly-used word taking the form and position of a conjunction but really being a postp. or commitative case-sign of the meaning "with ཞ." Thus ལུག་དང་ར་མོ་དང་མཛོ is not properly "sheep and she-goats and yak," but "yak with she-goats with sheep." However, in such enumerations, the rendering "and" is legitimate, as well as in mere couplings, *e.g.*, སྐྲ་དང་ཁ་སྤུ་འབྲེག་པ shaving the hair and moustache. Acc. to Thon-mi-Sambhoṭa, the father of Tibetan literature, this word has the following five significations:—(1) ཚིག་ཟླ་ཕྱི་ཕྱོགས་གཅིག་ཏུ་སྡུད་པ as a conj. for connecting a word with another following it. (2) སོ་སོར་འབྱེད་པ as an analytic term to separate one word from another:—དབང་པོ་རྣམས་ནི་མིག་དང་རྣ་བ་དང་སྣ་དང་ལྕེ་དང་ལུས་སོ the *Dwaṅ-po* or the organs of sense are the eye and ear and nose and tongue and the body. (3) རྒྱུ་མཚན་ཏེ་རྒྱུ་མཚན་ཉིད་ཀྱི་དོན because of, on account of, by reason of: སྨན་ཟོས་པ་དང་ནད་སོས་སོ because of having taken medicine the disease was cured; ཆོས་མང་དུ་ཐོས་པ་དང་ལྷག་མཐོང་འཕེལ་ལོ on account of hearing many religious discourses his perceptive faculty increased; དུ་བ་མཐོང་བ་དང་མེར་ཤེས་སོ by seeing smoke he could know (there was) fire. (4) དུས་བརྗོད་པ་ཆེ་སྐབས་ཀྱི་དོན when, as soon as, occasion, opportunity: རྒྱ་སྐར་རྒྱལ་འཆར་བ་དང་ཡུལ་དུ་ཆས་སོ he proceeded to the country when the constellation Puṣyā appeared; ཉི་མ་ལ་ལ་ཤར་བ་དང་ཆོས་རྫོན་དངས as soon as the sun rose on the mountain-pass he performed the religious service. (5) གདམས་ངག་བརྗོད་པའི་དོན་ལ་འཇུག་གོ it is used to signify exhortation, advice or entreaty: ལེགས་པར་སློབ་དང do learn well; ཁ་ཏོན་གྱིས་དང་ and read loudly (*Situ.*). This last usage, namely, the annexation of *daṅ* to the imperative, has become common with certain verbs in the colloq. being then used almost as a sign of the imperative. Thus ལྟོས་དང་ "*toi tang*" look, see! ལྟོ་ཟོས་དང་ eat food. That "with" is the general signification is evident from many phraseological usages of *daṅ*:—in using མཉམ་དུ "in equality, on a level," *daṅ* connects that word with the consequent, *e.g.*, ཁོ་རང་ཁྱེད་དང་མཉམ་དུ་འགྲོ་དགོས he must go with you;

so with the formative ལྡན་པ *ldan-pa* signifying "possessed of," "provided with," *e.g.*, ནོར་དང་ལྡན་པ provided with wealth, wealthy; བུ་ལྔ་དང་ལྡན་པའི་རྒྱལ་པོ a king possessed of (or with) five sons. More explicitly in its true sense does it occur with many verbs:—མི་སེར་དང་འཕྲད་པ to meet with the husbandman; ཇག་པ་དང་ཐུག་པ to fall in with robbers; རྒྱལ་པོའི་སྐུ་དང་མཇལ་བ to salute the king's person; གཞན་གྱི་ཡིད་དང་མཐུན་པ to agree with another's opinion; ཐམས་ཅད་དང་གྲུབས་མཐུན་པ to be in harmony with all; ས་བདག་དང་འགལ་བ to be in opposition to or with the local god; དགྲ་དང་འཐབ་བ to fight with an enemy; ཁ་ཆུབ་དང་འཐབ་པ to struggle with a snow-storm; སྔ་ཏེ་འཁོར་ལོ་ལ་བླ་མ་དང་རྩོད་པ་བྱས made dispute with the lama about the prayer-wheel; ཡ་མཚན་ལ་གྲུབ་ཐོབ་དང་འགྲན་པ to contend in miracles with the saint; བུད་མེད་དང་ཉལ་བ to lie with a woman; གྲོང་ཁྱེར་དང་ཉེ་བ near the town; དེ་དང་འདྲ་བ equal to that. Some particular ways of using དང་ *dań* are the following:—གསེར་དང་དངུལ་དང་ལྕགས་ལ་སོགས་པ gold, and silver, and iron, and the other (metals); whence note that in enumerations དང་ is employed in different ways, arbitrarily, *e.g.*, after every single noun or pronoun except the last one, or also after the last; it is used or omitted just as the metre may require it; or when a sum is mentioned, in the following manner:—འབྱུང་བ་བཞི་ནི the four elements; ས་དང་ཆུ་དང་མེ་དང་རླུང་དང་བཞི་འོ *sa-dań chu-dań me-dań rluń-dań bshiho* earth, and water, and fire, and air, or esp. in col. language, thus ས་དང་གཅིག, ཆུ་དང་གཉིས, etc.—དང་ is frequent also in the sense of "from," especially with certain verbs which cannot indeed be used apart from it. Of these are འབྲལ་བ to be separated དང་ from, *e. g.*, འདོད་ཆགས་དང་བྲལ་ཡིན was separated from lust; also འཕྲལ་བ *hphral-wa* to divide དང་ from; again: ཁང་པ་དང་རིང་བ far from the house. In general, however, ལས or ནས is the sign of "from." A further employment of དང་ very habitual in the classical treatises is in the manner of a continuative particle at the end of subordinate and co-ordinate sentences; so it is annexed to the verbal participle which concludes the clause, but never in the older works to the root of a verb standing thus; it can often, of course, be rendered by "and" as if it belonged to the following clause, but not always so. One example of this very common usage will here suffice: དེའི་ཚེ་ན་སྦྲུལ་གྱིས་ཁྱིམ་བདག་དེ་དངང་བར་བྱེད་པ་དང་། མི་དེ་དང་ལྷན་གཅིག་ཏུ་ཁྱེའུ་གཉིས་སྐད་འདེབས་ཏེ་བྲོས་སོང་ thereupon the snake terrifying the householder, two boys together with that man, throwing up cries, escaped. Finally, the one conclusion derivable from the various usages of དང་ is that the word must be always technically regarded as belonging to the words or clause which may precede it and not to any word or clause subsequent; which thus negatives the notion that it is a true conjunction.

དང་ II: a meadow.

དང་ག *dań-ga* (col.=དང་ཁ *dań-kha*) appetite: ངའི་དང་ག་འགགས my appetite is gone; དང་ག་མི་བདེ want of appetite (though wishing to eat, cannot eat); དང་ག་བདེ་བ *dań-ga bde-wa* good appetite.

Syn. ལྟོ་ཆེ *lto-che*; གྲོད་པ་ཆེ *grod-che*; དང་ཁ་བདེ *dań-kha bde*; ཚིམ་མེད *tshim-med*; ཆོག་པ་མེད་པ *chog-pa med-pa* (*Mńon.*).

དང་དུ་བླང་བ *dań-du blań-wa* or དང་ལེན་པ. to receive a command or missive with readiness, to do a work with earnestness: བཀའ་རྩལ་དང་དུ་བླངས་པས་ཚུལ་བཞིན *bkah-rtsal dań-du blańs-pas tshul-bshin* the behest he received as a work of first importance (*i.e.*, considering it as the first of duties). དང་དུ་མི་ལེན *dañ-du mi-len* does not accept; does not apprehend.

དང་པོ *dañ-po* आदि, पूर्व्वं, उपक्रम, आदिम, प्राक्, पुरस्तात्, अग्रतः, पुरतस्, प्रमुख, प्रथम 1. the first, earliest, with respect to number, time, rank: དང་པོའི་སངས་རྒྱས आदिबुद्ध the first or the earliest Buddha; དང་པོའི་གཏམ་དེ་སུས་ཟེར who spoke (raised) the first rumour? who was it that first got up the rumour? དང་པོའི་ཉིན་པར on the very first day; ན་ཚོད་དང་པོ་ལ་གནས་པ being still in the prime of life; དང་པོ་གཉིས the two first. 2. the first beginning, outset; also signifies aboriginal, fundamental: ཉིན་མོའི་དང་པོ་ལ at the beginning of the day; དང་པོ་ཉིད་དུ in the first place, above all, at the very commencement; དང་པོ་ནས from the beginning; ལས་དང་པོ་པ *las dañ-po-pa* a beginner; ལས་དང་པོ་པའི་དུས་སུ as long as he is only a beginner; དང་པོ་དང་ཐ་མ *dañ-po dañ tha-ma* the first and the last; དང་པོའི་རྒྱུ *dañ-pohi rgyu* निदान the original or primary cause; དང་པོའི་སྒྲ *dañ-pohi sgra* preceding word; དང་པོ་སྨྲ་བ་བརྗོད་པ་རྗེས་མའི་དོན་ཤེས he knows the meaning from the context. 3. as adv. དང་པོར firstly, in the first place; at first; in the beginning; དང་པོར་བདེ happy from the beginning.

དང་པོའི་དུལ་ཅན *dañ-pohi dul-can* a bride (just passed out of virginhood) (*Mñon.*); དང་པོའི་དུལ་ཅན་མ a maiden; a girl at puberty.

Syn. བུ་མོ་དར་མ *bu-mo dar-ma*; ཁེངས་ལྡན་མ *kheñs ldan-ma*; ལང་ཚོ་ཅན་མ *lañ-tsho can-ma* (*Mñon.*).

དང་པོའི་བདག *dañ-pohi bdag* महात्म [1. a noble man]*S.* 2. in Gram. प्रथम पुरुष the first person.

དང་བ *dañ-wa* मं, पव 1. to be pure; to be clear; gen. as adj. pure, clear; འབྲས་དང་བ cleaned or sifted rice. 2. sincere, single-hearted, guileless: སེམས་ཅན་ཀུན་ལ་རབ་དང་བ truly sincere towards all creatures; དགེ་སེམས་དང་བ a pure, sincere disposition to virtue (S. o.). དང་བ་ཉིད *dañ-wa ñid* संमन devotion, purity of heart. དང་བའི་གསལ་བ *dañ-wahi gsal-wa* (ཁ་དོག་སྐྱ་བ) प्रसन्न, चेत to be cheerful; of open countenance; of bright appearance.

དང་ཙེ *dañ-tse* 1. n. of a kind of Chinese satin. 2. in *W.* a field-terrace (*Jä.*).

དང་ཟས་མ་ཟ *dañ-zas ma-za* अविश्रम्भभोजिन् do not eat with a doubt; also do not entertain doubt [a suspicious man]*S.*

དང་ར *dañ-ra* stable for cattle, in *C.* and *W.* (*Jä.*).

卐 **དང་ལ** *Dañ-la* 1. ཆུ་ཡི་རྫིང་བུ a tank, a pond. 2. acc. to *Sch.* a tract of land abounding in springs. 3. n. of a long and lofty mountain range in N. E. Tibet, running from long. 90° to long. 96° E. and keeping mainly to the 33rd parallel of latitude. Travellers to Lhasa from the N. E. must cross this range. It is Father Huc's "Tant-la."

དྭངས *dwañs* or དྭངས་པ *dwañs-pa* 1. sbst. glare, lustre: དྭངས་མི་འདུག it has no brightness or glitter; དྭངས་ཆེན་པོ very glittering. 2. force of language; also pronunciation (colloq. ལབ་དངས); དྭངས་པོ་ཉིད *dwañs-po ñid* sbst. brightness, lustre, glare, clearness. 3. adj. sparkling, pure, clean, clear: ཆུ་དྭངས་པ sparkling water; སེམས་དྭངས unpolluted heart; ཁམས་དྭངས་པ (of the body) perfect health, looking bright; གནམ་དྭངས a clear sky, fine weather; དྭངས་ཤེལ་མེ་ལོང n. of a code called "the clear crystal mirror" or directions for the guidance of government officials.

དྭངས་མ *dwaṅs-ma*＝ཁུ་བ *khu-wa* रस juice, gravy; fig. relish, taste: ཟས་ཀྱི་དྭངས་མ the relish of food (*M̱ṅon.*).

དད་པ *daḏ-pa* श्रद्धा, भक्ति, छन्द: 1. sbst. faith, devotion. 2. vb. to believe, to have faith; acc. to *Jä.* a secondary form of འདོད་པ to wish; hence in compounds: སྐོམ་དད thirst, etc. Referring to this word *Milaraṣpa* remarks: དད་པ་དང་འདོད་པ་གཉིས་ནོར་དོགས་ཡོད་པས, དེ་གཉིས་དང་དད་པ་བྱ་བའི་ཡུལ་ཡང་མ་ནོར་བ་གལ་ཆེ as it is to be feared that དད་པ may be mistaken for འདོད་པ, it is important that these two and the object of one's དད་པ or faith should not be confounded. The first is what may be called divine love, the second, *i.e.*, འདོད་པ, is love for one's wife, children, and worldly things. དད་པ་མེད་པའི་མི་རྣམས་ལ, དཀར་པོའི་ཆོས་རྣམས་མི་བྱུང་ངོ། to men who are devoid of faith, holy thoughts (religious ideas) would not occur (*Lam-rim. 25*). དེ་ལ་དད་པ་ཐམས་ཅད་ཤིག་པར་མི་འགྱུར་གྱི། མཐར་མེད་པའི་སྲོག་ཐོབ་པར་བྱའོ all believing in him shall not be destroyed, but shall obtain everlasting life. There are three kinds of དད་པ *daḏ-pa*, viz:—(1) དང་བའི་དད་པ भक्ति sincere faith; (2) ཡིད་ཆེས་པའི་དད་པ trust, full confidence; (3) ཕྱིར་མི་ལྡོག་པའི་དད་པ unflagging devotion, unalterable belief. དད་པ་ཉིད *daḏ-pa ñiḏ* sbst. श्रद्धा faith, love, devotion; དད་གུས *daḏ-guṣ* reverence and faith: ཁོང་གི་ཡོན་ཏན་ཐོས་པ་ལ་བརྟེན་ནས་དད་གུས་སྒོམ on hearing of his high virtues I meditated reverentially on faith (*Ḫbrom.* ཁ *2*). དད་པ་ལོག་པ *daḏ-pa log-pa* श्रद्धाविपन्न impaired faith, want of faith [also, the man who is wanting in faith]*S*; དད་པ་ཕྱིར་བསྒྱུར་བ *daḏ-pa phyirḇsgyur-wa* དད་པ་ཉམས་པ छन्द: प्रत्युद्धार change or modification of one's opinion, (regarding another person). དད་པ་བྱེད་པ *daḏ-pa byeḏ-pa* to confide in, to believe; དད་བཞིན་དུ in faith; དད་པ་འབུལ་བ *daḏ-pa ḫbul-wa* offer of faith; དད་པ་མི་ཕྱེད་པ *daḏ-pa mi-phyeḏ-pa* unflagging faith.

དད་གུས་ལྡན *daḏ-guṣ ḻdan* भक्त, श्रद्धावान्, श्रद्धायुक्त, श्रद्धालु faithful, loyal, devout, respectful.

Syn. གུས་པར་བྱེད *guṣ-par byeḏ*; གུས་ལྡན *guṣ-ḻdan*; ཤེ་ས་བྱེད *she-sa byeḏ*; མངོན་པར་ལྡང *m̱ṅon-par ḻdaṅ*; སྟེན་བྱེད *ṣten-byeḏ*; ཀུན་ཏུ་བསྟེན *kun-tu ḇsten*; རབ་ཏུ་བསྟེན *rab-tu ḇsten*; མོས་ལྡན *moṣ-ḻdan*; དད་ལྡན *daḏ-ḻdan*; དད་ཆགས་ཅན *daḏ-chagṣ-can*; དད་པ་ཅན *daḏ-pa can*; གཅིག་ཏུ་སེམས *gcig-tu semṣ*; དང་བ *daṅ-wa*; མོས་པ *moṣ-pa*; གུས་པ་ཕྱག་བྱེད་པ *guṣ-pa phyag byeḏ-pa*; བན་དྷ་རུ *ban-dā-ru* वन्दारु (*M̱ṅon.*).

དད་དམ་འཕོ་མེད་ཀྱི་འདུན་པ *daḏ-dam ḫpho-meḏ-kyi ḫdun-pa* love with unflagging faith and unflinching devotion; as in ས་ཐག་འཁྱུང་གིས་བཅད་པས་དད་དམ་འཕོ་མེད་ཀྱི་འདུན་པ་ཆེད་མེད་པ in a remote land though separated by distance his unfailing love and devotion remained undiminished.

དད་འདུན *daḏ-ḫdun* love, faith, devotion, reverence, veneration. དད་འདུན་མེད་པ *daḏ-ḫdun meḏ-pa* faithless, irreverent, unbelieving.

དད་པ་གསུམ *daḏ-pa gsum* the three kinds of དད་པ *daḏ-pa* or faith acc. to Bon:—མངོན་འདོད་ཀྱི་དད་པ; དང་བའི་དད་པ; ཡིད་ཆེས་ཀྱི་དད་པ; but acc. to Buddhism, there are two kinds of དད་པ (1) འཇིག་རྟེན་པའི་དད་པ faith in a worldly sense; (2) འཇིག་རྟེན་ལས་འདས་པའི་དད་པ faith in a spiritual sense (*K. d.* ན *310*).

དད་པའི་རྗེས་སུ་འབྲང་བ *daḏ-paḫi ṛjeṣ-su ḫbraṅ-wa* श्रद्धानुसारी one of the stages of a Buddhist monk who is a *Çrāvaka*. དད་པའི་གསོ་སྦྱོང་བྱ་བར་གསོལ་བ་འདེབས་པ छन्दश: पोषधमारोचयति to pray to perform the *uposatha* (religious fasting) in faith; དད་པས་མོས་པ श्रद्धायुक्त one of the twenty stages which a Buddhist monk attains to in the order of *Çrāvaka*.

དན་གོང་ *dan-goṅ* balls mado of wood, cloth, stone, or glass, with which children play (*K. du.* ད *146*).

དན་ཏ *dan-ta* n. of a fruit yielding a medicinal drug.

དན་ཉེག *dan-ñeg* in tho dialect of Amdo: precious, important.

དན་ཐུ་ལི་ཀ *dan-thu li-ka* n. of a kind of grass which grows as quickly as it is cut (*K. my.* ཀ *228*).

དན་ད *dan-da* n. of a modicinal herb.

དན་ད་ལི *dan-da-li* in *Ld.* a sieve, gen. consisting of perforated leather or a wooden frame; རས་དན་དལ *ras dan-dal* a sieve made of cloth (*Jä.*).

དན་འདྲ *dan-ḥdra* एरण्ड n. of a medicinal fruit. [the castor-oil plant]*S.*

དན་བག *Dan-bag* or དམ་བག *Dam-bag* n. of hamlet situated below the great monastery of འབྲས་སྤུངས *Ḥbras spuṅs* or Daipung near Lhasa, about 4 miles to the W. of that city (*Loṅ* ཟ *3*).

དན་རོག *dan-rog* जयपाल *Croton euphorbia;* or rather its medicinal fruit: དན་རོག་ནང་ནད་དྲག་པོ་སྦྱོང་བ་བྱེད *dan-rog naṅ-nad drag-po sbyoṅ-wa byed* croton heals serious internal maladies.

‡ དན་ཊ་ཨུ་ཏ་པ་ལ *Danda u-ta pa-la* दण्ड-उत्पल n. of a medicinal plant: དན་ཊ་ཨུ་ཏ་པ་ལ་རྩ་བ་དང་། བ་ཡི་མར་དང་བཙུང་ཕྱམ། དུས་ལྡན་དུས་ལ་བུམ་པར་འགྱུར from the root of the plant called Danda Utpala taken with cow's butter a woman will in proper time become pregnant (*K. g.* ཙ *44*).

དམ *dam* bound fast: དམ་ཁས་བླངས་པར་འོས་པ fit or suitable to be bound by promise or under an oath, v. ཁས་བླངས *khas-blaṅs*; དམ་དུ་བཅིང་བ *dam-du bciṅ-pa* विबन्ध well bound; also bound tightly. དམ་དུ་བཟུང་བ *dam-du bzuṅ-wa* to hold tightly, hold fast; ཡི་དམ *yi-dam* or ཐུགས་དམ *thugs-dam* a solemn promise, vow, oath, confirmation by oath; དམ་ལ་གནས་པ *dam-la gnas-pa* to abide by one's own promise or words; དམ་ཉམས *dam-ñams* a violation of promise; a violator of promises; དམ་ཉམས་ཀྱི་ལས་རྣམས violations of duty. དམ་ལ་འདོགས་པ to exorciso demons, to bind them under solemn oath, etc.

དམ་ཁ *dam-kha* = ཐེའུ་ཙེ *thehu-tse* a seal; དམ་ཁ་རྒྱབ་པ to seal, stamp. དམ་ག *dam-ga* = ཐམ་ཁ *tham-kha* (*Cs.*).

དམ་ཕྲུག *dam-prhug* = ཕྱག་དམ or ཐེའུ་ཙེ *thehu-tse* a seal (*Mṅon.*).

དམ་བཅའ *dam-bcah* or དམ་བཅའ་བ *dam-bcah-wa* नियम, वृत, संविद्, सं गर, बन्ध a promise, a vow; the act of promising; almost equivalent to what we might term a sacrament. དམ་བཅའ་འབུལ་བ *dam-bcah hbul-wa* to give assurance; to make a promise; མི་འབབ་པའི་དམ་བཅའ *mi-hbab-pahi dam-bcah* a promise from which one will not shrink.

དམ་ཅན་རྡོ་རྗེ་ལེགས་པ *Dam-can rdo-rje legs-pa* is a Tantrik deity introduced by Padma S'ambhawa and mentioned in *Pth.* He is of the དྲག་གཤེད or terrific class of deities and is usually portrayed riding either on the Tibetan imaginary form of lion or on a he-goat. He is known also as *Rdor-legs.* Probably the same as that in the next paragraph.

དམ་ཆེན་ཆོས་རྒྱལ *Dam-chen chos-rgal* is the tutelary deity of the Grand Lama of Tashi-lhunpo, and is supposed to be under a solemn oath to defend Buddhism against all infidels.

དམ་བཅས་པ *dam bcas-pa* a promise made; to make a promise; དམ་སྲུང་བ *dam sruṅ-wa* to keep one's word or vow; དམ་བཅས་པ་དང་མི་འགལ་བ not to violate one's promise.

དམ་དུམ *dam-dum* 1.= ཕྲན་བུ *phran-bu* or ཉུང་ཉུང་ *ñuṅ-ñuṅ* small; a little quantity or bit. 2. various (*Sch.*).

དམ་པ *dam-pa* उत्तम, परम, सत्, दृढ 1. excellent, superior, the best. 2. steady or firm, tight. 3. holy, sacred; which is the most frequent usage of the word: བླ་མ་དམ་པ་བྱོན་བྱུང་ a holy lama has come; དམ་པ་ཉི་མཆོག་ཏུ་གྱུར་བ་ཡིན he is a holy one who has become the very best; དམ་པའི་བློ་གྲོས *dam-pahi blo-gros* holy intention, pious inclination. 4. seems to be also used as a term resp. for: the deceased, the late, *e.g.*, ཡབ་དམ་པ་དེ་ཉིད he my deceased father; སློབ་དཔོན་དམ་པ་དེ་ཉིད the late teacher himself, etc. 5. also sbst. the good, the holy, holiness: དམ་པ་རྣམས་ཀྱི of the holy ones.

དམ་པ་རྒྱལ *dam-pa rgyal* for སྐྱེས་བུ་དམ་པ་ཐམས་ཅད་ལས་རྒྱལ

དམ་པ་ཏོག་དཀར *Dam-pa tog-dkar* n. of a Deva-puttra; acc. to some Gautama Buddha bore this name in the Gahdan heavens.

དམ་པ་མི་ལྡན *dam-pa mi-ldan*=དམ་པ་མ་ཡིན་པ.

དམ་པའི་གྲིབ་བསིལ་དང་ལྡན་པ *dam-pahi grib-bsil-daṅ ldan-pa* सच्छाय possessed of the grateful shade of sanctity.

དམ་པའི་ཆོས *dam-pahi chos* or དམ་ཆོས सद्धर्म holy religion, Buddhism: དམ་པའི་ཆོས་དང་ཚེ་འདིའི་འདུན་མ་གཉིས མཉམ་དུ་འགྲུབ་པ་སུ་ཡང་ཡོད་པ་མིན both holy religion and worldly wishes there is none that can accomplish these two together (*Lo.* 7). དམ་པའི་ཆོས་པདྨ་དཀར་པོའི་མདོ *Dam-pahi chos pad-ma dkar-pohi mdo* सद्धर्मपुण्डरीकसूत्र n. of one of the well-known scriptures of the *Mahāyāna* school.

དམ་པའི་གཟུགས་བརྙན *dam-pahi gzugs-brñan* the image of holiness.

དམ་པོ *dam-po* दृढ 1. strict, firm, strong, tight; adv. as in དམ་པོར་འཛིན་པ to hold firmly, to seize securely. 2. acc. to *Jä.* narrow. དམ་པོ་མ་ཡིན *dam-po ma-yin* शिथिल not strong-willed; not strict; relaxed; དམ་པོར་བྱེད་པ *dam-por byed-pa* or སྲ་བར་བྱེད་པ दृढीक्रियते making firm, tight, or strict.

དམ་འབྱར *dam-hbyar* 1. = ལུགས་སྲོལ custom, usage, official practice: ལོ་གསར་ཐོབ་གཞི་དམ་འབྱར་དང་བླར the customary allowances of the new year, etc. (*Rtsii*). 2. the affixing a seal; also a letter to which a seal has been fixed.

དམ་ཚིག *dam-tshig* word of honour, a sacred or solemn vow; words or engagement made solemnly; དམ་ཚིག་ཉིད *dam-tshig ñid* promise solemnly undertaken.

དམ་རྫས *dam-rdsas* or དམ་ཚིག་གི་རྫས *dam-tshig-gi rdsas* objects or articles of religious utility which one carries about; for instance, the bell and the dorje are the དམ་རྫས of a *Tantrik* lama or a Buddhist exorcist which he always carries with him: རྣལ་འབྱོར་མ་ལ་ཐུགས་དམ་མཛད་པས་དེའི་རྫས་ཆང་གཅིག་སྦས་པས because he consulted the holy opinion of the *naljorma* (female ascetic of the *Tantrik* school); her desideratum (དམ་རྫས) which was beer was kept concealed (*A.* 61).

འདམ་བུའི་ཚལ *Hdam-buhi tshal* n. of a place beyond Suvarṇa-bhūmi (ancient Pegu); it is located: རྒྱ་མཚོ་ཆེན་པོ་བརྒལ་མ་ཐག་ཏུ་གསེར་གླིང་ནོན་ཤིང་གི་ནུབ་ཕྱོགས soon after crossing the ocean to the west of the groves of Suvarṇa-bhūmi (*A.* 20).

དམ་སྲག་རྫོང་ *Dam-srag rdsoṅ* described as as being a district in Tibet (*Rtsii.*).

དམ་སྲི *dam-sri* a species of gnome mentioned in *Pth.* as causing plague and cattle-disease.

དའུ *dah̲u* a kind of fever (typhoid): ཚད་པ་དའུམ་ཐེབས་ནས being laid up with typhoid fever. དའུ་བུ་ཚ *dah̲u bu-tsha* = དྭའུ་བུ་ཚ *dwah̲u bu-tsha* an orphan boy, orphan.

དར I: *dar* कौम, राग, पट्टक silk; also a flag: མཇལ་དར lit. meeting-scarf, is resp. for ཁ་བཏགས silk-scarf presented on meeting; presentation scarf; རྒྱ་དར Chinese or Indian silk; དར་དཀར white or plain silk scarf; དར་གོས silk stuff or dress. འཕྱར་དར *h̲phyar-dar* a hoisted flag; དར་ཆུང a small flag; མདུང་དར *m̲duń-dar* a silken strip attached to the top of a lance. དར་སྐུད *dar-s̲kud̲* रागसूत्र silk-thread: གོས་མེད་དར་སྐུད་འདྲ without dress; naked like a silk thread (stark-naked). དར་ཁྲ *dar-khra* चित्रपट painted or coloured satin; satin with figures on it; དར་ཕོན *dar-phon* a coarse kind of silk; དར་ཁྲུ *dar-khru* small square or triangular flag (made originally of silk); དར་གྱི་ལྡ་ལྡིང་ *dar-gyi l̲da-l̲diń* पट्टदाम silk-lace or fringes: དར་གྱི་ལྡ་ལྡིང་མང་པོ་བཏགས་པ *dar-gyi l̲da-l̲diń mań-po b̲tags-pa* पट्टदामकलाप decorated with a large number of silk fringes, lace, &c. དར་ཟབ *dar-zab* कौम the finest satin, silk-stuff; embroidered silk *kincob*; དར་ཟབ་སྣུམས་ལས་བྱུང་བ (དང་པོ་ལས་བྱུང་བ) कौशेय the finest satin: དར་ཟབ་གོས་ཐིངས (གོས་ཆེན་གྱི་གདན) ཟླ་བའི་སྙིང་པོ་ཞོག (*A. 4*) let Chandragarbha sit on the satin-robe spread out. རིན་པོ་ཆེའི་དར་ཟབ་སོགས་ཕྲུད་གཟིགས་མང་ཚམ a large present consisting of the finest embroidered satin, etc. (*R̲tsii.*): དར་རི་མོ་ཅན *dar ri-mo-can* चित्रपट्टक figured satin imported from China.

དར་ལ *dar-la* पट, (གོས་ཞིག) अवस्त्रापट्ट [a kind of satin cloth used for protection against frost]*S.*

དར་གྱི་འབུ *dar-gyi h̲bu* or དར་གྱི་སྲིན་བུ *dar-gyi s̲rin-bu* कौषकीट silk-worm.

Syn. སྐུད་པའི་འབུ *s̲kud̲-pahi h̲bu*; དར་གྱི་འབུ *dar-gyi h̲bu* (*M̲ṅon.*).

དར་ལྕོག *dar-l̲cog* a flag-staff about 10 or 12 feet high (with inscribed flag) fixed on house-tops, piles of stone, or on votive cairns.

Syn. དར་པོ་ཆེ *dar-po che.*

དར་བཏགས་པ *dar-b̲tags-pa* to bind silk scarves to the neck or throw them on the necks of parties to be blessed.

དར་ཐོགས་པ *dar-thogs-pa* one with a scarf in his hand; དམག་དཔོན་དར་ཐོགས་པ the general (when given command of an army) being presented with a silk scarf as a token of office (*D.R.*).

དར་འཐག་མཁན *dar h̲thag-m̲khan* silk-weaver; དར་འཐག་མཁན་གྱི་བུ་མོ daughter of a silk-weaver.

དར་བུ *dar-bu* a kind of red cloth made of either coarse silk or cotton, manufactured in Amdo (*S. kar. 174*).

དར་བུབས *dar-bubs* a whole piece of silk-stuff rolled together.

དར་དཔྱངས *dar-d̲pyańs* or དར་ཡུག *daryug* पट्टक a narrow ribbon-like piece of silk, a kind of silken ornament. 2. the silk scarves or coloured cotton cloth attached to a flag-staff (*R̲tsii.*)..

Syn. དར་བུ *dar-bu*; དར་ཆུང་ *dar-chuń* (*Jä.*).

དར II: ice, not glacial ice, but that on ponds, streams and lakes; དར་ཆགས *dar-chags* icy formation, ice in formation: མཚོ་ལ་དར་ཆགས་འདུག an incrustation of ice has formed on the lake. དར་ཟམ *dar-zam* ice-bridge.

དར III : यौवन youth; དར་བབས or དར་ལ་བབས་པ मध्यम; युवा youth; youthful age; also=སྐྱེས་ཕྲན *skyes-phran*. དར་ཕྱེད *dar-phyed* or དར་ཡོལ *dar-yol* आजीर्ण, गतयौवन one past his youth, *i.e.*, after the middle age, *i.e.*, from the 49th to the 60th year in man.

དར་གཅིག *dar-gcig*=ཐུང་ཙམ or རེ་ཞིག a little while, a moment; དར་གཅིག་སོང་བ་ན after a while; adverbially: for a little while, for a moment, directly, instantly, in a moment; དར་ཙམ *dar-tsam* about a moment.

དར་བ *dar-wa* vb. 1. to be diffused, grown up; to spread, spreading; ཆེས་དར་བ to gain much ground, to increase exceedingly; དར་དུ་འཇུག་པ to extend, enlarge; དར་རྒུད spreading and decaying; increase and decrease; ཡུལ་དར་བ a growing place or country. 2.=དར་ར (Beng.) घोल sbst. whey; milk from which butter has been churned out; དར་བའི་ཆང wine made of fermented whey.

Syn. ཆུ་སྐྱ *chu-skya*; ཆབ་སྐྱ *chab-skya* (*Mṅon.*).

དར་བབ་མ *dar bab-ma*=བུ་མོ་དར་མ तरुणी a maiden; a damsel.

དར་བབས *dar-babs*=དར་ལ་བབས་པ youthful.

དར་རྒྱས་གླིང *Dar-rgyas gliṅ* n. of a Buddhist monastery in Upper Tibet. *Jä.* mentions this also as another n. for Darjeeling.

དར་སྒ *dar-sga* the walnut-tree.

དར་དིར *dar-dir* किलकिलायित humming or buzzing; wailing, lamenting (*Jä.*).

དར་རྡོ *dar-rdo*=དར་རྡོ *rdar-rdo*, གྲི་སོགས་རྡར་བྱེད a stone on which any steel implement is sharpened; grinding stone.

‡ **དར་དྷི** *dar-dhi*, v. ཀུ་ཤ *ku-ça* (*Mṅon.*).

དར་པོ *dar-po* an adult.

དར་པོ་ཆེ *dar-po che*, v. དར་ལྕོག *dar-lcog* sail; large flag fastened to a flag-staff: ཊིངས་དེ་ཡར་དར་པོ་ཆེ་རླུང་གིས་བསྒྱོད་པ་བཞིན་དུ་འདར་བ་དང་ and that ship quivered like as a flag when moved by the wind (*A. 16*).

དར་མ I : *Dar-ma* n. of a district in the province of *Hphan-yul*, with a small fort (*Rtsii.*).

དར་མ II : तारुण्य, संरूढ़, तरुण, also प्रौढ़, middle age (in man or woman) after the 40th year.

དར་མའི་སྟོབས *dar-mahi stobs* the strength of full-grown man, that of an adult.

དར་མའི་ལུས *dar-mahi lus* उक्षशरीर the body of a bull; youthful body (like that of growing bull).

དར་མ་རིན་ཆེན *Dar-ma rin-chen* also called རྒྱལ་ཚབ་རྗེ the disciple and successor of Tsong-khapa; དར་མ་བསོད་ནམས *Dar-ma bsod-nams* n. of a disciple of Tsong-khapa (*Loñ.* ཧ *11*).

དར་མོ *Dar-mo* an abbreviated n. of a Tibetan physician called དར་མོ་སྨན་རམས་པ; his work on medicine is still extant in Tibet.

དར་དམང་པ *dar dmañ-pa* raw-silk (*Schtr.*).

དར་སྨན *dar-sman*=དར་ཚུར alum.

དར་ཙམ *dar-tsam*=རེབ་ཙམ or སྐྱིབ་ཙམ or དར་གཅིག a moment; very short time.

དར་བཙག *dar-btsag*=རས་བཙག cloth used for sifting and filtering: གྲོ་ཞིབ་དར་བཙག་བྱུང་པ་ནས་དང་འདྲ sifted wheat is like barley (in price) (*Rtsii.*).

དར་རྩེ་མདོ *Dar-rtse-mdo* Darchendo, otherwise Ta-chien-lu, situated in the south-easternmost corner of Tibet and practically out of all Tibetan jurisdiction. It is the transport place from whence brick tea is brought into Tibet.

དར་ཚིལ *dar-tshil* 1. the fat of youthful growth. 2. acc. to *Sch.* grain.

དར་ཡ་ཀན *dar-ya kan* a medicinal herb growing in clefts of rocks: དར་ཡ་ཀན་གྱི་བྲང་ཁོག་ཆུ་སེར་གླ་མ་མགོ་བའི་དུམ་ཚག་སྦྱོར་ཞིང་ལྷ་བ་འཛིན།

དར་ཡབ *dar-yab* a silk-fan.

དར་ཤམ *dar-çam* 1. the lower border of a silk dress (*Jä.*). 2.=केरा n. of a plant, prob. the plantain.

དར་ཤིང་ *dar-çiñ* 1. a medicinal fruit. 2.= དར་ལྕོག་ཤིང་ flag-staff. 3. ཤིང་རྒྱ་ལེགས་པ a very fine wood (*Jig.*), prob. the satin-wood.

དར་སར་བྱེད་པ *dar-sar byed-pa* to keep observances where religion flourishes.

དར་སང་ *dar-sañ* a thin satiny muslin used for door-curtains and screens by lamas and great personages to prevent the public gazing on any ceremony or entertainment.

དར་ཧན *dar-han* a Mongol word signifying a man who is exempt from the duty of furnishing labour, &c., to the State, and also from supplying ponies, &c., to those who travel under official authority.

དལ मन्द adj. slow, leisurely; དལ་རྐང་ *dal-ṛkañ* slowly walking; དལ་ཁོམ་མེད་པ *dal-khom med-pa*=འོང་མེད་པ without leisure or rest: བྱ་རོག་དང་ཕྲིའུ་སོགས་ཁ་དལ་ཁོམ་མེད་པར the mouths of crows and little birds, etc., have little rest (*Khrid. 45*). དལ་གྱིས *dal-gyis*= ཀ་ལེ slowly, softly, gently.

དལ་གྱིས་འབབ་པ *dal-gyis ḥbab-pa* मन्दाकिनी n. of the river Ganges in the Himalaya; any sluggish or glacial stream. Also *dal-babs*.

དལ་འགྲོ *dal-ḥgro* or དལ་གྱིས་འགྲོ मन्दाकिनी, प्रतिलम्बित, शनैश्वर slowly or gradually moving; that moves in a prostrate position. Met. for the planet Saturn, the white swan, or a tortoise. དལ་འགྲོའི་རྒྱུན་བཞིན *dal-ḥgroḥi ṛgyun-bshin* meandering, as great rivers of the plains which flow sluggishly: བཀའ་མཆིད་ཡེབས་ཚོགས་ཀྱང་དལ་འགྲོའི་རྒྱུན་བཞིན་ཡོད་པ་མཁྱེན (*Yig. k. 15*) pray permit your instructions (letters) to come to me uninterruptedly, like the flow of a river.

དལ་འགྲོས *dal-ḥgros* 1. a mode of dancing v. རྐང་པའི་འདུ་བྱེད. 2. described as ཀ་ལེ་ཀ་ལེ་འགྲོ་བ to walk or move slowly.

དལ་རྒྱུ *dal-ṛgyu* slowly moving, sluggish stream.

དལ་ཅིག *dal-cig*=ལན་ཅིག *lan-cig* 1. once: དལ་ཅིག་ང་ཡོང་རྒྱུ་ཡིན I shall be coming over once. 2. क्षण a moment, cf. དར་གཅིག *dar-gcig* a little while.

དལ་རྟེན *dal-ṛten*=མི་ལུས the human body (which is very slowly evolved).

དལ་ཐོག་འཇུག་པ *dal-thog ḥjug-pa* to attack, disperse an enemy (*Sch.*).

དལ་དག *dal-dag* this term and དལ་རྐང་ and དལ་འགྲོས occur in astrological calculations of གཟའ་ལྔ the five planets (which term probably implies the planet Saturn).

དལ་དུ་འཕངས་པ *dal-du phañs-pa* fig. to work or to study assiduously; not to be lazy or indolent: ད་ན་དལ་དུ་འཕངས་རིག་པ་སློབས་ཟེར he said: but then learn some science not to remain idle (*A. 32*).

དལ་པོ *dal-po* शनैः=*dal* sluggish, slow, relaxed; weak, with but little energy.

Syn. ལྷོད་པོ *lhod-po*; ཤུགས་ཆུང་བ *çugs chuñ-wa*; བུལ་བ *bul-wa* (*Mñon.*).

དལ་བ *dal-wa*=ཁོམ་པ क्षण, जिह्म, विलम्बित languor, ease, quietude, leisure; also the state of *dalwa*, and so the being at ease or in state of leisurely comfort or repose: བུགས་དལ་དུས when at leisure, when the mind is disengaged or at ease, *dolce far niente*.

སྤྱིར་མི་ཁོམ་པའི་གནས་བརྒྱད་དུ་མ་སྐྱེས་པར་དམ་པའི་ཆོས་བསྒྲུབ་ཁོམ་པ་ནི་དལ་བ་ཞེས་བྱ generally, not being born in any of the eight states of restless existence, one who finds rest by religious practice is said to be *Dal-wa* (*S̱ñiñ.*).. དལ་བ་བརྒྱད the eight states in which living beings are at ease and happy as being possessed of many blessings; they are: (1) ཆོས་བྱེད་པའི་མི a religious person; (2) དབང་པོ་ཚང་བ one who is fully developed both physically and mentally; (3) ལྟ་བ་མ་ལོག not a heretic, *i.e.*, one who is a Buddhist; (4) as a ལྷ *lha* or god; (5) as a ལྷ་མ་ཡིན *lha-ma yin* or *Asura* an antagonist of the gods; (6) an enlightened man (*i.e.*, not a savage or wildman); (7) and (8) those not born in space or in any animated nature outside humanity. These are also called ཁོམ་པ་བརྒྱད. The following are མི་ཁོམ་པ་བརྒྱད *mi-khom-pa ḇrgyaḏ* अष्टाक्षणाः, *i.e.*, the states in which living beings have no ease or rest who suffer from continual work, and are therefore called restless ones or མི་ཁོམ་པ:—(1) དམྱལ་བ नरकोपपत्ति hell-beings; (2) ཡི་དྭགས प्रेतलोकोपपत्ति those born in the form of pretas; (3) དུད་འགྲོ तिर्यगुपपत्ति those in the animal kingdom (humanity excluded); (4) ཡུལ་མཐའ་འཁོབ प्रत्यन्तजनपदोपपत्ति wild tribes living in the border countries, *i.e.*, outside the pale of civilization; (5) ཀླ་ཀློ *ḵla-ḵlo* म्लेच्छ, or यवन lit. one of indistinct speech, *i.e.*, Moslems; (6) ལྷ་ཚེ་རིང་པོ दीर्घायुर्देवोपपत्ति the gods who on account of desire to live long are born in spheres of the heavens where there is no opportunity of entering the state of *Nirvāṇa*; (7) དབང་པོ་མ་ཚང་བ इन्द्रियविकलता those who are defective in their internal or external organs; (8) ལྟ་བ་ལོག་པ मिथ्यादृष्टि those who are heretics or infidels, *i.e.*, not Buddhists. In Sanskṛt and Pali works we find चित्तोत्पादविरागिता indifference with respect to the purification of heart, instead of (5).

དལ་བའི་ལྷ་ལྡན་མ *dal-waḥi lha-ḻdan-ma* रोहिणीनक्षत्र the lunar mansion in which there are five star-gods, a constellation appearing in the shape of a chariot.

Syn. བི་རྗི *bi-ṟji*; སྐར་མ་སྣར་མ *s̱kar-ma s̱nar-ma* (*M̱ñon.*).

དལ་བར་དགའ་བ *dal-war ḏgaḥ-wa* to like doing things slowly, not rashly.

དལ་བུ *dal-bu*=དལ་བ *dalwa* मन्द slow: དལ་བུས་འགྲོ་མ मन्दगामिनी she who moves slowly. དལ་བུས=ཁྱད་ཀྱིས slowly; gently.

དལ་བོན *Dal-bon* a sect of the Bon: དལ་བོན་ལུ་གུ་གར་དལ་ཁམས་དང་ཚམས་པ་དང་ the Dal-Bon came from the soft regions where the lambs dwell (*D.R.*).

དལ་འབབ་རྣམ་བཞི *dal-ḥbab ṟnam-ḇshi* the four great rivers which have issued from the glaciers are:—(1) सिन्धु the Indus; (2) གང་གཱ गङ्गा the Ganges; (3) པཀྵུ पक्षु the Pakshu; acc. to some authors, the Yamunā; (4) སི་ཏཱ सिता the Oxus; acc. to some authors the Brahmaputtra: ཡིག་ཚོགས་ཀྱང་དལ་འབབ་རྣམ་པ་བཞིའི་རྒྱུན་བཞིན་ཡོད་པ་མཆིས (*Yig. k. 28*) may your letters also be like the flowing streams of the four *Mandākinī* rivers.

དལ་འབྱོར *dal-ḥbyor* an abbr. of དལ་བ་བརྒྱད and འབྱོར་བ་བཅུ; and when these eighteen conditions are complete in a *Sattva*, *i.e.*, in an animate being, it becomes a human being: བདག་ནི་དལ་འབྱོར་མི་དབང་ལུས་ཐོབ་ཅིང་ I having obtained the noble body of a *dal-ḥbyor* man (*A. 3*). དལ་འབྱོར་རྙེད་པར་དཀའ་བ *dal-ḥbyor ṟñeḏ-par dkaḥ-wa* humanity, *i.e.*, the state in which the eighteen blessings are with difficulty acquired.

དལ་སྦྱིན་མ *dal s̱byin-ma* क्षणदा 1. n. of a festival. [2. night, giving relaxation or rest]*S.*

དལ་མ *dal-ma*=གར་མཁན་མ a nautch-girl or dancing-woman (*M̱ñon.*).

དལ་མོ *dal-mo* quiet, calm; also the chine, loin (*Jä.*).

དལ་མོ *dal-mo*=ག་ལེ slowly: ཁྱོད་རང་དལ་མོ་འགྲོ you walk slowly, proceed slowly. དལ་མྱུར་མཐོ་དམན་གྱི་འགྲོས *dal-myur mtho-dman-gyi hgros* slow and quick, upward or downward movement (*B. ch.*).

དལ་བཙོང་ *dal-btson* དལ་ཚོང་ 1. one selling articles at his own residence, who has not to move here and there for their disposal; བཙོང *btson* is pf. of འཚོང་ *htshon*. 2. in *W.* the people of མངའ་རིས་སྐོར་གསུམ are not seldom forced by their rulers to take goods from them at fixed prices. When this is done underlings appear before the tents or houses with a quantity of goods (which nobody else will buy) and throwing them down tell the owner of the house or tent that he now owes so much to the Government for things received. This is called དལ་ཚོང་ orthogr. of དལ not certain, but it appears to mean to spread, distribute—to spread trade by force.

དལ་འཛིན་ *dal-hdsin*=དལ་འབབ or དལ་འབྱིན་ मन्दधार flowing in a low stream. དལ་འཛིན་ང་རྒྱལ *dal-hdsin na-rgyal* मानमन्धर the pride of Mandhara; the pride that I am more happy than another person; དལ་འཛིན་ལྟོ་དགའ *dal-dsin lto-dgah* मन्दोदरीप्रिय the lover of Mandodari, Rāvana; དལ་འཛིན་གནས་བཟང་ *dal-hdsin gnas-bzan* the superb mansion of heaven.

དལ་ཡམས *dal-yams*=ནད་རིམས་ངན་པ a pestilence of the worst kind, with the following symptoms:—གཟེར་ཐུང་ *gzer-thun*; ཁྲག་ནད *khrag-nad*; ལྟག་འགྱེལ *ltag-hgyel*; ཅོག་འགྱེལ *cog-hgyel*; མཁྲིས་རིམས *mkhris-rims*; སྨྱོ་རིམས *smyo-rims*, etc. (*Sman. 119*).

དི *di* num. fig. 41.

དི་ཀི *di-ki* in mysticism=an assemblage; all or some brought in together (*K. g.* ག *215*).

དི་མར *di-mar* a certain worm or insect (*Sch.*).

དི་རི་རི *di-ri-ri* the howling noise of the wind, the rattle of thunder; also buzz, murmur, hum, low confused noise as of crowds, of number of praying people, of wailing prisoners, of birds on the wing. (*Glr.*, *Jä*).

དི་ཧི *di-hi*=ར་རོ་ཅན drunk (mystic) (*K. g.* ག *215*).

དིག *dig* in ཁ་དིག or ཁ་དིག་པ, v. དིག་པ.

དིག་སྙན *dig-snan* कपोत a pigeon.

Syn. ཕུག་རོན *phug-ron*; ཅ་ཅོ་སྒྲོག *ca-co sgrog*; འཕྲུལ་བའི་མིག་ཅན *hphrul-wahi mig-can* (*Mnon.*).

དིག་པ *dig-pa* खक्खल 1. to stammer, also ཁ་དིག་པ a stammerer: སྨྲ་ཆ་བཤད་དུས་ཁ་དིག་པ he at the time of speaking stammers (*Ya-sel. 35*); cf. འདིག་པ *hdig-pa.* 2. staggering, intoxicated (*Jä.*).

དིང་ *din* for དིང་སང་ *din-san*.

དིང་ཁྲི *din-khri* a descendant of *Gnah-khri btsan-po*, the first historical king of Tibet (*J. Zan.*).

དིང་དིང *din-din* the sound of the drum; acc. to *Schr.* གད་མོ་དིང་དིང་=laughing aloud (*Tā. 158-4*).

དིང་ཕོན *din-phon* n. of a superior kind of Chinese satin embroidered and worked with needle: གནམ་ཡོལ་དིང་ཕོན་ཁོ་ན་བྱས་པ་རབ the canopy or ceiling made only of *Din-phon* satin is better (*Jig.*). Also དིང་གོས *din-gos* id. (*S. kar. 179*).

དིང་ཧུར *din-hur* नाद a sound, noise.

དིང་རི *Din-ri* n. of an extensive table-land situated N. E. of the confines of Nepal in Tibet and where there is stationed a Chinese militia. It is commonly called Tingri Maidān. Is more than once mentioned by Milaras-pa in his Nam-thar.

དིང་སང་ *diṅ-saṅ* सम्प्रति, abbr. དེ་རིང་ and སང་ to-day and to-morrow, hence just now, now-a-days; also written as དེང་སང་.

དིང་གསལ་བའོ་དཔག་སུ་རུམ་ཕྱུང་ཁྱབ་པས this passage was explained as: སྟོན་པས་ཁྱིམ་ཕྱུང་རབ་ཏུ་བྱུང་བའི་ཞེ་ན the stage wherein the teacher renouncing his home enters the religious life (*D.R.*).

དུ I: *du* 1. num. fig. 71. 2. terminative case-sign after final ང, ད, ན, མ, ར, ལ. 3. how many, how much: དུ་ ཡོད how much is there? སྣོབས་ནས་ཟླ་བ་དུ་སོན how many months ago was it that he came? སངས་རྒྱས་སྐུ་ངན་ལས་འདས་ནས་ལོ་དུ་ཙམ་ལགས་ཞུས་པས (*A. 93*) he asked how many years have passed since the *Nirvāṇa* of Buddha.

Syn. ག་ཙམ *ga-tsam*; ཅི་ཙམ *ci-tsam*; ཇི་ཙམ *ji-tsam* (*Mṅon.*).

དུ་དུ *du-du* how much, how many each time?

དུ་མ *du-ma* अनेक, नाना many; also various, several; ཞག་དུ་མ many days: དུ་མར་ཕྱེ it divided itself into several (parts); ལན་དུ་མར many a time, often. Occurs for "many" in *Mil. Gurbum* 79*b*. 2 and 182*a*. 3.

དུ་ཤིག *du-shig* about how much?

དུ་རུ *du-ru* how much, what extent? རྒྱུས་མེད་ཡུལ་འདིར་མགོ་བོ་འཁོར, དེ་ཕྱིར་བོད་ཀྱི་ཡུལ་འདི་ན, ཡུལ་གྱི་མ་དཔྱད་དུ་རུ་སྨིན (*Loṅ.* ཤ *4*) I am confused being a stranger in this country; for that reason the nature and extent of this country of Tibet (pray describe).

དུ II: in mystic sense 1.=རོ taste (རོ also=dead body). 2. a woman of bad morals (*K. g.* ཕ *179*).

‡ དུ་ཀུ་ལའི་རས *du-ku-laḫi ras* or དུ་ཀུ་ལའི་རས दौकूलकं the finest kind of silk cloth manufactured in very early times in India.

‡ དུ་པ་ཏྲི་ཡ *du-pa tri-ya* (mystic) a cloud (*K. g.* ཕ *28*).

དུ་བ *du-wa* धूम smoke; དུ་བ་མཐུལ *du-wa mthul* धूमायते it smokes; དུ་བ་ཕྱུར་བ་བྱེད *du-wa phyur-wa byed* smoke rises; ཧོར་དུ *hor-du* "Turk's smoke," signifying the Turkoman Lob-nor or nomad's tents each containing a stove from which smoke rises.

དུ་བ་འཇུག་རིང *du-wa mjug-riṅ* केतु comet.

Syn. ཕོད་ཅན *phod-can*; མཇུག་ཕོད་ཅན *mjug-phod-can*; གཙུག་ཕུད་ཅན *gtsug-phud-can*; སྦྲུལ་ཅན *sbrul-can*; སྐག་ལས་སྐྱེས *skag-las-kges*; སྐྲ་གཉིས་པ *skra-gñis-pa* (*Mṅon.*).

དུ་བ་པ *du-wa-pa* acc. to *Jä.*: in *Spiti* very poor people that pay but a trifling tax; proletarians ('smoke people') that have nothing but the smoke of their fire.

དུ་བ་མི་ཟད་པ *du-wa-mi zad-pa*=དམྱལ་བ n. of a hell (in the Bon mythology).

དུ་བ་འཚུབས *du-wa ḫtshubs* भङ्ग the hornet.

དུ་བའི་སྐྱེ་གནས *du-waḫi skye-gnas* 1. धूमयोनि fire (as the source of smoke). 2. acc. to *Mṅon.*=སྤྲིན *sprin* cloud.

དུ་བའི་ཏོག *du-waḫi tog* धूमकेतु a comet.

དུ་ཤག *du-shag* acc. to *Jä.* the smoke or vapour hanging over towns and large villages in the morning.

‡ **དུ་རུ་ཀ** *du-ru-ka* 1. a kind of fir from the sap of which a resinous incense is produced; སང་རྩི་ནི་སྦྱིན་སྲེག་ལ་བཟང (*K. g.* ད *338*) the resin is considered good for the sacrificial fire. 2. རྒྱ་དུ་རུ་ཀའི་ཡུལ *rgya duru-kaḫi yul* n. of a place in China inhabited by Musalmans (*Loṅ.* ཤ *12*).

‡ དུ་ཧཾ *du-ham* གྲོང་ཁྱེར་ཞེས་སྨྲ་བའི་ལན་ནོ a reply saying "it is a town" (a phrase used in mysticism) (*K. g.* ཕ *27*).

དུ་ཧར་ནག་པོ་ *Du-har nag-po*, n. of a celebrated Chinese astronomer and mathematician (*Rtsii.*).

‡ དཱུ་པ་ཀཱ་ཡ *dū-pa kā ya* स्तूपकाय 1.= མཆོད་རྟེན་གྱི་སྐུ an image either inscribed on or deposited in a *stûpa* or chaitya. 2. a name of the great temple in the Daipung monastery near Lhasa.

དུག *dug* poison, which is of several kinds, viz:—རང་བཞིན་གྱི་དུག *i.e.*, natural poison, such as snake venom, vegetable and also moral poisons; གྱུར་བའི་དུག substances that have been converted into poison; are སྦྱར་བའི་དུག poisons applied and also made by mixture; མཐོང་བའི་དུག sight-poison, poisons which are visible as such; རེག་པའི་དུག poisons of contagion and infection, those of fatal or ruinous consequences. The four figurative poisons in Budh. are:—རིག་སྔགས་ལོག་པར་ཤེས་པ་དུག a *mantra* or charm known in a wrong manner is poison; ནད་ལ་བཏང་སྙོམས་བྱས་པ་དུག indifference to an illness is poison; རྒན་པོས་གཞོན་ནུ་མ་བསྟེན་པ་དུག an old man's keeping company with a young woman is poison; དབུལ་པོ་ཉིན་པར་ཉལ་བ་དུག a poor man's sleep during the day-time is poison (*Ç. doṅ.*). In medical works: ཉི་མ་ཚ་བ་པགས་པའི་དུག the hot sun acts as a poison to the skin; ཆང་ནི་ཤ་ཡི་དུག་ཡིན་ཏེ beer acts as poison to the flesh; ཚྭ་ནི་རུས་པའི་དུག་ཡིན་པ table-salt acts as poison to the bones. Again, we read of དུག་གསུམ་ནི *dug-gsum-ni* the three poisons:—འདོད་ཆགས་ काम [lust]*S.* ཞེ་སྡང་ क्रोध [hatred]*S.* གཏི་མུག मोह [ignorance]*S.* (*A. K. 111-21*). Acc. to the Bon there are five moral poisons:—(1) ང་རྒྱལ pride originating from an inordinate sense of one's acquirements; (2) འདོད་ཆགས love and lust originated from objects that fascinate the mind; (3) ཞེ་སྡང་ anger as the poison of the mind which embitters everything that would otherwise be charming; (4) ཕྲག་དོག jealousy which does not allow the mind to bear the sight of another's prosperity; (5) གཏི་མུག= མོངས་པ darkness of the mind. The five gods who acc. to the Bon can suppress the above five poisons are:—(1) གཉེན་ལྷ་འོད་དཀར, (2) གང་གསལ་བཙན་པོ (3) དགོད་གསལ་ཁམས་པ, (4) གསལ་རྗེ་མང་པོ, (5) གནམ་གསལ་དབྱིང་ཆུམ.

དུག་གིས་བྱུག་པ་ཅན་ *dug-gis byug-pa-can* whatever has been poisoned or besmeared with poison (as an arrow point) (*Mṅon.*).

དུག་གི་མེ་ཏོག *dug-gi me-tog* 1. generally the plant *Vangueria spinosa*, the blue-lotus, 2. also अतसी *Linum usitatissimum.*

དུག་གི་སྨན *dug-gi sman* or དུག་སྨན aconite; poison used as medicine. དུག་གི་སྨན་པ *dug-gi sman-pa* जाङ्गुलवैद्य a physican or medicine-man using poisonous drugs in diseases.

དུག་སྔགས *dug-sṅags* poison charm; the following poison-charm is carried in amulet cases inscribed on cloth, paper, or birch-bark, as a protection against poison: ༀ་ཧུམ་པེ་ལེ ཧུམ་པེ་ལེ ཕྲ་ཧུམ་པེ ནད་ཧི སུར་ཏ་ཏེ ཀེ་པ་ ཏ་ཏེ ཧུ་ན་ཡེ, ས་མ་ཡེ ད་ན་ཏེ *da-na-te* དན་ཏི་ཝེ ཏི་ཝེ ཏི་ཝ་ཀེ་ཤེ ཕུ་ཝེ་ཕུ་ལ་ཀོ་ཊེ ༀ་ལེ *o-le* ཧུང་གེ་ལེ་སྭཱ་ཧཱ (*K. du.* ཙ *116*).

དུག་ཅན *dug-can* poisonous; དུག་ཅན་པ *dug-can-pa* = ཐལ་ཧྲུགས་པ also= सागर the ocean; anything poisonous or mischievous; དུག་ཅན་མཚོ *dug-can mtsho* सागर the ocean (which is believed to contain poison).

དུག་བཅོམ *dug-bcom* हतविष an epithet of Buddha; one who has made poison ineffectual, (*M.V.*).

དུག་ཆགས *dug-chags* mischievous; colloq. མི་འདི་དུག་ཆགས་རེད "*mi di duk-chak re,*" that man is very mischievous.

དུག་འཇོམས *dug-hjoms* गुडुच, विषघ्ना, विषघातिन्, a kind of twining shrub used as an antidote against poison, *Muispermum cordifolium.*

དུག་འཇོམས་ལྡན་ *dug hjoms-ldan* गरुड़ the golden eagle which Vishnu is said to ride.

དུག་གཉེན་ *dug-gñen* an antidote to poison.

དུག་ཏི་ *dug-ti* in Tsang: so, thus, in this manner=ཅུག་ཏི་ (*Jä.*).

དུག་པ་ *dug-pa* or དུག་པོ་ old coat or garment patched up and mended (*Mṅon.*). Acc. to *Jä.* coat, garment, dress.

དུག་འཕྲོག་ *dag-hphrog* विषापहा poison-repelling, antidote against poison, n. of a species of tree, *Aristolochia Indica.*

དུག་དམར་ *dug-dmar*=མཚན་ལ་མེ་སྟོན་པོ.

དུག་མོ་ཉུང་ *dug-mo ñuñ* or དུག་མོ་ཉུང་གི་ཤིང་ཏོག medicinal fruit akin to *Karaya*: ཀ་རུ་ཉ་ཡ དུག་མོ་ཉུང་གིས་མཁྲིས་སེལ་ཚ་འབྲུ་གཅོད *Karaya* or *Dugma-ñuñ* stops dysentery and cures biliousness.

Syn. བཅད་སྐྱེ *bcad-skye*; སྤུ་ཅན *spu-can*; རི་ཡི་ཕྲེང *ri-yi-phreñ*; བེའུ་ཅན *behu-can*; ཤིང་སྐྱ *çiñ-skya*.

དུག་མོ་ཉུང་གི་འབྲུ་ *dug-mo ñuñ-gi hbru* कलिक described as ནས་འབྲས་བཟང་ *nas hbras-bzañ* fine-fruiting barley.

དུག་རྩ་ *dug-rtsa* (བོང་ནག) a species of aconite.

དུག་རབ་འཇོམས་ *dug rab-hjoms* 1. पद्म, विषप्रायुध the lotus; that which destroys the effect of poison. 2. शिरीष the poison-destroying, the tree *Mimosa sirissa.*

དུག་རྦ་ཅན་ *dug rba-can* विषशृङ्गिन् hornet or insect having a poison-sting.

དུག་ལོ་ *dug-lo* 1. poisonous leaf. 2. न्यग्रोध the banyan tree; *Ficus religiosa.* དུག་ལོ་ལྗོན་པའི་མདོ་ *Dug-lo ljon-pahi mdo* n. of a Bon religious work called 'the tree of poisonous leaves.'

དུག་ཤོག་ *dug-çog* poisonous paper, or *daphne* bark paper of Tibet arsenicated to prevent its being eaten up by moth.

དུག་སེལ་ *dug-sel* 1. श्रीकण्ठ that which neutralizes the effect of poison; an epithet of Mahâdeva. 2. n. of a medical author of ancient India. 3. སྐྱུ་རུ the fruit of *Emblic myrobalan.*

‡ དུག་ཧ་ལཱ་ཧ་ལ་ *dug-ha-lā ha-la* हलाहल, or हलहल, कालकूट, a deadly poisonous drug.

དུགས I: *dugs* inflamation; in medical works of Tibet are named two kinds of དུགས, viz.:—བསིལ་དུགས inflamation from cold, and དྲོད་དུགས inflamation from heat.

དུགས II: 1. gentle warmth; acc. to *Schtr.* heat: ཚད་པའི་དུགས་ཀྱིས by the heat of fever; རྡོ་དུགས warmth from heated stone; ལྕུམས་དུགས སྦངས་དུགས warmth from the fresh dung of animals; ཡོས་དུགས parched corn before it has lost its warmth. 2. revenge, grudge, rancour (*Jä.*).

དུགས་པ *dugs-pa* vb. 1. to make warm, to warm. 2. to light, to kindle (*Jä.*).

དུང་ *duñ* कम्बु, शङ्ख, जलज, कम्बोज any shell, the conch-shell (used as a vessel for offerings; or, when perforated at one end, for blowing as a horn); a horn, trumpet (to call the monks of a monastery to a service); དུང་འབུད་པ to blow a shell; ཁྲིམས་དུང་ trumpet used in courts of justice; ཆོས་དུང་ church-trumpet, trumpet used in religious services; དམག་དུང་ war-trumpet; ཞེངས་དུང་ hunting bugle; རྐང་དུང་ a trumpet made of a hollow thigh-bone; ཟངས་དུང་ a copper trumpet; རག་དུང་ a brass tube about eight feet long used as a trumpet; དབང་དུང་ a similar instrument but shorter and smaller in size; རུ་དུང་ a horn trumpet; དུང་གི་ཚོགས *duñ-gi-tshogs* a series of conch-shells. དུང་གི་ལག་འཁོར་=དུང་འཁོར the conch-shell ornament worn in Tibet on the wrist by the women; དུང་གི་ལག शङ्खकर an arm adorned with the conch-shell; དུང་སྐད *duṅ-skad* the sound of the conch-shell trumpet; དུང་སྐད་ཡིན་ཕྱིར་རོལ་ཆ་ཀུན་ལས་མཐོ a conch-shell on account of its sound is higher than all musical instruments (*Loṅ.* ཎ *2*); དུང་ཆེན *duṅ-chen* large trumpets made of copper or brass used in religious services; the human skull; རྐང་དུང *rkaṅ-duṅ* the thigh-bone trumpet; དུང་ཆོས *duṅ-chos* शङ्ख religious service with the music of the church shell-trumpets; also the damning of religious faith or inclination in the mind.

Syn. ཤམ་ཀ *çamka*; ཆུ་སྲིན་གཤེད *chu-srin gçed*.

དུང་གི་ཐོར་ཅོག་ཅན *Duṅ-gi thor-cog can* n. of a celebrated physician of Tibet who lived in the 4th century A. D: སྨན་པ་དུང་གི་ཐོར་ཅོག་ཅན་གྱི་ལྷ་ཐོ་རི་དང་དེའི་སྲས་ཁྲི་སྙན་གཟུགས་ཅན་གཉིས་ཀའི་བླ་སྨན་མཛད་དོ the physician Dungi-thor-chog-chan served as physician-lama to king Thori and his son Khri-sñan-gzugs-can (*Gyu.* *33*).

དུང་གི་ལྡེམ་ཤིང་དཀར་པོ *duṅ-gi ldem-çiṅ dkar-po* white-wood tree to make images, the wood resembling a conch-shell in appearance; prob. birch-tree (*D.R.*). དུང་གི་སྒྲ་སེ་མི་སེ་མི་ཉམས་དུ་བའི་རྒྱ་མཚོ n. of a mythological ocean situated beyond the great mountain of *Rtsed-mohi Phreṅ-wahi ri* (*K. d.* ར *330*).

དུང་སྐྱོང *duṅ-skyoṅ* n. of a Nāga Rājā who resides in the ocean and protects the shells (*Mṅon.*).

དུང་དཀར་རག་གཤོག་མ *duṅ-dkar rag-gçog-ma* lit. white conch with brass wings; a conch-shell trumpet or vessel mounted with brass, with brass-wings (*Rtsii.*).

དུང་དཀར་གཡས་འཁྱིལ *duṅ-dkar gyas-hkhyil* दक्षिणावर्तशङ्ख a conch-shell with its coil reverting to the right instead of to the left: གཡས་འཁྱིལ་གསུང་སྐད་ཐོས་པས་ནད་རིགས་སེལ། ཁྱིམ་དུ་བཅང་ན་འཐབ་རྩོད་མེད་ཅིང་མཐུན། the sound of the *Dakṣiṇā vartta* conch-shell cures various diseases and if one is kept in the house it removes quarrels, strife, and brings in harmony (*Loṅ.* ཎ *2*).

Syn. དུང་ མཆོག *duṅ-mchog*; རྒྱལ་པོ་འཁྱིལ་བ *rgyal-po hkhyil-wa*; བཀྲ་ཤིས་དུང་ *bkraçis duṅ*; སྐྱེ་བ་ལྔ་པ *skye-wa lṅa-pa* (*Mṅon.*).

དུང་གཡོན་འཁྱིལ *duṅ gyon-hkhyil* the ordinary conch-shell of which the coil is from left to right; དུང་དམར *duṅ-dmar* रक्तशङ्ख=དོག་ཅན red conch-shell; conch-shell vermilion dyed; དུང་ཚེར་མ་ཅན *duṅ tsher-ma can* कण्टकशङ्ख; དུང་རྭ་བ་ཅན horned conch-shell or one with bristle-like excrescences.

དུང་མཁན *duṅ-mkhan*, v. དུང་བཟོ་བ

དུང་མཆོག *duṅ-mchog*, v. དུང་དཀར་གཡས་འཁྱིལ *duṅ-dkar gyas-hkhyil*.

དུང་རྡོ *duṅ-rdo* fossil-shell.

དུང་མདོག་ཅན *duṅ-mdog-can* possessed of conch-shell colour, conch-like colour;=མི་ཐོད་པ the human skull (*Sman. 348*).

དུང་འབྲས *duṅ-hbras* शङ्खफल a kind of stone which joins fracture: དུང་འབྲས་རུས་སྐོར་དངུལ་ཆུ་འཆིང་བར་བྱེད.

དུང་མཚོ་དཀར་མོ *duṅ-mtsho dkar-mo* n. of a great white ocean abounding in conch-shells (*J. Zaṅ.*).

དུང་གཡས་འཁྱིལ *duṅ gyas-hkyil*, v. དུང་དཀར་གཡས་འཁྱིལ.

དུང་ངེ *duṅ-ṅe* defined as འདོད་པ or དད་པ་མངོན་སུམ་སྐྱེས་པ the growth of real attachment or regard; also སེམས་དུང་ངེ or ཡིད་དུང་ངེ id. དུང་ངེ་བ *duṅ-ṅe-wa* constant, continual (*Jä.*).

དུང་ཅན་མ *Duṅ-can-ma* शङ्खिनी n. of a Khadoma sprite.

དུང་དུང་ *duṅ-duṅ*=ཟུམས་ཟུམས 1. with བྱེད་པ=to yearn: ཆགས་ལྟོགས་ཀྱང་དུང་དུང་མ་བྱེད even if you starve, do not yearn after a thing; གཉེན་ལ་སེམས་དུང་དུང་བྱེད་པ he yearns for his relations. 2. staggering, reeling, loitering, wavering (*Sch.*).

དུང་པན *duṅ-pan* a Chinese word Tibetanized=a washing bowl, basin.

དུང་ཕྱུར *duṅ-phyur* (གྲངས) शङ्कु, अर्बुद, मध्य acc. to *Sch.* and *Jä.* 100 millions.

དུང་ལུང་ *Duṅ-luṅ* n. of a sacred place in Tibet (*Deb. 43*): དུང་ལུང་དུ་མཁའ་འགྲོ་མའི་སྒྲ་ཐོས at Dunlung he heard the voice of a *Dākini*.

དུང་ལོ་ལྗོན་པའི་མདོ *Duṅ-lo ḷjon-paḥi ṃdo* n. of a Bon religious work (*B. Nam.*).

དུང་སེམས *duṅ-semṣ* lit. white heart, sincerity, candidness: ཁོ་བོ་ཡང་དུང་སེམས་ཇོ་ཇེའི་ཚོམ་ནས་མི་འདོར་བའི་མོལ་ཚོམ་ཡང་ཀྱང་ཡང་བྱེད། (*Yig. k. 88*) I shall again and again sincerely hold intercourse with you on appropriate subjects so as not to be discarded.

དུངས་པ *duṅṣ-pa* a secondary form of གདུངས་པ love, དད་པ་དང་དུངས་པ་ཞིག་སྐྱེས་ཏེ some faith and love having grown. ཡིད་དུངས་=སྙིང་བརྩེ་བ loving, affectionate.

དུད་པ I: *duḍ-pa* 1.=ཞུམ་པ नम्र adj. humble, sbst. mildness, humility, also respect, homage. 2. vb. to lie, to knit, v. འདུད་པ. 3. pf. of འདུད་པ to stoop, bend, to bow down.

དུད་འགྲོ *duḍ-ḥgro* पशु that which walks bending; opposite to man who walks upright; a quadruped, beast, and sometimes used as a general name for all animals except man. Duḍo are of two kinds:—(1) བྱིངས་ན་གནས་པ་ those that live hidden, such as in the sea, underground, &c. 2. ཁ་འཐོར་བ those that live scattered in the abodes of men and gods. དམྱལ་བ་དང་ཡི་དྭགས་ཀྱི་གནས་སུ་ཡང་དུད་འགྲོ་ཡོད it is said that there are Duḍo also in hell and in the region of the *Preta* (ghosts) (*K. d.* འ *2*).

དུད་པ II: (མེ་ཡི་དུ་བ) धूम 1. smoke. 2. कज्जल soot mixed with butter which is applied to the eye-lashes in the East. དུད་ཁ *duḍ-kha* acc. to *Sch.*: (1) having the colour of smoke. (2) a family; household, as smoke-emitters. (3) chimney; དུད་གྲངས *duḍ-grañṣ* number of houses counted by the smoke coming out from each: ཁྲི་བསྐོར་རྣམས་ཀྱི་དུད་གྲངས the number of households or families of *Ŭ* and Tsang under the *Khri-ḅskor* rule. (*Yig.*). དུད་པ་སྔོན *duḍ-pa ṣṅon* the smoke preceding the flames; དུད་བལ *duḍ-bal* soot; དུད་རྩི *duḍ-ṛtsi* id.

དུད་དམག *duḍ-ḍmag* 1. fight or dispute among householders. 2. soldiers recruited from among villagers.

དུད་ཚང *duḍ-tshañ*=མི་ཚང་ a family, a household; དུད་འཚོ *duḍ-ḥtsho*=གྲོང་ཚོ a village, hamlet; དུད་འཚོ་ཁག་བཅུ་གཉིས twelve villages or hamlets.

དུན་པ *dun-pa* (for འདུན་པ) great diligence, assiduity; འདུན་པ་དག་པོ very diligent; in *W.* (cf. འདུན་པ and རྟུན).

དུབ་པ *dub-pa* क्लिन or ལུས་དུབ་པ vb., pf. དུབ་པ to be fatigued, to be tired; ལུས་སེམས་དུབ་པར་མ་གྱུར་ཏམ have you not become fatigued in mind and body (*A. 23.*); adj. tired, fatigued; also དུབ་ཅན; sbst. fatigue; མི་དུབ་པ untired ones; ངལ་ཞིང་དུབ་ནས being fatigued: ལུས་དང་ངག་ཡིད་དུབ he is tired in body, speech, and mind.

དུམ *dum* 1. a small plate or vessel: དུམ་གཅིག་གཏོར་མས་བཀང་བ་ཐོགས་ནས carrying one plate filled with torma offerings (*A. 29*). 2. a small quantity, a little, a bit: དུམ་ཙམ་སྡོད wait just a short while.

དུམ་པ *dum-pa* 1. किञ्चित् some: དུམ་པ་སྟེ it being a little, somewhat. 2. a division, or volume, in the dialect of Amdo: འབུམ་དུམ་པ་བཅུ་གཉིས the twelve volumes of the Bum (scriptures).

དུམ་པོ *dum-po* a large piece, a fragment.

དུམ་བུ *dum-bu*=དམ་དུམ खण्ड a fraction, small piece, a part, a quantity. དུམ་བུར་གཅོག་པ, གཅོད་པ or བྱེད་པ to break, to cut to pieces: ནོར་རྫས་གང་ཡོད་ཐམས་ཅད་དུམ་བུ་གསུམ་ལ་བཏང་ནས་དུམ་བུ་གཉིས་ཕ་མ་ལ་ཐོབ, དུམ་བུ་གཅིག་བུ་ལ་ཐོབ all properties and effects whatever there may be should be divided into three parts—the parents will get two parts and the son one part. དུམ་བུ་ཅན *dum-bu can* fractional; དུམ་བུ་མིན *dum-bu min* दलं, अखण्ड entire. དུམ་བུ་གསུམ *dum-bu gsum* त्रिखण्डक three parts, triple division; དུམ་བུར་གྱུར་པ *dum-bur gyur-pa* divided into parts; དུམ་བུར་བྱེད་པ *dum-bur byed-pa* छिदा to divide.

དུམ་བྲག *Dum-brag* n. of a rock-cavern (*Deb.* ག *21*).

དུམ་ཡང *dum-yañ* in Sikk.=ལས་དཔོན head workman, one who supervises work.

དུམ་བུ་གསུམ་པ *dum-bu gsum-pa*, v. དུར་བྱིད.

དུར་བ *dur-wa* vb. 1. to dispose of the dead, to keep a dead body. 2. དུར *dur* or དུར་ས tomb, grave; དུར་དུ་འཇུག་པ to bury, to inter, to put in the grave; དུར་རྐོ་བ to dig a grave; དུར་ཁུང *dur-khuñ* a grave, tomb.

དུར་ཁྲོད *dur-khrod* श्मशान a cemetery or any place where the dead are disposed of (being buried, cremated, or else cut into pieces for distribution to birds, dogs, etc.). In the N. E. and E. suburbs of Lhasa are two large "dur-t'oi" or cemeteries, attended to by the notorious Rogya-pa or scavengers of the city, whose huts built of bones and horns stand in rows hard by. The different systems of dealing with the dead in East Tibet on the Chinese border, which in the main are identical with the methods in vogue at Lhasa, are fully described by Mr. W. W. Rockhill in his interesting work "The Land of the Lamas."

Syn. འཇིགས་གནས *hjigs-gnas*; སྲེག་གནས *sreg-gnas*; རོ་ཡི་གནས *ro-yi gnas*; ཤི་བའི་གནས *shi-wahi gnas*; ཕ་མེས་ནགས *pha-mes nags*; གཤིན་གྱི་ནགས *gçin-gyi nags* (*Mñon.*).

དུར་ཁྲོད་ཆེན་པོ་བརྒྱད *dur-khrod chen-po brgyad* the eight great historical cemeteries of Magadha mentioned in Mahâyāna works: (1) གཏུམ་དྲག lies in a forest where the fragrant sandal tree abounded; (2) ཚང་ཚིང་འཁྲིགས་པ in a forest of *Bodhi* trees where the sacred fig-tree abounded; (3) འབར་འཁྲིགས་པ in a forest where *Jonesia asoka* abounded; 4. ཀེང་རུས་ཅན in a forest where the བ་རུ་ར myrobalan abounded. 5. བཀྲ་ཤིས་ཚལ or བསིལ་བའི་ཚལ (*Çitavana*) where the species of sandal tree *kasañja* abounded; (6) མུན་པ་ནག་པོ the forest where the glomerous fig-tree abounded; (7) ཀི་ལི་ཀི་ལིར་སྒྲ་སྒྲོག་པ *ki-li ki-lir sgra sgrog-pa* where the *Arjuna* tree abounded; (8) ཧ་ཧ་རྒོད་པ where the banyan tree abounded.

དུར་ཁྲོད་པ *dur-khrod-pa* श्माशानिक a *Tantrik* lama, one who resides in a cemetery for propitiating spirits.

དུར་ཁྲོད་མ *dur-khrod-ma* श्माशानिका an epithet of the goddess Paldan Lhamo.

དུར་རྒྱས *dur-rgyas* अन्तखाद्य the food which is given to a dying man.

དུར་སྒམ *dur-sgam* or དུར་སྒྲོམ coffin.

དུར་རྡོ *dur-rdo* stones piled over one's grave or place of cremation.

དུར་སྤྱང *dur-spyań* lit. "grave-wolf"; perhaps a species of hyena that digs out dead bodies to devour them.

† དུར་བ *dur-wa* 1. to hurry, hasten; དུར་ཏེ་རྒྱུག་པ to run towards a place or object; in colloq. to hasten to: ཟས་ལ་དུར་བ to hasten to dinner; ལས་ལ་དུར་བ to hasten to work; cf. ངམ་དུར་ཅན. 2. दूर्वा, रसाला a kind of grass with syn. ནུས་པ་སྟོང་ལྡན *nus-pa stoń-ldan*; ངན་སྤོང་སྐྱེས *ńan spoń-skyes*; སྐྱེས་ལྡན *skyes-ldan*; མཐའ་ཡས *mthah-yas*; ཚིག་བརྒྱ་བ *tshig brgya-wa*; ས་ཡི་འདབ *sa-yi hdab*; ལྗང་སེར་ཅན *ljań-ser can*; ཚེ་འཕེལ་རྫས *tshe-hphel-rdsas* (*Mńon.*).

དུར་བ་དཀར་པོ *dur-wa dkar-po* 1. भार्गवी the blue or white flowering *dūrwā*; *Panicum dactylon*. 2. गण्डाली, सिता दूर्वा other white species of *durwā*.

Syn. བརྩོན་འགྲུས་བརྒྱ་བ *brston-hgrus brgya-wa*; གླང་སྤུ་སྐྱེས *glań-spu skyes*; བྱ་ཡི་མིག *bya-yi mig*.

དུར་བས་འཆི *dur-was hchi* a scorpion.

Syn. སྡིག་པ་རྦ་ཅན *sdig-pa rba-can* (*Mńon.*).

དུར་བོན *Dur-bon* (lit. the Bon of the cemeteries) one of the earlier sects of Bon-pa which originating in Shang-Shung and Brutsha at last spread into the Tibetan central provinces during the reign of king གྲི་གུམ་བཙན་པོ, the son of སྲིབ་ཁྲི་བཙན་པོ *srib-khri btsan-po*; Lońam his minister under the instigation of the Dur-bon priests assassinated the king with a sword, whence he was called by the historians of Tibet གྲི་གུམ་བཙན་པོ the sword-assasinated king. (*J. Zań.*).

དུར་བྱ *dur-bya* कङ्क 1. also དུར་བྱ་རྒྱབ་དཀར Brahminy kite with white back (*Mńon.*). 2. acc. to *Sch.* a paring-axe, a hoe.

དུར་བྱིད *dur-byid*, (སྨན) त्रिपुटा, कुम्भ 1. the castor-oil plant, *Ricinus communis*. དུར་བྱིད་ཚ་གྲང་ནད་ཀུན་སྦྱོང་བར་བྱེད the root of *dur-byid* ejects all diseases arising from heat or cold. 2. (acc. to *Vai. sń.*) त्रिवृता *Ipomoea turpethum* [a plant of valuable purgative properties, commonly called Tëori, and distinguished into two species, white and black (*Convulvulus turpethum*)] *S*.

Syn. མདའ་འཇོམས *mdah-hjoms*; ཚངས་གསུམ *tshańs-gsum*; དོར་བྱེད་མ *dor byed-ma*; ཕུར་མ་གསུམ་པ *phur-ma gsum-pa*; ཀུན་རྗེས་འབྱུང *kun-rjes-hbyuń*; རྡུལ་ཅན *rdul-can*; ལོ་མ་གསུམ་པ *lo-ma gsum-pa*; དུམ་བུ་གསུམ་པ *dum-bu gsum-pa* (*Mńon.*).

དུར་བྱེད *dur-byed* रेचनी, विषघ्न, निकुम्भ, काल the plant *Croton polyandrum*.

དུར་བྱང *dur-byań* an inscription placed on a tomb.

དུར་ཚུན *dur-tshun*, དུར་ཚོད *dur-tshod* food offered to the dead (*Cs.*).

དུར་མཚེད *dur-mtshed* a place for burying dead bodies (*Sch.*).

དུར་ཡུ *dur-yu*=ཕྱི་རོལ out side, beyond, foreign (mystic) (*K. g.* ཤ 26).

དུར་ལེན *dur-len* (lit. that takes away from the cemetery) a sort of vampire.

དུལ *dul* is perf. root of the trs. vb. འདུལ་བ *hdul-wa* to tame, *q. v.*

དུལ་གནས *dul-gnas* or དུལ་བའི་གནས place of conversion or of one's discipline.

དུལ་བ दम discipline; དུལ་བ་ལེགས sādhudama [good discipline] *S*.

དུལ་བ་པ *dul-wa-pa* दमक a tamer, discipliner. དུལ་བ་ལྷ विनीत देव one of the early Buddhist sages and authors of India.

དུལ་བ་འཛིན *dul-wa hdsin*=བསྒྲུབ་པ་ལ་ཉན་པ obedient, holding to discipline; one who observes the rules of *Vinaya* (*Mńon.*).

འདུལ་བར་འདོད་ *dul-war ḥdod* साहस courage.

དུལ་མ་ *dul-ma* 1. powdered or pulverized by burning, grinding, pounding, etc.; གསེར་དུལ་མ་ gold-dust, also oxidized powder of gold; སྨན་དུལ་མ་ medicinal powders. 2. acc. to *Jä.* a kind of water-colour made of pulverized gold and silver, for painting and writing. Really an erroneous form of རྡུལ་ *rdul.*

དུལ་མོ་ *dul-mo* tender-mouthed, tame, manageable, tractable (*Jä.*).

དུས *dus* काल, समय, वेला, युग 1. time in general, season. 2. =རན a certain time, the time or occasion for a thing to happen; right time, proper season: དུས་ཁྱད་པར་ཅན་ཚེས་བཅུ་ནམ་ཐུང་བའི་ཐུན་མོ་སྔོན་གྱི་དང་པོ་ལ་སྐུ་ལ་དར་ནག་གོས་བེར་གསོལ taking the 10th day of the month as the most appropriate time, when night came on, in the first hour of dusk he would equip himself with a black silk robe and a staff (*Pth. 129*). དུས *dus* adv. for a while, sometimes; དེའི་དུས་སུ at the time; དུས་དེ་ཙ་ན at that time; དེ་དུས, དུས་དེར then, at this time; དུས་དེ་ཉིད་དུ in that very time; དང་ པོའི་དུས་ཉིད་དུ in the very first time; དུས་སུ or དུས་དུས་སུ at times; དུས་འགའ་རེ sometimes, now and then; དེ་དང་དུས་མཉམ་དུ simultaneously with that; དེ་ནས་དུས་རེ་ཞིག་གི་ཚེ then on occasion; དུས་གཅིག་ན on a certain time, once; དུས་གཅིག་ཏུ or དུས་གཅིག་ལ at one and the same time, together; དུས་ཕྱིས་ཞིག་ན some future day. The statement that the time had arrived for anything is always phrased: it came down to the time དུས་ལ་བབ་སོང་; the time will arrive: དུས་ལ་འབབ་ཡོང་ it will descend to the time. དུས or དུས་ན after a genit. inf. or verbal root=when, after: ཞག་གཉིས་སོང་དུས when two days had, or will have passed; ང་བུ་མོའི་དུས་ན་ཡིན་ཏེ when I was still a girl; མགུ་དུས་མེད the time of merriment never arrives; བཙའ་དུས་ཏེ being the time of giving birth; འགྲོ་བའི་དུས་འདེབས་པ to fix a time for going; དུས་ད་ནས henceforth, from this time forward; དུས་ཀྱི་ཁྱད་པར *dus-kyi khyad-par* कालविशेष special time, special occasion.

དུས་ཀྱི་འཁོར་ལོ *Dus-kyi ḥkhor-lo* कालचक्र 1. the famous Kala-chakra system of Buddhism which introduced the worship of a Supreme Deity under the designation of Adi-buddha or ཐོག་མའི་སངས་རྒྱས. It arose in the 11th century A.D. in Shambala, a city said to have been located near the river Oxus in Central Asia; and both Atis'a and the historian Buston belonged to this cult. Under the appellation *Tsakun Kürden* it is popular with the Mongols. Varieties of the cult in India gave to S'iva or to Ganes'a the position of Adi-Buddha. 2. ནང་དུས་ཀྱི་འཁོར་ལོ=སེམས་ཅན animated nature or living beings; གཞན་དུས་ཀྱི་འཁོར་ལོ=ནང་གི་བསྒོམ meditation. 3. v. དུས་འཁོར *dus-ḥkhor*.

དུས་ཀྱི་ཆ་ཤས *dus-kyi cha-ças* the divisions of time—such as ལོ year; ཟླ་ར་བ season; ཟླ month; ordinarily the year ལོ is divided into four seasons, each of three months; but according to the *Vinaya* school the seasons are six, divided in reference to the *Uposatha* observances, and are:—དཔྱིད་ཀ་གཉིས two spring months, སོས་ཀ་གཉིས two summer months, དབྱར་གཉིས two rainy months, སྟོན་གཉིས two autumn or harvesting months, དགུན་གཉིས two winter months, དགུན་སྨད་གཉིས two deep-winter months. Tibetans also divide the year into three seasons, counting དཔྱིད་སོས spring and summer together, དབྱར་སྟོན rains and autumn together, and དགུན་སྟོད and དགུན་སྨད anterior winter and posterior winter together.

དུས་ཀྱི་ཆོས་ཉིད *dus-kyi chos-ñid* कालधर्म met. death (*Mñon.*).

དུས་ཀྱི་རྗེས་སུ་འགྲོ་བ *dus-kyi rjes-su hgro-wa* कालानुसारि one who behaves or changes according to the occasion; a wind-cock. [also, it is a phrase signifying benzoin or benjamin]S.

དུས་ཀྱི་རྗེས་སུ་འབྲང་བའི་ཙན་དན *dus-kyi rjes-su hbrañ-wahi tsan-dan* कालानुसारिचन्दन yellow sandal.

དུས་ཀྱི་བདག་པོ *dus-kyi bdag-po* met. the sun, the lord of time (*Mñon.*).

དུས་ཀྱི་གནས *dus-kyi gnas* ऋतुवृत्ति [revolution of the seasons; a year]S.

དུས་ཀྱི་དབྱིད་པ *dus-kyi dbyid-pa* कालदण्ड [the staff of time, death]S.

དུས་ཀྱི་བྱེད་པོ *dus-kyi byed-po* कालकृत्, सूर्य the sun; the maker of time.

དུས་ཀྱི་བར *dus-kyi-bar* during; आकालिक [momentary]S.

དུས་ཀྱི་མེ་ཏོག *dus-kyi me-tog*, v. མཐིང་ *mthiñ* deep blue (*Mñon.*).

དུས་ཀྱི་བརྩི་ཚུལ *dus-kyi brtsi-tshul* the manner of counting time:—120 of དུས་མཐའི་སྐད་ཅིག་པ *dus-mthahi skad-cig-pa* (the smallest conceivable division of time) make one བྱ་རྫོགས་ཀྱི་སྐད་ཅིག་མ *bya rdsogs-kyi skad-cig-ma* (སེ་གོལ་གཏོགས་པ *se-gol gtogs-pa*); 60 of this latter make one ཐང་ *thañ*; 30 ཐང་ *thañ* make a ཡུད་ཙམ *yud-tsam*; and 30 ཡུད *yud* make one ཞག *shag* or day. Acc. to the system of counting adopted by Tibetan astronomers (སྐར་རྩིས་པ *skar rtsis-pa*) four drawings of breath in an adult make one ཆུ་སྲང་ *chu-srañ*, 60 ཆུ་སྲང་ *chu-srañ* make one ཆུ་ཚོད *chu-tshod*, 60 ཆུ་ཚོད *chu-tshod* make one ཞག *shag* (day and night); sixty years make one རབ་བྱུང་ *rab-byuñ* or cycle.

དུས་ཀྱི་ཚིགས *dus-kyi-tshigs* कालसन्द [a summons by the angel of death]S.

དུས་བཀག་པ *dus bkag-pa* explained as ཡོད་པ་ལག་དང་མེད་པ་དུས *yodpa-lag dañ med-pa dus*.

དུས་སྐབས *dus-skabs* v. སྐབས *skabs*.

དུས་སྐྱེས *dus-skyes* कालज, कुसुम=སྐྱེར་ཤིང་ *skyer-çiñ* prob. *Berberis vulgaris* called སྐྱེར་པ *skyer-pa* or ཤིང་སེར *çiñ-ser* the yellow plant.

དུས་འཁོར *dus-hkhor* कालचक्र [the wheel of time]S.

Syn. མཆོག་གི་དང་པོའི་སངས་རྒྱས *mchog-gi dañ-pohi sañs-rgyas*; ཐབས་ཤེས་བདག་ཉིད *thabs-çes bdag-ñid*; རྡོ་རྗེ་སེམས་དཔའ *rdo-rje sems-dpah*; ཨེ་ཝཾ་ཡི་གེ་རིགས་མེད་པ *e-wam yi-ge rigs med-pa*; ཤེས་དང་ཤེས་བྱའི་བདག་ཉིད་མཆོག *çes-dañ çes-byahi bdag-ñid mchog*; ཞི་བ་སྡོམས་ལ་འདུས་པ *shi-wa sdoms-la hdus-pa*; འཕོ་མེད *hpho-med*; ཐོག་མེད *thog-med*; ཐ་མ་མེད *tha-ma med*; རིགས་ཀུན་ཁྱབ་དག *rigs-kun khyab-dag*; བྱང་ཆུབ་སེམས *byañ-chub sems*; རྣལ་འབྱོར་རྣམ་པ *rnal-hbyor rnam-pa*; རྣམ་ཀུན་མཆོག་ལྡན *rnam-kun mchog-ldan*; ཐོག་མའི་མགོན་པོ *thog-mahi mgon-po*; གཉིས་སུ་མེད *gñis-su med*; ཁམས་གསུམ་འཁོར་ལོས་བསྒྱུར་བ *khams-gsum hkhor-los bsgyur-wa*. (*Mñon.*).

དུས་འཁོར་པཎྜི་ཏ *Dus-hkhor pandita* n. of a celebrated lama born in Mongolia who was recognised as an incarnation by the Emperor of China. He founded the monastery of *Pad-dkar cho-gliñ* now harbouring three thousand monks.

དུས་འགྱུར *dus-hgyur* ऋतुपरिवर्त्त; change of season.

དུས་ཅན *dus-can* कालिक; n. of a flower; དུས་ཅན་ཆེན་པོ महाकालिक n. of a flower (*K. my.* ཀ *20*).

དུས་གཅིག་སྐྱེས་པའི་མ་བུ *dus-gcig skyes-pahi ma-bu*=མགྲོན་བུ་བུ་མ (mystic) (*Miñ-rda. 4*).

དུས་ཆད་པ་མེད་པ *dus chad-pa med-pa* कालिक in proper time, timely; time without interruption, continually.

དུས་ཆེན་དགེ་བ་འབུམ་འགྱུར *dus-chen dge-wa hbum hgyur* the days when one work of merit done produces one hundred thousand merits; they are: the 8th lunar day of the month of *Vaiçakha* when Gautama Buddha renounced the world; the 15th or full moon of the same month when he was conceived; the day when he became a Buddha; the day he entered *Nirvāṇa*; the day of his preaching the *Dharma*; the day when he descended from among the gods. དུས་ཆེན་བཞི *dus-chen bshi* or དུས་ཆེན་པོ་བཞི the great periods of time or *Yuga*.

དུས་མཆོད *dus-mchod* ऋत्विक्, कालाय religious service observed at certain prescribed periods [a priest for performing a sacrifice]*S*.

དུས་སྟོན *dus-ston* or དགའ་སྟོན उत्सव a festival (*Mñon.*). དུས་སྟོན་དགུ the nine festivals observed by Buddhists:—དུས་སྟོན་ཆེན་པོ *dus-ston chen-po* महोत्सव great festival; བཙས་སྟོན जातकर्म birth festival; རལ་པ་འབྲེག་པའི་དུས་སྟོན गोदान the festival of cutting the hair; གཙུག་ཕུད་ཀྱི་དུས་སྟོན चूडाकरण-उत्सव festival of forming the crest; ལོ་ལྔའི་དུས་སྟོན festival at the fifth year of child; ལོ་དྲུག་གི་དུས་སྟོན the sixth year festival; གཙུག་ལག་ཁང་གི་དུས་སྟོན the monastic or *vihāra* festival; དགའ་སྟོན आनन्द-उत्सव festive rejoicing. དུས་སྟོན་བྱེད་པ *dus-ston byed-pa* to keep a festival.

དུས་བཏབ་པ *dus btab-pa* to fix time (for meeting, etc.). དུས་བཏབ་མ *dus btab-ma*=བུད་མེད་འདོད་ལྡན་མ a passionate woman (*Mñon.*).

དུས་མཐའི་རླུང *dus-mthahi rluṅ*=བསྐལ་པ་འཇིག་པའི་རླུང་ प्रलयवायु the wind that will destroy the world.

དུས་དང་མི་སྦྱོར་བར་རྣམ་པར་གྲོལ་བ असमय-विमुक्त one of the 20 stages a monk of the *Çrāvaka* school reaches [delivered at a wrong time]*S*.

དུས་དུས་སུ *dus-dus-su* at times, occasionally.

དུས་འདས *dus-ḥdas* ऊर्ध्वं, अतीत, कालातीत; past time, past tense; time elapsed.

དུས་ལྡན *Dus-ldan* कालिक n. of one of the 16 *sthavira* or གནས་བརྟན; also: goddess; sandal-wood.

དུས་ལྡན་མ *dus-ldan-ma* a woman in menstruation (*Mñon.*).

དུས་ན་དགའ་བ་ཤེས་བྱ་བའི་རི *Dus-na dgaḥ-wa shes bya-wahi ri* a mountain in the fabulous continent of Uttara Kuru (*K. d.* ར *315*).

དུས་རྣམ་པ་ཀུན *dus rnam-pa kun* all times; with ལ, as adv. always, at all times (*Mñon.*).

དུས་བབས *dus-babs* appointed time; the natural course of events.

དུས་སྦྱོར *dus-sbyor* लग्न, विलग्न [the particular time in which a man is born]*S*. དུས་སྦྱོར་པ *dus-sbyor-pa* an astrologer. དུས་སྦྱོར་བྱེད་པ *dus-sbyor byed-pa* होरा [the hour in which a man is born]*S*. དུས་འབྱོར་པ *dus-sbyor-pa* लग्न junction of periods, time, &c. [the particular sign of the zodiac under which a man is born]*S*.

དུས་མ་ཡིན་པར་ཟ་བ *dus ma-yin-par za-wa* अकाल-भोजन taking food untimely, *i.e.*, not at the fixed or prescribed time or hour; དུས་མིན་ཤེས་པ *dus-min çes-pa* समयज्ञ one who knows the fixed times or seasons; a cock; an astrologer.

དུས་མེ *dus-me* कालाग्नि lately said to=universal conflagration at the end of time.

དུས་ཚིགས *dus-tshigs* ऋतु season. དུས་ཚིགས་ཀུན་འགྲོ=བྱ་འཇོལ་མོ the jolmo bird (*Mñon.*). དུས་ཚིགས་གསར་བ *dus-tshigs gsar-wa*=དུས་འགྱུར་བ change of time, season; also fresh provision, produce of the year, etc.

དུས་ཚོད *dus-tshod* 1. a division of time equal to two English hours: ཉིན་རེ་ལ་དུས་ཚོད་བཅུ་གཉིས in each day are twelve *dus-tshod*. Acc. to the Chinese method each of these has a separate name attached to it, viz:—(1) ནམ་ལངས day-break, called ཡོས yoş rabbit; (2) ཉི་ཤར sun-rise, called ḥbrug (ḍuk) dragon; (3) ཉི་དྲོས morning, called şbrul (ḍul) serpent; (4) ཉི་ཕྱེད ñi-phyeḍ noon called, ṛta horse; (5) ཕྱེད་ཡོལ afternoon, called lug sheep; (6) evening, called şprel monkey; (7) ཉི་ནུབ sunset, called bya bird; (8) ས་སྲོས dusk, called khyi dog; (9) སྲོད་འཁོར fore-night, called phag pig; (10) ནམ་ཕྱེད mid-night, called byi-wa mouse; (11) ཕྱེད་ཡོལ after-night, called གླང glañ ox; (12) ཐོ་རངས dawn, called ştag tiger. These twelve names are also given to the succeeding years of the 60 years cycle in various combinations with the names of five so-called elements, viz., earth, fire, water, wood, iron, v. ལོ lo.

དུས་ཚོད་ཉེས་པ duş-tshoḍ ñeş-pa evil-hour, bad time=དུས་ཚོད་ནོར་བ wrong or inauspicious time or hour.

དུས་མཚན duş-mtshan: कलिङ्गराज the king of Kalinga, a descendant of Chakravarti raja.

དུས་མཚམས duş-mtshamş सन्ध्या, सन्ध्यावेला junction of day and night; period, epoch.

དུས་བཞི duş-bshi the four seasons, viz:—དབྱར the summer; དགུན the winter; སྟོན the autumn; དཔྱིད the spring time; also ནང morning or day; ནུབ evening or night; ཉིན day-time, and མཚན night.

དུས་བཞིའི་ཕང་ལོ duş-bshiḥi phañ-lo=འཁོར་ལོ the four times wheel; a cycle of years.

དུས་བཞིའི་ལྷ་མོ Duş-bshiḥi lha-mo or རྒྱལ་མོ the goddesses presiding over the four seasons:—དཔྱིད་ཀྱི་རྒྱལ་མོ་སྐྱ་མདོག་དཀར the white fair queen of spring; དབྱར་གྱི་རྒྱལ་མོ་སྔོན་མོ the blue queen of the summer season; སྟོན་གྱི་རྒྱལ་མོ་མདོག་སེར་མོ the yellow queen of the autumn; དགུན་གྱི་རྒྱལ་མོ་སྐྱ་མདོག་ནག the black queen of the winter season (*B. ch.*).

དུས་ཟིང duş-ziñ time of depravity (*Sch.*).

དུས་ཡོལ་བ duş yol-wa पर्यवनुप्राप्त lit. time passed; too late.

དུས་རིང་པོ duş riñ-po चिरान्तर long delayed.

དུས་རླབས duş-ṛlabş वेला wave of time, *i.e.*, ebb and flow of time.

དུས་ལ་དགའ་བ duş-la dgaḥ-wa सूर्य्य, कालप्रिय that delights in time; an epithet of the sun (*Mñon.*).

དུས་ལོག duş-log a year yielding no crops; a sterile year (*Jä.*).

དུས་ཤེས་པ duş-çeş-pa कालज्ञ an astronomer or astrologer; རྩིས་པ ṛtsiş-pa (*Mñon.*).

དུས་སུ་སྐྱེ་བ duş-su şkye-wa mature; born or grown at the proper time.

དུས་སུ་ཐོབ་པ duş-su thob-pa to get at the opportune time or hour.

དུས་སུ་འོས་པ duş-su ḥoş-pa कालसदृश suiting the occasion, opportune; དེ་དུས་སུ་འོས་པ तत्कालसदृश as suited the occasion.

དུས་སུ་རུང་བ duş-su ruñ-wa कालिक timely.

དུས་གསུམ duş-gsum त्रिकाल the three times, viz:—(1) སྔ་ཕྱི་ད early, after and now, described as མ་འོངས་པ future, འདས་པ the past, and ད་ལྟ་བ the present. དུས་གསུམ་མཁྱེན་པ duş-gsum mkhyen-pa त्रिकालज्ञ a general epithet of a Buddha. དུས་གསུམ་མཚམས duş-gsum mtshamş त्रिसन्धि the three junctions of time.

དེ I: de तत्, सः 1. that, that one; he, she, it; དེ་བཞིན like that; གང་ཡིན་པ་དེ that which is; དེ་ལས་གུང་གཞན other than that; དེའི་ཕྱིར for that; དེའི་འོག་ཏུ under that, after that; དེའི་དུས་སུ at that time; སྔོན་ལ་སོང་བ་དེ he that has gone before. 2. དེ frq. stands in the place of the definite article—the: ལུག་འདི་ཁྲིད་འོངས་པའི་ཤན་པ་དེ་ངའི་ལྷམ་ཅག་རྐུ་སོང *lug-ḥdi khriḍ-ḥonş-paḥi çan-pa de ñaḥi lham-cag ṛku-soñ* the butcher who brought the sheep stole my boots; གཞོན་ནུ་དེ་ན་རེ the younger one said, or the youth replied; also sometimes in the plural: དེ་ཁྱེད་ཅག་ཡིན་ནམ་ཞེས་སྨྲས་པས he said—were you they or those ones (*Hbrom. 55*).

དེ II: (in mystic) a term for she; དེ་ཞེས་བྱ་བ་བུད་མེད་ཡིན the term 'de' is a woman (*K. g.* ཁ *1;9*).

དེ་ཀ *de-ka* or དེ་ཁ *de-kha* that, the very same; གང་ཟག་དེ་ཀ་ང་ཡིན that very person was I myself; དེ་ཀ་ལྟར just so; དེ་ཀ་ཡོད (in answer to a question) indeed! that is so; དེ་ཀ་ལགས just that.

དེ་ཁ *de-kha* = དེ་ཀ: དེ་ཁ་སྤུན་ཚོང་ནས from those same public bodies.

དེ་ཁུལ *de-khul* = དེ་ཁོངས or དེ་འོག that jurisdiction; also under that, included in that.

དེ་ཁོ་ན *de kho-na* तत, एवं; cf. ཁོ་ན; = the col. དེ་རང་ the very same, that itself. དེ་ཁོ་ན་ཉིད *de kho-na ñid* तत्त्व; = སྟོང་ཉིད *Sūnyatā*, essence, nature; སེམས་ཀྱི་དེ་ཁོ་ན་ཉིད the essence of the soul. དེ་ཁོ་ན་ཉིད་བསྡུས་པ *de kho-na ñid bdus-pa* तत्त्वार्थसमोह n. of a Buddhist metaphysical work: ཞི་བ་འཚོའི་བརྟན་བཅོས་དེ་ཁོ་ན་ཉིད་བསྡུས་པ་ཞེས་བྱ་བ་བོད་དུ་བསྣམས་ནས་བྱོན he proceeded in the direction of Tibet carrying with him the religious work called *Tattva-samuccaya* by Santi-jīva (*A. 33*). དེ་ཁོ་ན་ཉིད་རྟོགས་པ *de kho-na ñid rtogs-pa* तत्त्वभूत to meditate on the real *tattva* or secrets of religion.

དེ་ག *de-ga* colloq. that, that one; precisely so, just so; དེ་གར *de-gar* = དེ་རུ or དེར there, in that place.

དེ་ཉིད *de-ñid* तदेव, सएव that itself; དེ་ཉིད་སྨྲ་བ *de-ñid smra-wa* तत्त्ववादिन one who expounds the truth.

དེ་སྙེད *de-sñed* = དེ་སྙེད तावत so many: མི་ཇི་སྙེད་ཡོད་པ་དེ་སྙེད་ཀྱི་སྐལ་བ་དགོས so many men as there are so many shares are required.

དེ་ལྟ *de-lta* like that; so; is fig. in books, but in colloq. དེ་འདྲ is used instead: ཕ་ནི་དེ་ལྟ་མ་ཡིན་ཏེ not being so with the father; དེ་ལྟ་འདུ་ཤེས་པས *de lta-hdu çes-pas* तत्सत्ज्ञाया: being known as that; དེ་ལྟ་ན *de-lta-na* like this; དེ་ལྟ་བུ *de-lta-bu* एवंरूप of that kind, quality, or manner; such; དེ་ལྟ་བུ་བྱུང་བར་བརྗོད་པ इतिहास history, oral account, narration of accounts; དེ་ལྟ་མོད་ཀྱི *de-lta mod-kyi* तथापि, किन्तर्हि yet, notwithstanding that; དེ་ལྟ་ཡང་ *de-lta-yañ* अथच and yet; དེ་ལྟ་ལ *de-lta-la* = འོན་ཀྱང although.

དེ་ཅིའི་ཕྱིར་ཞེ་ན *de-cihi-phyir-she-na* is a curious paraphrase, used chiefly in the older classical writings, but not quite disused still, to express the conjunctions "for" and "because" at the beginning of a consequent clause or sentence. It is sometimes varied to དེ་ཅིའི་སླད་དུ་ཞེ་ན *de-cihi-slad-du she-na* (*K.* ང *3, etc.*), both meaning lit. "if asked, because of what is that." Curiously enough the Mongols have adopted in their sacred writings a similar phrase for the same conjunctions: *tere dzagun-u tula kemebessu.*

དེ་ལྟར *de-ltar* = དེ་སྐད इति, एवं, तथा, तादृक् like that, accordingly; དེ་ལྟར་གྱིས་ཤིག *de-ltar gyis-çig* एवं कुरु do accordingly; དེ་ལྟར་ན *de-ltar-na* एवंहि thus indeed; དེ་ལྟར་ཡང་ *de-ltar-yañ* अथच yet.

དེ་ཐད *de-thad* = དེ་ཕྱིར for that; also therefore: དེ་ཐད་རིམ་པར་བརྩི་བའི་ཚིག therefore, the words to be put together or in order (*Ya-sel. 34*).

དེ་དང་ *de-dañ* तेनैव by that very (thing) དེ་དང་འདྲ་བ *de-dañ hdra-wa* तत्सदृश like that.

དེ་དུས *de-dus* तत्काल that time; དེ་དུས་སུ་རུང་བ तत्कालसदृश fit for that time.

དེ་དེ *de-de* exactly that; that (emphatically); དེ་དེ་བཞིན་ནོ तत्, तथेति just according to that; yes, so it is.

དེ་དོན *de-don* तदर्थ for that.

དེ་ལྡན *de-ldan* सत्य truth.

དེ་འདྲ *de-hdra* is the modern and colloq. usage in place of དེ་ལྟ *de-lta* or དེ་ལྟ་བུ *de-lta-bu* like that, similar, similarly; དེ་འདྲ་མཐོང་ seen like that, seen so; དེ་འདྲ་ཕངས *de-hdra-phaṅs* विगर्ह an interj.: such a loss! so great a damage! དེ་འདྲ་མ *de-hdra-ma* तादृशी like that (applied to fem.).

དེ་ན *de-na* or དེ་ནས=དེ་རྗེ अथो, अथ therein, in that place; also thereafter, after that.

དེ་ནས་འདི་སྐད *de-nas hdi-skad* अथ एवं then for instance, then like this, then so.

དེ་ནི *de-ni* that, that one, it, those indeed: དེ་ནི་གནས་མ་ཡིན it is not the proper place.

དེ་པ *de-pa* one of that place; but in *C.* colloq.=there, thither; དེ་བས *de-was* ततः 1. than that, gen. after a comparative. 2. also for དེ་བས་ན therefore, consequently, now then.

དེ་པོ *de-po*=རབ་ཏུ, ཤིན་ཏུ well, excellent (*Yig. k. 88*).

དེ་ཕོ *de-pho* a cock.

དེ་འཕྲལ *de-hphral* तत्क्षणः immediately, at once. In colloq. in *C.* we hear དེ་ལྟ་འཕྲལ་དུ "*tanta t'el-tu*" immediately.

དེ་འཕྲོས *de-hphros*=དེ་ལྷག the remainder, excess thereof (*Ya-sel. 48*), the excess portion.

དེ་བས *de-was* than that; དེ་བས་ཀྱང་ *de-was kyaṅ* ततोऽपि more than that.

དེ་མ *de-ma* one of that place, sect, religion, etc. (*Cs.*); དེ་མ་ཐག་ཏུ *de-ma-thag-tu* सद्य at once, freshly, instantly; དེ་མ་ཐག་པ *de-ma-thag-pa* समनन्तर्य fresh, immediate; དེ་མ་ལགས *de-ma-lags*=དེ་མ་ཉིད *de-ma-ñid* not that, not the same; དེ་མ་ཐག་པའི་རྐྱེན समनन्तर प्रत्यय immediate cause or dependence, v. རྒྱུ་རྐྱེན་བཞི (*M.V.*).

卐 **དེ་མོ** *de-mo*=དགོས་པ necessity.

དེ་ཙམ *de-tsam* तन्मात्र, एतावान्, इयान्, तावि:, एतावत् so much, about that; དེ་ཙམ་ན=དེ་ཙ་ན then, at that time, at about that time; དེ་ཙུག *de-tsug* so, thus: དེ་ཙུག་ལགས=དེ་གང་འདྲ་རེད how is it? how is that? what is it like? (*Deb.* ག *38*).

དེ་ཚོ *de-tso*=དེ་དག or དེ་རྣམས those: དེ་ཚོ་ལ་ཉིད་རེ་འཛིན་ཕྱུར་ཕྱུམ་ཚོགས་པ་མངའ་བས they possessed perfect contemplative skill (*A. 124*).

དེ་མཚུངས *de-mtshuṅs*=དེ་འདྲ *de-hdra* सदृश like that, its match, equal.

དེ་འཛིན *de-hdsin* प्रतिग्रह=acceptance.

དེ་བཞིན་ཉིད *de-bshin ñid* तथता, एवं, तत्त्व identity, essence (*Was.*), lit. that-ness; དེ་བཞིན་དུ *de-bshin-du* एवमेव according to that, thus, so; acc. to *Jä.*=for it: དེ་བཞིན་དུ་གནང་ངོ he allowed it accordingly; དེ་བཞིན་ངོ་ཤེས་ནས *de-bshin ño-çes-nas* perceiving it as such; དེ་བཞིན་དུ་སྦྱར་བ *de-bshin-du sbyar-wa*=སྔོན་མ་བཞིན་དུ་སྦྱར་བ to apply as before, to adjust accordingly; དེ་བཞིན་བྱེད་པ *de-bshin byed-pa* एवं कृत to do accordingly; དེ་བཞིན་མིན *de-bshin min* अन्यथा not accordingly, differently.

དེ་བཞིན་གཤེགས་པ *de-bshin gçegs-pa* तथागत lit. he who is gone or passed away like as did that other one—like as did his predecessor; in other words, a Tathagata or evangelistic teaching Buddha. The Mongol synonym for the Tibetan term is *Tegün ehilen ireksen* "came like him." Shakya-thubpa or Gautama together with the six preceding terrestrial Buddhas form the seven pre-eminent Tathagatas. But we read of "thousands of Tathagatas" in the later Māhāyana writings. དེ་བཞིན་གཤེགས་པའི་སྙིང་རྗེ་ཆེན་པོ་བསྟན་པ तथागत महाकरुणा निर्देश n. of a religious work. དེ་བཞིན་གཤེགས་པ་སྐྱེ་བ་འབྱུང་བ་བསྟན་པ तथागतोत्पत्ति स्वभाव निर्देश n. of a religious work. དེ་བཞིན་གཤེགས་པ་ཐམས་ཅད་ཀྱི་ཡེ་ཤེས་ཀྱི་ཕྱག་རྒྱའི་ཏིང་ངེ་འཛིན सर्व्वतथागतज्ञानमुद्रा-समाधि n. of a religious work (*M.V.*).

དེ་ཟུག *de-zug* = དེ་ཙུག in *W.*

དེའི་ཆོས་ཅན *dehi chos-can* तद्धर्म्मा, तद्धर्म्मक possessed of that virtue; its attributes; of that quality.

དེའི་རྗེས་སུ་ཕྱོགས་པ *dehi rjes-su phyogs-pa* तदनुवर्त्तक imitating (considered as an inexcusible sin in a Budh. monk); following that; its follower.

དེའི་མོད་ལ *dehi mod-la* = དེའི་དུས་ལ or དེའི་ངང་ལ or དེའི་ཚེ at that time, during that time: དེའི་མོད་ལ་ནམ་ལངས་སོང་བས in the meantime the night was over (*Rdsa. 10*).

དེ་ཧོག *de-hog* ततः then, thereafter.

དེ་འང *de hañ* = དེ་ཡང.

དེ་ཡང *de-yañ* यथा 1. this also, or that too; he also. 2. namely, to wit, viz.; is used before any specification or detailed statement.

དེ་ཡན *de-yan* for དེ་ཡན་ཆད also that, preceding it (*Ya-sel. 35*).

དེ་རག *de-rag* directly, immediately (*Sch.*)

དེ་རང *de-rañ* = དེ་ཀོ་ན, དེ་རང་ཡིན that is just the thing! exactly! to be sure (*Jä.*).

དེ་རིང *de-riñ* = དེ་རིང་ཉི་མ अद्य colloq. to-day, this day. In *W. T.* འདི་རིང *hdi-ring* is more frq. དེ་རིང་བྱུང་བ *de-riñ byuñ-wa* अद्यतन a fresh occurrence; to day's outcome, produce, experience.

དེ་རུ *de-ru* = དེར into that, there, into that place, thither, that way.

དེ་ལ་རག་ལུས་པ་ཤེས *de-la rag-lus-pa shes* तद्विधेयत्वात् (བསྒོས་པ་བཞིན་བྱེད་པ) to do as directed, or as per design.

· དེ་ལས *de-las* ततः, तस्मात् from; out of; from that; after a comparative: and, other than that: དེ་ལས་སྐྱེས *de-las skyes* grown or born from or out of that; དེ་ལས་ཅི་འགྱུར་ཤེས what results from that? དེ་ལས་སྩོགས་པ *de-las stsogs-pa* एवंप्रमुखाः [having these as their mouth-pieces, *i.e.*, like these]*S.*

དེ་ཤོ *De-ço* n. of a tribe in Tibet. དེ་ཤོ་ལེགས n. of a king of Tibet (*J. Zañ.*).

དེ་སྲིད *de-srid* तावतिक, तावत् as much as that; thus far; also that is possible.

\+ དེག་གོ *deg-go* or ནོན་ནོ *non-no* used in ཡར་དེག་གོ keep it above, put it up.

དེང *deñ* also དེང to-day; དེང་ནས from this day forward; དེང་ཕྱིན་ཆད henceforth; དེང་གི་དུས = ད་ལྟ the present time or age. དེང་གསལ་འོད་དཔག་ཏུ་མེད་ཁྱབ་ལས = སྔོན་པས་ཁྲིམས་སྲུང་རབ་ཏུ་བྱུང་བའི་ལེ3. དེང་གི་ཆར་ཡང *deñ-gi char-yañ* = དེང་སང་གི་དུས་ནའང even at the present time, even now-a-days (*Yig. k. 14*). དེང་ཕན *deñ-phan* = དེ་ནས་ཕན་ཆད henceforth, henceforward.

དེངས་པ *deñs-pa* 1. or དེང་བ *deñ-wa*, pf. of འདེང་བ *hdeñ-wa* to go, to go away; མི་སོའི་གནས་སུ་དེངས went to their respective places; རང་སར་དེངས་སོ went each to his own place; ནམ་མཁར་དེང melted away into space, dissolved into air. 2. old, stale, worn.

དེང་སང *deñ-sañ* at present; for the present; now-a-days: དེང་སང་ལྷ་རྗེ *deñ-sañ lha-rje* the physician of the present day.

དེར *der* = དེ་རུ *de-ru* तत्रैव there; also as an adv.: then, at that time: དེར་ཟད དེར་བས that is all, there is nothing more (*Cs.*); དེར་གསལ *der-gsal* as mentioned, as stated therein; acc. to that. དེས *des* तेन, तया 1. instrum. of དེ; by that. དེས་ཆོག*des-chog*=དེ་ཡིས་ཆོག that is enough; that will do *Sch.* 2. for དེ་བས, v. དེ: ང་དེས་ཆོག that is enough for me (*A. 128*). དེས་ན་དེའི་ཕྱིར *des-na dehi-phyir* अतः, एतस्मात् कारणात् that then, on that very account then.

དེ་བ *de-wa* a medicinal herb: དེ་བས་རིམས་སེལ་རྒྱ་མཁྲིས་མཁྲིས་ནད་སེལ the *dewa*, removing the communicating cause, dispels biliousness.

དེ་བ་ས་ར *De-wa sa-rā* n. of a learned Singhalese nun who with ten companion-nuns visited China and preached Buddhism there (*Grub.* ཀ *6*).

དེ་བི་ཀོ་ཊ *De-bi ko-ṭa* an ancient city in India, probably near the cave temples of Ellora and Ajanta.

+ དེའུ *dehu*=ཆུང་བ small; adv. almost; ཆུ་བོ་གང་གཱའི་འགྲམ་ན་བྲག་དེའུ་ཞིག་ཡོད་པའི་སྟེང་དུ (*A. 59*) on a small rock standing on the bank of the river Gaṅgā; རྟ་ཆུར་མཆོངས་ཏེ་ཁུ་སྟོན་དེའུ་ཤི་སྐད the horse having leaped into the water, Khu-ston nearly died; དེའུ་མིན་ན *dehu-min-na*=ཏིག་ཙམ་མིན་ན but for a little; དེའུ་མིན་ན་ཐོག did hit (him) almost; དེའུ་ཚིག་ཙམ *dehu-tshig tsam*=དེའུ་མིན་ན་ལྷུང་ཙམ but for that, he had almost fallen down (*D.R.*); དེའུ་གཡེངས་ཙམ *dehu gyeṅs-tsam*=དེའུ་མིན་ན་གཡེང་བ (*D.R.*).

དེའུ་ར *dehu-ra* (vulg.) ཉུང་ཟད 1. a little, almost: ང་དེའུ་ར་མིན་ན་ཐོག་ཁ་ནས་ལྷུང་བ་ཡོད were it not for a little, I had fallen down from the roof. 2. acc. to *Jä.* one day, some future time.

དེད་འདྲེན *ded-hdren* वाहन (ཕྱུགས) n. of a large numerical figure (*Ya-sel. 57*). དེད་འདྲེན་ཆེན་པོ महावाहन n. of a still larger number than the above (*Ya-sel. 57*).

དེད་པ *ded-pa* driven, carried, moved, pursued; pf. of འདེད་པ *q. v.*

དེད་དཔོན *ded-dpon* सार्थवाह foreign-trader, master, captain of a ship. དེད་དཔོན་ཁང་པ=ཚོང་ཁང་ merchant's place, commercial building, shop (*Mṅon.*). དེད་དཔོན་ཆེན་པོ་ सुसार्थवाह merchant; དེད་དཔོན་དབྱངས་ལྡན=འདོད་ལྷའི་བུ an epithet of the son of Kāma (*Mṅon.*).

དེབ *deb* अक्षर, कोष or ཡི་གེའི་མཛོད library, archives, records; དངོས་པོའི་དཀར་ཆག a list or register of articles, &c.; དེབ་ཁང་ *deb-khaṅ* chancery, government office (*Schtr.*); དེབ་ཐེར *deb-ther* or དེབ་ཡིག register; documents, catalogues, anything recorded or put into writing or stitched together; བོ་རྒྱུས་རྣམས་གཅིག་ཏུ་དེབ་པ to register all accounts or put them together in one book; དེབ་ཐེར་མཁན *deb-ther mkhan* keeper of the archives or librarian (*Cs.*).

དེབ་ཐེར་སྔོན་པོ *Deb-ther sṅon-po* the n. of a historical work by *Gshon-nu dpal.*

དེབ་པ *deb-pa* 1. accounts cast into one place or shape; བོ་རྒྱུས་སོགས་གཅིག་ཏུ་དེབ་པ to cast all accounts or records into one place. 2. acc. to *Sch.*: poultice, cataplasm, applied to sores and inflamed parts of the body.

དེམ་ཙི *dem-tsi* a small, narrow bridge; foot-bridge (*Jä.*).

དེའུ *dehu*, or དེ་ཙར on any day, at some future time (*Mil.*).

+ དེས་པ *des-pa* གུ་རྣམས་པ་ पेशल 1. fine, brave, noble, chaste (*Cs.*); 2.=ངང་རྒྱུད་བཟང་བ or གཤིན་བཟང་བ of good nature; (*K. d.* ཚ *166*). དེས་པ་ཕུན་སུམ་ཚོགས་པ *des-pa phun-sum tshogs-pa* consummate.

དོ *do* 1. num. fig.: 131. 2. a pair or couple—used only in counting, weighing, measuring, etc.: ཞོ་དོ་རེ of *sho* two each.

3. this; དོ་ནུབ this evening, to-night: བདག་དོ་ནུབ་ཙམ་གྱི་མི I, a man only for to-day and to-morrow (*Jä.*); དོ་ཞག དོ་མོད to-day. 4. also དོ་མཉམ an equal, a match; དོ་བསྡོ་བ *do ḇsdo-wa* adversaries, rivals; དོ་བསྡོ་བ་རྣམས་ལ་དམག་གིས་ཚར་བཅད he exterminated his antagonists by war (*Sorig.*). དོ་སྙོན་པ *do non-pa* the equalizing of the load, by increasing or lessening it on one of the sides (*Jä.*). དོ་མ་ཡིན *do ma-yin* or དོ་མེད=འགྲན་ཟླ་མེད་པ match-less, unequalled: མི་ལུས་རིན་ཆེན་རྙེད་པ་འདི, ནོར་བུ་རྙེད་པའི་དོ་མ་ཡིན (*Khrid̲.*) the possession of this precious human body is not equalled by the gain of any gem.

+ **དོ་ཀེར** *do-ker*=ཐོར་ཚུགས or ཐོར་གཙུག also written as ཐོར་ཅོག luxuriant locks dressed neatly on the crown of the head, sometimes in fanciful designs as among the Burmese; Tibetan high officials of the lay-class also dress their hair in a prescribed form.

དོ་གར་ཁ *do-gar kha* in *W.* light-blue (*Jä.*).

དོ་གལ *do-gal* importance, weight; important: རང་ལ་དོ་གལ་གྱི་རྣམ་པའི་འགོར་བ་དང matters that are important to yourself should not be delayed (*Ya-sel. 4*). དོ་གལ་ཅན गौर्वी important; of weighty consequence (*Cs.*); དོ་གལ་ཆེ་བ=ཁག་ཆེ་བ very important.

དོ་ཆོད *do-choḏ*=གོ་ཆོད intelligent and useful.

དོ་དམ *do-dam* commission, charge, superintendence, care; དོ་དམ་པ an overseer, authorized person; དོ་དམ་བྱེད་པ to supervise, superintend.

དོ་པོ *do-po* 1. or ལག་དོ an assistant, a servant. 2. a load, for a beast of burden, cf. དོས (*Jä.*).

དོ་ཕྲུག *do-phrug* an orphan.

དོ་བ་རྫོང *Do-wa ṟdsoṅ* n. of a district in the province of *Lho-brag* in Tibet.

དོ་བའི་ཏོག་མ *do-wahi tog-ma* पिण्डालु; root of artichoke; also potatoe.

དོ་བོ *do-wo*=*doṣ-po* a load (*Ṟtsii.*).

དོ་མོད *do-moḏ*=འཕྲལ་དུ 1. quickly; དོ་མོད་ཏིང་ངེ་འཛིན་གསལ་བའི་དཀྱིལ་འཁོར་དམ་པ་རུ (place) quickly in the holy *maṇḍala* of unsullied contemplation. 2. to-day, this day (*Cs.*).

དོ་ཞག *do-shag* this day, presently: ཁྱད་པར་དུ་དང་དོ་ཞག་བློན་པོ་འདི་དག་སྔར་བས་དལ་བ and particularly to-day the ministers are more lazy than before (*Ḇbrom. 41*).

དོ་ཟླ *do-zla*=འགྲན་ཟླ *ḇgran-zla* 1. comrade, consort, fellow. 2. party in a law-suit. དོ་ཟླ་ཕན་ཚུན་ཞིབ་བྱེད་པ carefully to investigate (the right of) both parties (*Cs*). དོ་ཡ་གཅིག *do-ya-gcig* lit. one of the two or of a pair; half a load.

དོ་ར *do-ra* 1. a stage; a courtyard where dancing is performed=འཆམ་ར, བྲོ་འཁྲབ་ས. 2. an enclosed pasture land; a lawn.

དོ་ལོ *do-lo* or དོ་ལ: དོ་ལོ་བཅུ་ཤེལ་སྒྲོན་མོས་བྱས་པ a necklace, a string made of pearls or precious stones (worn hanging down from the neck); an ornament hanging down from the shoulders (*Jig.*).

དོ་ལོག *Do-log* a kind of worm: ཕྱིས་མ་སྲིན་བུ་དོ་ལོག་ཏུ་སྐྱེ་འོ in future life (he) would be born as the worm *Dolog* (*Ya-sel 7*).

དོ་ཤལ *do-çal* हार, अवहार, कण्ठ necklace. Syn. ཕྱང་འཕྲུལ *phyaṅ-phrul*; སེ་མོ་དོ *se-mo do*; བྲང་གི་རྒྱན *braṅ-gi ṟgyan* (*M̱ṅon.*). དོ་ཤལ་ཅན *do-çal-can* 1. one wearing a necklace. 2. n. of the residence of *Vaijayanta*. དོ་ཤལ་ཕྱེད་པ *do-çal phyed-pa* अर्द्धहार half-length string of pearls, &c., or half size necklace.

དོག *dog* 1. clod, clump, lump, loaf: ཀ་ར་དོག་གཅིག a lump of sugar. 2. capsule; སར་ཏེ་ཀའི་དོག་གཅིག capsule of the cotton plant (*Jä.*). 3. for དོག་པ *dog-pa* narrow.

དོག་པ I: *dog-pa* 1. सम्पक capsule: མེ་ཏོག་གི་འབྲུམ་བུ capsule of flower, *i.e.*, flower seed in one pod. 2. དོག bundle, skein, *i.e.*, of wool, as much as one can hold with the hand; ལག་དོག handful. 3. མགུལ་བརྒྱན་ལྷ་བུ as a neck ornament. 4. ear of corn དོག་པའི་སྙེ་མ; མེ་ཏོག་གི་དོག་པ पुष्पमञ्जरी flower shoots or buds; སྦྲང་རྩིའི་དོག་པ मधुमञ्जरी buds containing honey in their capsules.

དོག་པ II: also དོག་པོ or དོག་མོ 1. narrow, narrowness: དོག་པོ་མི་འདུག it is not narrow; དོག་པའི་གནས་ལ་ཐར་བ to get out of a narrow place; ཤིན་ཏུ་དོག་པར་གྱུར་ཏོ fig. they were kept within narrow bounds (*Glr.*, *Jä.*). 2. strict: ཁྲིམས་དོག་པོ *khrims dog-po* strict justice, also hard punishment. དོག་པོ་མེད not narrow, wide; ཁང་པ་དོག small narrow house; ས་ཆ་དོག narrow-place; གོས་དོག a robe that does not fit being narrow in dimensions. དོག་པོ *dog-po* or དོག་མོ adj. dense, thick; དོག་པོར densely, thickly: ཞིང་ཁམས་མཐའ་དག་དོག་པོར་ཁྱབ་པ all the regions were thickly filled up, *i.e.*, thickly inhabited (*Yig.*).

དོན་པ *don-pa*, v. འདོན་པ to bring out; ཁ་ནས་དོན་པ ejaculated; སྒོ་ནས་དོན་པ brought out by the door.

+ དོག་མ *dog-ma*=མདུན front, fore; also, resp. for མ (*Lex.*).

+ དོག་ལེ *dog-le*=ཆུ་བསྲོ་བའི་སྣོད *chu-bsro-wahi snod* acc. to *Jä.* an iron pan with a handle.

དོགས་པ I: *dogs-pa* for འདོགས་པ 1. प्रयोजन necessity, usefulness: ཕན་འདོགས usefulness; ཕན་འདོགས་མེད་པ useless, without usefulness. 2. fear, apprehension; ག་དོགས what fear! do not be afraid of; དོགས་པ་སྐྱེས་ཏེ fear having arisen; དོགས་གསལ་བ or དོགས་གཅོད་པ=ཐེ་ཚོམ་གཅོད་པ to remove doubt or clear misapprehension: དོན་ལྡན་ཡོད་པ་ཞིག་ཐྲིམ་གྱི་ཤོག་གང་འགའ་དོགས་གཅོད་དགོས་པའི་རིགས་རྣམས་ཞིབ་ཕྲིམ་བྱེད in a draft containing matters of some importance the points should be written carefully to avoid all that may be misapprehended (*D. çel. 20*). དོགས་པ་མེད or དོགས་མེད अशङ्क, निःशङ्क; without fear, fearlessly; རེ་དོགས hope and fear; དོགས་པ་དང་བཅས་པ संबाध, सशङ्क with apprehension; དོགས་པའི་ཟུམ་ང་བ dread of suspicion. 3.=ཐེ་ཚོམ scruple, doubt; དོགས་འགས in colloq. scrupulously, doubtfully; དོགས་མཐའ the limit of doubt (*A. 50*); དོགས་ཟོན scrupulous, also to take care, take heed, to be cautious: རྒྱལ་པོ་ཡིན་ཀྱང་དོགས་ཟོན་དགོས being a king he should be cautious. དོགས་སློང་པ *dogs-sloṅs-pa* to raise scruple, doubt; also to make another apprehensive, doubtful (*D. çel.* ང་ *20*).

དོགས་པ II: vb. to fear, not in the violent sense in which འཇིགས་པ is used, but to apprehend or dread anything happening: སེར་བ་འོང་དོགས་པའི་དུས་སུ at a time when he was apprehending that hail would come on; རྒྱལ་སྲིད་མ་ཐུབ་ཀྱིས་དོགས་ཏེ being afraid (the prince) might not be able to govern; ཡུམ་དེ་མ་མཐོང་དོགས་པས fearing lest he should not see the *sakli*; བུ་མིའི་མཐོང་གིས་དོགས་ནས dreading that his son might meet the view of the people; ཞེ་སྡང་འཕངས་དོགས་ཀྱང་རེ་གྱིས be on your guard lest anger should arise; take care not to grow angry! (*Jä.*).

དོང *doṅ*=ཁུང་ *khuṅ* गर्त, कूप 1. a deep hole, pit, trench: དོང་བརྐོས་པ་ལས་དེ་ཉིད་དུ་བླུགས་ན་མི་མཉམ་མོ in refilling the earth into the hole excavated, it will not be even with the surface (*K. du.* ད *113*). མེ་དོང=अग्निकुण्ड a firepit; acc. to *Sch.* crater; ས་དོང་ a hole in the ground; ཆུ་དོང་ a well, a deep cistern; དོང་ཞལ = a snake. 2. depth, deepness, profundity (*Jä.*). དོང་ཅན deep, full of trenches; དོང་མེད not deep, shallow (*Cs.*). 3. v. འདོང་བ.

དོང་ཀ *doṅ-ka* कर्णिकार the tree *Pterospermum acerifolium.* དོང་ཀའི་མེ་ཏོག कर्णिकार पुष्प flower of *Karnikāra.* དོང་ཀས་མཆིན་ནད་སེལ་ཞིང་འཇམ་པོར་འབྱུ the fruit of *doṅka* is a cure for liver disease and is a mild purgative.

Syn. མེ་ཏོག་འཕྲེང་བ *me-tog phreṅ-wa;* ལོ་མ་བཟང་ *lo-ma-bzaṅ;* ནད་འཇོམས *nad-hjoms;* འཁོར་ལོ་འདྲ *hkhor-lo hdra;* ཞི་བྱེད *shi-byed;* སོར་མོ་བཞི་པ *sor-mo bshi-pa;* རྒྱལ་པོའི་ཤིང་ *rgyal-pohi çiṅ* (*Mṅon.*).

དོང་ཁ *doṅ-kha* पाटीर [a kind of radish] *S.* དོང་ཁའི་འབྲུ पाटीरफल medicinal fruit.

+ དོང་སྟེ *doṅ-ste* = སོང་སྟེ *soṅ-ste.*

དོང་པ *doṅ-pa* padlock; དོང་པ་འཛུག་པ to put a padlock on (*Jä.*).

དོང་པོ *doṅ-po* = 1. སྦོང་བུ tube, any hollow cylindrical vessel. 2. སྦ་དོང་ a bamboo tube used as water or milk vessel in Sikkim, Bhutan, etc. མདའ་དོང་ a quiver (generally made of bamboo). ལྕགས་དོང་ iron tube; ཤིང་དོང་ wooden tube.

དོང་བ *doṅ-wa* = འགྲོ་བ, རྒྱུ་བ 1. to proceed, to go (*Mṅon.*), v. འདོང་བ. 2. इषुधि a quiver.

དོང་མོ *doṅ-mo* or ལྡོང་མོ a small churn for tea-making = ཕུར་ཕུར (*Jä.*).

དོང་ཙེ *doṅ-tse* or དོང་རྩེ *doṅ-rtse* कार्षापण 1. a copper coin in China. 2. piece of money of small value either in silver, gold, or copper; གསེར་གྱི་དོང་ཙེ gold coin. དོང་ཟེལ in *W. Corydalis meifolia* (*Jä.*).

དོང་ཟེ *doṅ-ze* wasp, acc. to *Cs.*

-དོད *dod* 1. definite; མ་དོད indefinite. 2. a substitute; an equivalent; དེའི་དོད་ཅི་འདུག་ཡོད what is the equivalent, what shall we get for it? བུ་དོད adopted son: ངེད་ཀྱི་བུའི་དོད་མཛོད pray, suffer yourself to be adopted by us. སྐད་དོད verbal equivalent, the original of a translation, a synonym; དོད་དུ as an equivalent, as payment for, instead of, at, *e.g.*, at a moderate price (*Jä.*); དོད་པོ *dod-po* one in the place of, a substitute, a representative; དོད་པོར་བྱས = ཚབ་བྱས represented, acted as a representative: མ་སྐྱེད་གཉིས་དགའ་ནས་རྣལ་འབྱོར་བ་དོད་པོར་བྱས་ཏེ་དེ་བ་གླང་རྫི་དངོས་མ་ཡིན་ཡང་དོད་པོ་ཡིན་པས both the mother and son being pleased, substituted the *yogi*, though he was not really the cow-herd, but one representing him (*A. 60*). དོད་པོར་བྱས་ཏེ *dod-por byas-te* acting as a substitute (*A. 59*).

དོད་པ *dod-pa* = བསྙེལ་བ *bsñel-wa* or དབྱེར་བ 1. to project, to be prominent. Often with འབུར་དུ; འབུར་དུ་དོད་པ elongated. གཟུགས་སུ་དོད་པ come out in relief; *skye-mched dod-pa* a child in the womb just when its nose and ears are being formed. 2. ཐོན་པ to come out, float up: ཆུས་གང་བའི་བར་བར་དུ་གླིང་རྣམས་དོད་པ (*Ya-sel. 36*) there arose islets in the midst of the flooded place.

དོན *don* 1. particle signifying: more than, over; བདུན་བཅུ་དོན་གཅིག one over seventy; བདུན་ཅུ་དོན་གཉིས two over seventy, etc.

དོན II: अर्थ, संज्ञा, उद्देश, मूल 1. the sense or signification of anything; དོན་གོ་བ to understand the meaning; བརྗོད་བྱའི་དོན the meaning to be expressed; དོན་འགྲེལ་བ to elucidate, explain the meaning; དོན་རྟོགས་པར་དཀའ་བའི་ཡིག་འབྲུ individual letter, the meaning of which is not easily understood; དོན་མི་འདུག it has no sense; འདིའི་དོན་ཅི་ཡིན what does this mean? དོན་དང་ལྡན་པ full of meaning; also one who is a sensible man; དོན་བྲལ་ཚིག meaningless words, ravings;

དོན་དེ་ལ་སོམས do think over the meaning of this (*Mil.*); དོན་ལ་ལྟ་ན col. in truth, in fact, really, surely, indeed! 2. reason, purpose, profit, advantage; object: སོང་སོང་བའི་དོན་མེད going on is to no purpose; འགྲོ་བའི་རང་གི་དོན་ལབ *hgro-wahi rañ-gi don lab* tell me your reason for going; ཡོང་གི་དོན་གང་བྱེད་བྱུང་ངམ what has been his object in coming? དོན་སྒྲུབ་པ *don sgrub-pa* to gain one's object; དོན་གནད་རྣམས *don gnad-rnams* real reasons. 3. in a general sense: affair, concern, business; རང་གི་དོན one's own affairs, one's own interest; གཞན་གྱི་དོན interest of others; དོན་མང་བས on account of much business (*Dzl.*). 4. welfare, advantage, the good of a person; མིའི་དོན་བྱེད་པ to promote a man's welfare; འགྲོ་བའི་དོན་བྱེད་པ to work for the welfare of all living beings; ཕན་པའི་དོན a useful thing; བདེ་བའི་དོན a gift of fortune (*Jä.*). དངོས་གྲུབ་མཆོག་གི་དོན the substantial benefit of the highest perfection.

དོན III: a document: ཚད་དོན 1. a special request or object (in writing a letter to a subordinate or one in subordinate position). 2. a written contract, agreement; also a letter to an inferior person. ངེས་དོན the certain or real meaning, also positive order or instruction. དྲང་དོན the proper or plain meaning; distinct order or instruction. ཞུ་དོན application, petition, request. ཚིག་དོན literal meaning, grammatical signification.

དོན་ལ་གཡེང་བ *don-la gyeñ-wa* to change or divert the thoughts from the three causes which disturb the mind.

དོན་ཀུན *don-kun* सर्व्वार्थ the interest or well-being of all; public good, cause, object, etc. དོན་ཀུན་གྲུབ་པ *don-kun grub-pa* सर्व्वार्थसिद्ध 1. to accomplish or fulfil all objects, purposes; one who has done them. 2. the early name of Buddha S'ākya-Muni which was given him by his father. དོན་ཀུན་སྒྲུབ་པ *don-kun sgrub-pa* सर्व्वार्थ-साधक one who performs service for the good of the public, *i.e.*, does public good.

དོན་གྱི་ཁོག་ཕུབ་པ *don-gyi khog-phub-pa* as in སྙིང་འགྲུལ་གྱི་བང་མཛོད་ཀྱིས་དོན་གྱི་ཁོག་ཕུབ (*G. Bon.*) to penetrate into the real import.

དོན་གྱི་སྤྱི *don-gyi spyi* अर्थसामान्य general sense, ordinary meaning, common object.

དོན་གྲུབ *Don-grub* = དོན་ཀུན་གྲུབ *don kun-grub* 1. Amoghasiddha, v. དོན་ཡོད་གྲུབ་པ post. 2. कदम्ब assemblage. 3. common personal name in use in Tibet and Sikkim.

དོན་འགལ *don-hgal* = དོན་མི་མཐུན་པ *don-mi mthun-pa* contrary sense, opposite meaning, going against the purpose or interest of (*Mñon.*).

དོན་ལྔ *don-lña* in anatomy the five functionaries of the human body: (1) སྙིང་ *sñiñ* the heart; (2) གློ *glo* lungs; (3) མཆིན་པ *mchin-pa* liver; (4) མཆེར་བ *mcher-wa* spleen; (5) མཁལ་མ *mkhal-ma* kidney.

དོན་ཅན *don-can* = དོན་ལྡན *don-ldan* अर्थिक 1. useful, meaningful, profitable, expedient. 2. enjoying an advantage. 3. having a certain sense.

དོན་གཅོད *don-gcod* or དོན་གཅོད་པ *don gcod-pa* (དོན་ཐག་གཅོད་མཁན *don-thag gcod-mkhan*) one commissioned, a commissioner; one specially appointed for the performance of a certain object: དོན་གཅོད་དམིགས་གསལ་འགྲོ་དགོས་བྱུང་ it necessitated the going of a commissioner (*Rtsii.*).

དོན་ཉམས་པ *don ñams-pa* = དོན་དུ་ཆུང་འགྲོ་བ failure, ill-success; also the decrease of interest or importance (*Mñon.*).

དོན་གཉེར *don-gñer* (ཆོས་ལྡུ་ཁྲ) प्रार्थन, अर्थन 1. prayer. 2. the care-taker of a place, the custodian of the property in a temple.

དོན་གཉིས *don-gñis* in Budh. རང་གི་དོན་ आत्मार्थ for one's self, one's own affair; གཞན་གྱི་དོན་ परार्थ another's business: དེ་ངའི་དོན་མི་འདུག་གཞན་གྱི་དོན་ཡིན that is not my but another's business. Acc. to the Bon *don* is of two kinds: (1) བདག་དོན self-interest which is ལྷུན་གྲུབ inherent, and (2) དོན་གཞན interest for others. མཐར་དོན the final interest for self emancipation.

དོན་སྙིང་ *don-sñiṅ* or དོན་གྱི་སྙིང་པོ the real object, the chief object of a petition or prayer, etc.

དོན་རྟོགས་པ *don ṟtogs-pa*=དོན་གོ་བ to comprehend the meaning; also to reflect on the sense of a term or passage, or on any subject.

དོན་སྟོང་གི་ཚིག *don stoṅ-gi tshig* a word of empty meaning, nonsense; a meaningless expression.

དོན་སྟོང་པ *don stoṅ-pa*=དོན་མེད་པ or དོན་མ་གྲུབ་པ निरर्थक objectless; unfulfilled purpose; void of meaning; for nothing (*M̱ñon.*).

དོན་མེད་བཞིན་དུ *don-meḏ ḇshin-du* without seeing the use of it, without understanding the purpose (with the genit. of the noun).

དོན་མཐུན *don-m̱thun* lit. one having common interest or purpose to serve; originally a number of traders who would make a voyage to Ceylon for buying pearls, &c. གྲུ་ནང་དུ་འཇུག་པའི་སྤྱི་པོ सार्थवाह merchant (generally those who make sea voyages), hence a boat passenger (*M̱ñon.*). དོན་མཐུན་པ *don m̱thun-pa*=དོན་དང་མཐུན་པ 1. (ཚོགས) समानार्थ an assembly having a common interest. 2. अन्वर्थ business men.

དོན་དག *don-dag* lit. good or pure intention = purpose, object, interest; commission, business, affairs.

དོན་དམ *don-dam* 1. the true sense; subjectively: good, earnest; col. in *W.* ཡངས་པ་མིན་དོན་དམ་ཡིན it is not said in jest but in right earnest; objectively; དོན་དམ་པར་དབྱེར་མེད in truth, after all, upon the whole. 2.=ཐར་པ emancipation, liberation (from worldly troubles) (*M̱ñon.*). But དོན་དམ་བདེན་པ *don-dam ḇden-pa* or དོན་དམ་པའི་བདེན་པ परमार्थसत्य =absolute truth, *i.e.*, སྟོང་པ་ཉིད *stoṅ-pa ñiḏ* शून्यता emptiness, voidity.

དོན་དམ་པ *don dam-pa* परमार्थ [the highest truth]*S.* 1. དེ་ཁོ་ན, तत्त्व [essence, the very truth]*S.* 2. ཡང་དག་པའི་མཐའ, भूतकोटि [the culminating point for all beings; voidness, vacuity, absolute nonentity)]*S.* 3. དེ་བཞིན་ཉིད, तथता; [that-ness, true essence]*S.* 4. མ་ནོར་དེ་བཞིན་ཉིད, अवितथता [unmistakable truth]*S.* 5. གཞན་མ་ཡིན་པ་དེ་བཞིན་ཉིད, अनन्यतथता [non-alternate truth]*S.* 6. སྟོང་པ་ཉིད, शून्यता [emptiness itself]*S.* 7. ཆོས་ཀྱི་དབྱིངས, धर्म्मधातु [the essence of existence]*S.* 8. ཆོས་མི་འགྱུར་བ་ཉིད, धर्म्मान्यमयता [unalterable entity]*S.* 9. བསམ་གྱི་མི་ཁྱབ་པའི་དབྱིངས, अचिन्त्यधातु [unthinkable entity]*S.* 10. ཕྱིན་ཅི་མ་ལོག་པ་དེ་བཞིན་ཉིད, अविपर्यासतथता irreversible truth]*S.*; 11. གཉིས་སུ་མེད་པ, अद्वय [non-separable]*S.* 12. གཉིས་སུ་བྱར་མེད་པ, अद्वैधीकार [non-divisible]*S.* 13. ཆོས་གནས་པ་ཉིད, धर्म्मस्थिति [substratum of existence]*S.* 14. ཆོས་ཀྱི་དབྱིངས་ཀྱི་ཚུལ་ནི་གནས་པ་ཉིད་དོ. 15. དེ་བཞིན་ཉིད་འདི་ནི་གཅིག་པ་ཉིད་དོ. 16. ཆོས་ཀྱི་དབྱིངས་ འཇིག་པ་མེད་པས་དབྱེར་མེད་པ, धर्म्मधातु असम्भेद [indestructible essence of existence]*S.* 17. འདི་ནི་གཉིས་སུ་མེད་དེ་གཉིས་སུ་དབྱེར་མེད་ཅིང་ཐ་མི་དད་དེ་བཅད་དུ་མེད.

དོན་དུ *don-du* postp. c. genit. 1. for, for the good of. 2. for the sake of, on account of; c. genit. of inf. in order to, that. 3. rarely, in the place of, instead of, for.

དོན་འདོད་པ *don doḏ-pa* (སྤྲང་པོ) a needy person, a beggar (*M̱ñon.*).

དོན་ལྡན *don-ldan* with some object or design; in Budh. abbr. of དོན་ཆོས་དགེ་བ་དང་ལྡན་པ possessed of religion and piety; མི་ལུས་དོན་ལྡན་སྒྲུབ་པ་སྙིང་པོ་མཛོད make it essential to acquire while you are a human being (*Rdsa. 23*).

དོན་རྣམ་པ་གསུམ *don rnam-pa gsum* the three kinds of *don*, *i.e.* of significations: (1) ཚིག་འབྲུའི་དོན the literal meaning or signification of a word; (2) དོན་གྱི་དོན the meaning of a meaning, real import; (3) ཁམས་ཀྱི་དོན this includes དེ་ཁོ་ནའི་མཚན་ཉིད, ཡོངས་སུ་ཤེས་པའི་མཚན་ཉིད, etc., the meaning of the root and also that of physical things and spirit, also ཁམས་ཀྱི་དོན་ལ་འཇིག་རྟེན་གྱི་ཁམས, སེམས་ཅན་གྱི་ཁམས, etc. (*K. d.* ཙ *47*).

དོན་དཔྱོད་སྔོན་གནང *don-dpyod sṅon-gnaṅ* the pioneer investigator; the first man who inquires into any subject or case; དོན་དཔྱོད་པ *don dpyod-pa* an investigator, inquirer.= ཨ་ཙུ་ར हरितकी *Arjuna*.

དོན་མེད *don-med* निरर्थक; useless, in vain, for no purpose, silly manner: ཉིན་པར་མར་མེ་སྦྱར་བ་དོན་མེད་དོ it is useless to light lamps in the day time; འགྲངས་ལ་སྟོན་མོ་བྱིན་པ་དོན་མེད་དོ to entertain one who has eaten to the full is useless; སྐྱེ་བོ་ངན་པ་བསྟེན་པ་དོན་མེད་དོ it is useless to stick to a bad man or mean person (*K. du.* ད *200*). དོན་མེད་དཀྲོག་རྐྱེན *don med-dkrog-rkyen* quarrel for nothing or without any cause.

དོན་མེད་གཏམ *don-med gtam* विप्रलाप vain, idle talk.

Syn. ངག་འཆལ་གཏམ *ṅag-hchal gtam;* དོན་སྟོང་ཚིག *don stoṅ-tshig;* དོན་བྲལ་ཚིག *don bral-tshig.*

དོན་རྩ *don-rtsa* (དོན་གྱི་རྩ་བ) the real meaning, reason; also result.

དོན་ཞགས *Don-shags* seems to be a Tantrik manifestation of Avalokites'vara.

དོན་བཟང་ཡེ་ཤེས་སྙིང་པོའི་རྒྱུད *don-bzaṅ ye-çes sñiṅ-pohi rgyud* n. of a Bon work on mysticism.

དོན་ཡོད་གྲུབ་པ *Don-yod grub-pa* अमोघसिद्ध lit. one who does a real work successfully; n. of the fifth Dhyani Buddha, the ruler of the heaven situated to the north. In Tantrik ceremonial he is generally painted green and is often represented with a Khadoma fairy as his *Sakti* (Tib. ཡུམ་མ). Is styled དོན་གྲུབ *Don-grub* for short.

དོབ་དོབ *dob-dob* 1. one who dresses tying his breeches above the knees, in the manner of a Bhutanese. 2. stuff, nonsense (*Sch.*).

དོམ *dom* भल्लुक, ऋक्ष the tawny bear, *Ursus pruinosus* of Blyth, found near Lhasa and elsewhere: དོམ་གྱི་མཆེ་བས་ཁྲག་ནོར་གཅོད་པར་བྱེད the teeth of the bear (made into paste) stops bleeding; དོམ་གྱི་ཀླད་པས་མགོ་རྨ་གསོ the bear's brains heal sores on the head; དོམ་གྱི་ཤ་ཡིས་གདོན་གྱི་ནད་ལ་ཕན the flesh of the bear is useful in the diseases caused by evil spirits. དོམ་མཁྲིས *dom-mkhris* bear's bile (it is used as a medicine).

Syn. ཕུག་ཉལ *phug-ñal;* མིག་སྨན་ལུས་ཅན *mig-sman lus-can;* རབ་དཀར་སྙིང *rab dkar-sñiṅ;* གཏུམ་དྲག་ཞེ་སྡང་ཅན *gtum-drag she-sdaṅ-can;* སྡིག་པའི་ལྟོ་ཅན *sdig-pahi lto-can* (*Mṅon.*).

དོར *dor* a pair of draught cattle; གླང་དོར *glaṅ-dor* a yoke of oxen (*Jä.*).

དོར་བ *dor-wa* pf. and imp. of འདོར་བ *hdor-wa* to throw out, cast out; བྱ་བ་ངན་པ་དོར give up bad actions or behaviour; དོར་བར་གྱུར *dor-war gyur* विरराम left, cast out (*A. K. 1*).

དོར་བྱེད་མ *dor byed-ma* = དུར་བྱིད་སྨན *dur-byid-sman.*

དོར་མ *dor-ma* breeches, trowsers; དོར་ཐུང་ short breeches; དོར་རིང་ long drawers; སྣམ་དོར breeches made of thick sergo cloth; དོར་རྟ *dor-ṛta* that part of the breeches which covers the privy parts.

དོལ I: *dol* 1. ཉ་རྒྱ fishing-net (*Mṅon.*); ཉ་དོལ་པ a fisherman, cf. གདོལ་པ *gdol-pa*. 2. *W.* stew-pan (*Jä.*). 3. in དོལ་གཅོད་པ to split, to cleave (*Sch.*).

དོལ II: n. of a place in the province of Lhokha in Tibet: དེ་ནས་དོལ་དུ་སྣ་བོ་ལ་ཁ་ནས་དུང་ བུས then arriving at Dol from *Ṣna-bola kha* he blew the conch-shell (trumpet) (*A. 90*). དོལ་གྱི་གདོང་སྣ *Dol-gyi doṅ-ṣna* n. of a village in Dol (*Deb.* ག *34.*). དོལ་རྣམ་རྒྱལ་རྫོང་ *Dol-ṛnam ṛgyal-dsoṅ* the head-quarters of Dol (*Ṛtsii*). དོལ་པ *Dol-pa* a native or resident of Dol; དོལ་པ་རིན་པོ་ཆེ *dol-pa rin-po-che* n. of a celebrated lama of this place (*Loṅ.* ཟ *2*); དོལ་བུ་བ *Dol-bu-wa* the name by which that lama was usually called (*Ya-sel. 37*).

དོལ་བོན. *dol-bon* a sect of the Bon (*J. Zaṅ.*):

དོས *doṣ* or དོས་པོ=ཁུར་པོ a load that is carried by man or beast; *khal-doṣ* ཁལ་དོས load carried by a beast of burden; ཇ་དོས a load of tea carried in this manner; དོས་འགེལ་བ to load, to pack; དོས་འབོགས་པ to unload. དོས་སྐྱབ a guard in charge of loads, one in charge of loads carried by beasts of burden and walking behind; ཁམས་སོགས་ཐག་རིང་པོའི་ དོས་སྐྱབ caravan-guard coming from Khams and other distant places (*Ṛtsii*).

དོས་ཆེ. *doṣ-che*=འབོར་ཆེ་བ. *ḥbor che-wa* or ཐངས་ཆེ་བ (*Jig.*).

དོས་དྲག *doṣ-drag*=ཚ་དྲག *tsha-drag* (*D.R.*) =ཧ་ཅང་བྲེལ་ཚ་བོ *ha-caṅ brel tsha-wo* urgent, impatient; calling for inquiry.

དོས་དྲག་པ *doṣ drag-pa* 1. hard compulsory service. 2. severe in exacting it, *e.g.*, a feudal lord (*Jä.*).

དོས་པ *doṣ-pa* one who carries loads, a coolie; དོས་པོ *doṣ-po*=ཁུར་པོ a load; དོས་དཔོན the leader of a caravan of such loads. དོས་ཚད=དོས་ཀྱི་ཚད the weight that can becarried by a man or beast. In Tibet 12 *khal* is the usual *doṣ-po* or load for a cooly (*Rtsii.*).

དྲ *dra* signifies (mystically) སྐྱེས་བུ *ṣkyeṣ bu* a person, a personage (*K. g.* ཁ *179*).

དྲ་ཅི *dra-ci* or དྲང་ཅི *draṅ-ci* in *Pur.* a flat basket (*Jä.*); དྲ་ཆུང *dra-chuṅ* a small bag made of net cloth (*Cs.*); དྲ་ཕད *dra-phad* a bag of net-cloth.

དྲ་ཕྱེད *dra-phyed* 1. अर्द्धहार half-necklace, half-chain. 2. half-lattice-work; a kind of silk ornament.

དྲ་བ I: *dra-wa* 1. a tailor who cuts robes, shirts, etc. 2. to cut, clip, lop, dress, prune, pare with knife or scissors; also fig. ཕའི་མིང་ནས་དྲས་ཏེ borrowing (a syllable) from the father's name; གོས་དྲས cloth cut out for a garment (*Cs.*): བཟོ་རིག་པ་ནི, དྲ་བ་དང་ ཚེམ་པ་དང in handicraft (he knew) tailoring, cutting and sewing (*A. 34*); དྲ་གྲིད scissors (*Sch.*). 3. a small copper coin used in the Western Himalaya; called also *Dabu*.

དྲ་བ II: sbst. 1. हार necklace (of pearls, gold etc.), chain worn as an ornament. 2. जाल web, net, lattice, grate, net-work: ལུས་ལ་དྲ་བར་འབྲེལ (the veins) are spread throughout the body like net-work (*S.g.*). དྲ་བའི་ཐག་པ *dra-waḥi thag-pa* rope or string of a net or trap. དྲ་བའི་རྐང་ལྡན *dra-waḥi ṛkaṅ-ldan* web-footed; a goose, duck, swan. རུས་པའི་དྲ་བ the frame-work of bones, the skeleton; ལྕགས་དྲ iron lattice; ཤིང་དྲ wooden rails, fencing; ལྕགས་ཀྱི་དྲ་མིག iron trellis; gridiron; འོད་ཟེར་གྱི་དྲ lattice-work of rays. 3. लकुट [a club] *S.*

དྲ་བ་འཁྲོལ་བ *dra-wa hkhrol-wa*=དྲ་མིག་གྲོལ་བ.

དྲ་བ་ཅན *dra-wa-can* 1. जालक latticed, grated. 2. met. a spider. 3.=གོ་ཁྲབ a coat of mail (*Mñon.*). 4.=ཀུ་བ a gourd (*Mñon.*). དྲ་བ་ཅན་མ *dra-wa can-ma* (བུད་མེད་སྒོ་ལྡན་མ) a clever and skilful woman (*Mñon.*).

དྲ་བ་དྲ་ཕྱེད *dra-wa dra-phyed* laced curtains or ornamental silken frills, hangings embroidered and with pendant strings: མུ་ཏིག་གི་དྲ་བ་དྲ་ཕྱེད་དེ་རྣམས་བཏགས་ནས having put on certain ornaments with pearls and pendant tassels (*A. 141*).

དྲ་བ་འཛིན *dra-wa-hdsin* met. a fisherman; one who holds or uses fishing-net (*Mñon.*).

དྲ་མ *dra-ma* 1.=ཡ་རབས nobility, generally applied to the लिच्छवी Licchabi race of Vais'ali. 2. experienced, practised, learned. 3.=རྩི་ཤིང *rtsi-çiñ* a board or slate for counting and writing figures upon.

དྲ་མ་སྤྲུལ་པའི་གླིང *Dra-ma sprul-pahi gliñ* n. of a fancied continent or island.

དྲ་མིག *dra-mig* or དྲ་བའི་མིག the openings or "eyes" in a net-work or lattice.

དྲག *drag* seems to be a root with two distinct significations: 1. advisable, better, best; where two or more courses offer, that which is the more or most expedient: འགྲོ་ན་དྲག *hgro-na drag* it is better to go; སྡོད་ན་དྲག *sdod-na drag* better to sit, to stay (*Mñon.*); ང་ཅི་ལྟར་བྱས་ན་དྲག what course would be expedient? Also any improvement may be expressed by *drag*: དྲག་སོང has improved, become better; ཁྱོད་ཆོས་ལྡན་དུ གཤེགས་པ་དྲག your entering into a religious life is better (*A. 127*); དྲག་སྐྱེས *drag-skyes* growing better, is improving; is in the way of improvement (*Yig.*); colloq. better, that is better, well done. 2. vehement, forcible; and so, fierce, violent. In this sense is gen. applied to the powerful and violent aspect of certain Tantrik deities; other compounds of this root, however, are being more frequently employed.

དྲག་གིས *drag-gis* firmly; དྲག་གིས་དད to believe firmly.

དྲག་སྔགས་འདུས་པ་རྡོ་རྗེ་ཟ་བའི་རྒྱུད n. of a *Tantra* used by the *Rñiñ-ma* sect (*K. g.* ཤ *349*).

དྲག་ཅན *drag-can* तीव्र, उग्र strong, vehement. Term applied to terrifying deities.

དྲག་ཆར *drag-char* झीकर heavy rain, heavy rain or downpour.

དྲག་འཇིང *drag-hjiñ* n. of Indra's horse (*Sorig.*).

དྲག་ཏུ *drag-tu*=ཤུགས་ཆེ་བ or ལྷག་པར་དུ adv. strongly, earnestly, vehemently, violently; moreover: གནས་འདི་ཉིད་དུ་བཞུགས་ཞུ་ཞེས་གསོལ་དྲག་ཏུ་བཏབ་པས he implored him to stay in that place (*Hbrom. 106*). དྲག་ཏུ་འཐེན་པ *drag-tu hthen-pa* to pull violently, with great force.

དྲག་སྡེབས *drag-sdebs*=མི་དྲག་པ་རྣམས་ཀྱི་གྲས rank or class of better people; higher class or order: ལས་བྱེད་ནང་ཟན་དྲག་སྡེབས་ལ་ཟླ་ཆེས་ཐོག་རྩིས account of monthly allowance to the better or higher class of domestic servants and workmen (*Rtsii.*).

དྲག་ནད *drag-nad* a serious illness, gen.=དྲེག་ནད *dreg-nad* gout.

དྲག་པ *drag-pa* 1. from the root *drag* and thus signifying: the better sort of persons, and so: noble, of noble birth, superior, respectable, of superior quality or order; མི་དྲག་པ a nobleman, gentleman, respectable man; རྫས་ལ་དྲག་པ articles of superior quality; དྲག་རིགས nobility, gentry; དྲག་པར་བྱེད་པ to raise to nobility; དྲག་པར་འགྱུར་བ་ to become a nobleman. 2. vehement, powerful, severe; བརྩོན་འགྲུས་དྲག་པ་འབད་པ to exert with assiduity; དྲག་པ་འདུད་པ unbending, unwearied application; སྐད་དྲག་པ a powerful voice; ཁྲིམས་དྲག་པ a severe punishment; སྙིང་རྗེ་དྲག་པ yearning compassion. *Drag-pa* implies in fact possessing any quality in a high degree; དུག་དྲག་པ very poisonous, virulent poison.

དྲག་པའི་ཆོས་པ *drag-paḥi chos-pa* a performer of *Tantrik* rites and religious observances, in which fierce deities are either coerced or propitiated.

དྲག་པའི་ཐོད *drag-paḥi thod* described as ཆུ་བོ་གང་གཱའི་མིང उग्रशेखरी an epithet of the river Ganges (*Mṅon.*).

དྲག་པོ *drag-po* also དྲགས་པོ *drags-po* (*A. K. 1-34*), तीव्र, घोर, उग्र, चण्ड, रौद्र 1. fierce, terrible, fearful, violent; and is the term specially attached to deities in their aspect of anger as defenders of Buddhism; is thus synonymous with ཁྲོ་བོ as used in that sense. 2. sbst. any terrific deity; a *Bhairava*.

དྲག་པོ་དབལ་སློག་ཅན *drag-po dwal-slog-can* n. of a Bon deity (*D.R.*).

དྲག་པོའི་མིག रुद्राक्ष 1. n. of a fabulous animal. 2. species of tree, *Elæocarpus ganitrus;* the berry of this tree used for rosaries.

དྲག་པོའི་གཙུག་རྒྱན *drag-poḥi gtsug-rgyan* an epithet of the moon (*Mṅon.*).

དྲག་པོའི་ཤུགས་འགྲོ *drag-poḥi çugs-ḥgro* उग्रगति that which moves with vehement speed, like a shooting arrow.

དྲག་མོ *drag-mo* 1. उग्रा a fearful woman. an amazon (*Mṅon.*). 2. रुद्राणी Rudra's wife, an epithet of the goddess Durgā.

དྲག་རྩལ་ཅན *drag rtsal-can*=དྲག་པོ acc. to the Bon, possessing the terrific attitude and powers of deities.

དྲག་རྩུབ་བསྐལ་པ *drag-rtsub bskal-pa* the rough or rude age, a name of this present period of time which is called སྙིགས་དུས་བསྐལ་པ.

དྲག་ཚང་ཆོང་ཅན *drag-tshañ choñ-can* acc. to the Bon: in whom are all manner of perfections, good qualities.

དྲག་ཞན *drag-shan* strong and weak, *i.e.*, the relative force of sound; also with respect to rank, superior and inferior or good and bad.

དྲག་ཤུལ *drag-çul* fierce, also frightfulness; དྲག་ཤུལ་ཅན *drag-çul can* उग्र, रौद्र frightful, terrible, powerful, cruel; also one of the ten tones of music (*M.V.*). དྲག་ཤུལ་ཆེ *drag-çul che*, དཔའ་བོ་ལྟ་བ *dpaḥ-bo lta-wa* fierce, terrible; also like a hero, chivalrous, heroic: ཁྱོད་ནི་གཏུམ་ཆེ་ལ་དྲག་ཤུལ་ཆེ thou art heroic and fearful (*Rtsii. 30*). དྲག་ཤུལ་སྤྱོད *drag-çul spyod* a mystical practice=སྤྱོད་པ་རྩུབ་པ आभिचारक।

དྲག་གཤེད *Drag-gçed* is not, as *Jä* has it, a single deity but indicates a group of fierce and redoubtable gods, of which there are said to be eight. See Grünwedel's *Mythologie des Buddhismus, 164.* The Mongols style the Drag-shed group *Dokshit;* and a special robe and hat are worn by exorcists who deal with the group. Each Dhyani Buddha, moreover, is held to have a *drag-shed* in his retinue.

དྲག་གསུམ *Drag-gsum* the three fierce ones (the Bon trinity).

དྲགས *drags*=ཆེས་པ, ལྷག་པ or ཐལ་པ *thal-pa* =excess: ཟས་ཟ་དྲགས་ན་མ་ཞུ་བའི་ནད་ཡོང eating in excess will cause the illness of indigestion; མང་དྲགས *maṅ-drags* very much, in excess; as adj. much, strong, intense. དྲགས་བྱེད *drags-byed* दर्पक a bragadacio, one who brags much.

དྲང་ *draṅ* 1. a kind of beer (*Sch.*). 2. सरल honest, straightforward, upright. དྲང་འགྲོ *draṅ-ḥgro* = མདའ, शर an arrow, a shot (lit. that which goes straight) (*Mṅon.*); དྲང་གཏམ plain language; དྲང་པོ *draṅ-po* ऋजु, सरल, सम्मित right, truthful, straight (མ་ཁྱོག་པ not crooked or bent), sincere, honest. དྲང་ལམ *draṅ-lam* short road, straight-road, straightforward, not deviating from the direct course; upright; ལམ་དྲང་པོ good actions, righteous deeds; ཁྲིམས་དྲང་པོ righteous judgment, justice. དྲང་བཤག་གི་བཟོས་སྒོ *draṅ bshag-gi bzos-sgo* settlement, good arrangement—also described as བཟོས་སྒོ་ནི་སྔར་ཕན་ཐོགས་པ་དང་དྲིན་ཆེ་བ་ལ་བཟང་ལན་བྱེད་པ to return good to one who has done kindness or good service before (*Yig.*).

དྲང་དོན *draṅ-don* ordinary signification; དྲང་དོན་དང་ངེས་དོན་གྱི་ཁྱད་པར the difference between the general and real significations; ངེས་དོན (भावार्थ) the sense or spirit of an expression or word: ཀུན་རྫོབ་ཀྱི་ཆ་ནས་དྲངས་པ་ཐམས་ཅད་དྲང་དོན་དུ་འདོད་པ་ཡིན significations drawn from unrealities or phenomena are to come within the term *draṅ-don*; དོན་དམ་པའི་ཆ་ནས་དྲངས་པ་ཐམས་ཅད་ངེས་དོན a meaning derived from the spirit or spiritual sense is ངེས་དོན, *i.e.*, the certain or absolute meaning. (*Beḥu. 37*).

དྲང་པོར *draṅ-por* adv. straight; དྲང་པོར་འཇོག་པ *draṅ-por ḥjog-pa* to place, put straight; དྲང་པོར་འདོད་པ *draṅ-por ḥdod-pa* wishing frankly; དྲང་པོར་སྨྲ་བ *draṅ-por smra-wa* to speak plainly, to be candid, to speak the truth.

དྲང་བ *draṅ-wa* आकर्षण, नेय. 1. abstract noun to དྲང་པོ *draṅ-po*. 2. pf. to འདྲེན་པ.

དྲང་སྲོང་ *draṅ-sroṅ* ऋषि, मुनि, गुणिकर; རིག་བྱེད་ཀློག་པ a reciter of sacred hymns, an inspired sage; originally the authors or rather seers of the Vedic hymns; a saint; an anchorite. *Jä.* says: at present the lama that offers *sbyin-sreg* is stated to bear this name, and whilst he is attending to the sacred rites he is not allowed to eat anything but དཀར་ཟས white food, *i.e.*, milk, curds and cheese. The terms cognate to དྲང་སྲོང *draṅ-sroṅ* but not exactly synonymous with it are the following: ཐུབ་པ, བརྟུལ་ཞུགས་ཅན, དབང་པོ་ཐུལ་བ, སྨྲེས་བརྩོན, ཀུན་ཏུ་རྒྱུ, དགེ་བར་སྤྱོང, ཕ་རོལ་འདོད་པ, སྨྲ་བ་བཅད་པ, ངག་བསྡམས་པ, མི་སྨྲ་བ, ཁྲུས་ཀྱི་བརྟུལ་ཞུགས་ཅན, གཙང་བར་གནས་པ, དཀའ་ཐུབ་སྤྱོད་པ, ཚངས་པར་སྤྱོད་པ, ཉོན་མོངས་ཐུལ, བདེན་སྨྲ (*Mṅon.*).

དྲང་སྲོང་བདུན *draṅ-sroṅ bdun* सप्तर्षि the seven sages; also the constellation of the Great-Bear. Acc. to Bon the seven are:—(1) དྲང་སྲོང་ཁྲི་ལྡེ་འོད; (2) ལྷང་ལྷང་བཙུག; (3) ཐག་ཡིད་རིང; (4) ཟུགས་དཀར་ཡེ་ཤེས; (5) དཔུང་རྒྱམ་ཡེ་ཤེས; (6) འོད་གསལ་འབར; (7) རྫུ་འཕྲུལ་ཡེ་ཤེས (*G. Bon.*). དྲང་སྲོང་རིགས་བཅུ *draṅ-sroṅ rigs-bcu* ten kinds of Rishi, acc. to Budh.: (1) ས་ལ་རྒྱུ་བའི་དྲང་སྲོང་ Rishi that move on earth; (2) འཕུར་འཕྱོའི་དྲང་སྲོང་ flying Rishi; (3) རྣམ་པར་རོལ་ཞིང་རྒྱུ་བའི་དྲང་སྲོང་ the Rishi that walk in a dancing mode; (4) མཁའ་ལ་རྒྱུ་བའི་དྲང་སྲོང་ Rishi that travel in the sky; (5) ལྷ་ཡུལ་དུ་འགྲོ་བའི་དྲང་སྲོང་ Rishi that travel to the celestial regions; (6) རྫུ་འཕྲུལ་གྱིས་འགྲོ་བའི་དྲང་སྲོང་ Rishi who move miraculously; (7) དངོས་ཁྱབ་གྱིས་འགྲོ་བའི་དྲང་སྲོང་ Rishi that can take an enchanted form; (8) སྣང་བས་འགྲོ་བའི་དྲང་སྲོང་ Rishi that can vanish in light; (9) བཅུད་ཀྱིས་འགྲོ་བའི་དྲང་སྲོང་ Rishi that can move as embodied forms of anything; (10) ཐུབ་པར་དུ་འགྲོ་བའི་དྲང་སྲོང་ Rishi who have attained to excellence.

དྲང་སྲོང་ལྷུང་བ *d̤raṅ-sroṅ lhuṅ-wa* ऋषिपतन one of the 36 sacred places of Buddhists in ancient India, the site of modern Sarnath, near Benaros, where Buddha first preached the *Saddharma*.

དྲངས *d̤raṅs* v. འདྲེན་པ

དྲན་པ *d̤ran-pa* I: 1. in Budh. དམིགས་པ་མངོན་པར་བརྗོད་པ་ཉིད་དེ, སེམས་མྱོངས་པ་མེད་པའོ (*K. d.* ན *355*) the stato of the expression of आवलम्ब, i.e., dependence of a thing upon another, indicating that the mind is freo from darkness. 2. स्मृति, संज्ञा recollection, remembrance, memory: དྲན་པ་གསལ་པོ clear recollection; ཟུགས་དྲན་མེད་དུ་ཤོར་བ to lose one's memory or senses; དྲན་མེད་དུ་འགྱེལ་བ to swoon, to fall down uneonscious; དྲན་འཛིན་མེད་པ being out of one's senses (with joy) (*Jä.*). 3. self-recollection, consideration: སེམས་ཅན་སྨྱོན་པ་དག་དྲན་པ་སོ་སོར་རྙེད insane persons regained the respective faculties of their minds; དྲན་པ་གཞུངས་པ quickness of apprehension, good capacity (*Jä.*). 4. स्मर an epithet of Kāmadeva.

དྲན་པ II: 1. vb. to think of, pender; gen. to remember, recollect with ཡིད་ལ: དཀོན་མཆོག་དྲན་པ to think of, to remember Buddha, Dharma and Saṅgha: སྡུག་པོ་ཡོང་བ་དེ་མ་དྲན་པ་ཡིན do not think of, do not trouble yourself about, future evils; བསྐྱིས་པར་མི་དྲན་ནོ I do not reeollect having taken anything on credit (*Jä.*); དྲན་པ་ཙམ་གྱིས as soon one thinks of it; quick as thought; རྗེས་སུ་དྲན་པར་བྱེད་པ *r̤jes-su d̤ran-par byed̤-pa*=དྲན་དུ་འཇུག་པ, *d̤ran-du ḥjug-pa* also to be reminded of, to put in mind of; དྲན་སྐུལ་བྱེད་པ to recall to the mind. 2. to become conscious; དྲན་པར་འགྱུར་པ to recover one's senses, to be one's self again; དྲན་མེད་པ unconscious; མི་དྲན་པའི་རྗེས་སུ after they had become insensible (*Jä.*). 3. to think of with love or affection, to be attached to, to long for.

དྲན་མཆོག་རྗེ *d̤ran-m̤chog r̤je* dearest sir (*Jä.*).

དྲན་ཉམས་པ *d̤ran ñams-pa* निःसंज्ञा 1. unconscious, senseless. 2.=དྲན་པ་གསལ་པོ་མེད་པ faint recollection; weak-minded.

དྲན་པ་ཉེ་བར་བཞག་པ་བཞི *d̤ran-pa ñe-war b̤shag-pa b̤shi* चत्वारि स्मृत्युपस्थानानि the four essential recollections, which are—(1) ལུས་དྲན་པ་ཉེ་བར་བཞག་པ कायस्मृत्युपस्थान [the body is impermanent]*S.*; (2) ཚོར་བ་དྲན་པ་ཉེ་བར་བཞག་པ वेदनास्मृत्युपस्थान [the evils of sensation]*S.*; (3) སེམས་དྲན་པ་ཉེ་བར་བཞག་པ चित्तस्मृत्युपस्थान [the evanescence of thought]*S.*; (4) ཆོས་དྲན་པ་ཉེ་བར་བཞག་པ धर्मस्मृत्युपस्थान [the conditions of existence]*S.*

དྲན་ཐོ *d̤ran-tho* a memo, a note for refreshing the memory.

དྲན་དྲི *d̤ran-d̤ri* abbr. of དྲན་པ་དང་དྲི་བ.

དྲན་པའི་ཀ་བ *d̤ran-paḥi ka-wa*=ཕོ་དབང་ or ཕོ་མཚན the glans penis, the male organ.

དྲན་པ་བཅུ *d̤ran-pa b̤cu* or རྗེས་སུ་དྲན་པ the ten remembrances, viz.:—(1) སངས་རྒྱས་རྗེས་སུ་དྲན་པ; (2) ཆོས་རྗེས་སུ་དྲན་པ; (3) དགེ་འདུན་རྗེས་སུ་དྲན་པ the constant remembrance of Buddha, Dharma and Saṅgha; (4) ཚུལ་ཁྲིམས་རྗེས་སུ་དྲན་པ the bearing in mind monastie vows of morality; (5) གཏོང་བ་རྗེས་སུ་དྲན་པ remembrance to givo away in charity; (6) ལྷ་རྗེས་སུ་དྲན་པ remembrance of one's tutelary deity; (7) དབུགས་ཕྱི་ནང་དུ་རྒྱུ་བ་རྗེས་སུ་དྲན་པ recollection of breathing in and out in the practice of *yoga*; (8) ལུས་ཀྱི་རྣམ་པ་རྗེས་སུ་དྲན་པ the remembrance of the various constituents of the body; (9) སྐྱེ་བ་རྗེས་སུ་དྲན་པ *skye-wa r̤jes-su d̤ran-pa* bearing in mind that one has to be reborn (in any of the six states of existence); (10) འཆི་བ་རྗེས་སུ་དྲན་པ the remembrance of death (as a certain and unavoidable fact) (*Ḥbum.* ཀ *93*).

དྲན་པ་འཇོམས་ *Dran-pa hjoms* स्मर-ध्वंसी the subduer of Dod-lha, *i.e.*, of the desire of procreation, an epithet of Buddha; also n. of an Arhat, &c.

དྲན་པའི་ཁྲོན་པ་ *dran-pahi khron-pa* स्मरकूपक the female organ of generation.

དྲན་པའི་དབང་པོ་ *dran-pahi dwaṅ-po* 1.= མཁས་པ་ *mkhas-pa* a learned man (*Mṅon.*). 2. स्मृतीन्द्रिय the faculty of recollection; memory as one of the five faculities, v. དབང་པོ་ལྔ་.

དྲན་པའི་གཟུགས་ *dran-pahi gzugs* a handsome woman, a beauty (*Mṅon.*).

དྲན་པའི་ཤིང་རྟ་ *dran-pahi çiṅ-rta* स्मररथ an epithet of Kamadeva or Dod-lha.

དྲན་པོ་ *dran-po* स्मर, चेतन awake, one in his senses, conscious.

དྲན་མ་ *dran-ma* the mind, memory: དྲན་མ་བཟང་ good memory; དྲན་ལས་ *dran-las* स्मरणतः from memory, from consciousness; conscious state; དྲན་ཧད་ཀྱི་ཟིན་པ་ *dran had-kyi zin-pa* sudden recollection; remembering all on a sudden.

དྲན་ཤ *dran-ça* the meat of an animal that was slaughtered three days ago; the flesh of an animal after the third day of its death (consciousness is said to linger in the body until life has been extinct for three days; it is therefore that the human body is not disposed of until after the third day of death in Tibet).

དྲན་སེམས་ *dran-sems* in *W.* love, affection, attachment (*Jä.*).

དྲལ *dral* 1. v. ལྷུམ་མོ. 2. v. འདྲལ་བ. 3. for གྲལ་ *gral.*

དྲལ་པོ་ *dral-po* (སྲན་མ་སོགས་རྡུམ་བུ་ཁ་ཤས་ལ་བཏང་བ་རྡལ་རྡལ) (*Rtsii.*) grain or peas that have been split by beating.

དྲལ་བ་ *dral-wa* भेद्य, विदार्य्यन्ते to split with a blow; ཕན་ཚུན་དྲལ་བ་ to split assunder, splitting, rending; བསླབ་པ་དྲལ་བ་ one whose observance (of a religious study or vow) has been broken; དྲལ་གྱིས་ཤུས་པའི་རྗེས་བཞིན་ཁོ་ན་རུ *dral-gyis shus-pahi rjes-bshin kho-na ru* scar or mark left on human body by striking (*D.R.*).

དྲལ་ཙེ་ *dral-tse* a kind of courier or messenger (*Cs.*).

དྲས་ *dras* གོས་སོགས་དྲས་ཚར་བ་ cloth cut out for making a robe or coat, etc., v. དྲ་བ *dra-wa.*

དྲི *dri* 1. आमोद, गन्ध, घ्राण odour, smell, scent; དྲི་ཅན་ sweet-smelling; དྲི་ངན་པ་ *dri ṅan-pa* दुर्गन्ध bad smell, stench, offensive smell; དྲི་མེད་ *dri-med* निर्गन्ध without smell; odourless; bright (*A. K. 1-2*); དྲི་མེད་ཆུ= ཆུ་གཙང་མ་ water (*Mṅon.*). 2. मल ordure, for དྲི་མ. དྲི་མེད་རྣམ་དག་ལྷ་ཁང་ n. of a sacred shrine at Lhar-ṭse in Tsang (*Jig.*). དྲི་མེད་འོད་ཟེར་ n. of a work (*Ya-sel. 34*). དྲི་མེད་གཤེས་གཉེན་ विमलमित्र n. of an Indian pandit who worked in the Buddhist propaganda in Tibet in the 8th century, A.D. དྲི་མེད་ལྡན་པོ་ n. of a *Rñiṅ-ma* lama (*S. kar. 182*).

དྲི་སྐྱེ་མ་ *dri skye-ma* गन्ध-जननी produced of smell, a kind of insect come into existence from dirt or གཤེར་དྲོད་ moisture and warmth.

དྲི་འཁོར་ *dri-hkhor* changing or fading of colour of a dress by use or age: གོས་གསར་བབས་དང་དྲི་འཁོར་བཅས་རིམ་པ་གཉིས་པ (*Rtsii.*).

དྲི་མགྱོགས་ *dri-mgyogs*=སྤོས་དྲི་ *spos-dri* आघ्रा-गन्ध strong scent; incense; དྲི་ང་བ་ *dri-ṅa-wa* bad smell; དྲི་ང་བ་མེད་པ་ निरामगन्ध odourless, free from bad smell.

དྲི་ངད་ *dri-ṅad* vapour, exhalations; དྲི་ངད་འཇམ་པ་ *dri-ṅad hjam-pa* मृदुगन्धिक very agreeable scent; fig. virtue, laudable merit, qualification: ཚུལ་ཁྲིམས་དྲི་དང་དང་ལྡན་པ་ཞེས་བྱ་བ་བི་ཀྲ་མ་ཤཱི་ལ the monastery of Vikrama'sila was so called, (its monks) being possessed of purity in morals (*A. 61*).

དྲི་ངའི་འདབ་ཆགས *dri-ṅahi ḥdab-chags* met. the hoopoe (*Mṅon.*).

དྲི་ལྔ *dri-lṅa* the five perfumes used in offerings to saints and gods.

དྲི་ཅན་ལྟེ་བ *dri-can lte-wa*=ཐ་རི a pod of musk (mystic) (*Miṅ-rda. 3*).

དྲི་ཆབ *dri-chab* scented water; scent, perfumery.

དྲི་ཆུ *dri-chu*=གཅིན मूत्र urine, also abbr. དྲི་མ *dri-ma* ordure and ཆུ urine; ཆུ water when written with དྲི conveys the meaning of urine.

དྲི་ཆུ་གསིལ་བ *dri-chu gsil-wa*=ཆབ་གསིལ or གཅིན་གཏོང་བ to make water, to piss (*Ṅag. 68*).

དྲི་ཆེན *dri-chen*=སྐྱག་པ पुरीष ordure, filth, dung (*Sman.*).

དྲི་མཆོག *dri-mchog*, དྲི་རབ सौगन्ध excellent smell, sweet scent, fragrance (*Mṅon.*).

དྲི་མཉམ་པ *dri mñam-pa* समगन्ध of uniform smell as of incense-sticks of China.

དྲི་བཏུལ *dri-btul*=དྲི་ངན་པ་དུལ་བ suppression of stench.

དྲི་དང་འཕྲེང་བས་མཆོད་པ *dri-daṅ ḥphreṅ-was mchod-pa* गन्धमाल्येन महीयते worshipping with offerings of garlands and frankincense.

དྲི་ལྡན *dri-ldan* 1. गन्धिक having the smell of. 2. राजहंस a gander or ངང་པའི་རྒྱལ་པོ (*Mṅon.*).

དྲི་ལྡན་པ *dri ldan-pa* there are acc. to the Bon cult seven classes of scent:—(1) ས་དྲི་དང་ལྡན་པ་མུ་ཟི་ལྟ་བུ earthy smell such as sulphur; (2) ཆུ་དྲི་དང་ལྡན་པ་འགར་རྟེ་གཟིང་ལྟ་བུ; (3) མེའི་དྲི་དང་ལྡན་པ་གསུར་དུད་ལྟ་བུ; (4) ཤ་དྲི་དང་ལྡན་པ་གླ་རྩི་ལྟ་བུ fleshy musky smell; (5) འབྲུ་དྲི་དང་ལྡན་པ་འབྲུ་རྩི་ཟི་ལྟ་བུ; (6) ཁྲག་དྲི་དང་ལྡན་པ་གླང་ཆེན་གྱི་ཁྲག་ལྟ་བུ; (7) ག་བུར་ལྟ་བུ (*D.R.*).

དྲི་ལྡན་མ *Dri ldan-ma* (མ་ཆ) गन्धवती n. of a place in ancient India.

དྲི་སྣོམ་པ *dri snom-pa* pf. བསྣམས *bsnams* =དབུགས་ལེན་པ to smell, to inhale an odour (*Mṅon.*).

དྲི་ཕོག *dri-phog* gen. དྲི་ངན་ཕོག་པ clothes soiled with spots and bad smell (*Rtsii.*).

དྲི་བྲལ *dri-bral* or དྲི་མ་བྲལ *dri-ma-bral* निर्मल free from bad smell; that which is not soiled; fig.=སྐྱོན་མེད་པ *skyon-med-pa* blameless, without any defect (*A. K. 1-2*). དྲི་བྲལ་ལྷག་བསམ་གྱི་སྦྲུན་ཟླ = སྐྱོན་བྲལ་སེམས་དཀར་པའི་ཁ་བཏགས a white scarf presented as a token of pure heart and good wishes.

དྲི་མ *dri-ma* व्यालक, मल, पुरीष filth, excrement, manure; སྣ་དྲི *sna-dri* nose-mucus; དྲི་མ་ཀུན་ཟད་ནས *dri-ma kun-zad-nas* after all impurities have been put off; དྲི་མ་དཀུ *dri-ma dku* or དྲི་མི་ཞིམ་པ कटुक bad or offensive smell; དྲི་མ་འགགས་པའི་ནད *dri-ma ḥgags-paḥi nad* the disease of obstruction of the bowels. དྲི་མ་ཅན *dri-ma-can* 1. dirty, sluttish (as to dress). དྲི་མ་དང་བཅས་པ *dri-ma daṅ bcas-pa* समल with smell, stain or defilement. དྲི་མ་དང་བྲལ་བ *dri-ma daṅ bral-wa* (དྲི་བྲལ.) washed, bleached, cleansed—དྲི་མ་མེད་པར་བྱས and དྲི་མ་སུན་ཕྱུང་བ signify the same 2. मलमास interlocutary month in the lunar calendar (*Mṅon.*).

དྲི་མ་དྲུག *dri-ma drug* in Budh. the six sorts of defilement, namely:—(1) the feeling that I am superior to my spiritual teacher; (2) want of regard for religion and one's spiritual guide; (3) ཆོས་ལ་དོན་གཉེར་མེད་པ neglect of religious observances; (4) སེམས་ཕྱི་རོལ་གྱི་ཡུལ་ལ་རྣམ་པར་གཡེང་བ the mind wandering over external objects, in deviation from the observance of religious duties; (5) དབང་པོའི་སྒོ་ལྔ་ནང་དུ་སྡུད་པ concentrating attention upon the working of the five senses; (6) ཆོས་ལུན་རིང་དུབ་པ་སོགས་ཀྱིས་སྐྱོ་བ tiring of continued application to religion (*Khrid. 6*).

དྲི་མ་ལྡན་མ *dri-ma ldan-ma*=བུད་མེད་འདོད་ལྡན་མ a voluptuous woman (*Mṅon.*).

དྲི་མ་འཕྱི་བའི་མ་མ *dri-ma hphyi-wahi ma-ma* मलधात्री a child's wet-nurse; a woman who attends to infants' cleanliness.

དྲི་མ་མི་མངའ *dri-ma mi-mṅah* अमल not touched or affected by filth; unblemished, throughly pure.

དྲི་མ་མེད་པ *dri-ma med-pa* विमल 1. the third stage of *Bodhisattva* perfection or མེ་ཏོག་གི་དྲི་ལྟ་བུ pure as smell of flowers; निर्मल without defilement, an epithet of Buddha (*M.V.*). 2. शिव pure, holy, all-good; clean, cleanly.

དྲི་མ་མེད་པའི་དྲིམ་ལན་རིན་པོ་ཆེའི་ཕྲེང་བ a treatise by Achārya Amogha (*Tan. d.* གོ *117*).

དྲི་མ་མེད་པར་གྲགས་པས་བསྟན་པའི་མདོ विमलकीर्त्तिनिर्देश n. of a Sutra (*K. d.* ཕ *224*).

དྲི་མ་གསུམ *dri-ma-gsum* the three impurities or filths:—བ་ཤང་ ordure, གཅི urine, རྔུལ *rṅul* sweat (*Sman.*); fig. ཉེས་པའི་དྲི་མ also ཉོན་མོངས་པའི་དྲི་མ and ཁ་ན་མ་ཐོ་བའི་དྲི་མ.

དྲི་མས་ནོགས་པ *dri-mns nogs-pa* blemished, stained, spoiled.

Syn. ནག་ནོག *nag-nog*; དྲི་ལྡན *dri-ldan* དྲི་མ་ཅན *dri-ma can*; དྲི་མས་སུན་ཕྱུང་ *dri-mas sun-phyuṅ*; དྲི་མ་གོས *dri-ma gos* (*Mṅon.*).

དྲི་གཙང་ཁང་ *dri-gtsaṅ khaṅ* गन्धकुटीर, गन्धोल prob. गन्धालय a sacred place, the principal chapel in a monastery.

Syn. གཙུག་ལག་ཁང་ *gtsug-lag khaṅ* (*Mṅon.*).

+ དྲི་བཙུང་ *dri-brtsuṅ*=དྲི་བསུང་ good smell, fragrance.

དྲི་འཛིན་སྐྱེས *dri-hdsin skyes*=སྣའི་རྣམ་ཤེས·

དྲི་ཞིབ་དཀར *dri-shib dkar* clear and definite instruction or direction.

དྲི་ཞིམ་པ *dri shim-pa* or དྲི་ཞིམ་པོ 1. an agreeable smell, sweet fragrance; adj. fragrant. 2.=གུར་གུམ कुङ्कुम saffron.

Syn. of 1. རྣམ་ཉིད་སྦྱར་སྤོས *rnam-ñid sbyar-spos*; སྙིང་འབབ་དྲི *sñiṅ-hbab dri*; ཀུན་མོས་དྲི་བཟང་ *kun-mos dri-bzaṅ*; བཞོན་པ་ཅན *bshon-pa can*; ཤིན་ཏུ་ཡིད་འཕྲོག *çin-tu yid-hphrog*; རིང་ནས་འགུགས *riṅ-nas hgugs*; འདོད་པའི་དྲི *hdod-pahi dri*; སྣ་ཚིམ་བྱེད *sna-tshim byed*; འབོད་བྱེད *hbod-byed*; ངད་བཟང་ *ṅad-bzaṅ*; རིང་དུ་ཁྱབ *riṅ-du khyab*; ལེགས་པར་འཐུལ *legs-par hthul* (*Mṅon.*).

དྲི་ཞིམ་བྱས *dri-shim byas* वासित perfumed, scented.

དྲི་ཞོན *dri-shon* गन्धवह met. for wind (*Mṅon.*).

དྲི་ཟ *dri-za* गन्धर्व lit. eaters of smells, a class of demi-gods supposed to orignate from the zone of scents in Gandhamādna in the Himalayas; are also celestial musicians. Acc. to *Jä.*: "the *Dri-za* are not only supposed to be fond of flowers and other fragrant objects, but also to visit dung-hills, flaying places, shambles, etc. The insects swarming about such place, the Tibetan believes, to be incarnated *Dri-za.*" དྲི་ཟ་ག་བུར་ནུ་ཞོ་ཅན *dri-za ga-bur nu-sho-can* དབྱི་མོང་རིགས་གཉིས *dbyi-moṅ rigs-gñis* names of two species of vegetable medicine black and white (*Sman. 109*).

དྲི་ཟའི་གྲོང་ཁྱེར *dri-zahi groṅ-khyer* a mirage; explained as མེད་པ་གསལ་སྣང་ཅན་དུ་ཤར་བ an illusory phenomenon appearing as a reality: སྐྱི་ལམ་ཇི་བཞིན་སྒྱུ་མ་བཞིན, དྲི་ཟའི་གྲོང་ཁྱེར་ཇི་བཞིན་དུ, དེ་བཞིན་སྐྱེ་དང་དེ་བཞིན་གནས, དེ་བཞིན་དུ་ཡང་འཇིག་པ་གསུངས (Buddha) has said that like as a dream or illusion or in the manner of a mirage are we born, live, and die (*Theg. 44*).

དྲི་ཟའི་གླུ་དབྱངས་ *dri-zahi glu-dbyaṅs* गन्धर्वे, संगीति melodies of the dri-za musicians.

དྲི་བཟང་སྐྱེས་ *dri-bzaṅ skyes* lit. born of fragrance; an insect; the rose-bug.

དྲི་བཟང་དབང་པོ་ *dri-bzaṅ dwaṅ-po* musk-deer.

Syn. གླ་བ་ *gla-wa*; གླ་རྩི་ཅན་ *gla-rtsi-can* (*Mṅon.*).

དྲི་བཟང་ཁང་པ་ *dri-bzaṅ khaṅ-pa* पद्म lotus flower (*Mṅon.*).

དྲིའི་སྲས་པོ་ *drihi sras-po* a kind of insect believed to grow from smell.

Syn. སྤང་སྤོས་ *spaṅ-spos*; འབྱུང་པོའི་རལ་པ་ *hbyuṅ-pohi ral-pa*; སྤུ་ཅན་ *spu-can* (*Mṅon.*).

དྲིའི་བཅུད་ *drihi bcud* flower, lotus; the virtue or nutriment of དྲི་ scent, smell; substances like camphor, assafoetida, &c.

དྲི་བླང་བ་ *dri-blaṅ-wa* घ्राण to smell.

དྲི་ལ་འཁོར་ *kri-la hkhor* a bee, that which roves round or is attracted by fragrance.

དྲི་བ *dri-wa* for འདྲི་བ pf. དྲིས་ *dris*; = དྲིས་སྐད་ཆ་དྲི་བ to ask, to make inquiry, to interrogate; also sbst. प्रश्न, पृच्छा question, inquiry. + དྲི་བ་རྣ་ལ་གཟོན་པ་ *dri-wa rna-la gzon-pa* = དྲི་བ་དངོས་སུ་དྲང་པོར་མི་བཤད་པ not asking to the point but in an artful manner; དྲི་བ་ལོག་པ་ *dri-wa log-pa* to ask irrelevantly; wrong or contrary questions; དྲི་བ་འདྲི་བ་ *dri-wa hdri-wa* to ask a question.

དྲིང་ *driṅ* 1. looking to; care, regard; dependance upon; = བལྟོས་པ་ or རག་ལུས་པ་: གཞན་དྲིང་མི་འཇོག་ཅེ་ན if you place no regard in others, if (you) do not care for others. 2. acc. to *Cs.* = དྲིན.

དྲིན་ *drin* resp. བཀའ་དྲིན་ rarely སྐུ་དྲིན་ kindness, favour, grace; དྲིན་ཅན་ *drin-can* kind, gracious, benevolent; also benefactor; དྲིན་ཅན་ཕ་མ the parents, the benefactors (*Jä.*); དྲིན་དྲན་པ vb., to acknowledge a kindness, to feel obliged: དྲིན་དྲན་པས as I shall always feel greatly obliged to you; དེང་བཀའ་དྲིན་དྲན་ཅིང་ being now full of thankfulness to him; དྲིན་བརྗེད་པ to forget kindness received, unmindful of obligations.

དྲིན་ཆེ་བ་ *drin che-wa* or དྲིན་ཆེན་ very kind, great boon, the great or greatest benefactor. བཀའ་དྲིན་ཆེ་ *bkah-drin-che* is a very frequent phrase of thanks equivalent to our "most kind of you," "many thanks"; it is often repeated twice and is a common expression of ceremonious thanks in letters. བཙུན་པ་ཚེ་འདི་ལ་དྲིན་ཆེ་ཤོས་རང་གི་མ་ཡིན the greatest benefactress for this life is one's own mother; བོད་ལ་བཀའ་དྲིན་ཆེ་བ་ལགས་སོ this turned out the greatest benefit for Tibet; ཨ་མ་དྲིན་ཅན kindest mother.

དྲིན་གཟོ་བ་ *drin gzo-wa* or དྲིན་དུ་གཟོ་བ to show one's self grateful; དྲིན་གཟོ་ཤིང་ལན་བྱུར you shall not have done it for nothing.

དྲིན་ལན་ *drin-lan* gratitude; དྲིན་ལན་པ to be grateful; དྲིན་ལན་དུ in return for kindness received; དྲིན་ལན་ལོག་པ ingratitude, ungratefulness: ནམ་ཞིག་དྲིན་ལན་ལོག་པ་ཡིས, ཐ་མ་སྒོམ་ཆེན་ཁྲིམས་ལ་སྦྱོར one night because of his ungratefulness, the hermit was punished at last (*Rdsa. 19*); དྲིན་ལན་བསམས་པ to be grateful.

དྲིན་ལོག་པ་ *drin log-pa* or དྲིན་ལན་ལོག་པ lit. to reverse a favour, to return evil for good or for kindness; ingratitude: ད་ནི་དྲིན་ལོག་པར་འཕལ་ནས་ང་ལ་ངན་བྱས་པ now, having met with ingratitude, he did me wrong (*Rdsa. 10*).

དྲིབ་ཤིལ་ *drib-çil* acc. to *Jä.* a corrupt form for དྲིལ་བུ་གཤིལ in *Ld.* = གཡེར་ཁ.

དྲིམ *drim* stump, trunk of a tree or plant; pollarded (in *Ld.*).

དྲིའུ *drihu* v. དྲེ *dre*; prob. for དྲེལ་ཕྲུག a young mule.

དྲིལ *dril* 1. roll or rounded thing: ཤོག་དྲིལ a roll of paper. 2. for དྲིལ་བུ a bell.

དྲིལ་བུ *dril-bu* घण्टा a bell; དྲིལ་བུ་པ one who rings the bell. དྲིལ་བུ་སྒྲ a member of the S'ākya race whose daughter was married to Siddhartha (*Yig.*). དྲིལ་བུ་གཡེར་ཁའི་འདུ་བ་འཁྲོལ་བ किङ्किणी, जालसुखरा sounding like a small bell.

དྲིལ་ཁང་ *dril-khañ* bell-tower, belfry; དྲིལ་སྒྲ the sound of a bell. དྲིལ་སྒྲ་ལས་བསྒྲགས་པ *dril-sgra las bsgrags-pa* घण्टाघोषण proclamation by ringing the bell; དྲིལ་སྒྲོག་པ *dril sgrog-pa* to ring the bell; to publish by ringing a bell; དྲིལ་སྒྲོགས=ཁྲིམས་ཁང་ a place of justice (*Mñon.*). དྲིལ་ལྕེ *dril-lce* the tongue of a bell, the clapper; དྲིལ་ཆུང་ *dril-chuñ* घर्घरिका a small bell; དྲིལ་སྟེགས *dril-stegs* a bell stand, or a piece of cloth on which bells stand; the frame of timber in which bells are suspended.

དྲིལ་བ *dril-wa*, v. འདྲིལ་བ *hdril-wa*.

དྲིས་པ *dris-pa*, v. འདྲི་བ *hdri-wa*. དྲིས *dris* पृष्ट, प्रश्न asked, an interrogation. དྲིས་ནས परिपृच्छा having asked; ཡང་དག་དྲིས सम्पृष्ट well asked; asked carefully.

དྲིས་པ་གཏན་ལ་ཕབ *dris-pa gtan-la phab* [प्रश्ननिर्णय decision of questions]*S.*

དྲིས་པའི་ཐོ *dris-pahi tho* बुद्ध;=སྐད་ཆ་དྲིས་པའི་ཐོ.

དྲི་བོ *dri-bo* an enchanter, sorcerer, magician; དྲི་མོ *dri-mo* enchantress, witch (*Jä.*).

དྲིས་མ *dris-ma* पृष्टवान् one who has asked; having asked.

དྲིས་ལན *dris-lan* प्रश्नोत्तर answer to a question.

དྲུ་གུ *dru-gu* a ball or skein of thread.

དྲུ་བུ *dru-bu* a clew or ball; སྐུད་པའི་དྲུ་བུ a ball of thread or of wool; དྲུ་བུ་འཛིངས་པ་ལྟ་བུ गुडगुन्दिकभूता like the clew of a thread mixed up or confused.

དྲུག *drug* 1. षट् num. six. 2.=བཟང་པོ good. 3. symbolic of རོ་བ the kinds of taste which are six, also of the six quarters (མཚམས), *i.e.*, the four cardinal points besides above and below; also that of the six ornaments or རྒྱན (*Rtsii.*). དྲུག་དཀར *drug-dkar* a superior kind of turquoise. དྲུག་བརྒྱ *drug-brgya* six hundred (600). དྲུག་སྒྲ *drug-sgra* in Gram. the so-called article presenting itself in the following six forms; པ, བ, མ, པོ, བོ, མོ. དྲུག་ཅུ *drug-cu* or དྲུག་ཅུ་ཐམ་པ षष्टि the num. sixty (60); དྲུག་ཅུ་རེ་གཅིག एकषष्टि num. sixty-one (61). དྲུག་ཅུ་སྐོར *drug-cu skor* the Vṛhaspati cycle or the cycle of sixty years. དྲུག་ཆ *drug-cha* one-sixth, one-sixth part; དྲུག་སྟོང་ *drug-stoñ* six thousand (6,000). དྲུག་ལྡན་མ *drug ldan-ma* षष्ठी an epithet of the goddess Gaurī (*Mñon.*). དྲུག་པ *drug-pa* or དྲུག་པོ *drug-po* षष्ठ the sixth one. དྲུག་དམར *drug-dmar* a very fine kind of turquoise supposed to be one-sixth part red in tint. དྲུག་ཞོ *drug-sho* six *khal* (mule load) of barley grain for one *sho* (*Rtsii.*).

དྲུག་སྡེ *drug-sde* षड्वर्गिक 1. the early disciples of Buddha:—དགའ་བོ नन्द; ཉེ་དགའ उपनन्द; ནབས་སོ पुनर्वसु; འདུན་པ छन्दः; འགྲོ་མགྱོགས अश्वक; འཆར་ཀ उदायी. 2. a class of dissenting monks who being of a discordant disposition often brought troubles to the early congregation of S'ākya Muni.

དྲུག་མདོ *drug-mdo* back joint, spinal joint; hence དྲུག་མདོ་བ=རྒྱལ་གྱི་རྒྱུད་འཛིན a follower. (*Mñon.*).

དྲུང་ *druñ* resp. 1. निकट, सन्निधान, समीप adv. and postp. near to, beside, at, to; དྲུང་ནས་འབྱིན *druñ-nas hbyin* आचेपण: drawn from near; ཕོ་བྲང་གི་དྲུང་གང་ན་བ་དེར་འདུག་ནས having alighted on the place before the palace. But the ordinary form in which the word is found is as the postp. and adv. དྲུང་དུ नैकटिक

at, near to, in front of, before; རྒྱལ་པོའི་དྲུང་དུ to the king, before the king; དྲུང་དུ་རྟོག་པ to examine personally, face to face; དྲུང་དུ་འགྲོ་བ to go near or up to; ཤིང་གི་དྲུང་དུ near or under the tree. 2. a title or address of honour generally intended for the sons of noblemen; སྐུ་ཞབས་དྲུང་ your honour; ཨ་ནེ་དྲུང་ honourable miss. 3. civil officer, official; དྲུང་ཆེན, དྲུང་འཁོར་ཆེན་པོ high official; དྲུང་ཡིག *druṅ-yig* private secretary; དྲུང་དཀྱུས་མ *druṅ dkyus-ma* an inferior official, a common clerk (*Rtsii.*); དྲུང་འཁོར *druṅ-ḥkhor* gen. lay-officials under the government of Tibet; དྲུང་གནས་པ *druṅ gnas-pa* a companion, an associate; དྲུང་འབྲིང་བ *druṅ ḥbriṅ-wa* or དྲུང་འཁོར་འབྲིང་པ a middle-class official (*Rtsii.*); དྲུང་སྤྱི *druṅ-spyi* civil officers in general.

དྲུང་གྲགས་པ *druṅ grags-pa* names of officials under Phag-mo Grub hierarchy.

དྲུང་དྲག *druṅ-drag* superior rank of officials: དྲུང་དྲག་ལན་རྒྱུན་གཡེལ་ཆེ་བ་དང་སྐྱེར་དུ་བཀའ་དྲིན་བསྐྱངས་རིགས those superior officials who are of much importance for public service and are especially favoured, etc. (*D. çel. 11*).

དྲུང་ན་མོ *druṅ na-mo* आसन्न imminent, very near, close to, impending.

Syn. ཐག་ཉེ་བ *thag ñe-wa*; ཉེ་འཁོར *ñe-ḥkhor* (*Mṅon.*).

དྲུང་ནམ་མཁའ་བཟང་པོ *Druṅ Nam-mkaḥ bzaṅ-po* (*Loṅ. ཀ 15*) n. of a Government secretary of Lhasa.

卐 **དྲུང་པ** *druṅ-pa* or སྐུ་དྲུང་པ=སྐུ་མདུན་པ secretary, lit. one standing near, waiting in the presence of a great man, an aide-de-camp.

དྲུང་པོ *druṅ-po*=1. སྒྲུང་པོ or སྒྲུང་པོ चतुर clever, skilful. Acc. to *Jä.* prudent, wise, judicious, sensible. 2. sincere, candid.

དྲུང་འཚོ་བ *druṅ ḥtsho-wa* private physician, physician in ordinary (*Cs.*).

དྲུང་ཡིག་པ *druṅ-yig-pa* कायस्थ a clerk, specially the clerk of a superior officer, a writer.

དྲུངས *druṅs* root (of misery, sin, disease, etc., also that of a tree, etc.). དྲུངས་ནས་ཕྱུང उन्मूल exterminated or destroyed from the root; radically cured.

དྲུངས་པ *druṅs-pa* 1.=དྲུངས་པོ bright, sparkling. 2. acc. to *Cs.* clarified, clear. 3. beer, resp. བཞེས་དྲུངས beer for the use of a great man.

དྲུད *drud* v. འདྲུད་པ निर्मोचित 1. divested: ཕ་ཡིས་སྟག་བསད, བུ་ཡིས་སྟག་གི་དྲུད་ the father killed a tiger, the son pulled off its skin. 2. དྲུད་དྲུད *drud-drud* a pelican (*Sch.*).

卐 **དྲུབ་པ** *drub-pa* or དྲུབས་པ v. འདྲུབ་པ= བཙེམས་པ (anything) sewn.

དྲུམ་པ *drum-pa* or ཆགས་དྲུམ passion; acc. to *Sch.* to have a strong desire, to long, languish, pine for.

དྲུས་མ *drus-ma* 1. in foal, as བ་དྲུས་མ a cow about to bring forth. 2. millet (*Sch.*).

དྲེ *dre* acc. to *Jä.* a mule; prob. col. of དྲེལ. དྲེ་མོ, མོ་དྲེ she-mule; དྲེ་ཕོ, ཕོ་དྲེ mule.

དྲེ་བོ *dre-wo* in *W.* the elbow (*Jä.*).

དྲེག་པ *dreg-pa* grime, incrusted dirt, soot: སྒྲོན་དྲེག *sgron-dreg* lamp-black; སླང་དྲེག *slaṅ-dreg* soot on the frying-pan; དྲེག་ནད or དྲེག་གྲུམ *dreg-grum* gout; དྲེག་ལྡན *dreg-ldan* अवलेप coating of dirt on anything; དྲེག་བྱེད་རྡོ་བ *dreg-byed rdo-wa* (?).

དྲེགས *dregs* or དྲེགས་པ *dregs-pa* दर्प मदकल, आडम्बर, उद्धत pride, haughtiness, arrogance; ཁེངས་དྲེགས id. དྲེགས་ཚིག *dregs-tshig*= ཁེངས་གཏམ haughty expressions or words;

boasting (*Mñon.*). དྲེགས་ལྡན་མ *dregs ldan-ma*=ཁེངས་ལྡན་མ a youthful female, a damsel who on account of the charms of her youth is proud. In Budh. fifteen kinds of pride are mentioned:—(1) ཚུལ་ཁྲིམས་ཀྱིས་དྲེགས་པ the pride of moral purity; (2) ཐོས་པས་དྲེགས་པ pride from much hearing; (3) སྤོབས་པས་དྲེགས་པ pride of courage; (4) རྙེད་པས་དྲེགས་པ pride of acquirements; (5) བཀུར་སྟི་ས་དྲེགས་པ pride of honours; (6) རིག་གནས་མཁས་པས་དྲེགས་པ pride of intellect; (7) དབེན་གནས་ཀྱིས་དྲེགས་པ pride of residence in solitude; (8) སྦྱངས་པའི་ཡོན་ཏན་གྱིས་དྲེགས་པ pride in attainments; (9) ཡོ་བྱད་ཉུང་བས་དྲེགས་པ pride of having few necessaries of life; (10) གཟུགས་བཟང་བས་དྲེགས་པ pride of personal appearance; (11) ལོངས་སྤྱོད་ཀྱིས་དྲེགས་པ pride of wealth; (12) དབང་ཆེ་བས་དྲེགས་པ pride of power; (13) འཁོར་གཡོག་མང་བས་དྲེགས་པ pride in possessing many servants and retainers; (14) བསམ་གཏན་མངོན་ཤེས་ཀྱིས་ of dhyāna and fore-knowledge; (15) ལྷ་ཀླུ་སོགས་ཀྱི་བསྟོད་པས་དྲེགས་པ pride from the praises of gods and nāga. (*K. d.* ཕ *78* and *Loñ.*).

དྲེགས་བྱེད *dregs-byed* met. for a devil.

དྲེད *dred*, generally དྲེད་མོ *dred-mo*, indicates the red or snow bear (*Ursus isabellinus*); but is often indiscriminately applied to other species found in Tibet.

དྲེད་པོ *dred-po* 1. a wild-man, a savage; one who is brute-like and irreligious. མི་རུ་སྐྱེས་ཀྱང་དགེ་མེད་དྲེད་པོར་སྐྱེས though born as a human being, he has grown an impious savage (*D.R.*); acc. to *Sch.*: evasive, lazy; he quotes the passage: ཆོས་མེད་དྲེད་པོ་ཟོལ་ཟོག་གཡོ་སྒྱུ་ཅན a savage without religion, full of deceit and cunning. 2. a yellow male-bear; དྲེད་ཚང་ *dred-tshañ* a bear's den.

དྲེད་མོ *dred-mo* 1. one who has gone astray from a religious life; one who has abandoned a righteous life. 2. a yellow bear.

དྲེད་མོ *dred-mo* species of bear peculiar to the mountainous plains of Amdo and the Kökö Nor region, the *Ursus lagomyarius* of Prejevalski. It preys upon *lagomys* and marmots, as described by "A. K." in his *Report on a Journey in Tibet and Mongolia.*

དྲེའུ *drehu* प्रखर, वेसर a young or small mule.

+ དྲེའུ་རྔོག *drehu-rñog*; དྲེའུའི་རྔོག་མ 1. the mane of a mule. 2.=སྟན་ཁྲ་བོ a spotted seat, or cushion. 3. a kind of long-haired cloth.

དྲེལ *drel* a full grown mule. དྲེལ་གདང་= དྲེལ་ར *drel-ra* stall for mule, the rope for tethering mules (*Rtsii.*).

དྲེས་མ *dres-ma* a kind of grass, of which ropes and shoe-soles are made in Tibet. དྲེས་མ་གེ་སར the filaments of དྲེས་མ; དྲེས་འབྲུ *dres-hbru* or དྲེས་འབྲུམ *dres-hbrum* the seeds of དྲེས་མ grass; དྲེས་ཤུན *dres-çun* rope made of དྲེས་མ grass (*Rtsii.*).

དྲོ *dro* 1. the hot time of the day. སྔ་དྲོ *sña-dro* the morning from 8 A.M. to 10 A.M. ཕྱི་དྲོ *phyi-dro* afternoon from 3 P.M. to 5 P.M. in India and Tibet. 2. acc. to *Jä.*, lunch, a meal taken about noon; དྲོ་བཏབ་པ to lunch. དྲོ has also the general meaning of any meal: ཉི་མ་གཅིག་ལ་དྲོ་གསུམ in one day three meals; ང་ཉི་མ་གཅིག་ལ་དྲོ་ལྔ་གཏོང་འདུག "give to (the labourers) five meals a day" (said a rich man who was building a house).

དྲོ་འཇམ *dro-hjam* (col. *tonjam*) tepid.

དྲོ་དོད *dro-dod*=comfortable accommodation (of travellers) under road-bill.

དྲོ་བ *dro-wa* 1. vb. and adj. to be warm; warm, as distinguished from hot. 2.=བྲོ་བ *bro-wa* of which it is an incorrect form.

དྲོ་བ་རྣོན་པོ *dro-wa rnon-po* तीव्ररस very acrid taste; pungent.

དྲོ་ལུག *dro-lug* a sheep intended for food; དྲོ་ཤ་ *dro-ça* meat intended for such a purpose.

དྲོགས *drogs* (*Sch.*) packed up, made up into a pack or parcel.

དྲོང་ *droṅ* or དྲོངས *droṅs* v. འདྲེན་པ *hdren-pa*.

དྲོང་མ *droṅ-ma* a large basket or dosser provided with a lid and carried on the back.

དྲོད *drod* ऊष्मा 1. sbst. warmth; གོས་ཀྱི་དྲོད warmth (derived from clothes); མེ་དྲོད warmth from fire. 2. animal heat. ཁ་དྲོད་ཟུང་གཅིག a small piece of food=ཁ་ཟས, prob. for ཁ་དྲོད enjoyment of the mouth. (*Jä.*); དྲོད་ཅན *drod-can* ऊष्मक possessed of warmth, warm.

+ དྲོད་ཉུལ *drod-ñul*=བློ་ཡི་གདེང་ཚད matching one's desires, in accordance with design, &c.

དྲོད་ཕེབས་དུས *drod phebs-dus*=དཔྱིད་ཀ *dpyid-ka*, the warm season, *i.e.*, the spring (*Mṅon.*).

དྲོད་སྨན *drod-sman*=དྲོད་སྐྱེད་བྱེད stimulant; དྲོད་སྨན་བཟང་པོ་གསུམ the three stimulant medicines are *Piper longum*, cardamom, and a smaller species of cardamom (*Mih-rdla. 3*).

དྲོད་འོངས *drod-hoṅs* ऊष्मागम the coming of the hot season, the summer. དྲོད་ཡལ་བ *drod yal-wa* the vanishing or diminishing of warmth or heat.

དྲོད་རིག་པ *drod rig-pa* मन्त्रज्ञान the science of mysticism, occultism, charms. *Jä.* has: well-versed in measures.

དྲོད་གཤེར *drod-gçer* संस्वेद 1. sweat, perspiration. 2. acc. to *Jä.*: warmth and moisture. དྲོད་གཤེར་ལས་སྐྱེས་པ संस्वेदजा vermin, insect, etc., produced by heat and moisture.

དྲོན་པོ *dron-po* col. for དྲོ་པོ *dro-wo*.

དྲོན་མ *dron-ma* or དྲོན་མོ gentle warmth, gen. equalling དྲོ་འཇམ *dro-hjam* ཟན་དྲོན warm food; ཁྲག་དྲོན་མོ *khrag dron-mo* warm blood. (*Hbrom. 41*).

དྲོལ *drol* v. འདྲོལ་བ *hdrol-wa*.

དྲོས I: *dros* (*Sch.*)=དྲོ *dro*, དྲོས་ཆེན noon, midday; དྲོས་ན when it is getting warm.

དྲོས II: sometimes written for བྲོས.

དྲོས་པ *dros-pa* 1. अवतप्त heated, grown warm, esp. of the ground by the heat of the sun or of men by warm clothing. མ་དྲོས་པ *Ma dros-pa* अनवतप्त is the n. of a lake, *i.e.*, of Tsho Mapham, the eastern one of the two Manasarowar lakes in S. W. Tibet; also a Naga king. 2. (གོས་ལྷ་བྱ) cutting cloth to make a dress.

གདག *gdag* or གདགས *gdags* 1. fut. of འདོགས་པ, प्रज्ञप्ति; མིང་གདགས་པ to attach or give a name; གདགས་གཞི the man about to be given the name; གདགས་ཆོས the doctrine that one should be attached to (*Rdo. 46*). 2. acc. to *Jä.* day-light, opp. to སྲིབས. 3. in *Stg.* གདགས་པ occurs frq. as a translation of प्रज्ञा wisdom (*Jä.*).

གདང *gdaṅ* or གདང་བུ (གོས་འགེལ་བའི་གདང་) आलम्बक clothes-horse, rack; the rail on which a bird perches is called བྱ་གདང་. 2. a peg or nail for clothing. 3. སྐས་ཀྱི་གདང་བུ the rail of a ladder; but acc. to *Jä.*, the step of a ladder. གསེར་གྱི་གདང་བུ་ལ་ར་ལྤགས་ནག་པོ་བཀལ་ནས་ཡོད། on a golden rack there was placed a black goat-skin (*Hbrom. 142*).

གདང་བ *gdaṅ-wa* pf. གདངས་པ *gdaṅs-pa* संजृम्भ; ཁ་གདང་བ to gape, to open wide (the mouth and nostrils); to stretch; ལག་པ་གདངས stretched apart the arms; བསྙུང་གཞི་གདངས *bsñuṅ gshi gdaṅs* cured of disease.